the Next EXIT®

2016

THE MOST ACCURATE INTERSTATE HIGHWAY SERVICE GUIDE EVER PRINTED™

the Next EXIT® will save time, money and frustration.

This tool will help you find services along the USA Interstate Highways like nothing you have ever used.

GAS STATIONS • RESTAURANTS • RV CAMPING • HOTELS • AND MUCH MORE

PO Box 888
Garden City, UT 84028
www.theNextExit.com

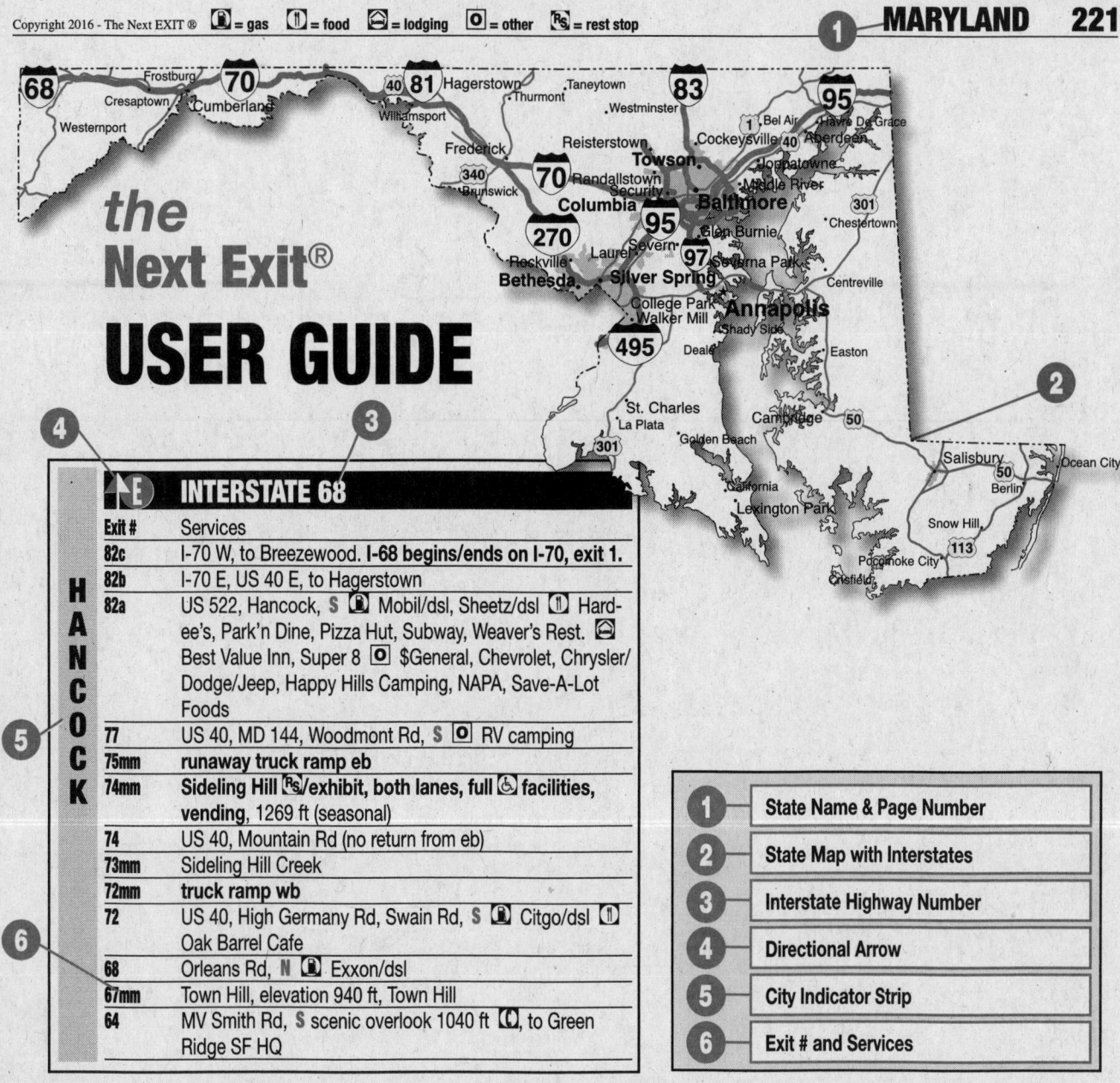

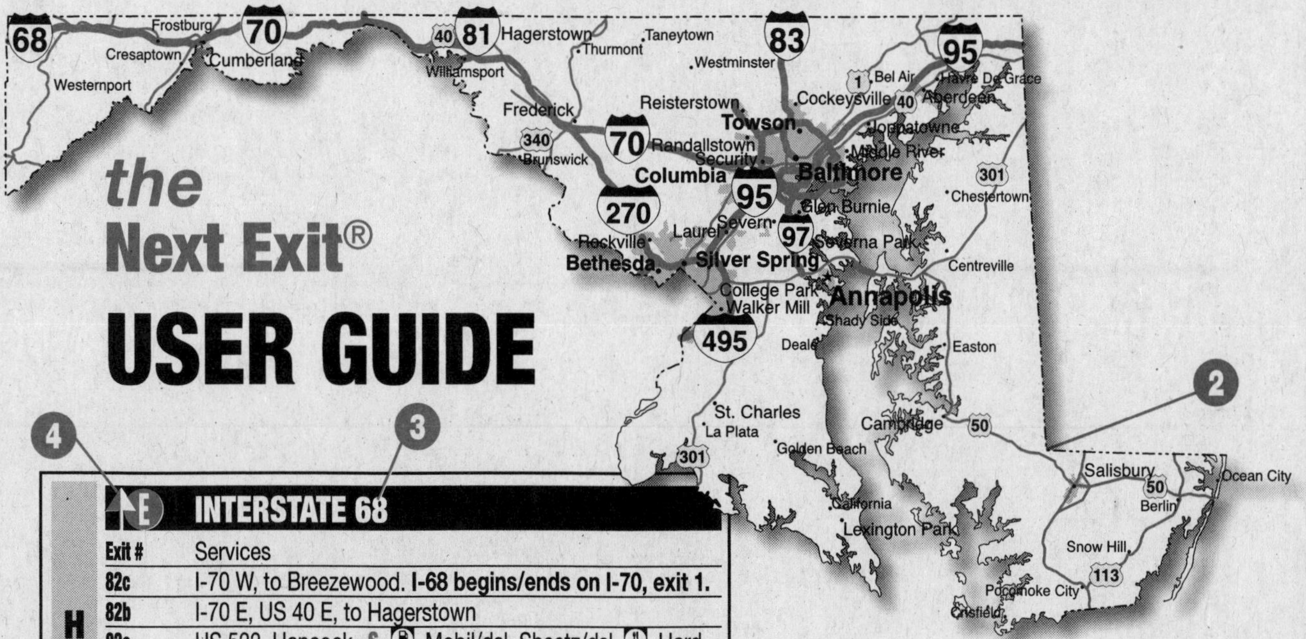

the Next Exit®

USER GUIDE

HANCOCK

INTERSTATE 68 (E)

Exit #	Services
82c	I-70 W, to Breezewood. **I-68 begins/ends on I-70, exit 1.**
82b	I-70 E, US 40 E, to Hagerstown
82a	US 522, Hancock, S [gas] Mobil/dsl, Sheetz/dsl [food] Hardee's, Park'n Dine, Pizza Hut, Subway, Weaver's Rest. [lodging] Best Value Inn, Super 8 [other] $General, Chevrolet, Chrysler/Dodge/Jeep, Happy Hills Camping, NAPA, Save-A-Lot Foods
77	US 40, MD 144, Woodmont Rd, S [other] RV camping
75mm	**runaway truck ramp eb**
74mm	**Sideling Hill [rest stop]/exhibit, both lanes, full [handicap] facilities, vending**, 1269 ft (seasonal)
74	US 40, Mountain Rd (no return from eb)
73mm	Sideling Hill Creek
72mm	**truck ramp wb**
72	US 40, High Germany Rd, Swain Rd, S [gas] Citgo/dsl [food] Oak Barrel Cafe
68	Orleans Rd, N [gas] Exxon/dsl
67mm	Town Hill, elevation 940 ft, Town Hill
64	MV Smith Rd, S scenic overlook 1040 ft [phone], to Green Ridge SF HQ

1. State Name & Page Number
2. State Map with Interstates
3. Interstate Highway Number
4. Directional Arrow
5. City Indicator Strip
6. Exit # and Services

Exit

Most states number exits by the nearest mile marker(mm). A few states use consecutive numbers, in which case mile markers are given in ( ). Mile markers are the little green vertical signs beside the interstate at one mile intervals which indicate distance from the southern or western border of a state. Odd numbered interstates run north/south, even numbered run east/west.

Services

Services are listed alphabetically by category [gas]**=gas** [food]**=food** [lodging]**=lodging** [rest stop]**=rest stop** [other]**=other** services including camping.

"[H]" indicates an exit from which a hospital may be accessed, but it may not be close to the exit.

Services located away from the exit may be referred to by "access to," or "to" and a distance may be given.

A directional notation is also given, such as **N**, **S**, **E** or **W**

Directional Arrows

Follow exits DOWN the page if traveling from North to South or East to West, UP the page if traveling South to North or West to East.

Additional copies may be ordered by using the form supplied in the back of this book, or by visiting online at ***www.theNextExit.com***
the Next EXIT, inc. makes no warranty regarding the accuracy of the information contained in this publication. This information is subject to change without notice.

TABLE OF CONTENTS

Abbreviations & Symbols used in the Next EXIT ®

AFB ....Air Force Base
B&B ....Bed&Breakfast
Bfd............Battlefield
CNG..........Compressed Natural Gas
Ctr ....Center
Coll ....College
Cyn ....canyon
dsl.............diesel
$................Dollar
EVC ....Electric Vehicle Charger
LNG ....Liquid Natural Gas
Mem ....Memorial
Mkt ....Market
Mtn ....Mountain
mm ....mile marker
N ....north side of exit
S................south side of exit
E................east side of exit
W...............west side of exit

NM............National Monument
NHS..........Nat Hist Site
NWR.........Nat Wildlife Reserve
NF.............National Forest
[H] ....Hospital
[airport symbol]............Airport
[picnic symbol]............Picnic Tables
NP.............National Park
NRA..........Nat Rec Area
pk ....park
pkwy.........parkway
rest. ....restaurant
nb ....northbound
sb ....southbound
eb ....eastbound
wb.............westbound
SP.............state park
SF ....state forest
Sprs..........springs

st ....street, state
sta ....station
TPK...........Turnpike
USPO ....Post Office
vet ....veterinarian
whse.........warehouse
@..............truckstop (full service)
red print....RV accessible
[handicapped symbol] ....Handicapped accessible
[telephone symbol]............Telephone
[gas symbol] ....Gas
[food symbol] ....Food
[lodging symbol] ....Lodging
[O] ....Other
[RS]............Rest Stop / Rest Area

For Trans Canada Highway (TCH) information and more, please visit us on the web at ***www.thenextexit.com***

I, Crop Duster

Mark Watson - Winter 2016

I raced a yellow crop duster across Iowa last summer. He had the short term advantage since I could not travel at 180 mph, but the smooth concrete surface of Interstate 80 enabled me to cruise safely by trees and underneath power lines without much trouble. After sparring back and forth for several miles, our directions diverged when he turned to take another swipe at the corn and I continued west.

Do you remember how you decided what your life's work would be? I don't either, exactly. A fortunate few find a satisfying occupation early but many of us take a more tortuous track to a career, testing several areas before finally discovering what makes us happy while paying the bills. Retrospection is seldom satisfying, but every time I pass through farming country and see little airplanes spraying crops from above I am reminded of what might have been. I have worked as a middle manager, owner of small businesses, a doctor and company president, and except for a couple of twists I could have been a crop duster. Let me explain.

Whenever our father announced the crop duster would be coming to spray the cotton or soy beans my brother and I could hardly wait for him to get there. We listened for the hum of his engine and studied the horizon beyond the trees bordering our farm, anxiously anticipating his arrival. Our place was small and it did not take many passes for him to finish the job and leave, so we had to be ready if we didn't want to miss anything. By and by we would be rewarded with our own little air show as "Flyboy" dove past the electric lines, flattened out, turned on the spray and headed for the woods, all at astonishing speed and five feet above the ground. At the last possible instant he would pull up just in time to avoid the trees at the end of the field. It was exciting, even thrilling, and looked like a job you could love doing every day of your life, especially if you got paid for it.

Besides the crop dusters our experience with flying had been limited to a brief excursion in a Piper Cub courtesy of my mother's cousin, and a similar ride in our scoutmaster's airplane. One day, during the US Army's war game "Swift Strike", a US Air Force jet made several strafing dives directly at our home, prompting my wise older brother to declare that we were his primary target. We were delighted to think our place was important enough to be in his sights and relieved to realize he was only firing blanks, but that incident filed a note in my mind regarding future career choices. If you could streak through the air at tremendous speed, avoiding all perils and commanding awe and respect from everybody below you, just about anything was possible.

Then one day Dad told us boys to get into the truck, we were going to get haircuts. Not just any haircut, but a 25 cent haircut administered by a back porch barber over in Oats Community. It was the kind of place your elders took you to before you got your own ideas of who you wanted messing with your hair and how you wanted it to look when they were done. The humid shop hung heavy with the smell of talcum powder, Vitalis, a hint of Butch Hair Wax and featured a solid chair which could be elevated by pumping a

Continued Next Page

handle on its side. When the barber was in, there was a waiting line of local men with much conversation on many subjects. On such an excursion you never knew what might be said by the older gentlemen there, so into the truck we went.

When we arrived, my brother, a fair storyteller himself, amused the barbershop crowd with one of his comical tales while we awaited our turn. One by one we moved up the queue until each of us had undergone the shears that improved and simplified our grooming. As later customers appeared every one contributed news or topics of his own, giving the banter fresh life with each arrival. It was a scene that might have been duplicated in rural barber shops all over America.

After a while word came that a crop duster had crashed earlier right there in Oats only a couple of miles from where we sat. Nobody knew more than that, so since we were finishing up and heading home anyhow, we pestered Dad into riding over to take a look. He agreed and we found our way to the site of the accident. Turning down a farm road heading into the woods, we were waved off by the ambulance attendants who were loading a gurney into the back of their vehicle. Although we saw little else and did not know the pilot, we understood that one of our heroes had fallen victim to the power lines, the trees or some other obstacle. An equipment failure, miscalculation or mistake had led to this horrific event and we were stunned by the sobering consequences.

Following next month's haircut we revisited the spot where the plane had gone down. This time, only the broken trees and pieces of charred canvas were there to remind us of the tragedy, but they were enough to impact how I looked at this type of professional flying.

In the 1950's, the mortality rate for crop dusters was between 6 and 8 percent annually because surplus WW II aircraft, never intended for such duty as crop dusting, were commonly used. Compared to other pilots and related occupations this statistic was shocking, and improved only when the aviation industry began designing and building better planes. Afterwards, it was still dangerous but more modern equipment and training along with experience decreased fatalities dramatically.

In the years after, we heard of other crop dusters going down. A friend's pilot father developed a heart problem and was going to be grounded, so he went up for one last time. That final trip ended in a crash. On the other side of the county another flyer fell and a few years later his son did as well. "Flyboy" eventually retired, but not before walking away from a dozen wrecked airplanes and cracking a vertebrae while jumping out of another just ahead of the flames. Somewhere in the numbers that began to add up I had an epiphany. Two wonders of the modern world are overcoming inertia with automobiles and gravity by way of airplanes, but neither is without its hazards.

The yellow Iowa crop duster swooped down, turned on the mist and levelled off for most of a mile, crossing cleanly between a set of high power lines and the ground beneath. Toward the end of the field he rose up, narrowly avoiding a row of trees and a grain silo. Taking a wide loop, he repeated the same action again from the opposite direction, making the entire exercise seem smooth and easy. He was paying close attention to the transmission lines and by now I was once again focusing on the traffic of Interstate 80. The whole affair made quite an impression on me but he never even knew we were competing.

ALABAMA

INTERSTATE 10

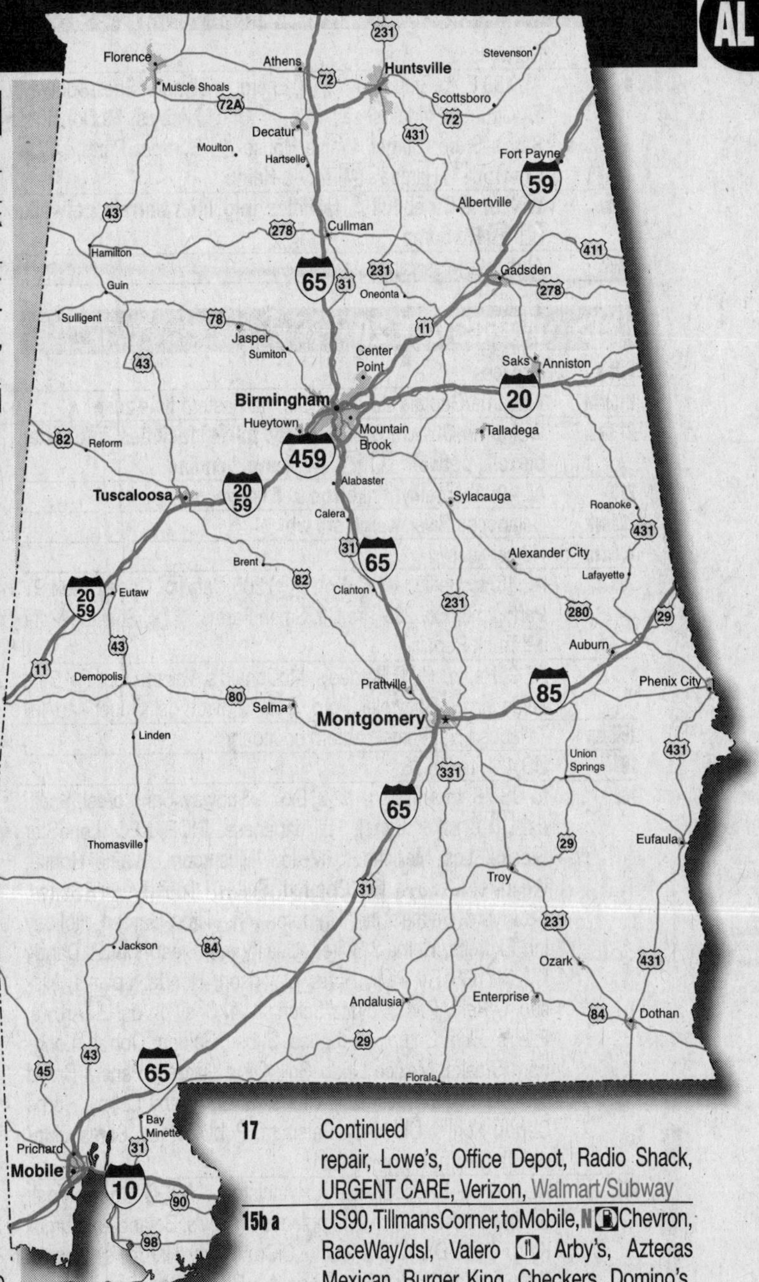

Exit #	Services
66.5mm	Alabama/Florida state line
66mm	**Welcome Ctr full facilities, litter barrels, petwalk vending**
53	Rd 64, Wilcox Rd, N BP/Oasis/Chester's/Stuckey's/Subway/dsl/scales/24hr/ @ Riverside RV Park, Styx River Resort, S Chevron/dsl, Outpost/dsl Azalea Acres RV Park, fireworks, Hilltop RV Park (1.5 mi), Wilderness RV Park
44	AL 59, Loxley, N Loves /Arby's/dsl/scales/24hr Bay Inn, S Chevron/dsl, Exxon/dsl, RaceWay/dsl Burger King, Hardee's, McDonald's, Waffle House Loxley Motel (3mi), WindChase Inn to Gulf SP
38	AL 181, Malbis, N CA Dreaming, Chick-fil-A, Cracker Barrel, Hibachi Grill, Logan's Roadhouse, McDonald's, Moe's SW Grill, Olive Garden, Panera Bread, Poor Mexican, Ruby Tuesday, Starbucks, Stix Asian, Taco Bell, Wendy's, Wintzell's Oyster House Best Western, Country Inn&Suites, Holiday Inn Express, La Quinta $Tree, Advance Parts, Barnes&Noble, Belk, Best Buy, Dillard's, Goodyear/auto, Michael's, Old Navy, Petsmart, Publix, Ross, Tuesday Morning, Verizon, Walgreens, World Mkt, S Chevron/dsl, Shell/LA Subs, Texaco/dsl Burger King, Don Carlos, Firehouse Subs, Mellow Mushroom, Zaxby's Malbis Motel (1mi), ValuePlace AT&T, Honda, Hyundai, Lowe's, Nissan, Sam's Club/gas, Toyota/Scion, URGENT CARE, Walmart
35	US 90, US 98, N BP, Shell Beef O'Brady's, China Fun Courtyard, Fairfield Inn Bass Pro Shops, Books-A-Million, JC Penney, Kohl's, Rite Aid, USPO, S Exxon/dsl, Shell 5 Guys Burgers, Arby's, Bangkok Thai, Baumhower's, Burger King, Domino's, Dragon City Buffet, El Rancho Mexican, Firehouse Subs, Grand Buffet, Hooters, IHOP, Longhorn Steaks, Los Tacos, Marble Slab, McAlister's Deli, McDonald's, O'Charley's, Papa John's, Pizza Hut, S China Rest., Smoothie King, Starbucks, Subway, Taco Bell, Top of the Bay, Waffle House, Wendy's, Zaxby's Comfort Suites, Eastern Shore Motel, Hampton Inn, Hilton Garden, Homewood Suites, Microtel H, AT&T, Dick's, GNC, Hancock Fabrics, Hobby Lobby, Home Depot, Office Depot, Radio Shack, SteinMart, TJ Maxx, to Blakeley SP
30	US 90/98, Battleship Pkwy, same as 27
27	US 90/98, Battleship Pkwy, Gov't St, S Capt's Table Seafood, Felix's Fish Camp, R&R Seafood, Tacky Jack's Rest, Word's Rest Battleship Inn Lap's Grocery, to USS Alabama
26b	Water St, Mobile, downtown, N Adventure Inn, Hampton Inn, Holiday Inn, Quality Inn, Renaissance, to Visitors Ctr
26a	Canal St (from eb), same as 26b
25b	Virginia St, Mobile, N Shell/dsl
25a	Texas St (from wb, no return)
24	Broad St, to Duval St, Mobile, N Chevron
23	Michigan Ave, N Shell/dsl $General
22b a	AL 163, Dauphin Island Pkwy, N Citgo Family$, S Exxon/Subway, Shell/dsl Checker's, Chester's, Hart's Chicken, Kim's Palace, Waffle House $General
20	I-65 N, to Montgomery
17	AL 193, Tillmans Corner, to Dauphin Island, N Chevron Boiling Pot, Crazy Hibachi, Firehouse Subs, Five Guys, Golden Corral, IHOP, Ruby Tuesday, Zaxby's H, AT&T, auto
17	Continued repair, Lowe's, Office Depot, Radio Shack, URGENT CARE, Verizon, Walmart/Subway
15b a	US90, Tillmans Corner, to Mobile, N Chevron, RaceWay/dsl, Valero Arby's, Aztecas Mexican, Burger King, Checkers, Domino's, Godfather's, Hooters, KFC, King's Buffet, Little Caesar's, McDonald's, Papa John's, Popeye's, Russell's BBQ, Shrimp Basket, Subway, Taco Bell, Waffle House Baymont Inn, Best Inn, Best Value Inn, Comfort Suites, Days Inn, EconoLodge, Hampton Inn, Holiday Inn, InTown Suites, La Quinta, Motel 6, Quality Inn, Rodeway Inn, Super 8, Wingate Inn $General, $Tree, AutoZone, BigLots, CarQuest, Family$, Firestone/auto, Mike's Transmissions, O'Reilly Parts, PepBoys, Rite Aid, vet, Walgreens, Winn-Dixie, S Chevron/Circle K, Exxon, RaceWay/dsl, Shell/dsl Hardee's, Waffle House Advance Parts, auto repair, B&R Campers, Johnnys RV Ctr, Peterbilt, tires, transmissions, USPO, vet
13	to Theodore, N Clark/dsl, Pilot/Wendy's/dsl/scales/24hr, Shell/Subway, Texaco/McDonald's Burger King, Church's, Waffle House Advance Parts, auto repair, Family$, Greyhound Prk, Rite Aid, Rouse's Mkt, transmissions, S Chevron/dsl Bellingraf Gardens, I-10 Kamping, Paynes RV Park
10	Rd 39, Bayou La Batre, Dawes, N Waffle House Kenworth

MOBILE

THEODORE

AL

INTERSTATE 10 Cont'd

Exit #	Services
4	AL 188 E, to Grand Bay, N Energize/Blimpie, Shell/Subway, TA/Country Pride/dsl/scales/24hr/ @ Arby's, McDonald's, Sam's Super Burger, Waffle House Bumper Parts, S Chevron Hardee's Trav-L-Kamp
1mm	**Welcome Ctr eb full facilities, info, litter barrels, petwalk, RV dump**
0mm	Alabama/Mississippi state line

INTERSTATE 20

Exit #	Services
215mm	Alabama/Georgia state line, Central/Eastern time zone
213mm	**Welcome Ctr wb, 24hr security, full facilities, info, litter barrels, petwalk RV dump, vending**
210	AL 49, Abernathy, N fireworks, S fireworks
209mm	Tallapoosa River, **weigh sta wb**
208mm	No services
205	AL 46, to Heflin, N BP/dsl 205 Cafe Cane Creek RV Park (2mi), Exit 205 Tire Ctr, Smith Farms, S Shell/dsl/24hr Truck Repair
199	AL 9, Heflin, N Hardee's, McDonald's, Vallarta Grill Best Value Inn Chevrolet, Ford, S Chevron/dsl, SuperMart/dsl
198mm	Talladega Nat Forest eastern boundary
191	US 431, to US 78
188	to US 78, to Anniston, N Exxon/Subway, Samco/dsl, Shell/dsl Cracker Barrel, Fuji Japanese, IHOP, KFC, LoneStar Steaks, Los Mexicanos, Mellow Mushroom, Waffle House, Wendy's, Zaxby's Comfort Suites, Country Inn&Suites, Courtyard, Fairfield Inn, Hampton Inn, Hilton Garden, Holiday Inn Express, Home 2 Suites, Quality Inn, Sleep Inn Dandy RV Ctr, GS RV Park, Harley-Davidson, Honda, Lowe's, Nissan, O'Reilly Parts, Toyota/Scion, S Chevron/dsl Arby's, Ezell's Fish Camp, Firehouse Subs, Golden Corral, Longhorn Steaks, Mexico Lindo Grill, Olive Garden, Panera Bread AAA, AT&T, Best Buy, Dick's, GNC, Hobby Lobby, Home Depot, Kohl's, Old Navy, Petsmart, Publix, Ross, Sams Club/dsl, Target, TJ Maxx, Verizon
185	AL 21, to Ft McClellan, to Anniston, N Chevron/dsl, GrubMart/dsl, Texaco Applebee's, Arby's, Bojangles, Burger King, Capt D's, China Luck, CiCi's Pizza, Hardee's, HoneyBaked Ham, Jack's Rest., Logan's Roadhouse, Los Mexicanos, McAlister's Deli, McDonald's, O'Charley's, Pizza Hut, Red Lobster, Red Pepper Grill, Shoney's, Sonic, Starbucks, Super Buffet, Taco Bell, Waffle House, Western Sizzlin Best Value Inn, Liberty Inn, Red Carpet Inn $General, Advance Parts, Aldi Foods, BooksAMillion, CVS Drug, Dillard's, Firestone/auto, Ford, JC Penney, Martin's Foods, Rite Aid, Sears/auto, S Chevron/dsl, Kangaroo/dsl/scales, Murphy USA/dsl, RaceWay, Valero/Subway/dsl Chick-fil-A, Jefferson's Rest, Outback Steaks, Waffle House, Wendy's Comfort Inn, EconoLodge, Key West Inn, Motel 6, Super 8 H, $Tree, Cobb Automotive, Walmart
179	AL 202, to US 78, to Munford, Coldwater, N Chevron/Subway/dsl China King, Jack's Rest $General, Anniston Army Depot, Rite Aid, Winn Dixie, S Texaco/dsl
173	AL 5, Eastaboga, S MapCo/cafe Stuckey's to Speedway/Hall of Fame
168	AL 77, to Talladega, N Citgo/dsl, Marathon/KFC/Taco Bell, QV/Domino's Jack's Rest, Waffle House, S AOC/Burger King, Chevron/Subway/dsl, Race City TC/diner/dsl/scales

ANNISTON

Exit #	Services
168	Continued McDonald's, MT Grill, Rana's Mexican Comfort Inn, Day Inn, Lincoln Inn Hall of Fame, to Speedway
165	Embry Cross Roads, N Hi-Tech/dsl, Pilot/Subway/ds scales/24hr Paradise Island RV Park, S 165 TP/Hudd House/dsl, I-20TrkStp/rest./dsl/scales/24hr Doghouse Gr McCaig Motel
164mm	Coosa River
162	US 78, Riverside, N Safe Harbor RV Park, S Texaco/d Best Value Inn/rest.
158	US 231, Pell City, N Marathon/dsl, Murphy USA/d Arby's, Chick-fil-A, Cracker Barrel, El Cazador, Golden Ru BBQ, Jade E Chinese, Krystal, Wendy's, Zaxby's Comfo Suites, Hampton Inn, Holiday Inn Express H, $Tree, Ci Tire, Home Depot, Radio Shack, URGENT CARE, Walgreens Walmart/Subway, S Shell/dsl, Texaco/dsl, Valero Akit Japanese, Burger King, Dunkin Donuts/Baskin Robbins, Hard ee's, Jack's Rest., KFC, Little Caesar's, McDonald's, Pell Cit Steaks, Pizza Hut, Subway, Taco Bell, Waffle House Qual ity Inn $General, AutoZone, CVS Drug, Ford, O'Reilly Parts Verizon
156	US 78 E, to Pell City, S Chevron/dsl, Shell/dsl
153	US 78, Chula Vista
152	Cook Springs
147	Brompton, N Citgo, Valero TC/dsl/scales/24hr, S Loves/McDonalds/Subway/dsl/scales/24hr, Valero/dsl/del
144	US 411, Leeds, N Marathon/dsl, RaceWay/dsl, Shell/Subway Arby's, Bojangles, Burger King, Cracker Barrel, Krystal Logan's Roadhouse, Milo's Burgers, Pizza Hut, Ruby Tuesday Waffle House, Wendy's, Zaxby's Best Western, Comfort Inn Super 8 $Tree, Food Giant, Verizon, S Chevron, Race Way/dsl Capt D's, Chick-fil-A, El Cazador Mexican, Guadalajara Jalisco Mexican, Hardee's, KFC, Little Caesar's, McDonald's, Supreme East Buffet, Taco Bell, Waffle House Days Inn $General, Advance Parts, AT&T, AutoZone, Lowe's, O'Reilly Parts, Radio Shack, Walgreens, Walmart/Subway
140	US 78, Leeds, N Distinctive Outlets/Famous Brands, S Chevron, Marathon Subway Best Value Inn, Hampton Inn Bass Pro Shop
139mm	Cahaba River
136	I-459 S, to Montgomery, Tuscaloosa
135	US 78, Old Leeds Rd, N Shell/dsl B'ham Race Course
133	US 78, to Kilgore Memorial Dr, (wb return at 132), N Chevron, Exxon/dsl Golden Rule BBQ, Hamburger Heaven, Jack's, Krystal, Waffle House Best Value Inn, Siesta Motel same as 132, S Shell McDonald's Hampton Inn, Holiday Inn Express, Quality Inn, Rime Inn/Suites Sam's Club/dsl, Tire Engineers
132b a	US 78, Crestwood Blvd, N Chevron, Exxon/dsl Golden Rule BBQ, Hamburger Heaven, Jack's, Krystal, Subway, Villa Fiesta Mexican, Waffle House Best Value Inn, Siesta Motel $General, Aamco, O'Reilly Parts, same as 133, S Chevron, Exxon, Marathon/dsl, Murphy Express/dsl, Shell, Texaco/dsl Arby's, Bojangles, Burger King, Capt D's, Chick-fil-A, Domino's, El Cazador Mexican, Hacienda Mexican, Honeybaked Ham, IHOP, KFC, Logan's Roadhouse, Los Arcos Mexican, McDonald's, Milo's Burgers, New China Buffet, Olive Garden, Pizza Hut, Starbucks, Taco Bell, Zaxby's Comfort Inn, Delux Inn,

PELL CITY

LEEDS

AL

INTERSTATE 20 Cont'd

BIRMINGHAM

132b a	Continued Garden Suites, $Tree, Advance Parts, Aldi Foods, Burlington Coats, Firestone/auto, Food Smart, Home Depot, Office Depot, Ross, TJ Maxx, Tuesday Morning, URGENT CARE, Verizon, Walgreens, Walmart
130b	US 11, 1st Ave, N Chevron, Marathon, Petro AutoZone, Family$, Piggly Wiggly, S Exxon/dsl McDonald's, Pacific Seafood Relax Inn, Sky Inn
130a	I-59 N, to Gadsden
I-59 S and I-20 W run together from B'ham to Meridian, MS	
129	Airport Blvd, N Clarion airport, S BP, Shell/dsl, Shell/dsl Hardee's, Kabob House Best Inn, Holiday Inn
128	AL 79, Tallapoosa St, N Exxon/Wings/dsl, Kangaroo/Subway/dsl/scales
126b	31st St, N Shell/dsl, Texaco/dsl McDonald's Family$
126a	US 31, US 280, 26th St, Carraway Blvd, N Church's, KFC, Rally's
125b	22nd St, N Subway Sheraton, Westin
125a	17th St, to downtown
124b a	I-65, S to Montgomery, N to Nashville
123	US 78, Arkadelphia Rd, N Chevron, Jet-Pep, Pilot/Wendy's/dsl/scales/24hr (0.5mi), Shell/dsl Popeye's Days Inn, S to Legion Field
121	Bush Blvd (from wb, no return), Ensley, N Exxon, Marathon
120	AL 269, 20th St, Ensley Ave, N Jet-Pep KFC Honda, S Chevron, Toyota/Scion
119b	Ave I (from wb)
119a	Lloyd Noland Pwky, N Chevron/dsl, Sunoco/dsl Burger King, Fairfield Seafood, McDonald's, Subway, S Mobil, Texaco
118	AL 56, Valley Rd, Fairfield, S Shell Papa John's Best Inn Advance Parts, Home Depot, URGENT CARE
115	Allison-Bonnett Memorial Dr, N Marathon/dsl, RaceWay/dsl, Shell/dsl Church's, Jack's, Los Reyes, Subway, Zaxby's Advance Parts, O'Reilly Parts, USPO

BESSEMER

113	18th Ave, to Hueytown, S Chevron/dsl, Marathon McDonald's
112	18th St, 19th St, Bessemer, N RaceWay/dsl, Shell Jack's Rest. tire/repair, S Chevron, Sunoco/dsl KFC, Muffaletta's Italian, Rally's, Subway, Sykes BBQ Advance Parts, FMS Drug, Lowe's, NAPA, O'Reilly Parts, Walgreens
110	AL Adventure Pkwy, N Splash Adventure Funpark, S
108	US 11, AL 5 N, Academy Dr, N Marathon Applebee's, Carnation Buffet, Catfish Cabin, Cracker Barrel, Waffle House Best Western, Comfort Inn, Country Inn&Suites, Fairfield Inn, Holiday Inn Express, Quality Inn, ValuePlace Chevrolet, Chrysler/Dodge/Jeep, Nissan, S Marathon, Texaco/Church's/dsl Burger King, Domino's, Jade Garden, Little Caesars, McDonald's, Milo's Burgers, Ruby Tuesday, Sonic, Wendy's, Zaxby's Economy Inn, Hampton Inn, Knights Inn, Motel 6, $Tree, BigLots, Ford, PepBoys, Radio Shack, to civic ctr, Verizon, Walmart/Subway
106	I-459 N, to Montgomery
104	Rock Mt Lake, S FLYING J/Subway/dsl/LP/24hr
100	to Abernant, N Loves/McDonald's/Subway/dsl/scales/24hr, S Exxon, Marathon, Petro/Valero/Iron Skillet/Popeyes/dsl/scales/24hr/ @ $General, Tannehill Ironworks Camping, Tannehill SP (3mi)

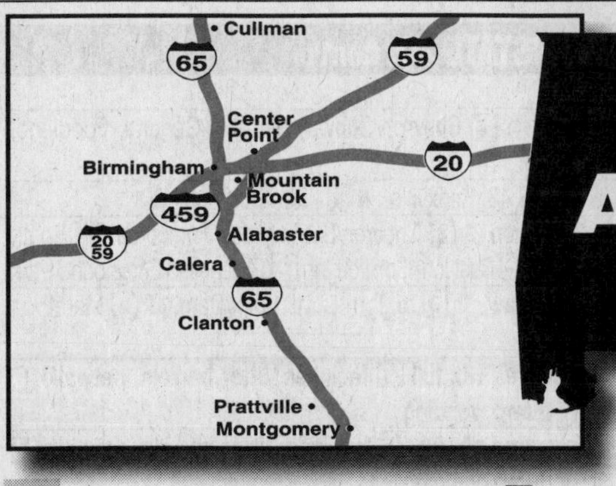

TUSCALOOSA

97	US 11 S, AL 5 S, to W Blocton, S Chevron/KFC/dsl, Exxon/Subway/dsl, Texaco/dsl Jack's Rest., La Tortilla Grill Cahaba River NWR
89	Mercedes Dr, N Greystone Inn, S Mercedes Auto Plant
86	Vance, to Brookwood, N Marathon/Huddle House/Subway/dsl, Shell/dsl/rest./24hr
85mm	**rest area both lanes, full facilities, litter barrels, petwalk, , , RV dump, vending**
79	US 11, University Blvd, Coaling, S Chevron/dsl, Texaco/dsl
77	Cottondale, N Chevron/McDonald's, TA/BP/Taco Bell/dsl/scales/24hr/@, Wilco/Wendy's/dsl/scales/24hr Arby's, Pizza Hut, Ruby Tuesday Hampton Inn, Microtel Blue Beacon, SpeedCo, USPO, S Chevrolet
76	US 11, E Tuscaloosa, Cottondale, N Chevron, Marathon, Shell/dsl Burger King, Cracker Barrel, Waffle House Centerstone Inn, Howard Johnson, ValuePlace, Western Motel, Wingate Inn Sunset 2 RV Park, transmissions, S Pilot/Subway/dsl/scales/24hr, Texaco/dsl Rodeway Inn
73	US 82, McFarland Blvd, Tuscaloosa, N BP, Chevron/dsl, Marathon, RaceWay 5 Guys Burgers, Applebee's, Arby's, Buffalo Wild Wings, Burger King, Capt D's, Chick-fil-A, Chipotle, Full Moon BBQ, Jason's Deli, Krystal, Longhorn Steaks, Moe's SW Grill, O'Charley's, Olive Garden, Panera Bread, Popeyes, Red Lobster, Shrimp Basket, Starbucks, TCBY, Waffle House Best Value Inn, Best Western, Comfort Suites, Guest Lodge, Holiday Inn Express, Masters Inn, $General, Aamco, Advance Parts, AT&T, Barnes&Noble, Belk, Best Buy, CVS Drug, Firestone/auto, Gander Mtn, Goodyear/auto, Home Depot, JC Penney, Michael's, OK Tire, Old Navy, PepBoys, Rite Aid, Ross, Sears/auto, SteinMart, Target, Verizon, vet, S Jet-Pep/dsl, Marathon Buffet City, Checkers, Cheddar's, Chili's, Hardee's, KFC, Logan's Roadhouse, McDonald's, Papa John's, Pizza Hut, Sonic, Subway, Taco Bell, Taco Casa, Trey Yuen Cinese Ambassador Inn, Candlewood Suites, Country Inn&Suites, Days Inn, EconoLodge, La Quinta, Motel 6, Quality Inn, Ramada Inn, Super 8 $General, $Tree, Chrysler/Dodge/Jeep, NAPA, Office Depot, Rite Aid, Sam's Club/gas, TJ Maxx, U-Haul, Walmart/Subway
71b	I-359, Al 69 N, to Tuscaloosa, N, to Stillman Coll, U of AL
71a	AL 69 S, to Moundville, S Chevron, Citgo/dsl, Mapco/Quiznos/dsl, Shell/dsl Arby's, Baumhower's Rest., Chick-fil-A, Costa BBQ, Hooters, IHOP, LoneStar Steaks, OutBack Steaks, Pizza Hut, Ryan's, Waffle House, Wendy's, Zaxby's Baymont Inn, Courtyard, Fairfield Inn, Hilton Garden Advance Parts, Goodyear/auto, Kia/Mazda/VW, K-Mart, Lowe's, O'Reilly Parts, PepBoys, to Mound SM, URGENT CARE
68	Northport-Tuscaloosa Western Bypass
64mm	Black Warrior River

[gas] = gas [food] = food [lodging] = lodging [other] = other [RS] = rest stop

AL

INTERSTATE 20 Cont'd

Exit #	Services
62	Fosters, N [gas] Chevron/Subway/dsl [other] $General, Foodland, USPO, vet
52	US 11, US 43, Knoxville, N [gas] Marathon/dsl
45	AL 37, Union, S [gas] Chevron/Subway/dsl, Texaco/dsl [food] South Fork Rest [lodging] Best Inn, Comfort Inn [other] Greene Co Greyhound Park
40	AL 14, Eutaw, N [other] to Tom Bevill Lock/Dam, S [gas] Marathon [other] [H]
39mm	**[RS] rest area wb, full [handicapped] facilities, litter barrels, petwalk [phone] [picnic] RV dump, vending**
38mm	**[RS] rest area eb, full [handicapped] facilities, litter barrels, petwalk [phone] [picnic] RV dump, vending**
32	Boligee, N [gas] Marathon/rest./dsl/24hr, S [gas] Chevron/Subway/dsl
27mm	Tenn-Tom Waterway, Tombigbee River
23	Rd 20, Epes, to Gainesville
17	AL 28, Livingston, S [gas] Chevron/Subway/dsl, Exxon/L&B/dsl/24hr, Shell/dsl, Spirit [food] Burger King, Diamond Jim's/Mrs Donna's, McDonald's, Pizza Hut [lodging] Comfort Inn, Western Inn [other] repair/24hr
8	AL 17, York, S [gas] Marathon/New Orleans Grill/dsl/scales/@ [lodging] Best Inn
1	to US 80 E, Cuba, S [gas] Chevron/dsl, Citgo/rest./dsl
.5mm	**Welcome Ctr eb, full [handicapped] facilities, litter barrels, petwalk [phone] [picnic] RV dump, vending**
I-20 E and I-59 N run together frm Meridian, MS to B'ham	
0mm	Alabama/Mississippi state line

INTERSTATE 22 (Future)

Exit #	Services
96	I-65, N to Nashville, S to Birmingham, **I-22 begins/ends**
93	Rd 77
91	Rd 105, to Brookside
89	Rd 65, to Adamsville, Graysville
87	Rd 112, to Graysville
85	US 78, Birmingham
81	Rd 45, W Jefferson
78	Rd 81, Dora, Sumiton, N [gas] TJ's/dsl
72	Rd 61, Cordova
70	Rd 22, Cordova, Parish
65	Bevill Ind Pkwy, Jasper, N [lodging] Hampton Inn (3mi) [other] [H], to Walker Co Lake, S [gas] Love's /McDonald's/Subway/dsl/scales/24hr [food] Cracker Barrel [lodging] Sleep Inn [other] Buick/Cadillac/Chevrolet/GMC
63	AlL 269, Jasper, Parish, N [gas] Chevron/deli/dsl
61	AL 69, Jasper, Tuscaloosa, N [gas] RJ's [food] Deano's Hickory Pit
57	AL 118 E, Jasper, N [gas] Chevron, Shell/dsl [food] The Barn Rest.
53	to AL 118
52	to 118, Carbon Hill
46	Rd 11, Carbon Hill, Nauvoo, S [gas] Chevron/dsl, Shell
39	AL 13, Natural Bridge, Eldridge
34	AL 233, Glen Allen, Natural Bridge
30	AL 129, Brilliant, Winfield, S [gas] Chevron/deli/dsl, [food] Huddle House [lodging] Hampton Inn
26	AL 44, Brilliant, Guin, S [lodging] Holiday Inn Express [other] [H]
22	Rd 45
16	US 43, US 278, Hamilton, Guin, S [gas] Shell/deli/dsl
14	Hamilton, N [gas] Texaco/dsl [food] Huddle House [lodging] Days Inn (1mi), EconoLodge (1mi), Keywest Inn
11	AL 17, Hamilton, Sulligent, N [gas] Citgo/dsl [other] [H]
7	Hamilton, Weston, N [other] [H]
3	Rd 33
0mm	Alabama/Mississippi State Line

FT PAYNE

GADSDEN

INTERSTATE 59

Exit #	Services
241.5mm	Alabama/Georgia state line, Central/Eastern time zone
241mm	**Welcome Ctr sb, full [handicapped] facilities, litter barrels, petwalk [phone] [picnic] RV dump, vending**
239	to US 11, Sulphur Springs Rd, E [other] camping
231	AL 40, AL 117, Hammondville, Valley Head, E [other] camping (5mi), DeSoto SP, W [gas] Victory Fuel
224	49th St, to Ft Payne
222	US 11, to Ft Payne, E 1 mi [gas] Delta [food] Arby's, Hardee's, Jack's Rest., KFC, Krystal, Pizza Hut, SteviB's Pizza, Subway, Toke Thai Grill, Wingstop [lodging] Quality Inn [other] Chevrolet, Foodland/dsl, W [gas] Citgo/dsl, JetPep/dsl [food] Waffle King
218	AL 35, Ft Payne, E [food] Capt D's, Don Chico Mexican, DQ, Jack's, Jefferson's Burgers, McDonald's, New China, Papa John's, Sonic, Taco Bell, Western Sizzlin, Zaxby's [other] $General, Advance Parts, Alabama Museum, AutoZone, BigLots, Buick/GMC, Chrysler/Dodge/Jeep, O'Reilly Parts, URGENT CARE, W [gas] Kangaroo/dsl, MapCo, Murphy USA/dsl, Victory Fuel [food] Burger King, Chow King, Cracker Barrel, Hardee's, Huddle House, Los Arcos, Ruby Tuesday, Ryan's, Santa Fe Steaks, Subway, Waffle House [lodging] Days Inn, EconoLodge, Hampton Inn, Holiday Inn Express [other] [H] $Tree, AT&T, Ford/Lincoln, GNC, Lowe's, Verizon, Walgreens, Walmart, Will's Creek RV Park
205	AL 68, Collinsville, E [gas] Delta [food] Jack's Rest. [lodging] Travelers Inn [other] to Little River Canyon, Weiss Lake, W [gas] BP/dsl, MapCo
188	AL 211, to US 11, Gadsden, E [gas] Jet-Pep [other] Noccalula Falls Camping, W [gas] Clean Fuels/dsl/E85
183	US 431, US 278, Gadsden, E [gas] Jet-Pep/dsl, Shell, Texaco/dsl [food] Magic Burger, Waffle House [lodging] Days Inn, HomeLodge, Rodeway Inn [other] st police, W [gas] Chevron, Exxon, Jet-Pep [food] McDonald's, Pizza Hut, Subway, Taco Bell
182	I-759, to Gadsden
181	AL 77, Rainbow City, to Gadsden, E [gas] Petro/Popeye's/dsl/scales/24hr/ @ [lodging] Days Inn, W [gas] Kangaroo/dsl, Murphy Express/dsl [food] Arby's, Bubba Rito's SW Grill, Cracker Barrel, Domino's, Hardee's, Los Arcos, Lucky Wok, McDonald's, Old Mexico Grille, Ray's BBQ, Ruby Tuesday, Subway, Waffle House, Wendy's [lodging] Best Western, Comfort Suites, Fairfield Inn, Hampton Inn, Holiday Inn Express [other] $General, $Tree, O'Reilly Parts, Radio Shack, Verizon, Walmart/Papa John's
174	to Steele, E [gas] Love's /Subway/Chester's/dsl/scales/24hr, W [gas] JetPep/dsl, Shell/rest/dsl
168mm	**[RS] sb, full [handicapped] facilities, litter barrels, petwalk [phone] [picnic] RV dump, vending**
166	US 231, Whitney, to Ashville, E [gas] BP, W [gas] Texaco/dsl [food] Huddle House, Jack's Rest., Subway
165mm	**[RS] nb, full [handicapped] facilities, litter barrels, petwalk, [phone] [picnic] RV dump, vending**
156	AL 23, to US 11, Springville, to St Clair Springs, W [gas] Murphy USA/dsl, Shell /dsl [food] Azteca's Mexican, China Stix, Hardee's, Pizza Hut, Taco Bell, Waffle House [other] $Tree, AT&T, Walmart/Subway
154	AL 174, Springville, to Odenville, E [gas] Exxon/dsl, W [gas] Chevron, Citgo, MapCo, Shell/dsl, Valero/Subway [food] Choppin Block Rest., Jack's Rest., McDonald's, Sal's Rest., Smokin Grill BBQ [other] vet

 [gas] = gas [food] = food [lodging] = lodging [other] = other [RS] = rest stop

AL

INTERSTATE 59 Cont'd

Exit #	Services
148	to US 11, Argo, E [gas] Shell [food] Jack's, Subway
143	Mt Olive Church Rd, Deerfoot Pkwy, E [gas] Chevron/dsl/CNG, Shell/dsl (1mi) [food] Munoz Mexica [other] Publix (1mi)
141	to Trussville, Pinson, E [gas] Bama/dsl, Shell/Subway/dsl, Texaco/dsl [food] Applebee's, Cracker Barrel, Guthrie's, LoneStar Steaks, McDonald's, Papa John's, Pizza Hut, Taco Bell, Waffle House, Wendy's [lodging] Comfort Inn, Holiday Inn Express, Quality In [other] Harley-Davidson, W [gas] BP, Chevron, Shell/dsl [food] Arby's, Buffalo Wild Wings, Burger King, Chick-fil-A, Costa's Italian, DQ, East Buffet, Frontera Grill, Jack's, Konomi Japanese, Krystal, Little Caesars, Milo's Burgers, Moe's SW Grill, Momma Goldberg's Deli, Palace Asian, Paul's Hotdogs, Ruby Tuesday, Seafood&Chicken Box, Whataburger, Zaxby's [other] $Tree, Ace Hardware, Advance Parts, Aldi Foods, AT&T, BigLots, CVS Drug, GNC, K-Mart, Kohl's, Marshalls, Office Depot, Petsmart, Radio Shack, Sam's Club/gas, Verizon, vet, Walgreens, Walmart/Subway
137	I-459 S, to Montgomery, Tuscaloosa
134	to AL 75, Roebuck Pkwy, W [gas] Chevron, Marathon/Kangaroo, Murphy USA/dsl, Shell/dsl [food] Arby's, Burger King, Chick-fil-A, China Buffet, Hardee's, Los Arcos, McDonald's, Milo's Burgers, Pizza Hut, Subway, Taco Bell, Waffle House [lodging] Best Inn [other] [H], $Tree, Aldi Foods, AT&T, CVS Drug, GNC, Honda, NTB, O'Reilly Parts, Rite Aid, URGENT CARE, V Tires, Walgreens, Walmart/Burger King
133	4th St, to US 11 (from nb), W [food] Papa John's [other] $General, same as 134, USPO
132	US 11 N, 1st Ave, E same as 131, W [gas] Chevron, Shell/dsl [food] Krispy Kreme [other] city park
131	Oporto-Madrid Blvd (from nb), E [gas] Chevron, Marathon/Subway [food] Church's, Little Caesars, Rally's [other] CVS Drug, Family$, O'Reilly Parts, same as 132, U-Haul
130	I-20, E to Atlanta, W to Tuscaloosa

I-59 S and I-20 W run together from B'ham to Mississippi. See Alabama Interstate 20, exit 129-1.

INTERSTATE 65

Exit #	Services
366mm	Alabama/Tennessee state line
365	AL 53, to Ardmore, E [gas] Pure [lodging] Budget Inn
364mm	**W Welcome Ctr sb, full [handicapped] facilities, info, litter barrels, petwalk, [phone] [picnic] RV dump, vending**
361	Elkmont, W [gas] BP/dsl, HQ/rest./dsl [food] Momma D's Rest. [other] antiques, repair
354	US 31 S, to Athens, W [gas] Chevron/dsl, Texaco/dsl [food] Capt D's, China Dragon, Domino's, Jack's Rest., Little Caesars, McDonald's, Pizza Hut, Rooster's Cafe, Subway [lodging] Mark Motel [other] [H] $General, Advance Parts, city park, CVS Drug, HomeTown Mkt, K-Mart, Northgate RV Park, Rite Aid, Walgreens
351	US 72, to Athens, Huntsville, E [gas] Exxon, RaceWay/dsl, Shell/Subway, Texaco/dsl [food] Burger King, Casa Blanca Mexican, Clark's Rest, Cracker Barrel, Jack's, Las Tejanas Mexican, Lawler's BBQ, McDonald's/RV Parking, New China Buffet, Pepper's Deli, Waffle House, Wendy's [lodging] Country Hearth Inn, Hampton Inn, Quality Inn, Travel Inn [other] $General, AT&T, Publix, Russell Stover, Verizon, vet W [gas] BP, Chevron/dsl, Citgo/dsl, Murphy USA [food] Applebee's, Arby's, Bojangles, Burger King, Catfish Cabin, Chick-fil-A, DQ, Firehouse Subs, Hardee's, IHOP, KFC, Krystal, Logan's Roadhouse, Papa John's, Papa Murphy's,

ATHENS

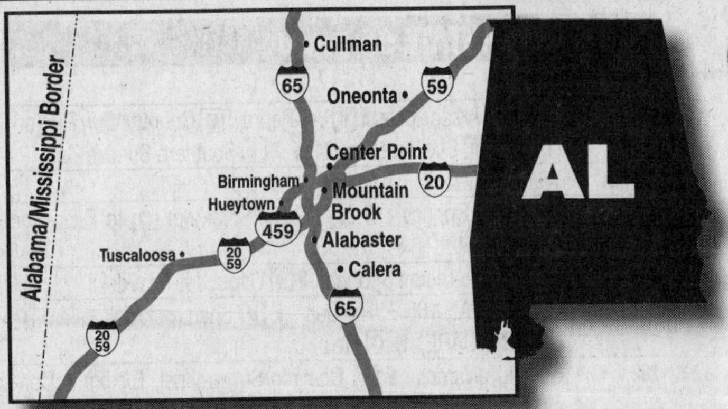

DECATUR

Exit #	Services
351	Continued Pizza Hut, Ruby Tuesday, Shoney's, Sonic, Starbucks, SteakOut, Subway, Taco Bell, Zaxby's [lodging] Best Western, Days Inn, Fairfield Inn, Holiday Inn Express, Sleep Inn, Super 8 [other] [H] $General, $Tree, Advance Parts, Big 10 Tire, Big Lots, Chevrolet, Chrysler/Dodge/Jeep, Ford, Goodyear/auto, Lowe's, O'Reilly Parts, Pepboys, Radio Shack, SaveALot Foods, Staples, to Joe Wheeler SP, Tuesday Morning, Verizon, Walmart
347	Brownsferry Rd, Huntsville, Swan Creek RV Park
340b	I-565, to Huntsville, E to Alabama Space & Rocket Ctr
340a	AL 20, to Decatur, W [gas] Chevron/dsl, RaceWay [lodging] Courtyard, Hampton Inn, Holiday Inn
337mm	Tennessee River
334	AL 67, Priceville, to Decatur, E [gas] BP/dsl, RaceWay/dsl [food] JW's Steaks [lodging] Days Inn, Super 8 [other] $General, Family$, Foodland, W [gas] Chevron/dsl, Pilot/Subway/Wendy's/dsl/scales/24hr [food] Burger King, DQ, Hardee's, Krystal, McDonald's/playplace, Pizza Hut, Smokehouse BBQ, Taste of China, Waffle House [lodging] Comfort Inn [other] [H] Hood RV Ctr
328	AL 36, Hartselle, E [food] Cracker Barrel, W [gas] Cowboys/dsl, Jet-Pep/dsl, Shell/dsl, Ztrac [food] Huddle House [lodging] Best Value Inn [other] vet
325	Thompson Rd, to Hartselle
322	AL 55, to US 31, to Falkville, Eva, E [gas] BP/Chester's/dsl, W [gas] Chevron, Loves/McDonald's/Subway/dsl/scales/24hr [food] Momma's Grill [other] $General
318	US 31, to Lacon, E [gas] BP/Stuckey's [lodging] Lacon Motel
310	AL 157, Cullman, West Point, E [gas] Chevron, Conoco/Subway/dsl, Marathon/dsl, Shell/dsl, Texaco/Wendy's/dsl [food] Arby's, Backyard Burger, Burger King, Cracker Barrel, Denny's, KFC, Logan's Roadhouse, McDonald's, New China, Ruby Tuesday, Taco Bell, Waffle House [lodging] Best Western, Comfort Suites, Hampton Inn, Holiday Inn Express, Quality Inn, Sleep Inn [other], Buick/GMC, Ford/Lincoln, Piggly Wiggly, W [gas] BP/dsl, Exxon/dsl [lodging] Best Value Inn
308	US 278, Cullman, E [lodging] Days Inn [other] Smith Farms, W [gas] Chevron [other] Chrysler/Dodge/Jeep, flea mkt
304	AL 69 N, Good Hope, to Cullman, E [gas] Exxon/dsl, Jet-Pep/dsl, Shell/rest/dsl/scales, Wilco/Hess/Wendy's/Dunkin Donuts/dsl/scales/24hrs [food] Hardee's, Jack's Rest., Waffle House [lodging] EconoLodge [other] [H] dsl/rv repair, Good Hope Camping, Kountry Mile RV Ctr, W [gas] Jet-Pep, to Smith Lake Camping [other] $General
301mm	**E [RS] both lanes full [handicapped] facilities, litter barrels, petwalk [phone] [picnic] RV dump, vending**
299	AL 69 S, to Jasper, E [gas] Sunoco/dsl [other] Millican RV Ctr, repair/tires, W [gas] HQ, Petro/Conoco/Iron Skillet/dsl/scales/24hr, Shell/McDonald's/dsl, Texaco/dsl [food] Jack's Rest., Subway [other] $General, Parts City

CULLMAN

[gas] = gas [food] = food [lodging] = lodging [other] = other [RS] = rest stop

INTERSTATE 65 Cont'd

Exit #	Services
291	AL 91, to Arkadelphia, E [gas] Jet-Pep/dsl [other] Country View RV Park (1mi), W [gas] Shell/rest./dsl/24hr/ @ [food] Southern Sunrise Cafe
291mm	Warrior River
289	to Blount Springs, W [gas] BP/DQ/Stuckey's [other] to Rickwood Caverns SP
287	US 31 N, to Blount Springs, E [gas] Citgo, Jet-Pep/dsl
284	US 31 S, AL 160 E, Hayden, E [gas] Shamrock/dsl, Valero [other] URGENT CARE, W [other] tires
282	AL 140, Warrior, E [gas] Chevron/Subway/dsl, Exxon/McDonald's, FuelZ/Dunkin Donuts/Little Caesars/dsl [food] Hardee's, Pizza Hut, Taco Bell, W [gas] BP
281	US 31, to Warrior, E [other] Chevrolet
280	to US 31, to Warrior, E [gas] Chevron/dsl [other] Chevrolet, vet
279mm	Warrior River
275	to US 31, Morris
272	Mt Olive Rd, E [gas] Shell/dsl [other] LDS Temple, W [gas] BP/dsl, Chevron/dsl [food] Jack's Rest. [other] $General
271	Fieldstown Rd, E [gas] BP/Circle K, Chevron/dsl, Exxon, Murphy USA/dsl, RaceWay/dsl [food] Arby's, Buffalo Wild Wings, Capt D's, Chick-fil-A, DQ, Guthrie's Diner, Habanero's Mexican, Jim'n Nick's BBQ, KFC, Little Caesars, McDonald's, Milo's Burgers, Panera Bread, Pasquales Pizza, Pizza Hut, Ryan's, Sonic, Subway, Taco Bell, Waffle House, Wendy's, Zaxby's [lodging] Microtel [other] $General, $Tree, Advance Parts, AT&T, AutoZone, CVS, Hobby Lobby, Kia, NAPA, PepBoys, Publix, Radio Shack, URGENT CARE, Verizon, Walgreens, Walmart/McDonald's, W [gas] Shell/dsl [food] Cracker Barrel [lodging] Best Western
267	Walkers Chapel Rd, to Fultondale, E [gas] Chevron/dsl, Jet-Pep, Murphy Express/dsl, Shell/Subway/dsl [food] 5 Guys Burgers, Applebee's, Arby's, Bojangles, Burger King, Casa Fiesta, Chick-fil-A, Chili's, Domino's, Firehouse Subs, Fullmoon BBQ, Hardee's, Jack's Rest., Jalisco Mexican, Logan's Roadhouse, McDonald's, O'Charley's, Outback Steaks, Stix Asian, Waffle House, Whataburger, Zaxby's [lodging] Comfort Suites, Fairfield Inn, Hampton Inn, Holiday Inn Express, La Quinta [other] $General, AAA, Aldi Foods, AT&T, Best Buy, Books-A-Million, CVS Drug, GNC, JC Penney, Lowe's, O'Reilly Parts, Rite Aid, Ross, Target, URGENT CARE, USPO, Verizon, Volvo/Mack Trucks, Winn-Dixie, W [gas] Chevron/dsl [food] Porky's Pride BBQ
266	US 31, Fultondale, E [gas] Chevron/dsl [lodging] Days Inn, Super 8
265	I-22 W, to Memphis
264	41st Ave, W [gas] FLYING J/Denny's/dsl/LP/scales/24hr, LNG
263	33rd Ave, E [gas] Chevron/dsl, W [gas] Exxon
262b a	16th St, Finley Ave, E [gas] Chevron, Marathon/dsl, Sunoco/dsl [other] Kenworth, W [gas] Chevron, Fuel City/dsl [food] Capt D's, McDonald's, Popeye's
261b a	I-20/59, E to Gadsden, W to Tuscaloosa
260b a	6th Ave N, E [gas] Citgo, Shell, Texaco [food] Mrs Winner's [lodging] Tourway Inn [other] Chevrolet, Chrysler/Dodge/Jeep, Hyundai, Nissan, Subaru, W [gas] Chevron/dsl [other] Tire Pros, to Legion Field
259b a	University Blvd, 4th Ave, 5th Ave, E [gas] Chevron/dsl [food] Capt D's, McDonald's, Ted's Cafeteria [other] H, W [gas] Chevron/dsl [other] Goodyear
258	Green Springs Ave, E [gas] Chevron, Shell, Sunoco/dsl [food] Exotic Wings
256b a	Oxmoor Rd, E [gas] Exxon, Marathon, Mobil/dsl, Shell [food] Acapulco Grill, Alfredo's Pizza, Burger King, Domino's, Firehouse Subs, Hunan Rest., KFC, McDonald's, Papa Murphy's, Paw Paw Patch, Popeyes, Purple Onion, San Miguel Mexican, Taco
256b a	Continued Bell, The Baskits, Zaxby's [lodging] Howard Johnson [other] $Tree, Aldi Foods, AutoZone, BigLots, Firestone/auto, Food World, Fred's, K-Mart, Midas, Office Depot, Omega Tire Pros, PepBoys, Publix, Tire Engineers, Tuesday Morning, URGENT CARE, Walgreens, Walmart Mkt, W [gas] Chevron, Texaco/dsl [food] Hamburger Heaven, Hardee's, Jim'n Nick's BBQ, Waffle House [lodging] Best Inn, Best Value Inn, Comfort Inn, EconoLodge, Motel 6, Quality Inn, Super [other] Batteries+, Valley Tire, vet
255	Lakeshore Dr, E [gas] BP/Circle [other] H, to Samford U, URGENT CARE, W [gas] Chevron, Shell [food] Arby's, Chick-fil-A, Chili's, Costas BBQ, Hooters, IHOP, La Catrina Mexican, Landry's Seafood, McAlister's Deli, McDonald's, Milo's Burger, Moe's SW Grill, Mr Wang's, O'Charley's, Okinawa Grill, Outback Steaks, Starbucks, Subway, Taco Bell, Taco Casa, Wendy's [lodging] Best Western, Candlewood Suites, Country Inn&Suites, Drury Inn, Extended Stay, Hampton Inn, Hilton Garden, Holiday Inn, La Quinta, Residence Inn, TownePlace Suite [other] $Tree, AT&T, Goodyear/auto, Hobby Lobby, Lowe's, Radio Shack, Sam's Club/gas, Verizon, Walmart/Subway
254	Alford Ave, Shades Crest Rd, E [gas] Chevron [other] vet, W [gas] BP/dsl, Shell/dsl
252	US 31, Montgomery Hwy, E [gas] Chevron, Shell, Sunoco, Texaco/dsl [food] Arby's, Backyard Burger, Bruster's, Capt D's, Chuck-ECheese's, Hardee's, Ichiban Japanese, Milo's Burger, Waffle House [lodging] Baymont Inn, Days Inn [other] H Aamco, GMC, NAPA, PepBoys, Verizon, vet, Volvo, VW, W [gas] Exxon/dsl, Shell/dsl, Sunoco/dsl [food] Burger King, Chick-fil-A, FishMkt Rest., Full Moon BBQ, Golden Rule BBQ, Habanero's Mexican, Krispy Kreme, Krystal, Mandarin House, McDonald's, Outback Steaks, Papa John's, Papa Murphy's, Purple Onion, Salvatore's Pizza, Starbucks, Subway, Waffle House [lodging] EconoLodge [other] $Tree, Acura, Advance Parts, AutoZone, Cadillac, Chevrolet, Chrysler/Dodge/Jeep, Firestone, Goodyear/auto, Honda, Hyundai, Mr Transmission, Nissan, Publix, Rite Aid, Staples, TJ Maxx, vet
250	I-459, to US 280
247	Rd 17, Valleydale Rd, E [gas] BP/Circle K [food] Hardee's, Jeffersons Wing [other] Goodyear/auto, Lowe's, W [gas] Marathon, RaceWay/dsl, Shell/dsl [food] Arby's, Backyard Burger, IHOP, Milo's Burgers, Papa John's, RagTime Café, Subway, Waffle House, Zapatas Mexican [lodging] Homewood Suites, InTown Suites, La Quinta [other] Publix, Rite Aid, vet, Walgreens
246	AL 119, Cahaba Valley Rd, E [other] to Oak Mtn SP, W [gas] Chevron, Kangaroo/Subway/dsl/scales, Murphy USA/dsl, RaceWay/dsl, Shell/dsl [food] 2 Pesos Mexican, Applebee's, Arby's, Burger King, Capt D's, Chick-fil-A, Cracker Barrel, DQ, Dunkin Donuts, Golden Corral, Hooters, Johnny Ray's BBQ, KFC, Krystal, Margarita Grill, McAlister's Deli, McDonald's, Pizza Hut, Purple Onion, Ruby Tuesday, Sonic, Taco Bell, TX Roadhouse, Waffle House, Wendy's, Whataburger [lodging] Best Western, Comfort Suites, Fairfield Inn, Hampton Inn, Holiday Inn Express, Quality Inn, Ramada, Sleep Inn, Travelodge, ValuePlace [other] H $Tree, Advance Parts, AutoZone, Firestone/auto, Harley-Davidson, Kia, Mazda, NAPA, O'Reilly Parts, Verizon, Walmart
242	Rd 52, Pelham, E [gas] Chevron/dsl, Exxon/dsl, Shell/dsl [food] Johnny Ray's BBQ, Subway [other] CVS Drug, Publix W [lodging] Shelby Motel (2mi) [other] H Good Sam Camping (1mi)
238	US 31, Alabaster, Saginaw, E [gas] Murphy USA/dsl [food] Arby's, Buffalo Wild Wings, Chick-fil-A, DQ, Firehouse Subs, Full Moon BBQ, Habanero's Mexican, HoneyBaked Ham, Jim'n Nick's BBQ, Longhorn Steaks, McDonald's, Mizu Japanese, Moe's SW Grill, Momma Goldberg Deli, O'Charley's, Olive Garden, Panda House,

FULTONDALE

BIRMINGHAM

HOOVER

PELHAM

INTERSTATE 65 Cont'd

238 Continued
Panera Bread, Ruby Tuesday, Starbucks, Steak'n Shake, Taco Bell Candlewood Suites $Tree, AT&T, Belk, Best Buy, Books-A-Million, Dick's, GNC, JC Penney, Lowe's, NTB, Old Navy, Petsmart, Radio Shack, Ross, Target, TJ Maxx, URGENT CARE, Walmart/Subway, **W** Chevron/dsl, Shell/dsl Waffle House, Whataburger Shelby Motel

234 Shelby County **E** BP/Subway/dsl, **W** Chevron/dsl, Shell/dsl Buick/GMC, Camping World RV Ctr

231 US 31, Saginaw, **E** GasBoy, Murphy USA/dsl, Shell/dsl Bojangles, Capt D's, Cracker Barrel, Ezell's Catfish Cabin, McDonald's, Milo's Burgers, Pizza Hut, Subway, Taco Bell, Waffle House, Zaxby's, Zopapan Mexican Hampton Inn, Quality Inn $Tree, AT&T, Burton RV Ctr, Publix, Radio Shack, Rolling Hills RV Park, URGENT CARE, Verizon, Walmart/Subway

228 AL 25, to Calera, **E** Marathon/dsl, Shell/dsl Calera Inn, **W** Chevron/dsl Little Caesar's, Subway $General, Family$, to Brierfield Iron Works SP (15mi)

227mm Buxahatchie Creek

219 Union Grove, Thorsby, **E** Chevron/dsl, Exxon/Subway/dsl Peach Queen Camping, **W** Shell/dsl Jack's Rest., Smokey Hollow Rest.

213mm **both lanes full facilities, litter barrels, petwalk RV dump, vending**

212 AL 145, Clanton, **E** Chevron/dsl Nissan, Toyota/Scion, **W** Headco/dsl, Texaco/Subway H, Buick/Chevrolet/GMC, Chrysler/Dodge/Jeep, One Big Peach

208 Clanton, **E** Loves/Arby's/dsl/scales/24hr Higgins Ferry RV Park (8mi), **W** Exxon/dsl Shoney's Clanton Inn Dandy RV Park/Ctr, Heaton Pecans, KOA

205 US 31, AL 22, to Clanton, **E** Jet-Pep/dsl/E85, Shell/dsl, Texaco/dsl McDonald's, Waffle House, Whataburger Best Western, Days Inn, Holiday Inn Express, Scottish Inn Peach Park, to Confed Mem Park (9mi), **0-2 mi W** Chevron/dsl, Murphy USA/dsl, Shell/dsl Boomerang's Grill, Burger King, Capt D's, Jack's Rest., KFC, New China Buffet, Papa John's, Pizza Hut, San Marcos Mexican, Subway, Taco Bell, Wendy's, Zaxby's Key West Inn $General, $Tree, auto repair, Durbin Farms Mkt, Verizon, Walmart

200 to Verbena, **E** Texaco/dsl, **W** Sunoco

195 Worlds Largest Confederate Flag

186 US 31, Pine Level, **E** Confederate Mem Park (13mi), **W** Chevron/dsl, Exxon/dsl, Texaco/Subway/dsl Shann's Kitchen H

181 AL 14, to Prattville, **E** Chevron/dsl, Entec/dsl Jack's, **W** BP, Marathon/Kangaroo, QV, Shell/DQ/dsl Cracker Barrel, Los Toros, McDonald's, Ruby Tuesday, Subway, Waffle House, Wendy's EconoLodge, Hometowne Suites, La Quinta, Quality Inn, Super 8 H

179 US 82 W, Millbrook, **E** Chevron/dsl Country Inn&Suites, Key West Inn, Sleep Inn K&K RV Ctr/Park, **0-2 mi W** Liberty/dsl, Murphy Express/dsl, RaceWay/dsl, Shell/dsl Applebee's, Arby's, Beef'O'Brady's, Bruster's, Burger King, Capt. D's, Chappy's Deli, Chick-fil-A, Chipotle, CiCi's Pizza, City Buffet, El Patron, Five Guys, Hardee's, IHOP, Jim'n Nick's BBQ, KFC, Krystal, Las Casitas Mexican, Logan's Roadhouse, Longhorn Steaks, McAlister's Deli, McDonald's, Mellow Mushroom, Mexico Tipico, Moe's SW Grill, O'Charley's, Olive Garden, Outback Steaks, Panda Express, Popeyes, Ryan's, Shoney's, Sonic, Starbucks, Steak'n Shake, Subway, Waffle House, Zaxby's Courtyard,

CLANTON

MILLBROOK

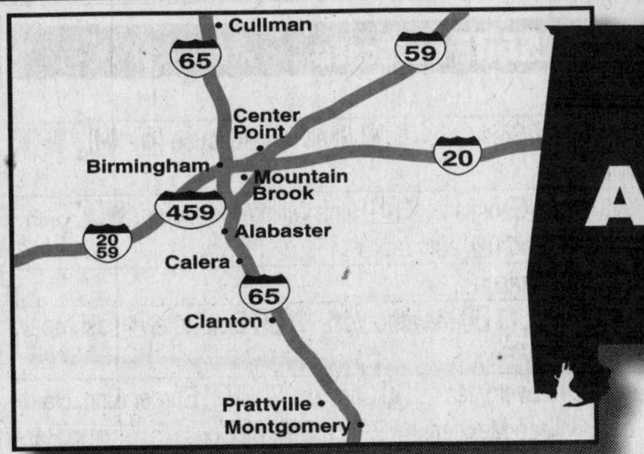

179 Continued
Days Inn, Hampton Inn, Holiday Inn Express, Howard Johnson, Rodeway Inn $General, $Tree, AT&T, AutoZone, Bass Pro Shops, Belk, Best Buy, BigLots, Books-A-Million, Chevrolet, CVS Drug, Firestone/auto, Ford, GNC, Hobby Lobby, Home Depot, JC Penney, K-Mart, Kohl's, Lowe's, Michael's, Office Depot, O'Reilly Parts, PepBoys, Petsmart, Publix, Ross, Target, TJ Maxx, URGENT CARE, Verizon, vet, Walmart

176 AL 143 N (from nb, no return), Millbrook, Coosada

173 AL 152, North Blvd, to US 231

172mm Alabama River

172 Clay St, Herron St, **E** Embassy Suites, Hampton Inn, Renaissance Hotel, **W** Chevron/dsl

171 I-85 N, Day St

170 Fairview Ave, **E** Citgo/Subway, Sunoco/dsl Church's, McDonald's, Wing Master Advance Parts, AutoZone, CVS Drug, Family$, O'Reilly Parts, Piggly Wiggly, Rite Aid, **W** Exxon/dsl Calhoun Foods, Family$

169 Edgemont Ave (from sb), **E** Liberty

168 US 80 E, US 82, South Blvd, **E** Entec/dsl, Kangaroo/dsl, TA/Marathon/Country Pride/dsl/24hr/ @ Arby's, Burger King, Capt D's, KFC, McDonald's, Pizza Hut, Popeye's, Taco Bell, Waffle House Best Inn, Economy Inn H The Woods RV Park, **W** Chevron/dsl, RaceWay/dsl, Shell/Subway/dsl DQ, Hardee's, Wendy's Candlelight Inn, Comfort Inn, KeyWest Inn

167 US 80 W, to Selma

164 US 31, Hyundai Blvd, Hope Hull, **E** Liberty, Saveway/dsl/scales/24hr, Shell/dsl El Amigo Mexican auto repair, Montgomery Camping, **W** BP, Chevron, Liberty/Subway Burger King, McDonald's, Waffle House Best Western, Comfort Suites, Fairfield Inn, Hampton Inn, Holiday Inn, Motel 6 auto repair

158 to US 31, Tyson, **E** BP/DQ/Stuckey's Montgomery South RV Park, **W** FLYING J/Denny's/dsl/scales/24hr

151 AL 97, to Letohatchee, **E** Marathon/dsl, **W** BP, PaceCar/dsl

142 AL 185, to Ft Deposit, **E** Petro+/dsl Priester's Pecans, Subway auto parts, **W** Chevron

133mm **both lanes full facilities, litter barrels, petwalk RV dump, vending**

130 AL10 E, AL 185, to Greenville, **E** Chevron/dsl, PaceCar/dsl, Shell Arby's, Capt D's, China Town, Hardee's, KFC, McDonald's, Old Mexico, Papa John's, Pizza Hut, Waffle House, Wendy's Days Inn, Quality Inn $General, $Tree, Advance Parts, CVS Drug, Fred's Store, O'Reilly Parts, Super Foods, to Sherling Lake Park, Walgreens, **W** Exxon/Subway/dsl, Murphy USA/dsl, QV, Texaco/dsl Bates Turkey Cafe, Burger King, Cracker Barrel, Krystal, Ruby Tuesday, Shoney's, Sonic, Taco Bell Baymont Inn, Best Western, Comfort Inn, Hampton Inn, Holiday Inn Express AT&T, Chevrolet, Verizon, Walmart/Subway

MONTGOMERY

GREENVILLE

= gas = food = lodging = other = rest stop

AL

INTERSTATE 65 Cont'd

EVERGREEN

Exit #	Services
128	AL 10, to Greenville, E Shell/Smokehouse, W Marathon
114	AL 106, to Georgiana, E Hank Williams Museum, W Chevron, Marathon auto repair
107	Rd 7, to Garland
101	to Owassa, E Marathon/dsl, W Exxon/dsl dsl repair, Owassa RV Park
96	AL 83, to Evergreen, E Chevron, Shell Burger King, Hardee's, Jalisco Mexican, KFC/Taco Bell, McDonald's, Shrimp Basket Sleep Inn vet W Spirit/Subway/dsl Black Angus Rest., Bubba's BBQ, Waffle House Best Value Inn, EconoLodge, Quality Inn, Pizza Hut
93	US 84, to Evergreen, E Liberty/dsl, W BP/dsl, Loves Arby's/dsl/scales/24hr
89mm	**sb full facilities, litter barrels, petwalk RV dump, vending**
85mm	**nb full facilities, litter barrels, petwalk RV dump, vending**
83	AL 6, to Lenox, E Marathon/dsl RV Park (4mi)
77	AL 41, to Range W Shell/dsl
69	AL 113, to Flomaton, E Chevron/dsl, Jet-Pep/Subway/dsl, Shell/dsl/scales/24hr dsl repair, Magnolia Branch Camping

ATMORE

Exit #	Services
57	AL 21, to Atmore, E Chevron/dsl, Shell/dsl Hardee's, Heritage Steaks, McDonald's, Waffle House Hampton Inn, Holiday Inn Express, Muskogee Inn Wind Creek Indian Gaming, W BP/ds to Kelley SP
54	Escambia Cty Rd 1, E BP/Subway/dsl to Creek Indian Res, W Shell/diner/dsl $General
45	to Perdido, W Chevron/dsl
37	AL 287, Gulf Shores Pkwy, to Bay Minette, E BP/dsl
34	to AL 59, to Bay Minette, Stockton
31	AL 225, to Stockton, E Confederate Mem Bfd, to Blakeley SP, W Shell/Subway/dsl Landing RV Park (2mi)
29mm	Tensaw River
28mm	Middle River
25mm	Mobile River
22	Creola, E River Delta RV Park (1mi)
19	US 43, to Satsuma, E Chevron/dsl/24hr, Pilot/Arby's/dsl/scales/24hr McDonald's, Waffle House La Quinta, W Chevron/dsl, Shell I-65 RV Park (1.5mi)
15	AL 41, E Chevron, Shell/Pizza Inn/DQ/dsl China Chef, Church's, Godfather's Pizza, Pizza Hut Family$, O'Reilly Parts, Rite Aid, Rouse's Mkt, Walgreens, W Circle K, Shell/Subway/dsl $General
13	AL 158, AL 213, to Saraland, E Murphy USA/dsl, Shell/dsl Goldberg's Deli, Krystal, Marble Slab, Rotolo's Pizza, Ruby Tuesday, Waffle House, Wintzell's Oyster House Best Western, Comfort Suites, Country Inn Suites, Days Inn, EconoLodge, Microtel, Quality Inn $Tree, AT&T, Radio Shack, URGENT CARE, Walmart/McDonald's, W Exxon/Subway Hampton Inn, Holiday Inn Express to Chickasabogue Campground
10	W Lee St, E Kangaroo, Shell/Subway Huddle House Best Inn
9	I-165 S, to I-10 E, to Mobile
8b a	US 45, to Prichard, E Chevron/Circle K/dsl, Shell/dsl, Texaco/dsl Church's Star Motel $General, Family$, tires/repair, W 1st Stop, BP, Energize/dsl, Pride Trkstp/dsl/scales, RaceWay/dsl, Texaco/dsl Burger King, Domino's, Golden Egg

MOBILE

Exit #	Services
8b a	Continued Café, McDonald's $General, Advance Parts, CVS Drug, Family$, O'Reilly Parts
5b	US 98, Moffett Rd, E Exxon/dsl, Texaco/dsl BJ's BBQ, Burger King, Church's, McDonald's, Sub King AutoZone, Family$, PepBoys, W Hardee's Super 8 auto repair
5a	Spring Hill Ave, E Burger King, Dreamland BBQ, McDonald's , Mr Transmission, PepBoys, W Chevron/dsl, Shell/dsl Hibachi Express, Starbucks, Subway, Waffle House, Zaxby's Extended Stay America, Wingate Inn
4	Dauphin St, E BP/Circle K/dsl, Shell/dsl Checkers, Chick-fil-A, Cracker Barrel, Krystal, McDonald's, Taco Bell, Taco Bell, Waffle House, Wendy's Comfort Suites, Jameson Inn, Red Roof Inn, Rodeway Inn $General, Buick/GMC, Food-Champs, Lowe's, Mercedes, same as 3 & 5a, Walmart/McDonald's W
3	Airport Blvd, E Shell Burger King, Cane's, Logan's Roadhouse, Macaroni Grill, McDonald's, Morrison's Cafeteria, Santa Fe Grill, Starbucks, Waffle House, Wendy's Marriott $Tree, Acura, Belk, Best Buy, BigLots, Cadillac, Dillard's, Firestone/auto, Ford, Goodyear/auto, Harley-Davidson, Honda, Infiniti, Land Rover, mall, Marshalls, Michaels, Nissan, Old Navy, Sam's Club/gas, Sears/auto, Staples, Target, Verizon, W BudgetZone/dsl, Shell/dsl Arby's, Bamboo Japanese, Baumhowers, Boiling Pot, Burger King, Carrabba's, Cheddar's, China Doll, Chipotle, ChuckECheese, Denny's, Dunkin Donuts, Firehouse Subs, Goldberg's Deli, Honeybaked Ham, Hooters, IHOP, Jason's Deli, Lenny's Subs, Los Rancheros Mexican, Marble Slab, Melting Pot, Moe's SW Grill, Newk's Cafe, O'Charley's, Olive Garden, Osaka Japanese, Outback Steaks, Panda Express, Panera Bread, Popeye's, Red Lobster, Ruby Tuesday, Starbucks, Subway, Taco Bell, Waffle House Ashberry Suites, Baymont Inn, Best Value Inn, Comfort Inn, Courtyard, Drury Inn, EconoLodge, Fairfield Inn, Family Inn, Hampton Inn, Hilton Garden, Holiday Inn, Homewood Suites, InTowne Suites, La Quinta, Motel 6, Quality Inn, Residence Inn, ValuePlace $General, $Tree, AT&T, BooksAMillion, Fresh Mkt Foods, Hancock Fabrics, Home Depot, Jo-Ann Fabrics, Office Depot, PepBoys, Petsmart, Radio Shack, Ross, SteinMart, TJ Maxx, to USAL, U-Haul, vet, Walgreens
1b a	US 90, Government Blvd E Raceway/dsl, Snell/dsl McAlister's Deli, Steak'n Shake Audi/Porsche/VW, BMW, Chevrolet, Dodge, Family$, Kia, Lexus, Lincoln/Volvo, Mazda, Subaru, Toyota/Scion, W Shell/dsl Waffle House
0mm	I-10, E to Pensacola, W to New Orleans, **I-65 begins/ends on I-10.**

INTERSTATE 85

LANETT

Exit #	Services
80mm	Alabama/Georgia state line, Chattahoochee River
79	US 29, to Lanett E Murphy USA, Shell/Circle K Arby's, Burger King, Capt D's, Chuck's BBQ, KFC, Krystal, Little Caesars, McDonald's, Pizza Hut, Popeyes, San Marcos Mexican, Subway, Taco Bell, Waffle House, Wendy's, Wing Stop $General, $Tree, Advance Parts, repair, to West Point Lake, Verizon, Walmart, W JetPep, QV, RaceWay/dsl Domino's, Jin Japanese Steaks, Sonic Days Inn, EconoLodge AutoZone, CVS Drug, Kroger, O'Reilly Parts, vet
78.5mm	**Welcome Ctr sb, full facilities, info, litter barrels, petwalk RV dump, vending**

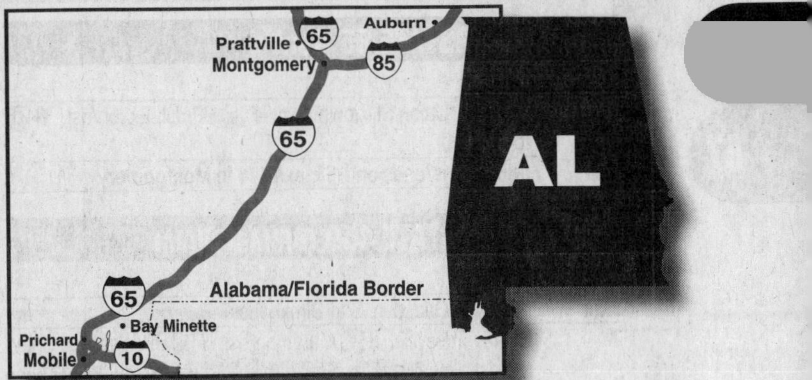

IINTERSTATE 85 Cont'd

OPELIKA

AUBURN

Exit #	Services
77	AL 208, to Huguley, E Jet Pep/Church's/dsl, Shell/Circle K/dsl Waffle House Holiday Inn Express Chevrolet, Chrysler/Dodge/Ford/Lincoln, W Hampton Inn fireworks
76mm	Eastern/Central time zone
70	AL 388, to Cusseta, E BigCat/dsl, Trvl Plaza/Shell/Subway/dsl/scales/24hr/ @, W fireworks
66	Andrews Rd, to US 29
64	US 29, to Opelika, E Sunoco/dsl, W Tiger/dsl
62	US 280/431, to Opelika, E Big Cat/dsl, Chevron/dsl, Eagle/dsl, Shell/Circle K/Church's/dsl Burger King, Durango Mexican, McDonald's, Subway, Wasabi Japanese, Wok'n Roll Rest. Best Value Inn, Budget Inn, Days Inn, EconoLodge, Motel 6, Quality Inn Lakeside RV Park (4.5mi), W GrubMart, JetPep Capt. D's, Cracker Barrel, Sizzlin Steaks, Waffle House Comfort Inn, Travelodge Buick/Chevrolet/GMC, Chrysler/Dodge/Jeep, Ford, H&W Tire, Harley-Davidson, USA Stores/Famous Brands
60	AL 51, AL 169, to Opelika, E RaceWay/dsl Hardee's $General, W H auto repair
58	US 280 W, to Opelika, E Hampton Inn, Holiday Inn Express golf, museum, W Shell/Subway/dsl Arby's, Brick Oven Pizza, Buffalo Wild Wings, Chick-fil-A, El Patron Mexican, Huddle House, Jersey Mike's, Jim Bob's, Logan's Roadhouse, Longhorn Steaks, Marble Slab, McDonald's, Moe's SW Grill, New Tokyo, Newk's Eatery, O'Charley's, Olive Garden, Sonic, Starbucks, Steak'n Shake, Waffle House, Zaxby's Fairfield Inn, Microtel, Motel 6 H Best Buy, Books-A-Million, Dick's, Hobby Lobby, Home Depot, Kohl's, Kroger/dsl, Lowe's, Office Depot, Old Navy, PetCo, Ross, Target, TJ Maxx, URGENT CARE, World Mkt
57	Bent Creek Rd W Mapco, QV Bob's Victory Grille, Shakey's Pizza, Venditori's Italian, Waffle House, Wendy's Hilton Garden, Sleep Inn Sam's Club/gas
51	US 29, to Auburn E Chevron/dsl, Grub Mart Hampton Inn Cadillac/Chevrolet, Leisure Time RV Park/Camping, Nissan, to Chewacla SP, Toyota/Scion, vet W Chevron/Subway/dsl, Murphy USA Arby's, Burger King, Dunkin Donuts, El Dorado Mexican, Firehouse Subs, Jack's, Jim'n Nick's BBQ, KJ's Fish Camp, Krystal, Little Caesars, McDonald's, Ozzio's Italian, Philly Connection, Pizza Hut, Ruby Tuesday, Shrimp Basket, Sonic, Taco Bell, Waffle House, Wendy's, Zaxby's Clarion, EconoLodge, Holiday Inn Express, Microtel, Pannie George's Kitchen, Quality Inn, Sleep Inn $General, Advance Parts, Ford/Lincoln, Kia, tires/repair, to Auburn U, URGENT CARE, Walmart, Winn-Dixie
50	Cox Rd
44mm	**both lanes, 24hr security, full facilities, litter barrels, petwalk RV dump, vending**
42	US 80, AL 186 E, Wire Rd E dsl repair/tires, to Tuskegee NF, W Torch 85/rest./dsl/24hr
38	AL 81, to Tuskegee, E to Tuskegee NHS, Tuskegee University
32	AL 49 N, to Tuskegee, E Sunoco/dsl
26	AL 229 N, to Tallassee, E Shell/Guthrie's/dsl, W H
22	US 80, to Shorter, E BP/dsl, Marathon/dsl, Petro/Valero/rest./dsl/scales/24hr Days Inn Wind Drift RV Park
16	Waugh, to Cecil, E BP/Subway/ds auto repair
11	US 80, AL 110, to Mitylene, to Mt Meigs, E Exxon/Subway/dsl, Liberty/dsl, Murphy USA/dsl Anthony's Rest., Bruster's, Burger King, Cracker Barrel, Jose's Grill, McDonald's, Taco Bell, Top China, Waffle House Candlewood Suites, Comfort Inn, Country Inn&Suites, Fairfield Inn, Holiday Inn Express, Sleep Inn

MONTGOMERY

Exit #	Services
11	Continued auto repair, Home Depot, Walmart/Subway W Chevron/dsl Microtel
9	AL 271, to AL 110, to Auburn U/Montgomery, E 5 Guys Burgers, Arby's, BoneFish Grill, Chick-fil-A, Chili's, Chipotle Mexican, Del Taco, Firebirds Grill, Genghis Grill, Ixtapa Mexican, La Jolla Rest., Moe's SW Grill, Panera Bread, Red Robin, Ruby Tuesday, Sonic, Starbucks, Taziki's Cafe, TX Roadhouse, Wendy's, Zoe's Kitchen Hampton Inn, Staybridge Suites AT&T, Books-A-Million, Costco/gas, Dick's, Dillard's, Earth-Fare Foods, Firestone/auto, Jo-Ann Fabrics, Kohl's, Michael's, Old Navy, Petsmart, Radio Shack, Ross, Target, URGENT CARE, Verizon, vet, World Mkt, W H
6	US 80, US 231, AL 21, East Blvd, **0-2 mi** E Chevron, Exxon/dsl, RaceWay/dsl, Shell Arby's, Baumhowers Rest., Burger King, Carrabba's, Chick-fil-A, Gangnam Grill, Golden Corral, Hardee's, Jason's Deli, KFC, Longhorn Steaks, Los Cabos, Los Vaqueros Mexican, McDonald's, Ming's Garden, Olive Garden, Piccadilly Cafe, Popeyes, Rock Bottom Cafe, Schlotzsky's, Starbucks, Subway, Sushiyama, Taco Bell, Waffle House, Wendy's, Zaxby's Arlington Lodge, Best Inn, Comfort Inn, Country Inn&Suites, Courtyard, Extended Stay America, Home-Towne Suites, La Quinta, Quality Inn, Quality Roof Inn, Residence Inn, Sleep Inn, Springhill Suites, ValuePlace, Wingate Inn $General, $Tree, Acura, Best Buy, Books-A-Million, Family$, Ford/Lincoln, Fresh Mkt Foods, Home Depot, Honda, Hyundai, Lowe's, Office Depot, Pepboys, PetCo, Radio Shack, Subaru, TJ Maxx, Tuesday Morning, UHaul, USPO, Walmart/McDonald's, Winn-Dixie, W Chevron, Liberty, Mapco/dsl, Shell Arby's, Capt D's, Hardee's, Hibachi Buffet, IHOP, Jan's Rest., Krispy Kreme, Krystal, McDonald's, Outback Steaks, Red Lobster, Saigon Bistro, Taco Bell, Waffle House Alabama Hotel, Baymont Inn, Comfort Suites, Drury Inn, Express Inn, Motel 6, Ramada Inn $General, Audi/VW, BMW, Buick/Cadillac/GMC, Chevrolet, Chrysler/Dodge/Jeep, Firestone/auto, Fred's Store, Infiniti, JC Penney, Kia, Lexus, mall, Mercedes, Nissan, Sam's Club/gas, Sears/auto, to Gunter AFB, Toyota/Scion, Volvo
4	Perry Hill Rd, E Chappy's Deli, Marco's Pizza Fresh Mkt, W Cannon/dsl, Chevron Hardee's, Subway Hilton Garden, Homewood Suites $General, Express Oil Change, Rite Aid, vet
3	Ann St, E Big Cat/dsl, Chevron Arby's, Capt D's, Country's BBQ, Domino's, KFC, Krystal, McDonald's, Taco Bell, Waffle House, Wendy's, Zaxby's Days Inn Pepboys, W Entec, Murphy USA/dsl, PaceCar, Ztec Burger King, Chick-fil-A, CiCi's Pizza, Hardee's, Popeye's Stay Lodge $Tree, AT&T, Office Depot, O'Reilly Parts, Radio Shack, Ross, Verizon, Walmart/Subway
2	Forest Ave, E CVS Drug, W H

AL AZ

INTERSTATE 85 Cont'd

Exit #	Services
1	Court St, Union St, downtown, E BP/dsl, Exxon/dsl, W to Ala St U
0mm	**I-85 begins/ends on I-65, exit 171 in Montgomery**

INTERSTATE 459 (BIRMINGHAM)

Exit #	Services
33b a	I-59, N to Gadsden, S to Birmingham
32	US 11, Trussville, N Marathon/dsl, S BP/Wendy's, Chevron/dsl, RaceWay/dsl, Shell/dsl Arby's, Bojangles, Burger King, Cajun Steamer, Chili's, China Palace, Coldstone, Dunkin Donuts, El Cazador Mexican, Firehouse Subs, Five Guys, Habanero's Rest., Hooters, Jack's Rest., Jim'n Nick's BBQ, KFC, La Bamba Mexican, Logan's Roadhouse, McDonald's, Mizu Japanese, Olive Garden, Red Lobster, Red Robin, Starbucks, Subway, Taziki's Mediterranean, Waffle House, Zaxby's Courtyard, Hampton Inn, Hilton Garden AT&T, Belk, Best Buy, Books-A-Million, Buick/GMC, GNC, Home Depot, JC Penney, Lowe's, Mazda, Michael's, Pepboys, Staples, Target, TJ Maxx, Verizon
31	Derby Parkway, N B'ham Race Course
29	I-20, E to Atlanta, W to Birmingham
27	Grants Mill Rd, N Hampton Inn Fiat, S Chevron/dsl Audi/Porsche, BMW, Chrysler/Dodge/Jeep, Land Rover, Lexus, Mini
23	Liberty Parkway, S Billy's Grill, DQ, Taziki's Greek Hilton Garden
19	US 280, Mt Brook, Childersburg, N Chevron/dsl CA Pizza Kitchen, Cheesecake Factory, Chuy's Mexican, Flemings Rest., Johnny Rockets, Lime Tex Mex, Macaroni Grill, Panera Bread, PF Chang's, Seasons Grille, Village Tavern, Which Wich?, Zoe's Kitchen AT&T, Barnes&Noble, Belk, Old Navy, Verizon, **0-3 mi S** BP/Circle K, Chevron, Marathon, Shell Arby's, Asian Rim, Black Pearl Asian, Buffalo Wild Wings, Burger King, Carrabba's, Chick-fil-A, Chili's, Chipotle Mexican, Cracker Barrel, Edgar's Rest., Full Moon BBQ, Jason's Deli, Jimmy John's, Kobe Japanese, Logan's Roadhouse, Longhorn Steaks, McDonald's, Milo's Burgers, Mooyah Burgers, Newk's Eatery, Pablo's, Papa John's, Pappadeaux, Pizza Hut, Schlotzsky's, Starbucks, Steak'n Shake, Subway, Superior Grill, Suriname 280, Taco Bell, Taziki's Greek, Tilted Kilt, Wendy's, Zaxby's Courtyard, Days Inn, Drury Inn, Extended Stay America, Hampton Inn, Hilton, Homewood Suites, Hyatt Place, La Quinta, Marriott, Quality Inn, Residence Inn, SpringHill Suites AT&T, Autozone, Best Buy, CVS Drug, Firestone/auto, Fresh Mkt Foods, Goodyear/auto, Home Depot, Kohl's, NTB, Radio Shack, Staples, Target, vet, Walgreens, Winn-Dixie, World Mkt
17	Acton Rd, N Shell/dsl Krystal, McDonald's, S Comfort Inn
15b a	I-65, N to Birmingham, S to Montgomery
13	US 31, Hoover, Pelham, N Exxon/dsl, Shell/dsl, Sunoco/dsl Burger King, Chick-fil-A, Fish Mkt Rest., Full Moon BBQ, Golden Rule BBQ, Habanero's, Krispy Kreme, Krystal, McDonald's, Outback Steaks, Papa John's, Purple Onion, Salvatori's Pizza, Starbucks, Subway Econolodge $Tree, Acura, AutoZone, Cadillac, Chevrolet, Firestone/auto, Goodyear/auto, Honda, Hyundai, Mr Transmission, Nissan, Publix, Rite Aid, Staples, TJ Maxx, vet, S Exxon, Jet-Pep, Shell/dsl Arby's, Bonefish Grill, CA Pizza Kitchen, Chick-fil-A, Chipotle Mexican, Firebird's Grill, Firehouse Subs, J Alexander's Rest., Jason's

BIRMINGHAM

HOOVER

Exit #	Services
13	Continued Deli, Jim'n Nicks BBQ, La Paz, McDonald's, Moe's BBQ, Moe's SW Grill, Newk's Eatery, Olive Garden, Panera Bread, Pizza Hut, Ruby Tuesday, Steak'n Shake, Stix Asian, Sumo Japanese, Taco Bell, Twin Peaks Rest., Wendy's Courtyard, Days Inn, Embassy Suites, Hampton Inn, Hyatt Place, Hyatt Regency/Wynfrey Hotel Barnes&Noble, Belk, Best Buy, Costco/gas, Dick's, GNC, Hancock Fabrics, Home Depot, Infiniti, JC Penney, Jo-Ann Fabrics, Macy's, mall, Mercedes, Michael's, NTB, Office Depot, PepBoys, Petsmart, Ross, Sam's Club/gas, Sears/auto, Tuesday Morning, Verizon, Walgreens, World Mkt
10	AL 150, Waverly, N Beef o Brady's, Frontera Mexican Grill, Jimmy John's, McDonald's, Starbucks $Tree, Kohl's, Marshall's, PetCo, Sprouts Mkt, Target, URGENT CARE, S Marathon/Kangaroo/dsl, Shell Hampton Inn, Hyatt Place Ford/Lincoln, Publix/deli, Toyota, Walgreens
6	AL 52, to Bessemer, N Shell/dsl, S Chevron/dsl, Jet-Pep, Texaco/Taco Bell Arby's, China Wok, Domino's, Fish Hook Rest., McDonald's, Pizza Hut, Railroad Cafe, Subway, Waffle House, Wendy's Sleep Inn $General, CVS Drug, RV Camping, Winn-Dixie
1	AL 18, Bessemer, N Exxon/dsl, Shell/dsl Burger King, Chick-fil-A, Firehouse Subs, Full Moon BBQ, Habanero's Mexican, Logan's Roadhouse, McAlister's Deli, Taco Bell AAA, AT&T, GNC, JC Penney, Michaels, Petsmart, Publix, Ross, Target, URGENT CARE, S Sunoco/dsl Bojangles, China King, McDonald's, San Antonio Grill, Subway, Zaxby's Advance Parts, CVS Drug, Meineke, Piggly Wiggly, to Tannehill SP, Verizon
0mm	**I-459 begins/ends on I-20/59, exit 106.**

BESSEMER

ARIZONA

INTERSTATE 8

Exit #	Services
178b a	I-10, **I-8 begins/ends on I-10, exit 199**, E to Tucson, W to Phoenix
174	Trekell Rd, to Casa Grande, **2-4 mi N**
172	Thornton Rd, to Casa Grande, **5-8 mi N** Francisco Grande Resort, Holiday Inn
171mm	Santa Cruz River
169	Bianco Rd
167	Montgomery Rd
163mm	Santa Rosa Wash
161	Stanfield Rd
151	AZ 84 E, Maricopa Rd, to Stanfield, S Vija Trkstp/dsl Saguaro RV Park
151mm	**litter barrels, picnic area wb**
149mm	**litter barrels, picnic area eb**
144	Vekol Rd
140	Freeman Rd
119	Butterfield Trail, to AZ 85, I-10, Gila Bend, **3 mi N** Shell/dsl/scales, Shell/Subway/dsl/scales/RV Park/24hr Little Italy, Subway America's Choice Inn, Best Western, Knights Inn, Space Age/rest, Yucca Motel $General, Augie's RV Park, Sanborn RV Resort
117mm	Sand Tank Wash
115	AZ 85, to Gila Bend, N Circle K, Loves/Taco Bell/dsl/scales/24hr, Texaco/dsl Burger King, Carl's Jr, Don Jose Mexican, McDonald's Best Western, El Coronado Motel, Yucca Motel Avila Bend Mkt, Family$, Goodyear/auto, NAPA

GILA BEND

AZ

INTERSTATE 8 Cont'd

Exit #	Services
111	Citrus Valley Rd
106	Paloma Rd
102	Painted Rock Rd, N [other] Painted Rock Petroglyph Site (11mi)
87	Aqua Caliente Rd, Sentinel Rd, Sentinel, Hyder, N [gas] Sentinel Gen Store/dsl [other] RV Camping
85mm	[RS] eb, full [handicapped] facilities, litter barrels, petwalk [phone] [picnic] wb, vending
84mm	[RS] eb, full [handicapped] facilities, litter barrels, petwalk [phone] [picnic] wb, vending
78	Spot Rd
73	Aztec, S [other] Oasis RV Park/dump (4mi)
67	Dateland, S [gas] Texaco/Quiznos/dsl [other] Oasis RV Park/dump (2mi)
56mm	[RS] both lanes, full [handicapped] facilities, litter barrels, petwalk [phone] [picnic] vending
54	Ave 52 E, Mohawk Valley
42	Ave 40 E, to Tacna, N [gas] Chevron/dsl [food] Jac's Whistlestop Cafe [lodging] Chaparral Motel [other] USPO, S [other] Copper Mtn RV Park
37	Ave 36 E, to Roll
30	Ave 29 E, Wellton, N [gas] Circle K/dsl [food] Geronimo Mexican [lodging] Desert Motel [other] NAPA, Tier Drop RV Park, USPO, S [gas] Chevron/dsl [food] Chen's Chinese, Dusty's Pizza & Wings, Fusion Deli, Jack-in-the-Box [lodging] Microtel
24mm	Ligurta Wash
23mm	Red Top Wash
22mm	[other] Parking area/litter barrels both lanes
21	Dome Valley, N [other] Ligurta Sta RV park, Yuma Proving Ground (16mi)
17mm	Insp sta eb
15mm	Fortuna Wash
14	Foothills Blvd, N [other] Sundance RV Park, S [food] Domino's, Foothills Eatery, Mi Fajita [other] auto/RV care/lube ctr, Family$, Foothill Hardware, Foothills RV Park, Hank's IGA/dsl
12	Fortuna Rd, to US 95 N, N [gas] Chevron/dsl, FLYING J/Giant/dsl/scales/24hr [food] DayBreakers Cafe, Jack-in-the-Box, Las Palapas Tacos, McDonald's, Pizza Hut, Starbucks, Taco Bell [lodging] Comfort Inn, Courtesy Inn [other] Caravan RV Park, Oasis RV Park, Shangri La RV Park, S [gas] Shell/Burger King/dsl, SP/dsl [food] A&W/KFC, Applebee's, Daboyz Pizza, Denny's, DQ, Little Caesar's, Subway [lodging] Microtel [other] $General, 99cents Store, Big O Tire, CVS Drug, Family$, Fry's Foods/dsl, GNC, O'Reilly Parts, Radio Shack, URGENT CARE, USPO, Walgreens
9	32nd St, to Yuma, S [food] Del Taco, Panda Express [other] RV Parks, Verizon, Walmart/McDonald's
7	AZ 195, Araby Rd, N [gas] Circle K/dsl, S [gas] Chevron/Jack-in-the-Box/dsl, Circle K/dsl [other] RV Parks, RV World, to AZWU
3	AZ 280 S, Ave 3E, N [gas] Arby's [lodging] Candlewood Suites, Holiday Inn Express, S [gas] Loves/Chester's/Subway/dsl/scales/24hr [other] CarQuest, Harley-Davidson, to Marine Corp Air Sta
2	US 95, 16th St, Yuma, N [gas] Circle K [food] Ah-So Steaks, Buffalo Wild Wings, Burrito Grill, Chick-fil-A, Chili's, Chipotle Mexican, ChuckeCheese, Coldstone Creamery, Cracker Barrel, Del Taco, Denny's, Famous Dave's BBQ, Firehouse Subs, Five Guys, Hawaiian BBQ, In-N-Out, Jack-in-the-Box, Kneaders, Lin's Chinese, Logans Roadhouse, Mimi's Cafe, Olive Garden, Panda Express, Penny's Diner, Pita Pit, Red Lobster, Starbucks, Subway [lodging] Best Western, Days Inn, Fairfield Inn, Hampton Inn, Holiday Inn, Homewood Suites, La Fuente Inn, Motel 6, OakTree Inn, Shilo Inn, SpringHill Suites, TownePlace Suites, Wingate Inn [other] AT&T, Best Buy, Dillards, GNC, JC Penney, Jo-Ann Fabrics, Kohl's, Marshall's, Old Navy, PetsMart, Ross, Sam's Club/gas, Target, Verizon, S [gas] 76/dsl, Arco/dsl, Chevron/Blimpie/dsl, Shell [food] Applebee's, Burger King, Carl's Jr, Chretin's Mexican, Golden Corral, IHOP, Jack-in-the-Box, McDonald's, Subway, TX Roadhouse, Village Inn Pizza, Wendy's [lodging] Comfort Inn, Motel 6, Radisson, Super 8 [other] [H], BigLots, Family$, Home Depot, Radio Shack, Staples
1.5mm	weigh sta both lanes

WELLTON

YUMA

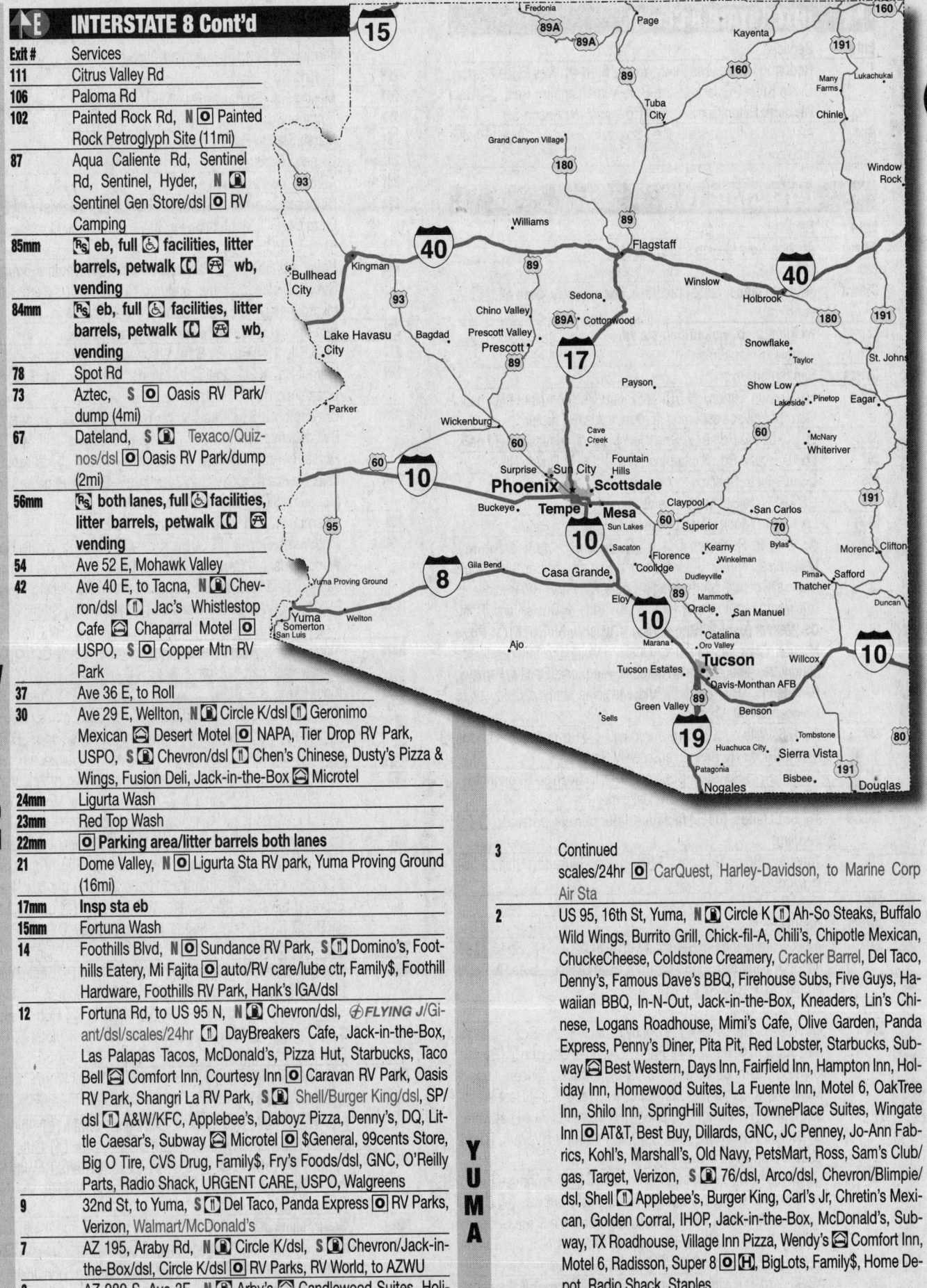

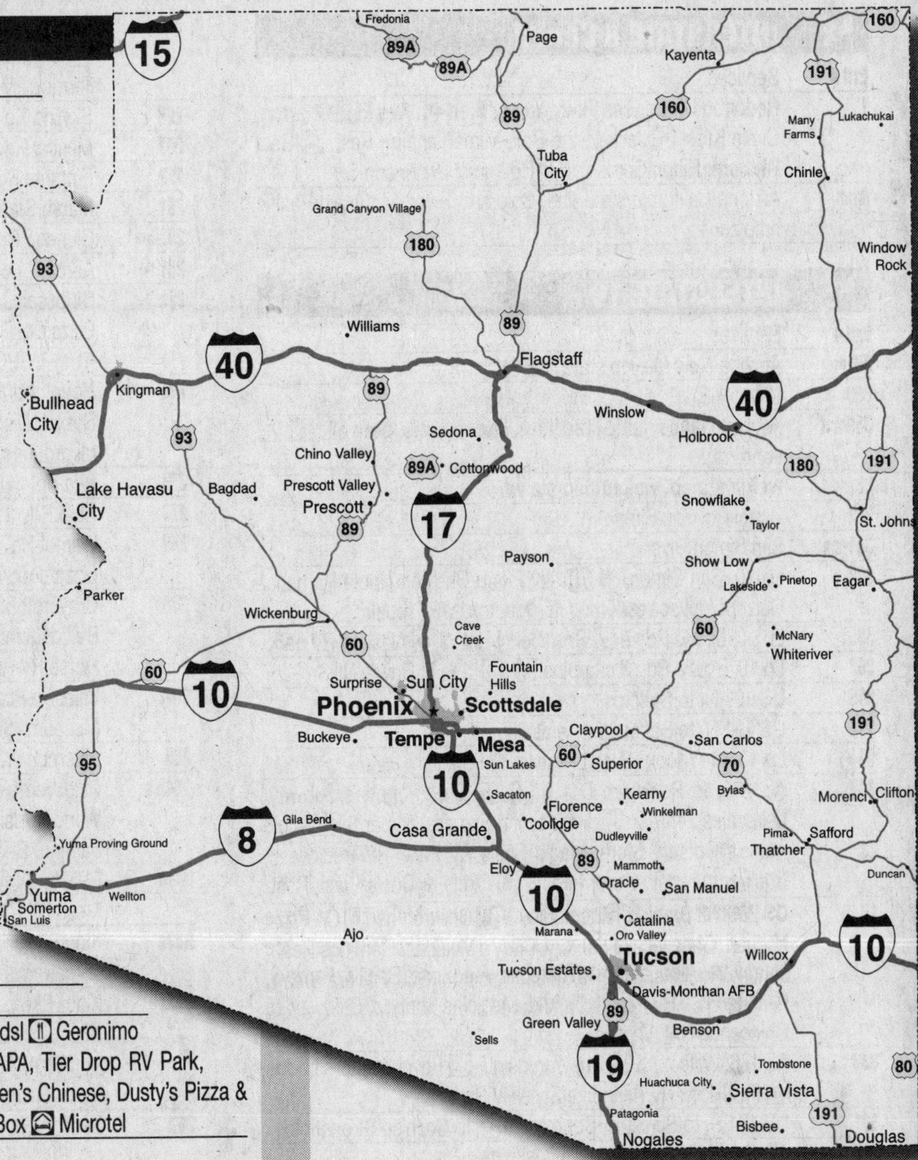

Y U M A

INTERSTATE 8 Cont'd

Exit #	Services
1	Redondo Ctr Dr, Giss Pkwy, Yuma, **S on 4th Ave E** 🛢 Chevron, Circle K/dsl 🍽 Jack-in-the-Box, Yuma Landing Rest. 🛏 Best Western, Hilton Garden, **N** ⊡ to Yuma Terr Prison SP
0mm	Arizona/California state line, Colorado River, Mountain/Pacific time zone

INTERSTATE 10

Exit #	Services
391mm	Arizona/New Mexico state line
390	Cavot Rd
389mm	🆁ₛ **both lanes, full** ♿ **facilities, litter barrels, petwalk** ☎ 🖼 **vending**
383mm	**weigh sta eb, weigh/insp sta wb**
382	Portal Rd, San Simon
381mm	San Simon River
378	Lp 10, San Simon, **N** 🛢 4K Trkstp/Chevron/Noble Romans/ Quiznos/dsl/scales/24hrs/ @ ⊡ auto/dsl/RV repair
366	Lp 10, Bowie Rd, **N** 🛢 Shell/Jerky/dsl, **S** ⊡ Alaskan RV park
362	Lp 10, Bowie Rd, **N** camping 🛢 🛏 **S** to Ft Bowie NHS
355	US 191 N, to Safford
352	US 191 N, to Safford, same as 355
344	Lp 10, to Willcox, **N** ⊡ Lifestyle RV Park
340	AZ 186, to Rex Allen Dr, **N** 🛢 TA/Shell/Popeye's/Subway/ dsl/scales/24hr/ @ 🛏 Holiday Inn Express, Super 8 ⊡ Apple Annie's Country Store, Magic Circle RV Park, RV/Truckwash, truck/auto repair, visitor info, **S** 🛢 Circle K, Doc's/Plaza Rest/ dsl, Texaco/dsl 🍽 Burger King, Carl's Jr, McDonald's, Pizza Hut 🛏 Days Inn, Motel 6, Quality Inn ⊡ 🅗 $General, Ace Hardware, Alco, auto/tire/RV repair, AutoZone, Beall's, Family$, Grande Vista RV Park, KT's Mkt, Medicine Shoppe, Safeway, to Chiricahua NM, Verizon
336	AZ 186, Willcox, **S** 🛢 Chevron/dsl/LP 🛏 Royal Western Lodge ⊡ Ft Willcox RV Park, Life Style RV Park
331	US 191 S, to Sunsites, Douglas, **S** ⊡ to Cochise Stronghold
322	Johnson Rd, **S** 🛢 Shell/DQ/dsl/gifts
320mm	🆁ₛ **both lanes, full** ♿ **facilities, litter barrels, petwalk** ☎ 🖼 **vending**
318	Triangle T Rd, to Dragoon, **S** ⊡ Amerind Museum (1mi), camping, lodging
312	Sibyl Rd
309mm	Adams Peak Wash
306	AZ 80, Pomerene Rd, Benson, **1-2 mi S** 🛢 Circle K, Shell 🍽 86 Cafe ⊡ CarQuest, El Rio RV Park, Pato Blanco Lakes RV Park, repair, San Pedro RV (2mi)
305mm	San Pedro River
304	Ocotillo St, Benson, **N** 🍽 Denny's, Jack-in-the-Box 🛏 Days Inn, Super 8 ⊡ Benson RV Park, KOA, **S** 🛢 Chevron 🍽 Beijing Chinese, Farmhouse Rest, Galleano's Italian-American, Lupe's Mexican, Magaly's Mexican, Subway, Wendy's 🛏 Best Western, QuarterHorse Inn/RV Park ⊡ 🅗, $General, Ace Hardware, Butterfield RV Resort, Dillon RV Ctr, Pardner's RV Park, Radio Shack, Safeway, Walmart
303	US 80 (eb only), to Tombstone, Bisbee, **S** 🍽 Farmhouse Rest., Little Caesar's, Pablo's Steaks, Reb's Rest., Subway 🛏 Quarter Horse Motel/RV Park ⊡ auto/dsl/repair, Medicine Shoppe, O'Reilly Parts, Pardners RV Park, to Douglas NHL, to Tombstone Courthouse SHP (26mi), Verizon, Walmart
302	AZ 90 S, to Ft Huachuca, Benson, **S** 🛢 ♥Loves/Chester's/ Subway/dsl/scales/24hr, Shell/dsl 🍽 KFC/Taco Bell, McDonald's

W I L L C O X

B E N S O N

T U C S O N

Exit #	Services
302	Continued 🛏 Comfort Inn, Motel 6 ⊡ AZ Legends RV Resort, Cochise Terrace RV Park, Ft Huachuca NHS (25mi)
299	Skyline Rd
297	Mescal Rd, J-6 Ranch Rd, **N** 🛢 QuickPic/dsl
292	Empirita Rd
291	Marsh Station Rd
288mm	Cienega Creek
281	AZ 83 S, to Patagonia
279	Colossal Cave Rd, Wentworth Rd, **N** 🛢 QuikMart/dsl 🍽 AZ Pizza Co, DQ, Montgomery's Grill, Quizno ⊡ to Colossal Caves (7mi), USPO
275	Houghton Rd, **N** 🍽 Panda Express ⊡ Adventure Bound RV Resort, Discount Tire, to Saguaro NP (10mi), Walmart, **S** ⊡ to fairgrounds (1mi)
273	Rita Rd, **N** 🛢 Conoco (2mi), **S** ⊡ fairgrounds
270	Kolb Rd, **S** ⊡ Bay RV Resort, Voyager RV Resort
269	Wilmot Rd, **N** 🛢 Chevron/A&W/dsl 🛏 Travel Inn, **S** 🛢 Shell/ pizza/subs/dsl
268	Craycroft Rd, **N** 🛢 Circle K, Mr T/dsl/LP, ▐Pilot▌/Subway/Taco Bell/dsl/lp/scales/24hr @, TTT/rest/dsl/scales/24hr ⊡ Crazy Horse RV Park, Frieghtliner, truck/RV wash, **S** ⊡ dsl repair
267	Valencia Rd, **N** 🛢 Chevron/Jack-in-the-Box ⊡ Pima Air&Space Museum, **S** 🛢 Valero/ds ⊡ airport
265	Alvernon Way, **N** ⊡ Davis-Monthan AFB
264b a	Palo Verde Rd, **N** 🛢 Circle K/dsl 🍽 Denny's, Waffle House, Wendy's/dsl 🛏 Crossland Suites, Days Inn, Fairfield Inn, Holiday Inn, Red Roof Inn ⊡ Camping World RV Resort, Freedom RV Ctr, **S** 🍽 Arby's, McDonald's 🛏 Quality Inn, Studio 6 ⊡ La Mesa RV Ctr, Lazy Days RV Ctr/Resort, Pedata RV Ctr
263b	Kino Pkwy N, **N** 🛢 Chevron/dsl 🍽 Culver's, In-N-Out ⊡ Costco/gas, Walmart/Subway
263a	Kino Pkwy S, **S** 🛢 Arco/dsl, Shamrock 🍽 Burger King, KFC, Little Caesar's, Mandarin Buffet, Papa John's, Taco Bell ⊡ $Tree, AutoZone, Family$, Food City, Fry's Foods, O'Reilly Parts, Radio Shack, to Tucson Intn'l Airport, Walgreens
262	Benson Hwy, Park Ave, **S** 🛢 Arco/dsl, Chevron/McDonald's/ dsl, Circle K/dsl 🍽 Carl's Jr. 🛏 Best Value Inn, Motel 6, Rodeway Inn, Western Inn ⊡ Mack/Volvo Trucks, USPO
261	6th/4th Ave, **N** 🛢 GasCo 🍽 Little Caesars, Los Portales 🛏 EconoLodge ⊡ Discount Tire, Family$, Food City, USPO, **S** 🛢 Circle K/dsl 🍽 Church's, El Indio, Jack-in-the-Box, Panda Express, Silver Saddle Steaks, Whataburger 🛏 Lazy 8 Motel ⊡ Big O Tire, El Super Foods, Family$, Midas, O'Reilly Parts
260	I-19 S, to Nogales
259	22nd St, Starr Pass Blvd, **N** 🛢 Circle K/dsl, **S** 🍽 Kettle, Waffle House 🛏 Clarion, Regal Inn, Silverbell Inn, Super 8, Travel Inn
258	Congress St, Broadway St, **N** 🛢 Circle K 🛏 Hotel Tuscan, **S** 🍽 Carl's Jr 🛏 Days Inn, Howard Johnson, Motel 6, River Park Inn, Travelodge
257a	St Mary's Rd, **N** ⊡ 🅗 **S** 🛢 Shell/dsl 🍽 Burger King, Church's, Denny's, Eegee's Cafe, Furr's Cafeteria, Jack-in-the-Box, Little Caesar's, Whataburger 🛏 Country Inn&Suites, Ramada Ltd ⊡ Family$, Food City, Pima Comm Coll
257	Speedway Blvd, **N** 🛏 Best Western, EconoLodge ⊡ 🅗 U of AZ, Victory Motorcycles, **S** 🛢 Arco/dsl ⊡ museum, Old Town Tucson
256	Grant Rd, **N** 🛢 Circle K 🍽 auto/dsl repair, Burger King, Jack-in-the-Box, Sonic ⊡ Walgreens, **S** 🛢 Circle K, QT/dsl, Shell/ dsl 🍽 Arby's, Del Taco, Eegee's Cafe, IHOP, Waffle House 🛏 Comfort Inn, Grant Inn, Hampton Inn, Holiday Inn Express, Super 8 ⊡ Ace Hardware, Safeway, Walgreens

AZ

INTERSTATE 10 Cont'd

TUCSON

Exit #	Services
255	AZ 77 N, to Miracle Mile
254	Prince Rd, N Circle K, Valero/dsl $General, O'Reilly Parts, Walgreens, S golf, Kenworth, Prince of Tucson RV Park
252	El Camino del Cerro, Ruthrauff Rd, N Arco Ruthrauff RV Ctr, S Chevron/Jack-in-the-Box/dsl
251	Sunset Rd
250	Orange Grove Rd, N Arco/dsl, Circle K/dsl Burger King, Culver's, Domino's, Firehouse Subs, Golden Corral, Little Caesar's, Subway, Tulioberto's, Wendy's Big O Tire, Costco/gas, diesel repair, Home Depot, Petsmart, South Forty RV Park, Sprouts Mkt, Staples, URGENT CARE, vet
248	Ina Rd, N Chevron/dsl, Circle K/dsl, Shell/dsl Bisbee Breakfast Club, Carl's Jr, ChickeNuevo, Chuy's Mesquite, DQ, Eegee's Cafe, Five Guys, Hooters, Jack-in-the-Box, Jade Garden, Losbetos Cafe, Lupita's Cafe, McDonald's, Miss Saigon, Molinitas Mexican, Papa John's, Peter Piper's Pizza, Pollo Loco, Starbucks, Subway, Taco Bell, Waffle House InTown Suites, Motel 6 $Tree, 99cents Store, auto repair, AutoZone, BigLots, CarQuest, CVS Drug, Discount Tire, Firestone/auto, Fry's Foods/dsl, Goodyear/auto, Hancock Fabrics, Lowe's, Michael's, Midas, O'Reilly Parts, PepBoys, Radio Shack, Target, U-Haul, Walgreens, Walmart Mkt, S Circle K Denny's, Starbucks Best Western, Red Roof Inn, Travelodge Ace Hardware, Freedom RV Ctr, Harley-Davidson
246	Cortaro Rd, N Circle K/Arby's/dsl, QT/dsl IHOP, Wendy's, S Shell/dsl Boston's Rest, Burger King, Chili's, Chopstix, Cracker Barrel, Eegee's Rest., In-N-Out, KFC/Taco Bell, Little Caesars, McDonald's, Nana's Mexican, Native New Yorker, New Town Asian, Panda Express, Starbucks, Subway, TX Roadhouse Comfort Inn, Days Inn, Holiday Inn Express, La Quinta, Super 8 access to RV camping, Ace Hardware, AT&T, Batteries+, GNC, Kohl's, O'Reilly Parts, USPO, Verizon, Walmart/McDonald's
244	Twin Peaks Rd, N Tucson Outlets/famous brands
242	Avra Valley Rd, S airport, RV camping, Saguaro NP (13mi)
240	Tangerine Rd, to Rillito, N A-A RV Park, S USPO
236	Marana, S Chevron/dsl/LP, Circle K/dsl McDonald's, R&R Pizz auto repair, Family$, Sun RV Park
232	Pinal Air Park Rd, S Pinal Air Park (3mi)
228mm	to frontage rd, wb pulloff
226	Red Rock, S USPO
219	Picacho Peak Rd, N Shell/DQ, Shell/Subway/dsl, S Ostrich Ranch, Pichaco Peak RV Park, to Picacho Peak SP
212	Picacho (from wb), S KOA
211b	AZ 87 N, AZ 84 W, to Coolidge, S KOA
211a	Picacho (from eb), S KOA, state prison
208	Sunshine Blvd, to Eloy, N Pilot/Subway/DQ/dsl/scales/24hr dsl repair, S FLYING J/Denny's/dsl/scales/24hr Blue Beacon
203	Toltec Rd, to Eloy, N Circle K/dsl, Shell/McDonald's/playplace/24hr Carl's Jr, El Caballito Mexican Best Value Inn, Super 8 Desert Valley RV Park, dsl/tire repair, S TA/A&W/Taco Bell/dsl/RV dump/24hr/ @ Pizza Hut golf, truckwash
200	Sunland Gin Rd, Arizona City, N Petro/Iron Skillet/dsl/scales/24hr/ @, Pride/Subway/dsl/24hr Burger King, Eva's Mexican Days Inn, Travelodge

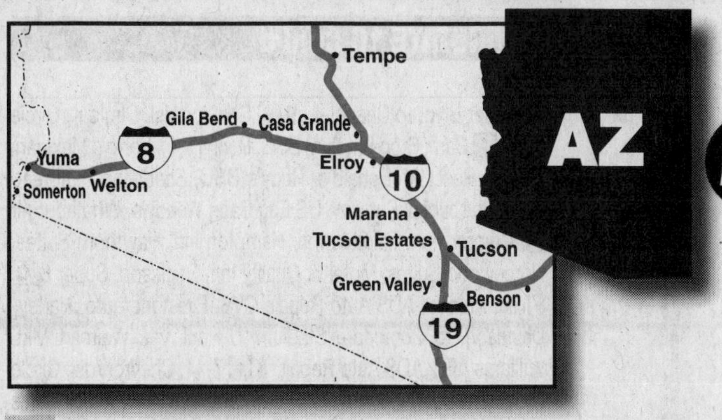

CASA GRANDE

Exit #	Services
200	Continued Blue Beacon, Eagle Truckwash, Las Colinas RV Park, S Loves/Arby's/Baskin-Robbins/dsl/24hr Golden 9 Rest Motel 6 Speedco Lube
199	I-8 W, to Yuma, San Diego
198	AZ 84, to Eloy, Casa Grande, N Robson Ranch Rest./golf (3mi), S Casa Grande Outlets/famous brands
194	AZ 287, Florence Blvd, to Casa Grande, N Tesla Buffalo Wild Wings, Cactus Moon Grill, Cane's, Chick-fil-A, Culver's, In-N-Out, Krispy Kreme, Mimi's Cafe, Olive Garden, Rubio's, Subway Dillard's, GNC, JC Penney, Kohl's, Marshall's, Michael's, Petsmart, Radio Shack, Ross, Sam's Club/dsl, Staples, Sunscape RV Park (7mi), Target, Verizon, Walgreens, World Mkt, **0-2 mi** S 76/DQ, Arco/dsl, Chevron/Little Caesars/dsl, Circle K/gas Arby's, Burger King, Carl's Jr, Chili's, China Buffet, Chipotle Mexican, Church's, Coldstone, Cracker Barrel, Del Taco, Denny's, Eegee's, Filiberto's Mexican, Golden Corral, IHOP, Jack-in-the-Box, JB's, Jimmy John's, LJ Silver/Taco Bell, Macayo's Mexican, McDonald's, Panda Express, Papa John's, Papa Murphy's, Peter Piper Pizza, Sonic, Starbucks, Subway, T&M Italian, Wendy's Best Western, Comfort Inn, Holiday Inn Express, Legacy Suites, Mainstay Suites, Super 8 H $Tree, 99cents Store, AT&T, AutoZone, Big Lots, Big O Tire, CVS Drug, Discount Tire, Encore Camping (2mi), Family$, Fiesta Grande RV Resort, Food City, Fry's Food/drug/dsl, Goodyear/auto, Home Depot, Jo-Ann Fabrics, K-Mart, Lowe's, U-Haul, URGENT CARE, Verizon, vet, Walgreens, Walmart/McDonalds
190	McCartney Rd, N to Central AZ Coll, S Barro's Pizza (3mi)
185	AZ 387, to Casa Grande, Casa Grande Ruins NM, S Eva's Mexican (6mi) Fransisco Grande (6mi), Holiday Inn (6mi) Fry's Food/gas (6mi), hwy patrol, to Casa Grande Ruins NM, Val Vista RV camping (3mi)
183mm	**wb, full facilities, litter barrels, petwalk vending**
181mm	**eb, full facilities, litter barrels, petwalk, vending**
175	AZ 587 N, Casa Blanca Rd, Chandler, Gilbert, S Shell/dsl
173mm	Gila River
167	Riggs Rd, to Sun Lake, N Shell/dsl Akimel Smoke Shop
164	AZ 347 S, Queen Creek Rd, to Maricopa, N to Chandler Airport
162b a	Wild Horse Pass Rd, Sundust Rd, N Loves/Arby's/dsl/scales/24hr McDonald's, S Chevron/dsl Sheraton Resort, Wildhorse Pass Hotel/Casino Firebird Sports Park, Gila River Casino, Phoenix Outlets/famous brands
161	AZ 202 E, Pecos Rd

E INTERSTATE 10 Cont'd

CHANDLER

Exit #	Services
160	Chandler Blvd, to Chandler, N [gas] Chevron/dsl, Circle K, Circle K/dsl [food] Can't Stop Smokin' BBQ, Denny's, Filiberto's Mexican, Marie's Rest., McDonald's, Rudy's BBQ, Sandella's Flatbread Cafe, Starbucks, Subway, US Egg Cafe, Wendy's, Whataburger [lodging] Comfort Inn, Fairfield Inn, Hampton Inn, Hawthorn Suites, Homewood Suites, Motel 6, Quality Inn, Radisson, Super 8 [other] $Tree, Aamco, ADS Auto Repair, CVS, Firestone/auto, Harley-Davidson, to Compadre Stadium, U-Haul, vet, Walmart Mkt, Williams AFB, ADS Auto Repair, S [gas] 7-11, Chevron/dsl, Circle K/dsl, Shell/dsl [food] Bell Italian Pizza, Brazilian Bull Steaks, Carl's Jr, Cracker Barrel, Del Taco, Dunkin Donuts, Hong Kong Buffet, Jersey Mike's, Qdoba, Spinato's Pizzaria, Starbucks, Tukee's Grille, Waffle House, Wendy's [lodging] Extended Stay America, Holiday Inn Express, InTown Suites, La Quinta [other] [H] AT&T, AutoZone, Discount Tire, Kohl's, URGENT CARE
159	Ray Rd, N [gas] Circle K, Shell [food] Buca Italian, Carrabba's, Charleston's Rest., Chipotle Mexican, Fleming's Steaks, Frederico's Mexican, Genghis Grill, Habit Burger, In-N-Out, Jason's Deli, Jimmy John's, Longhorn Steaks, McDonald's, Nabers Rest., Outback Steaks, Paradise Cafe, Pei Wei Asian, Red Lobster, Roy's Hawaiian, Rumbi Grill, Sandbar Mexican, Starbucks, Subway, Tejas, Zoe's Kitchen [lodging] Courtyard [other] AJ's Fine Foods, Audi, BMW, Chevrolet, Ford, Home Depot, Lexus, Lowe's Whse, Mercedes, PetsMart, Sam's Club/gas, Verizon, S [gas] Circle K/dsl [food] Barro's Pizza, Boston Mkt, Chick-Fil-A, Five Guys, Honeybaked Ham, IHOP/24hr, Jack-in-the-Box, Kneaders Cafe, Mellow Mushroom, Mimi's Café, Native Grill, Neo Tokyo, On-the-Border, Peter Piper Pizza, Pizza Hut, Rubio's, Subway, Uncle Bear's Grill, Vincent's Pizza, Wendy's [lodging] Extended Stay America [other] AT&T, auto repair, Barnes&Noble, Best Buy, Fresh&Easy Mkt, Hobby Lobby, JC Penney, Jo-Ann Fabrics, Marshall's, Michael's, PetCo, Ross, Sprouts Mkt, Target, Verizon
158	Warner Rd, N [gas] Circle K/dsl, QT [food] Carl's Jr, Dunkin Donuts, Forefathers Cheesteaks, Port of Subs, Topical Smoothie [lodging] Drury Inn [other] Dick's, IKEA, S [gas] Circle K/dsl, Minute Mart/dsl [food] AZ Sandwich Co., Burger King, ChuckeCheese, DQ, Hillside Spot Cafe, Macayo's Mexican, McDonald's, Nello's Pizza, Panda Garden, Ruffino's Italian, Taco Bell, Zipp's Grill [other] Ace Hardware, Basha's Foods, Big O Tire, Goodyear/auto, vet
157	Elliot Rd, N [gas] Chevron/dsl, QT/dsl, Shell/Circle K/dsl [food] Applebee's, Arby's, Burger King, Crackers Cafe, Crazy Buffet, Fuddrucker's, Jimmy John's, Kabab Palace, Kobe Japanese, McDonald's, Olive Garden, Oregano's Pizza Bistro, Panda Express, Red Robin Rest., Sonic, Starbucks, Subway, Taco Bell, Wendy's, YC Mongolian Grill [lodging] Days Inn&Suite [other] $Tree, Acura, Buick, Cadillac/GMC, Chrysler/Dodge/Jeep, Costco/gas, Discount Tire, Fiat, Honda, Hyundai, Kia, Mazda, Mini, NAPA, Nissan, PetsMart, Ross, Savers, Staples, Toyota/Scion, URGENT CARE, Volvo, Walmart, S [gas] Shell/Circle K/dsl [food] Biscuits, Cactus Jack's, Niros Gyros, Original Burrito, Pacific Gardens Asian, Starbucks, Sub Factory, Subway [lodging] Clarion, Sheraton [other] auto repair, O'Reilly Parts, Safeway, vet, Walgreens
155	Baseline Rd, Guadalupe, N [gas] Circle K/dsl, Shell/Circle K/Popeye's/dsl [food] Carl's Jr, ClaimJumper, Ell Pollo Loco, Joe's Crabshack, KFC, McDonald's, Poliberto's Tacos, Rainforest Cafe, Subway, Taco Bell, Waffle House, Wendy's [lodging] Best Western, Candlewood Studios, Holiday Inn Express, InnSuites,

PHOENIX

Exit #	Services
155	Continued Ramada, Residence Inn, SpringHill Suites, TownePlace Suites [other] AutoZone, AZ Mills/Famous Brands, CVS Drug, Food City, Home Depot, Marshall's, Parts Authority, Ross, Walgreens, S [gas] 7-11, Arco/dsl, QT [food] Aunt Chilada's Mexican, China Town, Denny's, Little Caesar's, Sonic, Subway [other] Fry's Electronics, Fry's Foods, URGENT CARE
154	US 60 E, AZ 360, Superstition Frwy, to Mesa, N [other] to Camping World (off Mesa Dr)
153b	Broadway Rd E, N [food] Denny's [lodging] Comfort Suites, Extended Stay America, La Quinta, Quality Inn, Red Roof Inn, Sheraton [other] to Diablo Stadium, S [gas] Chevron/dsl, Shell/Circle K/Del Taco/24hr [food] Goodcents Deli, Panda Express, Papa John's, Pizza Hut, Port of Subs, Taco Bell, Whataburger [lodging] Country Inn & Suites, Homewood Suite [other] Staples
153a	AZ 143 N, N [food] Denny's [lodging] Courtyard, Fairfield Inn, Hilton, Holiday Inn, La Quinta, Sleep Inn [other] to Diablo Stadium, S same as 153b
152	40th St, N [gas] Shell/dsl [other] U Phoenix, S [gas] Shell/Circle K [food] Burger King, Quiznos
151mm	Salt River
151b a	28th St, 32nd St, University Ave, N [food] Waffle House [lodging] Drury Inn, Extended Stay America, Hilton Garden, Holiday Inn Express [other] AZSU, U Phoenix, S [gas] Circle K/dsl, QT/dsl [food] McDonald's
150b	24th St E (from wb), N [lodging] Motel [other] Air Nat Guard, S [lodging] Best Western/rest.
150a	I-17 N, to Flagstaff
149	Buckeye Rd, N [other] Sky Harbor Airport
148	Washington St, Jefferson St, N [gas] Chevron/dsl, Shell, Tiemco/dsl [food] Carl's Jr, McDonald's [lodging] Motel 6, Sterling Hotel [other] to Sky Harbor Airport, S [gas] Circle K [other] [H]
147b a	AZ 51 N, AZ 202 E, to Squaw Peak Pkwy
146	16th St (from sb), N [gas] Shell/Circle K [food] Filiberto's Mexican, S [gas] Circle K, Shamrock/dsl [food] Church's, Jack-in-the-Box, Little Caesar's, Salsita's Mexica [other] [H] O'Reilly Parts, Ranch Mkt
145	7th St, N [food] Chicos Tacos, McDonald's, Sonic, Starbucks, Subway, Taco Bell, Whataburger [other] Safeway Foods, Walgreens, S [gas] Circle K, Shell, Sinclair/dsl [food] Jimmy John's [lodging] Holiday Inn Express, Hyatt, Sheraton, Springhill Suites [other] [H], to Chase Field
144	7th Ave, N [gas] Circle K [food] Chipotle, Five Guys, Habit Burger, Jersey Mike's, NY Pizza, Peiwei Asian, Potbelly, Starbucks, Zoe's Kitchen, S [gas] Circle [other] central bus dist
143c	US 60, 19th Ave (from wb), downtown
143b a	I-17, N to Flagstaff, S to Phoenix
142	27th Ave (from eb, no return), N [lodging] Comfort Inn
141	35th Ave, N [food] Jack-in-the-Box, Rita's Mexican, S [gas] Shell/Circle K
140	43rd Ave, N [gas] 7-11, Circle K/dsl, Shell [food] Filberto's Mexican, KFC, Little Caesar's, Pizza Hut, Salsita's Mexican, Subway [lodging] ValuePlace Hotel [other] AutoZone, Family$, Food City, Fry's Mercado/gas, Radio Shack, Walgreens
139	51st Ave, N [gas] Chevron/dsl, Circle K [food] Burger King, Domino's, El Pollo Loco, McDonald's, Sonic [lodging] Best Value Inn, Budget Inn, Crossland Suites, Holiday Inn, InTown Suites, La Quinta, Motel 6, Red Roof Inn, Travelodge [other] Food City, S [gas] QT/dsl/scales, Shell/dsl [food] Carl's Jr, Filiberto's Mexican, IHOP, Port of Subs, Taco Bell [lodging] Comfort Inn, Days Inn, Super 8, Travelers Inn
138	59th Ave, N [gas] Circle K, Valero [food] Los Armandos Mexican, Papa John's, Subway [other] 7-11, AutoZone, Family$, O'Reilly

INTERSTATE 10 Cont'd

138	Continued
	Parts, URGENT CARE, Walgreens, **S** Q Liberty/Chester's/ dsl/24hr 🍴 Waffle House O Blue Beacon/scales
137	67th Ave, **N** Q Circle K/dsl, QT, Shell/dsl 🍴 Church's, **S** Q *FLYING J*/Denny's/dsl/LP/24hr
136	75th Ave, **N** Q Chevron/dsl, Circle K 🍴 A&W/LJ Silver, CiCi's Pizza, Coco's, Denny's, Hooters, IHOP, Lin's Buffet, Longhorn Steaks, McDonald's, Olive Garden, Pizza Hut/Taco Bell, Red Lobster, Starbucks, Subway, TX Roadhouse, Wendy's, Whataburger O $Tree, AT&T, Big Lots, Big O Tire, Dillards, Home Depot, La Mesa RV Ctr, Lowe's, Radio Shack, Ross, Sears, Target, Walmart, **S** Q Arco
135	83rd Ave, **N** Q Circle K, QT 🍴 Burger King, Jack-in-the-Box, Waffle House 🏠 Best Western, Premier Inn, Victory Inn O K-Mart, Sam's Club/gas
134	91st Ave, Tolleson, **N** Q Circle K/dsl
133b	Lp 101 N
133a	99th Ave, **N** Q Chevron/dsl 🍴 Cafe Rio, Cane's, Carrabba's, Chick-fil-A, China City, Chipotle Mexican, ClaimJumper, HoneyBaked Ham, Ichiban Rest., Island's Burgers, Jimmy John's, McDonald's, Native Grill, Panda Express, Paradise Cafe, Peter Piper Pizza, Pita Kitchen, Red Robin, Rumbi Grill, Smashburger, Starbucks, Subway, Taco Bell, Village Inn 🏠 Courtyard O Best Buy, Costco/gas, Discount Tire, GNC, Hobby Lobby, Marshall's,
	Old Navy, PetCo, Ross, URGENT CARE, Verizon, **S** 🍴 *Pilot*/ Subway/Wendy's/dsl/scales/24hr O CarMax, Chevrolet
132	107th Ave, **N** O Walgreens, **S** O Camping World RV Ctr, Chrysler/Jeep, Dodge/Ram, Fiat, Honda, Hyundai, Kia, Mazda, Nissan, Toyota/Scion, VW
131	Avondale Blvd, to Cashion, **N** Q Circle K/dsl, **S** 🍴 Culver's, Jack-in-the-Box, Panda Express, Ruby Tuesday 🏠 Hilton Garden, Homewood Suite O CVS Drug, to Phoenix Intnl Raceway
129	Dysart Rd, to Avondale, **N** Q Chevron/dsl, Shell/Circle K/dsl 🍴 Buffalo Wild Wings, Chick-fil-A, ChuckECheese, Fiesta Mexican, In-N-Out, Jack-in-the-Box/24hr, Manuel's Mexican, Mimi's Cafe, Nakomo Japanese, NYPD Pizza, Ono Hawaiian BBQ, Panda Express, Peiwei Asian, Starbucks, Subway, Taco Bell, Tomo Japanese 🏠 Holiday Inn Express O $Tree, AT&T, AutoZone, Discount Tire, Fry's Foods, JC Penney, Jo-Ann Fabrics, Kohl's, Lowe's, PetsMart, Sprouts Mkt, Tuesday Morning, Verizon, vet, Walmart, **S** Q QT 🍴 AZ Frybread, Black Bear Diner, Del Taco, Golden Corral, IHOP, KFC, McDonald's, Peter Piper Pizza, Subway, Waffle House, Whataburger 🏠 Quality Inn, Super 8 O Brakemasters, Food City, Home Depot, Pepboys, S&S Tire/repair, Sam's Club/gas, Walgreens
128	Litchfield Rd, **N** Q Circle K/dsl 🍴 Applebee's, Black Angus Steaks, Caballero, Carl's Jr, Chili's, Chipotle Mexican, Cracker Barrel, Denny's, Five Guys, Freddy's Steakburger, Gus' NY Pizza, Hayashi Japanese, Jimmy John's, Macaroni Grill, Macavo's Mexican, McDonald's, Raul&Theresa's Mexican, Starbucks, Subway, Wendy's, Wildflower Bread Co. 🏠 Hampton Inn, Holiday Inn Express, Residence Inn O H, Barnes&Noble, Best Buy, Michael's, Ross, Target, to Luke AFB, URGENT CARE, Wigwam Resort/rest (3mi), **S** Q Circle K/dsl 🍴 Arby's, Burger King, Eggs&More, Little Caesar's, Ramiro's Mexican, Rudy's BBQ, Schlotsky's 🏠 Best Western, TownePlace Suite O AutoZone, BigLots, Buick/GMC, Ford, O'Reilly Parts
127	Bullard Ave, **N** 🍴 PF Chang's, Red Robin
126	PebbleCreek Pkwy, to Estrella Park, **N** 🍴 Ah-So Steaks, Aribba Mexican, Barro's Pizza, Native Grill, Olive Garden, Paradise Cafe, Red Lobster, Rubio's, Taco Bell, TX Roadhouse O $Tree, Cal Ranch, Firestone/auto, Old Navy, PetCo, Staples, TJ Maxx, Walgreens, **S** Q QT/dsl 🍴 Augie's Grill, Austin's Rest., Burger Joint, Filiberto's Mexican, McDonald's, Panda Express, Pizza Hut, Senor Taco, Starbucks, Subway, Yan's Chinese 🏠 Comfort Suites O Ace Hardware, Fletcher Tire, Radio Shack, Safeway Foods/dsl, Verizon, vet, Walgreens, Walmart
125	Sarival Ave, Cotton Lane (from wb)
125mm	Roosevelt Canal
124	AZ 303
123	Citrus Rd, to Cotton Ln, **S** O Phoenix RV Park
122	Perryville Rd
121	Jackrabbit Trail, **N** Q Chevron/dsl, **S** Q Circle K/ds O CarQuest
120	Verrado Way
117	Watson Rd, **S** Q Circle K/dsl 🍴 Carl's Jr, Chipotle Mexican, Cracker Barrel, Denny's, Dunkin Donuts, El Pollo Loco, Federico's Mexican, Jack-in-the-Box, KFC, Little Caesar's, McDonald's, Native NY Grill, Palermo's Pizza, Panda Express, Papa John's, Peter Piper Pizza, Subway, Taco Bell, Wendy's O $Tree, AT&T, AutoZone, Discount Tire, Fletcher's Tire, Fry's Foods/dsl, Lowe's, PetsMart, URGENT CARE, Verizon, vet, Walgreens, Walmart/McDonald's
114	Miller Rd, to Buckeye, **S** Q Chevron Travel Ctr/Sams Deli/ grill/dsl/E85/LP/24hr, *Loves*/Chester's/Subway/dsl/ scales/24hr, QT/dsl 🍴 Burger King 🏠 Days Inn O Leaf Verde RV Park
112	AZ 85, to I-8, Gila Bend, **S** 🍴 Subway (3mi)
109	Sun Valley Pkwy, Palo Verde Rd
104mm	Hassayampa River
103	339th Ave, **S** Q TA/Country Pride/Pizza Hut/Shell/Subway/ Taco Bell/dsl/scales/LP/24hr/ @ O truckwash
98	Wintersburg Rd
97mm	Coyote Wash
95.5mm	Old Camp Wash
94	411th Ave, Tonopah, **S** Q Chevron/dsl, Mobil/dsl, Shell/Cafe Charro/Noble Roman's/Subway/dsl/LP/24hr 🍴 Oscar's Place Cantina O Saddle Mtn RV Park, tires/repair, USPO
86mm	Rs both lanes, full 🧑‍🦽 facilities, litter barrels, petwalk 📞 🚮 vending
81	Salome Rd, Harquahala Valley Rd
69	Ave 75E
53	Hovatter Rd
52mm	Rs both lanes, full 🧑‍🦽 facilities, litter barrels, petwalk 📞 🚮 vending

P H O E N I X

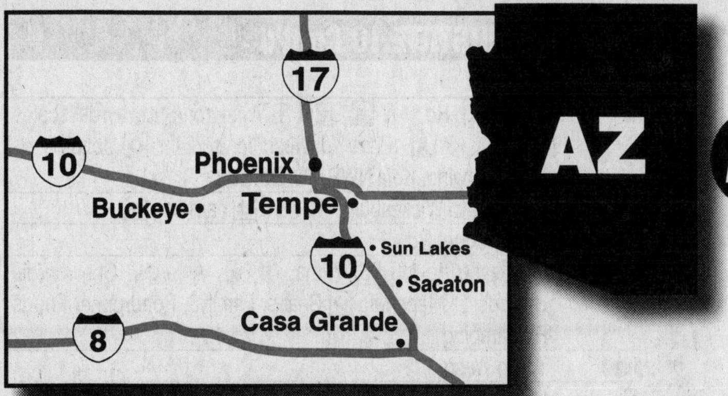

AZ

QUARTZSITE

INTERSTATE 10 Cont'd

Exit #	Services
45	Vicksburg Rd, N [gas] Zip TC/Chevron/Subway/dsl/scales/LP/24hr, S [gas] Pride /dsl/rest./scales/24hr [other] Jobski's dsl Repair/towing, Kofa NWR, RV Park, tires
31	US 60 E, to Wickenburg, **12 mi** N [other] camping [food]
26	Gold Nugget Rd
19	Quartzsite, to US 95, Yuma, N [gas] Arco/dsl, Chevron/dsl, Shell/dsl [food] Taco Mio [other] Beall's, Family$, Roadrunner Foods, RV camping
18mm	Tyson Wash
17	US 95, AZ 95, Quartzsite, N [gas] Mobil/Burger King/LP/dsl, Pilot/DQ/Subway/dsl/scales/24hr [food] Carl's Jr, McDonald's, Quartzsite Yacht Grill, Times 3 Rest. [lodging] Stagecoach Motel/rest [other] $General, RV camping, tires/repair, S [gas] Loves/Chester's/Subway/dsl/24hr [lodging] Super 8 [other] Desert Gardens RV Park, Lifestyles RV Ctr
11	Dome Rock Rd
5	Tom Wells Rd, N [gas] Texaco/SunMart/Quizno's/dsl/scales
4.5mm	**[rest stop] both lanes, full [handicapped] facilities, litter barrels, petwalk [phone] [picnic] vending**
3.5mm	AZ Port of Entry, weigh sta
1	Ehrenberg, to Parker, N [gas] Texaco [other] River Lagoon RV Resort, S [gas] FLYING J/Wendy's/dsl/LP/scales/lube/repair/tires/24hr [lodging] Best Western
0mm	Arizona/California state line, Colorado River, Mountain/Pacific time zone

INTERSTATE 15

Exit #	Services
29.5mm	Arizona/Utah state line
27	Black Rock Rd
21mm	turnout sb
18	Cedar Pocket, S [other] **parking area**, Virgin River Canyon RA/camping
16mm	**truck parking both lanes**
15mm	**truck parking nb**
14mm	**truck parking nb**
10mm	**truck parking nb**
9	Desert Springs
8.5mm	Virgin River
8	Littlefield, Beaver Dam, E [other] RV park, **1 mi** W [other] camping, food, gas/dsl, lodging
0mm	Arizona/Nevada state line, Pacific/Mountain time zone

INTERSTATE 17

FLAGSTAFF

Exit #	Services
341	McConnell Dr, **I-17 begins/ends**, N [gas] Chevron/dsl, Circle K, Conoco/dsl, Giant/dsl, Mobil/dsl, Shell, Texaco/Wendy's/dsl [food] 5 Guys Burgers, Arby's, August Moon Chinese, Baskin-Robbins, Buffalo Wild Wings, Burger King, Buster's Rest., Cafe Rio, Carl's Jr, Chick-fil-A, Chili's, China Garden, Chipotle Mexican, Coco's, Coldstone, Del Taco, Denny's, Domino's, DQ, Freddy's Steakburgers, IHOP, Jack-in-the-Box, Jimmy John's, KFC, Little Caesars, Mandarin Buffet, McDonald's, Native New Yorker, Ni Marco's Pizza, Olive Garden, Panda Express, Papa John's, Papa Murphy's, Peter Piper Pizza, Picazzo's Pizza, Pizza Hut, Quiznos, Red Lobster, Sizzler, Starbucks, Subway, Taco Bell [lodging] Best Inn, Budget Inn, Canyon Inn, Comfort Inn,
341	Continued Courtyard, Days Inn, Drury Inn, EconoLodge, Embassy Suites, Fairfield Inn, Hampton Inn, Knights Inn, La Quinta, Motel 6, Quality Inn, Ramada Ltd, Rodeway Inn, SpringHill Suites, Super 8 [other] $Tree, AT&T, Barnes&Noble, Basha's Foods, Discount Tire, Hastings Books, Jo-Ann Crafts, Kohl's, Michael's, O'Reilly Parts, Petsmart, Ross, Safeway, Sprouts Mkt, Staples, Target, Verizon, Walgreens, Walmart
340b a	I-40, E to Gallup, W to Kingman
339	Lake Mary Rd (from nb), Mormon Lake, E [gas] Circle K/dsl [lodging] AZ Mtn Inn [other] access to same as 341
337	AZ 89A S, to Sedona, Ft Tuthill RA, W [other] camping
333	Kachina Blvd, Mountainaire Rd, E [food] Mountainaire Rest. (1mi) [lodging] Abineau B&B, W [gas] Shell/Subway/dsl [other] county park
331	Kelly Canyon Rd
328	Newman Park Rd
326	Willard Springs Rd
322	Pinewood Rd, to Munds Park, E [gas] Shell/dsl, Woody's/dsl [food] Lone Pine Rest. [other] golf, Motel in the Pines, W [gas] Chevron/dsl [other] Munds RV Park
322mm	Munds Canyon
320	Schnebly Hill Rd
317	Fox Ranch Rd
316mm	Woods Canyon
315	Rocky Park Rd
313mm	Scenic view sb, litter barrels
306	Stoneman Lake Rd
300mm	**runaway truck ramp sb**
298	AZ 179, to Sedona, Oak Creek Canyon, **7-15 mi** W [food] Burger King, Cowboy Club Rest., Joey's Bistro [lodging] Belrock Inn, Diamond Resort, Hilton, La Quinta, Radisson/cafe, Wildflower Inn [other] Rancho Sedona RV Park
297mm	**[rest stop] both lanes, full [handicapped] facilities, litter barrels, petwalk [phone] [picnic] vending**
293mm	Dry Beaver Creek
293	Cornville Rd, McGuireville Rd, to Rimrock, E [gas] McGuireville [food] Nikki's Grill, W [gas] 76/dsl, Conoco/Beaver Hollow/dsl [food] El Patio Grill
289	Middle Verde Rd, Camp Verde, E [gas] Chevron/dsl [food] Sonic, The Gathering Rest. [lodging] Cliff Castle Hotel/casino/rest. [other] to Montezuma Castle NM, W [other] Distant Drums RV Park
288mm	Verde River
287	AZ 260, to AZ 89A, Cottonwood, Payson, E [gas] Shell/Subway/dsl/RV dump/LP/24hr [food] Burger King, Carl's Jr, Denny's, DQ, Gabriela's Mexican, Los Betos Mexican, McDonald's, Starbucks, Taco Bell [lodging] Comfort Inn, Days Inn, Super 8 [other] Territorial RV Park (1mi), Trails End RV Park, Zane Grane RV Park (9mi), W [gas] Chevron/Wendy's/dsl/24hr [other] RV camping, to Jerome SP
285	Camp Verde, Gen Crook Tr, **3 mi** E [food] Rio Verde Mexican [lodging] Territorial Town Inn [other] to Ft Verde SP, Trail End RV Park, Zane Gray RV Park (9mi)
281mm	**safety pullout area nb**
278	AZ 169, Cherry Rd, to Prescott
269mm	Ash Creek
268	Dugas Rd, Orme Rd
265.5mm	Agua Fria River
263b a	AZ 69 N, Cordes Jct Rd (262 from nb), to Prescott, E [gas] Chevron, Shell/Noble Roman's/Subway/dsl/LP/24hr [food] Cafe Charo, McDonald's [lodging] Cordes Jct Motel/RV Park [other] Family$
259	Bloody Basin Rd, to Crown King, Horse Thief Basin RA
256	Badger Springs Rd

SEDONA

CAMP VERDE

INTERSTATE 17 Cont'd

Exit #	Services
252	**Sunset Point, /scenic view both lanes, full facilities, picnic tables, litter barrels vending**
248	Bumble Bee, W Horsethief Basin RA
244	Squaw Valley Rd, Black Canyon City, E Chilleen's on 17 BBQ/Steaks, W Shell Beni's Pizza Mountain Breeze Motel Bradshaw Mtn RV Resort (2mi), Family$
243.5mm	Agua Fria River
242	Rock Springs, Black Canyon City, E KOA (1mi), W 76/dsl, Shell Beni's Pizza, Rock Springs Cafe Bradshaw Mtn RV Resort, Mtn Breeze Motel Ron's Mkt
239.5mm	Little Squaw Creek
239mm	Moore's Gulch
236	Table Mesa Rd
232	New River, E RoadRunner Rest.
231.5mm	New River
229	Anthem Way, Desert Hills Rd, E Circle K Hungry Howie's, McDonald's, Pizza Hut, Rosati's Pizza, Starbucks, Subway, Taco Bell, Wendy's CVS Drug, Safeway, URGENT CARE, W Chevron/dsl, Circle K/dsl Del Taco, Denny's, Fresca's Mexican, Subway Hampton Inn $Store, Anthem Outlets/famous brands/food court, Discount Tire, Harley-Davidson, Meineke, O'Reilly Parts, Tobias Auto, U-Haul, Walmart
227	Daisy Mtn Dr, E Circle K/dsl Cafe Provence, Domino's, Jack-in-the-Box, Roberto's Mexican, Starbucks, Streets of NY Deli, Streets of NY Deli, Subway CVS Drug, Fry's Foods, GNC, GNC, Verizon, vet
227mm	Dead Man Wash
225	Pioneer Rd, W Pioneer AZ Museum, Pioneer RV Park
223	AZ 74, Carefree Hwy, to Wickenburg, E Chevron AZool Grill, Chili's, Denny's, Good Egg Cafe, In-N-Out, McDonald's, Ray's Pizza, Starbucks, Subway, Taco Bell Albertson's/Osco, GNC, Home Depot, Kohl's, Staples, W Cibola Vista Camping (11mi)
222	Senora Blvd
220	Dixileta (from nb)
219	Jomax Rd
218	Happy Valley Rd, E Circle K/dsl, Shell Applebee's, Bajio, Buffalo Wild Wings, Burger King, Carl's Jr, Chipotle Mexican, Coldstone, IHOP, Jack-in-the-Box, Jersey Mike's Subs, Joey's Hotdogs, Johnny Rocket's, L&L Hawaiian BBQ, Logan's Roadhouse, Mellow Mushroom Pizza, Olive Garden, Panda Express, Paradise Cafe, PF Chang's, Rays Pizza, Red Robin, Sauce Pizza, Shane's Ribshack, Smash Burger, Starbucks, Subway, TGIFriday's, Zupas Courtyard, Hampton Inn, Homewood Suites, Residence Inn $Tree, Barnes&Noble, Best Buy, Big O Tire, Dick's, Lowe's, Old Navy, O'Reilly Parts, PetCo, Ross, Staples, TJ Maxx, Verizon, vet, Walmart, World Mkt, W to Meg&DeLyle's
217	Pinnacle Peak Rd, E Drury Inn, Hilton Garden Phoenix RV Park
215a	Rose Garden Ln, same as 215b
215b	Deer Valley Rd, E Shell/Circle K Arby's, Armando's Mexican, Culvers, Dunkin Donuts, Jack-in-the-Box, McDonald's, Sonic, Subway, Taco Bell, Wendy's Little Dealer RV Ctr, W Arco/dsl, Circle K/dsl Cracker Barrel, Denny's, Times Square Italian, Waffle House Days Inn, Extended Stay America H U-Haul
214c	AZ 101 loop

ANTHEM

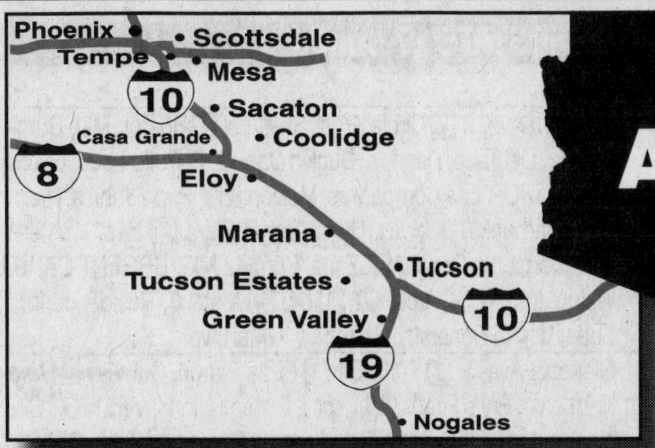

Exit #	Services
214b	Yorkshire Dr, W 7-11 Chick-fil-A, Chili's, In-N-Out, Jack-in-the-Box, Jimmy John's, Macaroni Grill, Pizza Hut, Wendy's Budget Suites H AT&T, Costco/gas, Michael's, Petsmart, Ross, Target
214a	Union Hills Dr, E Circle K/dsl, Valero, W Arco/dsl Comfort Inn, Sleep Inn, Studio 6
212b a	Bell Rd, Scottsdale, to Sun City, E Chevron/dsl, Circle K, QT, Shell/dsl Big Apple Rest., Caramba Mexican, IHOP, Jack-in-the-Box, LJ Silver, Manuel's Mexican, McDonald's, Schlotzsky's, Shenanigan's Grill, Waffle House Fairfield Inn, Motel 6, Super 8 Big O Tire, Chevrolet, Chrysler/Jeep/Dodge, Discount Tire, Fiat, Ford, Honda, Hyundai, Kohl's, Lincoln, Mazda, Nissan, O'Reilly Parts, Sam's Club/gas, Toyota/Scion, U-Haul, Volvo, Walmart, W Applebee's, Denny's, Native New Yorker, US Egg Breakfast Red Roof Inn Fry's Foods/dsl
211	Greenway Rd, E Embassy Suites, La Quinta 7-11
210	Thunderbird Rd, E Circle K/dsl, Valero/dsl/LP Asian Cafe, Barro's Pizza, Hong Kong Chinese, Jack-in-the-Box, Macayo's Mexican, Pizza Hut/Taco Bell, Subway, Wendy's CVS Drug, Home Depot, Walgreens, W QT Jamba Juice, McDonald's, Port of Subs, Whataburger Travelodge Best Buy, Fry's Electronics, Lowe's
209	Cactus Rd, W 7-11, Chevron/dsl, QT/dsl China Harvest, Tuliaberto's Mexican Holiday Inn
208	Peoria Ave, E Fajita's, First Watch Cafe, Native Grill, Outback Steaks, Pappadeaux, Sweet Tomatoes Candlewood Suites, Comfort Suites, Crowne Plaza, Extended Stay America, Homewood Suites, Hyatt Place, W QT/dsl Black Angus, Buffalo Wild Wings, Burger King, Cane's, Chili's, Chipotle Mexican, Coldstone, Culvers, Fat Burger, Filiberto's Mexican, Hibachi Grill, Hooters, In-N-Out, Jason's Deli, Longhorn Steaks, Mi Pueblo, Mimi's Cafe, Mongolian BBQ, Old Country Buffet, Olive Garden, Peter Piper Pizza, Red Lobster, Sizzler, Souper Salad, Starbucks, Subway, TX Roadhouse, Wendy's Metro Plaza, Premier Inn $Tree, AT&T, Barnes&Noble, Dillard's, Discount Tire, Firestone/auto, Macy's, mall, Michael's, PetCo, Petsmart, Ross, Sears/auto, Staples, Tire Pros/repair, URGENT CARE, Verizon
208.5mm	Arizona Canal
207	Dunlap Ave, E Circle K, Shell/dsl Blimpie, Domino's, Fajitas, First Watch Cafe, Fuddrucker's, Jack-in-the-Box, Native Grill, Outback Steaks, Steaken Burger, Subway, Sweet Tomatoes, Wong's Comfort Suites, Courtyard, Mainstay Suites, Sheraton, SpringHill Suites, TownPlace Suites Aamco, CVS Drug, URGENT CARE, W Chevron/dsl Bobby-Q's Rest., Denny's, Schlotzsky's, Subway ValuePlace Midas, repair, U-Haul

SCOTTSDALE

PHOENIX

INTERSTATE 17 Cont'd

17

AZ

PHOENIX

Services

- **[...]ern Ave**, E 🅿 Circle K/dsl, Shell/dsl 🍴 Boston Mkt, Burg[er] [K]ing, Del Taco, Denny's, Dunkin Donuts, El Pollo Loco, Gyros [H]ouse, IHOP, Los Compadres, McDonald's, Papa John's, Pizza Hut, Starbucks, Subway, Uncle Tony's Pizza 🛏 Best Western Ⓞ Albertson's/Osco, AutoZone, Sprouts Mkt, URGENT CARE, Walgreens, W 🅿 Arco, QT 🍴 DQ 🛏 Motel 6, Residence Inn, Super 8 Ⓞ $General, auto repair, K-Mart, vet

205 Glendale Ave, E 🅿 7-11, QT 🍴 Pizza Patron, Subway Ⓞ Ace Hardware, Fry's Foods/dsl, repair, transmissions, vet, W 🅿 Circle K/dsl 🍴 Jack-in-the-Box, Lenny's Burger Ⓞ 7-11, O'Reilly Parts, to Luke AFB, Walgreens

204 Bethany Home Rd, E 🅿 Arco, Chevron/dsl, Shell/Church's/dsl 🍴 Carl's Jr, Dunkin Donuts, KFC, Mandarin Buffet, McDonald's, Papa Joe's, Pizza Hut/Taco Bell, Subway, Tulioberto's Mexican, Whataburger Ⓞ Ⓗ $Tree, BigLots, Costco/gas, JC Penney, Petsmart, Radio Shack, Ross, Target, URGENT CARE, Walgreens, Walmart, W 🅿 Shell, Valero 🍴 Burger King, Familia Lorito, Great Dragon 🛏 Knights Inn Ⓞ auto repair, Food City, Jiffy Lube, Savers

203 Camelback Rd, E 🍴 Church's, Country Boy's Rest., Filiberto's Mexican, Little Caesars Ⓞ $General, Chrysler/Dodge/Jeep, Discount Tire, Family$, Hyundai, Kia, W 🅿 Circle K/dsl, QT 🍴 DQ, Jack-in-the-Box, McDonald's 🛏 Quality Inn Ⓞ AutoZone, to Grand Canyon U, USPO

202 Indian School Rd, E 🅿 Arco/dsl 🍴 Domino's, Federico's Mexican, Pizza Hut, Subway Ⓞ Ace Hardware, CVS Drug, Food City, Little RV Ctr, W 🅿 Shell, Sinclair/dsl, Valero/dsl 🍴 Lenny's Burgers 🛏 Motel 6, Travel Inn Ⓞ 7-11, Wide World of Maps

201 Thomas Rd, E 🅿 Chevron/McDonald's/playplace 🍴 Arby's, Denny's, Dunkin Donuts, Jack-in-the-Box, Starbucks 🛏 Days Inn, La Quinta Ⓞ Circle K, W 🅿 QT 🍴 Carl's Jr, Subway Ⓞ NAPA

200b McDowell Rd, Van Buren, E Ⓞ Purcell's Tire, W 🛏 Knights Inn

200a I-10, W to LA, E to Phoenix

199b Jefferson St (from sb), Adams St (from nb), Van Buren St (from nb), E 🅿 Circle K 🍴 Jack-in-the-Box Ⓞ to st capitol, W 🅿 Circle K/gas 🍴 La Canasta Mexican Ⓞ Penny Pincher Parts, PepBoys

199a Grant St

198 Buckeye Rd (from nb)

197 US 60, 19th Ave, Durango St, E 🍴 Jack-in-the-Box, to St Capitol, Whataburger Ⓞ $General, AutoZone

196 7th St, Central Ave, W 🅿 Shell/dsl

195b 7th St, Central Ave, E 🅿 Circle K/dsl 🍴 Jack-in-the-Box, McDonald's, Taco Bell 🛏 EZ 8 Motel Ⓞ Ⓗ NAPA Care

195a 16th St (from sb, no EZ return), E 🅿 Shell/Subway/dsl 🍴 Burger King Ⓞ to Sky Harbor Airport

194 I-10 W, to AZ 151, to Sky Harbor Airport

I-17 begins/ends on I-10, exit 150a.

⬆N INTERSTATE 19

Exit #	Services

I-19 uses kilometers (km)

101b a I-10, E to El Paso, W to Phoenix, **I-19 begins/ends on I-10, exit 260.**

99 AZ 86, Ajo Way, E 🅿 Circle K, Shell 🍴 Eegee's Cafe, Hamburger Stand, Peter Piper Pizza, Pizza Hut, Subway, Taco Bell,

TUCSON

99 Continued Wienerschnitzel Ⓞ auto repair, Family$, Fry's Foods, GNC, Goodyear/auto, U-Haul, URGENT CARE, vet, Walgreens, W 🅿 Circle K, QT/dsl, Shell/dsl 🍴 Burger King, Church's, Domino's, Little Caesars, Losbetos Mexican, McDonald's Ⓞ Ⓗ $General, city park, Family$, Food City, Jiffy Lube, museum, to Old Tucson

98 Irvington Rd, E 🅿 Arco/dsl 🍴 Jimmy John's, TX Roadhouse Ⓞ AutoZone, Fry's Foods/drug/dsl, W 🅿 Chevron, Circle K/dsl 🍴 Buffalo Wild Wings, China Olive Buffet, Coldstone, Five Guys, McDonald's, Olive Garden, Panda Express, Peter Piper Pizza, Red Lobster, Starbucks, Subway Ⓞ $Tree, AT&T, Best Buy, Discount Tire, Family$, Food City, Home Depot, JC Penney, Marshall's, Michael's, Old Navy, Petsmart, Ross, Target, Verizon

95b a Valencia Rd, E 🅿 Circle K, Shell 🍴 Chickenuevo, Church's, Donut Wheel, Eegee's Cafe, Jack-in-the-Box, Little Caesars, McDonald's, Peter Piper Pizza, Sonic, Subway, Whataburger, Yokohama Asian Ⓞ $General, $Tree, Aamco, AutoZone, Brake Masters, Family$, Food City, Jiffy Lube, O'Reilly Parts, to airport, USPO, Walgreens, W 🅿 Circle K/dsl 🍴 Arby's, Burger King, Carl's Jr, Casa Valencia, Chili's, China Dragon, Denny's, DQ, El Taco Tote, Golden Corral, Grand Buffet, Hamburger Stand, Little Caesars, Papa John's, Papa Murphy's, Pizza Hut, Subway, Taco Bell, Wendy's Ⓞ 99c Store, Big O Tire, BigLots, CVS Drug, Lowe's, Radio Shack, repair, transmissions, URGENT CARE, Walgreens, Walmart

92 San Xavier Rd, W Ⓞ to San Xavier Mission (2mi)

91.5km Santa Cruz River

87 Papago Rd

80 Pima Mine Rd, E 🍴 Agave Rest., Diamond Casino

75 Helmut Peak Rd, to Sahuarita, E 🅿 Shell/dsl/e-85 🍴 Asian Sky Rest, Dunkin Donuts/Baskin Robbins, Mama's Hawaiian BBQ, McDonald's, Starbucks, Subway Ⓞ Fry's Foods/drug, USPO, vet

GREEN VALLEY

69 US 89 N, Duval Mine Rd., Green Valley, E 🍴 50's Diner, Carl's Jr., Denny's, Little Caesars, Panda House, Pizza Hut, Rigoberto's, Subway Ⓞ 99cents Store, Ace Hardware, AutoZone, BigLots, Fletcher's Repair, Jo-Ann Fabrics, O'Reilly Parts, Petco, Radio Shack, Ross, Verizon, Walgreens, Walmart/Subway, W 🅿 Circle K 🍴 Arby's, Burger King, Domino's, Jerry Bob's Rest., Manuel's Mexican, Papa Murphy's, Starbucks, Taco Bell 🛏 Holiday Inn Express Ⓞ Big O Tire, Ford/Hyundai, Green Valley RV Resort, NAPA, Safeway/dsl, Titan Missile Museum, URGENT CARE, USPO, vet

65 Esperanza Blvd, to Green Valley, E 🅿 Shell/repair/dsl, W 🍴 AZ Family Rest., La Placita Mexican 🛏 Best Western/rest, Comfort Inn Ⓞ Ace Hardware, Walgreens

63 Continental Rd, Green Valley, E 🍴 Quail Creek Rest. (7mi) Ⓞ golf, San Ignacio Golf Club/rest., USPO, W 🅿 Chevron/Hot-Stuff Pizza 🍴 KFC, McDonald's, Starbucks Ⓞ CVS Drug, Merle's Parts, repair/tires, Safeway, to Madera Cyn RA, TrueValue, Verizon, Walgreens

56 Canoa Rd, W 🛏 San Ignacio Inn, Wyndham Resort

AMADO

54km Ⓡˢ both lanes, full ♿ facilities, litter barrels, petwalk 🍴 ♨ vending

48 Arivaca Rd, Amado, **2-3 mi** E 🛏 Amado Inn Ⓞ DeAnza RV Resort (2mi), Mtn View RV Park, W 🍴 Cow Palace Rest. Ⓞ Amado Mkt/gas, JJ's Auto Repair

42 Agua Linda Rd, to Amado, E Ⓞ Mtn View RV Park

40 Chavez Siding Rd, Tubac, E Ⓞ Tubac Golf Resort

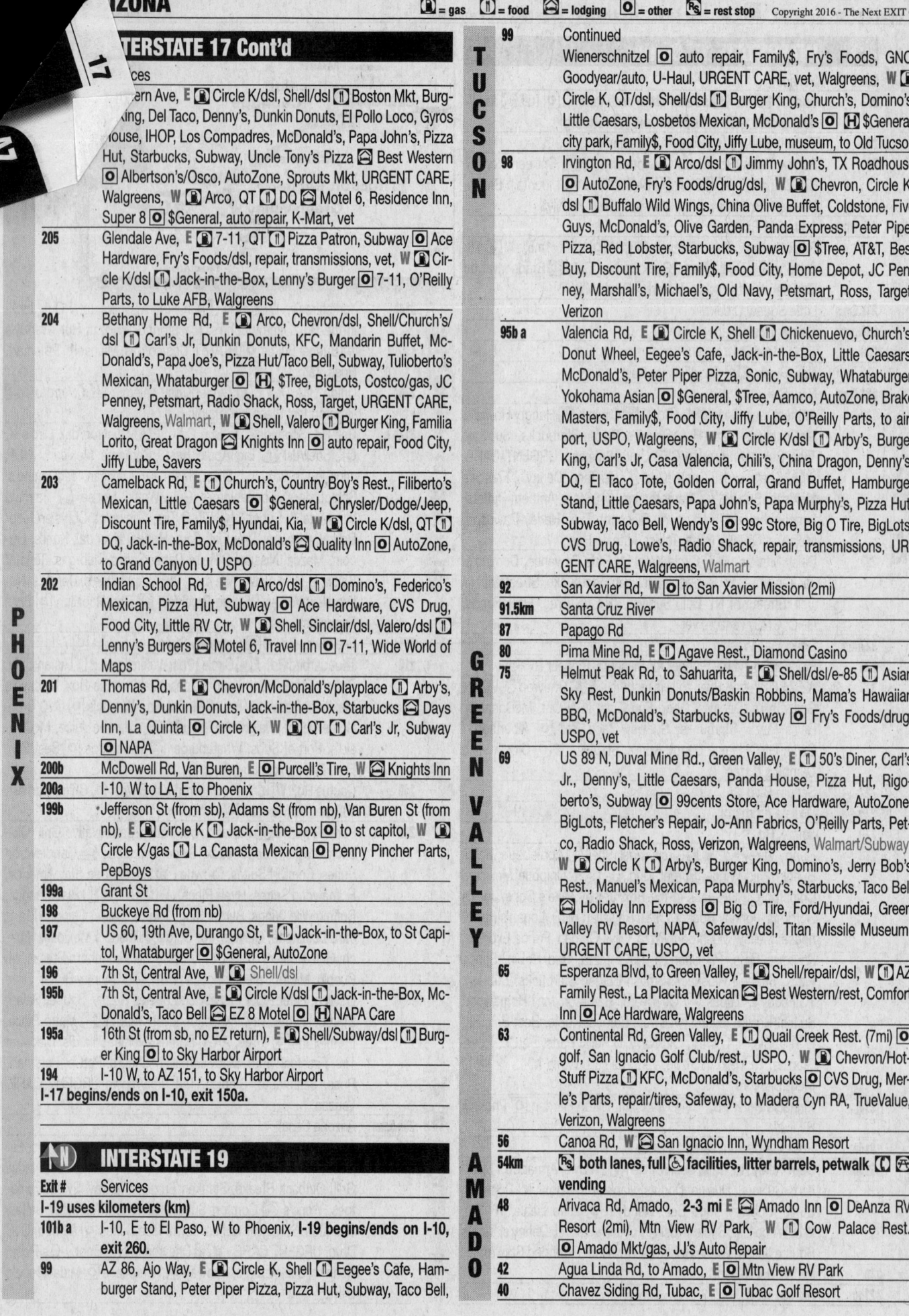

INTERSTATE 19 Cont'd

NOGALES

Exit #	Services
34	Tubac, E [gas] El Mercado [food] Elvira's Cafe, Tubac Deli, Tubac Hamburgers, Tubac Jack's Rest., Tubac Pizza [other] to Tubac Presidio SP, Tubac Golf Resort, Tubac Mkt, USPO
29	Carmen, Tumacacori, E [other] to Tumacacori Nat Hist Park, food, gas, lodging
25	Palo Parado Rd
22	Pec Canyon Rd
17	Rio Rico Dr, Calabasas Rd, W [gas] Chevron/dsl/LP [food] Hua Mei Chinese, Nickles Diner, Wood Oven Pizza [lodging] Esplendor Resort [other] IGA Foods, JC Auto Repair/Lube, USPO, vet
12	AZ 289, to Ruby Rd, E [gas] Pilot/Wendy's/dsl/scales/24hr, W [other] to Pena Blanca Lake RA
8	AZ 82 (exits left from sb, no return), Nogales, E [gas] Circle K [other] Mi Casa RV Park
4	AZ 189 S, Mariposa Rd, Nogales, E [gas] FasTrip/dsl [food] Bella Mia Rest., China Buffet, Chuyitos Hotdogs, City Salads, DQ, Dragon Buffet, Exquisito Mexican, Gorilla Pizza, Jack-in-the-Box, KFC, Little Caesars, McDonald's, Panda Express, Panda Express, Pizza Pollis, Subway, Toscanos [lodging] Mariposa Hotel, Motel 6 [other] $General, $Tree, Ace Hardware, AutoZone, Buick/GMC, Chevrolet, Ford, GNC, Home Depot, JC Penney, K-Mart, Petsmart, Radio Shack, Ross, Safeway, Walgreens, Walmart/McDonald's (N Grand Ave), W [gas] Circle K/dsl [food] Carl's Jr, IHOP [lodging] Best Western, Candlewood Suites, Holiday Inn Express [other] Mexico Insurance
1b	Western Ave, Nogales
1a	International St
0km	**I-19 begins/ends in Nogales, Arizona/Mexico Border, 1/2 mi** N [gas] Circle K, Jr's Fuel Depot/dsl, Shell [food] Church's, Denny's, Jack-in-the-Box, McDonald's, Peter Piper Pizza, Pizza Hut, Subway [other] AutoZone, CarQuest, Family$, Food City, museum, NAPA, O'Reilly Parts, PepBoys

INTERSTATE 40

CHAMBERS

Exit #	Services
359.5mm	Arizona/New Mexico state line
359	Grants Rd, to Lupton, N **Welcome Ctr/[RS] both lanes, full [handicapped] facilities, litter barrels, petwalk** [phone] [picnic], [gas] Speedy's/dsl/rest./24hr [other] Tee Pee Trading Post/rest., YellowHorse Indian Gifts
357	AZ 12 N, Lupton, to Window Rock, N [other] USPO
354	Hawthorne Rd
351	Allentown Rd, N [other] Chee's Indian Store, Indian City Gifts
348	St Anselm Rd, Houck, N [other] Ft Courage Food/gifts
347.5mm	Black Creek
346	Pine Springs Rd
345mm	Box Canyon
344mm	Querino Wash
343	Querino Rd
341	Ortega Rd, Cedar Point, N [gas] Armco/gas/gifts
340.5mm	**insp/weigh sta both lanes**
339	US 191 S, to St Johns, S [gas] Conoco/dsl [other] Family$, RV Park, USPO
333	US 191 N, Chambers, N [other] to Hubbell Trading Post NHS, USPO, S [gas] Mobil/dsl [lodging] Days Inn/rest.
330	McCarrell Rd
325	Navajo, S [gas] Shell/Subway/Navajo Trading Post/dsl/24hr

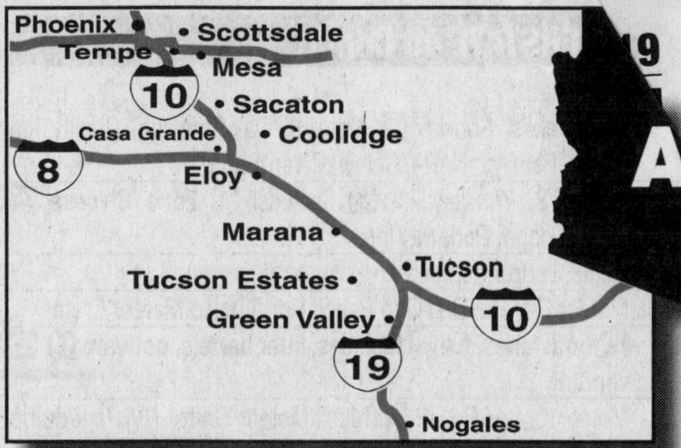

HOLBROOK

Exit #	Services
323mm	Crazy Creek
320	Pinta Rd
316mm	Dead River
311	Painted Desert, N [gas] Chevron [other] Painted Desert, Petrified Forest NP
303	Adamana Rd, N [other] Stewarts/gifts, S [other] Painted Desert Indian Ctr
302.5mm	Big Lithodendron Wash
301mm	Little Lithodendron Wash
300	Goodwater
299mm	Twin Wash
294	Sun Valley Rd, N [lodging] Root 66 RV camping, S [other] Knife City
292	AZ 77 N, to Keams Canyon, N [gas] Conoco/Burger King/dsl/24hr [other] dsl repair
289	Lp 40, Holbrook, N [gas] Chevron/dsl, Hatch's/dsl [food] Denny's, Jerry's Rest., Mesa Rest. [lodging] Best Western, Days Inn, EconoLodge, Howard Johnson, Motel 6, Quality Inn, Sahara Inn, Travelodge [other] Goodyear
286	Navajo Blvd, Holbrook, N [gas] 76/dsl, Circle K, Maverik/dsl [food] Aliberto's Mexican, Burger King, Carl's Jr, Hilltop Cafe, McDonald's, Pizza Hut, Taco Bell [lodging] 66 Motel, Lexington Inn, Super 8 [other] $General, KOA, OK RV Park, O'Reilly Parts, S [gas] Chevron/dsl, Fuel Express/dsl, MiniMart/gas, Speedy Dsl [food] DQ, Rte 66 Cafe [lodging] Best Value, El Rancho Motel/rest., Knights Inn [other] [H] Dodge/Ford/Lincoln, museum, rockshops, Scotty & Son Repair, SW Transmissions
285	US 180 E, AZ 77 S, Holbrook, **1 mi** S [gas] Giant/dsl [food] Butterfield Steaks, Wayside Mexican [lodging] Economy Inn, Globetrotter Hotel, Magnuson Hotel, Wigwam Motel [other] Best Hardware, Family$, repair, [RS] / [picnic] **/litter barrels**, Safeway, to Petrified Forest NP
284mm	Leroux Wash
283	Perkins Valley Rd, Golf Course Rd, S [gas] TA/Shell/Popeyes/dsl/scales/24hr/ @
280	Hunt Rd, Geronimo Rd, N [other] Geronimo Trading Post
277	Lp 40, Joseph City, N [gas] Loves/Chester's/Subway/scales/dsl/24hr, S [other] RV camping, to Cholla Lake CP
274	Lp 40, Joseph City, N [food] [gas] [lodging] RV camping
269	Jackrabbit Rd, S [other] Jackrabbit Trading Post
264	Hibbard Rd

WINSLOW

Exit #	Services
257	AZ 87 N, to Second Mesa, N [other] camping, to Homolovi Ruins SP, S [other] trading post
256.5mm	Little Colorado River
255	Lp 40, Winslow, N [gas] Winslow Fuel/dsl [lodging] Best Western [other] Mi Pueblo Mexican, Take-A-Rest RV Park, S [gas] FLYING J/Denny's/dsl/LNG/scales/RV Dump/24hr [food] Sonic [other] Chrysler/Dodge/Jeep, Nissan [RS]
253	N Park Dr, Winslow, N [gas] Chevron, Maverik/dsl [food] Capt Tony's Pizza, Pizza Hut [other] $General, Ford, O'Reilly Parts, tires/lube, Walmart/Subway, S [food] Alfonso's Mexican, LJ Silver/Taco Bell,

...STATE 40 Cont'd

	...ded
	...onald's, Subway Motel 6, Oak Tree Inn, Quality Inn H Family$, NAPA, Safeway, Verizon
	AZ 87 S, Winslow, S Shell/dsl Entre Chinese EconoLodge, Rodeway Inn
	AZ 99, Leupp Corner
	Meteor City Rd, Red Gap Ranch Rd, S to Meteor Crater
...5mm	**both lanes, full facilities, litter barrels, petwalk vending**
233	Meteor Crater Rd, S Mobil/Meteor Crater RV Park/dump to Meteor Crater NL
230	Two Guns
229.5mm	Canyon Diablo
225	Buffalo Range Rd
219	Twin Arrows, N Twin Arrows Casino
218.5mm	Padre Canyon
211	Winona, N Shell/dsl/repair
207	Cosnino Rd
204	to Walnut Canyon NM
201	US 89, Flagstaff, to Page, N 76/Express Stop/dsl, Chevron/dsl, Circle K/dsl, Maverik/dsl, Shell, VP/dsl Burger King, Del Taco, Denny's, Jack-in-the-Box, LJ Silver/Taco Bell, McDonald's, Pizza Hut, Sizzler, Village Inn, Wendy's Best Western, Days Inn, Hampton Inn, Howard Johnson, Luxury Inn, Super 8, Travelodge H auto repair, Best Buy, Chrysler/Dodge/Jeep, CVS Drug, Dillard's, Discount Tire, Family$, Family$, Goodyear/auto, Home Depot, Honda, JC Penney, KOA, mall, Marshall's, Nissan/Subaru, Old Navy, O'Reilly Parts, PetCo, Safeway/dsl, Sears/auto, Toyota/Scion, Tuesday Morning, VW, World Mkt, S Mobil/dsl Sonesta Suites, Wyndham Resort
198	Butler Ave, Flagstaff, N Chevron, Conoco/dsl, Shell Burger King, Country Host Rest., Cracker Barrel, Denny's, McDonald's, Outback Steaks, Sonic, Subway, Taco Bell EconoLodge, Holiday Inn Express, Howard Johnson, Motel 6, Quality Inn, Ramada, Rodeway Inn, Super 8 Autozone, NAPA, Sam's Club/gas, U-Haul, vet, Walgreens, Walmart, S Mobil, Sinclair/Little America/dsl/motel/ @ Black Bart's Steaks/RV Park
197.5mm	Rio de Flag
195b	US 89A N, McConnell Dr, Flagstaff, N Chevron/dsl, Circle K, Conoco/dsl, Giant/dsl, Mobil/dsl, Shell, Texaco/Wendy's/dsl 5 Guys Burgers, Arby's, August Moon Chinese, Baskin-Robbins, Buffalo Wild Wings, Burger King, Buster's Rest., Carl's Jr, Chili's, China Garden, Chipotle Mexican, Coco's, Coldstone, Del Taco, Denny's, Domino's, DQ, Freddy's Steakburgers, IHOP, Jack-in-the-Box, KFC, Little Caesars, Mandarin Buffet, McDonald's, Native New Yorker, Ni Marco's Pizza, Olive Garden, Panda Express, Papa John's, Papa Murphy's, Peter Piper Pizza, Picazzo's Pizza, Pizza Hut, Quiznos, Red Lobster, Sizzler, Starbucks, Subway, Taco Bell Best Inn, Budget Inn, Canyon Inn, Comfort Inn, Country Inn, Courtyard, Days Inn, Drury Inn, EconoLodge, Embassy Suites, Executive Inn, Fairfield Inn, Hampton Inn, Knights Inn, La Quinta, Motel 6, Quality Inn, Ramada Ltd, Rodeway Inn, SpringHill Suites, Super 8 H $Tree, AT&T, auto/RV repair, Barnes&Noble, Basha's Foods, Discount Tire, Hastings Books, Jo-Ann Crafts, Kohl's, Michael's, O'Reilly Parts, Petsmart, Ross, Safeway, Staples, Target, Verizon, Walgreens, Walmart
195a	I-17 S, AZ 89A S, to Phoenix
192	Flagstaff Ranch Rd

FLAGSTAFF

191	Lp 40, to Grand Canyon, Flagstaff, **5 mi** N Chevron, Maverik, Whistle Stop/dsl Galaxy Diner Best Value, Budget Host, Comfort Inn, Days Inn, EconoLodge, Radisson, Super 8, Travel Inn, Travelodge CarQuest, Chevrolet/Cadillac, Home Depot, Kia, Kit Carson RV Park, O'Reilly Parts, vet, Woody Mtn Camping
190	A-1 Mountain Rd
189.5mm	Arizona Divide, elevation 7335
185	Transwestern Rd, Bellemont, N Pilot/McDonald's/Subway/dsl/scales/24hr/ @ Motel 6, S Camping World, Harley-Davidson/Roadside Grill
178	Parks Rd, N Texaco/dsl
171	Pittman Valley Rd, Deer Farm Rd, S Mountain Ranch Resort
167	Garland Prairie Rd, Circle Pines Rd, N KOA
165	AZ 64, to Williams, Grand Canyon, N 76 (8mi), Shell/dsl (4mi) KOA (4mi), to Grand Canyon, S Super 8 (1mi)
163	Williams, N Chevron/dsl, Loves/Arby's/dsl/scales/24hr Quality Inn Canyon Gateway RV Park, S Circle K, Mobil/dsl, Mustang/dsl, Shell/dsl Jack-in-the-Box, KFC/Taco Bell, McDonald's, Old Town Rest., Pancho's Mexican, Pine Country Rest., Pizza Hut, Red Garter Rest, Rod's Steaks, Rte 66 Diner, Twisters Soda Fountain Canyon Motel/RV Park, EconoLodge, El Rancho Motel, Grand Canyon Railway Hotel, Howard Johnson, Knights Inn, Mountainside Motel, Ramada Inn, Rodeway Inn, Rodeway Inn, The Lodge Motel, Travelodge $General, same as 161, USPO
161	Lp 40, Golf Course Dr, Williams, N RV camping, **0-3 mi S** Circle K, Conoco/dsl/LP, Shell Buffalo Pointe Inn, DQ, Jessica's Rest., Maria's Tacos AZ Motel, Best Value, Best Western, Budget Host, Canyon Country Inn, Comfort Inn, Days Inn, Grand Canyon Hotel, Highlander Motel, Motel 6, Westerner Motel H Family$, Safeway, to Grand Canyon Railway
157	Devil Dog Rd
155.5mm	Litter barrels, safety pullout wb
151	Welch Rd
149	Monte Carlo Rd, N dsl repair
148	County Line Rd
146	AZ 89, to Prescott, Ash Fork, N Mobil/dsl, Shell/dsl Lulu Belle's BBQ, Ranch House Cafe Ash Fork Inn Family$
144	Ash Fork, N Ash Fork Inn Grand Canyon RV Park, museum/info, USPO, S Chevron/Piccadilly's/dsl, Texaco/dsl/RV Par auto/RV repair
139	Crookton Rd, to Rte 66
123	Lp 40, to Rte 66, to Grand Canyon Caverns, Seligman, N Chevron/A&W, Shell/dsl Copper Cart Cafe, Lilo's Rest., Pizza Joint, Snow Cap Burgers Canyon Lodge, Deluxe Inn, Stagecoach 66 Motel, Supai Motel KOA (1mi), repair, USPO, S Chevron/Subway/dsl, (same as 121)
121	Lp 40, to Rte 66, Seligman, N 76/dsl, Chevron/A&W Copper Cart Cafe, Lilo's Rest., Roadkill Cafe Canyon Lodge, Route 66 Motel/pizza, Supai Motel KOA (1mi), repair (same as 123), to Grand Canyon Caverns, USPO
109	Anvil Rock Rd
108mm	Markham Wash
103	Jolly Rd
96	Cross Mountain Rd
91	Fort Rock Rd
87	Willows Ranch Rd
86mm	Willow Creek
79	Silver Springs Rd
75.5mm	Big Sandy Wash
73.5mm	Peacock Wash
71	US 93 S, to Wickenburg, Phoenix

WILLIAMS

SELIGMAN

INTERSTATE 40 Cont'd

KINGMAN

Exit #	Services
66	Blake Ranch Rd, N Petro/Iron Skillet/dsl/scales/24hr/ @ Blake Ranch RV Park, SpeedCo Lube
60mm	Frees Wash
59	DW Ranch Rd, N Loves/Chester's/Subway/dsl/scales/24hr Hualapai Mtn Park (9mi), truckwash
57mm	Rattlesnake Wash
53	AZ 66, Andy Devine Ave, to Kingman, N FLYING J/Denny's/dsl/LP/scales/24hr, Chevron/dsl, Maverik/dsl, Terrible's/dsl, Texaco/dsl Arby's, Burger King, Denny's, Jack-in-the-Box, McDonald's, Pizza Hut, Taco Bell Days Inn, EconoLodge, Knights Inn, Motel 6, Super 8, Travelodge $General, Basha's Foods, Blue Beacon, dsl/tire repair, Freightliner, Goodyear, Harley-Davidson, K-Mart, KOA (1mi), S Mobil/dsl, Shell/dsl/repair ABC Chinese, JB's, Oyster's Mexican, Sonic Best Western, Comfort Inn, Days Inn, High Desert Inn, Holiday Inn Express, Magnuson, Rodeway Inn, Rte 66 Motel, SpringHill Suites Chrysler/Dodge/Jeep, Kia, NAPA, Sunrise RV Park, Uptown Drug
51	Stockton Hill Rd, Kingman, N Arco/dsl, Chevron, Circle K/dsl Carl's Jr, Chili's, Chipotle Mexican, Cracker Barrel, Del Taco, Domino's, Five Guys, Golden Corral, IHOP, In-N-Out, KFC, McDonald's, Panda Express, Papa John's, Papa Murphy, Plaza Bonita, Scotty's Rest., Sonic, Starbucks, Subway, Taco Bell Hampton Inn H, $General, $Tree, AutoZone, AZ RV Depot/repair, BigLots, BrakeMasters, Buick/Chevrolet, CVS Drug, Discount Tire, Ford/Lincoln, Home Depot, Honda, Hyundai, Oil Can Henry's, O'Reilly Parts, PetCo, Petsmart, Ross, Safeway/gas, Smith's Foods/dsl, Staples, Superior Tire, TrueValue, Verizon, vet, Walgreens, Walmart, S Circle K Kingman Co Steaks, Little Caesars, Paco's Mexican, Pizza Hut 99cents Store, CarQuest, Family$, Hastings Books, JC Penney, Radio Shack, Safeway/dsl, Sears

YUCCA

Exit #	Services
48	US 93 N, Beale St, Kingman, N 76/dsl, Chevron/dsl, Mobil/dsl, Shell/dsl, TA/Country Pride/Popeye's/dsl/scales/24hr/ @, Texaco/dsl, USA/Subway/dsl, Woody's Wendy's Budget Inn, Economy Inn, Tristate Inn 4A Tire/auto/RV repair, S Chevron/Quiznos/dsl Calico's Rest., Carl's Jr AZ Inn, Motel city park, Ft Beale RV Park, Mohave Museum
46.5mm	Holy Moses Wash
44	AZ 66, Oatman Hwy, McConnico, to Rte 66, S Crazy Fred's/café/dsl Canyon West RV Camping(3mi), truckwash
40.5mm	Griffith Wash
37	Griffith Rd
35mm	Black Rock Wash
32mm	Walnut Creek
28	Old Trails Rd
26	Proving Ground Rd, S AZ Proving Grounds
25	Alamo Rd, to Yucca, N USPO
23mm	**Rs both lanes, full facilities, litter barrels, petwalk vending**
21mm	Flat Top Wash
20	Santa Fe Ranch Rd
18.5mm	Illavar Wash
15mm	Buck Mtn Wash
13.5mm	Franconia Wash
13	Franconia Rd
9	AZ 95 S, to Lake Havasu City, Parker, London Br, S Chevron/dsl, Loves/Carl's Jr/Subway/dsl/scales/24hr, Pilot/Wendy's/dsl/scales/24hr Havasu RV Park, Prospectors RV Resort
4mm	**Weigh sta both lanes**
2	Needle Mtn Rd
1	Topock Rd, to Bullhead City, Oatman, N camping, food, gas, to Havasu NWR
0mm	Arizona/California state line, Colorado River, Mountain/Pacific time zone

ARKANSAS

INTERSTATE 30

MABLEVALE

Exit #	Services
	I-30 begins/ends on I-40, exit 153b.
143b a	I-40, E to Memphis, W to Ft Smith
142	15th St, S Super Stop/dsl
141b	US 70, Broadway St, downtown, N Exxon, U.S. Fuel Burger King U-Haul, Verizon Arena, S Phillips 66, Valero/dsl KFC/LJ Silver, McDonald's, Popeye's, Taco Bell, Wendy's Family$
141mm	Arkansas River
141a	AR 10, Cantrell Rd, Markham St (from wb), W to downtown
140	9th St, 6th St, downtown, N Phillips 66, Shel Pizza Hut Holiday Inn USPO, S SuperStop Comfort Inn
139b	I-630, downtown
139a	AR 365, Roosevelt Rd, N Exxon Sim's BBQ AutoZone, S Shell Family$, Kroger
138b	I-530 S, US 167 S, US 65 S, to Pine Bluff
138a	I-440 E, to Memphis, S airport
135	W 65th St, N Exxon/dsl, Shell/dsl, Valero/dsl Budget Host, S Rodeway Inn
134	Scott Hamilton Dr, S Exxon/dsl Best Value Inn, Motel 6
133	Geyer Springs Rd, N Exxon, Hess, Mobil Church's, Sims BBQ, Subway, S Citgo, Phillips 66, Shell Arby's, Burger King, El Chico, KFC, Little Caesar's, McDonald's, Panda Chinese, Rally's, Sonic, Taco Bell, Waffle House, Wendy's Best Western, Comfort Inn, Quality Inn, Rest Inn CVS Drug, Family$, Goodyear/auto, Kroger/gas, Walgreens
132	US 70b, University Ave, N RaceWay/dsl, SuperStop, Valero Best Value Inn, S Kum&Go/dsl O'Reilly Parts
131	McDaniel Dr, N U-Haul, S Economy Inn, Super 7 Inn Firestone
130	AR 338, Baseline Rd, Mabelvale, N Cimarron Inn, EconoLodge Harley-Davidson, S Shell/Popeye's/dsl Applebee's, China Buffet, Dixie Cafe, McDonald's, Pizza Hut, Sonic, Taco Bueno, Wendy's $Tree, Chevrolet, Crain RV Ctr, GNC, Home Depot, URGENT CARE, Walmart/Subway
129	I-430 N
128	Otter Creek Rd, Mabelvale West, N Loves /Hardee's/Subway/dsl/scales/24hr David's Burger AT&T, Bass Pro Shop, Cavender's, Little Rock Outlets/famous brands, S Exxon/dsl Super 8 Purcell Tire/auto
126	AR 111, County Line Rd, Alexander, N Shell/dsl, S Citgo/Subway Cherokee RV Park/dump (4mi)

AR

INTERSTATE 30 Cont'd

Exit #	Services
123	AR 183, Reynolds Rd, to Bryant, Bauxite, N 🚪 Murphy USA/dsl, Shell 🍴 Arby's, Backyard Burgers, Burger King, Casa Mexicana, Cracker Barrel, Dickey's BBQ, Domino's, Firehouse Subs, Great Wall Buffet, IHOP, KFC, Papa John's, Pasta Jack's Italian, Pizza Hut, Ruby Tuesday, Subway, Ta Molly's, Taste of D-Light, Waffle House, Whole Hog Cafe 🛏 Berkshire Inn, Best Value Inn, Comfort Inn, Hampton Inn, Holiday Inn Express, Hometown Hotel, La Quinta 🅾 $Tree, AT&T, AutoZone, CVS Drug, Tire Pros, vet, Walgreens, Walmart/Subway, S 🚪 Exxon/dsl, Kum&Go/dsl/e85, Mapco/dsl/e85, Valero/dsl 🍴 Bryant Cafe, Chick-fil-A, Dunkin Donuts, Hardee's, Little Caesar's, Logan's Roadhouse, McDonald's, Mi Ranchito, Sonic, Taco Bell, Wendy's, Zaxby's 🛏 Super 8 🅾 $General, Family$, Food Giant, Lowe's, O'Reilly Parts, USPO, vet
121	Alcoa Rd, N 🚪 Citgo, Pilot/Subway/dsl/scales/24hr/ @ 🍴 McDonald's, Slim Chickens, Sonic, Taco Bueno, Zaxby's 🅾 Chrysler/Dodge/Jeep, Fiat, Firestone/auto, Kroger, S 🍴 Chili's, McAlister's Deli, Moe's SW Grill, Sakura Japanese, Starbucks, Subway 🛏 Holiday Inn Express 🅾 AT&T, Best Buy, Buick/GMC, GNC, Kohl's, Old Navy, PetCo, Target, Verizon
118	Congo Rd, N 🍴 Applebee's, Brown's Rest., Dixie Café, Domino's, Gino's Grill 🛏 Fairfield Inn, Relax Inn 🅾 Chevrolet, Home Depot, Williams Tire, S 🚪 Exxon, Kum&Go/dsl/e85 🍴 Burger King, Popeye's 🛏 Days Inn 🅾 Ford, I-30 Travel Park, RV City, USPO
117	US 64, AR 5, AR 35, N 🚪 Shell 🍴 Papa John's, Waffle House 🛏 Best Inn, Best Western, EconoLodge, S 🚪 Exxon, Gulf/dsl, Murphy USA/dsl, Valero 🍴 Arby's, Backyard Burger, Buffet City, Burger King, Capt D's, Chicken Express, Colton's Steaks, IHOP, KFC, La Hacienda Mexican, Little Caesar's, Mazzio's, McDonald's, Pizza Hut, Rib Crib, Samuri Japanese, Smokey Joe's BBQ, Sonic, Subway, Taco Bell, Wendy's 🛏 Days Inn 🅾 H, $General, $Tree, Advance Parts, AT&T, AutoZone, BigLots, CVS Drug, GNC, Hastings Books, JC Penney, Kroger/dsl, Office Depot, O'Reilly Parts, Tuesday Morning, URGENT CARE, USPO, Verizon, Walgreens, Walmart/Subway
116	Sevier St, N 🚪 Citgo/dsl, Exxon 🛏 Troutt Motel, S 🚪 Phillips 66 🛏 Capri Inn
114	US 67 S, Benton, S 🚪 Valero/McDonald's/dsl 🍴 Sonic 🅾 $General
113mm	insp sta both lanes
111	US 70 W, Hot Springs, N 🅾 Cloud 9 RV Park, to Hot Springs NP
106	Old Military Rd, N 🚪 Alon/JJ's Rest./dsl/scales/ @, S 🅾 JB'S RV Park
99	US 270 E, Malvern, S 🅾 H
98b a	US 270, Malvern, Hot Springs, N 🚪 Valero/dsl 🛏 Super 8, S 🚪 Murphy USA/dsl, Phillips 66/dsl, Shell/dsl, Valero/Baskin-Robbins 🍴 Burger King, Chile Peppers, Cotija Mexican, El Parian, Great Wall Buffet, Larry's Pizza, McDonald's, Papa John's, Pizza Hut, Sonic, Subway, Taco Bell, Waffle House, Wendy's, Western Sizzlin 🛏 Best Value Inn, Comfort Inn, Holiday Inn Express 🅾 H, $General, $Tree, AT&T, AutoZone, Chevrolet, Chrysler/Dodge/Jeep, city park, Ford, O'Reilly Parts, USPO, Verizon Walmart/Subway
97	AR 84, AR 171, N 🅾 Lake Catherine SP, RV camping
93mm	🆁 both lanes, full ♿ facilities, litter barrels, petwalk 🍴 🏧 vending
91	AR 84, Social Hill

Exit #	Services
83	AR 283, Friendship, S 🚪 Valero/dsl
78	AR 7, Caddo Valley, N 🚪 Pilot/PJ Fresh Deli/dsl/scales/24hr, Shell/dsl, Valero/dsl 🍴 Cracker Barrel 🛏 Holiday Inn Express 🅾 Arkadelphia RV Park, De Gray SP, to Hot Springs NP, S 🚪 Exxon/Subway/dsl, Phillips 66 🍴 Fat Boys Cafe, McDonald's, Taco Bell, TaMolly's Mexican, Waffle House, Wendy's 🛏 Best Value Inn, Best Western, Comfort Inn, Days Inn, EconoLodge, Hampton Inn, Motel 6, Super 8
73	AR 8, AR 26, AR 51, Arkadelphia, N 🚪 Phillips 66/dsl, Shell/Stuckey's 🍴 Allen's BBQ, Chicken Express, Domino's, Great Wall Buffet, McDonald's, Western Sizzlin 🅾 $Tree, AT&T, to Crater of Diamond SP, Verizon, Walmart/Subway, S 🚪 Exxon/dsl, Shell 🍴 Andy's Rest., Big Cheese Pizza, Burger King, El Torero's, Subway 🅾 H, $General, Ace Hardware, AutoZone, Brookshire Foods, O'Reilly Parts, vet, Walgreens
69	AR 26 E, Gum Springs
63	AR 53, Gurdon, N 🚪 South Fork Trkstp/Citgo/rest./dsl 🛏 Southfork Inn, S 🚪 Shell/dsl 🅾 to White Oak Lake SP
56mm	🆁 both lanes, full ♿ facilities, litter barrels, petwalk 🏧 vending
54	AR 51, Gurdon, Okolona
46	AR 19, Prescott, N 🚪 Valero/cafe/dsl/24hr 🅾 Crater of Diamonds SP (31mi), S 🚪 Loves/Hardee's/dsl/scales/24hr 🍴 Casa Carlos Mexican
44	AR 24, Prescott, N 🚪 TA/Country Pride/Subway/Taco Bell/dsl/scales/24hr/ @, S 🚪 Norman's 44 Trkstp/rest/dsl/scales/ @ 🛏 Best Value Inn 🅾 to S Ark U, truckwash
36	AR 299, to Emmett
31	AR 29, Hope, N 🚪 Shell/dsl 🛏 Relax Inn, Village Inn/RV park 🅾 st police, S 🚪 Exxon/dsl, Valero/dsl 🍴 KFC 🛏 Best Value Inn 🅾 H
30	AR 4, Hope, N 🚪 Mobil/dsl, Murphy USA/dsl 🍴 Dos Loco Gringos 🛏 Best Western, Hampton Inn, Holiday Inn Express, Super 8 🅾 Millwood SP, Verizon, Walmart/Subway, S 🚪 Exxon/Baskin-Robbins/Wendy's, Shell 🍴 Amigo Juan Mexican, Burger King, Little Caesar's, McDonald's, Pizza Hut, Roma's Italian, Sonic, Subway, Taco Bell, Waffle House 🛏 Days Inn 🅾 H, $Tree, AT&T, AutoZone, Buick/Chevrolet/GMC, Bumper Parts, Ford, Fred's, Old Washington Hist SP, O'Reilly Parts, Super 1 Foods/gas, Walgreens
26mm	weigh sta both lanes
18	Rd 355, Fulton, N 🚪 Red River Trkstp/dsl
17mm	Red River
12	US 67 (from eb), Fulton
7mm	Welcome Ctr eb full ♿ facilities, info, litter barrels, petwalk 🍴 🏧 vending
7	AR 108, Mandeville, N 🚪 Flying J/Denny's/dsl/LP/24hr 🛏 Sunrise RV Park 🅾 truckwash
3	I-49, N to Ft Smith, S to Shreveport
2	Four States Fair Pkwy, Texarkana, N 🚪 RoadRunner/dsl, Shell/Circle K/dsl, S 🚪 Camp I-30 Trkstp 🅾 Ferguson Fairpark, Nick's RV Ctr
1	US 71, Jefferson Ave, Texarkana, N 🍴 Copeland's Rest., Johnny Tamales 🛏 Best Western, Comfort Suites, Hampton Inn, Holiday Inn, Holiday Inn Express 🅾 KOA, S 🛏 Country Host Inn
0mm	Arkansas/Texas state line

INTERSTATE 40

Exit #	Services
285mm	Arkansas/Tennessee state line, Mississippi River

Side tab labels: ARKADELPHIA, HOPE, BENTON, MALVERN

AR

INTERSTATE 40 Cont'd

W E S T M E M P H I S

Exit #	Services
284mm	**weigh sta wb**
281	AR 131, S to Mound City
280	Club Rd, Southland Dr, **N** LNG, Pilot/Wendy's/dsl, **S** FLYING J/Denny's/dsl/LP/24hr, Loves/Subway/dsl, Petro/Iron Skillet/dsl/24hr/ @, Valero/dsl KFC/Taco Bell, McDonald's Best Western, Deluxe Inn, Express Inn, Super 8 Blue Beacon, SpeedCo Lube
279b	I-55 S (from eb)
279a	Ingram Blvd, **N** Margaritas Mexican Days Inn, Homegate Inn, Knights Inn, Red Roof Inn Ford, Southland Racetrack, **S** Citgo/dsl, Phillips 66, Shell/dsl Cross Creek Rest., Waffle House Best Value Inn, Clarion, EconoLodge, Hampshire Inn, Motel 6, Ramada, Relax Inn
278	AR 77, 7th St, Missouri St, **N Welcome Ctr/ full facilities, litter barrels, petwalk** Shell/dsl **S on Missouri** Exxon, MapCo, Phillips 66/dsl, Shell Applebee's, Burger King, Cracker Barrel, Domino's, Krystal, Lenny's Subs, Little Caesar's, McDonald's, Papa John's, Pizza Hut, Popeye's, Shoney's, Subway, Taco Bell, Wendy's Comfort Suites, Extend Suites, Quality Inn H $Tree, Goodyear/auto, Kroger/dsl, Walgreens, Walmart
277	I-55 N, to Jonesboro
276	AR 77, Rich Rd, to Missouri St (from eb, same as 278), **S** Exxon, MapCo, Murphy Express/dsl, Phillips 66/dsl, Shell Applebee's, Burger King, Domino's, Fusion Buffet, Krystal, Lenny's Subs, Little Caesar's, McDonald's, Mi Pueblo Mexican, Papa John's, Pizza Hut, Popeye's, Shoney's, Subway, Taco Bell, Wendy's Extend Suites H, $Tree, AT&T, Family$, Goodyear/auto, Kroger/dsl, Walgreens, Walmart
275	AR 118, Airport Rd, **S** Shell/DQ/dsl Huddle House city park, URGENT CARE
274mm	**parking area wb, weigh sta eb**
271	AR 147, to Blue Lake, **S** BP/dsl, Exxon/Chester's/dsl tires, to Horseshoe Lake
265	US 79, AR 218, to Hughes
260	AR 149, to Earle, **N** Citgo/Subway, TA/Country Pride/Burger King/Taco Bell/dsl/scales/24hr/ @, Valero/dsl Relax Inn Shell Lake Camping, **S** Shell dsl repair
256	AR 75, to Parkin, Parkin Archeological Park (12mi)
247	AR 38 E, to Widener
245mm	St Francis River
243mm	**wb, full facilities, litter barrels, petwalk vending**
242	AR 284, Crowley's Ridge Rd, **N** H camping, to Village Creek SP
241b a	AR 1, Forrest City, **N** Citgo/DQ/dsl, Shell/Popeye's/dsl Don Jose Mexican, HoHo Chinese, Wendy's Best Value Inn,

F O R R E S T C I T Y B R I N K L E Y

Exit #	Services
241b a	Continued Comfort Suites, Days Inn, Hampton Inn, Holiday Inn Express, Luxury Inn, Magnolia Inn, Sunrise Inn, Super 8 st police, **S** Citgo/dsl, Exxon/dsl, Murphy USA/dsl, Shell/dsl Ameca Mexican, Andrey Mexican, Burger King, Dragon China, KFC, McDonald's, Ole Sawmill Cafe, Pizza Hut, Sonic, Subway, Taco Bell, Waffle House Colony Inn $Tree, AT&T, Food Giant, Fred's, O'Reilly Parts, Save-A-Lot Foods, Verizon, Walgreens, Walmart
239	AR 1, to Wynne, Marianna
235mm	**eb, full facilities, litter barrels, petwalk vending**
234mm	L'Anguille River
233	AR 261, Palestine, **N** Loves/Chester's/Subway/dsl/scales/24hr Rest Inn, **S** Citgo/dsl Natty's Buffet Goodyear/tire repair
221	AR 78, Wheatley, **N** SweetPea/dsl/repair, **S** BP/Pitstop/diner/dsl, MapCo/Subway/dsl
216	US 49, AR 17, Brinkley, **N** Citgo, Mobil/dsl Best Inn, Days Inn, EconoLodge, Motel 6/RV Park dsl repair, KFC/Taco Bell, Los Piños Mexican, **S** Exxon/Baskin-Robbins/dsl, MapCo/dsl, Shell Gene's BBQ, McDonald's, New China, Pizza Hut, Sonic, Subway, Waffle House Heritage Inn/RV Park $General, AT&T, Bumper Parts, Family$, Fred's, Kroger, O'Reilly Parts
205mm	Cache River
202	AR 33, to Biscoe
200mm	White River
199mm	**both lanes, full facilities, litter barrels, no phones vending**
193	AR 11, to Hazen, **N** Exxon/Chester's/dsl, **S** Citgo/dsl, Shell/dsl El Amigo Mexican Super 8, Travel Inn T-rix RV Park

AR

INTERSTATE 40 Cont'd

Area	Exit #	Services
	183	AR 13, Carlisle, S Citgo, Conoco/dsl, Exxon/Subway/dsl, Valero/dsl Nick's BBQ, Pizza 'N More, Sonic Days Inn $General
LONOKE	175	AR 31, Lonoke, N Phillips 66, Valero/dsl Marachi Mexican, McDonald's, Waffle House Best Western, Days Inn, Economy Inn, Hampton Inn, Holiday Inn Express AT&T, Verizon, Walmart, S Shell/Subway KFC/Taco Bell, Pizza Hut, Sawbucks Mexican, Sonic Perry's Motel $General, Goodyear/auto, O'Reilly Parts
LONOKE	173	AR 89, Lonoke
LONOKE	169	AR 15, Remington Rd
LONOKE	165	Kerr Rd
	161	AR 391, Galloway, N Loves /Chester's/subs/dsl/scales/24hr Camping World RV Ctr, S IA-80 TruckOMat/dsl/scales, LNG, Petro/Iron Skillet/dsl/scales/24hr/ @, Pilot /Subway/Pizza Hut/dsl/scales/24hr Galloway Inn Blue Beacon, dsl repair, Freightliner, Southern Tire Mart, SpeedCo
	159	I-440 W, S
	157	AR 161, to US 70, N Exxon/dsl, S Citgo/dsl, Hess, Mobil/dsl, Shell/dsl Burger King, KFC/Taco Bell, McDonald's, Sonic Comfort Inn, Days Inn, EconoLodge, Red Roof Inn, Rest Inn, Super 8 Family$
	156	Springhill Dr, N Kum&Go/dsl, Mapco/dsl, Murphy USA/dsl Cracker Barrel Candlewood Suites, Fairfield Inn, Hilton Garden, Holiday Inn Express, Residence Inn, Walmart
LITTLE ROCK	155	US 67 N, US 167, to Jacksonville (exits left from eb), Little Rock AFB, **0-3 mi N on US 167/McCain Blvd** Murphy USA/dsl, Phillips 66/dsl, Shell, Valero/dsl Applebee's, Arby's, Bar Louie, BJ's Rest., Buffalo Wild Wings, Burger King, Cactus Jacks, Carino's Italian, Chick-fil-A, Chili's, ChuckECheese's, Chuy's TexMex, CiCi's Pizza, Corky's BBQ, David's Burgers, Dixie Cafe, El Porton Mexican, Firehouse Subs, Five Guys Burgers, Fox & Hound, Golden Corral, Hog Wild Cafe, Hooters, IHOP, Jason's Deli, Jimmy John's, Kanpai Japanese, McDonald's, Newk's Eatery, Old Chicago Pizza, Olive Garden, On-the-Border, Outback Steaks, Panera Bread, Pizza Hut, Popeyes, Rally's, Red Lobster, Saddle Creek Grill, Sonic, Subway, Super King Buffet, Taco Bell, Taziki's Mediterranean, TGIFriday's, TX Roadhouse, US Pizza, Waffle House, Wendy's Candlewood Suites, Comfort Inn, Courtyard, Hampton Inn, Hilton Garden, Holiday Inn Express, La Quinta, Super 8 H, $Tree, Aamco, AT&T, Barnes&Noble, Best Buy, BigLots, Books-A-Million, Buick/GMC, Chevrolet, Chrysler/Dodge/Jeep, Dillard's, Firestone/auto, Ford, Gander Mtn, Hancock Fabrics, Home Depot, Honda, Hyundai, JC Penney, Jo-Ann, Kia, Kroger, Lincoln, Lowe's, mall, Mazda, Michael's, Nissan, Office Depot, PepBoys, PetCo, Petsmart, Ross, Sam's Club/gas, Sears/auto, Steinmart, Target, TJ Maxx, Toyota/Scion, URGENT CARE, Verizon, vet, VW, Walgreens, Walmart/Subway
LITTLE ROCK	154	to Lakewood (from eb)
LITTLE ROCK	153b	I-30 W, US 65 S, to Little Rock
LITTLE ROCK	153a	AR 107 N, JFK Blvd, N Exxon, Mapco/dsl, Shell Schlotzsky's Best Value Inn vet, S Exxon Bogie's Grill, Royal Buffet Best Western, Bugetel, Clarion, Motel 6, Quality Inn H, USPO
LITTLE ROCK	152	AR 365, AR 176, Camp Pike Rd, Levy, S Shell Chicken King H, Family$, Kroger, Radio Shack, Save a Lot, N on Camp Robinson Rd Exxon, Shell Burger King, KFC, Little Caesars, McDonald's, Mexico Chiquito, Pizza Hut, Señor Tequila,
	152	Continued Sonic, Subway, Taco Bell, US Pizza, Waffle House, Wendy's $General, AutoZone, Family$, Fred's, Kroger/gas, O'Reilly Parts
	150	AR 176, Burns Park, Camp Robinson, S camping, info
	148	AR 100, Crystal Hill Rd, N Shell, S Citgo/dsl, Exxon/dsl KOA
	147	I-430 S, to Texarkana
	142	AR 365, to Morgan, N Phillips 66, Valero/dsl Days Inn Bumper Parts, Trails End RV Park, S Kum&Go/dsl, Shell/dsl KFC/Taco Bell, McDonald's, Razorback Pizza, Smokeshack BBQ, Subway, Waffle House Best Value Inn, Holiday Inn Express, Quality Inn $General, Autozone
	135	AR 365, AR 89, Mayflower, N Hess/dsl, S Exxon/dsl, Valero Sonic, Subway $General, Harp's Mkt
	134mm	**truck parking both lanes**
	129	US 65B, AR 286, Conway, N Kia, S Exxon/dsl, MapCo/Quiznos/dsl Subway H, Chevrolet, Chrysler/Dodge/Jeep, Honda, st police, to Toad Suck SP, Toyota/Scion
CONWAY	127	US 64, Conway, N Gulf/dsl, Shell, Valero/dsl Arby's, Buffalo Wild Wings, Chick-fil-A, Chili's, Golden Corral, Logan's Roadhouse, Las Palmas Mexican, Mulan's Buffet, Popeyes, Sonic, Starbucks, Subway, TGIFriday's, Waffle House Best Value Inn, Best Western, Comfort Suites, Country Inn&Suites, Days Inn, Economy Inn, Hampton Inn, Hilton Garden $General, AT&T, Belk, Best Buy, Buick/GMC, Dick's, Firestone/auto, Ford, GNC, Goodyear/auto, Harley-Davidson, Home Depot, Hyundai, Kohl's, Moix RV Ctr, NAPA, Nissan, Old Navy, O'Reilly Parts, Petsmart, repair/transmissions, Staples, Target, TJ Maxx, to Lester Flatt Park, Verizon, vet, S RaceWay, Shell/dsl, Valero/dsl Burger King, Church's, Colton's Steaks, Dunkin Donuts/Baskin Robbins, Jimmy John's, LJ Silver, McDonald's, Rally's, Saigon Rest., Taco Bell, Tacos 4 Life, Taziki's Mediterranean, Wendy's, Whole Hog Cafe Kings Inn AutoZone, BigLots, Family$, Fred's Drugs, Hancock Fabrics, Hobby Lobby, Kroger/gas, tires, Walgreens
CONWAY	125	US 65, Conway, N Conoco/dsl, Exxon/Subway/dsl China Town, Cracker Barrel, El Acapulco Mexican, McDonald's, MktPlace Deli Quality Inn $Tree, JC Penney, Office Depot, Sears, S Citgo, CNG, Horton's, Mobil/dsl, Murphy USA/dsl Burger King, Cast Iron Skillet, CiCi's Pizza, David's Burgers, Dixie Cafe, Firehouse Subs, Fuji Steaks, IHOP, Los Potrillos Mexican, McAlister's Deli, Mexico Chiquito, New China, Outback Steaks, Panera Bread, Ruby Tuesday, Russo's Italian Kitchen, Sonic, Starbucks, Subway, Waffle House, Wendy's Candlewood Suites, Comfort Inn, Fairfield Inn, Holiday Inn Express, Howard Johnson, La Quinta, Microtel, Motel 6, Super 8 H, Advance Parts, AT&T, Hastings Books, Lowe's, tires, Walmart
	124	AR 25 N, to Conway, S Hess/dsl DQ, KFC, Popeye's H vet
MORRILTON	120mm	Cadron River
MORRILTON	117	to Menifee
MORRILTON	112	AR 92, Plumerville, N Exxon/dsl, S Country Store/dsl USPO
MORRILTON	108	AR 9, Morrilton, S Murphy USA, Shell/Pizza Pro/dsl, Valero Chop Stix, Colton's Steaks, Hardees, Mama DeLuca's Pizza, McDonald's, Ortega's Mexican, Pizza Hut, Sonic, Subway, Waffle House, Wendy's Holiday Inn Express, Super 8 H, $General, Ace Hardware, AT&T, Chrysler/Dodge/Jeep, Kroger, NAPA, to Petit Jean SP (21mi), Verizon, vet, Walmart
MORRILTON	107	AR 95, Morrilton, N Shell/dsl Best Value Inn I-40/107 RV Park, S Loves /Subway/dsl/24hr, Shell

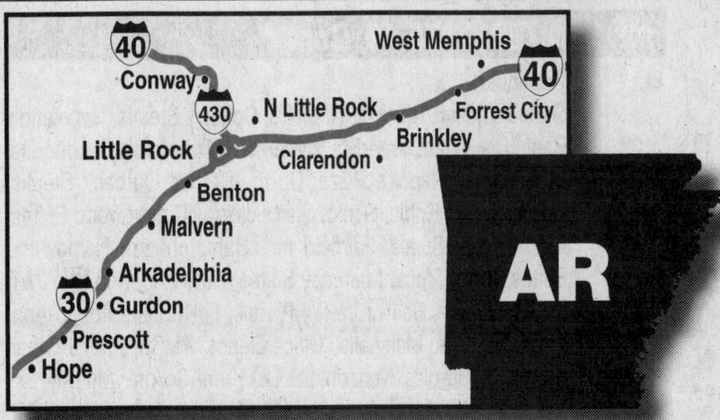

AR

INTERSTATE 40 Cont'd

107	Continued Mom&Pop's Waffles, Morrilton Drive Inn, Yesterdays Rest. Days Inn Bumper Parts
101	Blackwell, **N** Blackwell TrkStp/Citgo/Domino's/diner/dsl/scales/24hr Utility Trailer Sales
94	AR 105, Atkins, **N** Exxon/Subway/dsl, Shell/McDonald's/dsl Berky's Diner, El Parian Mexican, Sonic $General, **S** Casey's/dsl Cash Saver Foods
88	Pottsville, **S** $General, truck repair/wash
84	US 64, AR 331, Russellville, **N** FLYING J /Denny's/dsl/scales/LP/24hr, Shell/dsl Ivys Cove RV Retreat, **S** Phillips 66, Pilot/Subway/Wendy's/dsl/scales Chick-fil-A, CiCi's Pizza, Hardee's, McDonald's, Mulan's Buffet, Sonic, Waffle House Comfort Inn, Quality Inn $Tree, AT&T, Belk, Buick/Chevrolet/GMC, Chrysler/Dodge/Jeep, GNC, Hastings Books, Hobby Lobby, Hyundai, JC Penney, K-Mart, Lowe's, Nissan, Petsmart, Ross, Staples, TJ Maxx, Toyota, USPO
83	AK 326, Weir Rd, **S** Phillips 66/dsl, Walmart Gas/dsl Buffalo Wild Wings, DQ, McAlisters Deli, Popeye's, Starbucks, Subway, Sumo, Taco Bell, Taco John's Comfort Inn $General, AutoZone, Firestone/auto, Ford/Lincoln, Mazda, NAPA, O'Reilly Parts, Verizon, Walmart/McDonald's
81	AR 7, Russellville, **N** SuperStop/dsl CJ's Burgers Motel 6 $General, Outdoor RV Ctr/Park, **S** Exxon/dsl, Phillips 66/dsl, Shell Arby's, Burger King, Cagle's Mill Rest., Colton's Steaks, Cracker Barrel, Dixie Café, Firehouse Subs, IHOP, La Huerta Mexican, New China, Ruby Tuesday, Subway, Waffle House Best Value, Best Western, Clarion, Days Inn, Economy Inn, Fairfield Inn, Hampton Inn, La Quinta, Super 8 RV camping, to Lake Dardanelle SP
80mm	Dardanelle Reservoir
78	US 64, Russellville, **S** Fat Daddy's BBQ Darrell's Mkt, Mission RV Park, to Lake Dardanelle SP
74	AR 333, London
72mm	**wb, full facilities, litter barrels, petwalk vending**
70mm	**litter barrels, overlook wb lane**
68mm	**eb, full facilities, litter barrels, petwalk vending**
67	AR 315, Knoxville, **S** USPO
64	US 64, Clarksville, Lamar, **S** Dad's Dream RV Park
58	AR 21, AR 103, Clarksville, **N** Casey's/dsl, Shell, Valero Emerald Dragon Chinese, KFC, La Chiquita Mexican, McDonald's, Pasta Grill, Pizza Hut, Subway, Taco Bell, Waffle House Best Western, Executive Inn, Quality Inn, Super 8 $General, Buick/Chevrolet, **S** Murphy USA/dsl Arby's, China Fun, Wendy's $Tree, AT&T, Chrysler/Dodge/Jeep, Ford, Walmart/Subway
57	AR 109, Clarksville, **N** Fuel Stop/dsl Sonic, Subway Family$, Harp's Mkt, **S** Shell/Chester's/dsl Truckwash, TrueValue
55	US 64, AR 109, Clarksville, **N** Crosswoods Rest., Hardee's Hampton Inn, Holiday Inn Express, **S** Exxon/dsl Radio Shack, st police
47	AR 164, Coal Hill
41	AR 186, Altus, **N** Swiss Family Rest., **S** Wiederkehr Rest. (4mi) winery (4mi)
37	AR 219, Ozark, **S** Loves /Subway/dsl/scales/24hr, Shell/McDonald's/dsl KFC/Taco Bell Best Value Inn
36mm	**both lanes, full facilities, litter barrels, petwalk vending**
35	AR 23, Ozark, **N** Valero/Subway/dsl/scales Hillbilly Hideout Rest, **3 mi S** Hardee's, Subway Oxford Inn, Ozark Inn Aux Arc Park (5mi), to Mt Magazine SP (20 mi)
24	AR 215, Mulberry, **S** Vine Prairie Park
20	Dyer, **S** Phillips 66/dsl, Shell/dsl Mill Creek Inn
13	US 71 N, to Fayetteville, **N** Phillips 66/dsl, Shell Burger King, Catfish Hole, China Fun, Cracker Barrel, KFC, La Fiesta Mexican, Mazzio's, Pizza Parlor, Subway, Taco Bell Quality Inn $General, Crabtree RV Ctr/Park, KOA (2mi), Lake Ft Smith SP, O'Reilly Parts, to U of AR, **S** Murphy USA/dsl, Shamrock, Valero/dsl Braum's, Geno's Pizza, McDonald's, Pizza Hut, Sonic Days Inn AT&T, Coleman Drug, CV's Foods, Harp's Foods, Walgreens, Walmart
12	I-49 N, to Fayetteville, **N** to Lake Ft Smith SP
9mm	**weigh sta both lanes**
7	I-540 S, US 71 S, to Ft Smith, Van Buren, **S**
5	AR 59, Van Buren, **N** Conoco/dsl, Murphy USA/dsl, Phillips 66 Arby's, Burger King, Chili's, Domino's, Firehouse Subs, Frank's Italian, Golden Wok, La Fiesta Mexican, Little Caesar's, McDonald's, Papa Murphy's, Zaxby's Best Western, Hampton Inn $Tree, Advance Parts, AT&T, CVS Drug, Lowe's, NAPA, USPO, Verizon, Walmart/Subway, **S** Casey's/dsl, Shell/dsl Big Jake's Steaks, Braum's, Geno's Pizza, KFC/Taco Bell, La Fresas Mexican, Sonic, Subway, Waffle House, Wendy's Holiday Inn Express, Motel 6, Sleep Inn, Super 8 $General, CV's Foods, Grizzle Tire, Outdoor RV Park, truckwash, vet, Walgreens
3	Lee Creek Rd, **N** Shell/dsl Park Ridge Camping
2.5mm	**Welcome Ctr eb full facilities, info, litter barrels, petwalk vending**
1	to Ft Smith (from wb), Dora
0mm	Arkansas/Oklahoma state line

RUSSELLVILLE

CLARKSVILLE

VAN BUREN

INTERSTATE 49

Exit #	Services
93	US 71B, Bentonville, **I-49 begins/ends on US 71 N**
88	AR 72, Bentonville, Pea Ridge, **E** Casey's River Grille Courtyard, Simmon's Suites, **W** Kum&Go/dsl, Shell/dsl Smokin' Joe's Ribs Walmart Visitors Ctr
86	US 62, AR 102, Bentonville, Rogers, **E** TownePlace Suites Pea Ridge NMP, Sam's Club/gas, Walmart Mkt, **W** Shell/dsl Arby's, Dunkin Donuts, McDonald's, Sonic, Subway, Taco Bell ValuePlace
85	US 71B, AR 12, Bentonville, Rogers, **E** Conoco/dsl Abuelo's, Applebee's, Arby's, Atlanta Bread, Boar's Nest,

B E N T O N V I L L E

⬆N INTERSTATE 49 Cont'd

85	Continued
	Carino's Italian, Chick-fil-A, Chili's, Colton's Steaks, Copeland's Rest., Dixie Café, Freddy's Burgers, IHOP, Logan's Roadhouse, McDonald's, Napoli's Pizza, On-the-Border, Outback Steaks, Quiznos, Red Robin, Sonic, Starbucks 🛏 Candlewood Suites, Country Inn&Suites, Fairfield Inn, Hampton Inn, Homewood Suites, Hyatt Place, Mainstay Suites, Residence Inn 🅾 AT&T, Barnes&Noble, Beaver Lake SP, Belk, Firestone/auto, Jo-Ann, Kohl's, Lowe's, Marshalls, Office Depot, PetCo, Prairie Creek SP, Ross, Staples, Verizon, W 🅖 Kum&Go/dsl, Murphy Express/dsl, Shell 🍴 Azul Tequila Mexican, Billy Sims BBQ, Braum's, Buffalo Wild Wings, Chipotle, Cracker Barrel, Denny's, Firehouse Subs, HoneyBaked Ham, Jimmy John's, Joe's Italian, Jonny Brusco's Pizza, Krispy Kreme, Lenny's Subs, Lin's Garden, Mama Fu's Asian, McAlister's Deli, Panera Bread, Shogun Japanese, Smashburger, Starbucks, Subway, Taco Bueno, Taziki's Mediterranean Cafe, Village Inn, Waffle House, Whole Hog Cafe, Zaxby's 🛏 Best Western, Comfort Suites, Days Inn, DoubleTree Hotel, EconoLodge, Hilton Garden, Holiday Inn Express, La Quinta, Microtel, Motel 6, Sheraton, SpringHill Suites, Super 8 🅾 Ⓗ, BMW, Buick/GMC, Cadillac, Chevrolet, Christian Bros Auto, Chrysler/Dodge/Jeep, Honda, Hyundai, Kia, Mazda, Mercedes, Nissan, Toyota/Scion, URGENT CARE
83	AR 94 E, Pinnacle Hills Pkwy, E 🅖 Phillips 6 🍴 After 5 Grill, Bariola's Pizza, ChuckECheese's, Dickey's BBQ, Firehouse Subs, Five Guys, Genghis Grill, Jimmy John's, Maddio's Pizza, Mojitos Mexican, Olive Garden, Panda Express, Qdoba, Red Lobster, Slim Chickens, Starbucks, Steak'n Shake, Taco Bell 🅾 Ⓗ, Home Depot, Horse Shoe Bend Park, URGENT CARE, Walgreens, W 🍴 Bonefish Grill, Carrabba's, Coldstone, Crabby's Seafood Grill, Grub's Grille, Mellow Mushroom, Ruth's Chris Steaks, Subway, The Egg&I, Theo's, Tropical Smoothie 🛏 ALoft, Embassy Suites, Holiday Inn, Staybridge Suites
82	Promenade Blvd, E 🍴 Fish City Grill, Food Pavilion, Houlihan's, Longhorn Steaks, Mimi's Cafe, PF Chang's, Twin Peaks, TX Land&Cattle 🅾 Ⓗ, AT&T, Best Buy, Cabela's, Dillard's, Fresh Mkt, GNC, Gordman's, Hancock Fabrics, JC Penney, Old Navy, Petsmart, Target; TJMaxx, Verizon, W 🍴 Chuy's Mexican, Deluxe Cafe, Pei Wei, Roma Italian 🅾 Walmart Mkt/dsl
81	Pleasant Grove Rd, E 🅖 Murphy USA/dsl 🍴 Backyard Burger, Chick-fil-A, Golden Corral, Gusano's Pizzaria, McDonald's, Moe's SW, Papa Murphy's, Starbucks, Subway, Taco Bueno, Whataburger 🅾 Burlington, Cavender's, Firestone/auto, Walgreens, Walmart, W 🅖 Casey's/dsl
78	AR 264, Lowell, Cave Sprgs, Rogers, E 🅖 Kum&Go/dsl, Shell/dsl 🍴 Arby's, Dickey's BBQ, Domino's, DQ, KFC, LJ Silver, McDonald's, Sonic, Subway, Taco Bell 🅾 $General, auto repair, Camping World RV Ctr, Super 8, W 🅖 Kum&Go/dsl
76	Wagon Wheel Rd, E 🅖 Shell/Subway/dsl 🅾 to Hickory Creek Park
73	Elm Springs Rd, E 🅖 Kum&Go/dsl, VP/dsl 🍴 Eureka Pizza, Patrick's Burgers, Whataburger 🛏 ValuePlace 🅾 Chevrolet, Family$, W 🅖 Shell/dsl, Walmart/dsl 🍴 McDonald's, MJ Pizzaria, Panda Express 🅾 Walmart
72mm	weigh sta nb
72	US 412, Springdale, Siloam Springs, E 🅖 Citgo/dsl, Kum&Go/dsl, Phillips 66 🍴 Angus Jack's Burgers, Applebee's, Braum's, Denny's, Dickey's BBQ, Golden Dragon Buffet, Guadalajara Grill, Jimmy John's, Little Caesar's, McDonald's, Mkt Place Rest., Panda, Sonic, Subway, Sunset Grill, Taco Bell, Waffle

F A Y E T T E V I L L E

72	Continued
	House, Wendy's, Western Sizzlin 🛏 Comfort Inn, DoubleTree Hotel, Extended Stay America, Fairfield Inn, Hampton Inn, Holiday Inn, La Quinta, Residence Inn, Royal Inn, Sleep Inn, Super 8 🅾 $General, AT&T, Big O Tire , Harp's Mkt, Kenworth/Volvo Trucks, Lowe's, Office Depot, O'Reilly Parts, Radio Shack, URGENT CARE, Verizon, Walgreens, W 🅖 Casey's/dsl, Murphy Express/dsl, 🅿🅸🅻🅾🆃/Burger King/dsl/scales/24hr 🍴 Arby's, Buffalo Wild Wings, Cracker Barrel, Domino's, Flying Burrito, Jose's Mexican, McDonald's, Popeye's, Rib Crib, Subway, Taco Bueno, Tropical Smoothie 🅾 Buick/GMC, Harp's Mkt/dsl, Hobby Lobby, NW RV Ctr
71mm	weigh sta sb
70	Don Tyson Pkwy, E 🅖 Casey's/dsl, Walmart/dsl 🅾 Walmart Mkt
69	Johnson Mill Blvd, Johnson, E 🍴 Inn at the Mill Rest. 🛏 Inn at the Mill, TownePlace Suites
67	US 71B, Fayetteville, E 🅾 Ⓗ
66	AR 112, Garland Ave, E 🅖 Phillips 66/dsl, W 🅾 Acura, Chevrolet, Fiat, Honda, Hyundai, Sam's Club/dsl, Toyota/Scion
65	Porter Rd, W 🅾 Kia, Subaru
64	AR 16 W, AR 112 E, Wedington Dr, W 🅖 Citgo/McDonald's/dsl, Murphy Express/dsl 🍴 Boar's Nest BBQ, Dickey's BBQ, El Matador Mexican, Freddy's, Gusano's Pizza, Hunan Manor, IHOP, Slim Chickens, Sonic, Starbucks, Subway, Taco Bell 🛏 Comfort Inn, Hilton Garden, Holiday Inn Express, Homewood Suites 🅾 Harp's Food/gas, Walmart Mkt

F A R M I N G T O N

62	US 62, AR 180, Farmington, E 🅖 Citgo, Shell/dsl 🍴 Andy's Custard, Arby's, Braum's, Burger King, Chick-fil-A, Dunkin Donuts, Ginger Rice&Noodle, Hardee's, KFC, McDonald's, Mexico Viejo, Ozzys Cafe, Panda Express, Popeye's, Sonic, Starbucks, Subway, Taco Bell, Taco Bueno, Thai Wok, Waffle House, Wendy's, Whataburger, Zaxby's 🛏 Best Western, Candlewood Suites, EconoLodge 🅾 Bumper Parts, W 🅖 Murphy USA/dsl 🍴 Denny's, Firehouse Subs, Lucy's Diner, Papa Murphy's, Pavilion Buffet, Ruby Tuesday 🛏 Baymont Inn, Days Inn, Hampton Inn, Regency 7 Motel, Super 8, ValuePlace 🅾 $Tree, Aldi Foods, AT&T, AutoZone, Lowe's, Verizon, Walgreens, Walmart/McDonald's
61	US 71, to Boston Mtn Scenic Lp, sb only
60	AR 112, AR 265, Razorback Rd, E 🛏 Staybridge Suites 🅾 Southgate RV Park, to U of AR
58	Greenland, W 🅖 Phillips 66/McDonalds/dsl/scales/24hr 🍴 Sonic
53	AR 170, West Fork, E 🅖 Harp's/dsl 🅾 Harp's Mkt, Winn Creek RV Resort (4mi), W 🅾 to Devils Den SP
45	AR 74, Winslow, W 🅾 to Devils Den SP
41mm	Bobby Hopper Tunnel
34	AR 282, to US 71, Chester, W 🅾 USPO
29	AR 282, to US 71, Mountainburg, 1 mi E 🅾 $General, to Lake Ft Smith SP
24	AR 282, to US 71, Rudy, E 🅖 Shell/dsl 🍴 Red Hog BBQ 🅾 Boston Mtns Scenic Lp, KOA
21	Collum Ln
20	to I-40 (from sb) I-49 N begins/ends on I-40, exit 12.

⬆N INTERSTATE 49 (TEXARKANA)

Exit #	Services
42	**I-49 (Texarkana) begins/ends on US 59.**
41	Sanderson Ln
37b a	I-30, E to Little Rock, W to Dallas

INTERSTATE 49 (TEXARKANA) Cont'd

Exit #	Services
35	Arkansas Blvd, Four States Pkwy, E airport, fairgrounds, W Brangus Steaks, Park Place Rest. $General
32	US 82, 19th St, 9th St, E Shell/dsl, Valero/dsl Subway, TA Molly's Mexican $General, CashSaver
31	AR 196, Genoa Rd
29b a	US 71, Texarkana, US 59, to Houston, W Shell/dsl
26	AR 237
24	Rd 10, Ferguson
18	N Fouke Rd
16	US 71, Fouke
6	Rd 197, Spruell Rd
4	US 71, Doddridge
0mm	Arkansas/Louisiana state line

INTERSTATE 55

BLYTHEVILLE

Exit #	Services
72mm	Arkansas/Missouri state line
72	State Line Rd, **weigh sta sb**
71	AR 150, Yarbro
68mm	**Welcome Ctr sb full facilities, info, litter barrels, petwalk**
67	AR 18, Blytheville, E Mobil/dsl, Murphy Express/dsl Burger King, Hardee's, Las Brisas Mexican, Waffle Inn, Zaxby's Best Value Inn, Days Inn/RV park Chrysler/Dodge/Jeep, Lowe's, Verizon, Walmart/Subway, W Citgo/dsl, QuikStop/dsl, Shell El Puerto Mexican, GreatWall Chinese, Grecian Steaks, McDonald's, Olympia Steaks, Perkins, Pizza Hut, Pizza Inn, Sonic, Subway, Taco Bell, Wendy's Comfort Inn, Fairview Suites, Hampton Inn, Holiday Inn, Quality Inn, Super 8 H, AT&T, AutoZone, CarQuest, Family$, Ford/Nissan, JC Penney
63	US 61, to Blytheville, E Shearins RV Park (2mi), W Dodge's Store/dsl, Exxon/Baskin-Robbins/Chester's/Pizza Hut/dsl, Shell/McDonald's/dsl Deerfield Inn, Relax Inn H, truckwash
57	AR 148, Burdette, E NE AR Coll
53	AR 158, Victoria, Luxora
48	AR 140, to Osceola, E Mobil/dsl, Shell/Baskin-Robbins/Chester's/dsl McDonald's (3mi), Pizza Inn (3mi), Sonic (3mi), Subway3 (mi) Days Inn, Deerfield Inn, EconoLodge, Fairview Inn H, Cotton Inn Rest., Huddle House
45mm	**litter barrels, truck parking nb**
44	AR 181, Keiser
41	AR 14, Marie, E to Hampson SP/museum
36	AR 181, to Wilson, Bassett
35mm	**litter barrels, truck parking sb**
34	AR 118, Joiner
23b a	US 63, AR 77, to Marked Tree, Jonesboro, ASU, E Citgo/chicken/pizza
21	AR 42, Turrell, W Exxon/rest./dsl/scales/24hr
17	AR 50, to Jericho
14	Rd 4, to Jericho, E Citgo/dsl/scales/24hr, W Citgo/Stuckey's Chevrolet, KOA
10	US 64 W, Marion, E Citgo/Baskin-Robbins/Subway/scales, Shell/McDonald's KFC/Taco Bell, Sonic, Tops BBQ Comfort Inn, Hallmarc Inn $General, Family$, Mkt Place Foods, USPO, W JP Mkt, Shell Andrey Grill, Burger King, Colton's

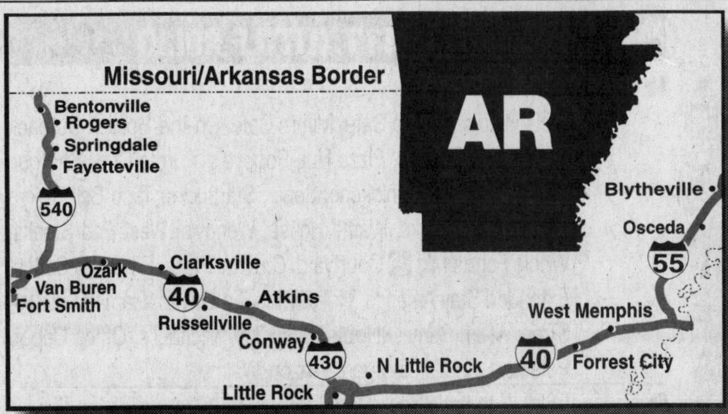

W MEMPHIS

Exit #	Services
10	Continued Steaks, Mi Pueblo, Tropical Cafe, Wendy's, Zaxby's Hampton Inn, Journey Inn, Motel 6 AutoZone, to Parkin SP (23mi)
9mm	**truck parking nb, weigh sta sb**
8	I-40 W, to Little Rock
I-55 and I-40 run together 3 mi. See I-40, exits 278-279b	
5	(279 a from I-40) Ingram Blvd, E **Welcome Ctr/ /full facilities, litter barrels, petwalk** Margaritas Mexican Days Inn, Homegate Inn, Knights Inn, Red Roof Inn Ford, Southland Racetrack, W Citgo/dsl, Phillips/dsl, Shell/dsl Cross Creek Rest., Waffle House Best Value Inn, Clarion Inn, EconoLodge, Hampshire Inn, Motel 6, Ramada, Relax Inn
4	King Dr, Southland Dr, E FLYING J/Denny's/dsl/LP/scales/RV dump, LNG, Loves/Subway/dsl/scales/ @, Petro/Iron Skillet/rest./dsl/24hr/ @, Pilot/Subway/Wendy's/dsl/scales/24hr, Valero/dsl KFC/Taco Bell, McDonald's Best Western, Deluxe Inn, Express Inn, Super 8 Blue Beacon, SpeedCo Lube, W Pancho's Mexican Sunset Inn
3b a	US 70, Broadway Blvd, AR 131, Mound City Rd (exits left from nb), W Budget Inn
2mm	**weigh sta nb**
1	Bridgeport Rd
0mm	Arkansas/Tennessee state line, Mississippi River

INTERSTATE 430 (LITTLE ROCK)

Exit #	Services
13b a	I-40. **I-430 begins/ends on I-40, exit 147.**
12	AR 100, Maumelle, W Kum&Go/dsl/e85 NAPA, O'Reilly Parts, vet
10mm	Arkansas River
9	AR 10, Cantrell Rd, W Maumelle Park, Pinnacle Mtn SP
8	Rodney Parham Rd, E Conoco/dsl, Kroger/dsl, Phillips 66/dsl, Shell Arby's, Baskin-Robbins, Dunkin Donuts, Firehouse Subs, McDonald's, Mt Fuji Japanese, Sonic, Starbucks, Subway, Taco Bell, Terri Lynn's BBQ, Tropical Smoothie Cafe, US Pizza La Quinta $General, AAA, Advance Parts, AutoZone, Drug Emporium, get, Kroger, TJ Maxx, Walgreens, W Exxon Burger King, Chili's, Dixie Cafe, Domino's, Franke's Café, Marco's Pizza, Olive Garden, Ponchito's Mexican, Shorty Small's Ribs, Starbucks, Wendy's Best Western Audi, Cadillac, Firestone/auto, GNC, K-Mart, Radio Shack, vet, Volvo
6b	Kanis Rd, Markham St, to downtown, E Shell Burger King, Kroger, Red Lobster, Subway Candlewood Suites, Comfort Inn, Motel 6, SpringHill Suites Burlington Coats, Ross, W Exxon/dsl Applebee's, Bobby's Country Cookin', Butcher Shop Steaks, Cactus Jack's, Chi Rest., Church's, Denny's, Famous Dave's BBQ, IHOP, Jason's Deli, KFC, Khalil's Grill, Kobe Japanese, Lenny's Subs, Macaroni Grill, McAlister's Deli,

AR

AR CA

LITTLE ROCK

INTERSTATE 430 (LITTLE ROCK)

6b Continued
McDonald's, Mexico Cafe, Mimi's Cafe, On-the-Border, Outback Steaks, PF Chang's, Pizza Hut, Popeye's, Purple Cow, Shotgun Dan's Pizza, Slim Chickens, Sonic, Starbucks, Taco Bell, Tokyo House, Twin Peaks, Waffle House, Wendy's, West End Steaks, Whole Foods Mkt Courtyard, Crowne Plaza, Embassy Suites, Extended Stay America, Holiday Inn, La Quinta, Ramada Ltd $Tree, AT&T, Barnes&Noble, Best Buy, Michael's, Office Depot, PetsMart, Sam's Club/gas, Verizon, Walmart

6a I-630, E to Little Rock, E H

5 Kanis Rd, Shackleford Rd, E Arby's, BJ's Rest., Chuck-ECheese, Copeland's Rest., Cracker Barrel, Longhorn Steaks, Panda Garden, Samurai Steaks, TX Roadhouse, Zangna Thai Comfort Suites, Home 2 Suites, La Quinta, Towneplace Suites AT&T, Gordman's, JC Penney, Jo-Ann, Verizon, Walmart/Subway, W Shell Dunkin Donuts, Krispy Kreme, Mooyah Burger, Panera Bread Extended Stay America, Hampton Inn, Hilton Garden, Residence Inn, Wingate Inn H Lexus

4 AR 300, Col Glenn Rd, E American Pie Pizza, Subway, Wendy's Holiday Inn Express, ValuePlace Hotel Toyota/Scion, W Valero/Burger King/dsl Sonic BMW,

4 Continued
Chrysler/Dodge/Jeep, Ford, Honda, Hyundai, Infiniti, Jaguar, Land Rover, Mazda, Mercedes, Nissan, Subaru, VW

1 AR 5, Stagecoach Rd, W Mapco/dsl/e85, Phillips 66, Valero/Domino's Down Home Rest., Subway $General, CB Tires, Walgreens

I-430 begins/ends on I-30, exit 129.

INTERSTATE 440 (LITTLE ROCK)

Exit #	Services
11	**I-440 begins/ends on I-40, exit 159.**
10	US 70, W Peterbilt
8	Faulkner Lake Rd
7	US 165, to England, S Valero/dsl Agricultural Museum, Toltec Mounds SP, Willow Beach SP
6mm	Arkansas River
5	Fourche Dam Pike, LR Riverport, N Exxon/dsl, Shell/Subway McDonald's Travelodge Kenworth, S Phillips 66/dsl, Valero/dsl
4	Lindsey Rd
3	Bankhead Dr, N Comfort Inn LR Airport, S Valero Boston's Rest., Waffle House Days Inn, Holiday Inn, Holiday Inn Express
0mm	**I-440 begins/ends on I-30, exit 138.**

CALIFORNIA

INTERSTATE 5

YREKA

Exit #	Services
797mm	California/Oregon state line
796	Hilt
793	Bailey Hill Rd
791mm	**inspection sta sb**
790	Hornbrook Hwy, Ditch Creek Rd
789	A28, to Hornbrook, Henley, E Chevron/dsl/LP Blue Heron RV Park/rest., , to Iron Gate RA
786	CA 96, Klamath River Hwy, W **both lanes, full facilities, info, litter barrels, petwalk** to Klamath River RA
782mm	Anderson Summit, elev 3067
780mm	vista point sb
779mm	Shasta River
776	Yreka, Montague, E Holiday Inn Express Yreka RV Park, W Mobil/dsl Casa Ramos Mexican, J&D Diner, Puerto Vallarta Mtn View Inn, Super 8 Grocery Outlet
775	Miner St, Central Yreka, W 76/dsl, Chevron/dsl China Dragon, Grandma's House, Purple Plum Rest., RoundTable Pizza, Subway Best Western, Budget Inn, EconoLodge, Klamath Motel, Relax Inn, Rodeway Inn, Yreka Motel H Ace Hardware, Baxter Parts, CarQuest, Clayton Tire, Honda, museum, Rite Aid, USPO
773	CA 3, to Ft Jones, Etna, E Les Schwab, tires, Trailer Haven RV Park, W Shell/dsl, Valero/dsl BlackBear Diner, Burger King, Carl's Jr, KFC, McDonald's, Pizza Factory, Siskiyou Roadhouse Grill, Starbucks, Subway, Taco Bell Baymont Inn, Comfort Inn, Motel 6 H $Tree, AAA, AT&T, CHP, Ford/Lincoln, JC Penney, NAPA, O'Reilly Parts, Radio Shack, Raley's Foods, Walmart
770	Shamrock Rd, Easy St, W Beacon/LP, Fuel 24/7/dsl RV camping

WEED

MT SHASTA

766	A12, to Gazelle, Grenada, E 76/dsl, W Texaco/dsl RV camping
759	Louie Rd
753	Weed Airport Rd, **both lanes, full facilities, litter barrels, petwalk**
751	Stewart Springs Rd, Edgewood, E Lake Shasta RA/RV camp (2mi), W RV camp (7mi)
748	to US 97, to Klamath Falls, Weed, E Chevron, Shell/dsl, Spirit/dsl Ellie's Cafe, Pizza Factory, Subway Hi-Lo Motel/rest., Motel 6, Summit Inn, Townhouse Motel auto repair, golf, NAPA, Ray's Foods, RV camping
747	Central Weed, E auto repair, same as 748, W Coll of Siskiyou
745	S Weed Blvd, E Chevron/dsl, Pilot/Subway/dsl/scales/24hr, Shell/dsl Burger King, Dos Amigos Mexican, McDonald's/RV parking, Silva's Rest., Taco Bell Comfort Inn, Quality Inn, Sis-Q Inn Friendly RV Park
743	Summit Dr, Truck Village Dr
742mm	Black Butte Summit, elev 3912
741	Abrams Lake Rd, E Schwab Tire, W Abrams Lake RV Park
740	Mt Shasta City (from sb), E Pacific Pride/dsl/LP, Shell/dsl/CFN Cold Creek Inn Tire Factory, vet
738	Central Mt Shasta, E Chevron/dsl, Shell/dsl/LP, Spirit/dsl BlackBear Diner, Burger King, KFC/Taco Bell, RoundTable Pizza, Subway Best Western/Treehouse Rest., Mt Shasta Inn, Travel Inn H Best Hardware, NAPA, O'Reilly Parts, Radio Shack, Ray's Foods, Rite Aid, USPO, visitors info, W Lake Siskiyou RV Park, Mt Shasta Resort/rest., Sisson Museum
737	Mt Shasta City (from nb), E Casa Ramos, LaiLai Chinese, Lily's Rest., Piemont Italian, Wayside Grill Alpine Lodge,

CA

N INTERSTATE 5 Cont'd

DUNSMUIR

737 Continued Choice Inn, Evergreen Lodge, Swiss Holiday Lodge [other] McCloud RV Park, same as 738

736 CA 89, to McCloud, to Reno, E [lodging] Swiss Holiday Lodge

735mm **weigh sta sb**

734 Mott Rd, to Dunsmuir

732 Dunsmuir Ave, Siskiyou Ave, E [food] Penny's Diner [lodging] Oak Tree Inn, W [gas] Chevron/dsl [lodging] Acorn Inn, Cedar Lodge

730 Central Dunsmuir, E [food] Burger Barn, Cornerstone Cafe, Dumsmuir Brewery Rest., Hot Dog Depot, Pizza Factory [lodging] Dunsmuir Inn, Hotel Dunsmuir/Rest [other] True Value, USPO, Value King Foods, W [gas] Chevron/dsl/LP [food] Hitching Post, Micki's Burgers [lodging] Cave Springs Motel [other] city park

729 Dunsmuir (from nb), E [gas] Manfredi's/deli/dsl [lodging] auto repair, Dunsmuir Lodge [other] to hist dist

728 Crag View Dr, Dunsmuir, Railroad Park Rd, W [other] Railroad Park Motel/RV Park

727 Crag View Dr (from nb), RV Camping

726 Soda Creek Rd, to Pacific Crest Trail

724 Castella, W [gas] Chevron/dsl [other] Castle Crags SP, RV camping, USPO

723mm vista point nb

723 Sweetbrier Ave

721 Conant Rd

720 Flume Creek Rd

718 Sims Rd, W [other] RV camping

714 Gibson Rd

712 Pollard Flat, E [gas] Pollard Flat/dsl/LP [food] Pollard Flat Diner

710 Slate Creek Rd, La Moine

707 Delta Rd, Dog Creek Rd, to Vollmers

705mm **[rest stop] sb, full [handicapped] facilities, litter barrels [phone] [picnic]**

704 Riverview Dr, E [food] Klondike Dine [lodging] Lakehead Lodge/RV Camping

702 Antlers Rd, Lakeshore Dr, to Lakehead, E [gas] Shell/Subway/dsl [lodging] Antlers RV Park, Lakehead Camping, Neu Lodge Motel [other] auto repair, USPO, W [gas] Jack's/dsl [food] Allyson's Rest., Bass Hole Rest. [lodging] Lakeshore Mkt, Shasta Lake Motel/RV [other] Villa RV Park

698 Salt Creek Rd, Gilman Rd, W [lodging] Salt Creek Resort/RV Park [other] Trail In RV Park

695 Shasta Caverns Rd, to O'Brien

694mm **[rest stop] both lanes, full [handicapped] facilities, litter barrels, petwalk [phone] [picnic]**

693 Packers Bay Rd (from sb)

692 Turntable Bay Rd

690 Bridge Bay Rd, W [food] Tail of a Whale Rest. [lodging] Bridge Bay Motel

689 Fawndale Rd, Wonderland Blvd, E [lodging] Fawndale Lodge, Fawndale Oaks RV Park, W [lodging] Wonderland RV Park

687 Wonderland Blvd, Mountain Gate, E [gas] Chevron/dsl/LP [food] La Fogata [other] Mountain Gate RV Park, Ranger Sta, W [gas] Shell/dsl/LP

685 CA 151, Shasta Dam Blvd, Project City, Central Valley, W [gas] 76/Circle K/dsl, Chevron/Burger King/dsl/LP, Valero/dsl [food] McDonald's, Pizza Factory, Taco Shop [lodging] Shasta Dam Motel [other] NAPA, Rite Aid, Sentry Foods, USPO, vet

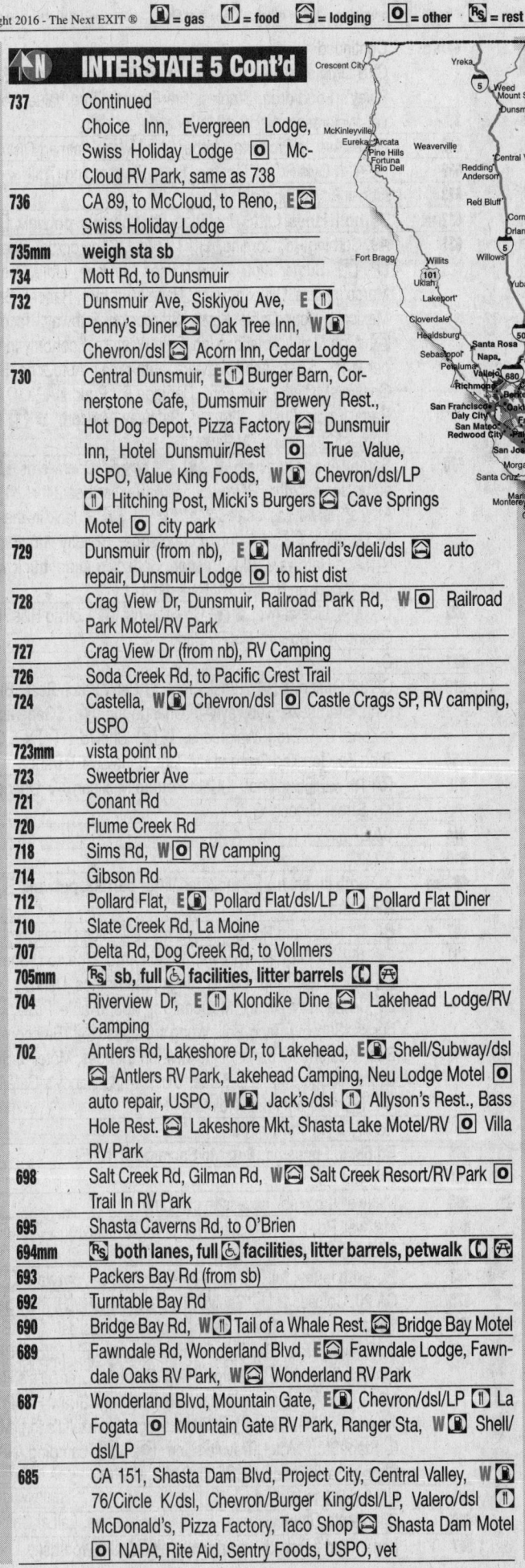

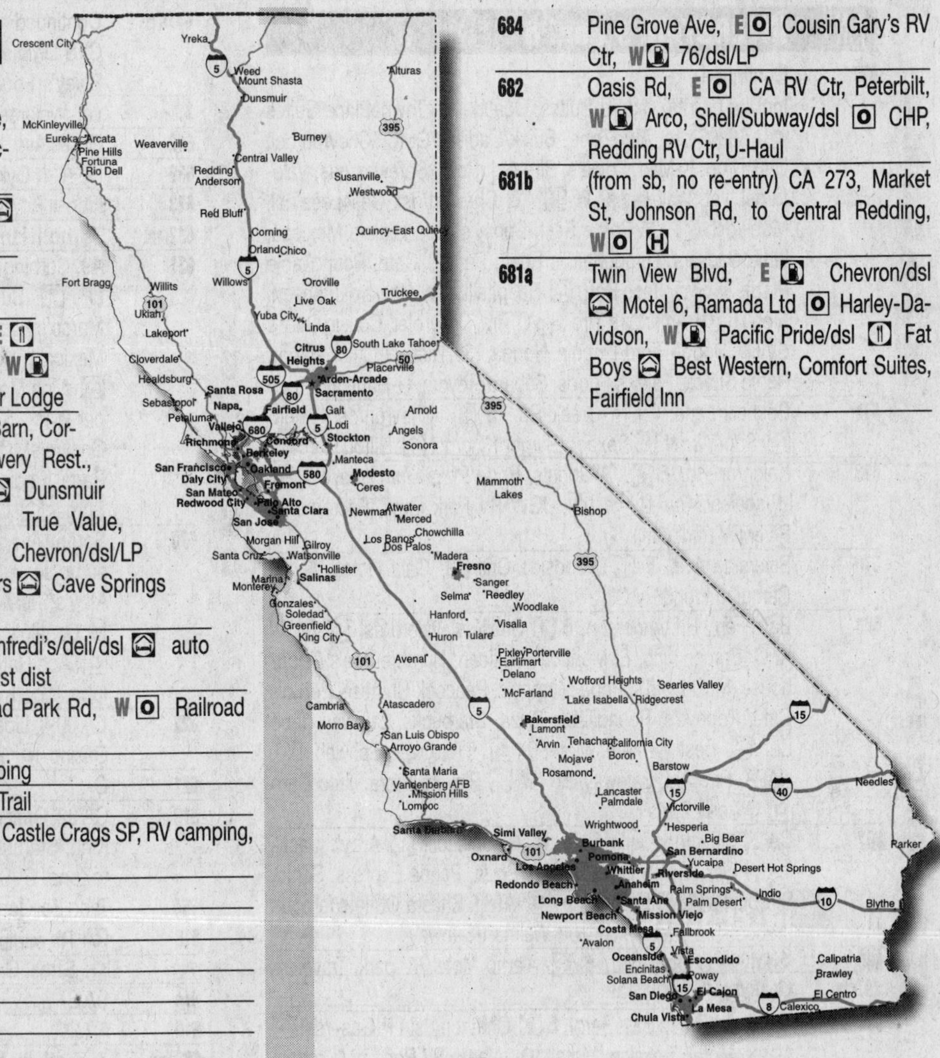

684 Pine Grove Ave, E [other] Cousin Gary's RV Ctr, W [gas] 76/dsl/LP

682 Oasis Rd, E [other] CA RV Ctr, Peterbilt, W [gas] Arco, Shell/Subway/dsl [other] CHP, Redding RV Ctr, U-Haul

681b (from sb, no re-entry) CA 273, Market St, Johnson Rd, to Central Redding, W [other] [H]

681a Twin View Blvd, E [gas] Chevron/dsl [lodging] Motel 6, Ramada Ltd [other] Harley-Davidson, W [gas] Pacific Pride/dsl [food] Fat Boys [lodging] Best Western, Comfort Suites, Fairfield Inn

REDDING

680 CA 299E, **1/2 mi** W [gas] Arco, Chevron/dsl [food] A&W/KFC, Carl's Jr, Giant Burger, Little Caesars, McDonald's, Papa Murphy's, Popeyes, RoundTable Pizza, Starbucks, Subway [other] AutoZone, O'Reilly Parts, Raley's Foods, Redding RV Camp, Redding RV Park, ShopKO, transmissions, Twin View RV Park, Walgreens

678 CA 299 W, CA 44, to Eureka, Redding, Burney, **E between Hilltop & Churncreek** [gas] Chevron/dsl, Shell [food] 5 Thai's, Applebee's, Carl's Jr, Casa Ramos, Chipotle Mexican, Chuck-eCheese, Coldstone, Famous Dave's, Five Guys, Hometown Buffet, In-N-Out, Jack-in-the-Box, Jamba Juice, Jersey Mike's, McDonald's, Olive Garden, Outback Steaks, Panda Express, Panda Express, Red Lobster, Red Robin, Starbucks, Strings Italian, Subway, Taco Bell [lodging] Motel 6, Red Lion Inn [other] AT&T, Barnes&Noble, Best Buy, BigLots, Costco, Dick's, FoodMaxx, Home Depot, JC Penney, Jo-Ann, Kohl's, Macy's, Michael's, Old Navy, O'Reilly Parts, PetCo, Petsmart, Schwab Tire, Sears/auto, Target, TJ Maxx, Trader Joe's, Verizon, Walmart/McDonald's, WinCo Foods, World Mkt

677 Cypress Ave, Hilltop Dr, Redding, E [gas] 76/dsl, Chevron/dsl, Valero/dsl [food] Black Bear Diner, Burger King, Carl's Jr, Cattlemen's Rest., Coldstone, Del Taco, Denny's, Gibb's Grille, Grand Buffet, IHOP, Jack-in-the-Box, Jade Garden, KFC, Logan's Roadhouse, Marie Callender's, McDonald's, Pizza Hut, Popeyes, Starbucks, Subway, Taco Bell, Togo's, Wendy's [lodging] Baymont Inn, Best Western, Comfort Inn, Hampton Inn, Holiday

CA

INTERSTATE 5 Cont'd

REDDING

677 Continued
Inn, La Quinta, Oxford Suites, Quality Inn, TownePlace Suites 99c Store, AutoZone, Buick/Cadillac/GMC, Chevron/dsl, CVS Drug, K-Mart, Lowe's, Rite Aid, Ross, Safeway/gas, Valero/dsl, vet, Walgreens, **W** 76, Chevron/dsl, Gas4Less/dsl, Mobil/dsl CA Cattle Rest, Denny's, Guadalajara Mexican, Little Caesars, Lumberjack's Rest., Perko's Cafe, RoundTable Pizza, Subway, Taco Barn Hospitality Inn, Howard Johnson, Motel 6 America's Tire, Big O Tire, Chevrolet, Cousin Gary's RV Ctr, Dodge, Ford/Lincoln, Honda, Kia, Nissan, Office Depot, Radio Shack, Raley's Foods, Subaru, Toyota, U-Haul, VW

675 Bechelli Lane, Churn Creek Rd, **E** Chevron/dsl, Valero Super 8, **W** Texaco/Burger King/dsl Hilton Garden

673 Knighton Rd, **E** TA/Country Pride/Pizza Hut/Popeye's/dsl/LP/scales/24hr/ @, **W** JGW RV Park (3mi), Sacramento River RV Park (3mi)

670 Riverside Ave, **E** Woodside Grill Gaia Hotel, **W** Camping World RV Ctr

ANDERSON

668 Balls Ferry Rd, Anderson, **E** Shell/dsl, Valero/dsl A&W/KFC, Burger King, El Mariachi Mexican, Humble Joe's Chophouse, McDonald's, Papa Murphy's, Peacock Chinese, Perko's Cafe, Popeye's, RoundTable Pizza, Starbucks, Subway, Taco Bell Best Western, Motel 6 $Tree, Les Schwab Tire, NAPA, Rite Aid, Safeway/dsl, **W** Players Pizza, Taco Barn O'Reilly Parts

667 CA 273, Factory Outlet Blvd, **W** Shell/dsl Arby's, Jack-in-the-Box, Luigi's Pizza, Mary's Pizza, Panda Express, Sonic, Starbucks Baymont Inn AT&T, Shasta Outlets/famous brands, Tire Factory, Verizon, Walmart/Subway

665 (from sb) Cottonwood, **E** Alamo Motel/RV park, Travelers Motel/RV Park

664 Gas Point Rd, to Balls Ferry, **E** Chevron/dsl/LP, Gas+/dsl Alamo Motel, Travelers Motel Alamo RV Park, auto repair, **W** Holiday/dsl, Sunshine/dsl Eagles Nest Pizza, Subway Ace Hardware, Holiday Foods, vet

662 Bowman Rd, to Cottonwood, **E** Chevron/dsl

660mm **weigh sta both lanes**

659 Snively Rd, Auction Yard Rd, (Sunset Hills Dr from nb)

657 Hooker Creek Rd, Auction Yard Rd

656mm **both lanes, full facilities, litter barrels, petwalk**

653 Jellys Ferry Rd, **E** RV Park/LP

652 Wilcox Golf Rd

RED BLUFF

651 CA 36W (from sb), Red Bluff, **W** Arco/dsl Holiday Inn Express same as 650

650 Adobe Rd, **W** Chevron/dsl Burrito Bandito, Casa Ramos Mexican, Starbucks Hampton Inn, Holiday Inn Express CHP, Home Depot

649 CA 36, to CA 99 S, Red Bluff, **E** Chevron/dsl, Red Bluff Gas, Shell/dsl Applebee's, Burger King, Del Taco, KFC, McDonald's, Perko's Cafe Best Western, Comfort Inn, Motel 6, **W** Mobil/dsl, Valero/dsl Denny's, Egg Roll King, Los Mariachis, Luigi's Pizza, Riverside Grill, RoundTable Pizza, Shari's, Subway Super 8, Travelodge AT&T, CVS Drug, Durango RV Resort, Foodmaxx, O'Nite RV Park, River's Edge RV Park, Verizon, vet

647a b S Main St, Red Bluff, **E** Valero/dsl Days Inn **W** Arco/dsl, Chevron/dsl, Shell/dsl Arby's, Baskin-Robbins, China Buffet, China Doll, Cozy Diner, Domino's, Jack-in-the-Box, Papa Murphy's, Starbucks, Subway, Wendy's American Inn, Best Value Inn, Triangle Motel AutoZone,

647a b Continued
CVS Drug, GNC, Grocery Outlet, O'Reilly Parts, Radio Shack Raley's Food/drug, Staples, Tire Factory, True Value, Verizon vet, Walgreens, Walmart/McDonald's

642 Flores Ave, to Proberta, Gerber, **1 mi E** Walmart Dist Ctr

636 Rd A11, Gyle Rd, to Tehama, **E** RV camping (7mi)

633 Finnell Rd, to Richfield

632mm **both lanes, full facilities, litter barrels, petwalk**

CORNING

631 A9, Corning Rd, Corning, **E** 76/dsl, Chevron/dsl, Shell/dsl, LP Burger King, Casa Ramos Mexican, Little Caesar's Marco's Pizza, Olive Pit Rest., Papa Murphy's, Rancho Grande Mexican, RoundTable Pizza, Starbucks, Subway, Taco Bell 7 Inn Motel, American Inn, Best Western, Economy Inn, Super 8 $Tree, Ace Hardware, auto repair, AutoZone, Buick/Chevrolet, Clark Drug, Ford, Heritage RV Park, NAPA, O'Reilly Parts, Radio Shack, Rite Aid, Safeway, Verizon, **W** Giant Burger Corning RV Park

630 South Ave, Corning, **E** Loves/Denny's/dsl/LP/RV dump/scales/24hr, Petro/Iron Skillet/dsl/scales/24hr/ @, TA/Arby's/Subway/dsl/scales/24hr/ @ Jack-in-the-Box, McDonald's CA Inn, Econolodge, Holiday Inn Express Ace Hardware, Blue Beacon, SpeedCo Lube, truck wash/lube, Woodson Br SRA/RV Park (6mi)

628 CA 99W, Liberal Ave, **W** Chevron/dsl Rolling Hills Hotel/Casino Rolling Hills RV Park

621 CA 7

619 CA 32, Orland, **E** 76/dsl, Arco Berry Patch Rest., Burger King, Starbucks, Subway Orlanda Inn $General, AutoZone, CVS Drug, Walgreens, **W** Shell/dsl I-5 Cafe, Taco Bell Old Orchard RV Park, Parkway RV Park

618 CA 16, **E** Shell/dsl El Potrero Mexican Orland Inn $Tree, Grocery Outlet

614 CA 27

610 Artois

608mm **both lanes, full facilities, litter barrels, petwalk RV dump**

607 CA 39, Blue Gum Rd, Bayliss, **2 mi E** Blue Gum Motel

603 CA 162, to Oroville, Willows, **E** Arco, Chevron, Shell/dsl Black Bear Diner, Burger King, Casa Ramos, Denny's, KFC, La Cascada Mexican, McDonald's, RoundTable Pizza, Starbucks, Subway, Taco Bell, Wong's Chinese Baymont Inn, Best Western/RV parking, Holiday Inn Express, Motel 6, Super 8, Travelodge $Tree, CHP, **W** Nancy's Café/24hr RV Park (8mi), Walmart

601 Rd 57, **E** Chevron/dsl

595 Rd 68, to Princeton, **E** to Sacramento NWR

WILLIAMS

591 Delevan Rd

588 Maxwell (from sb), access to camping

586 Maxwell Rd, **E** Delavan NWR, **W** Chevron Maxwell Inn/rest. Maxwell Parts

583 **both lanes, full facilities, litter barrels, petwalk**

578 CA 20, Colusa, **W** Shell/Orv's Cafe/dsl hwy patrol

577 Williams, **E** Shell/Baskin-Robbins/Togo's/dsl Carl's Jr, Subway, Taco Bell Ramada Inn, **W** 76/dsl, Chevron/dsl, Shell/dsl Burger King, Denny's, Granzella's Rest., Louis Cairo's Rest., McDonald's/RV parking, Straw Hat Pizza, Williams Chinese Rest. Econolodge, Granzella's Inn, Motel 6, StageStop Motel, Travelers Inn camping, NAPA, Shop'n Save Foods, URGENT CARE, USPO

575 Husted Rd, to Williams

569 Hahn Rd, to Grimes

567 frontage rd (from nb), to Arbuckle, **W** Chevron/dsl

INTERSTATE 5 Cont'd

Exit #	Services
566	to College City, Arbuckle, E Ace Hardware, USPO, W J&J/dsl $General
559	Yolo/Colusa County Line Rd
557mm	**both lanes, full facilities, litter barrels, petwalk**
556	E4, Dunnigan, E Chevron/dsl/LP Jack-in-the-Box Best Value Inn, Motel 6 Farmers Mkt Deli, W Camper's RV Park/golf (1mi)
554	Rd 8, E Pilot/Wendy's/dsl/scales/24hr Hacienda Motel HappyTime RV Park, Oasis Grill, W United TP/dsl
553	I-505 (from sb), to San Francisco, callboxes begin sb
548	Zamora, E Shell/dsl
542	Yolo, **1 mi** E
541	CA 16W, Woodland, **3 mi** W H
540	West St, W Arco Denny's
538	CA 113 N, E St, Woodland, E Valley Oaks Inn, W CFN/dsl, Chevron/dsl Perry's Best Western
537	CA 113 S, Main St, to Davis (same as 536), E Buick/Cadillac/Chevrolet/GMC, W Chevron/dsl Carl's Jr, Denny's, McDonald's, RoundTable Pizza, Starbucks, Subway, Taco Bell, Wendy's Days Inn, Motel 6, Quality Inn $Tree, Food-4Less
536	Rd 102 (same as 537), **E on Main St** Arco, Chevron/dsl Applebee's, Burger King, Jack-in-the-Box, McDonald's, Quiznos, Subway Hampton Inn, Holiday Inn Express America's Tire, Home Depot, museum, Staples, Walmart/McDonald's, W 76/Circle K/dsl In-N-Out, Panda Express, Red Robin, Spoon Me, Starbucks, Subway Best Buy, Best Buy, Costco/gas, Michael's, Target, Verizon
531	Rd 22, W Sacramento
530mm	Sacramento River
529mm	**sb, full facilities, litter barrels, petwalk**
528	Airport Rd, E Arco
525b	CA 99, to CA 70, to Marysville, Yuba City
525a	Del Paso Rd, E Chevron A&W/KFC, Chicken'n Waffles, Denny's, IHOP, In-N-Out, Jack-in-the-box, Malabar Rest., Panda Express, Panera Bread, Papa Murphy's, Sizzler, Sizzler, Taco Bell Hampton Inn, Holiday Inn Express, Homewood Suites Rite Aid, Safeway Foods/dsl, W Subway Sheraton Walgreens
524	Arena Blvd, E Papa John's, Subway Power Balance Arena, W RoundTable Pizza, Starbucks Bel-Air Food/Drug/dsl
522	I-80, E to Reno, W to San Francisco
521b	W El Camino Ave (from nb, no return), West El Camino, W Shell/dsl Carl's Jr, Jack-in-the-Box, Jamba Juice, Starbucks, Subway, Togo's/Baskin-Robbins Courtyard, Hilton Garden, Residence Inn, SpringHill Suites
521a	Garden Hwy, W Courtyard
520	Richards Blvd, E Chevron/dsl Denny's, McDonald's Governor's Inn, Hawthorn Suites, W Arco, Shell Nena's Mexican Best Value Inn, Best Western, Comfort Suites, Days Inn, La Quinta, Motel 6 waterfront park
519b	J St, Old Sacramento, E Holiday Inn, Vagabond Inn, W Embassy Suites Railroad Museum
519a	Q St, downtown, Sacramento, W Embassy Suites, to st capitol
518	US 50, CA 99, Broadway, E services downtown
516	Sutterville Rd, E 76/dsl, Chevron/dsl La Bou Cafe, Macau Cafe Sprouts Mkt, Wm Land Park, zoo

DAVIS

SACRAMENTO

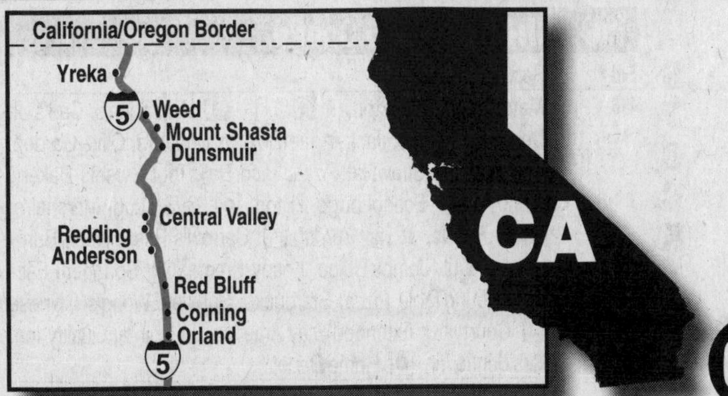

CA

Exit #	Services
515	Fruitridge Rd, Seamas Rd
514	43rd Ave, Riverside Blvd (from sb), E 76/repair
513	Florin Rd, E Arco, Chevron/dsl Rosalinda's Mexican, RoundTable Pizza $Tree, Bel Air Foods, CVS Drug, O'Reilly Parts, W Burger King, JimBoy's Tacos, L&L Hawaiian BBQ, Panda Garden, Shari's, Starbucks, Subway, Wings Stop Marshall's, Nugget Mkt, Radio Shack, Rite Aid
512	CA 160, Pocket Rd, Meadowview Rd, to Freeport, E Chargepoint, Shell/dsl, Valero/dsl Baskin Robbins/Togo's, IHOP, KFC, McDonald's, Starbucks, Wendy's AT&T, Home Depot, Staples, vet, Walgreens
510	Cosumnes River Blvd
508	Laguna Blvd, E 76/Circle K/dsl/LP, Chevron/Taco Bell/dsl, Shell A&W/KFC, Starbucks, Subway, Wendy's Extended Stay America, Hampton Inn Jiffy Lube, Laguna Auto/RV Repair, U-Haul
506	Elk Grove Blvd, E Arco/dsl, Chevron/dsl, Shell Carl's Jr, Flaming Grill Burger, Pete's Grill, Wasabi Grill Holiday Inn Express
504	Hood Franklin Rd
498	Twin Cities Rd, to Walnut Grove
493	Walnut Grove Rd, Thornton, E CFN/dsl, Chevron/Subway/dsl
490	Peltier Rd
487	Turner Rd
485	CA 12, Lodi, E FLYING J/Denny's/Subway/dsl/scales/24hr, Arco, Chevron/dsl, Loves/Arby's/dsl/scales/24hr, Shell/dsl, Sinclair/Rocky's Rest./dsl/scales/24hr Burger King, Carl's Jr, McDonald's, Taco Bell Best Western, Microtel Blue Beacon, Flag City RV Resort, Profleet Trucklube, W KOA (5mi)
481	Eight Mile Rd, W Chevron/Jack-in-the-Box/dsl Baskin-Robbins, Chipotle, Del Taco, Dickey's BBQ, El Pollo Loco, Hawaiian BBQ, Jamba Juice, McDonald's, MooMoo's Burgers, Panda Express, Panera Bread, RoundTable Pizza, Sonic, Starbucks, Strings Italian, Subway, Wendy's $Tree, AAA, AT&T, Jo-Ann Fabrics, Kohl's, Lowe's, Office Depot, Petsmart, Ross, Target, Verizon, Walmart/McDonald's, World Mkt
478	Hammer Lane, Stockton, E 76/Circle K/dsl, Arco Adalberto's Mexican, Carl's Jr, KFC, Little Caesar's, McDonald's, Subway AutoZone, Radio Shack, Raley's Foods, URGENT CARE, Walgreens, W Chevron/dsl, QuikStop Jack-in-the-Box, Taco Bell
477	Benjamin Holt Dr, Stockton, E Arco, Chevron/dsl Pizza Guys Motel 6 Quikstop, QwikStop, W 7-11 Eddie's Pizza, Fon Wong Chinese, Lumber Jack's Rest., Lyon's Rest., McDonald's, Starbucks, Subway/TCBY Ace Hardware, Marina Foods, vet

STOCKTON

INTERSTATE 5 Cont'd

STOCKTON

Exit #	Services
476	March Lane, Stockton, E 7-11 Applebee's, Carl's Jr, Denny's, El Torito, Jack-in-the-Box, McDonald's, Olive Garden, Red Lobster, StrawHat Pizza, Taco Bell, Toot Sweets Bakery, Wendy's EconoLodge, Hilton CVS Drug, Marshall's, SMart Foods, W 76/dsl Carrow's Rest., Habit Burger, In-N-Out, Jamba Juice, Krispy Kreme, Old Spaghetti Factory, RoundTable Pizza, Starbucks, Subway, Wong's Chinese Courtyard, Extended Stay America, La Quinta, Quality Inn, Residence Inn Home Depot
475	Alpine Ave, Country Club Blvd, same as 474 b
474b	Country Club Blvd (from nb), E Valero/dsl, W 7-11, Shell/dsl Papa Murphy's BigLots, Safeway/gas
474a	Monte Diablo Ave
473	Pershing Ave (from nb), W Arco Red Roof Inn
472	CA 4 E, to CA 99, Fresno Ave, downtown
471	CA 4 W, Charter Way, E Arco, Chevron/dsl, Shell Burger King, Denny's, Little Caesar's, McDonald's Days Inn $General Mkt, O'Reilly Parts, W 76/dsl/scales/24hr, Valero/Subway Jack-in-the-Box, Taco Bell Motel 6 Les Schwab Tire, truck repair
470	8th St, Stockton, W CA Stop/dsl, Shell/dsl I-5 Inn
469	Downing Ave, W China Express, Louie's Chinese, Mtn Mike's Pizza, Papa Murphy's, Subway $Tree, AutoZone, Food4Less/gas
468	French Camp, E 76/Togo's/dsl Pan Pacific RV Ctr, W H
467b	Mathews Rd, E J&L Mkt/dsl tires/repair, W H
467a	El Dorado St (from nb)
465	Roth Rd, Sharpe Depot, E FL/dsl Freightliner, Kenworth, truck/rv repair
463	Lathrop Rd, E Chevron/dsl/LP, Joe's Trkstp/Togo's/dsl/scales, TowerMart/dsl, Valero/dsl Baskin-Robbins, China Wok, CK Grill, Dickey's BBQ, Little Caesar's, Mi Kasa Japanese, Milan's Pizza, Papa Murphy's, Starbucks, Subway Comfort Inn, Days Inn, Days Inn, Holiday Inn Express Harley-Davidson, O'Reilly Parts, SaveMart Mkt, Walgreens, W Dos Reis CP, RV camping
462	Louise Ave, E Arco/dsl, Shell A&W/KFC, Carl's Jr, Denny's, Golden Bowl, Jack-in-the-Box, McDonald's, Mtn Mike's Pizza, Quiznos, Taco Bell Hampton Inn, Quality Inn, W Mossdale CP, Target
461	CA 120, to Sonora, Manteca, E Oakwood Lake Resort Camping, to Yosemite
460	Mossdale Rd, E Chevron/dsl, W fruit stand/cafe
458b	I-205, to Oakland (from sb, no return)
458a	11th St, to Tracy, Defense Depot, 2 mi W gas/dsl/food
457	Kasson Rd, to Tracy, W Valley Pacific/dsl
452	CA 33 S, Vernalis
449b a	CA 132, to Modesto, E The Orchard Campground
446	I-580 (from nb, exits left, no return)
445mm	**Westley both lanes, full facilities, litter barrels, petwalk RV dump**
441	Ingram Creek, Howard Rd, Westley, E 76/dsl, Chevron/dsl, Joe's Trvl Plaza/Denny's/dsl/scales/24hr, Westley Triangle TruckStp/dsl Antojito's Mexican, Carl's Jr, McDonald's, Subway Best Value Inn, Days Inn, EconoLodge, Holiday Inn Express, W Shell/dsl fruits, Ingram Creek Rest. truck repair

WESTLEY

SANTA NELLA

Exit #	Services
434	Sperry Ave, Del Puerto, Patterson, E 76/Subway/dsl, Chevron A&W/KFC, Apricot Wood BBQ, Carl's Jr, Denny's, El Rosal Mexican, Golden Lion Chinese, Jack-in-the-Box, Lamp Post Pizza, Starbucks Best Western Kit Fox RV Park
430mm	vista point nb
428	Fink Rd, Crow's Landing
423	Stuhr Rd, Newman, 5 mi E RV camping
422mm	vista point sb
418	CA 140E, Gustine, E Chevron/dsl, Shell/dsl
409	**weigh sta both lanes**
407	CA 33, Santa Nella, E Arco, Loves/Del Taco/dsl/scales/24hr, TA/Shell/Country Pride/Popeye's/dsl/scales/24hr/@ Andersen's Rest., Carl's Jr, Subway, Wendy's Best Western/Andersen's, Quality Inn, W 76/Circle K/Jack-in-the-Box/dsl, Chevron, Rotten Robbie/dsl/scales, Shell/Circle K/Jack-in-the-Box/dsl, Valero/dsl Denny's, In-N-Out, McDonald's, Panda Express, Starbucks, Taco Bell Hotel de Oro, Motel 6 Santa Nella RV Park
403b a	CA 152, Los Banos, 6 mi E H 1 mi W Petro/Shell/diner/dsl/24hr Motel 6 KOA
391	CA 165N, Mercy Springs Rd, E H W Shell
388	vista point (from nb)
386mm	**both lanes, full facilities, litter barrels, petwalk**
385	Nees Ave, to Firebaugh, W Chevron/CFN/Subway/dsl/scales
379	Shields Ave, to Mendota
372	Russell Ave
368	Panoche Rd, E Tesla, W 76/dsl, Chevron/McDonald's, Mobil/Taco Bell/dsl, Shell/dsl Apricot Tree Rest., Fosters Freeze, Subway Best Western country store
365	Manning Ave, to San Joaquin
357	Kamm Ave
349	CA 33 N, Derrick Ave
337	CA 33 S, CA 145 N, to Coalinga
334	CA 198, to Lemoore, Huron, E Shell/Subway/dsl/24hrs Harris Ranch Inn/rest., W 76, Chevron, Valero/Quiznos/dsl Burger King, Carl's Jr, Denny's, McDonald's, Oriental Express Chinese, Taco Bell Best Western, Motel 6, Travelodge H
325	Jayne Ave, to Coalinga, W Arco, Shell/Baja Fresh/dsl Sommerville RV Park/LP H
320mm	**both lanes, full facilities, litter barrels, petwalk**
319	CA 269, Lassen Ave, to Avenal, W Hillcrest TP/76/Subway/dsl/scales/24hr
309	CA 41, Kettleman City, E 76/Subway/TCBY, CFN/dsl, Chevron/McDonald's, Mobil/Starbucks/dsl/24hr, Shell/Baja Fresh/dsl, Valero/dsl Carl's Jr, Denny's, In-N-Out, Jack-in-the-Box, Pizza Hut/Taco Bell Best Value Inn, Best Western Bravo Farms Mercantile
305	Utica Ave
288	Twisselman Rd
278	CA 46, Lost Hills, E Buford Star Mart/dsl/LP to Kern NWR, W 76/Quiznos, Chevron/dsl, Loves/Arby's/dsl/scales/24hr, Mobil/McDonald's/dsl/LP, Pilot/Wendy's/dsl/scales/24hr, Shell/Pizza Hut/Subway/Taco Bell/dsl, Valero/dsl Carl's Jr, Denny's, Jack-in-the-Box Days Inn, Motel 6 Lost Hills RV Park, Royal Truck Wash/lube
268	Lerdo Hwy, to Shafter
262	7th Standard Rd, Rowlee Rd, to Buttonwillow
259mm	**Buttonwillow both lanes, full facilities, litter barrels, petwalk**

CA

INTERSTATE 5 Cont'd

BUTTONWILLOW

Exit #	Services
257	CA 58, to Bakersfield, Buttonwillow, **E** [gas] 76/Circle K/Quiznos/dsl, Arco/dsl, Chevron/dsl, Shell/dsl, Speedy Fuel/dsl/wash, TA/Mobil/Pizza Hut/Taco Bell/dsl/scales/24hr/ @ [food] Carl's Jr, Denny's, McDonald's, Starbucks, Subway, Tita's Mexican, Willow Ranch BBQ [lodging] EconoLodge, Motel 6, Super 8 [other] Castro's Tire/Truckwash, **W** [gas] Valero/dsl
253	Stockdale Hwy, **E** [gas] Chevron/Subway/dsl, Shell/dsl/24hr [food] IHOP, Jack-in-the-Box [lodging] Best Western, Vagabond Inn, **W** [other] Tule Elk St Reserve
246	CA 43, to Taft, Maricopa, [other] to Buena Vista RA
244	CA 119, to Pumpkin Center, **E** [gas] Mobil/dsl, **W** [gas] Chevron/dsl/LP
239	CA 223, Bear Mtn Blvd, to Arvin, **E** [other] Bear Mtn RV Resort, **W** [other] RV camping, to Buena Vista RA
234	Old River Rd
228	Copus Rd, **E** [other] Murray Farms Mkt
225	CA 166, to Mettler, **2-3 mi E** food, gas/dsl
221	I-5 and CA 99 (from nb, exits left, no return)
219b a	Laval Rd, Wheeler Ridge, **E** [gas] Shell/dsl, TA/Shell/Popeye's/Subway/scales/ @ [food] Black Bear Diner, Burger King, Carl's Jr, Pieology, Pizza Hut, Starbucks, Taco Bell [lodging] Microtel [other] Blue Beacon, Tejon Outlets/famous brands, **W** [gas] Chevron/dsl, Mobil/dsl, Petro/Iron Skillet/Subway/dsl/scales/24hr/ @ [food] Baskin-Robbins, Chipotle Mexican, Del Taco, In-N-Out, Mauricio's Mexican, McDonald's, Panda Express, Starbucks, Subway, Wendy's, Yogurtland [lodging] Best Western

FT TEJON

Exit #	Services
218	**truck weigh sta sb**
215	Grapevine, **E** [gas] Valero/dsl [food] Denny's, Jack-in-the-Box, **W** [gas] Shell/dsl [food] Don Perico Grill [lodging] Ramada Ltd
210	Ft Tejon Rd, **W** [other] to Ft Tejon Hist SP, towing/repair
209mm	**brake check area nb**
207	Lebec Rd, **W** [other] antiques, CHP, towing, USPO
206mm	[rest stop] **both lanes, full** (handicapped) **facilities, litter barrels, petwalk** (phone) (picnic) **vending**
205	Frazier Mtn Park Rd, **W** [gas] FLYING J dsl/LP/24hr/ @, Arco, Chevron/Subway/dsl/24hr, Shell/Quiznos/dsl/LP [food] Jack-in-the-Box, Los Pinos Mexican [lodging] Holiday Inn Express, Motel 6 [other] auto repair/towing, NAPA Autocare, to Mt Pinos RA
204	elev 4144, Tejon Pass, **truck brake insp sb**
202	Gorman Rd, to Hungry Valley, **E** [gas] 76/dsl, Chevron/dsl/LP [food] Carl's Jr, El Grullense, Ranch House Rest. [lodging] EconoLodge, **W** [gas] Shell/dsl [food] McDonald's [other] auto repair
199	CA 138 E, Lancaster Rd, to Palmdale
198b a	Quail Lake Rd, CA 138 E (from nb)
195	Smokey Bear Rd, Pyramid Lake, **W** [other] Pyramid Lake RV Park
191	Vista del Lago Rd, **W** [other] visitors ctr
186mm	**brake inspection area sb**, motorist callboxes begin sb

CASTAIC

Exit #	Services
183	Templin Hwy, **W** [other] Ranger Sta, RV camping
176b a	Lake Hughes Rd, Parker Rd, Castaic, **E** [gas] 7-11, Arco/dsl, Castaic Trkstp/dsl/24hr, Pilot/Wendy's/dsl/scales/24hr/@, Shell/dsl [food] Baskin-Robbins, Cajun Chicken, Carl's Jr, Denny's, Domino's, El Pollo Loco, Fosters Freeze, Jersey Mike's, McDonald's, Mike's Diner, Panda Express, PapaZ Burger, Pizza Factory, Popeye's, Red Dot Pizza, Starbucks, Subway, Waba Grill, Wok's Chinese [lodging] Castaic Inn, Days Inn, Rodeway Inn [other] $Tree, Benny's Tire/repair, Castaic Lake RV Park, O'Reilly Parts, to Castaic Lake, vet, **W** [gas] 76/repair, Mobil [food] Jack-in-the-Box, Taco Bell [other] auto repair, Walgreens
173	Hasley Canyon Rd, **W** [food] Pizza Hut, Subway [other] Ralph's Foods

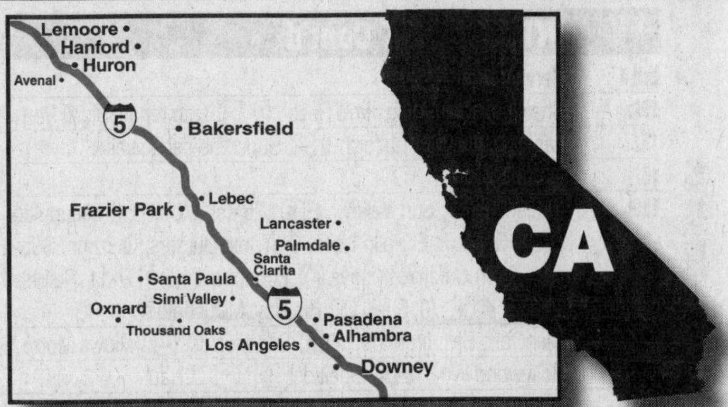

CA

SANTA CLARITA

Exit #	Services
172	CA 126 W, to Ventura, **E** [lodging] Courtyard, Embassy Suites
171mm	**weigh sta nb**
171	Rye Canyon Rd (from sb), **W** [gas] Chevron, Shell/dsl [food] Del Taco, Jack-in-the-Box, Jimmy Dean's, Starbucks, Subway, Tommy's Burgers [other] Six Flags
170	CA 126 E, Magic Mtn Pkwy, Saugus, **E** [food] Azul Tequila Mexican, Denny's, Rustic Eatery, Sam's Grille, Shrimp Haus, Starbucks [lodging] Best Western/rest., Holiday Inn Express, **W** [gas] Chevron/dsl [food] El Torito, Marie Callender's, Red Lobster, Wendy's [lodging] Hilton Garden [other] Six Flags of CA
169	Valencia Blvd, **W** [food] Fat Burger, Nick'n Willy's Pizza, Panda Express, Robeks, Starbucks, Subway [other] Verizon
168	McBean Pkwy, **E** [other] (H) **W** [food] Baskin-Robbins, Cabo Cabana, Chili's, ChuckeCheese, ClaimJumper, Jamba Juice, Jersey Mikes Subs, Macaroni Grill, Mamma Mia Italian, Mod Pizza, Pick up Stix, Starbucks, Subway, Urbane Cafe [other] Michael's, Old Navy, Verizon, Vons Foods, WorldMkt
167	Lyons Ave, Pico Canyon Rd, **E** [gas] 76/Circle K/dsl, Chevron/dsl, Shell/dsl [food] Burger King, Wendy's, **W** [gas] Arco, Shell/dsl [food] Cabo Cabana, Carl's Jr, Chuy's, Coco's, Del Taco, Denny's, El Pollo Loco, Fortune Express Chinese, Golden Spoon, IHOP, In-N-Out, Jack-in-the-Box, Jersey Mike's, McDonald's, Outback Steaks, Spumoni Italian, Taco Bell, Wood Ranch BBQ, Yamato Japanese [lodging] Comfort Suites, Extended Stay America, Fairfield Inn, Hampton Inn, La Quinta, Residence Inn [other] AT&T, Camping World RV Ctr, GNC, Jiffy Lube, Marshall's, Old Navy, Petsmart, Ralph's Foods, Ross, Staples, SteinMart, Walmart/McDonald's
166	Calgrove Blvd
162	CA 14 N, to Palmdale
161b	Balboa Blvd (from sb)
160a	I-210, to San Fernando, Pasadena

SYLMAR

Exit #	Services
159	Roxford St, Sylmar, **E** [gas] Chevron/dsl, Mobil/dsl [food] Denny's/24hr, McDonald's [lodging] Good Nite Inn, Motel 6
158	I-405 S (from sb, no return)
157b a	SF Mission Blvd, Brand Blvd, **E** [gas] 76, Arco, Chevron, Mobil/dsl, Shell [food] Carl's Jr, In-N-Out, Little Caesars, New Asia, Pollo Gordo, Popeye's, Subway, Taco Bell, Winchell's [other] (H) Honda, Rite Aid
156b	CA 118
156a	Paxton St, Brand Ave (from nb), **E** [gas] Shell/dsl [other] 7-11

ARLETA

Exit #	Services
155b	Van Nuys Blvd (no EZ nb return), **E** [gas] Eagle [food] Jack-in-the-Box, KFC/LJ Silver, McDonald's, Pizza Hut, Popeye's [other] Discount Parts, USPO, **W** [food] Domino's [other] auto repair
155a	Terra Bella St (from nb), **E** [gas] Arco
154	Osborne St, to Arleta, **E** [gas] Arco, Chevron/dsl [food] El Pollo Loco, Knight's Pizza, Papa's Tacos [other] AutoZone, BigLots, Food4Less, Superior Grocers, Target, **W** [gas] 76, Mobil/Burger King [other] 7-11
153b	CA 170 (from sb), to Hollywood

[gas] = gas [food] = food [lodging] = lodging [other] = other [RS] = rest stop

INTERSTATE 5 Cont'd

SUN VALLEY

Exit #	Services
152a	Sheldon St, E [food] Big Jim's Rest. [other] H auto repair, Big O Parts
152	Lankershim Blvd, Tuxford, E [gas] Superfine/dsl/scales
151	Penrose St
150b	Sunland Blvd, Sun Valley, E [gas] 76/dsl, Mobil [food] Acapulco Rest., Carl's Jr, El Pollo Loco, Old Time Burgers, Quiznos, Subway, Town Café, Yoshinoya [lodging] Economy Inn [other] 7-11, Ralph's Foods, W [gas] 76, Shell [food] Big Boy, McDonald's
150a	GlenOaks Blvd (from nb), E [gas] Superior/dsl [lodging] Willows Motel
149	Hollywood Way, W [gas] Shell/dsl [other] [airport], U-Haul
148	Buena Vista St, E [lodging] Hampton Inn, W [gas] 76/dsl [food] Jack-in-the-Box [lodging] Quality Inn, Ramada Inn
147	Scott Rd, to Burbank, E [gas] Sevan/dsl, W [food] Hometown Buffet, Krispy Kreme, Outback Steaks, Panda Express, Starbucks, Wendy's [lodging] Courtyard, Extended Stay America [other] Best Buy, Lowe's, Marshall's, Michael's, Staples, Target, Verizon
146b	Burbank Blvd, E [gas] 76/repair [food] Baskin-Robbins, CA Pizza Kitchen, Carl's Jr, Chevy's Mexican, ChuckECheese's, Corner Cafe, Harry's Rest., Hooters, IHOP, In-N-Out, McDonald's, Pizza Hut, Popeye's, Quiznos, Robek's Juice, Shakey's Pizza, Starbucks, Subway, Taco Bell, Tommy's Burgers, Yoshinoya [lodging] Holiday Inn [other] Barnes&Noble, Curves, CVS Drug, Henry's Mkt, K-Mart, Loehmanns, Macy's, Office Depot, Old Navy, Ralph's Foods, Ross, Sears, W [food] McDonald's, Subway [other] Costco/gas, Discount Tire
146a	Olive Ave, Verdugo, E [food] BJ's Rest., Black Angus [lodging] Holiday Inn [other] Radio Shack, USPO, W [other] H, 7-11, Chevrolet, Metro RV Ctr
145b	Alameda Ave, E [gas] Chevron [food] Baskin-Robbins/Togo's, Del Taco, Habit Burgers, Starbucks [other] CarMax, CVS Drug, Home Depot, Ralph's Foods, Trader Joes, Walgreens, W [gas] Arco, Shell [lodging] Burbank Inn [other] U-Haul
145a	Western Ave, W [other] Gene Autrey Museum
144b a	CA 134, Ventura Fwy, Glendale, Pasadena
142	Colorado St
141a	Los Feliz Blvd, E [other] H W [other] Griffith Park, zoo
140b	Glendale Blvd, E [gas] 76, Valero [food] Starbucks, Subway [other] auto repair, W [gas] Valero
140a	Fletcher Dr (from sb)
139b a	CA 2, Glendale Fwy
138	Stadium Way, Figueroa St, E [gas] Chevron, Thrifty, Valero [food] IHOP, McDonald's [other] Home Depot, W [other] to Dodger Stadium
137b a	CA 2, Glendale Fwy, W [gas] 76
136b	Broadway St (from sb), W [gas] 76
136a	Main St, E [gas] 76, Chevron/24hr [food] Chinatown Express, Jack-in-the-Box, McDonald's, Mr Pizza [other] H, Parts+
135c	I-10 W (from nb), Mission Rd (from sb), E [gas] 76/dsl, Chevron [food] Jack-in-the-Box, McDonald's [other] H
135b	Cesar Chavez Ave, W [other] H
135a	4th St, Soto St, E [gas] 76/dsl, Shell/Subway/dsl, W [gas] Arco/dsl [other] city park
134b	Ca 60 E (from sb), Soto St (from nb)
134a	CA 60 W, Santa Monica Fwy
133	Euclid Ave (from sb), Grand Vista (from nb), E [gas] Arco, USA/dsl, W [gas] Mobil, Shell [other] H
132	Calzona St, Indiana St, E [gas] Arco/dsl
131b	Indiana St (from nb), E [gas] Arco/dsl, Valero/dsl
131a	Olympic Blvd, E [food] McDonald's, W [food] Jack-in-the-Box, King Taco [other] H
130c b	I-710 (exits left from nb), to Long Beach, Eastern Ave, E [food] McDonald's
130a	Triggs St (from sb), E [other] outlet mall, W [food] Denny's/24hr [lodging] Destiny Inn
129	Atlantic Blvd N, Eastern Ave (from sb), E [food] Carl's Jr, Fresca's Mexican, Panda Express, Ruby's Diner, Starbucks, Subway [lodging] Doubletree [other] Hyundai, outlets/famous brands, W [food] Denny's, Steven's Steaks
128b	Washington Blvd, Commerce, E [gas] Chevron/dsl/repair/24hr [food] McDonald's [lodging] Crowne Plaza Hotel/casino, Doubletree [other] Costco, outlets/famous brands, W [gas] Arco [food] Del Taco, Subway
128a	Garfield Blvd, E [lodging] Commerce/Hotel/casino [other] Home Depot, Office Depot, W [gas] 76
126b	Slauson Ave, Montebello, E [gas] Shell, Valero/dsl [food] Ozzie's Diner, Quiznos, Starbucks [lodging] Quality Inn, Super 8, W [gas] Arco [food] Denny's [lodging] Budget Inn, Ramada Inn
126a	Paramount Blvd, Downey, E [gas] Shell/Jack-in-the-Box/dsl
125	CA 19 S, Lakewood Blvd, Rosemead Blvd, E [gas] Mobil, Thrifty [food] Arthurs Cafe, Foster's Freeze, Sam's Burgers, Starbucks, Taco Bell [lodging] EconoLodge, W [food] China Wok, Chris&Pitt's BBQ, McDonald's, Subway [other] Ralph's Foods
124	I-605
123	Florence Ave, to Downey, E [gas] Mobil, W [other] Honda, repair
122	Imperial Hwy, Pioneer Blvd, E [gas] Chevron [food] Applebee's, Habit Burgers, IHOP, Jack-in-the-Box, McDonald's, Subway, Wendy's, Wood Grill Buffet [other] Firestone/auto, Rite Aid, Target, W [gas] 7-11, Chevron [food] Alberts Mexican, Denny's, HongKong Express, Panda King, Pizza Hut, Rally's, Shakey's Pizza, Sizzler, Wienerschnitzel [lodging] Comfort Inn, Keystone Motel, Rodeway Inn [other] Toyota/Scion, Walmart
121	San Antonio Dr, to Norwalk Blvd, E [food] IHOP, Jack-in-the-Box, McDonald's, Outback Steaks, Starbucks, Wood Grill Buffet [lodging] Doubletree Inn [other] Rite Aid, Target, W [gas] 76 [other] auto repair
120b	Firestone Blvd (exits left from nb)
120a	Rosecrans Ave, E [gas] Valero/dsl [food] Jim's Burgers, KFC, Little Caesars, Starbucks, Taco Joe [other] H BigSaver Foods, W [gas] Arco/24hr [food] El Pollo Loco, Fosters Freeze [lodging] Guesthouse Inn [other] Camping World RV Ctr, El Monte RV Ctr, Tune-Up Masters
119	Carmenita Rd, Buena Park, E [gas] Arco [food] Burger King [other] Ford Trucks, Lowe's, W [food] Galaxy Burgers [lodging] Budget Inn, Dynasty Suites
118	Valley View Blvd, E [food] Carl's Jr, Elephant Bar Rest, In-N-Out, Northwoods Rest, Red Robin, Subway [lodging] Extended Stay America, Holiday Inn Select, Residence Inn [other] Staples, W [gas] Chevron [food] Burger King, El Pollo Loco [other] Thompson's RV Ctr, to Camping World
117	Artesia Blvd, Knott Ave, E [gas] 76/24hr, Chevron [lodging] Extended Stay America [other] CarMax, W [other] Chrysler, Knotts Berry Farm, to Camping World RV Ctr
116	CA 39, Beach Blvd, E [gas] Chevron [other] H Acura, BMW, Buick/GMC, CarMax, Honda, Hyundai, Mercedes, Nissan, Toyota/Scion, VW, W [gas] Chevron [food] Arby's, Black Angus, Denny's, Fuddruckers, KFC, Pizza Hut, Subway, Wendy's [lodging] Holiday Inn, Red Roof Inn [other] Stater Bros, Target, to Knotts Berry Farm
115	Manchester (from nb), same as 116
114b	CA 91 E, Riverside Fwy, W to [airport]
114a	Magnolia Ave, Orangethorpe Ave, E [gas] Mobil/dsl [food] Burger King, Burger Town, Taco Bell [other] Harley-Davidson
113c	CA 91 W (from nb

LOS ANGELES AREA

NORWALK

INTERSTATE 5 Cont'd

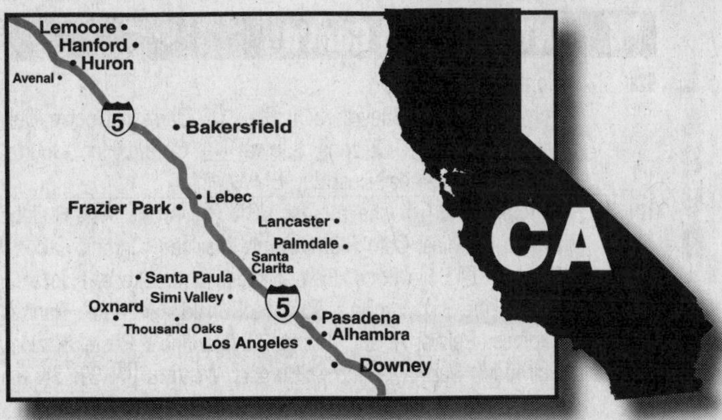

ANAHEIM

Exit #	Services
113b a	Brookhurst St, LaPalma, E [gas] Chevron/dsl [food] Subway, W [gas] Arco, Texaco/dsl [food] Carl's Jr, Quiznos, Starbucks [other] Home Depot, Staples
112	Euclid St, E [gas] Arco [food] IHOP, Marie Callender's, McDonald's, Starbucks, Taco Bell, Wendy's [other] 7-11, AAA, PetCo, Ross, TJ Maxx, Walmart, W [gas] 76, Mobil [food] Burger King, Charley's Subs, Denny's, KFC/LJ Silver, Subway [other] Radio Shack, Target, Verizon
111	Lincoln Ave, to Anaheim, E [food] El Triunfo Mexican, La Casa Garcia Mexican, Ruby's Diner, Starbucks, Subway [other] vet, W [other] Discount Auto Repair
110b	Ball Rd (from sb), E [gas] 7-11, Chevron/dsl, Shell [food] Burger King, El Pollo Loco, McDonald's, Shakey's Pizza, Starbucks, Subway, Taco Bell [lodging] Best Inn, Best Value Inn, Days Inn, Hotel Menage [other] Anaheim RV, Traveler's World RV Park, W [gas] Arco/24hr, Shell/dsl [lodging] Best Western, Budget Inn, Holiday Inn, Rodeway Inn, Sheraton, Travelodge [other] Camping World RV Ctr, Disneyland, USPO
110a	Harbor Blvd, E [gas] Chevron, Shell [food] Carrow's, Shakey's Pizza, Taco Bell [lodging] Days Inn, EconoLodge, Frontier Harbor Hotel, Hotel Menage, Ramada Ltd [other] Anaheim Harbor RV Park, **0-2 mi** W [food] Acapulco Mexican, Captain Kidd's, Coldstone, Del Sol, Dennys, IHOP, McDonald's, Millie's Rest., Mimi's Cafe, Mortons Steaks, Overland Sage BBQ, Quiznos, Tony Roma's [lodging] Anaheim Resort, Best Inn, Best Western, Camelot Inn, Candy Cane Inn, Carousel Inn, Castle Inn Suites, Clarion, Courtyard, Desert Inn, Fairfield Inn, Hampton Inn, Hilton Garden, Howard Johnson, ParkVue Inn, Portofino Inn, Ramada Inn, Red Lion, Saga Inn, Sheraton, Travelodge, Tropicana Inn [other] same as 109, to Disneyland
109	Katella Ave, Disney Way, E [gas] Arco [food] Baskin-Robbins, Carl's Jr, Catch Seafood, Denny's, El Torito, McDonald's, Mr Stox Dining, Panda Express, Subway, Togo's [lodging] Angel Inn, TownePlace Suites [other] Angels Stadium, W [gas] Chevron [food] Bubba Gump Shrimp, CA Pizza Kitchen, Cheesecake Factory, Del Taco, McCormick&Schmick, PF Chang's, Roy Roy's, Subway [lodging] Arena Inn, Best Value Inn, Comfort Inn, Desert Palms Suites, Extended Stay America, Hilton, Holiday Inn Express, Little Boy Blue, Marriott, Peacock Suites, Ramada Inn, Residence Inn, Riviera Motel, Staybridge Suites, Super 8, Worldmark [other] 7-11, to Disneyland
107c	St Coll Blvd, City Drive, E [food] Del Taco [lodging] Hilton Suites, W [lodging] Doubletree Hotel
107b a	CA 57 N, Chapman Ave, E [food] Burger King, Del Taco, Denny's [lodging] Holiday Inn, Motel 6, Quality Inn, W [gas] Chevron [food] Krispy Kreme, Lucille's BBQ, Taco Bell, Wendy's [lodging] Ayer's Inn, DoubleTree [other] [H] Best Buy
106	CA 22 W (from nb), Garden Grove Fwy, Bristol St
105b	N Broadway, Main St, E [gas] 7-11 [food] Baskin-Robbins, CA Pizza Kitchen, Carl's Jr, Chili Pepper Mexican, Corner Bakery, El Torito, FoodCourt, Habit Burgers, Jamba Juice, Manhattan Steaks, McCormick&Schmicks, Papa Johns, Pat&Oscars, Polly's Café, Rubio's Grill, Starbucks, Subway, Taco Bell, Togo's [lodging] Days Inn, Red Roof Inn [other] [H] Barnes&Noble, CVS Drug, JC Penney, Macy's, mall, Nordstrom's, Staples, Verizon, W [lodging] Golden West Motel, Travel Inn [other] Bowers Museum
105a	17th St, E [gas] 76/dsl/24hr [food] Hometown Buffet, IHOP, McDonald's [other] Chevrolet, CVS Drug, Food4Less, same as 104b, Walgreens, W [gas] Chevron [food] YumYum Donuts [other] 7-11

TUSTIN

IRVINE

Exit #	Services
104b	Santa Ana Blvd, Grand Ave, E [food] Denny's, Hometown Buffet, IHOP, KFC/LJ Silver, Marie Callender, McDonald's, Pizza Hut/Taco Bell, Popeye's, Starbucks, Subway, Taco Sinaloa [other] $Tree, Big O Tire, CVS Drug, Goodyear, O'Reilly Parts, Target, vet, Walgreens, W [other] KIA, Suzuki
104a	(103c from nb), 4th St, 1st St, to CA 55 N, E [gas] 76, Chevron, Shell [food] Del Taco
103b	CA 55 S, to Newport Beach
103a	CA 55 N (from nb), to Riverside
102	Newport Ave (from sb), W [gas] Arco
101b	Red Hill Ave, E [gas] Mobil/dsl, Shell/repair [food] Del Taco, Denny's, Starbucks, Subway, Wendy's [lodging] Key Inn [other] BigLots, U-Haul, W [gas] 76, Arco/24hr, Chevron/24hr [food] Pizza Shack, Taco Bell [other] 7-11, Stater Bros
101a	Tustin Ranch Rd, E [food] McDonald's [other] Acura, Buick/GMC, Cadillac, Chrysler/Dodge/Jeep, Costco, Ford/Lincoln, Hyundai, Infiniti, Lexus, Mazda, Nissan, Toyota/Scion
100	Jamboree Rd, E [gas] Shell [food] Baja Fresh, BJ's Rest., Buca Italian, Burger King, CA Pizza, Carl's Jr, Chick-fil-A, Corner Bakery, Daphne's Greek, DQ, El Pollo Loco, IHOP, In-N-Out, Jamba Juice, JinJin Asian, Lazy Dog Cafe, Macaroni Grill, On the Border, Panda Express, Panera Bread, Pick-up Stix, Quiznos, Red Robin, Rubio's, Starbucks, Subway, Taco Bell, Taco Rosa [other] AAA, AT&T, Barnes&Noble, Best Buy, Costco, Dick's, Henry's Mkt, Home Depot, Loehmann's, Lowe's, Old Navy, Petsmart, Radio Shack, Ralph's Foods, Rite Aid, Ross, Target, TJ Maxx, Verizon
99	Culver Dr, E [gas] Shell/24hr [other] vet
97	Jeffrey Rd, E [gas] Arco [food] Baskin-Robbins, Juice-it-Up, La Salsa, Starbucks, Subway [other] Albertson's, Kohl's, W [gas] 76/dsl [food] Thai Cafe [other] Ranch Mkt Foods, Verizon, vet
96	Sand Canyon Ave, Old Towne, W [gas] 76/dsl [food] Denny's, Jack-in-the-Box, Knowlwood Burgers, Tiajuana's Rest. [lodging] La Quinta [other] [H] Traveland USA RV Park
95	CA 133 (toll), Laguna Fwy, N to Riverside, S Laguna Beach
94b	Alton Pkwy, E [gas] Shell/Subway/dsl [food] Cabo Grill, Carl's Jr, Homestead Suites, Quiznos, Starbucks, W [food] CA Pizza, Cheesecake Factory, Chipotle Mexican, Dave&Buster's, Johnny Rockets, Panda Express, PF Chang's, Wahoo's Fish Tacos, Wood Ranch, Yardhouse Rest. [lodging] Doubletree Inn [other] Barnes&Noble, Macy's, Nordstrom, Old Navy, Target
94a	I-405 N (from nb)
92b	Bake Pkwy, same as 92a
92a	Lake Forest Dr, Laguna Hills, E [gas] Chevron/24hr, Shell/dsl [food] Buffalo Wild Wings, Del Taco, Jack-in-the-Box, McDonald's, Panera Bread, Pizza Hut, RoundTable Pizza, Subway, Taco Bell, The Hat [lodging] Best Value Inn, Holiday Inn, Irvine Suites Hotel, Quality Inn [other] America's Tire, Buick/GMC, Chrysler/Dodge/Jeep, Ford/Lincoln, Honda, Hyundai, Mazda, Nissan, Subaru,

= gas = food = lodging = other = rest stop

CA

INTERSTATE 5 Cont'd

LAGUNA HILLS

Exit	Services
92a	Continued Volvo, VW, W Chevron/24hr, Shell Carl's Jr, Coco's, Del Taco, McDonald's, Quiznos, Subway Comfort Inn, Courtyard AZ Leather, Best Buy, BMW/Mini
91	El Toro Rd, E Chevron/dsl, USA Arby's, Asia Buffet, Baskin-Robbins, Cafe Rio, Chipotle Mexican, Chronic Tacos, Denny's, El Pollo Loco, Flamebroiler, Fuddrucker's, Hooters, Jack-in-the-Box, Lucille's BBQ, McDonald's, Mr Wok, Panda Express, PeiWei Asian, Quiznos, Scarantino's Rest., Sizzler, Starbucks, Subway, Tommy's Burgers, Wendy's 99c Store, CVS Drug, Firestone/auto, Home Depot, PetCo, Petsmart, Ralph's Foods, Ross, Staples, W 76/Circle K, Chevron/dsl/24hr, Shell/24hr BJ's Rest., Carrow's, El Torito, In-N-Out, King's Fishhouse, LoneStar Steaks, Nami Seafood, Starbucks, Woody's Diner Laguna Hills Lodge CVS Drug, Firestone/auto, JC Penney, Just Tires, Macy's, mall, Marshall's, Sears/auto, Trader Joe's, USPO, Walgreens

MISSON VIEJO

Exit	Services
90	Alicia Pkwy, Mission Viejo, E Del Taco, Denny's, Subway $Tree, Albertson's, America's Tire, CVS Drug, Kragen Parts, Target, W 76/dsl, Chevron Carl's Jr, It's a Grind, Togo's, Wendy's AAA, BigLots, Mazda, vet
89	La Paz Rd, Mission Viejo, E Arco/24hr, Shell Chronic Tacos, Pizza Hut, Starbucks, Taco Bell, TK Burgers Albertson's/Sav-On, vet, W 76 Claim Jumper Rest., DQ, Flamingos Mexican, Hot Off the Grill, Jack-in-the-Box, Krispy Kreme, La Salsa, McDonald's, Outback Steaks, Spasso's Italian, Starbucks, Subway, Villa Roma, Wienerschnitzel, Yamato Japanese Hills Hotel 7-11, Best Buy, Curves, Goodyear/auto, Jo-Ann Fabrics, PetCo, to Laguna Niguel Pk, URGENT CARE
87	Oso Pkwy, Pacific Park Dr, E 76/dsl/repair, Chevron/repair Carl's Jr, Starbucks, Subway Fairfield Inn golf
86	Crown Valley Pkwy, E 76, Arco, Chevron Buffalo Wild Wings, Chili's, Coco's, Islands Grill Macy's, mall, vet, W Chevron/dsl Aamco, Costco/gas
85b	Avery Pkwy, E Shell/dsl Alberto's Mexican, Carrow's, Del Taco, Jack-in-the-Box, Mongolian BBQ, Papa John's, Starbucks, Subway Acura, America's Tire/auto, Audi/Infiniti, Jaguar/Land Rover, Lexus, Parts+, World Mkt, W Chevron, Shell/dsl/24hr A's Burgers, Carl's Jr, In-N-Out Best Value Laguna Inn Aamco, Cadillac/GMC, Costco/gas, Firestone/auto, Hyundai, Mercedes
85a	CA 73 N (toll)
83	Junipero Serra Rd, to San Juan Capistrano, W Shell, Spirit/service/dsl

CAPISTRANO

Exit	Services
82	CA 74, Ortego Hwy, E 76, Chevron/dsl, Shell Bad to the Bone BBQ, Ballpark Pizza, Bravo Burgers, Denny's, Subway Best Western vet, W Chevron/24hr Arby's, Carl's Jr, Del Taco, Jack-in-the-Box, KFC, Marie Callender's, McDonald's, Oeeshi Japanese, Pedro's Tacos, Quiznos, RoundTable Pizza, Ruby's Cafe, Starbucks, Taco Bell Cedar Creek Inn, Mission Inn Capistrano Trading Post, GNC, Marshall's, Ralph's Foods, Ross, San Juan Capistrano Mission, TrueValue
81	Camino Capistrano, E VW, **W on Capistrano** Chevron El Adobe Rest., El Pollo Loco, Eng's Chinese, KFC, Papa John's, Pizza Hut, Ricardo's Mexican, Starbucks Aamco, BigLots, CHP, Costco, Ford, Goodyear/auto, Honda, KIA, Nissan, PetCo, Petsmart, Radio Shack, Rite Aid, Ross, San Juan Capistrano SP (1mi), Staples, Toyota/Scion, URGENT CARE, Vons Foods
79	CA 1, Pacific Coast Hwy, Capistrano Bch, Capistrano, **1 mi** W 76/dsl, Arco/24hr A's Burgers, Carl's Jr, Del Taco Denny's, Jack-in-the-Box, JuiceSpot, McDonald's, Rib Joint Subway DoubleTree, Harbor Inn, Holiday Inn Express Ralph's Foods, Rite Aid, USPO, vet

SAN CLEMENTE

Exit	Services
78	Camino de Estrella, San Clemente, E 76/dsl Carl's Jr, China Well, Coldstone, Crispins, Flame Broiler, Jamba Juice, Melting Pot, Papa Murphy's, RoundTable Pizza, Rubio's, Starbucks, Subway, Wahoo's Fish Taco AT&T, CVS Drug Ralph's Foods, Stater Bros Foods, Trader Joe's, vet, W Arco/dsl Las Golondrinas BigLots, Kragen Parts, Sears Essentials
77	Ave Vista Hermosa
76	Ave Pico, E Mobil Buono Pizza, Carrow's, Golden Spoon, Juice it Up, McDonald's, Panda Express Albertson's/Sav-On, GNC, W Chevron, Shell/dsl Bad to the Bone BBQ, BurgerStop, Del Taco, Denny's/24hr, Pick-up-Stix, Pizza Hut, Stuft Pizza, Subway Holiday Inn Express 99c Store, Curves, Staples, tires/repair, Tuesday Morning, USPO, vet
75	Ave Palizada, Ave Presidio, W Valero Baskin-Robbins, Coffee Bean, Mr. Pete's Burgers, Sonny's Pizza, Starbucks, Subway, Taka-O Japanese Holiday Inn 7-11, TrueValue
74	El Camino Real, E Chevron/dsl/24hr El Mariachi Rest., Pipes Cafe Budget Lodge, San Clemente Inn, Tradewinds Motel same as 75, vet, W 76/dsl, Exxon FatBurger, KFC, Pizza Hut/Taco Bell, Subway, Taste Of China, Tommy's Rest./24hr 7-11, Kragen Parts, Radio Shack, Ralph's Foods
73	Ave Calafia, Ave Magdalena, E 76/dsl, Shell Jack-in-the-Box, Molly Bloom's Cafe, Pedro's Tacos, Sugar Shack Cafe Budget Inn, Calafia Beach Motel, C-Vu Inn, Hampton Inn, LaVista Inn, San Clemente Motel, Travelodge 7-11, repair, San-O Tire, W to San Clemente SP
72	Cristianitios Ave, E Cafe Del Sol, Carl's Jr. Carmelo Motel, Comfort Suites San Mateo RV Park/dump, W to San Clemente SP
71	Basilone Rd, W San Onofre St Beach
67mm	**weigh sta both lanes**
66mm	viewpoint sb
62	Las Pulgas Rd
59mm	**Aliso Creek both lanes, full facilities, litter barrels, petwalk RV dump, vending**

OCEANSIDE

Exit	Services
54c	Oceanside Harbor Dr, W Chevron, Mobil Burger King (1mi), Del Taco, Denny's/24hr GuestHouse Inn, Holiday Inn Express, Sandman Hotel, The Bridge Motel, Travelodge to Camp Pendleton
54b	Hill St (from sb), to Oceanside, W Chevron, Mobil Carrow's Rest., Denny's GuestHouse Inn, Holiday Inn Express, Travelodge
54a	CA 76 E, Coast Hwy
53	Mission Ave, Oceanside, E Arco/24hr, Mobil/dsl Alberto's Mexican, Arby's, Armando's Tacos, Burger King, China Star, Jack-in-the-Box, KFC, McDonald's, Mission Donuts Quality Inn, Ramada CarQuest, NAPA, PepBoys, Valu+ Foods, W El Pollo Loco, Panda Express, Subway, Wendy's 99c Store, Office Depot, Radio Shack
52	Oceanside Blvd, E Alberto's Mexican, Domino's, IHOP, McDonald's, Papa John's, Pizza Hut, Starbucks, Subway, Taco Bell, Wienerschnitzel Boney's Foods, CHP, CVS Drug, Ralph's Foods, W Oceanside/dsl Best Western Oceanside

INTERSTATE 5 Cont'd

Exit #	Services
51c	Cassidy St (from sb), W [gas] 7-11, 76, Mobil [other] [H]
51b	CA 78, Vista Way, Escondido, E [gas] 76/Circle K, Chevron/dsl/24hr, Shell [food] Applebee's, Boston Mkt, Burger King, Carl's Jr, Chili's, ChuckECheese's, Fuddrucker's, Golden Taipei, Hooters, Macaroni Grill, McDonald's, Mimi's Café, Olive Garden, Outback Steaks, QuikWok, Rubio's, Starbucks, Subway, Wendy's [lodging] Holiday Inn Express [other] $Tree, Best Buy, CVS Drug, Firestone, Henry's Mkt, JC Penney, Macy's, Marshall's, Michael's, PetCo, Sears/auto, Staples, Stater Bros Foods, Target, Tuesday Morning, Vons Foods, Walmart/auto, World Mkt, W [food] Hunter Steaks
51a	Las Flores Dr
50	Elm Ave, Carlsbad Village Dr, E [gas] Shell/24hr [food] Lotus Thai Bistro, W [gas] Carlsbad/dsl/LP, Valero [food] Al's Cafe, Carl's Jr, Denny's/24hr, Jack-in-the-Box, KFC/Taco Bell, Mikko Japanese [lodging] Extended Stay America, Motel 6 [other] Albertson's, TrueValue
49	Tamarack Ave, E [gas] 76/dsl, Chevron/24hr [food] Village Kitchen [lodging] Comfort Inn, Rodeway Inn, Travel Inn [other] GNC, Rite Aid, Vons Foods, W [gas] Arco [food] Hensley's Grill
48	Cannon Rd, Car Country Carlsbad, E [other] Acura, Buick, Cadillac/Chevrolet, Ford, Honda, Lexus, Lincoln, Mazda, Mercedes, Toyota, VW
47	Carlsbad Blvd, Palomar Airport Rd, E [gas] 7-11, Chevron, Mobil/dsl [food] BJ's Rest., Carl's Jr, Islands Burgers, Panda Express, Pat&Oscar's Rest., PF Chang's, Strauss Brewery Rest., Subway, Taco Bell, TGIFriday's [lodging] Holiday Inn, Motel 6 [other] Carlsbad Ranch/Flower Fields, Chrysler/Dodge/Jeep, Costco/gas, Ford, outlet mall, W [gas] Shell/dsl [food] ClaimJumper Rest., Marie Callender's, McDonald's [lodging] Hilton Garden [other] S Carlsbad St Bch
45	Poinsettia Lane, W [gas] Chevron [food] Benihana, El Pollo Loco, Golden Spoon, Jack-in-the-Box, Pick-Up Stix, Starbucks, Subway [lodging] La Quinta, Motel 6, Quality Inn, Ramada [other] Ace Hardware, Porsche/Volvo, Ralph's Foods, Rite Aid
44	La Costa Ave, E vista point, W [gas] Chevron/dsl
43	Leucadia Blvd, E [lodging] Howard Johnson, W [gas] Shell/service
41b	Encinitas Blvd, E [gas] Chevron/dsl, O'Brien Sta., Valero [food] Coco's Cafe, Del Taco, Gusto Trattoria, HoneyBaked Ham, Oggi's Pizza [other] CVS Drug, NAPA, to Quail Botanical Gardens, vet, W [gas] Shell [food] Denny's, Little Caesar's, Subway, Wendy's [lodging] Best Western/rest., Days Inn [other] PetCo
41a	Santa Fe Dr, to Encinitas, E [gas] Shell [food] Carl's Jr, El Nopalito, Papa Toni's Pizza [other] 7-11, W [food] Today's Pizza [other] [H] Rite Aid, vet, Vons Foods
40	Birmingham Dr, E [gas] Chevron, Valero [food] Mandarin City [lodging] Holiday Inn Express, W [gas] Arco/24hr
39mm	viewpoint sb
39	Manchester Ave, E [gas] 76 [other] to MiraCosta College
37	Lomas Santa Fe Dr, Solana Bch, E [food] Baskin-Robbins, Pizza Nova, Samurai Rest., Starbucks [other] Ross, Vons Foods, We-R-Fabrics, W [gas] Mobil [food] Carl's Jr, Golden Spoon, Jamba Juice, Panda Express, Panera Bread, RoundTable Pizza, Starbucks, Togo's [other] CVS Drug, Discount Tire, GNC, Henry's Foods, Marshall's, Staples
36	Via de La Valle, Del Mar, E [gas] Chevron, Mobil [food] Chevy's Mexican, Coffee Bean, McDonald's, Milton's Deli, Pappachino's Italian, Paradise Grille, Pasta Pronto, Pick-Up Stix, Taste of Thai [other] Albertson's/SavOn, PetCo, Radio Shack, W [gas] Arco/24hr,

CARLSBAD

ENCINITAS

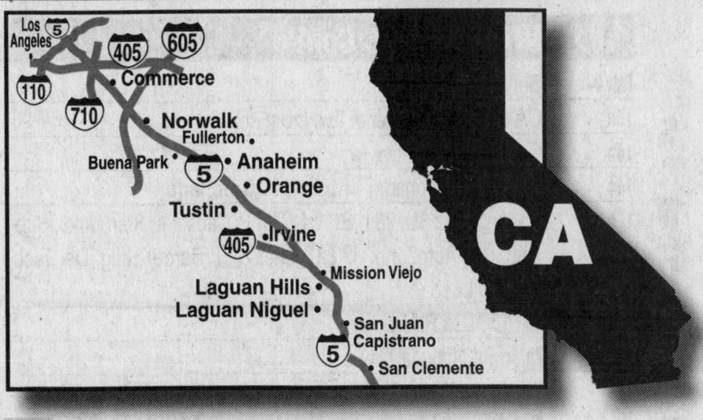

CA

Exit #	Services
36	Continued Shell/dsl [food] Denny's, FishMkt Rest., Red Tracton's Rest. [lodging] Hilton [other] racetrack
34	Del Mar Heights Rd, E [gas] Shell/dsl, W [gas] 7-11 [food] Elijah's Rest., Jack-in-the-Box, Mexican Grill [other] CVS Drug, vet, Vons Foods
33	Carmel Mtn Rd, E [gas] Arco, Shell/repair [food] Taco Bell, Tio Leo's Mexican [lodging] DoubleTree Hotel, Hampton Inn, Marriott
32	CA 56 E, Carmel Valley Rd
31	I-805 (from sb)
30	Sorrento Valley Rd
29	Genesee Ave, E [other] [H]
28b	La Jolla Village Dr, E [food] Italian Bistro [lodging] Embassy Suites, Hyatt, Marriott [other] [H] to LDS Temple, W [gas] Mobil/dsl [food] BJ's Grill, CA Pizza Kitchen, Chipotle Mexican, Dominos, El Torito, Elijah's Deli, Flame Broiler, Islands Burgers, Mrs Gooch's, Pick-Up Stix, RockBottom Café, Rubio's, TGIFriday's [lodging] Sheraton [other] [H] AT&T, Best Buy, CVS Drug, Marshall's, PetsMart, Radio Shack, Ralph's Foods, Ross, Staples, Trader Joe's, Whole Foods Mkt
28a	Nobel Dr (from nb), E [lodging] Hyatt [other] LDS Temple, W same as 28b
27	Gilman Dr, La Jolla Colony Dr
26b	CA 52 E
26a	La Jolla Rd (from nb)
23b	CA 274, Balboa Ave, 1 mi E [gas] Shell [food] Del Taco [other] Albertson's, W [gas] 7-11, 76/repair, Mobil [food] In-N-Out, McDonald's, Rubio's, Wienerschnitzel [lodging] Days Inn, Holiday Inn Express, Mission Bay Inn, San Diego Motel [other] [H], Discount Tire, Express Tire, Ford, Mission Bay Pk, Nissan, Toyota/Scion
23a	Grand Ave, Garnet Ave, same as 23b
22	Clairemont Dr, Mission Bay Dr, E [gas] Arco, Shell [lodging] Best Western [other] Chevrolet/VW, W to Sea World Dr
21	Sea World Dr, Tecolote Dr, E [gas] Shell [lodging] Seaside Inn [other] Aamco, CarQuest, Circle K, PetCo, W [lodging] Hilton [other] Old Town SP, Seaworld
20	I-8, W to Nimitz Blvd, E to El Centro, CA 209 S (from sb), to Rosecrans St
19	Old Town Ave, E [gas] Arco/24hr, Shell [lodging] Courtyard, La Quinta
18b	Washington St, E [lodging] Comfort Inn
18a	Pacific Hwy Viaduct, Kettner St
17b	India St, Front St, Sassafras St, E [gas] Mobil, Rte 66 Gas, W [other] [airport] civic ctr
17a	Hawthorn St, Front St, W [gas] Exxon/dsl [lodging] Holiday Inn, Motel 6, Radisson [other] [H]
16b	6th Ave, downtown
16a	CA 163 N, 10th St, E [other] AeroSpace Museum, W [gas] Shell [food] Del Taco, Jack-in-the-Box, McDonald's [lodging] Days Inn, Downtown Lodge, El Cortez Motel, Holiday Inn, Marriott [other] [H]
15c b	CA 94 E (from nb), Pershing Dr, B St, civic ctr

LA JOLLA

SAN DIEGO AREA

= gas = food = lodging = other = rest stop

CA

INTERSTATE 5 Cont'd

SAN DIEGO AREA

Exit #	Services
15a	CA 94 E, J St, Imperial Ave (from sb),
14b	Cesar Chavez Pkwy
14a	CA 75, to Coronado, **W toll rd to Coronado**
13b	National Ave SD, 28th St, E Little Caesar's, Starbucks, Subway AutoZone, W Shell Burger King, Del Taco, El Pollo Loco
13a	CA 15 N, to Riverside
12	Main St, National City
11b	8th St, National City, E Arco, Shell/24hr Jack-in-the-Box Holiday Inn, Howard Johnson, Ramada Inn, Super 8, Value Inn, W Chevron/dsl
11a	Harbor Dr, Civic Center Dr
10	Bay Marina, 24th St, Mile of Cars Way, **1/2 mi E** Denny's, In-N-Out
9	CA 54 E
8b	E St, Chula Vista, E Motel 6, W Anthony's Fish Grotto GoodNite Inn
8a	H St
7b	J St (from sb)
7a	L St, E 7-11, 76, Shell/dsl Mandarin Chinese Best Western AutoZone, NAPA, Office Depot, Parts+
6	Palomar St, E Arco China King, Del Taco, DQ, HomeTown Buffet, KFC, Little Caesar's, McDonald's, Subway Palomar Inn 7-11, Costco/gas, **E on Broadway**, Food4Less, Jack-in-the-Box, KFC, Michael's, Office Depot, Panda Express, Quizno's, Ross, Target, Walmart, Yoshinoya
5b	Main St, to Imperial Beach, E Arco AZ Chinese
5a	CA 75 (from sb), Palm Ave, to Imperial Beach, E Arco Armando's Mexican, Papa John's, Wahshing Chinese 7-11, Discount Tire, Soto's Transmissions, W 7-11, Arco, Shell/repair/24hr, Thrifty Boll Weevil Diner, Burger King, Carl's Jr, Carrow's, Coldstone Creamery, El Chile Mexican, Los Pancho's Tacos, McDonald's, Rally's, Red Hawk Steaks, Roberto's Mexican, Subway, Taco Bell, Wienerschnitzel Super 8, Travelodge 99c Store, AutoZone, CVS Drug, Home Depot, Jiffy Lube, Von's Foods

SAN YSIDRO

Exit #	Services
4	Coronado Ave (from sb), E Chevron/service, Shell/service Denny's, Taco Bell EZ 8 Motel 7-11, W Shell/dsl Days Inn to Border Field SP
3	CA 905, Tocayo Ave, W 7-11
2	Dairy Mart Rd, E Arco/24hr, Circle K Burger King, Carl's Jr, Coco's, KFC, McDonald's, Roberto's Mexican Americana Inn, Best Value, Super 8, Valli-Hi Motel CarQuest, Pacifica RV Resort, Radio Shack
1b	Via de San Ysidro, W Chevron, Mobil/dsl Denny's Knights/RV park, Motel 6, Travelodge
1a	I-805 N (from nb), Camino de la Plaza (from sb), E Burger King, El Pollo Loco, Jack-in-the-Box, KFC, McDonald's, Subway Holiday Motel AutoZone, W Achiato Mexican, IHOP, Iron Wok, McDonald's, Starbucks, Sunrise Buffet $Tree, Baja Duty-Free, border parking, factory outlet, K-Mart, Marshall's, Old Navy, Ross, TJ Maxx
0	California state line, US/Mexico Border, customs, **I-5 begins/ends.**

INTERSTATE 8

YUMA

Exit #	Services
172.5mm	California/Arizona state line, Colorado River, Pacific/Mounta time zone
172	4th Ave, Yuma, N Paradise Casino, S Chevron, Circ K/dsl Jack-in-the-Box, Yuma Landing Rest. Best Western, Hilton Garden to Yuma SP
170	Winterhaven Dr, S Rivers Edge RV Park
166	CA 186, Algodones Rd, Andrade, S Cocopah RV Resort/gol Quechan Hotel/Casino, to Mexico
165mm	**CA Insp/weigh sta**
164	Sidewinder Rd, N st patrol, S Shell/LP/dsl Pilo Knob RV Park
159	CA 34, Ogilby Rd, to Blythe
156	Grays Well Rd, N Imperial Dunes RA
155mm	**both lanes (exits left), full facilities, litter barrels, pet walk**
151	Gordons Well
146	Brock Research Ctr Rd
143	CA 98, to Calexico, Midway Well
131	CA 115, VanDerLinden Rd, to Holtville, **5 mi N** food, gas lodging, RV camping
128	Bonds Corner Rd
125	CA 7 S, Orchard Rd, Holtville, **4 mi N** food, gas/dsl
120	Bowker Rd
118b a	CA 111, to Calexico, N Country Life RV Park
116	Dogwood Rd, S Arco/dsl Burger King, Carino's, Chili's ChuckeCheese, Denny's, Famous Dave's BBQ, Fortune Garden, Jack-in-the-Box, Olive Garden, Sombrero Mexican, Starbucks, Subway Fairfield Inn, TownePlace Suites $Tree 99c, Americas Tire, Best Buy, Dillard's, JC Penney, Kohl's Macy's, mall, Marshall's, Michael's, PetCo, Ross, Sears/auto Staples

EL CENTRO

Exit #	Services
115	CA 86, 4th St, El Centro, N 7-11/dsl, Arco/dsl, Chevron/dsl FillCo/dsl, Shell/dsl Carl's Jr, Exotic Thai, Jack-in-the-Box Las Palmitas Tacos, Lucky Chinese, McDonald's Holiday Inn Express, Motel 6 Family$, O'Reilly Parts, U-Haul, S 7-11/Subway, Mobil/dsl/scales IHOP, In-N-Out, Johnny's Burritos, Panda Express, Taco Bell Best Western, Comfort Inn, Rodeway Inn AutoZone, Buick/Chevrolet/GMC/Cadillac, Desert Trails RV Park, Home Depot, Honda, Hyundai, Lucky Foods
114	Imperial Ave, El Centro, N 7-11/dsl, Arco, Chevron/dsl Chevron/dsl, USA/dsl Applebee's, Broken Yolk Cafe Burger King, Carl's Jr, Carrow's, Church's, Coldstone, Del Taco Denny's, Domino's, El Pollo Loco, Farmer Boys, Golden Corral, Jack-in-the-Box, Jack-in-the-Box, KFC, La Resaca, Little Caesars, McDonald's, Mexicali Grill, Papa John's, Pizza Hut Rally's, Sizzler, Sonic, Starbucks, Subway, Taco Bell, Tastee-Freez Burgers, Wendy's Clarion, Crown Motel, Super 8, SuperStar Inn, Vacation Inn/RV Park, Value Inn $General Mkt, $Tree, 99c Store, Chrysler/Dodge/Jeep, Costco/gas, Discount Tire, Food4Less, Ford, Goodyear/auto, Jo-Ann, K-Mart, Lowe's, Nissan, O'Reilly Parts, PepBoys, Radio Shack, Rite Aid, st patrol, Target, Toyota/Scion, Verizon, Von's Foods, Walgreens, Walmart
111	Forrester Rd, to Westmorland
108mm	**Sunbeam both lanes, full facilities, litter barrels, petwalk RV dump**
107	Drew Rd, Seeley, N Sunbeam RV Park, to Sunbeam Lake, S Rio Bend RV Park

CA

INTERSTATE 8 Cont'd

Exit #	Services
101	Dunaway Rd, Imperial Valley, N st prison, elev 0 ft
89	Imperial Hwy, CA 98, Ocotillo, N Red Feathers Mkt/Cafe, RV camping, USPO, S Chevron/dsl Desert Museum
87	CA 98 (from eb), to Calexico
81mm	**eb, runaway truck ramp**
80	Mountain Springs Rd
77	In-ko-pah Park Rd, N towing
75mm	**brake insp area eb,**
73	Jacumba, S Chevron/dsl, Shell/Subway/dsl/24hr RV camping
65	CA 94, Boulevard, to Campo, S MtnTop/dsl Back Country Inn auto repair, to McCain Valley RA (7mi), USPO
63mm	elev 4140 ft, Tecate Divide
62mm	Crestwood Summit, elev 4190 ft
61	Crestwood Rd, Live Oak Springs, S Golden Acorn Trkstp/casino/dsl Live Oak Sprs Country Inn info
54	Kitchen Creek Rd, Cameron Station, S RV camping
51	Rd 1, Buckman Spgs Rd, to Lake Morena, **both lanes, full facilities, litter barrels, petwalk RV dump** S gas/dsl/LP, , Lake Morena CP (7mi), Potrero CP (19mi), RV camping
48	**insp sta, wb**
47	Rd 1, Sunrise Hwy, Laguna Summit, elev 4055 ft, N to Laguna Mtn RA
45	Pine Valley, Julian, N Calvin's Rest., Frosty Burger, Major's Diner Pine Valley Inn city park, Mtn Mkt, Pine Valley/gas, to Cuyamaca Rancho SP, USPO, vet
44mm	Pine Valley Creek
42mm	elev 4000 ft
40	CA 79, Japatul Rd, Descanso, N Descanso Rest. to Cuyamaca Rancho SP
37mm	elev 3000 ft, vista point eb
36	E Willows, N Alpine Sprs RV Park, casino, Viejas Indian Res
33	W Willows Rd, to Alpine, N Alpine Sprs RV Park, casino, same as 36, Viejas Outlets/famous brands, S ranger sta
31mm	elev 2000 ft
30	Tavern Rd, to Alpine, N Chevron/dsl, Shell/dsl, S 76/Circle K American Grill, Carl's Jr, Greek Village Grill, La Carreta, Little Caesars, Mananas Mexican, Mediterraneo Grill, Panda Machi Chinese, Subway Ayre's Lodge Ace Hardware, city park, CVS Drug, Farmers Mkt, Rite Aid
27	Dunbar Lane, Harbison Canyon, N Flinn Sprgs CP, RV camping
25mm	elev 1000 ft
24mm	
23	Lake Jennings Pk Rd, Lakeside, N Arco/Jack-in-the-Box/dsl/24hr, to Lake Jennings CP RV camping, S 7-11 Burger King, Karla's Mexican, Marechiaro's Pizza
22	Los Coches Rd, Lakeside, N 7-11, Eagle/dsl/LP, East County Gas Albert's Mexican, Giant Pizza, Laposta Mexican RV camping/dump, S Shell/dsl Denny's, GiantNY Pizza, McDonald's, Panda Express, Subway, Taco Bell Radio Shack, Vons Foods, Walmart
20b	Greenfield Dr, to Crest, N Chevron/dsl, Sky Fuel/dsl Jack-in-the-Box, Marieta's Mexican, McDonald's, Panchos Tacos, Subway 7-11, 99c Store, Albertson's, auto repair, AutoZone, Ford, RV camping, st patrol, URGENT CARE, vet, S Mobil/dsl/LP
20a	E Main St (from wb, no EZ return), N Budget Inn Ford, repair, Vacationer RV Park, S Arco Cadillac

EL CAJON

Exit #	Services
19	2nd St, CA 54, El Cajon, N 76/dsl, Arco, Chevron/dsl Marechio's Italian, Pancake House CVS Drug, Meineke, USPO, Vons Foods, Walgreens, S Gas Depot, Golden State/dsl, Shell Arby's, Baskin-Robbins, Burger King, Carl's Jr, Estrada's Mexican, IHOP, Jack-in-the-Box, KFC, Little Caesar's, McDonald's, Popeye's, Subway, Taco Bell, Taco Shop, Wings n Things Best Value Inn $Tree, 7-11, CarQuest, Firestone/auto, Jiffy Lube, PepBoys, PetCo, Radio Shack, Sprouts Mkt, Walgreens, Walmart Mkt
18	Mollison Ave, El Cajon, N Chevron Denny's Best Western, Days Inn, S Arco, QuickTrip/dsl Los Garcia's EconoLodge
17c	Magnolia Ave, CA 67 (from wb), to Santee, N Arco Del Taco, El Pollo Loco, Jack-in-the-Box, Jersey Mike's, Panda Express, Starbucks AT&T, Food4Less, Target, S Shell/service New East Buffet, Panda Express, Perry's Cafe, Rubio's Motel 6, Super 8 Nudo's Drug, Ross
17b	CA 67 (from eb), same as 17 a&c
17a	Johnson Ave (from eb), N Applebee's, Boston Mkt, Burger King, Carl's Jr, Coco's, Five Guys, Hacienda Mexican, Jamba Juice, KFC, Little Caesar's, LJ Silver, McDonald's, New Century Buffet, On the Border, O's American Kitchen, Rubio's, Ruby's Diner, Subway $Tree, Best Buy, CVS Drug, Dick's, Goodyear/auto, Home Depot, Honda, JC Penney, Lexus, Macy's, mall, Marshall's, Mazda, Office Depot, PetsMart, Sears/auto, Subaru, Toyota/Scion, Walmart, S Aamco, KIA, vet
16	Main St, N Arco Denny's, Sombrero Mexican Relax Inn 7-11, S Chevron/dsl, Super Star brakes/transmissions, Nissan
15	El Cajon Blvd (from eb), N Quality Inn, S 76/dsl Wrangler BBQ BMW
14c	Severin Dr, Fuerte Dr (from wb), N USA/dsl Anthony's Fish Grotto, Charcoal House Rest., La Casa Blanca Holiday Inn Express, S Brigantine Seafood Rest.
14b a	CA 125, to CA 94
13b	Jackson Dr, Grossmont Blvd, N Chevron Arby's, BJ's Rest., Casa de Pico, Chili's, ChuckeCheese, ClaimJumper, Fuddrucker's, Olive Garden, Panera Bread, Red Lobster, Shakey's Pizza, Starbucks H $Tree, Best Buy, CVS Drug, Macy's, mall, O'Reilly Parts, Staples, Target, USPO, Verizon, vet, Walmart, World Mkt, S 76 Honeybaked Ham, Jack-in-the-Box Discount Tire, Ford, Hyundai, Ross, Walmart Mkt
13a	Spring St (from eb), El Cajon Blvd (from wb), S El Pollo Loco, Starbucks, Subway Hitching Post 99c Store, AutoZone
12	Fletcher Pkwy, to La Mesa, N Shell/dsl Carl's Jr, Chipotle Mexican, McDonald's, Pick Up Stix Heritage Inn 7-11, Costco, S El Torito, Starbucks, Subway Motel 6 99c Store, Chevrolet, San Diego RV Resort

= gas = food = lodging = other = rest stop

CA

SAN DIEGO AREA

INTERSTATE 8 Cont'd

Exit #	Services
11	70th St, Lake Murray Blvd, N Shell/dsl Subway, S Shell/7-11/dsl Aiken's Deli, Denny's, Marie Callender's H auto repair, URGENT CARE
10	College Ave, N Chevron/dsl Windmill Farms Mkt, S H to SDSU
9	Waring Rd, N Days Inn, Rodeway Inn
8	Fairmount Ave (7 from eb), to Mission Gorge Rd, N 7-11, Mobil, Sky/dsl, USA/dsl Arby's, Black Angus, Carl's Jr, Chili's, Coco's, El Pollo Loco, Filippi's Pizza, Jack-in-the-Box, Jamba Juice, Jersey Mike's, McDonald's, Roberto's Tacos, Rubio's, Sombrero Mexican, Starbucks, Subway, Szechuan Chinese, Togo's, Wendy's Motel 6 H AutoZone, CVS Drug, Discount Tire, Home Depot, Honda, Radio Shack, Rite Aid, Toyota/Scion, Tuesday Morning, Vons Foods
7b a	I-15 N, CA 15 S, to 40th St
6b	I-805, N to LA, S to Chula Vista
6a	Texas St, Qualcomm Way, N Dave&Buster's, same as 5
5	Mission Ctr Rd, N Chevron Broken Yolk Cafe, Chipotle Mexican, Corner Cafe, El Pollo Loco, Fuddrucker's, Gordon Biersch Rest., Habit Burger, Hooters, In-N-Out, King's Fishouse, Lazy Dog Rest., Mimi's Cafe, On The Border, Outback Steaks, Panda Express, Peiwei Asian, Pick-Up Stix, Robek Juice, Rubio's, Sammy's Woodfired Pizza, Starbucks, Subway, Taco Bell, Tilted Kilt Marriott, Sheraton AT&T, Best Buy, Chevrolet, Lincoln, Macy's, mall, Marshall's, Michael's, Nordstrom Rack, Old Navy, Staples, Target, Trader Joe's, S Arco Benihana, Denny's, Fuji Japanese, Mission Valley Cafe, Wendy's Comfort Suites, Hilton, La Quinta, Sheraton Buick/GMC/Cadillac, Chrysler/Dodge/Jeep, Mazda
4c b	CA 163, Cabrillo Frwy, S to downtown, zoo
4a	Hotel Circle Dr (from eb), CA 163 (from wb)
3a	Hotel Circle, Taylor St, N Hunter Steaks Comfort Suites, Crowne Plaza, Handlery Hotel, Motel 6, Town&Country Motel golf, S Adam's Cafe, Albie's Rest., Ricky's Rest., Valley Kitchen Best Western, Candlewood Suites, Comfort Inn, Courtyard, Days Hotel, DoubleTree Inn, Extended Stay America, Hampton Inn, Howard Johnson, King's Inn/rest., Mission Valley Hotel, Residence Inn, Super 8, Travelodge, Vagabond Inn vet
2c	Morena Blvd (from wb)
2b	I-5, N to LA, S to San Diego
2a	Rosecrans St (from wb), CA 209, S Shell Chipotle Mexican, ChuckECheese, Del Taco, Denny's, In-N-Out, Panda Express, Starbucks, Subway Goodnite Inn, Hampton Inn Staples
1	W Mission Bay Blvd, Sports Arena Blvd (from wb), N to SeaWorld, S Arby's, Buffalo Wild Wings, Chick-fil-A, Chili's, Jack-in-the-Box, McDonald's, Phil's BBQ, Red Lobster, Wendy's Ramada Ltd, Wyndham Garden Dick's, Home Depot, Ralph's, Target, U-Haul, Von's
0mm	**I-8 begins/ends on Sunset Cliffs Blvd, 1/4 mi W** 76, Shell/repair Jack-in-the-Box, Kaiserhof Cafe, N Mission Bay Park

POINT LOMA

BLYTHE

INTERSTATE 10

Exit #	Services
245mm	California/Arizona state line, Colorado River, Pacific/Mountain time zone
244mm	**inspection sta wb**
243	Riviera Dr, S Riviera RV Park
241	US 95, Intake Blvd, to Needles, Blythe, N Mobil/dsl, Shell dsl Lalo's Mexican, Steaks'n Cakes Rest. Days Inn Relax Inn, Rodeway Inn auto/RV repair/24hr, Burton's RV Park, S Hampton Inn McIntyre Park
240	7th St, N 76/dsl, EZ Mart China Garden Blue Line Motel, Budget Inn, Knights Inn, Solar City Inn $General Albertson's, AutoZone, Ford, repair, Rite Aid, S Buick/Chevrolet, Chrysler/Dodge/Jeep
239	Lovekin Blvd, Blythe, N Mobil/dsl, Shell/Quiznos Carl's Jr, Del Taco, Domino's, Jack-in-the-Box, McDonald's Pizza Hut, Popeye's, Rebel BBQ, Rosita's Mexican, Sizzler Starbucks, Wang's Chinese Best Value Inn, Best Western Budget Host, Clarion, Regency Inn, Willow Inn H $Tree, Ace Hardware, Goodyear/auto, K-Mart/Little Caesars, O'Reilly Parts, Radio Shack, Verizon, S 76/dsl, Chevron/dsl, USA/Chester's/dsl, Valero/Circle K Burger King, Denny's, Red Cactus Grill, Subway, Taco Bell Comfort Suites, Motel 6, Quality Inn, Super 8 city park
236	CA 78, Neighbours Blvd, to Ripley, N Valero/dsl, S to Cibola NWR
232	Mesa Dr, N 76/dsl/rest./scales/24hr/ @, Valero/dsl Airport
231	weigh sta wb
222mm	Wileys Well Rd, N **both lanes, full facilities, litter barrels, petwalk** S to st prison
217	Ford Dry Lake Rd
201	Corn Springs Rd
192	CA 177, Rice Rd, to Lake Tamarisk, N camping, USPO
189	Eagle Mtn Rd
182	Red Cloud Rd
177	Hayfield Rd
173	Chiriaco Summit, N Chevron/Foster's Freeze/dsl/24hr Chiriaco Rest Patton Museum, truck/tire repair
168	to Twentynine Palms, to Mecca, Joshua Tree NM
162	frontage rd
159mm	**Cactus City both lanes, full facilities, litter barrels, petwalk**
147mm	0 ft elevation
146	Dillon Rd, to CA 86, to CA 111 S, Coachella, N Chevron, Loves /Carl's Jr/dsl/24hr Del Taco, S Chevron/Jack-in-the-Box, TA/Shell/Country Pride/Taco Bell/dsl/24hr/ @ Spotlight Casino, truckwash
145	CA 86 S (from eb)
144	CA 111 N, CA 86 S, Indio, N Holiday Inn Express, Quality Inn Classic RV Park, Fantasy Sprgs Casino/Hotel/Cafe
143	Jackson St, Indio, N Arco/dsl IHOP, KFC, La Casita Mexican, McDonald's, Panda Express, Starbucks, Subway, Taco Bell $Tree, AT&T, AutoZone, BigLots, CVS Drug, GNC, Home Depot, Marshall's, PetCo, Ramona Tire/auto, Ross, Target, Verizon, Walgreens, WinCo Foods, S 7-11
142	Monroe St, Central Indio, N RV camping, Walmart, S 76, Circle K, Shell/dsl/LP Mexicali Cafe, Subway, Taco Jalisco Best Value Inn $General
139	Jefferson St, Indio Blvd, N hwy patrol, Shadow Hills RV Resort

INDIO

INTERSTATE 10 Cont'd

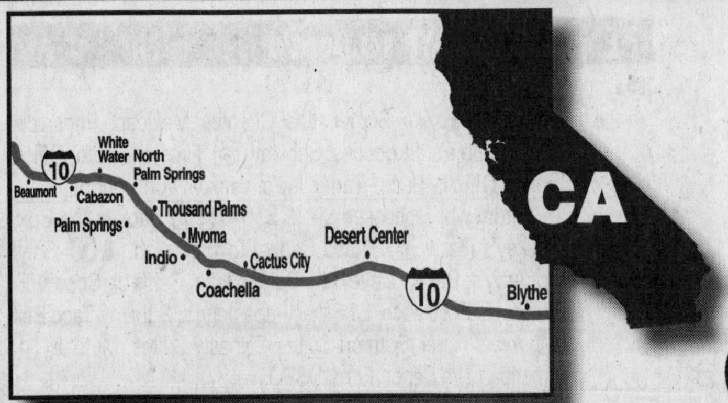

CA

PALM SPRINGS

BANNING

Exit #	Services
137	Washington St, Country Club Dr, to Indian Wells, N [gas] Arco, Chevron/dsl [food] Burger King, Coco's, Del Taco, Legends and Icons Grill, Mario's Italian, Papa John's, Popeye's, Starbucks, Winchell's [lodging] Comfort Suites, Motel 6 [other] 1000 Trails RV Park, Buick/GMC, Ford, Honda, McMahon's RV Ctr, Rite Aid, Stater Bros, Toyota/Scion, TrueValue, VW, Walgreens, S [gas] 76/Circle K, Mobil/Circle K [food] Carl's Jr, China Wok, Domino's, Goody's Cafe, La Casita Mexican, Lili's Chinese, Pizza Hut, Pronto Mexican, Quiznos, Subway, TJ's Mexican, ToGo's/Baskin-Robbins, Wendy's [other] Firestone/auto, Goodyear/auto
134	Cook St, to Indian Wells, S [gas] Arco, Mobil/Circle K/dsl [food] Applebees, Carl's Jr, Coldstone, Firehouse Grill, Goody's Cafe, Jack-in-the-Box, Pueblo Viejo Grill, Starbucks, Subway [lodging] Courtyard, Hampton Inn, Hilton/Homewood Suites, Residence Inn [other] vet
131	Monterey Ave, Thousand Palms, N [gas] Arco [food] Jack-in-the-Box, S [food] Clark's Cafe/Food Mkt, Del Taco, El Pollo Loco, Hibachi City, IHOP, Maracas Cantina, McDonald's, Panda Express, Red Robin, Santana's Mexican, Starbucks, Subway, Wendy's [other] $Tree, 99c Store, America's Tire, Costco/gas, Goodyear/auto, Home Depot, Kohls, Lowe's, PetsMart, Sam's Club/gas, Walmart
130	Ramon Rd, Bob Hope Dr, N [gas] FLYING J/dsl/LP/rest./24hr, Chevron/dsl, Shell/dsl, Valero/dsl [food] Carl's Jr, Del Taco, Denny's, Domino's, Goody's Cafe, In-N-Out, McDonald's, San Miguel Mexican [lodging] Red Roof Inn [other] truckwash, S [other] [H] Agua Caliente Casino/rest.
126	Date Palm Dr, Rancho Mirage, S [gas] Arco/dsl, Mobil, Valero [other] Walgreens
123	Palm Dr, to Desert Hot Sprgs, N [gas] Arco/dsl, Chevron/Jack-in-the-Box/dsl [other] Caliente Springs Camping, S [other] to Gene Autry Trail (3mi)
120	Indian Ave, to N Palm Sprgs, N [gas] 76/Circle K, Arco/dsl, Shell/dsl [lodging] Motel 6 [other] Harley-Davidson, S [gas] Chevron, Pilot/Wendy's/dsl/scales/24hr [food] Del Taco, Jack-in-the-Box [other] [H]
117	CA 62, to Yucca Valley, Twentynine Palms, to Joshua Tree NM
114	Whitewater, many windmills
113mm	**[rest stop] both lanes, full [handicapped] facilities, litter barrels, [phone] [picnic]**
112	CA 111 (from eb), to Palm Springs
110	Haugeen-Lehmann
106	Main St, to Cabazon, N [gas] Shell/dsl [food] Burger King, S [gas] Valero/Circle K/dsl
104	Cabazon, same as 103
103	Fields Rd, N [gas] Chevron, Morongo/dsl [food] In-N-Out, McDonald's, Ruby's Diner [other] Hadley Fruit Orchards, Morongo Reservation/casino, Premium Outlets/famous brands
102.5mm	Banning weigh sta both lanes
102	Ramsey St (from wb)
101	Hargrave St, Banning, N [gas] 76/Church's, Arco/dsl [lodging] Country Inn, Stagecoach Motel [other] tires
100	CA 243, 8th St, Banning, N [gas] Chevron/dsl [food] IHOP, Jack-in-the-Box, Subway [other] Rite Aid
99	22nd St, to Ramsey St, N [gas] Arco/dsl, Shell/dsl [food] Carl's Jr, Carrow's, Chelos Tacos, Del Taco, Fishermans Grill, KFC, Little Caesar's, McDonald's, Pizza Hut, Russo's Italian, Sizzler, Starbucks, Wall Chinese [lodging] Days Inn, Super 8, Travelodge [other] $General, Banning RV Ctr, Family$, Goodyear/auto

BEAUMONT

REDLANDS

Exit #	Services
98	Sunset Ave, Banning, N [gas] Chevron/dsl [food] Domino's, Gramma's Kitchen, Gus Jr #7 Burger [lodging] Holiday Inn Express [other] $Tree, AutoZone, BigLots, Buick/Chevrolet/GMC, Ray's RV Ctr, repair, Rio Ranch Mkt, vet
96	Highland Springs Ave, N [gas] Arco, Chevron/dsl, Shell/dsl [food] Applebee's, Burger King, Denny's, FarmHouse Rest., Guy's Italian, Jack-in-the-Box, Little Caesar's, Orchid Thai, Papa John's, Subway, Wendy's [lodging] Hampton Inn [other] [H] Best Hardware, Food4Less, O'Reilly Parts, Stater Bros Foods, Walgreens, S [gas] Mobil [food] Carl's Jr, Chili's, Dickey's BBQ, El Pollo Loco, FarmerBoys, Good China, La Casita, McDonald's, Palermo's Pizza, Quiznos, Starbucks, Taco Bell, Wienerschnitzel [other] $Tree, Albertson's, Best Buy, GNC, Home Depot, hwy patrol, Kohls, PetCo, Ramona Tire/auto, Rite Aid, Ross, Verizon, Walmart/Subway
95	Pennsylvania Ave (from wb), Beaumont, N [food] Country Jct Rest., Jasmine Thai, Marla's Rest. [lodging] Rodeway Inn [other] AutoZone, Meineke, Miller RV Ctr
94	CA 79, Beaumont, N [gas] 76/dsl, USA [food] Baker's DriveThru, BMG Mexican, Casa Palacios, McDonald's, Popeye's, YumYum Donuts [lodging] Best Value Inn, Best Western [other] Family$, NAPA, O'Reilly Parts, S [gas] Arco/dsl, Shell/Circle K/dsl [food] Del Taco, Denny's, Jack-in-the-Box, Subway [other] RV camping, vet
93	CA 60 W, to Riverside
92	San Timoteo Canyon Rd, Oak Valley Pkwy, N [gas] Chevron/dsl [food] Sand Trap Grill, Subway [lodging] Holiday Inn Express [other] golf, Rite Aid, S [other] golf
91mm	**[rest stop] wb, full [handicapped] facilities, litter barrels, petwalk [phone] [picnic]**
90	Cherry Valley Blvd, N [other] truck/tire repair
89	Singleton Rd (from wb), to Calimesa
88	Calimesa Blvd, N [gas] Arco/dsl, Chevron/dsl, Shell/dsl [food] Best Wok, Burger King, Carl's Jr, Denny's, Isabella's Italian, McDonald's, NY Pizzaria, Subway, Taco Bell, Tang's Chinese [lodging] Calimesa Inn [other] Fresh&Easy Foods, Stater Bros Foods, Walgreens, S [food] Big Boy, Jack-in-the-Box
87	County Line Rd, to Yucaipa, N [gas] FasTrip/dsl, Shell/dsl [food] Baker's DriveThru, Del Taco [lodging] Best Value [other] $General, auto repair/tires, SavALot Foods, USPO, vet
86mm	**Wildwood [rest stop] eb, full [handicapped] facilities, litter barrels, petwalk [phone] [picnic]**
85	Live Oak Canyon Rd, Oak Glen
83	Yucaipa Blvd, N [gas] Arco/dsl, Chevron/dsl, Mobil [food] Baker's DriveThru, Starbucks, S [food] Subway
82	Wabash Ave (from wb)
81	Redlands Blvd, Ford St, S [gas] 76
80	Cypress Ave, University St, N [other] [H] to U of Redlands
79b a	CA 38, 6th St, Orange St, Redlands, N [gas] Chevron, USA [food] Redlands Rest. [lodging] Budget Inn, Stardust Motel [other] Stater Bros Foods, S [gas] 76, Shell [food] Chipotle Mexican, Corner Cafe,

[gas] = gas [food] = food [lodging] = lodging [other] = other [RS] = rest stop

CA

SAN BERNARDINO

INTERSTATE 10 Cont'd

79b a Continued
Domino's, Eureka Burger, Las Cuentes Mexican, Phoenicia Greek, Rubio's, Starbucks, Subway [other] Firestone/auto, Office Depot, O'Reilly Parts, Trader Joe's, Verizon, Von's Foods

77c (77b from wb) Tennessee St, N [gas] 7-11 [food] Jack-in-the-Box, Shakey's Pizza [other] Home Depot, Toyota/Scion, S [gas] Shell [food] Arby's, Bakers DriveThru, Burger King, Carl's Jr, Coco's, El Burrito, El Pollo Loco, LJ Silver, Papa John's, Subway, Taco Bell [lodging] Ayers Hotel, Comfort Suites, Dynasty Suites, Motel 6 [other] American Tire Depot, Ford, USPO, vet

77b (77c from wb) CA 210, to Highlands

77a Alabama St, N [gas] 76/Circle K/dsl [food] Buffet Star, Cafe Rio, Chick-fil-A, Chili's, Coldstone Creamery, Denny's, Famous Dave's BBQ, Five Guys, Hawaiian BBQ, Jamba Juice, Jersey Mike's, Macaroni Grill, Magic Wok, Noodle 21 Asian, Red Robin, Starbucks, Subway, Tom's Charburgers [lodging] Best Value Inn, Motel 7 West, Super 8 [other] AT&T, Barnes&Noble, GNC, JC Penney, Jo-Ann Superstore, Kohl's, Marshall's, Michael's, PetCo, Target, U-Haul, Verizon, World Mkt, S [gas] Chevron, Shell [food] Del Taco, IHOP, McDonald's, Nick's Burgers, Old Spaghetti Factory, Pizza Hut, Zabella's Mexican [lodging] Country Inn&Suites, GoodNite Inn [other] $Tree, 7-11, 99c Store, BigLots, Chevrolet, CVS Drug, Discount Tire, Goodyear/auto, K-Mart, Lowe's, Midas, Nissan, PepBoys, Ross, Tuesday Morning

76 California St, N [food] Mill Creek Rest. [other] funpark, museum, S [gas] Arco, Shell/LP/dsl [food] Applebee's, Bravo Burger, Jack-in-the-Box, Jose's Mexican, Little Caesar's, Panda Express, Red Chili Szechuan, Subway, Wendy's, Wienerschnitzel [other] AT&T, AutoZone, Food4Less, Just Tires, Mission RV Park, Radio Shack, Walmart

75 Mountain View Ave, Loma Linda, N [gas] Valero/dsl, S [food] Domino's, FarmerBoys Burgers, Lupe's Mexican, Subway

74 Tippecanoe Ave, Anderson St, N [food] BJ's Rest., Chipotle Mexican, El Pollo Loco, Hawaiian BBQ, In-N-Out, Jack-in-the-Box, Jamba Juice, Panera Bread, Pick-Up Stix, Pollo Campero, Starbucks, Subway, Tasty Goody [lodging] Fairfield Inn, Hampton Inn, Homewood Suites, Residence Inn [other] Costco/gas, Sam's Club/gas, Staples, S [gas] 76/dsl [food] Baker's DriveThru, Del Taco, HomeTown Buffet, KFC, Napoli Italian, Wienerschnitzel [other] auto repair, Honda, Hyundai, to Loma Linda U

73b a Waterman Ave, N [gas] 76, Shell/dsl [food] Baja Fresh, Black Angus, Buffalo Wild Wings, Chili's, ChuckeCheese, ClaimJumper, Coco's, El Torito, Five Guys, IHOP, King Buffet, Lotus Garden Chinese, Mimi's Café, Olive Garden, Outback Steaks, Panda Express, Red Lobster, Sizzler, Souplantation, Subway, TGIFriday's, Togo's [lodging] Best Western, Days Inn, Hilton Garden, La Quinta, Quality Inn, San Bernardino Hotel, Super 8 [other] 7-11, Best Buy, Home Depot, Office Depot, PetsMart, S [gas] Arco [food] Burger King, Carl's Jr, Gus Jr Burger #8, McDonald's, Popeye's, Starbucks, Taco Bell [lodging] Motel 6 [other] Camping World RV Ctr, El Monte RV Ctr, repair

72 I-215, CA 91

71 Mt Vernon Ave, Sperry Ave, N [gas] 7-11, Trkstp/dsl/LP [food] Alberto's Mexican [lodging] Colony Inn, Colton Motel, Comfort Inn [other] repair

70b 9th St, N [gas] Mobil [food] Denny's, Domino's, McDonald's, P&G Burgers, Starbucks, Subway [lodging] Holiday Inn Express [other] NAPA, Stater Bros Foods, USPO

70a Rancho Ave, N [food] Del Taco, Jack-in-the-Box, KFC/Taco Bell, Wienerschnitzel

ONTARIO

69 Pepper Dr, N [gas] Valero [food] Baker's DriveThru

68 Riverside Ave, to Rialto, N [gas] Chevron/dsl, I-10 Trkstp/dsl/scales, USA [food] Burger King, Burger King, Coco's, El Pollo Loco, HomeTown Buffet, Jack-in-the-Box, McDonald's, Panda Express, Starbucks, Subway, Taco Joe's [lodging] American Inn, Days Inn, ValleyView Inn [other] dsl repair, Midas, Pepboys, Walmart, S [gas] Shell/Circle K/dsl

66 Cedar Ave, to Bloomington, N [gas] Arco, Valero/dsl [food] Baker's DriveThru, Burger King, DQ, FarmerBoys Burgers, Subway, Taco Bell, S [other] 7-11

64 Sierra Ave, to Fontana, N [gas] Arco, Mobil, Shell, Valero/dsl [food] Arby's, Billy J's Rest., China Cook, China Panda, ChuckeCheese, Del Taco, Denny's, El Gallo Giro, Hawaiian BBQ, IHOP, In-N-Out, Jack-in-the-Box, KFC, Little Caesars, Little Caesar's, McDonald's, Pancho Villa's, Papa John's, Pizza Hut/Taco Bell, Popeye's, Sizzler, Sub Shop, Subway, Wendy's, Wienerschnitzel, Yoshinoya [lodging] Best Value Inn, EconoLodge, Motel 6, Valley Motel [other] [H] $Tree, AutoZone, BigLots, Cardenas Foods, CVS Drug, Food4Less, GNC, Just Tires, K-Mart, PepBoys, Radio Shack, Rite Aid, Stater Bros Foods, Verizon, S [gas] Chevron/dsl [food] Alvaro's Mexican, Brandon's Diner, China Buffet, Circle K, Del Taco, Los Jalapeños, Shakey's Pizza, Shrimp House, Subway, Tasty Goody [lodging] Hilton Garden [other] AutoZone, Ross, Target, TJ Maxx

63 Citrus Ave, N [gas] 76, Gasco [food] Baker's DriveThru, Subway [other] Ford, S [gas] 7-11/dsl, Arco/dsl

61 Cherry Ave, N [gas] Arco, Chevron, Fontana Trkstp/dsl/24hr, Valero/dsl [food] Carl's Jr, Del Taco, Jack-in-the-Box [other] Mack/Volvo, truck sales, S [gas] 3 Sisters Trkstp/dsl/ @, 76/Circle K, North American Trkstp/dsl [food] Farmer Boy's Rest., La Chaquita [other] Peterbilt

59 Etiwanda Ave, Valley Blvd

58b a I-15, N to Barstow, S to San Diego

57 Milliken Ave, N [gas] 76/dsl, Arco/24hr, Chevron, Mobil/Albertos Mexican/dsl, Shell [food] Applebee's, Arby's, Baja Fresh, BJ's Rest., Boston's, Burger King, Carl's Jr, Chevy's Mexican, Chipotle, Coco's, Coldstone, Dave&Buster's, Del Taco, El Pollo Loco, Famous Dave's BBQ, Fat Burger, Fuddruckers, Hooters, IHOP, In-n-Out, Jack-in-the-Box, Jamba Juice, KFC, Krispy Kreme, McDonald's, Mkt Broiler, New City Buffet, NY Grill, Olive Garden, Outback Steaks, Rain Forest Cafe, Red Lobster, Rubio's, Sonic, Starbucks, Subway, Tokyo Tokyo, Wendy's, Wienerschnitzel, Wing Place [lodging] Ayre's Suites, Country Inn&Suites, Courtyard, Hampton Inn, Hilton Garden, Holiday Inn Express, Homewood Suites, Hyatt, TownePlace Suites [other] America's Tire, Best Buy, Big O Tire, Carmax, Costco/gas, JC Penney, Jo-Ann Fabrics, Kohl's, Marshalls, Ontario Mills Mall, Petsmart, Sam's Club/gas, Staples, Target, Verizon, S [gas] TA/Shell/Pizza Hut/Subway/Taco Bell/dsl/rest./24hr/ @ [lodging] Rodeway Inn

56 Haven Ave, Rancho Cucamonga, N [gas] Mobil [food] Benihana, Black Angus, Pizza Factory [lodging] Aloft Hotel, Best Western, Extended Stay America, Hilton, La Quinta, Ontario Grand Suites, S [food] Panda Chinese, TGIFriday's [lodging] Fairfield Inn

55b a Holt Blvd, to Archibald Ave, N [gas] Arco, Mobil/dsl [food] Baker's Drive-thru, Burgertown USA, Hawaiian BBQ, Subway, Weinerschnitzel

54 Vineyard Ave, N [gas] 76/Circle K [food] Carl's Jr, Del Taco, El Pollo Loco, Great China, Pizza Hut/Taco Bell, Popeye's, Quiznos, Rocky's Pizza [other] AutoZone, Ralph's Foods, Rite Aid, Stater Bros Foods, S [gas] 76, Mobil, Valero [food] Basil Rest., Cowboy Burgers, Denny's, Garden Square Rest., In-N-Out, Jack-in-the-Box, Marie Callenders, Quiznos, Rosa's Italian, Spires Rest.,

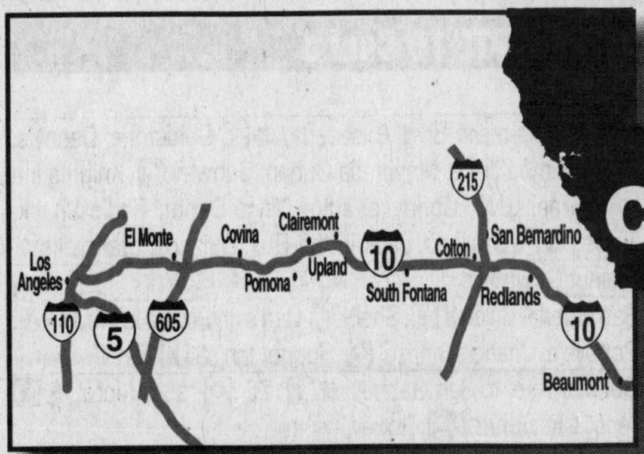

INTERSTATE 10 Cont'd

MONTCLAIR

54 Continued
Wendy's, Yoshinoya Japanese Ayers Suites, Best Western, Comfort Suites, Countryside Suites, DoubleTree Inn, Holiday Inn, Motel 6, Ontario Airport Inn, Quality Inn, Ramada Inn, Red Roof Inn, Residence Inn, Sheraton Buick/Cadillac/Chevrolet/GMC, to Airport, USPO

53 San Bernardino Ave, 4th St, to Ontario, N 7-11, 76, Arco, Shell Burger King, Carl's Jr, Jack-in-the-Box EconoLodge, Motel 6 K-Mart, Radio Shack, S 76, Arco/24hr, Valero Denny's, Little Caesars, Subway, YumYum Donuts Days Inn, Rodeway Inn city park, Jax Mkt

51 CA 83, Euclid Ave, to Ontario, Upland, N H

50 Mountain Ave, to Mt Baldy, N Chevron, Mobil/dsl, Shell/dsl Carrow's, Denny's, El Torito, Fresh&Easy, HoneyBaked Ham, Mi Taco, Mimi's Café, Rubio's, Subway, Trader Joe's, Wendy's Super 8 $Tree, AT&T, CVS Drug, Home Depot, Kohl's, Michaels, Radio Shack, Staples, S 76/dsl Baskin-Robbins, Carl's Jr, Chopstix, Coldstone, Jo-Anne's Cafe, Pizza Hut, Quiznos, Roundtable Pizza, Starbucks, Wingnuts Albertsons, Rite Aid, USPO, vet

49 Central Ave, to Montclair, N Carl's Jr., Chipotle Mexican, Del Taco, El Pollo Loco, Hometown Buffet, John's Incredible Pizza, McDonald's, Panda Garden Buffet, Pizza Hut, Quiznos, Starbucks, Subway, Taco Bell 99c Store, America's Tire, AT&T, AutoZone, Barnes&Noble, Best Buy, Firestone/auto, Giant RV Ctr, Goodyear/auto, Harley-Davidson, JC Penney, Just Tires, Macy's, mall, PepBoys, PetCo, Ross, same as 48, Sears/auto, Target, Tuesday Morning, vet, S Chevron, Thrifty Alberto's Mexican, Fulin Chinese, Jack-in-the-Box, LJ Silver, Subway, Wienerschnitzel 7-11, Acura/Honda/Infiniti, Costco/gas, Nissan, Stater Bros

48 Monte Vista, N Shell Acapulco Mexican, Applebee's, Black Angus, Chilis, Elephant Bar Rest., Macaroni Grill, Olive Garden, Red Lobster H Macy's, mall, Nordstrom's, same as 49

47 Indian Hill Blvd, to Claremont, N Mobil BC Cafe, Garden Square Claremont Lodge, Howard Johnson, S 76/dsl, Chevron/McDonald's Burger King, Carl's Jr, Denny's, In-N-Out, Norm's Rest., RoundTable Pizza, Starbucks, World Famous Grill 7-11, Toyota/Scion

46 Towne Ave, N 7-11, 76/dsl Jack-in-the-Box

45b Garey Ave, to Pomona, N Arco H vet, S Chevron, Shell/dsl Del Taco

45 White Ave, Garey Ave, to Pomona

44 (43 from eb)Dudley St, Fairplex Dr, N Arco/dsl Denny's LemonTree Motel, Sheraton, S Chevron/24hr Jack-in-the-Box, McDonald's, Starbucks 7-11

42b CA 71 S (from eb), to Corona

42a to I-210, CA 57 S

41 Kellogg Dr, S to Cal Poly Inst

40 Via Verde

38b Holt Ave, to Covina, N Hamiltons Steaks Radisson

38a Grand Ave, N Arco/dsl, United Baily's Rest, Denny's Best Western

37b Barranca St, Grand Ave, N 76, Shell/dsl BJ's Rest., Carinos, Carl's Jr, Chili's, Chipotle Mexican, Dockside Grill, El Torito, Habit Burgers, Hooters, Islands Burgers, Marie Callender, Mariposa Mexican, Starbucks Best Western, Clarion, Fairfield Inn, Hampton Inn Albertsons, CVS Drug, Dick's, IKEA, Marshalls, Office Depot, Old Navy, Petsmart, Target,

COVINA

37b Continued
Verizon, S In-N-Out, McDonald's 5 Star Inn, Days Inn, same as 37a

37a Citrus Ave, to Covina, N Chevron Buffalo Wild Wings, Burger King, Del Taco, IHOP, Jack-in-the-Box, Millie's Rest., Starbucks, Subway, TGIFriday's, Yum Yum Donuts Acura, Albertsons, Baja Ranch Foods, Buick/GMC, CVS Drug, KIA, Marshall's, Nissan, VW, S 76/autocare Classic Burger H Cadillac, same as 37b

36 CA 39, Azusa Ave, to Covina, N 76/dsl, Arco/24hr Dennys, Green Field Brazillian, McDonald's, Norm's Rest., Papa John's, Quiznos, Subway BigLots, Chrysler/Dodge/Jeep, CVS Drug, Food4Less, Stater Bros, S Mobil, Shell/dsl Carrow's Audi, Chevrolet, Ford, Honda, Hummer, Mercedes, Toyota

35 Vincent Ave, Glendora Ave, N 76/dsl/autocare, S 76 Applebee's, Baja Fresh, CA Pizza Kitchen, Elephant Bar Rest., Fresh&Easy, Grand Buffet, Jamba Juice, Panera Bread, Pizza Hut, Red Robin, Starbucks, Subway, Weinerschnitzel Best Buy, Big O Tire, Firestone, JC Penney, Macy's, mall, Sears/auto, USPO, Verizon

34 Pacific Ave, N 76, S Mobil, Valero H Discount Tire, K-Mart, mall, same as 35, Sears Outlet

33 Puente Ave, N Chevron Denny's, Farmer Boy's, Guadalajara Grill, McDonald's, Panda Express, Sizzler, Starbucks Courtyard, Motel 6 AT&T, Home Depot, Verizon, Walmart, S Valero/dsl Jack-in-the-Box Regency Inn Harley-Davidson, U-Haul

32b Francisquito Ave, to La Puente, N V&G hwy patrol, S 76 Carl's Jr, In-N-Out, Wienerschnitzel Grand Park Inn

32a Baldwin Pk Blvd, N Chevron/McDonald's Burger King, Fronteiras, IHOP, Jack-in-the-Box, Papa Johns, Pizza Hut/Taco Bell, Starbucks, Subway, Wok'n Go, Yum Yum Donuts H CVS Drug, Food4Less, Target, transmissions, S In-N-Out

EL MONTE

31c (31b from wb) Frazier St, N 7-11

31b a (31a from wb) I-605 N/S, to Long Beach

30 Garvey Ave, S Rte 66

29b Valley Blvd, Peck Rd, N Chevron Baskin-Robbins, Carl's Jr., Denny's, Hometown Buffet, Jamba Juice, KFC, Papa Johns, Shakey's Pizza, Subway, Taco Bell, Yoshinoya Motel 6 Honda, Hyundai, Lexus, Nissan, Radio Shack, Sears Essentials, Staples, Toyota/Scion, Walgreens, S McDonald's, Pepe's Seafood, Tommy's Burgers

29a S Peck Rd (from eb)

28 Santa Anita Ave, to El Monte, S 76/dsl 7-11, vet

27 Baldwin Avenue, Temple City Blvd, S Arco/24hr Denny's, same as 26b a

CA

LOS ANGELES AREA / SANTA MONICA

INTERSTATE 10 Cont'd

Exit #	Services
26b	CA 19, Rosemead Blvd, Pasadena, N [food] Coldstone, Denny's, IHOP, Jamba Juice, Mayumba Cuban, Subway [lodging] Knights Inn [other] $Tree, GNC, Goodyear/auto, Office Depot, Radio Shack, Target, S [food] Del Taco, Jack-in-the-Box, Quiznos, Starbucks
26a	Walnut Grove Ave
25b	San Gabriel Blvd, N [gas] Shell [food] Carl's Jr, Pizza Hut/Taco Bell, Popeye's, Wienerschnitzel [lodging] Budget Inn, S [gas] 7-11
25a	Del Mar Ave, to San Gabriel, N [gas] 76 [other] auto repair, S [gas] Arco, Chevron/dsl [lodging] Rodeway Inn
24	New Ave, to Monterey Park, N [food] KFC, to Mission San Gabriel
23b	Garfield Ave, to Alhambra, S [gas] Arco [lodging] Grand Inn [other] [H]
23a	Atlantic Blvd, Monterey Park, N [gas] 76, Mobil [food] Pizza Hut, Popeye's, Starbucks [other] [H] S [lodging] Best Western [other] auto repair, Ralph's Foods
22	Fremont Ave, N [other] [H] tuneup, S [food] Papa Johns [other] 7-11
21	I-710, Long Beach Fwy, Eastern Ave (from wb)
20b a	Eastern Ave, City Terrace Dr, S [gas] Chevron/service, Mobil [food] Burger King, McDonald's
19c	Soto St (from wb), N [gas] Chevron/dsl [food] Burger King [other] [H] city park, S [gas] 76, Mobil
19b	I-5 (from wb), US 101 S, N to Burbank, S to San Diego
19a	State St, N [other] [H]
17	I-5 N
16b	I-5 S (from eb)
16a	Santa Fe Ave, San Mateo St, S [gas] 76/dsl [other] industrial area, Penske Trucks
15b	Alameda St, N [gas] 76/dsl [food] Jack-in-the-Box, to downtown, S industrial area
15a	Central Ave, N [gas] Shell/repair
14b	San Pedro Blvd, S industrial
14a	LA St, N [other] conv ctr, S [food] El Pollo Loco, McDonald's [other] 99c Store, O'Reilly Parts, Radio Shack, Rite Aid, URGENT CARE
13	I-110, Harbor Fwy
12	Hoover St, Vermont Ave, N [gas] Mobil [food] Burger King, McDonald's, Subway [other] AutoZone, Honda, PepBoys, Rite Aid, S [gas] 76, Arco, Chevron [food] Jack-in-the-Box, Papa Johns, Yoshinoya [other] Ralph's Foods
11	Normandie Ave, Western Ave
10	Arlington Ave, N [gas] 76, Chevron
9	Crenshaw Blvd, S [gas] 76, Chevron, Mobil, Thrifty [food] El Pollo Loco, McDonald's, Pizza Hut/Taco Bell, Subway, Yoshinoya [other] U-Haul
8	La Brea Ave, N [gas] Valero/dsl [other] USPO, S [gas] Chevron [other] AutoZone
7b	Washington Blvd, Fairfax Ave, S [gas] Mobil, same as 8
7a	La Cienega Blvd, Venice Ave (from wb), N [gas] Chevron/24hr, Mobil [food] Carl's Jr., Del Taco [other] Firestone/auto, S [food] Subway [other] Aamco
6	Robertson Blvd, Culver City, N [gas] Chevron, Valero [food] Domino's, Taco Bell [other] EZ Lube, Goodyear, S [food] Del Taco [other] Albertsons, CVS Drug, Ross
5	National Blvd, N [gas] 76, United Oil [food] Starbucks, Subway, Taco+ [other] Rite Aid, Von's Foods, S [gas] Arco
4	Overland Ave, S [gas] Mobil/dsl
3b a	I-405, N to Sacramento, S to Long Beach
2c b	Bundy Dr, N [gas] Chevron, Shell/dsl [food] Taco Bell [other] Cadillac/GMC, Staples
2a	Centinela Ave, to Santa Monica, N [food] Taco Bell, S [food] McDonald's, Trader Joe's [lodging] Santa Monica Hotel
1c	20th St (from wb), Cloverfield Blvd, 26th St (from wb), N [gas] 76, dsl, Arco, Shell/repair [other] [H]
1b	Lincoln Blvd, CA 1 S, N [gas] Mobil [food] Arbys, Denny's, Jack-in-the-Box, McDonald's, Norm's Rest., Starbucks [lodging] Holiday Inn [other] BrakeMasters, Jo-Ann Fabrics, Sears, Toyota, Tuesday Morning, USPO, Vons Foods, S [gas] 76, Chevron/dsl, Mobil Shell, World Gas [food] Dominos, Hawaiian BBQ, Jack-in-the-Box, Subway, Taco Bell, Tommy's Burgers [lodging] Doubletree Suites [other] 7-11, EZ Lube, Firestone/auto, U-Haul
1a	4th, 5th, (from wb), N [other] mall, Sears
0	Santa Monica Blvd, to beaches, **I-10 begins/ends on CA 1.**

BAKER / BARSTOW

INTERSTATE 15

Exit #	Services
298	California/Nevada state line, facilities located at state line, Nevada side
291	Yates Well Rd
286	Nipton Rd, E Mojave Nat Preserve, to Searchlight
281	Bailey Rd
276mm	**brake check area for trucks, nb**
272	Cima Rd, E [gas] Shell/cafe/dsl/towing
270mm	**Valley Wells [RS] both lanes, full [handicapped] facilities, litter barrels, petwalk [phone] [picnic]**
265	Halloran Summit Rd
259	Halloran Springs Rd
248	to Baker (from sb), same as 246
246	CA 127, Kel-Baker Rd, Baker, to Death Valley, W [gas] 76/dsl, Arco, Chevron/Taco Bell, Shell/Jack-in-the-Box/dsl, Valero/A&W/Pizza Hut/Subway/TCBY, Valero/DQ/Quiznos/dsl [food] Arby's, Big Boy Rest., Burger King, Carl's Jr, Del Taco, Dennys, IHOP, Mad Greek Cafe [lodging] BunBoy Hotel, Will's Fargo Motel [other] Alien Fresh Jerky, Baker Mkt Foods, Country Store, repair, USPO, World's Tallest Thermometer
245	to Baker (from nb), same as 246
239	Zzyzx Rd
233	Rasor Rd, E [gas] Shell/Rasor Sta/dsl/towing/24hr
230	Basin Rd
221	Afton Rd, to Dunn, W [other] Mini Mkt
217mm	**[RS] both lanes, full [handicapped] facilities, litter barrels, petwalk [phone] [picnic]**
213	Field Rd
206	Harvard Rd, to Newberry Springs
198	Minneola Rd, W [gas] /dsl
197mm	**agricultural insp sta sb**
196	Yermo Rd, Yermo
194	Calico Rd
191	Ghost Town Rd, E [gas] Arco/24hr, Mohsen Oil Trkstp/dsl/24hr [food] Jack-in-the-Box, Peggy Sue's 50s Diner, Penny's Diner [lodging] OakTree Inn, W [gas] 76, Shell/dsl/24hr [other] Calico Ghost-Town (3mi), KOA
189	Ft Irwin Rd
186	CA 58 W, to Bakersfield, W [food] Idle Spur Steaks
184	E Main, Barstow, Montera Rd (from eb), to I-40, E [gas] 76/dsl [food] Grill It, McDonald's, Mega Tom's Burgers, Popeye's, Starbucks, Subway [lodging] Arco, Best Western, Travelodge [other] Walmart/McDonald's/auto, W [gas] Chevron, Circle K, Shell/dsl, USA/dsl [food] Alberto's, Burger King, Carl's Jr, China Town Buffet, Del Taco, Denny's, Di Napoli's Italian, IHOP, Jack-in-the-Box, Jenny's Grill, Little Caesar's, LJ Silver, Wienerschnitzel [lodging] Astrobudget Motel, Best Motel, Budget Inn, CA Inn, Days Inn, Desert Inn, EconoLodge, Economy Inn, Motel 6, Quality Inn/rest., Ramada Inn, Rodeway Inn, Super 8 [other] $Tree, 99Cent Store, AutoZone,

INTERSTATE 15 Cont'd

LENWOOD

Exit	Services
184	Continued Family$, O'Reilly Parts, Radio Shack, U-Haul/LP, URGENT CARE, Von's Foods
184a	I-40 E (from nb), **I-40 begins/ends**
183	CA 247, Barstow Rd, E Circle K, Valero/dsl Jimenez Mexican, Pizza Hut, Subway $General, Rite Aid, W Shell H Food4Less, Mojave River Valley Museum, st patrol
181	L St, W Main, Barstow, W Arco/dsl, Chevron, USA Foster's Freeze Sleep Inn Firestone/auto, Home Depot, NAPA, tires/towing
179	CA 58, to Bakersfield
178	Lenwood, to Barstow, E FLYING J/Denny's/dsl/24hr, 76/dsl, Arco/dsl, Chevron, Shell/dsl, Valero Arby's, Big Boy, Burger King, Carl's Jr, Chili's, Chipotle Mexican, Del Taco, El Pollo Loco, In-N-Out, Jack-in-the-Box, Panda Express, Starbucks, Subway, Tommy's Burgers Comfort Suites, Country Inn&Suites, Hampton Inn, Holiday Inn Express Blue Beacon, Old Navy, Tanger Outlet/famous brands/food ct, W Loves/Chester's/Godfather's/dsl/scales/24hr/ @, Pilot/Subway/dsl/scales/24hr, TA/Shell/Country Fare/Subway/dsl/scales/24hr/ @ McDonald's Days Inn repair, truckwash, Zippy Lube
175	Outlet Ctr Dr, Sidewinder Rd
169	Hodge Rd
165	Wild Wash Rd
161	Dale Evans Pkwy, to Apple Valley
157	Stoddard Wells Rd, to Bell Mtn
154	Stoddard Wells Rd, to Bell Mtn, E Shady Oasis Camping/LP, W 76/dsl, Mobil Franky's Diner Motel 6, Queens Motel
153.5mm	Mojave River
153b	E St
153a	CA 18 E, D St, to Apple Valley, E Arco H repair, W Arco/Subway/dsl
151b	Mojave Dr, Victorville, E Gasmart/dsl Rodeway Inn, W Valero/dsl Economy Inn, Sunset Inn
151a	La Paz Dr, Roy Rogers Dr, E Chevron, Shell/dsl Burger King, Carl's Jr, El Pollo Loco, HomeTown Buffet, IHOP, Jack-in-the-Box, McDonald's, Wendy's, Wienerschnitzel $General, $Tree, 99c Store, AutoZone, BigLots, Costco/gas, Fiat, Food4Less, Goodyear/auto, Harley-Davidson, Pepboys, Radio Shack, Rite Aid, Toyota/Scion, W Arco Carl's Jr, Dickey's BBQ, Domino's, Farmer Boys, Golden ChopStix, Hawaiian BBQ, In-N-Out, Panda Express, Papa John's, Starbucks, Subway Americas Tire, Buick/GMC, Chrysler/Dodge/Jeep, Home Depot, Honda, Kia, Nissan, Stater Bros, Verizon, Walgreens, WinCo Foods
150	CA 18 W, Palmdale Rd, Victorville, E Baker's Drive-Thru, Burger King, Denny's, KFC, Richie's Diner Greentree Inn, Red Roof Inn, W 76/dsl, Arco, Circle K Coco's, Del Taco, House of Joy, La Casita Mexican, McDonald's, Pizza Hut, Raul's Mexican, Starbucks, Subway, Taco Bell, Tom's Rest. Budget Inn, Days Inn, Holiday Inn H $General, Aamco, AutoZone, CVS Drug, Ford, Hyundai, Kamper's Korner RV, Mazda, Target, Town&Country Tire, vet
148	La Mesa Rd, Nisquali Rd, E Red Roof Inn, W Baskin-Robbins, Buffalo's, ChuckeCheese, Fatburger AT&T, Petsmart

VICTORVILLE

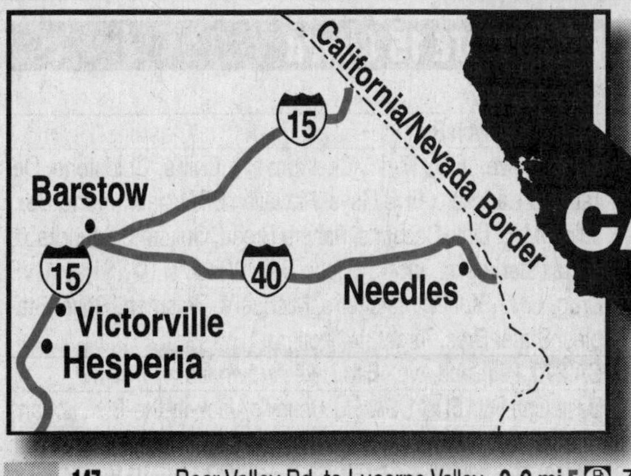

CA

HESPERIA

Exit	Services
147	Bear Valley Rd, to Lucerne Valley, **0-2 mi** E 76/Circle K/dsl, Arco, Chevron, Mobil Arby's, Baker's Drive-Thru, Burger King, Carl's Jr, Del Taco, Dragon Express, John's Pizza, KFC, Los Alazanes Mexican, Los Toritos, Marie Callender's, McDonald's, Panda Express, Red Robin, Starbucks, Steak'n Shake, Steer'n Stein, Tacos Mexico, Tilted Kilt, Wienerschnitzel Best Value Inn, Comfort Suites, Day&Night Inn, EconoLodge, Extended Studio Hotel, Hilton Garden, La Quinta, Travelodge Affordable RV Ctr, America's Tire, AutoZone, Firestone/auto, Home Depot, Michael's, O'Reilly Parts, Range RV, Rite Aid, Scandia Funpark, Tire Depot, Vallarta Foods, vet, Walmart/McDonald's/auto, W 76/Circle K, Arco, Chevron/dsl, Valero/dsl Applebee's, Archibald's Drive-Thru, Baja Fresh, Carino's, Chili's, Chipotle Mexican, Del Taco, El Pollo Loco, El Tio Pepe Mexican, Farmer Boy's Rest., Freddy's Custard, Giuseppe's, Jack-in-the-Box, Little Caesar's, McDonald's, Mimi's Cafe, Olive Garden, Outback Steaks, Pancho Villa's, Red Lobster, RoadHouse Grill, Sonic, Starbucks, Subway, Tokyo Steaks, Wendy's Hawthorn Suites 99c Store, AAA, Barnes&Noble, Best Buy, CVS Drug, Dick's, Goodyear/auto, Hobby Lobby, JC Penney, Kohl's, Lowe's, Macy's, mall, Rite Aid, Stater Bros., Verizon, Walgreens, Walmart
143	Main St, to Hesperia, Phelan, E Chevron/dsl, Mobil/Alberto's, Shell/Popeye's/dsl Arby's, Burger King, Chipotle, Del Taco, Denny's, IHOP, In-N-Out, Jack-in-the-Box, Panda Express, Quiznos, Starbucks Courtyard, SpringHill Suites Walmart/Subway, W 76/dsl, Arco/dsl Baker's Drive-thru, Farmer Boys, Golden Corral, Subway Holiday Inn Express, Motel 6 Desert Willow RV Park, GNC, Jo-Ann Fabrics, Marshall's, Radio Shack, Ross, SuperTarget, URGENT CARE, Verizon
141	US 395, Joshua St, Adelanto, W Arco/dsl, Pilot/Wendy's/dsl/scales/24hr Outpost Café repair, RV supply ctr, truck/RV wash, Zippy Lube
140	Ranchero Rd
138	Oak Hill Rd, E Chevron/dsl Summit Inn Café, W Oak Hills RV Village/LP
137mm	brake check sb, Cajon Summit, elevation 4260
131	CA 138, to Palmdale, Silverwood Lake, E Chevron McDonald's Silverwood SRA, W 76/Circle K/Del Taco/LP, Shell/Subway/dsl/LP Best Western
130mm	elevation 3000, **weigh sta both lanes**
129	Cleghorn Rd
124	Kenwood Ave
123	I-215 S, to San Bernardino, E Arco to Glen Helen Park
122	Glen Helen Parkway
119	Sierra Ave, W Arco/dsl, Chevron/dsl, Shell/Del Taco/dsl, Valero/dsl Jack-in-the-Box, McDonalds to Lytle Creek RA

INTERSTATE 15 Cont'd

Exit #	Services
118	Duncan Canyon Rd
116	Summit Ave, E [gas] 7-11, Chevron [food] Chili's, Coldstone, Del Taco, El Ranchero, Five Guys, Hawaiian BBQ, Jack-in-the-Box, Juice It Up, Little Caesar's, Panera Bread, Quiznos, Roundtable Pizza, Starbucks, Subway, Taco Bell, Wendy's [other] $Tree, CVS Drug, GNC, Kohl's, Marshall's, Michael's, Petsmart, Ross, Staples, Stater Bros, Target, Verizon
115b a	CA 210, Highland Ave, E to Lake Arrowhead
113	Base Line Rd, E [gas] USA [food] Denny's, Jack-in-the-Box, Logans Roadhouse, Pizza Hut, Rosa Maria's, Starbucks [lodging] Comfort Inn

CUCAMONGA

Exit #	Services
112	CA 66, Foothill Blvd, E [gas] Chevron [food] Asia Buffet, Claim-Jumper, Golden Spoon, In-N-Out, Panda Express, Subway, Taco Bell, Wienerschnitzel [other] $City, Food4Less, Jiffy Lube, Radio Shack, Walmart, **1-2 mi** W [gas] 76/dsl, Chevron/dsl [food] Baker's, Buffalo Wild Wings, Carino's, Cheesecake Factory, Chick-fil-A, Chipotle Mexican, Del Taco, Denny's, El Pollo Loco, El Torito, Flemings Steaks, Islamadora Fish Co, Jack-in-the-Box, Joe's Crab Shack, Johnny Rockets, Kings Fishouse, Lucille's BBQ, Old Spagetti Factory, Paisano's Rest., PF Chang's, Popeyes, Red Robin, Richie's Diner, Shakey's Pizza, Starbucks, TGIFriday's, The Hat Grill, Wendy's [lodging] Sheraton 4 Points [other] AT&T, AutoZone, Bass Pro Shops, Best Buy, Fresh&Easy Mkt, Home Depot, JC Penney, Macy's, Office Depot, Sears Grand
110	4th St, E [gas] Arco/dsl [food] Baker's, Subway, W [gas] 76/dsl, Arco, Chevron/Alberto's Mexican/dsl, Shell/dsl [food] Applebee's, Arby's, Baja Fresh, Baskin-Robbins, BJ's Rest., Boston's, Burger King, Carl's Jr, Chevy's Mexican, Chick-fil-A, Chipotle, Chop Sticks, Coco's, Daphne's Greek, Del Taco, Denny's, El Pollo Loco, Famous Dave's BBQ, Fat Burger, Fuddruckers, Hooters, IHOP, In-N-Out, Jack-in-the-Box, Jamba Juice, Juice It Up, KFC, Krispy Kreme, Lazy Dog Cafe, McDonald's, Mkt Broiler, New City Buffet, NY Grill, Olive Garden, Outback Steaks, Panera Bread, Rain Forest Cafe, Red Brick Pizza, Red Lobster, Rubio's, Sonic, Starbucks, Subway, Tokyo Tokyo, Wendy's, Wienerschnitzel, Wing Place [lodging] Ayre's Suites, Country Inn&Suites, Courtyard, Hampton Inn, Hilton Garden, Holiday Inn Express, Homewood Suites, Hyatt Place, TownePlace Suites [other] $Tree, America's Tire, Costco/gas, JC Penney, Jo-Ann Fabrics, Kohl's, Marshall's, Ontario Mills Mall, Petsmart, Sam's Club/gas, Staples, Target, Tire Pros, Verizon

ONTARIO

Exit #	Services
109b a	I-10, E to San Bernardino, W to LA
108	Jurupa St, E [gas] Chevron/dsl [food] Burger King, Del Taco, El Gran Burrito, Starbucks, Subway [other] Affordable RV, BMW, Chrysler/Dodge/Jeep, Family RV Ctr, Fiat, Honda, Hyundai, Lexus, Mazda, Mini, Nissan, Subaru, Toyota/Scion, Volvo, VW, W [gas] Arco [food] Carl's Jr [other] Ford, Kia, Scandia funpark
106	CA 60, E to Riverside, W to LA
105	Cantu-Galleano Ranch Rd
103	Limonite Ave, E [food] Asado Grill, Carl's Jr, Del Taco, Denny's, Five Guys, Hawaiian BBQ, Jamba Juice, Subway [other] Lowe's, Michael's, PetCo, Ross, W [gas] Chevron [food] Applebee's, Carino's, Coldstone, El Gran Burrito, Farmer Boys, Golden Chop Sticks, Golden Spoon, Johnny Rockets, L&L BBQ, Little Caesars, McDonald's, On-the-Border, Panda Express, Pick Up Stix, Quiznos, Red Brick Pizza, Starbucks, Subway, Taco Bell, Tasty Chinese, Tutti Frutti Yogurt, Wendy's [other] AT&T, Best Buy, GNC, Home Depot, Kohl's, Nestle Tollhouse, Petsmart, Radio Shack, Ralph's Foods/gas, Staples, Target, TJ Maxx, URGENT CARE, Verizon, Vons Foods/gas, Walgreens

NORCO

Exit #	Services
100	6th St, Norco Dr, Old Town Norco, E [gas] 76/dsl, Chevron [food] Jack-in-the-Box, McDonald's, Starbucks [other] Rite Aid, W [gas] Arco, Valero/dsl [food] Big Boy, Norco's Burgers, Senior Tacos, Wienerschnitzel, Zaky's Kabob [lodging] Knights Inn [other] Brake Masters, Jiffy Lube, USPO, vet
98	2nd St, W [gas] Mobil, Shell/dsl, Thrifty [food] Baja Fish Tacos, Burger Basket, Burger King, Carl's Jr, Del Taco, Domino's, In-N-Out, Magic Wok, Pizza Hut, Polly's Cafe, Sizzler, Subway [other] $Tree, 7-11, Ace Hardware, America's Tire, Mazda, Norco Tires, Stater Bros
97	Yuma Dr, Hidden Valley Pkwy, E [gas] 7-11 [food] Baja Fresh, Chick-fil-A, Fat Burger, Hot Dog Shoppe, Shogun Japanese, Starbucks, Subway [other] Kohl's, Stater Bros, Walgreens, W [gas] 76/dsl, Chevron, Shell/dsl [food] 5 Guys Burgers, Alberto's Mexican, Burger City Grill, Carl's Jr, Chipotle, Denny's, Domino's, DQ, Hawaiian BBQ, Hickory Joe's BBQ, Jack-in-the-Box, Jamba Juice, Jersey Mikes, KFC, Magic Wok, McDonald's, Miguel's Jr, Papa John's, Pizza Hut/Taco Bell, Rodrigo's Mexican, Rubio's, Starbucks [lodging] Hampton Inn, Howard Johnson Express [other] Albertson's/Sav-On, America's Tire, AT&T, AutoZone, Big-Lots, GNC, K-Mart, O'Reilly Parts, Radio Shack, Staples, Target, Verizon, Walgreens

EL CERRITO

Exit #	Services
96b a	CA 91, to Riverside, beaches
95	Magnolia Ave, E [gas] Chevron/Jack-in-the-Box/dsl [food] Islands Burgers, Lonestar Steaks, Shamrock's Grill [lodging] Residence Inn [other] AAA, Lowe's, Office Depot, W [gas] Mobil/Circle K, Shell [food] Baskin-Robbins, Burger King, Coco's, Golden China, Jersey's Pizza, Little Caesars, McDonald's, Sizzler, Subway [lodging] Holiday Inn Express [other] $Tree, AT&T, CVS Drug, El Tapatio Mkt, O'Reilly Parts, Rite Aid, Stater Bros Foods
93	Ontario Ave, to El Cerrito, E [gas] Shell/dsl [food] Sombrero Mexican, Starbucks [other] Mtn View Tire, vet, W [gas] 76/Circle K, Arco, Chevron [food] Chopstix, Denny's, Eatza Pizza, El Pollo Loco, Hawaiian BBQ, In-N-Out, Jack-in-the-Box, Juice It Up, KFC, Magic Wok, McDonald's, Miguel's Jr, Papa John's, Porky's Pizza, Quiznos, Rubio's, SpringHill Suites, Subway, Taco Bell, Tommy's Burgers, Wienerschnitzel [other] Albertson's/Sav-On, America's Tire, AutoZone, CVS Drug, Fresh&Easy Mkt, Home Depot, Long's Drug, Radio Shack, Sam's Club/gas, USPO, vet, Walmart
92	El Cerrito Rd
91	Cajalco Rd, E [food] 5 Guys Burgers, BJ's Grill, Bubba Jack's Roadhouse, Buffalo Wild Wings, Chick-fil-A, Chili's, Jamba Juice, King's Fish House, Macaroni Grill, Panera Bread, Starbucks, Wendy's [other] AT&T, Barnes&Noble, Best Buy, Kohl's, Marshall's, Michael's, Old Navy, PetCo, Ross, See's Candies, Staples, Target, World Mkt, W [gas] Mobil/dsl [food] Jack-in-the-Box, Juice It Up, NY Pizza, Subway [other] Stater Bros, vet
90	Weirick Rd, Dos Lagos Dr, E [gas] Arco/dsl [food] Citrus City Grille, Miguel's, Tap's Rest., TGIFriday's, Wood Ranch BBQ [other] 7 Oaks Gen Store, Trader Joe's
88	Temescal Cyn Rd, Glen Ivy, E [gas] Shell, W [gas] Arco/dsl [food] Carl's Jr, Tom's Farms/BBQ
85	Indian Truck Trail, W [food] Pizza Hut, Starbucks, Subway [other] CVS Drug, Von's Foods/dsl
81	Lake St
78	Nichols Rd, W [gas] Arco/dsl [other] Outlets/famous brands
77	CA 74, Central Ave, Lake Elsinore, E [gas] Arco, Chevron, Mobil/Circle K/dsl [food] Archibald's, Burger King, Chili's, Del Taco, Douglas Burgers, Hawaiian BBQ, Juice It Up, Panda Express, Submarina, Taco Del Mar, Tom's ChiliBurgers, Wendy's [other] $Tree, AT&T, Costco/gas, Lowe's, Petsmart, Staples, Valvoline,

INTERSTATE 15 Cont'd

LAKE ELSINORE

77 Continued
W [food] El Pollo Loco, Farmer Boys, Golden Chop Stix, IHOP, McDonald's, Papa John's, Starbucks, Subway, Wienerschnitzel [other] 99c Store, Home Depot, PetCo, Target, Verizon, Walgreens

75 Main St, Lake Elsinore, W [gas] Main St Gas/dsl [food] Gina's Rest. [other] Circle K, tires/repair

73 Railroad Cyn Rd, to Lake Elsinore, E [gas] 76/7-11, Shell/Circle K/dsl [food] Alberto's Mexican, Denny's, El Pollo Loco, In-N-Out, KFC, Peony Chinese, Starbucks [lodging] Holiday Inn Express [other] Albertson's, GNC, Jiffy Lube, O'Reilly Parts, URGENT CARE, Verizon, vet, Von's Foods, Walmart/McDonald's, W [gas] Arco, Chevron, Mobil/Circle K/dsl [food] Annie's Cafe, Cafe China, Carl's Jr, Coco's, Del Taco, Don Jose's Mexican, King Kabob, Kokoro Japanese, Los Gallos Mexican, McDonald's, My Buddies Pizza, Pizza Hut, Sizzler, Subway, Taco Bell, Vincenzo's [lodging] Best Western Lake Elsinore, Quality Inn, Travel Inn [other] 7-11, AutoZone, BigLots, Buick/GMC, Chevrolet, CVS Drug, Express Tire/auto, Firestone/auto, Ford, NAPA, Radio Shack, Rite Aid, Stater Bro's, vet, Walgreens

71 Bundy Cyn Rd, W [gas] Arco [food] Jack-in-the-Box

69 Baxter Rd, E [food] Pizza Factory

68 Clinton Keith Rd, E [gas] Chevron/dsl, USA [food] Denny's, Golden Spoon, Los Jilbetos Tacos, Los Reyes Grill, McDonald's, Panda Express, Starbucks, Subway [other] [H] Ace Hardware, Albertsons/Sav-on, W [gas] 7-11, Arco/dsl [food] Arriba Grill, Checkerboard Deli, D'Canter's Grill, Del Taco, Jack-in-the-Box, KFC/LJ Silver, Stadium Pizza, Starbucks, Submarina, Tresino's Italian, Yellow Basket Burgers [other] Baron's Mkt, Rite Aid, Stater Bro's

MURRIETA

65 California Oaks Rd, Kalmia St, E [gas] 76/Circle K/dsl, Chevron, Shell/7-11/dsl [food] Big Cheese Pizza, Burger King, Carl's Jr, Chili's, Chiptole Mexican, DQ, Jade Chinese, Jamba Juice, Jersey's, Jimenez Mexican, KFC, Little Caesars, Papa John's, Starbucks, Subway, Wings'N Things [lodging] Comfort Inn [other] $Tree, Albertson's/Sav-On, AutoZone, Express Tire, O'Reilly Parts, Radio Shack, Ralphs, Rite Aid, Target, Tuesday Morning, vet, Walgreens, W [gas] Arco/dsl, Chevron [food] Applebee's, Carrow's, Chick-fil-A, Farmer Boys, Jack-in-the-Box, Juice it Up, Pick Up Stix, Sizzlin Steer, Subway, Taco Bell [other] America's Tire, fun ctr, Giant RV Ctr, Kohl's, Lowe's, Office Depot, PetCo, Verizon

64 Murrieta Hot Springs Rd, to I-215, E [gas] 7-11, Shell/dsl [food] Buffalo Wild Wings, Carl's Jr, El Pollo Loco, Hungry Bull, Richie's Diner, Rubio's, Sizzler, Starbucks, Wendy's [other] Ralph's Foods, Rite Aid, Ross, Sam's Club/gas, Walgreens, W [gas] 7-11, Shell/Popeye's/dsl [food] Arby's, Chuy's, Coldstone, Denny's, IHOP, Jersey Mike's Subs, McDonald's, Panda Express, Starbucks, Subway, Tom's Burgers, Wienerschnitzel [other] 99c Store, AAA, American Tire Depot, AT&T, Best Buy, BigLots, Home Depot, Petsmart, Staples, Walmart/McDonald's

63 I-215 N (from nb), to Riverside

62 French Valley Pkwy (from sb, no return), W [food] Los Cabos [other] BMW, O'Reilly Parts, VW

61 CA 79 N, Winchester Rd, E [gas] 76/dsl, Chevron [food] 5 Guys Burgers, Baja Fresh, Baskin-Robbins/Togo's, BF Greek Rest., BJ's Rest., Burger King, CA Pizza Kitchen, Chick-fil-A, Chipotle Mexican, Coldstone, Corner Cafe, Del Taco, Dickey's BBQ, El Torito, Famous Dave's, Fatburger, Freebirds Burrito, Harry's Grill, Hometown Buffet, Islands Burgers, Jamba Juice, Lazy Dog Cafe, Lucille's BBQ, Macaroni Grill, McDonald's, Mimi's Cafe, Ming's, Olive Garden, Outback Steaks, Panda Express, Panera Bread, PF Chang's, Red Ginger Chinese, Red Lobster,

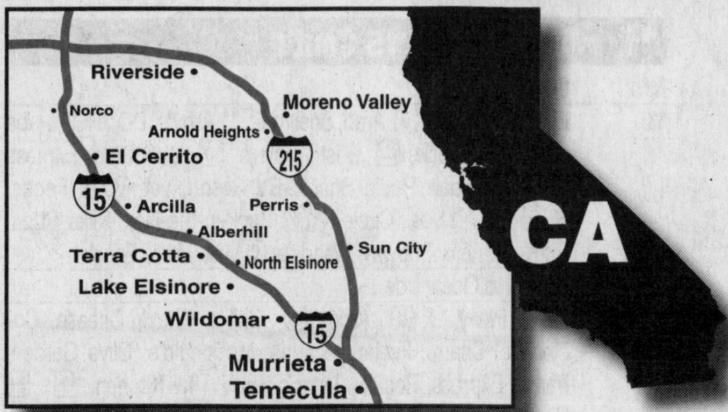

TEMECULA

61 Continued
Red Robin, Shakey's Pizza, Shogun Chinese, Souplantation, Starbucks, Subway, Taco Bell, TGIFriday's, Tilted Kilt, Wahoo's, Yellow Basket Hamburgers [other] $Tree, 99c Store, America's Tire, AT&T, AutoZone, Barnes&Noble, Costco/gas, CVS Drug, Express Tire, Express Tire, Food4Less, GNC, Hobby Lobby, Hyundai, JC Penney, Jo-Ann Fabrics, K-Mart, Lowe's, Macy's, Nissan, Office Depot, Old Navy, PepBoys, PetCo, Radio Shack, Ramona Tire, Roots Mkt, Sears/auto, See's Candies, TJ Maxx, Trader Joe's, Verizon, WinCo Foods, World Mkt, W [gas] Arco, Chevron/dsl [food] Arby's, Banzai Japanese, Chin's Gourmet Chinese, Del Taco, El Pollo Loco, Farmer Boys, In-N-Out, Jack-in-the-Box, Patsy's Country Kitchen, Serrano's Grill, Starbucks, Subway, Super China, Tacos El Gallo, Vail Ranch Steakhouse, Wendy's [lodging] Best Western, Extended Stay America, Fairfield Inn, Holiday Inn Express, La Quinta, Quality Inn [other] NAPA, Richardson's RV Ctr, st patrol, tires/repair, vet

59 Rancho California Rd, E [gas] Arco, Mobil/Circle K/dsl, Shell/dsl [food] Black Angus, Chili's, ClaimJumper, Del Taco, Golden Spoon, Jilberto's Mexican, Little Caesars, Marie Callender's, Pat&Oscar's Rest., Peony Chinese, Pizza Hut, RoundTable Pizza, Rubio's, Starbucks, Subway, Times Square NY Pizza [lodging] Embassy Suites [other] BigLots, CVS Drug, Ford, Mazda, Michael's, Subaru, Target, URGENT CARE, Verizon, vet, Von's Foods, W [gas] 76/Circle K/dsl, Chevron [food] Alberto's Mexican, Denny's, McDonald's, Mr Kabob Grill, Penfold's Cafe, Rosa's Café, Starbucks, Vince's Spaghetti [lodging] Hampton Inn, Motel 6, Rancho California Inn, Rodeway Inn, SpringHill Suites [other] to Old Town Temecula, USPO

58 CA 79 S, to Indio, Temecula, E [gas] Mobil/Circle K/dsl, Valero/Circle K/dsl [food] Carl's Jr, Del Taco, Domino's, Domino's, Francesca's Italian, Golden Bowl Asian, In-N-Out, Los Jilberto's, Starbucks, Utopizza, Wing-n-Things [other] 7-11, Ace Hardware, America's Tire, CVS Drug, Valvoline, W [gas] Arco, Shell/dsl [food] Baskin-Robbins, Eldorado Mexican, Garage Rest., Hungry Howie's, Leinzo Charro Mexican, Wienerschnitzel [lodging] Ramada Inn [other] Express Tire, Harley-Davidson

55mm **check sta nb**

54 Rainbow Valley Blvd, **2 mi** E [other] food, gas, W [other] CA Insp Sta

51 Mission Rd, to Fallbrook, W [other] [H]

46 CA 76, to Oceanside, Pala, E [other] RV camp, W [gas] Mobil/Circle K [food] McGrath's Grill [lodging] Quality Inn [other] Pala Meas Mkt

44mm San Luis Rey River

43 Old Hwy 395

41 Gopher Canyon Rd, Old Castle Rd, **1 mi** E [lodging] Welk Resort [other] gas, RV camping

37 Deer Springs Rd, Mountain Meadow Rd, W [gas] Arco

34 Centre City Pkwy (from sb)

INTERSTATE 15 Cont'd

Exit #	Services
	ESCONDIDO
33	El Norte Pkwy, **E** [gas] Arco, Shell/dsl [food] Arby's, DQ, IHOP, Papa John's, Starbucks [lodging] Best Western [other] CVS Drug, Express Tire/auto repair, Radio Shack, RV Resort, vet, Von's Foods, **W** [gas] 76/7-11/dsl, Circle K [food] Jack-in-the-Box, Killer Pizza, Rita's Custard, Subway, Wendy's [other] vet, Von's Foods
32	CA 78, to Oceanside
31	Valley Pkwy, **E** [gas] Arco [food] Chili's, ChuckeCheese, Cocina del Charro, Firehouse Subs, McDonald's, Olive Garden, Panda Express, Rock'N Jenny's Subs, Thai Kitchen [other] [H] Barnes&Noble, Meineke, Michael's, PetCo, URGENT CARE, **W** [gas] Express [food] 5 Guys Burgers, Applebee's, Burger King, Carl's Jr, Chipotle Mexican, Coco's, Del Taco, El Pollo Loco, In-N-Out, Jamba Juice, Mike's BBQ, Panera Bread, Pick Up Stix, Port of Subs, Primo's Mexican, Soup Plantation, Starbucks, Subway, Wendy's [lodging] Comfort Inn, Holiday Inn Express [other] 7-11, Albertson's, AT&T, BigLots, CVS Drug, Dick's, GNC, Home Depot, Lexus, Ross, Staples, Target, TJ Maxx, Verizon, World Mkt
30	9th Ave, Auto Parkway, **E** [other] Infiniti, Mercedes, **W** same as 31
29	Felicita Rd
28	Centre City Pkwy (from nb, no return), **E** [food] Center City Cafe [lodging] Escondido Lodge [other] vet
27	Via Rancho Pkwy, to Escondido, **E** [gas] Chevron/dsl, Shell [food] BJ's Rest., Cheesecake Factory, Macaroni Grill, On-the-Border, Panera Bread, Red Robin [other] JC Penney, Macy's, Nordstrom, San Diego Animal Park, Sears/auto, Target, **W** [gas] Shell/Quiznos/dsl [food] McDonald's, Starbucks, Subway [other] Verizon
26	W Bernardo Dr, to Highland Valley Rd, Palmerado Rd
24	Rancho Bernardo Rd, to Lake Poway, **E** [gas] Arco, Mobil/Circle K [food] Chef Chin, Cojita's Taco, Pizza Hut, Soup Plantation, Starbucks, Stirfresh, Sub Marina, Subway [lodging] Hilton Garden [other] AT&T, Barons Mkt, GNC, Von's Foods, **W** [gas] 76/Circle K, Chevron/7-11 [food] Elephant Bar Rest., Starbucks [lodging] Holiday Inn Express, Radisson
23	Bernardo Ctr Dr, **E** [gas] Chevron [food] Burger King, Carl's Jr, Coco's, Denny's, Hibachi Buffet, Jack-in-the-Box, Little Caesars, McDonald's, Quiznos, Robeks Juice, RoundTable Pizza, Rubio's [other] 7-11, CVS Drug, Express Tire/auto, Firestone/auto, Radio Shack, vet
	CARMEL MTN
22	Camino del Norte
21	Carmel Mtn Rd, **E** [gas] Chevron, Shell/dsl [food] Athens Greek, Baskin-Robbins, Boston Mkt, Broken Yolk Cafe, CA Pizza Kitchen, Carl's Jr, Chick-fil-A, China Fun, Chipotle Mexican, ClaimJumper, DQ Orange Julius, El Pollo Loco, Habit Burgers, In-N-Out, Islands Burgers, Jamba Juice, Little Tokyo, Marie Callender's, McDonald's, Olive Garden, O's American Kitchen, Panda Express, Panera Bread, Rubio's, Sombrero Mexican, Subway, Taco Bell, TGIFriday's, Wendy's, Which Wich? [lodging] Residence Inn [other] AT&T, Barnes&Noble, Best Buy, Costco/gas, GNC, Home Depot, Marshall's, Michael's, PetCo, Radio Shack, Ralph's Foods, Rite Aid, Ross, Sears Outlet, See's Candies, Sprouts Mkt, Staples, TJ Maxx, Trader Joe's, USPO, Valvoline, Verizon, **W** [gas] Chevron [food] Jack-in-the-Box, Starbucks [other] 7-11, Albertson's, Big O Tire, Office Depot
19	CA 56 W, Ted Williams Pkwy
18	Rancho Penasquitos Blvd, Poway Rd, **E** [gas] Arco [food] Alvero's Mexican, Papa John's [other] AAA, **W** [gas] 76/dsl, Mobil/dsl [food] IHOP, McDonald's, Mi Ranchito Mexican, MXN Cafe, NY Pizza, Starbucks, Subway [lodging] La Quinta [other] 7-11
17	Mercy Rd, Scripps Poway Pkwy, **E** [gas] USA/dsl [food] Chili's, Wendy's, Yanni's Grill [lodging] Residence Inn, SpringHill Suites **W** [gas] Chevron [food] KFC, Que Pasa Mexican, Starbucks
	MIRAMESA
16	Mira Mesa Blvd, to Lake Miramar, **E** [food] Bruski Burgers, ChuckeCheese, Denny's, Filippi's Pizza, Filippi's Pizza, Gyu-Kaku Japanese, Lucio's Mexican, Nok Thai, Pizza Hut, Shozen BBQ [lodging] Comfort Suites, Holiday Inn Express [other] Trader Joe's, USPO, **W** [gas] Arco, Shell [food] Applebee's, Arby's, Buca Italian, Coldstone, El Patron, In-N-Out, Islands Burgers, Jack-in-the-Box, Jamba Juice, Jersey Mike's Subs, McDonald's, Mimi's Café, MXN Mexican, On the Border, Panera Bread, Pick Up Stix, Popeye's, Rubio's, Starbucks, Subway, Wings n Things [other] Albertson's/Sav-On, AutoZone, Barnes&Noble, Best Buy, BigLots, CVS Drug, Discount Tire, GNC, Home Depot, Old Navy, Ralph's Foods, Rite Aid, Ross, USPO, Verizon
15	Carroll Canyon Rd, to Miramar College, **E** [food] Carl's Jr, Subway
14	Pomerado Rd, Miramar Rd, **W** [gas] Chevron/dsl, Mobil, Shell/dsl, USA/dsl [food] Carl's Jr, Chin's Rest., IHOP, Rice King, Subway [lodging] Best Western, Holiday Inn, Quality Inn [other] Audi/Porsche, aviation museum, Land Rover, vet
13	Miramar Way, US Naval Air Station
12	CA 163 S (from sb), to San Diego
11	to CA 52
10	Clairemont Mesa Blvd, **W** [food] Boll Weevil Rest., Carl's Jr, China Express, Giovanni's, Giovanni's Pizza, Jack-in-the-Box, Jersey Mike's, La Salsa, McDonald's, Panda Express, Primo's Mexican, Robeks, Rubio's, Spice House Cafe, Starbucks, Subway, Sunny Donuts, Taco Bell, Taco Bell, Togo's, Wendy's [other] 7-11, vet
9	CA 274, Balboa Ave
8	Aero Dr, **W** [gas] Arco, Chevron/dsl [food] Baskin-Robbins/Togo's, Jack-in-the-Box, McDonald's, Papa John's, Pick Up Stix, Rubio's, Sizzler, SmashBurger, Starbucks, Submarina, Subway, Taco Bell [lodging] Holiday Inn [other] $Tree, AT&T, Express Tire/auto, Fry's Electronics, Petsmart, Radio Shack, Verizon, Von's Foods, Walmart/McDonald's
	SAN DIEGO AREA
7b	Friars Rd W, **W** [food] Coldstone, Dragon Chinese, IHOP, Islands Burgers, Luna Grill, McDonald's, Oggi's Pizza, Playa Grill, Starbucks, Subway [other] Costco/gas, Lowe's, San Diego Stadium
7a	Friars Rd E
6b	I-8, E to El Centro, W to beaches
6a	Adams Ave, downtown
5b	El Cajon Blvd, **E** [gas] Pearson/dsl/E85/NG [food] Subway [other] Carquest, Ford, **W** [gas] Chevron/dsl, United Oil [food] Church's [other] PepBoys
5a	University Ave, **E** [gas] Chevron/dsl [food] Burger King, Jack-in-the-Box
3	I-805, N to I-5, S to San Ysidro
2b	(2c from nb)CA 94 W, downtown
2a	Market St, downtown
1c	National Ave, Ocean View Blvd
1b	(from sb) I-5 S, to Chula Vista
1a	(from sb) I-5 N. **I-15 begins/ends on I-5.**

INTERSTATE 40

Exit #	Services
155	California/Arizona state line, Colorado River, Pacific/Mountain time zone
153	Park Moabi Rd, to Rte 66, **N** boating, camping
149mm	**insp both lanes**
148	5 Mile Rd, to Topock, Rte 66 (from eb)

INTERSTATE 40 Cont'd

NEEDLES

Exit #	Services
144	US 95 S, E Broadway, Needles, N Chevron/dsl, Mobil, Shell/dsl/LP Domino's 99cStore, Harris Repair/towing, Rite Aid, S Best Value Inn $Tree, Stout Tires/repair
142	J St, Needles, N J St Gas, Valero/dsl Jack-in-the-Box, McDonald's Rodeway Inn Big O Tire, NAPA, S Denny's Days Inn, Motel 6 H
141	W Broadway, River Rd, Needles, N River City Pizza Best Motel, Desert Mirage Inn, River Valley Motel, S Chevron/dsl, Mobil/dsl, Shell/DQ/dsl Carl's Jr, Panda Garden, River Cafe, Taco Bell, Wagon Wheel Rest. Best Western, Budget Inn, Knights Inn, Relax Inn, Rio Del Sol Inn auto/RV/tire/repair
139	River Rd Cutoff (from eb), N Desert View RV Park, KOA, Hist Rte 66, rec area
133	US 95 N, to Searchlight, to Rte 66
120	Water Rd
115	Mountain Springs Rd, elev 2770, High Springs Summit
107	Goffs Rd, Essex, N gas/dsl/food, Hist Rte 66
106mm	**both lanes, full facilities, litter barrels, petwalk**
100	Essex Rd, Essex, N Mitchell Caverns, to Providence Mtn SP
78	Kelbaker Rd, to Amboy, E Mojave Nat Preserve, Kelso, S RV camping (14mi), Hist Rte 66
50	Ludlow, N 76/DQ, S Chevron/dsl Ludlow Cafe Ludlow Motel
33	Hector Rd, to Hist Rte 66
28mm	**both lanes, full facilities, litter barrels, petwalk vending**
23	Ft Cady Rd, to Newberry Spgs, N Mobil/Circle K/dsk, S Newberry Mtn RV Park, Twins Lake RV Park (8mi)
18	Newberry Springs, N Valero/dsl, S Chevron/Subway/dsl/LP
12	Barstow-Daggett Airport, N
7	Daggett, N RV camping (2mi), to Calico Ghost Town
5	Nebo St (from eb), to Hist Rte 66
2	USMC Logistics Base, N Pennywise Inn

BARSTOW

Exit #	Services
1	E Main St, Montara Rd, Barstow, **1 mi** N Chevron, Circle K, Circle K/dsl, Shell/dsl, Travelodge, USA/dsl, Valero Burger King, Carl's Jr, China Town Buffet, Del Taco, Denny's, Di Napoli's Italian, Grill It, Hollywood Subs, IHOP, Jack-in-the-Box, Jenny's Grill, Little Caesar's, LJ Silver, McDonald's, Panda Express, Popeye's, Starbucks, Taco Bell, Tom's Burgers, Wienerschnitzel Astrobudget Motel, Best Motel, Best Western, Budget Inn, CA Inn, Days Inn, Desert Inn, EconoLodge, Economy Inn, Motel 6, Quality Inn/rest., Ramada Inn, Rodeway Inn, Super 8 $Tree, 99Cent Store, AutoZone, Family$, O'Reilly Parts, Radio Shack, U-Haul/LP, Von's Foods, S Arco Walmart/McDonald's/auto
0mm	**I-40 begins/ends on I-15 in Barstow.**

INTERSTATE 80

Exit #	Services
208	California/Nevada state line
201	Farad
199	Floristan
194	Hirschdale Rd, N Stampede Dam, to Boca Dam, S RV Park
191	(from wb), **inspection sta, weigh sta**
190	Overland Trail

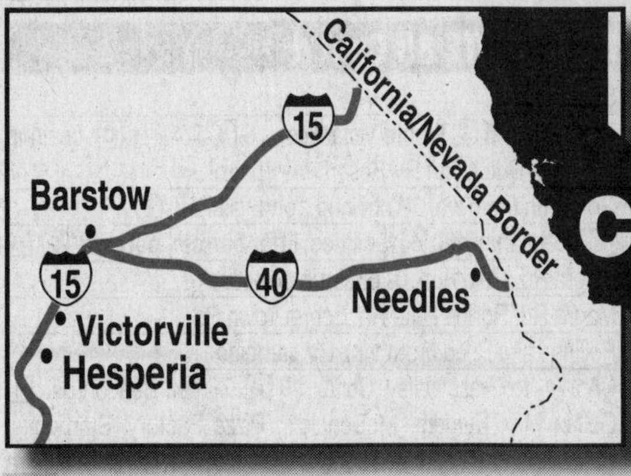

CA

TRUCKEE

Exit #	Services
188	CA 89 N, CA 267, to N Shore Lake Tahoe, N Coachland RV Park, USFS, S same as 186
186	Central Truckee (no eb return), S 76/dsl, Beacon Burger Me, Casa Baeza Mexican, El Toro Bravo Mexican, Jax Truckee Diner, Marg's Taco Bistro, Wagon Train Cafe Hilltop Lodge, Truckee Hotel
185	CA 89 S, to N Lake Tahoe, N DQ, El Sancho, Jiffy's Pizza, Panda Express, Port of Subs, RoundTable Pizza, Starbucks, Zano's Pizza H 7-11, Ace Hardware, hwy patrol, NAPA, New Moon Natural Foods, Rite Aid, Safeway Foods, URGENT CARE, Verizon, S Shell/dsl Bill's Rotisseire, McDonald's, Subway, Village Pizzaria auto repair, CVS Drug, O'Reilly Parts, RV camping, SaveMart Foods, to Squaw Valley
184	Donner Pass Rd, Truckee, N Shell/dsl La Bamba Mexican, Smokey's Kitchen, Taco Station Sunset Inn vet, S 76, Chevron/dsl Taco Bell Truckee Donner Lodge chain service, RV camp/dump, to Donner SP
181mm	vista point both lanes
180	Donner Lake (from wb), S Donner Lake Village Resort
177mm	Donner Summit, elev 7239, **both lanes, full facilities, litter barrels, petwalk view area**
176	Castle Park, Boreal Ridge Rd, S Boreal Inn/rest. Pacific Crest Trailhead, skiing
174	Soda Springs, Norden, S Sugar Bowl/dsl Summit Rest. Donner Summit Lodge chain services
171	Kingvale, S Shell
168	Rainbow Rd, to Big Bend, S Rainbow Lodge/rest. RV camping
166	Big Bend (from eb), no facilities
165	Cisco Grove, N RV camp/dump, skiing, snowmobiling, S Chevron/dsl chain services
164	Eagle Lakes Rd
161	CA 20 W, to Nevada City, Grass Valley
160	Yuba Gap, S boating, camping, phone, picnic tables, skiing, snowpark
158	Laing Rd, S Sierra Woods Lodge/café USPO
157mm	**brake check area, wb**
158a	Emigrant Gap (from eb), S Sierra Woods Lodge/café USPO
156	Nyack Rd, Emigrant Gap, S Shell/Burger King/dsl Nyack Café USPO
156mm	**brake check area**
155	Blue Canyon
150	Drum Forebay
148b	Baxter, N chainup services, food, phone, RV camping
148a	Crystal Springs
146	Alta

CA

INTERSTATE 80 Cont'd

COLFAX

Exit #	Services
145	Dutch Flat, N [food] Monte Vista Rest., S [gas] 76/dsl [other] chainup services, Dutch Flat RV Resort, hwy patrol
144	Gold Run (from wb), N chainup, food, gas/dsl [phone]
143mm	[RS] both lanes, full [handicap] facilities, litter barrels, petwalk [phone] [picnic]
143	Magra Rd, Gold Run, N chainup services
140	Magra Rd, Rollins Lake Rd, Secret Town Rd
139	Rollins Lake Road (from wb), RV camping
135	CA 174, to Grass Valley, Colfax, N [gas] 76/dsl, Beacon/dsl [food] Colfax Max Burgers, McDonald's, Pizza Factory, Starbucks, Taco Bell, TJ's Roadhouse [lodging] Colfax Motel [other] NAPA, Sierra Mkt Foods, S [gas] Chevron/dsl, Valero/dsl [food] Shang Garden Chinese, Subway
133	Canyon Way, to Colfax, S [food] Dine'n Dash Cafe [other] Chevrolet, Plaza Tire
131	Cross Rd, to Weimar
130	W Paoli Lane, to Weimar, S [gas] Weimar Store/dsl
129	Heather Glen, elev 2000 ft
128	Applegate, N [gas] Valero/dsl/LP [other] chainup services
125	Clipper Gap, Meadow Vista
124	Dry Creek Rd, [other]
123	Bell Rd
122	Foresthill Rd, Ravine Rd, Auburn, N [other] RV camping/dump, S [food] Burger King, La Bonte's Rest., Sizzler, Starbucks, Subway [lodging] Best Western, Quality Inn [other] same as 121
121	Lincolnway (from eb), Auburn, N [gas] Flyers/dsl, Mobil, Valero/dsl [food] Denny's, JimBoy's Tacos, Starbucks, Taco Bell, Wienerschnitzel [lodging] Comfort Inn, Foothills Motel, Motel 6, Super 8, S [gas] Arco, Beacon/dsl, Chevron/dsl, Gas&Shop, Shell/dsl [food] Black Bear Diner, Burger King, Burrito Shop, Carl's Jr, Hawaiian BBQ, Jack-in-the-Box, Joe Caribe Bistro, KFC, La Bonte's Rest., McDonald's, Pete's Grill, Sierra Grill, Sizzler, Starbucks, Subway [lodging] Best Western, Quality Inn [other] Ikeda's Mkt, Raley's Foods, Verizon
120	Russell Ave (from wb), same as 121, to Lincolnway from eb
119c	Elm Ave, Auburn, N [gas] 76/dsl, Shell/dsl [food] Foster's, Starbucks [lodging] Holiday Inn [other] CVS Drug, Grocery Outlet, Rite Aid, SaveMart Foods, Staples, Verizon
119b	CA 49, to Grass Valley, Auburn, N [gas] 76/dsl, Shell/dsl [food] In-N-Out [lodging] Holiday Inn [other] RV Connection, Staples
119a	Maple St, Nevada St, Old Town Auburn, S [gas] Valero [food] Cafe Delicias, Mary Belle's, Tio Pepe Mexican [other] USPO
118	Ophir Rd (from wb)
116	CA 193, to Lincoln
115	Indian Hill Rd, Newcastle, N [other] transmissions, USPO, S [gas] Flyers/dsl, Valero/dsl [food] Denny's [other] CHP
112	Penryn, N [gas] 76/dsl, Valero/dsl [food] Ground Cow Rest., Subway
110	Horseshoe Bar Rd, to Loomis, N [food] Burger King, RoundTable Pizza, Starbucks, Taco Bell [other] Raley's Food
109	Sierra College Blvd, N [gas] 7-11/dsl, Arco/dsl, Chevron/McDonald's/dsl [food] Blast Pizza, Carl's Jr, Chipotle, Noodles&Co, Panera Bread, Subway [other] Camping World RV Ctr, Rocklin RV Ctr, Ross, Steinmart, Target, Tesla, Verizon, S [food] Starbucks [other] Petsmart, Walmart
108	Rocklin Rd, N [gas] Valero/dsl [food] A&W/KFC, Adalberto's Mexican, Arby's, Baskin-Robbins, Denny's, Golden Dragon, Jack-in-the-Box, Jamba Juice, Milo's, Mongolian BBQ, Papa Murphy's, RoundTable Pizza, Starbucks, Subway, Taco Bell [lodging] Days Inn, Heritage Inn, Howard Johnson [other] CVS Drug, GNC, Land Rover, Mercedes, Porsche, Radio Shack, Safeway Foods, S [gas] Arco [food] Little Caesar's [lodging] Rocklin Park Hotel [other] vet
106	CA 65, to Lincoln, Marysville, 1 mi N on Stanford Ranch R [gas] 76, Arco, Shell [food] Black Bear Diner, Carl's Jr, Cheesecak Factory, Chipotle, IHOP, Jack-in-the-Box, KFC, Olive Garde On-the-Border, PF Changs, TGIFriday [lodging] Holiday Inn Expres [other] AutoZone, Barnes&Noble, Best Buy, Costco, Goodyea auto, JC Penney, Macy's, Marshall's, Michael's, Nordstrom's Old Navy, Ross, Sears/auto, Sprouts Mkt, Staples
105b	Taylor Rd, to Rocklin (from eb), N [food] Cattlemen's Rest., S [gas] 76/Burger King/dsl, Chevron [food] Islands Burgers, Subwa Tahoe Joe's [lodging] Courtyard, Fairfield Inn, Hilton Garden, Holida Inn Express, Larkspur Suites, Residence Inn [other] [H] funpark
105a	Atlantic St, Eureka Rd, S [gas] 76/7-11/dsl, Shell/Circle K [food] Brookfield's Rest., Chicago Fire Rest, In-N-Out, Taco Bell, Wendy's [other] [H] Acura, America'sTire, Buick/GMC, Carmax, Chevrolet, Chrysler/Dodge/Jeep, Fiat, Ford, Home Depot, Honda Hyundai, Infiniti, Kia, Lexus, Mazda, Nissan, Petsmart, Subaru Target, Toyota/Scion, VW
103b a	Douglas Blvd, N [gas] 76/dsl, Arco/dsl, Chevron/7-11, Shell/ds [food] Burger King, Carolina's Mexican, Claim Jumper, McDonald's Mongolian BBQ, Popeyes, Starbucks, Subway [lodging] Best Western, Extended Stay America, Heritage Inn [other] $Tree, Ace Hardware, Autozone, Big O Tire, BigLots, BrakeMasters, Goodyea Grocery Outlet, Midas, O'Reilly Parts, Rite Aid, Trader Joe's, S [food] Carl's Jr, Carrow's, Chevy's, Del Taco, Denny's, Jack-in-the-Box Lorenzo's Mexican, Outback Steaks, Panera Bread, Rubio's, Sizzler, Subway [lodging] Best Western, Hampton Inn [other] [H], Fry's Electronics, Hobby Lobby, Office Depot, Ross, Target
102	Riverside Ave, Auburn Blvd, to Roseville, N [gas] Arco/dsl, Valero/dsl [food] Starbucks [other] auto repair, Meineke, S [gas] Chevron/7-11, Shell, Towne Mart [food] Back 40 TX BBQ, Baskin-Robbins, CA Burgers, Jack-in-the-Box, Subway, The Statior Bistro [other] $General, auto repair, AutoZone, BMW Motorcycles, Camping World RV Ctr, K-Mart, NAPA, Schwab Tire
100	Antelope Rd, to Citrus Heights, N [gas] 76 [food] Carl's Jr, Extreme Hummus, Giant Pizza, McDonald's, Papa Murphy's, Popeye's, RoundTable Pizza, Subway, Taco Bell, Wendy's [other] $Tree, 7-11, O'Reilly Parts, Raley's Foods, vet
100mm	weigh sta both lanes
98	Greenback Lane, Elkhorn Blvd, Orangedale, Citrus Heights, N [food] Baskin Robbins, Carl's Jr, Little Caesar's, McDonald's, Pizza Hut, Subway, Taco Bell [other] $General, CVS Drug, Radio Shack, Safeway Foods
96	Madison Ave, N [gas] Chevron/dsl, Valero/dsl [food] Brookfield's Rest., Denny's, El Malecon Mexican, Jack-in-the-Box, Mongolian BBQ, Starbucks [lodging] Motel 6, Super 8 [other] funpark, to McClellan AFB, S [gas] Arco, Shell/dsl [food] Boston Mkt, Burger King, Chipotle Mexican, El Pollo Loco, IHOP, In-N-Out, Jack-in-the-Box, McDonald's, Panda Express, Starbucks, Strings Italian, Subway, Wienerschnitzel [lodging] Crowne Plaza, La Quinta [other] 7-11, Acura, AT&T, Chevrolet, Firestone/auto, Ford, Office Depot, PepBoys, Schwab Tire, Target, Verizon, Walgreens
95	CA 99 S
94b	Auburn Blvd
94a	Watt Ave, N [gas] 76/dsl, Arco [food] Carl's Jr, Golden Corral, Jack-in-the-Box, KFC, McDonald's, Panda Express, Starbucks, Subway, Taco Bell [lodging] Courtyard Inn, Mega Inn [other] $Tree, Firestone/auto, McClellan AFB, Walmart, S [gas] 76/dsl, Arco, Chevron, Shell [food] China Taste, Denny's, Jimboy's Tacos, Kim Long Noodle House, Quiznos, Starbucks, Wendy's [lodging] Economy Inn

AUBURN

ROCKLIN

CITRUS HEIGHTS

SACRAMENTO

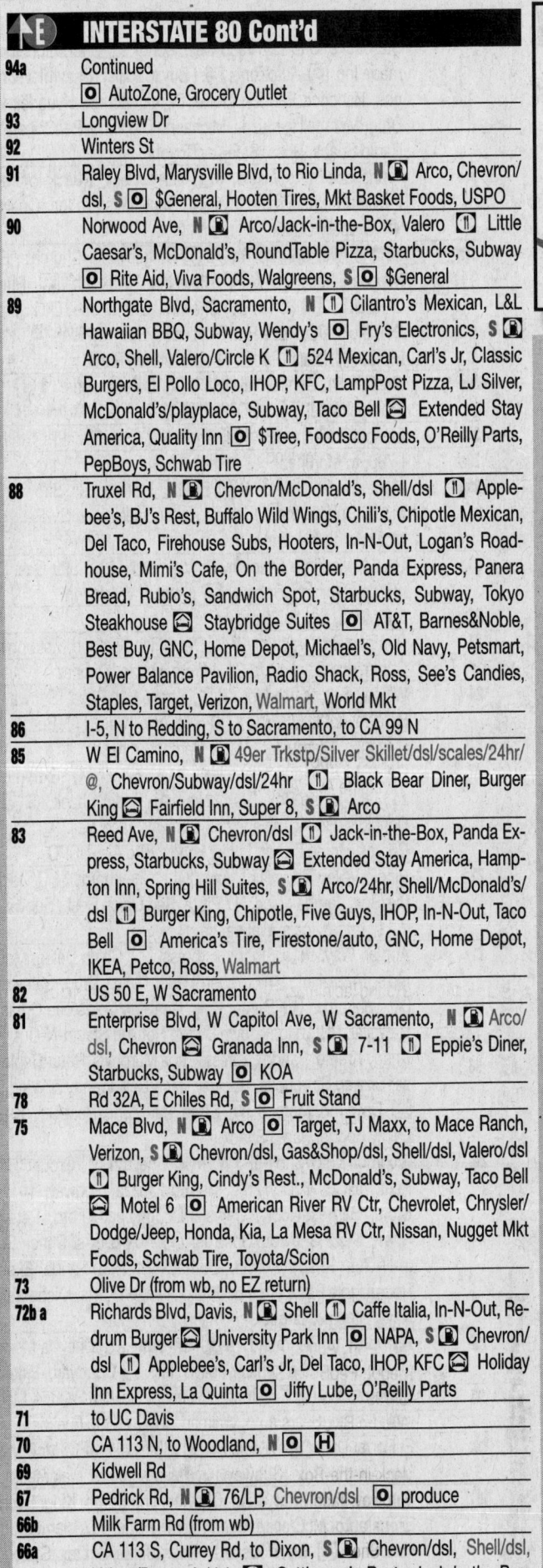

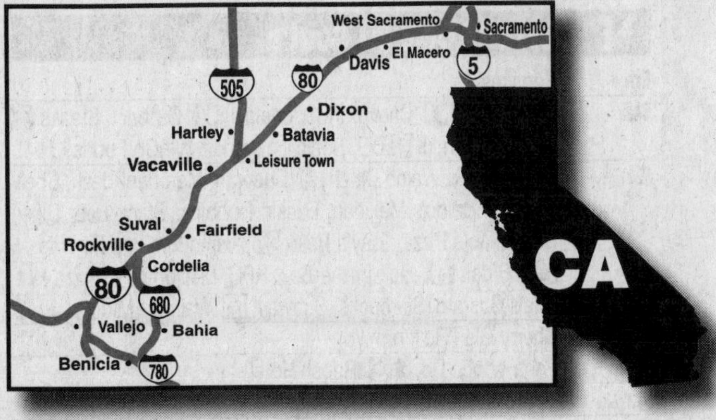

E INTERSTATE 80 Cont'd

SACRAMENTO

94a Continued
[other] AutoZone, Grocery Outlet

93 Longview Dr

92 Winters St

91 Raley Blvd, Marysville Blvd, to Rio Linda, N [gas] Arco, Chevron/dsl, S [other] $General, Hooten Tires, Mkt Basket Foods, USPO

90 Norwood Ave, N [gas] Arco/Jack-in-the-Box, Valero [food] Little Caesar's, McDonald's, RoundTable Pizza, Starbucks, Subway [other] Rite Aid, Viva Foods, Walgreens, S [other] $General

89 Northgate Blvd, Sacramento, N [food] Cilantro's Mexican, L&L Hawaiian BBQ, Subway, Wendy's [other] Fry's Electronics, S [gas] Arco, Shell, Valero/Circle K [food] 524 Mexican, Carl's Jr, Classic Burgers, El Pollo Loco, IHOP, KFC, LampPost Pizza, LJ Silver, McDonald's/playplace, Subway, Taco Bell [lodging] Extended Stay America, Quality Inn [other] $Tree, Foodsco Foods, O'Reilly Parts, PepBoys, Schwab Tire

88 Truxel Rd, N [gas] Chevron/McDonald's, Shell/dsl [food] Applebee's, BJ's Rest, Buffalo Wild Wings, Chili's, Chipotle Mexican, Del Taco, Firehouse Subs, Hooters, In-N-Out, Logan's Roadhouse, Mimi's Cafe, On the Border, Panda Express, Panera Bread, Rubio's, Sandwich Spot, Starbucks, Subway, Tokyo Steakhouse [lodging] Staybridge Suites [other] AT&T, Barnes&Noble, Best Buy, GNC, Home Depot, Michael's, Old Navy, Petsmart, Power Balance Pavilion, Radio Shack, Ross, See's Candies, Staples, Target, Verizon, Walmart, World Mkt

86 I-5, N to Redding, S to Sacramento, to CA 99 N

85 W El Camino, N [gas] 49er Trkstp/Silver Skillet/dsl/scales/24hr/@, Chevron/Subway/dsl/24hr [food] Black Bear Diner, Burger King [lodging] Fairfield Inn, Super 8, S [gas] Arco

83 Reed Ave, N [gas] Chevron/dsl [food] Jack-in-the-Box, Panda Express, Starbucks, Subway [lodging] Extended Stay America, Hampton Inn, Spring Hill Suites, S [gas] Arco/24hr, Shell/McDonald's/dsl [food] Burger King, Chipotle, Five Guys, IHOP, In-N-Out, Taco Bell [other] America's Tire, Firestone/auto, GNC, Home Depot, IKEA, Petco, Ross, Walmart

82 US 50 E, W Sacramento

81 Enterprise Blvd, W Capitol Ave, W Sacramento, N [gas] Arco/dsl, Chevron [lodging] Granada Inn, S [gas] 7-11 [food] Eppie's Diner, Starbucks, Subway [other] KOA

78 Rd 32A, E Chiles Rd, S [other] Fruit Stand

DAVIS

75 Mace Blvd, N [gas] Arco [other] Target, TJ Maxx, to Mace Ranch, Verizon, S [gas] Chevron/dsl, Gas&Shop/dsl, Shell/dsl, Valero/dsl [food] Burger King, Cindy's Rest., McDonald's, Subway, Taco Bell [lodging] Motel 6 [other] American River RV Ctr, Chevrolet, Chrysler/Dodge/Jeep, Honda, Kia, La Mesa RV Ctr, Nissan, Nugget Mkt Foods, Schwab Tire, Toyota/Scion

73 Olive Dr (from wb, no EZ return)

72b a Richards Blvd, Davis, N [gas] Shell [food] Caffe Italia, In-N-Out, Redrum Burger [lodging] University Park Inn [other] NAPA, S [gas] Chevron/dsl [food] Applebee's, Carl's Jr, Del Taco, IHOP, KFC [lodging] Holiday Inn Express, La Quinta [other] Jiffy Lube, O'Reilly Parts

71 to UC Davis

70 CA 113 N, to Woodland, N [other] [H]

69 Kidwell Rd

67 Pedrick Rd, N [gas] 76/LP, Chevron/dsl [other] produce

66b Milk Farm Rd (from wb)

66a CA 113 S, Currey Rd, to Dixon, S [gas] Chevron/dsl, Shell/dsl, Valero/Popeye's/dsl [food] Cattlemen's Rest., Jack-in-the-Box,

66a Continued
La Cocina, Papa Murphy's, Subway, Wendy's [lodging] Country Inn Suites [other] Schwab Tires, Walmart

64 Pitt School Rd, to Dixon, S [gas] Chevron/24hr, Valero/24hr [food] Arby's, Asian Garden, Baskin Robbins, Burger King, Capital China, Denny's, IHOP, Little Caesar's, Maria's Mexican, Mary's Pizza, McDonald's, Pizza Guys, Solano Bakery, Starbucks, Subway, Taco Bell [lodging] Best Western, Motel 6 [other] Safeway/dsl

63 Dixon Ave, Midway Rd, N [gas] Truck Stp/dsl, S [gas] Arco/LP/lube, Chevron/dsl [food] Alheli's Drive Thru, Carl's Jr, Mr Taco [lodging] Super 8 [other] Dixon Fruit Mkt

60 Midway Rd, Lewis Rd, Elmyra, N [other] Produce Mkt, RV camping (3mi)

59 Meridian Rd, Weber Rd

57 Leisure Town Rd, N [other] [H] Camping World, S [gas] 76/McDonald's, Arco, Chevron/dsl, QuikStop [food] Black Oak Rest., Clay Oven Grill, Hideaway Grill, Jack-in-the-Box, King's Buffet, Popeye's, Starbucks, Subway, Taco Bell [lodging] Comfort Suites, Extended Stay America, Fairfield Inn, Holiday Inn Express, Motel 6, Quality Inn, Residence Inn [other] Buick/GMC, Chevrolet, Chrysler/Dodge/Jeep, Harley-Davidson, Home Depot, Honda, Kohl's, Mazda, Nissan, Toyota, VW

VACAVILLE

56 I-505 N, to Winters

55 Nut Tree Pkwy, Monte Vista Dr, Allison Dr, N [gas] 7-11, 76/Circle K, Chevron [food] Boudin SF Sourdough, Buckhorn BBQ, Buffalo Wild Wings, Burger King, Chipotle, Denny's, El Pollo Loco, Fenton's Creamery, Firehouse Subs, Five Guys, Food Court, Habit Burger, Hawaiian BBQ, Hisui Japanese, IHOP, Jamba Juice, Krispy Kreme, McDonald's, Murillo's Mexican, Nations Burger, Noodles&Co, Panda Express, Panera Bread, Pelayo's Mexican, Pieology Pizza, Round Table Pizza, Rubio's, Starbucks, Subway, Taco Bell, Wendy's, Yen King Chinese [lodging] Best Value Inn, Best Western, Super 8 [other] America's Tire, Best Buy, Big O Tire, CVS Drug, Firestone/auto, Lowe's Whse, Michael's, Nugget Foods, Old Navy, Petsmart, See's Candies, U-Haul, Verizon, World Mkt, S [gas] Arco/24hr, Chevron/24hr [food] Applebee's, BJ's Grill, Black Oak Rest., Carl's Jr, Chick-fil-A, Chili's, Coldstone Creamery, Dickey's BBQ, Favela's Mexican Grill, Freebirds Burrito, Grocery Outlet, Home Towne Buffet, In-N-Out, Jack-in-the-Box, Jamba Juice, Mel's Diner, Olive Garden, Popeye's, Red Robin, Starbucks, Starbucks, String's Italian, Subway, Tahoe Joe's Steaks, Togo's [lodging] Comfort Suites, Courtyard, Fairfield Inn, Holiday Inn Express, Motel 6, Residence Inn [other] [H] GMC, GNC, Jo-Ann Fabrics, Marshall's, PetCo, Ross, Safeway, Sam's Club/dsl, Staples, Target, Vacaville Stores/famous brands, Walmart/McDonald's

54b Mason St, Peabody Rd, N [gas] Chevron/7-11, Conservative Fuel/dsl [lodging] Hampton Inn [other] CVS Drug, NAPA, O'Reilly Parts, Schwab Tire, S [gas] Shell [food] Carl's Jr, Domino's, Starbucks, Subway [other] $Tree, 7-11, Costco/gas

= gas = food = lodging = other = rest stop

CA

INTERSTATE 80 Cont'd

Exit #	Services
54a	Davis St, N Chevron/McDonald's Outback Steaks Hampton Inn, S DQ, Sonic repair, WinCo Foods
53	Merchant St, Alamo Dr, N Chevron, Merchant/desk, Shell/dsl Baldo's Mexican, Baskin-Robbins, Black Bear Diner, RoundTable Pizza, Tony's Rest. Alamo Inn BigLots, S 76/dsl Jack-in-the-Box, KFC, McDonald's, Pizza Hut, Rita's Custard, Starbucks, Subway Walmart Mkt
52	Cherry Glen Rd (from wb)
51b	Pena Adobe Rd, S Ranch Hotel
51a	Lagoon Valley Rd, Cherry Glen
48	N Texas St, Fairfield, S Arco/24hr, Chevron, Shell El Pollo Loco, Jim Boy's Tacos, Panda Express, RoundTable Pizza, Starbucks, Subway, Texas Roadhouse Longs Drugs, Raley's Foods
47	Waterman Blvd, N Dynasty Chinese, Loard's Icecream, RoundTable Pizza, Starbucks, Strings Italian Chevrolet/Cadillac, Safeway, to Austin's Place, S museum, to Travis AFB
45	Travis Blvd, Fairfield, N Arco/24hr, Chevron/24hr Baskin-Robbins, Burger King, Denny's, In-N-Out, McDonald's, Peking Rest., Subway, Taco Bell Courtyard, Motel 6 CHP, Ford, Harley-Davidson, Hyundai, Nissan, PetCo, Raley's Foods, S BizWiz Tasty Burgers, Carino's Italian, Chevy's Mexican, Chipotle Mexican, Coldstone Creamery, FreshChoice Rest., Marie Callender's, Mimi's Café, Panda Express, Quizno's, Red Lobster, Redbrick Pizza, Starbucks Hilton Garden H Barnes&Noble, Best Buy, Cost+, JC Penney, Macy's, mall, Michael's, Ross, Sears/auto, Trader Joe's, World Mkt
44	W Texas St, same as 45, Fairfield, N Shell/dsl, Valero/dsl ChuckeCheese, Gordito's Mexican, Starbucks Extended Stay America Staples, S Valero Baldo's Mexican, McDonald's, Paleyo's Mexican, Scenario's Pizza Acura/Honda, Chrysler/Jeep/Dodge, FoodMaxx, Home Depot, Hyundai, Infiniti, Mitsubishi, Nissan, Target, Toyota, Volvo, Walgreens
43	CA 12 E, Abernathy Rd, Suisun City, S Budweiser Plant, Walmart
42mm	**weigh sta both lanes**
41	Suisan Valley Rd, N Homewood Suites, Staybridge Suites, S 76/dsl/24hr, Arco/24hr, Chevron, Shell/dsl, Valero Arby's, Bravo's Pizza, Burger King, Carl's Jr, Denny's, Green Bamboo, Jack-in-the-Box, McDonald's, Starbucks, Subway, Taco Bell, Wendy's Best Western, Comfort Inn, Days Inn, Fairfield Inn, Holiday Inn Express Ray's RV Ctr, Scandia FunCtr
40	I-680 (from wb)
39b	Green Valley Rd, I-680 (from eb), N Hawaiian BBQ, Peloyas Mexican, RoundTable Pizza, Starbucks, Sticky Rice Bistro, Subway Homewood Suites, Staybridge Suites Costco/gas, Longs Drug, Safeway, TJ Maxx, S Arco
39a	Red Top Rd, N 76/Circle K/24hr Jack-in-the-Box
36	American Canyon Rd
34mm	**wb, full facilities, info, litter barrels, petwalk vista parking**
33b a	CA 37, to San Rafael, Columbus Pkwy, N Chevron/dsl Baskin-Robbins, Carl's Jr. Best Western, Courtyard funpark, S same as 32
32	Redwood St, to Vallejo, N 76 Denny's, Panda Garden Best Inn, Motel 6 H S Arco, BonFair, Shell Applebee's, Black Angus, Chevy's Mexican, Coldstone Creamery, IHOP, Jamba Juice, Lyon's Rest., McDonald's, Mtn. Mike's Pizza, Olive Garden, Panda Express, Red Lobster, Rubio's,
32	Continued Starbucks, Subway, Taco Bell, Wendy's Comfort Inn, Ramada Inn AutoZone, Best Buy, Cadillac/Chevrolet, Costco gas, Hancock Fabrics, Home Depot, Honda, Hyundai, Longs Drug, Marshall's, Mazda, Michael's, Old Navy, PepBoys, PetCo Radio Shack, Ross, Safeway, Toyota
31b	Tennessee St, to Vallejo, S Valero/dsl Jack-in-the-Box Pacifica Pizza, Pizza Guys Great Western Inn, Quality Inn Grocery Outlet
31a	Solano Ave, Springs Rd, N Burger King, Church's, El Rey Mexican, Taco Bell Deluxe Inn, Relax Inn Rite Aid U-Haul, S Chemco, Chevron, Grand Gas, QuikStop Domino's, DQ, Pizza Hut, Starbucks, Subway, Wok Islander Motel Island Pacific Foods, Kragen Parts
30c	Georgia St, Central Vallejo, N Safeway/gas, S Shell/Starbucks/dsl McDonald's California Motel
30b	Benicia Rd (from wb), S Shell/dsl McDonald's, Starbucks
30a	I-780, to Martinez
29b	Magazine St, Vallejo, N BPG Starbucks, Subway 7 Motel, Budget Inn, El Rancho Tradewinds RV Park, S McDonald's Travel Inn 7-11
29a	CA 29, Maritime Academy Dr, Vallejo, N 5 Star Gas, Chevron/dsl/24hr Subway Motel 6, Vallejo Inn
28mm	**toll plaza, pay toll from eb**
27	Pomona Rd, Crockett, N Dead Fish Seafood, vista point
26	Cummings Skyway, to CA 4 (from wb), to Martinez
24	Willow Ave, to Rodeo, N Straw Hat Pizza, Subway Safeway/24hr, USPO, S 76/Circle K/dsl Burger King, Mazatlan, Starbucks, Willow Garden Chinese
23	CA 4, to Stockton, Hercules, N Shell Extreme Pizza, Jack-in-the-Box, Starbucks Radio Shack, S McDonald's, RoundTable Pizza, Subway, Taco Bell BigLots, Curves, Home Depot, Lucky Foods, Rite Aid, USPO
22	Pinole Valley Rd, S Arco/24hr, Chevron/dsl Jack-in-the-Box, Jamba Juice, NY Pizza, Red Onion Rest., Subway 7-11, Trader Joe's, Walgreens
21	Appian Way, N Pinole Express China Delite, McDonald's, Pizza Hut Kragen Parts, Longs Drug, Safeway, S Valero/dsl Burger King, Carl's Jr, Coldstone Creamery, Hawaiian BBQ, HomeTown Buffet, HotDog Sta, In-N-Out, KFC, Krispy Kreme, Panda Express, Papa Murphy's, RoundTable Pizza, Sizzler, Starbucks, Subway, Taco Bell, Wendy's, Wing Stop Days Inn, Motel 6 $Tree, AutoZone, Best Buy, K-Mart, Lucky Foods, Radio Shack
20	Richmond Pkwy, to I-580 W, N Chevron Ground Round Rest., IHOP, McDonald's, Me&Ed's Pizza, Subway 99c Store, Barnes&Noble, Chrysler/Dodge/Jeep, Ford, Petsmart, Ross, S Chevron, Shell/dsl Applebee's, Chuck Steak, In-N-Out, Krispy Kreme, Outback Steaks, Panda Express, RoundTable Pizza FoodMaxx, Kragen Parts, Michael's, Old Navy, Staples, Target
19b	Hilltop Dr, to Richmond, N Chevron Chevy's Mexican, Olive Garden, Red Lobster, Tokyo Rest. Courtyard, Extended Stay America Firestone, JC Penney, Jo-Ann Fabrics, Macy's, mall, Nissan, Sears/auto, Walmart, S Hilltop Fuel/dsl
19a	El Portal Dr, to San Pablo, S SMP KFC, McDonalds, Mtn. Mike's Pizza, Subway Raley's Foods, Walgreens
18	San Pablo Dam Rd, N Chevron Burger King, Denny's, El Pollo Loco, Empire Buffet, Jack-in-the-Box, Jamba Juice, Nations Burgers, Popeye's, RoundTable Pizza, Starbucks, Subway, Taco Bell Holiday Inn Express H $Tree,

FAIRFIELD

VALLEJO

RICHMOND

INTERSTATE 80 Cont'd

18	Continued AutoZone, FoodMaxx, Lucky Foods, Walgreens, S CamperLand RV Ctr
17	Macdonald Ave (from eb), McBryde Ave (from wb), Richmond, N Arco/24hr Burger King, Church's, S Chevron/24hr Wendy's auto repair, Safeway
16	San Pablo Ave, to Richmond, San Pablo, S Chevron KFC, LJ Silver, Subway, Wendy's Safeway
15	Cutting Blvd, Potrero St, to I-580 Br (from wb), to El Cerrito, N Arco Panda Express Target, S Chevron Carrow's Rest., Church's, Denny's, IHOP, Jack-in-the-Box, Little Caesar's, McDonald's, Starbucks $Tree, Home Depot, Honda, Staples, Walgreens
14b	Carlson Blvd, El Cerrito, N 76 40 Flags Motel, S Best Value Inn
14a	Central Ave, El Cerrito, S 76, Valero Burger King, KFC, Nations Burgers
13	to I-580 (from eb), Albany
12	Gilman St, to Berkeley, N Golden Gate Fields Racetrack, S Target
11	University Ave, to Berkeley, S 76, University Gas La Quinta to UC Berkeley
10	CA 13, to Ashby Ave
9	Powell St, Emeryville, N Shell Chevy's Mexican Hilton Garden, S 76 Burger King, CA Pizza Kitchen, Denny's, Elephant Bar/Grill, Jamba Juice, PF Chang's, Starbucks, Togo's Courtyard, Sheraton, Woodfin Suites Barnes&Noble, Old Navy, Ross, Trader Joe's
8c b	Oakland, to I-880, I-580
8a	W Grand Ave, Maritime St
7mm	**toll plaza wb**
5mm	SF Bay
4a	Treasure Island (EXITs left)
2c b	Fremont St, Harrison St, Embarcadero (from wb)
2a	4th st (from eb), S Shell
1	9th st, Civic Ctr, downtown SF
1b a	**I-80 begins/ends on US 101 in SF.**

BERKELEY

INTERSTATE 110 (LOS ANGELES)

Exit #	Services
21	**I-110 begins/ends on I-10**
20c	Adams Blvd, E Chevron Audi, Chrysler/Dodge/Jeep, LA Convention Ctr., Mercedes, Nissan, Office Depot, VW
20b	37th St, Exposition Blvd, W Chevron/McDonald's Radisson Chevrolet
20a	MLK Blvd, Expo Park, W Chevron McDonald's, Subway
19b	Vernon Ave, E Mobil Tacos El Gavilan, W 76/24hr, Shell Burger King, Jack-in-the-Box Rite Aid, Ross
18b	Slauson Ave, E Mobil, W 76
18a	Gage Blvd, E Arco Church's, Hercules Burgers
17	Florence Ave, E Shell Jack-in-the-Box, W Chevron, Valero Burger King, Little Caesars, McDonald's, Pizza Hut, Subway
16	Manchester Ave, E Arco El Pollo Loco, Little Caesars, McDonald's, Subway, Winchell's AutoZone, W 76/Circle K Church's, Jack-in-the-Box, Popeye's, Tam's Burgers
15	Century Blvd, E Arco, Shell/Subway/dsl Burger King, McDonald's, W 76/dsl
14b	Imperial Hwy, W Chevron/dsl Jack-in-the-Box, McDonald's

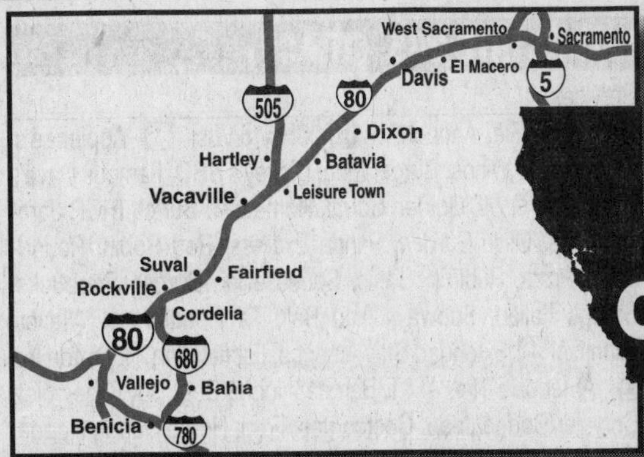

CA

LA AREA

14a	I-105
13	El Segundo Blvd, E Dominos, Taco Bell, W Mobil, Shell Executive Inn
12	Rosecrans Ave, E Arco/24hr, Valero, W Chevron/McDonald's, Valero Jack-in-the-Box, KFC/LJ Silver, Pizza Hut, Popeye's, Subway, Yoshinoya 7-11, AutoZone, casino
11	Redondo Beach Blvd, E McDonald's, W Mobil casino
10b a	CA 91, 190th St, W Arco Carl's Jr, Jack-in-the-Box, Krispy Kreme, McDonald's, Pizza Hut/Taco Bell, Subway Food4Less, Ranch Mkt, Sam's Club
9	I-405, San Diego Fwy
8	Torrance Blvd, Del Amo, E Burger King, Chile Verde, Hawaiian BBQ, Starbucks K-mart, W Mobil, Shell/Subway/dsl
7b	Carson St, E KFC Cali Inn vet, W 76, Shell FatBurger, Hong Kong Deli, In-N-Out, Jack-in-the-Box, Louis Burgers, McDonalds, Pizza Hut, Polly's Pies, Starbucks, Subway, Wienerschnitzel Autozone, Carson Drug, Costsaver Mkt, O'Reilly Parts, Rite Aid
5	Sepulveda Blvd, E McDonald's Albertson's, Home Depot, Staples, Target, W Arco/24hr, Chevron, Mobil Burger King, Carl's Jr, McDonald's, Pizza Hut/Taco Bell, Popeye's, Starbucks, Subway Motel 6 $Tree, 99c Store, AT&T, Food4Less, Rite Aid, Ross
4	CA 1, Pacific Coast Hwy, E 76, Arco Jack-in-the-Box, Pizza Hut, Wienerschnitzel, W Circle K, United/dsl Del Taco, Denny's, El Pollo Loco, Subway Best Western Discount Parts, PepBoys, Rite Aid, transmissions
3b	Anaheim St, W Mobil/dsl, Thrifty Conoco/Phillips Refinery, radiators
3a	C St
1b	Channel St, W Arco, Chevron Subway 7-11, Home Depot, Target
1a	CA 47, Gaffey Ave
0mm	**I-110 begins/ends.**

INTERSTATE 205 (TRACY)

Exit #	Services
12	**I-205 begins wb, ends eb**, accesses I-5 nb
9	MacArthur Dr, Tracy, S Chevron/Jack-in-the-Box/Subway/dsl Tracy Outlet Ctr/famous brands
8	Tracy Blvd, Tracy, N 76/Mean Gene's Burger/dsl, Chevron, Shell/dsl Denny's Holiday Inn Express, Motel 6, S Arco Arby's, Burger King, In-N-Out, Lyon's Rest., McDonald's, Milano Pizza, Nations Burgers, Pizza Guys, Starbucks, Straw Hat Pizza, Subway, Wendy's Best Western, Microtel, Quality Inn CHP, CVS Drug, Mi Pueblo Mkt, O'Reilly Parts

CA

INTERSTATE 205 (TRACY)

TRACY

Exit #	Services
6	Grant Line Rd, Antioch, N [gas] Chevron/dsl [food] Applebee's, Buffalo Wild Wings, Burger King, Dickey's BBQ, Famous Dave's BBQ, Five Guys, Golden Corral, Hometown Buffet, IHOP, Jamba Juice, Olive Garden, Panda Express, Red Robin, Round-Table Pizza, Rubio's, Sonic, Squeeze Inn Burger, Starbucks, Strings Italian, Subway, Taco Bell, TX Roadhouse, Wienerschnitzel [lodging] Extended Stay America, Fairfield Inn, Hampton Inn [other] America's Tire, AT&T, Barnes&Noble, Best Buy, Chevrolet, Chrysler/Dodge/Jeep, Costco/gas, Ford, Home Depot, Honda, Hyundai, JC Penney, Les Schwab Tire, Macy's, mall, Marshall's, Michael's, Nissan, Petsmart, Ross, Sears/auto, See's Candies, Staples, Target, Toyota/Scion, Verizon, VW, Walmart/McDonald's/auto, WinCo Foods, World Mkt, World Mkt, S [gas] 7-11, 76/Subway/dsl, Arco, Shell/dsl [food] A&W/KFC, Black Bear Diner, Carl's Jr, Chili's, Hawaiian BBQ, Mtn Mike's Pizza, Popeye's [other] Rite Aid
4	11th St (from eb), to Tracy, Defense Depot
2	Mtn House Pkwy, to I-580 E
0mm	**I-205 begins eb/ends wb, accesses I-580 wb.**

INTERSTATE 210 (PASADENA)

SAN DIMAS

Exit #	Services
85a	**I-210 begins/ends on I-10, EXIT 77.**
84	San Bernardino Ave, W [food] Habit Burger [other] Hobby Lobby, Old Navy, Ross, TJ Maxx
83	W 5th St, Greenspot Rd, E [gas] Chevron/dsl [food] Del Taco, Dickey's BBQ, In-N-Out, Subway, Waba Grill [other] AT&T, Lowe's, Staples
82	Base Line Rd, E [gas] Arco, Valero [food] Carl's Jr, KFC/Taco Bell, McDonald's, Subway, Wendy's [other] Albertson's, CVS Drug, Walgreens, W [gas] 76/dsl [food] Baker's, Popeye, Starbucks [other] AutoZone, CVS Drug, Family$
81	CA 330 N, to Big Bear
79	Highland Ave, N [gas] Chevron/Subway, Shell/dsl [food] Baker's, Coco's, IHOP, Taco Bell, Wienerschnitzel/Tastee Freez, S [food] Del Taco, El Pollo Loco, KFC [other] $Tree, 99c Store, O'Reilly Parts, Rite Aid, Target, Walmart Mkt
78	Del Rosa Ave, N [gas] 7-11, Shell [food] Del Taco, S [gas] Circle K, Exxon, Valero [food] Jack-in-the-Box, McDonald's [other] CVS Drug, Stater Bros, Walgreens
76	Waterman Ave, S [gas] Mobil/7-11/dsl [other] [H]
75	CA 259 (from wb), H St
74	I-215 N to Barstow S to San Bernardino
73	State St, University Pkwy, N [gas] American, USA [other] $General
71	Riverside Ave, N [gas] Chevron [food] Carl's Jr, Del Taco, Panda Paradise, Starbucks, Subway [other] GNC, Ralph's Foods, Rite Aid, Verizon, Walgreens, S [gas] Arco [food] Chipotle, In-N-Out, Jack-in-the-Box [other] 7-11, URGENT CARE
70	Ayala Dr, S [other] city park
68	Alder Ave, N [gas] Arco/Subway/dsl
67	Sierra Ave, N [food] Applebee's, Boston's, Carl's Jr, Dickie's BBQ, El Pollo Loco, Jamba Juice, McDonald's, Mimi's Cafe, Panda Express, Papa Murphy's, Pizza Hut, Starbucks, Subway, Tio's Mexican, Waba Grill [other] $Tree, Costco/gas, Jo-Ann, Lowe's Whse, Petco, Schwab Tire, Verizon, car repair, 7-11, S [other] Chevrolet, Honda, Nissan
66	Citrus Ave, N [food] El Ranchero, FarmerBoys Rest., Jimmy John's, Juice It Up, Pick Up Stix, Popeye's, Red Brick Pizza,
66	Continued Taco Bell [other] America's Tire, AutoZone, Home Depot, Ralph's Foods, Walgreens, S [gas] Arco/dsl
64	Cherry Ave
63	I-15 N to Barstow, S to San Diego
62	Day Creek Blvd, S [gas] Arco/dsl, Shell [food] Chinese Food, Jack in-the-Box, Starbucks, Subway, Wendy's [other] Ralph's Foods
60	Milliken Ave, S [gas] Mobil/Circle K/dsl [food] Subway, Taco Bel [other] Albertsons, CVS Drug, vet
59	Haven Ave, N [gas] 7-11, 76, Mobil [food] Corky's Kitchen, De Taco, Domino's, Jack-in-the-Box, McDonald's, Subway, Tio's Mexican [other] Trader Joe's, vet, Vons Foods, Walgreens
58	Archibald Ave, S [food] Bamboo Garden, Barboni's Pizza, Carl's J [other] Stater Bros, vet
57	Carnelion St, S [gas] 76 [food] Baskin-Robbins, Del Taco, El Ranchero Mexican, Juice It Up, Papa John's, Starbucks, Subway [other] Radio Shack, Rite Aid, Vons Foods, Walgreens
56	Campus Ave, N [gas] Arco/dsl, S [food] Carl's Jr, Chick-fil-A, Chili's, Chipotle, El Pollo Loco, Golden Spoon Yogurt, Habit Burger, Hawaiian BBQ, Jersey Mike's, Magic Wok, Panera Bread, Pick Up Stix, Pieology Pizza, Qdoba Mexican, Starbucks, Subway, Which Wich? [other] AT&T, Dick's, GNC, Goodyear/auto, Haggen Mkt, Home Depot, Kohl's, Office Depot, Petsmart, Target, TJ Maxx, Verizon
54	Mtn Ave, Mount Balde
52	Baseline Rd
50	Towne Ave
48	Fruit St, Via Verde, S [gas] Shell [food] Chipotle, El Pollo Loco, In-N-Out, Jersey Mike's, Jimmy John's, McDonald's, Myabi Japanese, Panda Express, Panera Bread, Pizza Hut, Round Table Pizza, Rubio's Grill, Starbucks, Subway [other] Kohl's, Marshall's, Staples, Target, U of LaVerne, vet
47	Foothill Blvd, LaVerne, N [gas] Mobil [food] Mr D's, S [gas] 76/dsl [food] IHOP, Jack-in-the-Box, Starbucks, The Grill House, Togo's [other] GNC
46	San Dimas Ave, San Dimas, N San Dimas Canyon CP
45	CA 57 S
44	Lone Hill Ave, Santa Ana, N [food] Panda Express, S [gas] Chevron [food] Baja Fresh, Chili's, Chipotle, Coco's, Corner Bakery Cafe, In-N-Out, Olive Garden, Subway, Wendy's [other] Barnes&Noble, Best Buy, Chevrolet, Chrysler/Dodge/Jeep, Costco/gas, Ford, Home Depot, Hyundai, Kohl's, Old Navy, Petsmart, Sam's Club/gas, Staples, Toyota, Verizon, Walmart/auto
43	Sunflower Ave
42	Grand Ave, to Glendora, N [gas] 76, Valero/dsl [food] Carl's Jr, Denny's, El Pollo Loco [other] [H]
41	Citrus Ave, to Covina
40	CA 39, Azusa Ave, N [gas] Arco/24hr, Chevron/dsl, Mobil/dsl, Shell/Del Taco [food] Jack-in-the-Box [lodging] Rodeway Inn, Super 8, S [gas] Chevron [food] In-N-Out [lodging] Best Value [other] 7-11, Family$, Rite Aid
39	Vernon Ave (from wb), same as 38
38	Irwindale, N [gas] Arco, Shell/Subway/dsl [food] Carl's Jr, Farmer-Boys Rest., McDonald's, Taco Bell [other] Costco/gas
36b	Mt Olive Dr, N [gas] Mobil/dsl [food] Subway [other] CVS, Fresh&Easy Mkt
36a	I-605 S
35b a	Mountain Ave, N [gas] Arco, Chevron [food] Del Taco, Denny's, Old Spaghetti Factory, Qdoba, Sonic, Taco Bell, Tommy's Hamburgers, Wienerschnitzel [lodging] Oak Park Motel [other] Best Buy, BMW/Mini, Buick/Chevrolet, CarMax, Chrysler/Dodge/Jeep, Fiat, Ford, Goodyear/auto, Honda, Infiniti, Mazda, Staples,

INTERSTATE 210 (PASADENA) Cont'd

MONROVIA

35b a	Continued Subaru, Target, Walgreens, S IHOP, Panda Express, Subway Home Depot, Ross, Verizon, Walmart/McDonald's
34	Myrtle Ave, S 76, Chevron/dsl Jack-in-the-Box
33	Huntington Dr, Monrovia, N Shell/dsl Applebee's, Black Angus, Burger King, Chili's, Chipotle, ChuckeCheese, Domenico's Italian, Domino's, Jack-in-the-Box, Jersey Mike's, Jimmy John's, LeRoy's Rest., McDonald's, Mimi's Cafe, Panda Express, Panera Bread, Papa Murphy's, Popeye's, RoundTable Pizza, Rubio's, Smashburger, Starbucks Courtyard Baja Ranch Foods, GNC, Kohl's, Marshall's, Pepboy's, Petsmart, Rite Aid, Sprouts Mkt, Trader Joe's, vet, Walgreens, S 76 Baja Fresh, BJ's Grill, Capistrano's, Capital Seafood, Claim-Jumper, Derby Rest., Golden Dragon, Olive Garden, Outback Steaks, Pieology, Red Lobster, Robeks Juice, Soup Plantation, Starbucks, Subway, Taisho Rest., Togo's, Tokyo Wako, Zen Buffet DoubleTree, Embassy Suites, Extended Stay America, Extended Stay America (2), Hampton Inn, Hilton Garden, OakTree Inn, Residence Inn, SpringHill Suites Verizon
32	Santa Anita Ave, Arcadia, N 76, Arco McDonald's, Pizza Hut, Subway Ralph's Foods, Rite Aid, Walgreens, S Chevron/dsl In-N-Out carwash, vet
31	Baldwin Ave, to Sierra Madre
30b a	Rosemead Blvd, N 76/dsl, Arco Baskin Robbins, ChuckeCheese, Corner Bakery Cafe, Del Taco, Habit Burger, Island Burger, Jamba Juice, Panda Express, Panera Bread, Pick Up Stix, Starbucks, Subway AT&T, CVS Drug, Marshall's, Ralph's Foods, Rite Aid, Sears/auto, Toyota/Scion, Verizon, Whole Foods Mkt, S 76 Coco's, Jack-in-the-Box Best Value Inn, Best Western Big O Tires, Sprouts Mkt, Staples, World Mkt

PASADENA

29b a	San Gabriel Blvd, Madre St, N 76 Chipotle Mexican, El Torito, Pizza Rey, Starbucks, Togo's Best Buy, Dick's, Old Navy, Petsmart, Ross, S 76 Subway Best Western, Holiday Inn Express, Hotel La Reve Buick/Chevrolet/GMC, Cadillac, Land Rover Staples, Target
28	Altadena Dr, Sierra Madre, S Chevron, Mobil Just Tires
27b	Allen
27a	Hill Ave
26	Lake Ave, N Mobil/Circle K/dsl AutoZone
25b	CA 134, to Ventura
25a	Del Mar Blvd, CA Blvd, CO Blvd (EXITs left from eb)
24	Mountain St
23	Lincoln Ave, S Lincoln Motel tire service
22b	Arroyo Blvd, N Jack-in-the-Box, S to Rose Bowl
22a	Berkshire Ave, Oak Grove Dr
21	Gould Ave, S Arco, Chevron McDonald's, RoundTable Pizza, Subway, Trader Joe's Firestone/auto, Just Tires, La Canada Automotive, Petco, Ralph's Foods
20	CA 2, Angeles Crest Hwy, S 76, Shell
19	CA 2, Glendale Fwy, S H
18	Ocean View Blvd, to Montrose
17b a	Pennsylvania Ave, La Crescenta Ave, La Crescenta, N 76, Shell/7-11, Valero Baja Fresh, Burger King, Domino's, Little Caesar's, Starbucks, Subway, Togo's, Wienerschnitzel Office Depot, O'Reilly Parts, Ralph's Foods, Rite Aid, Toyota/Scion, USPO, Verizon, vet, Vons Foods, Walgreens, S Gardenia Mkt/deli
16	Lowell Ave
14	La Tuna Cyn Rd

11	Sunland Blvd, Tujunga, N Chevron, Mobil/dsl, Shell Coco's, Jack-in-the-Box, Panda Express, Pizza Hut, Starbucks, Subway, Yum Yum Donuts 7-11, city park, O'Reilly Parts, Ralph's Foods, Rite Aid, Verizon
9	Wheatland Ave
8	Osborne St, Lakeview Terrace, N Ranch Side Cafe 7-11
6a	Paxton St
6b	CA 118
5	Maclay St, to San Fernando, S 76/dsl, Chevron El Pollo Loco, KFC, McDonald's, Quizno's, Subway, Taco Bell Home Depot, Office Depot, Radio Shack, Sam's Club
4	Hubbard St, N Chevron Denny's, Yum Yum Donuts 99c Store, AutoZone, Fresh&Easy, Radio Shack, S Mobil/dsl, Shell El Caporal Mexican, Jack-in-the-Box, Shakey's Pizza, Starbucks, Subway USPO, Von's Foods
3	Polk St, S Arco, Chevron/dsl KFC H 7-11
2	Roxford St, N Arco/dsl Fresh&Fast Mexican H Jiffy Lube, S Travelodge
1c	Yarnell St
1b a	**I-210 begins/ends on I-5, EXIT 160.**

INTERSTATE 215 (RIVERSIDE)

SAN BERNARDINO

Exit #	Services
55	**I-215 begins/ends on I-15.**
54	Devore, E Arco/dsl, Shell, W Tony's Diner
50	Palm Ave, Kendall Dr, E 7-11, Arco Albertacos, Burger King, Mi Cocina Mexican, Starbucks, Subway, W Denny's
48	University Pkwy, E 76/Circle K, Chevron/dsl Alberto's, Baskin Robbins/Togo's, Carl's Jr, Del Taco, Domino's, IHOP, KFC, Little Ceasars, McDonald's, Papa John's, Starbucks, Subway, Wienerschnitzel AT&T, Jiffy Lube, Radio Shack, Ralph's Foods, Staples, W Arco, Mobil/dsl/LP Don Martin Grill, Jack-in-the-Box, Taco Bell Days Inn, Motel 6 Verizon, Walmart/Subway
46c a	CA 210, Redlands, to Pasadena, E golf, W golf
46b	Highland Ave
45a	CA 210 E, Highlands
45	Baseline Rd, E 76, Arco
44a	CA 66 W, 5th St, E In-N-Out Best Value Inn, Country Inn, Golden Star Inn, Leisure Inn, Rodeway Inn
43	2nd St, Civic Ctr, E Chevron/dsl Del Taco, Honeybaked Ham, In-N-Out, McDonald's, Starbucks, Subway, Taco Bell Best Value Inn $Tree, Food4Less, Ford, Marshall's, Ross
42b	Mill St, E Carl's Jr, Jack-in-the-Box AutoZone, W Shell Yum-yum Donuts
42a	Inland Ctr Dr, E Chevron/dsl Carl's Jr, Jack-in-the-Box, Wienerschnitzel AutoZone, Macy's, mall, O'Reilly Parts, Sears/auto, W Arco/dsl

[gas] = gas [food] = food [lodging] = lodging [other] = other [RS] = rest stop

CA

INTERSTATE 215 (RIVERSIDE) Cont'd

(N)

Exit #	Services
41	Orange Show Rd, E [gas] 76/dsl, World [food] Burger Mania, ChuckECheese, Jose's Mexican, Subway, Sundowners Rest., Viva Villa Grill [lodging] Knights Inn, Orange Show Inn [other] 7-11, 99c Store, BigLots, Chrysler/Dodge/Jeep, Firestone/auto, Kelly Tire, Radio Shack, Target, W [other] AT&T, Kia, Mitsubishi, Nissan, Subaru, Toyota/Scion, VW
40b a	I-10, E to Palm Springs, W to LA
39	Washington St, Mt Vernon Ave, E [gas] 5 Point/repair, 76/Circle K, Arco [food] Baker's Drive-Thru, China Town, DQ, George's Burgers, Siquio's Mexican, Starbucks, Taco Joe's [lodging] Colton Inn [other] BigLots, Goodyear/auto, Jiffy Lube, W [food] Buffet Star, Carl's Jr, Church's, Del Taco, Denny's, Graziano's Pizza, Jack-in-the-Box, McDonald's, Starbucks, Subway, Taco Patron [lodging] Red Tile Inn [other] 99c Store, GNC, multiple RV dealers, Radio Shack, Ross, Walmart/auto
38	Barton Rd, E [gas] Arco, Shell/Circle K/dsl [food] Miguel's Mexican, Quiznos [other] AutoZone, Stater Bros., W [food] Demetri's Burgers [other] vet
37	La Cadena Dr, (Iowa Ave from sb), E [gas] Shell/dsl [food] Jack-in-the-Box, YumYum Rest. [lodging] Holiday Inn Express
36	Center St, to Highgrove, E [gas] Chevron/Subway/dsl, W [gas] Valero/dsl
35	Columbia Ave, E [gas] Arco/dsl, W [other] Circle K
34b a	CA 91, CA 60, Main St, Riverside, to beach cities
33	Blaine St, 3rd St, E [gas] 76, Shell, Valero [food] Baker's Drive-Thru, Jack-in-the-Box, Starbucks [other] K-Mart, Stater Bros., Valvoline
32	University Ave, Riverside, W [gas] Mobil/dsl, Shell, Thrifty [food] Canton Chinese, Carl's Jr, Coco's, Denny's, Domino's, Fatburger, Gus Jr, IHOP, Jack-in-the-Box, Jersey Mike's, Little Ceasars, Mandarin Chinese, Papa John's, Pizza Hut, Rubio's, Santana's Mexican, Shakey's Pizza, Starbucks, Subway, Taco Bell, Wienerschnitzel [lodging] Comfort Inn, Courtyard, Motel 6 [other] $Tree, AT&T, Food4Less, O'Reilly Parts, Radio Shack, Rite Aid, USPO, Walgreens
31	MLK Blvd, El Cerrito
30b	Central Ave, Watkins Dr
30a	Fair Isle Dr, Box Springs, E [other] Marjon RV Ctr, W [gas] 76/Circle K/Subway/dsl [food] Jack-in-the-Box [other] Ford, Nissan
29	CA 60 E, to Indio, E [gas] Arco, Shell/dsl [food] Applebee's, Baffalo Wild Wings, Baker's Drive-Thru, BJ's Rest., Burger Boss, Carl's Jr, Chick-fil-A, Chili's, Chipotle Mexican, El Pollo Loco, Five Guys, Golden Chop Stix, Hawaiian BBQ, Home Town Buffet, Hooters, Jamba Juice, Jason's Deli, Jersey Mike's, John's Pizza, McDonald's, Miguel's Mexican, Mimi's Cafe, Olive Garden, Outback Steaks, Panda Express, Panera Bread, Portillo's Hot Dogs, Round Table Pizza, Rubio's, Starbucks, Subway, Waba Grill, Wendy's, Wienerschnitzel [lodging] Ayres Hotel, Hampton Inn [other] $Tree, 99c Store, Best Buy, Costco/gas, JC Penney, Jo-Ann Fabrics, Lowe's, Macy's, mall, Marshall's, Michael's, Old Navy, PetCo, Petsmart, Ross, Sears/auto, Staples, Target, TJ Maxx, Verizon, Walmart, WinCo Foods, World Mkt
28	Eucalyptus Ave, Eastridge Ave, E [food] Bravo Burgers, Hooters [other] Sam's Club/gas, Target, Walmart, [other] same as 29
27b	(27c from sb) Alessandro Blvd, E [gas] Arco/dsl [other] auto repair, Big O Tire, W [gas] Chevron [food] Farmer Boys
27a	Cactus Ave to March ARB, E [gas] 76/Circle K/dsl, Chevron/dsl [food] Carl's Jr, Gus Jr
25	Van Buren Blvd, E [other] March Field Museum, W [other] Riverside Nat Cem
23	Harley Knox Blvd

RIVERSIDE

PERRIS

Exit #	Services
22	Ramona Expswy, E [gas] Arco, Chevron/dsl, Mobil/Circle K, Shell/Subway/dsl [food] Farmer Boys, Harry's Cafe, McDonald's, Papa John's, Starbucks, Subway, Valentino's Pizza, W [gas] 76/Circle K/dsl/LP, Arco/dsl/scales/24hr [food] Jack-in-the-Box
19	Nuevo Rd, E [gas] Arco, Chevron/dsl, Mobil/Circle K [food] Baskin-Robbins, Burger King, Carl's Jr, China Palace, Del Taco, El Pollo Loco, IHOP, Jenny's Rest., McDonald's, Pizza Hut, Sizzler, Starbucks, Subway [other] AutoZone, Food4Less, GNC, Radio Shack, Rite Aid, Stater Bros Foods, Walmart
17	CA 74 W, 4th St, to Perris, Lake Elsinore, E [gas] Shell, W [gas] Chevron [food] Del Taco, Denny's, Jack-in-the-Box, Jimenez Mexican, Little Caesar's, Popeye's [lodging] Holiday Inn Express [other] AutoZone, Chrysler/Dodge/Jeep/Kia
15	CA 74 E, Hemet, E [food] Jack-in-the-Box [lodging] Sun Leisure Motel
14	Ethanac Rd, E [food] KFC/Taco Bell [other] Richardson's RV, W [gas] 76/dsl, Circle K/dsl [food] Carl's Jr, Del Taco, Ono Hawaiian BBQ, Starbucks, Subway [other] Home Depot, Just Tires, Verizon, WinCo Foods
12	McCall Blvd, Sun City, E [gas] Valero/dsl [food] Wendy's [lodging] Best Value Inn, Motel 6 [other] [H] W [gas] Chevron/dsl, United Oil [food] Coco's, Domino's, McDonald's, Papa Murphy's, Santana's Mexican, Subway [other] $Tree, Rite Aid, Stater Bros, Von's Foods, Walgreens
10	Newport Rd, Quail Valley, E [gas] Shell/Del Taco/dsl [food] Cathay Chinese, Jack-in-the-Box, Papa John's, Subway, Taco Bell [other] $Tree, AutoZone, GNC, Ralph's Foods, Ross, vet, W [gas] Circle K/dsl [food] Applebee's, Baskin-Robbins, BJ's Rest., Chipotle Mexican, In-N-Out, Miguel's Mexican, NY Pizza, Panda Express, Panera Bread, Red Robin, Starbucks, Subway, TX Roadhouse, Yellow Basket Cafe [other] AT&T, Best Buy, CVS Drug, Kohl's, Lowe's, Michael's, Old Navy, PetCo, Radio Shack, Staples, SuperTarget, TJ Maxx, URGENT CARE, Verizon, vet
7	Scott Rd, E [gas] 7-11, Arco/dsl [food] Carl's Jr, Del Taco, Jack-in-the-Box, Submarina, Subway, Wood Rock Fire Pizza [other] Albertson's/SavOn, Verizon, vet, Walgreens, W [food] Marco's Pizza
4	Clinton Keith Rd, W [gas] Arco/dsl [food] Del Taco, Jersey Mike's, Juice It Up, Starbucks, Subway [other] Mtn View Tire, Target, URGENT CARE, Verizon, Walgreens
2	Los Alamos, E [gas] Shell [food] Board'z Grill, Cojito's Mexican, In-N-Out, Miguel's Jr Mexican, Peony Chinese, Starbucks, Taco Bell [other] USPO, W [gas] Mobil/Circle K/dsl [food] ChuckeCheese, Jack-in-the-Box, McDonald's, Pizza Hut, Starbucks, Subway, TJ's Pizza [other] CVS Drug, Stater Bros., vet
1	Murrieta Hot Springs, E [gas] 7-11, Shell/dsl [food] Alberto's Mexican, Buffalo Wild Wings, Carl's Jr, El Pollo Loco, Habit Burger, Hungry Bull, Richie's Diner, Rubio's, Sizzler, Starbucks, Submarina, Wendy's [other] $Tree, Dick's, Ralph's Foods, Rite Aid, Ross, Sam's Club/gas, Verizon, vet, Walgreens, W [food] Richie's Diner, Starbucks
0mm	**I-215 begins/ends on I-15.**

MURRIETA

INTERSTATE 280 (BAY AREA)

(E)

Exit #	Services
58	4th St, **I-280 begins/ends,** N [other] Whole Foods Mkt, S [gas] Shell
57	7th St, to I-80, downtown
56	Mariposa St, downtown
55	Army St, Port of SF
54	US 101 S, Alemany Blvd, Mission St, E [gas] Shell
52	San Jose Ave, Bosworth St (from nb, no return)
51	Geneva Ave

CA

INTERSTATE 280 (BAY AREA) Cont'd

SAN FRANCISCO

Exit #	Services
50	CA 1, 19th Ave, W [gas] Chevron [other] SFSU, to Bay Bridge
49	Daly City, Daly City, E [gas] 76/dsl/LP [other] Toyota, Walgreens, W [gas] Arco [food] Carl's Jr, Domino's, IHOP, In-N-Out, Krispy Kreme, McDonald's, Val's Rest. [lodging] Hampton Inn
47a	Serramonte Blvd, Daly City (from sb), E [gas] Silver Gas [other] Cadillac, Chevrolet, Ford, Home Depot, Honda, Nissan, Target, W [gas] 76, Olympian [food] Boston Mkt, Elephant Bar Rest., McDonald's, Sizzler, Starbucks [other] Longs Drugs, Macy's, Office Depot, PetsMart, Ross, Target
47b	CA 1, Mission St (from nb), Pacifica, E [food] Hawaiian BBQ, RoundTable Pizza, Sizzler [other] [H] Chrysler/Jeep/Dodge, Drug Barn, Fresh Choice Foods, Home Depot, Infiniti, Isuzu, Jo-Ann Fabrics, Lexus, mall, Mitsubishi, Nordstrom's, PetCo, Target
46	Hickey Blvd, Colma, E [gas] Chevron/dsl/24hr, Shell, W [gas] Shell/dsl/24hr [food] Boston Mkt, Celia's Rest., Koi Palace, Moonstar, Outback Steaks, Sizzler [other] 7-11, Ross
45	Avalon Dr (from sb), Westborough, W [gas] Arco/24hr, Valero/dsl [food] Denny's, McDonald's, Subway [other] Pak'n Save Foods, Skyline Coll, Walgreens/24hr
44	(from nb)
43b	I-380 E, to US 101, to SF Airport
43a	San Bruno Ave, Sneath Ave, E [food] Au's Kitchen, Baskin-Robbins, Carl's Jr, Jamba Juice, Quizno's, Starbucks, Taco Bell [other] GNC, Longs Drugs, Mollie Stones Mkt, Radio Shack, W [gas] 76, Chevron [food] Baker's Square [other] 7-11
42	Crystal Springs (from sb), county park
41	CA 35 N, Skyline Blvd (from wb, no EZ return), to Pacifica, **1 mi** W [gas] Chevron
40	Millbrae Ave, Millbrae, E [gas] Chevron
39	Trousdale Dr, to Burlingame, E [other] [H]
36	Black Mtn Rd, Hayne Rd, W [other] vista point, golf
36mm	**Crystal Springs [RS] wb, full [handicapped] facilities, litter barrels, petwalk [phone] [picnic]**
35	CA 35, CA 92W (from eb), to Half Moon Bay
34	Bunker Hill Dr
33	CA 92, to Half Moon Bay, San Mateo
32mm	vista point both lanes
29	Edgewood Rd, Canada Rd, to San Carlos, E [other] [H]
27	Farm Hill Blvd, E [other] Cañada Coll, phone
25	CA 84, Woodside Rd, Redwood City, **1 mi** W [gas] Chevron/dsl [food] Buck's Rest., John Bentley's Rest. [other] Robert's Mkt, USPO
24	Sand Hill Rd, Menlo Park, **1 mi** E [gas] Shell [food] Starbucks [other] Longs Drug, Safeway
22	Alpine Rd, Portola Valley, E [other] [H] W [gas] Shell/autocare [food] Red Lotus Cafe, RoundTable Pizza [other] Curves
20	Page Mill Rd, to Palo Alto, E [other] [H] to Stanford U
16	El Monte Rd, Moody Rd
15	Magdalena Ave
13	Foothill Expswy, Grant Rd, E [gas] Chevron/24hr [food] Starbucks, Woodpecker Grill [other] Rite Aid, Trader Joe's, W [other] to Rancho San Antonio CP
12b a	CA 85, N to Mtn View, S to Gilroy
11	Saratoga, Cupertino, Sunnyvale, E [gas] Chevron [food] Carl's Jr, Quizno's [lodging] Cupertino Inn [other] Goodyear, Michael's, repair, Rite Aid, TJ Maxx, W [gas] 76, Chevron, Dianza Gas, USA [food] BJ's Rest., Outback Steaks [lodging] Cypress Hotel [other] Apple Computer HQ, PetsMart
10	Wolfe Rd, E [gas] Arco/24hr [food] Starbucks, Teppan Steaks [lodging] Courtyard, Hilton Garden [other] Ranch Mkt, W [gas] 76 [food] Alexan

SAN JOSE

Exit #	Services
10	Continued der Steaks, Benihana, Vallco Dynasty Chinese [other] FreshChoice Foods, JC Penney, Jiffy Lube, Sears/auto, Vallco Fashion Park
9	Lawrence Expswy, Stevens Creek Blvd (from eb), N [food] El Pollo Loco, McDonalds, Mtn Mikes Pizza, Panda Express, Quizno's, Starbucks [other] Land Rover, Marshalls, Nissan, Safeway, S [gas] 76, Rotten Robbie [food] IHOP, Subway [lodging] 7-11, Woodcrest Hotel
7	Saratoga Ave, N [gas] Arco/24hr, Chevron/24hr [food] Black Angus, Burger King, Garden City Rest., Happi House, Lion Rest., McDonald's, Taco Bell [other] 7-11, Cadillac, Chevrolet, Ford, Goodyear, Jiffy Lube, PepBoys, S [gas] 76, Shell, Valero [food] Applebee's, Tony Roma's [lodging] MoorPark Hotel
5c	Winchester Blvd, Campbell Ave (from eb)
5b	CA 17 S, to Santa Cruz, I-880 N, to San Jose
5a	Leigh Ave, Bascom Ave
4	Meridian St (from eb), N [gas] 76 [other] Big O Tire, FoodMaxx, S [gas] Chevron [food] KFC, Subway, Wienerschnitzel [other] 7-11
3b	Bird Ave, Race St
3a	CA 87, N [lodging] Hilton, Holiday Inn, Hotel Sainte Claire, Marriott
2	7th St, to CA 82, N conv ctr
1	10th St, 11th St, N [other] 7-11, to San Jose St U
0mm	**I-280 begins/ends on US 101.**

INTERSTATE 405 (LOS ANGELES)

LOS ANGELES AREA

Exit #	Services
73	I-5, N to Sacramento, I-5, S to LA
72	Rinaldi St, Sepulveda, E [gas] 76, Chevron/dsl [food] Arby's, McDonald's, Presidente Mexican, Subway [other] [H] Nissan, Toyota, W [gas] Shell [lodging] Best Value Inn
71	CA 118 W, Simi Valley
70	Devonshire St, Granada Hills, E [gas] 76, Arco, GasMart/dsl [food] Holiday Burger, Millie's Rest., Papa John's, Quiznos, Safari Room Rest, Subway [other] Bare's RV Ctr, Radio Shack, Ralph's Foods, Rite Aid, Verizon, Vons Foods
69	Nordhoff St, E [gas] Mobil/dsl [food] 7 Mares, China Wok, Coldstone, Del Taco, KFC, Panda Express, Pollo Campero, Starbucks [lodging] Hillcrest Inn [other] 7-11, Marshalls, Vallarta Foods, Walgreens, W [gas] 76/dsl, Arco [food] Jack-in-the-Box, Pizza Hut
68	Roscoe Blvd, to Panorama City, E [gas] 76/dsl, Shell [food] Burger King, Country Folks Rest., Denny's, Galpin Rest., Jack-in-the-Box, Little Caesars, McDonald's, Panda Express, Taco Bell, Yoshinoya [lodging] Holiday Inn Express [other] 7-11, AutoZone, Ford, Jaguar/Volvo, Lincoln, U-Haul, W [gas] Chevron/dsl, Shell/dsl [food] Tommy's Burgers [lodging] Motel 6
66	Sherman Blvd, Reseda, E [gas] Chevron, Mobil/LP [food] Golden Chicken, KFC, McDonald's, Starbucks [lodging] Motel 6 [other] BigLots

Legend: 🅿 = gas 🍴 = food 🛏 = lodging ⊙ = other ⛺ = rest stop Copyright 2016 - The Next EXIT

LOS ANGELES AREA

CA

INTERSTATE 405 (LOS ANGELES) Cont'd

Exit	Description
66	Continued CVS Drug, Jon's Foods, W 🅿 76/dsl/24hr 🍴 Taco Bell ⊙ Ⓗ USPO
65	Victory Blvd, Van Nuys, E 🍴 Carl's Jr, El Pollo Loco, Jack-in-the-Box, Subway, Wendy's ⊙ Costco/gas, CVS Drug, El Monte RV Ctr, Office Depot, PepBoys, Staples, W 🅿 Arco/24hr ⊙ Ⓗ
64	Burbank Blvd, E 🅿 Chevron, Shell 🍴 Denny's 🛏 Best Western, Hampton Inn ⊙ Target
63b	US 101, Ventura Fwy
63a	Ventura Blvd (from nb), E 🅿 Mobil 🍴 Cheesecake Factory, El Pollo Loco ⊙ mall, Whole Foods Mkt, W 🅿 76 🍴 Ameci Pizza, CA Chicken Cafe, Corner Bakery Cafe, IHOP, McDonald's 🛏 Courtyard, Valley Inn
63a	Valley Vista Blvd (from sb)
61	Mulholland Dr, Skirvall Dr
59	Sepulveda Blvd, Getty Ctr Dr, W ⊙ to Getty Ctr
57	Sunset Blvd, Morega Dr, E 🅿 76/dsl, Chevron/24hr ⊙ to UCLA, W 🛏 Luxe Hotel
56	Waterford St, Montana Ave (from nb)
55c b	Wilshire Blvd, E downtown, W ⊙ Ⓗ
55a	CA 2, Santa Monica Blvd, E 🅿 Chevron, Mobil, Shell, Thrifty 🍴 Coffee Bean, Jack-in-the-Box, Jamba Juice, Quiznos, Starbucks, Winchell's, Yoshinoya, Zankau Chicken ⊙ 7-11, Firestone/auto, LDS Temple, Staples, vet, W 🅿 76/24hr, Chevron/dsl 🍴 Subway 🛏 Holiday Inn Express
54	Olympic Blvd, Peco Blvd, E 🅿 Mobil 🍴 Islands Burgers, Jack-in-the-Box, La Salsa, Norm's Rest., Stabucks ⊙ Barnes&Noble, Nordstroms, W 🍴 Big Tomy's Rest. ⊙ Best Buy, Marshall's, USPO
53	I-10, Santa Monica Fwy
52	Venice Blvd, E 🅿 Chevron/service, Shell/dsl 🍴 Carl's Jr, Subway 🛏 Ramada ⊙ 7-11, services on Sepulveda, W 🅿 SP/dsl 🍴 FatBurger
51	Culver Blvd, Washington Blvd, E 🍴 Dear John's Café, Taco Bell ⊙ vet, W 🅿 76/repair
50b	CA 90, Slauson Ave, to Marina del Rey, E 🅿 Arco/24hr 🍴 Del Taco, El Pollo Loco, HoneyBaked Ham, Shakey's Pizza, Winchell's ⊙ $Tree, BigLots, Firestone/auto, Goodyear/auto, Just Tires, Office Depot, Old Navy, Staples, transmissions, W 🅿 76 🍴 Denny's ⊙ Albertson's
50a	Jefferson Blvd (from sb), E 🍴 Coco's, Jack-in-the-Box ⊙ PetsMart, Rite Aid, Target, W to LA Airport
49	Howard Hughes Pkwy, to Centinela Ave, E 🅿 Chevron/dsl, Mobil/dsl 🍴 BJ's Brewhouse, Quiznos, Sizzler 🛏 Courtyard, Sheraton ⊙ Best Buy, CVS Drug, Ford, Honda, JC Penney, Macy's, mall, Marshall's, Target, W 🅿 Chevron 🍴 Dinah's Rest., Habuki Japanese, Islands Burgers, Marie Callender's, Rubio's, Starbucks, Subway, Wild Thai 🛏 Extended Stay America, Radisson ⊙ Howard Hughes Ctr, Nordstrom
48	La Tijera Blvd, E 🅿 Mobil/sl 🍴 Burger King, ChuckeCheese, El Pollo Loco, Jamba Juice, KFC, McDonald's, Starbucks, Subway, Taco Bell, TGIFridays 🛏 Best Western ⊙ 99c Store, CVS Drug, Ralph's Foods, Ross, Vons Foods, W 🅿 76/Circle K, Chevron/dsl/24hr 🍴 Buggy Whip Rest., Wendy's ⊙ USPO
47	CA 42, Manchester Ave, Inglewood, E 🅿 76/Circle K/dsl/24hr 🍴 Carl's Jr, Subway 🛏 Best Western, Economy Inn ⊙ 7-11, repair, W 🅿 76, Arco, Circle K, Shell, Valero 🍴 Arby's, Burger King, Denny's, El Pollo Loco, Jack-in-the-Box, Louis Burgers 🛏 Days Inn ⊙ CarMax, Chrysler/Dodge/Jeep, Home Depot, Hyundai

HAWTHORNE / TORRANCE

Exit	Description
46	Century Blvd, E 🅿 Chevron/dsl 🍴 Casa Gamino Mexican, El Pollo Loco, Flower Drum Chinese, Hawaiian BBQ, Little Caesars, Panda Express, Rally's 🛏 Best Value Inn, Best Western, Comfort Inn, Motel 6, Tivoli Hotel ⊙ 7-11, LAX Transmissions, W 🅿 76/Circle K, Arco/24hr, Chevron/dsl, Shell 🍴 Carl's J Denny's, McDonald's, Pizza Hut/Taco Bell 🛏 Hampton Inn, Hilton, Holiday Inn, La Quinta, Marriott, Travelodge, Westin Hotel ⊙ to LAX
45	I-105, Imperial Hwy, E 🅿 76/dsl, Shell, Valero 🍴 El Pollo Loco, El Tarasco Mexican, Jack-in-the-Box, KFC/Taco Bell, McDonald's 🛏 Best Value Inn, Candlewood Suites, Holiday Inn Express ⊙ J&S Transmissions, repair, W 🍴 Wild Goose Rest./Theater (1mi)
44	El Segundo Blvd, to El Segundo, E 🅿 Chevron/24hr, Thrifty, Valero 🍴 Burger King, Christy's Donuts, Cougars Burgers Jack-in-the-Box, Jase Burgers, Subway 🛏 El Segundo Inn ⊙ transmissions, W 🍴 Denny's 🛏 Ramada Inn
43b a	Rosecrans Ave, to Manhattan Beach, E 🅿 76, Shell 🍴 Denny's, El Pollo Loco, Pizza Hut, Starbucks, Subway ⊙ Best Buy, CVS Drug, Food4Less, Ford/Lincoln, Home Depot, Marshall's, Michael's, Office Depot, Ross, W 🅿 Thrifty 🍴 Cafe Rio, Carl's Jr, Chipotle Mexican, Flemings Rest., Hawaiian BBQ, Houston's, Luigi's Rest., Macaroni Grill, McDonald's, Qdoba Mexican, Robeks Juice, Sansai Japanese, Starbucks, Subway 🛏 Ayres Hotel, Hyatt, SpringHill Suites, TownePlace Suites ⊙ AT&T, Barnes&Noble, Costco/gas, CVS Drug, Fresh&Easy Nissan, Office Depot, Old Navy, Staples, Trader Joe's, VW
42b	Inglewood Ave, E 🅿 Shell 🍴 Baskin-Robbins, Del Taco, Denny's, Domino's, In-N-Out, Quiznos ⊙ CVS Drug, Marshall's, PetCo, Vons Foods, W 🅿 76, Shell/dsl/24hr 🍴 La Salsa Mexican, Subway ⊙ 99c Store, repair
42a	CA 107, Hawthorne Blvd, E 🅿 Chevron 🍴 Carl's Jr, Jack-in-the-Box, Little Caesars, McDonald's, Panda Express, Papa John's, Wendy's, Wienerschnitzel 🛏 Baymont Inn, Best Western, Days Inn ⊙ 99c Store, CVS Drug, Kragen Parts, PepBoys, Radio Shack, Value+ Foods, vet, W 🅿 Arco/24hr, Chevron/dsl, Thrifty 🍴 Boston Mkt, Marie Callendar's, Quiznos, Sizzler, Starbucks, Subway, Taco Bell, Yoshinoya ⊙ AutoZone, Macy's, Nordstom
40b	Redondo Beach Blvd (no EZ sb return), Hermosa Beach, E 🅿 76, Arco/24hr 🍴 ChuckeCheese, Jack-in-the-Box ⊙ golf, W 🍴 RoundTable Pizza, Starbucks ⊙ AutoZone, Curves, CVS Drug, URGENT CARE
40a	CA 91 E, Artesia Blvd, to Torrance, W 🅿 Chevron ⊙ Carl's Jr, Starbucks, YumYum Donuts
39	Crenshaw Blvd, to Torrance, E 🅿 Arco/24hr, Shell 🍴 Burger King, El Pollo Loco, McDonald's ⊙ Ralph's Foods, USPO, W 🅿 Mobil/dsl, Shell/Subway/dsl ⊙ Jiffy Lube
38b	Western Ave, to Torrance, E 🅿 76/dsl, Arco, Chevron 🍴 Del Taco, Denny's, Hong Kong Express, Local Place, Papa John's, Quiznos, Starbucks, Wendy's, Yorgo's Burgers 🛏 Dynasty Inn ⊙ Albertson's/Sav-On, Curves, GNC, Toyota/Scion, W 🅿 Mobil 🍴 Mill's Rest. 🛏 Courtyard ⊙ Lexus
38a	Normandie Ave, to Gardena, E 🛏 Comfort Inn, W 🅿 Shell/dsl 🍴 Big Island BBQ, Carl's Jr, Chile Verde Mexican, Hong Kong Cafe, Pizza Hut/Taco Bell, Quiznos, Starbucks, Subway, Wienerschnitzel 🛏 Extended Stay America ⊙ $Tree, Walmart
37b	Vermont Ave (from sb), W 🛏 Holiday Inn ⊙ hwy patrol
37a	I-110, Harbor Fwy
36	Main St (from nb)
36mm	**weigh sta both lanes**

INTERSTATE 405 (LOS ANGELES) Cont'd

CARSON

Exit #	Services
35	Avalon Blvd, to Carson, E[gas] Chevron, Mobil [food] 5 Guys Burgers, Carson Buffet, Chili's, ChuckeCheese, Denny's, Food-Court, Jack-in-the-Box, Jamba Juice, McDonald's, Panda Express, Panera Bread, Pizza Hut, Quiznos, Sensai Grill, Shakey's Pizza, Sizzler, Starbucks, Tokyo Grill, Tony Roma, WingStop [lodging] Clarion [other] America's Tire, AT&T, Bestway Foods, Firestone/auto, Goodyear/auto, Ikea, JC Penney, Just Tires, mall, PepBoys, Radio Shack, Sears/auto, Target, USPO, Verizon, W[gas] Arco/24hr, Mobil [food] Carl's Jr, McDonald's [other] Kia, O'Reilly Parts, Ralph's Foods
34	Carson St, to Carson, E[lodging] EconoLodge, W[gas] 76/dsl/24hr, Mobil [food] Carl's Jr, Jack-in-the-Box, Subway [lodging] DoubleTree Inn
33b	Wilmington Ave, E[gas] Mobil/dsl [food] Carson Burgers, W[gas] Chevron/Jack-in-the-Box/dsl, Shell/Subway/dsl [food] Del Taco, Spires Rest. [other] Chevrolet/Hyundai, Honda, Nissan, Toyota/Scion
33a	Alameda St
32d	Santa Fe Ave (from nb), E[gas] Arco/24hr, W[gas] Chevron/24hr, United/dsl [food] Fantastic Burgers
32c b	I-710, Long Beach Fwy
32a	Pacific Ave (from sb)
30b	Long Beach Blvd, E[gas] Arco/dsl [food] Subway [other] 7-11, W[gas] Exxon [other] [H]
30a	Atlantic Blvd, E[gas] Chevron/dsl [food] Arby's, Carl's Jr, Denny's/24hr, El Torito, Jack-in-the-Box, Polly's Cafe [other] CVS Drug, NAPACare, Staples, Target, vet, Walgreens, W[other] [H] $Tree, Home Depot, PetCo, Ross
29c	Orange Ave (from sb), W[other] Dodge/GMC/Nissan
29b a	Cherry Ave, to Signal Hill, E[gas] Mobil/dsl [food] Fantastic Burgers [other] auto repair, Ford, Lincoln, Mazda, W[gas] 76 [other] America's Tire, Best Buy, BMW/Mini, Buick, Dodge, Firestone, Honda, Mercedes, Nissan
27	CA 19, Lakewood Blvd, E[lodging] Marriott [other] [symbol] W[gas] Chevron, Shell/24hr [food] Spires Rest. [lodging] Extended Stay America, Holiday Inn, Residence Inn [other] [H] Ford, Goodyear/auto
26b	Bellflower Blvd, E[gas] 76 [food] Burger King, Carl's Jr, Denny's, Jamba Juice, KFC, Papa John's, Subway, Togo's [other] Ford, K-Mart, Lowe's, W[gas] Chevron, Mobil/dsl, Shell [food] Baja Fresh, Hof's Hut, IHOP, McDonald's, Pick-Up Stix, Quiznos, Wendy's [other] [H] BigLots, CVS Drug, Goodyear/auto, Rite Aid/24hr, Sears, See's Candies, Target, USPO
26a	Woodruff Ave (from nb)
25	Palo Verde Ave, W[gas] 76 [food] Dave's Burgers, Del Taco, Domino's, Pizza Hut/Taco Bell, Starbucks, Subway
24b	Studebaker Rd (from sb)
24a	I-605 N
23	CA 22 W, 7th St, to Long Beach
22	Seal Beach Blvd, Los Alamitos Blvd, E[gas] 76/dsl, Chevron/repair/24hr, Mobil/dsl [food] Baja Fresh, CA Pizza Kitchen Daphne's Greek, Hot Off the Grill, Islands Burgers, Jamba Juice, KFC, Kobe Japanese, Macaroni Grill, Marie Callenders, Peiwei Asian, Pick-Up Stix, Quiznos, Rubio's, Spaghettini Grill, Starbucks, Z Pizza [lodging] Ayres Hotel [other] AT&T, CVS Drug, GNC, Kohl's, Marshall's, Ralph's Foods, Sprouts Mkt, Target, **1 mi W** [gas] 76/dsl, Chevron [food] Carl's Jr, Del Taco, Domino's [lodging] Hampton Inn
21	CA 22 E, Garden Grove Fwy, Valley View St, E[other] Ford

COSTA MESA

19	Westminster Ave, to Springdale St, E[gas] 76/Circle K, Arco/24hr, Chevron/dsl, Thrifty [food] Café Westminster, Carl's Jr, In-N-Out, KFC, McDonald's [lodging] Knights Inn, Motel 6, Travelodge [other] 7-11, America's Tire, AutoZone, BigLots, Home Depot, O'Reilly Parts, Radio Shack, Rite Aid, Ross, W[gas] Chevron/dsl/24hr [food] Ranchito Mkt, Starbucks, Subway [lodging] Best Western, Courtyard Inn
18	Bolsa Ave, Golden West St, W[gas] 76, Mobil/dsl [food] Coco's, El Torito, IHOP, Jack-in-the-Box, Outback Steaks, Rodrigo's Mexican, Starbucks, Wendy's [other] $Tree, CVS Drug, JC Penney, JoAnn Fabrics, Jons Foods, Macy's, mall, Sears/auto, Target
16	CA 39, Beach Blvd, to Huntington Bch, E[gas] Chevron, Shell [food] Jack-in-the-Box, Subway [lodging] Super 8 [other] [H] PepBoys, Toyota, U-Haul, W[gas] Mobil/service [food] Arby's, BJ's Rest., Buca Italian, Burger King, CA Pizza Kitchen, Chipotle Mexican, Islands Burgers, Jack-in-the-Box, Macaroni Grill, Marie Callender's, McDonald's, Panera Bread, Popeye's, Quiznos, Starbucks, Subway [lodging] Comfort Suites [other] AT&T, Barnes&Noble, Big O Tire, Chrysler/Dodge/Jeep, Firestone/auto, Kohl's, Office Depot, See's Candies, Staples, Target, Verizon, Whole Foods Mkt
15b a	Magnolia St, Warner Ave, E[food] Del Taco, Sizzler [other] Fresh&Easy, W[gas] Chevron, Mobil [food] Carrow's, Magnolia Café, Starbucks, Tommy's Burgers [lodging] Days Inn [other] 7-11, CVS Drug, Grocery Outlet, Tuesday Morning, Winchell's
14	Brookhurst St, Fountain Valley, E[gas] Arco/24hr, Chevron, Mobil, Shell [food] Alerto's Mexican, Carl's Jr, Coco's, Del Taco, KFC, Taco Bell [lodging] Courtyard, Residence Inn [other] America's Tire, Sam's Club/gas, Thompson's RV Ctr, W[gas] 76/dsl, Arco, Shell/dsl [food] Applebee's, Black Angus, Chop Stix, ClaimJumper, Coco's, Coldstone, Corner Bakery Cafe, Islands Burgers, Mandarin, Mimi's Cafe, Quiznos, Rubio's, Starbucks, Subway, Togo's, Wendy's [other] [H] Albertson's, Office Depot, Ralph's Foods, Rite Aid, TJ Maxx, vet
12	Euclid Ave, E[food] Cancun Fresh, Carl's Jr, Coffee Bean, FlameBroiler, Panda Express, Pita Fresh Grill, Quiznos, Souplantation, Starbucks, Subway, Taco Bell, Z Pizza [other] [H] $Tree, Big Lots, Costco/gas, PetsMart, Staples, Tire Whse
11b	Harbor Blvd, to Costa Mesa, E[food] Hooters [lodging] La Quinta, W[gas] 7-11, Arco, Chevron, Mobil, Shell/dsl [food] Burger King, Denny's, Domino's, El Pollo Loco, IHOP, Jack-in-the-Box, KFC, LJ Silver, McDonald's, Subway [lodging] Costa Mesa Inn, Motel 6, Super 8, Vagabond Inn [other] Acura/Dodge, Albertson's, Big O Tire, Buick, Cadillac, Chevrolet, Ford/Lincoln, Honda, Infiniti, JustTires, Mazda, Radio Shack, Rite Aid, Target, Vons Foods, Winchell's
11a	Fairview Rd, E[other] Barnes&Noble, Best Buy, Marshall's, Nordstrom's, Old Navy, W[gas] 76, Chevron, Shell [food] Del Taco, Jack-in-the-Box, Round Table Pizza, Taco Bell [other] CVS Drug, O'Reilly Parts, Stater Bros
10	CA 73, to CA 55 S (from sb), Corona del Mar, Newport Beach

CA

INTERSTATE 405 (LOS ANGELES) Cont'd

IRVINE

Exit #	Services
9b	Bristol St, E Chevron/dsl Antonello's Italian, Baja Fresh, Baskin-Robbins, Boudin SF Cafe, Capital Grill, Carrow's, Chick-fil-A, China Olive, Chipotle Mexican, ClaimJumper, Corner Bakery, Darya Persian, In-N-Out, Jack-in-the-Box, Jade Palace, Maggiano's Rest., McDonald's, Morton's Steaks, Pat&Oscar's, Pizza Hut, Quiznos, Red Robin, Sabores Mexican, Scott Seafood, South Coast Rest, Starbucks, Subway, Z Pizza, Ztejas Rest Marriott Suites, Westin Hotel BigLots, Bloomingdale's, CVS Drug, Firestone/auto, GNC, Macy's, mall, Michael's, Office Depot, PetCo, Radio Shack, Rite Aid, Ross, Sears/auto, Staples, Target, TJ Maxx, Trader Joe's, Vons Foods, World Mkt, W 76/Circle K/dsl, Chevron/dsl Del Taco/24hr, El Pollo Loco, McDonald's, Orchid Rest., Subway, Wahoo's Fish Taco Hanford Hotel, Hilton 7-11, PepBoys, vet
9a	CA 55, Costa Mesa Fwy, to Newport Bch, Riverside
8	MacArthur Blvd, E Chevron, Mobil/Subway Carl's Jr, El Torito, McCormick&Schmick's, McDonald's, Quiznos, Starbucks Crowne Plaza, Embassy Suites Pepperdine U, W Chevron El Torito, Gulliver's Ribs, IHOP Atrium Hotel, Hilton, to
7	Jamboree Rd, Irvine, E Shell Andrei's Rest., Burger King, Soup Plantation Courtyard, Hyatt, Residence Inn, W CA Pizza Kitchen, Daily Grill, FatBurger, Flamebroiler, Houston's, Melting Pot, Ruth's Chris Steaks, Starbucks, Subway, Taleo Mexico, Wahoo's Fish Taco Marriott Office Depot
5	Culver Dr, W Alfie's Gas, Chevron/dsl Carl's Jr, Subway Ace Hardware, Rite Aid, Wholesome Foods Mkt
4	Jeffrey Rd, University Dr, E Chevron, Circle K/gas Baja Fresh, Coffee Bean, Daphney's Greek, El Cholo Cantina, El Pollo Loco, Golden Spoon, Juice It Up, McDonald's, NY Pizza, Pei-wei Asian, Pick-Up Stix, Pomodoro Italian, Starbucks, Togo's, Z Pizza H Ace Hardware, CVS Drug, Gelson's Mkt, Office Depot, Ralph's Foods, Walgreens, W Mobil/dsl IHOP, Korean BBQ, Subway Curves, Ralph's Foods, vet
3	Sand Canyon Ave, E H W Arco/dsl Crystal Jade Asian, Lucca Cafe, Mitsui Grill, Red Brick Pizza, Sharkey's Mexican, Starbucks, Subway, Thai Bamboo Albertson's, CVS Drug, Starbucks
2	CA 133, to Laguna Beach, E DoubleTree Inn
1c	Irvine Center Dr, E Cheesecake Factory, Chipotle Mexican, Dave&Buster's, Oasis Cafes, Panda Express, PF Chang's, Wahoo's Fish Tacos Barnes&Noble, Macy's, Nordstrom, Target, W 7-11 Burger King, La Salsa, NY Deli Big O Tire
1b	Bake Pkwy, W Carmax, Toyota
1a	Lake Forest
0mm	**I-405 begins/ends on I-5, EXIT 132.**

INTERSTATE 505 (WINTERS)

Exit #	Services
33	I-5. **I-505 begins/ends on I-5.**
31	CR 12A
28	CR 14, Zamora
24	CR 19
21	CA 16, to Esparto, Woodland, W Guy's Food/fuel La Plazita
17	CR 27
15	CR 29A
11	CA 128 W, Russell Blvd, W Arco/dsl, Chevron/24hr RoundTable Pizza, Subway, Taco Bell $General, Lorenzo's Mkt
10	Putah Creek Rd, **no crossover...same as 11**
6	Allendale Rd
3	Midway Rd, E RV camping
1c	Vaca Valley Pkwy, E H W Vaca Valley TC/Chevron/Blimpie/dsl
1b	I-80 E. **I-505 begins/ends on I-80.**

INTERSTATE 580 (BAY AREA)

LIVERMORE

Exit #	Services
79	**I-580 begins/ends**, accesses I-5 sb.
76b a	CA 132, Chrisman Rd, to Modesto, E 76/dsl RV camping (5mi)
72	Corral Hollow Rd
67	Patterson Pass Rd, E Subway, W Shell/7-11/dsl
65	I-205 (from eb), to Tracy
63	Grant Line Rd, to Byron
59	N Flynn Rd, S Brake Check Area, many wind-turbines, Altamont Pass, elev 1009
57	N Greenville Rd, Laughlin Rd, Altamont Pass Rd, to Livermore Lab, S 76/7-11/dsl Best Western, La Quinta Harley-Davidson
56mm	**weigh sta both lanes**
55	Vasco Rd, to Brentwood, N 7-11, Arco, Chevron/dsl, Gas&Shop/dsl, QuikStop/dsl A&W/KFC, Country Waffles, McDonald's, Wienerschnitzel/Tastee Freez Toyota/Scion, S 7-11, Valero/dsl Jack-in-the-Box, Taco Bell Quality Inn
54	CA 84, 1st St, Springtown Blvd, Livermore, N Chevron/dsl Zpizz DoubleTree, Motel 6, Springtown Inn 7-11, S 76, Chevron, Shell, Valero/Circle K Applebee's, Burger King, Chili's, Chipotle, IHOP, Jamba Juice, McDonald's, Panda Express, Panera Bread, Peking Chinese, Starbucks, Subway, Taco Bell, Togo's America's Tire, Big Lots, CVS Drug, GNC, Lowe's Whse, Petco, Ross, Safeway/gas, Target, TJ Maxx, vet
52	N Livermore Ave, S 7-11, Chevron Baja Fresh, Coldstone, Denica's Kitchen, In-N-Out, Jack-in-the-Box, Popeye's, Quizno's, String's Italian Hawthorn Suites AT&T, Home Depot, Honda, Kohl's, Schwab Tire, Subaru, USPO, Walmart/Subway
51	Portola Ave, Livermore (no EZ eb return), S Ford/Lincoln
50	Airway Blvd, Collier Canyon Rd, Livermore, N Chevron/dsl Wendy's Comfort Inn, Courtyard, Hampton Inn, Hilton Garden, Holiday Inn Express, Residence Inn Costco/gas, S Carl's Jr, Cattlemen's Rest., Cholula's, Starbucks, Subway Extended Stay America 7-11
48	El Charro Rd, O'Fallon Rd, N Chevron/dsl BJ's Rest., Fresh Pixx, Jersey Mike's, Panera Bread, Starbucks Dick's, Target, S Chrysler/Dodge/Jeep, SF Outlets/famous brands
47	Santa Rita Rd, Tassajara Rd, N Baja Fresh, Buffalo Wild Wings, Coco Cabana Buick/GMC, GNC, Kia, Lowe's, Safeway, S Shell McDonald's, Ozora Steaks, Pizza Guys, Subway $Tree, Acura, AutoZone, BMW/Mini, Chevrolet/Cadillac, CVS Drug, Goodyear/auto, Lexus, Ranch Mkt, Trader Joe's
46	Hacienda Dr, Pleasanton, N Shell Applebee's, Black Angus, Chipotle, Five Guys, Fuddruckers, Habit Burger, Lazy Dog Rest., Mimi's Cafe, On-the-Border, Papa John's, Quiznos,

INTERSTATE 580 (BAY AREA) Cont'd

PLEASANTON

46	Continued Starbucks, Urban Plates Hyatt Place Barnes&Noble, Best Buy, Old Navy, TJ Maxx, Toyota/Scion, Verizon, Whole Foods Mkt, S Red Robin, Subway H Kohl's, Walmart/McDonald's
45	Hopyard Rd, Pleasanton, N 76, Chevron/dsl, Shell/dsl IHOP, Subway La Quinta America's Tire, El Monte RV Ctr, Fiat, Honda, Hyundai, Mazda, Nissan, Office Depot, O'Reilly Parts, U-Haul, VW, S Chevron/dsl, Shell/dsl Arby's, Black Bear Diner, Burger King, Chili's, Denny's, Faz Rest., In-N-Out, Nations Burgers, Specialty's Cafe Bakery, Starbucks, Taco Bell Best Western, Courtyard, Doubltree, Larkspur Landing, Motel 6, Sheraton Home Depot, Mercedes, Verizon
44b	I-680, N to San Ramon, S to San Jose
44a	Foothills Rd, San Ramon Rd, W Sheraton, N 76/dsl, Chevron/dsl, Shell/dsl, Valero Baskin Robbins, Burger King, Casa Orozco, Chipotle Mexican, ChuckeCheese, Country Waffles, Elephant Bar Rest., Frankie Johnnie & Luigi's Too, Freebirds Burrito, Habit Burger, Hana Japan, Hooters, Korean BBQ, McNamara's Steaks, Outback Steaks, Panda Express, Panera Bread, Popeye's, RoundTable Pizza, Starbucks, Subway, Togo's Holiday Inn $Tree, Big Lots, CVS Drug, Hobby Lobby, Jo-Ann, Marshall's, Michael's, O'Reilly Parts, PetCo, PetsMart, Ranch Mkt Foods, REI, Ross, Safeway/gas, Sprouts, Target, S Baja Fresh, CA Pizza Kitchen, Cheesecake Factory, PF Chang's Marriott, Residence Inn JC Penney, Macy's, mall, Nordstrom, Sears

CASTRO VALLEY

39	Eden Canyon Rd, Palomares Rd, S rodeo park
37	Center St, Crow Canyon Rd, S 76/dsl, Arco/24hr, Chevron/dsl/, Quikstop McDonald's, Starbucks, Subway, same as 35
35	Redwood Rd (from eb), Castro Valley, N 76/dsl, Chevron, Shell/dsl Baker's Square, Chipotle Mexican, KFC, McDonald's, Quizno's, RoundTable Pizza, Sizzler, Taco Bell, Wendy's Comfort Suites, Goodyear, Holiday Inn Express, Longs Drug, Lucky Foods, NAPA, Radio Shack, Rite Aid, Safeway, Walgreens
34	I-238 W, to I-880, CA 238, **off I-238** W Jack-in-the Box, McDonald's 99c Store, Chrysler/Jeep
33	164th Ave, Miramar Ave, E Chevron/dsl, Valero Fairmont Inn
32	150th Ave, Fairmont, E H W 76/dsl, Shell Arby's, Burger King, Carrows, Chili's, Denny's, McDonald's, RoundTable Pizza, Starbucks, Tito's Cafe Goodyear, Kohl's, Long's Drug, Macy's, Pepboys, Staples, Target
31	Grand Ave (from sb), Dutton Ave, W Coast Rite Aid
30	106th Ave, Foothill Blvd, MacArthur Blvd, W Arco Church's
29	98th Ave, Golf Links Rd, E Shell Oakland Zoo, W 76, Valero
27b	Keller Ave, Mtn Blvd, E repair
27a	Edwards Ave (from sb, no EZ return), E US Naval Hospital
26a	CA 13, Warren Fwy, to Berkeley (from eb)
26b	Seminary Rd, E Observatory/Planetarium, W Arco/24hr
25b a	High St, to MacArthur Blvd, E 76 Razzo's Pizza, Subway Lucky Foods, O'Reilly Parts, USPO, W 76 Walgreens
24	35th Ave (no EZ sb return), E 76 Taco Bell, W 76, Chevron, QuikStop

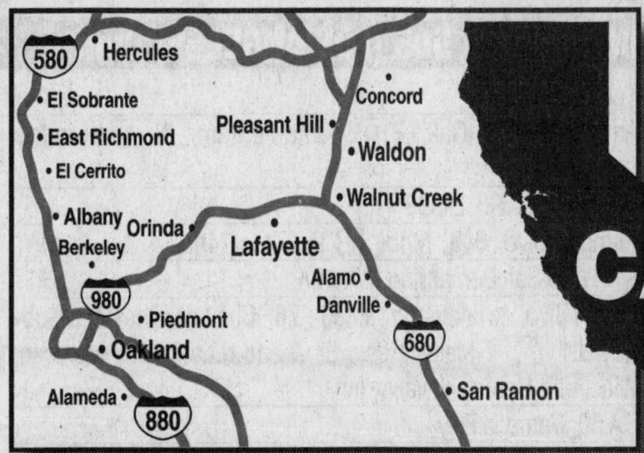

CA

OAKLAND AREA

23	Coolidge Ave, Fruitvale, E Shell/24hr China Gourmet, McDonald's, Subway Farmer Joe's, Longs Drug, Radio Shack
22	Park Blvd, E Shell, W Arco, Quikstop H
21b	Grand Ave, Lake Shore, E 76/24hr, Chevron/dsl KFC, Subway Long's Drug, Trader Joe's, USPO, Walgreens, W Chevron/dsl/24hr
21a	Harrison St, Oakland Ave, E Quikstop, W Honda
19d c	CA 24 E, I-980 W, to Oakland
19b	West St, San Pablo Ave, E Extended Stay America Best Buy, Home Depot, Jo-Ann Fabrics, Michael's, Office Depot
19a	I-80 W
18c	Market St, to San Pablo Ave, downtown
18b	Powell St, Emeryville, E 76 Burger King, CA Pizza Kitchen, Denny's, Elephant Bar/Grill, Jamba Juice, PF Chang's, Starbucks, Togo's Courtyard, Sheraton, Woodfin Suites Barnes&Noble, Old Navy, Ross, Trader Joe's, W Shell Chevy's Mexican Hilton Garden
18a	CA 13, Ashby Ave, Bay St, same as 18b
17	University Ave, Berkeley, E 76, University Gas La Quinta to UC Berkeley
16	Gilman St, E Golden Gate Fields Race Track, W Target
13	Albany St, Buchanan St (from eb)
12	Central Ave (from eb), El Cerrito, E Shell, Valero Costco/gas
11	Bayview Ave, Carlson Blvd, E 76
10b	Regatta Blvd, E Golden Gate/dsl
10a	S 23rd St, Marina Bay Pkwy, E Stop and Save/dsl Subway, W Cafe Tiatro, El Molchaete, Quizno's, Wing Stop Longs Drugs
9	Harbour Way, Cutting Blvd, E Arco, W Burger King
8	Canal Blvd, Garrard Blvd, W Chevron/dsl Days Inn
7b	Castro St, to I-80 E, Point Richmond, downtown industrial
7a	Western Drive (from wb), Point Molate
5mm	Richmond-San Rafael Toll Bridge
2a	Francis Drake Blvd, to US 101 S, E Extended Stay Deluxe BMW, Home Depot
1b	Francisco Blvd, San Rafael, E Beacon, Circle K, Francisco Burger King, La Croissant Motel 6, Travelodge Mazda, tires, U-Haul, W Subway, Wendy's Office Depot, to San Quentin, USPO
1a	US 101 N to San Rafael, **I-580 begins/ends on US 101.**

INTERSTATE 605 (LOS ANGELES)

Exit #	Services
27c	Huntington Dr. **I-605 begins/ends.** Mobil/dsl Subway CVS Drug, Fresh&Easy Foods
27	I-210

CA

LOS ANGELES AREA

INTERSTATE 605 (LOS ANGELES) Cont'd

Exit #	Services
26	Arrow Hwy, Live Oak, E [other] Santa Fe Dam, W [other] Irwindale Speedway
24	Lower Azusa Rd, LA St
23	Ramona Blvd, E [gas] Mobil [food] Del Taco/24hr
22	I-10, E to San Bernardino, W to LA
21	Valley Blvd, to Industry, E [gas] 76, Chevron/Chester's/Subway/dsl [food] 7 Mares Rest., El Charro, Las Milpas Mexican, Winchell's Donut [lodging] Valley Inn
19	CA 60, Pamona Fwy
18	Peck Rd, E [gas] Shell, W [other] Ford Trucks
17	RoseHills Rd, W [other] Sports Arena
16	Beverly Blvd
15	Whittier Blvd, E [gas] 76/dsl, Arco [food] Carl's Jr, Taco Bell, YumYum Donuts [lodging] GoodNite Inn [other] 7-11, W [gas] Chevron, Shell [food] DQ, Pizza Hut, Shakey's Pizza, Starbucks, Subway, Taco's Mexico, Tommy's Burgers [lodging] Howard Johnson [other] AutoZone, Rite Aid
14	Washington Blvd, to Pico Rivera, E [other] Firestone/auto
13	Slauson Ave, E [gas] Arco, Mobil [food] Denny's [lodging] Motel 6, W [other] [H]
12	Telegraph Rd, to Santa Fe Springs, E [gas] 76, Chevron [food] Del Taco, Jack-in-the-Box, KFC, Subway, Taco Bell, Yoshinoya [other] URGENT CARE, W [gas] Arco/dsl
12mm	I-5
11	Florence Ave, to Downey, E [gas] Mobil [other] Cadillac, Chevrolet, Honda
10	Firestone Blvd, E [gas] 76 [food] ChuckeCheese, KFC, McDonald's, Norm's Burgers, Sam's Burgers, Subway [lodging] Best Western [other] 99c Store, Audi/BMW/Porsche, Costco, Food4Less, Staples, Verizon, Walgreens, W [gas] Chevron/repair [food] Starbucks [other] Chrysler/Dodge/Jeep, Office Depot, Target
8	I-105, Imperial Hwy, E [gas] 76 [food] Domino's, KFC, LJ Silver, McDonald's, Pizza Hut/Taco Bell [other] CVS Drug, Food4Less, W [gas] Arco
9	Rosecrans Ave, to Norwalk, E [gas] Chevron, Mobil [food] Del Taco, Little Caesars, McDonald's, Subway [other] [H] Food Basket Foods, Fresh&Easy, vet, Walgreens, W [food] Carrow's Rest. [lodging] Motel 6
7	Alondra Blvd, E [gas] 7-11, Chevron [food] A&W, Alondra's Mexican, Frantone's Rest., KFC, Red Chili [other] CVS Drug, Home Depot, Staples, W [gas] Shell/Subway/24hr [food] Del Taco
6	CA 91
5	South St, E [food] 5 Guys, BJ's Rest., CA Pizza Kitchen, Carl's Jr, Chick-fil-A, Coco's, Coldstone, Hometown Buffet, Jamba Juice, Lazy Dog Cafe, Luecille's BBQ, Panda Express, Panera Bread, Quiznos, Red Robin, Starbucks [other] AT&T, Firestone, Macy's, mall, Nordstrom's, Sears/auto, Target, Verizon, W [gas] Shell/service, Valero [other] Acura, Buick/GMC, Chevrolet, Chrysler/Dodge/Jeep, Ford, Honda, Hyundai, Infiniti, KIA, Lexus, Mazda, Nissan, Smartcar, Suzuki, Toyota/Scion, VW
4	Del Amo Blvd, to Cerritos, E [food] Del Taco, Omega Burgers, Starbucks [other] Ralph's Foods, W [gas] Mobil
3	Carson St, E [gas] 76, Price Saver/dsl [food] Alberto's Mexican, Jack-in-the-Box, KFC, Little Caesar's, McDonald's, Pizza Hut, Popeye's, Subway, Taco Bell, Wienerschnitzel [lodging] Lakewood Inn [other] 7-11, CVS Drug, Food4Less, O'Reilly Parts, Price Right Foods, W [gas] Chevron/Subway/dsl [food] Carl's Jr, Chick-fil-A, Del Taco, Denny's, El Pollo Loco, El Torito, FoodCourt, In-N-Out, Island's Burgers, Jack-in-the-Box, Leucille's BBQ, Panda
3	Continued Express, Roadhouse Grill, Starbucks, SuperMex, TGIFriday's, Yashi Japanese [other] America's Tire, Barnes&Noble, Lowe's, Michael's, Old Navy, Petsmart, Radio Shack, Ross, Sam's Club, Staples, Walmart/auto
1	Katella Ave, Willow St, E [gas] Shell [food] Madera's Steaks, McDonald's, Polly's Cafe, Starbucks [other] [H] Rite Aid, W Eldorado Regional Park
0mm	**I-605 begins/ends on I-405.**

CONCORD

INTERSTATE 680 (BAY AREA)

Exit #	Services
71b a	I-80 E, to Sacramento, W to Oakland, **I-680 begins/ends on I-80.**
70	Green Valley Rd (from eb), Cordelia, N [gas] Arco am/pm [other] Costco/gas, Longs Drug, Safeway
69	Gold Hill Rd, W [gas] TowerMart/dsl
65	Marshview Rd
63	Parish Rd
61	Lake Herman Rd, E [gas] Arco/Jack-in-the-Box/dsl, W [gas] Gas City/dsl, Shell/Carl's Jr/dsl/24hr [other] vista point
60	Bayshore Rd, industrial park
58	I-780, to Benicia, toll plaza
56	Marina Vista, to Martinez
55mm	Martinez-Benicia Toll Br
54	Pacheco Blvd, Arthur Rd, Concord, W [gas] 76, Shell/dsl
53	CA 4 E to Pittsburg, W to Richmond, Pittsburg
52	CA 4 E, Concord, Pacheco, E [food] Hometown Buffet, Marie Callender's, Starbucks, Taco Bell [lodging] Crowne Plaza, Holiday Inn [other] Chevrolet, Ford, Hyundai, Infiniti/VW, Sam's Club, Toyota, Trader Joe's, USPO, W [gas] 76, Grand Gas, Shell/24hr [food] Denny's, McDonald's, Wendy's [other] AutoZone, Barnes&Noble, Firestone, K-Mart, Kragen Parts, Pepboys, Safeway Foods, Schwab Tire, Target, Toyota
51	Willow Pass Rd, Taylor Blvd, E [food] Benihana Rest., Buffet City, Claim Jumper, Denny's, El Torito, Elephant Bar Rest., Fuddruckers, Grissini Italian, Jamba Juice, Panera Bread, Quizno's, Sizzler [lodging] Hilton [other] Cost+, Old Navy, Willows Shopping Ctr, W [food] Baja Fresh, Red Robin [other] JC Penney, Macy's, Sears/auto
50	CA 242 (from nb), to Concord
49b	Monument Blvd, Gregory Lane (from sb), E [gas] Valero/dsl [food] Country Waffles, Panda Express, Rubio's, Starbucks [other] Kohl's, Marshall's, W [gas] Chevron [food] Boston Mkt, Jack-in-the-Box, McDonald's, Nations Burgers, Pizza Hut, Red Brick Pizza, Taco Bell [lodging] Courtyard, Hyatt [other] Big O Tire, Grocery Outlet, Lucky Foods, Michael's, Radio Shack, Rite Aid, Ross, Safeway Foods, Staples, Tuesday Morning
49a	Contra Costa Blvd (from nb)
48	Treat Blvd, Geary Rd, E [gas] Chevron [food] Back 40 BBQ, Heavenly Cafe, Subway [lodging] Embassy Suites, Extended Stay America [other] 7-11, Best Buy, Office Depot, W [gas] Chevron, Shell [food] Black Angus, Primavera Pasta, Quizno's, Starbucks, Wendy's, Yan's China Bistro [other] Walgreens
47	N Main St, to Walnut Creek, E [gas] Chevron [food] Fuddrucker's, Jack-in-the-Box, Taco Bell [lodging] Marriott, Motel 6, Walnut Cr Motel [other] Cadillac, Chevrolet, Chrysler/Dodge/Jeep, Harley-Davidson, Honda, Jaguar, Land Rover, Mercedes, Nissan, Target, W [gas] 76/7-11/dsl/24hr [food] Domino's [other] NAPA, Porsche
46b	Ygnacio Valley Rd
46a	SR-24 W

INTERSTATE 680 (BAY AREA) Cont'd

SAN RAMON

Exit #	Services
45b	Olympic Blvd, Oakland
45a	S Main St, Walnut Creek, E [other] [H]
44	Rudgear (from nb)
43	Livorna Rd
42b a	Stone Valley Rd, Alamo, W [gas] Chevron, Shell/dsl [food] Papa Murphy's, Starbucks, Subway, Taco Bell, Xenia's [other] 7-11, Curves, Longs Drugs, Rite Aid, Safeway, vet
41	El Pintado Rd, Danville
40	El Cerro Blvd
39	Diablo Rd, Danville, E [gas] 76/24hr [food] Chinese Cuisine, Taco Bell [other] Mt Diablo SP (12mi), Walgreens, W [gas] Diablo
38	Sycamore Valley Rd, E [gas] Shell [food] Denny's [lodging] Best Western, W [gas] 76/dsl, Valero/dsl
36	Crow Canyon Rd, San Ramon, E [gas] Shell/dsl [food] Baskin Robbins, Burger King, Carl's Jr, Cheese Steak Shop, Chili's, Dickey's BBQ, Habit Burger, Jamba Juice, On Fire Pizza, Panda Express, Panera Bread, Primavera Ristorante, Round Table Pizza, Ruggie's Rest., Starbucks, Starbucks (2), Subway, Zachary's Pizza [lodging] Extended Stay America [other] [H] Big O Tire, Costco, GNC, Marshall's, Office Depot, PetCo, Radio Shack, Rite Aid, Sea's Candies, Sprouts, W [gas] 76, Chevron/dsl, Shell/autocare, Valero [food] Chipotle Mexican, Giuseppe's Italian, In-N-Out, McDonald's, Nation's Burger's, Subway, Taco Bell, Togo's [lodging] Hyatt House Hotel [other] 7-11, CVS Drug, Home Depot, Safeway, Staples, Verizon, vet
34	Bollinger Canyon Rd, E [gas] Valero [food] Baja Fresh, Buffalo Wild Wings, Izzy's Steaks, Jimmy John's, Pasta Pomodoro [lodging] Marriott, Residence Inn [other] AT&T, CVS Drug, Target, Whole Foods Mkt, W [gas] Chevron/dsl [food] Chevy's Mexican, Clementine's Grill [lodging] Courtyard, Extended Stay America
31	Alcosta Blvd, to Dublin, E [gas] 76/dsl [other] 7-11, W [gas] Chevron, Shell/dsl [food] DQ, McDonalds, Papa Murphy's, Peking Delight, Subway, Taco Bell [other] Lucky Foods, Walgreens
30	I-580, W to Oakland, E to Tracy
29	Stoneridge, Dublin, E [lodging] DoubleTree, W [food] Baja Fresh, Cheesecake Factory, PF Chang's, Taco Bell [lodging] Sheraton [other] JC Penney, Macy's, mall, Nordstrom, Sears
26	Bernal Ave, Pleasanton, E [gas] Shell/Jack-in-the-Box [food] Lindo's Mexican
25	Sunol Blvd, Pleasanton
21b a	CA 84, Calvaras Rd, Sunol, W to Dumbarton Bridge
20	Andrade Rd, Sheridan Rd (from sb), E [gas] Sunol Super Stp/dsl
19mm	**weigh sta nb**

FREMONT

Exit #	Services
19	Sheridan Rd (from nb)
18	Vargas Rd
16	CA 238, Mission Blvd, to Hayward, E [gas] Shell [food] McDonald's, W [other] [H]
15	Washington Blvd, Irvington Dist, E [gas] QuikStop
14	Durham Rd, to Auto Mall Pkwy, W [gas] 76/Circle K/Subway/24hr, Shell/Jack-in-the-Box [other] Fry's Electronics, Home Depot, Walmart
12	CA 262, Mission Blvd, to I-880, Warm Springs Dist, W [gas] 76, Valero [food] Burger King, Carl's Jr, Denny's, KFC, RoundTable Pizza, Starbucks, Subway, Taco Bell [lodging] Extended Stay America [other] 7-11, GNC, Longs Drug, Radio Shack, Ross, Safeway, Walgreens
10	Scott Creek Rd
9	Jacklin Rd, E [other] Bonfare Mkt, W [gas] Shell

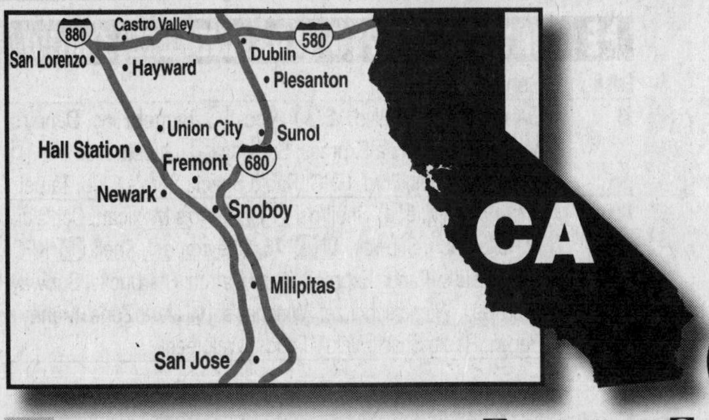

CA

SAN JOSE

Exit #	Services
8	CA 237, Calaveras Blvd, Milpitas, E [gas] 76, Shell/repair [food] Domino's, Flames CoffeeShop, RoadTable Pizza, Sizzler, Subway [lodging] Exectuive Inn [other] 7-11, Oceans SuperMkt, W [gas] Shell [food] El Torito, Giorgio's Italian, It's a Grind, Lyon's Rest., McDonald's, Red Lobster [lodging] Embassy Suites, Extended Stay America [other] Longs Drug, Lucky Foods, Safeway, Staples
6	Landess Ave, Montague Expswy, E [gas] 76, Arco, Chevron [food] Burger King, Jack-in-the-Box, McDonald's, Taco Bell, Togo's, Wienerschnitzel [other] Firestone, Lucky Foods, Radio Shack, Rite Aid, Target, Walgreens
5	Capitol Ave, Hostetter Ave, E [gas] Shell [food] Carl's Jr, Popeye's [other] SaveMart Foods, W [gas] Valero [other] Jiffy Lube
4	Berryessa Rd, E [gas] Arco/24hr, USA, Valero/repair [food] Denny's, Lee's Sandwiches, McDonald's, Taco Bell [other] AutoZone, Longs Drug, Safeway
2b	McKee Rd, E [gas] 76, Chevron, Shell [food] Burger King, HomeTown Buffet, Pizza Hut, Quizno's, Starbucks, Togo's, Wienerschnitzel [other] $Tree, PaknSave Foods, Ross, Target, Walgreens, W [gas] World Gas [food] Baskin-Robbins, Foster's Freeze, Lee's Sandwiches, McDonald's, RoundTable Pizza, Wendy's, Yum Yum Doughnut [other] [H] Kohl's
2a	Alum Rock Ave, E [gas] Shell/dsl/24hr [food] Jack-in-the-Box, Taco Bell, W [gas] 76/24hr, Chevron [food] Carl's Jr
1d	Capitol Expswy
1c	King Rd, Jackson Ave (from nb), E [gas] L&D Gas, Shell [food] El Gallo Giro, Jamba Juice, Kings Burger, Panda Express, Starbucks, Super Buffet, Taco Bell [other] Target, Walgreens
1b	US 101, to LA, SF
1a	(EXITs left from sb) **I-680 begins/ends on I-280.**

INTERSTATE 710 (LOS ANGELES)

L.A. AREA

Exit #	Services
23	**I-710 begins/ends on Valley Blvd,** E [gas] Arco
22b a	I-10
20c	Chavez Ave
20b	CA 60, Pamona Fwy, E [food] King Taco, Monterrey Hill Rest., W [gas] Shell
20a	3rd St
19	Whittier Blvd, Olympic Blvd, W [gas] Shell [food] McDonald's
17b	Washington Blvd, Commerce, W [gas] Commerce Trkstp/dsl/rest.
17a	Bandini Blvd, Atlantic Blvd, industrial
15	Florence Ave, E [food] Alfredo's Mexican, Applebee's, Coldstone, El Pescador Mexican, El Pollo Loco, IHOP, KFC, McDonald's, Panda Express, Quiznos, Red Brick Pizza, Starbucks, Subway, Taco Bell, Yoshinoya [lodging] Comfort Inn [other] $Tree, casino, Food-4Less, Marshall's, Rite Aid, Ross, W [other] truck repair

[gas] = gas [food] = food [lodging] = lodging [other] = other [rest stop] = rest stop

CA

INTERSTATE 710 (LOS ANGELES) Cont'd

LOS ANGELES AREA

Exit #	Services
13	CA 42, Firestone Blvd, E [gas] Arco [food] Burger King, Denny's, McDonald's, Panda Express, Subway [lodging] Guesthouse Inn [other] El Super Foods, Ford, GNC, Radio Shack, Sam's Club, Target
12b a	Imperial Hwy, E [gas] Shell/dsl [food] Abierto's Mexican, Carl's Jr., El Pollo Loco, Subway, W [gas] 76, Chevron/dsl, Shell [food] KFC, McDonald's, Panda Express, Pizza Patron, Starbucks, Subway, Taco Bell, Wienerschnitzel, Winchell's [other] AutoZone, Manny's Repair, Radio Shack, Valu+ Foods, Walgreens
11b a	I-105
10	Rosecrans Ave
9b a	Alondra Ave, E [gas] Chevron/dsl [food] Jack-in-the-Box [other] Home Depot
8b a	CA 91
7b a	Long Beach Blvd, E [gas] Chevron, Mobil, United/dsl, Valero [food] El Ranchito Mexican, McDonald's, Sizzler [other] CVS Drug, W [gas] Arco/24hr [food] Jack-in-the-Box, Mocasalitos, Subway [lodging] Luxury Inn
6	Del Amo Blvd
4	I-405, San Diego Freeway
3b a	Willow St, E [gas] Arco, Chevron [food] Baskin-Robbins, Chee Chinese, Dominos, Pizza Hut [other] Radio Shack, Walgreens, W [gas] 76, Arco [food] KFC, Little Caesars, Popeye's [other] AutoZone, Big Saver Foods
2	CA 1, Pacific Coast Hwy, E [gas] 76/dsl, Arco/mart, Chevron, Mobil [food] Hong Kong Express, KFC, McDonald's [lodging] Beacon Inn, Don Chente Tacos, King Taco, La Mirage Inn, Travel Eagle Inn [other] auto repair, Ranch Mkt, W [gas] 76/service, PCH Trkstp/dsl, Shell/Carl's Jr/dsl [food] Alberto's Mexican, Golden Star Rest., Jack-in-the-Box, McDonald's, Taco Bell, Tom's Burgers, Winchell's [lodging] Hiland Motel, SeaBreeze Motel [other] truckwash, TrueValue
1d	Anaheim St, W [gas] Speedy Fuel [other] dsl repair/scales
1c	Ahjoreline Dr, Piers B, C, D, E, Pico Ave
1b	Pico Ave, Piers F-J, Queen Mary
1a	Harbor Scenic Dr, Piers S, T, Terminal Island, E [lodging] Hilton

I-710 begins/ends in Long Beach.

INTERSTATE 780 (VALLEJO)

BENICIA

Exit #	Services
7	**I-780 begins/ends on I-680.**
6	E 5th St, Benicia, N [gas] Fast&Easy, S [gas] Citgo/7-11, Valero/dsl [food] China Garden [other] Big O Tire, repair, vet
5	E 2nd St, Central Benicia, N [gas] Valero [lodging] Best Western, S [food] McDonald's, Pappa's Rest.
4	Southampton Rd, Benicia, N [food] Asian Bistro, Burger King, Coldstone Creamery, Country Waffles, Jamba Juice, Rickshaw Express, RoundTable Pizza, Starbucks, Subway [other] Ace Hardware, Radio Shack, Raley's Foods, vet
3b	Military West
3a	Columbus Pkwy, N [gas] Shell [food] Burger King, Napoli Pizza, Subway [other] Jiffy Lube, Longs Drugs, S to Benicia RA
1d	Glen Cove Pkwy, N [other] Hwy Patrol, S [food] Baskin-Robbins, Subway, Taco Bell [other] Safeway
1c	Cedar St
1b a	**I-780 begins/ends on I-80.**

INTERSTATE 805 (SAN DIEGO)

SAN DIEGO AREA

Exit #	Services
28mm	I-5 (from nb), **I-805 begins/ends on I-5.**
27.5	CA 56 E (from nb)
27	Sorrento Valley Rd, Mira Mesa Blvd
26	Vista Sorrento Pkwy, E [gas] Mobil/dsl [food] Chili's, Flame Broiler, Jamba Juice, McDonald's, Quizno's, Rubio's, Starbucks, Subway [lodging] Country Inn, Courtyard, Extended Stay America, Holiday Inn Express, Hyatt House [other] Staples
25b a	La Jolla Village Dr, Miramar Rd, **1 mi** E [gas] 76/dsl [other] Discount Tire, Firestone, W [food] Corner Cafe, Cozymel's Cantina, Donovan's Grill, Harry's Grill, PF Chang's, Seasons Fresh Grill [lodging] Embassy Suites, Marriott [other] [H] Macy's, mall, Nordstom's, Sears
24	Governor Dr
23	CA 52
22	Clairemont Mesa Blvd, E [gas] 7-11/dsl, Chevron/dsl, Mega/Subway/dsl, Shell [food] Arby's, Burger King, Carl's Jr, Chipotle Mexican, Coco's, Godfather Rest., Jersey Mike's, McDonald's, Rubio's Grill, Souplantation, Starbucks, Subway, Tommy's Burgers [other] Food4Less, Ford/Kia, Nissan, Ranch Mkt, Verizon, Walmart, W [gas] Gas [food] Buga Korean BBQ, Subway [lodging] Best Western, CA Suites, Motel 6
21	CA 274, Balboa Ave, E [gas] 7-11, 76, Arco/dsl, Chevron/dsl [food] Applebee's, Islands Burger, Jack-in-the-Box [other] CarMax Chevrolet, Chrysler/Dodge/Jeep, Jaguar, VW
20	CA 163 N, to Escondido
20a	Mesa College Dr, Kearney Villa Rd, W [other] [H]
18	Murray Ridge Rd, to Phyllis Place
17b	I-8, E to El Centro, W to beaches
16	El Cajon Blvd, E [gas] Arco, Ultra [other] Pancho Villa Mkt, W [gas] 76 [food] Carl's Jr, Jack-in-the-Box, Rudford's Rest., Subway, Wendy's [other] O'Reilly Parts
15	University Ave, E [gas] Chevron [food] Subway [other] Radio Shack, W [gas] 76/dsl, USA/dsl [food] Starbucks [other] CVS Drug, Fresh&Easy Mkt, Walgreens
14	CA 15 N, 40th St, to I-15
13b	Home Ave, MLK Ave
13a	CA 94
12b	Market St
12a	Imperial Ave, E [gas] Homeland Gas/dsl, United, W [food] Asia Wok, Cojita's Taco, Domino's, KFC/LJ Silver, Sizzler, Subway [other] 99c Store, Home Depot
11b	47th St
11a	43rd St, W [food] Giant Pizza, Jack-in-the-Box, Subway [other] AutoZone, CVS Drug, Northgate Mkt
10	Plaza Blvd, National City, E [food] Chow King, McDonald's, Pizza Hut, Popeye's, Starbucks, Subway, Winchell's [other] [H], AutoZone, Firestone/auto, Vallarta Foods, vet, Walgreens, Well's Drug, W [gas] USA [food] Bistro City Chinese, Carl's Jr, Family House Rest., IHOP, Jubilee Chicken/burgers, Little Caesar's, Papa John's, Subway, Wings n Things [lodging] Holiday Inn Express, Motel 6, Stardust Inn [other] AT&T, Big Lots, CVS Drug, Discount Tire, Firestone/auto, Jo-Ann Fabrics, O'Reilly Parts, Walmart
9	Sweetwater Rd, E [food] Applebee's, Outback Steaks [lodging] Sweetwater Inn [other] 7-11, JC Penney, Macy's, W [gas] Chevron/7-11/dsl [food] Ben's Rest., Carl's Jr, Denny's, Hanaoka Japanese, Mike's NY Pizza, Pizza Hut, Pizza Hut, Starbucks, Subway, Taco Bell [other] CVS Drug, Food4Less, Goodyear/auto, Staples
8	CA 54

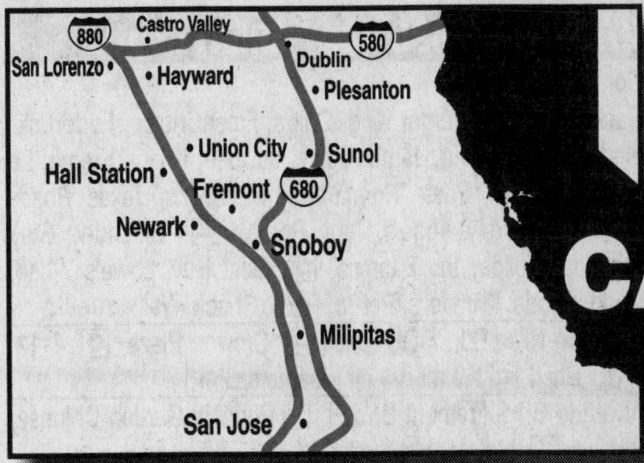

CA

INTERSTATE 805 (SAN DIEGO) Cont'd

7c	E St, Bonita Rd, E on Bonita Plaza Rd Applebee's, El Torito, Outback Steaks, Red Robin, Starbucks, Subway JC Penney, Macy's, mall, Target, W Chevron/dsl, Circle K, Shell/dsl Burger King, Denny's, La Tequila Mexican Comfort Inn, La Quinta
7b a	H St, E Shell China China, Coldstone, Daphne's CA Greek, D'Lish Pizza, Honeybaked, Jack-in-the-Box, Robeks Juice, Subway, Taco Bell CVS Drug, Marshall's, Radio Shack, Vons Foods, W Caffe Tazza
6	L St, Telegraph Canyon Rd, E Arco/dsl Little Caesar's, Mandarin Canyon, McDonald's, Starbucks, Subway H, Olympic Training Ctr, Rite Aid, vet, Von's Foods, W 76/ Circle K/dsl, USA Canada Steakburger 7-11
4	Orange Ave, E Olympic Training Ctr
3	Main St, Otay Valley Rd, E Shell/dsl Panda Express, Souplantation Ford/Kia, Honda, Kohl's, Nissan, PetsMart, Staples, Toyota/Scion, W Circle K/dsl Best Western
2	Palm Ave, E Arco, Chevron Carl's Jr, Hometown Buffet, Starbucks, Subway, Taco Bell AT&T, Home Depot, Meineke, Radio Shack, Tire Pros, USPO, Von's Foods, Walmart/McDonald's, W Chevron Golden House Chinese, KFC, Little Caesar's, McDonald's
1b	CA 905, E Brown Field Airport, Otay Mesa Border Crossing
1a	San Ysidro Blvd, E Shell/dsl, Valero Church's 99c Store, CVS Drug, Factory2U, O'Reilly Parts, W 76, Chevron, Mobil/dsl, Shell Denny's, McDonald's Motel 6

I-805 begins/ends on I-5.

INTERSTATE 880 (BAY AREA)

Exit #	Services
46b a	I-80 W (EXITs left). I-80 E/580 W.
44	7th St, Grand Ave, downtown
42b a	Broadway St, E KFC Marriott, W Jack London Inn to Jack London Square
41a	Oak St, Lakeside Dr, downtown
40	5th Ave, Embarcadero, E Burger King, W Quizno's, Starbucks Executive Inn, Homewood Suites, Motel 6
39b a	29th Ave, 23rd Ave, to Fruitvale, E Shell Boston Mkt, Burger King, DonutStar, Popeye's, Starbucks AutoZone, Lucky Foods, Office Depot, Radio Shack, W 7-11
38	High St, to Alameda, E Bay Breeze Inn, Coliseum Motel El Monte RV Ctr, W Shell/dsl McDonald's Home Depot
37	66th Ave, Zhone Way, E coliseum
36	Hegenberger Rd, E Arco/24hr, Shell/dsl Burger King, Chubby Freeze, Denny's, Jack-in-the-Box/24hr, McDonald's, Taco Bell Day's Hotel, Fairfield Inn, La Quinta, Motel 6, Quality Inn Freightliner, GMC/Volvo, Pak'n Save Foods, W 76/Circle K/dsl, Shell Carrows Rest., Francesco's Rest., Hegen Burger, In-N-Out, Jamba Juice, Panda Express, Quizno's, Red Barn Pizza, Starbucks, Subway, Wing Stop Best Western, Courtyard, Econolodge, Hilton, Holiday Inn, Holiday Inn Express, Marriott, Park Plaza Motel /auto, Harley-Davidson, Infiniti, Lexus, to Oakland Airport, Walmart
35	98th Ave, W

OAKLAND AREA

34	Davis St, W Shell/Burger King Hawaiian BBQ, Jamba Juice, Starbucks, Togo's /McDonald's, Costco/gas, Home Depot, Office Depot, See's Candy, Walmart/ McDonalds
33b a	Marina Blvd, E Valero Jack-in-the-Box, La Salsa Mexican, Panda Express, Starbucks, Taco Bell Buick/ GMC, Chevrolet, Ford, Honda, Hyundai, Kia, Marshall's, Nissan, Nordstrom's, Radio Shack, Volvo, W Flyers/dsl A&W/KFC, DairyBelle, Denny's
32	Washington Ave (from nb), Lewelling Blvd (from sb), W 76, Arco, TechCo Hometown Buffet, Jack-in-the-Box, McDonald's, Papa Murphy's, Subway Nimitz Motel 99c Store, Big Lots, Big O Tire, Food Maxx, GNC, Home Depot, Longs Drugs, Radio Shack, Safeway/24hr, same as 30, Walgreens/24hr
31	I-238 (from sb), to I-580, Castro Valley
30	Hesperian Blvd, E 76 In-N-Out, KFC, Quizno's, Starbucks O'Reilly Parts, Walmart, Wheelworks Repair, W 76, Arco, Chevron Black Angus, Hometown Buffet Hilton Garden, Nimitz Inn 99c Store, BigLots, Food Maxx, Longs Drugs, Lucky Foods, Radio Shack, same as 32, USPO, vet
29	A St, San Lorenzo, E 76/Circle K McDonald's Best Western Costco, tires/repair, W 76/Circle K, KB/ dsl, Valero Burger King, Carrow's, Chef Ming, Hawaiian BBQ, Jamba Juice, Pizza Hut, Starbucks, Subway Days Inn, Heritage Inn, La Quinta, MainStay Suites, Phoenix Lodge $Tree, Home Depot, Mi Pueblo Foods, Target
28	Winton Ave, W Chevron, Valero/dsl Applebee's, Coldstone, Elephant Grill, Hawaiian BBQ, Hometown Buffet, Marie Callendar's, Mimi's Cafe, Olive Garden, Panda Express, Panera Bread, Sizzler, Subway Firestone/auto, Goodyear/auto, JC Penney, Macy's, mall, O'Reilly Parts, Ross, Sears/auto
27	CA 92, Jackson St, E 76, Beacon, Valero/24hr Asian Wok, Baskin-Robbins, Hawaiian BBQ, Mnt Mike's Pizza, Nations Burgers, Papa Murphy's, Popeye's, Starbucks, Subway, Taco Bell 7-11, Grocery Outlet, Longs Drug, Lucky Foods, Radio Shack, Safeway, Walgreens, W San Mateo Br
26	Tennyson Rd, E 76, All American/dsl Jack-in-the-Box, KFC, RoundTable Pizza Kragen Parts, Walgreens, W 76 H
25	Industrial Pkwy (from sb), E Industrial/dsl Lite Wok, Quizno's, Starbucks, W Pheonix Lodge
24	Whipple Rd, Dyer St, E 76, Chevron/dsl/24hr Country Waffles, Del Taco, Denny's, McDonald's, Panda Express, Taco Bell, Wing Stop Best Value Inn, Motel 6 FoodMaxx, Home Depot, PepBoys, Target, W Shell Applebee's,

INTERSTATE 880 (BAY AREA) Cont'd

FREMONT

24 Continued
Baskin-Robbins, Burger King, Chili's, FreshChoice, Fuddrucker's, IHOP, In-N-Out, Jamba Juice, Jollibee, Krispy Kreme, La Salsa Mexican, Pasta Pormadora, Starbucks, Texas Roadhouse, TGIFriday, Togo's, Tony Roma's Extended Stay America, Holiday Inn Express Best Buy, Lowe's Whse, Lucky Foods, Michael's, PetCo, Radio Shack, Walmart/auto

23 Alvarado-Niles Rd, E Shell Crowne Plaza 7-11, W Shell Walmart/auto, (same as 24)

22 Alvarado Blvd, Fremont Blvd, E Phoenix Garden Chinese, Subway Motel 6 Lucky Foods

21 CA 84 W, Decoto Rd to Dumbarton Br, E 7-11 McDonald's Walgreens

19 CA 84 E, Thornton Ave, Newark, E U-Haul, W Chevron/dsl/24hr, Shell Carl's Jr, KFC, Mtn Mike's Pizza, Taco Bell 7-11, BigLots, Home Depot

17 Mowry Ave, Fremont, E 76/Circle K, Chevron/dsl, QuikStop, Valero Applebee's, Burger King, Chinese Buffet, Denny's, HoneyBaked Ham, KFC, Olive Garden, Starbucks, Subway, T&D Sandwiches Best Western, Extended Stay Deluxe, Residence Inn H Lucky Foods, W 76 Arby's, BJ's Rest., Bombay Garden, El Burro Mexican, Jack-in-the-Box, McDonald's, Red Robin, Subway, Taco Bell, TK Noodles Chase Suites, Comfort Inn, EZ 8 Motel, Homewood Suites, Motel 6, Towneplace Suites Firestone, Goodyear/auto, JC Penney, Jiffy Lube, Lion Mkt., Macy's, mall, Mazda, Sears/auto, Target, TJ Maxx

16 Stevenson Blvd, E Arco/dsl, Shell Jack-in-the-Box, Outback Steaks, W Chevron Chevy's Mexican, ChuckeCheese, Palm Gardens Rest., Starbucks, Togo's Hilton FoodMaxx, Ford, Harley-Davidson, Nissan, Tuesday Morning, Walmart

15 Auto Mall Pkwy, E Arco, Chevron Subway, W Shell/dsl Applebee's, Asian Pearl, Carino's, Chipotle Mexican, ClaimJumper, Coldstone Creamery, Dickey's BBQ, Hawaiian BBQ, In-N-Out, Jamba Juice, Panda Express, Panera Bread, PF Chang's, Quizno's, Rubio's, Starbucks, Subway, Tandoori Grill, Wendy's, Wing Stop BMW, Chrysler/Dodge/Jeep, Costco/gas, Honda, Jaguar, Jo-Ann Fabrics, Kia, Kohl's, Land Rover, Lexus, Lowes Whse, Mercedes, Office Depot, Old Navy, Porsche, Radio Shack, Staples, Toyota, Volvo

14mm **weigh sta both lanes**

13 Fremont Blvd, Irving Dist, W Valero/Subway McDonald's, SmartBrew GoodNite Inn, Homestead Suites, La Quinta, Marriott

SAN JOSE

13a Gateway Blvd (from nb), E Holiday Inn Express

12 Mission Blvd, E 76, Valero Carl's Jr, Denny's, Jack-in-the-Box, KFC, Togo's Holiday Inn Express, Quality Inn 7-11, Longs Drugs, Safeway, Walgreens, to I-680, W Courtyard, Hampton Inn, Hyatt Place

10 Dixon Landing Rd, E McDonald's Residence Inn 7-11

8b CA 237, Alviso Rd, Calaveras Rd, to McCarthy Rd, Milpitas E 76, CA Fuel Burger King, Carl's Jr, Chili Palace Denny's, Lee's Sandwiches, Marie Callender's Best Western, Days Inn, Travelodge 7-11, BigLots, O'Reilly Parts SaveMart Foods, vet, Walgreens, **W on McCarthy Rd** Chevron, Applebee's, Black Angus, Happi House, HomeTown Buffet, In-N-Out, Jamba Juice, Macaroni Grill, McDonald's, On the Border, Pasta Pomodoro, RedBrick Pizza, Starbucks, Subway, Taco Bell Crowne Plaza, Hampton Inn, Hilton Garden, Homestead Suites, Larkspur Landing Hotel, Staybridge Suites Best Buy, Chevron, GNC, Michael's, Petsmart, RanchMkt Foods, Ross, Walmart/McDonald's/auto

8a Great Mall Parkway, Tasman Dr, E Toyota

7 Montague Expswy, E Shell/dsl, Valero Jack-in-the-Box Sleep Inn U-Haul, W Chevron/dsl Dave&Buster's Beverly Heritage Hotel, Sheraton

5 Brokaw Rd, E Lowe's Whse, W CHP, Ford Trucks, Fry's Electronics

4d Gish Rd (nb only), W auto/dsl repair/transmissions

4c b US 101, N to San Francisco, S to LA

4a 1st St, E 76, Shell/repair Subway, W 76 Cathay Chinese, Denny's/24hr, Empire Buffet, Genji Japanese Clarion, Comfort Suites, Days Inn, Executive Inn, EZ 8 Motel, Holiday Inn Express, Homestead Suites, Radisson, Red Roof Inn, Vagabond Inn, Wyndham Garden 7-11

3 Coleman St, E Valero/dsl Quizno's, W

2 CA 82, The Alameda, W Shell/repair Starbucks, Subway, Taco Bell Best Western, Santa Clara Inn, St. Francis Hotel, Sterling Motel, Valley Inn Safeway, Santa Clara U

1d Bascom Ave, to Santa Clara, W Rotten Robbie/dsl, Valero Burger King

1c Stevens Creek Blvd, San Carlos St, E Valero/dsl, Valley/dsl Valley Park Hotel H W 76 Arby's, CheeseCake Factory, Jack-in-the-Box, RoundTable Pizza 7-11, Audi/VW, Best Buy, Ford, Goodyear/auto, Lexus, Longs Drugs, Macy's, mall, Nordstrom's, Old Navy, Safeway, Subaru

1b I-280. **I-880 begins/ends on I-280.**

1a Ca 17 to Santa Cruz

COLORADO

INTERSTATE 25

Exit #	Services
299	Colorado/Wyoming state line
296	point of interest both lanes
293	to Carr, Norfolk
288	Buckeye Rd
281	Owl Canyon Rd, E KOA Campground, truck repair
278	CO 1 S, to Wellington, W Kum&Go/dsl, Loaf'N Jug/dsl, Shell/dsl Burger King, Domino's, McDonald's, Subway, Taco John's Days Inn Bella Mkt, Family$, USPO, vet
271	Mountain Vista Dr, W Budweiser Brewery
269b a	CO 14, to US 87, Ft Collins, E CF&G Cookhouse, McDonald's Best Value Inn, W Shell/dsl Denny's, Hacienda Real, Waffle House 9 Motel, Comfort Inn, Days Inn, EconoLodge, La Quinta, Motel 6, Red Lion Inn, Rodeway Inn, Super 8 to CO St U, vet
268	Prospect Rd, to Ft Collins, W H **Welcome Ctr/ both lanes, full facilities, litter barrels, petwalk**
267mm	**weigh sta both lanes**

INTERSTATE 25 Cont'd

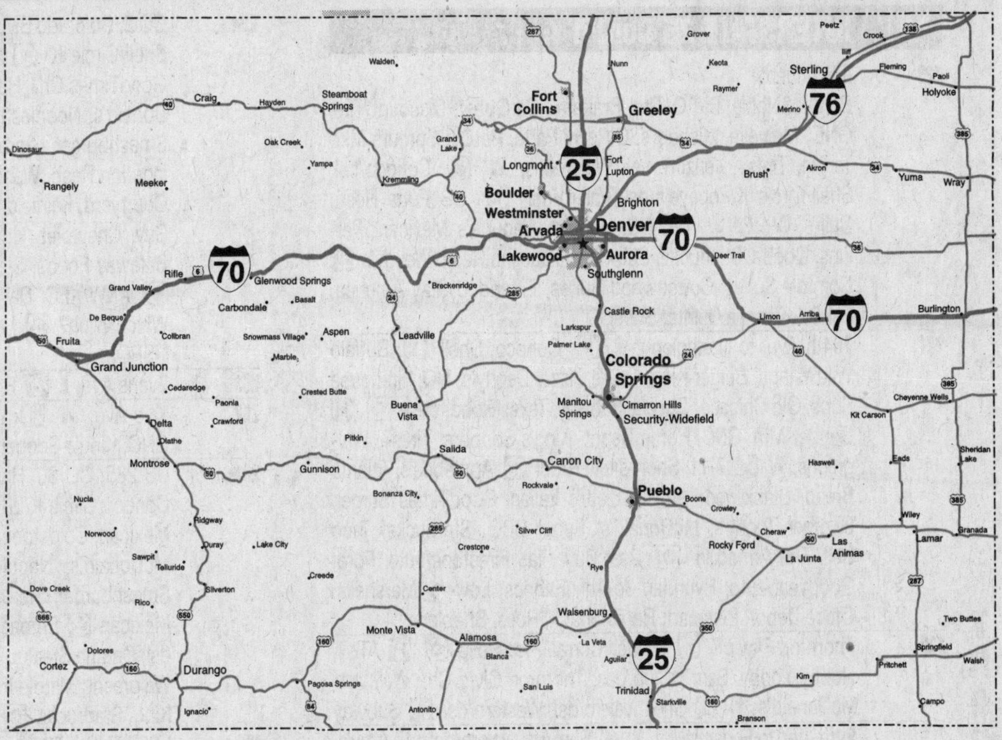

Exit #	Services
266mm	E [other] st patrol
265	Harmony Rd, Timnath, E [gas] Murphy USA/dsl [food] Freddy's [other] Costco/dsl, Walmart/Subway, 2-3 mi W [gas] Shell/dsl [food] Austin's Grill, BJ's Rest., Carrabba's, Chipotle, Famous Dave's, Firehouse Subs, Five Guys, HuHot, IHOP, Jersey Mike's, Macaroni Grill, McAlister's Deli, Old Chicago, Outback Steaks, Panera Bread, Papa John's, Qdoba, Red Robin, Rustic Oven, SmashBurger, Sprouts Mkt, Starbucks, Subway, Texas Roadhouse, Tom+Chee, Village Inn, Wahoo's, Which Wich? [lodging] Cambria Suites, Comfort Suites, Courtyard, Hampton Inn, Hilton Garden, Holiday Inn Express, Homewood Suites, Residence Inn [other] [H] Kohl's, Lowe's, Office Depot, Safeway/gas, Sam's Club, Staples, Target, Verizon, Walgreens, World Mkt
262	CO 392 E, to Windsor, E [gas] 7-11/dsl, Shell/Subway/dsl [food] Arby's, Pueblo Viejo, Taco John's [lodging] AmericInn [other] vet, W [other] Powder River RV Ctr
259	Crossroads Blvd, E [gas] 7-11/dsl, Shell/dsl [food] Boot Grill, Carl's Jr, Nordy's, Palomino Mexican, Perkins, Qdoba Mexican, Subway [lodging] Candlewood Suites, Embassy Suites, Holiday Inn Express, ValuePlace Inn, W [food] Hooters [other] BMW, Buick/GMC, CarMax, Chevrolet, Harley-Davidson, Hyundai, Mercedes, Mini, Subaru, to [airport]
257b a	US 34, to Loveland, E [gas] 7-11/dsl, Shell/dsl [food] Bent Fork Grill, Biaggi Italian, BoneFish Grill, Culver's, East Coast Pizza, On-the-Border, PF Chang's, Qdoba, Red Robin, Rock Bottom Rest., Starbucks [other] AT&T, Barnes&Noble, Best Buy, Dick's, GNC, Macy's, See's Candies, Verizon, W [gas] Conoco/dsl [food] Buffalo Wild Wings, Carino's Italian, Chick-fil-A, Chili's, Chipotle Mexican, Cracker Barrel, IHOP, Jimmy John's, KFC/Taco Bell, LoneStar Steaks, McDonald's, Mimi's Cafe, Noodles&Co, Old Chicago, Panera Bread, Starbucks, Subway, Wendy's [lodging] Best Western, Fairfield Inn, Hampton Inn, Residence Inn [other] [H] JoAnn Fabrics, Loveland Outlets/famous brands, Loveland RV Resort, Marshall's, museum, Old Navy, Petsmart, Ross, Sportsman's Whse, Staples, Target, to Rocky Mtn NP
255	CO 402 W, to Loveland
254	to CO 60 W, to Campion, E [gas] Johnson's Corner/Sinclair/café/dsl/scales/motel/24hr [lodging] Budget Host [other] RV retreat/service
252	CO 60 E, to Johnstown, Milliken, W [gas] Loaf'n Jug/Subway/dsl
250	CO 56 W, to Berthoud, W [other] to Carter Lake
245	to Mead
243	CO 66, to Longmont, Platteville, E [gas] Conoco/dsl, Kum&Go/dsl, Shell/7-11 [food] Rancheros Rest., Red Rooster Rest. [other] Camping World/K&C RV Ctr, tires, vet, W [other] to Estes Park, to Rocky Mtn NP

LOVELAND

Exit #	Services
241mm	St Vrain River
240	CO 119, to Longmont, E [gas] Shell/7-11/dsl [food] Burger King, Carl's Jr, Del Taco, Good Times Grill, Pizza Hut, Popeye's, Qdoba, Starbucks, Wendy's [lodging] Best Western, Comfort Suites, Value Place Inn [other] Century RV Ctr, Home Depot, Kia, Lexus, Toyota/Scion, Transwest RV Ctr, W [gas] 7-11/Subway/dsl, Conoco/dsl/scales/24hr, Shell/Circle K/dsl [food] Arby's, McDonald's, Pizza Hut/Taco Bell, Waffle House [lodging] 1st Inn, Best Value Inn, Quality Inn, Super 8, Travelodge [other] museum, to Barbour Ponds SP, truckwash, Valley Camper RV Ctr
235	CO 52, Dacono, E [gas] Kum&Go/dsl [other] Ford, Infiniti, W [gas] Conoco/dsl/LP [food] McDonald's, Pepper Jacks Grille, Starbucks, Subway [other] Harley-Davidson, to Eldora Ski Area
232	to Erie, Dacono
229	CO 7, to Lafayette, Brighton, E [food] Buffalo Wild Wings, Chick-fil-A, Chili's, Famous Dave's BBQ, Goodtimes Burgers, Gunther Toody's, La Fogata, Starbucks, Subway, Village Inn [other] AT&T, Costco/gas, Dick's, Home Depot, Petsmart, Sears Grand
228	E-470 (**tollway**), to Limon
226	144th Ave, E [gas] Murphy Express/dsl [food] Firehouse Subs, Freddy's [other] Cabela's, Hobby Lobby, W [food] HuHot Mongolian, Mimi's Cafe, Mooyah Burgers, Panera Bread, Red Robin, Rusty Bucket, Starbucks, Which Wich? [other] [H] $Tree, AT&T, JC Penney, Macy's, Marshall's, Old Navy, REI, Ross, Staples, Target, Verizon
225	136th Ave, W [gas] Valero/dsl [food] Big Burrito, Carl's Jr, KFC/LJ Silver, Starbucks, Subway [other] Advance Parts, Firestone/auto, Lowe's, URGENT CARE, Walmart/McDonald's
223	CO 128, 120th Ave, to Broomfield, E [gas] Conoco, Valero/dsl [food] Applebee's, Bad Daddy's Burger Bar, Burger King, Café Rio, Chick-fil-A, Chipotle Mexican, Coldstone, Fazoli's, First Watch Cafe, Jimmy John's, Jim'N Nick's BBQ, Krispy Kreme, LoneStar Steaks, Longhorn Steaks, McDonald's, Olive Garden, Outback Steaks, Panda Express, Panera Bread, Smashburger, Sonic, Starbucks, Subway, Taziki's Cafe, Tequila's Mexican, TGIFriday's [lodging] DoubleTree, EconoLodge, Hampton Inn, Holiday Inn Express, Ramada Inn [other] $Tree, Albertson's, AT&T,

BROOMFIELD

CO

CO

INTERSTATE 25 Cont'd

THORNTON

223 Continued Barnes&Noble, Big O Tire, Brakes+, CarQuest, Discount Tire, GNC, Meineke, Michael's, O'Reilly Parts, PetCo, Sprouts Mkt, Target, Tires+, Verizon, vet, Walgreens, W Conoco/dsl, Shell/Circle K/Popeye's/dsl, Valero/dsl CB Potts Rest., Chili's, Cracker Barrel, DQ, Hooters, Laguna's Mexican, Perkins, Qdoba, Starbucks, Subway, Village Inn Rest., Wendy's Comfort Suites, Cottonwood Suites, Extended Stay America, Fairfield Inn, La Quinta, Super 8

221 104th Ave, to Northglenn, E Conoco, Shell Buffalo Wild Wings, Burger King, CiCi's Pizza, Denny's, DQ, Firehouse Subs, Old Chicago, Qdoba, Subway, Texas Roadhouse H Gander Mtn, GNC, Home Depot, King's Soopers, Tires+, Walgreens, W 7-11, Shell/Circle K/dsl Applebee's, Atlanta Bread, Blackeyed Pea, Cinzzetti's Italian, GoodTimes Burger, Gunther Toody's, McDonald's, Seoul BBQ, Starbucks, Taco Bell, The Armadillo Best Buy, Fiat, Firestone/auto, Ford, Goodyear/auto, Hyundai, Jo-Ann Fabrics, Lowe's, Marshalls, Office Depot, Petsmart, Radio Shack, Ross, Sheplar's

220 Thornton Pkwy, E Golden Corral, Rico Pollo H AT&T, Hobby Lobby, Sam's Club/gas, Thornton Civic Ctr, Walmart/McDonald's, W Shell, Valero/dsl, Western/dsl Subway

219 84th Ave, to Federal Way, E Shell/dsl, Valero/dsl Arby's, McDonald's, Quiznos, Sonic, Starbucks, Subway, Taco Bell, Taco Star, Waffle House O'Reilly Parts, W Econogas, Valero/dsl Burger King, DQ, El Fogon, McDonald's, Popeye's, Santiago's Mexican, Village Inn Rest. Motel 6 H AutoZone, CarQuest, Discount Tire, Meineke, Save-A-Lot, vet

217 US 36 W (exits left from nb), to Boulder, W Ammco Subway Chevrolet, Toyota/Scion

DENVER AREA

216b a I-76 E, to I-270 E

215 58th Ave, E Burger King, McDonald's, Steak Escape, Subway, Wendy's Comfort Inn URGENT CARE, W Conoco/dsl, Shamrock/dsl Super 8 O'Reilly Parts

214c 48th Ave, E airport, coliseum, W Village Inn Rest. Quality Inn, Ramada

214b a I-70, E to Limon, W to Grand Junction

213 Park Ave, W 38th Ave, 23rd St, downtown, E Conoco Domino's, McDonald's, Starbucks La Quinta, W Town&Country Motel

212c 20th St, downtown, Denver

212b a Speer Blvd, E museum, downtown, W Conoco/dsl, Shell/dsl Starbucks, Subway Hampton Inn, Ramada, Residence Inn, Super 8 AutoZone, Walgreens

211 23rd Ave, E funpark

210c CO 33 (from nb)

210b US 40 W, Colfax Ave, W Denny's, KFC Ramada Inn/rest., Red Lion Inn Mile High Stadium

210a US 40 E, Colfax Ave, E civic center, U-Haul, downtown

209c 8th Ave

209b 6th Ave W, US 6, W Shell/dsl

209a 6th Ave E, downtown, Denver

208 CO 26, Alameda Ave (from sb), E Shamrock/dsl Burger King, Denny's Home Depot, same as 207b, W Conoco/dsl

207b US 85 S, Santa Fe Dr, same as 208

207a Broadway, Lincoln St, E Griff's Burgers USPO

206b Washington St, Emerson St, E Whole Foods Mkt, W H

206a Downing St (from nb)

205b a University Blvd, W to U of Denver

DENVER AREA

204 CO 2, Colorado Blvd, E Conoco/dsl, Loaf'n Jug, Shamrock Shell/Circle K Arby's, Black Eyed Pea, Chili's, Domino's GoodTimes Grill, Hacienda Colorado, IHOP, Jimmy John's, McDonald's, Noodles&Co, Old Chicago Pizza, Pizza Hut, Qdoba Smashburger, Starbucks, Subway, Taco Bell, Tokyo Joe's, Village Inn Rest., Wahoo's, Whole Foods Mkt Belcaro Motel, Courtyard, Fairfield Inn, Hampton Inn Barnes&Noble, Best Buy, Chevrolet, Home Depot, Mercedes/BMW, Petco, Ross, Safeway Foods, Staples, vet, VW, Walgreens, W Conoco A&W/KFC, Dave&Buster's, McDonald's, Pei Wei, Perkins, Which Wich? La Quinta Natural Grocers, Office Depot, USPO

203 Evans Ave, E Rockies Inn, W Cameron Motel Ford

202 Yale Ave, W BeauJo's CO Pizza, Chipotle Mexican GNC, King's Sooper, Michaels, Petsmart

201 US 285, CO 30, Hampden Ave, to Englewood, Aurora, E Conoco/Circle K/LP, Shamrock, Shell Chick-fil-A, Chipotle Mexican, Coldstone, Domino's, Firehouse Subs, Jimmy John's, McDonald's, Noodles&Co, NY Deli, Panera Bread, Qdoba, Smashburger, Starbucks, Subway, Wahoos Fish Taco, Zanitas Mexican Embassy Suites Discount Tire, King's Sooper/dsl, Omaha Steaks, Petco, Target, URGENT CARE, Verizon, vet, Walgreens, Whole Food Mkt, W Conoco/7-11 Burger King, Starbucks Safeway

200 I-225 N, to I-70

199 CO 88, Belleview Ave, to Littleton, E Baker St Grill, Chipotle Mexican, Cool River Cafe, Fiocchi's Pizzeria, Fornaio Rest., Garcia's Mexican, Great Northern Rest., Noodles&Co, Pancake House, Panera Bread, Qdoba, Starbucks, Wendy's, Which Wich? Hampton Inn, Hilton Garden, Hyatt Place, Marriott, W Conoco, Shamrock McDonald's, Pappadeaux Café, Pizza Hut/Taco Bell Extended Stay Am, Extended Stay America Lexus

198 Orchard Rd, E Del Frisco's Steaks Shepler's, W Shell/Circle K/dsl Subway DoubleTree vet

197 Arapahoe Blvd, E Conoco/dsl, Shell/Circle K/dsl A&W/KFC, Bros BBQ, Burger King, Chick-fil-A, Del Taco, Dickie's BBQ, Domino's, El Parral, El Tapatio Mexican, Gunther Toody's Rest., Hoong's Palace, McDonald's, Outback Steaks, Pat's Cheesesteak, Pizza Hut, Qdoba, Schlotsky's, Smashburger, Sonic, Starbucks, Subway, Volcano Chinese, Wendy's Best Western, Courtyard, Extended Stay America, Hawthorn Suites, Hyatt House, LaQuinta, Motel 6, Sleep Inn Chrysler/Jeep, Discount Tire, Ford, Home Depot, Honda, Hyundai, Kia, Lowe's Whse, Mazda, Nissan, Subaru, Target, Toyota/Scion, USPO, Walmart, W Phillips 66/dsl, Shell/dsl, Valero/dsl Arby's, Boston Mkt, CB & Potts, Chipotle Mexican, DQ, Elephant Bar Rest., Five Guys, Garbanzo Grill, Goodtimes, Jamba Juice, Jimmy John's, Macaroni Grill, McDonald's, Papa Murphy's, Qdoba, Red Robin, Starbucks, Subway, Taco Bell, Twin Peaks Grill Residence Inn, Wingate Inn Advance Parts, AT&T, Big O Tire, Brakes+, Firestone/auto, GNC, Goodyear/auto, Office Depot, Safeway, Sprouts Mkt, URGENT CARE, vet

196 Dry Creek Rd, E IHOP, Landry's Seafood, Maggiano's Italian, Purple Ginger Asian Comfort Suites, Days Inn, Extended Stay America, Holiday Inn Express, La Quinta, Quality Inn, Sheraton, Staybridge Suites, W 7-11/dsl Bono's BBQ Drury Inn

195 County Line Rd, E Fleming's Courtyard, Homewood Suites, Residence Inn, W Conoco Buffalo Wild Wings, Burger King, CA Pizza Kitchen, Chick-fil-A, Chipotle Mexican, Earl's Kitchen, Firehouse Subs, G enghis Grill, J Alexander's, Jason's Deli, Panda Express, PF Changs, Red Lobster, Red

INTERSTATE 25 Cont'd

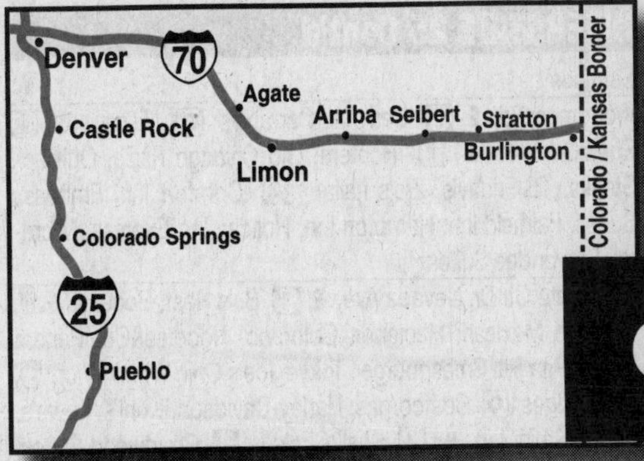

CO

CASTLE ROCK

195 Continued Robin, Rock Bottom Brewery/Cafe, Smashburger, Starbucks, TGIFriday's, Thai Basil, Tokyo Joe's [lodging] Hyatt Place [other] AT&T, Barnes&Noble, Best Buy, Costco/gas, Dick's, Dillard's, Home Depot, JC Penney, Jo-Ann Fabrics, Macy's, Marshall's, Michaels, Nordstrom, Old Navy, PetsMart, REI, Ross, Verizon

194 CO 470 W, CO 470 E (**tollway**)

193 Lincoln Ave, to Parker, **E** [gas] 7-11/dsl, Conoco, Valero/dsl [food] Carl's Jr, Hacienda Colorado, Starbucks, Subway [lodging] Candlewood Suites, Hilton Garden, **W** [gas] Conoco/dsl [food] Chili's, Chipotle Mexican, Firehouse Subs, Five Guys, Garbanzo Grill, Heidi's, KFC, McDonald's, Noodles&Co, Papa John's, Papa Murphy's, Pizza Hut/Taco Bell, Qdoba, Starbucks, Subway [lodging] Hampton Inn, Marriott [other] [H] Discount Tire, GNC, Safeway, Sprouts Mkt, Target

192 Ridgegate Pkwy, **W** [other] [H] Cabela's

191 no services

190 Surrey Ridge, Surrey Ridge

188 Castle Pines Pkwy, **W** [gas] Conoco/dsl, Shell/Circle K/Taco Bell/dsl [food] La Dolce Vita, Las Fajitas Mexican, Papa John's, Papa Murphy's, Starbucks, Subway, Wendy's [other] Big O Tires, Discount Tire, King's Sooper/dsl, Safeway, URGENT CARE, vet, Walgreens

187 Happy Canyon Rd, **W** [other] **services 2 mi**

184 Founders Pkwy, Meadows Pkwy, to Castle Rock, **E** [gas] Conoco/dsl, Shell/Circle K/dsl [food] A&W/KFC, Applebee's, Baskin-Robbins, Chick-fil-A, Chipotle Mexican, Coldstone, Five Guys, Goodtimes Grill, Jimmy John's, Little Caesars, Noodles&Co, Outback Steaks, Panera Bread, Parry's Pizza, Qdoba, Red Robin, Sonic, Starbucks, Subway, Taco Bell, Wendy's [other] $Tree, Advance Parts, AT&T, Brakes+, Discount Tire, Firestone/auto, GNC, Goodyear/auto, Grease Monkey, Home Depot, Just Brakes, King's Sooper, Kohl's, Michael's, Natural Grocers, Office Depot, O'Reilly Parts, Petsmart, Radio Shack, Sprouts Mkt, Target, Verizon, vet, Walgreens, Walmart, **W** [gas] Loaf'n Jug/dsl [food] Arby's, Blackeyed Pea, Chili's, Food Court, Freddy's Steakburger, IHOP, McDonald's, Rockyard Grill [lodging] Best Western, Comfort Suites, Days Inn, Hampton Inn, Holiday Inn Express [other] Castle Rock Outlet/famous brands, Lowe's, Midas, st patrol

182 CO 86, Castle Rock, Franktown, **E** [gas] 7-11/dsl, Conoco/dsl, Phillips 66/dsl [food] Augustine Grill, B&B Cafe, Castle Cafe, El Meson Mexican [lodging] Castle Pines Motel [other] vet, **W** [gas] Shell/Circle K/dsl, Valero/dsl [food] Burger King, Domino's, Guadalajara Mexican, Jack-in-the-Box, McDonald's, Old West BBQ, Santiago's Mexican, Village Inn, Waffle House, Wendy's [lodging] Castle Inn, LaQuinta, Super 8 [other] NAPA

181 CO 86, Wilcox St, Plum Creek Pkwy, Castle Rock, **E** [gas] Conoco, Valero/dsl, Western/dsl [food] Blimpie, DQ, El Meson Mexican, Papa John's, Papa Murphy's, Pizza Hut, Quiznos, Starbucks, Stumpy's Pizzaria, Subway, Taco Bell [lodging] Castle Rock Motel [other] AutoZone, Big O Tire, Buick/Chevrolet/GMC, Chrysler/Dodge/Jeep, Ford, Midas, Safeway/dsl, Tuesday Morning, URGENT CARE, USPO, Walgreens

LARKSPUR

174 Tomah Rd, **W** [other] Yogi Bear's Campground

173 Larkspur (from sb, no return), **3 mi W** [gas] Conoco/Larkspur Cafe/dsl/ [phone]

172 Upper Lake Gulch Rd, Larkspur, **2 mi W** [gas] Conoco/dsl/ [phone] [food] Larkspur Pizza Cafe, Spur Grill [other] USPO

167 Greenland

163 County Line Rd

162.5mm Monument Hill, elev 7352

162mm **weigh sta both lanes**

161 CO 105, Woodmoor Dr, **E** [gas] Conoco [food] 3 Margaritas Mexican, Papa John's [lodging] Sundance Mtn Lodge/rest [other] CO Hts RV Park (2mi), **W** [gas] 7-11, Conoco/Circle K/dsl [food] Arby's, Domino's, La Casa Fiesta New Mexican, McDonald's, Rosie's Diner, Starbucks, Subway, Taco Bell, Village Inn [other] Big O Tire, Natural Grocers, Safeway/dsl, USPO, Walgreens

158 Baptist Rd, **E** [gas] Shell/Circle K/Popeye's/dsl/24hr [food] Borriello Bros. Pizza, Carlos Miguel's, Chili's, Coldstone, Freddy's Steakburgers, McDonald's, Papa Murphy's, Subway, TX Roadhouse [lodging] Fairfield Inn [other] AutoZone, Christian Bros. Auto, Discount Tire, GNC, Home Depot, King's Sooper, Kohl's, O'Reilly Parts, Petsmart, Staples, URGENT CARE, Verizon, Walgreens, Walmart/Subway car repair Jiffy Lube, **W** [gas] Shamrock/dsl/scales, **N** [food] Mexican Grill

156b N Entrance to USAF Academy, **E** [food] Bourbon Bros Kitchen, C B & Potts Rest., Jimmy John's [other] Bass Pro Shops, **W** [other] visitors center

156a Gleneagle Dr, **E** [other] mining museum

153 InterQuest Pkwy, **E** [gas] Kum&Go/dsl [food] Cheddar's, CO Mtn Brewery/rest. [lodging] Hampton Inn, Residence Inn

152 scenic overlook on sb

151 Briargate Pkwy, **E** [gas] 7-11 [food] Biaggi's, CA Pizza Kitchen, Garbanzo Grill, Marco's Pizza, Panera Bread, PF Changs, Qdoba, Salsa Brava Mexican, Starbucks, Ted's MT Grill [lodging] Hilton Garden, Homewood Suites [other] AT&T, to Black Forest

150b a CO 83, Academy Blvd, **E** [gas] Shamrock/dsl, Shell/Circle K/dsl [food] 5 Guys Burgers, A&W, Amanda's Fonda, Applebee's, Baskin-Robbins, Buffalo Wild Wings, Burger King, Chick-fil-A, Chipotle Mexican, Coldstone, Cracker Barrel, Crave Burgers, Culver's, Del Taco, Denny's, Drifters Hamburgers, Egg&I Café, Elephant Bar Rest., Extreme Pizza, Famous Dave's, Firehouse Subs, HuHot Mongolian, IHOP, Jason's Deli, Jimmy John's, KFC, McDonald's, Mimi's Café, Noodles&Co, Olive Garden, Olive Garden, On-the-Border, Panera Bread, Pei Wei, Qdoba, Red Robin, Salt Grass Steaks, Schlotzsky's, Sonic, Starbucks, Steak'n Shake, Subway, Tokyo Joe's Grill, Wendy's [lodging] Academy Hotel, Comfort Suites, Days Inn, Drury Inn, EconoLodge, Howard Johnson, Super 8 [other] $Tree, Advance Parts, AT&T, Barnes&Noble, Best Buy, Chevrolet, Dick's, Dillard's, Firestone/auto, Ford, Hobby Lobby, Home Depot, Hyundai, JC Penney, Kia, King's Sooper, Macy's, Marshall's, Michael's, Midas, Natural Grocers, Old Navy, O'Reilly Parts, PepBoys, Petsmart, REI, Ross, Sam's Club/gas, Sears/auto, to Peterson AFB, URGENT CARE, Verizon, VW, Walmart/Subway, Whole Foods Mkt, **W** S Entrance to USAF Academy

= gas = food = lodging = other = rest stop

INTERSTATE 25 Cont'd

CO

COLORADO SPRINGS

Exit #	Services
149	Woodmen Rd, E Carl's Jr, Carraba's Nissan, W Shell/Circle K/dsl Hooters, Old Chicago Pizza, Outback Steaks, TGIFriday's, Zio's Italian Comfort Inn, Embassy Suites, Fairfield Inn, Hampton Inn, Holiday Inn Express, Microtel, Staybridge Suites
148	Corporate Ctr Dr, Nevada Ave, E BJ's Rest, Bonefish Grill, Chipotle Mexican, Hacienda Colorado, Noodles&Co, Panera Bread, Pita Pit, Smashburger, Tokyo Joe's Grill, Which Wich The Lodges Costco/gas, Harley-Davidson, Kohl's, Lowe's, Petco, SteinMart, W Shell/Circle K Crestwood Suites, Extended Stay America, Hyatt House, Marriott to Rodeo Hall of Fame
146	Garden of the Gods Rd, E Conoco/7-11, Shell/Circle K/dsl Carl's Jr, Caspian Cafe, Drifter's Burgers, McDonald's Best Value Inn, La Quinta Aamco, W 7-11, Conoco/Circle K, Shamrock/dsl, Shell/dsl Applebee's, Arby's, Arceo's Mexican, Blackeyed Pea, Chick-fil-A, Freddy's Steakburgers, Jimmy John's, Mollica's Italian, Sonic, Souper Salad, Subway, Taco Bell, Village Inn, Wendy's Days Inn, Hyatt Place, Quality Inn, Super 8 $Tree, AutoZone, Discount Tire, to Garden of Gods, vet
145	CO 38 E, Fillmore St, E 7-11, Shamrock/dsl, Western/dsl Arby's, Burger King, Carl's Jr, DQ, Lucky Dragon, McDonald's, Subway, Taco Bell Budget Host H Advance Parts, Walgreens, W Waffle House Motel 6, Super 8
144	Fontanero St
143	Uintah St, E 7-11 Uintah Fine Arts Ctr
142	Bijou St, Bus Dist, E Hilton Firestone/auto, visitor info, W Denny's Clarion, Quality Inn 7-11
141	US 24 W, Cimarron St, to Manitou Springs, W Conoco/dsl, Shell/7-11/dsl Arby's, Capt D's, La Casita Mexican, McDonald's, Popeye's, Sonic, TX Roadhouse Acura, Audi, AutoZone, Brakes+, Buick/GMC, Cadillac, Chevrolet, Chrysler/Dodge/Jeep, Discount Tire, Ford, Grease Monkey, Hobby Lobby, Hyundai, Infiniti, Kia, Land Rover/Jaguar, Lexus, Lincoln, Mazda, Meineke, Mercedes, NAPA, Office Depot, Porsche, Radio Shack, Subaru, to Pikes Peak, Toyota/Scion, Volvo, VW, Walmart/McDonald's
140b	US 85 S, Tejon St, E Peerless Tires, W Conoco/dsl access to same as 141
140a	Nevada Ave, E Kum & Go/dsl Chateau Motel, Howard Johnson repair, W 7-11, Shamrock Arceo's Mexican, Burger King, China Kitchen, Chipotle Mexican, IHOP, KFC, McDonald's, Noodles&Co, On the Border, Panda Express, Panera Bread, Rancho Alegre Mexican, Red Robin, Schlotzsky's, Starbucks, Subway, Taco Bell, Taco Express, Wendy's Rodeway Inn, Sunsprings Motel, Travel Star Inn $Tree, access to auto dealers at 141, Big O Tire, Family$, Michael's, Midas, Natural Grocers, Office Depot, O'Reilly Parts, Petsmart, Ross, Safeway Foods, Sears, Tuesday Morning, Walgreens
139	US 24 E, to Lyman, Peterson AFB
138	CO 29, Circle Dr, E Conoco, Shell/Circle K/dsl McDonald's Days Inn, Hotel Elegante, Super 8 airport, Kohl's, URGENT CARE, zoo, W 7-11 Arby's, Buffalo Wild Wings, Burger King, Carl's Jr, Carrabba's, Chili's, ChuckeCheese, Culver's, Denny's, Fazoli's, Flatiron Grill, Macaroni Grill, Outback Steaks, Smoothie King, Subway, Village Inn Best Western, Comfort Inn, Courtyard, DoubleTree Hotel, Fairfield Inn, Hampton Inn, La Quinta, Residence Inn AT&T, GNC, PetCo, Radio Shack, Target
135	CO 83, Academy Blvd, E to , to Cheyenne Mtn SP, W F Carson, Sam's Club/dsl, Walmart/Subway
132	CO 16, Wide Field Security, E Loves/Subway/dsl Camping World RV Ctr, KOA
128	to US 85 N, Fountain, Security, E 7-11, Loaf'n Jug/Subway/dsl Family$, USPO, W Tomahawk/Shell/rest/dsl/24hr/@ Fountain Inn, Super 8 Freightliner
125	Ray Nixon Rd
123	no services
122	to Pikes Peak Meadows, W Pikes Peak Intn'l Raceway
119	Rancho Colorado Blvd, Midway
116	county line rd
115mm	**nb, full facilities, litter barrels, petwalk**
114	Young Hollow
112mm	**sb, full facilities, litter barrels, petwalk**
110	Pinon
108	Purcell Blvd, Bragdon, E racetrack, W KOA
106	Porter Draw
104	Eden, W Loves/Chester's/Subway/dsl/scales/24hr Peterbilt
102	Eagleridge Blvd, E Loaf'n Jug/dsl Burger King, Subway, TX Roadhouse Holiday Inn Express Big O Tire, Home Depot, Sam's Club/gas, W Shell/dsl Buffalo Wild Wings, Cactus Flower Mexican, Chili's, Cracker Barrel, IHOP, Starbucks, Taco Star, Village Inn, Wonderful Bistro Best Western, Comfort Inn, EconoLodge, Hampton Inn, La Quinta, Ramada, Wingate Inn Best Buy, frontage rds access 101, Harley-Davidson, Kohl's, Old Navy, PetCo
101	US 50 W, Pueblo, E Capt D's, Coldstone, Country Buffet, Denny's, Margaritas Mexican, Ruby Tuesday, Souper Salad Sleep Inn Barnes&Noble, CO Tire, Dillard's, JC Penney, Jo-Ann, mall, Petsmart, Ross, Sears/auto, Target, TJ Maxx, U-Haul, Verizon, Walmart/Subway, W 7-11, Loaf'n Jug/dsl, Shell/dsl, Valero/dsl Applebee's, Arby's, Arriba Mexican, Blackeyed Pea, Carl's Jr, China Rest., Chipotle Mexican, Country Kitchen, DJ's Steaks, Domino's, DQ, Fazoli's, Golden Corral, Jack-in-the-Box, Little Caesars, Manhattan's Pizza, McAlister's Deli, McDonald's, Noodles&Co, Olive Garden, Papa John's, Papa Murphy's, Pass Key Rest., Pizza Hut, Popeye's, Red Lobster, Starbucks, Subway, SW Grill, Taco Bell, Wendy's Clarion, Days Inn, Motel 6, Quality Inn, Rodeway Inn, Super 8 Aamco, Advance Parts, Albertson's, AT&T, AutoZone, Brakes+, Chevrolet, Chrysler/Dodge/Jeep, Discount Tire, EmergiCare, Ford/Lincoln, frontage rds access 102, Hyundai, Kia/Mazda, K-Mart, Lowe's, Midas, NAPA, Nissan, O'Reilly Parts, Staples, Subaru, Toyota, vet, Walgreens
100b	29th St, Pueblo, E Country Buffet, Mongolian Grill $Tree, Car Dr, Hobby Lobby, King's Sooper Foods, Natural Grocers, Peerless Tires, Tuesday Morning, W Conoco Sonic USA Motel Grease Monkey, Safeway
100a	US 50 E, to La Junta, E Loaf'n Jug/dsl, Shell Little Caesars, McDonald's, Pizza Hut, Wendy's Advance Parts, AutoZone, Belmont Tire/repair, Family$, Save-A-Lot Foods, Walgreens
99b a	Santa Fe Ave, 13th St, downtown, W Subway, Taco Bell, Wendy's Bramble Tree Inn, Travelers Motel H Buick/Cadillac/GMC, CarQuest, Honda
98b	CO 96, 1st St, Union Ave Hist Dist, Pueblo, W Loaf'n Jug/dsl Carl's Jr Courtyard
98a	US 50E bus, to La Junta, W Sonic
97b	Abriendo Ave
97a	Central Ave, W Alta/dsl McDonald's $General
96	Indiana Ave, W H

PUEBLO

INTERSTATE 25 Cont'd

Exit #	Services
95	Illinois Ave (from sb), W [other] to dogtrack
94	CO 45 N, Pueblo Blvd, W [gas] Loaf'n Jug/dsl, Western/dsl [food] Subway, Taco Bell [lodging] Hampton Inn, Microtel [other] fairgrounds/racetrack, Forts RV Park, to Lake Pueblo SP
91	Stem Beach
88	Burnt Mill Rd
87	Verde Rd
83	no services
77	Hatchet Ranch Rd, Cedarwood
74	CO 165 W, Colo City, E [gas] Shamrock/deli/dsl/24hr [food] Obie's BBQ [other] KOA, W [RS] **both lanes, full [handicapped] facilities, litter barrels, petwalk [phone] [picnic] vending** [gas] Sinclair/Subway/dsl [food] Los Cuervo's [lodging] Days Inn
71	Graneros Rd
67	to Apache
64	Lascar Rd
60	Huerfano
59	Butte Rd
56	Redrock Rd
55	Airport Rd
52	CO 69 W, to Alamosa, Walsenburg, W [gas] Conoco/A&W/dsl, Loaf'n Jug/dsl (2mi), Western/dsl [food] Carl's Jr (2mi), George's Rest., KFC/Taco Bell, Subway (2mi) [lodging] Best Western, Budget Host [other] Country Host RV Park, Dakota RV Park/camping, Family$ (2mi), San Luis Valley, to Great Sand Dunes NM
50	CO 10 E, to La Junta, W [other] [H] tourist info
49	Lp 25, to US 160 W, Walsenburg, **1 mi** W [gas] Loaf'n Jug/dsl [food] Carl's Jr., Subway [other] Lathrop SP, to Cuchara Ski Valley
42	Rouse Rd, to Pryor
41	Rugby Rd
34	Aguilar
30	Aguilar Rd
27	Ludlow, W [other] Ludlow Memorial
23	Hoehne Rd
18	El Moro Rd, W [RS] **both lanes, full [handicapped] facilities, litter barrels, petwalk** [picnic]
15	US 350 E, Goddard Ave, E [food] Burger King, Pizza Hut [lodging] Super 8 [other] [H] AutoZone, Big R Ranch Store, Family$, W [gas] Shell/dsl [lodging] Frontier Motel/café
14	Commercial St, downtown, Trinidad, same as 13b
13b	Main St, Trinidad, E **CO Welcome Ctr**, [gas] Shell/dsl [food] KFC/Taco Bell, McDonald's, Sonic [lodging] Days Inn [other] CarQuest, Safeway Foods/dsl, Trinidad Motor Inn, W [gas] Conoco/dsl [other] Monument Lake, RV camping, to Trinidad Lake
13a	Santa Fe Trail, Trinidad, E [other] RV camping
11	Starkville, E [gas] Shell/Wendy's/dsl/24hr [food] Tequila's Mexican [lodging] Budget Host/RVPark, Holiday Inn, Rodeway Inn [other] Summit RV Park, to Santa Fe Trail, **weigh/check sta**, W [lodging] La Quinta, Quality Inn/rest. [other] Big O Tire, Grease Monkey, O'Reilly Parts, Toyota, Walmart
8	Springcreek
6	Gallinas
2	Wootten
1mm	scenic area pulloff nb
0mm	Colorado/New Mexico state line, Raton Pass, elev 7834, **weigh sta sb**

WALSENBURG

TRINIDAD

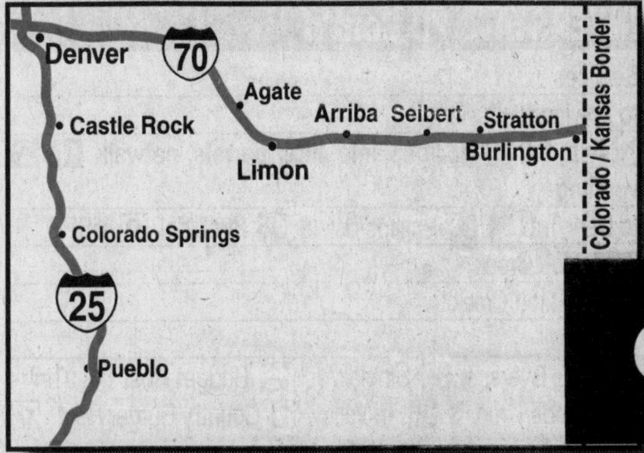

CO

INTERSTATE 70

Exit #	Services
450mm	Colorado/Kansas state line
438	US 24, Rose Ave, Burlington, N [gas] Conoco/dsl [lodging] Hi-Lo Motel, Sloan's Motel [other] [H] $General, Buick/Cadillac/Chevrolet/GMC, CarQuest, Family$, Ford/Lincoln, NAPA, O'Reilly Parts, Outback RV Park, Safeway Foods, S [gas] Shell/Reynaldo's Mexican/dsl/24hr [other] truck repair
437.5mm	**Welcome Ctr wb, full [handicapped] facilities, historical site, info, litter barrels, petwalk** [phone] [picnic]
437	US 385, Burlington, N [gas] Conoco/dsl, Western/dsl [food] Arby's, Burger King, Denny's, McDonald's, Pizza Hut, Route Steaks, Subway [lodging] Best Value Inn, Burlington Inn, Chaparral Motel, Quality Inn, Western Motel [other] [H] ShopKO, S [gas] Loves/Carl's Jr/dsl/scales/24hr@ [lodging] Best Western/rest., Fairfield Inn, Woodbridge Suites
429	Bethune
419	CO 57, Stratton, N [gas] Cenex/dsl, Conoco/dsl [food] Dairy Treat [lodging] Claremont Inn/café, Rodeway Inn [other] Marshall Ash Village Camping, Trails End Camping
412	Vona, **1/2 mi** N [other] [gas], [phone]
405	CO 59, Seibert, N [other] Shady Grove Camping/RV dump, S [gas] Conoco/dsl [other] tire repair
395	Flagler, N [gas] Loaf'N Jug/dsl [food] I-70 Diner, Subway [lodging] Little England Motel [other] Flagler SWA, G&B RV camping, NAPA, S [gas] Cenex/dsl [other] golf
383	Arriba, N [gas] DJ/café/dsl, motel, S [RS] **both lanes, full [handicapped] facilities, litter barrels, petwalk** [picnic] **point of interest, RV camping**
376	Bovina
371	Genoa, N food, gas, [phone], point of interest, S [other] [H]
363	US 24, US 40, US 287, to CO 71, to Hugo, Limon, **13 mi** S [other] [H]
361	CO 71, Limon, N [other] Ace Hardware, Chrysler/Dodge/Jeep, S [gas] Conoco/dsl, Shell/Wendy's/dsl [food] Golden China, Pizza Hut [lodging] 1st Inn Gold, Coyote Motel [other] KOA, RV camping, st patrol
360.5mm	**weigh/check sta both lanes**
359	to US 24, to CO 71, Limon, N [gas] FLYING J/IHOP/dsl/scales/LP/24hr [other] dsl repair, RV camping, S [gas] Phillips 66, Qwest/dsl, TA/Shell/Subway/Country Pride/dsl/scales/24hr/ @ [food] Arby's, Denny's, McDonald's, Oscar's Grill [lodging] Comfort Inn, EconoLodge, Holiday Inn Express, Quality Inn, Super 8, TS Inn [other] camping
354	no services
352	CO 86 W, to Kiowa
348	to Cedar Point
340	Agate, **1/4 mi** S gas/dsl [phone]

BURLINGTON

LIMON

INTERSTATE 70 Cont'd

Exit #	Services
336	to Lowland
332mm	Ⓡs wb, full ♿ facilities, info, litter barrels, petwalk ⊙ 📷 vending
328	to Deer Trail, N 📷 Phillips/dsl, S 📷 Shell/dsl ⊙ USPO
325mm	East Bijou Creek
323.5mm	Middle Bijou Creek
322	to Peoria
316	US 36 E, Byers, N 📷 Sinclair/dsl 🛏 Budget Host ⊙ Thriftway Foods/Drug, S 📷 Tri Valley 🍴 Country Burger Rest. ⊙ USPO
310	Strasburg, N 📷 Conoco/dsl 🍴 Coronas Mexican, KT's BBQ, Patio Cafe, Subway ⊙ Country Gardens RV Camping (3mi), dsl/auto repair, KOA, NAPA, Radio Shack, USPO, vet, Western Hardware
306mm	Kiowa , Bennett, N Ⓡs both lanes, full ♿ facilities, litter barrels, petwalk ⊙ 📷
305	Kiowa (from eb)
304	CO 79 N, Bennett, N 📷 Conoco/Hotstuff Pizza/dsl, ♥ Loves /McDonald's/dsl/scales/24hr 🍴 China Kitchen, High Plains Diner, Starbucks, Subway, Taco Bell ⊙ Family$, King Soopers Foods/dsl, O'Reilly Parts, USPO, S ⊙ Ace Hardware
299	CO 36, Manila Rd, S 📷 Shamrock/dsl
295	Lp 70, Watkins, N 📷 Shell/Tomahawk/rest/dsl/24hr/ @ 🍴 Biscuit's Cafe, Lulu's Cafe 🛏 Country Manor Motel ⊙ USPO
292	CO 36, Airpark Rd
289	E-470 Tollway, 120th Ave, CO Springs
288	US 287, US 40, Lp 70, Colfax Ave (exits left from wb)
286	CO 32, Tower Rd, N 📷 Murphy Express/dsl 🍴 Chick-fil-A, Chili's, Chipotle Mexican, Del Taco, DQ, Firehouse Subs, McAlister's Deli, Noodles&Co, Panda Express, Starbucks, Wendy's ⊙ $Tree, AT&T, Best Buy, Brakes+, Discount Tire, GNC, Home Depot, Les Schwab Tire, Office Depot, O'Reilly Parts, PetCo, Verizon, Walmart/Subway
285	Airport Blvd, N ⊙ Denver Int Airport, S 📷 ♦FLYING J / Denny's/dsl/scales/24hr, Conoco/McDonald's/dsl 🛏 Comfort Inn, Quality Inn ⊙ Harley-Davidson
284	I-225 N (from eb)
283	Chambers Rd, N 📷 Conoco, Shell/Circle K/Popeye's 🍴 A&W/ KFC, Anthony's Pizza, Applebees, Chicago Grill, Jimmy John's, LJ Silver/Taco Bell, Outback Steaks, Pizza Hut, Qdoba, Sonic, Subway, Ted's MT Grill, Urban Sombrero, Wendy's, Zume Asian 🛏 A Loft, Cambria Suites, Country Inn&Suites, Crowne Plaza, Econolodge, Hampton Inn, Hilton Garden, Homewood Suites, Hyatt Place, Marriott, Residence Inn, TownePlace Suites, Woolley's Suites ⊙ Tires+, U-haul, S 📷 Shamrock 🍴 Burger King, Jack-in-the-Box 🛏 Crossland Suites, ValuePlace Inn ⊙ RV America, URGENT CARE
282	I-225 S, to Colorado Springs
281	Peoria St, N 📷 7-11, Conoco/dsl, Shell/dsl 🍴 Ajua Mexican, Burger King, Del Taco, Domino's, GoodTimes Burgers, McDonald's, Peoria Grill, Quizno's, Starbucks, Subway 🛏 Holiday Inn Express, La Quinta, Rodeway Inn, Timbers Motel ⊙ Big O Tire, Family$, S 📷 Conoco/dsl, Shamrock/dsl 🍴 Bennett's BBQ, Denny's, Ho Mei Chinese, Taco Bell, Taco Mex 🛏 Motel 6, Rodeway Inn, Star Hotel, Stay Inn ⊙ auto/RV repair, Goodyear/auto
280	Havana St, N 🛏 Embassy Suites
279b	Central Ave, N 🛏 Drury Inn
279	I-270 W, US 36 W (from wb), to Ft Collins, Boulder
278	CO 35, Quebec St, N 📷 Sapp Bros/Sinclair/Subway/ @, TA/dsl/rest./24hr/ @ 🍴 Bar Louie, Coldstone, Del Taco, Islamorada Fish Co, Jim'n Nick's BBQ, La Sandia Cantina, Marco's Pizza, Olive Garden, Qdoba, Red Lobster, Red Robin, Starbucks, Subway, TGIFriday's, TX Roadhouse, Wahoo's, Which Wich? 🛏 Best Inn, Comfort Inn, Staybridge Suites ⊙ Bass Pro Shops, JC Penney, Macys, Old Navy, Super Target, S 🍴 Arby's, Buffalo Wild Wings, Country Buffet, Famous Dave's BBQ, IHOP, Jimmy John's, La Mariposa, McDonald's, Panda Express, Panera Bread, Papa John's, Smashburger, Sonic, Subway 🛏 Best Western, Courtyard, DoubleTree Hilton, DoubleTree Hotel, Holiday Inn, Renaissance Inn, Super 8 ⊙ AT&T, GNC, Home Depot, Office Depot, Petsmart, Radio Shack, Ross, Sam's Club/gas, Tires+, Walgreens, Walmart/ Subway
277	to Dahlia St, Holly St, Monaco St, frontage rd
276b	US 6 E, US 85 N, CO 2, Colorado Blvd, S 📷 Conoco/Subway/ dsl 🍴 Carl's Jr, Domino's, KT'S BBQ, Starbucks
276a	Vasquez Ave, N 📷 Pilot/Wendy's/dsl/scales/24hr 🛏 Western Inn ⊙ Blue Beacon, Ford Trucks, Peterbilt, S 📷 7-11 🍴 Burger King
275c	York St (from eb)
275b	CO 265, Brighton Blvd, Coliseum, N 📷 7-11
275a	Washington St (from wb), N 📷 7-11 🍴 Pizza Hut, S 📷 Conoco/dsl 🍴 McDonald's
274b a	I-25, N to Cheyenne, S to Colorado Springs
273	Pecos St, N 📷 Conoco/7-11/dsl ⊙ Family$, SavALot Foods, S 📷 7-11 🍴 Quiznos ⊙ Autocare
272	US 287, Federal Blvd, N 📷 Conoco/dsl, Sinclair 🍴 Burger King, Goodtimes Burgers, Little Caesar's, McCoy's Rest., McDonald's, Pizza Hut, Rico Pollo, Subway, Taco Bell, Village Inn, Wendy's, Winchell's 🛏 Motel 6 ⊙ $Tree, 7-11, Advance Parts, Family$, tires, S 📷 Conoco/Mkt/dsl 🍴 El Padrino Mexican, Popeye's, Starbucks 🛏 Travelers Inn
271b	Lowell Blvd, Tennyson St (from wb)
271a	CO 95, S ⊙ funpark
270	Sheridan Blvd, N 📷 Shell/dsl, S 📷 Murphy Express/dsl 🍴 El Paraiso Mexican, Grammy's Pizza ⊙ Family$, Firestone/ auto, fun park, Schwab Tire, Walmart
269b	I-76 E (from eb), to Ft Morgan, Ft Collins
269a	CO 121, Wadsworth Blvd, N 📷 7-11, Conoco, Shell/dsl 🍴 Anthony's Pizza, Applebee's, BeauJo's, Bennet's BBQ, Chick-fil-A, Chipotle Mexican, Coldstone, Country Buffet, El Tapatio Mexican, Fazoli's, HuHot, IHOP, Jimmy John's, Kukoro Japanese, McDonald's/playplace, Red Robin, Ruby Tuesday, Smiling Moose Deli, Starbucks, Subway, Taco Bell, TX Roadhouse ⊙ $Tree, Advance Parts, Big O Tire, city park, Costco/gas, Discount Tire, Home Depot, Lowe's, Petsmart, Radio Shack, Sam's Club, Tires+, URGENT CARE
267	CO 391, Kipling St, Wheat Ridge, N 📷 Conoco, Shell/Carl's Jr/Circle K/dsl 🍴 Burger King, Denny's, Einstein Bros, Jack-in-the-Box, Lil Nick's Pizza, Margarita's Mexican, Panda Express, Popeye's, Qdoba, Quiznos, Starbucks, Subway 🛏 American Inn, Motel 6 ⊙ 7-11, AT&T, Cadillac/Chevrolet, GNC, NAPA, Natural Grocers, repair, Target, Verizon, vet, S 📷 Conoco/ Mkt/dsl, Shell 🍴 3 Agaves Mexican, Taco Bell, Village Inn, Winchell's 🛏 Affordable Inn, Best Value Inn, Comfort Inn, Holiday Inn Express, Super 8 ⊙ Ketelesen RV Ctr
266	CO 72, W 44th Ave, Ward Rd, Wheat Ridge, N 📷 Conoco/dsl ⊙ transmissions, S 📷 Shamrock/dsl, TA/Country Pride/dsl/ scales/24hr/ @ 🛏 Howard Johnson ⊙ Trailer Source RV Ctr
265	CO 58 W (from wb), to Golden, Central City

Sidebar (vertical): **DENVER AREA** — **WHEAT RIDGE**

Left margin (vertical): **CO**

INTERSTATE 70 Cont'd

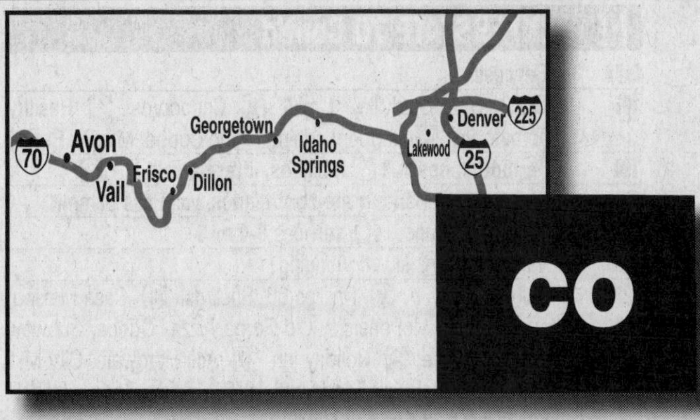

Exit #	Services
	LAKEWOOD
264	Youngfield St, W 32nd Ave, N Conoco/mkt Denny's, GoodTimes Burgers La Quinta, S Abrusci's Italian, Chili's, Chipotle, DQ, McDonald's, Noodles&Co, Pizza Hut, Pizza Hut/Taco Bell, Qdoba, SmashBurger, Starbucks, Subway Four Seasons RV Ctr, King's Sooper/24hr, Petsmart, Tuesday Morning, Walgreens, Walmart/Subway
263	Denver West Blvd, N Marriott/rest., S Coldstone, Freddy's, Jamba Juice, Keg Steaks, Macaroni Grill, Mimi's Cafe, Noodles&Co, Olive Garden, Qdoba, Twin Peaks Barnes&Noble, Best Buy, Old Navy, same as 262, Whole Foods Mkt
262	US 40 E, W Colfax, Lakewood, N Sinclair/dsl El Señor Sol Mexican, Jack-in-the-Box, Lil' Ricci's Cafe, Subway Hampton Inn, Holiday Inn Express Buick/GMC, Camping World RV Ctr, Chrysler/Jeep, Dodge, Home Depot, Honda, Hyundai, Kohl's, PetCo, Staples, Subaru, transmissions, U-Haul, vet, S Shell/Circle K/dsl/LP Bonefish Grill, Cafe Rio, Carrabba's, Chick-fil-A, Chipotle Mexican, Five Guys, Garbanzo Grill, Jamba Juice, Jimmy John's, Mimi's Cafe, Mod Mkt Eatery, Native Foods Cafe, On-the-Border, Outback Steaks, Panera Bread, Pei Wei Asian, Pieology, Wendy's, Which Wich?, Yard House Courtyard, Days Inn/rest., Mtn View Inn, Residence Inn Chevrolet, Lexus, mall, Marshall's, Old Navy, same as 263, Target, Toyota, Verizon, World Mkt
261	US 6 E (from eb), W 6th Ave, to Denver
260	CO 470, to Colo Springs
259	CO 26, Golden, N Shamrock/dsl Hampton Inn (2mi), Holiday Inn Express (2mi) Heritage Sq Funpark, S Music Hall, to Red Rocks SP
257mm	**runaway truck ramp eb**
256	Lookout Mtn, N to Buffalo Bill's Grave
254	Genesee, Lookout Mtn, N to Buffalo Bill's Grave, S Conoco/Genesee Store Chart House Rest., Guido's Pizza, Hideaway Cafe vet
253	Chief Hosa, S RV Camping, phone
252	(251 from eb), CO 74, Evergreen Pkwy, S Conoco El Señor Sol, Illegal Burger, McDonald's, Qdoba, Starbucks Comfort Suites Big O Tire, Echo Mtn Ski Area, Home Depot, King Sooper (2mi), Walmart/Subway
248	(247 from eb), Beaver Brook, Floyd Hill, S antiques
244	US 6, to CO 119, to Golden, Central City , Eldora Ski Area
243	Hidden Valley
242mm	tunnel
	IDAHO SPRINGS
241b a	Rd 314, Idaho Springs West, N Conoco/McDonald's/dsl, Shell/dsl, Sinclair, Western/dsl/e85 Carl's Jr, Cherry Blossom Chinese, Marion's Rest., Picci's Pizzaria, Smokin' Yards BBQ, Starbucks, Subway, Wildfire Rest. 6&40 Motel, Argo Inn, Columbine Inn, H&H Motel, Idaho Springs Hotel, JC Motel CarQuest, Safeway Foods/Drug, USPO
240	CO 103, Mt Evans, N Kum&Go/dsl, Shell/dsl, Sinclair/dsl 2 Bros Deli, Azteca Mexican, Beaujo's Pizza, Buffalo Rest., Jiggie's Cafe, Main St Rest., Tommy Knocker Grill, West Winds Cafe same as 241, vet, S to Mt Evans
239	Idaho Springs, S camping
238	Fall River Rd, to St Mary's Glacier
235	Dumont (from wb)
234	Downeyville, Dumont, N Conoco/Subway/dsl Starbucks, Taco Bell ski rentals, S **weigh sta both lanes**
233	Lawson (from eb)
232	US 40 W, to Empire, N Rocky Mtn NP, to Berthoud Pass, Winterpark/Sol Vista ski areas
228	Georgetown, S Conoco/Subway/dsl, Shell/dsl, Valero/dsl Blue Sky Cafe, Mountain Buzz Cafe Chateau Chamonix, Super 8 Family$, visitors ctr
226.5mm	scenic overlook eb
226	Georgetown, Silver Plume Hist Dist, N repair
221	Bakerville
220mm	Arapahoe NF eastern boundary
219	**parking area (eb only)**
218	no services
216	US 6 W, Loveland Valley, Loveland Basin, ski areas
214mm	Eisenhower/Johnson Tunnel, elev 11013
213mm	**parking area eb**
	SILVERTHORNE
205	US 6 E, CO 9 N, Dillon, Silverthorne, N 7-11, Kum&Go/dsl, Shell/7-11/dsl, Sinclair/dsl Cafe Toro, Chipotle Mexican, Dominos, Mint Cafe, Mtn Lyon Café, Murphy's Cafe, Old Chicago, Quiznos, Wendy's, Which Wich? 1st Interstate Inn, Days Inn, La Quinta, Luxury Suites, Quality Inn, Silver Inn AutoZone, Buick/Cadillac/Chevrolet/GMC, CarQuest, Chrysler/Dodge/Jeep, Ford, Lowe's, Murdoch's, Outlets/famous brands, Subaru, Target, TrueValue, S Conoco, Shell/dsl Arby's, Bamboo Garden, Blue Moon Deli, Burger King, Chimayo Burrito, Dam Brewery/Rest., DQ, Fiesta Mexican, Jimmy John's, McDonald's, Nick'n Willy's Pizza, Noodles&Co, Nozawa Japanese, Pizza Hut, Qdoba, Red Mtn Grill, Ruby Tuesday, SmashBurger, Smiling Moose Cafe, Starbucks, Subway, Sunshine Cafe Comfort Suites, Dillon Inn, Hampton Inn, Super 8 AT&T, City Mkt Foods/gas, GNC, Natural Grocers, Outlets/famous brands, Petco, Tuesday Morning, Verizon, vet, Walgreens
203.5mm	scenic overlook both lanes
	FRISCO
203	CO 9 S, to Breckenridge, Frisco, S 7-11, Conoco/Wendy's/dsl, Shell/dsl, Valero/dsl Hacienda Real Mexican, KFC, Q4U BBQ, Rio Grande Mexican, Spinelli's Pizza/Subs, Sporting News Grill, Starbucks, Subway, Szechuan Chinese, Taco Bell Alpine Inn, Baymont Inn, Holiday Inn, Ramada Ltd, Summit Inn Big O Tire, Meadow Creek Tire/auto, NAPA, RV Resort (6mi), Safeway Foods, to Breckenridge Ski Area, Verizon, Walmart, Whole Foods Mkt
201	Main St, Frisco, S Loaf N' Jug Backcountry Brew Pub, Bagali's Italian, Blue Spruce Inn, Boatyard Pizzaria, Butterhorn Cafe, Frisco Emporium, Greco's Pastaria, Log Cabin Cafe, Lost Cajun Rest., Moosejaw Cafe, Rainbow Ct Rest. Frisco Lodge, Hotel Frisco, Snowshoe Motel museum/visitor info, RV camping, to Breckenridge Ski Area, USPO
198	Officers Gulch, emergency callbox
196mm	scenic area (wb only)

= gas = food = lodging = other = rest stop

INTERSTATE 70 Cont'd

Exit#	Services
195	CO 91 S, to Leadville, **1 mi S** Conoco/dsl Healthy Tomato Deli Copper Lodging to Copper Mtn Ski Resort
190	**both lanes, full facilities, litter barrels**
189mm	elev 10662 ft, **parking area both lanes**, Vail Pass Summit
180	Vail East Entrance, services **3-4 mi S**
176	Vail, **S** ski info/lodging
173	Vail Ski Area, **N** Phillips 66, Shell/dsl Casa Mexico, May Palace, McDonald's, Old Forge Pizza, Qdoba, Subway, Westside Cafe Holiday Inn Ace Hardware, City Mkt Foods/deli, Safeway Food/Drug, USPO, **S** Conoco/dsl/LP Marriott/Streamside Hotel
171	US 6 W, US 24 E, to Minturn, Leadville, **N** Ski Cooper ski area, **2 mi S** Shell Magusto's Italian, Minturn Steaks Minturn Inn RV Camping, USPO
169	Eaglevale, (from wb), no return
168	William J. Post Blvd, **S** Castle Peak Grill Home Depot, Verizon, Walmart/McDonald's
AVON	
167	Avon, **N** Conoco/7-11/dsl, Shell Northside Kitchen vet, **S** Boxcar Rest., Burger King, Domino's, Fiesta Jalisco Mexican, Gondola Pizza, Montana's Smokehouse, Pazzo's Pizza, Starbucks, Subway Avon Ctr Lodge, Christie Lodge, Comfort Inn, Sheraton, Westin City Mkt/drugs, GNC, Radio Shack, ski info, to Beaver Creek/Arrowhead Ski, URGENT CARE, USPO, Walgreens
163	Edwards, **S both lanes, full facilities, litter barrels, RV dump,** Conoco/dsl, Shell/Wendy's/dsl Cafe Milano, Dive Cafe, East Asian, Fiestas Cafe, Gashouse Rest., Gore Range Brewery, Henry's Chinese, Main St Grill, Marble Slab Creamery, Marko's Pizza, Old Forge Pizza, Smiling Moose, Starbucks, Subway, Zino's Italian Riverwalk Inn AT&T, to Arrowhead Ski Area, USPO, Village Mkt
162mm	scenic area eb
159mm	Eagle River
157	CO 131 N, Wolcott, **N** to Steamboat Ski Area
EAGLE	
147	Eagle, **N** Kum&Go/dsl Burger King, Roberto's Italian, Starbucks AmericInn, Comfort Inn, Holiday Inn Express City Mkt Foods, **S both lanes, full facilities, info** Conoco/dsl, Shell/dsl, Sinclair/Subway/dsl Eagle Diner, Gourmet China, Grand Ave Grill, Moe's Original BBQ, Pazzo's Pizzaria, Primavera Mexican, Taco Bell, Wendy's Best Western, Eagle Lodge&Suites, Hawthorn Suites AutoZone (3mi), Costco/gas (3mi),USPO, vet
140	Gypsum, **S** Conoco, Kum&Go/dsl, Shell/dsl Buffalo Grill, Columbine Mkt Deli, Gypsum Grill, Tu Casa Mexican airport, Family$, River Dance Resort camping, USPO
134mm	Colorado River
133	Dotsero, **N** River Dance RV Camping (3mi)
129	Bair Ranch, **S both lanes, full facilities, litter barrels, petwalk**
128.5mm	**parking area eb**
127mm	tunnel wb
125mm	tunnel
125	to Hanging Lake (no return eb)
123	Shoshone (no return eb)
122.5mm	exit to river (no return eb)
121	to Hanging Lake, Grizzly Creek, **S both lanes, full facilities, litter barrels,**
119	**No Name both lanes, full facilities, rafting, RV camping**
118mm	tunnel
GLENWOOD SPRINGS	
116	CO 82 E, to Aspen, Glenwood Springs, **N** Kum&Go/dsl, Shell/dsl Chomp's Rest., Fiesta Guadalajara, KFC, Qdoba, Subway, Tequilas Rest., Village Inn Best Western, Glenwood Springs Inn, Hampton Inn, Holiday Inn Express, Hotel Colorado, Hotel Glenwood Springs, Ramada Inn, Silver Spruce Motel, Starlight Motel Hot Springs Bath, Land Rover, **0-2 mi S** Conoco, Phillips 66/dsl, Shamrock/dsl, Shell, Sinclair 19th St Diner, Chang Thai Cuisine, China Town, Domino's, Jimmy John's, McDonald's, Pizza Hut, Starbucks, Subway, Taco Bell, Taipei Japanese, Wendy's Caravan Inn, Cedar Lodge, Frontier Lodge, Hotel Denver 7-11, Alpine Tire, AutoZone, B.Thornal DDS, Chrysler/Dodge/Jeep, City Mkt Foods, city park, Midas, NAPA, Office Depot, Rite Aid, Safeway Foods, to Ski Sunlight, USPO, Walmart
114	W Glenwood Springs, **N** 7-11, Loco/Fazoli's/dsl, Shell/dsl Burger King, Jilberito's Mexican, Rte 6 Grill House, Vicco's Charcoal Burger Affordable Inn, Hanging Lake Inn, Ponderosa Motel, Red Mtn Inn, Rodeway Inn Big O Tire, Carquest, Chevrolet, Discount Tire, Ford, Honda, JC Penney, mall, O'Reilly Parts, Radio Shack, Ross, Subaru, Toyota, Verizon, **S** Kum&Go/DQ/dsl Chili's, Moe's SW Grill, Russo's Pizza, Starbucks, Zheng Asian Courtyard, Glenwood Suites, Quality Inn, Residence Inn AT&T, Audi/VW, Harley-Davidson, Lowe's, Natural Grocers, PetCo, Target, URGENT CARE, Verizon
111	South Canyon
109	Canyon Creek
108mm	**parking area both lanes**
105	New Castle, **N** Conoco/dsl, Kum&Go/dsl Hong's Garden, McDonald's, New Castle Diner, Subway Econolodge City Mkt Foods/deli, Elk Creek Campground (4mi), **S** Best Hardware
RIFLE	
97	Silt, **N** Conoco/dsl, Kum&Go/dsl, Phillips 66/dsl Brickhouse Italian Red River Inn $General, to Harvey Gap SP, **S** Holiday Inn Express Heron's Nest RV Park, KOA
94	Garfield County Airport Rd
90	CO 13 N, Rifle, **N both lanes, full facilities, litter barrels,NF info RV dump,** Conoco/dsl, Kum&Go/dsl, Phillips 66/dsl, Shell Dickey's BBQ Gateway Lodge Rifle Gap SP (10mi), USPO, **S** Kum&Go/dsl, Phillips 66/Subway/dsl Burger King, Domino's, Little Caesar's, McDonald's/playplace, Rib City Grill, Sonic, Starbucks, Subway, Taco Bell Comfort Inn, Hampton Inn, La Quinta, Rodeway Inn AutoZone, O'Reilly Parts, Radio Shack, Verizon, Walmart/Subway
87	to CO 13, West Rifle
81	Rulison
PARACHUTE	
75	Parachute, **N both lanes, full facilities, info, litter barrels, petwalk** CNG, Shell/Wienerschnizel/dsl, Sinclair/dsl El Tapatio Mexican, Hong's Garden Chinese, Outlaws Rest., Subway Comfort Inn, Parachute Inn NAPA, Radio Shack, USPO, Verizon, vet, **S** Phillips 66/Domino's/dsl, Shell/Wendy's/dsl Candlewood Suites, Days Inn Family$, RV Park (4mi)
72	US 6, W Parachute
63mm	Colorado River
62	De Beque, **N** Kum&Go/Subway/dsl
50mm	Colorado River, **parking area eastbound**, tunnel begins eastbound
49mm	Plateau Creek
49	CO 65 S, to CO 330 E, to Grand Mesa, Powderhorn Ski Area
47	Island Acres St RA, **N** CO River SP, RV camping, **S** Conoco/rest./dsl

INTERSTATE 70 Cont'd

Exit #	Services
46	Cameo
44	Lp 70 W, to Palisade, **3 mi S** [other] food, gas, lodging
43.5mm	Colorado River
42	US 6, Palisade, **S** [gas] [lodging] Wine Country Inn [other] Fruitstand/ store, wineries
37	to US 6, to US 50 S, Clifton, Grand Jct, **0-1 mi S** [gas] Conoco/dsl, Maverik/dsl, Shamrock/dsl, Shell/dsl, Sinclair/dsl [food] Burger King, Chin Chin Oriental, China Jade, Denny's, Dos Hombres, Enzo's Pizza, Jimmy John's, KFC, Little Caesar's, McDonald's/playplace, Papa John's, Papa Murphy's, Pizza Hut, Qdoba, Sonic, Starbucks, Starvin Arvin's Steaks, Subway, Taco Bell, Taco John's, Wendy's [lodging] Best Western [other] Ace Hardware, AutoZone, City Mkt Food/dsl, Family$, GNC, Murdoch's Store, O'Reilly Parts, repair, RV Ranch, URGENT CARE, USPO, vet, Walgreens, Walmart (2mi)
31	Horizon Dr, Grand Jct, **N** [gas] Shell/dsl [food] Enzo's Pizza, Pantuso Mexican, Peppers Rest., Tepanyaki Rest., Village Inn, Wendy's [lodging] Best Value Inn, Clarion, Comfort Inn, Courtyard, Econolodge, Grand Vista Hotel, Holiday Inn, La Quinta, Motel 6, Ramada Inn, Residence Inn [other] airport, Harley-Davidson, Zarlingo's Repair, **S** [gas] Conoco/Subway/dsl, Shell/dsl [food] Applebee's, Burger King/playland, Denny's, Good Pastures Rest., Nick'n Willy's Pizza, Pizza Hut, Sang Garden, Starbucks, Sushi&Rok, Taco Bell [lodging] Affordable Inn, Days Inn, Doubletree Hotel, Mesa Inn, Quality Inn, Super 8, Super 8, Travelodge [other] [H] CO NM, golf, Safeway Food/drug/gas, to Mesa St Coll, **visitors ctr**
28	Redlands Pkwy, 24 Rd, **N** [other] Kenworth, **0-2 mi S** [lodging] Candlewood Suites, city park, same as 26, ValuePlace [other] Subaru, VW
26	US 6, US 50, Grand Jct, **N** [gas] Loves/Carl's Jr/dsl/scales/ Lp/24hr, Pilot/PJ Fresh/dsl/scales/24hr [other] Hyundai, Jct W RV Park, **0-4 mi S** [gas] Conoco/A&W/dsl [food] Boston's Grill, Buffalo Wild Wings, Burger King, Cafe Rio, Chick-fil-A, Chili's, Chipotle Mexican, ChuckeCheese, Citrolas Italian, Coldstone, Costa Vida, Del Taco, Famous Dave's BBQ, Genghis Grill, Golden Corral, Grand Buffet, Honeybaked Ham, IHOP, Jimmy John's, McDonald's/playplace, Mi Mexico, Noodles&Co, Olive Garden, Outback Steaks, Papa Murphys, Qdoba, Red Lobster, Red Robin, Schlotzky's, Sonic, Starbucks, Subway, Taco Bell, Tequila's, Wendy's, Which Wich? [lodging] Holiday Inn Express, West Gate Inn [other] $Tree, AT&T, AutoZone, Barnes&Noble, Best Buy, Big O Tire, Buick/Chevrolet, Cabela's, Chrysler/Dodge/Jeep, City Mkt/dsl, Ford, Freightliner, Herberger's, Hobby Lobby, Home Depot, JC Penney, Kohl's, Lowe's, mall, Michael's, Mobile City RV Park, Natural Grocers, Nissan, Office Depot, Old Navy, PetCo, Petsmart, Ross, Sam's Club/dsl, Scott RV Ctr, Sears/auto, Sprouts Mkt, Target, TJ Maxx, Toyota, Verizon, Walmart/McDonald's
19	US 6, CO 340, Fruita, **N** [gas] Conoco/dsl [food] Burger King, Munchie's Burgers/Pizza [lodging] Balanced Rock Motel [other] [H] City Mkt Foods/deli/24hr, city park, NAPA, USPO, Walgreens, **S Welcome Ctr eb full [handicapped] facilities, litter barrels, petwalk [phone] [picnic] RV dump** [gas] Conoco/Subway/dsl/24hr, LNG, Shell/ Wendy's/dsl/24hr [food] El Tapatio Mexican, FeedLot Rest., McDonald's/playplace, Pablo's Pizza, Rib City Grill, Taco Bell [lodging] Comfort Inn, La Quinta, Super 8 [other] dinosaur museum, Monument RV Park, Peterbilt/Volvo, to CO NM, vet
17mm	Colorado River
15	CO 139 N, to Loma, Rangely, **N** gas/dsl, phone, to Highline Lake SP

GRAND JCT

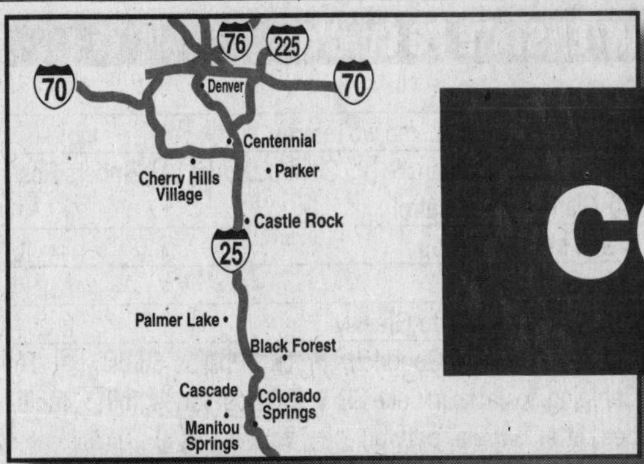

CO

Exit #	Services
14.5mm	**weigh/check sta both lanes [phone]**
11	Mack, **2-3 mi N** [other] food, gas/dsl
2	Rabbit Valley, **N** [other] to Trail Through Time
0mm	Colorado/Utah state line

INTERSTATE 76

Exit #	Services
185mm	**I-76 begins/ends on NE I-80, exit 102**
184mm	Colorado/Nebraska state line
180	US 385, Julesburg, **N Welcome Ctr/[RS] both lanes, full [handicapped] facilities, info, RV dump,** [gas] Shell [food] Subway [lodging] Budget Host [other] [H] **S** [gas] Conoco/dsl
172	Ovid
165	CO 59, to Haxtun, Sedgewick, **N** [food] Lucy's Cafe
155	Red Lion Rd
149	CO 55, to Fleming, Crook, **S** [gas] Sinclair/dsl/café
141	Proctor
134	Iliff
125	US 6, Sterling, **0-3 mi N** [RS] **both lanes, full [handicapped] facilities, litter barrels, petwalk [phone] [picnic] vending, RV dump,** [gas] Cenex/dsl, HR/dsl [food] Arby's, Bamboo Garden, Burger King, Domino's, DQ, KFC/LJ Silver, Little Caesar's, McDonald's, Mi Ranchito, Old Town Bistro, Papa Murphy's, Pizza Hut, Sonic, Subway, Taco Bell, Taco John's, Village Inn, Wendy's [lodging] 1st Interstate Inn, Best Western [other] [H] $Tree, AutoZone, Buick/Chevrolet, Chrysler/Dodge/Jeep, Family Food Mkt, Ford/Lincoln, Home Depot, museum, N Sterling SP, NAPA, O'Reilly Parts, Radio Shack, st patrol, USPO, Verizon, vet, Walgreens, Walmart, **S** [gas] Reata/dsl [food] Country Kitchen [lodging] Comfort Inn, Ramada Inn, Super 8, Traveler Inn [other] RV Camping
115	CO 63, Atwood, **N** [gas] Sinclair/dsl [other] [H] **S** [food] Steakhouse
102	Merino
95	Hillrose
92	to US 6 E, to US 34, CO 71 S
90b a	CO 71 N, to US 34, Brush, **N** [gas] Brush Trkstp/Shell/Subway/ dsl/24hr [food] China Buffet, Pizza Hut, Wendy's [lodging] Econolodge, **S** [gas] Conoco/dsl [food] McDonald's [lodging] Microtel
89	Hospital Rd, **S** [other] [H] golf
86	Dodd Bridge Rd
82	Barlow Rd, **N** [food] Maverick's Grill [lodging] Comfort Inn, Rodeway Inn [other] Silver Spur Camping, **S** [gas] Reata/dsl/scales, USA/ dsl [food] Burger King [other] $Tree, Walmart/Subway
80	CO 52, Ft Morgan, **N** [other] City Park, Golf, RV Camping, **S** [gas] Conoco/dsl, Maverik/dsl, Sinclair/dsl, Western/dsl [food] Arby's, DQ, El Jacal Mexican, McDonald's, Sonic, Subway, Taco Bell, Taco John's, Wonderful House Chinese [lodging] Central Motel, Hampton Inn, Sands Inn, Super 8 [other] [H] AutoZone, Family$, Toyota, Verizon, Walgreens

STERLING

FT MORGAN

= gas = food = lodging = other = rest stop

CO

INTERSTATE 76 Cont'd

Exit #	Services
79	CO 144, to Weldona, (no wb return)
75	US 34 E, to Ft Morgan, S Shell/pizza/dsl Embers Rest. Clarion st patrol
74.5mm	**weigh sta both lanes**
73	Long Bridge Rd
66b	US 34 W (from wb), to Greeley
66a	CO 39, CO 52, to Goodrich, N Phillips 66/dsl RV Camping, to Jackson Lake SP, S **both lanes, full facilities, litter barrels, petwalk vending** Sinclair/cafe/dsl/e-85
64	Wiggins
60	to CO 144 E, to Orchard
57	Rd 91
49	Painter Rd (from wb)
48	to Roggen, N Conoco/dsl, S USPO
39	Keenesburg, S Shell/dsl Dos Hijos Mexican Keene Motel Family$, Tim's Car Clinic
34	Kersey Rd
31	CO 52, Hudson, N Loves/Subway/Carl's Jr/scales/24hr/dsl , S Conoco/dsl, Shell/dsl El Faro Mexican, Pepper Pod Rest. Pepper Pod Camping, USPO
25	CO 7, Lochbuie, N Shell/dsl
22	Bromley, N Valero/dsl KFC/LJ Silver, Wendy's Hampton Inn (4mi) Lowe's, S Barr Lake SP
21	144th Ave, Eagle Blvd, N Buffalo Wild Wings, Chick-fil-A, Chili's, McDonald's, Subway, Taco Bell Candlewood Suites, Holiday Inn Express $Tree, AT&T, Dick's, GNC, Home Depot, JC Penney, Kohl's, Michael's, Office Depot, Petsmart, Ross, Target, Verizon
20	136th Ave, N Barr Lake RV Park, same as 21
18	**E-470 tollway**, to Limon (from wb)
16	CO 2, Sable Blvd, Commerce City, N Shell/diner/dsl/24hr/@ , to Denver Airport
12	US 85 N, to Brighton (exits left from eb), Greeley
11	96th Ave, N dsl repair, S Buick/GMC
10	88th Ave, N Shell/dsl La Quinta, Super 8, S flea mkt
9	US 6 W, US 85 S (no EZ wb return), Commerce City, S Shell/dsl st patrol, transmissions
8	CO 224, 74th Ave (no EZ eb return), **1 mi** N NAPA
6b a	I-270 E, to Limon, to airport, to I-25 N
5	I-25, N to Ft Collins, S to Colo Springs
4	Pecos St
3	US 287, Federal Blvd, N Shamrock/dsl, S Advance Parts, Family$, vet
1b	CO 95, Sheridan Blvd
1a	CO 121, Wadsworth Blvd, N 7-11/gas, Conoco, Shell/dsl Anthony's Pizza, Applebee's, BeauJo's, Bennet's BBQ, Chick-fil-A, Chipotle Mexican, Coldstone Creamery, Country Buffet, El Tapatio Mexican, Fazoli's, HuHot, IHOP, Jimmy John's, Kukoro Japanese, McDonald's/playplace, Red Robin, Ruby Tuesday, Smiling Moose, Starbucks, Subway, Taco Bell, TX Roadhouse $Tree, Advance Parts, Big O Tire, Costco/gas, Discount Tire, Home Depot, Lowe's Whse, Petsmart, Radio Shack, Sam's Club, Tires+, URGENT CARE

I-76 begins/ends on I-70, exit 269b

INTERSTATE 225 (DENVER)

Exit #	Services
12b a	I-70, W to Denver, E to Limon
10	US 40, US 287, Colfax Ave, E Conoco/dsl, Shell/dsl, Sinclai Burger King, Del Taco, Domino's, DQ, El Pelicano Seafood KFC, McDonald's, Pizza Hut/Taco Bell, Popeye's, Starbucks Subway, Village Inn, Wendy's 7-11, Aamco, Advance Parts Chevrolet, Family$, King's Sooper/gas, K-Mart, NAPA, Walgreens, W Conoco/dsl, Shamrock/dsl Caribou Coffee Chipotle Mexican, Noodles&Co, Panera Bread, Smashburger Which Wich? SpringHill Suites U-Haul
9	Co 30, 6th Ave, E Conoco/dsl Denny's Travelodge, ValuePlace Inn, W Shell/dsl
8	Alameda Ave, E Valero/dsl Atlanta Bread, BJ's Rest., Chick-fil-A, Chili's, Coldstone, FatBurger, Jamba Juice, Jimmy John's, L&L BBQ, Macaroni Grill, Mimi's Cafe, Panda Express, Sabor Mexican, Starbucks, TGIFriday, Wingstop AT&T, Barnes&Noble, Dillards, Hobby Lobby, JC Penney, Macy's, Michael's, Petsmart, Ross, Sears/auto, Super Target, W Conoco/dsl, Shell/Circle K $Tree
7	Mississippi Ave, Alameda Ave, E Arby's, Burger King, Chubby's Mexican, ChuckeCheese, CiCi's, Fazoli's, Guadalajara Mexican, McAlister's Deli, Schlotsky's, Sonic, Starbucks, Subway, Tokyo Joe's, Village Inn Best Western, Holiday Inn Express, La Quinta Best Buy, Burlington Coats, Home Depot, JoAnn Fabrics, Sam's Club/gas, Tires +, Verizon, Walmart, W IHOP, McDonald's, Mirage Rest., Senor Ric's, Waffle House 7-11, AutoZone, Pepboys
5	Iliff Ave, E 7-11 Ajuua Mexican, Applebee's, Boston Mkt, Carrabba's, Hibachi Japanese, Joe's Crabshack, Outback Steaks, Real de Minas Mexican, Rosie's Diner, Ruby Tuesday, Sweet Tomatoes, TX Roadhouse Comfort Inn, Crestwood Suites, Extended Stay America, Extended Stay America (2), Fairfield Inn, Motel 6 Gander Mtn, W Conoco Dragon Boat, Legends Grill, Subway DoubleTree 7-11
4	CO 83, Parker Rd, E Radisson Cherry Creek SP, W Shell/dsl Big Burrito, DQ, Little Caesar's, Popeye's, Starbucks, Subway, Taco Bell, Wendy's $Tree, 7-11, Firestone/auto, King Sooper/dsl
2b	Yosemite St
2	DTC Blvd, Tamarac St, W Conoco/7-11 Fel Fel Mediterranean, La Fogata Mexican, Sonic, South Garden Chinese, Subway $Tree, Goodyear/auto
1b a	**I-25. I-225 begins/ends on I-25, exit 200**

INTERSTATE 270 (DENVER)

Exit #	Services
4	I-70
3	N TA/Burger King/Country Pride/Popeye's/Pizza Hut/dsl/24hr/ @ , S Sapp Bros/Sinclair/Subway/dsl/ @
2b a	US 85, CO 2, Vasquez Ave, N Arby's, Carls Jr, Chipotle Mexican, Jack-in-the-Box, KFC/LJ Silver, McDonald's, Taco Bell, Wendy's TDS Tire, Walgreens, Walmart
1b	York St
1a	I-76 E, to Ft Morgan
1c	I-25 S, to Denver

CONNECTICUT

INTERSTATE 84

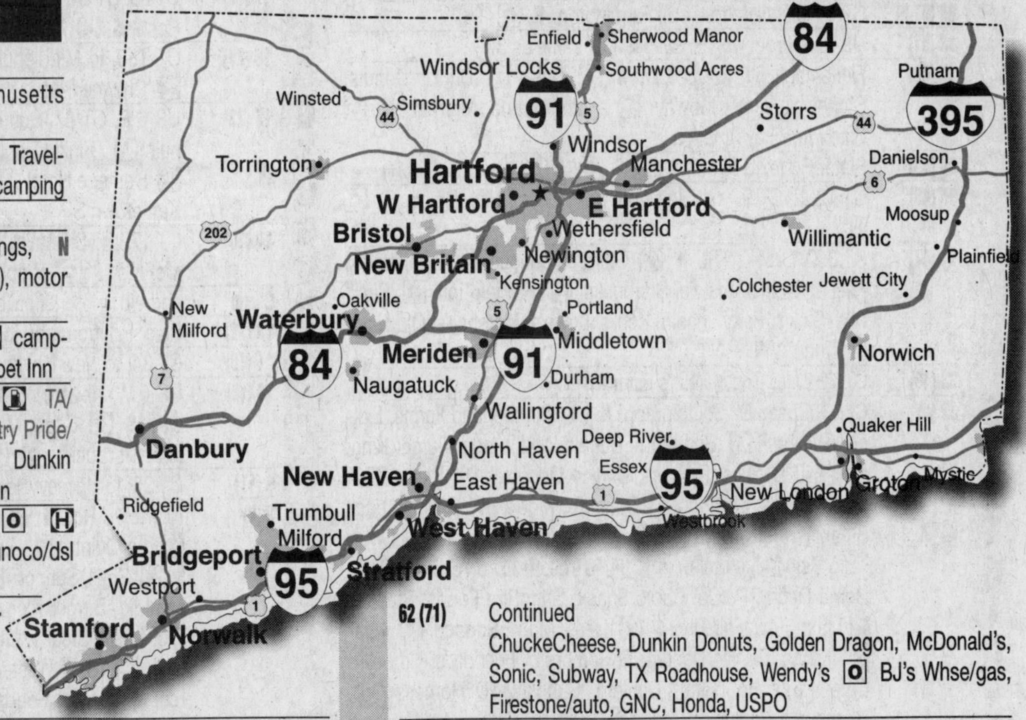

Exit #	Services
98mm	Connecticut/Massachusetts state line
74 (97)	CT 171, Holland, S food Traveler's Book Rest. other RV camping
95mm	weigh sta wb
73 (95)	CT 190, Stafford Springs, N other camping (seasonal), motor speedway, st police
72 (93)	CT 89, Westford, N lodging camping (seasonal), Red Carpet Inn
71 (88)	CT 320, Ruby Rd, S gas TA/Shell/Burger King/Country Pride/dsl/scales/24hr/ @ food Dunkin Donuts lodging Rodeway Inn
70 (86)	CT 32, Willington, N other H S gas Mobil/dsl, Sunoco/dsl other RV Camping
85mm	rest stop both lanes, campers, full facilities, litter barrels, petwalk vending
69 (83)	CT 74, to US 44, Willington, S food, gas, RV camping, st police
68 (81)	CT 195, Tolland, N gas Gulf/dsl, Mobil food Dunkin Donuts, Papa T's Rest., Subway other NAPA, RV camping, S gas Citgo other Big Y Foods, Radio Shack
67 (77)	CT 31, Rockville, N gas Mobil, Shell food Beni's Grill, Burger King, China Taste, Dunkin Donuts, McDonald's, Subway other H RV Camping, S other Nathan Hale Mon
66 (76)	Tunnel Rd, Vernon
65 (75)	CT 30, Vernon Ctr, N gas Mobil/dsl, Shell food Brick Oven Pizza, Burger King, Joy Luck, KFC, Lotus Rest., Oki Asian, Rein's Deli, Vernon Diner lodging Howard Johnson, Quality Inn other CarQuest, Firestone/auto, K-Mart, Meineke, Stop&Shop/gas
64 (74)	Vernon Ctr, N gas Mobil/24hr, Sunoco food 99 Rest., Angellino's Italian, Anthony's Pizza, Denny's, Dunkin Donuts, Friendly's, McDonald's, Rita's Custard, Taco Bell, Wood'n Tap lodging Holiday Inn Express other $Tree, AutoZone, CVS Drug, GNC, Goodyear/auto, PriceChopper, Staples, TJ Maxx, vet, S lodging Motel 6
63 (72)	CT 30, CT 83, Manchester, S Windsor, N food Applebee's, Azteca Mexican, Chipotle Mexican, Dunkin Donuts, HomeTown Buffet, Longhorn Steaks, McDonald's, Outback Steaks, Panera Bread, Red Robin, Starbucks, TGIFriday's lodging Courtyard, Residence Inn other AT&T, Barnes&Noble, Best Buy, Dick's, JC Penney, Macy's, Marshall's, PetCo, same as 62, Sears/auto, Walgreens, Walmart, S gas Shell/dsl, Sunoco/dsl, Xtra food Misaki Buffet, Shea's Grill lodging Baymont Inn, Best Value Inn, Extended Stay America, Motel 6 other H Big Y Mkt, Hyundai, Kohl's, Nissan, Subaru, Toyota/Scion, U-Haul
62 (71)	Buckland St, N gas Mobil/Dunkin Donuts/dsl food Bonefish Grill, Boston Mkt, Boston's, Chili's, Friendly's, Hooters, Johnny Rocket's, KFC, Moe's SW Grill, Olive Garden, Starbucks, Taco Bell, Ted's MT Grill, Tullycross Tavern lodging Fairfield Inn, Hampton Inn other $Tree, BigLots, Home Depot, Jo-Ann Fabrics, Lowe's, mall, Michael's, PetsMart, same as 63, Sam's Club, Target, S gas Xtra/dsl food Buffalo Wild Wings, Carrabba's,
62 (71)	Continued ChuckeCheese, Dunkin Donuts, Golden Dragon, McDonald's, Sonic, Subway, TX Roadhouse, Wendy's other BJ's Whse/gas, Firestone/auto, GNC, Honda, USPO
61 (70)	I-291 W, to Windsor
60 (69)	US 6, US 44, Burnside Ave (from eb)
59 (68)	I-384 E, Manchester
58 (67)	Roberts St, Burnside Ave, N food Margarita's Grill lodging Comfort Inn, Ramada, S gas Mobil, Sunoco food Dunkin Donuts other Cabelas
57 (66)	CT 15 S, to I-91 S, Charter Oak Br
56 (65)	Governor St, E Hartford, S other airport
55 (64)	CT 2 E, New London, downtown
54 (63)	Old State House, N other Chevrolet, Ford, Lexus, Lincoln
53 (62)	CT Blvd (from eb), S lodging Holiday Inn
52 (61)	W Main St (from eb), downtown
51 (60)	I-91 N, to Springfield
50 (59.8)	to I-91 S (from wb), N lodging Ramada, S lodging Hilton, Residence Inn
48 (59.5)	Asylum St , downtown, N lodging Ramada, S lodging Holiday Inn Express other H
47 (59)	Sigourney St, downtown, N other Hartford Seminary, Mark Twain House
46 (58)	Sisson St, downtown (from wb, exits left), S other UConn Law School
45 (57)	Flatbush Ave (from wb, exits left)
44 (56.5)	Prospect Ave, N gas Mobil, Shell/dsl food Burger King, D'angelo's, Hibachi Grill, McDonald's, Prospect Pizza, Wendy's other ShopRite Foods
43 (56)	Park Rd, W Hartford, N other to St Joseph Coll
42 (55)	Trout Brk Dr (exits left from wb), to Elmwood
41 (54)	S Main St, Elmwood, S other American School for the Deaf
40 (53)	CT 71, New Britain Ave, S gas Shell, Sunoco food Brio Grille, Burger King, CA Pizza, Chili's, China Pan, Chipotle Mexican, Dunkin Donuts, McDonald's, Olive Garden, Panera Bread, PF Chang's, Red Robin, Starbucks, Subway, Wendy's lodging Courtyard other Barnes&Noble, Best Buy, JC Penney, Macy's, mall, Michael's, Nordstrom, Office Depot, Old Navy, PetCo, Radio Shack, Sears/auto, Target, TJ Maxx, Trader Joe's, Verizon

VERNON CTR WINDSOR

HARTFORD

↑E INTERSTATE 84 Cont'd

Exit #	Services
39a (52)	CT 9 S, to New Britain, Newington, **S** ☐ Ⓗ
39 (51.5)	CT 4, (exits left from eb), Farmington, **N** ☐ Ⓗ
38 (51)	US 6 W (from wb), Bristol, **N** ⛽ same as 37
37 (50)	Fienemann Rd, to US 6 W, **N** ⛽ Shell 🍴 Dunkin Donuts, Stonewell Rest., Subway 🛏 Hampton Inn, Marriott, **S** 🛏 Extended Stay America
36 (49)	Slater Rd (exits left from eb), **S** ☐ Ⓗ
35 (48)	CT 72, to CT 9 (exits left from both lanes), New Britain, **S** ☐ Ⓗ
34 (47)	CT 372, Crooked St, **N** ⛽ Gulf/dsl, Sunoco 🍴 Applebee's, Friendly's, McDonald's, Starbucks 🛏 Fairfield Inn ☐ Big Y Mkt, Dick's, Ford/Lincoln, Kohl's, Lowe's, Marshall's, Old Navy, Petsmart, VW
33 (46)	CT 72 W, to Bristol (exits left from eb)
32 (45)	Ct 10, Queen St, Southington, **N** ⛽ Cumberland Farms, Exxon, Shell/dsl 🍴 Bertucci's, Buffalo Wild Wings, Burger King, Chili's, D'angelos, Denny's, Dunkin Donuts, JD's Rest., KFC, Liberty Pizza, Luenhop, McDonald's, Moe's SW Grill, Outback Steaks, Puerto Vallarta, Ruby Tuesday, Starbucks, Subway, Taco Bell 🛏 Motel 6 ☐ Ⓗ $Tree, 7-11, CVS Drug, GNC, Home Depot, PetCo, Radio Shack, ShopRite Foods, Staples, TJ Maxx, TownFair Tire, **S** ⛽ Hess, Mobil, Sunoco 🍴 Aziagos Italian, Dunkin Donuts, El Sombrero, Friendly's, Nordelli's Cafe, Pizza Hut, Rita's Custard, Subway, TD Homer's Grill, Wendy's, Wood'n Tap Grill 🛏 Days Inn, Holiday Inn Express, Knights Inn ☐ Advance Parts, AT&T, Firestone, Midas, Monro, PriceChopper Foods, Rite Aid, Walmart
31 (44)	CT 229, West St, **N** ⛽ Mobil, Sunoco/dsl ☐ Lowe's, Target, **S** ⛽ Citgo, Valero 🍴 Dunkin Donuts, Giovanni's Pizza, Subway 🛏 Residence Inn
30 (43)	Marion Ave, W Main, Southington, **N** ☐ ski area, **S** ⛽ Mobil/dsl ☐ Ⓗ
29 (42)	CT 10, from wb, exits left, Milldale (exits left from wb)
41.5mm	🅿 eb, full ♿ facilities, info, litter barrels, petwalk ☐ 🚶
28 (41)	CT 322, Marion, **S** ⛽ Fleet/dsl, Mobil, TA/Country Pride/Pizza Hut/Popeye's/Taco Bell/dsl/scales/24hr/ @ 🍴 Blimpie, Burger King, DQ, Dunkin Donuts, Manor Inn Rest., Subway, Young Young Chinese 🛏 Comfort Suites, EconoLodge ☐ Home Depot, repair
27 (40)	I-691 E, to Meriden
26 (38)	CT 70, to Cheshire, **N** 🍴 Blackie's Cafe
25a (37)	Austin Rd, **N** ⛽ Winzz/dsl 🍴 Asian Garden, Subway ☐ Costco/gas, funpark, Kohl's
25 (36)	Harper's Ferry Rd, Reed Dr, Scott Rd, E Main St, **N** ⛽ Gulf/dsl, Mobil/dsl 🍴 Dunkin Donuts, Subway ☐ NAPA, **S** ⛽ Gulf 🍴 Burger King, Dunkin Donuts, Friendly's, Golden Wok, McDonald's, Nino's Rest., Subway 🛏 Quality Inn ☐ Aldi Foods, BJ's Whse/gas, Cadillac/Chevrolet, CVS Drug, Super Stop&Shop/gas
23 (33.5)	CT 69, Hamilton Ave, **N** 🍴 Bertucci's, Buffalo Wild Wings, Chili's, HomeTown Buffet, IHOP, McDonald's, Olive Garden, TGIFriday's ☐ Ⓗ Barnes&Noble, JC Penney, Macy's, mall, Michael's, Save-a-Lot Foods, Sears/auto, **S** ⛽ Shell 🍴 Dunkin Donuts
22 (33)	Baldwin St, Waterbury, **N** ⛽ Gulf 🛏 Courtyard ☐ Ⓗ same as 23, USPO
21 (33)	Meadow St, Banks St, **N** ⛽ 7-11, Citgo, **S** ⛽ Exxon/dsl ☐ Home Depot, PetsMart
20 (32)	CT 8 N (exits left from eb), to Torrington

Exit #	Services
19 (32)	CT 8 S (exits left from wb), to Bridgeport
18 (32)	W Main, Highland Ave, **N** 🍴 Dunkin Donuts, Lena's Deli, Subway 🛏 Hampton Inn ☐ Ⓗ CVS Drug
17 (30)	CT 63, CT 64, to Watertown, Naugatuck, **N** 🍴 Maggie McFly's Rest., **S** ⛽ Mobil/dsl 🍴 Leo's Rest., Maples Rest., Subway
16 (25)	CT 188, to Middlebury, **N** ⛽ Mobil 🍴 Patty's Pantry Del 🛏 Crowne Plaza
15 (22)	US 6 E, CT 67, Southbury, **N** ⛽ Citgo/deli, Mobil, Shell/repair 🍴 Dunkin Donuts, Friendly's (1mi), McDonald's, Subway 🛏 Heritage Hotel ☐ K-Mart, Stop&Shop, TJ Maxx, **S** ☐ to Kettletown SP
14 (20)	CT 172, to S Britain, **N** ⛽ Mobil 🍴 Dunkin Donuts, Maggie McFly's, **S** ☐ st police
20mm	end wb, motorist callboxes begin eb
13 (19)	River Rd (from eb), to Southbury
11 (16)	CT 34, to New Haven
10 (15)	US 6 W, Newtown, **N** 🍴 Fig's Rest., Foundry Kitchen, Subway, **S** ⛽ Citgo, Mobil/dsl 🍴 Blue Colony Diner, Pizza Palace, Starbucks ☐ Ⓗ
9 (11)	CT 25, to Hawleyville, **S** 🍴 McGuire's Alehouse
8 (8)	Newtown Rd, **N** ⛽ Global, Mobil/dsl 🍴 Outback Steaks 🛏 La Quinta ☐ Best Buy, Harley-Davidson, Lowe's, Volvo, **S** ⛽ Shell, Sunoco 🍴 Bangkok Thai, Bertucci's Italian, Boston Mkt, Burger King, Chili's, Denny's, Dunkin Donuts, Friendly's, Ichiro Steaks, Little Caesars, McDonald's, Subway, Taco Bell 🛏 Best Western, Days Inn, Hampton Inn, Holiday Inn/rest. ☐ Aldi Foods, Buick, Chrysler/Jeep, Goodyear/auto, Marshall's, Radio Shack, Staples, Stop&Shop, Target, Town Fair Tire, Verizon, Walmart
7 (7)	US 7N/202E, to Brookfield (exits left from eb), New Milford, **1 mi N on Federal Rd** ⛽ Mobil, Shell, Sunoco 🍴 5 Guys Burgers, Applebee's, Arby's, KFC, McDonald's, Panera Bread, Pizza Hut, Starbucks, Subway, Wendy's ☐ Bj's Whse/gas, CVS Drug, Firestone, Ford, GNC, Harley-Davidson, Home Depot, Jo-Ann Fabrics, Kohl's, Michael's, ShopRite Foods, Stew Leonards, Subaru, TJ Maxx, Town Fair Tire, Toyota/Scion, Walgreens
6 (6)	CT 37 (from wb), New Fairfield, **N** ⛽ Gulf 🍴 Burger King, Castello's Italian, Dunkin Donuts, Elmer's Diner, Grand Century Buffet, KFC, McDonald's, Moon Star Chinese ☐ $Tree, A&P Foods, Radio Shack, Rite Aid, **S** ⛽ Citgo, Valero 🍴 KFC
5 (5)	CT 37, CT 39, CT 53, Danbury, **N** ⛽ Gulf/dsl, Shell 🛏 Best Value Inn, **S** ⛽ Mobil 🍴 Dunkin Donuts, Taco Bell ☐ Ⓗ to Putnam SP
4 (4)	US 6 W/202 W, Lake Ave, **N** ⛽ Exxon, Gulf/dsl, Shell/dsl 🍴 Dunkin Donuts, McDonald's 🛏 Ethan Allen Hotel, Maron Hotel, Super 8 ☐ CVS Drug, Stop&Shop Foods, **S** 🍴 Chuck's Steaks 🛏 Residence Inn, to mall
3 (3)	US 7 S (exits left from wb), to Norwalk, **S** ⛽ Mobil 🍴 Brio Grille, Buffalo Wild Wings, Cheesecake Factory, Chucke-Cheese, Coldstone, Olive Garden, Panera Bread, Red Lobster ☐ Barnes&Noble, Dick's, JC Penney, LL Bean, Macy's, mall, Petco, Sears/auto
2b a (1)	US 6, US 202, Mill Plain Rd, **N** ⛽ Mobil/dsl 🍴 Desert Moon Café, Rosy Tomorrows, Starbucks, Tuscanero's Pizza 🛏 Hilton Garden, Holiday Inn Express ☐ Rite Aid, Staples, Trader Joe's, **S** Welcome Ctr/weigh sta eb full ♿ facilities, info, litter barrels, ☐ 🚶 vending 🛏 SpringHill Suites ☐ to Old Ridgebury
1 (0)	Saw Mill Rd, **N** 🛏 Hilton Garden, Holiday Inn Express, Maron Hotel
0mm	Connecticut/New York state line

INTERSTATE 91

Exit #	Services
58mm	Connecticut/Massachusetts state line
49 (57)	US 5, to Longmeadow, MA, E Pride/dsl, Valero Backyard Grille, McDonald's Holiday Inn Meineke, repair, W Sunoco/dsl Baco's Pizza, Cloverleaf Café, DQ, Dunkin Donuts, Pizza Palace $General, Chrysler/Dodge
48 (56)	CT 220, Elm St (same as 47), E Mobil/dsl Arby's, Burger King, Denny's, Dunkin Donuts, Figaro, Friendly's, Jason's Seafood, McDonald's, Outback Steaks, Oyama Japanese, Panera Bread, Ruby Tuesday, TGIFriday's, Wendy's $Tree, AutoZone, Best Buy, Costco/gas, Dick's, Firestone/auto, Home Depot, Honda, Hyundai, Jo-Ann Fabrics, Kohl's, Macy's, Nissan, Radio Shack, Sears/auto, Target, TownFair Tire, Toyota, USPO, VW
47 (55)	CT 190, to Hazardville (same as 48), E 99 Rest., Acapulcos Mexican, Cheng's Garden, Chipotle, D'angelo, Domino's, Dunkin Donuts, Longhorn Steaks, McDonald's, Moe's SW Grill, Olive Garden, Pizza Hut, Plaza Azteca Mexican, Red Robin, Starbucks, Subway, Taco Bell Hampton Inn, Motel 6, Red Roof Inn H Advance Parts, Aldi Foods, AT&T, Barnes&Noble, Big Y Foods, CVS Drug, Ford, Goodyear, Marshall's, Michael's, NAPA, Old Navy, PetCo, Petsmart, Rite Aid, ShopRite, Staples, Stop&Shop/gas, URGENT CARE, Verizon, Walgreens
46 (53)	US 5, King St, to Enfield, E Mobil Astro's Rest., W Hacienda Del Sol Enfield Inn
45 (51)	CT 140, Warehouse Point, E Shell Burger King, Chen's Chinese, Cracker Barrel, Dunkin Donuts, Friendly's, Jake's Burgers, Sofia's Rest., Subway Comfort Inn to Trolley Museum, W Sunoco/dsl Clarion Advance Parts
44 (50)	US 5 S, to E Windsor, E Sunoco/dsl Dunkin Donuts, KFC, Sky Diner, Taco Bell, Wendy's Baymont Inn Walmart
49mm	Connecticut River
42 (48)	CT 159, Windsor Locks, E Longview RV Ctr, W same as 41
41 (47)	Center St (exits with 39), W Ad's Pizzaria HillPoint Hotel
40 (46.5)	CT 20, W Old New-Gate Prison
39 (46)	Kennedy Rd (exits with 41), Community Rd, E vet, W Shell/dsl Charkoon, Chili's $Tree, GNC, PetCo, Radio Shack, Stop&Shop Foods, Target
38 (45)	CT 75, to Poquonock, Windsor Area, E Mobil/dsl Buffalo Wild Wings, Buffalo Wild Wings, China Sea, Dunkin Donuts, Izote SW Grill, Pizzarama, Subway AT&T, PriceChopper Foods, to Ellsworth Homestead, W River City Grill Courtyard, Hilton Garden, Hyatt House Suites, Marriott
37 (44)	CT 305, Bloomfield Ave, Windsor Ctr, E Mobil/dsl McDonald's, W Sunoco Residence Inn
36 (43)	CT 178, Park Ave, to W Hartford
35b (41)	CT 218, to Bloomfield, to S Windsor, E food, gas/dsl
35a	I-291 E, to Manchester
34 (40)	CT 159, Windsor Ave, E Shell/dsl, W Citgo/dsl Flamingo Inn, RanchHouse Rest. H
33 (39)	Jennings Rd, Weston St, E Cadillac, Fiat, Jaguar, VW, W Mobil, Sunoco/dsl Burger King, Dunkin Donuts, McDonald's, Subway Super 8, Travel Inn CarMax, Honda, Hyundai, Infiniti, Mazda, Mercedes, Midas, Nissan, Subaru, Toyota/Scion
32b (38)	Trumbull St (exits left from nb), W Crowne Plaza, Hilton H Goodyear, to downtown
32a	(exit 30 from sb), I-84 W
29b (37)	I-84 E, Hartford
29a (36.5)	US 5 N, CT 15 N (exits left from nb), W H, capitol, civic ctr, downtown
28 (36)	US 5, CT 15 S (from nb), W Citgo Burger King, Dunkin Donuts, Wendy's
27 (35)	Brainerd Rd, Airport Rd, E Mobil/Dunkin Donuts/Subway/dsl, Shell/Dunkin Donuts/dsl McDonald's, USS Chowder Days Inn, Hartford Suites Ford Trucks, to Regional Mkt
26 (33.5)	Marsh St, E CT MVD, Silas Deane House, Webb House
25 (33)	CT 3, Glastonbury, Wethersfield
24 (32)	CT 99, Rocky Hill, Wethersfield, E Phillips 66/dsl, Sunoco Algarve Grill, Chuck's Steaks, Dakota Steaks, Dunkin Donuts, McDonald's, On-the-Border, Rita's Custard, Rockyhill Pizza, Saybrook Seafood, Subway Hampton Inn, Howard Johnson, Super 8 Aldi Foods, Kohl's, Meineke, Monro, W Mobil, Shell/dsl, Valero/dsl Buffalo Wild Wings, Burger King, D'Angelo, Denny's, Dunkin Donuts, Friendly's, Ginza Cuisine, HomeTown Buffet, KFC, Ming Dynasty, Panera Bread, Pizza Hut, Red Lobster, Sake Japanese, Sophia's Pizzaria, Starbucks, Subway, Tamarind Rest., Tilted Kilt, Townline Diner, Wendy's, Wood-n-Tap Grill Comfort Inn, Motel 6 $Tree, AT&T, CVS Drug, Goodyear/auto, Marshalls, Office Depot, Radio Shack, Stop&Shop, TJMaxx, TownFair Tire, TrueValue, Verizon, Walgreens, Walmart/Subway
23 (29)	to CT 3, West St, Rocky Hill, Vet Home, E Sheraton to Dinosaur SP, W Mobil, Valero/dsl Dunkin Donuts, Michelangeo's Pizza, Papa John's, Subway Residence Inn IGA Foods
22 (27)	CT 9, to New Britain, Middletown
21 (26)	CT 372, to Berlin, Cromwell, E Sunoco/dsl/repair Crowne Plaza, Quality Inn Krauszer's Foods, Lowe's, W Citgo/Subway/dsl, Mobil/dsl Baci Grill, Burger King, Chili's, Cromwell Diner, Dunkin Donuts, McDonald's, Nordelli's, Oyama Japanese Courtyard, Super 8 $Plus, Firestone/auto, Price Rite Foods, Verizon, vet, Walmart
20 (23)	Country Club Rd, Middle St
22mm	**/weigh sta nb, full facilities, info, litter barrels, petwalk RV dump, vending**
19 (21)	Baldwin Ave (from sb)
18 (20.5)	I-691 W, to Marion, access to same as 16 & 17, ski area
17 (20)	CT 15 N (from sb), to I-691, CT 66 E, Meriden
16 (19)	CT 15, E Main St, E Gulf/dsl, Mobil/dsl, Valero American Steaks, Gianni's Rest., Huxley's Cafe, Kings Garden Chinese, Olympos Diner, Subway Hampton Inn, Hawthorn Inn, The Meridan Inn URGENT CARE, Volvo, W Getty/dsl, Gulf/repair, Shell/dsl Boston Mkt, Boston Mkt, Burger King, Dominos, Dunkin Donuts, KFC, Les' Dairy Bar, Little Caesar's, McDonald's, Nordelli's, Subway, Taco Bell, Wayback Burgers,

WINDSOR AREA

ROCKY HILL

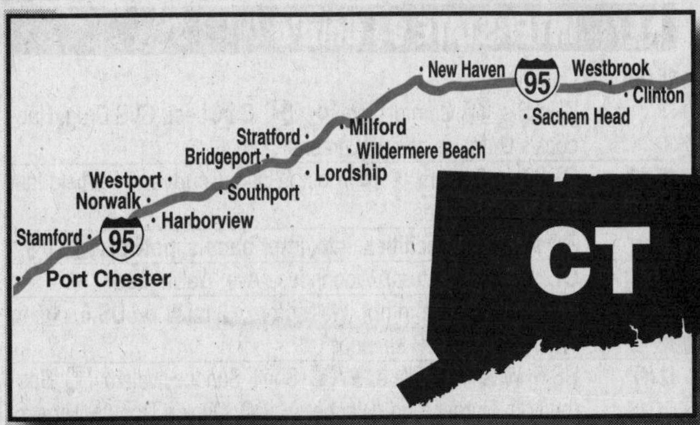

CT

= gas = food = lodging = other = rest stop

INTERSTATE 91 Cont'd

16 (19) Continued
Wendy's Comfort Inn H CarQuest, CVS Drug, Hancock's Drug, Verizon, Walgreens

WALLINGFORD

15 (16) CT 68, to Durham, E golf, W Courtyard, Fairfield Inn, Homewood Suites

15mm **sb, full facilities, info, litter barrels, petwalk**

14 (12) CT 150 (no EZ return), Woodhouse Ave, Wallingford

13 (10) US 5 (exits left from nb), Wallingford, **2 mi W on US 5** to Wharton Brook SP, services

12 (9) US 5, Washington Ave, E Shell, Sunoco, Valero Boston Mkt, Burger King, D'angelo's, DQ, Dunkin Donuts, Hibachi Buffet, McDonald's, Popeyes, Starbucks, Subway, Wendy's CVS Drug, Stop&Shop Food, Town Fair Tire, URGENT CARE, USPO, Walgreens, W Citgo, Gulf/dsl, Mobil Arby's, Athena II Diner, Dunkin Donuts, Outback Steaks Best Western/Harry's Grill Advance Parts, BigY Foods/drug, vet

11 (7) CT 22 (from nb), North Haven, same as 12

10 (6) CT 40, to Cheshire, Hamden

NEW HAVEN

9 (5) Montowese Ave, W Berkshire/dsl, Sunoco Buffalo Wild Wings, Dunkin Donuts, Dynasty Chinese, Friendly's, Longhorn Steaks, McDonald's, Olive Garden, Panera Bread, Red Lobster, Ruby Tuesday, Subway, Wendy's $Tree, AT&T, Barnes&Noble, Best Buy, BigLots, BJ's Whse/gas, GNC, Home Depot, Michael's, Nissan/Jeep, PetCo, Petsmart, Radio Shack, Target, TJMaxx, URGENT CARE, Verizon

8 (4) CT 17, CT 80, Middletown Ave, E 7-11, Citgo, Global/dsl, Mercury/dsl, Shell, Sunoco Burger King, Country House Rest., Dunkin Donuts, Exit 8 Diner, KFC, McDonald's, Taco Bell Days Inn Advance Parts, Aldi Foods, AutoZone, Lowe's, vet, Walgreens, Walmart/Subway

7 (3) Ferry St (from sb), Fair Haven, W Hess/dsl NAPA

6 (2.5) Willow St (exits left from nb), Blatchley Ave, E repair

5 (2) US 5 (from nb), State St, Fair Haven

4 (1.5) State St (from sb), downtown

3 (1) Trumbull St, downtown, W Peabody Museum

2 (.5) Hamilton St, downtown, New Haven

1 (.3) CT 34W (from sb), New Haven, W H downtown

0mm **I-91 begins/ends on I-95, exit 48.**

INTERSTATE 95

Exit # Services

94mm Connecticut/Rhode Island state line

93 (111) CT 216, Clarks Falls, E Shell/dsl/repair Dunkin Donuts, Subway, to Burlingame SP, W Mobil/Dunkin Donuts/dsl, Pilot/Shell/Stuckey's/Roy Rogers/Sbarro's/dsl/scales/24hr McDonald's Budget Inn, Stardust Motel

92 (107) CT 2, CT 49 (no EZ nb return), Pawcatuck, E Shell Dunkin Donuts La Quinta H Stop&Shop, W Cedar Park Suites FoxWoods (8mi), KOA

MYSTIC

91 (103) CT 234, N Main St, to Stonington, E H

90 (101) CT 27, Mystic, E Mobil/Domino's/Dunkin Donuts/dsl 5 Guys Burgers, Boathouse Rest., Equinox Diner, Friendly's, Go Fish, McDonald's, Starbucks, Steak Loft, Ten Clams EconoLodge, Hilton, Holiday Inn Express, Howard Johnson, Hyatt Place aquarium, Curves, Mystic Outlet Shops, Verizon, W Shell/Subway/dsl Dunkin Donuts, Jakes Burgers, Pizza Grille, Thai 1 Comfort Inn, Days Inn, Hampton Inn, Ramada Inn, Residence Inn Chevrolet, Chrysler/Dodge/Jeep, Ford, RV camping, TrueValue, VW

89mm scenic overlook

89 (99) CT 215, Allyn St, W camping (seasonal)

GROTON

88 (98) CT 117, to Noank, E airport, W Octagon Steaks, Starbucks Marriott

87 (97) Sharp Hwy (exits left from sb), Groton, E Hampton Inn airport, to Griswold SP

86 (96) Rd 184 (exits left from nb), Groton, E 99 Rest., Applebees Hampton Inn, Knights Inn Walgreens, W Cory's/dsl, Hess, Mobil, Shell/dsl Chinese Kitchen, Dunkin Donuts, Flanagan's Diner, Groton Rest., KFC, NY Pizza, Russell's Ribs, Subway, Taco Bell Best Western, Groton Inn, Super 8 $Tree, Advance Parts, GNC, Honda, Kia, Kohl's, Midas, Stop&Shop, to US Sub Base, Verizon

85 (95) US 1 N, Groton, downtown, E NAPA

84 (94) CT 32 (from sb), New London, downtown

83 (92) CT 32, New London, E to Long Island Ferry

82a (90.5) frontage rd, New London, E Mobil Panda Buffet, Pizza Hut AutoZone, NSA Foods, Radio Shack, same as 82, Staples, TownFair Tire, Verizon, W Chili's, ChuckeCheese, Outback Steaks Clarion, SpringHill Suites Marshall's, Petsmart, same as 82, ShopRite Foods

82 (90) CT 85, to I-395 N, New London, W Mobil/Dunkin Donuts Coldstone, FoodCourt, Longhorn Steaks, Olive Garden, Panera Bread, Ruby Tuesday, Subway, Wendy's Best Buy, Dick's, Home Depot, JC Penney, Macy's, mall, Michael's, PetCo, Sears/auto, Target, Verizon

90mm **weigh sta both directions**

81 (89.5) Cross Road, W Rodeway Inn BJ's Whse/gas, Lowe's, Walmart/McDonald's

80 (89.3) Oil Mill Rd (from sb), W Rodeway Inn

76 (89) I-395 N (from nb, exits left), to Norwich

75 (88) US 1, to Waterford

NIANTIC

74 (87) Rd 161, to Flanders, Niantic, E Citgo/dsl, Cory's/repair, Mobil Burger King, Country Gourmet, Dunkin Donuts, Illiano's Grill, Quiznos, Shoreline Rest., Starbucks Best Value Inn, Hilltop Inn, Motel 6, Sleep Inn Ford, Stop&Shop, Tires+, W Shell 5 Guys Burgers, Flanders Pizza, Flanders Seafood, Kings Garden Chinese, McDonald's, Nanami Japanese, Shack Rest., Smokey O'Grady's BBQ, Yummy Yummy Pizza Curves, CVS Drug, IGA Foods, Rite Aid, RV camping, TrueValue, vet

73 (86) Society Rd

72 (84) to Rocky Neck SP, **2 mi E** food, lodging, RV camping, to Rocky Neck SP

71 (83) 4 Mile Rd, River Rd, to Rocky Neck SP, **1 mi E** camping (seasonal), beaches

70 (80) US 1, CT 156, Old Lyme, W Shell/dsl Morning Glory Cafe, Subway Old Lyme Inn/dining Big Y Foods, Griswold Museum, Rite Aid, USPO, vet

69 (77) US 1, CT 9 N, to Hartford, W Bangkok Sushi Comfort Inn antiques, vet

68 (76.5) US 1 S, Old Saybrook, E Irving/dsl, Mobil Cloud 9 Deli, Pat's Country Kitchen, W Buick/GMC, Chevrolet/Nissan, Chrysler/Dodge/Jeep, Kia, Mazda, NAPA, VW

67 (76) CT 154, Elm St (no EZ sb return), Old Saybrook, E Pasta Vita Itaian, same as 68

66 (75) to US 1, Spencer Plain Rd, E Citgo/dsl Blue Crab Steaks, Brick Oven Pizza, Cuckoo's Nest Mexican, DQ, Dunkin Donuts, Fogo Grill, Luigi's Italian, Mike's Deli, Pizza Palace, Sal's Pizza, Samurai Japanese, Siagon City, Tiberio's Italian Days Inn, EconoLodge, Saybrook Motel, Super 8 Benny's Mkt, transmissions, vet

INTERSTATE 95 Cont'd

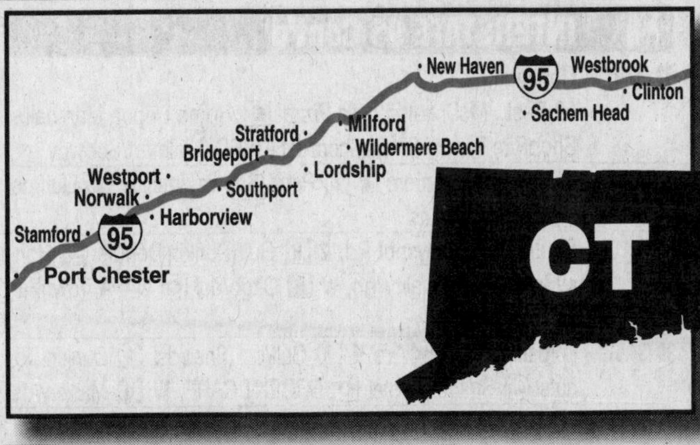

MADISON

Exit #	Services
74mm	[rest stop] sb, full [handicapped] facilities, st police
65 (73)	Rd 153, Westbrook, E [gas] Mobil/Dunkin Donuts, Valero [food] Cafe Rotier, Cristy's Rest., Denny's, Subway, Westbook Deli [other] Honda, Old Navy, Tanger Factory Stores/famous brands, Toyota/Scion, USPO, Walgreens
64 (70)	Rd 145, Horse Hill Rd, Clinton
63 (68)	CT 81, Clinton, E [gas] Shell, Shell/dsl/LP, Sunoco/dsl [food] Chips Rest., McDonald's, Piccadeli Sta. [other] CVS Drug, USPO, vet, W [food] Coldstone, Dunkin Donuts [other] AT&T, Clinton Crossing Premium Outlets/famous brands, PetCo
62 (67)	E [other] RV camping, to Hammonasset SP, beaches
66mm	**service area both lanes,** [gas] Mobil/dsl [food] McDonald's [other] atm
61 (64)	CT 79, Madison, E [gas] Gulf, Shell, Sunoco [food] Cafe Allegre, Starbucks, Subway, Village Pizza [other] CVS Drug, Stop&Shop, USPO
60 (63.5)	Mungertown Rd (from sb, no return), E [food] [lodging]
61mm	East River
59 (60)	Rd 146, Goose Lane, Guilford, E [gas] Citgo, Mobil/24hr, Shell/DQ/dsl [food] Avest Pizza, Dunkin Donuts, First Garden Chinese, McDonald's, Nick&Tony's Pizza, Shoreline Diner, Splash American Grill, The Whole Enchilada, Wendy's [lodging] Comfort Inn, Tower Motel [other] NAPA, transmissions, W [other] st police, URGENT CARE
58 (59)	CT 77, Guilford, E on US 1 [food] BP, Hess, Mobil, Sunoco/dsl [other] CVS Drug, to Henry Whitfield Museum, Walgreens, W [other] st police
57 (58)	US 1, Guilford, E [other] Extra/Dunkin Donuts/dsl, W [other] Land Rover
56 (55)	Rd 146, to Stony Creek, E [lodging] Rodeway Inn, W [gas] Mobil, Shell/dsl, TA/Popeye's/Starbucks/Subway/dsl/scales/24hr/ @ [food] Dunkin Donuts, Friendly's, USS Chowderpot [lodging] Baymont Inn, Best Value Inn [other] Freightliner, Stop&Shop Foods, Verizon
55 (54)	US 1, E [gas] Branford/repair, Cumberland, Global [food] Hornet's Nest Deli, Lynn's Rest, Marco Pizzaria, Rita's Custard, Sapori d'Italia, TNT Seafood Grill [lodging] Holiday Inn Express, Motel 6 [other] Ford, vet, Walgreens, W [gas] Gulf, Mobil/Dunkin Donuts/dsl [food] Brother's Deli, Chuck's Margarita Grill, Gourmet Wok, Parthenon Diner, Su Casa Mexican [lodging] Days Inn
54 (53)	Cedar St, Branford, E [gas] Citgo/repair, Mobil [food] Dragon East Chinese, Dunkin Donuts, La Luna Ristorante [other] AAA, Hyundai, Staples, Subaru, W [other] Krauszer's Foods
52mm	**service area both lanes,** [gas] Mobil/dsl/24hr [food] McDonald's, pizza [other] atm\52 (50) Rd 100, North High St, E [other] to Trolley Museum, W [other] st police
51 (49.5)	US 1, Easthaven, E [gas] Hess/dsl, Sunoco, Valero/dsl [food] Boston Mkt, Chili's [lodging] Quality Inn [other] Chevrolet, Lexus, TJ Maxx, Verizon, W [food] Dunkin Donuts, Wendy's [other] AutoZone, CarMax, Home Depot, USPO
50 (49)	Woodward Ave (from nb), E [other] Ft Nathan Hale, US Naval/Marine Reserve
49 (48.5)	Stiles St (from nb)
48 (48)	I-91 N, to Hartford
47 (47.5)	CT 34, New Haven, W [gas] Mobil/Dunkin Donuts/dsl [food] Brazi's Italian, Greek Olive Diner [lodging] La Quinta [other] Ikea, Long Wharf Theater, same as 46
46 (47)	Long Wharf Dr, Sargent Dr, E [food] Lenny & Joe's Rest., W [gas] Mobil/Dunkin Donuts/dsl [food] Brazi's Italian, Greek Olive Diner [lodging] La Quinta [other] Ikea, Long Warf Theater
45 (46.5)	CT 10 (from sb), Blvd, W [food] Dunkin Donuts, McDonald's [other] same as 44
44 (46)	CT 10 (from nb), Kimberly Ave, E [lodging] Super 8, W [food] DQ, Dunkin Donuts, McDonald's, Popeyes [other] same as 45
43 (45)	CT 122, 1st Ave (no EZ return), West Haven, W [gas] 1st Fuel/dsl, Xtra [other] [H] NAPA, to U of New Haven, vet
42 (44)	CT 162, Saw Mill Rd, E [food] Pizza Hut [lodging] EconoLodge, W [gas] Shell [food] American Steaks, Denny's, Dunkin Donuts, Starbucks, Subway, TX Roadhouse, Uncle Willie's BBQ [lodging] Best Western, Hampton Inn [other] Aldi Foods, Firestone/auto, Walmart/Subway
41 (42)	Marsh Hill Rd, to Orange
41mm	**service area both lanes,** [gas] Mobil/dsl [food] Dunkin Donuts, McDonald's, Subway
40 (40)	Old Gate Lane, Woodmont Rd, E [gas] Citgo/dsl, Pilot/Wendy's/dsl/scales/24hr, Shell, Sunoco [food] Cracker Barrel, Duchess Rest., Dunkin Donuts, Gipper's Rest., Popeyes, Titlted Kilt [lodging] Hilton Garden, Holiday Inn Express, Mayflower Motel, Milford Inn [other] Blue Beacon, Lowe's, Midas
39 (39)	US 1, to Milford, E [gas] Cumberland Farms/dsl [food] Athenian Diner, Chicago Grill, Dunkin Donuts, Friendly's, Hooters, Mama Teresa's [lodging] Howard Johnson, Super 8 [other] $Tree, CVS Drug, Firestone/auto, Mazda/Volvo, ShopRite Foods, URGENT CARE, vet, Walgreens, W on US 1 [gas] Mobil [food] Boston Mkt, Boston Mkt, Buffalo Wild Wings, Burger King, Chili's, Chipotle Mexican, DiBella Subs, Domino's, Dunkin Donuts, Hometown Buffet, HoneyBaked Ham, McDonald's, Panera Bread, Sonic, Starbucks, Subway, Taco Bell, Villano's Rest. [other] Acura, Advance Parts, AT&T, Barnes&Noble, BigLots, Chrysler/Dodge/Jeep, Costco/gas, Dick's, JC Penney, Jo-Ann Fabrics, Macy's, mall, Marshall's, Michael's, Old Navy, PetCo, Rite Aid, Sears/auto, Shop&Shop/gas, Staples, Target, TownFair Tire, Walmart/Subway, Whole Foods Mkt
38 (38)	CT 15, Merritt Pkwy, Cross Pkwy
37 (37.5)	High St (no ez nb return), E [gas] Gulf, Sunoco, USA [food] Subway [other] 7-11, Toyota/Scion, vet
36	Plains Rd, E [food] Dunkin Donuts, Gusto Italian [lodging] Hampton Inn [other] Aldi Foods
35 (37)	Bic Dr, School House Rd, E [gas] Citgo [food] Wendy's [lodging] Fairfield Inn [other] AutoZone, Buick/GMC, Chevrolet, CVS Drug, Dennis' Parts, Ford/Lincoln, Honda, Kia, Land Rover, Nissan, Stop&Shop Foods/gas, Subaru, Walgreens, W [lodging] Red Roof Inn, Residence Inn, SpringHill Suites
34 (34)	US 1, Milford, E on US 1 [food] Dunkin Donuts, McDonald's, Pizza Hut, Subway, Taco Bell [lodging] Devon Motel [other] $Tree, Hyundai, K-Mart, Radio Shack, Walgreens
33 (33.5)	US 1 (from nb, no EZ return), CT 110, Ferry Blvd, E [gas] Shell/dsl, Sunoco/dsl [food] Danny's Drive-In, Lumi Rest., Riverview Bistro, Subway [other] $Tree, BJ's Whse, PetCo, Staples, W [food]

BRANFORD

NEW HAVEN

MILFORD

CT

CT

INTERSTATE 95 Cont'd

33 (33.5)	Continued 99 Rest., McDonalds, Villa Pizza [other] Home Depot, Marshall's, ShopRite Foods, Stop&Shop/dsl, USPO, Walmart/Subway
32 (33)	W Broad St, Stratford, E [gas] Petra/Subway/dsl, W [gas] Gulf/dsl [food] Dunkin Donuts
31 (32)	South Ave, Honeyspot Rd, E [gas] Gulf/Dunkin Donuts [lodging] HoneySpot Motel, Quality Inn, W [gas] Citgo/dsl [other] NAPA, TownFair Tire
30 (31.5)	Lordship Blvd, Surf Ave, E [gas] Gulf/dsl, Shell/dsl [food] Dunkin Donuts [lodging] Stratford Hotel [other] URGENT CARE, W [gas] Massey/dsl
29 (31)	Rd 130, Stratford Ave, Seaview Ave, W [other] [H]
28 (30)	CT 113, E Main St, Pembrook St
27 (29.5)	Lafayette Blvd, downtown, W [food] Dunkin Donuts [other] [H] Barnum Museum
27a (29)	CT 25, CT 8, to Waterbury
26 (28)	Wordin Ave
25 (27)	CT 130 (from sb, no EZ return), State St, Commerce Dr, Fairfield Ave, E [other] Audi, Infiniti, Mercedes, Porsche, USPO, W [food] McDonald's
24 (26.5)	Black Rock Tpk, E [food] Blackrock Oyster Bar, Fairfield Pizza, Rio Bravo, Sweet Basil [lodging] Best Western [other] BJ's Whse/Subway, Lexus, Porsche, Staples, USPO, Verizon, W [gas] Gulf [other] Firestone/auto, Nissan
23 (26)	US 1, Kings Hwy, E [gas] Sunoco/dsl [food] Chipotle, Five Guys [other] CVS Drug, Home Depot, Petco, Whole Foods Mkt
22 (24)	Round Hill Rd, N Benson Rd
23.5mm	**service area both lanes,** [gas] Mobil/dsl [food] FoodCourt (sb), McDonald's
21 (23)	Mill Plain Rd, E [gas] Citgo/dsl, Mobil/dsl [food] Avellino's Italian, DQ, Geronimo SW Grill, Kiraku Japanese, Rawley's Drive-In, Starbucks, Subway, Wilson's BBQ [other] Hemlock Hardware, Rite Aid
20 (22)	Bronson Rd (from sb)
19 (21)	US 1, Center St, W [gas] BP, Shell/dsl [food] Athena Diner, Baskin-Robbins/Dunkin Donuts, Panera Bread, Subway [lodging] Westport Inn [other] Balducci's Mkt, Honda, Stop&Shop, TownFair Tire, Walgreens
18 (20)	to Westport, E [other] beaches, Sherwood Island SP, st police, **1 mi W on US 1** [gas] Gulf, Mobil [food] Angelina's Trattoria, Arby's, Bertucci's Italian, Fresh Mkt, McDonald's, Sakura Japanese, Sherwood Diner, Starbucks, Subway [other] Barnes&Noble, Radio Shack, Toyota/Scion, URGENT CARE, Walgreens
17 (18)	CT 33, Rd 136, Westport
16 (17)	E Norwalk, E [gas] Citgo, Gulf, Mobil/dsl, Shell/dsl [food] Baskin-Robbins/Dunkin Donuts, Eastside Café, Penny's Diner, Subway [other] Rite Aid
15 (16)	US 7, to Danbury, Norwalk, E [gas] Shell [other] Walgreens, W [gas] Exxon, Sunoco
14 (15)	US 1, CT Ave, S Norwalk, E [other] st police, W [gas] Shell/Dunkin Donuts [food] Burger King, Dunkin Donuts, Post Road Diner, Silver Star Diner, Subway, Wendy's [other] [H], Barnes&Noble, Best Buy, CVS Drug, Kohl's, Old Navy, Petsmart, Radio Shack, same as 13, ShopRite Foods, Stop&Shop, TJ Maxx, TownFair Tire
13 (13)	US 1 (no EZ return), Post Rd, Norwalk, W [gas] Mobil, Shell, Sunoco [food] American Steaks, Bertucci's, Chipotle Mexican, Darien Diner, Friendly's, KFC, McDonald's, Palmwich [lodging] DoubleTree Hotel [other] AT&T, Costco, Home Depot, Mini, same as 14, Staples, vet, Walmart

NORWALK

12.5mm	**service area nb,** [gas] Mobil/dsl [food] Dunkin Donuts [food] McDonald's, Subway
12 (12)	Rd 136, Tokeneke Rd (from nb, no return), W [food] deli
11 (11)	US 1, Darien, E [gas] Exxon [lodging] Chuck's Steaks [other] Chevrolet, Nissan, repair, vet, W [gas] Gulf [food] Panera Bread [other] BMW, Whole Foods Mkt
10 (10)	Noroton, W [gas] Shell, Standard [other] vet
9.5mm	**service area sb,** [gas] Mobil/dsl [food] McDonald's, Subway
9 (9)	US 1, Rd 106, Glenbrook, E [lodging] Best Value Inn, W [gas] Gulf [food] Dunkin Donuts, McDonald's, Subway [other] Advance Parts, Meineke
8 (8)	Atlantic Ave, Elm St, E [other] U-Haul, W [gas] Sunoco [lodging] Marriott [other] [H]
7 (7)	CT 137, Atlantic Ave, W [food] PF Chang's [lodging] Hampton Inn, Marriott [other] Barnes&Noble, same as 8, USPO
6 (6)	Harvard Ave, West Ave, E [gas] Gulf [food] City Limits Diner, Starbucks [lodging] La Quinta [other] Advance Parts, Petsmart, Subaru, USPO, W [gas] Shell [lodging] Super 8 [other] [H]
5 (5)	US 1, Riverside, Old Greenwich, W [gas] BP, Mobil, Shell [food] Boston Mkt, Corner Deli, Hunan Cafe, McDonald's, Starbucks, Taco Bell, Valbello Ristorante [lodging] Hyatt Regency [other] A&P Mkt, CVS Drug, GNC, Staples, USPO, Walgreens
4 (4)	Indian Field Rd, Cos Cob, W [other] Bush-Holley House Museum
3 (3)	Arch St, Greenwich, E [other] Bruce Museum, W [gas] Shell [other] [H] Lexus
2mm	**weigh sta nb**
2 (1)	Delavan Ave, Byram
0mm	Connecticut/New York state line

GREENWICH

INTERSTATE 395

Exit #	Services
55.5mm	Connecticut/Massachusetts state line
100 (54)	E Thompson, to Wilsonville
99 (50)	Rd 200, N Grosvenor Dale, E [other] W Thompson Lake Camping (seasonal)
98 (49)	to CT 12 (from nb, exits left), Grosvenor Dale, same as 99
97 (47)	US 44, to E Putnam, E [food] Dunkin Donuts, Empire Buffet, McDonald's/playplace, Subway, Wendy's [other] $Tree, Advance Parts, BigLots, CVS Drug, Giant Pizza, GNC, Radio Shack, Sears Essentials, Stop&Shop/gas, W [gas] Shell/dsl/repair, Sunoco [other] Walmart/Subway
96 (46)	to CT 12, Putnam, W [food] Casa Mariachi [lodging] King's Inn [other] [H]
95 (45)	Kennedy Dr, to Putnam, E [other] Ford, W [other] [H]
94 (43)	Ballouville, W [food] Gold Eagle Rest. [lodging] Comfort Inn [other] truck parts
93 (41)	CT 101, to Dayville, E [gas] Shell/dsl [food] Burger King, China Garden, Domino's, Dunkin Donuts, Nuccio's Pizza, Subway, Yamoto Japanese, Zip's Diner [other] $Tree, Aldi Foods, Walgreens, Wibberley Tire/repair, W [gas] Mobil/dsl, Xtra/dsl [food] 99 Rest., Dunkin Donuts, McDonald's, Mozzarella's Grill [other] AT&T, city park, GNC, Lowe's, Michael's, PetCo, Staples, Stop&Shop, Target, TJ Maxx, Verizon
92 (39)	to S Killingly, W [food] Dunkin Donuts, Giant Pizza [other] Bonneville Drug, st police
91 (38)	US 6 W, to Danielson, to Quinebaug Valley Coll
90 (36)	to US 6 E (from nb), to Providence
35mm	[rest stop] **both lanes, full** [handicapped] **facilities,** [gas] Mobil/dsl
89 (32)	CT 14, to Sterling, Central Village, E [gas] Best Way, Gulf/repair [food] Johnny's Rest., Pizza Pizzaz [other] Rite Aid, RV camping, USPO, W [gas] 7-11/dsl, Shell/Dunkin Donuts/dsl [food] Music Lady Cafe, Subway [lodging] Knights Inn [other] transmissions

PUTNAM

INTERSTATE 395 Cont'd

PLAINFIELD / NORWICHTOWN

Exit #	Services
88 (30)	CT 14A to Plainfield, E RV camping (seasonal), W Mobil
87 (28)	Lathrop Rd, to Plainfield, E Shell/Domino's/dsl Dunkin Donuts, HongKong Star Chinese, Subway, Wendy's Holiday Inn Express, Quality Inn Big Y Foods, Ford, Hyundai, Mazda, Mercedes, Radio Shack, W Gulf, Sunoco/dsl Bakers Dozen Cafe, Eli's Steaks, McDonald's Advance Parts, Curves, CVS Drug
86 (24)	Rd 201, Hopeville, E Hopeville Pond SP, RV camping
85 (23)	CT 164, CT 138, to Pachaug, Preston, E Petro Max/Dunkin Donuts/dsl $Tree, Curves, RV camping, W AmericInn
84 (21)	CT 12, Jewett City, E Chili's, Panera Bread, Ruby Tuesday Aldi Foods, AT&T, Dick's, GNC, Home Depot, Kohl's, Lowe's, PetCo, Target, Verizon, Walmart/Dunkin Donuts, W Gulf/dsl, Mobil/dsl, Shell/dsl McDonald's Val-U Foods
83a (20)	CT 169 (from nb), Lisbon, E RV camping
83 (18)	Rd 97, Taftville, E BP/dsl, W 7-11
82 (14)	to CT 2 W, CT 32 N, Norwichtown, E Friendly's tires, W BP/Dunkin Donuts/dsl, Mobil/dsl, Shell/dsl Buddy's Dugout, Illiano's Grill, Prime Rest., Subway Courtyard, Rosemont Suites Ace Hardware
81 (14)	CT 2 E, CT 32 S, Norwich, E H to Mohegan Coll
80 (12)	CT 82, Norwich, E Mobil, Shell, Xtra/dsl 99 Rest., Burger King, Chinese Buffet, Dunkin Donuts, Friendly's, KFC/Taco Bell, McDonald's, Mr Pizza, Papa Gino's, Subway, Wendy's Jo-Ann Fabrics, Rite Aid, ShopRite Foods, Staples, TJ Maxx, TownFair Tire, Verizon, W Holiday Inn Big Y Foods, RV Camping, Walmart
79a (10)	CT 2A E, to Ledyard, E to Pequot Res
8.5mm	nb, full facilities, Mobil/dsl st police
79 (6)	Rd 163, to Uncasville, Montville, 1 mi E Mobil/dsl Dunkin Donuts, Friendly Pizza, McDonald's, Subway repair, Rite Aid, Tri-Town Foods
78 (5)	CT 32 (from sb, exits left), to New London, RI Beaches
77 (2)	CT 85, to I-95 N, Colchester, 1/2 mi E Dunkin Donuts, Shell/dsl Oakdell Motel
I-95. I-395 begins/ends on I-95, exit 76.	

INTERSTATE 691

MERIDEN

Exit #	Services
I-691 begins/ends on I-91	
12 (12)	Preston Ave
11 (11)	I-91 N, to Hartford
10 (11)	I-91 S, to New Haven, CT 15 S, W Cross Pkwy
9	Berlin Tpk
8 (10)	US 5, Broad St, N HH Gas, Irving, Shell/dsl Broad St Pizza, DQ
7 (9)	downtown (no ez wb return), Meriden (from wb), S Citgo
6 (8)	Lewis Ave (from wb, no EZ return), to CT 71, N Ruby Tuesday H Best Buy, Dick's, Macy's, mall, Old Navy, Sears/auto, Target, TJ Maxx, S 7-11 Subway
5 (7)	CT 71, to Chamberlain Hill (from eb, no EZ return), N H Best Buy, mall, Target, S 7-11/gas Subway
4 (4)	CT 322, W Main St (no re-entry from eb), N Sunoco Dunkin Donuts, Hubbard Park Pizza H
3mm	Quinnipiac River
3 (1)	CT 10, to Cheshire, Southington, N Sam's Clams Rest., Tony's Rest.
2 (0)	I-84 E, to Hartford
1 (0)	I-84 W, to Waterbury
I-691 begins/ends on I-84	

CT DE

DELAWARE

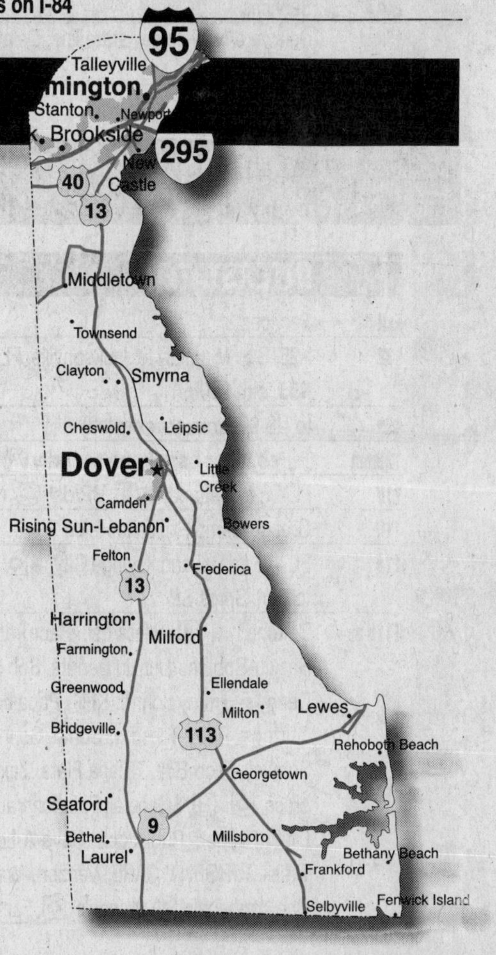

INTERSTATE 95

Exit #	Services
23mm	Delaware/Pennsylvania state line, motorist callboxes for 23 miles sb
11 (22)	to I-495 S, DE 92, Naamans Rd, E China Star $General, Burlington Coats, Jo-Ann Fabrics, K-Mart, WaWa, W Gulf/dsl KFC/Taco Bell, Quiznos Holiday Inn Select Home Depot, Radio Shack, Rite Aid
10 (21)	Harvey Rd (no nb return)
9 (19)	DE 3, to Marsh Rd, E Dunkin Donuts, Lamberti's Italian, Starbucks Rockwood Museum, st police, to Bellevue SP
8b a (17)	US 202, Concord Pike, to Wilmington, E Home Depot, to Brandywine Park
7b a (16)	DE 52, Delaware Ave
6 (15)	DE 4, MLK Blvd, E Joe's Crabshack, McDonald's AAA, Fresh Grocer Foods, Rite Aid, W Gulf Family$
5c (12)	I-495 N, to Wilmington, to DE Mem Bridge
5b a (11)	DE 141, to US 202, to New Castle, Newport, E Quality Inn (3mi)
4b a (8)	DE 1, DE 7, to Christiana, E Brio Tuscan Grille, CA Pizza Kitchen, Cheesecake Factory, Don Pablo, FoodCourt, JB Dawson's Rest., Panera Bread, Ruby Tuesday Barnes&Noble, Costco, Dick's, JC Penney, Macy's, mall, Michael's, Nordstrom, PetCo, Target, W Applebee's, Bugaboo Creek Steaks,

NEWARK

DE FL

INTERSTATE 95 Cont'd

4b a (8) Continued
Cheeseburger Paradise, Chili's, Dunkin Donuts, Firebird's Grill, Marble Slab Creamery, Michael's Rest., Old Country Buffet, Olive Garden, Quiznos, Red Lobster [lodging] Country Inn&Suites, Courtyard, Days Inn, Fairfield Inn, Hilton, Homestead Suites, Red Roof Inn [other] [H] AAA, Best Buy, casino/racetrack, Home Depot, Office Depot, Petsmart, TJ Maxx, Verizon

3b a (6) DE 273, to Newark, Dover, **E** [gas] BP, Exxon/dsl [food] Bertucci's, Bob Evans, Boston Mkt, Ciao Pizza, Famous Dave's BBQ, Olive Grill Italian, Red Robin, Shell Hammer's Grille, Wendy's [lodging] Ramada Inn, Residence Inn, Staybridge Suites, TownePlace Suites [other] Acme Foods, Boscov's, Jo-Ann Fabrics, Old Navy, Staples, Walgreens, **W** [gas] Getty, Shell/dsl [food] Denny's, Dunkin Donuts, Pizza Hut [lodging] Comfort Inn, EconoLodge, Holiday Inn Express [other] 7-11

5mm [RS] **both lanes (exits left from both lanes),** [gas] Sunoco/dsl [food] Baja Fresh, Burger King, Famiglia, Popeye's, Starbucks [other] info, Z-Mkt

1b a (3) DE 896, to Newark, to U of DE, Middletown, **W** [gas] Exxon, Gulf/dsl, Shell/dsl, Sunoco [food] 896 Diner, Boston Mkt, China Garden, Dunkin Donuts, Friendly's, Mario's Pizza, Matilda's Rest, McDonald's, TGIFriday's [lodging] Best Value Inn, Courtyard (3mi), Embassy Suites, Homewood Suites, Howard Johnson, Sleep Inn [other] DE Tire Ctr

1mm toll booth, st police

0mm Delaware/Maryland state line, motorist callboxes for 23 miles nb

INTERSTATE 295 (WILMINGTON)

Exit #	Services
15mm	Delaware/New Jersey state line, Delaware River, Delaware Memorial Bridge
14.5mm	**toll plaza**
14	DE 9, New Castle Ave, to Wilmington, **E** [gas] BP, Citgo [food] Giovanni's Cafe [other] Advance Parts, Family$, Firestone/auto, Harley-Davidson/rest., Rite Aid, SuperFresh Foods, **W** [gas] Shell, Super/dsl [food] Dunkin Donuts, McDonald's [lodging] Budget Inn, Motel 6, SuperLodge
13	US 13, US 40, to New Castle, **E** [gas] BP, Hess, Shell/dsl, Sunoco/dsl, WaWa [food] Applebee's, Arby's, Arner's Rest, Burger King, DogHouse, Dove Diner, Dunkin Donuts, Hadfield's Seafood, Hooters, IHOP, KFC, Lonestar Steaks, McDonald's, Pizza Hut, Popeye's, Season's Pizza, Subway, Taco Bell, TGIFriday's, Wendy's [lodging] EconoLodge, Quality Inn, Super 8 [other] $Tree, 7-11, Acura, AutoZone, BJ's Whse/gas, Chevrolet, Chrysler, Jeep/Dodge, Cottman Transmissions, Fiat, Ford, Home Depot, Hyundai, Lincoln, Mazda, Nissan, PathMark Foods, PepBoys, Radio Shack, repair, Ross, Save-a-Lot, Staples, Toyota/Scion, Walgreens, Walmart, **W** [gas] WaWa/dsl [food] Dunkin Donuts [lodging] Clarion [other] Ford Trucks, Freightliner, Lowe's
12	I-495, US 202, N to Wilmington

I-295 begins/ends on I-95.

INTERSTATE 495

Exit #	Services
11mm	I-95 N. **I-495 begins/ends on I-95**
5 (10)	US 13, Phila Pike, Claymont, **W** [gas] BP, Exxon/dsl, Sunoco/dsl [food] Arby's, Boston Mkt, Dunkin Donuts, McDonald's [lodging] Milan Motel [other] Family$, Food Lion, USPO
4 (5)	US 13, Rd 3, Edgemoor Rd, to Fox Point Park
3 (4)	12th St
2 (3)	Rd 9A, Terminal Ave, Port of Wilmington
1 (1)	US 13, **E** [gas] WaWa/dsl [food] Dunkin Donuts [lodging] Clarion [other] Ford Trucks, Lowe's
0mm	I-95 S. **I-495 begins/ends on I-95**

FLORIDA

INTERSTATE 4

Exit #	Services
132	I-95, S to Miami, N to Jacksonville, FL 400. **I-4 begins/ends on I-95, exit 260b.**
129	to US 92 (from eb, exits left)
126mm	[RS] **eb, litter barrels, no security**
118	FL 44, to DeLand, **N** [gas] BP/dsl [lodging] Howard Johnson [other] [H]
116	Orange Camp Rd, Lake Helen
114	FL 472, to DeLand, Orange City, **N** [other] Clark Campground (1mi), to Blue Sprgs SP
111b a	Deltona, **N** [gas] Hess/dsl, RaceTrac/dsl, Shell/Circle K [food] Baskin-Robbins/Dunkin Donuts, Bob Evans, Chick-fil-A, Chili's, Denny's, Jimmy John's, KFC, Papa John's, Perkins, Pizza Hut, Quiznos, Ruby Tuesday, Sonic, Sonny's BBQ, Steak'n Shake, Subway, Taco Bell, Tijuana Flats, Zaxby's [lodging] Holiday Inn Express [other] [H], $General, Firestone/auto, Home Depot, Lowe's, Office Depot, Publix/deli, Save-A-Lot Foods, Tire Kingdom, Tires+, URGENT CARE, Verizon, Walgreens, Walmart, **S** [gas] Chevron/repair [food] Wendy's [other] Family$, Publix, Walgreens
108	Dirksen Dr, DeBary, Deltona, **N** [gas] Chevron [food] Burger King, IHOP [lodging] Hampton Inn, **S** [gas] Kangaroo [food] McDonald's, Subway, Waffle House [lodging] Best Western [other] Publix (2mi)
104	US 17, US 92, Sanford, **N** [food] Captains Cove Rest. [other] La Mesa RV Ctr, **S** [gas] Citgo/Subway
101c	Rd 46, to Mt Dora, Sanford, **N** [gas] 7-11 [food] Tijuana Flats [other] Ace Hardware, Ford, **S** [gas] 7-11, Chevron/dsl, Mobil, Murphy USA/dsl, RaceTrac [food] Baskin-Robbins/Dunkin Donuts, Big Boy, Burger King, Cracker Barrel, Denny's, Don Pablo, Firehouse Subs, Hooters, Joe's Crabshack, LJ Silver/Taco Bell, Logan's Roadhouse, McDonald's, Olive Garden, Outback Steaks, Panda Express, Panera Bread, Red Brick Pizza, Red Lobster, Rte 46 Smokehouse, Smokey Bones BBQ, Steak'n Shake, Subway, Wendy's [lodging] Comfort Inn, Days Inn, SpringHill Suites, Super 8 [other] [H], $Tree, Aldi Foods, Beall's, Belk, Best Buy, Big 10 Tire, BJ's Whse/gas, Books-A-Million, CVS Drug, Dillard's, GNC, Goodyear/auto, Harley-Davidson, JC Penney, Jo-Ann Fabrics, Macy's, mall, Marshall's, Michael's, Old Navy, PetCo, Ross, Sears/auto, Target, Tire Kingdom, Tuffy Auto, URGENT CARE, Verizon, Walmart, World Mkt
101a b	Rd 46a, FL 417 (**toll**), FL 46, Sanford , Heathrow, **N** [food] Applebee's, Carlos'n Charley's, Crisper's, FishBones, Moe's SW

INTERSTATE 4 Cont'd

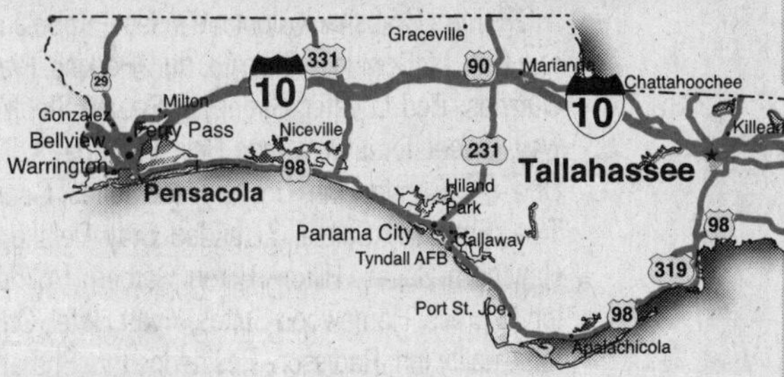

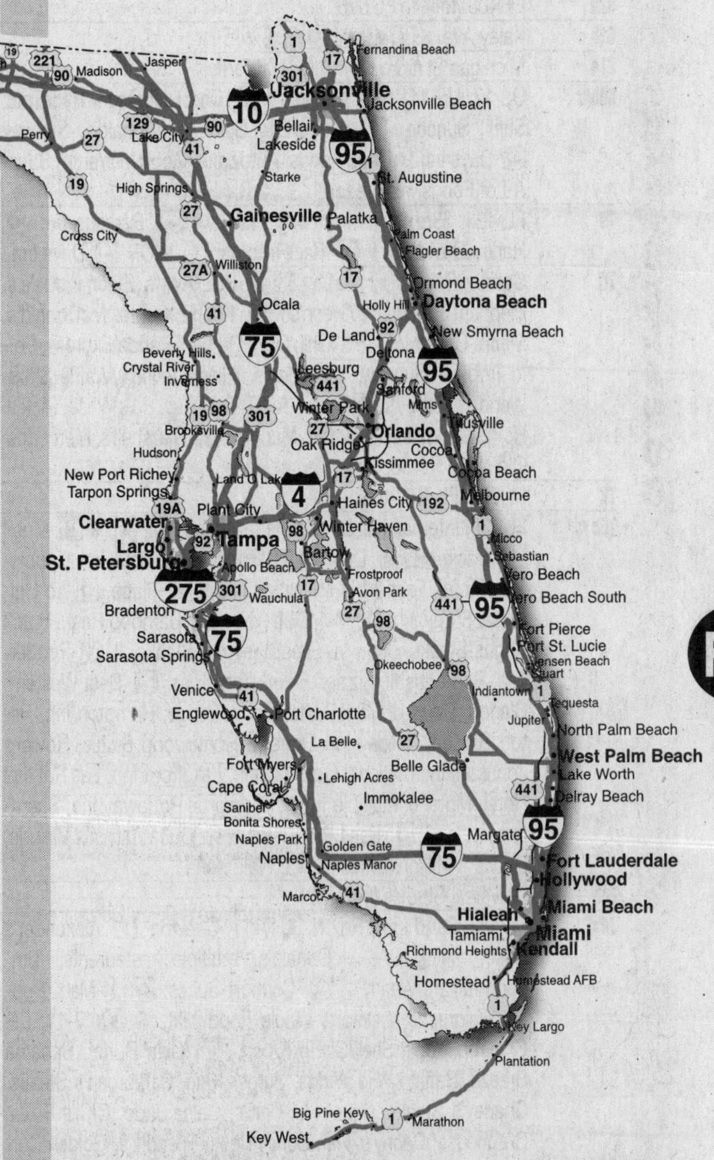

101a b Continued Grill, Papa Joe's Pizza, Rikka Asian Bistro, Ruth's Chris Steaks, Shula's 347 Grill, Subway, Vamonos [lodging] Hampton Inn, Marriott, Residence Inn, Westin [other] Publix, URGENT CARE, Walgreens, **S** [other] 7-11, Acura, CarMax, CVS Drug, Honda, Kohl's, Sam's Club/gas, Toyota/Scion

98 Lake Mary Blvd, Heathrow, **N** [gas] Shell [food] Luigino's Italian, Panera Bread, Peach Valley Cafe, Stonewood Grill, Subway [lodging] Courtyard, Hyatt Place [other] CVS Drug, Verizon, Walgreens, Winn-Dixie, **S** [gas] 7-11, BP/24hr, Chevron/24hr, Citgo, Mobil/dsl [food] Arby's, Baskin-Robbins/Dunkin Donuts, Bob Evans, Boston Mkt, Burger King, Checkers, Chick-fil-A, Chili's, Chipotle Mexican, Chop Stix, Domino's, Firehouse Subs, Frank&Naomi's, KFC, Krystal, Longhorn Steaks, Macaroni Grill, McDonald's, Panera Bread, Papa Joe's Pizza, Papa John's, Pizza Hut/Taco Bell, Quiznos, Starbucks, Steak'n Shake, Subway, Taste of China, Uno, Wendy's, WingZone [lodging] Candlewood Suites, Extended Stay America, Hilton Garden, Homestead Suites, Homewood Suites, La Quinta [other] Advance Parts, Albertsons, AT&T, Family$, Gander Mtn, Goodyear, Home Depot, K-Mart, mall, Office Depot, Petsmart, Publix, Radio Shack, Staples, Target, Tires+, TJ Maxx, USPO, vet, Walgreens

H
E
A
T
H
R
O
W

95mm [rest stop] **both lanes, 24 hr security, full [handicapped] facilities, litter barrels, petwalk [phone] [picnic] vending**

94 FL 434, to Winter Springs, Longwood, **N** [gas] 7-11, Hess/dsl, Mobil/dsl [food] Burger King, East Buffet, Imperial Dynasty, Kobe Japanese, Melting Pot Rest., Miami Subs, Panera Bread, Papa Joe's Pizza, Starbucks, Tijuana Flats, Wendy's [lodging] Comfort Inn [other] CVS Drug, Publix, **S** [food] Bonefish Grill, Boston Mkt, Carmela's Rest., Crisper's, Pickle's NY [lodging] Candlewood Suites [other] [H]

92 FL 436, Altamonte Springs, **N** [gas] 7-11, Shell/Circle K/dsl [food] Bojangles, Boston Mkt, Checkers, Chick-fil-A, Chipotle Mexican, ChuckeCheese, Cracker Barrel, Kobe Japanese, Little Caesars, Longhorn Steaks, McDonald's, Olive Garden, Perkins, Pollo Tropical, Popeye's, Red Lobster, Sweet Tomatoes, Taco Bell, TGIFriday's, Waffle House, WingHouse [lodging] Days Inn, Hampton Inn, Hotel Altamonte, Quality Suites, Remington Inn, Residence Inn, SpringHill Suites [other] Best Buy, CVS Drug, Family$, Firestone/auto, Goodyear/auto, Tire Kingdom, U-Haul, URGENT CARE, Walgreens, **S** [gas] BP, Citgo, Hess/dsl, Mobil/dsl [food] 5 Guys Burgers, Bahama Breeze, Burger King, Chili's, Denny's, Dunkin Donuts, Elephant Bar, Jason's Deli, Mimi's Cafe, Moe's SW Grill, Orlando Alehouse, Panda Express, Pizza Hut, Starbucks, Steak'n Shake, Subway, Wendy's [lodging] Embassy Suites, Hilton, Homestead Suites [other] [H] Advance Parts, Albertsons, Barnes&Noble, CVS Drug, Dillard's, JC Penney, Marshall's, Michael's, Office Depot, PetCo, Publix, Ross, Sears/auto, TJMaxx, vet

A
L
T
A
M
O
N
T
E

S
P
R
I
N
G
S

90b a FL 414, Maitland Blvd, **N** [gas] 7-11 [food] Applebee's, Chick-fil-A, Oak Grill, Wendy's [lodging] Extended Stay America, Extended Stay Deluxe, Homewood Suites, Sheraton, **S** [other] Maitland Art Ctr

88 FL 423, Lee Rd, **N** [gas] 7-11 [food] Arby's, Burger King, Del Frisco, IHOP, Little Caesars, LJ Silver/Taco Bell, McDonald's, Nick&Gina's Italian, Popeye's, Quiznos [lodging] Countryside Inn, InTown Suites, La Quinta, Motel 6 [other] Aamco, Family$, Firestone/auto, Home Depot, Land Rover, Mini, Ross, Save-A-Lot Foods, Tires+, VW, **S** [gas] Chevron/dsl, Sunoco [food] Denny's [other] BMW

87 FL 426, Fairbanks Ave (no eb re-entry), **N** [gas] Hess/Blimpie/Dunkin Donuts/Godfather's/dsl, **1mi S** [food] Burger King, Chick-fil-A, Chipotle Mexican, Pizza Hut/Taco Bell, Popeye's, Steak'n Shake, Subway, Wendy's [other] Walgreens

86 Par St (from eb, no re-entry), **S** [gas] Shell/Circle K

85 Princeton St, **S** [gas] 7-11, Chevron [other] [H]

84 FL 50, Colonial Dr, Ivanhoe Blvd, **N** [lodging] Crowne Plaza

83b US 17, US 92, FL 50, Amelia St (from eb), **N** [lodging] Crowne Plaza

83a FL 526 (from eb), Robinson St, **N** [lodging] Sheraton

83 South St (from wb), downtown

82c Anderson St E, Church St Sta Hist Dist, downtown

82b Gore Ave (from wb), **S** [other] [H], downtown

FL

FL

INTERSTATE 4 Cont'd

Exit #	Services
82a	FL 408 (**toll**), to FL 526
81b c	Kaley Ave, S 🅖 Mobil 🅞 🄷
81a	Michigan St (from wb), N 🅖 Citgo/dsl
80b a	US 17, US 441 S, US 92 W, S 🅖 Chevron, Citgo, RaceTrac, Shell, Sunoco 🍴 Checkers, Gyros, McDonald's, Subway 🛏 Days Inn 🅞 Aldi Foods, AutoZone, Goodyear/auto, Save-A-Lot Foods, Walgreens
79	FL 423, 33rd St, John Young Pkwy, N 🛏 Ramada Inn 🅞 Harley-Davidson, S 🅖 RaceTrac/dsl 🍴 IHOP 🛏 Days Inn
78	Conroy Rd, N 🅖 7-11, S 🍴 BJ's Rest., Bloomingdale's, Elephant Bar Rest., Green's Grill, Krispy Kreme, McDonald's, Mimi's Cafe, Moe's SW Grill, Olive Garden, Panda Express, Pollo Tropical, Subway, TGIFriday's, Village Tavern, Waffle Shop, Wendy's, Zaxby's 🅞 $Tree, AT&T, Best Buy, BJ's Whse, Dick's, Home Depot, Infiniti/Smart, Macy's, mall, Marshall's, Mercedes, Old Navy, PetCo, Super Target
77	FL 527, FL TPK (**toll**)
75b a	FL 435, International Dr (exits left from both lanes), N 🅖 Mobil 🍴 Cracker Barrel, Denny's, TGIFriday's 🛏 Days Inn, DoubleTree Motel, Fairfield Inn, Holiday Inn, Hyatt Place 🅞 to Universal Studios, S 🅖 7-11, Chevron 🍴 Bamboo Rest., Black Angus Steaks, Denny's, Great Western Steaks, IHOP, Ponderosa, Red Lobster, Sizzler, Sweet Tomatoes 🛏 Best Western, Clarion, Court of Flags Hotel, EconoLodge, Hampton Inn, Hilton Garden, Holiday Inn Express, Homewood Suites, Howard Johnson, International Gateway Inn, Lakefront Inn, Las Palmas Hotel, Motel 6, multiple hotels & resorts, Rodeway Inn, Sheraton, Super 8 🅞 Bass Pro Shops, Belz Outlet/famous Brands, Books A Million, Office Depot, Walgreens
74b	Universal Studios (from wb)
74a	FL 482, Sand Lake Rd, N 🅖 7-11, Chevron 🍴 Alexander's Rest., Chick-fil-A, McDonald's, multiple restaurants, Timpano Italian, Wendy's 🛏 Comfort Suites 🅞 K-Mart, Publix, Walgreens, Walmart, Whole Food Mkt, S 🅖 7-11, BP, Chevron,Mobil, Shell/Circle K/dsl 🍴 Asian Buffet, Bahama Breeze, Buffalo Wild Wings, Burger King, Cattleman's Steaks, Charley's Steaks, Checkers, Chili's, China Jade, CiCi's Pizza, Crabhouse, Denny's, Fish Bones Rest., Friendly's, Golden Corral, Houlihan's, IHOP, Italianni's, Kobe Japanese, Lobster Feast, McDonald's, Miller's Alehouse, Ming Court, Olive Garden, Perkins, Pizza Hut, Ponderosa, Popeye's, Sizzler, TGIFriday's, Tony Roma, Uno, Vito's Chophouse, Wendy's, Wild Bean Cafe 🛏 Best Western, Castle Hotel, Comfort Inn, Courtyard, Crowne Plaza, EconoLodge, Embassy Suites, Fairfield Inn, Hampton Inn, Holiday Inn, Homewood Suites, Howard Johnson, Hyatt Place, La Quinta, Marriott, Masters Inn, Microtel, Peabody Hotel, Quality Inn, Radisson Inn, Ramada Inn, Red Roof Inn, Residence Inn, Rodeway Inn, Rosen Suites, Staybridge Suites, Wyndham Garden 🅞 🄷, Harley-Davidson, Ripley's Believe-it-or-not!, RV Park, Stouffer Resort, Walgreens
72	FL 528 E (**toll, no eb re-entry**), to Cape Canaveral, N 🅞 USPO, S 🅞 to 🖻
71	Central FL Pkwy (from eb no re-entry), S 🅖 Chevron 🍴 Wendy's 🛏 Hilton Garden, Renaissance Resort, Residence Inn, to SeaWorld
68	FL 535, Lake Buena Vista, N 🅖 7-11, Mobil/dsl, Shell/Circle K/dsl 🍴 AleHouse, Amici Italian, Black Angus Steaks, Buffalo Wild Wings, Burger King, Chevy's Mexican, Chili's, China Buffet, CiCi's Pizza, Denny's, Dragon Super Buffet, El Patron, Flipper's

ORLANDO

Exit #	Services
68	Continued
	Pizzaria, Fuddrucker's, Giordano's, Havana's Cuisine, Hooter⸱ IHOP, Joe's Crabshack, Johnnie's Rest., Kobe Japanese, Macaroni Grill, McDonald's, Olive Garden, Perkins, Pizza Hut, Qdoba⸱ Quiznos, Red Lobster, Shoney's, Sizzler, Steak'n Shake, Sub⸱ way, Sweet Tomatoes, Taco Bell, TGIFriday's, The Crabhous⸱ Uno 🛏 Comfort Inn, Country Inn&Suites, Courtyard, Double⸱ Tree, Embassy Suites, Extended Stay Deluxe, Hampton In⸱ Hawthorn Suites, Hilton, Hilton Gargen, Holiday Inn, Holida⸱ Inn Express, Homewood Suites, Hyatt Hotel, Orlando Vista Ho⸱ tel, Quality Inn, Radisson, Residence Inn, Sheraton, StayBridg⸱ Suites 🅞 Gooding's Foods/drug, USPO, Walgreens, S 🅖 7-11, Chevron, Shell/dsl 🍴 Applebee's, Bahama Breeze, Ca⸱ rabba's, Chick-fil-A, CiCi's Pizza, Dunkin Donuts, Golden Co⸱ ral, Landry's Seafood, LoneStar Steaks, Panera Bread, Sant⸱ Fe Steaks, Starbucks, Wendy's 🛏 Blue Heron Resort, Buen⸱ Vista Suites, Courtyard, Fairfield Inn, Holiday Inn Resort, Marr⸱ ott Village, Residence Inn, Sheraton, SpringHill Suites 🅞 CV⸱ Drug, Orlando Premium Outlets, Verizon, Walgreens
67	Fl 536, to Epcot, N 🅞 DisneyWorld, **1 mi** S 🅖 7-11 🍴 Asia⸱ Harbor 🛏 Buena Vista, Marriott 🅞 CVS Drug, multiple re⸱ sorts, to 🖻
65	Osceola Pkwy, to FL 417 (**toll**), N 🅞 Animal Kingdom, Epcot⸱ to DisneyWorld, Wide World of Sports
64b a	US 192, FL 536, to FL 417 (**toll**), to Kissimmee, N 🅖 7-11⸱ MGM, to DisneyWorld, **0-3 mi** S 🅖 7-11, Mobil/dsl, Race⸱ Trac/dsl 🍴 Applebee's, Arby's, Bob Evans, Boston Lobste⸱ Feast, Burger King, Charley's Steakhouse, Checkers, Chick⸱ fil-A, Chili's, Chinese Buffet, CiCi's Pizza, Cracker Barre⸱ Denny's, Domino's, Dunkin Donuts, Golden Corral, IHOP, Joe"⸱ Crabshack, Kabuki Oriental, KFC, Kobe Japanese, Krisp⸱ Kreme, Logan's Roadhouse, Longhorn Steaks, Macaroni Gril⸱ McDonald's, Ocean 11 Rest., Olive Garden, Pacino's Italiar⸱ Panda Express, Papa John's, Perkins, Pizza Hut, Ponderosa⸱ Quiznos, Red Lobster, Rio Mexican Grill, Ruby Tuesday, Sizzli⸱ Grill, Smokey Bones BBQ, Starbucks, Subway, Taco Bell, TGI⸱ Friday's, Uno, Waffle House, Wendy's 🛏 Best Inn, Celebratio⸱ Suites, Comfort Suites, Days Inn, Holiday Inn, Howard John⸱ son, Knight Inn, Masters Inn, Mona Lisa Hotel, Motel 6, Orlando⸱ Palms, Parkway Resort, Quality Suites, Radisson, Ramada, Re⸱ Roof Inn, Rodeway Inn, Seralago Hotel, Sun Inn, Super 8, Trav⸱ elodge 🅞 🄷, $General, AT&T, Camping World RV Ctr, CVS⸱ Drug, factory outlet/famous brands, Harley-Davidson, Jo-An⸱ Fabrics, Marshall's, Publix, Target, USPO, Walgreens
62	FL 417 (**toll, from eb**), World Dr, N 🅞 to DisneyWorld, S 🅞⸱ Celebration, to 🖻
60	Fl 429 N (**toll**), Apopka
58	FL 532, to Kissimmee, N 🅖 7-11, BP 🍴 Chili's, China One⸱ McDonald's, Pizzaria, Subway 🛏 Championship Gate Resor⸱ 🅞 Publix, Walgreens, S 🍴 Dunkin Donuts (1mi) 🛏 Reunio⸱ Resort (2mi)
55	US 27, to Haines City, N 🅖 7-11, Sunoco/dsl 🍴 Burger King⸱ Cracker Barrel, Denny's, McDonald's, Waffle House, Wendy's⸱ 🛏 Comfort Inn, Hampton Inn, Holiday Inn Express, Super ⸱ 🅞 FL Camp Inn (5mi), Ford, S 🅖 7-11, BP/dsl, Marathon⸱ RaceWay/dsl, Shell/dsl/service 🍴 Bob Evans, CiCi's Pizza⸱ Grand China, Perkins, Sake Steaks, Subway 🛏 Days Inn, Mi⸱ crotel, Quality Inn, Southgate Inn 🅞 🄷 $Tree, Belk, Best Buy⸱ Books-A-Million, Deer Creek RV Resort, Dick's, GNC, JC Pen⸱ ney, KOA, Michael's, Petsmart, Ross, Staples, Target, Them⸱ World RV Park, to Cypress Gardens, tourist info, Verizon
48	Rd 557, to Winter Haven, Lake Alfred, S 🅖 BP/dsl

INTERSTATE 4 Cont'd

LAKELAND

Exit #	Services
46mm	**Welcome Ctr eb, 24 hr security, full [handicapped] facilities, info, litter barrels, petwalk [phone] [picnic] vending**
44	FL 559, to Auburndale, **S** [gas] BP/dsl/scales/24hr, Love's/Arby's/dsl/scales/24hr
41	FL 570 W **toll**, Auburndale, Lakeland
38	FL 33, to Lakeland, Polk City
33	Rd 582, to FL 33, Lakeland, **N** [gas] 7-11, BP, Exxon/24hr [food] 5 Guys Burger, Applebee's, Cracker Barrel, McDonald's, Starbucks, Wendy's [lodging] Country Inn&Suites, Crestwood Suites, Days Inn, Hampton Inn, Jameson Inn, La Quinta, Quality Inn, Ramada, Sleep Inn [other] BMW, CVS Drug, GNC, Publix, **S** [gas] BP/dsl [food] Waffle House [lodging] ValuePlace [other] [H] Harley-Davidson, Lakeland RV Resort, Nissan
32	US 98, Lakeland, **N** [gas] 7-11, BP, Mobil, Murphy USA/dsl [food] Asian Buffet, Checkers, Chili's, ChuckeCheese, CiCi's Pizza, Domino's, DQ, Dunkin Donuts, Golden Corral, Hooters, IHOP, KFC, Ling's Buffet, LJ Silver, McDonald's, Moe's SW Grill, Olive Garden, Outback Steaks, Panera Bread, Papa John's, Place Garden, Red Lobster, Smokey Bones BBQ, Sonny's BBQ, Starbucks, Steak'n Shake, Subway, Taco Bell, TGIFriday's, Wendy's, Zaxby's [lodging] Comfort Inn, La Quinta, Royalty Inn [other] $General, (2mi), Advance Parts, Aldi Foods, AT&T, AutoZone, Barnes&Noble, Beall's, Belk, Best Buy, CVS Drug, Dillard's, Firestone/auto, Goodyear/auto, JC Penney, JoAnn Fabrics, Lowe's, Macy's, PepBoys, PetCo, Publix, Sam's Club/gas, Sears/auto, Staples, Sweetbay Foods, Target, Tire Kingdom, Tires+, Verizon, vet, Walgreens, Walmart, **S** [gas] 7-11, Coastal, RaceTrac/dsl, Sunoco/dsl [food] Bob Evans, Burger King, Denny's, LJ Silver, McDonald's, Popeye's, Waffle House [lodging] Howard Johnson, Motel 6 [other] [H], AutoZone, Beall's, Chrysler/Dodge, Family$, Home Depot, NAPA, U-Haul
31	FL 539, to Kathleen, Lakeland, **N** [gas] Shell/Circle K [food] Romeo's Pizza, Suwbay, Wendy's [other] Publix/dsl, Walgreens, **S** hist dist
28	FL 546, to US 92, Memorial Blvd, Lakeland (from eb re-entry), **S** [gas] Shell/Circle K/dsl, Sunoco [food] Hardee's
27	FL 570 E **toll**, Lakeland
25	County Line Rd, **S** [gas] Citgo/dsl, Shell/Circle K/Subway [food] McDonald's, Wendy's [lodging] Fairfield Inn [other] FL Air Museum
22	FL 553, Park Rd, Plant City, **N** [other] Chevrolet, **S** [gas] Shell/Circle K/Subway [food] Arby's, Burger King, Denny's, Popeye's [lodging] Comfort Inn, Holiday Inn Express
21	FL 39, Alexander St, to Zephyrhills, Plant City, **S on FL 39** [gas] BP/dsl, Shell/dsl [lodging] Days Inn, Red Rose Inn/rest.
19	FL 566, to Thonotosassa, **N** [gas] BP, **S** [gas] RaceTrac/dsl [food] Applebee's, BuddyFreddy's Rest., Carrabba's, Lin's Chinese, Little Caesars, McDonald's, Mi Casa, OutBack Steaks, Pizza Hut/Taco Bell, Sonny's BBQ, Starbucks, Subway, Waffle House [other] [H], $General, AT&T, Publix, Walgreens
17	Branch Forbes Rd, **N** [gas] Marathon, Sunoco [other] Dinosaur World, **S** [gas] BP, Shell/Circle K/Subway/dsl [other] Advance Parts, AutoZone
14	McIntosh Rd, **N** [gas] BP/dsl [other] Longview RV Ctr, Windward RV Park (2mi), **S** [gas] 7-11/dsl, RaceWay/dsl [food] Burger King, McDonald's/playplace [other] Bates RV Ctr, East Tampa RV Park
12mm	**both lanes, weigh sta**
10	Rd 579, Mango, Thonotosassa, **N** [gas] FLYING J/Denny's/dsl/LP/scales/24hr, Sunoco, TA/Arby's/Popeye's/dsl/scales/24hr/@ [food] Bob Evans, Cracker Barrel [lodging] Country Inn&Suites, Hampton Inn [other] Camping World RV Ctr, Ford/Lincoln, Hillsboro River

MANGO

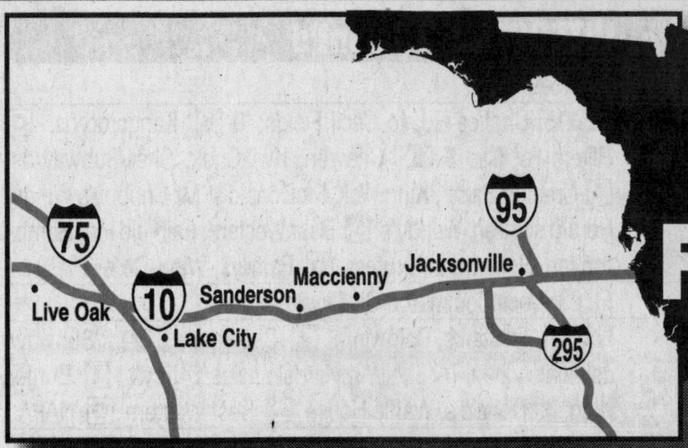

TAMPA

Exit #	Services
10	Continued SP, Lazy Day's RV Ctr, Rally RV Park, **S** [gas] Shell/Circle K/dsl [food] Hardee's, Subway, Wendy's [lodging] Masters Inn
9	I-75, N to Ocala, S to Naples
7	US 92W, to US 301, Hillsborough Ave, **N** [gas] Chevron/dsl, Mobil [food] Waffle House [other] Hard Rock Hotel/casino, Knights Inn, **S** [gas] BP, Citgo, Hess/Dunkin Donuts/Quiznos [food] 5 Guys Burgers, WingHouse [lodging] Comfort Suites, Holiday Inn Express, La Quinta, Red Roof Inn [other] FL Expo Fair
6	Orient Rd (from eb)
5	FL 574, MLK Blvd, **N** [food] McDonald's [other] truck/rv wash, **S** [gas] BP, Mobil, Sunoco/Subway [food] Wendy's [lodging] Fairfield Inn [other] Kenworth
3	US 41, 50th St, Columbus Dr (exits left from eb), **N** [gas] Chevron/dsl, Shell/Subway/dsl [lodging] Best Value Inn, Days Inn, Quality Inn [other] to Busch Gardens, **S** [gas] Sunoco/dsl [food] Checkers, Church's, KFC, McDonald's, Salem's Subs, Subway, Taco Bell [lodging] Howard Johnson [other] Advance Parts, Family$, Save-A-Lot, Sweetbay Foods, URGENT CARE
1	FL 585, 22nd, 21st St, Port of Tampa, **S** [gas] Sunoco [food] Burger King, McDonald's [other] museum

I-4 begins/ends on I-275, exit 45b.

INTERSTATE 10

JACKSONVILLE

Exit #	Services
363mm	**I-10 begins/ends on I-95, exit 351b.**
362	Stockton St, to Riverside, **S** [gas] BP, Gate [other] [H]
361	US 17 S (from wb), **S** [gas] BP, Gate
360	FL 129, McDuff Ave, **S** [gas] BP [food] Popeye's
359	Luna St, to Lenox Ave (from wb)
358	FL 111, Cassat Ave, **N** [gas] Hess/Godfather's/Quiznos/dsl, Shell/Subway/dsl [food] Burger King, McDonald's, Popeye's, Wendy's [other] AutoZone, Mr Transmission, **S** [gas] BP, RaceWay/dsl [food] Baskin-Robbins/Dunkin Donuts, Domino's, Gorgi's BBQ, Pizza Hut, Taco Bell, Wendy's [other] Advance Parts, Discount Tire, Lowe's, Walgreens
357	FL 103, Lane Ave, **N** [gas] Hess/dsl [food] Andy's Sandwiches [lodging] Knights Inn, Stars Rest Inn, **S** [gas] BP, Shell/dsl [food] Applebee's, Cross Creek Steaks, Hardee's, KFC, Lee's Dragon, McDonald's, Piccadilly's [lodging] Diamond Inn, Executive Inn, Sleep Inn [other] Carquest, CVS Drug, Firestone/auto, Home Depot, Office Depot, PepBoys
356	I-295, N to Savannah, S to St Augustine
355	Marietta, **N** [gas] Exxon, **S** [gas] Hess/Dunkin Donuts/Godfather's/Quiznos/dsl, Shell/dsl [food] Domino's

FL

LAKE CITY

LIVE OAK

INTERSTATE 10 Cont'd

Exit #	Services
351	FL 115, Chaffee Rd, to Cecil Fields, N Kangaroo/dsl Rivers RV Ctr, S Chevron, KwikChek, Shell/Subway/dsl Cracker Barrel, King Wok, McDonald's, Mr Chubby's Wings, Perard's Italian, Wendy's Best Western, Fairfield Inn, Hampton Inn, Holiday Inn Express Family$, Winn-Dixie
350	FL 23, Cecil Commerce Ctr Pkwy
343	US 301, to Starke, Baldwin, S Chevron, Pilot/Subway/dsl/scales/24hr, TA/Shell/Arby's/dsl/scales/24hr/ @ Burger King, McDonald's, Waffle House Best Western NAPA
336	FL 228, to Maxville, Macclenny, N Murphy USA/dsl Starbucks H, fireworks, Walmart/Subway
335	FL 121, to Lake Butler, Macclenny, N BP/dsl, Kangaroo China Dragon, Crystal River Seafood, Domino's, Hardee's, KFC, McDonald's, Pier 6, Pizza Hut, Subway, Taco Bell, Waffle House, Wendy's, Woody's BBQ, Zaxby's American Inn H $General, $Tree, Advance Parts, AutoZone, repair, Save-A-Lot Foods, USPO, Verizon, Walgreens, Winn-Dixie, S Exxon/dsl, RaceWay/dsl Burger King, China Buffet, San Jose Mexican EconoLodge, Travelodge
333	Rd 125, Glen Saint Mary, N Citgo/dsl/24hr
327	Rd 229, to Raiford, Sanderson, 1 mi N gas
324	US 90, to Olustee, Sanderson, S Citgo/dsl, Osceola NF, to Olustee Bfd
318mm	**both lanes, 24hr security, full facilities, litter barrels, petwalk vending**
303	US 441, Lake City, N Chevron/dsl Lake City Camping (1mi), Oaks'n Pines RV Park, S Shell/dsl, Sunoco/dsl Huddle House Days Inn H
301	US 41, to Lake City, N Busy Bee/dsl to Stephen Foster Ctr, S H
296b a	I-75, N to Valdosta, S to Tampa
294mm	**both lanes, 24hr security, full facilities, litter barrels, petwalk vending**
292	Rd 137, to Wellborn
283	US 129, to Live Oak, N Penn/dsl , to Boys Ranch, S BP, Chevron/dsl, Exxon/dsl, Murphy USA/dsl, Shell/dsl China Buffet, Huddle House, Krystal, McDonald's, Subway, Taco Bell, Waffle House, Wendy's, Zaxby's Best Western, EconoLodge, Holiday Inn Express H, $Tree, Lowe's, Verizon, Walmart
275	US 90, Live Oak, N to Suwannee River SP, S H
271mm	truck insp sta both lanes
269mm	Suwannee River
265mm	**both lanes, 24 hr security, full facilities, litter barrels, petwalk vending**
264mm	**weigh sta both lanes**
262	Rd 255, Lee, N to Suwannee River SP, S Jimmy's/Chevron/Red Onion Grill/dsl/scales/24hr/ @, Loves/Arby's/dsl/scales/24hr
258	FL 53, N Chevron/McDonald's/dsl, Mobil/DQ/Subway/Wendy's/dsl/scales/24hr Denny's, Waffle House Best Western, Days Inn, Super 8 H S Deerwood Inn Jellystone Camping, Madison Camping
251	FL 14, to Madison, N Mobil/Arby's/24hr H
241	US 221, Greenville, N Mobil/DQ
234mm	**both lanes, 24hr security, full facilities, litter barrels, petwalk**
233	Rd 257, Aucilla, N Shell/dsl

TALLAHASSEE

QUINCY

Exit #	Services
225	US 19, to Monticello, N Camper's World Camping, S BP, Chevron/McDonald's/dsl, Mobil/Arby's/dsl, Sunoco/c Huddle House Days Inn, Super 8 A Stones Thro RV Park, dogtrack, KOA
217	FL 59, Lloyd, S BP/rest/dsl/scales/24hr, Shell/Subway/d EconoLodge truckwash
209b a	US 90, Tallahassee, N Staybridge Suites, S Circle dsl, Shell/Subway/dsl Eastern Chinese, Waffle House Best Western, Country Inn&Suites auto museum, Publi Tallahassee RV Park
203	FL 61, US 319, Tallahassee, N BP/dsl, Shell/Circle K, US 5 Guys Burgers, Applebee's, Baskin-Robbins/Dunkin Do nuts, Bonefish Grill, Firehouse Subs, Genghis Grill, Jimm John's, McDonald's, Moe's SW Grill, Panda Buffet, Pane Bread, Popeye's, Sonny's BBQ, Starbucks, Subway, Taco Be Waffle House, Wendy's $Tree, (3mi), AT&T, Books-A-M lion, CVS Drug, Discount Tire, Fresh Mkt Foods, GNC, Hobb Lobby, Publix, Radio Shack, SteinMart, SuperLube, TJ Max Walgreens, Walmart, S BP, Citgo Calico Jack's Oyst Bar, Carrabba's, Chick-fil-A, Los Amigos, McDonald's, Osak Japanese, Outback Steaks, Steak'n Shake, Subway, Ted's M Grill, TGIFriday's, Village Inn, Zaxby's Cabot Lodge, Cour yard, Hampton Inn, Hilton Garden, Residence Inn, Sherato Studio+ H, Advance Parts, Goodyear/auto, Home Depo Infiniti, Office Depot, Petsmart, U-Haul, URGENT CARE, vet
199	US 27, Tallahassee, N Chevron/dsl, Kangaroo/dsl, McKenzie/dsl Burger King, Domino's, McDonald's, Papa John' Pizza Hut, Subway, Taco Bell, Waffle House Baymont In Country Inn&Suites, Days Inn, Fairfield Inn, Holiday Inn, Microtel, Quality Inn $General, Ace Hardware, Advance Part Big Oak RV Park (2mi), CVS Drug, Family$, USPO, vet, Wa greens, Walmart, Winn-Dixie, S Chevron/dsl, Shell/Circl K, USA/dsl Arby's, Boston Mkt, Chick-fil-A, China Buffe ChuckECheese, Cracker Barrel, Crystal River Seafood, Denny's DQ, El Jalisco, Firehouse Subs, Golden Corral, Hooters, IHO Julie's Rest, Kacey's Rest, KFC, Krispy Kreme, Little Caesar Longhorn Steaks, McDonald's, Melting Pot, Ole Times Buffe On-the-Border, Papa John's, Red Lobster, Shoney's, Soni Sonny's BBQ, Starbucks, Subway, TCBY, Wendy's, Whataburg er, Zaxby's Best Value Inn, EconoLodge, Guesthouse In Howard Johnson, La Quinta, Red Roof Inn, Rodeway Inn, Supe 8 $Tree, Advance Parts, AT&T, AutoZone, Barnes&Nobl Belk, city park, CVS Drug, PepBoys, Publix, Staples, Sun Tir Tuffy Auto, U-Haul, Verizon, vet, Walgreens
196	FL 263, Tallahassee, S Chevron/dsl, Inland/dsl, Shell/ds Stop'n Save Gas Applebee's, Checker's, Dunkin Donut Firehouse Subs, KFC, McDonald's, Sonic, Steak'n Shak Subway, Taco Bell, Waffle House, Wendy's, Zaxby's Slee Inn Advance Parts, , Chrysler/Dodge/Jeep, Harley-Da vidson, Home Depot, Lowe's, Mazda, Toyota, VW, Walgreen Walmart
194mm	**both lanes, 24hr security, full facilities, litter barrels petwalk vending**
192	US 90, to Tallahassee, Quincy, N FLYING J /Denny's dsl/LP/scales/24hr , BP Comfort Inn, Howard Johnso Camping World RV Ctr (2mi), S Pilot/Subway/ds scales/24hr Waffle House Best Western
181	FL 267, Quincy, 1 mi N Murphy USA/dsl Domino's Mayflower Chinese H, Walmart, S BP/dsl, Pur Hampton Inn, Holiday Inn Express, Parkway Inn, to Lak Talquin SF
174	FL 12, to Greensboro, N BP/dsl, Shell/Burger King/dsl

INTERSTATE 10 Cont'd

Exit #	Services
166	Rd 270A, Chattahoochee, N [other] to Lake Seminole, to Torreya SP, S [gas] Shell/dsl [other] KOA (1mi)
161mm	**[rest stop] both lanes, 24hr security, full [handicapped] facilities, litter barrels, petwalk [phone] [picnic] vending**
160mm	Apalachicola River, central/eastern time zone
158	Rd 286, Sneads, N [other] Lake Seminole, to Three Rivers SP
155mm	**weigh sta both lanes**
152	FL 69, to Grand Ridge, Blountstown, N [gas] BP, Exxon/dsl
142	FL 71, to Marianna, Oakdale, N [gas] Murphy USA/dsl, Pilot/Arby's/dsl/scales/24hr [food] Beef'O'Brady's, Burger King, Firehouse Subs, Hong Kong Chinese, KFC, Pizza Hut, PoFolks, Ruby Tuesday, San Marco's Mexican, Sonny's BBQ, Waffle House [lodging] American Inn, Comfort Inn, Days Inn, Fairfield Inn, Marianna Inn, Microtel, Quality Inn, Super 8 [other] [H] $Tree, AT&T, Lowe's, to FL Caverns SP (8mi), Verizon, Walmart/Subway, S [gas] Chevron/dsl, Sunoco/dsl, TA/Pizza Hut/Popeye's/Taco Bell/dsl/scales/24hr/ @ [food] DQ, McDonald's [lodging] Best Value Inn [other] Dove Rest RV Park
136	FL 276, to Marianna, N [other] to FL Caverns SP (8mi)
133mm	**[rest stop] both lanes, 24hr security, full [handicapped] facilities, litter barrels, petwalk [phone] [picnic]**
130	US 231, Cottondale, N [gas] BP/dsl, Chevron [food] Hardee's, Subway, S [gas] Loves/Chester's/McDonald's/dsl/scales/24hr/ @ , RaceWay/dsl
120	FL 77, to Panama City, Chipley, N [gas] BP/dsl, Exxon/Burger King/Stuckey's, Murphy USA/dsl, Shell/dsl [food] Arby's, Cancun Mexican, Hardee's, Hungry Howie's, JinJin Chinese, KFC, McDonald's, Pizza Hut, Sonic, Subway, Waffle House, Wendy's [lodging] Comfort Inn, Days Inn/rest., Executive Inn, Quality Inn, Super 8 [other] [H] $General, $Tree, Advance Parts, NAPA, O'Reilly Parts, Save-A-Lot Foods, Verizon, Walmart, S [other] Falling Water SP
112	FL 79, Bonifay, N [gas] Chevron, Citgo/Tom Thumb/dsl, Exxon/dsl [food] Burger King, Hardee's, Hungry Howie, McDonald's, Pizza Hut, Simbo's Rest, Subway, Waffle House [lodging] Bonifay Inn, Economy Lodge, Holiday Inn Express, Tivoli Inn [other] [H], FL Springs RV Camping, Fred's, repair, S Panama City Beach
104	Rd 279, Caryville
96	FL 81, Ponce de Leon, N [other] $General, to Ponce de Leon SRA, Vortex Spring Camping (5mi), S **[rest stop] both lanes, 24hr security, full [handicapped] facilities, litter barrels, petwalk [phone] [picnic]**, [gas] 87 Depot/Subway/dsl, BP/dsl, Exxon/dsl [lodging] Ponce de Leon Motel
85	US 331, De Funiak Springs, N [gas] Chevron/dsl, Murphy USA/dsl [food] Arby's, Beef O'Brady's, Burger King, Hungry Howie's, McLain's Steaks, Pizza Hut, Sonic, Subway, Waffle House [lodging] Best Value Inn, Regency Inn, Sundown Inn, Super 8 [other] [H] $General, $Tree, AT&T, Lowe's, Verizon, Walgreens, Walmart, winery, Winn-Dixie, S [gas] 87 Depot/dsl, BP, Emerald Express/dsl [food] KFC, McDonald's, Whataburger [lodging] Best Western [other] [H] camping (3mi)
70	FL 285, to Ft Walton Bch, Eglin AFB, N [gas] RaceWay/dsl, S [lodging] Rodeway Inn [other] Dixie RV Ctr, repair
60mm	**[rest stop] both lanes, 24hr security, full [handicapped] facilities, litter barrels, petwalk [phone] [picnic] vending**
56	FL 85, Crestview , Eglin AFB, N [gas] BP/dsl, Mobil/Chester's/dsl [food] Applebee's, Beef O'Brady's, Burger King, Capt D's, Chill Frozen Yogurt, China 1, Dunkin Donuts, Golden Asian, Hungry Howie's, Hunon Chinese, Lenny's Subs, McDonald's, Mia's Italian, Ryan's, Sonic, Starbucks, Steve&Joe's Diner, Taco Bell [lodging] Country Inn&Suites, EconoLodge [other] [H] $General, Advance

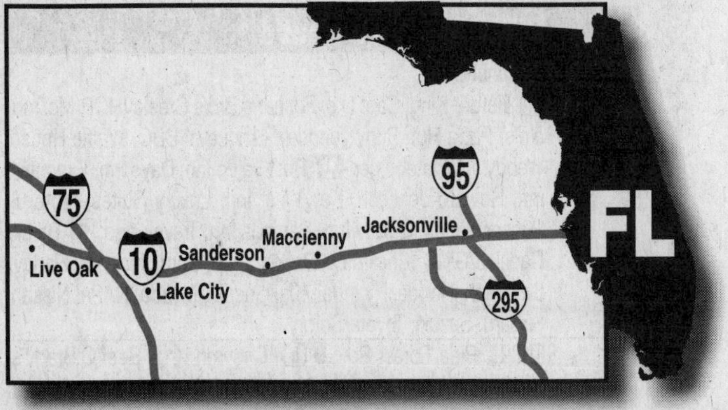

Exit #	Services
56	Continued Parts, AT&T, AutoZone, BigLots, GNC, Lowe's, Publix, Radio Shack, Staples, URGENT CARE, Verizon, Walgreens, Walmart, S [gas] Citgo/Tom Thumb/dsl, Exxon/dsl [food] Arby's, Coach-n-Four Steaks, Cracker Barrel, Hardee's, Hooters, LaRumba Mexican, Waffle House, Wendy's, Whataburger [lodging] Baymont Inn, Best Value Inn, Comfort Inn, Hampton Inn, Holiday Inn Express, Jameson Inn, Rodeway Inn, Super 8 [other] Buick/GMC, Chevrolet, Ford, museum, RV camping
45	Rd 189, to US 90, Holt, N [gas] Chevron (1mi) [other] Eagle's Landing RV Park, to Blackwater River SP, S [other] River's Edge RV Park (1mi)
31	FL 87, to Ft Walton Beach, Milton, N [gas] Exxon/dsl [food] Waffle House [lodging] Holiday Inn Express [other] Blackwater River SP, KOA, S [gas] BP, Shell/dsl [lodging] Comfort Inn, Red Carpet Inn
31mm	**[rest stop] both lanes, 24hr security, full [handicapped] facilities, litter barrels, petwalk [phone] [picnic]**
28	Rd 89, Milton, N [other] [H]
27mm	Blackwater River
26	Rd 191, Bagdad, Milton, N [gas] Shell/Circle K/dsl [other] [H] $General, S [gas] Chevron/DQ/Stuckey's [other] Pelican Palms RV Park
22	N FL 281, Avalon Blvd, N [gas] RaceWay/dsl, Tom Thumb [food] Capt Pete's Oyster House, McDonald's, S [gas] Shell/Circle K/Subway/dsl [food] Waffle House [lodging] Red Roof Inn [other] Avalon Landing RV Park (3mi)
18mm	Escambia Bay
17	US 90, Pensacola, N [gas] BP/dsl, S [gas] Exxon/DQ [lodging] Quality Inn/rest.
14mm	**truck inspection sta**
13	FL 291, to US 90, Pensacola, N [gas] BP, Exxon, Shell/dsl [food] Arby's, Capt D's, Denny's, DQ, La Hacienda Mexican, McDonald's, Santino's Cafe, Subway, Taco Bell, Waffle House [lodging] Comfort Inn, Holiday Inn, La Quinta, Motel 6, Villager Lodge [other] $Tree, CVS Drug, Food World, Ross, U-Haul, Walgreens, S [food] ChuckECheese, Fazoli's, HoneyBaked Ham, Los Rancheros Mexican, Shrimp Basket Rest, Waffle House, Wendy's, Whataburger [lodging] Baymont Inn, Best Value Inn, Courtyard, Extended Stay America, Fairfield Inn, Hampton Inn, Mainstay Suites, Red Roof Inn, Super 6 Inn, TownePlace Suites [other] [H] $General, Belk, Books-A-Million, Firestone/auto, Hobby Lobby, JC Penney, Jo-Ann Fabrics, PepBoys, Petsmart, Radio Shack, Sears/auto, TJ Maxx, U-Haul
12	I-110, to Pensacola, Hist Dist, Islands Nat Seashore
10b a	US 29, Pensacola, N [gas] Kangaroo/dsl/scales , Murphy USA/dsl [food] Church's, Hardee's, Ryan's, Sonic, Vallarta Mexican, Waffle House [other] $Tree, Advance Parts, AT&T, AutoZone, Carpenter's RV Ctr, GNC, Office Depot, O'Reilly Parts, Radio Shack, Tires+, Walmart, **0-2 mi** S [gas] RaceWay/dsl, Shell/Circle K, Tom Thumb

CHIPLEY

CRESTVIEW

PENSACOLA

FL

PENSACOLA

INTERSTATE 10 Cont'd

10b a Continued
Burger King, Capt D's, Founaris Bro's Greek, IHOP, McDonald's, Pizza Hut, Ruby Tuesday, Smokey's BBQ, Waffle House, Wendy's, Whataburger Best Value Inn, Days Inn, Executive Inn, Howard Johnson, Key West Inn, Luxury Suites, Motel 6, Pensacola Inn, Quality Inn, Ramada Inn, Travelodge Buick/Cadillac/GMC, Chevrolet, Dodge/Jeep, Ford, funpark, Harley-Davidson, Honda, Hyundai, Kia, Lincoln, Mazda, NAPA, Nissan, Subaru, Suzuki, Toyota/Scion

7b a Fl 297, Pine Forest Rd, N Chevron Beef'O'Brady's, Starbucks, Wendy's Best Western, Comfort Inn, Garden Inn, Value Place Publix, Tall Oaks Camping, transmissions, S BP, Raceway/dsl, Tom Thumb Burger King, Cracker Barrel, Figaro's Pizza, Hardee's, McDonald's, Ruby Tuesday, Sonny's BBQ, Subway, Waffle House, Wayne's Diner Country Inn&Suites, Holiday Inn Express, Microtel, Quality Inn, Red Roof Inn Big Lagoon SRA (12mi), Food World/24hr, museum

5 US 90 A, N Kangaroo/Subway/dsl , Shell/Circle K Beef'O Brady's, Hershey's Ice Cream, Starbucks, Wendy's AT&T, Publix/gas, Walgreens, S Leisure Lakes Camping

4mm **Welcome Ctr eb, 24hr security, full facilities, info, litter barrels, petwalk vending**

3mm **weigh sta both lanes**

1mm **inspection sta eb**

0mm Florida/Alabama state line, Perdido River

FL

LAKE CITY

INTERSTATE 75

Exit #	Services
471mm	Florida/Georgia state line, Motorist callboxes begin sb.
469mm	**Welcome Ctr sb full facilities, info, litter barrels, petwalk vending**
467	FL 143, Jennings, E Budget Lodge, W Exxon/dsl Jennings House Inn, N Florida Inn fireworks, Jennings Camping
460	FL 6, Jasper, E BP/Burger King, Indian River Fruit/gas, Penn Oil/Huddle House/dsl 7 Oaks Inn, W Shell/dsl, Sunoco/dsl Sheffield's Country Kitchen Scottish Inn Suwanee River SP
451	US 129, Jasper, Live Oak, E Love's /Arby's/dsl/scales/24hr, Mobil/DQ/Subway/dsl, W BP/Lester's Grill/dsl Suwanee Music Park (4mi), to FL Boys Ranch
448mm	**weigh sta both lanes**
446mm	**insp sta both lanes**
443mm	Historic Suwanee River
439	to FL 136, White Springs, Live Oak, E Gate/dsl/e-85 , Shell/dsl McDonald's Lee's Camping (3mi), Suwanee RV Camping (4mi), to S Foster Ctr, W Best Value Inn
435	I-10, E to Jacksonville, W to Tallahassee
427	US 90, to Live Oak, Lake City, E BP/dsl, Chevron/dsl, Exxon, Gas'n Go, Murphy USA/dsl, Shell/dsl Applebee's, Arby's, Burger King, Cedar River Seafood, Cracker Barrel, Domino's, El Potro, Elliano's Coffee, Firehouse Subs, Gondolier Italian, Hardee's, IHOP, Ken's BBQ, Krystal, McDonald's, Moe's SW Grill, Ole Times Buffet, Papa John's, Pizza Hut, Player's Club, Red Lobster, Ruby Tuesday, Sonny's BBQ, Starbucks, Steak'n Shake, Subway, Taco Bell, TX Roadhouse, Waffle House, Wasabi, Wendy's, Zaxby's Best Inn, Budget Inn, Cypress Inn, Days Inn, Driftwood Inn, Holiday Inn, Jameson Inn, Piney Woods Motel,
427	Continued Ramada Ltd, Rodeway Inn, Scottish Inn H Advance Parts, AT&T, AutoZone, Belk, BigLots, CVS Drug, Ford/Lincoln, Home Depot, Inn&Out RV Park, JC Penney, Kia, Lowe's, mall, Petsmart, Publix, Radio Shack, Tire Kingdom, TireMart, TJ Maxx, Toyota/Scion, Verizon, Walgreens, Walmart, W BP, Chevron/dsl, Shell, Sunoco Bob Evans, China One, Waffle House Best Value Inn, Best Western, Cabot Lodge, Comfort Suites, Country Inn&Suites, EconoLodge, Fairfield Inn, Gateway Inn, Hampton Inn, Red Roof Inn, Travelodge $General, Cadillac/Chevrolet, Camping World RV Ctr, Carquest, Chrysler/Dodge/Jeep, Family$, Harvey's Foods, Nissan, vet
423	FL 47, to Ft White, Lake City, E Shell/dsl Mack/Volvo Trucks, W BP/dsl, Exxon/dsl, Stop-N-Go/USPO Little Caesars, Subway Motel 8, Super 8 $General, Casey Jones RV Park, Freightliner
414	US 41, US 441, to Lake City, High Springs, E Chevron/dsl, Exxon, Pitstop Traveler's Inn, Travelodge, W BP/dsl, Shell/Wendy's/dsl Subway antiques, tires/repair, to O'Leno SP (5 mi)
413mm	**both lanes, full facilities, litter barrels, petwalk vending**
409mm	Santa Fe River
404	Rd 236, to High Springs, E Chevron/fruits/gifts, Citgo/dsl, Sunoco, W High Springs Camping
399	US 441, to High Sprs, Alachua, E BP, Kangaroo Domino's, McDonald's, Moe's SW Grill, Pizza Hut, Sonny's BBQ, Subway, Taco Bell, Waffle House EconoLodge, Quality Inn $General, Advance Parts, AT&T, CVS Drug, Family$, Hitchcock's Foods, Lowe's, Traveler's Campground (1mi), vet, Walgreens, W Chevron, Kangaroo/Wendy's, Mobil/PizzaVito/dsl KFC, Mason's Grill Best Value Inn, Royal Inn
390	FL 222, to Gainesville, E Chevron/dsl, Kangaroo/Subway/dsl, Marathon/McDonald's/dsl Burger King, La Fiesta Mexican, Pomodoro Cafe, Sonny's BBQ, Wendy's Publix, Walgreens, W BP/DQ/Dunkin Donuts/dsl Best Western Harley-Davidson, vet
387	FL 26, to Newberry, Gainesville, E BP, Chevron/dsl, Shell/dsl, Sunoco BJ's Rest., Bono's BBQ, Boston Mkt, Burger King, Dunkin Donuts, FoodCourt, HoneyBaked Ham, Jason's Deli, LJ Silver, Macaroni Grill, McAlister's Deli, McDonald's, Mr Tequila's Grill, Perkins, Red Lobster, Ruby Tuesday, Starbucks, Subway, Wendy's La Quinta H Belk, Books-A-Million, Dillard's, JC Penney, Macy's, mall, Office Depot, PetCo, Sears/auto, SteinMart, to UF, Verizon, W BP, Chevron/dsl, Exxon/dsl, Marathon/dsl Asian Cafe, El Norteno's Mexican, Hardee's, Krystal, Moe's SW Grill, Napolatanos Rest., Pizza Hut, Taco Bell, Waffle House Baymont Inn, Days Inn, EconoLodge, Gainesville Hotel $Tree, Advance Parts, Goodyear/auto, Home Depot, Jo-Ann Fabrics, K-Mart, PepBoys, Publix, tires/repair, TJ Maxx, vet, Walgreens
384	FL 24, to Archer, Gainesville, E Chevron/dsl, Exxon/dsl, Shell 5 Guys Burgers, Arby's, Asian Wok, Backyard Burger, BoneFish Grill, Burger King, Checkers, Chick-fil-A, Chili's, Chipotle Mexican, Chuy's Mexican, CiCi's Pizza, Cody's Roadhouse, Coldstone, DQ, Dunkin Donuts, Firehouse Subs, Gainesville Alehouse, Genghis Grill, KFC, McAlister's Deli, McDonald's, Moe's SW Grill, Olive Garden, Outback Steaks, Panera Bread, Papa John's, Pizza Hut, Sonny's BBQ, Starbucks, Steak'n Shake, Subway, Taco Bell, TGIFriday's, Tijuana Flats, TX Roadhouse, Waffle House, Wendy's, Willy's Mexican Grill, Wing House, Zaxby's Cabot Lodge, Comfort Inn, Courtyard,

GAINESVILLE

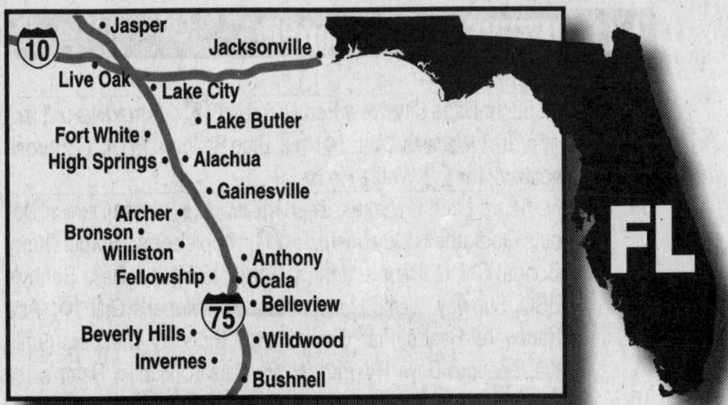

INTERSTATE 75 Cont'd

GAINESVILLE

384 Continued
Extended Stay America, Hampton Inn, Hilton Garden, Homewood Suites, Motel 6, Red Roof Inn, Residence Inn, Sleep Inn, SpringHill Suites, Super 8 [other] $Tree, Barnes&Noble, Best Buy, CarQuest, CVS Drug, Discount Tire, Firestone/auto, GNC, Kohl's, Lowe's, Michael's, Old Navy, Petsmart, Publix, Radio Shack, Ross, Target, Tuffy Auto, Verizon, Walgreens, Walmart, **W** [gas] Marathon/dsl [food] Cracker Barrel [lodging] Country Inn&Suites, Holiday Inn Express [other] Sunshine RV Park, to Bear Museum

382 FL 121, to Williston, Gainesville, **E** [gas] Marathon/dsl, Mobil/dsl [food] 1st Wok, Little Caesars, McDonald's, Subway [other] Publix, USPO, **W** [gas] BP/dsl, Chevron/dsl, Kangaroo/dsl [food] 43rd St Deli [lodging] Quality Inn, Rodeway Inn, ValuePlace [other] Fred Bear Museum

381mm **[RS] both lanes, 24 hr security, full facilities, litter barrels, petwalk vending**

374 Rd 234, Micanopy, **E** [gas] BP, Chevron/dsl [other] antiques, to Paynes Prairie SP, **W** [lodging] Micanopy Inn [other] repair

368 Rd 318, Orange Lake, **E** [gas] Chevron, Jim's/BBQ, Petro/BP/Iron Skillet/dsl/scales/24hr/ @ [food] Wendy's [other] Grand Lake RV Park (3mi), **W** [other] Ocala N RV Camping

358 FL 326, **E** [gas] Marathon/McDonald's/dsl, Pilot/Arby's/dsl/scales/24hr, Pilot/Wendy's/dsl/scales/24hr, Sunoco/FL Citrus Ctr/dsl [other] auto/truck repair, Freightliner, **W** [gas] Chevron/dsl, Love's/Chester's/Subway/dsl/scales/24hr [food] DQ

OCALA

354 US 27, to Silver Springs, Ocala, **E** [gas] BP/dsl, RaceTrac/dsl [food] Burger King, Rascal's BBQ [lodging] Golden Palms Inn, **W** [gas] BP/dsl, Chevron/dsl, Shell/dsl [food] Blanca's Cafe, China Taste, McDonald's, Roma Rest, Subway, Swampy's Grill [lodging] Budget Host, Comfort Suites, Days Inn, Howard Johnson, Ramada [other] $General, AT&T, Family$, GNC, Nelson's Trailers, Oaktree Village Camping, Publix, Walgreens, Winn-Dixie

352 FL 40, to Silver Springs, Ocala, **E** [gas] Chevron, Mobil/dsl, RaceTrac/dsl, Sunoco/dsl [food] Dunkin Donuts, McDonald's, Pizza Hut/Taco Bell, Subway, Wendy's, Zaxby's [lodging] Amadeus Inn, Days Inn/café, Economy Inn, Motor Inn/RV [other] Family$, to Silver River SP (8mi), **W** [gas] Shell/dsl, Texaco/dsl [food] Denny's, Golden Coast Buffet, Waffle House [lodging] Red Roof Inn, Super 8, Travelodge [other] Gander Mtn, Holiday Trav-L Park

350 FL 200, to Hernando, Ocala, **0-2 mi E** [gas] BP/dsl, Citgo/dsl, Texaco/dsl [food] 5 Guys Burgers, Applebee's, Arby's, Bob Evans, Boston Mkt, Burger King, Carrabba's, Checkers, Chick-fil-A, Chili's, ChuckECheese, City Buffet, Cody's Roadhouse, Coldstone, Crispers, Domino's, El Toreo Mexican, Firehouse Subs, Golden Corral, Guadalajara Mexican, Hardee's, House of Japan, Krystal, Lee's Chicken, Logan's Roadhouse, McDonald's, Moe's SW Grill, Ocean Buffet, Olive Garden, Outback Steaks, Panera Bread, Papa John's, Red Lobster, Ruby Tuesday, Shane's Rib Shack, Smoothie King, Sonic, Sonny's BBQ, Starbucks, Stevie B's Pizza, Subway, Taco Bell, Wendy's, Zaxby's [lodging] Country Inn&Suites, Hilton, La Quinta [other] [H], $Tree, Acura, Advance Parts, Aldi Foods, Belk, Best Buy, Books-A-Million, Chevrolet, CVS Drug, Discount Tire, Goodyear/auto, Hobby Lobby, Home Depot, Honda, Hyundai, JC Penney, Jo-Ann Fabrics, Kia, Lowe's, Macy's, Mazda, Michael's, Nissan, Office Depot, O'Reilly Parts, PepBoys, Petsmart, Publix, Ross, Sears/auto, Staples, SteinMart, Target, Tire Kingdom, TJ Maxx, Toyota, Tuffy Auto, URGENT CARE, Verizon, Walgreens, Walmart, **W** [gas] BP/dsl, Chevron [food] Bonefish Grill, Burger King, Cracker Barrel,

350 Continued
Dunkin Donuts, KFC, McAlister's Deli, McDonald's, Mimi's Cafe, Panera Bread, Starbucks, Steak'n Shake, Tijuana Flats, Waffle House, Yamato Japanese [lodging] Best Western, Courtyard, Fairfield Inn, Hampton Inn, Holiday Inn, Homewood Suites, Residence Inn [other] [H], AT&T, Barnes&Noble, BMW, Buick/GMC, Cadillac, Camper Village RV Park, Dick's, Dillard's, Kohl's, Ocala RV Park, Old Navy, PetCo, Porsche, Sam's Club/gas, Tires+, Verizon, vet, VW, Walgreens

346mm **[RS] both lanes, 24hr security, full facilities, litter barrels, petwalk vending**

341 Rd 484, to Belleview, **E** [gas] Chevron/fruit, Citgo/Baskin-Robbins/Dunkin Donuts, Exxon/dsl, Shell/dsl [food] Cracker Barrel, KFC/Taco Bell, Sonny's BBQ, Zaxby's [lodging] Microtel, Sleep Inn [other] drag racing museum, FL Citrus Ctr, **W** [gas] Pilot/DQ/Wendy's/dsl/scales/24hr [food] McDonald's, Subway, Waffle House [lodging] Hampton Inn [other] Ocala Sun RV Resort, outlets

INVERNESS

338mm **weigh sta both lanes**

329 FL 44, to Inverness, Wildwood, **E** [gas] Marathon/dsl, Sunoco/DQ, Wilco/Hess/Steak'n Shake/dsl/scales/24hr [food] Burger King, McDonald's, Waffle House, Wendy's [other] FL Citrus Ctr, Wild Wood RV Park, **W** [gas] Citgo/dsl/repair/24hr, Pilot/dsl/scales/24hr, TA/BP/Pizza Hut/Popeye's/Subway/dsl/scales/24hr/ @ [food] IHOP, KFC [lodging] Best Value Inn, Days Inn, Super 8, Villager Lodge [other] truck repair, truckwash

328 FL TPK (from sb), to Orlando

321 Rd 470, to Sumterville, Lake Panasoffkee, **E** [gas] Spirit/deli/dsl/scales/24hr [other] Coleman Correctional, **W** [gas] Chevron/7-11/dsl, Mobil/Hardee's/Subway/dsl

314 FL 48, to Bushnell, **E** [gas] Citgo, Murphy USA/dsl, Shell/Circle K/Subway, Texaco [food] Hong Kong Chinese, KFC/Taco Bell, McDonald's, Wendy's [lodging] Rodeway Inn [other] $Tree, AutoZone, BlueBerry Hill RV Camp, Red Oaks Camp (1mi), to Dade Bfd HS, Verizon, vet, Walmart, **W** [gas] Shell/dsl, Sunoco/dsl [food] Beef'O'Brady's, Sonny's BBQ, Waffle House [lodging] Microtel [other] Flagship RV Ctr

DADE CITY

309 Rd 476, to Webster, **E** [other] Breezy Oaks RV Park (1mi), Sumter Oaks RV Park (1mi)

307mm **[RS] both lanes, 24hr security, full facilities, litter barrels, petwalk**

301 US 98, FL 50, to Dade City, **E** [gas] RaceTrac/dsl [food] Beef'O'Brady's, Cracker Barrel, Denny's, McDonald's, Quinzos, Subway, Waffle House, Wendy's [lodging] Days Inn, Holiday Inn Express [other] $General, Advance Parts, Tall Pines RV Park, Winn-Dixie, **W** [gas] Chevron/dsl [food] Burger King [lodging] Hampton Inn, Microtel, Quality Inn [other] [H]

293 Rd 41, to Dade City, **E** [gas] Citgo (2mi) [other] to Sertoma Youth Ranch, **W** [other] Travelers Rest Resort RV Park

= gas = food = lodging = other = rest stop

FL

INTERSTATE 75 Cont'd

TAMPA

Exit #	Services
285	FL 52, to Dade City, New Port Richey, E FLYING J /Denny's/dsl/LP/scales/24hr Blue Beacon, W Citgo/dsl/scales/24hr Waffle House
279	FL 54, to Land O' Lakes, Zephyrhills, E Hess/Dunkin Donuts/Godfather's/Quiznos/dsl Applebee's, Burger King, Gonna China, Papa's John's, Pizza Hut/Taco Bell, Sonny's BBQ, Subway, Waffle House, Wendy's, Winner's Grill Ace Hardware, Beall's, Fiat, Ford, Happy Days RV Camping (9mi), Kia, Leasure Days RV Park (7mi), Nissan, Publix, Ralph's RV Camping (7mi), to Hillsborough River SP (18mi), Toyota/Scion, vet, Walgreens, W 7-11, Marathon, Mobil/Dunkin Donuts, Shell/Circle K/dsl Beef'O'Brady's, Buffalo's, Cracker Barrel, DQ, Hungry Howie's, Marco's Pizza, McDonald's, Outback Steaks, Remington's Steaks, Shanghai Chinese Best Western, Comfort Inn, Holiday Inn Express, Sleep Inn $Tree, Advance Parts, AT&T, Best Buy, CVS Drug, Dick's, Encore RV Camping, GNC, Goodyear/auto, Honda, Hyundai, Mazda, Michael's, Petsmart, Quail Run RV Camping, Ross, Tire Kingdom, TJ Maxx, Tuffy Auto, URGENT CARE, Verizon
277mm	**both lanes, 24hr security, full facilities, litter barrels, petwalk**
275	FL 56, Land O Lakes, Tarpon Springs, E BP/Dunkin Donuts/dsl TX Roadhouse Hampton Inn Mini, Publix (2mi), W Shell/dsl Walgreens
274	I-275 (from sb), to Tampa, St Petersburg
270	Rd 581, Bruce B Downs Blvd, E 7-11, Hess/dsl, Mobil, Shell/Circle K/Taco Bell/dsl Baskin-Robbins/Dunkin Donuts, Boston Mkt, Chick-fil-A, Chili's, Coldstone, DQ, Firehouse Subs, Jimmy John's, KFC, Kobe Japanese, Liang's Asian Bistro, Macaroni Grill, McDonald's, Moe's SW Grill, Panera Bread, Papa John's, Pizza Hut, Ruby Tuesday, Selmon's Cafe, Starbucks, Steak'n Shake, Subway, TGIFriday's, Tijuana Flats, Wendy's Holiday Inn Express, Wingate Inn Best Buy, CVS Drug, GNC, Home Depot, Kauffman Tire, Michael's, Publix, Radio Shack, Tires+, URGENT CARE, Verizon, Walgreens, Walmart, W 7-11 McDonald's, Olive Garden, Panda Buffet, Red Lobster, Stonewood Grill SpringHill Suites $Tree, BJ's Whse/gas, CVS Drug, Jo-Ann Fabrics, Lowe's, Petsmart, Ross, Staples, USPO
266	Rd 582A, Fletcher Ave, W Shell/Circle K/dsl Baskin-Robbins/Dunkin Donuts, Bob Evans, Lenny's Subs, Starbucks, Wendy's Courtyard, Extended Stay America, Fairfield Inn, Hampton Inn, Hilton Garden, Holiday Inn Express, Residence Inn, Sleep Inn
265	FL 582, Fowler Ave, Temple Terrace, E flea mkt, Happy Traveler RV Park, W BP, Sunoco, Value/dsl IHOP, Marco's Pizza Ramada Inn to Busch Gardens, to USF
261	I-4, W to Tampa, E to Orlando
260b a	FL 574, to Mango, Tampa, E Chevron, Citgo/dsl, Shell/Circle K/Subway Baskin-Robbins/Dunkin Donuts, China Wok, Quiznos, Waffle House SweetBay Foods, Walgreens, W BP, Mobil Residence Inn, Sheraton, Staybridge Suites
257	FL 60, Brandon, E Chevron, Citgo/dsl, Mobil, Mobil/dsl, Shell/Circle K, Sunoco 5 Guys Burgers, Anthony's Pizza, Arby's, Boston Mkt, Brandon Ale House, Buca Italian, Buffalo Wild Wings, Burger King, Checkers, Cheddars, Cheescake Factory, Chick-fil-A, Chili's, ChuckECheese, Crispers, Denny's, DQ, Dunkin Donuts, Firehouse Subs, Grill Smith Grill, Jesse's Steaks, Jimmy John's, Kabuki Japanese, KFC, Kobe Japanese,

BRANDON

Exit #	Services
257	Continued Krispy Kreme, Little Caesars, LJ Silver, Longhorn Steaks, Macaroni Grill, McDonald's, McDonald's, Moe's SW Grill, Olive Garden, Outback Steaks, Panda Express, Panera Bread, Papa John's, Popeye's, Qdoba, Quiznos, Red Lobster, Salad Works, Smokey Bones BBQ, Smoothie King, Starbucks, Steak'n Shake, Steak'n Shake, Subway, Tia's TexMex, Tops China Buffet, Tres Amigos Mexican, Waffle House, Wendy's, Wing House Holiday Inn Express, HomeStead Suites, La Quinta $General, $Tree, Aamco, Advance Parts, AT&T, AutoZone, Barnes&Noble, Best Buy, Books-A-Million, Cadillac, Costco/gas, CVS Drug, Dick's, Dillard's, Family$, Fiat, Firestone/auto, JC Penney, Jo-Ann Fabrics, Kia, K-Mart, Kohl's, Kohl's, Lowe's, Macy's, mall, Marshall's, Michael's, Office Depot, PepBoys, PetCo, Petsmart, Petsmart, Publix, Publix, Radio Shack, Ross, Sam's Club/gas, Sears/auto, Staples, Target, Tires+, TJ Maxx, Tuffy Auto, U-Haul, URGENT CARE, Walgreens, Walmart, W Citgo/dsl, Marathon, Shell Beef O'Brady's, Bob Evans, Burger King, Hooters, McDonald's, Sonny's BBQ, Subway, Sweet Tomatoes, Wendy's Best Western, Comfort Suites, Country Inn&Suites, Courtyard, Embassy Suites, Fairfield Inn, Homewood Suites, La Quinta, Motel 6, Red Roof Inn, SpringHill Suites Buick/GMC, Chevrolet, Chrysler/Dodge/Jeep, Ford, Harley-Davidson, Home Depot, Honda, Hyundai, Mazda, Nissan, Office Depot, Toyota/Scion, VW
256	FL 618 W (**toll**), to Tampa
254	US 301, Riverview, E RaceTrac/dsl Panda Express, Steak'n Shake CVS Drug, Firestone, Home Depot, Target, W 7-11/dsl China 1, Crazy Cafe, McDonald's Hilton Garden Publix
250	Gibsonton Dr, Riverview, E RaceWay/dsl Beef'O'Brady's, Burger King, DQ, Hungry Howie's, Little Caesars, Lucky Buffet, McDonald's, Pizza Hut, Ruby Tuesday, Subway, Taco Bell, Wendy's $Tree, Alafia River RV Resort, Beall's, CVS Drug, Family$, Hidden River RV Resort (4mi), Lowe's, Save-a-Lot, USPO, Walgreens, Winn-Dixie, W Murphy USA/dsl Walmart/McDonald's
246	Rd 672, Big Bend Rd, Apollo Bch, E 7-11, Hess/Dunkin Donuts/Godfather's Pizza/Quiznos/dsl 5 Guys Burgers, Applebee's, Beef'O'Brady's, Buffalo Wild Wings, Burger King, China Taste, East Coast Pizza, Little Caesars, McDonald's, Panera Bread, Pita, Poppi's Pizza, Qdoba, Sakura Japanese, Sonic, Starbucks, Subway, Village Inn, Wendy's $Tree, Ace Hardware, Advance Parts, AT&T, AutoZone, Beall's, Firestone/auto, GNC, Goodyear/auto, Publix, Sam's Club/gas, Sweetbay Foods, Tire Choice, Tuffy Auto, URGENT CARE, Verizon, vet, Walgreens, W Shell/Dunkin Donuts/dsl
240b a	FL 674, Sun City Ctr, Ruskin, E Shell Beef'O'Brady's, Bob Evans, Burger King, Denny's, Hungry Howie's, Pizza Hut, Seafood Dive, Sonny's BBQ, Subway, Taco Bell, Wendy's Comfort Inn Beall's, GNC, Home Depot, Radio Shack, SunLake RV Resort (1mi), to Little Manatee River SP, W Circle K/dsl, Hess/dsl, RaceTrac/dsl China Wok, KFC, McDonald's Ruskin Inn auto repair, BigLots, NAPA
237mm	**both lanes, 24hr security, full facilities, litter barrels, petwalk vending**
229	Rd 683, Moccasin Wallow Rd, to Parrish, E Little Manatee Sprs SRA (10mi), W Circle K, Fiesta Grove RV Park (3mi), Frog Creek RV Park (3mi), Terra Ceia RV Village (2mi), Winterset RV Park (3mi)
228	I-275 N, to St Petersburg

INTERSTATE 75 Cont'd

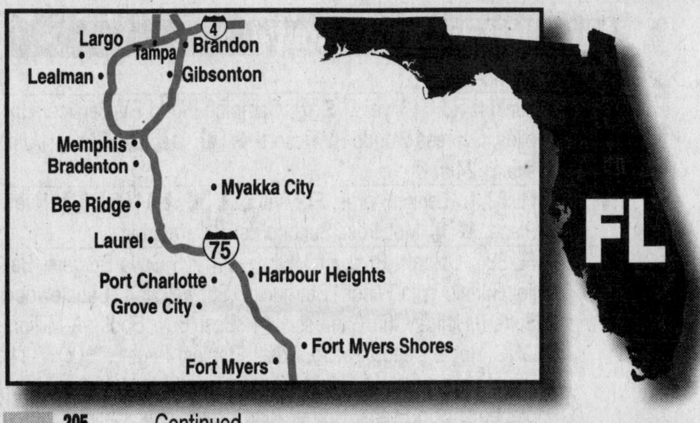

BRADENTON

Exit #	Services
224	US 301, to Bradenton, Ellenton, E gas Mobil, RaceWay/dsl, Shell/Circle K/dsl food Applebee's, Checkers, GioPizza, Hungry Howie's, Kings Wok, McDonald's, Peach's Rest., Ruby Tuesday, Subway, Wendy's, Woody's River Grill lodging Hampton Inn, Sleep Inn other $General, $Tree, Ace Hardware, Beall's, Ellenton Outlets/famous brands, GNC, Just Brakes, K-Mart, Publix, USPO, Walgreens, W gas Pilot/dsl food Anna Maria's, Crabtrap Seafood, Waffle House lodging GuestHouse Inn, Ramada Ltd
220b a	FL 64, to Zolfo Springs, Bradenton, E other Lake Manatee SRA, W gas BP/dsl, Citgo/dsl, RaceTrac/dsl, Shell/Circle K/dsl food Burger King, Cracker Barrel, D. Americo's Pizza, Dunkin Donuts, KFC/LJ Silver, McDonald's, Sonny's BBQ, Subway, Waffle House, Wendy's lodging Best Western, Comfort Inn, Days Inn, EconoLodge, Motel 6 other H Dream RV Ctr, Encore RV Resort (1mi), Harley-Davidson, Toyota/Scion, Walmart
217b a	FL 70, to Arcadia, E gas Hess/Godfather's/Quiznos/dsl food Burger King, Crispers lodging Wingate Inn other Goodyear/auto, Sweetbay Foods, Walmart/Subway, W gas 7-11/dsl, BP/Dunkin Donuts/dsl, Shell/Circle K food Applebee's, Arby's, Bangkok Tokyo, Bob Evans, Bogey's Rest., Chick-fil-A, Dawson's Rest, DQ, Hungry Howie's, LJ Silver/Taco Bell, McDonald's, Papa John's, Peppermill Eatery, Rice Bowl, Starbucks, Subway lodging Country Inn&Suites other $Tree, Beall's, CVS Drug, Lowe's, Pleasant Lake RV Resort, Publix, Tire Kingdom, Tires+, Tuffy Auto, Verizon, vet

SARASOTA

Exit #	Services
213	University Parkway, to Sarasota, E gas Mobil/dsl food Chili's, Monty's Pizza, Ms JC Garden, Pizza Hut, Quiznos lodging Fairfield Inn, Holiday Inn other H GNC, Publix, URGENT CARE, Walgreens, W food 5 Guys Burgers, Bellacino's, BoneFish Grill, Buffalo Wild Wings, Carrabba's, Chipotle Mexican, Jason's Deli, Jersey Mike's Subs, Jimmy John's, John Dough Cafe, Moe's SW Grill, Pei Wei, Red Elephant Grill, Ruby Tuesday, Selmon's Rest., Starbucks, Stonewood Grill, Sweet Tomatoes, Tijuana Flats, Wendy's lodging Comfort Suites, Hampton Inn other $Tree, Beall's, Best Buy, BJ's Whse/gas, CVS Drug, Fresh Mkt Foods, Home Depot, Jo-Ann Fabrics, Kohl's, Marshall's, Michael's, Old Navy, PetCo, Ross, SteinMart, Target, to Ringling Museum, Verizon
210	FL 780, Fruitville Rd, Sarasota, E other Sun-N-Fun RV Park (1mi), W gas BP/dsl/LP, Mobil/7-11/dsl, RaceTrac/dsl, Sav-On/dsl, Shell food Applebee's, Bob Evans, Burger King, Cafe Italia, Checkers, Chick-fil-A, Don Pablo's, Dunkin Donuts, Firehouse Subs, KFC, Longhorn Steaks, McDonald's, Peking Tokyo, Perkins, Starbucks, Subway, Super Buffet, Taco Bell, Trader Vic's Grill lodging AmericInn, Homewood Suites (2mi) other $Tree, Advance Parts, AT&T, CVS Drug, GNC, Lowe's, Office Depot, Publix, Radio Shack, Sam's Club, Target, Tire Kingdom, Tuffy Auto, Verizon, Winn-Dixie
207	FL 758, Sarasota, W gas BP/Subway/dsl, Marathon/Dunkin Donuts/Subway food Arby's, Cafe Amalfi, Chili's, Fortune Buffet, MadFish Grill, McDonald's, Panera Bread, Pizza Hut, Sarasota Alehouse, Starbucks, Steak'n Shake, Taco Bell lodging Hampton Inn other H, Beall's, Home Depot, Publix, Radio Shack, to Selby Botanical Gardens (8mi), Verizon, vet, Walgreens, Walmart
205	FL 72, to Arcadia, Sarasota, E other Myakka River SP (9mi), W gas BP/dsl, Mobil/7-11/dsl, Shell/Circle K food Applebee's, Burger King, Chick-fil-A, Dunkin Donuts, Gecko's Grill, Just Pizza, KFC, McDonald's, Quiznos, Starbucks, Subway, Waffle House, Wendy's, Wings&Weenies lodging Comfort Inn, Days Inn, Holiday Inn Express other Acura, AT&T, Beall's, BMW, CVS Drug,

VENICE

Exit #	Services
205	Continued Jaguar, Land Rover, Lexus, Lotus, Mercedes/Smart, Publix, Tire Kingdom, Turtle Beach Camping (8mi), UPSO, vet, Walgreens, Windward Isle RV Park
200	FL 681 S (from sb), to Venice, Osprey, Gulf Bchs
195	Laurel Rd, Nokomis, E gas BP/USPO/dsl food Subway other CVS Drug, W other Encore RV Park (2mi), Scherer SP (6mi)
193	Jaracanda Blvd, Venice, W gas Hess/Godfather's/Quiznos/dsl, RaceTrac/dsl food BrewBurgers, Cracker Barrel, McDonald's, Ping's Chinese lodging Best Western, Fairfield Inn, Holiday Inn Express other H CVS Drug, Publix, Verizon
191	Rd 777, Venice Rd, to Englewood, W other Encore RV Park (3mi), KOA (6mi), to Myakka SF (9mi)
182	Rd 771, Sumter Blvd, to North Port
179	Rd 779, Toledo Blade Blvd, North Port, **1-2 mi** W gas Mobil/Subway/dsl, Shell/Burger King other H Publix
170	Rd 769, to Arcadia, Port Charlotte, E gas 7-11/dsl, Murphy USA/dsl, RaceTrac/dsl food Applebee's lodging Hampton Inn, Holiday Inn Express other Lettuce Lake Camping (7mi), Riverside Camping (5mi), Walmart, W gas Hess/dsl, Mobil/Circle K/DQ/dsl, Shell/Circle K/Dunkin Donuts food Burger King, Cracker Barrel, Domino's, DQ, McDonald's, Peach Garden, Quiznos, Starbucks, Subway, Taco Bell, Top China, Waffle House, Wendy's lodging Country Inn&Suites, La Quinta, Sleep Inn other H $General, $Tree, Ace Hardware, Advance Parts, Beall's, Curves, CVS Drug, Publix, USPO, vet, Walgreens, Winn-Dixie

PUNTA GORDA

Exit #	Services
167	Rd 776, Port Charlotte
164	US 17, Punta Gorda, Arcadia, E gas Chevron/7-11/dsl, RaceWay/dsl, Shell/Circle K/dsl food King House Chinese, RV camping, Subway, vet other $General, Winn-Dixie, W food Fisherman's Village Rest. (2mi) other H
161	Rd 768, Punta Gorda, E other rest stop **both lanes, 24hr security, full facilities, litter barrels, petwalk** (phone) (vending), W gas BP/DQ/Subway, Murphy USA/dsl, Pilot/Arby's/dsl/scales/24hr, Sunoco/dsl food Burger King, McDonald's, Pizza Hut, Waffle House, Wendy's lodging Best Value Inn, Knights Inn other Encore RV Park (2mi), Walmart
160mm	**weigh sta both lanes**
158	Rd 762, Tropical Gulf Acres, Tuckers Grade, E other Babcock-Wells Wildlife Mgt Area
143	FL 78, to Cape Coral, N Ft Myers, E gas Marathon/dsl other Seminole Camping (1mi), Up the River Camping, W lodging Encore RV Camping
141	FL 80, Palm Bch Blvd, Ft Myers, E gas Marathon, Sunoco/dsl food Cracker Barrel, Waffle House lodging Comfort Inn, ValuePlace, W gas 7-11, Hess/Dunkin Donuts/dsl, Mobil food Domino's, Hardee's, KFC, Papa John's, Popeye's, Sonny's BBQ, Subway, Taco Bell other $General, BigLots, CVS Drug, North Trail RV Ctr, Radio Shack, Save-A-Lot, USPO, vet

FL

INTERSTATE 75 Cont'd

FT MYERS / CAPE CORAL / ESTERO

Exit #	Services
139	Luckett Rd, Ft Myers, E Camping World RV Service/supplies, Cypress Woods RV Resort, W Pilot/Subway/dsl/scales/24hr/ @
138	FL 82, to Lehigh Acres, Ft Myers, E 7-11/dsl Hyatt Place, W Mobil/dsl, Sunoco/dsl Peterbilt
136	FL 884, Colonial Blvd, Ft Myers, E 5 Guys Burgers, Bajio, Buffalo Wild Wings, Starbucks, Subway Candlewood Suites, Holiday Inn Express Best Buy, Books-A-Million, GNC, Home Depot, PetCo, Ross, Staples, Target, W 7-11, BP, Marathon/dsl, Murphy USA/dsl, Shell/Circle K/dsl Applebee's, Bob Evans, Burger King, Chick-fil-A, Chili's, Golden Corral, LJ Silver/Taco Bell, McDonald's, Panda Express, Steak'n Shake, Subway, TX Roadhouse ValuePlace H $Tree, AT&T, Beall's, BJ's Whse/gas, Hobby Lobby, Kohl's, Lowe's, Petsmart, Publix, Tire Choice/auto, Verizon, Walmart/McDonald's
131	Rd 876, Daniels Pkwy, to Cape Coral, E **both lanes, 24hr security, full facilities, litter barrels, petwalk** BP/Dunkin Donuts/Subway/dsl, RaceTrac/dsl Cracker Barrel, Fat Katz Comfort Inn, Floridian Inn, Grand Stay CVS Drug, Porsche, W 7-11, Hess/Dunkin Donuts/dsl, RaceWay/dsl, Shell/Circle K/dsl Arby's, Beef'O'Brady's, Burger King, Denny's, DQ, Mac Daddy's, McDonald's, New China, Papa John's, Rib City, Sports Page Grill, Subway, Taco Bell, Waffle House, Wendy's Baymont Inn, Best Western, Hampton Inn, La Quinta, Quality Inn, SpringHill Suites, Travelodge H, CVS Drug, Dream RV Ctr, Publix, Tire Choice/auto, Tuffy Auto, Walgreens
128	Alico Rd, San Carlos Park, E 7-11 Aurelio's Pizza, Bar Louie, Carrabba's, Chick-fil-A, Connor's Steaks, Elevation Burger, Famous Dave's BBQ, Longhorn Steaks, McDonald's, Miller's Alehouse, Moe's SW Grill, Olive Garden, Outback Steaks, Pincher's Crabshack, Pita Pit, Red Robin Courtyard, Hilton Garden, Holiday Inn, Homewood Suites, Residence Inn $Tree, AT&T, Bass Pro Shop/Islamorada Fish Co, Belk, Best Buy, Costco/gas, Dick's, GNC, JC Penney, Jo-Ann Fabrics, Marshall's, PetCo, Ross, Staples, Target, Verizon, W 7-11/dsl, Hess/Dunkin Donuts/dsl
123	Rd 850, Corkscrew Rd, Estero, E BP/Dunkin Donuts/dsl, Chevron/7-11/dsl Beef'O'Brady's, China Gourmet, Marsala's Italian, McDonald's, Naples Flat Bread, Perkins, Subway CVS Drug, Johnson Tire/auto, Miramar Outlet/famous brands, Publix, W 7-11, Hess/Dunkin Donuts/dsl, Shell/Blimpie/dsl Applebee's, Arby's, Rib City, Ruby Tuesday, Subway Embassy Suites, Hampton Inn Chevrolet, Koreshan SHS (2mi), Lowe's, Tire Choice/auto, Woodsmoke RV Park (4mi)
116	Bonita Bch Rd, Bonita Springs, E Mobil, Valero/7-11/dsl Subway Advance Parts, AT&T, Publix, Tire Choice/auto, W Chevron/dsl, Hess/Dunkin Donuts/dsl, Shell/McDonald's Waffle House Best Western CVS Drug, Home Depot, Imperial Bonita RV Park, Tire Kingdom, to Lovers Key SP (11mi), Walgreens
111	Rd 846, Immokalee Rd, Naples Park, E 7-11, Mobil/dsl Bob Evans, Burger King, Chili's, L'Appetite Pizza, Panera Bread Hampton Inn Staples, Target, World Mkt, W Shell/Circle K/dsl Bella's Pizza, Subway H Publix, to Delnor-Wiggins SP, Verizon, Walmart/McDonald's
107	Rd 896, Pinebridge Rd, Naples, E BP/McDonald's/dsl China Garden, Giovanni Ristorante, Starbucks, Subway H Publix, vet, Walgreens, W Chevron/dsl, RaceTrac/dsl, Shell/

NAPLES

Exit #	Services
107	Continued Circle K/dsl 5 Guys Burgers, Burger King, Hooters, IHOP, Perkins, Senor Tequilas, Sophia's Rest., Starbucks, Waffle House Best Western, Hawthorn Suites, Spinnaker Inn Harley-Davidson, Johnson Tire/auto, Nissan, Tire Choice/auto, vet
105	Rd 886, to Golden Gate Pkwy, Golden Gate, E Subway CVS Drug, W to , zoo
101	Rd 951, to FL 84, to Naples, E BP/Subway/pizza Fairfield Inn, SpringHill Suites H W BP/dsl, Circle K, Mobil/dsl, Shell/dsl BBQ Place, Cracker Barrel, McDonald's, Subway, Taco Bell, Waffle House Comfort Inn, Days Inn, La Quinta, Super 8 $Tree, AT&T, Club Naples RV Ctr, Endless Summer RV Park (3mi), KOA
100mm	**toll plaza eb**
80	FL 29, to Everglade City, Immokalee, W Big Cypress NR, Everglades NP, Smallwoods Store
71mm	Big Cypress Nat Preserve, hiking, no security
63mm	W **both lanes, 24hr security, full facilities, litter barrels, petwalk**
49	Rd 833, Snake Rd, Big Cypress Indian Reservation, E Miccosukee Service Plaza/deli/dsl museum, swamp safari
41mm	**litter barrels, picnic tables, rec area eb**
38mm	**litter barrels, picnic tables, rec area wb**
35mm	W **/rec area both lanes, 24hr security, full facilities, litter barrels, petwalk**
32mm	**litter barrels, picnic tables, rec area both lanes**
25mm	motorist callboxes begin/end, **toll plaza wb**
23	US 27, FL 25, , Miami, South Bay
22	FL 84 W, NW 196th, Glades Pkwy, W Publix, same as 21
21	FL 84 W (from nb), Indian Trace, W BP/dsl Las Rikuras, Papa John's, Spain's Cuisine $Days
19	I-595 E, FL 869 (**toll**), Sawgrass Expswy
15	Royal Palm Blvd,, Weston, Bonaventure, W Chevron, Mobil Carolina Ale House, El Mariachi, Flanigan's Rest, Il Toscano Rest., La Granja, Lucille's Cafe, Offerdahl's Grill, Pollo Tropical, Sir Pizza, Wendy's Comfort Suites, Courtyard, Residence Inn H Meineke, Tires+, USPO
13b a	Griffin Rd, E Shell/dsl Burger King, Donato's Rest., DQ, Outback Steaks, Subway, Waffle House Goodyear/auto, Publix, vet, W 7-11/dsl, Tom Thumb/dsl Anthony's Pizza, Bone Fish Grill, Chick-fil-A, Chili's, Coldstone, Domino's, Dunkin Donuts, HoneyBaked Ham, Jimmy John's, McDonald's, Panera Bread, Pei Wei, Pizza Heaven, Starbucks, Weston Diner AT&T, Fiat, Home Depot, Honda, Hyundai, Nissan/Volvo, Office Depot, Publix, Radio Shack, Toyota/Scion, vet, Walgreens
11b a	Sheridan St, E Chevron Cracker Barrel, Wendy's Hampton Inn, Holiday Inn Express Audi, BMW, H (3mi), Piccolo Park, W Shell/dsl Applebee's, Bistro 555, China One, Coldstone, Little Caesars, McDonald's, Original Pancake House, Romeus Cuban, Subway, TGIFriday's Firestone/auto, GNC, Lowe's, Publix, URGENT CARE, Verizon, vet, Walgreens
9b a	FL 820, Pine Blvd, Hollywood Blvd, E BP, Shell Boston Mkt, Brimstone Woodfire Grill, Brio Italian, Cheesecake Factory, Chick-fil-A, Chili's, Fuddrucker's, HoneyBaked Ham, Jason's Deli, La Granja, Latin-American Grill, Lime Mexican Grill, Macaroni Grill, McDonald's, RA Grill, Sal's Italian, Starbucks, Stir Crazy, Subway, The Pub, Tijuana Flats, Village Tavern, Wendys H Barnes&Noble, BJ's Whse/gas, Dick's, Dodge, Mercedes, Old Navy, Petsmart, Publix, Radio Shack, USPO, Verizon, Walgreens, Walmart, W BP/dsl, Citgo/dsl, Shell Burger

INTERSTATE 75 Cont'd

9b a	Continued King, Chick-fil-A, Chipotle Mexican, Elevation Burger, KFC/Taco Bell, La Granja, Las Vegas Cuban, Marco's Pizza, McDonald's, Panda Express, Sal's Italian, SmashBurger, Starbucks, Sweet Tomatoes, Wendy's Acura, Advance Parts, AT&T, AutoZone, Costco/gas, CVS Drug, GNC, Lexus, Publix, Sedano's Foods, Subaru, Tires+, Walgreens, Whole Foods Mkt
7b a	Miramar Pkwy, E Chevron Baskin-Robbins/Dunkin Donuts, Cancun Grill, La Carreta, McDonald's, Pollo Tropical, Quiznos, Sal's Italian, Starbucks, Subway, Tijuana Flats, Wendy's Courtyard, Hilton Garden, Residence Inn, Wingate Inn $Tree, Publix, USPO, Walgreens, W Shell Benihana, Chick-fil-A, Chili's, Coldstone, McDonald's, Orient Chef, Panera Bread, Starbucks, Subway, Yummy Asian H AT&T, city park, CVS Drug, Home Depot, Marshall's, Office Depot, Ross, SuperTarget, Winn-Dixie
5	to FL 821 (from sb), FL TPK (toll)
4	FL 860, NW 186th, Miami Gardens Dr, E BP, Chevron Carrabba's, Chicken Kitchen, Dunkin Donuts, McDonald's, Starbucks, Subway AT&T, CVS Drug, GNC, Publix/deli, Sedanos Foods, vet
2	NW 138th, Graham Dairy Rd, W Mobil, Shell/dsl China Casa, China Wok, IHOP, Latin Cuban Cafe, Little Caesars, McDonald's, Starbucks, Subway, Wendy's H GNC, Publix, vet, Walgreens
1b a	**I-75 begins/ends on FL 826, Palmetto Expswy, multiple services on FL 826.**

MIAMI

INTERSTATE 95

Exit #	Services
382mm	Florida/Georgia state line, St Marys River, motorist callboxes begin/end.
381mm	**inspection sta both lanes**
380	US 17, to Yulee, Kingsland, E Osprey RV Park, W Shell American Inn
378mm	**Welcome Ctr sb full facilities, info, litter barrels, petwalk vending**
376mm	**weigh sta both lanes**
373	FL 200, FL A1A, to Yulee, Callahan , Fernandina Bch, E Flash/Krystal, Sunoco Burger King, DQ, KFC/Pizza Hut, McDonald's, Wendy's Comfort Inn, Holiday Inn Express, Nassau Holiday Motel (3mi) RV Camping (3mi), to Ft Clinch SP (16mi), W BP/Subway/dsl, Exxon/dsl
366	Pecan Park Rd, W Flea&Farmer's Mkt, Pecan Park RV Camping
363b a	Duval Rd, E Mobil/7-11 5 Guys Burgers, Arby's, Boston's, Buffalo Wild Wings, Buffalo's Philly, Chick-fil-A, Chili's, Coldstone, Cracker Barrel, Green Papaya, Hardee's, Jimmy John's, Logan's Roadhouse, McDonald's, Olive Garden, Panda Express, Panera Bread, Pollo Tropical, Red Lobster, Salsaritas, Starbucks, Sticky Fingers, Subway, Taco Bell, Wasabi A Loft $Tree, AT&T, AutoZone, Best Buy, Dick's, Discount Tire, Gander Mtn, GNC, Goodyear/auto, Lowe's, Marshall's, Michael's, Old Navy, Petsmart, Ross, URGENT CARE, Verizon, Walgreens, Walmart/Subway, W BP/dsl, Chevron, Exxon/dsl, Sunoco/Subway Denny's, Longhorn Steaks, Millhouse Steaks, Ruby Tuesday, Waffle House, Zaxby's Inn, Best Western, Comfort Suites, Country Hearth Inn, Courtyard, Crowne Plaza, Fairfield Inn, Hampton Inn, Hilton Garden, Hyatt

JACKSONVILLE

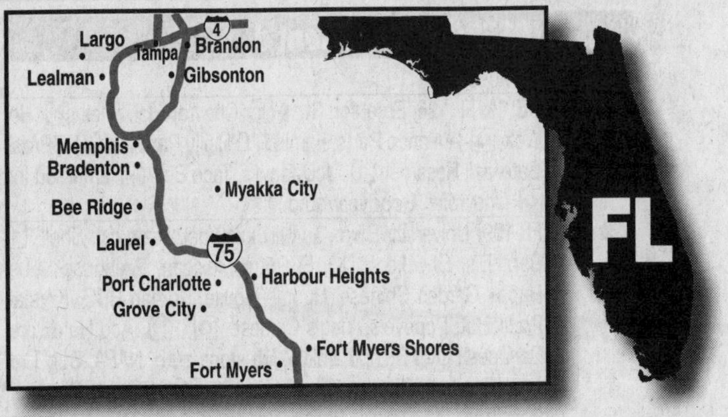

363b a	Continued Place, Jacksonville Plaza Hotel, Jaxport Inn, Microtel, Quality Inn, Red Roof Inn, Residence Inn, SpringHill Suites, Travelodge, Wingate Inn , Gore's RV Ctr
362b a	I-295 S, FL 9A, to Blount Island, Jacksonville
360	FL 104, Dunn Ave, Busch Dr, E Gate/dsl Hardee's, Waffle House Executive Inn Sam's Club/gas, USPO, W BP/dsl, Chevron, Hess, RaceTrac/dsl, Shell/dsl Arby's, Burger King, Capt D's, Checker's, China Buffet, Country Cabin Rest., Firehouse Subs, KFC, Krystal, Little Caesars, McDonald's, New China, Pizza Hut, Popeye's, Sonny's BBQ, Starbucks, Subway, Taco Bell, Wendy's EconoLodge, La Quinta, Motel 6 $Tree, Aamco, Advance Parts, BigLots, CVS Drug, Family$, Marshall's, Office Depot, PepBoys, Publix, Radio Shack, Tires+, Walgreens
358b a	FL 105, Broward Rd, Heckscher Dr, E zoo, W BP/dsl USA Inn
357mm	Trout River
357	FL 111, Edgewood Ave, W BP/dsl, Texaco/dsl
356b a	Fl 115, FL 117, Lem Turner Rd, Norwood Ave, E Hardee's, W BP/dsl, Hess/Dunkin Donuts, RaceWay/dsl, Shell Burger King, Checker's, Golden EggRoll, Ho-Ho Chinese, Krystal, Popeye's, Subway, Taco Bell Advance Parts, Save-A-Lot, Tires+, Walgreens
355	Golfair Blvd, E Shell McDonald's Publix, W Chevron/dsl, RaceWay/dsl
354b a	US 1, 20th St, to Jacksonville, to AmTrak, MLK Pkwy
353d	FL 114, to 8th St, E McDonald's H Walgreens
353c	US 23 N, Kings Rd, downtown
353b	US 90A, Union St, Sports Complex, downtown
353a	Church St, Myrtle Ave, Forsythe St, downtown
352d	I-10 W, Stockton St (from sb), Lake City
352c	Monroe St (from nb), downtown
352b a	Myrtle Ave (from nb), downtown
351d	Stockton St, H downtown
351c	Margaret St, downtown
351b	I-10 W, to Tallahassee
351a	Park St, College St, H to downtown
351mm	St Johns River
350b	FL 13, San Marco Blvd, E H
350a	Prudential Dr, Main St, Riverside Ave (from nb), to downtown, E BP Extended Stay America, Hampton Inn, Wyndham, W Panera Bread Hilton Garden
349	US 90 E (from sb), to beaches, W Super 8, downtown
348	US 1 S (from sb), Philips Hwy, W Scottish Inn, Super 8 Volvo

FL

📗 = gas 🍴 = food 🛏 = lodging ⊙ = other 🆁🆂 = rest stop Copyright 2016 - The Next EXIT®

J A C K S O N V I L L E

⬆N INTERSTATE 95 Cont'd

Exit #	Services
347	US 1A, FL 126, Emerson St, **E** 📗 Chevron/dsl, Shell 🍴 Hot Wok ⊙ Advance Parts, Family$, O'Reilly Parts, **W** 📗 BP/dsl, Gate/dsl, Hess/dsl 🍴 McDonald's, Taco Bell 🛏 Emerson Inn ⊙ Chevrolet, Goodyear/auto
346b a	FL 109, University Blvd, **E** 📗 Exxon/dsl, Hess/dsl, Shell 🍴 Capt D's, Checkers, DQ, El Potro Mexican, Firehouse Subs, Happy Garden Chinese, Huddle House, Korean BBQ, Krystal, Pizza Hut, Popeye's, Ying's Chinese ⊙ Ⓗ Ace Hardware, CarQuest, CVS Drug, Family$, Firestone/auto, NAPA, Sun Tire, Tire Kingdom, Tires+, Winn-Dixie, **W** 📗 BP/dsl, Chevron, RaceTrac 🍴 Arby's, Baskin-Robbins/Dunkin Donuts, Burger King, Famous Amos, KFC, McDonald's, Papa John's, Sonny's BBQ, Taco Bell, Wendy's, Whataburger, Woody's BBQ 🛏 Days Inn, Ramada Inn, Super 8 ⊙ auto repair, Family$, U-Haul
345	FL 109, University Blvd (from nb), **E** 📗 Chevron, Gate/dsl/24hr, Hess/Blimpie/Godfather's Pizza/dsl 🍴 Bono's BBQ, Schnitzel House ⊙ Ⓗ
344	FL 202, Butler Blvd, **E** 📗 Gate/dsl 🍴 Dave&Buster's 🛏 Best Western, Candlewood Suites, EconoLodge, Holiday Inn Express, Homestead Suites, Howard Johnson, Marriott, Radisson ⊙ Ⓗ USPO, **W** 📗 BP/dsl, Shell 🍴 Applebee's, Baskin-Robbins/Dunkin Donuts, Chick-fil-A, Cracker Barrel, Hardee's, McDonald's, Quiznos, Sonic, Starbucks, Waffle House, Wendy's, Whataburger/24hr, Zaxby's 🛏 Courtyard, Extended Stay Deluxe, Fairfield Inn, Jameson Inn, La Quinta, Microtel, Red Roof Inn, Wingate Inn
341	FL 152, Baymeadows Rd, **E** 📗 BP/dsl, Gate/dsl, Shell/dsl 🍴 Arby's, Chili's, CiCi's Pizza, Hardee's, Krystal, Omaha Steaks, Panda Express, Quiznos, Subway 🛏 Bay Meadows Inn, Comfort Suites, Embassy Suites, Holiday Inn, HomeStead Suites ⊙ Advance Parts, Tires+, Walgreens, Winn-Dixie, **W** 📗 Kangaroo, Shell 🍴 Al's Pizza, Bamboo Creek, Chicago Pizzaria, Denny's, Gator's Seafood, IHOP, KFC, Larry's Subs, Little Caesars, McDonald's, Pagoda Chinese, Red Lobster, Taco Bell, Wendy's, Woody's BBQ 🛏 Best Inn, Homewood Suites, La Quinta, Motel 6, Quality Inn, Residence Inn, Sheraton, Studio 6, Sun Suites ⊙ $Tree, BJ's Whse/gas, CVS Drug, Discount Tire, Goodyear/auto, Harley-Davidson, Lowe's, Office Depot
340	FL 115, Southside Blvd (from nb), **E** on FL 115 📗 Kangaroo/dsl 🍴 5 Guys Burgers, Longhorn Steaks ⊙ AT&T, Home Depot, Michael's, Petsmart, same as 339, Target
339	US 1, Philips Hwy, **E** 📗 Kangaroo/dsl, RaceTrac 🍴 Arby's, Bono's BBQ, Buca Italian, Burger King, Chick-fil-A, Coldstone, McDonald's, Mikado, Moe's SW Grill, Olive Garden, Ruby Tuesday, Starbucks, Taco Bell ⊙ $Tree, Belk, Best Buy, Chevrolet, Dillard's, Ford, JC Penney, mall, Mazda, Nissan, Sears/auto, Tire Kingdom, Toyota, Walmart, **W** 📗 BP/dsl 🍴 Benito's Italian, Steak&Subway
337	I-295 N, to rd 9a, Orange Park, Jax Beaches
335	Old St Augustine Rd, **E** 🍴 Applebee's, Starbucks 🛏 Courtyard ⊙ Ⓗ **W** 📗 Gate/dsl, Shell 🍴 5 Guys Burgers, Bamboo Wok, Bono's BBQ, Chili's, Daruma Steaks, McDonald's, Panera Bread, Subway, Tijuana Flats, Zaxby's 🛏 Hampton Inn ⊙ AT&T, GNC, Goodyear/auto, Kohl's, Publix, Verizon, vet, Walgreens
331mm	🆁🆂 both lanes, 24hr security, full ♿ facilities, litter barrels, petwalk 🅲 ♻ vending
329	Rd 210, Green Cove Springs, Ponte Vedra Beach, **E** 📗 🍴/McDonald's/dsl/scales/24hr, Sunoco/fruit, TA/Shell/Subway/dsl/scales/24hr/@ 🍴 Waffle House, **W** 📗 BP/Sub

S T A U G U S T I N E

P A L M C O A S T

Exit #	Services
329	Continued
	way/dsl/USPO, Marathon/Kangaroo/dsl, Shell 🍴 Burger Kin, China Wok, Domino's, Dunkin Donuts, Firehouse Subs, Jenk Pizza, Starbucks, Tropical Smoothie, Yummy Asian ⊙ AT& CVS Drug, fireworks, vet, Winn-Dixie
323	International Golf Pkwy, **E** 📗 BP/dsl/USPO, Shell/Subway/d 🛏 Comfort Suites, **W** 🍴 Cino's Pizza, King Wok, Village Gril Subs 🛏 Renaissance Resort ⊙ vet, World Golf Village
318	FL 16, Green Cove Sprgs, St Augustine, **E** 📗 BP/DQ/dsl, Gat dsl/fruit, Kangaroo/dsl, Shell 🍴 Burger King, Dunkin Donut Krystal, McDonald's, NY Diner, Subway 🛏 Best Value In Comfort Inn, Courtyard, Fairfield Inn, Holiday Inn Express, L Quinta, Quality Inn ⊙ Cadillac, Camping World RV Ctr, For Lincoln, Gander Mtn, Gore's RV Ctr, St Augustine Outlets/Fa mous Brands, **W** 📗 Exxon, RaceTrac/dsl 🍴 A-1 Chines Cracker Barrel, Denny's, Giovanni's Italian, IHOP, KFC, Lemon Grass Asian, Ruby Tuesday, Sonny's BBQ, Taco Bell, Wendy 🛏 Best Western, Days Inn, Hampton Inn, Ramada Ltd, Sup 8, Wingate Inn ⊙ funpark, RV camping, St Augustine Outlet Verizon
311	FL 207, St Augustine, **E** 📗 Chevron, Hess/Subway/dsl, Rac Trac/dsl ⊙ Ⓗ flea mkt/fireworks, Indian Forest RV Park (2m Indian River Fruit, KOA (7mi), St Johns RV Park, to Anastasia S **W** 📗 Mobil/dsl/repair 🛏 Quality Inn
305	FL 206, to Hastings, Crescent Beach, **E** 📗 ✈FLYING J/Den ny's/Subway/dsl/LP/scales/24hr ⊙ to Ft Matanzas NM, truc repair, **W** ⊙ truck repair
302mm	🆁🆂 both lanes, 24hr security, full ♿ facilities, litter barrel petwalk 🅲 ♻
298	US 1, to St Augustine, **E** 📗 BP/dsl, Indian River Fruit, Sunoc ⊙ to Faver-Dykes SP, **W** 📗 Mobil/DQ/dsl, Sunrise/dsl
289	to FL A1A (toll br), to Palm Coast, **E** 📗 Kangaroo/dsl, Mo bil/7-11, RaceTrac/dsl, Shell 🍴 China Express, Colletti Italian, Cracker Barrel, Denny's, Dunkin Donuts, Grand Ch na, KFC, McDonald's, Salsa's Mexican, Starbucks, Wendy 🛏 Best Western, Fairfield Inn, Microtel, Sleep Inn ⊙ Beall' CVS Drug, Publix, Staples, vet, Walgreens, **W** 📗 Chevro Citgo, Kangaroo/dsl, Shell 🍴 Baskin-Robbins/Dunkin Donut Bob Evans, Brusters, China King, China One, Golden Corra HoneyBaked Ham, Houligan's, Joe's NY Pizza, Nathan's Caf Outback Steaks, Perkins, Ruby Tuesday, Sakura Japanes Sonny's BBQ, Steak'n Shake, Subway, Taco Bell, Wendy's 🛏 Days Inn ⊙ $General, Advance Parts, AutoZone, Beall's, Bel CVS Drug, Ford, Home Depot, Kohl's, Lowe's, Publix, Rad Shack, Tire Kingdom, Tuffy Auto, USPO, Verizon, Walgreen Walmart, Winn-Dixie
286mm	weigh sta both lanes, 🅲
284	FL 100, to Bunnell, Flagler Beach, **E** 📗 Mobil/dsl, Valero/d 🍴 Burger King, Domino's, McDonald's, Oriental Garden, Sub way, Woody's BBQ 🛏 Hampton Inn, Holiday Inn Express ⊙ Ace Hardware, Curves, Russell Stover's, vet, Winn-Dixie, **W** 📗 BP 🛏 Hilton Garden ⊙ Ⓗ Chevrolet, Chrysler/Dodge/Jee Dunkin Donuts, Panera Bread, Red Lobster
278	Old Dixie Hwy, **E** 📗 7-11 🍴 King Chinese, Plantation Grill ⊙ Bulow RV Park (3mi), Publix, to Tomoka SP, **W** 📗 BP/dsl 🍴 Joe's Pizza 🛏 Country Hearth Inn ⊙ Holiday Travel Park, ve
273	US 1, **E** 📗 Chevron, RaceTrac/dsl 🍴 McDonald's, Waff House 🛏 Econo Inn, La Quinta ⊙ fruit/fireworks, Gia Rec RV Ctr, **W** 📗 Exxon/Burger King, ♥Love's/Arby dsl/scales/24hr 🍴 Daytona Pig Stand BBQ, DQ, Houligan

FL

INTERSTATE 95 Cont'd

ORMOND BEACH

273 Continued
Days Inn, Daytona Hotel, Motel 6, Scottish Inn, Super 8
Encore RV Park, Harley-Davidson

268 FL 40, Ormond Beach, E Chevron/dsl, Hess/dsl Applebee's, Boston Mkt, Chick-fil-A, Chili's, Crispers, Denny's, Dustin's BBQ, Houligan's, Mama Mia's Pizza, Papa John's, Starbucks, Steak'n Shake, Subway, Taco Bell, Takeya Steaks, The Dish, Wendy's, Wok&Roll Sleep Inn H $General, $Tree, AT&T, Beall's, Discount Tire, GNC, Lowe's, Publix, Ross, Tire Kingdom, to Tomoka SP, USPO, vet, Walmart, Whole Foods Mkt, W 7-11, BP/Dunkin Donuts, Mobil/dsl, RaceTrac/dsl, Texaco Cracker Barrel, Little Italy, McDonald's, Salsa's Mexican Hampton Inn, Jameson Inn Walgreens

265 LPGA Blvd, Holly Hill, Daytona Beach, E 7-11, Shell/Circle K/Dunkin Donuts/dsl Vince Carter Rest, Wendy's CVS Drug, W Holiday Inn BMW, Chrysler/Dodge/Jeep, Fiat, Ford, Lincoln, Mazda, Nissan, VW

DAYTONA

261b a US 92, to DeLand, Daytona Bch, E 7-11, Citgo/dsl, Hess/Quiznos/Dunkin Donuts/dsl, RaceTrac, RaceWay/dsl, Sunoco 5 Guys Burgers, Applebee's, Asian Grill, BJ's Rest., Bob Evans, Buffalo Wild Wings, Burger King, Carrabba's, Checkers, Chick-fil-A, Chili's, Chipotle Mexican, Cracker Barrel, Daytona Ale House, Denny's, Dickey's BBQ, Firehouse Subs, Gators, Hooters, Jersey Mike's Subs, Jimmy John's, KFC, Krystal, Longhorn Steaks, McDonald's, Olive Garden, Outback Steaks, Panera Bread, Piccadilly, Quiznos, Red Lobster, Ruby Tuesday, Subway, Taco Bell, Tijuana Flats, Waffle House, Wendy's, Winghouse Comfort Suites, Hampton Inn, Hilton Garden, Holiday Inn Express, Homewood Suites, La Quinta, Quality Inn, Ramada Inn, Residence Inn H, $Tree, AT&T, Barnes&Noble, Beall's, Best Buy, BigLots, Books-A-Million, Dick's, Dillard's, Firestone/auto, Hobby Lobby, Home Depot, JC Penney, Jo-Ann Fabrics, K-Mart, Macy's, mall, Marshall's, Michael's, Old Navy, PepBoys, PetCo, Petsmart, Sears/auto, Staples, SteinMart, Target, TJMaxx, to Daytona Racetrack, Tuesday Morning, Verizon, World Mkt, W BP/dsl IHOP, McDonald's Days Inn, Super 8 flea mkt, KOA

260b a I-4, to Orlando, FL 400 E, to S Daytona, E Chevron/dsl, Citgo/7-11

256 FL 421, to Port Orange, E BP, Shell/Circle K Applebee's, Bob Evans, Boston Mkt, Burger King, Chick-fil-A, Chili's, Daily Grind Burgers, Denny's, Dustin's BBQ, Golden Corral, KFC, Marble Slab Creamery, McDonald's, Monterrey Grill, Panera Bread, Papa John's, Quiznos, Smoothie King, Sonny's BBQ, Stonewood Grill, TGIFriday's, Tijuana Flats Country Inn&Suites, La Quinta BigLots, CVS Drug, Daytona Beach RV Park, Home Depot, Lowe's, Save-a-Lot, Super Target, Tuffy Auto, vet, Walgreens, Walmart, W 7-11, BP, Citgo 5 Guys Burgers, China Chef, Coldstone, Gatti's Pizza, Malibu Beach Grill, McDonald's, Olive Garden, Red Brick Pizza, Red Robin, Subway, Takara Steaks, TX Roadhouse, Wendy's $Tree, AT&T, Belk, GNC, Kohl's, Marshall's, Michael's, PetCo, Publix, Walgreens, Whole Foods Mkt

249b a FL 44, to De Land, New Smyrna Beach, E Shell/dsl/fruit New Smyrna RV Camp (3mi), W Chevron/dsl McDonald's Walmart/Subway

244 FL 442, to Edgewater, E BP/dsl truck repair

231 Rd 5A, Scottsmoor, E BP/Stuckey's/dsl Crystal Lake RV Park

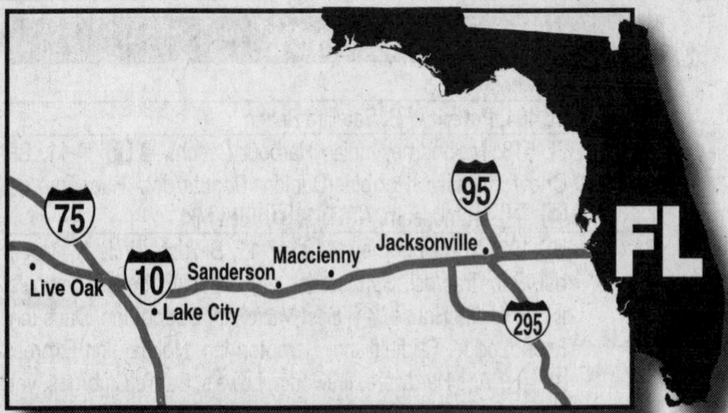

227mm sb, 24hr security, full facilities, litter barrels, petwalk

225mm bn, 24hr security, full facilities, litter barrels, petwalk

TITUSVILLE

223 FL 46, Mims, E Chevron (2mi), RaceWay/dsl McDonald's, W BP, Shell KOA/LP, Seasons RV Park

220 FL 406, Titusville, E BP/dsl, Shell/Hungry Howie's/dsl 1st Wok, Beef'O'Brady's, Kelsey's Pizza, McDonald's, Subway, Valentino's Rest, Wendy's Super 8 H, $General, Advance Parts, AT&T, GNC, Publix, Tires+, to Canaveral Nat Seashore, Walgreens

215 FL 50, to Orlando, Titusville, E BP/KFC/dsl, Circle K, Mobil/Subway/dsl, Murphy USA/dsl, Shell/DQ/dsl Buddy Freddy's, Burger King, Denny's, Durango Steaks, McDonald's, Panda Express, Quiznos, Sonny's BBQ, Taco Bell, Waffle House, Wendy's Best Western, Ramada Inn Aldi Foods, Ford, GNC, Home Depot, Lowe's, Marshall's, PetCo, Radio Shack, Staples, Target, Tire Kingdom, to Kennedy Space Ctr, Walmart, W Cracker Barrel, IHOP Days Inn, Fairfield Inn, Hampton Inn, Holiday Inn, Quality Inn Christmas RV Park (8mi), Great Outdoors RV/golf Resort

212 FL 407, to FL 528 toll (no re-entry sb)

208 Port St John

205 FL 528 (**toll** 528), to Cape Canaveral & Cape Port AFS, City Point

202 FL 524, Cocoa, E Shell/dsl Museum of History&Science, W BP/dsl Days Inn

201 FL 520, to Cocoa Bch, Cocoa, E BP/dsl, Chevron, Pilot/Subway/dsl/scales/24hr IHOP, Waffle House Best Western, Motel 6 H fireworks, Sams Club/gas, W Chevron/dsl, Shell/Burger King, Sunoco/dsl McDonald's Holiday Inn Express Camping World RV Ctr

195 FL 519, Fiske Blvd, E 7-11, Mobil/dsl Dominico Italian, Ruby Tuesday Swiss Inn H Discount Tire, Lowe's, Space Coast RV Park

191 Rd 509, to Satellite Beach, Viera, E 7-11, BP, Hess/dsl, Sunoco/dsl Bob Evans, Carrabba's, Chick-fil-A, Denny's, Domino's, DQ, Firehouse Subs, McDonald's, Papa John's, Perkins, Sonny's BBQ, Tropical Smoothie, Uno Grill, Wendy's Hampton Inn, Holiday Inn AT&T, CVS Drug, Publix, Radio Shack, Tires+, to Patrick AFB, Tuffy Auto, URGENT CARE, Walgreens, zoo, W Chevron/dsl, Murphy USA 5 Guys Burgers, Asian Too, Asian Wok, Burger King, Chili's, Coldstone, Cracker Barrel, Longhorn Steaks, Melting Pot, Mimi's Cafe, Moe's SW Grill, Panera Bread, Pita Pit, Pizza Gallery, Starbucks, Steak'nShake, Subway La Quinta H, $Tree, AT&T, Belk, Books-A-Million, GNC, Hobby Lobby, Kohl's, Lexus, Michael's, Office Depot, Old Navy, PetCo, Ross, SuperTarget, Tire Kingdom, Verizon, Walmart/McDonald's, World Mkt

FL

MELBOURNE · PALM BAY · OKEECHOBEE

INTERSTATE 95 Cont'd

Exit #	Services
188	FL 404, Patrick AFB, Satellite Beach
183	FL 518, Melbourne, Indian Harbour Beach, E [gas] 7-11, BP, Chevron/Baskin-Robbins/Dunkin Donuts/dsl, RaceTrac/dsl [other] H art museum, AT&T, W [other] Flea Mkt
180	US 192, to Melbourne, E [gas] 7-11, BP/dsl, Circle K, Mobil/dsl, RaceTrac/dsl, Sunoco/dsl [food] ChuckECheese, Denny's, IHOP, Waffle House [lodging] Best Value Inn, Budget Inn, Days Inn, EconoLodge, Fairfield Inn, Hampton Inn, Holiday Inn Express [other] H Ace Hardware, fireworks, Lowe's, Sam's Club/gas, vet, Volvo
176	Rd 516, to Palm Bay, E [gas] 7-11, BP/dsl, Citgo, Murphy USA/dsl [food] Baskin Robbins/Dunkin Donuts, Bob Evans, Chick-fil-A, Cracker Barrel, Denny's, Golden Corral, Starbucks [lodging] Jameson Inn [other] Aldi Foods, BJ's Whse/gas, GNC, Harley-Davidson, Office Depot, vet, Walgreens, Walmart, W [gas] 7-11, Mobil/dsl, Shell [food] 5 Guys Burgers, Buffalo Wild Wings, Burger King, Long Doggers, Longhorn Steaks, McDonald's, Michelli's Pizzeria, Moe's SW Grill, Panera Bread, Subway, Wendy's [other] $Tree, AT&T, CVS Drug, Discount Tire, Kohl's, Marshall's, Michael's, PetCo, Publix, Ross, Target, Walgreens
173	FL 514, to Palm Bay, E [gas] RaceTrac/dsl, Shell, Sunoco/dsl [lodging] Holiday Inn Express [other] H Firestone/auto, Ford, truck/RV repair, W [gas] Hess/Quiznos, Mobil/dsl, Sunoco [food] Arby's, Burger King, IHOP, Japanese Buffet, McDonald's/playplace, Panda Express, Sonny's BBQ, Subway, Taco Bell, TX Roadhouse, Waffle House, Wendy's [lodging] Comfort Suites, Motel 6 [other] $General, Advance Parts, Beall's, BigLots, CVS Drug, Home Depot, Lowe's, Publix, Tire Kingdom, URGENT CARE, USPO, Verizon, Walgreens, Walmart
168mm	**[rest stop] both lanes, 24hr security, full [handicapped] facilities, litter barrels, petwalk [phone] [picnic]**
156	Rd 512, to Sebastian, Fellsmere, E [gas] BP/DQ/Stuckey's/dsl, Chevron/McDonald's, RaceWay/dsl [other] H Encore RV Park, Sebastian Inlet SRA, Vero Bch RV Park (8mi), W [other] Marsh Landing Camping, St Sebastian SP
147	FL 60, Osceola Blvd, E [gas] 7-11, BP/Dunkin Donuts/dsl, Citgo/dsl, Mobil/dsl, Sunoco, TA/BP/Popeye's/Subway/dsl/scales/24hr/ @, Texaco/dsl, Valero/dsl [food] IHOP, Wendy's [lodging] Best Value Inn, Comfort Suites, Howard Johnson, Knights Inn, Vero Beach Resort [other] H Hyundai, USPO, vet, W [gas] Shell/dsl [food] Cracker Barrel, McDonald's, Steak'n Shake [lodging] Country Inn&Suites, Hampton Inn, Holiday Inn Express [other] Vero Beach Outlets/famous brands
138	FL 614, Indrio Rd, **3 mi** E [other] Oceanographic Institute
133mm	**[rest stop] both lanes, 24hr security, full [handicapped] facilities, litter barrels, petwalk [phone] [picnic]**
131b a	FL 68, Orange Ave, E [other] H to Ft Pierce SP, W [gas] FLYING J/Denny's/Subway/dsl/LP/scales/24hr, Love's/Hardee's/dsl/scales/24hr [other] Blue Beacon
129	FL 70, to Okeechobee, E [gas] Citgo, Hess/dsl, Murphy USA, RaceTrac/dsl, Shell/Circle K, Sunoco/dsl [food] Applebee's, Cowboys BBQ, Golden Corral, Sonic, Waffle House [other] H $General, $Tree, Advance Parts, Firestone/auto, Home Depot, Radio Shack, truck tires, URGENT CARE, Walgreens, Walmart, W [gas] BP/scales/dsl, Chevron, Love's/Arby's/dsl/24hr/ @, Mobil/Dunkin Donuts/Subway, Pilot/McDonald's/dsl/scales/24hr [food] Burger King, Cracker Barrel, KFC, La Granja, LJ Silver, McDonald's, Red Lobster, Steak'n Shake, Waffle House, Wendy's [lodging] Best Value Inn, Best Western,
129	Continued Comfort Suites, Fairfield Inn, Hampton Inn, Holiday Inn Expres[s], La Quinta, Motel 6, Quality Inn, Rodeway Inn, Sleep Inn, Trea[s]ure Coast Inn [other] Indian River Fruit, to FL TPK, Treasure Coa[st] RV Park, UF R&E Ctr
126	Rd 712, Midway Rd, E [gas] BP/Subway/dsl
121	St Lucie West Blvd, E [gas] 7-11, BP/Dunkin Donuts, Mobil/7-1[1], Murphy USA/dsl, Shell/Subway/dsl [food] Arby's, Bob Evan[s], Burger King, Carrabba's, Chili's, Chipotle Mexican, Duffy's Gri[ll], Frank&Al's Pizza, Friendly's, Hokkaido, Hurricane Grill, IHO[P], Jimmy John's, KFC, Little Caesars, McDonald's, Moe's SW Gri[ll], Outback Steaks, PA BBQ, Panda Express, Panera Bread, Rub[y] Tuesday, Starbucks, Stevi B's Pizza, Taco Bell, TGIFriday's, Wendy's [lodging] Hampton Inn, Holiday Inn Express, Residence Inn, SpringHill Suites [other] H $Tree, AT&T, Beall's, CVS Drug, Outdoor Resorts Camping (2mi), PetCo, Publix/deli, Ross, Staples, SteinMart, Tire Kingdom, Tires+, URGENT CARE, USPO, Verizon, Walgreens, Walmart, W [gas] Mobil/dsl [lodging] Hilton Garden, MainStay Suites, Sheraton Resort [other] PGA Village
120	Crosstown Pkwy
118	Gatlin Blvd, to Port St Lucie, E [gas] BP/dsl/LP, Chevron/Dunkin Donuts/Subway/dsl, Shell, Sunoco/e-85 [food] McDonald's, Taco Bell [other] AutoZone, Home Depot, Sam's Club/gas, Tires+, vet, Walgreens, Walmart, W [food] Longhorn Steaks, McDonald's, Olive Garden, Subway, Tropical Smoothie [lodging] Homewood Suites [other] H GNC, Michael's, Old Navy, Petsmart, Publix, Radio Shack, Target, TJ Maxx
114	Becker Rd
112mm	**weigh sta sb**
110	FL 714, to Martin Hwy, Palm City, E [other] H
106mm	**[rest stop] both lanes, 24hr security, full [handicapped] facilities, litter barrels, petwalk [phone] [picnic]**
102	Rd 713, High Meadow Ave, Palm City
101	FL 76, to Stuart, Indiantown, E [gas] Chevron/dsl, Sunoco/ds[l] [food] Baskin-Robbins/Dunkin Donuts, Cracker Barrel, McDonald's [lodging] Courtyard, Holiday Inn Express [other] H city park, Publix, Walgreens, W [gas] Marathon/DQ/dsl, Valero/dsl [other] RV camping
96	Rd 708, to Hobe Sound, E [other] Dickinson SP (11mi), RV camping
92mm	**weigh sta nb**
87b a	FL 706, to Okeechobee, Jupiter, E [gas] Citgo, Mobil/dsl, Shell/dsl, Sunoco [food] 5 Guys Burgers, Applebee's, Cheeseburgers&More, Duffy's Rest., Dunkin Donuts, Giuseppe's, IHOP, Jersey Mike's Subs, KFC, McDonald's, Panera Bread, Pollo Tropical, Rancho Chico, Sonny's BBQ, Starbucks, Subway, Taco Bell, Tomato Pie, YumYum [lodging] Comfort Inn, Fairfield Inn [other] H Advance Parts, BMW, Books-A-Million, GNC, hist sites, Home Depot, museum, PepBoys, Publix, Tire Kingdom, to Dickinson SP, URGENT CARE, vet, Walgreens, Walmart, Winn-Dixie, W [gas] Sunoco [other] RV camping, to FL TPK
83	Donald Ross Rd, E [gas] BP/Subway, Shell/deli [food] McDonald's [lodging] Hampton Inn, Holiday Inn Express, Homewood Suites [other] H AT&T, CVS Drug, stadium, Walgreens
79c	FL 809 S (from sb), Military Tr, W same services as 79b, to FL TPK
79a b	FL 786, PGA Blvd, E [gas] Shell [food] Chili's, TGIFriday's, Yardhouse Rest [lodging] Hilton Garden, Marriott [other] H Best Buy, Michael's, PetCo, Publix, Whole Foods Mkt, W [gas] Shell/dsl [food] 3 Forks Rest, Cantina Laredo, China Kitchen, Chipotle Mexican, J Alexanders, Outback Steaks [lodging] DoubleTree Hotel, Embassy Suites [other] CVS Drug, Publix
77	Northlake Blvd, to W Palm Bch, E [gas] BP, Hess/Dunkin Donuts, Shell/dsl [food] Aladdin Grill, Applebee's, Arby's, Burger King,

W PALM BEACH

INTERSTATE 95 Cont'd

77 Continued
Checkers, Chick-fil-A, Giovanni's Rest, Jimmy John's, KFC, La Granja, Little Caesars, McDonald's, Miami Subs, Panera Bread, Pollo Tropical, Starbucks, Taco Bell [other] H $Tree, AT&T, Buick/Chevrolet/GMC, Chrysler/Dodge/Jeep, Costco, CVS Drug, Family$, Ford, Gander Mtn, Home Depot, Hyundai, K-Mart, Lowe's, PepBoys, Ross, Staples, Target, Verizon, vet, VW, Walgreens, **W** [gas] Chevron/dsl, Shell, Sunoco/dsl, Valero [food] Duffy's Grill, Dunkin Donuts, Original Pancakes, Papa John's, Pizza Hut, Wendy's [lodging] Inn of America [other] Advance Parts, CVS Drug, Publix, Radio Shack, Verizon, vet, Winn-Dixie

76 FL 708, Blue Heron Blvd, **E** [gas] BP/dsl, Shell/dsl [food] Wendy's [lodging] Travelodge [other] Honda, Kia, Nissan, Walgreens, **W** [gas] BP, Chevron/dsl, Cumberland Farms, RaceTrac/dsl, Texaco/dsl [food] Burger King, Denny's, McDonald's [lodging] Super 8

74 FL 702, 45th St, **E** [food] Burger King, IHOP [lodging] Days Inn [other] H Cadillac, URGENT CARE, Walgreens, **W** [gas] RaceTrac [food] Cracker Barrel, McDonald's, Pollo Tropical, Subway, Taco Bell, Wendy's [lodging] Courtyard, Extended Stay Deluxe, Holiday Inn Express, Homewood Suites, Red Roof Inn, Residence Inn, SpringHill Suites [other] Family$, FoodTown, Goodyear/auto, Harley-Davidson, Sams Club/gas, Walmart

PALM BEACH

71 Lake Blvd, Palm Beach, **E** [gas] BP, Mobil/7-11/dsl [food] McDonald's, Wendy's [lodging] Best Western [other] H Best Buy, Firestone/auto, Home Depot, JC Penney, Target, Tire Kingdom, **W** [gas] Texaco/dsl, Valero [food] Carrabba's, Chick-fil-A, Chipotle Mexican, Hooters, Manzo Italian, Palm Tree Cafe, Sweet Tomatoes [lodging] Comfort Inn, La Quinta [other] URGENT CARE, vet, Walgreens

70b a FL 704, Okeechobee Blvd, **E** [food] McCormick&Schmick, Ruth's Chris Steaks [lodging] Marriott [other] museum, **W** [gas] BP/dsl, Chevron/dsl, Hess, Mobil/dsl, Shell, Texaco/dsl, Valero/dsl [food] Arby's, Burger King, Checkers, Denny's, Firehouse Grill, IHOP, McDonald's, Pizza Hut, Pollo Tropical, Starbucks, Subway, Taco Bell [other] $Tree, AT&T, Audi/Porsche, BMW/Mini, Chevrolet, Firestone/auto, GNC, Hyundai, Mercedes, Michael's, Office Depot, Old Navy, Petsmart, Staples, Verizon, VW

69b **W** [other] to [airport]

69a Belvedere Rd, **W** [gas] BP, Shell [food] Burger King, IHOP, Wendy's [lodging] Best Western, Courtyard, Crowne Plaza, DoubleTree, Hampton Inn, Hilton Garden, Holiday Inn/rest., Studio 6

68 US 98, Southern Blvd, **E** [gas] Texaco [other] CVS Drug, Publix, Radio Shack, **W** [lodging] Hilton

66 Forest Hill Blvd, **W** [gas] Chevron/dsl, Sunoco [food] Bellante's Pizza [other] Advance Parts

64 10th Ave N, **W** [gas] BP, Citgo [food] China Empire, Dunkin Donuts, Flanigans Grill, Wendy's [other] CarQuest, CVS Drug, Family$, Ford, President Foods, Ross, Tires+, vet, Walgreens, Walmart/Subway

63 6th Ave S, **W** [other] H

61 FL 812, Lantana Rd, **E** [gas] Shell [food] Domino's, Dunkin Donuts, Golden Wok, KFC, Little Caesars, McDonald's, Pearl's Rest, Riggin's Crabhouse, Subway [lodging] Motel 6 [other] $General, 7-11, Ace Hardware, CVS Drug, Publix, **W** [other] H, Costco/gas

60 Hypoluxo Rd, **E** [gas] BP, Mobil/dsl, Shell/dsl [food] IHOP, Popeye's, Subway, Taco Bell, Wendy's [lodging] Best Value Inn, Comfort Inn, Super 8 [other] Family$, Sam's Club, Tire Kingdom, Tire Pros, Tires+, Winn-Dixie, **W** [gas] Valero/dsl [food] Anchor Inn Rest [other] Advance Parts

59 Gateway Blvd, **W** [gas] Mobil/7-11/dsl [food] Bonefish Grill, Boynton Alehouse, Carrabba's, Chili's, Firehouse Subs, Friendly's,

59 Continued
Golden Phoenix Chinese, Greek Cafe, McDonald's, Starbucks, Subway, Tropical Smoothie [lodging] Hampton Inn [other] AT&T, CarMax, CVS Drug, Kohl's, Publix, Ross, Tuesday Morning, vet

57 FL 804, Boynton Bch Blvd, **E** [gas] Marathon/dsl [food] KFC [lodging] Boynton Beach Inn [other] H USPO, **0-2 mi W** [gas] BP, Mobil, Shell [food] Applebee's, Burger King, Checkers, Chick-Fil-A, Dunkin Donuts, Golden Corral, KFC, La Granja, Little Caesars, Sonic, Starbucks, Steak'n Shake, Subway, TGIFriday's, Wendy's [other] 7-11, Barnes&Noble, BJ's Whse/gas, CVS Drug, Dick's, Dillard's, GNC, JC Penney, Macy's, Office Depot, Old Navy, PetCo, Petsmart, Publix, Radio Shack, Sears, SteinMart, TJ Maxx, USPO, vet, Walmart

56 Woolbright Rd, **E** [gas] Shell, Valero [food] Boynton Diner, McDonald's, Subway [other] H 7-11, Jo-Ann Fabrics, Publix, vet, Walgreens, Winn-Dixie, **W** [gas] RaceTrac/dsl [food] Burger King, Cracker Barrel, Dunkin Donuts [other] Advance Parts, Bravo Foods, Home Depot, Lowe's, Staples, Walgreens

52b a FL 806, Atlantic Ave, **W** [gas] Chevron/dsl, Shell/dsl [food] Dunkin Donuts, Sandwich Man, Silver Wok [other] H, Tires+, transmissions, Verizon, vet, Walgreens

51 Rd 782, Linton Blvd, **E** [gas] Shell [food] Applebee's, Arby's, Chipotle Mexican, DQ, Duffy's Grill, IHOP, KFC, McDonald's, Outback Steaks, Pollo Tropical, Steak'n Shake, Subway, Taco Bell, Wendy's [other] AT&T, Chevrolet, Ford, Home Depot, Marshall's, Mercedes, Michael's, Petsmart, Publix, Ross, Staples, Target, Tire Kingdom, Verizon, **W** [gas] Shell [food] Little Caesars [other] H, Family$, Monterrey's Mkt, URGENT CARE

50 Congress Ave, **W** [gas] Mobil [lodging] Hilton Garden, Residence Inn

48b a FL 794, Yamato Rd, **E** [gas] Mobil [food] Panera Bread [other] CVS Drug, vet, **W** [gas] Chevron/dsl, Mobil [food] Blue Fin, Dunkin Donuts, Jersey Mike's Subs, Jimmy John's, McDonald's, Miller's Alehouse, Quiznos, Sal's Italian, Starbucks, Subway, Wendy's [lodging] DoubleTree, Embassy Suites, Guest Suites, Hampton Inn, SpringHill Suites, TownePlace Suites

45 FL 808, Glades Rd, **E** [gas] Chevron/dsl [food] J Alexander's Rest, Jamba Juice, PF Changs [lodging] Fairfield Inn [other] Barnes&Noble, CVS Drug, museum, Whole Foods Mkt, **W** [gas] BP [food] Brewzzi Cafe, Brio Italian Grill, CA Pizza Kitchen, Capital Grille, Cheesecake Factory, Chili's, Chipotle Mexican, Coldstone, Hooters, Houston Rest., Macaroni Grill, Maggiano's Italian, Moe's SW Grill, Morton Steaks, Pinon Grill, Quiznos, Rosso Italian, Season's Rest, Starbucks, Stephane's, Stir Crazy, Subway, Wendy's [lodging] Courtyard, Holiday Inn, Marriott, Wyndham Garden [other] Macy's, Nordstrom, Publix, Sears/auto

44 Palmetto Park Rd, **E** [gas] Valero/dsl [food] Denny's, Dunkin Donuts, Red's BBQ, Subway, Taco Bell, Tomasso's Pizza [other] AT&T, K-Mart, museums, Publix, **W** [food] McDonald's (2mi)

FL

[gas] = gas [food] = food [lodging] = lodging [other] = other [rest stop] = rest stop

POMPANO BEACH

FT LAUDERDALE

FL

INTERSTATE 95 Cont'd

Exit #	Services
42b a	FL 810, Hillsboro Blvd, E [gas] BP, Shell/dsl [food] Hook Fish&Chicken, McDonald's, Popeye's, Wendy's [lodging] Hampton Inn, Hilton, La Quinta [other] Advance Parts, W [gas] Chevron/dsl, Mobil/dsl [food] Boston Mkt, Checkers, Dunkin Donuts, Subway [lodging] Holiday Park Hotel, La Quinta [other] CVS Drug, Home Depot, Walgreens
41	FL 869 (**toll**), SW 10th, to I-75, E [gas] Mobil/7-11 [food] Cracker Barrel, Pizza Express [lodging] Extended Stay America, W [lodging] Best Western, Comfort Suites
39	FL 834, Sample Rd, E [gas] BP, Chevron/dsl, Hess/dsl, Shell/dsl [food] Taco Bell [other] [H] $General, Save-A-Lot, U-Haul, W [gas] Chevron, Citgo/dsl, Mobil/dsl, Solo/dsl, Sunoco/dsl [food] Burger King, Checkers, IHOP, La Granja, McDonald's, Miami Subs, Subway [other] 7-11, CarMax, Costco/gas, CVS Drug, Family$, Seabra Foods, vet
38b a	Copans Rd, E [gas] BP/7-11 [food] McDonald's, Subway [other] Land Rover, Mercedes, PepBoys, Porche/Audi, Walmart, W [gas] Chevron, Valero/dsl [other] Home Depot, NAPA
36b a	FL 814, Atlantic Blvd, to Pompano Beach, E [gas] RaceTrac/dsl [food] KFC/Pizza Hut/Taco Bell, Miami Subs, **1 mi** W [gas] BP, Chevron, Mobil/dsl, Murphy USA/dsl [food] Baskin-Robbins/Dunkin Donuts, Burger King, Golden Corral, KFC/LJ Silver, McDonald's, Pollo Tropical, Subway, Wendy's [other] $Tree, Chevrolet/Mazda, CVS Drug, Power Line Rd has many services, Radio Shack, to FL TPK, USPO, Walgreens, Walmart
33b a	Cypress Creek Rd, E [gas] 7-11, BP, Hess [food] Duffy's Diner [lodging] Extended Stay America, Hampton Inn, Westin Hotel, W [gas] Hess, Shell/repair [food] 5 Guys Burgers, Arby's, Burger King, Carlucci's Italian, Champp's Grill, Chili's, Hooters, Longhorn Steaks, McDonald's, Moonlite Diner, Subway, Sweet Tomatoes, Wendy's [lodging] Courtyard, La Quinta, Marriott, Sheraton Suites [other] AT&T, GNC, Jaguar, Office Depot, Tires+, URGENT CARE
32	FL 870, Commercial Blvd, Lauderdale by the Sea, Lauderhill, E [food] Subway, W [gas] BP, Circle K, Mobil/dsl, Shell, Sunoco/dsl [food] Dunkin Donuts, KFC, McDonald's, Miami Subs, Subway, Waffle House [lodging] Holiday Inn Express, Red Roof Inn, Universal Palms Motel [other] Advance Parts, auto repair, BJ's Whse/gas, Tire Kingdom
31b a	FL 816, Oakland Park Blvd, E [gas] 7-11, Chevron, Mobil/dsl, Petro America/dsl [food] 24 Diner, BBQ Jacks, Burger King, Checkers, Denny's, Domino's, Dunkin Donuts, Little Caesars, McDonald's, Miami Subs, Primanti Bros, Subway, Taco Bell, Wendy's [other] Advance Parts, K-Mart, Lowe's, Publix, Radio Shack, Walgreens, W [gas] BP/dsl, RaceTrac/dsl, Shell, Texaco, Valero [food] Baskin-Robbins/Dunkin Donuts, Burger King, Checkers, IHOP, KFC, McDonald's, Pizza Hut, Subway [lodging] Days Inn [other] $General, Home Depot, Toyota/Scion, USPO, vet, Walgreens
29b a	FL 838, Sunrise Blvd, E [gas] BP, Shell, Sunoco/dsl/e-85, Valero/dsl [food] Burger King, Krystal, Miami Subs, Popeye's [other] Advance Parts, auto repair/tires, AutoZone, Family$, to Birch SP, Winn-Dixie, W [gas] BP, Exxon/dsl, Marathon, Shell, Valero [food] China Bowl, Church's, KFC, McDonald's, Snapper's Fish&Chicken, Subway [other] [H] Family$
27	FL 842, Broward Blvd, Ft Lauderdale, E [other] [H]
26	I-595 (from sb), FL 736 (from nb), Davie Blvd, W [other] to [airport]
25	FL 84, E [gas] 7-11, Marathon/dsl, RaceTrac/dsl, Sunoco/dsl, Texaco, Valero [food] Dunkin Donuts, Li'l Red's BBQ, McDonald's, Ruby Chinese, Subway, Wendy's [lodging] Best Western, Candlewood Suites, Holiday Inn Express, Motel 6, Sky Motel

HOLLYWOOD

Exit #	Services
25	Continued [other] $Tree, BigLots, Firestone/auto, Radio Shack, U-Haul, Winr Dixie, W [lodging] Ramada Inn, Red Carpet Inn, Rodeway Inn
24	I-595 (from nb), to I-75, E [other] to [airport]
23	FL 818, Griffin Rd, E [lodging] Hilton, Sheraton, W [gas] Mob [food] Subway [lodging] Courtyard, Fairfield Inn, Homewood Suite [other] Bass Pro Shops, N Trail RV Ctr, Publix
22	FL 848, Stirling Rd, Cooper City, E [gas] Mobil [food] AleHous Grill, Burger King, Chipotle Mexican, Dave&Buster's, McDonald's, Moonlite Diner, Quiznos, Red Lobster, Sal's Italian, Swee Tomatoes, Taco Bell, TGIFriday's, Wendy's, Yum Berry Yogu [lodging] Comfort Inn, Hampton Inn, Hilton Garden, Hyatt House, Hyatt Place, La Quinta, SpringHill Suites [other] Advance Parts, BJ' Whse, GNC, Home Depot, K-Mart, Marshall's, Michael's, Ol Navy, Petsmart, Radio Shack, Ross, to Lloyd SP, Verizon, W [food] Las Vegas Cuban, Mr M's Sandwiches, Subway [lodging] Best Western [other] CVS Drug, PepBoys, Tire Kingdom, vet, Walgreens Winn-Dixie
21	FL 822, Sheridan St, E [gas] BP, Chevron/dsl, Cumberlanc Farms/gas, same as 22, W [gas] Shell [food] Denny's [lodging] Days Inn Holiday Inn
20	FL 820, Hollywood Blvd, E [gas] Shell [food] IHOP, Miami Subs [lodging] Hollywood Gateway Inn [other] Goodyear/auto, Office Depot U-Haul, vet, W [gas] BP, Chevron/dsl [food] Boston Mkt, China Hollywood, Coldstone, Firehouse Subs, Mama Fu's Asian, McDonald's, Offerdahl's Grill, Quiznos, Starbucks, Subway, Taco Bell Waffle Works, Wendy's [other] [H] Publix, Radio Shack, Target Verizon, Walgreens
19	FL 824, Pembroke Rd, E [gas] Shell, W [gas] Giant
18	FL 858, Hallandale Bch Blvd, E [gas] 7-11, Exxon, Shell [food] Baskin-Robbins/Dunkin Donuts, Burger King, Denny's, IHOP KFC, La Granja, Little Caesars, McDonald's, Miami Subs, Pollo Tropical, Subway, Wendy's, Won Ton Garden [lodging] Best Westerr [other] [H] Family$, Goodyear/auto, Tire Kingdom, vet, Walgreens, Winn-Dixie, W [gas] BP/dsl, RaceTrac/dsl [other] Advance Parts
16	Ives Dairy Rd, E [other] [H], mall, W [gas] BP/7-11 [food] Subway
14	FL 860, Miami Gardens Dr, N Miami Beach, E [other] [H] Oleta River SRA, W [gas] BP, Valero/dsl
12c	US 441, FL 826, FL TPK, FL 9, E [gas] 7-11, BP, Chevron, Hess/dsl, Valero [food] Baskin-Robbins/Dunkin Donuts, Burger King, McDonald's, Wendy's [lodging] Holidays Hotel [other] [H], PepBoys
12b	US 441 (from nb), same as 12c
12a	FL 868 (from nb), FL TPK N
11	NW 151st (from nb), W [gas] Sunoco/dsl [food] McDonald's [other] Advance Parts, services on US 441 N, Winn-Dixie
10b	FL 916, NW 135th, Opa-Locka Blvd, W [gas] Chevron, CR/dsl, Liberty [food] Checkers, Subway
10a	NW 125th, N Miami , Bal Harbour, W [gas] Shell [food] Burger King, Wendy's
9	NW 119th (from nb), W [gas] BP/McDonald's [food] KFC, Pollo Tropical, Popeye's [other] Advance Parts, AutoZone, CVS Drug, Family$, Walgreens, Winn-Dixie
8b	FL 932, NW 103rd, E [gas] Shell, Texaco [other] 7-11, W [gas] BP, Sunoco [food] $General, Baskin-Robbins/Dunkin Donuts, Bravo Foods
8a	NW 95th, E [gas] BP, W [gas] CR/dsl, Mobil/dsl [food] McDonald's [other] [H], Advance Parts, Walgreens
7	FL 934, NW 81st, NW 79th, E [gas] BP/dsl, Chevron/dsl, W [gas] Sunoco [food] Checkers
6b	NW 69th (from sb)
6a	FL 944, NW 62nd, NW 54th, W [food] China Town, McDonald's, Subway, Wing Stop [other] Family$, Presidente Mkt, Walgreens

MIAMI

INTERSTATE 95 Cont'd

Exit #	Services
4b a	I-195 E, FL 112 W (**toll**), Miami Beach, **E** downtown, **W** [other] [airport]
3b	NW 8th St (from sb)
3a	FL 836 W (**toll**) (exits left from nb), **W** [other] [H], to [airport]
2d	I-395 E (exits left from sb), to Miami Beach
2c	NW 8th, NW 14th (from sb), Miami Ave, **E** [other] Port of Miami
2b	NW 2nd (from nb), downtown Miami
2a	US 1 (exits left from sb), Biscayne Blvd, downtown Miami
1b	US 41, SW 7th, SW 8th, Brickell Ave, **E** [gas] Chevron, Citgo [food] Burger King, Graziano's, McDonald's, Munchies, Subway, Wendy's [lodging] Extended Stay America, Hampton Inn [other] CVS Drug, GNC, Publix, **W** [gas] Shell [food] Papa John's, Pepper's Mexican Grill
1a	SW 25th (from sb), downtown, to Rickenbacker Causeway, **E** [other] museum, to Baggs SRA
0mm	**I-95 begins/ends on US 1, 1 mi S** [gas] BP [food] Quiznos

TAMPA

INTERSTATE 275 (TAMPA)

Exit #	Services
59mm	**I-275 begins/ends on I-75, exit 274.**
53	Bearss Ave, **E** [gas] Citgo/dsl [other] Carmax, **W** [gas] Chevron/dsl, Marathon/Dunkin Donuts, RaceTrac/dsl, Shell [food] Burger King, IHOP, McDonald's, Subway [lodging] Vista Inn [other] Aldi Foods, Big-Lots, CVS Drug, GNC, Ross
52	Fletcher Ave, **E** [gas] BP, Citgo/dsl, Hess, RaceTrac/dsl, Shell/dsl, Sunoco [food] Arby's, Bruno's Pizza, Church's, DQ, Hoho Chinese, Krystal, Little Caesars, McDonald's, Popeye's [lodging] Days Inn [other] [H] Aldi Foods, AutoZone, Family$, to USF, Toyota/Scion, **W** [gas] BP, Citgo, Mobil [food] Dunkin Donuts [lodging] Super 8 [other] Advance Parts, Cadillac, Family$, Jaguar, Save-A-Lot, Sweetbay Foods
51	FL 582, Fowler Ave, **E** [gas] BP, Citgo/dsl, GK, Mobil/dsl, Shell/Circle K [food] 5 Guys Burgers, A&W/LJ Silver, Baskin-Robbins/Dunkin Donuts, Burger King, Checkers, Chili's, China Buffet, Chipotle Mexican, Denny's, Firehouse Subs, Jason's Deli, Jimmy John's, KFC, Longhorn Steaks, McAliter's Deli, McDonald's, Panera Bread, Pizza Hut, Quiznos, Sonic, Steak'n Shake, Subway, Taco Bell, TGIFriday's, Tia's TexMex, Waffle House, Wendy's [lodging] Clarion, Embassy Suites, Howard Johnson, Hyatt Place, La Quinta, Wingate Inn [other] $General, $Tree, 7-11, Advance Parts, AT&T, CarQuest, CVS Drug, Family$, Firestone/auto, Macy's, O'Reilly Parts, Sears/auto, Sweetbay Foods, Verizon, Walgreens, **W** [lodging] Economy Inn, Motel 6, Rodeway Inn [other] Audi, BMW
50	FL 580, Busch Blvd, **E** [gas] BP, Chevron, Citgo [food] Arby's, McDonald's, Olive Garden, Popeye's, Red Lobster, Sonny's BBQ, Subway, Taco Bell [lodging] Days Inn, Holiday Inn Express, La Quinta, Red Roof Inn [other] $General, AutoZone, Busch Gardens, Family$, Walgreens, **W** [gas] Chevron/dsl [food] Burger King, Pizza Hut [other] $Tree, Advance Parts, CVS Drug, Firestone/auto, Home Depot, Meineke, Radio Shack, Walmart Mkt
49	Bird Ave (from nb), **W** [gas] Shell [food] Checkers, KFC, McDonald's, Wendy's [other] $General, K-Mart, Save-A-Lot
48	Sligh Ave, **E** [gas] BP, Sunoco [other] USPO, **W** [other] zoo
47b a	US 92, to US 41 S, Hillsborough Ave, **E** [gas] Circle K, Marathon, Mobil/dsl [food] Burger King, Checkers, McDonald's, Popeye's, Subway, Wendy's [other] Advance Parts, Ross, vet, Walgreens, **W** [gas] BP, Shell/Circle K [food] Papa John's, Starbucks [lodging] Dutch Motel

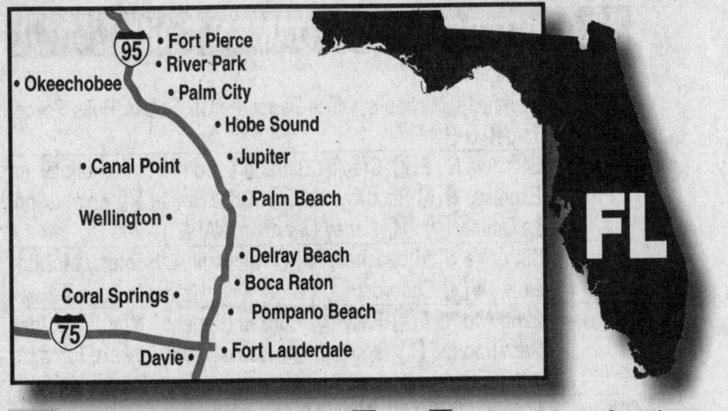

Exit #	Services
46b	FL 574, MLK Blvd, **E** [gas] BP [other] Advance Parts, Sweetbay Foods, Walgreens, **W** [gas] Chevron/dsl [food] McDonald's [other] [H]
46a	Floribraska Ave (from sb, no return)
45b	I-4 E, to Orlando, I-75
45a	Jefferson St, downtown E
44	Ashley Dr, Tampa St, downtown W
42	Howard Ave, Armenia Ave, **W** [gas] Texaco/dsl [food] Popeye's
41c	Himes Ave (from sb), **W** [other] RJ Stadium
41b a	US 92, Dale Mabry Blvd, **E** [gas] BP, Marathon, Mobil/dsl, Shell/Circle K [food] Brickhouse Grill, Burger King, Carrabba's, Chick-Fil-A, Don Pan Cuban, Donatello Italian, Grill Smith, IHOP, J.Alexanders Rest, Jersey Mike's Subs, Little Caesars, Pei Wei, Pizza Hut, Red Elephant Cafe, Ruby Tuesday, Shells Rest., Starbucks, Subway, Village Inn [lodging] Best Western, Courtyard, Quality Inn, Tahitian Inn/cafe [other] AT&T, Barnes&Noble, CVS Drug, Hancock Fabrics, Office Depot, Tire Kingdom, to MacDill AFB, Verizon, **W** [gas] Marathon/Dunkin Donuts [food] Burger King, Chili's, China 1, Crazy Buffet, Denny's, Jimmy John's, Joe's Pizza, Longhorn Steaks, Macaroni Grill, McDonald's, Moe's SW Grill, Sonic, Sonny's BBQ, Subway, Sweet Tomatoes, Wendy's [lodging] Hilton, Howard Johnson, Residence Inn, Stadium Inn [other] Best Buy, Chrysler/Dodge/Jeep, Family$, Home Depot, K-Mart, Petsmart, Staples, SweetBay Foods, Target, to RJ Stadium, Walmart, Whole Foods Mkt
40b	Lois Ave, **W** [gas] Marathon/dsl [food] Charley's Rest. [lodging] DoubleTree Hotel, Sheraton
40a	FL 587, Westshore Blvd, **E** [gas] BP, Chevron/dsl, Citgo/Subway [food] Burger King, Chipotle Mexican, Gogo's Greek, Maggiano's Rest., McDonald's, Panera Bread, PF Chang's, Season's Grill, Starbucks, Taco Bell, Waffle House [lodging] Crowne Plaza, Embassy Suites [other] Goodyear, JC Penney, Macy's, Old Navy, PetCo, Sears/auto, Walgreens, **W** [gas] Shell/Subway [food] Blue Water Grill, Hurricane Grill [lodging] Hampton Inn, Marriott, Ramada Inn, SpringHill Suites, Wyndham
39b a	FL 60 W, **W** [food] Outback Steaks [other] to [airport]
32	Fl 687 S, 4th St N, to US 92 (no sb re-entry)
31b a	9th St N, MLK St N (exits left from sb), [other] [airport], info
30	FL 686, Roosevelt Blvd, **0-2mi W** [food] Bascom's Chophouse, Bob Evans, Burger King, Chil-fil-A, Cracker Barrel, Kingfish Grill, McDonald's, Panchero's Mexican, Subway, Taco Bell [lodging] Courtyard, EconoLodge, Executive Inn, Extended Stay America, Fairfield Inn, Hampton Inn, Holiday Inn, La Quinta, Marriott, Quality Inn, Sleep Inn, SpringHill Suites [other] CVS Drug, Publix
28	FL 694 W, Gandy Blvd, Indian Shores, **0-2mi W** [gas] Citgo, Hess/dsl, WaWa/dsl [food] Applebee's, BJ's Brewhouse, Bob Evans, Chili's, Cracker Barrel, Dunkin Donuts, Firehouse Subs, Godfather's, McDonald's, Pollo Tropical, Sonny's BBQ, Taco Bell, Wendy's [lodging] La Quinta [other] Bentley, Cadillac, Home Depot,

INTERSTATE 275 (TAMPA) Cont'd

ST PETERSBURG

28 Continued
Marshall's, Michael's, Office Depot, PetCo, Publix, Rolls Royce, Target, U-Haul

26b a 54th Ave N, E [gas] Cracker Barrel [lodging] Comfort Inn, Holiday Inn Express, W [gas] RaceTrac/dsl [food] Waffle House [lodging] Knights Inn, La Quinta [other] [H] Harley-Davidson, NAPA

25 38th Ave N, to beaches, E [food] Chick-fil-A, Hooters, McDonald's, W [gas] Citgo/dsl [food] Burger King, Hardee's

24 22nd Ave N, E [gas] Rally [other] Sunken Gardens, W [gas] Citgo/dsl, RaceTrac/dsl [food] Taco Son [other] Home Depot, Lowe's, Tommy's Auto Service

23b FL 595, 5th Ave N, E [other] [H]

23a I-375, E [other] The Pier, Waterfront, downtown

22 I-175 E, Tropicana Field, W [other] [H]

21 28th St S, downtown

20 31st Ave (from nb), downtown

19 22nd Ave S, Gulfport, W [gas] Chevron, Citgo, Shell [food] Church's, KFC [other] Bravo Foods, Family$

18 26th Ave S (from nb)

17 FL 682 W, 54th Ave S, Pinellas Bayway, **services W on US 19 (34th St)** [gas] 7-11, Sunoco/dsl [food] Beef'O'Brady's, Bob Evans, Burger King, China Wok, Denny's, Domino's, Dunkin Donuts, IHOP, McDonald's, Papa John's, Portofino Italian, Subway, Taco Bell, Wendy's [lodging] Bayway Inn, Crystal Inn [other] $Tree, AT&T, Beall's, CVS Drug, GNC, Publix, Radio Shack, St Pete Beach, to Ft DeSoto Pk, Walmart/McDonald's

16 Pinellas Point Dr, Skyway Lane, to Maximo Park, E [lodging] Holiday Inn Resort, W [other] marina

16mm **toll plaza sb**

13mm N Skyway Fishing Pier, W [RS] **both lanes, full [handicapped] facilities, litter barrels, petwalk** [phone] [picnic]

10mm Tampa Bay

7mm S Skyway Fishing Pier, E [RS] **both lanes, full [handicapped] facilities, litter barrels, petwalk** [phone] [picnic]

6mm **toll plaza nb**

5 US 19, Palmetto, Bradenton

2 US 41, (last nb exit before toll), Palmetto, Bradenton, E [other] Circle K, Fiesta Grove RV Resort, Frog Creek Campground, Terra Ceia Village Campground, Winterset RV Resort, W [gas] BP/DQ/Subway/dsl

0mm **I-275 begins/ends on I-75, exit 228.**

INTERSTATE 295 (JACKSONVILLE)

JACKSONVILLE

Exit # Services

61b a **I-295 begins/ends on I-95, exit 337**

60 US 1, Philips Hwy, E [gas] RaceTrac/dsl [other] Buick/GMC, Honda, VW, W [gas] BP [other] Chevrolet, Ford, Mazda, Nissan

58 FL 9b

56 FL 152, Baymeadows Rd, E [lodging] Holiday Inn [other] Chrysler/Dodge/Jeep, W [gas] Shell [food] Bubba Burger, Carrabba's, Hampton Inn, Hurricane Grill, Outback Steaks, Sticky Fingers, Tequila's Mexican, Tony D's Pizza, Wendy's [other] Publix, SteinMart, URGENT CARE, Verizon, vet, Walgreens

54 Gate Pkwy, W [food] Joey's Pizzeria, Melting Pot

53 FL 202, Butler Blvd, **1 mi W on Gate Pkwy** [gas] Shell [food] Bahama Breeze, BJ's Rest, Bono's BBQ, Brio Grille, Capital Grill, Cheesecake Factory, Chipotle Mexican, Maggiano's Italian, Mimi's Cafe, Panda Express, Panera Bread, Pei Wei, PF Chang's, Pollo Tropical, Seasons Rest, Wasabi, Wendy's,

53 Continued
Zaxby's [lodging] Sheraton [other] Barnes&Noble, Best Buy, Costco, CVS Drug, Dick's, Dillard's, Target

52 U of NF Dr, Town Center Pkwy, same as 53

51 US 90, Beach Blvd, E [gas] Citgo [food] Burger King, Dunkin Donuts, Gene's Seafood, Jimmy John's, W [gas] Shell [food] Arby's, KFC, McDonald's, Pizza Hut, Sonic, Taco Bell [lodging] InTown Suites [other] $Tree, Advance Parts, Walgreens, Winn-Dixie

49 St John's Bluff Rd (from nb), E [gas] BP, Shell [food] Papa John's [lodging] Holiday Inn Express, InTown Suites [other] Nissan

48 FL 10, to Atlantic Blvd

47 Monument Rd, E [gas] Marathon/Kangaroo/dsl [food] Mudville Grille [other] vet, W [gas] Gate/dsl [food] Ruby Tuesday [lodging] Courtyard, Hampton Inn [other] Walmart

46 FL 116 E, Wonderwood Connector, Merrill Rd, E [lodging] Candlewood Suites

44mm St John's River

41 FL 105, Heckscher Dr, Zoo Pkwy, E [gas] Gate/dsl, W [gas] Chevron/Kangaroo/dsl [food] Wendy's [lodging] Holiday Inn Express [other] zoo

40 Alta Dr, E [food] 3 Lions Grill, Viva Mexican

37 Pulaski Rd, E [gas] Kangaroo/dsl

36 US 17, Main St, E [gas] Kangaroo/dsl [food] DQ, McDonald's [other] Winn-Dixie, W [food] Subway

35b a I-95, S to Jacksonville, N to Savannah.

33 Duval Rd, W [airport]

32 FL 115, Lem Turner Rd, E [food] China Wok, Larry's Subs, McDonald's (1mi), Subway, Wendy's [other] Home Depot, Radio Shack, Walmart, W [other] Flamingo Lake RV Resort, Lakeside Cabins/RV Park

30 FL 104, Dunn Ave, E [gas] Gate/dsl, Shell (1mi) [food] McDonald's (1mi), Wendy's (4mi), W [other] Big Tree RV Park

28b a US 1, US 23, to Callahan, Jacksonville, E [gas] Kangaroo, W [gas] auto repair, BP/DQ/dsl, Chevron/Subway/dsl, RaceTrac/dsl

25 Pritchard Rd, W [gas] Kangaroo/Subway/deli/dsl/24hr

22 Commonwealth Ave, E [gas] BP/dsl [food] Burger King, Hardee's, Waffle House [lodging] Holiday Inn [other] dogtrack, W [food] Wendy's [lodging] Comfort Suites, Country Inn&Suites

21b a I-10, W to Tallahassee, E to Jacksonville

19 FL 228, Normandy Blvd, E [gas] BP/dsl/24hr, Murphy USA/dsl [food] Arby's, Burger King, El Potro, Firehouse Subs, Golden Corral, Hot Wok, McDonald's, Panda Express, Papa John's, Sonic, Wendy's [other] $Tree, CVS Drug, Radio Shack, st patrol, Walgreens, Walmart, W [gas] BP, Hess/dsl, RaceTrac/dsl, Shell [food] Famous Amos, Golden China, Hardee's, KFC, McDonald's, Pizza Hut, Popeye's, Whataburger [other] Advance Parts, Curves, CVS Drug, Family$, K-Mart, Publix, Walgreens, Winn-Dixie

17 FL 208, Wilson Blvd, E [gas] BP/Subway/dsl, Hess/Dunkin Donuts/dsl [food] China Wok, Hardee's, McDonald's (1mi) [other] $General, Advance Parts, FL RV Ctr, W [gas] Kangaroo

16 FL 134, 103rd St, Cecil Field, E [gas] BP, Gate/dsl, Hess, Shell/dsl [food] Applebee's, Arby's, Capt D's, Firehouse Subs, Krystal, Papa John's, Popeye's, Red Apple Asian, Sonic, Wendy's, Ying's Chinese [lodging] [H] ity Inn [other] $General, Advance Parts, CVS Drug, Goodyear/auto, NAPA, Radio Shack, Save-A-Lot Foods, Tires+, U-Haul, Walmart/McDonald's, W [gas] BP, Chevron, Exxon/dsl, Kangaroo, Shell [food] Burger King, DQ, Dunkin Donuts, IHOP, KFC, Little Caesars, McDonald's, Pizza Hut, Rosy's Mexican, Subway, Taco Bell [other] Aamco, AutoZone, Family$, Goodyear/auto, O'Reilly Parts, Publix, SavRite Foods, Sun Tires, vet, Walgreens

FL

INTERSTATE 295 (JACKSONVILLE) Cont'd

Exit #	Services
12	FL 21, Blanding Blvd, E [gas] BP, Hess/Blimpie/Dunkin Donuts/ Godfather's/dsl, RaceWay/dsl, Texaco [food] Burger King, Larry's Subs, McDonald's, Pizza Hut, Subway, Sunrise Cafe [other] $General, Acura, Audi, Best Buy, Buick/GMC, Cadillac, Chrysler/ Dodge/Jeep, CVS Drug, Ford, Honda, Hyundai, Lexus, Lincoln, Mazda, Mercedes, Nissan, Office Depot, Petsmart, Subaru, U-Haul, USPO, VW, Walgreens, W [gas] 5 Guys Burgers, Arby's, BP, Buffalo's, Burger King, Carrabba's, Chick-fil-A, Chili's, China Buffet, Chipotle Mexican, ChuckeCheese, Denny's, El Potro, food: Applebee's, HoneyBaked Ham, Hooters, Kangaroo/dsl, KFC, Kyodai Steaks, Longhorn Steaks, Olive Garden, Orange Park Ale House, Outback Steaks, Panda Express, Panera Bread, Papa John's, Red Lobster, Ruby Tuesday, Shell, Smokey Bones, Sonic, Starbucks, Steak'n Shake, Sweet Tomatoes, Taco Bell, Ted's MT Grill, TGIFriday's, Thai Garden [lodging] Country Inn&Suites, Hampton Inn, La Quinta, Motel 6, Red Roof Inn, Suburban Lodge, Super 8 [other] [H], $Tree, Advance Parts, AT&T, Belk, Books-A-Million, Dick's, Dillard's, Discount Tire, Goodyear/auto, Home Depot, JC Penney, Jo-Ann Fabrics, mall, Michael's, Old Navy, O'Reilly Parts, PepBoys, Publix, Sam's Club/ gas, Sears/auto, Target, Tire Kingdom, Tires+, TJMaxx, Toyota, Verizon, Walgreens
10	US 17, FL 15, Roosevelt Blvd, Orange Park, E [lodging] Best Western, W [gas] BP, Chevron/dsl/24hr, Hess, RaceTrac/dsl [food] Aron's Pizza, Cracker Barrel, Krystal, McDonald's, Ramirez Rest., Subway, Waffle House, Wendy's [lodging] Comfort Inn, Days Inn, Fairfield
10	Continued Inn, Hilton Garden, Holiday Inn, Rodeway Inn [other] [H] $General, CVS Drug, General RV Ctr, Harley-Davidson, Save-A-Lot Foods, Sun Tire, vet, Winn-Dixie
7mm	St Johns River, Buckman Br
5b a	FL 13, San Jose Blvd, E [gas] Chevron/DQ/dsl, Hess [food] 5 Guys Burgers, Arby's, Bob Evans, Bono's BBQ, Carrabba's, Domino's, Famous Amos, Firehouse Subs, HoneyBaked Ham, Krystal, McDonald's, Outback Steaks, Popeye's, Red Elephant Pizza, Smoothie King, Starbucks, Steak'n Shake, Subway, Tijuana Flats, Village Inn, Wendy's [lodging] La Quinta, Ramada Inn [other] Aamco, Advance Parts, auto repair, BigLots, CVS Drug, Firestone/auto, K-Mart, Office Depot, PepBoys, Publix, Sun Tire, Target, Tire Kingdom, Tires+, URGENT CARE, Verizon, vet, Walgreens, Whole Foods Mkt, W [gas] BP, Citgo, Shell (1mi) [food] Al's Pizza, Brooklyn Pizza, Bruster's, Chili's, Chipotle Mexican, Golden China, Golden Corral, Hardee's, Krispy Kreme, Lee's Chicken, Mama Fu's, Mandarin Ale House, McDonald's, Moe's SW Grill, Osaka Grill, Panera Bread, Papa John's, Papa Murphy's, Pizza Hut, Subway, Taco Bell [other] $Tree, Ace Hardware, Advance Parts, AT&T, AutoZone, Barnes&Noble, Books-A-Million, Goodyear/auto, Marshall's, Michael's, NAPA, PetCo, Publix, Radio Shack, Staples, SteinMart, Tire Kingdom, TJMaxx, U-Haul, Walmart, Winn-Dixie, World Mkt
3	Old St Augustine Rd, E [gas] BP, Shell [food] Burger King, Little Caesars, Little China, McDonald's, Taco Bell, Wendy's [lodging] Holiday Inn Express [other] $General, $Tree, CVS Drug, Family$, GNC, Hobby Lobby, Publix/deli, Winn-Dixie, W [gas] Gate/dsl, Kangaroo/dsl [food] Firehouse Subs, KFC, Rosy's Mexican, Subway, Vino's Pizza [other] Lowe's, vet, Walgreens

FL
GA

GEORGIA

INTERSTATE 16

Exit #	Services
167b a	W Broad, Montgomery St, Savannah, **0-1 mi** N [gas] Chevron, Enmark, Parker's [lodging] Best Western, Courtyard, DoubleTree, Fairfield Inn, Hampton Inn, Hilton Garden, Holiday Inn, Quality Inn, Residence Inn, Springhill Suites, S [food] Burger King, Popeye's, Wendy's [other] **I-16 begins/ends in Savannah.**
166	US 17, Gwinnet St, Savannah, Savannah Visitors Ctr
165	GA 204, 37th St (from eb), to Ft Pulaski NM, Savannah College
164b a	I-516, US 80, US 17, GA 21
162	Chatham Pkwy, S [gas] Shell/dsl [food] Kan Pai Japanese, Larry's Subs, Nicky's Pizza, Sunrise Rest. [other] Chrysler/Dodge/Jeep, Kia, Lexus, Subaru, Toyota/Scion
160	GA 307, Dean Forest Rd, N [gas] Pilot/Subway/dsl/scales, Shell/dsl [food] Ronnie's Rest., Waffle House
157b a	I-95, S to Jacksonville, N to Florence
155	Pooler Pkwy, N [gas] Murphy USA/dsl [food] Jalapeno's Mexican, Papa John's, Subway, Wasabi Fusion [other] Lowe's, to [airport] Verizon, S [gas] BP/dsl
152	GA 17, to Bloomingdale
148	Old River Rd, to US 80
144mm	**weigh sta both lanes**
143	US 280, to US 80, S [gas] El Cheapo/dsl, Gas'n Go/Subway/dsl
137	GA 119, to Pembroke, Ft Stewart
132	Ash Branch Church Rd

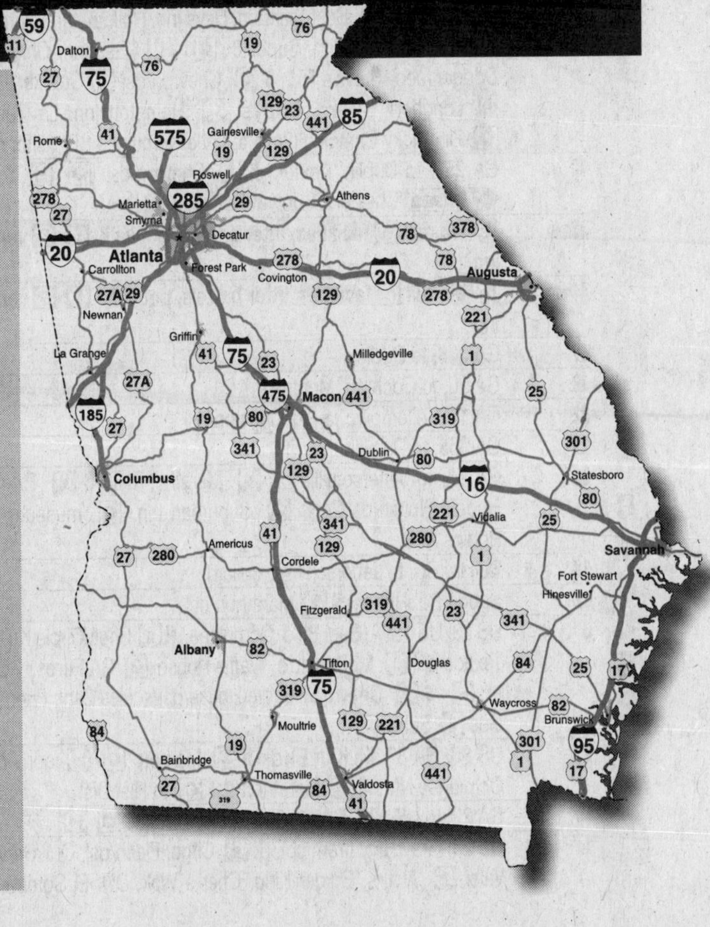

INTERSTATE 16 Cont'd

	Exit #	Services
	127	GA 67, to Pembroke, Ft Stewart, N BP/dsl, Shell/dsl Bay South Rest., Gator Rest. antiques
	116	US 25/301, to Statesboro, N Chevron/rest/dsl/scales/24hr Magnolia Springs SP (45 mi), to GA S U, S Patriot Inn
	111	Pulaski-Excelsior Rd, S Citgo/Grady's Grill/dsl Beaver Run RV Park, tires/repair
METTER	104	GA 22, GA 121, Metter, N BP/dsl/scales/24hr, Exxon, Parker's/dsl, Shell/dsl Bevrick's Grille, Burger King, Chinese Buffet, DQ, El Mariachi, Jomax BBQ, KFC/Taco Bell, McDonald's, Papa Buck's BBQ, Pizza Hut, Pond House Grill, Shogun, Subway, Waffle House, Zaxby's American Inn, Days Inn, Econo Inn, Garden Inn H Chevrolet, info, O'Reilly Parts, Rite Aid, to Smith SP, S Marathon/dsl, Phillips 66/dsl Ford
	101mm	Canoochee River
	98	GA 57, to Stillmore, S BP/dsl/24hr, Chevron/dsl to Altahama SP
	90	US 1, to Swainsboro, N Gasco/Subway/dsl, Marathon/dsl
	88mm	Ohoopee River
	84	GA 297, to Vidalia, N truck sales
	78	US 221, GA 56, to Swainsboro
	71	GA 15, GA 78, to Soperton, N Chevron/dsl
	67	GA 29, to Soperton, S Chevron/dsl, Marathon/dsl Huddle House
	58	GA 199, Old River Rd, East Dublin
	56mm	Oconee River
	54	GA 19, to Dublin, S Chevron/dsl
DUBLIN	51	US 441, US 319, to Dublin, N BP/Stuckey's/Subway/dsl, Flash/gas, Neighbor's/dsl, Pilot/dsl/scales/24hr Arby's, Burger King, KFC, King's Inn/rest., McDonald's, Ruby Tuesday, Sanchez Border Grill, Taco Bell, Waffle House, Wendy's Baymont Inn, Best Western, Days Inn, Holiday Inn Express, Quality Inn, Relax Inn, Super 8 H $General, Chrysler/Dodge/Jeep, Steve's RV, S Chevron/dsl Cracker Barrel, Longhorn Steaks, Zaxby's Hampton Inn, La Quinta Pinetucky Camping (2mi), to Little Ocmulgee SP, visitor ctr
	49	GA 257, to Dublin, Dexter, N Chevron/dsl H S Loves/Chester's/Subway/dsl/scales/24hr
	46mm	**wb, full facilities, litter barrels, petwalk vending**
	44mm	**eb, full facilities, litter barrels, petwalk vending**
	42	GA 338, to Dudley
	39	GA 26, to Cochran, Montrose
	32	GA 112, Allentown, S Chevron/dsl
	27	GA 358, to Danville
OCMULGEE	24	GA 96, to Jeffersonville, N Marathon/dsl, S Exxon/Huddle House/dsl/24hr Suburban Inn museum, to Robins AFB
	18	Bullard Rd, to Jeffersonville, Bullard
	12	Sgoda Rd, Huber, N Marathon/dsl
	6	US 23, US 129A, East Blvd, Ocmulgee, N Shell/Circle K/DQ, Texaco/dsl McDonald's, Waffle House GA Forestry Ctr, to S Chevron/Huddle House/dsl/scales/24hr, Friendly Gus Subway
	2	US 80, GA 87, MLK Jr Blvd, N Marriott H conv ctr, Ocmulgee NM, S Marathon/dsl to Hist Dist
	1b	GA 22, to US 129, GA 49, 2nd St (from wb), S H
	1a	US 23, Gray Hwy (from eb), N Citgo, Flash/dsl, QuikServe, Valer Arby's, Burger King, Chen's Wok, DQ, El Sombrero
MACON	1a	Continued Mexican, Fincher's BBQ, Hardee's, Hong Kong Express, Krispy Kreme, Krystal, Little Caesar's, McDonald's, Papa John's, Subway, Taco Bell, Wendy's H Attaway Tire, CVS Drug, Family$, Kroger, O'Reilly Parts, U-Haul, Walgreens, S Jumbo's Sunoco/dsl Burger King, Checker's, Krystal, Pizza Hut, Waffle House, Zaxby's
	0mm	I-75, S to Valdosta, N to Atlanta. **I-16 begins/ends on I-75, exit 165 in Macon.**

INTERSTATE 20

	Exit #	Services
	202mm	Georgia/South Carolina state line, Savannah River
	201mm	**Welcome Ctr wb full facilities, info, litter barrels, petwalk vending**
	200	GA 104, Riverwatch Pkwy, Augusta, N Pilot/Wendy's/dsl/scales/24hr Waffle House Baymont Inn, Candlewood Suites, Comfort Suites, Jameson Inn, Microtel, Quality Inn, Sleep Inn, ValuePlace Freightliner, S Cabela's, Costco/gas
AUGUSTA	199	GA 28, Washington Rd, Augusta, **0-3 mi** N BP, RaceWay, Shell/Circle K, Sprin Applebee's, Baskin-Robbins/Dunkin Donuts, Burger King, CA Dreaming, Capt D's, Checkers, Chick-fil-A, Denny's, Domino's, DQ, Fujiyama Japanese, Krystal, Longhorn Steaks, McDonald's, Mi Rancho Mexican, Piccadilly, Pizza Hut, Rhinehart's Seafood, Starbucks, Steakout, Veracruz Mexican, Waffle House, Wife Saver Rest, Wild Wing Cafe Clarion, Courtyard, Econolodge, Hampton Inn, Hilton Garden, Holiday Inn Express, Homewood Suites, La Quinta, Masters Inn, Scottish Inn, Sheraton, Sunset Inn, Super 8, Travelodge $Tree, AutoZone, Buick/GMC, Chevrolet, Chrysler/Dodge/Jeep, Hancock Fabrics, Hyundai, Infiniti, Lexus, Mercedes, NAPA, Nissan, Toyota/Scion, Tuesday Morning, S BP, Circle K/dsl, Shell/Circle K/dsl 5 Guys Burgers, Arby's, BoneFish Grill, Carrabba's, Crazy Turk's Pizza, HoneyBaked Ham, Hooters, Krispy Kreme, McDonald's, Moe's SW Grill, New Peking, Olive Garden, Outback Steaks, Red Lobster, Roadrunner Cafe, Shangri La, Straw Hat Pizza, Subway, Taco Bell, T-Bonz Steaks, Teresa's Mexican, TGIFriday's, Thai Jong Rest., TX Roadhouse, Vallarta Mexican, Waffle House, Wendy's, Zaxby's Best Western, Country Inn&Suites, Knights Inn, Magnolia Inn, Motel 6, Parkway Inn, Staybridge Suites, Westbank Inn $Tree, AT&T, CVS Drug, Firestone/auto, Fresh Mkt Foods, Goodyear/auto, Kroger/dsl, Midas, PepBoys, Publix, SteinMart, Tire Kingdom, Verizon, Walgreens, Whole Food Mkt
	196b	GA 232 W, N Enmark, Murphy Express/dsl Checkers, Golden Corral, Krystal, Salsa's Grill, Stevi B's Pizza Baymont Inn, Travel Inn Aldi Foods, Discount Tire, GNC, Home Depot, Lowe's, O'Reilly Parts, Sam's Club/gas, Tire Kingdom, URGENT CARE, Walgreens, Walmart
	196a	I-520, Bobby Jones Fwy, S Atlanta Bread Co, Buffalo Wild Wings, Carolina Alehouse, Chick-fil-A, Chili's, Dunkin Donuts, Genghis Grill, Logan's Roadhouse, Macaroni Grill, McDonald's, O'Charley's, Panera Bread, Starbucks, Sticky Fingers, Subway, Waffle House DoubleTree Hotel H, Best Buy, Hobby Lobby, Michael's, Office Depot, Old Navy, Petsmart, Rite Aid, Staples, Target, Tires+, to Verizon, vet
	195	Wheeler Rd, N Sprint CarMax, Gander Mtn, S Shell/Circle K/Blimpi Guiseppe's Pizza, Sonic Days Inn H BP/dsl, Harley-Davidson, Rite Aid, URGENT CARE

GA

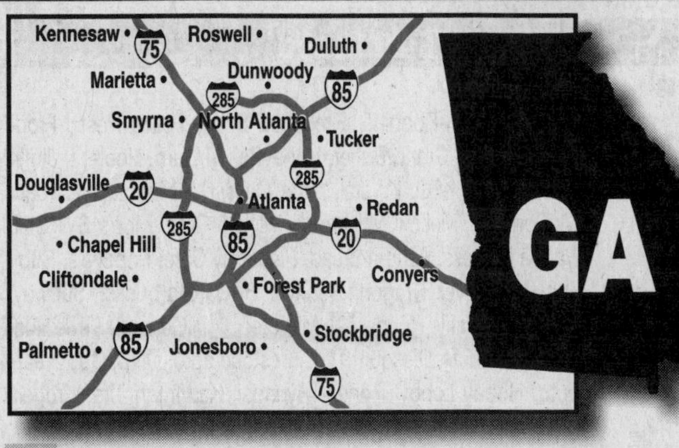

INTERSTATE 20 Cont'd

Exit #	Services
194	GA 383, Belair Rd, to Evans, N Shell/Circle K/dsl, Sprint Bojangles, Burger King, Hungry Howie's, Popeye's, Sun Kwong Chinese, Taco Bell, Waffle House, Wendy's GA Inn Family$, Food Lion, Fun Park, S BP/DQ/dsl, Fuel Express, Pilot/Subway/dsl/scales/24hr Cookout, Cracker Barrel, McDonald's, Steak'n Shake, Waffle House Augusta Inn, Best Suites, Best Value Inn, Best Western, Comfort Inn, Hampton Inn, Hawthorn Suites, Holiday Inn, Howard Johnson, Quality Inn, Red Roof Inn, Super 8, Wingate Inn Goodyear/auto, Kenworth
190	GA 388, to Grovetown, N TPS/dsl/scales/24hr Waffle House, S Murphy Express/dsl Applebee's, Arby's, Jersey Mike's, Mi Rancho Verizon, Walmart
189mm	**weigh sta both lanes**
183	US 221, to Harlem, Appling, S Exxon/dsl to Laurel&Hardy Museum
182mm	**both lanes, 24hr security, full facilities, litter barrels, petwalk RV dump, vending**
175	GA 150, N Chevron/rest/dsl/24hr Express Inn to Mistletoe SP
172	US 78, GA 17, Thomson, N Loves/Chester's/Subway/dsl/scales/24hr Waffle House Chrysler/Dodge/Jeep S BP/DQ/dsl, BP/dsl, Circle K/Blimpie/dsl, M&A/dsl, RaceWay/dsl Arby's, Bojangles, Burger King, Checkers, Domino's, Habaneros Mexican, Kiosco Mexican, Krystal, LJ Silver, Lucky Chinese, McDonald's, MingWah Chinese, Pizza Hut, Popeye's, Ryan's, Taco Bell, Waffle House, Wendy's, Zaxby's Comfort Inn, EconoLodge, Hampton Inn, Scottish Inn, White Columns Inn H $General, Advance Parts, AutoZone, Bi-Lo, Family$, O'Reilly Parts, URGENT CARE, Verizon, Walgreens
169	Thomson
165	GA 80, Camak
160	E Cadley Rd, Norwood
154	US 278, GA 12, Barnett
148	GA 22, Crawfordville, N BP to Stephens SP
138	GA 77, GA 15, Siloam, N FLYING J/Denny's/dsl/LP/scales/24hr, S BP/dsl H
130	GA 44, Greensboro, N BP/dsl, Valero/Subwa DQ, McDonald's, Pizza Hut, Waffle House, Wendy's, Zaxby's Holiday Lodge, Jameson Inn H $General, Buick/Chevrolet, Greensboro Tire/repair, S Chevron/dsl Home Depot/gas, **weigh sta**
121	to Lake Oconee, Buckhead, S Chevron/dsl Museum of Art (3mi)
114	US 441, US 129, to Madison, N Chevron/Subway/dsl, Citgo/dsl, Pilot/Huddle House/dsl/scales/24hr, RaceWay/dsl Arby's, Burger King, Chick-fil-A, Cracker Barrel, Hong Kong Buffet, KFC, Krystal, McDonald's, Pachos Mexican, Pizza Hut, Steak'n Shake, Taco Bell, Waffle House, Wendy's, Zaxby's Comfort Inn, Hampton Inn, Quality Inn H $General, $Tree, Advance Parts, AutoZone, Ingles Foods/gas, Lowe's, O'Reilly Parts, Rite Aid, Verizon, Walmart, S Flash/dsl, Shell, TA/BP/Country Pride/Popeye's/dsl/scales/24hr/ @ Waffle House Deerfield Inn, Super 8, Wingate Inn Country Boys RV Park (1mi), truckwash/service
113	GA 83, Madison, N BP/dsl H st patrol
108mm	**N wb, full facilities, litter barrels, petwalk RV dump, vending**
105	Rutledge, Newborn, N Valero/pizza/dsl Hard Labor Creek SP
103mm	**S wb, full facilities, litter barrels, petwalk RV dump, vending**
101	US 278
98	GA 11, to Monroe, Monticello, N Blue Willow Inn (4mi), S BP/Blimpie/dsl, Marathon
95mm	Alcovy River
93	GA 142, Hazelbrand Rd, N Home Depot, S QT/dsl Bullrito's Cafe, IHOP, McDonald's, Shane's Rib Shack, Subway, Taco Bell, Waffle House, Wendy's Hampton Inn, Travelodge H $Tree, Aldi Foods, AT&T, Kauffman Tire, Verizon, Walmart/Subway
92	Alcovy Rd, N Chevron/dsl, Shell/dsl Waffle House Baymont Inn, Best Value Inn, Covington Lodge, Days Inn, Super 8, S H
90	US 278, GA 81, Covington, S Citgo/dsl, QT, RaceWay/dsl Applebee's, Arby's, Bojangles, Burrito Loco, Capt D's, Checkers, Chick-fil-A, Church's, Covington Diner, DQ, Dunkin Donuts/Baskin-Robbins, Firehouse Subs, Hardee's, Just Dogs/Burgers, KFC, Krystal, Little Caesars, LJ Silver, Longhorn Steaks, Mama Maria's, McDonald's, Moe's SW Grill, Pacho's Mexican, Papa John's, Pizza Hut, Stalvey's Rest., Stevi B's Pizza, Subway, Taco Bell, Waffle House, Wendy's, Zaxby's Holiday Inn Express $General, Ace Hardware, Advance Parts, AutoZone, BigLots, Chevrolet, CVS, Family$, Food Depot, GNC, Ingles Foods, K-Mart, Kroger/dsl, O'Reilly Parts, Radio Shack, Rite Aid, vet, Walgreens
88	Almon Rd, to Porterdale, N Chevron/dsl, S BP, Libert McDonald's, Subway (2mi) Riverside Estates RV Camp, transmissions/repair
84	GA 162, Salem Rd, to Pace, N BJ's Whse/gas, Marathon/dsl Chrysler/Dodge/Jeep, S Citgo, QT, RaceWay/dsl, Shell/dsl Baskin-Robbins, Burger King, Dunkin Donuts, Hardee's, KFC, Los Bravos Mexican, McDonald's, Quiznos, Subway, Taco Bell, Waffle House, Wendy's Advance Parts, Family$, Food Depot, Ingles/gas, Olympic Auto, O'Reilly Parts, PepBoys, Rite Aid
82	GA 138, GA 20, Conyers, N BP/dsl, QT Applebee's, Bruster's, Chili's, ChuckECheese, Coldstone, Cracker Barrel, Don Tello's, Golden Corral, IHOP, O'Charley's, Outback Steaks, Red Lobster, Sonic, Subway Country Inn&Suites, Days Inn, Hampton Inn, Holiday Inn Express, Jameson Inn, La Quinta, Super 8 AT&T, Belk, Chevrolet/Buick/GMC, Courtyard, Ford, Harley-Davidson, Home Depot, Jo-Ann, Kohl's, Michael's, Office Depot, Old Navy, Petsmart, Staples, Tires+, TJ Maxx, U-Haul, Walmart, S Chevron, Shell/dsl Blimpie, Burger King, Capt D's, Checkers, Chick-fil-A, CiCi's Pizza, Dunkin

THOMSON

MADISON

COVINGTON

CONYERS

GA

GA

INTERSTATE 20 Cont'd

LITHONIA

82 Continued
Donuts/Baskin-Robbins, Firehouse Subs, Folk's Rest., Frontera Mexican, Grand Buffet, HoneyBaked Ham, Hooters, Jim'n Nick's BBQ, KFC, Krystal, Little Caesar's, Mandarin Garden, McDonald's, Mellow Mushroom, Milano Cafe, Moe's SW Grill, Panda Express, Panera Bread, Piccadilly Cafe, Popeye's, Ruby Tuesday, Silver Dragon, Sonny's BBQ, Starbucks, Subway, Taco Bell, Waffle House [lodging] Microtel [other] $General, $Tree, Aldi Foods, BigLots, Discount Tire, Firestone/auto, GNC, Goodyear/auto, Hobby Lobby, Honda, Hyundai, Kauffman Tire, Kroger/gas, NTB, PepBoys, Publix, Radio Shack, Ross, Target, USPO, Verizon, Walgreens

80 West Ave, Conyers, N [gas] Shell/dsl, Valero/dsl [food] Domino's, DQ, Subway, Waffle House [lodging] Best Value Inn, Motel 6 [other] Conyers Drug, Family$, Meineke, Piggly Wiggly, S [gas] QT/dsl, Texaco/dsl [food] Fish House, Longhorn Steaks, McDonald's [lodging] Comfort Inn [other] Nissan, vet

79mm **parking area eb**

78 Sigman Rd, N [gas] Shell/dsl, Texaco [food] Waffle House

75 US 278, GA 124, Turner Hill Rd, N [gas] BP/dsl, Citgo/dsl, S [food] Applebee's, Arizona's, Bruster's, Buffalo Wild Wings, Chicken&Waffles, Chick-fil-A, Chili's, Don Tello's Mexican, Firehouse Subs, Grand China, IHOP, Kampai's Steaks, McDonald's, Olive Garden, Panera Bread, Smokey Bones BBQ, Steak n'Shake, Steak'n Shake, Subway, Taco Bell, TGIFriday, Zaxby's [lodging] Comfort Inn, Comfort Suites, Fairfield Inn, Hilton Garden, Holiday Inn Express, Hyatt Place [other] $Tree, AT&T, Best Buy, Big Lots, Dillard's, JC Penney, Kia, Kohl's, Macy's, mall, Marshalls, PetCo, Rite Aid, Ross, Sam's Club/gas, Sears/auto, Staples, Target, Tires+, Toyota/Scion, Verizon, Walmart

74 Evans Mill Rd, GA 124, Lithonia, N [gas] BP/Circle K, Chevron, Shell [food] Capt D's, McDonald's, Pizza Hut, SoulFood Rest., Subway, Wendy's [other] Advance Parts, CVS Drug, O'Reilly Parts, S [gas] Citgo/dsl [food] Da-Bomb Wings/Seafood, DQ, Dudley's Rest., Krystal, Waffle House [lodging] Microtel [other] $General

71 Hillandale Dr, Farrington Rd, Panola Rd, N [gas] QT/dsl, Shell/dsl [food] Burger King, Checkers, KFC, McDonald's, Rib Tips, Waffle House, Wings&Philly [lodging] Budgetel, Quality Inn, Super 8 [other] Family$, S [gas] BP/dsl, Citgo, Murphy USA/dsl, Shell/dsl [food] Dunkin Donuts, IHOP, Marco's Pizza, New China, Popeye's, Ruby Tuesday, Subway, Taco Bell/LJ Silver, Town Wings, Wendy's [lodging] Red Roof Inn [other] Lowe's, Publix, Radio Shack, Tires+, Verizon, Walgreens, Walmart/McDonald's

68 Wesley Chapel Rd, Snapfinger Rd, N [food] Capt D's, Checkers, Chick-fil-A, China Cafeteria, Church's, Dunkin Donuts, KFC, Little Caesar's, New China, Subway, Taco Bell, Waffle House [lodging] Economy Inn [other] $General, DJ's Repair, Home Depot, Kroger, NTB, S [gas] Chevron/dsl, Mobil, QT, Shell/dsl [food] Dragon Chinese, JJ's Fish& Chicken, McDonald's, Popeye's [lodging] Super Inn [other] Family$, USPO

67b a I-285, S to Macon, N to Greenville

66 Columbia Dr (from eb, no return), N [gas] Chevron

65 GA 155, Candler Rd, to Decatur, N [gas] Chevron, Citgo, Marathon/dsl [food] Pizza Hut, Popeye's, Red Lobster, Wendy's [lodging] Best Value Inn [other] CVS Drug, U-Haul, S [gas] BP, Chevron, Shell/dsl, Texaco [food] Baskin-Robbins/Dunkin Donuts, Burger King, Checkers, Church's, DQ, KFC, McDonald's, Subway, Taco Bell, Waffle King [lodging] Country Hearth Inn [other] BigLots, Firestone/auto, Macy's

ATLANTA AREA

63 Gresham Rd, N [gas] Chevron, Citgo/dsl [food] American D [other] Walmart/Subway, S [gas] Citgo, Marathon, Shell, Texaco/ [food] Church's

62 Flat Shoals Rd (from eb, no return)

61b GA 260, Glenwood Ave, N [gas] Chevron, Texaco/dsl

61a Maynard Terrace (from eb, no return)

60b a US 23, Moreland Ave, N [gas] Exxon, Valero [lodging] Atlanta Mo [other] Advance Parts, S [gas] Citgo/dsl, Shell [food] Checkers, Kryst LJ Silver, McDonald's, Wendy's

59b Memorial Dr, Glenwood Ave (from eb)

59a Cyclorama, N [gas] Chevron/Blimpie/dsl [other] MLK Site, S [gas] B Subway [other] Confederate Ave Complex, CVS

58b Hill St (from wb, no return), N [gas] Shell [food] Mrs. Winners

58a Capitol St (from wb, no return), N to GA Dome, S Capital In downtown

57 I-75/85

56b Windsor St (from eb), [other] to Turner Field

56a US 19, US 29, McDaniel St (eb only), N [gas] Chevron/dsl

55b Lee St (from wb), Ft McPherson, S [gas] Exxon, Shell [food] Church Popeye's, Taco Bell, West Inn Food Court [other] $Family, Maxwa Sav-A-Lot

55a Lowery Blvd, S [gas] Exxon/dsl, Shell [food] Church's, Popeye's, Tac Bell, West Inn Food Court [other] Family$, Maxway, Sav-A-Lot

54 Langhorn St (from wb), to Cascade Rd

53 MLK Dr, to GA 139, N [gas] Chevron, Shell/dsl, S [gas] Texaco/d [other] auto repair

52b a GA 280, Holmes Dr, High Tower Rd, S [gas] Chevron, Exxon/d [food] Hong Kong Chinese, McDonald's, Wendy's [other] AutoZon CVS Drug, Family$

51b a I-285, S to Montgomery, N to Chattanooga

49 GA 70, Fulton Ind Blvd, N [gas] Citgo/dsl, Shamrock/d [food] Wendy's [lodging] Days Inn, Majestick Lodge [other] [airport] S [gas] BP dsl, Chevron/dsl, Texaco/dsl, Valero [food] Grand Buffet, McDo ald's, Waffle House [lodging] Fairview Inn, Red Roof Inn [other] U-Ha

48mm Chattahoochee River

47 Six Flags Pkwy (from wb), N [gas] BP [lodging] EconoLodge, S [lodging] Knights Inn, Sleep Inn, Wingate Inn [other] Six Flags Funpark

46b a Riverside Parkway, N [gas] Citgo/Church's, Marathon, Q [food] Hong Kong Buffet, Waffle House [lodging] Super 8 [other] Family$ S [gas] Citgo [food] Wendy's [lodging] Knights Inn, Sleep Inn, Wingat Inn [other] Six Flags Funpark

44 GA 6, Thornton Rd, to Lithia Springs, N [gas] BP, QT, RaceTrac dsl, Shell/dsl, Valero [food] Applebee's, BBQ House, Bojangles Burger King, Chick-fil-A, Church's, Domino's, Firehouse Subs Golden Dragon Chinese, Hardee's, IHOP, KFC, Krystal, Mc Donald's, Olive Tree Rest., Popeye's, Ruby Tuesday, Shoney's Sonic, Subway, Taco Bell, Waffle House, Wendy's, Zaxby' [lodging] Budget Inn, Holiday Inn Express, InTowne Suites, Qualit Inn [other] $General, AT&T, Atlanta West Camping (2mi), Autozone Carmax, Chevrolet, Ford, Harley Davidson, Home Depot, Hon da, Hyundai, Kroger/gas, Midas, Nissan, Office Depot, Tires+ Verizon, vet, VW, Walgreens, S [gas] Shell [food] Bei Jin China Cracker Barrel, Fiesta Mexican [lodging] Candlewood Suites, Coun try Inn&Suites, Courtyard, Fairfield Inn, Hampton Inn, Hilto Garden, Motel 6, SpringHill Suites [other] Chrysler/Dodge/Jeep Kia, to Sweetwater Creek SP, Toyota/Scion, Walmart

42mm **weigh sta eb**

41 Lee Rd, to Lithia Springs, N [gas] Marathon/dsl

37 GA 92, to Douglasville, N [gas] RaceTrac/dsl, Shell/dsl [food] Blimpie Checker's, Chick-fil-A, Church's, DQ, Kenny's Rest., Krystal, Longhorn Steaks, Martin's Rest., McDonald's, Pizza Hut, Popeye's

INTERSTATE 20 Cont'd

DOUGLASVILLE

37 Continued
Subway, Taco Bell, Waffle House, Wendy's Best Value Inn, Comfort Inn, Days Inn, EconoLodge, Quality Inn, Ramada Ltd, Royal Inn H, AutoZone, CVS Drug, Family$, Kroger/dsl, NAPA, O'Reilly Parts, Tires+, Walgreens, S Chevron/dsl, QT, Texaco/dsl Domino's, Waffle House $General, Aamco, Advance Parts, Ingles Foods

36 Chapel Hill Rd, N H S QT, Shell/dsl 5 Guys Burgers, Arby's, Carrabba's, China Garden, Coldstone, Daruma, Joe's Crabshack, Johnny's Subs, Logan's Roadhouse, McDonald's, O'Charley's, Olive Garden, Outback Steaks, Panda Express, Provino's Italian, Shane's Rib Shack, Starbucks, Subway, TX Roadhouse, Waffle House Hampton Inn $Tree, Aldi Foods, Belk, BigLots, Dillard's, Discount Tire, Firestone/auto, Hobby Lobby, JC Penney, Kohl's, Macy's, Marshall's, Michael's, Old Navy, Petsmart, Rite Aid, Ross, Sears/auto, Target, Verizon

34 GA 5, to Douglasville, N RaceTrac/dsl, Texaco/dsl Atlantic Grill, Cracker Barrel, Stevie B's Pizza, Waffle House, Williamson Bros BBQ, Zaxby's Holiday Inn Express, La Quinta, Sleep Inn $Tree, Kauffman Tires, Sam's Club, URGENT CARE, Walmart, S Chevron/dsl, Circle K, Shell/dsl Applebee's, Bruster's, Buffalo Wild Wings, Burger King, Chick-fil-A, ChuckECheese, DQ, Dunkin Donuts, El Tio Mexican, Fiesta Mexican, Folk's Rest., Golden Corral, HoneyBaked Ham, IHOP, KFC, King Buffet, Krystal, La Salsa, LJ Silver, McDonald's, Moe's SW Grill, Monterrey Mexican, Papa John's, Pizza Buffet, Popeyes, Quiznos, Red Lobster, Seabreeze Seafood, S'more BBQ, Sonic, Steak'n Shake, Subway, Taco Bell, Taco Mac, Waffle House, Wasabi Japanese, Wendy's InTown Suites Advance Parts, AT&T, Batteries+, Best Buy, Goodyear/auto, Home Depot, Jo-Ann Crafts, Kroger/dsl, Lowe's, Meineke, NTB, Office Depot, O'Reilly Parts, PepBoys, Publix, Tuesday Morning, U-Haul, vet, Walgreens

30 Post Rd, S Shell/dsl

VILLA RICA

26 Liberty Rd, Villa Rica, N Shell/dsl, Swifty/dsl China Wok, Johnny's Pizza, McDonald's, Mex-Grill, Olive Tree Rest., Subway, Sumo Japanese, Waffle House H, $General, Publix, vet, Walgreens, S Chevron, Wilco/Hess/Godfather's Pizza/Subway/dsl/scales/24hr American Inn

24 GA 101, GA 61, Villa Rica, N BP/dsl, RaceTrac/dsl, Shell/dsl Arby's, Chick-fil-A, Hardee's, KFC/Taco Bell, Krystal, Lin's Garden Chinese, McDonald's, Pizza Hut, Romero's Italian, Sonic, Stix Grill, Subway, Waffle House, Wendy's Comfort Inn, Days Inn, EconoLodge, Super 8 H, Advance Parts, AT&T, AutoZone, CVS Drug, Ingles Foods, Rite Aid, Walgreens, S QT, Shell/dsl Bojangles, Burger King, Capt D's, Domino's, El Ranchito Mexican, O'Charley's, Papa John's, Waffle House, Zaxby's $Tree, Chevrolet, GNC, Home Depot, Radio Shack, to W GA Coll, URGENT CARE, Verizon, Walmart/Subway

21mm Little Tallapoosa River

19 GA 113, Temple, N FLYING J/dsl/scales/24hr, Pilot/Subway/Wendy's/dsl/scales/24hr/ @ El Tapatio's, Fortune Star Chinese, Hardee's, McDonald's, Temple Pizza, Waffle House Ingles Foods/gas

BREMEN

15mm **weigh sta wb**

11 US 27, Bremen, Bowdon, N Chevron/dsl, Marathon/dsl, Murphy USA/dsl, Valero/Domino's/dsl Arby's, Capt D's, Checker's, Chopsticks Chinese, Cracker Barrel, Juanito's, KFC/Taco Bell, McDonald's, Papa John's, Subway, Waffle House, Wendy's, Zaxby's Bridgeview Inn, Hampton Inn, Holiday Inn

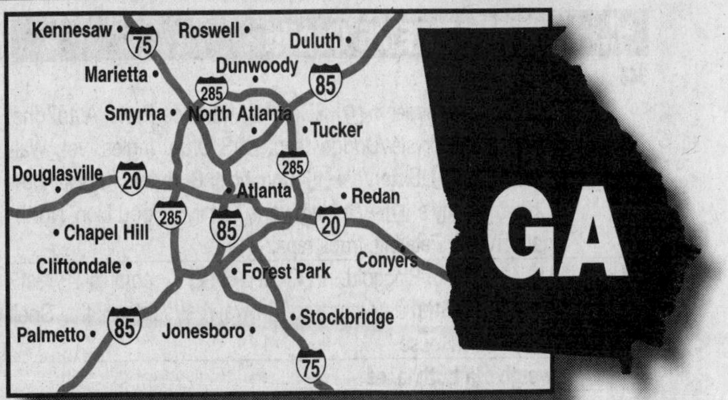

11 Continued
Express, Microtel, Quality Inn H $General, Advance Parts, Ford, Ingles Foods/gas, URGENT CARE, Verizon, Walmart/McDonald's, S BP/dsl, Kangaroo/dsl John Tanner SP

9 Waco Rd, N Loves/Chesters/Subway/dsl/scales/24hr Jellystone RV Park (2mi)

5 GA 100, Tallapoosa, N Citgo/dsl/24hr, Victory/dsl Waffle House Big Oak RV park, S Newborn TrkStp/rest/dsl/24hr/ @, Pilot/KFC/Taco Bell/dsl/scales/24hr, Robinson/Subway DQ, GA Diner Super 8 to John Tanner SP, truck repair/wash

1mm **Welcome Ctr eb full facilities, info, litter barrels, petwalk vending**

0mm Georgia/Alabama state line, Eastern/Central time zone

GA

INTERSTATE 59

Exit # Services

I-59 begins/ends on I-24, exit 167. For I-24, turn to Tennessee Interstate 24.

20mm I-24, W to Nashville, E to Chattanooga

17 Slygo Rd, to New England, W Midnite/dsl KOA (2mi)

11 GA 136, Trenton, E Chevron/dsl, Exxon/dsl, Marathon/Kangaro Asian Garden, Guthrie's, Hardee's, McDonald's, Pizza Hut, Subway Days Inn Advance Parts, CVS Drug, Family$, Fred's Drug, Ingles, O'Reilly Parts, to Cloudland Canyon SP, W BP, Citgo/dsl, Marathon/Kangaroo/dsl Huddle House, Krystal, Little Caesars, Taco Bell, Wendy's $General, BiLo, Food Outlet

4 Rising Fawn, E Citgo, W BP/dsl, Pilot/Subway/dsl/scales/24hr camping

0mm Georgia/Alabama state line, eastern/central time zone

INTERSTATE 75

Exit # Services

355mm Georgia/Tennessee state line

354mm Chickamauga Creek

353 GA 146, Rossville, E Cloud Springs Lodge, W BP/Subway/dsl, Shell/dsl Cabela's, Costco/gas

352mm **Welcome Ctr sb, full facilities, info, litter barrels, petwalk vending**

350 GA 2, Bfd Pkwy, to Ft Oglethorpe, E Chevron/dsl, Kangaroo/dsl Hampton Inn, Hometown Inn, W RaceTrac/dsl Subway H, KOA, to Chickamauga NP

348 GA 151, Ringgold, E BP/Kangaroo/dsl, Mapco Cracker Barrel, Hardee's, KFC, Los Maguey Mexican, McDonald's, Pizza Hut, Sonic, Subway, Taco Bell, Waffle House Holiday

INTERSTATE 75 Cont'd

DALTON

348 Continued
Inn Express, Super 8 $General, Advance Parts, AutoZone, Chevrolet, Chrysler/Dodge/Jeep, CVS Drug, Ingles, vet, Walgreens, W Exxon/dsl Domino's, Guthries, Krystal, New China, Wendy's Ace Hardware, Family$, Food Lion, Northgate RV Ctr, Peterbilt, truck repair

345 US 41, US 76, Ringgold, E BP, W Cochran's TP/rest./dsl/scales/24hr/@, Kangaroo/Subway/dsl/scales/24hr, Shell Waffle House

343mm **weigh sta both lanes**

341 GA 201, to Varnell, Tunnel Hill, W BP/Mapco, Chevron carpet outlets

336 US 41, US 76, Dalton, Rocky Face, E Mapco, Murphy USA/dsl, RaceTrac/dsl Checkers, Waffle House Ford/Lincoln, Home Depot, Kohl's, PetCo, Verizon, Walmart/Subway, W BP/dsl, Exxon Los Pablos, Tijuana Mexican, Wendy's Baymont Inn, carpet outlets, Econolodge, Guest Inn, Motel 6, Staylodge

333 GA 52, Dalton, E BP/dsl, Exxon/dsl, RaceTrac/dsl Applebee's, Bruster's, Burger King, Capt D's, Chick-fil-A, CiCi's Pizza, Cracker Barrel, DQ, El Patron Mexican, Five Guys Burgers, Fuji Japanese, IHOP, Jersey Mike's Subs, KFC, Las Palmas Mexican, LJ Silver, Longhorn Steaks, McDonald's, O'Charley's, Outback Steaks, Panda Express, Panera Bread, Pizza Hut, Schlotzsky's, Shoney's, Sonic, Starbucks, Steak'n Shake, Subway, Taco Bell, Tony's Italian, Waffle House Days Inn, Hampton Inn, Red Roof Inn $Tree, AT&T, BigLots, Chevrolet, Chrysler/Dodge/Jeep, Harley-Davidson, K-Mart, Kroger/dsl, TJ Maxx, Tuesday Morning, Walgreens, W Chili's, Red Lobster, Zaxby's Comfort Inn, Country Inn Suites, Courtyard, Holiday Inn, Holiday Inn Express, Howard Johnson, La Quinta, Quality Inn, Super 8 NW GA Trade/Conv Ctr

GA

328 GA 3, to US 41, E BP/Kangaroo/dsl, Pilot/Arby's/dsl/scales/24hr Waffle House, Wendy's Best Value Inn, W carpet outlets

326 Carbondale Rd, E LNG, Pilot/McDonald's/Subway/dsl/scales, W BP

RESACA

320 GA 136, to Lafayette, Resaca, E FLYING J/Denny's/dsl/LP/24hr truck repair/parts

319mm **sb, full facilities, litter barrels, Oostanaula River, petwalk RV dump, vending**

318 US 41, Resaca, E Hess/Wilco/DQ/Wendy's/scales/dsl/24hr Hardee's Rodeway Inn, W Pure, Shell/dsl Chuckwagon Rest. Best Inn, Budget Inn, Duffy's Motel, Executive Inn

317 GA 225, to Chatsworth, E New Echota HS, Vann House HS, W Marathon (1mi) Express Inn

CALHOUN

315 GA 156, Redbud Rd, to Calhoun, E Subway, Waffle House Food Lion, KOA (2mi), W BP/dsl Arby's, Shoney's Ramada Rite Aid, URGENT CARE

312 GA 53, to Calhoun, E Shell/dsl Applebee's, Cracker Barrel, Longhorn Steaks, Wendy's Country Inn&Suites, Days Inn, Fairfield Inn, La Quinta Calhoun Outlets/famous brands, W BP/Arby's, Chevron/dsl, Marathon/Kangaroo, Murphy USA, RaceTrac/dsl Bojangles, Burger King, Capt D's, Checkers, Chick-fil-A, China Palace, Church's, DQ, Dunkin Donuts, Eastern Buffet, El Nopal Mexican, Gondolier Pizza, Hibachi Buffet, Huddle House, IHOP, KFC, Krystal, Little Caesars

ADAIRSVILLE

312 Continued
LJ Silver, McDonald's, Pizza Hut, Popeyes, Ruby Tuesday, Starbucks, Subway, Taco Bell, Tokyo Steaks, Waffle House, Zaxby's Baymont Inn, Holiday Inn Express, Motel 6, Scottish Inn, Super 8 $General, Advance Parts, AT&T, AutoZone, GNC, Goodyear/auto, Home Depot, Ingles, Kroger/dsl, NAPA, Office Depot, Verizon, vet, Walmart

308mm **nb, full facilities, litter barrels, petwalk RV dump, vending**

306 GA 140, Adairsville, E Click/dsl, Patty's Tkstp/rest./dsl, QT/dsl/scales/24hrs, Valero/dsl Cracker Barrel, Wendy's Hampton Inn truck repair, W Adairsville TP/dsl/scales, BP/dsl, Chevron/dsl, Exxon/dsl Burger King, Hardee's, McDonald's, Subway, Taco Bell, Waffle House, Zaxby's Magnuson Hotel, Quality Inn, Ramada Ltd Advance Parts, AT&T, AutoZone, Family$, Food Lion, Harvest Moon RV Park

296 Cassville-White Rd, E Pilot/McDonald's/Subway/dsl/scales, Pure, TA/BP/Burger King/Pizza Hut/Popeye's/Taco Bell/dsl/scales/24hr/ @, Texaco/dsl Cartersville North Inn truckwash, W Chevron, Marathon/dsl, Shell/dsl Country Hearth Inn KOA

293 US 411, to White, E Sunoco/dsl, Texaco/dsl Quality Inn, W Chevron/dsl, Marathon AJ's Cafe, Waffle House Clarion Harley-Davidson, mineral museum, RV camping, st patrol

290 GA 20, to Rome, E Chevron/dsl, Exxon/Subway/dsl, Kangaroo/dsl Arby's, McDonald's, Wendy's Best Value Inn, Best Western, Country Inn Suites, EconoLodge, Motel 6, Red Roof Inn, Super 8, W BP/dsl, Murphy USA (1.5mi), Shell/dsl Cracker Barrel, Shoney's, Waffle House, Zaxby's Days Inn, Hampton Inn $Tree, Lowe's, Rite Aid, RV camping (7mi), Walmart/McDonald's

288 GA 113, Cartersville, **0-2 mi** W Exxon/Subway/dsl, Kangaroo/dsl Applebee's, Bojangles, Bruster's, Burger King, Chick-Fil-A, Chili's, CiCi's, Gondolier Pizza, IHOP, KFC, Krystal, Larry's Subs, Longhorn Steaks, Los Reyes Mexican, McDonald's, McDonald's, Ming Moon, Moe's SW Grill, Papa John's, Red Lobster, Starbucks, Steak'n Shake, Subway, Taco Bell, Waffle House, Wendy's Fairfield Inn, Hilton Garden, Knights Inn $General, $Tree, AT&T, Belk, Big Lots, Chrysler/Dodge/Jeep, GNC, Goodyear/auto, Hobby Lobby, Honda, Kohl's, Kroger/dsl, O'Reilly Parts, Publix, Staples, Target, TJ Maxx, to Etowah Indian Mounds (6mi), USPO, Verizon

286mm Etowah River

285 Emerson, E Sunoco Red Top Mtn Lodge to Red Top Mtn SP, W to Allatoona Dam

283 Allatoona Rd, Emerson, E camping (2mi), W Loves /McDonald's/Subway/dsl/scales/24hr Chick-fil-A, Wendy's Hampton Inn, Loves Hotel

280mm Allatoona Lake

ACWORTH

278 Glade Rd, to Acworth, E Marathon/dsl, Shell Best Value McKinney Camping (3mi), to Glade Marina, W Marathon/dsl, RaceTrac/dsl Bojangles, KFC, Krystal, Papa John's, Pizza Hut, Subway, Taco Bell, Waffle House Best Inn AutoZone, Ingles/cafe, O'Reilly Parts, Rite Aid

277 GA 92, Acworth, E BP/Dunkin Donuts/dsl, RaceTrac/dsl Hardee's, Waffle House Days Inn, Holiday Inn Express, La Quinta Cabela's, W Chevron/dsl, Shell/DQ/dsl Bamboo Garden, China Chef, Domino's, La Bamba Mexican, McDonald's, Sonic, Subway, Waffle House, Wendy's, Zaxby's Best Western, Econolodge, Quality Inn, Super 8 $General,

INTERSTATE 75 Cont'd

277 Continued
Advance Parts, CVS Drug, Family$, Goodyear/auto, Publix, Walgreens

273 Wade Green Rd, E [gas] BP/dsl, RaceTrac/dsl [food] Arby's, Burger King, Dunkin Donuts, Firehouse Subs, Happy Panda, Las Palmas Mexican, Marco's Pizza, McDonald's, Papa John's, Sam's Eatery, Subway, Taco Bell, Waffle House [lodging] Magnuson Motel, Sleep Inn [other] BigLots, GNC, Goodyear/auto, O'Reilly Parts, Publix, Rite Aid, Tires+, W [gas] Shell, Texaco/dsl [food] BBQ Street, Donny's Rest., Johnny's Pizza/Subs, Mandarin Cafe, Starbucks, Wendy's, Wing Zone [other] $Tree, Home Depot, Kauffman Tire, Kroger/gas, Verizon, Walgreens

271 Chastain Rd, to I-575 N, E [gas] Chevron [food] CA Dreaming, Chick-Fil-A, Cookout, Cracker Barrel, Del Taco, Dunkin Donuts/Baskin Robbins, Firehouse Subs, Five Guys Burgers, Los Reyes, Maddio's Pizza, O'Charley's, Panda Express, Panera Bread, Ruth's Chris Steaks, Starbucks, Taco Mac, Tin Lizzy Cantina, Zaxby's [lodging] Best Western, Comfort Suites, Embassy Suites, Fairfield Inn, Residence Inn, W [gas] Shell/dsl, Swifty Save Gas/Blimpie [food] Arby's, Jimmy John's, Mellow Mushroom, Taco Bell, Waffle House, Wendy's [lodging] Baymont Inn, SpringHill Suites, Sun Suites [other] museum

269 to US 41, to Marietta, E [gas] Shell/dsl [food] Applebee's, Fuddrucker's, Fujihana, Honey Baked Ham, Jimmy John's, Longhorn Steaks, McDonald's, Olive Garden, Penang Asian, Provino's, Red Lobster, Shogun Japanese, Smashburger, Smoothie King, Starbucks, Subway, Twin Peaks [lodging] Comfort Inn, Holiday Inn Express, La Quinta, Red Roof Inn [other] Belk, Firestone/auto, Home Depot, JC Penney, Macy's, mall, Marshall's, Midas, Pepboys, Sears/auto, TJ Maxx, Verizon, W [gas] BP/dsl, Exxon [food] Bahama Breeze, Burger King, Carrabbas, Chick-fil-A, Chili's, Chipotle, ChuckeCheese, Chuy's Mexican, Coldstone, Copelands Grill, Golden Corral, Jason's Deli, Joe's Crabshack, Melting Pot, On-the-Border, Outback Steaks, Panera Bread, Pollo Tropical, Rafferty's, Starbucks, Steak'n Shake, Sweet Tomato, Ted's MT Steaks, TGIFriday, Tilted Kilt, Willy's Mexican [lodging] Courtyard, Day's Inn, Hampton Inn, Hilton Garden, Homewood Suites, Quality Inn, Wingate Inn [other] Best Buy, Buick/GMC, CarMax, Chevrolet, Costco/gas, Dick's, Ford/Lincoln, Hobby Lobby, Jo-Ann Fabrics, Kia/Toyota, Michaels, Nissan, NTB, Old Navy, PetsMart, REI, Subaru, Target, to Kennesaw Mtn NP, VW

MARIETTA

268 I-575 N, GA 5 N, to Canton

267b a GA 5 N, to US 41, Marietta

265 GA120, N Marietta Pkwy, W [gas] Chevron/dsl, Shell/dsl [lodging] Days Inn [other] Advance Parts, Family$, Office Depot, O'Reilly Parts

263 GA 120, to Roswell, E [gas] Chevron, QT, Shell, W [gas] Exxon/dsl, QT [food] Applebee's, China Kitchen, DQ, Hardee's, Haveli Rest., Piccadilly's, Subway, Tasty China [lodging] Econolodge, Hampton Inn, Ltd Suites, Radisson, Super 8 [other] U-Haul, Verizon

261 GA 280, Delk Rd, to Dobbins AFB, E [gas] Exxon/dsl, RaceTrac/dsl, Shell, Shell/Subway/dsl [food] China Wok, Cosmopolitan Cafeteria, Hardee's, KFC/Taco Bell, Little Caesar's, Marco's Pizza, McDonald's, Ruby Tuesday, Waffle House [lodging] Courtyard, Drury Inn, Howard Johnson, Motel 6, Ramada, W [gas] BP, Chevron/dsl [food] Cracker Barrel, Dave&Busters [lodging] Baymont Inn, Days Inn, Holiday Inn Express, Marietta Hotel, Quality Inn

260 Windy Hill Rd, to Smyrna, E [gas] BP/dsl [food] Boston Mkt, Frontera Mex, Fuddrucker's, Houston's Rest., Jersey Mike's Subs, NY Pizza, Pappadeaux Seafood, Pappasito's Cantina,

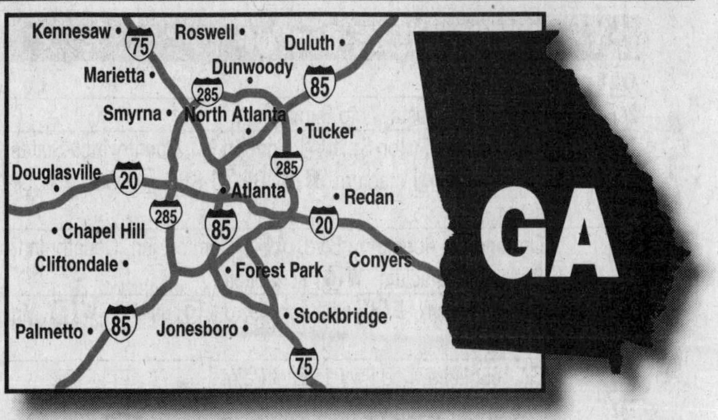

SMYRNA

260 Continued
Rose&Crown, Schlotzsky's, Subway [lodging] Best Value Inn, Country Hearth Inn, Extended Stay America, Hilton Garden, Hyatt, Marriott [other] CVS Drug, USPO, W [gas] Chevron, Conoco, Gulf/dsl, Shell [food] Arby's, Chick-fil-A, McDonald's, Panda Express, Popeye's, Starbucks, Subway, Waffle House, Wendy's [lodging] Comfort Inn, Country Inn&Suites, Courtyard, Days Inn, DoubleTree, Masters Inn, Red Roof Inn, Sky Suites [other] [H], Target

259b a I-285, W to Birmingham, E to Greenville, Montgomery

258 Cumberland Pkwy, E [lodging] Hyatt House, W [food] Chick-fil-A, Chipotle Mexican, Copelands Rest, Firehouse Subs, Hooters, Longhorn Steaks, Moe's SW Grill, Shane's Ribshack, Subway [lodging] Homewood Suites [other] Krogers

257mm Chattahoochee River

256 to US 41, Northside Pkwy

255 US 41, W Paces Ferry Rd, E [gas] Chevron, Shell/dsl [food] Blue Ridge Grill, Caribou Coffee, Chick-fil-A, Flying Biscuit Cafe, Houston's Rest., McDonald's/playplace, OK Café, Pero's Pizza, Smoothie King, Starbucks, Steak'n Shake, Taco Bell, Willy's Mexicana [other] [H], Ace Hardware, CVS Drug, Publix, W [gas] Exxon

ATLANTA

254 Moores Mill Rd

252b Howell Mill Rd, E [gas] Shell/auto [food] Chick-fil-A, Chipotle, Domino's, Jersey Mike's, McDonald's, Willy's Grill [other] Goodyear/auto, Publix, Rite Aid, USPO, W [gas] Shell [food] Arby's, Chin Chin Chinese, La Parrilla Mexican, Piccadilly, Starbucks, Subway, Taco Bell, Waffle House, Wendy's [other] Ace Hardware, Firestone/auto, GNC, Kroger, NTB, Office Depot, Petsmart, Ross, TJ Maxx, Verizon, Walmart

252a US 41, Northside Dr, E [other] [H] W [gas] Shell [food] Little Zio's [lodging] InTown Suites

251 I-85 N, to Greenville

250 Techwood Dr (from sb), 10th St, 14th St, E [lodging] Travelodge

249d 10th St, Spring St (from nb), E [gas] BP, Chevron/24hr [food] Checker's, Domino's, Pizza Hut, The Varsity [lodging] Fairfield Inn, Regency Suites, Renaissance Hotel, Residence Inn, W [food] McDonald's [lodging] Comfort Inn, Courtyard [other] [H], to GA Tech

249c Williams St (from sb), [other] to GA Dome, downtown

249b Pine St, Peachtree St (from nb), downtown, W [lodging] Hilton, Marriott

249a Courtland St (from sb), downtown, W [lodging] Hilton, Marriott [other] GA St U

248d Piedmont Ave, Butler St (from sb), downtown, W [lodging] Courtyard, Fairfield Inn, Radisson [other] [H], Ford, MLK NHS

248c GA 10 E, Intn'l Blvd, downtown, W [lodging] Hilton, Holiday Inn, Marriott Marquis, Radisson

248b Edgewood Ave (from nb), W [other] [H] downtown, hotels

248a MLK Dr (from sb), W st capitol, to Underground Atlanta

GA

= gas = food = lodging = other = rest stop

INTERSTATE 75 Cont'd

ATLANTA

Exit #	Services
247	I-20, E to Augusta, W to Birmingham
246	Georgia Ave, Fulton St, E Comfort Inn, Country Inn& Suites, Holiday Inn stadium, W BP KFC GSU, to Coliseum
245	Ormond St, Abernathy Blvd, E Comfort Inn, Country Inn& Suites stadium, W st capitol
244	University Ave, E Chevron, Exxon NAPA, W Mrs Winner's
243	GA 166, Lakewood Fwy, to East Point
242	I-85 S, to airport
241	Cleveland Ave, E BP, Chevron/Subway/dsl Checkers, Church's, McDonald's Advance Parts, W Citgo/dsl, ExpressZone, Marathon Ameican Deli, Burger King, Krystal, Papa John's American Inn $Tree, AutoZone, Big Lots, CVS Drug, Family$, Kroger, Walgreens
239	US 19, US 41, E Chevron/dsl Waffle House USPO, W Texaco Chick-fil-A, IHOP, McDonald's, Wendy's Best Western to airport
238b a	I-285 around Atlanta
237a	GA 85 S (from sb)
237	GA 331, Forest Parkway, E BP, Chevron/dsl, Shell/McDonald's, SunPetro/dsl Burger King, Mr Taco, Subway, Waffle House Econolodge Farmer's Mkt, W BP, Exxon/Subway/dsl Quizno's Atlanta Inn, Ramada Ltd Lee Tires/repair
235	US 19, US 41, GA 3, Jonesboro, E Chevron/dsl, Circle K/Subway/dsl, Texaco/dsl Super 8, Travelodge, W Chevron/dsl, Citgo, Texaco/dsl Applebee's, Burger King, Checkers, ChuckeCheese, Dunkin Donuts, Hibachi Grill, Hooters, Little Caesar's, McDonald's, Popeye's, Red Lobster, Waffle House, Zaxby's Amercan Inn, Econolodge, Motel 6 H, $General, $Tree, Little Giant Farmers Mkt, Office Depot, O'Reilly Parts

MORROW

Exit #	Services
233	GA 54, Morrow, E BP/dsl, Citgo, Gulf Cookout, Cracker Barrel, IHOP, Krystal, Taco Bell, Waffle House, Wendy's Best Western, Comfort Suites, Days Inn, Drury Inn, Red Roof Inn Walmart, W Chevron/dsl, Exxon/dsl, QT/dsl China Café, Golden Buddha, KFC, Lenny's Subs, Olive Garden, Subway, Three$ Cafe, Waffle House, Wendy's Hampton Inn, Quality Inn Acura, Buick/GMC/Mazda, Burlington Coats, Cadillac, Costco/gas, Fiat, Harley-Davidson, Kia, Macy's, Nissan, Sam's Club/gas, Sears/auto, TJ Maxx, Toyota/Scion
231	Mt Zion Blvd, E QT Chrysler/Dodge/Jeep, Ford/Lincoln, Honda, W BP/Circle K/Subway/dsl, Chevron, Texaco/dsl Arby's, Atlanta Bread, Bruster's, Burger King, Carrabba's, Chili's, China King, Chipotle, City Cafe Diner, Joe's Crabshack, Longhorn Steaks, McDonald's, Moe's SW Grill, Mo-Jo's Wings, Panda Express, Papa John's, Pizza Hut, Skyboxx Rest., Steak'n Shake, Taco Bell, TGIFriday, Truett's Rest., Waffle House, Wendy's, Wok Asian, Zaxby's Best Value Inn, Country Inn&Suites, Extended Stay America, Sun Suites AT&T, Barnes & Noble, Best Buy, Hancock Fabrics, Home Depot, NTB, Petsmart, Publix, Ross, Verizon

JONESBORO

Exit #	Services
228	GA 54, GA 138, Jonesboro, E Raceway/dsl Applebee's, Broadway Diner, Chick-fil-A, Frontera Mexican, Golden Corral, Honeybaked Ham, IHOP, Krystal, Marco's Pizza, O'Charley's, Piccadilly's, Stevi B's Pizza, Subway, Taco Mac, Tokyo Seafood
228	Continued Waffle House, Wing Nuts Comfort Inn, Day's Inn, Express Inn, Hampton Inn, Holiday Inn, La Quinta, Red Roof Inn H Kroger/dsl, Lowes Whse, Office Depot, Tires+, URGENT CARE, Verizon, W Marathon, Mobil, Raceway/Wendy's/dsl Dragon Garden Chinese, McDonald's, Ranchero's Mexican Fairfield Inn CarMax, CVS Drug, Kohl's
227	I-675 N, to I-285 E (from nb)
224	Hudson Bridge Rd, E Shell/dsl, Texaco/dsl Chick-fil-A, China Wok, DQ, Italian Oven, Johnny's NY Pizza, KFC, La Hacienda, Outback Steaks, Pueblo Mio, Serafino Itlian, Starbucks, Sticky Cactus Mexican, Subway, Waffle House, Wendy's Quality Inn H, Kauffman Tire, Publix, Rite Aid, Walgreens, W Murphy USA/dsl, QT Arby's, China Cafe, Firehouse Subs, McDonald's, Mellow Mushroom, Taco Bell, Zaxby's Super 8 $Tree, AT&T, AutoZone, Discount Tire, GNC, Verizon, Walmart
222	Jodeco Rd, E Citgo, Shell, Texaco Hardee's, W Fifteenth St Pizza Atlanta So. RV Camping
221	Jonesboro Rd, E QT/dsl, Shell/dsl Kauffman Tire, Kroger/gas (2mi), W American Deli, Arby's, Burger King, Cheddar's, Chili's, Firehouse Subs, Golden Corral, Hong Kong Cafe, Hooters, La Parrilla, Logan's Roadhouse, Longhorn Steaks, Marble Slab Creamery, McDonald's, Mike's Burger, O'Charley's, Olive Garden, Red Lobster, Rocky's Pizza, Starbucks, Subway, Truett's Grill, Wendy's, Wild Wing Cafe, Yuki Hibachi Courtyard, Fairfield Inn, Home 2 Suites AT&T, AutoZone, Belk, Best Buy, Books-A-Million, Dick's, Gander Mtn, Home Depot, Marshall's, Michael's, Old Navy, PetsMart, Radio Shack, Ross, Sam's Club/gas, Staples, Target, Verizon

MC DONOUGH

Exit #	Services
218	GA 20, GA 81, McDonough, E BP/dsl, Murphy USA/dsl, QT, Texaco American Deli, Applebee's, Arby's, Burger King, China King, China Star, Cracker Barrel, DQ, IHOP, KFC, Maritza&Frank's Rest., McDonald's, Mesquite Mexican, Moe's SW Grill, Montego Bay Cafe, OB's BBQ, Pizza Hut, Popeye's, Ruby Tuesday, Sakura Hibachi, South Side Diner, Taco Bell, Three $ Cafe, Waffle House, Zaxby's Baymont Inn, Best Western, Economy Inn, Howard Johnson, Super 8 $General, $Tree, Aamco, Discount Tire, Goodyear, Lowe's Whse, Office Depot, Rite Aid, URGENT CARE, Walmart, W RaceTrac/dsl, Shell Chick-fil-A, Dunkin Donuts, El Agade Mexican, Firehouse Subs, Folks Rest., Freddy's, Hardee's, Ichiban Express, Jimmy John's, Starbucks, Subway, Waffle House Comfort Suites, Econolodge, Fair Bridge Inn, Hampton Inn, Hilton Garden, Holiday Inn Express, Motel 6 Advance Parts, AT&T, Hobby Lobby, Honda, JC Penney, Kia, Kohl's, NTB, TJ Maxx, Toyota/Scion, Verizon
216	GA 155, McDonough, Blacksville, E Shell/dsl, Sunoco Honk Kong Express, Sonic Best Value, Day's Inn, Rodeway Inn Chevrolet/Buick/GMC, Ford, GMC, Hyundai, Tire South, W BP, Chevron, Citgo/dsl/24hr, Exxon/dsl, QT Bass BBQ, Da Vinci's Pizza, El Jimador, Graffiti's Oizza, Krystal, Kuma Japanese, Steve's Cafe, Subway, Waffle House Country Inn&Suites, Quality Inn, Sleep Inn
212	to US 23, Locust Grove, E BP/McDonald's/dsl, Chevron/Burger King, Marathon/Quizno's, Murphy USA/dsl, QT/dsl, Shell/dsl American Deli, Capt D's, Denny's, Hamburger Mike's, IHOP, KFC/Taco Bell, Koji Japanese, Little Caesar's, Pizza Hut, San Diego Mexican, Shane's Ribshack, Subway, Sunrise China, Waffle House, Wendy's, Zaxby's Executive Inn, La Quinta, Ramada, Red Roof Inn $Tree, Advance Parts, AT&T, Ingles/gas, NapaCare, Tanger Outlet/famous brands,

INTERSTATE 75 Cont'd

212 Continued
Verizon, Walmart, W Exxon/dsl, Shell/DQ/dsl Subway Comfort Suites, Scottish Inn, Sundown Lodge, Super 8 Bumper Parts

205 GA 16, to Griffin, Jackson, E BP, W Chevron/Subway/dsl Hogfather's BBQ Forest Glen RV Park

201 GA 36, to Jackson, Barnesville, E Loves/McDonald's/dsl/grill/scales/24hr, TA/Subway/Taco Bell/dsl/scales/24hr/@, Wilco/Hess/DQ/Stuckey's/Wendy's/dsl/scales/24hr/ @ Blue Beacon, W FLYING J/Denny's/dsl/LP/24hr, BP/dsl Waffle House Speedco Lube, truckwash

198 Highfalls Rd, E Exxon (1mi) High Falls BBQ High Falls Lodge High Falls SP, HighFalls RV Park (1mi)

193 Johnstonville Rd, W Marathon/dsl

190mm **weigh sta both lanes**

188 GA 42, E Shell Budget Inn, Hill Top Garden Inn RV camping, to Indian Springs SP

FORSYTH

187 GA 83, Forsyth, E Econolodge, Regency Inn KOA, W Citgo/dsl, Exxon/Circle K, Marathon, Shell, Valero/dsl Burger King, Capt D's, DQ, Hardee's, McDonald's, Subway, Taco Bell, Waffle House, Wendy's Day's Inn $Tree, Advance Parts, Family$, Freshway Foods, O'Reilly Parts, Verizon, Walmart/dsl

186 Tift College Dr, Juliette Rd, Forsyth, E Jarrell Plantation HS (18mi), KOA, W BP/dsl, Chevron/dsl, Marathon Waffle House Holiday Inn Express, Motel 6, Super 8 H, CVS Drug, Ingles/Deli

185 GA 18, E L&D RV Park (2mi), W Exxon/Circle K, Shell/dsl Shoney's Comfort Inn Ford, st patrol

181 Rumble Rd, to Smarr, E BP/dsl

179mm **sb, full facilities, litter barrels, petwalk RV dump, vending**

177 I-475 S around Macon (from sb)

175 Pate Rd, Bolingbroke (from nb, no re-entry)

MACON

172 Bass Rd, E McDonald's, Zaxby's Bass Pro Shop, W Citgo/dsl, Flash/DQ/dsl Chick-fil-A, Genghis Grill, Homewood Suites, Magarita's Mexican, Mellow Mushroom, Natalia's Rest., Subway, Taco Bell, Zheng's Wok Microtel, Value-Place CVS, Publix, to Museum of Arts&Sciences

171 US 23, to GA 87, Riverside Dr, E BP, Marathon/dsl Barbarito's Cantina, Bonefish Grill, Buca Italian, Chili's, Firehouse Subs, GA Bob's BBQ, Jersey Mike's, La Parrilla, TX Roadhouse, Wild Wing Cafe SpringHill Suites Acura, AT&T, Barnes & Noble, Belk, BMW, Dick's, Dillard's, GNC, Hobby Lobby, Jo-Ann, Mercedes, Petsmart, Subaru, Verizon, Volvo, W Lexus, Toyota/Scion

169 to US 23, Arkwright Dr, E Shell/Circle K/24hr Carrabba's, Logan's Roadhouse, Outback Steaks, Waffle House, Wager's Grill Candlewood Suites, Comfort Inn, Country Inn & Suites, Courtyard, Fairfield Inn, Hampton Inn, Holiday Inn, Home 2 Suites, La Quinta, Red Roof Inn, Residence Inn, Sleep Inn Buick/Cadillac/GMC, W Chevron/dsl, Marathon/dsl Arby's, Buffalo Wild Wings, Burger King, Cheddar's, Chick-fil-A, Chipotle, Cracker Barrel, Dunkin Donuts, Five Guys, Guitarras Mexican, Hooters, IHOP, Joy's Buffet, KFC, Krystal, Little Caesar's, Longhorn Steaks, Mandarin Chinese, McDonald's, Panda Express, Panera Bread, Papa John's, Starbucks, Steak'n Shake, Steve B's Pizza, Subway, Taco Bell, Waffle House, Wendy's Baymont Inn, Budgetel, Days Inn, Extended Stay America, Quality Inn, Rodeway Inn, Travelodge, Wingate Inn

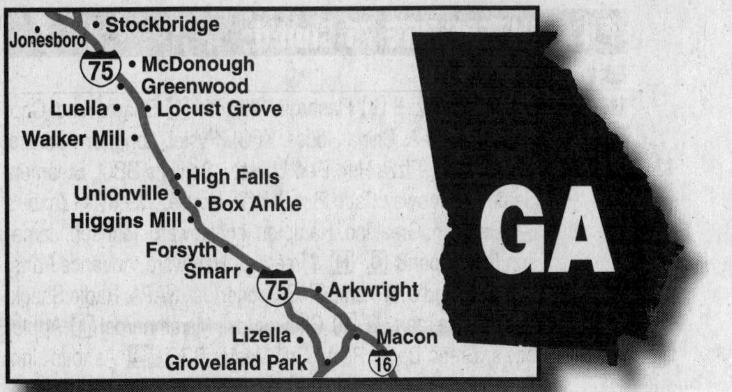

169 Continued
H, $General, $Tree, Ace Hardware, Chrysler/Jeep/Dodge, GNC, Goodyear/auto, Hyundai, Kia, K-Mart, Kroger/dsl, Mazda, O'Reilly Parts, Publix, Tuesday Morning

167 GA 247, Pierce Ave, E United Inn, W Exxon, Fastrip/dsl, Shell/Circle K/dsl, Shell/dsl Applebee's, Loco's Grill, Marco's Pizza, Metropolis Mediterranean, S&S Cafeteria, Shogun Japanese, SteakOut, Waffle House Best Western/rest., Holiday Inn Express, Howard Johnson, Magnuson Hotel, Palmtree Extended Stay Firestone/auto, Rite Aid

165 I-16 E, to Savannah

MACON

164 US 41, GA 19, Forsyth Ave, Macon, E Sid's Rest. H, hist dist, W Citgo/dsl museum

163 GA 74 W, Mercer U Dr, E Hilton Garden to Mercer U, W Citgo

162 US 80, GA 22, Eisenhower Pkwy, W Citgo/dsl, Lo-lo Gas, Sunoco/dsl Burger King, Capt D's, Checker's, Krispy Kreme, Krystal, McDonald's, Mrs Winners, Overtyme Grill, Subway, Wendy's InTown Suites $Tree, O'Reilly Parts, PepBoys, Save-A-Lot Foods, Walgreens

160 US 41, GA 247, Pio Nono Ave, E Flash/dsl, RaceWay/Dunkin Donuts/dsl Waffle House, W BP, Enmark/dsl Arby's, DQ, KFC, McDonald's, Subway, Waffle House $General, Advance Parts, Family$, O'Reilly Parts, Piggly Wiggly, Raffield Tire, Roses

156 I-475 N around Macon (from nb)

155 Hartley Br Rd, E BP/KFC/dsl/24hr Subway, Waffle House, Wendy's Kroger/dsl, Verizon, W Citgo/dsl, Exxon/dsl, Flash/DQ/dsl McDonald's, Zaxby's Best Value Inn Advance Parts, CVS Drug

153 Sardis Church Rd

149 GA 49, Byron, E Chevron/dsl, Marathon/dsl, Shell/dsl Burger King, Denny's, GA Bob's BBQ, Krystal, McDonald's, Pizza Hut, Subway, Waffle House, Wendy's, Zaxby's Best Western, Comfort Suites, Holiday Inn Express, Super 8 antiques, Campers Inn RV Ctr, Mid-State RV Ctr, Peach Stores/famous brands, W Citgo/dsl/24hr, Flash/dsl, Marathon/dsl, RaceWay/dsl, Texaco/dsl DQ, Huddle House, Waffle House Budget Inn, Days Inn, EconoLodge, Quality Inn Ace Hardware, Bumper Parts, Camping World RV Ctr, Chevrolet, Ford, O'Reilly Parts, USPO, Verizon

146 GA 247, to Centerville, E Exxon, Flash/dsl, Shell Subway, Waffle House EconoLodge, Knights Inn H, museum, to Robins AFB, W Pilot/Arby's/dsl/24hr

144 Russel Pkwy, E aviation museum, Robins AFB

142 GA 96, Housers Mill Rd, E Chevron/dsl Ponderosa RV Park

138 Thompson Rd, E Valero/dsl H W airport

GA

[gas] = gas [food] = food [lodging] = lodging [other] = other [RS] = rest stop

INTERSTATE 75 Cont'd

PERRY

Exit #	Services
136	US 341, Perry, E [gas] Flash/dsl, Shell/dsl [food] Burger King, Capt D's, Chick-fil-A, China House, KFC, Krystal, Longhorn Steaks, McDonald's, Pizza Hut, Red Lobster, Sonny's BBQ, Steamers Seafood, Subway, Taco Bell, Waffle House, Wendy's, Zaxby's [lodging] Best Inn, Great Inn, Hampton Inn, Howard Johnson, Jameson Inn, Super 8 [other] [H] $Tree, Ace Hardware, Advance Parts, AT&T, Boland's RV Park, GNC, Kroger/dsl, NAPA, Radio Shack, Verizon, Walmart, W [gas] Chevron/dsl, Marathon/dsl [food] Applebee's, Green Derby Rest., Grill Master BBQ [lodging] Ashburn Inn, EconoLodge, Knights Inn, Passport Inn, Quality Inn, Ramada Inn, Roadway Inn
135	US 41, GA 127, Perry, E [gas] Flash/dsl, Marathon, Shell, Texaco [food] Cracker Barrel, DQ, Subway, Waffle House [lodging] Best Western, Comfort Inn, Red Carpet Inn, Relax Inn, Travelodge [other] Chrysler/Dodge/Jeep, GA Nat Fair, Kia, W [other] Fair Harbor RV Park, st patrol
134	South Perry Pkwy, W [gas] Marathon [lodging] Microtel [other] Buick/Chevrolet/GMC, Priester's Pecans
127	GA 26, Henderson, E [other] Twin Oaks Camping, W [gas] Chevron
122	GA 230, Unadilla, E [gas] Chevron/dsl [other] Chevrolet/Ford, W [lodging] Red Carpet Inn
121	US 41, Unadilla, E [gas] Borum/repair, Danfair, Flash/DQ/Stuckey's/dsl, Shell [food] Country Boys BBQ, Subway [lodging] Economy Inn, Scottish Inn [other] $General, Carquest, Family$, Firestone, Piggly Wiggly, Southern Trails RV Resort, W [gas] Citgo/rest./dsl/scales/24hr
118mm	**[RS] sb, full [accessible] facilities, litter barrels, petwalk [phone] [picnic] RV dump, vending**
117	to US 41, Pinehurst
112	GA 27, Vienna
109	GA 215, Vienna, E [gas] Pilot/McDonalds/dsl/scales/24hrs, W [gas] Citgo/dsl, Shell/Subway/dsl/e-85, Sunoco [food] Huddle House, Popeye's [lodging] Executive Inn [other] [H], antiques, Cotton Museum
108mm	**[RS] nb, full [accessible] facilities, litter barrels, petwalk [phone] [picnic] RV dump, vending**

CORDELE

Exit #	Services
104	Farmers Mkt Rd, Cordele
102	GA 257, Cordele, E [gas] Sunoco/dsl, W [food] Pecan House [other] [H]
101	US 280, GA 90, Cordele, E [gas] Chevron, Pilot/Arby's/dsl/scales/24hr, Shell [food] Denny's, Golden Corral, Waffle House [lodging] Days Inn, Fairfield Inn, Holiday Inn Express, Ramada Inn [other] Ford/Lincoln, st patrol, W [gas] Flash, Gas'n Go, Pacecar Express, Sunoco [food] Burger King, Capt D's, Cracker Barrel, Cutter's Steaks, Domino's, DQ, Hardee's, KFC, Krystal, Little Caesars, Los Compadres, McDonald's, New China, Pizza Hut, Sonic, Subway, Taco Bell, TJ's Rest, Wendy's, Zaxby's [lodging] Ashburn Inn, Athens 8 Motel, Best Western, Comfort Inn, Hampton Inn, Quality Inn, Travelodge [other] $General, $Tree, Ace Hardware, Advance Parts, AutoZone, Belk, Harvey's Foods, Home Depot, J Carter HS, NAPA, O'Reilly Parts, Radio Shack, Save-A-Lot, to Veterans Mem SP, Verizon, Walgreens, Walmart

WENONA

Exit #	Services
99	GA 300, GA/FL Pkwy, E [food] Citgo/DQ/dsl, W [food] Waffle House [lodging] Country Inn&Suites [other] to Chehaw SP
97	to GA 33, Wenona, E [other] Cordele RV Park, dsl repair, W [other] KOA, truckwash
92	Arabi, E [gas] Shell/Plantation House, W [gas] Citgo/dsl [other] Southern Gates RV Park
85mm	**[RS] nb, full [accessible] facilities, litter barrels, petwalk [phone] [picnic] RV dump, vending**

ASHBURN

Exit #	Services
84	GA 159, Ashburn, W [gas] Chevron/DQ/Subway/dsl/24hr [lodging] Ashburn Inn/RV Park
82	GA 107, GA 112, Ashburn, W [gas] BP, Shell, Sunoco/dsl [food] KFC, McDonald's, Pizza Hut, Shoney's, Waffle House, Zaxby's [lodging] Best Value Inn, Best Western, Days Inn, Super 8 [other] $General, Auto Value Parts, Buick/Chevrolet/GMC, Fred's, O'Reilly Parts, Piggly Wiggly, Rite Aid, to Chehaw SP
80	Bussey Rd, Sycamore, W [other] Allen's Tires
78	GA 32, Sycamore, E to Jefferson Davis Mem Pk (14mi)
76mm	**[RS] sb, full [accessible] facilities, litter barrels, petwalk [phone] [picnic] RV dump, vending**
75	Inaha Rd
71	Willis Still Rd, Sunsweet, W [gas] BP/dsl
69	Chula-Brookfield Rd, E [gas] Sunoco/dsl [lodging] Chula Carpet Inn
66	Brighton Rd

TIFTON

Exit #	Services
64	US 41, Tifton, E [gas] BP/dsl [other] [H], $General, Harvey's Foods, W [gas] Shell
63b	8th St, Tifton, E [gas] Flash/dsl/e-85 [food] Los Compadres [other] Publix, W [food] Pit Stop BBQ [other] GA Museum of Agriculture
63a	2nd St, Tifton, E [gas] BP, Marathon [food] Asahi Xpress, Checker's, El Cazador Mexican, Krystal, McDonald's, Pizza Hut, Ranchero's Grill, Red Lobster, Stevi B's Pizza, Subway, Taco Bell, Waffle House [lodging] EconoLodge, Super 8 [other] $General, $Tree, Belk, Buick/Cadillac/GMC, JC Penney, K-Mart, W [gas] Bob's/dsl [food] Coyoacan Mexican [lodging] Quality Inn, Travelodge
62	US 82, to US 319, Tifton, E [gas] BP, Citgo, Flash/dsl [food] Applebee's, Charles Seafood, Chili's, Cracker Barrel, DQ, Golden Corral, King Buffet, Logan's Roadhouse, Ole Times, Sonic, Tokyo Japanese, Waffle House, Zaxby's [lodging] Comfort Inn, Country Inn&Suites, Fairfield Inn, Hampton Inn, Microtel, Tifton Inn [other] $Tree, Advance Parts, AutoZone, BigLots, Bumper Parts, Family$, Ford/Lincoln, NAPACare, O'Reilly Parts, Pecan Outlet, Save-A-Lot, Staples, W [gas] Exxon/Burger King, EZ Mart, Flash/dsl, Murphy USA/dsl, RaceWay/dsl, Shell/dsl [food] Capt D's, Chick-fil-A, HogBones BBQ, Lin's Garden, Little Caesars, Loco's Grill, Longhorn Steaks, McDonald's, Oishi Japanese, Ruby Tuesday, Shoney's, Starbucks, Subway, Waffle House, Wendy's [lodging] Days Inn, Hilton Garden, Rodeway Inn [other] $General, Chevrolet, Chrysler/Dodge/Jeep, Honda, Lowe's, Radio Shack, Toyota, URGENT CARE, Verizon, Walmart/Subway
61	Omega Rd, E [other] Nissan, W [gas] Shell/Stuckey's/Country Diner/pizza/dsl/24hr [lodging] Motel 6 [other] Harley-Davidson, Pines RV Park
60	Central Ave, Tifton, E [gas] Chevron [food] Dragon 1 Chinese, W [gas] Pilot/Steak'n Shake/Subway/dsl/scales/24hr [other] Blue Beacon, KOA
59	Southwell Blvd, to US 41, Tifton, E [gas] Loves/Hardee's/dsl/24hr
55	to Eldorado, Omega, E [gas] Shell/Magnolia Plantation/dsl
49	Kinard Br Rd, Lenox, E [gas] Dixie/dsl [lodging] Knights Inn, W [gas] BP/dsl/24hr [other] repair
47mm	**[RS] both lanes, full [accessible] facilities, litter barrels, petwalk [phone] [picnic] RV dump, vending**

ADEL

Exit #	Services
45	Barneyville Rd, E [lodging] Economy Inn
41	Rountree Br Rd, E [gas] Citgo, W [other] to Reed Bingham SP
39	GA 37, Adel, Moultrie, E [gas] Citgo/dsl, Dixie Gas, Quick Gas, Shell/McDonald's/dsl [food] DQ, Hardee's, Subway, Waffle House [lodging] Scottish Inn, Super 8 [other] [H] $General, Ace Hardware, Advance Parts, Family$, Harvey's Foods, O'Reilly Parts, Piggly Wiggly, Rite Aid, W [gas] BP, Citgo/dsl/scales [food] Burger King, Capt D's, China Buffet, IHOP, Taco Bell, Wendy's, Western Sizzlin [lodging] Days Inn, Hampton Inn [other] to Reed Bingham SP

GA

INTERSTATE 75 Cont'd

VALDOSTA

Exit #	Services
37	Adel
32	Old Coffee Rd, Cecil, E Citgo Stagecoach Inn, W Chevron Cecil Bay RV Park
29	US 41 N, GA 122, Hahira, Sheriff's Boys Ranch, E Subway NAPA, W Big Foot TC/cafe/dsl/24hr, Citgo/dsl Hahira Inn
23mm	**weigh sta both lanes**
22	US 41 S, to Valdosta, E BP, Shell/Subway/dsl Waffle House Best Western Buick/Chevrolet/GMC, golf, Mazda, W Citgo/Stuckey's Burger King, DQ Days Inn, Howard Johnson
18	GA 133, Valdosta, E Citgo/dsl, Exxon, Flash, Mobil Applebee's, Arby's, Atl. Bread Co, Brusters, Buffalo Wild Wings, Burger King, Chick-fil-A, Chili's, Chow Town, CiCi's Pizza, Cracker Barrel, Crystal River Seafood, Denny's, El Potro Mexican, El Toreo, Fazoli's, Green Iguana Cafe, Honeybaked Ham, Hooters, KFC, Krystal, Little Caesars, Longhorn Steaks, Marble Slab, McAlister's Deli, McDonald's, Olive Garden, Outback Steaks, Quiznos, Red Lobster, Ruby Tuesday, Sonny's BBQ, Starbucks, Steak'n Shake, Subway, Taco Bell, TX Roadhouse, Waffle House, Wendy's, Zaxby's Comfort Suites, Country Inn&Suites, Courtyard, Drury Inn, Hilton Garden, Holiday Inn Express, InTown Suites, Jameson Inn, Jolly Inn, La Quinta, Quality Inn $Tree, AT&T, Belk, Best Buy, Books-A-Million, Family$, Harvey's Foods, Hobby Lobby, Home Depot, JC Penney, Kohl's, Lowe's, mall, Michael's, Office Depot, Old Navy, Petsmart, Publix, repair, Ross, Sears/auto, Target, TJ Maxx, Tuesday Morning, Verizon, Walgreens, W BP/dsl, RaceWay/dsl, Shell Days Inn, EconoLodge, Sleep Inn, Super 8 RiverPark Camping, Toyota/Scion
16	US 84, US 221, GA 94, Valdosta, E Big Foot/dsl, BP/dsl, Citgo/DQ/dsl, Danfair Express, Murphy Express/dsl, Pure/dsl, Shell/dsl Aligatou Japanese, Bojangles, Bubba Jax Crab Shack, Burger King, Cheddar's, IHOP, McDonald's, Pizza Hut, Sonic, Waffle House, Wendy's Days Inn, Fairfield Inn, Hampton Inn, Holiday Inn, Motel 6, New Valdosta Inn, Quality Inn, Stay Inn, Super 8, Wingate Inn NAPA, repair, Sam's Club/gas, to Okefenokee SP, Walmart/Subway, W Horizon/Backyard Burger/pizza, Shell/dsl/24hr Austin's Steaks Clarion, Knights Inn
13	Old Clyattville Rd, Valdosta, W Wild Adventures Park
11	GA 31, Valdosta, E Pilot/Subway/dsl/24hr/ @, Wilco/Hess/Dunkin Donuts/Stuckey's/dsl/scales/24hr Waffle House Travelers Inn truckwash, W BP Big Ed's BBQ $General
5	GA 376, to Lake Park, E Citgo, Flash Foods/Stuckey's/dsl, RaceWay/dsl, Shell Chick-fil-A, Domino's, Farmhouse Rest., Krystal, Lin's Garden Chinese, Rodeo Mexican, Sonny's BBQ, Subway, Waffle House, Zaxby's Guesthouse Inn, Quality Inn $Tree, antiques, Eagles Roost Camping, Family$, Fred's, Horizon RV Ctr, USPO, Winn-Dixie, W Citgo/dsl, Exxon/dsl, Shell/dsl Cracker Barrel, McDonald's, Pizza Hut, Taco Bell, Wendy's Ashburn Inn, Days Inn, Hampton Inn, Super 8 KOA
3mm	**Welcome Ctr nb full facilities, info, litter barrels, petwalk vending**
2	Lake Park, Bellville, E Mobil/DQ, Shell/dsl, TA/BP/Arby's/dsl/scales/24hr/ @ SpeedCo, W FLYING J/Denny's/Subway/dsl/LP/scales/24hr Motel 6 lube/tires/wash
0mm	Georgia/Florida state line

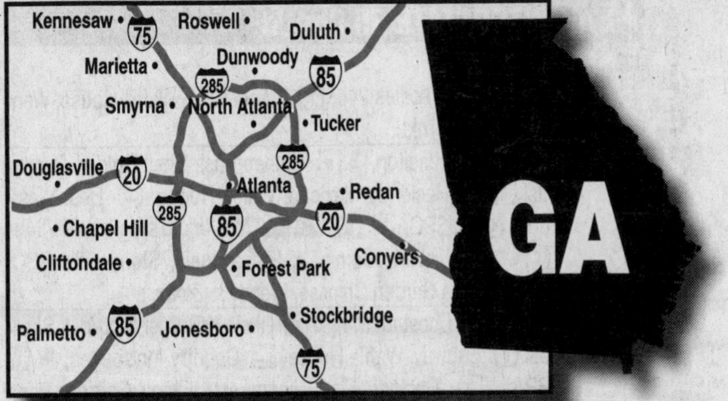

INTERSTATE 85

LAVONIA

COMMERCE

Exit #	Services
179mm	Georgia/South Carolina state line, Lake Hartwell, Tugaloo River
177	GA 77 S, to Hartwell, E BP/gifts/dsl Dad's Grill to Hart SP, W Tugaloo SP
176mm	**Welcome Ctr sb full facilities, info, litter barrels, petwalk vending**
173	GA 17, to Lavonia, E Raceway/dsl Bojangles, La Cabana Mexican, McDonald's, Subway, Taco Bell, Waffle House Magnuson Hotel $General, Lavonia Foods, Rite Aid, W Chevron/dsl, Exxon/dsl Burger King, DQ, Hardee's, J Peters Grill, Pizza Hut, Shoney's, Zaxby's Hampton Inn, Holiday Inn Express, Super 8 Chrysler/Dodge/Jeep, Ford, to Tugaloo SP
171mm	**weigh sta nb**
169mm	**weigh sta sb**
166	GA 106, to Carnesville, Toccoa, E Exxon/dsl, Wilco/Hess/DQ/Wendy's/dsl/scales/24hr Subway, W Echo Trkstp/Chevron/Echo Rest./dsl/scales/24hr
164	GA 320, to Carnesville, E Chevron/dsl
160	GA 51, to Homer, E Marathon/Subway/dsl/24hr Sterling RV Ctr, to Russell SP, Ty Cobb Museum, Victoria Bryant SP, W FLYING J/dsl/24hr, Petro/BP/Iron Skillet/dsl/scales/24hr @ Blue Beacon
154	GA 63, Martin Br Rd
149	US 441, GA 15, to Commerce, Homer, E Murphy USA, QT/dsl, TA/Shell/Country Pride/dsl/scales/24hr/ @ Bojangles, Capt D's, El Azteca, Grand Buffet, Koji Japanese, Krispy Kreme, Longhorn Steaks, Outback Steaks, Papa John's, Sonny's BBQ, Taco Bell, Waffle House, Zaxby's Days Inn, Hampton Inn, Red Roof Inn, Scottish Inn $General, $Tree, AT&T, Chrysler/Dodge/Jeep, Funopolis, GNC, O'Reilly Parts, Radio Shack, vURGENT CARE, Walmart/Subway, W BP/Krystal/dsl, RaceTrac/dsl, Valero/dsl Applebee's, Arby's, Burger King, Chick-fil-A, Cracker Barrel, DQ, Five Guys Burgers, Hawg Wild BBQ, La Hacienda, McDonald's, Pizza Hut, Ruby Tuesday, Ryan's, Sonic, Starbucks, Subway, Wendy's Best Inn, Best Western, Comfort Suites, Fairfield Inn, Holiday Inn Express, Howard Johnson, Motel 6, Quality Inn, Super 8, Travelodge Home Depot, Pritchett Tires, Tanger Outlet/famous brands, Verizon
147	GA 98, to Commerce, E FLYING J/Dunkin Donuts/dsl/24hr, Valero/dsl W Gulf
140	GA 82, Dry Pond Rd, E Freightliner, W RV & Truck Repair
137	US 129, GA 11 to Jefferson, E RaceTrac/dsl Arby's, Bojangles, El Jinete Mexican, KFC/Taco Bell, McDonald's, Waffle House, Zaxby's Quality Inn museum,

GA

JEFFERSON

INTERSTATE 85 Cont'd

137 Continued
W QT/dsl/scales/24hr Burger King, Waffle House, Wendy's flea mkt

129 GA 53, to Braselton, E Chevron/dsl, Shell/Golden Pantry/dsl La Hacienda Mexican, Waffle House Best Western USPO, W Pilot/McDonald's/dsl/scales/24hr Cracker Barrel, Domino's, El Centinela, Stonewall's BBQ, Subway, Tea Garden Chinese, Wendy's, Zaxby's

126 GA 211, to Chestnut Mtn, E Circle K/Burger King/dsl, Shell/dsl Subway, Waffle House Country Inn&Suites, W BP/dsl Chateau Elan Winery/rest., China Garden, Papa John's Holiday Inn Express Publix, vet

120 to GA 124, Hamilton Mill Rd, E BP, QT/dsl Arby's, Buffalo's Café, Burger King, Caprese Rest., Firehouse Subs, Five Guys Burgers, McDonald's, Moe's SW Grill, Riverside Pizza, Starbucks, Subway, Wendy's, Zaxby's Aldi Foods, auto repair, Home Depot, Kohl's, Publix/Deli, RV World of GA (1mi), vet, W Chevron, Murphy USA/dsl, Shell/dsl Barbarito's, Chick-fil-A, Chili's, El Molcajate, Hardee's, Italy's Pizza, Little Caesars, Taco Bell $Tree, AT&T, CVS Drug, O'Reilly Parts, Tires+, USPO, Verizon, Walmart/Subway

GA

115 GA 20, to Buford Dam, E QT Waffle House Pepboys, W Arby's, Atlanta Bread, Bonefish Grill, Bruster's, Burger 21, Burger King, Cheesecake Factory, Chick-fil-A, Chili's, Chipotle, ChuckeCheese, East Coast Wings, Einstein's Bagels, Firehouse Subs, Genghis Grill, Honeybaked Ham, Kani House, Krispy Kreme, Longhorn Steaks, Macaroni Grill, Maddio's Pizza, McDonald's, Mimi's Cafe, Moe's SW Grill, O'Charley's, Olive Garden, On-the-Border, Panda Express, Panera Bread, PF Chang's, Provino's Italian, Red Lobster, Shogun Japanese, Sonny's BBQ, Starbucks, Steak n' Shake, Subway, Taco Mac, Ted's MT Grill, TGIFriday's, Tilted Kilt, Waffle House, Wendy's, Which Wich? Country Inn&Suites, Courtyard, Hampton Inn, SpringHill Suites, Wingate Inn $Tree, AT&T, Barnes&Noble, Belk, Best Buy, Buick/GMC, Costco/gas, Dick's, Dillard's, Discount Tire, Fiat, Firestone/auto, Hancock Fabrics, Honda, Hyundai, JC Penney, Lowe's, Macy's, Mall of GA, Marshall's, Mazda, Michael's, Nissan, Nordstrom Rack, PetCo, Petsmart, Radio Shack, REI, Ross, Sam's Club/gas, Staples, SteinMart, Target, TJ Maxx, to Lake Lanier Islands, Toyota/Scion, Tuesday Morning, Verizon, Von Maur, VW, Walmart

SUWANEE

113 I-985 N (from nb), to Gainesville

111 GA 317, to Suwanee, E BP/dsl, Valero/dsl Applebee's, Arby's, Checker's, Chick-fil-A, Cracker Barrel, Dunkin Donuts, Orient Garden, Outback Steaks, Philly Connection, Pizza Hut, Pizza Hut/Taco Bell, Schlotsky's, Subway, Waffle House, Wendy's Comfort Suites, Courtyard, Fairfield Inn, Motel 6, Quality Inn, Sun Suites CVS Drug, GNC, O'Reilly Parts, W Chevron/dsl, Murphy USA/dsl, QT/dsl, Raceway/dsl, Shell Dunkin Donuts, Greek Island, HoneyBaked Ham, IHOP, Jimmy John's, KFC, McDonald's, Moe's SW Grill, Sonic, Subway, Taco Mac Red Roof Inn, Super 8 $Tree, Advance Parts, AT&T, Lowe's, Office Depot, Walmart

DULUTH

109 Old Peachtree Rd, E QT McAlister's, McDonald's, Mi Casa Mexican Hampton Inn, Homewood Suites Bass Pro Shops, Publix, W Arena Tavern, Carrabba's, Chick-fil-A, China Delight, Firehouse Subs, Five Guys Burgers, Jim&Nicks BBQ, Starbucks, Subway, Tilted Kilt, Waffle House Hilton Garden, Holiday Inn, Residence Inn Home Depot

ATLANTA AREA

108 Sugarloaf Pkwy (from nb), E Hampton Inn, Homewo Suites, W Carrabba's, Chick-fil-A, Tin Lizzy Canti Hilton Garden, Holiday Inn Gwinnett Civic Ctr

107 GA 120, to GA 316 E, Athens, E Shell Burger Kir Carino's, Dave&Busters, Dunkin Donuts, Subway, Zaxb Bass Pro Shops, Books-a-Million, Burlington Coats, D count Tire, Rite Aid, Ross, Saks 5th Ave, Sears, Suburban Ti W BP/dsl, Chevron Bojangles, China Gate, McDonald Subway, Waffle House La Quinta, Suburban Lodge

106 Boggs Rd (from sb, no return), Duluth, W QT/dsl/24 Mercedes

104 Pleasant Hill Rd, E Chevron/e85, QT/dsl, Shell/dsl, Vale dsl Bahama Breeze, Burger King, Chick-fil-A, Costas Naya itas, Don Pedro Mexican, East Pearl, Fung Mei Chinese, C Diner, Golden House, Joe's Crabshack, McDonald's, Popeye Schlotsky's, Stevie B's Pizza, Subway, Super Buffet, TGIF day's, Waffle House, Wendy's Best Western, Candlewoo Suites, Comfort Suites, Fairfield Inn, Hampton Inn Suites, Ho day Inn Express, Residence Inn, Sonesta $General, $Tre Advance Parts, Best Buy, Family$, Home Depot, Publix, U GENT CARE, Walgreens, W BP/Dunkin Donuts/dsl, Che ron/dsl, Valero/dsl Applebee's, Arby's, Barnacle's, Bruster' Burger King, Checker's, Chili's, Chipotle Mexican, Hooter IHOP, Jimmy John's, KFC, Krispy Kreme, McDonald's, Meltin Pot, Olive Garden, On the Border, Panda Express, Red Lob ster, Starbucks, Steak'n Shake, Subway, Taco Bell, Wendy's Courtyard, Extended Stay America, Hyatt Place, Jameson In Quality Inn, Wingate Inn, Wyndham Garden AT&T, Aud Batteries+, Belk, BMW, Buick/GMC, Firestone/auto, For Fry's Electronics, Goodyear/auto, Honda, Hyundai, Infiniti, J Penney, Jo-Ann Fabrics, Kia, Macy's, mall, Marshall's, Nissa PetCo, Rite Aid, Sears/auto, Staples, Subaru, TJ Maxx, Toyota Scion, Verizon

103 Steve Reynolds Blvd (from nb, no return), W QT/dsl, She Dave&Buster's, Waffle House InTown Suites $Tree Big Lots, Costco/gas, Kohl's, Petsmart, same as 104, Sam' Club

102 GA 378, Beaver Ruin Rd, E QT, Shell/dsl, Valero/ds Subway, W Citgo

101 Lilburn Rd, E QT, Shell/dsl Blimpie, Bruster's, Burge King, Domino's, Hong Kong Buffet, Jimmy John's, KFC, Krys tal, McDonald's/playplace, Starbucks, Taco Bell, Waffle Hous Guesthouse Inn, InTown Suites, Super 8 Jones R Park, W Chevron, Marathon/dsl, QT Arby's, China Pan da, El Taco Veloz, Papa John's, Pizza Plaza, Subway, Waffl House, Wendy's Knights Inn, Red Roof Inn CarMax Chrysler/Dodge/Jeep, Lowe's

99 GA 140, Jimmy Carter Blvd, E Shell/dsl Checker's, Chick-fil-A, Cracker Barrel, Denny's, Dunkin Donuts, McDonald's, Papa John's, Pizza Hut/Taco Bell, Pollo Campero, Subway Congress Suites, Courtyard, Horizon Inn, La Quinta, Motel 6, Rite4Us Inn Advance Parts, Aldi Foods, Family$, U-Haul, Walgreens, W Chevron/dsl, QT/dsl, Valero/ds Hibachi Grill, Hong Kong Buffet, Pappadeaux Steak/seafood, Sonic, Waffle House, Wendy's Country Inn&Suites, Days Inn, Microtel, Rodeway Inn AutoZone, CarQuest, NTB, O'Reilly Parts, PepBoys

96 Pleasantdale Rd, Northcrest Rd, E Burger King, Pleasantdale Chinese, W Exxon/dsl, QT/dsl Subway Atlanta Lodge

95 I-285

INTERSTATE 85 Cont'd

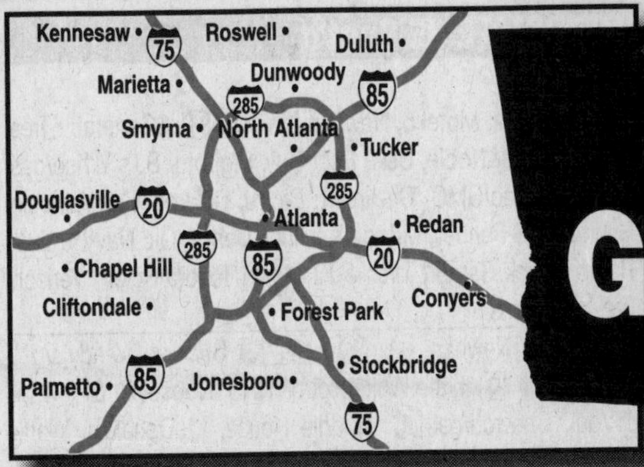

ATLANTA AREA

Exit #	Services
94	Chamblee-Tucker Rd, E [gas] Chevron/Subway/dsl, Shell/dsl [other] to Mercer U, W [gas] QT/dsl [food] DQ, Waffle House [lodging] Motel 6, Super 8
93	Shallowford Rd, to Doraville, E [gas] Shell [food] Hop Shing Chinese, Marco's Pizza, Subway [other] Publix, U-Haul, W [gas] Shell/dsl [lodging] Quality Inn
91	US 23, GA 155, Clairmont Rd, E [gas] Chevron/dsl, QT/dsl [food] IHOP, Mo's Pizza, Popeye's [other] repair, URGENT CARE, W [gas] BP [food] McDonald's, Waffle House [lodging] Extended Stay America, Holiday Inn Express, Marriott [other] NTB, Sam's Club/dsl
89	GA 42, N Druid Hills, E [gas] Chevron/Subway/dsl, QT, Shell/dsl [food] Arby's, Boston Mkt, Burger King, Chick-fil-A, El Torero, Fortune Cookie, Grub Burger, Jersey Mike's, McDonald's, Moe's SW Grill, Newk's Eatery, Panera Bread, Penn Sta Subs, Piccadilly's, Starbucks, Taco Bell, Tin Roof Cantina, Willy's Mexicana, Zoe's Kitchen [lodging] Courtyard [other] $Tree, Firestone/auto, GNC, Target, Walgreens, W [gas] Chevron/dsl, Exxon/dsl, Shell [food] HoneyBaked Ham, Krystal, McDonald's, Waffle House [lodging] DoubleTree, Hampton Inn, Red Roof Inn [other] CVS Drug, Just Brakes
88	Lenox Rd, GA 400 N, Cheshire Br Rd (from sb), E [gas] Valero/dsl [food] McDonald's [lodging] La Quinta
87	GA 400 N (from nb)
86	GA 13 S, Peachtree St, E [gas] BP, Chevron [food] Papa John's, Wendy's [lodging] Intown Inn [other] Sprouts Mkt, vet
85	I-75 N, to Marietta, Chattanooga
84	Techwood Dr, 14th St, E [gas] BP, Shell [food] CheeseSteaks, La Bamba Mexican, Thai Cuisine, VVV Ristorante Italiano [lodging] Best Western, Hampton Inn, Marriott, Sheraton, Travelodge [other] Woodruff Arts Ctr, W [food] Blimpie [lodging] Courtyard, Knights Inn [other] CVS Drug, Dillard's, Office Depot, to Georgia Tech
77	I-75 S
76	Cleveland Ave, E [gas] Citgo/dsl [food] Burger King, Papa John's [other] (H), $Tree, AutoZone, BigLots, CVS Drug, Family$, Kroger, Walgreens, W [gas] Shell/dsl, Texaco/dsl [food] Chick-fil-A, Church's [other] CVS, O'Reilly Parts
75	Sylvan Rd, E [gas] Shell/dsl
74	Loop Rd, [other] Aviation Commercial Center
73b a	Virginia Ave, E [gas] Citgo/dsl [food] Jimmy John's, Jonny's Pizza, Landmark Diner, Malone's Grill, McDonald's, Pizza Hut, Ruby Tuesday, Schlotsky's, Spondivit's Rest., Waffle House, Wendy's, Willy's Mexican [lodging] Courtyard, Drury Inn, Hilton, Motel 6, Renaissance Hotel, Residence Inn, W [gas] Chevron/Subway, Shell [food] Arby's, BBQ Kitchen, Blimpie, Giovanna's Italian, Happy Buddha Chinese, KFC, La Fiesta Mexican, Waffle House [lodging] Country Inn&Suites, Crowne Plaza, DoubleTree, EconoLodge, Fairfield Inn, Hampton Inn, Hilton Garden, Holiday Inn, Homewood Suites, Hyatt Place, Palms Hotel, Staybridge Inn, Wellesley Inn
72	Camp Creek Pkwy
71	Riverdale Rd, Atlanta [airport] E [food] Ruby Tuesday [lodging] Courtyard, Fairfield Inn, Hampton Inn, Holiday Inn, Hyatt Place, La Quinta, Microtel, Sheraton/grill, Sleep Inn, Super 8, W [lodging] Days Inn, Embassy Suites, Hilton Garden, Holiday Inn Express, Marriott, Westin Hotel
70	I-85 (from sb)
69	GA 14, GA 279, E [gas] Chevron/dsl, Citgo, Exxon/dsl, Valer [food] Blimpie, Bojangles, Burger King, Checker's, China Cafe, Church's, Cozumel, KFC, Krystal, McDonald's, Piccadilly

FAIRBURN

NEWNAN

Exit #	Services
69	Continued Cafeteria, Subway, Taco Bell, Waffle House, Wendy's [lodging] Comfort Inn, Days Inn, Quality Inn, Super 8, Travelodge, Windsor Atl Hotel [other] AutoZone, Family$, U-Haul, URGENT CARE, W [gas] Chevron/dsl, Texaco [food] Waffle House [lodging] EconoLodge
68	I-285 Atlanta Perimeter (from nb)
66	Flat Shoals Rd, W [gas] BP, Chevron/dsl, Shell/Blimpie [food] King's Rest., Waffle House [lodging] Motel 6
64	GA 138, to Union City, E [gas] BP/dsl, RaceTrac/dsl [food] Waffle House [lodging] EconoLodge, Western Inn [other] BMW/Mini, Chevrolet, Chrysler/Dodge/Jeep, CVS Drug, Ford/Lincoln, Honda, Infiniti, Kia/Nissan, Lexus, Toyota/Scion, VW, W [gas] Chevron/dsl, QT, Shell/dsl [food] Arby's, Burger King, Capt D's, China Garden, China King, Corner Cafe, Dunkin Donuts, IHOP, KFC, Krystal, McDonald's, Papa John's, Pizza Hut, Sonic, Southern Grill, Subway, Taco Bell, Wendy's, Zaxby's [lodging] Best Western, Comfort Inn, Country Hearth Inn, Garden Inn, La Quinta, Magnuson Hotel, Microtel [other] $Tree, Advance Parts, AT&T, BigLots, Firestone/auto, Kroger/dsl, NTB, O'Reilly Parts, PepBoys, Radio Shack, vet, Walgreens, Walmart/Subway
61	GA 74, to Fairburn, E [gas] BP/Huddle House/dsl/scales/24hr, Los Mariachis, QT/dsl, RaceWay/dsl, Shell [food] Chick-fil-A, Cracker Barrel, Dunkin Donuts, Hardee's, McDonald's, Taco Bell, Waffle House, Wendy's, Zaxby's [lodging] Country Inn&Suites, Hampton Inn, Holiday Inn Express, Sleep Inn, Wingate Inn [other] Tire Depot, vet, W [gas] Chevron/dsl, Citgo/dsl [lodging] Efficiency Motel
56	Collinsworth Rd, W [gas] Marathon/dsl, Shell [food] Frank's Rest. [other] South Oaks Camping
51	GA 154, to Sharpsburg, E [gas] Phillips 66/dsl, Texaco/Blimpie/dsl [food] Hardee's, W [gas] Chevron/dsl, Shell/Subway/dsl [food] Waffle House
47	GA 34, to Newnan, E [gas] BP, Chevron/dsl, Marathon/Subway/dsl, QT, Shell/dsl [food] Applebee's, Arby's, Asian Chef, Capt D's, Chin Chin, Dunkin Donuts, Fried Tomato Buffet, Hooters, La Hacienda, Longhorn Steaks, Marco's Pizza, Moe's SW Grill, Panda Express, Red Lobster, Ruby Tuesday, Sprayberry's BBQ, Steak'n Shake, Stevi B's Pizza, TX Roadhouse, Waffle House, Wendy's [lodging] Country Inn&Suites, Hampton Inn, Quality Inn, Springhill Suites [other] GNC, Goodyear/auto, Hobby Lobby, Home Depot, Jo-Ann, Kauffman Tire, Kohl's, Lowe's, Petsmart, Ross, Walmart/McDonald's, W [gas] RaceTrac/dsl [food] 5 Guys Burgers, Burger King, Checkers, Chick-fil-A, Coldstone, Cracker Barrel, Firehouse Subs, Goldberg's Deli, Golden Corral, HoneyBaked Ham, IHOP, Jimmy John's, KFC, Krystal, La Parrilla Mexican, Newk's Cafe, O'Charley's, Olive Garden, Panera Bread, Red Robin, Rockback Pizza, Shane's BBQ, Shoney's, Starbucks, Taco Bell, Taco Mac, Thai Heaven, Tokyo Japanese, Yogli Mogli, Zaxby's [lodging] Best Western, Comfort

GA

INTERSTATE 85 Cont'd

47 Continued
Inn, La Quinta, Motel 6, Newnan Inn H, $General, $Tree, AT&T, Barnes&Noble, Belk, Best Buy, BigLots, BJ's Whse/gas, Buick/Cadillac/GMC, Chevrolet, Dick's, Dillards, Ford/Lincoln, Hyundai, JC Penney, Michael's, Office Depot, Old Navy, Publix, Radio Shack, Target, Tires+, TJ Maxx, Toyota/Scion, Verizon, vet, Walgreens

41 US 27/29, Newnan, E Pilot/Subway/Wendy's/dsl/scales/24hr Little White House NHS, Roosevelt SP, W BP/dsl, Chevron/dsl Huddle House, McDonald's, Waffle House Best Value Inn, Economy Inn, Home Lodge, Super 8 $General, repair

35 US 29, to Grantville, W BP/dsl, Phillips 66/dsl

28 GA 54, GA 100, to Hogansville, E Valero/dsl, W Chevron/dsl, Loves/Arby's/dsl/scales/24hr, Shell/dsl Intnat'l Cafe, McDonald's, Nachos Mexican, Roger's BBQ, Subway, Waffle House, Wendy's Garden Inn, Woodstream Inn Ingles

23mm Beech Creek

22mm **weigh sta both lanes**

21 I-185 S, to Columbus

18 GA 109, to Mountville, E Marathon/Domino's Red Roof Inn, Wingate Inn Little White House HS, to FDR SP, W BP/dsl, Circle K/dsl, RaceTrac/dsl, Shell/dsl, Texaco/dsl Applebee's, Banzai Japanese, Burger King, Chick-fil-A, Cracker Barrel, IHOP, Juanito's Mexican, Longhorn Steaks, Los Nopales, McDonald's, Mi Casa Mexican, Moe's SW Grill, Starbucks, Subway, Waffle House, Wendy's, Zaxby's Baymont Inn, Comfort Inn, Holiday Inn Express, La Quinta, Lafayette Garden Inn, Quality Inn, Super 8 AT&T, Belk, Chrysler/Dodge/Jeep, Ford/Lincoln, Home Depot, Honda, Hyundai, JC Penney, mall, RV Park (3mi), TJ Maxx, Verizon

14 US 27, to La Grange, W Pure, Shell, Summit/dsl Hampton Inn

13 GA 219, to La Grange, E Waffle House Days Inn, W Pilot/Subway/dsl/scales/24hr, Shell/dsl Arbys, McDonald's H

10mm Long Cane Creek

6 Kia Blvd, W Kia Plant

2 GA 18, to West Point, E Shell/dsl, Summit/dsl Best Value, W Subway (1.5) camping, to West Point Lake

0.5mm **Welcome Ctr nb full facilities, info, litter barrels, petwalk vending**

0mm Georgia/Alabama state line, Chattahoochee River

INTERSTATE 95

Exit # Services

113mm Georgia/South Carolina state line, Savannah River

111mm **Welcome Ctr/weigh sta sb, full facilities, info, litter barrels, petwalk vending**

109 GA 21, to Savannah, Pt Wentworth, Rincon, E Enmark/dsl, Pilot/McDonald's/Subway/dsl/scales/24hr Waffle House Best Western, Country Inn&Suites, Hampton Inn, Mulberry Grove Inn Freightliner, W Flash/dsl, Murphy Express/dsl, Shell/Circle K/Blimpie/dsl Bojangles, Dunkin Donuts, El Ranchito, Happy Wok, Island Grill, Port Side Seafood, Sweet Tea Grill, Wendy's, Zaxby's Comfort Suites, Days Inn, Holiday Inn Express, Palm Extended Stay, Quality Inn, Savannah

109 Continued
Inn, Sleep Inn, Super 8 CVS Drug, Family$, Food Lio
Whispering Pines RV Park (3mi)

107mm Augustine Creek

106 Jimmy DeLoach Pkwy

104 Savannah E BP, Shell/Wendy's/dsl Sam Snee Grill, Waffle House, Waffle House Candlewood Suite Comfort Suites, Country Inn&Suites, DoubleTree, Fairfield In Hampton Inn, Hilton Garden, Holiday Inn Express, Hyatt Plac SpringHill Suites, Staybridge Suites, TownePlace Suites, Win ate Inn to W Murphy USA, Parkers/dsl, She Subwa Arby's, Buffalo Wild Wings, Cheddar's, Chick-fil- Chili's, Chipotle, CookOut, DQ, Fatz Cafe, Firehouse Subs, Fiv Guys, Hilliard's Rest., IHOP, Jalapeños, Jersey Mike's, Jimm John's, Little Caesar's, Logan's Roadhouse, Longhorn Steak McAlister's Deli, McDonald's, Mellow Mushroom, Moe's SW, O ive Garden, Panera Bread, Ruby Tuesday, Shane's Rib Shac Sonic, Starbucks, Steak'n Shake, Wild Wing Cafe, Zaxby's Embassy Suites, Red Roof Inn, Residence Inn AT&T, GN Goodyear, Home Depot, Michael's, Petsmart, Publix, Ros Sam's Club/gas, Savannah Tire, Tanger Outlets/famous brand TJ Maxx, URGENT CARE, Verizon, Walmart/McDonald's

102 US 80, to Garden City, E El Cheapos/Baldinos Subs, En market/dsl, Flash/dsl Bojangles, Cracker Barrel, Dickey' BBQ, Guerrero Mexican, Hiranos Steaks, Jersey Style Subs KFC, Krystal, Larry's Subs, Los Bravos Mexican, McDonald's Peking Chinese, Spanky's, Subway, Taco Bell, Waffle Hous Best Western, Microtel, Motel 6, Quality Inn, Travelodg Camping World RV Ctr, Family$, Food Lion, museum, t Ft Pulaski NM, W Gate/dsl, Marathon, Shell Burge King, Domino's, El Potro Mexican, Hardee's, Italian Pizza, Pizz Hut, Wendy's, Western Sizzlin EconoLodge, Holiday Inn, L Quinta, Magnolia Inn, Ramada, Sleep Inn $General

99b a I-16, W to Macon, E to Savannah

94 GA 204, to Savannah, Pembroke, E BP/dsl, Exxon, Murphy USA/dsl (2mi), Shell/dsl Applebee's, Cracker Barrel, Denny's, Hardee's, Houlihan's, IHOP, McDonald's, Perkins, Ruby Tuesday, Sonic, Tony Popa's Baymont Inn, Best Inn, Best Western, Clarion, Comfort Suites, Days Inn, EconoLodge, Fairfield Inn, Hampton Inn, Holiday Inn Express, Howard Johnson, La Quinta, Quality Inn, Red Roof Inn, San's Boutique Hotel, Scottish Inn, Sleep Inn, SpringHill Suites, Wingate Inn H, Factory Stores/Famous Brands, GNC, Walmart (2mi), W Chevron/dsl, Shell Hooters, JT's Grill, Shellhouse Rest, Subway, Waffle House Heritage Inn, Knights Inn, Microtel, Travel Inn Harley-Davidson, Savannah Oaks RV Park (2mi)

91mm Ogeechee River

90 GA 144, Old Clyde Rd, to Ft Stewart, Richmond Hill SP, E Exxon/dsl, Parker DQ, Jalapeno's, Pizza Hut, Starbucks, Subway, Zaxby's AT&T, Kroger/deli/dsl, URGENT CARE, Verizon, W Loves/McDonald's/dsl/scales/24hr, Shell/dsl Gore's RV Ctr

87 US 17, to Coastal Hwy, Richmond Hill, E BP, Chevron/dsl, RaceWay/dsl China 1, Denny's, Domino's, Fuji Japanese, Papa Murphy's, Smokin' Pig BBQ, Southern Image Rest., Steamer's Rest., Subway, Waffle House Days Inn, Motel 6, Royal Inn, Scottish Inn, Travelodge Food Lion, URGENT CARE, W El Cheapo, Exxon/McDonald's/dsl, Shell/dsl, TA/BP/Pizza Hut/Popeye's/dsl/scales/24hr/ @ Arby's, KFC/Taco Bell, Waffle House, Wendy's Best Western, Comfort Suites, EconoLodge, Hampton Inn, Quality Inn, Savannah South Inn KOA

INTERSTATE 95 Cont'd

Exit #	Services
85mm	Elbow Swamp
80mm	Jerico River
76	US 84, GA 38, to Midway, Sunbury, E hist sites, W El Cheapo/dsl/scales, Parker's/dsl Holton's Seafood, Huddle House
67	US 17, Coastal Hwy, to S Newport, E Chevron/Subway/dsl, Citgo/dsl, El Cheapo, Shell/McDonald's Jones BBQ Harris Neck NWR, S Newport Camping (2mi), W Texaco
58	GA 99, GA 57, Townsend Rd, Eulonia, E BP/dsl, Citgo $General, USPO, W Chevron/dsl, El Cheapo, Shell/Stuckey's/dsl 7 Townsend Inn, Magnuson Inn Lake Harmony RV Park, McIntosh Lake RV Park
55mm	**weigh sta both lanes**
49	GA 251, to Darien, E Chevron, Mobil/dsl DQ, McDonald's, Waffle House Cathead RV Park, Ford, Inland Harbor RV Park, W BP, El Cheapo/Larry's Subs/dsl/scales, Shell/Stuckey's/dsl Burger King, KFC/Taco Bell, Ruby Tuesday, Wendy's Comfort Inn, Days Inn, Hampton Inn, Quality Inn, Super 8 Darien Outlets/famous brands
47mm	Darien River
46.5mm	Butler River
46mm	Champney River
45mm	Altamaha River
42	GA 99, E to Hofwyl Plantation HS
41mm	**sb, full facilities, litter barrels, petwalk RV dump, vending**
38	US 17, GA 25, N Golden Isles Pkwy, Brunswick, E RaceTrac/dsl Comfort Suites, Country Inn&Suites, Embassy Suites (2mi), Fairfield Inn, Hawthorn Inn, Holiday Inn, Microtel Nissan, W BP, Chevron/dsl, Flash, Shell/dsl China Town, Denny's, Huddle House, Logan's Roadhouse, Subway, Toucan's, Waffle House Best Western, Courtyard, EconoLodge, Guest Cottage Motel, Hampton Inn, Quality Inn,Sleep Inn $General, Family$, Harley-Davidson, Harvey's Foods, Toyota/Scion
36b a	US 25, US 341, to Jesup, Brunswick, E Chevron/Subway/dsl, Exxon/dsl, RaceWay/dsl Cracker Barrel, IHOP, KFC, Krystal, McDonald's, Pizza Hut, Starbucks, Taco Bell, Wendy's Brunswick Park Motel, Days Inn, Howard Johnson, La Quinta, Red Roof Inn Jack's Tires, transmissions, W Mr Pete's/dsl, Parker's/dsl, Sunoco/dsl Capt Joe's Seafood, China Lee, Huddle House, Larry's Subs, Sonny's BBQ, Waffle House Clarion, Comfort Inn, Magnuson Inn, Ramada Inn, Rodeway Inn, Super 8 $General, Advance Parts, CVS Drug, Family$, Fred's, Winn-Dixie
33mm	Turtle River
30mm	S Brunswick River
29	US 17, US 82, GA 520, S GA Pkwy, Brunswick, E Citgo/Church's/dsl, Exxon, Loves/Steak'n Shake/Subway/dsl/scales/24hr Huddle House, Krystal, McDonald's, Zaxby's Comfort Suites Blue Beacon, SpeedCo, W Citgo, FLYING J/Denny's/dsl/LP/scales/24hr, Goasis/BP/Burger King/Starbucks/Subway/dsl/24hr, Shell/dsl Domino's, Larry's Subs, Waffle House, Zachry's Rest EconoLodge, Microtel, Super 8 $General, Family$, Golden Isles Camping, Harvey's Foods, TA Truck Service
27.5mm	Little Satilla River
26	Dover Bluff Rd, E Mobil/Stuckey's/dsl
22	Horse Stamp Church Rd

DARIEN

BRUNSWICK

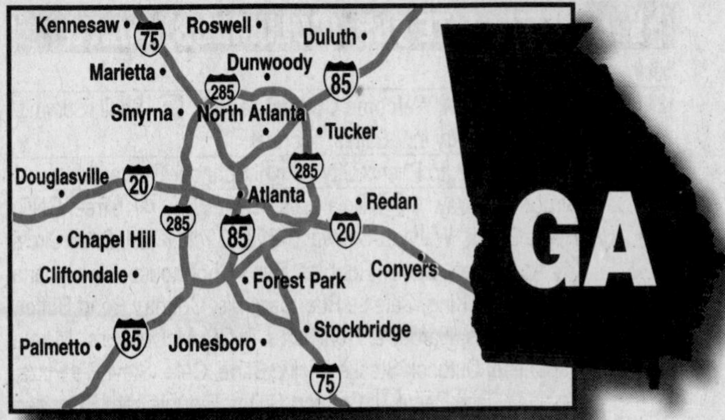

Exit #	Services
21mm	White Oak Creek
19mm	Canoe Swamp
15mm	Satilla River
14	GA 25, to Woodbine, W Chevron/Sunshine/rest/dsl/scales/24hr Stardust Motel (3mi)
7	Harrietts Bluff Rd, E Exxon/dsl, Shell/Subway/e-85, W BP/dsl Walkabout Camping/RV Park
6.5mm	Crooked River
6	Laurel Island Pkwy, E Green Cedar/Shell/dsl
3	GA 40, Kingsland, to St Marys, E BP/dsl, Chevron, El Cheapo, Exxon/Krystal, Mobil, Murphy USA/dsl, Shell/Subwa Applebee's, Burger King, Chick-fil-A, China Wok, DQ, Dunkin Donuts, Hong Kong Buffet, KFC, Little Caesars, Longhorn Steaks, McDonald's, Papa John's, Ruby Tuesday, Sonny's BBQ, Taco Bell, Waffle House, Wendy's, Zaxby's Best Value Inn, Best Western, Comfort Inn, Country Inn&Suites, Days Inn, Fairfield Inn, Hawthorn Suites, Magnolia Inn, Microtel, Red Roof Inn, Rodeway Inn, Sleep Inn $Tree, Buick/Chevrolet, Chrysler/Dodge/Jeep, CVS Drug, Ford, GNC, K-Mart, Lowe's, NAPA, Publix, Radio Shack, Suzuki, Tire Kingdom, to Crooked River SP, to Submarine Base, URGENT CARE, Verizon, Walgreens, Walmart, Winn-Dixie, W **Welcome Ctr/info** Flash/dsl, Petro/Popeye's/dsl/scales/24hr/ @, RaceWay/dsl, Shell/dsl Cracker Barrel, Domino's, IHOP, Millhouse Steaks, Subway, Waffle House Clean Stay USA, Country Hearth Inn, EconoLodge, Hampton Inn, Jameson Inn, La Quinta, Springfield Suites Ace Hardware, Fred's, Kiki RV Park
1	St Marys Rd, to Cumberland Is Nat Seashore, E **Welcome Ctr nb full facilities, info, litter barrels, petwalk vending,** Shell/dsl W BP/dsl, Chevron/dsl, Wilco/Hess/Dunkin Donuts/Wendy's/dsl/scales/24hr Jack's BBQ GS RV Park, KOA
0mm	Georgia/Florida state line, St Marys River

ST MARYS

INTERSTATE 185 (COLUMBUS)

Exit #	Services
48	I-85. **I-185 begins/ends on I-85.**
46	Big Springs Rd, E Shell/dsl, W tires
42	US 27, Pine Mountain, E Shell/dsl, Summit/dsl Waffle House Little White House HS, Pine Mtn Camping, to Callaway Gardens
34	GA 18, to West Point, E to Callaway Gardens
30	Hopewell Church Rd, Whitesville, W Shell/dsl
25	GA 116, to Hamilton, W RV camping
19	GA 315, Mulberry Grove, W Chevron/dsl
14	Smith Rd

GA

[gas] = gas [food] = food [lodging] = lodging [other] = other [RS] = rest stop

COLUMBUS

INTERSTATE 185 (COLUMBUS) Cont'd

Exit #	Services
12	Williams Rd, **W Welcome Ctr/rest rooms** [gas] Shell, Summit/dsl [lodging] Country Inn&Suites, Microtel
10	US 80, GA 22, to Phenix City, **W** [other] Springer Opera House
8	Airport Thruway, **E** [food] Bojangles, Great Wall [other] $Tree, GNC, Home Depot, Walmart/Subway, **W** [gas] Circle K/dsl, Shell/Circle [food] Applebee's, Baskin Robbins, Ben's Chophouse, Blue Iguana Grill, Burger King, Cafe Le Rue, Capt D's, Country Road Buffet, Fuddruckers, Hardee's, Houlihan's, IHOP, McDonald's, Mikata Japanese, Outback Steaks, Pickle Barrel Cafe, Stevi B's Pizza, Subway, Taco Bell [lodging] Comfort Suites, DoubleTree, Extended Stay America, Hampton Inn, Sleep Inn [other] AAA, BigLots, Hancock Fabrics, K-Mart, Office Depot
7	45th St, Manchester Expswy, **E** [food] Applebee's, Burger King, Carino's Italian, Krystal, Ruby Tuesday [lodging] Courtyard, La Quinta, Super 8 [other] Best Buy, Cadillac/Chevrolet, Dillard's, JC Penney, Macy's, mall, **W** [gas] BP/dsl, Chevron/dsl, Circle K/dsl, Marathon [food] Arby's, China Express, Dunkin Donuts, Goldberg's Deli, Golden Corral, Jimmy John's, KFC, Little Caesar's, Logan's Roadhouse, Lucky China, McDonald's, Pizza Hut, Ryan's, Shogun Japanese, Sonic, Starbucks, SteakOut, Subway, Waffle House [lodging] Fairfield Inn, Holiday Inn, TownePlace Suites [other] [H], $General, Advance Parts, Big T Tire/repair, Civil War Naval Museum, Midas, Mr Transmission
6	GA 22, Macon Rd, **E** [gas] Chevron/dsl, Circle K/dsl [food] Bruster's, Burger King, DQ, Little Caesars, Taco Bell, Waffle House [lodging] Best Western, Comfort Inn, Days Inn [other] $General, Rite Aid, U-Haul, vet, Walgreens, **W** [gas] Chevron/dsl, Shell/dsl [food] American Deli, Capt D's, ChuckeCheese, Cici's, Country's BBQ, Denny's, DunkinDonuts/Baskin Robbins, Firehouse Subs, Jimmy John's, Longhorn Steaks, McDonald's, Subway, Zaxby's [lodging] Efficiency Lodge, La Quinta [other] AT&T, CVS Drug, Fred's, GNC, Goodyear/auto, K-Mart, Publix, Radio Shack, TJ Maxx, Tuesday Morning, Verizon
4	Buena Vista Rd, **E** [gas] BP, Circle K, Solo [food] Burger King, Capt D's, Checkers, Church's, Krystal, McDonald's, Papa John's, Pizza Hut, Subway, Taco Bell, Waffle House, Zaxby's [other] $Tree, AutoZone, Family$, Firestone/auto, Goodyear/auto, O'Reilly Parts, Rainbow Foods, repair, USPO, vet, Walgreens, Walmart, Winn-Dixie, **W** [gas] Marathon
3	St Marys Rd, **E** [food] Domino's [lodging] Microtel [other] Family$, **W** [gas] FuelTech/dsl, Shell/dsl [food] Hardee's, Shark Seafood/Chicken [other] $General, Ace Hardware, Piggly Wiggly
1b a	US 27, US 280, Victory Dr, **0-3 mi W** [gas] Chevron/dsl, Circle K, Liberty, RaceWay/dsl [food] Burger King, Capt D's, Checkers, Krystal, McDonald's, Papa John's, Sonic, Subway, Taco Bell, Waffle House, Wendy's [lodging] Candlewood Suites, Columbus Inn, EconoLodge, Holiday Inn Express, Motel 6, Suburban Lodge [other] $General, Advance Parts, AutoZone, CVS Drug, Family$, O'Reilly Parts, Piggly Wiggly, Verizon
0mm	**I-185 begins/ends on Victory Dr**

GA

ATLANTA AREA

INTERSTATE 285

Exit #	Services
62	GA 279, S Fulton Hwy, Old Nat Hwy, **N** [gas] Chevron/dsl, Texaco [food] Waffle House [lodging] Econolodge, **S** [gas] Chevron, Citgo, Exxon, Shell, Valer [food] American Deli, Blimpie, Bojangles, Burger King, Checker's, China Cafeteria, Church's, Cozumel Mexican, KFC, Krystal, McDonald's, Piccadilly Cafeteria, Subway, Taco
62	Continued Bell, Waffle House, Wendy's [lodging] Baymont Inn, Day's Inn, Qu ity Inn, Super 8, Travelodge, Windsor Atl Hotel [other] AutoZo Family$, Midas, O'Reilly Parts, U-Haul
61	I-85, N to Atlanta, S to Montgomery
60	GA 139, Riverdale Rd, **N** [lodging] Fairfield Inn (2mi), Microtel (2r Wingate Inn (2mi), **S** [gas] QT/dsl, Shell/dsl, Valero/dsl [food] Che ers, Church's, McDonald's, Papa John's, Waffle House [lodging] B Western, Day's Inn, Quality Hotel [other] $General, Advance Pa Family$
59	Clark Howell Hwy, **N** [other] air cargo
58	I-75, N to Atlanta, S to Macon (from eb), to US 19, US 41, Hapeville, **S** [gas] BP/dsl, Citgp/dsl, Exxon/dsl [food] American D Jimmy John's, Subway, Tijuana Joe's, Waffle House, Wend [lodging] Home Lodge Motel
55	GA 54, Jonesboro Rd, **N** [lodging] Super 8, **S** [gas] BP/dsl, Citg dsl, Shell/dsl, Texaco/dsl [food] DaiLai Vietnamese, McDonal [other] Family$, Home Depot, repair
53	US 23, Moreland Ave, to Ft Gillem, **N** [gas] BP/dsl, Citgo/dsl, [gas] Chevron/dsl, Citg [food] Wendy's [lodging] EconoLodge [other] USF
52	I-675, S to Macon
51	Bouldercrest Rd, **N** [gas] BP, Pilot/Wendy's/dsl/24hr [Checkers, Domino's, Hardee's, KFC, WK Wings [other] Family Wayfield Foods, **S** [gas] Exxon/dsl, Shell/Blimpie/dsl, Texaco/d
48	GA 155, Flat Shoals Rd, Candler Rd, **N** [gas] BP, Chevron, Citg dsl, Shell/dsl, Texaco/dsl [food] Burger King, Checkers, Church DQ, Dunkin Donuts/BR, KFC, McDonald's, Taco Bell, Waf King, WK Wings [lodging] Gulf American Inn [other] BigLots, Macy **S** [gas] Citgo, QT, Texaco/dsl [food] Burger King, China One, Son Subway [other] Family$
46b a	I-20, E to Augusta, W to Atlanta
44	GA 260, Glenwood Rd, **E** [gas] Sunoco/dsl [lodging] EconoLodg **W** [gas] Exxon/dsl, Texaco/dsl, Valero
43	US 278, Covington Hwy, **E** [gas] Chevron/Subway, Citgo/d [food] Waffle House [other] U-Haul, **W** [gas] BP, QT, RaceTrac/ds Shell/dsl, Texaco/dsl [food] HoneyBaked Ham, Mrs Winner' Wendy's [lodging] Best Inn [other] Advance Parts, Family$
42	(from nb), [other] Marta Station
41	GA 10, Memorial Dr, Avondale Estates, **E** [gas] Citgo, Shell/d [food] Applebee's, Baskin-Robbins/Dunkin Donuts, Burger Kin Church's, DQ, IHOP, Pancake House, Pizza Hut, Subway, Tac Bell, Waffle House, Wendy's [lodging] Aloha Inn, Savannah Suite United Suites [other] $Tree, Advance Parts, Atl Tires, AutoZon Family$, Firestone/auto, GNC, Office Depot, Ross, transmis sions, U-Haul, URGENT CARE
40	Church St, to Clarkston, **E** [gas] Chevron, Shell/dsl, Texac [other] auto repair, **W** [other] [H]
39b a	US 78, to Athens, Decatur
38	US 29, Lawrenceville Hwy, **E** [gas] Phillips 66, QT/dsl, RaceTrac dsl [food] Waffle House [lodging] Knights Inn, Super 8 [other] [H] **W** [gas] Citgo/dsl [food] Bruster's [lodging] Masters Inn, Motel 6 [other] AutoZone CVS Drug
37	GA 236, to LaVista, Tucker, **E** [gas] Chevron/dsl, Texaco [food] Checkers, Folks Rest., IHOP, O'Charley's, Piccadilly's, Waffle House [lodging] Comfort Suites, Days Inn [other] Firestone, Target **W** [gas] BP/repair, Chevron, Citgo/dsl, Shell/dsl [food] Arby's, Black eyed Pea, Blue Ribbon Grill, Capt D's, Chick-fil-A, Chipotle, City Cafe, Coco Cabana Cuban, Dunkin Donuts, Eduardo's Mexican, HoneyBaked Ham, Jason's Deli, Kacey's Rest., Lucky Key Chinese, Madios Pizza, McDonald's, Mellow Mushroom, Panda Express, Red Lobster, Smoothie King, Starbucks, Wendy's

 [gas] = gas [food] = food [lodging] = lodging [other] = other [RS] = rest stop

INTERSTATE 285 Cont'd

37 Continued
[lodging] Courtyard, DoubleTree, Holiday Inn, Quality Inn [other] $Tree, AT&T

Best Buy, Goodyear/auto, JC Penney, Kohl's, Kroger, Macy's, mall, Michael's, Office Depot, Petsmart, Publix, Sears/auto, TJ Maxx, Verizon

34 Chamblee-Tucker Rd, E [gas] Chevron, Texaco [food] $3 Cafe, Galaxy Diner, Hunan Chinese, Jersey Mike's Subs, KFC/Taco Bell, Moe's SW Grill, S&S Cafeteria, Wendy's [lodging] Motel 6 [other] Advance Parts, Goodyear, Kroger, Rite Aid, Verizon, W [gas] Citgo, Shell [food] Little Cuba, McDonald's, Subway [other] BigLots, vet

33b a I-85, N to Greenville, S to Atlanta

32 US 23, Buford Hwy, to Doraville, E [gas] BP/dsl [food] Burger King/playland, Checkers, Chick-fil-A, McDonald's, Waffle House, White Windmill Café, Zaxby's [other] Advance Parts, auto repair, Firestone/auto, Marshalls, PepBoys, W [gas] Citgo, QT/dsl [food] McDonald's, Monterrey Mexican, Pestones Cuban, Subway, Tostones Cuban, Waffle House [lodging] Comfort Inn [other] $Tree, Meineke, transmissions

31b a GA 141, Peachtree Ind, to Chamblee, W [gas] Citgo/dsl, QT [food] Arby's, Baskin-Robbins/Dunkin Donuts, Chick-fil-A, IHOP, McDonald's, Pizza Hut, Subway, Wendy's [other] Acura, Advance Parts, Audi/VW, Brands Mart, Buick/GMC, Chevrolet, CVS Drug, Fiat, Firestone/auto, Ford, Honda, Hyundai, Kia, Lexus, Mazda, Mini, Office Depot, Porsche Toyota, Walgreens

30 Chamblee-Dunwoody Rd, N Shallowford Rd, to N Peachtree Rd, N [gas] BP, Shell, Texaco/dsl [food] Bagel&Co. Deli, Burger King, Guthrie's, Marco's Pizza, McDonald's, Starbucks, Subway, Waffle House [other] Kroger, Tuesday Morning, S [gas] Exxon/Blimpie/dsl, Mobil, Phillips 66/dsl, Shell, Valero/dsl [food] Bombay Grill, La Botana Mexican, Mad Italian Rest., Papa John's, Taco Bell, Wendy's, Wild Ginger Thai [lodging] Holiday Inn Select, Residence Inn [other] vet

29 Ashford-Dunwoody Rd, N [gas] BP, Exxon/Subway [food] Brio Tuscan, Broken Egg, CA Pizza Kitchen, Capital Grille, Cheesecake Factory, Chili's, Firebird's Rest., Goldfish, J. Alexander's, Jason's Deli, Maddio's Pizza, Maggiano's Little Italy, McCormick&Schmick's, McDonald's, McKendrick Steaks, Olive Garden, PF Chang's, Popeye's, Schlotzsky's, Seasons 32 Grill, Starbucks [lodging] Crowne Plaza [other] Barnes&Noble, Best Buy, Dillard's, Goodyear/auto, Hobby Lobby, Macy's, mall, Marshalls, Nordstrom, Old Navy, USPO, Walmart, S [other] Hilton Garden

28 Peachtree-Dunwoody Rd (no EZ return wb), N [food] 5 Guys Burgers, Arby's, Chequer's Grill, Chipotle, Chuy's Mexican, Fleming's Steaks, Fuddrucker's, Genghis Grill, Mimi's Café, Panera Bread, Shane's Rib Shack, Taco Mac, Uncle Julio's Mexican [lodging] Comfort Suites, Courtyard, Extended Stay America, Extended Stay Deluxe, Fairfield Inn, Hampton Inn, Hilton Suites, Holiday Inn Express, Homestead Suites, La Quinta, Marriott, Microtel, Residence Inn, Sheraton, Westin [other] Costco/gas, Firestone/auto, Home Depot, mall, Petsmart, Publix, Rite Aid, Ross, Target, TJ Maxx, Verizon, S [other] [H]

27 US 19 N, GA 400, **2 mi** N [other] LDS Temple

26 Glenridge Dr (from eb), Johnson Ferry Rd

25 US 19 S, Roswell Rd, Sandy Springs, N [gas] BP, Shell/dsl [food] 5 Guys Burgers, Applebee's, Bobbys Burgers, Boston Mkt, Burger King, Chick-fil-A, Chipotle Mexican, Domino's, Dunkin Donuts, Egg Harbor Café, El Azteca Mexican, Firehouse Subs, Hudson Grille, IHOP, Jason's Deli, Jimmy John's, Longhorn Steaks, Mandarin House, McDonald's, Mellow Mushroom,

ATLANTA AREA

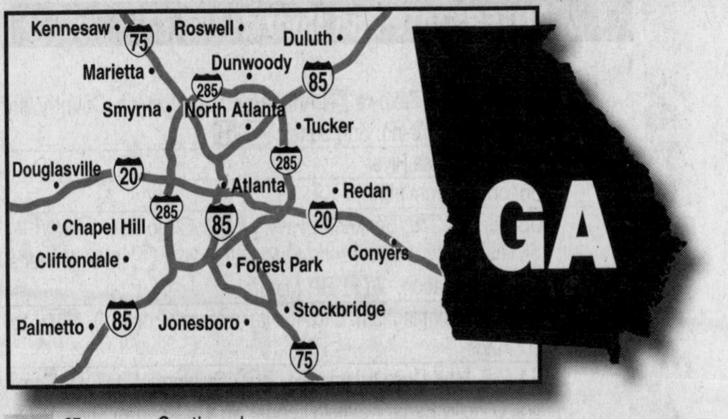

25 Continued
Moe's SW Grill, Pizza Hut, Ray's NY Pizza, Roasters, Ruth's Chris Steaks, SeaBass Kitchen, Smash Burger, Starbucks, Steak'n Shake, Subway, Taco Bell, Waffle House, Wendy's [lodging] Comfort Inn [other] [H], $Tree, Aldi Foods, AT&T, CVS Drug, DeKalb Tire, Hancock Fabrics, Lowe's, Marshalls, Mr Transmission, NAPA AutoCare, Office Depot, PepBoys, PetCo, Publix, Radio Shack, Target, Toyota, Trader Joe's, Tuesday Morning, URGENT CARE, Verizon, Walgreens, Whole Foods Mkt, S [gas] Chevron/dsl, Citgo, Shell [food] Barberitos, El Taco Veloz, Kobe Steaks, Seasons Rest., Starbucks, Subway, Taco Mac [other] Publix, Staples, Target, URGENT CARE

24 Riverside Dr

22 New Northside Dr, to Powers Ferry Rd, N [gas] Shell/Subway/dsl, S [gas] BP, Chevron/dsl [food] Blimpie, McDonald's, Peter Cheng's Chinese, Ray's Rest., Waffle House [lodging] Candlewood Suites, Hawthorn Suites, Homestead Suites, Wyndham [other] CVS Drug, Publix, vet

21 (from wb), N [gas] Shell [food] Harry's Pizza, Homestead Village [other] BMW/Mini

20 I-75, N to Chattanooga, S to Atlanta (from wb), to US 41 N

19 US 41, Cobb Pkwy, to Dobbins AFB, N [gas] BP, Chevron/24hr, Citgo, Shell [food] Arby's, BBQ, Bruster's, Carrabba's, Chuck-eCheese, Denny's, Dunkin Donuts, Hardee's, IHOP, Jade Palace, Joe's Crabshack, KFC, McDonald's, Olive Garden, Papa John's, Pizza Hut, Red Lobster, Steak'n Shake, Subway, Sunny's BBQ, The Border Mexican, Waffle House, Wendy's, Wingate Inn [lodging] Hilton, Holiday Inn Express [other] Best Buy, Buick/Subaru, Cadillac, Chevrolet, Honda, Hyundai, Lexus, Marshall's, Michael's, Office Depot, PetsMart, Ross, Target, Walgreen, S [gas] Chevron/24hr [food] Buffalo's Café, Cheese Factory, Chick-fil-A, Chipotle Mexican, El Toro Mexican, Hooters, Jason's Deli, Johnny Rocket's, Longhorn Steaks, Maggiano's Italian, Malone's Grill, Olde Mill Steaks, PF Chang, Pizza Hut, Ruby Tuesday, Schlotsky's [lodging] Courtyard, Homewood Suites, Renaissance Motel, Sheraton Suites, Stouffer Waverly Hotel, Sumner Suites [other] A&P, Barnes&Noble, Costco/gas, JC Penney, Macy's, mall, Sears/auto, USPO

18 Paces Ferry Rd, to Vinings, N [food] Panera Bread [lodging] Fairfield Inn, La Quinta, S [gas] QT/24hr [food] Chick-fil-A, Subway, Willy's Grill [lodging] Extended Stay Deluxe, Hampton Inn, Wyndham [other] Goodyear/auto, Home Depot, Publix

16 S Atlanta Rd, to Smyrna, N [food] Five Guys Burgers, Waffle House, Zio's Italian [lodging] Holiday Inn Express [other] [H] S [gas] Pilot/Wendy's/dsl/scales/24hr, Shell/dsl, Texaco [other] Kroger

15 GA 280, S Cobb Dr, E [lodging] Microtel [other] U-Haul, W [gas] BP/dsl, RaceTrac, Shell [food] Arby's/Mrs Winners, Checker's, Chick-fil-A, China Buffet, IHOP, Krystal/24hr, McDonald's, Subway, Taco

GA

⛽ = gas 🍴 = food 🛏 = lodging ⓞ = other RS = rest stop

ATLANTA AREA

INTERSTATE 285 Cont'd

15	Continued Bell, Wendy's, Zaxby's lodging AmeriHost, Comfort Inn, Country Inn Suites, Knight's Inn, Sun Suites other H
14mm	Chattahoochee River
13	Bolton Rd (from nb)
12	US 78, US 278, Bankhead Hwy, E gas Citgo/dsl, Petro/Iron Skillet/dsl/rest./scales/24hr/@, Shell/dsl/24hr food Mrs Winner's other Blue Beacon, W gas BP, Marathon
10b a	I-20, W to Birmingham, E to Atlanta (exits left from nb), W other to Six Flags
9	GA 139, MLK Dr, to Adamsville, E gas Quikmart, Shell other Family$, O'Reilly Parts, Wayfield Foods, W gas Chevron, Shell, Texaco/dsl food Checker's, Church's, KFC/Taco Bell, McDonald's other $General, Family$
7	Cascade Rd, E gas Exxon/dsl food Papa John's other Kroger, W gas BP/dsl, Shell/dsl food Applebee's, China Express, KFC, Little Caesar's, McDonald's, Pizza Hut, Starbucks, Subway, Wendy's other GNC, Home Depot, Publix, Radio Shack, Tires+, Walgreens, Walmart
5b a	GA 166, Lakewood Fwy, E gas Chevron, Shell food Burger King, Capt D's, Checker's, KFC, Little Caesar's, Subway, Wendy's other CVS Drug, Firestone, Goodyear/auto, Kroger, Macy's, mall, W gas BP, RaceWay/dsl, Shell/dsl, Texaco/dsl, Valer food Church's lodging Deluxe Inn other AutoZone, Family$, O'Reilly Parts
2	Camp Creek Pkwy, to ✈ E gas Exxon/dsl, Texaco food Checker's, Church's, McDonald's, W gas RaceTrac/dsl food American Deli, Bruster's, Carino's, Chick-fil-A, Chili's, China 1, Five Guys, Jason's Deli, LongHorn Steaks, Moe's SW, Panda Express, Papa John's, Popeyes, Red Lobster, Ruby Tuesday, Starbucks, Taco Bell, TGIFriday, Wendys, Zaxby's lodging Courtyard, Hampton Inn, Holiday Inn Express other $Tree, AT&T, Barnes&Noble, BJ's Whse/gas, Lowes Whse, Marshall's, Old Navy, PetsMart, Publix, Ross, Staples, Target, TJ Maxx, Verizon, Walgreens
1	Washington Rd, E gas Texaco/dsl, W gas Chevron/dsl

GA

MACON

INTERSTATE 475 (MACON)

Exit #	Services
16mm	**I-475 begins/ends on I-75, exit 177.**
15	US 41, Bolingbroke, **1 mi** E gas Exxon/dsl/LP, Marathon/dsl
9	Zebulon Rd, E gas Marathon/dsl, Shell/Circle K/24hr food Applebee's, Buffalo's Café, Chick-fil-A, Johnny's NY Pizz, Krystal, Macon Pizza Co, Margarita's Mexican, McAlister's Deli, McDonald's, Moe's SW, NU Way Wieners, Papa John's, Pizza Hut, Sonic, Subway, Taco Bell, Taki Japanese, Tutti Frutti, Waffle House, Wendy's lodging Baymont Inn, Comfort Suites, Fairfield Inn, Sleep Inn other H, Goodyear/auto, Kohl's, Kroger/dsl, Lowe's, URGENT CARE, USPO, Verizon, Walgreens, Walmart/Subway, W gas Marathon/dsl, Sunoco/dsl food Marco's Pizza, Polly's Cafe, Zaxby's other Advance Parts, CVS Drug
8mm	**RS nb, full ♿ facilities, litter barrels, petwalk ☎ picnic RV dump, vending**
5	GA 74, Macon, E gas RaceWay/dsl food Waffle House other Harley-Davidson, to Mercer U, W gas Flash/Subway/dsl, Texaco/Church's/dsl food Capt D's lodging A1 Economy other $General, Tires+, to Lake Tobesofkee, vet
3	US 80, Macon, **0-2 mi** E gas Marathon/dsl, Murphy USA/dsl, RaceWay, Shell/Circle K/Subwa food Aldi Foods, Applebee's, Burger King, Chick-fil-A, China Buffet, Cracker Barrel, DQ, Firehouse Subs, Golden Corral, JL's BBQ, Margarita's Mexican,
3	Continued McAlister's Deli, McDonald's, Papa John's, S&S Cafeteria, Silver Bay Seafood, Smokin' Pig BBQ, Taco Bell, Waffle House, Zaxby's lodging Best Inn, Best Western, Bridgeview Inn, Comfort Suites, Days Inn, Discovery Inn, EconoLodge, Hampton Inn, Holiday Inn Express, La Quinta, Motel 6, Quality Inn, Ramada Inn, Red Roof Inn, Super 8, ValuePlace other $Tree, AT&T, Best Buy, BigLots, CVS Drug, Dick's, Discount Tire, Firestone/auto, GNC, Home Depot, Honda, JC Penney, Kroger/gas, Lowe's, Macy's, mall, Marshall's, Michael's, Nissan, Office Depot, Old Navy, Petsmart, Ross, Sam's Club/gas, Staples, Target, Verizon, vet, VW, Walmart/Subway, W gas Shell/Circle K, Sunoco/dsl food Burger King lodging Best Value Inn, Windsor Economy Inn
1	Hartley Bridge Rd, same as I-75 exit 156
	I-475 begins/ends on I-75, exit 156.

CANTON

WOODSTOCK

INTERSTATE 575

Exit #	Services
30mm	**I-575 begins/ends on GA 5/515.**
27	GA 5, Howell Br, to Ball Ground
24	Airport Dr
20	GA 5, to Canton, E gas BP food Bojangles, Buffalo's Cafe, Casey's Rest., Chick-fil-A, Dos Margaritas Mexican, Jin's Buffet, Stevi B's Pizza, Waffle Wouse, Wendy's lodging Econolodge, Homestead Inn, Motel 6 other AT&T, Chevrolet, Chrysler/Dodge/Jeep, GNC, Toyota, Verizon, Walmart, W gas RaceTrac/dsl, Shell/Subway, Texaco/dsl food Applebee's, Arby's, Cracker Barrel, Five Guys, Honeybaked Ham, Longhorn Steaks, McDonald's, O'Charley's, Okinawa Steaks, Outback Steaks, Panda Express, Provino's, Red Lobster, Seven Tequilas Mexican, Starbucks, Zaxby's lodging Best Western, Hampton Inn, Holiday Inn Express other H, Belk, Home Depot, Michaels, Publix, Ross
19	GA 20 E, Canton, E food Bobby's Burgers, Chick-fil-A, Chipotle, IHOP, Jimmy John's, La Parrilla Mexican, Maddio's Pizza, McDonald's, Olive Garden, Starbucks, Subway, Taco Mac, Waffle House, Which Wich?, Zaxby's other Best Buy, BooksAMillion, Dick's, Goodyear/auto, Kohl's, Lowe's, NTB, Petsmart, Target, TJ Maxx
17	GA 140, to Roswell (from sb), Canton
16	GA 20, GA 140, W gas Citgo, RaceTrac/dsl food Burger King, KFC, Mandarin House, Papa John's, Subway, Taco Bell, Waffle House other $General, Advance Parts, Rite Aid
14	Holly Springs, E gas Texaco/dsl food Domino's, Ichiban Buffet, Las Palmas Mexican, Pizza Hut lodging Pinecrest Motel other vet, Walmart/Subway, W gas Chevron, Shell/dsl food Dunkin Donuts, Golden China, McDonald's, Subway, Taste of Italy, Viva Mexico, Wendy's, Zaxby's other Autozone, Family$, Kauffman Tire, Kroger/dsl, Publix, Verizon, Walgreens
11	Sixes Rd, E gas Chevron/dsl, QT food Shane's Ribshack, Zaxby's other Home Depot, Verizon
9	Ridgewalk Pkwy, E food Applebee's, Chick-fil-A, Five Guys, McDonald's, Panda Express other outlets/famous brands
8	Towne Lake Pkwy, to Woodstock, E gas Shell/dsl food Subway, Waffle House other Ford, W gas Phillips 66, QT food Chili's, Longhorn Steaks other Tuesday Morning, Walgreens
7	GA 92, Woodstock, E gas Chevron, QT food Arby's, Bubba Q's Rest., Burger King, Capt D's, Checker's, Chick-fil-A, Chin Chin, Del Taco, DQ, Dunkin Donuts, Firehouse Subs, Folk's Kitchen, Honeybaked Ham, Maddio's Pizza, McDonald's, Moe's SW Grill, O'Charley's, Resturante Mexico, Ruby Tuesday, Starbucks, Stevi B's Pizza, Subway, Taco Bell, Waffle House lodging Comfort Suites, Hampton Inn, InTown Suite other Camping World,

INTERSTATE 575 Cont'd

7	Continued Firestone/auto, Goodyear/auto, W [gas] Texaco/dsl [food] Hacienda Vieja Mexican, IHOP, Jimmy John's, Schlotzky's, Steak'n Shake, Taco Mac [lodging] Microtel [other] AT&T, Atlanta Bread, Big Lots, BJ's Whse/gas, Discount Tire, GNC, Home Depot, Honda, Kohl's, Lowe's Whse, Old Navy, Petsmart, Target, Verizon
4	Bells Ferry Rd, W [gas] QT, RaceTrac/dsl, Shell/dsl [food] Arby's, Burger King, Dunkin Donuts, Pizza Hut, Ralph's Grill, Subway, Waffle House [other] Pepboys, Publix, Walgreens
3	Chastain Rd, to I-75 N, W [gas] Chevron [food] CA Dreaming, Cookout, Cracker Barrel, Del Taco, Firehouse Subs, Five Guys, Los Reyes, Maddio's Pizza, Marlow's Tavern, O'Charley's, Panda Express, Papa's Cuban, Ruth's Chris Steks, Starbucks, Taco Mac [lodging] Best Western, Comfort Suites, Embassy Suites, Fairfield Inn, Residence Inn, Springhill Suites [other] to Kennesaw St Coll
1	Barrett Pkwy, to I-75 N, US 41, E [gas] Murphy USA/dsl, QT [food] Bobby's Burgers, Buffalo Wild Wings, Burger King, Moe's SW Grill, Pacific Grill, Starbucks, Stevi B's Pizza, Texas Roadhouse, Twisted Kitchen, Waffle House, Wendy's, Zaxby's [other] $Tree, AT&T, Barnes&Noble, CVS Drug, Kauffman Tire, Petco, Publix, Ross, SteinMart, Tuesday Morning, Walmart/Subway, W [gas] Shell/dsl [food] Applebee's, Fuddrucker's, Fujihana, Honeybaked Ham, Jimmy John's, Longhorn Steaks, McDonald's, Olive Garden, Provino's Italian, Red Lobster, Shogun Japanese, Smashburger, Starbucks, Subway, Twin Peaks [lodging] Comfort Inn, Holiday Inn Express, La Quinta, Red Roof Inn [other] Belk, Firestone/auto, Home Depot, mall, Marshall's, Midas, Pepboys, TJ Maxx, Verizon
0mm	**I-575 begins/ends on I-75, exit 268.**

INTERSTATE 675

Exit #	Services
10mm	I-285 W, to Atlanta [airport] E to Augusta. **I-675 begins/ends on I-285, exit 52.**
7	Anvil Block Rd, Ft Gillem, E [gas] Chevron/dsl [food] Waffle House, Wendy's [other] $Tree, Walmart/Subway, W [gas] Exxon/dsl
5	Forest Pkwy, E [gas] Texaco/dsl, W [gas] BP/dsl, QT/dsl/scales, Texaco/dsl [food] McDonald's, Waffle House
2	US 23, GA 42, E [gas] BP, Texaco, Valero/Subway/dsl El Granero Mexican, W [gas] Chevron/dsl, Citg [food] Waffle House [other] Family$, Food Depot, GoodTime/auto, Rite Aid, USPO
1	GA 138, to I-75 N, Stockbridge, E [gas] Citgo/dsl, Exxon/dsl, Murphy USA/dsl, QT, Sunoco/dsl [food] Burger King, Capt D's, Checker's, Church's Chicken, DQ, Dunkin Donuts, Golden Corral, Hibachi Buffet, KFC, Krispy Kreme, Little Caesar's, McDonald's, Olympia Pizza, Papa John's, Popeye's, Taco Bell, Waffle House, Wendy's, Zaxby's [lodging] Best Value, Econolodge, Knights Inn, Magnolia Inn, Quality Inn, Sleep Inn, Stay Inn, Stockbridge Inn [other] $General, $Tree, Advance Parts, Aldi Foods, BigLots, CVS Drug, Goodyear/auto, NAPA, Pepboys, Radio Shack, Walmart, W [gas] Raceway/dsl [food] Applebee's, Broadway Diner, Chick-fil-A, Frontera Mexican, Honeybaked Ham, IHOP, Krystal, O'Charley's, Piccadilly's, Subway, Taco Mac, Tokyo Seafood, Waffle House [lodging] Comfort Inn, Day's Inn, Express Inn, Hampton Inn, Holiday Inn, La Quinta, Red Roof Inn [other] Kroger/dsl, Lowes Whse, Office Depot, Tires+, URGENT CARE, Verizon
0	**I-675 begins/ends on I-75, exit 227.**

STOCKBRIDGE

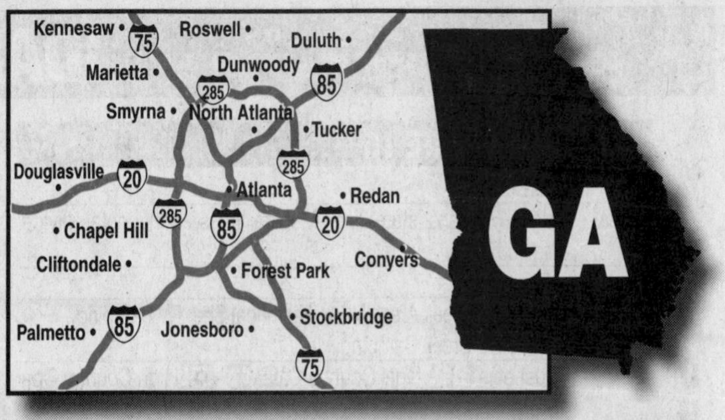

GAINESVILLE

INTERSTATE 985 (GAINESVILLE)

Exit #	Services
	I-985 begins/ends on US 23, 25mm.
24	to US 129 N, GA 369 W, Gainesville, N [gas] QT/dsl [food] McDonald's, Papa John's, Taco Bell [other] [H], Autozone, Kroger/dsl, S [gas] BP/dsl, Chevron/dsl [food] Double B Burger, Rabbittown Cafe, Subway
22	GA 11, Gainesville, N [gas] QT/dsl, Shell/dsl [food] Burger King, S [gas] Chevron/dsl, ΔShell/dslΔ [food] Waffle House [lodging] Motel 6 [other] $General
20	GA 60, GA 53, Gainesville, N [gas] RaceTrac/dsl, S [gas] Kangaroo/Subway/dsl [food] Waffle House
17	GA 13, Gainesville
16	GA 53, Oakwood, N [food] Arby's, Burger King, Capt D's, DQ, Dunkin Donuts, El Sombrero Mexican, Firehouse Subs, Hardee's, KFC, McDonald's, Napoli's Pizza, Pizza Hut, Steak'n Shake, Taco Bell, Waffle House, Zaxby's [lodging] Best Western, Jameson Inn [other] $Tree, Aldi Foods, Camping World RV Ctr, Chrysler/Dodge/Jeep, Sam's Club/dsl, Walmart/Subway, S [gas] QT/dsl [food] Buffalo's Cafe, Chick-Fil-A, Krystal, La Parilla Mexican, Sonic, Sonny's BBQ, Subway, Waffle House, Wendy's [lodging] Quality Inn [other] Ace Hardware, AutoZone, Kauffman Tire, O'Reilly Parts, Publix, Slack Parts, Toyota/Scion, Walgreens
12	Spout Springs Rd, Flowery Branch, N [gas] Exxon/dsl, S [gas] Chevron/dsl, Marathon/Subway/dsl [food] Burger&Shake, Chick-fil-A, Chili's, China Garden, CrossRoads Grill, Domino's, El Sombrero Mexican, Firehouse Subs, Little Caesar's, Napoli's Pizza, Shane's Ribshack, Shogun Japanese [lodging] Hampton Inn [other] AT&T, GNC, Home Depot, Kohl's, Petsmart, Publix, Rite Aid, Ross, Target, TJ Maxx, Verizon, Walgreens
8	GA 347, Friendship Rd, Lake Lanier, N [gas] Chevron/dsl, QT/dsl, Shell/dsl [food] Blimpie, Burger King, Cracker Barrel, McDonald's, Mykonos Cafe, Shoney's, Subway, Vinny's NY Grill, Waffle House, Wendy's, Zaxby's [lodging] Holiday Inn Express [other] $General, Advance parts, Family$, O'Reilly Parts, Publix, URGENT CARE, Verizon, vet, S [other] Camper City RV Ctr, Harley Davidson
4	US 23 S, GA 20, Buford, N [gas] QT, Shell/dsl [food] Arby's, Bojangles, Burger King, Capt D's, Golden Buddah, Golden Corral, Hardee's, IHOP, KFC, McDonald's, Pizza Hut, Subway, Taco Bell, Waffle House, Wendy's, Zaxby's [lodging] Best Value Inn, Holiday Inn Express [other] Ace Hardware, Chrysler/Dodge/Jeep, Hobby Lobby, Home Depot, Kia, NAPA Autocare, NTB, O'Reilly Parts, S [gas] Chevron/dsl, Exxon/dsl, Mtn Express/dsl [food] Asia Buffet, Sonny's BBQ, Stevi B's Pizza, Viva Mexico [other] $Tree, Firestone/auto, Honda, Kauffman Tire, Lowes Whse, Walmart
0mm	**I-985 begins/ends on I-85.**

GA

IDAHO

INTERSTATE 15

Exit #	Services
196mm	Idaho/Montana state line, Monida Pass, continental divide, elev 6870
190	Humphrey
184	Stoddard Creek Area, E Historical Site, RV camping, W Stoddard Creek Camping
180	Spencer, E Opal Country Café/ High Country Opal Store
172	no services
167	ID 22, Dubois, E **both lanes, full facilities, litter barrels, petwalk** , Phillips 66/dsl Dubois Cafe city park, USPO, W Nez Pearce Tr, to Craters NM
150	Hamer, E Ron's Tire, USPO, W Camus NWR
143	ID 33, ID 28, to Mud Lake, Rexburg, W Sacajawea Hist Bywy, **weigh sta both lanes**
142mm	hist site, roadside parking
135	ID 48, Roberts, E Exxon/cafe/dsl/LP city park
128	Osgood Area, E Osgood/dsl camping (6mi)
119	US 20 E, to Rexburg, Idaho Falls, E **on Lindsay** Sinclair/dsl Denny's, Jaker's Steaks, Outback Steaks, Sandpiper Rest. Best Western, Guesthouse Inn, Hampton Inn, Hilton Garden, Hotel on the Falls, LeRitz Hotel, Safari Inn, Shilo Inn/rest., South Fork Inn, Super 8 LDS Temple, same as 118, Snake River RV Park/camping, W Chevron/dsl
118	US 20, Broadway St, Idaho Falls, E Phillips 66/dsl Applebee's, Arctic Circle, Buffalo Wild Wings, Carl's Jr, Cedric's Rest., Chili's, Domino's, Famous Dave's BBQ, Jimmy John's, MacKenzie River Grill, Olive Garden, Panda Express, Shari's Rest., Smitty's Pancakes, Starbucks, Wendy's Candlewood Suites, Fairfield Inn, Hampton Inn, Hilton Garden, Residence Inn H Candy Jct, Ford, Harley-Davidson, LDS Temple, same as 119, tires, URGENT CARE, Verizon, Walmart/Subway, W Exxon/dsl, Phillips 66/dsl, Sinclair/McDonald's 5 Buck Pizza, Arby's, Burger King, Fiesta Ole, Hong Kong Rest., Jack-in-the-Box, Los Adalaberto's Mexican, O'Brady's, Papa Murphy's, Pizza Hut, Subway Comfort Inn, Motel 6, Motel West Albertsons, AutoZone, O'Reilly Parts, Walgreens
116	US 26, Sunnyside Rd, Ammon, Jackson, E H Chevrolet, Honda, Sunnyside Acres RV Park, Toyota/Scion, VW, zoo, W Exxon/diesel DoubleDown Grill Sleep Inn
113	US 26, to Idaho Falls, Jackson, E Blu/dsl/LNG, Chevron/Burger King/dsl, Loves/McDonald's/dsl/scales/24hr, Sinclair/Dad's/dsl/24hr/ @ Subway H Jack's Tires, Peterbilt, Sunnyside RV Park, Targhee RV Park
108	Shelley, Firth Area, **1 mi** E RV Park/dump
101mm	**both lanes, full facilities, geological site, litter barrels, petwalk**
98	Rose-Firth Area
94.5mm	Snake River
93	US 26, ID 39, Blackfoot, E Chevron/dsl, Maverik/dsl, Stinker/dsl Arby's, Burger King, Domino's, Golden China, Homestead Rest., Hong Kong Garden, Italiano's, Little Caesars, McDonald's, Papa Murphy's, Pizza Hut, Roberto's Mexican, Subway, Taco Bell, Taco Time, Wendy's, Wingers Best Western, Super 8 AutoZone, Bealls, Chrysler/Dodge/Ford/Jeep, city park, GNC, Kesler's Foods, O'Reilly Parts, Radio Shack, Ridley's Mkt, Schwab Tire, Tire Factory, URGENT CARE
93	Continued Verizon, Walgreens, Walmart/Subway, W Sinc lair/A&W/dsl Riverside Boot/saddleshop (4mi)
90.5mm	Blackfoot River
89	US 91, S Blackfoot, W Sinclair/Sage Cafe/dsl
80	Ft Hall, W Phillips 66/rest./dsl/casino Shoshone Bannock Hotel/casino
72	I-86 W, to Twin Falls
71	Pocatello Creek Rd, Pocatello, E Chevron/Burger King/dsl, Phillips 66/dsl, Shell/dsl Applebee's, Jack-in-the Box, Perkins, Sandpiper Rest., Subway AmeriTel, Best Western, Clarion, Comfort Inn, Red Lion Inn, Super 8 KOA (1mi), **0-2 mi** W Exxon, Maverik/dsl Arby's, Bamboo Garden, Butter Burr's Rest., Café Rio, Carl's Jr, Changs Garden Chinese, Coldstone, El Caparal, Golden Corral, Jamba Juice, KFC, Mandarin House, McDonald's, Papa Murphy's, Pizza Hut, Ridley's Mkt, Schlotzsky's, Senor Iguana's Mexican, SF Pizza, Sizzler, Sonic, Subway, Taco Bell, Taco Time, Thai Kitchen, Wendy's, Winger's $Tree, AutoZone, BigLots, Buick/GMC, Chevrolet, Fred Meyer/dsl, Harley-Davidson, Honda, O'Reilly Parts, Radio Shack, Subaru, Toyota, Tuesday Morning, Walgreens, WinCo Foods
69	Clark St, Pocatello, E Chevron/cafe/dsl, Maverik/dsl, Sinclair/Arctic Circle/dsl Ruby Tuesday Hampton Inn, Holiday Inn Express, TownePlace Suites H W museum, to ID St U
67	US 30/91, 5th St, Pocatello, E Exxon/dsl, **1/2 mi** W Chevron/dsl, Shell/dsl Elmer's Dining, Goody's Deli, Jimmy John's, McDonald's, Pizza Hut, Subway, Taco Bell Rodeway Inn, Thunderbird Motel H city park, info, museum, Old Fort Hall, RV dump
63	Portneuf Area, W RV camp/dump, to Mink Creek RA
59mm	**weigh sta both lanes**
58	Inkom (from sb), **1/2 mi** W Sinclair/café/dsl Bisharat's Mkt, Pebble Creek Ski Area, repair, USPO
57	Inkom (from nb), same as 58
47	US 30, to Lava Hot Springs, McCammon, E FLYING J/dsl/scales/LP/RV dump/24hr, Chevron/A&W/Taco Time/dsl Subway Lava Hot Springs RA, McCammon RV Park, to KOA
44	Lp 15, Jenson Rd, McCammon, E access to food
40	Arimo, E USPO
36	US 91, Virginia
31	ID 40, to Downey, Preston, E Shell/Flags West/café/dsl/motel/24hr/ @ Downata Hot Springs RV camping (6mi)
25mm	**sb, full facilities, litter barrels, petwalk**
24.5mm	elev 5574, Malad Summit
22	to Devil Creek Reservoir, E RV camping
17	ID 36, to Weston, to Preston
13	ID 38, Malad City, W Chevron/Burger King, Phillips 66/café/dsl, Texaco/dsl Me&Lou's Rest., Pines Rest., Sperow's BBQ, Subway Village Inn Motel H 3R's Tire, Family$, pioneer museum, repair, RV dump
7mm	**Welcome Ctr nb, full facilities, info, litter barrels, petwalk** **vending**
3	to Samaria, Woodruff
0mm	Idaho/Utah state line

DUBOIS

IDAHO FALLS

POCATELLO

ID

INTERSTATE 84

Exit #	Services
275mm	Idaho/Utah state line
270mm	**[rest stop] both lanes, full [handicap] facilities,geological site, litter barrels, petwalk [phone] [picnic] vending**
263	Juniper Rd
257mm	Sweetzer Summit, elev 5530, Sweetzer Summit
254	Sweetzer Rd
245	Sublett Rd, to Malta, N [gas] Middle of Nowhere/dsl/café
237	Idahome Rd
234mm	Raft River
229mm	**[rest stop] weigh sta both lanes, full [handicap] facilities, litter barrels, petwalk [phone] [picnic]**
228	ID 81, Yale Rd, to Declo
222	I-86, US 30, E to Pocatello
216	ID 77, ID 25, to Declo, N [gas] Phillips 66/Food Court/dsl [other] [hospital] to Walcott SP, Village of Trees RV Park, S [gas] Shell/Pit Stop Grill/dsl
215mm	Snake River
211	ID 24, Heyburn, Burley, N [gas] Sinclair/A&W/café/dsl [food] Wayside Cafe [lodging] Tops Motel [other] [hospital] Country RV Village/park, S [gas] Love's/Carl's Jr./dsl/scales/24hr [other] Riverside RV Park, truck repair, truck wash
208	ID 27, Burley, N [gas] Phillips 66/dsl [food] Conner's Cafe [lodging] Super 8 [other] Kenworth, S [gas] Chevron/Subway/dsl/24hr, Maverik/dsl, Shell/dsl, Sinclair/dsl [food] Aguila's Mexican, Arby's, Burger King, Denny's, El Caporal, Guadalajara Mexican, Jack-in-the-Box, KFC, Little Caesar's, McDonald's, Morey's Steaks, Perkins, Taco Bell, Wendy's [lodging] Best Western, Budget Motel, Fairfield Inn [other] [hospital] $Tree, Beall's, Buick/GMC, Cal Ranch Store, CarQuest, Chrysler/Dodge/Jeep, Commercial Tire, JC Penney, NAPA, O'Reilly Parts, to Snake River RA, URGENT CARE, Verizon, Walmart
201	ID 25, Kasota Rd, to Paul, N [other] Kasota RV Park
194	ID 25, to Hazelton
188	Valley Rd, to Eden
182	ID 50, to Kimberly, Twin Falls, N [gas] Sinclair/dsl [other] Gary's RV Ctr/park/dump, S [gas] Shell/Blimpie/Taco Time/dsl/scales/24hr/ @ [food] Garden of Eden Cafe [lodging] Amber Inn [other] [hospital] auto/truck/ rv repair, to Shoshone Falls scenic attraction
173	US 93, Twin Falls, N [gas] FLYING J /dsl/LP/24hr/ @ [food] Subway [lodging] Comfort Inn, Days Inn [other] Blue Beacon, Freightliner, KOA (1mi), to Sun Valley, **5 mi** S [gas] Chevron/Subway/dsl, Maverik/dsl, Phillips 66/dsl, Shell/dsl, Sinclair, Walmart Fuel/ dsl [food] Applebee's, Arby's, Arctic Circle, Baskin-Robbins, Buffalo Wild Wings, Burger King, Cafe Rio, Carino's, Chick-fil-A, Chili's, Coldstone, Culver's, Denny's, Dickey's BBQ, DQ, Five Guys, Golden Corral, Idaho Joe's, IHOP, IHOP, Jack-in-the-Box, Jakers Grill, Jamba Juice, Jimmy John's, KFC, La Fiesta, Mandarin Chinese, McDonald's, Noodles&Co, Outback Steaks, Panda Express, Papa John's, Papa Murphy's, Perkins, Pizza Hut, River Rock Grill, Shari's, Sizzler, Sonic, Starbucks, Subway, Taco Bell, Tomato's Italian, Wendy's, Wok In Grill [lodging] Best Western, Fairfield Inn, Hampton Inn, Hilton Garden, Holiday Inn Express, La Quinta, Motel 6, Quality Inn, Red Lion, Shilo Inn, Super 8 [other] [hospital] $Tree, AT&T, AutoZone, Barnes&Noble, Best Buy, Buick/GMC, Chevrolet, Chrysler/Dodge/Jeep, Coll of S ID, Commercial Tire, Costco/gas, Dick's, Ford/Lincoln, Fred Meyer/dsl, Hancock Fabrics, Hastings Books, Home Depot, Honda, Hyundai, JC Penney, Jo-Ann Fabrics, LDS Temple, Les Schwab Tire, Lowe's, Macy's, Mazda/VW, Michael's, Nissan,

BURLEY

TWIN FALLS

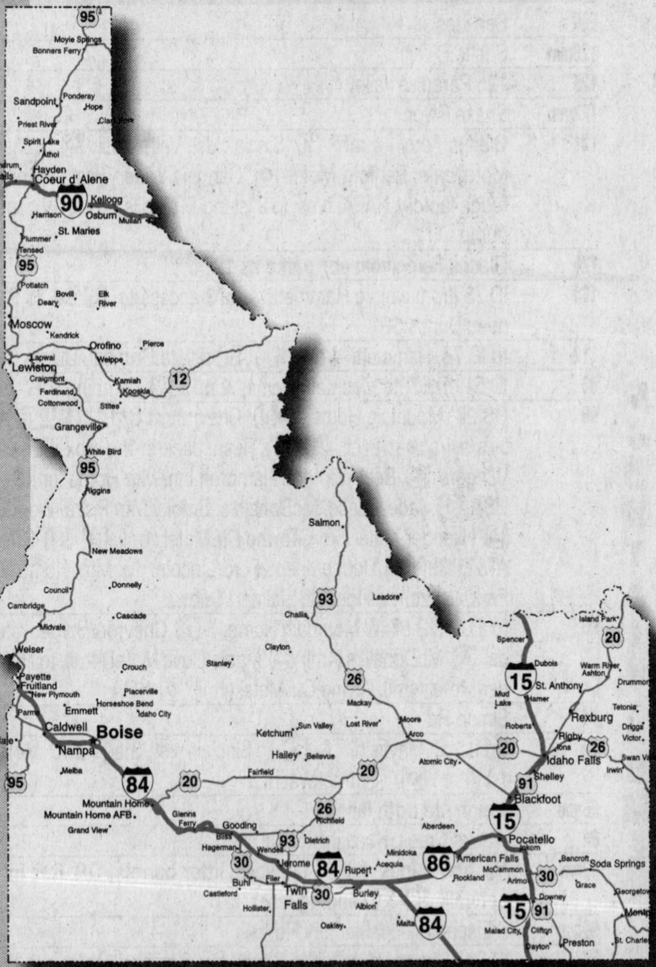

Exit #	Services
173	Continued Old Navy, O'Reilly Parts, Petco, Petsmart, Ross, Sears/auto, ShopKO, Sportsmans Whse, Target, Tire Factory, TJ Maxx, Verizon, visitors ctr, Walgreens, Walmart/Subway, WinCo Foods
171mm	**[rest stop] weigh sta eb, full [handicap] facilities, litter barrels, petwalk [phone] [picnic] vending**
168	ID 79, to Jerome, N [gas] Blu/LNG/dsl, Chevron/dsl , Shell/ Wendy's/dsl, Tesoro/dsl [food] Burger King, Domino's, DQ, Garibaldi's Mexican, Little Caesar's, McDonald's, Pizza Hut [lodging] Best Western, Crest Motel, Holiday Motel [other] [hospital] $Tree, AutoZone, Brockman RV Ctr, Family$, Les Schwab Tire, NAPA, O'Reilly Parts, Verizon, Walmart/Subway, S [food] Subway [other] Chevrolet
165	ID 25, Jerome, N [gas] Sinclair/dsl [lodging] Holiday Motel (1mi) [other] [hospital] RV camping/dump, vet
157	ID 46, Wendell, **1 mi** N [food] Subway [other] [hospital] CarQuest, Family$, Intermountain RV Park, S [gas] Phillips 66/dsl [food] Farmhouse Rest.
155	ID 46, to Wendell, N [other] Intermountain RV Camp/ctr
147	to Tuttle, S [other] High Adventure RV Park/cafe, to Malad Gorge SP
146mm	Malad River
141	US 26, to US 30, Gooding, N [other] [hospital] S [gas] Phillips 66/café/dsl, Sinclair/dsl [lodging] Amber Inn, Hagerman Inn (9mi) [other] Hagerman RV Village (8mi)
137	Lp 84, to US 30, to Pioneer Road, Bliss, **2 mi** S [gas] Sinclair/ Stinker/dsl/24hr [other] camping
133mm	**[rest stop] both lanes, full [handicap] facilities, info, litter barrels, petwalk [phone] [picnic]**
129	King Hill

ID

INTERSTATE 84 Cont'd

MOUNTAIN HOME · BOISE · EAGLE · NAMPA · CALDWELL · ID

Exit #	Services
128mm	Snake River
125	125 Paradise Valley
122mm	Snake River
121	Glenns Ferry, **1 mi S** [gas] Sinclair/dsl, Veltex/dsl [lodging] Hansen Motel/cafe, Redford Motel [other] Carmela Winery/rest., Family$, fudge factory, NAPA, tires, to 3 Island SP, Trails Break RV camp/dump
120	Glenns Ferry (from eb), **same as 121**
114	ID 78 (from wb), to Hammett, **1 mi S** access to [gas]/dsl, to Bruneau Dunes SP
112	to ID 78, Hammett, **1 mi S** [food] [gas]/dsl, to Bruneau Dunes SP
99	ID 51, ID 67, to Mountain Home, **2 mi S** [lodging] camping
95	US 20, Mountain Home, **N** [gas] Chevron/KFC/dsl, Pilot/Arby's/dsl/scales/24hr [food] AJ's Rest., Jack-in-the-Box, Subway, Wingers [lodging] Best Western, Hampton Inn, Mtn Home Inn, **S** [gas] USA [food] Jade Palace, McDonald's, Smoky Mtn Pizza, Wendy's [lodging] Hilander Motel (1mi), Towne Ctr Motel (1mi) [other] [H] $Tree, AT&T, Chrysler/Dodge/Jeep, Ford/Lincoln, to Mtn Home RV Park, Verizon, visitors ctr, Walmart/Subway
90	to ID 51, ID 67, W Mountain Home, **S** [gas] Chevron/Burger King/dsl [food] McDonald's (4mi) [lodging] Maple Cove Motel (4mi), to Hilander Motel (4mi), Towne Ctr Motel (4mi) [other] KOA
74	Simco Rd
71	Orchard, Mayfield, **S** [gas] Sinclair/rest./StageStop Motel/dsl/24hr [other] [C] truckwash
66mm	**weigh sta both lanes**
64	Blacks Creek, Kuna, historical site
62mm	[rest stop] **both lanes, full [handicapped] facilities, litter barrels, OR Trail info, petwalk [C] [vending] vending**
59b a	S Eisenman Rd, Memory Rd
57	ID 21, Gowen Rd, to Idaho City, **N** [gas] Sinclair [food] Jack-in-the-Box, McDonald's, Quiznos, Subway, Taco Del Mar [lodging] Best Western/NW Lodge [other] Albertsons/Sav-On, Peterbilt, to Micron, **S** [gas] Chevron/dsl [food] Burger King, FoodCourt [other] Boise Stores/famous brands, ID Ice World
54	US 20/26, Broadway Ave, Boise, **N** [gas] FLYING J /dsl/LP/24hr, Chevron/dsl, Fred Meyer/dsl, Shell/dsl [food] A&W/KFC, Arby's, Fiesta Mexican, IHOP, Jack-in-the-Box, Mongolian Noodles, Pizza Pie Cafe, Port Of Subs, Sonic [lodging] Courtyard (3mi) [other] Big O Tire, Firestone/auto, Fred Meyer, Goodyear/auto, Home Depot, Jo-Ann Fabrics, O'Reilly Parts, PetCo, Radio Shack, Ross, ShopKO, to Boise St U, vet, Walgreens, **S** [gas] TA/Country Pride/Taco Bell/Subway/dsl/24hr/ @ [lodging] Shilo Inn [other] Bretz RV Ctr, Kenworth, Mtn View RV Park
53	Vista Ave, Boise, **N** [gas] Shell/dsl, Texaco/dsl [food] Applebee's, Pizza Hut [lodging] Comfort Suites, Extended Stay America, Fairfield Inn, Hampton Inn, Holiday Inn/rest., La Quinta, Super 8, Wyndham Garden [other] museums, st capitol, st police, zoo, **S** [gas] Chevron/dsl [food] Denny's, Kopper Kitchen [lodging] Best Western, InnAmerica, Motel 6, Quality Inn, Rodeway Inn [other] [airport]
52	Orchard St, Boise, **N** [gas] Maverik/dsl, Shell/dsl [food] Subway [other] BMW Motorcycles, Fiat, GMC
50b a	Cole Rd, Overland Rd, **N** [gas] Chevron/dsl, Shell, Sinclair [food] Cancun Mexican, Cobby's Sandwiches, Eddie's Rest., McDonald's, Outback Steaks, Pizza Hut, Subway, Taco Bell, Taco Time [other] Grocery Outlet, LDS Temple, transmissions, **S** [gas] Phillips 66/dsl, Shell/dsl [food] A&W/KFC, Black Bear Diner, Burger King, Carino's, Carl's Jr, Chapala Mexican, Chuck-a-Rama, Cracker Barrel, Del Taco, Fuddruckers, Goodwood BBQ, Jimmy John's, Lucky Palace Chinese, McGrath's FishHouse, Nato's Mexican,
50b a	Continued On the Border, Panda Express, Papa John's, Sonic, Starbucks, Tucano's Brazilian Grill, Twin Peaks [lodging] Hampton Inn, Hilton Garden, Homewood Suites, Howard Johnson's, Oxford Suites [other] Commercial Tire, Costco/gas, Dillon RV Ctr, Discount Tire, Einstein Oilery, Les Schwab Tire, Lowe's, Meineke, USPO, Verizon, vet, Walmart/McDonald's
49	I-184 (exits left from eb), to W Boise, **N** [other] [H]
46	ID 55, Eagle, **N** [gas] Chevron/McDonald's/dsl [food] Buffalo Wild Wings, Del Taco, Ling&Louie's, Los Beto's, Mi Casa, Smash Burger, Starbucks, Subway [lodging] Hampton Inn, Holiday Inn Express, La Quinta [other] [H] **S** [gas] Chevron/dsl [food] Beef'O'Brady's, Chicago Connection, Dickey's BBQ, Dutch Bros Coffee, Happy Teriyaki, Jack-in-the-Box, Jimmy John's, Joy Garden, Panda Garden, Pita Pit, Qdoba, Rudy's Grill, Sakana Japanese, Subway, Taco Bell, TCBY, The Griddle [lodging] Candlewood Suites, Courtyard, TownePlace Suites [other] AAA, Harley-Davidson, Indian Motorcycles, URGENT CARE, vet
44	ID 69, Meridian, **N** [gas] Chevron/dsl, Sinclair [food] 50's Cafe, A&W/KFC, Blimpie, China Wok, DQ, McDonald's, Panda Express, Pizza Hut, Shari's, Starbucks, Subway, Taco Bell, Taco Time, Wendy's [lodging] Best Western, Motel 6 [other] AT&T, Home Depot, Johnny's Autocare, Les Schwab Tire, Sierra Trading Post, Verizon, WinCo Foods, **S** [gas] Shell/dsl [food] Carl's Jr, JB's, Papa John's [lodging] Mr Sandman Inn [other] Camping World RV Ctr, Ford, Lowe's, O'Reilly Parts, Walgreens, Walmart, waterpark
42	Ten Mile Rd
38	Garrity Blvd, Nampa, **N** [gas] Chevron/dsl, Walmart Gas/dsl [food] Dutch Bros Coffee, Jack-in-the-Box, Los Betos, Port of Subs, Sonic [lodging] Hampton Inn [other] Buick/GMC, Cadillac/Chevrolet, Chrysler/Dodge/Jeep, Ford, Hyundai, Infiniti, Kia, Nissan, Toyota/Scion, Walmart/Subway, **S** [gas] Phillips 66/dsl, Shell/dsl [food] Fiesta Guadalajara, Jimmy John's, McDonald's, Panda Express, Pizza Hut, Popeye's, Starbucks, Subway [lodging] Holiday Inn Express [other] [H] Discount Tire, Freddy's, Garrity RV Park, JC Penney, Macy's, Verizon, War Hawk Museum
36	Franklin Blvd, Nampa, **N** [gas] Blu/LNG/dsl, Maverik/dsl [food] Jack-in-the-Box [lodging] Shilo Inn/rest., **S** [gas] Chevron/dsl, Shell/Subway/dsl/RV dump/scales/4hr [lodging] Sleep Inn [other] [H] Bish's RV Ctr, Freightliner, Honda, Mason Cr RV Park
35	ID 55, Nampa, **S** [gas] Shell/dsl [food] Denny's [lodging] Nampa Inn, Rodeway Inn, Super 8
33b a	ID 55 S, Midland Blvd, Marcine, **N** [food] Cracker Barrel, Dickey's BBQ, McDonald's, Olive Garden, Panera Bread, Port of Subs, Qdoba Mexican, Sonic, Subway, TGIFriday's, Winger's [lodging] Fairfield Inn [other] AT&T, Best Buy, Costco/gas, Dick's, Discount Tire, Eistein's Oilery, Gordmans, Hobby Lobby, [H] Kohl's, Michael's, Old Navy, PetCo, Petsmart, Sportsmans Whse, Target, TJ Maxx, Verizon, World Mkt, **S** [gas] Shell/dsl [food] Applebee's, Arby's, Baskin-Robbins, Blimpie, Buffalo Wild Wings, Carl's Jr, Chipotle, Coldstone, Costa Vida, DQ, Golden Corral, IHOP, Jack-in-the-Box, Jade Garden, Jalapeno's Grill, Jimmy John's, Mongolian BBQ, Outback Steaks, Papa Murphy's, Pizza Hut, Red Robin, Shari's Rest, Skipper's, Smokey Mtn Grill, Starbucks, Subway, Taco Bell, TX Roadhouse, Wendy's [other] $Tree, Big O Tire, Hastings Books, Home Depot, Jo-Ann Fabrics, K-Mart, Lowe's, NAPA, Ross, Savers, Shopko, Staples, Tire Factory, U-Haul, Verizon, Verizon (2), vet, Walgreens, WinCo Foods
29	US 20/26, Franklin Rd, Caldwell, **N** [gas] FLYING J /Denny's/dsl/LP/scales/24hr [other] Ambassador RV camping, RV dump, **S** [gas] Sage/Sinclair/cafe/dsl/24hr [food] Burger King, Magic Recipe [lodging] Best Western, La Quinta

INTERSTATE 84 Cont'd

Exit #	Services
28	10th Ave, Caldwell, N Maverik/dsl city park, U-Haul, S Chevron/dsl, Shell/dsl Carl's Jr, Fiesta Mexican, Jack-in-the-Box, Mr V's Rest., Pizza Hut, Subway, Wendy's Sundowner Motel AutoZone, Paul's Food/Drug, Tire Factory, Walgreens
27	ID 19, to Wilder, **1 mi** S Conoco/dsl **visitor info**
26.5mm	Boise River
26	US 20/26, to Notus, N Caldwell Campground, S Sinclair/dsl RV Resort
25	ID 44, Middleton, N Sinclair/dsl 44 Burgers/shakes, S **Insp sta eb**
17	Sand Hollow, N Sinclair/Sand Hollow Café/dsl Country Corners RV Park
13	Black Canyon Jct, S Sinclair/rest./motel/dsl/scales/24hr phone
9	US 30, to New Plymouth
3	US 95, Fruitland, N Chevron/A&W/dsl Neat Retreat RV Park (5mi), to Hell's Cyn RA (26mi)
1mm	**Welcome Ctr eb full facilities, info, litter barrels, petwalk**
0mm	Idaho/Oregon state line, Snake River

INTERSTATE 86

POCATELLO

Exit #	Services
63b a	I-15, N to Butte, S to SLC. **I-86 begins/ends on I-15, exit 72.**
61	US 91, Yellowstone Ave, Pocatello, N Exxon, Maverik/dsl, Shell/dsl 5 Mile Café, Arby's, Arctic Circle, Burger King, Chapala Mexican, Lei's BBQ, Papa Murphy's, Pizza Hut, Subway, Wendy's Motel 6, Ramada Inn $Tree, Crossroads RV Ctr, Family$, O'Reilly Parts, Smith's Foods/dsl, Tire Discounters, vet, S Exxon/dsl, Phillips 66/dsl 5 Guys Burgers, Buffalo Wild Wings, Chili's, Costa Vida, Denny's, Great Wall, IHOP, Jimmy John's, MacKenzie River Grill, McDonald's, Panda Express, Pizza Pie Café, Red Lobster, Starbucks, Taco John's, TX Roadhouse AT&T, Cal Ranch Store, Costco/gas, Dick's, Ford/Lincoln, Herbergers, Home Depot, JC Penney, Jo-Ann Fabrics, K-Mart/Little Caesars, Lowe's, PetCo, Radio Shack, Ross, Schwab Tire, ShopKo, Staples, TJ Maxx, Verizon, Walgreens, Walmart
58.5mm	Portneuf River
58	US 30, W Pocatello, N Batise Springs RV Park/dump (1mi-seasonal)
56	N Pocatello Reg Airport, S Sinclair/dsl/24hr
52	Arbon Valley, S Phillips 66/Bannock Peak/dsl casino
51mm	Bannock Creek
49	Rainbow Rd
44	Seagull Bay
40	ID 39, American Falls, N Phillips 66/dsl (1mi), Sinclair/dsl (1mi), Texaco Pizza Hut, Subway, Tres Hermanos Mexican American Motel Alco, auto repair, Family$ (1mi), Jiffy Lube, NAPA, Schwab Tire, to Am Falls RA, Willow Bay RV Park/dump, S Hillview Motel
36	ID 37, to Rockland, American Falls, **2 mi** N Shell/dsl Falls Motel **2 mi** S Indian Springs RV Resort
33	Neeley Area
31mm	**wb, full facilities, hist site, litter barrels, petwalk vending**

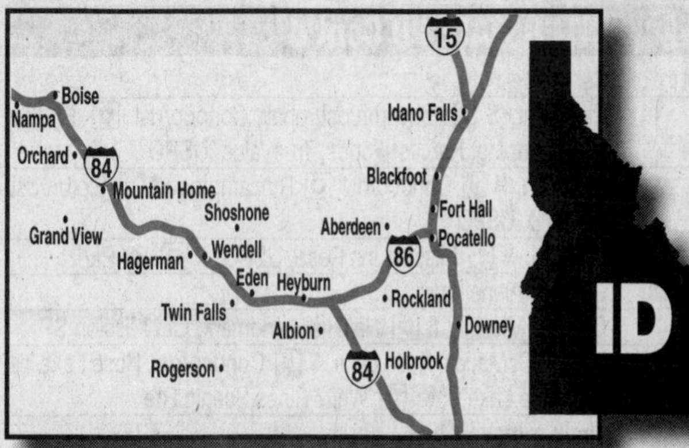

28	N Register Rock Hist Site, RV camping/dump, to Massacre Rock SP
21	Coldwater Area
19mm	**eb, full facilities, hist site, litter barrels, petwalk vending**
15	Raft River Area
1	I-84 E, to Ogden **I-86 begins/ends on I-84, exit 222.**

INTERSTATE 90

WALLACE

KELLOGG

Exit #	Services
74mm	Idaho/Montana state line, Lookout Pass elev 4680, Pacific/Central time zone
73mm	scenic area/hist site wb
72mm	scenic area/hist site eb
71mm	**runaway truck ramp wb**
70mm	**runaway truck ramp wb**
69	Lp 90, Mullan, N Sinclair/dsl Lookout Motel (1mi) Mullan Trail grocery/RV Park, museum, USPO
68	Lp 90 (from eb), Mullan, same as 69
67	Morning District
66	Gold Creek (from eb)
65	Compressor District
64	Golconda District
62	ID 4, Wallace, S Conoco Pizza Factory, Smokehouse Rest. Brooks Hotel, Stardust Motel Depot RV Park, Harvest Foods, museum, TrueValue
61	Lp 90, Wallace, S Conoco/dsl Pizza Factory, Red Light Garage, Smokehouse Rest., Wallace Sta Rest./gifts Brooks Hotel/rest., Molly B-Damm Inn, Wallace Inn auto repair, info ctr, same as 62
60	Lp 90, Silverton, S Molly B-Damm Inn RV camping
57	Lp 90, Osburn, S 76/dsl Blue Anchor RV Park, Stein's Foods, USPO
54	Big Creek, N hist site
51	Lp 90, Division St, Kellogg, N Conoco/dsl Trail Motel Buick/Cadillac/Chevrolet/GMC, Chrysler/Dodge/Jeep, Schwab Tire, Stein's Foods, Sunnyside Drug, vet, S In Cahoots Cafe, Moose Creek Grill USPO
50	Hill St (from eb), Kellogg, N Humdinger Drive-In Trail Motel Ace Hardware, NAPA, Stein's Foods, Sunnyside Drug, tires, S Conoco/dsl Greek Deli museum, Silver Mtn Ski/summer resort/rec area, Yoke's Foods
49	Bunker Ave, N Conoco/dsl McDonald's, Sam's Drive-In, Subway Silverhorn Motel/rest. S Noah's Canteen, Silver Mtn Rest. GuestHouse Inn, Morning Star Lodge city park, museum, RV dump, Silver Mtn RA
48	Smelterville, S O'Reilly Parts, Tire Factory, USPO, Walmart

ID

INTERSTATE 90 Cont'd

Exit #	Services
45	Pinehurst, S Chevron/dsl/repair, Conoco/dsl By-the-way Camping, Harvest Foods, TrueValue, USPO
43	Kingston, N Conoco/dsl RV camping, S Exxon/dsl/rv dump, USPO
40	Cataldo, N Mission Inn Rest., USPO, S RV Park
39.5mm	Coeur d'Alene River
39	Cataldo Mission, S Nat Hist Landmark, Old Mission SP
34	ID 3, to St Maries, Rose Lake, S Conoco/dsl, Rose Lake/dsl Rose Lake Cafe White Pines Scenic Rte
33	**chain removal eb**
32mm	**chainup area/weigh sta wb**
31.5mm	4th of July Creek, eastern boundary, Idaho Panhandle NF
28	4th of July Pass RA, elev 3069, Mullan Tree HS, ski area, snowmobile area, turnout both lanes
24mm	**chainup eb, removal wb**
22	ID 97, to St Maries, L Coeur d' Alene Scenic ByWay, Wolf Lodge District, Harrison, **1 mi** N Wolf Lodge Camping, S Lake Coeur d'Alene RV Park, Squaw Bay Resort (7mi)
20.5mm	Lake Coeur d' Alene
17	Mullan Trail Rd
15	Lp 90, Sherman Ave, Coeur d' Alene, N forest info, Lake Coeur D' Alene RA/HS, S Exxon/dsl, Tesoro/dsl/LP, Texaco Jeffrey's Rest., Jimmy's Cafe, Michael D's Eatery, O'Shay's Rest., Roger's Burgers, Subway, Zip's Rest. Bates Motel, BudgetSaver Motel, Cedar Motel/RV park, El Rancho Motel, Flaming Motel, Holiday Motel, Japan House Suites, La Quinta, State Motel auto repair, Peterson's Foods, tourist info
14	15th St, Coeur d' Alene, S TAJ Mart Jordon's Grocery
13	4th St, Coeur d' Alene, N A&D/dsl Atilano's Mexican, Baskin Robbins, Carl's Jr, Davis Donuts, Denny's, DQ, Fiesta Mexican, IHOP, Jimmy John's, Little Caesars, Original Mongolian BBQ, Panda Express, Satay Bistro, Starbucks, Subway, Taco Time, Uva Trattoria, Wendy's Comfort Inn AutoZone, BigLots, CarQuest, Costco/gas, Hastings Books, NAPA, Radio Shack, same as 12, Schwab Tire, S Exxon/dsl Thai Bamboo
12	US 95, to Sandpoint, Moscow, N Exxon/dsl, Holiday/dsl, Mobil/dsl Applebee's, Arby's, Buffalo Wild Wings, Burger King, Cafe Rio, Chili's, Del Taco, Dragon House Chinese, Elmer's, Golden Corral, JB's Rest., Jimmy John's, MacKenzie River Pizza, McDonald's, Olive Garden, Panda Express, Papa Murphy's, Pizza Hut, Qdoba, Red Lobster, Skipper's, Taco Bell, Tomato St., TX Roadhouse Best Western, Guesthouse Inn, Motel 6, Quality Inn, Shilo Suites, Super 8 $Tree, Albertson's, AT&T, Best Buy, Buick/GMC, Cadillac, Cour d' Alene RV, Discount Tire, Ford/Lincoln, Fred Meyer/dsl, Grocery Outlet, Home Depot, JC Penney, Jo-Ann Fabrics, Kia, K-Mart, Kohl's, Michael's, Natural Grocers, O'Reilly Parts, PetCo, Ross, RVs NW, Safeway/dsl, Sears/auto, Subaru, Super 1 Foods, Target, TireRama, TJ Maxx, Toyota/Scion, Tuesday Morning, U-Haul, URGENT CARE, Verizon, Walgreens, Walmart/Subway, S Conoco/dsl, Tesoro Asian Twist, Jack-in-the-Box, Jamba Juice, Papa Murphy's, Qdoba Mexican, Quiznos, Schlotzsky's, Shari's, Starbucks La Quinta H Albertson's, AT&T, GNC, Rite Aid, same as 13, ShopKO/drugs, Staples
11	Northwest Blvd, N Conoco/dsl Jack-in-the-Box, Subway Lowe's, WinCo Foods, S Exxon/dsl, Texaco Azteca Mexican, Bullman's Woodfired Pizza, Coldstone, McDonald's, Outback Steaks, Porky G's BBQ, Red Robin,
11	Continued SF Sourdough, Starbucks, Ugly Fish Rest. Days Inn, Hampton Inn, Holiday Inn Express, Springhill Suites H Honda Riverwalk RV Park, Verizon
8.5mm	**Welcome Ctr/weigh sta eb, full facilities, info, litter barrels, petwalk**
7	ID 41, to Rathdrum, Spirit Lake, N 76/dsl Burger King Del Taco, La Cocina Mexican, NY Pizza, Papa Murphy's, Pita Pit, Pizza Factory, Quiznos, Sonic, Starbucks, Subway, Wendy's $Tree, AT&T, auto repair, Chevrolet, Chrysler/Dodge/Jeep, Couer d'Alene RV Park, Hyundai, Mazda, Nissan, Radio Shack, VW, Walmart/Subway, S Chevron/dsl, Coleman/dsl A&W/KFC, Capone's Grill, DQ Comfort Inn Robins RV Ctr, truck repair, Verizon, vet
6	Seltice Way, N 7-11 La Cabana Mexican, Paul Bunyan Burgers, Pizza Hut NAPA, Super 1 Foods, Walgreens, S Conoco/dsl/LP Denny's, Fuki Japanese, Lide St Cafe, Little Caesars, McDonald's, Moons Mongolian, Old European Cafe, Rancho Viejo Mexican, Taco Bell Ace Hardware, O'Reilly Parts, TireRama, Trading Co Foods, USPO, vet
5	Lp 90, Spokane St, Treaty Rock HS, N 76/dsl, Exxon/dsl Corner Cafe, Domino's, Hunter's Rest., Rob's Seafood/burgers, Subway, WhiteHouse Grill AutoZone, Blue Dog RV Ctr, Meineke, Perfection Tire/repair, Schwab Tire, S Handy Mart/Pacific Pride/dsl Red Lion Inn visitors ctr
2	Pleasant View Rd, N FLYING J/Conoco/Subway/dsl/LP/scales/24hr, Exxon/dsl, Loves/Carl's Jr/dsl/scales/24hr McDonald's, Toro Viejo Mexican Silver Stone Inn RV/truckwash, Suntree RV Park, S Exxon/dsl Zip's Drive-in Riverbend Inn, Sleep Inn dogtrack
1	Beck Rd, N Cabela's, Walmart/Subway, S greyhound track
0mm	Idaho/Washington state line

INTERSTATE 184 (BOISE)

Exit #	Services
6mm	**I-184 begins/ends on 13th St**, downtown, Shell Bonefish Grill, Chandler's Steaks, Five Guys, PF Chang's Hampton Inn, Safari Inn, The Grove Office Depot, USPO
5	River St (from eb), W Chevron McDonald's Red Lion
4.5mm	Boise River
3	Fairview Ave, to US 20/26 E, W Joe's Crabshack, Tepanyaki Japanese Boise Inn, Cottonwood Suites, Riverside Hotel Commercial Tire
2	Curtis Rd, to Garden City, E Shell H
1b a	Cole Rd, Franklin Rd, E Chevron/Subway/dsl Acura, Chrysler/Dodge/Jeep, Honda, Jaguar, Land Rover, Mercedes, Volvo, W Chevron/dsl, Sinclair/dsl Applebee's, Cafe Ole, Cafe Rio, Carl's Jr, Cheesecake Factory, Chick-fil-A, Chili's, Chipotle, Dave&Buster's, Fujiyama Japanese, Golden Corral, IHOP, Jalapeno's, McDonald's, Noodles&Co, Old Chicago Pizza, Olive Garden, Port of Subs, Quiznos, Red Lobster, Red Robin, Rumbi Island Grill, Shari's, Sizzler, Smash Burger, Starbucks, Wendy's Candlewood Suites, La Quinta, Residence Inn AT&T, AT&T, Audi/VW, Best Buy, Cabela's, Dick's, Dillard's, JC Penney, Kohl's, Macy's, mall, Michael's, Old Navy, PetCo, Petsmart, Petsmart, REI, Ross, Sears/auto, Target, TJ Maxx, Tuesday Morning, Verizon
0mm	**I-184 begins/ends on I-84, exit 49.**

ILLINOIS

INTERSTATE 24

Exit #	Services
38mm	Illinois/Kentucky state line, Ohio River
37	US 45, Metropolis, N **both lanes, full facilities, litter barrels, petwalk vending**, S BP/Quiznos/dsl China House, McDonald's, Pizza Hut, Sonic Best Value Inn, Holiday Inn Express, Metropolis Inn, Motel 6, Super 8 H, $General, Buick/Chrysler/Dodge/GMC/Jeep, camping, Chevrolet, Ft Massac SP, O'Reilly Parts, Plaza Tire, to Riverboat Casino
27	to New Columbia, Big Bay
16	IL 146, Vienna, N Gambit Golf, S BP/dsl, FastStop, Roc/dsl DQ, Jumbo Grill, McDonald's, Subway, Vienna Diner Limited Inn vet
14	US 45, Vienna, S camping
7	to Goreville, Tunnel Hill, N winery (7mi), S camping, to Ferne Clyffe SP
1	I-57, N to Chicago, S to Memphis. **I-24 begins/ends on I-57, exit 44.**

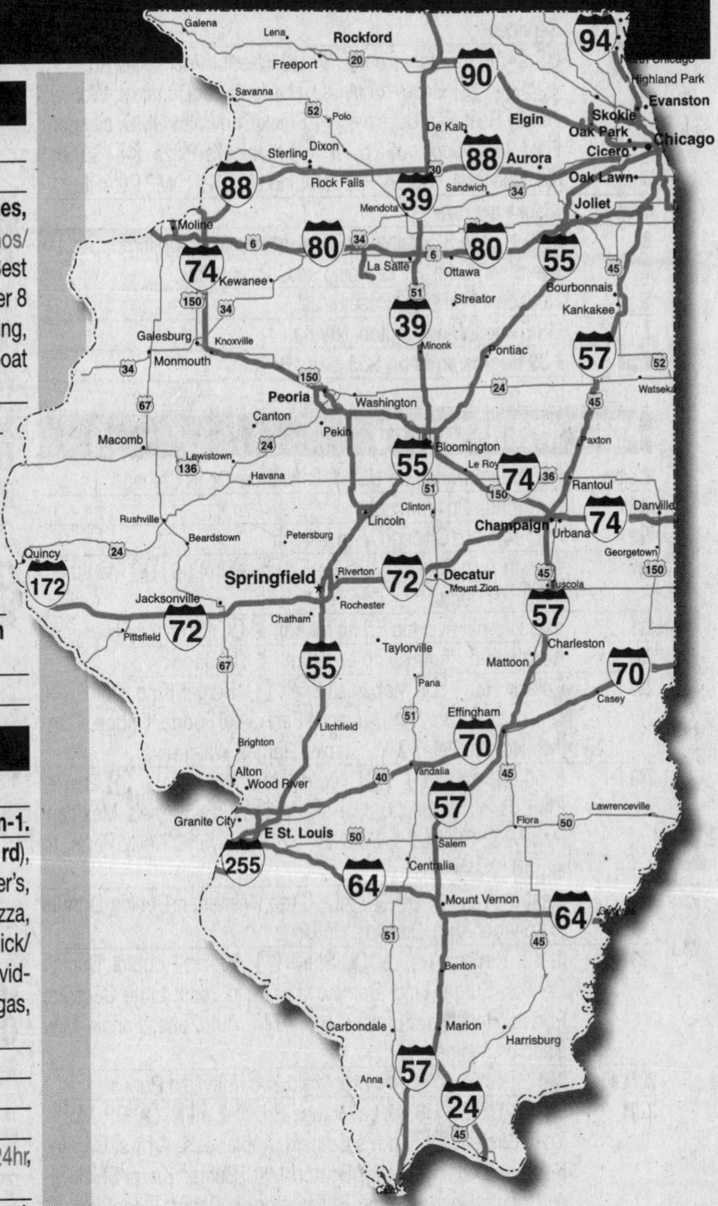

IL

INTERSTATE 39

Exit #	Services
	I-39 & I-90 run together into Wisconsin. See Illinois I-90, exits 15mm-1.
122b a	US 20 E, Harrison Ave, to Belvidere (**last nb exit before toll rd**), W Mobil, Road Ranger/Subway/dsl Arby's, Bergner's, Burger King, DQ, Granite City Rest., Lung Fung, Rosati's Pizza, Sonic, Taco Bell, TGIFriday's Barnes&Noble, BMW, Buick/Chevrolet/GMC, Collier RV Ctr, Goodyear/auto, Harley-Davidson, JC Penney, Macy's, mall, Menards, Schnuck's Foods/gas, Sears/auto, Tires+, vet, VW, Walgreens
119	US 20 W, Alpine Rd, to Rockford
116.5mm	Kishwaukee River
115	Baxter Rd, E Shell/Subway/dsl/scales/24hr/ @
111	IL 72, to Monroe Center, E BP/Sunrise Family Rest./dsl/24hr, Marathon (1mi)
104	IL 64, to Oregon, Sycamore, W Grubsteakers Rest/truck parking (2mi)
99	IL 38, to De Kalb, Rochelle, **0-2 mi** W Murphy USA/dsl, Petro/Iron Skillet/dsl/scales/RV Dump/ @, Phillips 66/dsl, Road Ranger/Pilot/Subway/dsl/scales/24hr, Shell/dsl Arby's, Butterfly Rest, Culver's, DQ, Jimmy John's, Little Ceasar's, McDonald's, New China, Pizza Hut, Subway, Taco Bell, Wendy's Comfort Inn, Holiday Inn Express, Red Roof Inn, Super 8 H $General, Blue Beacon, GNC, O'Reilly Parts, Sullivan's Foods, Verizon, Walgreens, Walmart
97b a	**I-88 tollway**, to Moline, Rock Island, Chicago
93	Steward
87	US 30, to Sterling, Rock Falls, E to Shabbona Lake SP, W Yogi Bear Camping (16mi)
84.5mm	**both lanes, full facilities, litter barrels, petwalk playground, vending**
82	Paw Paw, **3 mi** E Casey's (3mi), W many wind turbines
72	US 34, to Mendota, Earlville, W BP/Cindy's/dsl/scales/24hr, Road Ranger/Pilot/dsl/scales/24hr KFC/Taco Bell, McDonald's Comfort Inn, Super 8/truck parking H
67.5mm	Little Vermilion River
66	US 52, Troy Grove, E KOA (1mi)
62.5mm	Tomahawk Creek
59b a	I-80, E to Chicago, W to Des Moines
57	US 6, to Peru, La Salle, **1-2 mi** W Casey's Daniel's Motel city park
56mm	Abraham Lincoln Mem Bridge, Illinois River
54	Oglesby, E BP/dsl, Casey's, Phillips 66/dsl, Shell Burger King, Delaney's Rest., KFC/Taco Bell, McDonald's, Root Beer Stand, Subway Best Western, Days Inn Starved Rock SP, W Loves/Hardee's/dsl/scales/24hr
52	IL 251, to La Salle, Peru
51	IL 71, to Hennepin, Oglesby
48	Tonica, E Casey's city park
41	IL 18, to Streator, Henry
35	IL 17, to Wenona, Lacon, E BP/dsl, Casey's (2mi), Fast&Fresh/Burger King/dsl/RV dump Subway, Sunrise Rest. Super 8/truck parking NAPA Autocare
27	to Minonk, E Casey's (2mi), Pilot/Road Ranger/Subway/Woody's Rest./dsl/24hr Motel 6 NAPA
22	IL 116, to Peoria, Benson

ROCKFORD

OGLESBY

INTERSTATE 39

Exit #	Services
14	US 24, to El Paso, Peoria, E Freedom/dsl, Shell/Subway/dsl/24hr Casey's/dsl, DQ, Hardee's, McDonald's, Woody's Family Rest. Days Inn Buick/Chevrolet/GMC, city park, Ford, IGA Foods, USPO, W Monical's Pizza Super 8 $General, Hickory Hill Camping (4mi), PROMPT CARE
9mm	Mackinaw River
8	IL 251, Lake Bloomington Rd, E Lake Bloomington, W Evergreen Lake, RV camping, to Comlara Park
5	Hudson, **1 mi** E Casey's/dsl
2	US 51 bus, Bloomington, Normal
0mm	**I-39 begins/ends on I-55, exit 164**

INTERSTATE 55

CHICAGO AREA

295mm	**I-55 begins/ends on US 41**, Lakeshore Dr, in Chicago.
293a	to Cermak Rd (from nb)
292	I-90/94, W to Chicago, E to Indiana
290	Damen Ave, Ashland Ave (no EZ nb return), E Marathon, Shell Target
289	to California Ave (no EZ nb return), E Citgo, Speedway/dsl
288	Kedzie Ave, (from sb no ez return), E Citgo
287	Pulaski Rd, E Mobil/dsl, Shell Burger King, Domino's, Quiznos, Subway Advance Parts, Aldi Foods, Dodge, Family$, Honda, Pete's Mkt, Staples, Target, Walgreens
286	IL 50, Cicero Ave, E Citgo/dsl, Marathon, Mobil Burger King, Dunkin Donuts, JJ Fish, McDonald's, Pepe's Mexican, Popeye's, Starbucks, Subway Family$, O'Reilly Parts, to airport, Walgreens
285	Central Ave, E BP/dsl , Citgo, Marathon/Dunkin Donuts Burger King, Donald's HotDogs
283	IL 43, Harlem Ave, E Shell Baskin-Robbins/Dunkin Donuts, Burger King, Domino's, El Pollo Loco, Little Caesars, Portillo HotDogs, Subway AT&T, AutoZone, Fannie May Candies, Walgreens
282b a	IL 171, 1st Ave, W Brookfield Zoo, Mayfield Park
279b	US 12, US 20, US 45, La Grange Rd, **0-2 mi** W BP, Mobil, Shell/Circle K Andy's Custard, Applebee's, Arby's, Baskin-Robbins/Dunkin Donuts, Boston Mkt, Burger King, Chick-fil-A, Cocula Rest., Dragon Buffet, Dunkin Donuts, Hooters, JC Georges Rest., Jimmy John's, Ledo's Pizza, LoneStar Steaks, McDonald's, Nonno's Pizza, Panda Express, Pizza Hut, Popeye's, Starbucks, Subway, Taco Bell, Taco Tico, Time Out Grill, TX Roadhouse, Via Bella, Wendy's, White Castle Best Western, Holiday Inn $Tree, Aldi Foods, Best Buy, Buick/Cadillac/GMC, Chevrolet, Chrysler/Dodge/Jeep, Discount Tire, Firestone/auto, Ford, GNC, Harley Davidson, Home Depot, Honda, Jo-Ann Fabrics, Kohl's, Mazda, Menards, NAPA, Nissan, NTB, O'Reilly Parts, PepBoys, PetCo, Petsmart, Sam's Club/gas, Subaru, Target, Toyota/Scion, Verizon, VW, Walmart
279a	La Grange Rd, **to I-294 toll**, S to Indiana
277b	**I-294 toll (from nb)**, S to Indiana
277a	**I-294 toll**, N to Wisconsin
276c	Joliet Rd (from nb)
276b a	County Line Rd, E Capri Rest., China King, Ciazzi's Cafe, Cooper's Hawk, Max&Erma's, Moon Dance Diner, Salerno's Pizza, Starbucks, Subway, Topaz Rest. Extended Stay America, Marriott, Quality Inn Brookhaven Mkt, Tuesday Morning, W SpringHill Suites
274	IL 83, Kingery Rd, E Shell, W 7-11, Mobil/dsl, Phillips 66/dsl, Shell Bakers Square, Barnelli's Pasta, Buffalo

BOLINGBROOK

274	Continued Wild Wings, Burger King, Chipotle Mexican, Denny's, Domino's, Dunkin Donuts, Jamba Juice, Jimmy John's, Papa John's, Patio BBQ, Pei Wei, Portillo's HotDogs, Potbelly's Rest., Starbucks, Subway, Wendy's Holiday Inn, La Quinta, Red Roof Inn, Super 8 AT&T, Firestone, Ford/KIA, K-Mart, Michael's, Radio Shack, Staples, Target, Verizon
273b a	Cass Ave, W Shell La Notte Due Rest., Rosati's Pizza, Uncle Mao's Chinese vet
271b a	Lemont Rd, E Extended Stay America, W Shell
269	**I-355 toll**, to W Suburbs
268	(from sb only), Joliet, same as 267
267	IL 53, Bolingbrook, E BP, Phillips 66/55 Trkstp/rest./dsl/scales/24hr/ @ McDonald's La Quinta, Ramada Ltd, Super 8 Chevrolet, W Shell/Circle K, Speedway/dsl A&W/LJ Silver, Burger King, Cheddar's, Culver's, Denny's, Dunkin Donuts, El Burrito Loco, Family Square Rest., Golden Chopsticks, Golden Corral, IHOP, Margarita's Rest., McDonald's, Popeye's, Rancho Santa Fe Mexican, Starbucks, Subway, Wendy's, White Castle AmericInn, Hampton Inn, Holiday Inn, SpringHill Suites $Tree, AAA, Aldi Foods, CarQuest, Family$, Fiesta Mkt, Food-4-Less/gas, Just Tires, Menards, NAPA, O'Reilly Parts, U-Haul, Walgreens, Walmart
266mm	**weigh sta both lanes**
263	Weber Rd, E 7-11, BP/dsl, Speedway/Dunkin Donuts/dsl/e85 Applebee's, Burger King, Burrito's, Culver's, Giovanny's Pizza, KFC, Little China, McDonald's, Michal's Pizza, Popeye's, Starbucks, Todake Steaks, White Castle Best Western Ace Hardware, Discount Tire, Dominick's Food/gas, GNC, Walgreens, W 7-11, Shell/Circle K Arby's, Cracker Barrel, Wendy's Comfort Inn, Country Inn&Suites, Extended Stay America
261	IL 126 (from sb), to Plainfield

JOLIET

257	US 30, to Joliet, Aurora, E Shell/Circle K Applebee's, Baskin-Robbins/Dunkin Donuts, Burger King, ChuckeCheese, Denny's, Diamand's Rest., Hooters, KFC, LoneStar Steaks, McDonald's, Old Country Buffet, Outback Steaks, Panera Bread, Pizza Hut, Red Lobster, Steak'n Shake, Subway, Taco Bell, TGI Friday's, TX Roadhouse, Wendy's Comfort Inn, Fairfield Inn, Hampton Inn, Holiday Inn Express, Motel 6, Super 8 AutoZone, Barnes&Noble, Best Buy, Discount Tire, Firestone/auto, Gander Mtn, Home Depot, Honda, JC Penney, JoAnn Fabrics, Macy's, NTB, Old Navy, Petsmart, Sears/auto, Target, Verizon, W Mobil/dsl Blue's BBQ, Luigi's Pizza Chevrolet, Ford
253b a	US 52, Jefferson St, Joliet, E Citgo/dsl, Mobil/dsl, Shell Joe's Rest., KFC/Pizza Hut, McDonald's Best Budget Inn, Best Western, Elk's Motel, Joliet Inn, Wingate Inn H, airport, Ford, Freightliner, Harley-Davidson, Rick's RV Ctr, W BP/dsl Al's Beef, Burger King, Casa Maya, DQ, Louie's Chophouse, Nancy's Pizza, Rosati's Pizza, Subway H, 7-11, Chrysler/Dodge/Jeep, Jewel-Osco/gas, NAPA
251	IL 59 (from nb), to Shorewood, access to same as 253 W
250b a	I-80, W to Iowa, E to Toledo
248	US 6, Joliet, E Pilot/Dunkin Donuts/Subway/dsl/24hr, Speedway/dsl Taco Burrito King Manor Motel, W BP/McDonald's Lone Star Rest. (2mi) to Ill/Mich SP
247	Bluff Rd
245mm	Des Plaines River
244	Arsenal Rd, E Exxon/Mobil Refinery
241	to Wilmington
241mm	Kankakee River

IL

INTERSTATE 55 Cont'd

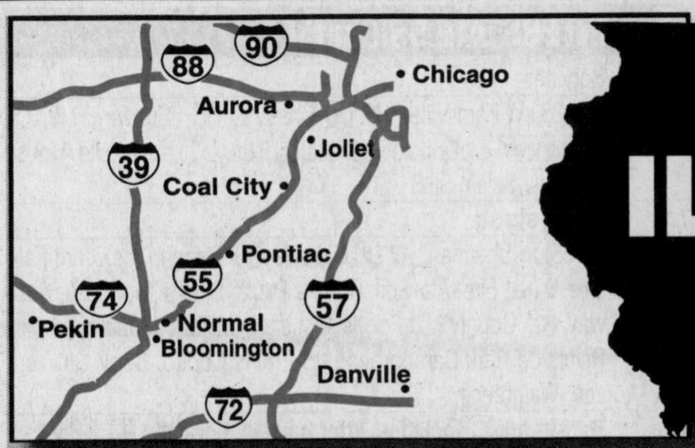

Exit #	Services
240	Lorenzo Rd, E BP/dsl, W Mobil/pizza/dsl/scales/24hr River Rest. Knights Inn
238	IL 129 S, to Wilmington (from nb), Braidwood
236	IL 113, Coal City, E Good Table Rest. Fossil Rock Camping, W Casey's, Shell/DQ/dsl KFC/Taco Bell, Los 3 Burritos, WhistleStop Cafe EZ Living RV Ctr
233	Reed Rd, E Marathon/dsl Jones-sez BBQ, W antiques
227	IL 53, Gardner, E Casey's Gardner Rest., Subway $General, truck/tire repair, W Shell/dsl
220	IL 47, Dwight, E BP/Burger King/dsl, Love's/Hardee's/dsl/scales/24hr, Marathon/Circle K/dsl/24hr Arby's, Dwight Chinese, Dwight Pizza, McDonald's, Pete's Rest., Subway Classic Motel, Super 8
217	IL 17, Dwight, E Casey's, Shell/Circle K/dsl/24hr DQ, Rte 66 Rest. Best Hardware, Doc's Drug, Family$, NAPA, ShopKO
213mm	Mazon River
209	Odell, E BP USPO
201	IL 23, Pontiac, 0-3 mi E Marathon DQ, La Mex 4H RV Camp (seasonal) RV Ctr, W truck repair
198mm	Vermilion River
197	IL 116, Pontiac, E BP/dsl, Freedom, Shell/dsl, Thornton's/dsl Arby's, Baby Bull's Rest., Burger King, Cafe Fontana, KFC, LJ Silver, McDonald's, Monical's Pizza, Pizza Hut, Subway, Taco Bell, Wendy's Best Western, Fiesta Motel (1mi), Quality Inn, Super 8 $General, $Tree, Aldi Foods, AT&T, AutoZone, Big R Store, Buick/Chevrolet, Cadillac/GMC, Chrysler/Dodge/Jeep, Firestone/auto, Lincoln, st police, Verizon, Walgreens, Walmart/Subway, W Mobil/dsl H
193mm	**both lanes, full facilities, litter barrels, petwalk vending**
187	US 24, Chenoa, E Casey's, Phillips 66/McDonald's/dsl, Shell/Subway/dsl Best Value Inn, Chenoa Family Rest.
179mm	Des Plaines River
178	Lexington, E BP/McDonalds/dsl, Freedom/dsl Subway $General, W Chevrolet
178mm	Mackinaw River
171	Towanda, E FastStop/dsl
167	Lp 55 S Veterans Pkwy, to Normal, 0-3 mi E BP/Circle K, Marathon/Circle K/dsl Alexander's Steaks, Applebee's, Bandana's BBQ, Biaggi's Ristorante, Bob Evans, Burger King, Carlos O'Kelly's, Chili's, Chipotle Mexican, ChuckeCheese, Coldstone, Destihl Rest., DQ, Fazoli's, Fiesta Ranchera Mexican, FlatTop Grill, Hardee's, IHOP, Jason's Deli, Jimmy John's, Krispy Kreme, Logan's Roadhouse, Lonestar Steaks, McDonald's, Monical's Pizza, Noodles&Co, Olive Garden, Outback Steaks, Panda Express, Panera Bread, Papa John's, Pizza Hut, Pizza Ranch, Popeyes, Potbelly, Qdoba Mexican, Red Lobster, Schlotzsky's, Smashburger, Sonic, Starbucks, Steak'n Shake, Subway, Taco Bell, Tony Roma's, Wendy's, Wild Berries Rest. Baymont Inn, Candlewood Suites, Chateau, Comfort Suites, Courtyard, Hampton Inn, Holiday Inn Express, Motel 6, Quality Inn, Super8 H, $Tree, Advance Parts, Aldi Foods, AT&T, AutoZone, Barnes&Noble, Best Buy, Cub Foods, CVS Drug, Dick's, Fresh Mkt, GNC, Goodyear/auto, Gordman's, Hobby Lobby, Home Depot, Honda, Hyundai, JC Penney, Jewel-Osco, Jo-Ann Fabrics, K-Mart, Kohl's, Kroger/dsl, Lowe's, Macy's, mall, Meijer/dsl, Meineke, Menards, Michael's, Midas, Mitsubishi, Office Depot, Old Navy, PetCo, Sam's Club/gas, Schnuck'sFoods, Sears/auto, Target, TJ Maxx, to airport,
167	Continued Tuesday Morning, Tuffy, Verizon, Von Maur, Walgreens, Walmart/Subway
165b a	US 51 bus, to Bloomington, E BP/Circle K, Mobil/Arby's/dsl, Qik-n-EZ, Shell/Burger King/dsl Denny's, Dunkin Donuts, McDonald's, Moe's SW Grill, Rosati's Pizza, Smoothie King, Steak'n Shake, Subway, Uncle Tom's Pancakes, Wendy's Best Value Inn, Motel 6, Super 8 H, $General, $Tree, Discount Tire, Schuncks Foods, to Ill St U, Walgreens, W dsl repair
164	I-39, US 51, N to Peru
163	I-74 W, to Peoria
160b a	US 150, IL 9, Market St, Bloomington, E BP/Circle K, Freedom/dsl, Pilot/Wendy's/dsl/scales/24hr, Shell/repair, TA/Country Pride/dsl/scales/24hr/ @ Arby's, Cracker Barrel, Culver's, JJ Fish&Chicken, KFC, McDonald's, Popeye's, Subway, Taco Bell Days Inn, EconoLodge, Hawthorn Suites, La Quinta, Quality Suites, Red Roof Inn H, Advance Parts, Blue Beacon, Family$, Peterbilt, W Marathon/Circle K/dsl, Murphy USA/dsl Bob Evans, Fiesta Ranchera Mexican, Steak'n Shake/24hr Comfort Suites, Country Inn&Suites, Fairfield Inn, Hampton Inn, Holiday Inn Express, Ramada Ltd Aldi Foods, Farm&Fleet, Walmart
157b	Lp 55 N, Veterans Pkwy, Bloomington, E H, to airport
157a	I-74 E, to Indianapolis, US 51 to Decatur
154	Shirley
149	W **both lanes, full facilities, litter barrels, petwalk playground, vending**
145	US 136, E Quality RV Ctr, W Dixie/Pilot/Road Ranger/Subway/dsl/scales/24hr, Shell-dsl McDonald's, Rte 66 Drive Thru Super 8
140	Atlanta, E RV camping (3mi), W Casey's/dsl Country-Aire Rest. Atlanta Inn $General, NAPA
133	Lp 55, Lincoln, 2 mi E H Camp-A-While Camping
127	I-155 N, to Peoria
126	IL 10, IL 121 S, Lincoln, 0-2 mi E BP/Arby's/dsl/24hr, Thornton's/Pilot/dsl/scales/24hr Bonanza Steaks, Burger King, Cracker Barrel, Culver's, Daphne's Rest., DQ, El Mazatlan Mexican, Hardee's, McDonald's, Pizza Hut, Rio Grande Grill, Steak'n Shake, Subway, Taco Bell, Wendy's EconoLodge, Hampton Inn, Holiday Inn Express, Super 8 H $General, $Tree, Aldi Foods, AT&T, AutoZone, Chrysler/Dodge/Jeep, CVS Drug, Ford/Lincoln, Kroger, O'Reilly Parts, Radio Shack, Russell Stover, Verizon, Walgreens, Walmart/Subway
123	Lp 55, to Lincoln, E H
119	Broadwell
115	Elkhart

PONTIAC NORMAL BLOOMINGTON LINCOLN

INTERSTATE 55 Cont'd

SPRINGFIELD

Exit #	Services
109	IL 123, Williamsville, E Casey's Subway, W Love's/McDonalds/dsl/scales/24hr Huddle House New Salem SHS
107mm	**weigh sta sb**
105	Lp 55, to Sherman, W Casey's Cancun Mexican, Fairlane Diner, Fire&Ale Grill, Ricco's Pizza, Sam's Too Pizza, Subway County Mkt Foods, hist sites, Military Museum, repair, Riverside Park Campground, to Prairie Capitol Conv Ctr, Verizon, Walgreens
103mm	**sb, full facilities, litter barrels, petwalk vending**
102mm	Sangamon River
102mm	**nb, full facilities, litter barrels, petwalk vending**
100b	IL 54, Sangamon Ave, Springfield, W BP/Circle K, Marathon/Circle K, Murphy USA/dsl, Shell/dsl Arby's, Buffalo Wild Wings, Burger King, Culver's, DQ, Hickory River BBQ, Jimmy John's, McDonald's, Parkway Cafe, Penn Sta Subs, Royal Buffet, Sonic, Steak'n Shake, Taco Bell, Thai Basil, Wendy's, Wings Etc, Xochimilco Mexican, Yummy House Northfield Suites, Ramada airport, Aldi Foods, AT&T, GNC, Harley-Davidson, Lowe's, Menards, to Vet Mem, Verizon, Walmart/Subway
100a	Il 54, E to Clinton, E Road Ranger/Pilot/Subway/dsl/scales/24hr Kenworth/Ryder/Volvo, truckwash
98b	I-72, IL 97, Springfield, W BP/Circle K, Casey's, Shell/dsl Chesapeake Seafood House, Freddy's Steakburger, Hardee's, Mario's Pizza, McDonald's, Starbucks, Subway Best Western, Lincoln's Lodge H, city park, Ford Trucks, K-Mart/Little Caesar's, to Capitol Complex, Walgreens
98a	I-72 E, US 36 E, to Decatur
96b a	IL 29 N, S Grand Ave, Springfield, W Marathon/dsl, Road Ranger/dsl Burger King, Godfather's, Popeye's Red Roof Inn, Super 8 $General, Advance Parts, AutoZone, Buick/GMC, Hyundai, JC Penney, museum, O'Reilly Parts, Shop'n Save
94	Stevenson Dr, Springfield, E KOA (7mi), W BP/Circle K/Dsl, Mobil/Subway/dsl, Shell/dsl Applebee's, Arby's, Bob Evans, Cancun Rest., Cheddar's, Denny's, Gallina Pizza, Hardee's, Hooters, IHOP, La Fiesta Mexican, LJ Silver, Luca Pizza, McDonald's, Outback Steaks, Panera Bread, Papa John's, Red Lobster, Smokey Bones BBQ, Steak'n Shake, Taste of Thai Candlewood Suites, Comfort Suites, Country Inn Suites, Crowne Plaza, Drury Inn, Hampton Inn, Hilton Garden, Holiday Inn Express, Microtel, Residence Inn $General, auto repair, BigLots, CVS Drug, GNC, Walgreens, zoo (4mi)
92b a	I-72 W, US 36 W, 6th St, Springfield, W Road Ranger/dsl, Thornton's Arby's, Burger King, Chadito's Tacos, Cozy Drive In, Golden Corral, Jimmy John's, KFC, McDonald's, New China, Pizza Hut, Pizza Ranch, Sgt. Pepper's Cafe, Starbucks, Subway, Taco Bell Comfort Inn, La Quinta, Route 66 H Aldi, AutoZone, CarX, County Mkt Foods, Lincoln, Mazda, Walgreens, Walmart/McDonald's
90	Toronto Rd, E Qik-n-EZ/Wendy's/dsl, Shell/Circle K Antonio's Pizza, China Express, Cracker Barrel, Head West Subs, Hen House, McDonald's, Subway, Taco Bell Baymont Inn, Day's Inn, Motel 6, W Pilot/Road Ranger/dsl/24hr
89mm	Lake Springfield
88	E Lake Dr, Chatham, E KOA, to Lincoln Mem Garden/Nature Ctr, W JJ RV Park/camping (2mi)
83	Glenarm, W JJ RV Park/camping (4mi)
82	IL 104, to Pawnee, E to Sangchris Lake SP, W Mobil/Auburn Trvl Ctr/Subway/scales/dsl/rest/24hr Myra's Rest antiques/crafts
80	Hist 66, Divernon, W antiques
72	Farmersville, W Phillips 66/Subway/dsl/24hr, Shell/24hr
65mm	**both lanes, full facilities, litter barrels, petwalk playground, vending**
63	IL 48, IL 127, to Raymond
60	IL 108, to Carlinville, E Kamper Kampanion RV Park, W Shell/dsl/LP/café Magnuson Grand Hotel/cafe antiques, to Blackburn Coll
56mm	**weigh sta nb**

LITCHFIELD

Exit #	Services
52	IL 16, Hist 66, Litchfield, E BP, Casey's, Conoco/Jack-in-the-Box/dsl, Faststop/deli/dsl/scales, Murphy USA/dsl, Shell A&W/LJ Silver, Arby's, Ariston Café, Burger King, China Town, Denny's, DQ, El Rancherito Mexican, Jubelt's Rest., KFC, Maverick Steaks, McDonald's, Pizza Hut, Ruby Tuesday, Subway, Taco Bell, Wendy's Best Value Inn, Hampton Inn, Holiday Inn Express, Quality Inn, Super 8 H $General, $Tree, Aldi Foods, AT&T, Buick/Cadillac/Chevrolet/GMC, Ford, Goodyear/auto, IGA Foods, NAPA, O'Reilly Parts, Radio Shack, Rte 66 Museum, Verizon, vet, Walgreens, Walmart/Subway, W st police
44	IL 138, to Benld, Mt Olive, E Crossroads Diner, Sunset Rest. Mother Jones Mon
41	to Staunton, E Country Classic Cars, W Casey's DQ, Las Cabanas Mexican Super 8 H $General
37	Livingston, New Douglas, W Shell/dsl Gasperoni's Café Country Inn/cafe IGA Foods, NAPA AutoCare, USPO
33	IL 4, to Staunton, Worden
30	IL 140, Hamel, E Love's/McDonald's/Subway/dsl/scales/24hr Innkeeper Motel, W Shell Weezy's Grill
28mm	**both lanes, full facilities, litter barrels, petwalk vending**
23	IL 143, Edwardsville, E Phillips 66/dsl, W Red Barn Camping (apr-oct)
20b	I-270 W, to Kansas City
20a	I-70 E, to Indianapolis
19	**I-55 S and I-70 W run together 18 mi**

COLLINSVILLE

Exit #	Services
18	IL 162, to Troy, E Casey's/dsl, Phillips 66/Circle K/dsl, Pilot/Arby's/dsl/scales/24hr, TA/BP/Country Pride/dsl/scales/24hr/ @ , ZX Alfonzo's Pizza, Burger King, China King, Domino's, DQ, Dunkin Donuts, El Potro Mexican, Jack-in-the-Box, Little Caesar's, McDonald's/playplace, Pizza Hut, Subway, Troy Rest. H, $General, Ace Hardware, Speedco, SuperValu Foods, truckwash, USPO, vet, Walgreens, W Mobil Cracker Barrel, Joe's Pizza, Taco Bell Holiday Inn Express, Motel 6, Red Roof Inn, Super 8 Freightliner, Verizon
17	US 40 E, to Troy, to St Jacob
15b a	IL 159, Maryville, Collinsville, **0-2 mi** E Phillips 66/Circle K/dsl, Shell, Zx Gas Asia Garden, Carisillo's Mexican, KFC, McDonald's, Sonic, Subway $General, Advance Parts, Aldi Foods, AutoZone, CVS Drug, Ford/Lincoln, O'Reilly Parts, vet, Walgreens, W Rodeway Inn
14mm	**weigh sta sb**
11	IL 157, Collinsville, E Casey's A&W/LJ Silver, Denny's, Golden Corral, Little Caesar's, McDonald's, Penn Sta Subs, Qdoba Mexican, St Louis Bread Co, Starbucks, Waffle House,

INTERSTATE 55 Cont'd

11	Continued Wendy's Best Value Inn AT&T, Dobbs Tire, GNC, Home Depot, Midas, Radio Shack, Verizon, Walgreens, Walmart/Subway, W Motomart/dsl/24hr Applebee's, Arby's, Bandana's BBQ, Bob Evans, Burger King, Culver's, DQ, Pizza Hut, Ponderosa, Porter's Steaks, Ruby Tuesday, Steak'n Shake, White Castle/24hr, Zapata's Mexican Comfort Inn, Days Inn, DoubleTree Inn, Drury Inn, Extended Stay Suites, Fairfield Inn, Hampton Inn, Super 8 Buick/GMC, st police
10	I-255, S to Memphis, N to I-270
9	Black Lane (from nb, no return), E Fairmount RaceTrack
6	IL 111, Great River Rd, Fairmont City, E Phillips 66 Relax Inn, Royal Budget Inn auto repair, W Horseshoe SP
5mm	motorist callboxes begin at 1/2 mi intervals nb
4b a	IL 203, Granite City, E BP/dsl Western Inn, W Pilot/Subway/Taco Bell/dsl/scales/24hr/ @ Gateway Int Raceway
3	Exchange Ave
2	I-64 E, IL 3 N, St Clair Ave
2b	3rd St
2a	M L King Bridge, to downtown E St Louis
1	IL 3, to Sauget (from sb)
I-55 N and I-70 E run together 18 mi	
0mm	Illinois/Missouri state line, Mississippi River

INTERSTATE 57

Exit #	Services
358mm	I-94 E to Indiana, **I-57 begins/ends on I-94, exit 63 in Chicago.**
357	IL 1, Halsted St, E BP, Mobil auto repair, W Citgo/dsl, Shell/Dunkin Donuts McDonald's, Shark's, Subway Walgreens
355	111th St, Monterey Ave, W BP, Citgo
354	119th St, W Citgo/Dunkin Donuts Chili's, Harold's Chicken, Panda Express, Subway $Tree, Jewel-Osco, Marshall's, PetCo, Staples, Target
353	127th St, Burr Oak Ave, E Citgo, Marathon, Shell Burger King, Dillinger's Drive-In, McDonald's, Wendy's Motel 6, Plaza Inn, Red Roof Inn H Ace Hardware, Advance Parts, Aldi Foods, Family$, Walgreens, W BP, Citgo/dsl JJ Fish&Chicken
352mm	Calumet Sag Channel
350	IL 83, 147th St, Sibley Blvd, E Marathon/dsl Checker's, Dunkin Donuts, Harold's Chicken, McDonald's, Subway Aldi Foods, Family$, O'Reilly Parts, W USPO
348	US 6, 159th St, E BP/dsl, Clark, Marathon/dsl Baskin-Robbins/Dunkin Donuts, Burger King, McDonald's, Popeye's, Subway, Taco Bell, White Castle $Tree, AutoZone, U-Haul, Walgreens, W Gas Depot/dsl, Mobil/dsl
346	167th St, Cicero Ave, to IL 50, E BP, Citgo/dsl Applebee's, Baskin-Robbins/Dunkin Donuts, Bee's Steaks, Harold's Chicken, McDonald's, Panda Express, Shark's Fish&Chicken, Sonic, Subway, Thom's BBQ, Wendy's Best Western Oak Forest Radio Shack, Verizon, Walmart/Subway, W Shell 7-11
345b a	I-80, W to Iowa, E to Indiana, to **I-294 N toll to Wisconsin**
342	Vollmer Rd, E Shell/Circle K/dsl H
340b a	US 30, Lincoln Hwy, Matteson, E BP, Citgo/dsl A&W/LJ Silver, Afusion Asian, Applebee's, Bocce's Grill, Burger King, Chuck-eCheese, Cracker Barrel, Culver's, Dusties Buffet, Fuddrucker's,

CHICAGO

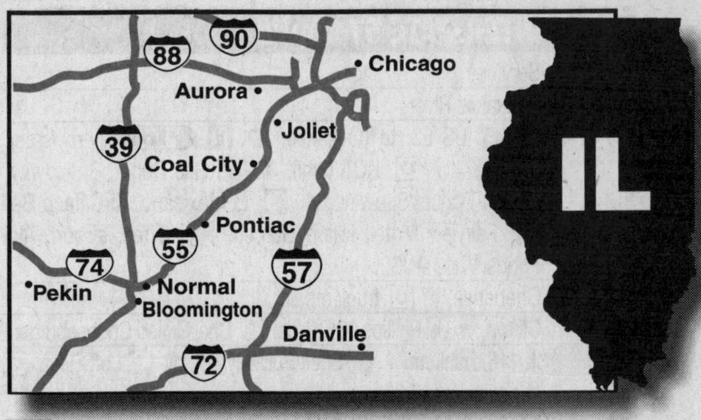

MATTESON

340b a	Continued Hibachi Grill, IHOP, Jimmy John's, KFC, Knock-Outs Rest., McDonald's, Michael's Rest., Mr Benny's Rest., Olive Garden, Panda Express, Panera Bread, Pepe's, Perros Bros Gyros, Pizza Hut, Quiznos, Red Lobster, Shark's, Starbucks, Subway, Taco Bell, Wendy's, White Castle Best Value Inn, Country Inn&Suites, Hampton Inn, La Quinta, Matteson Hotel $Tree, Aldi Foods, AT&T, Best Buy, Chrysler/Dodge/Jeep, Discount Tire, Dominick's Foods, Firestone/auto, Home Depot, JC Penney, Marshall's, Menards, NTB, Old Navy, PepBoys, Petsmart, Radio Shack, Sam's Club/gas, Sears/auto, Target, USPO, Verizon, Walgreens, Walmart, W Buick/Cadillac/GMC, Ford/Lincoln, Honda, Hyundai, Kia, Nissan, Toyota/Scion, Walgreens
339	Sauk Trail, to Richton Park, E BP, Citgo/dsl Domino's, McDonald's, Uncle John's BBQ/Ribs Walgreens
335	Monee, E BP/Dunkin Donuts/Subway/dsl, Petro/Iron Skillet/dsl/e-85/scales/24hr/ @, Pilot/McDonald's/dsl/scales/24hr Burger King, Lucky Burrito, Quiznos, Schoops Rest. Best Western, Country Host Motel, Red Roof Inn, Super 8 Blue Beacon
332mm	**Prairie View both lanes, full facilities, litter barrels, petwalk vending**
330mm	**weigh sta both lanes**
327	to Peotone, E Casey's, Shell/Circle K Bierstube German, McDonald's/RV parking
322	Manteno, E Phillips 66/Subway, Shell/McDonald's Jimmy John's, KFC/Pizza Hut/Taco Bell, Monical's Pizza, Wendy's Country Inn&Suites, Howard Johnson Curves, Harley-Davidson, W BP/dsl
315	IL 50, Bradley, E F&F, Shell/Circle K/Burger King Buffalo Wild Wings, Cracker Barrel, LoneStar Steaks, McDonald's, Red Lobster, Ruby Tuesday, TGIFriday's, Tucci's Rest., White Castle Best Inn, Fairfield Inn, Hampton Inn, Holiday Inn Express Barnes&Noble, Best Buy, Chrysler/Dodge/Jeep, Dick's, JC Penney, Kohl's, mall, Marshall's, Michael's, PetCo, Petsmart, Sears/auto, Staples, Target, Verizon, Walmart/Subway, W Phillips 66/dsl, Shell/Circle K/dsl, Speedway/dsl Applebee's, Arby's, Bakers Square, Coyote Canyon, Denny's, El Campesino Mexican, IHOP, LJ Silver, Mancino's Pizza, McDonald's, Oberweis Ice Cream, Old Country Buffet, Panda Express, Pizza Hut/Taco Bell, Starbucks, Steak'n Shake, Subway, VIP's Rest., Wendy's Motel 6, Quality Inn, Super 8 $Tree, Aldi Foods, AutoZone, Brown RV Ctr, Buick/GMC, Chevrolet, Hobby Lobby, Honda, Hyundai, Jo-Ann Fabrics, Kia, K-Mart, Lowe's, Menards, Nissan, to Kankakee River SP, Verizon, vet
312	IL 17, Kankakee, E Twin River's Camping, W BP/dsl, Marathon/dsl, Shell/Circle K Capt Hook's Fish&Chicken, McDonald's/RV parking, PoorBoy Rest. H Advance Parts, auto repair, Family$, Walgreens

BRADLEY

K A N K A K E E / **R A N T O U L**	**INTERSTATE 57 Cont'd**

Exit #	Services
310.5mm	Kankakee River
308	US 45, US 52, to Kankakee, **E** 🅿 ♥Loves/Arby's/dsl/scales/24hr Ⓞ KOA (3mi), **W** 🅿 Gas Depot, Speedway/Dunkin Donuts/Subway/dsl 🍴 El Mexicano, KFC/Taco Bell 🛏 Fairview Motel, Hilton Garden Ⓞ $Tree, airport, Aldi Foods, Walmart/Subway
302	Chebanse, **W** Ⓞ truck repair
297	Clifton, **W** 🅿 Phillips 66/DQ/dsl 🍴 CharGrilled Cheeseburgers
293	IL 116, Ashkum, **E** 🅿 Shell/Subway/dsl, **W** 🍴 Loft Rest. Ⓞ st police, tires
283	US 24, IL 54, Gilman, **E** 🅿 Apollo/Marathon/dsl/scales/24hr, K&H Trkstp/BP/dsl/scales/24hr/@, Shell/dsl 🍴 Burger King, DQ, McDonald's, Monical's Pizza, Red Door Rest. 🛏 Motel 6, Super 8, **W** 🅿 Shell/Subway/dsl
280	IL 54, Onarga, **E** 🅿 Casey's, Phillips 66 Ⓞ USPO, **W** Ⓞ Lake Arrowhead RV camping
272	to Roberts, Buckley
268.5mm	🆁🆂 both lanes, full 🦽 facilities, litter barrels, petwalk Ⓒ 🖾 vending
261	IL 9, Paxton, **0-1 mi E** 🅿 Casey's, Phillips 66/dsl 🍴 Hardee's, Monical's Pizza, Pizza Hut, Subway Ⓞ Buick/Cadillac/Chevrolet/GMC, Family$, IGA Foods, TrueValue, USPO, **W** 🅿 BP, Marathon 🍴 Country Garden Rest. 🛏 Paxton Inn
250	US 136, Rantoul, **0-1 mi E** 🅿 BP/Circle K, Casey's/dsl 🍴 Arby's, Baskin-Robbins/Dunkin Donuts, Burger King, Hardee's, KFC/Taco Bell, LJ Silver, McDonald's, Monical's Pizza, Papa John's, Red Wheel Rest., Subway 🛏 Best Western, Days Inn, Super 8 Ⓞ $General, camping, Chrysler/Dodge/Jeep, Ford, NAPA, to Chanute AFB, vet, Walgreens, Walmart/Subway
240	Market St, **E** 🅿 Road Ranger/🍴/McDonald's/dsl/scales Ⓞ D&W Lake Camping/RV Park, Kenworth/Volvo, truck/tire repair
238	Olympian Dr, to Champaign, **W** 🅿 Mobil/dsl 🍴 DQ 🛏 Microtel Ⓞ RV/dsl repair
237b a	I-74, W to Peoria, E to Urbana
235b	I-72 W, to Decatur
235a	University Ave, to Champaign, **E** Ⓞ Ⓗ, U of Ill
232	Curtis Rd
229	to Savoy, Monticello, **E** 🅿 Marathon/dsl
221.5mm	🆁🆂 both lanes, full 🦽 facilities, litter barrels, petwalk Ⓒ 🖾 vending
220	US 45, Pesotum, **E** Ⓞ st police
212	US 36, Tuscola, **E** 🅿 FuelMart/dsl , **W** 🅿 Phillips 66/Circle K, 🍴/Road Ranger/dsl/scales/24hr 🍴 Amish Land Country Buffet, Big Red Barn Rest., Burger King, Denny's, DQ, McDonald's, Monical's Pizza, Pantry Cafe, Pizza Hut, Subway, Tuscany Steaks 🛏 Baymont Inn, Holiday Inn Express, Super 8 Ⓞ Ford, IGA Foods, Radio Shack, ShopKO, Tanger Outlets/Famous Brands, Verizon
203	IL 133, Arcola, **E** 🛏 Best Western, **W** 🅿 Phillips 66/Subway/dsl, Sunrise/dsl 🍴 DQ, Hen House, La Cazuela's, Mexican, Monical's Pizza 🛏 Arcola Inn, Comfort Inn, Knights Inn Ⓞ $General, city park, NAPA, Rockome Gardens (5mi), vet
192	Cty Rd 1000 N, Rd 18
190b a	IL 16, to Mattoon, **E** 🅿 BP/dsl Ⓞ Ⓗ Fox Ridge SP, to **E** IL U, **W** 🅿 Huck's, Murphy USA/dsl, Phillips 66/Subway/dsl 🍴 A&W/LJ Silver, Alamo Steaks, Arby's, Buffalo Wild Wings, Cody's Roadhouse, Cracker Barrel, Domino's, Don Sol Mexi-

M A T T O O N / **E F F I N G H A M** / **S A L E M**	

Exit #	Services
190b a	Continued can, DQ, Fast Freddy's, Jumbo Buffet, KFC, Lee's Chick McDonald's/playplace, McHugh's, Papa Murphy's, Pizza H Quiznos, Stadium Grill, Steak'n Shake, Super Jumbo Buf Taco Bell, Wendy's 🛏 Baymont Inn, Comfort Suites, D Inn, Hampton Inn, Holiday Inn Express, Super 8 Ⓞ $Gene $Tree, Aldi Foods, BigLots, CVS Drug, Home Depot, JC Penn Petsmart, Sears, Staples, Verizon, Walgreens, Walmart/Subw
184	US 45, IL 121, to Mattoon, **E** 🅿 Phillips 66/Subway/dsl, **W** 🍴 McDonald's 🛏 Budget Inn, Quality Inn Ⓞ to Lake Shelbyv
177	US 45, Neoga, **E** 🅿 FuelMart/Subway/dsl/e-85 Ⓞ NA **W** 🅿 Casey's (1mi) Ⓞ $General
166.5mm	🆁🆂 both lanes, full 🦽 facilities, litter barrels, petwalk Ⓒ vending
163	I-70 E, to Indianapolis

I-57 S and I-70 W run together 6 mi

Exit #	Services
162	US 45, Effingham, **E** 🅿 Motomart Ⓞ Harley-Davidson, **W** 🅿 🍴/McDonald's/dsl/scales/24hr 🍴 Subway Ⓞ Ca Lakewood (2mi), truck repair
160	IL 33, IL 32, Effingham, **E** 🍴 Domino's, Jimmy John's, L eStar Steaks, Papa John's, Pizza Hut 🛏 Delta Inn, Fairfi Inn, Quality Inn Ⓞ Ⓗ $General, Aldi Foods, AutoZone, Mart, Save-a-Lot, Verizon, vet, **W** 🅿 ⒻFLYING J/Denny dsl/LP/scales/24hr, BP/dsl, Murphy USA/dsl, TA/Popeye's/c @ 🍴 Arby's, Buffalo Wild Wings, Burger King, Cracker Bar Denny's, El Rancherito Mexican, Firefly Grill, Fujiyama Stea LJ Silver, McDonald's, Panda Express, Ruby Tuesday, Ryan Starbucks, Steak'n Shake, Taco Bell, TGIFriday's, Wend 🛏 Baymont Inn, Country Inn&Suites, Days Inn, Hampton I Holiday Inn, Rodeway Inn, Super 8 Ⓞ $Tree, AT&T, Blue B con, Camp Lakewood RV Park, Ford/Lincoln, Kohl's, Menar Peterbilt, SpeedCo, Verizon, Walmart/Subway
159	US 40, Effingham, **E** 🅿 Conoco/dsl, Phillips 66/dsl 🍴 Ch Buffet, Culver's, Hardee's, Little Caesars, Niemerg's Rest, S way 🛏 Abe Lincoln Motel, Best Value Inn, Comfort Suit EconoLodge, Lexington Inn Ⓞ Honda, O'Reilly Parts, tir repair, Walgreens, **W** 🅿 Petro/Iron Skillet/dsl/24hr/@ 🛏 B Western Ⓞ Blue Beacon

I-57 N and I-70 E run together 6 mi

Exit #	Services
157	I-70 W, to St Louis
151	Watson, **5 mi E** Ⓞ Percival Springs RV Park
150mm	Little Wabash River
145	Edgewood, **E** 🅿 Phillips 66
135	IL 185, Farina, **E** 🅿 BP/Subway/dsl Ⓞ $General, Ford
127	to Kinmundy, Patoka
116	US 50, Salem, **E** 🅿 Huck's/dsl, Shell/Circle K/dsl, Sw 🍴 Burger King, Domino's, Hardee's, La Cocina Mexican, Silver, McDonald's, Pizza Hut, Pizza Man, Subway, Taco B Village Garden, Wendy's Ⓞ Ⓗ AutoZone, Chrysler/Dod Jeep, CVS Drug, GMC, NAPA, O'Reilly Parts, Save-A-L to Forbes SP, USPO, **W** 🅿 Murphy USA/dsl, Phillips 66/ 🍴 Applebee's, Arby's, Denny's, KFC 🛏 Comfort Inn, Gue house Inn, Salem Inn, Super 8 Ⓞ $Tree, AT&T, Buick/Chev let, Carlisle Lake (23mi), Ford, Salem Tires, Walmart
114mm	🆁🆂 both lanes, full 🦽 facilities, litter barrels, petwalk Ⓒ playground, vending
109	IL 161, to Centralia, **W** 🅿 Biggie's General Store/cafe/dsl
103	Dix, **E** 🍴 Austin's Rest 🛏 Red Carpet Inn
96	I-64 W, to St Louis
95	IL 15, Mt Vernon, **E** 🅿 Hucks, Phillips 66/Circle K/dsl 🍴 Agave Mexican, Asian Buffet, Bandana's BBQ, El Ranche Mexican, Fazoli's, Hardee's, Hardee's, KFC, Little Caesa

INTERSTATE 57 Cont'd

MT VERNON

95	Continued LJ Silver, McDonald's, Moe's SW Grill, Panda Express, Papa John's, Pizza Hut, Steak'n Shake, Subway, Taco Bell, Waffle Co, Wendy's [lodging] Best Inn, Best Value Inn, Comfort Suites, Drury Inn, Motel 6, Super 8 [other] [H] Aldi Foods, AutoZone, Big Lots, Chevrolet/Cadillac, Chrysler/Dodge/Jeep, CVS Drug, Ford/Lincoln, Harley-Davidson, Hobby Lobby, JC Penney, K-Mart, Kroger/dsl, Midas, O'Reilly Parts, Prompt Care, Radio Shack, Ross, Verizon, Walgreens, **W** [gas] FLYING J/Hucks/Country Cookin/dsl/scales/24hr, Pilot/Denny's/dsl/scales/24hr, Shell/Circle K/dsl, TA/Country Pride/Popeye's/dsl/24hr/@ [food] Applebee's, Arby's, Bob Evans, Buffalo Wild Wings, Burger King, Chili's, Cracker Barrel, Jimmy John's, Kriger's Grill, LoneStar Steaks, McDonald's, Ryan's, Sonic, Subway [lodging] Days Inn, Fairfield Inn, Hampton Inn, Holiday Inn, Quality Inn [other] $Tree, Archway RV Park, Buick/GMC, Freightliner, Kohl's, Lowe's, NAPA, Staples, Toyota, truckwash, Verizon, Walmart
94	Veteran's Memorial Dr, [other] [H]
92	I-64 E, to Louisville
83	Ina, **E** [gas] Love's/McDonald's/dsl/scales [food] Uncle Joe's BBQ [other] Sherwood Camping (2mi), tire/trailer repair, **W** [other] to Rend Lake Coll
79mm	**[RS] sb, full [handicap] facilities, info, litter barrels, petwalk [phone] [picnic] playground, vending**
77	IL 154, to Whittington, **E** [gas] Shell/dsl [lodging] Lake Cove Resort [other] Whittington Woods RV Park, **W** [food] Birdies Grille [lodging] Seasons at Rend Lake Lodge/rest. [other] golf, to Rend Lake, Wayne Fitzgerrell SP
74mm	**[RS] nb, full [handicap] facilities, litter barrels, petwalk [phone] [picnic] playground, vending**
71	BENTON IL 14, Benton, **E** [gas] Phillips 66/dsl [food] Arby's, Hardee's, KFC/Taco Bell, Pizza Hut [lodging] Econolodge, Gray Plaza Motel, Magnuson Hotel [other] [H] AutoZone, CVS Drug, KOA (1.5mi), O'Reilly Parts, Plaza Tire, **W** [gas] Murphy USA/dsl, Phillips 66/dsl [food] Applebee's, Burger King, McDonald's, Subway [other] $Tree, AT&T, Radio Shack, to Rend Lake, Verizon, Walmart
65	IL 149, W Frankfort, **E** [gas] Gas-4-Less, Phillips 66/dsl, ROC/dsl [food] China Star, Dixie Cream Deli, Don Luna Mexican, Hardee's, La Fiesta Mexican, LJ Silver, Mike's Drive-In, Miranda's Rest., Sonic, Subway [lodging] Gray Plaza Motel [other] CVS Drug, MadPricer Foods, NAPA, **W** [gas] Casey's/dsl [food] McDonald's, Pizza Hut [lodging] Best Value Inn [other] $General, $Tree, AT&T, Buick/Chevrolet/GMC, Chrysler/Dodge/Jeep, K-Mart, Kroger, VF Factory Stores
59	to Herrin, Johnston City, **E** [gas] ROC/dsl/e85, ZX/dsl [food] DQ, McDonald's, Subway [other] $General, Bandy Drug, camping (2mi), NAPA, **W** [other] [H] camping (4mi)
54b a	MARION IL 13, Marion, **E** [gas] Phillips 66/dsl [food] Arby's, Fazoli's, Hardee's, KFC, La Fiesta Mexican, Little Caesar's, LJ Silver, Papa John's, Pizza Hut, Subway, Tequila's Mexican, Wendy's [lodging] EconoLodge [other] $General, Advance Parts, Aldi Foods, AutoZone, Ford/Hyundai/Lincoln, Kroger/gas, Plaza Tire, Radio Shack, Sav-A-Lot Foods, USPO, Walgreens, **W** [gas] Huck's/dsl, Pilot/Subway/dsl/scales/24h [food] 17th St Grill, Applebee's, Asian Bistro, Backyard Burger, Bob Evans, Burger King, Hong Kong BBQ, Logan's Roadhouse, Mackie's Pizza, McAlister's Deli, McDonald's, O'Charley's, Panera Bread, Red Lobster, Ryan's, Sonic, Steak'n Shake, Taco Bell, Wok'n Roll Buffet [lodging] Best Inn, Comfort Inn, Country Inn&Suites, Drury Inn, Fairfield Inn, Hampton Inn, Holiday Inn Express, Super 8 [other] [H] $Tree, AT&T, Buick/Chevrolet/GMC, Chrysler/Dodge/Jeep,

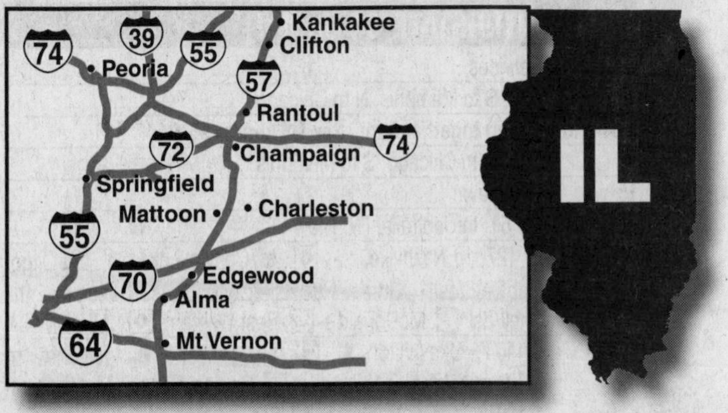

54b a	Continued Dillard's, Harley-Davidson, Home Depot, Honda, mall, Menards, Mercedes, Nissan, Sam's Club/gas, Sears/auto, Subaru, Target, Toyota/Scion, Verizon, Walmart/Subway
53	Main St, Marion, **E** [gas] Casey's/dsl [food] DQ [lodging] Motel Marion [other] [H] Marion Camping/RV Park, NAPA, **W** [gas] Motomart [food] Cracker Barrel, HideOut Steaks [lodging] Best Western, Comfort Suites, Quality Inn
47mm	**weigh sta both lanes**
45	IL 148, **1 mi E** [gas] King Tut's Food/dsl [lodging] Lake Tree Inn [other] camping, dsl repair, vet
44	I-24 E to Nashville
40	Goreville Rd, **E** [other] camping, Ferne Clyffe SP, scenic overlook
36	Lick Creek Rd, **W** [other] vineyards
32mm	**Trail of Tears [RS] both lanes, full [handicap] facilities, info, litter barrels, petwalk [phone] [picnic] playground, vending**
30	IL 146, Anna, Vienna, **W** [gas] Fast Stop/dsl [other] [H] auto/RV repair
25	US 51 N (from nb, exits left), to Carbondale
24	Dongola Rd, **E** [other] $General, **W** [gas] BP/dsl
18	Ullin Rd, **W** [gas] Fast Stop/dsl [food] EEE BBQ [lodging] Best Value Inn [other] Chevrolet, st police
8	Mounds Rd, to Mound City, **E** [other] K&K AutoTruck/dsl/repair
1	IL 3, to US 51, Cairo, **E** [lodging] Belvedere Motel (2mi), Days Inn [other] $General, camping, Mound City Nat Cem (4mi), **W** [other] camping
0mm	Illinois/Missouri state line, Mississippi River

INTERSTATE 64

Exit #	Services
131.5mm	Illinois/Indiana state line, Wabash River
131mm	**Skeeter Mountain Welcome Ctr wb, full [handicap] facilities, litter barrels, petwalk [phone] [picnic] vending**
130	IL 1, to Grayville, **N** [gas] Casey's (2mi), Pilot/Road Ranger/dsl/scales/24hr, Shell/dsl/24hr [food] Season's Grill, Subway [lodging] Super 8, Windsor Oaks Inn/rest. [other] Beall Woods SP (10mi)
124mm	Little Wabash River
117	Burnt Prairie, **S** [gas] CountryMark/dsl [food] ChuckWagon Charlie's Café [other] antiques
110	US 45, Mill Shoals
100	IL 242, to Wayne City, **N** [gas] Citgo/dsl
94	Veterans Memorial Drive, **N** [other] [H]
89	to Belle Rive, Bluford
86mm	**[RS] wb, full [handicap] facilities, litter barrels, petwalk [phone] [picnic] vending**
82.5mm	**[RS] eb, full [handicap] facilities, litter barrels, petwalk [phone] [picnic] vending**
80	IL 37, to Mt Vernon, **2 mi N** [gas] Hucks/dsl/24hr, Phillips 66/Circle K/Burger King/dsl [other] $General

IL

O'FALLON COLLINSVILLE

INTERSTATE 64 Cont'd

Exit #	Services
78	I-57, S to Memphis, N to Chicago
I-64 and I-57 run together 5 mi. See I-57, exits 95-94.	
73	I-57, N to Chicago, S to Memphis
69	Woodlawn
61	US 51, to Centralia, Richview
50	IL 127, to Nashville, N to Carlyle Lake, S Citgo/rest/E-85/dsl, Little Nashville/Conoco/rest/dsl/scales/24hr, Shell/dsl McDonald's Best Western H
41	IL 177, Okawville, S Pilot/Road Ranger/dsl/24hr Burger King, DQ, Subway Original Springs Motel, Super 8 $General, truck repair, USPO
37mm	Kaskaskia River
34	to Albers, 3 mi N Casey's
27	IL 161, New Baden, N Casey's/dsl, Shell/dsl China King, Four Corners Pizza, Good Ol Days Rest., McDonald's, Subway $General, Chevrolet, S Loves/Hardee's/dsl/scales/24hr
25mm	**both lanes, full facilities, litter barrels, petwalk RV dump, vending**
23	IL 4, to Mascoutah, N Mobil/dsl, Phillips 66/Huddle House/dsl/RV dump Best Western, S airport
20	Reader Rd
19b a	US 50, IL 158, N Motomart/dsl Amore Italian, Subway Super 8 H S to Scott AFB
18mm	**weigh sta eb**
16	to O'Fallon, Shiloh, N Bella Milano, Sonic, The Egg & I Hilton Garden CVS Drug, Harley-Davidson, URGENT CARE, S Motomart/dsl 54th St. Grille, Applebee's, Arby's, Aroy Thai, Buffalo Wild Wings, China King, Coldstone, Cracker Barrel, Golden Corral, Jersey Mike's, Jimmy John's, La Casa Mexicana, Little Caesar's, McAlister's Deli, McDonald's, Qdoba, Ravanelli's Rest., St. Louis Bread Co., Starbucks, Subway, TX Roadhouse, White Castle Drury Inn, Holiday Inn Express AT&T, Dierbergs Foods, Dobb's Tire, Menard's, Michael's, Radio Shack, Target, vet, World Mkt
14	O'Fallon, N Motomart, Phillips 66/Circle K, Shell/dsl IHOP, Japanese Garden, Steak'n Shake, Subway Country Inn&Suites, Extended Stay America, La Quinta, Sleep Inn, Suburban Inn Cadillac, Chevrolet, Ford, O'Reilly Parts, S Chevy's Mexican, Culver's, Hardee's, Jack-in-the-Box, KFC, La Parrilla Mexican, McDonald's, O'Charley's, Panda Express, Papa Murphy's, Sake Grill, Schiappa's Pizza, Syberg's Rest., Taco Bell Candlewood Suites, Days Inn, Quality Inn Aldi Foods, BMW, Home Depot, Honda, Hyundai, Kia, Mazda, Nissan, Petsmart, Sam's Club/gas, Toyota, VW, Walmart
12	IL 159, to Collinsville, N Shell/Circle K Agostino's, Applebee's, Bob Evans, Houlihan's, Joe's Crabshack, Lotawata Creek Grill, Olive Garden, Red Lobster, Shogun Japanese Best Value Inn, Comfort Suites, Drury Inn, Fairfield Inn, Hampton Inn, Holiday Inn, Sheraton, Super 8 Fiat, Gordman's, S BP/dsl, Motomart/dsl 5 Guys Burgers, Arby's, Boston Mkt, Burger King, Capt D's, Cheddar's, Chick-fil-A, Chili's, Chipotle Mexican, ChuckECheese, Domino's, Dunkin Donuts,Fazoli's, Firehouse Subs, Honeybaked Ham, Hooters, Imo's Pizza, Jimmy John's, Krispy Kreme, Little Caesar's, LJ Silver, Logan's Roadhouse, Longhorn Steaks, McAlister's Deli, McDonald's, Popeye's, Red Robin, Ruby Tuesday, Smokey Bones BBQ, St. Louis Bread, Steak'n Shake, Subway, Taco Bell, Wasabi, Wendy's, White Castle $General, $Tree,
12	Continued Aamco, Advance Parts, AT&T, Barnes&Noble, Best Buy, B Lots, Burlington Coats, CarX, Dillard's, Dobb's Tire, Firesto auto, Hobby Lobby, JC Penney, Jo-Ann Fabrics, Kohl's, Lowe Macy's, Marshall's, Meineke, Midas, NTB, Old Navy, O'Re Parts, PetCo, Ross, Russell Stover, Schnuck's Foods, Sea auto, TJ Maxx, Tuesday Morning, Verizon, vet, Walgreens
9	IL 157, to Caseyville, N Huck's/dsl, Phillips 66/Subw Hardee's Western Inn, S BP Cracker Barr Domino's, DQ, McDonald's, Pizza Hut/Taco Bell Best In Motel 6, Quality Inn, Rodeway Inn
7	I-255, S to Memphis, N to Chicago
6	IL 111, Kingshighway, N BP, Mobil/ Ray's Re Econo Inn
5	25th St
4	15th St, Baugh
3	I-55 N, I-70 E, IL 3 N, to St Clair Ave, to stockyards
2b a	3rd St, S
1	IL 3 S, 13th St, E St Louis, N Casino Queen
0mm	Illinois/Missouri state line, Mississippi River

INTERSTATE 70

Exit #	Services
156mm	Illinois/Indiana state line
154	US 40 W
151mm	**weigh sta wb**
149mm	**wb, full facilities, info, litter barrels, petwalk vending**
147	IL 1, Marshall, N Pilot/Road Ranger/Church's/d scales/24hr Crossroads Rest., S Casey's (1mi), D Marathon/Arby's/dsl, Phillips 66/Jiffy/dsl Burger King, L Tres Caminos, McDonald's, Pizza Hut, Sam's Steaks, Subwa Wendy's Lincoln Suites, Relax Inn, Super 8 antique camping, Ford, Lincoln Trail SP, Walmart
136	to Martinsville, S Phillips 66/dsl/24hr
134.5mm	N Fork Embarras River
129	IL 49, Casey, N KOA (seasonal), RV service, S Casey DQ, Marathon/Circle K/dsl, Phillips 66/dsl Hacienda Mex can, McDonald's, Pizza Hut, Prairie Fire Smokehouse BB Subway Days Inn $General, IGA Foods
119	IL 130, Greenup, S Casey's/dsl Backyard BBQ, D Subway Budget Host, Greenup Motel $General, h sites, NAPA
105	Montrose, N Spring Creek Camping (1mi), S BP/d Phillips/dsl Red Carpet Inn
98	I-57, N to Chicago
I-70 and I-57 run together 6 mi. See I-57, exits 159-162.	
92	I-57, S to Mt Vernon
91mm	Little Wabash River
87mm	**both lanes, full facilities, info, litter barrels, petwa playground, RV dump, vending**
82	IL 128, Altamont, N Casey's, Fast Stop/dsl, Phillips 6 Subway/dsl/24hr Dairy Bar, Joe's Pizza/pasta, McDonal Altamont Motel $General, city park, S Super 8
76	US 40, St Elmo, N Casey's Waldorf Motel Timbe line Camping (2mi)
71mm	**weigh sta eb**
68	US 40, Brownstown, N Okaw Valley Kamping, S tru repair
63.5mm	Kaskaskia River

INTERSTATE 70 Cont'd

Exit #	Services
63	US 51, Vandalia, N Chuck Wagon Cafe, LJ Silver Best Value Inn, S BP/Burger King/24hr, Casey's, Phillips 66 Arby's, China Buffet, DQ, McDonald's, Pizza Hut, Rancho Nuevo Mexican, Sonic, Subway, Wendy's Economy Inn, Jay's Inn Aldi Foods, city park, County Mkt Foods, hist site
61	US 40, Vandalia, N Fast Stop/Denny's/dsl/scales/24hr, S Murphy USA/dsl China King, Embers Pizza, Huddle House, KFC/Taco Bell, Ponderosa Holiday Inn Express, Ramada $Tree, AT&T, AutoZone, Verizon, Walmart
52	US 40, Mulberry Grove, N Timber Trail Camp-In (2mi), tires, S Cedar Brook Camping (1mi)
45	IL 127, Greenville, N Love's/Subway/dsl/scales/24hr, Phillips 66/Domino's/dsl, Shell/dsl Chang's Buffet, Cunetto's Rest., Huddle House, KFC/Taco Bell, Lu-Bob's Rest., McDonald's EconoLodge, Red Carpet Inn, Super 8 S La Hacienda Mexican Comfort Inn American Farm Heritage Museum, RV Service, to Carlyle Lake
41	US 40 E, to Greenville
36	US 40 E, Pocahontas, S BP/dsl, Phillips 66/dsl Funderburk's Grill Lighthouse Lodge, Powhatan Motel/rest., Tahoe Motel truck/tire repair
30	US 40, IL 143, to Highland, S Shell/dsl/wifi Blue Springs Café Tomahawk RV Park (7mi)
26.5mm	**Silver Lake both lanes, full facilities, litter barrels, petwalk vending**
24	IL 143, Marine, **4 mi** S Ponderosa Holiday Inn Express
21	IL 4, Troy
15b a	I-55, N to Chicago, S to St Louis, I-270 W to Kansas City, **I-70 and I-55 run together 18 mi. See I-55, exits 3-18.**
19mm	motorist callboxes begin wb every 1/2mile
0mm	Illinois/Missouri state line, Mississippi River

INTERSTATE 72

Exit #	Services
183mm	**1 mi E on University** Gas Depot, Thornton's/dsl Arby's, Burger King, Garcia's Pizza, Ichiban Buffet, Jimmy John's, KFC, La Bamba Mexican, McDonald's, Monical's Pizza, Original Pancakes, Papa John's, Pizza Hut, Sonic, Subway, Taco Bell, TX Roadhouse, Za's Italian $General, Advance Parts, AutoZone, Big Lots, County Mkt Foods, CVS Drug, O'Reilly Parts, Schnuck's Foods/e85, Walgreens
182b a	I-57, N to Chicago, S to Memphis, to I-74
176	IL 47, to Mahomet
172	IL 10, Lodge, Seymour
169	White Heath Rd
166	IL 105 W, Market St, N Ford, S Mobil/Subway/dsl Red Wheel Rest. Best Western, Foster Inn city park, railway museum
165mm	Sangamon River
164	Bridge St, **1 mi** S Mobil/Circle K/dsl China Star, DQ, Hardee's, McDonald's, Monical's Pizza, Pizza Hut, Subway $General, Buick/Chevrolet, Chrysler/Dodge/Jeep, USPO
156	IL 48, to Weldon, Cisco, N Friends Creek Camping (may-oct) (3mi).
153mm	**both lanes, full facilities, litter barrels, petwalk RV dump, vending**
152mm	Friends Creek

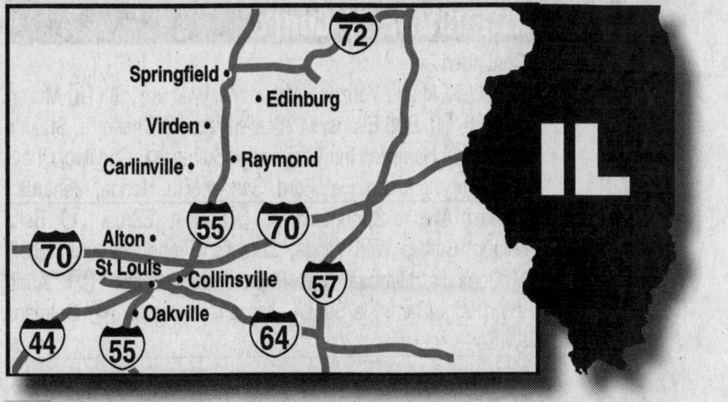

DECATUR

Exit #	Services
150	Argenta
144	IL 48, Oreana, S Pilot/McDonald's/Subway/dsl/scales/24hr Sleep Inn Chrysler/Dodge/Jeep, Honda, Hyundai, Pressley RV Ctr (3mi)
141b a	US 51, Decatur, N Shell/Circle K Applebee's, Buffalo Wild Wings, Cheddar's, Cracker Barrel, HomeTown Buffet, McDonald's, O'Charley's, Pizza Hut, Red Lobster, Steak'n Shake, Subway, Taco Bell, TX Roadhouse Baymont Inn, Country Inn&Suites, Fairfield Inn, Hampton Inn, Homewood Suites, Quality Inn, Ramada Ltd, Residence Inn $Tree, AT&T, Bergner's, Best Buy, Buick/Cadillac/GMC, Harley-Davidson, Hobby Lobby, Kohl's, Lowe's, Menards, Petsmart, Ross, Verizon, Von Maur, S Arby's, Burger King, El Rodeo Mexican, Fuji Japanese, La Fondita, Monical's Pizza, Olive Garden, Panera Bread, Papa Murphy's, Starbucks Jo-Ann Fabrics, Radio Shack, Sam's Club, Target, Verizon, Walgreens, Walmart/Subway
138	IL 121, Decatur, S
133b a	US 36 E, US 51, Decatur, S Phillips 66/Subway/dsl Best Value Inn, Decatur Hotel/rest.
128	Niantic
122	to Mt Auburn, Illiopolis, N FastStop/dsl
114	Buffalo, Mechanicsburg, **2 mi** S Gas Depot/dsl USPO
108	Riverton, Dawson
107mm	Sangamon River
104	Camp Butler, **2 mi** N McDonald's, Starbucks, Subway Best Rest Inn, Best Western, Lincoln Inn, Park View Motel golf
103b a	I-55, N to Chicago, S to St Louis, Il 97, to Springfield

I-72 and I-55 run together 6 mi. See I-55, exits 92-98.

SPRINGFIELD

Exit #	Services
97b a	6th St, I-55 S, Loop 55 N (from eb), 6th St, I-55 S, N Road Ranger Golden Corral, McDonald's, Pizza Ranch Comfort Inn, La Quinta, Rte 66 Aldi Foods, Lincoln, Mazda, Walmart
96	MacArthur Blvd, N Tesla EVC Engrained Brewing Co Scheels
93	IL 4, Springfield, N Hucks, Thorntons/dsl Applebee's, Arby's, Bakers Square, Burger King, Chili's, Chipotle Mexican, Cooper's Hawk Rest., Denny's, Five Guys, Ginger Asian, Jersey Mike's, Jimmy John's, Longhorn Steaks, Los Agaves Mexican, Los Rancheros Mexican, McDonald's, Noodles&Co, Olive Garden, Panda Express, Panera Bread, Penn Sta Subs, Popeye's, Qdoba, Red Robin, Sonic, Starbucks, Subway, Taco Bell, TGIFriday's, TX Roadhouse, Wasabi Japanese, Wendy's Courtyard, Fairfield Inn, Quality Inn, Sleep Inn Aldi Foods, AT&T, Barnes&Noble, Bergner's, Best Buy, County Mkt Foods, Dick's, Discount Tire, Gordman's, Hobby Lobby, Jo-Ann Fabrics, K-Mart, Kohl's, Lowe's, Macy's, Michael's, Office Depot, Old Navy, PetCo, Petsmart, Ross, Sam's Club/gas, Sears/auto, Staples,

IL

INTERSTATE 72 Cont'd

93 Continued
Target, TJ Maxx, Verizon, Walgreens, Walmart, S Meijer/dsl/E85 Bob Evans, Monical's Pizza, O'Charley's, Steak'n Shake Hampton Inn, Staybridge Suites Cadillac, Chevrolet, Chrysler/Jeep, Fiat, Ford, Gander Mtn, Honda, Menards

91 Wabash Ave, to Springfield, N Qik-n- EZ/dsl Bella Milano, Buffalo Wild Wings, Culver's, Firehouse Subs, IHOP, McDonald's, Mimosa Thai, Papa Frank's Italian Audi/VW, Dodge/Ram, Kia/Subaru, Nissan, Toyota, S Colmans RV Ctr

82 New Berlin, S Pilot/Road Ranger/Subway/dsl $General

76 IL 123, to Ashland, Alexander

68 to IL 104, to Jacksonville, 2 mi N BP/Circle K, Casey's/dsl H

64 US 67, to Jacksonville, 2 mi N BP/Circle K/dsl, Casey's, FastStop/dsl, Qik-n-EZ/Subway/dsl KFC, Little Caesar's, McDonald's Baymont Inn, Comfort Inn, Holiday Inn Express H $General, CVS Drug, Family$, Hopper RV Ctr, Walgreens

60 to US 67 N, to Jacksonville, 6 mi N on IL 104 H food, gas, lodging

52 to IL 106, Winchester, N golf, 2 mi S

46 IL 100, to Bluffs

42mm Illinois River

35 US 54, IL 107, to Pittsfield, Griggsville, 4 mi N , S H, Jellystone Camping (6mi), st police

31 to Pittsfield, New Salem, 5 mi S H Jellystone Camping,

20 IL 106, Barry, S FastStop/dsl/24hr, Shell/dsl a Subway, Wendy's Ice House Inn

10 IL 96, to Payson, Hull

4a I-172, N to Quincy

1 IL 106, to Hull

0mm Illinois/Missouri state line, Mississippi River.

Exits 157 & 156 are in Missouri.

157 to Hannibal, MO 179, S Ayerco, BP, Phillips 66, Shell/dsl Mark Twain Dinette, Subway Best Value Inn, Best Way Inn, Best Western, Hotel Mark Twain auto repair, visitor info

156 US 61, New London, Palmyra. **I-72 begins/ends in Hannibal, MO on US 61,** N BP, Casey's/dsl, Conoco/dsl, Murphy USA/dsl Burger King, Country Kitchen, Domino's, Gabriella's Mexican, Golden Corral, Hardee's, LJ Silver, McDonald's, Mi Mexico, Pizza Hut, Royal Garden, Rustic Oak Grill, Sonic, Subway, Taco Bell $General, $Tree, Aldi Foods, BigLots, Ford, JC Penney, Lowe's, Walmart, 0-2 mi S Ayerco, Shell/dsl Cassano's Subs, China King, DQ, Gran Rio Mexican, Hardee's, Jimmy John's, KFC, Logue's Rest, Wendy's Days Inn, EconoLodge, Hannibal Inn, Holiday Inn Express, Motel 6, Super 8 $General, AT&T, AutoZone, Buick/Chevrolet, Chrysler/Dodge/Jeep, County Mkt Foods, CVS Drug, O'Reilly Parts, Walgreens

INTERSTATE 74

Exit # Services

221mm Illinois/Indiana state line, Central/Eastern Time Zone

220 Lynch Rd, Danville, N Marathon/dsl (1mi), Shell/dsl Big Boy Best Western, Hampton Inn, Holiday Inn Express, Motel 6, Quality Inn, Red Roof Inn, Sleep Inn, Super 8

DANVILLE

216 Bowman Ave, Danville, N Mobil/dsl, Phillips 66, Godfather's, KFC, McDonald's city park, CVS Dr Walgreens

215b a US 150, IL 1, Gilbert St, Danville, N Casey's/dsl, Circle K Arby's, El Toro, La Potosina, LJ Silver, McDonald's, Pi Hut, Steak'n Shake, Subway, Taco Bell Best Western, D Inn H, Aldi Foods, BigLots, S Casey's/dsl, Marath Circle K/dsl Burger King, Green Jade Chinese, Mike's G Monical's Pizza, Rich's Rest. $General, AutoZone, Big Buick/Chevrolet/GMC, Country Mkt, Family$, Forest Glen P serve Camping (11mi), Toyota/Scion

214 G St, Tilton

210 US 150, MLK Dr, 2 mi N Marathon Little Nugget Ste H, to Kickapoo SP

208mm **Welcome Ctr wb, full facilities, info, litter barrels, p walk vending**

206 Oakwood, S Casey's (1mi), Phillips 66/Subway/dsl/scal Pilot/PJ Fresh/dsl/scales/24hr McDonald's $Gen

200 IL 49 N, to Rankin

197 IL 49 S, Ogden, S Phillips 66/Godfather's/dsl Ric Rest. city park

192 St Joseph, S Casey's, Shell/dsl DQ, Monical's Piz Subway antiques

185 IL 130, University Ave

184 US 45, Cunningham Ave, Urbana, N F&F Hyundai, K Mazda, Toyota/Scion, VW, S Marathon/Circle K/Subw dsl, Shell/dsl Arby's, Cracker Barrel, Hickory River BB McDonald's, Steak'n Shake, Toro Loco, Wendy's Eastla Suites, Motel 6 $General, auto repair, vet

183 Lincoln Ave, Urbana, S Circle K/dsl, Marathon/Circle dsl Urbana Garden Rest. Comfort Suites, Holiday Express, Knights Inn, Ramada Inn, Sleep Inn, Wyndham Garc H Harley-Davidson, to U of IL

182 Neil St (same as 181), Champaign, N Alexander's Stea Bob Evans, Buca Italian, Buca Italian, Food Court, McDonal Old Chicago, Olive Garden, Panera Bread, Taco Bell, TGIFriday TGIFriday's, Za's Italian Baymont Inn, La Quinta, Quality I Red Roof Inn, Super 8 Barnes&Noble, Bergner's, Cadill Chevrolet, Chrysler/Dodge/Jeep, Dick's, Dick's, Field&Strea Field&Stream, Gordman's, Hobby Lobby, Kohl's, Macy's, m Mercedes/Volvo, Office Depot, Sears Hometown, Sears Hom town, TJ Maxx, Verizon, Verizon, S Mobil/Circle K

CHAMPAIGN

181 Prospect Ave (same as 182), Champaign, N Murphy US dsl Applebee's, Best Wok, Buffalo Wild Wings, Burg King, Chili's, China Town, Chipotle, Chipotle, Culver's, Denny Denny's, Fazoli's, Firehouse Subs, Firehouse Subs, Five Gu Five Guys, Hometown Buffet, Longhorn Steaks, O'Charley Oishi Asian, Outback Steaks, Panda Express, Penn Sta Sub Red Lobster, Ruby Tuesday, Ryan's, Starbucks, Steak'n Sha Subway, Super Niro's Gyros, Super Niro's Gyros, Wendy's Candlewood Suites, Country Inn&Suites, Courtyard, Drury In Extended Stay America, Fairfield Inn, Residence Inn, Residen Inn, ValuePlace Hotel, Wingate Inn $Tree, Advance Par Aldi Foods, Aldi Foods, AT&T, Best Buy, Ford/Lincoln, Fo Lincoln, Gander Mtn, Jo-Ann, Jo-Ann, Lowe's, Meijer/dsl, Me ards, Michael's, Nissan, Nissan, Petsmart, Radio Shack, Sar Club/gas, Staples, Target, Tires+, Verizon, Verizon, Walma Subway, S Freedom/dsl, Marathon/Circle K, Mobil/Jim John's, Phillips 66/dsl, Phillips 66/dsl Arby's, Dos Rea Mexican, Dunkin Donuts, LJ Silver, McDonald's, McDonald Popeye's, Popeye's Best Value Inn, Best Value Inn, Da

INTERSTATE 74 Cont'd

181	Continued
	Inn [O] $General, CarX, Home Depot, NAPA, Tire Barn, Walgreens
179b a	I-57, N to Chicago, S to Memphis
174	Lake of the Woods Rd, Prairieview Rd, N [gas] BP, Casey's, Mobil/Circle K/dsl [O] $General, auto repair, Lake of the Woods SP, Tin Cup RV Park, S [gas] Marathon/Subway/dsl [food] McDonald's
172	IL 47, Mahomet, N [O] R&S RV Sales, S [gas] Mobil/dsl, Shell/Domino's/dsl [food] Arby's, Azteca, DQ, El Toro Mexican, HenHouse Rest., Monical's Pizza, Peking House, Subway, The Wok [lodging] Heritage Inn [O] Ace Hardware, CVS Drug, IGA Foods, NAPA, Walgreens
166	Mansfield, S [gas] Phillips 66/dsl [O] Mansfield Gen. Store/Rest.
159	IL 54, Farmer City, S [gas] Casey's/dsl, Huck's/Godfather's/dsl [food] Imo's Cafe, Subway [lodging] Budget Motel, Days Inn [O] $General, NAPA, to Clinton Lake RA, USPO
156mm	**[RS] both lanes, full [handicapped] facilities, litter barrels, petwalk [phone] [picnic] playground, vending**
152	US 136, to Heyworth
149	Le Roy, N [gas] Freedom/dsl, Love's/Arby's/dsl/scales/24hr [food] Jack's Cafe, McDonald's, Roma Pizza, Subway [lodging] Holiday Inn Express [O] $General, Doc's Drug, IGA Foods, NAPA, to Moraine View SP, TrueValue, S [gas] Shell/Woody's Rest./dsl/scales/24hr [lodging] Days Inn [O] camping, Clinton Lake
142	Downs, N [gas] BP/Pizza/Subs/dsl/24hr [O] USPO
135	US 51, Bloomington, N [gas] Huck's/dsl, Mobil/Circle K/dsl [food] McDonald's, Pizza Hut [O] $General, S [gas] FastStop/dsl
134b[157]	N [O] [H] to airport, Bloomington, Veterans Pkwy
134a	I-55, N to Chicago, S to St Louis, I-74 E
I-74 and I-55 run together 6 mi. See I-55 exits 157b-160b a.	
127[163]	I-55, N to Chicago, S to St Louis, I-74 W to Peoria
125	US 150, to Bloomington, Mitsubishi Motorway
123mm	**weigh sta wb**
122mm	**weigh sta eb**
120	Carlock, N [gas] BP/dsl/repair [food] Carlock Rest., S [O] Kamp Komfort Camping (Apr-Oct)
114.5mm	**[RS] both lanes, full [handicapped] facilities, litter barrels, petwalk [phone] [picnic] vending**
113.5mm	Mackinaw River
112	IL 117, Goodfield, N [gas] Shell/Subway/dsl [food] Busy Corner Rest. [O] Eureka Coll, Jellystone Camping (1mi), Reagan Home, to Timberline RA, USPO
102b a	Morton, N [gas] BP/rest./dsl, Mobil/Arby's/dsl/scales/24hr [food] Burger King, Cracker Barrel, Culver's, Hardee's, Ruby Tuesday, Steak'n Shake, Taco Bell [lodging] Baymont Inn, Best Value Inn, Best Western, Holiday Inn Express, Quality Inn, Travelodge [O] Chrysler/Dodge/Jeep, Farm&Fleet, Freightliner, Walmart/Subway , S [gas] BP/Circle K, Marathon/Circle K, Shell/Subway/dsl/24hr [food] China Dragon, Domino's, Great Harvest Bread, Jimmy John's, KFC, La Fiesta, Lin's Buffet, McDonald's, Monical's Pizza, Pizza Hut, Pizza Ranch [O] $Tree, Buick/GMC, CVS Drug, Ford, K-Mart, Kroger/dsl, O'Reilly Parts, Verizon
101	I-155 S, to Lincoln
99	I-474 W, [O] airport
98	Pinecrest Dr
96	95c (from eb), US 150, IL 8, E Washington St, E Peoria, N [gas] Fast Stop/dsl [food] Subway, Super Gyros [lodging] Super 8 [O] O'Reilly Parts
95b	(from eb) IL 116, to Metamora, N [gas] Shell/dsl [food] Burger King [lodging] Hampton Inn, Paradise Hotel [O] casino

BLOOMINGTON

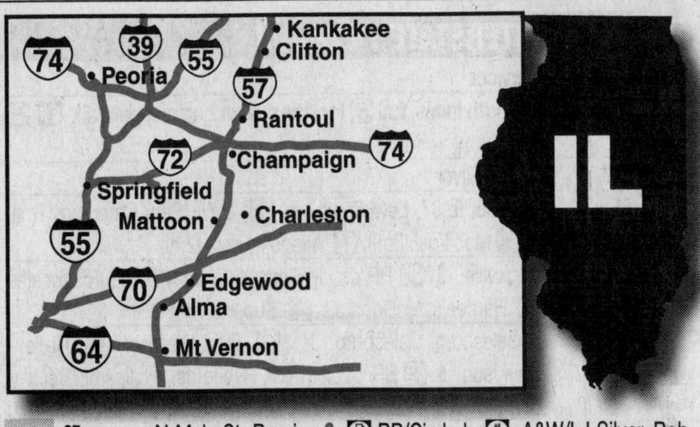

95a	N Main St, Peoria, S [gas] BP/Circle k [food] A&W/LJ Silver, Bob Evans, Chipotle Mexican, Firehouse Pizza/subs, Grand Village Buffet, Hardee's, IHOP, Jersey Mikes, Jimmy John's, Johnny's Italian Steaks, McDonald's, Noodles&Co, Panda Express, Papa Murphy's, Pizza Hut, Popeyes, Potbelly, Red Robin, Subway, Taco Bell, Tequilas Grill [lodging] Best Western, Fairfield Inn, Holiday Inn, Motel 6 [O] $Tree, Advance Parts, Aldi Foods, AT&T, Costco/gas, CVS Drug, GNC, Goodyear/auto, Gordman's, Kohl's, Kroger, Ross, Target, Verizon, Walgreens
94	IL 40, RiverFront Dr, S [gas] Hucks/Godfather's/dsl [food] Applebee's, Arby's, Buffalo Wild Wings, Chili's, Culver's, Granite City Grill, Logan's Roadhouse, Lorena's Mexican, Ming's Rest., Panera Bread, Papa John's, Qdoba Mexican, Steak'n Shake, TX Roadhouse, Uncle Buck's Grill [lodging] Embassy Suites [O] Bass Pro Shop, Lowe's, PetsMart, Radio Shack, Verizon, Walmart/Subway
93.5mm	Illinois River
93b	US 24, IL 29, Peoria, N [gas] BP, S [lodging] Mark Twain Hotel [O] civic ctr
93a	Jefferson St, Peoria, N [gas] BP, S [food] Two 25 Grill [lodging] Mark Twain Hotel, Marriott, Sheraton [O] to civic ctr
92b	Glendale Ave, Peoria, S [O] [H] downtown
92a	IL 40 N, Knoxville Ave, Peoria, S [lodging] Sheraton [O] [H]
91	University St, Peoria
90	Gale Ave, Peoria, S [gas] Marathon [O] to Bradley U
89	US 150, War Memorial Dr, Peoria, **N on War Memorial** [gas] BP/Circle K, Marathon/dsl, Shell [food] Arby's, Avanti's Rest., Baskin-Robbins/Dunkin Donuts, Biaggi's Ristorante, Bob Evans, Burger King, Chick-fil-A, Chipotle Mexican, ChuckeCheese, Dunkin Donuts, Five Guys, Golden Corral, Hokkaido Hibachi, Hometown Buffet, IHOP, Mango Grill, McDonald's, Panda Express, Panera Bread, Papa Murphy's, Perkins, Red Lobster, Sonic, Steak'n Shake, Subway, Wendy's, Wild Berries Rest. [lodging] Baymont Inn, Comfort Suites, Courtyard, EconoLodge, Extended Stay America, Grand Hotel, Quality Inn, Red Roof Inn, Residence Inn, SpringHill Suites, Super 8 [O] $Tree, Aldi Foods, AT&T, AutoZone, Barnes&Noble, Best Buy, Chevrolet/Cadillac, Hobby Lobby, JC Penney, Lowe's, Macy's, mall, Midas, NAPA, PetsMart, Ross, Sears/auto, Shop'n Save Foods, Target, The Fresh Mkt, Tires+, U-Haul, Verizon, vet, Walgreens, Walmart/Subway
88	to US 150, War Memorial Dr, same as 89
87b a	I-474 E, IL 6, N to Chillicothe, S [O] airport
82	Edwards Rd, Kickapoo, N [gas] Mobil/dsl/service, Shell/Subway/dsl [food] Jubilee Café [O] to Jubilee Coll SP, S [O] USPO, Wildlife Prairie SP
75	Brimfield, Oak Hill, N [gas] Casey's/dsl
Exit #	**Services**
71	to IL 78, to Canton, Elmwood

PEORIA

IL

= gas = food = lodging = other = rest stop

INTERSTATE 74 Cont'd

GALESBURG

Exit #	Services
62mm	**both lanes, full facilities, litter barrels, petwalk RV dump, vending**
61.5mm	Spoon River
54	US 150, IL 97, Lewistown, N TravL Park Camping (1mi), S Mobil/dsl (2mi) Alfano's Pizza (2mi)
51	Knoxville, S BP/dsl, Phillips 66/Charley's Subs/dsl/scales Hardee's, McDonald's Super 8
48b a	E Galesburg, Galesburg, N Best Western Harley-Davidson, S BP/Circle K/dsl, HyVee/dsl, Phillps 66/Beck's/dsl DQ, Hardee's, Jalisco Mexican, KFC, Marco's Pizza, McDonald's, Pizza Hut, Subway, Taco Bell Holiday Inn Express Family$, Firestone, HyVee Foods, Lincoln-Douglas Debates, Sav-A-Lot Foods, to Sandburg Birthplace, Walgreens
46b a	US 34, to Monmouth, N Nichol's dsl Service, **1 mi** S Buffalo Wild Wings, Crazy Buffet H Aldi Foods, Menards, Radio Shack, Toyota/Scion, Verizon, vet, Walmart/Subway
32	IL 17, Woodhull, N BP/dsl Subway, S Pilot/dsl/scales/24hr Shady Lakes Camping (8mi)
30mm	**wb, full facilities, litter barrels, petwalk playground, RV dump, vending**
28mm	**eb, full facilities, litter barrels, petwalk playground, RV dump, vending**
24	IL 81, Andover, N camping, Casey's (2mi)
14mm	I-80, E to Chicago, I-80/I-280 W to Des Moines
8mm	**weigh sta wb**
6mm	**weigh sta eb**

MOLINE

Exit #	Services
5b	US 6, Moline, S Shell/dsl Bare Bones BBQ, McDonald's, MT Jack's Best Inn, Country Inn&Suites, Hampton Inn, Holiday Inn Express, La Quinta, Motel 6, Quality Inn
5a	I-280 W, US 6 W, to Des Moines
4b a	IL 5, John Deere Rd, Moline, N BP/7-11, Phillips 66, Shell/dsl Applebee's, Burger King, Chipotle Mexican, Culver's, Hungy Hobo, Osaka Buffet, Panera Bread, Ryan's, Starbucks, Steak'n Shake, Subway, Wendy's Residence Inn $Tree, Cadillac, Farm&Fleet, Honda, Hyundai, Lowe's, Menard's, Radio Shack, Sam's Club/dsl, Staples, Subaru, Tires+, Toyota/Scion, Volvo, Walmart/Subway, S BP/7-11 A&W/LJ Silver, Arby's, Buffalo Wild Wings, China Cafe, Denny's, KFC, Los Agaves, McDonald's, New Mandarin Chinese, Qdoba Mexican, Taco Bell Best Western, Comfort Inn, Fairfield Inn, Motel 6 $General, Best Buy, Buick/GMC, Chevrolet, Chrysler/Dodge/Jeep, Dillards, Firestone/auto, Ford/Lincoln, Goodyear/auto, Gordman's, Hancock Fabrics, JC Penney, mall, Mazda, Nissan, PetCo, Von Maur, Walgreens, Younkers
3	23rd Ave, Moline, N Economy Inn
2	7th Ave, Moline, S QuikStop La Casa Mexican riverfront, to civic ctr, USPO
1	3rd Ave (from eb), Moline, S QuickStop Stoney Creek Inn
0mm	Illinois/Iowa state line, Mississippi River, **Exits 4-1 are in Iowa.**

BETTENDORF

Exit #	Services
4	US 67, Grant St, State St, Bettendorf, N Hardee's, McDonald's, Ross' Rest./24hr, Subway Twin Bridges Motel, Waterfront Conv Ctr CarQuest, S Village Inn Rest. City Ctr Motel $General
3	Middle Rd, Locust St, Bettendorf, S BP/dsl China Taste, Grinders Rest., McDonald's, Pizza Ranch, Red Ginger Asian, Starbucks, Subway Hilton Garden H AT&T,
3	Continued Burlington Coats, Hobby Lobby, Home Depot, Marshall's, Schuck's Foods, Verizon, Walgreens
2	US 6 W, Spruce Hills Dr, Bettendorf, N BP/dsl, Phillips 66 Domino's, Old Chicago Pizza Courtyard, EconoLodge, Ramada Inn, Super 8, The Lodge Hotel/rest. U-Haul, S Hyvee Gas Applebee's, KFC, Panera Bread, Red Lobster Days Inn, Fairfield Inn, Holiday Inn, La Quinta Buick/GMC, Gander Mtn, Gordman's, Kohl's, Lowe's, PetCo, Sam's Club/gas, st patrol
1	53rd St, Hamilton, N BP Bad Boyz Pizza, Biaggi's Italian, Buffalo Wild Wings, Chili's, Coldstone, Granite City Rest., Los Agaves, Maggie Moo's, Osaka Steaks, Panchero's Mexican, Red Lantern Chinese, Red Robin, TX Roadhouse Hampton Inn, Staybridge Suites H Harley-Davidson, HyVee Foods, Michael's, Old Navy, TJ Maxx, Walgreens, S Murphy USA/dsl, Shell/dsl Arby's, Azteca Mexican, Burger King, Chick-fil-A, China Cafe, Chipotle Mexican, DQ, Dynasty Buffet, Golden Corral, HuHot, Hungry Hobo, IHOP, La Rancherita, Noodles&Co, PepperJax Grill, Quiznos, Sonic, Starbucks, Steak'n Shake, Subway, Taco Bell, Village Inn Rest., Wendy's Sleep Inn $Tree, Aldi Foods, AT&T, Best Buy, Dick's, Discount Tire, Meineke, PetsMart, Staples, Target, Verizon, Walmart

I-74 begins/ends on I-80, exit 298. Exits 1-4 are in Iowa.

INTERSTATE 80

CHICAGO AREA

Exit #	Services
163mm	Illinois/Indiana state line
161	US 6, IL 83, Torrence Ave, N BP Burger King, Chili's, Culver's, Dixie Kitchen, Hooters, IHOP, Kenny's Ribs, Liang's Garden, New China Buffet, Oberweiss, Olive Garden, Shark's, Taco-Burrito's, Wendy's Comfort Suites, Days Inn, Extended Stay America, Holiday Inn Express, Howard Johnson Express, Red Roof Inn, Sleep Inn, Super 8 $General, $Tree, Aldi Foods, AT&T, Best Buy, CarEx, Chrysler/Jeep, Curves, Dunkin Donuts, Fannie May Candies, Firestone/auto, Home Depot, Honda, JustTires, K-Mart, PepBoys, Radio Shack, Ultra Foods, Walmart, S Citgo, Marathon, Mobil Burger King, China Chef, DQ, Dunkin Donuts, Jonny's K's Cafe, McDonald's/playplace, Mr Gyros, Popolono's Italian, Subway Pioneer Motel Chevrolet, Petsmart, SunRise Foods, Tuesday Morning, vet, Walgreens
160b	I-94 W, to Chicago, **tollway begins wb, ends eb**
160a	IL 394 S, to Danville
159mm	**Oasis,** Mobil/dsl McDonald's, Panda Express, Starbucks, Subway
157	IL 1, Halsted St, N Citgo/dsl, Marathon/dsl Burger King Chicago Southland Hotel, Clarion, Comfort Inn, Comfort Suites, EconoLodge, Regency Inn, S Citgo, Delta Sonic, Shell, Speedway Applebee's, Arby's, Athens Gyros, Boston Mkt, Burger King, Chili's, Dunkin Donuts, Fannie May Candies, KFC, McDonald's, Panda Express, Pizza Hut, Popeye's, Starbucks, Subway, Taco Bell, Washington Square Rest., Wendy's, White Castle Homewood Hotel, Super 8 $Tree, Aldi Foods, AT&T, Best Buy, Chevrolet, Discount Tire, Fanny May Candies, Firestone/auto, Goodyear/auto, Home Depot, Jewel-Osco, Jo-Ann Fabrics, K-Mart, Kohl's, Menards, PepBoys, PetCo, Radio Shack, Target, TJ Maxx, Walgreens
156	Dixie Hwy (from eb, no return), S Mobil Leona's Rest. golf
155	I-294 N, **Tri-State Tollway, toll plaza**

IL

INTERSTATE 80 Cont'd

Exit #	Services
154	Kedzie Ave (from eb, no return), N [gas] Speedway, S [O] [H]
151b a	I-57 (exits left from both directions), N to Chicago, S to Memphis
148b a	IL 43, Harlem Ave, N [gas] Speedway/dsl [food] Al's Beef, Buffalo Wild Wings, Burger King, Cracker Barrel, Culver's, Dunkin Donuts, Eggi Grill, Hamada of Japan, Pop's Italian Beef, Quizno's, Taco Fresco, Tin Fish Grill, Wendy's [lodging] Comfort Suites, Fairfield Inn, Hampton Inn, Holiday Inn, La Quinta, Sleep Inn, Wingate Inn, S [food] Arby's, Boston's Grill, Subway, Taco Bell, TGIFriday's [O] ampitheater, Best Buy, Carmax, Kohl's, Michael's, PetsMart, SuperTarget
147.5mm	**weigh sta wb**
145b a	US 45, 96th Ave, N [food] 4K Asian, Arby's, Arrenello's Pizza, Baskin-Robbins/Dunkin Donuts, Quizno's, Tokyo Steaks, TX Roadhouse [lodging] Country Inn&Suites, Hilton Garden [O] Harley-Davidson, **0-2 mi** S [gas] BP, Clark, Gas City, Shell/Circle K/dsl/24hr [food] A&W, Applebee's, Beggar's Pizza, Denny's, DQ, KFC, Mindy's Ribs, Nick's Rest., Rising Sun Chinese, Stoney Pt Grill, Subway, Wendy's, White Castle [lodging] Super 8 [O] Brookhaven Foods, CVS Drug, repair, Tuesday Morning
143mm	**weigh sta eb**
140	SW Hwy, **I-355 N Tollway**, US 6 S
137	US 30, New Lenox, N [food] Williamson's Rest. [O] K-Mart, S [gas] Speedway/dsl [food] Beggar's Pizza, Burger King, KFC, LJ Silver/Papa Joe's, McDonald's/playplace, Paisono's Pizza, Pizza Hut, Subway, Taco Bell [O] Ace Hardware, city park, Goodyear/auto, Jewel-Osco/dsl, vet, Walgreens
134	Briggs St, N [gas] Citgo, Speedway [O] [H] S [gas] Shell/dsl, Valero/dsl [O] EZ Lube, Martin Camping, US RV Ctr
133	Richards St
132b a	US 52, IL 53, Chicago St
131.5mm	Des Plaines River
131	US 6, Meadow Ave, N [O] to Riverboat Casino
130b a	IL 7, Larkin Ave, N [gas] Clark, Delta Sonic/dsl, Marathon/24hr, Mobil, Shell/24hr, Speedway [food] A&W/KFC, Baskin-Robbins/Dunkin Donuts, Bellagio Pizzaria, Bob Evans, Boston Mkt, Burger King, DQ, JJ Fish&Chicken, McDonald's, Quizno's, Steak'n Shake, Subway, Taco Bell, Wendy's, White Castle [lodging] Budget Inn, Comfort Inn, Holiday Inn, Motel 6, Red Roof Inn, Super 8 [O] [H] 7-11, Aldi Foods, Cadillac/Chevrolet, Discount Tire, Ford, Goodyear/auto, K-Mart, Pepboys, Radio Shack, Sam's Club/gas, to Coll of St Francis, vet, S [gas] Citgo [O] auto repair
127	Houbolt Rd, to Joliet, N [gas] 7-11, BP/deli [food] Arby's, Burger King, China Kitchen, Cracker Barrel, Dunkin Donuts, Heros Sports Grill, Jimmy John's, McDonald's, Papa&Nana's Pizza [lodging] Fairfield Inn, Hampton Inn, Ramada Inn [O] Riverboat Casino
126b a	I-55, N to Chicago, S to St Louis
125.5mm	Du Page River
122	Minooka, N [gas] Citgo/dsl, S [gas] BP, Pilot/Arby's/scales/dsl/24hr [food] 2-Fers Pizza, Baskin-Robbins/Dunkin Donuts, KFC, McDonald's/playplace, Rosati's Pizza, Subway, Taco Bell, Wendy's [O] $General, 7-11
119mm	**[RS] wb, full [handicapped] facilities, litter barrels, petwalk [phone] [picnic] playground, vending**
117mm	**[RS] eb, full [handicapped] facilities, litter barrels, petwalk [phone] [picnic] playground, vending**
116	Brisbin Rd
112	IL 47, Morris, N [gas] Marathon/dsl, Pilot/Subway/dsl/scales/24hr, TA/BP/Quiznos/scales/dsl/24hr/ @ [food] Bellacino's, Chili's, IHOP [lodging] Comfort Inn, Days Inn, Holiday Inn Express, Quality Inn [O] $General, Menards, URGENT CARE, S [gas] BP/dsl, Mobil/dsl, Shell, Spirit [food] Burger King, Culver's, DQ, Dunkin Donuts, Hong Kong Chinese, KFC/LJ Silver, Little Caesar's, Maria's Ristorante, McDonald's, Morris Diner, Pizza Hut, Rosati's Pizza, Subway, Taco Bell, Wendy's [lodging] Park Motel, Sherwood Oaks Motel, Super 8 [O] [H] $Tree, Aldi Foods, AT&T, AutoZone, Big R Store, Buick/Cadillac/Chevrolet, Chrysler/Dodge/Jeep, Fisher Parts, Ford, GMC, GNC, Jewel-Osco, Radio Shack, to Stratton SP, transmissions/repair, Verizon, Walgreens, Walmart/Subway

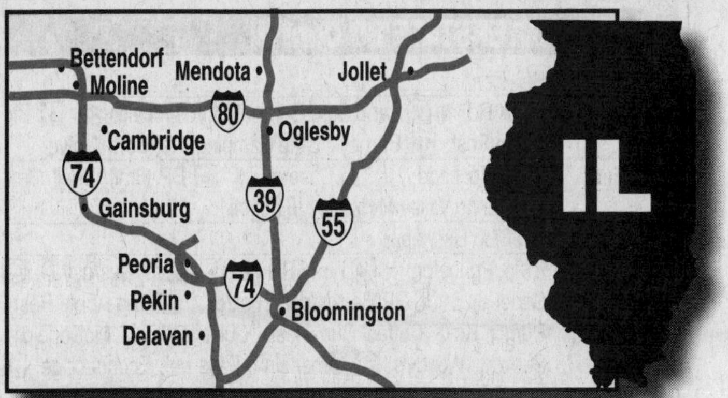

MORRIS

Exit #	Services
112	Continued
105	to Seneca
97	to Marseilles, S [gas] Shell/dsl [O] Four Star Camping (5mi), Glenwood Camping (4mi), to Illini SP
93	IL 71, Ottawa, N [gas] Pilot/Road Ranger/Subway/dsl/scales/24hr, Shell/rest./dsl, S [food] Hank's Farm Rest., New Chiam [O] [H]
92.5mm	Fox River
90	IL 23, Ottawa, N [gas] BP/Subway [food] Arby's, Cracker Barrel, Taco Bell [lodging] Hampton Inn, Holiday Inn Express [O] AT&T, F&F, Honda, Toyota/Scion, Walmart/McDonald's, S [gas] BP/dsl/LP, Thornton's/dsl [food] Culver's, Dunkin Donuts, Hardee's, KFC/LJ Silver, Papa Murphy's, Sunfield Rest. [lodging] EconoLodge, Fairfield Inn, Super 8, Surrey Motel [O] [H], $Tree, Aldi Foods, Ford/Lincoln/Kia, Harley-Davidson, Kroger, O'Reilly Parts, Radio Shack, USPO
81	IL 178, Utica, N [gas] Loves/McDonald's/Subway/dsl/scales/24hr [O] Hickory Hollow Camping, KOA (2mi), S [gas] Shell/Jimmy Johns/dsl [lodging] Starved Rock Inn [O] repair, to Starved Rock SP, visitor info
79b a	I-39, US 51, N to Rockford, S to Bloomington
77.5mm	Little Vermilion River
77	IL 351, La Salle, S [gas] FLYING J/Denny's/dsl/scales/24hr [food] UpTown Grill (3mi) [lodging] Daniels Motel (1mi) [O] st police
75	IL 251, Peru, N [gas] BP, Shell/rest./dsl/24hr [food] 4Star Rest., Arby's, McDonald's, Olive Garden, Starbucks, Taco Bell [lodging] Holiday Inn Express, Quality Inn, Super 8 [O] Kohl's, Petsmart, Walmart/Dunkin Donuts/Subway, S [gas] BP, Shell [food] Applebee's, Buffalo Wild Wings, Burger King, Culver's, DQ, IHOP, Jalepeno's Mexican, Jimmy John's, Master Buffet, McDonald's/Mi Margarita, Papa John's, Pizza Hut, Red Lobster, Steak'n Shake, Subway, Wendy's [lodging] Fairfield Inn, Hampton Inn, La Quinta [O] [H] $Tree, Advance Parts, Aldi Foods, AT&T, AutoZone, BigLots, Buick/GMC, Chevrolet/Mercedes, Chrysler/Dodge/Jeep, CVS Drug, Ford/Hyundai/Lincoln, Goodyear/auto, Hobby Lobby, Home Depot, HyVee Food/dsl, JC Penney, Jo-Ann Fabrics, Marshall's, Menards, Mercedes, Midas, NAPA, Nissan, O'Reilly Parts, Sears/auto, Staples, Target, Verizon, Walgreens

PERU

CHICAGO AREA

INTERSTATE 80 Cont'd

Exit #	Services
73	Plank Rd, N Sapp Bros/Burger King/dsl/scales/ @ Big Apple Rest. Barney's Lake Camping, Kenworth/Volvo
70	IL 89, to Ladd, N Casey's, S BP (3mi), Shell (3mi) Spring Valley Motel golf
61	I-180, to Hennepin
56	IL 26, Princeton, N Road Ranger/[illegible]/scales/dsl/ @ Super 8, S BP/Beck's/dsl, Shell/dsl Big Apple Rest., Burger King, Coffee Cup Rest., Culver's, KFC, McDonald's, Subway, Wendy's AmericInn, Days Inn, EconoLodge $General, antiques, AutoZone, Buick/Cadillac/Chevrolet, O'Reilly Parts, Pennzoil, Sullivan's Food/gas/E-85, vet, Walmart
51mm	**both lanes, full facilities, litter barrels, petwalk playground, RV dump, vending**
45	IL 40, N antiques, to Ronald Reagan Birthplace (21mi), S Hennepin Canal SP
44mm	Hennepin Canal
33	IL 78, to Kewanee, Annawan, N Shabbona RV Ctr/Camp (3mi), S Cenex/dsl, FS/dsl/E-85, Shell/Subway/dsl Best Western to Johnson-Sauk Tr SP
27	to US 6, Atkinson, N Casey's (1mi)
19	IL 82, Geneseo, N BP/dsl, Casey's/dsl Culvers, DQ, Happy Joe's Pizza, Hardee's, McDonald's, New China, Pizza Hut, Subway, Sweet Pea's Grill Best Western, Super 8 (2 mi) $General, Ford, SaveALot Foods, Verizon, Walgreens, Walmart, S Los Ranchitos Mexican
10	I-74, I-280, W to Moline, E to Peoria
9	US 6, to Geneseo, N Lavender Crest Winery/Cafe, S Niabi Zoo
7	Colona, N Shell/dsl Country Fixins Rest.
5mm	Rock River
4a	IL 5, IL 92, W to Silvis, S Lundeen's Camping, st police
4b	I-88, IL 92, E to Rock Falls
2mm	**weigh sta both lanes**
1.5mm	**Welcome Ctr eb full facilities, info, litter barrels, petwalk scenic overlook**
1	IL 84, 20th St, Great River Rd, E Moline, N BP/dsl Bros Rest. camping, The Great River Rd, **3 mi** S camping
0mm	Illinois/Iowa state line, Mississippi River

INTERSTATE 88

Exit #	Services
139.5mm	**I-88 begins/ends on I-290.**
139	I-294, S to Indiana, N to Milwaukee
138mm	**toll plaza**
137	IL 83 N, Cermak Rd, N Clubhouse Rest., Ditkas Rest., McDonald's Marriott, Renaissance Inn Barnes&Noble, Lord&Taylor, Macy's, Nieman-Marcus
136	IL 83 S, Midwest Rd (from eb), N Shell/Circle K All-Stars Rest., Burger King, Capri Ristorante, Chipotle Mexican, Denny's, Dunkin Donuts, Eggstacy, Giordano's Rest., Jamba Juice, McDonalds, Noodles&Co, Quizno's, Redstones, Star bucks, Subway, Subway Holiday Inn, La Quinta AT&T, Costco/gas, Home Depot, Nordstrom's, Old Navy, TJ Maxx, Walgreens, World Mkt
134	Highland Ave (no EZ wb return), N Baker's Square, Bouna Beef, Brio Grille, Buca Italian, Burger King, Capital Grille, Champps Grill, Cheeseburger Paradise, Cici's, Claimjumper Rest., Fuddruckers, Harry Caray's, Hooters, Joe's Crabshack,
134	Continued Kona Grill, Kyoto, McCormick & Schmick's, Miller's Steakhous Olive Garden, Panera Bread, PF Chang's, Portilo's Hotdog Potbelly's, Qdoba, Red Lobster, Rockbottom Brewery, Ru Tuesday, Starbucks, Subway, Taylor Brewing Co, TGIFriday Uncle Milio's, Weber Grill Comfort Inn, Embassy Suite Holiday Inn Express, Homestead Studios, Hyatt Place, Marrio Red Roof Inn, Westin Hotel Best Buy, Firestone/au Home Depot, JC Penney, Kohl's, mall, Marshall's, PetsMa Vonmaur, S Parkers Ocean Grill
132	I-355 N (from wb)
131	I-355 S (from eb)
130	IL 53 (from wb), **1 mi** N BP, Mobil McDonald Walmart
127	Naperville Rd, N Mullen's Grill Hilton, Wyndam, S Mobil Buona Beef, Froots, HoneyBaked Ham, Jason's De Maggiano's, McDonald's, Morton's Steaks, Pizza Hut, Subway, Taco Fresco, TGIFriday's, Wendy's, White Chocolate Gr Best Western, Courtyard, Days Inn, Fairfield Inn, Hampto Inn, Holiday Inn Select Dodge, Ford, Kia, Office Depo Radio Shack, Subaru
125	Winfield Rd, N BP, Mobil Hamton Inn Walgreens, S Arby's, Atlanta Bread, Buffalo Wild Wings, C Pizza Kitchen, Chipotle Mexican, Corner Bakery Cafe, GoRoma, Jamba Juice, Max&Erma's, McDonald's, Potbelly's, Re Robin, Rockbottom Brewery, Starbucks, StirCrazy Grill Hilton Garden, Springhill Suites SuperTarget
123	IL 59, N Gas City/dsl Omega Rest Carmax, S BP, Mobil/dsl, Speedway Baskin Robbins/Dunkin Donut Caribou Coffee, Cracker Barrel, Danny's Grill, Jimmy John's Lee's Garden, Oberweis, Spicy Pickle, Starbucks, Steak Shake, Subway, TX Roadhouse, Wendy's Extended Sta America, Fairfield Inn, Red Roof Inn, Sleep Inn, SpringHi Suites, Towneplace Suites 7-11, CVS Drug, Walgreens
119	Farnsworth Ave, N BP, Shell McDonald's, Millet's Gri Papa Bear Rest., Quizno's, Sonic, Starbucks Fox Valley In Motel 6 Firestone/auto, Premium Outlets/Famous Brand Walmart, S Marathon, Phillips 66/dsl, Shell, Speedwa Baskin-Robbins/Dunkin Donuts, Drive-Thru, Little Caesars, Mc Donald's, Mike&Denise's Pizza, Subway, Taco Be 7-11, AutoZone, Family$, Goodyear, Walgreens
118mm	**toll plaza**
117	IL 31, IL 56, to Aurora, Batavia, N Citgo/dsl A&W 7-11, S Mobil, Thornton's Arby's, Baskin-Robbins Dunkin Donuts, Burger King, Culver's, Denny's, KFC, LJ Silve McDonald's, Nikary's, Popeye's, Quizno's, Rest., Subway, Taco Bell, White Castle Baymont Inn $Store, Ace Hardware, AutoZone, Cermak Foods, Firestone, GNC, Jewel/Osco Murray's Parts, Radio Shack, U-Haul, Walgreens
115	Orchard Rd, N McDonald's, Subway Best Buy, Chrysler/Dodge/Jeep, Ford/Lincoln, Hyundai, JC Penney, Michaels Nissan, PetCo, Subaru, Target, Woodman's/dsl, **0-2 mi** S 7-11 A&W/KFC, Arby's, Buffalo Wild Wings, Chili's, Col Stone, IHOP, Jimmy John's, Panera Bread, Papa Saverio's, Pizza Hut, Quizno's, Starbucks, Wendy's Candlewood Suite Hampton Inn, Holiday Inn AT&T, CVS Drug, Discount Tire Home Depot, Lowe's Whse, Office Depot, T-Moble
114	IL 56W, to US 30 (from wb, no EZ return), to Sugar Grove
109	IL 47 (from eb), Elburn
94	Peace Rd, to IL 38, N
93mm	**Dekalb Oasis/24hr both lanes,** Mobil/dsl McDonald's Panda Express, Subway

IL

INTERSTATE 88 Cont'd

DEKALB

Exit #	Services
92	IL 38, IL 23, Annie Glidden Rd, to DeKalb, **2-3 mi N** [gas] BP, Marathon, Road Ranger/dsl, Shell [food] Aldorado, Baskin-Robbins, Blackstone Rest, Burger King, Chipotle Mexican, El Burrito Loco, Gyro's, Happy Wok Chinese, Jct Rest., KFC, LJ Silver, Lukulo's Rest., McDonald's, Molly's Eatery, Pagliai's Pizza, Pancake Rest., Panda Express, Papa John's, Pizza Hut, Pizza Pros, Pizza Villa, Potbelly, Quizno's, Starbucks, Subway, Taco Bell, Tom&Jerry's, Topper's Pizza, Vinny's Pizza, Wendy's [lodging] Best Western, Magneson Inn, Super 8, Travelodge [other] $General, Ford, Illini Tire, Schnuck's Food/Drug, to N IL U, Walgreens
86mm	**toll plaza**
78	I-39, US 51, S to Bloomington, N to Rockford
76	IL 251, Rochelle, **N** [gas] BP, Casey's, Shell [food] Olive Branch Rest. [other] [H] Ford, GMC, tires/repair
56mm	**toll plaza**

DIXON

Exit #	Services
54	IL 26, Dixon, **N** [gas] BP/Subway/scales/dsl, Murphy USA/dsl [food] Culver's, Hardee's, Panda Chinese, Pizza Hut [lodging] Comfort Inn, Quality Inn, Super 8 [other] [H] $Tree, to John Deere HS, to Ronald Reagan Birthplace, to St Parks, Verizon, Walmart
44	US 30 (last free exit eb), **N** [other] Leisure lake RV Ctr (2mi), food, gas, lodging

E MOLINE

Exit #	Services
41	IL 40, to Sterling, Rock Falls, **1-2 mi N** [gas] Marathon, Mobil/dsl, Shell [food] American Grill, Arby's, Arthur's Deli, Burger King, Candlelight Rest., Culver's, El Tapatio Mexican, First Wok Chinese, Gazi's Rest., Hardee's, KFC, McDonald's/playplace, Perna's Pizza, Pizza Hut, Red Apple Rest., Subway [lodging] All Seasons Motel, Candlelight Inn, Country Inn&Suites, Holiday Inn, Super 8 [other] [H] $General, AutoZone, Country Mkt Foods, Curves, Harley-Davidson, O'Reilly Parts, Sav-a-Lot, Walgreens, Walmart
36	to US 30, Rock Falls, Sterling
26	IL 78, to Prophetstown, Morrison, **N** [other] to Morrison-Rockwood SP
18	to Albany, Erie
10	to Port Byron, Hillsdale, **S** [gas] Phillips 66/dsl, Shell/Mama J's Rest./scales/dsl/24hr
6	IL 92 E, to Joslin, **N** [food] Jammerz Roadhouse (2mi), **S** [other] Sunset Lake Camping (1mi)
2	Former IL 2
1b a	I-80, W to Des Moines, E to Chicago
0mm	IL 5, IL 92, W to Silvis. Lundeen's Camping, to Quad City Downs. **I-88 begins/ends on I-80, exit 4b.**

INTERSTATE 90

Exit #	Services
0mm	Illinois/Indiana state line, **Chicago Skyway Toll Rd begins/ends**
1mm	US 12, US 20, 106th St, Indianapolis Blvd, **N** [gas] Citgo, Mobil, Shell/dsl [other] casino, **S** [food] Burger King, KFC, McDonald's [other] Aldi Foods, auto repair, Jewel-Osco
2.5mm	[gas] Skyway Oasis [food] McDonald's [other] **toll plaza**
3mm	87th St (from wb)
4mm	79th St , services on 79th St and Stoney Island Ave
5.5mm	73rd St (from wb)
6mm	State St (from wb), **S** [gas] Citgo
7mm	I-94 N (mile markers decrease to IN state line)
I-90 E and I-94 E run together. See I-94, exits 43b - 59a.	
84	I-94 W Lawrence Ave, **N** [gas] BP/dsl

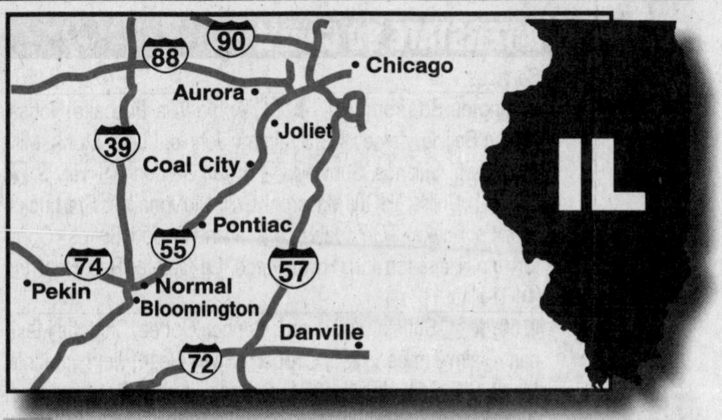

CHICAGO AREA

Exit #	Services
83b a	Foster Ave (from wb), **N** [gas] BP [food] Elly's Pancakes, Subway [other] Advance Parts, Firestone/auto, Walgreens
82c	Austin Ave, to Foster Ave
82b	Byrn-Mawr (from wb)
82a	Nagle Ave
81b	Sayre Ave (from wb)
81a	IL 43, Harlem Ave, **S** [gas] Gas Depot, Shell [food] Dunkin Donuts, Popeye's, Sally's Pancakes, Wendy's [other] $Tree, AutoZone
80	Canfield Rd (from wb), **N** [other] Walgreens
79b a	IL 171 S, Cumberland Ave (from wb), **N** [gas] 7-11, Mobil [food] Al's Burgers, Dunkin Donuts/Baskin Robbins, Hooters, McDonald's, Nancy's Pizza, Outback Steaks [lodging] Marriott, SpringHill Suites, Westin Hotel [other] Hampton Inn, Mariano's Mkt, **S** [food] Bar Louie's, Starbucks [lodging] Holiday Inn, Hyatt, Renaissance
78mm	I-294, I-190 W, **S** [other] to O'Hare Airport
76mm	IL 72, Lee St (from wb), **N** [food] Buona, Chili's, Chipotle, Culver's, IHOP, Jimmy John's, Longhorn Steaks, Panda Express, Steak'n Shake, Subway [lodging] Extended Stay America, Radisson, Residence Inn [other] Target, **S** [food] McDonald's [lodging] Best Western, Holiday Inn Express, Holiday Inn Select, Sheraton Gateway
73.5mm	Elmhurst Rd (from wb), **S** [gas] Shell [food] McDonald's [lodging] Best Western, Comfort Inn, Days Inn, La Quinta, Microtel, Motel 6
70.5mm	Arlington Hts Rd, **S** [gas] Mobil, Shell [food] Subway [lodging] Sheraton, N on Algonquin [gas] Shell [food] Arby's, Baja Fresh, Birch River Grill, Buona Beef, Caribou Coffee, Chicago Pizza, Chili's, Chipotle Mexican, Denny's, Honey Baked Ham, Jimmy Johns, Magnum Steaks, McDonald's, Old Country Buffet, Panda Express, Pappadeaux Rest., Potbelly's, Steak'n Shake, Subway, Yanni's Greek Rest. [lodging] Courtyard, DoubleTree, Hyatt, Jameson Suites, Motel 6, Radisson, Red Roof Inn [other] AT&T, GNC, Lowe's Whse, Meijer, NTB, Staples, vet, Walmart

SCHAUMBURG

Exit #	Services
68mm	I-290, IL 53, **N on Algonquin** [lodging] Best Western, Embassy Suites, Holiday Inn, Holiday Inn Express, Renaissance Inn [other] mall, **1 mi S on Golf Rd** [food] CA Pizza Kitchen, Cheesecake Factory, Hooters, Joe's Crabshack, Moretti's Italian, Olive Garden, Panera Bread, Red Robin, Ruby Tuesday, Starbucks, Subway, TGI Friday's, Uno [lodging] Extended Stay America, Hyatt, Residence Inn [other] AT&T, Firestone, JC Penney, Lord&Taylor, Macy's, Marshall's, Nordstrom, Sears/auto
65.5mm	Roselle Rd (from wb, no return), **N** [other] Medieval Times Funpark, **S** [gas] Mobil [food] Boston Mkt, Caribou Coffee, Chipotle Mexican, Denny's, Fox&Hound, Jimmy John's, KFC, La Magdalena, Melting Pot, Outback Steaks, Panda Express, Subway, Wendy's [lodging] Country Inn&Suites, Extended Stay America, Holiday Inn Express, Homestead Suites [other] 7-11, Advance Parts, Audi, AutoZone, Buick/GMC, Carmax, Chrysler/Dodge/Jeep, Firestone, Hancock Fabrics, Jewel-Osco, Lexus, Mazda, Office Depot, O'Reilly Parts, PetCo, TJ Maxx, Walgreens

IL

INTERSTATE 90 Cont'd

Exit #	Services
62mm	Barrington Rd (from wb), N food Apple Villa Pancake House, Hunan Beijing, Jersey's Grill, Jimmy John's, Lucky Monk, Millrose Rest., Quiznos, Subway lodging Hilton Garden other vet, S gas BP food Chili's, IHOP, Macaroni Grill, McDonald's, Starbucks, Steak'n Shake, TGIFriday's lodging Candlewood Suites, Comfort Inn, Hampton Inn, Hyatt Place, La Quinta, Red Roof Inn other U-Haul
59.5mm	IL 59, N food Buffalo Wild Wings, Caribou Coffee, Chipotle Mexican, Claim Jumper Rest., Cooper's Hawk Rest., Jimmy John's, Moe's SW Grill, Noodles&Co, Panda Express, Panera Bread, Potbelly's, Red Robin, Ruth's Chris Steaks, Subway, Which Wich lodging Marriott other AT&T, Cabela's, CVS Drug, GNC, Michael's, Petsmart, Ross, Target, TJ Maxx, to Poplar Creek Music Theatre, Verizon, World Mkt
58mm	Beverly Rd (from wb)
56mm	IL 25, N lodging Lexington Inn, S gas BP/dsl, Citgo, Shell/dsl, Speedway/dsl food Arby's, Baker Hill Pancakes, Wendy's other H Advance Parts, city park, NAPA AutoCare
54.5mm	IL 31 N, N gas BP, Thornton's food Alexander's Rest., Baskin-Robbins/Dunkin Donuts lodging Courtyard, Hampton Inn, Holiday Inn, Quality Inn, Super 8, TownePlace Suites, S food One for the Road Hotdogs
54mm	**Elgin Toll Plaza**
52mm	Randall Rd, N gas Shell food Big Sammy's Hot Dogs, Burnt Toast, Cafe Roma, DQ, Jimmy John's, Jimmy's Charhouse, Mr Wok, Panera Bread, Rookies Grill, Starbucks, Tilted Kilt, Village Pizza lodging Comfort Suites, Country Inn&Suites other Honda, S gas 7-11 lodging Candlewood Suites other H
46.5mm	IL 47, to Woodstock, N other Ford, General RV Ctr, Huntley Outlets/famous brands
42.5mm	US 20, Marengo, N gas Citgo/Arrowhead Rest/dsl/scales/24hr, Pilot/Road Ranger/Subway/dsl/scales/24hr, TA/BP/Burger King/Popeye's/dsl/scales/24hr/ @ food McDonald's, Wendy's lodging Super 8 other access to services at exit 46 (6mi), Ford, Huntley Outlets, museums
38mm	**Marengo Toll Plaza (from eb)**
25mm	Genoa Rd, to Belvidere, N gas Murphy USA/dsl food Applebee's, Rosati's Pizza, Starbucks, Subway other camping, Verizon, Walmart/Blimpie
24mm	**Belvidere Oasis both lanes,** gas Mobil/7-11/dsl/24hr food Food Court, McDonald's, Panda Express, Starbucks, Subway, Taco Bell other phone
23.5mm	**Belvidere Toll Plaza**
18mm	Kishwaukee River
17.5mm	I-39 S, US 20, US 51, to Rockford, S funpark
15	US 20, State St, N gas Mobil/dsl, Phillips 66/Subway/dsl food Cracker Barrel lodging Baymont Inn, Clocktower Resort, Days Inn, **0-2 mi** S gas Mobil/dsl, Road Ranger/dsl food 5 Guys Burgers, Applebee's, Buffalo Wild Wings, Burger King, Chick-fil-A, Chili's, Chipotle Mexican, City Buffet, Coldstone, Culver's, Denny's, Dos Reales, Fiesta Cancun, Gerry's Pizza, Giovanni's Rest., Hoffman House Rest., Hooters, IHOP, Jason's Deli, JerseyMike's, Jimmy John's, KFC/LJ Silver, Lino's Italian, LoneStar Steaks, Longhorn Steaks, Machine Shed Rest, McDonald's, Noodles&Co, Old Chicago Grill, Olive Garden, Outback Steaks, Panda Express, Panera Bread, Panino's Drive-Thru, Perkins, Pizza Hut/Taco Bell, PotBelly, Red Lobster, Red Robin, Ruby Tuesday, Starbucks, Steak'n Shake, Stone Eagle Tavern, Subway, ThunderBay Grille, TX Roadhouse, Wendy's
15	Continued lodging Candlewood Suites, Comfort Inn, Courtyard, Extended S America,Fairfield Inn, Hampton Inn, Hilton Garden, Holiday I Motel 6, Quality Suites, Radisson, Red Roof Inn, Residence I Sleep Inn, Staybridge Suites, Super 8 other H $Tree, Advar Parts, Aldi Foods, AT&T, Best Buy, BigLots, Burlington Coa Cadillac, Chrysler/Dodge/Jeep, Dick's, Discount Tire, GM Gordman's, Hancock Fabrics, Hobby Lobby, Home Dep Hyundai, JoAnn Fabrics, K-Mart, Kohl's, Lowe's, Marsha Mazda, Michael's, Nissan, Old Navy, Old Time Pottery, Pet Petsmart, Radio Shack, Ross, Sam's Club/gas, Schnuc Foods, Subaru, Target, Tuesday Morning, Valli Foods, Veriz Walgreens, Walmart/McDonald's
12	E Riverside Blvd, Loves Park, **0-2 mi** S gas BP, Mobil/c Phillips 66/dsl, Road Ranger/Pilot/Subway/dsl, Shell/c food 2nd Cousin's Grill, Arby's, BeefARoo, Ciaobella, Culve DQ, Greenfire Rest., India House, Japanese Express, KFC, M Donald's, RBI Rest., Rosatti's Pizza, Sam's Ristorante, Sing pore Grill, Subway, Taco Bell, Wendy's lodging Holiday Inn Expre Quality Inn other Audi/Honda/Mercedes, Autowerks, Farm&Fle funpark, Lexus, to Rock Cut SP, Toyota/Scion, Tuffy Au Walgreens
9	IL 173, S to Rock Cut SP
3.5mm	phone, S Beloit Toll Plaza
3	Rockton Rd, S gas Loves/Hardee's/dsl/scales/24hr
1.5mm	**Welcome Ctr/Rest Area eb full facilities, info, litter ba rels, petwalk playground, RV dump**
1	US 51 N, IL 75 W, S Beloit, N gas Road Ranger/McDonald dsl, S gas FLYING J/Denny's/dsl/scales/24hr, Road Range Pilot/Subway/dsl/E85/scales/24hr lodging Best Western, To way Inn other Finnegan's RV Ctr, Pearl Lake camping (2mi)
0mm	Illinois/Wisconsin state line

INTERSTATE 94

Exit #	Services
77mm	Illinois/Indiana state line
I-94 and I-80 run together 3 mi. See I-80, exit 161.	
74[160]b	I-80/I-294 W
74a	IL 394 S, to Danville
73b a	US 6,159th St, N gas Mobil food Applebee's, Buffalo Wild Wing Fuddrucker's, Outback Steaks, Panda Express, Quiznos, R Ribs, Sonic, Starbucks, Taco Bell, White Castle other BigLot Hyundai, JC Penney, Kia, Lincoln, Macy's, Marshall's, M chael's, Nissan, Office Depot, Old Navy, PetCo, Target, Toyot Scion, USPO, vet, S gas BP, Marathon food Harold's Chicke McDonald's, Popeye's, Rally's, Shark's, Subway lodging Cher Lane Motel other Aldi Foods, Jewel-Osco, Stanfa Tire/repair
71b a	Sibley Blvd, N gas Citgo, Mobil/dsl, Valero/dsl food McDonald' Nicky's Gyros, Popeye's, Quiznos, Shark's, Subway lodging Bay mont Inn other Family$, Pete's Mkt, S gas Clark, Marathon/ds Shell food Baskin-Robbins/Dunkin Donuts, Burger King, Fam ily Wendy's, KFC, Snapper's Chicken, White Castle lodging Be Motel other $General, Advance Parts, AutoZone, Fairplay Food Food4Less/gas, Menards, Radio Shack, Walgreens
70b a	Dolton
69	Beaubien Woods (from eb), Beaubien Woods Forest Preserve
68b a	130th St
66b	115th St, S food McDonald's
66a	111th Ave, S gas Citgo/dsl, Shell other H Firestone/auto
65	103rd Ave, Stony Island Ave
63	I-57 S (exits left from wb)

ELGIN

ROCKFORD

ROCKFORD

CHICAGO AREA

IL

INTERSTATE 94 Cont'd

CHICAGO AREA

Exit #	Services
62	Wentworth Ave (from eb), N [gas] Citgo, Mobil [food] Subway
61b	87th St, N [gas] BP, Shell [food] Burger King, McDonald's, S [food] Stabucks, Subway [other] $Tree, AutoZone, Best Buy, Burlington Coats, Food4Less, Home Depot, Jewel-Osco, Marshall's, O'Reilly Parts, Staples, Verizon
61a	83rd St (from eb), N [gas] Shell [food] Subway [other] st police
60c	79th St, N [gas] Mobil, Shell [food] Brown's Chicken [other] Walgreens, S [gas] Citgo/dsl [food] Church's
60b	76th St, N [gas] BP, Mobil, Shell [other] Walgreens, S [food] KFC/Pizza Hut, Popeye's
60a	75th St (from eb), N [gas] BP, Mobil, Shell [other] Aldi Foods, S [food] KFC, Pizza Hut, Popeye's [other] Walgreens
59c	71st St, N [gas] BP, S [food] McDonald's
59a	I-90 E, **to Indiana Toll Rd**
58b	63rd St (from eb), N [gas] Citgo, S [gas] Mobil
58a	I-94 divides into local and express, 59th St, S [gas] BP
57b	Garfield Blvd, N [food] Al's Beef, Checker's, Grand Chinese Kitchen, Subway [other] Family$, Walgreens, S [gas] Citgo, Mobil, Shell/24hr [food] Wendy's [other] [H]
57a	51st St
56b	47th St (from eb)
56a	43rd St, S [gas] BP/Subway/dsl, Citgo/dsl
55b	Pershing Rd
55a	35th St, S [other] to New Comiskey Park
54	31st St
53c	I-55, Stevenson Pkwy, N to downtown, Lakeshore Dr
53b	I-55, Stevenson Pkwy, S to St Louis
52c	18th St (from eb), [other] Dominick's Foods
52b	Roosevelt Rd, Taylor St (from wb), N [gas] Citgo [other] Best Buy, Home Depot, Walgreens, Whole Foods Mkt
52a	Taylor St, Roosevelt Rd (from eb), N [gas] Citgo
51h-i	I-290 W, to W Suburbs
51g	E Jackson Blvd, downtown
51f	W Adams St, downtown
51e	Monroe St (from eb), downtown, S [lodging] Crowne Plaza [other] Dominick's Foods, Walgreens
51d	Madison St (from eb), S [lodging] Crowne Plaza [other] Dominick's Foods, Walgreens, downtown
51c	E Washington Blvd, downtown
51b	W Randolph St, downtown
51a	Lake St (from wb)
50b	E Ohio St, S [gas] Marathon, downtown
50a	Ogden Ave
49b a	Augusta Blvd, Division St, N [other] Lexus, S [gas] BP, Shell [food] Pizza Hut
48b	IL 64, North Ave, N [gas] BP, S [gas] Valero [other] Mercedes
48a	Armitage Ave, N [other] Best Buy, Kohl's, S [gas] Shell [other] Jaguar, Land Rover, Volvo
47c b	Damen Ave, N [gas] car/vanwash, Citgo
47a	Western Ave, Fullerton Ave, N [gas] Citgo [food] Burger King, Dunkin Donuts, Popeye's, Starbucks, Subway [other] Costco/gas, Home Depot, Jo-Ann Fabrics, Pepboys, Petsmart, Staples, Target, S [gas] Marathon
46b a	Diversey Ave, California Ave, N [gas] Citgo, S [food] IHOP/24hr, Popeye's [other] Walgreens
45c	Belmont Ave, N [food] Wendy's
45b	Kimball Ave, N [gas] Marathon/dsl, S [gas] Valero [food] Dunkin Donuts, Pizza Hut, Subway [other] Aldi Foods, Best Buy, Radio Shack, Walgreens
45a	Addison St

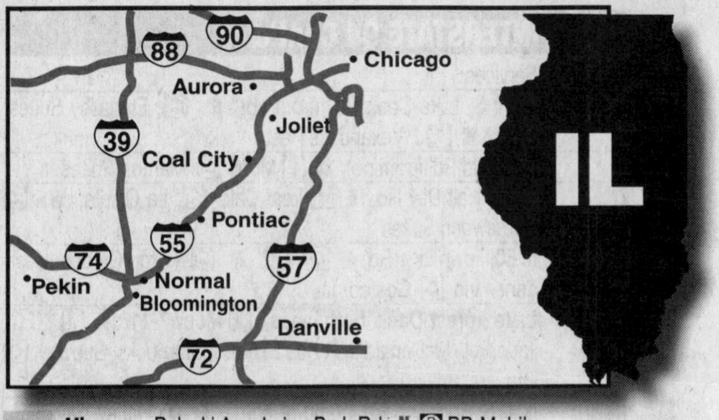

CHICAGO AREA

Exit #	Services
44b	Pulaski Ave, Irving Park Rd, N [gas] BP, Mobil
44a	IL 19, Keeler Ave, Irving Park Rd, N [gas] BP, Shell/24hr [other] to Wrigley Field
43c	Montrose Ave
43b	I-90 W
43a	Wilson Ave
42	W Foster Ave (from wb), S [gas] Marathon/service, Mobil [food] Subway
41mm	Chicago River, N Branch
41c	IL 50 S, to Cicero, to I-90 W
41b a	US 14, Peterson Ave, N [other] Whole Foods Mkt
39b a	Touhy Ave, N [gas] BP/dsl, Shell/Circle K [other] Cassidy Tire, Toyota/Scion, S [gas] BP, Citgo, Mobil, Shell [food] Bar Louie's, Baskin-Robbins/Dunkin Donuts, Brickhouse Rest., Buffalo Wild Wings, Burger King, Chili's, Chipotle Mexican, ChuckeCheese, Corner Bakery Cafe, Jersey Mike's, Jimmy John's, McDonald's, Noodles&Co, Outback Steaks, Panda Express, Penn Sta Subs, Red Robin, Sander's Rest., Shallot's Bistro, Starbucks, Subway, Tilted Kilt [lodging] Holiday Inn [other] Barnes&Noble, Best Buy, Dick's, Fresh Farms Mkt, GNC, Jewel-Osco, Michael's, Nissan, PepBoys, Petsmart, Ross, Tuesday Morning, vet, Walgreens, Walmart
37b a	IL 58, Dempster St, N [gas] Shell [food] Panda Express, Subway, S [gas] BP/dsl, Shell [food] Pizza Hut [other] Midas
35	Old Orchard Rd, N [gas] BP, Shell [food] Bloomingdale's, Buffalo Wild Wings, CA Pizza Kitchen, CheeseCake Factory, McCormick&Schmick's Rest [other] [H] Lord&Taylor, Macy's, mall, Nissan, Nordstrom's, S [food] Ruby Tuesday [lodging] Extended Stay America, Hampton Inn, Residence Inn
34c b	E Lake Ave, N [gas] BP/dsl [food] Corner Bakery Cafe, Five Guys, Panda Express, Starbucks, Subway [other] Fresh Mkt Foods, GNC, Walgreens, S [gas] Shell [food] DQ, Jimmy John's, Starbucks [other] auto repair
34a	US 41 S, Skokie Rd (from eb)
33b a	Willow Rd, S [gas] Shell [food] Dunkin Donuts, Starbucks [other] Mariano's Mkt, USPO, Walgreens
31	E Tower Rd, S [other] BMW, Carmax, Infiniti, Land Rover, Mercedes, Toyota/Scion, vet, Volvo
30b a	Dundee Rd (from wb, no EZ return), S [gas] Citgo/dsl [food] Barnaby's Rest., Chipotle, Morton's Steaks, Noodles&Co, Panera Bread, Potbelly, Roti Mediterranean, Ruth's Chris Steaks, Starbucks [lodging] Renaissance [other] Mariano's Mkt
29	US 41, to Waukegan, to Tri-state tollway
28	IL 43, Waukegan Rd (from eb), N [gas] BP, Shell [food] Dunkin Donuts/Baskin Robbins, Mod Pizza, Noodles&Co, Starbucks [lodging] Courtyard, Embassy Suites, Red Roof Inn [other] Hobby Lobby, Home Depot, Jewel-Osco, Just Tires

▲E INTERSTATE 94 Cont'd

Exit #	Services
25	I-294 S, Lake-Cook Rd (from sb), **E** 🛏 Embassy Suites, Hyatt, **W** 🍴 J Alexander's Rest.
24	Deerfield Rd (from nb), **W** ⒢ Mobil 🛏 Marriott Suites
21	IL 22, Half Day Rd, **E** 🍴 Leaf Cafe 🛏 La Quinta, **W** 🛏 Homewood Suites
19	IL 60, Town Line Rd, **E** ⊙ Ⓗ **W** 🛏 Hilton Garden, Residence Inn ⊙ Costco/gas
18mm	**Lake Forest Oasis both lanes**, ⒢ Mobil/7-11/dsl 🍴 KFC/Taco Bell, McDonald's, Panda Express, Starbucks, Subway ⊙ info
16mm	IL 176, Rockland Rd (no nb re-entry), **E** ⊙ Harley-Davidson, to Lamb's Farm
14mm	IL 137, Buckley Rd, **E** ⊙ Chicago Med School, to VA Ⓗ
11mm	IL 120 E, Belvidere Rd (no nb re-entry), **E** ⊙ Ⓗ
10mm	IL 21, Milwaukee Ave (from eb, no eb re-entry), **E** ⊙ Ⓗ Six Flags
8mm	IL 132, Grand Ave, **E** ⒢ Speedway/dsl 🍴 Baskin-Robbins/Dunkin Donuts, Burger King, ChuckeCheese, Cracker Barrel, Cravings Red Hots, Culver's, Golden Corral, Ichibahn, IHOP, Jimmy John's, Joe's Crabshack, KFC/LJ Silver, Mama K's Zpizza, McDonald's, Oberweiss, Old Chicago Red Hots, Olive Garden, Outback Steaks, Rosati's Pizza, Starbucks, Subway 🛏 Baymont Inn, Country Inn&Suites, Extended Stay America, Hampton Inn, Key Lime Cove Resort, La Quinta, Super 8 ⊙ Six Flags Park, **0-2 mi W** ⒢ Shell/Circle K 🍴 Bakers Square, Boston Mkt, Buffalo Wild Wings, Chili's, Chipotle Mexican, Denny's, Five Guys, Giordano's Pizza, Jersey Mike's Subs, Jimano's Pizza, LoneStar Steaks, McDonald's, Noodles&Co, Panda Express, Panera Bread, Penn Sta Subs, Pizza Hut, Portillo's, Potbelly's, Red Lobster, Red Robin, Ruby Tuesday, Starbucks, Steak'n Shake, Taco Bell, TGIFriday's, Uno Grill, Wendy's, White Castle 🛏 Comfort Inn, Fairfield Inn, Holiday Inn ⊙ $Tree, AT&T, AutoZone, Bass Pro Shops, Best Buy, Buick/GMC, Chrysler/Dodge/Jeep, Goodyear, Gurnee Mills Outlet Mall/famous brands, Home Depot, Honda, Hyundai, Jewel-Osco, Kohl's, Macy's, Mariano's Mkt, Marshall's, Menards, Michael's, Old Navy, Petsmart, Ross, Sam's Club, Sears Grand/auto, Target, TJ Maxx, Tuesday Morning, Verizon, VW, Walgreens, Walmart
5mm	**Waukegan toll plaza** 🅲
2	IL 173 (from nb, no return), Rosecrans Ave, **E** ⊙ to IL Beach SP
1b	US 41 S, to Waukegan (from sb)
1a	Russell Rd, **E** ⊙ I-94 RV Ctr, **W** ⒢ Citgo/dsl/scales, TA/Country Pride/dsl/scales/24hr/ @ ⊙ Peterbilt
0mm	Illinois/Wisconsin state line

▲N INTERSTATE 255 (ST LOUIS)

Exit #	Services
	I-255 begins/ends on I-270, exit 7.
30	I-270, W to Kansas City, E to Indianapolis
29	IL 162, to Glen Carbon, to Pontoon Beach, Granite City
26	Horseshoe Lake Rd, **E** st police
25b a	I-55/I-70, W to St Louis, E to Chicago, Indianapolis
24	Collinsville Rd, **E** ⒢ BP/24hr 🍴 Jack-in-the-Box ⊙ Shop'n Save, **W** ⊙ Fairmount Racetrack
20	I-64, US 50, W to St Louis, E to Louisville, **services 1 mi E off I-64, exit 9.**
19	State St, E St Louis, **E** 🛏 Western Inn ⊙ Holten SP
17b a	IL 15, E St Louis, to Belleville, Centreville, **E** ⒢ ✈FLYING J/Denny's/dsl/scales/24hr , **W** ⒢ Phillips 66

Exit #	Services
15	Mousette Lane, **E** ⊙ Ⓗ **W** ⊙ Peterbilt
13	IL 157, to Cahokia, **E** ⒢ Phillips 66, **W** ⒢ BP/24hr, Q🍴 Capt D's, China Express, Classic K Burgers, Domino's, DC Hardee's, Jade Garden, KFC, McDonald's, Pizza Hut, Popeye's Rally's, Subway ⊙ Holiday Inn Express ⊙ $General, Advance Parts, Aldi Foods, AutoZone, Buick/GMC, Cahokia RV Park, Cahokia RV Parque (2mi), CarQuest, Curves, Dobb's Tires, Family$ Schnuck's, Shop'n Save Foods, Walgreens, Walmart/drugs
10	IL 3 N, to Cahokia, E St Louis, **W** ⒢ ZX/Subway/dsl
9	to Dupo, **W** ⒢ BP
6	IL 3 S, to Columbia (exits left from sb), **E** ⒢ Phillips 66, She dsl/24hr 🛏 Hampton Inn (2mi) ⊙ Chevrolet
4mm	Missouri/Illinois state line, Mississippi River
3	Koch Rd
2	MO 231, Telegraph Rd, **N** ⒢ Conoco, Shell/Circle K 🍴 Mc Donald's, Pizza Hut/Taco Bell, Steak'n Shake, Waffle Hous ⊙ $Tree, Advance Parts, Jefferson Barracks Nat Cem, Radi Shack, Walmart, **S** ⒢ CFM/dsl, Mobil, QT, Shell 🍴 Chin Wok, DQ, Imo's Pizza
1d c	US 50, US 61, US 67, Lindbergh Blvd, Lemay Ferry Rd, ac cesses same as I-55 exit 197 E, **N** ⒢ Phillips 66 🍴 Apple bee's, Arby's, Buffalo Wild Wings, ChuckeCheese, CiCi's Pizza Dillard's, Hometown Buffet, HoneyBaked Ham, Hooters, IHO Imo's Pizza, Krispy Kreme, McAlister's Deli, Noodles&Co, Pen Sta Subs, Qdoba Mexican, Starbucks, Steak'n Shake, Subwa Taco Bell, Tucker's Place, Wendy's 🛏 Holiday Inn ⊙ AT& Best Buy, Chrysler/Dodge/Jeep, Costco/gas, CVS Drug, Dick's Ford/Lincoln, Home Depot, JC Penney, K-Mart, Macy's, mal Marshall's, NTB, Sears/auto, Verizon, vet, **S** ⒢ Phillips 6 🍴 Jack-in-the-Box, McDonald's, Rich & Charlie's Italian, Whi Castle ⊙ $General, BigLots, Firestone, Old Navy, Petsma Sam's Club/gas, Walgreens
1b a	I-55 S to Memphis, N to St Louis. **I-255 begins/ends on I-5 exit 196.**

INTERSTATE 270

See Missouri Interstate 270 (St Louis)

▲E INTERSTATE 294 (CHICAGO)

Exit #	Services
	I-294 begins/ends on I-94, exit 71. Numbering descends from we to east.
	I-294 & I-80 run together 5 mi. See exits 155-160.
5mm	I-80 W, access to I-57
5.5mm	167th St, **toll booth** 🅲
6mm	US 6, 159th St, **E** ⒢ Citgo, Exxon/dsl, Marathon, Mob dsl, Shell/dsl ⊙ $Tree, AutoZone, Family$, **W** ⒢ BP/d 🍴 Baskin-Robbins/Dunkin Donuts, Burger King, McDon ald's, Popeye's, Subway, Taco Bell, White Castle 🛏 Chicag Inn&Suites ⊙ $Tree, AutoZone, U-Haul, Walgreens
11mm	Cal Sag Channel
12mm	IL 50, Cicero Ave, **E** ⒢ BP, Shell/dsl 🍴 Dunkin Donuts, Sub way, White Castle ⊙ Home Depot, O'Reilly Parts, **W** ⒢ BP, Shell/dsl 🍴 Applebee's, Boston Mkt, Chipotle, Culver's IHOP, Lone Star Steaks, Panda Express, Pizza Hut, Popeye's Portillo's Dogs, Potbelly, Starbucks, Subway 🛏 Baymont Inn Days Inn, DoubleTree, Holiday Inn Express ⊙ AT&T, Best Buy GNC, Jo-Ann, Kohl's, NTB, PepBoys, Petsmart, Ross, Targe TJ Maxx, Ultra Foods, Walgreens, Walmart/Subway
18mm	US 12/20, 95th St, **E** ⒢ Marathon 🍴 Buffalo Wild Wings Chick-fil-A, Starbucks, TX Corral ⊙ Ⓗ CarMax, Discour Tire, mall, Mazda, Sears/auto, **W** ⒢ 7-11, BP, Shell, Speed way/dsl 🍴 Arby's, Baskin-Robbins, Burger King, Denny's

CHICAGO AREA
GURNEE

IL

CHICAGO AREA

CHICAGO AREA

INTERSTATE 294 (CHICAGO) Cont'd

18mm Continued
Dunkin Donuts, Jimmy John's, Les Bros Rest., McDonald's, Papa John's, Prime Time Rest., Subway, Taco Bell, The Pit Rib-house, Wendy's [lodging] Motel 6 [other] $Tree, AutoZone, Jewel-Osco, Walgreens

20mm **toll booth** [phone]

22mm 75th St, Willow Springs Rd

23mm I-55, Wolf Rd, to Hawthorne Park

25mm **Hinsdale Oasis both lanes,** [gas] Mobil/7-11/dsl [food] KFC/Taco Bell, McDonald's, McDonald's, Panda Express, Sbarro, Subway

28mm US 34, Ogden Ave, **E** [other] zoo, **W** [gas] BP, Shell/deli [food] Dunkin Donuts, McDonald's, Starbucks [other] [H] Ferrari/Maserati, Firestone/auto, LandRover, Whole Foods Mkt

28.5mm Cermak Rd (from sb, no return)

29mm **I-88 tollway**

30mm **toll booth** [phone]

31mm IL 38, Roosevelt Rd (no EZ nb return), **E** [gas] Shell/dsl [lodging] Hillside Manor Motel [other] vet

32mm I-290 W, to Rockford (from nb)

34mm I-290 (from sb), to Rockford

38mm **O'Hare Oasis both lanes,** [gas] Mobil/7-11/dsl [food] KFC, McDonald's, Panda Express, Sbarro, Starbucks, Subway, Taco Bell, TCBY

39mm IL 19 W (from sb), Irving Park Rd, **E** [gas] Citgo, Marathon/dsl, Shell/dsl [food] Dunkin Donuts, McDonald's, Starbucks, Subway, Wendy's [lodging] Comfort Suites [other] 7-11, Aldi Foods, Walgreens, **W** [gas] BP/Subway/desk [food] Mirage Rest. [lodging] Candlewood Suites, Hampton Inn, Sheraton

40mm I-190 W, **E** [gas] Mobil [food] Basil's Kitchen, McDonald's, Starbucks [lodging] Courtyard, Doubletree, Embassy Suites, Hampton Inn, Hilton, Hilton Garden, Holiday Inn, Hyatt, Hyatt Regency, Marriott, Rosemont Suites, Westin

41mm **toll booth** [phone]

42mm Touhy Ave, **W** [gas] Mobil/service [food] Tiffany's Rest. [lodging] Comfort Inn, Radisson

43mm Des Plaines River

44mm Dempster St (from nb, no return), **E** [food] Wendy's [other] [H] CVS Drug, **W** [food] Dunkin Donuts, Subway

46mm IL 58, Golf Rd, **E** [gas] Mobil/Dunkin Donuts/dsl, Shell/Subway/dsl [food] Omega Rest. [lodging] Wyndham [other] CVS Drug, Golf Mill Mall, Meineke, Meijer, Target, **W** [other] [H]

49mm Willow Rd, **W** [gas] BP/Subway/dsl [food] Chipotle, Jimmy John's, McDonald's, Pie Five Pizza, Starbucks, TGIFriday's [lodging] Best Western, Country Inn Suites, Courtyard, Motel 6 [other] CVS Drug, Mariano's Mkt

53mm Lake Cook Rd (no nb re-entry), **E** [lodging] Embassy Suites, Hyatt, **W** [food] J Alexander's

I-294 begins/ends on I-94.

INTERSTATE 355

Exit # Services

30mm **I-355 begins/end on I-290.**

29 US 20 W Lakes St, **E** [gas] Citgo/dsl, Marathon, Shell [food] Applebee's, Baskin-Robbins/Dunkin Donuts, Culver's, Famous Dave's BBQ, Home Run Rest, IHOP, Jimmy John's, La Hacienda Mexican, Nana Hotdogs, Panera Bread, Ristorante de Marco's, Starbucks, Wok'n Fire, Zaza's Steaks [lodging] Hampton Inn [other] Midas, Verizon, Walmart, **W** [gas] Shell [food] Venuti's Rest

28 IL 64, E North Ave, **E** [gas] BP/Subway/dsl, Burger King, Comfort Suites, Fairfield Inn, McDonald's, Shell/Circle K, **W** [gas] Phillips

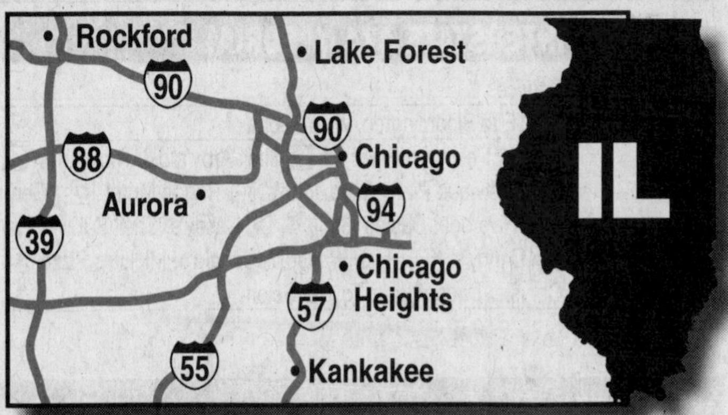

28 Continued
66, Speedway/dsl [lodging] Hilton Garden, Ramada [other] Art's RV Ctr, Goodyear

25 Roosevelt, **E** [gas] Mobil [food] Boston Mkt, Buffalo Wild Wings, Jimmy John's, Odyssey Greek, Pizza Hut, Roundhead Pizza, Starbucks, White Castle, Wolfy's Dogs [lodging] Crowne Plaza [other] $General, AutoZone, Cadillac, Jewel-Osco, K-Mart, Toyota/Scion, **W** [other] NAPA

22 IL 56, Butterfield Rd, **E** [food] Arby's, Brick House Rest., Burger King, Chama Gaucha Brazilian, Chipotle Mexican, Fuddrucker's, Hooters, Melting Pot, Olive Garden, Panera Bread, Portillo's, Red Lobster, Ruby Tuesday, Starbucks, Subway, Zoup! [lodging] Comfort Inn, Extended Stay America, Holiday Inn Express, Marriott, Red Roof Inn [other] $Tree, Best Buy, Kohl's, Michael's, Petsmart, Ross, Verizon, **W** [food] Carlucci Italian [lodging] DoubleTree Suites [other] 7-11, Home Depot

20mm **I-88 E/I-355 run together**

19 US 34, Ogden Ave, **E** [gas] Shell [food] Culver's, Jimmy John's, McDonald's [lodging] InTown Suites [other] AT&T, Buick/GMC, Chrysler/Dodge/Jeep, Ford, **W** [food] Baskin-Robbins/Dunkin Donuts [lodging] Extended Stay America [other] Chevrolet, Speedway/dsl, vet

18 Maple Ave, **1 mi W** [gas] BP, Mobil, Shell/Circle K [food] KFC/Taco Bell, McDonald's [other] Jewel Osco, Walgreens

16 63rd St, Hobson Rd, **E** [gas] Mobil/dsl, Thornton's/McDonald's/dsl [food] Steven's Rest, Subway [other] AutoZone, Familia Fresk Mkt, GNC, Target, Walgreens

15 W 75th St, **E** [gas] Mobil [food] Arby's, Bakers Square Rest [other] Hobby Lobby, Home Depot, JC Penney, Sam's Club/gas, **W** [gas] Marathon [food] Dunkin-Donuts, El Burro Loco, McDonald's, Pizza Italiano [other] Jewel-Osco

14 87th St, Baughton Rd, **E** [gas] BP, Shell [food] Al's Pizza, Dunkin-Donuts, McDonald's, Oberweiss, Subway, Wendy's [other] Costco/gas, CVS Drug, **W** [gas] Mobil [food] Bar Louie, Buffalo Wild Wings, Famous Dave's BBQ, Five Guys, IHOP, Jimmy John's, Longhorn Steaks, Panda Express, Panera Bread, Potbelly, Starbucks, Ted's MT Grill [lodging] ALoft [other] AT&T, Barnes&Noble, Bass Pro Shops, Discount Tire, IKEA, Macy's, Meijer/gas, Verizon, Walgreens

12 I-55

8 127th St, **E** [food] Burger King, Jimmy John's, KFC, McDonald's, Starbucks, Subway, Taco Bell [other] Aldi Foods, AT&T, Firestone/auto, Jewel-Osco, Jiffy Lube, Pepper's Autocare, USPO, Verizon, Walgreens

6 IL 171, Archer Ave, 143rd St, **E** [other] Kohl's, Target, vet

4 159th Ave, IL 7, Orland Park, Homer Glen, **E** [gas] Citgo/dsl, **W** [gas] URGENT CARE

3mm **toll booth both directions**

1 US 6, **E** [gas] Rte 6 Food'n Fuel/Dunkin Donuts/dsl, **W** [other] [H]

0mm I-80 E, W, **I-355 begins/ends on I-80 exit 140**

IL

PEORIA

INTERSTATE 474 (PEORIA)

Exit #	Services
15	I-74, E to Bloomington, W to Peoria
9	IL 29, E Peoria, to Pekin, N Shell/Arby's/dsl, Thornton's DQ, Driftwood Pizza, Taco John's Ragon Motel $General, Riverboat Casino (6mi), S Casey's, Shell/Subway/dsl Denny's, KFC, Lian Wang, McDonald's, Mickie's Pizza Chrysler/Dodge/Jeep, Toyota/Scion
8mm	Illinois River
6b a	US 24, Adams St, Bartonville, S BP/dsl, Shell/dsl Ha ee's, KFC, McDonald's, Tyroni's Café
5	Airport Rd, S Phillips 66/e-85/dsl airport
3a	to IL 116, Farmington, S Wildlife Prairie Park
0b a	I-74, W to Moline, E to Peoria. **I-474 begins/ends on I- exit 87.**

INDIANA

IL IN CORYDON

INTERSTATE 64

Exit #	Services
124mm	Indiana/Kentucky state line, Ohio River
123	IN 62 E, New Albany, N Marathon/dsl, Shell/Circle K DQ H, Family$, Firestone/auto, Save-A-Lot, S Shell/Circle K, Valero Daisy's Cafeteria, Subway, Waffle House Best Western, Hampton Inn
121	I-265 E, to I-65 (exits left from eb), N access to H
119	US 150 W, to Greenville, N Marathon Bean St Cafe, Bearno's Buffet, Beef O'Brady's, China Cafe, Domino's, DQ, El Nopal, McDonald's, Papa John's, Sam's Family Rest., Subway, Taco Bell, Tumbleweed SW Grill AutoZone, JayC Foods, Rite Aid, URGENT CARE, Walgreens
118	IN 62, IN 64W, to Georgetown, N Marathon/dsl/24hr, Shell/Circle K Korner Kitchen, McDonald's Motel 6 CashSaver Foods, Mr. Hardware, S Marathon/dsl
115mm	**Welcome Ctr wb, full facilities, litter barrels, vending**
113	to Lanesville
105	IN 135, to Corydon, N Marathon/dsl, Shell Big Boy Comfort Inn, S 5 Star, BP/dsl Alberto's Italian, Arby's, Beef O'Brady's, Burger King, Cracker Barrel, Culver's, Domino's, DQ, El Nopal Mexican, Hong Kong Buffet, KFC, Lee's Chicken, LJ Silver, McDonald's, O'Charley's, Papa John's, Papa Murphy's, Pizza Hut, Ryan's, Subway, Taco Bell, Waffle House, Wendy's, White Castle Baymont Inn, Hampton Inn, Holiday Inn Express, Super 8 H $Tree, Advance Parts, AT&T, AutoZone, Big O Tire, Buick/Chevrolet, Chrysler/Dodge/Jeep, CVS Drug, Family$, Ford, Radio Shack, RV camping, Verizon, Walgreens, Walmart/Subway
100mm	Blue River
97mm	**parking area both lanes**
92	IN 66, Carefree, N Marengo Caves, S Marathon/dsl/rest./24hr, Pilot/Subway/dsl/scales/24hr Big Dadd's Rest., Country Style Rest. Old Stone Lodge/Grill Carefree Truckwash, Harrison Crawford SF, repair, to Wyandotte Caves
88mm	Hoosier Nat Forest eastern boundary
86	IN 37, to Sulphur, N to Patoka Lake, S scenic route
79	IN 37, to Tell City, St Croix, S Marathon/Subshop/pizza/dsl phone, Rec. Facilities, to Hoosier NF, to OH River Br
76mm	Anderson River
72	IN 145, to Birdseye, N to Patoka Lake, S St Meinrad Coll, winery (2mi), gas
63	IN 162, to Ferdinand, N Sunoco/dsl China Garden, McDonald's, Subway, Wendy's Comfort Inn, Super 8 CVS Drug, Ferdinand SF, S Lake Rudolph RV Camping (8mi)
58mm	**both lanes, full facilities, info, litter barrels vending**
57	US 231, to Dale, Huntingburg, N H S Chuckles/ Denny's, Wendy's Baymont Inn, Motel 6 Linc Boyhood Home, Lincoln SP
54	IN 161, to Holland, Tennyson
39	IN 61, Lynnville, N Marathon Monterrey Mexic USPO
32mm	N Wabash & Erie Canal
29b a	I-69 N, IN 57 N&S, to Evansville
25b a	US 41, to Evansville, N FLYING J/Denny's/d scales/24hr, Loves/Wendy's/dsl/24hr, Pilot/Subwa Taco Bell/dsl/24hr Baymont Inn Blue Beacon, tru repair/lube, S Marathon/dsl Arby's, Denny's, McDo ald's, Stoll's Amish Rest. Apar Inn, Comfort Inn, Gatew Inn, Super 8 st police, to U S IN
18	IN 65, to Cynthiana, S Motomart/dsl/24hr
12	IN 165, Poseyville, S CountryMark/Subway/dsl R Wagon Rest NAPA, New Harmonie Hist Area/SP
7mm	**Black River Welcome Ctr eb, full facilities, litter barre petwalk**
5mm	Black River
4	IN 69 S, New Harmony, Griffin, **1 mi** N USPO, S Harmo St Park
2mm	Big Bayou River
0mm	Indiana/Illinois state line, Wabash River

INTERSTATE 65

Exit #	Services
262	I-90, W to Chicago, E to Ohio, **I-65 begins/ends on US 12, U 20.**
261	15th Ave, to Gary, E Mack/Volvo Trucks, W Clark
259b a	I-94/80, US 6W
258	US 6, Ridge Rd, E Marathon/dsl, Speedway/dsl Cou try Lounge Diner, Diner's Choice Rest., W Clark, Save Ga
255	61st Ave, Merrillville, E Speedway/dsl, Thornton's A by's, Cracker Barrel, McDonald's, Pizza Hut/Taco Bell, Wendy $Inn, Comfort Inn, EconoLodge H, Chevrolet, I-6 Repair, Menards, Mr Tire, **1 mi** W Shell Burger Kin Subway
253b	US 30 W, Merrillville, W Mobil/dsl, Shell, Speedway/dsl Abuelo's Mexican, Applebee's, Barnelli's Rest., Baskin-Rob bins/Dunkin Donuts, Denny's, DQ, Gino's Rest., Golden Corra Hooters, House of Kobe, Ichiban Steaks, Johnnie's Rest., KFC La Carreta's, Maloney's Grill, McDonald's, Old Chicago Pizz Oriental Buffet, Outback Steaks, Panda Express, Panera Brea

INTERSTATE 65 Cont'd

MERRILLVILLE

253b Continued
Pepe's Mexican, Pizza Hut, Portillo's Hot Dogs, Starbucks, Steak'n Shake, Subway, TX Corral Steaks, Wendy's, White Castle Courtyard, Deluxe Inn, Fairfield Inn, Hampton Inn, Holiday Inn Express, Radisson, Red Roof Inn, Residence Inn H $Tree, Aldi Foods, Buick/GMC, Cadillac, CarQuest, CarX, Chrysler/Dodge/Jeep, Discount Tire, Fanny May Candies, Ford, Goodyear/auto, Hyundai, Jo-Ann Fabrics, K-Mart, Lincoln, Mazda, Meijer/dsl, Midas, Mr Tire, NTB, Old Time Pottery, Staples, Subaru, U-Haul, Verizon, Walgreens

253a US 30 E, E BP/Noble Romans, Speedway/dsl Arby's, Bakers Square, Bob Evans, Buffalo Wild Wings, Chick-fil-A, Chili's, Chipotle Mexican, ChuckeCheese, Culver's, Don Pablo, IHOP, Jamba Juice, Jimmy John's, Joe's Crabshack, KFC/LJ Silver, Longhorn Steaks, McDonald's, Olive Garden, Peking Buffet, Popeye's, Potbelly, Red Lobster, Red Robin, Ruby Tuesday, Sheffield's Rest., Starbucks, Taco Bell, Taco Depot, TGI-Friday's, Wendy's Best Value Inn, Best Western, Candlewood Suites, Comfort Suites, Country Inn&Suites, Economy Inn, Extended Stay America, Hilton Garden, La Quinta, Motel 6, Quality Inn, Super 8 AT&T, Audi/VW, AutoZone, Best Buy, BigLots, Carmax, Costco/gas, Dick's, Firestone/auto, Gander Mtn, Hobby Lobby, Home Depot, Honda, JC Penney, Kia, Kohl's, Lowe's, Macy's, mall, Michael's, Nissan, Office Depot, Old Navy, PetCo, Petsmart, Sam's Club/gas, Sears/auto, Target, Tire Barn, TJ Maxx, Toyota/Scion, Tuesday Morning, vet, Walmart/McDonald's

249 109th Ave, W Beggars Pizza, China Garden, Golden Apple Rest., Jimmy John's, Oberweis Icecream GNC, Verizon, Walgreens

247 US 231, Crown Point, W Mobil/dsl H Vietnam Vet Mem

241mm **weigh sta sb**

240 IN 2, Lowell, E FLYING J/Denny's/dsl/24hr/ @, Mobil/Burger King, Pilot/McDonalds/dsl/scales/24hr Arby's, Subway Comfort Inn, Super 8 truck wash, W st police

234mm Kankakee River

231mm **both lanes, full facilities, info, litter barrels, petwalk vending**

230 IN 10, Roselawn, E Gas City/Kozy Kitchen/dsl/scales/24hr, Loves/Arby's/dsl/scales/24hr, W Family Express/e85, Marathon/Subway China Wok, J&J Pizza, Sycamore Drive-In $General, CarQuest, CVS Drug, Fagen Drug, IGA Foods, Lake Holiday Camping, Oak Lake Camping, TrueValue

220 IN 14, Winamac, W BP/Subway/dsl Fair Oaks Farms Store

215 IN 114, Rensselaer, E Family Express/dsl/e85/24hr Arby's, DQ, KFC, McDonald's, Rensselear Rest. Holiday Inn Express, Knights Inn H W Marathon/Trail Tree Rest./dsl/24hr Burger King Economy Inn fireworks, tires/repair/towing/24hr

212mm Iroquois River

205 US 231 Remington, E BP/dsl, Crazy D/dsl H to St Joseph's Coll

201 US 24/231, Remington, E Caboose Lake RV Camping, W Petro/Shell/Iron Skillet/dsl/scales/24hr/ @, Pilot/Subway/dsl/scales/24hr KFC, McDonald's Sunset Inn, Super 8

196mm **both lanes, full facilities, info, litter barrels, petwalk vending**

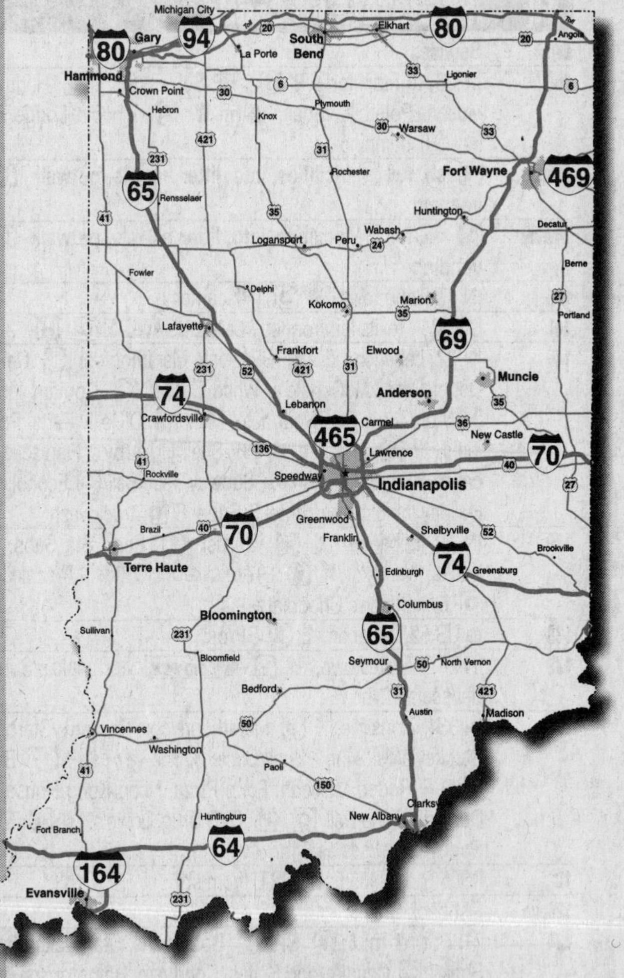

LAFAYETTE

193 US 231, to Chalmers, E BP/DQ/Stuckey's

188 IN 18, to Brookston, Fowler, many windmills

178 IN 43, W Lafayette, E GA/Taco Bell, Phillips 66/Subway/dsl McDonald's, Wendy's EconoLodge museum, st police, to Tippecanoe Bfd, W to Purdue U

176mm Wabash River

175 IN 25, Lafayette, E BP/dsl, Family Express/dsl/e85, W H

172 IN 26, Lafayette, E Cracker Barrel, DQ, El Rodeo, Starbucks, Steak'n Shake, Subway, Taj Mahal, White Castle Baymont Inn, Candlewood Suites, Comfort Inn, Comfort Suites, Days Inn, La Quinta, Motel 6, TownePlace Suites Meijer/dsl/e85, visitor's ctr, W BP/Circle K/dsl/24hr, Citgo, Speedway/dsl Arby's, Bob Evans, Burger King, Camille's Cafe, Chick-fil-A, Chili's, ChuckeCheese, Country Cafe, Culvers, Denny's, Don Pablo, Fazoli's, Golden Corral, Grindstone Charlie's, Hour Time Rest., IHOP, Jimmy John's, KFC, Logan's Roadhouse, McAlister's Deli, McDonald's, Moe's SW Grill, Mt Jack's, Olive Garden, Outback Steaks, Pizza Hut, Sonic, Spageddie's, Starbucks, Steak'n Shake, Subway, Taco Bell, TGIFriday's Best Western, Clarion, Courtyard, Fairfield Inn, Hampton Inn, Homewood Suites, Knights Inn, Quality Inn, Red Roof Inn, Super 8 H $General, $Tree, Aamco, Chevrolet, CVS Drug, Discount Tire, Gordman's, Hobby Lobby, Home Depot, Hyundai, Lowe's, Marsh Foods, Nissan, Office Depot, Sam's Club/gas, Target, TJ Maxx, to Purdue U, Toyota, USPO, Verizon, vet, Walgreens, Walmart/Subway

168 IN 38, IN 25 S, Dayton, E BP/Subway, Pantry/dsl

⬆N INTERSTATE 65 Cont'd

Exit #	Services
158	IN 28, to Frankfort, **E** 🅖 BP/Subway/dsl 🅞 Harley-Davidson, Peterbilt, repair, **2 mi W** 🛏 Lincoln Lodge Motel 🅞 🄷, camping
150mm	🅡ₛ sb, full 🚻 facilities, info, litter barrels, petwalk Ⓒ 🅰 vending
148mm	🅡ₛ nb, full 🚻 facilities, info, litter barrels, petwalk Ⓒ 🅰 vending
146	IN 47, Thorntown, **W** 🅞 🄷, camping
141	US 52 W (exits left from sb), Lafayette Ave, **E** 🅞 🍴
140	IN 32, Lebanon, **E** 🅖 BP/repair, Marathon/dsl 🍴 Denny's, Depot Rest., McDonald's, White Castle 🛏 Comfort Inn 🅞 🄷 AutoZone, Goodyear/auto, Menards, O'Reilly Parts, Pomp's Tires, **W** 🅖 McClure/dsl/e85, Shell 🍴 Arby's, Flapjacks Pancakes, KFC, Steak'n Shake, Subway, Taco Bell 🛏 EconoLodge, Holiday Inn Express, Motel 6, Super 8 🅞 truckwash
139	IN 39, Lebanon, **E** 🅖 GA/dsl 🍴 Penn Sta Subs, Starbucks, Wendy's, **W** 🅖 ⚡FLYING J/IHOP/dsl/LP/scales/24hr 🅞 Donaldson's Chocolates
138	to US 52, Lebanon, **E** 🅖 BP/dsl
133	IN 267, Whitestown, **W** 🅖 ◆Loves/McDonald's/Subway/dsl/scales/24hr
130	IN 334, Zionsville, **E** 🅖 Marathon/Noble Roman's/Starbucks/Stuckey's/dsl/24hr, Shell/Circle K/Subway/dsl 🍴 Burger King, El Rodeo Mexican, Fox's Pizza, Hong Kong House, McDonald's, Taco Bell 🅞 🄷 CVS Drug, Lowe's, **W** 🅖 TA/BP/Popeye's/dsl/scales/24hr/ @
129	I-865 E, to I-465 E, US 52 E (from sb)
126mm	Fishback Creek
124	71st St, **1 mi E** 🅖 BP 🍴 Bob Evans, Starbucks, Steak'n Shake 🛏 Candlewood Suites, Courtyard, Hampton Inn, Hilton Garden, Residence Inn, Wingate Inn, **W** 🅞 Eagle Creek Park
123	I-465 S, **S** 🅞 to 💲
121	Lafayette Rd, **E** 🅖 GA, Speedway/dsl 🛏 Quality Inn, **W** 🅖 Shell/Circle K 🍴 Applebee's, Arby's, Church's, Fazoli's, La Bamba Burritos, Wendy's 🛏 Best Value Inn 🅞 🄷 $Tree, Batteries+, Discount Tire, Family$, Kia, Mazda, NAPA, Nissan, PepBoys, same as 119, Tire Barn, Toyota/Scion, Verizon, Walmart/Subway
119	38th St (no nb return), Dodge, **W** 🅖 Speedway/dsl 🍴 ChuckeCheese, Fiesta Mexican, Hooters, KFC, McDonald's, O'Charley's, Papa John's, Penn Sta Subs, Pizza Hut, Popeye's, Red Lobster, Taco Bell, WTT Buffet 🅞 Aldi Foods, Best Buy, Chevrolet, CVS Drug, Honda, Hyundai, Meijer/dsl, Radio Shack, same as 121, Staples, Tires+
117.5mm	White River
117	MLK St (from sb), **W** 🅖 Marathon/dsl
116	29th St, 30th St (from nb), **W** 🅞 Marian Coll
115	21st St, **E** 🅖 Shell/Circle K 🅞 🄷 **W** 🅞 museums, zoo
114	MLK St, West St, downtown
113	US 31, IN 37, Meridian St, to downtown, **E** 🅞 🄷
112a	I-70 E, to Columbus
111	Market St, Michigan St, Ohio St, **E** 🍴 Hardee's, **W** 🅞 City Market, museum
110b	I-70 W, to St Louis
110a	Prospect St, Morris St, East St
109	Raymond St, **E** 🅞 🄷 **W** 🅖 BP, Speedway/dsl 🍴 Little Caesars, White Castle 🅞 CVS Drug, Family$, Safeway
107	Keystone Ave, **E** 🅖 Mystik 🛏 Best Value Inn 🅞 🄷 **W** 🅖 Phillips 66/dsl, Speedway/dsl, Valero 🍴 Big Kahuna

Exit #	Services
107	Continued Pizza, Burger King, Denny's, McDonald's, Subway, Wendy 🛏 Comfort Inn 🅞 $General, U of Indianapolis, Walmart Mk
106	I-465 and I-74
103	Southport Rd, **E** 🍴 BP/McDonald's, Shell/Circle K 🍴 A by's, Chicago Grill, Chick-fil-A, El Puerto, Hardee's, Hong Kon Jimmy John's, Longhorn Steaks, Noble Roman's, O'Charley Panda Express, Panera Bread, Penn Sta Subs, Qdoba, Qui nos, Rally's, Starbucks, Taco Bell 🅞 Aldi Foods, AT&T, Fire stone/auto, Harley-Davidson, Home Depot, Kohl's, Meijer/ds e85, Menards, Radio Shack, Staples, Target, Verizon, **W** Marathon/Circle K, Phillips 66, Speedway/dsl 🍴 Bob Evan Burger King, Carrabba's, Cheeseburger Paradise, Cracker Ba rel, JT Johnson's Grill, KFC, McDonald's, Starbucks, Steak Shake, Subway, TX Roadhouse, Waffle House, Wendy's 🛏 Best Western, Comfort Suites, Country Inn&Suites, Courtyar Fairfield Inn, Hampton Inn, Jameson Inn, Quality Inn, Super 🅞 🄷, 7-11
101	CountyLine Rd, **E** 🍴 Candlewood Suites, **W** 🅖 Murph USA/dsl 🍴 Buffalo Wild Wings, El Mason Mexican, Firesid Rest., Little Mexico, Pasquale's Pizza, Tokyo Buffet 🛏 Hilto Garden, Holiday Inn Express, Value Place Hotel 🅞 🄷 Gand Mtn, Kroger, Verizon, Walmart/Subway
99	Greenwood, **E** 🅖 Road Ranger/◆Pilot◆/Subway/ds scales/24hr, **W** 🅖 Marathon, Shell/Circle K, Sunoco 🍴 A by's, Bob Evans, Byrd's Cafeteria, China Wok, Denny's, McDo ald's, Oaken Barrel Rest., Puerto Vallarta, Starbucks, Subwa Taco Bell, Waffle House, White Castle 🛏 Baymont Inn, InTow Suites, Red Carpet Inn, Red Roof Inn 🅞 🄷, Camping Worl RV Ctr, Sam's Club, vet
95	Whiteland, **E** 🅖 ⚡FLYING J/Denny's/scales/dsl/LF RV dump/24hr 🅞 Blue Beacon, SpeedCo, tires, **W** 🅖 ◆Loves/Arby's/dsl/scales/24hr, ◆Pilot◆/McDonald's/ds scales/24hr/ @ 🅞 Family RV Ctr
90	IN 44, Franklin, **W** 🅖 Marathon/Chester's/Subway/dsl, Shel Circle K 🍴 Burger King, El Torito, McDonald's/RV Parking Waffle House 🛏 Comfort Inn, Howard Johnson, Quality Inr Red Carpet Inn, Super 8 🅞 🄷, golf
85mm	Sugar Creek
82mm	Big Blue River
80	IN 252, to Flat Rock, Edinburgh, **W** 🅖 Shell/dsl, Sunoco/dsl
76b a	US 31, Taylorsville, **E** 🅖 Shell/Circle K/dsl, Speedway/dsl 🍴 A&W/KFC, Burger King, El Toreo Mexican, Waffle House 🛏 Red Roof Inn 🅞 🄷 $ General, Buick/Cadillac/Chevrolet GMC, Toyota, **W** 🅖 Marathon, Thornton's/café/dsl 🍴 Arby's Cracker Barrel, Hardee's, Max&Erma's, McDonald's, MT Mikes Ruby Tuesday, Snappy Tomato Pizza, Subway, Taco Bell 🛏 Best Western, Comfort Inn, Hampton Inn, Hilton Garden, Holi day Inn Express 🅞 antiques, Driftwood RV Camp, Goodyea Harley-Davidson, Premium Outlets/famous brands, repair
73mm	🅡ₛ both lanes, full 🚻 facilities, info, litter barrels, petwalk Ⓒ 🅰 vending
68mm	Driftwood River
68	IN 46, Columbus, **E** 🅖 Shell/Circle K, Speedway/dsl 🍴 Buffa lo Wild Wings, Burger King, Coldstone, Culver's, Dimitri's Rest. IHOP, Jimmy John's, McDonald's, RuYi Asian, Snappy Tomat Pizza, Starbucks, Subway, Wendy's 🛏 Comfort Inn&Suites Holiday Inn/rest., Sleep Inn, Super 8 🅞 🄷 AT&T, Menards Sam's Club/gas, Verizon, Walgreens, Walmart/Subway, **W** 🅖 BP, Swifty 🍴 Arby's, Bob Evans, Casa del Sol, Denny's, E Nopal Mexican, KFC, Noble Roman's, Papa's Grill, Taco Bel 🛏 Courtyard, Days Inn, La Quinta, Motel 6, Residence In 🅞 $General, CVS Drug, Jay-C Foods, to Brown Co SP

Side labels: **LEBANON** / **INDIANAPOLIS AREA** (left column); **GREENWOOD** / **COLUMBUS** (right column)

INTERSTATE 65 Cont'd

Exit #	Services
64	IN 58, Walesboro, W Marathon/dsl to RV camping
55	IN 11, to Jonesville, Seymour
54mm	White River
51mm	**weigh sta both lanes**
50b a	US 50, Seymour, E Marathon/Circle K/dsl, Swifty, TA/BP/Country Pride/dsl/24hr/ @ McDonald's, Waffle House Allstate Inn, Days Inn, EconoLodge, Motel 6, Super 8, W Citgo/dsl, Shell/Circle K/dsl, Speedway/dsl, Sunoco/dsl Applebee's, Arby's, Buffalo Wild Wings, Buffet China, Burger King, Capt D's, Chili's, Cracker Barrel, Domino's, DQ, El Nopal Mexican, Hardee's, KFC, Little Caesars, LJ Silver, McDonalds, Papa John's, Pizza Hut, Rally's, Ryan's, Steak'n Shake, Subway, Taco Bell, Tumbleweed Grill, Wendy's, White Castle Fairfield Inn, Hampton Inn, Holiday Inn Express, Knights Inn, Quality Inn H, $General, $Tree, Advance Parts, Aldi Foods, AT&T, AutoZone, BigLots, Buick/Cadillac/Chevrolet/GMC, Chrysler/Dodge/Jeep, CVS Drug, Ford, GNC, Home Depot, Jay-C Foods, JC Penney, O'Reilly Parts, Radio Shack, Russell Stover Candies, st police, Staples, Walgreens, Walmart/Subway
41	IN 250, Uniontown, E tires, W UnionTown/rest./dsl auto/truck repair
36	US 31, Crothersville, E Shell, W Marathon/dsl
34a b	IN 256, Austin, E Shell/Circle K Clifty Falls SP, to Hardy Lake, W Fuelmart/dsl/scales, Sunoco/Huddle House/dsl
29b a	IN 56, to Salem, Scottsburg, E MotoMart, Speedway/dsl Burger King, Cracker Barrel, KFC, Mariann Rest., Papa John's, Ponderosa, Sonic, Subway, Taco Bell Best Value Inn, Holiday Inn Express H, Ace Hardware, Advance Parts, AutoZone, CVS Drug, O'Reilly Parts, W Marathon, Murphy USA, Shell/Circle K Arby's, LJ Silver, McDonald's, Pizza Hut, Roadhouse USA, Waffle House, Wendy's Hampton Inn, Quality Inn, Super 8 Big O Tire, Jellystone Camping (4mi), Radio Shack, Verizon, Walmart/Subway
22mm	**both lanes, full facilities, info, litter barrels, petwalk vending**
19	IN 160, Henryville, E Marathon/Subway/dsl, Shell/Circle K Schuler's Rest. Family$
16	Memphis Rd, Memphis, E Loves/McDonald's/Subway/dsl/scales/24hr Fill'n Station Cafe, W Pilot/Arby's/dsl/scales/24hr/ @ Customers 1st RV Ctr
9	IN 311, to New Albany, Sellersburg, E 5 Star Gas, BP, Shell/Circle K, Swifty Arby's, Cracker Barrel, DQ, Quiznos, Waffle House Ramada Inn Carmerica/repair, Ford, O'Reilly Parts, st police, W Marathon/Circle K Burger King, El Nopal Mexican, McDonald's, Taco Bell Comfort Inn city park
7	IN 60, Hamburg, E Clark/dsl, W Cricket's Cafe, KFC/Pizza Hut Days Inn
6b a	I-265 W, to I-64 W, IN 265 E, New Albany
5	Veterans Parkway, E Shell/Circle K Beef'O Brady's H, Tire Discounters, W Buffalo Wild Wings, Cheddars, Chick-fil-A, Chuy's Mexican, DQ, Famous Dave's, IHOP, Krispy Kreme, Longhorn Steaks, McAlister's Deli, Moe's SW Grill, Olive Garden, Panera Bread, Papa Murphy's, Pizza Hut, Ruby Tuesday, Stevie B's Burgers, Studio Pizza, Subway, Taco Bell AT&T, Bass Pro Shops, Best Buy, Chevrolet, Lowe's, Michael's, Old Navy, Old Time Pottery, Petsmart, Rite Aid, Sam's Club/gas, Staples, Target, Verizon, Walmart/Subway

SEYMOUR

SCOTTSBURG

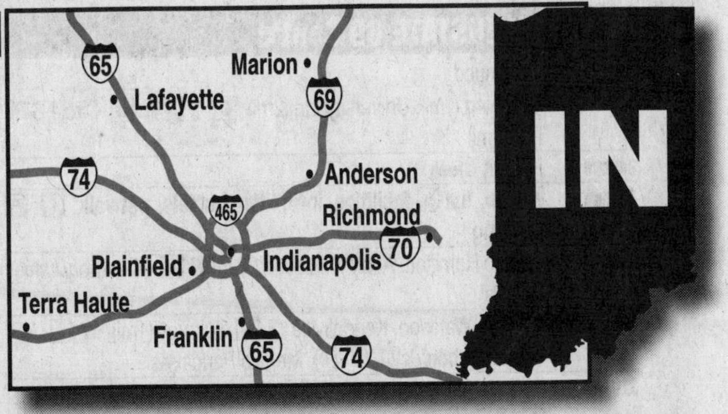

CLARKSVILLE

Exit #	Services
4	US 31 N, IN 131 S, Clarksville, New Albany, E Thorntons/Dunkin Donuts/dsl White Castle Value Place Inn Raben Tire, W Speedway/dsl Applebee's, Arby's, Bob Evans, Burger King, Capt D's, ChuckeCheese, Denny's, Don Pablo, El Caporal, Fazoli's, Frisch's, Golden Corral, Hooters, Iguana Rest., LJ Silver, Logan's Roadhouse, McDonald's, O'Charley's, Outback Steaks, Papa John's, Rally's, Red Lobster, Steak'n Shake, Wendy's Best Western, Candlewood Suites, Hampton Inn, Suburban Lodge $Tree, AT&T, AutoZone, BigLots, Books-A-Million, Buick/GMC, Dick's, Dillard's, Firestone/auto, Ford, Hobby Lobby, Home Depot, Honda, JC Penney, Jo-Ann Fabrics, Kia, Kroger/gas, Office Depot, O'Reilly Parts, PepBoys, Sears/auto, Toyota/Scion, Tuesday Morning, USPO, VW, Walgreens
2	Eastern Blvd, Clarksville, E Comfort Suites, Days Inn, Motel 6, Super 8 H, U-Haul, W Shell/Circle K Best Inn
1	US 31 S, IN 62, Stansifer Ave, E Thorntons DQ H Advance Parts, info ctr, Walgreens, W Holiday Inn Stinnett RV Ctr
0	Jeffersonville, E Thornton/Dunkin Donuts Hardee's, McDonald's, Waffle House H Chrysler/Jeep, Hyundai, Nissan, to Falls of OH SP, Walgreens, W Subway Fairfield Inn, Sheraton, TownePlace Suites
0mm	Indiana/Kentucky state line, Ohio River

IN

INTERSTATE 69

Exit #	Services
358mm	Indiana/Michigan state line
357	Lake George Rd, to IN 120, Fremont, Lake James, E Petro/Iron Skillet/dsl/LP/scales/24hr/ @ Comfort Inn, Hampton Inn, Travelers Inn Freightliner/Western Star Truck Repair, golf/rest, Kenworth, W Marathon/dsl, Pilot/Wendy's/dsl/scales/24hr, Shell/Subway/dsl McDonald's, Red Arrow Rest. Holiday Inn Express, Redwood Inn Freemont Outlets/Famous Brands, GNC, Jellystone Camping (5mi), to Pokagon SP
356	**I-80/90 Toll Rd**, E to Toledo, W to Chicago
354	IN 127, to IN 120, IN 727, Fremont, Orland, E Budgeteer Motel, Comfort Inn, Hampton Inn, Ramada, Travelers Inn golf, Oak Hill RV camp, W Marathon/dsl Holiday Inn Express Freemont Outlets/Famous Brands, Jellystone Camping (4mi), to Pokagon SP
350	Rd 200 W, to Lake James, Crooked Lake, E Sunoco/Subway/dsl fireworks, W Marathon, Shell Caruso's Rest., Tasty Pizza Marine Ctr
348	US 20, to Angola, Lagrange, E Marathon/Subway/dsl, Speedway/Taco Bell/dsl McDonald's Happy Acres

INTERSTATE 69 Cont'd

AUBURN

348	Continued Camping (1mi), University Inn (2mi) W Circle B RV Prk (2mi)
345mm	Pigeon Creek
344mm	**sb, full facilities, info, litter barrels, petwalk vending**
340	IN 4, to Hamilton, Ashley, Hudson, **1 mi** W Marathon/Ashley Deli/dsl
334	US 6, to Waterloo, Kendallville, E Subway (1mi), W BP/dsl, Marathon/dsl/24hr Maria's Pancakes
329	IN 8, to Garrett, Auburn, E BP, GA, Lassus, Speedway/dsl Applebee's, Arby's, Bob Evans, Burger King, China Buffet, DQ, KFC, Little Caesars, McDonald's, Papa John's, Peking Buffet, Penguin Point Rest., Pizza Hut, Ponderosa, Richard's Rest., Starbucks, Steak'n Shake, Subway, Taco Bell, Wendy's Comfort Suites, Days Inn, Holiday Inn Express, La Quinta, Quality Inn, Super 8 $General, $Tree, Ace Hardware, Advance Parts, AT&T, AutoZone, Buick/Chevrolet/RV Ctr, Chrysler/Dodge/Jeep, CVS Drug, Ford, GNC, Kroger/dsl, museum, Radio Shack, Staples, Walmart/Subway, W Marathon/dsl Buffalo Wild Wings, Cracker Barrel, Paradise Buffet Hampton Inn Home Depot, Verizon
326	Rd 11A, to Garrett, Auburn, E Kruse Auction Park, W camping
321	**nb, full facilities, info, litter barrels vending**
317	Union Chapel Rd,
316	IN 1 N, Dupont Rd, E Lassus/Elmo's/dsl, Phillips 66/Burger King Arby's, Culver's Comfort Suites, Hampton Inn W Speedway/dsl Bandito's Mexican, Bob Evans, Cozy Nook Cafe, Jimmy John's, Mancino's Grinders, McDonald's, Pine Valley Grill, Starbucks, Trolley Grill Baymont Inn, La Quinta
315	I-469, US 30 E, W Value Place Hotel
312b a	Coldwater Rd, E BP/dsl, Marathon, Sunoco Arby's, Chappell's, Chili's, Cork'N Cleaver, Hall's Factory Rest., Hunan Chinese, IHOP, Jimmy John's, Koto Japanese, Papa John's, Quiznos, Rally's, Red Lobster, Red River Steaks, Steak'n Shake, Taco Bell, Wendy's Hotel Ft Wayne, Hyatt Place $Tree, Hobby Lobby, Hyundai, JoAnn Fabrics, NAPA, O'Reilly Parts, PetCo, Tuesday Morning, Tuffy Auto, U-Haul, Walmart/Subway, W Dunkin Donuts
311b a	US 27 S, IN 3 N, E Shell/dsl, Sunoco/dsl Arby's, Cheddar's, ChuckECheese's, DQ, Fazoli's, Golden Corral, Hall's Rest., McDonald's, Olive Garden, Quaker Steak&Lube, TGIFriday's Candlewood Suites, Stay Inn, TownePlace Suites Aldi Foods, Barnes&Noble, Chevrolet, Chrysler/Dodge/Jeep, Costco/gas, Discount Tire, Fiat, Ford/Lincoln, Hancock Fabrics, Honda, Infiniti, JC Penney, Macy's, Nissan, Sears, Toyota/Scion, Verizon, W Lassus/Elmo's Pizza/dsl, Marathon Applebee's, Burger King, Cracker Barrel, Culver's, Golden China, IHOP, Logan's Roadhouse, McDonald's, Panda Express, Starbucks, Subway, Taco Bell, TX Roadhouse Best Value Inn,County Inn&Suites, Courtyard, Days Inn, EconoLodge, Extended Stay America, Fairfield Inn, Guesthouse Motel, Hampton Inn, Quality Inn, Super 8 CVS Drug, Gander Mtn, Home Depot, Lowe's, Meijer/dsl/E85, Sam's Club/gas, URGENT CARE, VW, Walgreens
309b a	US 33, Goshen Rd, Ft Wayne, E Pilot/dsl/scales/24hr, Sunoco/dsl Liberty Diner, McDonald's, Pace Rest. Clarion, Country Hearth Inn, Guest House Inn, Knights Inn,

FT WAYNE

309b a	Continued Motel 6, Red Roof Inn, Travel Inn auto/dsl repair, Blu Beacon, NAPA
305b a	IN 14 W, Ft Wayne, E Lassus, Murphy USA, Shell/Subway dsl, Speedway/dsl/LP Arby's, Biaggi's, Bob Evans, Burger King, Chick-fil-A, Chipotle Mexican, Coldstone, Eddy Merlo Rest., Firehouse Subs, Flat Top Grill, Great Wall Buffet, Logan's Roadhouse, McAlister's Deli, Noodles&Co., O'Charley's, Panda Express, Panera Bread, Papa Murphy's, Penn Sta Subs, Qdoba Smokey Bones BBQ, Starbucks, Steak'n Shake, Subway, Tilted Kilt Eatery, Wendy's Klopfenstein Suites $Tree Acura, Advance Parts, AT&T, Audi/Porsche, Barnes&Noble Best Buy, BigLots, BMW, Buick/GMC, Cadillac, Chevrolet Chrysler/Dodge/Jeep, Dick's, Ford/Lincoln, Hancock Fabrics Harley-Davidson, Kia, Kohl's, Lexus, Lowe's, mall, Marshalls Mazda, Meijer/dsl, Menards, Michael's, NAPA, Old Navy Petsmart, Radio Shack, Staples, Subaru, Target, to St Francis U, Toyota/Scion, Tuesday Morning, Verizon, vet, Volvo, Walmart
302	US 24, to Jefferson Blvd, Ft Wayne, E Subway (1mi), Taco Bell (1mi) Extended Stay America, Hampton Inn, Residence Inn to IN Wesleyan U, W Lassus, Marathon dsl Applebee's, Arby's, Bob Evans, Buffalo Wild Wings Carlos O'Kelly's, Coventry Tavern Rest., McDonald's, Naked Chopstix, Outback Steaks, Pizza Hut, Sara's Rest., Starbucks Wendy's, Zesto Drive-In Best Western Luxbury, Comfort Suites, Hilton Garden, Holiday Inn Express, Homewood Suites Staybridge Suites Kroger, Meineke, st police, Walgreens
299	Lower Huntington Rd, E to
296b a	I-469, US 24 E, US 33 S, E to
286	US 224, to Huntington, Markle, E Marathon (1mi), Phillips 66/Subway/dsl Daily Diner, DQ, Vinatelli's Guesthouse Inn, Super 8 repair/tires, W Roush Lake, to Huntington Reservoir
280mm	**weigh sta sb/parking area nb**
278	IN 5, to Warren, Huntington, E Phillips 66/dsl Huggy Bear Motel, W Marathon/Subway/dsl, Sunoco/Home TownDiner/dsl/scales/24hr McDonald's, Ugalde's Rest. Best Value Inn, Comfort Inn fireworks, RV Camping, to Salamonie Reservoir
276mm	Salamonie River
273	IN 218, to Warren
264	IN 18, to Marion, Montpelier, E Loves/McDonalds dsl/scales/24hr, W BP/Subway/dsl Arby's Best Value Inn Chrysler/Jeep, Harley-Davidson
260mm	Walnut Creek
259	US 35 N, IN 22, to Upland, E Valero/Subway Burger King, Casa Grande Mexican, China 1, Cracker Barrel Best Western, Super 8 Mar-Brook Camping, Taylor U, W Marathon/dsl, McClure Trkstp/dsl/24hr, Phillips 66/dsl Hardee's, KFC/Taco Bell, Starbucks Holiday Inn Express to IN Wesleyan
255	IN 26, to Fairmount
250mm	**both lanes, full facilities, info, litter barrels, petwalk vending**
245	US 35 S, IN 28, to Alexandria, Albany, E Petro/Shell/Iron Skillet/Subway/dsl/scales/24hr/ @ RV Camping
241	IN 332, to Muncie, Frankton, E BP/dsl to Ball St U
234	IN 67, to IN 32, Chesterfield, Daleville, E Pilot/Subway/dsl/scales/24hr, Shell Arby's, Pizza Hut, Smokehouse BBQ, Taco Bell, Waffle House, White Castle Budget Inn W McClure/dsl/E85, Pilot/Denny's/dsl/scales/24hr, Speedway/dsl 3rd Generation Pizza, McDonald's, Subway,

IN

INTERSTATE 69 Cont'd

234	Continued Wendy's Travel Inn flea mkt, Timberline Valley Camping (3mi)
226	IN 9, IN 109, to Anderson, E A&W/KFC, Culver's, Golden Corral, MT Mike's Deluxe Inn, Hampton Inn, Holiday Inn Express, Quality Inn Meijer/dsl, Menards, visitors ctr, W BP, Marathon/dsl, PayLess/dsl, Speedway/dsl Applebee's, Arby's, Bob Evans, Buffalo Wild Wings, Burger King, Cracker Barrel, Fazoli's, IHOP, Jimmy John's, LoneStar Steaks, Mayo Mexican, McDonald's, Olive Garden, Panda Express, Panera Bread, Papa Murphy's, Penn Sta Subs, Perkins, Pizza Hut, Poblanos Mexican, Qdoba, Quiznos, Red Lobster, Ruby Tuesday, Starbucks, Steak'n Shake, Subway, Taco Bell, Waffle House, Wendy's, White Castle Best Western, Comfort Inn, Days Inn, Fairfield Inn, Motel 6, Super 8 H $General, $Tree, Aldi Foods, AT&T, Cadillac/Chevrolet, Chrysler/Dodge/Jeep, Freightliner, GNC, Hobby Lobby, Kohl's, Lowe's, Marshalls, Office Depot, Old Navy, O'Reilly Parts, Petsmart, Radio Shack, Target, Tire Barn, to Anderson U, to Mounds SP, Toyota/Scion, Verizon, Walgreens, Walmart/Subway
222	IN 9, IN 67, to Anderson, W Speedway/dsl Skyline Chili H, st police
219	IN 38, Pendleton, E Marathon Burger King, McDonald's, Subway, W Pine Lakes Camping
214	IN 13, to Lapel, E BP Waffle House, W Pilot/Subway/dsl/scales/24hr camping
210	IN 238, to Noblesville, Fortville, E BP DQ, Starbucks, Taco Bell, Wendy's H W 5 Guys Burgers, BBQ, Bella Pizzeria, Coldstone, Famous Dave's, Houlihan's, McAlister's Deli, McDonald's, Mo's Cafe, Olive Garden, Panda Express, Paradise Cafe, Qdoba, Red Robin, Stone Creek Rest. Cambria Suites $Tree, AT&T, CVS Drug, Dick's, Earth Fare Foods, Firestone/auto, GNC, JC Penney, Old Navy, Radio Shack, Sleepy Bear Camping, Steinmart, Verizon
205	IN 37 N, 116th St, to Noblesville, Fishers, E ~~BP~~ La Fuente Mexican, Penn Sta Subs, Sunrise Cafe Fresh Mkt, Kroger, URGENT CARE, W Shell/Circle K, Speedway 5 Guys Burgers, Coldstone, Friaco's Mexican Grill, Greek Pizzaria, Handel's Ice Cream, Happy Dragon, Jet's Pizza, Marco's Pizza, Maya Mexican, McAlister's Deli, McDonald's, Moe's SW Grill, O'Charley's, Qdoba, Starbucks, Steak'n Shake, Subway, Wendy's, Wild Ginger Asian Hampton Inn AT&T, CVS Drug, Firestone/auto, Target
203	96th St, E Marathon/dsl, Murphy USA/dsl, Shell/Circle K Applebee's, Blimpie, Cracker Barrel, Donato's Pizza, Dunkin Donuts, Extreme Pizza, IHOP, Jimmy John's, McDonald's, Noodles&Co., Panda Express, Panera Bread, Qdoba, Ruby Tuesday, Sahm's Grill, Starbucks, Steak'n Shake, Subway, Tiawana Flats, Wendy's AmericInn, Baymont Inn, Hilton Garden, Holiday Inn, Studio 6 AT&T, Fry's, GNC, Kohl's, Marsh Food, Meijer/dsl, PepBoys, PetCo, Radio Shack, Staples, Tuesday Morning, Verizon, Walmart, W Marathon/dsl Arby's, Bob Evans, Burger King, Cheeseburger Paradise, Culver's, DJ's Hotdogs, Izakya Japanese, La Cabana, Panda Express, Peterson's Steaks/seafood, Quiznos, Starbucks, Taco Bell, Wolfie's Grill Comfort Suites, Residence Inn, SpringHill Suites, Staybridge Suites $Tree, Aldi Foods, Home Depot, Menards, NAPA, Sam's Club/gas
201	82nd St, Castleton, E Shell Boston Mkt, Burger King, Golden Corral, Jet's Pizza, O'Charley's $Inn, Drury Inn, Extended Stay, Hilton, Super 8 H CVS Drug, Lowe's,

ANDERSON

INDIANAPOLIS AREA

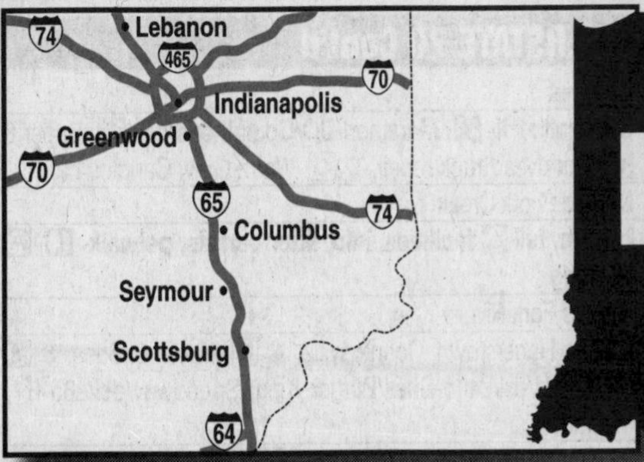

234	Continued Walgreens, W Speedway/dsl Applebee's, Arby's, Burger King, Castleton Grill, Charleston's Rest., Denny's, Domino's, Fazoli's, Formosa Buffet, Hooters, Houlihan's, Jimmy John's, Joe's Grille, KFC, LJ Silver, Longhorn Steaks, Los Cabos Mexican, McDonald's, Olive Garden, Penn Sta Subs, Pizza Hut, Rally's, Red Lobster, Skyline Chili, Starbucks, Stir Crazy, Subway, Taco Bell, Wendy's Candlewood Suites, Days Inn, Hampton Inn, Magnuson Hotel, Motel 6 $Tree, Aamco, Advance Parts, AutoZone, Best Buy, CarX, Dick's, Discount Tire, Firestone/auto, fireworks, Goodyear/auto, JC Penney, Macy's, mall, Midas, O'Reilly Parts, Sears/auto, Tire Barn, Verizon
200mm	I-465 around Indianapolis. **I-69 begins/ends on I-465, exit 37, at Indianapolis.**

INTERSTATE 70

Exit #	Services
156.5mm	Indiana/Ohio state line, **weigh sta**
156b a	US 40 E, Richmond, N Petro/BP/Iron Skillet/dsl/24hr/@ Fairfield Inn Blue Beacon, S BP/White Castle, Murphy USA/dsl, Shell/dsl, Speedway/dsl A&W/LJ Silver, Applebee's, Arby's, Big Boy, Bob Evans, Buffalo Wild Wings, Buffalo Wings&Rings, Burger King, Chili's, Chipotle Mexican, Cracker Barrel, El Rodeo Mexican, Fazoli's, Galo's Italian, Golden Corral, IHOP, Jade House Chinese, KFC, McDonald's, MCL Cafeteria, O'Charley's, Olive Garden, Papa Murphy's, Pizza Hut, Rally's, Red Lobster, Starbucks, Steak'n Shake, Subway, Taco Bell, TX Roadhouse, Yamato Japanese Days Inn, EconoLodge, Hampton Inn, Holiday Inn, Motel 6, Quality Inn $General, $Tree, Advance Parts, Aldi Foods, AT&T, Best Buy, Big Lots, Buick/GMC, CarQuest, Chevrolet, Chrysler/Dodge/Jeep, Dick's, Dillard's, Firestone/auto, Ford, Hastings Books, Hobby Lobby, JC Penney, Jo-Ann Fabrics, Kohl's, Kroger/dsl, Lowe's, Menards, O'Reilly Parts, Save-A-Lot Foods, Tires+, TJ Maxx, Toyota/Scion/Nissan, U-Haul, Verizon, Walgreens, Walmart/Subway
153	IN 227, to Whitewater, Richmond, **2 mi** N KOA, car repair, Grandpa's Farm RV Park (seasonal)
151b a	US 27, to Chester, Richmond, N Fricker's Rest. Honda, KOA, S Shell Bob Evans, Burger King, Carver's Rest., China Buffet, McDonald's, Rally's, Subway, Taco Bell, Wendy's Comfort Inn, Super 8 H CVS Drug, Harley-Davidson, Meijer/dsl/E85
149b a	US 35, IN 38, to Muncie, N Loves/Hardee's/dsl/scales/24hr, S Shell/dsl Camping World RV Ctr
148mm	**weigh sta wb**

RICHMOND

IN

= gas = food = lodging = other = rest stop

INTERSTATE 70 Cont'd

Exit #	Services
145	Centerville, N Marathon/DQ/Godfather's/dsl Super 8 Goodyear/truck repair, S Warm Glow Candles/cafe
145mm	Nolands Fork Creek
144mm	**wb, full facilities, info, litter barrels, petwalk vending**
141mm	Greens Fork River
137	IN 1, to Hagerstown, Connersville, N Amish Cheese, S BP/Arby's/dsl/24hr, Shell/Burger King, Speedway/dsl/e85 McDonald's
131	Wilbur Wright Rd, New Lisbon, S Shell/Pizza Hut/Taco Bell/dsl/scales/24hr/ @ New Lisbon RV park
126mm	Flatrock River
123	IN 3, to New Castle, Spiceland, N All American Inn (3mi), Holiday Inn Express (3mi) S FLYING J/Denny's/Subway/dsl/LP/scales/24hr, Mr Fuel/rest./dsl/scales/24hr Montgomery's Steaks tires/repair
117mm	Big Blue River
115	IN 109, to Knightstown, Wilkinson, N Loves/McDonald's/Subway/dsl/scales/24hr, Speedway/rest./dsl/scales/24hr Burger King Jellystone Camping
107mm	**both lanes, full facilities, litter barrels, petwalk vending**
104	IN 9, Greenfield, Maxwell, N Speedway/dsl, S Murphy USA/dsl, Shell/Circle K, Speedway/dsl, Sunoco/dsl Applebee's, Arby's, Bamboo Garden, Bob Evans, Burger King, Chicago's Pizza, China Inn, Cracker Barrel, Culver's, Firehouse Subs, Hardee's, Jimmy John's, KFC, Little Caesars, McDonald's, Mi Casa Mexican, Mozzi's Pizza, MT Mike's Steaks, O'Charley's, Papa John's, Papa Murphy's, Penn Sta Subs, Pizza Hut, Ponderosa, Popeye's, Qdoba, Starbucks, Steak'n Shake, Subway, Taco Bell, Waffle House, Wasabi, Wendy's, White Castle, Wings Etc Comfort Inn, Country Inn&Suites, Greenfield Inn, Hampton Inn, Holiday Inn Express, Quality Inn, Super 8 $General, $Tree, Advance Parts, Aldi Foods, AutoZone, Big Lots, CVS Drug, Gander Mtn, GNC, Home Depot, Kroger/dsl, Marsh Foods, Verizon, Walgreens, Walmart
96	Mt Comfort Rd, N Pilot/Pizza Hut/dsl/scales/24hr, Speedway/Subway/dsl Burger King, Wendy's, S Shell/Circle K McDonald's KOA (seasonal), Mt Comfort RV Ctr
91	Post Rd, to Ft Harrison, N Mobil/Circle K Cracker Barrel, Denny's, Outback Steaks, Steak'n Shake, Wendy's InTown Suites, La Quinta Lowe's, st police, S Admiral, BP/dsl, Shell/dsl, Speedway Hardee's, Jack-in-the-Box, KFC/Taco Bell, Little Caesar's, Subway, Waffle House Country Hearth Inn, Days Inn CVS Drug, Family$, Home Depot, Marsh Foods
90	I-465 (from wb)
89	Shadeland Ave, I-465 (from eb), N Marathon/dsl Bob Evans Comfort Inn, Hampton Inn, Holiday Inn Express, Motel 6 Toyota/Scion, U-Haul, S Admiral/dsl, Circle K, Marathon, Shell, Speedway/dsl Arby's, Burger King, Damon's, Four Seasons Diner, Jimmy John's, Lincoln Sq Rest., McDonald's, Papa John's, Penn Sta Subs, Rally's, Red Lobster, Starbucks, Subway, Taco Bell, TX Roadhouse, Wendy's, Zelma's Rest. Always Inn, Best Value Inn, Candlewood Suites, Fairfield Inn, Knights Inn, La Quinta, Marriott, Quality Inn $General, CarX, Chevrolet, Chrysler/Dodge/Jeep, CVS Drug, Honda, Kia, Kroger/gas, Mazda, Nissan
87	Emerson Ave, N BP/McDonald's, Speedway/dsl, S Shell
85b a	Rural St, Keystone Ave, N fairgrounds
83b (112)	I-65 N, to Chicago
83a (111)	Michigan St, Market St, S Hardee's, downtown
80 (110a)	I-65 S, to Louisville
79b	Illinois St, McCarty St, downtown
79a	West St, N Speedway/dsl Comfort Suites, Holiday Inn Express, Hyatt, JW Marriott, Staybridge Suites Gov Ctr, Lucas Oil Stadium, zoo
78	Harding St, to downtown, S Marathon/Subway Wendy's
77	Holt Rd, N Phillips 66/dsl Rally's, Steak'n Shake, S Shell/dsl McDonald's Ford /Volvo Trucks
75	Expswy, to Raymond St (no EZ wb return), N Marathon/dsl, Speedway/dsl Indy's Rest., Jimmy John's, Library Rest., Subway, Waffle House Candlewood Suites, Courtyard, Extended Stay America, Fairfield Inn, Hyatt Place, La Quinta, Quality Inn, Ramada, Residence Inn, Super 8, Wyndham NAPA, to Airport Expressway
73b a	I-465 N/S, I-74 E/W
69	(only from eb) to I-74 E, to I-465 S
68	Six Points Rd, N Hampton Inn , S Subway Hilton Garden, Holiday Inn
66	IN 267, to Plainfield, Mooresville, N Blu/dsl, BP, Shell/Circle K, Speedway/dsl, Thornton's/dsl Arby's, Bob Evans, Burger King, Coachman Rest., Cracker Barrel, Golden Corral, McDonald's, Narita Japanese, Steak'n Shake, Subway, Taco Bell, Waffle House, White Castle Baymont Inn, Best Western, Budget Inn, Cambria Suites, Comfort Inn, Days Inn, Hampton Inn, Holiday Inn Express, Homewood Suites, La Quinta, Quality Inn, Staybridge Suites, Super 8, ValuePlace Inn, Wingate Inn Buick/GMC, Chateau Thomas Winery, Harley-Davidson
65mm	**both lanes, full facilities, info, litter barrels, petwalk vending**
59	IN 39, to Belleville, N Loves/McDonald's/Subway/dsl/scales/24hr, S TA/Country Pride/dsl/scales/24hr/ @ truckwash
51	Rd 1100W, S Koger's/Sunoco/dsl/rest./24hr repair/towing/24hr
41	US 231, to Greencastle, Cloverdale, S BP/dsl, Casey's (2mi), Marathon/dsl/scales/24hr Arby's, Chicago's Pizza, El Cantarito, KFC, McDonald's, Subway, Taco Bell Days Inn, EconoLodge, Holiday Inn Express, Motel 6, Super 8 $General, Family$, Jordan's Carcare, NAPA, Taylor's Hardware, to Lieber SRA, Value Mkt Foods
37	IN 243, to Putnamville, S Marathon/dsl Misty Morning Campground (4mi), to Lieber SRA
23	IN 59, to Brazil, N Pilot/McDonald's/Subway/dsl/scales/24hr truck repair, S BP/dsl, Petro/Iron Skillet/dsl/scales/24hr/ @, Road Ranger/Pilot/Subway/dsl/scales Burger King, Family Table Rest. Best Western, Knights Inn
15mm	Honey Creek
11	IN 46, Terre Haute, N Pilot/Subway/dsl/scales/24hr, Thornton/dsl Burger King, Holiday Inn Express, McDonald's, Real Hacienda, Sonic, Taco Bell $Tree, , GNC, Meijer/dsl, Verizon, Walmart, S KOA
7	US 41, US 150, Terre Haute, N Casey's/dsl, Marathon/dsl, Thornton's/dsl Applebee's, Bob Evans, Coyote's Mexican, Cracker Barrel, East Star Buffet, Fazoli's, IHOP, Moe's SW Grill, NewDay Cafe, Pizza Hut, Real Hacienda Mexican, Starbucks, Steak'n Shake, TX Roadhouse, Wise Pies Comfort Suites,

GREENFIELD

INDIANAPOLIS AREA

TERRE HAUTE

ID

INTERSTATE 70 Cont'd

TERRE HAUTE

7	Continued Days Inn, Drury Inn, Fairfield Inn, PearTree Inn, Red Roof Inn, Super 8 AT&T, AutoZone, Chrysler/Jeep, Kia, Mike's Mkt, O'Reilly Parts, URGENT CARE, S Speedway/dsl, Thornton's/dsl Arby's, Baskin-Robbins, Buffalo Wild Wings, Burger King, Cheddar's, Chick-fil-A, Chili's, Denny's, DQ, Five Guys, Fuddrucker's, Golden Corral, Hardee's, Jimmy John's, KFC, Little Caesar's, LJ Silver, Los Tres Caminos, McDonald's, Monical's Pizza, Olive Garden, Outback Steaks, Panda Express, Panda Garden, Panera Bread, Papa John's, Penn Sta Subs, Qdoba, Rally's, Red Lobster, Ruby Tuesday, Ryan's, Starbucks, Subway, Taco Bell, TGIFriday's, Wendy's, White Castle Hampton Inn, Holiday Inn, Motel 6, SpringHill Suites H $Tree, Aldi Foods, AT&T, Best Buy, Big O Tire, BigLots, BooksAMillion, Buick/Cadillac/GMC, Burlington Coats, Chevrolet, Dodge, Ford, Gander Mtn, Goodyear/auto, Harley-Davidson, Hobby Lobby, Hyundai, JC Penney, Jo-Ann Fabrics, K-Mart/gas, Kohl's, Kroger/dsl, Lowe's, Macy's, NAPA, Nissan, Old Navy, Petsmart, Sam's Club/gas, Sears/auto, Staples, Tire Barn, TJ Maxx, Verizon, Walgreens, Walmart
5.5mm	Wabash River
3	Darwin Rd, W Terre Haute, N to St Mary of-the-Woods Coll
1.5mm	**Welcome Ctr eb, full facilities, info, litter barrels, petwalk vending**
1	US 40 E (from eb, exits left), to Terre Haute, W Terre Haute
.5mm	**eb only, weigh sta**
0mm	Indiana/Illinois state line

INTERSTATE 74

GREENSBURG

Exit #	Services
171.5mm	Indiana/Ohio state line
171mm	**weigh sta wb**
169	US 52 W, to Brookville
168.5mm	Whitewater River
164	IN 1, St Leon, N Exxon/Noble Romans, Shell/dsl, S BP/Blimpie/dsl Skyline Chili
156	IN 101, to Sunman, Milan, S Exxon/dsl KOA (2mi)
152mm	**both lanes, full facilities, info, litter barrels, petwalk vending**
149	IN 229, to Oldenburg, Batesville, N Marathon, Shell/dsl China Buffet, McDonald's, Pizza Hut, Pizza King, Subway, Toros Mexican, Wendy's Hampton Inn $General, Advance Parts, Kroger/dsl, ShopKo, URGENT CARE, Verizon, S BP Arby's, DQ, KFC/Taco Bell, La Rosa's Pizza, Skyline Chili, Steak'n Shake Comfort Inn H, CVS Drug, O'Reilly Parts
143	to IN 46, New Point, N Petro/Iron Skillet/Subway/dsl/scales/24hr/@, S BP Hwy 46 Inn
134b a	IN 3, to Rushville, Greensburg, S BP/dsl, Marathon/DQ/Subway, Speedway/dsl A&W, Arby's, Big Boy, Buffalo Wings&Rings, Burger King, Chili's, El Chile Poblano, El Reparo Mexican, Great Wall Buffet, Jimmy John's, KFC/LJ Silver, Lincoln St Grill, Little Caesars, McDonald's, Papa John's, Pizza Hut, Taco Bell, Waffle House, Wendy's Baymont Inn, Holiday Inn Express, Quality Inn $General, $Tree, Aldi Foods, AT&T, AutoZone, Buick/Chevrolet, Chrysler/Dodge/Jeep, CVS Drug, Ford, GNC, O'Reilly Parts, TrueValue, Verizon, Walgreens, Walmart/Subway
132	US 421, to Greensburg, S BP/dsl, CNG Hampton Inn, Holiday Inn Express (2mi)
130mm	Clifty Creek

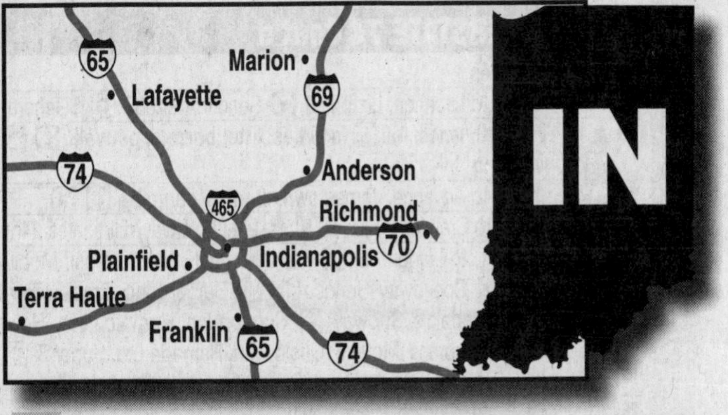

SHELBYVILLE

123	Saint Paul, S Loves/McDonald's/Subway/dsl/scales/24hr camping, repair
119	IN 244 E, to Milroy
116	IN 44, to Shelbyville, Rushville, N Marathon/Circle K/dsl, S BP/dsl, Country Mark/dsl, Marathon, Murphy USA/dsl, Sunoco/dsl Agustin's Mexican, Applebee's, Arby's, Bellacino's, Bob Evans, Buffalo Wild Wings, Burger King, China Wok, Cholula Mexican, Denny's, Domino's, DQ, Dunkin Donuts, Fazoli's, Jimmy John's, KFC, King Buffet, McDonald's, Papa John's, Penn Sta Subs, Pizza Hut, Rally's, Starbucks, Subway, Taco Bell, Wendy's, White Castle Quality Inn H, $General, $Tree, Ace Hardware, Advance Parts, Aldi Foods, AT&T, AutoZone, BigLots, Chevrolet, Ford, GNC, Kroger/dsl, Midas, O'Reilly Parts, Verizon, Walgreens, Walmart/Subway
115mm	Little Blue River
113mm	Big Blue River
113	IN 9, to Shelbyville, N Speedway/dsl Cracker Barrel, TX Corral, Wendy's, S Shell, Shell/Circle K/Subway/dsl McDonald's, Waffle House Comfort Inn, EconoLodge, Hampton Inn, Holiday Inn Express, Super 8 H
109	Fairland Rd, N Pilot/McDonald's/dsl/scales/24hr Indiana Downs/casino, S Brownie's Marine
103	London Rd, to Boggstown
102mm	Big Sugar Creek
101	Pleasant View Rd, N Country Mark/dsl/repair
99	Acton Rd
96	Post Rd, N Marathon/Subway/dsl/24hr McDonald's, S Shell/Circle K/dsl Wendy's Chevrolet
94b a	I-465/I-74 W, I-465 N, US 421 N.

I-74 and I-465 run together 21 miles. See I-465 exits 2-16, and 52-53.

BROWNSBURG

73b	I-465 N, access to same services as 16a on I-465
73a	I-465 S, I-74 E
71mm	Eagle Creek
68	Ronald Reagan Pkwy
66	IN 267, Brownsburg, N Citgo/dsl, Shell/Circle K Applebee's, Asia Wok, Buffalo Wild Wings, Dunkin Donuts, Hardee's, Papa's Pizzaria, Steak'n Shake, Subway, Tequila Mexican Hampton Inn, Quality Inn Big O Tire, Midas, S BP/dsl, Speedway/dsl Arby's, Bob Evans, Burger King, China's Best, Elegance Rest., Firehouse Subs, Five Guys, HoWah, IHOP, Jimmy John's, KFC, Little Caesar's, McDonald's, Mediterranean Pizza, Papa Murphy's, Penn Sta Subs, Starbucks, Taco Bell, The Toros Mexican, Wendy's, White Castle Comfort Suites, Super 8 AT&T, Firestone/auto, Ford, GNC, K-Mart,Kohl's, Kroger/gas, Lowe's, O'Reilly Parts, Radio Shack, USPO, Verizon, Walmart/Subway
61	to Pittsboro, S Loves /Godfather's/Subway/dsl/scales/24hr

IN

[gas] = gas [food] = food [lodging] = lodging [other] = other [rest stop] = rest stop

INTERSTATE 74 Cont'd

Exit #	Services
58	IN 39, to Lebanon, Lizton, **S** [gas] Sunoco/dsl/e85 [other] $General
57mm	**[rest stop] both lanes, full [handicapped] facilities, litter barrels, petwalk [phone] [picnic] vending**
52	IN 75, to Advance, Jamestown, **2 mi S** camping [food] [gas]
39	IN 32, to Crawfordsville, **S** [gas] Pilot/Subway/dsl/scales/24hr
34	US 231, to Linden, **S** [gas] Marathon/dsl, McClure/dsl, Mobil/Circle K, Speedway, Sunoco/dsl [food] Burger King, Cracker Barrel, McDonald's, Subway [lodging] Comfort Inn, Hampton Inn, Holiday Inn Express, Motel 6, Quality Inn, Ramada Ltd, Super 8 [other] [H], KOA (1mi), Sugar Creek Campground (4mi)
25	IN 25, to Wingate, Waynetown
19mm	**weigh sta eb/parking area wb**
15	US 41, to Attica, Veedersburg, **1 mi S** [gas] Casey's/dsl, Marathon/dsl, Valero/Subway [food] Apple Tree Diner [other] camping, Family$, to Turkey Run SP
8	Covington, **N** [gas] Marathon/dsl, Valero/dsl [food] Benjamin's, Overpass Pizza, Snoddy's Mill Grill [other] fireworks, Ford
7mm	Wabash River
4	IN 63, to Newport, **N** [gas] Pilot/Arby's/dsl/scales/24hr, Shell/Wendy's [food] Beefhouse Rest.
1mm	**Welcome Ctr eb, full [handicapped] facilities, info, litter barrels, petwalk [phone] [picnic] vending**
0mm	Indiana/Illinois state line, Eastern/Central Time Zone

INTERSTATE 80/90

Exit #	Services
157mm	Indiana/Ohio state line
153mm	**toll plaza,** litter barrels
146mm	**TP both lanes,** [gas] Mobil/dsl [food] McDonald's
144	I-69, US 27, Angola, Ft Wayne, **N** [gas] Petro/BP/dsl/scales/@, Pilot/Wendy's/dsl/scales, Shell/Subway/dsl [food] Clay's Family Rest., Lake George Rest., McDonald's, Red Arrow Rest. [lodging] Redwood Inn [other] Freightliner/Western Star/truck repair, **S** [gas] Marathon/dsl [other] Freemont Outlet Shops/famous brands, GNC, **Services on IN 120 E** [lodging] Comfort Inn, Hampton Inn, Holiday Inn Express, Travelers Inn [other] golf/rest, **W** to Pokagon SP, Jellystone Camping (5mi)
131.5mm	Fawn River
126mm	**Ernie Pyle TP both lanes,** [gas] Mobil/dsl [food] Hardee's, Red Burrito [other] gifts, RV dump
121	IN 9, to Lagrange, Howe, **2 mi N** [gas] Golden Buddha, Marathon, Murphy USA/dsl, Speedway/dsl [food] Applebee's, Burger King, Fiesta Mexican, Hot'n Now, KFC, King Dragon, Little Caesar's, McDonald's, Pizza Hut, Subway, Taco Bell, Wendy's [lodging] American Inn, Best Western, Country Hearth Inn, Hampton Inn, Regency Inn, Sturgess Inn, Travel Inn [other] $Tree, AT&T, Cadillac/Chevrolet, CarQuest, Family$, Ford, GNC, [H] (4mi), K-Mart, Kroger, Radio Shack, Rite Aid, Walgreens, Walmart/Subway, **S** [gas] Valero/dsl [lodging] Holiday Inn Express, Super 8 [other] [H] (8mi)
120mm	Fawn River
108mm	**[rest stop] both lanes, trucks only**
107	US 131, IN 13, to Middlebury, Constantine, **0-3 mi N** [gas] Marathon/dsl, Speedway [food] Country Table Rest., McDonald's [lodging] Patchwork Quilt Inn, Plaza Motel, Tower Motel [other] $General, Family$, **1 mi S** [gas] BP/Blimpie/dsl [food] Yup's DairyLand [lodging] McKenzie House B&B [other] Eby's Pines RV Park, KOA (Apr-Nov)
101	IN 15, to Goshen, Bristol, **0-2 mi S** [gas] 7-11, Speedway/dsl [food] River Inn Rest., Subway [other] Eby's Pines Camping (3mi), USPO

ELKHART

MISHAWAKA

SOUTH BEND

Exit #	Services
96	Rd 1, E Elkhart, **2 mi S** [gas] 7-11, BP/dsl, Marathon [food] Arby's, China Star, DQ, McDonald's, Subway, Taco Bell [other] Ace Hardware, RV/MH Hall of Fame
92	IN 19, to Elkhart, **N** [gas] 7-11, Marathon, Phillips 66/Subway/dsl [food] Applebee's, Cracker Barrel, Golden Egg Pancakes, Perkins, Steak'n Shake [lodging] Best Western, Candlewood Suites, Comfort Suites, Country Inn&Suites, Diplomat Motel, EconoLodge, Fairway Inn, Hampton Inn, Hilton Garden, Holiday Inn Express, Microtel, Quality Inn, Sleep Inn, Staybridge Suties, Turnpike Motel [other] $General, Aldi Foods, CVS Drug, Elkhart Campground (1mi), GNC, K-Mart, Martin's Foods, tires, transmissions, Walgreens, **0-2mi S** [gas] Marathon/dsl, Shell, Speedway [food] Arby's, Bob Evans, Burger King, Callahan's, Chicago Grill, Chubby Trout, Culver's, Da Vinci's Pizza, DQ, El Camino Royal, Jimmy John's, KFC, King Wha Chinese, LJ Silver, Marco's Pizza, Matterhorn Rest., McDonald's, North Garden Buffet, Olive Garden, Papa John's, Pizza Hut, Red Lobster, Ryan's, Subway, Taco Bell, Texas Roadhouse, Wendy's, Wings Etc. [lodging] Budget Inn, Days Inn, Jameson Inn, Red Roof Inn, Super 8 [other] [H], $Tree, Ace Hardware, Advance Parts, AT&T, AutoZone, CarQuest, Family$, Lowe's, Menards, O'Reilly Parts, Radio Shack, Verizon, vet, Walmart
91mm	Christiana Creek
90mm	**Schricker TP both directions,** [gas] Phillips 66/dsl [food] Burger King, Pizza Hut, Starbucks [other] RV Dump, USPO, Z Mkt
83	to Mishawaka, **N** [gas] BP/dsl, Phillips 66/Subway/dsl [food] Applebee's, Moe's SW Grill, [lodging] Country Inn&Suites, Hampton Inn, Red Roof Inn, [other] $Tree, CVS Drug, Marshall's, Martin's Foods/gas, Menards, PetCo, Target, vet, Walgreens, **N 1-2 mi in IN 23 W** [food] 5 Guys Burgers, Barlouie, Famous Dave's BBQ, Granite City Grill, King's Buffet, Olive Garden, Papa Murphy's, Pizza Hut, Subway, Wendy's, Wings Etc. [lodging] Fairfield Inn, Holiday Inn Express, Super 8 [other] Barnes&Noble, Best Buy, JC Penney, KOA (mar-nov), Macy's, mall, Michael's, Sears/auto, **S 2 mi on Grape Rd & Main St (off IN 23W)** [food] Arby's, Bob Evans, Buffalo Wild Wings, Burger King, Carraba's, Chick-fil-A, Chili's, Chipotle Mexican, CiCi's Pizza, Culver's, Del Taco, Hacienta Mexican, Hooters, Houlihan's, IHOP, Jimmy John's, Krispy Kreme, Logan's Roadhouse, Mancino's Pizza, Max&Erma's, McDonald's, Old Country Buffet, Outback Steaks, Panera Bread, Papa Vino's Italian, Quiznos, Red Lobster, Red Robin, Sonic, Starbucks, Steak'n Shake, Subway, Taste of Asia, TGIFriday's [lodging] Comfort Inn, Courtyard, Extended Stay America, Hyatt Place Hotel, Residence Inn, SpringHill Suites, Studio+ [other] [H], Aldi Foods, Barnes&Noble, Buick/GMC/Hyundai, Christmas Tree Shop, Discount Tire, Hobby Lobby, Home Depot, Honda, Jo-Ann Fabrics, Kohl's, Lexus, Lowe's, Meijer/dsl, Meijer/gas, Mercedes, Nissan, Office Depot, Old Navy, Petsmart, Sam's Club, TJ Maxx, VW, Walmart
77	US 33, US 31B, IN 933, South Bend, **N** [gas] Admiral, Mobil/dsl, [food] Arby's, DQ, Eleni's Rest., Fazoli's, Marco's Pizza, McDonald's, Papa John's, Ponderosa, Starbucks, Steak'nShake, Subway [lodging] Comfort Suites, Hampton Inn, Motel 6, Suburban Lodge, Waterford Lodge [other] AutoZone, BMW/Mazda, NAPA, O'Reilly Parts, TrueValue, Walgreens, **2 mi N on frtge rd** [gas] Murphy USA/dsl, [food] Applebee's, Burger King, Hacienda Mexican, Jimmy John's, KFC, McDonald's, Pizza Hut, Sonic, [other] $Tree, Aldi Foods, Meijer/dsl/24hr, Walmart/Subway, **S** [gas] Marathon, Phillips 66/Subway/dsl [food] American Pancake House, Bob Evans, HoPing House Chinese, King Gyros, Perkins, Pizza King, Taco Bell, Wendy's [lodging] Best

INTERSTATE 80/90 Cont'd

77 Continued
Value Inn, Econolodge, Hilton Garden, Holiday Inn Express, Microtel, Quality Inn, St Marys Inn CarX, to Notre Dame

76mm St Joseph River

72 US 31, to Niles, South Bend, **N** Pilot/Subway/dsl/scales/24hr, Speedway/Subway/dsl Bruno's Pizza, El Arriero, Taco Bell, **S**, to Potato Creek SP (20mi)

62mm Eastern Time Zone/Central Time Zone

56mm **TP both lanes,** Phillips 66/dsl DQ, McDonald's litter barrel RV dump

49 IN 39, to La Porte, **N** Hampton Inn, **3 mi S** Family Express, Phillips 66/dsl DQ, El Bracero Mexican Best Western, Blue Heron Inn, Cassidy Inn & RV, Holiday Inn Express, Travelodge

39 US 421, to Michigan City, Westville, **S** Purdue U North Cent

38mm **trucks only, both lanes, litter barrels**

31 IN 49, to Chesterton, Valparaiso, **N** Family Express/dsl, Phillips 66, Speedway/dsl AJ's Pizza, Bob Evans, Clock Rest., Culver's Hilton Garden CVS Drug, Sand Creek RV Park (3mi, Apr-Oct), Strack&Van Til Mkt, Tire Pros, to IN Dunes Nat Lakeshore, **S** Hampton Inn (8mi), Super 8 (8mi)

24mm **toll plaza**

PORTAGE

23 Portage, Port of Indiana, **0-2 mi N** Marathon, Shell Denny's, Mark's Grill $Inn, Best Western, Comfort Inn, Country Inn&Suites, Days Inn, Holiday Inn Express, Super 8, **S** BP, Speedway/dsl Burger King, CiCi's Pizza, DQ, Dunkin Donuts, El Contarito Mexican, Jimmy John's, KFC, Little Caesar's, McDonald's, Rosewood Rest., Starbucks, Subway, Wendy's Ace Hardware, Advance Parts, AutoZone, Family$, GNC, O'Reilly Parts, Town&Country Mkt, USPO, Verizon, Walgreens

22mm **TP both lanes,** Phillips 66/dsl Hardee's, Red Burrito info, scales

21mm **I-90 and I-80 run together eb, separate wb. I-80 runs with I-94 wb. For I-80 exits 1 through 15, see Indiana Interstate 94.**

21 I-94 E to Detroit, I-80/94 W, US 6, IN 51, Lake Station, **S** FLYING J/Denny's/dsl/scales/24hr/ @, Mr Fuel/dsl/scales/24hr, Pilot/Road Ranger/Subway/dsl/scales, TA/BP/Popeye's/dsl/scales/24hr/ @ Blue Beacon

17 I-65 S, US 12, US 20, Dunes Hwy, to Indianapolis

14b IN 53, to Gary, Broadway, **S** Citgo

14a Grant St, to Gary, **S**

10 IN 912, Cline Ave, to Gary, **N**, casino

5 US 41, Calumet Ave, to Hammond, **S** Nice'n Easy, Race-Co, Speedway/dsl Arby's, Aurelio's Pizza, Dunkin Donuts, Johnel's Rest., KFC, McDonald's, Subway, Taco Bell, White Castle Quality Inn, Ramada Inn, Super 8 Aldi Foods, AutoZone, Murray's Parts, Walgreens

3 IN 912, Cline Ave, to Hammond, **S** BP, to Gary Reg

1.5mm toll plaza

1mm US 12, US 20, 106th St, Indianapolis Blvd, **N** Citgo, Mobil, Shell/dsl casino, **S** Burger King, KFC, McDonald's Aldi Foods, auto repair, Jewel-Osco

0mm Indiana/Illinois state line

INTERSTATE 94

Exit #	Services
46mm	Indiana/Michigan state line

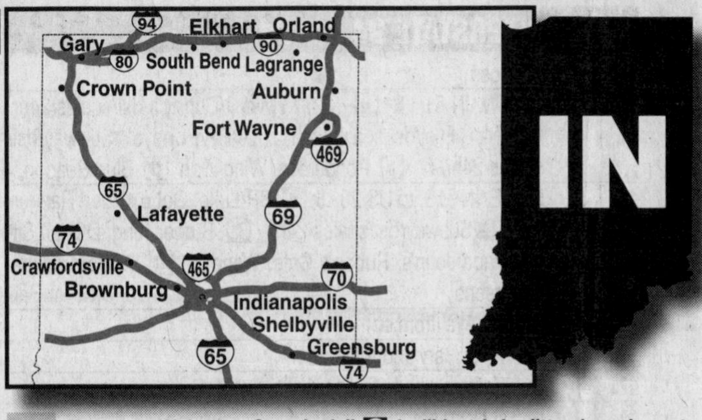

43mm **Welcome Ctr wb, full facilities, info, litter barrels, petwalk vending**

40b a US 20, US 35, to Michigan City, **N** McDonald's (3mi) **S** Speedway/dsl

34b a US 421, to Michigan City, **N** BP/dsl, Family Express/e-85, Speedway/dsl, Speedway/White Castle/dsl Arby's, Baskin-Robbins/Dunkin Donuts, Buffalo Wild Wings, Burger King, Chili's, Crawford's Eatery, Culver's, Denny's, El Bracero Mexican, Fiesta Cantina, Hibachi Buffet, IHOP, Jimmy John's, KFC, LJ Silver, McDonald's, Olive Garden, Panda Express, Panera Bread, Pizza Hut/Taco Bell, Red Lobster, Ryan's, Schoop's Rest., Sophia's Pancakes, Starbucks, Steak'n Shake, Subway, TX Corral, Wendy's ABC Motel, Baymont Inn, Clarion, Comfort Inn, Country Inn&Suites, Hampton Inn, Knights Inn, Microtel, Red Roof Inn, Super 8, Travel Inn $General, $Tree, Advance Parts, Aldi Foods, AT&T, AutoZone, Big R, Big-Lots, Family$, Fannie May Candies, Ford/Lincoln, GNC, Hobby Lobby, JC Penney, Jo-Ann Fabrics, Kohl's, Lowe's, Meijer/dsl, Menards, Midas, Petsmart, Radio Shack, Ross, Save-a-Lot, Sears/auto, TJ Maxx, Verizon, Walgreens, Walmart/Subway, **S** Speedway/Subway/dsl/scales/24hr Buick/Chevrolet/GMC, Harley-Davidson

29mm **weigh sta both lanes**

26b a IN 49, Chesterton, **N** to IN Dunes SP, **S** BP/White Castle, Speedway/dsl A&W/KFC, Applebee's, Arby's, Burger King, DQ, Dunkin Donuts, El Salto Mexican, Gelsosomo's Pizza, Happy Wok, Jimmy John's, Lemon Tree Grill, Little Caesar's, LJ Silver, McDonald's, Papa John's, Pizza Hut, Subway, Taco Bell, Tao Chen's, Third Coast Cafe, Wendy's Best Western, EconoLodge, Hilton Garden (3mi), Lakeside Inn, Quality Inn Advance Parts, AutoZone, Jewel-Osco, K-Mart, Sand Cr Camping (5mi), to Valparaiso, Verizon, Walgreens

22b a US 20, Burns Harbor, **N** Shell/Subway/dsl/scales/LP, TA/BP/Country Pride/Pizza Hut/Popeye's/Taco Bell/dsl/scales/24hr/ @ Comfort Inn fireworks, **S** Luke/dsl, Pilot/McDonald's/Subway/dsl/scales/24hr Camp-Land RV Ctr, Chevrolet, fireworks, Ford, Kia, Nissan, repair, Toyota/Scion

19 IN 249, to Port of IN, Portage, **N** Family Express/dsl/e-85 Corner Bistro, DQ, Longhorn Steaks, McDonald's, Quaker Steak&Lube, Starbucks, Subway Affordable Suites, Country Inn&Suites Bass Pro Shops, **S** Marathon/dsl, Shell/Luke Denny's, Shenanigans Grill Best Western, Days Inn, Dollar Inn, Hampton Inn, Super 8, Travel Inn

16 access to **I-80/90 toll road E, I-90 toll road W,** IN 51N, Ripley St, same as 15b&a

I-94/I-80 run together wb.

IN

GARY AREA

INTERSTATE 94 Cont'd

Exit #	Services
15b	US 6W, IN 51, N [gas] FLYING J/Denny's/dsl/scales/24hr/@, Mr Fuel/dsl/scales/24hr, TA/BP/Popeye's/Subway/dsl/scales/24hr/ @ [food] Ponderosa, Wing Wah [other] Blue Beacon,
15a	US 6E, IN 51S, to US 20, S [gas] BP/Luke, GoLo, Road Ranger/Pilot/Subway/dsl/scales/24hr [food] Burger King, DQ, LJ Silver, Papa John's, Ruben's Café, Wendy's [other] Ace Hardware, Walgreens
13	Central Ave (from eb)
12b	I-65 N, to Gary and toll road
12a	I-65 S (from wb), to Indianapolis
11	I-65 S (from eb)
10b a	IN 53, Broadway, N [gas] Citgo, Gas for Less [food] JJ Fish, S [gas] Mobil [food] DQ, Rally's
9	Grant St, N [gas] Clark [food] Chicago Hotdogs [other] County Mkt Foods, Sav-a-Lot Foods, Walgreens, S [gas] Citgo, Loves/Denny's/dsl/scales/LP/24hr/ @, Steel City/dsl/scales/rest./24hr [food] A&W/KFC, Burger King, Church's, Dunkin Donuts, J&J Fish, McDonald's, Subway [other] $Tree, Aldi Foods, AutoZone, CarX, Fagen Drug, Firestone/auto, Midas
6	Burr St, N [gas] Pilot/Subway/dsl/scales/24hr/ @, TA/Chester's/Pizza Hut/Taco Bell/dsl/scales/24hr/ @ [food] J&J Fish & Chicken, Philly Steaks, Rico's Pizza [other] SpeedCo, S [gas] Citgo/dsl/24hr
5	IN 912, Cline Ave, S [gas] BP, Clark, Marathon, Speedway [food] Arby's, DQ, Jedi's Garden Rest., KFC, McDonald's, Pizza Hut, Popeye's, Taco Bell, Wendy's, White Castle [lodging] Best Western, Hometowne Lodge, Motel 6, Super 8 [other] $Tree, Fannie May Candies, K-Mart, Radio Shack
3	Kennedy Ave, N [gas] Clark, Mobil/dsl, Speedway [food] Burger King, Domino's, McDonald's [other] repair, Walgreens, S [gas] Citgo [food] Cholie's Pizza, Cracker Barrel, Squigi's Pizza, Subway, Wendy's [lodging] Courtyard, Fairfield Inn, Residence Inn [other] IN Welcome Ctr, USPO
2	US 41S, IN 152N, Indianapolis Blvd, N [gas] GoLo, Luke, SavAStop [food] Arby's, Dunkin Donuts, House Of Pizza, La Rosa, Papa John's, Pizza Hut, Popeye's, Rally's, Schoop's Burgers, Taco Bell, Wheel Rest., Woodmar Rest. [other] CarEx, Goodyear, Midas, vet, S [gas] Pilot/scales/dsl/24hr [food] White Castle [lodging] Hammond Inn [other] Aldi Foods, Cabela's
1	US 41N, Calumet Ave, N [gas] BP/dsl, Gas City [food] Barton's Pizza, Baskin-Robbins/Dunkin Donuts, Subway [other] Walgreens, S [gas] BP, Marathon, Mobil/dsl, Shell [food] Arby's, Baskin-Robbins/Dunkin Donuts, Boston Mkt, Burger King, Canton House Chinese, Edwardo's Pizza, Fortune House, Munster Gyros, Subway, Taco Bell, Wendy's [other] $Jct, Jewel-Osco, Radio Shack, Staples, Target, vet
0mm	Indiana/Illinois state line

IN

INDIANAPOLIS AREA

INTERSTATE 465 (INDIANAPOLIS)

Exit #	Services
	I-465 loops around Indianapolis. Exit numbers begin/end on I-65, exit 108.
53b a	I-65 N to Indianapolis, S to Louisville
52	Emerson Ave N [gas] BP/dsl, Marathon, Shell/Circle K, Speedway/dsl [food] Burger King, Domino's, El Mariachi, KFC, LJ Silver, Subway, Taco Bell, Waffle House [lodging] Motel 6 [other] [H] $General, S [gas] Murphy USA/dsl, Speedway/dsl [food] Arby's, Bamboo House, China Buffet, DJ's Hotdogs, DQ, Egg Roll, El
52	Continued Puerto Mexican, Fazoli's, Firehouse Subs, Fujiyama, Hardee' Jets Pizza, Jimmy John's, Little Caesar's, McDonald's, Pap John's, Papa Murphy's, Pizza Hut, Ponderosa, Rally's, Star bucks, Steak'n Shake, Subway, Taco Bell, Wendy's, White Cas tle [lodging] Holiday Inn Express, La Quinta, Red Roof Inn, Super [other] $Tree, Advance Parts, AT&T, AutoZone, CarX, GNC, Good year/auto, K-Mart, Kroger/dsl, Lowe's Whse, Meineke, O'Reill Parts, Verizon, vet, Walgreens, Walmart/Subway
	I-74 W and I-465 S run together around S Indianapolis 21 miles
49	I-74 E, US 421 S
48	Shadeland Ave (from nb)
47	US 52 E, Brookville Rd, E [gas] Marathon/Burger King, Speedway/dsl [food] Bugsy's Grill, McDonald's, Subway [lodging] Baymon Inn [other] CVS Drug, vet
46	US 40, Washington St, E [gas] Marathon, Phillips 66, Shell/dsl Speedway [food] Arby's, Blueberry Hill Pancakes, China Buffet Church's, LJ Silver, Olive Garden, Skyline Chili, Steak'n Shake Yen Ching Chinese [other] $General, Advance Parts, AutoZone Ford, Meineke, O'Reilly Parts, Radio Shack, Target, W [gas] Thornton's [food] Applebee's, Bob Evans, Fazoli's, McDonald's Subway [lodging] Best Western [other] Buick/GMC, Hyundai, K-Mar PepBoys
44b	I-70 E, to Columbus
44a	I-70 W, to Indianapolis
42	US 36, IN 67 N, Pendleton Pike, E [food] Chile Verde, Hardee's, Papa's Rest., Popeye's, Wendy's [other] $General, Family$ Meineke, Save-A-Lot Foods, U-Haul, W [gas] Speedway/dsl Thornton's [food] Arby's, Café Heidelberg, Domino's, Dunki Donuts, KFC, LJ Silver, Los Rancheros, McDonald's, Pizz Hut/Taco Bell, Rally's, Subway, Waffle House, White Castl [other] [H] Advance Parts, Aldi Foods, CVS Drug, Family$, Men ards, O'Reilly Parts
40	56th St, Shadeland Ave, E [gas] Marathon, to Ft Harrison SP
37b a	I-69, N to Ft Wayne, IN 37, W [other] [H] services on frontage rd
35	Allisonville Rd, N [food] Bravo Italian, Buca Italian, Buffalo Wil Wings, Dave&Buster's, Hardee's, Max&Erma's, MCL Cafeteria Melting Pot, On-the-Border, Outback Steaks [lodging] Courtyar [other] Costco/gas, Firestone/auto, Gander Mtn, JC Penney, Jo Ann Fabrics, Macy's, mall, Sear/auto, Target, Tires+, Van Mau S [gas] Shell, Speedway/dsl [food] 5 Guys Burgers, China Buf fet, ChuckeCheese, Panera Bread, Papa John's, Perkins/24h Qdoba, White Castle [lodging] Jameson Inn [other] Marsh Foods, Mi chael's, Petsmart, Radio Shack, TJ Maxx, Trader Joe's
33	IN 431, Keystone Ave, N [gas] BP/McDonald's, Marathon/ds [food] Arby's, Bob Evans, Burger King, Penn Sta Subs, Ruth Chris Steaks, Subway [other] Acura, Audi, BMW/Mini, Chevrolet, Ford Harley-Davidson, Honda, Hyundai, Infiniti, Nissan, Porsche Scion/Toyota, Subaru, S [food] Blimpie, Champ's, Cheesecak Factory, El Torito Grill, Fleming's Steaks, LePeep's Rest, Lulu' Rest, Maggiano's, Maggie Moo's Icecream, McAlister's Deli, PF Changs, Pizza Hut, Shanghai Lil, Starbucks, Sullivan's Steaks TGIFriday's [lodging] Hyatt Place, Marriott, Sheraton [other] Kohl's mall, Nordstrom's
31	US 31, Meridian St, N [lodging] Courtyard, Jameson Inn, Radissor [other] [H] Cadillac, S [gas] Shell/Circle K/dsl [food] Arby's, Granite City Rest, La Margarita, McAlister's Deli, McDonald's, Paradise Bakery/Cafe, Starbucks
27	US 421 N, Michigan Rd, N [gas] Marathon, Phillips 66/dsl, Speedway/dsl [food] Applebee's, Bajio Mexican, Burger King HoneyBaked Ham, Jimmy John's, Maggie Moo's Icecream McDonald's, Noble Roman's, Red Robin, Subway, Wendy's Wings Etc [lodging] Country Inn&Suites, Red Roof Inn [other] AT&T

INTERSTATE 465 (INDIANAPOLIS)

INDIANAPOLIS AREA

27 Continued
Best Buy, Buick/GMC, Chevrolet, Chrysler/Dodge/Jeep, Ford, Home Depot, Kohl's, Marshall's, PetCo, Target, Walgreens, S [gas] Citgo/dsl, Shell/Circle K [food] Arby's, Burger King, Chic-fil-A, China Buffet, Chipotle Mexican, Cici's, Cracker Barrel, Denny's, El Meson Mexican, Famous Dave's, Hardee's, McAlister's Deli, McDonald's, Noodles&Co, O'Charley's, Outback Steaks, Panda Express, Papa Murphy's, Pizza Hut, Qdoba, Rally's, Ruby Tuesday, Steak'n Shake, Subway, Taco Bell, TX Roadhouse, Wendy's, White Castle, Yen Ching Chinese [lodging] Best Western, Comfort Inn, Days Inn, Drury Inn, Embassy Suites, Extended Stay America, Extended Stay Deluxe, Holiday Inn, Homewood Suites, InTown Suites, La Quinta, Microtel, Residence Inn, Super 8 [O] $General, $Tree, Aamco, Aldi Foods, BigLots, Costco/gas, Discount Tire, Firestone, GNC, JC Penney, Lowe's Whse, Office Depot, Radio Shack, Sam's Club/gas, Staples, Walgreens, Walmart

25 I-865 W, I-465 N to Chicago

23 86th St, E [gas] BP, Speedway/dsl [food] Abuelo's, Applebee's, Arby's, Chili's, Coldstone Creamery, Jimmy John's, Longhorn Steaks, Macaroni Grill, Monical's Pizza, Noodles&Co, Panera Bread, Quizno's, Starbucks, Steak'n Shake, Subway, Taco Bell, Ted's MT Grill, Traders Mill Grill, Wendy's [lodging] Fairfield Inn, Homestead Suites, InTown Suites [O] [H] AT&T, Big-O Tires, BookAMillion, Marsh Foods, Michael's, Old Navy, Petsmart

21 71st St, E [gas] BP [food] Bella Chino's Italian, Hardee's, McDonald's, Steak'n Shake, Subway [lodging] Candlewood Suites, Clarion Inn, Courtyard, Hampton Inn, Holiday Inn Express, TownePlace Suites [O] Curves, W [food] Bob Evans, LePeep's Rest, Los Agave's Mexican, Max&Erma's, Quizno's, Starbucks [lodging] Hilton Garden, Residence Inn, Wingate Inn

20 I-65, N to Chicago, S to Indianapolis

19 56th St (from nb), E [gas] Marathon, Speedway/dsl

17 38th St, E [gas] BP, Marathon/dsl, Shell/Circle K/24hr, Speedway [food] ChuckeCheese, Domino's, DQ, El Maguey Mexican, Ginzo Japanese, Golden Corral, Hooters, Little Caesar's, LJ Silver, LoneStar Steaks, Machu Pichu Peruvian, O'Charley's, Penn Sta Subs, Popeye's, Red Lobster, Starbucks, Steak'n Shake, Subway, White Castle, World Buffet [lodging] Best Value Inn [O] $Tree, AutoZone, Best Buy, Chevrolet, CVS Drug, Family$, Ford, Home Depot, Kroger/gas, Meijer, O'Reilly Parts, Radio Shack, Staples, Walgreens, W [food] Arby's, Burger King, Chili's, Cracker Barrel, McDonald's, Mike's Subs, Pizza Hut/Taco Bell, Ruby Tuesday, TGIFriday's [lodging] Jameson Inn, Ramada Ltd [O] Marsh Foods, Target

I-74 W and I-465 S run together around S Indianapolis 21 miles

16b I-74 W, to Peoria

16a US 136, to Speedway, E [gas] Circle K, Shell/Circle K, Thornton's/dsl [food] Applebee's, Arby's, Buffalo Wild Wings, Denny's, El Rodeo, Firehouse Subs, Grindstone Charley's, Hardee's, Jimmy John's, KFC, LJ Silver, McDonald's, Papa Murphy's, Pizza Hut, Subway, Taco Bell, White Castle [lodging] $Inn [O] $General, $Tree, Advance Parts, AT&T, Big Lots, CarX, CVS Drug, Firestone/auto, GNC, Goodyear/auto, Kohl's, Kroger/dsl, PetCo, Radio Shack, TJ Maxx, Tuesday Morning, W [gas] BP/dsl [lodging] Clarion

14b a 10th St, E [food] Peking Chinese, Penn Sta, Pizza Hut, Wendy's [O] [H], Lowe's Whse, Walmart Mkt, W [gas] Shell/Circle K, Speedway/dsl [food] Arby's, Fazoli's, Flapjacks, Marco's Pizza, McDonald's, Rally's, Starbucks, Taco Bell [O] CVS Drug, Marsh Foods, Walgreens

INDIANAPOLIS AREA

13b a US 36, Rockville Rd, E [gas] Mobil [food] Kazablanka Grill [lodging] Holiday Inn Express, Microtel, Motel 6, Wingate Inn [O] Sam's Club, W [gas] Speedway/dsl [food] Bob Evans [lodging] Best Western

12b a US 40 E, Washington St, E [gas] BP/dsl [food] Burger King, China Inn, Church's, Fazoli's, McDonald's, Papa John's, Pizza Hut, Taco Bell, Wendy's, White Castle [O] $General, $Tree, $Tree, Ace Hardware, Advance Parts, AutoZone, CVS Drug, Family$, Kroger/gas, O'Reilly Parts, Speedway Parts, U-Haul, vet, W [gas] Circle K/dsl, Phillips 66/dsl, Thornton's/dsl [food] Arby's, Hardee's, Jimmy John's, LJ Silver, McDonald's, Steak'n Shake, Subway [lodging] Regal 8 Inn [O] $General, CarX, Goodyear/auto, K-Mart, Save-A-Lot Foods

11b a Sam Jones Expwy, E [gas] Marathon/dsl, Speedway/dsl [food] Indy's Rest., Jimmy John's, Library Rest., Subway, Waffle House [lodging] Candlewood Suites, Courtyard, Extended Stay America, Fairfield Inn, Hyatt Place, La Quinta, Quality Inn, Ramada Inn, Residence Inn, Super 8, Wyndham, W [lodging] Crowne Plaza, Radisson

9b a I-70, E to Indianapolis, W to Terre Haute

8 IN 67 S, Kentucky Ave, E [gas] Phillips 66/dsl [O] [H] W [gas] BP/McDonald's/dsl, Shell/Subway/dsl, Speedway/dsl [food] Burger King, Culver's, Denny's, KFC, Rally's [lodging] Country Inn&Suites [O] Walmart Mkt

7 Mann Rd (from wb), E [O] [H]

4 IN 37 S, Harding St, N [gas] Mr Fuel/dsl/scales, Pilot/Subway/dsl/scales/24hr [food] Omelette Shoppe [lodging] Best Inn, Quality Inn [O] [H] Blue Beacon, S [gas] FLYING J/Denny's/dsl/LP/scales/24hr/ @, Marathon [food] Hardee's, McDonald's, Taco Bell, Waffle House, White Castle [lodging] Knight's Inn [O] Freightliner, SpeedCo, TruckoMat/scales

2b a US 31, IN 37, N [gas] BP/dsl, Marathon/Dunkin Donuts/dsl [food] Arby's, China Garden, CiCi's, Domino's, El Azabache, Golden Wok, KFC, King Gyros, Little Caesar's, LJ Silver, MCL Cafeteria, Penn Sta Subs, Pizza Hut, Qdoba, Steak'n Shake, White Castle [O] $General, $Tree, Advance Parts, Aldi Foods, AT&T, AutoZone, CarQuest, Family$, Firestone/auto, GNC, Kroger/gas, Marshall's, Meineke, Midas, Save-A-Lot, U-Haul, S [gas] BP/dsl, Speedway/dsl [food] 8 Lucky Buffet, Bob Evans, El Jalapeño, McDonald's, Red Lobster, Subway, Taco Bell, Wendy's [lodging] Comfort Inn, Holiday Inn Express, Indy Lodge, Super 8, Travel Inn [O] CVS Drug, Walgreens

I-465 loops around Indianapolis. Exit numbers begin/end on I-65, exit 108.

INTERSTATE 469 (FT WAYNE)

Exit #	Services
31c b a	I-69, US 27 S, Auburn Road. **I-469 begins/ends.**
29.15mm	St Joseph River

IN

R = gas ⊤ = food ⌂ = lodging O = other Rs = rest stop Copyright 2016 - The Next EXIT

⬆N INTERSTATE 469 (FT WAYNE) Cont'd

Exit #	Services
29b a	Maplecrest Rd, W R Lassus/DQ/Subway/dsl, Marathon/dsl
25	IN 37, to Ft Wayne, W R Murphy USA/dsl ⊤ Antonio's Pizza, Applebee's, Bob Evans, Buffalo Wild Wings, Cracker Barrel, DQ, Golden Corral, Steak'n Shake, Subway, Vince's Rest., Wendy's, Wings Etc, Zianos Italian O AT&T, Discount Tire, Kohl's, Marshall's, Meijer/dsl, Menards, Michael's, Office Depot, Petsmart, Walgreens, Walmart/McDonald's
21	US 24 E
19b a	US 30 E, to Ft Wayne, E R FLYING J/Huddle House/Subway/dsl/LP/scales/24hr, Sunoco/Taco Bell/dsl O Freightliner, Mack, Peterbilt, truck/tire repair, W R Marathon ⊤ Garno's

Exit #	Services
19b a	Continued
	Italian, Golden Gate Chinese, Mancino's Grinders, Richards Rest., Salvatori's Mexican, Zesto Drive-In ⌂ Holiday Inn Express
17	Minnich Rd
15	Tillman Rd
13	Marion Center Rd
11	US 27, US 33 S, to Decatur, Ft Wayne, E R BP/Subway/dsl
10.5mm	St Marys River
9	Winchester Rd
6	IN 1, to Bluffton, Ft Wayne, E O KOA, W O to ☺
2	Indianapolis Rd, W O to ☺
1	Lafayette Ctr Rd

IOWA

⬆N INTERSTATE 29

SIOUX CITY

Exit #	Services
152mm	Iowa/South Dakota state line, Big Sioux River
151	IA 12 N, Riverside Blvd, E R Casey's O $General, Fareway Foods, Pecaut Nature Ctr, Riverside Park, to Stone SP
149	Hamilton Blvd, E R Conoco ⊤ Horizon Rest ⌂ Rodeway Inn O JiffyLube, to Briar Cliff Coll, W Iowa Welcome Ctr sb, full facilities ⊤ Bev's on the River Rest. ⌂ Hilton Garden O Riverboat Museum
148	US 77 S, to S Sioux City, Nebraska; W R Casey's, Conoco/dsl, Sam's ⊤ DQ, McDonald's, MiFamilia, Pizza Hut, Taco Bell ⌂ Marina Inn, Regency Inn O Advance Parts, camping/picnic area, Family $, O'Reilly Parts
147b	US 20 bus, Sioux City, E R Sam's ⊤ Arby's, Burger King, Chili's, Famous Dave's BBQ, Hardee's, IHOP, Perkins ⌂ Holiday Inn, Ramada, Stoney Creek Inn O H Chevrolet, USPO, Walgreens
147a	Floyd Blvd, E R Valero O Home Depot, W O to Riverboat Casino
146.5mm	Floyd River
144b	I-129 W, US 20 W, US 75 S
144a	US 20 E, US 75 N, to Ft Dodge, 1 mi E on Lakeport Rd R Casey's, Shell ⊤ 5 Guys Burgers, A&W/LJ Silver, Applebee's, Black Bear Diner, Buffalo Wild Wings, Burger King, Carlos'o Kelly's, ChuckeCheese, Golden Corral, Hardee's, HuHot Chinese, Iron Hill Grill, Jimmy John's, McDonald's, Olive Garden, Outback Steaks, Red Lobster, Red Robin, Starbucks, Taco Del Mar, Tokyo Japanese, TX Roadhouse ⌂ Comfort Inn, Fairfield Inn, Holiday Inn Express, Quality Inn O Barnes&Noble, Best Buy, Buick/Honda, Gordman's, Hobby Lobby, Hy-Vee Foods/gas, JC Penney, Jiffy Lube, Kohls, Lowe's, Michael's, Old Navy, Petsmart, Scheel's, Sears/auto, Staples, Target, URGENT CARE, Verizon, Younkers
143	US 75 N, Singing Hills Blvd, E R Cenex/dsl, Murphy USA/dsl, PILOT/Moe's SW Grill/Subway/dsl/scales/24hr ⊤ China Buffet, Culver's, Eldon's Rest., KFC, McDonald's, Pizza Hut, Quiznos, Taco John's ⌂ AmericInn, Days Inn, Victorian Inn O $Tree, AT&T, Cadillac/GMC, Ford/Kia, Mazda, Nissan, Sam's Club/gas, Sgt Floyd Mon, Subaru, Suzuki, Toyota/Scion, URGENT CARE, Verizon, vet, Walmart/Subway, W R Loves/Subway/dsl/scales/24hr @ ⊤ Wendy's ⌂ Super 8 O Peterbilt, truckwash/repair

MO VALLEY

Exit #	Services
141	D38, Sioux Gateway ☺, E R Cenex, Phillips 66/dsl, Shell dsl ⊤ Aggies Rest., Pizza Ranch, Puerto Vallarta Mexican Subway ⌂ EconoLodge O $General, W ⌂ Motel O airport, museum
139mm	Rs both lanes, full ♿ facilities, info, litter barrels ⦿ ▤ RV dump, wireless internet
135	Port Neal Landing
134	Salix, W O camping
132mm	Rs parking only nb, weigh sta sb, litter barrels
127	IA 141, Sloan, E R Casey's, Kum&Go/Subway/dsl ⌂ Homestead Inn, WinnaVegas Inn O RV Park, 3 mi W R Heritage Express O to Winnebago Indian Res/casino
120	to Whiting, W O camping
112	IA 175, Onawa, E R Conoco/Subway/dsl, Phillips 66/dsl ⊤ DQ, McDonald's, Michael's Rest. ⌂ Super 8 O H NAPA, On-Ur-Wa RV Park, Pamida, repair, 2 mi W O Keelboat Exhibit, KOA, Lewis&Clark SP
110mm	Rs both lanes, full ♿ facilities, info, litter barrels, petwalk ⦿ ▤ RV dump, wireless internet
105	E60, Blencoe
96mm	Little Sioux River
95	F 20, Little Sioux, E O Loess Hills SF (9mi), gas, W O Woodland RV Park
92mm	Soldier River
91.5mm	Rs both lanes, litter barrels, parking only
89	IA 127, Mondamin, 1 mi E R Jiffy Mart/dsl ⊤ K Crossing Cafe
82	F50, Modale, 1 mi W R Cenex/dsl
79mm	Rs both lanes, full ♿ facilities, info, litter barrels ⦿ ▤ RV dump, wireless internet
75	US 30, Missouri Valley, E Iowa Welcome Ctr (5mi) R Shell/dsl/24hr ⊤ Arby's, McDonald's, Penny's Diner, Subway ⌂ Oaktree Inn O H (2mi), to Steamboat Exhibit, W R BP/dsl, Phillips 66/Jctn Cafe/dsl ⊤ Burger King, Taco John's ⌂ Days Inn, Rath Inn, Super 8 O Buick/Chevrolet
72.5mm	Boyer River
72	IA 362, Loveland, E R Phillips 66/dsl, W O to Wilson Island SP (6mi)
71	I-680 E, to Des Moines,
	I-29 S & I-680 W run together 10 mi.
66	W O RV Camping, Honey Creek
61b	I-680 W, to N Omaha, W Mormon Trail Ctr
	I-29 N & I-680 E run together 10 mi
61a	IA 988, to Crescent, E to ski area

INTERSTATE 29 Cont'd

COUNCIL BLUFFS

Exit #	Services
56	IA 192 S (sb only, exits left), Council [H]
55	N 25th, Council Bluffs, **E** [gas] Cenex/dsl, Sinclair
54b	N 35th St (from nb), Council Bluffs
54a	G Ave (from sb), Council Bluffs
53b	I-480 W, US 6, to Omaha (exits left from nb)
53a	9th Ave, S 37th Ave, Council Bluffs, **E** [gas] Phillips 66, Shell [food] Hog Stop BBQ [lodging] Days Inn, **W** [other] camping, Harrah's Hotel/Casino, RiverBoat Casino
52	Nebraska Ave, **E** [gas] Phillips 66/dsl [food] Quaker Steak, Ruby Tuesday [lodging] Comfort Suites, Holiday Inn Express, Microtel, SpringHill Suites, ValuePlace Inn [other] Bass Pro Shops, **W** [lodging] AmeriStar Hotel/casino, Hampton Inn, Holiday Inn
51	I-80 W, to Omaha
I-29 and I-80 run together 3 miles. See Iowa I-80, exits 1b-3.	
48	I-80 E (from nb), to Des Moines, **E** [other] [H]
47	US 275, IA 92, Lake Manawa, **E** [other] Iowa School for the Deaf, **W** [food] Buffalo Wild Wings, Famous Dave's, Firehouse Subs, Freddy's, Longhorn Steaks, Olive Garden, Panda Express, Panera Bread, Pepperjax Grill, Pizza Ranch, Qdoba, Starbucks [other] $Tree, Dick's, Hobby Lobby, Kohl's, Petsmart, Target, TJ Maxx, Verizon
42	IA 370, to Bellevue, **W** [other] K&B Saddlery, to Offutt AFB, truck parts
38mm	[rest stop] **both lanes, full [handicapped] facilities, info, litter barrels, petwalk [phone] [RV] RV dump, wireless internet**
35	US 34 E, to Glenwood, **E** [food] McDonalds (4mi) [lodging] Western Inn (4mi) [other] RV Park, **W** [gas] BP/rest/dsl [lodging] Bluff View Motel [other] Harley-Davidson
32	US 34 W, Pacific Jct, to Plattsmouth
24	L31, to Tabor, Bartlett
20	IA 145, Thurman
15	J26, Percival, **1-2 mi E** [gas]/dsl
11.5mm	**weigh sta nb**
10	IA 2, to Nebraska City, Sidney, **E** [other] to Waubonsie SP (5mi), **W** Cenex/Godfathers/dsl E85, Pilot/Subway/dsl/scales/24hr, Sapp Bros/Apple Barrel Rest/dsl/scales/24hr [food] Wendy's [lodging] Best Value Inn, Super 8 [other] antiques, dsl/tire repair, IA Info, Lewis&Clark Ctr (3mi), to Arbor Lodge SP, Victorian Acres RV Park (3mi)
1	IA 333, Hamburg, **1 mi E** [gas] Casey's/dsl [food] Blue Moon Grill [lodging] Hamburg Motel [other] [H], NAPA, Soda Fountain
0mm	Iowa/Missouri state line

INTERSTATE 35

Exit #	Services
219mm	Iowa/Minnesota state line
214	Rd 105, to Northwood, Lake Mills, **E** [lodging] Royal Motel (7mi), **W Welcome Ctr both lanes, full [handicapped] facilities, gas, litter barrels, petwalk [RV] RV dump, vending, wireless internet,** [gas] BP/Burger King/dsl [lodging] Country Inn&Suites, Holiday Inn Express [other] casino
212mm	[rest stop] **sb, litter barrels, [RV], weigh sta sb**
208	Rd A38, to Joice, Kensett, windmills

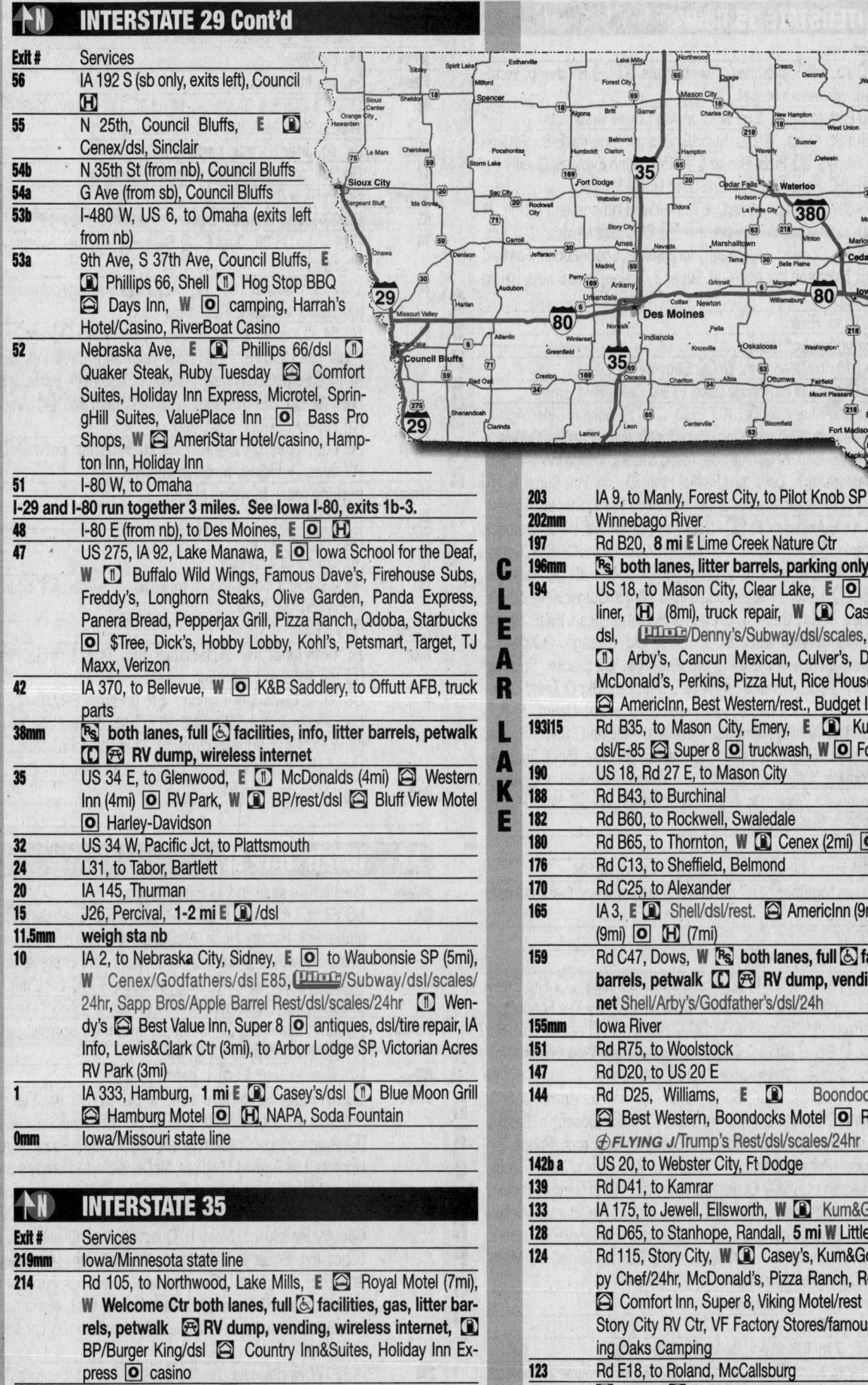

CLEAR LAKE

Exit #	Services
203	IA 9, to Manly, Forest City, to Pilot Knob SP
202mm	Winnebago River
197	Rd B20, **8 mi E** Lime Creek Nature Ctr
196mm	[rest stop] **both lanes, litter barrels, parking only**
194	US 18, to Mason City, Clear Lake, **E** [other] Chevrolet, Freightliner, [H] (8mi), truck repair, **W** [gas] Casey's/dsl, Kum&Go/dsl, Pilot/Denny's/Subway/dsl/scales, Shell/Wendy's/dsl [food] Arby's, Cancun Mexican, Culver's, DQ, KFC/Taco Bell, McDonald's, Perkins, Pizza Hut, Rice House Chinese, Subway [lodging] AmericInn, Best Western/rest., Budget Inn, Microtel
193ß15	Rd B35, to Mason City, Emery, **E** [gas] Kum&Go/Taco John's/dsl/E-85 [lodging] Super 8 [other] truckwash, **W** [other] Ford, to Clear Lake SP
190	US 18, Rd 27 E, to Mason City
188	Rd B43, to Burchinal
182	Rd B60, to Rockwell, Swaledale
180	Rd B65, to Thornton, **W** [gas] Cenex (2mi) [other] camping
176	Rd C13, to Sheffield, Belmond
170	Rd C25, to Alexander
165	IA 3, **E** [gas] Shell/dsl/rest. [lodging] AmericInn (9mi), Hampton Motel (9mi) [other] [H] (7mi)
159	Rd C47, Dows, **W** [rest stop] **both lanes, full [handicapped] facilities, info, litter barrels, petwalk [phone] [RV] RV dump, vending, wireless internet** Shell/Arby's/Godfather's/dsl/24h
155mm	Iowa River
151	Rd R75, to Woolstock
147	Rd D20, to US 20 E
144	Rd D25, Williams, **E** [gas] Boondocks Trkstp/cafe/dsl [lodging] Best Western, Boondocks Motel [other] RV camping, **W** [gas] FLYING J/Trump's Rest/dsl/scales/24hr
142b a	US 20, to Webster City, Ft Dodge
139	Rd D41, to Kamrar
133	IA 175, to Jewell, Ellsworth, **W** [gas] Kum&Go/Subway/dsl
128	Rd D65, to Stanhope, Randall, **5 mi W** Little Wall Lake Pk
124	Rd 115, Story City, **W** [gas] Casey's, Kum&Go/dsl [food] DQ, Happy Chef/24hr, McDonald's, Pizza Ranch, Royal Cafe, Subway [lodging] Comfort Inn, Super 8, Viking Motel/rest [other] antiques, Ford, Story City RV Ctr, VF Factory Stores/famous brands, Whispering Oaks Camping
123	Rd E18, to Roland, McCallsburg
120mm	[rest stop] **nb, full [handicapped] facilities, info, litter barrels [phone] [RV] RV dump/scenic prairie area sb, vending, wireless internet**

IA

[gas] = gas [food] = food [lodging] = lodging [other] = other [RS] = rest stop

INTERSTATE 35 Cont'd

AMES

Exit #	Services
119mm	**[RS] sb, full [H] facilities, litter barrels [phone] [picnic] RV dump, vending, wireless internet**
116	Rd E29, to Story, **2 mi W** Story Co Conservation Ctr
113	13th St, Ames, **W** [gas] Kum&Go/Burger King/dsl/E-85, Phillips 66/Arby's [food] Pizza Ranch [lodging] Holiday Inn Express, Quality Inn [other] [H], Harley-Davidson, ISU, to USDA Vet Labs
111b a	US 30, to Nevada, Ames, **E** Twin Acres Campground (11mi), **W** [gas] Kum&Go/DQ/Subway/dsl [food] El Azteca Mexican [lodging] AmericInn, Comfort Inn, Country Inn&Suites, EconoLodge, Fairfield Inn, Hampton Inn, Microtel, Super 8, TownePlace Suites [other] to IA St U
109mm	S Skunk River
106mm	**weigh sta both lanes**
102	IA 210, to Slater, **3 mi W** [food] Subway
96	to Elkhart, **W** Saylorville Lake, to Big Creek SP (11mi)
92	1st St, Ankeny, **W** [gas] Kum&Go, QT [food] Ankeny Diner, Applebee's, Arby's, Burger King, Cazador Mexican, Fazoli's, Guadalajara Mexican, KFC, Quiznos, Tokyo Steaks, Village Inn [lodging] Best Western/rest., Days Inn, Fairfield Inn, Quality Inn, Super 8 [other] [H], auto repair, Goodyear/auto, O'Reilly Parts, Staples, Tires+
90	IA 160, Ankeny, **E** [gas] Casey's [food] Chip's Diner, Outback Steaks [lodging] AmericInn, Comfort Inn, Country Inn&Suites, Courtyard, Holiday Inn Express [other] Buick/GMC, **W** [gas] Casey's/dsl [food] B-bops Rest., Buffalo Wild Wings, Burger King, Chili's, China Buffet, Culver's, El Charro, HuHot Chinese, IHOP, Jimmy John's, Marble Slab, McDonald's, Old Chicago, Panchero's Mexican, Panera Bread, SmashBurger, Starbucks, Subway, Tasty Tacos, Wendy's [other] AT&T, Best Buy, Big O Tires, Chevrolet, Chrysler/Dodge/Jeep, Ford, GNC, Home Depot, Jo-Ann Fabrics, Kohl's, Menards, Michael's, Petsmart, Radio Shack, Staples, Target, TJ Maxx, to Saylorville Lake (5mi), Tuesday Morning, Tuffy Auto, Verizon, vet, Walgreens, Walmart/Subway
89	Corporate Woods Dr, **E** [lodging] Hampton Inn, **W** [lodging] ValuePlace
87b a	I-235, I-35 and I-80
86	Exits 124-136
72c	(124 from I-80) University Ave, **See I-80, exit 124.**
I-35 and I-80 run together 14 mi around NW Des Moines. See I-80 exits 124-136	
72b	I-80 W
72a	I-235 E, to Des Moines
70	Civic Pkwy, Mills, **E** [gas] Kum&Go/McDonald's [food] Fire Creek Grill, Legend's Grill, Quiznos, Starbucks [other] Hy-Vee Foods/gas, Verizon, vet, Walgreens, **W** [gas] Casey's/dsl [food] Applebee's, Bar Louie, BoneFish Grill, Bravo Italiana, Buffalo Wild Wings, Caribou Coffee, Cheesecake Factory, Chick-fil-A, Draught House 50, Fleming's Rest., Fuddruckers, Iron Wok, Jimmy John's, Joe's Crabshack, Johnny's Italian Steaks, Joseph's Steaks, Monterrey Mexican, Noodles&Co, On-the-Border, Panda Express, Panera Bread, PF Chang's, Red Robin, Tasty Tacos, Wellman's Grill [lodging] Courtyard, Drury Inn, Hilton Garden, Holiday Inn, Residence Inn [other] [H], $Tree, Aldi Foods, Barnes&Noble, Best Buy, Costco/gas, Dick's, Dillards, Firestone/auto, Kohl's, Lowe's, Old Navy, PetCo, Scheel's Sports, Target, TJ Maxx, Trader Joe's, Verizon, Walmart, Younkers
69b a	Grand Ave, W Des Moines
68.5mm	Racoon River
68	IA 5, **7 mi E** to airport, to Walnut Woods SP
65	G14, to Norwalk, Cumming, **14 mi W** John Wayne Birthplace, Madison Co Museum
61mm	North River
56	IA 92, to Indianola, Winterset, **W** [gas] Kum&Go/dsl [food] Hitchi Post Grill [other] Diamond Trail RV Ctr
56mm	Middle River
53mm	**[RS] nb, litter barrels,**
52	G50, St Charles, St Marys, **14 mi W** [gas] Casey's/dsl [other] John Wayne Birthplace, Kum&Go, museum
51mm	**[RS] sb, litter barrels, parking only**
47	Rd G64, to Truro, **W** [gas] Kum&Go (1mi)
45.5mm	South River
43	Rd 207, New Virginia, **E** [gas] Kum&Go/Subway/dsl
36	Rd 152, to US 69, **3 mi E** [lodging] Blue Haven Motel, Evergreen Inn **W** st patrol
34	Clay St, Osceola, **W** [gas] Pilot/Subway/dsl/scales/24hr [other] Lakeside Casino Resort/camping
33	US 34, Osceola, **E** [gas] Casey's/dsl/scales [food] McDonald's, Pizza Hut, Subway [lodging] Best Value Inn, Days Inn, Super 8 [other] [H], Ford, Goodyear, Hy-Vee Foods, O'Reilly Parts, st patrol, tires, **W** [gas] BP/Arby's/dsl [food] KFC/Taco Bell [lodging] AmericInn [other] Harley-Davidson, Walmart
32mm	**[RS] both lanes, full [H] facilities, litter barrels, petwalk [phone] [picnic] RV dump, vending, wireless internet**
31mm	**parking area sb, weigh sta nb**
29	Rd H45
22	Rd J14, Van Wert
18	Rd J20, to Grand River
12	Rd 2, Decatur City, Leon, **5 mi E** [gas] Shell/dsl [lodging] Little River Motel [other] [H]
7.5mm	Grand River
7mm	**[RS] both lanes, full [H] facilities, info, litter barrels, petwalk [phone] [picnic] RV dump, vending, wireless internet**
4	US 69, to Davis City, Lamoni, **E** to 9 Eagles SP (10mi), **W** [gas] Casey's (2mi), Kum&Go/dsl/E-85 [food] Maid-Rite Cafe, Pizza Hut (2mi), QC Rest, Subway (2mi) [lodging] Best Value Inn, Chief Lamoni Motel [other] auto/truck repair, CarQuest, IA Welcome Ctr
0mm	Iowa/Missouri state line

ANKENY · DES MOINES · OSCEOLA

INTERSTATE 80

DAVENPORT

Exit #	Services
307mm	Iowa/Illinois state line, Mississippi River
306	US 67, to Le Claire, **N** [gas] BP/A&W (2mi), Shell/dsl [food] Bierstube Grill, Hungry Hobo, McDonald's, Pizza Hut, Steventon's Rest., Subway [lodging] Comfort Inn, Holiday Inn Express, Super 8 [other] Buffalo Bill Museum, Slagles Foods, **S** [gas] BP (2mi)
301	Middle Rd, to Bettendorf
300mm	**[RS] both lanes, full [H] facilities, info, litter barrels, petwalk [phone] [picnic] RV dump, vending, wifi**
298	I-74 E, to Peoria, **S** [other] st patrol, to [H]
295b a	US 61, Brady St, to Davenport, **N** [gas] BP/dsl [other] Fiat, Sears Auto Ctr, to Scott CP, **0-2 mi S** [gas] BP, KwikStar/dsl, Shell [food] Burger King, Cracker Barrel, Happy Joe's Pizza, Hardee's, Hooters, Los Agaves Mexican, McDonald's, Mo Brady's Steaks, Olive Garden, Papa John's, ThunderBay Grille, Village Inn Rest. [lodging] Baymont Inn, Best Western, Casa Loma Suites, Clarion, Country Inn&Suites, Motel 6, Quad City Inn, Quality Inn, Residence Inn, Super 8, Travelodge, Wickliffe Inn [other] $General, AutoZone, Ca rQuest, Firestone/auto, Hancock Fabrics, Honda, Hyundai, JC Penney, K-Mart, Lexus, mall, Menards, Nissan, Sears/auto, Tires+, Toyota, US Adventures RV Ctr, vet, Von Maur, VW
292	IA 130 W, Northwest Blvd, **N** [gas] FLYING J/Denny's/dsl/LP/scales/24hr, Loves/Arby's/dsl/scales/24hr [lodging] Comfort Inn [other] Farm&Fleet, Interstate RV Park (1mi), Peterbilt, truck

IA

INTERSTATE 80 Cont'd

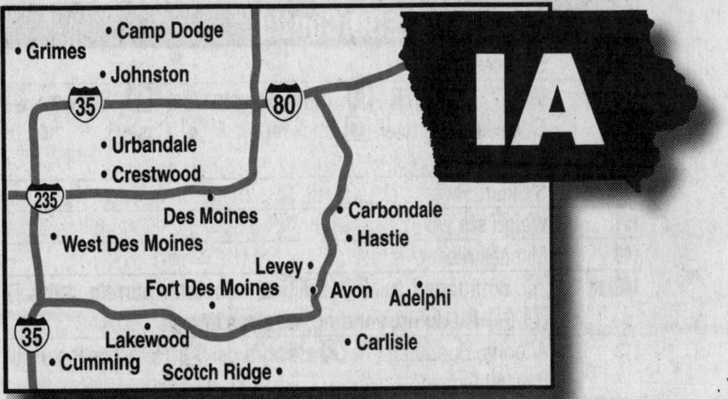

292 Continued wash, S BP/McDonald's/dsl, Sinclair Machine Shed Rest. Days Inn Freightliner

290 I-280 E, to Rock Island

Exit # Services

284 Y40, to Walcott, N Pilot/Arby's/dsl/24hr/scales, TA/IA 80/BP/DQ/Pizza Hut/Taco Bell/Wendy's/dsl/scales/24hr/ @ Checkered Flag Grille, Gramma's Rest. Best Value Inn, Comfort Inn Blue Beacon, IA 80 Trucking Museum, IA 80 Truck-o-Mat, SpeedCo Lube, tires, S Pilot/Subway/dsl/24hr McDonald's Days Inn Cheyenne Camping Ctr, Walcott CP

280 Y30, to Stockton, New Liberty

277 Durant, 2 mi S Casey's/dsl, Fifth St Petro/dsl Subway

271 US 6 W, IA 38 S, to Wilton

270mm **both lanes, full facilities, info, litter barrels, petwalk RV dump, vending, wifi**

268mm **parking areas**

267 IA 38 N, to Tipton, N Kum&Go/Subway/dsl/e85 Cedar River Camping

266mm Cedar River

265 to Atalissa, S Pilot/dsl only/scales/24hr

259 to West Liberty, Springdale, S BP/dsl EconoLodge Little Bear Camping

254 X30, West Branch, N BP/Quiznos/dsl, Casey's Hoover NHS, Jack&Jill Foods, USPO, S Kum&Go Casa Tequila Mexican, McDonald's Days Inn Chrysler/Dodge/Jeep

249 Herbert Hoover Hwy, N winery (2mi), S Wildwood Smokehouse golf

246 IA 1, Dodge St, N BP/Subway/dsl Jimmy John's, Joensy's Clarion URGENT CARE, S Sinclair Bob's Pizza Travelodge

244 Dubuque St, Iowa City, N Coralville Lake, S H, museum, to Old Capitol

242 to Coralville, N River City Grille Hampton Inn, Holiday Inn, S BP, Kum&Go/dsl 30 Hop Cafe, Applebee's, Arby's, Back Pocket Brewing, Bandana's BBQ, Burger King, Casa Azul, DQ, Dunkin Donuts, Edge Water Grill, Hardee's, IA Riverpower Rest., McDonald's, Milio's Sandwiches, Mondo's Cafe, Monica's Rest., Old Chicago Grill, Panera Bread, Papa John's, Peking Buffet, Perkins, Sparti's Gyros, Subway, Taco John's, Wig&Pen Rest. Baymont Inn, Best Western, Big Ten Inn, Comfort Inn, Heartland Inn, Homewood Suites, IA Lodge, Marriott, Quality Inn, Super 7, Super 8 H, auto repair, vet, Von Maur, Walgreens

240 IA 965, to US 6, Coralville, N Liberty, N BP, Casey's/dsl Buffalo Wild Wings, Cheddar's, Culver's, Jimmy John's, La Cava Mexican, McDonald's, Steak'n Shake, TX Roadhouse, Village Inn, Wendy's AmericInn, Country Inn&Suites, Suburban Lodge Colony Country Camping (3mi), Costco/gas, Gordman's, Harley-Davidson, Kohl's, Michael's, PetCo, TJ Maxx, URGENT CARE, Walgreens, Walmart/Subway, S Casey's/dsl Caribou Coffee, Chili's, Coldstone, Food Court, Huhot Mongolian, IHOP, Jimmy John's, Longhorn Steaks, Mellow Mushroom, Noodles&Co, Olive Garden, Panchero's Mexican, Papa Murphy's, Pizza Hut, Red Lobster, Starbucks, Taste of China, Which Wich? Comfort Suites, Holiday Inn Express, Residence Inn Ace Hardware, Advance Parts, Barnes&Noble, Best Buy, Dillard's, Discount Tire, Hobby Lobby, HyVee Foods/dsl, JC Penney, Lowe's, mall, Old Navy, Scheel's Sports, Target, Tires+, U-Haul, Verizon, Younkers

239b I-380 N, US 218 N, to Cedar Rapids

IOWA CITY

239a US 218 S

237 Tiffin, N Kum&Go/Subway/dsl Jon's Rest (1mi) (seasonal)

236mm **both lanes, full facilities, litter barrels, petwalk RV dump, vending, wireless internet**

230 W38, to Oxford, N Sleepy Hollow Camping, S Kalona Village Museum (15mi)

225 US 151 N, W21 S, N Heritage Inn, to Amana Colonies, S Casey's 7 Villages Rest., MaidRite Cafe Motel 6, Ramada

220 IA 149 S, V77 N, to Williamsburg, N BP, Casey's/Landmark Rest./dsl Arby's, McDonald's, Subway Cozy House Inn, Crest Motel, Super 8 factory outlets/famous brands, GNC, Old Navy, S Days Inn $General, Williamsburg Tire/auto

216 to Marengo, N Kum&Go/Subway/dsl H (8mi)

211 to Ladora, Millersburg, S Lake IA Park (5mi)

208mm **both lanes, full facilities, info, litter barrels, petwalk RV dump, vending, wireless internet**

205 to Victor

201 IA 21, to Deep River, N Pilot/Subway/dsl/scales/24hr Pleasant Stay Inn, S KwikStar/Pinecone Rest./dsl/scales/24hr/ @, truck repair

197 to Brooklyn, N TA/Country Pride/Dunkin Donuts/dsl/scales/24hr/@

191 US 63, to Montezuma, S to Diamond Lake SP (9mi)

182 IA 146, to Grinnell, 0-2 mi N Casey's, Kum&Go/Subway/dsl/24hr Casa Margaritas, Grinnell Steakhouse, KFC/Taco Bell, McDonald's, Pizza Ranch Best Western, Comfort Inn, Country Inn, Quality Inn, Super 8 $General, Ace Hardware, Buick/Chevrolet/GMC, Chrysler/Dodge/Jeep, H (4mi), HyVee Foods, O'Reilly Parts, Verizon, vet, Walmart

180mm **both lanes, full facilities, litter barrels, petwalk playground, RV dump (eb), wireless internet, vending, weather info**

179 IA 124, to Oakland Acres, Lynnville

175mm N Skunk River

173 IA 224, Kellogg, N Phillips 66/Best Burger/dsl/24hr Kellogg RV Park, Rock Creek SP (9mi), S Pella Museum

168 SE Beltline Dr, to Newton, 1 mi N Casey's/dsl, Murphy USA/dsl Arby's $Tree, KOA (seasonal), Walmart, S Loves/Chester's/McDonald's/dsl/scales, Valero/dsl AmericInn, Boulders Inn Iowa Speedway

164 US 6, IA 14, Newton, N Casey's/dsl, Phillips 66/Subway/dsl Culver's, KFC/Taco Bell, MT Mikes, Okoboji Grill, Perkins, Pizza Ranch Days Inn, EconoLodge, Quality Inn, Super 8 H, museum, S Best Value Inn Cadillac/Chevrolet, Chrysler/Jeep/Dodge, Ford/Lincoln, to Lake Red Rock

159 F48, to Jasper, Baxter

NEWTON

IA

INTERSTATE 80 Cont'd

Exit #	Services
155	IA 117, Colfax, N BP/McDonald's/dsl Subway Colfax Inn, Microtel truck repair, S Casey's, Kum&Go/pizza/dsl/e85/24hr
153mm	S Skunk River
151	**weigh sta wb**
149	Mitchellville
148mm	**both lanes, full facilities, info, litter barrels, petwalk RV dump, vending, wireless internet**
143	Altoona, Bondurant, S Casey's/dsl Hampton Inn, Holiday Inn Express
142b a	US 65, Hubble Ave, Des Moines, S BP, FLYING J/Max's Diner/dsl/scales/24hr/ @, Git'n Go Bianchi Boys Pizza, Big Steer Rest., Burger King, Culver's, Jethro's BBQ, KFC/Taco Bell, McDonald's/playplace, Perkins, Pizza Hut, Subway, Taco John's Adventureland Inn, Best Western, Comfort Inn, Motel 6, Quality Inn Adventureland Funpark, Blue Beacon, camping, casino, Freightliner, Peterbilt
141	US 6 W, US 65 S, Pleasant Hill, Des Moines, S Uncle Buck's Grill Bass Pro Shops
137b a	I-35 N, I-235 S, to Des Moines

I-80 W and I-35 S run together 14 mi.

Exit #	Services
136	US 69, E 14th St, Camp Sunnyside, N BP/dsl, Casey's Bonanza Steaks, MT Mikes Budget Inn, Comfort Inn, Motel 6, Rodeway Inn Allied Tire, antiques, Volvo, **0-1 mi** S Casey's/dsl, QT/Burger King/dsl/scales/24hr, Star Gas Arby's, Fazoli's, Hardee's, KFC, McDonald's, Papa Murphy's, Pueblo Viejo Mexican, Subway, Taco Bell, Taco John's, Village Inn, Wendy's Baymont Inn, Travelodge $General, Advance Parts, Aldi Foods, AutoZone, CarX, Family$, O'Reilly Parts, Tires+, TruckLube, USPO
135	IA 415, 2nd Ave, Polk City, N Smokey D's BBQ antiques, Harley-Davidson, Ryder Trucks, S Git'n Go, QT, Shop&Save Earl's Tire, NAPA, st patrol
133mm	Des Moines River
131	IA 28 S, NW 58th St, N Casey's, QT Bandit Burrito, Chopsticks, DQ, El Mariachi Mexican, Greenbriar Rest., Jimmy John's, Pagliai's Pizza, Panera Bread, Sonic, Subway, VanDee's Icecream/Sandwiches AmericInn Ace Hardware, Acura, Audi/VW, Goodyear/auto, Hy-Vee Food/dsl, USPO, vet, S BP/dsl/LP/24hr, Casey's, QT Applebee's, Arby's, Bamboo Buffet, Bennigan's, Buffalo Wild Wings, Burger King, Carlos O'Kelly's, Chipotle Mexican, Cici's Pizza, Dunkin Donuts, Famous Dave's BBQ, Fazoli's, Hardee's, IHOP, Jimmy John's, KFC, McDonald's, Noodles&Co, Old Chicago, Panda Express, Perfect Taco, Perkins, Pita Pit, Popeye's, Starbucks, Subway, Taco John's, Wendy's Days Inn, EconoLodge, Holiday Inn, Quality Inn, Ramada/Rest., Super 8 $Tree, Advance Parts, AT&T, Big Lots, BigLots, CarX, Chevrolet, Dahl's Food/Fuel, Firestone/auto, Ford, Goodyear/auto, Hobby Lobby, Kia, Kohl's, mall, NAPA, Nissan, Office Depot, Old Navy, PriceChopper, Sears/auto, Staples, Target, Toyota/Scion, URGENT CARE, Verizon, vet, Younkers
129	NW 86th St, Camp Dodge, N Kum&Go Burger King, Legends Grill, McDonald's, Okoboji Grill, Panchero's Mexican, Planet Sub, Starbucks, TX Roadhouse, Village Inn Hilton Garden, Stoney Creek Inn, TownePlace Suites Dahl's Foods, Verizon, S Casey's, Kum&Go/dsl Arby's, B-Bops Burgers, Culver's, Friedrich's Coffee, Overtime Grill, Papa Murphy's, Pizza Ranch, Ruby Tuesday, Subway, Viva La Bamba
129	Continued Fairfield Inn, Hampton Inn, Holiday Inn Express, Microtel Walgreens
127	IA 141 W, Grimes, N BP/dsl, QT/dsl MaidRite Cafe, McCoy's Grill, Subway to Saylorville Lake, Toyota/Scion, S Kum&Go/dsl/e85 McDonald's, Quiznos Firestone/auto, Home Depot, Target
126	Douglas Ave, Urbandale, E Casey's/dsl EconoLodge, Extended Stay America Chevrolet, W Kum&Go/dsl, Pilot/Subway/dsl/scales/24hr/ @ Mama Lacona'sß
125	US 6, Hickman Rd, E IA Machine Shed Rest., Subway Hotel Renovo, Sleep Inn CarMax, Fiat, Honda, Hyundai, to Living History Farms, W Kum&Go/dsl, Loves/Denny's/dsl/scales/LP/24hr Chrysler/Dodge/Jeep, Menards, S Starbucks Clive Hotel
124	**(72c from I-35 nb)**, University Ave, E Git'n Go/dsl Applebee's, Bakers Square, Chili's, Chuck-fil-A, Huhot Mongolian, Jason's Deli, KFC, Little Caesars, McDonald's, Mi Mexico, Outback Steaks, Qdoba Mexican, RockBottom Rest./brewery, Starbucks, TCBY, Twin Peaks, Wobbly Boots BBQ Courtyard, Days Inn, Sheraton, Sterling Suites, Super 8, Wildwood Lodge AT&T, Barnes&Noble, Best Buy, Home Depot, Kohl's, Lowe's, Marshall's, Office Depot, Petsmart, Target, Verizon, Whole Foods Mkt, World Mkt, W Kum&Go/Burger King, QT Biaggi's Rest, Caribou Coffee, Cracker Barrel, El Rodeo Mexican, Jersey Mike's, Other Place Grill, Panera Bread, Red Rossa Pizza, Wendy's, Z'Marik's Cafe Best Western, Country Inn&Suites, La Quinta H, Granite City Food, Walgreens, S Mi Mexico,

I-80 E and I-35 N run together 14 mi

Exit #	Services
123b a	I-80/I-35 N, I-35 S to Kansas City, I-235 to Des Moines
122	(from eb)60th St, W Des Moines, N H, same as 121
121	74th St, W Des Moines, N Biaggi's Rest., Panera Bread, Red Rossa Pizza Hampton Inn, Staybridge Suites H, Granite City Foods, HyVee Food/gas, Walgreens, S Kum&Go/Subway Arby's, Burger King, CK's, Culver's, McDonald's, Perkins, Quiznos, Taco John's Candlewood Suites, Fairfield Inn, Marriott, Motel 6, SpringHill Suites, vet
118	Alices Rd, to Waukee
117	R22, Booneville, Waukee, N Kum&Go/dsl/e85 Organic Farm Rest. Timberline Camping (2mi), S Rube's Steaks, Waveland Rest. (2mi)
115mm	**weigh sta eb**
113	R16, Van Meter, **1 mi** S Casey's Veteran's Cemetary
112mm	N Racoon River
111mm	Middle Racoon River
110	US 169, to Adel, DeSoto, N camping (6mi), S Casey's/dsl, Kum&Go/dsl/e85 Countryside Inn, Edgetowner Motel $General, John Wayne Birthplace (14mi), USPO
106	F90, P58, N KOA (Apr-Oct)
104	P57, Earlham, S Casey's (1mi)
100	US 6, to Redfield, Dexter, N Casey's (2mi) Drew's Chocolate (2mi)
97	P48, to Dexter, N camping, Casey's (2mi)
93	P28, Stuart, N Casey's/dsl/scales, Kum&Go/dsl/e85 Burger King, McDonald's/playplace, Subway AmericInn, Best Value a Inn $General, camping (7mi), Chevrolet, city park, Hometown Foods, S Phillips 66/dsl Country Kitchen Economy Inn NAPA
88	P20, Menlo
86	IA 25, to Greenfield, Guthrie Ctr, N to Spring Brook SP, S Hospital (13mi)
85mm	Middle River

INTERSTATE 80 Cont'd

Exit #	Services
83	N77, Casey, **1 mi N** [gas] Kum&Go [other] camping
80.5mm	**[RS] both lanes, full [handicap] facilities, info, litter barrels, petwalk [phone] [picnic] RV dump, vending, wireless internet**
76	IA 925, N54, Adair, **N** [gas] Casey's/dsl, Kum&Go/Subway/dsl [food] Chuck Wagon Rest. [lodging] Adair Budget Inn, Super 8 [other] camping, city park
75	G30, to Adair
70	IA 148 S, Anita, **S** to Lake Anita SP (6mi)
64	N28, to Wiota
61mm	E Nishnabotna River
60	US 6, US 71, to Atlantic, Lorah, **S** [gas] Conoco/dsl/24hr [lodging] Sunset Inn
57	N16, to Atlantic, **N** [other] Nelsen RV Ctr, **S** [other] [H] (7mi)
54	IA 173, to Elk Horn, **6 mi N Welcome Ctr/wifi** [lodging] Tivoli Inn [other] Windmill Museum
51	M56, to Marne
46	M47, Walnut, **N** [gas] Cenex/McDonald's/dsl [food] Emma Jean's Rest. [lodging] Super 8 [other] to Prairie Rose SP (8mi), **S** [gas] Kum&Go/pizza/dsl [lodging] EconoLodge/RV Park, tires/repair
44mm	**weigh sta wb/parking area eb**
40	US 59, to Harlan, Avoca, **N** [gas] FLYING J /Taco John's/MaidRite Cafe/dsl/24hr/scales [food] Subway [lodging] Cobblestone Inn [other] [H] (12mi), truckwash, **S** [gas] Casey's/dsl, Shell/dsl [food] Embers Rest. [lodging] Acova Motel, Capri Motel [other] Avoca Foods, Farmall-Land Museum (seasonal), Nishna Museum
39.5mm	W Nishnabotna River
34	M16, Shelby, **N** [gas] BP/rest./dsl/e85, Shell/Cornstalk Cafe/dsl [food] DQ, Godfather's [lodging] Shelby Country Inn/RV Park, **S** [gas] Loves /McDonald's/Chester's/dsl/scales/24hr
32mm	**rest area both lanes, parking only**
29	L66, to Minden, **S** [gas] Casey's/dsl [lodging] Midtown Motel (2mi) [other] winery (4mi)
27	I-680 W, to N Omaha
23	IA 244, L55, Neola, **S** [gas] Kum&Go/dsl/e85 [other] camping, to Arrowhead Park
20mm	**Welcome Ctr eb/[RS] wb, full [handicap] facilities, litter barrels, petwalk [phone] [picnic] RV dump, vending, wireless internet**
17	G30, Underwood, **N** [gas] Phillips 66/Subway/dsl/24hr [lodging] Underwood Motel [other] truck/tire repair
8	US 6, Council Bluffs, **N** [gas] Phillips 66/dsl (1mi) [other] $General, [H] (3mi), K-Mart, **S** [other] st patrol
5	Madison Ave, Council Bluffs, **N** [gas] BP/dsl [food] Burger King, FoodCourt, Great Wall Chinese, KFC, McDonald's, Papa Murphy's, Starbucks, Subway [lodging] AmericInn [other] HyVee Foods/drug, Sears/auto, Verizon, Walgreens, **S** [gas] Cenex/DQ/dsl, Phillips 66 [food] Puerto Vallarta, Sam&Louie's Pizza, Village Inn Rest. [lodging] Western Inn [other] No Frills Mkt, TrueValue
4	I-29 S, to Kansas City
3	IA 192 N, Council Bluffs, **N** [other] to Hist Dodge House, **S** [gas] Casey's/dsl, Shell/dsl, TA/Valero/Country Pride/dsl/scales/24hr @ [food] Applebee's, Beijing Rest., Burger King, Cracker Barrel, Dickey's BBQ, DQ, Fazoli's, Golden Corral, Hardee's, Huhot Mongolian, La Mesa Mexican, LJ Silver, McDonald's, Perkins, Red Lobster, Subway, Taco Bell [lodging] Days Inn, Fairfield Inn, Motel 6, Red Roof Inn [other] Advance Parts, Aldi Foods, Best Buy, Buick/GMC, Cadillac/Chevrolet, Chrysler/Dodge/Jeep, Ford, Freightliner, Gordman's, Home Depot, Hyundai/Subaru, Kia, Menards, Nissan, Outdoor Recreation RV, Sam's Club/gas, truck/dsl repair, U-Haul, Walmart/Subway

COUNCIL BLUFFS

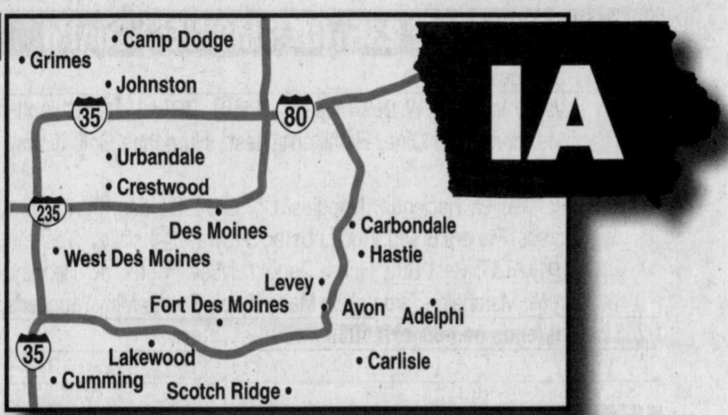

Exit #	Services
1b	S 24th St, Council Bluffs, **N** [gas] BP, Casey's, Pilot/Arby's/scales/dsl/24hr, Sapp Bros/Burger King/dsl [food] Famous Dave's BBQ, Hooters, Quaker Steak&Lube, Ruby Tuesday, Uncle Buck's [lodging] American Inn, Best Western, Country Inn&Suites, Hilton Garden, Holiday Inn Express, Microtel, SpringHill Suites, Super 8 [other] Bass Pro Shop, Blue Beacon, Camping World RV Ctr, casino, Horseshoe RV Park, Peterbilt, SpeedCo, **S Welcome Ctr, full facilities** [food] Culver's, TX Roadhouse [other] JC Penney, PetCo, ShopKO,
1a	I-29 N, to Sioux City
0mm	Iowa/Nebraska state line, Missouri River

INTERSTATE 235 (DES MOINES)

Exit #	Services
15	I-80, E to Davenport
12	US 6, E Euclid Ave, **E** [gas] Casey's [food] Burger King, Dragon House Chinese, Papa John's, Perkins, Tasty Tacos [other] $Tree, HyVee Foods/drug, Radio Shack, Walgreens, **W** [gas] QT/dsl [other] Midas, NAPA
11	Guthrie Ave, **W** [gas] Kum&Go/dsl [other] CarQuest
10b a	IA 163 W, E University Ave, Easton Dr
9	US 65/69, E 14th, E 15th, **N** [food] Subway [other] Walgreens, **S** [gas] QT [food] McDonald's, Quiznos, Tasty Tacos [other] [H], st capitol, URGENT CARE, zoo
8b	E 6th St, Penn Ave (from wb), **N** [other] [H]
8a	3rd St, 5th Ave, **N** [lodging] Holiday Inn [other] [H], **S** [lodging] Embassy Suites, Marriott, Quality Inn [other] Conv Ctr
7	Keo Way
6	MLK Blvd/31st St, **N** [other] Drake U, **S** [other] airport, Governor's Mansion
5b	42nd St, Science & Art Ctr, **N** [gas] Git'n Go [food] Papa John's [other] Drake Automotive
5a	56th St (from wb), **N** [other] golf
4	IA 28, 63rd St, to Windsor Heights, **S** [other] Historic Valley Jct, zoo
3	8th St, W Des Moines, **N** [gas] Kum&Go [food] B-Bop's Café, Burger King, Papa Murphy's, Starbucks [other] HyVee Foods, PetCo, Sam's Club/gas, Walmart/Subway, **S** [gas] BP, Kum&Go/dsl/e85 [food] Dunkin Donuts, Jimmy John's, Lemon Grass Thai, Tacos Andreas [lodging] Days Inn
2	22nd St, 24th St, W Des Moines, **N** [gas] BP, Casey's/dsl, Kum&Go/dsl, QT/dsl [food] Arby's, ChuckeCheese, Culver's, Famous Dave's BBQ, Hardee's, Hibachi Buffet, Jethro's BBQ, McDonald's, SmashBurger, Taco Bell, Village Inn [other] $Tree, CarX, Firestone/auto, Gordman's, Hancock Fabrics, Meineke, Michael's, Midas, Walgreens

DES MOINES

INTERSTATE 235 (DES MOINES) Cont'd

Exit #	Services
1b	Valley West Dr, W Des Moines, N BP/dsl Chipotle Mexican, Cozy Cafe, Hamilton's Rest., Hurricane Grill, Jimmy
1b	Continued John's, La Hacienda, Noodles&Co, Olive Garden, Panda Express, Panera Bread, Red Lobster, Subway Valley West Inn AT&T, Best Buy, Home Depot, HyVee Foods, JC Penney, mall, Marshall's, Target, Von Maur, Whole Foods Mkt, Younker's

I-235 begins/ends on I-80, exit 123.

INTERSTATE 280 (DAVENPORT)

Exit #	Services
18b a	I-74, US 6, Moline, S Shell/dsl Bare Bones BBQ, McDonald's, MT Jack's Best Inn, Country Inn&Suites, Hampton Inn, Holiday Inn Express, La Quinta, Motel 6, Quality Inn airport
15	Rd, Milan, 1 mi N Hardee's, MaidRite Café, McDonald's, Subway auto repair, Buick/Chevrolet, Firestone
11b a	IL 92, to Andalusia, Rock Island, S Jumer's Hotel/casino/rest. KOA Camping
9.5mm	Iowa/Illinois state line, Mississippi River
8	Rd 22, Rockingham Rd, to Buffalo
6	US 61, W River Dr, to Muscatine, W camping,
4	Locust St, Rd F65, 160th St, E H, St Ambrose U, to Palmer Coll, W Shell/Subway/dsl
1	US 6 E, IA 927, Kimberly Rd, to Walcott, 3 mi E Murphy USA/dsl Applebee's, Culver's, Harlan's Rest., Steak'n Shake, Subway, Wendy's Discount Tire, GNC, Walmart

I-280 begins/ends on I-80, exit 290.

INTERSTATE 380 (CEDAR RAPIDS)

WATERLOO

Exit #	Services
73mm	**I-380 begins/ends on US 218, 73mm in Waterloo** E BP/dsl, W Clark Pizza Hut
72	San Marnan Dr, W A&W/LJ Silver, Applebee's, Bonanza, Burger King, Carlos O'Kelly's, Coldstone, Godfather's, Golden China, Hardee's, IHOP, Jimmy John's, Olive Garden, Panera Bread, Pizza Hut, Red Lobster, Starbucks, Subway, Taco John's Baymont Inn, Candlewoods Suites, Comfort Inn, Country Inn&Suites, Days Inn, Fairfield Inn, Hampton Inn, Holiday Inn Express, Super 8 $General, Advance Parts, Aldi Foods, Barnes&Noble, Best Buy, Chevrolet, Chrysler/Dodge/Jeep, CVS Drug, Dillards, Ford, Gordman's, Hobby Lobby, HyVee Foods, JC Penney, Jo-Ann Fabrics, KIA, Menards, Old Navy, PetCo, PetsMart, Radio Shack, Sears/auto, Staples, Target, Tires+, TJ Maxx, Walmart
71	I-380, US 20, IA 27, Cedar Rapids, Cedar Falls, Dubuque, US 18 S Isle Hotel/Casino
70	River Forest Rd
68	Elk Run Heights, Evansdale Dr, E FLYING J/Denny's/dsl/scales/24hr, Pilot/RR/Junie's/Subway/dsl/scales/24hr/ @ Arby's, McDonald's Days Inn Freightliner, Paine's RV Ctr, truckwash/repair
66	Gilbertville, Raymond
65	US 20 E, Dubuque
62	Rd d-38, Gilbertville
55	Rd v-65, Jesup, La Port, W Hickory Hills Park, McFarlane Park
54mm	**weigh sta sb**
51mm	**weigh sta nb**
49	Rd d-48, Brandon, **1 mi** W
43	IA 150, Independence, Vinton, E Phillips 66/dsl/24hr Inn Suites truckwash
41	Urbana, E Lazy Acres RV Park, W Casey's/dsl
35	Rd w-36, Center Point, E BP, Casey's, Sinclair/McDonald's/Subway/dsl/scales/24hr, W Pleasant Creek SRA (5mi)
28	Rd e-34, Robins, Toddville, W Wickiup Outdoor Learning Ctr (5mi)

CEDAR RAPIDS

Exit #	Services
25	Boyson Rd, Hiawatha, E Ketelsen RV Ctr, W BP, Casey's/Blimpie/Pizza Culver's, Pizza Wagon Toyota/Scion/VW
24	IA 100, Blairs Ferry Rd, E KwikShop/dsl Happy Chef, Hardee's, KFC, La Glorias Mexican, McDonald's Days Inn, Hawthorn Suites CVS Drug, HyVee Foods, W Road Ranger Arby's, Burger King, Metro Buffet, Pizza Hut, Subway, Taco Bell Aldi Foods, AutoZone, GNC, Lowe's, Sam's Club/gas, Walmart
22	Glass Rd, 32nd st, E KwikShop/dsl Papa Johns
21	H St, Cedar Rapids, downtown
20b	7th St E, Cedar Rapids, E H, downtown
20a	US 151 Bus., E Crowne Plaza
19b	1st Ave W, W Best Western NAPA
18	Wilson Ave, museums
17	33rd ave SW, Hawkeye Downs, W Casey's Burger King, McDonald's, Sonic, Taco Bell, Wendy's Clarion, Comfort Inn, Economy Inn, Hampton Inn, Heartland Inn, Holiday Inn Express, Motel 6, Red Roof Inn, Super 8
16	US 30 W, US 151 S, US 218 N, Tama
13	Ely, W Casey's/A&W/dsl, Casey's/dsl/scales McDonald's AmericInn, Country Inn&Suites
12mm	**both lanes, full facilities, info, litter barrels, petwalk RV dump, vending, wireless internet**
10	Rd f-12, Shueyville, Swisher, E BP/dsl Lake Mcbride SP, W Amana Colonies
8mm	Iowa River
4	Rd f-28, North Liberty, E BP/dsl, Casey's/Blimpie, Kum&Go/dsl (2mi) Sleep Inn Colony Country RV Park (5mi)
0b a	I-80 E to Iowa City, W to Des Moines, **I-380 begins/ends on I-80.**

NOTES

IA

KANSAS

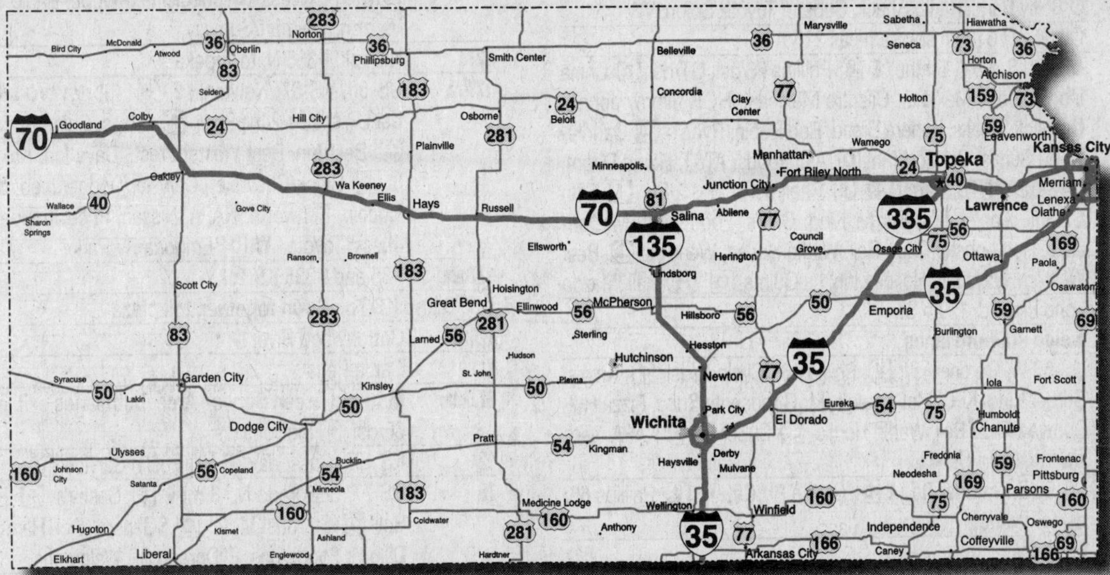

INTERSTATE 35

Exit #	Services
235mm	Kansas/Missouri state line
235	Cambridge Circle
234b a	US 169, Rainbow Blvd, E Phillips 66, QT Applebee's, Arby's, Burger King, McDonald's, Rosedale BBQ, Sonic, Wendy's Best Western, Sun Inn KU MED CTR, W KFC, LJ Silver, Taco Bell
233a	SW Blvd, Mission Rd
233b	37th Ave (from sb)
232b	US 69 N, E QT Cici's, McDonald's, Taco Bell
232a	Lamar Ave, E QT ValuePlace Inn
231b a	I-635 (exits left from sb)
230	Antioch Rd (from sb), E QT
229	Johnson Dr, E Phillips 66 Arby's, Bob Evans, Chili's, Chipotle Mexican, McDonald's, Papa John's, Starbucks GNC, Hen House Mkt, Home Depot, Marshall's, Old Navy, Petsmart, Walgreens, W Cenex/dsl
228b	US 56 E, US 69, Shawnee Mission Pkwy, E Shell Caribou Coffee, Denny's, IHOP, Krispy Kreme, Pizza Hut, Taco Bell Drury Inn, Homestead Suites, Winsteads Suites BMW/Mini, Sears Grand, W Valero A&W, LJ Silver, Panera Bread, Pizza Hut, Subway, Wendy's Cotman's Transmissions, Firestone, Ford, Goodyear/auto, Jo-Ann Fabrics, Office Depot, O'Reilly Parts, Russell Stover, Walgreens
228a	67th St, E Quality Inn CarMax, W Phillips 66/Circle K/dsl Hyundai, Jaguar, Land Rover, Maserati, Mercedes, Porsche Smart, Toyota/Scion
227	75th St, E McDonald's Extended Stay America H, Acura, vet, Walmart, W QT/dsl 2 Amigos Mexican, Domino's, Sonic, Subway, Taco Bell, Wendy's Hampton Inn Hyundai
225b	US 69 S (from sb), Overland Pkwy
225a	87th St, E Phillips 66 Green Mill Rest Holiday Inn, W Phillips 66/Circle K/dsl Taco Bell, Zarda BBQ auto repair
224	95th St, E Phillips 66/Circle K, Shell Applebee's, BD Mongolian BBQ, Burger King, Chick-fil-A, Chipotle Mexican,
224	Continued Denny's, Houlihan's, KFC, McDonald's, Mimi's Café, On-the-Border, Outback Steaks, Panda Express, Subway, Taco Bell, TGIFriday's, Winstead's Cafe Comfort Inn, Crowne Plaza, Days Inn, Extended Stay America, Knight's Inn, La Quinta, Motel 6, Super 8 H, Advance Parts, Barnes&Noble, Best Buy, Dillard's, Firestone/auto, Hy-Vee Foods, JC Penney, Kohl's, Macy's, mall, Nordstrom, Office Depot, PetCo, Sam's Club/gas, Target, W Phillips 66 Mi Ranchito Costco/gas, O'Reilly Parts, U-Haul
222b a	I-435 W & E
220	119th St, E Conoco/7-11, Phillips 66/Circle K, Shell 5 Guys Burgers, A&W, Buffalo Wild Wings, Burger King, Chick-fil-A, Chipotle Mexican, Coldstone, Cracker Barrel, Dodge City Steaks, Firehouse Subs, Granite City Cafe, Greek Rest., Haru's Steak, IHOP, Jersey Mike's, Jimmy John's, Joe's Crabshack, La Parrilla, LJ Silver, Longhorn Steaks, McDonald's, Noodles&Co, OK Joe's BBQ, Old Chicago, Olive Garden, Panda Express, Panera Bread, Papa Murphy's, Pei Wei, Planet Sub, Popeye's, Red Lobster, Ruby Tuesday, Schlotzsky's, Starbucks, Steak'n Shake, Subway, Taco Bell, TX Roadhouse, Wei's Buffet, Zio's Italian Comfort Suites, Fairfield Inn, Hampton Inn, Hilton Garden, Residence Inn, SpringHill Suites, ValuePlace Inn AT&T, Best Buy, Chrysler/Dodge/Jeep, Dick's, Fiat, GNC, Goodyear/auto, Home Depot, Honda, Marshall's, Mazda, Michael's, NTB, Old Navy, Petsmart, Radio Shack, Target, U-Haul, Verizon, W Houlihan's, Jason's Deli, Longhorn Steaks, Starbucks Bass Pro Shops
218	135th, Santa Fe St, Olathe, E Phillips 66/dsl, QT Applebee's, Burger King, Chapala Mexican, China Buffet, Chuck-eCheese, Church's, Garozzo's Italian, McDonald's, Other Place Grill, Papa John's, Perkins, Pizza St, Quiznos, Sheridan's Custard, Subway, Taco Bell $General, $Tree, Ace Hardware, Aldi Foods, AutoZone, BigLots, CVS Drug, Ford/Lincoln, GNC, Goodyear, Hobby Lobby, Hy-Vee Foods, K-Mart, Kohl's, Lowe's, Office Depot, PriceChopper Foods, Tuesday Morning, vet, W QT El Camino Real, Taco Bell, Waffle House, Wendy's Rodeway Inn Aamco, Advance Parts, Buick/

KANSAS CITY AREA

OLATHE

INTERSTATE 35 Cont'd

218	Continued GMC, Chevrolet, Harley-Davidson, Hyundai, Kia, Meineke, O'Reilly Parts, Radio Shack, Subaru, Toyota/Scion, VW
217	Old Hwy 56 (from sb), same as 215
215	US 169 S, KS 7, Olathe, E Phillips 66/dsl, QT/dsl China Inn, Chipotle Mexican, Cilantro Mexican, IHOP, Jimmy John's, Outback Steaks, Panera Bread, Red Robin, Ryan's Candlewood Suites, Comfort Inn Aldi Foods, AT&T, Home Depot, Jiffy Lube, NTB, Target, W Shell/dsl/scales/24hr 54th St Grill, Applebee's, Burger King, Chili's, FoodCourt, McDonald's, Red Lobster, Taco Bell, Waffle House, Wendy's Best Western, Days Inn, Holiday Inn, La Quinta H, mall, Mazda
214	Lone Elm Rd, 159th St
213mm	**weigh sta both lanes**
210	US 56 W, Gardner, W Phillips 66/Circle K/dsl Arby's, Burger King, KFC, McDonald's, Mr Goodcents Subs, Pizza Hut, Subway, Taco Bell, Waffle House Super 8 NAPA, Verizon, Walmart/Subway
207	US 56 E, Gardner Rd, E Olathe RV Ctr, W Phillips 66/dsl, Shell/dsl
202	Edgerton
198	KS 33, to Wellsville, W
193	Tennessee Rd, Baldwin
188	US 59 N, to Lawrence
187	KS 68, Ottawa, W Zarco/Phillips 66/dsl/E-85 Central RV Ctr, vet
185	15th St, Ottawa
183	US 59, Ottawa, E Loves/Hardee's/dsl/scales/24hr, W BP, Conoco/dsl, Ottawa/dsl Applebee's, Burger King, KFC, McDonald's, Old 56 Rest, Pizza Hut, Sirloin Stockade, Taco Bell, Wendy's Best Western, Comfort Inn, Days Inn, EconoLodge, Super 8 H, $General, $Tree, Advance Parts, CountryMart Foods, Walmart
182b a	US 50, Eisenhower Rd, Ottawa
176	Homewood, W RV camping
175mm	**both lanes, full facilities, litter barrels, petwalk RV dump, vending, wireless internet**
170	KS 273, Williamsburg, W
162	KS 31 S, Waverly
160	KS 31 N, Melvern
155	US 75, Burlington, Melvern Lake, E BP/Subway/dsl, TA/Shell/Wendy's/dsl/scales/24hr/@ Beto Jct Rest. Wyatt Earp Inn dsl repair
148	KS 131, Lebo, E Casey's, Cenex/dsl Lebo Diner Universal Inn, W to Melvern Lake
141	KS 130, Neosho Rapids, E NWR (8mi)
138	County Rd U
135	County Rd R1, W RV camping/
133	US 50 W, 6th Ave, Emporia, **1-3 mi** E Casey's McDonald's, Pizza Hut Budget Host
131	KS 57, KS 99, Burlingame Rd, E Conoco/dsl Hardee's, Mr Goodcents Subs Dillon's Food, repair, tires
130	KS 99, Merchant St, E Phillips 66/dsl Subway Emporia SU, Lyon Co Museum
128	Industrial Rd, E FL Arby's, Bruff's Steaks, Burger King, China Buffet, Gambino's Pizza, House of Ma, Spangles, Subway EconoLodge, GuestHouse Inn, Motel 6 H, $General, Aldi Foods, AT&T, CarQuest, Family$, JC Penney, Walgreens, W Phillips 66/Wendy's/dsl/LP Applebee's, Braum's, Golden Corral, KFC, McDonald's, MT Mike's Steaks,
128	Continued Pizza Hut, Pizza Ranch, Planet Sub, Starbucks, Taco Bell, Village Inn Candlewood Suites, Comfort Inn, Fairfield Inn, Holiday Inn Express Medicine Shoppe, Radio Shack, Staples, Verizon, Walmart/Subway
127c	KS Tpk, I-335 N, to Topeka
127b a	US 50, KS 57, Newton, E FLYING J/Huddle House/dsl/LP/scales/24hr, Shell Arby's, China Buffet, Papa John's Best Inn, Best Western/rest., Days Inn, Knights Inn, Super 8 Buick/Chevrolet, Chrysler/Dodge/Jeep, dsl repair, Ford/Lincoln, Kenworth, NAPA, Nissan, PriceChopper Foods, Tires-4Less, Toyota, W Emporia RV Park
127mm	I-35 and I-335 KS Tpk
	I-35 S and KS Tpk S run together, toll plaza
125mm	Cottonwood River
111	Cattle Pens
97.5mm	**Matfield Green Service Area (both lanes exit left),** Phillips 66/dsl McDonald's
92	KS 177, Cassoday, E Fuel'n Service
76	US 77, El Dorado N, **3 mi** E Casey's Pizza Hut, Taco Bell Stardust Motel $General, Ace Hardware, city park, Dillon's Foods/gas, El Dorado SP, Walgreens
71	KS 254, KS 196, El Dorado, E Conoco/dsl, Phillips 66/dsl, QT Arbys, Braum's, Burger King, China Star Buffet, DD Family Rest, Freddy's Frozen Custard, Gambino's Pizza, KFC, Kountry Kettle, LJ Silver, McDonald's, Papa Murphy's, Pizza Hut, Playa Azul Mexican, Sonic, Spangles, Subway, Taco Tico Best Western, Heritage Inn, Holiday Inn Express, Sunset Inn, Super 8 H, $General, Buick/Cadillac, Bumper Parts, Deer Grove RV Park, KS Oil Museum, O'Reilly Parts, Radio Shack, Walmart
65mm	**Towanda Service Area (both lanes exit left),** Phillips 66/dsl McDonald's
62mm	Whitewater River
57	21st St, Andover, W golf, phone
53	KS 96, Wichita, **1 mi on Kellogg** W Phillips 66
50	US 54, Kellogg Ave, E McConnell AFB, **W on Kellogg Ave East** Conoco/Wendy's/dsl Beijing Bistro, Burger King, Golden Corral, IHOP, McDonald's, Panda Express, Pizza Hut, Sonic, Subway, Taco Bell Acura, AT&T, CarMax, Infiniti, Jaguar/Porsche, Lexus, Lowe's, Mazda, Michael's, Nissan, Suzuki, Verizon, VW, Walmart/Subway, **W on Kellogg Ave West** BJ's Rest, Carlos Kelly's, Chipotle Mexican, Denny's, Green Mill Rest., LJ Silver, Logan's Roadhouse, Old Chicago Pizza, Red Lobster, Scotch&Sirloin Steaks, Super Buffet Best Western, Comfort Inn, Days Inn, EconoLodge, Fairfield Inn, GuestHouse Inn, Hampton Inn, Hawthorn Suites, Holiday Inn, La Quinta, Marriott, Motel 6, Studio+, Super 8, Wichita Inn, Wichita Suites BMW, Bosley Tires, Buick/GMC, Cadillac/Chevrolet, CarQuest, Chrysler/Dodge/Jeep, Dillard's, Fiat, Firestone/auto, Ford, Hancock Fabrics, Honda, JC Penney, Kia, Lincoln, Radio Shack, Ross, Sears/auto, Target, TJ Maxx, Toyota/Scion, VA H, Von Maur
45	KS 15, Wichita, E Spirit Aero Systems
44.5mm	Arkansas River
42	47th St, I-135, to I-235, Wichita, W Phillips 66, QT Applebee's, Braum's, Burger King, Carlos O'Kelly's, Godfather's, Heritage Rest, KFC, LJ Silver, McDonald's, Mr Goodcents, New China, Papa John's, Pizza Hut, Spangles Rest., Subway, Taco Bell, Wild Hog BBQ AmericInn, Best Western, Days Inn, Quality Inn, Springfield Inn, ValuePlace $General, $Tree,

OTTAWA

EMPORIA

WICHITA

KS

INTERSTATE 35 Cont'd

42	Continued AutoZone, Dillon's Foods/dsl, K-Mart, O'Reilly Parts, Radio Shack
39	US 81, Haysville, **W** [lodging] Haysville Inn
33	KS 53, Mulvane, **E** [other] Mulvane Hist Museum, **W** [lodging] Kansas Star Casino/Hotel [other] Wyldewood Winery
26mm	**Belle Plaine Service Area (both lanes exit left),** [gas] Phillips 66/dsl [food] McDonald's
19	US 160, Wellington, **3 mi W** [food] KFC, McDonald's, Penny's Diner [lodging] OakTree Inn, Sunshine Inn [other] KOA
17mm	**I-35 N and KS TPK N run together, toll plaza**
4	US 166, to US 81, South Haven, **E** [lodging] Motel 6 [other] repair/tires, **W** [other] Oasis RV Park
1.5mm	**weigh sta nb**
0mm	Kansas/Oklahoma state line

INTERSTATE 70

KANSAS CITY

Exit #	Services
423b	3rd St, James St
423a	5th St
422d c	Central Ave, service rd
422b a	US 69 N, US 169 S
421b	I-670
421a	**S** [other] railroad yard
420b a	US 69 S, 18th St Expswy, **N** [gas] Cenex/dsl, Sinclair/Subway/dsl [food] China Town, Jack-in-the-Box, Little Caesar's, Tapatio Mexican [other] GNC, SunFresh Foods
419	38th St, Park Dr, access to 10 motels
418b	I-635 N (eb only)
418a	I-635 S
417	57th St
415a	KS 32 E (from eb)
415b	to US 24 W, State Ave, Kansas City, **N on US 24** [food] Papa John's, Taco Bell [lodging] Gables Motel [other] Chrysler/Jeep/Dodge, Lowe's
414mm	**parking area both lanes** [phone]**, vehicle insp sta wb**
414	78th St, **N on US 24** [gas] Phillips 66, QT/dsl [food] Arby's, Burger King, Capt D's, Hardee's, KFC, Krispy Kreme, Little Caesar's, Lucky Chinese, McDonald's, Papa John's, Papa Murphy's, Sonic, Subway, Taco Bell, Wendy's [lodging] Days Inn [other] [H], $Tree, Advance Parts, BigLots, Buick/GMC, CVS Drug, Firestone/auto, K-Mart, Marshall's, O'Reilly Parts, Petsmart, PriceChopper Foods, Radio Shack, SavALot, Tires+, Walgreens, XPress/auto/tire, **S** [gas] BP [lodging] American Motel, Comfort Inn
411b	I-435 N, [other] to KCI Airport, access to Woodlands Racetrack
411a	I-435 S
410	110th St, **N** [lodging] Chateau Avalon, Great Wolf Lodge [other] Cabela's, KS Speedway
225mm	**I-70 W and KS TPK W run together**
224	KS 7, to US 73 (**last free exit wb before KS TPK**), Bonner Springs, Leavenworth, **N** [gas] Phillips 66/7-11/dsl, QT/dsl [food] el Potro Mexican, KFC/Taco Bell, Waffle House [lodging] Holiday Inn Express, Super 8 [other] museum, **S** [gas] BP [food] Arby's, Burger King, Goodcents Subs, Lin's Chinese, McDonald's, Papa Murphy's, Pizza Hut, Taco John's [other] $Tree, AutoZone, Cottonwood RV Camp, Ford, PriceChopper Foods, Radio Shack, TrueValue, Walgreens, Walmart/Subway
217mm	**toll booth**
212	Eudora, Tonganoxie

BONNER SPGS

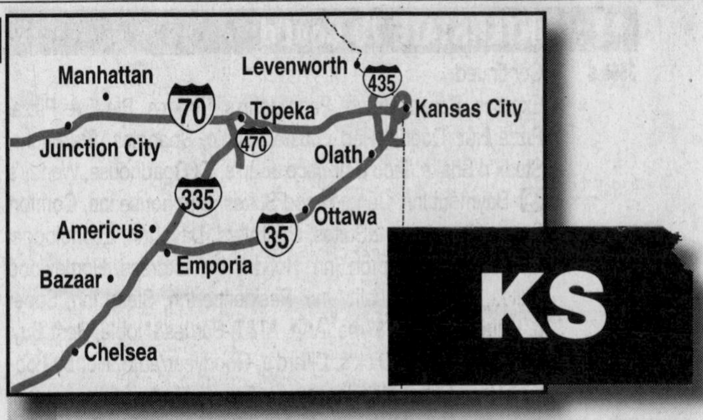

LAWRENCE

209mm	**Lawrence Service Area (both lanes exit left), full facilities,** [gas] Phillips 66/dsl [food] McDonald's
204	US 24, US 59, to E Lawrence, **S** [gas] Phillips 66/Subway [food] Burger King, Sonic [lodging] Motel 6, SpringHill Suites (1mi) [other] $General, O'Reilly Parts
203mm	Kansas River
202	US 59 S, to W Lawrence, **S on US 40** [gas] Conoco, Phillips 66/dsl, Snappy, Zarco/dsl [food] Burger King, Domino's, Dunkin Donuts, Jimmy John's, Kobe Japanese, McDonald's, Panda Garden, Sonic, Subway, Taco Bell, Taco John's, Wendy's [lodging] Baymont Inn, Comfort Inn, Days Inn, EconoLodge, Hampton Inn, Holiday Inn, Quality Inn, Rodeway Inn [other] [H], $General, Advance Parts, CarQuest, Dillon's Foods/gas, O'Reilly Parts, to Clinton Lake SP, to U of KS, vet, Walgreens
197	KS 10, Lecompton, Lawrence, **N** [other] Perry Lake SP, **S** [other] Clinton Lake SP
188mm	**Topeka Service Area, full** [handicapped] **facilities,** [gas] Phillips 66/dsl [food] Dunkin Donuts, Hardee's, Pizza Hut, Taco Bell
183	I-70 W (from wb), to Denver
367mm	**toll plaza**
366	I-470 W, to Wichita
	I-70 E and KS TPK E run together
365	21st St, Rice Rd, access to Shawnee Lake RA
364b	US 40 E, Carnahan Ave, to Lake Shawnee
364a	California Ave, **0-1 mi S** [gas] BP/dsl, Phillips 66/dsl [food] Arby's, Baskin-Robbins, Burger King, Domino's, DQ, McDonald's, Pizza Hut, Subway, Tacos Mexicano [other] $General, Ace Hardware, Advance Parts, AutoZone, Dillon's Food/gas, Family$, O'Reilly Parts, repair, TrueValue, vet, Walgreens, Walmart/Subway
363	Adams St, downtown
362c	10th Ave (from wb), **N** [lodging] Ramada Inn, **S** [other] st capitol
362b a	to 8th Ave, **N** [lodging] Ramada, **S** [other] to St Capitol, downtown
361b	3rd St, Monroe St
361a	1st Ave, **S** Ryder
359	MacVicar Ave, **S** [other] Kenworth
358b a	Gage Blvd
357b a	Fairlawn Rd, 6th Ave, **S** [gas] Conoco/dsl, Phillips 66 [lodging] Best Western, Motel 6, Ramada/rest. [other] $General, NAPACare, vet, zoo-rain forest
356b a	Wanamaker Rd, **N** [food] Red Robin [lodging] Hyatt Place [other] KS Museum of History, **S** [gas] BP, Murphy Express/dsl, Phillips 66/dsl [food] Applebee's, Arby's, Buffalo Wild Wings, Burger King, Chili's, Chipotle Mexican, Chow Time Buffet, ChuckECheese, CiCi's Pizza, Coldstone, Coyote Canyon Café, Cracker Barrel, Denny's, Famous Dave's BBQ, Five Guys, Freddy's Steakburgers, Golden Corral, Hardee's, Hooters, HuHot Chinese, IHOP, Jason's Deli, Jersey Mike's Subs, Jimmy John's, Jose Pepper's, Longhorn Steaks, McAlister's, McDonald's, Noodles&Co, Old Chicago, Olive Garden, On-the-Border, Outback Steaks, Panda

TOPEKA

INTERSTATE 70 Cont'd

356b a Continued
Express, Panera Bread, Papa John's, Perkins, Pie Five Pizza, Pizza Hut, Qdoba, Red Lobster, Sonic, Spangles, Starbucks, Steak'n Shake, Taco Bell, Taco John's, TX Roadhouse, Wendy's Baymont Inn, Candlewood Suites, Clubhouse Inn, Comfort Suites, Country Inn&Suites, Courtyard, Days Inn, Econolodge, Fairfield Inn, Hampton Inn, Holiday Inn Express, Homewood Suites, Motel 6, Quality Inn, Residence Inn, Sleep Inn, Super 8, ValuePlace $Tree, AAA, AT&T, Barnes&Noble, Best Buy, Burlington Coats, Dick's, Dillard's, Goodyear/auto, Hobby Lobby, Home Depot, JC Penney, Jo-Ann, K-Mart, Kohl's, Lowe's, mall, Menards, Michael's, Natural Grocers, Office Depot, Old Navy, PetCo, Radio Shack, Sam's Club/gas, Sears/auto, Target, TJ Maxx, Tuesday Morning, Verizon, Walmart/Subway

355 I-470 E, US 75 S, to VA MED CTR, Topeka, **1 mi** S same as 356, air museum

353 KS 4 W, to Auburn Rd

351 frontage rd (from eb), Mission Creek

350 Valencia Rd

347 West Union Rd

346 Carlson Rd, to Rossville, Willard

343 Ranch Rd

342 Keene-Eskridge Rd, access to Lake Wabaunsee

341 KS 30, Maple Hill, S 24-7/Subway/café/dsl/RV dump

338 Vera Rd, S Valero/Baskin-Robbins/dsl

336mm **(exits left from both lanes), full facilities, info, litter barrels, petwalk RV parking, wireless internet**

335 Snokomo Rd, Paxico, Skyline Mill Creek Scenic Drive

333 KS 138, Paxico, N Mill Creek RV Park, winery

332 Spring Creek Rd

330 KS 185, to McFarland

329mm **weigh sta both lanes**

328 KS 99, to Alma, S Wabaunsee Co Museum

324 Wabaunsee Rd, N Grandma Horners Store&Factory

322 Tallgrass Rd

318 frontage rd

316 Deep Creek Rd

313 KS 177, to Manhattan, **8 mi** N Phillips 66 Chili's, IHOP, Longhorn Steaks, McAlister's Deli, McDonald's, Olive Garden, Sonic, Taco Bell, TX Roadhouse, Wendy's Best Western, Candlewood Suites, Comfort Inn, Fairfield Inn, Hampton Inn, Hilton Garden, Motel 6, Quality Inn, Super 8 Aldi Foods, JC Penney, Sears/auto, to KSU, Walmart/Subway

311 Moritz Rd

310mm **both lanes, full facilities, info, litter barrels, petwalk RV dump**

307 McDowell Creek Rd, scenic river rd to Manhattan

304 Humboldt Creek Rd

303 KS 18 E, to Ogden, Manhattan, N to KSU

301 Marshall Field, N Cavalry Museum, Custer's House, KS Terr Capitol, to Ft Riley

300 US 40, KS 57, Council Grove, S hist church

299 Flinthills Blvd, to Jct City, Ft Riley, N Phillips 66/dsl Stacy's Rest EconoLodge, Grandview Plaza Inn, Great Western Inn

298 Chestnut St, to Jct City, Ft Riley, N Shell/dsl/24hr Arby's, Cox Bros BBQ, Cracker Barrel, Family Buffet, Freddy's Steakburgers, La Fiesta, Pizza Hut, Qdoba, Starbucks, Taco Bell Best Western, Candlewood Suites, Courtyard, Holiday

JCT CITY

298 Continued
Inn Express, Quality Inn $General, $Tree, CVS Drug, Verizon, Walmart/Subway

296 US 40, Washington St, Junction City, N Casey's, Cenex/dsl, Phillips 66, Shell/dsl IHOP, McDonald's, Munson's Prime, Peking Chinese, Sonic, Subway Budget Host/RV park, Comfort Inn, Express Inn, Hampton Inn, Super 8, ValuePlace Cadillac/Chevrolet, Haas Tire, Harley-Davidson, vet

295 US 77, KS 18 W, Marysville, to Milford Lake, N Phillips 66/Sapp Bros/A&W/dsl/24hr Motel 6 H, Ford/Lincoln/Kia/Chrysler/Dodge/Jeep, RV Ctr, S Owls Nest Camping, truckwash

294mm **both lanes, full facilities, litter barrels, petwalk RV dump**

290 Milford Lake Rd

286 KS 206, Chapman, S Casey's/dsl, Cenex/dsl $General, Chapman Creek RV Park, KS Auto Racing Museum

281 KS 43, to Enterprise, N Shell/dsl 4 Seasons RV Ctr/Park

277 Jeep Rd

275 KS 15, to Clay Ctr, Abilene, N DQ Brookville Hotel/rest., Holiday Inn Express, S 24-7/dsl, KwikShop, Sips Burger King, M&R Grill, McDonald's, Pizza Hut, Sonic, Subway Best Value Inn, Budget Inn, Super 8 H, $General, Auburn Drug, AutoZone, Buick/Cadillac/Chevrolet, CountryMart Foods, O'Reilly Parts, ShopKO, to Eisenhower Museum

272 Fair Rd, to Talmage, S Russell Stover Candies

266 KS 221, Solomon

265mm **both lanes, full facilities, litter barrels, petwalk RV dump, vending**

264mm Solomon River

260 Niles Rd, New Cambria

253mm Saline River

253 Ohio St, N RV park, S FLYING J/Huddle House/dsl/LP/scales/24hr, LNG H, Harley-Davidson, Kenworth

252 KS 143, 9th St, Salina, N 24-7/Subway/dsl/24hr, Petro/Shell/Starbucks/Wendy's/dsl/24hr/ @ IHOP, Iron Skillet, McDonald's Days Inn, Holiday Inn Express, Howard Johnson, La Quinta, Motel 6, Rodeway Inn, Super 8 Blue Beacon, dsl repair, Freightliner, KOA, S Pilot/Grandma Max/dsl/scales/24hr/ @ EconoLodge

250b a I-135, US 81, N to Concordia, S to Wichita

249 Halstead Rd, to Trenton

244 Hedville, S Rolling Hills Park (2mi)

238 to Brookville, Glendale, Tescott

233 290th Rd, Juniata

225 KS 156, to Ellsworth, S D&S/dsl Ft Harker Museum, Ft Larned HS

224mm **both lanes, full facilities, litter barrels, petwalk RV dump**

221 KS 14 N, to Lincoln

219 KS 14 S, to Ellsworth, S Conoco/dsl

216 to Vesper

209 to Sylvan Grove

206 KS 232, Wilson, N Travel Shoppe/rest. Wilson Lake (6mi), S RV camping

199 Dorrance, N to Wilson Lake, S Agco/dsl/food

193 Bunker Hill Rd, N Conoco/Quiznos/dsl/24hr, to Wilson Lake WA

189 US 40 bus, Pioneer Rd, Russell

187mm **both lanes, litter barrels, petwalk RV dump**

ABILENE

SALINA

KS

INTERSTATE 70 Cont'd

	Exit #	Services
RUSSELL	184	US 281, Russell, N 24-7/dsl, Phillips 66/Fossil Sta./dsl A&W, McDonald's, Meridy's Rest., Pizza Hut, Sonic, Subway Days Inn, Fossil Creek Hotel, Russell's Inn, Super 8 H, $General, Bumper Parts, CarQuest, Fossil Creek RV Park, JJJ RV Park, Klema Mkt, st patrol
	180	Balta Rd, to Russell
	175	Gorham, 1 mi N Co-Op/dsl
	172	Walker Ave
	168	KS 255, to Victoria, S 255 Diner/dsl, to Cathedral of the Plains
	163	Toulon Ave
	161	Commerce Parkway
HAYS	159	US 183, Hays, N Qwest/dsl Applebee's, Golden Corral, IHOP, Wendy's Best Western, Comfort Inn, Fairfield Inn, Hampton Inn, Holiday Inn Express, Sleep Inn Chrysler/Dodge/Jeep, Ford/Lincoln, Harley-Davidson, Home Depot, Radio Shack, Tesla EVP, Toyota, Verizon, Walmart/Subway, S 24-7/dsl, Conoco/dsl/24hr, Loves, Phillips 66/dsl, Valero/dsl Arby's, Burger King, China Garden, Freddy's Steakburgers, Jimmy John's, KFC, LJ Silver, Lucky Buffet, McDonald's, Pheasant Run Pancakes, Pizza Hut, Qdoba, Sonic, Subway, Taco Bell, Taco Grande, Thirsty's Grill, Vernie's Hamburger House, Wendy's, Whiskey Creek Grill Ambassador Hotel, Baymont Inn, Best Value Inn, Days Inn, EconoLodge, Motel 6, Quality Inn, Super 8 H, Ace Hardware, Advance Parts, Chevrolet, Dillon's Foods/gas, Firestone/auto, Hastings Books, Hobby Lobby, JC Penney, O'Reilly Parts, st patrol, Tires 4 Less, Verizon, Walgreens
	157	US 183 S byp, to Hays, N Peterbilt, S museum, to Ft Hays St U, tourist info
	153	Yocemento Ave
ELLIS	145	KS 247 S, Ellis, S Casey's, Loves/DQ/Subway/dsl/scales/24hr Cancun Mexican Days Inn Railroad Museum, RV camping, to Chrysler Museum, USPO
	140	Riga Rd
	135	KS 147, Ogallah, N Frontier Selfserve/dsl, S to Cedar Bluff SP (13mi)
	132mm	**both lanes, full facilities, litter barrels, petwalk RV dump**
WAKEENEY	128	US 283 N, WaKeeney, N Super 8
	127	US 283 S, WaKeeney, N Jake & Chet's Cafe, Pizza Hut, Tropical Mexican Best Western, KS Kountry Inn $General, S 24-7/McDonald's/dsl/24hr, Conoco/Subway/dsl EconoLodge antiques, auto repair, KOA
	120	Voda Rd
	115	KS 198 N, Banner Rd, Collyer
	107	KS 212, Castle Rock Rd, Quinter, N Sinclair/dsl First Inn/rest. H, S Conoco/dsl/24hr DQ, Pizza Sta
	99	KS 211, Park, 1 mi N Sinclair/dsl
	97mm	**both lanes, full facilities, litter barrels, petwalk RV dump, vending**
	95	KS 23 N, to Hoxie
	93	KS 23, Grainfield, N Sinclair/dsl
	85	KS 216, Grinnell
	79	Campus Rd
	76	US 40, to Oakley, S TA/Shell/Buckhorn Rest./Subway/dsl/e-85/scales/24hr/ @ Relax Inn, Rodeway Inn (2mi), Sleep Inn H, Blue Beacon, Fick Museum

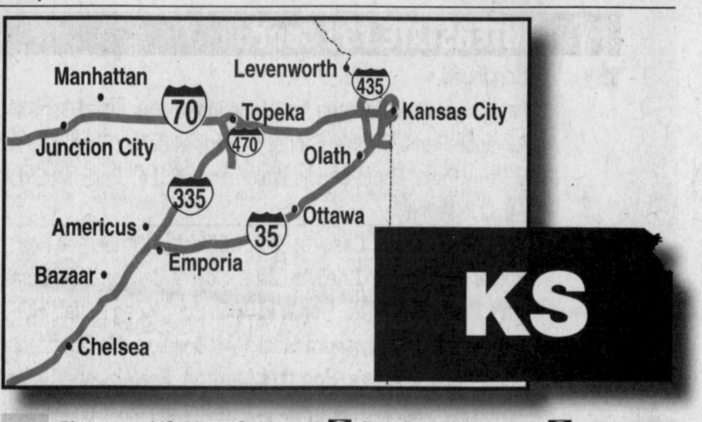

COLBY	70	US 83, to Oakley, N Free Breakfast Inn, S Cenex/dsl Colonial Steaks H, antiques, Fick Museum, High-Plains RV Park
	62	Rd K, Mingo, S gas/dsl/phone
	54	Country Club Dr, Colby, N LNG, Pilot/Subway/dsl/scales/24hr Hampton Inn H, truck/dsl repair
	53	KS 25, Colby, N 24-7/Subway/dsl Arby's, Burger King, China Buffet, McDonald's, MT Mike's Steaks, Pizza Hut, Sonic, Subway, Taco John's Days Inn, Holiday Inn Express, Motel 6, Quality Inn, Sleep Inn, Super 8 H,$General, Dillon's Foods/dsl, dsl repair, Ford/Lincoln, Haas Tire, Prairie Museum, Quilt Cabin, Radio Shack, RV park/antiques, visitors ctr, Walmart, S Petro/Phillips 66/scales/dsl/ @ City Limits Grill, Qdoba, Quiznos, Starbucks, Village Inn Comfort Inn, Knights Inn Chrysler/Dodge/Jeep, truck repair
	48.5mm	**both lanes, full facilities, litter barrels, petwalk RV park/dump, vending**
	45	US 24 E, Levant
	36	KS 184, Brewster, N Fuel Depot/dsl
	35.5mm	Mountain/Central time zone
	27	KS 253, Edson
GOODLAND	19	US 24, Goodland, N Pizza Hut $General, High Plains Museum, KOA, NAPA
	17	US 24, KS 27, Goodland, N Cenex/dsl, Conoco, Phillips 66/dsl DQ, McDonald's, Reynaldo's Mexican, Sonic, Subway, Taco John's Best Value Inn, Comfort Inn, Motel 6, Sunset Inn, Super 8 H, CarQuest/Firestone, Chevrolet/GMC, Ford, Walmart, S 24-7/dsl/scales Steak'n Shake Holiday Inn Express Mid-America Camping, Tesla EVP
	12	Rd 14, Caruso
	9	Rd 11, Ruleton
	7.5mm	**Welcome Ctr eb/rest area wb, full facilities, info, litter barrels, petwalk RV dump, vending**
	1	KS 267, Kanorado, N
	0.5mm	**weigh sta eb**
	0mm	Kansas/Colorado State Line

KS

INTERSTATE 135

Exit #	Services
95b a	**I-135 begins/ends on I-70, exit 250.** US 81 continues nb, I-70, E to KS City, W to Denver.
93	KS 140, State St, Salina, art ctr, museum
92	Crawford St, E 24-7/dsl, Gas4Less/dsl, KwikShop, Shell, Sinclair Arby's, Braum's, Cotijas Mexican, Daimaru Steaks, Great Wall Chinese, Gutierrez Mexican, Hickory Hut BBQ, Jim's Chicken, KFC, McDonald's, Russell's Rest., Spangles, Subway, Taco Bell, Western Sizzlin AmericInn, Days Inn, Fairfield

ⓖ = gas ⓕ = food ⓛ = lodging ⓞ = other Ⓡ = rest stop Copyright 2016 - The Next EXIT ®

⬆N INTERSTATE 135 Cont'd

92	Continued
	Inn, Knights Inn, Ramada Inn, Value Inn&Suites ⓞ $General, Advance Parts, Dillon's Foods, K-Mart, Midwest Tires, NAPA, O'Reilly Parts, Radio Shack, Walgreens, **W** ⓖ Phillips 66/dsl ⓛ Quality Inn
90	Magnolia Rd, **E** ⓖ Casey's, Phillips 66/dsl ⓕ AppleTree Rest., Burger King, Carlos O'Kelly's, Chili's, Coyote Canyon Café, Domino's, Freddy's Burgers, Hog Wild BBQ, Hong Kong Buffet, IHOP, Jalisco Mexican, Longhorn Steaks, McDonald's, Mr Goodcents Subs, Papa Murphy's, Poncho's Mexican, Schlotzsky's, Sonic, Spangles, Starbucks, Subway ⓛ Best Value Inn, Candlewood Suites ⓞ $General, $Tree, Aldi Foods, AutoZone, BigLots, Cadillac/Chevrolet, Dick's, Dillard's, Dillon's Foods/dsl, Hobby Lobby, Honda, JC Penney, Jo-Ann Fabrics, Kohl's, Menard's, Old Navy, O'Reilly Parts, PetCo, Sears/auto, Subaru, Toyota, Tuesday Morning, Verizon, vet, **W** ⓖ Cenex/dsl
89	Schilling Rd, **E** ⓖ KwikShop/dsl ⓕ Applebee's, Daimaru Steaks, Logan's Roadhouse, Olive Garden, Pizza Hut, Popeye's, Red Lobster, Tucson's Steaks, Wendy's ⓛ Country Inn&Suites, Courtyard, Hampton Inn ⓞ Lowe's, Sam's Club/gas, Target, Walmart/Subway, **W** ⓖ Casey's ⓛ Best Western, Comfort Suites, Super 8
88	Water Well Rd, **E** ⓛ Sleep Inn ⓞ Ford, Nissan
86	KS 104, Mentor, Smolan
82	KS 4, Falun Rd, Assaria, **E** ⓞ RV Camping
78	KS 4 W, Lindsborg, **E** ⓞ to Sandz Gallery/Museum
72	Lindsborg, **4 mi E** ⓞ Maxwell WR, McPherson St Fishing Lake, **W** ⓞ Ⓗ, camping, food, gas, lodging, museum
68mm	Ⓡ (both lanes exit left), full ⓰ facilities, info, litter barrels ⓒ ♿ RV dump
65	Pawnee Rd
60	US 56, McPherson, Marion, **W** ⓖ Midway Gas/dsl, Phillips 66/dsl ⓕ Applebee's, Arby's, Braum's, Freddy's Burgers, Golden Dragon Chinese, Hunan Chinese, KFC/LJ Silver, La Fiesta Mexican, McDonald's, MT Mike's, Perkins, Pizza Hut, Subway, Taco Bell, Taco John's, Woodie's BBQ ⓛ Best Value Inn, Best Western, Days Inn, EconoLodge, Holiday Inn Express ⓞ Ⓗ, AutoZone, Buick/Cadillac/GMC, Chrysler/Dodge/Jeep, Ford, Walgreens, Walmart
58	US 81, KS 61, to Hutchinson, McPherson
54	Elyria
48	KS 260 E, Moundridge, **2 mi W** ⓕ Block 2 Eatery, gas
46	KS 260 W, Moundridge, **2 mi W** ⓞ truck repair, food, gas
40	Lincoln Blvd, Hesston, **E** ⓕ Panda Kitchen ⓛ AmericInn ⓞ Cottonwood Grove RV Camping, **W** ⓖ Casey's/dsl/24hr ⓕ El Cerrito Grill, Lincoln Perk Coffee, Pizza Hut, Sonic, Subway ⓛ Best Value Inn ⓞ city park
34	KS 15, N Newton, to Abilene, KS 15, **E** ⓞ RV camping, **W** ⓕ Subway (1mi), Taco Bell (1mi) ⓞ Kauffman Museum
33	US 50 E, to Peabody (from nb)
31	1st St, Broadway St, **E** ⓖ Conoco/dsl, Newell TC/dsl/ @ ⓕ Applebee's, CJ's Rest., Huddle House, KFC ⓛ 1st Inn, Days Inn, EconoLodge, Holiday Inn Express ⓞ Cadillac/Chevrolet, Chrysler/Dodge/Jeep, Ford/Lincoln, **W** ⓕ Braum's, MT Mike's ⓛ Best Western/rest., Comfort Inn
30	US 50 W, KS 15 (exits left from nb), to Hutchinson, Newton, **W** ⓖ KwikShop/dsl ⓕ Arby's, Papa Murphy's, Pizza Hut, Sonic, Subway ⓞ Ⓗ, $Tree, AutoZone, Buick/GMC, Dillon's Foods, R Tires, Radio Shack, Verizon, Walmart
28	SE 36th St, **W** ⓖ Phillips 66/dsl ⓕ Burger King ⓞ Chisholm Trail Outlets/famous brands
25	KS 196, to Whitewater, El Dorado
23mm	Ⓡ both lanes, full ⓰ facilities, litter barrels, petwalk ⓒ ♿ RV dump, vending
22	125th St
19	101st St, **W** ⓞ RV camping
17	85th St, **E** ⓞ KS Coliseum, Valley Ctr
16	77th St, **E** ⓛ Sleep Inn ⓞ Wichita Greyhound Park
14	61st St, **E** ⓖ QT/dsl ⓕ Applebee's, Chopstix, Cracker Barrel, Pizza Hut, Spangles Rest., Subway, Taco Bell, Wendy's ⓛ Comfort Inn ⓞ Chevrolet, TrueValue, vet, **W** ⓖ Phillips 66/dsl ⓕ KFC, McDonald's ⓛ Quality Inn, Super 8 ⓞ Goodyear/auto
13	53rd St, **E** ⓞ Freightliner, Harley-Davidson, Mack Trucks, **W** ⓖ Phillips 66/dsl ⓕ Country Kitchen ⓛ Best Western, Days Inn
11b	I-235 W, KS 96, to Hutchinson
11a	KS 254, to El Dorado
10b	29th St, Hydraulic Ave
10a	KS 96 E
9	21st St, **E** ⓕ Sonic ⓞ $General, Wichita St U
8	13th St, ⓕ Dad's BBQ, Mel's Carryout, Pig In Pig Out BBQ
7b	8th St, 9th St, Central Ave., **E** ⓞ School of Medicine
7a	downtown
6b	1st St, 2nd St, downtown
5b	US 54, US 400, Kellogg Ave, **E** ⓖ QT/dsl ⓕ Burger King, Chipotle Mexican, Jimmy John's, Subway, Taco Bueno ⓛ Wichita Suites
5a	Lincoln St, **E** ⓕ DQ, **W** ⓖ QT
4	Harry St, **1 mi E** ⓖ QT ⓕ Arby's, Bionic Burger, Burger King, Church's, Denny's, Jimmie's Diner, Jimmy's Egg, Little Caesars, LJ Silver, McDonald's, NuWay Drive-Thru, Poblano Mexican, Shanghai Chinese, Spangles Rest., Subway, Taco Bell, Wendy's ⓞ Ⓗ, BigLots, CVS Drug, Firestone/auto, Goodyear/auto, **W** ⓖ BD-C/dsl
3	Pawnee Ave, **E** ⓖ QT ⓞ Family$, O'Reilly Parts, **W** ⓖ Jumpstart/dsl ⓕ Burger King, Pizza Hut, Spangles ⓛ Pawnee Inn (1mi) ⓞ $General, AutoZone
2	Hydraulic Ave, **E** ⓖ QT, **W** ⓕ McDonald's, Subway
2mm	Arkansas River
1c	I-235 N, **2 mi W** ⓛ Hilton
1b a	US 81 S, 47th St, **E** ⓖ QT ⓛ Days Inn, Quality Inn, Super 8, **W** ⓖ Phillips 66 ⓕ Applebee's, Braum's, Burger King, Carlos O'Kelly's, Godfather's, Goodcents Subs, Heritage Rest, Hog Wild BBQ, KFC, LJ Silver, McDonald's, New China, Papa John's, Pizza Hut, Spangles Rest., Subway, Taco Bell ⓛ Best Western, Springfield Inn, ValuePlace ⓞ $Tree, Air Capital RV Park, AutoZone, Dillon's Foods/dsl, K-Mart, O'Reilly Parts, Radio Shack

I-135 begins/ends on I-35, exit 42.

KENTUCKY

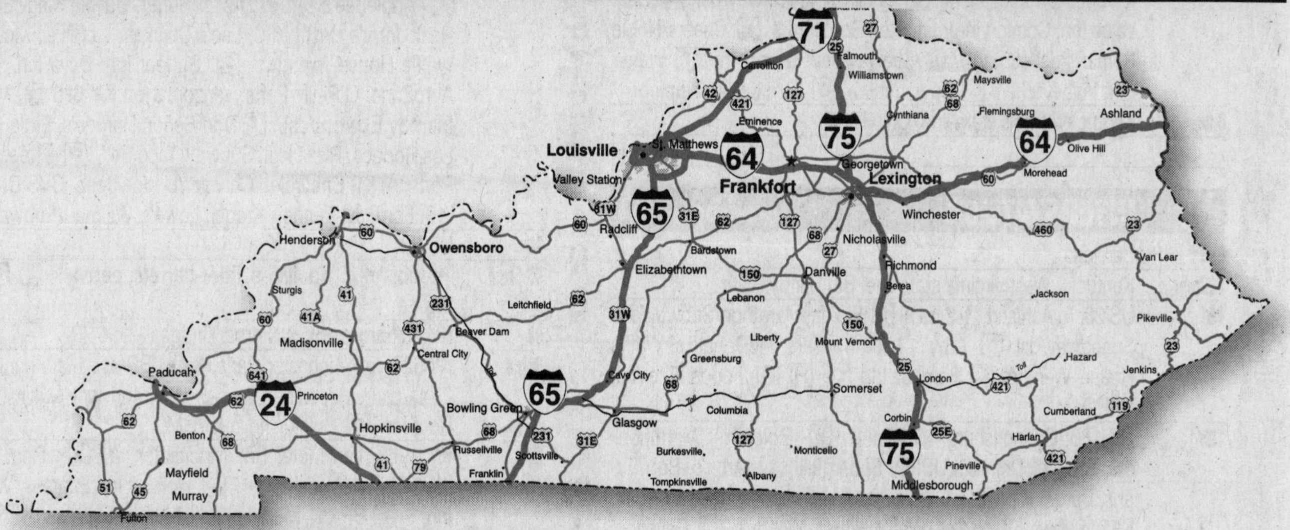

INTERSTATE 24

Exit #	Services
93.5mm	Kentucky/Tennessee state line
93mm	**Welcome Ctr wb, full facilities, litter barrels, petwalk vending**
91.5mm	Big West Fork Red River
89	KY 115, to Oak Grove, N to Jeff Davis Mon St HS, S Pilot/McDonald's/dsl/scales/24hr, Shell/Subway/dsl truck repair
86	US 41A, to Ft Campbell, Pennyrile Pkwy, Hopkinsville, N Marathon/Chester's/dsl/scales/24hr, S FLYING J/Denny's/dsl/LP/scales/24hr, Exxon/dsl, Pilot/Subway/Wendy's/dsl/scales/24hr McDonald's, Waffle House Candlewood Suites, Comfort Suites, Days Inn, Holiday Inn Express, Quality Inn, Sleep Inn H, truck wash
81	Pennyrile Pky N, to Hopkinsville
79mm	Little River
73	KY 117, to Gracey, Newstead
65	US 68, KY 80, to Cadiz, S BP/dsl, Marathon/dsl, Shell/dsl Cracker Barrel, KFC, McDonald's, Subway, Taco Bell, Wendy's Econolodge, Knights Inn, Super 7 Inn, Super 8 H, Chevrolet, golf, to NRA
56	KY 139, to Cadiz, Princeton, S Marathon/dsl KOA (9mi), NRA
47mm	Lake Barkley
45	KY 293, to Princeton, Saratoga, S Marathon/dsl Mineral Mound SP, RV Camping, to KY St Penitentiary
42	I-69 to W KY Pkwy, Elizabethtown
40	US 62, US 641, Kuttawa, Eddyville, N Regency Inn (2mi), Relax Inn camping, Mineral Mound SP, S BP/Wendy's/dsl/24hr, Exxon, Pilot/Huck's/Quiznos/dsl/scales/24hr Huddle House, SW Grill Days Inn, Hampton Inn camping, KY Lake Rec Areas, to Lake Barkley
36mm	**weigh sta both lanes**
34mm	Cumberland River
31	KY 453, to Grand Rivers, Smithland, N BP/dsl Patti's Inn, S Exxon/dsl Miss Scarlett's Best Value Inn, Grand Rivers Resort (3mi), Lighthouse Landing Resort Exit 31 RV Park, NRA
29mm	Tennessee River
27	US 62, to KY Dam, Calvert City, N BP/dsl, Marathon/dsl Cracker Barrel, DQ, KFC, McDonald's, Waffle House Days Inn, KY Dam Motel, Super 8 Cypress Lakes Camp, Freightliner, KOA, vet, S Loves/Arby's/dsl/scales/24hr Subway Econolodge truck repair
25b a	to Calvert City, Carroll/Purchase Pkwy, N services **1 mi** S to KY Lake RA
16	US 68, to Paducah, S BP/Southern Pride/Subway/dsl/scales/24hr flea mkt
11	Rd 1954, Husband Rd, to Paducah, N BP/dsl, FiveStar/dsl Best Western Duck Creek RV Park, S Harley-Davidson
7	US 45, US 62, to Paducah, N FiveStar/dsl Burger King, Taco Bell H, S **Welcome Ctr both lanes, full facilities, litter barrels, petwalk vending** BP, Marathon/dsl Arby's, Backyard Burger, Chong's Chinese, Domino's, Hardee's, KFC, Los Amigo's Mexican, McDonald's, Pap John's, Popeye's, Sonic, Subway, Waffle House, Wendy's Travelers Inn AT&T, Banks Mkt/gas, CVS Drug, Family$, K-Mart, O'Reilly Parts, Plaza Tires, Verizon,
4	US 60, to Paducah, N BP Applebee's, Bob Evans, Burger King, McDonald's, O'Charley's, Outback Steaks, Rafferty's Auburn Place, Candlewood Suites, Courtyard, Days Inn, Drury Inn, Fairfield Inn, Hampton Inn, Holiday Inn Express, La Quinta, Residence Inn, Westowne Inn Hancock Fabrics, Toyota/Scion, S BP, Murphy USA/dsl Arby's, Backyard Burger, Buffalo Wild Wings, Capt D's, Chick-fil-A, Chong's Chinese, ChuckeCheese, Coldstone, Cracker Barrel, Domino's, Fazoli's, Firehouse Subs, Gondolier Italian, Hananoki Hibachi, Hardee's, IHOP, Logan's Roadhouse, Los Amigos, Los Garcia's, McAlister's Deli, Olive Garden, Panchero's, Panera Bread, Penn Sta. Subs, Pizza Hut, Red Lobster, Ryan's, Sonic, Steak'n Shake, Taco Bell, Taco John's, TGIFriday's, Tokyo Hibachi, TX Roadhouse, Wendy's Comfort Suites, Country Inn&Suites, Drury Suites, Motel 6, PearTree Inn, Super 8, Thrifty Inn $General, $Tree, AAA, Advance Parts, Aldi Foods, AT&T, Best Buy, Books-A-Million, Dick's, Dillard's, Gander Mtn, Goodyear/auto, Hobby Lobby, Home Depot, JC Penney, Kohl's, Lowe's, mall, Michael's, Office Depot, Old Navy, Petsmart, Plaza Tire, Sam's Club/gas, Sears/auto, TJ Maxx, Tuesday Morning, Verizon, Walmart

PADUCAH

= gas = food = lodging = other = rest stop

INTERSTATE 24 Cont'd

Exit #	Services
3	KY 305, to Paducah, N Shell/dsl, Superway/dsl Best Value Inn, Comfort Inn/rest., Red Roof Inn, S Cheers/Noble Romans/dsl/e85, Pilot/Subway/dsl/scales/24hr Waffle Hut, Yu's Kitchen Baymont Inn Fern Lake Camping
0mm	Kentucky/Illinois state line, Ohio River

INTERSTATE 64

Exit #	Services
192mm	Kentucky/West Virginia state line, Big Sandy River
191	US 23, to Ashland, 1-2 mi N Exxon, Marathon/Subway/dsl, Speedway/dsl Arby's, Little Caesars, McDonald's, Waffle House, Wendy's Ramada Ltd H, IGA Foods, Rite Aid, USPO
185	KY 180, Cannonsburg, 0-3 mi N Exxon/dsl, Marathon/dsl, Shell/McDonald's/USPO, Superquik Arby's, Bob Evans, Burger King, DQ, Gatti's Pizza, Hermanos Nunez Mexican, KFC, Subway, Taco Bell, Waffle House, Wendy's Days Inn, Fairfield Inn, Hampton Inn, Holiday Inn Express $Tree, st police, Walmart/Subway, S FLYING J/Denny's/dsl/LP/scales/24hr Hidden Valley Camping
181	181 US 60, to Princess, N BP/dsl, S Marathon/dsl
179	Rd 67, Industrial Pkwy, N KOA @
174mm	**eb, full facilities, litter barrels, petwalk vending**
173mm	**wb, full facilities, litter barrels, petwalk vending**
172	Rd 1, Rd 7, Grayson, N Marathon/dsl, Superquik/dsl/24hr A&W/LJ Silver, Huddle House, KFC, Pizza Hut, Subway Days Inn, Guesthouse Inn, Quality Inn $General, $Tree, Chrysler/Dodge/Jeep, Ford, K-Mart, Save-A-Lot Foods, URGENT CARE, S BP, Exxon, Exxon/Hardees, Loves/Wendy's/scales/dsl/24hr, Marathon, Shell/dsl, Speedway/dsl Arby's, Biscuit World, China House, DQ, Little Caesar's, McDonald's, Papa John's, Taco Bell, Toro Loco Super 8 $General, Advance Parts, AT&T, AutoZone, Family$, Food Fair, Rite Aid, Verizon
161	US 60, to Olive Hill, N BP Spanish Manor Motel camping, to Carter Caves SP
156	Rd 2, to KY 59, to Olive Hill, S BP
148mm	**weigh sta wb**
141mm	**both lanes, full facilities, litter barrels, petwalk vending**
137	KY 32, to Morehead, N BP/dsl, Speedway/dsl CiCi's Pizza, DQ, Huddle House, Reno's Roadhouse AT&T, Big Lots, Kroger/dsl, Lowe's, Walmart/Subway, S BP/McDonald's/dsl/24hr, Marathon/dsl China Star, Cracker Barrel, Domino's, Don Señor, Hardee's, Lee's Chicken, Ponderosa Days Inn, Hampton Inn, Holiday Inn Express, Red Roof Inn, Super 8 H, $General, Ace Hardware, auto repair, AutoZone, Radio Shack, st police
133	Rd 801, to Sharkey, Farmers, N Shell/dsl, S BP/Subway/dsl Comfort Inn Outpost RV Park (4mi)
123	US 60, to Salt Lick, Owingsville
121	KY 36, to Owingsville, N BP/dsl, Exxon/dsl, Valero/dsl DQ, McDonald's, Subway $General, Family$, S Save-a-Lot Foods
113	US 60, to Mt Sterling, N Shell/dsl, S Pilot/McDonald's/Subway/dsl/scales/24hr
110	US 460, KY 11, Mt Sterling, N Shell/Krystal/Subway/dsl, Valero/dsl Cattleman's Roadhouse, Cracker Barrel Fairfield Inn, Ramada Ltd, S Marathon/dsl, Speedway/dsl Applebee's, Arby's, Asian Buffet, Burger King, El Camino Real, Jerry's Rest., KFC, Lee's Chicken, LJ Silver, McDonald's, Waffle House, Wendy's Budget Inn, Days Inn H, AutoZone, O'Reilly Parts, Verizon, S **on KY 686** Marathon, Murphy Express/dsl, Don Señor, Hardee's, Little Caesar's, Los Rodeos, Pizza Hut, Subway, Taco Bell, $Tree, Advance Parts, AT&T, Chevrolet, Chrysler/Dodge/Jeep, CVS Drug, Family$, Ford, JC Penney, Kroger, Lowe's, Walmart/Subway
101	US 60
98.5mm	**eb, full facilities, litter barrels, petwalk vending**
98	KY 402 (from eb), S Natural Bridge Resort SP
96b a	KY 627, to Winchester, Paris, N BP/dsl, Marathon/96 Truck Plaza/dsl/rest./scales, S Hampton Inn, Quality Inn, Red Roof Inn Buick/Chevrolet/GMC
94	KY 1958, Van Meter Rd, Winchester, N Road Ranger/dsl/24hr, Shell/scales/dsl Holiday Inn Express, Value Stay Inn, S BP/dsl, Marathon/dsl, Murphy Express/dsl, She'll/dsl, Speedway/dsl Applebee's, Arby's, Big Boy, Burger King, Capt D's, Domino's, Don Senor, DQ, El Camino Real, Fazoli's, Golden Corral, Great Wall Chinese, Hardee's, Jade Garden Chinese, KFC, Little Caesar's, McDonald's, Papa John's, Pizza Hut, Puerta Grande, Rally's, Sakura Express, Sir Pizza, Sonic, Starbucks, Subway, Taco Bell, Taste Of China, Waffle House, Wendy's H, $Tree, Advance Parts, AT&T, auto repair, AutoZone, Chrysler/Dodge/Jeep, Kroger/dsl, Lowe's, Office Depot, O'Reilly Parts, Radio Shack, Rite Aid, Tire Discounters, to Ft Boonesborough Camping, Verizon, Walgreens, Walmart/Subway
87	KY 859, Blue Grass Sta
81	I-75 S, to Knoxville

I-64 and I-75 run together 7 mi. See KY I-75, exits 113-115.

Exit #	Services
75	I-75 N, to Cincinnati, access to KY Horse Park
69	US 62 E, to Georgetown, N antiques (6mi), to Georgetown Coll., S Equus Run Vineyards (2mi)
65	US 421, Midway, S Shell/dsl McDonald's
60mm	**both lanes, full facilities, litter barrels, petwalk, vending**
58	US 60, Frankfort, N BP/dsl, Shell/dsl, Speedway/dsl Arby's, Buffalo Wild Wings, Capt. D's, Cattleman's Roadhouse, DQ, KFC, McDonald's, Miguel's Mexican, Starbucks, Subway, Taco Bell, Waffle House, Wendy's, White Castle, Zaxby's Best Western, Bluegrass Inn, Fairfield Inn $General, $Tree, Buick/Chevrolet/GMC, Chrysler/Dodge/Jeep, Dick's, ElkHorn Camping (5mi), Ford/Lincoln, GNC, Honda, Kohl's, Kroger/gas, KYSU, Michael's, Nissan, TireDiscounters, TJMaxx, to KY St Capitol, to Viet Vets Mem, Toyota/Scion, Walgreens, S Cracker Barrel, Logan's Roadhouse
55mm	Kentucky River
53b a	US 127, Frankfort, N Marathon, Speedway/dsl, Speedway/dsl Applebee's, Arby's, Baskin-Robbins, Beef O'Brady's, Big Boy, Burger King, Capt D's, Carino's Italian, Chili's, China Buffet, CookOut, DQ, Fazoli's, Ginza Japanese, Hardee's, KFC, Longhorn Steaks, McDonald's, My Guadalajara, O'Charley's, Panera Bread, Penn Sta Subs, Qdoba Mexican, Sonic, Starbucks, Staxx BBQ, Steak'n Shake, Subway, Taco Bell, Tacos n More, Wendy's Best Value Inn, Days Inn, Hampton Inn, Holiday Inn Express H, $General, Advance Parts, Ancient Age Tour, AT&T, AutoZone, BigLots, Big-O Tire, Family$, GNC, Goodyear/auto, JC Penney, K-Mart, Kroger/gas, Lowe's,

GRAYSON

MT STERLING

WINCHESTER

FRANKFORT

INTERSTATE 64 Cont'd

SHELBYVILLE

53b a Continued
Midas, Office Depot, Petco, Radio Shack, Rite Aid, st police, Staples, to KY St Capitol, URGENT CARE, USPO, Verizon, Walgreens, Walmart/Subway, S BP/dsl

48 KY 151, to US 127 S, S BP/dsl, Valero/dsl

43 KY 395, Waddy, N FLYING J/Denny's/dsl/LP/scales/24hr, S Loves/McDonald's/Subway/dsl/scales/24hr

38.5mm **weigh sta eb**

35 KY 53, Shelbyville, N Marathon/dsl, Shell/Circle K/dsl, Speedway/dsl Cracker Barrel, KFC, Little Caesar's, McDonald's (1mi), Subway, Taco Bell, Waffle House $General, Advance Parts, Family$, Ford, Kroger/deli/dsl, Lake Shelby Camping (3mi), vet, S Huck's/White Castle/dsl, Valero/Subway/dsl Holiday Inn Express golf

32b a KY 55, Shelbyville, **1-2 mi N** Murphy USA/dsl, Valero/dsl Arby's, Asian Buffet, Firefresh BBQ, Hardee's, McDonald's, Pizza Hut, Salgado's FreshMex, Subway, Waffle House, Wendy's, Zaxby's Best Western, Country Hearth Inn, Red Roof Inn H, $Tree, AutoZone, Big O Tire, Buick/Chevrolet/GMC, Chrysler/Dodge/Jeep, CVS Drug, Lowe's, Rolling Hills Camping (16mi), Verizon, Walgreens, Walmart, S Cattleman's Roadhouse Ramada Taylorsville Lake SP

28mm **RS eb, full facilities, info, litter barrels, petwalk vending**

28 KY 1848, Veechdale Rd, Simpsonville, N Pilot/Wendy's/dsl/scales/24hr DQ, Subway golf, S Bob Evans, Culver's Blue Grass Outlets/famous brands

19b a I-265, Gene Snyder Fwy, N to Tom Sawyer SP

LOUISVILLE

17 S Blankenbaker, N Shell/Circle K/dsl Mellow Mushroom Pizza, Zaxby's Staybridge Suites Harley-Davidson, S Marathon, Speedway/Subway/dsl, Thornton's/dsl Arby's, BackYard Burger, Burger King, Cracker Barrel, El Caporal Mexican, HomeTown Buffet, KFC, Kingfish Rest., LJ Silver/Taco Bell, Logan's Roadhouse, McDonald's, Penn Sta Subs, Qdoba, Ruby Tuesday, Starbucks, Waffle House, Wendy's Comfort Suites, Country Inn&Suites, Extended Stay America, Fairfield Inn, Hampton Inn, Hawthorn Suites, Hilton Garden, Holiday Inn Express, La Quinta, Microtel, Quality Inn, Sleep Inn, ValuePlace, Wingate Inn Lexus, Sam's Club/gas

15 Hurstbourne Pkwy, Louisville, **0-2 mi N** Shell/Circle K/dsl, Speedway, Thorton's/dsl Arby's, Bob Evans, Bonefish Grill, Carrabba's, Chili's, Fazoli's, Firehouse Subs, IHOP, Jimmy John's, Macaroni Grill, McDonald's, Mimi's Cafe, Momma's BBQ, Noodles&Co, Olive Garden, Panda Express, Panera Bread, Papa John's, PF Changs, Pita Pit, Qdoba, Sichuan Garden, Skyline Chili, Smashburger, Starbucks, Subway, Waffle House Baymont Inn, Courtyard, Days Inn, Drury Inn, Holiday Inn, Hyatt Place, Red Roof Inn, Residence Inn Barnes&Noble, Kroger/gas, Lowe's, Towery's Auto, Tuesday Morning, Walgreens, S Applebee's, BoomBozz Pizza, Buca Italian, Buffalo Wild Wing, Burger King, Cattleman's Roadhouse, Chick-fil-A, ChuckeCheese, Coldstone, DQ, El Marlin Seafood, El Torazo Mexican, Famous Daves, Happy China, Home Run Burgers, J Gumbo's Cajun, Jason's Deli, Jumbo Buffet, Kansai Japanese, Longhorn Steaks, McAlister's Deli, McDonald's, Melting Pot, Moe's SW Grill, O'Charley's, Old Chicago, Panera Bread, Penn Sta. Subs, Pizza Hut, Qdoba, Shogun Japanese, Smokey Bones BBQ, Starbucks, Steak'n Shake, Taco Bell, Tumbleweed SW Grill, Wendy's, White Castle, Yen Ching Best Western, Extended Stay America, Marriott, Ramada, Red Carpet Inn $Tree, Autozone, BMW, Buick/GMC, Cadillac,

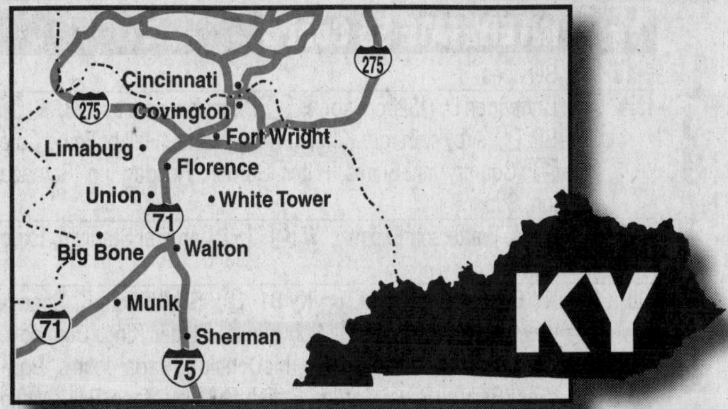

15 Continued
Carmax, Chevrolet, Discount Tire, GNC, Hancock Fabrics, Home Depot, Honda, Infiniti, Kroger/gas, Michael's, Office Depot, Radio Shack, Staples, Subaru, Target, Verizon, Volvo, VW, Walgreens, Walmart

12b I-264 E, Watterson Expswy, **1 exit N on US 60** Thornton's/dsl Arby's, Big Boy, Bravo Cucina Italin, Buffalo Wild Wings, CA Pizza, Cheesecake Factory, Chick-Fil-A, Chuy's Mexican, Jason's Deli, Logan's Roadhouse, McDonald's, Outback Steaks, Panera Bread, Red Robin, Speedway/dsl, Taco Bell, Wendy's Acura, Best Buy, Dick's, Dillard's, Ford/Lincoln, Goodyear/auto, Hyundai, JC Penney, Jo-Ann, Kia, Kohl's, Macy's, mall, Old Navy, Sears/auto, Staples, SteinMart, Toyota/Scion, Von Maur, Whole Foods Mkt

12a I-264 W, access to H

10 Cannons Lane

8 Grinstead Dr, Louisville, S gas Jim Porter's Rest., KT Cafe

7 US 42, US 62, Mellwood Ave, Story Ave

6 I-71 N (from eb), to Cincinnati

5a I-65, S to Nashville, N to Indianapolis

5b 3rd St, Louisville, N Joe's CrabShack, S Galt House Hotel, Marriott H

4 9th St, Roy Wilkins Ave, S KY Art Ctr, science museum, downtown

3 US 150 E, to 22nd St, S Marathon/dsl, Shell/Circle K DQ, McDonald's Family$

1 I-264 E, to Shively, S zoo

0mm Kentucky/Indiana state line, Ohio River

INTERSTATE 65

LOUISVILLE

Exit #	Services
138mm	Kentucky/Indiana state line, Ohio River
137	I-64 W, I-71 N, I-64 E, W to Galt House, downtown
136c	Jefferson St, Louisville, E H, Walgreens, W Shell McDonald's, Papa John's, Subway, White Castle Courtyard, EconoLodge, Fairfield Inn, Hampton Inn, Hyatt, Marriott, SpringHill Suites Tires+
136b	Broadway St, Chestnut St (from nb), E H, NAPA, Walgreens, W Shell, Thornton's McDonald's, Rally's, Subway, White Castle Courtyard, Fairfield Inn, Hampton Inn, Hyatt, Marriott, Springhill Suites same as 136c, Tires+
135	W St Catherine, E Shell
134b a	KY 61, Jackson St, Woodbine St, W Shell/Circle K Days Inn, Quality Inn Harley-Davidson
133b	US 60A, Eastern Pkwy, Taylor Blvd, E Denny's, Pizza Mia, Snappy Tomato Pizza, Subway, W Marathon Cracker Barrel, McDonald's, Papa John's Country Hearth Inn Churchill Downs, museum, U of Louisville

KY

LOUISVILLE

INTERSTATE 65 Cont'd

Exit #	Services
133b	Crittenden Dr (132from sb), E Denny's, same as 133, W BP Arby's, Burger King, Cracker Barrel, Hall of Fame Cafe Country Inn&Suites, Hilton Garden, Holiday Inn, Ramada Inn, Super 8
131b a	I-264, Watterson Expswy, W Cardinal Stadium, Expo Center
130	KY 61, Preston Hwy, E on Ky 61 Shell/Circle K, Speedway/dsl, Thornton's Bob Evans, Burger King, Domino's, Fazoli's, KFC, Little Caesars, McDonald's, Papa John's, Popeyes, Rally's, Royal Garden Buffet, Subway, Taco Bell, Waffle House, Wendy's EconoLodge, Red Roof Inn, Super 8 $General, Aamco, AutoZone, Big O Tire, BigLots, Chevrolet/Kia, Dodge, Ford, O'Reilly Parts, PepBoys, Radio Shack, Sav-A-Lot Foods, Staples, Tires+, U-Haul
128	KY 1631, Fern Valley Rd, E BP, Marathon/Circle K, Thornton's/dsl Arby's, Big Boy, El Nopal Mexican, Hardee's, Indi's Rest., McDonald's, Outback Steaks, Shoney's, Subway, Taco Bell, Waffle House, Wendy's, White Castle Comfort Suites, Days Inn, Fern Valley Hotel, Holiday Inn, InTown Suites, Jameson Inn Sam's Club/gas, Walgreens, W UPS Depot
127	KY 1065, outer loop, E TX Roadhouse, W McDonald's/RV Parking, to Motor Speedway
125b a	I-265 E, KY 841, Gene Snyder Fwy
121	KY 1526, Brooks Rd, E BP, Marathon Arby's, Burger King, Cracker Barrel, McDonald's, Tumbleweed Grill Comfort Inn, Fairfield Inn, Holiday Inn Express H, Tinker's RV Ctr, W BP/dsl, Pilot/Subway/Taco Bell/dsl/scales/24hr Waffle House Baymont Inn, EconoLodge, Hampton Inn, Quality Inn
117	KY 44, Shepherdsville, E Gulf Bearno's Pizza, Denny's Best Western/rest., Days Inn KOA (2mi), W Marathon, Speedway/dsl Arby's, Big Boy, Cattlelands Roadhouse, China Buffet, DQ, El Nopal, Fazoli's, KFC, Little Caesars, LJ Silver, McDonald's/playplace, Mr Gatti's, Quiznos, Sonic, Subway, Taco Bell, Triple Crown Steaks, Waffle House, Wendy's, White Castle Country Inn&Suites, Motel 6, Sleep Inn, Super 8 $General, Advance Parts, auto repair, AutoZone, BigLots, Family$, Kroger/gas, Lowe's, Radio Shack, Rite Aid, Sav-a-Lot, Walgreens
116.5mm	Salt River
116	KY 480, to KY 61, E Loves/Chester's/Subway/dsl/scales/24hr, Shell/dsl House of Quilts, W Marathon/dsl Grandma's RV Park/flea mkt
114mm	**[RS] sb, full [handicap] facilities, litter barrels, petwalk [phone] [picnic] vending**
112	KY 245, Clermont, E Shell/dsl Bernheim Forest, Jim Beam Outpost, to My Old Kentucky Home SP
105	KY 61, Lebanon Jct, W 105 QuikStop/dsl, /McDonald's/Subway/dsl/scales/24hr/ @ Vegas Lou's BBQ
102	KY 313, to KY 434, Radcliff, W to Patton Museum
94	US 62, Elizabethtown, E BP/dsl, Marathon/dsl Denny's, Waffle House, White Castle Comfort Inn, Days Inn, Super 8, W BP/dsl, Speedway/dsl Arby's, Burger King, Chalupa's Mexican, Cracker Barrel, Gatti's Pizza, HoneyBaked Ham, KFC/Taco Bell, McDonald's, Papa John's, Ruby Tuesday, Ryan's, Shoney's, Snappy Tomato Pizza, Stone Hearth, Subway, TX Outlaw Steaks, TX Roadhouse, Wendy's Baymont Inn, Best Western, Comfort Suites, Fairfield Inn, Hampton Inn, Holiday Inn Express, Howard Johnson, La Quinta, Motel 6, Ramada Inn H, $General, $Tree, Advance Parts, AutoZone,

KY

ELIZABETHTOWN

BOWLING GREEN

Exit #	Services
94	Continued Crossroads Camping, Kroger/gas, Skagg's RV Ctr, st police, USPO, visitors ctr, Walgreens
93	to Bardstown, to BG Pky, E Maker's Mark Distillery, to My Old KY Home SP
91	US 31 W, KY 61, WK Pkwy, Elizabethtown, E Marathon/dsl LJ Silver, Subway Bluegrass Inn, Budget Motel, Commonwealth Lodge $General, to Lincoln B'Place, W Doug's/dsl, Marathon Jerry's Rest. KY Cardinal Inn, Roadside Inn H
90mm	**weigh sta sb only**
86	KY 222, Glendale, E Pilot/McDonalds/dsl/scales/24hr Glendale Camping, trk repair, W Petro/Dunkin Donuts/dsl/scales/24hr/ @ Glendale Economy Inn Blue Beacon
83mm	Nolin River
81	KY 84, Sonora, E Marathon/dsl, Pilot/Subway/dsl/scales/24hr Blue Beacon, to Lincoln B'Place, W BP/dsl
76	KY 224, Upton, E Marathon/dsl, W to Nolin Lake
75mm	eastern/central time zone
71	KY 728, Bonnieville
65	US 31 W, Munfordville, E BP/Subway/dsl, FiveStar/dsl DQ, El Mazatlan, King Buffet, McDonald's, Pizza Hut, Sonic Super 11 $General, Advance Parts, Family$, Fred's Store, IGA Foods, Pamida, Save-A-Lot, W Marathon/dsl, Shell Country Kitchen, to Nolin Lake
61mm	**[RS] both lanes, full [handicap] facilities, Green River, info, litter barrels, petwalk [phone] [picnic] vending**
58	KY 218, Horse Cave, E Loves/McDonald's/dsl/scales/24hr/ @ H, W Gulf/dsl, Marathon/dsl/repair Country Hearth Inn, Hampton Inn KOA, to Mammoth Cave NP
53	KY 70, KY 90, Cave City, E BP/dsl, Gulf/dsl/repair, JR's, Marathon/dsl, Shell A&W/LJ Silver, Cracker Barrel, El Mazatlan, El Patron, KFC, McDonald's, Pizza Hut, Subway, Wendy's Best Value Inn, Best Western, Comfort Inn, Days Inn/rest., EconoLodge, Sleep Inn, Super 8 H, $General, Barren River Lake SP (24mi), W Watermill Rest. Jellystone Camping, Mammoth Cave NP, Onyx Cave
48	KY 255, Park City, E Shell/dsl $General, Park Mammoth Resort, W Diamond Caverns Resort, to Mammoth Cave NP
43	Nun/Cumberland Pky, to Barren River Lake SP
38	KY 101, Smiths Grove, W Exxon/dsl/scales, Marathon/Subway/dsl, Shell Bestway Pizza, McDonald's, Wendy's Bryce Motel $General, auto repair, city park, IGA Foods, Larry's Parts
36	US 68, KY 80, Oakland, (no nb return)
28	Rd 446, to US 31 W, Bowling Green, W Shell/dsl Hardee's, Jerry's Rest., Wendy's Continental Inn, Country Hearth Inn, Super 8, Value Lodge H, Corvette Museum/cafe, to WKYU
26	KY 234, Bowling Green, W Shell/dsl Subway H, IGA Foods
22	US 231, Bowling Green, E Exxon/dsl Keystop Gas, Shell Catfish House, Cracker Barrel, Culver's, Denny's, Domino's, Godfather's, Hardee's, Mancino's Pizza, Motor City Grill, Ryan's, Sonic, Waffle House, Zaxby's Best Value Inn, Best Western, Comfort Inn, Days Inn, EconoLodge, Fairfield Inn, HomeTowne Suites, La Quinta, Microtel, Quality Inn, Ramada Inn, Sleep Inn $General, Camping World/Gander Mtn, Harley-Davidson, URGENT CARE, USPO, W Gulf/dsl, Race

INTERSTATE 65 Cont'd

BOWLING GREEN

22	Continued Way, Shell/dsl, Speedway/dsl Applebee's, Arby's, Beijing Chinese, Bob Evans, Bruster's, Buffalo Wild Wings, Burger King, Capt D's, Chick-fil-A, China Buffet, ChuckeCheese, Double-Dog's Chowhouse, Fazoli's, Great Harvest Bread, Guadalajara Grill, KFC, Krystal, Kyoto Steaks, Linzie's Sandwiches, Logan's Roadhouse, Longhorn Steaks, McDonald's, Moe's SW Grill, MT Grille, O'Charley's, Olive Garden, Outback Steaks, Panera Bread, Pizza Hut, Rafferty's, Red Lobster, Ruby Tuesday, Shogun Japanese, Smokey Bones BBQ, Sonic, Starbucks, Steak'n Shake, Subway, Taco Bell, TGIFriday's, Toots Rest., Waffle House, Wendy's, White Castle, Zaxby's Baymont Inn, Candlewood Suites, Country Inn&Suites, Courtyard, Drury Inn, Hampton Inn, Hilton Garden, Holiday Inn, Motel 6, News Inn, Red Roof Inn H, $General, Advance Parts, AT&T, Barnes&Noble, Best Buy, BMW/Mercedes, Buick/GMC, Chevrolet, Chrysler/Jeep, Curves, CVS Drug, Dillard's, Fisher Parts, Ford/Lincoln, Goodyear/auto, Hancock Fabrics, Hobby Lobby, Home Depot, Honda, JC Penney, Kia, K-Mart, KOA, Kohl's, Kroger/gas, Lowe's, mall, Nissan, Office Depot, Old Navy, PetCo, Sam's Club/gas, Sears, Staples, Target, TJ Maxx, Toyota, U-Haul, URGENT CARE, Walgreens, Walmart/McDonald's
20	**WH Natcher Toll Rd**, to Bowling Green, access to W KY U, st police
6	KY 100, Franklin, E BP/dsl, Shell/dsl/24hr truckwash, W Pilot/Subway/dsl/scales/24hr, Pilot/Wendy's/dsl/scales/24hr Comfort Inn, Days Inn, Knights Inn H, Bluegrass RV Park, Petrolube, SpeedCo, truck&tires/repair, truckwash
4mm	**weigh sta nb**
2	US 31 W, to Franklin, E FLYING J/Denny's/dsl/LP/scales/24hr, Keystop/Marathon/Burger King/dsl/24hr, W BP/dsl Cracker Barrel, McDonald's, Oasis SW Grill, Waffle House Best Western, EconoLodge, Hampton Inn, Holiday Inn Express, Quality Inn, Super 8 H, antiques
1mm	**Welcome Ctr nb, full facilities, info, litter barrels, petwalk vending**
Kentucky/Tennessee state line	

FRANKLIN

INTERSTATE 71

Exit #	Services
100	Kentucky/Ohio state line, Ohio River
I-71 and I-75 run together 19 miles. See I-75, exits 175-192.	
77 [173]	I-75 S, to Lexington
75mm	**weigh sta sb**
72	KY 14, to Verona, E BP/dsl, Marathon/dsl Oak Creek Camping (5mi)
62	US 127, to Glencoe, E 62 TrkPlaza/rest./dsl, W Valero/dsl/rest. 127 Motel
57	KY 35, to Sparta, E Marathon/dsl Eagle Valley Camping (10mi), Sparta RV Park (3mi), W BP/dsl Ramada KY Speedway
55	KY 1039, W Loves/McDonald's/Subway/dsl/scales/24hr casino, KY Speedway
44	KY 227, to Indian Hills, W Marathon/dsl, Marathon/dsl, Murphy USA/dsl, Valero/dsl Arby's, Burger King, El Nopal, Hometown Pizza, KFC, McDonald's, Mi Viejo Mexican, New China, Sonic, Subway, Taco Bell, Waffle House Best Western, Hampton Inn, Holiday Inn Express, Quality Inn, Super 8

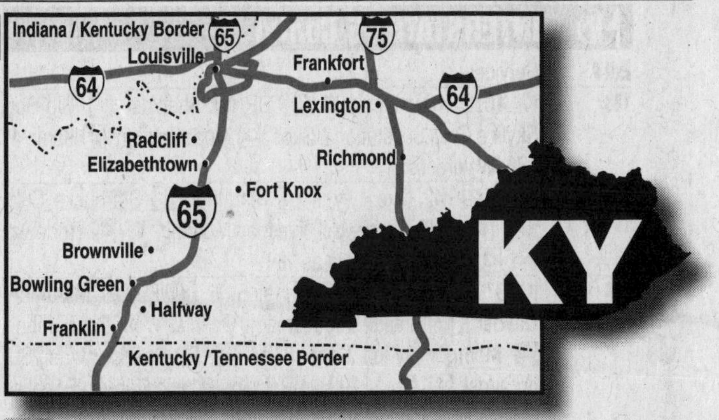

44	Continued H, $General, $Tree, AutoZone, Chevrolet, Ford, Gen. Butler SP, Kroger/dsl, Save-a-Lot Foods, URGENT CARE, Verizon, Walmart
43.5mm	Kentucky River
43	KY 389, to KY 55, English
34	US 421, New Castle, Campbellsburg, W Marathon/dsl, Valero/Subway/dsl st police
28	KY 153, KY 146, to US 42, Pendleton, E Pilot/Subway/dsl/scales/24hr/ @, Valero/dsl, W Pilot/McDonald's/scales/dsl/24hr truck repair
22	KY 53, La Grange, E Speedway/Rally's/dsl, Valero/dsl Applebee's, Beef O'Brady's, Burger King, Jumbo Buffet, Papa John's, Papa Murphy's, Ponderosa, Subway, Waffle House, Wendy's Best Western-Ashbury, Comfort Inn H, $General, AT&T, Big-O Tire, GNC, Kroger/gas, Radio Shack, Towery's Tire/auto, Verizon, Walgreens, Walmart/Subway, W Marathon/dsl Arby's, Cracker Barrel, Domino's, DQ, El Nopal, Hometown Pizza, KFC, LJ Silver, McDonald's, Taco Bell Comfort Suites, Super 8 $Tree, Advance Parts, Buick/Chevrolet/GMC, Lee Tires, NAPA, Rite Aid, USPO, vet
18	KY 393, Buckner, W Marathon/dsl Subway Ford
17	KY 146, Buckner, W Thornton's/dsl/24hr st police, USPO
14	KY 329, Crestwood, Pewee Valley, Brownsboro, E BP/dsl DQ, Hometown Pizza, McDonald's, Sonic, Starbucks, Subway
13mm	**both lanes, full facilities, litter barrels, petwalk vending**
9b a	I-265, KY 841, Gene Snyder Fwy, E Hilton Garden Cabela's, Costco/gas, H, to Sawyer SP
5	I-264, Watterson Expswy (exits left from sb), E to Sawyer SP
2	Zorn Ave, E VA H, W Shell/dsl, Valero El Nopal Mexican, KingFish Rest. Ramada Inn WaterTower Art Museum
1b	I-65, S to Nashville, N to Indianapolis

LOUISVILLE

INTERSTATE 75

Exit #	Services
193mm	Kentucky/Ohio state line, Ohio River
192	5th St (from nb), Covington, E BP/dsl, Shell/Circle K, Speedway/dsl Big Boy, Burger King, GoldStar Chili, McDonald's, Popeyes, Riverfront Pizza, Skyline Chili, Subway, Taco Bell, Waffle House, Wendy's, White Castle Courtyard, Extended Stay America, Holiday Inn, Radisson Lexus, Riverboat Casino, W Hampton Inn
191	12th St, Covington, E H, museum, same as 192

= gas = food = lodging = other = rest stop

INTERSTATE 75 Cont'd

COVINGTON

Exit #	Services
189	KY 1072, Kyles Lane, W BP/dsl, Shell/dsl Big Boy, Skyline Chili, Substation II Subs Rodeway Inn same as 188, Walgreens
188	US 25, US 42, Dixe Hwy, E Marathon Starbucks, Subway GNC, Kroger/dsl, Tuesday Morning, W Rodeway Inn Mercedes, same as 189
186	KY 371, Buttermilk Pike, Covington, E BP/dsl, Marathon/DQ/dsl Graeter's Ice Cream, Oriental Wok, Papa John's Montgomery Inn, Super 8, W BP, Speedway/dsl, Sunoco/dsl Arby's, Baskin-Robbins/Dunkin Donuts, Bonefish Grill, Burger King, Cancun Mexican, Chipotle Mexican, Domino's, Empire Buffet, Firehouse Subs, GoldStar Chili, Jimmy John's, La Rosa's Pizza, Marco's Pizza, McDonald's, Miyako Steaks, Outback Steaks, Skyline Chili, Subway, Sweet Basil Thai $Tree, Field & Stream, Home Depot, Petco, Remke Foods, Staples, Verizon, Walgreens
185	I-275 E and W, W to
184	KY 236, Donaldson Rd, to Erlanger, E BP, Erlanger/Dunkin Donuts Double Dragon Oriental, W Racers/Subway/dsl, Speedway/dsl Peecox Grill, Waffle House Country Hearth Inn, EconoLodge, Red Roof Inn, Wingate Inn Goodyear/auto
182	KY 1017, Turfway Rd, E BP/dsl, Shell/dsl Bamboo Garden, Big Boy, China City, Lee's Chicken, McDonald's, Papa John's, Subway, Taco Bell Baymont Inn, Courtyard, Days Inn, ValuePlace BigLots, CVS Drug, Family$, Office Depot, Remke Foods, USPO, W Applebee's, Chick-fil-A, Chili's, CiCi's Pizza, Cracker Barrel, Famous Dave's BBQ, Firebowl Grill, Longhorn Steaks, Noodles&Co., O'Charley's, Potbelly, Rafferty's, Skyline Chili, Steak'n Shake, Subway, Wendy's Comfort Inn, Extended Stay America, Hampton Inn, Hilton, Hyatt Place, La Quinta, SpringHill Suites H, Best Buy, Dick's, Home Depot, Jo-Ann, Kohl's, Lowe's, Meijer, Michael's, Petsmart, Radio Shack, Sam's Club, Target, Turfway Park Racing
181	KY 18, Florence, E Speedway/dsl, TA/Valero/Pizza Hut/Popeye's/Subway/dsl/24hr/ @ Kiwha Korean, Waffle House Best Value Inn, Best Western, Heritage Inn Chevrolet, W BP/dsl, Marathon/dsl, Speedway/dsl Buffalo Wild Wings, Cheddar's, Chipotle Mexican, Chuy's Mexican, City BBQ, Currito Burrito, El Rio Grande, Fazoli's, Firehouse Subs, Fuji Steaks, Hooters, IHOP, Jersey Mike's, La Rosa's, Laughing Noodle, Logan's Roadhouse, Miyoshi Japanese, Panda Express, Panera Bread, Red Robin Homewood Suites, Stay Lodge AT&T, Buick/GMC, Chrysler/Jeep/Dodge, Ford, Honda, Hyundai, Mazda, Nissan, Tire Discounters, Toyota/Scion, URGENT CARE, Verizon, VW, Walmart/Subway
180a	Mall Rd (from sb), W Asian Buffet, BJ's Rest., Buca Italian, ChuckeCheese, GoldStar Chili, HoneyBaked Ham, Jimmy John's, Olive Garden, Pizza Hut, Qdoba, Quaker Steak, Skyline Chili, Smokey Bones BBQ, Starbucks, Subway, Taco Bell, Which Wich? $General, $Tree, AT&T, Barnes&Noble, Harley Davidson, Hobby Lobby, JC Penney, Kroger/dsl, Macy's, mall, Old Navy, same as 180, Sears/auto, Staples, TJ Maxx, Tuesday Morning
180	US 42, US 127, Florence, Union, E BP/dsl, Speedway/dsl Big Boy, Bob Evans, Capt D's, Chipotle Mexican, El Nopal Mexican, Mai Thai, McDonald's, Penn Sta Subs, Rally's, Red Lobster, Subway, Wendy's Holiday Inn, Howard Johnson, Knights Inn, Motel 6, Quality Inn, Super 8 Cadillac, funpark,

FLORENCE

KY

Exit #	Services
180	Continued Subaru, W Marathon/dsl, Murphy USA/dsl, Speedway/dsl Arby's, KFC, Little Caesars, LJ Silver, Ponderosa, Waffle House, White Castle Magnuson Hotel, Travelodge CarX, Midas, O'Reilly Parts, PepBoys, Tire Discounters, Tires+, Walgreens
178	KY 536, Mt Zion Rd, E Marathon/Rally's/dsl, Speedway/dsl, Sunoco/Subway/dsl Buffalo Bob's, Chopsticks, GoldStar Chili, Hot Head Burritos, Jersey Mike's Subs, La Fuentes Mexican, La Rosa's Pizza, Mad Mike's Burgers, Sonic, Steak'n Shake, Taco Bell AutoZone, Goodyear/auto, Kroger
177mm	**Welcome Ctr sb/ nb, full facilities, litter barrels RV dump, vending**
175	KY 338, Richwood, E Pilot/Subway/dsl/24hr, TA/BP/Country Pride/Taco Bell/dsl/24hr/ @ Arby's, Burger King, White Castle Richwood Inn RV Park, W BP/dsl, Pilot/Subway/dsl/scales/24hr, Shell/dsl GoldStar Chili, Gourmet Cafe, Hong Kong Cafe, McDonald's, Papa Dino's Pizza, Penn Sta Subs, Skyline Chili, Snappy Tomato Pizza, Waffle House, Wendy's EconoLodge, Holiday Inn Express to Big Bone Lick SP
173	I-71 S, to Louisville
171	KY 14, KY 16, to Verona, Walton, E BP/dsl, Marathon/DQ/dsl China Moon, El Toro Mexican, McDonald's, Pizza Hut, Starbucks, Subway, Waffle House AT&T, AutoZone, Kohl's, Kroger/dsl, Tire Discounters, URGENT CARE, Walton Drug, W FLYING J/Denny's/dsl/scales/24hr Blue Beacon, Delightful Days RV Ctr, Oak Creek Camping (1mi), to Big Bone Lick SP, vet
168mm	**weigh sta/rest haven sb**
166	KY 491, Crittenden, E BP/dsl, Marathon/dsl McDonald's Chrysler/Dodge/Jeep, Cincinnati S Camping (2mi), W Marathon/dsl, Shell/Gold Star Chili China Castle, Subway, Wendy's $General, Grant Co Drugs
159	KY 22, to Owenton, Dry Ridge, E BP, Shell/dsl, Speedway/dsl Arby's, Burger King, Happy Dragon Chinese, KFC/Taco Bell, La Rosa's, LJ Silver, McDonald's, Pizza Hut, Skyline Chili, Subway, Waffle House, Wendy's Microtel, Value Stay H, $General, Buick/Chevrolet, O'Reilly Parts, Radio Shack, Verizon, Walmart, W Road Ranger/dsl, Speedway/dsl Country Grill, Cracker Barrel, El Rio Grande Mexican Comfort Inn, Hampton Inn Camper Village, Dry Ridge TowneCtr, Sav-A-Lot, Tire Discounters, Toyota/Scion
156	Barnes Rd, E H
154	KY 36, Williamstown, E Marathon/dsl, Shell/dsl H, to Kincaid Lake SP, W Marathon/dsl El Jalisco Mexican Best Value Inn, Sunrise Inn
144	KY 330, to Owenton, Corinth, E Marathon/dsl, Noble's Trk Plaza/rest./dsl camping, W BP Gary's Grill Inn 3 Springs Motel
136	KY 32, to Sadieville, E Loves/Hardee's/dsl/scales/24hr
130.5mm	**weigh sta nb**
129	Rd 620, Cherry Blossom Wy, E Pilot/Wendy's/dsl/scales/24hr/ @ Waffle House Days Inn, Motel 6, W Pilot/McDonald's/dsl/scales/24hr, Shell Whispering Hills RV Park (3mi)
127mm	**both lanes, full facilities, litter barrels, petwalk vending**
126	US 62, to US 460, Georgetown, E Marathon/dsl, Murphy USA/dsl Applebee's, Asian Royal Buffet, Big Boy, Buffalo Wild Wings, Gold Star Chili, Golden Corral, Jimmy John's, McDonald's, O'Charley's, Papa John's, Penn Sta Subs, Pepe's Mexican, Qdoba, Starbucks, Steak'n Shake, Subway Holi-

GEORGETOWN

▲N INTERSTATE 75 Cont'd

126 Continued
day Inn Express ◉ AT&T, Kohl's, Lowe's, Tire Discounters, URGENT CARE, Verizon, Walmart/Subway, **W** 🚇 Marathon, Shell/Subway, Speedway/dsl 🍴 Chick-fil-A, Cracker Barrel, Fazoli's, KFC, Ruby Tuesday, Waffle House 🛏 Baymont Inn, Best Western, Comfort Suites, Country Inn&Suites, Fairfield Inn, Hampton Inn, Hilton Garden, Microtel, Super 8 ◉ Ⓗ, Buick/Chevrolet, Chrysler/Dodge/Jeep, same as 125, to Georgetown Coll

125 US 460 (from nb), Georgetown, **E** 🚇 Gulf, Shell 🍴 FatKats Pizza 🛏 Knights Inn, **W** 🚇 Swifty/dsl, Valero/dsl 🍴 Arby's, DQ, Little Caesars, LJ Silver, Taco Bell, Wendy's 🛏 Winner's Circle Motel ◉ $Tree, Advance Parts, BigLots, K-Mart, Midas, Outlets/Famous Brands, Radio Shack, same as 126

120 Rd 1973, to Ironworks Pike, KY Horse Park, **E** ◉ KY Horse Park Camping, **W** 🚇 Shell/dsl ◉ Ⓗ

118 I-64 W, to Frankfort, Louisville

LEXINGTON

115 Rd 922, Lexington, **E** 🚇 Shell/Subway/dsl 🍴 Cracker Barrel, McDonald's, Waffle House 🛏 Fairfield Inn, Knights Inn, La Quinta, Sheraton ◉ SaddleHorse Museum (4mi), **W** 🚇 Marathon/dsl 🍴 Cortland's Kitchen, Denny's, Happy Dragon Chinese 🛏 Clarion, Embassy Suites, Marriott/rest. ◉ museum

113 US 27, US 68, to Paris, Lexington, **E** 🚇 BP/dsl, Speedway/dsl 🍴 Waffle House 🛏 Ramada Inn, **W** 🚇 Marathon/dsl, Shell, Shell/dsl 🍴 Arby's, Burger King, Capt D's, Donato's Pizza, DQ, Fazoli's, Golden Corral, Hardee's, Horseshoes Grill, Little Caesars, McDonald's, Penn Sta Subs, Rally's, Subway, Taco Bell, Wendy's, Zaxby's 🛏 Catalina Motel, Days Inn, Red Roof Inn ◉ Advance Parts, AutoZone, Bluegrass RV Ctr, Chevrolet, CVS Drug, Northside RV Ctr, O'Reilly Parts, Rupp Arena, to UK, Walmart

111 I-64 E, to Huntington, WV

110 US 60, Lexington, **W** 🚇 Murphy USA/dsl, Shell/dsl, Speedway/dsl, Thorntons/dsl 🍴 A&W Cafe, Arby's, Bob Evans, Calistoga Cafe, Cane's Chicken, Cracker Barrel, FirstWatch Cafe, McDonald's, Smashing Tomato, Starbucks, Tom+Chee Rest., Waffle House, Wendy's 🛏 Baymont Inn, Comfort Inn, Country Inn&Suites, Guesthouse Inn, Hampton Inn, Holiday Inn Express, Howard Johnson, Microtel, Motel 6, Quality Inn, Super 8 ◉ Ⓗ, Hobby Lobby, Lowe's, Rite Aid, Walmart/Subway

108 Man O War Blvd, **E** 🚇 Shell ◉ Cabela's, Costco/gas, Rite Aid, **W** 🚇 Marathon/dsl, Meijer/dsl, Shell/KFC/Pizza Hut/Wendy's/dsl 🍴 Applebee's, Arby's, Asuka Grill, Backyard Burger, BD Mongolian Grill, Big Boy, BoneFish Grill, Carino's, Carrabba's, Cheddar's, Chick-fil-A, Chipotle Mexican, Coldstone, Culver's, Fazoli's, GoldStar Chili, IChing Asian, Logan's Roadhouse, Malone's, McDonald's, Old Chicago, Outback Steaks, Qdoba, Quiznos, Rafferty's, Red Lobster, Saul Good Rest., Starbucks, Steak'n Shake, Subway, Taco Bell, Ted's MT Grill, TGIFriday's, Waffle House 🛏 Courtyard, Hilton Garden, Homewood Suites, Hyatt Place, Residence Inn, Sleep Inn, TownePlace Suites ◉ Ⓗ, AT&T, Audi, Barnes&Noble, Best Buy, BigLots, Dick's, GNC, Gordmans, Harley-Davidson, Kohl's, Marshall's, Michael's, Old Navy, Petsmart, Radio Shack, Ross, Staples, Target, Tire Discounters, Verizon, Walgreens

104 KY 418, Lexington, **E** 🚇 BP/Arby's/dsl, Shell/McDonald's 🍴 Waffle House 🛏 Best Western, Comfort Inn, Days Inn, EconoLodge, La Quinta, **W** 🚇 Marathon/dsl, Speedway/dsl 🍴 Wendy's ◉ Ⓗ

99 US 25 N, US 421 N, Clays Ferry

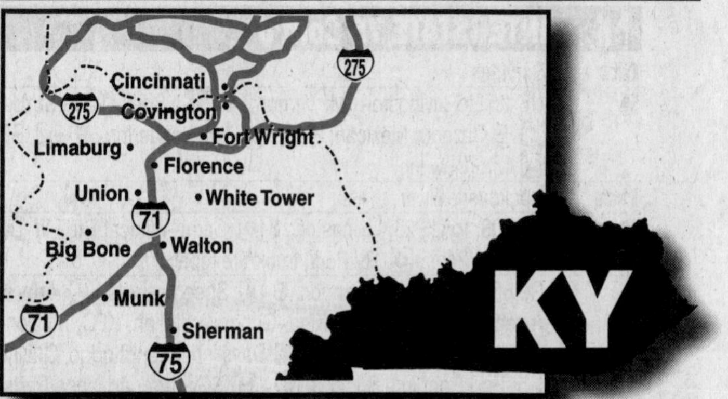

RICHMOND

98mm Kentucky River

97 US 25 S, US 421 S, Clay's Ferry

95 Rd 627, to Boonesborough, Winchester, **E** 🚇 BP/dsl, Love's/Arby's/dsl/scales/24hr ◉ camping, Ft Boonesborough SP, **W** 🚇 Shell/Subway/dsl

90 US 25, US 421, Richmond, **E** 🚇 Shell 🍴 Cracker Barrel 🛏 La Quinta, Red Roof Inn, Relax Inn, Super 7, **W** 🚇 BP, Exxon/Arby's/dsl, Marathon, Shell 🍴 Big Boy, DQ, Hanger's Rest., Hardee's, McDonald's, Pizza Hut, Subway, Waffle House, Wendy's 🛏 Days Inn, Super 8 ◉ $General, vet

87 Rd 876, Richmond, **E** 🚇 BP/dsl, Marathon/dsl, Shell/dsl, Speedway/dsl 🍴 A&W/LJ Silver, Arby's, Casa Fiesta Mexican, CookOut, Domino's, Fazoli's, Fong's Chinese, Hardee's, Hooters, King Buffet, Lee's Chicken, Little Caesars, McAlister's Deli, McDonald's, Papa John's, Qdoba, Rally's, Subway, Taco Bell, Waffle House, Wendy's 🛏 Best Western, Country Hearth Inn, Quality Quarters Inn ◉ Ⓗ, $General, Aamco, Ace Hardware, AT&T, BigLots, Goodyear/auto, Rite Aid, to EKU, vet, **W** 🚇 Marathon/Circle K, Shell/dsl 🍴 Bob Evans, Buffalo Wild Wings, Burger King, Cane's, Chick-fil-A, Culver's, Firehouse Subs, IHOP, Koto Japanese, Logan's Roadhouse, Olive Garden, Panera Bread, Ryan's, Starbucks, Steak'n Shake, Subway 🛏 Comfort Suites, Hampton Inn, Holiday Inn Express, Quality Inn ◉ Belk, Dick's, GNC, Hastings Books, JC Penney, Meijer/dsl, Michaels, Petsmart, Radio Shack, Tire Discounters, TJ Maxx, Verizon

83 to US 25, rd 2872, Duncannon Ln, Richmond, **E** ◉ Bluegrass Army Depot

BEREA

77 Rd 595, Berea, **E** ◉ Ⓗ, KY Artisan Ctr/Cafe/Travelers Ctr, to Berea Coll, **W** 🚇 Shell/dsl, Valero/Subway/dsl 🍴 Back Porch BBQ, Dino's Italian, Smokehouse Grill 🛏 Motel 6, Red Roof Inn

76 KY 21, Berea, **E** 🚇 BP, Marathon/Circle K, Shell/Burger King, Speedway/dsl 🍴 A&W/LJ Silver, Arby's, Cracker Barrel, Dinner Bell Rest., Gondolier Italian, Hong Kong Buffet, KFC, Mario's Pizza, McDonald's, Old Town Amish Rest., Papa John's, Pizza Hut, Subway, Taco Bell, WanPen Chinese/Thai, Wendy's 🛏 Best Value Inn, Holiday Motel, Knights Inn ◉ Ⓗ, $General, $Tree, Radio Shack, URGENT CARE, Walmart, **W** 🚇 76 Fuel/dsl, BP/dsl, Marathon/dsl 🍴 Lee's Chicken 🛏 Comfort Inn, EconoLodge, Fairfield Inn ◉ Oh! Kentucky Camping, tires, Walnut Meadow RV Park

62 US 25, to KY 461, Renfro Valley, **E** 🚇 Derby City/rest./dsl, Shell 🍴 Hardee's, Little Caesar's 🛏 Heritage Inn ◉ KOA (2mi), Renfro Valley RV Park/rest, **W** 🚇 BP, Marathon/dsl, Marathon/Wendy's/dsl, Shell 🍴 Arby's, Denny's, Godfather's/Subway, KFC, Limestone Grill, McDonald's, Taco Bell 🛏 Days Inn, EconoLodge ◉ Ⓗ, Lake Cumberland, Rite Aid, to Big South Fork NRA

= gas = food = lodging = other = rest stop

INTERSTATE 75 Cont'd

Exit #	Services
59	US 25, to Livingston, Mt Vernon, E Shell, TravelCtr/dsl El Cazador Mexican, Pizza Hut Kastle Inn, W BP Mtn View Inn
51mm	Rockcastle River
49	KY 909, to US 25, Livingston, E Camp Wildcat Bfd, W 49er/dsl/24hr RV Park, truck/tire repair
41	Rd 80, to Somerset, London, E Speedway/dsl Arby's, Azteca Mexican, Burger King, Gondolier Italian, KFC, McDonald's, Subway, White Castle Days Inn, EconoLodge, Quality Inn, Red Roof Inn, Super 8 H, $General, Advance Parts, AutoZone, CVS Drug, Kroger/deli, Parsley's Tire/repair, st police, W BP/Home Cooker/dsl/24hr, Marathon/McDonald's, Shell/pizza, Sunoco/dsl, Valero/dsl Cheddar's, Cracker Barrel, LJ Silver, Old Town Grill, Shiloh Roadhouse, Subway, Taco Bell, Waffle House, Wendy's Budget Host, Hampton Inn Dog Patch Ctr, Westgate RV Camping
38	Rd 192, to Rogers Pkwy, London, E BP/dsl, Marathon, Shell/Mama's Subs/dsl, Speedway/dsl Big Boy, Burger King, Capt D's, Dino's Italian, Domino's, DQ, El Dorado Mexican, Fazoli's, Golden Corral, Great Wall Chinese, Hardee's, Huddle House, Krystal, McDonald's, Penn Sta Subs, Pizza Hut, Ruby Tuesday, Starbucks, Steak'n Shake, Subway, Sun Buffet, Taco Bell Baymont Inn, Comfort Suites, Country Inn&Suites, Holiday Inn Express, Microtel $Tree, Advance Parts, , camping, E Kentucky RV Ctr, K-Mart, Kroger/dsl, Lowe's, NAPA, Nissan, Office Depot, Peterbilt, Radio Shack, Rogers Pkwy to Manchester/Hazard, to Levi Jackson SP, USPO, Verizon, Walgreens, Walmart/Subway, W H, to Laurel River Lake RA
34mm	**truck haven, weigh sta both lanes**
30.5mm	Laurel River
29	US 25, US 25E, Corbin, E Marathon, Murphy USA, McDonald's/Subway/dsl/scales/24hr, Spur Oil David's Steaks, DQ, Huddle House, Mi Jalisco Mexican, Taco Bell Super 8 Aldi Foods, AutoZone, Blue Beacon, Lowe's, to Cumberland Gap NP, Walmart/Subway, W BP/Krystal/dsl, Loves/Hardee's/dsl/scales/24hr/ @, Marathon, Shell/dsl Cracker Barrel, Sonny's BBQ Baymont Inn, Comfort Suites, Fairfield Inn, Hampton Inn, Knights Inn KOA, tires/repair, to Laurel River Lake RA
25	US 25W, Corbin, E Speedway/dsl Applebee's, Burger King, Cayenne SW Grill, CB's Grill, Dino's Italian, McDonald's, Wendy's Country Inn&Suites, EconoLodge, Holiday Inn Express, Landmark Inn H, auto repair/tires, W Shell Arby's, El Dorado Mexican, Subway, Waffle House Best Western to Cumberland Falls SP
15	US 25W, to Williamsburg, Goldbug, W Xpress/dsl Cumberland Falls SP
14.5mm	Cumberland River
11	KY 92, Williamsburg, E BP/dsl, Shell Arby's, El Dorado Mexican, Hardee's, KFC, Little Caesars, McDonald's, Pizza Hut, Subway, Taco Bell Cumberland Inn, Scottish Inn, Super 8 $General, Advance Parts, AutoZone, Family$, museum, Sav-A-Lot, Windham Drug, W Wendy's/dsl/scales/24hr, Shell Burger King, DQ, Huddle House, Krystal, LJ Silver Hampton Inn $Tree, Radio Shack, to Big South Fork NRA, Walmart
1.5mm	**Welcome Ctr nb, full facilities, litter barrels, petwalk vending**
0mm	Kentucky/Tennessee state line

L
O
N
D
O
N

C
O
R
B
I
N

KY

INTERSTATE 275 (CINCINNATI)

Exit #	Services
84	I-71, I-75, N to Cincinnati, S to Lexington, Louisville
83	US 25, US 42, US 127, S Shell/Circle K/dsl, Thornton's/dsl Abuelo's Mexican, Buffalo Wings&Rings, Carrabba's, Chipotle, Coldstone, Dewey's Pizza, Donato's Pizza, First Watch Cafe, Five Guys, Gold Star Chili, Jimmy John's, KFC, Max&Erma's, McAlister's Deli, McDonald's, Moe's SW Grill, Panera Bread, Starbucks, Subway, Taco Bell, The Pub, Wendy's $Tree, CarX, Dillard's, GNC, K-Mart, Verizon, Walgreens
82	rd 1303, Turkeyfoot Rd, S TGIFriday's H
80	KY 17, Independence, N Speedway/dsl, United/dsl Arby's, Big Boy, Bob Evans, Buffalo Wild Wings, Burger King, El Ranchero Mexican, Golden Corral, Hot Head Burrito, Penn Sta Subs, Snappy Tomato Pizza, Subway, Taco Bell, TX Roadhouse, Wendy's, White Castle AT&T, Petco, TireDiscounters, Verizon, Walmart/Subway, S Thornton's/dsl McDonald's, Waffle House
79	KY 16, Taylor Mill Rd, N BP, Marathon, Speedway/dsl Domino's, Goldstar Chili, McDonald's, Peking Chinese, Subway, Wendy's $General, $Tree, Big Lots, Burlington Coats, CVS Drug, Kroger/gas, URGENT CARE, Walgreens, S BP/dsl El Jinete Mexican, Graeter's Rest., KFC/Taco Bell, La Rosa's Pizza, Marco's Pizza, McDonald's, Original Wok, Skyline Chili, Subway Remke's Mkt, Verizon, vet
77	KY 9, Maysville, Wilder, N Hampton Inn, S Speedway/dsl, Thorntons/dsl, UDF/dsl DQ, Goldstar Chili, McDonald's, Mellow Mushroom Pizza, Subway, Waffle House Country Inn Suites
76	Three Mile Rd
74a	Alexandria, (exits left from sb), to US 27
74b	I-471 N, Newport, Cincinnati, N H
73mm	OH River, OH/KY state line
72	US 52 W, Kellogg Ave, S Marathon(2mi) Coney Island Funpark
71	US 52 E, New Richmond
69	5 Mile Rd, W BP/dsl Big Boy, Carrabba's, Firehouse Subs, IHOP, La Rosa's Mexican, McDonald's, Moe's SW Grill, Outback, TGIFriday's H, CVS, Kroger/gas, TireDiscounters
65	OH 125, Beechmont Ave, Amelia, E Shell, Speedway, UDF/dsl Hibachi Grill, Los Cazadores, Red Lobster, Ron's Chinese, Tender Towne, Wendy's Beechmont Motel CarX, Family$, Ford, Lowe's, Tires+, Walgreens, W BP, Marathon, Speedway/dsl Big Boy, Bob Evans, Burger King, Butterbee's Grille, Chick-fil-A, Chipotle Mexican, McDonald's, Olive Garden, Peking Chinese, Skyline Chili, Smashburger, Starbucks, Waffle House, White Castle Best Western, Days Inn, Red Roof Inn $Tree, Aldi Foods, AT&T, Audi, AutoZone, BigLots, Goodyear/auto, Hancock Fabrics, Home Depot, Honda, Kroger, O'Reilly Parts, Staples, Sumerel Tire/repair, Target, TireDiscounters, TJ Maxx, Toyota/Scion, Tuesday Morning, Verizon
63b a	OH 32, Batavia, Newtown, E UDF Applebee's, Big Boy, Bob Evans, Burger King, Chick-fil-A, China Buffet, Chipotle, ChuckECheese, City BBQ, Firehouse Subs, Five Guys, Fuji Steaks, Golden Corral, Hwy 55 Cafe, Jimmy John's, KFC, LaRosa's Pizza, LJ Silver, Logan's Roadhouse, Longhorn Steaks, McDonalds, O'Charley's, Panera Bread, Penn Sta Subs, Pizza Hut, Popeye's, Skyline Chili, Skyline Chili, Sonic, Starbucks, Steak'n Shake, Taco Bell, Wendy's, White Castle Comfort Inn, Fairfield Inn, Hampton Inn, Holiday Inn $Tree, Advance Parts, Aldi Foods, AT&T, Best Buy, Dick's, Dillard's,

INTERSTATE 275 (CINCINNATI) Cont'd

63b a Continued
Firestone/auto, Hobby Lobby, JC Penney, Jo-Ann Fabrics, Jungle Jim's Mkt, Kohl's, Kroger/dsl, Marshall's, Meijer/dsl, PepBoys, Petsmart, Sam's Club/gas, Sears, URGENT CARE, Walmart/Subway, W Marathon, Speedway/dsl, Sunoco Gold Star Chili, Gramma's Pizza Kroger, Midas

59 OH 452, US 50, Milford Pkwy, Hillsboro, S UDF/dsl Buffalo Wild Wings, Cracker Barrel, Dos Amigos, Goldstar Chili, Mint Bistro, Quaker Steak&Lube, Red Robin, Roney's Rest., Ruby Tuesday, Subway, TX Roadhouse, Wendy's Homewood Suites Office Depot, Petsmart, Target, Verizon, Walmart

57 OH 28, Blanchester, Milford, 0-1 mi N Arby's, Burger King, Chipotle Mexican, Donato's Pizza, DQ, Dunkin Donuts, Goldstar Chili, IHOP, KFC, Panera Bread, Papa John's, Penn Sta Subs, Skyline Chili, Sonic, Steak'n Shake, Subway, Taco Bell, Wendy's, White Castle GNC, Home Depot, Kroger/dsl, Lowe's, Meijer/dsl, Petco, URGENT CARE, S Thornton's/dsl Bob Evans, Cazadore's Mexican, Putter's Grill, Roosters Grill Holiday Inn Express Goodyear/auto, vet

54 Wards Corner Rd, N BP, S UDF/dsl Big Boy, Dominos, Goldstar Chili, Subway Hilton Garden

53mm Little Miami River

52 Loveland, Indian Hill, N Marathon/Circle K/dsl, Shell, Speedway/dsl Arby's, Burger King, Penn Sta Subs, Pizza Hut, Skyline Chili, Starbucks, Subway, Taco Bell, Wendy's CVS Drug, Indian Motorcycles, URGENT CARE, Verizon, vet, Walgreens

50 US 22, OH 3, Montgomery, N Shell Buffalo Wild Wings, Chili's, deSha's Tavern, Dewey's Pizza, Donato's Puzza, DQ, Johnny Chan's, Melting Pot, Panera Bread, Starbucks, Subway, Taco Casa, Which Wich? Acura, AT&T, Fresh Thyme Mkt, GNC, Hyundai, Kroger/dsl, TJ Maxx, S BP/dsl, Shell/Subway/Dunkin Donuts El Jinete, Goldstar Chili, McDonald's, Merlot's Rest., Skyline Chili, Wendy's H

49 I-71 N to Columbus, S to Cincinnati

47 Reed Hartman Hwy, Blue Ash, S Chipotle, Jersey Mike's, Jimmy John's, Kanpai Japanese, Ruby Tuesday, Smashburger, Starbucks, Tropical Cafe DoubleTree, Hyatt Place, Quality Inn, Residence Inn

46 US 42, Mason, N BP Chipotle, KFC, Marie's Scrambler, Max&Erma's, McDonald's, Skyline Chili, Taco Bell, Wendy's, White Castle Holiday Inn, Motel 6, ValuePlace Advance Parts, CVS Drug, Goodyear/auto, Kroger/dsl, Walgreens, S Marathon/dsl, Shell, Speedway/dsl, UDF/dsl Arby's, El Rancho Grande, Waffle House Days Inn Midas, Mr Transmission, Tire Discounters

44 Mosteller Rd, N Subway, S Homewood Suites

43b a I-75, N to Dayton, S to Cincinnati

42 OH 747, Springdale, Glendale, N Sunoco, Thorntons $General, Staples, S Shell/dsl BJ's Brewhouse, Blue Agave Mexican, Chick-fil-A, Chipotle, Firehouse Subs, La Rosa's Pizza, McDonald's, Noodles&Co, Panera Bread, Steak'n Shake, TGIFriday's BigLots, Chevrolet, Chrysler/Dodge/Jeep, Dillard's, Hancock Fabrics, Hobby Lobby, Lowe's, Macy's, Michael's, Office Depot, Petsmart, Sears/auto, TJ Maxx, Verizon

41 OH 4, Springdale Pkwy, N Shell, Speedway/dsl, Sunoco/dsl Burger King, Hooters, Olive Garden, Pappadeaux, Rib City, Skyline Chili, SmoQ Rest., Wendy's La Quinta, S BP, UDF/dsl Beef'O'Brady's, DJ's Tavern, DQ, Goldstar

41 Continued
Chili, Outback Steaks, Penn Sta Subs, Subway, White Castle Extended Stay America, Howard Johnson, Super 8 CVS Drug, Family$, O'Reilly Parts

39 Winton Rd, Winton Woods, N BP Asian Buffet, Chipotle, Golden Corral, IHOP, McDonald's, Old Spaghetti Factory, Panera Bread, Red Lobster, Steak'n Shake Comfort Suites, Hampton Inn Bass Pro Shops, CarMax, Home Depot, Kohl's, Meijer/dsl, Tire Discounters, S Marathon/dsl, Shell/dsl, UDF/dsl Big Boy, Cancun Mexican, China Garden, Cracker Barrel, Izzy's Cafe, Jade House Chinese, Jax Tavern, KFC, La Fiesta Mexican, Papa John's, Penn Sta Subs, Popeye's, Skyline Chili, Starbucks, Subway, Taco Bell, Wendy's Quality Inn, SpringHill Suites $Tree, AAA, Aldi Foods, AutoZone, Kroger/gas, Tires+, vet, Walmart

36 US 127, Hamilton, Mt Healthy, N Marathon/Circle K/dsl, Speedway Wendy's CVS Drug, S Shell/dsl, Sunoco, UDF Big Boy, China Island, La Rosa's Pizza, Little Caesars, McDonald's, Rally's, Subway, Taco Bell Advance Parts, Family$, O'Reilly Parts

33 US 27, US 126, Colerain Ave, N Speedway/dsl Burger King, Skyline Chili, Steak'n Shake, Wendy's Dick's, Jo-Ann, Lowe's, Petsmart, TireDiscounters, Walmart/Subway, S Shell Applebee's, Arby's, Big Boy, Bob Evans, Buffalo Wild Wings, Burger King, Cheddar's, Chipotle, Five Guys, Honeybaked Ham, IHOP, KFC, La Piñata Mexican, La Rosa's Pizza, LJ Silver, Logan's Roadhouse, Longhorn Steaks, McDonald's, Olive Garden, Outback Steaks, Panera Bread, Pizza Hut, Popeye's, Potbelly, Qdoba, Quaker Steak, Red Lobster, Starbucks, Taco Bell, TGIFriday's, White Castle Aldi Foods, AT&T, Best Buy, GNC, Hobby Lobby, JC Penney, Kroger, Macy's, Marshalls, Meijer/dsl, Michael's, Old Navy, Sumerel Tire/auto, Tires+, Tuesday Morning, URGENT CARE, Verizon, Walgreens

31 Ronald Reagan Hwy, Blue Rock Rd

28 E to Cincinnati, I-74, US 52, W to Indianapolis

25 E to Cincinnati, I-74, W to Indianapolis

21 Kilby Rd, Indian Springs Camping(3mi)

18mm Ohio/Indiana State Line, Ohio/Indiana State Line

16 US 50, Greendale, Lawrenceburg, W Ameristop/dsl, Marathon/dsl, Shell/Circle K/Subway Buffalo Wings&Rings, Burger King, KFC, La Rosa's Pizza, Maverick's Grill, McDonald's, Taco Bell, Waffle House, White Castle Comfort Inn, Holiday Inn Express, Modern Inn, Riverside Inn casino, Chevrolet, Chrysler/Dodge/Jeep, Ford, TireDiscounters, Walgreens

14mm Kentucky/Indiana state line, Ohio River

11 Petersburg

8b a KY 237, Hebron, N Marathon/DQ/dsl, UDF/dsl Agave Mexican, Arby's, China Wok, Hebron Grille, Jets Pizza, Jimmy

INTERSTATE 275 (CINCINNATI) Cont'd

8b a Continued
John's, Longnecks Grill, Papa John's, Penn Sta Subs, Pizza Hut, Strong's Pizza, Wendy's Remke's Mkt, URGENT CARE, S Speedway/Subway/dsl Burger King, Goldstar Chili, Skyline Chili, Sonic, Waffle House

4a b KY 212, KY 20, N Shell/dsl Comfort Suites, Country Inn&Suites, Hampton Inn, Marriott, S DoubleTree (2mi) H, airport

2 Mineola Pike, N Mobil/Rally's/Subway/dsl Holiday Inn, Quality Inn, S Shell/dsl Hot Head Burrito, Subway Courtyard Inn, Residence Inn

LOUISIANA

INTERSTATE 10

Exit # Services

274mm Louisiana/Mississippi state line, Pearl River

272mm West Pearl River

270mm **Welcome Ctr wb full facilities, info, litter barrels, petwalk RV dump**

267b I-12 W, to Baton Rouge

267a I-59 N, to Meridian

SLIDELL

266 US 190, Slidell, N RaceTrac/dsl, Shell/dsl, TA/Country Pride/dsl/scales/24hr/ @, Valero/dsl Arby's, Baskin-Robbins, Cane's Rest., Carreta's Mexican, Chesterfield Grill, Chick-fil-A, Copeland's Rest., Golden Dragon Chinese, KFC, Los Tres Amigos, McDonald's, NOLA Southern Grill, Panda Express, Retro Grill, Rotolo's Pizza, Shoney's, Sonic, Subway, Taco Bell, Wendy's, Zydecos Rest. Best Value Inn, Best Western, Deluxe Motel, Motel 6 H, CVS Drug, Firestone/auto, Freightliner, GNC, Harley-Davidson, Hobby Lobby, Office Depot, O'Reilly Parts, PepBoys, Petco, Radio Shack, Rouse's Mkt, U-Haul, Walgreens, S Chevron/Subway/dsl, Murphy USA/dsl, RaceTrac/dsl Applebee's, Big Easy Diner, Cracker Barrel, Fuji Yama Hibachi, Hooters, McAlister's Deli, Outback Steaks, Ruby Tuesday, Sonic, Starbucks, TX Roadhouse, Waffle House Days Inn, La Quinta, Value Inn, Wingate Inn H, $General, $Tree, AT&T, CVS, Home Depot, Lowe's, repair/transmissions, Rite Aid, vet, Walmart/Subway

265 US 190, Fremaux Ave, N Shell/Purple Cow/dsl Cheddar's, Felipe's Mexican, Longhorn Steaks, Panera Bread, Starbucks Best Buy, Dick's, Kohl's, Michaels, Petsmart, TJ Maxx, Verizon

263 LA 433, Slidell, N Exxon/Circle K/dsl, Shell/dsl, Valero Oishii Buffet, Waffle House Hampton Inn, Super 8 repair, S Kangaroo/Subway/scales/dsl, Valero/dsl McDonald's, Taco Bell, Wendy's Holiday Inn Buick/GMC, Chevrolet/Cadillac, Chrysler/Dodge/Jeep, Ford, Honda, Hyundai, Kia, Mazda, Nissan, NO East RV Park (1mi), Pinecrest RV Park, Toyota/Scion

261 Oak Harbor Blvd, Eden Isles, N Exxon/Circle K/dsl Waffle House Sleep Inn, S Shell/Subway/dsl Bayou Country Store

255mm Lake Pontchartrain

254 US 11, to Northshore, Irish Bayou, S Texaco/dsl

251 Bayou Sauvage NWR, S swamp tours

248 Michoud Blvd

246b a I-510 S, LA 47 N, S to Chalmette, N to Little Woods

245 Bullard Ave, N Chevron/dsl, Shell/dsl Southern Smoque Diner, Waffle House Comfort Suites, Holiday Inn Express Family$, Honda, S Chevron/dsl, Shell Burger King, IHOP, KFC/Taco Bell, McDonald's, Papa John's, Super Cajun Seafood Baymont Inn, Motel 6 Chrysler/Dodge/Jeep, Home Depot, Nissan, PepBoys, Rite Aid, Tire Kingdom, Toyota/Scion, Walgreens, Walmart

NEW ORLEANS AREA

244 Read Blvd, N Shell/dsl McDonald's Walgreens, S EZ Stop/dsl Popeye's, Subway, Waffle House, Wendy's Clarion, Days Inn, Knights Inn H, CVS, Lowe's, SaveALot Foods

242 Crowder Blvd, N Chevron, S Crowder Ctr, Exxon/dsl Subway Quality Inn Walgreens

241 Morrison Rd, N Big E-Z/dsl, FuelXpress/dsl

240b a US 90 E, Chef Hwy, Downman Rd, N Shell/dsl Super 8 Chevrolet, U-Haul, USPO, S Chevron/dsl, DZ/dsl Delta Tires

239b a Louisa St, Almonaster Blvd, N Big Easy TP/rest./dsl, Chevron/dsl, Exxon/dsl, FuelZone/dsl Burger King, Church's, McDonald's, Min Moon Chinese, Popeyes, Rally's, Subway, Taco Bell, Waffle House, Wendy's EconoLodge, Motel 6 $General, Family$, Goodyear/auto, Walgreens, Walmart, Winn-Dixie, S Day&Night/dsl

238b I-610 W (from wb)

237 Elysian Fields Ave, N Mardi Gras Trkstp/Subway/dsl Lowe's

236c St. Bernard Ave

236b LA 39, N Claiborne Ave

236a Esplanade Ave, downtown

235a Orleans Ave, to Vieux Carre, French Qtr, S Chevron/dsl Clarion, Marriott, Sheraton

235b Poydras St, N H, S to Superdome, downtown

234a US 90A, Claiborne Ave, to Westbank, S Superdome

232 US 61, Airline Hwy, Tulane Ave, N Burger King, S Exxon, Shell McDonald's, Popeye's, Rallys, Subway, Wendy's Costco/gas, CVS, Family$, Firesrone/auto, Pepboys, to Xavier U, USPO, vet

231b Florida Blvd, WestEnd

231a Metairie Rd

230 I-610 E (from eb), to Slidell

229 Bonnabel Blvd

228 Causeway Blvd, N Exxon/dsl, Shell/dsl Buffalo Wild Wings, Cheesecake Factory, Cucina Italiana, Outback Steaks, PF Chang's, Red Lobster, Ruth's Chris Steaks, TGIFriday's Best Western, Hampton Inn, Ramada Dick's, Dillard's, JC Penney, Macy's, Whole Foods Mkt, S DZ, Exxon/Circle K IHOP, Little Tokyo Courtyard, Days Inn, Extended Stay America, Holiday Inn, La Quinta, Residence Inn, Sheraton

226 Clearview Pkwy, Huey Long Br, N Chevron/dsl, Exxon/Circle K/dsl Cafe Dumonde, Cane's, Chili's, Copeland's Cheesecake Bistro, Corky's BBQ, Don's Seafood Hut, Hooters, Houston's Rest., Izzo's Burrito, Jimmy John's, Popeye's, Romano Italian, Starbucks, Taco Bell, Taco Tico, Zea Rotisserie Sleep Inn Hancock Fabrics, Sears/auto, Target, Tire Kingdom,

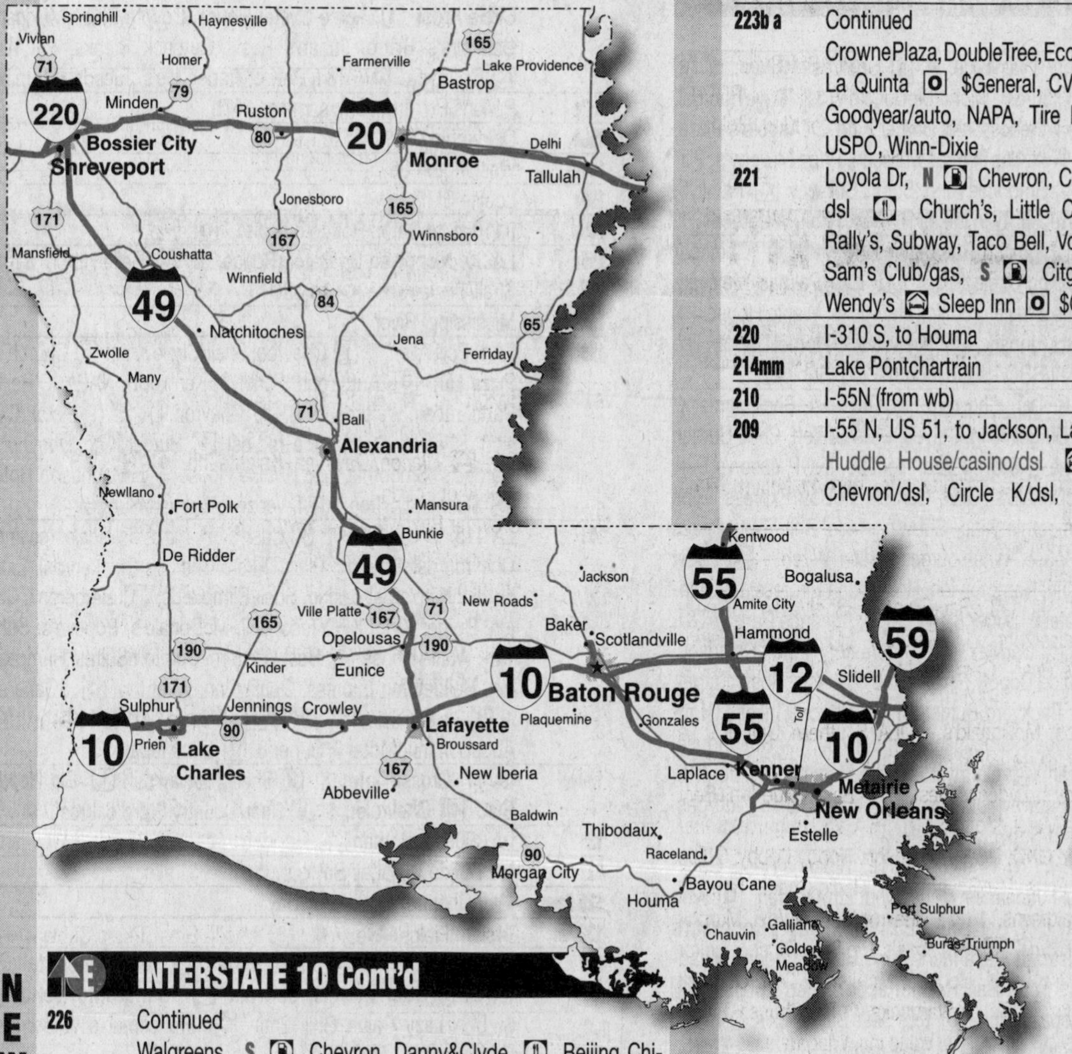

NEW ORLEANS AREA

INTERSTATE 10 Cont'd

226 Continued
Walgreens, **S** Chevron, Danny&Clyde Beijing Chinese, Burger King, Piccadilly, Smoothie King, Subway Sun Suites, Super 8 AT&T, Buick/GMC, Firestone/auto

225 Veterans Blvd, **N** Chevron, DZ/dsl, Shell Bonefish, Burger King, Coyote Blues, Denny's, Hooters, McDonald's, Panera Bread, Pei Wei La Quinta CVS Drug, Honda, Hyundai, Radio Shack, Rite Aid, Rouses Mkt, URGENT CARE, **S** Shell/dsl Burger King, Casa Garcia, ChuckeCheese, Little Caesars, Louisiana Purchase Kitchen, New Orleans Burgers, O'Henry's, Popeye's, Starbucks, Subway, Tiffin Pancakes, Wendy's Evergreen Inn, Sheraton $General, Acura, Best Buy, BigLots, BMW, Chevrolet, GNC, Home Depot, JoAnn Fabrics, Kia, K-Mart, Lexus, Michaels, Nissan, Office Depot, PepBoys, Petsmart, TJ Maxx, Verizon, vet, VW, Walgreens, Walmart

224 Power Blvd (from wb)

223b a LA 49, Williams Blvd, **N** DZ/dsl, Exxon/dsl, Shell/dsl Cafe Dumonde, Cane's Chicken, Casa Tequila, Fisherman's Cove, IHOP, Papa's Pizza, Popeye's, Rally's, Subway, Taco Bell, Wendy's Fairfield Inn $Tree, AutoZone, Dillards, Family$, Ford, Macy's, Office Depot, PetCo, Save-a-Lot Foods, Target, TrueValue, Walmart Mkt, **S** Exxon/Circle K/dsl, Shell American Pie Diner, Brick Oven, Don Jose's Grill, Dot's Diner, KFC/LJ Silver, McDonald's, Pollo Campero, Prime Time Steaks/Seafood, Quiznos, Sonic, Subway, Taco Tico Airport Inn, Comfort Suites, Contempra Inn, Country Inn&Suites,

223b a Continued
CrownePlaza, DoubleTree, EconoLodge, ExtendedStayAmerica, La Quinta $General, CVS Drug, Family$, Firestone/auto, Goodyear/auto, NAPA, Tire Kingdom, Toyota/Scion, U-Haul, USPO, Winn-Dixie

221 Loyola Dr, **N** Chevron, Circle K, Exxon/Circle K/dsl, Shell/dsl Church's, Little Caesar's, McDonald's, Popeye's, Rally's, Subway, Taco Bell, VooDoo BBQ Advance Parts, Sam's Club/gas, **S** Citgo/dsl, DZ Michelle's Rest., Wendy's Sleep Inn $General, Family$, info

220 I-310 S, to Houma

214mm Lake Pontchartrain

210 I-55N (from wb)

209 I-55 N, US 51, to Jackson, LaPlace, Hammond, **N** Shell/Huddle House/casino/dsl Suburban Lodge, **S** Chevron/dsl, Circle K/dsl, Pilot/Subway/dsl/24hr/scales Burger King, McDonald's, Waffle House, Wendy's Best Western, Days Inn, Hampton Inn, Holiday Inn Express, Quality Inn

207mm **weigh sta both lanes**

206 LA 3188 S, La Place, **S** Citgo/dsl, Shell/dsl Chrysler/Dodge/Jeep, Ford, Goodyear/auto

194 LA 641 S, to Gramercy, **4-6 mi S** Chevron, Shell, Taylors/dsl Golden Grove Rest, McDonald's, Popeye's plantations

187 US 61, N to Sorrento, S to Gramercy

182 LA 22, Sorrento, **N** Shell/Popeye's/dsl, Texaco/dsl, **S** Chevron/Subway/dsl/scales/24hr, SJ/dsl McDonald's, Waffle House tourist info

179 LA 44, Gonzales, **1 mi N** Exxon/Popingo's Cafe/dsl, Murphy USA/dsl Alabasha Cafe, Subway $General, Buick/GMC, Fred's Store, Walgreens

177 LA 30, Gonzales, **N** Cracker Barrel/dsl, Shell/dsl Burger King, El Paso Mexican, Jack-in-the-Box, McDonald's, Outback Steaks, Taco Bell, Taco Bell, Waffle House Best Inn, Best Western, Budget Inn, Clarion, Highland Inn, Western Inn Home Depot, **S** Chevron/dsl, RaceTrac/dsl, Shell/dsl Chili's, Cracker Barrel, Don's Seafood Hut, KFC, Logan's Roadhouse, Popeye's, Sonic, Starbucks, Subway, Tang Buffet, Wendy's Comfort Suites, Hampton Inn, Holiday Inn Express, La Quinta, SpringHill Suites, Supreme Inn, TownePlace Suites Cabela's, Tanger/famous brands, Vesta RV Park

LA

= gas = food = lodging = other = rest stop

INTERSTATE 10 Cont'd

Exit #	Services
173	LA 73, to Geismar, Prairieville, N Shell/dsl vet, S Chevron/dsl, Exxon/dsl, Mobil/McDonald's/dsl, RaveTrac/dsl, Sunoco/dsl Athenos Cafe, Burger King, DeAngelo's Pizza, Griffin Grill, Hot Wok, Las Palmas Mexican, Papa Murphy's, Pizza Hut, Popeye's, Smoothie King, Sonic, Subway Family$, Harvest Foods, repair, Twin Lakes RV Park (1mi), Walgreens
166	LA 42, LA 427, Highland Rd, Perkins Rd, N Chevron/Church's/dsl, Exxon/Circle K/dsl Las Palmas Mexican, Popeye's, Ruffino's Italian, Sonic, Starbucks, Waffle House Alexander's Mkt, funpark, Goodyear/auto, Home Depot, Tire Pros, S Shell/BBQ/dsl, Texaco/dsl Subway
163	Siegen Lane, N Chevron, RaceTrac/dsl, Shell/Circle K/dsl Arby's, Burger King, Cane's, CC's Coffee, Chee Burger, Chick-fil-A, China 1, CiCi's Pizza, Hooters, IHOP, Jason's Deli, McAlister's, McDonald's, Olive Garden, PoBoy Express, Ribs Chophouse, Smoothie King, Subway, Taco Bell, Twin Peaks Rest., Waffle House, Whataburger, Which Witch? Best Western, Days Inn, Hampton Inn, Holiday Inn Express, La Quinta, Microtel, Motel 6, Super 8 $Tree, Advance Parts, AT&T, BigLots, Cadillac, CarMax, Firestone/auto, Harley-Davidson, Honda, Kia, Office Depot, PetCo, Radio Shack, Ross, Target, Verizon, S Backyard Burger, Chili's, ChuckeCheese, Honeybaked Ham, Joe's Crabshack, Teppanyaki, TX Roadhouse, Zapata's Mexican Courtyard, Residence Inn Jo-Ann, Kohl's, Lowe's/Subway, Old Navy, Petsmart, Sam's Club/gas, TJ Maxx, Walmart/Subway, World Mkt
162	Bluebonnet Rd, N Chevron/dsl Albasha Rest., Cadillac Cafe, Kabuki Japanese Wyndham Garden vet, S Raceway Bar Louie, BJ's Brewhouse, Copeland's Cheesecake Bistro, J Alexander's, King Buffet, Logan's Roadhouse, Pluckers Wing Bar, Ralph&Kacoo's, Red Lobster Hyatt Place, Renaissance H, Best Buy, Dick's, Dillard's, JC Penney, Macy's, Mall of LA, Sears/auto
160	LA 3064, Essen Lane, S Exxon/Circle K/dsl, RaceTrac/dsl, Valero Burger King, Copeland's Bistro, Domino's, Gatti's Pizza, Ichiban Japanese, India's Rest., McDonald's, Omi Japanese, Piccadilly, Popeye's, Quiznos, Smoothie King, Subway, Taco Bell, Times Grill, Wendy's Drury Inn, Fairfield Inn, Springhill Suites H, $General, Albertson's, O'Reilly Parts, Rite Aid, Tire Kingdom, URGENT CARE, Walgreens
159	I-12 E, to Hammond
158	College Dr, Baton Rouge, N Valero Broken Egg Cafe, Cane's, Firehouse Subs, Hooters, Izzo's Grill, Jason's Deli, Koto Rest., Mansurs Rest., Marble Slab Creamery, Melting Pot, On-the-Border, Pelican House Rest., Subway, Sullivan's Rest., Waffle House, Wendy's Best Western, Chase Suites, Extended Stay America, Homewood Suites, Marriott H, Barnes&Noble, Meineke, Midas, S Chevron, Exxon/ dsl, Shell/Circle K Casa Maria Mexican, Chick-fil-A, Chili's, Gino's Rest., IHOP, Jingdu Japanese, Marina's Mexican, McDonald's, Ninfa's Mexican, Panda Express, Ruth's Chris Steaks, Sporting News Grill, Starbucks, Station Grill, Subway, Taco Bell Aspen Suites, Comfort Inn, Comfort Suites, Crowne Plaza, DoubleTree, Embassy Suites, Hampton Inn, Holiday Inn, Holiday Inn Express $Tree, Albertson's/Sav-On, AutoZone, Hobby Lobby, Office Depot, Radio Shack, USPO, Verizon, Walgreens, Walmart/Subway
157b	Acadian Thwy, N Chevron/dsl, Shell/Circle K Mestizo Grill, Rib's Rest. La Quinta, Radisson H, S Shell/
157b	Continued Circle K/dsl Acme Oyster House, Coyote Blues Mexican, Galatoire's Bistro, Juban's Rest., Outback Steaks, Pei Wei Courtyard AT&T, PetCo, Trader Joe's, Tuesday Morning
157a	Perkins Rd (from eb), same as 157b
156b	Dalrymple Dr, S to LSU
156a	Washington St
155c	Louise St (from wb)
155b	I-110 N, to Baton Rouge bus dist,
155a	LA 30, Nicholson Dr, Baton Rouge, N Belle Hotel, S Shell/Circle K/dsl to LSU
154mm	Mississippi River
153	LA 1, Port Allen, N Chevron, Shell/Circle K/dsl Church's, Pizza Hut AutoZone, Family$, Kenworth, NAPA, O'Reilly Parts, repair, Walgreens, S Chevron, LA 1S TP/Exxon/Casino/dsl/scales/24hr, RaceTrac/dsl Burger King, Domino's, Hardee's, Smoothie King, Waffle House Magnuson Hotel $General, $Tree, AT&T, Verizon, Walmart/Subway
151	LA 415, to US 190, N Cash's Trk Plaza/dsl/scales/casino, Chevron/dsl, Emerald Plaza Trkstp/Champs Chicken/dsl, Exxon/dsl, Nino's/dsl/casino, Shell/Blimpie/dsl Bergeron's Cajun, Burger King, KFC/Taco Bell, McDonald's, Popeye's, Subway, Waffle House Best Western, Comfort Suites, Hampton Inn, Holiday Inn Express, Quality Inn, West Inn $General, S Valero/dsl/24hr, Loves/Arby's/dsl/scales/24hr Audubon Inn, Motel 6, Super 8 truck repair
139	LA 77, Grosse Tete, N Shell/Subway/dsl Big Heads BBQ Chevrolet, S Tiger/Country Store/dsl/rest./ @
135	LA 3000, to Ramah
127	LA 975, to Whiskey Bay
126.5mm	Pilot Channel of Whiskey Bay
122mm	Atchafalaya River
121	Butte La Rose, N **Visitors Ctr/ both lanes, full facilities, litter barrels, petwalk, tourist info, vending,** S Lazy Cajun Grill (2mi) Frenchman's Wilderness Campground (.5mi)
115	LA 347, to Cecilia, Henderson, N Shamrock/dsl, Texaco/dsl Chicken on the Bayou, Landry's Seafood Holiday Inn Express casinos, S Chevron/dsl, Exxon/Subway/dsl, Shell/McDonald's/dsl, Texaco/dsl, Valero/dsl Popeye's, Waffle House, Exxon/dsl/24hr
109	LA 328, to Breaux Bridge, N Shell/dsl, Texaco/Quiznos/dsl/casino Microtel, S Conoco/dsl, Exxon/Domino's/dsl, Murphy USA/dsl, Pilot/Arby's/dsl/scales/24hr, Valero/Popeye's/dsl Burger King, City Buffet, Crazy Bout Cajun, Hacienda Real, McDonald's, Pizza Hut, Sonic, Taco Bell, Waffle House, Wendy's, Zapote Mexican, Zeus Sona Inn, Super 8 $General, $Tree, AT&T, AutoZone, Chevrolet, Chrysler/Dodge/Jeep, city park, Family$, Ford/Lincoln, O'Reilly Parts, Pioneer RV Park, USPO, Verizon, Walgreens, Walmart/Subway, Winn-Dixie
108mm	**weigh sta both lanes**
104	Louisiana Ave, S Chick-fil-A, McDonald's, Subway, Taco Bell AT&T, GNC, JC Penney, Office Depot, PetCo, Ross, Target, Verizon
103b	I-49 N, to Opelousas
103a	US 167 S, to Lafayette, S Chevron/dsl, Murphy USA/dsl, RaceTrac/dsl, Shell/dsl, Valero Checkers, McDonald's, Pizza Hut, Popeye's, Subway, Taco Bell, Waffle House, Wendy's Baymont Inn, Best Value Inn, Best Western, Comfort Inn, EconoLodge, Fairfield Inn, Holiday Inn, Howard Johnson, La Quinta, Ramada, Super 8, TravelHost Inn H, $Tree, CVS

BATON ROUGE

LA

INTERSTATE 10 Cont'd

LAFAYETTE

103a Continued
Drug, Home Depot, Radio Shack, repair, Super 1 Foods/gas, transmissions, Walmart/Subway

101 LA 182, to Lafayette, N Chevron/McDonald's, Shell/dsl, TA/Country Pride/dsl/scales/24hr/ @, Valero/Subway/dsl Burger King, Waffle House, Whataburger Red Roof Inn, S Exxon, RaceTrac/dsl, Shell/dsl, Shell/dsl, Texaco Cracker Barrel, Popeyes Days Inn, Drury Inn, Hilton Garden (2mi), Motel 6, Peartree Inn H, $General, Advance Parts, Family$, Kia, O'Reilly Parts

100 Ambassador Caffery Pkwy, N Exxon/Subway/dsl Gauthier's RV Ctr, Peterbilt, Ryder Trucks, S Chevron/dsl, RaceTrac/dsl, Shell/dsl Burger King, McDonald's, Pizza Hut/Taco Bell, Sonic, Waffle House, Wendy's Ambassador Inn, Hampton Inn, Microtel, Sleep Inn H, Southern Tire Mart

97 LA 93, to Scott, S Chevron/McDonald's, Shell/Church's/dsl Billy's Cracklings, Fezzo's Seafood, Huddle House, Popeyes, Rochetto's Pizza Comfort Inn, Holiday Inn Express, Howard Johnson Harley-Davidson, KOA

92 LA 95, to Duson, N Exxon/dsl/casino/RV dump/scales/24hr, Loves/Chester's/Wendy's/dsl/scales/24hr, S Chevron/dsl, Roadies/cafe/dsl/casino, Shell/Subway/dsl/casino Super 8 Frog City RV Park

CROWLEY

87 LA 35, to Rayne, N Chevron/dsl, Shell/Subway/casino/dsl Burger King, Chef Roy's Rest., McDonald's Days Inn $General, RV camping, S Frog City/Exxon/Cajun Rest./dsl, Mobil/dsl, Shop Rite, Valero/dsl Candyland Ice Cream, DQ, Gabe's Café, Great Wall Chinese, Pizza Hut, Popeye's, Sonic Best Western H, Advance Parts, Family$, O'Reilly Parts, Walgreens, Winn-Dixie

82 LA 1111, to E Crowley, S Chevron/dsl, Murphy USA Chili's, Wendy's H, $Tree, AT&T, GNC, Lowe's, Radio Shack, Walgreens, Walmart/Subway

80 LA 13, to Crowley, N Conoco/Exit 80/dsl/rest./24hr Fezzo's Seafood/steaks, Waffle House Crowley Inn, Days Inn, La Quinta Buick/Chevrolet, vet, S Chevron/dsl, Exxon, Raceway/dsl, Tobacco+/gas, Valero/dsl Asian Buffet, Burger King, Cajun Way, China Dragon, El Dorado Mexican, Gatti's Pizza, Golden Seafood, McDonald's, Pizza Hut, PJ's Grill, Popeye's, Sonic, Subway, Taco Bell $General, $General, AutoZone, Family$, Ford, O'Reilly Parts, Verizon, Winn-Dixie

76 LA 91, to Iota, S Petro/Shell/Subway/dsl/scales/24hr

72 Egan, N Cajun Haven RV Park

JENNINGS

65 LA 97, to Jennings, S Shell/dsl/casino Howard Johnson

64 LA 26, to Jennings, N Los Tres Potrillos LA Oil & Gas Park, RV Park, S Exxon/dsl, EZ Mart, Jennings Trvl Ctr/dsl/casino, Murphy USA/dsl, Valero/dsl Burger King, Gatti's Pizza, General Wok Chinese, La Rumba Mexican, McDonald's, Pizza Hut, Popeye's, Shoney's, Sonic, Subway, Taco Bell, Waffle House, Wendy's Days Inn, Hampton Inn, Red Carpet Inn H, $General, $Tree, AT&T, AutoZone, Buick/GMC, Chrysler/Dodge/Jeep, Fred's Store, O'Reilly Parts, Radio Shack, Verizon, Walgreens, Walmart/Subway

59 LA 395, to Roanoke, N Petos TrvlCtr/Chevron/dsl/scales/24hr

54 LA 99, Welsh, S Cajun Lunch/dsl, Citgo/Perky's Pizza, Exxon/dsl/24hr Cajun Tales Seafood, DQ

48 LA 101, Lacassine, S Exxon

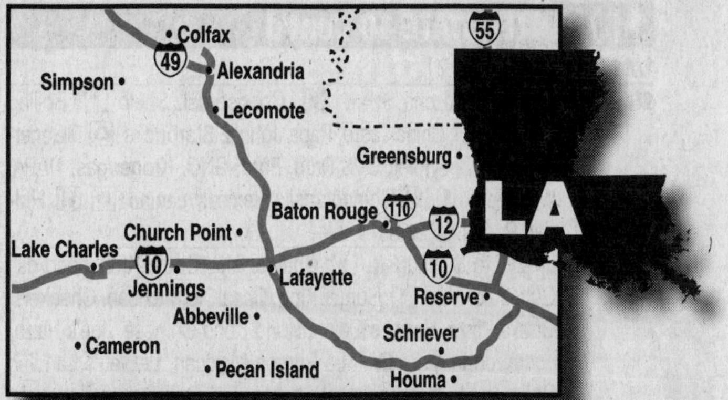

LAKE CHARLES

44 US 165, to Alexandria, N Quiet Oaks RV Park (10mi), S Rabideaux's Cajun RV Park

43 LA 383, to Iowa, N Exxon/Pit Grill/Quiznos/dsl/24hr, Loves/Hardee's/dsl/scales/24hr Burger King Howard Johnson Express, La Quinta United RV Ctr, S Citgo/dsl, Shell/McDonald's/dsl, Valero Boudreaux's Cajun, Sonic, Subway $General, I-10 Outlet/famous brands, RV park

36 LA 397, to Creole, Cameron, N I-10 RV Camping, Jean Lafitte RV Park (2mi), Jellystone Camping, S Cash Magic/grill/dsl/RV Dump, Chevron/dsl Red Roof Inn casino, RV Camping

34 I-210 W, to Lake Charles

33 US 171 N, N Chevron/dsl, Conoco/dsl, Exxon/dsl, Raceway/dsl/E85, Shell/ dsl Burger King, Church's, Subway, Taco Bell Best Value, Best Western, Comfort Suites, Lake Charles Inn, Richmond Suites $General, AutoZone, Family$, O'Reilly Parts, to Sam Houston Jones SP, S EconoLodge, Holiday Inn Express, Motel 6

32 Opelousas St, N Exxon, S EconoLodge, Holiday Inn Express, Motel 6

31b US 90 E, Shattuck St, to LA 14, N Shell/Subway/dsl/casino, S Valero/dsl

31a US 90 bus, Enterprise Blvd, S Popeye's

30b downtown

30a LA 385, N Lakeshore Dr, Ryan St, N Exxon Steamboat Bill's Rest., Waffle House Days Inn, Oasis Inn, S Wendy's Best Suites

29 LA 385 (from eb), same as 30a

28mm Calcasieu Bayou, Lake Charles

27 LA 378, to Westlake, N Chevron/dsl, Conoco/dsl, Shell/dsl, Valero Burger King, El Tapatia Mexican, McDonald's, Popeye's, RoundTop Burger, Sonic, Subway $General, Bumper Parts, Family$, Fred's, MarketBasket, O'Reilly Parts, to Sam Houston Jones SP (6mi), S Inn at the Isle Riverboat Casinos

26 US 90 W, Southern Rd, Columbia, N Exxon/dsl

25 I-210 E, to Lake Charles

SULPHUR

23 LA 108, to Sulphur, N Chevron, Circle K, Exxon/dsl, Murphy USA, Shell Burger King, Cane's, Chili's, China Wok, Hollier's Cajun Diner, Japanese Steaks, McDonald's, Popeye's, Subway, Taco Bell, Wendy's Quality Inn $General, $Tree, AT&T, Bumper Parts, Lowe's, Radio Shack, Verizon, Walgreens, Walmart/Subway, S Chevron/Jack-in-the-Box/dsl, Citgo/Cash Magic/dsl, Sulphur Trkstp/Shell/Subway/dsl/casino Cracker Barrel, Waffle House Best Western, Comfort Suites, Crossland Suites, Days Inn, Holiday Inn Express, Studio 6, Super 8 Southern Tire Mart

INTERSTATE 10 Cont'd

Exit #	Services
21	LA 3077, Arizona St, N Conoco/dsl, Shell Boiling Point Cajun, China Taste, Papa John's, Starbucks $General, AT&T, Chevrolet, CVS Drug, Ford, GNC, Kroger/gas, NAPA, Walgreens, S Chevron/dsl, Valero/dsl/casino H, Hidden Ponds RV Park
20	LA 27, to Sulphur, N Chevron/dsl, Circle K, Conoco/dsl, Gulf, Valero/dsl Burger King, Casa Ole Mexican, Checkers, Gatti's Pizza, Hollier's Cajun, Hong Kong Chinese, Joe's Pizza/pasta, Johnny T's Grill, La Rumba Mexican, LeBleu's Landing Cajun, Little Caesar's, McDonald's, Pitt Grill Cajun, Popeye's, Subway, Taco Bell, Wendy's Best Value, Hampton Inn, Motel 6 Brookshire Bros/gas, Family$, Firestone/auto, Goodyear/auto, Jiffy Lube, S Conoco/dsl, Shell/dsl Navroskey's Burgers, Pizza Hut, Sonic, Waffle House Baymont Inn, Candlewood Suites, Fairfield Inn, Holiday Inn, La Quinta, Super Inn, Wingate Inn H, casino, Stine, to Creole Nature Trail
8	LA 108, Vinton, N Chevron/dsl, Exxon/dsl Cajun Cowboy's Rest. V RV Park
7	LA 3063, Vinton, N Exxon/dsl Burger King, Sonic, Subway $General, casino, S Love's/Arby's/dsl/scales/24hr
4	US 90, LA 109, Toomey, N Cash Magic/dsl/grill/casino, Chevron/dsl/casino truck repair, S Exxon/dsl, Shell/dsl/rest Subway casinos, RV Park
2.5mm	**weigh sta wb lanes**
1.5mm	**Welcome Ctr eb, full facilities, info, litter barrels, petwalk**
1	(from wb), Sabine River Turnaround
0mm	Louisiana/Texas state line, Sabine River

INTERSTATE 12

Exit #	Services
85c	I-10 E, to Biloxi. **I-12 begins/ends on I-10, exit 267.**
85b	I-59 N, to Hattiesburg
85a	I-10 W, to New Orleans
83	US 11, to Slidell, N Exxon/dsl, Valero/dsl Burger King, McDonald's, Sonic, Waffle House, S RaceTrak/dsl, Shell/Subway/dsl H
80	Airport Dr, North Shore Blvd, N Kangaroo/Krystal/dsl Dickey's BBQ, IHOP, PJ's Coffee, Sonic Comfort Inn AT&T, Petsmart, Ross, Target, S Chevron, Shell/dsl Burger King, Chili's, ChuckECheese's, Domino's, McDonald's, Olive Garden, Starbucks, Subway, Taco Bell, Waffle House, Wendy's, Zea Grill Candlewood Suites, Holiday Inn Express, Homewood Suites, La Quinta $Tree, Burlington, Dillard's, Goodyear/auto, Home Depot, JC Penney, Jo-Ann, mall, Marshalls, Sam's Club/gas, Walgreens, Walmart
74	LA 434, to Lacombe, N Chevron/Subway/dsl H, Steve's RV Ctr, S Big Branch Marsh NWR
68	LA 1088 to Mandeville
65	LA 59, to Mandeville, N Chevron/dsl, Exxon/Danny&Clyde's/cafe/dsl, Shell/dsl Fat Spoon Cafe, Popeye's, Smoothie King, Sonic, Subway, Waffle House Comfort Suites, S Kangaroo/Arby's/dsl, Valero/Domino's/dsl El Rancho Mexican, Liu's Wok, McDonald's, PJ's Coffee, Quiznos camping, to Fontainebleau SP, vet, Winn-Dixie

COVINGTON

Exit #	Services
63b a	US 190, Covington, Mandeville, N Chevron/dsl, Exxon, RaceTrac, Shell/Circle K Acme Oyster House, Applebee's, Burger King, Cane's, Chick-fil-A, Copeland's Grill, Dakota Rest., Don's Seafood, Dunkin Donuts, Four Seasons Chinese, HoneyBaked Ham, IHOP, Jimmy John's, Johnny's Pizza, La Carreta, Lee's Hamburgers, McAlister's Deli, Mellow Mushroom Cafe, North Shore Empress Asian, Osaka Japanese, Outback Steaks, Papi's Fajita Factory, Piccadilly, Sonic, Starbucks, Subway, Thai Chili, Waffle House, Wendy's, Zea Rotisserie Best Western, Clarion, Comfort Inn, Country Inn&Suites, Courtyard, Hampton Inn, Hilton Garden, Holiday Inn, Homewood Suites, Residence Inn, Staybridge Suites, Super 8 Ace Hardware, AT&T, AutoZone, Chevrolet, Chrysler/Dodge/Jeep, CVS Drug, Firestone/auto, GNC, Home Depot, Honda, Hyundai, Lowe's, Nissan, Office Depot, Petsmart, Rouse's Mkt, Subaru, Toyota/Scion, Verizon, Walmart/McDonald's, S H, st police, **to New Orleans via toll causeway**
60	Pinnacle Pkwy, to Covington, same as 59
59	LA 21, to Covington, Madisonville, N Chevron/dsl, Kangaroo, Shell/dsl Buffalo Wild Wings, Cafe Du Monde, Carreta's Grill, Chili's, Cracker Barrel, Firehouse Subs, Five Guys, Golden Wok, Isabella's Pizza, Italian Pie, Izzo's Burrito, Jimmy John's, McDonald's, Olive Garden, Panda Buffet, Panera Bread, PJ's Coffee, Safa Mediterranean, Sake Steaks, Seafood Grill, Smoothie King, Steak'n Shake, Subway, TX Roadhouse La Quinta H, $Tree, AT&T, AutoZone, CVS Drug, Hobby Lobby, Kohl's, Petco, URGENT CARE, Walgreens, Winn-Dixie, S Valero/Domino's Chick-fil-A, ChuckECheese's, Dickey's BBQ, Habaneros Mexican, Longhorn Steaks, Pardo's Grill, Taco Bell, Wendy's, Which Wich?, Zoe's Kitchen Holiday Inn Express Belk, Best Buy, Fairview Riverside SP, GNC, JC Penney, Marshall's, Michael's, Ross, Sam's Club/dsl, Target, Verizon, World Mkt
57	LA 1077, to Goodbee, Madisonville, S QuickWay/PoBoys/dsl Best Wok, Pizza Hut, PJ's Coffee, Subway to Fairview Riverside SP, vet
47	LA 445, to Robert, **1-3 mi** N Jellystone Camping, to Global Wildlife Ctr
42	LA 3158, to Airport, N Chevron/Quiznos/dsl/24hr, Texaco/dsl McDonald's, Popeye's Friendly Inn, S Shell/Subway/dsl H, Berryland RV Ctr
40	US 51, to Hammond, N RaceTrac/dsl, Shell/Circle K Burger King, Cane's, Chick-fil-A, China Garden, Church's, Coldstone, Don's Seafood, East of Italy, IHOP, Jimmy John's, McDonald's, Nagoya Rest., Olive Garden, Ryan's, Santa Fe Steaks, Shane's Rib Shack, Smoothie King, Sonic, Subway, Taco Bell, Wendy's, Which Wich? Best Western, Courtyard, Holiday Inn, Quality Inn AT&T, Best Buy, Books-A-Million, Dillard's, GNC, Harley-Davidson, JC Penney, mall, Rite Aid, Sears/auto, Target, TJ Maxx, U-Haul, Verizon, Walgreens, S Petro/Mobil/Subway/dsl/scales/24hr/ @, Pilot/Arby's/dsl/scales/24hr, Shell/dsl Waffle House Colonial Inn, Days Inn, La Quinta H, $General, Blue Beacon, SpeedCo

HAMMOND

Exit #	Services
38b a	I-55, N to Jackson, S to New Orleans
37mm	**weigh sta both lanes**
35	Pumpkin Ctr, Baptist, N Texaco/dsl $General, Dixie Camping World RV Service/Supplies, Punkin RV Park (2mi) S Chevron/Bayou Boyz/Subway/dsl
32	LA 43, to Albany, N Chevron/Subway/dsl, Exxon/dsl, Shell/Big River/dsl McDonald's, S to Tickfaw SP (11mi) tourist info
29	LA 441, to Holden, N Sunoco/dsl Berryland Campers

LA

INTERSTATE 12 Cont'd

Exit #	Services
22	LA 63, to Frost, Livingston, N Chevron/dsl Pizza Hut, Subway, Wayne's BBQ Carters Foods, Family$, Thrift Town Drug, USPO, S Lakeside RV Park (1mi)
19	to Satsuma, Colyell, N Exxon/dsl Subway
15	LA 447, to Walker, N Murphy Express/dsl, Shell/Subway/dsl, Texaco/dsl Burger King, China Wok, Domino's, Foochow Buffet, Jack-in-the-Box, McDonald's, Papa John's, Papa Murphy's, Pizza Hut, Popeye's, Quiznos, Sherwood PoBoy's, Sombrero Mexican, Sonic, Taco Bell, Waffle House, Wendy's La Quinta $General, $Tree, AT&T, AutoZone, NAPA, O'Reilly Parts, Verizon, Walgreens, Walmart/Subway, Winn-Dixie, S Chevron/dsl H
12	LA 1036, Juban Rd, N Marble Slab, Moe's SW Belk, Kohl's, Michael's, Old Navy, Petsmart, Ross, Rouse's Mkt, TJ Maxx, Verizon, S Shell/dsl
10	LA 3002, to Denham Springs, N Chevron, Exxon, RaceTrac/dsl, Shell/Circle K/dsl Arby's, Baskin-Robbins, Burger King, Cactus Café, Cane's, Chili's, Church's, Domino's, Don's Seafood, Gatti's Pizza, IHOP, McDonald's, Papa John's, Papi's Fajita, Pizza Hut, Popeye's, Ron's Seafood, Ryan's, Sonic, Starbucks, Subway, Taco Bell, Waffle House, Wendy's Best Value Inn, Candlewood Suites, Carom Inn, Comfort Suites, Hampton Inn, Motel 6 $General, $Tree, Advance Parts, Albertsons, AT&T, AutoZone, CVS Drug, Home Depot, Meineke, NTB, Office Depot, O'Reilly Parts, PetCo, Radio Shack, Rite Aid, Tire Pros, Walgreens, Walmart/Subway, S Pilot/Subway/dsl/scales/24hr, Shell Cafe Phoenicia, El Rancho Mexican, Hardee's, Hooters, Islamorada Fish Co, Longhorn Steaks, Piccadilly, Rotolo's Pizza, VooDoo BBQ Days Inn, Highland Inn Bass Pro Shops, Cavender's, Chrysler/Dodge/Jeep, Ford, KOA, Sam's Club/dsl, Walgreens
8.5mm	Amite River
7	O'Neal Lane, N Mobil, RaceTrac/dsl La Quinta, Quality Inn Hobby Lobby, Toyota/Scion, S Murphy USA/dsl, RaceTrac/dsl, Shell, Texaco/Subway/dsl China King, Hardee's, Las Palmas Mexican, Little Caesar's, LoneStar Steaks, McDonald's, Popeye's, Rice Bowl, Sonic, Taco Bell, Waffle House, Wendy's H, $Tree, AutoZone, O'Reilly Parts, Walgreens, Walmart/Subway
6	Millerville Rd, N Chevron/dsl Chick-fil-A, Chili's Best Buy, Lowe's, Office Depot, Petsmart, Super Target, S Texaco/dsl Rotolo's Pizza, Subway Ace Hardware
4	Sherwood Forest Blvd, N Exxon, Shell/Circle K/dsl Burger King, ChuckECheese, Egg Roll King, Jack-in-the-Box, McDonald's, Pizza Hut, Popeye's, Sonic, Subway, Taco Bell, Waffle House Crossland Suites, Red Roof Inn, Super 8, Value Place Fred's, Goodyear/auto, Rite Aid, S RaceTrac/dsl, Shell/dsl Cane's, DQ, Dunkin Donuts, Hardee's, Nagoya, Piccadilly, Podnuh's BBQ, Sherwood PoBoys Calloway Inn AT&T, auto care
2b	US 61 N, N Chevron/dsl, Mobil/dsl, Rende's/dsl, Shell/Circle K Applebee's, Chinese Inn, Cracker Barrel, Little Caesar's, McDonald's, Taco Bell Days Inn, Holiday Inn, Knights Inn, Magnuson Hotel, Microtel, Motel 6, Sleep Inn $Tree, Albertsons/gas, Burlington Coats, Dodge/Ram, GNC, Marshall's, Michael's, Nissan, PepBoys, SteinMart, Toyota/Scion, Walgreens, Walmart Mkt
2a	US 61 S, S Circle K, Exxon/Circle K/dsl Burger King, China 1, Fernando's Mexican, Isabella's Pizza, Jimmy John's,

BATON ROUGE

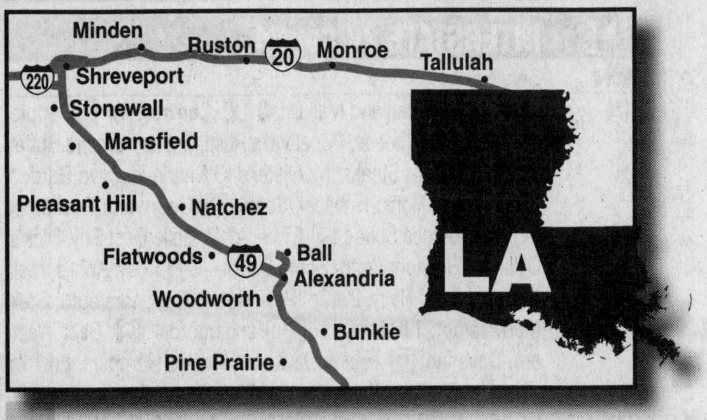

Exit #	Services
2a	Continued McDonald's, Subway, Waffle House $Tree, Costco/gas, Home Depot, Hyundai, Volvo
1b	LA 1068, to LA 73, Essen Lane, N Shell/Circle K/dsl Cane's, China Wok, McDonald's, VooDoo BBQ Family$, Hancock Fabrics, Le Blanc's Mkt, S H
1a	I-10 (from wb). **I-12 begins/ends on I-10, exit 159 in Baton Rouge**

INTERSTATE 20

Exit #	Services
189mm	Louisiana/Mississippi state line, Mississippi River
187mm	**weigh sta both lanes**
186	US 80, Delta, S Chevron/Subway/dsl/24hr
184mm	**wb, full facilities, info, litter barrels, petwalk RV dump**
182	LA 602, Mound
173	LA 602, Richmond
171	US 65, Tallulah, N Chevron/Subway/dsl, Kangaroo/dsl Chopsticks Buffet, McDonald's, Wendy's Days Inn, Super 8 H, S Exxon/dsl/scales, Loves/Arby's/dsl/scales/24hr, TA/Country Pride/dsl/scales/24hr/ @, Texaco Red Top Grill
164mm	Tensas River
157	LA 577, Waverly, N Tiger Trkstp/rest./dsl/24hr to Tensas River NWR, S Chevron/Hunt Bros Pizza/dsl/24hr, Shell/rest./dsl/24hr Casino
155mm	Bayou Macon
153	LA 17, Delhi, N Chevron/Subway, Texaco/dsl Boomers, Burger King, Pizza Hut, Sonic H, $General, AT&T, Brookshire's Foods, Family$, Fred's, USPO, S Valero/dsl Best Western, Executive Inn
148	LA 609, Dunn
145	LA 183, Rd 202, Holly Ridge
141	LA 583, Bee Bayou Rd
138	US 425, Rayville, N Bud's, Pilot/Wendy's/dsl/scales/24hr Fox's Pizza, McDonald's, Sonic Days Inn H, $General, $Tree, AutoZone, Brookshire's Foods, Buick/Chevrolet, Family$, repair, Verizon, Walmart, S Chevron/Subway/dsl/24hr, Exxon/Circle K/Quiznos/dsl, RaceWay/dsl Big John's Rest., Popeye's, Waffle House Super 8
135mm	Boeuf River
132	LA 133, Start, N Exxon/dsl
128mm	Lafourche Bayou
124	LA 594, Millhaven, N EZ Mart/dsl st police, to Sage Wildlife Area

RAYVILLE

LA

= gas = food = lodging = other = rest stop

INTERSTATE 20 Cont'd

Exit #	Services
120	Garrett Rd, Pecanland Mall Dr, N Chevron/dsl Applebee's, ChuckECheese, Copeland's Rest., Eastern Empire Buffet, IHOP, Longhorn Steaks, McAlister's, O'Charleys, Olive Garden, Red Lobster, Ronin Habachi, Sonic Courtyard, Residence Inn, TownePlace Suites $Tree, AT&T, Belk, Best Buy, Dick's, Dillard's, Firestone/auto, Home Depot, JC Penney, Kohl's, mall, Michael's, Old Navy, PetCo, Petsmart, Ross, Sears/auto, Stein Mart, Target, TJ Maxx, S Kangaroo/dsl Best Western, Days Inn Harley-Davidson, Hope's Campers, Lowe's, Ouachita RV Park, Pecanland RV Park, Sam's Club/gas
118b a	US 165, N Valero/dsl Clarion, Motel 6, Stratford House Inn Hyundai, Kia, Nissan, to NE LA U, S Chevron, Conoco/dsl, Exxon, Now Save/dsl, Shell/Circle K Burger King, Capt D's, Church's, KFC, McDonald's, Popeye's, Sonic, Subway, Taco Bell, Wendy's Comfort Suites, Hampton Inn, Motel 6, Super 8
117b	LA 594, Texas Ave, N Now Save/deli/dsl
117a	Hall St, Monroe, N H, Civic Ctr
116b	US 165 bus, LA 15, Jackson St, N H
116a	5th St, Monroe
115	LA 34, Mill St, N Chevron
114	LA 617, Thomas Rd, N Murphy USA, RaceWay/dsl 5 Guys Burgers, Burger King, Cane's, Capt D's, Cheddar's, Chick-fil-A, El Chico, El Chile Verde, Grandy's, Hibachi Grill, IHOP, KFC, McAlister's Deli, McDonald's, Podnuh's BBQ, Popeye's, Subway, Taco Bell, Waffle House, Wendy's Best Value Inn, Super 8, Wingate Inn H, AT&T, BigLots, Hobby Lobby, Office Depot, Rite Aid, Walgreens, Walmart/McDonald's, S Chevron, Exxon/Circle K/Subway/dsl Buffalo Wild Wings, Chili's, Cracker Barrel, El Sombrero, Four Bros Rest., Genghis Grill, Hooters, Logan's Roadhouse, Outback Steaks, Peking Chinese, Pizza Hut, Ronin Hibachi, Sonic, Waffle House Best Western, Comfort Inn, Motel 6, Quality Inn, Red Roof Inn Radio Shack
113	Downing Pines Rd, S Hampton Inn, Hilton Garden, Holiday Inn Express Chrysler/Dodge/Jeep
112	Well Rd, N Conoco, Shell/Circle K/dsl, Texaco/dsl Burger King, McDonald's, Sam's Eatery, San Francisco Tex-Mex, Sonic, Subway, Taco Bell, Waffle House, Zaxby's Advance Parts, CVS Drug, Mac's Fresh Mkt, vet, Walgreens, S Pilot/Subway/Wendy's/dsl/scales/24hr Pavilion RV Park
108	LA 546, to US 80, Cheniere, N Shell/dsl, Smart/dsl
107	Camp Rd, Rd 25, Cheniere
103	US 80, Calhoun, N Chevron, Shell/rest/dsl/24hr Johnny's Pizza (1mi) Avant Motel
101	LA 151, to Calhoun, S Chevron/Huddle House/Subway/dsl, Exxon Sonic
97mm	**wb, full facilities, litter barrels, petwalk RV dump**
95mm	**eb, full facilities, litter barrels, petwalk RV dump**
93	LA 145, Choudrant, S American camping, Jimmy Davis SP
86	LA 33, Ruston, N Murphy USA, RaceWay/dsl, Shell/Circle K/Quiznos/dsl, Texaco/dsl Arby's, Cane's Chicken, Cheeburger Cheeburger, Chili's, El Jarrito Mexican, Hot Rod BBQ, Huddle House, Log Cabin Grill, Logan's Roadhouse, Portico Grill, Ronin Hibachi, Ryan's, Sonic, Taco Bell, Whataburger, Z Buffet Comfort Inn, Days Inn $Tree, AT&T, Buick/GMC, Cadillac/Chevrolet, Chrysler/Dodge/Jeep, Ford/Lincoln, Fred's,
86	Continued GNC, Lowe's, Toyota, vet, Walmart/Subway, S Spirit/ds Fairfield Inn, Holiday Inn Express
85	US 167, Ruston, N Chevron/Subway, Exxon, Shell/Circle K Applebee's, Burger King, Capt D's, Little Caesars, McDonald's, Peking Chinese, Wendy's Hampton Inn, Relax Inn $General, Office Depot, Radio Shack, Super 1 Foods, TrueValue, Walgreens, S Texaco, Valero/dsl Pizza Hut Best Value Inn, Sleep Inn H, Advance Parts, Verizon
84	LA 544, Ruston, S Chevron/dsl, Exxon Domino's Johnny's Pizza, Pizza Inn, Smoothie King, Starbucks, Subway Waffle House Super 8
81	LA 149, Grambling, S Chevron/Church's/dsl, Exxon to Grambling St U
78	LA 563, Industry, S Texaco/dsl
77	LA 507, Simsboro
69	LA 151, Arcadia, N Mobil/Burger King/dsl La Fogata Mexican, S Exxon/dsl, Gulf/dsl, Shell/Church's/dsl El Jarrito Mexican, McDonald's, Sonic, Subway Days Inn H, $General, Brookshire Foods, Bumper Parts, Factory Stores/famous brands, Fred's, tires/repair
67	LA 9, Arcadia, N to Lake Claiborne SP, S Shell/dsl/repair
61	LA 154, Gibsland, N to Lake Claibourne SP
55	US 80, Ada, Taylor
52	LA 532, to US 80, Dubberly, N Exxon/dsl, Texaco/CJ's Diner/dsl
49	LA 531, Minden, N Loves/Arby's/dsl/scales/24hr Minden TrkStp/Shell/dsl/rest./24hr, Murphy USA, QuickDraw Subway/dsl KFC (3mi), Pizza Hut (3mi), Taco Bell (3mi) Walmart (3mi), S truck/tire repair
47	US 371 S, LA 159 N, Minden, N Chevron/dsl, Exxon/dsl Valero/dsl Beanie&Bubba's Grill Best Western, Exacta Inn/rest., Holiday Inn Express, Southern Inn H, Ford, S camping, to Lake Bistineau SP
44	US 371 N, Cotton Valley, N Exxon/Huddle House/dsl Crawfish Hole #2, Nicky's Cantina, Sonic Minden Motel (2mi) Cinnamon Creek RV/camping, Family$, Lakeside RV Camping
38	Goodwill Rd, S Gulf/Rainbow Diner/dsl/24hr Ammo Plant, truck/trailer repair
33	LA 157, Fillmore, N Texaco, S Exxon, Pilot/Arby's/dsl/scales/24hr Pizza Hut, Waffle House $General Family$, Fred's, Lake Bistineau SP, USPO
26	I-220, Shreveport, 1 mi N RaceWay/dsl Comfort Suites, Holiday Inn, Springhill Suites Casino
23	Industrial Dr, N Exxon/dsl, Shell/Circle K, Valero/dsl McDonald's, Popeye's, Sue's Country Kitchen, Taco Bell, Wendy's Ramada Inn O'Reilly Parts, RV Repair, st police S Mobil/dsl EconoLodge Peterbilt, Southern RV Ctr
22	Airline Dr, N Citgo/dsl, Mobil/McDonald's/dsl, Shell/Circle K, Valero/dsl Applebee's, Arby's, Burger King, Chili's China Flag, DQ, Five Guys, Gatti's Pizza, IHOP, Johnny's Pizza, Logan's Roadhouse, Notini's Italian, Popeye's, Red Lobster, Shogun Steaks, Sonic, Starbucks, Subway, Taco Bell, TX Street Steaks, Waffle House Country Hearth Inn, Crossland Suites, Rodeway Inn, Super 8 H, Albertsons, BigLots Books-A-Million, CVS Drug, Dillard's, Firestone/auto, Hancock Fabrics, JC Penney, K-Mart, mall, Meineke, Michael's, Office Depot, PepBoys, Sears/auto, Tuesday Morning, Verizon, Walgreens, S Exxon/dsl Beard's Catfish/seafood, Capt John's, Church's, Griff's Burgers, Outback Steaks, Quizno's

MONROE

RUSTON

MINDEN

INTERSTATE 20 Cont'd

22	Continued Microtel, Quality Inn, Red Carpet Inn AutoZone, Fred's, Super1 Foods, to Barksdale AFB
21	LA 72, to US 71 S, Old Minden Rd, N Shell/Circle K/dsl, Valero DAQ's Grill, Denny's, Johnny's Pizza, McDonald's, Pancho's Mexican, Podnah's BBQ, Posado's Mexican, Ralph&Kacoo's, Subway, TX Roadhouse, Whataburger Best Value Inn, Hampton Inn, Hilton Garden, Homewood Suites, La Quinta, MainStay Suites, TownePlace Suites $General, Bayou RV Ctr, O'Reilly Parts, USPO, VW, S RaceWay Waffle House, Wendy's Days Inn, Motel 6, ValuePlace Inn visitor info
20c	to US 71 S, to Barksdale Blvd
20b	LA 3, Benton Rd, same as 21
20a	Hamilton Rd, Isle of Capri Blvd, N Circle K Comfort Inn, Wingate Inn, S Exxon Bossier Inn, Travelodge casino
19b	Traffic St, Shreveport, N Courtyard Bass Pro Shop, casino, Chevrolet, S casino, downtown
19a	US 71 N, LA 1 N, Spring St, Shreveport, N Best Western, Hilton, Shreveport Hotel
18b-d	Fairfield Ave (from wb), S H, downtown Shreveport
18a	Line Ave, Common St (from eb), S 1st Stop H, downtown
17b	I-49 S, to Alexandria
17a	Lakeshore Dr, Linwood Ave
16b	US 79/80, Greenwood Rd, N H, S Citgo/dsl El Chico Travelodge
16a	US 171, Hearne Ave, N Shell/dsl Subway H, vet, S Raceway/dsl KFC, Wendy's Cajun Inn
14	Jewella Ave, Shreveport, N Clark/dsl, Phillips 66/dsl, Valero Burger King, Church's, McDonald's, Popeye's, Sonic, Subway, Whataburger AutoZone, County Mkt Foods, Family$, O'Reilly Parts, Rite Aid, Super 1 Foods, Walgreens
13	Monkhouse Dr, Shreveport, N Bro's Cafe Days Inn, Ramada, Residence Inn, Super 8, Value Inn, S Citgo/dsl, Exxon/Subway/dsl, Valero/dsl Waffle House Baymont Inn, Hampton Inn, Holiday Inn Express, Merryton Inn, Moonrider Inn, Motel 6, Quality Inn, Regency Inn to
11	I-220 E, LA 3132 E, to I-49 S
10	Pines Rd, N Chevron/dsl DQ, Johnny's Pizza, Pizza Hut, Popeye's, Sam's Eatery, Subway Meineke, S Circle K, Exxon/dsl, Murphy USA/dsl, Shell/Circle K/Quiznos/dsl Burger King, CiCi's Pizza, Cracker Barrel, Domino's, Dragon Chinese, Great Wall Chinese, IHOP, KFC, McDonald's, Nicky's Mexican, Papa John's, Sonic, Taco Bell, Waffle House, Wendy's, Whataburger Comfort Suites, Courtyard, Fairfield Inn, Hilton Garden, Holiday Inn, Homewood Suites, Howard Johnson, La Quinta, Sleep Inn, ValuePlace Inn $Tree, CVS Drug, Family$, GNC, Home Depot, O'Reilly Parts, Radio Shack, Rite Aid, USPO, Verizon, Walgreens, Walmart/Subway
8	US 80, LA 526 E, N Motel 6 Freightliner, repair, tires, S Chevron/dsl, Citgo/dsl, Petro/Shell/Iron Skillet/dsl/scales/@ Wendy's Blue Beacon, Camper's RV Ctr/park, Tall Pines RV Park (1mi)
5	US 79 N, US 80, to Greenwood, N Outpost Travel Ctr/dsl, TA/Valero/Country Pride/Subway/dsl/scales/24hr/@ Country Inn, Mid Continent Motel RV park, S Pizza Hut $General, Southern Living RV Park

SHREVEPORT

GREENWOOD

3	US 79 S, LA 169, Mooringsport, S FLYING J/Denny's/dsl/LP/scales/24hr, Loves/Arby's/dsl/scales/24hr Sonic Alligator RV Park (4mi), SpeedCo
2mm	**Welcome Ctr eb, full facilities, litter barrels, petwalk RV dump**
1mm	**weigh sta both lanes**
0mm	Louisiana/Texas state line

INTERSTATE 49

Exit #	Services
246.5mm	Louisiana/Arkansas state line
245	LA 168, Ida, Rodessa
241	Rd 16, Mira Myrtis Rd, to Mira
237	LA 2, Plain Dealing, Hosston
234	US 71, Gilliam, Hosston
231	LA 170, Gilliam, Vivian, W H
228	LA 530, Belcher, Oil City
223	LA 169, Mooringsport
221	LA 173, Dixie, Blanchard
215	LA 1, N Market St (**I-49 begins/ends**), E Dickey's BBQ Family$, vet
I-49 begins/ends in Shreveport on I-20, exit 17	
206	I-20, E to Monroe, W to Dallas
205	King's Hwy, E Cane's, McDonald's, Piccadilly's, Taco Bell Dillard's, mall, Sears/auto, W Valero/dsl Burger King, LJ Silver, Subway Sleep Inn H
203	Hollywood Ave, Pierremont Rd, W Chevron/dsl
202	LA 511, E 70th St, E RaceWay/dsl, W Circle K SC Chicken $General, Family$
201	LA 3132, to Dallas, Texarkana
199	LA 526, Bert Kouns Loop, E Chevron/Arby's/dsl/24hr, Exxon/Circle K Burger King, KFC, Taco Bell, Wendy's Comfort Inn Home Depot, W RaceWay/dsl, Shell/dsl McDonald's, Sonic, Starbucks, Subway, Waffle House Brookshire Foods, Verizon
196	Southern Loop
196mm	Bayou Pierre
191	LA 16, LA 3276, to Stonewall, W Chevrolet/Buick
186	LA 175, to Frierson, Kingston, E Trailerhood RV Park (3mi), W Relay Sta./rest./casino/dsl/scales Heart of Haynesville RV Park (7mi)
177	LA 509, to Carmel, E Texaco/Eagles Trkstp/casino/dsl/rest., W Hwy 509 RV Park (4mi)
172	US 84, to Grand Bayou, Mansfield, W Civil War Site, New Rockdale RV Park (4mi)
169	Asseff Rd
162	US 371, LA 177, to Evelyn, Pleasant Hill

SHREVEPORT

LA

= gas = food = lodging = other = rest stop

INTERSTATE 49 Cont'd

Exit #	Services
	NATCHITOCHES
155	LA 174, to Ajax, Lake End, **W** Country Livin' RV Pk, Cowboys/dsl
148	LA 485, Powhatan, Allen
142	LA 547, Posey Rd
138	LA 6, to Natchitoches, **E** French Mkt/cafe/dsl, RaceWay/dsl Cane's (5mi), IHOP, Popeye's, Wendy's Best Western, Comfort Suites, Days Inn, Fairfield Inn, Holiday Inn Express H, Walmart (5mi), **W** Chevron/dsl, Exxon, Texaco/dsl Burger King, El Patio Mexican, Huddle House, McDonald's, Subway EconoLodge, Hampton Inn, Quality Inn Nakatosh RV Park, to Kisatchie NF
132	LA 478, Rd 620
127	LA 120, to Cypress, Flora, **E** Exxon/dsl to Cane River Plantations
119	LA 119, to Derry, Cloutierville, **E** to Cane River Plantations
113	LA 490, to Chopin, **E** Express Mart TrkStp/dsl
107	to Lena, **E** USPO
103	LA 8 W, to Flatwoods, **E** Shell/dsl, **W** RV camping, to Cotile Lake
99	LA 8, LA 1200, to Boyce, Colfax, **6 mi W** Cotile Lake RV Camping
98	LA 1 (from nb), to Boyce
94	Rd 23, to Rapides Sta Rd, **E** Rapides/dsl, **W LA Welcome Ctr, full facilities, litter barrels, petwalk vending** Alexandria RV Park (2mi), I-49 RV Ctr
	ALEXANDRIA
90	LA 498, Air Base Rd, **W** Chevron/dsl/CNG/24hr, Exxon/Subway/dsl, Shell/dsl, Texaco/Eddie's BBQ/dsl Burger King, Cracker Barrel, McDonald's Comfort Suites, Hampton Inn, La Quinta, Rodeway Inn, Super 8 Cabana RV Park
86	US 71, US 165, MacArthur Dr, **0-2 mi W** Chevron, Conoco/dsl, Exxon/dsl, Mobil/dsl, Shell/Circle K/dsl, Texaco/dsl, Valero/dsl Applebee's, Burger King, Cajun Landing Rest., Cane's, Chick-fil-A, Church's, CiCi's Pizza, Dominos, DQ, Eddie's BBQ, El Paso Mexican, El Reparo Mexican, Golden Corral, Little Caesar's, McDonald's, Outlaw's BBQ, Piccadilly, Popeye's, Schlotzsky's, Sonic, Subway, Taco Bell, Taco Bueno, TX Roadhouse Alexandria Inn, Best Value Inn, Best Western, Candlewood Suites, Comfort Inn, EconoLodge, Guesthouse Inn, Holiday Inn Express, Magnuson Inn, Motel 6, Quality Inn, Ramada Ltd, Super 8, Value Place Inn $General, $Tree, Advance Parts, AutoZone, BigLots, Buick/GMC, Family$, Hastings Books, Kia, Kroger/gas, NAPA, O'Reilly Parts, Petco, Rite Aid, Staples, Super 1 Foods, Tuesday Morning
85b	Monroe St, Medical Ctr Dr (from nb), **E** H
85a	LA 1, 10th St, MLK Dr, downtown
84	US 167 N, LA 28, LA 1, Pineville Expswy, no ez return nb
83	Broadway Ave, **E** Conoco, Valero $General, **1 mi W** Murphy USA/dsl Checker's, Little Caesar's, Sonic, Wendy's $Tree, AutoZone, Harley-Davidson, Walmart
81	US 71 N, LA 3250, Sugarhouse Rd, MacArthur Dr (from sb), **W** same as 80 and 83
80	US 71 S, US 167, MacArthur Dr, Alexandria, **0-3 mi W** Chevron/dsl, Exxon/dsl, Shell Buffalo Wild Wings, Burger King, Capt D's, Carino's Italian, Chili's, Copeland's Rest., IHOP, KFC, Logan's Roadhouse, McDonald's, Outback Steaks, Pizza Hut, Popeye's, Sonic, Subway, Taco Bell Courtyard $General, Albertsons, Best Buy, Dillard's, Family$, Ford/Lincoln, Hyundai, JC Penney, mall, Marshall's, Mazda, Michael's, Old Navy, Petsmart, Sam's Club/gas, U-Haul
73	LA 3265, Rd 22, to Woodworth, **W** Chevron/dsl LA Cont Ctr, RV camping, to Indian Creek RA
66	LA 112, to Lecompte, **E** Chevron/dsl Burger King **W** Exxon/dsl museum (10mi)
61	US 167, to Meeker, **E** to Loyd Hall Plantation (3mi), Turkey Creek
56	LA 181, Cheneyville
53	LA 115, to Bunkie, **E** Sammy's/Chevron/dsl/casino/24hr Howard Johnson
46	LA 106, to St Landry, **W** to Chicot SP
40	LA 29, to Ville Platte, **E** Exxon/Cafe Mangeur/casino/dsl
35mm	**/rec area both lanes, full facilities, litter barrels, petwalk RV dump, vending**
	OPELOUSAS
27	LA 10, to Lebeau
25	LA 103, to Washington, Port Barre, **W** Citgo, Mobi Family$
23	US 167 N, LA 744, to Ville Platte, **E** Chevron/Subway/Stuckey's/dsl/scales/casino, Valero/dsl/casino, **W** Exxon/dsl/casino visitors ctr
19b a	US 190, to Opelousas, **E** Evangeline Downs Racetrack, **W** Chevron/dsl, Exxon/dsl, RaceTrac/dsl, Valero H, CVS Drug, Lowe's, USPO
18	LA 31, to Cresswell Lane, **E** Murphy USA/dsl Casa Ole's, Little Caesar's, Sombreros, Waffle House Comfort Inn, Holiday Inn $Tree, Chrysler/Dodge/Jeep, Ford/Lincoln, Radio Shack, URGENT CARE, Verizon, Walmart/Subway, **W** Chevron/dsl, Shell, Valero/dsl Burger King, Cane's, Cresswell Lane, Domino's, Gatti's Pizza, Hacienda Mexican, McDonald's, Peking Buffet, Pizza Hut, Subway, Taco Bell, Wendy's Days Inn, Super 8 AT&T, Buick/GMC, Danny's Tires, Family$, Nissan, Piggly Wiggly, repair, Save-A-Lot, Walgreens
17	Judson Walsh Dr, **E** Texaco/dsl, Valero/dsl
15	LA 3233, Harry Guilbeau Rd, **W** Regency Inn H, Courvelle RV Ctr, Toyota/Scion
	CARENCRO
11	LA 93, to Grand Coteau, Sunset, **E** Chevron, Citgo/rest./dsl/24hr, Exxon/Popeye's/dsl, Valero/dsl Beau Chere Rest., McDonald's Primeaux RV Ctr, vet, **W** Subway $General, Family$, Janise's Foods
7	LA 182, **W** Primeaux RV Ctr
4	LA 726, Carencro, **E** Popeye's, Rotolo's Pizza, Taco Bel GNC, Super 1 Foods/gas, URGENT CARE, **W** Chevron/dsl, Texaco/dsl Burger King, King Wok, McDonald's Economy Inn $General, Champagne's Mkt, Family$, Fred's, USPO
2	LA 98, Gloria Switch Rd, **E** Chevron/deli/dsl Chili's, IHOP, Prejean's Rest., Wendy's Lowe's, **W** Shell/Church's/dsl Domino's, Great Wall Buffet, Picante Mexican, Subway
1c	Pont Des Mouton Rd, **E** Exxon/dsl/LP, Texaco/dsl, Valero/dsl Buffalo Wild Wings, Burger King Motel 6, Plantation Inn CVS, Walgreens, **W** Firestone/auto, Ford
0b a	I-10, W to Lake Charles, E to Baton Rouge, **US 167 S** Chevron/dsl, Murphy USA/dsl, RaceTrac/dsl, Shell, Shell/dsl, Valero Checker's, McDonald's, Pizza Hut, Popeye's, Subway, Taco Bell, Waffle House, Wendy's Baymont Inn, Best Value Inn, Best Western, Comfort Inn, EconoLodge, Fairfield Inn, Holiday Inn, Howard Johnson, La Quinta, Ramada, Super 8, Travel Host Inn H, $Tree, Home Depot, Radio Shack, repair, Super 1 Foods/gas, transmissions, Walmart/Subway

I-49 begins/ends on I-10, exit 103

LA

INTERSTATE 55 (N)

Exit #	Services
66mm	Louisiana/Mississippi state line
65mm	**Welcome Ctr sb, full [handicapped] facilities, litter barrels, petwalk [phone] [picnic] tourist info**
64mm	**weigh sta nb**
61	LA 38, Kentwood, E [gas] Chevron/dsl, Texaco [food] Jam Chicken, Popeye's, Sonic [O] [H], $General, AutoZone, Family$, Fred's, IGA Foods, Super$, W [gas] Kangaroo/dsl, Kangaroo/Subway/dsl
58.5mm	**weigh sta sb**
57	LA 440, Tangipahoa, E [O] to Camp Moore Confederate Site
53	LA 10, to Greensburg, Fluker, W [O] [H]
50	LA 1048, Roseland, E [gas] Chevron/dsl [food] Subway (1mi)
46	LA 16, Amite, E [gas] Exxon/dsl, Murphy USA/dsl, RaceTrac/dsl [food] Burger King, Master Chef, McDonald's, Mike's Catfish, Panda Garden, Popeye's, Sonic, Subway, Waffle House, Wendy's [lodging] Comfort Inn [O] [H], $Tree, AutoZone, Fred's, O'Reilly Parts, to Bogue Chitto SP, Walgreens, Walmart/Subway, Winn-Dixie, W [gas] Amite Trkstp/grill/dsl (2mi) [food] Ardillo's [lodging] Colonial Inn, Holiday Inn Express [O] Buick/Chevrolet/GMC
40	LA 40, Independence, E [gas] Best Stop [O] [H], W [O] Indian Cr Camping (2mi)
36	LA 442, Tickfaw, E [gas] Chevron/dsl [O] camping, to Global Wildlife Ctr (15mi), W [gas] Exxon/dsl
32	LA 3234, Wardline Rd, E [gas] Chevron, Kangaroo/dsl, Texaco [food] Burger King, McDonald's, Popeye's, Sarita Grill, Sonic, Subway, Taco Bell, Wendy's [lodging] Lexington Inn [O] Tony's Tire
31	US 190, Hammond, E [gas] Exxon/dsl, Murphy USA/dsl, RaceTrac/dsl, Shell/dsl/scales/24hr [food] Applebee's, Baskin-Robbins, Buffalo Wild Wings, Burger King, Cane's, Chili's, CiCi's Pizza, Cracker Barrel, Firehouse Subs, Hi-Ho 1 BBQ, McDonald's, Pizza Hut, Sonic, Starbucks, Taco Bell, Voodoo BBQ, Waffle House, Wendy's [lodging] Comfort Inn, Hampton Inn, Super 8, ValuePlace, Western Inn [O] [H], $General, $Tree, Advance Parts, AT&T, AutoZone, Chrysler/Dodge/Jeep, CVS Drug, Family$, Hobby Lobby, LeBlanc's Foods Lowe's, Lowe's, Office Depot, Radio Shack, Ross, Sav-A-Lot Foods, Tuesday Morning, URGENT CARE, Walgreens, Walmart/Subway, Winn-Dixie
29b a	I-12, W to Baton Rouge, E to Slidell
28	US 51 N, Hammond, E [gas] Exxon, RaceTrac/dsl [food] Don's Seafood/Steaks, Great Wall Chinese [lodging] Magnuson Hotel, Motel 6 [O] [H], Buick/GMC, dsl repair, Mitchell RV Ctr, Toyota/Scion
26	LA 22, to Springfield, Ponchatoula, E [gas] Chevron/dsl, Exxon/dsl, Shell/dsl [food] Burger King, China King, Hi-Ho BBQ, McDonald's/playplace, Papa John's, Pizza Hut, Popeye's, Smoothie King, Sonic, Subway, Waffle House, Wendy's [lodging] Microtel [O] AutoZone, Bohning's Foods, CVS Drug, Family$, Ford, O'Reilly Parts, Walgreens, Winn-Dixie, W [gas] Kangaroo/Domino's/dsl [O] Tickfaw SP (13mi)
23	US 51, Ponchatoula
22	frontage Rd (from sb)
15	Manchac, E [food] Middendorf Café [O] phone, swamp tours
7	Ruddock
1	US 51, to I-10, Baton Rouge, La Place, S [gas] Circle K/dsl, Pilot/Subway/dsl/24hr/scales, Shell/Huddle House/casino/dsl [food] Bully's Seafood, Burger King, McDonald's, Shoney's, Waffle House, Wendy's [lodging] Best Western, Days Inn, Hampton Inn, Holiday Inn Express, Quality Inn, Suburban Lodge

I-55 begins/ends on I-10, exit 209

AMITE

HAMMOND

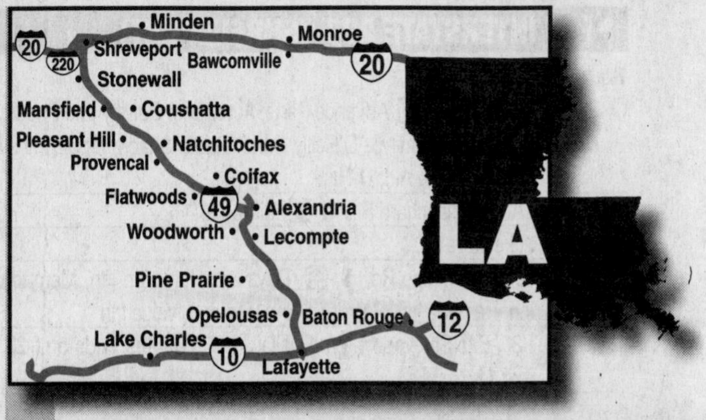

INTERSTATE 59 (N)

Exit #	Services
11	W to Bogue Chito NWR, Pearl River Turnaround
5b	Honey Island Swamp
5a	LA 3081, Pearl River, E Riverside TrvlCtr/dsl
3	US 11 S, LA 1090, Pearl River, **0-1 mi** W [gas] Chevron/dsl, Interstate Fuels/dsl, Shell/Subway/dsl, Texaco, [food] McDonald"s, Sonic, Waffle House, [lodging] Microtel, Autozone, Family$, Jubilee Foods/drug, NAPA
1.5mm	**Welcome Ctr sb, full [handicapped] facilities, info, litter barrels, petwalk [phone] [picnic] RV dump**
1c b	I-10, E to Bay St Louis, W to New Orleans
1a	I-12 W, to Hammond. **I-59 begins/ends on I-10/I-12.**

INTERSTATE 220 (SHREVEPORT) (E)

Exit #	Services
	I-220 begins/ends on I-20, exit 26.
17b	I-20, W to Shreveport, E to Monroe
17a	US 79, US 80, N [gas] RaceWay/dsl, Shell/Circle K [food] Taco Bell, Waffle House [lodging] Comfort Suites, Holiday Inn, SpringHill Suites [O] Racetrack/casino, S [gas] Chevron/Huddle House/dsl [food] Silver Star Smokehouse
15	Shed Rd
13	Swan Lake Rd
12	LA 3105, Airline Dr, N [food] Baskin-Robbins, Chick-fil-A, Dickey's BBQ, Firehouse Subs, Izzo's Burrito, McAlister's Deli, Newk's Eatery, Olive Garden, Papa Murphy's, Santa Fe Steaks, Starbucks, Subway, TaMolly's [O] [H], AT&T, Belk, Best Buy, GNC, Old Navy, Petsmart, Ross, Sam's Club/gas, Target, Verizon, Walgreens, S [gas] Exxon/dsl, Murphy USA/dsl, Valero/dsl [food] Applebee's, Burger King, Cane's, Capt D's, China Flag, McDonald's, Nicky's Rest., Panda Express, Ruby Tuesday, Ryan's, Smashburger, Sonic, Taco Bell, Trejo's Mexican, Wendy's [lodging] Hampton Inn [O] $Tree, Gateway Tire, Hobby Lobby, Home Depot, Kroger/dsl, Lowe's, vet, Walmart
11	LA 3, Bossier City, N [gas] RaceWay/dsl [O] [H], Buick/GMC, Ford, Harley-Davidson, Lexus, RV Park, Subaru, Suzuki, Toyota/Scion, S [gas] Valero/dsl [O] Chrysler/Dodge/Jeep, Nissan
7b a	US 71, LA 1, Shreveport, N [gas] Exxon/dsl, Shell/dsl [food] Checkers, Domino's, Johnny's Pizza, Papa John's, Pizza Hut, Sonic, Subway, Waffle House, Whataburger/24hr [O] Brookshire Foods/gas, Family$, Walgreens, S [gas] RaceWay/dsl, Shell, Valero/dsl [food] Burger King, Carl's Jr, Church's, KFC, McDonald's, Podnah's BBQ, Popeye's, Taco Bell, Wendy's

SHREVEPORT

LA

INTERSTATE 220 (SHREVEPORT)

7b a	Continued Royal Inn Advance Parts, AutoZone, County Mkt Foods, CVS Drug, Family$, O'Reilly Parts, Radio Shack, repair/transmissions, Rite Aid, U-Haul
5	LA 173, Blanchard Rd, N Citgo/dsl
2	Lakeshore Dr
1a	Jefferson Paige Rd, S Days Inn, Hampton Inn, Merryton Inn, Ramada Inn, Residence Inn, Super 8, Value Inn
1b c	I-20, E to Shreveport, W to Dallas. **I-220 begins/ends on I-20, exit 11.**

INTERSTATE 610 (NEW ORLEANS)

Exit #	Services
I-610 begins/ends on I-10	
4	Franklin Ave (from eb)
3	Elysian fields, S B Express, Shell Burger King, McDonald's, Waffle House Lowe's
2b	US 90, N Broad St, New Orleans St (from wb)
2c	Paris Ave (from wb, no return), S Jimmy's, Shell/24 Popeye's
2a	St Bernard Ave (from eb), to LSU School of Dentistry, auto race track
1a	Canal Blvd
1b	I-10, to New Orleans
I-610 begins/ends on I-10	

MAINE

INTERSTATE 95

Exit #	Services
305mm	US/Canada border, Maine state line, US Customs. **I-95 begins/ends.**
305	US 2, to Houlton, E DFA Duty Free Shop, Houlton Airport
303mm	Meduxnekeag River
302	US 1, Houlton, E Irving/Circle K/dsl/24hr Amato's, Burger King, McDonald's, Pizza Hut, Tang's Chinese , IGA Foods, Mardens, O'Reilly Parts/VIP Service, Rite Aid, W **both lanes, full facilities, petwalk, litter barrels** , Citgo/Subway/dsl, Irving/Circle K/dsl/scales/ @, Shell/Dunkin Donuts/dsl Tim Hortons/Coldstone Ivey's Motel, Shiretown Motel Arrowstook SP, Family$, Ford, Shop'n Save, Toyota, Walmart
301mm	B Stream
291	US 2, to Smyrna, E Brookside Motel/rest.
286	Oakfield Rd, to ME 11, Eagle Lake, Ashland, W Irving/Circle K/dsl, Valero/dsl A Place To Eat USPO
277mm	Mattawamkeag River, W Branch
276	ME 159, Island Falls, E Dysarts Fuel, Porter's/rest. Bishop's Mkt, USPO, W RV camping, to Baxter SP (N entrance)
264	to ME 11, Sherman, E Shell/dsl/LP/rest., W Irving/Circle K/dsl Katahdin Valley Motel to Baxter SP (N entrance)
259	Benedicta (from nb, no re-entry)
252mm	scenic view Mt Katahdin, nb
247mm	Salmon Stream
244	ME 157, to Medway, E Millinocket, W Irving/Circle K/dsl The Bridge Rest. Gateway Inn , city park, Pine Grove Camping (4mi), to Baxter SP (S entrance), USPO, vet
244mm	Penobscot River
243mm	**both lanes, full facilities, litter barrels, petwalk**
227	to US 2, ME 6, Lincoln, **4 mi** E , RV camping, food, gas, lodging
219mm	Piscataquis River
217	ME 6, Howland, E Irving/95 Diner/dsl 95er Towing/repair, camping, LP
201mm	Birch Stream
199	ME 16 (no nb re-entry), to LaGrange
197	ME 43, to Old Town, E /dsl
196mm	Pushaw Stream
193	Stillwater Ave, to Old Town, E Citgo/dsl, Gulf/Subway/dsl, Irving/Circle K/dsl Burger King, China Garden, Dunkin Donuts, Governor's Rest., McDonald's, Tim Horton, Wendy's Black Bear Inn $Tree, IGA Foods, O'Reilly Parts/VIP Servic
191	Kelly Rd, to Orono, **2-3 mi** E camping,
187	Hogan Rd, Bangor Mall Blvd, to Bangor, E Citgo Denny's Courtyard, Hampton Inn, Hilton Garden, Towne Place Suites , Audi/VW, Buick/GMC, Cadillac/Chevrole Chrysler/Dodge/Jeep, Firestone/auto, Ford, Honda, Hyunda Mazda, Mercedes, Nissan, Sam's Club/gas, Subaru, Volvo W Citgo/dsl, Irving/Circle K/dsl Applebee's, Arby's Buffalo Wild Wings, Bugaboo Creek Café, Burger King, Chicag Grill, Chili's, Dunkin Donuts, Five Guys, Green Tea Japanese Happy China, KFC, Kobe Japanese, Las Palapas, Longhor Steaks, McDonald's, Miguel's Mexican, Olive Garden, Pap Johns, Pizza Hut, Quiznos, Ruby Tuesday, Starbucks, Subway, TX Roadhouse, Wendy's Bangor Motel, Comfort Inn Country Inn, Quality Inn $Tree, Advance Parts, AT&T, Bes Buy, BigLots, BooksAMillion, Dick's, Goodyear/auto, Hannaford Foods, Harley-Davidson, Hobby Lobby, Home Depot, JC Penney, Jo-Ann Fabrics, Kia, K-Mart/Little Caesars, Kohl's, L Bean, Lowe's, Macy's, mall, Old Navy, O'Reilly Parts/VIP Service, PetCo, Petsmart, Sears/auto, Staples, Target, Town Fa Tire, URGENT CARE, Verizon, Walmart
186	Stillwater Ave, same as 187
185	ME 15, to Broadway, Bangor, E Irving/Circle K/ds Tri-City Pizza , W Citgo Amato's, BoBo Chinese, China Light, Coldstone/Tim Hortons, Governor's Rest. KFC, McDonald's, Moe's BBQ, Pizza Hut, Subway, Taco Be CarQuest, Family$, Hannaford Foods, Rite Aid, TJ Maxx Walgreens
184	ME 222, Union St, to Ohio St, Bangor, E Citgo, Irving Rite Aid, W Citgo, Gulf, Shell/dsl Burger King Capt Nick's Rest., Dunkin Donuts, McDonald's, Nicky's Rest. Wendy's Sheraton $Tree, Hannaford Foods, Marshall's Midas, RV Camping, to
183	US 2, ME 2, Hammond St, Bangor, E Citgo, She Angelo's Pizza, Papa Gambino's Pizza, Whoopie Pie Cafe Corner Store, Fairmont Mkt, NAPA, TrueValue, W
182b	US 2, ME 100 W, W Irving/Subway/dsl, Shell/ds Dunkin Donuts, Ground Round, Tim Hortons Days Inn

HOULTON

BANGOR

N INTERSTATE 95 Cont'd

182b Continued
EconoLodge, Fairfield Inn, Holiday Inn, Howard Johnson, Motel 6, Ramada Inn, Super 8, Travelodge [other] O'Reilly Parts/VIP Service, RV camping, Tire Whse

182a I-395, to US 2, US 1A, Bangor, downtown

180 Cold Brook Rd, to Hampden, E [gas] Citgo [food] Angler's Rest. (1mi), W [gas] Citgo/dsl/24hr/ @, Dysarts Fleet Fuel/dsl [lodging] Best Western [other] dsl repair, Mack, Volvo

178mm **[rest stop] sb, full [handicapped] facilities, info, litter barrels, petwalk [phone] [picnic] vending, wireless internet**

177mm Soudabscook Stream

176mm **[rest stop] nb, full [handicapped] facilities, info, litter barrels, petwalk [phone] [picnic] vending, wireless internet**

174 ME 69, to Carmel, E [gas] Citgo/dsl, W [other] RV camping

167 ME 69, ME 143, to Etna

NEWPORT

161 ME 7, to E Newport, Plymouth, W [other] LP, RV camping

159 Ridge Rd (from sb), to Plymouth, Newport

157 to US 2, ME 7, ME 11, Newport, W [gas] Irving/Circle K/dsl/24hr, Shell/dsl [food] Burger King, China Way, Dunkin Donuts, McDonald's, Pando Italian American, Pizza Hut, Sawyers Dairy Bar, Subway, Tim Hortons [lodging] Lovley's Motel [other] Aubuchon Hardware, Auto Value Parts, AutoZone, CarQuest, Chrysler/Dodge/Jeep, Rite Aid, Shop'n Save, Verizon, Walmart/Dunkin Donuts

151mm Sebasticook River

150 Somerset Ave, Pittsfield, E [gas] Irving/dsl [food] Subway [lodging] Pittsfield Motel [other] [H], CarQuest, Chevrolet, Family$, Rite Aid, Shop'n Save Foods

138 Hinckley Rd, Clinton, W [gas] 95 One-Stop/dsl

134mm Kennebec River

133 US 201, Fairfield, E [food] Purple Cow Pancakes

WATERVILLE

132 ME 139, Fairfield, W [gas] Irving/Circle K/Subway/dsl/scales/24hr

130 ME 104, Main St, Waterville, E [gas] Citgo [food] Cappza's Pizza, Coldstone, Dunkin Donuts, Friendly's, Governor's Rest., Little Caesar's, McDonald's, Ruby Tuesday, Starbucks, Subway, Tim Horton, Wendy's [lodging] Best Western, Comfort Inn, Fireside Inn [other] [H], Advance Parts, Audi/Mazda/VW, GNC, Hannaford Foods, Home Depot, JC Penney, K-Mart, O'Reilly Parts/VIP Service, Radio Shack, Staples, Verizon, Walmart

129mm Messalonskee Stream

127 ME 11, ME 137, Waterville, Oakland, E [gas] Irving/dsl/24hr, Xpress/dsl [food] Applebee's, Burger King, DQ, Dunkin Donuts, KFC/Taco Bell, McDonald's, Pad Thai, Papa John's, Pizza Hut, Sam's Italian, Subway, Super Buffet, Weathervane Seafood [lodging] Budget Host, EconoLodge, Hampton Inn [other] [H], AutoZone, Buick/Chevrolet, Chrysler/Dodge/Jeep, CVS Drug, Hannaford Foods, Jo-Ann Fabrics, Marden's, Shaw's Foods/Osco Drug, Tire Whse, TJ Maxx, Toyota/Scion, Verizon, W [gas] Shell/dsl [other] Aubuchon Hardware, CarQuest, Ford/Lincoln

120 Lyons Rd, Sidney

117mm **weigh sta both lanes**

113 ME 3, Augusta, Belfast

112 ME 27, ME 8, ME 11, Augusta, E [gas] Citgo [food] Denny's, DQ, Dunkin Donuts, Longhorn Steaks, Olive Garden, Panera Bread, Red Robin, Rooster's, Ruby Tuesday, Sam's Italian, Subway [lodging] Best Western [other] Barnes&Noble, Dick's, GNC, Home Depot, Kohl's, Michaels, Old Navy, Radio Shack, Sam's Club, TownFair Tire, Verizon, Walmart, W [gas] Irving/Circle K/dsl/24hr [food] 99 Rest., Great Wall Chinese, KFC/Taco Bell, Wendy's [lodging] Comfort Inn, Fairfield Inn [other] Advance Parts

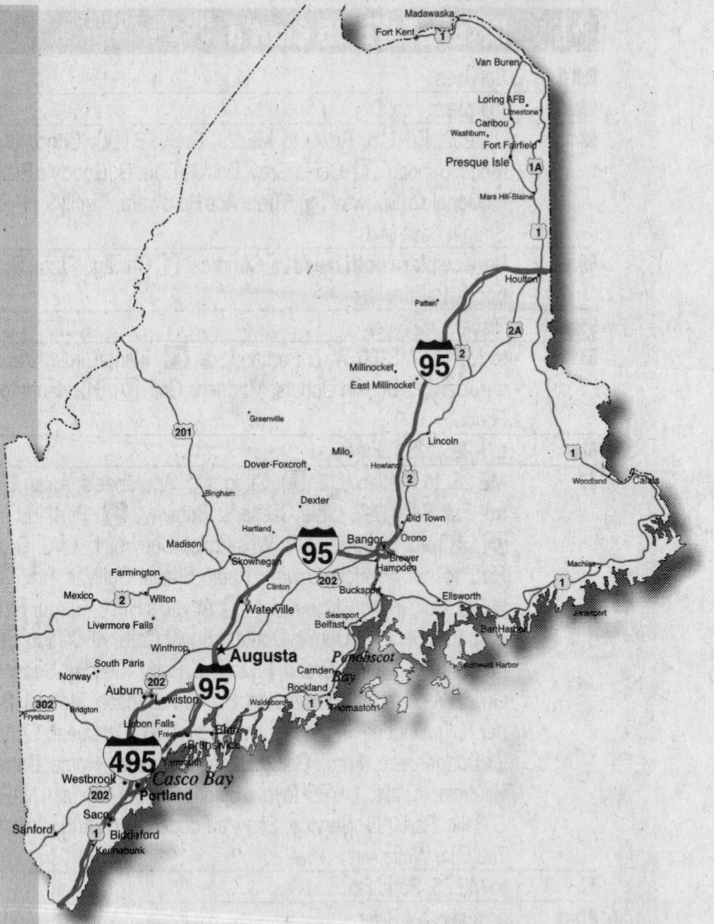

AUGUSTA

109 US 202, ME 11, ME 17, ME 100, Augusta, E [gas] Citgo/Dunkin Donuts/dsl, Irving/Circle K/dsl [food] Amato's Rest., Applebee's, Arby's, Burger King, China King, Damon's Italian, Domino's, DQ, Friendly's, KFC, Little Caesars, McDonald's, Pizza Hut, Subway, Tim Horton, Wendy's [lodging] Senator Inn [other] $Tree, Best Buy, BigLots, Family$, K-Mart, Lowe's, O'Reilly Parts/VIP Service, Petsmart, Radio Shack, Shaw's Foods/Osco Drug, Staples, Target, U-Haul, USPO, vet, Walgreens, W [gas] Valero [food] Margarita's Mexican, TX Roadhouse [lodging] Hampton Inn, Motel 6, Quality Inn, Super 8 [other] CarQuest, Chrysler/Dodge, Hannaford Foods, Honda, Hyundai, Jeep, Kia, Nissan, PetCo, Sears/auto, Subaru, TJ Maxx, Toyota/Scion

103 to I-295 S (from sb), ME 9, ME 126, to Gardiner, **service plaza** [gas] Citgo [food] Burger King, Hersheys, Quiznos, Starbucks [other] ZMkt

102 to I-295 S (from nb), Rd 9, Rd 106, **service plaza** [gas] Citgo [food] Burger King, Hersheys, Quiznos, Starbucks [other] ZMkt

100mm **toll plaza**

86 to ME 9, Sabattus

84mm Sabattus Creek

LEWISTON

80 ME 196, Lewiston, **W on ME 196** [gas] Coast Fuels, Gendron's/dsl, Mobil, Shell/dsl, Sunoco, XPress/dsl [food] Burger King, Cathay Hut Chinese, D'Angelo, Dunkin Donuts, Governor's Rest., KFC/Taco Bell, McDonald's, Papa John's, Pepper&Spice Thai, Sam's Italian, Subway [lodging] Advance Parts, Motel 6, Ramada Inn, Super 8 [other] [H], $Tree, Family$, NAPA, Rite Aid, Staples, USPO

78mm Androscoggin River

75 US 202, Rd 4, Rd 100, to Auburn, E [gas] Irving/Circle K/dsl, Mobil/Subway/dsl [food] Danny Boy's Rest., Dunkin Donuts, Peking Chinese [lodging] Fireside Inn [other] RV Camping, W [other] [H]

71mm Royal River

INTERSTATE 95 Cont'd

PORTLAND

Exit #	Services
66mm	**toll plaza**
63	US 202, Rd 115, Rd 4, to ME 26, Gray, **E** [gas] Citgo, Gulf, Mobil, Sunoco [food] China Gray, Dunkin Donuts, Goody's Pizza, McDonald's, Subway [other] $Tree, Ace Hardware, Family$, NAPA, Shop'n Save Mkt
59mm	**Service plaza both lanes** [gas] Citgo/dsl [food] Chicago Pizza, Starbucks [other] atm
55mm	Piscataqua River
53	to ME 26, ME100 W, N Portland, **E** [gas] Irving/Circle K/Subway/dsl [food] Dunkin Donuts, Maddens Grill [other] [H], Hannaford Foods
52	to I-295, US 1, Freeport
48	ME 25, to Portland, **E** [gas] Citgo [food] Applebee's, Asian Bistro, Full Belly Deli, Little Caesar's, Subway [lodging] Portland Inn [other] $Tree, BigLots, BJ's Whse/gas, Chevrolet, CVS Drug, Fiat, Jo-Ann Fabrics, Lowe's, Radio Shack, Sullivan Tire, vet, **W** [gas] Gulf, Irving/Circle K/dsl [food] Amato's Rest., Burger King, Chipotle, Denny's, Dunkin Donuts, Egg&I Cafe, KFC/Taco Bell, McDonald's, Panera Bread, Pizza Hut, Ruby Tuesday, Seasons Grille, Wendy's [lodging] Fireside Inn, Howard Johnson, Motel 6, Super 8, Travelodge [other] Advance Parts, AT&T, CarQuest, Chrysler/Dodge/Jeep, Ford, GNC, Harley-Davidson, Home Depot, Hyundai, Kohl's, Lexus/Toyota/Scion, Lincoln, Midas, NAPA, O'Reilly Parts/VIP Service, Shaw's Foods/Osco Drug, Sullivan Tire, Tire Whse, vet
47	to ME 25, Rand Rd
47mm	Stroudwater River
46	to ME 22, Congress St, same as 45
45	to US 1, Maine Mall Rd, S Portland, **E** [gas] Citgo/dsl, Sunoco/dsl [food] Bugaboo Creek Steaks, Burger King, Chili's, Chipotle Mexican, Cracker Barrel, Dunkin Donuts, Five Guys, Food Court, Friendly's, Great Wall Chinese, Hokkaido Japanese, HomeTown Buffet, IHOP, Imperial China, Jimmy the Greek Rest., Longhorn Steaks, Macaroni Grill, McDonald's, Newick's Lobster House, Olive Garden, On the Border, Panera Bread, Pizza Hut, Qdoba, Ruby Tuesday, Sebago Brewing Rest., Starbucks, Tim Horton/Coldstone, UNO Pizzaria, Weathervane Seafood, Wendy's [lodging] Comfort Inn, Courtyard, Days Inn, DoubleTree, EconoLodge, Fairfield Inn, Hampton Inn, Homewood Suites [other] $Tree, Best Buy, BonTon, BooksAMillon, Dick's, Hannaford Foods, Honda, JC Penney, Macy's, mall, Michael's, Nissan, Old Navy, PetCo, Sears/auto, Staples, TJ Maxx, TownFair Tire, Verizon, **W** [food] Applebee's, Starbucks [lodging] Holiday Inn Express, Marriott [other] Target
44	I-295 N (from nb), to S Portland, Scarborough, **1 mi E on ME 114** [gas] Cumberland [food] Chia Sen Chinese, KFC/Taco Bell, Little Caesars, Red Robin, Shogun Japanese, Subway, TX Roadhouse [lodging] Homewood Suites, Residence Inn, TownePlace Suites [other] [H], AT&T, Lowe's, NAPA, O'Reilly/VIP Parts/service, Sam's Club/gas, Shaw's Foods/Osco Drug, Walmart/Dunkin Donuts
42mm	Nonesuch River
42	to US 1, **E** [food] Famous Dave's, Portland Pie [other] Cabela's, Scarborough Downs Racetrack (seasonal)
36	I-195 E, to Saco, Old Orchard Beach, **E** [lodging] Hampton Inn [other] KOA, Paradise Park Resort RV
35mm	**E** [lodging] Ramada Inn/Saco Hotel Conference Ctr
33mm	Saco River

BIDDEFORD

KITTERY

Exit #	Services
32	ME 111, to Biddeford, **E** [gas] Irving/Circle K/Subway/dsl [food] Amato's Sandwiches, Dunkin Donuts, Ruby Tuesday, Wendy's [lodging] Best Value Inn, Holiday Inn Express [other] [H], AAA, AutoZone, O'Reilly/VIP Parts/Service, Osco Drug, Shaw's Foods, Walmart, **W** [gas] Cumberland/dsl [food] Applebees, Casa Fiesta Mexican, Kobe Japanese, Longhorn Steaks, Olive Garden, Panera Bread [other] GNC, Home Depot, Kohl's, MarketBasket Foods, Michaels, Petsmart, Staples, Target, TJ Maxx, TownFair Tire, Verizon
25mm	Kennebunk River
25	ME 35, Kennebunk Beach, **E** [lodging] Turnpike Motel
24mm	**Service plaza both lanes** [gas] Citgo/dsl [food] Burger King, Hersheys, Popeye's, Starbucks [other] atm, Z Mkt
19.5mm	Merriland River
19	ME 9, ME 109, to Wells, Sanford, **W** [other] to Sanford RA
7mm	**Maine Tpk begins/ends, toll booth**
7	**last exit before toll Rd nb**, ME 91, to US 1, The Yorks, **E** [gas] Gulf, Irving/Circle K/dsl, Mobil/dsl, Shell [food] China Bistro, Norma's Rest., Ruby's Grill, Wild Willy's Burgers, York 54 Cafe [lodging] Best Western, Microtel, York Corner Inn [other] [H], Ford, Hannaford Foods, NAPA, Rite Aid, TrueValue, vet
5.5mm	**weigh sta nb**
5mm	York River
4mm	**weigh sta sb**
3mm	**Welcome Ctr nb, full [handicapped] facilities, info, litter barrels, petwalk** [phone] [picnic] **vending,** [other] wireless,
2	(2 & 3 from nb), US 1, to Kittery, **E on US 1** [gas] 7-11/dsl, Irving/Circle K/dsl/scales [food] Burger King, DQ, McDonald's, Robert's Maine Grill, Starbucks, Subway, Sunrise Grill, Tasty Thai, Weathervane Seafood Rest. [lodging] Blue Roof Motel, Days Inn, Northeaster Hotel, Ramada Inn [other] Outlets/Famous Brands, vet
1	ME 103 (from nb, no re-entry), to Kittery
0mm	Maine/New Hampshire state line, Piscataqua River

INTERSTATE 295

Exit #	Services
I-295 begins/ends on I-95 exit 103	
51	ME 9, ME 126, to Gardiner, Litchfield, **toll plaza**, **W service plaza**, [gas] Citgo [food] Burger King, Hersheys, Quiznos, Starbucks [other] ZMkt
49	US 201, to Gardiner
43	ME 197, to Richmond, **E** [gas] Irving/Quincey's Deli/dsl [food] Dunkin Donuts, Subway, **W** [other] KOA (5mi)
37	ME 125, Bowdoinham
31b a	ME 196, to Lisbon, Topsham, **E** [gas] Gibbs/dsl, Irving/Circle K/Dunkin Donuts/Subway [food] 99 Rest., Arby's, Fairground Cafe, Firehouse Subs, Little Caesars, McDonald's, Panera Bread, Romeo's Pizza, Ruby Tuesday, Starbucks, Tim Horton's, Wendy's [other] $Tree, AT&T, Best Buy, Dick's, Hannaford Foods, Home Depot, Jo-Ann Fabrics, Meineke, Nissan, O'Reilly Parts/VIP Service, PetCo, Radio Shack, Rite Aid, Target, Tire Whse, Town Fair Tire, Toyota/Scion, Verizon, **W** [gas] Xpress Stop/dsl
30mm	Androscoggin River
28	US 1, Bath, **1 mi E on US 1** [gas] Cumberland/dsl, Irving/dsl, Mobil/dsl, Shell [food] Amato's, Dunkin Donuts, McDonald's, Subway [lodging] Best Value Inn, Comfort Inn, Fairfield Inn, Knights Inn, Travelers Inn [other] [H], Chevrolet/Mazda, Chrysler/Dodge/Jeep, Ford
24	to Freeport (from nb), **services 1 mi E on US 1**
22	ME 125, to Pownal, **1 mi E on US 1** [gas] Irving/Circle K [food] Azure Cafe, Corsican Rest., Jameson Rest., Linda Bean's M

ME

FREEPORT

INTERSTATE 295 Cont'd

22	Continued Kitchen, McDonald's, Sam's Italian, Starbucks, Subway, Tuscan Bistro [lodging] Harraseeket Inn, Hilton Garden [other] CVS Drug, LL Bean, outlets/famous brands, USPO, **W** to Bradbury Mtn SP
20	Desert Rd, Freeport, **E** [gas] Irving/Circle K [food] Antonia's Pizza, Buck's BBQ, Dunkin Donuts, Thai Garden Rest. [lodging] Comfort Suites, Econolodge, Hampton Inn, Holiday Inn Express, Super 8 [other] RV camping, Shaw's Foods
17	US 1, Yarmouth, **E** [rest stop] **both lanes, full** [handicapped] **facilities, info,** [food] Day's Takeout, Muddy Rudder Rest. [lodging] Best Western [other] Delorme Mapping, Ford, **W** [gas] Citgo/dsl, Cumberland/dsl [food] McDonald's, Pat's Pizza [other] Ace Hardware, Hannaford Foods, O'Reilly Parts/VIP Service, Tire Whse
15	US 1, to Cumberland, Yarmouth, **W** [gas] Irving/dsl, Mobil [food] 233 Grill, Chopstick Asian, Romeo's Pizza, Subway [other] AT&T, Rite Aid
11	to I-95, ME Tpk (from sb)
10	US 1, to Falmouth, **E** [gas] Citgo/dsl, Irving/dsl [food] Dunkin Donuts, Foreside Rest., House of Pizza, Leavitt & Sons Deli, McDonald's, Orchid Thai, Ricetta's Pizza, Starbucks, Subway, Wendy's [lodging] Falmouth Inn [other] Ace Hardware, Audi/VW, Goodyear/auto, Mazda, Radio Shack, Rite Aid, Shaw's Foods, Staples, vet, Walmart
9mm	Presumpscot River
9	US 1 S, ME 26, to Baxter Blvd
8	ME 26 S, Washington Ave, **E** [other] U-Haul
7	US 1A, Franklin St, **E** [food] Miss Portland Diner [other] AAA Car Care, AT&T, CarQuest, NAPA, Trader Joe's, Verizon, Walgreens, Whole Foods Mkt
6b a	US 1, Forest Ave, **E** [gas] Citgo [other] [hospital], Firestone/auto, USPO, **W** [gas] Mobil/dsl [food] Burger King, Leonardo's Pizza, Pizza Hut, Stavro's Pizza, Subway [other] CVS Drug, Hannaford Foods, U of SME, Walgreens
5b a	ME 22, Congress St, **E** [food] Amato's Rest., D'Angelos, Denny's, Dunkin Donuts, Lang's Chinese, McDonald's, Subway [lodging] La Quinta [other] [hospital], Sullivan Tire, **W** [gas] Gulf/Dunkin Donuts, Mobil/dsl [food] Anania's Italian [lodging] Clarion
3mm	Fore River
4	US 1 S, to Main St, to S Portland, US 1 S, **services E on US 1**
3	ME 9, to Westbrook St, no sb return, **W** [gas] Citgo/dsl, Irving/Circle K/dsl [food] Buffalo Wild Wings, El Rodeo Mexican, Olive Garden, Seadog Brew Co., Subway, Wild Willy's Burger [other] Chevrolet, Home Depot, Marshalls
2	to US 1 S, S Portland, **services E on US 1** [gas] 7-11, Irving/Circle K/dsl, Mobil [food] Dunkin Donuts [lodging] Howard Johnson, Super 8, Best Western, Knights Inn
1	to I-95, to US 1, **multiple services E on US 1**, same as 2

I-295 begins/ends on I-95, exit 44.

MARYLAND

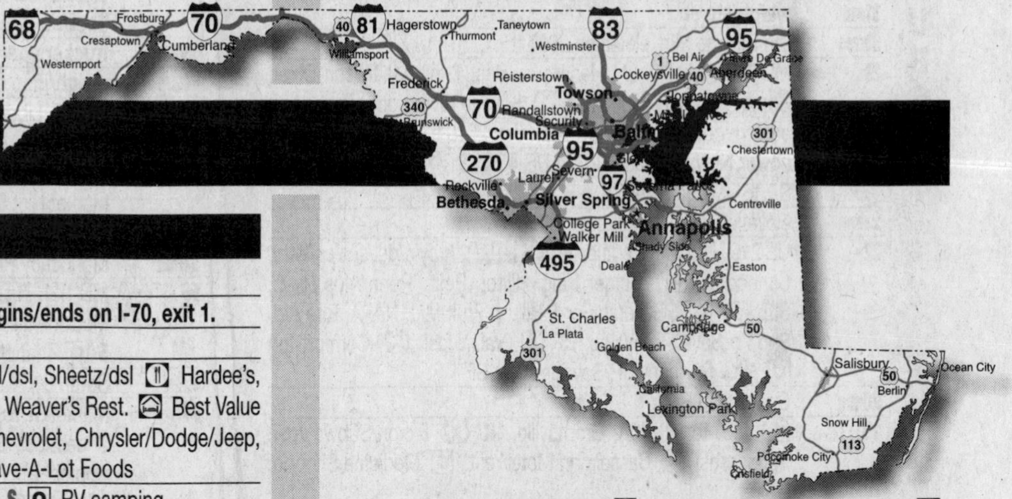

HANCOCK

INTERSTATE 68

Exit #	Services
82c	I-70 W, to Breezewood. **I-68 begins/ends on I-70, exit 1.**
82b	I-70 E, US 40 E, to Hagerstown
82a	US 522, Hancock, **S** [gas] Mobil/dsl, Sheetz/dsl [food] Hardee's, Park'n Dine, Pizza Hut, Subway, Weaver's Rest. [lodging] Best Value Inn, Super 8 [other] $General, Chevrolet, Chrysler/Dodge/Jeep, Happy Hills Camping, NAPA, Save-A-Lot Foods
77	US 40, MD 144, Woodmont Rd, **S** [other] RV camping
75mm	**runaway truck ramp eb**
74mm	**Sideling Hill** [rest stop]**/exhibit, both lanes, full** [handicapped] **facilities, vending,** 1269 ft (seasonal)
74	US 40, Mountain Rd (no return from eb)
73mm	Sideling Hill Creek
72mm	**truck ramp wb**
72	US 40, High Germany Rd, Swain Rd, **S** [gas] Citgo/dsl [food] Oak Barrel Cafe
68	Orleans Rd, **N** [gas] Exxon/dsl
67mm	Town Hill, elevation 940 ft, Town Hill
64	MV Smith Rd, **S** scenic overlook 1040 ft [phone], to Green Ridge SF HQ
62	US 40, 15 Mile Creek Rd, **N** [other] Billmeyer Wildlife Mgt Area
58.7mm	Polish Mtn, elevation 1246 ft
57mm	Town Creek
56mm	Flintstone Creek
56	MD 144, National Pike, Flintstone, **S** [gas] Billie's Gas&Grub [lodging] Seven C's Lodge [other] USPO
52	MD 144, Pleasant Valley Rd (from eb), National Pike
50	Pleasant Valley Rd, **N** [food] Lakeside Grill, Signature's Grill [lodging] Rocky Gap Lodge/golf/rest. [other] to Rocky Gap SP
47	US 220 N, MD 144, Dehaven Rd (from wb), Old National Pike, Bedford, **S** [gas] Loves/Arby's/dsl/scales/24hr
46	US 220 N, Dehaven Rd, Baltimore Pike, Naves Crossroads, **N** [gas] Sheetz/dsl [lodging] Cumberland Motel [other] $General, Advance Parts, **S** [gas] Loves/Arby's/dsl/scales/24hr [food] Puccini's Rest.
45	Hillcrest Dr, **S** [gas] Sunoco/dsl
44	US 40A, Baltimore Ave, Willow Brook Rd, to Allegany Comm Coll, **S** [other] [hospital], to Allegany Comm Coll
43d	Maryland Ave, **N** [lodging] Ramada [other] USPO, **S** [gas] Gulf/7-11 [food] Chick-fil-A, Papa John's [other] [hospital], AT&T, AutoZone, Martin's Foods/gas
Exit #	Services
43c	downtown, same as 43b
43mm	Youghiogheny River
43b	MD 51, Industrial Blvd, **N** [food] McDonald's, Subway [lodging] Ramada [other] Family$, SaveALot Foods, **S** [gas] Gulf/dsl [food] Roy Rogers, Taco Bell, Wendy's [lodging] Fairfield Inn

ME

MD

INTERSTATE 68 Cont'd

FROSTBURG

Exit #	Services
43a	to WV 28A, Beall St, Industrial Blvd, to Cumberland, Johnson St, N [gas] Sheetz
42	US 220 S, Greene St, Ridgedale
41	Seton Dr (from wb, no directory turn)
41mm	Haystack Mtn, elev 1240 ft
40	US 220 S, to US 40A, Vocke Rd, La Vale, N [gas] BP/dsl, Sunoco [food] Arby's, Asian Garden, Bob Evans, Burger King, D'Atri Rest., Denny's, DQ, Grand China, KFC, LJ Silver, McDonald's, Pizza Hut, Rio Grande Mexican, Rita's Custard, Ruby Tuesday, Subway, TX Grill, Wendy's [lodging] Best Western/rest, Comfort Inn, Holiday Inn Express, Slumberland Motel, Super 8 [other] $General, Advance Parts, AT&T, AutoZone, CVS Drug, Harley-Davidson, Jo-Ann Fabrics, Lowe's, Mr Tire, NAPA, st police, Staples, URGENT CARE, S [food] Applebee's, Dragon China Buffet, Ponderosa, Wasabi Japanese [lodging] EconoLodge [other] $Tree, Aldi Foods, BonTon, JC Penney, Kohl's, mall, Martin's Foods/gas, Sears/auto, TJ Maxx, Walmart/McDonald's
39	US 40A (from wb), same as 40
34	MD 36, to Westernport, Frostburg, N [gas] Sheetz/dsl, Valero/dsl [food] Burger King, Fox's Pizza, Mario's Italian, McDonald's, Pizza Hut, Subway [lodging] Days Inn, Hampton Inn [other] [H], $General, Food Lion, Rite Aid, Save-A-Lot, S [other] to Dans Mtn SP
33	Midlothian Rd, to Frostburg, N [other] [H], S [other] to Dans Mt SP
31mm	**weigh sta eb**
30mm	Big Savage Mtn, elevation 2800 ft
29	MD 546, Finzel, N [food] Hen House Rest. (2mi) [other] Mason-Dixon Camping (4mi/seasonal), S [food] Savage River Lodge/rest. (4mi)
25.8mm	eastern continental divide, elevation 2610 ft
24	Lower New Germany Rd, to US 40A, S [other] to New Germany SP, to Savage River SF
23mm	elevation 2780 ft, Meadow Mtn
22	US 219 N, to Meyersdale, N [gas] Pilot/Arby's/dsl/scales/24hr, Sunoco/dsl [food] Burger King, Hilltop Rest., Penn Alps Rest., Subway [other] $General, Ford, Hilltop Fruit Mkt, NAPA, Rite Aid, Shop'n Save, TrueValue, S [gas] Valero/dsl [lodging] Comfort Inn [other] New Germany SP, Savage River SF
20mm	Casselman River
19	MD 495, to US 40A, Grantsville, N [gas] Exxon/Subway/dsl, Sunoco/dsl [lodging] Casselman Motel/rest. [other] Medicine Shoppe, USPO
15mm	Mt Negro, elevation 2740 ft
14mm	Keyser's Ridge, elevation 2880 ft
14b a	US 219, US 40 W, Oakland, N [gas] Liberty/Ridge/rest./dsl, Sunoco/7-11/dsl [food] McDonald's, repair
6mm	**Welcome Ctr eb, full [handicapped] facilities, info, litter barrels, petwalk [phone] [picnic] vending**
4.5mm	Bear Creek
4	MD 42, Friendsville, N [gas] Liberty/dsl, Marathon/dsl [lodging] Yough Valley Motel [other] S&S Mkt, USPO, S [lodging] Sunset Inn [other] camping, to Deep Creek Lake SP
0mm	Maryland/West Virginia state line

INTERSTATE 70

BALTIMORE / FREDERICK

Exit #	Services
	I-70 begins/ends in Baltimore at Cooks Lane.
94	Security Blvd N, S [gas] Shell
91b a	I-695
87b a	US 29 (exits left from wb)to MD 99, Columbia, **2 mi S on US 40** [gas] BP/dsl, Exxon/dsl, Gulf, Shell/dsl, Sunoco [food] Arby's,
87b a	Continued Baskin-Robbins/Dunkin Donuts, Boston Mkt, Burger King, Checkers, Domino's, Jimmy John's, McDonald's, Papa John's, Pizza Hut, Qdoba, Starbucks, Subway [other] 7-11, Acura, Advance Parts, Cadillac/Chevrolet, Carmax, CVS Drug, Giant Foods, Goodyear/auto, H Mart Foods, Home Depot, Honda, Infiniti, Kia, Mars Foods, Midas, Mr Tire, Nissan, Rite Aid, Safeway Foods, Verizon, Walgreens, Walmart
83	US 40, Marriottsville (no EZ wb return), **2 mi S** [lodging] Turf Valley Hotel/Country Club/rest.
82	US 40 E (from eb), same as 83
80	MD 32, Sykesville, N [other] golf, S [gas] High's/dsl [food] Subway, Tony's Pizzeria
79mm	**weigh/insp sta wb** [phone]
76	MD 97, Olney, S [gas] High's/dsl [food] Subway
73	MD 94, Woodbine, N [gas] High's/dsl [food] Baskin Robbins, China Yee, Dunkin Donuts, Harvest Chicken, McDonald's, Pizza Hut, Subway [other] $Tree, Food Lion, Ramblin Pines RV Park (6mi), Verizon, S [gas] BP/dsl, Citgo [food] Town Grill
68	MD 27, Mt Airy, N [gas] 7-11, Liberty/dsl [food] Arby's, Baskin-Robbns/Dunkin Donuts, Burger King, Chipotle, Chong Yet Yin Chinese, Domino's, Five Guys, J&P Pizza, Jersey Mike' Subs, KFC/Taco Bell, Ledo's Pizza, McDonald's, Papa John's, Pizza Hut, Rita's Custard, Starbucks, Subway [other] Ace Hardware, Advance Parts, AT&T, Food Lion, GNC, Goodyear, Mr Tire, Radio Shack, Rite Aid, Safeway, Verizon, Walmart, S [gas] Exxon/dsl, Shell/dsl [lodging] Budget Inn
66mm	**truckers parking area eb**
64mm	**weigh/insp sta eb**
62	MD 75, Libertytown, N [gas] Falcon Fuels, High's/dsl [food] Asian Bistro, Baskin Robbins, Burger King, Domino's, Dunkin Donuts, McDonald's, Morgan's Grill [other] CVS Drug, Food Lion, New Market Hist Dist
59	MD 144
57mm	Monocacy River
56	MD 144, N [gas] BP, Sheetz [food] Beijing, Burger King, JR's Pizza, McDonald's, Roy Rogers, Taco Bell, Wendy's [other] to Hist Dist, S [other] Triangle RV Ctr
55	South St, **1 mi N** [gas] BP, Sheetz/dsl [other] same as 56
54	Market St, to I-270, N [gas] Costco/gas [lodging] Super 8, S [gas] 7-11, Sheetz/dsl, Shell/dsl, SouStates/dsl, Valero/dsl, Wawa/dsl [food] Applebee's, Arby's, Bob Evans, Burger King, Checker's, Chuck-eCheese, Cracker Barrel, KFC/Taco Bell, Longhorn Steaks, McDonald's, Panera Bread, Papa John's, Peking Gourmet, Pizza Hut, Popeye's, Red Robin, Ruby Tuesday, Sonic, Subway, Tilted Kilt, Waffle House [lodging] Country Inn Suites, Courtyard, Days Inn, EconoLodge, Extended Stay America, Fairfield Inn, Hampton Inn, Hilton Garden, Holiday Inn, Residence Inn, Sleep Inn [other] $Tree, AAA, Aamco, Audi, Barnes&Noble, Best Buy, Buick, GMC, Chrysler/Dodge/Jeep, Dick's, Home Depot, Honda, Hyundai, JC Penney, Kia, Kohl's, Lincoln, Lowe's, Macy's, mall, Michael's, Mr Tire, Nissan, Office Depot, Petsmart, Ross, Sam's Club/dsl, Sears/auto, Staples, Target, Tires+, TJMaxx, Toyota, Scion, Volvo, Walmart
53b a	I-270 S, US 15 N, US 40 W, to Frederick
52b a	US 15 S, US 340 W, Leesburg
49	US 40A, Braddock Heights, S [other] camping, to Washington Mon SP, **N on US 40** [gas] Citgo/dsl, Exxon/dsl, Freestate/dsl, GetGo, Shell/dsl, Sunoco [food] Arby's, Bob Evans, Boston Mkt, Burger King, Carrabba's, Casa Rico Mexican, Denny's, Domino's, Dunkin Donuts, Famous Dave's BBQ, Flaming Grill, Fritchie's Rest., Ground Round, HoneyBaked Ham, KFC, Los Trios, McDonald's, McDonald's, Mtn View Diner, Outback Steaks,

E INTERSTATE 70 Cont'd

HAGERSTOWN

Exit	Services
49	Continued Pizza Hut, Popeye's, Red Horse Rest., Red Lobster, Roy Rogers, Ruby Tuesday, Starbucks, Subway, Taco Bell, Wendy's [lodging] Comfort Inn, Motel 6 [other] H, $General, 7-11, Aldi Foods, AT&T, AutoZone, Boscov's, CVS Drug, Giant Eagle Foods, Home Depot, K-Mart, Merchant Tire, Mr Tire, PepBoys, PetCo, st police, Subaru, Toyota, Verizon, Weis Foods
48	US 40 E, US 340 (from eb, no return), **1 mi N** same as 49
42	MD 17, Myersville, **N** [gas] Exxon, Sunoco/dsl [food] Burger King, McDonald's, Old Town Diner [other] Greenbrier SP (4mi), to Gambrill SP (6mi), **S** [gas] Crown/dsl [food] Subway
39mm	**[RS] both lanes, full [handicapped] facilities, litter barrels, petwalk [phone] [picnic] vending**
35	MD 66, to Boonsboro, **S** [gas] Sheetz/dsl (1mi) [other] camping, to Greenbrier SP
32b a	US 40, Hagerstown, **N** [gas] 7-11, BP, Exxon/dsl, Sheetz/dsl, Sunoco [food] Baskin-Robbins/Dunkin Donuts, Bob Evans, Burger King, Cancun Cantina, Checkers, Denny's, DQ, El Ranchero Mexican, Family Diner, Five Guys, Jimmy John's, KFC, Ledo's Pizza, McDonald's, Papa John's, Pizza Hut, Popeye's, Sonic, Subway, Supreme Buffet, Taco Bell, TX Roadhouse [lodging] Best Western, Clarion, Comfort Inn, Comfort Suites, Days Inn, Hampton Inn, Rodeway Inn, Super 8 [other] H, $General, Advance Parts, Aldi Foods, AT&T, AutoZone, Cadillac/Chevrolet, Chrysler/Dodge/Jeep, CVS Drug, Family$, Firestone/auto, Martin's Foods, Mercedes, Midas, Mr Tire, Nissan, Tires+, Toyota/Scion, URGENT CARE, Walgreens, Weis Foods, **S** [other] Buick/GMC, Honda, Kia, Subaru/Mazda/VW
29b a	MD 65, to Sharpsburg, **N** [gas] Exxon/Subway/dsl, Sheetz/dsl [food] FoodCourt, Longhorn Steaks [other] H, Prime Outlets/famous brands, st police, **S** [gas] Liberty/7-11/dsl [food] Burger King, Cracker Barrel, McDonald's, Waffle House, Wendy's [lodging] Sleep Inn [other] Jellystone Camping, to Antietam Bfd
28	MD 632, Hagerstown
26	I-81, N to Harrisburg, S to Martinsburg
24	MD 63, Huyett, **N** [gas] Pilot/Subway/dsl/24hr, Sheetz/dsl (2mi), **S** [lodging] Red Roof Inn [other] C&O Canal, KOA (2mi)
18	MD 68 E, Clear Spring, **N** [gas] BP/dsl, Liberty [food] McDonald's [lodging] Sleep Inn, **S** [gas] Exxon/dsl [food] Wendy Hill Café
12	MD 56, Indian Springs, **S** [gas] Exxon/dsl [other] Ft Frederick SP
9	US 40 E (from eb, exits left), Indian Springs
5	MD 615 (no immediate wb return), **N** [other] Log Cabin Rest. (2mi)
3	MD 144, Hancock (exits left from wb), **S** [gas] ACT/Exxon/dsl, Liberty/rest./dsl/24hr [food] Hardee's, Park'n Dine [lodging] Hilltop Inn [other] Blue Goose Mkt
1b	US 522 (exits left from both lanes), Hancock, **S** [gas] Mobil/dsl, Sheetz/dsl [food] Hardee's, Park'n Dine, Pizza Hut, Subway, Weaver's Rest. [lodging] Best Value Inn, Super 8 [other] $General, Chevrolet, Chrysler/Dodge/Jeep, Happy Hills Camp, NAPA, Save-A-Lot Foods
1a	I-68 W, US 40, W to Cumberland
0mm	Maryland/Pennsylvania state line, Mason-Dixon Line

N INTERSTATE 81

HAGERSTOWN

Exit #	Services
12mm	Maryland/Pennsylvania state line
10b a	Showalter Rd, **E** [other] [airport]
9	Maugans Ave, **E** [gas] BP, Sheetz/dsl, Shell/Domino's/dsl [food] Fox's Pizza, Hometown Diner, McDonald's, Papa Murphy's, Pizza Hut, Pollo Loco, Quiznos, Subway, Taco Bell, Waffle House [lodging] Hampton Inn [other] $General, AutoZone, CVS Drug, Food Lion, Martin's Foods/gas, Meineke, vet, Walgreens, **W** [food] Burger King, Dunkin Donuts [lodging] Microtel [other] Kenworth, Volvo
7b a	MD 58, Hagerstown, same as 6
6b a	US 40, Hagerstown, **E** [gas] Shell [other] H, **W** [food] Arby's, Chipotle Mexican, Five Guys, IHOP, Jersey Mike's Subs, KFC, McDonald's, Number One Chinese, Panera Bread, Ryan's, Starbucks, Subway, TGIFriday's, Uno Pizza, Wendy's [other] $Tree, AT&T, Best Buy, Dick's, GNC, Home Depot, Marshall's, Petsmart, Walmart
5b a	Halfway Blvd, **E** [gas] AC&T/dsl [food] Bob Evans, Boston Mkt, Boston Mkt, Buffalo Wild Wings, Burger King, Chick-fil-A, ChuckECheese's, CiCi's Pizza, Cinco de Mayo, Coldstone, El Ranchero Mexican, Fireside Rest., Golden Corral, Hard Times Cafe, Jimmy John's, McDonald's, Nikko Japanese, Noodles&Co, Olive Garden, Outback Steaks, Papa John's, Pizza Hut, Popeye's, Red Lobster, Red Robin, Roy Rogers, Ruby Tuesday, Sakura Steaks, Starbucks, Taco Bell, Tilted Kilt, Wendy's [lodging] Country Inn&Suites, Courtyard, Holiday Inn Express, Homewood Suites, Motel 6, Ramada, SpringHill Suites [other] $Tree, BigLots, BonTon, CVS Drug, Firestone/auto, Ford, Hobby Lobby, Hyundai, JC Penney, K-Mart, Kohl's, Lowe's, Macy's, mall, Martin's Foods/gas, Michael's, PetCo, Ross, Sam's Club/gas, Sears/auto, Staples, Target, **W** [gas] Exxon/dsl/scales/24hr, Pilot/McDonald's/Subway/dsl/scales/24hr [lodging] Super 8 [other] Freightliner
4	I-70, E to Frederick, W to Hancock, to I-68
2	US 11, Williamsport, **E** [gas] AC&T/dsl, **W** [gas] Exxon/dsl, Sunoco/dsl [food] China 88, McDonald's, Subway, Waffle House [lodging] Red Roof Inn [other] auto repair, KOA (4mi)
1	MD 63, MD 68, Williamsport, **E** [gas] Bowman/dsl [other] Jellystone, KOA, to Antietam Bfd, **W** [gas] Citgo [other] $General, NAPA
0mm	Maryland/West Virginia state line, Potomac River

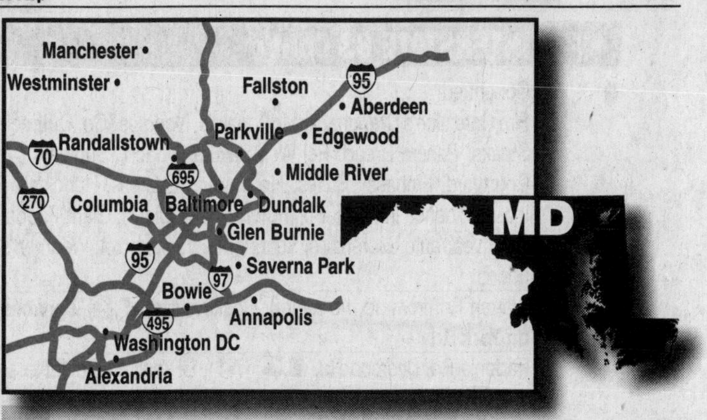

N INTERSTATE 83

Exit #	Services
38mm	Maryland/Pennsylvania state line, Mason-Dixon Line
37	to Freeland (from sb)
36	MD 439, Bel Air, **W** [gas] Filler-Up [food] Maryland Line Inn Grill [other] Holiday Travel Park (5mi), Morris Meadows Camping (5mi)
35mm	**weigh/insp sta sb**
33	MD 45, Parkton, **E** [other] USPO
31	Middletown Rd, to Parkton, **E** [other] golf
27	MD 137, Mt Carmel, Hereford, **E** [gas] Exxon/dsl [food] Michael's Pizza, Monkton Grill, Subway [other] 7-11, Graul's Foods, Hereford Drug, Mt Carmel Drug, USPO, vet
24	Belfast Rd, to Butler, Sparks
20	Shawan Rd, Hunt Valley, **E** [gas] Exxon/dsl, Mobil [food] Burger King, CA Pizza, Carrabba's, Chick-fil-A, Chipotle Mexican, Coal

INTERSTATE 83 Cont'd

BALTIMORE

20	Continued Fire Cafe, Joe's Crabshack, McDonald's, Noodles&Co, Outback Steaks, Panera Bread, Pei Wei, Sakura Hibachi, Subway Courtyard, Embassy Suites, Holiday Inn Express, Hunt Valley Inn, Residence Inn Burlington Coats, Dick's, Giant Foods, Goodyear/auto, Marshall's, Sears/auto, Verizon, vet, Wegman's Foods
18	Warren Rd (from nb, no return), Cockeysville, E **services on York Rd**
17	Padonia Rd, Deereco Rd, E 7-11, BP/dsl, Gulf/dsl, Hess/dsl Applebee's, Bob Evans, Chili's, Macaroni Grill, Wendy's Extended Stay America, Hampton Inn, Holiday Inn Audi/VW, Chevrolet, Goodyear/auto, Lowe's Whse, Mars Mkt, Mr Tire, Porsche, Rite Aid, Sam's Club, services E on York Rd, Subaru, Target, USPO
16b a	Timonium Rd, E **on York Rd** Sunoco/dsl Baja Fresh, Firehouse Subs, Little Caesar's, McDonald's N Baltimore Plaza Hotel, Red Roof Inn Infiniti/Nissan, Petsmart, REI, Rite Aid, ShopRite Foods
14	I-695 N
13	I-695 S, Falls Rd, H, st police
12	Ruxton Rd (from nb, no return)
10b a	Northern Parkway, E Exxon, Shell, W H
9b a	Cold Spring Lane
8	MD 25 N (from nb), Falls Rd
7b a	28th St, E H, W Baltimore Zoo
6	US 1, US 40T, North Ave, downtown
5	MD Ave (from sb), downtown
3	Chase St, Gilford St, downtown
2	Pleasant St (from sb), downtown
1	Fayette St, **I-83 begins/ends, downtown Baltimore**

INTERSTATE 95

Exit #	Services
110mm	Maryland/Delaware state line
109b a	MD 279, to Elkton, Newark, E FLYING J/Patriot Farms/dsl/scales/24hr/ @, Shell/dsl Cracker Barrel, KFC/Taco Bell, McDonald's, Waffle House Days Inn, Elkton Lodge, Hampton Inn, Knights Inn, La Quinta, Motel 6 H, Blue Beacon, W 7-11, TA/Subway/dsl/24hr/ @, WaWa Comfort Suites to U of DE
100	MD 272, to North East, Rising Sun, E FLYING J/Denny's/dsl/LP/24hr, Sunoco/dsl Burger King, Dunkin Donuts, Empire Rest., Frank's Pizza, McDonald's, Waffle House, Wendy's Comfort Inn, Holiday Inn Express $General, $Tree, Advance Parts, AT&T, auto repair, Food Lion, PetCo, Rite Aid, st police, to Elk Neck SP, Verizon, Walgreens, Walmart/Subway, W Citgo Best Western zoo
96mm	**Chesapeake House service area** (exits left from both lanes) Exxon/dsl, Sunoco/dsl Burger King, Popeye's, Quiznos, Starbucks gifts
93	MD 275, to Rising Sun, US 222, to Perryville, E Exxon/dsl, Pilot/Subway/dsl/scales/24hr Denny's, KFC/Taco Bell Ramada Inn H, Perryville Outlets/famous brands, Riverview Camping
92mm	**weigh sta/toll booth**
91.5mm	Susquehanna River
89	MD 155, to Havre de Grace (last nb exit before toll), **1-3 mi** E Burger King, Chesapeake Grill, Dunkin Donuts, Mac

ABERDEEN

89	Continued Gregor's Rest., McDonald's, Waffle House Best Budget Inn Super 8, Van Divers B&B H, W to Susquehanna SP
85	MD 22, to Aberdeen, E 7-11, BP/dsl, Royal Farms/dsl Shell/dsl Applebee's, Arby's, Baskin-Robbins/Dunkin Donuts, Bob Evans, Burger King, Durango's, Family Buffet, KFC Korea House, Little Caesars, Mamie's Cafe, McDonald's, Olive Tree Italian, Panera Bread, Papa John's, Pizza Hut, Rita's Custard, Subway, Taco Bell, Wendy's Clarion, Courtyard Days Inn, Hilton Garden, Holiday Inn, La Quinta, Red Roof Inn Residence Inn, Super 8, Travelodge $General, $Tree, auto repair, Home Depot, Mars Foods, museum, Radio Shack, Rite Aid, ShopRite Foods, Target, Verizon, Walgreens
81mm	**MD House service area** (exits left from both lanes) Exxon/dsl, Sunoco/dsl Phillips Seafood, Roy Rogers, Sbarro's Starbucks, TCBY gifts
80	MD 543, to Riverside, Churchville, E 7-11, BP/Burger King Shell/Quiznos/dsl, Sunoco Arby's, China Moon, Cracker Barrel, McDonald's, Pizza Hut, Riverside Crabs, Riverside Grille Riverside Pizzeria, Ruby Tuesday, Subway, Waffle House Candlewood Suites, Country Inn&Suites, Extended Stay America, Homewood Suites, SpringHill Suites, Wingate Inn Bar Harbor RV Park (4mi), Rite Aid, ShopRite Foods, Verizon
77b a	MD 24, to Edgewood, Bel Air, E BP/dsl, Citgo/dsl, Exxon/dsl, Royal Farms/dsl Denny's, Dimitri's Pizza, El Rodeo, My 3 Sons Rest., Waffle House Best Western, Days Inn, Hampton Inn, Holiday Inn Express, Ramada Inn, Sleep Inn URGENT CARE, W Exxon/dsl, WaWa/dsl Chick-fil-A, KFC/Taco Bell, McDonald's, Starbucks H, $Tree, BJ's Whse, Lowe's, Target, Walmart/Subway, Wegman's Foods
74	MD 152, Fallston, Joppatowne, E BP/dsl, Citgo/dsl, Exxon/dsl, Sheetz, Shell/dsl, WaWa/dsl Dunkin Donuts, Friendly's, KFC, Subway, Venitian Palace, Wendy's Edgewood Motel, Super 8 H, Toyota (1mi), W Royal Farms/dsl
70mm	Big Gunpowder Falls
67b a	MD 43, to White Marsh Blvd, US 1, US 40, E **on MD 7** BP/dsl 5 Guys Burgers, Chick-fil-A, McDonald's, Noodles&Co, Panera Bread, Qdoba Mexian, Starbucks, Subway Best Buy, Carmax, Chevrolet, Dick's, Lowe's, Michael's, Nissan, Target, Tire Discounters, W **on White Marsh Blvd** 7-11, Exxon/dsl Bertucci's, Buffalo Wild Wings, Burger King, Chili's, China Wok, Coldstone, Don Pablo, Lin's Chinese, McDonald's, Olive Garden, PF Chang's, Red Brick Sta., Red Lobster, Red Robin, Ruby Tuesday, Starbucks, Taco Bell, TGIFriday's, Wendy's, Zack's Hotdogs, Z-Burger Fairfield Inn, Hampton Inn, Hilton Garden, Residence Inn AT&T, Barnes&Noble, Giant Foods, JC Penney, Macy's, mall, Old Navy, Sears/auto, Staples, to Gunpowder SP, USPO, Verizon

BALTIMORE

64b a	I-695 (exits left), E to Essex, W to Towson
62	to I-895 (from sb)
61	US 40, Pulaski Hwy, E BP, Shell/dsl McDonald's
60	Moravia Rd
59	Eastern Ave, W BP/dsl, Exxon, Royal Farms/dsl, WaWa Broadway Diner, McDonald's, Subway, Wendy's H, AT&T, Shoppers Foods
58	Dundalk Ave, (from nb), E Citgo, Sunoco
57	O'Donnell St, Boston St, E TA/Buckhorn/Subway/dsl/scales/motel/ @ McDonald's Best Western
56	Keith Ave
56mm	McHenry Tunnel, **toll plaza** (north side of tunnel)
55	Key Hwy, to Ft McHenry NM, **last nb exit before toll**
54	MD 2 S, to Hanover St, W H, Harris Teeter, downtown
53	I-395 N, to MLK, W Oriole Park, downtown

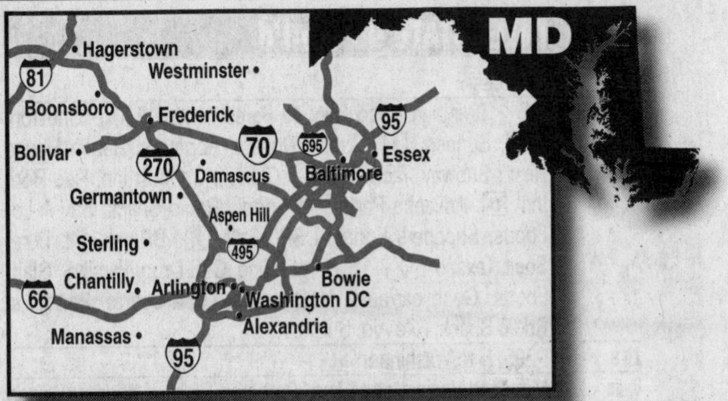

INTERSTATE 95 Cont'd

COLUMBIA

52 Russell St N, W [other] [H]

51 Washington Blvd

50.5mm **inspection sta nb**

50 Caton Ave, E [gas] Hess/dsl, Shell/dsl, US/dsl [food] Caton House, Loafers Grill, McDonald's [lodging] Motel 6 [other] 7-11, Aldi Foods, auto repair, Midas, Toyota/Scion, W [other] [H]

49b a I-695, E to Key Bridge, Glen Burnie, W to Towson, to I-70, to I-83

47b a I-195, to MD 166, to BWI Airport, to Baltimore

46 I-895, to Harbor Tunnel Thruway

43b a MD 100, to Glen Burnie, **1 mi E on US 1** [gas] Exxon/Wendy's/dsl, Xtra [lodging] Best Western

41b a MD 175, to Columbia, E [gas] BP/dsl, Exxon/dsl, Shell/dsl, TA/Country Pride/Subway/dsl/scales/24hr/ @ [food] Arby's, Burger King, Frank's Diner, IHOP, McDonald's, Panda Express, Starbucks [lodging] Comfort Suites, Holiday Inn, La Quinta, Red Roof Inn, Sleep Inn, Super 8 [other] $Tree, Advance Parts, Mom's Organic Mkt, W [gas] Exxon [food] Bob Evans, Fat Burger, Houlihan's, Jersey Mike's, McDonald's, Mimi's Cafe, Olive Garden, On the Border, TGIFriday's [lodging] Extended Stay America, Homewood Suites [other] [H], Best Buy, Costco/gas, CVS Drug, Lowe's, Loyola U, Office Depot, Royal Farms, to Johns Hopkins U, Trader Joe's

38b a MD 32, to Ft Meade, **2 mi E on US 1** [gas] BP/dsl, Exxon/Wendy's/dsl, Royal Farms, Shell/dsl [food] Burger King, Dunkin Donuts, McDonald's, Subway, Taco Bell [lodging] Comfort Inn, Extended Stay America [other] [H], to BWI Airport

37mm **Welcome Ctr both lanes, full [handicapped] facilities, info, litter barrels, petwalk [phone] [picnic] RV dump, vending**

35b a MD 216, to Laurel, E [gas] Exxon, Shell/dsl [food] McDonald's, Subway [other] Weis Food/drug

34mm Patuxent River

33b a MD 198, to Laurel, E [gas] Exxon [other] [H], W [gas] Exxon/Blimpie/dsl, Shell [food] Outback Steaks [lodging] Holiday Inn

31 MD 200 **(toll)**

29 MD 212, to Beltsville, W [gas] Exxon/Blimpie/dsl [food] Baskin-Robbins, Danny's Subs, KFC, McDonald's, Sierra Mexican, Taco Bell, The Villa Rest., TJ's Rest., TJ's Rest., Wendy's [lodging] Comfort Inn, Sheraton [other] CVS Drug, Giant Foods

27 I-495 S around Washington

25b a US 1, Baltimore Ave, to Laurel, College Park, E [gas] 7-11, BP/dsl, Chevron, Exxon/dsl, Shell/24hr [food] 3 Bro's Rest., Arby's, Buffalo Wild Wings, Burger King, Dickey's BBQ, Domino's, El Mexicano, Jerry's Subs, KFC, McDonald's, Moose Creek Steaks, Papa John's, Pizza Hut/Taco Bell, Potbelly's, Quizno's, Subway, Wendy's [lodging] Holiday Inn [other] Advance Parts, Costco, CVS Drug, PetCo, Radio Shack, Rite Aid, URGENT CARE, US Agri Library, Verizon, W [gas] BP/24hr, Shell, Xtra [food] Burger King, China Buffet, College Park Diner, Dunkin Donuts, Hard Times Cafe, IHOP, Pizza Hut, Starbucks, Taco Bell [lodging] Clarion, Comfort Inn, Days Inn, EconoLodge, Hampton Inn, Howard Johnson, Ramada Ltd, Super 8 [other] GNC, Home Depot, Honda, Hyundai, Nissan, Shoppers Foods, to U of MD, vet, VW

24 (from sb), to metro

23 MD 201, Kenilworth Ave, **1 mi E** [lodging] Marriott/rest., **1 mi W on Greenbelt** [food] Atlanta Bread, Boston Mkt, Checker's, Chipotle Mexican, KFC, McDonald's, Popeye's, Quizno's, Silver Diner, TGIFriday's, Wendy's, William's Bistro [lodging] Courtyard, Hilton Garden, Residence Inn, Shell [other] Cadillac, CVS Drug, Giant Food/drug, Jo-Ann Fabrics, Marshall's, Staples, Target

22 Baltimore-Washington Pkwy, E [other] to NASA

WASHINGTON DC AREA

20b a MD 450, Annapolis Rd, Lanham, E [food] Burger King, Jerry's Subs, McDonald's, Red Lobster [lodging] Best Western, Days Inn/rest., Red Roof Inn [other] Ford/KIA, W [gas] 7-11, BP, Chevron/dsl, Liberty, Shell, Sunoco/24hr, Texaco [food] 5 Guys Burgers, Bojangles, Domino's, Dunkin Donuts, El Gran Chaparral, IHOP, KFC, Manny&Olga's Pizza, Popeye's, Quizno's, Subway, Wendy's [lodging] Sheraton [other] [H], $Value, Aamco, Advance Parts, Chevrolet, Chrysler/Dodge/Jeep, Curves, CVS Drug, Foodway Foods, Giant Foods, JustTires, Lincoln, Lowe's, Office Depot, Radio Shack, Shoppers Foods, Staples

19b a US 50, to Annapolis, Washington

17 MD 202, Landover Rd, to Upper Marlboro, E [food] Jasper's Rest., Outback Steaks, Ruby Tuesday [lodging] Holiday Inn Express, Radisson, W [other] FedEx Center, Sears/auto

16 Arena Dr, E [food] 5 Guys Burgers, 5 Guys Burgers, Bugaboo Creek Steaks, Bugaboo Creek Steaks, Carolina Kitchen, Carolina Kitchen, Chick-fil-A, Chick-fil-A, ChuckeCheese, ChuckeCheese, Golden Corral, Golden Corral, Kobe Japanese, Kobe Japanese, Momma Rosa, Momma Rosa, Panda Express, Panda Express, Qdoba, Qdoba, Quizno's, Quizno's, Stonefish Grill, Stonefish Grill, W [other] to Arena

15 MD 214, Central Ave, E [lodging] Extended Stay America, Hampton Inn [other] to Six Flags, W [gas] Exxon/dsl, Liberty, Shell, Texaco/dsl [food] A&W/LJ Silver, Checker's, Dunkin Donuts, IHOP, Jerry's Subs, KFC, McDonald's, Panda Express, Pizza Hut, Subway, Taco Bell, Wendy's [lodging] Comfort Inn, Country Inn&Suites [other] Family$, Goodyear/auto, Home Depot, NTB, Staples, U-Haul, URGENT CARE

13 Ritchie-Marlboro Rd, Capitol Hgts, W [gas] WaWa [food] Chick-fil-A [other] BJ Whse/gas

11 MD 4, Pennsylvania Ave, to Upper Marlboro, W [gas] Exxon, Shell, Sunoco [food] 5 Guys Burgers, Applebee's, Arby's, Domino's, IHOP, LJ Silver, Old Country Buffet, Pizza Hut, Starbucks, Subway, Taco Bell, Wendy's [other] $Tree, CVS Drug, Hancock Fabrics, JC Penney, Marshall's, PetCo, Shoppers Foods, st police, Staples, Target

9 MD 337, to Allentown Rd, E [gas] Shell/repair, Texaco [food] Arby's, Checker's, Dunkin Donuts, McDonald's, Popeye's [lodging] Days Inn, Quality Inn, Super 8 [other] [H], to Andrews AFB, U-Haul, W [gas] Sunoco

7 MD 5, Branch Ave, to Silver Hill, E [gas] Exxon, Getty, Sunoco [food] Dunkin Donuts, Wendy's, W [gas] Shell/Subway/dsl [food] Red Lobster [lodging] Holiday Inn Express [other] [H], BMW, Chrysler/Dodge/Jeep, Ford, KIA, Lincoln, Nissan, Scion/Toyota, VW

4b a MD 414, St Barnabas Rd, Marlow Hgts, E [gas] Citgo/dsl, Zip-in [food] Burger King, Checker's, IHOP, KFC, McDonald's, Outback Steaks, Wendy's [lodging] Red Roof Inn [other] $Tree, CVS Drug, GNC, Home Depot, K-Mart, Old Navy, Petsmart, Safeway Foods, Staples, W [gas] Exxon/dsl, Shell/autocare [food] China Best, McDonald's, Subway [other] Family$

= gas = food = lodging = other = rest stop

INTERSTATE 95 Cont'd

Exit #	Services
3b a	MD 210, Indian Head Hwy, to Forest Hgts, E Chevron, Shell, Sunoco Dunkin Donuts, Popeye's, Ranch House Rest., Subway, Taco Bell Clarion, Comfort Inn, Red Roof Inn Advance Parts, Aldi Foods, Radio Shack, Sav-A-Lot Foods, Shoppers Foods, USPO, W BP/dsl/24hr, Pure, Shell, Texaco 7-11, Burger King, CVS Drug, Family$, Giant Foods, Goodyear/auto, McDonald's, Papa John's, Popeye's, Radio Shack, Rite Aid, Subway
2b a	I-295, N to Washington
0mm	Maryland/Virginia state line, Potomac River, Woodrow Wilson Bridge

INTERSTATE 97

GLEN BURNIE

Exit #	Services
17	I-695. **I-97 begins/ends on I-695.**
16	MD 648, Ferndale, Glen Burnie, E BP, Shell Hong Kong Cafe, KFC, McDonald's, Rita's Custard, Wendy's $General, Giant Foods, W Citgo
15b a	MD 176 W, Dorsey Rd, Aviation Blvd, E BP, Shell KFC, McDonald's, Wendy's, W st police, to BWI
14b a	MD 100, Ellicott City, Gibson Island
13b a	MD 174, Quarterfield Rd, E 7-11, AP/dsl, Gulf Subway, The Grill WaWa, W Shell/dsl Chick-fil-A, Pizza Hut, Quiznos AT&T, Kohl's, Lowe's, Rite Aid, Sam's Club/dsl, Shoppers Foods, Walmart
12	MD 3, New Cut Rd, Glen Burnie, E Exxon, Sunoco Burger King, Fortune Cooky, Friendly's, Hardee's, Squisto NY Pizza, Subway, Wendy's H, Ace Hardware, Giant Foods, Goodyear/auto, Target, Walgreens, **E on Veterans Hwy** BP, Gulf, Royal Farms, WaWa Domino's, KFC, McDonald's, Taco Bell CVS Drug, vet
10b a	Benfield Blvd, Severna Park, E BP/dsl, Exxon/Quiznos/dsl, Transit/dsl/scales Baskin-Robbins/Dunkin Donuts, Hella's Rest., Ledo's Pizza 7-11, access to same as 12, KOA
7	MD 3, MD 32, Bowie, Odenton, E motel
5	MD 178 (from sb, no EZ return), Crownsville

I-97 begins/ends on US 50/301.

INTERSTATE 270

FREDERICK

Exit #	Services
32	**I-270 begins/ends on I-70, exit 53.**
31b a	MD 85, N 7-11, Sheetz/24hr, Shell/dsl, SouStates/dsl, Valero/dsl, Wawa/dsl Applebee's, Arby's, BJ's Rest., Bob Evans, Burger King, Checker's, Chick-fil-A, ChuckeCheese, Golden Corral, Jersey Mike's, KFC/Taco Bell, Longhorn Steaks, McDonald's, Olive Garden, Panera Bread, Papa John's, Peking Gourmet, Pizza Hut, Popeye's, Red Robin, Roy Rogers, Ruby Tuesday, Smashburger, Sonic, Subway, Tilted Kilt, UNO Grill, Waffle House Country Inn Suites, Days Inn, EconoLodge, Holiday Inn, Sleep Inn, Super 8 $Tree, AAA, Aamco, Audi, Barnes&Noble, Best Buy, Buick/GMC, CarMax, Chrysler/Dodge/Jeep, Costco/gas, Dick's, Harley-Davidson, Home Depot, Hyundai, JC Penney, Kohl's, Lincoln, Lowe's, Macy's, mall, Michael's, Mr Tire, Nissan, Office Depot, Petsmart, Ross, Sam's Club/dsl, Sears/auto, Staples, Target, Tires+, TJ Maxx, Verizon, Volvo, Walmart, S BP Cafe Rio, Chipotle Mexican, Cici's, Cracker Barrel, Firehouse Subs, Five Guys, IHOP, Jimmy John's, Macaroni Grill, McDonald's, Noodles&Co, Panda Express, Starbucks, TGIFriday's, TX Roadhouse Comfort Inn, Courtyard, Extended Stay America, Fairfield Inn, Hampton Inn, Hilton Garden, Homewood Suites, MainStay Suites, Residence Inn, TownePlace Suites Honda, Toyota/Scion
30mm	Monocacy River
28mm	scenic view wb, no rest rooms
26	MD 80, Urbana, N 7-11, Exxon Buffalo Wild Wings, China Taste, Dunkin Donuts, Foster's Grill, Ledo's Pizza, McDonald's, Waffle House
22	MD 109, to Barnesville, Hyattstown, N BP/dsl Hyattstown Deli Food+
21mm	**weigh/insp sta both lanes**
18	MD 121, to Clarksburg, Boyds, N camping, gas, Little Bennett Pk, S Blackhill Pk
16	MD 27, Father Hurley Blvd, to Damascus, N Chevron, Exxon, Free State/dsl, Sunoco Applebee's, Bob Evans, Burger King, Jersey Mike's Subs, McDonald's, Starbucks, Subway Extended Stay America, Hampton Inn AT&T, Best Buy, Giant Foods, GNC, Home Depot, Kohl's, Michael's, PepBoys, Petsmart, Target, TJ Maxx, Verizon, Walmart, S 7-11, BP, Exxon, Shell, Sunoco 5 Guys Burgers, Bailey's Grill, Baja Fresh, Burger King, Carrabba's, Chick-fil-A, Domino's, Dunkin Donuts, Hardtimes Cafe, IHOP, Jerry's Subs, Longhorn Steaks, McDonald's, Mi Rancho, Panera Bread, Pizza Hut, Quizno's, Red Robin, Ruby Tuesday, Starbucks, Subway, Taco Bell, Wendy's Fairfield Inn, Homestead Suites Giant Foods, Mercedes, NAPA, NTB, Office Depot, PetCo, Rite Aid, Safeway Foods, same as 15, SmartCar, USPO
15b a	MD 118, to MD 355, S Honda, Nissan, same as 16
13b a	Middlebrook Rd (from wb)
11	MD 124, Quince Orchard Rd, N Exxon, Shell Boston Mkt, ChuckeCheese, Honeybaked Ham, Ichiban Rest., KFC, McDonald's, Panera Bread, Popeye's, Subway Hilton, Holiday Inn, TownePlace Suites, Wyndham Garden Aamco, Acura, AT&T, Costco, CVS Drugs, Ford, Hyundai, JC Penney, JustTires, Lincoln, Lord&Taylor, Macy's, mall, Mazda, NAPA, Nissan, Ross, Sam's Club, Sears/auto, Toyota, VW, S Shell/dsl Chevy's Mexican, CiCi's Pizza, Jerry's Subs, Rita's Ice Cream, Starbucks Motel 6 Advance Parts, Chevrolet, Chrysler/Dodge/Jeep, Giant Foods, JoAnn Fabrics, McGruder's Foods, Rite Aid, Seneca Creek SP, Staples
10	MD 117, Clopper Rd (from wb), same as 11
9b a	I-370, to Gaithersburg, Sam Eig Hwy, **S on Washington Blvd** Chevron Joe's Crabshack, Macaroni Grill, Pizza Hut, Red Rock Grill, Subway, Uncle Julio's Courtyard Barnes&Noble, Kohl's, Target, Weis Mkt
8	Shady Grove Rd, N Chevron, Shell/dsl Bugaboo Creek Steaks, Burger King, Red Lobster Sheraton 7-11, AT&T, Best Buy, Home Depot, Office Depot, vet, S Thatsamore Courtyard, Crowne Plaza, Marriott, Residence Inn, Sleep Inn, SpringHill Suites H
6b a	MD 28, W Montgomery Ave, N H, S Shell Best Western
5b a	MD 189, Falls Rd
4b a	Montrose Rd, N gas, S Starbucks Harris Teeter, Walgreens, st police
2	I-270/I-270 spur diverges eb, converges wb
1b a	(I-270 spur) Democracy Blvd, E Marriott, W Exxon/dsl, Shell/dsl Macy's, mall, Nordstrom's, Sears
1	MD 187, Old Georgetown Rd, S Exxon Hamburger Hamlet H, Balducci's Foods, Giant Foods, GNC

I-270 begins/ends on I-495, exit 35.

GAITHERSBURG ROCKVILLE

MD

INTERSTATE 495 (DC)

See Virginia Interstate 495 (DC)

INTERSTATE 695 (BALTIMORE)

Exit #	Services
48mm	Francis Scott Key Br, Patapsco River
44	MD 695 (from nb)
43mm	**toll plaza**
42	MD 151 S, Sparrows Point (last exit before toll sb), E [gas] Citgo/dsl [other] North Point SP
41	MD 20, Cove Rd, W [gas] Royal Farms, WaWa [food] Burger King, McDonald's, Subway
40	MD 150, MD 151, North Point Blvd, (nb only)
39	Merritt Blvd, W [gas] BP [food] Burger King, McDonald's [other] $Tree, Aldi Foods, Ford, Giant Foods, Honda, Hyundai, JC Penney, Mazda, Mr Tire, Walmart
38b a	MD 150, Eastern Blvd, to Baltimore, E [gas] Royal Farms, W [food] Applebee's, Arby's, Burger King, Cactus Willy's Steaks, Checker's, Chick-fil-A, Dunkin Donuts [other] AT&T, Kia/Nissan, mall, Sears/auto, Staples, Walgreens
36	MD 702 S (exits left from sb), Essex
35	US 40, N [gas] Sunoco, WaWa/gas [food] Arby's, Bateman's Bistro, Chipotle Mexican, DQ, Dunkin Donuts, Grand Buffet, Longhorn Steaks, Panda Express, Panera Bread [other] Aldi Foods, Best Buy, Harley-Davidson, Home Depot, NTB, Office Depot, PetCo, same as 34, Sam's Club/gas, U-Haul, Walmart
34	MD 7, Philadelphia Rd, N [food] McDonald's, Wendy's [lodging] La Quinta [other] [H], $General, $Tree, Giant Foods, Goodyear/auto, Marshall's, S [gas] Exxon [other] same as 35, Walgreens
33b a	I-95, N to Philadelphia, S to Baltimore
32b a	US 1, Bel Air, N [gas] Exxon [food] Arby's, Bob Evans, Burger King, Denny's, Dunkin Donuts, Golden Corral, IHOP, McDonald's, Taco Bell [other] $Tree, 7-11, BJ's Whse, Giant Foods, K-Mart, Merchants Tire/auto, Mr Tire/auto, Toyota/Scion, Verizon, vet, S [gas] Shell [food] Baskin-Robbins/Dunkin Donuts, Carrabba's, McDonald's, Rita's Custard, Subway, Szechuan Taste [other] 7-11, Goodyear/auto
31c	MD 43 E (from eb, exits left)
31b a	MD 147, Harford Rd, N [gas] 7-11, BP, CF/dsl, Shell/dsl [food] Dunkin Donuts, Wendy's [other] Chrysler/Jeep, CVS Drug, Goodyear/auto, Honda, Mars Foods, VW, Walgreens
30b a	MD 41, Perring Pkwy, N [gas] Shell [food] 5 Guys Burgers, Burger King, Checker's, Chick-fil-A, Denny's, Dunkin Donuts, KFC, McDonald's, Popeye's, Rita's Custard, Subway, Taco Bell [other] Advance Parts, Chevrolet, Ford, Home Depot, Jo-Ann Fabrics, K-Mart, NTB, Office Depot, Ross, Safeway Foods, Shoppers Foods, Tuesday Morning, Verizon
29b	MD 542, Loch Raven Blvd, S [gas] BP, Gulf, Hess [food] Bel-Loch Diner, Hooters, McDonald's, Pizza Hut, Subway [lodging] Comfort Inn, Ramada Inn [other] Mr Tire, PepBoys
29a	Cromwell Bridge Rd, S [lodging] Best Western
28	Providence Rd, S [gas] Citgo [other] Royal Farms
27b a	MD 146, Dulaney Valley Rd, N [other] Hampton NHS, S [gas] Exxon [food] Bahama Breeze, Cheesecake Factory, PF Chang's, Starbucks, Stoney River Steaks [lodging] Sheraton [other] Barnes&Noble, Fresh Mkt, Macy's, mall
26b a	MD 45, York Rd, Towson, N [gas] BP, Exxon/dsl, Oceanic, Sunoco/dsl [food] Dunkin Donuts, Friendly's, Ocean Pride Rest., Pizza Hut, Subway [other] Best Buy, Kia, Mr Tire, NTB, Rite Aid, S [gas] Exxon, Shell [food] 5 Guys Burgers, Burger King, McDonald's

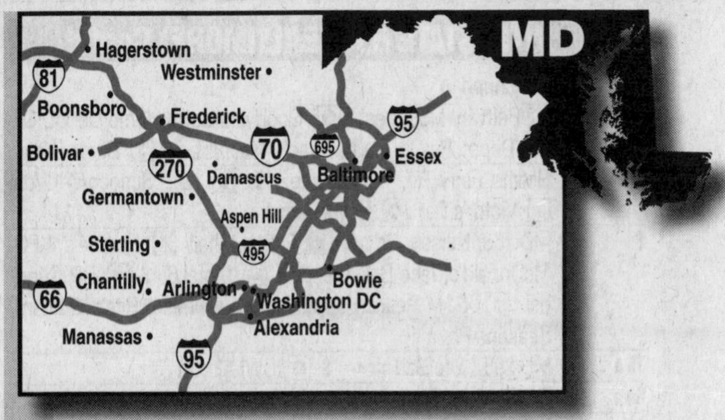

Exit #	Services
26b a	Continued [other] CVS Drug, Goodyear/auto, Honda, Hyundai, Lexus, Safeway Foods, vet, Walgreens
25	MD 139, Charles St, S [other] [H]
24	I-83 N, to York
23b	MD 25, Falls Rd, Baltimore, N [gas] Exxon/dsl
23a	I-83 S, MD 25 N, Baltimore
22	Greenspring Ave
21	MD 129, to Stevenson Rd, Park Hghts Rd
20	MD 140, Reisterstown Rd, Pikesville, N [gas] Exxon/7-11/dsl [food] Chipotle Mexican [other] AT&T, Barnes&Noble, Trader Joe's, S [gas] BP/dsl, Shell/dsl, Sunoco/Subway [food] McDonald's, Olive Branch Italian [lodging] Hilton, Ramada Inn [other] Target, vet
19	I-795, NW Expswy
18b a	MD 26, Randallstown, Lochearn, E [gas] Shell/dsl, Sunoco/dsl [food] Baskin-Robbins/Dunkin Donuts, KFC, Subway [other] $General, Family$, W [gas] BP, Exxon/dsl Shell [food] Burger King, Dunkin Donuts, McDonald's, Sonic, Subway, Taco Bell [other] [H], 7-11, auto repair, Firestone/auto, Giant Foods, Shoppers Foods, Walgreens
17	MD 122, Security Blvd, E [gas] BP/repair, Shell [food] City View Grill, Dunkin Donuts, McDonald's, Subway, Wendy's [lodging] Days Inn, Motel 6, Quality Inn [other] Chevrolet, Family$, Nissan, PriceRite Foods, Rite Aid, W [gas] Exxon/dsl, Sunoco [food] 5 Guys Burgers, Burger King, McDonald's, Panera Bread, Popeye's, Quiznos, Rita's Custard [lodging] Best Western [other] Best Buy, Ford, Macy's, mall, Old Navy, Rite Aid, Sears/auto
16b a	I-70, E to Baltimore, W to Frederick
15b a	US 40, Ellicott City, Baltimore, E [gas] BP [food] Burger King, Checker's, Chick-fil-A, ChuckECheese's, KFC, McDonald's, Panda Express, Quiznos, Shirley's Diner, Subway [lodging] Comfort Inn [other] $Tree, BigLots, CVS Drug, Dodge, Firestone/auto, Lowe's, Marshall's, Rite Aid, Ross, Safeway Foods/gas, Sam's Club/gas, Shoppers Foods, U-Haul, Walgreens, W [gas] BP/dsl, Exxon, Gulf, Shell [food] Applebee's, Bob Evans, CiCi's Pizza, McDonald's, Old Country Buffet, Popeye's, Starbucks, Subway, Taco Bell, TT Diner [lodging] Ramada Ltd [other] $Tree, Aamco, Chrysler/Jeep, Firestone/auto, Giant Foods, Goodyear/auto, Home Depot, Hyundai, Mr Tire, NTB, Office Depot, PepBoys, Petsmart, Staples, Toyota/Scion, Verizon, Walgreens, Walmart/McDonald's
14	Edmondson Ave, E [gas] Sunoco [food] Grilled Cheese&Co [other] Royal Farms, W [gas] CF [food] Papa John's
13	MD 144, Frederick Rd, Catonsville, W [gas] BP, CF, Gulf [food] Baskin-Robbins/Dunkin Donuts, McDonald's, Subway [other] 7-11
12c b	MD 372 E, Wilkens, E [other] [H]
11b a	I-95, N to Baltimore, S to Washington
10US 1	Washington Blvd (from wb only), E [gas] Royal Farms/dsl [food] 3 Bros Pizza, Chick-fil-A, Dunkin Donuts, Quiznos, Wendy's

MD

INTERSTATE 695 (BALTIMORE) Cont'd

10US 1	Continued Beltway Motel/rest. Goodyear/auto, Home Depot, Office Depot, PetCo, Radio Shack, Walmart, W Burger King
9	Hollins Ferry Rd, Lansdowne, E BP, Sunoco/7-11/dsl Victor's Deli Royal Farms
8	MD 168, Nursery Rd, N Exxon, Shell Hardee's, KFC, McDonald's, Taco Bell, Wendy's Motel 6, S BP, Citgo/dsl G&M Rest., Happy Garden Chinese, Rita's Custard, Seasons Pizza
7b a	MD 295, N to Baltimore, S BWI Airport
6b a	Camp Mead Rd (from eb)
5	MD 648, Ferndale, Shell, Xtra/7-11/dsl Checker's, Dunkin Donuts, Hot Wok Comfort Inn NAPA, police
4b a	I-97 S, to Annapolis
3b a	MD 2, Brooklyn Park, S Exxon, Hess, Royal Farms/dsl, Shell, Sunoco 5 Guys Burgers, Best Buffet, Bob Evans, BoneFish Grill, Checker's, Chick-fil-A, ChuckECheese's, Coldstone, Denny's, Golden Corral, HipHop Fish&Chicken, KFC, McDonald's, Panera Bread, Pappas Rest., Pizza Hut, Qdoba, Quiznos, Starbucks, Subway, Taco Bell Days Inn, Extended Stay America, Hampton Inn, La Quinta $Tree, Aamco, Advance Parts, Aldi Foods, Best Buy, BigLots, Buick/GMC, Dick's, Giant Foods, Hyundai, Just Tires, Lowe's, Office Depot, PetCo, Radio Shack, Salvo Parts, ShopRite Foods, Subaru, Target, Tuesday Morning, Verizon, Walgreens, Walmart
2	MD 10, Glen Burnie
1	MD 174, Hawkins Point Rd, S Citgo/deli/dsl

MASSACHUSETTS

STURBRIDGE

INTERSTATE 84

Exit #	Services
4 (11)	**I-84 begins/ends on I-90, Exit 9.**
3b a (9)	US 20, Sturbridge, **0-2 mi** N Citgo, Cumberland Farms Admiral O'Brien's, Burger King, Dunkin Donuts, Empire Village, Friendly's, McDonald's, Rovezzi's Ristorante, Smokehouse BBQ, Thai Place, Village Pizza EconoLodge, Hampton Inn, Quality Inn, Sturbridge Country Inn, Super 8 H, USPO, vet, **0-2 mi** S NE TrkStp/dsl, S&S, Shell/Dunkin Donuts/Subway Applebee's, Cracker Barrel, Uno Pizzaria, Wendy's Comfort Inn Marshall's, Michael's, Staples, Stop&Shop, Verizon, vet, Walmart
2 (5)	MA 131, to Old Sturbridge Village, Sturbridge, **2 mi** S Publick House, RV camping
4mm	wb, litter barrels
1 (3)	Mashapaug Rd, to Southbridge, S Mobil/dsl, Pilot/deli/dsl/scales/24hr/ @ Roy Rogers, Sbarro's Days Inn H
2mm	**weigh sta both lanes**
0.5mm	eb
0mm	Massachusetts/Connecticut state line

BOSTON AREA

INTERSTATE 90

Exit #	Services
140mm	**I-90 begins/ends near Logan Airport**
25	to I-93, to downtown Boston
24	to I-93, to downtown Boston
22 (134)	Presidential Ctr, downtown
20 (132)	MA 28, Alston, Brighton, Cambridge, N Courtyard, Doubletree Inn H, S Sunoco
131mm	**toll plaza**
19 (130)	MA Ave (from eb), N IHOP, McDonald's Day's Inn
17 (128)	Centre St, Newton, N Sheraton Cadillac, Chevrolet, Honda, Nissan
16 (125)	MA 16, W Newton, S Mobil/repair
15 (124)	I-95, N Marriott
123mm	**toll plaza**
14 (122)	MA 30, Weston
117mm	**Natick Travel Plaza eb,** Gulf/dsl Dunkin Donuts, McDonald's info
13 (116)	MA 30, Natick, S Getty, Gulf, Shell Bickford's, Boston Mkt, Bugaboo Creek Steaks, Burger King, Harvard's Steaks, Lotus Flower Chinese, McDonald's, Panera Bread, Papagino's, Quizno's Best Western, Red Roof Inn H, BJ's Whse, Home Depot, Isuzu, Kohl's, Lowe's, Macy's, mall, Marshalls, Target, USPO, Walmart
114mm	**Framingham Travel Plaza wb,** Gulf/dsl Boston Mkt, McDonald's info
12 (111)	MA 9, Framington, N Getty, Hess Acapulco Mexican, Dunkin Donuts, Molly Malone's Grill, Tin Alley Grill Motel 6, Sheraton H, S Chef Orient Chrysler/Isuzu/Jeep, mall, Target, Toyota/Scion
11a (106)	I-495, N to NH, S to Cape Cod
105mm	**Westborough Travel Plaza wb,** Gulf/dsl Boston Mkt, D'angelo, Dunkin Donuts, Papagino's gifts
11 (96)	MA 122, to Millbury, N UMA Med Ctr
10a (95)	MA 146
94mm	Blackstone River
10 (90)	I-395 S, to Auburn, I-290 N, Worcester, N Shell Piccadilly's Comfort Inn, Holiday Inn Express, S Shell/repair/24hr Applebee's, D'angelo's, Dunkin Donuts, Friendly's, Wendy's Fairfield Inn H, CVS Drug, Hyundai, Park'n Shop, TJ Maxx
84mm	**Charlton Travel Plaza wb** Gulf/dsl McDonald's info
80mm	**Charlton Travel Plaza eb** Exxon/dsl McDonald's st police, info
79mm	**toll plaza**
9 (78)	I-84, to Hartford, NYC, Sturbridge, access to H
67mm	Quaboag River
8 (62)	MA 32, to US 20, Palmer, **S on MA 32** Hess/Godfather's, Pride, Shell/dsl Jenny Chan's Chinese, McDonald's, Subway, Wendy's H, Big Y Foods, Chevrolet, CVS Drug, repair/transmissions, Rite Aid
58mm	Chicopee River
56mm	**Ludlow Travel Plaza wb** Gulf/dsl Boston Mkt, D'angelo
55mm	**Ludlow Travel Plaza eb** Gulf/dsl McDonald's

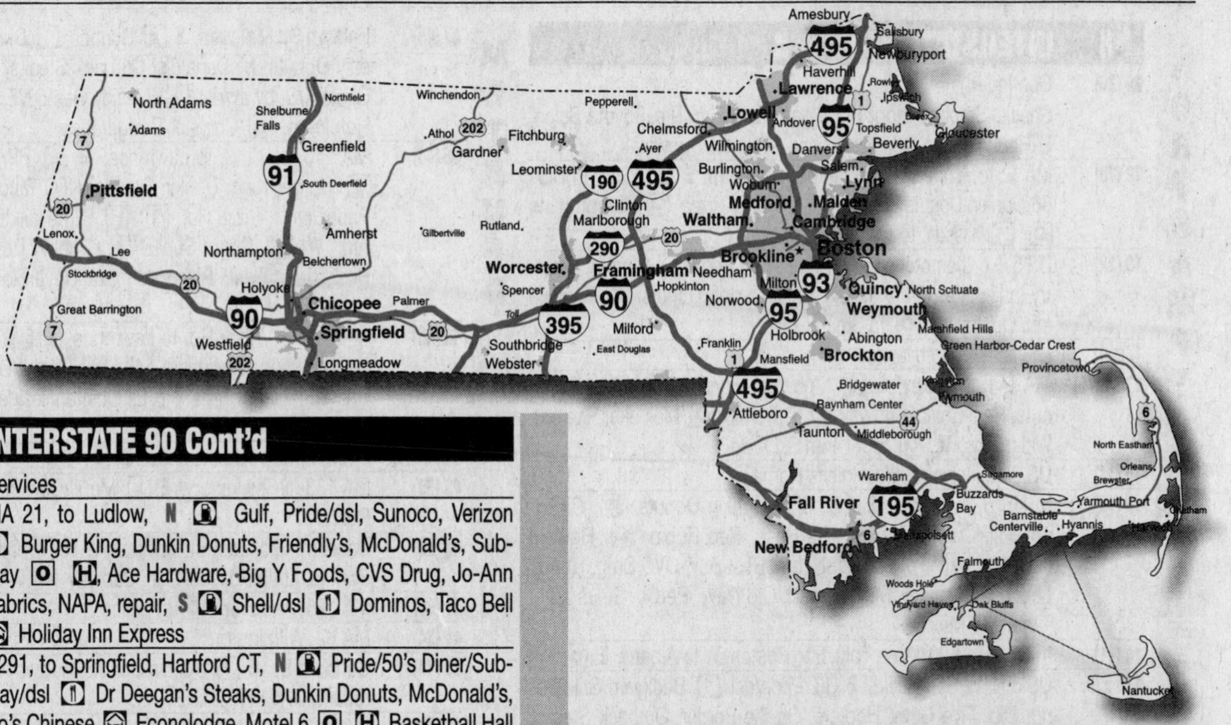

INTERSTATE 90 Cont'd

Exit #	Services
7 (54)	MA 21, to Ludlow, N Gulf, Pride/dsl, Sunoco, Verizon Burger King, Dunkin Donuts, Friendly's, McDonald's, Subway H, Ace Hardware, Big Y Foods, CVS Drug, Jo-Ann Fabrics, NAPA, repair, S Shell/dsl Dominos, Taco Bell Holiday Inn Express
6 (51)	I-291, to Springfield, Hartford CT, N Pride/50's Diner/Subway/dsl Dr Deegan's Steaks, Dunkin Donuts, McDonald's, Po's Chinese Econolodge, Motel 6 H, Basketball Hall of Fame, to Bradley Int Airport
5 (49)	MA 33, to Chicopee, Westover AFB, N 99 Rest., Applebee's, Arby's, Chipotle Mexican, Denny's, Dunkin Donuts, Friendly's, Panera Bread, Popeye's, Royal Buffet, Starbucks, Subway, Wendy's Days Inn, Hampton Inn, Quality Inn, Residence Inn $Tree, Aldi Foods, Big Y Foods, BJ's Whse/gas, Chrysler/Dodge/Jeep, Home Depot, Honda, Marshall's, Monroe, Nissan, Staples, Stop&Shop/gas, TownFair Tire, U-Haul, Walmart, S Pride/Dunkin Donuts/Subway/dsl Buick/GMC
46mm	Connecticut River
4 (46)	I-91, US 5, to Holyoke, W Springfield, N on US 5 Shell Dunkin Donuts Welcome Inn, S on US 5 Pride/dsl 5 Guys, Donut Dip, Hooters, On the Border, Outback Steaks, Piccadilly's, Subway Knights Inn, Red Roof Inn, Springfield Inn, Super 8 AAA, BMW, Honda/Lexus/Toyota/Scion, repair
41mm	st police wb
3 (40)	US 202, to Westfield, N Mobil Amalfi Pizza, Dunkin Donuts, S Citgo/Subway/dsl Friendly's, Wendy's EconoLodge, Holiday Inn Express H, repair
36mm	Westfield River
35.5mm	**runaway truck ramp eb**
29mm	**Blandford/Ludlow Travel Plaza wb,** Gulf/dsl McDonald's info, vending
20mm	1724 ft, highest point on MA Tpk
14.5mm	Appalachian Trail
2 (11)	US 20, to Lee, Pittsfield, N Citgo, Shell/dsl, Sunoco Arizona Pizza, Athena's Rest., Dunkin Donuts, Friendly's, McDonald's, Red Apple Chinese, Subway Morgan House/rest., Pilgrim Inn, Sunset Motel, Super 8 PriceChopper Foods, Rite Aid, True Value, S Orient Taste, Simply Grillicious, Subway, Villa Pizza Big Y Foods, Lee Outlets/famous brands
10.5mm	Hoosatonic River
8mm	**Lee Travel Plaza both lanes,** Gulf/dsl McDonald's atm, info, vending
4mm	**toll booth**
1 (2)	MA 41 (from wb, no return), to MA 102, W Stockbridge, the Berkshires, N Pleasant Valley Motel to Bousquet Ski Area
0mm	Massachusetts/New York state line

GREENFIELD

PITTSFIELD

INTERSTATE 91

Exit #	Services
55mm	Massachusetts/Vermont state line, call boxes
54mm	**parking area both lanes,**
28 (51)	US 5, MA 10, Bernardston, E Fox Inn, W Sunoco Antonio's II Ristorante, Four-leaf Clover Rest., Hillside Organic Pizza Country Corner Store, RV camping, USPO
27 (45)	MA 2 E (exits left from sb), Greenfield, E US 5 Gulf, Hess/Dunkin Donuts, Stop&Shop, Sunoco/dsl Burger King, Denny's Pantry, Domino's, Dunkin Donuts, Goodies Rest., McDonald's, Subway H, $General, Aubuchon Hardware, AutoZone, Bond Parts, Chrysler/Dodge/Jeep, Honda, Walgreens
26 (43)	MA 2 W, MA 2A E, Greenfield, E Planet/dsl, Shell/dsl Applebee's, Athens Pizza, China Gourmet, D'Angelo, Dunkin Donuts Quality Inn H, Chevrolet, Ford/Lincoln, Toyota, W Irving/Circle K, Valero 99 Rest., Asian Buffet, Friendly's, KFC/Pizza Hut/Taco Bell, McDonald's, Subway Days Inn, Hampton Inn $Tree, Big Y Foods, BJ's Whse, Family$, Home Depot, Radio Shack, Staples, to Mohawk Tr, Verizon
39mm	Deerfield River
37mm	**weigh sta both lanes**
25 (36)	MA 116 (from sb), S Deerfield, camping, hist dist, same as 24
24 (35)	US 5, MA 10, MA 116, Deerfield (no EZ return), E Irving/Circle K/Dunkin Donuts/Subway/dsl Red Roof Inn Final Markdown, vet, Yankee Candle Co, W Roady's Trkstp/diner/dsl/24hr 24hr Diner
34.5mm	**parking area both lanes**
23 (34)	US 5 (from sb), E Tom's Hot Dog Orchard Trailers, Rainbow Motel/camping
22 (30)	US 5, MA 10 (from nb), N Hatfield, W Diamond RV Ctr
21 (28)	US 5, MA 10, Hatfield, W Sunoco/dsl Subway Scottish Inn st police
20 (26)	US 5, MA 9, MA 10 (from sb), Northampton, W Hess/dsl, Pride/Dunkin Donuts/dsl Burger King, D'angelo's, KFC, McDonald's, PapaGino's Italian, Taco Bell H, AutoZone, Big Y Food/Drug, BigLots, Chevrolet, CVS Drug, Firestone/auto, Ford, Goodyear/auto, Honda, Hyundai, Kia, NAPA, Radio

INTERSTATE 91 Cont'd

NORTHAMPTON

20 (26)	Continued Shack, Staples, Stop&Shop/gas, TownFair Tire, Toyota/Scion, U-Haul, Verizon, VW, Walgreens, Walmart/Subway
19 (25)	MA 9, to Amherst, Northampton, **0-2 mi E** [gas] Gulf, Phillips 66/Dunkin Donuts, Shell/dsl [food] Primo Pizza [lodging] Hampton Inn [other] [H], Nissan, to Elwell SP, vet
18 (22)	US 5, Northampton, **E** [food] Page's Loft Rest. [lodging] Clarion, Country Inn&Suites (5mi), **W** [gas] Shell/Dunkin Donuts [lodging] Fairfield Inn, Quality Inn [other] to Smith Coll
18mm	scenic area both lanes
17b a (16)	MA 141, S Hadley, **E** [gas] Mobil/dsl, Shell/dsl [food] Dunkin Donuts, Real China, Subway [lodging] Days Inn [other] Meineke, Rite Aid, Walgreens, **W** [other] to Mt Tom Ski Area
16 (14)	US 202, Holyoke, **W** Soldier's Home
15 (12)	to US 5, Ingleside, **E** [gas] Shell/Dunkin Donuts [food] Chicago Grill, Cracker Barrel, JP's Rest., Red Robin [lodging] Howard Johnson [other] [H], Barnes&Noble, Best Buy, CVS Drug, Hobby Lobby, JC Penney, Macy's, mall, Old Navy, PetCo, Sears/auto, Target, TJ Maxx

SPRINGFIELD

14 (11)	to US 5, to I-90 (Mass Tpk), E to Boston, W to Albany, **E** [other] [H]
13b a (9)	US 5 N, W Springfield, **E** [gas] Pride/dsl [food] Backyard Grill, Donut Dip, Five Guys, Hooters, On-the-Border, Outback Steaks, Shallot Thai, Subway [lodging] Knights Inn, Red Roof Inn, Residence Inn, Springfield Inn, Super 8 [other] BMW, Lexus/Toyota/Scion, **W** [gas] Mobil/dsl, Pride/dsl [food] 99 Rest., Arby's, Bertucci's, Burger King, Cal's Grill, Carrabba's, Chili's, D'angelo's, Friendly's, IHOP, KFC, Longhorn Steaks, McDonald's, Nippon Grill, Olive Garden, Panera Bread, Pizza Hut, Tokyo Cuisine [lodging] Bel Air Inn, Candlewood Suites, Clarion, Days Inn, EconoLodge, Hampton Inn, Quality Inn, Red Carpet Inn, Travelodge [other] $Tree, Aldi Foods, AT&T, Chrysler/Dodge/Jeep, Costco, CVS Drug, Dick's, Fiat, GNC, Home Depot, Honda, Kohl's, Mazda, Michael's, Nissan, Staples, Stop&Shop, Subaru, TownFair Tire, Verizon
12 (8.5)	I-391 N, to Chicopee
11 (8)	Birnie Ave (from sb), **E** [gas] Mobil [other] [H]
10 (7.5)	Main St (from nb), Springfield, **E** [gas] Mobil
9 (7)	US 20 W, MA 20A E (from nb), **E** [food] McDonald's, **W** [gas] Pride/Subway/dsl
8 (6.5)	I-291, US 20 E, to I-90, **E** downtown
7 (6)	Columbus Ave (from sb), **E** [gas] Pride/Subway/dsl [lodging] Marriott, Sheraton, **W** [other] to Basketball Hall of Fame
6 (5.5)	Springfield Ctr, **E** [gas] Pride/Dunkin Donuts/Subway/dsl [food] Starbucks, **W** [food] Coldstone, Plan B Burger [other] Basketball Hall of Fame
5 (5)	Broad St, **E** [gas] Mobil/dsl [lodging] Hampton Inn [other] Hyundai, **W** [gas] Sunoco/dsl [food] Chicago Grill, Subway [lodging] Hilton Garden [other] Buick/GMC, same as 4
4 (4.5)	MA 83, Broad St, Main St, **E** [gas] Mobil/dsl [food] Antonio's Grinders [other] Hyundai, **W** [gas] Sunoco/dsl [food] Chicago Grill, Subway [lodging] Buick/GMC, Chevrolet, Hilton Garden, same as 5
3 (4)	US 5 N, to MA 57, Columbus Ave, W Springfield, **E** [gas] Sunoco [food] Antonio's Pizza, **W** [other] Chevrolet
2 (3.5)	MA 83 S (from nb), to E Longmeadow, **E** [food] Friendly's
1 (3)	US 5 S (from sb)
0mm	Massachusetts/Connecticut state line, callboxes begin/end

INTERSTATE 93

Exit #	Services
47mm	Massachusetts/New Hampshire state line, callboxes begin/end
48 (46)	MA 213 E, to Methuen, **E** [other] [H]

METHUEN

47 (45)	Pelham St, Methuen, **E** [gas] Sunoco [food] Dunkin Donuts, Heavenly Donuts, McDonald's, Outback Steaks, **W** [gas] BP, Irving/Circle K/Subway/dsl [food] Fireside Rest., NE Seafood [lodging] Day's Hotel/rest. [other] Chrysler/Dodge/Jeep
46 (44)	MA 110, MA 113, to Lawrence, **E** [gas] BP/repair, Mobil, Shell [food] Burger King, Dunkin Donuts, KFC/Taco Bell, McDonald's, PapaGino's, Pizza Hut [other] [H], $Tree, MktBasket Foods, Rite Aid, **W** [gas] Citgo, Super [food] Dunkin Donuts, Irish Cottage Rest., Jules Rest., Riverside Pizza, Royal Roast Beef [lodging] Passport Inn
45 (43)	Andover St, River Rd, to Lawrence, **E** [lodging] Courtyard, Homewood Suites, Wyndham, **W** [gas] Mobil/Dunkin Donuts [food] Chateu Italian, Chili's [lodging] La Quinta, Residence Inn, SpringHill Suites [other] vet
44b a (40)	I-495, to Lowell, Lawrence, **E** [other] [H]
43 (39)	MA 133, N Tewksbury, **E** [gas] Mobil/Dunkin Donuts, **W** [food] 99 Rest.
42 (38)	Dascomb Rd, East St, Tewksbury, **W** [gas] Citgo/dsl [food] Dunkin Donuts, Luna Rossa Italian, Subway [other] 7-11
41 (35)	MA 125, Andover, [other] st police
40 (34)	MA 62, Wilmington

BOSTON AREA

39 (33)	Concord St, **E** [food] Dunkin Donuts, Subway [other] Shriners Auditorium, URGENT CARE
38 (31)	MA 129, Reading, **W** [gas] Mobil/Dunkin Donuts/Subway/dsl [food] Burger King, Pacific Grove Chinese, Red Heat Tavern
37c (30)	Commerce Way, Atlantic Ave, **W** [food] Chipotle Mexican, Firehouse Subs, Starbucks [lodging] Red Roof Inn, Residence Inn [other] PetCo, Petsmart, Target, Verizon
37b a (29)	I-95, S to Waltham, N to Peabody
36 (28)	Montvale Ave, **E** [gas] Mobil [food] Deli Works, Dunkin Donuts, Kiotoya Japanese [lodging] Courtyard, **W** [gas] BP, Gulf [food] Bickford's Grille, Dunkin Donuts, McDonald's, Polcari's Italian, Wendy's [lodging] Best Western, Comfort Inn [other] [H]
35 (27)	Winchester Highlands, Melrose, **E** [other] [H] (no EZ return to sb)
34 (26)	MA 28 N (from nb, no EZ return), Stoneham, **E** [gas] Mobil [food] Friendly's [other] [H]
33 (25)	MA 28, Fellsway West, Winchester, **E** [other] [H]
32 (23)	MA 60, Salem Ave, Medford Square, **W** [lodging] Hyatt Place [other] [H], to Tufts U
31 (22)	MA 16 E, to Revere (no EZ return sb), **W** [gas] Fred's Gas, Mr. C's/dsl [food] Avellino's Italian, Burger King, Dunkin Donuts, Pizza Hut [other] AutoZone, Chrysler/Dodge/Jeep, Kia, Nissan, Staples
30 (21)	MA 28, MA 38, Mystic Ave, Somerville, **W** [gas] Mr. C's/dsl [food] Burger King [other] AutoZone, Lincoln
29 (20)	MA 28 (from nb), Somerville, **E** [food] 99 Rest., Dunkin Donuts [lodging] La Quinta [other] Home Depot, K-Mart, mall, Staples, TJ Maxx, **W** [gas] Gulf, Hess [other] Radio Shack, same as 30, Stop&Shop
28 (19)	Sullivans Square, Charles Town, downtown

BOSTON AREA

27	US 1 N (from nb)
26 (18.5)	MA 28 N, Storrow Dr, North Sta, downtown
25	Haymarket Sq, [other] Gov't Center
24 (18)	Callahan Tunnel, **E** [other] [airport]
23 (17.5)	High St, Congress St, **W** [lodging] Marriott
22 (17)	Atlantic Ave, Northern Ave, South Sta, [other] Boston World Trade Ctr
21 (16.5)	Kneeland St, ChinaTown
20 (16)	I-90 W, to Mass Tpk
19 (15.5)	Albany St (from sb), **W** [gas] Mobil/dsl [other] [H]
18 (15)	Mass Ave, to Roxbury, **W** [other] [H]
17 (14.5)	E Berkeley (from nb), **E** [other] New Boston Food Mkt
16 (14)	S Hampton St, Andrew Square, **W** [food] Applebee's, Olive Garden [lodging] Holiday Inn Express [other] Best Buy, Home Depot, Marshall's, Old Navy, Stop&Shop/gas, Target, TJ Maxx

INTERSTATE 93 Cont'd

BOSTON AREA

15 (13)	Columbia Rd, Everett Square, **E** [lodging] DoubleTree [other] JFK Library, to UMA, **W** [gas] Shell
14 (12.5)	Morissey Blvd (from nb no return), **E** [other] JFK Library, **W** [gas] Shell
13 (12)	Freeport St, to Dorchester, (from nb), **W** [gas] 7-11, BP [food] Boston Mkt, D'Angelo's, Deadwood Cafe, Freeport Tavern [lodging] Comfort Inn, Ramada [other] CVS Drug, Lambert's Mkt, NAPA-Care, Stop&Shop, Toyota/Scion
12 (11.5)	MA 3A S (from sb, no EZ return), Quincy, **E** [gas] repair, Shell, **W** [gas] Gulf/Dunkin Donuts, Hess [food] PapaGino's [other] AutoZone, CVS Drug, Lincoln, Staples, Verizon, Walgreens
11b a (11)	to MA 203, Granite Ave, Ashmont
10 (10)	Squantum Ave (from sb), Milton, **W** [other] [H]
9 (9)	Adams St, Bryant Ave, to N Quincy, **E** [gas] Milton Fuel [food] Dunkin Donuts, **W** [gas] Shell/repair
8 (8)	Brook Pkwy, to Quincy, Furnace, **E** [gas] Gulf/dsl, Mobil/dsl
7 (7)	MA 3 S, to Cape Cod (exits left from sb), Braintree, **E** [lodging] Marriott
6 (6)	MA 37, to Holbrook, Braintree, **E** [gas] Mobil/24hr [food] 99 Rest., Boardwalk Café, CA Pizza Kitchen, Cheesecake Factory, Chicago Grill, D'angelo's, Legal Seafood, TGIFriday's, Tokyo Japanese [other] Lord&Taylor, Macy's, mall, Nordstom's, Sears/auto, Target, **W** [gas] Citgo [food] Ascari Café, Wood Road Deli [lodging] Candlewood Suites, Extended Stay America, Hampton Inn, Holiday Inn Express [other] Ford, VW
5b a (4)	MA 28 S, to Randolph, Milton, **E** [gas] Citgo, Mobil/dsl, Mutual, Shell/dsl/24hr [food] Domino's, Dunkin Donuts, La Scala, Lombardo's, Picadilly's Pub, Randolph Cafe, Sal's Calzone Rest., Stash's Pizza, Wong's Chinese [lodging] Comfort Inn [other] AT&T
4 (3)	MA 24 S (exits left from sb), to Brockton
3 (2)	MA 138 N, to Ponkapoag Trail, Houghtons Pond
2b a (1)	MA 138 S, to Stoughton, Milton, **E** [other] golf, **W** [gas] BlueHill/dsl, Mobil, Shell/dsl [food] Dunkin Donuts [lodging] Homewood Suites
1 (0)	I-95 N, S to Providence. **I-93 begins/ends on I-95, exit 12.**

INTERSTATE 95

AMESBURY

Exit #	Services
89.5mm	Massachusetts/New Hampshire state line, **Welcome Ctr/[RS] sb, full [handicap] facilities, info, litter barrels [picnic]**
60 (89)	MA 286, to Salisbury, beaches, **E** [gas] Mobil/dsl [food] Cosmos Rest., Dunkin Donuts, Lena's Seafood Rest. [other] Black Bear Camping (seasonal)
59 (88)	I-495 S (from sb)
58b a (87)	Rd 110, to I-495 S, to Amesbury, Salisbury, **E** [gas] Sunoco/Dunkin Donuts/Subway/dsl [food] China Buffet, Niko's Place, Sylvan St Grille, Winner's Circle Rest. [other] Ford, U-Haul, vet, **W** [gas] Irving Gas/Circle K, Mobil, Sunoco/dsl [food] Acapulco's Mexican, Burger King, Dunkin Donuts, Friendly's, McDonald's, PapaGino's [lodging] Fairfield Inn [other] AT&T, Chevrolet, Stop&Shop, Verizon
57 (85)	MA 113, to W Newbury, **E** [gas] Mobil/dsl, Shell/dsl/repair, Sunoco [food] China One, D'angelo, Dunkin Donuts, Dunkin Donuts, Giuseppe's Italian, Hana Japan, McDonald's, Panera Bread, PapaGino's, Sal's Pizza, Wendy's [other] [H], 7-11, GNC, K-Mart, Marshall's, Midas, MktBasket Foods, Radio Shack, Rite Aid, Shaw's Foods, Verizon, Walgreens
56 (83)	Scotland Rd, to Newbury, **E** [other] st police
55 (82)	Central St, to Byfield, **E** [food] Gen Store Eatery, Parker River Grille, **W** [gas] Prime/dsl/repair
54b a (78)	MA 133, E to Rowley, W to Groveland, **E** [other] vet

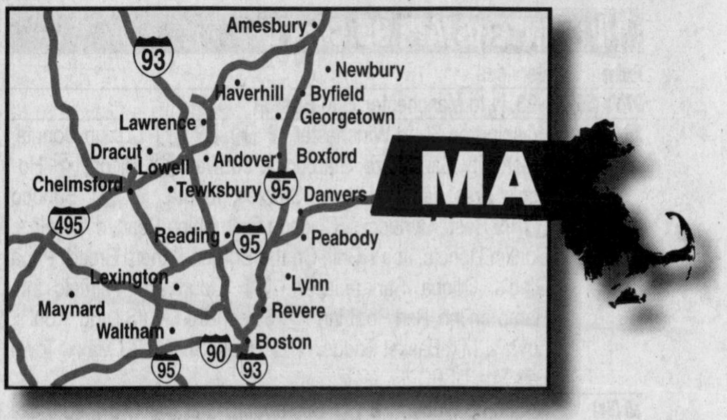

PEABODY

77mm	weigh sta both lanes
53b a (76)	MA 97, S to Topsfield, N to Georgetown
52 (74)	Topsfield Rd, to Topsfield, Boxford
51 (72)	Endicott Rd, to Topsfield, Middleton
50 (71)	US 1, to MA 62, Topsfield, **E** [gas] Gulf/dsl, Mobil/dsl [other] Honda, **W** [gas] S&S [food] Supino's Rest., Timothy's Rest., TX Roadhouse [lodging] DoubleTree, Knights Inn [other] CVS Drug, st police, Staples, Stop&Shop
49 (70)	MA 62 (from nb), Danvers, Middleton, **W** same as 50
48 (69)	Hobart St (from sb), **W** [food] Calitri's Italian [lodging] Comfort Inn, Extended Stay America, Motel 6 [other] Home Depot
47b a (68)	MA 114, to Middleton, Peabody, **E** [gas] Gulf/Dunkin Donuts, Sunoco [food] Dunkin Donuts, Honey Dew Donuts, McDonald's, Olive Garden, Outback Steaks, PapaGino's, Pizza Hut, Subway [other] Audi, Chevrolet, Chrysler/Dodge/Jeep, Infiniti, Lexus, Lowe's, NTB, [gas], Petsmart, Porsche, Subaru, TJ Maxx, Toyota/Scion, Trader Joe's, Verizon, vet, VW, Walmart, **W on US 1** [gas] Hess/dsl [food] Chili's, Hardcover Rest., TGIFriday's [lodging] Motel 6, Residence Inn, TownePlace Suites [other] Costco/gas, Home Depot, LandRover, Meineke, NAPA
46 (67)	to US 1, **W** [gas] Best, Global, Gulf/dsl, Sunoco/dsl [food] Dunkin Donuts, Honey Dew Donuts [other] auto repair
45 (66)	MA 128 N, to Peabody
44b a (65)	US 1 N, MA 129, **W** [gas] 7-11, Shell, Sunoco [food] Bertucci's, Bros Kouzina Rest., Carrabba's, Dunkin Donuts, Marco's Italian, Santarpio's Pizza, Sonic, Wendy's [lodging] Hampton Inn, Holiday Inn, Homewood Suites, Plaza Motel, SpringHill Suites [other] [H]
43 (61)	Walnut St, Lynnfield, **E** [other] to Saugus Iron Works NHS (3mi), **W** [lodging] Sheraton [other] golf
42 (62)	Salem St, Montrose, **E** [gas] Irving/Circle K/Subway, Sunoco [food] Dunkin Donuts, **W** [lodging] Sheraton
41 (60)	Main St, Lynnfield Ctr, **E** [gas] Shell

READING

40 (59)	MA 129, Wakefield Ctr, N Reading, **E** [food] Bellino's Italian, Honey Dew Donuts [other] city park, vet, **W** [gas] Gulf [food] Dunkin Donuts, Mandarin Chinese [other] Chevrolet, Mazda, REI
39 (58)	North Ave, Reading, **E** [lodging] Clarion [other] city park, Subaru, Volvo, **W** [gas] Shell/dsl [food] Bertucci's, Chili's, Fuddrucker's, Longhorn Steaks, Macaroni Grill, Oye's Rest., Starbucks [other] [H], Home Depot, Honda, Mkt Basket Foods, Staples, Stop&Shop Foods, URGENT CARE, Verizon
38b a (57)	MA 28, to Reading, **E** [gas] Gulf/repair, Hess/dsl, Mobil [food] 5 Guys Burgers, 99 Rest., Burger King, Burger King, D'Angelo's/PapaGino's, Dunkin Donuts, Dunkin Donuts, Subway, Uno Fresco Cafe [other] Advance Parts, AutoZone, CVS Drug, Ford, GNC, Marshall's, Michaels, Radio Shack, Stop&Shop/gas, Walgreens, **W** [gas] Eleven Variety, Mobil/dsl, Shell, Sunoco [food] Anthony's Roastbeef, Burger King, Calariso's Farm Stand, Domino's, Dunkin Donuts, Harrow's Chicken Pies, McDonald's, Sam's Bistro, Starbucks [other] Meineke

N INTERSTATE 95 Cont'd

Exit #	Services
37b a (56)	I-93, N to Manchester, S to Boston
36 (55)	Washington St, to Winchester, E [gas] BP [food] Dunkin Donuts, Fresh City, Sal's Pizza, Starbucks, Subway [lodging] Hilton [other] Hogan's Tires, Jaguar, Nissan, Staples, Toyota, W [gas] Sunoco [food] 99 Rest., Bertucci's, Chicago Grill, China Pearl, d'Angelo's, Dunkin Donuts, Joe's Grill, On the Border, Panera Bread, Papa Gino's, Qdoba, Sarku Japan [lodging] Courtyard, Fairfield Inn, Hampton Inn, Red Roof Inn [other] $Tree, AT&T, CVS Drug, Kohl's, Lowe's, Mkt Basket Foods, NTB, Radio Shack, TJ Maxx, Town Fair Tire, USPO
35 (54)	MA 38, to Woburn, E [food] Scoreboard Grill [lodging] Crowned Plaza [other] [H], W [gas] Mobil/dsl [food] Applebee's, Dunkin Donuts, Sichuan Garden [lodging] Extended Stay America [other] city park, CVS Drug, Stop&Shop Foods
34 (53)	Winn St, Woburn
33b a (52)	US 3 S, MA 3A N, to Winchester, E [food] Bickford's Grille, Café Escadrille, Capital Grille, ChuckeCheese, Dunkin Donuts, Outback Steaks, Panera Bread, Paparazzi's, Subway [other] [H], AAA, CVS Drug, Honda, Marshall's, Michael's, Roche Bro's Foods, W [gas] Hess, Prime [lodging] Marriott [other] [H], Audi/Porsche, Kia, repair
32b a (51)	US 3 N, MA 2A S, to Lowell, E [gas] Mobil, Shell [food] Burger King, d'Angelo's, Dunkin Donuts, McDonald's, Subway [lodging] Hilton Garden [other] Best Buy, Mkt Basket Foods, Old Navy, PetCo, Trader Joe's, Verizon, W [food] Border Cafe, Cheesecake Factory, Chicago Grill, Chili's, Legal Seafoods, Macaroni Grill, Pizzaria Regina [lodging] Candlewood Suites, Homestead Suites [other] Barnes&Noble, Macy's, mall, Nordstrom, Sears/auto, Staples
31b a (48)	MA 4, MA 225, Lexington, E [gas] Gulf, Mobil/dsl/repair [food] Alexander's Pizza, Starbucks [other] Curves, Stop&Shop, Walgreens, W [gas] Gulf, Shell [food] d'Angelo's, Dunkin Donuts, Firebox BBQ, Friendly's, Margarita's, McDonald's, Papa Gino's [lodging] Bedford Plaza Hotel, Quality Inn, Travelodge [other] Staples, TJ Maxx, vet
30b a (47)	MA 2A, Lexington, E [gas] Sunoco/Dunkin Donuts/dsl [other] [H], W [lodging] ALoft, Element Hotel [other] Hanscom AFB, to MinuteMan NP
46.5mm	**travel plaza nb** [gas] Gulf/dsl [food] Honey Dew Donuts, McDonald's [other] gifts
29b a (46)	MA 2 W, Cambridge
28b a (45)	Trapelo Rd, Belmont, E [gas] Gulf/dsl, Mobil/dsl [food] Boston Mkt, Burger King, Dunkin Donuts, Friendly's, McDonald's, Panera Bread, Papa Gino's [other] AT&T, city park, Radio Shack, Shaw's Foods/Osco Drugs
27b a (44)	Totten Pond Rd, Waltham, E [gas] Shell [food] Naked Fish Rest. [lodging] Best Western, Courtyard, Hilton Garden, Holiday Inn Express, Home Suites, Westin Hotel, W [food] Bertucci's Rest., Green Papaya Thai [lodging] Embassy Suites/The Grill [other] AT&T, Costco, Home Depot
26 (43)	US 20, to MA 117, to Waltham, E [gas] Sunoco/dsl, W [gas] Mobil/dsl [food] Chicago Grill [other] NTB, vet
25 (42)	I-90, MA Tpk
24 (41)	MA 30, Newton, Wayland, E [gas] Hess [lodging] Marriott/rest.
23 (40)	Recreation Rd (from nb), to MA Tpk
22b a (39)	Grove St, E [lodging] Holiday Inn Express [other] golf
38.5mm	**travel plaza sb** [gas] Gulf/dsl [food] Honey Dew Donuts, McDonald's [other] gifts
21b a (38)	MA 16, Newton, Wellesley, E [other] [H], W [gas] Sunoco [food] Dunkin Donuts, House of Pizza, Paparazzi, Starbucks
20b a (36)	MA 9, Brookline, Framingham
19 (35)	Highland Ave, Newton, Needham, E [gas] Hess [food] Acupulcos, Chipotle Mexican, D'Angelo's, Mandarin Cuisine, Mighty Subs,
19 (35)	Continued Panera Bread, Pronto Bistro, Starbucks [lodging] Sheraton/rest. [other] AAA, CVS Drug, Marshall's, PetCo, Radio Shack, Staples, TJ Maxx, W [food] Bickford's [other] Chevrolet, Ford
18 (34)	Great Plain Ave, W Roxbury
33.5mm	**parking area sb, litter barrels** [phone]
17 (33)	MA 135, Needham, Wellesley
32mm	**truck turnout sb**
16b a (31)	MA 109, High St, Dedham, W [gas] Mobil/dsl
15b a (29)	US 1, MA 128, **0-2 mi** E [gas] Gulf, Monro/service [food] Bugaboo Creek Steaks, Chili's, Domino's, Joe's Grill, Panera Bread, PapaGino's, PF Chang's, TGIFriday's [lodging] Fairfield Inn, Holiday Inn, Residence Inn [other] AT&T, Best Buy, BJ's Whse, Costco, CVS Drug, Lincoln, LL Bean, NTB, PepBoys, PetCo, Staples, Star Foods, Tuesday Morning, Verizon, vet, Volvo, Walgreens, Whole Foods Mkt, **0-2 mi** W [gas] Irving/dsl, Shell/dsl/24hr [food] Burger King, Dunkin Donuts, Jade Chinese, McDonald's [lodging] Budget Inn [other] AAA, AT&T, Audi/Porsche, Buick/GMC, Chevrolet, Chrysler/Dodge/Jeep, Fiat, Honda, Kia, Mercedes, Toyota/Scion
14 (28)	East St, Canton St, E [lodging] Hilton
27mm	[RS] **sb, full** [handicapped] **facilities, litter barrels** [phone] [picnic]
13 (26.5)	University Ave
12 (26)	I-93 N, to Braintree, Boston, motorist callboxes end nb
11b a (23)	Neponset St, to Canton, E [gas] Citgo/repair, Sunoco [food] Dunkin Donuts, Rosario's Grill, **2 mi** W **on US 1** [gas] Gulf, Sunoco [food] Jake&Joe's [lodging] Hampton Inn, The Chateau [other] [H], Chevrolet, Ferrari, Hyundai, Maserati, Nissan
22.5mm	Neponset River
10 (20)	Coney St (from sb, no EZ return), to US 1, Sharon, Walpole, **1 mi** W **on US 1** [gas] Mobil [food] 5 Guys Burgers, 99 Rest., Bertucci's, Chili's, Chipotle Mexican, Dunkin Donuts, Friendly's, HoneyDew Donuts, IHOP, McDonald's, Old Country Buffet, Outback Steaks, Panda Express, Panera Bread, PapaGino's, Pizza Hut, Starbucks, Subway, Taco Bell, TGIFriday's, TX Roadhouse [lodging] Courtyard, Residence Inn, Sheraton [other] Acura, Advance Parts, Barnes&Noble, CVS Drug, Home Depot, Kohl's, Lexus, mall, Old Navy, PetCo, Radio Shack, Staples, Stop&Shop, TownFair Tire, VW, Walgreens
9 (19)	US 1, to MA 27, Walpole, W [gas] Gulf, Mobil/dsl [food] Applebee's, Asia Treasures, Dunkin Donuts, Starbucks [lodging] Boston View, EconoLodge, Holiday Inn Express [other] BigY Foods/drug, same as 10, Stop&Shop, Walmart
8 (16)	S Main St, Sharon, E [food] Dunkin Donuts [other] Rite Aid, Shaw's Foods, whaling museum
7b a (13)	MA 140, to Mansfield, E [food] 99 Rest., Domino's, Piccadilly's [lodging] Comfort Inn, Courtyard, Holiday Inn, Red Roof Inn, Residence Inn., W [gas] Shell/HoneyDew Donuts/dsl [food] Dunkin Donuts, PapaGino's [other] AT&T
6b a (12)	I-495, S to Cape Cod, N to NH
10mm	**Welcome Ctr/**[RS] **nb, full** [handicapped] **facilities, info, litter barrels, petwalk** [phone] [picnic]
9mm	**truck parking area sb**
5 (7)	MA 152, Attleboro, E [other] [H], W [gas] Gulf/dsl [food] Bill's Pizza, Piccadilly Rest., Wendy's [other] Shaw's Foods/Osco Drug
4 (6)	I-295 S, to Woonsocket
3 (4)	MA 123, to Attleboro, E [gas] Shell/dsl [food] Dunkin Donuts [other] [H], zoo
2.5mm	**parking area/weigh sta both lanes, litter barrels, no restrooms**
2b a (1)	US 1A, Newport Ave, Attleboro, E [gas] Mobil/dsl, Shell [food] Archie's Pizza, HoneyDew Donuts, McDonald's, Olive Garden,

LEXINGTON

NEWTON

DEDHAM

ATTLEBORO

INTERSTATE 95 Cont'd

2b a (1)	Continued Spumoni's Italian [other] Home Depot, K-Mart, Monroe's Service, W [gas] BP
1 (.5)	US 1 (from sb), E [lodging] Days Inn [other] Kia, Rite Aid, Volvo, W [gas] Hess
0mm	Massachusetts/Rhode Island state line

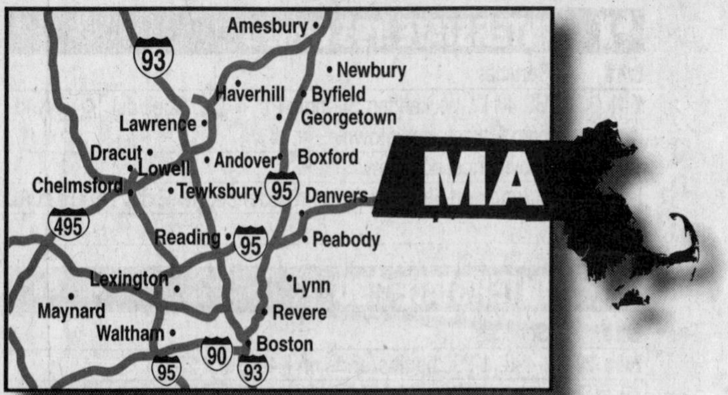

INTERSTATE 195

Exit #	Services
22 (41)	I-495 N, MA 25 S, to Cape Cod. **I-195 begins/ends on I-495, exit 1.**
21 (39)	MA 28, to Wareham, N [gas] Maxi/dsl/24hr [food] Longhorn Steaks, Pomodore's Italian, Qdoba Mexican, Red Robin [other] Best Buy, JC Penney, LL Bean, Lowe's, Michaels, Old Navy, PetCo, Staples, Target, TJ Maxx, S [gas] Irving/dsl, Mobil/Dunkin Donuts/dsl [other] [H], repair
37mm	**parking area eb, boatramp, info,**
36mm	Sippican River
20 (35)	MA 105, to Marion, S [other] RV camping (seasonal)
19b a (31)	to Mattapoisett, S [gas] Mobil [food] Nick's Pizza, Panino's Rest., Ying Dynasty [other] USPO
18 (26)	MA 240 S, to Fairhaven, **1 mi** S [gas] 7-11, Valero/dsl [food] 99 Rest., Burger King, Dunkin Donuts, Jake's Diner, McDonald's, PapaGino's, Pasta House, Pizza Hut, Subway, Sweet Ginger Asian, Taco Bell, Wendy's [lodging] Hampton Inn [other] $Tree, AutoZone, Brahman Handbags, Buick/GMC, GNC, K-Mart, Marshalls, Mazda, Radio Shack, Shaw's Foods, Staples, Stop&Shop/gas, Sullivan Tire, TownFair Tire, Verizon, Walgreens, Walmart
25.5mm	Acushnet River
17 (24)	Coggeshall St, (from wb only), New Bedford, N [gas] 7-11/gas, Petro, Sunoco [food] Dunkin Donuts, HoneyDew Donuts, McDonald's, Papa Johns, Subway [other] Market Basket Foods, same as 16
16 (23)	Washburn St (from eb), N [gas] Sunoco [food] McDonald's, Papa John's
15 (22)	MA 18 S, New Bedford, S [gas] Lukoil [lodging] Fairfield Inn [other] hist dist, to downtown, Whaling Museum
14 (21)	Penniman St (from eb), New Bedford, downtown
13b a (20)	MA 140, N [other] [airport], S [gas] 1 Stop, Sunoco [food] Dunkin Donuts [other] [H], Buttonwood Park/zoo, CVS Drug, Honda, Shaw's Foods, Walgreens
12b a (19)	N Dartmouth, S [gas] Hess, Mobil/dsl [food] 5 Guys Burgers, 99 Rest., Applebee's, Azuma Asian, Burger King, ChuckeCheese, Coldstone, Dunkin Donuts, Friendly's, IHOP, Jimmy's Pizza, McDonald's, Old Country Buffet, Olive Garden, Panera Bread, PapaGino's, Peking Garden, Quiznos, Rose&Vicki's Bistro, Ruby Tuesday, Subway, Taco Bell, TGIFriday's, Tropical Smoothie, TX Roadhouse, Wendy's [lodging] Residence Inn [other] $Tree, AT&T, Barnes&Noble, Best Buy, BJ's Whse/gas, Chevrolet, Curves, Dick's, Firestone/auto, JC Penney, Kohl's, Lowe's, Macy's, mall, Michael's, Nissan, Old Navy, PetCo, Sears/auto, st police, Stop&Shop/gas, Target, TJ Maxx, TownFair Tire, Toyota/Scion, USPO, Verizon, Walgreens, Walmart
11b a (17)	Reed Rd, to Dartmouth, **2 mi** S [gas] Shell
10 (16)	MA 88 S, to US 6, Westport, S [gas] Gulf [other] CVS Drug, same as 9
9 (15.5)	MA 24 N (from nb), Stanford Rd, Westport, S [gas] Rte 6 Gas, Supreme, Valero [food] Dunkin Donuts, Galley Grill [lodging] Hampton Inn [other] White's Hospitality
8b	MA 24 N, (exits left from eb)

FALL RIVER

8a (15)	MA 24 S, Fall River, Westport
7 (14)	MA 81 S, Plymouth Ave, Fall River, N [gas] BP, Hess [food] 99 Rest., Boston Mkt, Burger King, D'angelo's Rest., Dunkin Donuts, HoneyDew Donuts, KFC, Subway, Wendy's [other] [H], CVS Drug, S [gas] Gulf, Shell [food] Applebee's, McDonald's [other] Stop&Shop, Sullivan Tire, Walgreens
6 (13.5)	Pleasant St, Fall River, downtown
5 (13)	MA 79, MA 138, to Taunton, S [gas] 7-11, Hess [food] Dunkin Donuts
12mm	Assonet Bay
4b a (10)	MA 103, to Swansea, Somerset, N [gas] BP [food] Rogers Rest. [other] repair, vet, S [gas] Shell/24hr [food] Jillian's Grill [lodging] Quality Inn, Super 8
3 (8)	US 6, to MA 118, Swansea, Rehoboth, N [gas] Citgo/dsl, Hess, Mobil/Dunkin Donuts [food] Friendly's, McDonald's, Subway, Thai Taste, Wendy's [other] $Tree, BigLots, CarQuest, Firestone/auto, Jo-Ann Fabrics, Macy's, mall, Marshall's, Old Navy, Price Rite Foods, Radio Shack, Sears/auto, Target, S [gas] Gulf [food] Anthony's Seafood [lodging] Swansea Motel [other] Kia, NAPA
6mm	[RS] **eb, full [handicapped] facilities, litter barrels, petwalk [phone] [picnic]**
5.5mm	**parking area wb**
2 (5)	MA 136, to Newport, S [gas] Mobil/24hr, Shell/24hr [food] Cathay Pearl Chinese, Dunkin Donuts, McDonald's, Michael's Rest., Subway [other] CVS Drug
3mm	**weigh sta both lanes**

SEEKONK

1 (1)	MA 114A, to Seekonk, N [gas] Citgo, Gulf, Shell/24hr [food] 99 Rest., Dunkin Donuts, HoneyDew Donuts, Lums Sandwiches, Newport Creamery [lodging] Motel 6 [other] vet, S [gas] Hess/dsl, Mobil/24hr, Stop&Shop Gas/repair [food] 1149 E Rest., 5 Guys Burgers, Applebee's, BigLots, Buca Italian, Burger King, Chili's, D'Angelo's, Dicky's BBQ, Diparma Italian, Dunkin Donuts, Friendly's, McDonald's, Old Country Buffet, Outback Steaks, Panera Bread, PapaGino's, Starbucks, Subway, Taco Bell, TGIFriday's, Wendy's [lodging] Best Western, Comfort Inn, Extended Stay America, Hampton Inn, Knights Inn, Mary's Motel, Ramada Inn, Town&Country Motel [other] $Tree, Acura, Advance Parts, AT&T, Best Buy, BigLots, Bob's Stores, Dick's, Firestone/auto, Home Depot, Kohl's, Lowe's, Michael's, PepBoys, PetCo, Sam's Club, Staples, Stop&Shop Foods, Target, TJMaxx, TownFair Tire, Tuesday Morning, Verizon, Walmart
0mm	Massachusetts/Rhode Island state line. **Exits 8-1 are in RI**

PROVIDENCE

8 (5)	US 1A N, Pawtucket, S [gas] Mobil/dsl [food] Subway [other] CVS Drug
7 (4)	US 6 E, CT 114 S, to Barrington, Seekonk
6 (3)	Broadway Ave, N [gas] Speedy AutoService, S [gas] Shell, Sunoco/dsl
5 (2.5)	RI 103 E, Warren Ave
4 (2)	US 44 E, RI 103 E, Taunton Ave, Warren Ave, N [gas] Sunoco
3 (1.5)	Gano St, N [other] Wyndham Garden

INTERSTATE 195 Cont'd

Exit #	Services
2 (1)	US 44 W, Wickenden St, India Pt, N Shell/dsl Wyndham Garden, downtown
1 (.5)	Providence, downtown

I-195 begins/ends on I-95, exit 20 in Providence, RI. Exits 1-8 are in RI.

INTERSTATE 290

Exit #	Services
26b a (20)	I-495. **I-290 begins/ends on I-495, exit 25.**
25b a (17)	Solomon Pond Mall Rd, to Berlin, N Bertucci's, Olive Garden, TGIFriday's Comfort Inn, Residence Inn Best Buy, JC Penney, Macy's, mall/foodcourt, Old Navy, Sears/auto, Target, S Guiseppe's Grill
24 (15)	Church St, Northborough
23b a (13)	MA 140, Boylston, N Citgo/Dunkin Donuts/dsl
22 (11)	Main St, Worchester, N Dunkin Donuts
21 (10)	Plantation St (from eb), N Dunkin Donuts, same as 20
20 (8)	MA 70, Lincoln St, Burncoat St, N Gulf/Subway 5 Guys Burgers, 5&Diner, Crown Chicken, Denny's, Dunkin Donuts, KFC, McDonald's, PapaGino's, Plaza Azteca, Ruby Tuesday, Taco Bell, TX Roadhouse, Wendy's Quality Inn $Tree, Aldi Foods, AutoZone, Barnes&Noble, CVS Drug, Dick's, Lowe's, Radio Shack, Staples, Stop&Shop, Target, USPO, Walgreens
19 (7)	I-190 N, MA 12
18	MA 9, Framington, Ware, N H, Worcester Airport
16	Central St, Worcester, N 99 Rest., Starbucks Crowne Plaza, Hilton Garden, mall
14	MA 122, Barre, Worcester, downtown
13	MA 122A, Vernon St, Worcester, downtown
12	MA 146 S, to Millbury
11	Southbridge St, College Square, N Shell/dsl Golden House Chinese, Wendy's Family$
10	MA 12 N (from wb), Hope Ave
9	Auburn St, to Auburn, E BP, Shell Arby's, Auburn Town Pizza, Dunkin Donuts, McDonald's, PapaGino's, Starbucks, Yong Shing Comfort Inn, Holiday Inn Express (1mi), La Quinta Acura, Macy's, mall, Sears/auto, Shaw's Foods, TownFair Tire
8	MA 12 S (from sb), Webster, W Shell Holiday Inn Express
7	I-90, E to Boston, W to Springfield. **I-290 begins/ends on I-90.**

WORCESTER

INTERSTATE 395

Exit #	Services
	I-395 begins/ends on I-290, exit 10.
7 (12)	to I-90 (MA Tpk), MA 12, E Shell Piccadilly's Holiday Inn Express
6b a (11)	US 20, E BP, Gulf Frank&Nancy's Cafe Honda/VW, NAPA, truck tires/repair, W Shell Chuck's Steakhouse, Dunkin Donuts, Friendly's Fairfield Inn, Hampton Inn BJ's Whse, Buick/Cadillac/GMC, Chevrolet, Ford, Home Depot, Nissan, TJ Maxx, transmissions
5 (8)	Depot Rd, N Oxford
4b a (6)	Sutton Ave, to Oxford, E MktBasket Foods, W Cumberland Farms, Mobil/24hr Dunkin Donuts, McDonald's, NE Pizza, Subway, Veranda Cafe Cahill's Tire/repair, CVS Drug, Home Depot, MktBasket Foods, Verizon
3 (4)	Cudworth Rd, to N Webster, S Oxford
2 (3)	MA 16, to Webster, E RV Camping, Subaru, W BP/repair, Gulf, Hi-Lo Gas, Sunoco Burger King, D'angelo's, Dunkin Donuts, Empire Wok, Friendly's, HoneyDew Donuts, KFC/Taco Bell, McDonald's, PapaGino's H, Advance Parts, AT&T, Consumer Parts, CVS Drug, Ford, PriceChopper Foods, Rite Aid, Verizon, vet, Walgreens
1 (1)	MA 193, to Webster, E H, W Citgo/dsl Golden Greek Rest., Wind Tiki Chinese Goodyear/auto
0mm	Massachusetts/Connecticut state line

OXFORD

MA

INTERSTATE 495

Exit #	Services
119	**I-495 begins/ends on I-95 exit 59.**
55 (119)	MA 110 (from nb, no return), to I-95 S, E Irving/Circle K, Mobil, Sunoco/dsl Acupulco Mexican, Burger King, Dunkin Donuts, Friendly's, McDonald's, PapaGino's Fairfield Inn AT&T, Chevrolet, Stop&Shop, Verizon, W Gulf CVS, NAPA
54 (118)	MA 150, to Amesbury, W RV camping
53 (115)	Broad St, Merrimac, W Citgo/repair Dunkin Donuts
114mm	**parking area sb (6am-8pm)**, litter barrels, restrooms
	52 (111) MA 110, to Haverhill, E Seafood Etc H, W Racing Mart Biggart Ice Cream, Dunkin Donuts
52 (111)	MA 110, to Haverhill, E Seafood Etc H, W Racing Mart Biggart Ice Cream, Dunkin Donuts
110mm	**parking area nb, litter barrels**
51 (109)	MA 125, to Haverhill, E Gulf Bros Pizza, China King, Dunkin Donuts H, Family$, W Mobil/dsl Applebee's, Burger King, Dunkin Donuts, Friendly's, Li's Asian, Longhorn Steaks, Lucky Corner Chinese, McDonald's, Mr Mikes Grill, Starbucks, Taco Bell, Tuscan House Pizza, Wendy's Monro Service
50 (107)	MA 97, to Haverhill, W Ford, Target
49 (106)	MA 110, to Haverhill, E Gulf, Sunoco 99 Rest., Athens Pizza, Dunkin Donuts, McDonald's, Oriental Garden, PapaGino's Best Western, Hampton Inn Buick/Chevrolet/GMC, Chrysler/Dodge/Jeep, CVS Drug, Marshall's, MktBasket Foods, Walgreens
105.8mm	Merrimac River
48 (105.5)	MA 125, to Bradford, E BJ's Whse/gas
47 (105)	MA 213, to Methuen, **1-2 mi** W Burger King, ChuckeCheese, Friendly's, Joe's Crabshack, McDonald's, New Tokyo, Olive Garden, OrangeLeaf, Santana Rae's Mexican, Starbucks, TGIFriday's, Wendy's H, Home Depot, Marshalls, MktBasket Foods, Old Navy, Radio Shack, Stop&Shop, Target, The Mann Orchards/Bakery, Walmart/Subway
46 (104)	MA 110, E Giovanni's Deli, Pleasant Valley Gas, Sunoco, W H
45 (103)	Marston St, to Lawrence, W Chevrolet, Honda, Kia, Nissan, VW
44 (102)	Merrimac St, to Lawrence
43 (101)	Mass Ave
42 (100)	MA 114, E Gulf, Mobil, Wave Bertucci's, Boll Wood Grill, Boston Mkt, Burger King, Burtons Grill, Chipotle Mexican, Dunkin Donuts, Friendly's, Lee Chin Chinese, Panera Bread Holiday Inn Express Ace Hardware, CVS Drug, Kohl's, MktBasket Foods, PetCo, Staples, TJ Maxx, Walgreens, W Denny's, Dunkin Donuts, KFC, Little Caesar's, Pizza Hut/Taco Bell, Subway, Wendy's H, Advance Parts, Family$, Marshall's, Monroe Service, O'Reilly Parts/VIP Service, vet
41 (99)	MA 28, to Andover, E Dunkin Donuts Cadillac/Chevrolet
40b a (98)	I-93, N to Methuen, S to Boston

HAVERHILL

INTERSTATE 495 Cont'd

LOWELL

Exit #	Services
39 (94)	MA 133, to Dracut, E Hess Longhorn Steaks, McDonald's Extended Stay America, W Mobil/dsl Cracker Barrel, Wendy's Fairfield Inn, Holiday Inn/rest., Residence Inn
38 (93)	MA 38, to Lowell, E Petroil/dsl, Shell/dsl 99 Rest., Applebee's, Burger King, Dunkin Donuts, IHOP, Jade East, Waffle House Motel 6, Motel Caswell Home Depot, Honda/VW, TownFair Tire, Walmart, W Citgo, Mobil, Sunoco, USA/dsl Dunkin Donuts, Jillie's Rest., McDonald's, Milan Pizza, Wendy's Buick/GMC, Chevrolet, Chrysler/Dodge/Jeep, CVS Drug, Hannaford Foods, Marshalls, Mazda, MktBasket Foods, Sears Essentials, Staples
37 (91)	Woburn St, to S Lowell, W Gulf/Dunkin Donuts/Subway
35c (90)	to Lowell SP, Lowell ConX, **0-2 mi W on US 3** Burger King, Chili's, McDonald's, Outback Steaks, Wendy's Courtyard Kia, Lowe's, Shop&Save, Walgreens
35b a (89)	US 3, S to Burlington, N to Nashua, NH
34 (88)	MA 4, Chelmsford, E Ampet, Mobil, Sunoco Cafe Madrid, Domino's, Dunkin Donuts, Jimmy's Pizza, PapaGino's Radisson CVS Drug, Walgreens, W Shell Moonstone's Rest. Best Western
33	MA 4, N Chelmsford (from nb)
87mm	**both lanes (8am-8pm), full facilities, litter barrels vending**
32 (83)	Boston Rd, to MA 225, E Cumberland Farms, Gulf, Mobil Applebee's, British Beer Co Rest., Burger King, Chili's, D'angelo's, Dunkin Donuts, McDonald's, PapaGino's, Starbucks, Subway, Westford Grill Hampton Inn, Residence Inn H, CVS Drug, Jo-Ann Fabrics, MktBasket Foods, Radio Shack, Rite Aid, to Nashoba Valley Ski Area, Walgreens
31 (80)	MA 119, to Groton, E Gulf, Mobil/dsl/24hr, Shell Dunkin Donuts, Littleton's Subs, Subway, Tre Amici Ristorante Aubuchon Hardware, CVS Drug, Donelan's Foods, Toyota/Scion, Verizon, vet
30 (78)	MA 110, to Littleton, **1 mi E** Shell/Dunkin Donuts CVS Drug, RV Camping, USPO, vet, W Shell/Dunkin Donuts H, vet
29b a (77)	MA 2, to Leominster, E to Walden Pond St Reserve
28 (75)	MA 111, to Boxborough, Harvard, E Gulf/Dunkin Donuts Holiday Inn
27 (70)	MA 117, to Bolton, E Mobil/dsl Subway, W Bolton Pizza vet
26 (68)	MA 62, to Berlin, E Gulf/Dunkin Donuts Holiday Inn Express H, BJ's Whse/gas, Lowe's, W Shell/dsl Berlin Farms Cafe
66mm	Assabet River
25b (64)	I-290, to Worchester
25a	to MA 85, Marlborough, **1 mi E** Gulf, Mobil/dsl 99 Rest., Applebee's, Burger King, Checkerboards Rest., Domino's, HoneyDew Donuts, KFC/Taco Bell, PapaGino's $Tree, AutoZone, Chevrolet, CVS Drug, Family$, Hannaford Foods, PetCo, Stop&Shop/gas, TJ Maxx, Verizon, Walgreens
24b a (63)	US 20, to Northboro, Marlborough, E Mobil Allora Rest., D'angelo's, Dunkin Donuts, Lake Williams Pizza Holiday Inn, W Gulf, Shell 5 Guys Burgers, 99 Rest., Boston Mkt, China Taste, Chipotle Mexican, Japan 1, Longhorn Steaks, McDonald's/playplace, Panera Bread, PapaGino's, Quiznos, Starbucks, Tandoori Grill, Wendy's Best Western,

MARLBORO

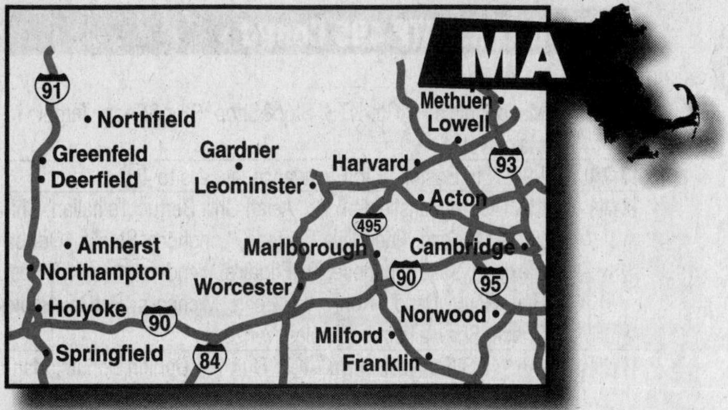

MILFORD

Exit #	Services
24b a (63)	Continued Courtyard, Embassy Suites, Hampton Inn, Homestead Suites $Tree, GNC, Hannaford Foods
23c (60)	Simrano Dr, Marlborough
23b a (59)	MA 9, to Shrewsbury, Framingham, E Cumberland/Dunkin Donuts, Gulf Wendy's Red Roof Inn, **0-2 mi W** Mobil/dsl/24hr, Shell Bertucci's, Burger King, Chateau Rest., Chengdu, Chipotle Mexican, D'angelo's, Dunkin Donuts, Friendly's, Harry's Rest., McDonald's, Piccadilly Cafe, Ruby Tuesday, Starbucks Doubletree Inn, Extended Stay America, Extended Stay Deluxe, Residence Inn H, Buick/GMC, Chrysler/Dodge/Jeep, Marshall's, Staples, Stop&Shop, VW
22 (58)	I-90, MA TPK, E to Boston, W to Albany
21b a (54)	MA 135, to Hopkinton, Upton, E Cumberland, Mobil Dino's Pizza, Dynasty Chinese, Golden Spoon Rest.
20 (50)	MA 85, to Milford, W Gulf/dsl/LP, Mobil/dsl 99 Rest., Pizza 85/deli, TGIFriday's, Wendy's Comfort Inn, Courtyard, Fairfield Inn, Holiday Inn Express H, Best Buy, Lowe's, PetCo, Staples, Stop&Shop, Target, TJ Maxx, Toyota/Scion
19 (48)	MA 109, to Milford, W Mobil/Dunkin Donuts/dsl, Shell 5 Guys Burgers, Alamo Mexican, Applebee's, Bugaboo Cr Steaks, Burger King, D'angelo's, Friendly's, KFC/Pizza Hut, Maria's Italian, McDonald's/playplace, Panera Bread, PapaGino's, Subway Doubletree, La Quinta $Tree, AutoZone, CVS Drug, Hannaford Foods, Jo-Ann Fabrics, K-Mart, Kohl's, Radio Shack, Rite Aid, TownFair Tire
18 (46)	MA 126, to Bellingham, E Chili's, Coldstone, McDonald's Barnes&Noble, Michael's, MktBasket Foods, Old Navy, Staples, Verizon, Walmart/Subway, Whole Foods Mkt, W Hess/dsl, Mobil/24hr, Sunoco/dsl Chicago Grill, DQ, Dunkin Donuts, Outback Steaks Home Depot, Petsmart
17 (44)	MA 140, to Franklin, Bellingham, E Mobil/dsl, Shell, Sunoco Burger King, D'angelo's, Dunkin Donuts, Franklin Cafe, HoneyDew Donuts, Longhorn Steaks, Panera Bread, PapaGino's, Pepper Terrace Thai, Subway, Taco Bell, Tepanyaki Asian AT&T, AutoZone, Buick/GMC, CVS Drug, GNC, Marshalls, Radio Shack, Stop&Shop, W 99 Rest., Encontro Rest. Residence Inn H, BJ's Whse/Subway/gas
16 (42)	King St, to Franklin, E Sunoco Dunkin Donuts, Joe's Grill, King St Cafe, Spruce Pond Creamery Hampton Inn, W Hawthorn Inn
15 (39)	MA 1A, to Plainville, Wrentham, E Shell Assisi Pizza H, W Mobil/dsl Chicago Grill, Cracker Barrel, Dunkin Donuts, Friendly's, Ruby Tuesday Premium Outlets/famous brands
14b a (37)	US 1, to N Attleboro, E Interstate/D'angelo's/PapaGino's/dsl Luciano's Rest. Arbor Motel Bass Pro Shops (4mi), W Citgo/dsl, Mobil Chili's, Dunkin Donuts, Panera Bread, The Tavern Holiday Inn Express Lowe's,

MA

MI

INTERSTATE 495 Cont'd

14b a (37)	Continued Macdonald's RV Ctr, NTB, Stop&Shop, Stop&Shop, Target, TJ Maxx, vet
13 (32)	I-95, N to Boston, S to Providence, access to H
12 (30)	MA 140, to Mansfield, E Asian Grill, Bertucci's Italian, Chipotle Mexican, Friendly's Express, Longhorn Steaks, Qdoba Mexican, Sake Japanese, TGIFriday's, Wendy's AT&T, Best Buy, Home Depot, Kohl's, LL Bean, Michael's, PetCo, Radio Shack, Shaw's Foods, Staples, Verizon
11 (29)	MA 140 S (from sb), **1 mi** W Gulf Dunkin Donuts, Mandarin Chinese, McDonald's, Subway $Tree
10 (26)	MA 123, to Norton, E Dunkin Donuts QuickStop, W H
9 (24)	Bay St, to Taunton, E Chateau Rest., W Dunkin Donuts, Jaybo Cafe, NE Hotdog, Ruby Tuesday, Subway, Wendy's Extended Stay America $Tree, BJ's Whse, Tadeschi Foods, Watson Pond SP
8 (22)	MA 138, to Raynham, E Hess/dsl, Mobil/dsl Christopher's Pizza, HoneyDew Donuts, Yummyhouse Rest., W Gulf/dsl, Shell/dsl/repair, Stop'n Go/dsl Brothers Pizza, Cape Cod Cafe, China Garden, D'angelos, Dunkin Donuts, HoneyDew Donuts, Lucky Corner Chinese, McDonald's, Subway H, Ace Hardware, CVS Drug, Mkt Basket Foods, USPO, vet
7b a (19)	MA 24, to Fall River, Boston, **1/2 mi** E Mobil/dsl Burger King
18mm	**weigh sta both lanes**
17mm	Taunton River
6 (15)	US 44, to Middleboro, E Super/dsl Burger King, Dunkin Donuts, Fireside Grille, Friendly's, Hong Kong Taste, PapaGino's, Subway, W Mobil/Dunkin Donuts/dsl Fairfield Inn, Holiday Inn Express
5 (14)	MA 18, to Lakeville, E Shell, Super/dsl D'Angelo's, Dave's Diner, Fireside Grille, Harry's Grille, Lorenzo's Rest, PapaGino's, Persy's Place Cafe CVS Drug, Kelly's Tire, Stop&Shop, W Massasoit SP, RV camping (seasonal)
4 (12)	MA 105, to Middleboro, E Gulf/dsl, Shell/24hr, Sunoco/24hr China Sails, DQ, Dunkin Donuts, McDonald's, Tuttabella Pizza Days Inn AutoZone, Rite Aid
11mm	**parking area eb**
10mm	**parking area both lanes**
3 (8)	MA 28, to Rock Village, S Middleboro, E Irving/dsl Fred's Repair, W Mobil/Dunkin Donuts/Subway/dsl
2 (3)	MA 58, W Wareham, E RV camping, to Myles Standish SF, W 7-11
2mm	Weweantic River

I-495 begins/ends on I-195, MA 25 S.

MICHIGAN

INTERSTATE 69

Exit #	Services
	I-69 E and I-94 E run together into Port Huron. See I-94, exits 274-275mm.
199	Lp 69 (from eb, no return), to Port Huron, **0-2 mi S on Lp 69 S** Mobil/dsl, Speedway Arby's, Burger King, Jimmy John's, KFC, Little Caesar's, McDonalds, Subway, Taco Bell, Tim Horton's, Wendy's $General, Advance Parts, AutoZone, Kroger/gas, repair, Sam's Club/gas, to Port Huron, USPO
198	I-94, to Detroit and Canada
196	Wadhams Rd, N BP/Wendy's, Marathon, Speedy Q/dsl Hungry Howie's, McDonald's, Peking Kitchen, Subway, Taco Bell KOA (1mi), Vinckier Foods, Wadham's Drugs, S Pilot/Subway/dsl/scales/24hr golf
194	Taylor Rd, N Goodells CP, RV camping
189	Wales Center Rd, to Goodells, S golf
184	MI 19, to Emmett, N Citgo/dsl/scales/24hr repair, USPO, S Marathon/dsl/24hr
180	Riley Center Rd, N KOA
176	Capac Rd, N BP/McDonald's/dsl/scales Subway (2mi)
174mm	**wb, full facilities, litter barrels, petwalk vending**
168	MI 53, Imlay City, N BP/dsl, Speedway/dsl Big Boy, Burger King, DQ, Hungry Howie's, John's Country Kitchen, Little Caesar's, Lucky's Steaks, McDonald's, New China, Taco Bell, Wah Wong Chinese, Wendy's/Tim Horton Days Inn, M53 Motel, Super 8 AutoZone, Chevrolet, Chrysler/Dodge/Jeep, Ford, GNC, Kroger/dsl, NAPA, O'Reilly Parts, Radio Shack, Sav-On Drug, ShopKO, Verizon
163	Lake Pleasant Rd, to Attica
160mm	**eb, full facilities, litter barrels, petwalk vending**
159	Wilder Rd
158mm	Flint River
155	MI 24, Lapeer, **1 mi N** Speedy Q/dsl, Sunoco/dsl Apple Tree Rest., Applebee's, Arby's, Blind Fi sh Rest., Brian's Rest., Buffalo Wild Wings, Burger King, Checkers, DQ, Jet's Pizza, Jimmy John's, KFC, Leo's Coney Island, Little Caesar's, Mancino's, McDonald's, Nick's Grill, Sonic, Starbucks, Subway, Taco Bell, Tim Horton, Wah Wong Chinese, Wendy's Best Western, Holiday Inn Express H, $Tree, AT&T, AutoZone, Belle Tire, Home Depot, Kohl's, Kroger/gas, Meijer/dsl, Midas, Office Depot, O'Reilly Parts, Radio Shack, Rite Aid, st police, URGENT CARE, Verizon, vet, Walgreens, S Mobil/dsl Chrysler/Dodge/Jeep, Harley Davidson
153	Lake Nepessing Rd, S camping, golf, to Thumb Correctional
149	Elba Rd, N Torzewski CP, S Country Mkt, RV/truck repair
145	MI 15, Davison, N Marathon, Shell/dsl, Speedway/dsl Apollo Rest., Applebee's, Arby's, Big Boy, Big John's Rest., Burger King, Chee Kong Chinese, Flag City Diner, Hungry Howie's, Italia Gardens, Jimmy John's, KFC, Little Caesar's, Lucky's Steaks, McDonald's, Pizza Hut, Senor Lucky, Subway, Taco Bell, Tim Horton, Tropical Smoothie Best Western AutoValue Parts, Buick/GMC, Davison Automotive, GNC, Rite Aid, Valley Tire, Verizon, Walgreens, YaYa Chicken, S Mobil/dsl Sicilian Pizza vet

LAPEER

MA

MI

INTERSTATE 69 Cont'd

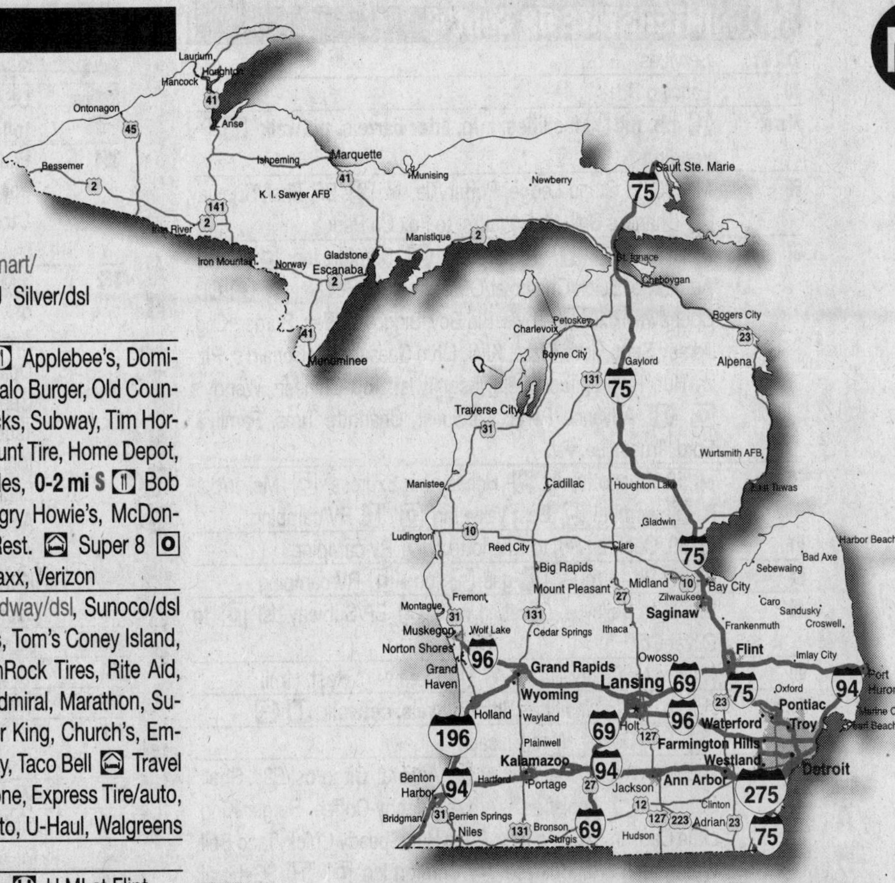

FLINT

Exit #	Services
143	Irish Rd, N Speedway/dsl Menard's, S Shell/McDonald's/24hr Meijer/dsl/e-85
141	Belsay Rd, Flint, N Marathon/Wendy's/dsl/24hr, Mobil Halo Burger, McDonald's, Subway, Taco Bell Walmart/Subway/auto, S Sunoco/A&W/LJ Silver/dsl O'Malley's Grill
139	Center Rd, Flint, N Speedway/dsl Applebee's, Domino's, El Cozumel Mexican, Empire Wok, Halo Burger, Old Country Buffet, Olympic Grill, Quiznos, Starbucks, Subway, Tim Horton Aldi Foods, AT&T, Big Lots, Discount Tire, Home Depot, JC Penney, Jo-Ann Fabrics, Lowe's, Staples, **0-2 mi** S Bob Evans, China 1, Coney Island, DQ, Hungry Howie's, McDonald's, Red Baron Rest., Subway, Walli's Rest. Super 8 $Tree, Belle Tire, Meijer/dsl, Target, TJ Maxx, Verizon
138	MI 54, Dort Hwy, N BP/dsl, Speedway/dsl, Sunoco/dsl Big John's Rest., KFC, Little Caesar's, Tom's Coney Island, YaYa's Chicken H, $General, KanRock Tires, Rite Aid, Save-a-Lot, Walgreens, **0-2 mi** S Admiral, Marathon, Sunoco Arby's, Big John Steak, Burger King, Church's, Empress of China, KFC, McDonald's, Subway, Taco Bell Travel Inn $General, Advance Parts, AutoZone, Express Tire/auto, Family$, O'Reilly Parts, Rite Aid, Tuffy Auto, U-Haul, Walgreens
137	I-475, UAW Fwy, to Detroit, Saginaw
136	Saginaw St, Flint, N Sunoco/dsl H, U MI at Flint
135	Hammerberg Rd, industrial area
133b a	I-75, S to Detroit, N to Saginaw, US 23 S to Ann Arbor
131	MI 121, to Bristol Rd, **1/2 mi N on Miller Rd** Bar Louie, BD Mongolian BBQ, Buffalo Wild Wing, Casa Real, Chili's, ChuckeCheese, Famous Dave's BBQ, Fortune Buffet, Golden Corral, Golden Moon Chinese, Halo Burger, Hooters, Leo's Coney Island, LJ Silver, Logan's Roadhouse, Olive Garden, Osaka Buffet, Outback Steaks, Panera Bread, Red Robin, Subway, Taco Bell, Telly's Coney Island, TX Roadhouse, Valley Diner $Tree, AT&T, Barnes&Noble, Belle Tire, Best Buy, BigLots, Discount Tire, Gander Mtn, Hobby Lobby, JC Penney, Jo-Ann Fabrics, Kohl's, Macy's, mall, Michael's, Old Navy, PetCo, Petsmart, Sears/auto, Target, TJ Maxx, USPO, Valley Tire, Verizon
129	Miller Rd, S Arby's, Burger King, McDonald's, Subway, Taco Bell, Wendy's Kroger/gas
128	Morrish Rd, N Meijer/dsl/e85, S Admiral, Mobil/dsl
126mm	**eb, full facilities, info, litter barrels, petwalk**
123	MI 13, to Saginaw, Lennon, N Speedway/dsl USPO
118	MI 71, to Corunna, Durand, N Durand Automotive, S Shell/dsl, Valero China House, Hungry Howie's, McDonald's, Subway, Wendy's Quality Inn Ace Hardware, CarQuest, Chevrolet, Family$, golf, Rite Aid
115mm	Shiawassee River
113	Bancroft, S BP/dsl (1.5mi) RV camping
105	MI 52, to Owosso, Perry, S Citgo/Subway/dsl, Exxon/7-11, Mobil/dsl, Sunoco/dsl/scales/24hr Burger King, Cafe Sports, China Garden, Hungry Howie's, McDonald's, Taco Bell Heb's Inn Family$, IGA Foods, Rite Aid, RV camping, truck repair (1mi), USPO
101mm	**wb, full facilities, info, litter barrels, petwalk**
98.5mm	Vermilion River
98	Woodbury Rd, to Laingsburg, Shaftsburg

LANSING

Exit #	Services
94	Lp 69, Marsh Rd, to E Lansing, Okemos, S Admiral/dsl, Speedway/dsl McDonald's Gillette RV Ctr, Meijer/Subway/dsl/e85, Monticello's Mkt
92	Webster Rd, Bath
89	US 127 S, to E Lansing
87	Old US 27, to Clare, Lansing, N Marathon, Speedway/dsl Arby's, Bob Evans, Burger King, China Gourmet, FlapJack Rest., Little Ceasars, Mancino's, McDonald's, Subway, Tim Horton Sleep Inn Annie Rae RV Ctr, Chevrolet, Meijer/dsl, Verizon, vet, S Speedway/dsl American Inn GNC
85	DeWitt Rd, to DeWitt
84	Airport Rd
91	I-96 (from sb), W to Grand Rapids, Grand River Ave, Frances Rd, W FLYING J/Denny's/dsl/24hr
93b a	MI 43, Lp 69, Saginaw Hwy, to Grand Ledge, **0-2 mi** N Shell, Speedway/dsl Applebee's, Buffalo Wild Wings, Burger King, Carrabba's, Cheddar's, Chipotle, Denny's, Fazoli's, Finley's Grill, Frank's Grill, Hibachi Grill, Honeybaked Ham, Houlihan's, Logan's Roadhouse, Longhorn Steaks, McDonald's, Outback Steaks, Panera Bread, Qdoba, Red Robin, Subway Comfort Inn, Fairfield Inn, Hampton Inn, Motel 6, Quality Inn, Ramada Inn, Red Roof Inn, Residence Inn H, $Tree, Aldi, AT&T, Barnes&Noble, Best Buy, BigLots, Chrysler/Dodge/Jeep, Hobby Lobby, JC Penney, Kohl's, Kroger/dsl, Macy's, Meijer/dsl/24hr, Target, TJ Maxx, vet, Walgreens, Younkers, S BP/Dunkin Donuts, QD, Sunoco/McDonald's Arby's, Biggby Coffee, Bob Evans, Cancun Mexican, Cracker Barrel, Culver's, Steak'n Shake SpringHill Suites Belle Tire, Buick/GMC, Discount Tire, Gander Mtn, Lowe's, Mazda/Volvo, Menards, Michael's, PetsMart, Staples, Walmart/Subway
95	I-496, to Lansing
72	I-96, E to Detroit, W to Grand Rapids

= gas = food = lodging = other = rest stop

INTERSTATE 69 Cont'd

Exit #	Services
70	Lansing Rd
68mm	**nb, full facilities, info, litter barrels, petwalk vending**
66	MI 100, to Grand Ledge, Potterville, W BP, Shell/Subway Charlie's Grill, McDonald's, to Fox Co Park
61	Lansing Rd, E Applebee's Comfort Inn $Tree, AutoZone, Buick/Chevrolet/GMC, Walmart/Subway, W QD, Speedway/dsl Arby's, Big Boy, Biggby Coffee, Burger King, Jersey Subs, Jet's Pizza, KFC, Little Caesars, McDonald's, Pizza Hut, Rally's, Taco Bell, Tasty Twist, Top Chinese, Wendy's H, Advance Parts, CarQuest, Charlotte Tires, Family$, Ford, TrueValue, vet
60	MI 50, Charlotte, E Holiday Inn Express Meijer/dsl, W Admiral Best Value Inn H, RV camping
57	Lp 69, Cochran Rd, to Charlotte, E RV camping
51	Ainger Rd, **1 mi** E gas food RV camping
48	MI 78, to Bellevue, Olivet, **1 mi** E BP/Subway/dsl to Olivet Coll
42	N Drive N, Turkeyville Rd, W Cornwell's Rest. (1mi)
41mm	**sb, full facilities, litter barrels, petwalk**
38	I-94, E to Detroit, W to Chicago
36	Michigan Ave, to Marshall, E Admiral, Citgo/dsl/E85, Shell/Subway Applebee's, Arby's, Biggby Coffee, Burger King, Little Caesars, McDonald's, Pizza Hut, Speedy Chick, Taco Bell, Wendy's, Yin Hai Chinese Comfort Inn H, $General, $Tree, Ace Hardware, AutoZone, Chevrolet, Family Fare Foods, K-Mart, NAPA, Radio Shack, Rite Aid, Save-A-Lot, Tuffy Auto, W Arbor Inn Chrysler/Dodge/Jeep
32	F Drive S, E Shell (3/4 mi) Moonraker Rest. (3mi), W RV Camping
25	MI 60, to Three Rivers, Jackson, E BP/dsl, Sunoco/dsl, TA/Shell/Country Pride/dsl/scales/24hr/ @ McDonald's, Subway $General, Auto Value Parts, auto/truck repair, RV camping
23	Tekonsha, W access to RV camping
16	Jonesville Rd, W Waffle Farm Camping (2mi)
13	US 12, to Quincy, Coldwater, E Speedway/dsl Applebee's, Biggby Coffee, Bob Evans, Buffalo Wild Wings, Grand Buffet, Papa Murphy's Hampton Inn, Red Roof Inn $Tree, Aldi Foods, AT&T, AutoZone, BigLots, Buick/Chevrolet/GMC, Gander Mtn, GNC, Haylett RV Ctr, Home Depot, Meijer/dsl, Radio Shack, Verizon, Walmart/Subway, Younkers, W Citgo, Speedway/dsl Arby's, Benedict's Steaks, Big Boy, Burger King, Coldwater Garden Rest., Cottage Inn Pizza, Culver's, Jimmy John's, KFC, Little Caesars, McDonald's, Pizza Hut, Ponderosa, Subway, Taco Bell, Wendy's Best Western, Comfort Inn H, Advance Parts, auto repair, Ford/Lincoln, Rite Aid, st police, Walgreens
10	Lp 69, Fenn Rd, to Coldwater
8mm	**weigh sta nb**
6mm	**Welcome Ctr nb, full facilities, litter barrels, petwalk vending**
3	Copeland Rd, Kinderhook, W BP/dsl camping
0mm	Michigan/Indiana state line

MARSHALL

COLDWATER

SAULT STE MARIE

INTERSTATE 75

Exit #	Services
395mm	US/Canada Border, Michigan state line, **I-75 begins/ends at toll bridge to Canada.**
394	Easterday Ave, E Citgo/dsl McDonald's Holiday Inn Express H, to Lake Superior St U, W **Welcome Ctr/rest area, info,** Admiral/dsl, Holiday/dsl/currency exchange Freighter's Rest (2mi) Ramada Inn (2mi)
392	3 Mile Rd, Sault Ste Marie, E Admiral/dsl, BP/dsl, Holiday/dsl, Marathon/dsl, Shell/dsl Ang-gio's Italian, Applebee's, Arby's, Buffalo Wild Wings, Burger King, Country Kitchen, Domino's, DQ, Great Wall Chinese, Indo China Garden, Little Caesars, McDonald's, Pizza Hut, Studebaker's Rest., Subway, Taco Bell, Wendy's Best Value Inn, Best Western, Comfort Inn, Days Inn, Park Inn, Plaza Motel, Skyline Motel, Soo Locks Lodge, Super 8, Superior Place Motel H, $Tree, Advance Parts, AT&T, BigLots, Buick/Chevrolet/GMC, Family$, Glen's Mkt, Goodyear/auto, JC Penney, Jo-Ann Fabrics, K-Mart, NAPA, Radio Shack, Save-a-Lot, Soo Locks Boat Tours, st police, TJ Maxx, Verizon, Walgreens, Walmart/Subway
389mm	**nb, full facilities, info, litter barrels, petwalk**
386	MI 28, W Clear Lake Camping (5mi), to Brimley SP
379	Gaines Hwy, E Clear Lake Camping, to Barbeau Area
378	MI 80, Kinross, E BP/dsl Frank&Jim's Diner golf, RV Camping, to Kinross Correctional
373	MI 48, Rudyard, **2 mi** W gas/dsl food lodging
359	MI 134, to Drummond Island, W National Forest Camping
352	MI 123, to Moran, Newberry
348	H63, to Sault Reservation, St Ignace, **0-2 mi** E Jose's Cantina Bavarian Haus, Bayview Motel, Bear Cove Inn, Best Value Inn, Birchwood Motel, Cedars Motel, Comfort Inn, Evergreen Motel, Great Lakes Motel, Holiday Inn Express, Kewadin Inn, NorthernAire Motel, Pines Motel, Quality Inn, Tradewinds Motel H, casino, Castle Rock Camping, st police, to Mackinac Trail, W Castle Rock Gifts
346mm	**/scenic turnout sb, full facilities, litter barrels, petwalk**
345	Portage St (from sb), St Ignace
344b	US 2 W, W BP/dsl, Holiday/dsl, Shell/dsl Big Boy, Burger King, Clyde's Drive-In, McDonald's, Subway, Suzy's Pasties 4 Star Motel, Quality Inn, Sunset Motel, Super 8 Ford, golf, Lakeshore RV Park
344a	Lp 75, St Ignace, **0-2 mi** E Shell BC Pizza, Bentley's Cafe, Galley Rest., Mackinac Grille, Marina Rest., Northern Lights Rest., Subway Aurora Borealis Motel, Boardwalk Inn, Colonial House, Moran Bay Motel, Normandy Motel, Thunderbird Motel, Village Inn/rest., Vitek's Motel, Voyager Motel H, Ace Hardware, Bay Drug, Doud's Mkt, Family$, Glen's Mkt, NAPA, public marina, Radio Shack, st police, Straits SP, to Island Ferrys, TrueValue, USPO
343mm	E **Welcome Ctr nb, full facilities, litter barrels** W museum, toll booth to toll bridge
341mm	Lake Huron, Lake Michigan, toll bridge
339	US 23, Jamet St, E Audie's Rest. Days Inn, EconoLodge, LightHouse View Motel, Parkside Motel, Riviera Motel, Super 8, W Shell Darrow's Rest., Mackinaw Cookie Co Holiday Inn Express, Vindel Motel Wilderness SP
338	US 23 (from sb), E Marathon/dsl BC Pizza, Burger King, Cunningham's Rest., DQ, KFC, Mama Mia's Pizza, Pancake Chef, Subway Baymont Inn, Court Plaza Hotel IGA Foods/supplies, Mackinaw Outfitters, same as 337, USPO, W Ft Mackinaw Motel, Holiday Inn Express

INTERSTATE 75 Cont'd

MACKINAW CITY

Exit #	Services
337	MI 108 (from nb, no EZ return), Nicolet St, Mackinaw City, E **Welcome Ctr/**, Citgo/dsl/LP Admiral's Table Rest, Anna's Country Buffet, Bell's Melody Motel, Blue Water Grill, Embers Rest., Lakeside Grill, Lighthouse Rest., Mackinaw Pastie&Cookie Co., Mancino's Pizza Anchor Inn, Bayside Inn, Beach House Cottages, BeachComber Motel, Best Inn, Best Value Inn, Best Western, Bridge Vista Beach Motel, Bridgeview Motel, Budget Inn, Capri Motel, Clarion, Clearwater Lakeshore Motel, Comfort Inn, Comfort Suites, Days Inn, EconoLodge, Fairview Inn, Grand Mackinaw Resort, Great Lakes Inn, Hamilton Inn, Hampton Inn, Mackinaw Inn, North Winds Motel, Quality Inn, Rainbow Motel, Ramada Ltd, Sundown Motel, Sunrise Beach Motel, Super 8, Thunderbird Inn, Waterfront Inn Harley-Davidson, Mackinaw Camping (2mi), Old Mill Creek SP, to Island Ferrys, W KOA, Wilderness SP
336	US 31 S (from sb), to Petoskey
328mm	**sb, full facilities, info, litter barrels, petwalk**
326	C66, to Cheboygan, E gas/dsl H, Sea Shell City/gifts, st police
322	C64, to Cheboygan, E H, LP, st police
317mm	**/scenic turnout nb, full facilities, info, litter barrels, petwalk**
313	MI 27 N, Topinabee, E Indian River RV Resort/Camping, Johnson Motel
311mm	Indian River
310	MI 33, MI 68, E Hometown Inn Jellystone Park (3mi), W Marathon, Shell/McDonald's Burger King, DQ, Paula's Cafe, Subway, Wilson's Rest Coach House Motel, Indian River Motel auto repair, Family$, Ken's Mkt/gas, to Burt Lake SP, to Indian River Trading Post/RV Resort
301	C58, Wolverine, E Marathon/dsl Whistle Stop Rest. Elkwood Campground (5mi), W Sturgin Valley Campground (3mi)
297mm	Sturgeon River
290	Vanderbilt, E BP/dsl/LP/RV dump, Spirit/dsl Elk Horn Grill USPO, Village Mkt Foods, W Mobil/dsl Black Bear Golf Resort (2mi)
287mm	**sb, full facilities, info, litter barrels**
282	MI 32, Gaylord, E Holiday, Speedway/dsl Arby's, Big Buck Steaks, Burger King, DQ, Gino's Italian, Jet's Pizza, KFC, La Senorita Mexican, McDonald's, Qdoba Mexican, Subway, Wendy's Alpine Lodge, Baymont Inn, Quality Inn H, Advance Parts, Ben Franklin, Family$, Glen's Mkt/gas, Harley-Davidson, Rite Aid, st police, W BP/dsl, Marathon/dsl, Mobil/dsl, Shell/dsl Applebee's, BC Pizza, Big Boy, Bob Evans, China 1, Coldstone/Tim Horton, Culver's, El Rancho Mexican, Little Caesars, Mancino's Pizza, Ponderosa, Ruby Tuesday, Taco Bell Hampton Inn, Holiday Inn Express $Tree, AT&T, BigLots, Chrysler/Dodge/Jeep, Hobby Lobby, Home Depot, International RV Ctr, Kenworth, Lowe's, Radio Shack, RV camping, Save-A-Lot Foods, tires, Verizon, Walgreens, Walmart/Subway
279mm	45th Parallel halfway between the equator and north pole
279	Old US 27, Gaylord, E Marathon/Subway/dsl, Mobil/dsl, Shell Burger King, Mama Leone's Best Value Inn Ace Hardware, Buick/GMC, Chevrolet, Ford, st police, transmissions, W Bennethums Rest, Stampede Saloon KOA (3mi), Marsh Ridge Motel (2mi)
277mm	**nb, full facilities, info, litter barrels, petwalk**

GAYLORD

GRAYLING

Exit #	Services
270	Waters, E BP/dsl Hilltop Rest., W Citgo/dsl, Waters Inn to Otsego Lake SP, USPO, Waters RV Ctr
264	Lewiston, Frederic, W access to food camping
262mm	**sb, full facilities, info, litter barrels, petwalk**
259	MI 93, E Hartwick Pines SP
256	(from sb), to MI 72, Grayling, access to same as 254
254	MI 72 (exits left from nb, no return), Grayling, **1 mi** W Admiral/dsl, Clark, Shell, Speedway, Valero Big Boy, Burger King, DQ, Keg'O'Nails, McDonald's, Pizza Hut, Subway, Taco Bell, Wendy's Days Inn, Ramada H, $General, 7-11, Ace Hardware, Auto Value Parts, Family$, Ford, Glen's Mkt, K-Mart, NAPA, Rite Aid, Save-A-Lot Foods, Walgreens
251mm	**nb, full facilities, info, litter barrels, petwalk**
251	4 Mile Rd, E Jellystone RV Park (5mi), skiing, W Marathon/Arby's/dsl/scales/RV Dump/24hr Super 8
249	US 127 S (from sb), to Clare
244	MI 18, Roscommon, **3 mi** E Mobil/dsl, Shell/dsl McDonald's, W Valero/dsl Higgins Lake SP, KOA (1mi), museum
239	MI 18, Roscommon, **S** Higgins Lake SP, **3 mi** E Marathon/McDonald's/dsl camping, W camping, Higgins Lake SP
235mm	**sb, full facilities, info, litter barrels, petwalk**
227	MI 55 W, Rd F97, to Houghton Lake, **5 mi** W food
222	Old 76, to St Helen, **2-4 mi** E food lodging camping
215	MI 55 E, West Branch, E Shell/dsl Wagon Wheel Rest. (6mi) H
212	MI 55, West Branch, E Citgo/7-11, Murphy USA/dsl, Shell/Subway/dsl Applebee's, Arby's, Big Boy, Burger King, KFC, Lumberjack Rest., McDonald's, Ponderosa, Taco Bell, Tim Horton, Wendy's Quality Inn, Super 8 H, Home Depot, st police, Tanger Outlet/famous brands, Walmart/Subway, W Jaxx Snaxx/dsl
210mm	**nb, full facilities, info, litter barrels, petwalk vending**
202	MI 33, to Rose City, Alger, E Mobil/jerky outlet/dsl, Narski's Mkt/gas (1/2mi), Shell/Subway/dsl camping
201mm	**sb, full facilities, info, litter barrels, petwalk vending**
195	Sterling Rd, to Sterling, **6 mi** E gas Riverview Camping (seasonal)
190	MI 61, to Standish, E H, Standish Correctional, W Marathon, Mobil/jerky
188	US 23, to Standish, **2-3 mi** E camping
181	Pinconning Rd, E Shell/McDonald's/dsl, XWay Cheesehouse Diner Pinconning Inn (2mi) Pinconning Camping, W Sunoco/pizza/dsl/24hr

INTERSTATE 75 Cont'd

Exit #	Services
175mm	**nb, full facilities, info, litter barrels, petwalk vending**
173	Linwood Rd, to Linwood, E Mobil/dsl/jerky Arby's (2mi)
171mm	Kawkawlin River
168	Beaver Rd, to Willard, E to Bay City SRA, W Mobil/jerky
166mm	Kawkawlin River
164	to MI 13, Wilder Rd, to Kawkawlin, E Cracker Barrel, Lucky Steaks, Ponderosa, Uno AmericInn, Holiday Inn Express KanRock Tire, Meijer/dsl, Menards
162b a	US 10, MI 25, to Midland
160	MI 84, Delta, E Mobil/Subway, W Citgo/7-11, Speedway Berger's Rest., Burger King, KFC/Taco Bell, McDonald's RV World Super Ctr, to Saginaw Valley Coll
158mm	**sb, full facilities, info, litter barrels, petwalk vending**
155	I-675 S, to downtown Saginaw, **4 mi** W Outback Steaks Hampton Inn
154	to Zilwaukee
153mm	Saginaw River
153	MI 13 E Bay City Rd, Saginaw, **2-3 mi** W lodging
151	MI 81, to Reese, Caro, E Sunoco/McDonald's/dsl Volvo Trucks, W FLYING J/Wendy's/dsl/LP/24hr
150	I-675 N, to downtown Saginaw, **6 mi** W Outback Steaks Hampton Inn
149b a	MI 46, Holland Ave, to Saginaw, W Speedway/dsl, Sunoco Arby's, Big John's Steaks, Burger King, McDonald's, Subway, Taco Bell, Texan Rest Best Value Inn, Motel 6, Super 7 Inn H, Advance Parts, Save-A-Lot Foods, USPO
144b a	Bridgeport, E Speedway/dsl Jellystone Camping (9mi), W Mobil/dsl/e-85, TA/Country Pride/dsl/scales/24hr/ @ Arby's, Big Boy, Cracker Barrel, Hungry Howie's, McDonald's, Subway, Taco Bell, Wendy's Baymont Inn, Knights Inn Family$, Kroger/gas, Rite Aid, st police, USPO
143mm	Cass River
138mm	**pull off both lanes**
136	MI 54, MI 83, Birch Run, E Mobil/dsl/24hr Exit Rest., Halo Burger, KFC, Subway Best Value Inn, Best Western, Comfort Inn, Hampton Inn, Holiday Inn Express CarQuest, General RV Ctr, Mejier/dsl/E-85, Totten Tires, W 7-11, Marathon, Sunoco/dsl A&W, Applebee's, Arby's, Big Boy, Bob Evans, Culver's, DQ, Little Caesars, McDonald's, Quiznos, Sonic, Starbucks, Taco Bell, Tony's Rest., Uno, Victor&Merek's Pizza, Wendy's Country Inn&Suites Birch Run Drug, Birch Run Outlet/famous brands, Buick/Chevrolet, GNC, Harley-Davidson, Old Navy, USPO
131	MI 57, to Montrose, E Citgo, Shell Arby's, Big John's Steaks, Burger King, DQ, KFC, McDonald's, Oriental Express, Subway, Taco Bell, Tim Horton, Twins Pizza, Wendy's AutoZone, Chevrolet, Chrysler/Dodge/Jeep, KanRock Tire, K-Mart, Tradewinds RV Ctr, vet, W BP, Mobil/Rally's/dsl, Murphy USA/dsl Big Boy, Lucky Steaks $Tree, Menards, Walmart/Subway
129mm	**both lanes, full facilities, litter barrels, petwalk vending**
126	to Mt Morris, E B&B/Halo Burger/dsl/scales/24hr, W BP/dsl
125	I-475 S, UAW Fwy, to Flint
122	Pierson Rd, to Flint, E BP, Marathon/dsl McDonald's, Papa's Coney's, Subway EconoLodge Kroger/gas, Murray's Parts, NW Tire, Tuffy Auto, W Citgo, Shell/dsl A&W/KFC, Applebee's, Arby's, Big John's Steaks, Bob Evans, Burger King, Cottage Inn Pizza, Cracker Barrel, Denny's, Halo Burger, LJ Silver, Red Lobster, Taco Bell, Tim Horton, Wendy's, YaYa Chicken Baymont Inn, Great Western Inn $Tree, Aldi Foods, AT&T, Discount Tire, Home Depot, Meijer/dsl
118	MI 21, Corunna Rd, E Sunoco Atlas Coney Island, Badawest Lebanese, Big John's Steaks, Burger King, Halo Burger, Hollywood Diner, Hungry Howie's, Little Caesar's, Taco Bell, Wing Fong Chinese, YaYa Chicken H, $Zone, CarQuest, Family$, Kroger/gas, Rite Aid, W BP/dsl, Mobil, Shell/Wendy's, Speedway, Valero A&W/KFC, Blue Collar Grill, Burger King, Fazoli's, Happy Valley Rest., McDonald's, Mega Diner, Tim Horton, White Castle Economy Motel $General, Aldi Foods, AutoZone, Buick, Chevrolet, GMC, Home Depot, KanRock Tire, Kroger/gas, Lowe's Whse, Rite Aid, Sam's Club/gas, st police, VG's Foods, Walgreens, Walmart/auto
117b	Miller Rd, to Flint, E Speedway/dsl, Sunoco/dsl Applebee's, Arby's, Cottage Inn, Don Pablo, Fuddrucker's, KFC, LoneStar Steaks, McDonald's, Pizza, Qdoba, Sonic, Subway, West Side Diner Comfort Inn, Motel 6, Sleep Inn Belle Tire, K-Mart, Tuffy Auto, URGENT CARE, W Admiral, Marathon Bar Louie, BD's Mongolian BBQ, Bob Evans, Casa Real, Chili's, ChuckeCheese, Famous Dave's BBQ, Golden Corral, Halo Burger, HoneyBaked Ham, Hooters, Italia Garden, Logan's Roadhouse, Olive Garden, Osaka Buffet, Outback Steaks, Pizza Hut, Red Robin, Salvatori's Ristorante, Starbucks, Subway, Taco Bell, Telly's Coney Island, TX Roadhouse, Valley Diner Red Roof Inn, Super 8 AT&T, Barnes&Noble, Best Buy, Big Lots, Dale's Foods, Discount Tire, Gander Mtn, Hobby Lobby, JC Penney, Jo-Ann Fabrics, Macy's, mall, Michael's, Office Depot, Old Navy, PetCo, Petsmart, Sears/auto, Target, U-Haul, Valley Tire, Verizon, vet
117a	I-69, E to Lansing, W to Port Huron
116	MI 121, Bristol Rd, E Citgo, Speedway/dsl Capitol Coney Island, KFC, McDonald's Days Inn, Rodeway Inn AutoZone, W Mobil/dsl
115	US 23 (from sb), **W on Hill Rd** Citgo, Mobil Arby's, McDonald's, Redwood Steaks, Subway, Taco Bell, Turkey Farm Deli AmericInn, Best Value Inn, Courtyard, Hampton Inn, Holiday Inn, Residence Inn $Tree, Meijer/dsl
111	I-475 N (from nb), UAW Fwy, to Flint
109	MI 54, Dort Hwy (no EZ return to sb)
108	Holly Rd, to Grand Blanc, E Sunoco/dsl Big Apple Bagels, Buffalo Wild Wings, Da Edoardo Ristorante, Quiznos, Taco Bell Comfort Inn, Holiday Inn Express BMW/Mercedes/Toyota, URGENT CARE, W BP/McDonald's/dsl Arby's H
106	Dixie Hwy (exits left from sb, no nb return), Saginaw Rd, to Grand Blanc
101	Grange Hall Rd, Ortonville, E Holly RA, KOA, st police, W Mobil/dsl RV camping, to Seven Lakes/Groveland Oaks SP
98	E Holly Rd, E Mobil/Subway/dsl/24hr Ford, golf
96mm	**nb, full facilities, info, litter barrels, petwalk vending**
95mm	**sb, full facilities, info, litter barrels, petwalk vending**

SAGINAW

FLINT

MI

INTERSTATE 75 Cont'd

Exit #	Services
93	US 24, Dixie Hwy, Waterford, E [gas] BP/dsl [other] Chrysler/ Dodge/Jeep, Kroger/gas (2mi), Nissan, **1-3 mi** W [gas] Speedway [food] Big Boy, McDonald's, Subway, Taco Bell, Wendy's [other] to Pontiac Lake RA, Walgreens
91	MI 15, Davison, Clarkston, E [gas] Sunoco/dsl [food] Bullfrog's (5mi), Subway (5mi) [other] camping, W [gas] BP [food] Mesquite Creek Café [other] [H], URGENT CARE
89	Sashabaw Rd, E [gas] Shell/dsl [food] Culvers, Ruby Tuesday, Tropical Smoothie Cafe [other] county park, W [gas] BP, Citgo [food] Caribou Coffee, Chicken Shack, Dunkin Donuts, E Ocean Chinese, Guido's Pizza, Hong Kong Chinese, Hungry Howie's, Jimmy John's, Leo's Coney Island, Little Caesars, McDonald's, Quiznos, Rio Wraps, Subway, Tim Horton, Wendy's [other] $Tree, CVS Drug, Kroger, vet
86mm	**weigh sta sb**
84b a	Baldwin Ave, E [gas] Shell [food] Arby's, Big Boy, Joe's Crabshack, Longhorn Steaks, Panera Bread, Taco Bell, Wendy's [other] $Tree, Best Buy, Costco/gas, Discount Tire, Kohl's, Michael's, Old Navy, PetCo, Staples, W [gas] Mobil [food] 5 Guys Burgers, Chili's, Jimmy John's, Kerry's Coney Island, Max&Erma's, McDonald's, On-the-Border, Oriental Forest Buffet, Qdoba Mexican, Quiznos, Rainforest Cafe, Starbucks, Steak'n Shake, Subway [other] AT&T, Bass Pro Shops, Batteries+, Great Lakes Crossing Outlet/famous brands, Hampton Inn, Holiday Inn Express, Marshall's, TJ Maxx, USPO, Vitamin Shoppe
83b a	Joslyn Rd, E [food] Applebee's, Logan's Roadhouse, Olive Garden [other] Belle Tire, Home Depot, Jo-Ann Fabrics, Meijer/dsl, Sam's Club/gas, Target, W [gas] BP
81	MI 24, Pontiac (no EZ return), E [other] The Palace Arena, to Bald Mtn RA
79	University Dr, E [gas] BP [food] BD Mongolian, Jimmy John's, Rio Wraps, Spargo Coney Island, Subway, Taste of Thailand [lodging] Homestead Suites, W [gas] Mobil, Speedway/dsl [food] A&W/KFC, Burger King, Lelli's Steaks, McDonald's, Taco Bell, Wendy's/Tim Horton [lodging] Candlewood Suites, Comfort Suites, Courtyard, Crowne Plaza, Extended Stay America, Extended Stay Deluxe, Fairfield Inn, Hampton Inn, Hilton, Hyatt Place, Rodeway Inn, Staybridge Suites, Wingate Inn [other] [H]
78	Chrysler Dr, E [other] Chrysler, Chrysler Museum, Oakland Tech Ctr
77b a	MI 59, to Pontiac, **2 mi E on Adams** [food] 112 Pizza, 5 Guys Burgers, Kerry's Cone Island, McDonald's, Panera Bread [other] GNC, Meijer/dsl, Petsmart, Radio Shack, Walmart
75	Square Lake Rd (exits left from nb), to Pontiac, W [other] [H], St Mary's Coll
74	Adams Rd
72	Crooks Rd, to Troy, W [food] Cedar Grill, Jimmy John's, Kerby's Coney Island, Loccino Italian, Papa Romano's Pizza, Red Robin, Starbucks [lodging] Embassy Suites
69	Big Beaver Rd, E [food] Champp's Grill, Kona Grill, Shula's Steaks, TGIFriday's [lodging] Drury Inn, Marriott, W [gas] BP [food] Benihana, Caribou Coffee, Chipotle Mexican, Granite City Rest, Maggiano's Italian, Melting Pot Rest., Morton's Steaks, Noodles&Co, Papa Romano's Pizza, PF Chang's, Potbelly's, Ruth's Chris Steaks, Starbucks [lodging] Somerset Inn [other] Macy's, mall, Neiman Marcus, Nordstrom
67	Rochester Rd, to Stevenson Hwy, E [gas] BP, Shell/dsl, Sunoco [food] Bahama Breeze, Burger King, Caribou Coffee, Dickey's BBQ, Domino's, El Charro, Hills Grille, Hooters, Hungry Howies,

AUBURN HILLS

TROY

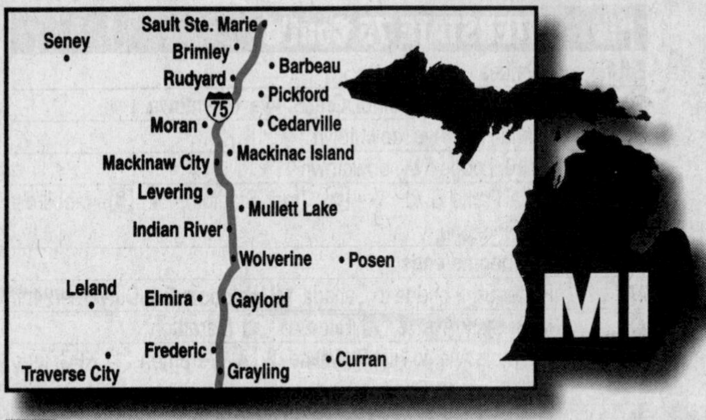

Exit #	Services
67	Continued Jimmy John's, McDonald's, Mr Pita, Ntl Coney Island, Orchid Cafe, Panera Bread, Papa John's, PeiWei, Picano's Italian, Pizza Hut/Taco Bell, Qdoba, Subway, Tim Hortons, Troy Deli, Wendy's [other] Discount Tire, Nordstrom Rack, Office Depot, Petsmart, Radio Shack, transmissions, vet, W [gas] BP [lodging] Courtyard, Quality Inn, Red Roof Inn [other] tires/repair
65b a	14 Mile Rd, Madison Heights, E [gas] Mobil, Shell [food] Azteca Mexican, Bob Evans, Burger King, Chili's, ChuckeCheese, CiCi's Pizza, Coldstone, Krispy Kreme, Logan's Roadhouse, McDonald's, Panera Bread, Pizza Papalis, Red Robin, Rio Wraps, Sonic, Steak'n Shake, Taco Bell, Wendy's [lodging] Motel 6, Red Roof Inn [other] AT&T, auto repair, Barnes&Noble, Belle Tire, Best Buy, BigLots, CVS Drug, Dick's, Firestone/auto, Ford, JC Penney, Jo-Ann Fabrics, Kohl's, Macy's, Sears/auto, Target, TJ Maxx, Verizon, W [gas] Mobil [food] Applebee's, Caribou Coffee, Dolly's Pizza, McDonald's, NY Coney Island, Outback Steaks [lodging] Courtyard, Days Inn, EconoLodge, Extended Stay America, Fairfield Inn, Hampton Inn, Residence Inn [other] Costco/gas, Value Ctr Foods
63	12 Mile Rd, E [gas] Marathon/dsl [food] Culver's, Green Lantern Rest., Marinelli's Pizza, McDonald's, Red Lobster, Sero's Rest., Starbucks, Tim Hortons, TX Roadhouse [other] Home Depot, K-Mart/foods, Lowe's, Midas, Radio Shack, Sam's Club/gas, Uncle Ed's Oil, USPO, W [gas] Marathon/Dunkin Donuts, Speedway [food] Col's Rest. [other] Chevrolet, Costco/gas
62	11 Mile Rd, E [gas] Mobil [food] Albert's Coney Island, Boodles Rest., Happy's Pizza, Jets Pizza, Telway Burgers [other] 7-11, Advance Parts, CVS Drug, repair/tires, Save-a-Lot, Tuffy Auto, vet, Walgreens, W [gas] BP, Marathon/dsl, Mobil [food] KFC, Taco Bell, Tim Hortons, Tubby's Subs [other] Belle Tire
61	I-696 E, to Port Huron, W to Lansing, to Hazel Park Raceway
60	9 Mile Rd, John R St, E [food] Checkers, China 1 Buffet, Coney Craver's Diner, DQ, Hardee's, McDonald's, Subway, Tim Hortons [other] CVS Drug, Kroger/gas, USPO, W [gas] Exxon, Marathon, Mobil [food] Tubby's Subs, Wendy's [other] Hasting's Parts, repair
59	MI 102, 8 Mile Rd, **3 mi** W [other] st fairgrounds
58	7 Mile Rd, W [gas] BP/dsl
57	McNichols Rd, E [gas] Citgo/dsl, Shell/dsl [food] LA Coney Island [other] Auto Parts/Repair
56b a	Davison Fwy
55	Holbrook Ave, Caniff St, E [gas] Mobil/dsl [food] Grandy's Coney Island
54	E Grand Blvd, Clay Ave, W [gas] BP/dsl
53b	I-94, Ford Fwy, to Port Huron, Chicago
53a	Warren Ave, E [gas] Mobil, Shell, W [gas] BP
52	Mack Ave, E [gas] Shell [food] McDonald's
51c	I-375 to civic center, tunnel to Canada, downtown

DETROIT AREA

MI

⬆ N INTERSTATE 75 Cont'd

Exit #	Services
51b	MI 3 (exits left from nb), Gratiot Ave, downtown
50	Grand River Ave, downtown
49b	MI 10, Lodge Fwy, downtown
49a	Rosa Parks Blvd, E Ⓞ Tiger Stadium, W ⛽ Mobil/dsl Ⓞ Firestone
48	I-96 begins/ends
47b	Porter St, E bridge to Canada, **MI Welcome Ctr**, DutyFree/24hr
47a	MI 3, Clark Ave, E ⛽ Citgo, W ⛽ Marathon
46	Livernois Ave, to Hist Ft Wayne, E ⛽ Marathon 🍴 KFC/Taco Bell, Livernois Coney Island
45	Fort St, Springwells Ave, E ⛽ BP/dsl, Pure Petro/dsl, W ⛽ Mobil 🍴 McDonald's
44	Deerborn St (from nb)
43b a	MI 85, Fort St, to Schaefer Hwy, E ⛽ BP, W ⛽ Marathon Refinery Ⓞ to River Rouge Ford Plant
42	Outer Dr, E ⛽ Marathon 🍴 Happy's Pizza Ⓞ URGENT CARE, W ⛽ BP/Subway/dsl Ⓞ Family$, truck tires
41	MI 39, Southfield Rd, to Lincoln Park, E 🍴 A&W, Tim Hortons, White Castle Ⓞ Aldi Foods, O'Reilly Parts, Walgreens, W ⛽ Citgo/Tim Hortons, Mobil 🍴 Burger King, Checker's, Hungry Howie, LJ Silver, McDonald's, Pizza Hut, Starbucks, Taco Bell, Wendy's 🛏 Sleep Inn Ⓞ AT&T, Belle Tire, Kroger/gas, Radio Shack, Rite Aid, Walgreens
40	Dix Hwy, E ⛽ Citgo, Future/A&W/dsl, Marathon/A&W/dsl, Sunoco, Welcome 🍴 Baskin-Robbins/Dunkin Donuts, Toma's Coney Island Ⓞ 7-11, CVS Drug, Meijer, repair, URGENT CARE, W ⛽ Future, Marathon 🍴 Big Boy, Burger King, Checker's, DQ, LJ Silver, McDonald's, Pizza Hut, Starbucks, Taco Bell, Wendy's Ⓞ AT&T, auto repair, Belle Tire, Family$, Kroger/gas, Rite Aid, Sears/auto, Walgreens
37	Allen Rd, North Line Rd, to Wyandotte, E ⛽ BP, Shell/Tim Hortons 🛏 Holiday Inn Ⓞ Ⓗ, Sam's Club/gas, W ⛽ Mobil, Sunoco 🍴 Arby's, Burger King, Mallie's Grill, McDonald's, Wendy's 🛏 Comfort Suites, La Quinta, Motel 6
36	Eureka Rd, E ⛽ BP 🍴 Bob Evans, Denny's, Fire Mtn Grill, Orleans Steaks 🛏 Ramada Inn, Super 8 Ⓞ vet, W 🍴 American Thai Grill, Big Boy, Coldstone, Culver's, HoneyBaked Ham, Hooters, Jimmy John's, Little Daddy's Rest., McDonald's, Ruby Tuesday, Starbucks, Subway, TX Roadhouse, Wendy's 🛏 Red Roof Inn Ⓞ AT&T, Belle Tire, Best Buy, Discount Tire, Home Depot, JC Penney, Kohl's, Macy's, mall, Meijer/dsl, Petsmart
35	US 24, Telegraph Rd, (from nb, exits left)
34b	Sibley Rd, Riverview, W ⛽ Sunoco/Baskin-Robbins/Dunkin Donuts/Subway Ⓞ General RV Ctr
34a	to US 24 (from sb), Telegraph Rd
32	West Rd, to Trenton, Woodhaven, E ⛽ ⊘FLYING J/Detroiter/IHOP/dsl/LP/scales/24hr/@, Speedway/dsl 🍴 5 Guys Burgers, Applebee's, Baskin-Robbins/Dunkin Donuts, Blue Margarita Mexican, Bob Evans, Christoff's Rest., Coldstone, IHOP, Jersey Subs, Panera Bread, Pizza Hut, Steak'n Shake, Subway, Taco Bell, Tim Hortons, Wendy's, White Castle Ⓞ Aldi Foods, Belle Tire, Chevrolet, Chrysler/Dodge/Jeep, Discount Tire, Firestone/auto, Ford, Home Depot, K-Mart, Kohl's, Kroger, Lowe's, Meijer/dsl, Michael's, Office Depot, O'Reilly Parts, Petsmart, Radio Shack, Target, transmissions, URGENT CARE, Verizon, Walmart, W ⛽ BP/Tim Hortons, Citgo, Shell 🍴 Andy's Pizza, Jimmy John's, Little Caesars, McDonald's, Milli's Rest, Subway 🛏 Best Western/rest., Holiday Inn Express, Westwood Inn Ⓞ Ⓗ, $Tree, CVS Drug, Kroger, SavOn Drug, Walgreens

Exit #	Services
29	Gilbralter Rd, to Flat Rock, Lake Erie Metropark, E ⛽ Citgo dsl 🍴 Cottage Inn Pizza, McDonald's, Peking Chinese, Subway, Wendy's Ⓞ Ⓗ, Curves, GNC, Kroger, W ⛽ Marathon dsl 🛏 Sleep Inn Ⓞ Ford, st police
28	Rd 85 (from nb), Fort St, E Ⓞ Ⓗ
27	N Huron River Dr, to Rockwood, E ⛽ Marathon/7-11/dsl 🍴 Benito's Pizza, Huron River Rest., Marco's Pizza Ⓞ Food Town Foods, Rite Aid, USPO, W ⛽ Speedway/dsl 🍴 Riverfront Rest.
26	S Huron River Dr, to S Rockwood, E ⛽ Sunoco/dsl 🍴 Dixie Cafe, Drift Inn Ⓞ USPO
21	Newport Rd, to Newport, E ⛽ BP/Subway/dsl Ⓞ repair W ⛽ Marathon/Burger King/dsl/24hr
20	I-275 N, to Flint
18	Nadeau Rd, W ⛽ 🛢PILOT🛢/Taco Bell/dsl/scales/24hr Ⓞ RV camping
15	MI 50, Dixie Hwy, to Monroe, E ⛽ Shell 🍴 Burger King, Red Lobster 🛏 Best Value Inn, Hampton Inn, Motel 6, Red Roof Inn Ⓞ to Sterling SP, W ⛽ 🛢PILOT🛢/Subway/dsl/scales/24hr, TA/BP/Country Pride/Pizza Hut/Popeye's/Tim Hortons/dsl/scales/24hr/@ 🍴 Big Boy, Cracker Barrel, Denny's, El Maguey, McDonald's, Wendy's 🛏 Knights Inn, Quality Inn Ⓞ Ⓗ, to Viet Vet Mem
14	Elm Ave, to Monroe
13	Front St, Monroe
11	La Plaisance Rd, to Bolles Harbor, W ⛽ Marathon/Taco Bell/dsl, Speedway 🍴 McDonald's, Wendy's 🛏 Baymont Inn, Comfort Inn, Harbor Town RV Resort Ⓞ Kroger/gas (2mi), st police
10mm	**Welcome Ctr nb, full ♿ services, info, litter barrels, petwalk** Ⓒ 🛏 vending
9	S Otter Creek Rd, to La Salle, W Ⓞ antiques
7mm	**weigh sta both lanes**
6	Luna Pier, E ⛽ Sunoco/dsl/scales 🍴 Beef Jerky UnLtd., Ganders Rest., Roma's Pizza 🛏 Super 8, W Ⓞ KOA, st police
5	to Erie, Temperance
2	Summit St
0mm	Michigan/Ohio state line

⬆ E INTERSTATE 94

Exit #	Services
275mm	**I-69/I-94 begin/end on MI 25, N Pinegrove Ave in Port Huron** ⛽ BP, Shell/dsl, Speedway/dsl 🍴 Arby's, McDonald's, Tim Horton, Wendy's 🛏 Days Inn, Quality Inn Ⓞ Family$, Honda, Rite Aid, **tollbridge to Canada**
274.5mm	Black River
274	Water St, Port Huron, N 🍴 Cracker Barrel 🛏 Best Western Ⓞ Lake Port SP, Port Huron RV Park, S ⛽ SpeedyQ/dsl 🍴 Bob Evans 🛏 Comfort Inn, Fairfield Inn, Hampton Inn, Holiday Inn Express Ⓞ Menard's, O'Reilly Parts
273mm	**Welcome Ctr/Ⓡˢ wb, full ♿ facilities, litter barrels, petwalk**
271	**I-69 E and I-94 E run together eb**, Lp I-69, 0-2 mi **S on Lp 69 S** ⛽ Mobil/dsl, Speedway 🍴 Arby's, Burger King, Jimmy John's, KFC, Little Caesar's, McDonalds, Subway, Taco Bell, Tim Horton's, Wendy's Ⓞ $General, Advance Parts, AutoZone, Kroger/gas, repair, Sam's Club/gas, to Port Huron, USPO
269	Dove St, Range Rd, N ⛽ Speedway/dsl 🍴 Theo's Rest. 🛏 Baymont Inn
266	Gratiot Rd, Marysville, 0-2 mi **S** ⛽ BP, Marathon/dsl/scales/24hr, Speedway/dsl 🍴 Arby's, Big Boy, Burger King,

D E T R O I T A R E A

M O N R O E

P O R T H U R O N

INTERSTATE 94 Cont'd

266 Continued
China Lite, Dairy Boy, Daliono's, Four Star Grille, Hungry Howie's, Jets Pizza, Jimmy John's, KFC, Little Caesars, McDonald's, Mr Pita, Pelican Café, Seros Rest., Subway, Taco Bell, Tim Horton [lodging] Super 8 [other] (H), $General, $Tree, AutoZone, CarQuest, CVS Drug, Meijer/dsl, O'Reilly Parts, Rite Aid, Verizon, vet, Wally's Foods

262 Wadhams Rd, N [other] camping, S [gas] Mobil/dsl

257 St Clair, Richmond, N [gas] Sunoco/dsl, S [gas] BP/dsl [other] st police

255mm [rest stop] eb, full facilities, info, litter barrels, petwalk

251mm [rest stop] wb, full facilities, info, litter barrels, petwalk

248 26 Mile Rd, to Marine City, N [food] McDonald's (2mi), S [gas] 7-11/gas, Speedy Q (1mi) [food] Asian Garden, My Place Cafe, Subway, Taco Bell, Tim Horton [other] Mejier/dsl

247mm Salt River

247 MI 19 (no eb return), New Haven

243 MI 29, MI 3, Utica, New Baltimore, N [gas] BP, Marathon/dsl, Sunoco/dsl [food] Applebee's, Arby's, Buffalo Wild Wings, Burger King, Chophouse, Coldstone, Coney Island, Dimitri's Rest., Dolly's Pizza, Eagles Grill, Father&Son Pizzaria, Happy's Pizza, Jersey Mike's, Little Caesars, McDonald's, Noodles&Co, Panera Bread, Qdoba, Ruby Tuesday, Starbucks, Stevie B's Pizza, Tim Horton, TX Roadhouse, Wendy's, White Castle [lodging] Chesterfield Motel [other] $Tree, AutoZone, Belle Tire, Best Buy, Big Lots, Dick's, Discount Tire, GNC, Hobby Lobby, Home Depot, JC Penney, Jo-Ann Fabrics, Kohl's, Lowe's, Meijer/Subway/dsl, Michael's, NAPA, Old Navy, O'Reilly Parts, PetCo, PetsMart, Rite Aid, Staples, Target, TJ Maxx, URGENT CARE, Verizon, Walgreens, S [gas] Marathon/dsl/24hr, Speedway/dsl/24hr [food] Big Boy, Buscemi's Pizza, Checkers, Taco Bell [lodging] Lodge-Keeper

241 21 Mile Rd, Selfridge, N [gas] Exxon/dsl/e85, Speedway/dsl [food] China King, Hungry Howie's, Jets Pizza, Jimmy John's [other] Advance Parts, AT&T, CVS Drug, same as 240, Verizon, vet

240 to MI 59, N [gas] 7-11/gas, BP, Mobil [food] Arby's, Bob Evans, Burger King, Coney Island, KFC, McDonald's, Taco Bell, Twisted Rooster [lodging] Hampton Inn, Holiday Inn Express [other] $Tree, Ford, Harley-Davidson, Hyundai/Mazda, Kia, Menard's, Subaru, Tuffy Auto, Walmart

237 N River Rd, Mt Clemens, N [gas] BP/dsl, Mobil/Subway/dsl [food] Captain's Landing Grill, McDonald's [other] (H), General RV Ctr, Gibraltar Trade Ctr

236.5mm Clinton River

236 Metro Parkway, S [food] Big Apple Bagels, Empire Chinese, Little Caesars, McDonald's, Subway [other] (H), CVS Drug, GNC, Kroger, URGENT CARE, Verizon

235 Shook Rd (from wb)

234b a Harper Rd, 15 Mile Rd, N [gas] BP/McDonald's, Marathon/dsl, SpeedyQ, Sunoco/dsl [food] Domino's, Gina's Cafe, Tim Horton's [other] Family$, vet, S [gas] Shell [food] China Moon, Subway, Travis Rest., Winners Grill [other] URGENT CARE

232 Little Mack Ave (from wb only), N [gas] Citgo, Marathon, Mobil, Shell, Sunoco [food] Coldstone, Denny's, Hooters, Longhorn Steaks, McDonald's, Pizza Hut, Red Robin [lodging] Hampton Inn, Holiday Inn Express, Red Roof Inn, Relax Inn, Super 8, Victory Inn [other] Advance Parts, Aldi Foods, Belle Tire, Discount Tire, Firestone, O'Reilly Parts, Sam's Club/gas, Sears/Auto, Staples, Target, Tuesday Morning, S [gas] Speedway/dsl

DETROIT AREA

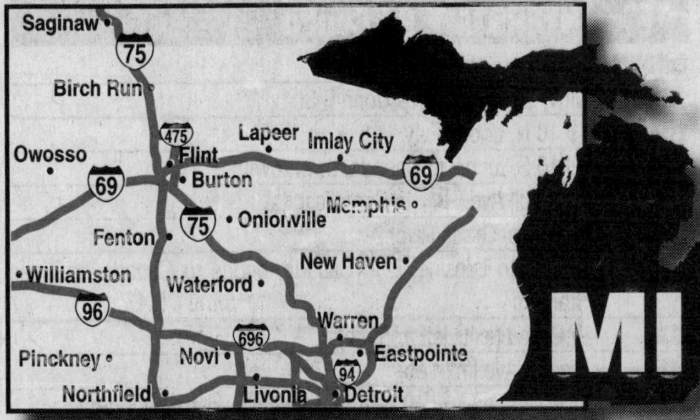

232 Continued
[food] Cracker Barrel, Culver's, IHOP [lodging] Baymont Inn [other] Home Depot, Jo-Ann Fabrics, Meijer/dsl/24hr, PetsMart, same as 231

231 (from eb), MI 3, Gratiot Ave, N [gas] Exxon/dsl, Marathon [food] Applebee's, Arby's, Bob Evans, Burger King, Chili's, Chipotle, ChuckeCheese, Del Taco, Denny's, Famous Dave's BBQ, Logan's Roadhouse, Longhorn Steaks, Marco's Italian, McDonald's, National Coney Island, Panera Bread, PetCo, Pizza Hut, Potbelly, Qdoba, Ruby Tuesday, Starbucks, Subway, Tim Horton, TX Roadhouse [lodging] Days Inn, Extended Stay America, Hampton Inn, Microtel [other] Belle Tire, Best Buy, Dick's, Discount Tire, Firestone/auto, Honda/Acura, Kia, Kohl's, Kroger, mall, Michael's, Nissan, Radio Shack, Sam's Club/gas, Staples

230 12 Mile Rd, N [gas] Mobil/dsl, Sunoco/dsl [food] BD's Mongolian, Jimmy John's, Outback Steaks, Starbucks, Taco Bell [other] $Tree, AT&T, CVS Drug, Marshall's, Verizon, Walmart/Subway, S [gas] Marathon

229 I-696 W, Reuther Fwy, to 11 Mile Rd, S [gas] Shell/dsl, Speedway/dsl [other] 7-11

228 10 Mile Rd, N [gas] 7-11, BP [food] Baskin-Robbins, Donna's Rest., Eastwind Chinese, Friendly Rest., Jet's Pizza, Little Italy Pizza, Sugarbush Rest. [other] Save Mor Drugs, URGENT CARE

227 9 Mile Rd, N [gas] Metro, Speedway/dsl, Sunoco [food] DQ, McDonald's, Milestone Grill, Popeye's, Subway, Taco Bell, Tim Horton's, Wendy's [other] $Tree, Aldi Foods, CVS Drug, Family$, Fresh Choice Foods, Office Depot, TrueValue, vet, S [gas] Mobil/dsl, Mobil/dsl [lodging] Shore Pointe Motel [other] Cadillac, Mercedes

225 MI 102, Vernier Rd, 8 Mile Rd, S [gas] BP/Subway, Mobil, Sunoco/dsl [food] Coney Island, KFC, Taco Bell, Wendy's [other] Kroger, Walgreens

224b Allard Ave, Eastwood Ave

224a Moross Rd, S [gas] Shell [other] (H), Family Foods

223 Cadieux Rd, S [gas] BP/Subway, Mobil, Shell/dsl, Sunoco [food] Checkers, McDonald's, Papa's Pizza, Popeye's, Tubby's Subs, Wendy's, White Castle [other] Family$, Rite Aid

222b Harper Ave (from eb), S [other] Hastings Auto

222a Chalmers Ave, Outer Dr, N [gas] BP/Subway/dsl, Clark [food] Coney Island, KFC, Little Caesars [other] Family$

220b Conner Ave, N [gas] BP, Sunoco

220a French Rd, S [gas] Citgo

219 MI 3, Gratiot Ave, N [gas] Clark, Marathon/Subway [food] Coney Island, McDonald's [other] Family$, Farmer John's Foods, USPO, S [gas] Citgo [food] Burger King

218 MI 53, Van Dyke Ave, N [gas] BP, Mobil/dsl

217b Mt Elliott Ave, S [gas] Citgo, Mobil/dsl [food] Royal BBQ

217a E Grand Blvd, Chene St, S [gas] Marathon

216b Russell St (from eb), to downtown

216a I-75, Chrysler Fwy, to tunnel to Canada

INTERSTATE 94 Cont'd

Exit #	Services
215c	MI 1, Woodward Ave, John R St
215b	MI 10 N, Lodge Fwy
215a	MI 10 S, tunnel to Canada, downtown
214b	Trumbull Ave, to Ford Hospital
214a	(from wb) Grand River Ave
213b	I-96 W to Lansing, E to Canada, bridge to Canada, to Tiger Stadium
213a	W Grand (exits left from eb)
212b	Warren Ave (from eb)
212a	Livernois Ave, S Marathon/Subway/dsl, Sunoco/dsl
211b	Cecil Ave (from wb), Central Ave
211a	Lonyo Rd, S Sunoco Ford
210	US 12, Michigan Ave, Wyoming Ave, N Mobil/dsl, S BP/dsl, Sunoco/dsl Checkers
209	Rotunda Dr (from wb)
208	Greenfield Rd, Schaefer Rd, N Mobil/dsl Wendy's/Tim Horton 7-11, S River Rouge Ford Plant
207mm	Rouge River
206	Oakwood Blvd, Melvindale, N Marathon, Shell Applebee's, Biggby Coffee, Carino's, Chili's, Coldstone, Coney Island, Five Guys, Jimmy John's, Little Caesar's, Longhorn Steaks, Olga's Kitchen, On-the-Border, Panda Express, Panera Bread, Potbelly, Qdoba, Starbucks, Subway, Taco Bell AAA, Barnes&Noble, Best Buy, GNC, Greenfield Village Museum, Home Depot, Jo-Ann Fabrics, Lowe's, Meijer, Michael's, Old Navy, PetCo, Staples, Target, TJ Maxx, USPO, Verizon, S BP/dsl Burger King, Hungry Howie's, McDonald's, Sabina's, Subway, Tim Horton's Best Western, Holiday Inn Express $General, $Tree, 7-11, CVS Drug, O'Reilly Parts, Rite Aid
205mm	Largest Uniroyal Tire in the World
204b a	MI 39, Southfield Fwy, Pelham Rd, N Marathon/dsl, Mobil, Valero/dsl 7-11, to Greenfield Village, S Exxon/dsl, Marathon/dsl, Marathon/dsl Walgreens
202b a	US 24, Telegraph Rd, N Citgo, Shell, Sunoco Burger King, Checkers, Dunkin Donuts, KFC, McDonald's, Pizza Hut, Ram's Horn Rest., Subway, Taco Bell, Wendy's Advance Parts, Aldi Foods, Rite Aid, Walgreens, **0-2 mi** S BP, Citgo/dsl, Marathon/dsl, Valero/dsl Arby's, Big Boy, Burger King, Dunkin Donuts, Hungry Howie's, Jimmy John's, KFC, Leon's Rest., Leo's Coney Island, Little Caesar's, LJ Silver, Marina's Pizza, McDonald's, New Hong Kong, Pancho's Mexican, Pizza Hut, Popeye's, Subway, Super China, Taco Bell, Teppanyaki, Tim Horton's/Coldstone, Wendy's Comfort Inn $Tree, AT&T, AutoZone, Family$, Firestone/auto, Home Depot, Radio Shack, Rite Aid, st police, U-Haul, Verizon, vet, Walgreens, Walmart/Burger King
200	Ecorse Rd, (no ez eb return), to Taylor, N Marathon/Subway/dsl/scales Tim Horton's, S Citgo/dsl, Rich
199	Middle Belt Rd, S BP/dsl Checkers, McDonald's, Wendy's Days Inn, Knights Inn, Quality Inn
198	Merriman Rd, N Citgo/dsl, Marathon, Speedway/Speedy Cafe/dsl Big Boy, Bob Evans, Capitol Bistro, Fortune Chinese, Leonardo's Italian, McDonald's, Merriman St Grill, Sporting News Grill, Subway, Toarmina's Pizza Baymont Inn, Best Value Inn, Clarion, Comfort Inn, Courtyard, Embassy Suites, Extended Stay America, Fairfield Inn, Hampton Inn, Hilton Garden, Holiday Inn, Holiday Inn Express, Howard Johnson, La Quinta, Magnuson Hotel, Marriott, Red Lion Inn, Rodeway

DETROIT AREA

Exit #	Services
198	Continued Inn, Sheraton, Sheraton Four Points, SpringHill Suites, Wyndham Garden Hotel, S Wayne Co
197	Vining Rd
196	Wayne Rd, Romulus, N Shell/dsl Little Caesar's, McDonald's, Taco Bell $General, S Mobil/dsl Burger King, Subway
194b a	I-275, N to Flint, S to Toledo
192	Haggerty Rd, N BP/Tubby's/dsl, Mobil/dsl, S Lower Huron Metro Park
190	Belleville Rd, to Belleville, N BP/Quizno's/dsl, Marathon Applebee's, Arby's, Asian Garden, Coney Island, Cracker Barrel, Culver's, Happy's Pizza, Hungry Howie's, McDonald's, Taco Bell, Tim Horton, Twisted Rooster, Wendy's Hampton Inn, Holiday Inn Express, Red Roof Inn $Tree, AT&T, AutoZone, Belle Tire, Camping World RV Ctr, CVS Drug, Firestone/auto, Ford, Meijer/dsl, National RV Ctr, O'Reilly Parts, Verizon, Walgreens, Walmart, S Shell Burger King, China City, Dos Pesos Mexican, Mike's Kitchen, Subway Comfort Inn, Super 8 URGENT CARE, USPO
189mm	**wb, full facilities, info, litter barrels, petwalk vending**
187	Rawsonville Rd, N Freightliner, S Mobil/dsl, Speedway/dsl Burger King, Denny's, KFC, Little Caesars, McDonald's, Pearl River Chinese, Pizza Hut, Taco Bell, Tim Horton, Wendy's $General, $Tree, Detroit Greenfield RV Park, GNC, K-Mart
185	US 12, Michigan Ave (from eb, exits left, no return), to frontage rds,
184mm	Ford Lake
183	US 12, Huron St, Ypsilanti, N Citgo/dsl H, to E MI U, S a Shell Buffalo Wild Wings, Coney Island, Jet's Pizza, McDonald's, Tim Horton's Marriott Kroger/dsl, st police
181b a	US 12 W, Michigan Ave, Ypsilanti, N Speedway/dsl Coney Island, Dunkin Donuts, Hong Kong Chinese, Roundtree Grill, Taco Bell, Tim Horton/Wendy's H, Aamco, BigLots, GNC, Radio Shack, Walmart/Subway, **0-2 mi** S Citgo/Subway/dsl, Mobil/Circle K, Sunoco/dsl Harvest Moon Cafe, McDonald's Sam's Club/gas
180b a	US 23, to Toledo, Flint
177	State St, N BP, Mobil Bravo Italiana, Buffalo Wild Wings, Burger King, CA Pizza, Chipotle, Graham's Steaks, Los Amigos, Macaroni Grill, Max&Erma's, Mediterrano Rest, Olive Garden, Panda Express, PF Chang's, Red Robin, Wendy's Comfort Inn, Courtyard, Extended Stay America, Extended Stay America, Fairfield Inn, Hampton Inn, Hilton Garden, Holiday Inn, Holiday Inn Express, Kensington Court Inn, Red Roof Inn, Residence Inn, Sheraton, TownePlace Suites Firestone/auto, Honda, JC Penney, Macy's, mall, Porsche, Sears/auto, to UMI, URGENT CARE, Von Maur, VW, World Mkt, S Citgo/Subway/dsl, Speedway/dsl Coney Island, McDonald's, Taco Bell, Tim Horton's Motel 6 Belle Tire, Costco/gas, U-Haul
175	Ann Arbor-Saline Rd, N Shell/Tim Horton's Applebee's, Bagger Dave's, Bella Italia, Dibella Subs, Moe's SW Grill, Old Carolina BBQ, Panera Bread, Subway, Tony Sacco's Pizza Candlewood Suites REI, to UMI Stadium, vet, Whole Foods Mkt, S ChuckECheese's, Five Guys, Joe's Crabshack, McDonald's, Outback Steaks, Panchero's, Subway, TGIFriday's AT&T, Best Buy, BigLots, Dick's, Jo-Ann Fabrics, Kohl's, Meijer/dsl/e-85, Petsmart, Target

ANN ARBOR

INTERSTATE 94 Cont'd

Exit #	Services
172	Jackson Ave, to Ann Arbor, N **on Stadium Ave** Marathon, Shell/dsl Burger King, Jersey Mike's, McDonald's, Noodles&Co, Quarter Rest., Subway, Taco Bell, Zingerman's Roadhouse H, $Tree, CVS, Goodyear/auto, Kroger, Midas, O'Reilly Parts, Plum Mkt, Rite Aid, Staples, TJ Maxx, Verizon, Walgreens, S Marathon Weber's Rest. Hampton Inn, Wyndham Garden Chevrolet/Cadillac, Ford, Hyundai, Mini, Nissan, Subaru, Toyota/Scion
171	MI 14 (from eb, exits left), Ann Arbor, to Flint by U.S. 23
169	Zeeb Rd, N BP/dsl Big Boy, Grand Traverse Pies Co, McDonald's, Metzger's Rest. Holiday Inn Express, S Citgo/dsl Arby's, Biggby Coffee, Burger King, Creekside Grill, Culver's, Domino's, Panera Bread, Pizza Hut, Subway, Taco Bell, Wendy's, Westside Grill CVS Drug, Discount Tire, Lowe's, Meijer/dsl, Menard's, vet
167	Baker Rd, Dexter, N Pilot/Subway/scales/dsl/24hr, S Pilot/Arby's/dsl/scales/24hr, TA/BP/Popeye's/dsl/scales/24hr/ @ McDonald's Blue Beacon
162	Jackson Rd, Fletcher Rd, S BP/Subway/dsl/24hr Stiver's Rest.
161mm	**eb, full facilities, litter barrels, petwalk vending**
159	MI 52, Chelsea, N Shell/dsl, Speedway/dsl, Sunoco/dsl Big Boy, Biggby Coffee, Chelsea Grill, China Garden, Chinese Tonite, Jimmy John's, KFC/Taco Bell, McDonald's, Subway, Uptown Coney Island, Wendy's Comfort Inn, Holiday Inn Express H, $Tree, Ace Hardware, AutoZone, Buick/Chevrolet, Chrysler/Dodge/Jeep, Country Mkt Foods/drug, CVS Drug, Travel Land RV Ctr, USPO, Verizon, S Buick/Chevrolet
157	Jackson Rd, Pierce Rd, N Gerald Eddy Geology Ctr
156	Kalmbach Rd, N to Waterloo RA
153	Clear Lake Rd, N Marathon/dsl
151.5mm	**weigh sta both lanes**
150	to Grass Lake, S Mobil/Dunkin Donuts/Subway/dsl
150mm	**wb, full facilities, litter barrels, petwalk vending**
147	Race Rd, N camping, to Waterloo RA, S lodging Holiday RV Camp
145	Sargent Rd, S BP McDonald's, Wendy's Colonial Inn
144	Lp 94 (from wb), to Jackson
142	US 127 S, to Hudson, **1 mi** S Meijer/dsl, Speedway/dsl Arby's, Bob Evans, KFC, McDonald's, Taco Bell, Wendy's $General, $Tree, Advance Parts, Kroger, Rite Aid, to MI Speedway, Verizon, Walgreens
141	Elm Rd, N Travelodge Chevrolet, Chrysler/Dodge/Jeep, Ford/Lincoln, Honda, Nissan, S H
139	MI 106, Cooper St, to Jackson, N st police/prison, S Citgo/Subway H, Meefhof Tire
138	US 127 N, MI 50, to Lansing, Jackson, N Red Lobster, Yen King Chinese Baymont Inn, Comfort Inn, Fairfield Inn, Hampton Inn, Super 8 vet, S Admiral, BP/dsl, Shell/dsl Arby's, Big Boy, Bob Evans, Burger King, Dunkin Donuts, Fazoli's, KFC, LJ Silver, Los Tres Amigos, McDonald's, Old Country Buffet, Outback Steaks, Panda Express, Panera Bread, Papa John's, Qdoba, Rally's, Starbucks, Subway, Wendy's Best Value Inn $Tree, Advance Parts, Aldi Foods, AT&T, AutoZone, Belle Tire, Best Buy, BigLots, Discount Tire, Family$, Home Depot, JoAnn Fabrics, Kohl's, Kroger/gas, Lowe's,

JACKSON

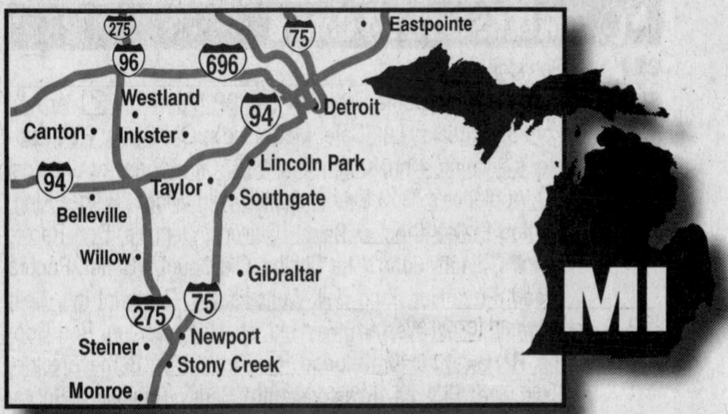

Exit #	Services
138	Continued Michael's, Midas, O'Reilly Parts, Petsmart, Sears/auto, Target, TJ Maxx, URGENT CARE, Verizon, Walgreens
137	Airport Rd, N Marathon/dsl, Shell/Taco Bell Burger King, Denny's, McDonald's, Steak'n Shake, Subway, Wendy's Holiday Inn 7-11, Meijer/dsl, S BP/dsl Cracker Barrel, Culver's, LoneStar Steaks, Olive Garden Holiday Inn Express K-Mart, Sam's Club/gas, Save-A-Lot Foods
136	Lp 94, MI 60, to Jackson
135mm	**eb, full facilities, litter barrels, petwalk vending**
133	Dearing Rd, Spring Arbor, S to Spring Arbor U
130	Parma
128	Michigan Ave, N BP/Burger King/scales/dsl/24hr RV camping
127	Concord Rd, N wineries
124	MI 99, to Eaton Rapids
121	28 Mile Rd, to Albion, N Mobil/Subway/dsl Arby's Days Inn, S AllStar/dsl, BP/dsl, Speedway/dsl Frosty Dan's, KFC, La Casa Mexican, Maria's Garden Rest., McDonald's, Pizza Hut Super 9 Inn H, $General, Albion Tire/auto, AutoZone, Buick/Chevrolet, Family Fare Foods, Family$, Ford, O'Reilly Parts
119	MI 199, 26 Mile Rd
115	22.5 Mile Rd, N Citgo/115 Rest./dsl/24hr
113mm	**wb, full facilities, litter barrels, petwalk vending**
112	Partello Rd, S Loves/Hardee's/scales/dsl/24hr Schuler's Rest.
110	Old US 27, Marshall, N Shell/Country Kitchen/Subway/dsl/24hr, S Citgo/dsl Denny's, Pizza Hut (2mi), Schuler's Rest. (2mi) Hampton Inn, Holiday Inn Express H, sheriff
108	I-69, US 27, N to Lansing, S to Ft Wayne
104	11 Mile Rd, Michigan Ave, N Pilot/McDonald's/dsl/scales/24hr, TA/Country Pride/dsl/scales/24hr/ @, S Citgo/Subway/dsl/e-85 Quality Inn/rest. casino
102mm	Kalamazoo River
100	Rd 294, Beadle Lake Rd, N Moonraker Rest., S Citgo/dsl/repair Binder Park Zoo
98b	I-194 N, to Battle Creek
98a	MI 66, to Sturgis, S Citgo/Tim Horton/dsl Chili's, Los Aztecas, McDonald's, Ruby Tuesday, Schlotzsky's, Starbucks, Steak'n Shake Courtyard, Holiday Inn AT&T, Best Buy, Discount Tire, Kohl's, Lowe's, Meijer/dsl, Menards, Michael's, PetCo, same as 97, Sam's Club/gas, Staples, TJ Maxx, Verizon, Walgreens, Walmart/Subway

MARSHALL

[gas] = gas [food] = food [lodging] = lodging [other] = other [RS] = rest stop

INTERSTATE 94 Cont'd

Exit #	Services
97	Capital Ave, to Battle Creek, N [gas] BP, Marathon [food] Arby's, LoneStar Steaks, Lux Cafe, McDonald's, Old China, Red Lobster [lodging] Comfort Inn, Knights Inn, S [gas] Citgo/Subway, Shell/dsl [food] Applebee's, Bob Evans, Buffalo Wild Wings, Burger King, Canton Buffet, Cracker Barrel, Culver's, Denny's, Don Pablo, Fazoli's, Jimmy John's, La Cocina, Old Country Buffet, Panera Bread, Pizza Hut, Taco Bell, Wendy's [lodging] Baymont Inn, Best Value Inn, Best Western, Fairfield Inn, Hampton Inn, Red Roof Inn, Rodeway Inn, Travelodge [other] $Tree, AAA, Barnes&Noble, Belle Tire, BigLots, Firestone/auto, Harley Davidson, Hobby Lobby, JC Penney, Jo-Ann Fabrics, Macy's, mall, Sears/auto, Target, Uncle Ed's Oil Shoppe, URGENT CARE, vet
96mm	**[RS] eb, full [handicapped] facilities, litter barrels, petwalk [phone] [vending] vending**
95	Helmer Rd, **2 mi** N [gas] Citgo/dsl [food] Arby's, Big Boy [other] Meijer/dsl/e-85, st police
92	Lp 94, rd 37, to Battle Creek, Springfield, N [gas] Citgo/Arlene's Trkstp/dsl/rest./24hr, Shell [other] RV camping, to Ft Custer RA
88	Climax, N [other] Galesburg Speedway
85	35th St, Galesburg, N [gas] Shell/dsl [food] McDonald's, Subway [other] Galesburg Speedway, River Oaks CP, to Ft Custer RA, S [other] Colebrook CP, RV camping, Scott's Mill CP, Winery Tours
85mm	**[RS] wb, full [handicapped] facilities, litter barrels, petwalk [phone] [vending] vending**
81	Lp 94 (from wb), to Kalamazoo
80	Cork St, Sprinkle Rd, to Kalamazoo, N [gas] Marathon/dsl, Speedway/dsl [food] Arby's, Bennucci's Grill, Burger King, Crew Rest., Denny's, Godfather's, Taco Bell [lodging] Baymont Inn, Clarion, Holiday Inn Express, Red Roof Inn, Sheraton [other] Monro, vet, S [gas] BP/dsl, Speedway/dsl [food] McDonald's, Michelle's Rest., Nob Hill Grill, Subway, Wendy's [lodging] Candlewood Suites, EconoLodge, Motel 6, Quality Inn
78	Portage Rd, Kilgore Rd, N [gas] Mobil/Circle K [food] China Hut, Summer Thyme Cafe [lodging] AmericInn [other] [H], repair, S [gas] Marathon/dsl, Shell, Speedway [food] Angelo's Italian, Biggby Coffee, Bravo Rest., Brewster's, Café Meli, CJ's Lubritorium, McDonald's, Pizza King, Subway, Taco Bell, Theo&Stacy's Rest. [lodging] Country Inn&Suites, Days Inn, Hampton Inn [other] AutoValue Parts, Fields Fabrics
76	Westnedge Ave, N [gas] Admiral, Meijer/dsl, Speedway/dsl [food] Burger King, Grand Traverse Pie Co, Hibachi Buffet, Hooters, IHOP, Lee's Chicken, McDonald's, Old Chicago Grill, Outback Steaks, Papa John's, Papa Murphy's, Pizza Hut, Qdoba, Riviera Mayo, Root Beer Stand, Steak'n Shake, Subway, Taco Bell, Theo&Stacy's Rest. [lodging] Courtyard, Homewood Suites [other] $Tree, Advance Parts, BigLots, Discount Tire, Earth Fare, Family$, Firestone/auto, Gander Mtn, Goodyear/auto, Lowe's, Meijer, Midas, Office Depot, Walgreens, S [gas] Shell [food] Antique Kitchen Rest., Applebee's, Biggby Coffee, Bilbo's Pizza, Bob Evans, Brann's Steaks, Burger King, Carrabba's, Chili's, ChuckECheese's, Coldstone, Culver's, Five Guys, HoneyBaked Ham, Jimmy John's, KFC, Little Caesars, LJ Silver, Logan's Roadhouse, Los Amigos Mexican, McDonald's, Moe's SW Grill, Noodles&Co, Olive Garden, Panchero's Mexican, Panera Bread, Penn Sta Subs, Pizza Hut, Qdoba Mexican, Red Lobster, Red Robin, Schlotzsky's, Subway, Taco Bell, Tim Horton, TX Roadhouse, Wendy's, Zoup! [lodging] Holiday Motel [other] $Tree, Aldi Foods, AT&T, AutoZone, Barnes&Noble, Belle Tire, Best Buy, Buick/Cadillac/GMC, Dick's, Fannie May Candies, Firestone/

KALAMAZOO

76	Continued auto, Harding's Foods, Hobby Lobby, Home Depot, JC Penney, JoAnn Fabrics, Kohl's, Macy's, mall, Menard's, Michael's, Monro, Old Navy, O'Reilly Parts, PepBoys, Petco, Sam's Club, gas, Sears/auto, Target, TJMaxx, Tuesday Morning, Tuffy Auto, Uncle Ed's Oil Shoppe, URGENT CARE, Verizon, Walgreens, World Mkt
75	Oakland Dr
74b a	US 131, to Kalamazoo, N [other] Kalamazoo Coll, to W MI U
72	9th St, Oshtemo, N [gas] Citgo/dsl, Speedway/dsl [food] Arby's, Culver's, McDonald's, Taco Bell, Wendy's [lodging] Hampton Inn, S [food] Cracker Barrel [lodging] Fairfield Inn, Microtel, Towne Place Suites
66	Mattawan, N [gas] Citgo/dsl, Speedway/Subway/dsl/scales/24hr [food] Mancino's Italian [other] Family$, Freightliner, R&S RV Service, Rossman Auto/repair, vet, S [gas] Shell/dsl [food] Pizza Hut, Subway [other] USPO, Wagoner's Foods
60	MI 40, Paw Paw, N [gas] Citgo, Speedway/dsl [food] Arby's, Burger King, Chicken Coop, Copper Grille, McDonald's, Pizza Hut, Red's Root Beer, Subway, Subway, Taco Bell, Wendy's [lodging] Comfort Inn, EconoLodge, Travelodge [other] [H], Advance Parts, AT&T, Buick/Chevrolet/GMC, Chrysler/Dodge/Jeep, Family Fare Foods, Ford, O'Reilly Parts, St Julian Winery, Walgreens, S [other] Walmart/Subway
56	MI 51, to Decatur, N [other] st police, S [gas] Citgo/dsl, Marathon/dsl
52	Lawrence
46	Hartford, N [gas] Shell/dsl [food] McDonald's, Panel Room Rest., Subway, S [other] fruit stand
42mm	**[RS] wb, full [handicapped] facilities, litter barrels, petwalk [phone] [vending] vending**
41	MI 140, to Niles, Watervliet, N [gas] Citgo, Marathon/dsl, Shell/dsl [food] Burger King, Chicken Coop, Frosty Boy, Mill Creek Charlie's Rest., Subway, Taco Bell [lodging] Fairfield Inn [other] [H], KOA (Apr-Oct) (7mi)
39	Millburg, Coloma, Deer Forest, **0-1 mi** N [gas] BP/dsl, Shell/dsl, Speedway/dsl, Wesco/dsl [food] DQ, El Asadero Mexican, Friendly Grill, McDonald's, Subway [other] Family$, Krenek RV Ctr, S [other] fruit mkt, Jollay Mkt, wine tasting
34	I-196 N, US 31 N, to Holland, Grand Rapids
33	Lp I-94, to Benton Harbor, **2-4 mi** N [other] [airport], sheriff's dept
30	Napier Ave, Benton Harbor, N [gas] Pilot/Wendy's/dsl/LP/24hr/ @, Shell/dsl [lodging] Knights Inn [other] [H], Blue Beacon
29	Pipestone Rd, Benton Harbor, N [food] Applebee's, Asian Grill, Burger King, Cravings Bistro, El Rodeo Mexican, IHOP, Mancino's Pizza, McDonald's, Sophia's Pancake House, Steak'n Shake, Subway, Super Buffet, TX Corral [lodging] Best Western, Days Inn, Hilton Garden, Motel 6, Red Roof Inn [other] Aldi Foods, Best Buy, Big Lots, Chrysler/Dodge/Jeep, Home Depot, JC Penney, Jo-Ann Fabrics, Lowe's, Meijer/dsl, NAPA Autocare, Staples, Walmart/Subway, S [gas] BP/dsl [food] Bob Evans [lodging] Comfort Suites, Holiday Inn Express
28	US 31 S, MI 139 N, Scottdale Rd, to Niles, N [gas] Citgo/dsl, Marathon/dsl [food] Burger King, Chicken Coop, Country Kitchen, DQ, Henry's Burgers, KFC, Little Caesars, Pizza Hut, Sonic, Subway, Taco Bell, Wendy's [lodging] Best Value Inn, Rodeway Inn [other] [H], $Tree, AutoZone, Belle Tire, Chevrolet/Buick/GMC, Family$, Kohl's, M&W Tire, Michael's, Midas, NAPA, O'Reilly Parts, Petsmart, radiators/repair/transmissions, Rite Aid, Save-A-Lot, Target, TJ Maxx, U-Haul, vet, Walgreens
27mm	St Joseph River

BENTON HARBOR

INTERSTATE 94 Cont'd

Exit #	Services
27	MI 63, Niles Ave, to St Joseph, N Citgo Nye's Apple Barn, S Tesla 45 Five Guys, Moe's SW Grill, Panera Bread Goodyear
23	Red Arrow Hwy, Stevensville, N Admiral, Marathon/dsl, Shell/dsl Big Boy, Burger King, Chicago Grill, Cracker Barrel, Culver's, DQ, LJ Silver, McDonald's, Papa John's, Rio's Mexican, Subway Baymont Inn, Candlewood Suites, Comfort Suites, Super 8 Honda, Walgreens, S Five O'Clock Grill Hampton Inn Meijer/dsl/e85
22	John Beers Rd, Stevensville, N Chalet on the Lake to Grand Mere SP, S Marathon/dsl
16	Bridgman, N BP/Quiznos/dsl camping, to Warren Dunes SP, S Citgo Lydia's Rest., McDonald's, Olympus Rest., Pizza Hut, Roma Pizza, Subway Bridgman Inn auto repair, Chevrolet, Chrysler/Dodge/Jeep, Ford/Mazda, st police, vet
12	Sawyer, N Marathon/deli/dsl/scales/24hr truck wash, S TA/Burger King/Popeye's/Taco Bell/scales/dsl/24hr/ @ Fitzgerald's Grill, Greenbush Brewing Super 8 USPO
6	Lakeside, Union Pier, N Round Barn Winery, St Julian Winery, S RV camping
4b a	US 12, to Three Oaks, New Buffalo, N Pizza Hut, Redamak's Hamburgers, Roma Pizza st police
2.5mm	**weigh sta both lanes**
1	MI 239, to Grand Beach, New Buffalo, **0-2 mi** N Shell/Quiznos/dsl Brewster's Italian, Casey's Grille, Jimmy's Grill, McDonald's, Nancy's, Rosie's Rest., Stray Dog Grill, Subway Baymont Inn, Comfort Inn, Fairfield Inn, Holiday Inn Express, Super Inn $General, S Plaza1/dsl/scales/24hr Wendy's casino
0.5mm	**Welcome Center eb, full facilities, info, litter barrels, petwalk vending**
0mm	Michigan/Indiana state line

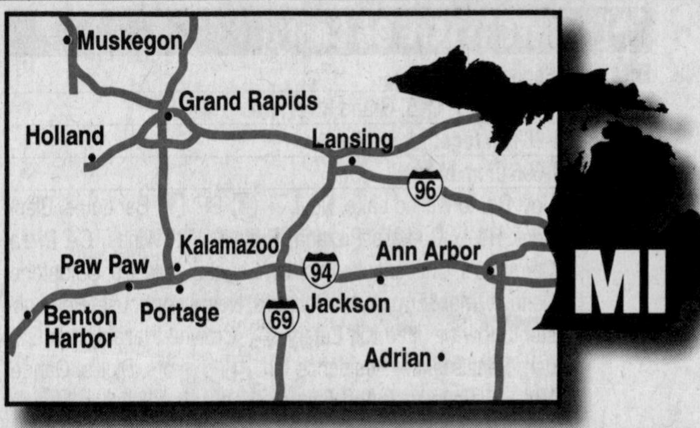

INTERSTATE 96

DETROIT AREA

Exit #	Services
	I-96 begins/ends on I-75, exit 48 in Detroit.
191	I-75, N to Flint, S to Toledo, US 12, to MLK Blvd, to Michigan Ave
190b	Warren Ave, N BP/dsl
190a	I-94 E, to Port Huron
189	W Grand Blvd, Tireman Rd, N BP/dsl, Mobil
188b	Joy Rd, N Church's
188a	Livernois, N Mobil, Shell/Subway Burger King, KFC, McDonald's, Wendy's
187	Grand River Ave (from eb)
186b	Davison Ave, I-96 local and I-96 express divide, no exits from express
186a	Wyoming Ave
185	Schaefer Hwy, to Grand River Ave, N Mobil, Shamrock Coney Island, McDonald's CVS Drug, S Sunoco/dsl
184	Greenfield Rd
183	MI 39, Southfield Fwy, exit from expswy and local
182	Evergreen Rd
180	Outer Dr, N BP/dsl/lube
180mm	I-96 local/express unite/divide
179	US 24, Telegraph Rd, N BP, Marathon/dsl Arby's, Baskin-Robbins/Dunkin Donuts, China King, Little Caesar's, McDonald's, Tim Horton's, White Castle AutoZone, Chevrolet, Family$, Family$, OReilly Parts, URGENT CARE, S Marathon/dsl, Shell/dsl
178	Beech Daly Rd, N gas
177	Inkster Rd, N BP/Tim Horton Subway Best Value Inn $General, 7-11, URGENT CARE
176	Middlebelt Rd, N Bob Evans, IHOP, Olive Garden Comfort Inn, **0-1 mi** S Applebee's, Biggby Coffee, Chili's, Culver's, Del Taco, Five Guys, Jimmy John's, Leo's Coney Island, Logan's Roadhouse, McDonald's, MOD Pizza, Noodles&Co, Outback, Panera Bread, Pizza Hut, Potbelly, Qdoba, Red Lobster, Starbucks Crossland Suites $Tree, AT&T, BigLots, Costco/gas, Dick's, Firestone/auto, GNC, Home Depot, Marshall's, Meijer, Menard's, Michael's, Office Depot, Petsmart, Target, URGENT CARE, Verizon, Walgreens, Walmart, car repair, Jo-Ann Fabrics
175	Merriman Rd, N Mobil/dsl, Speedway/dsl, S Exxon/dsl Blimpie, Prime Grill
174	Farmington Rd, N Mobil/dsl, Sunoco Looney Baker, S BP KFC
173b	Levan Rd, N H, to Madonna U
173a	Newburgh Rd
171mm	**I-275 and I-96 run together 9 miles**
170	6 Mile Rd, N Bar Louie, Big Boy, Buffalo Wild Wings, Jimmy John's, Panera Bread, Qdoba, Red Robin Best Western, Courtyard, Holiday Inn, Marriott H, Ace Hardware, Busch's Foods, GNC, mall, O'Reilly Parts, Rite Aid, URGENT CARE, Verizon, Walgreens, S Marathon, Mobil Applebee's, Brann's Steaks, Bravo Italian, Buca Italian, Charlie's Grille, Claddagh Rest., Fleming's, Food on Wood Grill, Jimmy John's, McDonald's, Mitchell's Fish Mkt, Noodles&Co, Panchero's, Papa Vino's, PF Chang, Potbelly, Subway, Tahini Grill, Tim Horton, Wendy's, Zoe's Pancakes Fairfield Inn, Residence Inn, TownePlace Suites Barnes&Noble, CVS, Kroger, Office Depot, Petsmart, REI
169b a	7 Mile Rd, N Dave&Buster's, Doc's Grill, Little Daddy's Embassy Suites, S Andiamo's Cafe, Bahama Breeze Rest., Burger Fi, Champp's Rest., Chipotle, Gaucho Brazilian, Granite City Grill, J Alexander's Rest., Macaroni Grill, Mod Pizza, Rusty Bucket Rest., Tom Chee Hyatt Place Home Depot
167	8 Mile Rd, to Northville, S BP/dsl, Speedway/dsl Aubree's Pizza, Benihana, Big Boy, Chili's, Five Guys, Kerry's Koney Island, McDonald's, On-the-Border, Panera Bread, Qdoba, Starbucks, Taco Bell, TGIFriday's, Zoup! Extended Stay America, Hampton Inn, Holiday Inn Express, Quality Inn, Sheraton Best Buy, Costco/gas, Dick's, Firestone/auto, Kohl's, Meijer/dsl, Target, to Maybury SP, Trader Joe's, Verizon

MI

INTERSTATE 96 Cont'd

Exit #	Services
165	I-696, I-275, MI 5, Grand River Ave.
I-275 and I-96 run together 9 miles	
163	I-696 (from eb)
162	Novi Rd, to Walled Lake, Novi, **N** [gas] BP [food] Bar Louie, Black Rock Rest., Buddy's Pizzaria, Buffalo Wild Wings, CA Pizza, Carrabba's, Cheesecake Factory, ChuckECheese's, Coldstone, Denny's, Max&Erma's, McDonald's, Novi Chophouse, Red Lobster, Subway, Tilted Kilt Eatery [lodging] Crowne Plaza, Hilton Garden, Renaissance, Residence Inn [other] BigLots, Dick's, Gander Mtn, JC Penney, JoAnn Fabrics, Kohl's, Lord&Taylor, Macy's, mall, Marshalls, Michael's, Midas, Nordstrom, Old Navy, Radio Shack, Sears/auto, **S** [gas] Mobil/dsl, Sunoco/dsl [food] Athenian Coney Island, Bagger Dave's Burgers, BD Mongolian BBQ, Big Salad, Biggby Coffee, Blaze Pizza, Bonefish Grill, Boston Mkt, Famous Dave's, Honeybaked Express, IHOP, Kim's Chinese, Maisano's Italian, Olive Garden, Panera Bread, Pei Wei, Potbelly, Qdoba, Red Robin, Rojo Mexican, Steve&Rocky's, TGIFriday's, Tony Sacco Pizza, Wasabi, Wendy's [lodging] Courtyard, DoubleTree, Towne Place Suites [other] [H], Advance Parts, AT&T, Belle Tire, Better Health Foods, Chevrolet, Discount Tire, Firestone/auto, Hobby Lobby, Kia, NAPA, O'Reilly Parts, TJ Maxx, URGENT CARE, Verizon, Walmart
160	Beck Rd, 12 Mile Rd, **S** [gas] Shell/Tim Horton [food] Applebee's, China King, Guido's Pizza, Halo Burger, La Herraduro Mexican, Lee's Coney Island, Olga's Kitchen, Outback Steaks, Subway, Zoup! [lodging] Hyatt Place, Staybridge Suites [other] [H], GNC, Home Depot, Kroger, Staples, to Maybury SP
159	Wixom Rd, Walled Lake, **N** [gas] Marathon/dsl, Sunoco/dsl [food] Culver's, Leon's Rest., Papa Romano's Pizza, Quiznos, Wendy's [lodging] Holiday Inn Express [other] General RV Ctr, Meineke, Menard's, to Proud Lake RA, **S** [gas] Mobil/dsl, Shell, Valero/dsl [food] A&W/KFC, Arby's, Baskin-Robbins/Dunkin Donuts, Biggby Coffee, Burger King, Don's Diner, Jimmy John's, La Roca Mexican, McDonald's, Red Olive Rest., Stinger's Grill, Taco Bell [lodging] Comfort Suites [other] AutoZone, Lincoln, Meijer/dsl, Sam's Club/gas, Target
155b a	to Milford, New Hudson, **N** [other] Camp Dearborn (5mi), Ford, to Lyon Oaks CP, **S** [gas] Sunoco [food] Applebee's, Arby's, Biggby Coffee, Jet's Pizza, Kensington Grill, Leo's Coney Island, McDonald's, Starbucks, Subway [other] AAA, AT&T, Belle Tire, Chevrolet, Discount Tire, Hyundai, Lowe's, URGENT CARE, Verizon, Walmart
153	Kent Lake Rd, **N** [other] Kensington Metropark, **S** [gas] BP/dsl [lodging] Country Meadows Inn (3mi)
151	Kensington Rd, **N** [other] Kensington Metropark, **S** [food] food [lodging] lodging [other] Island Lake RA
150	Pleasant Valley Rd (no return wb)
148b a	US 23, N to Flint, S to Ann Arbor
147	Spencer Rd, **N** [gas] Mobil/dsl [food] Cherry's Cafe [other] st police, **S** [food] Bagger Dave's Burgers (2mi) [other] to Brighton St RA
145	Grand River Ave, to Brighton, **N** [gas] BP, Shell/dsl [food] Arby's, Baskin-Robbins/Dunkin Donuts, Cracker Barrel, Outback Steaks, Pizza Hut [lodging] Courtyard [other] [H], $General, Buick/GMC, Ford, Honda, Mazda, URGENT CARE, vet, **S** [gas] Marathon/Subway [food] Big Boy, Border Cantina, Burger King, Chili's, Firehouse Subs, Gourmet Garden, Halo Burger, IHOP, Jimmy John's, Leo's Coney Island, Lil Chef, McDonald's, Olga's Kitchen, Panera Bread, Pi's Asian, Red Robin, Starbucks, Taco Bell, Tim Horton, Wendy's [lodging] Holiday Inn Express, Homewood Suites
145	Continued [other] $Tree, AAA, Advance Parts, Aldi Foods, AT&T, Belle Tire, Be Buy, Bob's Tire, CVS Drug, Home Depot, JoAnn Fabrics, Marshalls Meijer/dsl/E85, Michael's, O'Reilly Parts, Petsmart, Staple Target, to Brighton Ski Area, USPO, Verizon, Verizon, Walgreen
141	Lp 96 (from wb, return at 140), to Howell, **0-2 mi N** [gas] BP/ds Shell/Tim Horton/dsl, Speedway, Sunoco/dsl [food] Applebee's Arby's, Asian Fusian Buffet, Aubree's Pizzaria, Biggby Coffee Bluefin Steaks, Bob Evans, Buffalo Wild Wings, Jimmy John's KFC, Leo's Coney Island, Little Caesars, Los Tres Amigos, Mc Donald's, Qdoba, Subway, Taco Bell, Wendy's, White Castle [other] $Tree, AT&T, Belle Tire, Big Lots, Chevrolet, Discount Tire, GNC Home Depot, Kohl's, Lowe's, Meijer, O'Reilly Parts, TJ Max URGENT CARE, Walmart
140	S Latson Rd, same as 141
137	D19, to Pinckney, Howell, **N** [gas] Mobil/dsl, Shell, Speedway dsl, Sunoco/Baskin-Robbins/Dunkin Donuts/dsl [food] All Sta Coney Island, Bock Brewing Co, Hog Wild BBQ, Joanna's ToGo, Wendy's [lodging] Kensington Inn [other] [H], Parts+, Spar tan Tire, True Value, USPO, vet, **S** [food] Wooly Bully's Rest [lodging] Howell Inn
135mm	**[rest stop] eb, full [handicapped] facilities, litter barrels, petwalk [phone] [vending] vending**
133	MI 59, Highland Rd, **N** [gas] Marathon/McDonald's/dsl [food] Arby's, Leo's Coney Island [lodging] Baymont, Holiday Inn Expres [other] Tanger Outlets/famous brands
129	Fowlerville Rd, Fowlerville, **N** [gas] Marathon/dsl, Shell/dsl Sunoco/dsl [food] A&W/KFC, Great Lakes Rest., McDonald's Pizza Hut/Taco Bell, Wendy's [lodging] Magnuson Hotel [other] Chevrolet, O'Reilly Parts, Walmart, **S** [gas] Mobil/dsl [food] Subway [other] Chysler/Dodge/Jeep, Ford
126mm	**weigh sta both lanes**
122	MI 43, MI 52, Webberville, **N** [gas] Mobil/dsl/24hr [food] McDonald's [other] Sinclair Grill (2mi)
117	to Dansville, Williamston, **N** [gas] Marathon/Jersey's Giant Subs/dsl [food] Spag's Grill (3mi), **S** [gas] Sunoco/dsl
111mm	**[rest stop] wb, full [handicapped] facilities, litter barrels, petwalk [phone] [vending] vending**
110	Okemos, Mason, **N** [gas] Marathon/dsl, Shell/Jimmy John's/dsl, Sunoco/Dunkin Donuts [food] Applebee's, Arby's, Backyard BBQ, Big John's Steaks, Biggby Coffee, Coldstone/Tim Horton, Cracker Barrel, Culver's, Frank's Press Box Grille Gilbert&Blake's, Grand Traverse Pie Co., Leaf Salad Bar, Little Caesars, McDonald's, Ozzy Mediterranean, Panchero's Mexican, Starbucks, Stillwater Grill, Subway, Taco Bell [lodging] Comfort Inn, Fairfield Inn, Hampton Inn, Holiday Inn Express, Staybridge Suites [other] 7-11, BMW/Porsche, Mercedes, to stadium, Verizon
106b a	I-496, US 127, to Jackson, Lansing, **N** [other] St Police
104	Lp 96, Cedar St, to Holt, Lansing, **N** [gas] Admiral, Speedway/dsl [food] Applebee's, Arby's, Asia's Finest, Big John's, Biggby Coffee, Blimpie, Bob Evans, Boston Mkt, Burger King, China King, Domino's, Fazoli's, Finley's Rest., Happy's Pizza, Hooters, Jet's Pizza, KFC, Los Tres Amigos, Mikado Grill, Panda Gourmet, Pizza Hut, Steak'n Shake, Taco Bell, TX Roadhouse, Wendy's, Zeus Coney Island [lodging] Best Value Inn, Magnuson Hotel, Super 8 [other] [H], $Tree, Aldi Foods, AT&T, auto repair, Belle Tire, Cadillac, Chevrolet, Chrysler/Dodge/Jeep, Discount Tire, Family$, GNC, Hyundai, Kia, Lexus, Meijer/dsl, Menards, Sam's Club/gas, Target, Toyota/Scion, Tuffy Auto, vet, **S** [gas] Speedway/dsl [food] Aldaco's Taco Bar, Burger King, Champion's Grill, China East Buffet, Dairy Dan, Famous Dave's BBQ, Flapjack Rest., Hungry Howie's, McDonald's, Subway, Tim Horton/Coldstone [lodging] Causeway Bay Hotel [other] Advance Parts, AutoZone, Budget

LANSING

INTERSTATE 96 Cont'd

104 Continued
Tire, CVS Drug, Family$, Kroger/gas, Lowe's, NAPA, Rite Aid, URGENT CARE, Verizon

101 MI 99, MLK Blvd, to Eaton Rapids, **0-3 mi N** [gas] QD [food] Arby's, Tim Horton [O] Kroger/gas, Meijer/dsl, **S** [gas] Speedway/Subway/dsl [food] Coach's Grill, McDonald's, Wendy's

98b a Lansing Rd, to Lansing, **N** [food] Arby's, Wendy's [lodging] Comfort Inn, Holiday Inn Express [O] Harley-Davidson, **S** [O] st police

97 I-69, US 27 S, S to Ft Wayne, N to Lansing

95 I-496, to Lansing

93b a MI 43, Lp 69, Saginaw Hwy, to Grand Ledge, **0-2 mi N** [gas] Shell, Speedway/dsl [food] Applebee's, Buffalo Wild Wings, Burger King, Carrabba's, Cheddar's, Chipotle, Denny's, Fazoli's, Finley's Grill, Frank's Grill, Hibachi Grill, Honeybaked Ham, Houlihan's, Logan's Roadhouse, Longhorn Steaks, McDonald's, Outback Steaks, Panera Bread, Qdoba, Red Robin, Subway [lodging] Comfort Inn, Fairfield Inn, Hampton Inn, Motel 6, Quality Inn, Ramada Inn, Red Roof Inn, Residence Inn [O] [H], $Tree, Aldi, AT&T, Barnes&Noble, Best Buy, BigLots, Chrysler/Dodge/Jeep, Hobby Lobby, JC Penney, Kohl's, Kroger/dsl, Macy's, Meijer/dsl/24hr, Target, TJ Maxx, vet, Walgreens, Younkers, **S** [gas] BP/Dunkin Donuts, QD, Sunoco/McDonald's [food] Arby's, Biggby Coffee, Bob Evans, Cancun Mexican, Cracker Barrel, Culver's, Steak'n Shake [lodging] SpringHill Suites [O] Belle Tire, Buick/GMC, Discount Tire, Gander Mtn, Lowe's, Mazda/Volvo, Menards, Michael's, Petsmart, Staples, Walmart/Subway

92mm Grand River

91 I-69 N (from wb), US 27 N, to Flint

90 Grand River Ave, to [airport] (from wb), **S** [gas] FLYING J Denny's/dsl/24hr

89 I-69 N, US 27 N (from eb), to Flint

87mm **[RS] eb, full [handicap] facilities, litter barrels, petwalk [phone] [picnic] vending**

86 MI 100, Wright Rd, to Grand Ledge, **S** [gas] Mobil/McDonald's/dsl, Speedway/Subway/24hr

84 to Eagle, Westphalia

79mm **[RS] wb, full [handicap] facilities, info, litter barrels, petwalk [phone] [picnic] vending**

77 Lp 96, Grand River Ave, Portland, **N** [gas] BP/dsl, Shell/Subway, Speedway/dsl [food] Arby's, Biggby Coffee, Burger King, Little Caesar's, McDonald's, New China Buffet, Red Tomato Pizza [lodging] American Heritage Inn [O] CarQuest, Family$, Rite Aid, Tom's Foods, Verizon, **S** [gas] Tom's/dsl [food] Wendy's

76 Kent St, Portland

76mm Grand River

73 to Lyons-Muir, Grand River Ave

69mm **weigh sta both lanes**

67 MI 66, to Ionia, Battle Creek, **N** [gas] Pilot/Subway/dsl/scales/24hr [food] Corner Landing Grill [lodging] Midway Motel, Super 8 [O] [H], Alice Springs RV Park (3mi), Lakeside Camping, Meijer/dsl (4mi), st police, Walmart (4mi)

64 to Lake Odessa, Saranac, **N** [O] Ionia St RA, **S** [O] I-96 Speedway

63mm **[RS] eb, full [handicap] facilities, litter barrels, petwalk [phone] [picnic] vending**

59 Clarksville

52 MI 50, to Lowell, **N** [gas] Mobil/Subway/dsl [O] fairgrounds, **S** [gas] Marathon/Noble Roman's/dsl (2mi)

46mm Thornapple River

46 Rd 6, to Rd 37

44 36 St, **S** [O] [airport]

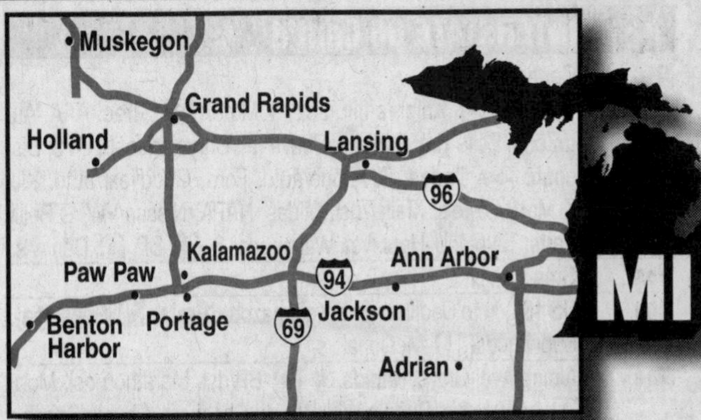

CASCADE

43b a MI 11, 28th St, Cascade, **N** [food] Bagger Dave's, Biggby Coffee, Brann's Steaks, Cascades Grill, Culver's, Dunkin Donuts/Baskin Robbins, Firehouse Subs, Georgio's Pizza, Jet's Pizza, Jimmy John's, Macaroni Grill, New Beginnings Rest., Pal's Diner, Panera Bread, Pit Stop BBQ, Pizza Hut, Qdoba, Subway, Sundance Grill, Tim Horton's, Wendy's [lodging] Baymont Inn, Best Western, Country Inn&Suites, Crowne Plaza, EconoLodge, Holiday Inn Express [O] Ace Hardware, AT&T, Audi/Porsche/Subaru, Fresh Mkt, GNC, Meijer/dsl, Mercedes/Volvo/VW, Subaru, Verizon, Walmart, **0-3 mi S** [gas] Citgo, Shell, Speedway/dsl [food] Applebee's, Arby's, Arby's, Arnie's Rest., Bob Evans, Burger King, Cantina Mexican, Carrabba's, Chili's, Chipotle Mexican, ChuckeCheese, Dave&Buster's, Denny's, Don Julio's, Five Guys, Grand Traverse Pie Co, Honey Baked Ham, IHOP, Jimmy John's, Krispy Kreme, Longhorn Steaks, McDonald's, Moe's SW Grill, Noodles&Co, Old Chicago, Olive Garden, Osaka Japanese, Outback Steaks, Panera Bread, Paulina's Mexican, Pizza Hut, Pizza Ranch, Potbelly, Red Lobster, Red Olive Rest., Red Sun Buffet, Smokey Bones, Starbucks, Steak'n Shake, Subway, Taco Bell, TX Roadhouse, Wendy's [lodging] Clarion, Comfort Inn, Courtyard, DoubleTree, Drury Inn, Extended Stay America, Fairfield Inn, Hampton Inn, Hawthorn Suites, Homewood Suites, Motel 6, Ramada, Red Roof Inn, Residence Inn, SpringHill Suites, Wyndham Garden [O] $General, $Tree, Aldi Foods, Belle Tire, Best Buy, Big Lots, CarQuest, Costco/gas, Dick's, Ford/Mazda, Gander Mtn, Hobby Lobby, Home Depot, Honda, Hyundai/Kia, Jo-Ann Fabrics, Lowe's, Michael's, Monro Auto, Nissan, Office Depot, Old Navy, Petsmart, Sam's Club/gas, Sears/auto, Staples, Target, TJ Maxx, Tuesday Morning, U-Haul, World Mkt

40b a Cascade Rd, **N** [gas] BP/dsl, Forrest Hills Fuel [food] Biggby Coffee, China Garden, Forrest Hills Rest., Great Harvest, Jets Pizza, Little Bangkok, Little Caesar's, Manna a Cafe, Subway [O] vet, Walgreens, **S** [gas] Shell/dsl, Speedway/dsl [food] Bonefish Grill, Jimmy John's, Zoup! [O] [H], Keystone Drug

39 MI 21 (from eb), to Flint

38 E Beltline Ave, to MI 21, MI 37, MI 44, **N** [gas] BP [food] Applebee's, Fuji Yama Japanese, Gus's Original, Red Hot Inn Rest., Wendy's [O] Meijer/dsl, RV camping, URGENT CARE, Verizon, **S** [food] Gravity Grille [lodging] Country Inn&Suites [O] [H]

37 I-196 (from wb, exits left), Gerald Ford Fwy, to Grand Rapids

36 Leonard St, **2 mi S** [food] Arby's, Jimmy John's, McDonald's [O] sheriff's dept

33 Plainfield Ave, MI 44 Connector, **N** [gas] Citgo/dsl, Speedway/dsl [food] Arby's, Biggby Coffee, Charlie's Grille, Cheers Grill, Dunkin Donuts, Fred's Italian, Golden Dragon, Jimmy John's, KFC, Little Caesar's, McDonald's, Pizza Hut, Rice Wok, Russ' Rest., Subway, Taco Bell, Tim Horton's, Tokyo Roadhouse,

INTERSTATE 96 Cont'd

33	Continued Wendy's [lodging] Knights Inn, Lazy T Motel [other] $Tree, AAA, AutoZone, Belle Tire, BigLots, Chevrolet, Chrysler/Jeep, CVS, Discount Tire, Dodge, Firestone/auto, Ford, Goodyear/auto, Kia, K-Mart, Lowe's, Meijer/dsl, Midas, NAPA, Nissan/VW, O'Reilly Parts, Toyota, U-Haul, vet, Walgreens, S [gas] BP [food] Denny's
31mm	Grand River
31b a	US 131, N to Cadillac, S to Kalamazoo, **1 mi N** [gas] Speedway/Subway/dsl [food] McDonald's
30b a	Alpine Ave, Grand Rapids, N [gas] BP/dsl, Marathon/dsl, Mobil [food] Applebee's, Buffalo Wild Wings, Checkers, ChuckeCheese, Cinco de Mayo, Coldstone, Culver's, El Burrito Mexican, Empire Buffet, Firehouse Subs, First Wok, Five Guys, Golden Corral, Hibachi Grill, IHOP, Jimmy John's, Little Caesar's, Logan's Roadhouse, McDonald's, Olive Garden, Outback Steaks, Panera Bread, Qdoba, Russ' Rest., Sonic, Starbucks, Steak'n Shake, Subway, Taco Bell, TGIFriday's, Three Happiness Chinese [lodging] Hampton Inn, Holiday Inn Express, SpringHill Suites [other] $Tree, Aldi Foods, AT&T, AutoZone, Belle Tire, Best Buy, CarQuest, Discount Tire, Ford, GNC, Hobby Lobby, Jo-Ann, Kohl's, Marshall's, Menards, Michael's, NAPA, PepBoys, PetCo, Sam's Club/gas, Target, TJ Maxx, Verizon, Walgreens, Walmart, S [gas] Admiral/dsl, Speedway/dsl [food] Arby's, Burger King, Fazoli's, KFC, LJ Silver, McDonald's, Papa John's, Pizza Hut, Wendy's [lodging] Best Value Inn [other] Goodyear/auto, Home Depot, Meijer/dsl, Midas, O'Reilly Parts, U-Haul, URGENT CARE
28	Walker Ave, S [gas] Meijer/dsl/24hr [food] Bob Evans, McDonald's [lodging] Baymont Inn, Quality Inn
26	Fruit Ridge Ave, N [gas] Citgo/dsl, S [gas] Citgo/deli/dsl
25mm	**[RS] eb, full [handicap] facilities, litter barrels, petwalk [phone] [picnic] vending**
25	8th Ave, 4Mile Rd (from wb), S [gas] Marathon/dsl [lodging] Wayside Motel
24	8th Ave, 4Mile Rd (from eb), S [gas] Marathon/dsl [lodging] Wayside Motel
23	Marne, N [other] tires, S [food] Depot Café, Rinaldi's Café [other] Ernie's Mkt, fairgrounds/raceway, USPO
19	Lamont, Coopersville, N [food] food, S [other] LP
16	B-35, Eastmanville, N [gas] Citgo/Subway/dsl, Shell/Burger King/dsl, Speedway/dsl/24hr [food] #1 Chinese, Arby's, Hungry Howie's, Little Caesar's, McDonald's, New Beginnings Rest., Taco Bell [lodging] Rodeway Inn [other] Buick/Chevrolet/Poniac, Family Fare Foods, Family$, Fun 'N Sun RV Ctr, Rite Aid, vet, S [gas] Pacific Pride/dsl [other] RV camping
10	B-31 (exits left from eb), Nunica, N [food] Turk's Rest., S [other] Conestoga RV camping, golf course/rest.
9	MI 104 (from wb, exits left), to Grand Haven, Spring Lake, S [gas] Marathon/dsl [other] to Grand Haven SP
8mm	**[RS] wb, full [handicap] facilities, litter barrels, petwalk [phone] [picnic] vending**
5	Fruitport (from wb, no return)
4	Airline Rd, S [gas] Speedway/dsl, Wesco/dsl [food] Burger Crest Diner, Dairy Bar, McDonald's, Subway, Village Inn [other] $General, auto/tire repair, Grover Drug, Orchard Mkt Foods, to PJ Hoffmaster SP, USPO, Water Park (5mi)
1c	Hile Rd (from eb), S [food] Arby's, Asian Buffet, Bob Evans, Brann's Grille, Buffalo Wild Wings, Burger King, ChuckeCheese, Five Guys, Golden Corral, Grand Traverse Pie Co, Kazumi Steaks, KFC/Taco Bell, Logan's Roadhouse, McDonald's, Olive Garden, Qdoba, Red Lobster, Red Robin, Starbucks, Subway, TX Roadhouse [lodging] Baymont Inn, Fairfield Inn, Hampton Inn [other] $Tree, AT&T, Barnes&Noble, Belle Tire, Best Buy, Dick's, Gordman's,
1c	Continued Hobby Lobby, JC Penney, Jo-Ann Fabrics, Kohl's, mall, Meijer/dsl, Menards, Old Navy, PetCo, Sears/auto, Target, TJ Maxx, Verizon, VW/Audi/Nissan/Subaru/Toyota/Scion, Younkers
1b a	US 31, to Ludington, Grand Haven, **2 mi N on Sherman Blvd** [food] Applebee's, Arby's, Fazoli's, Los Amigos, McDonald's, Panera Bread, Pizza Ranch, Red Wok, Subway, Wendy's [lodging] Airline Motel, Alpine Motel, Bel-aire Motel, Comfort Inn/rest. [other] [H], $Tree, All Seasons RV Ctr, Big Lots, GNC, Lowe's, Marathon/dsl, Norton Automotive, Petsmart, Sam's Club/gas, Staples, Walmart, S same as 1c

I-96 begins/ends on US 31 at Muskegon.

INTERSTATE 196 (GRAND RAPIDS)

Exit #	Services
81mm	**I-196 begins/ends on I-96, 37mm in E Grand Rapids.**
79	Fuller Ave, N [other] sheriff, S [gas] Shell/dsl, Speedway/dsl [food] Biggby Coffee, Bill's Rest., Checkers, Elbow Room, KFC, Subway, Taco Bell, Wendy's [other] [H], Ace Hardware, Family$, Verizon, Walgreens
78	College Ave, S [gas] Mobil/Circle K [food] McDonald's, Omelette Shop [other] [H], Ford Museum
77c	Ottawa Ave, S [other] Gerald R Ford Museum, downtown
77b a	US 131, S to Kalamazoo, N to Cadillac
76	MI 45 E, Lane Ave, S [other] Gerald R Ford Museum, John Ball Park&Zoo
75	MI 45 W, Lake Michigan Dr, N [other] to Grand Valley St U
74mm	Grand River
73	Market Ave, N [other] to Vanandel Arena
72	Lp 196, Chicago Dr E (from eb)
70	MI 11 (exits left from wb), Grandville, Walker, S [gas] BP/dsl, Shell [lodging] Days Inn [other] USPO, vet
69c	Baldwin St (from wb)
69b a	Chicago Dr, N [gas] Speedway [food] Biggby Coffee, Culver's, Domino's, Fazoli's, KFC, McDonald's, Peppino's Pizza, Subway, Taco Bell [other] $Tree, Advance a Parts, Aldi Foods, AutoZone, Meijer/dsl, O'Reilly Parts, USPO, Walgreens, S [gas] Admiral, Speedway/dsl [food] Adobe Mexican, Arby's, Brann's a Steaks, Little Caesar's, Rainbow Grill, Russ' Rest., Wings&More [lodging] Grand Village Inn, Holiday Inn Express [other] NAPA
67	44th St, N [gas] Mobil/dsl [food] Burger King, Cracker Barrel, Panera Bread, Steak'n Shake [lodging] Comfort Suites [other] Honda, Walmart/Subway, **0-2 mi S** [food] Applebee's, Bagger Dave's, Big Boy, Carrabba's, Famous Dave's, Great Harvest Bread Co, IHOP, Jimmy John's, Kobe Japanese, Logan's Roadhouse, Noodles&Co, Olive Garden, On the Border, Qdoba, Red Lobster, Red Robin, Starbucks, Subway, TGIFriday's, Tropical Smoothie, TX Roadhouse, Uccello's Ristorante, Wendy's [lodging] Residence Inn [other] $Tree, Barnes&Noble, Best Buy, Chrysler/Dodge/Jeep, Costco/gas, Dick's, Discount Tire, Family Fare Foods, Fiat, Gander Mtn, Gordman's, Hobby Lobby, Home Depot, JC Penney, Kohl's, Lowe's, Macy's, Marshall's, Meijer/zeal, Michael's, Old Navy, Petsmart, Sears/auto, Verizon, World Mkt, Younkers
64	MI 6 E, to Lansing (exits left from wb)
Exit #	Services
62	32nd Ave, to Hudsonville, N [gas] BP/dsl, Citgo/dsl [food] Arby's, Biggby Coffee, Burger King, Hudsonville Grille, Little Caesar's, McDonald's [lodging] Quality Inn [other] camping, Chevrolet, S [gas] Mobil/Subway/dsl/24hr [food] Rainbow Grill [lodging] Travelodge [other] Harley-Davidson, Harvest Foods

INTERSTATE 196 (GRAND RAPIDS) Cont'd

Exit #	Services
58mm	**eb, full facilities, litter barrels, petwalk vending**
55	Byron Rd, Zeeland, N Citgo/7-11 Blimpie, McDonald's to Holland SP
52	16th St, Adams St, **2 mi** N Speedway/dsl Burger King, Jimmy John's, Papa Murphy's, Pizza Ranch, Wendy's Meijer/dsl/e-85, S Mobil/Subway/dsl
49	MI 40, to Allegan, N BP/McDonald's/dsl Residence Inn, S Tulip City/Marathon/Subway/dsl/scales/24hr Rock Island Rest. truck repair, truck wash
44	US 31 N (from eb), to Holland, **3-5 mi** N Country Inn food, gas
43mm	**wb, full facilities, info, litter barrels, petwalk vending**
41	Rd A-2, Douglas, Saugatuck, N BP/dsl, Marathon/dsl, Shell/Subway/dsl Burger King, Dairy Dayz, Spectators Grill Best Western (1mi), Timberline Motel (3mi) $General, NAPA, to Saugatuck SP, S Belvedere Inn Rest. Red Barn Gifts
38mm	Kalamazoo River
36	Rd A-2, Ganges, N Shell Christo's Rest., Pizza Mambo, Saugatuck Brewing Co, Zing Rest. AmericInn, Blue Star Motel
34	MI 89, to Fennville, N to West Side CP, S Shell Cranes Pie Pantry (4mi, Lyons Farm Mkt, Winery Tours (seasonal)
30	Rd A-2, Glenn, Ganges, N to Westside CP (4mi)
28mm	**eb, full facilities, litter barrels, petwalk vending**
26	109th Ave, to Pullman, N Dutch Farm Mkt
22	N Shore Dr, N Cousin's RV Camping/rest., to Kal Haven Trail SP
20	Rd A-2, Phoenix Rd, N BP/dsl, Marathon/dsl Arby's, China Buffet, Taco Bell $Tree, AutoZone, Meijer/dsl, st police, Walgreens, S Murphy USA/dsl, Shell/dsl Big Boy, McDonald's, Sherman's Dairybar, Wendy's Baymont Inn, Comfort Suites, Hampton Inn, Holiday Inn Express $General, Aldi Foods, Menards, Walmart
18	MI 140, MI 43, to Watervliet, **0-2 mi** N Shell/dsl, Sunoco/dsl Burger King, Hungry Howie's, Little Caesar's, McDonald's, Pizza Hut Great Lakes Inn, LakeBluff Motel auto repair, AutoValue Parts, Buick/Cadillac/GMC, Chevrolet, Chrysler/Dodge/Jeep, Ford/Lincoln, st police, Village Mkt Foods, **7 mi** S KOA (Apr-Oct)
13	to Covert, N RV camping, to Van Buren SP
7	MI 63, to Benton Harbor, N DiMaggio's Pizza RV camping
4	to Coloma, Riverside, S Shell/dsl KOA (Apr-Oct)
2mm	Paw Paw River
1	Red Arrow Hwy, N SW Michigan Airport
0mm	I-94, E to Detroit, W to Chicago

I-196 begins/ends on I-94, exit 34 at Benton Harbor.

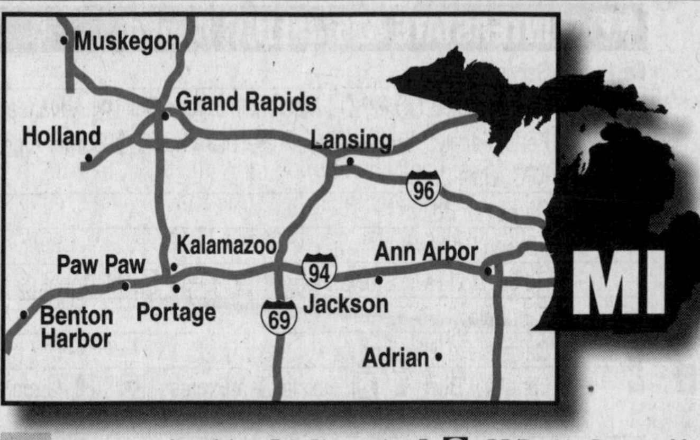

INTERSTATE 275 (LIVONIA)

LIVONIA

Exit #	Services
	I-275 and I-96 run together 9 miles. See Michigan I-96, exits 165-170.
29	I-96 E, to Detroit, MI 14 W, to Ann Arbor
28	Ann Arbor Rd, Plymouth, E BP/Dunkin Donuts, Mobil, Shell/dsl Denny's, Little Caesars, McDonald's Red Roof Inn $Tree, Verizon, vet, W Burger King, Firehouse Subs, Grand Traverse Pie Co., Lee's Coney Island Comfort Inn Cadillac, CVS Drug, K-Mart, Lincoln, URGENT CARE, vet
25	MI 153, Ford Rd, Garden City, E Hayden's Grill, Logan's Roadhouse, Parthenon Coney Island, Starbucks Home Depot, Sam's Club, Walmart, W BP, Speedway, Valero/dsl Applebee's, Basement Burger Bar, BD Mongolian BBQ, Black Rock Grill, Bob Evans, Boston Mkt, Bowery Grill, Buffalo Wild Wings, Burger King, Carrabba's, Carvel Ice Cream, Chili's, ChuckeCheese, Dunkin Donuts/Baskin-Robbins, Five Guys, JerseyMike's, Jimmy John's, KFC, Little Caesar's, McDonald's, Mexican Fiesta, Olga's Kitchen, Outback Steaks, Panera Bread, Pizza Hut, Potbelly, Subway, Taco Bell, TGIFriday's, Tilted Kilt, Tim Hortons/Coldstone, Wendy's, Wendy's, White Castle/Church's Comfort Suites, Extended Stay America, Fairfield Inn, Hampton Inn, La Quinta Advance Parts, Aldi Foods, Discount Tire, Firestone/auto, GNC, Hobby Lobby, IKEA, JC Penney, Jo-Ann, Kohl's, Lowe's, Marshall's, Meijer/dsl, Michael's, Midas, PetCo, Richardson's Drug, Target, Tuesday Morning, URGENT CARE, Verizon, vet, Walgreens
23	**nb, full facilities, info, litter barrels**
22	US 12, Michigan Ave, to Wayne, E BP/dsl, Mobil/dsl, Shell, Valero/dsl Arby's, Jonathan's Rest., McDonald's, Quiznos, Subway, Wendy's Days Inn, Fellows Cr Motel, Holiday Inn Express, Super 8, Willo Acres Motel, W Marathon/dsl Jimmy John's Kia, Nissan, URGENT CARE
20	Ecorse Rd, to Romulus, E 7-11, Shell/dsl, W BP/Burger King/scales/dsl/24hr
17	I-94, E to Detroit, W to Ann Arbor
15	Eureka Rd, E Shell
13	Sibley Rd, New Boston, W Fusion/Subway/dsl LC's Chicken to Lower Huron Metro Park
11	S Huron Rd, **1 mi** W Sunoco/Burger King/dsl Jacob's Rest RV LP (1mi)
8	Will Carleton Rd, to Flat Rock
5	Carleton, South Rockwood, W food
4mm	**sb, full facilities, litter barrels**
2	US 24, to Telegraph Rd, W lodging, Marathon/dsl
0mm	**I-275 begins/ends on I-75, exit 20.**

INTERSTATE 475 (FLINT)

Exit #	Services
17mm	**I-475 begins/ends on I-75, exit 125.**
15	Clio Rd, W BP Chevrolet

FLINT

INTERSTATE 475 (FLINT) Cont'd

Exit #	Services
13	Saginaw St, E gas BP food McDonald's, Taco Bell other Advanced Parts, Family$, Kroger/gas, W gas Marathon food Burger King, KFC, Little Caesars
11	Carpenter Rd
10	Pierson Rd
9	Rd 54, Dort Hwy, Stewart Ave, E gas Citgo food McDonald's
8mm	Flint River
8b	Davison Rd, Hamilton Ave
8a	Longway Blvd, W lodging Holiday Inn Express other H, farmers mkt, USPO
7	Rd 21, Court St, downtown Flint
6	I-69, W to Lansing, E to Port Huron
5	Atherton Rd (from sb), E gas Marathon/dsl
4	Hemphill Rd, Bristol Rd, E gas Speedway/dsl food Rally's, Subway other Rite Aid, W gas Speedway/dsl food Little Caesars, Tim Horton/Wendy's other Family$, Kroger/dsl, vet
2	Hill Rd, E gas Speedway food Applebee's, Bob Evans lodging Wingate Inn other vet, W gas Mobil/Tim Horton, Speedway/dsl food Arby's, Bangkok Peppers, Blimpie, Burger King, Burger St Grill, Little Caesars, McDonald's, Wendy's other Rite Aid

I-475 begins/ends on I-75, exit 111.

DETROIT

INTERSTATE 696 (DETROIT)

Exit #	Services
	I-696 begins/ends on I-94.
28	I-94 E to Port Huron, W to Detroit, 11 Mile Rd, E gas 7-11, BP/dsl, Shell/dsl
27	MI 3, Gratiot Ave, N gas BP, Marathon, Valero food Checkers, Firehouse Subs, McDonald's, National Coney Island, Tubby's Subs other Costco/gas, S gas Marathon, Mobil/McDonald's/dsl, Shell food Biggby Coffee, DQ, KFC, Subway, Taco Bell, Tim Horton's, White Castle other Belle Tire, Chrysler/Dodge/Jeep, Family$, GNC, Goodyear/auto, K-Mart, Kroger/gas, Rite Aid, Sav-A-Lot Foods, TJ Maxx
26	MI 97, Groesbeck Ave, Roseville, N gas BP/dsl, S food Omega Grill
24	Hoover Rd, Schoenherr Rd, N gas BP food Burger King, KFC, S gas BP/dsl, Mobil/7-11 food Boston Mkt, Del Taco, Doc's Rest., DQ, Little Caesar's, Red Lobster, Subway, Taco Bell, Tim Horton, Wendy's lodging Holiday Inn Express other $Tree, Advance Parts, CVS Drug, GNC, Home Depot, Kroger, Marshall's
23	MI 53, Van Dyke Ave, N gas BP, Marathon, Mobil/dsl food Applebee's, Arby's, Baskin-Robbins/Dunkin Donuts, Juliano's Rest., McDonald's, Subway other $General, Cadillac, Chrysler/Dodge/Jeep, Toyota, Walmart, S food Luca's Coney Island other Chevrolet/Buick/GMC, Discount Tire, Ford, Rite Aid, USPO, vet
22	Mound Rd, N gas BP/Burger King, Mobil/dsl
20	Ryan Rd, Dequindre Rd, N gas 7-11, Shell, Sunoco food Ponderosa lodging Knights Inn, Red Roof Inn other auto repair, BigLots, vet, S food Bob Evans, Church's, LA Coney Island, McDonald's lodging Best Inn, Victory Suites other transmissions
19	Couzens St, 10 Mile Rd, S other Hazel Park Racetrack
18	I-75, N to Flint, S to Detroit
17	Campbell Ave, Hilton Ave, Bermuda, Mohawk, S gas Marathon/dsl
16	MI 1, Woodward Ave, Main St, N other zoo, S gas Sunoco
14	Coolidge Rd, 10 Mile Rd, S gas Speedway food Hungry Howie's, Jade Palace Chinese, Little Caesar's, Sahara Grill, Subway other CVS Drug, Family$, URGENT CARE
13	Greenfield Rd, N gas Marathon, Mobil food Church's, L George Coney Island, McDonald's, Ponderosa, Popeye's, Subway, White Castle other $Tree, Aldi Foods, Family$, Save a Lot Foods, Sol's Automotive, URGENT CARE, S gas Shell, Sunoco food Baskin-Robbins/Dunkin Donuts, Front Page Deli, Pita Cafe, Starbucks other Rite Aid
12	MI 39, Southfield Rd, 11 Mile Rd, N other Discount Tire, S gas Shell food Happy's Pizza other AT&T, Verizon
11	Evergreen Rd, S gas Mobil, Speedway/dsl food Benito's Pizza, China Gourmet, Chipotle, Coldstone/Tim Horton's, Fuddrucker's, Jimmy John's, Potbelly, Qdoba, Subway, TGIFriday's lodging Hawthorn Suites, Holiday Inn Express
10	US 24, Telegraph Rd, N gas Marathon, Mobil, Sunoco food Biggby Coffee, Burger Joint, Chipotle, DiBella Subs, Fat Burger, Five Guys, Jimmy John's, Mezzanine Mediterranian, Noodles&Co, Panera Bread, Popeye's, Potbelly, Qdoba, Starbucks, Wendy's lodging Baymont Inn, Embassy Suites, Extended Stay America, Red Roof Inn, Springhill Suites other AT&T, Belle Tire, Best Buy, Buick/GMC, Chevrolet, Chrysler/Dodge/Jeep, Ford, Honda, Hyundai, Kia, Lexus, Lincoln, Lowe's, Meijer/dsl, Michael's, Mini, Nissan, Office Depot, Petsmart, Subaru, Verizon, S gas Mobil/7-11, Sunoco food Kerry's Koney Island, Tim Horton's lodging Candlewood Suites, Courtyard, Holiday Inn Express, Marriott, Quality Inn other AutoZone, Family$
8	MI 10, Lodge Fwy
7	American Dr (from eb), N lodging Embassy Suites, S lodging Extended Stay America, Hilton Garden
5	Orchard Lake Rd, Farmington Hills, N gas Marathon, Mobil/dsl, Valero food Arby's, Burger King, Camelia's Mexican, Coney Island, Hong Hua Chinese, Jet's Pizza, Jimmy John's, Kabuki Japanese, Marie's Scrambler, Ruby Tuesday, Starbucks, Subway, Wendy's lodging Comfort Inn, Courtyard, Extended Stay America, Fairfield Inn other CVS, Discount Tire, Holocaust Museum, Petco, to St Mary's Coll, Verizon
1	(from wb), I-96 W, I-275 S, to MI 5, Grand River Ave

NOTES

MINNESOTA

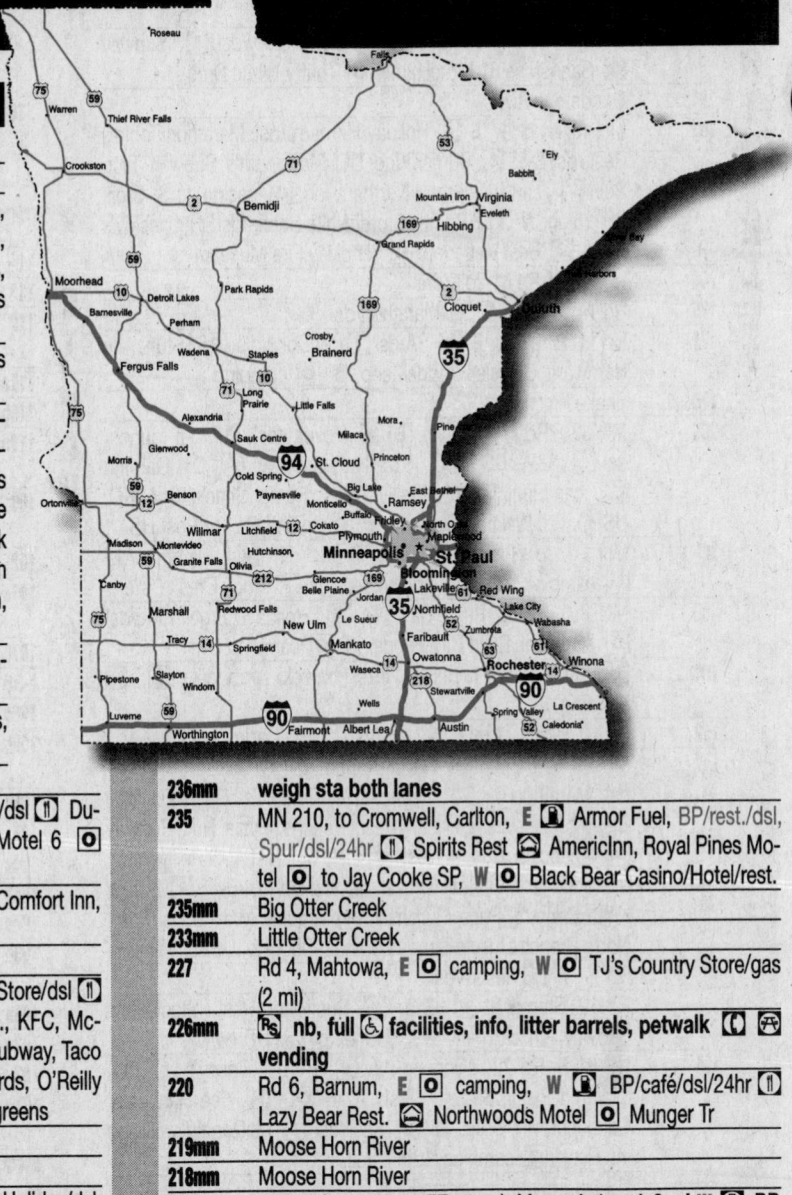

INTERSTATE 35

DULUTH

Exit #	Services
260mm	**I-35 begins/ends on MN 61 in Duluth.**
259	MN 61, London Rd, to Two Harbors, North Shore, W [gas] BP, Holiday/dsl, ICO/dsl [food] Blackwoods Grill, Burger King, Dunn Bros Coffee, KFC, McDonald's, Perkins, Pizza Hut, Subway, Taco John's, Wendy's [lodging] Edgewater Inn [other] vet
258	21st Ave E (from nb), to U of MN at Duluth, same as 259
256b	Mesaba Ave, Superior St, E [gas] ICO/DQ [food] Bellicio's, Caribou Coffee, Famous Dave's BBQ, Grandma's Grill, Greenmill Rest., Grizzly's, Little Angie's Cantina, Old Chicago, Red Lobster, Smokehouse Rest., Subway, Timberlodge Steaks [lodging] Canal Park Lodge, Comfort Suites, Hampton Inn, Hawthorn Suites, Inn at Lake Superior, Suites Motel, The Inn, W [lodging] Holiday Inn, Radisson, Sheraton
256a	Michigan St, E [other] waterfront, W [other] [H], downtown
255a	US 53 N (exits left from nb), W [other] Auto Value Parts, Kia, [other] mall, downtown
255b	I-535 spur, to Wisconsin
254	27th Ave W, W [gas] Holiday/Burger King/dsl, Spur/dsl [food] Duluth Grill, Little Caesars, Quiznos, Subway [lodging] Motel 6 [other] USPO
253b	40th Ave W, W [gas] BP/dsl/24hr [food] Perkins [lodging] Comfort Inn, Super 8
253a	US 2 E, US 53, to Wisconsin
252	Central Ave, W Duluth, W [gas] Holiday/dsl, Little Store/dsl [food] China King Buffet, Domino's, Jade Fountain Rest., KFC, McDonald's, Mr D's Grill, Pizza Hut, Sammy's Café, Subway, Taco John's [other] $Tree, Advance Parts, K-Mart, Menards, O'Reilly Parts, Save-a-Lot Foods, Super 1 Foods, vet, Walgreens
251b	MN 23 S, Grand Ave
251a	Cody St, E [lodging] Allyndale Motel [other] zoo
250	US 2 W (from sb), to Grand Rapids, **1/2 mi** W [gas] Holiday/dsl, Mobil/dsl/LP [food] Blackwoods Grill [lodging] AmericInn
249	Boundary Ave, Skyline Pkwy, E [gas] Holiday/McDonald's/dsl [lodging] Country Inn&Suites [other] to ski area, to Spirit Mtn RA, W [rest stop] **both lanes, full [handicapped] facilities, info, litter barrels [phone] [picnic] vending** [gas] Little Store/dsl/E-85/24hr [food] Blackwoods Grill [lodging] AmericInn, Best Value Inn
246	Rd 13, Midway Rd, Nopeming, W [gas] Armor/dsl [food] Dry Dock Rest.
245	Rd 61, E [food] Buffalo House Rest./camping
242	Rd 1, Esko, Thomson, E [gas] BP/dsl
239.5mm	St Louis River
239	MN 45, to Cloquet, Scanlon, E [other] Jay Cooke SP, KOA (May-Oct), W [gas] Holiday [food] Pantry Rest., Trapper Pete's Steaks [lodging] Golden Gate Motel [other] [H], camping, dsl repair
237	MN 33, Cloquet, **1 mi** W [gas] BP, Lemon Tree/dsl, Murphy USA/dsl [food] Applebee's, Arby's, DQ, Erbert&Gerberts, Little Caesars, McDonald's, Papa Murphy's, Perkins, Pizza Hut, South Gate Pizza, Subway, Taco John's/Stake Escape, Wendy's [lodging] AmericInn, Super 8 [other] [H], $Tree, AT&T, AutoZone, Chrysler/Dodge/Jeep, Family$, Ford, NAPA, Super 1 Foods, Verizon, Walmart/Subway, White Drug
236mm	**weigh sta both lanes**
235	MN 210, to Cromwell, Carlton, E [gas] Armor Fuel, BP/rest./dsl, Spur/dsl/24hr [food] Spirits Rest [lodging] AmericInn, Royal Pines Motel [other] to Jay Cooke SP, W [other] Black Bear Casino/Hotel/rest.
235mm	Big Otter Creek
233mm	Little Otter Creek
227	Rd 4, Mahtowa, E [other] camping, W [other] TJ's Country Store/gas (2 mi)
226mm	[rest stop] **nb, full [handicapped] facilities, info, litter barrels, petwalk [phone] [picnic] vending**
220	Rd 6, Barnum, E [other] camping, W [gas] BP/café/dsl/24hr [food] Lazy Bear Rest. [lodging] Northwoods Motel [other] Munger Tr
219mm	Moose Horn River
218mm	Moose Horn River
216	MN 27 (from sb, no EZ return), Moose Lake, **1-2 mi** W [gas] BP, Cenex/dsl, Holiday/dsl, Little Store (4mi), Rebel [food] Art's Café, DQ, Lazy Moose Grille, Poor Gary's Pizza [lodging] AmericInn (4mi), Moose Lake Motel [other] [H], 1918 Museum, Ace Hardware, AutoValue Parts, Ford, Mkt Place Foods, O'Reilly Parts, repair, to Munger Trail, vet
214	Rd 73 (no EZ return from nb), E [other] Alco, camping, Moose Lake SP (2mi), W [gas] Alco, Little Store/Subway/dsl/E-85 [lodging] AmericInn, Moose Lake Motel [other] [H], Munger Trail, Red Fox Camping
209	Rd 46, Sturgeon Lake, E [gas] Cenex [food] Doc's Cafe, W [food] Ernie's Rest. (seasonal) [lodging] Sturgeon Lake Motel [other] camping (3mi), [other] Sturgeon Lake
209mm	[rest stop] **sb, full [handicapped] facilities, litter barrels, petwalk [phone] [picnic] vending**
206.5mm	Willow River
205	Rd 43, Willow River, W [gas] BP/cafe/dsl [other] camping (2mi)
198.5mm	Kettle River
198mm	[rest stop] **nb, full [handicapped] facilities, litter barrels, petwalk [phone] [picnic] vending**
195	Rd 18, Rd 23 E, to Askov, E [gas] Cenex/cafe/dsl [food] Banning Jct Cafe [lodging] Best Value Inn [other] camping, to Banning SP, W [other] camping

[gas] = gas [food] = food [lodging] = lodging [other] = other [rest stop] = rest stop

MN

INTERSTATE 35 Cont'd

HINCKLEY

Exit #	Services
191	MN 23, Rd 61, Sandstone, E [gas] Victory/dsl [food] Subway [lodging] Sandstone 61 Motel (2mi) [other] Thrifty White Drug
184mm	Grindstone River
183	MN 48, Hinckley, E [gas] Holiday/Hardee's/dsl, Marathon/Tobie's Rest./dsl/E-85 [food] Burger King, DQ, McDonald's, Subway, Taco Bell [lodging] Days Inn, Grand Northern Inn [other] casino, to St Croix SP (15mi), W [gas] BP, Little Store/White Castle/dsl [food] Cassidy's Rest. [lodging] Best Value Inn [other] Hinckley Fire Museum
180	MN 23 W, Rd 61, to Mora
175	Rd 14, Beroun, E [gas] Marathon/dsl
171	Rd 11, Pine City, E [gas] SA/dsl [food] McDonald's [other] $Stuff, Ace Hardware, Chrysler/Dodge/Jeep, W [other] camping
170mm	Snake River
169	MN 324, Rd 7, Pine City, E [gas] Holiday/dsl, Pump-n-Munch/dsl [food] A&W, DQ, KFC, Pizza Hut, Subway [lodging] Old Oak Inn [other] camping, Ford, O'Reilly Parts, Radio Shack, ShopKO, USPO, vet, Walmart/Subway, W [other] to NW Co Fur Post HS
165	MN 70, to Grantsburg, Rock Creek, E [gas] Marathon/dsl [other] camping, W [gas] Heidelbergers/dsl [food] Rock Creek Cafe
159	MN 361, Rd 1, Rush City, E [gas] Holiday/Burger King/dsl [other] $General, Rush City Foods, W [other] camping (2mi)
154mm	**[rest stop] nb, full [handicapped] facilities, litter barrels, petwalk [phone] [picnic] vending**
152	Rd 10, Harris, **1 mi E** [gas] gas/dsl [food] Big Daddy's Grill
147	MN 95, to Cambridge, North Branch, E [gas] Casey's, Holiday/dsl, Marathon/dsl [food] China Taste, Domino's, DQ, KFC/Taco Bell, McDonald's, Oak Inn Rest, Perkins, Pizza Hut, Subway [lodging] AmericInn, Budget Host [other] Fisk Tire, NAPA, O'Reilly Parts, to Wild River SP (14mi), vet, W [gas] Holiday/dsl/E-85 [food] Burger King, Denny's, Papa Murphy's [other] County Mkt Foods, Ford, North Branch Outlets/famous brands, ShopKo, USPO, Verizon
143	Rd 17, E [gas] Tesoro/dsl
139	Rd 19, Stacy, E [gas] Gas+ [food] Rustic Inn Rest., Stacy Grill, Subway [other] city park, W [gas] Shell [other] A-1 Tires
135	US 61 S, Rd 22, Wyoming, E [gas] BP/dsl, Casey's [food] DQ, Linwood Pizza, Subway, Tasty Asia [other] [H], Ace Hardware, CarQuest, WY Drug, W [gas] Shell/dsl [food] McDonald's, Village Inn Rest. [other] camping (10mi), golf, vet
132	US 8 (from nb), to Taylors Falls
131	Rd 2, Forest Lake, E [gas] BP, Holiday/dsl, SA/dsl [food] Applebee's, Arby's, Burger King, Chueng Sing Chinese, Culvers, KFC, McDonald's, Papa John's, Perkins, Quack's Cafe, Subway, Taco Bell, White Castle [lodging] AmericInn [other] [H], AutoValue Parts, AutoZone, CarX, O'Reilly Parts, Rainbow Foods/24hr, RV/Auto repair, Target, Tires+, Walgreens, Walmart/Subway, W [gas] Holiday/dsl [food] Famous Dave's BBQ, Jimmy John's, Key's Cafe, Papa Murphy's, Starbucks, Taco John's, Wendy's [lodging] Country Inn&Suites [other] AT&T, Buick/GMC, Cadillac/Chevrolet, Chrysler/Dodge/Jeep, Cub Foods, GNC, Home Depot, Jiffy Lube, Menards, Radio Shack
131mm	**[rest stop] sb, full [handicapped] facilities, litter barrels, petwalk [phone] [picnic] vending**
129	MN 97, Rd 23, E [gas] Kwik Trip/dsl/E-85 [other] camping (6mi), W [gas] Holiday/dsl [other] camping (1mi), Coates RV Ctr, Gander Mtn.
128mm	**weigh sta both lanes**
127	I-35W, S to Minneapolis. See I-35W.
123	Rd 14, Centerville, E [gas] Kwik Trip [food] Blue Heron Grill, Papa Murphy's [other] Festival Foods, Otter Lake RV Ctr, vet, W [gas] Shell [food] Cadillac Grill, DQ, WiseGuys Pizza [other] NAPA
120	Rd J (from nb, no return)

FOREST LAKE

ST PAUL

Exit #	Services
117	Rd 96, E [gas] Marathon, SA/dsl [food] Burger King [lodging] AmericIn [other] Goodyear/auto, NAPA, W [gas] Holiday, PDQ [food] $5 Pizza Applebee's, Arby's, Asia's Finest, Caribou Coffee, Culver's, Little Caesars, McDonald's, Subway, Zen Asia [other] AutoZone, Cu Foods, Tires+, USPO, Valvoline, Walgreens
115	Rd E, E [gas] BP/repair, SA/dsl [food] Jimmy's Rest., Perkins [lodging] Country Inn&Suites, Holiday Inn Express, W [food] Chipotle Mexican, Dunn Bros Coffee, KFC/Pizza Hut, Mad Jack's Cafe, Panera Bread, Papa Murphy's, Thai Pan, Wendy's [other] $Tree, Curves Festival Foods, GNC, Radio Shack, Target, Walmart/auto
114	I-694 E (exits left from sb)
113	I-694 W
112	Little Canada Rd, E [gas] BP, W [gas] Clark/dsl [food] Porterhous Rest
111a/b	MN 36 E, to Stillwater/MN 36 W, to Minneapolis
110b	Roselawn Ave
110a	Wheelock Pkwy, E [gas] BP, Gulf [food] May's Deli, Roadside Pizza Subway, W [food] Champps Grill
109	Maryland Ave, E [gas] SA/dsl [food] Taco John's, W [food] Wendy's [other] K-Mart
108	Pennsylvania Ave, downtown
107c	University Ave, E [gas] Marathon/dsl, W [other] [H], to st capitol downtown
107b a	I-94, W to Minneapolis, E to St Paul.
I-35 and I-94 run together.	
106c	11th St (from nb), Marion St, downtown
106b	Kellogg Blvd (from nb), E [food] Eagle St. Grill, Subway [lodging] Holiday Inn [other] [H], downtown
106a	Grand Ave, E [other] [H]
105	St Clair Ave
104c	Victoria St, Jefferson Ave
104b	Ayd Mill Rd (from nb)
104a	Randolph Ave
103b	MN 5, W 7th St, E [food] Burger King, W [gas] SA/dsl [other] Midas USPO
103a	Shepard Rd (from nb)
102mm	Mississippi River
102	MN 13, Sibley Hwy, W [gas] BP, Holiday/Subway
101b a	MN 110 W, E [gas] BP [food] Caribou Coffee, McDonald's, Subway Teresa's Mexican [other] Tuesday Morning, W [gas] SA
99b a	I-494 W/I-494 E
98	Lone Oak Rd, E [lodging] Homestead Suites, Microtel [other] Sam's Club/gas, USPO, W [food] Joe Senser's Grill, Magic Thai Café [lodging] Hampton Inn, Residence Inn [other] Lone Oak Mkt/gas
97b	Yankee Doodle Rd, E [food] Applebee's, Arby's, Buffalo Wild Wings, Burger King, Coldstone, Culver's, DQ, Houlihan's, Jake's Grill, Jimmy John's, KFC, New China Buffet, Noodles&Co, Old Chicago Pizza, Panera Bread, Papa Murphy's, Perkins, Pizza Hut, Pizza Man, Pot Bellys, Savoy Pizza, Taco Bell [other] AT&T, Barnes&Noble, Best Buy, BigLots, Byerly's Foods, Firestone, Goodyear, Home Depot, Kohl's, Michael's, Office Depot, Old Navy, Petsmart, Radio Shack, Rainbow Foods, TJ Maxx, Walgreens, Walmart/Subway, W [gas] BP/dsl, SA/dsl [food] Al Baker's Rest., Dragon Palace Chinese, El Loro Mexican, Starbucks [lodging] Best Western, Extended Stay America [other] NAPA, Superior Auto
97a	Pilot Knob Rd, E [gas] Holiday, SA [food] Chili's, McDonald's, Wendy's [lodging] SpringHill Suites, TownePlace Suites [other] Excel Repair, Kohl's, Tires+, W [gas] BP, SA/dsl [lodging] Best Western, same as 97b
94	Rd 30, Diffley Rd, to Eagan, E [gas] Holiday/dsl [other] CVS Drug, Kowalski's Mkt/Starbucks, W [gas] Sinclair/Goodyear
93	Rd 32, Cliff Rd, E [gas] Holiday [food] Bonfire Grill, Subway [other] Ace Hardware, W [gas] Holiday/dsl [food] Burger King, Caribou

INTERSTATE 35 Cont'd

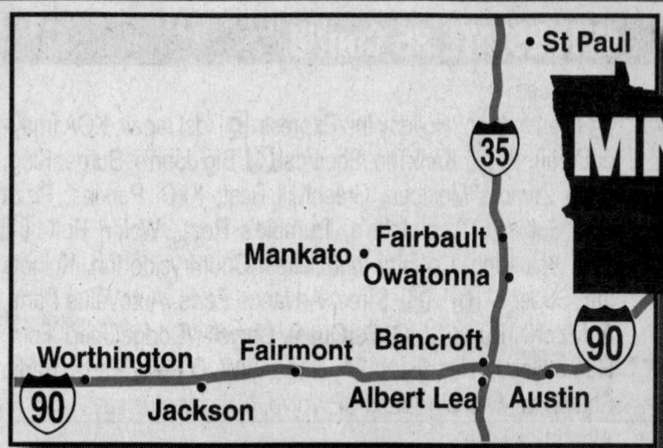

MN

93	Continued Coffee, Caspers's Rest., Chipotle Mexican, Dolittle's Grill, DQ, Hong Wong Chinese, KFC, Leeann Chin's, McDonald's, Pizza Hut, Quiznos, Starbucks, Taco Bell, Wendy's Hilton Garden, Holiday Inn Express, Staybridge Suites Cub Foods, O'Reilly Parts, Target, USPO, Walgreens
92	MN 77, Cedar Ave, **E** Zoo, **1 mi** **W** access to Cliff Rd services
90	Rd 11, **E** KwikTrip Subway Valley Natural Foods, **W** SA/dsl
88b	Rd 42, Crystal Lake Rd, **E** SA/dsl Caribou Coffee, Chianti Grill Byerly's Foods, Petsmart, Tuesday Morning, **W** BP, Holiday/dsl, PDQ, SA/dsl Applebee's, Arby's, Buca Italian, Burger Jones, Burger King, Cam Ranh Bay, Champp's Grill, Chipotle Mexican, Ernie's Grill, HoneyBaked Ham, IHOP, Jimmy John's, KFC, Kings Buffet, Little Caesars, Macaroni Grill, McDonald's, Noodles&Co, Old Country Buffet, Olive Garden, Outback Steaks, Panera Bread, Papa John's, Papa Murphy's, Porter Creek Grill, Red Lobster, Roasted Pear, Taco Bell, TGIFriday's, Wendy's Best Western, Days Inn, Fairfield Inn, Hampton Inn, InTown Suites H, Ace Hardware, AT&T, Barnes&Noble, Cadillac, Chevrolet, Cotco/gas, Cub Foods, Dick's, Discount Tire, Gordman's, Home Depot, JC Penney, K-Mart, Kohl's, Macy's, mall, Michael's, Office Depot, Old Navy, PetCo, Rainbow Foods, Sears/auto, Target, Tires+, TJ Maxx, USPO, Verizon, VW, Walgreens
88a	I-35W (from nb), N to Minneapolis. See I-35W.
87	Crystal Lake Rd (from nb), **W** Honda/Nissan, Mazda, to Beaver Mtn ski area, Toyota/Scion
86	Rd 46, **E** KwikTrip, SA/dsl KFC, Starbucks Harley-Davidson, **W** auto repair, O'Reilly Parts
85	MN 50, **E** F&F/dsl, SA/dsl Burger King, Caribou Coffee, Culver's, DQ, Greenmill Rest., Jimmy John's, Lakeville Chinese, Pizza Hut, Starbucks, Subway, Taco Bell, Wendy's Comfort Inn $Tree, CVS Drug, Goodyear/auto, NTB, O'Reilly Parts, Rainbow Foods, Verizon, Walgreens, **W** Holiday/dsl Cracker Barrel, Perkins, Pizza Ranch AmericInn Gander Mtn.
84	185th St W, Orchard Trail, **E** Applebee's, Buffalo Wild Wings, Caribou Coffee, Quiznos, SawaJapan Best Buy, Marshall's, Target
81	Rd 70, Lakeville, **E** Holiday/dsl Baldy's BBQ, McDonald's, Subway, Tacoville Holiday Inn/rest, Motel 6, **W** Harry's Cafe Walmart/Subway
76	Rd 2, Elko, **E** gas/dsl, **W** Endzone Grill Elko Speedway
76mm	**sb, full facilities, litter barrels, petwalk vending**
69	MN 19, to Northfield, New Prague, **7 mi** **E** KwikTrip Applebee's, Big Steer Rest., Caribou Coffee, McDonald's, Quarterback Rest., Subway, Taco Bell AmericInn, College City Motel, Country Inn&Suites, Super 8 H, Carleton Coll, St Olaf Coll, **W** FLYING J/Subway/dsl/scales/24hr
68mm	**nb, full facilities, litter barrels, petwalk vending**
66	Rd 1, to Dundas, **1 mi** **W** Boonie's Grill
59	MN 21, Faribault, **0-2 mi** **E** BP/rest./dsl/scales/24hr, KwikTrip A&W, Arby's, Burger King, DQ, Hardee's, Joe's Cafe, KFC, Pizza Hut, Taco Bell, Taco John's AmericInn, Best Value Inn, Days Inn, Grandstay Aldi Foods, AT&T, Buick/Chevrolet/GMC, Chrysler/Dodge/Jeep, O'Reilly Parts, repair, Satakah St Trail, vet, **W** camping, Harley-Davidson

FARIBAULT

56	MN 60, Faribault, **E** KwikTrip A&W, Arby's, Burger King, Great China Buffet, Hardee's, Jimmy John's, KFC, Little Caesars, McDonald's, Perkins, Pizza Hut, Subway, Taco John's H, $Tree, Aldi Foods, AutoValue Parts, Buick/Chevrolet/GMC, Chrysler/Dodge/Jeep, Curves, Dodge, Family$, Goodyear/auto, Hy-Vee Foods/gas, JC Penney, mall, O'Reilly Parts, Radio Shack, Tires+, TrueValue, Verizon, Walmart, **W** Petro/dsl Country Kitchen, DQ Regency Inn camping, Sakatah Lake SP, same as 59
55	Rd 48, (from nb, no return), **1 mi** **E** KwikTrip, Mobil/dsl, SA/dsl A&W, Arby's, Broaster Rest., Burger King, DQ, KFC, Pizza Hut, Southern China Cafe, Subway, Taco John's AmericInn
48	Rd 12, Rd 23, Medford, **W** McDonald's Outlet Mall/famous brands
45	Rd 9, Clinton Falls, **W** KwikTrip/dsl Caribou Coffee, Famous Dave's BBQ, Sportsman's Grille, Subway, TimberLodge Steaks, Wendy's Comfort Inn, Holiday Inn Cabela's Sporting Goods, museum, Russell-Stover Candies
43	Rd 34, 26th St, Owatonna, **E** Noble RV Ctr, **W** H
42b a	US 14 W, Rd 45, to Waseca, Owatonna, **E** Kernel Rest. Budget Host AutoZone, CashWise Foods, Chrysler/Dodge/Jeep, Ford/Lincoln, O'Reilly Parts, repair, vet, **W** KwikTrip/dsl Big 10 Rest., Buffalo Wild Wings, Culver's, Eastwind Buffet, McDonald's, Olivia's Rest., Perkins Best Budget Inn, Super 8 $Tree, GNC, Kohl's, Lowe's, Radio Shack, Verizon, Walmart/Subway
41	Bridge St, Owatonna, **E** Holiday/dsl Applebee's, Arby's, Asian Kitchen, Burger King, DQ, Jimmy John's, KFC, Papa Murphy's, Quiznos, Starbucks, Subway, Taco Bell AmericInn, Country Inn&Suites H, Verizon, **W** F&F/dsl Microtel Target
40	US 14 E, US 218, Owatonna, **1 mi** **E on Rd 6** El Tequila Mexican, Godfather's, Taco John's Oakdale Motel H, Buick/Chevrolet, Curves, Hy-Vee Foods/dsl, Walgreens, WholesaleTire
38mm	Turtle Creek
35mm	**both lanes, full facilities, litter barrels, petwalk vending**
34.5mm	Straight River
32	Rd 4, Hope, **1/2 mi** **E** camping, **1 mi** **W** gas food
26	MN 30, to Blooming Prairie, Ellendale, **E** Cenex/pizza/dsl
22	Rd 35, to Hartland, Geneva, **1 mi** **E** gas food
18	MN 251, to Hollandale, Clarks Grove, **W** BP/dsl/LP camping
17mm	**weigh sta both lanes**
13b a	I-90, W to Sioux Falls, E to Austin, **W** H
12	US 65 S (from sb), Lp 35, Albert Lea, same as 11
11	Rd 46, Albert Lea, **E** Loves/Wendy's/dsl/scales/24hr, TA/Coldstone/Pizza Hut/dsl/scales/24hr/ @ McDonald's

OWATONNA

MN

ALBERT LEA

INTERSTATE 35 Cont'd

11	Continued [lodging] Comfort Inn, Holiday Inn Express [other] dsl repair, KOA (may-oct/6mi), **W** [gas] KwikTrip, Shell/dsl [food] Big John's, Burger King, Casa Zamora Mexican, GreenMill Rest, KFC, Perkins, Pizza Hut, Subway, Taco John's, Trumble's Rest., Wok'n Roll [lodging] Best Value Inn, Country Inn&Suites, Countryside Inn, Knights Inn, Super 8 [other] [H], $Tree, Advance Parts, AutoValue Parts, AutoZone, Buick/GMC, CarQuest, Chrysler/Dodge/Jeep, Ford, Home Depot, Honda, NAPA, Nissan/VW, O'Reilly Parts, Radio Shack, to Myre-Big Island SP, Volvo, Walmart/Subway
9mm	Albert Lea Lake
8	US 65, Lp 35, Albert Lea, **2 mi W** [gas] Freeborn City Co-op/dsl [food] DQ, Hardee's
5	Rd 13, to Glenville, Twin Lakes, **3 mi W** [other] camping
2	Rd 5
1mm	**Welcome Ctr nb, full [handicapped] facilities, litter barrels, petwalk [phone] [picnic] vending**
0mm	Minnesota/Iowa state line

MINNEAPOLIS

IINTERSTATE 35 WEST

Exit #	Services
41mm	**I-35W begins/ends on I-35, exit 127.**
36	Rd 23, **E** [gas] Holiday/dsl [lodging] Country Inn&Suites, **W** [gas] US/dsl [food] Caribou Coffee, DQ, McDonald's, Subway [lodging] Hampton Inn [other] Discount Tire, Kohl's, Super Target
33	Rd 17, Lexington Ave, **1 mi E** [gas] F&F/dsl, Holiday [food] Burger King, McDonald's, **W** [food] Applebee's, Arby's, Bonfire Rest., Caribou Coffee, Green Mill Rest., Quizno's, Taco Bell/LJ Silver, Wendy's, Zantigo's Mexican [other] Cub Foods, GNC, Home Depot, Michael's, Radio Shack, Walgreens, Walmart
32	95th Ave NE, to Lexington, Circle Pines, **W** [other] Nat Sports Ctr
31b a	Lake Dr, **E** [gas] Shell/dsl [food] Quizno's, Red Ginger Asian, Steamin Bean Coffee [lodging] Country Inn&Suites
30	US 10 W, MN 118, to MN 65
29	Rd I
28c b	Rd 10, Rd H, **W** [gas] BP [food] KFC, LJ Silver/Taco Bell, McDonald's, Mermaid Café, RJ Riches Rest. [lodging] AmericInn, Days Inn [other] carwash, NAPA
28a	MN 96
27b a	I-694 E and W
26	Rd E2, **W** [gas] Exxon/dsl [food] Jimmy John's, Limu Coffee
25b	MN 88, to Roseville (no EZ return to sb), same as 25a
25a	Rd D (from nb), **E** [gas] BP/dsl [food] Blimpie [lodging] Courtyard, Fairfield Inn, Residence Inn, **W** [gas] PDQ, SA [food] Barley John's, Caribou Coffee, Jake's Café, McDonald's, New Hong Kong, Perkins/24hr, Sarpino's Italian, Subway
24	Rd C, **E** [food] Burger King, India Palace Rest., Joe Senser's Rest. [lodging] Days Inn, Motel 6, Radisson [other] USPO, **W** [lodging] Holiday Inn Express [other] Chevrolet/GMC, Chrysler/Dodge/Jeep, Volvo
23b	Cleveland Ave, MN 36
23a	MN 280, Industrial Blvd (from sb)
22	MN 280, Industrial Blvd (from nb), **E** [lodging] Ramada Plaza
21b a	Broadway St, Stinson Blvd, **E** [other] Ford/Isuzu Trucks, **W** [food] Baja Sol, Burger King, Caribou Coffee, Cousins Subs, Leeann Chin, McDonald's, Pizza Hut/Taco Bell [other] GNC, Home Depot, Old Navy, Rainbow Foods/24hr, Target
19	E Hennepin (from nb)
18	US 52, 4th St SE, University Ave, to U of MN, **E** [gas] BP/repair
17c	11th St, Washington Ave, **E** [lodging] Holiday Inn, **W** [gas] Mobil [other] [H], Goodyear, to Metrodome
17b	I-94 W (from sb)
17a	MN 55, Hiawatha
16b a	I-94 (from nb), E to St Paul, W to St Cloud, to MN 65
15	31st St (from nb), Lake St, **E** [food] McDonald's, Taco B[ell] [other] Auto Zone, **W** [other] [H]
14	35th St, 36th St
13	46th St
13mm	Minnehaha Creek
12b	Diamond Lake Rd
12a	60th St (from sb), **W** [gas] Mobil [other] Cub Foods
11b	MN 62 E, to [airport], [other] to [airport]
11a	Lyndale Ave (from sb)
10b	MN 62 W, 58th St
10a	Rd 53, 66th St, **E** [gas] SA
9c	76th St (from sb)
9b a	I-494, MN 5, to [airport], [other] to [airport]
8	82nd St, **E** [other] BMW, **W** [food] Caribou Coffee, Jimmy John['s], Red Lobster, Sonic, Timberlodge Steaks, Wendy's [lodging] Emba[s]sy Suites [other] Chevrolet, Chrysler/Dodge/Jeep, Hyundai, Infini[ti], Kia, Kohl's, TJ Maxx, Walgreens
7b	90th St
7a	94th St, **E** [other] Goodyear/auto, **W** [lodging] Holiday Inn
6	Rd 1, 98th St, **E** [gas] Holiday [food] Applebee's, Bakers Squa[re], Burger King, Coldstone, Domino's, Golden Wok, Jimmy John['s], Leeann Chen, McDonald's, Starbucks, Wendy's, White Cas[tle] [other] Bloomington Drug, Festival Foods, Ford, Radio Shack, U[R]GENT CARE, Walgreens, **W** [gas] SA/dsl [food] Denny's
5	106th St
5mm	Minnesota River
4b	113th St, Black Dog Rd
4a	Cliff Rd, **E** [other] Dodge, Subaru, **W** [other] VW
3b a	MN 13, Shakopee, Canterbury Downs, **E** [lodging] Select Inn
2	Burnsville Pkwy, **E** [gas] BP, Marathon [food] Bumpers Grill, **W** [gas] Holiday [food] Gourmet Chinese, Hooters, Perkins, TimberLod[ge] Steaks [lodging] Best Value Inn, LivInn, Prime Rate Motel, Travelod[ge] [other] Best Buy, Goodyear/auto, vet
1	Rd 42, Crystal Lake Rd, **E** [food] Chianti Grill [other] Byerly's Food[s], PetsMart, Tuesday Morning, **W** [gas] Holiday/dsl, SA [food] Applebee's, Arby's/Sbarro's, Azteca Mexican, Buca Italian, Burg[er] King, Cam Aranh Bay, Champp's Grill, Chili's, Dakota Coun[try] Grill, HoneyBaked Ham, IHOP, Jimmy John's, KFC, Kings Buffe[t], Macaroni Grill, McDonald's, Old Country Buffet, Olive Garde[n], Outback Steaks, Panera Bread, Papa John's, Papa Murphy['s], Qdoba Mexican, Red Lobster, Roasted Pear, Starbucks, Tac[o] Bell/Pizza Hut, TGIFriday's, Wendy's [lodging] Days Inn, Fairfie[ld] Inn, Hampton Inn, Holiday Inn, InTown Suites [other] [H], AT&[T], Barnes&Noble, Best Buy, Cadillac, Chevrolet, Cub Foods, Dis[count] Tire, Goodyear/auto, Home Depot, JC Penney, K-Ma[rt], Kohl's, Macy's, mall, Michael's, PetCo, Rainbow Foods, Sears auto, Target, Tires+, USPO, Walgreens

I-35W begins/ends on I-35, exit 88a.

INTERSTATE 90

Exit #	Services
278mm	Minnesota/Wisconsin state line, Mississippi River
276	US 14, US 61, to MN 16, La Crescent, **N** **Welcome Ctr wb, fu[ll] [handicapped] facilities, info, litter barrels, petwalk [phone] [picnic] vending** **S** [gas] Kwik Trip (1mi)
273b a	Dresbach
271	Dakota
270	US 14, US 61, to Winona (from wb), **N** to OL Kipp SP/camping

MN

E INTERSTATE 90 Cont'd

Exit #	Services
267	Rd 12, Nodine, N camping, Great River Bluffs SP, S Kwik Trip/Hearty Platter Rest./dsl/e-85/scales/24hr/ @
261mm	**weigh sta both lanes**
258	MN 76, to Houston, Ridgeway, Witoka, N gas, S camping
252	MN 43 N, to Winona, **7 mi** N Taco Bell Express Inn, Holiday Inn Express, Plaza Hotel, Quality Inn H, S vet
249	MN 43 S, to Rushford, N Peterbilt Trucks/repair
244mm	**eb, full facilities, litter barrels, petwalk vending**
242	Rd 29, Lewiston
233	MN 74, to Chatfield, St Charles, N Kwik Trip/LP/24hr (2mi) A&W (2mi), Subway (2mi) Whitewater SP, S BP/Amish Ovens Rest./dsl/RV dump/LP
229	Rd 10, Dover
224	MN 42, Rd 7, Eyota, N KwikTrip/dsl/E-85 (3mi) Country Cafe (3mi)
222mm	**wb, full facilities, litter barrels, petwalk vending**
218	US 52, to Rochester, S BP/dsl KOA (Mar-Oct) (1mi)
209b a	US 63, MN 30, to Rochester, Stewartville, **8-10 mi** N Clarion, Comfort Inn, EconoLodge, Hampton Inn, Holiday Inn, **1 mi** S KwikTrip/dsl DQ, Pizza Ranch, Subway Best Inn Family$, Verizon
205	Rd 6
202mm	**eb, full facilities, litter barrels, petwalk vending**
193	MN 16, Dexter, N BP/Oasis Rest./dsl, S Windmill Motel
189	Rd 13, to Elkton
187	Rd 20, S Jelly Stone Camping
183	MN 56, to Rose Creek, Brownsdale, S Freeborn County Co-op/dsl/LP
181	28th St NE
180b a	US 218, 21st St NE, to Austin, Oakland Place, S Shell Rodeway Inn
179	11th Dr NE, to Austin, N KwikTrip/dsl/24hr
178b	6th St NE, to Austin, S Spam Museum
178a	4th St NW, N Culver's, Jimmy John's, Perkins, Torge's Grille AmericInn, Days Inn, Holiday Inn AutoValue Parts, Buick/Chevrolet/GMC, S KwikTrip/dsl Burger King, Subway H
177	US 218 N, to Owatonna, Austin, Mapleview, N Applebee's, Arby's, China Star, El Patron Mexican, KFC, King Buffet, Pizza Ranch, Quiznos, Wendy's $Tree, Aldi Foods, AT&T, AutoZone, Hy-Vee Foods/gas, JoAnn Fabrics, mall, O'Reilly Parts, Radio Shack, ShopKO, Target, Verizon, Walmart/Subway, Younkers, S Sinclair/McDonald's/dsl Super 8
175	MN 105, Rd 46, to Oakland Rd, N Econolodge, S BP/dsl, Shell/dsl Chrysler/Dodge/Jeep, Ford/Lincoln, vet
171mm	**wb, full facilities, litter barrels, petwalk**
166	Rd 46, Oakland Rd, N golf (par3), KOA/LP
163	Rd 26, Hayward, S Freeborn County Co-op/dsl Pizza Hut (4mi), Trails Rest. (4mi) camping, Myre-Big Island SP
161.5mm	**eb, full facilities, litter barrels, petwalk**
159b a	I-35, N to Twin Cities, S to Des Moines
157	Rd 22, Albert Lea, N Kenworth, S HyVee/dsl Applebee's, Arby's, Caribou Coffee, DQ, KwikTrip/dsl, McDonald's, Pizza Ranch, Plaza Morina Mexican AmericInn, Best Western H, Ace Hardware, Chevrolet, Harley-Davidson, Herberger's, Hy-Vee Foods, mall, ShopKO, Verizon
154	MN 13, to US 69, to Manchester, Albert Lea, N SA/dsl, **3 mi** S BelAire Motel

AUSTIN

ALBERT LEA

Exit #	Services
146	MN 109, to Wells, Alden, S BP/dsl/rest., Freeborn Co-Op Gas/dsl/E-85 truck/dsl repair
138	MN 22, to Wells, Keister, N Casey's (6mi), S camping
134	MN 253, Rd 21, to Bricelyn, MN Lake, N camping
128	MN 254, Rd 17, Frost, Easton
119	US 169, to Winnebago, Blue Earth, S Shell/dsl, Sinclair/dsl Country Kitchen, DQ, McDonald's, Pizza Hut, Subway AmericInn, Super 8 H, $General, camping, Jolly Green Giant, Walmart
119mm	**both lanes, full facilities, litter barrels, petwalk playground**
113	Rd 1, Guckeen
107	MN 262, Rd 53, to East Chain, Granada, S camping (May-Oct) (1mi), gas/dsl
102	MN 15, to Madelia, Fairmont, N Verizon, Walmart/Subway, **0-2 mi** S BP, Cenex/dsl, SA/dsl/24hr Arby's, Bean Town a Grill, Burger King, Cina Buffet, DQ, Green Mill Rest., McDonald's, Perkins, Pizza Ranch, Ranch Family Rest., Subway Budget Inn, Comfort Inn, Hampton Inn, Holiday Inn, Super 8 H, $Tree, Ace Hardware, auto repair, camping, CarQuest, Chevrolet, Chrysler/Dodge/Jeep, Fareway Foods, Ford, Freightliner, Goodyear/auto, Hy-Vee Foods, JC Penney, NAPA, O'Reilly Parts, ShopKO, USPO, Walgreens
99	Rd 39, Fairmont
93	MN 263, Rd 27, Welcome, **1/2 mi** S camping, Casey's/dsl
87	MN 4, Sherburn, N Everett Park Camping (5mi), S Casey's/dsl, Kum&Go/Subway/dsl/E-85
80	Rd 29, Alpha
73	US 71, Jackson, N SA/dsl Burger King EconoLodge, Super 8 KOA, to Kilen Woods SP, S BP/DQ, Casey's/dsl Embers Rest., Pizza Ranch, Subway AmericInn, Earth Inn, Prairie Winds Motel H, Ace Hardware, Buick/Chevrolet, Chrysler/Dodge/Jeep, city park, Family$, Sunshine Foods, to Spirit Lake
72.5mm	W Fork Des Moines River
72mm	**wb, full facilities, litter barrels, petwalk vending**
69mm	**eb, full facilities, litter barrels, petwalk vending**
64	MN 86, Lakefield, N gas/dsl food H, camping, to Kilen SP (12mi)
57	Rd 9, to Heron Lake, Spafford
50	MN 264, Rd 1, to Brewster, Round Lake, S camping
47	Rd 3 (from eb), no return
46mm	weigh sta eb
45	MN 60, Worthington, N BP/Blueline Cafe/dsl/scales, S Holiday/dsl/scales/24hr camping, truckwash
43	US 59, Worthington, N Casey's/dsl Comfort Suites, Travelodge, S Casey's, Cenex/dsl, Shell Arby's, Burger King, DQ, Ground Round, Hardee's, KFC, McDonald's, Perkins,

FAIRMONT

WORTHINGTON

MN

INTERSTATE 90 Cont'd

43 Continued
Pizza Hut, Pizza Ranch, Subway, Taco John's [lodging] AmericInn, Holiday Inn Express [other] [H], $General, $Tree, Ace Hardware, CarQuest, Chevrolet, Fareway Foods, Ford, Hy-Vee Foods/dsl, NAPA, O'Reilly Parts, Radio Shack, ShopKO, Verizon, Walgreens, Walmart/Subway

42 MN 266, Rd 25, to Reading, S [lodging] Days Inn, Super 8

33 Rd 13, to Wilmont, Rushmore

26 MN 91, Adrian, S [gas] Cenex/dsl, Kum&Go/Subway/dsl/E-85/24hr [food] Countryside Steaks [other] Adrian Camping, city park

25mm [RS] wb, full [handicapped] facilities, litter barrels, petwalk [phone] [picnic]

24mm [RS] eb, full [handicapped] facilities, litter barrels, petwalk [phone] [picnic]

18 Rd 3, Kanaranzi, Magnolia, N [other] camping

12 US 75, Luverne, N [gas] BP/dsl/E-85, Casey's/dsl, Holiday/Subway/dsl [food] China Inn, McDonald's, Papa's Place Rest., Taco John's, Tasty Drive-In [lodging] Cozy Rest Motel (1mi), GrandStay Hotel, Quality Inn [other] [H], $General, Buick/Cadillac/Chevrolet/GMC, Chrysler/Dodge/Jeep, Ford, Lewis Drugs, Pipestone NM, Sturdevant's Parts, to Blue Mounds SP, S [food] Blue Stem Rest. [lodging] Super 8 [other] ShopKO

5 Rd 6, Beaver Creek, N [gas] Local/dsl

3 Rd 4 (from eb), Beaver Creek

1 MN 23, Rd 17, to Jasper, N [other] access to gas/dsl, to Pipestone NM

0mm Welcome Ctr eb, full [handicapped] facilities, info, litter barrels, petwalk [phone] [picnic], Minnesota/South Dakota state line

INTERSTATE 94

Exit #	Services
259mm	Minnesota/Wisconsin state line, St Croix River
258	MN 95 N, to Stillwater, Hastings, Lakeland, N [food] Bungalow Rest.
257mm	**Welcome Ctr wb, full [handicapped] facilities, litter barrels, petwalk [phone] [picnic] vending, weigh sta wb**
253	MN 95 S, Rd 15, Manning Ave, N [other] StoneRidge Golf, S [other] ski area, to Afton Alps SP
251	Rd 19, Keats Ave, Woodbury Dr, S [gas] KwikTrip, SA/dsl [food] Applebee's, Arby's, Asia Bistro, Burger King, Caribou Coffee, Chili's, Chipotle Mexican, Dino's Rest, Dunn Bros Coffee, Lakes Grill, Las Margaritas, LeeAnn Chin, McDonald's, Outback Steaks, Quiznos, Ray J's Grill, SmashBurger, Subway [lodging] Extended Stay America, Holiday Inn Express [other] $Tree, AT&T, Gander Mtn, Hancock Fabrics, Michael's, Sam's Club/gas, Staples, Target, Trader Joe's, Tuesday Morning, Walmart/Subway, Woodbury Lakes Outlets/famous brands
250	Rd 13, Radio Dr, Inwood Ave, N [food] 5 Guys Burgers, Baja Sol, Buffalo Wild Wings, Caribou Coffee, Machine Shed Rest., Milio's Rest., Olive Garden, Red Lobster [lodging] Hilton Garden, Wild Wood Lodge [other] Best Buy, S [gas] Holiday [food] Champp's, Domino's, DUK Vietnamese, Jamba Juice, Little Caesars, Pei Wei, Starbucks, Taco Bell, Wendy's, Wild Bill's Grill [other] Aldi Foods, BigLots, Cub Foods, CVS Drug, Dick's, Fannie May, GNC, Gordmans, Hepner's Auto Ctr, Home Depot, JC Penney, Jo-Ann, LandsEnd Inlet, Old Navy, Petsmart, Tires+, Verizon, vet
249	I-694 N & I-494 S
247	MN 120, Century Ave, N [food] Denny's [lodging] AmericInn, LivInn [other] Harley-Davidson, S [gas] SA [food] GreenMill Rest. [lodging] Country Inn/rest. [other] CarQuest, Chevrolet
246c b	McKnight Ave, N [other] 3M, S [lodging] Holiday Inn
246a	Ruth St (from eb, no return), N [gas] BP [food] Culver's, Domino's, Hoho Chinese, Jimmy John's [other] $Tree, Cub Foods, Firestone auto, GNC, Radio Shack, TJ Maxx
245	White Bear Ave, N [gas] BP, SA/dsl [food] Subway [lodging] Super [other] Walgreens, S [gas] BP [food] Arby's, Davanni's Pizza/subs Los Ocampo, McDonald's, Papa John's, Popeye's, Sonic, Taco Bell, Wendy's [other] Aldi Foods, Byerly's Foods, Family$, NAPA O'Reilly Parts, Target
244	US 10 E, US 61 S, [other] Mounds/Kellogg
243	US 61, Mounds Blvd, S River Centre
242d	US 52 S, MN 3, 6th St, (exits left from wb), N [gas] Holiday [food] Subway
242c	7th St, S [gas] SA
242b a	I-35E N, US 10 W, I-35E S (from eb)
241c	I-35E S (from wb)
241b	10th St, 5th St, to downtown
241a	12th St, Marion St, Kellogg Blvd, N [lodging] Best Western Kelly Inn S [other] St Paul's Cathedral
240	Dale Ave
239b a	Lexington Pkwy, Hamline Ave, N [gas] BP, SA [food] Hardee's Leeann Chin, Popeye's, White Castle [other] [H], AutoZone, Cub Foods, Discount Tire, Herberger's, O'Reilly Parts, Target
238	MN 51, Snelling Ave, N [food] Applebee's, Culver's, Jimmy John's Little Caesars, McDonald's, Perkins [other] CVS Drug, Family$ Radio Shack, Rainbow Foods, same as 239, Tires+, Walgreens Walmart
237	Cretin Ave, Vandalia Ave, to downtown
236	MN 280, University Ave, to downtown
235b	Huron Blvd
235mm	Mississippi River
235a	Riverside Ave, 25th Ave, N [gas] Tesoro [food] Starbucks, S [food] Perkins, Taco Bell
234c	Cedar Ave, downtown
234b a	MN 55, Hiawatha Ave, 5th St, N [lodging] Courtyard [other] to downtown
233b	I-35W N, I-35W S (exits left from wb)
233a	11th St (from wb), N downtown
231b	Hennepin Ave, Lyndale Ave, to downtown
231a	I-394, US 12 W, to downtown
230	US 52, MN 55, 4th St, 7th St, Olson Hwy, N [other] Metrodome S [other] [H], Int Mkt Square
229	W Broadway, Washington Ave, N [gas] Holiday/dsl, Old Colony dsl, S [gas] Winner [food] Broadway Pizza, Burger King, KFC, Little Caesars, McDonald's, Subway, Taco Bell, Wendy's [other] $Tree AutoZone, Cub Foods, Family$, Walgreens
228	Dowling Ave N
226	53rd Ave N, 49th Ave N
225	I-694 E, MN 252 N, to Minneapolis

I-94 & I-494 run together. See I-494/694, exits 28-34

216	I-94 W and I-494
215	Rd 109, Weaver Lake Rd, N [gas] SA/dsl, Shell [food] Anginos Broadway Pizza, Burger King, Caribou Coffee, Champps ChuckECheese's, Domino's, Don Pablo, DQ, El Rodeo Mexican, Famous Dave's BBQ, Frankie's Pizza, Great Harvest Bread Co., Jimmy John's, McDonald's, Old Country Buffet, Papa John's, Papa Murphy's, Starbucks, Subway, Taco Bell, Wendy's [other] AT&T, Barnes&Noble, Byerly's Foods, Cub Foods, Gander Mtn, GNC, Goodyear/auto, JC Penney, K-Mart, Kohl's, mall Michael's, Midas, Old Navy, PetCo, Radio Shack, same as 28 Tires+, USPO, Verizon, Walgreens, S [food] Applebee's, IHOP
214mm	**[RS] eb, full [handicapped] facilities, litter barrels [phone] [picnic]**
213	Rd 30, 95th Ave N, Maple Grove, N [gas] SA/dsl [food] Chipotle Mexican, Subway [lodging] Cambria Suites [other] [H], Aldi Foods

ST PAUL

MINNEAPOLIS

INTERSTATE 94 Cont'd

213 Continued
GNC, Home Depot, Target, **S** [gas] Holiday/dsl [food] Culver's, Leeann Chin, Little Caesars, McDonald's, Starbucks, Which Wich, White Castle [other] Apr-Oct), BigLots, Discount Tire, Firestone, Goodyear/auto, KOA (2mi, Menards, Rainbow Foods, Sam's Club/gas, Verizon, Walgreens, Walmart/Subway

207 MN 101, to Elk River, Rogers, **N** [gas] Holiday, SA/dsl, TA/Country Pride/dsl/scales/24hr/ @ [food] Applebee's, Arby's, Burger King, China Kitchen, Culver's, Davanni's Pizza, Denny's, Dickey's BBQ, Domino's, DQ, Hardee's, Jimmy John's, Maynard's, McDonald's, Noodles&Co, Starbucks, Subway, Taco Bell, Wendy's [lodging] Hampton Inn, Holiday Inn Express, Super 8 [other] $Tree, AT&T, Cabela's, Camping World, Cub Foods, Discount Tire, Gander Mtn, GNC, Kohl's, Lowe's, NAPA, NTB, O'Reilly Parts, Target, Tires+, Verizon, vet, Walgreens, **S** [gas] BP/Circle K/dsl, Holiday [food] BoBo Asian, Guadalajara Mexican, Harvest Grill, Minne's Diner [lodging] AmericInn [other] Chevrolet, CVS Drug, TrueValue, URGENT CARE

205.5mm Crow River

205 MN 241, Rd 36, St Michael, **S** [gas] QwikTrip/dsl, SA/dsl

202 Rd 37, Albertville, **N** [gas] Shell/dsl [food] Emma Krumbee's Rest., **S** [gas] BP/dsl, same as 201, Sunoco/dsl

201 Rd 19 (from eb), Albertville, St Michael, **N** [gas] Shell/dsl [food] Andy's Pizza, Burger King, Michael B's Grill, Perkins, Subway [lodging] Country Inn&Suites [other] Albertville Outlets/famous brands, Old Navy, **S** [gas] BP/dsl, Casey's, Mobil/Subway, Sunoco/dsl [food] Caribou Coffee, China Dragon, Culver's, Little Caesars, Papa Murphy's, Space Aliens Grill [other] Ace Hardware, auto repair, Coburn's/gas, Goodyear/auto, Verizon

MONTICELLO

194 Rd 18, Rd 39, Monticello, **N** [gas] Cruiser's/dsl, Marathon/dsl/E85 [food] Caribou Coffee, Little Caesars, McDonald's [other] [H], GNC, Home Depot, Petsmart, Target, Verizon

193 MN 25, to Buffalo, Monticello, Big Lake, **N** [gas] Holiday/dsl [food] 5 Buck Pizza, Burger King, Caribou Coffee, KFC, Papa Murphy's, Perkins, Poncho Villa Mexican, Quiznos, Rancho Grande Mexican, Taco Bell [lodging] AmericInn [other] AutoValue Parts, Cub Foods, Radio Shack, USPO, Walgreens, **S** [gas] Holiday/dsl, KwikTrip/dsl, SA/dsl [food] Applebee's, Arby's, Blue Stone Grill, Buffalo Wild Wings, Chatter's Grill, China Buffet, Culver's, DQ, Jimmy John's, McDonald's, Pizza Ranch, Subway, Taco John's [lodging] Best Western, Days Inn, Super 8 [other] $Tree, Buick/GMC, Chevrolet, Goodyear/auto, Lake Maria SP, NAPA, O'Reilly Parts, Verizon, vet, Walmart/Subway

187mm [RS] **eb, full [handicapped] facilities, litter barrels, petwalk [phone] [picnic] vending**

183 Rd 8, to Silver Creek, Hasty, Maple Lake, **S** [gas] BP/rest./dsl/scales/24hr/ @ [other] camping, to Lake Maria SP

178 MN 24, to Annandale, Clearwater, **N** [gas] Holiday/Petro/dsl/scales/24hr/ @ [food] Burger King, DQ, Keith's Kettle, Subway, Taco Gringo [lodging] Best Value Inn [other] Clearwater Hardware, Coburn's Foods/gas, GS Camping (1mi), Parts City, repair, USPO, vet, **S** [other] A-J Acres RV Camping (Apr-Oct)Recreation Outdoor RV Ctr

178mm [RS] **wb, full [handicapped] facilities, litter barrels, petwalk [phone] [picnic] vending**

173 Opportunity Dr

171 Rd 7, Rd 75, St Augusta, **N** [gas] Pilot/McDonald's/dsl/scales/24hr, Shell [food] Burger King, MadeRite Grill, RJ's Grill, Subway [lodging] AmericInn, Holiday Inn Express, Travelodge [other] [H], Goodyear/auto, **S** [other] Freightliner, Pleasureland RV Ctr

167b a MN 15, to St Cloud, Kimball, **4 mi N** [gas] Holiday, SA/dsl [food] 5 Guys Burgers, Applebee's, Arby's, Bonanza, Boulder Tap

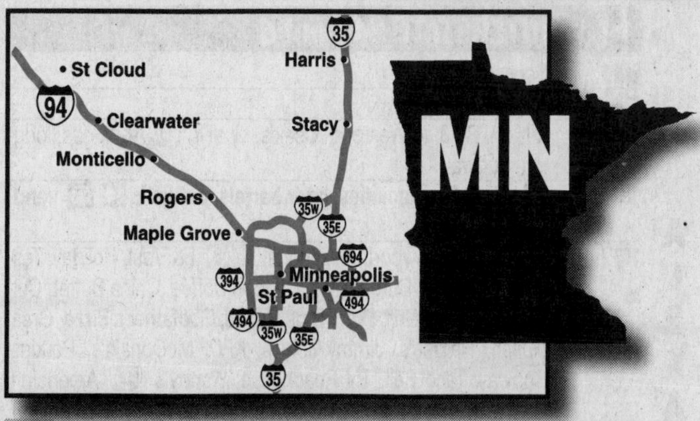

ST CLOUD

167b a Continued
house, Buffalo Wild Wings, Burger King, Caribou Coffee, Chipotle, ChuckECheese's, Domino's, Famous Dave's BBQ, Granite City Grill, Grizzly's Grill, IHOP, La Casita Mexican, McDonald's, Noodles&Co, Old Chicago Pizza, Old Country Buffet, Olive Garden, Panda Express, Perkins, Pizza Hut, Pizza Ranch, Qdoba, Red Lobster, Sammy's Pizza, Starbucks, Subway, Taco Bell, Taco John's, TGIFriday's, Wendy's, White Castle [lodging] Country Inn&Suites, Days Inn, Fairfield Inn, Hampton Inn, Holiday Inn, Homewood Suites, Quality Inn, Super 8 [other] [H], AT&T, Barnes&Noble, Best Buy, BigLots, CashWise Foods, Gander Mtn, Home Depot, JC Penney, Jo-Ann Fabrics, K-Mart, Kohl's, Macy's, Michael's, Office Depot, Old Navy, Petsmart, Sam's Club, Save-A-Lot, Scheel's Sports, Sears/auto, ShopKo, Subaru, Target, USPO, Walgreens, Walmart, **S** [gas] Shell/dsl (2mi)

164 MN 23, to St Cloud, Rockville, **4-6 mi N** [gas] Holiday [food] Culver's, IHOP, KFC, Subway, Taco Bell, Wendy's [lodging] Motel 6 [other] Discount Tire, Gander Mtn, Grande Depot Gourmet Foods, Hyundai, Kia, Menards, Petsmart, same as 167, Toyota/Scion

162.5mm Sauk River

160 Rd 2, to Cold Spring, St Joseph, **N** [gas] BP [lodging] Super 8 (3mi) [other] Coll of St Benedict

158 Rd 75 (from eb exits left), to St Cloud, **3 mi N** same as 160

156 Rd 159, St Joseph, **N** [other] St Johns U

153 Rd 9, Avon, **N** [gas] Shell/dsl, Tesoro/McDonald's/dsl [food] Joseph's Rest., Subway [lodging] Budget Host [other] city park, picnic area, USPO, **S** [other] El Rancho Manana Camping (10mi)

152mm [RS] **both lanes, full [handicapped] facilities, litter barrels, petwalk [phone] [picnic] vending**

147 MN 238, Rd 10, Albany, **N** [gas] Holiday/dsl, Shell/A&W/Subway/dsl [food] Chesters, DQ, Hillcrest Rest. [lodging] Norwood Inn&Suites [other] [H], golf, **S** [other] Chrysler/Dodge/Jeep, NAPA, vet

140 Rd 11, Freeport, **N** [gas] Cenex/dsl, Clark/dsl [food] Ackie's Pioneer Rest., Charlie's Café [other] auto repair, USPO, vet

137 MN 237, Rd 65, New Munich

137mm Sauk River

135 Rd 13, Melrose, **N** [gas] Clark/dsl/repair, Tesoro/Subway/dsl [food] Burger King, Cornerstone Buffet [other] [H], $General, **S** [gas] Casey's/dsl [food] DQ, El Portal Mexican [lodging] Super 8 [other] Save Foods, vet

132.5mm Sauk River

131 MN 4, to Paynesville, Meire Grove

128mm Sauk River

127 US 71, MN 28, Sauk Centre, **N** [gas] Casey's, Holiday/dsl [food] 4 Seas Buffet, DQ, Hardee's, McDonald's, Pizza Hut, Subway [lodging] AmericInn, Best Value Inn, Guesthouse Inn [other] [H], Ace Hardware, Coborn's Foods, Ford, Lewis Ctr/rest area, NAPA, O'Reilly Parts, Walmart/Subway, **S** [gas] Shell/café/dsl/scales/24hr/ @ [other] Buick/Chevrolet/Chrysler/Dodge/Jeep

124 Sinclair Lewis Ave (from eb), Sauk Centre

MN

MN

INTERSTATE 94 Cont'd

ALEXANDRIA / FERGUS FALLS

Exit #	Services
119	Rd 46, West Union
114	MN 27, Rd 3, to Westport, Osakis, **3 mi** N A&W, gas, lodging, Subway
105mm	**wb, full facilities, litter barrels, petwalk vending**
103	MN 29, to Glenwood, Alexandria, N F&F/dsl, Holiday, Tesoro Arby's, Burger King, Caribou Coffee, China Buffet, Culver's, Dolittle's Grill, Dunn Bros Coffee, Godfather's Pizza, Great Hunan, Hardee's, Jimmy John's, KFC, McDonald's, Perkins, Subway, Taco Bell, TN Roadhouse, Wendy's AmericInn, Best Western, Days Inn, Hampton Inn, Super 8 H, AT&T, Cadillac/Chevrolet/Mazda, County Mkt Foods, Goodyear/auto, Harley-Davidson, Jeep, Jo-Ann Fabrics, K-Mart, Menards, Radio Shack, Target, Tires+, Verizon, Walmart/Subway, S Holiday/dsl Country Inn&Suites, Holiday Inn Alexandria RV Ctr
100	MN 27, N Pilot/Subway/dsl/scales/24hr/ @ Best Inn/Alexandria RV Park H, S camping
100mm	Lake Latoka
99mm	**eb, full facilities, litter barrels, petwalk vending**
97	MN 114, Rd 40, to Lowry, Garfield
90	Rd 7, Brandon, S camping, ski area
82	MN 79, Rd 41, to Erdahl, Evansville, **2 mi** N BP/dsl, S H, camping
77	MN 78, Rd 10, to Barrett, Ashby, N gas/dsl Prairie Cove Camping (May-Sept), S camping
69mm	**wb, full facilities, litter barrels, petwalk vending**
67	Rd 35, Dalton, N camping, S camping
61	US 59 S, Rd 82, to Elbow Lake, N Tesoro/café/dsl/LP/24hr H, camping (4mi), Pine Plaza RV Ctr, S camping
57	MN 210 E, Rd 25, Fergus Falls, N H
55	Rd 1, to Wendell, Fergus Falls, N antiques
54	MN 210 W, Lincoln Ave, Fergus Falls, N Cenex/dsl, F&F/dsl, Tesoro/dsl Applebee's, Arby's, Burger King, Debbie's Kitchen, Family Diner, Hunan Spring Buffet, KFC, McDonald's, Papa Murphy's, Perkins, Pizza Hut, Pizza Ranch, Subway AmericInn, Best Value Inn, Best Western, Comfort Inn, Motel 7, Super 8 H, $Tree, AT&T, Chrysler/Dodge/Jeep, Ford/Lincoln, GMC, Herbergers, Home Depot, K-Mart, museum, NAPA, O'Reilly Parts, SunMart Foods, Target, Tires+, Toyota, S Mabel Murphy's Rest. Walmart
50	Rd 88, Rd 52, to US 59, to Fergus Falls, Elizabeth, camping
38	Rd 88, Rothsay, S Tesoro/cafe/dsl/24hr Ole&Lena's Pizza Comfort Zone Inn tires
32	MN 108, Rd 30, to Pelican Rapids, Lawndale, N **19 mi** Maplewood SP
24	MN 34, Barnesville, N Renee's Drive-in, **1 mi** S Cenex/dsl, Tesoro/dsl DQ, Subway motel city park, Wagner Park Camping (May-Oct)
22	MN 9, Barnesville, **1 mi** S Cenex/dsl, Tesoro/dsl DQ, Subway motel
15	Rd 10, Downer
8mm	Buffalo River
6	MN 336, Rd 11, to US 10, Dilworth, N to Buffalo River SP
5mm	**Red River weigh sta eb**
2b a	Rd 52, Moorhead, **2 mi** N Holiday/dsl/e-85, Tesoro Arby's, McDonald's, Perkins, Pizza Ranch, Subway, Taco Bell Travelodge H, antiques, CVS Drug, K-Mart, KOA, Menards, Radio Shack, Target, Walmart

MOORHEAD

Exit #	Services
2mm	**Welcome Ctr eb, full facilities, info, litter barrels vending**
1b	20th St, Moorhead (from eb, no return)
1a	US 75, Moorhead, N Clark/dsl Burger King, Crav Burger Co., Little Caesars, Papa Murphy's, Qdoba, Sarp nos Pizza, Starbucks, Village Inn Courtyard Curve SunMart Foods, Verizon, S Casey's, Orton's Gas DC Panchero's Mexican, Snapdragon Asian, Speak Easy Rest Subway Days Inn, Grand Inn, Super 8 CVS Drug, ve Walgreens
0mm	Minnesota/North Dakota state line, Red River

INTERSTATE 494/694

ST PAUL

Exit #	Services
I-494/I-694 loops around Minneapolis/St Paul.	
71	Rd 31, Pilot Knob Rd, N Courtyard, Fairfield Inn, S Lo neOak Café Best Western, Crowne Plaza
70	I-35E, N to St Paul, S to Albert Lea
69	MN 149, MN 55, Dodd Rd, N Ziggy's Deli, S Car bou Coffee, McDonald's, Subway Budget Host, Countr Inn&Suites
67	MN 3, Roberts St, **1 mi** N BP, Holiday, Mobil Acre Rest., Arby's/Sbarro's, Baker's Square, Buffalo Wings, Burge King, Chipotle Mexican, ChuckeCheese, Culver's, Grand Buffe KFC, Old Country Buffet, Pizza Hut, Taco Bell, Timber Lodg Steaks, White Castle Aamco, Best Buy, Buick, Checke Parts, Chevrolet, Cub Foods, Dodge, Ford, Jo-Ann Fabrics, Kia K-Mart, Lincoln, Mazda, NAPA, Nissan, Rainbow Foods/24h Target, Tires+, Toyota, VW, Walmart, S PDQ
66	US 52, S SA Old World Pizza, Outback Steak Country Inn&Suites, Microtel
65	7th Ave, 5th Ave
64b a	MN 56, Concord St, N Conoco/dsl Best Wester Drovers Ford Trucks, Goodyear, Peterbilt, S EZ Sto Chrysler/Jeep/Dodge, Parts+
63mm	Mississippi River
63c	Maxwell Ave
63b a	US 10, US 61, to St Paul, Hastings, S BP, SA Burge King, Subway Boyd's Motel NAPA
60	Lake Rd, E SA/dsl, W Country Inn&Suites
59	Valley Creek Rd, E BP/repair, SA/dsl/LP America' Burger, Applebees, Broadway Pizza, Chipotle Mexican, DQ Old Country Buffet, Papa Murphy's, Perkins, Potbelly's Rest. Yang's Chinese Red Roof Inn Barnes&Noble, Kohl's Marshall's, Office Depot, PetCo, Rainbow Foods, Target, USPO Walgreens, W PBQ Bonfire Rest., Burger King, Mc Donald's, Pizza Hut, Subway Hampton Inn H, Ac Hardware, Goodyear
58c	Tamarack Rd, E Paisano's Cafe, Woodbury's Caf Sheraton
58b a	I-94, E to Madison, W to St Paul. **I-494 S begins/ends, I-694 N begins/ends**
57	Rd 10, 10th St N, E SA IHOP, Quizno's Wing ate Inn, W Holiday Burger King, Hunan Buffet, KFC $Tree, K-Mart, mall, Rainbow Foods/24hr, vet
55	MN 5, E Target, W Holiday/dsl Subway Me nards, st patrol
52b a	MN 36, N St Paul, to Stillwater, W F&F/dsl
51	MN 120, E BP, SA/dsl Jethro's, Starbucks, W Ke lie's Corner/gas
50	White Bear Ave, E SA K-Mart, Sam's Club/gas W BP, Shell Acupulco Chicken, Arby's, Bakers Square

INTERSTATE 494/694 Cont'd

MINNEAPOLIS

50 Continued
Buffalo Wild Wings, Caribou Coffee, Chili's, Denny's, Great Moon Buffet, IHOP, Jake's Grill, Jimmy John's, KFC, McDonald's, Noodles&Co, North China, Old Country Buffet, Outback Steaks, Peiwei Asian, Perkins/24hr, Red Lobster, Taco Bell, TGI Friday, Wendy's [lodging] Emerald Inn [other] Aamco, Best Buy, Goodyear/auto, JC Penney, Jo-Ann Fabrics, Kohl's, Macy's, mall, Marshall's, Michael's, PetCo, Sears/auto, Tires+, Tuesday Morning, Walgreens

48 US 61, **E** [other] Acura, Chrysler/Dodge/Jeep, Ford, Honda, Hyundai, Isuzu/Subaru, Lincoln, **W** [food] Chili's, Gulden's Rest., McDonald's, Olive Garden [lodging] Best Western [other] [H], Audi/Porsche, Lexus, Mercedes, Toyota, Venburg Tire, Volvo

47 I-35E, N to Duluth

46 I-35E, US 10, S to St Paul

45 Rd 49, Rice St, **N** [gas] Gas+, Marathon/dsl [food] Papa John's, Subway, Taco Bell [other] Checker Parts, **S** [gas] Marathon/dsl [food] A&W, Burger King, Caribou Coffee, Taco John's [other] Kath Parts

43b Victoria St, **S** [other] Bill's Foods

43a Lexington Ave, **N** [food] Greenmill Rest., Red Robin [lodging] Hampton Inn, Hilton Garden, **S** [gas] Exxon, Sinclair [food] Blue Fox Grill, Burger King, Davanni's Pizza, Papa Murphy's, Perkins, Subway, Wendy's [lodging] Holiday Inn, Super 8 [other] Cub Foods, Goodyear/auto, Target, transmissions

42b US 10 W (from wb), to Anoka

42a MN 51, Snelling Ave, **1 mi S** [gas] Shell [food] Flaherty's Grill, Lindey's Steaks, McDonald's [lodging] Country Inn&Suites, Holiday Inn

41b a I-35W, S to Minneapolis, N to Duluth

40 Long Lake Rd, 10th St NW

39 Silver Lake Rd, **N** [gas] BP [food] Acupulco Mexican, Champps, McDonald's, Subway [other] Fairview Drug, Ford, U-Haul

38b a MN 65, Central Ave, **N** [gas] Holiday/dsl [food] Subway, **S** [gas] SA, SuperStop [food] A&W/KFC, Applebee's, Asia Rest., Big Marina Deli, Buffalo Wild Wings, Flameburger Rest., La Casita Mexican, McDonald's, Mr BBQ, Papa John's, Ricky's, Sonic, Subway, Taco Bell, Wendy's, White Castle [lodging] LivInn Hotel [other] $General, Advance Parts, AutoZone, Discount Tire, Menards, O'Reilly Parts, PetCo, Rainbow Foods, Target, Tires+, vet, Walgreens

37 Rd 47, University Ave, **N** [gas] Holiday, SA/dsl [food] Burger King, McDonald's, Papa Murphy's Pizza, Zantigo's Rest. [other] Cub Foods, CVS Drug, Goodyear, Home Depot, **S** [gas] Bona Bros/repair, Shell

36 E River Rd

35mm **I-494 W begins/ends, I-694 E begins/ends.**

35c MN 252, **N** [gas] Holiday, SA

35b a I-94 E to Minneapolis

34 to MN 100, Shingle Creek Pkwy, **N** [food] Denny's, Mr BBQ, Oak City Rest. [lodging] AmericInn, Comfort Inn, Country Inn&Suites, Crowne Plaza, Days Inn, Extended Stay America, Motel 6, Super 8, **S** [food] C1 Buffet, Global Kitchen, Ocean Buffet, Panera Bread [lodging] Embassy Suites [other] [H], AT&T, Curves, Kohl's, PepBoys, Target, Tires+, Walmart

33 Rd 152, Brooklyn Blvd, **N** [gas] SA/dsl, Shell [food] Culver's, Slim's Café, Subway [other] Buick/GMC, Chevrolet, Honda, Toyota/Scion, USPO, **S** [gas] BP [food] Applebee's, Arby's, IHOP, McDonald's, Popeye's, Starbucks, Subway, Taco Bell, Wendy's [other] AutoZone, Cub Foods, CVS Drug, Family$, NTB, Sun Foods, Walgreens

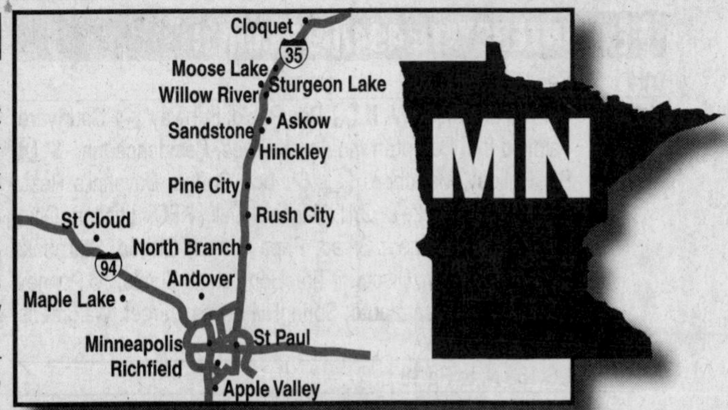

MN

MINNEAPOLIS

31 Rd 81, Lakeland Ave, **N** [gas] SA/dsl [food] Chipotle Mexican, Wagner's Drive-In, Wendy's [other] Target, U-Haul, **S** [lodging] Northstar Inn

30 Boone Ave, **N** [lodging] La Quinta, Marriott, **S** [other] Discount Tire, Home Depot

29b a US 169, to Hopkins, Osseo

28 Rd 61, Hemlock Lane, **N on Elm Creek** [food] 5 Guys Burgers, Arby's, Benihana, Biaggi's Italian, Boston's Grill, Buca Italian, CA Pizza Kitchen, Chick-fil-A, Chipotle Mexican, Coldstone, Dave&Buster's, Dickey's BBQ, Granite City Rest., Houlihan's, Leeann Chin, Malone's Grill, Mongo's Grill, Noodles&Co, Olive Garden, Panera Bread, PF Chang's, Pittsburgh Blue, Potbelly's, Red Lobster, Redstone Grill, Starbucks, Subway, TGIFriday's, Wild Bill's Café [lodging] Courtyard, Hampton Inn, Holiday Inn, Staybridge Suites [other] $Tree, Best Buy, Costco/gas, Dick's, Jo-Ann Fabrics, Lowe's, Marshalls, Office Depot, Old Navy, URGENT CARE, Whole Foods Mkt, **S** [gas] BP [food] Perkins [lodging] Asteria Suites

27 I-94 W to St Cloud, I-94/694 E to Minneapolis

26 Rd 10, Bass Lake Rd, **E** [gas] Freedom [food] Caribou Coffee, Culver's, McDonald's, Subway [lodging] Extended Stay America [other] mall, vet, **W** [gas] BP, Marathon/dsl [food] Dunn Bro's Cofee, Milio's Sandwiches, Pancake House, Pizza Hut [lodging] Hilton Garden [other] CVS Drug

23 Rd 9, Rockford Rd, **E** [gas] Holiday [food] Chili's, Peony's Chinese [other] GNC, O'Reilly Parts, PetsMart, Rainbow Foods, Target, TJ Maxx, vet, Walgreens, **W** [gas] PDQ [food] Cousins Subs, DQ, LeAnn Chin, Panchero's, Subway

22 MN 55, **E** [gas] Holiday/dsl [food] Broadway Pizza, Caribou Coffee, Green Mill Rest., Jimmy John's, McDonald's, Red Robin, Solos Pizza, Starbucks [lodging] Best Western Kelly, Radisson, Red Roof Inn, Residence Inn, **W** [gas] Holiday/dsl [food] Arby's, Burger King, Davanni's Rest., Jake's Rest., Perkins, Wendy's [lodging] Comfort Inn, Days Inn [other] Goodyear/auto, Tires+

21 Rd 6, **E** [gas] KwikTrip [other] Discount Tire, Home Depot

20 Carlson Pkwy, **E** [gas] Holiday/dsl [food] Pizza Hut, Subway, **W** [food] Woody's Grill [lodging] Country Inn&Suites

19b a I-394 E, US 12 W, to Minneapolis, **1 mi E off of I-394** [food] Applebee's, Wendy's [other] Barnes&Noble, Best Buy, Byerly's Foods, Ford, JC Penney, Jo-Ann Fabrics, Mazda, Mazerati, Mercedes, Sears/auto, Subaru, Target, Tires+, **1/2 mi W** [gas] BP, Holiday [food] KFC, McDonald's [other] BMW, Chevrolet, Lexus, Mitsubishi, Nissan

17b a Minnetonka Blvd, **W** [gas] US Gas [food] Cousin's Subs, Dunn Bros Coffee

16b a MN 7, **1 mi W** [gas] Marathon [food] Christo's Rest., Davanni's Rest., Famous Dave's BBQ, Taco Bell [other] Goodyear

13 MN 62, Rd 62

12 Valleyview Rd, Rd 39 (from sb)

11c MN 5 W, same as 11 a b

MN
MS

INTERSTATE 494/694 Cont'd

Exit #	Services
11b a	US 169 S, US 212 W, **N** Ⓕ Don Pablo, Subway Ⓛ Courtyard, Fairfield Inn, Hampton Inn, Hyatt Place, Residence Inn, **S** Ⓐ BP, Holiday, Marathon Ⓕ Caribou Coffee, Davanni's Rest., Fuddruckers, Jake's Grill, Jason's Deli, KFC, Leeann Chin, Old Chicago, Panera Bread, Papa John's, Qdoba, Starbucks Ⓛ Best Western, Discount Tire, Homestead Suites, JC Penney, Office Depot, Sears/auto, SpringHill Suites, Target, Walgreens, Walmart
10	US 169 N, to Rd 18
8	Rd 28 (from wb, no return), E Bush Lake Rd, same as 7 a b
7b a	MN 100, Rd 34, Normandale Blvd, **N** Ⓐ Shell/dsl Ⓕ Burger King, Caribou Coffee, Chili's, DQ, Subway, TGIFriday Ⓛ Days Inn, Sheraton, Sofatel, **S** Ⓕ Oak City Rest. Ⓛ Country Inn&Suites, Crowne Plaza, Hilton Garden, La Quinta, Staybridge Inn
6b	Rd 17, France Ave, **N** Ⓐ Mobil Ⓕ Cattle Co Rest., Chuck-eCheese, Fuddrucker's, Hot Wok, Macaroni Grill, McDonald's, Perkins, Quizno's Ⓛ Best Western, Le Bourget, Park Plaza Hotel Ⓞ Ⓗ, Michael's, Office Depot, **S** Ⓕ Denny's, Joe Senser's Grill, Olive Garden Ⓛ Hampton Inn, Hilton Ⓞ Buick/GMC, Ford, Mercedes, Nissan, Toyota/Scion
6a	Penn Ave (no EZ eb return), **N** Ⓛ Residence Inn Ⓞ Best Buy, Buick, Hyundai, Isuzu, **S** Ⓕ Applebee's, Atlantic Buffet, McDonald's, Starbucks, Steak&Ale, Subway Ⓛ Embassy Suites Ⓞ Chevrolet, Chrysler/Jeep/Plymouth, Dodge, Hancock

6a	Continued
	Fabrics, Herberger's, Kohl's, Rainbow Foods, Target, TJ Maxx
5b a	I-35W, S to Albert Lea, N to Minneapolis
4b	Lyndale Ave, **N** Ⓕ Boston Mkt, Chipotle Mexican, Don Pablo's, DQ, Eddie Cheng's, Papa John's, Subway Ⓛ Candlewood Suites, Hampton Inn, Ramada Inn Ⓞ Best Buy, Honda, Lands End, PetsMart, Tires+, **S** Ⓛ Extended Stay America Ⓞ Lincoln, Mazda, Subaru
4a	MN 52, Nicollet Ave, **N** Ⓐ SA/dsl Ⓕ Burger King, Ember's, Jumbo Chinese, Rest Ⓛ Candlewood Suites Ⓞ Honda, Menards, **S** Ⓐ Mobil, Shell Ⓕ Big Boy, Culver's, Kwik Mart, McDonald's Ⓛ La Quinta, Super 8 Ⓞ Home Depot, Sam's Club
3	Portland Ave, 12th Ave, **N** Ⓐ PDQ Mart, Phillips 66, Sinclair Ⓕ Arby's Ⓛ AmericInn, **S** Ⓐ BP Ⓕ Denny's, Outback Steaks, Subway Ⓛ Comfort Inn/rest., Holiday Inn Express, Microtel, Quality Inn, Residence Inn, Travelodge Ⓞ Walgreens, Walmart
2c b	MN 77, **N** Ⓛ Motel 6, **S** Ⓐ BP, SA Ⓛ AmeriSuites, Best Western, Courtyard, Embassy Suites, Exel Inn, Fairfield Inn, Grand Motel, Marriott, Sheraton Ⓞ Mall of America, Nordstrom's, Sears
2a	24th Ave, same as 2c b
1b	34th Ave, Nat Cemetery, **S** Ⓛ Embassy Suites, Hilton, Holiday Inn
1a	MN 5 E, **N** Ⓞ ✈
0mm	Minnesota River. **I-494/I-694 loops around Minneapolis/St Paul.**

MISSISSIPPI

INTERSTATE 10

MOSS POINT

Exit #	Services
77mm	Mississippi/Alabama state line, **weigh sta wb**
75	Franklin Creek Rd
75mm	**Welcome Center wb, full** Ⓗ **facilities, litter barrels, petwalk** Ⓒ Ⓡ **RV dump S** Ⓞ **weigh sta eb**
74mm	Escatawpa River
69	MS 63, to E Moss Point, **N** Ⓐ Raceway/dsl, Valero/Domino's/dsl/24hr Ⓕ Waffle House Ⓛ Best Value, Deluxe Inn, La Quinta, **S** Ⓐ Chevron/dsl, Exxon/Subway/dsl, Ⓟⓘⓛⓞⓣ/Moe's SW/dsl/scales/24hr, Shell Ⓕ Burger King, Cracker Barrel, Hardee's, KFC, McDonald's, Pizza Hut, Ruby Tuesday, San Miguel Mexican, Waffle House, Wendy's Ⓛ Best Western, Comfort Inn, Days Inn, Hampton Inn, Holiday Inn Express, Quality Inn, Shular Inn Ⓞ Ⓗ, Toyota
68	MS 613, to Moss Point, Pascagoula, **N** Ⓐ BP/Chester's, Chevron/dsl Ⓕ Coco Loco Mexican, Tugus' Rest. Ⓛ Super 8, **S** Ⓐ Marathon/dsl Ⓞ Ⓗ, Pelican Landing Conf Ctr
64mm	Pascagoula River
63.5mm	Ⓡⓢ **both lanes, 24hr security, full** Ⓗ **facilities, litter barrels, petwalk** Ⓒ Ⓡ **RV dump**
61	to Gautier, **N** Ⓞ MS Nat Golf Course, **1-3 mi S** Ⓐ Marathon/dsl Ⓕ Hardee's, KFC, McDonald's, Pizza Hut, Wendy's Ⓛ Best Western, Suburban Lodge Ⓞ Sandhill Crane WR, Shephard Camping
57	MS 57, to Vancleave, **N** Ⓐ Chevron/dsl Ⓕ Shed BBQ Ⓞ Journey's End Camping, tires/repair, **S** Ⓐ Exxon Ⓞ Ⓗ

BILOXI

50	MS 609 S, Ocean Springs, **N** Ⓐ Valero/Domino's/dsl Ⓕ Waffle House Ⓛ Best Western, Comfort Inn, Country Inn&Suites, Motel 6, Ramada Ltd, Scottish Inn, Super 8 Ⓞ Martin Lake Camping (1mi), tires/repair, **S** Ⓐ Chevron/McDonald's, Kangaroo/Subway/dsl, Marathon/dsl Ⓕ Denny's, El Rancho Mexican, Waffle House, Wendy's Ⓛ Comfort Suites, Days Inn, Hampton Inn, Holiday Inn Express, Quality Inn Ⓞ $General, Family$, Nat Seashore
46b a	I-110, MS 15 N, to Biloxi, **N** Ⓐ Chevron/dsl Ⓕ 5 Guys Burgers, Beef O'Brady's, Beijing Chinese, Buffalo Wild Wings, Chick-fil-A, Chili's, Dickey's BBQ, IHOP, Logan's Roadhouse, Moe's SW Grill, Newk's Cafe, Olive Garden, Osaka Japanese, Outback Steaks, Panda Palace, Papa John's, Red Lobster, Ruby Tuesday, Salsarita 's, Samurai, Sonic, Starbucks, Subway, Waffle House, Wendy's, Whataburger, Which Wich? Ⓛ Courtyard, Home2 Suites, Regency Inn, Wingate Inn Ⓞ AT&T, Best Buy, CVS, Dick's, GNC, Kohl's, Lowe's, Marshall's, Mercedes, Michaels, Office Depot, Petsmart, Radio Shack, Ross, Target, Tire Kingdom, URGENT CARE, Verizon, vet, VW, Walgreens, Walmart, **S** Ⓞ Ⓗ, to beaches
44	Cedar Lake Rd, to Biloxi, **N** Ⓐ Loves/Subway/dsl/scales/24hr Ⓞ Chevrolet, **S** Ⓐ Shell/dsl, Valero/dsl Ⓕ Applebee's, El Rey Mexican, El Saltillo, KFC/LJ Silver, McDonald's, Pop's Pizza, Sonic, Subway, Taco Bell, Waffle House Ⓛ La Quinta Ⓞ Ⓗ, $General, Biloxi Nat Cem, Cedar Lake Drug, Harley-Davidson, Home Depot, O'Reilly Parts, to Jeff Davis Shrine (Beauvoir), vet

INTERSTATE 10 Cont'd

Exit #	Services
41	MS 67 N, to Woolmarket, N Chevron/dsl, Texaco/dsl golf (6mi), S Freightliner, Mazalea RV Prk, Parkers Landing RV Prk, Reliable RV Ctr, Southern Tire Mart
39.5mm	Biloxi River
38	Lorraine-Cowan Rd, N Exxon/Subway, Kangaroo/dsl Capt Al's Cafe, Domino's, McDonald's, Sonic Toyota/Scion, S H, Baywood RV Park (3mi), Foxes RV Park (8mi), to beaches
34b a	US 49, to Gulfport, N Exxon, Kangaroo/dsl, Valero/dsl Burger King, Cane's Chicken, Chick-fil-A, Chili's, Chuck-eCheese, Cracker Barrel, Dickey's BBQ, Domino's, Five Guys, Golden Corral, Hardee's, KFC, Krystal, Little Caesars, Logan's Roadhouse, Longhorn Steaks, Marble Slab, McDonald's, Newk's Cafe, O'Charley's, O'Neal's PoBoy, Panda Palace, Papa John's, Pepper's Deli, Pizza Hut, Popeye's, Sicily's Italian Buffet, Sonic, Starbucks, Subway, Taco Bell, Taco Sombrero, TGIFriday's, Waffle House, Wendy's, Whataburger Hampton Inn, Sleep Inn H, $Tree, Advance Parts, AT&T, Barnes&Noble, Belk, Best Buy, Buick/Cadillac/Chevrolet, CVS Drug, Foley's RV Ctr, Food Giant/gas, Fred's Store, Goodyear/auto, Hobby Lobby, Honda, K-Mart, Michael's, Office Depot, Old Navy, Petsmart, Radio Shack, Rite Aid, Ross, Sam's Club/dsl, Tire Kingdom, TJ Maxx, URGENT CARE, USPO, Walgreens, Winn-Dixie, S Kangaroo/dsl, Murphy USA, RaceWay/dsl, Shell/dsl Applebee's, Arby's, Burger King, Dynasty Buffet, Food Court, Hibachi Express, Hooters, IHOP, KFC/LJ Silver, Krispy Kreme, Los Tres Amigos, McAlister's Deli, McDonald's, Morelia's Mexican, Shrimp Basket, Sonic, Taco Bell, Tres Amigos, Waffle House, Wendy's Best Value, Best Western, Clarion, Comfort Suites, Days Inn, EconoLodge, Fairfield Inn, Hilton Garden, Holiday Inn, Motel 6, Quality Inn, Ramada, Residence Inn, Sun Suites, Value Place Ford/Lincoln, GNC, Home Depot, Mazda, Nissan, Premium Outlets/famous brands, repair, Verizon, Walmart/McDonald's
31	Canal Rd, to Gulfport, N Clarks/Subway/dsl Bayberry RV Park, S FLYING J/Denny's/dsl/LP/scales/24hr, Pure Country/McDonald's/dsl/24hr Waffle House, Wendy's Legacy Inn, Magnolia Bay Inn Plantation Pines RV Prk
28	to Long Beach, S Chevron/dsl, Shell/dsl Subway NAPA, RV camping, tires/repair
27mm	Wolf River
24	Menge Ave, N Chevron/Subway/dsl/scales $General, S Texaco flea mkt/RV Park, golf, to beaches
20	to De Lisle, to Pass Christian, N Kin-Mart
16	Diamondhead, N Shell/Domino's, Valero/dsl Burger King, DQ, Fire Pit BBQ Grill, Pizza Hut, Red Zone Grill, Subway, Waffle House Diamondhead Resort Diamondhead Drug, Family$, repair, Rouse's Mkt, TrueValue, URGENT CARE, USPO, S Giterdone/dsl Harbor House Rest. EconoLodge, $Tree
15mm	Jourdan River
13	MS 43, MS 603, to Kiln, Bay St Louis, N McLeod SP, S Bay Fuel/dsl, Exxon/Subway/dsl Knights Inn (6mi) H, RV Camping (8-13mi)
10mm	**weigh sta eb**
2	MS 607, to Waveland, **Welcome Ctr both lanes, 24hr security, full facilities, litter barrels, petwalk RV dump,** S Buccaneer SP, camping, to beaches, NASA Visitor Ctr
1mm	**weigh sta wb**
0mm	Mississippi/Louisiana state line, Pearl River

GULFPORT

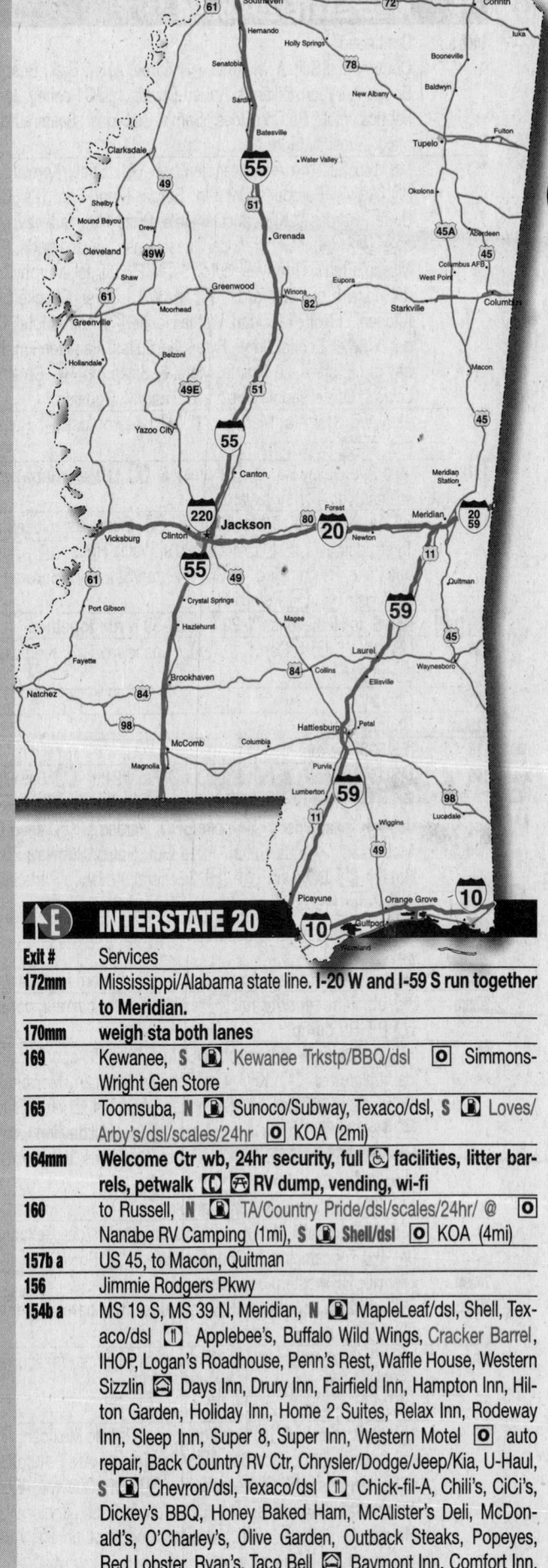

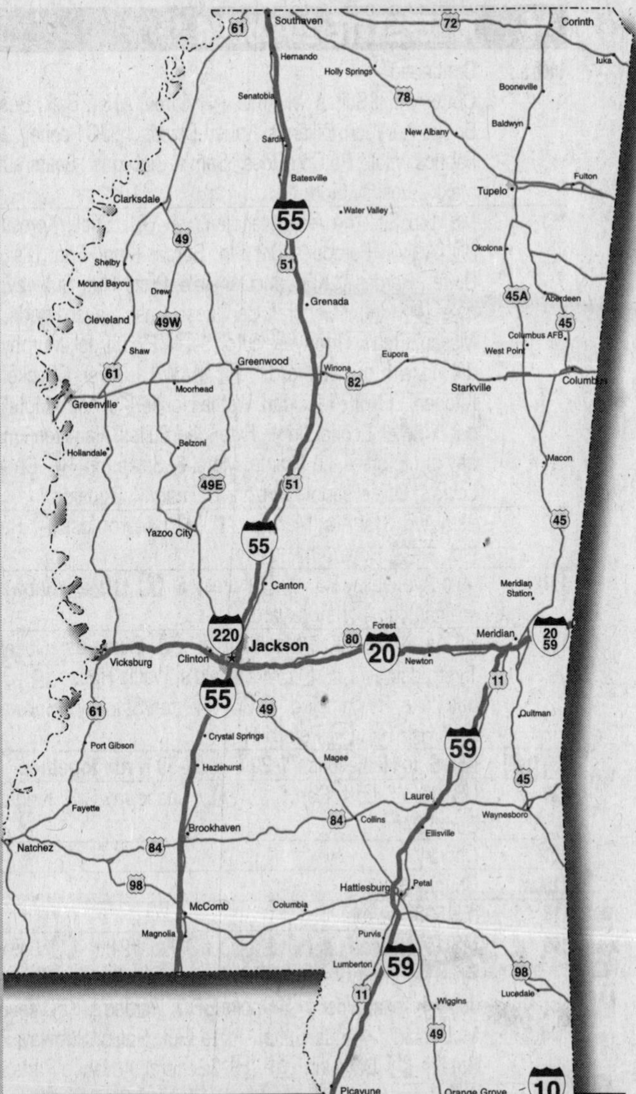

MS

INTERSTATE 20

Exit #	Services
172mm	Mississippi/Alabama state line. **I-20 W and I-59 S run together to Meridian.**
170mm	**weigh sta both lanes**
169	Kewanee, S Kewanee Trkstp/BBQ/dsl Simmons-Wright Gen Store
165	Toomsuba, N Sunoco/Subway, Texaco/dsl, S Loves/Arby's/dsl/scales/24hr KOA (2mi)
164mm	**Welcome Ctr wb, 24hr security, full facilities, litter barrels, petwalk RV dump, vending, wi-fi**
160	to Russell, N TA/Country Pride/dsl/scales/24hr/ @ Nanabe RV Camping (1mi), S **Shell/dsl** KOA (4mi)
157b a	US 45, to Macon, Quitman
156	Jimmie Rodgers Pkwy
154b a	MS 19 S, MS 39 N, Meridian, N MapleLeaf/dsl, Shell, Texaco/dsl Applebee's, Buffalo Wild Wings, Cracker Barrel, IHOP, Logan's Roadhouse, Penn's Rest, Waffle House, Western Sizzlin Days Inn, Drury Inn, Fairfield Inn, Hampton Inn, Hilton Garden, Holiday Inn, Home 2 Suites, Relax Inn, Rodeway Inn, Sleep Inn, Super 8, Super Inn, Western Motel auto repair, Back Country RV Ctr, Chrysler/Dodge/Jeep/Kia, U-Haul, S Chevron/dsl, Texaco/dsl Chick-fil-A, Chili's, CiCi's, Dickey's BBQ, Honey Baked Ham, McAlister's Deli, McDonald's, O'Charley's, Olive Garden, Outback Steaks, Popeyes, Red Lobster, Ryan's, Taco Bell Baymont Inn, Comfort Inn,

MS

INTERSTATE 20 Cont'd

Exit	Services
154b a	Continued Country Inn&Suites, Microtel [other] $Tree, AT&T, Belk, Best Buy, Books-A-Million, Dillard's, Harley-Davidson, JC Penney, Jo-Ann Fabrics, mall, PetCo, Ross, Sam's Club/gas, Sears/auto, TJ Maxx, Tuesday Morning
153	MS 145 S, 22nd Ave, Meridian, N [gas] Shell, Xpress Lane [food] Arby's, Bumper's Drive-In, Burger King, Capt D's, China Buffet, Hardee's, KFC, McDonald's, Pizza Hut, Subway, Wendy's [other] [H], $General, CarQuest, Cash Saver Foods, Ford/Nissan, Fred's, Goodyear/auto, S [gas] Exxon/dsl, Murphy USA/dsl, Texaco/dsl, Valero/dsl [food] A&W/LJ Silver, Checkerboard Kitchen, El Norte Mexican, Waffle House [lodging] Astro Motel, Budget 8 Motel, EconoLodge, Extended Suites, Hamilton Inn, Holiday Inn Express, La Quinta, Motel 6, Sleep Inn [other] Chevrolet, Lowe's, Office Depot, Verizon, Walmart/McDonald's
152	29th Ave, 31st Ave, Meridian, N [gas] Chevron/dsl [lodging] Ramada Ltd, S [lodging] Royal Inn
151	49th Ave, Valley Rd, N [other] tires, S [gas] Pilot/Subway/dsl/scales/24hr [other] stockyards
150	US 11 S, MS 19 N, Meridian, N [gas] Exxon/dsl, Queen City Trkstp/dsl/rest./ @ [food] McDonald's, Waffle House [other] Okatibbee Lake, RV camping, S [gas] Chevron/Stuckey's/Subway/dsl, Shell/dsl [other] [truck], Peterbilt
130 [149]	I-59 S, to Hattiesburg. **I-20 E and I-59 N run together.**
129	US 80 W, Lost Gap, S [gas] Spaceway/Grill King/dsl/RV Dump/24hr
121	Chunky
119mm	Chunky River
115	MS 503, Hickory
109	MS 15, Newton, N [gas] Shell/Jct Deli/dsl/24hr [food] Los Parrilleros [lodging] Thrifty Inn [other] lube/repair, S [gas] Chevron/dsl, Newton Jct/dsl, Texaco/dsl [food] Cooks BBQ, Hardee's, KFC/Taco Bell, McDonald's, Panda Buffet, Pizza Hut, Sonic, Subway, Zack's Steaks [lodging] Days Inn [other] [H], $General, Advance Parts, AT&T, AutoZone, Fred's, Piggly Wiggly, Walmart/Subway
100	US 80, Lake, Lawrence, N [gas] BP/rest/dsl
96	Lake
95mm	Bienville Nat Forest, Bienville Nat Forest, eastern boundary
90mm	**[RS] eb, 24hr security, full [handicapped] facilities, litter barrels, petwalk [phone] [picnic] RV dump**
88	MS 35, Forest, N [gas] Murphy USA/dsl, Shell, Texaco/Chester's/dsl, Valero/dsl [food] KFC, Las Parrillas Mexican, McDonald's, Popeye's, Taco Bell, Waffle House, Wendy's, Zhen's Garden [lodging] Best Value Inn, Days Inn, EconoLodge, Holiday Inn Express [other] [H], $Tree, AT&T, O'Reilly Parts, Walgreens, Walmart/Subway, S [gas] Chevron/dsl [food] Penn's Rest.
80	MS 481, Morton, S [other] RV Camping
77	MS 13, Morton, N [gas] Exxon/McDonald's/dsl, Texaco/dsl [other] [H], RV camping, to Roosevelt SP, S [gas] Shell/Subway/dsl
76mm	Bienville NF, western boundary
75mm	**[RS] wb, 24hr security, full [handicapped] facilities, litter barrels, petwalk [phone] [picnic] RV dump**
68	MS 43, Pelahatchie, N [gas] Chevron/Subway/dsl, Texaco/rest./dsl/24hr [other] Jellystone Camping, S [gas] BP/dsl
59	US 80, E Brandon, **2 mi** S [gas] Shell/dsl
56	US 80, Brandon, N [gas] Shell/dsl [food] El Potrillo Mexican, Krystal, Sonny's BBQ, Taco Bell [lodging] Microtel [other] AT&T, AutoZone, O'Reilly Parts, USPO, Verizon, S [gas] BP, Chevron, Exxon, Mac's Gas, Texaco/dsl [food] DQ, Penn's Rest., Sonic, Waffle House, Wendy's [lodging] Best Value Inn, Red Roof Inn [other] Auto+, to Ross Barnett Reservoir, vet
54	Crossgates Blvd, W Brandon, N [gas] Exxon, Kangaroo, Murphy USA [food] Abner's Chicken, Applebee's, Burger King, Chick-fil-A, China Buffet, Fernando's Fajita Factory, KFC, Little Caesars, Mazzio's, McAlister's Deli, McDonald's, Newk's Rest, Papa John's, Pizza Hut, Popeye's, Subway, Waffle House [other] [H], $Tree, BigLots, Buick/GMC, Chevrolet, CVS Drug, Ford/Lincoln, Fred's, GNC, Hancock Fabrics, Kroger/dsl, Nissan, Office Depot, Piggly Wiggly, Radio Shack, Scotty's Tire/repair, Toyota/Scion, Tuesday Morning, Walgreens, Walmart/Subway, S [gas] Exxon/dsl, Kangeroo/dsl, Valero/Domino's/dsl [food] Steak Escape, Wendy's [lodging] La Quinta [other] Home Depot, Honda, Tire Pros
52	MS 475, N [gas] RaceWay/dsl, Texaco/dsl, Valero/Subway/dsl [food] Waffle House [lodging] Quality Inn, Ramada, Sleep Inn, Super 8 [other] Peterbilt, to Jackson Airport
48	MS 468, Pearl, N [gas] Exxon/dsl, Snell/dsl, Texaco [food] Arby's, Baskin Robbins, Bumpers Drive-In, Cracker Barrel, Domino's, Dunkin Donuts, Jose's Rest., KFC, Kobe Japanese, Logan's Roadhouse, LoneStar Steaks, Los Parrilleros, McAlister's Deli, McDonald's, Mikado, Mikado Japanese, Moss Creek Fishouse, O'Charley's, Popeye's, Ruby Tuesday, Ryan's, Ryan's, Sonic, Subway, Waffle House, Wendy's [lodging] Baymont Inn, Best Western, Comfort Inn, Courtyard, Days Inn, Fairfield Inn, Hampton Inn, Hilton Garden, Holiday Inn Express, Motel 6 [other] AT&T, Car-Care, S [gas] Exxon/dsl, Valero/dsl [lodging] Candlewood Suites, Country Inn&Suites, La Quinta [other] $General, Family$
47b a	US 49 S, Flowood, N [gas] FLYING J/Denny's/dsl/LP/RV dump/24hr, Love's/Subway/dsl/scales/24hr [food] Western Sizzlin [lodging] Airport Inn, Holiday Inn [other] Bass Pro Shop, MS Outlets/famous brands, Sam's Club/dsl, SpeedCo, **2-3 mi** S [gas] RaceWay/dsl [food] Waffle House [other] Freightliner, Kenworth, tires
46	I-55 N, to Memphis
45b	US 51, State St, to downtown
45a	Gallatin St, to downtown, N [gas] BP/dsl, Petro/Iron Skillet/dsl/scales/24hr/ @, Shell [other] Blue Beacon, tires/truck repair, vet, S [gas] Pilot/McDonald's/dsl/scales/24hr [lodging] Hilltop Inn [other] Nissan
44	I-55 S (exits left from wb), to New Orleans
43b a	Terry Rd, N [gas] Exxon/dsl, Jasco [other] Apache RV Ctr
42b a	Ellis Ave, Belvidere, N [gas] BP, Citgo/dsl, Shell [food] Capt D's, Church's, McDonald's, Pizza Hut, Popeye's, Sonny's BBQ, Wendy's [lodging] Best Inn, Metro Inn, Scottish Inn, Super 8 [other] $Tree, Advance Parts, AutoZone, CarQuest, Family$, Firestone/auto, O'Reilly Parts, Sav-a-Lot Foods, transmissions, U-Haul, zoo, S [gas] Citgo/dsl, Exxon/dsl [food] DQ
41	I-220 N, US 49 N, to Jackson
40b a	MS 18 W, Robinson Rd, N [gas] Exxon/dsl, Jasco/dsl, Shell/dsl [food] Arby's, Krystal, Mazzio's, Piccadilly, Popeye's [other] $General, AT&T, Office Depot, USPO, S [gas] Chevron, Citgo/dsl, Murphy USA, RaceWay/dsl, Shell/Church's/dsl [food] Chan's Garden, IHOP, McDonald's, Subway, Waffle House, Wendy's [lodging] Quality Inn [other] [H], $Tree, GNC, Lowe's, Radio Shack, Walmart/Subway
36	Springridge Rd, Clinton, N [gas] Chevron/Burger King, Citgo/dsl, Murphy USA/dsl, Shell [food] Capt D's, Chick-fil-A, China Buffet, Chopstick Buffet, DQ, El Sombrero, Hungry Howie's, KFC, Kroger/dsl, Little Caesars, Mazzio's, McAlister's, McDonald's, Newk's Cafe, Smoothie King, Sonic, Starbucks, Subway, Taco Bell, Waffle House, Wendy's, Zaxby's [lodging] Comfort Inn, Days Inn [other] $Tree, Advance Parts, AT&T, BigLots, CVS Drug, Family$, Fred's, Home Depot, Kroger/gas, O'Reilly Parts, Radio Shack, Verizon, Walgreens, Walmart (2 mi), S [gas] Exxon/Baskin-Rob

NEWTON

BRANDON

PEARL

JACKSON

CLINTON

INTERSTATE 20 Cont'd

VICKSBURG

36	Continued bins/Quiznos/dsl, Valero/dsl Applebee's, Bonsai, Froghead Grill, Pizza Hut, Popeye's, Salsa's Mexican, Shoney's Best Western, Econolodge, Hampton Inn, Holiday Inn Express, Quality Inn, Super 8 $General, Davis Tire, Springridge RV Park, vet
35	US 80 E, Clinton, N Chevron, Shell/dsl, Valero/dsl vet
34	Natchez Trace Pkwy
31	Norrell Rd
27	Bolton, S Chevron/dsl
19	MS 22, Edwards, Flora, N Askew's Landing Camping (2mi), S Exxon/dsl, Shell/dsl Relax Inn
17mm	Big Black River
15	Flowers
11	Bovina, N Texaco/Subway/dsl/24hr RV camping
10mm	**weigh sta wb**
8mm	**weigh sta eb**
6.5mm	**parking area eb**
5b a	US 61, MS 27 S, N Exxon/dsl, Kangaroo/dsl Sonic, S same as 4a
4b a	Clay St, N Valero/Kangaroo Battlefield Inn, Hampton Inn, Motel 6, Quality Inn H, RV Park, to Vicksburg NP, S Texaco, Valero/dsl Bumper's Drive-In, China Buffet, Cracker Barrel, Little Caesars, McAlister's deli, Pizza Inn, Rowdy's Rest., Subway, Waffle House, Wendy's Baymont Inn, Beechwood Inn/rest., Comfort Suites, Courtyard, Econolodge, Holiday Inn Express, La Quinta, Scottish Inn $General, Outlet Mall/famous brands/deli, same as 5, Toyota
3	Indiana Ave, N Valero/Subway/dsl China King, McDonald's, Papa John's, Waffle House Best Western, Deluxe Inn Chevrolet, Chrysler/Dodge/Jeep, Corner Mkt Foods, Ford/Lincoln, Honda, Mazda, Nissan, Rite Aid, S Kangaroo/dsl Goldie's BBQ, Heavenly Ham, KFC Best Inn Buick/Cadillac/GMC, Family$
1c	Halls Ferry Rd, N Exxon/dsl Burger King, Sonic Travel Inn H, CVS Drug, Durst Drugs, S Kangaroo/dsl Asian Kitchen, Capt D's, Chick-fil-A, El Sombrero Mexican, Garfield's Rest., Goldie's Express, Little Caesars, Newk's Eatery, Pizza Hut, Popeye's, Shoney's, Subway, Taco Bell, Taco Casa, Wendy's, Whataburger Candlewood Suites, Fairfield Inn, Holiday Inn, Rodeway Inn, Super 8 $General, Advance Parts, AT&T, Belk, BigLots, Dillard's, Fred's, Hobby Lobby, Home Depot, JC Penney, Kroger/dsl, TJ Maxx, USPO, Walgreens
1b	US 61 S, S Kangaroo/Domino's/dsl, Murphy Express/dsl McDonald's, Panda Buffet, Waffle House $Tree, Radio Shack, same as 1c, Verizon, Walmart/Subway
1a	Washington St, Vicksburg, N **Welcome Ctr both lanes, full facilities**, Kangaroo/dsl, Shell/Subway/dsl AmeriStar Hotel/Casino/RV Park, S Waffle House Best Value Inn, Days Inn
0mm	Mississippi/Louisiana state line, Mississippi River

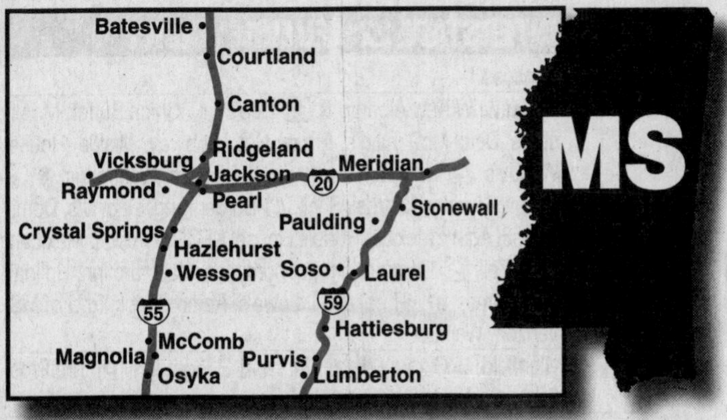

INTERSTATE 22 (FUTURE)

CORINTH

Exit #	Services
118mm	I-22, Alabama/Mississippi State Line
115mm	**Welcome Ctr/ wb, litter barrels, petwalk RV dump, vending**
113	Rd 23, Tremont, Smithville
108	Rd 25 N, Belmont, Iuka
106mm	**both lanes, weigh sta**
104	Rd 25 S, Fulton, Amory, N Shell/cafe/dsl/scales, Texaco/dsl Burger King, Hardee's, Homer's BBQ, Huddle House, McDonald's, Mi Toro Mexican, Sonic, Subway Days Inn, Holiday Inn Express $General, AutoZone, Food Giant/dsl, Fred's, O'Reilly Parts, RV camping, Whitten HS, Brown's Auto Repair, S Murphy USA/dsl Peking Palace AT&T, KFC, Los Compadres Mexican, Pizza Hut, URGENT CARE, Walmart, Wendy's
104mm	Tombigbee River/Tenn-Tom Waterway
101	Rd 178, Rd 363, Peppertown, Mantachie, N Bill's Foodmart, S Dorsey Fuel/dsl (2mi)
97	Fawn Grove Rd
94	Rd 371, Mantachie, Mooreville, N Woodchuck's/pizza/dsl
90	Auburn Rd, N Chevron/dsl
87	Veterans Blvd, N Shell/Chix Rest/dsl Huddle House Wingate Inn E. Presley Campground/Park, S Tombigbee SP
86	US 45 N, Tupelo, to Corinth, **1 exit** N Shell/dsl, Texaco, Valero Abner's Rest., Applebee's, Baskin Robbins, Buffalo Wild Wings, Burger King, Capt D's, Chick-fil-A, Chili's, ChuckeCheese, Cracker Barrel, Crossroads Rib Shack, D'Casa Grill, Dickey's BBQ, Five Guys, IHOP, Kyoto Japanese, Lenny's Subs, Logan's Roadhouse, Longhorn Steaks, Margaritas Mexican, McDonald's, Mt Fuji Japanese, New China Buffet, Newk's Eatery, O'Charley's, Olive Garden, Pizza Hut, Pizza Pro, Red Lobster, Ryan's, Sake Japanese, Sonic, Subway, Taco Bell, Thai Garden, Waffle House, Wendy's Best Inn, Best Western, Econolodge, Fairfield Inn, Hampton Inn $Tree, AT&T, AutoZone, Barnes&Noble, Belk, Best Buy, CarMax, Dick's, Ford/Lincoln, Hobby Lobby, Home Depot, Hyundai, JC Penney, JoAnn, Kohl's, Kroger/gas, Lowe's, Mazda, Midas, NAPA, Nissan, Old Navy, Petsmart, Ross, Sam's Club/gas, Sears, Staples, TJ Maxx, Toyota, Tuesday Morning, URGENT CARE, Verizon, Walgreens, Walmart
85	Natchez Trace Pkwy
82	Barnes Crossing Rd, Coley Rd
81	Rd 178, McCullough Blvd, N Loves/McDonald's/dsl/scales/24hr Executive Inn, S Exxon/dsl, Shell/dsl Old Venice Pizza, Sonic Super 8 $General, USPO
76	Rd 9 S, Sherman, Pontotoc, N Wild Bill's/dsl Sherman RV Ctr
73	Rd 9 N, Blue Springs
64	Rd 15, Rd 30 E, Pontotoc, Ripley, N Eagle/dsl, S Pilot/Arby's/scales/dsl/24hr, Shell/dsl
63	New Albany, N Dee's Oil/dsl Buick/Chevrolet/GMC, Ford
62mm	Tallahatchie River

MS

INTERSTATE 22 (FUTURE) Cont'd

Exit #	Services
61	Rd 30 W, W New Albany, N Dee's China Buffet, McAlister's Deli, McDonald's, Pizza Hut, Subway, Waffle House, Wendy's Hampton Inn H, Rite Aid, Walgreens, S Exxon, Murphy USA/dsl, Shell Burger King, Capt D's, Domino's, El Agave Mexicn, Huddle House, KFC, Mi Pueblo Mexican, Taco Bell Comfort Inn, Economy Inn, Hallmarc Inn, Holiday Inn Express $Tree, AT&T, Lowe's, Radio Shack, to U of MS, Verizon, Walmart
60	Glenfield, to Oxford, N Pure Budget Inn Tire Pros, S to U of MS
55	Myrtle
48	Rd 178, Hickory Flat, S Exxon/Trkstp/rest/dsl/24hr
41	Rd 346, Potts Camp, S Flicks/dsl $General, NAPA
41mm	Tippah River
37	Lake Center, N Chewalla Lake/RV camping
30	Rd 7, Rd 4, Holly Springs, Oxford, N Exxon, Shell/Chester's/BBQ Domino's, El Nopalito, Huddle House, KFC, Little Caesar's, McDonalds, Panda Buffet, Pizza Hut, Popeye's, Sonic, Subway, Taco Bell, Wendy's Magnolia Inn H, $General, AT&T, AutoZone, Liddy's Drug, O'Reilly Parts, Save-a-Lot, Wall Doxey SP/RV camping, S Shell/dsl Days Inn, Econolodge Walmart
26	W Holly Springs
21	Red Banks, N Dee's Oil/dsl, Texaco/dsl
18	Victoria, E Byhalia, N BP, S Victoria/dsl
14	Rd 309, Byhalia, N Exxon/dsl, Shell/dsl Best Value Inn Autozone, Fred's
10	W Byhalia
6	Bethel Rd, Hacks Crossroad, N FLYING J/Subway/dsl/scales/LP/RV dump/24hr, BP, Exxon/Baskin Robbins/dsl JR's Grill, Rancho Grande, Tops BBQ Best Western, Super 8 truck repair, S H
4	Rd 305, Olive Branch, Independence, N BP/dsl, Shell/Circle K, Valero/Huddle House Old Style BBQ, Pizza Hut Holiday Inn Express $General, Piggly Wiggly, USPO, S Exxon/dsl CVS Drug
3.5mm	**weigh sta, both lanes**
2	Rd 302, Olive Branch, N Abbay's Rest., Baskin-Robbins, Buffalo Wild Wings, Chick-fil-A, Chili's, Colton's Steaks, IHOP, Krystal, Lenny's Subs, McAlisters Deli, Mis Pueblos Mexican, O'Charley's, Starbucks, Wendy's Candlewood Suites, Comfort Suites $Tree, Ford, Home Depot, Lowe's, Radio Shack, Verizon, Walmart/Subway, S Chevron/dsl, Shell/Circle K Applebees, Backyard Burger, Burger King, Casa Mexicana, Honeybaked Ham, Hunan Chinese, McDonald's, Panera Bread, Papa John's, Steak Escape, Subway, Taco Bell, Waffle House, Zaxby's Comfort Inn, Hampton Inn AutoZone, CVS Drug, GNC, Goodyear/auto, Kroger/dsl, Petco
1	Craft Rd, N Candlewood Suites Camping World RV Ctr, Chevrolet, Hyundai, Suzuki
0mm	Mississippi/Tennessee state line, **I-22 (future) begins/ends. US 78 continues wb.**

OLIVE BRANCH

INTERSTATE 55

Exit #	Services
291.5mm	Mississippi/Tennessee state line
291	State Line Rd, Southaven, E Exxon, RaceWay/dsl, Shell/dsl Interstate BBQ, Little Caesars, Subway, Tops BBQ, Waffle House Days Inn, Holiday Inn Express, Quality Inn, Southern Inn, Super 8 Family$, Firestone/auto, Goodyear/auto, Kroger/dsl, Southaven RV Park, Walgreens, W Exxon Capt D's, Checker's, China Wok, Dales Rest, El Patron Mexican, Lucky China, Mainstreet Pizza, Sonic, Taco Bell, Wendy's BigLots, Fred's, Mainstreet Automotive, Rite Aid, tires, USPO
289	MS 302, to US 51, Horn Lake, E BP/Circle K, Shell Abbays Rest., Backyard Burger, Baskin-Robbins, Brusters, Buffalo Wild Wings, Burger King, Chick-fil-A, Chili's, Dunkin Donuts, Fazoli's, Firehouse Subs, Fox&Hound, Haru Japanese, Huey's Rest., Hunan Buffet, IHOP, Krystal, Kublai Khan, La Hacienda, Lenny's Subs, Logan's Roadhouse, Longhorn Steaks, Maria's Cantina, McDonald's, Mi Pueblo, Nagoya Japanese, O'Charley's, Olive Garden, On-the-Border, Outback Steaks, Red Lobster, Sonic, Starbucks, Steak'n Shake, Subway, TGIFriday's, Wendy's Comfort Suites, Courtyard, Fairfield Inn, Hampton Inn, Hilton Garden, Holiday Inn, Home2Suites, Residence Inn H, $Tree, Aldi Foods, AT&T, Best Buy, Books-A-Million, Buick/GMC, Chevrolet, Chrysler/Dodge/Jeep, CVS Drug, Dillards, Ford, GNC, Gordman's, Hancock Fabrics, JC Penney, Jo-Ann Fabrics, Kroger/dsl, Lowe's, Marshall's, Nissan, Office Depot, Old Navy, PetCo, Radio Shack, Sam's Club/gas, Tuesday Morning, URGENT CARE, Verizon, Walmart/Subway, W BP/Circle K, Phillips 66/dsl, Shell/Circle K/dsl Applebee's, Arby's, ChuckECheese's, Country Home Buffet, Cracker Barrel, Grand Buffet, Holiday Deli, Hooters, KFC, McDonald's, Memphis BBQ, Mrs Winner's, Papa John's, Pizza Hut, Popeye's, Ryan's, Sekisui Japan, Taco Bell, TX Roadhouse, Waffle House, Wendy's, Zaxby's Best Western, Comfort Inn, Drury Inn, EconoLodge, La Quinta, Motel 6, Ramada Ltd, Sleep Inn CVS Drug, Family$, Gateway Tires/repair, Home Depot, Kroger, Meineke, Save-a-Lot Foods, Target, Verizon, Walgreens
287	Church Rd, E Citgo/dsl Domino's, Wadford's Grill AutoZone, W Citgo/dsl, Shell/Circle K/dsl 3 Guys Pizza, Boiling Point Seafood, Casa Mexicana, McDonald's, Sonic, Subway, Taco Bell, Waffle House Keywest Inn, Magnolia Inn El Daze RV Camping (1mi), Family$, Fred's, Harley-Davidson, Jellystone Camping, Southaven RV Ctr, Walgreens
285mm	**weigh sta both lanes**
284	to US 51, Nesbit Rd, W Shell Happy Daze Dairybar USPO
283	I-69, MS 304, Tunica
280	MS 304, US 51, Hernando, E Exxon, Murphy USA/dsl Arby's, Asian Buffet, Capt D's, Dominos, Fins Grill, Guadalajara Mexican, KFC, Sonic, Steak Escape, Taco Bell, Zaxby's Days Inn, Hampton Inn $Tree, AT&T, Ultimate Tires/repair, URGENT CARE, Walgreens, Walmart, W Mobil, Shell/Circle K/dsl Brick Oven Rest., Coleman's BBQ, Lenny's Subs, Little Caesars, McDonald's, Mi Pueblo, Mr Chen's, Papa John's, Pizza Hut, Subway, Taco Felix, Waffle House, Wendy's Super 8 AutoZone, Bryant Repair, Desoto Museum, Family$, Fred's, Kroger/gas, Memphis S Camping (2mi), NAPA, to Arkabutla Lake, USPO
279mm	**Welcome Ctr sb, 24 hr security, full facilities, litter barrels, petwalk RV dump**
276mm	**Welcome Ctr nb, 24 hr security, full facilities, litter barrels, petwalk RV dump**
273mm	Coldwater River
271	MS 306, Coldwater, W Shell/dsl Subway Lake Arkabutla, Memphis S RV Park

SOUTHAVEN

INTERSTATE 55 Cont'd

Exit #	Services
265	MS 4, Senatobia, W BP/dsl, Exxon, Pilot/Huddle House/dsl/scales/24hr, Shell/dsl Backyard Burger, Coleman's BBQ, Domino's, KFC, McDonald's/playplace, New China Buffet, Pizza Hut, Popeye's, Rio Lindo Mexican, Sonic, Subway, Taco Bell, Waffle House, Wendy's Best Value Inn, Days Inn H, AT&T, CarQuest, City Drug, Curves, Fred's, Kaye Mkt, transmissions, truck repair, USPO
263	Rd 740, S Senatobia
257	MS 310, Como, E Dee's Oil N Sardis Lake, W Citgo/dsl Windy City Grille (1mi)
252	MS 315, Sardis, E Chevron/dsl, Local/dsl McDonald's Lake Inn, Super 8 NAPA, repair, RV camping, Sardis Dam, to Kyle SP, W BP/Chester's/dsl, Shell/dsl Sonic H, $General, Family$, Fred's
246	MS 35, N Batesville, E to Sardis Lake, W Loves/McDonald's/Subway/dsl/scales/24hr, Shell/dsl
243b a	MS 6, to Batesville, E BP/dsl, Murphy USA/dsl, Shell/dsl Backyard Burger, Chili's, Mi Pueblo Mexican, Zaxby's Comfort Suites H, $Tree, Lowe's, to Sardis Lake, U of MS, Walmart/Subway, W BP, Exxon/dsl, Phillips 66/dsl, Shell/dsl, Valero/Kangaroo/dsl Burger King, Burn's BBQ, Cafe Ole, Capt D's, Cracker Barrel, Domino's, Hardee's, Huddle House, KFC, McDonald's, New China, Pizza Hut, Popeye's, Sonic, Subway, Taco Bell, Waffle House, Wendy's, Western Sizzlin Days Inn, EconoLodge, Hampton Inn, Holiday Inn, Quality Inn, Ramada Ltd H, $General, AT&T, AutoZone, Curves, Factory Stores/famous brands, Family$, Fred's, Kroger, O'Reilly Parts, Piggly Wiggly, Save-a-Lot, URGENT CARE, USPO, Walgreens
240mm	**both lanes, 24hr security, full facilities, litter barrels, petwalk RV dump**
237	to US 51, Courtland, E Pure/dsl, W $General
233	to Enid Dam, E RV camping, to Enid Lake
227	MS 32, Oakland, E Sunrise RV Park, to Cossar SP, W Exxon/Chester's/dsl, Shell/dsl $General, antiques
220	MS 330, Tillatoba, E Conoco/rest./dsl/ @
211	MS 7 N, to Coffeeville, E Frog Hollow RV Park, W Shell/Chester's/dsl
208	Papermill Rd, E Grenada Airport
206	MS 8, MS 7 S, to Grenada, E Exxon/dsl, Shell/dsl Burger King, China Buffet, Church's, Clubhouse Rest., Domino's, Great Wall Chinese, Jake&Rip's Café, La Cabana Mexican, Lost Pizza Co., McAlister's Deli, McDonald's, Pizza Hut, Pizza Inn, Shoney's, Subway, Taco Bell, Wendy's, Western Sizzlin Baymont Inn, Best Value Inn, Days Inn, EconoLodge, Hampton Inn, Holiday Inn Express, Quality Inn; Relax Inn, Super 8 H, $General, $Tree, Advance Parts, AT&T, AutoZone, Chrysler/Dodge/Jeep, Curves, CVS Drug, GNC, O'Reilly Parts, Radio Shack, to Grenada Lake/RV camping, USPO, Walmart/McDonald's, W Exxon/Huddle House Waffle House Comfort Inn, Motel 6 Ford/Lincoln, Nissan, repair, Toyota
204mm	**parking area sb, litter barrels**
202mm	**parking area nb, litter barrels**
199	Troutt Rd, S Grenada, E to camp McCain
195	MS 404, Duck Hill, E to Camp McCain, W Conoco/dsl
185	US 82, Winona, E Exxon, Shell/Kangaroo/Baskin-Robbins/dsl Huddle House, KFC, McDonald's, Sonic, Subway, Waffle House Best Value Inn, Holiday Inn Express, Magnolia Lodge, Relax Inn H, W Pilot/Taco Bell/dsl/scales/24hr/ @

BATESVILLE

GRENADA

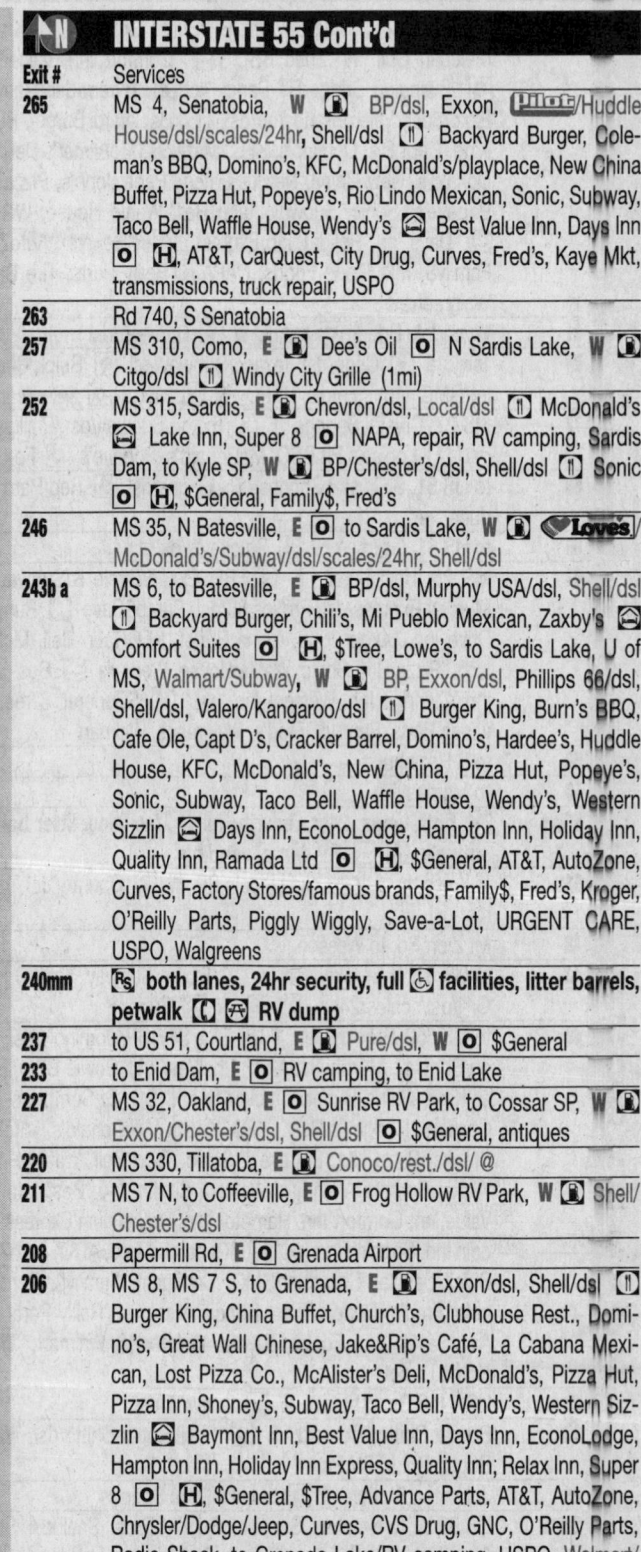

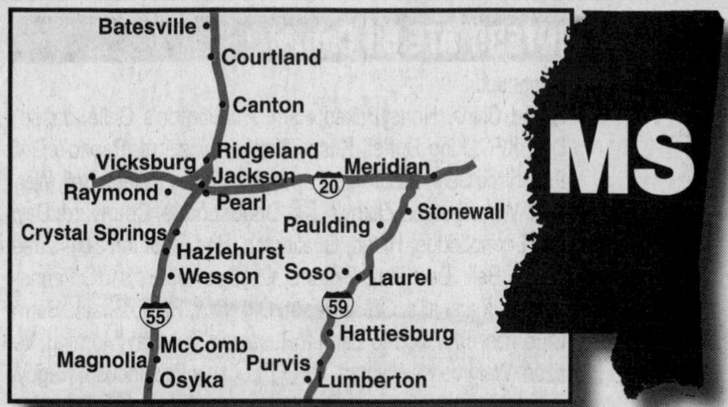

CANTON

MADISON

Exit #	Services
174	MS 35, MS 430, Vaiden, E 35-55 Trkstp/Chester's/dsl/scales/24hr, Chevron/dsl, Shell NAPA, Vaiden Camping, W Exxon/dsl
173mm	**sb, 24hr security, full facilities, litter barrels, petwalk RV dump**
164	to West, W West Trkstp/dsl
163mm	**nb, 24hr security, full facilities, litter barrels, petwalk RV dump**
156	MS 12, Durant, E Shell/Chester's/dsl Subway Durant Motel/rest. (3mi), Super 8, W H (7mi)
150	E Holmes Co SP, RV camping
146	MS 14, Goodman, W to Little Red Schoolhouse
144	MS 17, to Pickens, W BP/Baskin-Robbins/dsl/24hr to Little Red Schoolhouse
139	MS 432, to Pickens
133	Vaughan, E to Casey Jones Museum
128mm	Big Black River
124	MS 16, to N Canton
119	MS 22, to MS 16 E, Canton, E Canton Jct/dsl, Exxon, Kangaroo/Subway/dsl, Shell/Domino's, Valero/dsl El Sombrero Mexican, McDonald's, Pizza Hut, Popeye's, Sonic, Waffle House, Wendy's, Western Sizzlin Best Value Inn, Best Western, Brentwood Inn, Hampton Inn, Holiday Inn Express, La Quinta, Relax Inn, Studio 9 H, $General Mkt, Family$, O'Reilly Parts, to Ross Barnett Reservoir, W Chevron/KFC/dsl, Citgo, Loves/Arby's/dsl/scales/24hr/ @, Texaco/Penn's/dsl 2 Rivers Steaks, Bumpers Drive-In
118a b	Nissan Parkway, E to Nissan
114a b	Sowell Rd
112	US 51, Gluckstadt, E Exxon/Krystal/dsl Sonic Super 8 Goodyear/auto, W Camper Corral RV Ctr
108	MS 463, Madison, E Shell/dsl, Valero/dsl Applebee's, Backyard Burger, Burger King, Chick-Fil-A, Chili's, Coldstone, Corner Bakery Café, Dickey's BBQ, El Potrillo, Haute Pig Café, Little Caesars $Tree, AT&T, Best Buy, Dick's, GNC, Lowe's, Michael's, Office Depot, PetCo, SteinMart, Walmart, W Exxon/KFC/dsl BoneFish Grill, Nagoya Japanese, Papito's Grill, PieWorks, Pizza Inn, Subway, Tay's BBQ, Wendy's Hilton Garden H, CVS Drug, Home Depot, Kroger
105c b	Old Agency Rd, E Chevron/dsl Home2Suites Honda, Hyundai, W 5 Guys Burgers, Biaggi's Ristorante, Maggie Moo's, PF Changs, Ruth's Chris Steaks, Smoothie King, Sweet Peppers Cafe Hyatt Place Barnes&Noble, Fresh Mkt Foods
105a	Natchez Trace Pkwy
104	I-220, to W Jackson
103	County Line Rd, E Chevron, Exxon/dsl, Murphy Express/dsl Applebee's, Bop's Custard, Bulldog Grill, Burgers&Blues Cafe, Cane's, Chick-fil-A, ChuckECheese's, Cozumel Mexican,

INTERSTATE 55 Cont'd

103 Continued
Grand China, HoneyBaked Ham, Huntington's Grille, Jason's Deli, KFC, King Buffet, Krispy Kreme, Mazzio's, Papito's Grill, Peachtree Cafe, Pizza Hut, Popeye's, Shoney's, Taco Bell, Wendy's, Whataburger, Zaxby's 🛏 Cabot Lodge, Courtyard, Days Inn, EconoLodge, Hilton, Quality Inn, Red Roof Inn 🅞 $Tree, Acura, Belk, Best Buy, BigLots, Cadillac, Dillard's, JC Penney, Lowe's, Marshall's, Office Depot, Old Navy, Radio Shack, Sam's Club/gas, TJ Maxx, to Barnett Reservoir, Tuesday Morning, Verizon, Walgreens, Walmart, **W** 🍴 Logan's Roadhouse, Nagoya Japanese, Olive Garden, Red Lobster, Subway 🛏 Drury Inn, Holiday Inn Express, Motel 6, Studio 7 🅞 Fred's, Home Depot, Jo-Ann Fabrics, Office Depot, Petsmart, Target, Upton Tire

102b Beasley Rd, Adkins Blvd, **E** 🍴 Cracker Barrel, Outback Steaks, Twin Peaks Rest. 🛏 Super 8 🅞 Chevrolet, Ford, Nissan, Toyota/Scion, **W** 🅡 Exxon/dsl, Shell/dsl 🍴 Baskin-Robbins, Burger King, Chili's, IHOP, McDonald's 🛏 Baymont Inn, Best Western, Fairfield Inn, Hampton Inn, Harmony Court, Howard Johnson, InTown Suites 🅞 CarMax, frontage rds access 102a, Mercedes, Save-A-Lot Foods

102a Briarwood, **E** 🛏 La Quinta 🅞 Buick/GMC, **W** 🍴 Capt D's, Popeye's 🛏 Clarion, Hampton Inn 🅞 Chrysler/Dodge/Jeep, Porsche/Smart

100 North Side Dr W, **E** 🅡 BP/dsl, Chevron, Sprint 🍴 Burger King, Char Rest., Charokee Drive-In, McAlister's Deli, Papa John's, Piccadilly's, Pizza Hut, Starbucks, Subway, Wendy's 🛏 Extended Stay America 🅞 $Tree, AT&T, Audi, Books-A-Million, CVS Drug, Firestone/auto, Goodyear/auto, Jaguar/LandRover, Kroger/gas, Office Depot, SteinMart, vet, VW, Walgreens, **W** 🅡 Exxon/dsl FastLane, Shell 🍴 Domino's, Hooters, Waffle House 🛏 Select Motel, USA Inn

99 Meadowbrook Rd, Northside Dr E (from nb), **E** 🍴 Newk's Eatery

98c b MS 25 N, Lakeland Dr, **E** 🅡 Shell/dsl 🛏 Parkside Inn 🅞 LaFleur's Bluff SP, museum, **W** 🅞 🅷, 🚻

98a Woodrow Wilson Dr (exits left from nb), downtown

96c Fortification St, **E** 🛏 Studio 6 Suites, **W** 🅞 🅷, Bellhaven College

96b High St, Jackson, **E** 🅞 BMW, Chevrolet, Infiniti, Lexus, **W** 🅡 Shell/Subway/dsl, Valero/Kangaroo/dsl 🍴 Arby's, Chimneyville Cafe, Domino's, Popeye's, Shoney's, Taco Bell, Waffle House, Wendy's, Whataburger 🛏 Best Western, Comfort Inn, Days Inn, Hampton Inn, Jackson Hotel, Red Roof Inn, Regency Hotel, Travelodge 🅞 🅷, fairgrounds, Honda, museum, st capitol, Subaru/Volvo

96a Pearl St (from nb), Jackson, **W** access to same as 96b, downtown

94 (46 from nb), I-20 E, to Meridian, US 49 S

45b [I-20] US 51, State St, **N** 🅡 BP, Petro, Shell, **S** 🅡 🄿🄸🄻🄾🅃, to downtown

45a Gallatin St (from sb), **N** 🅡 BP, Petro/dsl, Shell, **S** 🅡 🄿🄸🄻🄾🅃/McDonald's/dsl 🅞 Nissan

92c (44 from sb), I-20 W, to Vicksburg, US 49 N

92b US 51 N, State St, Gallatin St

92a McDowell Rd, **E** 🅡 Petro/dsl, 🄿🄸🄻🄾🅃/McDonald's/dsl, **W** 🅡 BJ's/dsl, BP/dsl, Citgo/dsl, Exxon, Shell 🍴 McDonald's, Subway, Waffle House 🅞 Food Depot, Fred's, Rite Aid, Roses

90b Daniel Lake Blvd (from sb), **W** 🅡 Shell 🅞 Harley-Davidson

90a Savanna St, **E** 🅞 transmissions, **W** 🅡 BP 🅞 Caney Creek RV Ctr

88 Elton Rd, **W** 🅡 Exxon/dsl, Shell/Subway/dsl

85 Byram, **E** 🅡 Blue Sky/dsl, BP/Burns Grill/dsl 🍴 Krysta Mexican Grill, Tin Shed BBQ 🛏 Comfort Inn, ValuePlac 🅞 Swinging Bridge RV Park, **W** 🅡 Byram/dsl, Chevron Exxon/dsl, Valero/Kangaroo/dsl 🍴 Backyard Burger, Burge King, Capt D's, Domino's, KFC, Mazzio's, McAlister's Deli, Mc Donald's, New China, Newk's Eatery, Papa John's, Pizza Hu Popeye's, Sonic, Subway, Taco Bell, Waffle House, Wendy 🛏 Days Inn, Holiday Inn Express 🅞 $General, AutoZon Family$, Mkt Place Foods, NAPA, O'Reilly Parts, Tire Depo Walgreens

81 Wynndale Rd, **E** 🅞 repair, **W** 🅡 Chevron/dsl

78 Terry, **E** 🅡 Citgo/dsl, Texaco/Subway/dsl 🅞 Buick/Chevro let/GMC (1mi), Fred's, USPO, **W** 🅡 Mac's 🅞 $General

72 MS 27, Crystal Springs, **E** 🅡 Exxon/Subway/dsl, Phillips 66 dsl 🍴 Louise's Pit BBQ, McDonald's, Popeye's 🅞 Ford, ve

68 to US 51, S Crystal Springs, **E** 🅡 gas/dsl 🅞 Red Barn Pro duce, vet

65 to US 51, Gallman, **E** 🅡 Stuckey's/dsl

61 MS 28, Hazlehurst, **E** 🅡 BP, Exxon/Circle K/Subway/ds Murphy Express/dsl, Phillips 66/dsl, Pump&Save 🍴 Bumpe Drive Inn, Burger King, China Buffet, KFC/Taco Bell, McDor ald's, Pizza Hut, Sonic, Waffle House, Wendy's 🛏 Best Valu Inn, Claridge Inn, Western Inn 🅞 🅷, $General, $Tree, Ad vance Parts, Family$, Fred's, Walgreens, Walmart

59 to S Hazlehurst

56 to Martinsville

54mm 🆁🆂 both lanes, 24hr security, full 🅫 facilities, litter barrel petwalk 🄿 🄰 RV dump, vending

51 to Wesson, **E** 🅞 Lake Lincoln SP, **W** 🅡 Country Jct Trkstp rest/dsl

48 Mt Zion Rd, to Wesson

42 to US 51, N Brookhaven, **E** 🅡 Exxon/Subway, Shell/Gridirc Grill/dsl/scales/24hr 🅞 🅷, **W** 🛏 Super 8

40 to MS 550, Brookhaven, **E** 🅡 Blue Sky, BP/Domino's/dsl, Ex on/Subway, Murphy USA/dsl, Shell/dsl 🍴 Bowie BBQ, Burg er King, China Buffet, Cracker Barrel, DQ, El Sombrero Litt Caesars, Hudgey's Rest., KFC, Krystal, McDonald's, Mitchell Steaks, Pizza Hut, Popeye's, Sonic, Taco Bell, Waffle Hous Wards Burgers, Wendy's, Western Sizzlin 🛏 Best Inn, Be Value Inn, Comfort Inn, Hampton Inn, Holiday Inn Express, Lii coln Inn, Spanish Inn 🅞 🅷, $General, $Tree, AT&T, AutoZon Buick/Cadillac/Chevrolet/GMC, CarQuest, Family$, Ford/Lii coln, Fred's, Gene's Tires, Honda, Nissan, O'Reilly Parts, Ri Aid, Save-A-Lot Foods, Toyota, Walgreens, Walmart, **W** 🅞 Home Depot

38 US 84, S Brookhaven, **W** 🅡 Chevron/dsl

30 Bogue Chitto, Norfield, **E** 🅡 Shell/BogueChitto/dsl, **W** Bogue Chitto RV Park

24 Johnston Station, **E** 🅞 to Lake Dixie Springs

20b a US 98 W, to Natchez, Summit, **E** 🅡 BP/dsl, Shell/dsl, Stop Shop/dsl, **W** 🅡 Exxon/Subway/dsl, ShawnMart/dsl

18 MS 570, Smithdale Rd, N McComb, **E** 🅡 BP 🍴 Burg King, McDonald's, Piccadilly's, Ruby Tuesday 🛏 Holiday Ir Express 🅞 🅷, AT&T, Belk, JC Penney, Kia, Lowe's, ma Radio Shack, Walgreens, Walmart/Subway, **W** 🅡 Chevron/ds Whiskers/dsl 🍴 Applebee's, Arby's, El Dorado Mexican, San Fe Steaks 🛏 Deerfield Inn, Hampton Inn, Ramada 🅞 For Lincoln

17 Delaware Ave, McComb, **E** 🅡 Blue Sky, BP/Subway, Chevro dsl, Exxon/Penn's Rest., Pump&Savor, RaceWay/dsl 🍴 Bac yard BBQ, Burger King, Domino's, Golden Corral, Kyoto Steak Papa's Pizza, Popeye's, Smoothie King, Sonic, Taco Bell, Waf

(side tab) MS

(side tab) JACKSON

(side tab) BROOKHAVEN

(side tab) MCCOMB

INTERSTATE 55 Cont'd

17	Continued House, Wendy's [lodging] Best Western, Comfort Inn, Executive Inn [other] [H], $General, AutoZone, CVS Drug, Family$, Fred's, Kroger, Office Depot, O'Reilly Parts, Rite Aid, Verizon, **W** [lodging] Days Inn [other] Chrysler/Dodge/Jeep
15b a	US 98 E, MS 48 W, McComb, **1 mi E** [gas] BP, Citgo, Exxon/Subway, Presley QuikStop/dsl, Shell [food] Church's, KFC [lodging] Camellian Motel [other] $General, Advance Parts, Family$, tires, vet, **W** [gas] BP/dsl
13	Fernwood Rd, **E** [other] truck repair, **W** [gas] Loves/Chester's/McDonald's/dsl/scales/24hr/@ [other] golf, to Percy Quin SP
10	MS 48, Magnolia, **1 mi E** [gas] Exxon, Shell/dsl [food] Subway [other] RV camping
8	MS 568, Magnolia
4	Chatawa
3mm	**Welcome Ctr nb, 24hr security, full [handicapped] facilities, litter barrels, petwalk [phone] [picnic] RV dump**
2mm	**weigh sta nb**
1	MS 584, Osyka, Gillsburg
0mm	Mississippi/Louisiana state line

INTERSTATE 59

Exit #	Services
172mm	Mississippi/Alabama state line.
149mm	**I-59 N and I-20 E run together to AL state line. See I-20, exits 170mm-150.**
142	to US 11, Savoy, **W** to Dunns Falls
137	to N Enterprise, to Stonewall
134	MS 513, S Enterprise, **E** [gas] FastStop
126	MS 18, to Rose Hill, Pachuta, **E** [gas] BB/dsl, Pachuta TP/dsl
118	to Vossburg, Paulding
113	MS 528, to Heidelberg, **E** [gas] Chevron/dsl, Exxon/Subway/dsl, Shell [food] Ward's Burgers
109mm	**parking area sb, litter barrels, no restrooms**
106mm	**parking area nb, litter barrels, no restrooms**
104	Sandersville
99	US 11, **E** [other] Sleepy Hollow RV Park (1mi)
97	US 84 E, **E** [gas] Exxon/Huddle House/dsl/scales, Kangaroo/Subway/dsl [food] Hardee's, Ward's Burgers, **W** [gas] Shell [food] KFC, Vic's Rest.
96b	MS 15 S, Cook Ave
96a	Masonite Rd, 4th Ave
95d	(from nb)
95c	Beacon St, Laurel, **W** [food] Burger King, Church's, McDonald's, Panda Chinese, Popeye's [lodging] TownHouse Motel [other] $General, Family$, Firestone/auto, Grocery Depot, [H], JC Penney, museum of art, NAPA, USPO, Winn-Dixie
95b a	US 84 W, MS 15 N, 16th Ave, Laurel, **0-2 mi W** [gas] Alliance/dsl, Chevron, Exxon/dsl, Murphy Express/dsl, Pure, Shell [food] Applebee's, Arby's, Buffalo Wild Wings, Buffet City, Buffet Palace, Burger King, Cane's, Capt D's, Checkers, China Town, China Wok, Dickey's BBQ, Domino's, DQ, Eatza Pizza, Hardee's, IHOP, KFC, Laredo Grill, Little Caesar's, McDonald's, Mi Casita, Panda Express, Papa John's, Pizza Hut, Popeye's, Shipley's Donuts, Shoney's, Sonic, Subway, Sweet Peppers Deli, Taco Bell, Tokyo Grill, Waffle House, Ward's Burgers, Wendy's [lodging] Best Western, Comfort Suites, EconoLodge, Hampton Inn, Holiday Inn Express, Rodeway Inn, Super 8 [other] [H], $General, $Tree, Advance Parts, auto tech, AutoZone, BigLots, Buick/GMC, Chevrolet, Chrysler/Dodge/Jeep, CVS Drug,

LAUREL

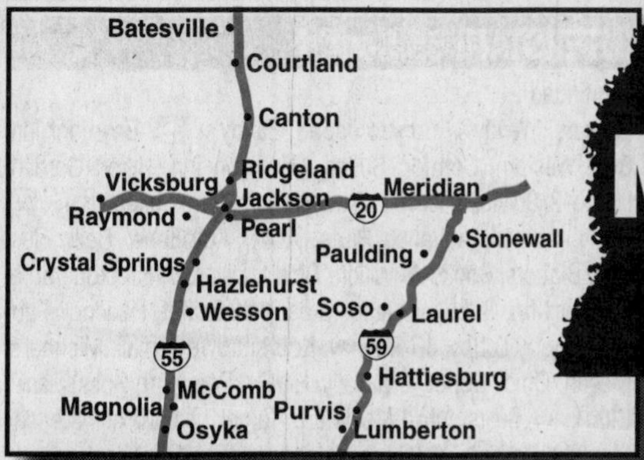

95b a	Continued Ford/Lincoln, Grocery Depot, Kia, Kroger/dsl, Lowe's, Nissan, Office Depot, O'Reilly Parts, Piggly Wiggly, Roses, Toyota, Tuesday Morning, Verizon, Walgreens, Walmart/Subway
93	US 11, S Laurel, **W** [gas] Exxon/Subway/dsl, Shell/dsl [food] Hardee's [other] Southern Tires
90	US 11, Ellisville Blvd, **E** [gas] Texaco/dsl [food] Huddle House, **W** [gas] Valero/dsl
88	MS 588, MS 29, Ellisville, **E** [gas] Chevron/dsl, Fast Mkt/dsl, Keith's/dsl [food] Domino's, KFC, Little Caesar's, McDonald's, Pizza Hut, Sonic, Subway, Ward's Burgers [other] $General, AutoZone, CashSaver, Ellisville Drug, Family$, NAPA, O'Reilly Parts, **W** [gas] Shell/dsl [lodging] Best Western
85	MS 590, to Ellisville
80	to US 11, Moselle, **E** [gas] Chevron/dsl
78	Sanford Rd
76	**W** [other] to Hattiesburg-Laurel Reg Airport
73	Monroe Rd, to Monroe
69	MS 42 E, Gandy Pkwy, to Petal, Eatonville
67b a	US 49, Hattiesburg, **E** [gas] Clark's/dsl, Exxon, Shell, Texaco, Valero/Kangaroo/dsl/scales [food] Arby's, Burger King, Cracker Barrel, DQ, Krystal, McDonald's, Waffle House [lodging] Budget Inn, Clarion, EconoLodge, Executive Inn, Motel 6, Quality Inn, Red Carpet Inn, Sleep Inn, Sunset Inn, Super 8 [other] $General, Hattiesburg Cycles, **W** [gas] Chevron, MapleLeaf/dsl, Pure/dsl, Shell/Subway, Stuckey's Express/dsl, Texaco [food] Sonic, Waffle House, Ward's Burgers, Wendy's [lodging] Candlewood Suites, Holiday Inn, Northgate Inn [other] URGENT CARE
65b a	US 98 W, Hardy St, Hattiesburg, **E** [gas] JR Mart, Shell/dsl [food] Applebee's, Baskin Robbins, Bop's Custard, Buffalo Wild Wings, Cane's, Checkers, Chinese Express, CiCi's Pizza, Domino's, Ed's Burger Joint, Firehouse Subs, IHOP, Izzo's Pizza, Jimmy John's, Kobe Japanese, Lenny's Subs, Little Caesar's, McDonald's, Papa John's, Pizza Hut, Purple Parrot Cafe, Qdoba, Smoothie King, Starbucks, Subway, Tabella Italian, Taco Bell, Ward's Burgers [lodging] Courtyard, Days Inn, Fairfield Inn, La Quinta, Residence Inn, Super 8, TownePlace Suites, Western Motel [other] Corner Mkt Foods, CVS Drug, Goodyear/auto, Home Depot, [H], to USM, URGENT CARE, Verizon, vet, Walgreens, **W** [gas] Exxon/Domino's, Kangaroo, Shell/Jimmy John's/dsl, Texaco [food] Arby's, Burger King, Cheddar's, Chesterfield's Rest., Chick-fil-A, Chili's, China Buffet, Chuck-ECheese's, Dickey's BBQ, FireHouse Subs, Five Guys, Gatti Town Pizza, Georgia Blue Rest., Golden Corral, Grand China, Hardee's, HoneyBaked Ham, Hooters, Krispy Kreme, Logan's Roadhouse, Longhorn Steaks, Marble Slab, McAlister's Deli, McDonald's, Newk's Eatery, O'Charley's, Olive Garden, Outback Steaks, Panda Express, Papa Murphy's, Pepper's Deli, Pizza Hut, Plaid Rhino Burger, Popeye's, Red Lobster, Super King Asian, Taco Bell, TGIFriday's, Waffle House, Ward's

HATTIESBURG

MS

MS
MO

INTERSTATE 59 Cont'd

HATTIESBURG

65b a	Continued Burgers, Wendy's, Yamato Japan, Zaxby's Baymont Inn, Best Western, Comfort Suites, Hampton Inn, Hilton Garden, Home 2 Suites, Microtel, Ramada Inn, Sun Suites H, $Tree, Aamco, Advance Parts, AT&T, AutoZone, Belk, Best Buy, BigLots, Books-A-Million, Dick's, Dillard's, Firestone/auto, Gander Mtn, Goodyear/auto, Great Wall Buffet, Hancock Fabrics, Hobby Lobby, JC Penney, Kohl's, Lowe's, mall, Michael's, Nissan, Office Depot, Old Navy, PetCo, Petsmart, Ross, Sam's Club/gas, Sears/auto, SteinMart, Target, TJ Maxx, Tuesday Morning, Verizon, Walgreens, Walmart, Winn-Dixie
60	US 11, S Hattiesburg, E Shell/dsl, W Kangaroo/Subway/dsl/24hr, Texaco, Valero/dsl Huddle House Freightliner, Peterbilt
59	US 98 E, to US 49, Lucedale, MS Gulf Coast
56mm	**parking area both lanes, litter barrels, no restrooms**
51	Rd 589, to Purvis, W Chevron/dsl, Pinebelt Oil/dsl, Shell/dsl (2mi) McDonald's (2mi), Pizza Hut (2mi), to Little Black Cr Water Park
48mm	Little Black Creek
41	MS 13, to Lumberton, W $General, to Little Black Cr Water Park
35	Hillsdale Rd, E Pitstop/dsl to Kings Arrow Ranch, to Lake Hillside Resort
32mm	Wolf River
29	Rd 26, to Poplarville, W Loves/Arby's/dsl/scales/24hr, Pure/dsl NAPA, tires/repair
27	MS 53, to Poplarville, Necaise, W Chevron/dsl McDonald's RV Camping (2mi)
19	to US 11, Millard
15	to McNeill, W McNeill Trkstop/rest./dsl
10	to US 11, Carriere, E Texaco/Huddle House/dsl Clearwater RV Camp (5mi)
6	MS 43 N, N Picayune, E Mi Sol Mexican, Paul's Pastries, W Chevron/dsl McDonald's, Sonic, Subway, Waffle House Super 8 H, $General, Claiborne Hill Mkt, CVS Drug, Family$, Walgreens, Winn-Dixie

PICAYUNE

4	MS 43 S, to Picayune, E Murphy USA/dsl, RaceTra dsl McDonald's, Rio Grande Mexican, Ryan's $Tre AT&T, Buick/Cadillac/Chevrolet/GMC, Chrysler/Dodge/Jee GNC, Home Depot, Nissan, Verizon, Walgreens, Walmar W Chevron/dsl, Exxon/dsl, Shell/dsl Applebee's, Burg King, Domino's, Don's Seafood, Hardee's, IHOP, Little Caesar' New Buffet City, Papa John's, Pizza Hut, Popeye's, Subwa Taco Bell, Tokyo Grill, Waffle House, Wendy's Days In EconoLodge, Heritage Inn, Holiday Inn Express H, $Ge eral, Advance Parts, AutoZone, Family$, Firestone/auto, For Lincoln, Fred's, O'Reilly Parts, Paw Paw's RV Ctr, Radio Shac Rite Aid, URGENT CARE, Winn-Dixie
3mm	**Welcome Ctr nb, full facilities, litter barrels, petwalk RV dump, vending**
1.5mm	**weigh sta both lanes**
1	US 11, MS 607, E NASA, W Chevron/dsl Subwa
0mm	Mississippi/Louisiana state line, Pearl River.

INTERSTATE 220 (JACKSON)

Exit #	Services
11mm	**I-220 begins/ends on I-55, exit 104.**
9	Hanging Moss Rd, County Line Rd, E BP
8	Watkins Dr, E Exxon/Subway, Shell/Chester's/dsl
5b a	US 49 N, Evers Blvd, to Yazoo City, E BP KFC, Soni Star Motel Family$, Food Depot/gas, W BP, Exxo Burger King, Gas+, Shell/Subway/dsl
3	Industrial Dr
2b a	Clinton Blvd, Capitol St, E to Jackson Zoo, W Race Way, Shell McDonald's, Popeye's, Sonic Family$
1b a	US 80, E BP, Citgo/dsl, Shell Capt D's, Hunan Garde KFC, McDonald's, Pizza Hut, Popeye's, Sonny's BBQ, Tac Bell, Wendy's Best Inn, Scottish Inn, Super 8 Mr Trans mission, W Exxon/dsl Arby's, Krystal $General
0mm	**I-220 begins/ends on I-20, exit 41.**

MISSOURI

INTERSTATE 29

Exit #	Services
124mm	Missouri/Iowa state line
123mm	Nishnabotna River
121.5mm	**weigh sta both lanes**
116	Rd A, Rd B, to Watson, W fireworks
110	US 136, Rock Port, Phelps City, E Sinclair/dsl fireworks, Rockport Inn, to NW MO St U, W Cenex/Godfather's/dsl/24hr, Phillips 66/Stuckey's/Subway/dsl/24hr Black Iron Grill, McDonald's, Trails End Rest. Super 8 fireworks, Rivers Edge RV Park, truck wash
109.5mm	**Welcome Ctr sb, full facilities, info, litter barrels, petwalk**
107	MO 111, to Rock Port
106.5mm	Rock Creek
102mm	Mill Creek
99	Rd W, Corning
97mm	Tarkio River
92	US 59, to Fairfax, Craig, W Sinclair/dsl
90.5mm	Little Tarkio Creek
86.5mm	Squaw Creek
84	MO 118, Mound City, E FL/Subway/dsl, Valero/ds Breadeaux Pizza, McDonald's, Quacker's Steaks, Shaker Icecream Audrey's Motel, Super 8 $General, Bumpe Parts, Chrysler/Dodge/Jeep, USPO, W BP/Baskin Robbins/dsl Big Lake SP (12mi)
82mm	**truck parking both lanes, limited facilities**
79	US 159, Rulo, E Phillips 66 Trkstp/dsl/rest/RV dump/ W to Big Lake SP (12mi), to Squaw Creek NWR (3mi)
78mm	Kimsey Creek
75	US 59, to Oregon
67	US 59 N, to Oregon
66.5mm	Nodaway River
65	US 59, Rd RA, to Fillmore, Savannah, E Conoco/ds antiques, fireworks
60	Rd K, Rd CC, Amazonia, W Hunt's Fruit Barn
58.5mm	Hopkins Creek
56b a	I-229 S, US 71 N, US 59 N, to St Joseph, Maryville

MO

INTERSTATE 29 Cont'd

ST JOSEPH

Exit #	Services
55mm	Dillon Creek
53	US 59, US 71 bus, to St Joseph, Savannah, E AOK Camping, W Phillips 66/dsl antiques, fireworks
50	US 169, St Joseph, King City, **1-3 mi W on Belt Hwy** Cenex/dsl, Conoco, Shell 54th St Grill, Bob Evans, Buffalo Wild Wings, Cheddar's, Chick-fil-A, Chili's, Chipotle Mexican, Coldstone, Culver's, Famous Dave's, Hardee's, IHOP, KFC, McDonald's, Olive Garden, Panda Express, Ryan's, Sonic, Starbucks, Subway, Taco Bell Candlewood Suites, Holiday Inn Express Advance Parts, Aldi Foods, AT&T, Autozone, Best Buy, Dick's, Home Depot, Kohl's, Lowe's, Michael's, Old Navy, Petco, Petsmart, Sam's Club/gas, Target, Tires+, TJ Maxx, Walgreens, Walmart/Subway
47	MO 6, Frederick Blvd, to Clarksdale, St Joseph, E Conoco Bandanas BBQ Days Inn, Drury Inn H, W Phillips 66/dsl, Sinclair/dsl Applebee's, Arby's, Burger King, Cracker Barrel, Denny's, Dunkin Donuts, El Maguey Mexican, Fazoli's, Five Guys, Golden Corral, LJ Silver, McAlister's Deli, McDonald's, New China Super Buffet, Pancheros, Panera Bread, Papa John's, Papa Murphy's, Perkins, Pizza Hut, Red Lobster, Rib Crib BBQ, Sonic, Starbucks, Subway, Taco Bell, TX Roadhouse, Wendy's, Whiskey Creek Steaks Best Value Inn, Comfort Suites, Hampton Inn, Motel 6, Ramada, Stoney Creek Inn $General, Apple Mkt Foods, BigLots, Buick/GMC, Chevrolet, CVS Drug, Dillard's, Firestone/auto, Ford/Lincoln, Hastings Books, Hobby Lobby, Honda, HyVee Foods/dsl, JC Penney, Jo-Ann Fabrics, Nissan, Office Depot, Radio Shack, Sears, Taco John's, Toyota/Scion, U-Haul, Verizon, vet, Walgreens
46b a	US 36, to Cameron, St Joseph, **1 mi W on US 169** BP/dsl, FP/dsl, Murphy USA/dsl, Roadstar/dsl, Sinclair/dsl Burger King, Jimmy John's, Pizza Hut, Taco John's, Wendy's $General, Ace Hardware, AT&T, CVS, KIA, Klein RV Ctr, O'Reilly Parts, to MO W St Coll, Walgreens, Walmart/Subway
44	US 169, to Gower, St Joseph, E Loves/Arby's/dsl/scales/24hr, Phillips 66 Nelly's Mexican, Subway Guesthouse Inn dsl repair, W Murphy USA/dsl, Shell/dsl/24hr DQ, McDonald's, Mr Goodcents, San Jose Steaks, Sonic, Taco Bell, Waffle House $Tree, Apple Mkt Foods, Chrysler/Dodge/Jeep, Harley-Davidson, Hyundai, Menards, Walmart/Subway
43	I-229 N, to St Joseph
39.5mm	Pigeon Creek
35	Rd DD, Faucett, W Farris Trkstp/dsl/motel/rest/24hr/ @
33.5mm	Bee Creek
30	Rd Z, Rd H, Dearborn, New Market, E Conoco/Subway/dsl/24hr
29.5mm	Bee Creek
27mm	**both lanes, full facilities, litter barrels, petwalk vending**
25	Rd E, Rd U, to Camden Point, E Phillips 66/dsl
24mm	**weigh sta nb/truck parking sb**
20	MO 92, MO 273, to Atchison, Leavenworth, W antiques, to Weston Bend SP
19.5mm	Platte River
19	Rd HH, Platte City (sb returns at 18), W Casey's, Platte-Clay Fuel/dsl DQ, Maria's Mexican, Pizza Hut, Red Dragon

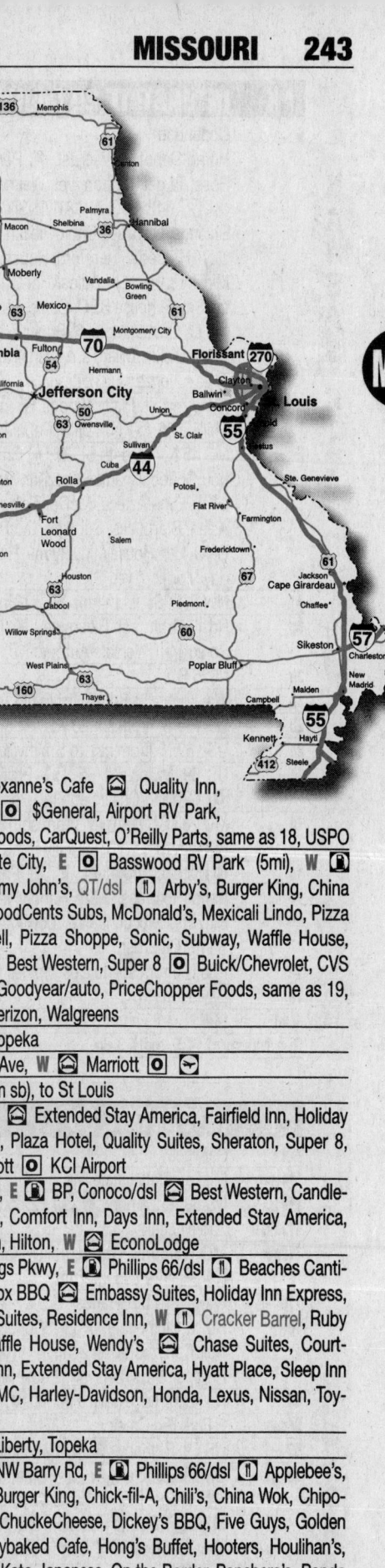

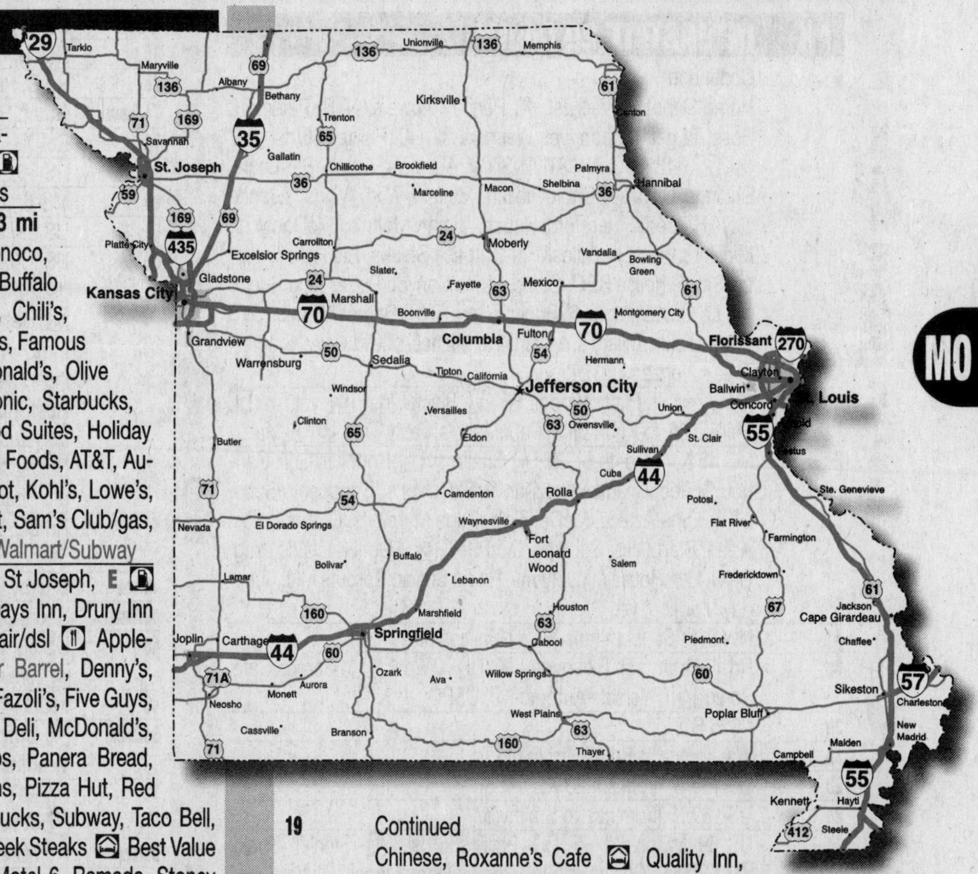

PLATTE CITY

Exit #	Services
19	Continued Chinese, Roxanne's Cafe Quality Inn, Travelodge $General, Airport RV Park, Apple Mkt Foods, CarQuest, O'Reilly Parts, same as 18, USPO
18	MO 92, Platte City, E Basswood RV Park (5mi), W Conoco/Jimmy John's, QT/dsl Arby's, Burger King, China Wok, DQ, GoodCents Subs, McDonald's, Mexicali Lindo, Pizza Hut/Taco Bell, Pizza Shoppe, Sonic, Subway, Waffle House, Wendy's Best Western, Super 8 Buick/Chevrolet, CVS Drug, Ford, Goodyear/auto, PriceChopper Foods, same as 19, TrueValue, Verizon, Walgreens
17	I-435 S, to Topeka
15	Mexico City Ave, W Marriott
14	I-435 E (from sb), to St Louis
13	to I-435 E, E Extended Stay America, Fairfield Inn, Holiday Inn, Microtel, Plaza Hotel, Quality Suites, Sheraton, Super 8, W Marriott KCI Airport
12	NW 112th St, E BP, Conoco/dsl Best Western, Candlewood Suites, Comfort Inn, Days Inn, Extended Stay America, Hampton Inn, Hilton, W EconoLodge
10	Tiffany Springs Pkwy, E Phillips 66/dsl Beaches Cantina, SmokeBox BBQ Embassy Suites, Holiday Inn Express, Homewood Suites, Residence Inn, W Cracker Barrel, Ruby Tuesday, Waffle House, Wendy's Chase Suites, Courtyard, Drury Inn, Extended Stay America, Hyatt Place, Sleep Inn Buick/GMC, Harley-Davidson, Honda, Lexus, Nissan, Toyota/Scion
9b a	MO 152, to Liberty, Topeka
8	MO 9, Rd T, NW Barry Rd, E Phillips 66/dsl Applebee's, Big Biscuit, Burger King, Chick-fil-A, Chili's, China Wok, Chipotle Mexican, ChuckeCheese, Dickey's BBQ, Five Guys, Golden Corral, Honeybaked Cafe, Hong's Buffet, Hooters, Houlihan's, Jason's Deli, Kato Japanese, On the Border, Panchero's, Panda Express, Panera Bread, Papa Murphy's, Rally House, Sheridan's Custard, Starbucks, Subway, Taco Bell, Wendy's, Winstead's Rest. H, $Tree, AutoZone, Best Buy, Ford, Hobby Lobby,

KANSAS CITY

INTERSTATE 29 Cont'd

8	Continued Home Depot, HyVee/dsl, JC Penney, Lowe's, NTB, Petsmart, Ross, Target, Verizon, vet, Walmart, W Phillips 66/dsl, QT/dsl 54th St Grill, A&W/LJSilver, Abuelo's, Arby's, Bar Louie, BoLings Chinese, Bravo Italian, Buffalo Wild Wings, Granite City, Hardee's, Hereford House, Jimmy John's, McDonald's, Minsky's Pizza, Noodles&Co, Outback Steaks, Rainbow Oriental, Smokehouse BBQ, Sonic, Stone Canyon Pizza, Taco Bueno La Quinta, Motel 6, Super 8 AT&T, Barnes&Noble, CVS Drug, Dick's, Dillard's, Marshall's, Michael's, Old Navy, Staples, Tires+, Verizon
6	NW 72nd St, Platte Woods, E Sinclair/dsl vet, W Phillips 66 Iron Wok, Papa John's, Tasty Thai K-Mart
5	MO 45 N, NW 64th St, W Shell/dsl Bonefish Grill, Caribou Coffee, Chamas Brazilian Grill, Culver's, Goodcents Subs, IHOP, Luna Azteca, McDonald's, Papa Murphy's, Quiznos, Saki Asian, Starbucks, Subway, Taco Bell $General, CVS Drug, GNC, Hen House Mkt, HyVee, Radio Shack, Sprouts Mkt, Tuesday Morning, vet
4	NW 56th St (from nb), W Phillips 66
3c	Rd A (from sb), Riverside, W QT/dsl Corner Café, Sonic Rverside Automotive, USPO
3b	I-635 S
3a	Waukomis Dr, Rd AA (from nb)
2b	US 169 S (from sb), to KC
2a	US 169 N (from nb), to Smithville
1e	US 69, Vivion Rd, E Phillips66/dsl Steak'n Shake Cadillac/Chevrolet, Fiat, Home Depot, Lincoln, Subaru
1d	MO 283 S, Oak Tfwy (from sb), W BP/dsl McDonald's, Subway CVS, O'Reilly Parts
1c	Gladstone (from nb), E Phillips 66 Arby's, Freddy's, Panda Express, Pizza Ranch, Taco Bueno, Wendy's H, BigLots, Discount Tire, Lowe's, Petco, PriceChopper Foods, Sam's Club/dsl
1b	I-35 N (from sb), to Des Moines
1a	Davidson Rd
8mm	I-35 N. I-29 and I-35 run together 6 mi.

See Missouri I-35, exits 3-8a.

INTERSTATE 35

Exit #	Services
114mm	Missouri/Iowa state line
114	US 69, to Lamoni, W Conoco/dsl/24hr
113.5mm	Zadie Creek
112mm	**MO Welcome Ctr sb, full facilities, litter barrels, petwalk wireless internet**
110	**weigh sta both lanes**
106	Rd N, Blythedale, E Conoco/fireworks, Phillips 66/Dinner Bell Cafe/motel/dsl/24hr/ @ camping, dsl repair, W Phillips 66/dsl/24hr Eagle Ridge RV Park (2mi), fireworks
99	Rd A, to Ridgeway, **5 mi** W camping
94mm	E Fork Big Creek
93	US 69, Bethany, W RV dump
92	US 136, Bethany, E FL/dsl KFC/Taco Bell, McDonald's Budget Inn, W BP/dsl, Casey's, Kum&Go/Wendy's/dsl, MFA Country Kitchen, DQ, Nopal Mexican, Sonic, Subway, TootToot Rest. Comfort Inn, Super 8 H, Russell Stover, Walmart
90mm	Pole Cat Creek
88	MO 13, to Bethany, Gallatin
84	Rds AA, H, to Gilman City, E Crowder SP (24mi)

BETHANY

81mm	**truck parking, limited facilities**
80	Rds B, N, to Coffey
78	Rd C, Pattonsburg, W Phillips 66/dsl
74.5mm	Grand River
72	Rd DD
68	US 69, to Pattonsburg
64	MO 6, to Maysville, Gallatin
61	US 69, Winston, Gallatin, E Shell/rest/dsl/24hr
54	US 36, Cameron, E Shell/Baskin-Robbins/Wendy's/dsl/24hr, Sinclair/dsl/scales/24hr McDonald's, Subwa Best Western, Budget Inn, Comfort Inn Crossroads R Park, W Valero/dsl Burger King, Chinese Chef, Domino's, DQ, El Maguey Mexican, KFC/Taco Bell, Ma&Pa's Kett Rest, Pizza Hut, Sonic Best Value Inn, Comfort Inn, Day Inn, EconoLodge, Super 8 H, Advance Parts, antique Buick/Chevrolet/GMC, CountryMart Foods, O'Reilly Parts, Radio Shack, tires, Twin Creeks Tire, USPO, Verizon, Walmart
52	Rd BB, Lp 35, to Cameron, E H, W Casey's, same a 54
49mm	Brushy Creek
48.5mm	Shoal Creek
48	US 69, Cameron, E to Wallace SP (2mi), W Shamroc fireworks
40	MO 116, Lathrop, E antiques
34.5mm	**both lanes, full facilities, litter barrels, petwalk vending**
33	Rd PP, Holt, E Hilltop Grill, W BP, Conoco/d American Eagle Inn
30mm	Holt Creek
26	MO 92, Kearney, E Casey's, Phillips 66/dsl, Shell/dsl China Wok, McDonald's, Pizza Hut, Sonic Comfort Inn, Super 8 CountryMart Foods, CVS Drug, Kramer Hardwar Red Cross Drug, to Watkins Mill SP, W Pilot/Taco Bel dsl/scales/24hr Arby's, Burger King, Hunan Garden Chinese, Pizza Shoppe, Stables Grill, Subway EconoLodg Quality Inn Curves, Goodyear/auto, John's Foods, O'Reil Parts, to Smithville Lake
22mm	**parking area sb, weigh sta nb**
20	US 69, MO 33, to Excelsior Springs, E H
17	MO 291, Rd A, **1 mi** E BP, QT A&W, Arby's, CiCi's LJ Silver, McDonald's, Minsky's Pizza, Papa John's, Papa Murphy's, Perkins, Sonic, Subway, Taco Bell $General, Chevrolet, Days Inn, Firestone, Lifestyle RV Ctr, O'Reilly Parts, sam as 16, Walgreens, W Phillips 66/dsl, QT McDonald's Nicky's Pizza, Sonic, Subway, Wasabi Japanese Sleep Inn ValuePlace Inn Price Chopper Foods, to KCI Airport, URGENT CARE, Walgreens
16	MO 152, Liberty, E Phillips 66 5 Guys Burgers, Baskin Robbins, Chick-fil-A, CiCi's Pizza, Culver's, IHOP, Jimmy John's Margarita's, Olive Garden, Perkins, Pizza Hut, Planet Sub, Re Robin, Starbucks, TX Roadhouse, Wendy's Days Inn, Super 8 H, Advance Parts, AutoZone, Chevrolet, CVS Drug Dick's, Firestone/auto, Ford, Hy-Vee Foods, K-Mart, Lowe's URGENT CARE, Walgreens, W Phillips 66/Circle K/ds 54th St Grill, Applebee's, Arby's, Bob Evans, Buffalo Wil Wings, Burger King, Chili's, Chipotle Mexican, Corner Cafe Cracker Barrel, Freddy's Burgers, Golden Corral, Jose Peppers KFC, LongHorn Steaks, McDonald's, Panda Express, Paner Bread, Schlotzsky's, SmokeBox BBQ, Steak'n Shake, Subway Taco Bell, Waffle House Comfort Suites, Fairfield Inn, Hampton Inn, Holiday Inn Express Aldi Foods, AT&T, Best Buy Christian Bros Auto, Ford, Home Depot, JC Penney, Jiffy Lube Kohl's, Michael's, NAPA, NTB, Office Depot, Petsmart, Radi Shack, Target, TJ Maxx, Verizon, Walmart/Subway

CAMERON KEARNEY LIBERTY

MO

INTERSTATE 35 Cont'd

Exit #	Services
14	US 69 (exits left from sb), Liberty Dr, to Glenaire, Pleasant Valley, E [gas] Phillips 66, Shell, Sinclair [other] I-35 RV Ctr, W [gas] QT/dsl
13	US 69 (from nb), to Pleasant Valley, E [gas] Phillips 66/dsl, Shell, Sinclair/24hr [food] KFC, McDonald's [other] auto repair, W [gas] QT/dsl
12b a	I-435, to St Louis
11	US 69 N, Vivion Rd, E [gas] BP/dsl, Shell/dsl [food] Church's, McDonald's, W [gas] QT [food] Sonic, Stroud's Rest.
10	N Brighton Ave (from nb), E [food] Church's, McDonald's
9	MO 269 S, Chouteau Trfwy, E [gas] Phillips 66 [food] IHOP, McDonald's, Ming Garden, Outback Steaks, Papa Murphy's, Popeye's, Subway, Wing Stop [other] AT&T, Food Festival, GNC, Harrah's Casino/rest., Radio Shack, Target, W [food] Wendy's (1mi)
8c	MO 1, Antioch Rd, E [gas] 7-11 [food] Domino's [lodging] Best Western [other] auto repair, W [gas] Phillips 66 [food] Catfish Rest., Waffle House [other] Walgreens
8b	I-29 N, US 71 N, KCI [airport]
I-35 S and I-29 S run together 6 mi.	
8a	Parvin Rd, E [gas] BP, Shell [other] O'Reilly Parts, W [lodging] Super Inn
6b a	Armour Rd, E [gas] Phillips 66/dsl [food] Arby's, Burger King, Denny's, McDonald's, Quiznos [lodging] EconoLodge, La Quinta [other] [H], repair, to Riverboat Casino, W [gas] Conoco/dsl, Phillips 66, QT [food] DQ, Lucky Dragon Chinese, Pizza Hut, Subway, Taco Bell, Wendy's [lodging] American Inn, Holiday Inn Express [other] USPO
5b	16th Ave, industrial district
5a	Levee Rd, Bedford St, industrial district
4.5mm	Missouri River
4b	Front St, E [other] Isle of Capri Riverboat Casino/rest.
4a	US 24 E, Independence Ave
3	I-70 E, US 71 S, to St Louis
2g	**I-35 N and I-29 N run together 6 mi**
2e	Oak St, Grand-Walnut St, E [gas] Phillips 66 [lodging] Marriott
2d	Main-Delaware, Wyandotte St, downtown
2a	I-70 W, to Topeka
2y	US 169, Broadway, to downtown
2w	12th St, Kemper Arena, to downtown
2v	14th St, to downtown
2u	I-70 E, to Broadway, E [food] Denny's
1e	US 69, Vivion Rd, E [gas] Phillips66/dsl [food] Steak'n Shake [other] Cadillac/Chevrolet, Chrysler/Jeep, Home Depot, Lincoln, Suzuki, W [gas] Shell [food] McDonald's, Subway
1d	20th St (from sb), W [gas] Phillips 66 [food] McDonald's
1c	27th St, SW Blvd, W Pennway (from nb), E [gas] Phillips 66 [food] CiCi's Pizza, Panda Express, Quiznos, Taco Bueno [other] [H], BigLots, Lowe's, Office Depot, PriceChopper Foods
1a	SW Trafficway (from sb)
0mm	Missouri/Kansas state line

KANSAS CITY

INTERSTATE 44

Exit #	Services
293mm	**I-44 begins/ends on I-70, exit 249 in St Louis.**
290a	I-55 S, to Memphis
290c	Gravois Ave (from wb), 12th St, S [food] Jack-in-the-Box
290b	18th St (from eb), downtown
289	Jefferson Ave, St Louis, N [gas] Phillips 66 [food] Subway [lodging] Holiday Inn Express, Residence Inn [other] Family$, SaveALot, S [gas] Conoco [food] Lee's Chicken, McDonald's [other] Family$

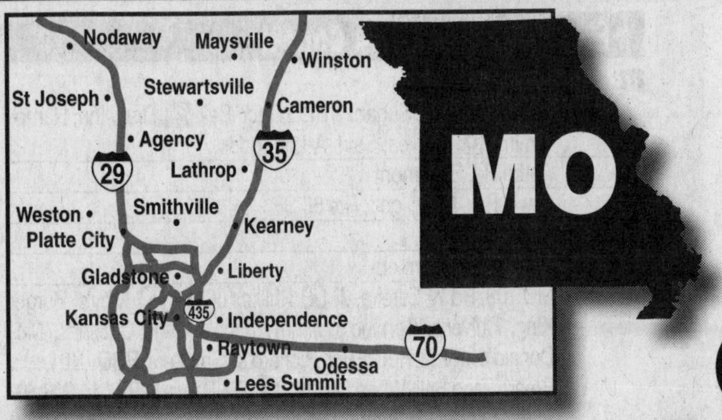

MO

ST LOUIS

Exit #	Services
288	Grand Blvd, St Louis, N [gas] BP [lodging] Water Tower Inn [other] [H], vet, S [food] Jack-in-the-Box, Qdoba, St Louis Bread, Starbucks, Subway [other] Family$
287b a	Kingshighway, Vandeventer Ave, St Louis, N [gas] BP, QT/dsl [other] [H], Jiffy Lube, U-Haul, S [gas] BP [other] Chevrolet, to MO Botanical Garden, Walgreens
286	Hampton Ave, St Louis, N [gas] BP, Mobil, Phillips 66, Shell/Circle K [food] Courtesy Diner, Denny's, Jack-in-the-Box, McDonald's, Steak'n Shake, Subway, Taco Bell [other] zoo, S [gas] Shell/Circle K/dsl [food] Bartolino's Rest., Hardee's, Wendy's [lodging] Drury Inn, Holiday Inn, Red Roof Inn [other] museums
285	SW Ave (from wb, no EZ return)
284b a	Arsenal St, Jamieson St
283	Shrewsbury (from wb), some services same as 282
282	Laclede Sta Rd, Murdock Ave (from eb), St Louis, N [gas] BP [food] Boardwalk Cafe, Front Row Grill, Hwy 61 Roadhouse, Imo's Pizza, McDonald's, Racanelli's Pizza, Starbucks, Stratton's Cafe, Subway, Webster Wok Chinese [other] Subaru, vet
280	Elm Ave, St Louis, N [gas] BP [food] Jamba Juice [other] Schnuck's Foods, **1 mi** S [gas] Shell/Circle K [food] Steak'n Shake [other] Walgreens
279	(from wb), Berry Rd
278	Big Bend Rd, St Louis, N [food] Culver's, Hardee's [other] [H], Sam's Club/gas, URGENT CARE, S [gas] Mobil/dsl, QT
277b	US 67, US 61, US 50, Lindbergh Blvd, N [food] Arby's, Buffalo Wild Wings, Chili's, Chipotle Mexican, Dunkin Donuts, Jason's Deli, O'Charley's, Sonic, Steak&Rice Chinese, TX Roadhouse, White Castle [lodging] Best Western [other] [H], $Tree, AT&T, Hancock Fabrics, Harley-Davidson, Hobby Lobby, Lowe's Whse, Office Depot, PetCo, Target, TJ Maxx, Verizon, Walmart, S [gas] Phillips 66/dsl, Shell/Circle K/dsl [food] Burger King, Chick-fil-A, Denny's, Five Guys, Fuddrucker's, Helen Fitzgerald's Grill, IHOP, Lion's Choice, Longhorn Steaks, Panda Express, Ruby Tuesday, St Louis Bread, Steak'n Shake, Subway [lodging] Days Inn/rest., EconoLodge, Hampton Inn, Holiday Inn [other] Dobb's Auto/Tire, GNC, Home Depot, Marshall's, Old Navy, Petsmart, Ross, Stein Mart
277a	MO 366 E, Watson Rd, access to same as 277b S
276b a	I-270, N to Chicago, S Memphis
275	N Highway Dr (from wb), Soccer Pk Rd, N [gas] Pilot/Road Ranger/rest/dsl
274a b	Bowles Ave, N [gas] Road Ranger/Pilot/Subway/dsl, S [gas] Phillips 66/dsl, QT/dsl, ZX/dsl [food] Bandana's BBQ, Cracker Barrel, Denny's, Jack-in-the-Box, Krispy Kreme, McDonald's, White Castle [lodging] Drury Inn, Fairfield Inn, Holiday Inn Express, Motel 6, PearTree Inn, Stratford Inn, Super 8, TownePlace Inn
272	MO 141, Fenton, Valley Park, N [gas] Motomart, S [gas] Phillips 66/dsl [food] Bob Evans, Burger King, Dickey's BBQ, Hardee's, Jimmy John's, McDonald's, Ruby Tuesday, Starbucks, Steak'n

MO

INTERSTATE 44 Cont'd

272 Continued
Shake, Subway, Sugarfire BBQ, Taco Bell [lodging] Drury Inn, Hampton Inn [other] Curves, Save-A-Lot Foods

269 Antire Rd, Beaumont

266 Lewis Rd, N [other] golf, Rte 66 SP

266mm Meramec River

265 Williams Rd (from eb)

264 MO 109, Rd W, Eureka, N [gas] Phillips 66/dsl [food] Arby's, Burger King, Culver's, Domino's, Jimmy John's, Little Caesar's, McDonald's, Pizza Hut, Poor Richard's, Smokers BBQ, St Louis Bread, Taco Bell, White Castle [other] AT&T, Byerly RV Ctr, O'Reilly Parts, Schnuck's Foods, to Babler SP, Valvoline, S [gas] QT/dsl [other] Walgreens

261 Lp 44, to Allenton, N [gas] Motomart/McDonald's/dsl [food] China King, Denny's, Imo's Pizza, Lion's Choice, Steak'n Shake, Subway [lodging] Best Inn, Holiday Inn, Super 8 [other] $Tree, AutoZone, GNC, Jellystone RV Camping, same as 264, to Six Flags, Walmart, S [gas] Shell/Circle K/dsl [other] KOA

257 (256 from eb) Lp 44, Pacific, N [gas] Phillips 66, Pilot/Subway/dsl/scales/24hr [lodging] Comfort Inn [other] fireworks, S [gas] BP/dsl, Mobil/dsl, Motomart [food] El Agave Mexican, Hardee's, KFC, McDonald's, New China, Pizza Hut, Taco Bell [lodging] Quality Inn [other] $General, Chrysler/Dodge/Jeep, CVS Drug, O'Reilly Parts, Queen's Foods, SaveALot, st police

253 MO 100 E, to Gray Summit, S [gas] Phillips 66/dsl [lodging] Travelodge [other] CarQuest, fireworks, Shaw Nature Preserve

251 MO 100 W, to Washington, N [gas] BP/dsl, Mr Fuel/dsl/scales, Phillips 66/Burger King/dsl [other] $General, antiques, [H] (11mi)

247 US 50 W, Rd AT, Rd O, to Union, N [other] Harley-Davidson, Pin Oak Creek RV Park, S [other] to Robertsville SP

247mm Bourbeuse River

242 Rd AH, to Hist Rte 66

240 MO 47, St Clair, N [gas] Phillips 66/Taco Bell/dsl [food] Burger King [other] tire/auto, S [gas] Mobil/dsl [food] Domino's, McDonald's, Subway [lodging] Budget Lodge, Super 8 [other] $General, Country Mart Foods, NAPA, Save-A-Lot Foods, USPO

239 MO 30, rds AB, WW, St Clair, N [other] repair, S [gas] Phillips 66/dsl

238mm **weigh sta both lanes**

235mm **[RS] both lanes (both lanes left exit), full [handicapped] facilities, litter barrels, petwalk [phone] [picnic] vending**

SULLIVAN

230 Rds W, Stanton, S [gas] Amstar/fireworks [other] KOA, Meramec Caverns Camping (3mi), USPO

226 MO 185 S, Sullivan, N [gas] Flying J/Denny's/dsl/LP/scales/24hr [other] vet, S [gas] Phillips 66/Burger King [food] Applebee's, Arby's, China Buffet, DQ, Imo's Pizza, KFC, McDonald's, Steak'n Shake, Subway, Taco Bell [other] $General, $Tree, Aldi Foods, AutoZone, Lowe's, O'Reilly Parts, same as 225, to Meramec SP, Verizon, Walmart

225 MO 185 N, Rd D, Sullivan, N [gas] Mobil, Phillips 66/dsl [food] Domino's, Du Kum Inn Rest [lodging] Baymont Inn, Best Value Inn, Family Inn, Super 8 [other] Chevrolet/Buick/GMC, Chrysler/Dodge/Jeep, Ford, S [gas] BP/Fas-Trip/dsl/café, ZX [food] Cracker Barrel, El Nopal Mexican, Jack-in-the-Box, Lion's Choice, Pizza Hut [lodging] Comfort Inn [other] [H], AT&T, city park, same as 226

218 Rds N, C, J, Bourbon, N [gas] ZX/dsl [lodging] Budget Inn, S [gas] Mobil/dsl [food] Planet Sub, Subway [other] $General, Blue Sprgs Camping (6mi), Bourbon RV Ctr, Riverview Ranch Camping (8mi), Town&Country Mkt

214 Rd H, Leasburg, N [gas] Mobil/dsl, S [food] Skippy's Rte 66 Rest. [other] to Onandaga Cave SP (7mi)

210 Rd UU, N [other] Meremac Valley Resort, S [food] MO Hick BBQ (2mi) [other] winery

CUBA

208 MO 19, Cuba, N [gas] Midwest/Phillips 66/Dotty's Rest./dsl/scales/24hr/ @ [food] Country Kitchen, Huddle House, Pizza Hut [lodging] EconoLodge, Super 8 [other] antiques, Blue Beacon, S [gas] Casey's, Mobil [food] East Sun Chinese, Hardee's, Jack-in-the-Box, McDonald's, Sonic, Subway [lodging] Chateau Inn [other] $General, Mace Foods, O'Reilly Parts, to Ozark Nat Scenic Riverways, Walmart

203 Rds F, ZZ, N [other] Ladybug RV Park, S [other] Rosatti Winery (2mi)

195 MO 8, MO 68, St James, Maramec Sprg Park, N [gas] BP/Circle K/dsl, Mobil/dsl [food] China King, McDonald's, Pizza Hut, Sonic, Subway [lodging] Economy Inn, Greenstay Inn [other] $General, Ford, O'Reilly Parts, Ray's Tires, to Maremac Winery, tours ctr, S [gas] Delano/dsl, Phillips 66/dsl [food] Burger King [lodging] Finn's Motel [other] CountryMart Foods

189 Rd V, Industrial Park Dr, Hypoint, N [gas] Loves/McDonald's/Subway/dsl/scales/24hr, S [other] Mule Trading Post

ROLLA

186 US 63, MO 72, Rolla, N [gas] Sinclair [food] Steak'n Shake [lodging] Drury Inn, Hampton Inn, Sooter Inn [other] Big O Tire, Kia, Kohl's, Lowe's, Nissan, Plaza Tire, S [gas] Mobil/dsl, Phillips 66 [food] Buffalo Wild Wings, Colton's Steaks, Donut King, Koi Chinese, Lee's Chicken, Panera Bread [lodging] Budget Motel [other] [H]

185 Rd E, to Rolla, N [other] hwy patrol, S [gas] Delano [food] Arby's, DQ, Gordoz Steaks, Hardee's, Huddle House, Jimmy John's, Kyoto Japanese, LJ Silver, Papa John's, Subway, Taco Bell, Wendy's [other] [H], CVS Drug, Ford, Kroger, UMO at Rolla

184 US 63 S, to Rolla, N [lodging] Comfort Suites, Holiday Inn Express, S [gas] Delano, MotoMart, Route 66 [food] Arby's, Bandana's BBQ, Burger King, Denny's, Little Caesars, LJ Silver, Los Cazadores, Lucky House Chinese, Maid-Rite, McDonald's, Penelope's Rest., Pizza Hut, Pizza Inn, Sirloin Stockade, Waffle House, Wendy's [lodging] Baymont Inn, Best Way Inn, Best Western, Days Inn, EconoLodge, Quality Inn, Sunset Inn, Super 8 [other] [H], Buick/Cadillac/GMC, Chevrolet, city park, CVS Drug, Kroger

179 Rds T, C, to Doolittle, Newburg, S [gas] Phillips 66/dsl [food] Cookin' From Scratch Rest. [other] $General

178mm **truck parking both lanes, restrooms,**

176 Sugar Tree Rd, S [lodging] Vernelle's Motel [other] Arlington River Resort Camping (2mi)

172 Rd D, Jerome, N [other] camping

169 Rd J

166 to Big Piney

164mm Big Piney River

163 MO 28, to Dixon, N [gas] Pilot/Road Ranger/Chesters/Subway/dsl/scales/24hr, S [gas] Phillips 66/dsl [food] Country Café, Sweetwater BBQ [lodging] Best Western, Country Hearth Inn, Days Inn [other] RV Park, Uranus Fudge a Factory

161b a Rd Y, to Ft Leonard Wood, N [gas] Mobil/dsl, Shell/dsl [food] Aussie Jack's, Cracker Barrel, Denny's, Domino's, Mama Mia Diner, Ocean Buffet, Papa Murphy's, Pizza Hut, Rte 66 Diner, Ruby Tuesday, Wendy's [lodging] Baymont Inn, Best Value Inn, Candlewood Suites, Comfort Inn, Fairfield Inn, Hampton Inn, Howard Johnson, Mainstay Suites, Red Roof Inn [other] AT&T, Kwik Kar, Lowe's, Toyota/Scion, visitors ctr, Walmart/Subway, S [gas] Cenex/dsl, Kum&Go/dsl [food] Arby's, Buffalo Wild Wings, Cantina Bravo, Colton's Steaks, Culver's, Hardee's, Little Caesar's, McDonald's, Panera Bread, Papa John's, Subway, Taco Bell, Waffle House [lodging] Budget Inn, EconoLodge, Holiday Inn Express, Liberty Lodge, Motel 6, Quality Inn, ZLoft Hotel [other] $General, $Tree, AutoZone, Chrysler/Dodge/Jeep, Family$, Ford/Lincoln, Mazda, NAPA, O'Reilly Parts, Verizon

159 Lp 44, to Waynesville, St Robert, N [gas] Road Star/dsl [food] DQ, Sonic [lodging] All Star Motel, Super 8 [other] auto repair, O'Reilly Parts, S [gas] Cenex/dsl [food] Don Jose [lodging] Alliance Inn [other] Big O Tire, Cadillac/GMC

INTERSTATE 44 Cont'd

Exit #	Services
158mm	Roubidoux Creek
156	Rd H, Waynesville, N BP, Express Stop/dsl/E-85, Kum&Go/dsl McDonald's, Subway $General, Chevrolet, Price Cutter+
153	MO 17, to Buckhorn, N Ft Wood Inn, S Shell/dsl Glen Oaks RV Park
150	MO 7, Rd P to Richland, S Roadhouse Steaks
145	MO 133, Rd AB, to Richland, N Sinclair/Oasis/cafe/dsl/24hr, S camping
143mm	Gasconade River
140	Rd N, to Stoutland, S Cenex/pizza/dsl
139mm	Bear Creek
135	Rd F, Sleeper
130	Rd MM, N Casey's /dsl, Conoco/dsl Angie's Place EconoLodge, Munger Moss Inn, S Kum&Go H
129	MO 5, MO 32, MO 64, to Hartville, Lebanon, N Applebee's, Arby's, Bamboo Garden, Bandana's BBQ, Burger King, DQ, Elm St Eatery, KFC, Little Caesars, LJ Silver, McDonald's, Papa Murphy's, Sonic, Steak'n Shake, Subway, Taco Bell, Wendy's Aldi Foods, AT&T, AutoZone, Chevrolet, Ford, O'Reilly Parts, repair, Rte 66 Museum, Smitty's Foods, to Bennett Sprgs SP, to Lake of the Ozarks, Verizon, Walgreens, Walnut Bowl Factory, S Conoco/dsl, Phillips 66/dsl Capt D's, Domino's, Hardee's, La Tolteca, Pizza Hut, T's Steaks H, $Tree, Lowe's, O'Reilly Parts, Sawyer Tire/auto, Walmart/Subway
127	Lp 44, Lebanon, N B&D/J Diner/dsl/scales/24hr, Phillips 66/dsl Dowd's Catfish&BBQ, El Sombrero Mexican, Great Wall Chinese, Subway, Waffle House Best Value Inn, Days Inn, Hampton Inn, Holiday Inn Express, Midwest Inn, Rte 66 Motel, Super 8 $General, Chrysler/Dodge/Jeep, Cutlery/Walnut Bowl Outlet, Firestone/auto, S Conoco/McDonald's/dsl Dickey's BBQ Buick/Cadillac/GMC, Harley-Davidson, Russell Stover
123	County Rd, S antiques, Happy Trails RV Ctr, Happy Trails RV Park
118	Rds C, A, Phillipsburg, S Phillips 66 Redmond's Gifts, tourist info
113	Rds J, Y, Conway, N Conoco/dsl Rockin Chair Café Budget Inn to Den of Metal Arts, S Sinclair/dsl $General, SummerFresh Foods, USPO
111mm	**both lanes, full facilities, litter barrels, petwalk playground, vending**
108mm	Bowen Creek
107	Sparkle Brooke Rd, Sampson Rd
106mm	Niangua River
100	MO 38, Rd W, Marshfield, N Murphy USA/dsl, Phillips 66 $Tree, auto repair, Chevrolet, Chrysler/Dodge/Jeep, Ford, Walmart/Subway, S Casey's/dsl, Conoco/dsl, Phillips 66/dsl DQ, El Charro, Golden China, Grillos Cafe, KFC/Rib Crib, McDonald's, Pizza Hut, Sonic, Subway, Taco Bell Holiday Inn Express $General, AutoZone, O'Reilly Parts, RV Express RV Park, Verizon, Walgreens
96	Rd B, Northview, N Paradise RV Park (2mi)
89mm	**weigh sta both lanes**
88	MO 125, to Fair Grove, Strafford, N Loves/Hardee's/dsl/scales/rv dump/24hr, TA/Subway/Taco Bell/dsl/scales/24hr/@ McDonald's Camping World RV Ctr, truckwash, S Breaktime/dsl, Kum&Go Fox's Pizza, Pizza Hut Super 8 $General, Strafford RV Park
84	MO 744, S Peterbilt

MARSHFIELD

MO

SPRINGFIELD

Exit #	Services
82b a	US 65, to Branson, Fedalia, S Kum&Go/dsl, Phillips 66/dsl Waffle House Bull Shoals Lake, Kenworth, st patrol, to Table Rock Lake
80b a	Rd H to Pleasant Hope, Springfield, N Conoco/rest./dsl/24hr, Kum&Go/dsl, Sinclair Waffle House Days Inn, Microtel, Super 8 $General, S Casey's, Kum&Go/dsl, Phillips 66/Circle K/dsl, Shell Andy's Custard, Applebee's, Bob Evans, Braum's, Buckingham BBQ, Cracker Barrel, Culver's, El Maguey Mexican, Fazoli's, Hardee's, Hong Kong Inn, Houlihan's, Ichiban Buffet, Jade East Chinese, Jose Locos, Little Tokyo, Little Tokyo, LJ Silver, McDonald's, Panda Express, Pizza Hut, Rib Crib, Royal Buffet, Ruby Tuesday, Schlotzsky's, Shanghai Inn, Sonic, Steak'n Shake, Subway, Taco Bell, Whole Hog Cafe, Ziggies Cafe Best Value Inn, Best Western, Budget Inn, Candlewood Suites, Comfort Inn, Dogwood Park Inn, Doubletree Hotel, Drury Inn, EconoLodge, Economy Inn, Flagship Motel, Hampton Inn, Holiday Inn, La Quinta, Lamplighter Hotel, Ozark Inn, Plaza Inn, Quality Inn, Ramada, Rancho Motel H, Aldi Foods, AutoZone, Big O Tire, K-Mart, O'Reilly Parts, PriceCutter Foods, Tire Express, U-Haul, Walmart/Subway
77	MO 13, KS Expswy, N Kum&Go/dsl/e-85 Lowe's, S Casey's/dsl, Phillips 66/dsl Arby's, Braum's, Buffalo Wild Wings, Chuckwagon BBQ, El Charro, Five Guys, Golden Corral, Goodcents, IHOP, Jimmy John's, McAlister's Deli, McDonald's, Moe's SW Grill, New China, Panera Bread, Papa John's, Papa Murphy's, Pizza Inn, Subway, Taco Bell, Waffle House $Tree, AT&T, BigLots, Drug Mart, GNC, Goodyear/auto, Hobby Lobby, PriceCutter Foods, Staples, Verizon, Walgreens, Walmart
75	US 160 W byp, to Willard, Stockton Lake, S Kum&Go/dsl Wendy's Courtyard, La Quinta
72	MO 266, to Chesnut Expwy, **1-2 mi** S Casey's, Cenex, Kum&Go/dsl Alli's Rest., Arby's, China Wok, Hardee's, KFC, LJ Silver, McDonald's, Plaza Mexico, Sonic, Subway, Taco Bell, Taco Bueno, Waffle House Best Budget Inn, Best Western, Redwood Motel $General, AutoZone, city park, PriceCutter Foods
70	Rds MM, B, N fireworks, S KOA (1mi), Wilson's Creek Nat Bfd (5mi)
69	to US 60, Springfield
67	Rds N, T, Bois D' Arc, to Republic, S Conoco/dsl AmericInn (5mi) art glass
66mm	Pond Creek
64.6mm	Dry Branch
64.5mm	Pickerel Creek
61	Rds K, PP, N Cenex/Hoods/dsl/scales/LP/24hr, Phillips 66 Hood I-44 Motel
58	MO 96, Rds O, Z, to Carthage, Halltown, S Shell/dsl truck repair

= gas = food = lodging = other = rest stop

MO

INTERSTATE 44 Cont'd

Exit #	Services
57	to Rd PP (from wb)
56.5mm	Turnback Creek
56mm	Goose Creek
52.5mm	**truck parking both lanes**
49	MO 174E, Rd CCW, Chesapeake
46	MO 39, MO 265, Mt Vernon, Aurora, N Casey's/dsl, Gulf/dsl, Kum&Go/dsl, TA/Conoco/46Diner/dsl/scales/24hr/ @ Bamboo Garden Chinese, El Azteca Mexican, KFC/LJ Silver, Mazzio's, McDonald's, Pizza Hut, Sonic, Subway, Taco Bell Best Western, USA Inn $General, Family$, O'Reilly Parts, PriceCutter Foods, True Value, S Conoco/dsl Best Value Inn to Table Rock Lake
44	Rd H, to Monett, Mt Vernon, N Subway (1mi) Mid-America Dental/Hearing, Walmart
43.5mm	Spring River
38	MO 97, to Stotts City, Pierce City, N gas/dsl/repair/tires, S U of MO SW Ctr (4mi)
33	MO 97 S, to Pierce City, S Hungry House Cafe
29	Rd U, to La Russell, Sarcoxie, N antiques, Beagle Bay RV Camping, OzarkLand Gifts, S Casey's (1mi), Kum&Go/Subway/dsl antiques
29mm	Center Creek
26	MO 37, to Reeds, Sarcoxie, N Bill's Truck/trailer repair
22	Rd 100 N, N Colaw RV Ctr, S Consignment RV Sales
21mm	Jones Creek
18b a	I-49 N, US 71 N, MO 59 S, to Carthage, Neosho, N Coachlight RV Ctr/Camping
15	MO 66 W, Lp 44 (from wb), Joplin, N Tara Motel
15mm	Grove Creek
14mm	Turkey Creek
13	Prigmore Ave
11b a	I-49 S, US 71 S, MO 249 N, to Neosho, Ft Smith, S FLYING J/Denny's/dsl/LP/scales/24hr/ @, Goodyear Tires/repair, Speedco Blue Beacon, Kenworth
8b a	US 71, to Neosho, Joplin, N Conoco/dsl, Kum&Go/dsl, Phillips 66/dsl Andy's Custard, Applebee's, Arby's, Billy Sims BBQ, Bob Evans, Braum's, Buffalo Wild Wings, Carino's Italian, Casa Montez Mexican, Cheddar's, Chick-fil-A, Chipotle, ChuckeCheese, CiCi's, Denny's, Domino's, El Vallarta Mexican, Firehouse Subs, Five Guys, Freddy's, Garfield's, Golden Corral, Golden Dragon, Hardee's, HuHot, IHOP, Jim Bob's Steaks, Jimmy John's, Jimmy's Egg, King Palace, Logan's Roadhouse, Longhorn Steaks, McAlister's, McDonald's, Noodle&Grill, Ocean Rest., Olive Garden, Outback Steaks, Panda Express, Pitcher's Grill, Pizza Hut, Popeye's, Qdoba, Red Hot&Blue Grill, Red Lobster, Rib Crib, Ruby Tuesday, Schlotzsky's, Sonic, Starbucks, Steak'n Shake, Subway, Taco Bell, TX Roadhouse, Waffle House, Wasab Steaks, Wendy's Baymont Inn, Best Western, Candlewood Suites, Comfort Inn, Days Inn, Drury Inn, Fairfield Inn, Hampton Inn, Hilton Garden, Homewood Suites, Joplin Hotel, La Quinta, Motel 6, Quality Inn, Residence Inn, Sunrise Inn, Super 8 $Tree, Aldi Foods, AT&T, AutoZone, Best Buy, Books-A-Million, Chrysler/Dodge/Jeep, Discount Tire, Firestone/auto, Food4Less, Ford/Lincoln, Freightliner, Goodyear/auto, Hobby Lobby, Home Depot, Honda, Hyundai, JC Penney, Jo-Ann Fabrics, Kia, Kohl's, Lowe's, Macy's, Mercedes, Michael's, Nissan, Office Depot, O'Reilly Parts, Petsmart, Ross, Sam's Club/gas, Target, TJ Maxx, Toyota/Scion, Verizon, Walgreens, Walmart/Subway, S Casey's Cracker Barrel, Fazoli's Microtel, TownePlace Suites vet, Wheelen RV Ctr
6	MO 86, MO 43 N, to Racine, Joplin, N Phillips 66 Moe's SW Grill, Schlotzsky's CVS Drug, Walgreens, S H, Harley-Davidson
5.5mm	Shoal Creek
4	MO 43 to Seneca, N Loves/Hardee's/dsl/scales/24hr, S Conoco/Subway/dsl, Petro/Iron Skillet/Pizza Hut/Taco Bell/dsl/scales/24hr/ @, Pilot/Wendy's/dsl/scales/24hr McDonald's Sleep Inn $General, fireworks, IA 80 Truckomat, KOA
3mm	**weigh sta both lanes**
2mm	**Welcome Ctr eb, truck parking wb, full facilities, litter barrels, restrooms vending**
1	US 400, US 166W, to Baxter Springs, KS, N Downstream/dsl Downstream Casino/RV Park, Downstream RV Park, S Sandstone Gardens
0mm	Missouri/Oklahoma state line

J O P L I N

INTERSTATE 49

Exit #	Services
184	I-435, I-470.
	I-49 begins/ends, continues N as US 71.
182	Red Bridge Rd, Longview Rd, E Phillips 66/dsl McDonald's auto repair, W 7-11, BP/dsl ValuePlace Inn
181	Blue Ridge Blvd, E Shell/dsl Church's Best Value Inn NAPA, U-Haul, W Applebee's, Arby's, Goodcents Subs, IHOP, KFC, Papa John's, Pizza Hut, Wendy's $Tree, Advance Parts, AutoZone, Burlington Coats, CVS, GNC, Price Chopper, Tires+, TrueValue
180	(from sb), same as 181 W, W Jerry's Auto Repair
179	Main St, E Conoco Burger King, Capestre Mexican, Capt D's, Little Caesar's, Popeye's, Providence Pizzeria $General, Firestone/auto, Holiday Inn Express, to Longview Lake CP, W Phillips 66/dsl Taco Bell, TJ's Cafe, Waffle House transmissions, USPO, Walgreens
178	140th St, W Phillips 66/dsl
177	MO 150, E QT/dsl, Shell/dsl Sonic, Subway Harley Davidson
176	155th St, to Belton, W Conoco Domino's
175	Rd Y, 163rd St, Belton, E Hampton Inn, W Conoco/dsl, QT/dsl Pizza Hut, Taco Bueno H, AutoZone, CVS, Menards, O'Reilly Parts, Price Chopper
174	MO 58, Belton, E QT, Shell/dsl Burger King, Church's, Golden Corral, KFC, Papa John's, Pizza Hut, Ryan's, Steak'n Shake, Taco Bell, Waffle House, Wendy's Comfort Inn Advance Parts, AT&T, Chrysler/Dodge/Jeep, Firestone/auto, H, Lowe's, NTB, Radio Shack, Sam's Club/dsl, Walmart/Subway, W A&W/LJ Silver, Applebee's, Arby's, Bob Evans, Buffalo Wild Wings, Chipotle, IHOP, Jimmy John's, Jose Pepper's, Little Caesar's, Longhorn Steaks, McDonald's, New China, Papa Murphy's, Pepper Jax Cafe, Ruby Tuesday, Starbucks, Subway EconoLodge $Tree, Aldi Foods, Discount Tire, Express Auto Service, GNC, Home Depot, HyVee/dsl, Jo-Ann, Kohl's, Petsmart, Target, Verizon, Walgreens
172	N Cass Pkwy
167	MO C, J, Peculiar, E Casey's, FLYING J/Denny's/dsl/Lp/scales/24hr Subway Peculiar RV Park, W Sonic CountryMart/dsl, USPO
160	MO 291 N, Harrisonville, E Casey's/dsl, Murphy USA, QT/dsl Applebee's, Arby's, Baskin Robbins, Bonsai Grill, Branding Iron BBQ, Capt D's, El Mezcal Mexican, Hardee's, KFC, McDonald's, Subway, Sunrise Chinese, Taco Bell, Wendy's

B E L T O N

INTERSTATE 49 Cont'd

HARRISONVILLE

Exit	Services
160	Continued [lodging] Caravan Motel, Harrisonville Inn [other] $Tree, GNC, [H], vet, Walmart, W [other] Ford, [lodging] Best Value Inn
159	MO 2 W, 7 N, Mechanic St, Harrisonville, E [gas] BP, Phillips 66/dsl [food] Burger King, China Wok, DQ, Jimmy John's, Papa Murphy's, Pizza Hut, Starbucks [other] Advance Parts, AT&T, CVS, DLS Tire/auto, Price Chopper, Verizon, vet, Walgreens
158	MO 2 E, Commercial Blvd, Harrisonville, E [gas] Conoco/dsl, Phillips 66 [food] Best Burrito [lodging] Comfort Inn [other] Russell Stover, Sutherland's
157mm	**weigh sta both lanes**
157	MO 7 S, to Clinton, E [other] [airport], W [gas] BP/dsl, Phillips 66 [lodging] Slumber Inn
153	307th St
148mm	S Grand River
147	MO A, B, Archie, Drexel, W [gas] Conoco/dsl, Phillips 66 [food] Mama's Kitchen
144	MO E, AA, Crescent Hill
141	MO 18, Adrian, to Clinton, W [gas] Casey's/dsl, Phillips 66/dsl [food] Old 71 Cafe [other] $General, NAPA
136	Rds D, F, Passaic, to Butler, W [other] McBee's Bratwurst/BBQ
131	MO 52 W, Butler, Amoret, E [gas] Conoco [food] McDonald's, Pizza Hut, Sonic, Subway, Taco Bell [lodging] Days Inn, Super 8 [other] $General, Chrysler/Dodge/Jeep/Ford, CountryMart, [H], Walmart, W [food] El Charro
130	US 71 Bus (from nb), to Butler
129	MO 52 E, Appleton City
120	Rds B, A, Rich Hill, to Osceola, W [gas] Phillips 66/dsl [food] Swope's Drive In [other] $General, Food Fair Mkt/drug
116	Rd TT, to Panama
112	Horton, W [other] Farm Mkt
110	Rd D, Stotesbury
107	Rd M, Compton Jct
103	Highland Ave, to Nevada, W [food] Breakfast Cafe [other] $General, Buick/Chevrolet/GMC, Osage Prairie RV Park
102b	49 Bus, W [other] same as 103

NEVADA

Exit	Services
102a	US 54, Nevada, to El Dorado Springs, W [gas] MFA/dsl/e85 [food] 54 Cafe, Rodeo Grill [other] Centennial Park, Highly Tires
101	Rd K, Nevada, to Camp Clark, E [gas] Conoco/dsl, W [gas] Hot Spot/dsl, Murphy USA/dsl, Pilot/dsl/scales/24hr [food] Burger King, Buzz's BBQ, Chinese Chef, Pizza Hut, Sonic, Subway [lodging] Best Value Inn, Country Inn&Suites, Holiday Inn Express, Nevada Inn, Super 8 [other] AutoZone, Chrysler/Dodge/Jeep/Ford, Verizon, Walmart/Subway, Wilson Tire
95	Rd E, Milo
91	Rds DD, BB, to Bellamy
88	Rds B, N, Sheldon, Bronaugh, E [other] to Stockton Lake (33 mi)
83	Rds C, V, Irwin
80	Rds EE, DD
77	US 160, Lamar, Mindenmines, E [gas] Phillips 66, Sinclair/dsl/scales/24hr [food] Bamboo House, KFC/Taco Bell, McDonald's, Pizza Hut, Sonic, Subway, Taco Palace [lodging] Blue Top Inn, Super 8 [other] $General, Blue Top Quiltshop, Family$, O'Reilly Parts, truck/trailer/tire repair, truckwash, W [gas] Conoco/Roady's/dsl, Murphy USA/dsl [food] DQ [other] [H], Lamar Truck/tire, Walmart
74	30th Rd
70	MO 126, Golden City, Pittsburg
66	Rds K, H, Jasper, W [gas] Conoco/dsl, Judy's Trkstp/Cafe/dsl [other] $General
63	Rds N, M
56	Garrison Ave (from sb), to Carthage, E [lodging] Best Inn (2 mi)
55	Civil War Rd, to Carthage

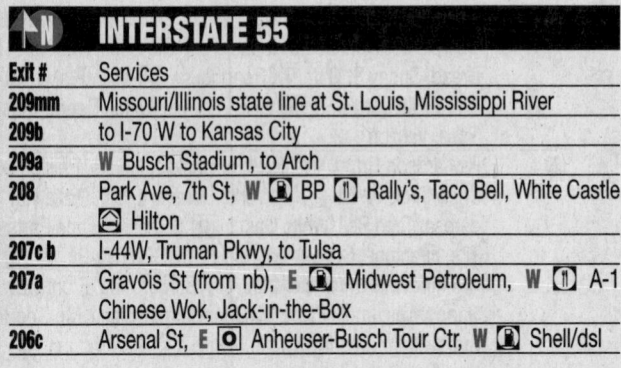

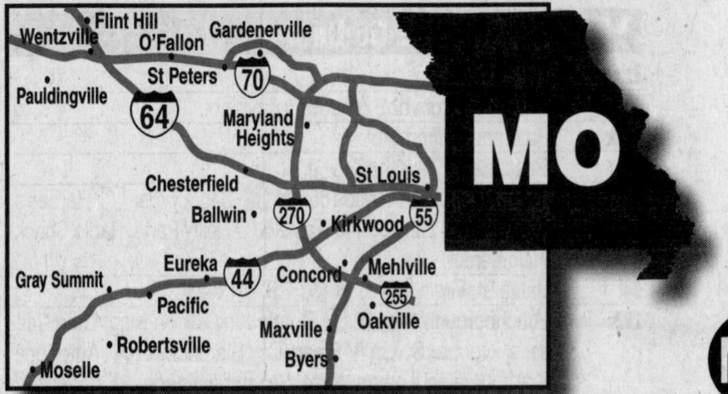

CARTHAGE

Exit	Services
53	MO 571 S, MO 96, MO 171 N, Central Ave, Carthage, E [gas] Casey's/dsl, Phillips 66/dsl [food] Arby's, Boomer's BBQ, Burger King, LJ Silver, McDonald's, Sirloin Stockade, Sonic, Subway [lodging] EconoLodge [other] $General, Price Cutter
51	Fairview Ave, to Carthage
50	Rd HH, Fir Rd, E [gas] Murphy USA, Phillips 66/McDonald's/dsl [food] Big Ben's BBQ, Hardee's, Iggy's Diner, Little Caesar's, Shakes Custard, Taco Bell, Wendy's [lodging] Best Western, Super 8 [other] $General, $Tree, Aldi Foods, Chrysler/Dodge/Jeep, Ford, Lowe's, Walgreens, Walmart/Subway, W [other] [H]
49	MO 571, Garrison Ave, to Carthage (from nb)
47	Cedar Rd, W [other] Coachlight RV Ctr/Park, Mid America RV Ctr
46mm	I-44, E to Springfield, W to Joplin. **I-49 and I-44 run together 7 mi. See I-44, exit 15.**
39b	I-44, E to Springfield, W to Joplin. **I-49 and I-44 run together 7 mi. See I-44, exit 15.**
39a	Rd FF, 32nd St, E [other] Kenworth, W [gas] FLYING J/Denny's/dsl/LP/scales/24hr [other] Blue Beacon, Goodyear Tires/repair, Speedco
35	Rd V, Diamond, E [other] G Washington Carver NM
33	MO 175, Gateway Dr, W [gas] Phillips 66/dsl/deli [other] Shoal Creek RV Park
30	Iris Rd
27	MO 86, to Neosho, Racine, E [gas] Love's/McDonald's/Subway/dsl/scales/24hr, Phillips 66/dsl
24	US 60, to Neosho, Seneca, E [gas] Kum&Go/dsl/e85, Murphy USA [food] Burger King, Denny's, El Charro, KFC, LJ Silver, Taco Bell [lodging] Best Western, Super 8 [other] $Tree, Lowe's, Verizon, Walmart, W [other] Whispering Woods RV Park (12 mi)
20	Rd AA
17	Rds C, B, to Goodman, E [other] truck repair
16	MO 59 (from sb), Kelley Springs
10	MO 76, to Anderson, W [gas] Conoco/Subway/dsl [lodging] EconoLodge
7	Rd EE, to Pineville, Lanagan
5	Rd H, to Pineville.

I-49 begins/ends, US 71 continues S, W [other] Bib Elk Camping (1 mi)

INTERSTATE 55

ST LOUIS

Exit #	Services
209mm	Missouri/Illinois state line at St. Louis, Mississippi River
209b	to I-70 W to Kansas City
209a	W Busch Stadium, to Arch
208	Park Ave, 7th St, W [gas] BP [food] Rally's, Taco Bell, White Castle [lodging] Hilton
207c b	I-44W, Truman Pkwy, to Tulsa
207a	Gravois St (from nb), E [gas] Midwest Petroleum, W [food] A-1 Chinese Wok, Jack-in-the-Box
206c	Arsenal St, E [other] Anheuser-Busch Tour Ctr, W [gas] Shell/dsl

INTERSTATE 55 Cont'd

Exit #	Services
206b	Broadway (from nb), Broadway (from nb)
206a	Potomac St (from nb)
205	Gasconade, W 🅾 hospital
204	Broadway, E 🅶 Phillips 66, W 🅶 Conoco/dsl 🍴 Hardee's, McDonald's, Subway 🅾 Family$, O'Reilly Parts, Radio Shack, Walgreens
203	Bates St, Virginia Ave, W 🅶 BP 🅾 7-11
202c	Loughborough Ave, W 🍴 Burger King, China King, Little Caesar's, Qdoba, St Louis Bread Co, Starbucks 🅾 AutoZone, Firestone/auto, Lowe's Whse, Schnuck's Foods
202b	Germania (from sb)
202a	Carondelet (from nb), Carondelet (from nb)
201b	Weber Rd
201a	Bayless Ave, E 🅶 BP 🍴 McDonald's, W 🅶 7-11/gas, Mobil/dsl 🍴 DQ, Jack-in-the-Box, Subway, Taco Bell 🅾 auto repair
200	Union Rd (from sb)
199	Reavis Barracks Rd, E 🅶 Shell/Circle K 🍴 STL BBQ 🅾 Hancock Fabrics
197	US 50, US 61, US 67, Lindbergh Blvd, E 🅶 Phillips 66 🍴 Applebee's, Arby's, Buffalo Wild Wings, ChuckeCheese, CiCi's, Dillard's, Hometown Buffet, HoneyBaked Ham, Hooters, IHOP, Imo's Pizza, KFC, Krispy Kreme, McAlister's, Noodles&Co, Penn Sta Subs, Qdoba, Starbucks, Steak'n Shake, Subway, Taco Bell, Tucker's Place, Wendy's 🛏 Holiday Inn 🅾 AT&T, Best Buy, Chrysler/Dodge/Jeep, CVS Drug, Dick's, Dobbs Tire, Ford/Lincoln, Home Depot, JC Penney, Jo-Ann Fabrics, K-Mart, Macy's, mall, Marshall's, NTB, Sears/auto, Verizon, vet, W 🅶 QT/dsl 🍴 Bob Evans, Culvers, Denny's, Golden Corral, O'Charley's, Panda Express, Pasta House 🛏 Best Value Inn 🅾 Aldi Foods, AT&T, CarMax, Chevrolet, Costco/gas, Honda, Hyundai, Kia, Mazda, Nissan, Target, VW
196b	I-270 W, to Kansas City
196a	I-255 E, to Chicago
195	Butler Hill Rd, E 🅶 Phillips 66 🛏 Hampton Inn 🅾 Advance Parts, Walgreens, W 🅶 Phillips 66 🍴 Burger King, Hardee's, Subway, Taco Bell, Waffle House 🅾 Schnuck's Foods, tires/repair
193	Meramec Bottom Rd, E 🅶 QT/dsl 🍴 Cracker Barrel 🛏 Best Western 🅾 Midwest RV Ctr
191	MO 141, Arnold, E 🅶 QT 🍴 54th St Grill, Applebee's, Arby's, Bandana's BBQ, Capt D's, Chick-fil-A, China King, Denny's, Dunkin Donuts/Baskin Robbins, Fazoli's, Five Guys, Jack-in-the-Box, Jimmy John's, Las Fuentes, Lee's Chicken, Lion's Choice, LJ Silver, McDonald's, Panda Express, Papa John's, Rally's, Starbucks, Steak'n Shake, Super China Buffet, Taco Bell, Terrazza Grill, Wendy's 🛏 Drury Inn, Pear Tree Inn 🅾 Aldi Foods, AT&T, CVS Drug, Dobbs Tire, Gordman's, Hobby Lobby, Kohl's, NAPA, O'Reilly Parts, PetCo, Shop'n Save Foods, vet, Walgreens, Walmart/Subway, W 🅶 Phillips 66/Circle K/dsl 🍴 Chili's, First Wok, Pasta House, Penn Sta Subs, Qdoba, St Louis Bread, Sunny St Cafe, TX Roadhouse 🛏 ValuePlace Hotel 🅾 $Tree, Dierberg's Foods, GNC, Lowe's, Office Depot, Petsmart, Ross, Verizon
190	Richardson Rd, E 🅶 BP/McDonald's, Hucks, Phillips 66/dsl, Shell/Circle K/dsl 🍴 Culver's, Domino's, DQ, Pizza Hut, Ponderosa, Taco Bell, White Castle 🅾 $Tree, Advance Parts, Auto Tire, Firestone, Save-A-Lot Foods, URGENT CARE, W 🅶 Phillips 66/dsl, Shell/Circle K/dsl 🍴 Burger King, Front Row Grill, Happy Wok, Imo's Pizza, McDonald's/playplace, Mr. Goodcents Subs, Ruby Tuesday, Waffle House 🛏 Comfort Inn 🅾 7-11,

190	Continued
	Aamco, AutoZone, GNC, Home Depot, Plaza Tire, Radio Shac, Schnuck's Foods, Target, Walgreens
186	Imperial, Kimmswick, E 🅶 Mobil, Shell/Circle K 🍴 Big Car BBQ, Blue Owl (1mi) 🅾 auto repair, W 🍴 Phillips 66/Jac in-the-Box/dsl 🍴 China Wok, Domino's, Ginono's Grill, Pa John's, Scottie's Grill, Subway 🅾 to Mastodon SP, USPO
185	Rd M, Barnhart, Antonia, W 🅶 Phillips 66, Phillips 66/c 🅾 Karsch's Mkt, USPO, Walgreens
184.5mm	weigh sta both lanes
180	Rd Z, to Hillsboro, Pevely, E 🅶 Mobil/dsl 🍴 Burger Kin Domino's, Main St BBQ, Pizza Hut, Subway, Taco Bell $General, Queens Foods; W 🅶 Mr Fuel/dsl, Phillips 66/M Donald's/dsl/scales 🛏 Super 8 🅾 auto repair, rv camping
178	Herculaneum, E 🅶 QT/Wendy's/dsl/scales, Shell/Circle K Cracker Barrel, DQ, Jack-in-the-Box, La Pachanga Mexica Subway 🅾 Toyota/Scion, W 🅾 Buick/GMC, Cadillac/Che rolet, Ford, vet
175	Rd A, Festus, E 🅶 Mobil, Murphy USA/dsl, Phillips 66/d 🍴 Arby's, Bob Evans, Burger King, Capt D's, China 1, Fazoli* Hibachi Grill, Imo's Pizza, Jack-in-the-Box, McDonald's/pla place, Oriental Buffet, Panda Express, Papa John's, Sonic, S Louis Bread Co, Steak'n Shake, Subway, Taco Bell, Tanglefo Steaks, White Castle 🛏 Drury Inn, Lexington 🅾 $Tree, Ad vance Parts, Aldi Foods, AT&T, AutoZone, CVS Drug, Dobb Tire, GNC, Home Depot, K-Mart, Plaza Tire, Radio Shac Schnuck's Foods/gas, URGENT CARE, Walgreens, Walmar W 🅶 7-11/dsl, Phillips 66/Domino's/dsl 🍴 Hardee's, Jin my John's, Ruby Tuesday, Waffle House, Whittaker's Pizz 🛏 Comfort Inn, Holiday Inn Express 🅾 Chrysler/Dodge/Jee Lowe's
174b a	US 67, Lp 55, Festus, Crystal City, E 🅶 Phillips 66/dsl 🅾 hospital
170	US 61, W 🅶 BP/dsl/LP 🍴 Gators Grill
165	Rd TT (from sb)
162	Rds DD, OO
160mm	🆁🆂 nb/weigh sta sb, full ♿ facilities, litter barrels, petwa 🍴 🖐 vending
157	Rd Y, Bloomsdale, E 🅶 Phillips 66/Subway, W 🅶 ❤Love /Chester's/McDonald's/dsl/scales/24hr
154	Rd O, to St Genevieve
150	MO 32, rds B, A, to St Genevieve, E 🅶 BP 🍴 DQ 🅾 hos pital, Hist Site (6mi), W 🅶 Phillips 66/dsl 🅾 Hawn SP (11m
143	Rds J, M, N, Ozora, W 🅶 Exxon/Subway/dsl/scales/24h 🛏 Econolodge 🅾 truckwash
141	Rd Z, St Mary
135	Rd M, Brewer
129	MO 51, to Perryville, E 🅶 MotoMart/McDonald's/dsl, Phillip 66/dsl 🍴 Burger King, KFC, Ponderosa, Taco Bell 🅾 hospi tal, Ford, W 🅶 Rhodes/dsl 🍴 5 Star Chinese, China Buffe Subway 🛏 Comfort Inn, Days Inn, Super 8 🅾 AT&T, Buick Chevrolet, Chrysler/Dodge/Jeep, Walmart
123	Rd B, Biehle, W 🅶 Rhodes/dsl
119mm	Apple Creek
117	Rd KK, to Appleton, E 🅾 Ron's Grocery
111	Rd E, Oak Ridge
110mm	🆁🆂 both lanes, full ♿ facilities, litter barrels, petwalk 🍴 🖐 vending
105	US 61, Fruitland, E 🅶 Casey's, Phillips 66/dsl, Rhodes/dsl 🅾 $General, Purcell Tires/repair, Trail of Tears SP (11mi), W 🅶 D-Mart/dsl 🍴 Bavarian Halle, DQ, Pizza Inn 🛏 Drury Inn
102	LaSalle Ave, E Main St

MO (side tab)

PERRYVILLE (vertical side text)

INTERSTATE 55 Cont'd

CAPE GIRARDEAU

Exit #	Services
99	US 61, MO 34, to Jackson, E RV camping, W Delmonico's Steaks Comfort Suites Hill Top RV, McDowell South RV Ctr
96	Rd K, to Cape Girardeau, E Phillips 66 Applebee's, Bob Evans, Buffalo Wild Wings, Burger King, Chick-fil-A, China Town, CiCi's Pizza, Cracker Barrel, Daddy's Cheesecake, Denny's, Dexter BBQ, DQ, El Acapulco, Firehouse Subs, Great Wall Chinese, Honey Baked Ham, IHOP, Logan's Roadhouse, O'Charley's, Olive Garden, Panera Bread, Papa Murphy's, Popeye's, Qdoba, Red Lobster, Ruby Tuesday, Ryan's, Starbucks, Steak'n Shake, Subway, Taco Bell, TX Roadhouse, Wendy's Auburn Place, Drury Lodge/rest., Hampton Inn, Holiday Inn Express, PearTree Inn hospital, AT&T, Barnes&Noble, Best Buy, BigLots, CVS Drug, Hancock Fabrics, Hobby Lobby, JC Penney, Macy's, Old Navy, Schnuck's Foods, to SEMSU, Verizon, W Shell McDonald's/playplace, Outback Steaks, Penn Sta Subs, White Castle Drury Suites, Quality Inn $Tree, Chrysler/Dodge/Jeep, Honda, Hyundai, Kohl's, Lowe's, Mazda, Nissan, PetCo, Plaza Tire, Sam's Club, Sears Grand, Staples, Target, TJ Maxx, Toyota, Walmart/Subway
95	MO 74 E, E Mercato/dsl Candlewood Suites URGENT CARE, W Menards
93a b	MO 74 W, Cape Girardeau, E diesel repair
91	Rd AB, to Cape Girardeau, E Rhodes/dsl Staxx Diner Harley-Davidson, tire repair, vet, W airport, Capetown RV Ctr
89	US 61, rds K, M, Scott City, E Rhodes Burger King, Ice Cream Corner, Las Brisas Mexican, Pizza Hut, Pizza Pro, Subway $General, Bob's Foods, Medicap Drug, NAPA, Plaza Tire/auto
80	MO 77, Benton, E Express/dsl, W Exxon/McDonald's/dsl/fireworks Subway antiques, winery (8mi)
69	Rd HH, to Sikeston, Miner, E Peterbilt, W hospital, golf
67	US 60, US 62, Miner, E Breaktime/dsl Best Value Inn, Best Western, Motel 6 Hinton RV Park, **0-2 mi W** Cenex, Hucks, Jasper's Gas, Mobil, QuickCheck Bo's BBQ, Buffalo Wild Wings, Burger King, Dexter BBQ, El Tapatio Mexican, Lambert's Rest., Little Caesars, McDonald's, Papa Murphy's, Pizza Hut, Pizza Inn, Ruby Tuesday, Sergio's Mexican, Sonic, Subway, Taco John's, Wendy's Comfort Inn, Country Hearth Inn, Drury Inn, PearTree Inn, Super 8 hospital, $General, AutoZone, Buick/Chevrolet, Cadillac/GMC, CVS Drug, Family$, Food Giant, Food Giant, Raben Tires, Sikeston Outlets/famous brands, Walgreens
66b	US 60 W, to Poplar Bluff, **3 mi W on US 61/62** Breaktime/E-85 A&W/LJ Silver, Applebee's, Arby's, China Buffet, Colton's Steaks, DQ, El Bracero Mexican, Hardee's, La Ruleta Mexican, McDonald's, Sonic, Taco Bell Days Inn, Holiday Inn Express $Tree, Aldi Foods, AT&T, Chrysler/Dodge/Jeep, Ford/Lincoln, GNC, JC Penney, Lowe's, O'Reilly Parts, Radio Shack, Walmart/Subway
66a	I-57 E, to Chicago, US 60 W
59mm	St Johns Bayou
58	MO 80, Matthews, E TA/Taco Bell/dsl/scales/24hr/ @ to Big Oak Tree SP (24mi), truck repair, W FLYING J/Denny's/dsl/LP/RV dump/scales/24hr, LNG, Loves/Chester's/Subway/dsl/scales/24hr repair
52	Rd P, Kewanee, E Mobil/BJ Trvl Ctr/BBQ/dsl
49	US 61, US 62, New Madrid, E Hunter-Dawson HS (3mi)
44	US 61, US 62, Lp 55, New Madrid, E hist site

MINER

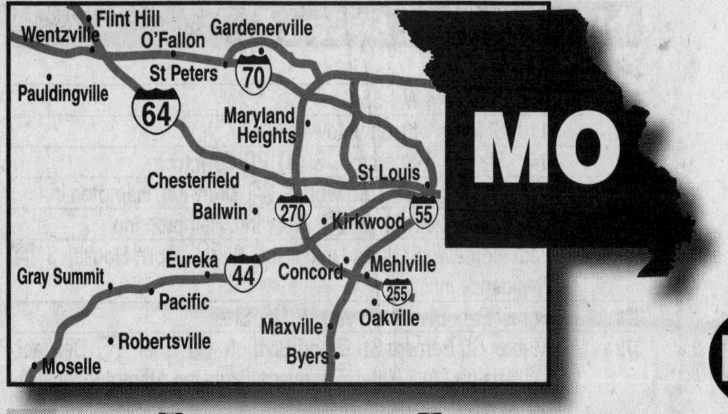

MO

HAYTI

Exit #	Services
42mm	**sb/truck parking nb, full facilities, litter barrels, petwalk restrooms, vending**
40	Rd EE, St Jude Rd, Marston, E Pilot/Subway/dsl/scales/24hr Hunter Lodge, W MFA Moore's Landing Suites
32	US 61, MO 162, Portageville, W Casey's, Phillips 66/dsl China King, McDonald's, Sonic, Subway $General
27	Rds K, A, BB, to Wardell, E RV camping (2mi), W Delta Research Ctr
20mm	**Welcome Ctr sb/ nb, full facilities, info, litter barrels, petwalk vending**
19	MO 84, Hayti, E Double Nickel/dsl, Pilot/Arby's/dsl/scales/24hr, Shell KFC/Taco Bell, McDonald's, Pizza Hut Comfort Inn/rest., M Motel Lady Luck Casino/camping, W BP/dsl, Exxon/Hayti Trvl Ctr/Subway/dsl, R&P/dsl Apple Barrel, Chubby's BBQ, Los Portales, Patty Ann's BBQ Drury Inn hospital, $General, CarQuest, Fred's Store, Hay's Foods, repair, USPO
17b a	I-155 E, US 412, to TN
14	Rds J, H, U, to Caruthersville, Braggadocio
10mm	**weigh sta nb**
8	US 61, MO 164, Steele, E truck repair, W Shell/Subway/dsl/scales Deerfield Inn
4	Rd E, to Holland, Cooter
3mm	**truck parking, restrooms**
1	US 61, Rd O, Holland, W Shell/dsl/24hr
0mm	Missouri/Arkansas state line

INTERSTATE 57

CHARLESTON

Exit #	Services
22mm	Missouri/Illinois state line, Mississippi River
18.5mm	**weigh sta both lanes**
12	US 62, MO 77, Charleston, E FLYING J/Huddle House/dsl/scales/24hr Eagle Inn JSH Towing/repair, W Casey's/dsl Las Brisas Mexican Super 8 vet
10	MO 105, Charleston, E Exxon/Boomland/dsl McDonald's, Wally's Eatery Boomland RV Park, W Casey's China Buffet, Pizza Hut, Subway Quality Inn city park, CountryMart Foods, Plaza Tire
4	Rd B, Bertrand
1b a	I-55, N to St Louis, S to Memphis.

I-57 begins/ends on I-55, exit 66.

INTERSTATE 64

Exit #	Services
41mm	Missouri/Illinois state line, Mississippi River
40b a	Broadway St, to Stadium, to the Arch, N Hilton, Sheraton, stadium, S Dobb's Tire

MO

ST LOUIS

INTERSTATE 64 Cont'd

Exit #	Services
40c	(from wb), I-44 W, I-55 S
39c	11th St (exits left), downtown
39b	14th St, N [lodging] Sheraton, S [gas] BP, downtown
39a	21st St, Market St (from wb), N [lodging] Drury Inn, Hampton Inn
38d	Chestnut at 20th St, N [lodging] Drury Inn, Hampton Inn
38c	Jefferson Ave, St Louis Union Sta, N [other] Joplin House, S [lodging] Residence Inn
38a	Forest Park Blvd (from wb), N [gas] Shell
37b a	Market St, Bernard St, Grand Blvd, N [gas] Shell [food] Del Taco [lodging] Adam's Mark Hotel, Courtyard, Drury Inn, Hampton Inn, Hyatt, Marriott
36d	Vandeventer Ave, Chouteau Ave
36b a	Kingshighway, N [other] [hospital], S [gas] BP
34d c	Hampton Ave, Forest Park, N [other] museums, zoo, S [gas] BP, Mobil, Phillips 66 [food] Courtesy Diner, Hardee's, Imo's Pizza, Jack-in-the-Box, Smokin' Al's BBQ, Steak'n Shake, Subway, Taco Bell [lodging] Hampton Inn
34a	Oakland Ave, N [gas] BP [food] Del Taco, Subway [other] [hospital]
33d	McCausland Ave, N [gas] BP [food] Del Taco
33c	Bellevue Ave, N [other] [hospital]
33b	Big Bend Blvd
32b a	Eager Rd, Hanley Rd, S [gas] Shell [food] Lion's Choice, Macaroni Grill, McDonald's, St Louis Bread Co, Subway [other] Best Buy, Dierberg's Foods, Home Depot, Target, Whole Foods Mkt
31b a	I-170 N, N [gas] Shell [food] Burger King, Dillard's, DQ, IHOP, KFC, Steak'n Shake, TGIFriday [other] mall, S [gas] BP [food] Macaroni Grill, Subway [other] Dierberg's Foods, Goodyear, Target
30	McKnight Rd
28c	Clayton Rd (from wb)
28b a	US 67, US 61, Lindbergh Blvd, S [gas] BP [food] Brio Grill, Fleming's Rest., Schneithouse Rest., Starbucks [lodging] Hilton [other] Honda, mall, Shnuck's Foods
27	Spoede Rd
26	Rd JJ, Ballas Rd, N [other] [hospital], S [other] [hospital]
25	I-270, N to Chicago, S to Memphis
24	Mason Rd, N [lodging] Courtyard, Marriott [other] hwy patrol, LDS Temple
23	Maryville Centre Dr (from wb), N [lodging] Courtyard, Marriott
22	MO 141, N [food] Regatta Grille [other] [hospital], S [food] 5 Guys Burgers, Pizza Hut
21	Timberlake Manor Pkwy
20	Chesterfield Pkwy (from wb), same as 19b a
19b a	MO 340, Chesterfield Pkwy, Olive Blvd, N [gas] BP, Shell [food] Applebee's, Pizzaria Uno, Sheridan's Custard, Taco Bell, Yaya's Cafe [lodging] DoubleTree Hotel, Hampton Inn, Homewood Suites, Residence Inn [other] Dobb's Tire, Schnucks Foods, USPO, Walgreens, S [gas] Mobil [food] Bacana Cafe, Bahama Breeze Rest., California Pizza Kitchen, Casa Gallardo's, Chili's, Houlihans, Macaroni Grill, PF Chang's [lodging] Drury Plaza Hotel [other] Dillard's, mall
17	Boones Crossing, Long Rd, Chesterfield Airport Rd, **1 mi** S [gas] Mobil [food] Bob Evans, Chick-fil-A, Coldstone, Cousins Subs, Culver's, East Coast Pizza, Emperor's Buffet, Fox&Hound, Golden China, Hardee's, Hometown Buffet, IHOP, IMO's Pizza, Joe's Crabshack, Kaldi's Coffee, Lion's Choice, Longhorn Steaks, Matador Cafe., McDonald's, Mimi's Cafe, O'Charley's, Old Country Buffet, Old Spaghetti Factory, Olive Garden, Original Pancakes, Qdoba Mexican, Quiznos, Red Lobster, Red Robin, SmokeHouse Rest., Sonic, Starbucks, Steak'n Shake, Subway, Taco Bell [lodging] Hampton Inn, Hilton Garden [other] $Tree,
17	Continued Best Buy, Dick's, Dobb's Tire, Firestone, Ford, Home Depot, KIA, Lowe's, Michael's, Petsmart, Radio Shack, Sam's Club, Target, vet, Walmart, WorldMkt
16	Long Rd (from wb)
14	Chesterfield Airport Rd (from eb), S [gas] Phillips 66 [lodging] Comfort Inn
13mm	Missouri River
11	Research Park Ctr Dr
10	MO 94 (from wb)
9	Rd K, O'Fallon, N [gas] Mobil, QT [food] Cracker Barrel, Ruby Tuesday, Starbucks [lodging] Holiday Inn Express, Residence Inn, Staybridge Suites [other] Chevrolet, Honda, Volvo
6	Rd DD, Wing Haven Blvd, N [gas] Phillips 66 [food] Bristol Seafood, Hunan King, Massa's Italian, Outback Steaks, Subway, VA BBQ [lodging] Hilton Garden
4	Rd N, N [gas] PetroMart, Phillips 66 [food] McDonald's, Qdoba Mexican, Red Robin, St. Louis Bread Co., Steak'n Shake [other] JC Penney, Shop'n Save, Target, S [gas] Murphy USA/dsl, Phillips 66 [food] Dragon Buffet, El Maguay, Jack-in-the-Box, McDonald's, Sonic, Starbucks, Subway, Taco Bell, Wendy's, White Castle [other] $Tree, Aldi Foods, AutoZone, Dobb's Tire, Firestone, GNC, Lowe's, Radio Shack, Walmart
2	Lake St. Louis Blvd, N [food] BC's Rest., Max&Erma's [other] Old Navy, Schnuck's Foods, Von Maur, Walgreens
1	Prospect Rd, N [gas] Shell
0mm	I-70 E to St Louis, W to Kansas City

CHESTERFIELD

INTERSTATE 70

Exit #	Services
251.5mm	Missouri/Illinois state line, Mississippi River
251a	I-55 S, to Memphis, to I-44, to downtown/no return
250b	Memorial Dr, downtown, S [gas] Shell [food] McDonald's [lodging] Days Inn [other] Stadium
250a	Arch, Riverfront, N [other] The Arch, S [lodging] Drury Inn, Hampton Inn, Hilton, Hyatt, Millineal Hotel, Renaissance [other] Edward Jones Dome
249b	Tucker Blvd, downtown St Louis, S [gas] Mobil/dsl
249a	I-44 W, I-55 S
248b	St Louis Ave, Branch St
248a	Salisbury St, McKinley Br, S [gas] BP, Phillips 66
247	Grand Ave, N [gas] BP, Phillips 66/Subway/dsl [lodging] Western Inn
246b	Adelaide Ave
246a	N Broadway, O'Fallon Park, N [gas] Loves/McDonald's/Subway/dsl/scales/24hr, Mobil/dsl [other] Freightliner, truck tires
245b	W Florissant
245a	Shreve Ave, S [gas] BP
244b	Kingshighway, S [gas] BP [food] Burger King, McDonald's, Subway [other] Walgreens
244a	Bircher Blvd, Union Blvd, N [gas] BP/dsl
243b	(243c from eb) Bircher Blvd
243a	Riverview Blvd
243	Goodfellow Blvd, N [gas] Phillips 66, Shell
242b a	Jennings Sta Rd, S [lodging] Western Inn
241b	Lucas-Hunt Rd, N [gas] Shell/Circle K, **3/4 mi** S [food] Church's, Lee's Chicken, McDonald's [other] Walgreens
241a	Bermuda Rd, S [other] [hospital]
240b a	Florissant Rd, N [gas] BP/McDonald's [other] Family$, Schnuck's Foods
239	N Hanley Rd, N [lodging] Hilton Garden, S [gas] BP
238c b	I-170 N, I-170 S, no return
238a	N [other] Lambert-St Louis Airport, S [lodging] Renaissance Hotel

INTERSTATE 70 Cont'd

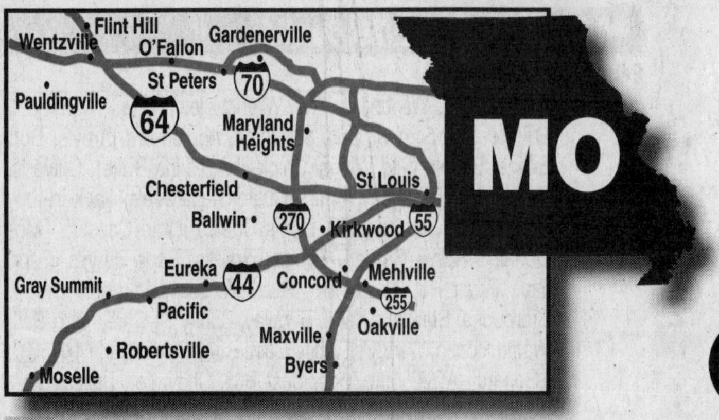

MO

ST LOUIS

Exit #	Services
237	Natural Bridge Rd (from eb), S [gas] Phillips 66, Shell [food] Church's, Jack-in-the-Box, Rally's, Steak'n Shake, Waffle House [lodging] Ramada Inn, Renaissance, Travelodge
236	Lambert-St Louis Airport, S [gas] BP/dsl [food] Bandana's BBQ, Golden Pancake, Lombardo's Café Rafferty's Rest., Subway [lodging] Best Value Inn, Drury Inn, Econolodge, Hampton Inn, Hilton, Holiday Inn, Holiday Inn Express, Marriott, Peartree Inn, Quality Inn
235c	Cypress Rd, Rd B W, N [other] to [airport]
235b a	US 67, Lindbergh Blvd, N [lodging] Airport Plaza Hotel, S [food] Lion's Choice Rest., TGIFriday's [lodging] Crowne Plaza, Embassy Suites, Extended Stay America [other] Menard's
234	MO 180, St Charles Rock Rd, N [gas] BP, Phillips 66/dsl [food] A&W/LJ Silver, Applebee's, Arby's, Chimi's Mexican, Chipotle, Fazoli's, HomeTown Buffet, Imo's Pizza, Jack-in-the-Box, Jimmy John's, LoneStar Steaks, McDonald's, New China Buffet, Pizza Hut, Ponderosa, Red Lobster, St Louis Bread, Subway, Taco Bell, Wendy's, White Castle, Ya Hala Mediterranean [other] [H], $Tree, Aldi Foods, AT&T, AutoZone, Best Buy, CVS Drug, Hobby Lobby, Kmart, Kohl's, Lowe's, Meineke, NTB, Office Depot, Petsmart, Save-A-Lot Foods, Target, Verizon, Walgreens, Walmart/Burger King, S [gas] QT [food] IHOP, Lion's Choice [other] Chrysler/Dodge/Jeep, Home Depot, Schnuck's, Shamel Tires/repair, Walgreens
232	I-270, N to Chicago, S to Memphis
231b a	Earth City Expwy, N [gas] Motomart, Phillips 66/Jack-in-the-Box/dsl [food] Malone's Grill, McDonald's [lodging] Candlewood Suites, Courtyard, Extended Stay America, Holiday Inn, Residence Inn, SpringHill Suites, S [gas] Mobil [food] Burger King, Dave&Buster's, Subway [lodging] Holiday Inn Express, Homewood Suites, Wingate Inn [other] Hollywood Casino/Hotel, Riverport Ampitheatre
230mm	Missouri River

ST CHARLES

Exit #	Services
229b a	5th St, St Charles, N [gas] BP, Mobil/dsl, Motomart/dsl [food] Bellacino's Italian, Buffalo Wild Wings, China House Buffet, Denny's, Dunkin Donuts, Firehouse Subs, Jack-in-the-Box, Lee's Chicken, Little Tokyo, McDonald's, Qdoba, Starbucks, TX Roadhouse, Waffle House [lodging] Best Value Inn, Best Western, Comfort Suites [other] Aldi Foods, Ameristar Casino, Bass Pro Shops, Gordman's, Walgreens, S [gas] QT/dsl [food] Bar Louie, Cracker Barrel, Five Guys, Tuscanos Brazilian [lodging] Embassy Suites, Fairfield Inn [other] malls
228	MO 94, to Weldon Springs, St Charles, N [gas] Mobil/dsl, QT/dsl [food] Arby's, DQ, Imo's Pizza, Papa John's, Steak'n Shake [other] Advance Parts, AutoZone, CVS Drug, GNC, NAPA, Schnuck's, Valvoline, S [gas] Mobil/dsl, QT [food] Chinese Express, ChuckECheese, Fazoli's, Gingham's Rest., Grappa Grill, Jimmy John's, McAlister's Deli, Outback Steaks, Pizza Hut, Tilted Kilt [lodging] Intown Suites [other] $General, access to 227, Dobb's Tire
227	Zumbehl Rd, N [gas] Phillips 66/dsl, ZX [food] Culpepper's Grill [lodging] Super 8 [other] Ford, Lowe's, Sav-A-Lot Foods, S [gas] BP, Hucks/dsl [food] Applebee's, Big Woody's BBQ, Bob Evans, Capt D's, El Mariachi Mexican, Fratelli's Ristorante, Golden Corral, Hardee's, Hoho Chinese, Jack-in-the-Box, McDonald's, Papa Murphy's, Penn Sta Subs, Shogun, Smashburger, St Louis Bread, Subway, Taco Bell [lodging] Red Roof Inn, TownePlace Suites [other] $Tree, access to 228, Dierberg's Foods, GNC, Jiffy Lube, Michael's, NTB, Petco, Petsmart, Radio Shack, Sam's Club/gas, Schnuck's Foods, URGENT CARE, vet, Walgreens, Walmart
225	Truman Rd, to Cave Springs, N [gas] Phillips 66/dsl [lodging] Hampton Inn, Rodeway Inn [other] Buick/GMC, Cadillac, Harley Davidson, Indian Motorcycles, Mazda, Subaru, U-Haul, VW, S [gas] Conoco, QT [food] Bandanas BBQ, Burger King, Chimi's Mexican,

ST PETERS

Exit #	Services
225	Continued Culver's, Denny's, Hibachi Grill, Hooters, IHOP, Jack-in-the-Box, KFC, Lion's Choice Rest., LJ Silver, Longhorn Steaks, Los Chavez Mexican, McDonald's, O'Charley's, Pasta House, Red Lobster, Steak'n Shake, Subway, Taco Bell, Thai Kitchen, Wendy's, White Castle [lodging] Country Inn&Suites, Courtyard [other] [H], Advance Parts, AT&T, Batteries+Bulbs, Chrysler/Dodge/Jeep, Firestone, Hobby Lobby, Home Depot, Kia, Office Depot, Shop'n Save, Target, TJ Maxx, URGENT CARE, Verizon
224	MO 370 E
222	Mid-Rivers Mall Dr, Rd C, St Peters, N [gas] QT/dsl/24hr [food] Burger King [other] CarMax, Chevrolet, Honda, Lincoln, Toyota/Scion, S [gas] Mobil/dsl [food] Arby's, Bob Evans, Buffalo Wild Wings, Chili's, China Wok, Domino's, Fazoli's, HoneyBaked Ham, Joe's Crabshack, Max & Erma's, McDonald's/playplace, Olive Garden, Planet Sub, Qdoba, Red Robin, Ruby Tuesday, St Louis Bread, Steak'n Shake, Subway, Taco Bell, Wendy's [lodging] Drury Inn, Extended Stay America [other] Aldi Foods, Barnes&Noble, Best Buy, BigLots, Costco/gas, Dick's, Dillard's, Hancock Fabrics, Hyundai/Nissan/VW, JC Penney, Jo-Ann Fabrics, Macy's, Marshall's, NTB, Sears/auto, Verizon
220	MO 79, to Elsberry, N [other] Cherokee Lakes Camping (7mi), S [gas] 7-11/gas, BP, Phillips 66/dsl [food] Caleco's Rest., El Mezon, Jack-in-the-Box, McDonald's/playplace, Pirrone's Pizzaria, Sonic, Subway [lodging] Days Inn [other] Dierberg's Foods, O'Reilly Parts, Walgreens

O'FALLON

Exit #	Services
219	T R Hughes Blvd, S [gas] QT [lodging] Comfort Inn
217	Rds K, M, O'Fallon, N [gas] Hucks/dsl [food] Baskin-Robbins, Burger King, Jack-in-the-Box, Piggy's BBQ, Pizza Hut/Taco Bell, Rally's, Sonic, Waffle House [other] Firestone, Jiffy Lube, O'Reilly Parts, Radio Shack, S [gas] Mobil/dsl, Phillips 66/dsl, QT [food] Applebee's, Arby's, Bob Evans, Cappuccino's, Domino's, Fazoli's, Golden Corral, Jimmy John's, KFC, Lion's Choice Rest., McDonald's/playplace, Pantera's Pizza, Papa John's, Pizza Hut, Red Robin, St Louis Bread, Stefanina's Pizza, Subway, TX Roadhouse, Wendy's [other] Advance Parts, Aldi Foods, Auto Tire, AutoZone, CVS Drug, GNC, Home Depot, Lowe's, Meineke, Midas, Schnuck's Foods, Shop'n Save Foods, Verizon, Walgreens, Walmart
216	Bryan Rd, N [lodging] Super 8 [other] Ford, Peterbilt, St Louis RV Ctr, S [gas] Conoco, Phillips 66/Jack-in-the-Box/dsl, QT [food] DQ, Little Caesar's, Mr. Goodcents, Wendy's
214	Lake St Louis, N [gas] Phillips 66/McDonald's/dsl, S [gas] Phillips 66/dsl, Shell/Circle K [food] Denny's, Hardee's [lodging] Best Value Inn [other] [H]
212	Rd A, N [lodging] Economy Inn, S [gas] Mobil [food] Pizzamenti's Cafe [lodging] Regency Plaza Hotel [other] Chrysler/Dodge/Jeep
210b a	to I-64, US 40 E, US 61 S, S [other] [H]
209	Rd Z, Church St, New Melle, N [food] DQ, S [gas] Phillips 66/dsl

MO

INTERSTATE 70 Cont'd

Exit #	Services
208	**WENTZVILLE** Pearce Blvd, Wentzville Pkwy, Wentzville, **N** [gas] Mobil/dsl, QT/dsl [food] 54th St Grill, 88 China, Applebee's, Arby's, Bob Evans, Buffalo Wild Wings, Chick-fil-A, China Buffet, Culver's, Domino's, El Maguey, Fritz's Custard, Hardee's, Jack-in-the-Box, Jimmy John's, KFC, Lion's Choice, Little Caesar's, McDonald's, Olive Garden, Panda Express, Papa John's, Penn Sta., Pizza Hut, Pizza Pro, Ruby Tuesday, St Louis Bread, Starbucks, Steak'n Shake, Subway, Sunny St Cafe, Taco Bell, Waffle House, Wendy's, White Castle [lodging] Fairfield Inn [other] [H], $General, AT&T, AutoZone, Best Buy, Chevrolet, Dick's, Dierberg's Foods, Dobb's Tire, GNC, Home Depot, Kohl's, Lowe's, Michael's, NAPA, O'Reilly Parts, Petsmart, Ross, Sam's Club/dsl, Save-A-Lot, Schnuck's Food, Target, URGENT CARE, Verizon, Walgreens, Walmart, **S** [gas] BP/dsl [food] Bandana's BBQ, Chimi's FreshMex, IHOP [lodging] Super 8 [other] Hyundai, Thomas RV Ctr
204mm	**weigh sta both lanes**
203	Rds W, T, Foristell, **N** [gas] Mr Fuel/dsl/scales, TA/BP/Pizza Hut/Popeye's/Taco Bell/dsl/scales/24hr/ @ [lodging] Quality Inn, **S** [gas] Phillips 66/McDonald's/dsl [other] dsl repair
200	Rds J, H, F (from wb), Wright City, **N** [gas] Phillips 66/dsl [food] Ruiz Castillo's Mexican (1mi), **S** [food] Subway [lodging] Super 7 Inn
199	Rd J, H, F, Wright City, **N** [gas] Shell/McDonald's/dsl [other] $General, **S** [lodging] Super 7 Inn [other] Volvo Trucks
198mm	[rest stop] **both lanes, full [icon] facilities, litter barrels, petwalk [icon] [icon]**
193	**WARRENTON** MO 47, Warrenton, **N** [gas] Mobil/dsl, Phillips 66/Chester's/dsl [food] 1st Wok, Applebee's, Burger King, China House, Dominos, DQ, El Jimador Mexican, Jack-in-the-Box, Little Caesar's, McDonald's, Pizza Hut, Subway, Waffle House, Wendy's [lodging] Best Value Inn, Holiday Inn Express, Super 8 [other] Aldi Foods, AT&T, Mosers Foods, Walmart, **S** [gas] BP/dsl, Conoco/dsl, Phillips 66/dsl [food] Denny's, Imo's Pizza, Papa John's, Taco Bell [lodging] Baymont Inn [other] AutoZone, CarQuest, Chevrolet, NAPA, O'Reilly Parts, Walgreens
188	Rds A, B, to Truxton, **S** [gas] FLYING J/Denny's/dsl/LP/RV Dump/scales/24hr [lodging] Budget Inn
183	Rds E, NN, Y, Jonesburg, **1 mi N** [other] Jonesburg Gardens Camping, **S** [gas] Phillips 66/Chester's/dsl [other] USPO
179	Rd F, High Hill, **S** [lodging] Budget Motel, Colonial Inn
175	MO 19, New Florence, **N** [gas] BP/dsl, Shell/dsl/24hr [food] Dad's Jct Cafe, McDonald's [lodging] Best Inn, Best Value Inn, Days Inn [other] auto repair, Stone Hill Winery/gifts (15mi)
170	MO 161, Rd J, Danville, **N** [gas] Sinclair/dsl [other] Kan-Do RV Park, to Graham Cave SP, **S** [other] Lazy Day RV Park
169.5mm	**truck parking**
168mm	Loutre River
167mm	**truck parking eb**
161	Rds D, YY, Williamsburg, **N** [gas] Cranes/mkt [food] Marlene's Rest. [other] USPO
155	Rds A, Z, to Calwood, **N** [other] antiques
148	US 54, Kingdom City, **N** [gas] BP/dsl, Phillips 66/Burger King/dsl [food] Taco Bell [other] MO Tourism Ctr, to Mark Twain Lake, **S** [gas] Conoco/Subway/dsl/scales/24hr, Petro/Mobil/Iron Skillet/dsl/scales/24hr/ @, Phillips 66/dsl, Shell/Gasper's/Arby's/dsl/scales/ @ [food] Denny's, McDonald's [lodging] Best Value Inn, Comfort Inn, Days Inn, Super 8 [other] Ozarkland Gifts, Wheeler's Truckwash
144	Rds M, HH, to Hatton, **S** [other] fireworks
137	Rds DD, J, to Millersburg, Stephens, **S** [food] Ranch House BBQ [other] antiques, Freightliner, to Little Dixie WA (4mi)
133	Rd Z, to Centralia, **N** [other] Camping World RV Ctr
131	**COLUMBIA** Lake of the Woods Rd, **N** [gas] BP, Phillips 66/Subway/dsl [food] Buckingham BBQ, George's Rest, Sonic [lodging] Super 8 [other] Harley-Davidson, **S** [gas] Conoco/dsl [food] Jimmy John's [lodging] Holiday Inn
128a	US 63, to Jefferson City, Columbia, **N** [gas] CNG, Mobil/dsl, QT [food] Bandanas BBQ, Bob Evans, Burger King, China Garden, Cracker Barrel, Golden Corral, Hooters, KFC, Lonestar Steaks, McDonald's, Pizza Hut, Ruby Tuesday, Steak'n Shake, Taco Bell, Wendy's, White Castle [lodging] Fairfield Inn, Hampton Inn, Hilton Garden, Red Roof Inn, Residence Inn, Super 8 [other] Bass Pro Shop, Home Depot, Menard's, Pine Grove RV Park, **S** [gas] BreakTime/dsl [food] 5 Guys Burgers, Applebee's, Baskin-Robbins, Chili's, Chipotle Mexican, CiCi's, Culver's, El Maguey, Firehouse Subs, Freddy's, Good Cents Subs, Houlihan's, IHOP, Kobe Japanese, Little Caesar's, Longhorn Steaks, Panda Express, Panera Bread, Sonic, Starbucks, Subway, TGIFriday's [lodging] Baymont Inn, Country Inn&Suites, Howard Johnson, Motel 6, Ramada, Staybridge Suites, Suburban Inn, Wingate Inn [other] [H], $Tree, HyVee Foods, Lowe's/Subway, Patricia's Foods, Sam's Club, Staples, Verizon, Walmart/McDonald's
128	Lp 70 (from wb), Columbia, **N** [gas] Shell [food] Hardee's [other] Honda, **S** [food] Cat's Kitchen [lodging] Eastwood Motel [other] [H], Big O Tire, NAPA, same as 128a
127	MO 763, to Moberly, Columbia, **N** [food] Waffle House [lodging] Budget Host [other] Chrysler/Dodge/Jeep, Fiat, Hyundai, Mazda, Toyota/Scion, transmissions, VW, **S** [gas] Phillips 66/dsl [lodging] Super 7 Motel
126	MO 163, Providence Rd, Columbia, **N** [gas] Phillips 66/dsl [food] Country Kitchen [lodging] Quality Inn, Red Roof Inn [other] CarQuest, McKnight Tire, same as 127, **S** [gas] BreakTime/dsl [food] Burger King, Carlito's Mexican, Church's, DQ, LJ Silver, McDonald's, Pizza Hut, Subway, Taco Bell [other] [H], AutoZone, Buick/Cadillac/Chevrolet/GMC, Nissan, O'Reilly Parts
125	Lp 70, West Blvd, Columbia, **N** [lodging] Comfort Suites, **S** [gas] Phillips 66/dsl [food] Agave Mexican, Cheddar's, Domino's, Fazoli's, Imo's Pizza, JJ's Cafe, Olive Garden, Teppanyaki Grill [lodging] Days Inn [other] Aldi Foods, BMW, Firestone/auto, Kia, Mercedes, Mosers Foods, same as 124, Subaru, U-Haul, vet
124	MO 740, Rd E, Stadium Blvd, Columbia, **N** [lodging] Extended Stay America, **S** [gas] BreakTime, Phillips 66/dsl [food] Applebee's, ChuckECheese, Denny's, Five Guys, Hardee's, Jazz Kitchen, KFC, Lee's Chicken, McDonald's, Pancheros, Panera Bread, Pizza Hut, Red Lobster, Ruby Tuesday, Smokehouse BBQ, Sports Zone Grill, Steak'n Shake, Subway, Taco Bell, TX Roadhouse, Wendy's [lodging] Best Value Inn, Drury Inn, Holiday Inn, La Quinta, Royal Inn [other] $Tree, AT&T, Barnes&Noble, Best Buy, Dick's, Dillard's, Ford, Hobby Lobby, JC Penney, Macy's, mall, Marshalls, Michael's, Natural Grocers, Old Navy, O'Reilly Parts, PetCo, Petsmart, Radio Shack, same as 125, Sears/auto, Target, to U of MO, URGENT CARE, Verizon
122mm	Perche Creek
121	US 40, Rd UU, Midway, **N** [gas] Midway/dsl/rest., Phillips 66 [lodging] Budget Inn [other] tires/repair, **S** [other] golf
117	Rds J, O, to Huntsdale, Harrisburg
115	Rd BB N, Rocheport, **N** [other] to Katy Tr SP, winery
114.5mm	Missouri River
111	MO 98, MO 179, to Wooldridge, Overton, **S** [gas] Phillips 66/dsl/repair [other] RV Park
106	MO 87, Bingham Rd, to Boonville, **S** [gas] Phillips 66/dsl
104mm	[rest stop] **both lanes, full [icon] facilities, litter barrels, petwalk [icon] [icon] vending**
103	Rd B, Main St, Boonville, **N** [gas] Breaktime, Casey's/dsl, Murphy USA/dsl [food] China One Buffet, La Hacienda Mexican, McDonald's, Pizza Hut, Sonic, Subway, Taco Bell [lodging] Days Inn,

B O O N V I L L E

INTERSTATE 70 Cont'd

103	Continued Super 8 H, NAPA, RV Express Camping, to Katy Tr SP, Walmart/Subway, S Cenex/dsl Rte B Cafe QT Inn
101	US 40, MO 5, to Boonville, N Pilot/Wendy's/dsl/24hr Arby's Comfort Inn, Holiday Inn Express, Isle of Capri Hotel (3mi) Buick/Cadillac/Chevrolet/GMC, Ford, Russell Stover Candies, S Loves/Hardee's/scales/dsl/24hr to Lake of the Ozarks
98	MO 41, MO 135, Lamine, N tires, to Arrow Rock HS (13mi), S Conoco/Ma's Kettle/dsl, Settlers/dsl repair
93mm	Lamine River
89	Rd K, to Arrow Rock, N to Arrow Rock HS
84	Rd J, N truck repair, Valero/DQ/Stuckey's
78b a	US 65, to Marshall, N Conoco/dsl fireworks, RV Park
77mm	Blackwater River
74	Rd YY, N Shell/Betty's/cafe/dsl/repair/24hr Welcome Motel
71	Rds EE, K, to Houstonia
66	MO 127, Sweet Springs, N H, S BreakTime/dsl, Casey's/dsl Brownsville Sta Rest. Rodeway Inn $General, Bumper Parts
65.5mm	Davis Creek
62	Rds VV, Y, Emma
58	MO 23, Concordia, N TA/Country Pride/Subway/dsl/scales/24hr/ @ McDonald's $General, NAPA, Patricia's Foods, truck/RV wash, S Breaktime/dsl, Casey's, Cenex/dsl, Conoco/dsl Dempsey's BBQ, Hardee's, Pizza Hut Budget Inn, Days Inn, Travelodge Bumper Parts
57.5mm	**both lanes, full facilities, litter barrels, petwalk vending**
52	Rd T, Aullville
49	MO 13, to Higginsville, N Casey's/dsl, Pilot/McDonald's/Subway/dsl/scales/24hr Camelot Inn/rest to Confederate Mem, S Super 8 Great Escape RV Park
45	Rd H, to Mayview
43mm	**weigh sta both lanes**
41	Rds O, M, to Lexington, Mayview
38	MO 131 (from wb), Odessa, S BP/dsl, Phillips 66/dsl, Shell, Sinclair McDonald's, Pizza Hut, Sonic, Subway, Taco John's, Thompson's Country Kitchen $General Mkt, camping, Family$, O'Reilly Parts, same as 37
37	MO 131, Odessa, N Country Gardens RV Park/dump, S BP/dsl, Shell, Sinclair El Camino Real, McDonald's, Pizza Hut, Sonic, Subway, Taco John's, Thompson's Country Kitchen Parkside Inn $General Mkt, Family$, fireworks, O'Reilly Parts, Patricia's Foods, same as 38
35mm	**truck parking both lanes**
31	Rds D, Z, to Bates City, Napoleon, N Bates City RV Camping, S Valero/dsl Bates City BBQ fireworks
29.5mm	Horse Shoe Creek
28	Rd H, Rd F, Oak Grove, N TA/Country Pride/Popeye's/dsl/scales/24hr/ @ Oak Grove Inn Blue Beacon, KOA, S Casey's, Petro/BP/Iron Skillet/DQ/Wendy's/scales/dsl/@, QT/dsl China Buffet, Hardee's, KFC/Taco Bell, McDonald's, Pizza Hut, PJ's Rest., Subway, Waffle House EconoLodge Cash Saver Foods, Lake Paradise RV/Camping (9mi), O'Reilly Parts, SpeedCo Lube, Walgreens, Walmart
24	US 40, Rds AA, BB, to Buckner, N Casey's/dsl Papa Murphy's Best Value Inn, Comfort Inn LifeStyle RV Ctr, vet, S Conoco/Subway/dsl/scales/24hr McDonald's, Sonic Advance Parts, Trailside RV Park/Ctr

C O N C O R D I A

O D E S S A

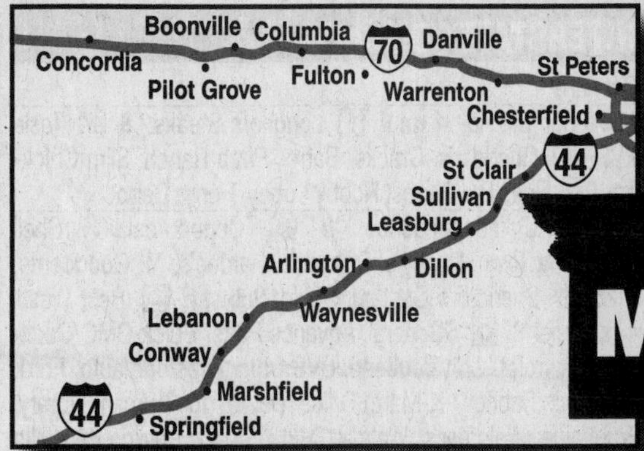

MO

21	Adams Dairy Pkwy, N Camping World RV Ctr (1mi), S Murphy USA/dsl, Phillips 66/Burger King/dsl Arby's, Chick-fil-A, Chipotle Mexican, Five Guys, Jersey Mike's, Olive Garden, Panda Express, Panera Bread, Pepper Jax Grill, Planet Sub, Sonic, Subway, Taco Bell, TX Roadhouse Courtyard AT&T, GNC, Gordman's, Home Depot, Kohl's, Michael's, NTB, PetCo, Ross, Target, TJ Maxx, Verizon, Walmart
20	MO 7, Blue Springs, N Phillips 66/dsl, QT/dsl Backyard Burger, Bob Evans, China 1, Custard's, Dunkin Donuts, Goodcents Subs, Minsky's Pizza, Papa Murphy's, Rancho Grande, Sonic, Subway Best Value Inn, Days Inn, Econolodge, Rodeway Inn $General, Ace Hardware, CVS Drug, NAPA, O'Reilly Parts, PriceChopper Foods, Walgreens, Walmart Mkt, S BP/dsl, QT, Valero/dsl Applebee's, Big Biscuit, Denny's, Firehouse Subs, Jack-in-the-Box, Jimmy John's, KFC, LJ Silver, McDonald's, Original Pizza, Starbucks, Subway, Taco Bell, Taco Bueno, Wendy's, Winsteads Cafe, Zarda's BBQ Hampton Inn, Quality Inn H, Advance Parts, Aldi Foods, AutoZone, BigLots, Chevrolet, Firestone/auto, Goodyear/auto, Hobby Lobby, Hy-Vee Foods/gas, Office Depot, Russell Stover, transmissions, URGENT CARE
18	Woods Chapel Rd, N BP American Inn, La Quinta, Night's Inn, Super 8 Harley-Davidson, S Conoco/dsl, Phillips 66/dsl, QT China Kitchen, KFC/Taco Bell, Las Playas Mexican, McDonald's, Pizza Hut, Sonic, Subway, Taco John's, Waffle House CVS Drug, Ford, Hyundai, Nissan, same as 20
17	Little Blue Pkwy, 39th St, N QT/dsl Buffalo Wild Wings, Coldstone, Hereford House, Jimmy John's, Joe's Crabshack, On the Border, Saints Grill, Sonic, Twin Peaks Hilton Garden H, mall entrance, World Mkt, S QT Arby's, BD Mongolian, Carrabba's, Chipotle Mexican, Corner Cafe, Culver's, Golden Corral, Hooters, IHOP, Kobe Steaks, McDonald's, Outback Steaks, Panera Bread, Red Robin, Rib Crib, Stroud's Rest., Subway, Wendy's Comfort Suites, Drury Inn, Holiday Inn Express Carmax, Costco/gas, Lowe's
16mm	Little Blue River
15b	MO 291 N, Independence, **1 exit N on 39th St** Phillips 66, QT 54th St Grill, Applebee's, Burger King, Chick-fil-A, Chili's, ChuckECheese, Famous Dave's, Fazoli's, Logan's Roadhouse, Longhorn Steaks, McDonald's, Noodles&Co, Perkins, Smokehouse BBQ, Starbucks, Taco Bell, Zio's Italian Fairfield Inn, Residence Inn, Staybridge Suites H, AT&T, AutoZone, Barnes&Noble, Best Buy, Dick's, Dillard's, JC Penney, Jo-Ann, Kohl's, Macy's, mall, Marshalls, NTB, Petsmart, Ross, Sam's Club/gas, Sears/auto, Target, Walmart
15a	I-470 S, MO 291 S, to Lee's Summit

B L U E S P G S

INTERSTATE 70 Cont'd

INDEPENDENCE

Exit #	Services
14	Lee's Summit Rd, **1 mi** N Longhorn Steaks, S Tesla EVP Cheddar's, Cracker Barrel, Pizza Ranch, Slim Chickens Bass Pro Shops, Hobby Lobby, Home Depot
12	Noland Rd, Independence, N Conoco/dsl, QT, Shell China Town, Denny's, Domino's, Hardee's, Mr Goodcents, Pizza St, Sheridan's Custard, Sonic, Subway Best Western, Super 8 $General, Advance Parts, Buick/GMC/Cadillac, Chevrolet, Chrysler/Jeep, CVS Drug, Firestone/auto, Ford, Hancock Fabrics, K-Mart, Office Depot, to Truman Library, TrueValue, Walgreens, Walmart Mkt, S Phillips 66/Kicks Arby's, Bandana's BBQ, Baskin Robbins, Burger King, HoneyBaked Ham, KFC/Taco Bell, Krispy Kreme, Ma Ma Garden, McDonald's, Olive Garden, Pizza Hut, Quiznos, Red Lobster, Ruby Tuesday, Steak'n Shake, Wendy's American Inn, Best Value Inn, Days Inn, Quality Inn, Super 6 Motel $Tree, BigLots, GNC, Gordman's, HyVee Foods/gas, Old Time Pottery, Petco, PriceChopper Mkt, Tires+, U-Haul
11	US 40, Blue Ridge Blvd, Independence, N QT A&W/LJ Silver, La Fuentes, Rosie's Cafe, Sonic, Subway, V's Italian, S 7-11, BP, Sinclair Applebee's, Big Boy Burgers, Chipotle Mexican, Church's, East Buffet, Firehouse Subs, IHOP, McDonald's, Papa John's, Samurai Chef, Starbucks Family$, GNC, Lowe's, O'Reilly Parts, Radio Shack, Verizon, vet, Walmart/Subway
10	Sterling Ave (from eb), same as 11
9	Blue Ridge Cutoff (from wb), N Denny's Drury Inn, Holiday Inn, ValuePlace Inn, S BP, Conoco/Subway Taco Bell Sheraton Sports Complex
8b a	I-435, N to Des Moines, S to Wichita
7b	Manchester Trafficway
7mm	Blue River
7a	US 40 E, 31st St
6	Van Brunt Blvd, N 7-11, Phillips 66/dsl, S BP McDonald's, Pizza Hut NAPA, VA H
5c	Jackson Ave (from wb)
5b	31st St (from eb)
5a	27th St (from eb)
4c	23rd Ave
4b	18th St
4a	Benton Blvd (from eb), Truman Rd, N Super Stop/Wendy's/dsl Subway Advance Parts, Save-A-Lot Foods
3c	Prospect Ave, N BP Church's, S McDonald's
3b	Brooklyn Ave (from eb), N BP Church's, Gates BBQ, S McDonald's
3a	Paseo St, S BP/dsl tires
2m	US 71 S, downtown
2l	I-670, to I-35 S
2j	11th St, downtown
2g	I-29/35 N, US 71 N, to Des Moines
2h	US 24 E, downtown
2e	MO 9 N, Oak St, S Phillips 66 Marriott
2d	Main St, downtown
2c	US 169 N, Broadway, S Phillips 66 Marriott
2b	Beardsley Rd
2a	I-35 S, to Wichita
0mm	Missouri/Kansas state line, Kansas River

KANSAS CITY

INTERSTATE 270 (ST LOUIS)

Exit #	Services
15b a	I-55 N to Chicago, S to St Louis. **I-270 begins/ends in Illinois on I-55/I-70, exit 20.**
12	IL 159, to Collinsville, **1 mi** N Conoco, QT/dsl Applebee's, Denny's, DQ, Hardee's, IHOP, Jack-in-the-Box, Jimmy John's, KFC, Little Caesar's, Papa John's, Subway Aldi Foods, AT&T, Chrysler/Dodge/Jeep, Home Depot, Lowe's, PetsMart, Sam's Club/dsl, Walgreens, Walmart, S H
9	IL 157, to Collinsville, N Quality Inn, S BP/dsl Hampton Inn
7	I-255, to I-55 S to Memphis
6b a	IL 111, N FLYING J/Denny's/dsl/scales/24hr Hen House Rest. Magnuson Hotel Blue Beacon/scales, Speedco, truck/trailer repair, S Mobil/dsl Denny's, McDonald's/playplace, Taco Bell Best Western, Days Inn, Fairfield Inn, La Quinta, Super 8 to Pontoon Beach
4	IL 203, Old Alton Rd, to Granite City
3b a	IL 3, N Riverboat Casino, S Phillips 66 Hardee's, Waffle House Budget Motel, EconoLodge, Economy Inn, Sun Motel KOA, MGM Camping
2mm	Chain of Rocks Canal
0mm	Illinois/Missouri state line, Mississippi River, motorist callboxes begin eb
34	Riverview Dr, to St Louis, N Moto Mart/Subway, **Welcome Ctr both lanes, full facilities, info, litter barrels**
33	Lilac Ave, N USPO, S Phillips 66/Jack-in-the-Box/dsl, QT/dsl/scales/24hr Hardee's
32	Bellefontaine Rd, N Mobil, QT, Shell China King, KFC, McDonald's, Pizza Hut, Steak'n Shake Economy Inn, Motel 6 Advance Parts, Firestone, Schnuck's Foods, S BP White Castle Aldi Foods
31b a	MO 367, N BP, QT/dsl Jack-in-the-Box, McDonalds, Subway H, $General, Chevrolet, Shop'n Save Foods, U-Haul, Walgreens
30b a	Hall's Ferry Rd, Rd AC, N Mobil/dsl, Phillips 66/dsl, QT, ZX Applebee's, Capt. D's, Popeye's, Waffle House, White Castle Knights Inn Ford/Lincoln, S BP/dsl, Conoco, Phillips 66 China Wok, Church's, CiCi's Pizza, Cracker Barrel, IHOP, Steak'n Shake, Subway $Buster, AutoZone, Family$, Home Depot, JoAnn Fabrics, O'Reilly Parts, Shop'n Save Foods
29	W Florissant Rd, N Jack-in-the-Box, Lion's Choice, Pasta House $General, Dobb's Tire/auto, Firestone, K-Mart, Office Depot, S Phillips 66 Arby's, Burger King, Krispy Kreme, Malone's Grill, McDonald's, Pantera's Pizza, Sonic $Tree, BigLots, Mazda, NTB, Radio Shack, Sam's Club/gas, Walgreens, Walmart
28	Elizabeth Ave, Washington St, N Phillips 66/dsl Jack-in-the-Box, Jerome's Pizza, Pizza Hut/Taco Bell, Subway Chevrolet, Schnuck's Foods, Walgreens, S BP
27	New Florissant Rd, Rd N, N BP, Shell/Circle K
26b	Graham Rd, N Hanley, N 7-11/dsl Arby's, LJ Silver, Starbucks Hampton Inn, Motel 6 H, S QT McDonald's Days Inn $General, Hancock Fabrics
26a	I-170 S
25b a	US 67, Lindbergh Blvd, N BP, Phillips 66, QT Bandana's BBQ, Burger King, China Wok, Church's, Del Taco, IHOP, Imo's Pizza, Jack-in-the-Box, McDonald's, Outback Steaks, Papa John's, Pizza Hut/Taco Bell, Pueblo Nuevo Mexican, Quiznos, Rally's, Sonic, Starbucks, Waffle House, Wendy's Comfort Inn, InTown Suites, La Quinta, Ramada Inn AutoZone, Cadillac, Dierberg's Deli, Family$, Firestone/auto, Ford, GNC, Goodyear, NAPA, Nissan, Radio Shack, Sav-a-Lot Foods, Schnuck's Foods, Toyota/Scion, Walgreens, S 7-11 Subway Budget Inn, EconoLodge, Extended Stay America, Studio+ Honda, transmissions, USPO, VW

ST LOUIS

MO

ST LOUIS

INTERSTATE 270 (ST LOUIS) Cont'd

Exit #	Services
23	McDonnell Blvd, E [food] Denny's, Quiznos [lodging] La Quinta, W [gas] BP, QT, ZX [food] Arby's, Jack-in-the-Box, Lion's Choice, McDonald's, Starbucks, Steak'n Shake [other] Buick/GMC
22b a	MO 370 W, to MO Bottom Rd
20c	MO 180, St Charles Rock Rd, E [gas] BP, Phillips 66/dsl [food] A&W/LJ Silver, Applebees, Arby's, Chimi's Mexican, Chipotle, Fazoli's, Hometown Buffet, Imo's Pizza, Jack-in-the-Box, Jimmy John's, Lonestar Steaks, McDonald's, New China Buffet, Pizza Hut, Ponderosa, Red Lobster, St. Louis Bread, Subway, Taco Bell, Wendy's, White Castle, Ya Hala Mediterranean [other] [H], $Tree, Aldi Foods, AT&T, AutoZone, Best Buy, CVS Drug, Hobby Lobby, K-Mart, Kohl's, Lowe's, Meineke, NTB, Office Depot, Petsmart, Save-a-Lot, Target, Verizon, Walgreens, Walmart/Burger, W [gas] QT [food] Bob Evans, Olive Garden, Waffle House [lodging] Best Value Inn, Motel 6, Super 8
20b a	I-70, E to St Louis, W to Kansas City
17	Dorsett Rd, E [gas] BP, QT [food] BBQ, Syberg's Grill [lodging] Best Western, Drury Inn, Hampton Inn, W [gas] Mobil, Phillips 66, Shell [food] Arby's, Denny's, Fuddrucker's, McDonald's, Steak'n Shake, Subway [lodging] Baymont Inn
16b a	Page Ave, Rd D, MO 364 W, E [gas] BP, CFM, Citgo/7-11, QT, Sinclair [food] Blimpie, Copperfield's Rest., Hardee's, Hooters, Malone's Grill, McDonald's, Stazio's Café [lodging] Comfort Inn, Courtyard, DoubleTree, Holiday Inn, Homestead Suites, Red Roof Inn, Residence Inn, Sheraton
14	MO 340, Olive Blvd, E [gas] BP, Mobil [food] Applebee's, Bristol Cafe, Denny's, Domino's, KFC, Lion's Choice Rest., McDonald's, Pasta House, Steakout [lodging] Courtyard, Drury Inn [other] [H], BMW/Land Rover/Cadillac, Chevrolet, Crysler/Jeep, Lexus, W [gas] Schnucks [food] Coldstone Creamery, Culpepper's Café, House of Wong, Subway, TGIFriday [other] Dierberg's Foods, Kohl's, Walgreens
13	Rd AB, Ladue Rd
12b a	I-64, US 40, US 61, E to St Louis, W to Wentzville, E [other] [H]
9	MO 100, Manchester Rd, E [gas] BP [food] Café America, Houlihan's Rest, IHOP, Lion's Choice Rest., McDonald's [other] Famous Barr, Galyan's, Lord&Taylor, mall, Nordstrom's, W [gas] Phillips 66, Shell [food] Applebee's, Casa Gallardo's Mexican, Olive Garden, Red Robin
8	Dougherty Ferry Rd, S [gas] Citgo/7-11, Mobil [food] McDonald's [other] [H]
7	Big Ben Rd, N [other] [H]
5b a	I-44, US 50, MO 366, E to St Louis, W to Tulsa
3	MO 30, Gravois Rd, N [gas] BP, Phillips 66 [food] Bandana BBQ, Olive Garden, Outback Steaks [lodging] Days Inn, Quality Inn [other] Ford
2	MO 21, Tesson Ferry Rd, N [gas] BP [food] El Muguey Mexican, Jimmy John's, Panda Chinese, Pizza Hut [other] Acura, AutoZone, Buick, Dobb's Auto, O'Reilly Parts, Scion/Toyota, vet, **N on Lindbergh** [gas] Mobil [food] 54th St Grill, Burger King, Church's, Jack-in-the-Box, Olive Garden, Outback Steaks, Quizno's, Red Lobster, Subway, Taco Bell, TGIFriday's, Waffle House, White Castle [other] Buick/GMC, Honda, Schnuck's Foods, Shop'n Save, Walgreens S [gas] Shell/Circle K/dsl [food] Little Caesar's, [other] Dierberg's Foods
1b a	I-55 N to St Louis, S to Memphis

KANSAS CITY

INTERSTATE 435 (KANSAS CITY)

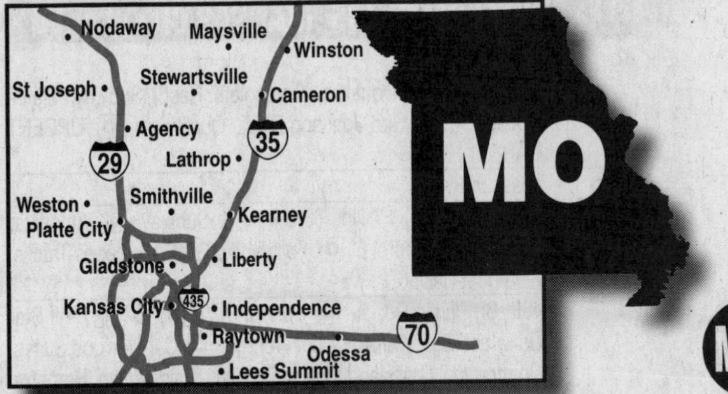

Exit #	Services
83	I-35, N to KS City, S to Wichita
82	Quivira Rd, Overland Park, N [food] Burger King, Cheddar's, Chick-fil-A, KFC, Mimi's Cafe, Outback Steaks, Sonic, Taco Bell [other] [H], AT&T, Dillard's, JC Penney, Macy's, Nordstrom's, Target, S [food] Boston Mkt, Domino's, McDonald's, Subway, Taco Bell, Wendy's [lodging] Extended Stay America [other] CVS Drug, Hen House Mkt
81	US 69 S, to Ft Scott
80	Antioch Rd
79	Metcalf Ave, N [gas] Conoco/7-11, Phillips 66/dsl/repair [food] Buffalo Wild Wings, Carrabba's, Chartroose Caboose, ChuckECheese, D'Bronx Pizza, Denny's, Fox&Hound, Hardee's, Hooters, Jack-in-the-Box, Jose Pepper's, Krispy Kreme, Subway [lodging] Comfort Inn, Days Inn, Embassy Suites, Extended Stay America, Hampton Inn, Homewood Suites, La Quinta, Motel 6, Overland Park Place Hotel, Super 8 [other] [H], AAA, Office Depot, vet, Walmart Mkt, S [food] Applebee's, McDonald's, Panera Bread [lodging] Drury Inn, Marriott, PearTree Inn
77b a	Nall Ave, Roe Ave, N [gas] QT [food] Brobeck's BBQ, Freddy's, Sonic, Winstead's Grill [lodging] Best Value Inn [other] USPO, S [food] Corner Bakery Cafe, Wendy's [lodging] Chase Suite Hotel, Courtyard, Extended Stay America, Hilton Garden, Holiday Inn, Hyatt Place, Sheraton [other] Walgreens
75b	State Line Rd, N [gas] Phillips 66 [food] Applebee's, Gate's BBQ, Jimmy John's, McDonald's, Taco Bell [other] Buick/GMC/Cadillac, Goodyear/auto, Midas, O'Reilly Parts, PriceChopper Foods, S [gas] QT/dsl [other] [H], city park
75a	Wornall Rd, N [gas] QT [food] Applebee's, China King, Coach's Grill, Dunkin Donuts, Fuzzy's Taco Shop, McDonald's, Panera Bread, Pizza Hut, Subway [other] Acura, Audi, Chevrolet, Honda, Nissan, Price Chopper, Toyota/Scion, VW
74	Holmes Rd, N [gas] Phillips 66/dsl [food] Subway, Thai House, S [lodging] Courtyard, Extended Stay America
73	103rd St (from wb)
71b a	I-470/US 50 E, I-49/US 71S
70	Bannister Rd, E [gas] Phillips 66 [food] Wendy's [other] Walgreens, W [food] Taco Bell [other] Firestone/auto, Home Depot
69	87th St., E [gas] Conoco/dsl, QT [food] McDonald's [lodging] Capital Inn [other] Advance Parts, W [lodging] Days Inn
67	Gregory Blvd (same as 66a b), W [other] Nature Ctr, zoo
66	MO 350 E, 63rd st
65	Eastwood Tfwy, W [gas] Conoco [food] Church's, McDonald's, Peachtree Rest.
63c	Raytown Rd, Stadium Dr (nb only), E [other] to Sports Complex
63b a	I-70, W to KC, E to St Louis
61	MO 78, **2 mi** E [food] Church's
60	MO 12 E, Truman Rd, 12th St, E [gas] Phillips 66/dsl, W [gas] QT
59	US 24, Independence Ave, E [gas] QT [other] to Truman Library, W [food] Hardee's [other] CarQuest
57	Front St, E [gas] FLYING J/Conoco/rest/dsl/scales/24hr [other] Blue Beacon, Kenworth, W [gas] Phillips 66/dsl, QT, Sinclair/dsl

MO

= gas = food = lodging = other = rest stop

MO MT

INTERSTATE 435 (KANSAS CITY) Cont'd

KANSAS CITY

57	Continued Denny's, McDonald's, Smugglers Rest., Subway, Waffle House Howard Johnson Plaza, Quality Inn URGENT CARE
56mm	Missouri River
55b a	MO 210, E Phillips 66/dsl Subway Ameristar Hotel/Casino, Motel 6 Ford/Volvo/GMC/Mercedes Trucks, Riverboat Casino
54	48th St, Parvin Rd, E Funpark, W QT All Star Grill, Taco Bell, Waffle House, Wendy's Candlewood Suites, Comfort Inn, Crossland Suites, Days Inn, Fairfield Inn, Hampton Inn, Holiday Inn, Super 8
52a	US 69, E Phillips 66/dsl, W McDonald's, Pizza Hut, Subway $General, Walgreens
52b	I-35, S to KC
51	Shoal Creek Dr, W LDS Temple
49b a	MO 152 E, to I-35 N, Liberty, **2 mi** E 54th St Grill, Applebee's, Bob Evans, Buffalo Wild Wings, Cracker Barrel, Longhorn Steaks, Steak'n Shake Best Western, Comfort Inn, Fairfield Inn, Hampton Inn, Holiday Inn Express, Super 8
47	NE 96th St
46	NE 108th St
45	MO 291, NE Cookingham Ave, E to I-35 N
42	N Woodland Ave
41b a	US 169, Smithville, **4 mi** N Kum&Go Burger King, McDonald's, Sonic Super 8
40	NW Cookingham
37	NW Skyview Ave, Rd C, N Cenex (1mi), S golf (3mi)
36	to I-29 S, to KCI Airport, N Cenex, S Extended Stay America, Fairfield Inn, Holiday Inn, Marriott, Microtel, Plaza Hotel, Quality Suites, Sheraton, Super 8
31	I-29 N, to St Joseph, S to KC, Prairie Creek
29	Rd D, NW 120th St
24	MO 152, Rd N, NW Berry Rd
22	MO 45, Weston, Parkville, E The Station/DiBella's Pizza/dsl
20mm	Missouri/Kansas state line, Missouri River
18	KS 5 N, Wolcott Dr, E to Wyandotte Co Lake Park
16	Donohoo Rd
15b a	Leavenworth Rd, E Conoco/Subway/dsl Comfort Suites Woodlands Racetrack
14b a	Parallel Pkwy, E Honda, Toyota/Scion, W Phillips 66/7-11/Subway/dsl Applebee's, Arby's, Bob Evans, Bryant BBQ, Carino's Italian, Chick-fil-A, Chili's, Chipotle Mexican, Chuisano's Brick Oven, Culver's, Danny's Grill, Dave&Buster's, Five Guys, Fuddrucker's, Granite City Rest, Hooters, IHOP, Jack-in-the-Box, Jose Pepper's Grill, Longhorn Sreaks, McDonald's, Olive Garden, Panda Express, Panera Bread, Pizza Hut, Red Lobster, Sheridan's Custard, Sonic, Starbucks, St Asian, Taco Bell, Taco Bueno, Wendy's Candlewood Suites, Country Inn&Suites, Holiday Inn Express, Residence Inn AT&T, JC Penney, Kohl's, NTB, Old Navy, Sam's Club/dsl, Target, TJ Maxx, Verizon, Walmart
13b a	US 24, US 40, State Ave, E Frontier Steaks water park, W Casa Agave, Famous Dave's BBQ, Lonestar Steak Best Western, Chateau Avalon, Great Wolf Lodge, Hampton Inn Cabela's, KS Race Track, Russell Stovers,
12b a	I-70, KS Tpk, to Topeka, St Louis
11	Kansas Ave
9	KS 32, KS City, Bonner Springs, W Phillips 66/dsl
8b	Woodend Rd, E Peterbilt, W Shell/Subway/dsl/scales
8.8mm	Kansas River
8a	Holliday Dr, to Lake Quivira
6c	Johnson Dr
6b a	Shawnee Mission Pkwy, E Chili's, Grand Wok, IHOP, McDonald's, Pizza Hut, Subway Aldi Foods, GNC, Home Depot, Kohl's, Lowe's, Michael's, NTB, Petsmart, Target, Walmart Subway
5	Midland Dr, Shawnee Mission Park, E Conoco, Phillips 66/7-11/Subway/dsl Barley's Brewhaus, Chen's Kitchen, Eggtc, Jose Pepper's Grill, Minsky's Pizza, Paula&Bill's Ristorante, Wendy's Hampton Inn, W Hereford House Courtyard, Holiday Inn Express
3	87th Ave, E BP, Phillips 66/dsl Freddy's, McDonald's, Panera Bread, Papa John's, Papa Murphy's, Sonic, Taco Bell Ace Hardware, Aldi Foods, Sprouts Mkt, Walgreens, W Gambino's Pizza, Grand St Cafe, Hen House Mkt, Subway Hyatt Place
2	95th St
1b	KS 10, to Lawrence
1a	Lackman Rd, N Phillips 66/dsl Suburban Lodge

I-435 begins/ends on I-35.

MONTANA

INTERSTATE 15

SHELBY

Exit #	Services
398mm	Montana/US/Canada Border
397	Sweetgrass, W **both lanes, full facilities, litter barrels, petwalk** , Gastrak Glocca Morra Motel/cafe Duty Free
394	ranch access
389	MT 552, Sunburst, W CFN/dsl Prairie Mkt/Chester Fried, Sunburst RV Park, USPO
385	Swayze Rd
379	MT 215, MT 343, to Kevin, Oilmont, W Four Corners Café
373	Potter Rd
369	Bronken Rd
366.5mm	**weigh sta sb**
364	Shelby, E Lewis&Clark RV Park, W
363	US 2, Shelby, to Cut Bank, Shelby, **0-1 mi** E Cenex, Pilot/Exxon/Country Skillet/dsl/scales/24hr, Sinclair/dsl Cowloon Chinese, Dash Drive-In, Dixie Inn Steaks, Pizza Hut, Subway, The Griddle Comfort Inn, Crossroads Inn, Glacier Motel/RV Park, O'Haire Motel H, Albertsons, CarQuest, city park, Mark's Tire, Parts+, TrueValue, USPO, visitor info, W Best Western ShopKo, to Glacier NP
361mm	**parking area nb**
358	Marias Valley Rd, to Golf Course Rd, E camping
357mm	Marias River
352	Bullhead Rd
348	Rd 44, to Valier, W Lake Frances RA (15mi)
345	MT 366, Ledger Rd, E to Tiber Dam (42mi)
339	Conrad, E **/weigh sta both lanes, full facilities, litter barrels** W Calumet/dsl, Cenex/dsl,

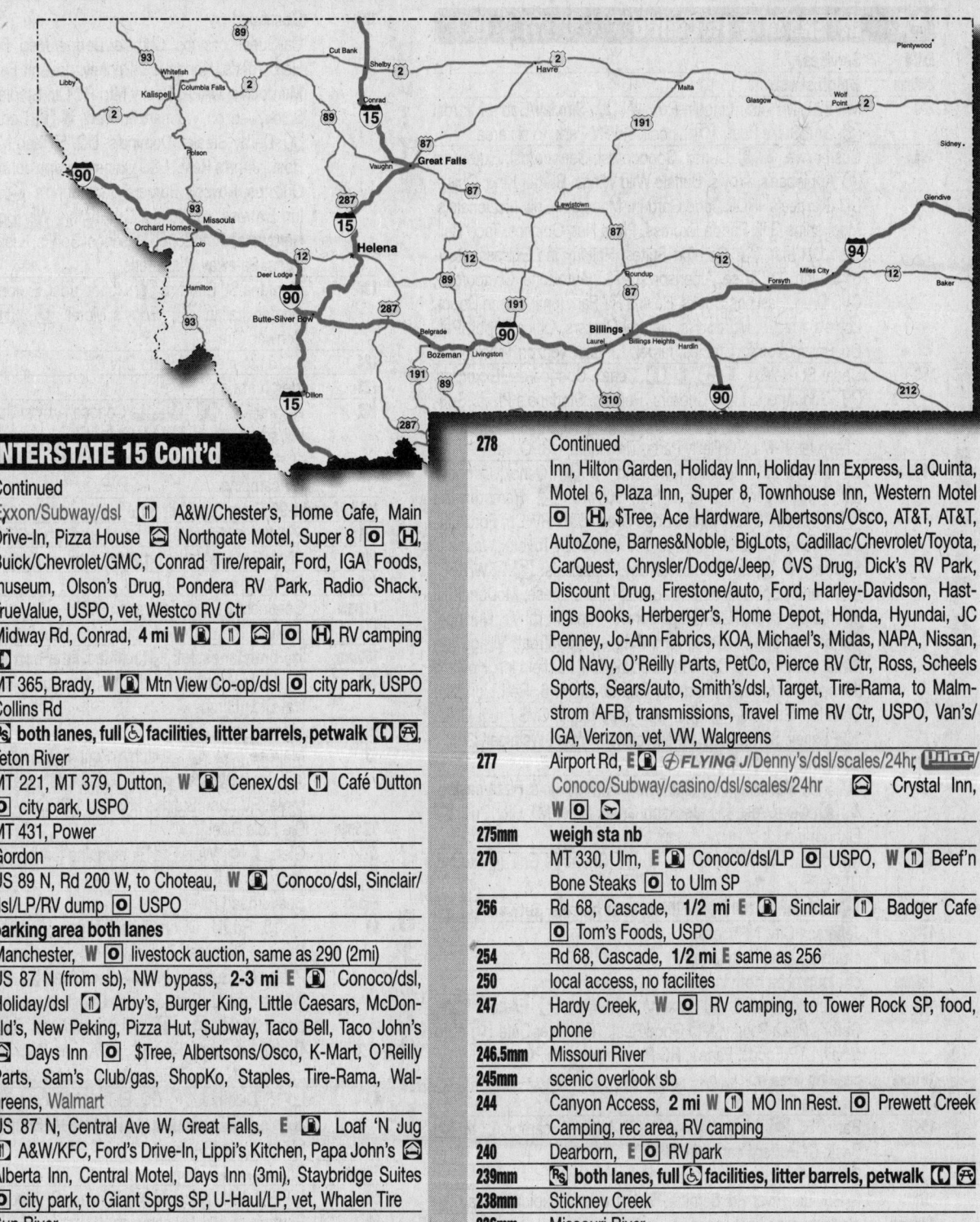

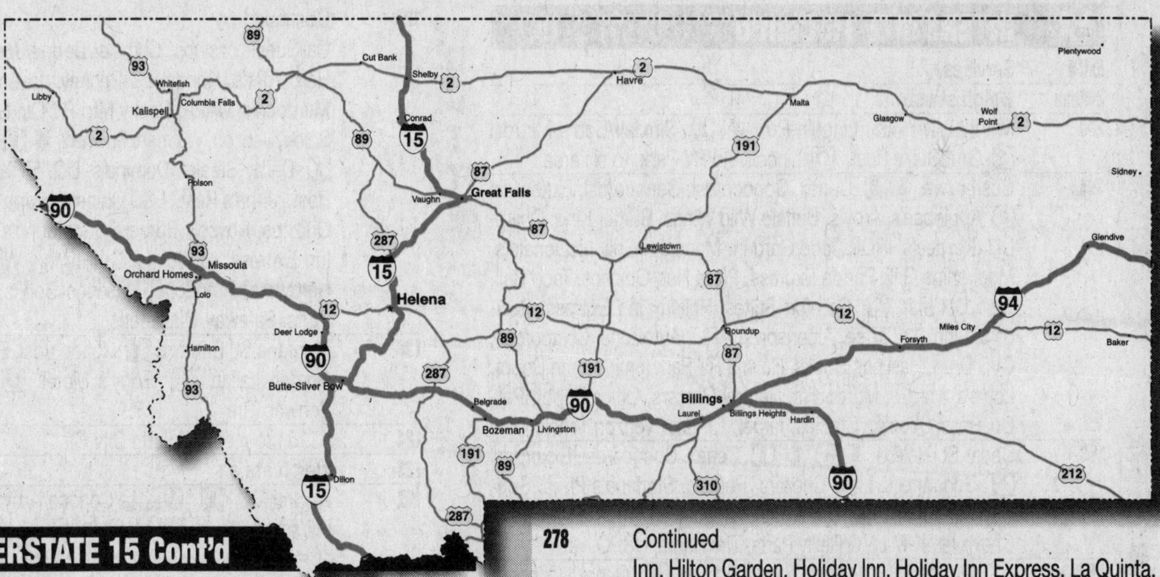

MT

INTERSTATE 15 Cont'd

CONRAD

339	Continued Exxon/Subway/dsl [food] A&W/Chester's, Home Cafe, Main Drive-In, Pizza House [lodging] Northgate Motel, Super 8 [other] [H], Buick/Chevrolet/GMC, Conrad Tire/repair, Ford, IGA Foods, museum, Olson's Drug, Pondera RV Park, Radio Shack, TrueValue, USPO, vet, Westco RV Ctr
335	Midway Rd, Conrad, **4 mi** **W** [gas] [food] [lodging] [other] [H], RV camping [phone]
328	MT 365, Brady, **W** [gas] Mtn View Co-op/dsl [other] city park, USPO
321	Collins Rd
319mm	**[rest stop] both lanes, full [handicapped] facilities, litter barrels, petwalk** [phone] [picnic], Teton River
313	MT 221, MT 379, Dutton, **W** [gas] Cenex/dsl [food] Café Dutton [other] city park, USPO
302	MT 431, Power
297	Gordon
290	US 89 N, Rd 200 W, to Choteau, **W** [gas] Conoco/dsl, Sinclair/dsl/LP/RV dump [other] USPO
288mm	**parking area both lanes**
286	Manchester, **W** [other] livestock auction, same as 290 (2mi)
282	US 87 N (from sb), NW bypass, **2-3 mi** **E** [gas] Conoco/dsl, Holiday/dsl [food] Arby's, Burger King, Little Caesars, McDonald's, New Peking, Pizza Hut, Subway, Taco Bell, Taco John's [lodging] Days Inn [other] $Tree, Albertsons/Osco, K-Mart, O'Reilly Parts, Sam's Club/gas, ShopKo, Staples, Tire-Rama, Walgreens, Walmart
280	US 87 N, Central Ave W, Great Falls, **E** [gas] Loaf 'N Jug [food] A&W/KFC, Ford's Drive-In, Lippi's Kitchen, Papa John's [lodging] Alberta Inn, Central Motel, Days Inn (3mi), Staybridge Suites [other] city park, to Giant Sprgs SP, U-Haul/LP, vet, Whalen Tire
280mm	Sun River
278	US 89 S, Rd 200 E, 10th Ave, Great Falls, **1-3 mi** **E** [gas] Calumet/dsl, Cenex/dsl, Conoco/dsl, Exxon/dsl, Holiday/Subway/dsl, Sinclair/dsl [food] 4B's Rest., Applebee's, Arby's, Baskin-Robbins, Beef'O'Brady's, Best Wok, Boston's Pizza, Burger King, Café Rio, Chili's, China Buffet, Classic 50s Diner/casino, Coldstone, DQ, Fiesta Jalicso, Fuddrucker's, Golden Corral, Hardee's, Jaker's Rest., JB's Rest., Jimmy John's, KFC, Little Caesars, MacKenzie River Pizza, McDonald's, Ming's Chinese, Moonshine Grill, Noodle Express, On-the-Border Mexican, Papa John's, Papa Murphy's, Pita Pit, Pizza Hut, PrimeCut Rest., Quiznos, Sonic, Starbucks, Subway, Taco Bell, Taco John's, Taco Treat, Wendy's, Wheat MT [lodging] Best Western, Comfort Inn, Extended Stay America, Fairfield Inn, Hampton

GREAT FALLS

278	Continued Inn, Hilton Garden, Holiday Inn, Holiday Inn Express, La Quinta, Motel 6, Plaza Inn, Super 8, Townhouse Inn, Western Motel [other] [H], $Tree, Ace Hardware, Albertsons/Osco, AT&T, AT&T, AutoZone, Barnes&Noble, BigLots, Cadillac/Chevrolet/Toyota, CarQuest, Chrysler/Dodge/Jeep, CVS Drug, Dick's RV Park, Discount Drug, Firestone/auto, Ford, Harley-Davidson, Hastings Books, Herberger's, Home Depot, Honda, Hyundai, JC Penney, Jo-Ann Fabrics, KOA, Michael's, Midas, NAPA, Nissan, Old Navy, O'Reilly Parts, PetCo, Pierce RV Ctr, Ross, Scheels Sports, Sears/auto, Smith's/dsl, Target, Tire-Rama, to Malmstrom AFB, transmissions, Travel Time RV Ctr, USPO, Van's/IGA, Verizon, vet, VW, Walgreens
277	Airport Rd, **E** [gas] FLYING J/Denny's/dsl/scales/24hr, Pilot/Conoco/Subway/casino/dsl/scales/24hr [lodging] Crystal Inn, **W** [other] [airport]
275mm	**weigh sta nb**
270	MT 330, Ulm, **E** [gas] Conoco/dsl/LP [other] USPO, **W** [food] Beef'n Bone Steaks [other] to Ulm SP
256	Rd 68, Cascade, **1/2 mi** **E** [gas] Sinclair [food] Badger Cafe [other] Tom's Foods, USPO
254	Rd 68, Cascade, **1/2 mi** **E** same as 256
250	local access, no facilites
247	Hardy Creek, **W** [other] RV camping, to Tower Rock SP, food, phone
246.5mm	Missouri River
245mm	scenic overlook sb
244	Canyon Access, **2 mi** **W** [food] MO Inn Rest. [other] Prewett Creek Camping, rec area, RV camping
240	Dearborn, **E** [other] RV park
239mm	**[rest stop] both lanes, full [handicapped] facilities, litter barrels, petwalk** [phone] [picnic]
238mm	Stickney Creek
236mm	Missouri River
234	Craig, **E** [food] Izaak's Cafe, Trout Shop Café/lodge [other] boating, camping, rec area
228	US 287 N, to Augusta, Choteau
226	MT 434, Wolf Creek, **E** [gas] Exxon/dsl [food] Oasis Café [other] camping, MT River Outfitters/lodge/flyshop, to Holter Lake, **W** [food] Frenchman&Me Café [other] USPO
222mm	**parking area both lanes**
219	Spring Creek, Recreation Rd (from nb), Spring Creek, [other] boating, camping
218mm	Little Prickly Pear Creek
216	Sieben
209	**E** [other] to Gates of the Mtns RA
205mm	turnout both directions

INTERSTATE 15 Cont'd

Exit #	Services
202mm	weigh sta sb
200	MT 279, MT 453, Lincoln Rd, W [gas] Sinclair/Bob's Mkt/dsl [food] GrubStake Rest. [other] Lincoln Rd RV Park, to ski area
194	Custer Ave, E [gas] Cenex, Conoco/dsl, Conoco/dsl, Exxon/dsl [food] Applebee's, Arby's, Buffalo Wild Wings, Burger King, Chili's, DQ, Hardee's, IHOP, Jade Garden, Macaroni Grill, McDonald's, Moonshine Grill, Panda Express, Pizza Hut, Quiznos, Taco Bell, Taco Del Mar [lodging] Comfort Suites, Holiday Inn Express, Residence Inn [other] $Tree, Albertson's, AT&T, AutoZone, Costco/gas, CVS Drug, Hastings Books, Helena RV Park (5mi), Home Depot, Lowe's, Macy's, Murdoch's, Natural Grocers, Office Depot, PetCo, Ross, ShopKo, Staples, Target, TJMaxx, Verizon, Whalen Tire
193	Cedar St, Helena, E [lodging], W [gas] Cenex, Conoco/dsl, Exxon/dsl [food] Godfather's, Little Caesars, Perkins, Steffano's Pizza, Subway, Taco John's [lodging] Quality Inn, Wingate Inn [other] Ace Hardware, Chevrolet, K-Mart, O'Reilly Parts, Tire Rama, USPO, vet
192b a	US 12, US 287, Helena, Townsend, E [gas] Cenex, Conoco/dsl [food] Burger King, Pizza Hut, Subway [lodging] Hampton Inn [other] Buick/GMC, Chrysler/Dodge/Jeep, D&D RV Ctr, Ford/Lincoln, Honda, Nissan, Schwab Tire, st patrol, Toyota, Walmart/Subway, W [gas] Exxon/dsl, Holiday, Sinclair/dsl [food] A&W/KFC, DQ, Hunan Chinese, Jimmy John's, L&D Chinese, McDonald's, Overland Express Rest., Papa John's, Papa Murphy's, Quiznos, Starbucks, Steve's Cafe, Taco John's, Taco Treat, Village Inn Pizza, Wendy's [lodging] Comfort Inn, Days Inn, Fairfield Inn, Howard Johnson, Jorgenson's Inn, La Quinta, Motel 6, Red Lion Inn, Shilo Inn, Super 8 [other] [H], AAA, Albertsons, CVS Drug, GNC, JC Penney, Safeway/dsl, Tire Factory, Verizon, Walgreens
190	S Helena, W [other] [H]
187	MT 518, Montana City, Clancy, E [food] Hugo's Pizza/casino, W [gas] Cenex/dsl [food] Jackson Creek Cafe, MT City Grill [lodging] Elkhorn Inn
182	Clancy, E [other] RV camping, W [food] Chubby's Grill [other] to NF, USPO
178mm	[rest stop] both lanes, full [access] facilities, litter barrels, petwalk [C] [RV]
176	Jefferson City, NF access
174.5mm	chain up area both lanes
168mm	chainup area both lanes
164	Rd 69, Boulder, E [gas] Exxon/dsl/casino [food] Elkhorn Cafe, Gator's Pizza Parlour, Mtn Good Rest., The River Café [other] auto repair, L&P Foods, Parts+, RC RV camping, USPO
161mm	parking area nb
160	High Ore Rd
156	Basin, E [other] Merry Widow Health Mine/RV camping, W [other] Basin Cr Pottery, camping, USPO
154mm	Boulder River
151	to Boulder River Rd, Bernice, W [other] camping, picnic area
148mm	chainup area both lanes
143.5mm	chainup area both lanes
138	Elk Park, W [other] Sheepshead Picnic Area, wildlife viewing
134	Woodville
133mm	continental divide, elev 6368
130.5mm	scenic overlook sb
129	I-90 E, to Billings

I-15 S and I-90 W run together 8 mi

127	Harrison Ave, Butte, E [gas] Cenex/dsl, Conoco/dsl, Exxon/dsl [food] 4B's Rest., A&W/KFC, Arby's, Burger King, MacKenzie River Pizza, McDonald's, MT Club Rest., Perkins, Pizza Hut, Silver Bow Pizza, Starbucks, Subway, Taco Bell, Wendy's [lodging] Best Western, Comfort Inn, Copper King Hotel, Hampton Inn, Super 8 [other] $Tree, American Car Care, Buick/Chevrolet/GMC,

127	Continued CarQuest, casinos, Chrysler/Dodge/Jeep, Ford, Hart's RV Ctr, Herberger's, Honda, JC Penney, Jo-Ann Fabrics, Kia, K-Mart, Murdoch's, NAPA, Rocky Mtn RV Ctr, Staples, Subaru, Toyota/Scion, Verizon, Walmart/Subway, W [gas] Cenex/dsl, Conoco/dsl [food] Derby Steaks, Domino's, DQ, El Taco Mexican, Hanging 5 Rest., John's Rest., L&D Chinese, Papa John's, Papa Murphy's, Quiznos, Royse's Burgers, Taco John's [lodging] Days Inn, Holiday Inn Express, La Quinta, Quality Inn, War Bonnet Inn [other] Ace Hardware, AutoZone, Hastings Books, Lisac's Tires, O'Reilly Parts, Safeway, Walgreens
126	Montana St, Butte, E [gas] Conoco/dsl, Exxon/dsl, W [food] Chef's Garden Italian [lodging] Eddy's Motel [other] [H], repair, Safeway, Schwab Tire
124	I-115 (from eb), to Butte City Ctr
123	weigh sta sb
122	Rocker, E [gas] [Pilot]/Conoco/Arby's/McDonald's/Subway/dsl/scales/24hr [lodging] Motel 6 [other] repair, weight sta nb, W [gas] [Flying J]/Exxon/rest./dsl/LP/24hr [lodging] Best Value Inn [other] RV camping

I-15 N and I-90 E run together 8 mi

121	I-90 W, to Missoula, W [other] 2 Bar Lazy-H RV Camping
119	Silver Bow, W [other] Port of MT Transportation Hub
116	Buxton
112mm	Continental Divide, elevation 5879
111	Feely
109mm	[rest stop] both lanes, full [access] facilities, litter barrels, petwalk [C] [RV]
102	Rd 43, to Wisdom, Divide, W [other] rv camping (2mi), to Big Hole Nat Bfd (62mi)
99	Moose Creek Rd
93	Melrose, W [food] Hitchin Post Rest., Melrose Café/grill/dsl [lodging] Great Waters Inn (5mi), Pioneer Mtn Cabins [other] Sportsman Motel/RV Park, Sunrise Flyshop, USPO
85.5mm	Big Hole River
85	Glen, E [other] Willis Sta RV camping (3mi)
74	Apex, Birch Creek
64mm	Beaverhead River
63	Lp 15, Rd 41, Dillon, Twin Bridges, E [gas] Cenex/dsl/LP/RV Dump, Exxon/dsl, Phillips 66/dsl [food] Lions Den, McDonald's, Pizza Hut, Subway, Whistlestop Diner [lodging] Best Value Inn, Best Western/rest., Comfort Inn, GuestHouse Inn, Motel 6, Sundowner Motel [other] [H], auto repair/tires, Buick/Chevrolet, CarQuest, city park, Family$, KOA, Les Schwab Tire, Murdoch's, museum, NAPA, O'Reilly Parts, Safeway/dsl, W MT U
62	Lp 15, Dillon, E [food] DQ, El Toro Mexican, Sparky's Rest., Taco John's [lodging] Flyshop Inn [other] [H], KOA, Southside RV Park, to W MT U, Van's/IGA Foods
60mm	Beaverhead River
59	MT 278, to Jackson, W [other] Bannack SP, Countryside RV Park/LP
56	Barretts, E [other] RV camping
55mm	parking area sb, litter barrels
52	Grasshopper Creek
51	Dalys (from sb, no return)
50mm	Beaverhead River
46mm	Beaverhead River
45mm	Beaverhead River
44	MT 324, E [food] Buffalo Lodge [other] Armstead RV Park, W [other] Clark Cyn Reservoir/RA, RV camping
38.5mm	Red Rock River
37	Red Rock
34mm	parking area both lanes, litter barrels, restrooms
29	Kidd
23	Dell, E [gas] Cenex/dsl [food] Yesterdays Calf-a [other] USPO

INTERSTATE 15 Cont'd

Exit #	Services
16.5mm	**weigh sta both lanes**
15	Lima, [rest stop] **both lanes, full [handicap] facilities, litter barrels, petwalk,** E [gas] Exxon/dsl [food] Jan's Café [lodging] Mtn View Motel/RV Park [other] ambulance, Big Sky Tire/auto, Ralph's Tire, USPO
9	Snowline
0	Monida, E [other] phone, to Red Rock Lakes
0mm	Montana/Idaho state line, Monida Pass, elevation 6870

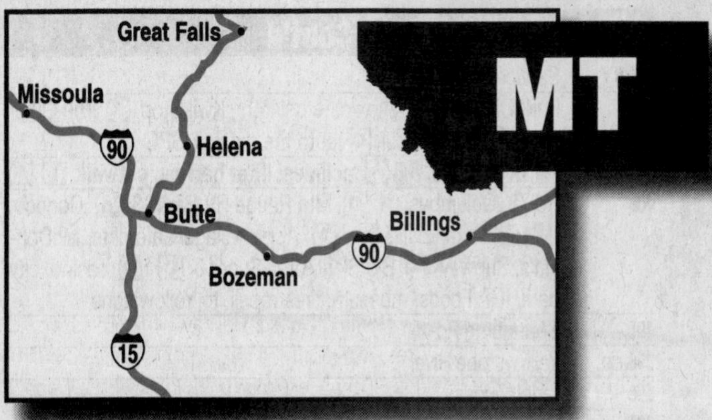

INTERSTATE 90

Exit #	Services
559.5mm	**weigh sta both lanes**
554.5mm	Montana/Wyoming state line
549	Aberdeen
544	Wyola
530	MT 463, Lodge Grass, **1 mi** S [gas] dsl, [food] [gas] [lodging]
517.5mm	Little Bighorn River
514	Garryowen, N [gas] Conoco/Subway [other] Custer Bfd Museum, S [other] 7th Ranch RV camp
511.5mm	Little Bighorn River
510	US 212 E, N [gas] Exxon/café/dsl/gifts [food] Crows Nest Café [other] [H], casino, to Little Bighorn Bfd, S [other] Little Bighorn RV Camp/dump
509.5mm	weigh sta both lanes, exit left
509.3mm	Little Bighorn River
509	Crow Agency, N [gas] Conoco, S [other] to Bighorn Canyon NRA
503	Dunmore
498mm	Bighorn River
497	MT 384, 3rd St, Hardin, S [lodging] Western Motel [other] [H], Bighorn Cty Museum, Casino Rest./lounge
495	MT 47, City Ctr, Hardin, N [gas] Cenex/dsl [food] Purple Cow Rest. [other] KOA, S [gas] Cenex/dsl, Exxon/dsl, FLYING J/Conoco/Subway/dsl/LP/24hr, Soco/dsl [food] DQ, Farwest Rest., McDonald's, Pizza Hut, Taco John's [lodging] Rodeway Inn, Super 8, Western Motel [other] [H], casinos, Chevrolet, Grand View Camping/RV Park, Sunset Village RV Park
484	Toluca
478	Fly Creek Rd
477mm	[rest stop] **both lanes, full [handicap] facilities, litter barrels, petwalk** [phone] [picnic]
469	Arrow Creek Rd
462	Pryor Creek Rd
456	I-94 E, to Bismarck, ND
455	Johnson Lane, N [gas] Pilot/Conoco/McDonald's/dsl/scales/24hr, S [gas] FLYING J/dsl/LP/scales/24hr, Exxon/A&W/dsl [food] Burger King, Domino's, DQ, Jin's Chinese, Subway [lodging] Holiday Inn Express [other] Bretz RV Ctr (1mi), Verizon, Whalen Tire
452	US 87 N, City Ctr, Billings, **2-4 mi on N US 87** [gas] Conoco/Arby's/dsl/LP, Exxon [food] Applebee's, Arby's, Bugz Rest./casino, Burger King, Domino's, DQ, Fuddrucker's, Golden Phoenix, Jimmy John's, KFC, Little Caesars, McDonald's, MT Jack's, Panda Express, Papa John's, Papa Murphy's, Pizza Hut, Shanghai Buffet, Sonic, Subway, Taco Bell, Taco John's, Wendy's [lodging] Best Western, Country Inn&Suites, Foothills Inn, Heights Motel [other] $Tree, Ace Hardware, Albertsons/Osco, American Spirit RV Ctr, AT&T, AutoZone, BigLots, CarQuest, Cenex/dsl, Conoco/dsl, CVS Drug, GNC, Holiday/dsl, Metra Rv Ctr, Office Depot, O'Reilly Parts, Radio Shack, Target, Tire Rama, transmissions, U-Haul, Verizon, vet, Walgreens, Walmart, S [gas] Cenex/dsl [other] RV Camping
451.5mm	Yellowstone River
450	MT 3, 27th St, Billings, N [gas] Conoco/dsl, Sinclair [food] Blondy's Cafe, Pizza Hut [lodging] Crowne Plaza, Vegas Motel [other] [H], CarQuest, city park, USPO, visitor ctr, S [other] KOA, Yellowstone River Camping
447	S Billings Blvd, N [gas] Conoco/Subway/dsl, Holiday/dsl [food] Burger King, DQ, El Corral Mexican, McDonald's [lodging] Best Western/Kelly, Days Inn, Extended Stay America, Hampton Inn, Sleep Inn, Super 8 [other] Cabela's Sporting Goods, NAPA, Sam's Club/gas, S [other] Billings RV Park (2mi), Freightliner, Kenworth, KOA (2mi), Yellowstone River Campground
446	King Ave, Billings, N **on 24th** [gas] Conoco/dsl, Conoco/dsl, Exxon, Exxon/Subway, Holiday/dsl/LP/RV dump [food] Applebee's, Arbys, Bruno's Italian, Buffalo Wild Wings, Burger King, Cactus Creek Steaks, Café Rio, Carino's Italian, ChuckECheese's, City Brew Coffee, Coldstone, Del Taco, Denny's, Dos Machos, DQ, Emporium Rest., Famous Dave's, Fuddrucker's, Golden Corral, Gusicks Rest., Hardee's, HuHot Mongolian, IHOP, Jade Palace, Jake's Grill, Japanese Steaks, KFC, Lemongrass Thai, Little Caesars, McDonald's, MooYah Burgers, Old Chicago, Olive Garden, Outback Steaks, Papa John's, Perkins, Pizza Hut, Pizza Ranch, Qdoba, Red Lobster, Rendezvous Grill, Starbucks, Subway, Taco Bell, Taco John's, TX Roadhouse, Wendy's [lodging] C'Mon Inn, Comfort Inn, Fairfield Inn, Hilton Garden, Lexington Inn, Quality Inn, Residence Inn, SpringHill Suites, Western Executive Inn [other] Albertsons/Osco, AutoZone, Barnes&Noble, Best Buy, Cadillac/GMC, Chevrolet, Chrysler/Dodge/Jeep, Costco/gas, Dillards, Ford, Hancock Fabrics, Hobby Lobby, Home Depot, JC Penney, JoAnn Fabrics, Kia, K-Mart, Lisac's Tire, Lowe's, mall, Mercedes, Michael's, Natural Grocers, Nissan, Office Depot, Old Navy, O'Reilly Parts, Petsmart, Ross, ShopKo, Subaru, Suzuki, Toyota, USPO, Verizon, Walmart/Subway, World Mkt, S [gas] Conoco/dsl [food] Cracker Barrel, Emporium Rest. [lodging] Billings Hotel, EconoLodge, Holiday Inn, Howard Johnson, Kelly Inn, Motel 6 [other] Volvo/Mack Trucks, water funpark
443	Zoo Dr, to Shiloh Rd, N [gas] Holiday/dsl [food] MT Rib/Chophouse [lodging] Bighorn Resort/waterpark, Hampton Inn, Holiday Inn Express, Homewood Suites [other] Honda, Pierce RV Ctr, zoo, S [other] Harley-Davidson, vet
439mm	**weigh sta both lanes**
437	E Laurel, S [gas] Sinclair/rest./dsl/scales/casino/motel/RV Park/24hr
434	US 212, US 310, to Red Lodge, Laurel, N [gas] Cenex/dsl, Conoco/dsl, Exxon/dsl [food] City Brew Coffee, Hardee's, McDonald's, Pitts Pizza, Pizza Hut, Subway, Taco John's [lodging] Best Western, Locomotive Inn [other] Ace Hardware, AutoZone, Chevrolet, CVS Drug, Ford, IGA Foods, O'Reilly Parts, Rapid Tire, Verizon, Walmart/Subway, S [other] Riverside Park/RV Camping, to Yellowstone NP, vet
433	Lp 90 (from eb), same as 434

HARDIN

BILLINGS

BILLINGS

MT

MT

INTERSTATE 90 Cont'd

Exit # Services

426 Park City, S Cenex/café/dsl/24hr, KwikStop The Other Cafe CJ's Motel auto/tire repair, USPO

419mm **both lanes, full facilities, litter barrels, petwalk**

408 Rd 78, Columbus, N Mtn Range RV Park, S Conoco, Pilot/Exxon/dsl/24hr Apple Village Café/gifts, McDonald's, Subway Big Sky Motel, Super 8 H, casino, city park, IGA Foods, museum, tires/repair, to Yellowstone

400 Springtime Rd

398mm Yellowstone River

396 ranch access

392 Reed Point, N Old West RV Park, USPO

384 Bridger Creek Rd

381mm **both lanes, full facilities, litter barrels, petwalk**

377 Greycliff, S KOA, Prairie Dog Town SP

370 US 191, Big Timber, **1 mi** N Cenex/dsl, Sinclair/dsl Grand Hotel, Lazy J Motel H, Spring Creek RV Ranch (4mi), USPO, vet

369mm Boulder River

367 US 191 N, Big Timber, N Conoco/dsl, Exxon/dsl Country Skillet River Valley Inn, Super 8 CarQuest, historic site/visitor info, Spring Creek Camping (3mi)

362 De Hart

354 MT 563, Springdale

352 ranch access

350 East End access

343 Mission Creek Rd, N Ft Parker HS

340 US 89 N, to White Sulphur Sprgs, S

LIVINGSTON

337 Lp 90, to Livingston, **2 mi** N services

333mm Yellowstone River

333 US 89 S, Livingston, N Clark's Rest., DQ, Mark's In&Out, Pizza Hut, Taco John's Best Western, Budget Host, Livingston Inn, Quality Inn, Rodeway Inn H, Chrysler/Dodge/Jeep, Radio Shack, RV Park, ShopKo, Town&Country Foods, Verizon, Western Drug, S Cenex/dsl, Conoco/dsl, Exxon/dsl Arby's, McDonald's, Rosa's Pizza, Subway Comfort Inn, Super 8 Albertsons/Osco, KOA (10mi), LP, Osen's RV Park, to Yellowstone, vet

330 Lp 90, Livingston, **1 mi** N Cenex/Yellowstone Trkstp/dsl/rest./24hr

326.5mm **chainup/chain removal area both lanes**

324 ranch access

323mm **chainup/chain removal area wb**

322mm Bridger Mountain Range

321mm turnouts/hist marker both lanes

319 Jackson Creek Rd

319mm **chainup area both lanes**

316 Trail Creek Rd

313 Bear Canyon Rd, S Bear Canyon Camping

BOZEMAN

309 US 191 S, Main St, Bozeman, N Subaru, Sunrise RV Park, VW, S Cenex/dsl, Exxon/dsl MT AleWorks Continental Motel, Ranch House Motel, Western Heritage Inn H, Heeb's Foods, repair, Tire Rama, to Yellowstone, vet

306 MT 205, N 7th, to US 191, Bozeman, N Cenex McDonald's, Panda Buffet Fairfield Inn, La Quinta, Microtel, Motel 6, Ramada Ltd, Super 8, TLC Inn Merdoch's, ski area, Whalen Tire, S Conoco/Arby's/dsl, Exxon Applebee's, Bar-3 BBQ, Dominos, DQ, Famous Dave's BBQ, Papa John's, Santa Fe Red's Cafe, Taco John's, Tarintino's Pizza, The Wok Chinese Best Western, Bozeman Inn, Comfort Inn, Days Inn, Hampton Inn, Holiday Inn, Homewood Suites, Royal 7 Inn

306 Continued
Big O Tire, Firestone/auto, K-Mart, Museum of the Rockie U-Haul, Walmart/McDonald's

305 MT412, N 19th Ave, N Exxon Mountainview Inn, 0- mi S **full facilities, litter barrels, petwalk** Conoco/dsl A&W/KFC, Baja Fresh, Buffalo Wild Wing Canyons Grill, Carino's Italian, City Brew Coffee, Clarks Fo Rest., IHOP, Jimmy John's, Mongolian BBQ, Old Chicago Pi. za, Olive Garden, Outback Steaks, Papa Murphy's, Starbuck Subway, Wasabi Grill, Wendy's C'mon Inn, Comfort Suite Hilton Garden, Holiday Inn Express, My Place Extended Sta Residence Inn AT&T, Costco/gas, Ford/Lincoln/RV C Home Depot, Lowe's, Michaels, Office Depot, Petsmart, Ra dio Shack, REI, Ross, Smith's Foods, Staples, Target, TJMax UPS, USPO, Verizon, vet, World MKT

BELGRADE

298 MT 291, Rd 85, Belgrade, N Cenex/dsl, Exxon/Subwa dsl Burger King, DQ, McDonald's, Papa Murphy's, Pizz Hut, Rosa's Pizza, Starbucks, Taco Time Holiday Inn Ex press Albertson's/Osco, Lee&Dad's Foods, NAPA, Verizo Whalen Tire, S FLYING J/Conoco/dsl/scales/LP L Quinta, Quality Inn, Super 8 Freightliner, Harley-Davidso KOA (9mi), repair, Tire Factory, to Yellowstone NP, truckwas TrueValue

292.5mm Gallatin River

288 MT 288, MT 346, Manhattan, N Conoco/Subway/d RV camping

283 Logan, S Madison Buffalo Jump SP (7mi)

279mm Madison River

278 MT 205, Rd 2, Three Forks, Trident, N Missouri Headwater SP, **1 mi** S Conoco/dsl Broken Spur Motel, Lewis&Clar Motel, Sacajawea Hotel camping, CarQuest,

277.5mm Jefferson River

274 US 287, to Helena, Ennis, N Conoco/dsl Wheat M Bakery/deli Ft 3 Forks Motel dsl repair, KOA (2mi), t Canyon Ferry SP, S Pilot/Exxon/Subway/dsl/scales/24h Camp 3 Forks, Lewis&Clark Caverns SP, to Yellowstone N

267 Milligan Canyon Rd

261.5mm **chain-up area**

257mm Boulder River

256 MT 359, Cardwell, S Cenex/dsl/RV Park Lewis&Clar Caverns SP, RV camping, to Yellowstone NP

249 Rd 55, to Rd 69, Whitehall, S Exxon/dsl A&W/KFC Subway Rodeway Inn camping, casino, Virginia Cit NHS

241 Pipestone

240.5mm **chainup/chain removal area both lanes**

238.5mm **runaway ramp eb**

237.5mm pulloff eb

235mm **truck parking both lanes, litter barrels, rest rooms**

233 Homestake, Continental Divide, elev 6393

230mm **chain-up area both lanes**

228 MT 375, Continental Dr, S Conoco/dsl 3 Bears Foods Harley-Davidson

BUTTE

227 I-15 N, to Helena, Great Falls

I-90 and I-15 run together 8 mi. See Montana I-15, exits 122-127.

123mm **weight sta wb**

219 I-15 S, to Dillon, Idaho Falls

216 Ramsay

211 MT 441, Gregson, **3-5 mi** S Fairmont RV Park (Apr-Oct), food lodging

210.5mm **Pintlar Scenic route info, parking area wb**

INTERSTATE 90 Cont'd

DEER LODGE

208 Rd 1, Pintler Scenic Loop, Georgetown Lake RA, Opportunity, Anaconda, **S** [rest stop] **both lanes, full [handicap] facilities, litter barrels, petwalk** [picnic], [other] [H], [food] [gas] [lodging], RV camp/dump, ski area

201 Warm Springs, **S** [other] MT ST [H]

197 MT 273, Galen, **S** [other] to MT ST [H]

195 Racetrack

187 Lp 90, Deer Lodge (no wb return), **2 mi S** [gas] Calumet/dsl [lodging] Budget Inn [other] [H], KOA (seasonal), Old MT Prison/auto museum, same as 184, Valley Foods

184 Deer Lodge, **0-1 mi S** [gas] Conoco/dsl/casino, Exxon/dsl/casino [food] 4B's Rest., A&W, McDonald's, Pizza Hut, Yak Yak Cafe [lodging] Travelodge, Western Big Sky Inn [other] [H], city park, Grant-Kohrs Ranch NHS, Indian Creek Camping, KOA, Safeway/deli, Schwab Tire, USPO

179 Beck Hill Rd

175 US 12 E, Garrison, **N** [other] hist site, phone, RiverFront RV Park

175mm Little Blackfoot River

174 US 12 E (from eb), **S** [food] Ranch House Cafe/RV Park, same as 175

170 Phosphate

168mm [rest stop] **both lanes, full [handicap] facilities, hist site litter barrels, petwalk** [phone] [picnic]

166 Gold Creek, **S** [other] Camp Mak-A-Dream, USPO

162 Jens

154 to MT 1 (from wb), Drummond, **S** [gas] Cenex/dsl, Conoco/dsl [food] Parker's Rest., Wagon Wheel Café [lodging] Drummond Motel, Sky Motel, Wagon Wheel Motel [other] city park, Front St Mkt, Georgetown Lake RA, Goodtime RV Park (3mi), Pintler Scenic Lp

153 MT 1 (from eb), **N** [other] Garnet GhostTown, Goodtime RV Park (3mi), **S** same as 154

150.5mm **weigh sta both lanes**

143mm [rest stop] **both lanes, full [handicap] facilities, hist site litter barrels, petwalk** [phone] [picnic]

138 Bearmouth Area, **N** [other] Chalet Bearmouth Camp/rest., food, lodging, to gas

130 Beavertail Rd, **S** [other] camping (seasonal), rec area, to Beavertail Hill SP

128mm **parking area both lanes, litter barrels/restrooms**

126 Rock Creek Rd, **S** [lodging] Rock Creek Lodge/gas/casino [other] rec area

120 Clinton, **N** [gas] Conoco/dsl [food] Poor Henry's Café (1mi W on frtg rd) [other] Clinton Market, **S** [other] USPO

113 Turah, **S** Turah RV Park/[gas]

109.5mm Clark Fork

109mm Blackfoot River

109 MT 200 E, Bonner, **N** [gas] Pilot/Exxon/Arby's/Subway/dsl/scales/casino/LP/24hr [food] River City Grill [other] hist site, USPO

108.5mm Clark Fork

MISSOULA

107 E Missoula, **N** [gas] Ole's Mkt/Conoco/diner/dsl, Sinclair [food] Reno Cafe [lodging] Aspen Motel [other] dsl repair

105 US 12 W, Missoula, **S** [gas] Cenex/dsl, Conoco/dsl, Sinclair/dsl [food] 5 Guys Burgers, Burger King, Finn &Porter Rest., McDonald's, Pizza Hut, Qdoba, Subway, Taco Bell [lodging] Budget Inn, Campus Inn, Comfort Inn, DoubleTree, Motel 6, Thunderbird Motel [other] Ace Hardware, Albertson's, Kingfisher Flyshop, O'Reilly Parts, U of MT, Verizon, Vietnam Vet's Mem

104 Orange St, Missoula, **S** [gas] Conoco/dsl [food] Pagoda Chinese, Subway, Taco John's [lodging] Best Value Inn, Red Lion Inn [other] [H], TireRama, to City Ctr

101 US 93 S, Reserve St, **N** [gas] Conoco/dsl [food] Cracker Barrel, MacKenzie River Pizza, Starbucks [lodging] Best Western, C'Mon Inn, Motel 6 [other] ski area, **0-2 mi S** [gas] Cenex/dsl/LP, Conoco/

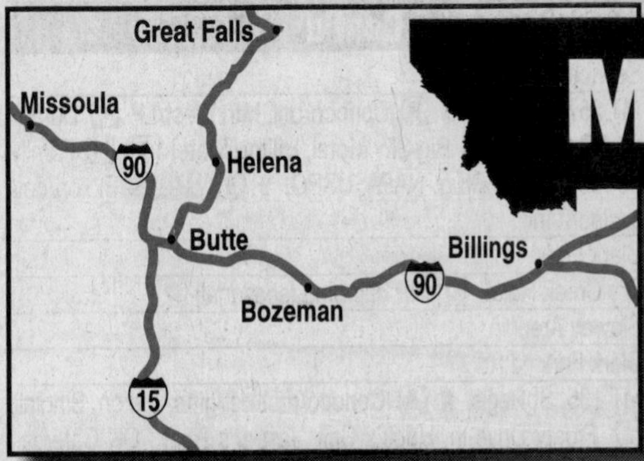

101 Continued
dsl, Exxon/Subway/dsl, Sinclair/dsl [food] Arby's, Buffalo Wild Wings, Burger King, Cafe Rio, Carino's, China Bowl, Coldstone, DQ, Famous Dave's BBQ, Fuddrucker's, HoagiVille, Hooters, IHOP, Jimmy John's, Little Caesars, McDonald's, MT Club Rest./casino, Outback Steaks, Perkins, Pizza Hut, Quiznos, Rowdy's Cabin Rest., Stone Of Accord, Taco Bell, Taco Time/TCBY, Wendy's [lodging] Courtyard, EconoLodge, Hampton Inn, Hilton Garden, Holiday Inn Express, La Quinta, Quality Inn, Ruby's Inn/rest., Staybridge Suites, Super 8, TownePlace Suites, Travelers Inn [other] Albertson's, Barnes&Noble, Best Buy, Bretz RV/Marine, casinos, Chevrolet/Cadillac, Costco/gas, dsl repair, Firestone/auto, GNC, Home Depot, Lowe's, Michael's, Old Navy, Petsmart, Radio Shack, Ross, Staples, Target, TJ Maxx, Verizon, VW, Walgreens, Walmart/Subway

99 Airway Blvd, **S** [gas] Mobil/dsl/24hr, Sinclair/dsl [lodging] Stone Creek Lodge, Wingate Inn [other] [airport], Chrysler/Dodge/Jeep, Harley-Davidson, Kia

96 US 93 N, MT 200W, Kalispell, **N** [gas] Conoco/rest./dsl/scales/24hr/ @, Flying J/Exxon/McDonald's/dsl/scales/24hr [food] WheatMT/deli [lodging] Days Inn/rest. [other] Jellystone RV Park (1mi), Jim&Mary's RV Park (1mi), Peterbilt, to Flathead Lake&Glacier NP, **S** [gas] Sinclair/dsl, TA/Sinclair/Country Pride/dsl/scales/24hr [lodging] Redwood Lodge [other] Kenworth

92.5mm **inspection sta both lanes**

89 Frenchtown, **N** [other] to Frenchtown Pond SP, **S** [gas] Conoco/dsl/café [food] Alcan Grill, Eugene's Cafe, Quiznos [other] Broncs Grocery/gas, USPO

85 Huson, **S** [gas] [food] [other] [phone]

82 Nine Mile Rd, **N** [food] Mile House Rest. [other] Hist Ranger Sta/info, [phone]

81.5mm Clark Fork

80mm Clark Fork

77 MT 507, Petty Creek Rd, Alberton, **S** [gas] access to [food] [gas] [lodging], [other] [phone]

75 Alberton, **N** [gas] Cenex/dsl [other] USPO, **S** [lodging] River Edge Rest [other] casino, motel, RV camp

73mm **parking area wb, litter barrels**

72mm **parking area eb, litter barrels**

70 Cyr

70mm Clark Fork

66 Fish Creek Rd

66mm Clark Fork

61 Tarkio

59mm Clark Fork

58mm [rest stop] **both lanes, full [handicap] facilities, litter barrels** [phone] [picnic] NF camping (seasonal)

55 Lozeau, Quartz

53.5mm Clark Fork

49mm Clark Fork

MT

INTERSTATE 90 Cont'd

Exit #	Services
47	MT 257, Superior, N [gas] Conoco/dsl, Mtn West/LP [food] Durango's Rest./gas [lodging] Big Sky Motel, Hilltop Motel [other] [H], Family Foods, Mineral Drug, NAPA, USPO, S [gas] Pilot/Exxon/dsl/casino/24hr
45mm	Clark Fork
43	Dry Creek Rd, N [other] NP camping (seasonal)
37	Sloway Area
34mm	Clark Fork
33	MT 135, St Regis, N [gas] Conoco/rest/dsl/gifts, Exxon, Sinclair [food] Frosty Drive-In, Huck's Grill, Jasper's Rest., OK Café/casino, Subway (seasonal) [lodging] Little River Motel, St Regis Motel, Super 8 [other] antiques, city park, Nugget Camground, St Regis Campground (seasonal), to Glacier NP, USPO
30	Two Mile Rd, S [other] fishing access
29mm	fishing access, wb
26	Ward Creek Rd (from eb)
25	Drexel
22	Camels Hump Rd, Henderson, N [other] antiques (1mi), camping (seasonal)
18	DeBorgia, N [food] O'aces Rest. [other] Black Diamond Guest Ranch, USPO
16	Haugan, N [gas] Exxon/dsl/24hr [lodging] 50000 Silver $/motel/rest./casino/RV park
15mm	**weigh sta both lanes exits left from both lanes**
10	Saltese, N [lodging] Mangold's Motel
10mm	St Regis River
5	Taft Area, access to Hiawatha Trail
4.5mm	[RS] **both lanes, chainup removal, full [handicap] facilities, litter barrels, petwalk**
0	Lookout Pass, [other] access to Lookout Pass ski area/lodge, info
0mm	Montana/Idaho state line, Lookout Pass elev 4680, Central/Pacific time zone

INTERSTATE 94

Exit #	Services
250mm	Montana/North Dakota state line
248	Carlyle Rd
242	MT 7 (from wb), Wibaux, S [RS] **both lanes, full [handicap] facilities, litter barrels [phone] [picnic],** [gas] Amsler's/dsl, Cenex/dsl/service [food] Tastee Hut [lodging] Beaver Creek Inn [other] RV camping,
241	MT 261 (from eb), to MT 7, Wibaux, S same as 242
240mm	**weigh sta both lanes**
236	ranch access
231	Hodges Rd
224	Griffith Creek, frontage road
222.5mm	Griffith Creek
	GLENDIVE
215	MT 335, Glendive, City Ctr, N [gas] Cenex [food] C's Family Café [lodging] Astoria Suites, Comfort Inn, Days Inn, Holiday Inn Express, Super 8, Yellowstone River Inn [other] Glendive Camping (apr-oct), museum, Running's Hardware, S [gas] Exxon/dsl, Holiday/dsl [food] Mexico Lindo, Subway, Taco John's [lodging] El Centro Motel, Glendive Inn, Guesthouse Inn [other] [H], Radio Shack, to Makoshika SP
215mm	Yellowstone River
213	MT 16, to Sidney, Glendive, N [other] Green Valley Camping, st patrol, S [gas] Cenex/dsl, Conoco/dsl, Sinclair/dsl [food] Dickey's BBQ, Pizza Hut [lodging] Riverside Inn [other] Albertson's/Osco, Ford, K-Mart, NAPA, Reynolds Mkt
211	MT 200S (from wb, no EZ return), to Circle
210	Lp 94, to Rd 200 S, W Glendive, S [gas] Cenex/dsl [other] Buick/Chevrolet, I-94 RV Park, Makoshika SP, Tire Rama
206	Pleasant View Rd
204	Whoopup Creek Rd
198	Cracker Box Rd
192	Bad Route Rd, S [RS] **/weigh sta both lanes, camping, full [handicap] facilities, litter barrels, petwalk [phone] [picnic] weather info**
187mm	Yellowstone River
185	MT 340, Fallon, S [food] café [other] [phone]
184mm	O'Fallon Creek
176	MT 253, Terry, N [gas] 4Corners/dsl, Conoco/dsl [food] Dizzy Diner [lodging] Kempton Hotel [other] [H], museum, Terry RV Oasis
170mm	Powder River
169	Powder River Rd
159	Diamond Ring
	MILES CITY
148	Valley Access
141	US 12 E, Miles City, N [other] RV Camping
138	Rd 59, Miles City, N [gas] Cenex/dsl, Conoco/dsl, Pilot/Exxon/dsl/24hr [food] 4B's Rest., Arby's, Boardwalk Rest., DQ, Gallagher's Rest., Little Caesars, McDonald's, Mexico Lindo, Pizza Hut, R&B Chophouse, Subway, Taco John's, Wendy's [lodging] Best Western, EconoLodge, Motel 6, Sleep Inn [other] [H], Ace Hardware, Albertsons/Osco, casinos, Meadows RV Park, Murdoch's, O'Reilly Parts, Verizon, Walmart, S [food] New Hunan Chinese [lodging] Comfort Inn, Guesthouse Inn, Holiday Inn Express, Super 8
137mm	Tongue River
135	Lp 94, Miles City, N [other] KOA (Apr-Oct)
128	local access
126	Moon Creek Rd
117	Hathaway
114mm	[RS] **eb, full [handicap] facilities, litter barrels, petwalk [phone] [picnic]**
113mm	[RS] **wb, full [handicap] facilities, litter barrels, petwalk [phone] [picnic]**
106	Butte Creek Rd, to Rosebud, N [food] [phone]
103	MT 446, MT 447, Rosebud Creek Rd, N [food] [phone]
	FORSYTH
98.5mm	**weigh sta both lanes**
95	Forsyth, N [gas] Exxon/dsl, Kum&Go [food] DQ, M&M Café [lodging] Magnuson Hotel [other] [H], Ford, museum, NAPA, to Rosebud RA, Van's/IGA, Yellowstone Drug, S [other] Wagon Wheel Camping
93	US 12 W, Forsyth, N [gas] Exxon/dsl, Kum&Go [food] Fitzgerald's Rest., Top That Eatery [lodging] Rails Inn, Restwel Inn, WestWind Motel [other] [H], museum, RV camping, Tire Factory/repair
87	Rd 39, to Colstrip
82	Reservation Creek Rd
72	MT 384, Sarpy Creek Rd
67	Hysham, **1-2 mi** N [gas] [food] [phone]
65mm	[RS] **both lanes, full [handicap] facilities, litter barrels, petwalk [phone] [picnic]**
63	ranch access
53	Bighorn, access to [phone]
52mm	Bighorn River
49	MT 47, to Hardin, Custer, S [food] Ft Custer Café [other] camping, to Little Bighorn Bfd
47	Custer, S [gas] Custer Sta/dsl [food] Jct City Saloon/café [other] USPO
41.5mm	[RS] **wb, full [handicap] facilities, litter barrels, petwalk [phone] [picnic]**
38mm	[RS] **eb, full [handicap] facilities, litter barrels, petwalk [phone] [picnic]**
36	frontage rd, Waco
23	Pompeys Pillar, N [other] Pompeys Pillar Nat Landmark
14	Ballentine, Worden, S [food] Long Branch Café/casino
6	MT 522, Huntley, N [gas] [phone] [food] Pryor Creek Café/casino [other] golf
0mm	I-90, E to Sheridan, W to Billings, **I-94 begins/ends on I-90, exit 456.**

NEBRASKA

INTERSTATE 80

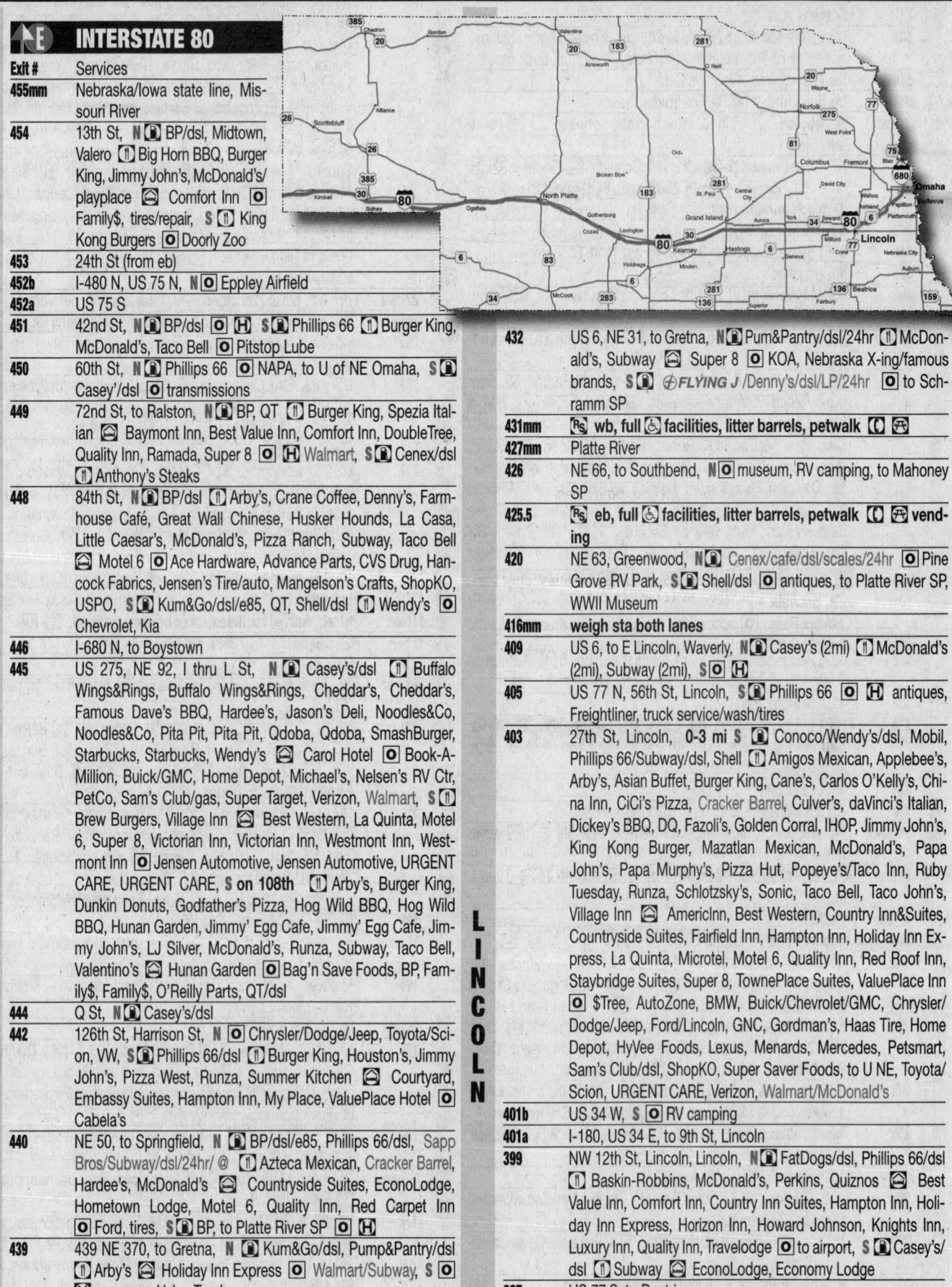

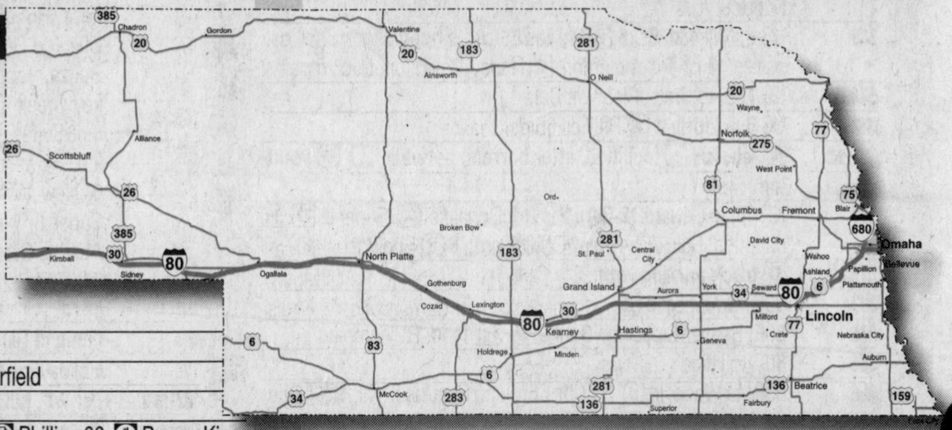

Exit #	Services
455mm	Nebraska/Iowa state line, Missouri River
454	13th St, N [gas] BP/dsl, Midtown, Valero [food] Big Horn BBQ, Burger King, Jimmy John's, McDonald's/playplace [lodging] Comfort Inn [other] Family$, tires/repair, S [food] King Kong Burgers [other] Doorly Zoo
453	24th St (from eb)
452b	I-480 N, US 75 N, N [other] Eppley Airfield
452a	US 75 S
451	42nd St, N [gas] BP/dsl [other] [H] S [gas] Phillips 66 [food] Burger King, McDonald's, Taco Bell [other] Pitstop Lube
450	60th St, N [gas] Phillips 66 [other] NAPA, to U of NE Omaha, S [gas] Casey'/dsl [other] transmissions
449	72nd St, to Ralston, N [gas] BP, QT [food] Burger King, Spezia Italian [lodging] Baymont Inn, Best Value Inn, Comfort Inn, DoubleTree, Quality Inn, Ramada, Super 8 [other] [H] Walmart, S [gas] Cenex/dsl [food] Anthony's Steaks
448	84th St, N [gas] BP/dsl [food] Arby's, Crane Coffee, Denny's, Farmhouse Café, Great Wall Chinese, Husker Hounds, La Casa, Little Caesar's, McDonald's, Pizza Ranch, Subway, Taco Bell [lodging] Motel 6 [other] Ace Hardware, Advance Parts, CVS Drug, Hancock Fabrics, Jensen's Tire/auto, Mangelson's Crafts, ShopKO, USPO, S [gas] Kum&Go/dsl/e85, QT, Shell/dsl [food] Wendy's [other] Chevrolet, Kia
446	I-680 N, to Boystown
445	US 275, NE 92, I thru L St, N [gas] Casey's/dsl [food] Buffalo Wings&Rings, Buffalo Wings&Rings, Cheddar's, Cheddar's, Famous Dave's BBQ, Hardee's, Jason's Deli, Noodles&Co, Noodles&Co, Pita Pit, Pita Pit, Qdoba, Qdoba, SmashBurger, Starbucks, Starbucks, Wendy's [lodging] Carol Hotel [other] Book-A-Million, Buick/GMC, Home Depot, Michael's, Nelsen's RV Ctr, PetCo, Sam's Club/gas, Super Target, Verizon, Walmart, S [food] Brew Burgers, Village Inn [lodging] Best Western, La Quinta, Motel 6, Super 8, Victorian Inn, Victorian Inn, Westmont Inn, Westmont Inn [other] Jensen Automotive, Jensen Automotive, URGENT CARE, URGENT CARE, S on 108th [food] Arby's, Burger King, Dunkin Donuts, Godfather's Pizza, Hog Wild BBQ, Hog Wild BBQ, Hunan Garden, Jimmy' Egg Cafe, Jimmy' Egg Cafe, Jimmy John's, LJ Silver, McDonald's, Runza, Subway, Taco Bell, Valentino's [lodging] Hunan Garden [other] Bag'n Save Foods, BP, Family$, Family$, O'Reilly Parts, QT/dsl
444	Q St, N [gas] Casey's/dsl
442	126th St, Harrison St, N [other] Chrysler/Dodge/Jeep, Toyota/Scion, VW, S [gas] Phillips 66/dsl [food] Burger King, Houston's, Jimmy John's, Pizza West, Runza, Summer Kitchen [lodging] Courtyard, Embassy Suites, Hampton Inn, My Place, ValuePlace Hotel [other] Cabela's
440	NE 50, to Springfield, N [gas] BP/dsl/e85, Phillips 66/dsl, Sapp Bros/Subway/dsl/24hr/ @ [food] Azteca Mexican, Cracker Barrel, Hardee's, McDonald's [lodging] Countryside Suites, EconoLodge, Hometown Lodge, Motel 6, Quality Inn, Red Carpet Inn [other] Ford, tires, S [gas] BP, to Platte River SP [other] [H]
439	439 NE 370, to Gretna, N [gas] Kum&Go/dsl, Pump&Pantry/dsl [food] Arby's [lodging] Holiday Inn Express [other] Walmart/Subway, S [other] [H] museum, Volvo Trucks
432	US 6, NE 31, to Gretna, N [gas] Pum&Pantry/dsl/24hr [food] McDonald's, Subway [lodging] Super 8 [other] KOA, Nebraska X-ing/famous brands, S [gas] FLYING J /Denny's/dsl/LP/24hr [other] to Schramm SP
431mm	**[RS] wb, full [handicapped] facilities, litter barrels, petwalk [phone] [picnic]**
427mm	Platte River
426	NE 66, to Southbend, N [other] museum, RV camping, to Mahoney SP
425.5	**[RS] eb, full [handicapped] facilities, litter barrels, petwalk [phone] [picnic] vending**
420	NE 63, Greenwood, N [gas] Cenex/cafe/dsl/scales/24hr [other] Pine Grove RV Park, S [gas] Shell/dsl [other] antiques, to Platte River SP, WWII Museum
416mm	**weigh sta both lanes**
409	US 6, to E Lincoln, Waverly, N [gas] Casey's (2mi) [food] McDonald's (2mi), Subway (2mi), S [other] [H]
405	US 77 N, 56th St, Lincoln, S [gas] Phillips 66 [other] [H] antiques, Freightliner, truck service/wash/tires
403	27th St, Lincoln, **0-3 mi** S [gas] Conoco/Wendy's/dsl, Mobil, Phillips 66/Subway/dsl, Shell [food] Amigos Mexican, Applebee's, Arby's, Asian Buffet, Burger King, Cane's, Carlos O'Kelly's, China Inn, CiCi's Pizza, Cracker Barrel, Culver's, daVinci's Italian, Dickey's BBQ, DQ, Fazoli's, Golden Corral, IHOP, Jimmy John's, King Kong Burger, Mazatlan Mexican, McDonald's, Papa John's, Papa Murphy's, Pizza Hut, Popeye's/Taco Inn, Ruby Tuesday, Runza, Schlotzsky's, Sonic, Taco Bell, Taco John's, Village Inn [lodging] AmericInn, Best Western, Country Inn&Suites, Countryside Suites, Fairfield Inn, Hampton Inn, Holiday Inn Express, La Quinta, Microtel, Motel 6, Quality Inn, Red Roof Inn, Staybridge Suites, Super 8, TownePlace Suites, ValuePlace Inn [other] $Tree, AutoZone, BMW, Buick/Chevrolet/GMC, Chrysler/Dodge/Jeep, Ford/Lincoln, GNC, Gordman's, Haas Tire, Home Depot, HyVee Foods, Lexus, Menards, Mercedes, Petsmart, Sam's Club/dsl, ShopKO, Super Saver Foods, to U NE, Toyota/Scion, URGENT CARE, Verizon, Walmart/McDonald's
401b	US 34 W, S [other] RV camping
401a	I-180, US 34 E, to 9th St, Lincoln
399	NW 12th St, Lincoln, Lincoln, N [gas] FatDogs/dsl, Phillips 66/dsl [food] Baskin-Robbins, McDonald's, Perkins, Quiznos [lodging] Best Value Inn, Comfort Inn, Country Inn Suites, Hampton Inn, Holiday Inn Express, Horizon Inn, Howard Johnson, Knights Inn, Luxury Inn, Quality Inn, Travelodge [other] to airport, S [gas] Casey's/dsl [food] Subway [lodging] EconoLodge, Economy Lodge
397	US 77 S, to Beatrice

LINCOLN

NE

INTERSTATE 80 Cont'd

Exit #	Services
396	US 6, West O St (from eb), S Sinclair/dsl Rodeway Inn, Super 8
395	US 6, NW 48th St, S Phillips 66/dsl, Shoemaker's/Shell/dsl/scales/ @ Cobbler Inn Harley-Davidson, truck repair
388	NE 103, to Crete, Pleasant Dale
382	US 6, Milford, S Phillips 66/dsl
381mm	**eb, full facilities, litter barrels, petwalk vending**
379	NE 15, to Seward, **2-3 mi** N McDonald's Super 8 antiques, Buick/Chevrolet/GMC, Ford, S Shell/dsl
375mm	**truck parking (wb)**
373	80G, Goehner, N
369	80E, Beaver Crossing, **3 mi** S food, RV camping
366	80F, to Utica
360	93B, to Waco, N Phillips 66/Waco Rest/dsl/24hr, S Double Nickel Camping
355mm	**wb, full facilities, litter barrels, petwalk vending**
353	US 81, to York, N Conoco/dsl, Pump-N-Pantry/e85, SappBros/Sinclair/Subway/scales/dsl, Shell/dsl Arby's, Burger King, China Buffet, Dickey's BBQ, Golden Gate Chinese, KFC/Taco Bell, McDonald's, Runza, Salsa's Mexican, Starbucks, Taco John's, The Kitchen, Wendy's Best Value Inn, Comfort Inn, Days Inn, Hampton Inn, Holiday Inn Express, New Victorian Inn, Super 8, Yorkshire Motel Buick/GMC, Chevrolet, Elms RV Park, Ford, Walmart/Subway, S Petro/Phillips 66/Iron Skillet/Pizza Hut/dsl/24hr/ @ Applebee's Best Western, Motel 6 Blue Beacon, Freightliner, tires/wash/lube
351mm	**eb, full facilities, litter barrels, petwalk vending**
348	93E, to Bradshaw
342	93A, Henderson, N Prairie Oasis Camping, S Henderson Trkstp/dsl Subway Sun Motel
338	41D, to Hampton
332	NE 14, Aurora, **2-3 mi** N Casey's McDonald's, Pizza Hut, Subway Budget Host to Plainsman Museum, S Loves/Arby's/dsl/scales/24hr
324	41B, to Giltner
318	NE 2, to Grand Island, S KOA (seasonal)
317mm	**wb, full facilities, litter barrels, petwalk vending**
315mm	**eb, full facilities, litter barrels, petwalk vending**
314mm	Platte River
314	Locust Street, to Grand Island, N **4-6 mi**
312	US 34/281, to Grand Island, N Bosselman/Sinclair/Little Caesar's/Max's/Subway/scales/dsl/24hr, Fat Dogs Quaker Steak Motel 6, USA Inn Mormon Island RA, to Stuhr Pioneer Museum, S Phillips 66/Arby's/dsl Days Inn, Quality Inn/Riverfront Grille Hastings Museum (15mi), Peterbilt
305	40C, to Alda, N Sinclair/dsl, TA/Country Pride/dsl/scales/24hr/ @, S Crane Meadows Nature Ctr/rest area
300	NE 11, Wood River, N to Cheyenne SRA, S Pilot/Subway/dsl/scales/24hr motel/RV park
291	10D, Shelton, N War Axe SRA
285	10C, Gibbon, N Petro Oasis/dsl RV camping, Windmill SP, S Country Inn
279	NE 10, to Minden, N Shell/dsl, S Pioneer Village Camping (13mi)
275	Kearney, E Entrance, N Great River Rd Mon
275mm	The Great Platte River Road Archway Monument
272	NE 44, Kearney, N Casey's, Casey's/dsl, Cenex/Subway/dsl, Pump&Pantry/dsl, Shell/dsl Amigo's, Arby's, Burger King, Carlos O'Kelly's, DQ, Egg&I, El Maguey, Gourmet House Japanese, Hunan's Rest., King's Buffet, LJ Silver, McDonald's, Old Chicago Rest, Perkins, Pizza Hut, Red Lobster, Ruby Tuesday, Runza, Taco Bell, Taco John's, USA Steaks, Wendy's, Whiskey Creek AmericInn, Boarders Inn, Comfort Inn, Country Inn&Suites, EconoLodge, Fairfield Inn, Hampton Inn, Holiday Inn, Howard Johnson, Microtel, Midtown Western Inn, Motel 6, New Victorian Inn, Quality Inn, Ramada Inn, Rodeway Inn, Super 8, Western Inn South, Wingate Inn $General, Apache Camper Ctr, Boogaart's Foods, Buick/Cadillac, Chevrolet, Chrysler/Dodge/Jeep, Kearney RV Park/camping, Museum of NE Art, to Archway Mon, U NE Kearney, Verizon, Walmart (3mi), S Qwest/dsl Skeeter's BBQ Best Western, Holiday Inn Express
271mm	**wb, full facilities, info, litter barrels, petwalk**
269mm	**eb, full facilities, info, litter barrels, petwalk**
263	Rd 10 b, Odessa, N Sapp Bros./Apple Barrel Rest./dsl UP Wayside
257	US 183, Elm Creek, N Pilot/Subway/dsl/scales/24hr Royal Inn Antique Car Museum, Sunny Meadows Camping, S Nebraska Prarie Museum (9mi)
248	Overton, N Jay Bros/dsl
237	US 283, Lexington, N Casey's, Cenex/dsl, Conoco/dsl, Phillips 66/dsl Arby's, Baskin-Robbins, Burger King, Delight Donuts, DQ, Hong Kong Buffet, Little Caesar's, McDonald's, Pizza Hut, San Pedro Mexican, Sonic, Wendy's Comfort Inn, Days Inn, Econolodge, Holiday Inn Express, Minute Man Motel $General, $Tree, Advance Parts, Buick/Chevrolet, Military Vehicle Museum, O'Reilly Parts, Plum Creek Foods, Verizon, Walmart/Subway, S Sinclair/dsl/ @ Kirk's Café Super 8 to Johnson Lake RA (6mi)
231	Darr Rd
227mm	**both lanes, full facilities, info, litter barrels, petwalk**
222	NE 21, Cozad, N Casey's/dsl, Cenex/dsl Burger King, DQ, El Paraiso Mexican, Panda Buffet, Pizza Hut, Runza, Subway Circle S Motel, Rodeway Inn $General, Alco, Firestone/auto, museum
211	NE 47, Gothenburg, N Cenex/dsl, Cenex/dsl/24hr China Cafe, Lasso Espresso, McDonald's, Mi Ranchito Mexican, NE Grill, Pizza Hut, Runza Comfort Suites, Howard Johnson, Travel Inn Buick/Chevrolet, Carquest, Pony Express Sta Museum (1mi), ShopKO, S KOA/Sinclair
199	Brady, N Brady 1 Stop/DQ/dsl
194mm	**both lanes, full facilities, info, litter barrels, petwalk**
190	Maxwell, N Sinclair/dsl, S RV camping, to Ft McPherson Nat Cemetary (2mi)
181mm	**weigh sta both lanes**
179	to US 30, N Platte, N Pump&Pantry/dsl La Quinta RV camping, S FLYING J /Denny's/dsl/scales/LP/RV dump/24hr, Loves/McDonald's/Subway/dsl/scales/24hr tire/lube/repair, truckwash
164	56C, Hershey, N Western/Western Cafe/dsl/24hr/ @ KJ's Ranch Store
160mm	**both lanes, full facilities, info, litter barrels, petwalk**
177	US 83, N Platte, N Cenex/dsl, Shell/dsl, Sinclair/dsl, U-Fillem Amigo's Rest., Applebee's, Arby's, Burger King, Coldstone, DQ, Dunkin Donuts, Hunan Moon, Jimmy John's, KFC, King Buffet, Little Caesar's, LJ Silver/Taco Bell, McDonald's,

YORK

AURORA

KEARNEY

LEXINGTON

N PLATTE

NE

INTERSTATE 80 Cont'd

177	Continued Penny's Diner, Perkins, Pizza Hut, Quiznos, Ruby Tuesday, Runza, San Pedro Mexican, Sonic, Starbucks, Subway, Wendy's, Whiskey Creek Steaks Blue Spruce Motel, Fairfield Inn, Hampton Inn, Howard Johnson, Knights Inn, Motel 6, Oak Tree Inn, Quality Inn H $General, $Tree, Advance Parts, Goodyear/auto, Harley-Davidson, Herberger's, Holiday RV Park, JC Penney, mall, museum, Staples, SunMart Foods, Tire Pros, to Buffalo Bill's Ranch, Verizon, Walgreens, Walmart/Subway, S Cenex, Conoco/Taco Bell/dsl/24hr, U-Fillem/dsl/RV dump Hunan Chinese, Taco John's Comfort Inn, Days Inn, Holiday Inn Express, Ramada Ltd, Super 8 Chevrolet/Cadillac, Chrysler/Dodge/Jeep, dsl repair, Ford/Lincoln, Honda, Menards, Nissan, to Lake Maloney RA, Toyota, vet, veterans memorial/info
158	NE 25, Sutherland, N Park Motel (1mi) RV camping, S Sinclair/Godfather's Pizza/dsl RV camping
149mm	Central/Mountain time zone
145	51C, Paxton, N Shell/dsl/24hr Days Inn RV camping
133	51B, Roscoe
132mm	**wb, full facilities, info, litter barrels, petwalk**
126	US 26, NE 61, Ogallala, N Cenex/dsl, Kwik Stop, PetroMart/dsl, Sapp Bros/Shell/dsl/24hr, Watering Hole/dsl, Western/dsl Arby's, Denny's, Front Street Cafe, Golden Village Chinese, Margarita's, McDonald's, Peking Chinese, Pizza Hut, Runza, Spur Steaks, Valentino's Days Inn, Holiday Inn Express, Quality Inn, Stagecoach Inn H $General, Alco, Buick/Chevrolet/GMC, Chrysler/Dodge/Jeep, Firestone/auto, Ford/Lincoln, NAPA, SunMart Foods, to Lake McConaughy, TrueValue, U-Save Drug, Verizon, S Conoco/Subway/dsl, TA/Country Pride/dsl/scales/24hr/ @ DQ, KFC/Taco Bell, Mi Ranchito Mexican, Wendy's Comfort Inn, Rodeway Inn, Super 8 Ace Hardware, Countryview Camping, ShopKO, Sleepy Sunflower RV Park, truck repair, Walmart/dsl
124mm	**eb, full facilities, info, litter barrels, petwalk**
117	51A, Brule, N Happy Jack's/dsl Riverside RV camping
107	25B, Big Springs, N Big Springs/dsl, FLYING J /Grandma Max's/Subway/dsl/scales/24hr/ @ Sam Bass' Steaks Motel 6 truckwash, S McGreer's Camping
102	I-76 S, to Denver
102mm	S Platte River
101	US 138, to Julesburg, S **truck parking**
99mm	**scenic turnout eb**
95	NE 27, to Julesburg
85	25A, Chappell, N Cenex/dsl/repair, Pump&Pantrydsl, Shell/dsl Creekside RV Park/Camping, Super Foods, USPO, wayside park
76	17F, Lodgepole, **1 mi** N gas/dsl, lodging
69	17E, to Sunol
61mm	**wb, full facilities, litter barrels, petwalk vending**
59	US 385, 17J, Sidney, N Conoco/dsl, Sapp Bros/Shell/dsl/24hr Arby's, Buffalo Point Rest., China 1 Buffet, DQ, McDonald's, Mi Ranchito Mexican, Perkins, Pizza Hut, Runza, Sonic, Subway Best Western, Comfort Inn, Days Inn, Hampton Inn, Motel 6 auto/dsl repair, Cabela's Outfitters/RV Park, Chrysler/Dodge/Jeep, Ford, Radio Shack, RV camping (2mi), **visitor ctr**, Walmart, S Love's/IHOP/dsl/scales/24hr, Shamrock/dsl Country Inn Suites auto tire/truck repair, truckwash
55	NE 19, to Sterling, Sidney

OGALLALA

SIDNEY

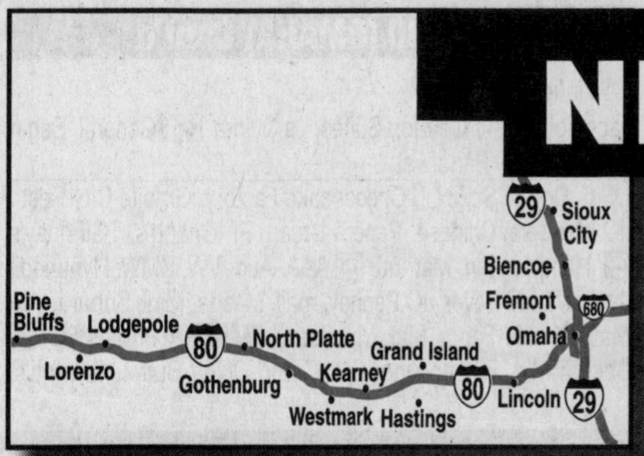

51.5mm	**/hist marker eb, full facilities, litter barrels, petwalk vending**
48	to Brownson
38	Rd 17 b, Potter, N Cenex/dsl/LP repair
29	53A, Dix, **1/2 mi** N gas
22	53E, Kimball, **1-2 mi** N Kwik Stop, Vince's/dsl Pizza Hut, Subway Days Inn, Motel Kimball, Sleep4Less Motel city park, Kimball RV Park (seasonal), Main St Mkt, NAPA
20	NE 71, Kimball, **0-2 mi** N Cenex/dsl, Kwk Stop, Vince's/dsl O'Henry's Diner, Pizza Hut, Subway 1st Interstate Inn, Days Inn, Motel Kimball, Sleep4Less Motel, Super 8 city park, Kimball RV Park (seasonal), Main St Mkt, NAPA, ShopKO
8	53C, to Bushnell
1	53B, Pine Bluffs, **1 mi** N RV camping
0mm	Nebraska/Wyoming state line

INTERSTATE 680 (OMAHA)

Exit #	Services
	I-680 begins/ends on I-80, exit 27
29b a	I-80, W to Omaha, E to Des Moines.
28	IA 191, to Neola, Persia
21	L34, Beebeetown
19mm	**wb, full facilities, info, litter barrels, petwalk**
16mm	**eb, full facilities, info, litter barrels, petwalk**
15mm	scenic overlook
71	I-29 N, to Sioux City
66	W Sinclair/dsl/rest. Iowa Feed&Grain Co Rest., Honey Creek
3b a	(61 b a from wb) I-29, S to Council Bluffs, IA 988, to Crescent, E Phillips 66 to ski area
1	County Rd
14mm	Nebraska/Iowa state line, Missouri River, Mormon Bridge
13	US 75 S, 30th St, Florence, E Shell/dsl Jimmy C's Cafe, Zesto Diner Mormon Trail Motel HyVee Drug, LDS Temple, Mormon Trail Ctr, vet, W Florence
12	US 75 N, 48th St, E Cenex/dsl Burger King (2mi), Taco Bell (2mi)
9	72nd St, **1-2 mi** E QuikShop Applebee's, Burger King, Famous Dave's BBQ, IHOP, Jimmy John's, Sonic, Taco Bueno, Village Inn H W Cunningham Lake RA
6	NE 133, Irvington, E Phillips 66 Burger King, Jimmy John's, Wings'n Things Walmart/Subway/drugs/24hr, W Legend's Grill, Zesto Cafe Holiday Inn Express
5	Fort St, W KwikShop CVS Drug, Goodyear/auto, HyVee Foods, URGENT CARE, USPO, Walgreens
4	NE 64, Maple St, E BP, W Kum&Go/dsl, Shell Burger King, China 1, Godfather's Pizza, Jimmy John's, KFC, La Mesa Mexican, McDonald's, Pizza Hut, Runza, Subway, Taco Bell,

OMAHA

NE

= gas = food = lodging = other = rest stop

INTERSTATE 680 (OMAHA) Cont'd

4 Continued
Taco John's Comfort Suites, La Quinta $General, Bag'n Save, O'Reilly Parts, vet

3 US 6, Dodge St, E Cheesecake Factory, Granite City Rest., JC Manderin Chinese, Panera Bread, PF Chang's, TGIFriday's Hampton Inn, Marriott AAA, Audi/VW, BMW, Hynundai, Jaguar/Land Rover, JC Penney, mall, Mazda, Mini, Subaru, Von Maur, Whole Foods Mkt, Younkers, W BP, Phillips 66 Boston Mkt, Burger King, DQ, Grand China Buffet, Grisanti's,

3 Continued
McDonald's, Starbucks Best Western, Crowne Plaza Motel Holiday Inn, Super 8, TownPlace Suites Bag'n Save Foods Cadillac, Chevrolet, Costco/gas, Ford, Hummer, Menards, Nissan, Toyota

2 Pacific St, E BP Regency Lodge

1 NE 38, W Center Rd, E Cenex/dsl Don Carmelo's, Don&Millie's Rest., W Phillips 66 Arby's, Burger King, Godfather's Pizza, Krispy Kreme, Ozark BBQ, Taco Bell, Wendy's $Tree, Baker's Foods, Haas Tire, TJ Maxx

I-680 begins/ends on I-80, exit 446.

NEVADA

INTERSTATE 15

NE NV

MESQUITE

Exit #	Services
123mm	Nevada/Arizona state line, Pacific/Mountain time zone
122	Lp 15, Mesquite, E **NV Welcome Ctr both lanes, full facilities, petwalk** Arco, Maverik/dsl, Shell/DQ/dsl Alberto's Mexican, Canton Chinese, Cucina Italiano, Dominos, Golden West Rest./casino, Jack-in-the-Box, KFC, Los Lupes, Panda Garden, Taco Bell Best Western $General, Ace Hardware, AutoZone, Big O Tire, CarQuest, city park, Radio Shack, Smith's/Subway/dsl, Sun Resort RV Park, USPO, Walgreens, W Rebel/dsl/LP/RV park McDonald's, Starbucks Eureka Motel/cassino, Virgin River Hotel/casino
120	Lp 15, Mesquite, Bunkerville, E Shell/dsl, Terrible's McDonald's Casablanca Resort/casino/RV Park, Oasis Resort RV Park USPO, W Chevron/dsl Del Taco, Popeye's, Roberto's Tacos Holiday Inn Express H $Tree, Beall's, Ford/RV Ctr, Verizon, Walmart/Subway
112	NV 170, Riverside, Bunkerville
110mm	**truck parking both lanes, litter barrels**
100	to Carp, Elgin
96mm	**truck parking both lanes, litter barrels**
93	NV 169, to Logandale, Overton, E Chevron (3mi) Lake Mead NRA, Lost City Museum
91	NV 168, Glendale, W Arco/dsl Muddy River Rest. USPO
90.5mm	Muddy River
90	NV 168 (from nb), Glendale, Moapa, W gas Moapa Indian Reservation, USPO
88	Hidden Valley
88mm	**litter barrels, parking area both lanes**
84	Byron
80	Ute
75	Valley of Fire SP, Lake Mead NRA, E Chevron/dsl casino, fireworks
64	US 93 N, Great Basin Hwy, to Ely, Great Basin NP, W Loves/Subway/Godfather's/dsl/scales/24hr
60mm	**livestock check sta sb**
58	NV 604, Las Vegas Blvd, to Apex, Nellis AFB
54	Speedway Blvd, Hollywood Blvd, E Petro/Valero/dsl/scales/24hr/ @ Race Day Cafe Las Vegas Speedway
52	Rd 215 W
50	Lamb Ave, **1-2 mi** E Shell/dsl Comfort Inn Hitchin Post RV Park
48	Craig Rd, E 7-11, Arco, Pilot/KFC/Pizza Hut/dsl/scales/24hr, Shell, Sinclair/Subway/dsl Burger King, Jack-in-the-Box, Zapata's Cantina Firestone, to Nellis AFB, W 7-11 Cannery Grill, Carl's Jr, Chipotle Mexican, Del Taco,

LAS VEGAS

48	Continued Famous Dave's BBQ, In-N-Out, Jamba Juice, Marble Slab, Mulligan's, Panda Express, Poppa's Grill, Quiznos, Sonic, Starbucks, Subway Best Western, Hampton Inn dsl repair, Freightliner, Just Brakes, Lowe's, Sam's Club/gas
46	Cheyenne Ave, E Arco/24hr CiCi's Pizza, Lucy's Grill, Marianna's Mkt, Panda Express, Starbucks, Subway $Tree, 7-11, NAPA, vet, W Mortons/dsl/LP/rest./24hr, 7-11, Sinclair/Jack-in-the-Box Denny's, McDonald's Comfort Inn Blue Beacon, dsl repair, Kenworth, Mack, SpeedCo, tires, Volvo
45	Lake Mead Blvd, E Chevron, Rebel/dsl Burger King, Carl's Jr., Jack-in-the-Box, McDonald's 7-11, PepBoys, W Arco/dsl Jack-in-the-Box, McDonald's CVS Drug
44	Washington Ave (from sb), E casinos
43	D St (from nb), same as 44
42b a	I-515 to LV, US 95 N to Reno, US 93 S to Phoenix
41b a	NV 159, Charleston Blvd, E 7-11, Arco/dsl antiques, Walgreens, W Rebel, Terrible's/E-85/dsl/casino Bentley's Coffee, Carl's Jr, Del Taco, McDonald's, Wendy's H CVS Drug, Smith's Foods
40	Sahara Ave, E Artisan Hotel, Vagabond Inn KOA, multiple casinos/hotels, NV Tire/Repair, The Strip, W 7-11, Chevron, Rebel/dsl, Shell Carl's Jr, Chipotle Mexican, El Pollo Loco, In-N-Out, Jack-in-the-Box, Jimmy Johns, KFC, Landry's Seafood, Los Tacos, Macaroni Grill, McDonald's, Panda Express, Pizza Hut, Shilla BBQ, Starbucks, TGIFriday's, Wendy's Palace Sta. Hotel/Casino casinos, CVS Drug, Food4Less, Office Depot, Ross, TJ Maxx, Von's Foods, Walgreens
39	Spring Mtn Rd (from sb), E multiple hotels/casinos, W Multiple Asian Cuisine, Quiznos, Starbucks Firestone/auto
38b a	Flamingo Rd, E multiple casinos/hotels, The Strip, to UNLV, W Chevron Burger King, McDonald's, Sonic, Starbucks, Subway, Taco Bell, TGIFriday's, Wendy's Gold Coast Hotel, Palms Hotel, Rio Hotel Discount Tire
37	Tropicana Ave, E Rebel Coco's Rest., McDonald's Bellagio, Excaliber Hotel, Hooters Hotel/casino, Mandalay Bay, MGM Grand, Monte Carlo, Motel 6, Tropicana Hotel multiple hotels/casinos, W Rebel/dsl, Shell/Subway, Standard, Texaco Burger King, Dennys, In-N-Out, Jack-in-the-Box, McDonald's, Taco's Mexico, Wendy's Budget Suites, Days Inn, Hampton Inn, La Quinta, Motel 6, Orleans Hotel, Siegel Suites
36	Russell Rd, E multiple hotels/casinos, to W Chevron/Herbst/dsl Courtyard, Fairfield Inn, Holiday Inn Express, Residence Inn, Staybridge Suites
34	to I-215 E, Las Vegas Blvd, to The Strip, E McCarran Airport
33	NV 160, to Blue Diamond, Death Valley, E 7-11/dsl, Chevron, Rebel/dsl Bootlegger Bistro, Buffalo Wild Wings, Burger

INTERSTATE 15 Cont'd

33	Continued King, Cane's Rest, Chili's, Chipotle Mexican, Dickey's BBQ, Dunkin Donuts, IHOP, McDonald's, Outback Steaks, Panda Express, Popeyes, Quizno's, Starbucks, Subway, Wienerschnitzel Budget Suites, Carib Resort, Crestwood Suites, Hilton Garden, Microtel CVS Drug, factory outlet/famous brands, Food4Less, Oasis RV Resort, Verizon, W Chevron/dsl, Fills/dsl, Shell, TA/Burger King/Subway/TacoTime/dsl/LP/scales/24hr/ @ Bilbo's Grill, Cafe Rio, Carl's Jr, Del Taco, Famous Dave's BBQ, In-N-Out, Jack-in-the-Box, Panda Express, Quiznos, Taco Bell Silverton Lodge/Casino $Tree, Albertson's, Bass ProShops, BigLots, Discount Tire, GNC, Kohl's, Office Depot, PetCo, Radio Shack, Ross, Target, Verizon, Walgreens, WorldMkt
31	Silverado Ranch Blvd, E Steak'n Shake South Point Hotel/Casino
27	NV 146, to Henderson, Lake Mead, Hoover Dam, **0-2 mi** E Arco, Chevron, Shell Jack-in-the-Box, Starbucks, Subway Hampton Inn, Wingate Inn Camping World, casino, USPO, W vet
25	NV 161, Sloan, **1 mi** E Camping World
24mm	**bus/truck check sta nb**
12	NV 161, to Goodsprings, Jean, E Shell/dsl Gold Strike Casino/hotel, NV Correctional, NV HP, skydiving, USPO, W Shell
1	Primm, E Chevron/dsl, Texaco/dsl Carl's Jr, Dennys, KFC, Mad Greek Cafe, McDonald's, Panda Express, Starbucks, Taco Bell, Tony Roma Buffalo Bill's Resort/casino, factory outlets, Primm Valley Resort/casino, W Chevron/dsl/scales Whiskey Pete's Hotel/casino
0mm	Nevada/California state line

JEAN

INTERSTATE 80

Exit #	Services
411mm	Nevada/Utah state line
410	US 93A, to Ely, W Wendover, S **NV Welcome Ctr/info, full facilities** Chevron/dsl, Pilot/Arby's/dsl/scales/24hr, Shell/Taco Time/dsl Burger King, McDonald's, Pizza Hut, Subway Knights Inn, Motel 6, Nugget Hotel/casino, Peppermill Hotel/casino/RV parking, Rainbow Hotel/casino, Red Garter Hotel/casino Best Hardware, city park, KOA, Smith's Foods/dsl
407	Ola, W Wendover
405mm	Pacific/Mountain time zone
398	to Pilot Peak
390mm	Silverzone Pass, elev 5940, Silverzone Pass
387	to Shafter
378	NV 233, to Montello, Oasis
376	to Pequop
373mm	Pequop Summit elev 6967, **both lanes, litter barrels, rest rooms**
365	to Independence Valley, N prison camp
360	to Moor
354mm	**parking area eb**
352b a	US 93, Great Basin Hwy, E Wells, N Chevron/Quiznos/dsl/LP, Petro/Sinclair/dsl/café/casino Bella's Diner, Burger King/Subway LoneStar Motel, Motel 6, Rest Inn Motel, Sharon Motel, Super 8 Crossroads RV Park, repair, Tire Factory, S FLYING J/dsl/scales/LP/casino/RV Dump/24hr, LNG, Loves/McDonalds/dsl/scales/24hr Great Basin NP
351	W Wells, N Wells/dsl/LP Family$, Mtn Shadows RV Park, Roy's Foods, USPO, Well's Hardware, S Angel Lake RV Park, to Angel Lake RA
348	to Beverly Hills, N RV camping
343	to Welcome, Starr Valley, N Welcome RV Park
333	Deeth, Starr Valley
328	to River Ranch
321	NV 229, Halleck, Ruby Valley
318mm	N Fork Humboldt River
317	to Elburz
314	to Ryndon, Devils Gate, N Sinclair/cafe/dsl, S RV camping
312mm	**check sta both lanes**
310	to Osino, **4 mi** S Valley View RV Park
303	E Elko, N Flyers/CFN/dsl, Sinclair/Arctic Circle/dsl/24hr Wingers TownePlace Suites, S Chevron/dsl, Conoco/dsl, Maverik/dsl, Sinclair/dsl, Tesoro/dsl Blue Moon Rest., Burger King, Chef Cheng's Chinese, Domino's, DQ, King Buffet, McDonald's/playplace, Monkey Sun Chinese, Pizza Barn, Pizza Hut, Quiznos, Subway, Taco Time, Toki Ona Diner, Wendy's Best Value Inn, Best Western, Budget Inn, Comfort Inn, Days Inn, High Desert Inn, Hilton Garden, Holiday Inn Express, Holiday Motel, Motel 6, Quality Inn, Red Lion Inn/casino, Super 8 H Albertson's, AT&T, Big O Tires, Buick/Cadillac/Chevrolet/GMC, Cal Ranch Store, city park, Double Dice RV Park, Ford, Gold Country RV Park, Goodyear/auto, Iron Horse RV Park, JC Penney, Kenworth, NE NV Museum, Valley View RV Park
301	NV 225, Elko, N Maverik/dsl 9 Beans/Burrito, Arby's, Burger King, Denny's, Greatwall Chinese, Jack-in-the-Box, Mattie's Grill, McDonald's/playplace, Papa Murphy's, Port of Subs, RoundTable Pizza OakTree Inn, Shilo Inn Suites AT&T, GNC, Home Depot, JoAnn Fabrics, K-Mart, Marshall's, Petco, Raley's Foods, Ross, Verizon, Walmart/Subway, S Shell, Shell/dsl Costa Vida, Dos Amigos, KFC, Little Caesar's, Sergio's Mexican, Starbucks, Subway, Taco Bell American Inn, Centre Motel, Economy Inn, Elko Inn, Esquire Inn, Manor Inn, Midtown Motel, Rodeway Inn, Scottish Inn, Stampede Motel, Stockmen's Hotel/casino, Thunderbird Motel H AutoZone, CarQuest, Cimarron West RV Park, CVS Drug, Family$, O'Reilly Parts, Smith's Foods/dsl, transmission, URGENT CARE, Verizon

WENDOVER

WELLS

ELKO

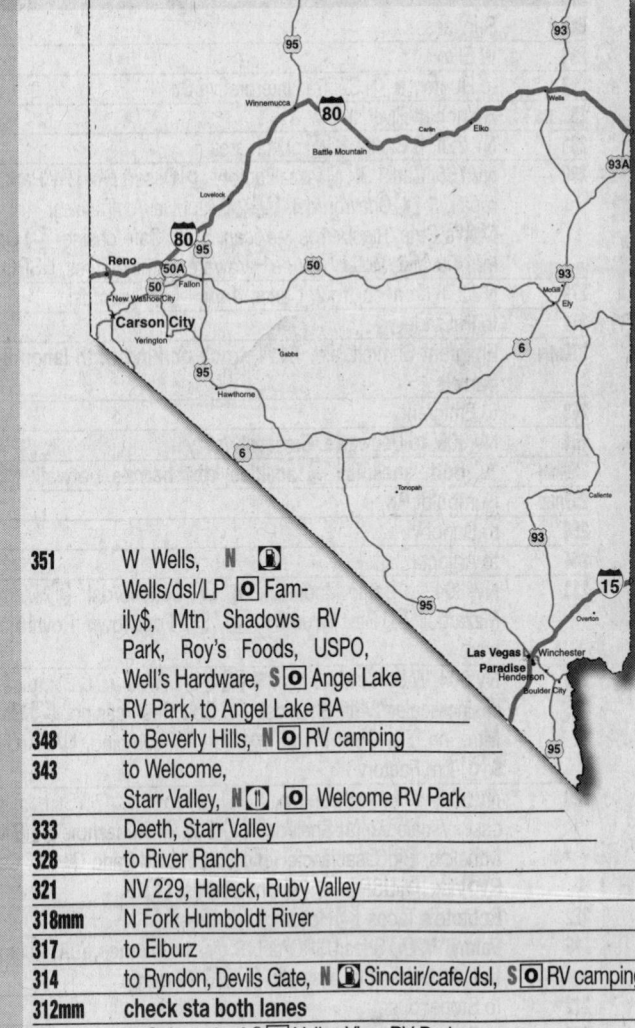

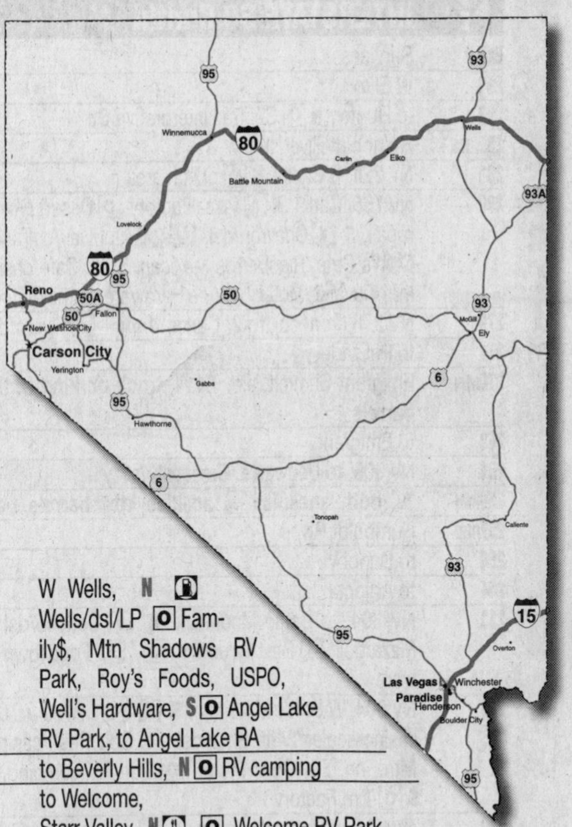

NV

INTERSTATE 80 Cont'd

CARLIN

Exit #	Services
298	W Elko
292	to Hunter, N CA Trail Interpretive Ctr
285mm	Humboldt River, tunnel
282	NV 221, E Carlin, N prison area
280	NV 766, Carlin, N Pizza Factory Desert Gold RV Park, dsl repair, S Chevron/dsl, Pilot/Subway/dsl/scales/24hr Chin's Cafe, Rigobertos Mexican, State Café/casino Carlin Inn, Cavalier Motel Ace Hardware, Family$, tires, USPO
279	NV 278 (from eb), to W Carlin, **1 mi** S Flyers/dsl
271	to Palisade
270mm	Emigrant Summit, elev 6114, **truck parking both lanes litter barrels**
268	to Emigrant
261	NV 306, to Beowawe, Crescent Valley
258mm	**both lanes, full facilities, litter barrels, petwalk**
257mm	Humboldt River
254	to Dunphy
244	to Argenta
233	NV 304, to Battle Mountain, N Conoco/dsl Mama's Pizza/deli Best Value Inn FoodTown, Royal Hardware
229	NV 304, W Battle Mountain, N FLYING J/76/Blimpie/dsl/casino/scales/24hr, Shell/dsl Colt Rest./casino Battle Mtn. Inn, Big Chief Motel Colt RV camping, NAPA Care, S Tire Factory
229	NV 304, W Battle Mountain, N FLYING J/76/Blimpie/dsl/casino/scales/24hr, Shell/dsl Colt Rest./casino Battle Mtn. Inn, Big Chief Motel Colt RV camping, NAPA Care, S Tire Factory
222	to Mote
216	Valmy, N Shell/USPO/dsl, S **both lanes, full facilities, litter barrels, petwalk RV dump**
212	to Stonehouse
205	to Pumpernickel Valley
203	to Iron Point
200	Golconda Summit, elev 5145, **truck parking area both lanes, litter barrels**
194	Golconda, N USPO
187	to Button Point, N **both lanes, full facilities, litter barrels, petwalk RV dump**
180	NV 794, E Winnemucca Blvd
178	NV 289, Winnemucca Blvd, Winnemucca, S Maverik/dsl, Sinclair/dsl Las Margaritas, Rte 66 Grill Budget Inn, Candlewood Suites, Cozy Motel, Frontier Motel, Valu Motel H CarQuest, carwash
176	US 95 N, Winnemucca, N Pacific Pride/dsl, S FLYING J/dsl/LP/RV dump/24hr, Chevron/dsl/24hr, Conoco/dsl, G Gas, Kwik Serv/dsl Arby's, Burger King, China Garden, Dos Amigos Mexican, Dotty's, Griddle Rest., Jack-in-the-Box, KFC/LJ Silver, McDonald's/playplace, Pig BBQ, Pizza Hut, Port of Subs, RoundTable Pizza, Sid's Rest., Subway, Taco Bell, Taco Time Best Western, Days Inn, Economy Inn, Holiday Inn Express, Holiday Motel, Model T Motel/casino/RVPark, Motel 6, Park Hotel, Pyrenees Motel, Quality Inn, Regency Inn, Santa Fe Inn, Scott Motel, Scottish Inn, Super 8, Winnemucca Inn/casino, Winner Hotel/casino H auto/truck repair, AutoZone, Ford, O'Reilly Parts, Raley's Foods, RV camping, Schwab Tire, Verizon, Walmart/Subway
173	W Winnemucca, N Pilot/Subway/dsl/scales/24hr, S airport
168	to Rose Creek, S prison area

WINNEMUCCA

LOVELOCK

Exit #	Services
158	to Cosgrave, S **both lanes, full facilities, litter barrels, petwalk vending**
151	Mill City, N TA/Subway/Taco Bell/Fork/dsl/casino/24hr/ @
149	NV 400, Mill City, **1 mi** N TA/Subway/Taco Bell/Fork/dsl/24hr/ @, S Star Point Gen. Store/RV camping
145	Imlay, S Star Peak RV Park
138	Humboldt
129	Rye Patch Dam, N to Rye Patch SRA, S Rye Patch Trkstp/dsl
119	to Rochester, Oreana
112	to Coal Canyon, S to correctional ctr
107	E Lovelock (from wb), same as 106
106	Main St, Lovelock, N 2 Stiffs, Chevron/dsl/LP, PJ's Gas/subs/dsl Black Rock Grill, Cowpoke Cafe, McDonald's, Pizza Factory Cadillac Inn, Covered Wagon Motel, Punch Inn/casino, Royal Inn, Super 10 Motel H auto care, city park/playground/restrooms, Family$, Lazy K Camping, Safeway Foods, USPO, S Conoco/Port of Subs/dsl24hr
105	W Lovelock (from eb), N Shell/dsl, Shop'n Go/dsl La Casita Mexican Lovelock Inn H Brookwood RV Park, museum, NAPA, same as 106
93	to Toulon, S
83	US 95 S, to Fallon, S **both lanes, full facilities, litter barrels**
78	to Jessup
65	to Hot Springs, Nightingale
50	NV Pacific Pkwy, Fernley
48	US 50A, US 95A, to Fallon, E Fernley, N FLYING J/Denny's/dsl/scales/Lp/24hr, S Shell/dsl, Silverado/dsl Bully's Rest., Burger King, Dotty's Grill, Jack-in-the-Box, KFC, Louie's China, McDonald's, Moto Japanese, Papa Murphy's, Pizza Hut, Silverado Rest./casino, Starbucks, Taco Bell Best Western, Super 8 $Tree, AutoZone, Lowe's, O'Reilly Parts, Scolari's Foods, tires, to Great Basin NP, URGENT CARE, USPO, Verizon, Walgreens, Walmart/Subway
46	US 95A, W Fernley, N Loves/Arby's/dsl/scales/24hr, S Pilot/DQ/Wendy's/dsl/scales/24hr Chukars Grill/Casino Comfort Suties Blue Beacon, SpeedCo
45mm	Truckee River
43	to Pyramid Lake, Wadsworth, N Pyramid Lake gas/dsl/RV camping
42mm	**check sta eb, wb, full facilities, litter barrels, petwalk vending, rest area wb, wireless internet**
40	Painted Rock
38	Orchard
36	Derby Dam
32	USA Pkwy, Tracy, Clark Station, S Golden Gate/Port of Subs/dsl/scales Phillys, Subway
28	NV 655, Waltham Way, Patrick
27mm	eb, scenic view
25mm	**check sta wb**
23	Mustang, S truck repair
22	Lockwood
21	Vista Blvd, Greg St, Sparks, N Chevron/McDonald's, Qwik-Stop Del Taco Fairfield Inn H S Petro/Iron Skillet/dsl/24hr/ @ Super 8 Peterbilt, truckwash
20	Sparks Blvd, Sparks, N 7-11, Shell/dsl BJ's Rest., Buffalo Wild Wings, Carl's Jr, Chipotle, Fuddruckers, Olive Garden, Outback Steaks, Panda Express, Popeye's, Starbucks, Subway, Taco Bell, Taco del Mar AT&T, Best Buy, Discount Tire, GNC, Lowe's, Old Navy, Scheel's Sports, Schwab Tire, Target, Tires+, TJ Maxx, water funpark, S Petro/Iron Skillet/dsl/scales/24hr/ @ Super 8 Freightliner

SPARKS

NV

INTERSTATE 80 Cont'd

SPARKS

Exit #	Services
19	E McCarran Blvd, Sparks, N Arco, Chevron/dsl, Sinclair/dsl, TA/Valero/Country Pride/dsl/scales/ @ Applebee's, Baskin-Robbins, BJ's BBQ, Black Bear Diner, Burger King, China King, Domino's, El Pollo Loco, Jack-in-the-Box, KFC, Little Caesar's, McDonald's, Pizza Hut, Pizza+, Port Of Subs, Sizzler, Taco Bell, Wendy's, Wienerschnitzel Aloha Inn, Sunrise Motel, Windsor Inn $Tree, 99c Store, AutoZone, BigLots, CVS Drug, Family$, O'Reilly Parts, Radio Shack, Ross, Savemart Foods, Victorian RV Park, S Denny's, Super Burrito Holiday Inn NAPA
18	NV 445, Pyramid Way, Sparks, N 7-11 In-N-Out Bourbon Square Casino, Nugget Courtyard, S Nugget Hotel/casino
17	Rock Blvd, Nugget Ave, Sparks, N Arco, Chevron, V/dsl Safari Motel, Victorian Inn, Wagon Train Motel casinos, O'Reilly Parts, S Nugget Hotel/casino
16	B St, E 4th St, Victorian Ave, N Arco Jack's Cafe Motel 6 Rail City Casino, S Chevron/repair
15	US 395, to Carson City, Susanville, **0-1 mi** S Best Western, Holiday Inn Express, Hyatt Place, La Quinta Costco/gas, Grand Sierra Resort, USPO, Walmart/McDonald's
14	Wells Ave, Reno, N Motel 6, S Chevron/dsl Carrow's Rest., Denny's America's Best Inn, Days Inn, Ramada Inn auto repair, Big O Tire, Goodyear
13	US 395, Virginia St, Reno, N Shell/dsl Giant Burger, S H Circus Circus, to downtown hotels/casinos, to UNVReno, Walgreens
12	Keystone Ave, Reno, N Arco Pizza Hut, Starbucks Gateway Inn, Motel 6 7-11, CVS Drug, Raley's Foods, S Chevron/dsl Burger King, Jack-in-the-Box, KFC, Little

RENO

Exit #	Services
12	Continued Caesar's, McDonald's, Port of Subs, Round Table Pizza, Taco Bell, Wendy's casinos, Keystone RV Park, Meineke, NAPA, O'Reilly Parts, Radio Shack, SaveMart/drug
10	McCarran Blvd, Reno, N 7-11/dsl, Arco Applebee's, Asian Wok, Baskin-Robbins, Bully's Grill, Burger King, Carl's Jr, Chili's, Del Taco, DQ, El Pollo Loco, Hacienda Mexican, Hawaiian BBQ, IHOP, Jack-in-the-Box, KFC, Little Caesar's, McDonald's, Papa Murphy's, Pizza+, Popeyes, Qdoba Mexican, RoundTable Pizza, Silver Chop Chinese, Starbucks, Subway, Taco Bell, Tacos el Rey $Tree, AT&T, AutoZone, Big O Tire, Discount Tire, Kohl's, O'Reilly Parts, Petsmart, Radio Shack, Ross, Safeway/dsl, SaveMart Foods, Staples, Tires+, Walgreens, Walmart/McDonald's, S 7-11 Home Depot, URGENT CARE, vet
9	Robb Dr, N Chevron/dsl, Maverik/dsl Bully's Grill, Burger Me, Casa Grande, China Kitchen, Dickey's BBQ, Domino's, Jimmy John's, Moxie's Cafe, Port Of Subs, Starbucks, Subway Hampton Inn CVS Drug, Raley's Foods/dsl, Scolari's Foods
8	W 4th St (from eb), Robb Dr, Reno, S RV camping
7	Mogul
6.5mm	**truck parking/hist marker/scenic view both lanes**
5	to E Verdi (from wb no return), N Backstop Grill
4.5mm	scenic view eb
4	Garson Rd, Boomtown, N Chevron/Boomtown Hotel/dsl/casino Peet's Rest. Cabela's, KOA/RV dump
3.5mm	**check sta eb**
3	Verdi (from wb)
2.5mm	Truckee River
2	Lp 80, to Verdi, N Sinclair/dsl/24hr Jack-in-the-Box Gold Ranch RV Resort/casino
0mm	Nevada/California state line

NV
NH

NEW HAMPSHIRE

INTERSTATE 89

LEBANON

Exit #	Services
61mm	New Hampshire/Vermont state line, Connecticut River
20 (60)	NH 12A, W Lebanon, E Sunoco 99 Rest., Chili's, Dunkin Donuts, KFC/Taco Bell, Lui Lui Pizza, Subway GNC, Hannaford Foods, Jo-Ann Fabrics, K-Mart, LL Bean, Rite Aid, Shaw's Foods, TJ Maxx, Town Fair Tire, USPO, W 7 Barrel Rest., Applebee's, Burger King, D'angelo's, Denny's, Five Guys, Friendly's, Koto Japanese, McDonald's, Moe's SW Grill, Panera Bread, Pizza Hut, Weathervane Seafood, Wendy's Baymont Inn, Fireside Inn $Tree, AT&T, Best Buy, BJ's Whse, BooksAMillion, CVS Drug, Home Depot, JC Penney, Kohl's, Midas, PriceChopper Foods, Radio Shack, Sears, Staples, Verizon, Walgreens, Walmart
19 (58)	US 4, NH 10, W Lebanon, E Gulf/dsl, Shell China Station AutoZone, Family$, Ford, Harley-Davidson, Honda, Pricechopper Foods, W Maplewoods/dsl, Sunoco/repair Bond Parts
57mm	**Welcome Ctr/ weigh sta sb, weigh sta nb, full facilities, litter barrels, petwalk vending**
18 (56)	NH 120, Lebanon, E Citgo/dsl/scales Courtyard (3mi), Days Inn, Residence Inn (2mi) H Cadillac/Chevrolet, Chrysler/Dodge/Jeep, Freightliner, Nissan, to Dartmouth Coll, Volvo/VW, Wilson Tire/repair, W Mobil/Subway/dsl, Shell U-Haul

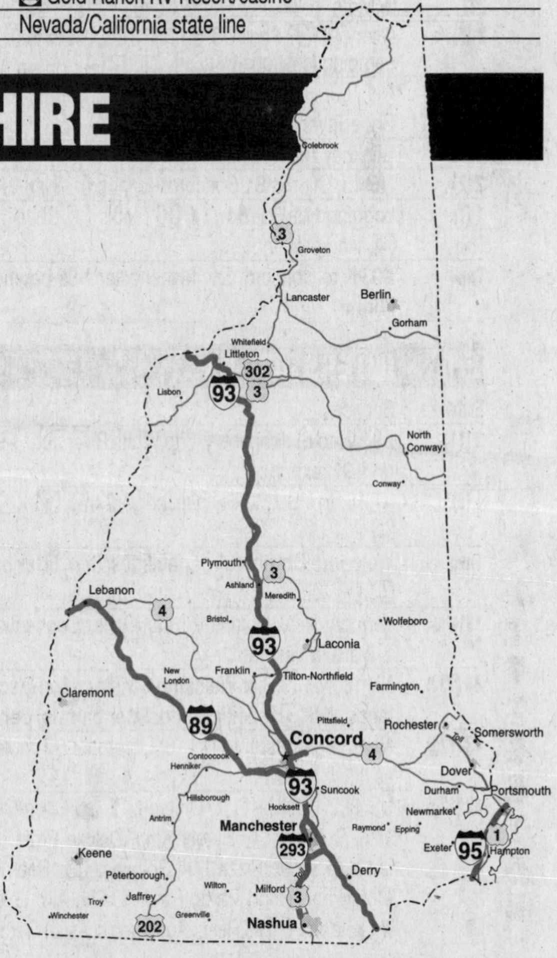

WARNER / LITTLETON *(side margin)*

⬆N INTERSTATE 89 Cont'd

Exit #	Services
17 (54)	US 4, to NH 4A, Enfield, E ◉ RV Camping, vet
16 (52)	Eastman Hill Rd, E 🅿 Gulf/Subway/dsl, W 🅿 Mobil/Dunkin Donuts/dsl ◉ Whaleback Ski Area
15 (50)	Montcalm
14 (47)	NH 10 (from sb), N Grantham
13 (43)	NH 10, Grantham, E 🅿 Irving/Gen Store/dsl, W 🅿 Irving/Circle K 🍴 Dunkin Donuts, Pizza Chef ◉ repair, vet
40mm	℞ₛ nb, full ♿ facilities, info, litter barrels, petwalk Ⓒ ⊠ vending
12A (37)	Georges Mills, W ◉ food, lodging, phone, RV camping, to Sunapee SP
12 (34)	NH 11 W, New London, 2 mi E 🅿 Irving/dsl 🍴 McKenna Rest. ⌂ Maple Hill Country Inn, New London Inn ◉ Ⓗ
11 (31)	NH 11 E, King Hill Rd, New London, 2-3 mi E 🍴 Hole in the Fence Cafe ⌂ Fairway Motel, New London Inn, ski area
10 (27)	to NH 114, Sutton, E ◉ to Winslow SP, 1 mi W ⌂ ◉ to Wadleigh SB
26mm	℞ₛ sb, full ♿ facilities, info, litter barrels, petwalk Ⓒ ⊠ vending
9 (19)	NH 103, Warner, E 🅿 Irving/Circle K/Dunkin Donuts/dsl, Shell/Subway/pizza 🍴 McDonald's ◉ Aubuchon Hardware, Mkt-Basket Foods, Rollins SP, W ◉ ski area, to Sunapee SP
8 (17)	NH 103 (from nb, no EZ return), Warner, 1 mi W 🅿 🍴 ◉ museum, to Rollins SP
15mm	Warner River
7 (14)	NH 103, Davisville, E ◉ camping, W ◉ Pleasant Lake Camping
12mm	Contoocook River
6 (10)	NH 127, Contoocook, E 🅿 Sunoco 🍴 Country Fair Cafe ◉ vet, W ◉ Elm Brook Park, Sandy Beach Camping (3mi)
5 (8)	US 202 W, NH 9 (exits left from nb), Hopkinton, W ◉ food, RV camping (seasonal)
4 (7)	NH 103, Hopkinton (from nb, no EZ return), E 🅿 ◉ Horse-Shoe Tavern
3 (4)	Stickney Hill Rd (from nb)
2 (2)	NH 13, Clinton St, Concord, E ◉ Ⓗ W ◉ NH Audubon Ctr
1 (1)	Logging Hill Rd, Bow, E 🅿 Mobil 🍴 Chen Yang Li Chinese ⌂ Hampton Inn
0mm	I-93 N to Concord, S to Manchester, **I-89 begins/ends on I-93, 36mm**

⬆N INTERSTATE 93

Exit #	Services
2 (11)	I-91, N to St Johnsbury, S to White River Jct. **I-93 begins/ends on I-91, exit 19.**
1 (8)	VT 18, to US 2, to St Johnsbury, 2 mi E 🅿 🍴 ⌂ camping, ⌂
1mm	Welcome Ctr nb, full ♿ facilities, info, litter barrels, petwalk Ⓒ ⊠ wifi
131mm	Vermont/New Hampshire state line, Connecticut River. **Exits 1-2 are in Vermont.**
44 (130)	NH 18, NH 135, W Welcome Ctr (8am-8pm)/scenic vista both lanes, full ♿ facilities, info, litter barrels, petwalk Ⓒ ⊠
43 (125)	NH 135 (from sb), to NH 18, Littleton, 1-2 mi W ◉ Ⓗ same as 42
42 (124)	US 302 E, NH 10 N, Littleton, E 🅿 Citgo/Quiznos, Gulf, Irving, Sunoco 🍴 Burger King, Deluxe Pizza, Dunkin Donuts, Littleton Diner, Pizza Hut, Subway ⌂ Beal House, Littleton Motel ◉ Bond Parts, Family$, Rite Aid, USPO, Walgreens, W 🅿 Mobil 🍴 99 Rest., Applebee's, Asian Garden, McDonald's

Exit #	Services
42 (124)	Continued ⌂ Hampton Inn ◉ $Tree, Aubuchan Hardware, Buick/Chevrolet, Chrysler/Dodge/Jeep, Home Depot, KOA (5mi), Lowe's, O'Reilly Parts/VIP Service, Shaw's Foods/Osco Drug, Staples, Tire Whse, TJ Maxx, Verizon, Walmart/Dunkin Donuts
41 (122)	US 302, NH 18, NH 116, Littleton, E 🅿 Irving/Circle K/dsl ⌂ Eastgate Motel/rest., Travel Inn ◉ Littleton Food Co-op, W ◉ NE Tire
40 (121)	US 302, NH 10 E, Bethlehem, E ⌂ Adair Country Inn/Rest. ◉ to Mt Washington
39 (119)	NH 116, NH 18 (from sb), N Franconia, Sugar Hill, W ⌂
38 (117)	NH 116, NH 117, NH 142, NH 18, Sugar Hill, E ⌂ Best Western, W 🍴 DutchTreat Rest., Wendle's Deli ◉ camping, Franconia Hardware, Franconia Village Store, Frost Museum, gifts, info, Mac's Mkt, USPO
37 (115)	NH 142, NH 18 (from nb), Franconia, ehem, W ⌂ Cannon Mtn View Motel, Hillwinds Lodge ◉ Franstead Camping
36 (114)	NH 141, to US 3, S Franconia, W 🍴 ⌂ ◉ golf
35 (113)	US 3 N (from nb), to Twin Mtn Lake
112mm	S Franconia, Franconia Notch SP begins sb
34c	NH 18, S Franconia, Echo Beach Ski Area, info, view area
34b	Cannon Mtn Tramway, W ◉ Boise Rock, Lafayette Place Camping, Old Man Viewing
109mm	trailhead parking
108mm	Lafayette Place Camping, trailhead parking
107mm	The Basin
34a	US 3, The Flume Gorge, camping (seasonal), info
104mm	Franconia Notch SP begins nb
33 (103)	US 3, N Woodstock, E 🅿 Irving/dsl 🍴 Dad's Rest., Fresolones Pizza, Longhorn Palace Rest., Notchview Country Kitchen ⌂ Beacon Lodge, EconoLodge, Franconia Notch Motel, Green Village Cottages, Indian Head Resort, Mt Coolidge Motel, Pemi Motel, Profile Motel, Rodeway Inn, Woodward's Resort/Rest. ◉ Indian Head viewing, to Franconia Notch SP, waterpark, W 🍴 Sunny Day Diner ⌂ Country Bumpkin Cottages/Camping, Cozy Cabins, Mt Liberty Cabins, White Mtn Motel/Cottages ◉ Arnold's NAPACare, Clark's Trading Post, Cold Springs Camping, Tim's Repair, vet
32 (101)	NH 112, Loon Mtn Rd, N Woodstock, E 🅿 Irving, Mobil, Tedeschi/dsl 🍴 3 Cultures Deli, Black Mtn Burger, Cafe Nacho's, Cheng Garden Chinese, Common Man Rest., Dunkin Donuts, Elvio's Pizza, Flapjack's Pancakes, GH Pizza, Gordi's Fish&Steaks, Gypsy Cafe, McDonald's, Subway, White Mtn Bagel Deli ⌂ Comfort Inn, Kancamagu's Lodge, Lincoln Sta. Lodge, Nordic Inn, South Mtn Resort ◉ Aubuchan Hardware, Family$, NAPA, PriceChopper Foods, Rite Aid, USPO, W 🅿 Citgo 🍴 Lafayette Dinner Train, Landmark II Rest., Peg's Café, Truant's Rest., Woodstock Inn Rest. ⌂ Alpine Lodge, Autumn Breeze Motel, Carriage Motel, Cascade Lodge ◉ candy/fudge/gifts, USPO
31 (97)	to NH 175, Tripoli Rd, E ◉ RV camping (seasonal), W ◉ KOA (2mi)
30 (95)	US 3, Woodstock, E 🍴 Lanterns End Grill, Tony's Rest. ⌂ Jack-O-Lantern Inn/rest. ◉ golf, W ◉ camping (seasonal)
29 (89)	US 3, Thornton, E ◉ Pemi River RV Park/LP, W ⌂ Gilcrest Motel
28 (87)	NH 49, Campton, E 🅿 Gulf, Mobil 🍴 Dunkin Donuts, Exit 28 Pizza ◉ Handy Man Hardware, RV camping, to ski area, USPO, W 🅿 Irving/dsl 🍴 Sunset Grill ◉ Branch Brook Camping, Chesley's Glory Sta., Mtn Vista RV Park, repair
27 (84)	Blair Rd, Beebe River, E 🍴 Country Cow Rest. ⌂ Days Inn, Red Sleigh Condos

WOODSTOCK *(side margin)*

INTERSTATE 93 Cont'd

Exit #	Services
26 (83)	US 3, NH 25, NH 3A, Tenney Mtn Hwy, W Common Man Inn, EconoLodge, Pilgrim Inn H
25 (81)	NH 175 (from nb), Plymouth, W Citgo/dsl, Irving/Circle K/dsl Downtown Pizza, Fracher's Diner, HongKong Garden, House of Pizza, Lucky Dog Grill, Subway, Thai Smile H Chase St Mkt, Plymouth State U, USPO
24 (76)	US 3, NH 25, Ashland, E Gulf, Irving/Circle K/dsl, Mobil Ashland Pizza, Burger King, Common Man Diner, Dot's Bistro, Dunkin Dounts, Lucky Dragon Chinese, Village Grill Comfort Inn Bob's Mkt, Jellystone RV Camp (4mi), repair, USPO
23 (71)	NH 104, NH 132, to Mt Washington Valley, New Hampton, E Irving/Circle K/dsl, Mobil/dsl Dunkin Donuts, Rossi Italian, Subway Clearwater Campground, info, Jellystone, USPO, W Homestead Rest. (2mi) RV Park (2mi), ski area
22 (62)	NH 127, Sanbornton, **1-5 mi** W H, /dsl
61mm	**sb, full facilities, info, litter barrels, petwalk vending**
20 (57)	US 3, NH 11, NH 132, NH 140, Tilton, E Irving/Circle K/dsl/24hr, Shell/Subway/dsl 99 Rest., Applebees, Burger King, Dunkin Donuts, Green Ginger Chinese, KFC, McDonald's, Starbucks, Thai Cuisine, Tilt'n Diner, UNO, UpperCrust Pizza, Wendy's Hampton Inn, Holiday Inn Express, Super 8 BJ's Whse/gas, Home Depot, Old Navy, O'Reilly Parts/VIP Service, Staples, Subaru, Tanger Outlet/famous brands, Walgreens, W Chili's, Pizza Hut Chrysler/Dodge/Jeep, Ford, Kohl's, Lowe's, MktBasket Foods, Nissan, USPO, VW, Walmart/Subway
56mm	Winnipesaukee River
19 (55)	NH 132 (from nb no ez return), Franklin, W Gulf Ciao Italian H antiques, NH Vet Home
51mm	**nb, full facilities, info, litter barrels, petwalk vending**
18 (49)	to NH 132, Canterbury, E Gulf to Shaker Village HS
17 (46)	US 4 W, to US 3, NH 132, Boscawen, **4 mi** W
16 (41)	NH 132, E Concord, E Mobil/dsl Quality Cash Mkt
15W (40)	US 202 W, to US 3, N Main St, Concord, W Citgo, Cumberland/Dunkin Donuts, Hess Domino's, Friendly's Courtyard/café
15E	I-393 E, US 4 E, to Portsmouth
14 (39)	NH 9, Loudon Rd, Concord, E Shell/dsl Boloco Burritos, Buffalo Wild Wings, Chicago Grill, El Rodeo Mexican, Five Guys, Moritomo Japanese, Panera Bread, Wok Inn, $Tree, AAA, Ace Hardware, AutoZone, BooksAMillion, CVS, GNC, Hannaford Foods, LLBean, Lowe's, Meineke, Midas, Mkt Basket Foods, PetCo, Radio Shack, Rite Aid, Shaws Foods/24hr, Staples, TJ Maxx, URGENT CARE, USPO, **1-2 mi E on Loudon Rd** Irving/Circle K/Subway/ dsl, Mobil, 7-11, Shell/dsl, Sunoco/dsl Applebee's, Arnie's Place, Burger King, D'angelo's, Dunkin Donuts, Friendly's, KFC, LJ Silver/Taco Bell, Longhorn Steaks, McDonald's, Newick's Lobster House, 99 Rest., Olive Garden, PapaGino's, Pizza Hut, Red Apple Buffet, Ruby Tuesday, Starbucks, Sunshine Oriental, TGIFriday's, Wendy's, Windmill Rest. Advance Parts, Best Buy, BonTon, Dick's, Home Depot, JC Penney, Michael's, Petsmart, Sam's Club/gas, Sears/auto, Shaw's Foods/Osco Drug, Target, Town Fair Tire, Verizon, Walgreens, Walmart, city park, W Citgo, Cumberland, Hess Domino's, Gas Lighter Rest., Nonni's Rest., Siam Orchid, Tea Garden Rest. Holiday Inn hist sites, Jo-Ann, Marshall's, MktBasket, museum, to state offices, vet
13 (38)	to US 3, Manchester St, Concord, E Cumberland, Sunoco/dsl/deli Beefside Rest., Brookside Pizza, Cityside Grille,

CONCORD

MANCHESTER

DERRY

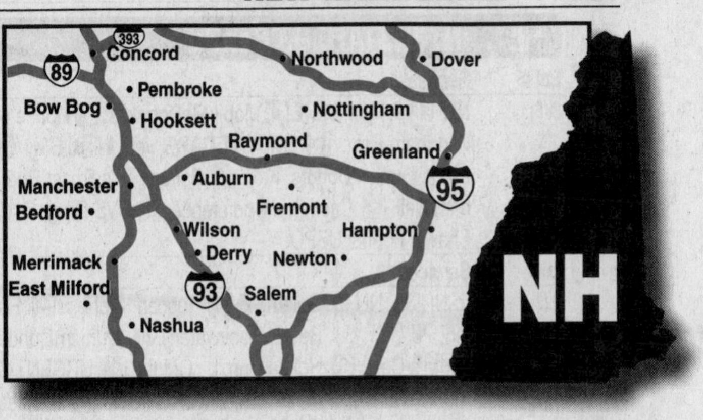

Exit #	Services
13 (38)	Continued Dunkin Donuts, Ichiban Japanese, Kaylen's Pizza, Red Blazer Rest., Veano's Italian Buick/GMC, Cadillac/Chevrolet, Chrysler/Dodge/Jeep, Harley-Davidson, Kia, Nissan, O'Reilly Parts/VIP Service, Outdoor RV Ctr Subaru, Subaru, Tire Whse, Volvo, W Hess/dsl, Mobil/dsl Burger King, Common Man Diner, D'angelo's, Dunkin Donuts, KFC, McDonald's Best Western, Comfort Inn, Fairfield Inn, Residence Inn H Aubuchon Hardware, CVS Drug, Firestone, Goodyear/auto
12N (37)	NH 3A N, S Main, E Gulf, Irving/Subway/dsl/24hr Dunkin Donuts Days Inn Ford, Honda, Hyundai, Mazda, Toyota/Scion, W H
12S	NH 3A S, Bow Junction
36mm	I-89 N to Lebanon, **toll road begins/ends**
31mm	**both lanes, full facilities, info, vending**
11 (28)	NH 3A, to Hooksett, **4 mi** E Pilot/dsl/rest. **toll plaza**
28mm	I-293, Everett Tpk
10 (27)	NH 3A, Hooksett, E Irving/Circle K/dsl Dunkin Donuts, Subway, Wendy's BJ's Whse, Home Depot, Kohl's, Petco, Target, W Irving/Circle K/Dunkin Donuts/dsl, Mr Gas Bass Pro Shop, MktBasket Foods, Walmart/Subway
26mm	Merrimac River
9N S (24)	US 3, NH 28, Manchester, E Irving/Dunkin Donuts/Circle K/dsl Fairfield Inn, W Manchester/dsl, Sunoco/dsl Burger King, Cheng Du Chinese, D'Angelo's, Happy Garden Chinese, La Carreta Mexican, Lusia's Italian, Mr Mac's Cafe, PapaGino's, Puritan Rest., Shorty's Mexican, Subway, Villaggio Ristorante H Chrysler/Dodge/Jeep, city park, Hannaford Foods, Kia, Lincoln, O'Reilly Parts/VIP Service, U-Haul
8 (23)	to NH 28a, Wellington Rd, W Currier Gallery, VA H
7 (22)	NH 101 E, to Portsmouth, Seacoast
6 (21)	Hanover St, Candia Rd, Manchester, E Dunkin Donuts, Wendy's vet, W Mobil/dsl, Shell Dunkin Donuts, McDonald's, Subway H GNC, Goodyear/auto, Hannaford Foods
19mm	I-293 W, to Manchester (from nb), to airport
5 (15)	NH 28, to N Londonderry, E Irving/Dunkin Donuts/dsl, Sunoco/dsl Poor Boy's Diner, W Shell/dsl Subway Sleep Inn
4 (12)	NH 102, Derry, E Mobil/dsl, Mutual, Shell/dsl, Sunoco/dsl, Super Burger King, Cracker Barrel, Derry Rest., Juliano's Pizza, Poorboys Drive-In, Subway H Advance Parts, R. Frost Farm, W 7-11, Global, Gulf/dsl/repair, Hess 99 Rest., Dunkin Donuts, Ginger Garden, KFC/Taco Bell, McDonald's, PapaGino's, Wendy's, Whippersnappers Rest. AT&T, Ford, GNC, Hannaford Foods, Home Depot, Mkt Basket Foods, O'Reilly Parts/VIP Service, Shaw's Foods, Staples, TJ Maxx, USPO, Verizon
7mm	**weigh sta both lanes**

= gas = food = lodging = other = rest stop

INTERSTATE 93 Cont'd

Exit #	Services
3 (6)	NH 111, Windham, **E** Mobil/McDonald's House of Pizza, Windham Rest. URGENT CARE, vet, **W** B&H Capri Pizza, Dunkin Donuts, Klemm's Bakery, TJ's Roast Beef, Windham Deli Castleton Conference Ctr, CVS Drug, Osco Drug, Shaw's Foods, USPO
Exit #	**Services**
2 (3)	to NH 38, NH 97, Salem, **E** Tuscan Kitchen Red Roof Inn, **W** A&A Rest., Blackwater Grill, Dunkin Donuts, Margarita's Cafe Holiday Inn, La Quinta URGENT CARE
1 (2)	NH 28, Salem, **E** BP/dsl, Citgo/dsl, Gulf 99 Rest., Bickfords, Burger King, Chili's, Denny's, Grand China, LJ Silver, McDonald's, PapaGino's, Taco Bell, T-Bones Park View Inn AT&T, Barnes&Noble, Best Buy, Home Depot, JC Penney, K-Mart, Kohl's, Lord&Taylor, Macy's, mall, Marshall's, Meineke, Michael's, MktBasket Foods, NTB, PetCo, Petsmart, racetrack, Radio Shack, Sears/auto, Shaw's Foods, Staples, Target, TJ Maxx, TownFair Tire, vet, Walgreens
1mm	**Welcome Ctr nb full facilities, info, litter barrels, petwalk vending**
0mm	New Hampshire/Massachusetts state line

SALEM

INTERSTATE 95

Exit #	Services
17mm	New Hampshire/Maine state line, Piscataqua River
7 (16)	Market St, Portsmouth, Port Authority, **E** Residence Inn, **0-2 mi W** BP, Mobil Applebee's, D'Angelo, Dunkin Donuts, Panera Bread, Qdoba, Ruby Tuesday, Starbucks, Wendy's Courtyard, Hampton Inn, Homewood Suites $Tree, BJ's Whse/gas, Marshall's, MktBasket Foods, PepBoys, PetCo, Rite Aid, Shaw's Foods, TJ Maxx, Verizon, vet, waterfront hist sites
6 (15)	Woodbury Ave (from nb), Portsmouth, **E** Best Inn, **W** same as 7
5 (14)	US 1, US 4, NH 16, The Circle, Portsmouth, **E** Gulf, Shell/dsl Roudabout Diner Anchorage Inn, Best Inn, Best Western, Fairfield Inn, Holiday Inn, Port Inn H Buick/Cadillac/GMC, Chevrolet, U-Haul, **W** Chipotle, Longhorn Steaks, McDonald's Hampton Inn, Motel 6, Residence Inn Barnes&Noble, Best Buy, Dick's, Ford/Lincoln, Home Depot, Kohl's, Mazda, Michael's, Nissan, Old Navy, Staples, Sullivan Tire, Trader Joe's
4 (13.5)	US 4 (exits left from nb), to White Mtns, Spaulding TPK, **E** H **W** to Pease Int Trade Port
3a (13)	NH 33, Greenland
3b (12)	NH 33, to Portsmouth, **E** H **0-2 mi W** Sunoco/dsl, TA/Country Pride/dsl/scales/24hr/@ Dunkin Donuts, McDonald's Lowe's, Mercedes, Target, VW
6.5mm	**toll plaza**
2 (6)	NH 101, to Hampton, **E** H
4mm	Taylor River
1 (1)	NH 107, to Seabrook, **toll rd begins/ends**, **E** BP, Irving/Circle K/dsl, Monster Energy, Prime, Richdale, Sunoco/Subway/dsl, Xtra 99 Rest., Applebees, Chili's, Dunkin Donuts, Five Guys, HoneyDew Donuts, KFC/Taco Bell, McDonald's, PapaGino's, Pizza Hut, Sal's Pizza, Starbucks, Wendy's Hampshire Inn, Holiday Inn Express $Tree, Advance Parts, AutoZone,
1 (1)	Continued CVS Drug, Dick's, GNC, Home Depot, Jo-Ann Fabrics, Kohl's, Lowe's, Meineke, MktBasket Foods, NTB, Petsmart, Radio Shack, Staples, Sullivan Tire, TJ Maxx, to Seacoast RA, Town Fair Tire, Verizon, Walmart, **W** Citgo McGrath's Dining Seabrook Inn NAPA, Sam's Club
.5mm	**Welcome Ctr nb full facilities, info, litter barrels, petwalk vending**
0mm	New Hampshire/Massachusetts state line

SEABROOK

NH

INTERSTATE 293 (MANCHESTER)

Exit #	Services
8(9)	I-93, N to Concord, S to Derry. **I-293 begins/ends on I-93, 28mm.**
7(6.5)	NH 3A N, Dunbarton Rd (from nb)
6(6)	Amoskeag Rd, Singer Park, Manchester, **E** Sunoco/dsl La Quinta, **W** Mobil, Shell/dsl Dunkin Donuts, Hot Stone Pizza H
5(5)	Granite St, Manchester(from nb, no EZ return), **E** World Sports Grill Radisson, **W** 7-11, Gulf Dunkin Donuts, Subway H tires, Walgreens
4 (4)	US 3, NH 3A, NH 114A, Queen City Br, **E** 7-11 Elliott H **W on US 3** Hess/dsl, Mobil/dsl, Z1 Gas/dsl Applebee's, Burger King, Chen's Garden, D'angelo's, DQ, Dunkin Donuts, Ipswich Clambake, KC's Rib Shack, KFC, Little Caesars, McDonald's, Panera Bread, Subway, Taco Bell, T-Bones, Wendy's Comfort Inn, EconoLodge Family$, Hannaford Foods, Subaru
3 (3)	NH 101, **0-2 mi on W US 3** Dunkin Donuts, IHOP Carrabba's, Chipotle, Fresh Mkt, Outback Steaks, Panera Bread, Starbucks Country Inn& Suites, Hampton Inn CVS Drug, Kohl's, Lexus, Lowe's, Macy's, Marshalls, Mini, O'Reilly Parts/VIP Service, Radio Shack, Rite Aid, Staples, Target, URGENT CARE, vet
2.5mm	Merrimac River
2 (2)	NH 3A, Brown Ave, **S** Mobil/dsl, Shell/Subway/dsl Airport Diner, Dunkin Donuts, McDonald's Holiday Inn, Super 8 Manchester Airport
1 (1)	NH 28, S Willow Rd, **N** Mobil/dsl, Sunoco/dsl 5 Guys Burgers, Boston Mkt, Burger King, Cactus Jack's, Chipotle Mexican, Coldstone, D'angelo's, Dunkin Donuts, Friendly's, McDonald's, Panera Bread, Papa John's, PapaGino's, Pizza Hut, Sal's Pizza, Starbucks, Subway, Taco Bell, Wendy's, Yee Dynasty Chinese Fairfield Inn, Holiday Inn Express, Sheraton H $Tree, AT&T, AutoZone, Batteries+Bulbs, Buick/GMC, Chevrolet, CVS Drug, Hannaford Foods, Harley-Davidson, Home Depot, Mazda, Mercedes, Michael's, PepBoys, PetCo, Petsmart, Radio Shack, Sam's Club, Sullivan Tire/repair, TJ Maxx, TownFair Tire, U-Haul, URGENT CARE, Verizon, vet, VW, **S** Shell 99 Rest., Bertucci's, ChuckeCheese, D'angelo's, FoodCourt, Great Buffet, La Carreta, Longhorn Steaks, Masa Japanese Steaks, Olive Garden, Red Robin, TGIFriday's, TX Roadhouse Courtyard, TownePlace Suites Barnes&Noble, Best Buy, BMW, Ford, Hobby Lobby, Honda, Hyundai, JC Penney, LL Bean, Macy's, mall, Nissan, NTB, Old Navy, Sears/auto, Staples, Toyota/Scion, Walmart/Subway
0mm	I-93, N to Concord, S to Derry. **I-293 begins/ends on I-93.**

NEW JERSEY

INTERSTATE 78

N E W A R K

Exit #	Services
58b a	US 1N, US 9N, NJ Tpk
57	US 1S, US 9S, N Doubletree, Ramada Inn, S Courtyard, Fairfield Inn, SpringHill Suites to Newark Airport
56	Clinton Ave (exits left from eb)
55	Irvington (from wb), N Hess/dsl Burger King, Wendy's, White Castle H, AutoZone
54	Hillside, Irvington (from eb), N Hess/dsl Burger King, Wendy's, White Castle H, AutoZone
52	Garden State Pkwy
50b a	Millburn (from wb), N BP, Exxon, Lukoil Manny's Wieners Best Buy, Firestone/auto, Ford/Lincoln, Home Depot Superstore, Target, USPO, Whole Foods Mkt
49b a	NJ 124 (from eb), to Maplewood, same as 50b a
48	to NJ 24, to I-287 N, (exits left from eb), Springfield
48mm	I-78 eb divides into express & local
45	NJ 527 (from eb), Glenside Ave, Summit
44	(from eb), to Berkeley Heights, New Providence
43	to New Providence, Berkeley Heights
41	to Berkeley Heights, Scotch Plains
40	NJ 531, The Plainfields, S Valero H
36	NJ 651, to Warrenville, Basking Ridge, N Exxon Dunkin Donuts A&P, S Exxon
33	NJ 525, to Martinsville, Bernardsville, N 3West Rest., LingLing Chinese, Starbucks Courtyard, Hotel Indigo, Somerset Hills Inn USGA Golf Museum, S Exxon/7-11 Panera Bread Goodyear/auto, Verizon
32mm	scenic overlook wb
29	I-287, to US 202, US 206, I-80, to Morristown, Somerville, S H
26	NJ 523 spur, to North Branch, Lamington
24	NJ 523, to NJ 517, to Oldwick, Whitehouse, **2-3 mi** S Exxon/dsl, Gulf/dsl Readington Diner, Starbucks, Subway Kings Mkt, Rite Aid
20b a	NJ 639 (from wb), to Cokesbury, Lebanon, S Exxon, Shell/dsl, Sunoco Cutting Board Deli, Dunkin Donuts, Janina Bistro, Kirsten's Italian Courtyard to Round Valley RA, vet
18	US 22 E, Annandale, Lebanon, N same as 17, S H, Honda
17	NJ 31 S, Clinton, N Exxon, Hess, Valero/dsl Baskin-Robbins/Dunkin Donuts, Blimpie, Country Griddle, Finnigal's, McDonald's STS Tire/auto, to Voorhees SP
16	NJ 31 N (from eb), Clinton, N same as 17
15	NJ 173 E, to Pittstown, Clinton, N Express/repair, Shell/dsl Subway Holiday Inn museum, S Cracker Barrel, Frank's Italian, Hunan Wok, Quiznos Hampton Inn H, GNC, ShopRite Foods, TJMaxx, Verizon, Walmart/Dunkin Donuts
13	NJ 173 W (from wb), N Clinton Sta Diner, same as 12
12	NJ 173, to Jutland, Norton, N Clinton/dsl, Exxon/Dunkin Donuts/dsl, Pilot/Subway/dsl/scales/24hr Grand Colonial Rest. to Spruce Run RA, vet, S Shell Bagelsmith Deli
11	NJ 173, West Portal, Pattenburg, N Mobil, Shell/pizza/dsl Chalet Rest., Landslide Rest. Jugtown Camping, st police
8mm	**both lanes, litter barrels, no restrooms**
7	NJ 173, to Bloomsbury, West Portal, N RV camping, S Citgo/deli, Pilot/Subway/dsl/scales/24hr, TA/Burger King/Country Pride/dsl/scales/24hr/ @

C L I N T O N

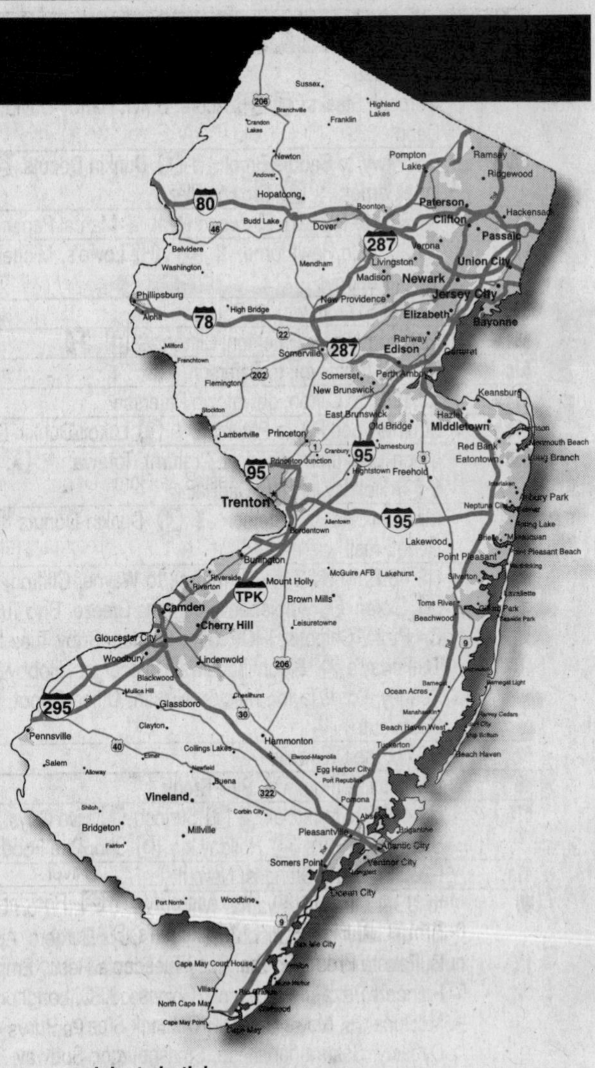

Exit #	Services
6mm	**weigh sta both lanes**
6	Warren Glen, Asbury (from eb)
4	Warren Glen, Stewartsville (from wb)
3	US 22, NJ 173, to Phillipsburg, **0-2 mi** N BP/dsl, Hess/dsl, Mobil/Subway/dsl, Penn Jersey Trkstp/dsl/scales/24hr, US/dsl, Wawa Applebee's, Burger King, Chick-fil-A, Dunkin Donuts, Frank's Trattoria, Friendly's, Key City Diner, McDonald's, Panera Bread, Perkins, Pizza Hut, Quaker Steak, Ruby Tuesday, Taco Bell, Teppanyaki, White Castle Best Value H, $Tree, Advance Parts, AutoZone, Best Buy, BonTon, Hobby Lobby, Home Depot, Honda, Kohl's, Lowe's, Marshall's, Meineke, Michael's, PetCo, Sears/auto, ShopRite Foods, Staples, Stop&Shop, Target, Walmart/Subway, S Hyundai
0mm	New Jersey/Pennsylvania state line, Delaware River

INTERSTATE 80

Exit #	Services
68	**I-80 begins/ends on I-95, exit 69.**
68b a	I-95, N to New York, S to Philadelphia, to US 46
68	Leonia, Teaneck, N Marriott H
67	to Bogota (from eb)
66	Hudson St, to Hackensack
65	Green St, S Hackensack
64b a	NJ 17 S, to US 46 E, Newark, Paramus, S BP/dsl Crow's Nest Rest. Hilton PathMark Foods, Stop&Shop
63	NJ 17 N, N BP, Exxon/dsl, Hess/dsl, Mobil/dsl, Sunoco, /dsl Burger King, Five Guys, Longhorn Steaks,

NJ

INTERSTATE 80 Cont'd

PATERSON

63	Continued Outback Steaks H, Acura, BMW, Harley-Davidson, Home Depot
62b a	GS Pkwy, to Saddle Brook, N Dunkin Donuts Holiday Inn, Marriott, S Crowne Plaza
61	NJ 507, to Garfield, Elmwood Park, N Marcal Paper Co
60	NJ 20, N to Hawthorne, N H, Lowe's, Michelin/Cooper Tires, Pepboys
59	Market St (from wb), to Paterson
58b a	Madison Ave, to Paterson, Clifton, S H
57c	Main St (from wb), to Paterson
57b a	NJ 19 S, to Clifton, downtown Paterson
56b a	Squirrelwood Rd, to Paterson, S Lukoil/Dunkin Donuts
55b a	Union Blvd (from wb, no EZ return), Totowa, N Shell/dsl, S Holiday Inn Cadillac
54	Minnisink Rd, to Paterson, S Dunkin Donuts Home Depot, mall
53	US 46 E, to NJ 3 (no eb return), to Wayne, Cliffton, **0-2 mi** S Exxon Applebee's, Bahama Breeze, Brio Tuscan Grill, CA Pizza, Chipotle, IHOP, Olive Garden, Ruby Tuesday, Sonic, TGIFriday's Bloomingdale's, Costco/gas, Hobby Lobby, JC Penney, Lord&Taylor, Macy's, Nissan, Office Depot, Old Navy, Sears/auto
52	US 46, the Caldwells
48	to Montville (from wb), Pine Brook
47b	US 46 W, to Montclair, N Sunoco Five Guys, Longhorn Steaks, Wendy's Holiday Inn ShopRite Foods
47a	I-280 E, to The Oranges, Newark
45	to US 46, Lake Hiawatha, Whippany, **0-2 mi** N **on US 46** BP/dsl, Gulf/dsl, Sunoco/dsl 5 Guys Burgers, Applebee's, Buffalo Wild Wings, Burger King, Eccola Rest., Empire Diner, Franco's Pizza, IHOP, Jasper Chinese, KFC, Longhorn Steaks, McDonald's, Moe's SW Grill, Outback Steaks, Pure Rest., Quin Dynasty, Sakura Japanese, Smashburger, Subway, Taco Bell, Wendy's Budget Inn, Holiday Inn/rest., Howard Johnson, Ramada Ltd, Red Roof Inn $Tree, Firestone, Home Depot, K-Mart, Michael's, PathMark Foods, PepBoys, PetCo, Radio Shack, ShopRite Foods, Staples, Verizon, Walgreens
43b a	I-287, to US 46, Boonton, Morristown
42b a	US 202, US 46, to Morris Plains, Parsippany, **0-1 mi** N **on US 46** 76/Dunkin Donuts/dsl, Exxon Fuddrucker's, McDonald's, TGIFriday's, Wendy's Courtyard, Days Inn, Fairfield Inn, Hampton Inn Marshall's, same as 39, Subaru
39	(38 from eb), US 46 E, to NJ 53, Denville, **0-2 mi** N **on US 46** Citgo/dsl, Enrite Gas, Exxon, Hess/Dunkin Donuts, Sunoco Burger King, Casa Bella Italian, Charlie Brown's Steaks, Dunkin Donuts, Moe's SW Grill, Paul's Diner, Wendy's H, Chevrolet, Verizon, Walgreens, S Delta
37	NJ 513, to Hibernia, Rockaway, N Exxon/dsl, Shell Barn Rest., Dunkin Donuts, Hibernia Diner Hampton Inn, Rockaway Hotel, S BP H
35b a	to Dover, Mount Hope, S Exxon Buffalo Wild Wings, Chipotle, Coldstone, Dunkin Donuts, La Salsa Mexican, Olive Garden, Quiznos, Red Robin, Tiff's Burger Hilton Garden, Homewood Suites H, Best Buy, JC Penney, Lord&Taylor, Macy's, mall, Michael's, Sears/auto, Verizon
34b a	NJ 15, to Sparta, Wharton, N Exxon/dsl Fortune Buffet Rite Aid, S Dunkin Donuts, Good 5 Chinese, Panera Bread, Qdoba, Starbucks, Townsquare Diner H, $Tree, Big Lots, Costco/gas, Dick's, Home Depot, Petsmart, ShopRite Foods, Target, Walmart
32mm	truck rest area wb

STANHOPE

30	Howard Blvd, to Mt Arlington, N Exxon/dsl Blosson Asian, Cracker Barrel, Davy's Hotdogs, Dunkin Donuts, Frank' Pizza, Wingman Courtyard, Holiday Inn Express Quick Chek Foods
28	US 46, to NJ 10, to Ledgewood, Lake Hopatcong, **1-2 mi on US 46, NJ 10** Delta Gas, Hess/dsl, Sunoco/dsl Boston Mkt, Domino's, Dunkin Donuts, Fuddruckers, KFC/L Silver, McDonald's, Muldoons Diner, Outback Steaks, Paner Bread, Pizza Hut, Red Lobster, Ruby Tuesday, Taco Bell, TG Friday's, Wendy's, White Castle AutoZone, Barnes&Noble BJ's Whse, CVS Drug, Home Depot, Jo-Ann, Kohl's, Petco ShopRite Foods, Walgreens, Walmart
27	US 206 S, NJ 182, to Netcong, Somerville, N Valero/ds Dunkin Donuts Ford, S Shell/dsl Apple bee's, Chili's, Longhorn Steaks, Macaroni Grill, McDonald's Panera Bread, Subway, Wendy's Extended Stay Americ $Tree, Lowe's, Michael's, Old Navy, Petsmart, Sam's Club TJMaxx, Walmart
26	US 46 W (from wb, no EZ return), to Budd Lake, S same a 27, Shell/dsl
25	US 206 N, to Newton, Stanhope, **1-2mi** N **on US 206** Exx on/dsl, Shell/dsl Blackforest Rest., Byram Diner, Byram Piz za, Dunkin Donuts, Empire Buffet, Frank's Pizza, McDonald's Subway Holiday Inn, Residence Inn CVS Drug, GNC Int Trade Ctr, Nissan, ShopRite Foods, STS tires/repair, to Wa terloo Village, vet
23.5mm	Musconetcong River
21mm	**picnic area both lanes, litter barrels, no facilities, pet walk, scenic overlook (eb)**
19	NJ 517, to Hackettstown, Andover, N Shell/dsl R camping, **1-2 mi** S Shell/dsl/repair Terranova Pizz Panther Valley Inn/rest. H, 7-11, Stephen's SP, USP
12	NJ 521, to Blairstown, Hope, N Mediterranean Dine Harley-Davidson, st police, S US Gas Hope Mk Deli Jenny Jump SF, Land of Make Believe, RV campin (5mi), USPO
7mm	**eb, full facilities, info, litter barrels, petwalk vending**
6mm	scenic overlook wb, no trailers
4c	to NJ 94 N (from eb), to Blairstown
4b	to US 46 E, to Buttzville
4a	NJ 94, to US 46 E, to Portland, Columbia, N TA/Pizza Hu Taco Bell/dsl/scales/24hr/@ McDonald's RV camping S USPO
3.5mm	Hainesburg Rd (from wb), accesses services at 4
2	**weigh sta eb**
1mm	Worthington SF
1	to Millbrook (from wb), N Worthington SF
0mm	New Jersey/Pennsylvania state line, Delaware River

INTERSTATE 95

Exit #	Services
124mm	New Jersey/New York state line, Hudson River, Geo Washingto Br
123mm	Palisades Pkwy (from sb)
73	NJ 67, Lemoine Ave, W Sunoco Five Guys, McDonald' A&P Mkt, GNC, Verizon, Walgreens
72 (122)	US 1, US 9, US 46, Ft Lee, E Doubletree, W Sunoc McDonald's
71 (121)	Broad Ave, Leonia, Englewood, E Lukoil, W Holiday Ir
70 (120)	to NJ 93, Leonia, Teaneck, W Marriott
69 (119)	I-80 W (from sb), to Paterson

NJ

TRENTON

INTERSTATE 95 Cont'd

Exit #	Services
68 (118)	US 46, Challenger Blvd, Ridgefield Park, E Exxon Lan Garden Chinese Day's Inn, Hampton Inn, Hilton Garden
I-95 and NJ Turnpike run together sb. See NJ TPK, exit 7a-18	
I-95 nb becomes I-295 sb at US 1.	
67b a	US 1, to Trenton, New Brunswick, E Shell Michael's Diner Howard Johnson, Sleepy Hollow Motel Acura, **0-3 mi W** Gulf, LukOil/dsl Applebee's, Big Fish Bistro, Cheeburger Cheeburger, Chevy's Mexican, Chili's, ChuckECheese's, Dunkin Donuts, Hooters, Houlihan's, Joe's Crabshack, Macaroni Grill, NY Deli, Olive Garden, On-the-Border, Panera Bread, PF Chang's, Princetonian Diner, Pure Rest., Red Lobster, Rita's Custard, Starbucks, Subway, TGIFriday's, Wendy's Clarion, Comfort Inn, Extended Stay America, Hyatt Place, Hyatt Regency, Red Roof Inn, Residence Inn AT&T, Barnes&Noble, Best Buy, Buick/Cadillac, Chevrolet, Dick's, Firestone/auto, Home Depot, JC Penney, Jo-Ann Fabrics, Kohl's, Lord&Taylor, Lowe's, Macy's, malls, Marshall's, Michael's, Mini, NTB, Office Depot, Old Navy, PepBoys, PetCo, Petsmart, Ross, Sam's Club, Sears/auto, ShopRite Foods, Staples, Target, TJ Maxx, Trader Joe's, Verizon, Walmart, Wegman's Foods, Whole Foods Mkt
8b a	NJ 583, NJ 546, to Princeton Pike
7b a	US 206, W LukOil/dsl Fox's Pizza, Tastee Subs
5b a	Federal City Rd (sb only)
4b a	NJ 31, to Ewing, Pennington, E Citgo/repair, Exxon/repair, LukOil/Dunkin Donuts/dsl SpringHill Suites 7-11, Robbins Drug, USPO, W Exxon, LukOil/Blimpie/dsl Mizuki Asian, Starbucks AT&T, ShopRite Foods, Stop&Shop Foods
3b a	Scotch Rd, E Courtyard, W H
2	NJ 579, to Harbourton, E LukOil (1mi) Dunkin Donuts, Red Star Pizza 7-11, W BP
1	1 NJ 29, to Trenton, **2 mi W** museum, st police
0mm	New Jersey/Pennsylvania state line, Delaware River

NEW JERSEY TURNPIKE

Exit #	Services
18 (117)	US 46 E, Ft Lee, Hackensack, last exit before toll sb
17 (116)	Lincoln Tunnel
115mm	**Vince Lombardi Service Plaza nb,** W Sunoco/dsl Burger King, Nathan's, Popeye's
114mm	**toll plaza,**
16W (113)	NJ 3, Secaucus, Rutherford, E Hess, Shell Hilton, M Plaza Hotel, W Sheraton Meadowlands
112mm	**Alexander Hamilton Service Area sb,** Sunoco/dsl Roy Rogers gifts
16E (112)	NJ 3, Secaucus, E Lincoln Tunnel
15W (109)	I-280, Newark, The Oranges
15E (107)	US 1, US 9, Newark, Jersey City, E Lincoln Tunnel
14c	Holland Tunnel
14b	Jersey City
14a	Bayonne
14 (105)	I-78 W, US 1, US 9, **2 mi W** Courtyard, Fairfield Inn, SpringHill Suites
102mm	**Halsey Service Area,** Sunoco/dsl Roy Rogers, services in Elizabeth
13a (102)	Elizabeth, E Country Inn Suites, Courtyard, Embassy Suites, Extended Stay America, Residence Inn, W McDonald's Crowne Plaza, Days Inn, Hampton Inn, Hilton, Rennaisance, services on US1/US9

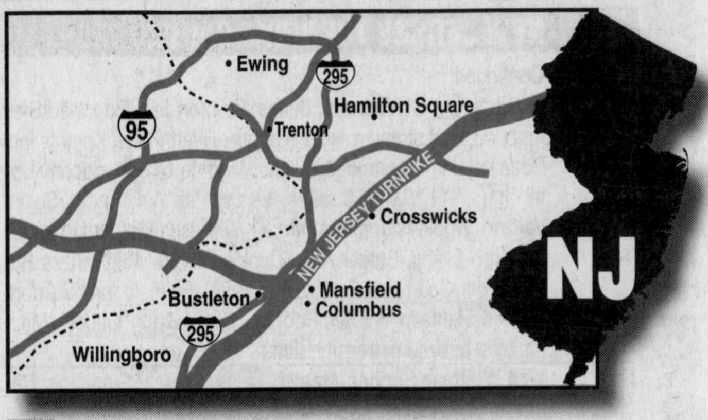

NEW JERSEY TURNPIKE

Exit #	Services
13 (100)	I-278, to Verrazano Narrows Bridge
12 (96)	Carteret, Rahway, E McDonald's Holiday Inn CVS Drug, Walgreens, W Executive Suites
93mm	**Cleveland Service Area nb** Nathans, Roy Roger's, Starbucks, **T Edison Service Area sb** Sunoco/dsl Burger King, Dunkin Donuts, Popeye's, Sbarro's, Starbucks
11 (91)	US 9, Garden State Pkwy, to Woodbridge, E McDonald's Hampton Inn Home Depot, Walmart
10 (88)	I-287, NJ 514, to Perth Amboy, E Courtyard, W Hess/dsl Holiday Inn
9 (83)	US 1, NJ 18, to New Brunswick, E Brunswick, E Gulf, Hess/dsl Bone Fish Grill, Boston Mkt, Burger King, Carrabba's, Dunkin Donuts, Grand Buffet, KFC, Perkins, Starbucks Days Inn, Motel 6 Best Buy, Goodyear/auto, Lowe's, Office Depot, Petsmart, Rite Aid, Sam's Club, Shopper's World Foods, ShopRite Foods, Staples, TJ Maxx, W Exxon Fuddruckers Hilton, Holiday Inn Express, Howard Johnson
79mm	**Kilmer Service Area nb** Burger King, Cookies and Creamery, Sbarro, Starbucks Sunoco/dsl
8a (74)	to Jamesburg, Cranbury, W Courtyard, Crowne Plaza
72mm	**Pitcher Service Area** Sunoco/dsl Arthur Treacher's, Cinnabon, Dick Clark's AB Grill, Nathan's, Roy Rogers, Starbucks
8 (67)	NJ 33, NJ 571, Highstown, E Hess/dsl, Petro/dsl, RaceWay, Shell/Dunkin Donuts Prestige Diner Days Inn, Hampton Inn, Holiday Inn CVS Drug, vet, W Quality Inn
7a (60)	I-195 W to Trenton, E to Neptune
59mm	**Woodrow Wilson Service Area nb** Burger King, Nathan's, Pizza Hut, Quiznos, Roy Rogers, Starbucks, TCBY, **Richard Stockton Service Area sb** Sunoco/dsl, Sunoco
7 (54)	US 206, to Bordentown, to Ft Dix, McGuire AFB, to I-295, Trenton, **Services W on US 206** Citgo, Delta/dsl, Exxon, Gulf, Loves/Wendy's/dsl/scales/24hr, Petro/Iron Skillet/dsl/scales/24hr/ @, Sunoco, Valero/dsl Denny's, Dunkin Donuts, McDonald's, Wendy's Best Western, Comfort Inn, Days Inn, Hampton Inn, Ramada Inn WaWa
6 (51)	I-276, to PA Tpk
5 (44)	to Mount Holly, Willingboro, E US Gas/dsl Applebee's, Charlie Brown's Steaks, Cracker Barrel, McDonald's, Recovery Grill Best Western, Hampton Inn, Hilton Garden, Quality Inn, W BP, Exxon/dsl, Valero/dsl Burger King, China House, ChuckECheese's, Dunkin Donuts, IHOP, Quiznos, Subway, TGIFriday's Courtyard, Holiday Inn Express $Tree, Home Depot, JC Penney, Kohl's, Sears/auto, Target, vet
39mm	**James Fenimore Cooper Service Area nb,** Sunoco/dsl Burger King, Cinnabon, Popeye's, Roy Rogers, TCBY gifts
4 (34)	NJ 73, to Philadelphia, Camden, E Exxon, WaWa/dsl Chick-fil-A, Chili's, Cracker Barrel, Denny's, Dunkin Donuts, Macaroni Grill, McDonald's, On-the-Border, Sage Rest., TGIFriday's,

NJ

= gas = food = lodging = other = rest stop

NEW JERSEY TURNPIKE Cont'd

4 (34)	Continued Wendy's Candlewood Suites, Comfort Inn, Extended Stay America, Hampton Inn, Hilton Garden, Hyatt Place, Knights Inn, Rodeway Inn, Staybridge Suites, Wingate Inn, Wyndham Hotel 7-11, BMW, Cadillac, Lexus, Rite Aid, Toyota/Scion, Verizon, Whole Foods Mkt, W Gulf/dsl, Hess, Lukoil, Shell Bob Evans, Burger King, Dunkin Donuts, KFC, Pizza Hut aLoft, Courtyard, DoubleTree Motel, Fairfield Inn, Marriott, Motel 6, Ramada Inn, Red Roof Inn, Super 8 Lincoln, Mazda, to st aquarium, transmissions
30mm	**Walt Whitman Service Area sb** Sunoco Cinnabon, Nathan's, Roy Rogers, TCBY gifts
3 (26)	NJ 168, Atlantic City Expwy, Walt Whitman Br, Camden, Woodbury, E 7-11, Pioneer, WaWa Antonietta's, Bella Rizzo's Pizza, Luigi's Pizza, Pat's Pizza, Phily Diner, Rita's Custard Comfort Inn, Runnymead Suites CVS Drug, Toyota/Scion, Walgreens, W Citgo, Gulf/repair, Shamrock/dsl, Shell/dsl Burger King, Club Diner, Dunkin Donuts, Italia Pizza, Wendy's Bellmawr Motel, Comfort Inn, EconoLodge, Holiday Inn, Howard Johnson, Motel 6, Red Roof Inn, Super 8 CVS Drug, transmissions, Walgreens
2 (13)	US 322, to Swedesboro, W Shell/Dunkin Donuts/dsl
5mm	**Barton Service Area sb,** Sunoco/dsl Burger King, Nathan's, Pizza Hut, Starbucks, TCBY **Fenwick Service Area nb,** Sunoco/dsl TCBY
1 (1.2)	Deepwater, W Gulf, Pilot/Subway/dsl/scales/24hr Comfort Inn, Friendship Motor Inn, Holiday Inn Express, Wellesley Inn
1mm	**toll road begins/ends**
2 (I-295)	**I-295 N divides from toll road, I-295 S converges with toll road,** W Shell/Dunkin Donuts/dsl
1 (I-295)	NJ 49, to Pennsville, E Exxon/dsl/repair Applebees, Burger King, Cracker Barrel, Dunkin Donuts, KFC/Taco Bell, McDonald's, Subway Hampton Inn, Super 8 Peterbilt, W Gulf, Pilot/Subway/dsl/scales/24hr Best Value, Comfort Inn, Friendship Motor Inn, Quality Inn, Seaview Motel
0mm	New Jersey/Delaware state line, Delaware Memorial BR, Delaware River

INTERSTATE 195

Exit #	Services
36	Garden State Parkway N. **I-195 begins/ends on GS Pkwy, exit 98.**
35b a	NJ 34, to Brielle, GS Pkwy S., Pt Pleasant, **0-2 mi** S Exxon/dsl, Getty, Lukoil/dsl Legends Japanese
31b a	NJ 547, NJ 524, to Farmingdale, N to Allaire SP
28b a	US 9, to Freehold, Lakewood, N LukOil/7-11/dsl Ivy League Grill, Stewart's Drive-In At 9 Motel, S Exxon, Getty, Gulf, LukOil, WaWa 5 Guys Burgers, Applebee's, Arby's, Baskin-Robbins/Dunkin Donuts, Boston Mkt, Burger King, Carino's, Chick-fil-A, China Moon, Coldstone, Domino's, Jersey Mike's Subs, Longhorn Steaks, Luigi's Pizza, McDonald's, Panera Bread, Pizza Hut, Rojo Loco, Ruby Tuesday, Sonic, Starbucks, Taco Bell Capri Inn Barnes&Noble, Best Buy, GNC, K-Mart, Kohl's, Lowe's, Michael's, PathMark Foods, PepBoys, PetCo, Petsmart, Radio Shack, repair, Staples, Stop&Shop, Target, TJ Maxx, USPO, Verizon, Walgreens, Walmart/McDonald's
22	to Jackson Mills, Georgia, N to Turkey Swamp Park, **2 mi** S McDonald's ShopRite Foods
21	NJ 526, NJ 527, to Jackson, Siloam
16	NJ 537, to Freehold, N Remington/dsl/LP, Sunoco DQ, FoodCourt, GianMarco's Pizza, Java Moon Café Jackson Outlets/famous brands, S WaWa/dsl Bella Pizzaria, Burger King, Chicken Holiday, Dunkin Donuts, KFC LJ Silver, McDonald's, McGinns Pizzaria, Rio Grande Mexica Tommy's Rest. 6Flags Themepark
11	NJ 524, Imlaystown, S to Horse Park of NJ
8	NJ 539, Hightstown, Allentown, S Shell (1mi), Valero/repa American Hero Deli Crosswicks HP, vet
7	NJ 526 (no eb return), Robbinsville, Allentown, **1 mi** S L Piazza Ristorante
6	NJ Tpk, N to NY, S to DE Memorial Br
5b a	US 130, N Delta/dsl/repair, Valero/dsl Domino's, Dunk Donuts, Rusert's Deli, ShrimpKing Rest. AAA, Harley-Davidson, vet, S GS Fuel/dsl Chick-fil-A, Chili's, Chin Grill, Cracker Barrel, DQ, Jersey Mike's Subs, Longhorn Steak McDonald's, Outback Steaks, Panera Bread, Red Robin, Rub Tuesday, Subway, TGIFriday's, Wendy's Hilton Garden $Tree, AT&T, Barnes&Noble, BJ's Whse, GNC, Hamilton Shops famous brands, Harry's Army Navy, Home Depot, Kohl's Lowe's, mall, Michael's, Old Navy, Petsmart, Ross, ShopRit Foods, Staples, to state aquarium, USPO, Verizon, Walmart
3b a	Hamilton Square, Yardville, N H
2	US 206 S, S Broad St, Yardville, N Rosa's Ristorante, S Shell, Valero Subway 7-11, CVS Drug, Rite Aid
1b a	US 206 (eb only), N Circle Deli, Taco Bell Advanc Parts, S Papa John's ShopRite Foods
0mm	**I-295, I-195 begins/ends.**

INTERSTATE 287

Exit #	Services
68mm	New Jersey/New York state line
66	NJ 17 S, Mahwah, **1-3 mi** E Gulf, Liberty/dsl, Mobil/ds Pilot/dsl, Sunoco/dsl, Valero/Subway/dsl Boston Mk Burger King, Dunkin Donuts, McDonald's Comfort Suites Courtyard, Doubletree, Hampton Inn, Homewood Suites, Sheraton, Super 8 Buick/GMC, Cadillac, Chrysler/Dodge/Jeep Home Depot, Honda, Hyundai
59	NJ 208 S, Franklin Lakes
58	US 202, Oakland, E Lukoil/dsl Jr's Pizza, Mike's Doghouse, Starbucks, Subway $Tree, Staples, USPO, Walgreens, W Exxon
57	Skyline Dr, Ringwood
55	NJ 511, Pompton Lakes, E Frank's Pizza, Quizno's, Starbucks, Subway, Thatcher McGhee Eatery, Wendy's A&P W Gulf/dsl Baskin-Robbins, Burger King, Dunkin Donuts Holiday Inn Express CVS Drug, Stop'n Shop
53	NJ 511A, Rd 694, Bloomingdale, Pompton Lakes, E Sunoco, Valero Blimpie USPO
52b a	NJ 23, Riverdale, Wayne, Butler, **0-3 mi** E Delta, Gulf, Hess dsl, Lukoil, Valero/dsl 23 Buffet, Moe's SW Grill, Pompto Queen Diner, Stefano's Pizza H, GNC, Honda, Pepboys Radio Shack, Stop&Shop, TJ Maxx, Toyota/Scion, VW, W Lukoil, Lukoil Applebees, Chili's, Dunkin Donuts, Mangia Pizza, NJ Buffet, Subway, Wendy's Best Buy, BJ's Whse Harley-Davidson, Home Depot, Jo-Ann, Lowes Whse, Staples Target, Walmart
47	US 202, Montville, Lincoln Park, E Exxon Harrigan' Rest., Montville Inn Rest.
45	Myrtle Ave, Boonton, W Hess, Shell/dsl Dunkin Donuts McDonald's, Subway A&P Mkt, Buick/Chevrolet, Walgreen

NEW JERSEY TURNPIKE

NJ

INTERSTATE 287 Cont'd

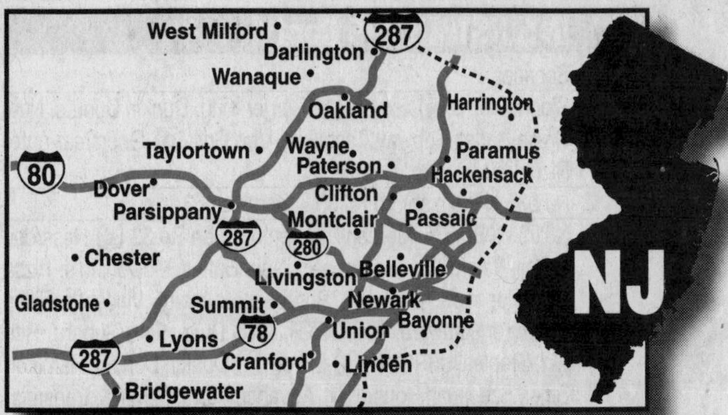

Exit #	Services
43	Intervale Rd, to Mountain Lakes, E Valero/dsl, W Dodge
42	US 46, US 202 (from sb only), W 76/Dunkin Donuts/dsl, Exxon Fuddrucker's, McDonald's, TGIFriday's, Wendy's Courtyard, Day's Inn, Embassy Suites, Fairfield Inn, Hampton Inn Marshall's, Subaru, USPO
41b a	I-80, E to New York, W to Delaware Water Gap
40	NJ 511, Parsippany Rd, to Whippany, W BP, Shell/dsl, Woroco Gas Frank&Son Pizza, Subway, Wok's Chinese Embassy Suites (1mi) vet
39b a	NJ 10, Dover, Whippany, E Exxon, Shell Brookside Diner, Dunkin Donuts, Jersey Mike's, Melting Pot, Pancake House, Scallopini Rest., Whippany Diner CVS Drug, Farmtastic Mkt, Tuesday Morning, W Liberty/dsl, Lukoil, Raceway Atlanta Bread, Dunkin Donuts, Panchero's Mexican, Smashburger, Subway, Wendy's EconoLodge, Hilton, Hyatt House, Marriott Barnes&Noble, Buick/GMC, GNC, Harley Davidson, Kohl's, Stop'n Shop, Verizon
37	NJ 24 E, Springfield
36b a	Rd 510, Morris Ave, Lafayette
35	NJ 124, South St, Madison Ave, Morristown, E Friendly's Richie's Country Store, vet, W Best Western H, Rite Aid, Walgreens
33mm	**E truck nb, full facilities, litter barrels, petwalk vending**
33	Harter Rd
30b a	to US 202, N Maple Ave, Basking Ridge, E Dolce Resort, W Gulf, Lukoil GrainHouse Rest., Vine Rest. Olde Mill Inn/rest.
26b a	Rd 525 S, Mt Airy Rd, Liberty Corner, **3 mi** E Exxon Courtyard, Somerset Hotel
22b a	US 202, US 206, Pluckemin, Bedminster, E Exxon, Exxon/dsl Burger King, Coldstone, Dunkin Donuts, Golden Palace, Panchero's, Rocco's Pizza, Starbucks, Subway CVS Drug, Fresh Mkt, King's Foods, URGENT CARE, Verizon
21b a	I-78, E to NY, W to PA
17	US 206 (from sb), Bridgewater, W Exxon, Hess Buffalo Wild Wings, CA Pizza, Cheescake Factory, Chipotle Mexican, Dunkin Donuts, KFC, La Catena Ristorante, Maggiano's Italian, McCormick&Schmick's, McDonald's, TGIFriday, Wendy's Marriott Best Buy, Bloomingdale's, Lord&Taylor, Macy's, mall
14b a	US 22, to US 202/206, E Hess/dsl Chevrolet/Lexus, W Sunoco/dsl, Valero/dsl Houlihan's, Red Lobster Day's Inn Acura, Chrysler/Dodge/Jeep, Fiat, Ford, Infiniti, Kia, Mercedes, Nissan, Volvo
13b a	NJ 28, Bound Brook, E 76/dsl, BP/dsl 25 Burgers, Burger King, Dunkin Donuts, Frank's Pizza, Girasole Rest., Little Caesar's 7-11, AT&T, AutoZone, QuickChek Mkt, Radio Shack, ShopRite Foods, Walgreens, W Applebees, ChuckeCheese, McDonald's, Panchero's Hilton Garden H, 7-11, Costco, Home Depot, Marshall's, Michael's, Old Navy, PepBoys, PetsMart, Target
12	Weston Canal Rd, Manville, E ShopRite (3mi), USPO, W Soho Grill La Quinta
10	NJ 527, Easton Ave, New Brunswick, E Hotel Somerset, W Exxon Dunkin Donuts, Lo Duca Pizza, Ruby Tuesday, Subway Candlewood Suites, Comfort Inn, Courtyard, Doubletree, EconoLodge, Extended Stay America, Fairfield Inn, Holiday Inn, Homewood Suites, Madison Suites, Residence Inn, Sonesta Suites H, Garden State Exhibit Ctr
9	NJ 514, River Rd, W Gulf Embassy Suites, Radisson
8.5mm	**weigh sta nb**
8	Possumtown Rd, Highland Park
7	S Randolphville Rd, Piscataway, E Lukoil/dsl
6	Washington Ave, Piscataway, E Shell/7-11/dsl Popeye's, W Applebees, Chand Palace, Gourmet Oizza, Healthy Garden, Longhorn Steaks, Olive Garden, Panera Bread, Piscataway Pizza, Starbucks, Subway, TGIFriday's, Thai Basil 99c Depot, Aldi Foods, GNC, Lowes Whse, PetCo, same as 5, ShopRite Foods, Walmart/McDonald's
5	NJ 529, Stelton Rd, Dunellen, E BP/dsl, Gulf/dsl, Lukoil/dsl Enzo's Pizza, KFC Ramada Ltd. Advance Parts, Goodyear/auto, Home Depot, Meineke, Stop'n Shop, STS Tire/auto, W Exxon, Gulf 365 Bistro, Brickhouse Rest., Burger King, Chipotle, Corner Cafe, Dunkin Donuts, Five Guys, Fontainbleu Diner, Friendly's, Gabrieles Grill, Gianni Pizza, IHOP, Joe's Crabshack, Panda Express, Pizza Hut, Red Lobster, Red Robin, Ruby Tuesday, Taco Bell, Villa Pizza, Wendy's, White Castle Best Western, Hampton Inn, Holiday Inn, Motel 6 $Tree, Burlington Coats, Dick's, Hobby Lobby, Kohl's, Macy's, Marshall's, NAPA, Pep Boys, Radio Shack, Staples, Target, Verizon, Walgreens
4	Durham Ave (from nb, no EZ return), S Plainfield, E Full One/dsl Subway H, Firestone/auto
3	New Durham Rd (from sb), E Shell, W Dunkin Donuts, Red Onion Chinese Fairfield Inn, Red Roof Inn Walgreens
2b a	NJ 27, Metuchen, New Brunswick, E Brownstone Grill, W BP, Lukoil Dunkin Donuts, Little Caesar's Costco/gas, Petsmart, USPO, Walmart/Subway
1b a	US 1, N Exxon/dsl, Raceway/dsl, Shell Benihana, Champp's, Cheesecake Factory, Dunkin Donuts, Famous Dave's BBQ, Houlihan's, IHOP, Macaroni Grill, McDonald's, Menlo Park Diner, Panera Bread, Seasons Grill, Sonic, Uno, White Castle Barnes&Noble, Firestone/auto, Goodyear/auto, Macy's, Midas, Nordstrom's, Target, S Shell/7-11/dsl Applebees, Boston Mkt, ChuckeCheese, McDonald's Comfort Inn, Quality Inn $Tree, BJ's Whse, Home Depot, Infiniti, Land Rover/Jaguar/Porche, Mercedes, Office Depot, PepBoys, PetCo, Sam's Club/gas, Staples, Stop&Shop Foods, Volvo
0mm	**I-287 begins/ends on NJ 440, I-95, NJ Tpk.**

INTERSTATE 295

Exit #	Services
67b a	US 1. **I-295 nb becomes I-95 sb at US 1. See NJ I-95, exit 67b a.**

NJ

= gas = food = lodging = other = rest stop

INTERSTATE 295 Cont'd

TRENTON

Exit #	Services
65b a	Sloan Ave, E Exxon Burger King, Dunkin Donuts, New China Buffet, Subway, Taco Bell, Uno Grill Goodyear/auto, Rizoldi's Mkt
64	NJ 535 N (from sb), to NJ 33 E, same as 63
63b a	NJ 33 W, Rd 535, Mercerville, Trenton, **E on Rd 33** Hess/dsl, Lukoil, Valero Applebee's, Asia Buffet, McDonald's, Pizza Hut, Popeye's, Stewart's Rootbeer, Subway, Vincent's Pizza Ace Hardware, auto repair, CVS Drug, Ford/Subaru, Rite Aid, Staples, USPO, W Exxon Dunkin Donuts, Hamilton Diner, Szechuan House Advance Parts, Family$, transmissions, Walgreens, WaWa
62	Olden Ave N (from sb, no return), W Delta
61b a	Arena Dr, White Horse Ave, W 7-11
60b a	I-195, to I-95, W to Trenton, E to Neptune
58mm	scenic overlook both lanes
57b a	US 130, to US 206, E Shell, Valero Denny's, McDonald's Best Western, Comfort Inn, Days Inn, EconoLodge, Hampton Inn Blue Beacon, W Candlewood Suites st police
56	to US 206 S (from nb, no return), to NJ Tpk, Ft Dix, McGuire AFB, E Loves/Wendy's/dsl/scales/24hr, Petro/Iron Skillet/dsl/scales/24hr/ @ Days Inn, Hampton Inn, same as 57, W Candlewood Suites st police
52b a	Rd 656, to Columbus, Florence, **3 mi E** Loves/Wendy's/dsl/scales/24hr, Petro/Iron Skillet/dsl/scales/24hr/ @
47b a	NJ 541, to Mount Holly, NJ Tpk, Burlington, E BP, Exxon/dsl, Valero/dsl Applebee's, Burger King, China House, ChuckECheese's, Coldstone, Cracker Barrel, Dunkin Donuts, IHOP, Quiznos, Recovery Grill, TGIFriday's Best Western, Budget Inn, Courtyard, Hampton Inn, Hilton Garden, Holiday Inn Express, Quality Inn $Tree, AT&T, Dick's, Home Depot, JC Penney, Kohl's, mall, Sears/auto, Target, vet, W Citgo/dsl, US Gas, WaWa/dsl Checker's, Friendly's, Subway, Villa Pizza, Wedgewood Farms Rest., Wendy's H, Acme Foods, AutoZone, Marshall's, Walmart
45b a	to Mt Holly, Willingboro, W LukOil H, auto repair
43b a	Rd 636, to Rancocas Woods, Delran, W Exxon Carlucci's Rest.
40b a	NJ 38, to Mount Holly, Moorestown, W Shell/dsl Arby's, Baja Fresh, Chick-fil-A, Dunkin Donuts, Panera Bread, Ruby Tuesday, Starbucks, Subway, TGIFriday's Residence Inn (4mi) H, Costco, GNC, Jo-Ann Fabrics, Petsmart, Radio Shack, Target, TJ Maxx, U-Haul, Wegman's Foods
36b a	NJ 73, to NJ Tpk, Tacony Br, Berlin, E Exxon, LukOil/dsl Bob Evans aLoft, Courtyard, EconoLodge, Fairfield Inn, Red Roof Inn, Super 8, W Citgo, Shell 5 Guys Burgers, Bertucci's, Boscov's, Boston Mkt, Chick-fil-A, Chipotle Mexican, Don Pablo, Dunkin Donuts, Friendly's, Mikado Japanese, Old Town Buffet, Panera Bread, PeiWei, Perkins, PJ Whelahin's, Popeye's, Uno Grill, Wendy's Bel-Air Motel, Crossland Suites, Homewood Suites, Motel 6, Quality Inn $Tree, Acura, AT&T, AutoZone, Barnes&Noble, Best Buy, Chevrolet, Dick's, Fiat, Firestone/auto, Ford/Lincoln, Home Depot, Infiniti, K-Mart, Lord&Taylor, Lowe's, Macy's, mall, Marshall's, Michael's, Old Navy, PepBoys, Petsmart, Ross, Sears/auto, ShopRite Foods, Staples
34b a	NJ 70, to Camden, Cherry Hill, E BP, Exxon, WaWa Big John's Steaks, Burger King, Dunkin Donuts, PJ Whelihans Extended Stay America Curves, Tires+, W Exxon, Gulf/dsl, LukOil, US Gas Dunkin Donuts, Famous Dave's BBQ, McDonald's, Mirabella Cafe, Norma's Cafe, Ponzio's Rest,

CHERRY HILL

NM

Exit #	Services
34b a	Continued Qdoba, Salad Works, Seasons Pizza, Starbucks, Steak&Al Subway Crowne Plaza (3mi) H, $Tree, AT&T, CV Drug, Goodyear/auto, Rite Aid, vet, WaWa
32	NJ 561, to Haddonfield, Voorhees, **3 mi E** LukOil/dsl Guys Burgers, Applebee's, Olive Garden, Panera Bread, Vitc Pizza Hampton Inn, Wingate Inn H, USPO, W Pioneer/dsl, Sunoco Burger King, Dunkin Donuts, Subw 7-11, Ford, vet
31	Woodcrest Station
30	Warwick Rd (from sb)
29b a	US 30, to Berlin, Collingswood, E Astro/dsl, Citgo/d Exxon, LukOil/dsl Arby's, Church's, Dunkin Donuts, M Donald's, Popeye's, Subway, Wendy's AutoZone, Hom Depot, Lowe's, PathMark Foods, Petsmart, Sears Essentials
28	NJ 168, to NJ Tpk, Belmawr, Mt Ephraim, E Citgo, Gu repair, Shamrock/dsl, Shell/dsl Burger King, Club Din Dunkin Donuts, Italia Pizza, Wendy's Bellmawr Mot Comfort Inn, EconoLodge, Holiday Inn, Howard Johnson, Mo 6, Red Roof Inn, Super 8 CVS Drug, transmissions, Wa greens, W BP, Exxon/LP, Hess/dsl, WaWa 5 Gu Burgers, Applebee's, Arby's, Black Horse Diner, Chick-fil- Domino's, Dunkin Donuts, Golden Corral, McDonald's, Soni Subway Acme Foods, AutoZone, Chrysler/Dodge, CV Drug, Firestone, Harley-Davidson, PepBoys, Staples, USP Walgreens, Walmart
26	I-76, NJ 42, to I-676 (exits left from sb), Walt Whitman Bridg Walt Whitman Bridge
25b a	NJ 47, to Westville, Deptford
24b a	NJ 45, NJ 551 (no EZ sb return), to Westville, E H, AutoZone, W WaWa Chevrolet, Family$
23	US 130 N, to National Park
22	NJ 644, to Red Bank, Woodbury, E LukOil, **1 mi W** Crown Point Trkstp/dsl/ @, WaWa Wendy's
21	NJ 44 S, Paulsboro, Woodbury, W WaWa, Wendy Westwood Motor Lodge
20	NJ 44, Rd 643, to National Park, Thorofare, E Best Western, W Red Bank Inn
19	to NJ 44, Rd 656, Mantua
18b a	Rd 667, to Rd 678, Clarksboro, Mt Royal, E BP/ds TA/Exxon/Buckhorn Rest./dsl/scales/ @ Dunkin Donut KFC/Taco Bell, McDonald's, Wendy's RV camping, W Valero, WaWa/dsl
17	Rd 680, to Mickleton, Gibbstown, W Burger King, Domino Motel 6 Advance Parts, Family$, GNC, Rite Aid, Shop Rite Foods, WaWa
16b	Rd 551, to Gibbstown, Mickleton
16a	Rd 653, to Paulsboro, Swedesboro
15	Rd 607, to Gibbstown
14	Rd 684, to Repaupo
13	US 130 S, US 322 W, to Bridgeport (from sb, no return)
11	US 322 E, to Mullica Hill
10	Ctr Square Rd, to Swedesboro, E BP/dsl, WaWa/d Applebee's, Dunkin Donuts, McDonald's, Subway, Wendy Hampton Inn, Holiday Inn Acme Foods/Sav-On, Firestone/auto, Rite Aid, W Camping World RV Supplies/servic
7	to Auburn, Pedricktown
4	NJ 48, Woodstown, Penns Grove
3mm	**weigh sta nb**
2mm	**nb, full facilities, info, litter barrels RV dum vending**
2c	to US 130 (from sb), Deepwater, E same as 2b, W FLYING J/Denny's/dsl/scales/LP/24hr, Sunoco/Dunkin Donuts/dsl/scales/24hr H

INTERSTATE 295 Cont'd

Exit #	Services
2b	US 40 E, to NJ Tpk, E Gulf, Pilot/Subway/dsl/scales/24hr Best Value, Comfort Inn, Friendship Motor Inn, Knights Inn, Quality Inn, W same as 2c
2a	to Delaware Bridge, US 40 W (from nb)
1c	NJ 551 S, Hook Rd, to Salem, E White Oaks Motel, W
1b	US 130 N (from nb), Penns Grove
1a	NJ 49 E, to Pennsville, Salem, E Exxon/dsl/repair Applebees, Burger King, Cracker Barrel, Dunkin Donuts, KFC/Taco Bell, McDonald's, Subway Hampton Inn, Super 8 Peterbilt, W Coastal/dsl Seaview Motel
0mm	New Jersey/Delaware state line, Delaware River, Delaware Memorial Br

NEW MEXICO

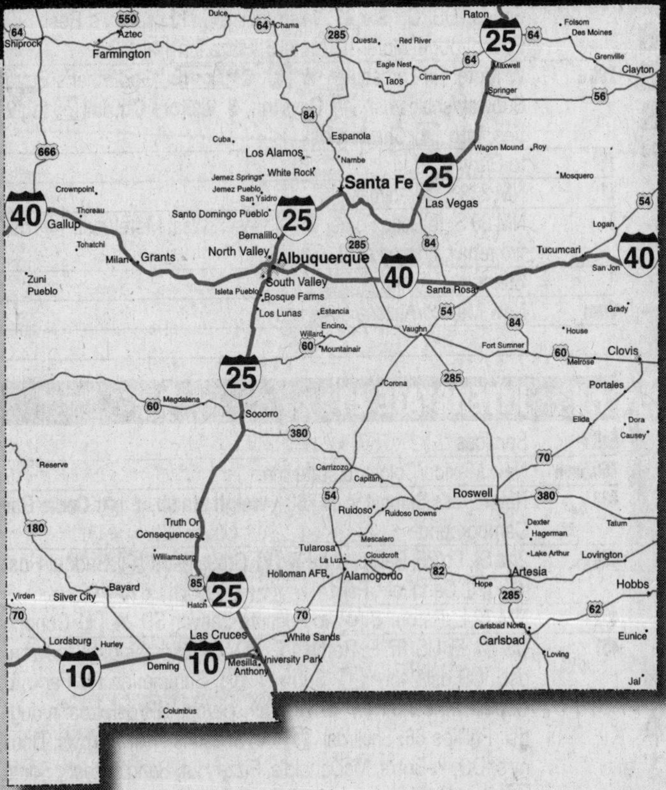

INTERSTATE 10

LAS CRUCES

Exit #	Services
164.5mm	New Mexico/Texas state line
164mm	**Welcome Ctr wb, full facilities, litter barrels, petwalk**
162	NM 404, Anthony, S Alon/dsl Family$, RV camping
160mm	weigh sta wb
155	NM 227 W, to Vado, N Western Sky's RV Park, S NTS/dsl/scales/24hr/ @, Texaco/El Viajero/dsl/scales/24hr $General, El Camino Real HS
151	Mesquite
144	I-25 N, to Las Cruces
142	Rd 188, Rd 101, Valley Dr, Las Cruces, N Chevron/dsl Chilito's Mexican, Dick's Cafe, Whataburger Best Western, EconoLodge, Holiday Inn Express, Motel 6, Quality Inn, Ramada Inn, Super 8, Teakwood Inn H, auto/RV repair/tires, Cadillac/Chevrolet, Dalmont's RV Camping, Ford/Lincoln, Honda, Hyundai, Mazda, Nissan, NMSU, vet, S Alon/dsl USPO
140	NM 28, to Mesilla, Las Cruces, N Alon/dsl Applebee's, Blake's Lotaburger, BurgerTime, Cracker Barrel, Domino's, McDonald's, Murry Express, Starbucks, Subway Best Value Inn, Days Inn, Drury Inn, Hampton Inn, La Quinta, SpringHill Suites Buick/GMC, Kia, Radio Shack, Toyota/Scion, VW, Walmart/McDonald's, S LunaRossa Pizza Comfort Inn Harley-Davidson, Holiday World RV Ctr, Siesta RV Park, United RV Ctr
139	NM 292, Amador Ave, Motel Blvd, Las Cruces, N Pilot/Subway/dsl/scales/24hr, TA/Burger King/Pizza Hut/Taco Bell/dsl/24hr/scales/ @, S PitStop Café Coachlight Inn/RV Park NAPACare
138mm	Rio Grande River
135.5mm	**eb, full facilities, litter barrels, petwalk RV dump, scenic view**
135	US 70 E, to W Las Cruces, Alamogordo, **1 mi N** KOA
132	N fairgrounds, to , S Love's/Subway/dsl/scales/24hr
127	Corralitos Rd, N Exxon Bowlin's Trading Post, to fairgrounds
120.5mm	**insp sta wb**
116	NM 549
111mm	**parking area wb, litter barrels**
102	Akela, N Exxon/dsl/gifts
85	East Motel Dr, Deming, S Chevron/dsl, Save Gas/dsl Hampton Inn, Holiday Inn Express, La Quinta, Motel 6, Quality Inn Buick/Cadillac/Chevrolet/GMC, Chrysler/Dodge/Jeep, Dreamcatcher RV Park
82b	Railroad Blvd, Deming, N Chevron/dsl, S Fina/dsl DQ, Golden Star Chinese, IHOP, KFC, Little Caesars, Ranchers Grill, Wendy's Days Inn, Grand Motel $General,

DEMING

Exit #	Services
82b	Continued $Tree, AutoZone, Big O Tire, Deming Visitors Ctr, Ford/Lincoln, K-Mart, Little Vinyard RV Park, NAPA, O'Reilly Parts, Roadrunner RV Park, st police, Sunrise RV Park, to Rock Hound SP, Verizon, Wagon Wheel RV Park, Walmart/Subway
82a	US 180, NM 26, NM 11, Deming, N Chevron/dsl Blake's Lotaburger, S Exxon, Phillips 66 Burger King, China Rest., Denny's, Domino's, KFC, Palma's Italian, Pizza Hut, Rancher's Grill, Si Senor Butterfield Stage Motel Budget Tire, CarQuest, museum, Radio Shack, Rockhound SP, to Pancho Villa SP, Walgreens
81	NM 11, W Motel Dr, Deming, S Deming Truck Terminal/cafe/dsl/scales/24hr/ @, Shamrock/dsl Benji's Rest, Burger Time, El Camino Real, McDonald's, Sonic, Subway, Taco Bell Best Western, Comfort Inn, Deming Motel, Executive Motel, Super 8, Western Motel 81 Palms RV Park, city park, Hitchin Post RV Park, Rock Hound SP, to Pancho Villa SP
68	NM 418, S Petro/Iron Skillet/Starbucks/dsl/scales/24hr, tires/repair
62	Gage, S Butterfield Station/Exxon/DQ/dsl
61mm	**wb, full facilities, litter barrels, petwalk vending**
55	Quincy
53mm	**eb, full facilities, litter barrels, petwalk vending**
51.5mm	Continental Divide, elev 4585
49	NM 146 S, to Hachita, Antelope Wells
42	Separ, S Bowlin's Continental Divide Trading Post/Gifts

NJ
NM

INTERSTATE 10 Cont'd

LORDSBURG

Exit #	Services
34	NM 113 S, Muir, Playas
29	no services
24	US 70, E Motel Dr, Lordsburg, N FLYING J/Denny's/dsl/LP/scales/RV Dump/24hr, Pilot/Arby's/dsl/scales/24hr American Motel Horseman RV Park
23.5mm	**weigh sta both lanes**
22	NM 494, Main St, Lordsburg, N McDonald's Comfort Inn, Hampton Inn $General, Family$, NAPA, Saucedo's Foods, USPO, S Valero/dsl Kranberry's Rest. EconoLodge, Motel 10, Motel 6, Plaza Inn KOA
20b a	W Motel Dr, Lordsburg, N Loves/Godfather's Pizza/Subway/scales/dsl Days Inn, S **Visitors Ctr, full facilities, info** Chevron/dsl
15	to Gary
11	NM 338 S, to Animas
5	NM 80 S, to Road Forks, S Desert West Motel/rest. dsl/tire repair, fireworks
3	Steins
0mm	New Mexico/Arizona state line

INTERSTATE 25

RATON

Exit #	Services
460.5mm	New Mexico/Colorado state line
460	Raton Pass Summit, elev 7834, **weigh sta sb,** E Cedar Rail Campground
454	2nd St, Lp 25, Raton, **2 mi** W Crossroads Budget Host H, CarQuest, Ford
452	NM 72 E, Raton, E to Sugarite Canyon SP, W Conoco
451	US 64 E, US 87 E, Raton, E 87 Express/dsl, Chevron/dsl, CR/dsl/24hr Subway Summerlan RV Park, to Capulin Volcano NM, W Conoco/dsl, CR/dsl, Loaf'n Jug/dsl, Phillips 66, Shell/dsl All Seasons Rest., Arby's, Denny's, DQ, K-Bob's, McDonald's, Pizza Hut, Sand's Rest., Sonic Best Value Inn, Best Western, Microtel, Motel 6, Oasis Motel/rest, Quality Inn, Robin Hood Motel, Super 8, Texan Motel, Travel Motel, Village Inn Motel H, $General, Ace Hardware, AutoZone, Family$, K-Mart, KOA, Super Save Foods, Visitor's Ctr/info
450	Lp 25, Raton, W Holiday Inn Express, Oasis Motel/rest. H, AutoZone, KOA, vet
446	US 64 W, to Cimarron, Taos, **4 mi** W camping, NRA Whittington Ctr
440mm	Canadian River
435	Tinaja
434.5mm	**both lanes, full facilities, litter barrels, petwalk weather info**
426	NM 505, Maxwell, W Maxwell Station/dsl to Maxwell Lakes, USPO
419	NM 58, to Cimarron, E Chevron/Russell's/Subway/dsl/scales/24hr/ @
414	US 56, Springer, **1 mi** E Conoco/dsl, Crossroads/dsl Minnie's Dairy Delite Oasis Motel Old Santa Fe Trail RV Park
412	US 56 E, US 412 E, NM 21, NM 468, Springer, **1 mi** E Alon Brown Hotel/cafe CarQuest, Springer Foods, USPO
404	NM 569, Colmor, Charette Lakes
393	Levy
387	NM 120, to Roy, Wagon Mound, E Conoco/dsl, Phillips 66/dsl
376mm	**sb, full facilities, litter barrels, petwalk RV camp**

LAS VEGAS

Exit #	Services
374mm	**nb, full facilities, litter barrels, petwalk RV camp**
366	NM 97, NM 161, Watrous, Valmora, W Ft Union NM, Santa Fe Trail
364	NM 97, NM 161, Watrous, Valmora
361	no services
360mm	**parking area both lanes, litter barrels**
356	Onava
352	E RV camping, W
347	to NM 518, Las Vegas, **0-2 mi** W Phillips 66/Burger King Pino/dsl/rest. Arby's, Hillcrest Rest., KFC, Little Moon Chinese, McDonald's, Sonic, Taco Bell, Wendy's Best Western Budget Inn, Comfort Inn, Days Inn, Palamino Inn, Regal Motel Super 8 H, Storrie Lake SP
345	NM 65, NM 104, University Ave, Las Vegas, E to Conchas Lake SP, W Allsups, Crossroads/dsl DQ, Hillcrest Rest. Johnny's Kitchen, KFC El Fidel, Knights Inn H, Hist Old Town Plaza
343	to NM 518 N, Las Vegas, E Garcia Tires, **0-2 mi** W Alon Phillips 66/dsl Holiday Inn Express, Thunderbird Motel auto repair
339	US 84 S, to Santa Rosa, Romeroville, E KOA, W Phillips 66/Subway/dsl
335	Tecolote
330	Bernal
325mm	**parking area both lanes, litter barrels, no restrooms**
323	NM 3 S, Villanueva, E La Risa (1mi) Madison Winery (6mi), to Villanueva SP/rv camping, USPO
319	San Juan, San Jose, W Pecos River Sta.
307	NM 63, Rowe, Pecos, W Hist Rte 66, Pecos NM, same as 299

SANTA FE

Exit #	Services
299	NM 50, Glorieta, Pecos, W Phillips 66 dsl (4mi), Shell (3mi) Glorieta Conf Ctr
297	Valencia
294	Apache Canyon, W KOA, Rancheros Camping (Mar-Nov) (3mi)
290	US 285 S, to Lamy, S to Clines Corners, W Cafe Fina KOA (3mi), Rancheros Camping (Mar-Nov)
284	NM 466, Old Pecos Trail, Santa Fe, W Chevron/Sunset Gen Store/dsl Harry's Roadhouse, Pecos Trail Inn/Cafe H museums
282	US 84, US 285, St Francis Dr, W Conoco/Wendy's/dsl, Giant/dsl Church's
278	NM 14, Cerrillos Rd, Santa Fe, E RV Ctr, **0-4 mi** W Giant/dsl, Murphy Express/dsl, Phillips 66/dsl, Shell Adelita's Mexican, Applebee's, Arby's, Blue Corn Cafe, Buffalo Wild Wings, Bumble Bee's Baja Grill, Burger King, Denny's, Domino's, Flying Tortilla, IHOP, KFC, Little Caesars, LJ Silver, Lotaburger, LuLu's Chinese, McDonald's, Olive Garden, Outback Steaks, Panda Express, Panera Bread, Papa Murphy's, Pizza Hut, Ranch House Steaks, Red Lobster, Schlotzsky's, Sonic, Starbucks, Taco Bell, Tortilla Flats Best Western, Comfort Inn, Comfort Suites, Courtyard, Days Inn, Doubletree, EconoLodge, Fairfield Inn, Hampton Inn, Holiday Inn Express, Hyatt Place, La Quinta, Motel 6, Quality Inn, Santa Fe Inn, Super 8, Tranquilla Inn AAA, Albertson's, AT&T, Best Buy, Big-Lots, BMW, Buick/GMC, Cadillac/Chevrolet, Chrysler/Dodge/Jeep, CVS Drug, Dillard's, Discount Tire, Firestone/auto, Ford/Lincoln, Harley-Davidson, Home Depot, Honda, JC Penney, Jo-Ann Fabrics, Kohl's, Land Rover, Lexus, Los Campos RV Park, Lowe's, Mazda, Mecedes/Smart, Meineke, Michaels, Natural Grocers, Peerless Tire, Penske, PepBoys, Petsmart, Ross, Sam's Club/gas, Santa Fe Outlets/famous brands, Sears/auto,

NM

INTERSTATE 25 Cont'd

278 Continued
Sprouts Mkt, Staples, Subaru/VW, Target, TJ Maxx, Tuesday Morning, Verizon, Volvo, Walgreens, Walmart

276b a NM 599, to NM 14, to Madrid, E Phillips 66/Allsup's Santa Fe Skies RV Park, **4 mi W** Shell Sunrise Springs

271 CR 50F, La Cienega

269mm **nb, full facilities, litter barrels, petwalk**

267 Waldo Canyon Rd, **insp sta., access to nb rest area**

264 NM 16, Pueblo, W to Cochiti Lake RA

263mm Galisteo River

259 NM 22, to Santo Domingo Pueblo, W Phillips 66/cafe/dsl to Cochiti Lake RA (11mi)

257 Budaghers, W Mormon Battalion Mon

252 San Felipe Pueblo, E Phillips 66/dsl San Felipe Casino/rest.

248 Rte 66, Algodones

242 US 550, NM 44 W, NM 165 E, to Farmington, Aztec, **0-2 mi W** Chevron/dsl, Conoco/dsl, M&M/Burger King/dsl, Phillips 66/dsl, Valero/dsl Denny's, Guang Dong Chinese, IHOP, KFC, Lotaburger, McDonald's, Pizza Hut, Sonic, Starbucks, Subway, Taco Bell, Twisters, Wendy's Days Inn, Holiday Inn Express, Motel 6, Super 8 $General, AutoZone, Casino, Home Depot, KOA, O'Reilly Parts, to Coronado SP, Walgreens, Walmart

240 NM 473, to Bernalillo, W Conoco/dsl Abuelita's Mexican, Range Café KOA, to Coronado SP, USPO, vet

234 NM 556, Tramway Rd, E Valero/Subway/dsl casino, W Phillips 66/dsl

233 Alameda Blvd, E Chevron Burger King Comfort Suites, Motel 6, Staybridge Suites Audi/Porsche, Lincoln, Meineke, Mercedes, Toyota/Scion, Volvo, W Phillips 66/Circle K/dsl Carl's Jr Best Value, Holiday Inn Express Balloon Fiesta Park, CarMax

232 Paseo del Norte, Paseo del Norte, E Chick-fil-A, China Luck, Chipotle Mexican, Five Guys, Freddy's Steakburgers, Jason's Deli, Jimmy John's, McDonald's, Panda Express, Panera Bread, Starbucks, Subway, Tomato Cafe, Wendy's Howard Johnson Aloha RV Ctr, AutoZone, Discount Tire, Kohl's, Lowe's, Office Depot, Target, Verizon, Walgreens, W Shell/Circle K Arby's Courtyard, Marriott

231 San Antonio Ave, E Alon/7-11 Cracker Barrel, Denny's, Lotaburger Comfort Suites, Hilton Garden, Homewood Suites, La Quinta, Quality Inn H, USPO, W Baymont Inn, Crossland Suites, LaQuinta Mazda, VW

230 San Mateo Blvd, Osuna Rd, Albuquerque, E Chevron, Circle K, Giant/dsl, Phillips 66/Circle K, Shell Applebee's, Arby's, Azuma Grill, Bob's Burgers, Burger King, Chick-fil-A, Chili's, Cici's Pizza, Firehouse Subs, Furrs Buffet, Golden Corral, Hayashi, Hooters, Jack-in-the-Box, KFC, LJ Silver, McDonald's, Olive Garden, Papa John's, Pizza Hut/Taco Bell, Popeyes, Schloztsky's, Sonic, Souper Salad, Starbucks, Subway, SweetTomatoes, Taco Bueno, Taco Cabana, Teriyaki Chicken, TX Roadhouse, Village Inn, Wendy's, Wienerschnitzel Nativo Lodge H, $Tree, Albertson's, AT&T, AutoZone, Brake Masters, Cadillac, CVS Drug, Fiat, Firestone, Firestone/auto, GNC, Just Brakes, Midas, NAPA, O'Reilly Parts, Peerless Tire, PepBoys, PetCo, Ross, Sprouts Mkt, Subaru, Tuesday Morning, U-Haul, Walgreens, W Circle K/dsl, Valero/dsl McDonald's, Quiznos, Weck's Breakfast/lunch, Whataburger Studio 6 BMW/Mini

229 Jefferson St, E Carrabba's, ClaimJumper, Landry's Seafood, Outback Steaks Holiday Inn H, same as 230,

ALBUQUERQUE

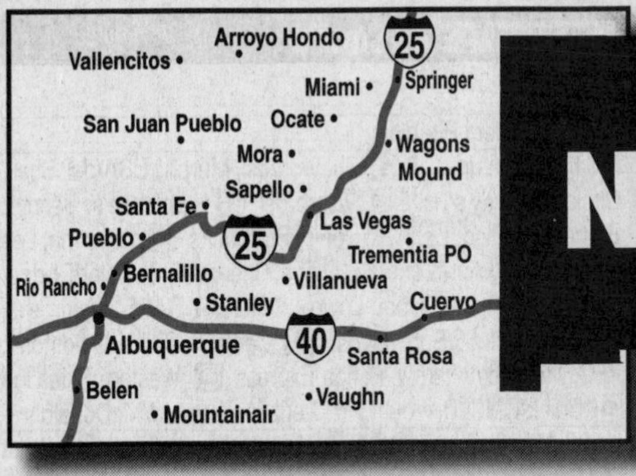

NM

W Boston's Pizza, Chama River Rest., Cheddar's, Chile Rio, Coldstone, Fox&Hound, Fuddrucker's, Genghis Grill, Mimi's Café, Nick&Jimmy's Grill, Pappadeaux, Pars Cuisine, PF Chang's, Plum Cafe Asian, Red Robin, Subway, Twin Peaks Rest., TX Land&Cattle Steaks Drury Inn, Hampton Inn, Residence Inn, TownePlace Suites Lexus

228 Montgomery Blvd, E Alon/7-11/dsl, Chevron/dsl, Conoco/dsl Fiestas Cantina, Lotaburger Best Western H, Discount Tire, W Shell/Circle K Arby's, Carl's Jr, IHOP, McDonald's, Panda Express, Starbucks, Wendy's InTowne Suite Acura, Costco/gas, Ford, Home Depot, Infiniti, Office Depot, Petsmart, REI, Sam's Club/gas, Sportsman's Whse

227b Comanche Rd, Griegos Rd, E UPS Depot

227a Candelaria Rd, Albuquerque, E Circle K/dsl, Pump'n'Save/dsl, Shell, TA/Valero/Country Pride/dsl/scales/24hr/ @ Applebee's, Little Anita's, Mesa Grill, Range Cafe, Subway, Village Inn Candlewood Suites, Crowne Plaza, Days Inn, Elegante Hotel, Fairfield Inn, Holiday Inn Express, La Quinta, Motel 1, Motel 76, Quality Inn, Rodeway Inn, Super 8, Travelodge Kenworth, W Chevron/dsl Ambassador Inn, Red Roof Inn Penske

226b a I-40, E to Amarillo, W to Flagstaff

225 Lomas Blvd, E Phillips 66 Plaza Inn/rest. Chevrolet, W FillUp, Shell/Circle K/McDonald's Burger King, Carl's Jr, Starbucks Embassy Suites H

224 Lead Ave, Coal Ave, Grand Ave, Central Ave, E Alon/7-11 66 Diner Crossroads Motel H, W M&M Best Value Inn, EconoLodge, Hotwl Parq Central, Knights Inn

223 Chavez Ave, E Motel 6 sports arena

222b a Gibson Blvd, E Phillips 66/dsl Applebee's, Buffalo Wild Wings, Burger King, Dion's Pizza, Fuddrucker's, IHOP, Subway, Village Inn, Waffle House AmericInn, Best Western, Comfort Inn, Country Inn&Suites, Courtyard, Days Inn, Extended Stay America, Fairfield Inn, Hawthorn Suites, Hilton Garden, Holiday Inn Express, La Quinta, Quality Suites, Ramada Inn, Residence Inn, Sleep Inn, TownePlace Suites H, Kirtland AFB, museum, vet, W Alon/7-11/dsl Church's, Lotaburger

221 Sunport, E Holiday Inn, Homewood Suites, Hyatt Place, Staybridge Suites USPO

220 Rio Bravo Blvd, Mountain View, E golf, **1-2 mi W** Shell/dsl, Valero/dsl Bob's Burgers, Burger King, Church's, KFC/Taco Bell, McDonald's, Pizza Hut, Subway Albertsons/Sav-On, Family$, O'Reilly Parts, vet, Walgreens

215 NM 47, E Isleta One Stop/dsl, Phillips 66/Subway/dsl casino, golf, st police, to Isleta Lakes RA/RV Camping

214mm Rio Grande

213 NM 314, Isleta Blvd, W Chevron/Subway/dsl $General, vet

ALBUQUERQUE

INTERSTATE 25 Cont'd

Exit #	Services
209	NM 45, to Isleta Pueblo
203	NM 6, to Los Lunas, E Chevron/dsl, Murphy USA/dsl, Shell/Circle K/Wendy's/dsl/24hr, Valero/dsl Applebee's, Benny's Burger, Del Taco, Denny's, Sonic, Starbucks Days Inn, Los Lunas Inn AutoZone, Big O Tire, Chevrolet, Chrysler/Dodge/Jeep, Ford, Home Depot, Lowe's, URGENT CARE, Walgreens, W Phillips 66/Subway/dsl Carl's Jr, Chili's, Coldstone, KFC, Mariscos Altamar, Panda Express Western Skies Inn Buick/GMC, Discount Tire, Verizon, Walmart/McDonald's
195	Lp 25, Los Chavez, **1 mi E** Roadrunner/grill/dsl Pizza Hut/Taco Bell Walmart/Subway
191	NM 548, Belen, **1 mi E** Conoco/dsl McDonald's, Pizza Hut Super 8 $General, USPO, Walgreens, W Rio Grande Diner Holiday Inn Express, RV park
190	Lp 25, Belen, **1-2 mi E** Conoco/dsl, Phillips 66 A&W/LJ Silver, McDonald's, Pizza Hut Super 8 $General, Affordable Tire/repair, AutoZone, USPO, Walgreens
175	US 60, Bernardo, E Salinas NM, W Kiva RV Park
174mm	Rio Puerco
169	E La Joya St Game Refuge Sevilleta NWR
167mm	**both lanes, full facilities, litter barrels, petwalk vending**
166mm	Rio Salado
165mm	**weigh sta/parking area both lanes**
163	San Acacia
156	Lemitar, W Phillips 66/dsl/24hr
152	Escondida, W to st police
150	US 60 W, Socorro, W Chevron/dsl, Exxon/dsl, Phillips 66/dsl, Valero/dsl Bodega Burger Co, Burger King, China Best, Denny's, Domino's, K-Bob's, Little Caesar's, Lotaburger, McDonald's, Pizza Hut, Socorro Springs Rest., Sofia's Kitchen, Sonic, Subway Best Value, Best Western, Comfort Inn, Days Inn, EconoLodge, Economy Inn, Holiday Inn Express, Sands Motel, Super 8 $General, Ace Hardware, AutoZone, Brooks Foods, CarQuest, Family$, Ford, NAPA, Radio Shack, Smith's Foods, to NM Tech, Verizon, vet, Walmart
147	US 60 W, Socorro, W Chevron/dsl, Conoco/dsl/LP, Pump-N-Save/dsl, Shell/Circle K/dsl Arby's Rodeway Inn H, repair/transmissions, Socorro RV Park, to
139	US 380 E, to San Antonio, E gas/food to Bosque Del Apache NWR
124	to San Marcial, E Ft Craig, to Bosque del Apache NWR
115	NM 107, E Truck Plaza/dsl/rest./24hr to Camino Real Heritage Ctr
114mm	**both lanes, full facilities, litter barrels, petwalk RV parking, vending**
107mm	Nogal Canyon
100	Red Rock
92	Mitchell Point
90mm	La Canada Alamosa
89	NM 181, to Cuchillo, to Monticello, RV Park (4mi)
83	NM 52, NM 181, to Cuchillo, **3 mi E** Ivory Tusk Inn& Tavern Elephant Butte Inn/rest. Elephant Lake Butte SP, RV Park
82mm	**insp sta nb**
79	Lp 25, to Truth or Consequences, E Chevron/dsl, Circle K, Shell/dsl Blakes's Lotaburger, Denny's, K-Bob's, La Cocina Mexican, Los Arcos Steaks, McDonald's, Pizza Hut, Sonic, Subway Ace Lodge, Comfort Inn, Desert View Motel, Holiday Inn Express, Hot Springs Inn, Motel 6, Oasis Motel H, $General, AutoZone, O'Reilly Parts, to Elephant Butte SP, USPO, Verizon, Walmart
76	(75 from nb) Lp 25, to Williamsburg, E Conoco/dsl, FillUp/dsl, Phillips 66/dsl, Shell/dsl Maria's Mexican Rio Grande Motel Alco, auto/tire repair, Buick/Chevrolet/GMC, Cielo Vista RV Park, city park, Rio Grande RV Park, RJ RV Park, Shady Corner RV Park
71	Las Palomas
63	NM 152, to Hillsboro, Caballo, E Lakeview RV Park/dsl/LP
59	Rd 187, Arrey, Derry, E to Caballo-Percha SPs
58mm	Rio Grande
51	Rd 546, to Arrey, Garfield, Derry
41	NM 26 W, Hatch, **1 mi W** Alon/Subway/dsl Burgers&More, Sparky's Cafe Kings Pillow Inn Chile Pepper Outlets, Franciscan RV Ctr, USPO
35	NM 140 W, Rincon
32	Upham
27mm	scenic view nb, **litter barrels, picnic tables**
26mm	**insp sta nb**
23mm	**both lanes, full facilities, info, litter barrels, petwalk vending**
19	Radium Springs, W Family$, Fort Selden St Mon, Leasburg SP, RV camping, USPO
9	Dona Ana, W Chucky's/dsl, Circle K/dsl Chachi's Mexican, Jake's Cafe $General, Family$, RV camping, USPO
6	US 70, to Alamogordo, Las Cruces, E Alon/dsl, Shell Domino's, IHOP, Outback Steaks, Papa Johns, Peter Piper Pizza, Pizzaria Uno, Red Brick Pizza, Ruby Tuesday, Starbucks, Subway Fairfield Inn, Holiday Inn Express, Motel 6, Staybridge Suites, Towneplace Suites H, AT&T, K-Mart, Sam's Club/gas, USPO, vet, W Alon/dsl, Chevron, Shell/dsl, Valero/dsl Burger King, BurgerTime, China Express, Domino's, DQ, Dunkin Donuts, KFC, Little Caesar's, Lotaburger, McDonald's, Sonic, Spanish Kitchen, Subway, Taco Bell, Whataburger/24hr, Wienerschnitzel $General, $Tree, Albertson's, AutoZone, CVS Drug, Family$, Kohl's, Lowe's, O'Reilly Parts, Radio Shack, Verizon, vet, Walgreens
3	Lohman Ave, Las Cruces, E Alon/dsl, Shell Applebee's, Buffalo Wild Wings, Burger King, Cattle Baron Steaks, Chili's, ChuckeCheese, Dumkin Donuts, Empire Buffet, Farley's Grill, Fidencio's Mexican, Five Guys, Genghis Grill, Golden Corral, Hooters, Jack-in-the-Box, Jason's Deli, KFC, McAlister's Deli, Olive Garden, Pecan Grill, Red Lobster, Sonic, Starbucks, Village Inn, Whataburger Hotel Encanto Albertsons, AutoZone, Barnes&Noble, Dick's, Dillard's, Discount Tire, Home Depot, JC Penney, mall, Marshalls, PetCo, Ross, Sears/auto, Target, W Giant/dsl, Valero/dsl Arby's, Carl's Jr, Corner Bakery Cafe, McDonald's, Papa Murphy's, Quiznos, Subway, Taco Bell, TX Roadhouse, Wendy's Hampton Inn AT&T, Best Buy, Big Lots, Brake Masters, Hastings Books, Hobby Lobby, NAPA, Old Navy, PepBoys, Petsmart, Staples, URGENT CARE, Verizon, vet, Walgreens, Walmart
1	University Ave, Las Cruces, E AlonSubway/dsl Hilton Garden H, golf, museum, st police, W Giant/dsl Dublin's Cafe, Lorenzo's Italian, McDonald's, Schlotsky's Comfort Suites, Sleep Inn, ValuePlace $Tree, Jo-Ann Fabrics, NMSU, Tuesday Morning
0mm	**I-25 begins/ends on I-10, exit 144 at Las Cruces.**

BELEN

SOCORRO

NM

LAS CRUCES

INTERSTATE 40

Exit #	Services
373.5mm	New Mexico/Texas state line, Mountain/Central time zone
373mm	**Welcome Ctr wb, full facilities, litter barrels, petwalk**

INTERSTATE 40 Cont'd

Exit #	Services
369	NM 93 S, NM 392 N, Endee, N Chevron/Russell's Truck&Travel/Subway/dsl/scales/24hr
361	Bard
358mm	**weigh sta both lanes**
356	NM 469, San Jon, N Dhillon/cafe/dsl repair, to Ute Lake SP, S Valero/dsl San Jon Motel city park, USPO
343	no services
339	NM 278, N
335	Lp 40, E Tucumcari Blvd, Tucumcari, N Conoco/dsl Best Value, EconoLodge, Motel 6, Quality Inn, Rodeway Inn, Super 8 Empty Saddle RV Park, to Conchas Lake SP, S KOA
333	US 54 E, Tucumcari, 0-1 mi N FLYING J/Phillips 66/dsl/LP/scales/24hr, Loves/Arbys/Chester's/Godfather's/dsl/scales Rockin Y's Roadhouse Tucumcari Inn city park, K-Mart, Mtn Rd RV Park, truck repair, truckwash
332	NM 209, NM 104, 1st St, Tucumcari, 0-2 mi N Phillips 66/Allsups, Shell/Circle K/Subway/dsl Blake's Lotaburger, K-Bob's, KFC, McDonald's, Pizza Hut, Sonic Best Western, Days Inn, Desert Inn, Holiday Inn Express, La Quinta H, $General, Ace Hardware, Dinosaur Museum, Family$, Lowe's Foods, st police, to Conchas Lake SP
331	Camino del Coronado, Tucumcari
329	US 54, US 66 E, W Tucumcari Ave
321	Palomas
311	Montoya
302mm	**both lanes, full facilities, litter barrels, petwalk RV dump**
300	NM 129, Newkirk, N Rte 66/dsl to Conchas Lake SP, USPO
291	to Rte 66, Cuervo, N Cuervo Gas/repair
284	no services
277	US 84 S, to Ft Sumner, N Phillips 66/dsl DQ, Silver Moon Café Best Western, Budget Inn, Comfort Inn, Hampton Inn, Holiday Inn Express, Motel 6, Quality Inn NAPA-Care, S Loves/Carl's Jr/dsl/24hr, TA/Shell/Subway/dsl/24hr/ @ truck/tire repair
275	US 54 W, Santa Rosa, N Phillips 66 McDonald's, Rte 66 Rest., Santa Fe Grill Days Inn, Econolodge, La Quinta, Motel 6 Santa Rosa Camping, st police, S Shell/Circle K/dsl Joseph's Grill, Papo's Pizza Laloma Motel/RV Park, Rodeway Inn, Sun'n Sand Motel/rest., Super 8, Tower Motel H, $General, CarQuest, city park, Family$, NAPA, USPO
273.5mm	Pecos River
273	US 54 S, Santa Rosa, N Santa Rosa Lake SP, S Phillips 66 Best Value Inn NAPACare, to Carlsbad Caverns NP
267	Colonias
263	San Ignacio
256	US 84 N, NM 219, to Las Vegas
252	no services
251.5mm	**both lanes, full facilities, info, litter barrels, petwalk RV dump**
243	Milagro, N Phillips 66/dsl
239	no services
234	N Exxon/Flying C/DQ/dsl/gifts
230	NM 3, to Encino, N to Villanueva SP
226	no services
220mm	**parking area both lanes, litter barrels**

TUCUMCARI — SANTA ROSA

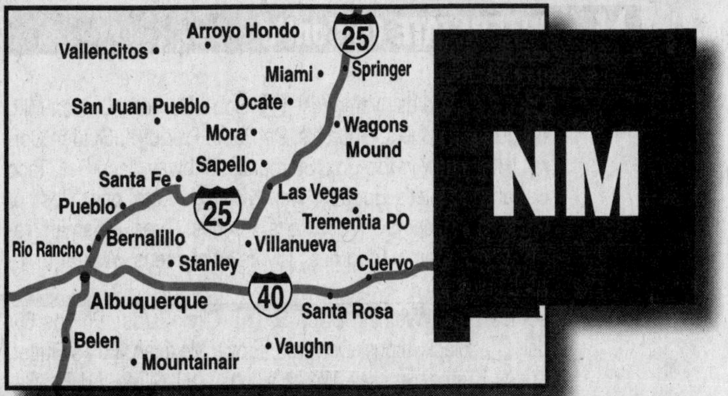

Exit #	Services
218b a	US 285, Clines Corners, N Conoco/dsl/24hr, Phillips 66/dsl Clines Corners Rest., Subway, S to Carlsbad Caverns NP
208	Wagon Wheel
207mm	**both lanes, full facilities, info, litter barrels, petwalk**
203	N RV Park
197	to Rte 66, Moriarty, S Lisa's TC/dsl/rest./ @ auto/RV repair, Glider Museum, same as 194
196	NM 41, Howard Cavasos Blvd, N Pilot/Subway/dsl/scales/24hr, S Phillips 66/Circle K/dsl Blakes Lotaburger Comfort Inn, Sunset Motel auto repair, city park, Family$, NAPA, to Salinas NM (35mi), USPO
194	NM 41, Moriarty, S Conoco/dsl, Pump'n Save/dsl, TA/Shell/Burger King/Country Pride/Pizza Hut/dsl/24hr/scales/ @ Arby's, Chili Hills Mexican, El Comedor Mexican, KFC/Taco Bell, McDonald's, Subway Best Value Inn, Best Western, Motel 6, Ponderosa Motel, Super 8 $General, Chevrolet/GMC, Moriarty Foods, RV Ctr, URGENT CARE
187	NM 344, Edgewood, N Conoco/DQ/dsl Walmart/McDonald's, S Phillips 66/dsl Chili Hills Mexican, China Chef, Domino's, McDonald's, Pizza Barn, Sonic, Subway auto/rv repair, AutoZone, Ford, O'Reilly Parts, RV Camping, Smith's Foods/dsl, USPO, Walgreens
181	NM 217, Sedillo, S Route 66/dsl
178	Zuzax, S Shelby's/dsl Hidden Valley RV Park, Leisure Mtn RV Park
175	NM 337, NM 14, Tijeras, N to Cibola NF, Turquoise Trail RV Park, S Subway USPO
170	Carnuel
167	Central Ave, to Tramway Blvd, S Alon/7-11, Phillips 66/Circle K/dsl, Pump-n-Save/dsl Blakes Lotaburger, KFC, Little Caesar's, McDonald's, Pizza Hut/Taco Bell, Starbucks, Subway, Waffle House Budget Host, Deluxe Inn, EconoLodge, Motel 6, Rodeway Inn, Suburban Lodge, Travelodge, Value Place $Tree, Rocky Mtn RV/marine, Smith's/gas, to Kirtland AFB, Valvoline
166	Juan Tabo Blvd, N Phillips 66/Circle K, Texaco/dsl AA Buffet, Dominos, Fedrico's Mexican, McDonald's, Olive Garden, Paul's Rest., Pizza Hut, Subway, Taco Bell, Twisters Diner, Village Inn Rest., Weck's Rest., Wendy's Best Value, Super 8 $General, Albertson's, Discount Tire, Family$, Hastings Books, Hobby Lobby, Midas, Sav-On Drug, Tire Factory, transmissions, Tuesday Morning, vet, S Sonic, Wienerschnitzel $General, Chisholm Trail RV Ctr, Holiday RV Ctr, KOA/LP, Myer's RV Ctr, repair
165	Eubank Blvd, N Chevron, Phillips 66/Circle K Applebee's, Owl Cafe, Panda Express, Sadie's Rest., Sonic Days Inn, Guesthouse Inn, Holiday Inn Express, Howard Johnson Best Buy, CarQuest, city park, PetCo, Radio Shack, Target,

MORIARTY — ALBUQUERQUE

NM

▣◆ INTERSTATE 40 Cont'd

165 **Continued**
S 🗔 Conoco/dsl, Valero/dsl 🍴 Bob's Burgers, Boston Mkt, Burger King, Chili's, Church's, Del Taco, Freddy's, Golden Corral, IHOP, Jack-in-the-Box, Starbucks, Subway, Taco Bell, Taco Cabana, Twister's Burritos, Wendy's 🅞 AutoZone, Costco/gas, Home Depot, O'Reilly Parts, Peerless Tires, Petsmart, repair, Ross, Sam's Club/gas, Toyota, Walgreens, Walmart/McDonald's

164 Lomas Blvd, Wyoming Blvd, **N** 🗔 Circle K/dsl, Phillips 66/dsl 🍴 Black Angus, Dominos, Eloy's Mexican, Furr's Buffet, Krispy Kreme, Subway, Wendy's 🅞 🇭 $Tree, NAPA, Radio Shack, Walgreens, Walmart, **S** 🅞 Chrysler/Dodge/Jeep, Ford, Harley-Davidson, Honda, Hyundai, Kirtland AFB, Mazda, Subaru, transmissions, VW

162b a Louisiana Blvd, **N** 🍴 BJ's Rest., Bonefish Grill, Bravo Italian, Buca Italian, CA Pizza Kitchen, Chili's, Chipotle, Dave & Buster', Elephant Bar Rest., Fuddrucker's, Garduno's Mexican, Genghis Grill, Jasons Deli, LePeep, Macaroni Grill, McAlister's Deli, Melting Pot, Ojos Locos, Panera Bread, Starbucks, Subway 🛏 Hilton Garden, Homewood Suites, Hyatt Place, Marriott, Sheraton 🅞 AT&T, Barnes&Noble, Big O Tire, Dillard's, Firestone/auto, JC Penney, Kohl's, Macy's, Sears/auto, Target, Trader Joe's, Verizon, **S** 🗔 Shell 🍴 Burger King 🅞 atomic museum

161b a San Mateo Blvd, Albuquerque, **N** 🗔 Giant/dsl, Shell 🍴 Bob's Burgers, Carl's Jr., Denny's, KFC, Pizza Hut, Starbucks, Subway, Taco Bell, Wendy's 🛏 Motel 6 🅞 $Tree, Office Depot, Old Navy, Walmart Mkt, **S** 🗔 Chevron/dsl 🍴 Starbucks

160 Carlisle Blvd, Albuquerque, **N** 🗔 Circle K/gas, Murphy Express/dsl, Pump'n Save, Shell, USA 🍴 Applebee's, Blakes Lotaburger, China Wok, Jack-in-the-Box, Little Anita's, McDonald's, Papa Murphy's, Pizza Hut, Range Cafe, Rudy's BBQ, Sonic, Subway, Twisters Grill, Village Inn Rest., Whataburger 🛏 Best Value Inn, Candlewood Suites, Days Inn, EconoLodge, Elegante Hotel, Hampton Inn, Holiday Inn Express, Hotel Cascada, Motel 6, Quality Inn, Residence Inn, Suburban Motel, Super 8 🅞 Autozone, Firestone/auto, Walgreens, Walmart, **S** 🗔 Chevron/dsl, Circle K 🍴 Burger King 🅞 🇭 K-Mart, Whole Foods Mkt

159b c I-25, S to Las Cruces, N to Santa Fe

158 6th St, 8th St, 12th St, Albuquerque, **N** 🗔 Loves/Subway/dsl 🅞 U-Haul, **S** 🗔 Chevron/dsl 🛏 Baymont Inn

157b 12th St (from eb), **N** 🗔 Four Winds/Burrito Co/dsl 🍴 McDonald's 🛏 Holiday Inn Express 🅞 Lowe's, Walgreens

157a Rio Grande Blvd, Albuquerque, **N** 🗔 Chevron, **S** 🗔 Shell 🍴 Ben Michaels, Blakes Lotaburger, Little Anita's, Starbucks 🛏 Best Western/grill, Hotel Albuquerque 🅞 repair

156mm Rio Grande River

155 Coors Rd, Albuquerque, **N** 🗔 Circle K, Duke City/dsl, Mobil, Valero/dsl 🍴 Applebee's, Arby's, Baskin-Robbins, Burger King, Chili's, Cracker Barrel, Golden Corral, IHOP, Krispy Kreme, McDonald's, Mimmo's Pizza, Panda Express, Papa Murphy's, Sonic, Starbucks, Subway, Taco Cabana, Twisters Burritos, Wendy's, Wing Stop 🅞 $Tree, AutoZone, Brake Masters, Brook's Foods, Family$, Firestone, GNC, Home Depot, Jiffy Lube, Midas, Radio Shack, Staples, Verizon, Walgreens, Walmart/Subway, **S** 🗔 Phillips 66/Circle K/dsl, Shell, Valero 🍴 Altimar's Mexican, Blakes Lotaburger, Buffalo Wild Wings, China Buffet, Del Taco, Denny's, Dion's, McDonald's, Papa John's, Pizza Hut/Taco Bell, Subway, Twisters Burritos, Village Inn Rest. 🛏 Days Inn, EconoLodge, Hampton Inn, La Quinta, Motel 6, Motel 76, Quality Inn, Rodeway Inn, Super 8 🅞 BigLots, Discount Tire, O'Reilly Parts

154 Unser Blvd, **N** 🗔 Valero 🅞 to Petroglyph NM

153 98th St, **S** 🗔 ⊕FLYING J/Denny's/dsl/LP/24hr, LNG, Valero-dsl 🍴 Burger King, Church's, Godfather's, Jack-in-the-Box, Little Caesars, McDonald's, Subway 🛏 Microtel 🅞 $Tree, AutoZone, truckwash/tire/lube

149 Central Ave, Paseo del Volcan, **N** 🅞 Camping World, Enchanted Trails RV Camping, Freightliner, LaMesa RV Ctr, to Shooting Range SP, **S** 🗔 Loves/Carl's Jr/dsl/scales 24hr 🅞 American RV Park, High Desert RV Park

140.5mm Rio Puerco River, **N** 🗔 66 Pit Stop

140 Rio Puerco, **N** 🗔 66 Pit Stop/dsl, **S** 🗔 Rte 66 TC/DQ/Road Runner Cafe/hotel/casino/dsl/ @

131 Canoncito

126 NM 6, to Los Lunas

120mm Rio San Jose, Rio San Jose

117 Mesita

114 NM 124, Laguna, **1/2 mi N** 🗔 66 Pit Stop/dsl

113.5mm scenic view both lanes, litter barrels

108 Casa Blanca, Paraje, **S** 🗔 Rte 66 TC/DQ/dsl/24hr 🅞 casino, Dancing Eagle Mkt, RV park

104 Cubero, Budville

102 Sky City Rd, Acomita, **N** 🗔 Sky City/McDonald's/hotel/casino/dsl 🍴 Huwak'a Rest. 🅞 casino, RV Park/laundry, **S** 🅡ₛ both lanes, full ♿ facilities, litter barrels ▣ 🏕, 🅞 🇭

100 San Fidel

96 McCartys

89 NM 117, to Quemado, **N** 🗔 Sky City/Subway/dsl/gifts, **S** 🅞 El Malpais NM

85 NM 122, NM 547, Grants, **N** 🗔 Alon/dsl, Phillips 66/dsl, Shell/dsl 🍴 Asian Buffet, Blakes Lotaburger, Canton Cafe, Denny's, Pizza Hut, Subway, Taco Bell 🛏 Comfort Inn, Days Inn, Holiday Inn Express, Motel 6, Quality Inn, Red Lion Hotel, Sands Motel, Super 8, Travelodge 🅞 🇭 $Tree, AutoZone, Delta Tire, O'Reilly Parts, repair/transmissions/towing, Walgreens, Walmart, **S** 🅞 Lavaland RV Park

81b a NM 53 S, Grants, **N** 🗔 Phillips 66/dsl 🍴 Domino's, KFC, McDonald's 🅞 🇭 Ford, NAPA, USPO, **S** 🅞 Blue Spruce RV Park, El Malpais NM, KOA/Cibola Sands RV Park

79 NM 122, NM 605, Milan, **N** 🗔 Chevron/dsl, Loves/Chester's/Subway/dsl/scales/24hr 🍴 DQ 🛏 Crossroads Motel 🅞 Bar-S RV Park, **S** 🗔 Petro/Iron Skillet/dsl/scales/24hr/ @ 🅞 dsl repair, Speedco Lube

72 Bluewater Village, **N** 🗔 Exxon/DQ/dsl

63 NM 412, Prewitt, **S** 🅞 to Bluewater Lake SP (7mi)

53 NM 371, NM 612, Thoreau, **N** 🗔 Giant/Blimpie/dsl 🅞 Family$, NAPA, USPO

47 **N** 🗔 Phillips 66 🅞 Continental Divide Trdg Post, towing/repair, **S** 🅞 USPO, 🅞 7275 ft, Continental Divide

44 Coolidge

39 Refinery, **N** 🗔 PILOT/Subway/Dennys/dsl/scales/24hr/ @

36 Iyanbito

33 NM 400, McGaffey, Ft Wingate, **N** 🅞 museum, RV camping, to Red Rock SP

26 E 66th Ave, E Gallup, **N** 🗔 Shell/Subway/dsl 🍴 Denny's 🛏 Comfort Suites, Holiday Inn Express, La Quinta, Sleep Inn 🅞 museum, Red Rock Camping, st police, to Red Rock SP, **S on Rte 66** 🗔 Conoco/dsl, Giant/dsl, Pronto Express, Shell/Ortega Gifts 🍴 Aurelie's Diner, Blakes Lotaburger, Burger King, KFC, McDonald's, Sonic, Wendy's 🛏 Days Inn, Fairfield Inn, Hacienda Motel, Roadrunner Motel 🅞 🇭 $General, Verizon

22 Montoya Blvd, Gallup, **N** 🅡ₛ both lanes, full ♿ facilities, info, **S on Rte 66** 🗔 Duke City/dsl, Gas Up, Giant/dsl, Phillips 66 🍴 Big Cheese Pizza, Church's, Domino's, DQ, Dragon Express, Earl's Rest., Hong Kong Buffet, LJ Silver, Panz Alegra,

A L B U Q U E R Q U E

NM

G R A N T S

G A L L U P

INTERSTATE 40 Cont'd

22	Continued Papa John's, Pizza Hut, Railway Cafe, Subway, Taco Bell Blue Spruce Motel, El Capitan Motel, El Rancho Motel/rest. Albertson's, O'Reilly Parts, Radio Shack, Shop'n Save, Walgreens
20	US 491, to Shiprock, Gallup, **N** Alon/dsl, Giant/dsl Applebee's, Arby's, Big Cheese Pizza, Blakes Lotaburger, Burger King, CA Chinese, Carl's Jr., Church's, ΔCracker BarrelΔ, Denny's, DQ, Golden Corral, KFC, King Dragon Chinese, Little Caesars, McDonald's, Pizza Hut, Sizzler, Sonic, Subway, Super Buffet, Taco Bell, Wendy's Comfort Inn, Hampton Inn, Hilton Garden, Quality Inn $Tree, AT&T, AutoZone, Beall's, Big Lots, CarQuest, Chrysler/Dodge/Jeep, Family$, Home Depot, JC Penney, mall, Nissan, O'Reilly Parts, PepBoys, Radio Shack, Safeway, Verizon, Walmart/McDonald's, **S on Rte 66** Phillips 66/dsl Badlands Grill, Blakes Lotaburger, Don Diego's, El Carrito, El Dorado Rest., El Sombrero Mexican, Garcia's Rest., McDonald's, Rte 66 Diner, Sonic Ambassador Motel, Best Value Inn, Days Inn, Desert Skies, Golden Desert Motel,
20	Continued Rodeway Inn, Royal Holiday Motel, Super 8 H, Ford/Lincoln, RV camping, Tire Factory
16	NM 118, W Gallup, Mentmore, **N** Loves/Chester's/Subway/dsl/24hr, Navajo/dsl/24hr, TA/Country Pride/dsl/scales/24hr/ @, USave Trkstp/dsl Blue Beacon, dsl repair, NKS Truck Repair, **S** Conoco/dsl, Phillips 66/Allsup's, Thrift Way Ranch Kitchen, Taco Bell, Virgie's Mexican Budget Inn, EconoLodge, Gallup Inn, Hampton Inn, Knights Inn, Microtel, Motel 6, Red Lion Hotel, Red Roof Inn, Travelodge USA RV Park
12mm	**inspection/weigh sta eb**
8	to Manuelito, no services
3mm	**Welcome Ctr eb, full facilities, litter barrels, petwalk**
0mm	New Mexico/Arizona state line

GALLUP

NEW YORK

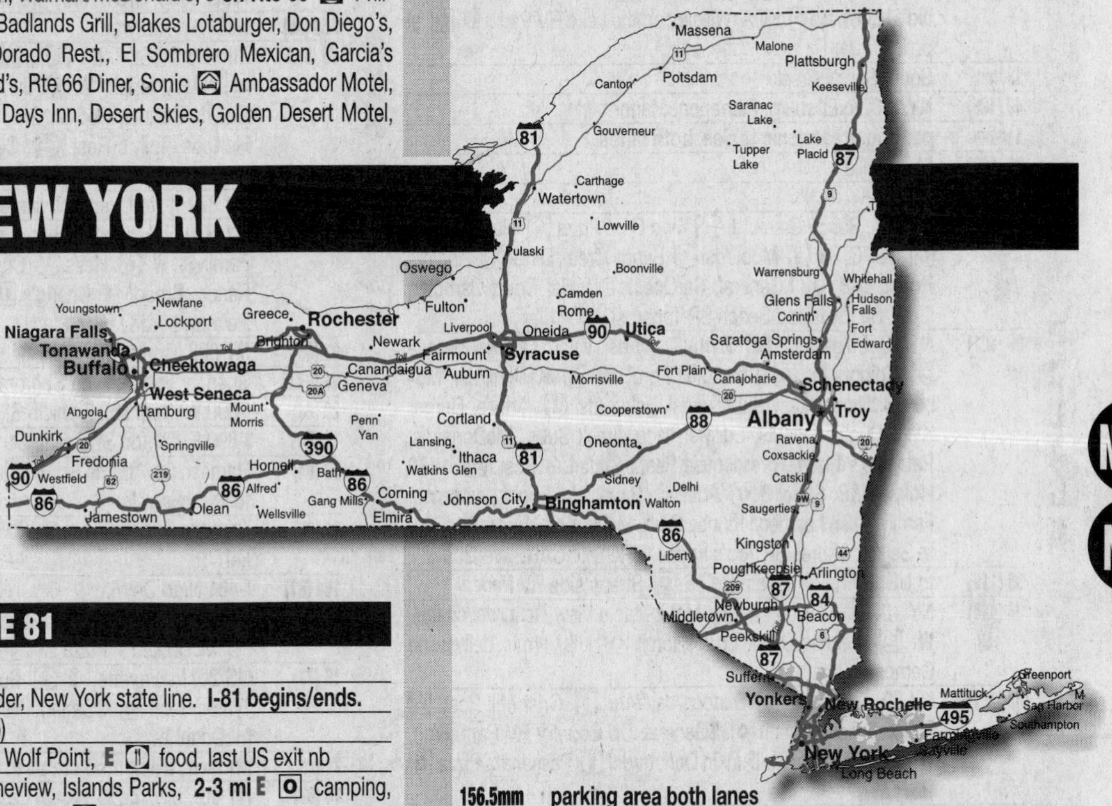

INTERSTATE 81

Exit #	Services
184mm	US/Canada border, New York state line. **I-81 begins/ends.**
183.5mm	US Customs (sb)
52 (183)	Island Rd, to De Wolf Point, **E** food, last US exit nb
51 (180)	Island Rd, to Fineview, Islands Parks, **2-3 mi E** camping, golf, USPO, **2-3 mi W** Seaway Island Resort, Thousand Islands Park
179mm	St Lawrence River
178.5mm	**Welcome Ctr/ sb, full facilities, litter barrels, petwalk , Thousand Islands Toll Bridge Booth**
50NS (178)	NY 12, E to Alexandria Bay, W to Clayton, **E** Sunoco/dsl Kountry Kottage Rest., Subway Bonnie Castle Rec Ctr, PineHurst Motel H, Chrysler/Dodge/Jeep, PriceChopper Mkt, st police, to Thousand Island Region, **W NY Welcome Ctr/rest area** Mobil Bridgeview Motel to RV camping, vet
174mm	**nb, full facilities, litter barrels, petwalk st police, vending**
49 (171)	NY 411, to Theresa, Indian River Lake, **E** Sunoco/dsl
168mm	**parking area sb**
161mm	**parking area nb**
48a	I-781, CR 16, to Ft Drum
48 (158)	US 11, NY 37, **E** Mirabito/dsl/scales, Nice'n Easy/dsl, Sunoco/Dunkin Donuts/dsl Longway's Diner Allen's Budget Motel, Royal Inn Long-Park Tire
156.5mm	**parking area both lanes**
47 (155)	NY 12, Bradley St, Watertown, **E** Nice'n Easy/Subway/dsl, Valero Frosty Dairy Bar H, **W** Rainbow Motel
154.5mm	Black River
46 (154)	NY 12F, Coffeen St, Watertown, **E** Mobil/Dunkin Donuts/dsl Cracker Barrel, Shorty's Diner Home Depot, URGENT CARE, **W** Nice'n Easy/dsl
45 (152)	NY 3, to Arsenal St, Watertown, **E** Mobil/Tim Horton/dsl, Sunoco Apollo Rest., Applebee's, Arby's, Buffalo Wild Wings, Burger King, Chipotle Mexican, CiCi's Pizza, Coldstone, Daily Buffet, Denny's, Dunkin Donuts, Five Guys, Friendly's, Japanese Steaks, Jreck Subs, KFC, McDonald's, Moe's SW Grill, Ponderosa, Riccardo's, Ruby Tuesday, Sonic, Starbucks, Taco Bell, Tilted Kilt Comfort Inn, EconoLodge, Fairfield Inn, Hampton Inn, Hilton Garden, Holiday Inn Express, Quality Inn $General, $Tree, Advance Parts, Aldi Foods, AT&T, AutoZone, BigLots, Jo-Ann Fabrics, Kost Tire, Mavis Discount Tire, Midas, Monro, PriceChopper Foods/24hr, Radio Shack, Staples, TJ Maxx, USPO, Walgreens, **W** Fastrac Bob Evans, Olive Garden, Panera Bread, Pizza Hut, Red Lobster,

WATERTOWN

NM NY

INTERSTATE 81 Cont'd

45 (152) Continued
Subway, TGIFriday's, TX Roadhouse Ramada Inn Best Buy, BonTon, Burlington Coats, Dick's, Gander Mtn, GNC, Hannaford Foods, JC Penney, K-Mart, Kohl's, Lowe's, mall, Michael's, Old Navy, PetCo, Sam's Club, Sears/auto, Target, to Sackets Harbor, Verizon, Walmart/Dunkin Donuts

149mm parking area nb, phone

44 (148) NY 232, to Watertown Ctr, **3 mi** E H

147mm **sb, full facilities, litter barrels, petwalk vending**

43 (146) US 11, to Kellogg Hill

42 (144) NY 177, Adams Center, E Nice'n Easy/Mama Mia's Pizza/dsl Depot Cafe Harley Davidson, Tugger's Camping (12mi)

41 (140) NY 178, Adams, E Sunoco/dsl Dunkin Donuts, McDonald's, Subway KOA, Willows on the Lake RV Park, W st police

138mm South Sandy Creek

40 (135) NY 193, to Ellisburg, Pierrepont Manor

134mm **parking area/picnic tables, both lanes**

39 (133) Mannsville

38 (131) US 11

37 (128) Lacona, Sandy Creek, E Two Bros Pizza Harris Lodge USPO, W Mobil/dsl Sandy Creek Diner Anglers Roost B&B $General, CarQuest, Colonial Court Camping (3mi), Sandy Island Beach SP, Tops/dsl

PULASKI

36 (121) NY 13, Pulaski, E Byrne Dairy/dsl, Valero Ponderosa Knights Inn Chevrolet, Ford, W KwikFill/dsl, Mobil/dsl, Nice'n Easy/Subway/dsl, Valero/dsl Arby's, Burger King, Dunkin Donuts, Eddy's Place, Jreck Subs, McDonald's, Paulanjo's Pizza, River House Rest., Stefano's Rest. 1880 House B&B, Super 8 Advance Parts, Aldi Foods, camping, Family$, fish hatchery, Kinney Drug, Mavis Tire, NAPA, Rite Aid, to Selkirk Shores SP, Top's Foods, URGENT CARE, Verizon

NY

35 (118) to US 11, Tinker Tavern Rd, E Streamside RV Park

34 (115) NY 104, to Mexico, E Mobil/Maple View Rest./dsl/scales, W Feeder Creek Lodge (5mi) J&J (4mi), Jellystone Camping (9mi)

33 (111) NY 69, Parish, E Sunoco/dsl/24hr Grist Mill Rest. E Coast Resort (4mi) $General, Up Country RV Park (8mi), W Gulf, Mirabito/Dunkin Donuts/dsl Passarella Pizza USPO

32 (103) NY 49, to Central Square, E Mirabito/dsl, Sunoco/Subway/dsl Good Golly's Rest. Murphy's Automotive, W Fastrac/gas Burger King, Dunkin Donuts, McDonald's $Tree, Advance Parts, Ford, NAPA, Rite Aid, st police, URGENT CARE, Verizon, Walmart/Subway

31 (99) to US 11, Brewerton, E Oneida Shores Camping, W Mirabito/Tim Hortons/dsl, Nice'n Easy/dsl Dunkin Donuts, Lin Li's Chinese, Little Caesars, McDonald's, Subway Days Inn $General, AT&T, Kinney Drugs, USPO, vet

30 (96) NY 31, to Cicero, E Fastrac/dsl, Hess/dsl Arby's, Cracker Barrel, Dunkin Donuts, McDonald's, Sapori Pizza Comfort Suites, Holiday Inn Express $Tree, Aldi, Gander Mtn, W Kwikfill Cicero Diner, Cicero Pizza 70's RV Ctr

29 (93) I-481 S, NY 481, to Oswego, Syracuse, **1 mi W on US 11** Hess Buffalo Wild Wings, Burger King, Copper Top Tavern, Denny's, Dunkin Donuts, Jimmy John's, KFC, Little Caesars, McDonald's, Moe's SW Grill, Panda Express, Panera Bread, Pizza Hut, Subway, Taco Bell, Tully's Rest., Wendy's $General, $Tree, Advance Parts, AT&T, Audi/Porsche/VW, AutoZone, BMW, Buick/GMC, Chevrolet, Chrysler/Dodge/Jeep, Firestone/

29 (93) Continued
auto, GNC, Goodyear/auto, Home Depot, Hyundai, Kia, Lexu Lincoln, Lowe's, Marshall's, Mavis Tire, Mazda, Midas, NAP Nissan, PepBoys, PriceChopper Foods, Rite Aid, Target, Toyota/Scion, Verizon, Walmart, Wegman's Foods

28 (91) N Syracuse, Taft Rd, E KwikFill, Sunoco/dsl U-Hau W Sunoco/dsl Auto Value Parts, USPO

27 (90) N Syracuse, E

26 (89) US 11, Mattydale, E Sunoco/Dunkin Donuts/dsl Hofmann Rest., Paladino's Pizza, Pizza Hut Red Carpet In $Tree, auto repair, BigLots, Dunn Tire/auto, Family$, GNC Goodyear/auto, K-Mart, PetCo, Rite Aid, W Delta Sonic/ds Applebee's, Arby's, Burger King, Denny's, Dunkin Donuts Gino&Joe's, Julie's Diner, McDonald's, Ponderosa, Roma's Italian, Subway, Taco Bell, Tim Hortons, Wendy's Candlewoo Suites, EconoLodge, Holiday Inn Express Advance Parts Aldi Foods, AT&T, Kost Tire, Monro Auto, Rite Aid, Top's Foods

SYRACUSE

25a (88) I-90, NY Thruway

25 (87.5) 7th North St, E Pilot/McDonald's/dsl/scales/24h NAPA, repair, W Sunoco/dsl Burger King, Denny's Dunkin Donuts, Flatiron Grill, Iamondo's Pizzeria, Subway, Tim Hortons, Tully's Rest. Comfort Inn, Hampton Inn, Maplewood Inn/cafe, Quality Inn, Ramada Inn, Super 8

24 (86) NY 370 W, to Liverpool, same as 23

23 (86) NY 370 E, Hiawatha Blvd, E Stella's Diner, Wendy's Family$, W Hess Cheesecake Factory, Dave&Busters Panera Bread, PF Chang's Best Buy, Bon Ton, Dick's, JC Penney, Lord&Taylor, Macy's, mall, TJ Maxx

22 (85) NY 298, Court St

21 (84.5) Spencer St, Catawba St (from sb), industrial area

20 (84) I-690 W (from sb), Franklin St, West St

19 (84) I-690 E, Clinton St, Salina St, to E Syracuse

18 (84) Harrison St, Adams St, E Crowne Plaza H, Civic Ct to Syracuse U

17 (82) Brighton Ave, S Salina St, W KwikFill, Valero/Chicken Basket

16a (81) I-481 N, to DeWitt

16 (78) US 11, to Nedrow, Onondaga Nation, **1-2 mi** W Valer McDonald's, Pizza Hut $General, Aldi

15 (73) US 20, La Fayette, E Sunoco/dsl La Fayette Inn, Old Tymes Rest. $General, NAPA, st police, USPO, vet, W McDonald's

71mm **phones, truck insp sta both lanes**

14 (67) NY 80, Tully, E Nice'n Easy/deli/dsl A Pizza More, Tasty China Best Western $General, Chevrolet, Kinney Drug USPO, W Burger King

13 (63) NY 281, Preble, E Mirabito/Dunkin Donuts/Subway/ds to Song Mtn Ski Resort

60mm **/truck insp nb, full facilities, litter barrels, petwalk vending**

CORTLAND

12 (53) US 11, NY 281, to Homer, W KwikFill, Sunoco/dsl, Valer Fabio's Italian, Little Italy H, $General, st police, to Fillmore Glen SP

11 (52) NY 13, Cortland, E Perkins Comfort Inn, Holiday Inn Express, Quality Inn, W Mobil/Dunkin Donuts/dsl Arby's China Moon, Crown City Rest., Denny's, Dickey's BBQ, Friendly's, McDonald's, Subway, Taco Bell, Wendy's Hampton Inn Ramada Inn Advance Parts, Family$, Jo-Ann Fabrics, Kost Tire, P&C Foods

10 (50) US 11, NY 41, to Cortland, McGraw, W Pitstop/Dunkin Donuts/Quesaritos/dsl, Sunoco/Subway/dsl/24hr Cortland Motel, Days Inn

9 (38) US 11, NY 221, W Sunoco/XtraMart/dsl/24hr, Valero NY Pizzaria Greek Peak Lodge, Three Bear Inn/rest. city

INTERSTATE 81 Cont'd

9 (38) Continued park, Country Hills Camping, Gregg's Mkt, Maple Museum, Robinson's Repair, st police, USPO

33mm **sb, full facilities, litter barrels, petwalk vending**

8 (30) NY 79, to US 11, NY 26, NY 206 (no EZ return), Whitney Pt, **E** Hess, Kwikfill, Sunoco Aiello's Ristorante, Arby's, Dunkin Donuts, McDonald's, Subway Hotel Griffin $General, Gregg's Mkt, NAPA, Parts+, Radio Shack, to Dorchester Park, USPO

7 (21) US 11, Castle Creek, **W** Mirabito/Subway/Tim Hortons/dsl

6 (16) US 11, to NY 12, I-88E, Chenango Bridge, **E on US 11** Gulf/dsl, Hess/dsl, Sunoco/dsl Arby's, Burger King, Denny's, Dunkin Donuts, Grande Pizza, Moe's SW Grill, Pizza Hut, Subway, Tokyo Buffet, Wendy's Advance Parts, Chrysler/Dodge/Jeep, CVS Drug, Kost Tire, Lowe's, Mavis Tire, Meineke, Monro, Radio Shack, Rite Aid, Staples, Valvoline, Verizon, Weis Foods, **W on US 11** KwikFill, Wave/dsl China Star, Friendly's, Nirchi's Pizza, Sonic, Spot Diner, Subway Comfort Inn, Howard Johnson, Motel 6 Aldi Foods, Harley Davidson

15mm **I-88 begins eb**

BINGHAMTON

5 (14) US 11, Front St, **1 mi W** Sunoco/McDonald's/dsl, Valero/dsl Applebee's, Coldstone, Cracker Barrel, Starbucks, TLC Pizza EconoLodge, Fairfield Inn, Red Roof Inn Cutler Botanical Garden

4 (13) NY 17, Binghamton

3 (12) Broad Ave, Binghamton, **W** Valero KFC CVS Drug, Weis Foods

3 (10) Industrial Park, same as 2

2 (8) US 11, NY 17, **1-2 mi W** Gulf/dsl, Loves/Wendy's/dsl/scales/24hr, TA/Country Pride/dsl/scales/24hr/ @ Arby's, Burger King, McDonald's, Subway, Taco Bell Del Motel

1 (4) US 11, NY 7, Kirkwood, **1-2 mi W** Mirabito/dsl, Xtra Hallo Berlin Rest. Kirkwood Motel

2mm **Welcome Ctr nb, full facilities, litter barrels, petwalk vending**

1mm **truck insp sta nb**

0mm New York/Pennsylvania state line

INTERSTATE 84

Exit # Services

71.5mm New York/Connecticut state line

21 (69) US 6, US 202, NY 121 (from wb), N Salem, same as 20

20N (67.5) NY 22, Palling, Palling, **N** Mobil, Shell/dsl, Valero Dunkin Donuts, Portofinos Cadillac/Chevrolet, Ford, Honda, Subaru

20S I-684, to NYC

19 (65) NY 312, Carmel, **N** st police, **S** Applebee's, Dunkin Donuts, Eveready Diner, Gaetano's Deli H, DeCicco's Mkt, Home Depot, Kohl's, Marshall's, Michael's, Verizon

18 (62) NY 311, Lake Carmel, **S** Lakeview Pizza

17 (59) Ludingtonville Rd, **S** Hess/Blimpie/dsl, Sunoco/dsl Cacciatore's Pizzaria, Cutiloo's Rest., Dunkin Donuts, Gappy's Pizza, Lou's Deli

56mm elevation 965 ft

55mm **both lanes, full facilities, litter barrels, petwalk vending**

16 (53) Taconic Parkway, N to Albany, S to New York

15 (51) Lime Kiln NY, **3 mi N** Mobil Dunkin Donuts Arbor Ridge Inn

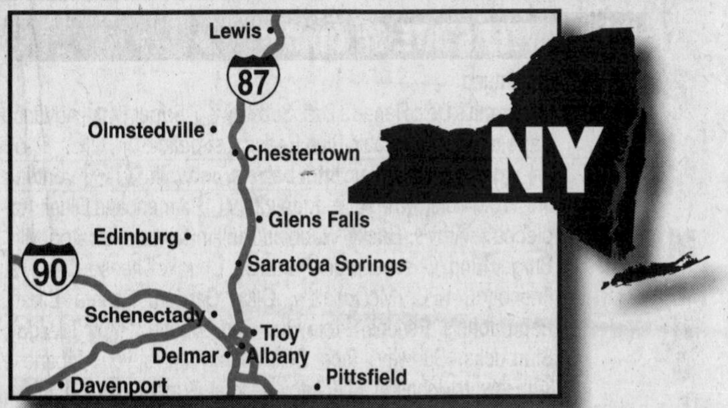

NEWBURGH

13 (46) US 9, to Poughkeepsie, **N** Flory's/deli, Mobil/dsl, Shell/dsl 5 Guys, A&W/KFC, Boston Mkt, Charlie Brown Steaks, Coldstone, Cracker Barrel, Fishkill Grill, Hudson Buffet, Izumi Japanese, Little Asia, Panera Bread, Pizza Shop, Red Line Diner, Ruby Tuesday, Starbucks, Subway, Taco Bell, Wendy's Comfort Inn, Courtyard, Days Inn, Extended Stay America, Hampton Inn, Hilton Garden, Holiday Inn Express, Hyatt House, Ramada Inn, Residence Inn AT&T, Sam's Club, Verizon, Walmart, **S** Hess/Blimpie/dsl Maya Cafe, McDonald's Home Depot

12 (45) NY 52 E, Fishkill, **N** Valero Golden Buddha, Green Garden, Sal's Pizza CVS Drug, **S** Mobil, Sunoco/dsl 84 Diner, Hometown Deli Quality Inn

11 (42) NY 9D, to Wappingers Falls, **1 mi N** Mobil/dsl, Shell

41mm **toll booth**

40mm Hudson River

10 (39) US 9W, NY 32, to Newburgh, **N** Citgo, Sunoco Alexis Diner, Andiamo Rest., Bonura's Little Italy, Burger King, Dunkin Donuts, Great Wall, Green Garden Chinese, KFC, McDonald's, New China, Pizza Hut, Subway $Tree, Advance Parts, BigLots, Family$, Firestone/auto, Monroe, PriceChopper Foods, Rite Aid, Shop Rite Foods, Walgreens, **S** Citgo/dsl, Sunoco H

8 (37) NY 52, to Walden, **N** Shell/dsl

7b (36) NY 300, Newburgh, **N** Mobil Daddy's Grill, DQ, Dunkin Donuts, Leo's Pizzaria, McDonald's, Newburgh Buffet, Perkins, Taco Bell, Wendy's $Tree, AT&T, AutoZone, BonTon, Marshall's, Mavis Tire, Midas, Office Depot, Sears/auto, Stop&Shop Foods, **S** Hess/dsl, Sunoco/dsl 5 Guys Burgers, Applebee's, Burger King, Chili's, China City, Cosimos Ristorante, Denny's, IHOP, Ikaros Diner, Longhorn Steaks, Neptune Diner, Panera Bread, Pizza Mia, Sonic, Starbucks, Steak'n Stein, Subway, TGIFriday's, Union Sq Rest., Yobo Asian Days Inn, Hilton Garden, Howard Johnson, Ramada Inn, Super 8 $General, Adam's Farm Mkt, Aldi Foods, Barnes&Noble, Buick/GMC, Cadillac/Chevrolet, Chrysler/Dodge/Jeep, Ford/Lincoln, Home Depot, Honda, Kohl's, Lowe's, Meineke, Michael's, Nissan, Orange County Choppers/cafe, PetsMart, Radio Shack, Target, Verizon, Walmart

7a (35) I-87, NY Thruway, Albany, to NYC

6 (34) NY 17K, to Newburgh, **N** Mobil, Pilot/Arby's/dsl/scales/24hr Airport Diner Comfort Inn, **S** Shell/dsl Courtyard, Days Inn, Hilton Garden, Howard Johnson

5a (33) NY 747, International Blvd, **S** Homewood Suites to Stewart Airport

5 (29) NY 208, Maybrook, **N** Mobil/dsl, Sunoco/dsl Burger King, Dunkin Donuts, McDonald's NAPA, Rite Aid, ShopRite Foods, Walgreens, Winding Hills Camping, **S** Hess/dsl, TA/Valero/Country Pride/Pizza Hut/dsl/scales/24hr/ @

NY

INTERSTATE 84 Cont'd

5 (29)	Continued [food] Prima's Deli, Renee's Deli, Subway [lodging] Super 8 [other] Advance Parts, auto/truck repair, Blue Beacon, st police
24mm	**[rest stop] wb, full [handicapped] facilities, litter barrels, petwalk [phone] [vending] vending**
4 (19)	NY 17, Middletown, **N** [gas] Mobil/24hr [food] Americana Diner, Applebee's, Arby's, Baskin-Robbins/Dunkin Donuts, Boston Mkt, Burger King, Cheeseburger Paradise, ChuckeCheese, Denny's, Friendly's, KFC, McDonald's, Olive Garden, Panera Bread, Papa John's, Perkins, Pizza Hut, Red Lobster, Ruby Tuesday, Starbucks, Subway, Taco Bell, Wendy's, Youyou Japanese [lodging] Howard Johnson, Middletown Motel, Super 8 [other] [H], $Tree, Aldi Foods, AutoZone, Best Buy, Big Lots, Firestone/auto, Gander Mtn, Hannaford Foods, Home Depot, Honda, JC Penney, Jo-Ann Fabrics, Kohl's, Lowe's, mall, Marshall's, Michael's, Old Navy, PetCo, PetsMart, PriceChopper Foods, Rite Aid, Sam's Club/gas, Sears/auto, ShopRite Foods, Staples, Tire Discount, TJ Maxx, U-Haul, URGENT CARE, Verizon, vet, Walmart/24hr, **S** [gas] Citgo/dsl [food] Chili's, El Bandido Mexican, Outback Steaks, TGIFriday [lodging] Courtyard, Hampton Inn, Holiday Inn, Microtel [other] st police
17mm	**[rest stop] eb, full [handicapped] facilities, litter barrels, petwalk [phone] [vending] vending**
3 (15)	US 6, to Middletown, **N** [gas] Citgo/dsl, Mobil, QuickChek/dsl, Shell, Valero [food] Bro Bruno's Pizza, Dunkin Donuts, IHOP, McDonald's, NY Buffet, Peking Chinese, Rita's Custard, Subway, Taco Bell, Wendy's [other] [H], Acura, AutoZone, Buick/Chevrolet, CarQuest, Family$, Goodyear, Mavis Discount Tire, Mazda, Meineke, Radio Shack, Rite Aid, ShopRite Foods, Subaru, Verizon, VW, **S** [gas] Citgo/dsl, Geo/Dunkin Donuts/dsl [lodging] Days Inn, Global Budget Inn [other] Kia, Nissan, Toyota/Scion
2 (5)	Mountain Rd, **S** [food] Greenville's Deli
4mm	1272 ft eb, elevation 1254 ft wb
3mm	**parking area both lanes**
1 (1)	US 6, NY 23, Port Jervis, **N** [food] Arlene'n Tom's Diner, Baskin-Robbins/Dunkin Donuts [lodging] Brookside Cottages [other] [H], Ford, **S** [gas] BP/dsl/LP, Citgo/dsl, Gulf/dsl, Pilot/Subway/dsl, Valero/dsl [food] DQ, McDonald's [lodging] Days Inn [other] [H], $Tree, GNC, ShopRite Foods, TJ Maxx
0mm	New York/Pennsylvania state line, Delaware River

MIDDLETOWN

INTERSTATE 86

Exit #	Services
	I-86 begins/ends on I-87, exit 16, toll booth.
131 (379)	NY 17, **N** [food] Applebee's [other] Outlets/famous brands, **S** [gas] Gulf/dsl [food] Chili's, Dunkin Donuts, KFC, Outback Steaks, Panera Bread, TGIFriday's, Uno Grill, Wendy's [lodging] Days Inn, Hampton Inn [other] $Tree, Best Buy, BJ's Whse, BMW, GNC, Home Depot, Kohl's, Michael's, Old Navy, Petsmart, Radio Shack, Staples, Target, TJMaxx, Verizon, Walmart/Subway
130a (378)	US 6, Bear Mtn, to West Point (from eb, no return)
130 (377)	NY 208, Monroe, Washingtonville, **N** [food] Rambler's Rest, **S** [gas] Mobil/dsl, Sunoco/dsl, Valero [food] Burger King, Dunkin Donuts, Monroe Diner [other] $Tree, ShopRite Foods, st police
129 (375)	Museum Village Rd
128 (374)	Rd 51 (only from wb), Oxford Depot
127 (373)	Greycourt Rd (from wb only), Sugar Loaf, Warwick
126 (372)	NY 94 (no EZ wb return), Chester, Florida, **N** [gas] Mobil, Shell, Sunoco/dsl [food] Bro Bruno Pizza, Chester Diner, Lobster Pier Rest, McDonald's, Wendy's [lodging] Holiday Inn Express [other] CVS Drug, GNC, Radio Shack, ShopRite Foods, USPO, **S** [other] Black Bear Camping, Lowe's
125 (369)	NY 17M E, South St, **N** [food] Hacienda Mexican
124 (368)	NY 17A, NY 207, **N** [gas] Gulf/Subway/dsl, Mobil/dsl [food] Burger King, Dunkin Donuts, Friendly's, Goshen Diner, Pizza H [other] [H], CVS Drug, Verizon, **S** [lodging] Comfort Inn [other] Chrysle Dodge/Jeep, Hyundai, URGENT CARE
123	US 6, NY 17M (wb only), Port Jervis
122a (367)	Fletcher St, Goshen
122 (364)	Rd 67, E Main St, Crystal Run Rd, **N** [food] Chili's, Outba Steaks, TGIFriday's [lodging] Courtyard, Hampton Inn, Holiday In Microtel [other] URGENT CARE, **S** [food] El Bandido Rest.
121 (363)	I-84, E to Newburgh, W to Port Jervis
120 (363)	NY 211, **N** [gas] Lukoil, Mobil, Sunoco [food] Buffalo Wild Wing Cosimo's Ristorante, Olive Garden, Perkins [lodging] Howard Johnson, Middletown Motel, Super 8 [other] Best Buy, Dick's, Gand Mtn, Hannaford's Foods, Honda, JC Penney, Lowe's, Macy' Mavis Discount Tire, Old Navy, PetCo, Sam's Club/gas, Sear Target, vet, **S** [gas] Mobil [food] 5 Guys Burgers, Americana Dine Applebee's, Arby's, Boston Mkt, Burger King, Cheeseburg Paradise, Denny's, Dunkin Donuts, Franko Di Roma Italia Friendly's, KFC, McDonald's, Panera Bread, Papa John's, Pizz Hut, Red Lobster, Ruby Tuesday, Starbucks, Subway, Taco Be TX Roadhouse, Wendy's, YouYou Chinese [other] $General, $Tre Aldi Foods, AT&T, AutoZone, BigLots, Firestone/auto, Hobb Lobby, Home Depot, Kohl's, Marshall's, Michael's, Mida Petsmart, PriceChopper, Rite Aid, ShopRite Foods, Staple Tire Discount Ctr, TJMaxx, U-Haul, Verizon, Walmart/Subway
119 (360)	NY 309, Pine Bush, **S** [gas] Citgo/dsl, Valero/Dunkin Donuts/d [food] Subway
118a (358)	NY 17M, Fair Oaks
118 (358)	Circleville, **N** [lodging] Economy Inn, **S** [gas] Citgo/dsl, Mobil/dsl
116 (355)	NY 17K, Bloomingburg, **N** [food] Mtn View Rest, **S** [gas] Citgo/d [food] Quickway Diner
115	Burlingame Rd
114	Wurtsboro, Highview (from wb)
113 (350)	US 209, Wurtsboro, Ellenville, **N** [gas] Mobil/dsl, Stewarts/ga [food] Custar's Last Stand, Danny's Steaks [lodging] Days Inn, Gold M Chalet, Honors Haven Resort, Valley Brook Motel [other] G-Ma Foods, Spring Glen Camping, **S** [food] Giovanni's Café (2mi)
112 (347)	Masten Lake, Yankee Lake, **N** [lodging] Days Inn, ValleyBrook Mot [other] Catskill Mtn Ranch Camping, Yankee Lake
111 (344)	(eb only), Wolf Lake, **S** [gas] Citgo/dsl
110 (343)	Lake Louise Marie
109 (342)	Rock Hill, Woodridge, **N** [gas] Citgo/dsl [food] Angelo's Kitche Dutch's Cafe, Krust Italian, Pizza Rock, RockHill Diner [lodging] Su livan Hotel [other] Ace Hardware, auto repair, Hilltop Farms Camp ing, Super Mkt Trading Post, USPO, **S** [gas] Mobil/dsl [food] Drago Garden Chinese
108 (341)	Bridgeville, same as 109
107 (340)	Thompsonville, **S** [food] Old Homestead Diner [other] Chevrole Chrysler/Dodge/Jeep, Toyota
106 (339)	(wb only), E. Broadway, **N** [other] Ford/Lincoln, **S** [gas] Mobil/d [lodging] Super 8 (2 mi) [other] GMC Trucks, Hyundai
105 (337)	NY 42, Monticello, **N** [gas] Mobil, Valero [food] Blue Horizon Dir er, Bro Bruno's Pizza, Burger King, China 1, Dunkin Donut Giovanni's Rest, KFC, McDonald's, Subway [other] AutoZon Home Depot, museum, Radio Shack, ShopRite Foods, Staple Walmart/McDonald's, **S** [gas] Citgo/dsl, Sunoco/dsl [food] Mis Monticello Diner, Nugget Rest, Pizza Hut, Pizza Hut, Stewart' Wendy's [lodging] EconoLodge, Heritage Inn, Super 8 [other] Advanc Parts, Family$, NAPA, Rite Aid
104 (336)	NY 17B, Raceway, Monticello, **S** [gas] Citgo/dsl, Mobil/d [food] Albella Rest, Bean Bag Cafe, Colosseo Rest. [lodging] Bes Western, Raceway Motel, Travel Inn [other] AT&T, Swinging Brid Camp, Woodstock Camping

MIDDLETOWN

NY

⬆E INTERSTATE 86 Cont'd

103	Rapp Rd (wb only)
102 (332)	Harris, **N** ⊙ Ⓗ
101 (327)	Ferndale, Swan Lake, **S** ⛽ Mobil/dsl ⊙ Swan Lake Camping (5mi)
100 (327)	NY 52 E, Liberty, **N** ⛽ Citgo, Sam's, Sunoco 🍴 Albert's Diner, Burger King, Dunkin Donuts, Last Licks Cafe, Liberty Diner, Mc-Donald's, Piccolo Italian, Pizza Hut, Subway, Taco Bell, Wendy's 🏨 Days Inn, Howard Johnson ⊙ $Tree, Ace Hardware, Advance Parts, Rite Aid, ShopRite Foods, USPO, **S** ⛽ XtraMart 🏨 Lincoln Motel ⊙ Buick/Cadillac, Chrysler/Dodge/Jeep, Ford/Lincoln, Southend Parts, Swan Lake Camping (5mi)
100a	NY 52 W (no wb return), Liberty, **S** 🍴 McCabe's Rest ⊙ K&K Drug, st police
99 (325)	NY 52 W, to NY 55, Liberty, **S** ⛽ Sunoco ⊙ Catskill Motel
98 (321)	Cooley, Parksville, **N** ⛽ Mobil/dsl 🍴 Dari-King
97 (319)	Morsston
96 (316)	Livingston Manor, **N** ⊙ Covered Bridge Camping, **S** ⛽ Citgo, Sunoco 🍴 Lazy Beagle Grill, Robinhood Diner 🏨 Lanza's Country Inn ⊙ Covered Bridge Camping, Mongaup Pond Camping, Peck's Mkt, to Covered Bridge, USPO
313mm	🅿 eb, full ♿ facilities, litter barrels, petwalk 🅲 🚚 truck insp. sta (eb), vending
94 (311)	NY 206, Roscoe, Lew Beach, **N** ⛽ Mobil/dsl, Sunoco/dsl 🍴 La Voglia, NYC Gyros, Raimondo's Diner, Roscoe Diner 🏨 Reynolds House Motel, Rockland House Motel, Roscoe Motel, Tennanah Lake Motel ⊙ Catskill Grocers, st police, **S** ⛽ Mobil/dsl ⊙ Beaverkill St Camping (8mi)
93 (305)	to Cooks Falls (from wb)
92 (303)	Horton, Cooks Falls, Colchester, **S** ⛽ Sunoco/dsl 🍴 Riverside Café/lodge ⊙ Russell Brook Camping
90 (297)	NY 30, East Branch, Downsville, **N** ⛽ Sunoco ⊙ Beaver-Del Camping, Oxbow Camping, Peaceful Valley Camping, **S** 🏨 E Branch Motel
295mm	🅿 wb, full ♿ facilities, litter barrels, petwalk 🅲 🚚 vending
89 (293)	Fishs Eddy
87a (288)	NY 268 (from wb, no ez-return), same as 87
87 (284)	NY 97, to NY 268, to NY 191, Hancock, Cadosia, **S** ⛽ Getty, Mirabito/Subway/dsl, Valero 🍴 Bluestone Grill, Little Italy Pizza, McDonald's, McTigues Rest, New China 🏨 Capra Inn, Colonial Motel, Starlight Lake Inn ⊙ Family$, Grand Union Foods, NAPA, Rite Aid
276mm	**parking area wb**
84 (274)	Deposit, **N** ⛽ Citgo/dsl 🍴 BC Pizza, Grand Stand Rest., Pines Rest., Wendy's 🏨 Deposit Motel, Laurel Bank Motel ⊙ Family$, st police
83 (272)	Deposit, Oquaga Lake
82 (270)	NY 41, McClure, Sanford, **N** 🍴 Cornerstone Cafe ⊙ Kellystone Park, **S** ⛽ Sun/dsl 🏨 Scott's Family Resort ⊙ Guestward Camping (3mi), Oquaga Creek SP
265mm	**parking area eb, litter barrels** 🚚
81 (263)	E Bosket Rd
80 (261)	Damascus, **N** ⛽ Gulf/Manley's/dsl ⊙ auto repair, Forest Hill Lake Park Camping
79 (259)	NY 79, Windsor, **N** ⛽ Extra, Sunoco/dsl 🍴 McBride's Rest, Subway, **S** 🍴 Marian's Pizza/Subs ⊙ Lakeside Camping (8mi)
78 (256)	Dunbar Rd, Occanum
77 (254)	W Windsor, **N** ⛽ Sunoco/dsl 🍴 McDonald's
76 (251)	Haskins Rd, to Foley Rd
75 (250)	I-81 S, to PA (exits left from wb)
	I-86/I-81 run together 4 miles

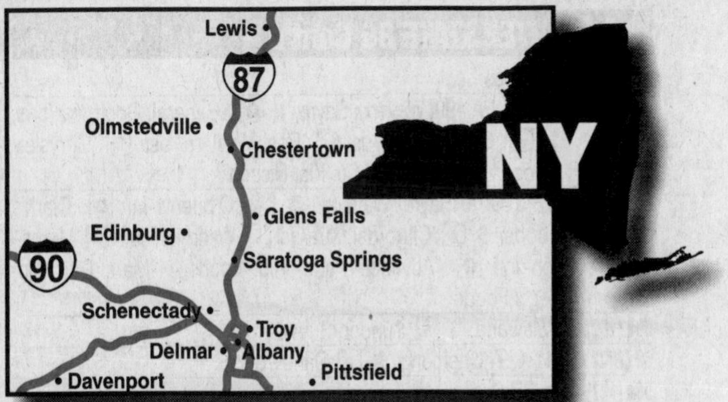

3	Colesville Rd (from eb), ⛽ ♥Loves/Wendy's, TA/dsl/scales/24hr
	I-86/I-81 run together 4 miles
3	Broad Ave (from wb, no return)
4NS	NY 7, **I-86/I-81 run together 4 miles**
72 (244)	I-81 N, US 11, Front St, Clinton St, (no wb re-entry), **S** ⊙ Aamco
71 (242)	Airport Rd, Johnson City, **S** ⛽ Valero ⊙ Walmart
70 (241)	NY 201, Johnson City, **N** ⛽ Hess/Blimpie/dsl, Valero 🍴 Arby's, Christy's Grill, Dunkin Donuts, Friendly's, Great China, Ground Round, Grub House Cafe, McDonald's, Papa John's, Pizza Hut, Ruby Tuesday, Taco Bell 🏨 Best Western, Hampton Inn, La Quinta, Red Roof Inn ⊙ Bon-Ton, JC Penney, Kost Tire, Macy's, mall, PetCo, Sears/auto, vet, Wegman's Foods, Wies Foods, **S** ⊙ Home Depot
69 (239)	NY 17C
238mm	Susquehanna River
68 (237)	NY 17C, Old Vestal Rd, (from eb, no re-entry)
67 (236)	NY 26, NY 434, Vestal, Endicott, **S on NY 434** ⛽ Hess, Stop'N Gas, Valero/dsl 🍴 A&W/LJ Silver, Arby's, Burger King, CA Grill, ChuckECheese, Dunkin Donuts, Friendly's, Grand Buffet, KFC, La Vita Bella, McDonald's, Moe's SW Grill, Old Country Buffet, Olive Garden, Outback Steaks, Panera Bread, Plaza Diner, Red Lobster, Starbucks, Subway, Taco Bell, TGIFriday's, Uno Grill, Wendy's 🏨 Comfort Suites, Courtyard, Hampton Inn, Holiday Inn Express, Homewood Suites, Parkway Motel, Vestal Motel ⊙ $General, $Tree, Advance Parts, Aldi Foods, AT&T, Barnes&Noble, Best Buy, BigLots, CarQuest, CVS Drug, Dick's, Firestone/auto, Ford/Lincoln, Jo-Ann Fabrics, Kohl's, Kost Tire, Lowe's, Meineke, Michael's, Nissan, Old Navy, Petsmart, Price Rite Foods, Radio Shack, Rite Aid, Sam's Club, Staples, Suzuki, Target, TJ Maxx, U-Haul, Verizon, vet, Volvo, Walmart/Blimpie, Wies Foods
66 (231)	NY 434, Apalachin, **S** ⛽ KwikFill, Mobil/dsl, Sunoco 🍴 Big Dipper Drive-In, Blue Dolphin Diner, Dunkin Donuts, McDonald's, Subway 🏨 Quality Inn
65 (225)	NY 17C, NY 434, Owego, **N** ⛽ Sunoco 🍴 A&W/KFC, Arby's, Panda Wok, Pizza Hut, Subway, Wendy's 🏨 Hampton Inn, Holiday Inn Express, Treadway Inn/rest. ⊙ $General, Buick/GMC, Hickories Park Camping, Kost Tire, Top's Foods, Verizon, **S** ⊙ st police
64 (223)	NY 96, Owego, **N** 🍴 Dunkin Donuts ⊙ AutoZone, CVS Drug, USPO, **S** ⛽ Valero
222mm	🅿 wb, full ♿ facilities, litter barrels, petwalk 🅲 🚚 vending
63 (218)	Lounsberry, **S** ⛽ Valero/rest./dsl/24hr
62 (214)	NY 282, Nichols, **S** ⛽ Citgo/pizza/dsl ⊙ Jim's RV Ctr, Tioga Downs Race Track (2mi)
212mm	🅿 eb, full ♿ facilities, litter barrels, petwalk 🅲 🚚 vending
208mm	Susquehanna River

VESTAL

OWEGO

WINDSOR

NY

= gas = food = lodging = other = rest stop

INTERSTATE 86 Cont'd

Exit #	Services
61 (206)	NY 34, PA 199, Waverly, Sayre, N $General, Goodyear/gas, S Gulf, Sunoco/dsl Best Western/rest. Chrysler/Dodge/Jeep, Joe's RV Ctr, Kia, Nissan
60 (204)	US 220, to Sayre, Waverly, N O'brien's Inn Clark's Foods, S Citgo/dsl, Xtra/dsl Wendy's (3mi) Hampton Inn Advance Parts, Aldi Foods, K-Mart, Rite Aid, Top's Foods
59a (202)	Wilawana, S Sunoco/Subway/dsl
59 (200)	NY 427, Chemung, N Dandy/dsl
58a (197)	to CR 60
57 (195)	Rd 2, Lowman, Wellsburg, N USPO, S Gardiner Hill Campsites (4mi), st police
56 (190)	Jerusalem Hill, S Citgo/dsl, KwikFill, Sunoco/Pizza Hut/Subway/dsl Hilltop Rest., McDonalds Coachman Motel, Holiday Inn, Mark Twain Motel
54 (186)	NY 13, to Ithaca
53 (185)	Horseheads, S Mobil, Sunoco Burger King, Dunkin Donuts, Guiseppe's Pizza, Lin Buffet, McDonald's, Subway, Wendy's Motel 6, Red Carpet Inn Advance Parts, Family$, K-Mart, Radio Shack, Rite Aid, Save-A-Lot Foods
52b (184)	NY 14, to Watkins Glen, N Friendly's Holiday Inn Express, Knights Inn, Landmark Inn, S Denny's
52a (183)	Commerce Ctr, S Buffalo Wild Wings, CiCi's Pizza, Cracker Barrel, Empire Buffet, TX Roadhouse Aldi Foods, AT&T, Dick's, Jo-Ann Fabrics, Kohl's, Mavis Discount Tire, Petsmart, Walmart/McDonald's
51a (182)	Chambers Rd, N Sunoco/Subway/dsl Bon Ton, Chili's, Dunkin Donuts, McDonald's, Olive Garden, Outback Steaks, Red Lobster, Ruby Tuesday Candlewood Suites, Country Inn&Suites, Hampton Inn, Hilton Garden Firestone/auto, JC Penney, Macy's, mall, Nissan, Sears/auto, S 5 Guys Burgers, Applebee's, Charley's Subs, Mt Fuji Japanese, Old Country Buffet, Panera Bread, Taco Bell, TGIFriday's, Wendy's EconoLodge $Tree, Barnes&Noble, Best Buy, Buick/GMC, Hobby Lobby, Hyundai, Kost Tire, Lowe's, Michael's, museum, Old Navy, PetCo, Sam's Club, Staples, Subaru/Suzuki, Target, TJ Maxx, Top's Foods, Toyota/Scion, URGENT CARE, Verizon
50 (180)	Kahler Rd, N to Airport
49 (178)	Olcott Rd, Canal St, Big Flats, N antiques, S Sunoco Picnic Pizza USPO
48 (171)	NY 352, E Corning, N Citgo Budget Inn, Gate House Motel
47 (174)	NY 352, Gibson, E Corning, N Budget Inn, Gate House Motel
46 (171)	NY 414, to Watkins Glen, Corning, N Ferenbaugh Camping (5mi), KOA (14mi), Watkins Glen Camping, S Sunoco Comfort Inn, Days Inn, Radisson, Staybridge Suites H, Corning Glass Museum
45 (170)	NY 352, Corning, S Fastrac Bob Evans, EnEn Chinese, Friendly's, Subway, Wendy's Fairfield Inn AT&T, AutoZone, CarQuest, Rite Aid
44a	US 15 S, NY 417 W, Gang Mills, N Sunoco McDonald's, S Citgo, Sunoco Applebee's, Arby's Best Value Inn, Corning Inn, Ramada Inn Aldi Foods, Buick/GMC, Chevrolet, Harley-Davidson, Home Depot, Walmart
43 (167)	NY 415, Painted Post, N Citgo Burger King $General, AutoValue Parts, Firestone/auto, Verizon, S Sunoco Denny's Hampton Inn
167mm	**parking area wb, litter barrels**
42 (165)	Coopers Plains, N st police
41 (161)	Rd 333, Campbell, N Camp Bell Camping (1mi), S Sunoco antiques, Cardinal Campsites (6mi)
160mm	**eb, full facilities, litter barrels, petwalk vending**
40 (156)	NY 226, Savona, N Mobil/dsl Savona Diner, Subway
39 (153)	NY 415, Bath, N Chat-a-Whyle Rest. (3mi) Holland American Country Inn, National Hotel, S Babcock Hollow Camping (2mi)
38 (150)	NY 54, to Hammondsport, Bath, N Citgo, KwikFill, Mobil, Sunoco/dsl Arby's, Burger King, Dunkin Donuts, Ling Ling Chinese, McDonald's/playplace, Pizza Hut, Ponderosa, Rico's Pizza, Subway Budget Inn, Days Inn, Microtel, Super 8 H, $General, Advance Parts, AT&T, Campers Haven Camping, Camping World RV Ctr, Family$, Hickory Hill Camping (3mi), K-Mart, museum, Rite Aid, st police, to Keuka Lake, Top's Foods/gas, Walgreens, winery
147mm	**wb, full facilities, litter barrels, petwalk vending**
37 (146)	NY 53, to Prattsburg, Kanona, S Pilot/Subway/dsl/scales/24hr/ @, Sunoco/Smokey's/dsl/scales st police, USPO, Wilkin's RV Ctr (1mi)
36 (145)	I-390 N, NY 15, to Rochester
35 (138)	Howard, S to Lake Demmon RA
34 (130)	NY 36, Hornell, Arkport, **0-2 mi** S KwikFill, Sunoco/dsl Applebee's, Country Kitchen, Dunkin Donuts, McDonald's, Subway Days Inn, EconoLodge, Sunshine Motel $General, $Tree, Advance Parts, Aldi Foods, Chrysler/Dodge/Jeep, Ford, GNC, Lowe's, NAPA, Radio Shack, Verizon, Walmart/Subway, Wegman's Foods
125mm	**scenic overlook eb, litter barrels**
33 (124)	NY 21, to Alfred, Almond, Andover, S Wilson Farms Kanakadea Camping, Lake Lodge Camping (8mi), USPO
117mm	2080 ft wb, elev 2110 ft eb, highest elevation on I-86
32 (116)	W Almond
31 (108)	Angelica, N Valero/dsl Angelica Inn B&B
30 (104)	NY 19, Belmont, Wellsville, N 6-S Camping (3mi), Letchworth SP (27mi), S Iron Kettle Rest. H, st police
101mm	**eb, full facilities, litter barrels, petwalk vending**
29 (99)	NY 275, to Bolivar, Friendship, S Miller&Brandes Gas, Mobil/Subway/dsl
28 (92)	NY 305, Cuba, N Moonwink's Rest. EconoLodge $General, Maple Lane RV Park, S Sunoco/dsl, Valero/dsl Charlie's Chicken Pizza, McDonald's, Subway H, Cuba Cheese Shop, Cuba Drug, Family$, Giant Foods
27 (84)	NY 16, NY 446, Hinsdale, N food, S gas lodging
26 (79)	NY 16, Olean, S Sunoco Burger King, Wendy's H
25 (77)	Buffalo St, Olean, S Citgo/dsl Country Fare H, **2 mi S on NY 417** Applebee's, Burger King, Coldstone/Tim Hortons, Domino's, Dunkin Donuts, Friendly's, Little Caesars, McDonald's, Perkins, Ponderosa, Subway Best Western, Country Inn&Suites, Microtel H, $Tree, Advance Parts, Aldi Foods, AT&T, BJ's Whse/gas, GNC, Home Depot, Jo-Ann Fabrics, K-Mart, KwikFill, NAPA, Old Navy, Radio Shack, St Bonaventure U, Staples, Tops Foods/gas, Verizon, Walmart/Subway
24 (74)	NY 417, Allegany, **1mi** S Mobil/7-11/dsl to St Bonaventure U
73mm	**wb, full facilities, litter barrels, petwalk vending**
23 (68)	US 219 S, N Allegany Jct./Subway/dsl
66mm	Allegheny River
21 (61)	US 219 N, Salamanca, S Red Garter Rest
20 (58)	NY 417, NY 353, Salamanca, N Antone's Gas, Nafco Quickstop/Burger King/24hr, Seneca OneStop/dsl/24hr, VIP Gas McDonald's Holiday Inn Express, Hotel Westgate AutoZone, Rail Museum, Seneca-Iroquis Museum, S casino
19 (54)	S Allegany SP, Red House Area

ELMIRA · CORNING · BATH · HORNELL · OLEAN · SALAMANCA · NY

INTERSTATE 86 Cont'd

JAMESTOWN

Exit #	Services
18 (51)	NY 280, S Allegany SP, Quaker Run Area
17 (48)	NY 394, Steamburg, N , RV camping, S Seneca, WW/dsl RV camping
16 (41)	W Main St, Randolph, N Mobil/dsl R&M Rest. RV camping
40mm	**parking area, picnic tables**
15 (39)	School House Rd
39mm	**parking area, picnic tables**
14 (36)	US 62, Kennedy, **1 mi** N Keystone Gas Office Pizza/Subs, S RV camping
32mm	Cassadaga Creek
13 (31)	NY 394, Falconer, S Mobil/dsl, Sunoco Burger King, McDonald's, Tim Hortons, Wendy's Budget Inn, Red Roof Inn CVS Drug, Harley-Davidson, Sugar Creek Stores
12 (28)	NY 60, Jamestown, N KwikFill/Dunkin Donuts/dsl, S Mobil/McDonald's/dsl Bob Evans Comfort Inn, Hampton Inn H, st police
11 (25)	to NY 430, Jamestown, S gas/dsl food lodging
22mm	**Welcome Ctr/ eb, full facilities, litter barrels, petwalk vending**
10 (21)	NY 430 W, Bemus Point
9 (20)	NY 430 E (no EZ eb return), N Mobil, S
19mm	Chautauqua Lake
8 (18)	NY 394, Mayville, N lodging, Mobil/dsl RV camping, USPO
7 (15)	Panama
6 (9)	NY 76, Sherman, N Keystone Gas Main Street Diner, Murdock's Rest Morse Hotel, Plum B&B city park, NAPA, Sherman Drug, USPO
4 (1)	NY 430, Findley Lake, N Holiday Inn Express, S gas food Peek'n Peak Conference Ctr RV camping, to Peek'n Peak Ski Area
0mm	New York/Pennsylvania state line. **Exits 3-1 are in PA.**
3	PA 89, North East, Wattsburg, N
1b a	I-90, W to Erie, E to Buffalo.

I-86 begins/ends on I-90, exit 37. I-390 begins/ends on I-86, exit 36.

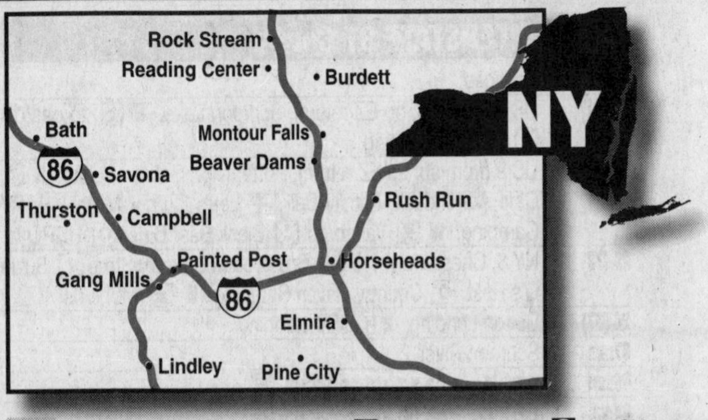

INTERSTATE 87

PLATTSBURGH

Exit #	Services
176mm	US/Canada Border, NY state line, **I-87 begins/ends**
43 (175)	US 9, Champlain, E Duty Free America, W Peterbilt Trkstp/deli/dsl/scales/24hr/ @ repair
42 (174)	US 11 S, to Rouse's Point, Champlain, E Irving/dsl, Sunoco/Subway China Buffet, J-reck Subs, Pizza+ Ace Hardware, Chevrolet (3mi), Kinney Drug, PriceChopper, Rite Aid, USPO, W Mobil/dsl, Valero/dsl Dunkin Donuts, McDonald's, Papa John's
41 (167)	NY 191, Chazy, E st police, W Miner Museum
162mm	**both lanes, full facilities, info, litter barrels, petwalk**
40 (160)	NY 456, Beekmantown, E Mobil/dsl Conroy's Organics Pt Auroche Lodge, Stonehelm Motel/café, W Twin Ells Camping
39 (158)	NY 314, Moffitt Rd, Plattsburgh Bay, E Mobil/dsl, Stewarts A&W, Dunkin Donuts, Gino's Pizza, Gus' Rest Rip van Winkle Motel, Super 8 Plattsburgh RV Park, to VT Ferry, W Shady Oaks Camping, to Adirondacks
38 (154)	NY 22, NY 374, to Plattsburgh, E Mobil/dsl Subway Kinney Drug
37 (153)	NY 3, Plattsburgh, E Stewarts, Sunoco #1 Chinese, Buffalo Wild Wings, Burger King, China Buffet, Chipotle, Domino's, Dunkin Donuts, Five Guys, Guiseppe's Pizza, Jade Buffet, KFC, Koto Japanese, McDonald's, Michigans+ Rest., Panera Bread, Perkins, Pizza Hut, Starbucks, Subway, Taco Bell, TX Roadhouse, Wendy's Comfort Inn, Holiday Inn H, Aldi Foods, BigLots, Buick/GMC, Family$, Ford, GNC, Kinney Drug, Michael's, Petsmart, Radio Shack, Rite Aid, Sam's Club, Staples, TJ Maxx, TrueValue, Verizon, vet, Walgreens, Walmart, W Mobil, Shell, Sunoco/Jreck Subs 99 Rest., Anthony's Rest., Applebee's, Butcher Block Rest., Dickey's BBQ, Dunkin Donuts, Friendly's, Ground Round, PriceChopper, Subway, Uno Best Value Inn, Best Western, Days Inn, EconoLodge, Hampton Inn, La Quinta, Microtel $Tree, Advance Parts, AT&T, AutoZone, Best Buy, Dick's, Gander Mtn, Harley-Davidson, Honda, JC Penney, Kinney Drug, K-Mart, Lowe's, Midas, Prays Mkt, Sears/auto, Target, vet
151mm	Saranac River
36 (150)	NY 22, Plattsburgh AFB, E Mobil/dsl st police, U-Haul, W Shell/Dunkin Donuts/dsl
146mm	**nb, full facilities, litter barrels, petwalk , truck insp sta both lanes**
35 (144)	NY 442, to Port Kent, Peru, **2-8 mi** E Iroquois/Ausable Pines Camping, to VT Ferry, W Mobil/Dunkin Donuts/Subway/dsl, Mobil/repair Livingood's Rest., McDonald's, Pasquale's Rest. Auchuban Hardware, Tops Foods, USPO, vet
143mm	emergency phones at 2 mi intervals begin sb/end nb
34 (137)	NY 9 N, Ausable Forks, E Sunoco/dsl Mac's Drive-in, Pleasant Corner Rest. vet, W Ausable River RV Camping, auto repair, Prays Mkt
136mm	Ausable River
33 (135)	US 9, NY 22, to Willsboro, E gas/dsl food lodging RV camping, to Essex Ferry
125mm	N Boquet River
32 (124)	Lewis, E RV Camping, W Lukoil/dsl, Pierce's/dsl Trkstp Diner RV Camping, st police
123mm	**both lanes, full facilities, info, no restrooms, petwalk**
120mm	Boquet River
31 (117)	NY 9 N, to Elizabethtown, Westport, E Mobil HillTop Motel RV camp/dump, W H, st police, vet
111mm	**nb, full facilities, litter barrels, petwalk vending**
30 (104)	US 9, NY 73, Keene Valley
99mm	**both lanes, full facilities, litter barrels, petwalk , truck insp. sta**
29 (94)	N Hudson, E Jellystone Camping, USPO, W Blue Ridge Falls Camping
28 (88)	NY 74 E, to Ticonderoga, Schroon Lake, E Mt Severance Country Store, Sunoco/dsl Maple Leaf Motel, Schroon Lake B&B RV camp/dump, services on US 9, st police

INTERSTATE 87 Cont'd

Exit #	Services
27 (81)	US 9 (from nb, no EZ return), Schroon Lake, E to gas/dsl food lodging
26 (78)	US 9 (from sb, no EZ return), Pottersville, Schroon Lake, E Cafe Adirondack, Family Deli Lee's Corner Motel RV Camping, W Valero/dsl Black Bear Diner USPO
25 (73)	NY 8, Chestertown, E Crossroads Country Store Suzie Q's Rest. Country Haven Camping, W Mobil/dsl
24 (67)	Bolton Landing, E RV camping
67mm	Schroon River
66mm	**parking area sb, no services**
64mm	**parking area nb, no services**
23 (58)	to US 9, Diamond Point, Warrensburg, W Citgo/dsl, Cumberland, Mobil/Dunkin Donuts/e85, Stewarts Dragon Lee Chinese, Geroge Henry's Rest., McDonald's, Subway Super 8 Central Adirondack Tr, Family$, Ford, PriceChopper Foods, Riverview Camping, Schroon River Camping (3mi), ski area, Tops Foods
22 (54)	US 9, NY 9 N, to Diamond Pt, Lake George, **E on US 9** Big Smoke BBQ, Gino&Tony's, Guiseppe's Pizza, Mario's Italian, Monte Cristo's, Moose Tooth Grill 7 Dwarfs Motel, Admiral Motel, Balsam Motel, Barberry Ct, Best Value Inn, Blue Moon Motel, Brookside Motel, EconoLodge, Georgian Lakeside Resort, Georgian Motel, Heritage Motel, Lake Crest Inn, Lake George Inn, Lake Haven Motel, Lake Motel, Marine Village Resort, Motel Montreal, Nordick's Motel, Oasis Motel, O'Sullivan's Motel, Park Lane Motel, Sundowner Motel, Surfside Motel multiple services, PriceChopper Foods, same as 21, **W parking area both lanes**
21 (53)	NY 9 N, Lake Geo, Ft Wm Henry, **E on US 9** Stewarts, Sunoco/dsl, Valero A&W, Adirondack Brewery, Barnsider BBQ, Blacksmith Rest., Dining Room, DJ's Cafe, Gaslight Grill, Jasper's Steaks, Lobster Pot, Mama Riso's Italian, McDonald's, Mezzaluna's, Pizza Hut Best Western, Ft William Henry Inn, Hampton Inn, Holiday Inn Resort, Lake View Inn, Lincoln Log Motel, Motel 6, Quality Inn, Rodeway Inn, Super 8, Tiki Hotel, Travelodge, Villager Motel, Windsor Hotel, Wingate Inn city park, Harley-Davidson, King Phillip Camping, Lake George Camping, multiple services, Rite Aid, same as 22, USPO, waterpark, W Mobil/dsl/LP Kathy's Cottages
51mm	W Adirondack Park
20 (49)	NY 149, to Ft Ann, **E on US 9 N** Mobil/Dunkin Donuts/dsl, Sunoco/dsl Blue Moose Rest., Frank's Pizza, Johnny Rocket's, Logjam Rest., Olde Post Grille, Subway Clarion, Comfort Suites, French Mtn Inn, Great Escape Lodge, Mohican Motel 6 Flags Funpark, Factory Outlets/famous brands, Ledgeview RV Park (3mi), st police, **E on US 9 S** waterpark
19 (47)	NY 254, Glens Falls, E Hess, Mobil/dsl, Sunoco 5 Guys Burgers, 99 Rest., Ambrosia Diner, Burger King, Chicago Grill, Dickey's BBQ, Dunkin Donuts, Friendly's, Giavano's Pizza, Golden Corral, KFC, Liberty Pizza, McDonald's, Moe's SW Grill, Mr B's Rest., Old China Buffet, Olive Garden, Outback Steaks, Panera Bread, Papa John's, Pizza Hut, Red Lobster, Silo Rest., Starbucks, Subway, Taco Bell/LJ Silver, Wendy's Alpen Haus Motel, Budget Inn, EconoLodge, Quality Inn, Red Roof Inn, Sleep Inn $Tree, Ace Hardware, Advance Parts, AT&T, AutoZone, Bon Ton, Dick's, Goodyear, Hobby Lobby, Home Depot, JC Penney, Jo-Ann Fabrics, mall, Meineke, Petco, Price Rite Foods, PriceChopper Foods, Radio Shack, Rite Aid, Sears/auto, Staples, Target, TJ Maxx, Tuesday Morning, USPO, Verizon, Walmart, W Mobil/Dunkin Donuts/Subway/dsl Ramada/rest. st police
18 (45)	Glens Falls, E Gulf/Subway/e-85/dsl, Hess/dsl, Sunoco/dsl Carl R's Café, Dunkin Donuts, Pizza Hut, Steve's Place Rest. Days Inn H, CVS Drug, Hannaford Foods, Toyota/Scion, U-Haul, Walgreens, W Stewarts McDonald's, Taco Bell Super 8
43mm	**both lanes, full facilities, litter barrels, petwalk vending**
42mm	Hudson River
17 (40)	US 9, S Glen Falls, E Citgo/dsl, Gulf, Hess/Blimpie/Dunkin Donuts, Sunoco/dsl, Valero/Subway/dsl Dunkin Donuts, Fitzgerald's Steaks Budget Inn, Landmark Motel (1mi) Adirondack RV Camp, auto/truck repair/transmissions, Suzuki, vet, W Moreau Lake SP
16 (36)	Ballard Rd, Wilton, E Coldbrook Campsites, golf, W Mobil, Stewart's, Sunoco/Scotty's Rest./dsl/scales/24hr Mt View Acres Motel Alpin Haus RV Ctr
15 (30)	NY 50, NY 29, Saratoga Springs, E Hess/dsl, Sunoco 5 Guys Burgers, 99 Rest., Applebee's, Burger King, Chicago Grill, Chipotle Mexican, Denny's, Dunkin Donuts, Friendly's, Golden Corral, KFC/Taco Bell, McDonald's, Moe's SW Grill, Osaka, Panera Bread, Subway, Sunny Wok, TGIFriday's Comfort Inn AT&T, Barnes&Noble, Best Buy, BJ's Whse, BonTon, Dick's, Ford, GNC, Hannaford Foods, Healthy Living Mkt, Home Depot, JC Penney, Kohl's, Lowe's, Mazda, Old Navy, Petsmart, PriceChopper Foods, Rite Aid, Sears/auto, Staples, Subaru, Target, TJ Maxx, Toyota/Scion, Walgreens, Walmart, W Residence Inn H
14 (28)	NY 9P, Schuylerville, **2 mi W** Hampton Inn, Holiday Inn H, museum, racetrack
13 (25)	US 9, Saratoga Springs, E Bentley's Rest., DeLucia's Deli, Saratoga Pizza Place Budget Inn, Locust Grove Motel Ballston Spa SP, Nissan, W Mobil/Dunkin Donuts/dsl, Stewarts Finish Line Rest., Hibachi Grill, Jack Dillon's Rest., PJ's BBQ Best Western, Hilton Garden (4mi), Roosevelt Inn/rest., Top Hill Hotel Saratoga SP, vet
12 (21)	NY 67, Malta, E Getty/dsl, Sunoco/dsl Bentley's Rest., Dunkin Donuts, KFC/Taco Bell, Malta Diner, McDonald's, Starbucks, Subway Fairfield Inn AT&T, CVS Drug, GNC, PriceChopper Foods, Saratoga NHP, st police, Stewart's, Verizon, W Hyatt Place URGENT CARE
11 (18)	Round Lake Rd, Round Lake, W Gulf/dsl, Sunoco/dsl Mulligan's Rest. Hannaford Foods, Rite Aid, Stewarts
10 (16)	Ushers Rd, E Hess/Dunkin Donuts/dsl, Xtra/dsl Ferretti's Rest. auto repair, W Stewarts
14mm	**nb, full facilities, info, litter barrels, petwalk vending**
9 (13)	NY 146, Clifton Park, E Hess/Dunkin Donuts/dsl, USA Burger King, Caputo's Pizza, Chili's, Cracker Barrel, Delmonico's Steaks, Giffy's BBQ, Harborhouse Fish Fry, Mr Subb, Peddler's Grill, Pizza Hut, Red Robin, Snyder's Rest., Subway, Wheatfields Bistro Comfort Suites, Holiday Inn Express, Residence Inn Advance Parts, Aldi Foods, BigLots, Goodyear/auto, Home Depot, Kohl's, Lowe's, Michael's, Midas, Petco, Rite Aid, Target, vet, W Mobil, Sunoco/dsl 5 Guys Burgers, 99 Rest., Bellini's Italian, Brick House Pizza, Buffalo Wild Wings, Chipotle Mexican, Dickey's BBQ, Dunkin Donuts, East Palace, East Wok, Friendly's, IHOP, La Fiesta, McDonald's, Moe's SW Grill, Olive Garden, Outback Steaks, Panera Bread, Pasta Pane, Ruby Tuesday, Salad Creations, Shane's Rib Shack, Starbucks, Subway, Taco Bell, TGIFriday's, Wendy's Best Western, Hampton Inn, Hilton Garden $Tree, AT&T, Chevrolet, CVS Drug, Firestone/auto, GNC, Hannaford Foods, JC Penney, Jo-Ann Fabrics, Marshall's, Petsmart, PriceChopper Foods, st police, Staples, Verizon, Walgreens

LAKE GEORGE

GLENS FALLS

SARATOGA SPGS

INTERSTATE 87 Cont'd

Exit #	Services
8a (12)	Grooms Rd, to Waterford
8 (10)	Crescent, Vischer Ferry, **E** Hess/Blimpie/Godfather's/dsl McDonald's USPO, **W** Gulf/NY Pizza/dsl, Sunoco Dunkin Donuts, Pancho's Mexican, Tufanos Pizza Ace Hardware, CVS Drug, Stewarts
8mm	Mohawk River
7 (7)	NY 7, Troy, **E on US 9 N** Hess/dsl Century House, Mr Subb Clarion, Comfort Inn, Days Inn, Holiday Inn Express, Sycamore Motel $General, Acura, Ford, Infiniti, Lexus, Nissan, Rite Aid, Volvo, **E on US 9 S** Sunoco Dunkin Donuts, McDonald's, Red Robin, Subway Hobby Lobby, Marshall's
6 (6)	NY 2, to US 9, Schenectady, **E** Hess, Mobil Applebee's, Boston Mkt, Chicago Grill, ChuckeCheese, Circle Diner, Firehouse Subs, Joe's Crabshack, Mr Subb, Panera Bread, Rafferty's, Red Robin, Sake Japanese, Starbucks, Wendy's Cocca's Inn, La Quinta, Travelodge $Tree, CVS Drug, GNC, Hannaford Foods, Home Depot, Lowe's, Mavis Discount Tire, Michael's, Mkt Bistro, Petsmart, same as 7, Sam's Club, Staples, Toyota/Scion, VW, Walmart, **W** Mobil/dsl, Stewart's Carrabba's, Chipotle Mexican, Denny's, DiBella's Subs, Dunkin Donuts, Kings Buffet, Ruby Tuesday, Subway Microtel, Quality Inn, Super 8 Goodyear/auto, Target, TJ Maxx, Verizon
5 (5)	NY 155 E, Latham, **E** DeeDee's Rest., Philly's Grill USPO
4 (4)	NY 155 W, Wolf Rd, **E on Wolf Rd** Hess/dsl, Mobil/Subway, Sunoco 99 Rest., Arby's, Buffalo Wagon, Burger King, Capital Buffet, Chipotle Mexican, CiCi's Pizza, Denny's, Dunkin Donuts, Macaroni Grill, Maxie's Grill, McDonald's, Moe's SW Grill, Olive Garden, Outback Steaks, Pizza Hut, Red Lobster, Reel Seafood Co, Samurai, Starbucks, Subway, Ted's Fishfry, TX Roadhouse, Wolf Rd Diner, Wolf Rd Diner, Wolfs 1-11 Best Western, Courtyard, Hampton Inn, Holiday Inn, Homewood Suites, Marriott, Red Roof Inn, Staybridge Suites Chevrolet, CVS Drug, Firestone/auto, Hannfords Foods, Trader Joe's, **W** Bluestone Bistro, Koto Japanese Desmond Hotel, Hotel Indigo to Heritage Park
2 (2)	NY 5, Central Ave, **E on Wolf Rd** Mobil/dsl, Sunoco Bonefish Grill, Bucca Italian, Cheesecake Factory, Chili's, Delma's Diner, Five Guys, Honeybaked Ham, Hooters, IHOP, Panera Bread, PF Chang's, Starbucks, Taco Bell, Wendy's Cocca's Inn, Comfort Inn, Scottish Inn, SpringHill Suites, Travelodge Barnes&Noble, BJ's Whse/gas, Goodyear/auto, Jo-Ann Fabrics, Kost Tire, LL Bean, Lowe's, Macy's, mall, Marshall's, PetCo, Sears/auto, Staples, Target, Whole Foods Mkt, **W** Gulf/dsl, Mobil, USA/dsl Delmonico's Steaks, Domino's, Dunkin Donuts, La Fiesta Mexican, McDonald's, Moe's SW Grill, Smokey Bones BBQ, Subway, Truman's Grill, Wendy's Days Inn, EconoLodge, Howard Johnson, Motel 6, Quality Inn, Super 8 Advance Parts, AT&T, Buick/GMC, Cadillac, Krause's Candy, Midas, PepBoys, ShopRite/gas, Subaru, Verizon, Walgreens
1W (1)	NY State Thruway (from sb), I-87 S to NYC, I-90 W to Buffalo
1E (1)	I-90 E (from sb), to Albany, Boston
1S (1)	to US 20, Western Ave, **E on US 20** Getty 5 Guys Burgers, 99 Rest., Burger King, Chipotle Mexican, Coldstone, Creo, Dunkin Donuts, Starbucks, TGIFriday's Best Western, CVS Drug, Days Inn, Holiday Inn Express AT&T, USPO, Verizon, vet, **W on US 20** Mobil, USA Capital City Diner, Dunkin

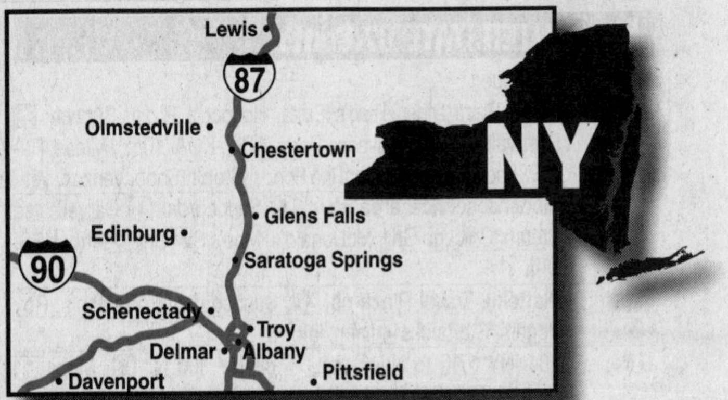

Exit #	Services
1S (1)	Continued Donuts, Hana Grill, Ichiban Japanese, McDonald's Adirondack Tires, PriceChopper Foods
1N (1)	I-87 N (from nb), to Plattsburgh
149	I-87 N to Montreal, **NY State Thruway goes west to Buffalo (I-90), S to NYC (I-87)**
24 (148)	I-90 and I-87 N
23 (142)	I-787, to Albany, US 9 W, **E on US 9 W** Cumberland Farms/Dunkin Donuts/dsl, Sunoco/dsl Comfort Inn to Knickerbocker Arena, transmissions, **W** Stewarts Days Inn
139mm	**parking area sb, litter barrel,**
22 (135)	NY 396, to Selkirk
21a (134)	I-90 E, to MA Tpk, Boston
127mm	**New Baltimore Travel Plaza both lanes,** Mobil/dsl Famous Famiglia, Quiznos, Roy Rogers, Starbucks, TCBY atm, info, wi-fi
21b (124)	US 9 W, NY 81, to Coxsackie, **W** Sunoco/dsl, Trvl Plaza/Citgo/rest./dsl/scales/24hr McDonald's Best Western, Budget Inn, Holiday Inn Express, Red Carpet Inn $Tree, Boat'n RV Whse, repair, vet
21 (114)	NY 23, Catskill, **E** Mobil, Sunoco/dsl Catskill Motel/rest. (2mi), Pelokes Motel (2mi) Home Depot, to Rip van Winkle Br, transmissions, visitors ctr, **W** Anthony's Banquet Hall Astoria Motel, Rip Van Winkle Motel to Hunter Mtn/Windham Ski Areas
103mm	**Malden Service Area nb,** Mobil/dsl Carvel Ice Cream, Hotdogs, McDonald's atm, parking area sb,
20 (102)	NY 32, to Saugerties, **E** Mobil/dsl, Stewarts, Sunoco Dunkin Donuts, Giordano's Pizza, McDonald's, Pizza Star, Starway Café, Subway Advance Parts, Big Lots, Chrysler/Dodge/Jeep, CVS Drug, Family$, PriceChopper Foods, Verizon, **W** Hess/Blimpie/Dunkin Donuts/dsl, Sunoco/dsl Land&Sea Grill, Saugerties Diner Comfort Inn, Howard Johnson/rest. Blue Mtn Campground (5mi), Brookside Campground (10mi), KOA (2mi), Rip Van Winkle Campground (3mi), to Catskills
99mm	**parking area nb, litter barrels**
96mm	**Ulster Travel Plaza sb,** Sunoco/dsl Nathan's, Pizza Hut, Roy Rogers, Starbucks, TCBY atm, phone, wi-fi
19 (91)	NY 28, Rhinecliff Br, Kingston, **E** QuickChek/dsl Blimpie, Olympic Diner, Picnic Pizza, Stadium Diner Garden Plaza Hotel, Super 8 access to I-587 E, Advance Parts, CVS Drug, Hannaford Foods, Kia, Radio Shack, Walgreens, **W** NY Pizza, Roudigan's Steaks Motel 19, Quality Inn, Rodeway Inn, SuperLodge access to US 209, Camping World RV Ctr, Ford, Nissan
18 (76)	NY 299, to Poughkeepsie, New Paltz, **E** Mobil, Shell/dsl College Diner 87 Motel, EconoLodge, Rodeway Inn Lowe's, to Mid-Hudson Br, **W** Sunoco Burger King, Dunkin Donuts, Gabaletos Seafood, McDonald's, Pasquale's

NY

ALBANY

= gas = food = lodging = other = rest stop

INTERSTATE 87 Cont'd

NEWBURGH

18 (76)	Continued Pizza, Plaza Diner, Rino's Pizza, Rococo's Pizza, Subway Best Value Inn Advance Parts, AT&T, KOA (10mi), Midas, Radio Shack, Rite Aid, ShopRite Foods, Stop'n Shop, Verizon, vet
66mm	**Modena service area sb,** Sunoco/dsl Carvel's Ice Cream, Chicago Grill, McDonald's, Moe's SW Grill atm, UPS, wi-fi
65mm	**Plattekill Travel Plaza nb,** Sunoco/dsl Nathan's, Roy Rogers, Starbucks atm, info, wi-fi
17 (60)	I-84, NY 17K, to Newburgh, **E on NY 300 N** Mobil Daddy's Grill, DQ, Dunkin Donuts, Joe's Deli, McDonald's, Newburgh Buffet, Perkins, Taco Bell, Wendy's $Tree, AT&T, AutoZone, BonTon, Marshall's, Mavis Tire, Midas, Office Depot, Sears/auto, Stop&Shop, **E on NY 300 S** Hess/dsl, Sunoco/dsl Applebee's, Burger King, Chili's, China City, Cosimos Ristorante, Denny's, Five Guys, IHOP, Ikaros Diner, Longhorn Steaks, Neptune Diner, Panera Bread, Pizza Mia, Sonic, Starbucks, Steak&Stein, Subway, TGIFriday's, Union Sq Rest., Yobo Asian Days Inn, Howard Johnson, Ramada Inn, Super 8 $General, Adam's Food Mkt, Aldi Foods, Barnes&Noble, Buick/GMC, Cadillac/Chevrolet, Chrysler/Dodge/Jeep, Ford/Lincoln, Home Depot, Honda, Kohl's, Lowe's, Meineke, Michael's, Nissan, Petsmart, Radio Shack, Target, Verizon, Walmart/McDonald's, **W on NY 17K** Hilton Garden
16 (45)	US 6, NY 17, to West Point, Harriman, **W** Gulf/dsl Applebee's, Chicago Grill, Chili's, Dunkin Donuts, KFC, Outback Steaks, Panera Bread, TGIFriday's, Wendy's Days Inn, Hampton Inn $Tree, Best Buy, BJ's Whse, BMW, GNC, Home Depot, Kohl's, Michaels, Old Navy, Petsmart, Radio Shack, st police, Staples, Target, TJ Maxx, Verizon, Walmart/Subway, Woodbury Outlet/famous brands
34mm	**Ramapo Service Area sb,** Sunoco/dsl Carvel, McDonald's, Uno Pizza atm, wi-fi
33mm	**Sloatsburg Travel Plaza nb,** Sunoco/dsl Burger King, Dunkin Donuts, Quiznos, Sbarro's atm, gifts, info
15a (31)	NY 17 N, NY 59, Sloatsburg
15 (30)	I-287 S, NY 17 S, to NJ. **I-87 S & I-287 E run together.**
14b (27)	Airmont Rd, Montebello, **E** Crowne Plaza, **W on NY9** Gulf/Dunkin Donuts/dsl Airmont Diner, Applebee's, Bagel Boys Cafe, Bella Vita Pizza, Friendly's, Pasta Cucina, Starbucks, Sutter's Mill Rest. Howard Johnson H, ShopRite Foods, Tall Man Tires, Walgreens, Walmart
14a (23)	Garden State Pkwy, to NJ, Chestnut Ridge
14 (22)	NY 59, Spring Valley, Nanuet, **E** Citgo/dsl, Shell/dsl, Valero/dsl Burger King, Deliziosa Pizza, Domino's, IHOP, McDonald's, Planet Wings, Subway Fairfield Inn BMW, CarQuest, GNC, Maserati/Ferrari, Michael's, Target, TJ Maxx, Verizon, **W** Citgo, Gulf Baskin-Robbins/Dunkin Donuts, Bonefish, ChuckeCheese, Corner Bakery Cafe, Dunkin Donuts, Franko's Pizza, KFC/Taco Bell, Nanuet Diner, Panera Bread, Red Lobster, Smashburger, Starbucks, White Castle Days Inn, Hampton Inn, Hilton Garden $Tree, AT&T, Barnes&Noble, Fairway Mkt, Home Depot, Hyundai, Macy's, Marshall's, Midas, PetCo, Sears/auto, Staples, Stop&Shop Foods, STS Tires, transmissions, Verizon
13 (20)	Palisades Pkwy, N to Bear Mtn, S to NJ
12 (19)	NY 303, Palisades Ctr Dr, W Nyack, **W** Mobil Cheesecake Factory, Outback Steaks, Panera Bread, Tony Roma's Nyack Motel Barnes&Noble, Best Buy, BJ's Whse, Dave&Buster's, Dick's, Home Depot, JC Penney, Lord&Taylor, Macy's, mall, Old Navy, Staples, STS Tire/repair, Target, Verizon

NYACK

11 (18)	US 9W, to Nyack, **E** Mobil, Shell/dsl Best Western Walgreens, **W** Shell/dsl Dunkin Donuts, McDonald's Super 8 H, J&L Repair/tire, Midas, Old World Food Mkt, VW
10 (17)	Nyack (from nb), same as 11
14mm	Hudson River, Tappan Zee Br
13mm	**toll plaza**
9 (12)	to US 9, to Tarrytown, **E** Hess/dsl, Shell CVS Drug **W** Mobil El Dorado West Diner DoubleTree Hotel Honda, Mavis Tire
8 (11)	I-287 E, to Saw Mill Pkwy, White Plains, **E** Hampton Inn, Marriott
7a (10)	Saw Mill River Pkwy S, to Saw Mill River SP, Taconic SP
7 (8)	NY 9A (from nb), Ardsley, **W** Ardsley Acres Motel H
6mm	**Ardsley Travel Plaza nb,** Sunoco/dsl Burger King, Popeye's vending

NYC AREA

5.5mm	**toll plaza**
6ba (5)	Stew Leonard Dr, to Ridge Hill, **W** Costco, Home Depot, Stew Leonard's Farmfresh Foods
6 (4.5)	Tuckahoe Dr, Yonkers, **E** Getty/repair Marcellino's Pizza, McDonald's, Subway Tuckahoe Motel ShopRite Foods/drug, **W** Gulf, Mobil/dsl Domino's, Dunkin Donuts, Kim Wei Chinese Ramada Inn, Royal Regency Hotel
5 (4.3)	NY 100 N (from nb), Central Park Ave, White Plains
4 (4)	Cross Country Pkwy, Mile Sq Rd, **E** Ford/Lincoln/Subaru, Macy's, Marshall's, Sears/auto, TJ Maxx, **W** BP, Shell/dsl, Shell/Dunkin Donuts/dsl Burger King Chevrolet, Mavis Tire
3 (3)	Mile Square Rd, **E** GNC, mall, Stop&Shop, Thriftway Drug, **W** BP, Citgo
2 (2)	Yonkers Ave (from nb), Westchester Fair, **E** Mobil Yonkers Speedway
1 (1)	Hall Place, McLean Ave, **E** Dunkin Donuts A&P Foods/Subway
0mm	**New York St Thruway and I-87 N run together to Albany**
14 (11)	McLean Ave, **E** A&P/dsl Dunkin Donuts, Subway
13 (10)	E 233rd, NE Tollway, **service plaza both lanes**/Gulf/Dunkin Donuts
12 (9.5)	Hudson Pkwy (from nb), Sawmill Pkwy
11 (9)	Van Cortlandt Pk S
10 (8.5)	W 230th St (from sb), W 240th (from nb), **W** Getty Dunkin Donuts H, Marshall's, Target
9 (8)	W Fordham Rd, **E** BP/dsl Dallas BBQ H
8 (7)	W 179th (from nb), **W** Roberto Clemente SP
7 (6)	I-95, US 1, S to Trenton, NJ, N to New Haven, CT
6 (5)	E 153rd t, River Ave, Stadium Rd, **E** Yankee Stadium
5 (5)	E 161st, Macombs Dam Br, (exit 4 from nb), **E** AT&T, Best Buy, Michael's, Target, Yankee Stadium
3 (3)	E 138th St, Madison Ave Br, **E** BP/dsl
2 (2)	Willis Ave, 3rd Ave Br, **E** Mobil/dsl, **W** McDonald's
1 (1)	Brook Ave, Hunts Point, **E** BP, Hess
0mm	**I-87 begins/ends on I-278.**

INTERSTATE 88

Exit #	Services
25a	I-90/NY Thruway. **I-88 begins/ends on I-90, exit 25a.**
117mm	**toll booth** (to enter or exit NY Thruway)
25 (116)	NY 7, to Rotterdam, Schenectady, **S** Pilot/Dunkin Donuts/Subway/dsl/scales/24hr **3 mi S** Gulf, Burger King, McDonald's, Peppino's Pizza, Top's Diner, Wagon Train BBQ L&M Motel, Quality Inn Frosty Acres Camping

NY

INTERSTATE 88 Cont'd

COBLESKILL

ONEONTA

Exit #	Services
24 (112)	US 20, NY 7, to Duanesburg, N Mobil, Stewarts Dunkin Donuts st police, S Duanesburg Diner USPO
23 (101)	NY 30, to Schoharie, Central Bridge, N Apple Food/dsl Holiday Motel Hideaway Camping, Locust Park Camping, S Mobil/Subway/dsl Dunkin Donuts Days Inn, Hyland House B&B (2mi), Wedgewood B&B (2mi)
22 (95)	NY 7, NY 145, to Cobleskill, Middleburgh, **2-5 mi** N Hess/dsl, Mobil, Sunoco Dunkin Donuts, Pizza Hut, Subway Colonial CT Motel, Holiday Motel, Super 8 H, $General, Advance Parts, Buick/Chevrolet/GMC, Chrysler/Dodge/Jeep, Howe Caverns Camping, PriceChopper Foods, to Howe Caverns, Walmart/McDonld's, S st police, Twin Oaks Camping (5mi)
21 (90)	NY 7, NY 10, to Cobleskill, Warnerville, **2-3 mi** N Hess/dsl, Mobil/dsl, Stewart's/dsl Arby's, Burger King, Dairy Deli, Delaney's Rest, KFC/Taco Bell, McDonald's, Pizza Hut, Red Apple Rest., Sub Express Best Western, Gables B&B H, $General, Ace Hardware, CarQuest, CVS Drug, NAPA, PriceChopper Foods, TrueValue, Walmart/McDonald's
20 (87)	NY 7, NY 10, to Richmondville, S Mobil/dsl, Sunoco/dsl Reinhardt's Deli, Sub Express Red Carpet Inn USPO
79mm	**wb, full facilities, litter barrels, petwalk vending**
19 (76)	to NY 7, Worcester, N Stewarts, Sunoco/dsl
18 (71)	to Schenevus, N Citgo Schenevus Rest.
17 (61)	NY 7, to NY 28 N, Colliersville, Cooperstown, **2 mi** N Sunoco Best Western (14mi), Red Carpet Inn to Baseball Hall of Fame
16 (59)	NY 7, to Emmons, N Arby's, Brooks BBQ, Farmhouse Rest., Morey's Rest., Pizza Hut, Sonny's Pizza Amber Life Motel, Rainbow Inn PriceChopper Foods, Rite Aid
15	NY 28, NY 23, Oneonta, N Citgo, Hess, KwikFill Dunkin Donuts, Friendly's, KFC Clarion, Townhouse Inn H, Advance Parts, to Soccer Hall of Fame, S Hess/Dunkin Donuts, Mirabito/dsl Applebee's, Burger King, Denny's, McDonald's, Neptune Diner/24hr, Quiznos, Sabatini's Italian, Subway, Taco Bell, Wendy's Budget Inn, Christopher's Lodge/rest., Holiday Inn, Sun Lodge, Super 8 $Tree, Aldi Foods, BJ's Whse/gas, Dick's, Ford, Hannaford Foods, Home Depot, JC Penney, Kost Tire, TJ Maxx, Verizon, Walmart
14 (55)	Main St (from eb), Oneonta, N Citgo, Stewarts, Sunoco Alfresco's Italian CarQuest
13 (53)	NY 205, **1-2 mi** N Citgo, Hess, Valero/dsl DQ, Dunkin Donuts, McDonald's Celtic Motel, Hampton Inn, Motel 88 Buick/Cadillac/Chevrolet/GMC, camping, Family$, Gilbert Lake SP (11mi), Honda, Jellystone Park Camping, Kia, NAPA, Nissan, Rite Aid, st police, Subaru, to Susquehanna Tr
12 (47)	NY 7, to Otego, S Mirabito/Subway/Tim Hortons/dsl/24hr
11 (40)	NY 357, to Unadilla,, Delhi, N KOA
39mm	**eb, full facilities, litter barrels, petwalk vending**
10 (38)	NY 7, to Unadilla, **2 mi** N KwikFill, Mirabito Country Motel (4mi) Great American Foods, st police, USPO
9 (33)	NY 8, to Sidney, N Hess/dsl, Mobil/dsl, Sunoco China Buffet, Little Caesars, McDonald's, Pizza Hut, Subway Algonkin Motel, Country Motel, Super 8 H, $General, Advance Parts, K-Mart, PriceChopper Foods, Tall Pines Camping, USPO
8 (29)	NY 206, to Bainbridge, N Sunoco Bob's Family Diner, Deli Joe's, Dunkin Donuts Algonkin Motel, Susquehanna

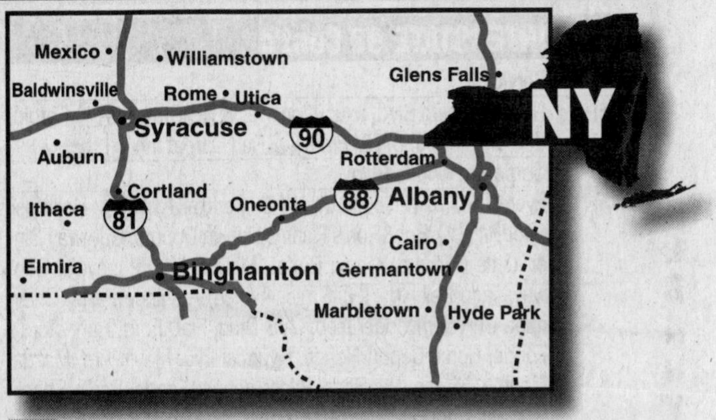

Exit #	Services
8 (29)	Continued Motel Chevrolet/GMC, Parts+, Riverside RV Park, to Oquage Creek Park, USPO
7 (22)	NY 41, to Afton, **1-2 mi** N Mobil, Sunoco/dsl River-Club Rest., Vincent's Rest. Afton Golf/rest., Kellystone Park, Smith-Hale HS
6 (16)	NY 79, to NY 7, Harpursville, Ninevah, S Mirabito/dsl Gramma's Country Cafe, Tim Hortons to Nathanial Cole Park, USPO
5 (12)	Martin Hill Rd, to Belden, N Manley's Trstp/dsl Belden Manor Camping
4 (8)	NY 7, to Sanitaria Springs, S Hess/dsl
3 (4)	NY 369, Port Crane, N to Chenango Valley SP, S Fastrac/dsl, KwikFill
2 (2)	NY 12a W, to Chenango Bridge, N Mirabito USPO
1 (1)	NY 7 W (no wb return), to Binghamton
0mm	I-81, N to Syracuse, S to Binghamton. **I-88 begins/ends on I-81.**

INTERSTATE 90

NY

Exit #	Services
B24.5mm	New York/Massachusetts state line
B3 (B23)	NY 22, to Austerlitz, New Lebanon, W Stockbridge, N Loves/Dunkin Donuts/Subway/dsl/scales/24hr, S Sunoco/dsl Berkshire Travel Lodge Woodland Hills Camp
B18mm	**toll plaza**
B2 (B15)	NY 295, Taconic Pkwy, **1-2 mi** S
B1 (B7)	US 9, NY Thruway W, to I-87, **toll booth**
12 (20)	US 9, to Hudson, N Pilot/McDonald's/Subway/dsl/scales/24hr, **0-3 mi** S to Van Buren NHS
18.5mm	**/weigh sta wb, full facilities, litter barrels, petwalk vending**
11 (15)	US 9, US 20, E Greenbush, Nassau, N Hess/dsl, Sunoco/dsl Dunkin Donuts st police, S Mobil (2mi), Stewarts Lighthouse Rest. Host Field Inn, Knights Inn repair, Rite Aid, vet
10 (10)	Miller Rd, to E Greenbush, S Mobil/dsl, Stewarts Dunkin Donuts Comfort Inn
9 (9)	US 4, to Rensselaer, Troy, N Mobil 5 Guys Burgers, Applebee's, Domino's, Dunkin Donuts, McDonald's, OffShore Pier Rest., Panera Bread, Starbucks, Subway, The Sports Grill Holiday Inn Express, Residence Inn $Tree, Home Depot, PetsMart, Radio Shack, Staples, Target, Walmart, S Mobil/dsl, Stewart's Cracker Barrel, Denny's, Dunkin Donuts Fairfield Inn
8 (8)	NY 43, Defreestville
7 (7)	Washington Ave (from eb), Rensselaer
6.5mm	Hudson River
6a	I-787, to Albany

[gas] = gas [food] = food [lodging] = lodging [other] = other RS = rest stop

INTERSTATE 90 Cont'd

ALBANY

Exit #	Services
6 (4.5)	US 9, Northern Blvd, to Loudonville, N Stewarts Forbidden City, Mr Subb, NY Pizza Red Carpet Inn H
5a (4)	Corporate Woods Blvd
5 (3.5)	Everett Rd, to NY 5, **S on NY 5, Central Ave** Hess/dsl, ShopRite Bob&Ron's Fishfry, Dunkin Donuts, Gateway Diner, Little Caesars, Mama Buffet, McDonald's, Popeye's, Subway, Taco Bell H, $Tree, Aamco, Advance Parts, Chevrolet, Chrysler/Dodge/Jeep, CVS Drug, Fiat, Ford, Hannaford's Foods, Home Depot, Honda, Hyundai, Kia, Mavis Tire, Mazda, Monroe, Nissan, PepBoys, PriceChopper Foods, Radio Shack, Rite Aid, ShopRite Foods
4 (3)	NY 85 S, to Slingerlands
3 (2.5)	N State Offices
2 (2)	Fuller Rd, Washington Ave, **S on Washington** Sunoco/Subway Dunkin Donuts Courtyard, CrestHill Suites, Extended Stay America, Fairfield Inn, Hilton Garden, Red Carpet Inn, TownePlace Suites same as 1S
1N (1)	I-87 N, to Montreal, to Albany Airport
1S (1)	US 20, Western Ave, S Mobil 5 Guys Burgers, 99 Rest., Burger King, Capital City Diner, Chipotle Mexican, Dunkin Donuts, Hana Grill, Ichiban Japanese, McDonald's, Moe's SW Grill, Panera Bread, Peaches Cafe, Starbucks, TGIFriday's, Uno Grill, Wendy's Holiday Inn Express, Residence Inn AT&T, Best Buy, CVS Drug, Dick's, Home Depot, JC Penney, Macy's, mall, Michael's, Old Navy, PetsMart, PriceChopper Foods, USPO, Verizon, vet, Walmart
24 (149)	I-87 N to Albany, Montreal, S to NYC
153mm	**Guilderland Service Area eb,** Mobil/dsl McDonald's
25 (154)	I-890, NY 7, NY 146, to Schenectady
25a (159)	I-88 S, NY 7, to Binghamton, Pilot/Dunkin Donuts/Subway/dsl/scales/24hr
26 (162)	I-890, NY 5 S, Schenectady
168mm	**Pattersonville Service Area wb,** Mobil/dsl Hershey's, Quiznos, Roy Rogers, Starbucks atm, wi-fi
172mm	**Mohawk Service Area eb,** Mobil/dsl McDonald's
27 (174)	NY 30, Amsterdam, **1 mi N** Mobil/dsl, Valero Best Value Inn, Super 8, Valleyview Motel Alpin Haus RV Ctr (3mi)
28 (182)	NY 30A, Fonda, N Citgo/rest/dsl/motel/24hr, Mobil (1mi), Sunoco/dsl, TA/Buck Hill Rest/dsl/motel/scales/24hr/ @ Dunkin Donuts, McDonald's Holiday Inn (7mi), Microtel, Riverside Motel, Super 8 (8mi) H, st police, truck repair
184mm	**parking area/truck insp area both lanes, litter barrels**
29 (194)	NY 10, Canajoharie, N Gulf, Stewarts McDonald's, Subway $General, Ace Hardware, BigLots, NAPA, Rite Aid, Riverfront Park, USPO, S Citgo/dsl, Lukoil/dsl, Sunoco Mercato Pizza, Village Rest. Rodeway Inn NAPA-Care, USPO
210mm	**Indian Castle Service area eb,** Hershey's Ice Cream, Roy Rogers, Starbucks atm, gifts, wi-fi **Iroquois Service Area wb,** Burger King, Dunkin Donuts, wi-fi
29a (211)	NY 169, to Little Falls, N Knights Inn (3mi) H, to Herkimer Home
30 (220)	NY 28, to Mohawk, Herkimer, N FasTrac/dsl, Mobil/Subway/dsl, Stewarts Applebee's, Burger King, Denny's, Dunkin Donuts, KFC/Taco Bell, McDonald's, Pizza Hut, Tony's Pizzaria, Vinny's Pizza Best Inn, Budget Motel, Herkimer Motel, Inn Towne Motel $General, $Tree, Advance Parts, Aubuchon Hardware, AutoZone, Goodyear, Rite Aid, Verizon, Walmart, S FasTrac Little Caesars, Red Apple Chinese Red Carpet Inn (2mi) Factory Depot, Family$, to Cooperstown (Baseball Hall of Fame)

UTICA

Exit #	Services
227mm	**Schuyler Service Area wb,** Mobil/dsl Breyer's, Fres Fudge, McDonald's atm, st police
31 (233)	I-790, NY 8, NY 12, to Utica, N Citgo/dsl, Fastrac, Sunoco Applebees, Burger King, Franco's Pizza, Good Frien Chinese $Tree, BigLots, BJ's Whse/gas, Curves, Lowe PriceChopper Foods, Rite Aid, Walmart/McDonald's, S Hess/dsl Babe's Grill, Delmonico's Steaks, Denny's, Dunk Donuts, Friendly's, Knock-Out Pizza, McDonald's, Pizza Hu Romeo's Italian, Subway, Taco Bell, Wendy's Best Wester Days Inn, Hampton Inn, Happy Journey Motel, Red Roof In Scottish Inn, Super 8 AT&T
236mm	I-790 (from eb), to Utica
237.5mm	Erie Canal
238mm	Mohawk River
32 (243)	NY 232, Westmoreland, **4-8 mi N** EconoLodge, Quality Inn Red Carpet Inn, Scottish Inn, **5 mi S** Hampton Inn
244mm	**Oneida Service Area eb,** Sunoco/dsl Burger King, Sbarro's, Starbucks atm, gifts
250mm	**parking area eb, litter barrels, phones, picnic tables**
33 (253)	NY 365, to Vernon Downs, Verona, N SavOn Gas/dsl Joel's Frontyard Steaks Inn at Turning Stone, S SavOn Gas/LP/repair Dunkin Donuts, Recovery Grill Fairfield Inn, La Quinta H, Turning Stone Casino
256mm	**litter barrel, parking area wb**
34 (262)	NY 13, to Canastota, S KwikFill, SavOn/dsl, Sunoco Dunkin Donuts, McDonald's Days Inn, Graziano Motel/rest Super 8 Boxing Hall of Fame, Verona Beach SP Camping
266mm	**Chittenango Service Area wb,** Sunoco/dsl Sbarro's Starbucks arm, wi-fi

SYRACUSE

Exit #	Services
34a (277)	I-481, to Syracuse, Chittenango
35 (279)	NY 298, The Circle, Syracuse, S Mobil, Valero/dsl Burger King, Denny's, Dunkin Donuts, East Wok, Green Onion Rest. Grimaldi's, Joey's Italian, Jreck Subs, Justin's Grill, McDonald's Ruby Tuesday, Weigh Lock Cafe Candlewood Suites, Comfort Inn, Courtyard, Cresthill Suites, Days Inn, Doubletree Inn Embassy Suites, Extended Stay America, Hampton Inn, Hilton Garden, Holiday Inn, John Milton Inn, Microtel, Motel 6, Quality Inn, Ramada Ltd, Red Roof Inn, Residence Inn, Super 8 Goodyear/auto
280mm	**Dewitt Service Area eb,** Sunoco/dsl Edy's Ice Cream, McDonald's
36 (283)	I-81, N to Watertown, S to Binghamton
37 (284)	7th St, Electronics Pkwy, to Liverpool, N Best Western, S Hess/Blimpie/Dunkin Donuts/Godfather's KFC/Taco Bell Holiday Inn, Homewood Suites, Knights Inn, Staybridge Suites Kinney Drug
38 (286)	NY 57, to Liverpool, Syracuse, N Fastrac/dsl, Hess, Kwik-Fill Bangkok Thai, Dunkin Donuts, Pier 57 Diner, Pizza Hut, Salsarita's Grill Hampton Inn (7mi), Super 8 $Tree, Aldi Foods, Midas, NAPA, Rite Aid
39 (290)	I-690, NY 690, Syracuse, N Comfort Inn/rest. Camping World RV Ctr, S Holiday Inn Express
292mm	**Warners Service Area wb,** Mobil/dsl Boston Pizza, Edy's Ice Cream, McDonald's
40 (304)	NY 34, to Owasco Lake, Weedsport, N Riverforest RV Park, S Fastrac, KwikFill, Sunoco/dsl Arby's, Arnold's Rest., Cj's Rest., DB's Drive-In, Dunkin Donuts, NY Pizzaria, Old Erie Diner, Peters Pizzaria Best Western, Days Inn, Holiday Inn (12mi) $General, Ace Hardware, Bass Pro Shops (12mi), Kinney Drug, NAPA, USPO, Weedsport Foods

INTERSTATE 90 Cont'd

Exit #	Services
310mm	**Port Byron Service Area eb,** Mobil/dsl Boston Pizza, Edy's Ice Cream, McDonald's
318mm	**parking area wb, litter barrels**
41 (320)	NY 414, to Cayuga Lake, Waterloo, S Nice'n Easy/dsl, Petro/Iron Skillet/dsl/scales/24hr/ @ MaGee Country Diner Hampton Inn (4mi), Holiday Inn (4mi), Microtel (4mi) Cayuga Lake SP/camping, Waterloo Outlets/famous brands (3mi)
324mm	**Junius Ponds Service Area wb,** Sunoco/dsl Dunkin Donuts, Roy Rogers atm, wi-fi
42 (327)	NY 14, to Geneva, Lyons, N RV camping, S Mobil/7-11/dsl/scales Belherst (6mi), Best Value Inn (6mi), Days Inn (6mi), Hampton Inn (6mi), Ramada Inn (6mi), Red Carpet Inn Junius Ponds RV Camping, Waterloo Outlets/famous brands (3mi)
337mm	**Clifton Springs Service Area eb,** Sunoco/dsl Roy Rogers, Starbucks atm, gifts
43 (340)	NY 21, to Palmyra, Manchester, N Hill Cumorah LDS HS (2mi), S Sunoco/dsl Grandpa Joe's Diner, McDonald's Manchester Inn KOA (6mi)
44 (347)	NY 332, Victor, S 7-11/dsl, Arrowmart/Subway, Hess, Sunoco/dsl Dunkin Donuts, KFC, McDonald's, Park Place Rest. Best Value Inn, Budget Inn, Comfort Inn, Travelodge $General, Aldi Foods, AutoZone, casino, CVS Drug, Family$, KOA (4mi), st police, Wade's Foods
350mm	**Seneca Service Area wb,** Mobil/dsl Checker's, Tim Hortons, Villa Pizza atm, wi-fi
45 (351)	I-490, NY 96, to Rochester, N Mobil/dsl Biaggi's Rest., BoneFish Grill, Champp's Grill, Distillery Rest., Five Guys, Longhorn Steaks, McDonald's, Moe's SW Grill, Olive Garden, Panera Bread, PF Chang's, Starbucks, Subway, TGIFriday's, Uno Grill Hampton Inn, Springdale Farm B&B $Tree, AT&T, Best Buy, BJ's Whse/gas, Dick's, GNC, Home Depot, JC Penney, K-Mart, Kohl's, Lord&Taylor, Macy's, Michael's, Old Navy, Petsmart, Rite Aid, Sears/auto, Staples, Target, Verizon, Von Maur, Walmart, S KwikFill/dsl Burger King, Chili's, Denny's, Taco Bell, Wendy's Best Western, Holiday Inn Express, Homewood Suites, Microtel, Royal Inn Ballantyne RV Ctr
353mm	**parking area eb, litter barrels**
46 (362)	I-390, to Rochester, **N on NY 253 W** Gulf/dsl, Hess/dsl, Sunoco/dsl McDonald's, Peppermint's Rest., Tim Hortons, Wendy's Country Inn&Suites, Days Inn, Fairfield Inn, Microtel, Red Roof Inn, Super 8 Buick/GMC
366mm	**Scottsville Service Area eb,** Mobil/dsl Arby's, Tim Horton atm, info, wi-fi
376mm	**Ontario Service Area wb,** Sunoco/dsl Boston Pizza, Edy's Ice Cream, McDonald's atm, wi-fi
47 (379)	I-490, NY 19, to Rochester, N Timberline Camping
48 (390)	NY 98, to Batavia, N Comfort Inn, Hampton Inn, Holiday Inn Express, S Citgo Applebee's, Bob Evans, Subway, Taco Bell, Tim Horton's, Yume Asian Bistro Best Western, Budget Inn, Clarion, Days Inn, La Quinta, Red Roof Inn, Super 8, Super 8 AT&T, AutoZone, BJ's Whse, Dick's, Home Depot, K-Mart, Kohl's, Marshall's, Michael's, PetCo, Radio Shack, Rite Aid, Target, Tops Foods, Verizon, Walmart/Subway
397mm	**Pembroke Service Area eb,** Sunoco/dsl Checker's, Tim Hortons atm, gifts wi-fi
48a (402)	NY 77, Pembroke, S FLYING J/Denny's/Subway/dsl/LP/scales/24hr, TA/Valero/Country Pride/dsl/scales/24hr/ @ Subway Darien Lake Lodge/camping, EconoLodge Sleepy Hollow Camping (8mi)

ROCHESTER

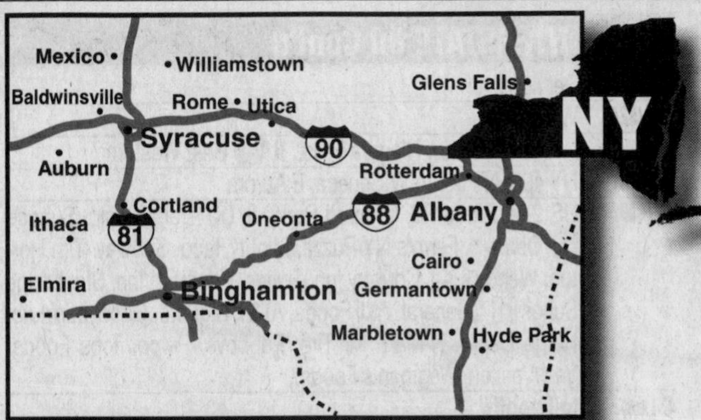

DEPEW

Exit #	Services
412mm	**Clarence Service Area wb, full facilities, info, wi-fi** Sunoco/dsl Arby's, Tim Hortons atm,
49 (417)	NY 78, Depew, **0-3 mi N** Delta Sonic, Mobil/dsl, Sunoco, Sunoco Applebee's, Arby's, Burger King, Carmine's Rest., Chili's, Chipotle, Coldstone, Cracker Barrel, Dave&Buster's, Dibella's Subs, DQ, Duff's Wings, Dunkin Donuts, Firehouse Subs, Five Guys, Friendly's, Garden Buffet, Jimmy John's, KFC, La Tolteca, McDonald's, Mighty Taco, Moe's SW Grill, Old Country Buffet, Olive Garden, Panera Bread, Picasso's Pizza, Pita Gourmet, Pizza Hut, Pizza Plant, Pomegranate, Protocol Rest., Quaker Steak&Lube, Red Lobster, Russel's Steaks, Salsarita's, Santora's Pizza, Shogun, Starbucks, Starbucks, Subway, Taco Bell, Ted's HotDogs, TGIFriday's, Tim Horton, Tully's Rest., Wendy's Clarion, Econolodge, Microtel, Motel 6, Salvatore's Hotel, Springhill Suites, Staybridge Suites, Super 8 $Tree, Acura, Advance Parts, Aldi Foods, AT&T, AutoZone, Barnes&Noble, Best Buy, BigLots, BJ's Whse/gas, BonTon, Buick/GMC, Chevrolet, Chrysler/Dodge/Jeep, Dick's, Dunn Tire, Firestone/auto, Ford, Goodyear/auto, Hobby Lobby, Home Depot, Honda, Hyundai, JC Penney, Jo-Ann Fabrics, Kohl's, Lowe's, Macy's, mall, Marshall's, Mavis Tire, Michael's, Office Depot, PetCo, PetsMart, Rite Aid, Sears/auto, SteinMart, Target, TJ Maxx, Top's Food/deli, Tuesday Morning, Verizon, vet, Walgreens, Walmart/Subway, Wegman's Foods, S Kwikfill, Mobil/dsl Bob Evans, China 1, Dunkin Donuts, Italian Village, John&Mary's Cafe, McDonald's, Salvatore's Italian, Subway, Tim Horton Garden Place Hotel, Hospitality Inn, La Quinta, Red Roof Inn $Tree, 7-11, Aamco, CarQuest, Top's Foods/gas
419mm	**toll booth**
50 (420)	I-290 to Niagara Falls
50a (421)	Cleveland Dr (from eb)
51 (422)	NY 33 E, Buffalo, S , st police
52 (423)	Walden Ave, to Buffalo, N Applebees, Burger King, Chipotle, Famous Dave's BBQ, IHOP, McDonald's, Ruby Tuesday, Starbucks, Subway, TGIFriday's, Tim Horton Hampton Inn, Holiday Inn Express, Residence Inn $Tree, Aldi Foods, AT&T, AutoZone, Firestone/auto, Ford, Goodyear/auto, Home Depot, Michael's, Office Depot, PetsMart, PriceRite Mkt, Target, Top's Foods, Walmart/Subway, S Delta Sonic, Jim's Trk Plaza/Sunoco/dsl/rest./scales/24hr, KwikFill Alton's Rest., Bar Louie's, Bravo Italiano, Cheesecake Factory, Dunkin Donuts, Gordon Biersch arrest., Jack Astor's Grill, Longhorn Steaks, McDonald's, Melting Pot, Mighty Taco, Milton's Rest., Olive Garden, Panera Bread, PF Chang's, Pizza Hut, Smokey Bones BBQ, Taco Bell, Texas de Brazil Steaks, Tim Horton, Zahng's Buffet Home 2 Suites, Millenium Hotel, Oak Tree Inn Best Buy, Burlington Coats, Cabela's, Dick's, Dunn Tire, JC Penney, K-Mart, Lord&Taylor, Macy's, mall, Marshall's, Mavis Tire, Niagara Hobby, Sam's Club, Sears/auto, Verizon

BUFFALO

NY

= gas = food = lodging = other = rest stop

NY

HAMBURG

INTERSTATE 90 Cont'd

Exit #	Services
52a (424)	William St
53 (425)	I-190, to Buffalo, Niagara Falls, N Best Western
54 (428)	NY 400, NY 16, to W Seneca, E Aurora
55 (430)	US 219, Ridge Rd, Orchard Park, S Delta Sonic, Sunoco Denny's, Ferro's NY Puzza, Mighty Taco, Subway, Tim Horton, Wendy's Country Inn&Suites, Hampton Inn, Staybridge Suites $General, Aldi Foods, AT&T, BigLots, Goodyear/auto, Home Depot, K-Mart, Mr Tire, Pepboys, Petco, Tops Foods/gas, Verizon, Wegman's Foods
431mm	toll booth
56 (432)	NY 179, Mile Strip Rd, N Gulf/dsl, Sunoco, Valero Blasdell Pizza, China King, DiPallo's Rest., Odyssey Rest., Whse Rest. EconoLodge $General, CarQuest, CVS Drug, repair, Rite Aid, SaveALot Foods, USPO, S Applebee's, Boston Mkt, Buffalo Wild Wings, Chipotle, ChuckeCheese, El Canelo Mexican, Firehouse Subs, Five Guys, Friendly's, McDonald's, Mongolian Buffet, Olive Garden, Outback Steaks, Panera Bread, Pizza Hut, Red Lobster, Ruby Tuesday, Starbucks, Subway, TGIFriday's, Wendy's $Tree, Aldi Foods, Barnes&Noble, Best Buy, BJ's Whse, BonTon, Firestone/auto, Hobby Lobby, Home Depot, JC Penney, Jo-Ann Etc, Macy's, mall, Old Navy, PepBoys, Sears, TJ Maxx, Wegman's Foods
57 (436)	NY 75, to Hamburg, N Mobil/Dunkin Donuts/dsl Arby's, Blasdell Pizza, Buffalo Grill, Denny's, McDonald's, Tim Horton, Uncle Joe's Diner, Waterstone Grill, Wendy's Comfort Inn, Holiday Inn Express, Motel 6, Red Roof Inn Ballentyne's RV Ctr, Chevrolet, Chrysler/Dodge/Jeep, Ford, Lowe's, repair, transmissions, Walmart, S Go Gas, Kwikfill/dsl, Mad J's Burger King, Hideaways Rest., Pizza Hut, Savory Cafe, Subway, Tim Horton Quality Inn, Super 8 $General, Advance Parts, AutoZone, Camping World, Carquest, Goodyear/auto, USPO, vet
442mm	**parking area both lanes, litter barrels**
57a (445)	to Eden, Angola, **2 mi** N Sunoco/dsl
447mm	**Angola Service Area both lanes,** Sunoco/dsl McDonald's, Moe's SW Grill, Subway atm, gifts, wi-fi
58 (456)	US 20, NY 5, to Silver Creek, Irving, N Kwikfill, Seneca Hawk Trkstp/dsl Burger King, Colony Rest., Dunkin Donuts, McDonald's, Millie's Rest., Primo's Rest., Subway, Sunset Bay, Sunset Grill, Tim Hortons, Tom's Rest. Lighthouse Inn H, auto repair, to Evangola SP, USPO
59 (468)	NY 60, Fredonia, Dunkirk, N Clarion (2mi), Dunkirk Motel (4mi) Lake Erie SP/camping (7mi), S Country Fair/dsl, Kwikfill/dsl Applebee's, Arby's, Azteca Cantina, Bob Evans, Burger King, Denny's, Dunkin Donuts, KFC/Taco Bell, Little Caesar's, McDonald's, Pizza Hut, Subway, Tim Hortons, Wendy's, Wing City Grille Best Western, Comfort Inn, Days Inn $General, $Tree, Advance Parts, Aldi Foods, AT&T, AutoZone, BigLots, Ford/Lincoln, GMC, GNC, Home Depot, Midas, Monroe, Radio Shack, Rite Aid, TJ Maxx, Tops Foods/gas, Verizon, Walmart/Subway
60 (485)	NY 394, Westfield, N Brookside Beach Camping, KOA, to Lake Erie SP/camping, S Holiday Motel, Webb's Motel H
494mm	toll booth
61 (495)	Shortman Rd, to Ripley, N Lakeshore RV Park
496mm	New York/Pennsylvania state line

INTERSTATE 95

Exit #	Services
32mm	New York/Connecticut state line

NYC AREA

22 (30)	Midland Ave (from nb), Port Chester, Rye, W Subway H, Home Depot, Staples
21 (29)	I-287 W, US 1 N, to White Plains, Port Chester, Tappan Zee
20 (28)	US 1 S (from nb), Port Chester, E Shell CVS Drug, Ford, Subaru, USPO
19 (27)	Playland Pkwy, Rye, Harrison
18b (25)	Mamaroneck Ave, to White Plains, E Hess, Shell Domino's A&P Foods, Mavis Tire
18a (24)	Fenimore Rd (from nb), Mamaroneck, E Citgo, Gulf
17 (20)	Chatsworth Ave (from nb, no return), Larchmont
19.5mm	**toll plaza**
16 (19)	North Ave, Cedar St, New Rochelle, E Applebee's, Buffalo Wild Wings, TX Roadhouse Radisson, Residence Inn ShopRite, Toyota, USPO, W H
15 (16)	US 1, New Rochelle, The Pelhams, E GasTrack/dsl, SuperGas AutoZone, Costco/gas, CVS Drug, Harley-Davidson, Home Depot, Walgreens, W repair
14 (15)	Hutchinson Pkwy (from sb), to Whitestone Br
13 (16)	Conner St, to Mt Vernon, E Gulf/dsl Ramada Inn, W BP McDonald's Holiday Motel H, Goodyear/auto, Pepboys
12 (15.5)	Baychester Ave (exits left from nb)
11 (15)	Bartow Ave, Co-op City Blvd, E Applebee's, Bartow Pizza, Burger King, Checker's, Dallas BBQ, Genarro's Pizza, McDonald's, Panera Bread, Popeye's, Red Lobster, Zinhi Chinese $Tree, AT&T, Barnes&Noble, JC Penney, K-Mart, Marshall's, Old Navy, PathMark Foods, Staples, Verizon, W BP/Dunkin Donuts, Sunoco/dsl, Wave/dsl ChuckeCheese, Dunkin Donuts, Pizza Hut, TGIFriday's Aldi Foods, Home Depot
10 (14.5)	Gun Hill Rd (exits left from nb), W Pelham Bay Hotel/diner
9 (14)	Hutchinson Pkwy
8c (13.5)	Pelham Pkwy W
8b (13)	Orchard Beach, City Island
8a (12.5)	Westchester Ave (from sb)
7c (12)	Pelham Bay Park (from nb), Country Club Rd
7b (11.5)	E Tremont (from sb), W Super FoodTown
7a (11)	I-695 (from sb), to I-295 S, Throgs Neck Br
6b (10.5)	I-278 W (from sb), I-295 S (from nb)
6a (10)	I-678 S, Whitestone Bridge
5b (9)	Castle Hill Ave, W Sunoco McDonald's
5a (8.5)	Westchester Ave, White Plains Rd
4b (8)	Bronx River Pkwy, Rosedale Ave, E BP
4a (7)	I-895 S, Sheridan Expsy
3 (6)	3rd Ave, W H
2b (5)	Webster Ave, W H
2a (4)	Jerome Ave, to I-87
1c (3)	I-87, Deegan Expswy, to Upstate
1b (2)	Harlem River Dr
1a (1)	US 9, NY 9A, H Hudson Pkwy, 178th St, downtown
0mm	New York/New Jersey state line, Hudson River, Geo Washington Br

INTERSTATE 190 (BUFFALO)

Exit #	Services
25.5mm	US/Canada Border, US Customs
25b a	R Moses Pkwy, NY 104, NY 265, Lewiston, E H
24	NY 31, Witmer Rd, E H, st police
23	NY 182, Porter Rd, Packard Rd, E Sunoco/dsl Applebees, Buffalo Wild Wings, Burger King, Chili's, Chipotle, DQ, Five Guys, Longhorn Steaks, Mighty Taco, Olive Garden, Subway, Tim Horton $Tree, Big Lots, CarQuest, Chrysler/Dodge/Jeep, Fashion Outlets/famous brands, Firestone/auto,

NIAGARA FALLS

INTERSTATE 190 (BUFFALO) Cont'd

23	Continued Goodyear/Auto, Hobby Lobby, Jo-Ann Fabrics, K-Mart, Marshall's, Mavis Tire, Mr Tire, NAPA, Petco, Sam's Club/gas, U-Haul, Verizon, Walmart/Subway, Wegman's, **W** [food] Wendy's [other] Aldi Foods
22	US 62, Niagara Falls Blvd, **E** [gas] Sunoco [food] Arby's, Bob Evans, Burger King, Denny's, Dunkin Donuts, Honey's Eatery, KFC, McDonald's, My Thai, Pizza Hut, Popeye's, Starbucks, Subway, Taco Bell, Wendy's [lodging] Beat Value Inn, Budget Host, Caravan Motel, Hampton Inn, Pelican Motel, Quality Inn, Red Carpet Inn, Super 8, Swiss Cottage Inn [other] $Tree, Advance Parts, AT&T, Dunn Tire, Ford, Rite Aid, Target, TJ Maxx, Top's Foods/gas, Walgreens, **W** [lodging] Econolodge, La Quinta [other] Home Depot
21a	La Salle Expswy
21	NY 384, Buffalo Ave, R Moses Pkwy, **E** [lodging] Ashram Hotel, Sheraton, **W** [gas] Gulf [other] American Falls, casino, to NF SP
20.5mm	Niagara River East, **toll booth sb**
20b a	Long Rd, **E** [lodging] Budget Motel [other] Kelly's Country Store
19	Whitehaven Rd, **E** [gas] Gulf/dsl, Noco Gas [food] McDonald's [lodging] Chateu Motel (2mi), Holiday Inn (4mi) [other] $Tree, funpark, KOA (1mi), Top's Foods/gas, **W** [other] Chevrolet, Hyundai, Toyota/Scion, vet
18b a	NY 324 W, Grand Island Blvd, **E** [gas] Gulf/dsl, NOCO/dsl, Sunoco/dsl [food] Burger King, McDonald's, Tim Horton, Wendy's [lodging] Chateu Motel, Grand Suites [other] $Tree, Advance Parts, Tops/gas, **W** [other] Beaver Island SP
17.5mm	Niagara River East, Niagara River East, **toll booth**
17	NY 266, last free exit nb
16	I-290 E, to I-90, Albany
15	NY 324, Kenmore Ave, **E** [gas] 7-11 [other] city park, **W** [other] U-Haul
14	Ontario St, **E** [gas] KwikFill [food] McDonald's, Tim Horton [other] Advance Parts, Family$
13	(from nb), same as 14
12	Amherst St, (from nb), downtown
11	NY 198, Buffalo, **E** [gas] First Line
9	Porter Ave, to Peace Bridge, Ft Erie
8	NY 266, Niagara St, **E** [lodging] Adams Mark Hotel, **W** [lodging] Courtyard, downtown
7	NY 5 W, Church St, Buffalo, downtown
6	Elm St, **E** [other] [H], downtown, **W** [other] Arena
5	Louisiana St, Buffalo, downtown
4	Smith St, Fillmore Ave, Buffalo, downtown
3	NY 16, Seneca St, from sb, **W** [other] CarQuest
2	US 62, NY 354, Bailey Ave, Clinton St
1	Ogden St, **E** [gas] Sunoco [food] Wendy's [lodging] Best Western, Comfort Inn [other] Big Lots, CVS Drug, Family$
0.5mm	**toll plaza nb**
0mm	I-90. **I-190 begins/ends on I-90, exit 53.**

BUFFALO

INTERSTATE 287 (NEW YORK CITY)

NYC AREA

Exit #	Services
12	I-95, N to New Haven, S to NYC. **I-287 begins/ends on I-95, exit 21.**
11	US 1, Port Chester, Rye, **N** [gas] BP, Mobil, Sunoco [food] Burger King, Domino's, Dunkin Donuts, KFC, McDonald's, Port Chester Diner, Subway, Wendy's [other] [H], Goodyear/auto, Kohl's, Mavis Discount Tire, Nissan, Petsmart, Staples, Verizon
10	Bowman Ave, Webb Ave
9N S	Hutchinson Pkwy, Merritt Pkwy, to Whitestone Br
9a	I-684, Brewster

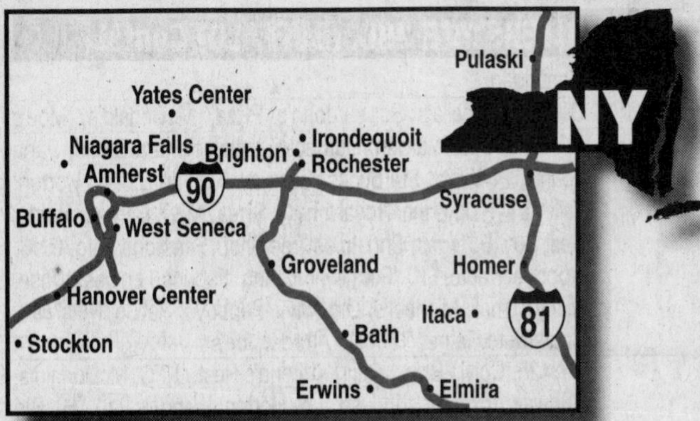

8	Westchester Ave, to White Plains, **S** [gas] BP, Cheesecake Factory, Mobil, Morton's Steaks, PF Chang's, Westchester Burger Co, White Plains Diner [other] Chrysler/Dodge/Jeep, Hyundai, Neiman Marcus, Nordstrom, Stop&Shop Foods, Westchester Mall Place, Whole Foods Mkt
7	Taconic Pkwy (from wb), to N White Plains
6	NY 22, White Plains
5	NY 100, Hillside Ave, **S** [gas] Citgo, Gulf, Lukoil [food] Applebee's, Dunkin Donuts, Papa John's, Planet Pizza, Subway [other] Aamco, AutoZone, Barnes&Noble, GNC, K-Mart, Lexus, Mazda, Radio Shack, vet
4	NY 100A, Hartsdale, **N** [gas] Shell [other] [H], **S** [food] Bamboo Garden Chinese, Burger King [other] BMW/Mini, Jaguar, Staples, Volvo
3	Sprain Pkwy, to Taconic Pkwy, NYC
2	NY 9A, Elmsford, **N** [gas] BP, Citgo, Mobil, Sunoco [food] Dunkin Donuts, KFC/Taco Bell, Subway [other] Mavis Discount Tire, NAPA, Sam's Club, **S** [gas] Shell [food] Wendy's
1	NY 119, Tarrytown, **N** [gas] Gulf/dsl [food] Ruth's Chris Steaks [lodging] Marriott, Sheraton, **S** [gas] Gulf/dsl [food] El Dorado Diner [lodging] Extended Stay America, Hampton Inn
0	**I-287 runs with I-87 N.**

NY

INTERSTATE 290 (BUFFALO)

BUFFALO

Exit #	Services
8	I-90, NY Thruway, **I-290 begins/ends on I-90, exit 50.**
7b a	NY 5, Main St, **N** [gas] Mobil/dsl, Sunoco [food] Coldstone, Dunkin Donuts, La Nova Pizza/Wings, McDonald's, Panera Bread, Subway, Tim Horton, Wendy's [lodging] Hampton Inn, Wyndham Garden [other] Tops Foods, Walgreens, **S** [gas] Valero [lodging] Hyatt Place
6	NY 324, NY 240, **N** [gas] Gulf/dsl [lodging] Courtyard [other] Cadillac, **S** [gas] Gas Stop [food] China Star, ChuckeCheese, Domino's, McDonald'd, Sheridan Rest., Subway [other] 7-11, Aamco, CVS Drug, Fiat, Hyundai/Subaru, KIA/Mazda, Lexus, Nissan, URGNT CARE, Walgreens
5b a	NY 263, to Millersport, **N** [gas] Gulf [food] Santora's Pizza, Zetti's Pizza [lodging] Candlewood Suites, Comfort Inn, DoubleTree, Marriott, Red Roof Inn, **S** [gas] Mobil [lodging] Homewood Suites [other] Scion/Toyota, VW, Walgreens
4	I-990, to St U
3b a	US 62, to Niagara Falls Blvd, **N** [gas] Mobil/7-11, Sunoco, Valero [food] Anderson's Rest., Blvd Grill, Bob Evans, Dunkin Donuts, Just Pizza, Pancake House, Roadhouse Grill, Ted's Hot Dogs [lodging] Econolodge, Extended Stay America, Holiday Inn, Knight's Inn, Red Carpet Inn, Rodeway Inn, Sleep Inn [other] Chrysler/Dodge/Jeep, Home Depot, Honda, John&Mary's Rest., NAPA, Rite Aid, URGENT CARE, vet, **S** [gas] Delta Sonic, Sunoco/dsl [food] Applebee's, Arby's, BoneFish Grill, Buffalo Wild Wings, Burger King, Carrabba's, Chili's, Chipotle, Corner Bakery Cafe,

INTERSTATE 290 (BUFFALO) Cont'd

3b a Continued
Denny's, Dibella's Subs, John's Pizza, McDonald's, Moe's SW Grill, Olive Garden, Outback Steaks, Panera Bread, Papa John's, Pl Pizza, Starbucks, Subway, TGIFriday, Tim Horton, Tulley's [lodging] Days Inn, Royal Inn [other] $Tree, AT&T, Barnes&Noble, Best Buy, BJ's/gas, Christmas Tree Shop, Firestone/auto, GNC, Goodyear/auto, JC Penney, Jo-Ann Fabrics, Lowes Whse, Macy's, mall, Michael's, Old Navy, Pepboys, PetCo, PetsMart, Sears/auto, Target, TJ Maxx, Trader Joe's

2 NY 425, Colvin Blvd, **N** [food] Athena's Rest., KFC, McDonald's, Subway, Texas Roadhouse, Tim Horton, Wendy's [other] [H], Big Lots, Family$, Gander Mtn, Top's Foods/gas, **S** [gas] KwikFill [food] Dunkin Donuts [other] Pepboys

1b a Elmwood Ave, NY 384, NY 265, **N** [gas] KwikFill [food] Franco's Pizza, John's Pizza/Subs, Subway, Touch of Italy [lodging] Center Way Motel [other] [H], $Tree, auto repair, Rite Aid, **S** [gas] Sunoco/dsl [food] Arby's

0mm I-190. **I-290 begins/ends on I-190 in Buffalo.**

INTERSTATE 390 (ROCHESTER)

ROCHESTER

Exit # Services

20b a I-490. **I-390 begins/ends on I-490 in Rochester**

18b a NY 204, Brooks Ave, **N** [lodging] Holiday Inn, **S** [lodging] Fairfield Inn [other] [airport]

19 (75) NY 33a, Chili Ave, **N** [food] Wishing Well Rest., **S** [gas] Sunoco [food] Burger King, Pizza Hut, Subway [lodging] Motel 6, Quality Inn [other] $General

17 (73) NY 383, Scottsville Rd, **S** [gas] Sunoco/Subway/dsl

16 (71) NY 15a, to E Henryetta, **S** [food] Basil's Rest [lodging] Courtyard, Hampton Inn [other] [H]

15 (70) I-590, Rochester

14 (68) NY 15a, NY 252, **E** [food] Domino's, Gray's Cafe, McDonald's, Outback Steaks, Papa John's, Perkins, Tully's Rest. [lodging] Extended Stay America [other] Staples, **W** [gas] Mobil/dsl [food] Boston Mkt, Dunkin Donuts, Starbucks, Subway, Taco Bell [lodging] Best Western, DoubleTree Inn [other] Big Lots, Office Depot, Radio Shack, Top's Foods

13 (67) Hylan Dr, **E** [food] Cracker Barrel [lodging] Comfort Suites, Homewood Suites, **W** [gas] Mobil/dsl [food] Bonton, ChuckECheese, IHOP, McDonald's, Olive Garden, Panera Bread, Tim Hortons, Uno Grill, Wendy's [other] Aldi Foods, Best Buy, BJ's Whse, Gander Mtn, Goodyear/auto, JC Penney, Lowe's, Macy's, Michael's, Old Navy, PepBoys, PetCo, Sam's Club/gas, Sears, Target, Walmart, Wegman's Foods

12 (66) I-90. NY Thruway, NY 253, **W** [gas] Gulf/dsl/scales, Hess, Sunoco/dsl [food] Lehigh Rest, McDonald's, Peppermint's Rest., Tim Hortons, Wendy's [lodging] Country Inn&Suites, Days Inn, Fairfield Inn, Microtel, Red Carpet Inn, Red Roof Inn, Super 8 [other] Buick/GMC

11 (62) NY 15, NY 251, Rush, Scottsville, **2 mi N** [food] McDonald's, Tim Hortons, Wendy's [lodging] Days Inn, Fairfield Inn, Red Roof Inn, RIT Inn

10 (55) US 20, NY 5, Avon, Lima, **N** [gas] Exxon [food] Countryside Diner [lodging] CrestHill Inn, Stratford Inn, **3 mi S** [gas] Sugar Creek/dsl [food] Avon Cafe, Dutch Hollow Cafe, McDonald's, Subway, Tom Wahls Cafe [lodging] Avon Cedar Lodge [other] Chrysler/Dodge/Jeep, Ford, Sugar Creek Camping

9mm scenic area wb

9 (52) NY 15, **N** [gas] Mobil/Dunkin Donuts/dsl [food] Fratelli's Rest., Lakeville Rest., McDonald's, Tee&Gee Cafe [lodging] Conesus Motel [other] Chevrolet

8 (48) US 20a, Geneseo, **N** [lodging] Oak Valley Inn [other] Conesus Lake Camp ing, **S** [food] Denny's, Dunkin Donuts, KFC/Taco Bell, McDonald's, Wendy's [lodging] Quality Inn

7 (39) NY 63, NY 408, Geneseo, **S** [gas] KwikFill, Mobil, Sunoco/dsl [food] Brian's Diner, McDonald's [lodging] Alligence B&B, Country Inn&Suites, Geneseo River Hotel/Rest., Greenway Motel [other] Bonadonna Auto, Family$, Letchworth SP, NAPA, Ridge Camping, Rite Aid, Save-A-Lot Foods, st police

38mm [rest stop] **both lanes, full [handicapped] facilities, litter barrels, petwalk [picnic] vending**

6 (33) NY 36, Mt Morris, Sonyea

5 (26) NY 36, Dansville, **N** [gas] KwikFill, Mobil/Subway [food] Arby's, Burger King, Dunkin Donuts, McDonald's, Pizza Hut, Subway [other] $Tree, Advance Parts, BigLots, Chevrolet, Chrysler/Dodge/Jeep, CVS Drug, Radio Shack, Rite Aid, Save-A-Lot Foods, Top's Foods/gas, Verizon, **S** [gas] TA/Valero/Country Pride/dsl/scales/24hr/ @ [lodging] TA Motel

4 (23) NY 36, Dansville, **N** [gas] Sunoco/dsl [lodging] Logan's Inn [other] [H], vet, **S** [other] Skybrook Camping, Stonybrook Park Camping, Sugar Creek Camping, Sunvalley Camping

3 (17) NY 15, NY 21, Wayland, **N** [food] Farmer's Kitchen Rest. (1mi) [other] CarQuest (1mi), Holiday Hill Campground (7mi), st patrol

2 (11) NY 415, Cohocton, Naples, **N** [gas] Mobil (2mi) [other] Tumble Hill Camping (3mi)

1 (2) NY 415, Avoca, **N** [other] truck/auto repair, USPO (2mi), **S** [gas] Mobil [lodging] Caboose Motel (3mi)

INTERSTATE 495 (LONG ISLAND)

RIVERHEAD

Exit # Services

I-495 begins/ends on NY 25.

73 Rd 58, Old Country Road, to Greenport, Orient, **0-2 mi S** [gas] Gulf, Hess/dsl, Lukoil/7-11, Mobil/dsl [food] Applebees, Boulder Creek Steaks, Panera Bread, Taco Bell, TGIFridays, Wendy's [lodging] Hilton Garden, Holiday Inn Express [other] AutoZone, Best Buy, Buick/GMC, Chevrolet, Chrysler/Jeep, Costco/gas, Curves, CVS Drug, Ford/Lincoln, Harley-Davidson, Home Depot, Honda, Kia/Mazda, Lowe's, Michael's, Nissan/Hyundai, PetCo, Stop&Shop, Subaru/VW, Tanger/famous brands, Target, Toyota/Scion, Volvo, Waldbaum's, Walgreens

72 NY 25, (no ez eb return), Riverhead, Calverton (no EZ eb return), **N** [other] funpark, **S** [gas] Hess [lodging] Hotel Indigo [other] Tanger/famous brands/foodcourt

71 NY 24, to Hampton Bays (no ez eb return), Calverton, **N** [gas] Hess/Subway/dsl

70 NY 111, to Eastport, Manorville, **S** [gas] 7-11, Mobil/dsl [food] McDonald's, Michelangelo's Rest., Starbucks [other] King Kullen Food/drug, Verizon

69 Wading River Rd, Center Moriches, to Wading River

68 NY 46, to Shirley, Wading River, **S** [other] 7-11, golf

67 Yaphank Ave

66 NY 101, Sills Rd, Yaphank, **N** [gas] Shell/24hr

65.5mm **parking area**

MEDFORD

65 Horse Block Rd, **N** [food] Baskin-Robbins/Dunkin Donuts, Kings Buffet [other] Ford/Kenworth/Mack, LI RV Ctr, **S** [other] funpark

64 NY 112, to Coram, Medford, **N** [gas] Citgo/dsl, Hess [food] Subway [other] 7-11, Lowe's, Michael's, Radio Shack, Sam's Club, Staples, Target, Walgreens, **S** [gas] BP, Gulf, USA/dsl [food] J&R Steaks, Quiznos, Rita's Custard, Starbucks [lodging] Comfort Inn, Fairfield Inn [other] 7-11, Aid Parts

63 NY 83, N Ocean Ave, **N** [gas] Hess/dsl [food] Applebee's, Burger King, McDonald's, Taco Bell, TGIFriday's [other] 7-11, CVS Drug,

NY

INTERSTATE 495 (LONG ISLAND) Cont'd

	Hampton Inn, K-Mart, Stop'n Shop, S Gulf/dsl, Lukoil/dsl Yogi's Grill Crowne Plaza
62	Nicolls Rd, Rd 97, to Blue Point, Stony Brook, N Gulf, S Charlie Brown's Steaks, Chili's, La Capannina Italian, Wendy's Residence Inn
61	Rd 19, to Patchogue, Holbrook, N Mobil, S Gulf/dsl, Hess/dsl China 4, Greek Islands Rest, Joe's Pizza/Pasta, Outback Steaks, Subway 7-11, CVS Drug, Waldbaums Foods
60	Ronkonkoma Ave, N Gulf, S Red Lobster, Smokey Bones BBQ Courtyard
59	Ocean Ave, to Oakdale, Ronkonkoma, S Gulf, Sunoco Hilton Garden (2mi) 7-11
58	Old Nichols Rd, Nesconset, N Gulf Hooters Marriott BJ's Whse, S BP
57	NY 454, Vets Hwy, to Hauppauge, N Exxon/dsl TGIFriday's, S Getty's, Gulf/dsl, Shell, Sunoco Dave&Buster's, Subway Hampton Inn 7-11, Radio Shack, Rite Aid, Stop&Shop Foods, TJ Maxx, Walmart
56	NY 111, Smithtown, Islip, N Gulf/Subway/Domino's/dsl, Mobil, S Mobil Café La Strada Holiday Inn Express
55	Central Islip, N Mobil, S Exxon/dsl
54	Wicks Rd, N BP Sheraton, S Mobil
53	Sunken Meadow Pkwy, to ocean beaches, Bayshore
52	Rd 4, Commack, N Mobil/dsl, Shell/repair Conca d'Oro Pizza, Ground Round Hampton Inn Costco
51.5mm	**parking area both lanes, litter barrels**
51	NY 231, to Northport, Babylon
50	Bagatelle Rd, to Wyandanch
49N	NY 110 N, to Huntington, N Marriott
49S	NY 110 S, to Amityville
48	Round Swamp Rd, Old Bethpage, S Mobil/dsl Old Country Pizza/deli Homewood Suites, Palace Hotel, Sheraton USPO
46	Sunnyside Blvd, Plainview, N Holiday Inn
45	Manetto Hill Rd, Plainview, Woodbury
44	NY 135, to Seaford, Syosset
43	S Oyster Bay Rd, to Syosset, Bethpage, N Mobil
42	Northern Pkwy, Rd N, Hauppauge
41	NY 106, NY 107, Hicksville, Oyster Bay, S BP, Mobil, Sunoco Boston Mkt, Boulder Creek Steaks, Broadway Diner, Burger King, Dunkin Donuts, McDonald's, On the Border Goodyear/auto, Sears/auto
40	NY 25, Mineola, Syosset, S BP, Exxon, Hess/dsl, Shell A&W, Burger King, Friendly's, IHOP, McDonald's, Wendy's Howard Johnson 7-11, Home Depot, Kohl's, Staples
39	Glen Cove Rd, N Mobil
38	Northern Pkwy E, Meadowbrook Pkwy, to Jones Beach

HICKSVILLE

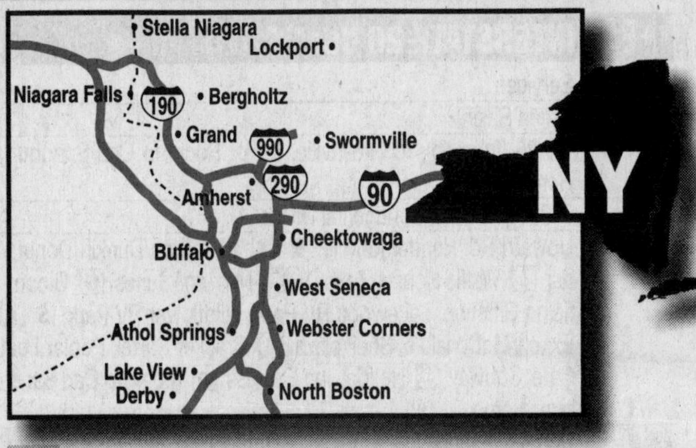

37	Willis Ave, to Roslyn, Mineola, N Gulf, Shell Dunkin Donuts, Skinny Pizza, S Mobil/dsl Tofu Chinese
36	Searingtown Rd, to Port Washington, S H
35	Shelter Rock Rd, Manhasset, S H
34	New Hyde Park Rd
33	Lakeville Rd, to Great Neck, N H
32	Little Neck Pkwy, N Gulf Centre Pizza, Jain Rest., KFC/Taco Bell, Panera Bread, Starbucks
31	Douglaston Pkwy, S BP/service Burger King, Grimaldi's Pizza, Pinecourt Chinese, Subway DR Drug, Macy's, USPO, Verizon, Waldbaum's Foods
30	E Hampton Blvd, Cross Island Pkwy
29	Springfield Blvd, S Citgo, Gulf/Dunkin Donuts McDonald's
27	I-295, Clearview Expswy, Throgs Neck, N 7-11, Gulf Blue Bay Diner drugstore
26	Francis Lewis Blvd
25	Utopia Pkwy, 188th St, N Citgo, Gulf, S Mobil, Quality/dsl, Savvy, Shell 5 Guys Burgers, Arby's, Baskin-Robbins, Dunkin Donuts, Subway Radio Shack, USPO
24	Kissena Blvd, N Gulf/dsl Baskin-Robbins, Dunkin Donuts, S Mobil
23	Main St, N Palace Diner
22	Grand Central Pkwy, to I-678, College Pt Blvd, N Holiday Inn Express
21	108th St, N BP/7-11, Mobil
19	NY 25, Queens Blvd, Woodhaven Blvd, to Rockaways, N McDonald's JC Penney, Macy's, mall, S BP 5 Guys Burgers, Applebees, Burger King, Dallas BBQ, Moe's SW Grill, Subway Aldi Foods, Costco, Kohl's, Marshall's, Old Navy, Rite Aid, Sears, TJ Maxx
18.5	69th Ave, Grand Ave (from wb)
18	Maurice St, N Exxon, S BP McDonald's Holiday Inn Express dsl repair
17	48th St, to I-278, N Queensboro Hotel
16	**I-495 begins/ends in NYC.**

NY
NC

NORTH CAROLINA

INTERSTATE 26

Exit #	Services
71mm	North Carolina/South Carolina state line
69mm	N Pacolet River
67.5mm	**Welcome Ctr wb full facilities, litter barrels vending**
67	US 74 E, to NC 108, Columbus, Tryon, N Shell//dsl, Vgo/dsl Cocula Mexican, Joy Wok, Larkin's Carolina Grill,
67	Continued Mc Donald's, Subway, Waffle House, Wendy's Advance Parts, CVS Drug, Family$, Food Lion, S Exxon/dsl KFC/Taco Bell, Mtn View Deli Days Inn H, $General, Bi-Lo
59	Saluda, N Saluda Mtn Lodge, S BP/dsl, Marathon/Subway/dsl Crust&Kettle Cafe, Saluda Rest. Orchard Inn B&B (2mi) $General, AppleMill Outlet, Atkins Fruit, camping, repair, vet

INTERSTATE 26 Cont'd

Exit #	Services
56mm	Green River
54	US 25 (from eb), to Greenville, E Flat Rock, to Carl Sandburg Home
53.5mm	2130 ft, Eastern Continental Divide
53	Upward Rd, Hendersonville, N Marathon/Dunkin Donuts/dsl Waffle House, Zaxby's Mtn Inn&Suites Bloomfields Giftshop, Lakewood RV Park, Wildflower RV Park, S Exxon/McDonald's, Shell/pizza Cracker Barrel, Poplar Leaf Cafe, Subway Holiday Inn Express repair, to Carl Sandburg Home
49b a	US 64, Hendersonville, N Marathon/dsl, Shell/dsl, Sunoco/dsl Chick-fil-A, Golden Corral, Jack-in-the-Box, Moose Cafe, O'Charley's, Sonic, Starbucks, Waffle House, Zaxby's Best Western, Hampton Inn, Quality Inn, Ramada Inn $Tree, Advance Parts, Ingles/gas, PetCo, Radio Shack, Sam's Club/gas, Staples, Walmart, World of Clothing, S Exxon/dsl/LP, Shell/dsl Applebee's, Arby's, Binion's Roadhouse, Bojangles, Burger King, China Buffet, Denny's, Fatz Café, Hardee's, Harry's Rest., HoneyBaked Ham, KFC, Krispy Kreme, LJ Silver, Lon Sen Chinese, McDonald's, Outback Steaks, Pizza Hut, Subway, Taco Bell, Tequila's Grill, Wendy's Days Inn, EconoLodge, Red Roof Inn H, Aldi Foods, Belk, BigLots, Bi-Lo Foods, Chrysler/Dodge/Jeep, Clark Tire/auto, CVS Drug, Family$, Home Depot, JC Penney, Jo-Ann, Lowe's, NAPA, TJ Maxx, Tuesday Morning, Verizon
46mm	**weigh sta both lanes**
44	US 25, Fletcher, N Exxon/dsl Hardee's, Subway flea mkt/campground, vet, S Citgo/dsl, Shell/DQ/dsl/scales/24hr, Sonny's/dsl Bojangles, Burger King, McDonald's, Valentina's Mexican Mountain Inn&Suites H, Camping World RV Ctr, USPO
41mm	**both lanes, full facilities, litter barrels vending**
40	NC 280, Arden, N Fastop/dsl, Shell/Arby's Bojangles, Carrabba's, Casa Torres, Chili's, Cracker Barrel, Firehouse Subs, IHOP, Jersey Mike's, Little Caesar's, Lonestar Steaks, McDonald's, Moe's SW Grill, Olive Garden, Ruby Tuesday, Sonic, Tamarind Thai, Tokyo Express Budget Motel, Clarion, Comfort Inn, Courtyard, EconoLodge, Hampton Inn, Knight's Inn Acura/Honda, Aldi Foods, Best Buy, BigLots, Dick's, Lowe's, Marshalls, Michael's, Old Navy, Petsmart, Ross, Rutledge Lake RV Park, Target, World Mkt, S Citgo/dsl Circle B Ranch BBQ, J&S Cafeteria Fairfield Inn Asheville Airport, BMW
37	NC 146, Skyland, N BP Arby's, Brixx Pizza, Broken Egg Cafe, Coldstone, Hickory Tavern, McDonald's, Neo Burrito, PF Changs, Starbucks, Waffle House, Which Wich Hilton, Quality Inn Barnes&Noble, CVS Drug, Ingles/gas, REI, S Chevrolet
34mm	French Broad River
33	NC 191, Brevard Rd, **2 mi** N Asheville Farmers Mkt, Bear Creek RV Camp, Toyota/Scion, S Citgo, HotSpot/dsl Apollo Flame, Harbor Inn Seafood, LJ Silver, McDonald's, Papa's Mexican, Ryan's, Shogun Buffet, Stoneridge Grill, Subway, Taco Bell, Waffle House Comfort Suites, Country Inn&Suites, Fairfield Inn, Hampton Inn, Holiday Inn Express, Rodeway Inn $Tree, Asheville Outlets, Belk, Dillards, Ingles Foods, Kia, K-Mart/Little Caesar's, PetCo, to Blue Ridge Pkwy
31b a	I-40, E to Statesville, W to Knoxville
27mm	I-240 E, Patton Ave

I-26 and I-240 run together 3 mi. See NC I-240 exits 1-4

Exit #	Services
25	Rd 251, N to UNCA
24	Elk Mtn Rd, Woodfin
23	Merrimon Ave, N Asheville, N Gulf/dsl, HotSpot Bellagio Bistro, Frank's Pizza, Moe's BBQ Days Inn camping, vet
21	New Stock Rd, N Citgo/dsl, Shell Domino's, Granny's Kitchen, Pizza Hut $General, Campfire Lodge RV Park, CVS, Ingles/gas
19a b	N US 25, W US 70, Marshall, N Shell/dsl Arby's, Bojangles, Burger King, Chapala Mexican, IHOP, KFC, La Careta Mexican, Little Caesars, McDonald's, Peking East, Subway, TCBY, Waffle House, Zaxby's Ace Hardware, Advance Parts, Aldi Foods, AutoZone, BigLots, Ingles/dsl, Roses, URGENT CARE, Verizon, S Shell/DQ/dsl Steak'n Shake $Tree, CVS, Lowe's, Walmart/Subway
18	Weaverville (no EZ return from eb)
17	to Flat Creek
15	Rd 197, to Jupiter, Barnardsville
13	Forks of Ivy, N Mkt Ctr/dsl, S Exxon/dsl
11	Rd 213, to Mars Hill, Marshall, N tires, S Exxon, Hardee's/dsl, TriCo Bojangles, Osaka Japanese, Subway, Waffle House, Wagon Wheel Rest. Comfort Inn $General, CVS, Ingles/dsl, NAPA
9	Burnsville, Spruce Pine, N to Mt Mitchell SP
7mm	**runaway truck ramp eb**, scenic overlook wb
6mm	**Welcome Ctr/ eb, full facilities**
5.5mm	**runaway truck ramp eb**
5mm	Buckner Gap, elev. 3370
3	to US 23 A, Wolf Laurel, N Exxon/dsl Little Creek Cafe to ski areas
2.5mm	**eb runaway truck ramp**
.5mm	**eb brake insp sta**
0mm	North Carolina/Tennessee state line

INTERSTATE 40

Exit #	Services
420mm	**I-40 begins/ends at Wilmington, Services N on US 17** Buffalo Wild Wings Hampton Inn CarQuest, Home Depot, Hyundai, Kia, Kohl's, Land Rover, Mazda, Nissan, Subaru, Toyota/Scion, Volvo, **Services on US 17 S** BP, Exxon/dsl, Hugo's, Murphy USA/dsl Arby's, Bojangles, Bonefish Grill, Carrabba's, Chick-fil-A, ChopStix, Church's, Cracker Barrel, Dunkin Donuts, Elizabeth's Pizza, Hardee's, Hooters, IHOP, Jason's Deli, McDonald's, Olive Garden, Sonic, Subway, Waffle House Best Western, Budgetel, Comfort Suites, Days Inn, EconoLodge, Extended Stay America, Holiday Inn, MainStay Suites, Quality Inn, Ramada Inn, Red Roof Inn, Sleep Inn, Travel Inn, Wingate Inn Advance Parts, AutoZone, Batteries+, Black's Tires/auto, Cadillac, Costco/gas, Marshall's, Petsmart, Radio Shack, Rite Aid, Target, Walgreens, Walmart, **Services 2-4 mi S on US 117/NC 132** BP/dsl, Exxon/dsl Applebee's, Bojangles, Burger King, Carolina Ale House, Chili's, CiCi's Pizza, College Diner, Cookout, Golden Corral, Hardee's, Hieronymus Seafood, HoneyBaked Ham, Jersey Mike's, Jimmy John's, Kickback Jack's, Little Caesars, McAlister's Deli, McDonald's, Mission BBQ, Okami Japanese, Outback Steaks, Starbucks, Taco Bell, Wendy's Baymont Inn, Comfort Inn, Country Inn Suites, Courtyard, Holiday Inn Express, Jameson Inn, Staybridge Suites $Tree, Acura/Honda, AT&T, Best Buy, Buick/GMC, Chevrolet, Chrysler/Dodge/Jeep, Dick's, Fiat, Harris-Teeter, Jo-Ann, K-Mart, Lowe's Foods, Lowe's Whse, Mercedes, Old Navy, PetCo, Ross, Sam's Club/gas, Staples, TJ Maxx, to UNCW, URGENT CARE, Verizon, VW

ASHEVILLE

ARDEN

WILMINGTON

NC

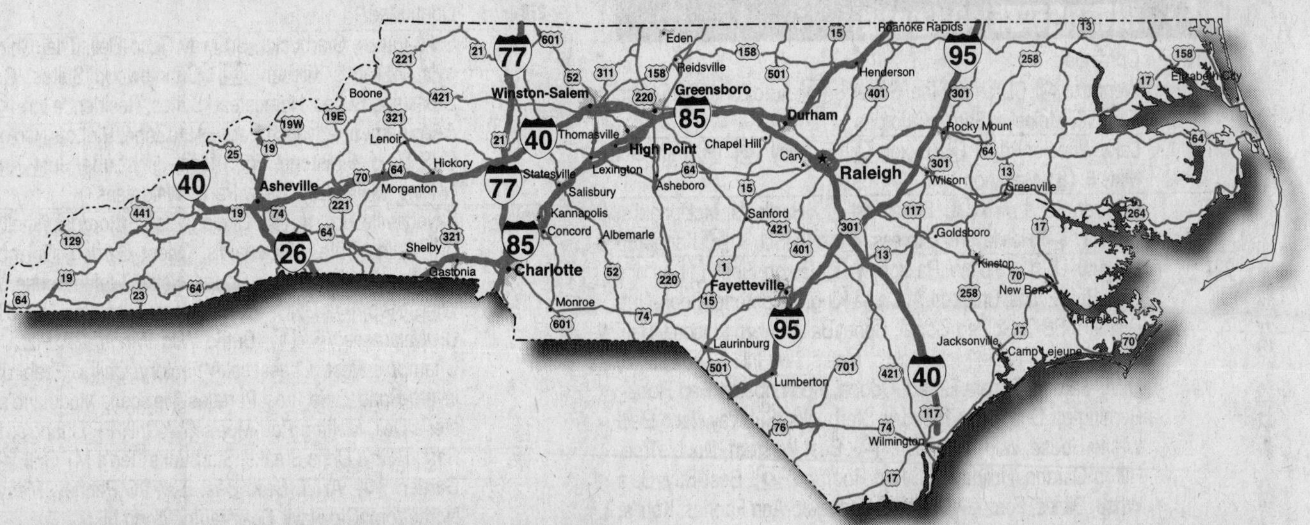

INTERSTATE 40 Cont'd

Exit #	Services
420b a	Gordon Rd, NC 132 N, **2 mi N** [gas] Hess/dsl, Kangaroo/dsl [food] Andy's, Domino's, Hardee's, KFC, McDonald's, Waffle House, Zaxby's [other] CVS Drug, KOA (4mi), Rite Aid, vet, Walgreens, **S** [gas] BP/dsl, Go Gas/dsl, Kangaroo/dsl [food] Carolina BBQ, China Wok, McDonald's, Subway [other] $General, Family$, Lowe's Foods, Rite Aid
416b a	I-140, US 17, to Topsail Island, New Bern, Myrtle Beach
414	Holly Shelter Rd, to Brunswick Co beaches, Castle Hayne, **S** [gas] BP, GoGas/dsl, Kangaroo/dsl [food] Carolina Cafe, Domino's, Hardee's, Subway [other] $General, Bo's Foods, CVS Drug, USPO
413mm	NE Cape Fear River
408	NC 210, **N** [other] Mack/Volvo/Isuzu, **S** [gas] Hess/Wendy's/dsl/cafe/scales/24hr, Phoenix TC/Exxon/Subway/dsl/scales, Shell/Noble Roman's/dsl [food] Hardee's, McDonald's [other] Advance Parts, Family$, Food Lion, to Moore's Creek Nat Bfd/camping, USPO
398	NC 53, Burgaw, **2 mi S** [gas] Carolina Petro [food] Hardee's, KFC, McDonald's, Subway [lodging] Burgaw Motel [other] [H], Advance Parts, camping, Family$, Food Lion
390	to US 117, Wallace
385	NC 41, Wallace, **N** [gas] Exxon/Village Subs [food] Bojangles, Mad Boar Rest. [lodging] Holiday Inn Express [other] Lake Leamon Camping, **1.5 mi S** [gas] Hess/dsl, Murphy USA/dsl [food] Burger King, Domino's, McDonald's, Subway, Taco Bell, Zaxby's [other] $General, $Tree, Food Lion, O'Reilly Parts, Verizon, Walgreens, Walmart/Subway
384	NC 11, Wallace
380	Rose Hill, **S** [gas] BP/Subway/dsl (1mi), Marathon (1mi), Pure [other] Duplin Winery
373	NC 24 E, NC 903, Magnolia, **N** [gas] BP/dsl, Exxon/dsl/e-85 [other] [H], Cowan Museum
369	US 117, Warsaw
364	NC 24, to NC 50, Clinton, [rest stop] **both lanes, full [handicapped] facilities, litter barrels, no overnight parking, petwalk [phone] [picnic] vending** **N** [gas] Wilco/Hess/Arby's/Dunkin Donuts/Stuckey's/dsl/24hr, **S** [gas] BP/dsl, Kangaroo/dsl, Marathon, Sunoco/Bojangles [food] KFC, McDonald's, Smithfield's BBQ, Subway, Waffle House, Wendy's [lodging] Days Inn, Quality Inn
355	NC 403, to US 117, Goldsboro, Faison, **3 mi N** [gas] Exxon
348	Suttontown Rd
343	US 701, Newton Grove, **1 mi N** [gas] Exxon/dsl, to Bentonville Bfd
341	NC 50, NC 55, to US 13, Newton Grove, **1.5 mi N** [gas] Exxon/dsl [food] Hardee's [other] Food Lion, **S** [gas] BP/McDonald's, Shell/Subway/dsl [food] Smithfield BBQ [other] Family Auto/tire
334	NC 96, Meadow, **S** [gas] Short Stop/dsl
328b a	I-95, N to Smithfield, S to Benson
325	NC 242, to US 301, to Benson, **S** [gas] Marathon/dsl
324mm	[rest stop] **both lanes, full [handicapped] facilities, litter barrels, no overnight parking, petwalk [phone] [picnic] vending**
319	NC 210, McGee's Crossroads, **N** [gas] BP/Papa's Subs&Pizza/dsl, Shell/BBQ/dsl/24hr [food] McDonald's [other] [H], vet, **S** [gas] Mobil/CW's Cafe [food] Bojangles, China Star, Italian Pizza/Pasta, KFC/Taco Bell, Subway, Wendy's [other] $General, AutoZone, Food Lion, USPO
312	NC 42, to Clayton, Fuquay-Varina, **N** [gas] Murphy Express/dsl, Wilco/Hess/Dunkin Donuts/Wendy's/dsl/24hr [food] Andy's, Applebee's, China King, Cookout, Cracker Barrel, Fiesta Mexicana, Golden Corral, Jersey Mike's Subs, King Chinese, Marco's Pizza, Papa Subs/Pizza, Pizza Inn, Ruby Tuesday, Smithfield BBQ [lodging] Comfort Inn, Holiday Inn Express, Super 8, ValuePlace Hotel [other] $Tree, JustTires, Lowe's, URGENT CARE, USPO, Verizon, Walmart/McDonald's, **S** [gas] BP/Subway/dsl, Exxon/Burger King, Marathon/dsl, Shell/dsl [food] American Hero Rest, Bojangles, Domino's, DQ, Jumbo China, KFC/Taco Bell, McDonald's, Snoopy's Hotdogs, Waffle House [lodging] Hampton Inn, Sleep Inn [other] CVS Drug, Food Lion, vet, Walgreens
309	US 70 E, Goldsboro, Smithfield
306b a	US 70 E bus, to Smithfield, Garner, Goldsboro, **1 mi N** [gas] Kangaroo/Subway/dsl, Shell/dsl [other] Chrysler/Dodge/Jeep, **S** [food] Buffalo Wild Wings, Chick-fil-A, Chili's, Coldstone, Kaze Japanese, La Cocina Mexican, Logan's Roadhouse, McDonald's, Moe's SW Grill, New Japan Express, Prima Vera Pizza, Subway, TGIFriday's, Wendy's [other] AT&T, Best Buy, BJ's Whse/gas, Dick's, GNC, Kohl's, Michael's, Petsmart, Ross, Staples, Target, TJ Maxx
303	Jones Sausage Rd, **N** [gas] Hess/Dunkin Donuts/dsl [food] Bojangles, Burger King, Smithfield BBQ, **S** [gas] Hess/Dunkin Donuts/dsl
301	I-440 E, US 64/70 E, to Wilson
300b a	Rock Quarry Rd, **N** [other] Kroger/gas, **S** [gas] Exxon, Valero [food] Burger King, Little Caesars, Subway [other] Food Lion, Rite Aid
299	Person St, Hammond Rd, Raleigh (no EZ return eb), **1 mi N** [gas] Exxon/dsl [other] to Shaw U
298b a	US 401 S, US 70 E, NC 50, **N** [gas] Shell/dsl [lodging] Red Roof Inn, **S** [gas] BP, Exxon/dsl, Hess/dsl, Hugo's, Raceway [food] Baskin-Robbins/Dunkin Donuts, Bojangles, Cinco de Mayo Mexican, Cook-Out, Domino's, Golden Seafood&Chicken, Taco Bell,

INTERSTATE 40 Cont'd

RALEIGH

298b a Continued
Wendy's Claremont Inn, Super 8 AutoZone, CarQuest, Family$, Meineke, Sam's Club/gas

297 Lake Wheeler Rd, N Exxon Subway H, Farmer's Mkt, S Marathon

295 Gorman St, **1 mi** N Exxon/dsl Hardee's, McDonald's, Subway Holiday Inn Express to NCSU, S Kangaroo

293 to I-440, US 1, US 64 W, Raleigh, S Exxon, Shell Astor's Grill, Bob Evans, Chick-fil-A, China King, Coldstone, Cook-Out, Dickey's BBQ, Golden Corral, HoneyBaked Ham, Jason's Deli, Jersey Mike's Subs, McDonald's, Moe's SW Grill, Noodles&Co, Olive Garden, Panera Bread, Qdoba, Red Lobster, Red Robin, Remington Grill, Ruby Tuesday, Starbucks, Subway, Taco Bell, Waffle House, Wild Wing Cafe Best Western, DoubleTree, Hilton Garden, Holiday Inn, Red Roof Inn Best Buy, BJ's Whse, Dick's, Ford, GNC, Home Depot, Jo-Ann Fabrics, Kohl's, Lincoln, Lowe's, Marshalls, Mazda, Michael's, NTB, Office Depot, Old Navy, PetCo, Petsmart, SteinMart, Target

CARY

291 Cary Towne Blvd, Cary, **1 mi** S Circle K 5 Guys Burgers, Burger King, China 1, DQ, Jersey Mike's, Macaroni Grill, McDonald's, Mimi's Cafe, On-the-Border, Pei Wei, Ragazzi's, S Asian, Starbucks, Tomyum Thai AT&T, Barnes&Noble, Belk, Dillard's, Firestone, Harris Teeter, JC Penney, Macy's, Sears, TJ Maxx

290 NC 54, Cary, N Sheetz/dsl McDonald's Hyatt Place, Wingate Inn, S Exxon (1mi) Hampton Inn

289 to I-440, Wade Ave, to Raleigh, N H, Carter-Finley Stadium, museum, S to fairgrounds

287 Harrison Ave, Cary, N to Wm B Umstead SP, S BP/dsl An Cuisine, Bonefish Grill, Burger King, BurgerFi, Carolina Cafe, Chick-fil-A, Maggie Moo's, McDonald's, Moe's SW Grill, NY Pizza, Ruth's Chris Steaks, Starbucks, Subway, Thai Cuisine, Wendy's Embassy Suites, Studio+, TownePlace Suites, Umstead Hotel Colony Tire

285 Aviation Pkwy, to Morrisville, N Sheetz/dsl Hilton Garden Raleigh/Durham Airport

284 Airport Blvd, N Capital City Chophouse Cambria Suites, Country Inn&Suites, Hyatt Place to RDU Airport, S BP/dsl, Mobil Bojangles, Cracker Barrel, Hooters, KFC/Taco Bell, TX Steaks, Waffle House, Wendy's Courtyard, Days Inn, Extended Stay America, Fairfield Inn, Hampton Inn, Holiday Inn, Holiday Inn Express, La Quinta, Microtel, Residence Inn, Sheraton, Staybridge Suites Morrisville Outlets/famous brands/food court

283 I-540 E, toll I-540 W, to US 70, Aviation Pkwy

282 Page Rd, S Arby's, Bojangles, Jimmy John's, McDonald's, Mez Cafe, Starbucks Comfort Suites, Hilton, Sheraton, Sleep Inn, Wingate Inn

281 Miami Blvd, N Extended Stay Deluxe, Hilton Garden, Marriott, S BP, Shell Arby's, Bojangles, Burger King, McDonald's, Quiznos, Randy's Pizza, Rudino's Grill, Subway, Tropical Smoothie, Wendy's, Wok'n Grill Extended Stay Deluxe, Holiday Inn Express, Homewood Suites, Hotel Indigo Office Depot

280 Davis Dr, N to Research Triangle, S Radisson

279b a NC 147 N, Triangle Expwy, to Durham, N H

278 NC 55, to NC 54, Apex, Foreign Trade Zone 93, N Marathon Sansui Grill, Waffle House Comfort Inn, DoubleTree, EconoLodge, La Quinta, Red Roof Inn, S BP, Exxon/dsl, Mobil/dsl Arby's, Backyard BBQ, Bojangles, Capt D's, Chick-fil-A, El Agave Mexican, El Dorado Mexican, Golden Corral, Hardee's, Little Caesars, Papa John's, Pizza Hut, Quiznos,

278 Continued
Sal's Italian, Starbucks, Subway, Taco Bell, Thai China, Wendy's, William's Kitchen Candlewood Suites, Courtyard, Crossland Suites, Homestead Suites, Residence Inn $Tree, AAA, Aamco, Advance Parts, AutoZone, BigLots, Colonial Tire, CVS Drug, Firestone, Food Lion, Jiffy Lube, Just Tires, Lube N'Tune, Meineke, O'Reilly Parts, Walgreens

CHAPEL HILL

276 Fayetteville Rd, N Circle K/dsl, Exxon/dsl, Shell/Circle K China Cafe, McDonald's, Orient Garden, Quiznos, Ruby Tuesday, Rudino's Pizza, Souper Salad, Waffle House, Wendy's, Wing Stop GNC, Harris-Teeter, Kroger/dsl, to NC Central U, Walgreens, S Bufflo Wild Wings, CA Pizza Kitchen, Champp's Rest, Cheesecake Factory, Chili's, Firebird's, Fork-in-the-Road Cafe, Los Portales Mexican, Maggiano's, McAlister's Deli, Melting Pot, Moe's SW Grill, PF Chang's, Rockfish Rest, Ruth's Chris Steaks, Starbucks, Ted's MT Grill Hilton Garden AT&T, Belk, Best Buy, JC Penney, Macy's, mall, Nordstrom, Old Navy, Sears/auto, World Mkt

274 NC 751, to Jordan Lake, N BP, Marathon Burger King, Char Grill, Dunkin Donuts, Jimmy John's, KFC, McDonald's, Taco Bell, Waffle House, Wendy's Advance Parts, CVS Drug, Harris Teeter, Honda, Lexus, Rite Aid, URGENT CARE, Walgreens, S BP Bonefish Grill, Chick-fil-A, Subway Sheraton Aldi Foods, Michael's, PetCo, Target

273 NC 54, to Durham, UNC-Chapel Hill, N BP/dsl, S BP, Shell/dsl Hardee's, Nantucket Grill Courtyard (2mi), Hampton Inn, Holiday Inn Express URGENT CARE, vet

270 US 15, US 501, Chapel Hill, Durham, N Applebee's, Bob Evans, Carrabba's, Dickey's BBQ, Firehouse Subs, Jason's Deli, Lonestar Steaks, Longhorn Steaks, McAlister's, Moe's SW Grill, NY Pizza, Outback Steaks, Panera Bread, Philly Steaks, Red Robin, Starbucks, Xank's Japanese Comfort Inn, Homewood Suites, SpringHill Suites, Staybridge Suites $Tree, AT&T, Barnes&Noble, Best Buy, Dick's, Home Depot, H, Kohl's, Kroger, Marshalls, Michael's, Old Navy, Petsmart, to Duke U, Verizon, Walmart/Subway, S BP, Exxon Boston Mkt, Chick-fil-A, Hardee's, K&W Cafeteria, La Hacienda Mexican, McDonald's, Subway, Wendy's Days Inn, Quality Inn, Red Roof Inn, Sheraton Acura, Advance Parts, BMW, Chevrolet, Dillard's, Food Lion, Harris Teeter, Kia, Lowe's, Subaru, Trader Joe's

266 NC 86, to Chapel Hill, **2 mi** S BP, Exxon, Hess/dsl Pop's Pizza, Subway

263 New Hope Church Rd

261 Hillsborough, **1.5 mi** N BP, Citgo/dsl, Shell Hardee's, KFC/Taco Bell, McDonald's, Subway, Waffle House, Wendy's Holiday Inn Express, Microtel

259 I-85 N, to Durham

I-40 and I-85 run together 30 mi. See I-85, exits 131-161.

227 to I-85 S, to I-73 N, to US 421, High Point, Charlotte

226 McConnell Rd, S Exxon

224 E Lee St, to US 29 N, to US 220 N, N BP/dsl, Shell/dsl Holiday Inn Express, Quality Inn

223 to N US 29, E US 70, N US 20, Reidsville

222 MLK Jr (from eb), Sanford, S Arby's, Biscuitville, Burger King, McDonald's, Subway, Taco Bell Advance Parts, CVS Drug, Food Lion, Hall Tire Co, Tom's Tire/auto

221 S Elm-Eugene St, N Citgo/dsl, Crown/dsl, Shell Homestead Lodge AutoZone, CarQuest, Family$, Food Lion, O'Reilly Parts, S BP, Shell/dsl EconoLodge, Super 8 Home Depot

220 Randleman Rd, US 220 S, to Greensboro, Ashboro, N BP, Solo Biscuitville, Church's, KFC, McDonald's, Pizza Hut, Sub Sta 2 Budget Inn Harley-Davidson, Rite Aid, Save-

NC

INTERSTATE 40 Cont'd

GREENSBORO

220 Continued
A-Lot, S [gas] BP, Kangaroo [food] Cook-Out, Mayflower Seafood, Waffle House, Wendy's

219 US 29 S, W US 70, Highpoint (exits left from wb), Charlotte

218 US 220, Freeman Mill Rd, Ashboro

217 Highpoint Rd, Koury Blvd (from wb), N [gas] Exxon, Shell/dsl [food] Biscuitville, Burger King, Chili's, China King, Fatz Cafe, Ham's Rest, Hooters, Little Caesars, Lonestar Steaks, Olive Garden, Sakura Japanese, Subway, Taco Bell [lodging] DoubleTree Hotel, Hampton Inn, Park Lane Hotel, Quality Inn, Red Roof Inn, Super 8 [other] $General, Office Depot, S [gas] Shell [food] Bonefish Grill, Carrabba's, Jimmy John's, Krispy Kreme, McDonald's, Smokey Bones BBQ, Waffle House, Wendy's [lodging] Baymont Inn, Comfort Suites, Drury Inn, Ramada Inn, Sheraton, Studio 6 [other] Dillard's, Discount Tire, Gander Mtn, JC Penney, O'Reilly Parts

216 (from eb), Greensboro, [other] coliseum

214 Wendover Ave, N [gas] Sheetz [food] Burger King, China Buffet, Coldstone, Mario's Pizza, Moe's SW Grill, Panera Bread, Penn Sta Subs, Waffle House [lodging] Extended Stay, Fairfield Inn, Hilton Garden, Holiday Inn Express, Microtel [other] Audi, Costco/gas, CVS Drug, Fiat, Ford, Nissan, PetCo, Staples, Verizon, VW, S [food] Applebee's, Arby's, Biscuitville, Bojangles, Chick-fil-A, Chipotle Mexican, Cracker Barrel, Elizabeth's Pizza, Fuddrucker's, Golden Corral, Golden Wok, IHOP, Jimmy John's, Kabuto Japanese, La Hacienda Mexican, Logan's Roadhouse, Longhorn Steaks, McDonald's, O'Charley's, Panda Express, Papa John's, Red Lobster, Steak'n Shake, Subway, Taco Bell, TGIFriday's, Tripp's Rest., Wendy's [lodging] Comfort Inn, Courtyard, Days Inn, Hyatt Place, La Quinta, Lodge America, SpringHill Suites, Studio+, Wingate Inn [other] $Tree, AT&T, Best Buy, Buick/GMC, Chevrolet, Dick's, GNC, Goodyear, Hobby Lobby, Home Depot, K-Mart/gas, Kohl's, Lowe's, Macy's, Mazda, Meineke, Michael's, Petsmart, Radio Shack, Ross, Sam's Club/gas, Target, Walmart

213 Guilford College Rd, N [gas] BP/dsl [lodging] Clarion, S [gas] same as 214, Sheetz

212b a I-73, US 241 S, to I-85, to Bryan Blvd, Ashboro, [other] to [airport]

211 Gallimore Dairy Rd, N [other] Freightliner

210 NC 68, to High Point, Piedmont Triad, N [gas] Shell [food] Arby's, Carolina's Diner [lodging] Days Inn, Embassy Suites, Fairview Inn, Homewood Suites, Sleep Inn, Wyndham Garden [other] Ford Trucks, Kenworth, to [airport], S [gas] Exxon/dsl [food] Bojangles, Fatz Cafe, McDonald's, Pizza Hut/Taco Bell, Pollo Pizza/Pasta, Ruby Tuesday, Shoney's, Subway, Wendy's [lodging] Best Western, Candlewood Suites, Comfort Suites, Courtyard, Extended Stay Deluxe, Fairfield Inn, Hampton Inn, Holiday Inn Express, Motel 6, Quality Inn, Red Roof Inn, Residence Inn

208 Sandy Ridge Rd, N [gas] Exxon/Subway/dsl, Hess/dsl [other] Camping World RV Ctr, S [gas] Shell/Circle K/dsl [other] Out Of Doors Mart

206 Lp 40 (from wb), to Kernersville, Winston-Salem, downtown

203 NC 66, to Kernersville, N [gas] Citgo/McDonald's/dsl, Hess/dsl, QM/Subway/dsl [food] Capt Tom's Seafood, Clark's BBQ, Wendy's [lodging] Sleep Inn [other] [H], Curves, Ford, Merchant Tire/repair, S [gas] Shell/dsl [lodging] Holiday Inn Express

201 Union Cross Rd, N [gas] Citgo/dsl, QM/dsl [food] Blue Naples Pizza, Burger King, China Café, Subway [other] $Mart, CVS Drug, Food Lion

196 US 311 S, to High Point

195 US 311 N, NC 109, to Thomasville, S [gas] Citgo, Hess/dsl [other] Family$

193b a US 52, NC 8, to Lexington, S [gas] Hess/dsl, Shell [food] Hardee's

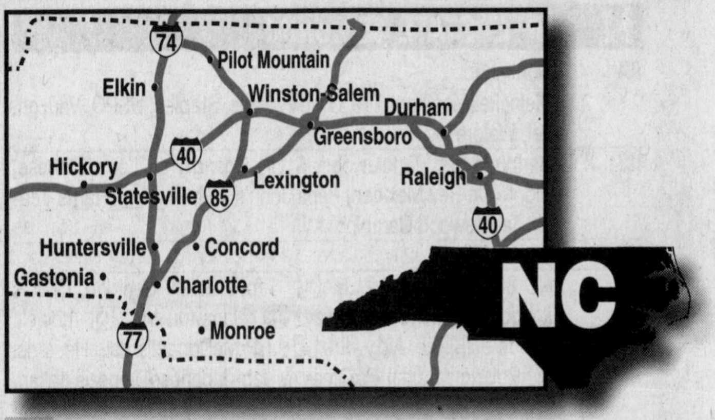

WINSTON • SALEM

193c Silas Creek Pkwy (from eb), same as 192

192 NC 150, to Peters Creek Pkwy, N [gas] Giant, Hess, Shell [food] Bojangles, Burger King, China Wok, Hero House Rest, Hong Kong Buffet, IHOP, KFC, Little Caesars, Monterrey Mexican, Mr BBQ, Sonic, Subway, Taco Bell, Tokyo Japanese, Tomo'E Steaks [lodging] Innkeeper [other] $General, $Tree, Acura/Subaru, Audi, AutoZone, BigLots, Ford, Hamrick's, Hyundai, Infiniti, Mazda, Office Depot, Radio Shack, Rite Aid, VW, S [gas] BP, QM [food] Arby's, Baskin-Robbins/Dunkin Donuts, Cook-Out, K&W Cafeteria, McDonald's, Papa John's, Pizza Hut, Waffle House, Wendy's [lodging] Holiday Inn Express [other] Advance Parts, Aldi Foods, BMW/Mini, CVS Drug, Family$, Food Lion, Hancock Fabrics, Honda, K-Mart, Mock Tire, Toyota/Scion

190 Hanes Mall Blvd (from wb, no re-entry), N [food] Chipotle Mexican, Coldstone, Elizabeth's Pizza, Jimmy John's, McDonald's, Ruby Tuesday, TGIFriday's, Tripp's Rest. [lodging] Quality Inn [other] [H], Belk, Dick's, Dillard's, Firestone/auto, JC Penney, Macy's, mall, Marshalls, same as 189, Sears/auto, S [food] Burger King, ChuckECheese, Outback Steaks, Starbucks, Subway [lodging] Comfort Suites, Microtel [other] Office Depot

189 US 158, Stratford Rd, Hanes Mall Blvd, N [food] Bojangles, Chili's, Golden Corral, Olive Garden, Red Lobster, Taco Bell, TX Roadhouse [lodging] Courtyard, Fairfield Inn [other] [H], Belk, Buick/GMC, Cadillac, Chevrolet, Dillard's, JC Penney, Jo-Ann Fabrics, Macy's, mall, Sears/auto, Walgreens, S [gas] BP, Shell [food] 5 Guys Burgers, Applebee's, Bleu Rest., Brixx Pizza, Buffalo Wild Wings, Chick-fil-A, Firebirds Grill, Fuddruckers, Hooters, Jason's Deli, KFC/LJ Silver, Lonestar Steaks, Longhorn Steaks, Macaroni Grill, Moe's SW Grill, Nuke's Cafe, Panera Bread, Qdoba, Subway, Village Tavern, Which Wich [lodging] Extended Stay America, Hampton Inn, Hilton Garden, La Quinta, Sleep Inn, SpringHill Suites [other] $Tree, AT&T, Barnes&Noble, Best Buy, Costco/gas, CVS Drug, Discount Tire, Food Lion, Home Depot, Kohl's, Lowe's, Michael's, Petsmart, Ross, Sam's Club/gas, Target, Verizon

188 US 421, to Yadkinville, to WFU (no EZ wb return), Winston-Salem, **1/2mi N off US 421** [gas] BP, Exxon, Kangaroo, Shell [food] Arby's, Burger King, Cook-Out, Dickey's BBQ, McDonald's, Starbucks, Subway, Waffle House, Wendy's [other] CarMax, Mercedes, vet, Walmart

CLEMMONS

184 to US 421, Clemmons, N [gas] Mobil, Shell [food] Applebee's, Dunkin Donuts, IHOP, K&W Cafe, KFC, Panera Bread, Steak Escape [lodging] Holiday Inn Express, S [gas] BP/dsl, Hess, Kangaroo [food] Arby's, Biscuitville, Brick Oven Pizza, Burger King, Cozumel Mexican, Cracker Barrel, Domino's, Kimono Japanese, Little Richard's BBQ, McDonald's, Mi Pueblo Mexican, Mtn Fried Chicken, Pizza Hut, Sonic, Starbucks, Subway, Taco Bell, Time to Eat Cafe, Waffle House, Wendy's [lodging] Super 8 [other] $Tree, Advance Parts, BigLots, CVS Drug, GNC, K-Mart, Lowe's Foods,

= gas = food = lodging = other = rest stop

INTERSTATE 40 Cont'd

MOCKSVILLE

184 Continued
Meineke, Merchant Tire, O'Reilly Parts, Staples, USPO, Verizon, vet, Walgreens

182 Bermuda Run, Tanglewood, S Chang Thai, Lee's Chinese, Monte De Rey Mexican, Papa John's, Subway Harris-Teeter, Tanglewood Camping

182mm Yadkin River

180 NC 801, Tanglewood, N Capt's Galley Seafood, Chilo's Mexican, Domino's, Subway Hampton Inn Lowe's Foods/dsl, Rite Aid, S BP/McDonald's/dsl, Hess/dsl Bojangles, Jimmy's Greek, Miyabi Japanese, Venezia Italian, Wendy's $General, Ace Hardware, CVS Drug, Food Lion, Radio Shack, Walgreens

177mm **both lanes, full facilities, info, litter barrels, petwalk vending**

174 Farmington Rd, N Shell/dsl antiques, S vineyards

170 US 601, Mocksville, N Citgo/dsl, Horn's TC/Marathon/DQ/Jersey Mike's/dsl/scales/24hr, Murphy USA/dsl JinJin Chinese, La Carreta Mexican, Moe's Cafe, Subway $Tree, Campers Inn RV Ctr, Verizon, Walmart, S Exxon, Hess/Taco Bell, Sheetz/dsl Arby's, Blackbeard's Seafood Shack, Bojangles, Burger King, China Grill, Dunkin Donuts, Dynasty Chinese, KFC, Marco's Pizza, McDonald's, Papa John's, Pier 601, Pizza Hut, Sagebrush Steaks, Shiki Japanese, Wendy's Days Inn, HighWay Inn, Quality Inn, Scottish Inn H, $General, Advance Parts, Lowe's, Mocksville Tire/auto, USPO, vet, Walgreens

168 US 64, to Mocksville, N Exxon/dsl Lake Myers RV Resort (3mi), S BP/dsl H

162 US 64, Cool Springs, N Lake Myers RV Resort (5mi), S Shell/dsl KOA

161mm S Yadkin River

STATESVILLE

154 to US 64, Old Mocksville Rd, N H, S Citgo/dsl Jaybee's Hotdogs repair/tires

153 US 64 (from eb), **1/2 mi** S Citgo/dsl Jaybee's Hotdogs repair/tires

152b a I-77, S to Charlotte, N to Elkin

151 US 21, E Statesville, N Hess/dsl, Marathon/DQ/dsl Applebee's, Baskin-Robbins/Dunkin Donuts, Bojangles, Chick-fil-A, Chili's, Cook-Out, Cracker Barrel, K&W Cafeteria, KFC, Logan's Roadhouse, McDonald's, Mi Pueblo Café, Red Lobster, Ruby Tuesday, Shiki Japanese, Sorrento's Italian, Taco Bell, Wendy's, Zaxby's Days Inn, Sleep Inn $Tree, Advance Parts, Aldi Foods, AutoZone, BigLots, Chevrolet, CVS Drug, GNC, Hobby Lobby, Home Depot, Lowe's, Meineke, Michael's, NTB, Petsmart, Staples, TJ Maxx, URGENT CARE, Verizon, Verizon, Walmart/Subway, S Exxon BJ Hibachi, Greg's BBQ, Lonestar Steaks, Olde 1847 Pizza&Wing, Sonic, Waffle House Holiday Inn Express, Masters Inn, Quality Inn H, $General, URGENT CARE

150 NC 115, Statesville, N BP/dsl, Citgo, Sheetz/dsl, Shell/Subway Amalfi's Italian, Little Caesar's, Ol'Bob's BBQ, Waffle Shop $General, CVS Drug, Food Lion, Fred's, museum

148 US 64, NC 90, W Statesville, N Citgo/dsl, Shell Arby's, BoxCar Grille, Burger King, McDonald's, Shiki Japanese, Subway, Village Inn Pizza Economy Inn $General, CVS Drug, Ingles Foods

146 Stamey Farm Rd, N truck repair

144 Old Mountain Rd, N Backyard's Troy's Rest., S BP/dsl, Shell/dsl

143mm **weigh sta both lanes**

141 Sharon School Rd, N Citgo/dsl

HICKORY

140mm Catawba River

138 NC 10 W, Oxford School Rd, to Catawba, N Valero/dsl

136mm **both lanes, full facilities, info, litter barrels, petwalk vending**

135 Claremont, S Shell/7-11 BoxCar Grille, Burger King, Hannah's BBQ, Hardee's, New Panda, Subway Rodeway Inn $General, Carolina Coach RV Ctr, Lowe's Foods

133 Rock Barn Rd, N Shell/dsl, S Wilco/Hess/Godfather's/Stuckey's/Subway/dsl/scales/24hr

132 to NC 16, Taylorsville, W Hwy 55 Cafe, N Marathon/Kangaroo, Murphy USA/dsl, Shell/dsl Burger King, Jin's Buffet, Subway, Zaxby's Holiday Inn Express $Tree, AT&T, AutoZone, Walmart

130 Old US 70, N Jack-in-the-Box, Subway repair, Verizon, vet, S Citgo, Pure USPO

128 US 321, Fairgrove Church Rd, Hickory, N BP, Marathon/dsl, Shell McDonald's, Waffle House H, S Citgo, Marathon/dsl Dos Amigos, Nagano Japanese, Papa Pesto's Greek/Italian, Wendy's Days Inn, La Quinta Chrysler/Dodge/Jeep, to Catawba Valley Coll

126 to US 70, NC 155, S Marathon/dsl Applebee's, Bob Evans, Buffalo Wild Wings, Chili's, East Coast Wings, IHOP, Jason's Deli, Krispy Kreme, McDonald's, O'Charley's, Olive Garden, Panera Bread, Popeye's, Taco Bell Holiday Inn Express Barnes&Noble, Discount Tire, Hickory Furniture Mart, Lowe's, Michael's, PetCo, Ross, Sam's Club/gas, URGENT CARE, Walmart/McDonald's

125 Hickory, N RaceWay/dsl Bojangles, Dickey's BBQ, Golden Corral, Hardee's, Kickback Jack's Grill, Mellow Mushroom, Rancho Viejo, Starbucks, TX Roadhouse Red Roof Inn $General, Aamco, Advance Parts, Firestone/auto, S Hess/dsl, Shell/dsl Arby's, Atlanta Bread, Burger Fi, Carrabba's, Chick-fil-A, Chipotle, ChuckECheese, CiCi's Pizza, Coldstone, Cracker Barrel, Five Guys, Hooters, J&S Cafeteria, Jack-in-the-Box, KFC, Kobe Japanese, Longhorn Steaks, NY Hibachi Buffet, Outback Steaks, PDQ Rest., Red Lobster, Ruby Tuesday, Tony's Pizza, Waffle House, Wendy's, Which Wich?, Wild Wok, Zaxby's Baymont Inn, Best Western, Courtyard, Crowne Plaza, Fairfield Inn, Hampton Inn, Hilton Garden, Quality Inn, Sleep Inn $Tree, Aldi Foods, AT&T, Belk, Best Buy, Carmax, Dick's, Dillard's, Food Lion, Ford, Hamrick's, Hancock Fabrics, Harley-Davidson, Home Depot, Honda, JC Penney, Kohl's, mall, Mazda, NAPA, Nissan, NTB, Office Depot, Old Navy, O'Reilly Parts, Petsmart, Sears/auto, Sunrise Camping Ctr, Suzuki, Target, TJ Maxx, Toyota/Scion, Verizon

123 US 70/321, to NC 127, Hickory

121 Long View, N Kenworth

119b a Hildebran, N Shell/Subway Bojangles, Hardee's $General

118 Old NC 10, N Pure, Shell/dsl

116 Icard, S Marathon/McDonald's/dsl Burger King, Granny's Kitchen Icard Inn USPO

113 Connelly Springs, N Citgo/dsl Patsy Ann's Rest, Subway H, CVS Drug, Ford/Hyundai, Walgreens

112 Mineral Springs Mtn Rd, Valdese

111 Valdese

107 NC 114, to Drexel

106 Bethel Rd, S Exxon/dsl Economy Inn/rest.

105 NC 18, Morganton, N Hess/Dunkin Donuts/dsl Abele's Rest., Arby's, Capt D's, Cracker Barrel, Fatz Café, Harbor Inn Seafood, Las Salsas, McDonald's, Sonic, Wendy's, Zaxby's, Zeko's Italian Hampton Inn H, Chevrolet/Buick/GMC, S Shell/dsl El Paso Mexican, Sagebrush Steaks, Waffle House Quality Inn, Sleep Inn to South Mtns SP

NC

MORGANTON

INTERSTATE 40 Cont'd

Exit #	Services
104	Enola Rd, S Chen's Garden $Tree, BigLots, Food Lion
103	US 64, Morganton, N Citgo/dsl, Exxon/dsl Allison's Rest., Chick-fil-A, Cook-Out, Village Inn Pizza Days Inn, S Marathon, RaceWay/dsl Bojangles, Butch's BBQ, Denny's, Hardee's, KFC, Subway, Taco Bell, Tokyo Diner Comfort Inn $General, Clark Tire/auto, Food Lion, Honda, Ingles Foods, Lowe's
100	Jamestown Rd, N BP/dsl Waffle Shop Chrysler/Dodge/Jeep, Ford/Lincoln
98	Causby Rd, to Glen Alpine, S B&B/food
96	Kathy Rd
94	Dysartsville Rd, Lake James, N Lake James SP
90	Lake James, Nebo, N Nebo/dsl to Lake James SP, S Marathon/dsl Springs Creek RV Ctr
86	NC 226, to Spruce Pine, Marion, N Exxon, Loves/Subway/Godfather's/dsl/scales/24hr Hardee's, KFC, Waffle House Jellystone RV Park (2mi)
85	US 221, Marion, N Hampton Inn to Mt Mitchell SP, S Marathon/dsl Best Value Inn, Super 8 $General
83	Ashworth Rd
82mm	**both lanes, full facilities, info, litter barrels, petwalk vending**
81	Sugar Hill Rd, to Marion, N BP/dsl, Murphy Express/dsl New China, Nopale's Mexican, Sixty Seven Pizza H, $Tree, Chrysler/Dodge/Jeep, GNC, Walmart/Subway, S Marion Travel Plaza/dsl
76mm	Catawba River
75	Parker Padgett Rd, S Exxon/Stuckey's/DQ/dsl
73	Old Fort, N BP/dsl Hardee's Auto+, S Sunoco/dsl McDonald's
72	US 70 (from eb), Old Fort, N B&B
71mm	Pisgah NF, eastern boundary
67.5mm	**truck rest area eb**
66	Ridgecrest, N B&B
65	(from wb), to Black Mountain, Black Mtn Ctr
64	NC 9, Black Mountain, N Exxon, Shell/Subway Pizza Hut BiLo/café, S BP/dsl Denny's, McDonald's, Phil's BBQ, Starbucks, Taco Bell, Wendy's Quality Inn Ingles Foods/gas, Rite Aid
63mm	Swannanoa River
59	Swannanoa, N BP/Subway, Shell/dsl Athens Pizza, Burger King, Don Chon Chinese, Papa John's Ace Hardware, CVS Drug, Family$, Harley-Davidson, Ingles Foods/gas, KOA (2mi), Miles RV Ctr/Park, to Warren Wilson Coll, USPO, vet, S Mama Gertie's Camping
55	US 70, E Asheville, N BP, Citgo/Subway, Mobil Arby's, Bojangles, Cocula Mexican, Domino's, Gondolier Italian, Waffle House, Zaxby's Days Inn, Holiday Inn, Motel 6, Quality Inn Family$, Folk Art Ctr, Go Groceries, Tap's RV park, to Mt Mitchell SP, VA H, vet
53b a	I-240 W, US 74 a, to Asheville, Bat Cave, S Shell/dsl Sonic, Subway CVS Drug, Ingles, to Blue Ridge Pkwy, N on Fairview Rd Ay Carumba Mexican, China Buffet, J&S Cafeteria, KFC, Little Caesars, McDonald's, Papa John's, Pizza Hut, Subway Ramada Inn $General, Advance Parts, Citgo/dsl, CVS Drug, Hamrick's, Hancock Fabrics, Home Depot, Meineke
51	US 25A, Sweeten Creek Rd, S Subway Brookstone Lodge
50	US 25, Asheville, N Market Ctr, Shell, Shell/dsl Arby's, Asaka Japanese, Chapala Mexican, Hardee's, Jimmy John's, LJ

ASHEVILLE

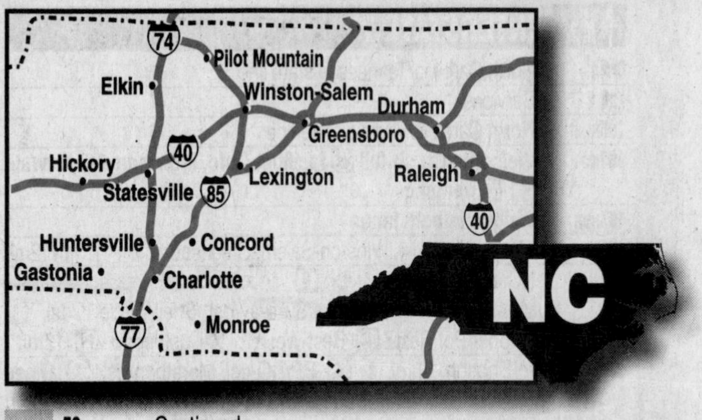

Exit #	Services
50	Continued Silver, McDonald's, Moe's SW Grill, Ruth's Chris Steaks, Starbucks, Subway, TGIFriday's, TX Roadhouse, Wendy's, Zoe's Kitchen Baymont Inn, Biltmore Village Lodge, Doubletree Inn, Grand Bohemian Hotel, Guesthouse Inn, Residence Inn H, to Biltmore House, URGENT CARE, S Hess/dsl Apollo Flame Rest., Atl Bread Co, Bojangles, Huddle House, Juicy Lucy's Advance Parts, Ingles/deli
47mm	French Broad River
47	NC 191, W Asheville, N Bear Creek RV Camping, S BP/Subway Moose Cafe Comfort Suites, Country Inn&Suites, Fairfield Inn, Hampton Inn, Holiday Inn Express, Rodeway Inn Audi/Porsche/VW, Farmer's Mkt, Ford, Nissan
46b a	I-26 & I-240 E, **2 mi** N multiple services from I-240
44	US 19, US 23, W Asheville, N BP, Hess/dsl, Shell/DQ/Quizno's/dsl Applebee's, Burger King, Cracker Barrel, Dunkin Donuts, El Chapala Mexican, Fatz Cafe, Hardee's, IHOP, Pizza Hut, Subway, Waffle House, Wendy's, Yao Grill Comfort Inn, Country Inn&Suites, Ramada Inn, Red Roof Inn, Rodeway Inn, Sleep Inn, Whispering Pines Motel Chevrolet, Chrysler/Dodge/Jeep, Family$, Ingles Foods, Lowe's, Mazda/Mercedes, S McDonald's, Zaxby's Budget Motel, Holiday Inn, ValuePlace Inn Bi-Lo Foods, CVS Drug, Home Depot
41mm	**weigh sta both lanes**
37	Candler, N BP, TA/Buckhorn Rest./dsl/scales/24hr/ @ Goodyear/truck tires, S Exxon/dsl Days Inn, Plantation Motel $General, KOA
33	Newfound Rd, to US 74, S Exxon
31	Rd 215, Canton, N Sagebrush Steaks Best Value Inn URGENT CARE, S BP/dsl, Marathon/DQ, Shell/dsl Arby's, Bojangles, Burger King, McDonald's, Starbucks, Subway, Taco Bell, Waffle House Comfort Inn Ford, Ingles Foods/dsl, RV/truck repair
27	US 19/23, to Waynesville, Great Smokey Mtn Expswy, **3 mi** S Burger King, Coffee Cup Cafe, Subway Super 8 H, $Tree, Food Lion, GNC, Lowe's, to WCU (25mi)
24	NC 209, to Lake Junaluska, N Pilot/Subway/dsl/scales/24hr/ @ Midway Motel, S Shell/cafe/dsl/24hr H
20	US 276, to Maggie Valley, Lake Junaluska, S BP/dsl, Exxon/dsl, Marathon (2mi) Creekwood RV Park, Pride RV Resort, Winngray RV Park
16mm	Pigeon River
15	Fines Creek
13mm	Pisgah NF eastern boundary
10mm	**both lanes, full facilities, info, litter barrels, petwalk vending**
7	Harmon Den
4mm	tunnel both lanes

NC

= gas = food = lodging = other = rest stop

INTERSTATE 77

ELKIN

0mm North Carolina/Tennessee state line

Exit # Services

105mm North Carolina/Virginia state line

105mm **Welcome Ctr sb full facilities, info, litter barrels, petwalk vending**

103mm **weigh sta both lanes**

101 I-74 E, to Mt Airy, Winston-Salem, Greensboro, E (12mi)

100 NC 89, to Mt Airy, E FLYING J/Brintle's Rest./dsl/scales/24hr/ @, Marathon/Subway/dsl, Shell/Circle K/dsl Copper Pot Rest. Best Western dsl repair, (12mi)

93 to Dobson, Surry, E BP/DQ/dsl, Marathon/dsl Diner, Harvest Grill (2mi), Putters Grill Hampton Inn, Surry Inn camping

85 NC 118, CC Camp Rd, to Elkin, **1-3 mi** W Murphy Express/dsl, Sheetz/dsl, Shell/7-11/dsl, Wilco/Hess/dsl Burger King, KFC, Mazzini's Italian, McDonald's, Sonic, Taco Bell, Zaxby's Fairfield Inn $Tree, AT&T, BigLots, Food Lion, Lowe's, Rite Aid, Walmart/Subway

83 US 21 byp, to Sparta (from nb)

82.5mm Yadkin River

82 NC 67, Elkin, E BP/Subway/dsl, Citgo/Case Outlet/dsl, Exxon/dsl Arby's, Cracker Barrel, Sixty Seven Pizza Best Western Holly Ridge Camping (8mi), W Wilco/Hess/Dunkin Donuts/dsl Bojangles, Capt Galley, McDonald's, Valentino's Pizza, Waffle House, Wendy's Comfort Inn, Days Inn, Hampton Inn $General, D-Rex Drug, Food Lion, URGENT CARE, vet

79 US 21 S, to Arlington, E Citgo/Subway/dsl Super 8, W BP/dsl Glenn's BBQ Best Value Inn

73b a US 421, to Winston-Salem, **1 mi** E Shell/Subway/7-11/dsl

72mm **nb, full facilities, litter barrels, petwalk vending**

65 NC 901, to Union Grove, Harmony, E Van Hoy Farms Camping, W BP/dsl, Shell/Subway/7-11/dsl Burger Barn B&B $General, Ace Hardware, Fiddler's Grove Camping (2mi)

NC

63mm **sb, full facilities, litter barrels, petwalk vending**

59 Tomlin Mill Rd, W Valero/dsl

56.5mm S Yadkin River

54 US 21, to Turnersburg, E Citgo, W Shell/7-11/dsl Arby's, Baskin-Robbins/Dunkin Donuts, Chick-fil-A, CookOut, Golden Corral, Zaxby's

STATESVILLE

51b a I-40, E to Winston-Salem, W to Hickory

50 E Broad St, Statesville, E Citgo, Kangaroo/dsl, Shell Arby's, Bojangles, Burger King, Charanda Mexican, Domino's, East Coast Grill, IHOP, Little Caesar's, McDonald's, Papa John's, Papa Murphy's, Pizza Hut, Shanghai Buffet, Starbucks, Subway, Taco Bell, Wendy's Brookwood Inn, Red Roof Inn $General, $Tree, AT&T, Belk, Bi-Lo, Food Lion, K-Mart, Rite Aid, URGENT CARE

49b a US 70, G Bagnal Blvd, to Statesville, E BP, Citgo/dsl, Citgo/dsl, Kangaroo/dsl, Shell, Solo KFC, Outback Steaks, Rice Fun Chinese, Subway, Village Inn Pizza, Waffle House Best Value Inn, Best Western, Comfort Inn, Courtyard, Hampton Inn, Motel 6, Ramada Inn auto repair, Camping World RV Ctr, Ford/Lincoln, Harley-Davidson, Honda, Nissan, Toyota/Scion, W Citgo/dsl, Exxon/dsl Microtel Buick/GMC, Carquest, Chrysler/Dodge/Jeep

45 to Troutman, Barium Springs, E KOA, RV Repair

42 US 21, NC 115, to Troutman, Oswalt, E Hess/Wilco/Subway/dsl/scales/24hr, Sheetz/dsl Bojangles, McDonald's,

MOORESVILLE

42 Continued
Wendy's AutoZone, Lowe's, W Citgo/dsl, CNC Arby's camping, to Lake Norman SP

39mm **both lanes, full facilities, litter barrels, petwalk vending**

36 NC 150, Mooresville, E Circle K/dsl, Exxon, QT/dsl, Shell/dsl Applebee's, CookOut, Denny's, Domino's, Fat Boys Rest., Hong Mei Buffet, Pizza Hut, Pomodoro's, Popeyes, Sonny's BBQ, Taco Bell, Waffle House, Wendy's, Zaxby's Days Inn, Fairfield Inn, Holiday Inn Express, Quality Inn $Tree, Belk, Big Lots, Cadillac/Chevrolet, Gander Mtn, GNC, Jo-Ann Fabrics, Kia, Kohl's, Subaru, Tuesday Morning, URGENT CARE, Walmart/Subway, W Circle K/dsl, Hess/dsl, Qt/dsl, Shell/dsl Baskin-Robbins/Dunkin Donuts, Bojangles, Buffalo Wild Wings, Charanda Mexican, Chick-fil-A, Chili's, Chipotle, Chopstix, Cracker Barrel, Duckworth's Grill, Firehouse Subs, Five Guys, Golden Corral, Hardee's, Hickory Tavern Grill, Hooters, IHOP, Iron Thunder Grill, LoneStar Steaks, McAlister's Deli, McDonald's, Moe's SW Cafe, Noodles&Co, O'Charley's, Panera Bread, Papa Murphy's, Red Robin, Rita's Custard, Sagebrush Steaks, Showmar's, Smoothie King, Sonic, Starbucks, Steak'n Shake, Subway Carolina Inn, Hampton Inn, Sleep Inn, Wingate Inn Advance Parts, AT&T, AutoZone, Best Buy, BJ's Whse/gas, CVS Drug, Dick's, Discount Tire, Food Lion, Hobby Lobby, Lowe's, Michael's, NTB, Old Navy, PetCo, Petsmart, Ross, Sam's Club/dsl, Staples, Target, TJ Maxx, Tuffy Auto, Verizon, vet, Walgreens, World Mkt

35 Brawley School Rd.

33 US 21 N, E Shell Brusco's Pizza, China Express, DQ, Iron Grill Japanese, Jeffrey's Rest, Jets Pizza, McDonald's, Starbucks, Subway Candlewood Suites, Hilton Garden, SpringHill Suites, TownePlace Suites , W Citgo/dsl, Marathon/dsl Arby's, Baskin-Robbins/Dunkin Donuts, Sauza's Mexican Food Lion, vet

31 Langtree Rd, W Shell/dsl

30 Davidson, E Exxon/dsl, Liberty Char-Grill, Ming's Chinese, Subway Homewood Suites Harris-Teeter, to Davidson College, Woodie's Auto Service, W North Harbor Rest

28 US 21 S, NC 73, Cornelius, Lake Norman, E Cashion/dsl, Citgo Acropolis Cafe Days Inn, Hampton Inn NAPA, vet, W Kangaroo Asiana, Bojangles, Chicago Dog, Choplin's Rest., Domino's, Dragon Buffet, Fresh Chef Cafe, Honeybaked Ham, Jersey Mike's, Jimmy John's, KFC, Little Caesar's, Mac's BBQ, McAlister's Deli, McDonald's, Pizza Hut, Starbucks, Subway, Taco Bell, Waffle House, Wendy's Clarion, Comfort Inn, EconoLodge, Microtel $Tree, Chrysler/Dodge/Jeep, Fresh Mkt, Goodyear/auto, Hyundai, Infiniti, SteinMart, USPO, Walgreens

CONCORD

25 NC 73, Concord, Lake Norman, E Shell/dsl Burger King, Chick-fil-A, Chili's, Duckworth's Grill, IHOP, Longhorn Steaks, McDonald's, Melting Pot, Moe's SW Grill, Panda Express, Panera Bread, Papa John's, Showmar's Rest., Starbucks, Subway, Zaxby's Country Inn&Suites, Holiday Inn Express, Quality Inn , AAA, Advance Parts, AT&T, GNC, Harris-Teeter, Home Depot, Kohl's, Lowe's, Marshall's, PetCo, Staples, Target, Tuffy Auto, Verizon, vet, W Shell/Circle K/dsl Bob Evans, Bojangles, Bonefish Grill, Carrabba's, Chipotle, Hickory Tavern Grill, House of Taipei, Jason's Deli, Jimmy John's, Kabuto Japanese, Outback Steaks, Qdoba, Red Rock's Cafe, Starbucks, Subway, Taco Mac, Viva Chicken, Which Wich?, Zoe's Kitchen Candlewood Suites, Courtyard, Sleep Inn Barnes&Noble, Dick's, Office Depot, to Energy Explorium, Walgreens, Whole Foods Mkt

INTERSTATE 77 Cont'd

Exit #	Services
23	Gilead Rd, to US 21, Huntersville, E BP, Pittstop, Shell Baskin-Robbins/Dunkin Dounuts, Bojangles, Chico's Mexican, CookOut, Hardee's, Huntersville Rest., Jersey Mike's, Little Caesar's, Rocky's Pizza, Romanello's Subs, Subway, Taco Bell, Waffle House, Wendy's Best Western, Comfort Suites, Hampton Inn, Super 8 AutoZone, Buick/GMC, Food Lion, Ford, Goodyear/auto, Hancock Fabrics, Honda, Mazda, O'Reilly Parts, Rite Aid, Toyota, Tuesday Morning, USPO, vet, VW, W Shell/7-11/dsl Domino's, Firehouse Subs, Five Guys, Fusion Asian, Groucho's Deli, Hawthorne's Pizza, Killington's Rest., McDonald's, Papa Murphy's, Pizza Hut, Starbucks H, Batteries+, CVS Drug, Earth Fare, GNC, Harris-Teeter, Publix, URGENT CARE, Walgreens
19b a	S I-485 Outer, Rd 115, to Spartanburg
18	Harris Blvd, Reames Rd, E BP/Arby's, Shell/7-11/dsl Azteca Mexican, Bob Evans, Hickory Tavern, Jack-in-the-Box, Jimmy John's, Subway, Waffle House Comfort Suites, Courtyard, Fairfield Inn, Hilton Garden, Holiday Inn Express, Suburban Lodge H, Advance Parts, Staples, to UNCC, Univ Research Park, URGENT CARE, W 5 Guys Burgers, Bravo Italian, Buffalo Wild Wings, Chick-fil-A, Chili's, East Coast Grill, Edomae Grill, Firebirds Grill, Firehouse Subs, Fox&Hound, Fox&Hound, Jersey Mike's, Mimi's Cafe, Moe's SW Grill, Olive Garden, Olive Garden, On-the-Border, Panera bread, PF Chang's, Red Robin, Shane's Rib Shack, TGI Friday's, Wendy's Drury Inn $Tree, AT&T, Belk, Best Buy, Dick's, Dillard's, Discount Tire, Lowe's, Macy's, mall, Old Navy, Petsmart, REI, Target, Verizon
16b a	US 21, Sunset Rd, E Circle K, QT/dsl, Shell/7-11/dsl Capt D's, Hardee's, KFC, McDonald's, Papa John's, Subway, Taco Bell, Wendy's Days Inn, Super 8 $General, AutoZone, Just$ave Foods, NAPA, O'Reilly Parts, W Circle K/dsl, Citgo/dsl, Shell/dsl/scales/24hr Baskin-Robbins/Dunkin Donuts, Bojangles, Bubba's BBQ, CookOut, Denny's, Domino's, Jack-in-the-Box, Little Caesar's, Subway, Waffle House Microtel, Sleep Inn Advance Parts, Aldi Foods, CVS Drug, Family$, Food Lion, Meineke, Walgreens
13b a	I-85, S to Spartanburg, N to Greensboro
12	La Salle St, W Marathon/dsl, Shell/dsl
11b a	I-277, Brookshire Fwy, NC 16
10b	Trade St, 5th St, E to Discovery Place, W Marathon Bojangles, Church's Family$
10a	US 21 (from sb), Moorhead St, downtown
9	I-277, US 74, to US 29, John Belk Fwy, downtown, E H, stadium
8	Remount Rd (from nb, no re-entry)
7	Clanton Rd, E Marathon/dsl EconoLodge, Super 8 Family$, W BP, Shell/7-11/dsl
6b a	US 521, Billy Graham Pkwy, E Citgo, QT/dsl, Shell/dsl Arby's, Azteca Mexican, Bojangles, Capt D's, Carolina Prime Steaks, Domino's, Dragon House, Firehouse Subs, HoneyBaked Ham, IHOP, KFC, Papa John's, Tres Pesos Grill, Waffle House Best Western, Days Inn, Ramada Ltd, Sheraton CVS Drug, Family$, Home Depot, TJ Maxx, to Queens Coll, Walgreens, W Kangaroo Omaha Steaks Courtyard, Embassy Suites, Extended Stay America, Hyatt House, InTowne Suites, La Quinta, Sleep Inn
5	Tyvola Rd, E Kangaroo, Shell Chili's, China King, Denny's, McDonald's, Sonny's BBQ, Subway Comfort Inn, Crowne Plaza, Extended Stay America, Hawthorn Suites, Hilton, Quality Inn, Residence Inn Costco/gas, Family$,

CHARLOTTE

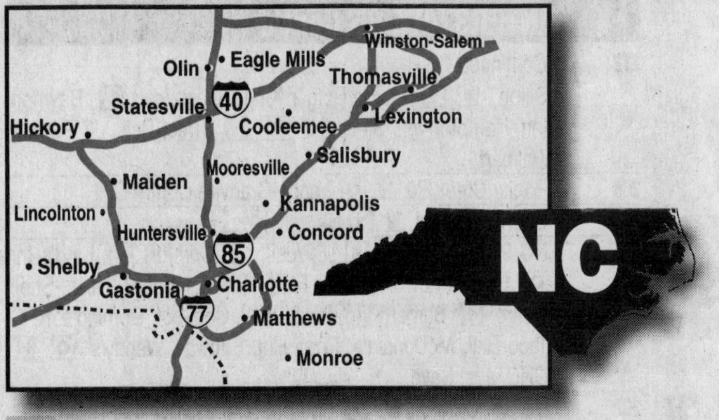

Exit #	Services
5	Continued Jaguar, Maserati, Meineke, Verizon, W Extended Stay America, Home2 Suites, Wingate Inn
4	Nations Ford Rd, E Citgo, Shell/Circle K Floyd's Rest. Knights Inn, La Casa Inn, W Shell/Burger King
3	Arrowood Rd, E Cafe South, Jack-in-the-Box, Sonic, Starbucks, Wendy's Courtyard, Fairfield Inn, Holiday Inn Express, Hyatt Place, Mainstay Suites, Sonesta Suites, TownePlace Suites, W Ruby Tuesday Hampton Inn
2	I-485
1.5mm	**Welcome Ctr nb, full facilities, info, litter barrels, petwalk vending**
1	Westinghouse Blvd, to I-485 (from nb), E BP/dsl Jack-in-the-Box, Subway, Waffle House Super 8, W Shell/7-11/dsl Burger King
0mm	North Carolina/South Carolina state line

INTERSTATE 85

Exit #	Services
234mm	North Carolina/Virginia state line
233	US 1, to Wise, E Budget Inn
231mm	**Welcome Ctr sb full facilities, litter barrels, petwalk vending**
229	Oine Rd, to Norlina, E BP, W SRA
226	Ridgeway Rd, W to Kerr Lake, to SRA
223	Manson Rd, E BP/dsl camping, W to Kerr Dam
220	US 1, US 158, Flemingtown Rd, to Middleburg, E Mobil/dsl, W Exxon/dsl/scales/truck wash Chex Motel/rest.
218	US 1 S (from sb exits left), to Raleigh
217	Nutbush Bridge, E auto repair, W Exxon/dsl Kerr Lake RA
215	US 158 BYP E, Henderson (no EZ return from nb), E Hess/dsl, Shell, Sunoco Burger King, Forsyth's BBQ, Nunnery-Freeman BBQ, Subway Budget Host, EconoLodge, Scottish Inn $General, Food Lion, repair/tires, Roses, services on US 158
214	NC 39, Henderson, E BP Waffle House Verizon, W Mobil/dsl, Shell to Kerr Lake RA
213	US 158, Dabney Dr, to Henderson, E Marathon, Valero Bamboo Garden, Big Cheese Pizza, Bojangles, Denny's, Ichibar Chinese, KFC, McDonald's, Papa John's, Pino's Italian, Subway, Wendy's Family$, Food Lion, Radio Shack, Roses, Save-a-Lot Foods, W Shell Chick-fil-A, Golden Corral, Mayflower Seafood, Pizza Hut, Ruby Tuesday, Smithfields BBQ, Taco Bell Holiday Inn Express Advance Parts, BigLots, Buick/Chevrolet/GMC, Chrysler/Dodge/Jeep, Ford/Lincoln, Lowe's, Rite Aid, Staples, Verizon
212	Ruin Creek Rd, E Shell/dsl Cracker Barrel, Mazatlan Mexican, Ribeye's, Waffle House Knight's Inn Toyota/

HENDERSON

NC

INTERSTATE 85 Cont'd

OXFORD

212 Continued
Scion, W gas Exxon/Burger King, Sheetz/dsl lodging Baymont Inn, Hampton Inn, Sleep Inn other H, $Tree, Belk, JC Penney, Walmart

209 Poplar Creek Rd, W other Vance-Granville Comm Coll

206 US 158, Oxford, W gas BP/dsl other

204 NC 96, Oxford, E gas BP/dsl lodging Comfort Inn, King's Inn other Buick/Chevrolet/GMC, Ford, Honda, W gas Hess, Shell, Valero food Burger King, China Wok, Cookout, Domino's, KFC/Taco Bell, McDonald's, Pizza Hut, Subway, Wendy's other H, GNC, Just Save

202 US 15, Oxford, W gas Murphy Express/dsl food Bojangles, Hibachi, HWY 55 lodging Crown Motel (2mi) other $Tree, Verizon, Walmart

199mm rest stop both lanes, full facilities, litter barrels, petwalk

198mm Tar River

BUTNER

191 NC 56, Butner, E gas BP/dsl, Hess/dsl food Betty Lue's Rest., Bob's BBQ, Bojangles, Domino's, El Rio Mexican, KFC/Taco Bell, McDonald's, Pizza Hut, Pizza Mia, Sonic, Subway, Taste of China, Wendy's lodging Creedmor Inn other $General, $Tree, Advance Parts, AutoZone, Food Lion, M&H Tires, Rite Aid, to Falls Lake RA, vet, W gas Exxon, Shell/dsl food Hardee's, Ribeye's lodging Best Western, EconoLodge, Ramada Ltd other auto repair

189 Butner, **1 mi** W gas BP/dsl, Citgo, Valero food Subway other repair

186b a US 15, to Creedmoor, E gas Variety Mart/dsl

185mm Falls Lake

183 Redwood Rd

182 Red Mill Rd, E gas Exxon/dsl other Kenworth/Isuzu Trucks

180 Glenn School Rd

179 E Club Blvd, E gas Exxon

DURHAM

178 US 70 E, to Raleigh, Falls Lake RA, Research Triangle, E other RDU Airport

177 Avondale Dr, NC 55, W gas BP, Shell food American Hero, Arby's, Hong Kong Buffet, Los Comales, McDonalds, Subway other Advance Parts, Family$

176b a Gregson St, US 501 N, E food Biscuitville, Burger King, Hugo's, PanPan Diner, Randy's Pizza, Ruby Tuesday, Tripp's Diner lodging Hampton Inn other Macy's, mall, Museum of Life&Science, Sears/auto, W other H, museum

175 Guess Rd, E gas Citgo food Doghouse Café, Hog Heaven BBQ lodging Holiday Inn Express, Super 8 other Rite Aid, W gas BP/dsl, Pure/dsl food Bojangles, Honey's Diner, IHOP, TX Roadhouse lodging Red Roof Inn other Family Dollar, GNC, Home Depot, Kroger, PetsMart, Ross, Verizon, vet

174a Hillandale Rd, W gas BP food Blue Olive, China King, El Corral, Pomodoro Italian lodging Comfort Inn, Courtyard other Kerr Drug, URGENT CARE

174b US 15 S, US 501 S

173 US 15, US 501, US 70, Colemill Rd, W Durham, E gas BP, Exxon/dsl, Mobil, Shell food Arby's, Biscuitville, Bojangles, Chick-fil-A, Cookout, Cracker Barrel, DogHouse Rest., Domino's, Japan Express, KFC/Taco Bell, McDonald's, Shanghai Chinese, Subway, Waffle House, Wendy's lodging Days Inn, Hilton, Motel 6, Quality Inn other H, $General, Advance Parts, Autozone, CVS Drug, Hancock Fabrics, Kroger, O'Reilly Parts, Rite Aid

172 NC 147 S, to US 15 S, US 501 S (from nb), Durham

170 to NC 751, to Duke U (no EZ return from nb), E lodging Durham Skyland Inn, Scottish Inn, W other to Eno River SP

165 NC 86, to Chapel Hill, E gas Eagles/Burger King/dsl food China Fuji, Hwy 55, Papa John's, Subway other Home Depot, Walmart, W gas BP/dsl other auto repair

164 Hillsborough, E gas BP, Citgo/dsl food McDonald's lodging Holiday Inn Express, W gas Shell food Bojangles, Domino's, Hardee's, KFC/Taco Bell, Pizza Hut, Pueblo Viejo Mexican, Russell's Steaks, Subway, Waffle House, Wendy's lodging Microtel other $General, $Tree, AutoZone, CarQuest, Food Lion, Ford, Goodyear/auto

163 I-40 E, to Raleigh.

I-85 S and I-40 W run together 38 mi.

161 to US 70 E, NC 86 N

160 to NC 86 N, Efland, W gas Exxon/dsl other Andrew's Repair

158mm **weigh sta both lanes**

MEBANE

157 Buckhorn Rd, E gas BP/dsl, Petro/Valero/Dunkin Donuts/Iron Skillet/dsl/scales/24hr/ @, W gas Citgo

154 Mebane-Oaks Rd, E gas Murphy USA/dsl, Sheetz/dsl food China Garden, Ciao Pizza, Subway, Wendy's, Zaxby's other $Tree, GNC, Radio Shack, Walmart/Subway, W gas BP, Hess/dsl, Shell/dsl food Biscuitville, Blue Ribbon Diner, Bojangles, La Fiesta Mexican, McDonald's, Roma Pizza, Sake Japanese, Waffle House lodging Budget Inn other Advance Parts, AutoZone, CVS Drug, Lowe's Foods, Tanger Outlets/famous brands, Verizon, vet, Walgreens

153 NC 119, Mebane, E gas BP/KFC/Pizza Hut/Taco Bell food Anna Maria's Pizza, Cracker Barrel, Jersey Mike's, Moe's SW Grill, Ruby Tuesday, Sakura Japanese, Smithfield's BBQ, Yogurt Café lodging Hampton Inn, Holiday Inn Express other $General, Lowe's, O'Reilly Parts, vet, W gas Exxon/Burger King food Domino's, La Cocina Mexican, Papa John's, Sonic, Subway, YumYum Chinese other Curves, Food Lion

152 Trollingwood Rd, E gas Pilot/McDonald's/dsl/scales/24hr

150 to Roxboro, Haw River, W gas FLYING J/Denny's/dsl/LP/scales/24hr, Hess/Wilco/DQ/Wendy's/dsl/scales/24hr, Speed-Co lodging Days Inn other Blue Beacon

BURLINGTON

148 NC 54, Graham, E gas BP/dsl, Marathon/dsl, Shell/dsl food Waffle House lodging Homestay Suites, W food AmMex 2 Cafe

147 NC 87, to Pittsboro, Graham, E gas BP, Sheetz/dsl food AnnaMaria's Pizzeria, Arby's, Bojangles, Burger King, Domino's, Great Wall Chinese, Guerrero Mexican, Lucky Bamboo, Pizza Hut, Subway, Wendy's other Advance Parts, AutoZone, Champion Tire/Repair, Curves, Family$, Food Lion, Ford, Just Save, O'Reilly Parts, Rite Aid, vet, W gas Citgo/dsl, Exxon/dsl, Shell/dsl food Biscuitville, Cook-Out, Golden China, McDonald's, Taco Bell, Zaxby's other H, $General, CVS Drug, Verizon, Walgreens

145 NC 49, Burlington, E gas Marathon/dsl, Shell/dsl food Capt D's lodging EconoLodge, Microtel, Motel 6 other Harley-Davidson, W gas BP/dsl food Biscuitville, Bojangles, Burger King, China Inn, Hardee's, KFC, Subway lodging Quality Inn, Red Carpet Inn, Royal Inn other $General, Chrysler/Dodge/Jeep, Family$, Food Lion, Radio Shack, Rite Aid

143 NC 62, Burlington, E gas Sav-Way food Hardee's, Waffle House, Wendy's other JR Outlet, to Alamance Bfd, W gas Marathon, Sheetz/dsl food Biscuitville, Cutting Board Rest, K&W Cafeteria lodging Ramada Inn other $General, auto repair, Cadillac, Chevrolet, Food Lion, Ford, Home Depot, Mazda, vet

141 Huffman Mill Rd, Burlington, E gas BP, Marathon/Kangaroo food IHOP, Mayflower Seafood, Outback Steaks lodging Hampton Inn, Holiday Inn Express other H, Nissan, W gas Raygo food 5 Guys Burgers, Andy's, Applebee's, Arby's, Biscuitville, Bojangles, Cancun Mexican, Chick-fil-A, China Gate, Cook-Out, Cracker Barrel, Golden Corral, Good Times Cafe, Grill 584, Hibachi Buffet, HoneyBaked Ham, Hooters, KFC, La Cocina Mexican, Longhorn Steaks, Mellow Mushroom, O'Charley's, Panera Bread, Ruby Tuesday, Sal's Italian, Starbucks, Steak'n Shake, Subway, Taco Bell, Village Grill, Wholly Guacamole lodging Best Western, Country Inn&Suites, Courtyard, Super 8 other $Tree,

NC

INTERSTATE 85 Cont'd

Exit	Services
141	Continued Hamrick's, Harris Teeter, Hyundai, K-Mart/gas, Lowe's, mall, Radio Shack, Sears/auto, TJ Maxx, to Elon Coll, Verizon, Walgreens, Walmart/McDonald's
140	University Ave, E [other] [H], Toyota/Scion, W [food] Brixx Pizza, Buffalo Wing Wings, Burger King, Chick-fil-A, Chili's, Coldstone, Jimmy John's, Little Italy, McDonald's, Mimi's Cafe, Moe's SW Grill, Olive Garden, Peking House, Qdoba, Red Bowl Asian, Red Lobster, Red Robin, Starbucks, TX Roadhouse [other] AT&T, Barnes&Noble, Belk, Best Buy, BJ's Whse/gas, Dick's, Dillard's, Discount Tire, GNC, Hobby Lobby, JC Penney, Kohl's, Michael's, Old Navy, Petsmart, Ross, Target, Verizon
139mm	**[RS] both lanes, full [handicapped] facilities, litter barrels [phone] [picnic] vending**
138	NC 61, Gibsonville, W [gas] TA/BP/Burger King/Popeye's/dsl/scales/24hr/ @ [other] truckwash
135	Rock Creek Dairy Rd, W [gas] Citgo, Marathon/Kangaroo [food] Bojangles, China 1, Ciao Italian, Domino's, Guacamole Mexican, Jersey Mike's Subs, McDonald's, Pizza Hut/Taco Bell, Subway [lodging] Comfort Suites [other] $General, Curves, CVS Drug, Food Lion, Midtown Drug, Verizon
132	Mt Hope Church Rd, E [gas] Citgo/Subway/dsl [food] McDonald's, Pascali's Pizza, W [gas] Exxon/dsl, Hess/Wendy's/dsl/24hr [lodging] Hampton Inn
131	to I-85 S, to I-73 N, to US 421, Highpoint, Charlotte
129	Youngsmill Rd, W [other] Greensboro Camping (4mi)
128	Alamance Church Rd, E [gas] Citgo/Subway/dsl
126b a	US 421, to Sanford, E [gas] Exxon/dsl, Hagan Stone Park Camping, Kangaroo/dsl
124	S Elm, Eugene St, W [gas] Murphy Express/dsl [food] Andy's, Bamboo Grill, Bojangles, Cracker Barrel, McDonald's, Mi Casa, Smithfield's BBQ, Starbucks, Subway, Waffle House, Wendy's [other] AT&T, Lowe's, Verizon, Walmart/McDonald's
122c b a	US 220, to Greensboro, Asheboro (from sb)
121	I-40 W, I-73 N, to Winston-Salem
120	N US 29, E US 70, to I-40 W
119	Groometown Rd, from nb, W [gas] Citgo/dsl
118	US 29 S, US 70 W, to High Point, Jamestown, W [lodging] Grandover Resort [other] [H]
115mm	Deep River
113c	I-74, US 311, Ashboro, to Winston-Salem
113a	NC 62, Archdale, E [gas] Citgo/dsl, W [gas] BP/dsl [lodging] Quality Inn
111	US 311, to High Point, Archdale, E [gas] Sheetz/dsl [food] Bamboo Garden, Bojangles, Hardee's, Pizza Hut, Subway, Wendy's [lodging] Days Inn [other] $General, CVS Drug, Food Lion, Lowe's Foods/24hr, W [gas] Citgo, Exxon/McDonald's, Marathon/dsl, Shell/Circle K/dsl [food] Biscuitville, J&S Cafe, Rancho Rest, Waffle House [lodging] Comfort Inn, Country Inn&Suites, Fairfield Inn, Hampton Inn, Holiday Inn Express [other] [H], O'Reilly Parts, tires, USPO, vet
108	Hopewell Church Rd, Trinity
106	Finch Farm Rd, E [gas] BP/dsl, W [gas] Sheetz/dsl [food] Smokey T's BBQ, Subway (1mi)
103	NC 109, to Thomasville, E [gas] Marathon/dsl, Murphy USA/dsl, Shell [food] Arby's, Chen's Kitchen, Cookout Burgers, Elizabeth's Pizza, Taco Bell [lodging] Hospitality Suites [other] $Tree, CVS Drug, Ingles Foods, K-Mart, Radio Shack, Walmart/McDonald's, W [gas] Exxon/Subway/dsl, Hess/Wilco/dsl, RaceWay, Shell [food] BBQ Shack, Biscuitville, Bojangles, Burger King, Captain Tom's, China Garden, Denny's, E Coast Grill, Hardee's, Hunan Chinese, KFC, La Carreta Mexican, Little Caesars, Mandarin Express, Mazatlan Mexican, McDonald's, Mr Gatti's, Papa John's, Pizza

GREENSBORO

THOMASVILLE

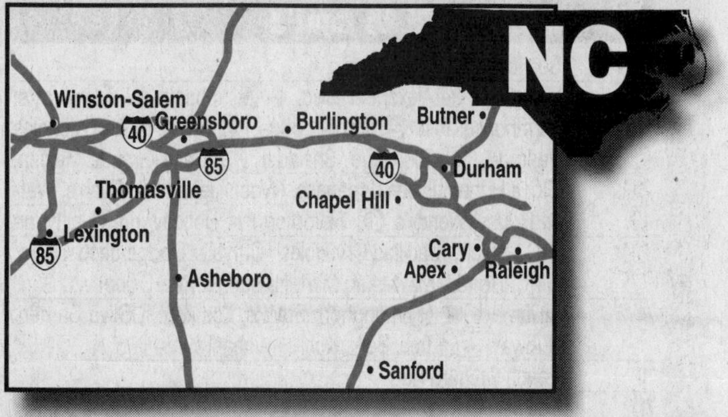

Exit	Services
103	Continued Hut, Ruby Tuesday, Sonic, Sunrise Diner, Waffle House, Wendy's [lodging] Davidson Lodge, Quality Inn [other] $General, Advance Parts, Aldi Foods, AutoZone, Family$, Food Lion, Merchant's Tire, Mighty$, NAPA, O'Reilly Parts, Peebles, Rite Aid, Verizon, Walgreens
102	Lake Rd, W [gas] Marathon/dsl, Sunoco/dsl [lodging] Comfort Inn, Microtel [other] [H]
100mm	**[RS] both lanes, full [handicapped] facilities, litter barrels, petwalk [phone] [picnic] vending**
96	US 64, to Asheboro, Lexington, E [gas] Exxon/dsl [other] Modern Tire, NC Zoo, W [gas] Citgo/dsl, Gulf/dsl [food] Randy's Rest. [other] to Davidson Co Coll
94	Old US 64, E [gas] Shell, W [other] Timberlake Gallery
91	NC 8, to Southmont, E [gas] BP/dsl, Mobil/7-11, Shell/dsl [food] Biscuit King, Chrissy's Doghouse, Christo Rest., Hunan Express, Jimmy's BBQ, Kabuki, KFC, McDonald's, Ocean View Seafood, Subway, Wendy's [lodging] Days Inn, Hwy 8 Motel [other] Food Lion, High Rock Lake Camping (7mi), Kerr Drug, Mock Tire, W [gas] Exxon/dsl, QM/dsl [food] Applebee's, Arby's, Burger King, Cagmey's Kitchen, Cracker Barrel, Golden Corral, La Carreta Mexican, Little Ceasars, Mi Pueblo, Pizza Hut (1mi), Subway, Taco Bell, Zaxby's [lodging] Country Hearth Inn, Quality Inn [other] [H], $Tree, Belk, GNC, Lowe's (1mi), Radio Shack, Walmart
88	Linwood, W [gas] Gulf/dsl [other] [H]
87	US 29, US 70, US 52 (from nb), High Point, W [other] [H], [airport]
86	Belmont Rd, W [gas] Bill's Trkstp/dsl/scales/24hr/ @
84	US 29 S, US 70 W, NC 150 (from nb), to Spencer
82	US 29, US 70 (from sb), to Spencer
81.5mm	Yadkin River
81	Long Ferry Rd, Spencer, E [gas] Liberty/dsl
79	Spencer Shops SHS, Spencer, E Spencer, **1 mile** W [gas] Citgo [food] Bojangles, Subway [other] $General, Food Lion, Kerr Drug
76b a	US 52, to Albemarle, Salisbury, E [gas] BP, Citgo, Pop Shoppe [food] Applebee's, Capriano's, ColdStone, E Coast Grill, Grand Asian, IHOP, Mr Gatti's Pizza, Pancho Villa Mexican, Top China, Zaxby's [lodging] Days Inn, Economy Inn, Happy Traveler Inn [other] $Tree, Aldi Foods, AT&T, CVS Drug, Food Lion, GNC, Harley-Davidson, Lowe's, Marshall's, Old Navy, Petsmart, Radio Shack, Rite Aid, Staples, Tire Kingdom, Verizon, vet, Walgreens, W [gas] Murphy Express/dsl, Shell/Circle K/dsl, Wilco/Hess/dsl [food] Blue Bay Seafood, Bojangles, Burger King, Capt D's, Chick-fil-A, China Buffet, Christo's Rest., Cookout, Cracker Barrel, Hardee's, HoneyBaked Ham, KFC, McDonald's, O'Charley's, Outback Steaks, Papa John's, Pizza Hut, Starbucks, Subway, Taco Bell, Tokyo Express, Wendy's [lodging] Comfort Suites, Courtyard [other] [H], Advance Parts, AutoZone, BigLots, Family$, Firestone/auto, Goodyear/auto, K-Mart, Office Depot, USPO, Walmart/Subway

SALISBURY

NC

INTERSTATE 85 Cont'd

Exit #	Services
75	US 601, Jake Alexander Blvd, E [gas] Sheetz/dsl [food] Arby's, Farmhouse Rest. [lodging] EconoLodge [other] NAPA, to Dan Nicholas Park, W [gas] BP, Citgo, Shell/dsl [food] Casa Grande Mexian, CiCi's Pizza, Ichiban Japanese, Nyoshi Japanese, Ryan's, Waffle House, Wendy's [lodging] Hampton Inn, Holiday Inn, Quality Inn [other] Buick, Cadillac/Chevrolet, Chrysler/Dodge/Jeep, Ford, GMC, Honda, Kia, Magic Mart, Nissan, Toyota/Scion
74	Julian Rd, W [food] Longhorn Steaks, Los Arcos, Olive Garden, Subway [other] $Tree, Belk, Kohl's, Michael's
72	Peach Orchard Rd
71	Peeler Rd, E [gas] Love's/Chester's/McDonald's/dsl/scales/24hr, W [gas] Hess/Wilco/Bojangles/Subway/dsl/scales/24hr [other] dsl repair
70	Webb Rd, E [other] flea mkt, W [gas] Shell/dsl [food] Bebops BBQ [other] st patrol
68	US 29, US 601, to Rockwell, China Grove, W [gas] BP [food] Domino's, Gary's BBQ, Hardee's, Jimmie's Rest, Pizza Hut, Subway [other] $General, AutoZone, Family$, Food Lion, Rite Aid
63	Kannapolis, E [gas] Pilot/Subway/dsl/scales [food] Waffle House [lodging] Motel 6
60	Earnhardt Rd, Copperfield Blvd, E [gas] Exxon/dsl, Marathon [food] Bojangles, Cracker Barrel, Waffle House [lodging] Country Inn&Suites, Hampton Inn, Sleep Inn [other] [H], Discount Tire, W [gas] Marathon/Kangaroo/dsl [food] Carino's Italian, Casa Grande Mexican, Dragon Wok, Firehouse Subs, Logan's Roadhouse, McDonald's, Ruby Tuesday, Steak'n Shake, Subway, Taco Bell, Wendy's [lodging] Holiday Inn Express [other] Hobby Lobby, Kohl's, Lowe's, Sam's Club/gas, URGENT CARE, Walmart
59mm	**[RS] both lanes, full [handicapped] facilities, litter barrels, petwalk [phone] [picnic] vending**
58	US 29, US 601, Concord, E [gas] BP, Marathon/dsl, Shell/dsl [food] Applebee's, Capt D's, Chick-fil-A, Chili's, El Vallarta Mexican, Golden Corral, Jimmy John's, Mayflower Seafood, McDonald's, Moe's SW Grill, Mr C's Rest., O'Charley's, Popeye's, Starbucks, Subway, Wendy's [lodging] Best Value Inn, Howard Johnson, Rodeway Inn [other] [H], Belk, Harris Teeter, JC Penney, mall, Sears/auto, st patrol, Staples, Verizon, Walgreens, W [gas] BP, Hess [food] CiCi's, IHOP [lodging] Econolodge, Fairfield Inn, Microtel [other] $General, Ford, Hancock Fabrics, Home Depot, vet
55	NC 73, to Davidson, Concord, E [gas] Shell [food] McDonald's, W [gas] Shell/Circle K/dsl [lodging] Days Inn
54	Kannapolis Pkwy, George W Lyles Pkwy, E [gas] Citgo [food] Bojangles, China Garden, Noodles&Co, Off-the-Grill [other] Advance Parts, AutoZone, CVS Drug, Firestone, Food Lion, Harris Teeter, URGENT CARE, vet, Walgreens, W [gas] Marathon/Kangaroo [food] Arby's, Asian Cafe, Buffalo Wild Wings, Chick-fil-A, Fatz Cafe, Jersey Mike's, McDonald's, Mi Pueblo, Starbucks [other] $Tree, Best Buy, Dick's, Goodyear/auto, Marshall's, Steinmart, Super Target
52	Poplar Tent Rd, E [gas] Shell/7-11/dsl [food] R&R BBQ [other] museum, to Lowe's Speedway, W [gas] Exxon/7-11/dsl
49	Bruton Smith Blvd, Concord Mills Blvd, E [gas] BP/McDonalds, Shell/7-11/dsl [food] 5 Guys Burgers, Bojangles, Camila's Mexican, Carrabbas, ChuckECheese, Cinco de Mayo Mexican, Cookout, Cracker Barrel, Firehouse Subs, Hooters, Jack-in-the-Box, KFC/Taco Bell, Quaker Steak, Ruby Tuesday, Sonic, Sonny's BBQ, Starbucks, Subway, Taco Bell, TX Land&Cattle Steaks, TX Roadhouse, Waffle House, Wendy's, Zaxby's [lodging] Comfort Suites, Courtyard, Embassy Suites, Great Wolf Lodge, Hampton Inn, Hilton Garden, Holiday Inn Express, Residence Inn, Sleep Inn, SpringHill Suites, Suburban Lodge, Wingate Inn
49	Continued [other] BJ's Whse/gas, Fleetwood RV camping (1.5mi), Harley-Davidson, Honda, to Lowe's Motor Speedway, Tom Johnson RV Ctr (1.5mi), Toyota/Scion, W [gas] Marathon/dsl, Texaco [food] Applebee's, Burger King, Charanda Mexican, Chick-fil-A, Foster's Grille, Jimmy John's, Mayflower Seafood, McAlisters Deli, Olive Garden, On-the-Border, Panera Bread, Razzoo's Cafe, Red Lobster, Steak'n Shake, Sticky Fingers, TGI Friday's [other] $Tree, AT&T, BassPro Shops, Best Buy, BooksAMillion, Concord Mills Mall, Discount Tire, Goodyear/auto, Lowe's, PetCo, Radio Shack, Ross, TJ Maxx, URGENT CARE, Verizon, Walmart/Subway
48	I-485, to US 29, to Rock Hill
46	Mallard Creek Church Rd, E [gas] Exxon/7-11, Hess/dsl, Kangaroo [food] China Cafe, Giacomos Pizza, Jack-in-the-Box, Wild Wing Cafe [other] Research Park, Tire Kingdom, vet, W [gas] Shell/Circle K [food] 5 Guys Burgers, Hickory Tavern, Rita's, Starbucks, Thai Taste [other] PetCo, Trader Joes
45b a	Harris Blvd, E [food] 360 Bistro, Applebee's, Bojangles, Buffalo Wild Wings, Burger King, Cheddar's, Chick-fil-A, Chili's, China Buffet, China Palace, Chipotle, Fuse Buffet, IHOP, Jersey Mike's Subs, Jimmy John's, Los Arcos, McDonald's, Nakato Steaks, Panera Bread, Papa John's, Picasso's Pizza, Qdoba, Shane's Rib Shack, Shoney's, Showmar's Rest, Smokey Bones, Starbucks, T. Mac Grill, Taco Bell, TGIFriday's [lodging] Country Inn&Suites, Courtyard, Drury Inn, Extended Stay America, Hampton Inn, Hilton, Holiday Inn, Homewood Suites, Microtel, Residence Inn, Sleep Inn [other] [H], Dick's, Food Lion, Kohl's, Michael's, Office Depot, Ross, Sam's Club, TJ Maxx, to Miz Scarlett's, to UNCC, U Research Park, Verizon, Walgreens, Walmart/McDonald's, **0-2 mi W** [food] Longhorn Steaks, Macaroni Grill, Red Robin, Tony's Pizza [lodging] SpringHill Suites, TownePlace Suites [other] Harris Teeter, Rite Aid
43	University City Blvd, E [gas] Marathon/Subway/dsl [food] Honey-baked Ham, Taco Bell, Zaxby's [lodging] Extended Stay America, InTowne Suites [other] Discount Tire, Firestone/auto, GNC, Hobby Lobby, IKEA, Marshall's, Old Navy, Petsmart, Walmart, World Mkt
42	US 29 (nb only)
41	Sugar Creek Rd, E [gas] RaceWay [food] Bojangles, McDonald's, Taco Bell, Wendy's [lodging] Brookwood Inn, Continental Inn, Motel 6, Travel Inn, W [gas] Shell/Circle K [food] Chicken Box Rest, Cook-out, TX Ranch Steaks [lodging] Days Inn, Red Roof Inn, Rodeway Inn, Sunset Inn, Super 8, S [gas] 7-11/gas
40	Graham St, E [gas] Exxon/7-11/dsl [lodging] Budget Inn [other] UPS, Volvo, Western Star, W [gas] Marathon/dsl [other] Freightliner, S [other] NAPA Autocare
39	Statesville Ave, E [gas] Pilot/Subway/dsl/scales/24hr [other] CarQuest, repair, W [gas] Citgo/dsl, Shell/dsl [food] Bojangles [other] Family$
38	I-77, US 21, N to Statesville, S to Columbia
37	Beatties Ford Rd, E [gas] Marathon, Shell/7-11/dsl [food] Burger King, McDonald's, Subway [other] CVS Drug, Family$, Food Lion, USPO, W [gas] Citgo
36	NC 16, Brookshire Blvd, E [lodging] Rodeway Inn [other] [H], repair, W [gas] Hari/dsl, RaceWay/dsl, Shell/7-11/dsl, Sunoco/dsl [food] Burger King, Jack-in-the-Box, Mr C's Rest., Subway [other] Family$, Griffin Tire
35	Glenwood Dr, E [lodging] Knights Inn, W [gas] Shell/dsl
34	NC 27, Freedom Dr, E [gas] Citgo/dsl, Shell/Circle K [food] Beauregard's Rest, Bojangles, Capt D's, Cookout, McDonald's, Pizza Hut, Showmar's, Subway, Taco Bell, Wendy's [other] $Tree, Advance Parts, Aldi Foods, AutoZone, Family$, Goodyear, Rite Aid, Save-A-Lot Foods, URGENT CARE, vet, Walgreens, W [lodging] Charlotte Express [other] JiffyLube

CONCORD

CHARLOTTE

NC

CHARLOTTE

INTERSTATE 85 Cont'd

Exit #	Services
33	US 521, Billy Graham Pkwy, E Shell/dsl Bojangles, KFC/Taco Bell, McDonald's, Wendy's Baymont Inn, Comfort Suites, Royal Inn, Sheraton, SpringHill Suites , W Exxon/dsl Cracker Barrel, Ichiban, Waffle House EconoLodge, La Quinta, Microtel, Motel 6, Quality Inn, Red Roof Inn, Super 8
32	Little Rock Rd, E Shell/7-11/dsl Airport Inn, Courtyard, Hampton Inn, Holiday Inn, W Citgo/dsl, Shell/7-11 Arby's, Bud's Chicken, Hardee's, Showmar's Rest., Subway Country Inn&Suites, Day's Inn, Wingate Inn Family$, Food Lion, Griffin Tire, Rite Aid
30b a	I-485, to 1-77, Pineville
29	Sam Wilson Rd, E BP (1mi) camping, W Shell/dsl
28mm	**weigh sta both lanes**
27.5mm	Catawba River
27	NC 273, Mt Holly, E BP/Dunkin Donuts/dsl, Murphy USA/dsl Arby's, Captain's Cap Seafood, Chick-fil-A, KFC, Pizza Hut, Sake Japanese, Subway, Taco Bell, Waffle House, Wendy's Big Lots, CVS Drug, Family$, Firestone/auto, Lowe's, NAPA, Walgreens, Walmart/Subway, W Citgo/dsl Holiday Inn Express
26	NC 7, E BP/dsl, Marathon/dsl Bojangles, Hardee's, King Buffet, McDonald's, New China, Papa John's Hampton Inn $Tree, Advance Parts, Aldi Foods, AT&T, AutoZone, BiLo, Ford, Verizon, W Belmont Abbey Coll
24mm	South Fork River
23	NC 7, McAdenville, W Exxon/dsl, Shell/Subway/dsl Hardee's, Hillbilly's BBQ/Steaks
22	Cramerton, Lowell, E Hess/dsl, Marathon Applebee's, Chick-fil-A, CiCi's, Jack-in-the-Box, Jersey Mike's Subs, Popeyes, Portofino's, Sakura Japanese, Schlotzsky's, Zaxby's Books-A-Million, Buick/Cadillac/Chevrolet/GMC, Gander Mtn, Honda, Kia, K-Mart, Kohl's, Lowe's, Old Navy, Petsmart, Sam's Club/gas, U-Haul
21	Cox Rd, E Marathon Akropolis Cafe, Buffalo Wild Wings, Cheddar's, Chili's, Chipotle, ChuckeCheese, Cookout, Dynasty Buffet, Firehouse Subs, Five Guys, Golden Corral, Hibachi Buffet, Krispy Kreme, La Fuente, Logan's Roadhouse, Longhorn Steaks, McAlister's Deli, McDonald's, Olive Garden, On the Border, Panera Bread, Peking Garden, Qdoba, Ruby Tuesday, Starbucks, Steak'n Shake, Subway, Tijuana Flats $Tree, AT&T, Best Buy, Chrysler/Dodge/Jeep, Dick's, Discount Tire, Ford/Subaru, GNC, Hobby Lobby, Home Depot, Lowes Foods, Mary Jo's Cloth, Michael's, Nissan, Office Depot, O'Reilly Parts, PepBoys, Petco, Ross, Target, Tire Kingdom, TJ Maxx, Verizon, vet, Walgreens, Walmart/Subway, W Marathon Arby's, Brixx Pizza, IHOP Super 8 H, $General, Medical Ctr Drug
20	NC 279, New Hope Rd, E United, World Capt D's, Jackson's Cafeteria, Los Arcos Mexican, McDonald's, O'Charley's, Pizza Hut, Red Lobster, Sake Japanese, Showmar's Rest, Taco Bell, Wendy's Advance Parts, AutoZone, Belk, Dillard's, Family$, Firestone/auto, JC Penney, Sears/auto, Tuesday Morning, W Bojangles, Cracker Barrel, Honeybaked Ham, KFC, Outback Steaks, TX Roadhouse, Waffle House Best Western, Comfort Suites, Courtyard, Fairfield Inn, Hampton Inn H, CarMax
19	NC 7, E Gastonia, E Shell
17	US 321, Gastonia, E Citgo/dsl/LP Los Arcos Mexican Days Inn, ValuePlace Family$, W Marathon/dsl,

GASTONIA

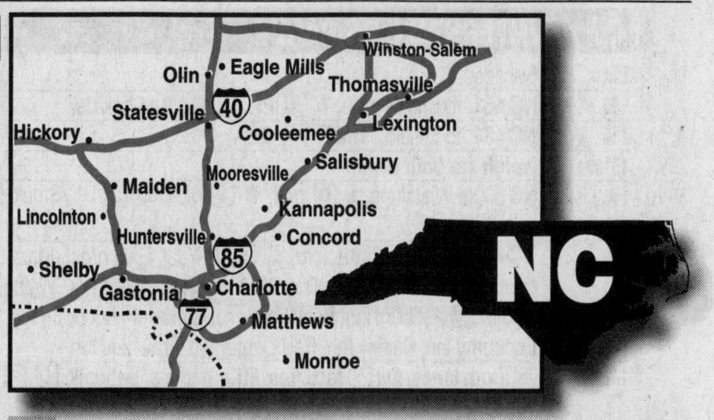

Exit #	Services
x	Continued QT/dsl Dunkin Donuts, Hardee's, Papa John's Holiday Inn Express, Motel 6, Red Carpet Inn
14	NC 274, E Bessemer, E Citgo/dsl, Murphy USA/dsl Walmart, W BP/Subway, Citgo/dsl Bojangles, Waffle House Express Inn
13	Edgewood Rd, Bessemer City, E to Crowders Mtn SP, W Exxon
10b a	US 74 W, US 29, Kings Mtn
8	NC 161, to Kings Mtn, E Holiday Inn Express camping, W BP/dsl McDonald's, Mi Pueblito Mexican, Subway, Taco Bell, Waffle House, Wendy's Quality Inn, Super 8 H, $General, Campers Inn RV Ctr
5	Dixon School Rd, E Citgo/dsl/24hr truck/tire repair
4	US 29 S (from sb)
2.5mm	**Welcome Ctr nb, full facilities, info, litter barrels, petwalk vending**
2	NC 216, Kings Mtn, E to Kings Mtn Nat Military Park
0mm	North Carolina/South Carolina state line

ROANOKE RAPIDS

INTERSTATE 95

Exit #	Services
181mm	**Welcome Ctr sb, full facilities, litter barrels, petwalk vending**, North Carolina/Virginia state line
180	NC 48, to Gaston, to Lake Gaston, Pleasant Hill, W Pilot/Subway/dsl/scales/24hr
176	NC 46, to Garysburg, W Shell/dsl Burger King Super 8
174mm	Roanoke River
173	US 158, Roanoke Rapids, Weldon, E BP/dsl, Shell/dsl Frazier's Rest., Ralph's BBQ, Waffle House Days Inn, Orchard Inn, W BP/dsl, Exxon/DQ/Stuckey's, Murphy USA/dsl, Shell/dsl Applebee's, Arby's, Bojangles, Burger King, Carolina BBQ, Chick-fil-A, China Lin, Cookout, Cracker Barrel, Hardee's, Ichiban, KFC, Little Caesar's, Logan's Roadhouse, Mayflower Seafood, McDonald's, New China, Papa John's, Pizza Hut, Popeyes, Ruby Tuesday, San Jose Mexican, Starbucks, Subway, Subway, Taco Bell, TX Steaks, Waffle House, Wendy's Hampton Inn, Holiday Inn Express, Motel 6, Quality Inn, Sleep Inn H, $General, $Tree, Advance Parts, AutoZone, Belk, BigLots, Firestone/auto, Food Lion, GNC, Harley-Davidson, Honda, Lowe's, O'Reilly Parts, Radio Shack, Rite Aid, Save a Lot Foods, Staples, Toyota, URGENT CARE, Verizon, Walgreens, Walmart
171	NC 125, Roanoke Rapids, E Hilton Garden Carolina Crossroads RV Resort, Roanoke Rapids Theater, W Shell/dsl Best Western st patrol
168	NC 903, to Halifax, E Exxon/Subway/dsl, Shell/Burger King/dsl, W Oasis/Dunkin Donuts/LP/dsl

INTERSTATE 95 Cont'd

Exit #	Services
160	NC 561, to Brinkleyville, E (gas) Exxon, W (gas) Shell/dsl
154	NC 481, to Enfield, 1mi W (other) KOA
151mm	**weigh sta both lanes**
150	NC 33, to Whitakers, E (other) golf, W (gas) BP/Subway/DQ/Stuckey's/dsl
145	NC 4, to US 301, Battleboro, E (gas) BP/dsl, Exxon/dsl, Marathon/dsl, Shell (food) Carolina BBQ, Denny's, Hardee's, Waffle House (lodging) Ashburn Inn, Best Western, Deluxe Inn, EconoLodge, Economy Inn, Quality Inn, Red Carpet Inn, Travelers Inn
142mm	**(RS) both lanes, full (handicapped) facilities, litter barrels, petwalk (phone) (picnic) vending**
141	NC 43, Red Oak, E (gas) BP/dsl, Exxon/dsl/LP (other) $General, Smith's Foods
138	US 64, **1 mi E on Winstead** (gas) BP/dsl, Hess/dsl (food) Bojangles, Cracker Barrel, Gardner's BBQ, Hardee's, Highway Diner, Outback Steaks, TX Steaks, Waffle House (lodging) Candlewood Suites, Comfort Inn, Country Inn&Suites, Courtyard, Doubletree, Hampton Inn, Holiday Inn, Residence Inn (other) (H), Buick/GMC, Harley-Davidson, Honda, Rite Aid, to Cape Hatteras Nat Seashore, URGENT CARE
132	to NC 58, E (gas) Pitstop/dsl, 1 mi W (gas) BP/dsl
128mm	Tar River
127	NC 97, to Stanhope, E (other) (airport)

WILSON

Exit #	Services
121	US 264a, Wilson, 0-4 mi E (gas) BP, Hess/dsl, Kangaroo/dsl/LP, Marathon, Murphy USA/dsl, Shell (food) Applebee's, Arby's, Buffalo Wild Wings, Burger King, Chick-fil-A, Chili's, Chopstix, Cookout, Denny's, El Tapatio, Golden Corral, Hardee's, Hibachi Buffet, Jersey Mike's, KFC/LJ Silver, Kobe Express, Mama Mia's Pizzaria, McDonald's, Moe's SW Grill, Olive Garden, Quizno's, Red Chileez Grill, Ruby Tuesday, San Jose Mexican, Sonic, Starbucks, Subway, Teppanyaki, TX Steaks, Waffle House, Wendy's, Zaxby's's (lodging) Candlewood Suites, Hampton Inn, Quality Inn (other) (H), $General, $Tree, Aldi Foods, AT&T, AutoZone, Belk, Best Buy, Big Lots, Chevrolet, Chrysler/Dodge/Jeep, Ford/Lincoln, GNC, Harris-Teeter, Hobby Lobby, Honda, Lowe's, Marshall's, Mr Tire, Nissan, O'Reilly Parts, Petsmart, Radio Shack, Ross, Staples, Target, Toyota/Scion, URGENT CARE, Verizon, vet, Walmart, White's Tires, W (gas) BP (food) Best-N-Burgers, Bojangles, Burger King, Cracker Barrel, McDonald's, Pino's Pizza (lodging) Comfort Suites, Country Inn&Suites, Fairfield Inn, Hampton Inn, Holiday Inn Express, Jameson Inn, Microtel, Sleep Inn (other) to Country Dr Museum
119b a	I-795 S, US 264, US 117
116	NC 42, to Clayton, Wilson, E (gas) Shell/dsl (other) (H), W (gas) BP/dsl (other) Rock Ridge Camping (2mi)

KENLY

Exit #	Services
107	US 301, Kenly, E (gas) BP/dsl, Citgo, Exxon/McDonald's/dsl, Fuel Doc, PitStop (food) Andy's Cafe, Golden China, Nik's Pizza, Norman's BBQ, Subway (lodging) Budget Inn, Deluxe Inn, Quality Inn (other) $General, CarQuest, Family$, Food Lion, Ford, O'Reilly Parts, Piggly Wiggly, Tobacco Museum
106	Truck Stop Rd, Kenly, E (gas) FLYING J/Denny's/dsl/LP/scales/24hr, W (gas) Kenly 95/Petro/DQ/Subway/Wendy's/dsl/scales/24hr/ @, Wilco/Hess/Arby's/dsl/scales/24hr (food) Waffle House (lodging) Days Inn, Motel 6 (other) Blue Beacon, Speedco Lube, Truck-o-Mat
105.5mm	Little River
105	Bagley Rd, Kenly, E (gas) Big Boys/Shell/105 Pizza/dsl/scales/24hr (food) Lowell Mill Rest.
102	Micro, W (gas) Shop'N-Go (food) Backdoor Cafe (other) $General, city park, USPO
101	Pittman Rd
99mm	**(RS) both lanes, full (handicapped) facilities, hist marker, litter barrel petwalk (phone) (picnic) vending**

SMITHFIELD

Exit #	Services
98	to Selma, E (other) RVacation
97	US 70 A, to Pine Level, Selma, E (gas) Mobil/dsl (food) Denny' Robbins Nest Rest. (lodging) Days Inn (other) J&R Outlet, W (gas) B dsl, Exxon/dsl, Shell/dsl (food) Bojangles, Cookout, Don Beto Tacos, KFC, McDonald's, Shoney's, Waffle House, Wendy's EconoLodge, Hampton Inn, Masters Inn, Quality Inn (other) (H)
95	US 70, Smithfield, E (lodging) Best Value Inn, Village Motel, W Hess/dsl, Sheetz/dsl, Sunoco/dsl (food) Bob Evans, Burger Kin Checker's, CiCi's Pizza, Coldstone, Cracker Barrel, El Sombre Mexican, Golden Corral, Outback Steaks, Ruby Tuesday, Sa Marcos Mexican, Subway, TX Steaks, Waffle House, Zaxby (lodging) Baymont Inn, Best Western, Comfort Inn, Fairfield Inn, Slee Inn, Super 8 (other) (H), Ava Gardner Museum, Carolina Premiu Outlets/famous brands, Harley-Davidson
93	Brogden Rd, Smithfield, W (gas) BP/dsl, Citgo (other) $General
91.5mm	Neuse River
90	US 301, US 701, to Newton Grove, E (gas) BP/dsl, Valero/d (lodging) Travelers Inn (other) Happy Trails RV Park, Raleigh Oaks F Resort, Ronnie's Tires, to Bentonville Bfd (14mi), W (gas) Exxo dsl (food) Holt Lake BBQ (lodging) Four Oaks Motel/RV Park
87	NC 96, Four Oaks, W (gas) BP/dsl, Hess/dsl, Walmart Expres dsl (food) McDonald's, Subway (other) $General
81b a	I-40, E to Wilmington, W to Raleigh
79	NC 50, to NC 27, to NC 242, Benson, Newton Grove, E Short Stop/dsl (food) Char-Grill, Waffle House (other) auto repa W (gas) Exxon/Burger King/dsl, Mule City/dsl (food) China 8, Don ino's, McDonald's, Pizza Hut, Subway, Taco Bell, White Swa BBQ (lodging) Days Inn (other) Advance Parts, auto repair, Family Food Lion, Walgreens
78mm	Neuse River, Neuse River
77	Hodges Chapel Rd, E (gas) Loves/Subway/dsl/scales/R dump/24hr
75	Jonesboro Rd, W (gas) Exxon/Milestone Diner, Pilot/She DQ/Quiznos/dsl/scales/24hr/ @

DUNN

Exit #	Services
73	US 421, NC 55, to Dunn, Clinton, E (food) Cracker Barrel, Mc Donald's, Mi Casita Mexican, Panda House Chinese, Steak Es cape (other) Chevrolet, Chrysler/Dodge/Jeep, Family$, Food Lio W (gas) Exxon/dsl, Hess/dsl, Shell (food) Bojangles, Burger King Dairy Freeze, El Charro Mexican, Hot Dog&Hamburger Heava Sagebrush Steaks, Subway, Taco Bell, Triangle Waffle (lodging) Bay mont Inn, Hampton Inn, Holiday Inn Express, Quality Inn, Su per 8 (other) Charlie C's IGA, museum, to Campbell U.
72	Pope Rd, E (lodging) Comfort Inn, Royal Inn, W (gas) BP, Pure/d (food) Brass Lantern Steaks (lodging) Fairfield Inn, Valley Motor In (other) Cadillac/GMC
71	Longbranch Rd, E (gas) Pilot/Kangaroo/Hardee's/ds scales/24hr, W (other) to Averasboro Bfd
70	SR 1811, E (lodging) Relax inn
65	NC 82, Godwin, E (other) Falcon Children's Home, W (gas) Epco dsl
61	to Wade, E (gas) 61 Trkstp/dsl (other) Fayetteville RV Resort Cottages, W (gas) Exxon/dsl
58	US 13, to Newton Grove, I-295 to Fayetteville, E (gas) Shell/ds scales (food) Quiznos, Waffle House (lodging) Days Inn
56	Lp 95, to US 301 (from sb), Fayetteville, W (gas) Epco/dsl, Kangaroo/dsl (other) (H), Pope AFB, to Ft Bragg
55	NC 1832, Murphy Rd, W (gas) Epco/dsl, Kangaroo/dsl
52	NC 24, Fayetteville, W (other) botanical gardens, museum, Pop AFB, to Ft Bragg
49	NC 53, NC 210, Fayetteville, E (gas) BP/dsl, Exxon/dsl, Kar garoo/dsl, Marathon (food) Burger King, McDonald's, Pizza Hu

INTERSTATE 95 Cont'd

FAYETTEVILLE

49	Continued Taco Bell, Waffle House Days Inn, Deluxe Inn, Motel 6, W BP/Subway/dsl, Exxon/dsl, Sunoco/dsl Cracker Barrel, Ruby Tuesday, Shoney's Comfort Inn, Country Hearth Inn, Doubletree, EconoLodge, Fairfield Inn, Hampton Inn, Holiday Inn, Quality Inn, Rodeway Inn, Sleep Inn, Super 8
48mm	**both lanes, full facilities, litter barrels, petwalk vending**
47mm	Cape Fear River
46b a	NC 87, to Fayetteville, Elizabethtown, W H, Civic Ctr, museum, to Agr Expo Ctr
44	Claude Lee Rd, W Lazy Acres Camping, to
41	NC 59, to Hope Mills, Parkton, E Kangaroo/Subway/dsl Bojangles, W BP/dsl Grandsons Buffet Lake Waldo's Camping, Spring Valley RV Park
40	Lp 95, to US 301 (from nb), to Fayetteville, services on US 301 (5-7mi)
33	US 301, St Pauls, E BP/dsl
31	NC 20, to St Pauls, Raeford, E BP, Marathon/Huddle House/dsl, Mobil/McDonald's, Valero Burger King, Hardee's Days Inn Volvo Trucks, Walgreens, Walmart Mkt, W Exxon/dsl, Sunoco Taco Bell Food Lion
25	US 301, E Sun-Do/dsl
24mm	**weigh sta both lanes**
22	US 301, E Exxon, Marathon, Shell/DQ Burger King, Chick-fil-A, China Wok, Denny's, Firehouse Subs, Golden Corral, Hardee's, IHOP, Outback Steaks, Papa John's, Pizza Hut, Ruby Tuesday, San Jose Mexican, Shogun, Smithfield BBQ, Starbucks, TX Steaks, Waffle House, Wendy's, Zaxby's Best Western, Comfort Suites, Hampton Inn, Holiday Inn, Super 8 $Tree, AT&T, Chrysler/Dodge/Jeep, Goodyear/auto, Honda, Lowe's, Lowe's Foods, Office Depot, Radio Shack, SaveALot Foods, st patrol, Toyota/Scion, URGENT CARE, Verizon, Walmart/Subway, W Gulf, Sun-Do/dsl, Sunoco/dsl Bojangles, Uncle George's Rest. Springhill Suites Ford/Lincoln, Sam's Club/gas

LUMBERTON

20	NC 211, to NC 41, Lumberton, E Exxon/dsl, Liberty/dsl Arby's, Arnold's Rest., Bojangles, Burger King, Cape Fear BBQ, Capt D's, CiCi's Pizza, Cook Out, Hardee's, Hong Kong Chinese, Kami Japanese, KFC, Little Caesar's, McDonald's, Shoney's, Sonic, Subway, Taco Bell, Tokyo Japanese, Tuscan Garden Italian, Village Sta. Rest., Waffle House Deluxe Inn, EconoLodge, Howard Johnson H, Advance Parts, AutoZone, Belk, city park, CVS Drug, Food Lion/deli, JC Penney, K-Mart, Nissan, O'Reilly Parts, Verizon, Walgreens, W Marathon/dsl, Sun-do/dsl Cracker Barrel, Fuller's BBQ Buffet, San Jose Mexican Best Value Inn, Comfort Inn, Country Inn&Suites, Days Inn/rest., Fairfield Inn, Quality Inn
19	Carthage Rd, Lumberton, E BP Rodeway Inn, W Valero/dsl Motel 6, Royal Inn
18mm	Lumber River
17	NC 72, Lumberton, Pembroke, E Atkinson's/dsl, BP/dsl, Dobbs, Dobb's/dsl, Go-Gas/dsl Burger King, Hardee's, Huddle House, Little China, McDonald's, Papa Bill's BBQ, Pizza Hut, Ruby Tuesday, Subway, Waffle House Atkinson Inn, Budget Inn, Southern Inn, Southern Inn $General, Advance Parts, AutoZone, CVS Drug, Family$, Food Lion, Walmart Mkt/dsl, W Sleepy Bear's RV Park (3mi)
13	I-74, US 74, Rockingham, Wilmington, E SE NC Beaches, U.S.S Wilmington
10	US 301, to Fairmont
7	to McDonald, Raynham

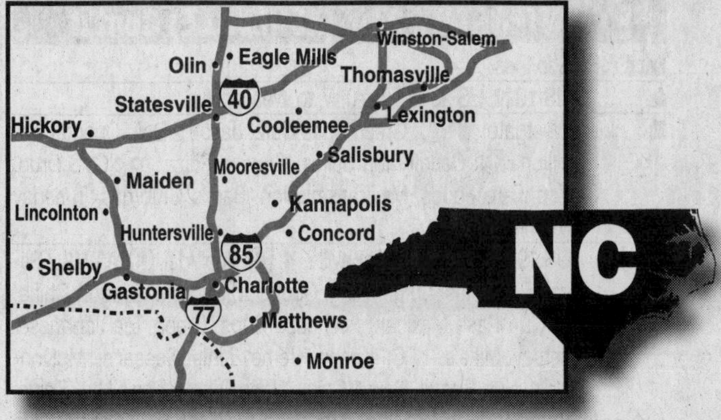

5mm	**Welcome Ctr nb, full facilities, litter barrels, petwalk vending**
2	NC 130, to NC 904, Rowland
1b a	US 301, US 501, Dillon, E Exxon, Mobil Hot Tamale Rest., Peddler Steaks, Porky's Truckstp, Sombrero Rest. Budget Motel, South of the Border Motel, South-of-the-Border Motel Pedro's Campground, W Shell/dsl Waffle House Night Inn, Super 8
0mm	North Carolina/South Carolina state line

INTERSTATE 240 (ASHEVILLE)

ASHEVILLE

Exit #	Services
9mm	**I-240 begins/ends on I-40, exit 53b a.**
8	Fairview Rd, N Shell/dsl Ay Carumba, Cheddar's, China Buffet, Coldstone, J&S Cafeteria, KFC, Little Caesar's, McDonald's, Papa John's, Subway Ramada Inn $General, Advance Parts, Aldi Foods, Bi-Lo Foods, CVS Drug, Discount Tire, Hamrick's, Hancock Fabrics, Kohl's, Petsmart, U-Haul, Walmart/McDonald's, S Citgo Pizza Hut Home Depot
7.5mm	Swannanoa River
7	US 70, N Enmark Best Western Hyundai, KIA, Subaru, S Shell/dsl Applebee's, Bonefish Grill, Buffalo Wild Wings, Burger King, Carrabba's, Chick-fil-A, Chili's, ChuckeCheese, Cici's Pizza, Cook Out, Cornerstone Rest., Cracker Barrel, DQ, Firehouse Subs, IHOP, Jersey Mike's Subs, Longhorn Steaks, McAlister's Deli, McDonald's, McDonald's, Mikado Japanese, O'Charley's, Olive Garden, Outback Steaks, Papa's Mexican, Red Lobster, Starbucks, Subway, Taco Bell, Waffle House, Wild Wok Country Inn&Suites, Courtyard, Days Inn, EconoLodge, Extended Stay America, Hampton Inn, Holiday Inn, Homewood Suites, InTown Motor Inn, Mountaineer Inn, SpringHill Suites, Super 8 $Tree, AT&T, Barnes&Noble, Belk, Best Buy, BigLots, Clark Tire/auto, Dick's, Dillards, Firestone/auto, Ingles Foods/gas, JC Penney, Jo-Ann, Lowe's, Michael's, Midas, Office Depot, Old Navy, Ross, Sears/auto, Target, TJ Maxx, Walgreens, Whole Foods Mkt
6	Tunnel Rd (from eb), same as 7
5b	US 70 E, US 74A, Charlotte St, N Exxon, Shell Charlotte St. Grill, Fuddruckers, Starbucks, Two Guys Hogi B&B vet, S Chop House Rest. Renaissance Hotel, Sheraton Civic Ctr
5a	US 25, Merrimon Ave, N Enmark, Exxon/dsl, Shell/dsl Bojangles, Chick-fil-A Green Life Foods, Harris Teeter, Staples, Trader Joe's
4c	Haywood St (no EZ return to eb), Montford, S Carmel's Rest., Isa's Bistro, Roman's Deli B&B, Hotel Indigo downtown
4b	Patton Ave (from eb), downtown

NC

🅔 INTERSTATE 240 (ASHEVILLE) Cont'd

Exit #	Services
4a	US 19 N, US 23 N, US 70 W, to Weaverville
3b	Westgate, **N** 🍴 Green Sage Cafe, Jason's Deli, Oriental Pavillion 🛌 Country Inn Suites, Crowne Plaza 🅾 CVS Drug, EarthFare Foods, Mr Transmission, Sam's Club/gas, Tuesday Morning
3a	US 19 S, US 23 S, W Asheville, **N** 🅡 Shell/dsl 🍴 A&W/LJ Silver, Bojangles, Burger King, CookOut, Denny's, Dragon China, El Que Pasa Mexican, Firehouse Subs, Green Tea Japanese, Jersey Mike's, KFC, Krispy Kreme, Little Caesar's, McDonald's, Neo Burrito, New 1 China, Papa John's, Pizza Hut, Sonic, Subway, Taco Bell, Wendy's, Yoshida Japanese, Zingers Cafe 🅾 $General, Advance Parts, Aldi Foods, AT&T, AutoZone, Clark Tire/auto, Ingles Foods, K-Mart, Radio Shack, Sav-Mor Foods, URGENT CARE, vet, Walgreens
2	US 19, US 23, W Asheville, **N** 🅡 Haywood Quickstop/dsl 🍴 Zia Mexican, **S** 🅾 B&B Drug
1c	Amboy Rd (from eb)
1b	NC 191, to I-40 E, Brevard Rd, **S** 🅾 camping, farmers mkt
1a	I-40 W, to Knoxville
0mm	I-240 begins/ends on I-40, exit 46b a.

🅔 INTERSTATE 440 (RALEIGH)

Exit #	Services
16	I-40
15	Poole Rd, **E** 🅡 Exxon 🍴 Quiznos, **W** 🅡 BP/dsl, Citgo/dsl 🍴 Burger King, Family$, Food Lion, KFC/Taco Bell, McDonald's, Subway
14	US 64, to Rocky Mount, limited access hwy
13b a	US 64, US 264 E, New Bern Ave, to Wilson, **0-2 mi E** 🅡 76/Circle K, BP, Caroco/dsl, Exxon, Micro Mart, Murphy USA/dsl, Shell/dsl 🍴 Bojangles, Burger King, Golden Corral, Jumbo China, McDonald's, Papa John's, Quiznos, Roh Buffet, Ruby Tuesday, Starbucks, Subway, Waffle House, Wendy's 🛌 Best Western, Comfort Suites, Holiday Inn Express, Microtel, Super 8 🅾 Advance Parts, AutoZone, CVS Drug, Firestone/auto, Food Lion, Kroger, Office Depot, O'Reilly Parts, RV Ctr, U-Haul, Walgreens, Walmart, **W** 🅾 🔣
12	Yonkers Rd, Brentwood Rd
11b a	US 1, US 401, Capital Blvd N, **N** 🅡 BP, Citgo, Exxon, Kangaroo/dsl, Mobil, Shell 🍴 Baskin-Robbins/Dunkin Donuts, Buffalo Bro's, Burger King, ChuckeCheese, Cici's, Cookout, IHOP, Mayflower Seafood, McDonald's, Outback Steaks, Perkins, Taco Bell, Vallerta Mexican, Waffle House 🛌 Best Western, Days Inn, EconoLodge, Holiday Inn, Lodge America, Quality Inn, Sleep Inn, Super 8, Wingate Inn 🅾 Aamco, AutoZone, Food Lion, Pepboys, Rite Aid, U-Haul, Walgreens
10	Wake Forest Rd, **N** 🍴 Bahama Breeze, Denny's 🛌 Days Inn, Hilton, Homestead Suites, Hyatt Place 🅾 🔣, CVS Drug, **S** 🅡 BP 🍴 Applebee's, Arby's, Biscuitville, Burger King, Courtney's Cafe, Jersey Mike's, Jimmy John's, Jumbo China, KFC/Taco Bell, McDonald's, Melting Pot Rest., Papa John's, Pizza Hut, Qdoba, Quiznos, Subway 🛌 Courtyard, Extended Stay America, Hampton Inn, Studio+ 🅾 Advance Parts, AutoZone, Buick/GMC, Costco/gas, Curves, Discount Tire, Hancock Fabrics, Hyundai, Mazda, Nissan, Staples, Subaru, Trader Joe's, VW
8b a	6 Forks Rd, North Hills, **N** 🅡 Exxon/repair 🍴 5 Guys Burgers, Bonefish Grill, Chick-fil-A, Firebirds Grill, Fox&Hound Grille, Moe's SW Grill, Panera Bread, Pig Shack, Ruths Chris

Exit #	Services
8b a	Continued Steaks, Starbucks, Tiola Pizza, Zoe's Kitchen 🛌 Renaissanc 🅾 AT&T, GNC, Harris Teeter, JC Penney, Kerr Drug, Targe
7b a	US 70, NC 50, Glenwood Ave, Crabtree Valley, **N** 🅡 BP, She 🍴 Brio Grill, Cheesecake Factory, Fleming's, McDonald's, Pl Chang's 🛌 Crabtree Inn, Embassy Suites, Holiday Inn, Mar riott, Residence Inn, Windsor Inn 🅾 Barnes&Noble, Belk, Bes Buy, Just Tires, Macy's, mall, McCormick&Shmicks, Old Navy Sears/auto
6	Ridge Rd (from nb), same as 7
5	Lake Boone Tr, **W** 🅡 Circle K 🍴 McDonald's, Starbucks Subway, Wendy's 🅾 🔣, Food Lion, Tuesday Morning
4b a	to I-40 W, Wade Ave, to RDU
3	NC 54, Hillsboro St, **E** 🅡 BP, Exxon, Hugo's, Pure 🍴 Ap plebee's, Arby's, Bean Sprout Chinese, Burger King, Marco' Pizza, Quiznos, Snoopy's Hotdogs, Subway, Waffle House, Za xby's 🅾 to Meredith Coll, to St Mary's, USPO
2b a	Western Blvd, **E** 🅡 76/Circle K, Hess, Hugo's 🍴 Bojangles Cookout, Dunkin Donuts, Greek Fiesta, McDonalds, Pizza Hut Subway, Taco Bell, Ten Ten Chinese, Wendy's 🅾 Advanc Parts, BigLots, Food Lion, Shaw U, to NCSU, **W** 🅾 K-Mart
1d	Melbourne Rd (from sb)
1c	Jones-Franklin Rd
1b a	I-40. **I-440 begins on I-40. 1-2 mi W on Walnut St** 🅡 Exxon Shell 🍴 Astor's Grill, Bob Evans, Chick-fil-A, China King, Cold stone, Cookout, Dickey's BBQ, Golden Corral, HoneyBakec Ham, Jasmin Bistro, McDonald's, Moe's SW Grill, Noodles&Cc Olive Garden, Panera Bread, Qdoba, Red Lobster, Red Robir Remington Grill, Ruby Tuesday, Starbucks, Subway, Taco Bel Waffle House 🛌 Best Western, Red Roof Inn 🅾 BJ's Whse Ford, GNC, Home Depot, Jo-Ann Fabrics, Kohl's, Lowe's, mal Marshall's, Michael's, NTB, Office Depot, Old Navy, PetsMar Steinmart

INTERSTATE 485 (CHARLOTTE)

Exit #	Services
67	I-77, US 21, to Charlotte, Columbia, **I-485 begins/ends.**
65	South Blvd, **N** 🅡 Kangaroo 🍴 Chick-fil-A, Golden Corral Hooters, McDonald's, Popeyes, Steak'n Shake, Wendy's 🅾 $Tree, Advance Parts, Big Lots, Chevrolet, Discount Tire, Hon da, Jo-Ann, Kohl's, Nissan, Old Navy, Petsmart, Ross, Subaru Target, Toyota/Scion, Verizon, VW, World Mkt, **S** 🍴 Arby's 🅾 Cadillac, CarMax, Mercedes, NAPA, TreadQtrs Auto/tire, vet
64b a	Rd 51, **N** 🅡 Exxon/dsl, Shell/Circle K/dsl 🍴 Bojangles Chili's, CiCi's, CookOut, Firehouse Subs, Jimmy John's, K&V Cafeteria, KFC, McDonald's, Outback Steaks, Pizza Hut, Star bucks, Wendy's 🛌 Extended Stay America 🅾 🔣, Ald Foods, AutoZone, Bi-Lo, Family$, Firestone/auto, **S** 🅡 Kan garoo, Shell/7-11 🍴 Applebee's, Buca Italian, Burger King Capt D's, China Buffet, Harper's Rest., IHOP, Jason's Deli Longhorn Steaks, McAlister's Deli, Olive Garden, Red Lobste Sky Asian, Subway, Taco Bell 🛌 Comfort Suites, Hampton Inn, Hilton Garden, Holiday Inn Express, Quality Inn 🅾 $Gen eral, Barnes&Noble, Belk, Best Buy, Dick's, Dillard's, Food Lion Home Depot, JC Penney, K-Mart, Macy's, Meineke, Midas Office Depot, REI, Rite Aid, Sam's Club/gas, Sears/auto SteinMart, Tire Kingdom, TJ Maxx
61b a	US 521 S, Johnston Rd, **N** 🍴 Global Rest., Hickory Tavern Red Robin, Ruby Tuesday, Sticky Fingers, Viva Chicken 🛌 Homewood Suites, SpringHill Suites 🅾 Earth Fare Foods **S** 🅡 Kangaroo/dsl 🍴 5 Guys Burgers, Duckworth's Grill Mellow Mushroom Rest., Pei Wei, Starbucks, Stone Mtr

NC

C H A R L O T T E

INTERSTATE 485 (CHARLOTTE) Cont'd

CHARLOTTE

61b a	Continued Grill, Subway, Tony's Pizza, Vine American Kitchen Ballantyne Hotel, Courtyard, Staybridge Suites CVS Drug
59	Rea Rd, E Exxon/7-11 1511 Cantina, Applebee's, Boneheads Grill, Chick-fil-A, City Tavern, Firebirds Grill, Marble Slab, Noodles Rest., Qdoba, Smashburger, Starbucks, True Pizza, Wendy's Residence Inn GNC, Goodyear/auto, Harris-Teeter, Michaels, Radio Shack, Target, vet
57	Providence Rd, Rd 16, E Kangaroo/Wendy's Hickory Tavern, Ilios Noche, Papa John's, Penn Sta, The Wok Harris-Teeter, USPO, W Exxon/7-11, Shell BBQ Shack, BT Burgers, Macaroni Grill, On the Border, Red Bowl Rest., Showmars Rest., Starbucks, Subway, Wolfman Pizza CVS Drug, Harris-Teeter, Home Depot, Lowes Whse, Rite Aid, Staples, SteinMart, vet
52	E John St, to Matthews
51b a	US 74, to Charlotte, Monroe, E Circle K/dsl, Shell/dsl Country Inn&Suites, InTown Suites, Quality Inn Country Camping RV Ctr, Toyota/Scion, W Citgo/dsl, Exxon/7-11, Shell Bojangles, Pizza Hut, TX Roadhouse, Wendy's Courtyard, EconoLodge, Microtel H, Aamco, AutoZone, Best Buy, Costco/gas, Firestone/auto, Goodyear/auto, Goodyear/auto, Lowe's Whse, Radio Shack, Sam's Club/gas, Target, Tuesday Morning
49	Idlewild Rd, E Exxon/7-11/dsl Cactus Rose Mexican, China Cafe, Mama's Pizza $Tree, GNC, Harris-Teeter, Meineke, Rite Aid
47	Lawyers Rd, E Gate/dsl Bellacino's Pizza, Best China, Carnita's Mexican, Domino's, McDonald's, Subway CVS Drug, Firestone/auto, Harris-Teeter, vet
44	Rd 218, to Mint Hill, W BP/dsl, Shell/7-11 $General, city park, CVS
43	Rd 51, to Mint Hill
41	Rd 24, Rd 27, to Albemarle, E Hess/dsl Bojangles
39	Harrisburg Rd, W BP China Garden, Papa John's, Wendy's Food Lion
36	Rocky River Rd, N Citgo/dsl, Gate/dsl Best China, Bojangles, Capriccio Pizza, Subway CVS Drug, Discount Tire, EMERGENCY, GNC, Harris-Teeter, Tuffy Auto
33	Rd 49, to Harrisburg, E USPO, W Arby's, Chopsticks, Domino's, N Hess/dsl Cici's Pizza Food Lion, S BP, Circle K/dsl, Exxon/7-11, Shell/7-11/dsl Little Caesar's, Wendy's Family$
32	US 29, N CVS Drug, S Exxon/7-11/dsl, Hess/dsl, Kangaroo Jack-in-the-Box H, Tire Kingdom
30b a	I-85, N to High Point, S to Charlotte
23c	Rd 115, to Huntersville, N Shell/7-11/dsl Audi, BMW, Lexus, Mercedes, Walmart
23b a	I-77, to Charlotte, Statesville

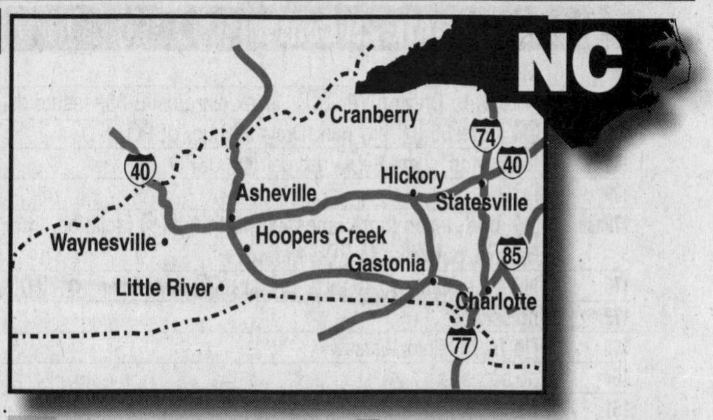

21	Rd 24, Harris Blvd, S 5 Guys Burgers, Bravo Italian, Buffalo Wild Wings, Chick-fil-A, Chili's, East Coast Grill, Edomae Grill, Firebirds Grill, Firehouse Subs, Fox&Hound, Jersey Mike's, McDonald's, Mimi's Cafe, Moe's SW Grill, Olive Garden, On-the-Border, Panera bread, PF Chang's, Red Robin, Shane's Rib Shack, TGI Friday's, Wendy's Drury Inn $Tree, AT&T, Belk, Best Buy, Dick's, Dillard's, Discount Tire, Lowe's Whse, Macy's, mall, Old Navy, Petsmart, REI, Target, Verizon
16	Rd 16, to Newton, Brookshire Blvd, E city park, W Bojangles, Bull&Barrister Grille, Chick-fil-A, Domino's, Los Arcos, McDonald's, Papa John's, Pizza Hut, Red Bowl Asian, Subway, Wendy's AT&T, AutoZone, Harris-Teeter, Rite Aid, URGENT CARE, vet, Walmart/Subway
14	Rd 27, to Mt Holly Rd, W BP (2mi) Sonic (2mi) Food Lion (2mi), Meineke (2mi)
12	Moores Chapel Rd, E Jin Jin Chinese, Subway Advance Parts, CVS Drug, Family$, Food Lion
10b a	I-85, to Spartanburg, Greensboro
9	US 29, US 74, Wilkinson Blvd, S BP camping
6	West Blvd
4	Rd 160, to Fort Mill, N Exxon/7-11/dsl CVS Drug, S BP/dsl Bojangles Charlotte Premium Outlets/famous brands
3	Arrowood Rd, S Quizno's, Siam Garden
1	S Tryon St, NC 49, N Citgo, Exxon/7-11 Arby's, Bojangles, Chick-fil-A, Chili's, Dragon Buffet, IHOP, Lenny's Subs, Luigi's Pizza, McDonald's, O'Charley's, Panera Bread, Qdoba, Showmars Rest., Waffle House, Zaxby's Family$, GNC, Lowe's Whse, Radio Shack, Rite Aid, Walmart, S Kangaroo/dsl, QT/dsl Mac's BBQ, Applebee's, Baskin-Robbins/Dunkin Donuts, Burger King, Domino's, Don Pedro Mexican, Firehouse Subs, Fortune Cookie, Hungry Howie's, Joe Momma's Pizza, KFC, McAlister's Deli, Pan China, Portofino's, Starbucks, Subway, Taco Bell, Wild Wing Cafe Hilton Garden, Homewood Suites $Tree, AT&T, AutoZone, Discount Tire, Food Lion, NAPA, Office Depot, Tire Kingdom, Tuffy Auto, URGENT CARE

NC

ND

NORTH DAKOTA

INTERSTATE 29

Exit #	Services
218mm	US/Canada border, North Dakota state line
217mm	US Customs sb
216mm	historical site nb, tourist info sb
215	ND 59, Rd 55, Pembina, E Gastrak/DutyFree Store/dsl, Gastrak/pizza/dsl/scales/24hr Pembina State Museum/info
212	no services
208	Rd 1, to Bathgate
203	US 81, ND 5, to Hamilton, Cavalier, to Icelandic SP (25 mi), **weigh sta both lanes**
200	no services
196	Rd 3, Bowesmont
193	no services
191	Rd 11, to St Thomas

INTERSTATE 29 Cont'd

GRAND FORKS

Exit #	Services
187	ND 66, to Drayton, E [gas] Cenex/pizza/dsl/E-85, Tesoro/dsl [lodging] Motel 66 [other] city park, Drayton Drug, USPO
184	to Drayton, **2 mi** E [gas] gas/dsl [other] USPO
180	Rd 9
179mm	**[rest stop] both lanes (both lanes exit left), full facilities, litter barrels, petwalk vending**
176	ND 17, to Grafton, **10 mi** W [gas] [food] [lodging] AmericInn [other] H
172	no services
168	Rd 15, to Minto, Warsaw
164	no services
161	ND 54, Rd 19, to Ardoch, Oslo
157	no services
152	US 81, to Gilby, Manvel, W [gas] Manvel/dsl/food
145	US 81 bus, N Washington St, to Grand Forks
141	US 2, Gateway Dr, Grand Forks, E [gas] Cenex, Loaf'N Jug/dsl, Univ. Sta/dsl [food] Al's Grill, Burger King, DQ, Greatwall Buffet, Little Caesars, McDonald's, Northside Cafe, Papa Murphy's, Subway, Taco John's [lodging] Best Value Inn, Budget Inn, Clarion, EconoLodge, Howard Johnson, Ramada Inn, Select Inn, Super 8 [other] H, AT&T, auto repair, Ford/Lincoln, Freightliner, Hugo's Foods, Kia, O'Reilly Parts, Subaru, to U of ND, transmissions, U-Haul, W [gas] Simonson/café/dsl/24hr, StaMart/Tesoro/dsl/RV dump/scales/24hr/ @ [food] Perkins [lodging] Settle Inn [other] Budget RV Ctr, dsl repair, Mack/Volvo, NW Tire, to AFB
140	DeMers Ave, E [gas] Cenex, Loaf'N Jug, Valley Dairy [food] Red Pepper Cafe [lodging] Canada Inn, Hilton Garden, Sleep Inn, Staybridge Suites [other] H, Alerus Ctr, to U of ND
138	US 81, 32nd Ave S, E [gas] Cenex, Holiday/dsl [food] 5 Guys Burgers, Arby's, Buffalo Wild Wings, Burger King, Cherry Berry Yogurt, China Garden, Coldstone, Culver's, Golden Corral, Ground Round, IHOP, Jimmy John's, McDonald's, Noodles&Co, Olive Garden, Papa Murphy's, Pizza Hut, Pizza Ranch, Qdoba Mexican, Quiznos, Red Lobster, Ruby Tuesday, Space Alien's Rest, Starbucks, Subway, TX Roadhouse, Village Inn, Wendy's [lodging] C'mon Inn, Country Inn&Suites, Days Inn, Fairfield Inn, Holiday Inn Express, Lakeview Inn, Quality Inn, Roadking Inn, SpringHill Suites [other] $Tree, AT&T, Best Buy, Chrysler/Dodge/Jeep, CVS Drug, Ford/Lincoln, Gordman's, Hugo's Foods, JC Penney, Jo-Ann Fabrics, Kohl's, Lowe's, Macy's, Menards, Michael's, Old Navy, PetCo, Sam's Club/gas, Super 1 Foods, Target, Tire 1, Tires+, TJ Maxx, Toyota/Scion, Verizon, vet, Walmart/Subway, White Drug, W [gas] FLYING J/Subway/dsl/LP/scales/RV dump/24hr [other] Grand Forks Camping
130	ND 15, Rd 81, Thompson, **1 mi** W [gas] gas [food] food
123	to Reynolds, E [other] to Central Valley School
118	to Buxton
111	ND 200 W, to Cummings, Mayville, W [other] Big Top Fireworks, to Mayville St U
104	Hillsboro, E [gas] Cenex/Burger King/dsl/LP/24hr, Tesoro/Stop-n-Go/dsl/24hr [food] Country Hearth Rest., Pizza Ranch, Subway [lodging] Hillsboro Inn [other] H, RV park, USPO
100	ND 200 E, ND 200A, to Blanchard, Halstad
99mm	**[rest stop] both lanes, full facilities, litter barrels, petwalk vending**
92	Rd 11, Grandin, W [gas] Stop&Shop/dsl
86	Gardner
78	Argusville
74.5mm	Sheyenne River
72	Rd 17, Rd 22, Harwood, E [gas] Cenex/pizza/dsl/LP/café/24hr
69	Rd 20

FARGO

Exit #	Services
67	US 81 bus, 19th Ave N, **1 mi** E [food] Applebee's, Buffalo Wild Wings, Burger King, McDonald's, Subway, Taco Bell [lodging] Candlewood Suites, Days Inn, Homewood Suites [other] CVS Drug, Hector Int Airport, VA H
66	12th Ave N, E [gas] StaMart/Tesoro/dsl/24hr/scales, Stop'n Go [other] H, to ND St U, tuck wash, W [gas] Cenex/dsl [food] Arby's [lodging] Super 8
65	US 10, Main Ave, W Fargo, E [gas] Tesoro/dsl [other] NAPA, OK Tire, True Value, vet, W [gas] Cenex/Subway/dsl, Simonson/dsl [food] Hardee's, O'Kelly's Rest, Season Buffet Chinese [lodging] Kelly Inn [other] CarQuest, Honda, Lincoln, Mac's Hardware, Mazda, O'Reilly Parts, Recreation RV Ctr, Subaru, Toyota/Scion
64	13th Ave, Fargo, E [gas] All-Stop, Don's, Kum&Go/dsl, PetroServe/dsl [food] Acapulco Mexican, Applebee's, Arby's, Buck's Rest, Burger King, ChuckeCheese, Dickey's BBQ, DQ, Erbert&Gerbert's Subs, Giant Panda Chinese, GreenMill Rest., Ground Round, Hooters, Little Caesars, Perkins, Quiznos, Subway, Taco John's, Wendy's [lodging] AmericInn, Best Western, Comfort Inn, Comfort Suites, Country Inn&Suites, Days Inn, EconoLodge, Grand Inn, Motel 6, Super 8 [other] AT&T, auto repair, CashWise Foods/drug/gas, CVS Drug, Family$, Goodyear/auto, O'Reilly Parts, Tires+/transmissions, Tuesday Morning, White Drug, W [gas] All-Stop/dsl, Cenex, Tesoro [food] Applebee's, Arby's, Buffalo Wild Wings, Chili's, Culver's, Denny's, Domino's, DQ, Happy Joe's Pizza, KFC, Kobe Japanese, Kroll's Diner, LoneStar Steaks, Longhorn Steaks, McDonald's, Olive Garden, Osaka Japanese, Panchero's Mexican, Paradiso Mexican, Pizza Hut, Red Lobster, Ruby Tuesday, Santa Lucia Cafe, Schlotzsky's, Spitfire Grill, Subway, Taco Bell, Taco John's, TGIFriday's, TX Roadhouse [lodging] Days Inn, EconoLodge, Fairfield Inn, Fargo Inn, Holiday Inn, Holiday Inn Express, Kelly Inn, Ramada Inn, Red River Lodge [other] $Tree, Audi/VW, Barnes&Noble, Best Buy, BigLots, Cadillac/Chevrolet, Chrysler/Dodge/Jeep, GNC, Gordman's, Herberger's, Hobby Lobby, Hornbacher's Foods, Hyundai, JC Penney, Jo-Ann Fabrics, Kohl's, Lowe's, Macy's, Menards, Michael's, Nissan, Office Depot, Old Navy, PetCo, Petsmart, Sam's Club/gas, Sears/auto, SunMart Foods, Target, TJ Maxx, USPO, Walgreens, Walmart/Subway
63b a	I-94, W to Bismarck, E to Minneapolis
62	32nd Ave S, Fargo, E [gas] F&F/dsl, Holiday, Tesoro [food] Arby's, Country Kitchen, Culver's, Jimmy John's, KFC, Little Caesars, Moe's SW Grill, Papa John's, Quiznos, Starbucks, Subway, Taco John's, Village Inn [other] H, Buick/GMC, Ford, Freightliner, JiffyLube, SunMart Foods, Verizon, W [gas] FLYING J/dsl/LP/scales/24hr/ @, Love's/McDonald's/Subway/dsl/scales/24hr [lodging] Motel 6 [other] Fargo Tire/repair, Peterbilt, Volvo
60	52nd Ave S, to Fargo, W [other] Walmart/Subway
56	to Wild Rice, Horace
54	Rd 16, to Oxbow, Davenport
50	Rd 18, Hickson
48	ND 46, to Kindred
44	to Christine, **1 mi** E [gas]
42	Rd 2, to Walcott
37	Rd 4, to Abercrombie, Colfax, E [other] to Ft Abercrombie HS, **3 mi** W [gas]
31	Rd 8, Galchutt
26	to Dwight
24mm	**weigh sta both lanes exit left**
23b a	ND 13, to Wahpeton, Mooreton, **10 mi** E [other] H, ND St Coll of Science
15	Rd 16, to Mantador, Great Bend
8	ND 11, to Hankinson, Fairmount, E [gas] Tesoro/dsl, **3 mi** W [other] camping

ND

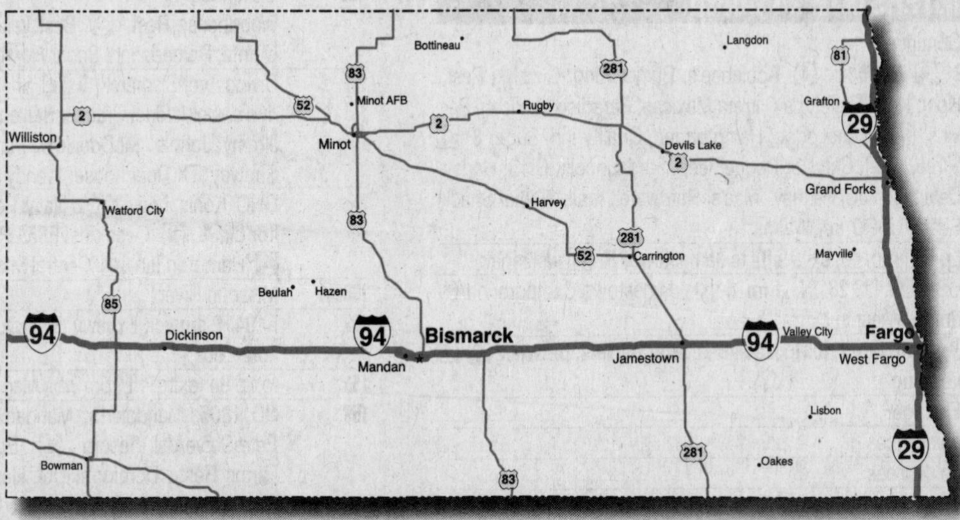

N INTERSTATE 29 Cont'd

Exit #	Services
3mm	**Welcome Ctr nb, full facilities, litter barrels, petwalk**
2	Rd 22
1	Rd 1E, E Dakota Magic Casino/Hotel/rest./gas/dsl
0mm	North Dakota/South Dakota state line

E INTERSTATE 94

FARGO

Exit #	Services
352mm	North Dakota/Minnesota state line, Red River
351	US 81, Fargo, N Loaf'n Jug, Stop'n Go Duane's Pizza, Great Harvest Breads, Great Wall Chinese, Taco Shop H, Hornbacher's Foods, Medicine Shoppe, Verizon, vet, S Stop'n Go, Tesoro/dsl A&W/LJ Silver, Burger King, Happy Joe's Pizza, McDonald's, Pepper's Café, Randy's Diner, Subway, Taco Bell Rodeway Inn, Vista Inn Hornbacher's/gas, K-Mart, O'Reilly Parts, USPO
350	25th St, Fargo, N Stop'n Go, S Cenex/dsl, Loaf'n Jug/dsl Dolittle's Grill, Ruby Tuesday
349b a	I-29, N to Grand Forks, S to Sioux Falls, services 1 mi N, exit 64
348	45th St, **N Visitor Ctr/full facilities, litter barrels,** Holiday/dsl, Petro/dsl/Lp/24hrs/@ Carino's, Coldstone, Culver's, Denny's, Dunn Bros Coffee, HuHot Mongolian, IHOP, Kroll's Diner, Little Caesar's, Longhorn Steaks, McDonald's, Noodles&Co, Papa Murphy's, Pizza Hut, Qdoba, Quaker Steak, Quiznos, Smashburger, Space Aliens Grill, Subway, Wendy's Best Western, C'Mon Inn, Expressway Suites, Hilton Garden, MainStay Suites, Ramada Inn, Red Roof Inn, Staybridge Suites, Wingate Inn Blue Beacon, Hobby Lobby, Home Depot, Kohl's, NAPA, Office Depot, Old Navy, Sam's Club, Scheel's Sports, Target, Tuffy Auto, Verizon, Walmart, S Holiday, Stop'n Go, Tesoro/DQ/dsl 5 Guys Burgers, Applebee's, Famous Dave's BBQ, Golden Corral, Hardee's, Korean BBQ, Mexican Village, Old Chicago Pizza, Pizza Ranch, Taco John's, Taco Shop Arbuckle Lodge, Comfort Suites, Hampton Inn, La Quinta, Residence Inn, Sleep Inn AT&T, Gander Mtn, Red River Zoo
347	9th St E, Veterans Blvd, S Stop-N-Go/dsl Taco Bell Costco/gas
346b a	to Horace, W Fargo, S repair, Tesoro/dsl
343	US 10, Lp 94, W Fargo, N Cenex/dsl Sunset Motel Adventure RV Ctr, Harley-Davidson, Pioneer Village

JAMESTOWN

Exit #	Services
342	no services
342mm	**weigh sta wb**
340	to Kindred
338	Mapleton, N Tesoro/dsl
337mm	**truck parking wb, litter barrels**
331	ND 18, to Leonard, Casselton, N Tesoro/Subway/dsl Country Kitchen Days Inn/RV park NAPA, repair
328	to Lynchburg
327mm	**truck parking eb, litter barrels**
324	Wheatland, to Chaffee
322	Absaraka
320	to Embden
317	to Ayr
314	ND 38 N, to Alice, Buffalo, **3 mi** N gas food
310	no services
307	to Tower City, N Cenex/café/dsl/RV Park/24hr, motel
304mm	**both lanes, full facilities, info, litter barrels, petwalk vending**
302	ND 32, to Fingal, Oriska, **1 mi** N city park
298	no services
296	no services
294	Lp 94, to Kathryn, Valley City, N H, camping
292	Valley City, N Tesoro/café/dsl Sabir's Rest. AmericInn, Super 8, Wagon Wheel Inn/rest. H, camping, to Bald Hill Dam, S Ft Ransom SP (35mi)
291	Sheyenne River
290	Lp 94, Valley City, N Tesoro/dsl Burger King, Kenny's Rest., Roby's Rest., Subway H, Chrysler/Dodge/Jeep, Family$, Firestone/auto, Ford, NAPA, Radio Shack, ShopKo
288	ND 1 S, to Oakes, S Fort Ransom SP (36 mi)
283	ND 1 N, to Rogers
281	to Litchville, Sanborn, **1-2 mi** N
276	Eckelson, S Prairie Haven Camping/gas/dsl
275mm	continental divide, elev 1490
272	to Urbana
269	Spiritwood
262	Bloom, N
260	Jamestown, N Stop'n Go, Tesoro/café/dsl/ @ Starlite Motel camping, to St H
259mm	James River
258	US 52 W, US 281, Jamestown, N Clark/TCBY/dsl, Tesoro/dsl Arby's, DQ, Hardee's, McDonald's, Pizza Ranch, Subway, Taco Bell Comfort Inn, Days Inn, Holiday Inn Express, Jamestown Motel H, Buffalo Herd/museum, Buick/Chevrolet/GMC, Firestone/auto, NW Tire, O'Reilly Parts, Toyota, vet,

ND

JAMESTOWN

INTERSTATE 94 Contd

258 Continued
S [gas] Shell/dsl [food] Applebee's, Burger King, Grizzly's Rest., Hong Kong Buffet, La Carreta Mexican, Paradiso Mexican, Perkins [lodging] EconoLodge, Hampton Inn, Quality Inn, Super 8 [other] $Tree, AT&T, Chrysler/Dodge/Jeep, Ford/Lincoln, GNC, Harley-Davidson, JC Penney, Mac's Hardware, mall, Radio Shack, Sears, USPO, vet, Walmart

257 Lp 94 (from eb, exits left), to Jamestown, N [other] dsl repair

256 US 52 W, US 281 N, **1 mi** S [other] Jamestown Campground/RV dump, Wiest truck/trailer repair

254mm **[RS] both lanes, full [handicapped] facilities, litter barrels, petwalk [phone] [picnic] vending**

251 Eldridge

248 no services

245 no services

242 Windsor

238 to Gackle, Cleveland

233 no services

230 Medina, **1 mi** N [gas] Famer's Union/dsl/LP [food] DairyTreat [other] city park, Medina RV Park, USPO

228 ND 30 S, to Streeter

224mm **[RS] wb, full [handicapped] facilities, litter barrels, petwalk [phone] [picnic] vending**

221 Crystal Springs

221mm **[RS] eb, full [handicapped] facilities, litter barrels, petwalk [phone] [picnic] vending**

217 Pettibone

214 Tappen, S [gas]/dsl/food

208 ND 3 S, Dawson, N [other] RV camping, **1/2 mi** S [gas] [food] [other] RV camping, to Camp Grassick

205 Robinson

200 ND 3 N, to Tuttle, Steele, S [gas] Cenex/dsl [food] Beary Tweet&Tasty [lodging] OK Motel [other] truckwash

195 no services

190 Driscoll, S [food] food

182 US 83 S, ND 14, to Wing, Sterling, S [gas] Cenex/dsl [lodging] Top's Motel (1mi)

176 McKenzie

170 Menoken, S [other] RV Park, to McDowell Dam

168mm **[RS] wb, full [handicapped] facilities, litter barrels, petwalk [phone] [picnic] vending, wifi**

BISMARCK

161 Lp 94, Bismarck Expswy, Bismarck, N [gas] Cenex/dsl/LP/24hr, Clark/dsl [lodging] My Place [other] Peterbilt, Toyota/Scion, S [gas] Tesoro/Marlin's Rest./dsl/scales/24hr [food] McDonald's [lodging] Ramada Ltd [other] Capital RV Ctr, Dakota Zoo, dsl repair, Freightliner, Kenworth, OK Tires, truckwash, Volvo

159 US 83, Bismarck, N [gas] Holiday/dsl, Simonson/dsl [food] Applebee's, Arby's, China Star, China Town, Golden Corral, Hooters, KFC, Kroll's Diner, Little Caesars, MacKenzie River Pizza, McDonald's, Olive Garden, Paradiso Mexican, Perkins, Pita Pit, Red Lobster, Ruby Tuesday, Space Alien Grill, Subway, Taco Bell, TCBY, Wendy's [lodging] AmericInn, Candlewood Suites, Comfort Inn, Comfort Suites, Country Suites, Fairfield Inn, Hampton Inn, Holiday Inn Express, Mainstay Suites, Motel 6, Residence Inn, Sleep Inn, Staybridge Suites, Wingate Inn [other] AT&T, Chevrolet, CVS Drug, Dan's Foods, Hancock Fabrics, Hobby Lobby, Jo-Ann Fabrics, K-Mart, mall, Menards, NW Tire, Sears/auto, UHaul, USPO, Verizon, Walmart/Subway, S [gas] PetroServe/dsl, Shell/dsl, Tesoro [food] Caspars Rest., DQ, Hardee's, Minerva's Rest., Pizza Hut, Schlotzsky's, Starbucks, Subway, Taco John's,

159 Continued
Woodhouse Rest. [lodging] Best Value Inn, Days Inn, Kelly Inn, La Quinta, Ramada Inn, Super 8 [other] [H], O'Reilly Parts

157 Divide Ave, Bismarck, N [gas] Shell/dsl [food] 5 Guys Burgers, Carino's, Coldstone, Cracker Barrel, Goodtimes Grill/Taco John's, Jimmy John's, McDonald's, Pancheros Mexican, Starbucks, Subway, TX Roadhouse, Wendy's [other] $Tree, AT&T, Best Buy, GNC, Kohls, Lowe's, Old Navy, Petsmart, TJ Maxx, Verizon, visitor ctr, S [gas] Cenex/dsl/E85/LP/RV Dump [food] Stadium Café [lodging] Hampton Inn [other] Central Mkt Foods

156mm Missouri River

156 I-194, Bismarck Expswy, Bismarck City Ctr, **1/2 mi** S [other] Dakota Zoo

155 to Lp 94 (exits left from wb), Mandan, City Ctr, same as 153

153 ND 1806, Mandan Dr, Mandan, **1/2 mi** S [gas] Cenex/dsl, PetroServe/dsl, Tesoro [food] Bonanza, Burger King, Dakota Farms Rest., Domino's, DQ, Hardee's, Papa Murphy's, Pizza Hut, Pizza Ranch, Subway, Taco John's [lodging] North Country Inn [other] Central Mkt Foods, Chevrolet, Dacotah Centennial Park, Family$, Ft Lincoln SP (5mi), Goodyear/auto, NAPA, NW Tire, O'Reilly Parts, Subaru, Verizon

152 Sunset Dr, Mandan, N [gas] Tesoro [food] MT Mike's Steaks [lodging] Best Western, Walmart, S [gas] Tesoro/RV dump [food] Fried's Rest. [other] [H]

152mm scenic view eb

147 ND 25, to ND 6, Mandan, S [gas] Tesoro/Subway/cafe/dsl/scales/24hr

140 to Crown Butte

135mm scenic view wb, litter barrel

134 to Judson, Sweet Briar Lake

127 ND 31 N, to New Salem, N [other] Knife River Indian Village (35mi), S [gas] Cenex/dsl, Tesoro/dsl [food] Sunset Cafe [lodging] Arrowhead Inn/café [other] DFC/dsl, Food Pride, Gaebe Drug, vet, World's Largest Cow

123 to Almont

120 no services

119mm **[RS] both lanes, full [handicapped] facilities, litter barrels, petwalk [phone] [picnic]**

117 no services

113 no services

HEBRON

110 ND 49, to Glen Ullin

108 to Glen Ullin, Lake Tschida, **3 mi** S [gas] [food] [lodging] [other] camping

102 Hebron, to Glen Ullin, to Lake Tschida, **3 mi** S [gas] [food] [lodging] [other] camping

97 Hebron, **2 mi** N [gas] [food] [lodging]

96.5mm central/mountain time zone

90 no services

84 ND 8, Richardton, N [gas] Cenex/dsl [other] [H], Schnell RA, to Assumption Abbey

78 to Taylor

72 to Enchanted Hwy, Gladstone

DICKINSON

64 Dickinson, S [gas] Cenex/Tiger Truckstop/rest./dsl/24hr, [food] Dakota Diner, [other] dsl repair, Ford/Lincoln, Honda, NW Tire, Toyota/Scion

61 ND 22, Dickinson, N [gas] Cenex/dsl/LP, Simonson/dsl [food] Applebee's, Arby's, Bonanza, Burger King, DQ, El Sombrero Mexican, Papa Murphy's, Pizza Ranch, Sakura Japanese, Sanford's Rest., Taco Bell, Taco John's, Wendy's [lodging] AmericInn, Astoria Suites, Best Western, Comfort Inn, Hampton Inn, Holiday Inn Express, Microtel, My Place, Ramada, Savannah Suites [other] AT&T, Chevrolet, Dan's Foods, Goodyear/auto, Herberger's, JC Penney, K-Mart, Midas, O'Reilly Parts, Runnings Hardware, USPO, Verizon, Walmart/Subway, White Drug, S [gas] Cenex/dsl, Conoco/repair, Holiday/dsl, Tesoro/dsl [food] A&W/KFC, Country

ND

INTERSTATE 94 Contd

61 Continued
Kitchen, Domino's, Don Pedro's Mexican, King Buffet, McDonald's, Perkins, Subway La Quinta, Quality Inn, Relax Inn, Select Inn, Super 8 H, Mac's Hardware, museum, visitor info

59 Lp 94, to Dickinson, N Extended Stay, ValuePlace, S camping, to Patterson Lake RA, services in Dickinson

51 South Heart

42 US 85, to Grassy Butte, Belfield, Williston, N MVP/dsl T Roosevelt NP (52mi), S Cenex/dsl/24hr, Conoco/dsl DQ, Trapper's Kettle Rest. Trapper's Inn info, NAPA

36 Fryburg

32 T Roosevelt NP

27 Lp 94, Historic Medora (from wb), T Roosevelt NP

24.5mm Little Missouri Scenic River

24 Medora, Historic Medora, S visitors ctr, Chateau de Mores HS, T Roosevelt NP

23 West River Rd (from wb)

22mm scenic view eb

18 Buffalo Gap, N Buffalo Gap Camping (seasonal)

10 Sentinel Butte, Camel Hump Lake, S

7 Home on the Range

1 ND 16, S **Welcome Ctr/, full facilities, litter barrels, petwalk vending** FLYING J/Subway/dsl/scales/LP/24hr, Cenex/dsl/LP/24hr Buckboard Inn H, Beach RV Park,

1mm **litter barrel, weigh sta eb**

0mm North Dakota/Montana state line

OHIO

INTERSTATE 70

Exit #	Services
225.5mm	Ohio/West Virginia state line, Ohio River
225	US 250 W, OH 7, Bridgeport, N Marathon, StarFire, Sunoco/dsl DQ, Papa John's, Pizza Hut Advance Parts, AutoZone, Family$, Meineke, NAPA, S Clark, Exxon/dsl Domino's
220	US 40, Rd 214, N Marathon, Sunoco/dsl Comfort Inn, S A Fuel Mart Days Inn vet
219	I-470 E, to Bel-Aire, Washington PA, (from eb)
218	Mall Rd, to US 40, to Blaine, N BP, Exxon/Subway/dsl Applebee's, Arby's, Buffalo Wild Wings, Burger King, DeFelice Pizza, Denny's, Eat'n Park, HoneyBaked Ham, King Buffet, Little Caesars, Outback Steaks, Pizza Hut, Red Lobster, Starbucks, Steak'n Shake, Taco Bell, Tlaquepaque Mexican, Undo's Rest., W Texas Steaks, Wendy's Best Value Inn, EconoLodge, Hampton Inn, Hawthorn Suites, Holiday Inn Express, Microtel, Red Roof Inn, Super 8 $General, $Tree, AAA, Advance Parts, Aldi Foods, AT&T, AutoZone, Buick/Cadillac/Chevrolet, CVS Drug, Kroger, Lowe's, Sam's Club, Staples, Stewarts RV Ctr, URGENT CARE, Verizon, Walmart/McDonald's, S Bob Evans, Chipotle, Cracker Barrel, Garfield's Rest., KFC/LJ Silver, Little Caesar's, Longhorn Steaks, McDonald's, Osaka Steaks, Panda Chinese, Panera Bread, Starbucks Candlewood Suites, Fairfield Inn, Residence Inn Boscov's, Chrysler/Dodge/Jeep, Elder-Beerman, Jo-Ann Fabrics, K-Mart, Macy's, mall, NTB, Sears/auto
216	OH 9, St Clairsville, N BP
215	National Rd, N Burger King, Domino's, WenWu Chinese NAPA, Riesbeck's Foods, USPO
213	OH 331, Flushing, S BP, Marathon/Subway/dsl, Sunoco/dsl
211mm	**both lanes, full facilities, litter barrels, petwalk vending**
208	OH 149, Morristown, N Exxon/McDonald's/dsl Schlepp's Rest. Arrowhead Motel (1mi), Days Inn
208	Continued $General, Cannonball Speedway, Ford/Lincoln, S Marathon/Quiznos/dsl, Pilot/Subway/dsl/scales/24hr Sleep Inn Barkcamp SP, Harley-Davidson
204	US 40 E (from eb, no return), National Rd
202	OH 800, to Barnesville, S Sunoco/dsl H
198	Rd 114, Fairview
193	OH 513, Middlebourne, N BP, FuelMart/dsl fireworks
189mm	**eb, full facilities, litter barrels, petwalk vending**
186	US 40, OH 285, to Old Washington, N Marathon/dsl, S GoMart/dsl, Speedway/dsl/scales/24hr
180b a	I-77 N, to Cleveland, to Salt Fork SP, I-77 S, to Charleston
178	OH 209, Cambridge, 0-1 mi N Marathon/dsl, Sheetz/dsl, Starfire/dsl Bob Evans, Coldstone/Tim Hortons, Cracker Barrel, Denny's, DQ, Forum Rest, KFC, McDonald's, Papa

ND OH

INTERSTATE 70 Cont'd

CAMBRIDGE

178 Continued
John's, Pizza Hut, Ruby Tuesday, Subway, Wendy's Comfort Inn, Days Inn, Hampton Inn, Holiday Inn Express, Microtel, Quality Inn, Sleep Inn, Southgate Hotel H, $General, Advance Parts, AutoZone, BigLots, Buick/Cadillac/GMC, Family$, O'Reilly a Parts, Riesbecks Foods, Verizon, S Murphy USA/dsl, Pilot/Subway/dsl/scales/24hr Arby's, Buffalo Wild Wings, Burger King, Great Chinese, Little Caesars, Taco Bell, Tlaquepaque Mexican Baymont Inn $Tree, Aldi Foods, AT&T, Chevrolet, Chrysler/Dodge/Jeep, K-Mart/gas, Radio Shack, Spring Valley RV Park (1mi), Verizon, Walmart/Subway

176 US 22, US 40, to Cambridge, N Sunoco/dsl Budget Inn RV camping, st patrol, vet, Western Shop

173mm **weigh sta both lanes**

169 OH 83, to Cumberland, New Concord, N Marathon/dsl Wall Hotel John&Annie Glen Historic Site, RV camping, to Muskingum Coll

164 US 22, US 40, Norwich, N BP Baker's Motel, Zane Gray Museum, S antiques, pottery

163mm **wb, full facilities, litter barrels, petwalk vending**

ZANESVILLE

160 OH 797, Airport Rd, N Love's/Arby's/dsl/scales/24hr, S BP, Exxon/Subway/dsl Denny's, McDonald's, Wendy's Best Western, Economy Inn, Motel 6 , st patrol

157 OH 93, Zanesville, N BP, S Marathon, Shell/dsl, st patrol

155 OH 60, OH 146, Underwood St, Zanesville, N Bob Evans, Olive Garden, Oriental Buffet, Red Lobster, Steak'n Shake, Tumbleweed Grill Comfort Inn, Fairfield Inn, Hampton Inn, Holiday Inn Express H, Riesbeck's Mkt, USPO, S Marathon/dsl Cracker Barrel, Subway, Wendy's Baymont Inn, EconoLodge, Travel Inn Rite Aid

154 5th St (from eb)

153b Maple Ave (no EZ return from wb), N BP DQ, Italian Eatery, Papa John's, Tee Jaye's Rest H, CVS Drug, Family$

153a State St, N Speedway/dsl to Dillon SP (8mi), USPO, S Marathon

153mm Licking River

152 US 40, National Rd, N Exxon/A&W/Blimpie/dsl, Starfire/dsl McDonald's Super 8

142 US 40 (from wb, no EZ return), Gratiot, N RV camping

141 OH 668, US 40 (from eb, no return), to Gratiot, same as 142

132 OH 13, to Thornville, Newark, N Dawes Arboretum (3mi), S BP, Shell Subway (2mi) RV camping

131mm **both lanes, full facilities, litter barrels, petwalk vending**

129b a OH 79, to Buckeye Lake, Hebron, N Best Western Advance Parts, Kroger/gas, S BP, Valero Donato's Pizza, McDonald's, Pizza Hut/Taco Bell, Subway, Wendy's EconoLodge Blue Goose Marina (2mi), CarQuest, KOA (2mi)

126 OH 37, to Granville, Lancaster, N Marathon/dsl, Pilot/Chester's/Subway/dsl/scales/24hr, S TA/BP/Popeye's/Sbarro's/dsl/scales/24hr/ @, Valero/dsl Deluxe Inn, Red Roof Inn IA 80 Truckomat/truckwash, KOA

122 OH 158, to Baltimore, Kirkersville, N Regal Inn, S FLYING J/Denny's/dsl/LP/scales/24hr fireworks

118 OH 310, to Pataskala, N BP/McDonald's, Shell/dsl, Speedway/dsl DQ, S BP/Duke's/Subway/dsl RCD RV Ctr

112c OH 204, to Blecklick Rd (from eb)

COLUMBUS AREA

112 OH 256, to Pickerington, Reynoldsburg, N BP, Shell McDonald's Buffalo Wild Wings, Chipotle Mexican, Culver's, Five Guys, IHOP, Logan's Roadhouse, Noodles&Co, O'Charley's, Olive Garden, Panera Bread, Penn Sta, Smokey Bones BBQ, Subway, TGIFriday's, Tim Horton's Fairfield Inn, Holiday Inn Express AT&T, Best Buy, Gander Mtn, Jo Ann Fabrics, Marshall's, NTB, Old Navy, Petco, Petsmart, Sam's Club/gas, Staples, Target, Tire Discounters, Verizon, Walgreens, Walmart/Subway, S Speedway/dsl Arby's, Bob Evans, Cane's, CiCi's Pizza, Classic's Diner, Cold Stone, Cracker Barrel, Feta Greek Cafe, Firehouse Subs, Iron Chef, Jimmy John's, KFC, La Fogata Mexican, LJ Silver, Longhorn Steaks, Max&Erma's, Omezzo Italian, Skyline Chili, Starbucks, Steak'n Shake, Tom+Chee, Uno, Wendy's Best Western, Comfort Inn, Hampton Inn Advance Parts, Barnes&Noble, Kohl's, Kroger/E85, Tuesday Morning, URGENT CARE, Verizon

110 Brice Rd, to Reynoldsburg, N Speedway/dsl, Sunoco Burger King, Donato's, Genji Japanese, Golden China, Popeye's, Subway, TeeJaye's Rest., Tim Horton's, Waffle House Days Inn, Extended Stay America, La Quinta, Red Roof Inn, Super 8 BigLots, Family$, Goodyear/auto, Home Depot, O'Reilly Parts, S BP, Speedway/dsl Applebee's, Arby's, Asian Star, Boston Mkt, Chipotle Mexican, KFC, McDonald's, Starbucks, Subway, Taco Bell, Waffle House Comfort Suites, Motel 6, Travelodge Acura, Advance Parts, Aldi Foods, Discount Tire, Family$, Fiat, Firestone/auto, GNC, Hobby Lobby, Honda, Lowe's, Michael's, NTB, Toyota, Scion, Walgreens

108b a I-270 N to Cleveland, access to H, I-270 S to Cincinnati

107a OH 317, Hamilton Rd, to Whitehall, S Shell/dsl Arby's, Burger King, Capt D's, ChuckeCheese, Eastland Buffet, Ichiban Japanese, McDonald's, Papa John's, Pizza Hut, Red Lobster, Steak'n Shake, Taco Bell AmeriVu Inn, Fort Rapids Resort, Hampton Inn, Hawthorn Inn, InTown Suites $General, AT&T, Macy's, PepBoys

105a US 33, to Lancaster, **2 mi** N Tat Italian

105b US 33, James Rd, Bexley, N Tat Italian

103b a Livingston Ave, to Capital University, N Exxon, Speedway/dsl Mr Hero Subs, Peking Dynasty, Popeye's, Subway, Taco Bell, Tim Horton's, Wendy's auto repair, Katz Tires, S Marathon, Shell McDonald's, Rally's, White Castle Family$

102 Kelton Ave, Miller Ave

101a I-71 N, to Cleveland

100b US 23, to 4th St, downtown

99c Rich St, Town St (exits left from wb)

99b OH 315 N, downtown

99a I-71 S, to Cincinnati

98b Mound St (from wb, no EZ return), S Speedway Little Caesar's, McDonald's, Rally's Aldi Foods, Family$

98a US 62, OH 3, Central Ave, to Sullivant, same as 98b

97 US 40, W Broad St, N Valero/dsl Arby's, Burger King, McDonald's, Subway, Taco Bell, Tim Horton's, Wendy's, White Castle Knights Inn, Travelodge Aamco, CVS Drug, U-Haul, USPO

96 I-670 (exits left from eb), to

95 Hague Ave (from wb), S Sunoco

94 Wilson Rd, N Marathon/Circle K/Subway/dsl, UDF, S BP, Pilot/Wendy's/dsl/scales/24hr, Shell/dsl, Speedway McDonald's, Waffle House EconoLodge vet

93b a I-270, N to Cleveland, S to Cincinnati

91b a to Hilliard, New Rome, N GetGo, Shell, Speedway/dsl Applebee's, Arby's, Buffalo Wild Wings, Burger King, Chick

ND

INTERSTATE 70 Cont'd

91b a	Continued fil-A, Chipotle, Cracker Barrel, Culver's, Donato's Pizza, El Vaquero Mexican, Fazoli's, Firehouse Subs, Five Guys, Golden Chopsticks, Hot Head Burrito, IHOP, KFC, McDonald's, Mikkado Japanese, Olive Garden, Outback Steaks, Panda Express, Panera Bread, Perkins, Red Robin, Rooster's Rest., Skyline Chili, Subway, Supreme Buffet, Taco Bell, Tim Horton's/Coldstone, Tom+Chee, TX Roadhouse, Wendy's, Which Wich?, White Castle, Wild Ginger Asian [lodging] Best Value Inn, Comfort Suites, Fairfield Inn, Hampton Inn, Hawthorn Inn, Holiday Inn, La Quinta, Motel 6, Red Roof Inn [other] Advance Parts, AT&T, Dick's, Discount Tire, Firestone/auto, Ford, Gander Mtn, Giant Eagle Foods/gas, GNC, Kohl's, Marshall's, Meijer/dsl, Michael's, Midas, Old Navy, Petsmart, Sam's Club/gas, Target, URGENT CARE, Verizon, Walmart/Subway, **S** [gas] BP/dsl, Marathon/dsl [food] Bob Evans, Handel's Ice Cream, Steak'n Shake [lodging] Best Western, Country Inn&Suites, Super 8
85	OH 142, to Plain City, W Jefferson, **N** [other] Prairie Oaks SP, **S** [other] Battelle Darby SP
80	OH 29, to Mechanicsburg, **S** [other] hwy patrol
79	US 42, to London, Plain City, **N** [gas] Pilot/Arby's/dsl/scales/24hr [food] Waffle House [other] Camping World RV Ctr, truck/auto repair, **S** [gas] Speedway/Subway/dsl, TA/BP/Pizza Hut/Popeye's/dsl/scales/24hr/ @ [food] McDonald's, Taco Bell, Wendy's [lodging] Holiday Inn Express, Motel 6 [other] [H]
72	OH 56, to London, Summerford, **N** [gas] Marathon/Subway/dsl, **4 mi S** [other] [H]
71mm	**[RS] wb, full [handicapped] facilities, litter barrels, petwalk [phone] [picnic] vending**
66	OH 54, to Catawba, South Vienna, **N** [gas] Fuelmart/dsl/scales, **S** [gas] Speedway/dsl
62	US 40, Springfield, **N** [lodging] Harmony Motel [other] [H], antiques, auto repair, Harmony Farm Mkt, to Buck Creek SP, **S** [other] Beaver Valley Camping
59	OH 41, to S Charleston, **N** [other] [H], Harley-Davidson, st patrol, **S** [gas] antiques, BP/dsl
54	OH 72, to Cedarville, Springfield, **N** [gas] BP/dsl, Shell, Speedway/dsl, Sunoco/dsl [food] A&W/LJ Silver, Arby's, Bob Evans, Burger King, Cassano's Pizza/subs, Cracker Barrel, Domino's, Dunkin Donuts, El Toro Mexican, Hardee's, Lee's Chicken, Little Caesars, McDonald's, Panda Chinese, Popeye's, Rally's, Rudy's Smokehouse, Subway, Taco Bell, Wendy's [lodging] Comfort Suites, Hampton Inn, Holiday Inn Express, Motel 6, Quality Inn, Ramada Ltd, Red Roof Inn, Super 8 [other] [H], Advance Parts, BigLots, Family$, Kroger/deli, Rite Aid, Walgreens, **S** [gas] Marathon/dsl
52b a	US 68, to Urbana, Xenia, **S** [other] to John Bryan SP
48	OH 4 (from wb), to Enon, Donnelsville, **N** [other] camping, **S** [gas] Speedway
47	OH 4 (from eb), to Springfield, **N** [other] Enon Beach Camping, **S** [gas] Speedway
44	I-675 S, Spangler Rd, to Cincinnati
43mm	Mad River
41b a	OH 4, OH 235, to Dayton, New Carlisle, **1 mi N** [gas] Shell/dsl [food] KFC, McDonald's, Wendy's [other] Freightliner, Kenworth
38	OH 201, Brandt Pike, **N** [gas] Marathon/dsl [other] Meijer/Subway/dsl/E85, **S** [gas] Shell, UDF/dsl [food] Bob Evans, Sonic, Tim Horton's, Waffle House, Wendy's [lodging] Best Value Inn, Comfort Inn [other] vet, Walmart
36	OH 202, Huber Heights, **N** [gas] Speedway/dsl [food] Applebee's, Big Boy, Dragon City, El Toro Grill, Fazoli's, Firehouse Subs, Osaka Japanese, Steak'n Shake, Taco Bell, Waffle House [lodging] Baymont Inn [other] $Tree, AT&T, Big Lots, Dick's, Elder Beerman, Gander Mtn, GNC, Hobby Lobby, Kia, Kohl's, Lowe's, Marshall's, Petsmart, Staples, Target, Verizon, vet, **S** [gas] BP/dsl, Marathon/dsl [food] Arby's, Buffalo Wild Wings, Burger King, Cadillac Jack's, Chipotle Mexican, CiCi's Pizza, La Rosa's Pizza, McDonald's, Rooster's Rest., Skyline Chili, Subway, TGIFriday's, TX Roadhouse [lodging] Days Inn, Hampton Inn, Holiday Inn Express [other] Kroger/gas

SPRINGFIELD

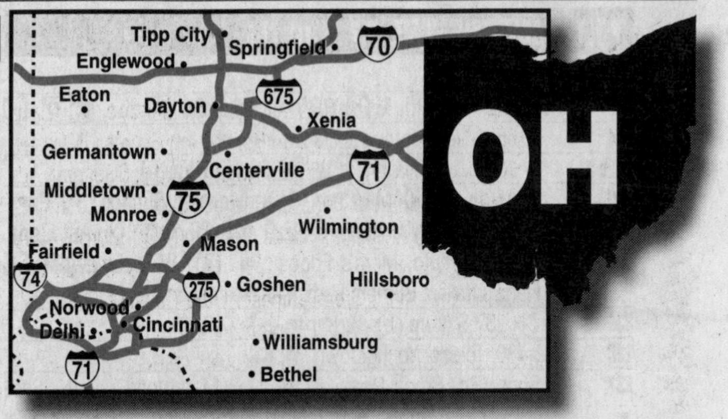

36	Continued
33b a	I-75, N to Toledo, S to Dayton
32	to US 40, Vandalia, **N** [other] to Dayton Intn'l Airport
29	OH 48, to Dayton, Englewood, **N** [gas] BP, Marathon/dsl, Speedway/dsl, Sunoco/dsl, Valero [food] Arby's, Big Boy, Bob Evans, Buffalo Wild Wings, Company BBQ, Hot Head Burrito, Lee's Chicken, Perkins, Pizza Hut, Ponderosa, Skyline Chili, Taco Bell, Tim Horton's, Tony's Italian, Wendy's, Yen Ching Chinese [lodging] Best Western, Clarion, Hampton Inn, Red Carpet Inn [other] Advance Parts, Aldi Foods, AutoZone, Family$, Grismer/auto, Midas, O'Reilly Parts, vet, **S** [food] Chipotle, El Toro, McDonald's, Steak'n Shake, Waffle House [lodging] Comfort Inn, Motel 6 [other] [H], Meijer/dsl/E85
26	OH 49 S, **N** [gas] Murphy USA/dsl [food] Bob Evans, La Rosa's Pizza, Sonic, Subway [other] Petco, URGENT CARE, Verizon, Walmart/Subway, **S** [gas] Shell/dsl [food] Wendy's
24	OH 49 N, to Greenville, Clayton, **N** [other] KOA (seasonal)
21	Arlington Rd, Brookville, **N** [gas] Speedway/Subway/dsl, **S** [gas] Speedway/dsl [food] Arby's, Brookville Grill, Great Wall Chinese, KFC/Taco Bell, K's Rest., Lee's Chicken, McDonald's, Pizza Hut, Rob's Rest., Subway, Waffle House, Wendy's [lodging] Brookville Inn, Holiday Inn Express [other] $General, Advance Parts, Brookville Parts, Chevrolet, Family$, IGA Foods, Rite Aid
14	OH 503, to West Alexandria, Lewisburg, **N** [gas] Marathon/Subway/dsl [food] Dari Twist [lodging] Super Inn [other] $General, **S** [gas] Valero/dsl
10	US 127, to Eaton, Greenville, **N** [gas] st patrol, TA/BP/Burger King/Subway/dsl/scales/24hr/ @, **S** [gas] Pilot/Subway/dsl/scales/24hr [lodging] Budget Inn
3mm	**Welcome Ctr/[RS] both lanes, full [handicapped] facilities, litter barrels, petwalk [phone] [picnic] vending**
1	US 35 E (from eb), to Eaton, New Hope
0mm	Ohio/Indiana state line, Welcome Arch, **weigh sta eb**

DAYTON

INTERSTATE 71

Exit #	Services
	I-71 begins/ends on I-90, exit 170 in Cleveland.
247b	I-90 W, I-490 E.
247a	W 14th, Clark Ave
246	Denison Ave, Jennings Rd (from sb)

OH

INTERSTATE 71 Cont'd

Exit #	Services
245	US 42, Pearl Rd, E [gas] BP/7-11, Gas&Go [other] zoo, W [other] H
244	W 65th, Denison Ave (exits left from nb)
242b a	W 130th, to Bellaire Rd, W [gas] Sunoco, Valero
240	W 150th, E [gas] Marathon, Speedway/dsl, Sunoco [food] Burger King, Denny's, Happy's Pizza [lodging] Marriott [other] AutoZone, Goodyear/auto, Marc's Foods, W [gas] BP/Subway/dsl [food] Nana's Italian, Somers Rest. [lodging] Holiday Inn, La Quinta
239	OH 237 S (from sb), W [other] to airport
238	I-480, Toledo, Youngstown, W [other] airport
237	Snow Rd, Brook Park, E [gas] BP, Marathon/Circle K, Shell [food] Arby's, Arby's, Bob Evans, Burger King, Dunkin Donuts, Garden Rest., Garden Rest., Goody's Rest., KFC, Little Caesar's, Little Caesar's, McDonald's, Rally's, Reddi's Pizza, Subway, Taco Bell [lodging] Best Western, Holiday Inn Express, Howard Johnson [other] $General, $Tree, $Tree, Advance Parts, AutoZone, Conrad Tire/repair, CVS Drug, CVS Drug, Giant Eagle, Giant Eagle, O'Reilly Parts, Rite Aid, W [other] to airport
235	Bagley Rd, E [food] Bob Evans [other] Mr Tire, vet, W [gas] BP/dsl, Shell, Speedway/dsl [food] Aladdin's a Eatery, Baskin-Robbins/Dunkin Donuts, Burger King, Capri a Pizza, Caribou Coffee, Chipotle, Craft Brew Garden, Five Guys, Jimmy John's, Little Hong Kong, Max&Erma's, McDonald's, Olive Garden, Panera Bread, Perkins, Pizza Hut, Taco Bell [lodging] Comfort Inn, Courtyard, Crowne Plaza, Days Inn, Extended Stay America, Hampton Inn, Motel 6, Red Roof Inn, Residence Inn, TownePlace Suites [other] H, Aldi Foods, K-Mart, Verizon
234	US 42, Pearl Rd, E [gas] Shell/dsl, Sunoco/dsl [food] Hunan Chinese, Jet's Pizza, Katherine's Rest., Mr Hero, Santo's Italian, Three Bros Pizza [other] Audi/Porsche, Honda, W [gas] Gas&Food/dsl, Sheetz/dsl [food] Buffalo Wild Wings, Jennifer's Rest., Mad Cactus Rest., McDonald's [lodging] Kings Inn, La Siesta Motel, Metrick's Motel [other] Home Depot, Lowe's, Walmart/Subway
233	I-80 and Ohio Tpk, to Toledo, Youngstown
231	OH 82, Strongsville, E [gas] Shell [lodging] Holiday Inn, Super 8 [other] Chevrolet, W [gas] BP/7-11/dsl, Marathon/Subway/dsl [food] Applebee's, Buca Italian, Chick-fil-A, Chipotle, DiBella's Subs, Firehouse Subs, Five Guys, Houlihan's, Longhorn Steaks, Macaroni Grill, Panera Bread, Red Lobster, Rockne's Grill, Rosewood Grill, Samurai Japanese, Starbucks, TGIFriday, Zoup! [other] $Tree, AAA, AT&T, Best Buy, Costco/gas, Dick's, Dillard's, Heinen's Mkt, JC Penney, Kohl's, Macy's, mall, Midas, NTB, Old Navy, PetCo, Sears/auto, Target, TJ Maxx, Verizon
226	OH 303, Brunswick, E [gas] Shell/dsl [food] Pizza Hut [other] Chrysler/Dodge/Jeep, Hyundai, Subaru, Toyota/Scion, vet, VW, W [gas] GetGo, Speedway/dsl, Sunoco/dsl [food] Applebee's, Arby's, Bob Evans, Burger King, Chipotle, Georgio's Pizza, House of Pearl, McDonald's, Muchos Buenos Mexican, Panera Bread, Panini's Grill, Pizza Hut, Sonic, Starbucks, Steak'n Shake, Subway, Taco Bell, Wendy's [lodging] Quality Inn [other] $General, Buehler's Foods, Ford, Giant Eagle Food, GNC, Home Depot, K-Mart, Marc's Mkt, Radio Shack, Verizon
225mm	[rest stop] nb, full facilities, litter barrels, petwalk
224mm	[rest stop] sb, full facilities, litter barrels, petwalk
222	OH 3, Medina, Hinckley, W [other] st patrol
220	I-271 N, (from nb) to Erie, Pa
218	OH 18, to Akron, Medina, E [gas] BP/dsl, Marathon/dsl, Sunoco/dsl [food] Alexandri's Rest., Baskin-Robbins/Dunkin Donuts, Burger King, DQ, Fresh Food Deli, Master Pizza [lodging] Holiday Inn Express, Quality Inn, Super 8 [other] Kia, Nissan, Verizon, W [gas] Speedway/dsl [food] Arby's, Bob Evans, Brown Derby, Buffalo
218	Continued Wild Wings, Denny's, McDonald's, Pizza Hut, Rocknes Rest., Taco Bell, Waffle House, Wendy's [lodging] Fairfield Inn, Hampton Inn, Motel 6, Red Roof Inn [other] H, Aldi Foods, Buehler's Foods, Buick/Cadillac/GMC, Chrysler/Dodge/Jeep, Firestone/auto, Harley-Davidson, Honda, Verizon
209	I-76 E, to Akron, US 224, W [gas] Pilot/Subway/dsl/scales/24hr, TA/Country Pride/Burger King/Popeye's/dsl/scales/24hr/ @ [food] Arby's, McDonald's, Starbucks [lodging] Super 8 [other] Blue Beacon, Chippewa Valley Camping (1mi), SpeedCo
204	OH 83, Burbank, E [gas] BP/dsl, Duke/dsl, Loves/Hardee's/dsl/scales/24hr [lodging] Plaza Motel, W [gas] Pilot/Wendy's/dsl/scales/24hr [food] Bob Evans, Burger King, KFC/Taco Bell, McDonald's [other] H, Lodi Outlets/famous brands
198	OH 539, W Salem
196mm	[rest stop] both lanes, full facilities, litter barrels, petwalk, vending
196	OH 301 (from nb, no re-entry), W Salem
186	US 250, Ashland, E [gas] Marathon [food] Grandpa's Village/cheese gifts, Perkins [other] Hickory Lakes Camping (7mi), W [gas] Goasis BP/Pizza Hut/Popeye's/Starbucks/Taco Bell/dsl/24hr, Marathon/Subway/dsl [food] Brian Buffet, Denny's, Dunkin Donuts, Jake's Rest., McDonald's, Wendy's [lodging] Ashland Inn, Holiday Inn Express, Quality Inn, Rodeway Inn, Super 8 [other] H, $Tree, Aldi Foods, AT&T, Buehler's Foods, GNC, Home Depot, st patrol, to Ashland U, URGENT CARE, Verizon, Walmart/Subway
176	US 30, to Mansfield, E [lodging] Heritage Inn [other] fireworks
173	OH 39, to Mansfield
169	OH 13, Mansfield, E [gas] Marathon/7-11/dsl, Murphy USA/dsl [food] Applebee's, Chipotle, Cracker Barrel, Steak'n Shake, Wendy's [lodging] Best Western, La Quinta [other] Mohican SP, Walmart/Subway, W [gas] BP/7-11 [food] Arby's, Bob Evans, Burger King, El Charrito Mexican, McDonald's, Subway, Taco Bell [lodging] Hampton Inn, Super 8, Travelodge [other] H, st patrol
165	OH 97, to Bellville, E [gas] BP, Shell/dsl, Speedway/dsl [food] Bucky Express Diner, Burger King, Der Dutchman, KC's Rib House, McDonald's [lodging] Comfort Inn, Days Inn, Economy Inn, Quality Inn [other] to Mohican SP, W [food] Wendy's
151	OH 95, to Mt Gilead, E [gas] Duke/BP/deli, Marathon [food] Buckeye Country Diner, McDonald's, Wendy's [lodging] Best Western [other] st patrol, W [gas] Shell/dsl, Sunoco/dsl/E85 [food] Subway [lodging] Knights Inn [other] H, Mt Gilead SP (6mi)
149mm	truck parking both lanes
140	OH 61, Mt Gilead, E [gas] Pilot/Arby's/dsl/scales/24hr, W [gas] BP/Taco Bell, Marathon/Subway [food] Farmstead Rest. [other] Cardinal Ctr Camping
131	US 36, OH 37, to Delaware, E [gas] FLYING J/Denny's/dsl/LP/scales/24hr/ @, Pilot/Subway/dsl/scales/24hr [food] Burger King [other] Harley-Davidson, W [gas] BP/dsl, Shell/Tim Horton [food] Arby's, Bob Evans, Cracker Barrel, KFC/LJ Silver, McDonald's, Panera Bread, Starbucks, Taco Bell, Waffle House, Wendy's, White Castle [lodging] Best Value Inn, Hampton Inn, Holiday Inn Express [other] H, Alum Cr SP, Cross Creek Camping (6mi)
128mm	[rest stop] both lanes, full facilities, litter barrels, petwalk, vending
121	Polaris Pkwy, to Gemini Pl, E [gas] BP, Mobil, Shell/dsl [food] Bonefish Grill, Buffalo Wild Wings, Canes, Carfagna's Kitchen, El Alcapulco, Firehouse Subs, Five Guys, McDonald's, Mellow Mushroom Pizza, Pei Wei, Polaris Grill, Skyline Chili, Starbucks, Steak'n Shake, Subway, Tim Horton's [lodging] Fairfield Inn, Four Points Sheraton, Hampton Inn, Holiday Inn Express, Homewood Suites [other] Firestone/auto, Mt Tire, W [gas] BP, Shell/Tim Horton [food] Applebee's, Arby's, Bar Louie, Benihana, BJ's

STRONGSVILLE

AKRON

MANSFIELD

OH

INTERSTATE 71 Cont'd

121	Continued Rest., Brio Grille, Carrabba's, Charley Subs, CheeseCake Factory, Chick-fil-A, Chipotle Mexican, Coldstone, Dave&Buster's, El Vaquero Mexican, Firebird's Grill, Genghis Grill, Honey Baked Ham, Hooters, Jason's Deli, Jersey Mike's, Jimmy John's, Krispy Kreme, Marcella's Italian, Matt the Miller's Tavern, Max&Erma's, McDonald's, Merlot's Rest., Mimi's Cafe, Mitchell Steaks, Molly Woo's, Noodles&Co, O'Charley's, Olive Garden, Panera Bread, Papa John's, Penn Sta Subs, Potbelly's, Qdoba, Quaker Steak, Red Lobster, Red Robin, Rooster's Grill, Smokey Bones BBQ, Sonic, Starbucks, Subway, Taco Bell, Tequilas Mexican, TGIFriday's, TX Roadhouse, Waffle House, Wendy's [lodging] Cambria Suites, Candlewood Suites, Comfort Inn, Extended Stay America, Hilton, Hilton Garden, Residence Inn [other] AT&T, AutoZone, Barnes&Noble, Best Buy, BigLots, Cabela's, Costco/gas, Dick's, Earth Fare Mkt, funpark, GNC, Hobby Lobby, JC Penney, Jo-Ann Etc, Kroger/gas, Lowe's, Macy's, mall, NTB, Old Navy, Petsmart, Sears/auto, Target, TireDiscounters, TJ Maxx, Verizon, Von Maur, Walgreens, World Mkt
119b a	I-270, to Indianapolis, Wheeling
117	OH 161, to Worthington, E [gas] BP/dsl, Shell, Speedway/dsl, Sunoco/dsl [food] Burger King, Carfagna's Italian, China Dynasty, Chipotle, Dunkin Donuts/Baskin Robbins, Happy's a Pizza, KFC, LJ Silver, Massey's Pizza, McDonald's, Popeye's, Rally's, Red Lobster, Subway, Super Seafood Buffet, Taco Bell, Wendy's, White Castle [lodging] Comfort Inn, Days Inn, Red Roof Inn [other] $General, auto repair, CVS Drug, Family$, Walgreens, W [gas] GetGo, Shell, Speedway/dsl [food] Asian Kitchen, Bob Evans, China Jade, Domino's, McDonald's, Pizza Hut, Skyline Chili, Subway, Tim Hortons, Waffle House, Wendy's [lodging] Continent Inn, Crowne Plaza, Extended Stay America, Hawthorn Suites, Lexington Inn&Suites, Motel 6, Super 8, ValuePlace [other] Advance Parts, AutoZone, Chevrolet, Family$, Giant Eagle Foods, Premier Tire
116	Morse Rd, Sinclair Rd, E [gas] BP, Marathon/dsl, Shell/dsl, Speedway/dsl, Turkey Hill/dsl [food] Chipotle, Jimmy John's, Little Caesars, McDonald's, Papa John's, Subway, Taco Bell, Tim Horton's [lodging] Extend Suites [other] $General, AT&T, Buick/GMC, Chrysler/Dodge/Jeep, CVS Drug, Family$, Firestone/auto, Ford, Kroger, Menard's, Mr Tire, PepBoys, Save-A-Lot Foods, URGENT CARE, W [gas] Sunoco [lodging] Best Value Inn, Motel 6 [other] NTB
115	Cooke Rd
114	N Broadway, W [gas] Sunoco/dsl [food] Broadway Mkt Cafe, Subway
113	Weber Rd, W [gas] Speedway/dsl [other] CarQuest
112	Hudson St, E [gas] Marathon, Shell/dsl [food] Wendy's [lodging] Holiday Inn Express [other] Family$, W [food] Big Boy [other] Aldi Foods, Lowe's, NTB
111	17th Ave, W [food] McDonald's [lodging] Comfort Suites, Days Inn
110b	11th Ave
110a	5th Ave, E [gas] Sunoco [food] Royal Fish&Chicken, White Castle, W [gas] Valero [food] Buckeye's Express, Church's, KFC, Wendy's [other] AutoZone
109a	I-670
109b	OH 3, Cleveland Ave
109c	Spring St (exits left from sb)
108b	US 40, Broad St, downtown, downtown
108a	Main St
101a [70]	I-70 E, US 23 N, to Wheeling
100b a [70]	US 23 S, Front St, High St, downtown
106a	I-70 W, to Indianapolis
106b	OH 315 N, Dublin St, Town St
105	Greenlawn, E [gas] BP [food] LJ Silver, White Castle [other] Berliner Park, W [gas] Shamrock
104	OH 104, Frank Rd
101b a	I-270, Wheeling, Indianapolis
100	Stringtown Rd, E [gas] BP [food] Bob Evans, Charley's Grilled Subs, Chick-fil-A, Chipotle, Coldstone, DQ, El Vaquero Mexican, Five Guys, Fusion Steaks, Jersey Mike's, Longhorn Steaks, O'Charley's, Olive Garden, Panda Express, Panera Bread, Red Robin, Roosters Grill, Smokey Bones BBQ, Sonic, Starbucks, Steak'n Shake, Subway, TX Roadhouse, White Castle [lodging] Best Western, Candlewood Suites, Courtyard, Drury Inn, Hampton Inn, Hilton Garden, Holiday Inn Express, La Quinta, Quality Inn, Red Roof Inn [other] AT&T, Best Buy, Dick's, Discount Tire, Firestone/auto, GNC, Hobby Lobby, Home Depot, Kohl's, Michael's, Petsmart, Staples, Target, TJ Maxx, Verizon, Walmart, W [gas] GetGo, Speedway/dsl, Sunoco/dsl, Turkey Hill/dsl [food] Applebee's, Arby's, Burger King, Cane's Chicken Fingers, China Bell, City BBQ, Cracker Barrel, Donato's Pizza, Fazoli's, Golden Corral, KFC, Mariachi Mexican, McDonald's, Papa John's, Pizza Hut, Rally's, Ruby Tuesday, Starbucks, Subway, Taco Bell, TeeJaye's Rest., Tim Horton, Waffle House, Wendy's [lodging] Comfort Inn, Days Inn, Motel 6, Travelodge [other] Advance Parts, Aldi Foods, AutoZone, BigLots, CVS Drug, Giant Eagle Foods, GNC, Goodyear/auto, K-Mart, Kroger/dsl, PetCo, Tuffy Auto, USPO, Walgreens
97	OH 665, London-Groveport Rd, E [gas] Marathon/Circle K [food] Arby's, Jimmy John's, McDonald's, Subway, Sunny St Cafe, Taco Bell, Tim Horton/Wendy's [other] $Tree, AT&T, Chevrolet, CVS Drug, Kroger/gas/E85, Meijer/E85, TireDiscounters, to Scioto Downs, URGENT CARE, Verizon, vet
94	US 62, OH 3, Orient, W [gas] Sunoco/Subway/dsl [other] Eddie's Repair
84	OH 56, Mt Sterling, E [gas] BP/Subway/dsl [other] to Deer Creek SP (9mi)
75	OH 38, Bloomingburg, E [other] fireworks, W [gas] Sunoco/dsl
69	OH 41, OH 734, Jeffersonville, E [gas] *FLYING J*/Denny's/dsl/scales/LP/24hr [other] [H], W [gas] BP, Shell/Subway/dsl [food] Arby's, Wendy's [lodging] Quality Inn [other] Family$, Walnut Lake Camping
68mm	**[RS] both lanes, full [handicapped] facilities, litter barrels, petwalk [phone] [picnic] vending**
65	US 35, Washington CH, E [gas] Shell/dsl, Speedway/dsl, TA/BP/Pizza Hut/Popeye's/dsl/scales/24hr/ @ [food] A&W/KFC, Bob Evans, Chipotle Mexican, LJ Silver/Taco Bell, McDonald's, Subway, Waffle House, Wendy's, Werner's BBQ [lodging] Baymont Inn, Fairfield Inn, Hampton Inn [other] [H], Tanger Outlets/famous brands, W [gas] Loves/Hardee's/dsl/scales/24hr [lodging] EconoLodge

COLUMBUS AREA

OH

= gas = food = lodging = other = rest stop

INTERSTATE 71 Cont'd

Exit #	Services
58	OH 72, to Sabina
50	US 68, to Wilmington, E H, W BP/dsl, Pilot/Subway/dsl/scales/24hr, Shell/dsl Max&Erma's, McDonald's, Wendy's Budget Inn, Holiday Inn, repair/tires Robert's Centre
49mm	**weigh sta nb**
45	OH 73, to Waynesville, E BP, Shell/dsl 73 Grill H, W Caesar Creek Camping (3mi), Caesar Creek SP (5mi), flea mkt
36	Wilmington Rd, E RV camping, to Ft Ancient St Mem
35mm	Little Miami River
34mm	**both lanes, full facilities, scenic view, litter barrels, petwalk scenic view, vending**
32	OH 123, to Lebanon, Morrow, E Marathon, Valero Country Kitchen Morgan's Riverside Camping, **3 mi** W Bob Evans, Skyline Chili
28	OH 48, S Lebanon, E Speedway/Speedy's Cafe/dsl Dickey's BBQ, Starbucks, White Castle $Tree, Kohl's, Lowe's, Petsmart, Target, Verizon, W hwy patrol, Lebanon Raceway (6mi)
25	OH 741 N, Kings Mills Rd, E Shell/Popeye's/Dunkin Donuts, Speedway/dsl Buffalo Wings&Rings, Chipotle, DQ, Jimmy John's, McDonald's, Outback Steaks, Ruby Tuesday, Taco Bell, Wendy's Comfort Suites, Great Wolf Lodge, Kings Island Resort Harley-Davidson, Verizon, W Ameristop/Subway, BP Arby's, Big Boy, Burger King, Perkins, Pizza Hut, Skyline Chili, Taste Wok, Waffle House Baymont Inn, Hampton Inn, Microtel, Super 8 CarX, CVS Drug, GNC, Kroger/dsl, vet
24	Western Row, King's Island Dr (from nb), E Sunoco Eli's Grill, Fantastic Wok King's Island Resort
19	US 22, Mason-Montgomery Rd, E Speedway/dsl Arby's, Big Boy, Boston Mkt, Burger King, Cracker Barrel, Dunkin Donuts, Firehouse Subs, Flipdaddy's Burgers, Fricker's, Golden Corral, HoneyBaked Ham, Iron Chef Grill, KFC, Longhorn Steaks, McDonald's, Olive Garden, Pizza Tower, Potbelly, Taco Bell, Wendy's, White Castle Comfort Inn, Red Roof Inn, SpringHill Suites, TownePlace Suites Aldi Foods, AT&T, AutoZone, Barnes&Noble, Best Buy, BigLots, Buick/GMC, Chevrolet, Chrysler/Dodge/Jeep, Costco/gas, Firestone/auto, Ford, GNC, Honda, Infiniti, JC Penney, Kia, Kohl's, Kroger, Lexus, Mazda, Meijer/dsl, Michael's, Nissan, Old Navy, Porsche, Sam's Club/gas, Subaru, Target, TireDiscounters, Tires+, Toyota/Scion, Tuffy Auto, USPO, Verizon, VW, Walgreens, W BP/dsl, Marathon/dsl, Shell/Dunkin Donuts Abuelo's Mexican, Applebee's, BD Mongolian Grill, Blaze Pizza, Bravo Italian, Burger King, Carrabba's, Chick-fil-A, Chipotle Mexican, DiBella Subs, Dickey's BBQ, Firebirds Grill, Five Guys, Fox&Hound Grill, Graeter's Cafe, IHOP, Jimmy John's, LoneStar Steaks, McAlister's Deli, Mimi's Cafe, Noodles&Co, Oasis Grill, O'Charley's, Panda Express, Panera Bread, Piada Italian, Qdoba, Red Robin, Remezo Greek, River City Grille, Rusty Bucket, Skyline Chili, Steak'n Shake, Subway, Waffle House, Wendy's, Zoup! Best Western, Hilton Garden, Holiday Inn Express, Homewood Suites, Hyatt Place, La Quinta, Marriott, Mason Inn Dick's, Hobby Lobby, Home Depot, Lowe's, Marshall's, NAPA, Staples, Tuesday Morning, URGENT CARE, vet, Walmart/Subway, Whole Foods Mkt
17b a	I-275, to I-75, OH 32
15	Pfeiffer Rd, E H, W BP, Shell/dsl, Sunoco/dsl Applebee's, Bob Evans, Buffalo Wild Wings, City BBQ, Firehouse

CINCINNATI AREA

Exit #	Services
15	Continued Grill, Subway Courtyard, Crowne Plaza, Embassy Suites, Hampton Inn, Holiday Inn Express, Red Roof Inn, Wingate Inn Office Depot
14	OH 126, Reagan Hwy, Blue Ash
12	US 22, OH 3, Montgomery Rd, E BP/dsl, Shell/Dunkin Donuts/Subway, Sunoco Arby's, Bob Evans, Chipotle Mexican, Chuy's, Coopers Hawk, Cucinova, Currito, Ember's, Fusian, Jimmy John's, Outback Steaks, Panera Bread, Penn Sta Subs, Red Lobster, TGIFriday Tuesday Morning, W BP, Marathon Burger King, Cheesecake Factory, Honeybaked Ham, IHOP, Jersey Mike's, Maggiano's, McDonald's, Noodles&Co, Potbelly, Ruby Tuesday, Starbucks, Wendy's Best Western H, AT&T, Barnes&Noble, Dick's, Dillard's, Firestone/auto, Fresh Mkt Foods, Macy's, mall, Old Navy, PepBoys, Staples, Taco Bell, TireDiscounters, TJ Maxx, Trader Joe's, Verizon
11	Kenwood Rd, (from nb), W H, same as 12
10	Stewart Rd (from nb), to Silverton, E BMW/Mini, W Marathon/dsl
9	Redbank Rd, to Fairfax, (no ez sb return), E UDF Rally's
8	Kennedy Ave, Ridge Ave W, E Meijer/dsl IHOP, Steak&Shake Motel 6 Fresh Thyme Mkt, Kroger/dsl, Petsmart, Sam's Club/gas, Target, W Marathon/dsl, Shell/Subway/dsl Gold Star Chili, Hooligan's, Jack-in-the-Box, LJ Silver, McDonald's, Wendy's, White Castle Days Inn $Tree, Aldi Foods, Big Lots, Buick/GMC, Burlington Coats, Family$, Home Depot, Lowes Whse, Office Depot, Remke Mkt, Tire Discounter
7	(from sb) OH 562, Ridge Ave E, Norwood
6	Edwards Rd, E BP, Shell/Popeye's/Dunkin Donuts, Speedway/dsl Boston Mkt, Bravo Italiana, Buca Italian, Buffalo Wild Wings, Capital Grille, Don Pablo's, Donato's, Five Guys, J Alexander's Rest., Jason's Deli, Longhorn Steaks, Marco's Pizza, Max&Erma's, PF Chang's, Potbelly, Qdoba, Rusty Bucket, Seasons Grill, Starbucks, The Pub Courtyard AT&T, GNC, Old Navy, REI, SteinMart, TJ Maxx, URGENT CARE, Whole Foods Mkt, W Shell
5	Dana Ave, Montgomery Rd, W Xavier Univ, Zoo
3	Taft Rd (from sb), W U of Cincinnati
2	US 42, Reading Rd, Gilbert ave (from sb), W H, art museum, ballpark stadium arena, downtown
1k j	I-471 S
1d	Main St, downtown
1c b	Pete Rose Way, Fine St, downtown, stadium
1a	I-75 N, US 50, to Dayton
I-71 S and I-75 S run together	
0mm	Ohio/Kentucky state line, Ohio River

INTERSTATE 74

Exit #	Services
20	I-75 (from eb), N to Dayton, S to Cincinnati, **I-74 begins/ends on I-75.**
19	Gilmore St, Spring Grove Ave
18	US 27 N, Colerain Ave
17	Montana Ave (from wb), N BP
14	North Bend Rd, Cheviot, N Shell, Speedway/dsl Big Boy, Dunkin Donuts, Jersey Mike's, Little Caesar's, McDonald's, Papa John's, Pizza Hut, Skyline Chili, Subway, Wendy's, White Castle

INTERSTATE 74 Cont'd

14	Continued Family$, Kroger, Petco, Sam's Club/gas, Tire Discounters, Verizon, Walgreens, S Shell Bob Evans vet
11	Rybolt Rd, Harrison Pike, S BP Chipotle, Longhorn Steaks, Marco's Puzza, McDonald's, Penn Sta Subs, Skyline Chili, Starbucks, Wendy's, White Castle Holiday Inn Express AT&T, Kohl's, Meijer/gas, Verizon
9	I-275 N, to I-75, N to Dayton, (exits left from eb)
8mm	Great Miami River
7	OH 128, to Hamilton, Cleves, N BP/dsl, Marathon/dsl Wendy's
5	I-275 S, to Kentucky
3	Dry Fork Rd, N BP/dsl, S Marathon/dsl, Shell/Dunkin Donuts/dsl
2mm	**weigh sta eb**
1	New Haven Rd, to Harrison, N BP/dsl Bob Evans, Buffalo Wild Wings, China Garden, Chipotle Mexican, Cracker Barrel, GoldStar Chili, Little Caesars, O'Charley's, Subway Best Western Ford, Home Depot, Kia, Remke Mkt, Staples, Tires+, URGENT CARE, Verizon, S Shell/Circle K, Speedway/dsl, Sunoco/White Castle, UDF A&W/KFC, Arby's, Big Boy, Burger King, Domino's, DQ, El Mariachi Cantina, Happy Garden, Harrison Rest., LJ Silver, McDonald's, Penn Sta Subs, Pizza Hut, Skyline Chili, Taco Bell, Waffle House, Wendy's Holiday Inn Express, Super 8 $General, $Tree, Advance Parts, AT&T, AutoZone, BigLots, CVS Drug, Family$, Firestone/auto, GNC, K-Mart, Kroger/dsl, Meineke, NAPA, O'Reilly Parts, Radio Shack, Sumerel Tire/auto, Tire Discounters, Walgreens
0mm	Ohio/Indiana state line

INTERSTATE 75

Exit #	Services
211mm	Ohio/Michigan state line
210	OH 184, Alexis Rd, to Raceway Park, W BP/Circle K/dsl, Pilot/Subway/dsl/scales/24hr Arby's, Bob Evans, Burger King, McDonald's, Taco Bell, Wendy's Fairfield Inn, Hampton Inn, Holiday Inn Express Aldi Foods, AutoZone, Meijer/dsl, Menards, URGENT CARE
210mm	Ottawa River
209	Ottawa River Rd (from nb), E BP, Sunoco China King, Little Caesars, Marco's Pizza, River Diner Kroger/E85, Rite Aid, Verizon
208	I-280 S, to I-80/90, to Cleveland
207	Stickney Ave, Lagrange St, E BP, S&G Arby's, McDonald's, Wendy's Family$, Rite Aid, Save-A-Lot Foods
206	to US 24, Phillips Ave, W auto repair, transmissions
205b	Berdan Ave, E H, W Valero/dsl Burger King, Subway $General
205a	to Willys Pkwy, to Jeep Pkwy
204	I-475 W, to US 23 (exits left fom nb), to Maumee, Ann Arbor
203b	US 24, to Detroit Ave, W AP, Gas Express/dsl KFC, McDonald's, Rally's, Wendy's Family$, Rite Aid, Save-A-Lot Foods, U-Haul
203a	Bancroft St, downtown
202	Washington St, Collingwood Ave (from sb, no EZ return), E H, $Tree, Art Museum, W McDonald's Family$
201b a	OH 25, Collingwood Ave, W Toledo Zoo
200	South Ave, Kuhlman Dr
200mm	Maumee River
199	OH 65, Miami St, to Rossford, E Days Inn
198	Wales Rd, Oregon Rd, to Northwood, E S&G/dsl, Shell/Subway/dsl Arby's, Arturo's Kitchen, China Wok, Coney Island Best Value Inn, BridgePointe Inn
197	Buck Rd, to Rossford, E Shell/dsl Tim Horton's, Wendy's, W BP, Sunoco/dsl Denny's, McDonald's, Subway American Inn, Knights Inn
195	to I-80/90, OH 795, OH Tpk (toll), Perrysburg, E BP/Subway/dsl Country Inn&Suites, Courtyard, Hampton Inn, Staybridge Suites Bass Pro Shops, Camping World RV Ctr
193	US 20, US 23 S, Perrysburg, E BP/dsl 1st Wok, Arby's, Big Boy, Bob Evans, Burger King, Chick-fil-A, Chili's, China City, Chipotle, Cocina de Carlos, Cracker Barrel, Five Guys, Fricker's, IHOP, Jimmy John's, KFC, McDonald's, Panera Bread, Penn Sta Subs, Sonic, Starbucks, Subway, Taco Bell, Tim Horton's, Wendy's Candlewood Suites, Comfort Suites, EconoLodge, Holiday Inn, Holiday Inn Express, Quality Inn $Tree, Aldi Foods, Belle Tire, Best Buy, Discount Tire, GNC, Hancock Fabrics, Hobby Lobby, Home Depot, KOA (7mi), Kohl's, Kroger/gas/E85, Lowe's, Meijer/dsl, Michael's, Petsmart, Target, TJ Maxx, Tuesday Morning, Tuffy, URGENT CARE, Walgreens, Walmart/Subway, W Speedway/dsl La Quinta AutoZone, Harley-Davidson
192	I-475, US 23 N (exits left from nb), to Maumee, Ann Arbor
187	OH 582, to Luckey, Haskins
181	OH 64, OH 105, to Pemberville, Bowling Green, E Holiday Inn Express Meijer/dsl/E85, W BP/dsl, Circle K/Subway/dsl, Speedway/dsl Big Boy, Bob Evans, Buffalo Wild Wings, Burger King, Chipotle Mexican, Coldstone/Tim Horton's, El Zarape Mexican, Fricker's Rest., Hunan Buffet, Jimmy John's, McDonald's, Penn Sta Subs, Starbucks, Waffle House, Wendy's Best Western, Days Inn, Hampton Inn, Victory Inn H, to Bowling Green State U, USPO, Verizon
179	US 6, to Fremont, Napoleon, W museum
179mm	**both lanes, full facilities, litter barrels, petwalk vending**
175mm	**weigh sta nb**
171	OH 25, Cygnet
168	Eagleville Rd, Quarry Rd, E FuelMart/dsl
167	OH 18, to Fostoria, North Baltimore, E Petro/BP/Iron Skillet/dsl/scales/24hr/ @ McDonald's truck repair, W Loves/Arby's/dsl/scales/24hr, Sunoco $General, Great Scot Mkt
165mm	Rocky Ford River
164	OH 613, to McComb, Fostoria, E RV camping, Van Buren SP, W Pilot/Subway/Taco Bell/dsl/scales/24hr
162mm	**weigh sta sb**
161	Rd 99, E Shell/Subway/dsl, Speedway/dsl Comfort Suites Ford/Lincoln, hwy patrol, Kia, URGENT CARE, VW, W antiques

TOLEDO

PERRYSBURG

OH

= gas = food = lodging = other = rest stop

INTERSTATE 75 Cont'd

FINDLAY

Exit #	Services
159	US 224, OH 15, Findlay, E BP/dsl, Marathon/dsl, Speedway/Speedy's Cafe/dsl Burger King, Culver's, Dakota Grill, Fin's Seafood Grill, Jimmy John's, KFC/LJ Silver, McDonald's, Ming's Great Wall, Pizza Hut, Ralphie's, Spaghetti Shop, Steak'n Shake, Subway, Taco Bell, Wendy's Drury Inn, Motel 6, Red Roof Inn, Rodeway Inn H, Advance Parts, W Murphy USA/dsl, Shell/dsl Bob Evans, Coldstone/Tim Horton's, Cracker Barrel, Denny's, Hokkaido Steaks, Jac&Do's Pizza, Landing Pad, Max&Erma's, Outback Steaks, Tony's Rest., TX Roadhouse, Waffle House Country Inn&Suites, Hampton Inn, Hilton Garden, Holiday Inn Express, Quality Inn AT&T, AutoZone, Best 1 Tires/repair, Chrysler/Dodge/Jeep, Peterbilt, Verizon, Walmart/Subway
158mm	Blanchard River
157	OH 12, Findlay, E Marathon/dsl, W Fricker's Rest. EconoLodge vet
156	US 68, OH 15, to Carey, E H
153mm	**both lanes, full facilities, litter barrels, petwalk vending**
145	OH 235, to Ada, Mount Cory, E KOA
142	OH 103, to Arlington, Bluffton, E Fairway Inn, W Marathon/Circle K/dsl, Shell Arby's, Burger King, McDonald's/rv parking, Subway, Subway, Taco Bell, Wendy's Comfort Inn $General, auto repair, to Bluffton U, vet
140	Bentley Rd, to Bluffton, W H
135	OH 696, to US 30, to Delphos, Beaverdam, E Speedway/Speedy's Cafe/dsl/24hr, W FLYING J/Denny's/dsl/scales/LP/24hr/ @, Pilot/McDonald's/Subway/dsl/24hr/ @ $General, Blue Beacon, SpeedCo, tires, truck repair
134	Napolean Rd (no nb re-entry), to Beaverdam
130	Bluelick Rd, E Clark
127b a	OH 81, to Ada, Lima, W Fuelstop/dsl, Valero/dsl Subway, Waffle House Comfort Inn
126mm	Ottawa River
125	OH 309, OH 117, Lima, E Murphy USA/dsl, Speedway/Speedy's Cafe/dsl Applebee's, Bob Evans, Burger King, Capt D's, China Bistro, China Buffet, Cracker Barrel, Hunan Garden, J's Grill, Lock Sixteen Steaks, McDonald's, Olive Garden, Panera Bread, Pizza Hut, Red Lobster, Skyline Chili, Subway, Taco Bell, TX Roadhouse, Wendy's Courtyard, Hampton Inn, Howard Johnson, Motel 6 AT&T, BigLots, Ford/Lincoln, K-Mart, Sam's Club/gas, Verizon, Walgreens, Walmart/McDonald's, W Arby's, Kewpee Hamburger's, Yamato Steaks Country Inn&Suites, Holiday Inn, Travelodge H, $General, Advance Parts, Best 1 Tires/repair, O'Reilly Parts, Rite Aid, Save-A-Lot Foods, Verizon
124	4th St, E Ford/Lincoln, hwy patrol
122	OH 65, Lima, E Speedway/dsl, W Marathon/Subway/dsl Freightliner, GMC, Mack, truck repair, vet, Volvo
120	Breese Rd, Ft Shawnee, W Shawnee Fuelstop/dsl Harley-Davidson
118	to Cridersville, W Fuelmart/Subway/dsl, Speedway/dsl Dixie Ley Diner $General, Community Mkt, vet
114mm	**both lanes, full facilities, litter barrels, petwalk vending**
113	OH 67, to Uniopolis, Wapakeneta
111	Bellefontaine St, Wahpakeneta, E TA/Hub Room Rest./dsl/scales/ @ Country Charm Rest. Knights Inn KOA, truck tires, W Clark/dsl, Murphy USA/dsl, Shell Arby's, Bob Evans, Burger King, Capt D's, DQ, El Azteca, Lucky Steer

LIMA

SIDNEY

Exit #	Services
111	Continued Rest., McDonald's, Pizza Hut, Subway, Taco Bell, Waffle House, Wendy's Best Western, Holiday Inn Express, Super 8 Advance Parts, Aldi Foods, CVS Drug, Lowe's, Neil Armstrong Museum, O'Reilly Parts, st patrol, URGENT CARE, Verizon, Walmart
110	US 33, to St Marys, Bellefontaine, E hwy patrol, KOA
104	OH 219, W Gulf/dsl, Marathon, Shell/Circle K/Subway/dsl Budget Host $General
102	OH 274, to Jackson Ctr, New Breman, E bicycle museum, W air stream tours
99	OH 119, to Minster, Anna, E 99/dsl, Marathon/dsl, W Shell, Speedway/Taco Bell/dsl Subway, Wendy's Family$, lube/wash/repair
94	Rd 25A, Sidney, E Marathon/deli
93	OH 29, to St Marys, Sidney, W Lake Loramie SP, RV camping
92	OH 47, to Versailles, Sidney, E Speedway/dsl Arby's, China Garden, Coldstone, Fuji Steakhouse, Little Caesar's, Subway, Time Horton's, Wendy's H, Advance Parts, AutoZone, CVS Drug, NAPA, Save-A-Lot Foods, URGENT CARE, Walgreens, W Murphy USA/dsl, Sunoco/dsl Applebee's, Big Boy, Bob Evans, Buffalo Wild Wings, Burger King, Cazadores Mexican, Culver's, Fricker's, Hong Kong Buffet, KFC, McDonald's, Perkins, Pizza Hut, Smokin Jo's BBQ, Taco Bell, Waffle House Comfort Inn, Country Hearth Inn, Days Inn, Holiday Inn Express, Travel Inn $Tree, Aldi Foods, AT&T, Buick/Cadillac/Chevrolet/GMC, Chrysler/Dodge/Jeep, Ford/Lincoln, Kroger/dsl, Lowe's, Menards, Verizon, Walmart/Subway
90	Fair Rd, to Sidney, E Sunoco/dsl, W Marathon/DQ/dsl Hampton Inn
88mm	Great Miami River
83	Rd 25A, Piqua, W Sunoco/MaidRite Cafe/Noble Roman's/dsl Chrysler/Dodge/Jeep, Sherry RV Ctr, to Piqua Hist Area
82	US 36, to Urbana, Piqua, E Marathon, Murphy USA/dsl A&W/LJ Silver, Arby's, China East, China Garden, DQ, El Sombrero, KFC, Subway, Taco Bell, Waffle House, Wendy's $Tree, Aldi Foods, BigLots, Harley-Davidson, Home Depot, JoAnn Fabrics, st patrol, Verizon, vet, Walmart/Subway, W Speedway Bob Evans, Buffalo Wings&Rings, Cracker Barrel, McDonald's, Red Lobster Budgetel, Comfort Inn, La Quinta Elder Beerman, JC Penney, Sears/auto
81mm	**both lanes, full facilities, litter barrels vending**
78	Rd 25A, E H
74	OH 41, to Covington, Troy, E BP/dsl Al's Pizza, China Garden, Little Caesars, McDonald's, Pizza Hut, Subway, Taco Bell to Hobart Arena, URGENT CARE, vet, W Shell, Speedway/dsl Applebee's, Big Boy, Bob Evans, Buffalo Wild Wings, Burger King, Chipotle Mexican, Culver's, Fazoli's, Jimmy John's, KFC, Logan's Roadhouse, Los Pitayos Mexican, Outback Steaks, Panera Bread, Penn Sta Subs, Ruby Tuesday, Sakai Japanese, Skyline Chili, Steak'n Shake Best Inn, Comfort Suites, Fairfield Inn, Hampton Inn, Holiday Inn Express, Residence Inn $General, $Tree, AT&T, AutoZone, GNC, Grismer Auto Service, Kohl's, Lowe's, Meijer/dsl, Petco, Radio Shack, Staples, Tire Discounters, Verizon, Walmart/Subway
73	OH 55, to Ludlow Falls, Troy, E BP, Shell Boston Stoker Coffee House, Honeybaked Ham, Hot Head Burrito, Lincoln Sq Rest., Papa John's, Subway, Waffle House, Wendy's Budget Inn, Motel 6, Royal Inn $General, Kroger/e85, Verizon

TROY

OH

INTERSTATE 75 Cont'd

Exit #	Services
69	Rd 25A, E Circle K/dsl, Gulf/dsl Arbogast RV Ctr, Buick/GMC, Chrysler/Dodge/Jeep, Ford
68	OH 571, to West Milton, Tipp City, E BP/dsl, Shell, Speedway/dsl Burger King, Cassano's Pizza, Domino's, Fox's Pizza, Greenfire Bustro, Hickory River BBQ, Hong Kong Kitchen, Hot Head Burritos, McDonald's, Subway, Taco Bell AT&T, CVS Drug, Family$, FoodTown, Goodyear/auto, Honda, O'Reilly Parts, W Speedway/dsl Arby's, Big Boy, Bob Evans, Tipp' O the Town Rest., Wendy's Holiday Inn Express, La Quinta Main St Parts, Menards, Performance Parts, vet
64	Northwoods Blvd, E El Toro Mexican, Emperial Palace $Tree, Kroger/dsl, W FLYING J/Subway/dsl/scales/RV dump/24hr
63	US 40, to Donnelsville, Vandalia, E Speedway/dsl Bunker's Grill, Dragon China, Fricker's AutoZone, repair, W BP/dsl, Shell, Speedway/dsl Arby's, Burger King, Domino's, Hot Head Burrito, KFC/LJ Silver, McDonald's, Pizza Hut, Rib House, Subway, Taco Bell, Waffle House, Wendy's Super 8 Goodyear/auto, Rexall Drug, Rite Aid
61b a	I-70, E to Columbus, W to Indianapolis, to Dayton Int Airport
59	Wyse Rd, Benchwood Rd, E El Rancho Grande, Little York Pizza, Shen's Hawthorn Suites, Knights Inn, Travelodge BMW/Volvo/VW, Discount Tire, W Speedway/dsl, Valero/dsl Arby's, Asian Buffet, Big Boy, Bob Evans, Cassano's Pizza, Chick-fil-A, Chipotle Mexican, Coldstone, Cousin Vinny's Puzza, Cracker Barrel, El Toro Mexican, Fazoli's, Fricker's, Golden Corral, Hooters, Longhorn Steaks, Max&Erma's, McAlister's Deli, McDonald's, O'Charley's, Olive Garden, Outback Steaks, Panera Bread, Red Lobster, Ruby Tuesday, Sake Japanese, Skyline Chili, SmashBurger, SmokeyBones BBQ, Steak'n Shake, Subway, Taco Bell, Tim Horton's Best Value Inn, Comfort Inn, Courtyard, Days Inn, Drury Inn, Extended Stay America, Fairfield Inn, Hampton Inn, Quality Inn, Red Roof Inn, Residence Inn, Springhill Suites, TownePlace Suites Office Depot, Radio Shack, Sam's Club/gas, Verizon, Walmart/Subway
58	Needmore Rd, to Dayton, E BP/dsl, Shell/McDonald's Hardee's Goodyear/auto, to AF Museum, W Marathon/dsl, Speedway/dsl, Sunoco/dsl A&W/LJ Silver, Church's, Domino's, Subway, Tim Horton's, Waffle House, Wendy's $General, $Tree, Advance Parts, auto repair, AutoZone, Family$, Kroger/gas, Midas, O'Reilly Parts, USPO, vet, Walgreens
57b	Wagner Ford Rd, Siebenthaler Rd, Dayton, E Marathon Ramada Inn
57a	Neva Rd
56	Stanley Ave, Dayton, E Shell, W Keowee Dragon City Chinese, Gold Star Chili, McDonald's, Pancake House, Taco Bell Dayton Motel
55b a	Keowee St, Dayton, downtown
54c	OH 4 N, Webster St, to Springfield, downtown
54mm	Great Miami River
54b	OH 48, Main St, Dayton, E Chevrolet, Honda, W H, Family$
54a	Grand Ave, Dayton, downtown
53b	OH 49, 1st St, Salem Ave, Dayton, downtown
53a	OH 49, 3rd St, downtown
52b a	US 35, E to Dayton, W to Eaton
51	Edwin C Moses Blvd, Nicholas Rd, E Courtyard, Marriott H, to U of Dayton, W BP/dsl, Love's/Hardee's/dsl/scales/24hr McDonald's, Wendy's SunWatch Indian Village

DAYTON

Exit #	Services
50b a	OH 741, Kettering St, Dryden Rd, E H, vet, W Marathon/dsl TJ's Rest. Super 8 U-Haul
47	Dixie Dr, W Carrollton, Moraine, E Shell/dsl Big Boy, Domino's, Waffle House $General, auto repair, transmissions, W Shell/dsl, Speedway/dsl El Meson, KFC, McDonald's, Pizza Hut, Sonic, Taco Bell, Wendy's $General, USPO
44	OH 725, to Centerville, Miamisburg, E BP/dsl, Shell, Speedway/dsl Applebee's, Baskin-Robbins, Big Boy, Bonefish Grill, Bravo Italiana, Burger King, ChuckeCheese, Dunkin Donuts, El Toro Mexican, Fazoli's, FirstWatch Cafe, Fricker's, Godfather's, Golden Corral, Hardee's, Jimmy John's, KFC, Logan's Roadhouse, Marion's Puzza, McDonald's, O'Charley's, Olive Garden, Panera Bread, Penn Sta Subs, PF Chang's, Qdoba, Red Lobster, Rooster's Grill, Rusty Bucket Grill, Saka Buffet, Sake Japanese, Skyline Chili, SmashBurger, Starbucks, Steak'n Shake, Subway, Taco Bell, TGIFriday's, Waffle House, Wendy's Comfort Suites, Courtyard, Days Inn, DoubleTree Suites, Extended Stay America, Hampton Inn, Hawthorn Suites, Homewood Suites, InTowne Suites, SpringHill Suites, Studio 6, ValuePlace H, $Tree, Advance Parts, Aldi Foods, AT&T, Audi/VW/Porsche/Jaguar, Barnes&Noble, Best Buy, Burlington Coats, Dick's, Discount Tire, Elder Beerman, Grismer Auto Service, Hobby Lobby, Home Depot, Honda/Nissan/Mazda, JC Penney, Jo-Ann Fabrics, Kia, Lowe's, Macy's, mall, Menard's, Michael's, Midas, Monro, NTB, Office Depot, PepBoys, Petsmart, Sears/auto, Target, Tire Discounters, Toyota/Scion, Verizon, vet, Walmart, W BP, Marathon, Shell/dsl Bob Evans, LJ Silver, Perkins, Tim Horton's Knights Inn, Quality Inn, Red Roof Inn, Super 8 H, $General, Aamco, CarMax, Chevrolet, Ford, NAPA
43	I-675 N, to Columbus
41	Austin Blvd, E BJ's Rest., Broken Egg Cafe, Chipotle, Chuy's, Coldstone, Dewey's Pizza, Firebirds, Five Guys, Noodles&Co, Panera Bread, Spicy Olive Hilton Garden AT&T, Field&Stream, Kohl's, Kroger/dsl, TJ Maxx
38	OH 73, Springboro, Franklin, E Shell, Speedway/dsl, Thornton's/dsl Applebee's, Arby's, Bob Evans, Burger King, China Garden, Chipotle Mexican, KFC, LJ Silver, McDonald's, Papa John's, Pizza Hut, Skyline Chili, Subway, Taco Bell, Tim Horton's, Waffle House, Wendy's Comfort Inn, Hampton Inn K-Mart, Kroger, O'Reilly Parts, Tire Discounters, USPO, vet, W Murphy USA/dsl, Shell, Speedway/dsl A&G Pizza, Big Boy, Cazadore's Mexican, Domino's, GoldStar Chili, Lee's Chicken, McDonald's EconoLodge, Holiday Inn Express $General, $Tree, Advance Parts, AutoZone, Brothers Automotive, Kemper Tire, KOI Parts, NAPA, URGENT CARE, USPO, Walgreens, Walmart
36	OH 123, to Lebanon, Franklin, E BP/Mom's Rest./dsl, Pilot/Subway/Pizza Hut/dsl/scales/24hr/ @, Shell/Wendy's/

(gas) = gas (food) = food (lodging) = lodging (other) = other (Rs) = rest stop

INTERSTATE 75 Cont'd

MIDDLETOWN

36 Continued
dsl (food) McDonald's, Waffle House (lodging) Motel 6, **W** (gas) Marathon/White Castle/dsl, Sunoco

32 OH 122, Middletown, **E** (food) McDonald's (lodging) Days Inn, Red Roof Inn, Super 8 (other) (H), CVS Drug, **W** (food) Applebee's, Arby's, Big Boy, Bob Evans, Cracker Barrel, El Rancho Grande, Golden Corral, GoldStar Chili, Hot Head Burritos, KFC, La Rosa's Pizza, LoneStar Steaks, O'Charley's, Olive Garden, Schlotzsky's, Sonic, Steak'n Shake, Wendy's, White Castle (lodging) Drury Inn, Fairfield Inn, Hampton Inn, Holiday Inn Express, Quality Inn (other) $General, Aldi Foods, AT&T, AutoZone, BigLots, Elder Beerman, Kohl's, Kroger/dsl, Lowe's, Meijer/dsl, Petco, Sears/auto, Staples, Tire Discounters, URGENT CARE, Verizon, Walmart/Subway

29 OH 63, to Hamilton, Monroe, **E** (gas) Shell/Popeye's/dsl, Stony Ridge/dsl (food) Burger King, Chipotle, Culver's, GoldStar Chili, Tim Horton/Wendy's, Waffle House (lodging) Comfort Inn (other) Premium Outlets/Famous Brands, Tire Discounters, Trader's World, **W** (gas) Speedway/dsl (food) Froggy Blue's, McDonald's, Richard's Pizza, Subway (lodging) Best Western, Wave Hotel (other) Honda

27.5mm (Rs) **both lanes, full (handicapped) facilities, info, litter barrels, petwalk (phone) (picnic) vending**

24 OH 129 W, to Hamilton, **W** (other) Dick's

22 Tylersville Rd, to Mason, Hamilton, **E** (gas) Sunoco, Thornton's/dsl (food) Arby's, Bob Evans, BoneFish Grill, Burger King, Cane's, Chick-fil-A, Chipotle, City BBQ, Firehouse Subs, Fricker's, Geisha, Graeter's Grill, Great Wall, IHOP, Jack-in-the-Box, Jimmy John's, KFC, LJ Silver, Longhorn Steaks, McAlister's Deli, McDonald's, Milano's, Noodles&Co, Panda Express, Panera Bread, Perkins, Pizza Hut, Skyline Chili, SmashBurger, Soho Japanese, Starbucks, Subway, Taco Bell, TGIFriday's, Twin Dragon, Waffle House, Wendy's (lodging) Economy Inn (other) (H), AT&T, Big Lots, Firestone/auto, Fresh Mkt, GNC, Goodyear/auto, Home Depot, Kohl's, Kroger, Michael's, Office Depot, Petsmart, Radio Shack, Target, Tires+, TJ Maxx, URGENT CARE, Verizon, Walgreens, **W** (gas) Speedway/dsl, Sunoco (food) O'Charley's (lodging) Wingate Inn (other) Aldi Foods, CarX, Lowe's, Meijer/dsl, Tire Discounters

21 Cin-Day Rd, **E** (food) Big Boy (lodging) Holiday Inn Express, **W** (gas) Marathon/dsl, Speedway/dsl, UDF/Subway/dsl (food) Arby's, Domino's, Dunkin Donuts, El Rancho Nuevo, La Rosa's Pizza, Little Caesar's, Papa John's, Sonic, Tikka Grill, Waffle House, Wendy's, White Castle (other) Ace Hardware, AutoZone, Walgreens, Walmart/Subway

19 Union Centre Blvd, to Fairfield, **E** (food) Bravo Italiana, Champps Rest., Mitchell's Fish Mkt, Original Pancakes, Panera Bread, PF Chang's, Red Robin, Smokey Bones BBQ, Steak'n Shake (other) AT&T, Barnes&Noble, Verizon, **W** (gas) BP/Subway/dsl, Marathon/Circle K, Shell (food) Aladdin's Eatery, Applebee's, Bob Evans, Buffalo Wild Wings, Burger King, Chipotle Mexican, Dingle House, Jag's Steaks, Jimmy John's, McDonald's, Mellow Mushroom, Rancho Nuevo, River City Grille, Skyline Chili, Starbucks, Subway, Tom+Chee, Uno, Wendy's (lodging) Comfort Inn, Courtyard, Hampton Inn, Hilton Garden, Holiday Inn, Homewood Suites, Marriott, Residence Inn, Staybridge Suites (other) IKEA, Mercedes, Monro, Volvo

16 I-275 to I-71, to I-74

15 Sharon Rd, to Sharonville, Glendale, **E** (gas) Sunoco, Thornton's/dsl (food) Big Boy, Bob Evans, Cracker Barrel, Jim Dandy BBQ, Ruby Tuesday, Skyline Chili, Subway, Waffle House (lodging) Baymont Inn, Drury Inn, Hawthorn Suites, Hilton Garden, Holiday Inn Express, La Quinta, Quality Inn, Red Roof Inn, Travel Inn,

CINCINNATI AREA

15 Continued
W on Kemper (gas) Sunoco (food) Burger King, Cane's, Chic fil-A, Chili's, ChuckeCheese, Five Guys, IHOP, LJ Silver, Ma aroni Grill, McDonald's, Panera Bread, Penn Sta Subs, Piz Hut, Subway, Taco Bell, Tokyo Japanese, Vincenzo's Italia Wendy's (lodging) Crossland Suites, EconoLodge, Extended St America, Fairfield Inn, LivInn Suites, Red Lion Hotel, Residen Inn (other) Best Buy, Costco/gas, Dick's, Lowe's, Nissan, Sam Club, Sears/auto, Sharonville Conv Ctr, Target

14 OH 126, to Woodlawn, Evendale, **E** (lodging) Wingate Inn (3n (other) GE Plant, **W** (gas) Shell/dsl

13 Shepherd Lane, to Lincoln Heights, **E** (other) GE Plant, **W** (food) Tac Bell, Wendy's

12 Wyoming Ave, Cooper Ave, to Lockland, **W** (gas) Marathon/ds

10a OH 126, Ronald Reagan Hwy

10b Galbraith Rd (exits left from nb), Arlington Heights

9 OH 4, OH 561, Paddock Rd, Seymour Ave, **E** (other) to Cincinna Gardens, **W** (other) fairgrounds

8 Towne St, Elmwood Pl (from nb)

7 OH 562, to I-71, Norwood, Cincinnati Gardens

6 Mitchell Ave, St Bernard, **E** (gas) Mobil, Shell, Sunoco (food) Whi Castle (lodging) Quality Inn (other) to Cincinnati Zoo, to Xavier U, Wa greens, **W** (gas) BP/Subway/dsl (food) Gold Star Chili, McDonald' Rally's (other) Advance Parts, Family$, Ford, Honda, Hyundai, Ki Kroger, Tires+

4 I-74 W, US 52, US 27 N, to Indianapolis

3 to US 27 S, US 127 S, Hopple St, **E** (food) Big Boy, White Cas tle (lodging) Budget Host (other) (H), U of Cincinnati, **W** (gas) She (food) Isadore's Italian, Wendy's

2b Harrison Ave, **W** (gas) BP/Subway (food) McDonald's (other) Family$ industrial district

2a Western Ave, Liberty St (from sb)

1g Ezzard Charles Dr ((from sb), **W** (lodging) Guest Inn

1f US 50W, Freeman Ave (from sb), **W** (gas) Marathon/dsl, Shell Subway (food) Big Boy, Taco Bell, Wendy's, White Castl (lodging) Guest Inn (other) Ford, NAPA, USPO

1e 7th St (from sb),, downtown

1c 5th St, **E** (lodging) Hilton, Hyatt, Millennial Hotel (other) Macy's, to Duk Energy Center, downtown

1a I-71 N, to Cincinnati, downtown, to stadium

0mm Ohio/Kentucky state line, Ohio River

INTERSTATE 76

Exit #	Services
	Ohio/Pennsylvania state line. **See OH TPK exits 232-234.**
60mm	I-76 eb joins Ohio TPK (toll)
57	to OH 45, Bailey Rd, to Warren
54	OH 534, to Newton Falls, Lake Milton, **N** (other) RV camping, **S** (gas) Sunoco/dsl (other) camping, to Berlin Lake
52mm	Lake Milton
48	OH 225, to Alliance, **N** (other) camping, to W Branch SP, **S** (other) to Berlin Lake, to Lake Milton SP
45mm	(Rs) **both lanes, full (handicapped) facilities, litter barrels, petwalk (phone) (picnic)**
43	OH 14, to Alliance, Ravenna, **N** (other) to W Branch SP, **S** (gas) Marathon/Subway/dsl (other) fireworks
38b a	OH 5, OH 44, to Ravenna, **N** (gas) BP/dsl, Speedway/ds (food) Arby's, McDonald's/rv parking, Wendy's, **S** (gas) Marathon Circle K/Subway (food) Cracker Barrel (other) (H), $General, auto parts, Giant Eagle Foods, RV camping
33	OH 43, to Hartville, Kent, **N** (gas) BP/dsl, Marathon (food) Salsita's Mexican (lodging) Comfort Inn, Days Inn, EconoLodge, Hampton Inn, Holiday Inn Express, Super 8 (other) to Kent St U, **S** (gas) Circle

OH

INTERSTATE 76 Cont'd

AKRON

33	Continued K, Speedway/dsl Gionino's Pizza, McDonald's, Pizza Hut, Subway, Wendy's $General, Goodyear Tire/brakes, vet
31	Rd 18, Tallmadge, N Murphy USA/dsl #1 Chinese, Applebee's, Beef'O'Brady's, DQ, La Terraza Mexican, Panera Bread $Tree, AT&T, GNC, Kohl's, Lowe's, Marshall's, Petco, Verizon, Walmart/Subway
29	OH 532, Tallmadge, Mogadore
27	OH 91, Canton Rd, Gilchrist Rd, N Bob Evans, S Marathon/Subway/dsl Hardee's Quality Inn
26	OH 18, E Market St, Mogadore Rd, N Marathon/dsl Hamad Tire/repair, S Arby's, McDonald's, Subway, Wendy's $General
25b a	Martha Ave, General St, Brittain, N Circle K/dsl Hilton Garden Mercedes, Toyota/Scion, S Goodyear HQ
24	Arlington St, Kelly Ave, S Goodyear HQ
23b	OH 8, Buchtell Ave, to Cuyahoga (exits left from eb), to U of Akron
23a	I-77 S, to Canton
22b	Grant St, Wolf Ledges, Akron, N USPO, S BP McDonald's Family$, downtown
22a	Main St, Broadway, downtown
21c	OH 59 E, Dart Ave, N H
21b	Lakeshore St, Bowery St (from eb)
21a	East Ave (from wb)
20	I-77 N (from eb), to Cleveland
19	Battles Ave, Kenmore Blvd
18	I-277, US 224 E, to Canton, Barberton
17b	OH 619, Wooster Rd, S Sunoco/dsl H, tires/repair
17a	(from eb, no return) State St, to Barberton, S Papa John's, Papa Roni's Pizza H, Walgreens
16	Barber Rd, S Rocky's/dsl/E85 DQ, Tomaso's Italian Chrysler/Dodge/Jeep, Fiat
14	Cleve-Mass Rd, to Norton, S BP/Blimpie/dsl, Circle K/dsl Arby's, Casa Del Mar Mexican, McDonald's, Pizza Hut, Subway, Wendy's $General, Ace Hardware, Acme Fresh Mkt, Advance Parts, CVS Drug, Family$, Radio Shack, Ritzman Drug, USPO, Verizon
13b a	OH 21, N to Cleveland, S to Massillon
11	OH 261, Wadsworth, N Speedway/dsl, S GetGo/E85, Giant Eagle Arabica Cafe, Beef'O'Brady's, Wayback Burger AAA, GNC, Kohl's, Lowe's, MC Sports, PetCo, Target, Verizon
9	OH 94, to N Royalton, Wadsworth, N Marathon/Circle K Applebee's, Arby's, Bob Evans, Burger King, China Express, Chipotle Mexican, Galaxy Rest., Marie's Cafe, McDonald's, Panera Bread, Patron's Mexican, Pizza Hut, Romeo's Pizza, Starbucks, Subway, Taco Bell, Wendy's Comfort Inn, Holiday Inn Express $General, $Tree, BigLots, Buehler's Foods, DrugMart, Goodyear/auto, Home Depot, NTB, Radio Shack, Verizon, Walmart/Subway, S Marathon/DQ/dsl, Sunoco Casa Del Rio, Dunkin Donuts, Papa John's Legacy Inn Advance Parts, auto repair, AutoZone, CVS Drug, NAPA, Rite Aid, vet
7	OH 57, to Rittman, Medina, N Marathon/dsl, S H,
6mm	**weigh sta eb**
2	OH 3, to Medina, Seville, N Marathon/Circle K/dsl DQ, Hardee's, Huddle House, Pizzazo's, Subway Comfort Inn, Hawthorn Suites Maple Lakes Camping (seasonal), S Clark, Shell/dsl #1 Chinese, E of Chicago Pizza, El Patron Mexican $General, Ritzman Drug, Verizon

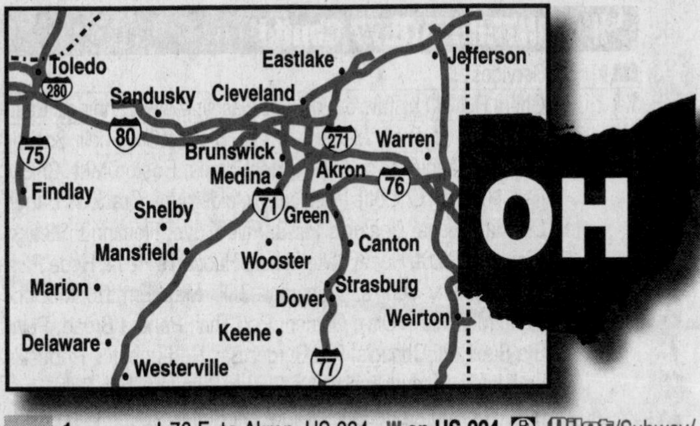

1	I-76 E, to Akron, US 224, W on US 224 Pilot/Subway/dsl/scales/24hr, TA/BP/Burger King/Popeye's/dsl/scales/24hr/@ Arby's, McDonald's, Starbucks Super 8 Blue Beacon, Chippewa Valley Camping (1mi), SpeedCo

I-76 begins/ends on I-71, exit 209.

INTERSTATE 77

CLEVELAND

Exit #	Services
	I-77 begins/ends on I-90 exit 172, in Cleveland.
163c	I-90, E to Erie, W to Toledo
163b	E 9th St, Tower City
162b	E 22nd St, E 14th St (from nb)
162a	E 30th St, Woodland Ave, Broadway St (from nb), W USPO
161b	I-490 W, to I-71, E 55th, E H
161a	OH 14 (from nb), Broadway St
160	Pershing Ave (from nb), W H
159b	Fleet Ave, E BP/7-11/dsl
159a	Harvard Ave, Newburgh Heights, W BP/Subway/dsl
158	Grant Ave, Cuyahoga Heights
157	OH 21, OH 17 (from sb), Brecksville Rd
156	I-480, to Youngstown, Toledo
155	Rockside Rd, to Independence, E Shell, Sunoco/dsl Aladdin's, Bob Evans, Bonefish Grill, Chipotle, Del Monico's Steaks, Denny's, DiBella's Subs, Jimmy John's, McDonald's, Melt Grill, Outback Steaks, Panera Bread, Potbelly's, Red Robin, Shula's Steaks, Starbucks, Wendy's, Winking Lizard Grill, Zoup Comfort Inn, DoubleTree, Embassy Suites, Holiday Inn, La Quinta, Red Roof Inn AT&T, Drugmart, to Cuyahoga Valley NP, Verizon, Walgreens, W BP/dsl Applebee's, Longhorn Steaks, Wasabi Steaks Courtyard, Crowne Plaza, Hampton Inn, Hyatt Place, Residence Inn
153	Pleasant Valley Rd, to Independence, 7 Hills
151	Wallings Rd
149	OH 82, to Broadview Heights, Brecksville, 1 mi E BP, Shell/dsl Austin's Grille, Panera Bread, Sakura Japanese, Simon's Rest., Starbucks, Subway CVS Drug, Marc's Foods, vet, Walgreens, W BP, GetGo/dsl Bob Evans, Chipotle Giant Eagle Foods
147	to OH 21, Miller Rd (from sb)
146	I-80/Ohio Tpk, to Youngstown, Toledo
145	OH 21 (from nb), E Pilot/Wendy's/dsl/scales Memories Rest., Subway Days Inn, Hampton Inn, Holiday Inn Express, Motel 6, Super 8
144	I-271 N, to Erie
143	OH 176, to I-271 S, W Shell McDonald's, Panda Chinese, Richfield Cafe, Subway, Teresa's Pizza
141mm	**both lanes, full facilities, litter barrels, petwalk vending**

OH

= gas = food = lodging = other = rest stop

INTERSTATE 77 Cont'd

FAIRLAWN

Exit #	Services
138	Ghent Rd, W Circle K/dsl Gasoline Ally, Lanning's Rest.
137b a	OH 18, to Fairlawn, Medina, E BP, GetGo, Shell, Speedway Applebee's, A-Wok, Bob Evans, Boston Mkt, Chick-fil-A, Chili's, Chipotle Mexican, Coldstone, Cracker Barrel, Cucina Italiana, Donato's Pizza, Five Guys, Fleming's Steaks, Gionino's Pizza, HoneyBaked Ham, Hudson's Rest., Hyde Park Grille, Jimmy John's, Macaroni Grill, Max&Erma's, McDonald's, Menchie's, Olive Garden, Pad Thai, Panera Bread, Penn Sta Subs, PF Chang's, Rail Burger Bar, Red Lobster, Robeck's FruitJuice, Starbucks, Steak'n Shake, Subway, Taco Bell, Wendy's, Winking Lizard Grill, Yellow Tail Buffet, Zoup! Courtyard, DoubleTree, EconoLodge, Hampton Inn, Hilton, Holiday Inn, Home 2 Suites, Homewood Suites, Motel 6, Quality Inn $Tree, Acme Fresh Mkt, Aldi Foods, AT&T, Barnes&Noble, Best Buy, Dick's, Dillard's, Earth Fare Foods, Ford, Giant Eagle Foods, Goodyear/auto, Hobby Lobby, Home Depot, JC Penney, Jo-Ann Fabrics, Lowe's, Macy's, Michael's, NTB, Old Navy, Petsmart, Sam's Club, Staples, TJ Maxx, Verizon, Walmart, World Mkt, W Sunoco Burger King, Hooley House Rest., Longhorn Steaks, Outback Steaks, TGIFriday's, Tres Potrillos, Wasabi Grill Baymont Inn, Best Western, Extended Stay America, Extended Stay America 2, Hawthorn Suites, Radisson, Residence Inn, Super 8 H
136	OH 21S, to Massillon (exits left from nb)
135	Cleveland-Massillon Rd (from nb, no return)
133	Ridgewood Rd, Miller Rd, E Circle K/dsl, W Old Carolina BBQ, Teresa's Pizza, Tiffany's Bakery Conrad's Automotive
132	White Pond Dr, Mull Ave
131	OH 162, Copley Rd, E Circle K China Star, Church's, Little Caesar's Save-A-Lot Foods, Walgreens, W BP/dsl McDonald's, Pizza Hut
130	OH 261, Wooster Ave, E Circle K, Valero/dsl Ann's Place, Burger King, Church's, McDonald's, New Ming Chinese, Rally's, Subway Advance Parts, AutoZone, Family$, O'Reilly Parts, W Chevrolet, Toyota/Scion, U-Haul
129	I-76 W, to I-277, to Kenmore Blvd, Barberton
I-77 S and I-76 E run together. See I-76, exits 21a-22b	
125b	I-76 E, to Youngstown, I-77 and I-76 run together
125a	OH 8 N, to Cuyahoga Falls, U of Akron
124b	Lover's Lane, Cole Ave
124a	Archwood Ave, Firestone Blvd (from sb), E BP
123b	OH 764, Wilbeth Rd, E DQ to
123a	Waterloo Rd (from sb), W BP, GetGo Burger King, House of Hunan, Hungry Howies, Mi Casa, Papa John's, Paramount Grille, Rally's, Subway, Waterloo Rest. $General, $Tree, American Automotive, Big Lots, Giant Eagle Foods, GNC, Marc's Mkt, Rite Aid, Walgreens
122b a	I-277, US 224 E, to Barberton, Mogadore
120	Arlington Rd, to Green, E Speedway/dsl Applebee's, Denny's, Golden Corral, IHOP, Jimmy John's, Mr Hero, Shogun, Starbucks, Waffle House Comfort Inn, Quality Inn, Red Roof Inn $General, AT&T, AutoZone, Home Depot, Kohl's, Staples, Walmart/Subway, W BP Bob Evans, Burger King, Chipotle Mexican, CiCi's Pizza, McDonald's, Panera Bread, Subway, Taco Bell, TGIFriday's, Tommy Li's, Wendy's Fairfield Inn, Hampton Inn, Holiday Inn Express, Residence Inn, ValuePlace Inn Aamco, Acura, Buick/GMC, Camping World RV Ctr, Chevrolet, GNC, Goodyear/auto, Honda, Hyundai, Infiniti, Lexus, Lowe's, Nissan, Subaru, Target, Verizon

AKRON

OH

CANTON

Exit #	Services
118	OH 241, to OH 619, Massillon, E Sheetz/dsl, Speedway/dsl Gionino's Pizza, Handel's Ice Cream, Hunan Chinese, Subway, W Circle K/dsl, GetGo Arby's, DQ, Dunkin Donuts, Hungry Howie's, Jimmy John's, Kasai Japanese, Lucky Star Chinese, McDonald's, Menche's Rest., Quizno's, Starbucks, Subway, Tom Chee Cafe Cambria Suites, Super 8 H, $General, Acme Fresh Mkt, Advance Parts, Conrad Automotive, CVS Dug, Giant Eagle Foods
113	W Hilton Garden Akron-Canton Airport, General RV Ctr (2mi)
112	Shuffel St, E Embassy Suites
111	Portage St, N Canton, E Circle K, Marathon/dsl, Sunoco/dsl, TA/Country Pride/dsl/scales/24hr/ @ Burger King, Geisen Haus, Jimmy's Rest., KFC, Palombo's Italian, Quaker Steak, Subway, Sylvester's Italian Mr Tire, TrueValue, W BP/dsl, Speedway/dsl Aladdin's Eatery, Bonefish Grill, Carrabba's, ChuckeCheese, Coldstone, Cracker Barrel, Dunkin Donuts/Baskin-Robbins, Five Guys, IHOP, Longhorn Steaks, McDonald's, Menchie's, Outback Steaks, Panera Bread, Pizza Hut, Red Robin, Rockne's Cafe, Romeo's Pizza, Samantha's Rest., Starbucks, Taco Bell, Wasabi Japanese, Wendy's, Zoup! Best Western, Microtel, Motel 6 AAA, At&T, Best Buy, BJ's Whse, Book A Million, Chevrolet, DrugMart, Gander Mtn, Giant Eagle Foods, Goodyear/auto, Harley-Davidson, Home Depot, Lowe's, Marshall's, Michael's, Old Navy, Sam's Club/gas, Walgreens, Walmart/Subway/auto
109b a	Everhard Rd, Whipple Ave, E Marathon/Subway/dsl, Speedway/dsl Denny's, Fazoli's, Waffle House Comfort Inn, Fairfield Inn, Hampton Inn, Home 2 Suites, Hyatt Place, La Quinta, Residence Inn, Staybridge Suites Buick/GMC, Ford, W Marathon A1 Japanese Steaks, Angry BBQ, Applebee's, Arby's, Bob Evans, Bravo Italiana, Brown Derby, Buffalo Wild Wings, Buffet Dynasty, Chick-fil-A, Chili's, Chipotle Mexican, CiCi's Pizza, DiBella Subs, Dunkin Donuts, Fox&Hound Grill, Golden Corral, HoneyBaked Ham, Jerzees Grille, Jimmy John's, Katanya Buffet, KFC, Max&Erma's, McDonald's, Mulligan's, Olive Garden, Panera Bread, Papa Bear's, Papa Gyros, Penn Sta Subs, Perkins, Potbelly, Red Lobster, Ruby Tuesday, Sahara Grill, Sakura Japanese, Starbucks, Steak'n Shake, Subway, Taco Bell, TGIFriday's, Tilted Kilt, TX Roadhouse, Wendy's Courtyard, Holiday Inn, Knights Inn, Quality Inn, Ramada, Red Roof Inn, Springhill Suites $Tree, Aamco, Aldi Foods, AT&T, Burlington Cots, Dick's, Dillard's, Firestone/auto, Goodyear/auto, Jo-Ann Fabrics, Kohl's, Macy's, mall, Marc's Foods, NTB, Petsmart, Sears/auto, Target, TJ Maxx, Tuesday Morning, Verizon, World Mkt
107b a	US 62, OH 687, Fulton Rd, to Alliance, E Marathon/Circle K/Subway city park, W Circle K/Dunkin Donuts Pro Football Hall of Fame, URGENT CARE
106	13th St NW, E H
105b	OH 172, Tuscarawas St, E McDonald's, W BP KFC, Subway AutoZone, CVS
105a	6th St SW (no EZ return from sb), E Sunoco McDonald's Ford, W Subway H, AutoZone
104b a	US 30, US 62, to E Liverpool, Massillon
103	OH 800 S, E Marathon/Subway/dsl, Speedway Arby's, DQ, Italo's Pizza, McDonald's, Peking Chinese, Taco Bell, Waffle House Advance Parts, auto repair, Family$, Goodyear/auto, Rite aid, Save-A-Lot Foods, W Firestone
101	OH 627, to Faircrest St, E Pilot/Subway/dsl/scales/24hr, Speedway/McDonald's Wendy's Fairfield Inn
99	Fohl Rd, to Navarre, W Sunoco KOA (4mi)

INTERSTATE 77 Cont'd

Exit #	Services
93	OH 212, to Zoar, Bolivar, E Speedway/dsl Georgio's Grill, McDonald's, Pizza Hut, Wendy's Sleep Inn $General, Giant Eagle Foods, NAPA, to Lake Atwood Region, vet, Zoar Tavern HS (3mi), W Marathon/DQ/Subway/dsl KOA
87	US 250W, to Strasburg, W Marathon/dsl Hardee's, Manor Rest., McDonald's, Subway Ramada Ltd Family$, Verizon
85	Schneiders Crossing Rd, to Dover, E Marathon Arby's, Subway Buehler's Mkt/gas
83	OH 39, OH 211, to Sugarcreek, Dover, E BP/dsl, Speedway/dsl Bob Evans, KFC, McDonald's, Shoney's, Wendy's 77 Inn/Grill H, Chrysler/Dodge/Jeep, Flynn's Tires, Ford, Honda, Lincoln, Nissan, W Comfort Inn, Country Inn&Suites
81	US 250, to Uhrichsville, OH 39, New Philadelphia, E Sheetz/dsl, Speedway Buffalo Wild Wings, Burger King, Denny's, El San Jose Mexican, Hog Heaven BBQ, LJ Silver, McDonald's, Pizza Hut, Taco Bell, TX Roadhouse Best Western, Hampton Inn, Holiday Inn Express, Knights Inn, New Philadelphia Inn, Schoenbrunn Inn $General, $Tree, Advance Parts, Aldi Foods, BigLots, O'Reilly Parts, Walmart/Subway, W Auto TP/rest./dsl/scales/24hr Harley-Davidson
73	OH 751, to Rd 53, Stone Creek, W Marathon/dsl
65	US 36, Port Washington, Newcomerstown, W BP, Duke TP/rest./dsl, Speedway/Wendy's McDonald's Hampton Inn, Super 8
64mm	Tuscarawas River
54	OH 541, Rd 831, to Plainfield, Kimbolton, W BP Jackie's Rest.
47	US 22, to Cadiz, Cambridge, E lodging RV camping, to Salt Fork SP (6mi), W BP/repair H, info, to Glass Museum
46b a	US 40, to Old Washington, Cambridge, W Marathon/Wendy's/dsl, Speedway/dsl Burger King, Hunan Chinese, Lee's Rest., LJ Silver, McDonald's Family$, Riesbeck's Food
44b a	I-70, E to Wheeling, W to Columbus
41	OH 209, OH 821, Byesville, W Circle K, Starfire McDonald's, Subway $General, Family$, museum, to Glenn HS
39mm	**nb, full facilities, litter barrels, petwalk vending**
37	OH 313, Buffalo, E BP Coutos Pizza, Subway to Senecaville Lake, UPSO
36mm	**sb, full facilities, litter barrels, petwalk vending**
28	OH 821, Belle Valley, E Sunoco/dsl RV camping, to Wolf Run SP, USPO
25	OH 78, Caldwel, E Marathon/dsl, Pilot/Arby's/dsl/scales/24hr, Sunoco/Subway/dsl DQ, Lori's Rest., McDonald's Best Western, Days Inn, Microtel, W Comfort Inn
16	OH 821, Macksburg
6	OH 821, to Devola, E Exxon/Subway/dsl, W Marathon/dsl/LP H, RV camping
3mm	**nb, full facilities, info, litter barrels, petwalk vending**
1	OH 7, to OH 26, Marietta, E GoMart/dsl/24hr DQ, Subway Best Western, Comfort Suites, Fairfield Inn, Quality Inn, Red Roof Inn $Tree, Aldi Foods, Buick/GMC, Cadillac/Chevrolet, Chrysler/Dodge/Jeep, Ford/Lincoln, GNC, Lowe's, Radio Shack, Toyota/Scion, Walmart/McDonald's, W BP/dsl,

CAMBRIDGE

MARIETTA

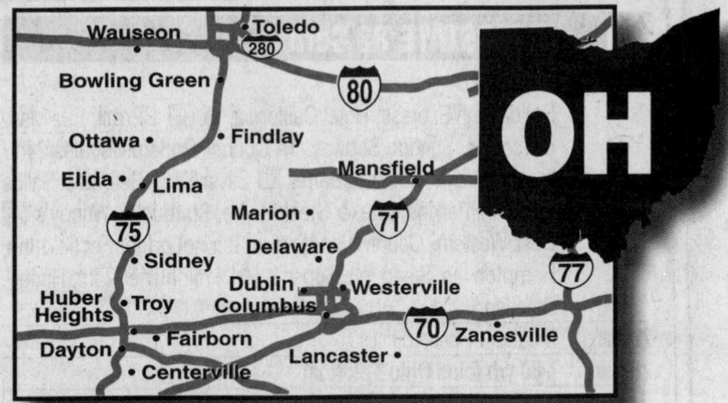

Exit #	Services
1	Continued GetGo/dsl, Marathon/dsl, Speedway/dsl Applebee's, Arby's, Bar-B-Cutie, Bob Evans, Burger King, Capt D's, China Fun, E Chicago Pizza, Empire Buffet, KFC, Las Trancas Mexican, Little Caesar's, LJ Silver, McDonald's, Napoli's Pizza, Papa John's, Pizza Hut, Qdoba, Shogun Hibachi, Shoney's, Subway, Taco Bell, Wendy's Hampton Inn, Microtel, Super 8 Advance Parts, AT&T, AutoZone, BigLots, Family$, Food4Less, JoAnn Fabrics, K-Mart, Kroger, Rite Aid, st patrol, TrueValue, Verizon, Walgreens
0mm	Ohio/West Virginia state line, Ohio River

INTERSTATE 80

Exit #	Services
237mm	Ohio/Pennsylvania state line
237mm	**Welcome Ctr wb, full facilities, info, litter barrels, petwalk vending**
234b a	US 62, OH 7, Hubbard, to Sharon, PA, Hubbard, N FLYING J/Denny's/dsl/LP/scales/24hr, Shell/rest./dsl/scales/motel/24hr/ @ Arby's, Burger King, Dunkin Donuts, McDonald's, Waffle House Best Western, Travelodge Blue Beacon, Homestead RV Ctr., tire/dsl repair, S Loves/Chester's/Subway/dsl/scales/24hr Chevrolet
232mm	**weigh sta wb**
229	OH 193, Belmont Ave, to Youngstown, N GetGo, Speedway/dsl Chad Anthony's Italian, Fortune Garden, Handel's Ice Cream, Sta Square Italian, Subway Hampton Inn, Motel 6, Super 8 Giant Eagle Foods, S BP/dsl, Shell Arby's, Bob Evans, Charley's Subs, Denny's, Fiesta Tapatia, Golden Hunan Chinese, Happy Buffet, Ianazones Pizza, Jimmy's Italian, KFC, Little Caesars, LJ Silver, McDonald's, Monteen's Southern Cuisine, Pizza Hut, Señor Jalapeño Mexican, Subway, Taco Bell, Uptown Pizza, Wendy's, Westfork Steaks, Youngstown Crab Co Days Inn, Quality Inn $General, Advance Parts, Aldi Foods, AutoZone, Family$, Firestone/auto, Goodyear/auto, O'Reilly Parts, Radio Shack, Rite Aid, SaveALot Foods, vet, Walgreens, Walmart/Subway
228	OH 11, to Warren (exits left from eb), Ashtabula
227	US 422, Girard, Youngstown, N Shell/dsl Burger King, DQ, Firegrill BBQ, JibJab Hotdogs, Subway
226	Salt Springs Rd, to I-680 (from wb), N BP/Dunkin Donuts/dsl, Sheetz/dsl McDonald's, Waffle House vet, S Mr Fuel/Road Rocket Diner/dsl/24hr, Petro/Shell/Iron Skillet/dsl/scales/24hr/ @, Pilot/Subway/dsl/scales/24hr Blue Beacon, dsl repair, Frank's Truckwash, SpeedCo
224b	I-680 (from eb), to Youngstown
224a	OH 11 S, to Canfield
223	OH 46, to Niles, N Country Fair/dsl, Pilot/McDonald's/dsl/scales/24hr Bob Evans, Dunkin Donuts, IceHouse Rest., Salsita's Mexican Candlewood Suites, Comfort Inn,

YOUNGSTOWN

OH

INTERSTATE 80 Cont'd

223	Continued Holiday Inn Express, Hotel California, S BP/dsl, FuelMart/dsl/scales, Sunoco/Subway, TA/Counry Pride/dsl/scales/24hr/@ Arby's, Cracker Barrel, LJ Silver/Taco Bell, Los Gallos Mexican, Perkins, Quaker Steak&Lube, Starbucks, Wendy's Best Western, Country Inn&Suites, EconoLodge, Fairfield Inn, Hampton Inn, Sleep Inn, Super 8 Freightliner/24hr, Harley-Davidson
221mm	Meander Reservoir
219mm	**I-80 wb joins Ohio Tpk (toll)**

For I-80 exits 2-218, see Ohio Turnpike.

INTERSTATE 90

Exit #	Services
244mm	Ohio/Pennsylvania state line
242mm	**/weigh sta wb, full facilities, info, litter barrels, petwalk**
241	OH 7, to Andover, Conneaut, N Burger King, McDonald's (2mi) Days Inn H, AutoZone, Evergreen RV Park, S Loves/McDonald's/Subway/dsl/scales/24hr Beef&Beer Café
235	OH 84, OH 193, to Youngstown, N Kingsville, N Grab&Go/gas, Marathon/Circle K Dav-Ed Motel Village Green Camping (2mi), S Circle K/Subway/dsl, TA/BP/Burger King/dsl/scales/24hr/@ Kay's Place Diner Kingsville Motel towing/repair
228	OH 11, to Ashtabula, Youngstown, N H (4mi)
223	OH 45, to Ashtabula, N FLYING J/Denny's/Shell/dsl/LP/scales/24hr Mr C's Rest. Best Value Inn, Holiday Inn Express, Ramada, Sleep Inn Buccaneer Camping, S Pilot/Subway/dsl/scales/24hr, SpeedCo Burger King, Clay St Grill, McDonald's, Waffle House Hampton Inn auto repair
218	OH 534, Geneva, N GetGo Best Friend's Grill, Chop's Grille, McDonald's, Pizza Hut, Wendy's Motel 6 H, Goodyear/repair, to Geneva SP, Willow Lake Camping (4mi), S KwikFill/Subway/dsl/scales/24hr Kenisse's Camping
212	OH 528, to Thompson, Madison, N McDonald's, Pizza Roto Mentor RV Ctr, S Marathon/dsl Heritage Hills Camping (4mi), radiator repair
205	Vrooman Rd, **0-2 mi** S BP/dsl, Marathon/dsl Capps Eatery, Subway Indian Point Park, Masons Landing Park
200	OH 44, to Painesville, Chardon, S BP/dsl, Sunoco/dsl McDonald's, Palmer's Bistro, Paninis Grill, Red Hawk Grille, Sunny St Cafe, Teresa's Pizzaria, Waffle House Comfort Inn, Quail Hollow Resort H, hwy patrol, Reider's Foods, URGENT CARE
198mm	**both lanes, full facilities, litter barrels, petwalk vending**
195	OH 615, Center St, Kirtland Hills, Mentor, **1-2 mi** N Best Western
193	OH 306, to Mentor, Kirtland, **0-2 mi** N BP/7-11/dsl, Shell McDonald's Best Value Inn H, S Speedway/dsl Burger King Days Inn, Red Roof Inn Kirtland Temple LDS Historic Site
190	Express Lane to I-271 (from wb)
189	OH 91, to Willoughby, Willoughby Hills, N BP/7-11/dsl, Shell/dsl Applebee's, Big Cheese Pizza, Bob Evans, Café Europa, Cracker Barrel, Eat'n Park, Peking Chef, Subway, TX Roadhouse, Wendy's Courtyard, Motel 6, Travelodge H, CVS Drug, Walgreens, S BMW/Mini, Lexus
188	I-271 S, to Akron
187	OH 84, Bishop Rd, to Wickliffe, Willoughby, S BP/7-11/dsl Shell Golden Mtn Chinese, McDonald's, Subway, Tony's Pizza Ramada Inn H, $Tree, Chevrolet, CVS Drug, Giant Eagle Foods, Marc's Foods, Mazda/VW, NTB, O'Reilly Parts
186	US 20, Euclid Ave, N Sunoco McDonald's Quality Inn Ford, radiators/transmissions, Subaru, S Shell Arby's, KFC, Popeye's, R-Ribs, Sidewalk Cafe, Taco Bell $General, Advance Parts, Family$, Firestone/auto, Save-a-Lot Foods
185	OH 2 E (exits left from eb), to Painesville
184b	OH 175, E 260th St, N Shell USPO, S auto/tire repair
184a	Babbitt Rd, N Buick/GMC
183	E 222nd St, N repair, Sunoco/dsl, S BP, Sunoco/dsl vet
182b a	185 St, 200 St, N BP/7-11/dsl Subway Home Depot, Honda, Hyundai, S Marathon/dsl, Shell/dsl, Speedway/dsl
181b a	E 156th St, S BP
180b a	E 140th St, E 152nd St
179	OH 283 E, to Lake Shore Blvd
178	Eddy Rd, to Bratenahl
177	University Circle, MLK Dr, N Cleveland Lake SP, S H, Rockefeller Park
176	E 72nd St
175	E 55th St, Marginal Rds
174b	OH 2 W, to Lakewood, downtown, N Browns Stadium, Rock&Roll Hall of Fame
174a	Lakeside Ave
173c	Superior Ave, St Clair Ave, N BP, downtown
173b	Chester Ave, S BP
173a	Prospect Ave (from wb), downtown
172d	Carnegie Ave, S Shell/dsl Burger King, KFC, McDonald's Cadillac, downtown
172c b	E 9th St, S H, to Cleveland St U
172a	I-77 S, to Akron
171b a	US 422, OH 14, Broadway St, Ontario St, N BP Hilton Garden
171	Abbey Ave, downtown
170c b	I-71 S, to I-490
170a	US 42, W 25th St, S Royal
169	W 44th St, W 41st St, N H
167b a	OH 10, West Blvd, 98th St, to Lorain Ave, N H, S BP/dsl CVS Drug
166	W 117th St, N BP/dsl, GetGo/dsl, Shell Penn Sta Subs Advance Parts, AutoZone, Giant Eagle Foods, Home Depot, Staples, Target, S Gas USA Monro
165	W 140th St, Bunts Rd, Warren Rd, S H
164	McKinley Ave, to Lakewood
162	Hilliard Blvd (from wb), to Westway Blvd, Rocky River, S BP, Shell Joe's Rest. USPO, vet
161	OH 2, OH 254 (from eb, no EZ return), Detroit Rd, Rocky River
160	Clague Rd (from wb), S H, same as 159
159	OH 252, Columbia Rd, N Carrabba's, Damon's Grill, Dave&Busters, Hooley House Grille, Outback Steaks Courtyard, Super 8, TownePlace Suites BMW, S BP/7-11 Houlihan's, Jets Pizza, KFC, McDonald's, Taco Bell, Urban Grill H, Chevrolet, NTB

EUCLID

CLEVELAND

INTERSTATE 90 Cont'd

Exit #	Services
156	Crocker Rd, Bassett Rd, Westlake, Bay Village, N BP, Shell DoublrTree, Extended Stay America, Holiday Inn Express, Red Roof Inn, Residence Inn, S BP/7-11, Speedway Aladdin's Eatery, Bar Louie, Bob Evans, Brio, Cheesecake Factory, Chipotle Mexican, Don Ramon Mexican, Five Guys, Jersey Mike's, Jimmy John's, Max&Erma's, McDonald's, Pizza by Robert, Starbucks, Subway, TGIFriday's, Vieng's Asian, Wendy's, Yardhouse a Grille, Zoup! Hampton Inn H, Aldi Foods, CVS Drug, Dick's, Giant Eagle, GNC, mall, Marc's Foods, Trader Joes, Verizon
155	Nagel Rd, Avon Lake, N GetGo/dsl Residence Inn, S Drugmart
153	OH 83, Avon Lake, N GetGo/dsl, Marathon/Circle K/Dunkin Donuts/dsl Arby's, Buffalo Wild Wings (2mi), Fujiyama, Istanbul Grill, King Yuan, Perkins, Rush Inn Grille, Wendy's Advance Parts, Ali Foods, AutoZone, Best Buy, Discount Tire, Firestone/auto, JC Penney, Lowe's, PetCo, Walmart, S Antonio's Pizza, Applebee's, Bob Evans, Burger King, Chipotle, CiCi's Pizza, Coldstone, Five Guys, IHOP, Jimmy John's, Mandarin House, Moe's SW Grill, Panera Bread, Red Robin, Starbucks, Subway, Winking Lizard Tavern, Zeppe's Pizza, Zoup! AT&T, Costco/gas, CVS Drug, GNC, Heinen's Mkt, Home Depot, Kohl's, Marc's Foods, Marshall's, Michael's, Old Navy, Target, USPO, Verizon, World Mkt
151	OH 611, Avon, N BP/7-11/dsl, Pilot/Subway/dsl/24hr McDonald's Fairfield Inn, Value Place Hotel Buick/GMC, Chevrolet, Goodyear/repair, Harley-Davidson, vet, S BJ's Whse/gas Mulligan's Grille
148	OH 254, Sheffield, Avon, N Quaker Steak&Lube Homewood Suites Ford, Kia, Mazda, Nissan, S BP, GetGo, Sheetz/dsl, Speedway/dsl Arby's, Burger King, China Star, Cracker Barrel, KFC, Marco's Pizza, McDonald's, Panera Bread, Pizza Hut, Ruby Tuesday, Sorrento Pizzaria, Steak'n Shake, Subway, Sugarcreek Rest., Taco Bell, Wendy's $General, $Tree, Aldi Foods, Drug Mart, Gander Mtn, Giant Eagle Mkt, Sam's Club/gas, Verizon
147mm	Black River
145	OH 57, to Lorain, I-80/Ohio Tpk E, Elyria, N Burger King, George's Rest. Country Inn&Suites $General, Save-a-Lot, U-Haul, vet, S Speedway/dsl Applebee's, Bob Evans, Buffalo Wild Wings, Burger King, Chipotle Mexican, Denny's, Golden Corral, Harry Buffalo, Honeybaked Ham, IHOP, McDonald's, Midway Diner, Olive Garden, Red Lobster, Subway, TX Roadhouse, Wasabi Grill, Wendy's Best Western, Hampton Inn, Quality Inn, Ramada Inn, Red Roof Inn $General, $Tree, AT&T, Best Buy, Conrad's Automotive, Dick's, Firestone/auto, Giant Eagle Mkt, Home Depot, Honda, Hyundai, JC Penney, Jo-Ann Fabrics, Lowe's, Macy's, Marc's Foods, Petsmart, Sears/auto, Staples, Target, Tuffy Repair, Verizon
144	OH 2 W(from wb, no return), to Sandusky

I-90 wb joins Ohio Tpk. WB exits to Ohio/Indiana state line are on Ohio Turnpike, exits 142-0.

AVON

INTERSTATE 270 (COLUMBUS)

Exit #	Services
55	I-71, to Columbus, Cincinnati
52b a	US 23, High St, Circleville, N Marathon/Circle K, Speedway/dsl, Turkey Hill/dsl Arby's, Bob Evans, Burger King,

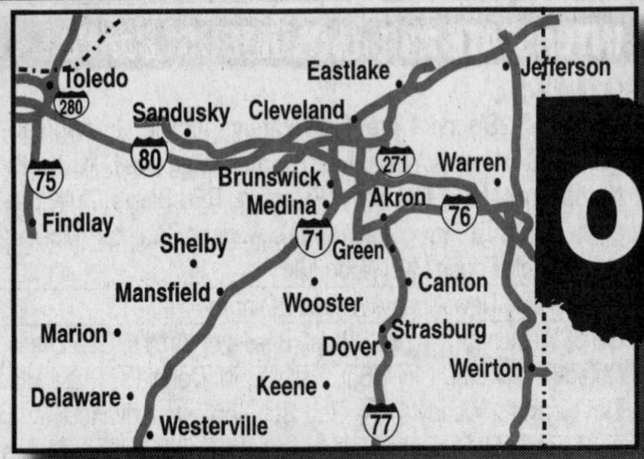

Exit #	Services
52b a	Continued China City, KFC, Little Caesar's, LJ Silver, Los Mariachis, McDon ald's, Pizza Hut, Ponderosa, Skyline Chili, Subway, Taco Bell, Tim Horton's, Waffle House, Wendy's, White Castle Kozy Inn $General, $Tree, Advance Parts, Aldi Foods, AutoZone, CVS Drug, Family$, Firestone/auto, Kroger/gas, Lowe's, NAPA, O'Reilly Parts, Walgreens, Walmart, S BP/dsl Kioto Downs
49	Alum Creek Dr, N BP/dsl, Shell/dsl, Thornton's/dsl Donato's Pizza, KFC/LJ Silver, Subway $General, Family$, S BP/dsl Arby's, McDonald's, Taco Bell, Wendy's Comfort Inn, Quality Inn
46b a	US 33, Bexley, Lancaster
43b a	I-70, E to Cambridge, W to Columbus
41b a	US 40, E Shell, Speedway Bob Evans, City BBQ, Honeybaked Ham, McDonald's, Outback Steaks, Rally's, Steak'n Shake, Taco Bell, Texas Roadhouse auto repair, AutoZone, Family$, K-Mart, NAPA, TJ Maxx, Verizon, Walgreens, W Shell/dsl, Speedway, UDF Golden Corral, Hunan Chinese, McDonald's, Mi Mexico, Poblanos Mexican, Subway $General, Family$
39	OH 16, Broad St, E GetGo, Speedway/dsl Arby's, Cane's, Chick-fil-A, Chipotle, Donato's Pizza, Dunkin Dontd, Five Guys, Hot Head Burrito, Jets Pizza, Jimmy John's, McDonald's, Noodles&Co, Panera Bread, Penn Sta Subs, Potbelly's, Sonic, Starbucks, Subway, Sunny St Cafe, Taco Bell, Tim Horton's, Waffle House, Wendy's, White Castle Comfort Suites H, Giant Eagle Mkt, Goodyear/auto, Grismer Auto Service, Kroger, Menard's, URGENT CARE, Verizon, Walgreens, W Shell, Speedway/dsl Chevrolet
37	OH 317, Hamilton Rd, E BP/dsl, Speedway/dsl Arby's, Big Boy, Bob Evans, Burger King, Chinese Express, Chipotle, Dunkin Donuts, Firehouse Subs, Jersey Mike's, McDonald's, Panera Bread, Penn Sta Subs, Rusty Bucket, Starbucks, Taco Bell, Tim Horton's Holiday Inn Express Firestone/auto, GNC, Kroger/dsl, W Fairfield Inn, Hampton Inn, Hilton Garden Buick/GMC, Subaru/Jaguar/Porsche, Volvo, VW/Audi
35b a	I-670W, US 62, E Speedway/dsl City BBQ, Little Caesar's, McDonald's, Tim Horton's Advance Parts, AutoZone, CVS Drug, Family$, W I-670
33	Easton Way
32	Morse Rd, E Marathon/DM, Speedway/dsl, UDF CVS Drug, Mazda, Nissan, Toyota/Scion, W BP, Shell/Subway, UDF/dsl Abuelo's, Applebee's, BJ's Rest., Champp's Grill, Donato's Pizza, HomeTown Buffet, J Akexander's, Kobe Japanese, Logan's Roadhouse, McDonald's, On-the-Border, Papa John's, Pei Wei, Red Robin, Sakura Steaks, Smokey Bones, Steak'n Shake, Taco Bell, Wendy's Courtyard, Extended Stay America, Hampton Inn, Holiday Inn Express, Residence Inn, ValuePlace AT&T, Best Buy, Cadillac, Carmax, Costco/

OH

INTERSTATE 270 (COLUMBUS) Cont'd

32	Continued gas, Dick's, Discount Tire, Field&Stream, Infiniti, Jo-Ann Fabrics, Lexus, Lowe's Whse, Macy's, mall, Mercedes, Michael's, Nordstrom's, NTB, Old Navy, Petsmart, REI, Sam's Club, Staples, Target, TJ Maxx, Trader Joe's, Verizon, Walmart/McDonald's, Whole Foods Mkt, World Mkt
30	OH 161 E to New Albany, W to Worthington
29	OH 3, Westerville, N [gas] BP/dsl, Shell [food] Arby's, Bob Evans, Chipotle Mexican, City BBQ, Fazoli's, McDonald's, Pizza Hut, Tim Horton's, Wendy's [lodging] Red Roof Inn [other] Advance Parts, AT&T, Big Lots, CarQuest, Firestone/auto, Kohl's, Kroger, Marc's Mkt, vet, Walmart, S [gas] Clark/dsl, Speedway/dsl [food] Carsoni's Italian, China House, Domino's, Subway [other] Aldi Foods, Family$, Grismer Tire/auto, Midas, Monro, USPO
27	OH 710, Cleveland Ave, N [gas] Speedway/dsl [food] Subway, Wendy's [lodging] Ramada Inn [other] $General, CVS Drug, NAPA Autocare, Tuffy, S [gas] Turkey Hill/dsl [food] El Rancho Allegre, McDonald's, O'Charley's [lodging] Embassy Suites [other] Home Depot
26	I-71, S to Columbus, N to Cleveland
23	US 23, Worthington, N [food] Bob Evans, Chipotle Mexican, Columbus Fish Mkt, Cucina Italiana, El Acapulco, Hyde Park Steaks, J Alexander's, J Gilbert's Steaks, Lotus Grill, Ruth's Chris Steaks, Starbucks, Subway, Sushiko Japanese, Winking Lizard [lodging] Courtyard, DoubleTree, Extended Stay America, Homewood Suites, Hyatt Place, Motel 6, Quality Inn, Red Roof Inn, Residence Inn, Sheraton, TownePlace Suites, ValuePlace, S [gas] BP [food] Aladdin's Eatery, Buca Italian, Cosi Grill, Jimmy John's, McDonald's, Panera Bread, Piada Italian, Starbucks [lodging] Econolodge, Holiday Inn [other] Kroger
22	OH 315, N [gas] BP/dsl, Marathon/dsl [food] Subway
20	Sawmill Rd, N [gas] BP, Marathon/dsl [food] Burger King, IHOP, Logan's Roadhouse, Max&Erma's, McDonald's, Olive Garden, Papa John's, Subway, Taco Bell, Wendy's [lodging] Fairfield Inn [other] Buick/GMC, CVS Drug, Ford, Hyundai, Kroger/gas, Lincoln, Mazda, NTB, Subaru, vet, S [gas] Shell, Speedway [food] Applebee's, Arby's, bd Mogolian, Blue Ginger Asian, Bob Evans, Bonchon, Burger King, Cane's, Charlie's Subs, Chick-fil-A, Chili's, Chipotle Mexican, ChuckeCheese, El Vaquero Mexican, Firehouse Subs, Genji Japanese, Golden Corral, HoneyBaked Cafe, Jimmy John's, Joe's Crabshack, KFC, Krispy Kreme, McDonald's, Mellow Mushroom, Panera Bread, Pizza Hut, Red Lobster, Ruby Tuesday, Starbucks, Steak'n Shake, Subway, Ted's MT Grill, Vicenzos Italian [lodging] Cloverleaf Suites, Hampton Inn, Quality Inn [other] $Tree, Advance Parts, AT&T, AutoZone, Barnes&Noble, Big Lots, Cadillac/Honda, CarMax, Dick's, Discount Tire, Firestone/auto, GNC, Hobby Lobby, Home Depot, Infiniti, Jo-Ann Fabrics, Kohl's, Lexus, Lowe's Whse, Meijer, Meineke, Michael's, Mr Tire, Old Navy, PetCo, Petsmart, Sam's Club/gas, Staples, SteinMart, Target, Toyota/Scion, Trader Joe's, Verizon, vet, Whole Foods Mkt
17b a	US 33, Dublin-Granville Rd, E [gas] Marathon, Sunoco [food] Bob Evans, Hyde Park Steaks, Jason's Deli, Max&Erma's, McDonald's, Pizza Hut, Subway [lodging] Courtyard, Crowne Plaza, Embassy Suites, Extended Stay America, Hilton Garden, Red Roof Inn, Residence Inn [other] CVS Drug, Fiat, Kroger, Mr Tire, USPO
15	Tuttle Crossing Blvd, E [gas] BP, UDF [food] BJ's Rest., Bob Evans, Boston Mkt, Chipotle Mexican, DiBella's Subs, House of Japan, Longhorn Steaks, Macaroni Grill, McDonald's, Noodles&Co, Panera Bread, PF Chang's, River City Grill, Taco Bell, Wendy's [lodging] Drury Inn, Homewood Suites, Hyatt Place, La Quinta, Marriott [other] JC Penney, Macy's, mall, Sears/auto, W [gas] Shell,
15	Continued Turkey Hill/Subway/dsl [food] Steak'n Shake, Uno Pizzeria [lodging] Staybridge Suites [other] Best Buy, NTB, vet, Walmart/Subway, World Mkt
13	Cemetery Rd, Fishinger Rd, E [gas] Exxon/Subway, Shell Speedway [food] Burger King, Carrabba's, Chipotle Mexican Damon's, Dave&Buster's, Donato's Pizza, KFC, Lunada Mexican, Panera Bread, Skyline Chili, Spageddie's, Starbucks Steak&Shake, Tim Horton's [lodging] Comfort Suites, Homewood Suites [other] $Tree, CVS Drug, Discount Tire, GNC, Home Depot Lowe's Whse, NTB, Staples, Tire Dicounters, Tuesday Morning W [gas] GetGo/dsl, Speedway [food] Bob Evans, Marie's Scrambler, Max&Erma's, McDonald's, Rusty Bucket Rest., Tim Horton's, Wendy's [lodging] Hampton Inn, Knights Inn [other] Giant Eagle Mkt, Nissan
10	Roberts Rd, E [gas] Marathon, Thornton's/dsl [food] Subway, Tim Horton's, Wendy's [lodging] ValuePlace, W [gas] Speedway/dsl [food] Tim Horton's, Waffle House [lodging] Courtyard, Quality Inn, Royal Inn [other] CVS Drug, Family$, O'Reilly Parts
8	I-70, E to Columbus, W to Indianapolis
7	US 40, Broad St, E [gas] BP, Speedway/dsl [food] Bob Evans, Boston Mkt, Burger King, ChuckeCheese, McDonald's, Peacock West, Popeye's, TeeJay's, White Castle [other] Advance Parts, Big Lots, Buick/GMC, Chevrolet, GNC, Radio Shack, Sears/auto, Target, W [gas] GetGo, Speedway/dsl, Thornton's [food] A&W/LJ Silver, Arby's, Canes, KFC, McDonald's, Papa John's, Tim Horton's, Waffle House [lodging] Red Roof Inn [other] H, CVS Drug, Family$, Giant Eagle Foods, Goodyear/auto, Home Depot, Jo-Ann Fabrics, O'Reilly Parts, Walgreens
5	Georgesville, E [gas] Shell/dsl, Sunoco/dsl, UDF/dsl [food] Jimmy John's, Starbucks [other] Verizon, Walmart, W [food] Applebee's, Arby's, Bob Evans, Buffalo Wild Wings, Chipotle Mexican, DQ, Fiesta Mariachi, KFC/LJ Silver, McDonald's, O'Charley's, Red Lobster, Steak'n Shake, Subway, Taco Bell, Wendy's, White Castle [other] Advance Parts, AT&T, Chrysler/Dodge/Jeep, GNC, Honda, Hyundai/Subaru, Kia, Kroger/gas, Lowe's Whse, NTB, TireDiscounters, Toyota/Scion, VW
2	US 62, OH 3, Grove City, N [gas] Turkey Hill/dsl [lodging] ValuePlace, S [gas] Marathon, Shell, Speedway/dsl [food] Big Boy, Burger King, Domino's, Donato's Pizza, Little Caesar's, McDonald's, Subway, Tim Horton/Wendy's, Waffle House, Wedgewood Pizza [other] CVS Drug, Verizon
0mm	I-71

INTERSTATE 271 (CLEVELAND)

Exit #	Services
39mm	**I-271 begins/ends on I-90, exit 188**
36	Wilson Mills Rd, Highland Hts, Mayfield, E [gas] Shell [food] Aladdin's a Eatery, Austin's Steaks, Jersey Mike's, Yours Truly Rest. [lodging] Hilton Garden, Holiday Inn [other] Chrysler/Dodge/Jeep, CVS Drug, Heinen's Mkt, vet, W [gas] Marathon/dsl [food] Burgers 2 Beer, Denny's, Hibachi Steaks, Panera Bread, Qdoba [other] Dick's, DrugMart, Home Depot, Kohl's, Tuesday Morning, Verizon
34	US 322, Mayfield Rd, E [gas] BP/7-11, Circle K [food] Chipotle, DiBella's Subs, Five Guys, Fox&Hound Grille, Georgio's Pizza, Jimmy John's, Marie's Scrambler, Piccolo Italian, Potbelly, Starbucks, Subway, Wendy's [other] H, CVS Drug, Marc's Foods, Michael's, Mr Tire, Old Navy, Rite Aid, Target, Tire Pros, Walmart, W [gas] Marathon, Shell, Speedway [food] Arby's, Bob Evans, Burger King, ChuckECheese, Dunkin Donuts, Firehouse Subs, Gaetano's Italian, McDonald's, Otani Japanese, Panera Bread,

COLUMBUS

OH

INTERSTATE 271 (CLEVELAND)

CLEVELAND

34	Continued Panini's Grill, Penn Sta Subs, Sonic, Subway, TGI Friday's, Two Bucks Cafe $Tree, AT&T, AutoZone, Best Buy, Conrad's Tire/auto, Costco/gas, CVS Drug, Ford/Lincoln, Giant Eagle Foods, GNC, JoAnn Fabrics, Marshalls, Midas, Nissan, NTB, O'Reilly Parts, Petsmart, Staples, Verizon, World Mkt
32	Brainerd Rd, E Burntwood Tavern, J Alexander's H, USPO
29	US 422 W, OH 87, Chagrin Blvd, Harvard Rd, E Mooney, Shell, Speedway Bahama Breeze, Bob Evans, Bravo Italian, Corky&Lenny's Rest., Firehouse Subs, Flemings, McDonald's, Mitchell's Fish Mkt, Paladar Latin Kitchen, Pancake House, Red Lobster, Starbucks, Stone Oven, Wasabi Japanese, Wendy's Courtyard, Extended Stay America, Extended Stay America, Fairfield Inn, Hampton Inn, Super 8 AT&T, Barnes&Noble, CVS Drug, Rite Aid, TJ Maxx, Trader Joe's, Verizon, Whole Foods Mkt, W BP/Subway, Shell/dsl Giovanni's Ristorante, Hyde Park Steaks, PF Chang's, Winking Lizard Tavern Clarion, DoubleTree, Embassy Suites, Homewood Suites, Hotel Indigo, Residence Inn H, Buick/GMC, Cadillac, Infiniti, NTB, Porsche
28b	Harvard Rd, E Red Robin, W Abuelo's, Buffalo Wild Wings, Chick-fil-A, Chipotle, DiBella's Subs, Five Guys, Olive Garden, Panera Bread, Piada Italian, River City Grille, Robeks Cafe, Zoup! Aloft, Marriott H, Verizon
28a	OH 175, Richmond Rd, Emery Rd, E BP, GetGo/dsl, Marathon/Circle K/Subway/dsl Baskin-Robbins/Dunkin Donuts, Don Ramon Mexican, Jimmy John's, McDonald's, Quiznos vet, W BJ's Whse
27b	I-480 W
27a	US 422 E, E CarMax, Lowe's
26	Rockside Rd, E Speedway/dsl, Sunoco/dsl Burger King, Subway Family$
23	OH 14 W, Forbes Rd, Broadway Ave, E Sunoco B&M BBQ, McDonald's, Wendy's Holiday Inn Express Sam's Club/dsl, W Marathon/Circle K/dsl
21	I-480 E, OH 14 E (from sb), to Youngstown
19	OH 82, Macedonia, E Speedway/dsl/E85 Papa John's, Penn Sta Subs, W Antonio's Ouzza, Applebee's, Arby's, Chick-fil-A, Chili's, Chipotle, Coldstone, Fuji Japanese, Golden Corral, Jersey Mike's, McDonald's, Outback Steaks, Panera Bread, Pizza Hut, Popeye's, Steak'n Shake, Taco Bell, Wendy's Aldi a Foods, AT&T, Best Buy, Chevrolet, Discount Tire, Giant Eagle Foods, GNC, Hobby Lobby, Home Depot, Kohl's, Lowe's, NTB, O'Reilly Parts, PetCo, Petsmart, Target, Verizon, Verizon, Walgreens, Walmart/Subway
18b a	OH 8, Boston Hts, to Akron, (exits left from sb), E BP/7-11/dsl, GetGo, Speedway/dsl Bob Evans, Pacific Chinese Country Inn&Suites, Knights Inn, La Quinta, Motel 6, W same as 19
12	OH 303, Richfield, Peninsula
10	I-77, to I-80, OH Tpk (from nb), to Akron, Cleveland
9	I-77 S, OH 176 (from nb), to Richfield
8mm	**both lanes, full facilities, litter barrels, petwalk**
3	OH 94, to I-71 N, Wadsworth, N Royalton, W PetroUSA/dsl
0mm	**I-271 begins/ends on I-71, exit 220.**

MACEDONIA

INTERSTATE 275 (CINCINNATI)

See Kentucky Interstate 275

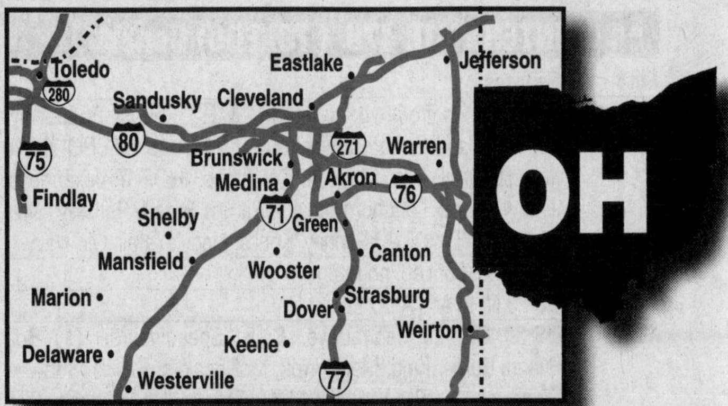

INTERSTATE 280 (TOLEDO)

TOLEDO

Exit #	Services
13	**I-280 begins/ends on I-75, exit 208**
12	Manhattan Blvd, E Sunoco, W Sunoco/dsl
11	OH 25 S, Eerie St, W Huntington Ctr
10mm	Maumee River
9	OH 65, Front St, E Sunoco Subway, Tony Packo's Cafe, W Sunoco/dsl
8	Starr Ave, (from sb only)
7	OH 2, Oregon, E Sunoco Arby's, Big Boy, Bob Evans, Burger King, Coldstone/Tim Horton's, Empire Chinese, McDonald's, Sonic, Taco Bell, Wendy's Comfort Inn, Hampton Inn H, Ford, K-Mart, to Maumee Bay SP, Walgreens
6	OH 51, Woodville Rd, Curtice Rd, E BP/dsl, Marathon Bob Evans, Burger King Menards, W Speedway/dsl Applebee's, Arby's, Big Boy, Gino's Pizza, KFC, LJ Silver, McDonald's, Subway, Taco Bell Sleep Inn H, $General, $Tree, Advance Parts, Meijer/dsl, O'Reilly Parts, Tires+
4	Walbridge
2	OH 795, Perrysburg, W Sunoco/Subway/dsl
1b	Bahnsen Rd, E FLYING J/Denny's/dsl/LP/scales/24hr Crown Inn, Regency Inn, W Loves/Arby's/dsl/scales/24hr, Petro/BP/Iron Skillet/dsl/scales/24hr/ @ Budget Inn Blue Beacon, SpeedCo, Super 8
1a	**I-280 begins/ends on I 80/90, OH Tpk, exit 71,** S Fuel-Mart/Subway/dsl/scales, Pilot/McDonald's/dsl/scales/24hr, TA/BP/Burger King/Taco Bell/dsl/scales/24hr/ @ KOA

INTERSTATE 475 (TOLEDO)

Exit #	Services
20	I-75. **I-475 begins/ends on I-75, exit 204.**
19	ProMedica Pky, Central Ave, S Burger King, Gino's Pizza, Subway H
18b	Douglas Rd (from wb)
18a	OH 51 W, Monroe St
17	Secor Rd, N Clark, Shell/dsl, Sunoco, Valero Applebee's, Bambino's Pizza, Bob Evans, Boston Mkt, Burger King, Famous Dave's BBQ, Hooters, KFC, Monroe St Diner, Penn Sta Subs, Red Robin, Rudy's Hot Dogs, Tim Horton's H, $Tree, AT&T, Barnes&Noble, Best Buy, Jo-AnnFabrics, Kohl's, Kroger/dsl, O'Reilly Parts, Walgreens, S BP Big Boy, Chipotle Mexican, Del Taco, El Vaquero, Five Guys, Jamba Juice, Marie's Scrambler, McDonald's, Original Pancakes, Piada Italian, Pizza Hut, Popeye's, Sonic, Starbucks, Subway, Taco Bell, Uncle John's Pancakes Hampton Inn, Holiday Inn Express, Quality Inn, Ramada Inn, Red Roof Inn Batteries+Bulbs, Costco/gas, Fresh Mkt, Home Depot, Radio Shack, Rite Aid, Sears/auto, Steinmart, U of Toledo

= gas = food = lodging = other = rest stop

INTERSTATE 475 (TOLEDO) Cont'd

Exit #	Services
16	Talmadge Rd (from wb, no return), N BP/dsl, Speedway/dsl Aladdin's Eatery, Bar Louie, bd Mongolian BBQ, Bravo Italiana, Chick-fil-A, Chipotle, Coldstone, IHOP, J Alexander's, Jimmy John's, Longhorn Steaks, Panera Bread, Potbelly, Starbucks Dick's, JC Penney, Kohl's, Macy's, mall, Old Navy
15	Corey Rd (from eb, no return)
14	US 23 N, to Ann Arbor
13	US 20, OH 120, Central Ave, E Speedway/dsl Bob Evans, Burger King, Magic Wok, McDonald's, Rally's, Subway, Wendy's BMW, Buick/GMC, Chrysler/Dodge/Jeep, Fiat, Ford, Honda, Hyundai, Kia, Nissan, Subaru, Toyota/Scion, Walmart, W BP, Shell, Speedway Buffalo Wild Wings, Jimmy John's, KFC, Tim Horton's Lowe's, Verizon, Walgreens
8b a	OH 2, E BP/dsl Don Pablo's, Penn Sta Subs, TGIFriday's, TX Roadhouse Extended Stay America, Hawthorn Suites, Knights Inn, Red Roof Inn H, Gander Mtn, Home Depot, Kohl's, Old Navy, to OH Med Coll, W BP, Shell/dsl, Speedway/dsl Arby's, Bob Evans, Boston Mkt, Burger King, Chick-fil-A, Chili's, Chinese Cuisine, Chipotle Mexican, IHOP, KFC, Little Caesar's, Mancino's Pizza, Marco's Pizza, McDonald's, Panera Bread, Starbucks, Subway, Taco Bell, Tim Horton's, Waffle House, Wendy's Courtyard, Quality Inn $Tree, Aldi Foods, Best Buy, BigLots, Dick's, Firestone/auto, GNC, Kroger/dsl, Menard's, Petsmart, Sam's Club/gas, Target, TJ Maxx, Verizon, Walmart/Subway
6	Dussel Dr, Salisbury Rd, to I-80-90/tpk, E BP Amaya's Mexican Grill, Applebee's, Arby's, Bankok Kitchen, Bluewater Grille, Buffalo Wild Wings, Coldstone, Cracker Barrel, Don Juan's, Gino's Pizza, Jimmy John's, Longhorn Steaks, Marie's Scrambler, Max&Erma's, McDonald's, Outback Steaks, Panera Bread, Sam's Diner, Smokey Bones BBQ, Subway, Wendy's, Yoko Japanese Country Inn&Suites, Courtyard, Extended Stay America, Fairfield Inn, Homewood Suites, Residence Inn, Super 8, W BP Bob Evans, Briarfield Café, Carrabba's, JoJo's Pizza Baymont Inn Churchill's Foods, vet
4	US 24, to Maumee, Napolean, N H, Toledo Zoo
3mm	Maumee River
2	OH 25, to Bowling Green, Perrysburg, N BP/dsl, Circle K/dsl, Shell American Table Rest., Arby's, Biggby Coffee, Buffalo Wild Wings, Charlie's Rest., Dave's Subs, El Vaquero, Gino's Pizza, Marco's Pizza, McDonald's, Subway, Wendy's Auto Value, Churchill's Mkt, Costco/dsl, GMC, Goodyear/auto, Hyundai, URGENT CARE, Volvo, VW, S Marathon, Speedway/dsl Bar Louie's, Biaggi's, Blue Pacific Grill, Bob Evans, Marie's Scrambler, Max&Erma's, Nagoya Japanese, Starbucks, Tea Tree Asian, Waffle House Economy Inn, Economy Inn, Hilton Garden AT&T, Books-A-Million, GNC, Mytee Automotive, Tireman/auto, URGENT CARE, Verizon, vet
0mm	**I-475 begins/ends on I-75, exit 192.**

INTERSTATE 480 (CLEVELAND)

Exit #	Services
42	I-80, PA Tpk, **I-480 begins/ends**, 0-2mi S BP, GetGo, Marathon/Circle K, Marathon/Circle K, Sheetz/24hr, Shell Applebees, Baskin Robbins/Dunkin Dounts, Bob Evans, Brown Derby Roadhouse, Buffalo Wild Wings, Burger King, China Chef, Chipotle, Denny's, DQ, El Campesino, Fun Buffet, Happy Moose Grill, Honeybaked Ham, Jimmy John's, KFC, Little
42	Continued Caesar's, McDonald's, Mr Hero, New Peking Chinese, Quino's, Rockne's Grill, Ruby Tuesday, Sonic, Starbucks, Steak Shake, Subway, Taco Bell Best Value Inn, Comfort In Econolodge, Fairfield Inn, Hampton Inn, Holiday Inn Expres Microtel, TownePlace Suites, Wingate Inn H, $Genera $Tree, Aldi Foods, All Seasons RV Ctr, AT&T, AutoZone, Def Tire/auto, Giant Eagle Mkt, GNC, Home Depot, Honda, Hyundai, Kia, K-Mart, Lowes Whse, Midas, NAPA, Nissan, NTI Save-a-Lot Foods, Staples, Target, to Kent St U, U-Haul, USPC Van's Tires, Verizon, vet, VW, Walgreens, Walmart
41	Frost Rd, Hudson-Aurora
37	OH 91, Solon, Twinsburg, N Arby's, Brewster's, Chipotl DQ, Mandarin Buffet, Panera Bread, Panini's Grill, Pizza Hu Taco Bell Comfort Suites, Gander Mtn, Giant Eagle Mk GNC, S BP/7-11
36	OH 82, Aurora, Twinsburg, N BP, McDonald's, Sheetz/d Burger King Super 8, S Bob Evans, Cracker Barre Get'n Go, Wendy's Blue Canyon Rest. Hilton Garden
26	I-271, to Erie, PA
25a b c	OH 8, OH 43, Northfield Rd, Bedford, S Marathon, She Sunoco Giant Eagle Mkt
24	Lee Rd (from wb)
23	OH 14, Broadway Ave, N Marathon Eldorado Mot H, S Freightliner
22	OH 17, Garanger, Maple Hts, Garfield Hts
21	Transportation Blvd, to E 98th St, N H, S GetG Applebee's, Chipotle, Penn Sta Subs, Starbucks, Steak' Shake AT&T, Giant Eagle Foods, Verizon
20b a	I-77, Cleveland
17	OH 176, OH 17, Cleveland
16	OH 94, to OH 17 S, State Rd, N auto repair, Convenier Mart, transmissions, S BP/7-11, Sunoco/dsl Kia
15	US 42, Ridge Rd, N Applebee's, Baskin-Robbins/Dunki Donuts, Boston Mkt, CiCi's Pizza, Coldstone Creamery, El Toltec ca Nexican, Hong Kong Buffet, McDonald's, Mr Hero, Penn St Subs, Pizza Hut, Rockne's Rest., Skyline a Chili, Starbucks TX Roadhouse $General, Giant Eagle Mkt, GNC, Lowe's Marc's Foods, Michael's, TJMaxx, URGENT CARE, USPO, Veri zon, S GetGo, Speedway/Speedy's Cafe/DSL Arby's Colonial Eatery, Denny's, DQ, Taco Bell, Wendy's $Tree Advance Parts, AT&T, Best Buy, Buick/GMC, Hyundai, Meineke Staples, Walgreens
13	Teideman Rd, Brooklyn, S BP/dsl, Sheetz/dsl, Speedway dsl Buffalo Wild Wings, Burger King, Carrabba's, Chipotl Mexican, Cracker Barrel, Golden Corral, Hooley House Grill, Ic House Grill, IHOP, LJ Silver, McDonald's, Panera Bread, Perkins, Steak 'n Shake, Subway, TGIFriday's, Wild Ginger China Bistro Extended Stay America, Hampton Inn Alc Foods, Home Depot, Jaguar, LandRover, Mazda, Sam's Club gas, Volvo, Walmart
12b	W 150th, W130th, Brookpark, N Marathon Family$ S Marathon/dsl, Shell/dsl Big Boy, Bob Evans, Subway Best Value Inn Acura, Chevrolet, Chrysler/Dodge/Jeep Infiniti, Lexus, Mini, Nissan, Toyota/Scion
11	I-71, Cleveland, Columbus
10	S Rd 237, Airport Blvd, (wb only)
9	OH 17, Brookpark Rd, N Subway Hilton Garden, ValuePlace H, S 100th Bomb Group Rest. Sheraton
7	(wb only) Clague Rd, to WestLake
6	OH 252, Great Northern Blvd, to N Olmsted, N BP, Shell Speedway/dsl Applebee's, Arby's, Bamboo Garden, Bob Evans, Boston Mkt, Brown Bag Burgers, Burger King, Chick

OH

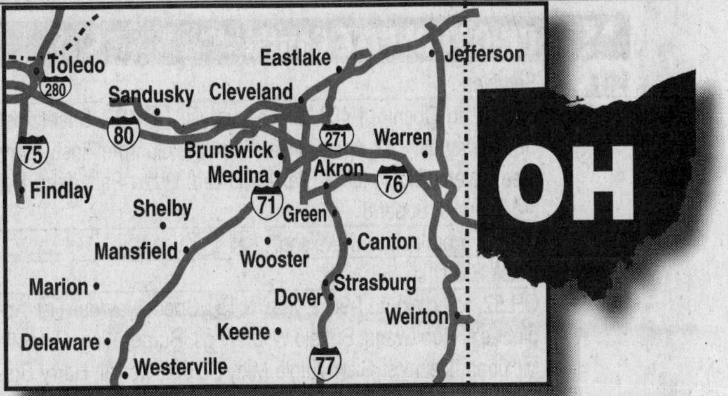

INTERSTATE 480 (CLEVELAND) Cont'd

6	Continued fil-A, Chili's, ChuckeCheese, Daishin Japanese, Denny's, Famous Dave's, Five Guys, Fox's Pizza, Frankie's Italian, Great Wall Buffet, Harry Buffalo, Jersey Mike's, Jimmy John's, Little Caesar's, Lonestar Steaks, Macaroni Grill, Marie's Scrambler, Moe's SW Grill, Olive Garden, Panera Bread, Penn Sta Subs, Popeye's, Rail Burger Bar, Red Lobster, Red Robin, Ruby Tuesday, Smokey Bones BBQ, Wendy's, Wild Mango Rest. Candlewood Suites, Courtyard, Extended Stay America, Extended Stay America, La Quinta, Radisson $Tree, Aldi Foods, AT&T, Best Buy, Big Lots, Buick/GMC/Cadillac, Chipotle Mexican, Conrad's Tire/auto, Dick's, Dillard's, Firestone/auto, Home Depot, Honda, Hyundai/VW, JC Penney, Jo-Ann Etc, Macy's, mall, Marc's Foods, Mr Tire, NAPA, NTB, Petsmart, Sears/auto, Subaru, Target, Toyota, Walmart, World Mkt
3	Stearns Rd, N H, S Razzle's Cafe CVS Drug
2	OH 10, Lorain Rd, to OH Tpk, S BP, Sheetz/dsl, Speedway/dsl Ace's Grille, Chipotle, Gourme Rest., Lone Tree Tavern, McDonald's, Panera Bread, Pizza Pan, Taco Bell Motel 6, Super 8
1	OH 10 W, to US 20 (from wb), Oberlin
0mm	OH 10, to Cleveland, **I-480 begins/ends on exit 151, OH Tpk**

INTERSTATE 680 (YOUNGSTOWN)

Exit #	Services
14	OH 164, to Western Reserve Rd, **I-680 begins/ends on OH Tpk, exit 234,** S Shell/Subway/dsl Cafe 422, Carmella's Cafe, Dunkin Donuts, McDonald's, Pizza Hut, Wendy's H
11b a	US 224, S BP, GetGo, Shell/dsl Applebee's, Burger King, Carabba's, Chick-fil-A, Chipotle, Dunkin Donuts, Honeybaked Ham, IHOP, KFC, LJ Silver, Longhorn Steaks, McDonald's, Nicolinni's Italian, O'Charley's, Olive Garden, Outback Steaks, Papa John's, Perkins, Red Lobster, Smokey Bones, Springfield Grill, Starbucks, Subway, Taco Bell, TGIFriday's, TX Roadhouse Best Western, Days Inn, Fairfield Inn, Hampton Inn, Holiday Inn, Red Roof Inn, Residence Inn H, $Tree, Aldi Foods, AT&T, Best Buy, Big Lots, Giant Eagle, GNC, K-Mart, Lowe's, Marc's Foods, NTB, Petsmart, Radio Shack, Sam's Club/gas, Staples, URGENT CARE, Walmart/Subway
9b a	OH 170, Midlothian Blvd, Struthers, S Shell/dsl, Speedway/dsl McDonald's, Subway $General, Rite Aid, Walgreens
8	Shirley Rd, downtown
7	US 62, OH 7, South Ave, downtown
6b a	US 62, OH 7, Mkt St, downtown
5	Glenwood Ave, Mahoning Ave, downtown
4b a	OH 193, to US 422, Salt Springs Rd, N H, museum
3c b	Belle Vista Ave, Connecticut Ave
3a	OH 711 E, to I-80 E
2	Meridian Rd, S Ford/Peterbilt Trucks
1	OH 11

OHIO TURNPIKE

Exit #	Services
241mm	Ohio/Pennsylvania state line
239mm	**toll plaza**
237mm	**Mahoning Valley Travel Plaza eb, Glacier Hills Travel Plaza wb,** Sunoco/dsl/24hr McDonald's gifts,
234	I-680 (from wb), to Youngstown
232	OH 7, to Boardman, Youngstown, N Sheetz, Valero/dsl DQ, Los Gallos Mexican, Rita's Custard, Steamer's Stonewall Tavern Best Value Inn, Budget Inn, Holiday Inn Express, Super 8 $General, antiques, S Pilot/McDonald's/dsl/scales/24hr Davis Motel, Liberty Inn
218	I-80 E, to Youngstown, Niles. **OH Tpk runs with I-76 eb, I-80 wb. Services S on Mahoning.**
216	Lordstown (from wb), N GM Plant
215	Lordstown (from eb), N GM Plant
210mm	Mahoning River
209	OH 5, to Warren, N Rodeway Inn, S Marathon/dsl EconoLodge, Holiday Inn Express
197mm	**Portage Service Plaza wb, Bradys Leap Service Plaza eb,** Sunoco/dsl/24hr McDonald's, Sbarro's, Starbucks gifts,
193	OH 44, to Ravenna
192mm	Cuyahoga River
187	OH 14 S, I-480, to Streetsboro, **0-2mi S** BP, GetGo, Marathon/Circle K, Marathon/Circle K, Sheetz, Shell Applebee's, Baskin Robbins/Dunkin Dounts, Bob Evans, Brown Derby Roadhouse, Buffalo Wild Wings, Burger King, China Chef, Chipotle, Denny's, DQ, El Campesino, Fun Buffet, Happy Moose Grill, Honeybaked Ham, Jimmy John's, KFC, Little Caesar's, McDonald's, Mr Hero, New Peking Chinese, Quiznos, Rockne's Grill, Ruby Tuesday, Sonic, Starbucks, Steak'n Shake, Subway, Taco Bell Best Value Inn, Comfort Inn, EconoLodge, Fairfield Inn, Hampton Inn, Holiday Inn Express, Microtel, TownePlace Suites, Wingate Inn H, $General, $Tree, Aldi Foods, All Seasons RV Ctr, AT&T, AutoZone, Defer Tire/auto, Giant Eagle Mkt, GNC, Home Depot, Honda, Hyundai, Kia, K-Mart, Lowe's, Midas, NAPA, Nissan, NTB, Save-a-Lot Foods, Staples, Target, to Kent St U, U-Haul, USPO, Van's Tires, Verizon, vet, VW, Walgreens, Walmart
180	OH 8, to I-90 E, N Baymont Inn, Clarion, S BP/dsl to Cuyahoga Valley NRA
177mm	Cuyahoga River
173	OH 21, to I-77, N Pilot/Wendy's/dsl/scales Holiday Inn Express, Motel 6, S Memories Rest., Subway Days Inn, Hampton Inn, Super 8
170mm	**Towpath Service Plaza eb, Great Lakes Service Plaza wb,** Sunoco/dsl/24hr Burger King, FoodCourt, Panera Bread, Pizza Hut, Starbucks gifts,
161	US 42, to I-71, Strongsville, **N on US 42** Mobil/dsl, Sheetz/dsl Buffalo Wild Wings, Jennifer's Rest., Mad Cactus Mexican, McDonald's Kings Inn, La Siesta Motel, Metrick's Motel Home Depot, Lowe's, vet, Walmart/Subway, **S on US 42** Elmhaven Motel Burger King, DQ, Fiat, J-Bella Rest., KFC, Marco's Pizza, Mr Hero, Olympia's Cafe, Staples, Tuesday Morning, vet

STREETSBORO

OH

= gas = food = lodging = other = rest stop

OHIO TURNPIKE Cont'd

E

Exit #	Services
152	OH 10, to Oberlin, I-480, Cleveland, N BP, Sheetz/dsl, Speedway/dsl Ace's Grille, Chipotle, Gourme Rest., Lone Tree Tavern, McDonald's, Panera Bread, Pizza Pan, Taco Bell Motel 6, Super 8
151	I-480 E (from eb), to Cleveland,
146mm	Black River
145	OH 57, to Lorain, to I-90, Elyria, N Speedway/dsl Applebee's, Bob Evans, Buffalo Wild Wings, Burger King, Chipotle Mexican, Denny's, Giant Eagle Mkt, Golden Corral, Harry Buffalo, Honeybaked Ham, IHOP, McDonald's, Midway Diner, Olive Garden, Red Lobster, Subway, TX Roadhouse, Wasabi Grill, Wendy's Best Western, Country Inn&Suites, Hampton Inn, Quality Inn, Ramada, Red Roof Inn $General, $Tree, AT&T, Best Buy, Conrad's Automotive, Dick's, Firestone/auto, Home Depot, Honda, Hyundai, JC Penney, Jo-Ann Fabrics, Lowe's, Macy's, Marc's Foods, Petsmart, Sears/auto, Staples, Target, Tuffy, Verizon, S Shell, Speedway/dsl Super 8
142	I-90 (from eb, exits left), OH 2, to W Cleveland
140	OH 58, Amherst, N Sunoco/Subway DQ, Moosehead Grill $General, Chrysler/Dodge/Jeep, S Ford
139mm	**Service Plaza both lanes,** Sunoco/dsl/24hr Burger King, Great Steak&Potato, Hershey's, Panera Bread, Popeye's, Starbucks gifts RV parking
135	Rd 51, Baumhart Rd, to Vermilion
132mm	Vermilion River
118	US 250, to Norwalk, Sandusky, N Circle K/dsl, Marathon/dsl McDonald's, Subway Country Inn Suites, Days Inn, Hampton Inn, Motel 6, Quality Inn, Red Roof Inn, Super 8 Milan RV Park, to Edison's Birthplace, S Colonial Inn
110	OH 4, to Bellevue
100mm	**Service Plaza both lanes,** Sunoco/dsl/24hr Burger King, Sbarro's, Starbucks
93mm	Sandusky River
91	OH 53, to Fremont, Port Clinton, N Days Inn, **0-2 mi S** BP/Subway/dsl/24hr, Murphy USA/dsl Applebee's, Bob Evans, Buffalo Wild Wings, Burger King, Fricker's, Grand American Buffet, Jimmy John's, McDonald's, Subway, Taco Bell Comfort Inn, Delux Inn, Hampton Inn, Holiday Inn Express, Quality Inn H, $Tree, Aldi Foods, AT&T, Ford/Lincoln, GNC, Lowe's, Rutherford B. Hayes Library, Staples, URGENT CARE, USPO, Verizon, vet, Walmart
81	OH 51, Elmore, Woodville, Gibsonburg
80.5mm	Portage River
77mm	**Service Plaza both lanes,** Sunoco/dsl/24hr Hardee's, Mancino's, Red Burrito

LORAIN

TOLEDO

Exit #	Services
71	I-280, OH 420, to Stony Ridge, Toledo, N FLYING J Denny's/dsl/scales/LP/24hr, Loves/Arby's/dsl/scales/24hr, Petro/BP/Iron Skillet/dsl/scales/24hr/ @ Budget Inn, Crown Inn, Regency Inn, Super 8 Blue Beacon, SpeedCo, S FuelMart/Subway/dsl/scales, Pilot/McDonald's/dsl/scales/24hr, TA/BP/Burger King/Taco Bell/dsl/scales/24hr/ @ KOA
64	I-75 N, to Toledo, Perrysburg, S BP/Subway/dsl, Country Inn&Suites, Courtyard, Hampton Inn, Staybridge Suites Bass Pro Shops, Camping World RV Ctr
63mm	Maumee River
59	US 20, to I-475, Maumee, Toledo, N Shell/dsl, Speedway/dsl Bob Evans, East of Chicago Pizza, Golden Lily, McDonald's, Nick's Cafe, Olive Garden, Steak'n Shake, Subway, Waffle House Motel 6 $Tree, Family$, Goodyear/auto, Jo-Ann Fabrics, NAPA, O'Reilly Parts, Rite Aid, Savers, to Toledo Stadium, Walgreens, S Shell/dsl, Speedway/dsl Big Boy, Chipotle Mexican, Deet's BBQ, Five Guys, Fricker's, Jed's BBQ, La Fiesta Mexican, Pizza Hut, Red Lobster, Schlotzsky's, Steak Escape, Taco Bell, Tim Horton's Best Value Inn, Budget Inn, Comfort Inn, Comfort Inn, Days Inn, Hampton Inn, Holiday Inn, Red Roof Inn antiques, AT&T, Ford, Honda, Kroger/dsl, Meijer/dsl, Toyota/Scion, Verizon, vet
52	OH 2, to Toledo, N Loma Linda Mexican, S Days Inn , RV/truck repair
39	OH 109, S Country Corral/Valero/Winchesters Rest/dsl/scales/wi-fi/24hr
34	OH 108, to Wauseon, S Shell/Subway/dsl/24hr Smith's Rest., Wendy's Arrowhead Motel, Best Western, Holiday Inn Express, Super 8 H, Woods Trucking/repair (1mi), **2 mi S on US 20A** BP/Circle K, Circle K, Marathon, Murphy USA/dsl, Valero, A&W/KFC, Arby's, Burger King, DQ, Grasshopper Rest., Kamwa Chinese, McDonald's, Pizza Hut, Subway, Taco Bell $General, Ace Hardware, AutoZone, O'Reilly Parts, Rite Aid, Walmart
25	OH 66, Burlington, N Harrison Lake SP, **3 mi S** Sauder Village Museum
24.5mm	Tiffen River
18	**Indian Meadow Service Plaza both lanes,** Sunoco/dsl Burger King, Sbarro's, Starbucks
13	OH 15, to Bryan, Montpelier, S Marathon/dsl, Sunoco 4Seasons Rest. EconoLodge, Holiday Inn Express, Rainbow Motel, Ramada Inn Hutch's dsl Repair
11.5mm	St Joseph River
3mm	**toll plaza**
2	OH 49, to US 20, N Burger King, Subway info, truck tires
0mm	Ohio/Indiana state line

OKLAHOMA

INTERSTATE 35

N

Exit #	Services
236mm	Oklahoma/Kansas state line
232	sb only, weigh sta
231	US 177, Braman, E Conoco/deli/dsl
230	Braman Rd
229mm	Chikaskia River
225mm	**Welcome Ctr sb, full facilities, litter barrels, petwalk vending**
222	OK 11, to Blackwell, Medford, Alva, Newkirk, E Conoco/dsl, Shell/dsl Braum's, KFC/Taco Bell, Los Potros Mexican, McDonald's, Plains Man Rest., Subway Best Way Inn, Best Western, Comfort Inn H
218	Hubbard Rd
217mm	**weigh sta both lanes**
214	US 60, to Tonkawa, Lamont, Ponka City, N OK Coll, W Casey's/dsl, Shell/dsl New Western Inn RV Park
213mm	Salt Fork of Arkansas River

OH

OK

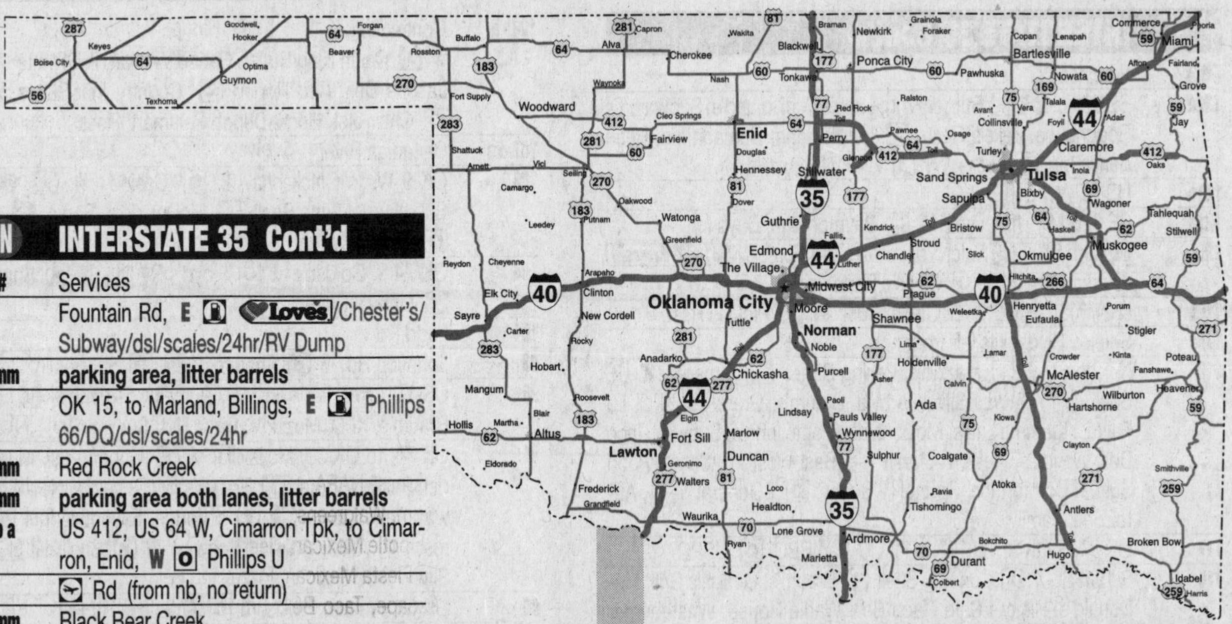

INTERSTATE 35 Cont'd

Exit #	Services
211	Fountain Rd, E [gas] Loves/Chester's/Subway/dsl/scales/24hr/RV Dump
209mm	**parking area, litter barrels**
203	OK 15, to Marland, Billings, E [gas] Phillips 66/DQ/dsl/scales/24hr
199mm	Red Rock Creek
195mm	**parking area both lanes, litter barrels**
194b a	US 412, US 64 W, Cimarron Tpk, to Cimarron, Enid, W [other] Phillips U
193	[airport] Rd (from nb, no return)
191mm	Black Bear Creek
186	US 64 E, to Fir St, Perry, E [gas] Mobil/Subway/dsl [food] Braum's, McDonald's, Taco Mayo [lodging] Super 8 [other] [H], museum, W [gas] Exxon/dsl [lodging] Comfort Suites, Holiday Inn Express, Regency Inn
185	US 77, to Covington, Perry, E [lodging] American Inn, W [gas] Phillips 66/rest/motel/dsl/24hr [other] RV camping
180	Orlando Rd
174	OK 51, to Stillwater, Hennessee, E [gas] Conoco/dsl [food] Smokey Pokey Cafe [lodging] Fairfield Inn (12mi), Hampton Inn (12mi), Motel 6 (12mi) [other] Lake Carl Blackwell RV Park, to OSU
173mm	**parking area sb, parking only, litter barrels**
171mm	**parking area nb, parking only, litter barrels**
170	Mulhall Rd
166mm	Cimarron River
157	OK 33, to Cushing, Guthrie, E [gas] Loves/Carl's Jr/dsl/scales/24hr, W [gas] K&L/dsl, Road Star, Shell/dsl, Valero [food] Arby's, Braum's, El Rodeo Mexican, KFC (2mi), LJ Silver, Mazzio's, McDonald's (3mi), Pizza Hut, Sonic, The Ribshack [lodging] Best Western, Holiday Inn Express, Interstate Motel, Sleep Inn [other] [H], Langston U, OK Terr Museum, RV camping
153	US 77 N (exits left from nb), Guthrie, W [food] McDonald's (3mi), Taco Bell (3mi) [other] Buick/Cadillac/GMC, Chevrolet, Chrysler/Dodge/Jeep
151	Seward Rd, E [gas] Shell/cafe/dsl [other] Lazy E Arena (4mi), Pioneer RV park
149mm	**weigh sta both lanes**
146	Waterloo Rd, E [gas] Shell/Subway/dsl
143	Covell Rd
142	Danforth Rd (from nb)
141	US 77 S, OK 66E, to 2nd St, Edmond, Tulsa, W [gas] Conoco/dsl, Phillips 66/dsl [lodging] Best Western, Comfort Suites, Fairfield Inn, Hampton Inn, Holiday Inn Express [other] [H], vet
140	SE 15th St, Spring Creek, Arcadia Lake, Edmond Park, W [gas] Phillips 66/Circle K/Subway [food] Braum's, McDonald's [other] Walmart/McDonald's
139	SE 33rd St
138d	Memorial Rd
138c	Sooner Rd (from sb)
138b	Kilpatrick Tpk
138a	I-44 Tpk E to Tulsa
I-35 S and I-44 W run together 8 mi.	
137	NE 122nd St, to OK City, E [gas] Shamrock/dsl, Shell/dsl [food] Charly's Rest., IHOP [lodging] Budget Lodge, Hampton Inn, Sleep Inn, W **Oklahoma Visitors Ctr/info/restrooms,** [gas] FLYING J/Huddle House/dsl/scales/LP/24hr, Loves/Godfathers/Subway/dsl/24hr, Phillips 66/dsl/scales [food] Cracker Barrel, McDonald's, Sonic, Waffle House [lodging] Best Value Inn, Comfort Inn, Days Inn, Economy Inn, Holiday Inn Express, Motel 6, Super 8 [other] Abe's RV Park, Frontier City Funpark, truckwash
136	Hefner Rd, W [gas] Conoco/dsl [other] same as 137
135	Britton Rd
134	Wilshire Blvd, W [lodging] Executive Inn [other] Blue Beacon
I-35 N and I-44 E run together 8 mi.	
133	I-44 W, to Amarillo, W [other] Cowboy Hall of Fame, st capitol
132b	NE 63rd St (from nb), **1/2 mi** E [gas] Conoco/dsl [food] Braum's [lodging] Remington Inn
132a	NE 50th St, Remington Pk, W [other] funpark, info, museum, zoo
131	NE 36th St, W [gas] Phillips 66/dsl/24hr [other] 45th Inf Division Museum
130	US 62 E, NE 23rd St, E [gas] Shell/dsl, W [other] to st capitol
129	NE 10th St, E [gas] Conoco/McDonald's/dsl
128	I-40 E, to Ft Smith
127	Eastern Ave, OK City, W [gas] JR's Trvl Ctr/Wendy's/dsl/scales/24hr/ @, Petro/rest/dsl/24hr/ @ [food] Waffle House [lodging] Best Western, Brick-Town Hotel, Central Plaza Hotel, EconoLodge, Quality Inn [other] Blue Beacon, Lewis RV Ctr
126a	I-40, W to Amarillo, I-235 N, to st capitol
126b	I-35 S to Dallas
125d	SE 15th St, E [gas] Conoco/dsl
125b	SE 22nd St (from nb)
125a	SE 25th, same as 124b
124b	SE 29th St, E [food] China Queen, Denny's, McDonald's, Sonic, Taco Bell [lodging] Best Value Inn, Days Inn, Plaza Inn, Royal Inn, W [gas] Phillips 66/Circle K [food] Mama Lou's Rest. [lodging] Executive Inn, same as 125a
124a	Grand Blvd, E [lodging] Studio 6, Super 8, W [lodging] Drover's Inn
123b	SE 44th St, E [gas] Shell [food] Domino's, Sonic [lodging] Best Value Inn, Courtesy Inn, Motel 6, W [gas] Phillips 66 [food] Subway, Taco Mayo [other] $General, Family$, USPO
123a	SE 51st St, E [gas] Conoco/dsl [lodging] Best Value Inn
122b	SE 59th St, E [gas] Phillips 66/dsl, W [gas] Shell, Valero/dsl [other] U-Haul

GUTHRIE

OK

[gas] = gas [food] = food [lodging] = lodging [other] = other [RS] = rest stop

INTERSTATE 35 Cont'd

OKLAHOMA CITY

Exit #	Services
122a	SE 66th St, E [food] Burger King, Luby's, McDonald's, Subway, TX Roadhouse, Zeke's Rest. [lodging] Fairfield Inn, Ramada Inn, Residence Inn [other] Tires+, W [gas] 7-11 [food] Arby's
121b	US 62 W, I-240 E
121a	SE 82nd St, (from sb), W [lodging] Baymont Inn, Days Inn
120	SE 89th St, E [gas] Valero/dsl/scales [lodging] Ford, W [gas] Loves /Subway/dsl/24hr [other] Classic Parts
119b	N 27th St, E [gas] Shell/Circle K/dsl, W [food] Pickles Rest.
119a	Shields Blvd (exits left from nb)
118	N 12th St, E [food] Mazzio's, Peking Buffet [lodging] Super 8, W [gas] Shell [food] A&W/LJ Silver, Arby's, Braum's, Grandy's, KFC, La Fajitas, Mamma Lou's, McDonald's, Papa John's, Subway, Taco Bell, Wendy's, Western Sizzlin [lodging] Best Western, Candlewood Suites, Comfort Inn, SpringHill Suites [other] $General, 7-11, AutoZone, Family$, vet
117	OK 37, S 4th St, W [gas] 7-11 [food] Van BBQ [other] USPO
116	S 19th St, E [gas] Conoco, Shell [food] Braum's, Genghis Grill, McDonald's, Ricky's Cafe, Taco Bell, Waffle House, Whataburger [other] AT&T, Best Buy, Firestone/auto, GNC, Hobby Lobby, JC Penney, Office Depot, Petsmart, Ross, W [gas] Murphy USA [food] 5 Guys Burgers, Alfredo's Mexican, Applebee's, Arby's, Buffalo Wild Wings, Burger King, Cane's, Carl's Jr, Chicken Express, Chick-fil-A, Chili's, China House, Earl's Ribs, Freddy's Custard, Furr's Buffet, Harry Bears, Hollies Steaks, IHOP, Jack-in-the-Box, Jersey's Mike's Subs, Jimmy's Egg, Mazzio's, McAlister's Deli, Panda Express, Poblano Grill, Qdoba Mexican, Quiznos, Schlotzsky's, Sonic, Starbucks, Subway, Taco Mayo [lodging] La Quinta [other] $Tree, Aldi Foods, AT&T, Discount Tire, Gordman's, Harley-Davidson, Home Depot, Kohl's, Lowe's, Radio Shack, Target, Tires+, Walmart
114	Indian Hill Rd, E [food] Double Dave's Pizza [lodging] ValuePlace Hotel [other] Cadillac, funpark
113	US 77 S (from sb, exits left), Norman
112	Tecumseh Rd, E [other] Nissan, Toyota/Scion, W [food] McDonald's, Sonic [other] H, CVS Drug, URGENT CARE
110b a	Robinson St, E [food] 5 Guys Burgers, Carl's Jr, Cheddar's, Logan's Roadhouse, Panda Express, Pei Wei, Qdoba Mexican, Taco Bell, Wing Stop, Zio's Italian [lodging] Embassy Suites, Motel 6 [other] H, $Tree, AT&T, Buick/GMC, Discount Tire, Ford, GMC, Homeland Foods/gas, Honda, Hyundai, Kohl's, Lincoln, Mazda, Office Depot, PetCo, Target, Tires+, TJ Maxx, Verizon, VW, W [gas] Conoco/Subway [food] Arby's, Braum's, Cafe Escondido, Chuy's Mexican, Cracker Barrel, Domino's, Jersey Mike's, Outback Steaks, Papa John's, Papa Murphy's, Pizza Hut, Rib Crib, Saltgrass Steaks, Waffle House, Yamato Steaks [lodging] Comfort Inn, Courtyard, Hilton Garden, Holiday Inn [other] 7-11, Kia, Suzuki
109	Main St, E [gas] Murphy USA, Phillips 66/dsl, Shell/Circle K, Sinclair [food] Chick-fil-A, Golden Corral, Panera Bread, Prairie Kitchen, Taco Cabana, Waffle House, Wendy's, Whataburger [lodging] EconoLodge, Guest Inn, Motel 6, Super 8, Travelodge [other] AT&T, AutoZone, Best Buy, BigLots, Cadillac, Chevrolet, Chrysler/Dodge/Jeep, Hastings Books, Hobby Lobby, Kwik Kar, Lowe's, Nissan, Tires+, Walmart/McDonald's, W [gas] Conoco/Circle K/dsl [food] Applebee's, BJ's Brewhouse, Burger King, Charleston's Rest. Chili's, McDonald's, Olive Garden, On the Border, Red Lobster [lodging] Fairfield Inn, Hampton Inn, La Quinta [other] Barnes&Noble, Dillard's, JC Penney, Michael's, Old Navy, Sam's Club, Sears/auto
108b a	OK 9 E, Norman, E [gas] Conoco/Circle K [food] Arby's, Braum's, Del Rancho Steaks, Schlotzsky's, Taco Bell [lodging] Sooner Legends Inn/rest [other] $General, NAPA, O'Reilly Parts, to U of OK,

NORMAN

OK

Exit #	Services
108b a	Continued W [food] Cajun King Buffet, Carino's Italian, IHOP, Interurban Grill, Jasons Deli, Red Robin [lodging] Country Inn&Suites, La Quinta [other] Chevrolet, Home Depot, Petsmart, Ross
107mm	Canadian River
106	OK 9 W, to Chickasha, E [other] Casino, W [gas] Loves/Subway/dsl/24hr, Shell [food] McDonald's, Sonic [lodging] Sleep Inn [other] casino, vet
104	OK 74 S, Goldsby, E [other] Floyd's RV Ctr, W [gas] Shamrock/dsl [food] Libby's Cafe
101	Ladd Rd
98	Johnson Rd, E [gas] Shamrock/dsl [other] Sooner RV Ctr
95	US 77 (exits left from sb), Purcell, **1-3 mi** E [gas] Shell [food] Braum's, KFC, Mazzio's, Pizza Hut, Subway [other] H, Ford
91	OK 74, to OK 39, Maysville, E [gas] Conoco/dsl, Murphy USA/dsl, Phillips 66/dsl [food] Braum's, McDonald's, New China, Subway, Taco Mayo [lodging] EconoLodge, Executive Inn, Ruby's Inn/rest. [other] AT&T, Walmart/Subway, W [gas] Shell/dsl [food] A&W/LJ Silver, Taco Bell
86	OK 59, Wayne, Payne, E [other] American RV Park
79	OK 145 E, Paoli, E [gas] Phillips 66
76mm	Washita River
74	Kimberlin Rd, to OK 19
72	OK 19, Paul's Valley, E [gas] Conoco/dsl, Murphy USA/dsl, Valero/dsl/rest/24hr [food] Arby's, Braum's, Chicken Express, Green Tea Chinese, Happy Days Diner, KFC/Taco Bell, McDonald's, Sonic, Stevenson BBQ, Subway, Taco Mayo, Tio's Mexican [lodging] American Inn, Best Value Inn, Comfort Inn, Days Inn, Holiday Inn Express, Relax Inn [other] AT&T, Buick/Cadillac/GMC, Chrysler/Dodge/Jeep, Ford/Lincoln, Walmart, W [gas] Phillips 66/dsl/24hr [other] truckwash
70	Airport Rd, E [gas] Loves/Burger King/dsl/LP/scales/24hr/ @ [other] H
66	OK 29, Wynnewood, E [lodging] Kent's Motel, W [gas] Shell/dsl
64	OK 17A E, to Wynnewood, E [other] GW Exotic Animal Park
60	Ruppe Rd
59mm	**[RS] both lanes, full [handicapped] facilities, litter barrels, petwalk [phone] [picnic] RV dump**
55	OK 7, Davis, E [gas] Conoco, Phillips 66/A&W/dsl/24hr [other] to Chickasaw NRA, Treasure Valley Casino/Inn, W [other] Chickasaw Nation Welcome Ctr, to Arbuckle Ski Area
54.5mm	Honey Creek Pass
53mm	**weigh sta both lanes**
51	US 77, Turner Falls, E [lodging] Arbuckle Mtn Motel, Mtnview Inn (3mi) [other] RV camping, to Arbuckle Wilderness, W [gas] Sinclair/rv park [food] Cliff Steaks [other] Botanic Gardens
49mm	scenic turnout both lanes
47	US 77, Turner Falls Area
46mm	scenic turnout both lanes
42	OK 53 W, Springer, Comanche, W [gas] Exxon/dsl
40	OK 53 E, Gene Autry, E [gas] Shell/dsl/café/24hr [food] Broaster Rest [other] Gene Autry Museum (8mi)
33	OK 142, Ardmore, E [gas] Phillips 66/dsl [food] IHOP, Jimmy's Egg Cafe [lodging] Guest Inn, Holiday Inn, La Quinta, SpringHill Suites, Super 8 [other] regional park, tires, W [gas] FLYING J/Huddle House/dsl/LP/scales/24hr
32	12th St, Ardmore, E [gas] Conoco/dsl, Shell [food] Braum's, CiCi's Pizza, Cotton Patch Cafe, Quiznos, Santa Fe Steaks, Starbucks, Whataburger [lodging] Candlewood Suites, Holiday Inn, La Quinta [other] $Tree, Hyundai, Lowe's, PetCo, Ross, Toyota, W [gas] Loves/Godfather's/Subway/dsl/24hr/ @ [food] McDonald's [lodging] Microtel

INTERSTATE 35 Cont'd

ARDMORE

Exit #	Services
31b a	US 70 W, OK 199 E, Ardmore, **E** [gas] Shell/dsl, Valero/dsl [food] 2Frogs Grill, Applebee's, Burger King, Cattle Rustlers, Denny's, El Chico, El Tapatio, Interurban Grill, Jack-in-the-Box, KFC, Mazzio's, McDonald's, Papa John's, Pizza Hut, Prairie Kitchen [lodging] Best Western, Comfort Inn, Days Inn, Motel 6, Quality Inn, Rodeway Inn [other] AutoZone, Honda, O'Reilly Parts, **W** [gas] Conoco/dsl [other] Ardmore RV Park, Chrysler/Dodge/Jeep, Ford/Lincoln, Nissan, vet
29	US 70 E, Ardmore, **E** [other] to Lake Murray SP/lodge (8mi), **W** [other] Hidden Lake RV Park
24	OK 77 S, **E** [other] Red River Livestock Mkt, to Lake Murray SP
22.5mm	Hickory Creek
21	Oswalt Rd, **W** [gas] Valero/dsl [other] Ardmore Marietta RV Park, Lazy Man's Corner RV Park
15	OK 32, Marietta, **E** [gas] Valero/dsl/24hr [food] Carl's Jr, McDonald's, Pizza Hut, Robertson's Sandwiches, Sonic, Subway [other] [H], $General, to Lake Texoma SP, **W** [gas] Phillips 66 [food] Hickory House BBQ
5	OK 153, Thackerville, **W** [other] Red River Ranch RV Park, Shorty's Foods/gas
3.5mm	**Welcome Ctr nb, full [handicapped] facilities, litter barrels, petwalk [phone] [picnic] vending**
1	US 77 N, **E** [gas] Phillips 66/dsl [lodging] Best Western, The Inn [other] RV park, Winstar Casino, **W** [other] Red River RV Resort (3mi)
0mm	Oklahoma/Texas state line, Red River

INTERSTATE 40

SALLISAW

Exit #	Services
331mm	Oklahoma/Arkansas state line
330	OK 64D S (from eb), Ft Smith
329mm	**weigh sta wb**
325	US 64, Roland, Ft Smith, **N** [gas] Cherokee Trkstp/Valero/Subway/dsl/scales/24hr [food] Four Star Diner [lodging] Best Value Inn, Cherokee Inn [other] casino, **S** [gas] Pilot/Wendy's/dsl/scales/24hr, Shell/dsl/scales, Valero/dsl [food] Arby's, El Celaya Mexican, Mazzio's, McDonald's, Sonic, Taco Bell [lodging] Interstate Inn [other] $General, Marvin's Foods, O'Reilly Parts
321	OK 64b N, Muldrow, **N** [food] Sonic (1mi), **S** [gas] Shell/dsl [lodging] Best Value Inn [other] auto/dsl repair
316mm	**[rest stop] eb, full [handicapped] facilities, info, litter barrels, petwalk [phone] [picnic] vending**
313mm	**[rest stop] wb, full [handicapped] facilities, info, litter barrels, petwalk [phone] [picnic] RV dump, vending**
311	US 64, Sallisaw, **N** [gas] Ed's Truckstop/Phillips 66/diner/dsl, FL/dsl [food] Hardee's, KFC/Taco Bell, Pizza Hut, Simple Simon's Pizza [lodging] Motel 6, Sallisaw Inn [other] [H], $General, AutoZone, Brushy Lake SP (10mi), NAPA, O'Reilly Parts, Sequoya's Home (12mi)
308	US 59, Sallisaw, **N** [gas] Murphy USA/dsl, Phillips 66/dsl [food] A&W/LJ Silver, Arby's, Asian Star, Braum's, Geno's Pizza, Mazzio's, McDonald's, Roma's Italian, Sonic, Taco Pronto, Western Sizzlin [lodging] Blue Ribbon Inn, Days Inn, Economy Inn, Golden Spur Motel, Super 8 [other] [H], $General, $Tree, AT&T, casino, Verizon, Walmart/Subway, **S** [gas] Shell/dsl [food] Chen's Garden [other] Buick/Chevrolet/GMC, Chrysler/Dodge/Jeep, Ford, KOA, to Kerr Lake, truck/tire repair
303	Dwight Mission Rd

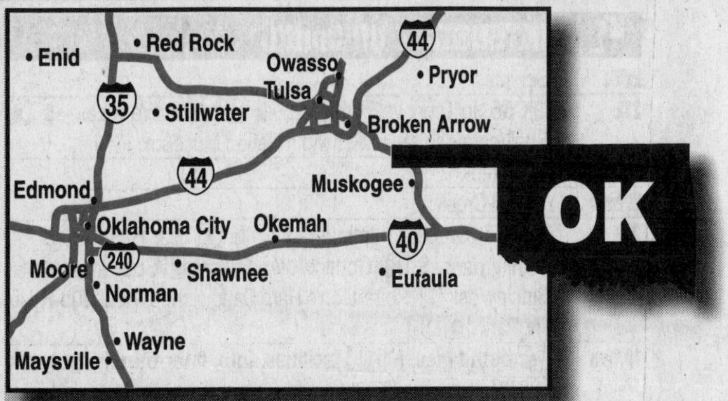

HENRYETTA

Exit #	Services
297	OK 82 N, Vian, **N** [gas] FL/dsl [food] Subway [other] Cherokee Landing SP (24 mi), IGA Foods, to Tenkiller Lake RA (12 mi), USPO, **S** [other] Sequoia NWR
291	OK 10 N, to Gore, **N** [other] Greenleaf SP (10mi), Tenkiller SP (21mi)
290mm	Arkansas River
287	OK 100 N, to Webbers Falls, **N** [gas] Loves/Burger King/Subway/dsl/24hr [food] Charlie's Chicken [other] Greenleaf SP, parts/tires/repair, Tenkiller SP
286	Muskogee Tpk, to Muskogee
284	Ross Rd
283mm	**parking area both lanes, litter barrels**
278	US 266, OK 2, Warner, **N** [gas] Conoco, Phillips 66/dsl, Sinclair/McDonald's/dsl [food] Cow Girls Drive Inn, Simon's Pizza, Sonic, Subway [lodging] Sleepy Traveler Motel [other] $General
270	Texanna Rd, to Porum Landing, **S** [gas] Sinclair
265	US 69 bus, Checotah, **N** [gas] Kwik'n Easy [food] Pizza Hut, Sonic, **S** [gas] Shell/dsl [lodging] Budget Inn [other] Chevrolet/Chrysler/Dodge/Jeep
264b a	US 69, to Eufaula, **1 mi N** [gas] FLYING J/Denny's/dsl/LP/scales/24hr, Casey's/dsl, Phillips 66/dsl/24hr [food] Charlie's Chicken, McDonald's, Simple Simon's Pizza [lodging] Best Value Inn [other] $General, AT&T, O'Reilly Parts, repair, TrueValue, Walmart/Subway
262	to US 266, Lotawatah Rd, **N** [gas] Sinclair
261mm	Lake Eufaula
259	OK 150, to Fountainhead Rd, **S** [gas] Shell/dsl [lodging] Lake Eufaula Inn [other] to Lake Eufaula SP
255	Pierce Rd, **N** [other] KOA
251mm	**rest area both lanes**
247	Tiger Mtn Rd, **S** [other] Quilt Barn/antiques
240b a	US 62 E, US 75 N, Henryetta, **N** [gas] Conoco/dsl, Loves/dsl, Phillips 66, Shell, Sinclair [food] Arby's, Braum's, Classic Diner, El Charro Mexican, KFC, Mazzio's, McDonald's, Sonic, Subway, Taco Bell [lodging] Best Value Inn, Colonial Motel, Days Inn, Economy Inn, Relax Inn [other] Chevrolet, Chrysler/Dodge/Jeep, Ford, O'Reilly Parts, tires/repair, Walmart, **S** [other] Indian Nation Tpk
237	US 62, US 75, Henryetta, **N** [gas] Shell/dsl [food] Cowboy Corner Rest. [lodging] Green Country Inn [other] [H], Henryetta RV Park (2mi), **S** [lodging] Super 8
231	US 75 S, to Weleetka, **N** [gas] Sinclair/dsl [food] Cowpoke's Cafe
227	Clearview Rd, **S** [other] casino
221	US 62, OK 27, Okemah, **N** [gas] Phillips 66/McDonald's, Valero/Subway/dsl/24hr [food] Mazzio's, Pepino's Mexican, Sonic [lodging] Days Inn [other] [H], $General, Chevrolet, Homeland Foods, NAPA, TrueValue, **S** [gas] Loves/Chester Fried/dsl/24hr, Shell/dsl [food] Kellogg's Rest [other] casino, truck repair
217	OK 48, to Bristow, Bearden, **S** [gas] gas/dsl
216mm	N Canadian River

INTERSTATE 40 Cont'd

SHAWNEE

Exit #	Services
212	OK 56, to Cromwell, Wewoka, N auto/tire repair, S Shell/cafe/dsl to Seminole Nation Museum
208mm	Gar Creek
202mm	Turkey Creek
200	US 377, OK 99, to Little, Prague, N Bar H Bar TC/Shell/dsl/RV park, S Conoco/dsl, Loves/Subway/dsl/24hr, Sinclair/dsl Robertson's Ham Sandwiches, Roundup Rest/RV Park H
197mm	both lanes, full facilities, info, litter barrels, petwalk
192	OK 9A, Earlsboro, S Valero/dsl/cafe
189mm	N Canadian River
186	OK 18, to Shawnee, N Phillips 66, Sinclair Denny's American Inn, Best Value Inn, Comfort Inn, Days Inn, La Quinta, Motel 6, Super 8, S Sinclair/DSL Carl's Jr, Golden Corral, Sonic, Subway, Van's BBQ Cadillac/Chevrolet/GMC, Chrysler/Dodge/Jeep, Ford, Homeland Foods
185	OK 3E, Shawnee Mall Dr, to Shawnee, N Murphy USA/dsl Buffalo Wild Wings, Chili's, KFC, Red Lobster, Santa Fe Steaks, Taco Bueno, Wendy's Holiday Inn Express $Tree, AT&T, Dillard's, JC Penney, Jo-Ann, Kohl's, mall, Radio Shack, Ross, Walgreens, Walmart/McDonald's, S Phillips 66/Circle K/Quiznos/dsl Braum's, Burger King, Cracker Barrel, Delta Cafe, IHOP, Mazzio's, McAlister's Deli, McDonald's, Popeye's, Rib Crib BBQ, Sonic, Starbucks, Subway, Taco Bell, Whataburger Hampton Inn CVS Drug, Kwik Kar, Lowe's, Staples, Verizon
181	US 177, US 270, to Tecumseh, S Shell/dsl Rosa's Mexican dsl repair
180mm	N Canadian River
178	OK 102 S, Dale, N Firelake/Subway/hotel/casino/dsl
176	OK 102 N, McLoud Rd, S Loves/Subway/dsl/24hr, Sinclair/dsl Curtis Watson Rest.
172	Newalla Rd, to Harrah
169	Peebly Rd
166	Choctaw Rd, to Woods, N Loves/McDonald's/Subway/dsl/scales/24hr KOA, S Pilot/Wendy's/dsl/scales/24hr Sonic to Lake Thunderbird SP (11mi)
165	I-240 W (from wb), to Dallas
162	Anderson Rd, N Leisure Time RV Ctr, LP
159b	Douglas Blvd, N OnCue/dsl, Shell/Circle K/dsl A&W/LJ Silver, Denny's, KFC, McDonald's, Pizza Hut, Sonic, Subway, Taco Bell, Whataburger Eastland Hills RV Park, S H, Tinker AFB
159a	Hruskocy Gate, N Chrysler/Dodge/Jeep, same as 157, U-Haul, S Tinker AFB, Gate 7
157c	Eaker Gate, Tinker AFB, same as 159
157b	Air Depot Blvd, N Shell/Circle K Cheddar's, Chick-fil-A, Chili's, Jack-in-the-Box, Logans Roadhouse, McAlister's Deli, Old Chicago Grill, Panda Express, Panera Bread, Qdoba Grill, Santa Fe Steaks, Starbucks, Steak&Shake AT&T, Best Buy, Dick's, Firestone/auto, GNC, JC Penney, Kohl's, Lowe's, Marshall's, Office Depot, Old Navy, Petsmart, Target, Verizon, S Tinker AFB, Gate 1
157a	SE 29th St, Midwest City, N PDQ/dsl, Shell/Circle K Best Western, Traveler's Inn O'Reilly Parts, S Ford, Sam's Club/gas
156b a	Sooner Rd, N Conoco/Circle K Primo's Rest., Waffle House Hampton Inn, Hawthorn Suites, Holiday Inn Express, La Quinta, Motel 6, Sheraton, Studio 6 Home Depot,

OKLAHOMA CITY

Exit #	Services
156b a	Continued Radio Shack, Walmart/Subway, S Best China, Buffalo Wild Wings, Carl's Jr, Garage Grill, Hungry Howie's, Ted's Mexican Candlewood Suites, Super 8 AT&T, Chevrolet/GMC, Discount Tire, Tires+, Toyota/Scion
155b	SE 15th St, Del City, N Valero/dsl Family$, Nissan
155a	Sunny Lane Rd, Del City, N Conoco/Subway/dsl Hyundai, U-Haul, S Braum's, Church's, Dunkin Donuts, Sonic $General
154	Reno Ave, Scott St, N Value Place Motel, S 7-11
152	(153 from wb)I-35 N, to Wichita
127	Eastern Ave (from eb), Okla City, N Checkers/Subway/dsl/scales/24hr, Petro/dsl/scales/rest./@, Shamrock Waffle House Bricktown Hotel, Econolodge, Motel 6 Lewis RV Ctr
151b c	I-35, S to Dallas, I-235 N, to downtown, st capitol
151a	Lincoln Blvd, N Conoco/Subway/Circle K/dsl Earl's Rib Palace, McDonald's, Sonic Hampton Inn, Homewood Suites, Residence Inn Bass Pro Shop, Bricktown Stadium
150c	Robinson Ave (from wb), OK City, N Spaghetti Whse, Zio's Italian Courtyard, Hilton Garden, Residence Inn U-Haul
150b	Harvey Ave (from eb), N Courtyard, Hilton Garden, Renaissance Hotel, Sheraton, downtown
150a	Shields Blvd (from eb), N to downtown
149b	Classen Blvd (from wb), same as 149a, to downtown
149a	Western Ave, Reno Ave, N Conoco/dsl, VP/Subway/dsl McDonald's, Sonic, Sweis Gyros, Taco Bell, S Shell/dsl
148c	Virginia Ave (from wb), to downtown
148b	Penn Ave (from eb), N Valero/dsl
148a	Agnew Ave, Villa Ave, N Phillips 66/dsl
147c	May Ave
147b a	I-44, E to Tulsa, W to Lawton
146	Portland Ave (from eb, no return), N Conoco/Subway/dsl
145	Meridian Ave, OK City, N Conoco/Circle K/dsl, Shell/Circle K/dsl Denny's, Earl's Ribs, Louie's Grill, McDonald's, On the Border, Portofinos Italian, Trapper's Rest. Best Western, Biltmore Hotel, Days Inn, Extended Stay America, Howard Johnson, Red Roof Inn, Residence Inn, Studio 6, Super 8, S Phillips 66/Circle K/dsl, Sinclair/dsl Arby's, Billy Sims BBQ, Burger King, Charleston Rest., Chili's, Cracker Barrel, Five Star Grill, Frosted Mug Grill, Golden Palace Chinese, IHOP, Mackie's Steaks, Rib Crib, San Marcos Mexican, Shorty Smalls Ribs, Sonic, Subway, Taco Bell, Taco Bueno, Waffle House, Whataburger, Zapata's, Zio's Italian AmericInn, Baymont Inn, Best Value Inn, Cambria Suites, Candlewood Suites, Comfort Suites, Country Inn&Suites, Courtyard, Embassy Suites, Fairfield Inn, Governors Suites, Hampton Inn, Hilton Garden, Holiday Inn, Holiday Inn Express, Hyatt Place, La Quinta, Meridian Inn, Motel 6, Oak Tree Inn, Quality Inn, Ramada, Sleep Inn, Staybridge Suites, TownePlace Suites, Wingate Inn, Wyndham Garden Celebration Sta., Shepler's
144	MacArthur Blvd, N Shell/Circle K/dsl Applebee's, Chick-fil-A, China One, Coldstone, Golden Corral, Jack-in-the-Box, Jimmy John's, KFC, Lin's Buffet, McDonald's, Olive Garden, Panda Express, Panera Bread, Qdoba, Sonic, Starbucks, Steak'n'Shake, Taco Bueno, Taco Cabana, Twin Peaks, TX Roadhouse SpringHill Suites $Tree, AT&T, GNC, Hobby Lobby, Office Depot, Petsmart, Radio Shack, Ross, Target, Verizon, Walmart/McDonald's, S Comfort Inn, Green Carpet Inn, Microtel, Travelers Inn Sam's Club/gas
143	Rockwell Ave, N Shell/dsl Buffalo Wild Wings, Jersey Mike's, Pizza Inn, Taco Bell Homewood Suites, Rodeway Inn Best Buy, Dick's, Discount Tire, Harley Davidson, Home

OK

INTERSTATE 40 Cont'd

143	Continued Depot, McClain's RV Ctr, Tires+, S Sands Motel/RV Park/ LP Rockwell RV Park
142	Council Rd, N Shell, Sinclair BJ's Rest, Braum's, McDonald's, Rib Shack, Ricky's Tacos, Subway, Whataburger Super 40 Inn dsl repair, S TA/Country Pride/dsl/ scales/24hr/ @ EconoLodge Council Rd RV Park, Ford/ Peterbilt, truckwash
140	Morgan Rd, N Pilot/McDonald's/dsl/24hr/ @, TA/ Popeye's/dsl/24hr/ @ Blue Beacon, S FLYING J /dsl/LP/scales/24hr, LNG, Loves/Subway/dsl/scales/24hr Ricky's Cafe, Sonic Speedco
139	Kilpatrick Tpk
138	OK 4, to Yukon, Mustang, N Catfish Cove Best Value Inn, Comfort Suites Chrysler/Dodge/Jeep, S Conoco/ Circle K/dsl Braum's, Burger King, Golden Chick, Hunan Express, IHOP, Interurban Grill, Mam Mo's Pizza, McDonald's,
138	Continued Sonic, Subway, Taco Bell Best Western, Hyatt Place, La Quinta Aamco, CVS Drug, Homeland Food/drug, Mustang Run RV Park, URGENT CARE
137	Cornwell Dr, Czech Hall Rd, N Homeland Food/drug
136	OK 92, Garth Brooks Blvd, Yukon, N Murphy USA/dsl, Shell/Circle K A&W/LJ Silver, Braum's, Chelino's Mexican, CiCi's Pizza, KFC, McDonald's, Primo's Italian, Subway, Taco Mayo, Waffle House, Wendy's, Wendy's, Yukon Buffet Hampton Inn $Tree, AutoZone, Big O Tire, GNC, Hancock Fabrics, Hastings Books, NAPA, Radio Shack, repair, Tuesday Morning, USPO, Verizon, Walgreens, Walmart, S Domino/dsl Alfredo's Mexican, Buffalo Wild Wings, Carino's Italian, Chick-fil-A, Chili's, Freddy's, Jersey Mike's, Jimmy's Egg Café, Logan's Roadhouse, Louie's Grill, McAlister's Deli, Pizza Hut, Quiznos, Rib Crib, Starbucks, Taco Bueno, Tokyo Moon, Top Shelf Grill Fairfield Inn, Holiday Inn Express H, Aldi, AT&T, Big Lots, Discount Tire, Ford, Hobby Lobby, Kohl's, Kwik Kar, Lowe's, PetsMart, Staples, Target, Tires+
132	Cimarron Rd, S
130	Banner Rd, N Shell/dsl/rest.
129mm	weigh st both lanes
125	US 81, to El Reno, N Conoco/dsl, Loves/Subway/dsl China King, Serapio's Mexican, Swadley's BBQ, Taco Mayo Economy Express, Ranger Motel, Super 8 $General, Buick/GMC, Chevrolet, Chrysler/Dodge/Jeep, Ford/Lincoln
123	Country Club Rd, to El Reno, N Murphy USA/dsl, Phillips 66, Shell/dsl, Valero/dsl Arby's, Braum's, Burger King, Greatwall Chinese, KFC, Little Caesar's, McDonald's, Pizza Hut, Subway, Taco Bell Motel 6 H, AT&T, AutoZone, Radio Shack, Walgreens, Walmart, S Denny's, MT Mikes Steaks Baymont Inn, Best Western/RV Park, Days Inn, Holiday Inn Express, Regency Motel
119	Lp 40, to El Reno
115	US 270, to Calumet
111mm	**picnic area eb, litter barrels**
108	US 281, to Geary, N Shell/Subway/dsl/24hr KOA/ Indian Trading Post, to Roman Nose SP, S Phillips 66/Pizza Inn/dsl
105mm	S Canadian River
104	Methodist Rd
101	US 281, OK 8, Hinton, N to Roman Nose SP, S Loves/Chester's/Godfather's/Sonic/dsl/scales Subway Hinton Travel Inn casino, Chevrolet, picnic area, to Red Rock Canyon SP

EL RENO

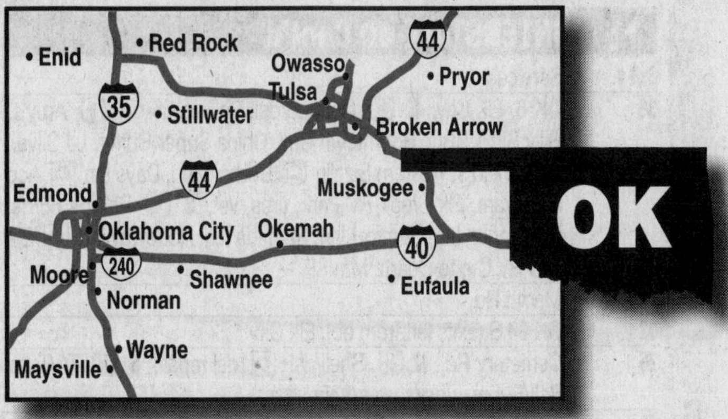

95	Bethel Rd
94.5mm	**picnic area wb, litter barrels**
88	OK 58, to Hydro, Carnegie
84	Airport Rd, N Phillips 66/dsl/CNG/scales/24hr Lucille's Roadhouse Holiday Inn Express, Travel Inn H, Buick/ Cadillac/Chevrolet/GMC, S Chrysler/Dodge/Jeep, Ford/ Lincoln, Stafford Aerospace Museum
82	E Main St, Weatherford, N Conoco/dsl, Phillips 66/dsl, Shell/dsl, Sinclair, Valero/dsl Arby's, BBQ Shed, Braum's, Carl's Jr, Double 6 Diner, El Patio Mexican, Hibachi Buffet, Jerry's Rest., KFC/Taco Bell, Little Caesars, Mark Rest., Mazzio's, McDonald's, Pizza Hut, Quiznos, Sonic, Subway, Taco Mayo, T-Bone Steaks, Vinicio's Mexican Best Western, Comfort Inn, Fairfield Inn, Scottish Inn H, $General, Ace Hardware, AT&T, GNC, O'Reilly Parts, to SW OSU, United Mkt, Walgreens, S Walmart/Subway
80a	(from eb), N Conoco/dsl Casa Soto Mexican
80	W Main St, Mountainview, Thomas, N Best Value Inn NAPAcare
71	Custer City Rd, N Loves/Subway/dsl/24hr Cherokee Trading Post/rest.
69	Lp 40 (from wb, no return), to Clinton
67.5mm	Washita River
66	US 183, Clinton, S Shell/dsl Buick/Chevrolet/GMC, Ford
65a	10th St, Neptune Dr, Clinton, N Branding Iron Rest., China King, Oakwood Steaks, Picante Grille, Pizza Hut Days Inn, Relax Inn, Super 8 United Foods, S Phillips 66/dsl EconoLodge, Holiday Inn Express Hargus RV Park
65	Gary Blvd, Clinton, N Conoco, Hutch/dsl, Shell/dsl Braum's, Del Rancho, Italian Villa, KFC/Taco Bell, LJ Silver, Mazzio's, McDonald's, MT Mike's, Palacios Mexican, Roberto's Mexican, Subway, Taco Mayo Hampton Inn, Motel 6, Ramada Inn, Tradewinds Inn H, $General, K-Mart, Rte 66 Museum, S Holiday Inn Express, La Quinta
62	Parkersburg Rd, S Hargus RV Ctr
61	Haggard Rd
57	Stafford Rd
53	OK 44, Foss, N to Foss SP, S Cenex/dsl
50	Clinton Lake Rd, N KOA/LP/dsl
47	Canute, S Shell/dsl Sunset Inn
41	OK 34 (exits left from eb), Elk City, N Hutch's/dsl, Loves /Subway/dsl Home Cooking Rest. Best Value Inn (3mi), Best Western (3mi), Elk City Motel, HomeTowne Inn, La Quinta, Motel 6, Sleep Inn, Super 8, Travel Inn H, Elk Run RV Park
40	E 7th St, Elk City, N Portobello Grill Holiday Inn Express Chrysler/Dodge/Jeep, S Hutch's/dsl/CNG Huddle House, Rib Crib Hampton Inn same as 41, Walmart/ McDonald's

WEATHERFORD

CLINTON

ELK CITY

OK

INTERSTATE 40 Cont'd

Exit #	Services
38	OK 6, Elk City, N Conoco/dsl, Phillips 66/dsl Arby's, Billy Sims BBQ, Boomtown Grill, China Super Buffet, LJ Silver, McDonald's, Western Sizzlin Bedford Inn, Days Inn Ace Hardware, Elk Creek RV Park, tires, vet, S Phillips 66/dsl Clarion Inn, Comfort Inn, Ramada Inn, Rodeway Inn Elk City RV Ctr, to Quartz Mtn SP
34	Merritt Rd
32	OK 34 S (exits left from eb), Elk City
26	Cemetery Rd, N Shell/dsl dsl repair, S TA/Taco Bell/Subway/dsl/scales/24hr/ @
25	Lp 40, Sayre, 1 mi N Hutch's/dsl/CNG Western Motel, Windgate Hotel H, $General, Bobcat Creek RV Park, Chevrolet/GMC, Ford
23	OK 152, Sayre, S Cenex/dsl
22.5mm	N Fork Red River
20	US 283, Sayre, N FLYING J/Denny's/dsl/LP/RV dump/scales/24hr McDonald's AmericInn to Washita Bfd Site (25mi), Truck lube, truckwash
Exit #	**Services**
14	Hext Rd
13.5mm	**check sta both lanes, litter barrels**
11	Lp 40, to Erick, Hext
10mm	**Welcome Ctr/ both lanes, full facilities, litter barrels, petwalk RV dump**
7	OK 30, Erick, N Premier Inn, S Loves/Subway/dsl/scales Simple Simon's Pizza Days Inn
5	Lp 40, Honeyfarm Rd
1	Texola, S gas/dsl/rest. RV camping
0mm	Oklahoma/Texas state line

INTERSTATE 44

Exit #	Services
329mm	Oklahoma/Missouri state line
321mm	Spring River
314mm	**Oklahoma Welcome Ctr wb, full facilities, info, restrooms**
313	OK 10, Miami, N Conoco, Loves/dsl, Phillips 66/dsl Donut Palace, Subway Best Value Inn, Deluxe Inn, EconoLodge, Hampton Inn, Holiday Inn Express, Legacy Inn, Microtel H, auto repair, casino, Miami RV Park, to NE OK A&M Coll, S Chrysler/Dodge/Jeep
312mm	Neosho River
302	US 59, US 69, Afton, S Buffalo Ranch/Subway/dsl Rte 66 Motel $General
289	US 60, Vinita, N Murphy USA/dsl Braum's, Clanton's Cafe, McDonald's, Pizza Hut, Sonic, Subway, Woodshed Deli Holiday Inn Express, Vinita Inn H, $General, Ace Hardware, Chevrolet, O'Reilly Parts, Radio Shack, st patrol, USPO, Walmart
288mm	**service plaza both lanes,** Kum&Go/dsl McDonald's, Subway
286mm	**toll plaza**
283	US 69, Big Cabin, N Big Cabin/Subway/dsl/scales/24hr/ @ Super 8 Cabin RV Park, trk repair
269	OK 28 (from eb, no re-entry), to Adair, Chelsea
255	OK 20, to Pryor, Claremore, 0-2 mi N Kum&Go/dsl/e-85, Murphy USA/dsl, QT/dsl Carl's Jr Hampton Inn, Holiday Inn Express, Super 8, Travel Inn, Will Rogers Inn H, $General, museum, to Rogers U, Walgreens, Walmart, Will Rogers Memorial
248	to OK 266, Port of Catoosa, N QT/dsl Comfort Inn (4mi), Hampton Inn (4mi), Microtel (2mi), Will Rogers Inn (4mi) Dave's RV Ctr
244mm	Kerr-McClellan Navigation System
241mm	**Will Rogers Tpk begins eb, ends wb**
241	OK 66 E, to Catoosa
240b	US 412 E, Choteau
240a	OK 167 N, 193rd E Ave, N IHOP, KFC/Taco Bell, McDonald's, Panda Express, Taco Bueno, Waffle House, Wendy's Cherokee Inn/Casino, Hampton Inn, Hardrock Hotel/Casino, La Quinta AT&T, Petco, Ross, Walgreens, Walmart, S QT Mazzio's, Port City Diner, Sonic, Subway Holiday Inn Express $General, O'Reilly Parts, tires/repair
238	161st E Ave, N Sinclair/rest./dsl/scales/24hr truckwash, **S Cherokee Nation Welcome Ctr** QT/dsl/scales/24hr Arby's, Burger King Microtel truckwash
236b	I-244 W, to downtown Tulsa, N
236a	129th E Ave, N FLYING J/Denny's/dsl/LP/24hr Southern Tire Mart, S McDonald's
235	E 11th St, Tulsa, N Mazzio's, Sonic, Subway Economy Inn, Executive Inn, Knights Inn, Super 8 $General, O'Reilly Parts, Walgreens, S QT Braum's, Taco Bueno Oak Tree Inn Whse Mkt
234b	same as 235
234a	US 169, N to Owasso, S to Broken Arrow, to
233	E 21st St, N Golden Corral Family$, S El Chico Comfort Suites Dean's RV Ctr, K-Mart
231	US 64, OK 51, to Muskogee, E 31st St, Memorial Dr, N QT/dsl Sonic, Speedy Gonzales Mexican, Subway Delux Inn, Motel 6, Ramada Inn, Tulsa Inn Walgreens, S Shell/Subway Cracker Barrel, IHOP, Jimmy's Egg, McDonald's, Pizza Hut, Ruby Tuesday, Village Inn Best Value Inn, Best Western, Comfort Suites, Country Inn Suites, Courtyard, EconoLodge, Embassy Suites, Extended Stay America, Fairfield Inn, Hampton Inn, Holiday Inn Express, Quality Inn, Sleep Inn, Super 8 Cavender's Boots, Chevrolet, Harley-Davidson, Nissan
230	E 41st St, Sheridan Rd, N Shell Carl's Jr, Chick-fil-A, Chipotle, Desi Wok, Flame Broiler, Jimmy John's, On-the-Border, Panera Bread, Schlotzsky's, Starbucks, Subway, TGIFriday's, Top That! Pizza, Whataburger AT&T, Barnes&Noble, Cartec Automotive, Dillard's, JC Penney, Jo-Ann Fabrics, Michael's, Old Navy, Petco, Petsmart, Reasor's Foods, Ross, Verizon, S Buffalo Wild Wings, Carino's Italian La Quinta Batteries+Bulbs, Best Buy, Home Depot
229	Yale Ave, Tulsa, N Shell El Chico, McDonald's, Subway Firestone/auto, JC Penney, Macy's, mall, PetCo, S Kum&Go/dsl/e85, Phillips 66/dsl, QT Andy's Custard, Applebee's, Arby's, Braum's, Bravo's Grill, Cane's, Delta Cafe, Jack-in-the-Box, Outback Steaks, Qdoba, Red Lobster, Smoothie King, Sonic, Taco Bell, Village Inn Baymont Inn, Hilton Garden, Holiday Inn Express, Knights Inn, Red Roof Inn H, Kia, vet
228	Harvard Ave, Tulsa, N QT/dsl El Tequila Mexican, McDonald's, NYC Pizza Tradewinds Motel, S Express A&W/LJ Silver, Chili's, Freckle's Frozen Custard, Jamil's Rest, Mario's Pizza, Papa John's, Starbucks, Subway Wingate Inn $Tree, Hobby Lobby, Reasor's Mkt, SteinMart
227	Lewis Ave, Tulsa, S Goldie's Grill Walgreens
226b	Peoria Ave, Tulsa, N Kum&Go/dsl, QT/dsl Arby's, Burger St., Charleston's Rest., China Wok, CiCi's, Egg Roll Express, Jimmy's Egg, KFC, Little Caesars, Mazzio's, Pizza Hut, Ron's Burgers/Chili, Sonic, Subway, Super Buffet, Taco Bell, Taco

E INTERSTATE 44 Cont'd

TULSA

226b	Continued Bueno Peoria Inn Harley-Davidson, O'Reilly Parts, Reasor's Mkt, Robertson Tire, Walmart Mkt, Whole Foods Mkt, S Braum's, Corner Cafe, Golden Palace, Golden Palace $General, AutoZone, Family$, Walgreens
226a	Riverside Dr
225mm	Arkansas River
225	Elwood Ave, N Chevrolet, Ford, S Budget Inn
224b a	US 75, to Okmulgee, Bartlesville, N QT/dsl Arnold's Burgers, KFC, Mazzio's, Sonic $General, vet, Whse Mkt, S Royal Inn Hurley RV Ctr
223c	33rd W Ave, Tulsa, N Braum's, Domino's, S Conoco Rib Crib BBQ
223b	51st St (from wb)
223a	I-244 E, to Tulsa, downtown
222c	(from wb), S Value Inn
222b	55th Place, N Capri Motel, Crystal Motel, S Best Value Inn, Economy Inn
222a	49th W Ave, Tulsa, N Carl's Jr, Kelly's Country Cooking, Monterey Mexican, Subway Gateway Motel, Interstate Inn, Motel 6 $General, BigLots, Mack Trucks, S QT/Kitchens/dsl/scales/24hr Arby's, McDonald's, Taco Bueno, Waffle House Comfort Inn, Super 8 Buick/GMC, Freightliner, Kenworth
221a	57th W Ave, (from wb), S Buick/GMC
221mm	Turner Tkp begins wb, ends eb
218	Creek Tpk E (from eb)
215	OK 97, to Sand Sprgs, Sapulpa, S Kum&Go/dsl/e85 Freddie's Rest., Subway, Three Amigos Super 8 H, Hunter RV Ctr, Route 66 RV Park
211	OK 33, to Kellyville, Drumright, S Heyburn Lake SP
207mm	**service plaza wb** Phillips 66/dsl
196	OK 48, Bristow, S Kenny's/dsl, Phillips 66/dsl Mazzio's, McDonald's, Pizza Hut, Sonic, Steak'nEgg Rest, Taco Mayo Carolyn Inn $General, $Tree, Ford, O'Reilly Parts, Walmart
182mm	**toll plaza**
179	OK 99, to Drumright, Stroud, N Best Western/rest., S Kids/dsl, Phillips 66/Subway/dsl 5Star BBQ, Cozumel Mexican, Mazzio's, McDonald's, Sonic Skyliner Motel, Sooner Motel H, auto/tire repair, USPO
178mm	**Hoback Plaza both lanes (exits left)** Phillips 66/dsl McDonald's
167mm	**service plaza (from eb)** S Phillips 66/dsl
166	OK 18, to Cushing, Chandler, S Phillips 66/dsl B's Rest., Sonic EconoLodge, Lincoln Motel Chandler Tire, Chevrolet/GMC, Ford
158	OK 66, to Wellston, N Kum&Go/Subway/dsl/24hr $General
146	Luther-Jones (from eb, no return)
138d	to Memorial Rd, to Enterprise Square
138a	I-35, I-44 E to Tulsa, Turner Tpk

I-44 and I-35 run together 8 mi, see I-35 exits 137-134.

OKLAHOMA CITY

130	I-35 S, to Dallas, access to services on I-35 S
129	MLK Ave, Remington Park, N Park Hill Inn Cowboy Museum, S McDonald's, Sonic, Subway Family$
128b	Kelley Ave, OK City, N Conoco, VP/Subway/dsl Gabriella's Italian
128a	Lincoln Blvd, S Lincoln Mart/dsl Lincoln Inn Express, Oxford Inn st capitol
127	I-235 S, US 77, City Ctr, Broadway St, **N on 63rd St** Conoco/Circle K, Shell/Circle K Best Western, Wyndham Garden URGENT CARE
126	Western Ave, S Sleep Inn

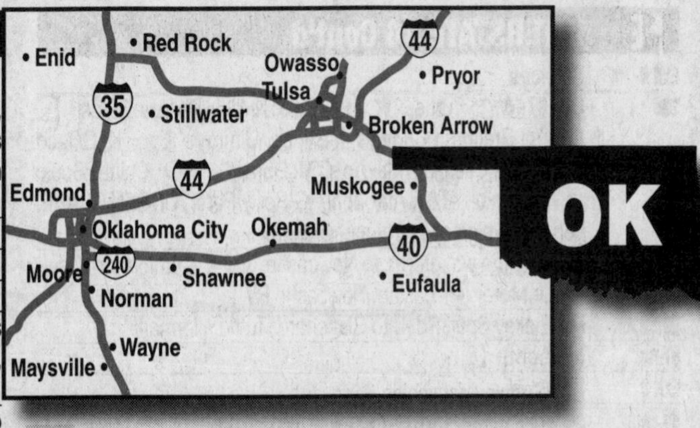

125c	NW Expressway (exits left from sb)
125	Classen Blvd, (exits left from wb), OK City, N Cheesecake Factory, Chili's, Freebirds Burrito, Jamba Juice, Milagro Mexican, Olive Garden, Pei Wei, Smashburger, Subway, Whiskey Cake Kitchen AT&T, Dillard's, JC Penney, Macy's, Old Navy, Ross, Verizon, Walmart/McDonald's, S IHOP, McDonald's Courtyard, Hyatt Place, Travelodge
125a	OK 3A, Penn Ave, to NW Expswy, N VP Express, S Shell/Circle K Braum's Habana Inn auto/tire repair, Family$
124	N May, N Shell/Circle K/Subway San Marco's Mexican Days Inn, Motel 6, Super 8 O'Reilly Parts, Sam's Club/dsl, S Valero Dunkin Donuts, Jersey Mike's, Starbucks, Wendy's Aamco, Advance Parts, Family$, Ford, Lowe's
123b	OK 66 W, NW 39th, to Warr Acres, N 7-11, Shell, Valero/McDonald's/dsl Braum's, Carl's Jr, Jimmy's Egg, Sonic Carlyle Motel, Hospitality Inn Family$, U-Haul
123a	NW 36th St, S Value Place Hotel
122	NW 23rd St, N 7-11, Conoco/dsl Church's, EggRoll King Tires+, S Conoco Arby's, Sonic Family$
121b a	NW 10th St, N Shell, S 7-11, Sinclair Subway $General, antiques, fairgrounds, Family$, Whittaker's Foods
120b a	I-40, W to Amarillo, E to Ft Smith
119	SW 15th St
118	OK 152 W, SW 29th St, OK City, E 7-11, Shamrock A&W/LJ Silver, Burger King, China Panda, CiCi's Pizza, KFC/Taco Bell, McDonald's, Pizza Hut, Sonic, Subway, Taco Bueno $General, $Tree, Advance Parts, AT&T, AutoZone, Buy-4-Less Foods, city park, O'Reilly Parts, Walgreens, W Alon/dsl city park, transmissions, U-Haul/LP
117	SW 44th St, W auto repair
116b	Airport Rd (exits left from nb), W
116a	SW 59th St, E Conoco/Circle K Pizza Inn, Subway, Taco Mayo Family$, W Will Rogers Airport
115	I-240 E, US 62 E, to Ft Smith
114	SW 74th St, OK City, E Nova, Valero/dsl Braum's, Burger King, Perry's Rest. Cambridge Inn, Knights Inn $General
113	SW 89th St, E 7-11, Love's/Subway/dsl, OG, Valero/dsl Sonic H, CVS Drug
112	SW 104th St, E Valero
111	SW 119th St, E Little Caesar's, Sonic
110	OK 37 E, to Moore, E H
109	SW 149th St, E JR's Grill
108mm	S Canadian River

[gas] = gas [food] = food [lodging] = lodging [other] = other [rest stop] = rest stop

INTERSTATE 44 Cont'd

CHICKASHA

Exit #	Services
108	OK 37 W, to Tuttle, W [gas] Conoco/dsl, Phillips 66/dsl [food] Arby's, Braum's, Carlito's Mexican, Jimmy's Egg, KFC/Taco Bell, Little Caesars, Mazzio's, McDonald's, New China, Sonic [other] $General, AT&T, AutoZone, O'Reilly Parts, URGENT CARE, Verizon, Walgreens, Walmart/Subway
107	US 62 S (no wb return), to Newcastle, E [lodging] Comfort Inn, Newcastle Motel [other] casino, Newcastle RV
99	H E Bailey Spur, Rd 4, to Blanchard, Tuttle, Norman
97mm	**toll booth** [icon]
Exit #	Services
85.5mm	**service plaza, both lanes exit left,** [gas] Phillips 66/dsl [food] McDonald's
83	US 62, Chickasha, W [gas] Jay's/dsl, Valero/dsl [other] Southern Plains Indian Museum
80	US 81, Chickasha, E [gas] Phillips 66/Circle K/dsl, Shell/dsl [food] Eduardo's Mexican, Jake's Rib, La Fiesta Mexican, Western Sizzlin [lodging] Best Value Inn, Hampton Inn, Holiday Inn Express, Maverick Inn, Super 8 [other] Buick/GMC, Cadillac/Chevrolet, Chrysler/Dodge/Jeep, vet, W [gas] Love's/dsl, Murphy USA/dsl, Valero [food] Arby's, Braum's, Chicken Express, China Dream, China Moon, Domino's, KFC, LJ Silver, Mazzio's Pizza, McDonald's, Napoli's Rest., New China, Pizza Hut, Sakura Japanese, Sonic, Subway, Taco Bell, Taco Mayo [lodging] Quality Inn, Ranch House Motel [other] [H], $General, Ace Hardware, AT&T, AutoZone, Chickasha RV Park, CVS Drug, Ford, Griffith's Repair, O'Reilly Parts, Ralph&Son's Tires/repair, Save-A-Lot Foods, Staples, Verizon, Walgreens, Walmart/Subway
78mm	**toll plaza** [icon]
62	to Cyril (from wb)
53	US 277, Elgin, Lake Ellsworth, E [gas] Shamrock, Valero/McDonald's/dsl [food] Billy Sim's BBQ, China Garden, Sonic, Subway [other] $General, Family$, tires
46	US 62 E, US 277, US 281, to Elgin, Apache, Comanche Tribe, last free exit eb
45	OK 49, to Medicine Park, W [gas] Love's/Subway/dsl/24hr [food] Burger King, Sonic [other] $General, Wichita NWR
41	to Ft Sill, Key Gate, W [other] Ft Sill Museum
40c	Gate 2, to Ft Sill
40a	to Cache
39	US 62 W, to Cache, E [gas] Alon/dsl, W [lodging] Knights Inn
39b	US 281 (from sb), [other] same as 39a
39a	US 281, Cache Rd (exits left from nb), Lawton, E [gas] Alon/dsl, **1-3 mi W** [gas] Shamrock/dsl, Valero/dsl [food] Subway [lodging] Knights Inn [other] $General
38	Cache Rd (exits left from nb)
37	Gore Blvd, Lawton, E [gas] Apache/dsl [food] Braum's, Los Tres Amigos, Marco's Pizza, Sonic, Taco Mayo [lodging] Apache Casino/Hotel, Best Western [other] casino, URGENT CARE, USPO, W [food] Cracker Barrel, Mike's Grille [lodging] Comfort Suites, Fairfield Inn, Holiday Inn Express, Homewood Suites, Sleep Inn, SpringHill Suites [other] Chrysler/Dodge/Jeep, Harley-Davidson
36a	OK 7, Lee Blvd, Lawton, E [gas] Phillips 66/dsl, W [gas] Alon/dsl/repair, Barefoot/dsl, Shamrock/dsl, WMS/dsl [food] Big Chef Rest., Braum's, Burger King, KFC/Taco Bell, Leo&Ken's Rest., McDonald's, Salas Mexican, Sonic [lodging] Motel 6 [other] [H], $General, Advance Parts, [icon], CVS Drug, vet, Walgreens
33	US 281, 11th St, Lawton, W [other] [icon]
30	OK 36 (last free exit sb), Geronimo
20.5mm	**Elmer Graham Plaza (both lanes exit left),** [gas] Phillips 66/dsl [food] McDonald's [other] info
20	OK 5, to Walters
19.5mm	**toll plaza**
5	US 277 N, US 281, Randlett, last free exit nb
1	OK 36, to Grandfield, E [gas] Comanche Nation TP/dsl, W [other] casino
0mm	Oklahoma/Texas state line, Red River

LAWTON

OK

INTERSTATE 240 (OKLAHOMA CITY)

OKLAHOMA CITY

Exit #	Services
16mm	**I-240 begins/ends on I-40.**
14	Anderson Rd, S [gas] Conoco/dsl
11b a	Douglas Blvd, N [other] Tinker AFB
9	Air Depot Blvd
8	OK 77, Sooner Rd, N [gas] Phillips 66/dsl/CNG/e85 [food] Sonic [other] URGENT CARE, S [gas] Phillips 66/Popeye's/dsl, Valero/McDonald's/dsl [other] [H]
7	Sunnylane Ave, S [gas] Valero/Subway/dsl [lodging] Value Place Motel
6	Bryant Ave
5	S Eastern Ave
4c	Pole Rd, N [food] Burger King, Subway, TX Roadhouse [lodging] Fairfield Inn, Magnuson Hotel, Residence Inn
4b a	I-35, N to OK City, S to Dallas, US 77 S, US 62/77 N
3b	S Shields, N [gas] Valero/dsl [food] Braum's [other] Chrysler/Dodge/Jeep, Home Depot, S [other] Discount Tire, Nissan, Subaru
3a	S Santa Fe, N [other] Kia, S [gas] Murphy USA/dsl [food] Chili's, IHOP, Jersey Mike's, Panda Express [other] Lowe's, Staples, Walmart/McDonald's
2b	S Walker Ave, N [gas] 7-11, Shell/Circle K [food] Johnnie's Broiler, Rib Crib, S [food] Burger Joint, Carino's, ChuckeCheese, City Bites, Jimmy's Egg Grill, On-the-Border [lodging] Holiday Inn Express [other] PepBoys
2a	S Western Ave, N [gas] 7-11, Conoco [food] Braum's, Burger King, CiCi's Pizza, House of Szechwan, Taste of China [other] $General, Advance Parts, Hyundai, Tires+, vet, S [gas] 7-11, Valero/dsl [food] A&W/LJ Silver, Chick-fil-A, Garage Burgers, Grandy's, Hibachi Buffet, Jimmy John's, KFC, McDonald's, Popeye's, Red Lobster [lodging] Best Western, Comfort Inn, Hampton Inn, Home 2 Suites, Quality Inn [other] Chevrolet, Honda, Office Depot
1c	S Penn Ave, N [gas] Conoco/dsl [food] Cane's, Carl's Jr, Charleston's Rest., Denny's, Golden Corral, Hooters, Old Chicago Pizza, Olive Garden, Outback Steaks, Pioneer Pies, SaltGrass Steaks, Schlotsky's [other] AT&T, Best Buy, BigLots, GNC, Green Acres Mkt, Hobby Lobby, Marshall's, Michaels, Old Navy, Petsmart, Radio Shack, Ross, Verizon, S [gas] Shell/Circle K [food] Hunan Buffet, Joe's Crabshack, Mazzio's, Papa John's, Starbucks, Subway, Taco Bueno, Western Sizzlin [other] $Tree, Hancock Fabrics, URGENT CARE
1b	S May Ave, N [gas] 7-11/gas [food] Abel's Mexican, Jack-in-the-Box, New Mandarin, Taco Bell, Waffle House [other] O'Reilly Parts, S [gas] Nova, Valero/dsl [food] Braum's, Burger King, Perry's Rest. [lodging] Cambridge Inn, Knights Inn [other] $General
1a	I-44, US 62, **I-240 begins ends on I-44.**

OREGON

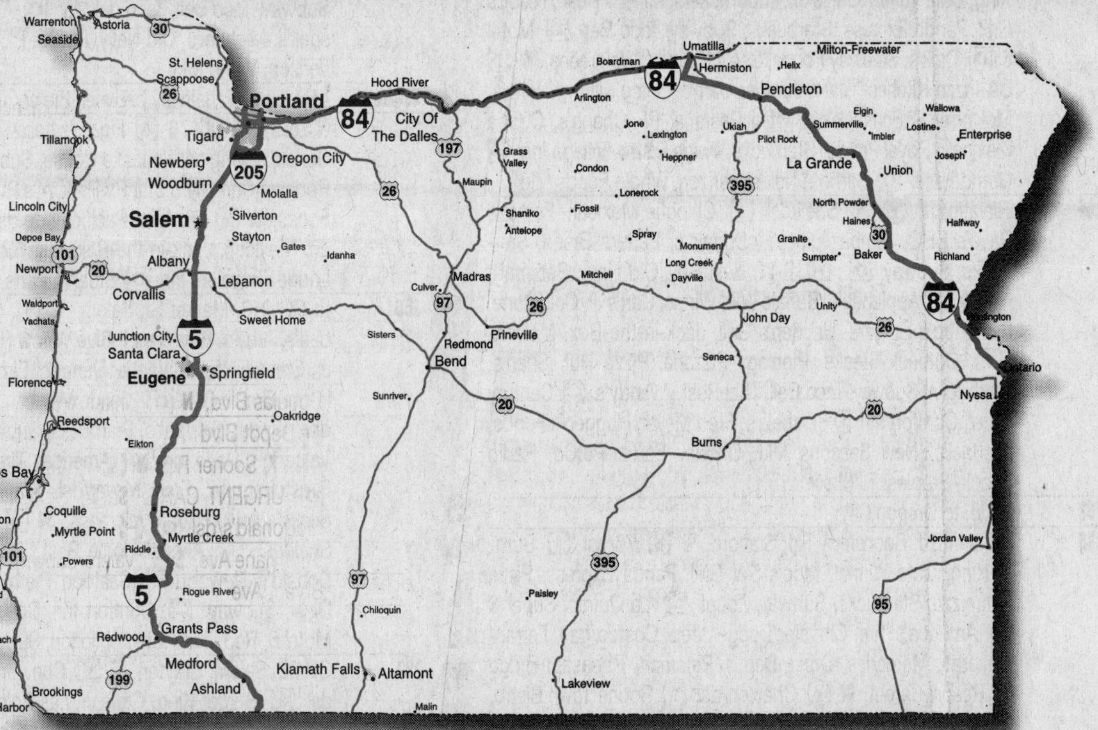

INTERSTATE 5

Exit #	Services
308.5mm	Oregon/Washington state line, Columbia River
308	Jansen Beach Dr, E Chevron/dsl Burger King, Hooters, Starbucks, Taco Bell Oxford Suites, Red Lion Safeway, W BJ's Rest., Bradley's Grill, CJ's Deli, Denny's, Jersey Mike's, Jimmy John's, McDonald's, Panera Bread, Stanford's Rest., Starbucks, Subway Best Buy, Burlington Coats, GNC, Home Depot, Jansen Beach RV Park, Michael's, Old Navy, PetCo, Ross, Staples, Target, TJ Maxx, Verizon
307	OR 99E S, MLK Blvd, Union Ave, Marine Dr (sb only), E 76/dsl, Jubitz Trvl Ctr/rest/dsl/@ Pizza Mia, Portland Cascade Grill, Subway Courtyard, Fairfield Inn, Portlander Inn, Residence Inn Blue Beacon, truck repair, W Expo Ctr
306b	Interstate Ave, Delta Park, E Arco Burger King, Burrito House, Elmer's, Mars Meadows Chinese, Shari's Best Western, Days Inn, Motel 6 $Tree, Baxter Parts, Dick's, Lowe's, Portland Meadows, vet, Walmart
306a	Columbia (from nb), same as 306b
305b a	US 30, Lombard St (from nb, no return), E Little Caesar's Knecht's Parts, W Astro/dsl, Shell/dsl Panda Express, Subway, Wendy's Fred Meyer
304	Rosa Parks Way, W 76/dsl, Arco Nite Hawk Cafe Viking Motel U of Portland
303	Alberta St, Swan Island, E H, W Subway, Taco Bell Monticello Motel, Westerner Motel CarQuest
302b	I-405, US 30 W, W to ocean beaches
302a	Rose Qtr, City Ctr, E 76/Circle K/dsl, Shell/dsl Bellagio's Pizza, Burger King, Chipotle Mexican, Jersey Mike's, McDonald's, Muchas Gracias, Qdoba Mexican, Starbucks, Wendy's Courtyard, Crowne Plaza, Shiloh Inn H, 7-11, Kia, Radio Shack, Schwab Tire, Toyota/Scion, Verizon, Walgreens, W coliseum
301	I-84 E, US 30 E, services E off I-84 exits
300	US 26 E (from sb), Milwaukie Ave, W Hilton, Marriott
299b	I-405, US 26 W, to city ctr
299a	US 26 E, OR 43 (from nb), City Ctr, to Lake Oswego
298	Corbett Ave
297	Terwilliger Blvd, W Baja Fresh, KFC, La Costita, Starbucks H, Fred Meyer, to Lewis and Clark Coll.
296b	Multnomah Blvd (from sb), W Safeway, same as 296a
296a	(from sb), Barbur, W 76/dsl, Chevron/dsl Bellagio's Pizza, Frack Burger, Subway Aladdin Inn, Budget Lodge, Capitol Hill Motel 7-11, AT&T, Schwab Tire
295	Capitol Hwy (from sb), Taylors Ferry Rd (from nb), E Shell/dsl McDonald's, Sho Japanese, Starbucks, Thai Orchid Hospitality Inn, W Taco Time, Wendy's Walgreens
294	Barbur Blvd, OR 99W, to Tigard, E Comfort Suites, W 76, Chevron, Shell Arby's, Baja Fresh, Banning's Rest., Baskin-Robbins, Burger King, Buster's BBQ, Carl's Jr, Chang's Mongolian Grill, Gators Eatery, Jimmy John's, Mazatlan Mexican, McDonald's, Starbucks, Subway, Taco Bell Quality Inn, Regency Inn $Tree, Americas Tire, auto repair, Baxter Parts, Costco, Fred Meyer, JoAnn Fabrics, NAPA, PetCo, Petsmart, Radio Shack, Schwab Tire, transmissions, U-Haul, vet, Walmart/Subway, Winco Foods
293	Haines St, W Ford/Lincoln
292	OR 217, Kruse Way, Lake Oswego, E Shell/dsl Applebee's, Chevy's Mexican, Chipotle, Olive Garden, Oswego Grill, Potbelly, Stanford's Rest., Starbucks Crowne Plaza, Fairfield Inn, Hilton Garden, Phoenix Inn, Residence Inn LDS Temple, W Extended Stay America Lowe's
291	Carman Dr, Carman Dr, W 76/dsl, Chevron Burgerville, Domino's, El Sol De Mexico, Starbucks, Subway, Sweet Tomatoes Courtyard, Holiday Inn Express Home Depot, Office Depot
290	Lower Boonsferry Rd, Lake Oswego, E Chevron/dsl, Space Age/dsl/LP Arby's, Baja Fresh, Baskin-Robbins, Burger

PORTLAND

OR

INTERSTATE 5 Cont'd

Exit	Services
290	Continued King, Cafe Yumm, Carl's Jr., Fuddruckers, Miller's Rest., Nicoli's Grill, Panda Express, Starbucks, Subway, Taco Bell Motel 6 Dick's, Safeway Foods, See's Kitchen, Walgreens, W CA Pizza Kitchen, Claim Jumper, Jamba Juice, Jimmy John's, McCormick&Schmick's, Pastini Pastaria, PF Chang's, Qdoba Mexican, Royal Panda, Starbucks, Twigs Bistro, Village Inn Grand Hotel Barnes&Noble, Verizon, Whole Foods Mkt
289	Tualatin, E 76, Shell/dsl Chipotle Mexican, Famous Dave's BBQ, Jamba Juice, McDonald's, Panera Bread, Starbucks, Subway H, 7-11, Best Buy, Old Navy, Petsmart, vet, W Applebee's, Buffalo Wild Wings, Carl's Jr, Coldstone, Dickie Jo's Burgers, Hayden's Grill, Jack-in-the-Box, McDonald's, Outback Steaks, Pieology Pizzaria, Pizza Hut, Shari's, Starbucks, Subway, Taco Bell, Thai Rest., Wendy's Century Hotel, Comfort Inn Cabela's, Fred Meyer, Haggen's Foods, Michael's, New Seasons Mkt, O'Reilly Parts, PetCo, Radio Shack, Staples, TJ Maxx
288	I-205, to Oregon City
286	Elligsen Rd, Boonsferry Rd, Stafford, E 76/dsl Burger King, Cafe Yumm!, Moe's SW Grill, Panda Express, Pizza Schmizza, Starbucks, Subway, Zoup! La Quinta, Super 8 America's Tire, Chrysler/Dodge/Jeep, Costco/gas, Ferrari/Maserati, Mercedes, Office Depot, Petsmart, Pheasant Ridge RV Resort, Target, W Chevron/dsl Boone Town Bistro, Carl's Jr Holiday Inn/rest. Audi, Camping World RV Ctr, Chevrolet, Nissan, Toyota/Scion
283	Wilsonville, E 76 Abella Italian, Arby's, Bellagio's Pizza, Denny's, Jamba Juice, Jimmy John's, Juan Colorado, McDonald's, Papa Murphy's, Red Robin, Shari's, Starbucks, Subway, Taco Bell, Thai Rest., Wanker's Café, Wendy's, Wong's Chinese GuestHouse Inn, Quality Inn, SnoozInn $Tree, Ace Hardware, AT&T, Fry's Electronics, funpark, GNC, Honda, Lamb's Mkt, NAPA, Rite Aid, Schwab Tire, URGENT CARE, USPO, vet, W Fred Meyer/dsl Baskin-Robbins, Biscuits Cafe, Boone's Jct Pizza, Burger King, Domino's, Hunan Kitchen, Little Caesar's, McMenamin's Rest., Oswego Grill, Perfect Pizza, Qdoba, RAM Rest., Sonic, Starbucks, Subway, Wow Burger Best Western Wilsonville 7-11, Albertson's, auto repair, Fred Meyer/dsl, O'Reilly Parts, Verizon, Walgreens
282.5mm	Willamette River
282	Charbonneau District, E Langdon Farms Rest. Langdon Farms Golf
281.5mm	**both lanes, full facilities, info, litter barrels, petwalk coffee, vending**
278	Donald, E 76/dsl/LP Aurora Acres RV Park, W FLYING J/Subway/dsl/scales/24hr, TA/Country Pride/Popeye's/dsl/scales/24hr/@ NAPA Truck Parts, SpeedCo Lube, to Champoeg SP, truckwash
274mm	**weigh sta both lanes**
271	OR 214, Woodburn, E Arco/dsl, Chevron Burger King, Denny's, DQ, KFC, McDonald's/playplace, Subway, Taco Bell, Yun Wah Chinese Best Western, Super 8 76/repair, vet, Walgreens, Walmart/McDonald's, Yun Wah Chinese, W Shell/dsl Arby's, Elmer's, Jack-in-the-Box, Jamba Juice, Starbucks La Quinta Ford, Woodburn Outlets/famous brands, Woodburn RV Park
263	Brooks, Gervais, E Chevron/dsl Brooks Mkt/deli, W Pilot/Subway/Taco Bell/dsl/LP/scales/24hr Chalet Rest. Antique Powerland Museum, Freightliner, Willamette Mission SP (4mi)
260b a	OR 99E, Chemawa Rd, Keizer, **2 mi** E Silver Spur RV Park, W Burger King, Jamba Juice, McDonald's, Outback Steaks, Panda Express, Panera Bread, RoundTable Pizza, Starbucks, Subway, Taco Bell, Taco del Mar AT&T, GNC, Lowe's, Marshall's, Michael's, Old Navy, PetCo, REI, Ross, Staples, Target, Verizon, World Mkt
259mm	45th parallel, halfway between the equator and N Pole
258	N Salem, E 76 Figaro's Italian, Guesthouse Rest., McDonald's, Original Pancake House, Subway Best Western, Rodeway Inn 5 Star RV Park, Al's RV Ctr, Hwy RV Ctr, Roth's Foods, W 76, Arco, Pacific Pride/dsl, Shell/dsl Don Pedro Mexican, Jack-in-the-Box, LumYuen Chinese Budget Lodge, Travelers Inn Stuart's Parts, to st capitol
256	to OR 213, Market St, Salem, E 5 Guys Burgers, Applebee's, Arby's, Baja Fresh, Blue Willow Rest., Burger King, Carl's Jr, China Buffet, Chipotle, Denny's, Elmer's, Izzy's Rest., Jack-in-the-Box, KFC, La Hacienda Mexican, McDonald's, Olive Garden, Sizzler, Skipper's, Starbucks, Subway, Taco Bell Best Value Inn, Days Inn Americas Tire, BigLots, Buick/GMC, Firestone/auto, Fred Meyer/dsl, Kia, Midas, Schwab Tires, Sears/auto, Verizon, Walgreens, W Arco, Pacific Pride/dsl, Shell/dsl Almost Home Rest., Baskin-Robbins, DQ, McDonald's, Newport Bay Seafood, Pietro's Pizza, Rockin-Rogers Diner, Subway Comfort Inn, DoubleTree, Holiday Lodge, Motel 6, Red Lion Hotel, Shilo Inn, Super 8 Mazda, vet
253	OR 22, Salem, Stayton, E Chevron, Shell/dsl, Space Age/dsl Burger King, Carls Jr, Las Polomas Mexican, McDonalds/playplace, Shari's, Subway $Tree, Home Depot, Salem Camping/RV Park, ShopKO, to Detroit RA, WinCo Foods, W Shell/dsl Carl's Jr, Denny's, DQ, Jack-in-the-Box, Panda Express, Popeyes, Taco Del Mar Best Western, Comfort Suites, Hampton Inn, La Quinta, Residence Inn H, AAA, Chrysler/Jeep, Costco/gas, K-Mart, Lowe's, Nissan, Schwab Tire, st police, Walmart
252	Kuebler Blvd
249	to Salem, **2 mi** W 76, Arco Arby's, Burger King, Carl's Jr, Kwan's Cuisine Phoenix Inn Safeway
248	Sunnyside, E Enchanted Forest Themepark, Willamette Valley Vineyards, W Pacific Pride/dsl
244	to N Jefferson, E Emerald Valley RV Park
243	Ankeny Hill
242	Talbot Rd
241mm	**both lanes, full facilities, info, litter barrels, petwalk**
240.5mm	Santiam River
239	Dever-Conner, Dever-Conner
238	S Jefferson, Scio
237	Viewcrest (from sb)
235	Millersburg
234	OR 99E, Albany, E Cascade Grill Comfort Suites, Holiday Inn Express , Knox Butte Camping/RV dump, W Chevron Burger King, Carl's Jr, DQ, Golden Town Buffet, McDonald's, Muchas Gracias, Subway, Taco Bell Budget Inn, La Quinta, Motel 6, Super 8 H, Costco/gas, Kohl's, NAPA, to Albany Hist Dist
233	US 20, Albany, E 76/dsl, Chevron/dsl/LP Denny's, LumYuen Chinese Best western, EconoLodge, Phoenix Inn Blue Ox RV Park, Chevrolet, Home Depot, Honda, Lassen RV Ctr, st police, Toyota/Scion, Walmart, W 76/dsl, Shell/dsl Abby's Pizza, Arby's, Baskin-Robbins, Burgerville, Carl's Jr, Elmer's, Fox Den Pizza, Golden Wok, Jack-in-the-Box, Los Dos Amigos, Los Tequilos Mexican, Original Breakfast Cafe, Pizza Hut, Sizzler, Skipper's, Starbucks, Sweetwaters Rest.,

WILSONVILLE

SALEM

ALBANY

INTERSTATE 5 Cont'd

233	Continued Taco Time, Wendy's Valu Inn H, $Tree, Bi-Mart, CarQuest, Chrysler/Dodge/Hyundai/Jeep/Subaru, Fred Meyer/dsl, Hyundai, JoAnn Fabrics, Knechts's Parts, Old Navy, O'Reilly Parts, Rite Aid, Ross, Schwab Tires, Staples, Target, Walgreens
228	OR 34, to Lebanon, Corvallis, E 76/dsl, Leather's/dsl Pine Cone Cafe Mallard Creek Golf/RV Resort, W Arco/dsl, Chevron/CFN/A&W/dsl, Shell/dsl Subway KOA (5mi), to OSU
222mm	Butte Creek
216	OR 228, Halsey, Brownsville, E 76/Pioneer Villa TrkStp/deli/dsl/24hr/ @ Travelodge, W Shell/dsl parts/repair/towing
209	to Jct City, Harrisburg, W Diamond Hill RV Park
206mm	**both lanes, full facilities, info, litter barrels, petwalk**
199	Coburg, E Fuel'n Go/dsl Premier RV Resort, W Shell/McDonald's/dsl, TA/Country Pride/Truck'n'Travel Motel/dsl/scales/24hr/ @ Coburg Crossing Cafe Camping World, dsl repair, Eugene Kamping RV Park, Evert RV Ctr, Freightliner, hist dist, Volvo
197mm	McKenzie River
195b a	N Springfield, E Arco, Chevron/dsl 5 Guys Burgers, Applebee's, Buffalo Wild Wings, Cafe Yummi, Carl's Jr, China Sun, Ciao Pizza, Denny's, Elmer's Rest., FarMan Chinese, Hacienda Amigo Mio, HomeTown Buffet, Hop Valley Rest., IHOP, Jack-in-the-Box, Jimmy John's, KFC, McDonald's, Outback Steaks, Panda Express, Quiznos, Roadhouse Grill, Shari's, Sizzler, Starbucks, Subway, Taco Bell, Taco Grande Best Western, Comfort Suites, Courtyard, Hilton Garden, Holiday Inn, Holiday Inn Express, Motel 6, Quality Inn, Super 8 H, Best Buy, Cabela's, Kohl's, mall, Michael's, Ross, Sears/auto, st police, Staples, Target, USPO, Walmart Mkt, W Taco Bell Costco/gas, Office Depot, Petsmart, ShopKO, to
194b a	OR 126 E, I-105 W, Springfield, Eugene, **1 mi** W 76, Chevron, Mobil Carl's Jr, PF Chang's, Starbucks La Quinta, Residence Inn Albertson's, Natural Grocers, Nissan, Old Navy, Subaru, U Of O
193mm	Willamette River
192	OR 99 (from nb), to Eugene, W 76 House Of Chen, Subway, Wendy's Best Western, Days Inn, Holiday Inn Express, University Inn Mkt Of Choice, to U of O
191	Glenwood, W 76/dsl, Shell/dsl/LP Denny's Comfort Suites, Motel 6
189	30th Ave S, Eugene, E Shell/dsl/LP Harley-Davidson, NW RV Supply, Shamrock RV Park, W Chevron/dsl, SeQuntial/dsl
188b	OR 99 S (nb only), Goshen
188a	OR 58, OR 99 S to Oakridge, E Deerwood RV Park, W Pacific Pride/dsl tires
186	Dillard Rd, to Goshen (from nb)
182	Creswell, E DQ, Subway Comfort Inn Bi-Mart, golf, OR RV Ctr, W 76/dsl, Arco/dsl China Wok, Creswell Cafe, Joe's Diner, My Boys Pizza, TJ's Rest. Super 8 Dari Mart, Knecht's Parts, NAPA, Sherwood Forest RV Park, Tire Factory
180mm	Coast Fork of Willamette River
178mm	**both lanes, full facilities, litter barrels, petwalk coffee**
176	Saginaw
175mm	Row River

SPRINGFIELD

EUGENE

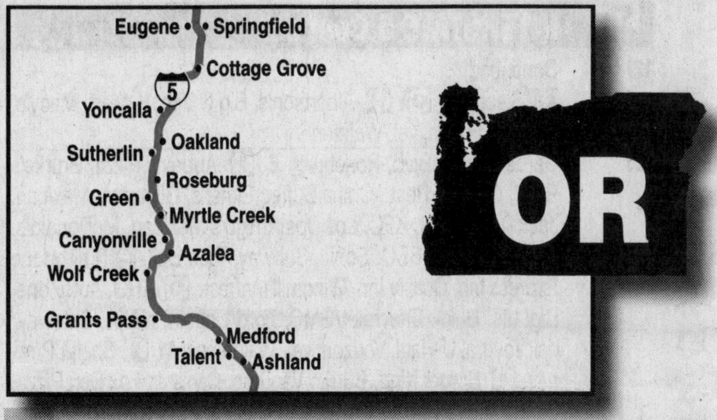

174	Cottage Grove, E Chevron/dsl/repair, Pacific Pride/dsl Chalerm Thai, Subway, Taco Bell Village Resort/RV park H, AutoZone, Chevrolet/GMC, Chrysler/Dodge/Jeep, Walmart, W 76/dsl, Chevron/dsl/LP, Shell/dsl Burger King, Carl's Jr, Domino's, Figaro's Pizza, Jack-in-the-Box, KFC, McDonald's/RV parking, Papa Murphy's, Pinocchio's Pizza, Torero's Mexican, Vintage Rest. Best Western, Comfort Inn, Relax Inn $Tree, Bi-Mart Foods, Grocery Outlet, Safeway/dsl, USPO, Walgreens
172	6th St (from sb), Cottage Grove Lake (from sb), **2 mi** W Cottage Grove RV Village
170	to OR 99, London Rd (nb only), Cottage Grove Lake, **6 mi** W Cottage Grove RV Village
163	Curtin, E Stardust Motel antiques, W Pass Creek Park/camping
162	OR 38, OR 99, to Drain, Elkton
161	Anlauf (from nb)
160	Salt Springs Rd
159	Elk Creek, Cox Rd
154	Yoncalla, Elkhead
150	OR 99, to OR 38, Yoncalla, Red Hill, W Trees of Oregon RV Park
148	Rice Hill, E Arco/LP, Pacific Pride/dsl, Pilot/Denny's/Subway/dsl/scales/24hr Ranch Rest. Motel 6, Ranch Motel Rice Hill RV Park, towing/dsl repair, W K-R Drive-In
146	Rice Valley
144mm	**sb, full facilities, litter barrels, petwalk**
143mm	**nb, full facilities, litter barrels, petwalk**
142	Metz Hill
140	OR 99 (from sb), Oakland, E Tolly's Rest. Oakland Hist Dist
138	OR 99 (from nb), Oakland, E Tolly's Rest. Oakland Hist Dist
136	OR 138W, Sutherlin, E 76/dsl, Chevron/A&W/dsl Abby's Pizza, Apple Peddler Rest., Burger King, Hong Kong Chinese, McDonald's, Papa Murphy's, Pedotti's Italian, Sol de Sutherlin Best Western, Guesthouse Inn, Relax Inn Autocare, I-5 RV Ctr, NAPA, W Shell/dsl Dakota St Pizza, DQ, Si Casa Flores, Subway, Taco Bell Hi-Way Haven RV Camp, Umpqua RV Park
135	Wilbur, Sutherlin, E CFN/dsl, Shell/dsl/LP vet
129	OR 99, Winchester, E Del Ray Cafe Kamper Korner RV Ctr (1mi), Rivers Edge RV Park, st police
129mm	N Umpqua River, N Umpqua River
127	Stewart Pkwy, Edenbower Rd, N Roseburg, E Shell/dsl Shari's Rest., Subway Motel 6, Super 8 Costco/gas, Home Depot, Lowe's, Mt Nebo RV Park, Verizon, W Mobil, Valero/dsl Applebee's, Del Taco, Jack-in-the-Box, McDonald's/playplace, Red Robin, Subway, Yummy Chinese

SUTHERLIN

INTERSTATE 5 Cont'd

ROSEBURG

127	Continued Sleep Inn (other) (H), Albertson's, Big O Tire, K-Mart, Macy's, Sherm's Foods, vet, Walmart
125	Garden Valley Blvd, Roseburg, E (food) Abbey's Pizza, Brutke's Rest., Casey's Rest., China Buffet, Elmer's, Gilberto's Mexican, Jack-in-the-Box, KFC, Los Dos Amigo's Mexican, McDonald's, Smokin' Friday BBQ, Sonic, Subway, Taco Bell (lodging) Fairbridge Express Inn, Quality Inn, Windmill Inn/rest. (other) AT&T, AutoZone, BigLots, Buick/Chevrolet/GMC, Ford/Lincoln, NAPA, Safeway/dsl, Toyota, U-Haul, Verizon, vet, Walgreens, W (gas) Shell/LP/repair (food) Burger King, Burrito Vaquero, Carl's Jr, Fox Den Pizza, Panda Express, Pita Pit, Rodeo Steaks, RoundTable Pizza, Si Casa Flores Mexican, Sizzler, Starbucks, TomTom Rest., Wendy's (lodging) Best Value Inn, Best Western (other) (H), $Tree, Bi-Mart Foods, Fred Meyer/dsl, JC Penney, JoAnn Fabrics, mall, Marshall's, Michael's, O'Reilly Parts, PetCo, Rite Aid, Ross, Staples, Walgreens
124	OR 138, Roseburg, City Ctr, E (gas) Chevron/dsl, Texaco/dsl (food) Chi's Chinese, Denny's (lodging) Dunes Motel, Holiday Inn Express, Rodeway Inn, Travelodge (other) Honda, Rite Aid, W (gas) 76/dsl, Shell/dsl (food) Charley's BBQ, Domino's, Gay 90's Deli, KFC/LJ Silver, Pete's Drive-In, Subway, Taco Time (other) Grocery Outlet, Harvard Ave Drug
123	Roseburg, E (other) camping, museum, to Umpqua Park
121	McLain Ave
120.5mm	S Umpqua River
120	OR 99 N (no EZ nb return), Green District, Roseburg, E (lodging) Shady Oaks Motel, W (other) auto repair
119	OR 99 S, OR 42 W, Winston, E (other) Ingram Dist., W (gas) Chevron/A&W/dsl, Loves/Arby's/dsl/scales/LP/24hr, Shell/dsl (food) McDonald's, Ocampos Mexican, Papa Murphy's, Subway (other) Ray's Foods, Rising River RV Park, Western Star RV Park
113	Clarks Branch Rd, Round Prairie, W (lodging) Quikstop Motel (other) On the River RV Park (2mi)
112.5mm	S Umpqua River, S Umpqua River
112	OR 99, OR 42, Dillard, E (other) Rivers West RV Park
111mm	**weigh sta both directions**
110	Boomer Hill Rd
108	Myrtle Creek, E (gas) Chevron (food) DQ, El Azteca, Golf Course Cafe, Subway (other) city park, Myrtle Creek RV Park, Ray's Foods
106	Weaver Rd
103	Tri City, Myrtle Creek, E (other) Tri-City RV Park, W (gas) Chevron/A&W/dsl, Pacific Pride (food) McDonald's

CANYONVILLE

102	Gazley Rd, E (other) Surprise Valley RV Park (1mi)
101.5mm	S Umpqua River, S Umpqua River
101	Riddle, Stanton Park, W (other) camping
99	Canyonville, E (rest stop), (gas) Penny Pincher (food) Burger King, El Paraiso (lodging) 7 Feathers Hotel/casino, Riverside Motel (other) Canyon Mkt, city park, W (gas) 7 Feathers Trkstp/café/dsl/scales/24hr/ @ (food) Creekside Rest. (lodging) Holiday Inn Express (other) 7 Feathers RV Resort
98	OR 99, Canyonville, Days Creek, E (gas) Arco/dsl, Shell/dsl (food) Ken's Cafe, Marla Kay's Cafe, Serafino's Italian, Subway (lodging) Leisure Inn (other) Ace Hardware, auto repair, NAPA, Ray's Foods, USPO, vet, W (other) museum
95	Canyon Creek
90mm	Canyon Creek Pass, elev 2020
88	Azalea
86	Barton Rd, Quine's Creek, E (other) Heaven on Earth Rest./rest., Meadow Wood RV Park (3mi)
83	Barton Rd (from nb), E (other) Meadow Wood RV Park/camping
80	Glendale, W (gas) Cow Creek/Lp/Rest.
79.5mm	Stage Road Pass, elev 1830
78	Speaker Rd (from sb)
76	Wolf Creek, W (gas) 76/deli/dsl, Pacific Pride/dsl, Shell/dsl (food) Wolf Creek Inn Rest. (other) Creekside RV park, USPO
74mm	Smith Hill Summit, elev 1730
71	Sunny Valley, E (other) Covered Bridge Store/gas, W (other) Sunny Valley RV Park
69mm	Sexton Mtn Pass, elev 1960
66	Hugo, E (other) Joe Creek Waterfalls RV Park, W (other) Pottsville Museum (3mi)
63mm	**(rest stop) both lanes, full (handicapped) facilities, info, litter barrels, petwalk (phone) (picnic) vending**
61	Merlin, W (gas) Shell/dsl (other) Almeda RV Park, Beaver Creek RV Resort (2mi), OR RV Ctr, Ray's Foods, repair

GRANTS PASS

58	OR 99, to US 199, Grants Pass, W (gas) 76/dsl/RV dump, CFN/dsl, Chevron, Fireball Gas, Shell/dsl/repair, Texaco/dsl, TownePump Gas (food) Angela's Mexican, Beacon Cafe, Black Bear Diner, Burger King, Carl's Jr, China Hut, Denny's, DQ, Jack-in-the-Box, McDonald's, Muchas Gracias Mexican, Orchid Thai, Papa Murphy's, Sizzler, Subway, Taco Bell, Wendy's (lodging) Best Way Inn, Buona Sera Inn, Comfort Inn, Hawks Inn, La Quinta, Motel 6, Redwood Motel, Royal Vue Motel, Shilo Inn, Sunset Inn, Super 8, SweetBreeze Inn, Travelodge (other) (H), $Tree, AutoZone, Chevrolet/Honda, Chrysler/Dodge/Jeep, Jack's RV Resort, Radio Shack, repair, Rouge Valley RV Park, Schwab Tire, st police, towing
55	US 199, Redwood Hwy, E Grants Pass, W (gas) Arco/dsl, Mobil/dsl (food) Abby's Pizza, Applebee's, Arby's, Carl's Jr, Elmer's, KFC, Kobe Buffet, La Burrita, McDonald's, Pizza Hut, Shari's, Si Casa Flores Mexican, Subway, Taco Bell (lodging) Best Western, Holiday Inn Express (other) (H), $Tree, Albertson's, AT&T, BigLots, Fred Meyer/dsl, Grocery Outlet, Home Depot, Jo-Ann, Moon Mtn RV Park (2mi), O'Reilly Parts, Petco, Rite Aid, RiverPark RV Park (4mi), Ross, Siskiyou RV Ctr, Staples, Verizon, Walmart
48	Rogue River, E (gas) 76/dsl, Chevron/Circle K/dsl (food) Abby's Pizza, Cottage Cafe, Homestead Rest. (other) Ace Hardware, auto repair, Rogue River RA, vet, W (food) La Guayacama, Mkt Basket Deli (lodging) Bella Rosa Inn, Best Western (other) Bridgeview RV Park, Chinook Winds RV Park, visitors ctr/info, Whispering Pines RV Park
45b	W **Valley of the Rogue SP/(rest stop) both lanes, full (handicapped) facilities, info, litter barrels, petwalk** (phone) (picnic), camping
45mm	Rogue River
45a	OR 99, Savage Rapids Dam, E (other) Cypress Grove RV Park
43	OR 99, OR 234, to Crater Lake, Gold Hill, E (lodging) Lazy Acres Motel/RV Park, RoadRiver B&B
40	OR 99, OR 234, Gold Hill, E (food) Figaro's Pizza (other) KOA, Lazy Acres Motel/RV Park, Running Salmon RV Park, W (gas) Dardanelle's/gas (other) Dardanelle's Trailer Park
35	OR 99, Blackwell Rd, Central Point, **2-4 mi** W (gas) gas (food) food (lodging) lodging (other) Jacksonville Nat Hist Landmark, st police
33	Central Point, E (gas) Chevron, LNG, Pilot/Subway/Taco Bell/dsl/scales/24hr (food) Burger King, KFC, Quiznos, Shari's Rest., Sonic (lodging) Candlewood Suites (2mi), Courtyard (2mi), Holiday Inn Express, Medford Inn, Super 8 (other) funpark, W (gas) 76/Circle K/dsl, Shell/dsl (food) Abby's Pizza, Little Caesar's, Mazatlan Mexican, McDonald's (other) Albertson's, AT&T, USPO
30	OR 62, to Crater Lake, Medford, E (gas) Arco, Chevron/dsl, Witham Trkstp/rest./dsl/24hr/ @ (food) Abby's Pizza, Applebee's, Asian Grill, Baskin Robbins, Buffalo Wild Wings, Burger King, Carl's Jr, Del Taco, Denny's, DQ, Elmer's, McDonald's, Olive Garden, Outback Steaks, Panda Express, Papa John's, Papa

OR

INTERSTATE 5 Cont'd (N)

MEDFORD

30	Continued Murphy's, Pita Pit, Pizza Hut, Red Robin, RoundTable Pizza, Si Casa Flores Mexican, Sizzler, Sonic, Starbucks, Subway, Taco Bell, Taco Delite, Thai Bistro, TX Roadhouse, Wayback Burger, Wendy's [lodging] Comfort Inn, Hampton Inn, Motel 6, Quality Inn, Ramada, Rogue Regency Hotel, Shilo Inn [other] [H], $Tree, AT&T, AutoZone, Barnes&Noble, Best Buy, BigLots, BiMart, Chevrolet/Buick/GMC, Costco/gas, Food4Less, Ford/Lincoln, Fred Meyer/dsl, JoAnn, Lowe's, Mazda, Mercedes, Michael's, NAPA, Office Depot, Old Navy, O'Reilly Parts, Petsmart, Radio Shack, Ross, Safeway, Schwab Tire, Sears/auto, st police, Subaru, TJ Maxx, Tuesday Morning, USPO, Verizon, vet, Walmart/Subway, **W** [gas] 76/dsl, Shell/dsl, Spirit/dsl [food] Chipotle, Jack-in-the-Box, Kaleidoscope Pizza, KFC, King Wah Chinese, Red Lobster, Wendy's [other] CarQuest, JC Penney, Kohl's, Macy's, mall, Natural Grocers, Petco, REI, Target, Toyota/Scion, Trader Joe's, Verizon
27	Barnett Rd, Medford, **E** [food] Blackbear Diner, DQ [lodging] Best Western, Days Inn/rest., Homewood Suites, Motel 6, Travelodge [other] [H], **W** [gas] 76/Circle K/dsl, Chevron/dsl, Texaco/dsl [food] Abby's Pizza, Arby's, Burger King, Carl's Jr, Domino's, El Arriero Mexican, HomeTown Buffet, Jack-in-the-Box, KFC, McDonald's, McGrath's FishHouse, Panda Express, Pizza Hut, Quiznos, Rooster's Rest., Shari's, Starbucks, Subway, Taco Bell, Wendy's [lodging] Comfort Inn, Holiday Inn Express, Medford Inn, Royal Crest Motel, Sovana Inn, SpringHill Suites, TownePlace Suites [other] $Tree, AT&T, Fred Meyer/dsl, GNC, Grocery Outlet, Harry&David's, O'Reilly Parts, Radio Shack, Staples, Verizon, Walgreens, Walmart/McDonald's, WinCo Foods
24	Phoenix, **E** [gas] Petro/Iron Skillet/dsl/scales/RV dump/24hr/ @, Shell/dsl [lodging] Best Inn/PearTree RV park [other] Home Depot, Peterbilt, **W** [gas] Chevron/Circle K/dsl [food] Angelo's Pizza, Jack-in-the-Box, Joe's Rest., McDonald's, Si Casa Flores Mexican [lodging] Bavarian Inn [other] CarQuest, Harley Davidson, Holiday RV Park, Ray's Foods, Tire Pros
22mm	**[RS] sb, full [handicap] facilities, litter barrels, petwalk [phone] [picnic] RV dump, vending**
21	Talent, **W** [gas] Chevron/dsl, Circle K/dsl [food] Subway [lodging] GoodNight Inn [other] American RV Resort, vet

ASHLAND

19	Valley View Rd, Ashland, **W** [gas] 76/dsl, Pacific Pride/dsl, Shell/dsl/LP [food] Burger King, El Tapatio Mexican [lodging] EconoLodge/RV Park, La Quinta [other] Acura, Chevrolet, Ford, Suzuki
18mm	**weigh sta both lanes**
14	OR 66, to Klamath Falls, Ashland, **E** [gas] 76/dsl/LP, Chevron/dsl, Valero/dsl [food] Caldera Rest., El Pariso Mexican, OakTree Rest. [lodging] Ashland Hills Inn & Suites, Best Western, Holiday Inn Express, Relax Inn [other] Emigrant Lake Camping (3mi), Glenyan RV Park (3mi), **W** [gas] Arco, Texaco [food] Little Caesar's, Panda Garden Chinse, Señor Sam's Mexican, Subway, Taco Bell, Wendy's, Wild Goose Cafe [lodging] Rodeway Inn, Super 8 [other] [H], $Tree, Albertson's, AT&T, Bi-Mart, NAPA, Radio Shack, Rite Aid, Schwab Tire, Shop'n Kart, U-Haul, vet
11	OR 99, Siskiyou Blvd (nb only, no return)
6	to Mt Ashland, **E** [lodging] Callahan's Siskiyou Lodge/rest. [other] [phone] ski area
4mm	Siskiyou Summit, elev 4310, **brake check both lanes**
1	to Siskiyou Summit (from nb, no return)
0mm	Oregon/California state line

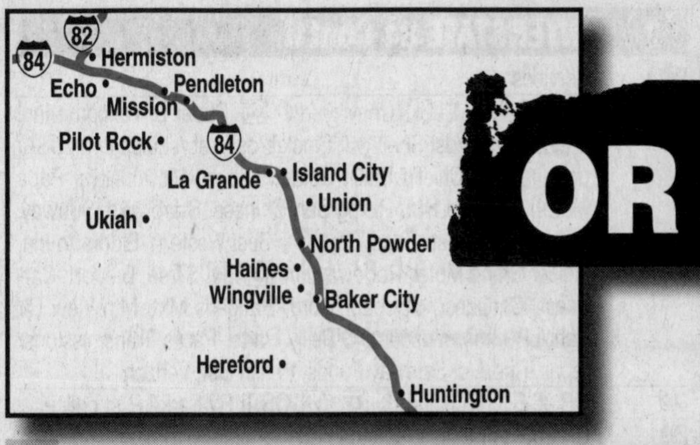

INTERSTATE 84 (E)

ONTARIO

Exit #	Services
378mm	Oregon/Idaho state line, Snake River
377.5mm	**Welcome Ctr wb, full [handicap] facilities, info, litter barrels, petwalk [phone] [picnic] vending**
376b a	US 30, to US 20/26, Ontario, Payette, **N** [gas] Chevron/dsl [food] A&W/KFC, Burger King, Carl's Jr, China Buffet, Country Kitchen, Denny's, Domino's, DQ, Dutch Bros Coffee, Little Caesar's, McDonald's, Panda Express, Subway, Taco Time, Wingers [lodging] Best Value Inn, Best Western, Clarion, Motel 6, Quality Inn, Sleep Inn [other] $Tree, AT&T, GNC, Home Depot, st police, Staples, Toyota/Scion, Verizon, Walgreens, Walmart/Subway, **S** [gas] Pilot/Arby's/dsl/scales/24hr, Sinclair/dsl [food] DJ's, East Side Cafe, Far East Chinese, Gandolfo's Deli, Ogawa's Japanese, Rusty's Steaks, Taco Bell [lodging] Economy Inn, Holiday Inn Express, OR Trail Motel, Stockman's Motel, Super 8 [other] [H], Commercial Tire, Les Schwab Tire, NAPA
374	US 30, OR 201, to Ontario, **N** [other] to Ontario SP, **2 mi S** [gas] Loves/Chester's/Subway/dsl/scales/24hr/ @, Pacific Pride [lodging] Budget Inn [other] [H]
373.5mm	Malheur River
371	Stanton Blvd, **2 mi S** [other] to correctional institution
362	Moores Hollow Rd
356	OR 201, to Weiser, ID, **3 mi N** [other] Catfish Junction RV Park, Oasis RV Park
354.5mm	**weigh sta eb**
353	US 30, to Huntington, **N** [other] info, RV camping, to Farewell Bend SP, **weigh sta wb**
351mm	Pacific/Mountain time zone
345	US 30, Lime, Huntington, **1 mi N** [gas] [food] [lodging] [other] to Snake River Area, Van Ornum BFD
342	Lime (from eb)
340	Rye Valley
338	Lookout Mountain
337mm	Burnt River
335	**[RS] both lanes, full [handicap] facilities, Oregon Trail info, litter barrels, petwalk [picnic] vending**
330	Plano Rd, to Cement Plant Rd, **S** [other] cement plant
329mm	pulloff eb
327	Durkee, **N** [gas] Co-op/dsl/LP/café
325mm	Pritchard Creek
321mm	Alder Creek
317	to Pleasant Valley (from wb)
315	to Pleasant Valley (from wb)
313	to Pleasant Valley (from eb)
306	US 30, Baker, **2-3 mi S** [gas] Chevron/dsl [lodging] Baker City Motel, Bridge Street Hotel, OR Trail Motel/rest. [other] [H], Les Schwab Tire, same as 304, to st police

OR

INTERSTATE 84 Cont'd

BAKER

Exit #	Services
304	OR 7, Baker, N Chevron/dsl Super 8, Welcome Inn, S Maverik/dsl, Shell/dsl, Sinclair/dsl/rest./scales/24hr, USA/dsl Big Chief's BBQ, Golden Crown, McDonald's, Papa Murphy's, Pizza Hut, Rising Sun Chinese, Starbucks, Subway, Sumpter Jct Rest., Taco Time Best Western, Eldorado Inn, Geiser Grand Motel, Rodeway Inn H, $Tree, Bi-Mart, Car-quest, CarQuest, city park, Ford, Haggens Mkt, Mtn View RV Park/LP (3mi), museum, O'Reilly Parts, Paul's Transmissions/repair, Rite Aid, Safeway Foods, to hist dist, Verizon
302	OR 86 E to Richland, S H, OR Tr RV Park/LP, st police
298	OR 203, to Medical Springs
297mm	Baldock Slough
295mm	**both lanes, full facilities, info, litter barrels, petwalk vending**
289mm	Powder River
287.5mm	45th parallel halfway between the equator and north pole
286mm	N Powder River
285	US 30, OR 237, North Powder, N North Powder Motel/cafe, S ski area, to Anthony Lakes
284mm	Wolf Creek
283	Wolf Creek Lane
278	Clover Creek
273	Frontage Rd
270	Ladd Creek Rd (from eb, no return)
269mm	**both lanes, full facilities, info, litter barrels, petwalk vending**
268	Foothill Rd
265	OR 203, LaGrande, N Eagles Hot Lake RV Park, S FLYING J/Shell/res./dsl/scales/24hr SmokeHouse Rest. (2mi) Freightliner

LA GRANDE

Exit #	Services
261	OR 82, LaGrande, N Chevron/dsl, Shell/dsl Denny's, Pizza Hut, Primo's Pizza, Starbucks, Taco Bell LaGrande Inn AT&T, Chrysler/Dodge/Jeep, Ford/Lincoln, Grocery Outlet, Thunder RV Ctr, Verizon, vet, Walmart/Subway, S 76/Baskin-Robbins/Subway/dsl, Chevron/dsl, Texaco/dsl Bear Mtn. Pizza, China Buffet, Domino's, DQ, Dutch Bro's Coffee, KFC, La Fiesta Mexican, McDonald's, Moy's Dynasty, Nell's Steakburger, Papa Murphy's, Taco Time, Wendy's Best Western, Royal Motel, Sandman Inn/Best Value, Super 8 H, $General, $Tree, Ace Hardware, E OR U, Rite Aid, Safeway/dsl, Schwab Tire, Wallowa Lake
260mm	Grande Ronde River
259	US 30 E (from eb), to La Grande, **1-2 mi** S Chevron/dsl, Shell/dsl Burger King Greenwell Motel/rest., Rodeway Inn, Royal Motel, same as 261
257	Perry (from wb)
256.5mm	**weigh sta eb**
256	Perry (from eb)
255mm	Grande Ronde River
254mm	scenic wayside
252	OR 244, to Starkey, Lehman Springs, S camping, chainup area, Hilgard SP
251mm	Wallowa-Whitman NF, eastern boundary
248	Spring Creek Rd, to Kamela, **3 mi** N Oregon Trail Visitors Park
246mm	Wallowa-Whitman NF, western boundary
243	Summit Rd, Mt Emily Rd, to Kamela, **2 mi** N Emily Summit SP, Oregon Trail info
241mm	Summit of the Blue Mtns, elev 4193
238	Meacham
234	Meacham, S Emigrant Sprs SP, RV camping
231.5mm	Umatilla Indian Reservation, eastern boundary
228mm	Deadman Pass, **both lanes, full facilities, Oregon Trail info, litter barrels, petwalk RV Dump (wb), vending**
227mm	**brake check area, weigh sta wb**
224	Poverty Flats Rd, Old Emigrant Hill Rd, to Emigrant Springs SP
223mm	wb viewpoint, no restrooms
221.5mm	eb viewpoint, no restrooms
220mm	**wb runaway truck ramp**

PENDLETON

Exit #	Services
216	Mission, McKay Creek, N Arrowhead Trkstp/Pacific Pride/McDonald's/dsl/24hr DQ, Subway Wildhorse Casino/RV Park
213	US 30 (from wb), Pendleton, **3-5 mi** N Chevron/dsl Travelers Inn Pendleton NHD
212mm	Umatilla Indian Reservation western boundary
210	OR 11, Pendleton, N museum, st police, S Chevron/Circle K/dsl, Sinclair/dsl/LP Shari's/24hr Best Western, Hampton Inn, Holiday Inn Express, Motel 6, Red Lion Inn/rest., Super 8 KOA
209	US 395, Pendleton, N Space Age Domino's, DQ, Jack-in-the-Box, KFC, Little Caesar's, Pizza Hut, Quiznos, Taco Bell Oxford Suites, Travelodge $Tree, AT&T, Dean's Mkt, Grocery Outlet, O'Reilly Parts, Radio Shack, Rite Aid, Safeway/dsl, Verizon, Walgreens, Walmart/Subway, S Astro/dsl, Sinclair/dsl Abby's Pizza, Burger King, Denny's, Dickey's BBQ, McDonald's, Rooster's Rest, Starbucks, Subway, Wendy's EconoLodge H, Les Schwab, Thompson RV Ctr
208mm	Umatilla River
207	US 30, W Pendleton, N Shell/dsl/LP Lookout RV Park, truck repair
202	Barnhart Rd, to Stage Gulch, N Woodpecker Truck Repair
199	Stage Coach Rd, Yoakum Rd
198	Lorenzen Rd, McClintock Rd, N trailer/reefer repair
193	Echo Rd, to Echo, Oregon Trail Site
188	US 395 N, Hermiston, N Pilot/Subway/McDonald's/dsl/24hr/RV park, **5 mi** N Chevron/dsl, Denny's/24hr, Jack-in-the-Box, McDonald's, Shari's/24hr Best Western, Economy Inn, Oak Tree Inn, Oxford Suites H, S Echo HS, Henrietta RV Park (1mi)
187mm	**both lanes, full facilities, info, litter barrels, petwalk**
182	OR 207, to Hermiston, N Space Age/A&W/dsl/LP/24hr Comfort Inn
180	Westland Rd, to Hermiston, McNary Dam, N trailer repair, S Western Express/dsl Freightliner
179	I-82 W, to Umatilla, Kennewick, WA
177	Umatilla Army Depot
171	Paterson Ferry Rd, to Paterson
168	US 730, to Irrigon, **8 mi** N Green Acres RV Park, Oasis RV Park, Oregon Trail info

BOARDMAN

Exit #	Services
165	Port of Morrow, S Pacific Pride/dsl
164	Boardman, N Chevron/Circle K/dsl, Sinclair/dsl C&D Drive-In, Lynard's Cafe, Sunrise Cafe, Village Rest. Knights Inn, Riverview Motel Boardman RV/Marina Park, city park, USPO, S Shell/dsl Subway NAPA, Oregon Trail Library, Rodeway Inn, Select Mkt, Tire Factory
161mm	**both lanes, full facilities, litter barrels, petwalk vending**
159	Tower Rd
151	Threemile Canyon
147	OR 74, to Ione, Blue Mtn Scenic Byway, Heppner, Oregon Trail Site
137	OR 19, Arlington, S Shell/Circle K/dsl Happy Canyon Cafe, Pheasant Grill, Rivers Edge Deli Rodeway Inn

INTERSTATE 84 Cont'd

137	Continued Arlington Hardware, Arlington RV Park/dump, city park, Thrifty Foods
136.5mm	view point wb, litter barrels
131	Woelpern Rd (from eb, no return)
129	Blalock Canyon, Lewis&Clark Trail
123	Philippi Canyon, Lewis&Clark Trail
114.5mm	John Day River
114	S LePage Park
112	N John Day Dam, **parking area both lanes, litter barrels**
109	Pendleton, N John Day Visitor Ctr, S Sinclair/dsl Bob's T-Bone, Bull Dog Diner Hillview Motel, Tyee Motel Ed's RV Park, Family Mkt/deli, Rufus RV Park
104	US 97, Biggs, N Des Chutes Park Bridge, Maryhill Museum, S 76/Circle K/Noble Roman's/dsl/24hr, Pilot/McDonald's/dsl/scales/24hr, Shell/Subway/dsl Linda's Rest. Dinty's Motel, Three Rivers Inn Dinty's Mkt, dsl/tire repair
100mm	Columbia River Gorge Scenic Area, Deschutes River
97	OR 206, Celilo, N Celilo SP, restrooms, S Deschutes SP, Indian Village
92mm	**pullout eb**
88	N to The Dalles Dam
87	US 30, US 197, to Dufur, N 76/dsl/24hr, Chevron/dsl McDonald's, Portage Grill Comfort Inn, Shilo Inn Columbia Hills RV Park, Lone Pine RV Park, st police, S Big Jim's Drive-In Celilo Inn
85	The Dalles, N **Riverfront Park, litter barrels, playground, restrooms** marina, S 76/dsl, Chevron, Shell Burgerville, Canton Wok, Clock Tower Rest., Domino's, River Tap Rest. Dalles Inn, Oregon Motel H, AJ's Radiators, Dalles Parts, to Nat Hist Dist, TrueValue, USPO
83	(84 from wb)W The Dalles, N Casa El Mirador Legends Hotel/Casino Tire Factory, S Astro/dsl, Chevron/dsl, Fred Meyer/dsl Burger King, Denny's, DQ, Dutch Bro's Coffee, Ixtapa Mexican, Jack-in-the-Box, KFC, McDonald's, Papa Murphy's, Pizza Hut, Shari's Rest., Skipper's, Starbucks, Subway, Taco Bell, Taco Time, The BBQ Cousin's Inn/rest., Fairfield Inn, Motel 6, Super 8 H, $Tree, AT&T, Buick/Chevrolet/GMC, Chrysler/Dodge/Jeep, Ford, Fred Meyer, Grocery Outlet, Honda, Jo-Ann Fabrics, K-Mart, Nissan, Oil Can Henry's, O'Reilly Parts, PetCo, Radio Shack, Rite Aid, Safeway/dsl, Staples, Subaru, Toyota/Scion, Verizon, Walgreens
82	Chenowith Area, S 76/dsl Spooky's Café Bi-Mart Foods, Columbia Discovery Ctr, Home Depot, museum, same as 83
76	Rowena, N Lewis & Clark info, Mayer SP, Memaloose SP, windsurfing
73mm	Memaloose SP, **both lanes, full facilities, litter barrels, petwalk RV dump** camping
69	US 30, Mosier, S USPO
66mm	N Koberg Beach SP, **wb, full facilities, litter barrels,**
64	US 30, OR 35, to White Salmon, Hood River, N Chevron/dsl, Shell McDonald's, Riverside Grill, Starbucks Best Western marina, museum, st police, visitors info
63	Hood River, City Ctr, N Valero/dsl Hampton Inn, S Astro 3 River's Grill, Andrew's Pizza, Big Horse Rest., Hood River Rest., Pietro's Pizza Hood River Hotel, Oakstreet Hotel H, USPO
62	US 30, Westcliff Dr, W Hood River, N Charburger, White Buffalo Rest. Columbia Gorge Hotel, Vagabond Lodge, S 76/dsl, Chevron/dsl/LP Domino's, DQ, Egg River Cafe, HoHo Chinese, McDonald's, Pelinti Cafe, Red Carpet Cafe,

THE DALLES

HOOD RIVER

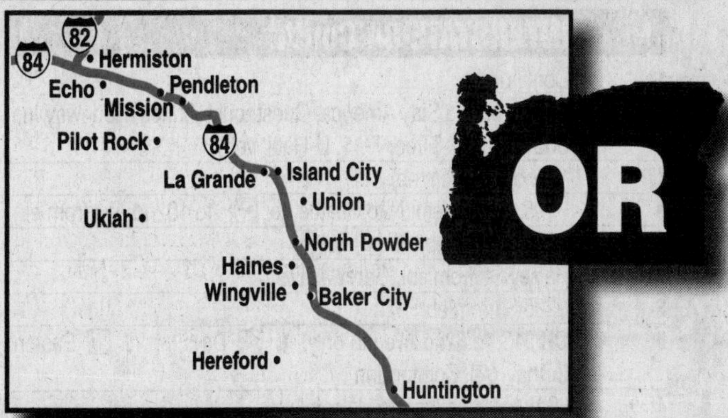

62	Continued Starbucks, Subway, Taco Bell Comfort Suites, Prater's Motel, Riverview Lodge H, AT&T, Les Schwab Tire, Oil Can Henry's, Rite Aid, Safeway, Verizon, Walmart
61mm	**pulloff wb**
60	service rd wb (no return)
58	Mitchell Point Overlook (from eb)
56	N phone, RV camping, Viento SP
55	Starvation Peak Tr Head (from eb), restrooms
54mm	**weigh sta wb**
51	Wyeth, S camping
49mm	**pulloff eb**
47	Forest Lane, Hermon Creek (from wb), camping
45mm	**weigh sta eb**
44	US 30, to Cascade Locks, N Chevron/dsl, Shell/dsl Bridgeside Rest., Cascade Inn Rest., Eastwind Drive-In, Waterfront Cafe Best Western, Bridge of the Gods Motel, Cascade Motel, Columbia Gorge Inn Columbia Mkt, KOA, Stern Wheeler RV Park, to Bridge of the Gods, USPO
41	Eagle Creek RA (from eb), to fish hatchery
40	N Bonneville Dam NHS, info, to fish hatchery
37	Warrendale (from wb)
35	Historic Hwy, Multnomah Falls, S Ainsworth SP, Fishery RV Park, scenic loop highway, waterfall area
31	Multnomah Falls (exits left from both lanes), S Multnomah Falls Lodge/Rest. (hist site) camping
30	S Benson SRA (from eb)
29	Dalton Point (from wb)
28	to Bridal Veil (7 mi return from eb), S USPO
25	N Rooster Rock SP
23mm	hist marker, viewpoint wb
22	Corbett, **2 mi** S Corbett Mkt View Point Rest. Crown Point RV Camping
19mm	Columbia River Gorge scenic area
18	Lewis&Clark SP, to Oxbow SP
17.5mm	Sandy River
17	Marine Dr, Troutdale, N DQ Comfort Inn, S Chevron/dsl, Loves/Chester's/dsl/LP/scales/24hr, TA/Shell/Country Pride/Popeye's/Subway/dsl/scales/24hr/ @ Arby's, McDonald's, Shari's/24hr, Subway, Taco Bell Holiday Inn Express, Motel 6 Premium Outlets/famous brands, Sandy Riverfront RV Resort
16	238th Dr, Fairview, N Arco/dsl/24hr Bronx Eatery, Burger King, Jack-in-the-Box Travelodge Camping World, Walmart/Subway, S 76 H
14	207th Ave, Fairview, N Shell/dsl Parkway Grill auto repair, Portland RV Park, Rolling Hills RV Park
13	181st Ave, Gresham, N Chevron/dsl Hampton Inn, S 76, Arco, Texaco Burger King, Canton Pearl, Carl's Jr, McDonald's, Pizza Hut, Shari's, Wendy's, Xavier's Days

PORTLAND

INTERSTATE 84 Cont'd

13	Continued Inn, Extended Stay America, Guesthouse Suites, Rodeway Inn, Sheraton [O] $Tree, 7-11, U-Haul, vet
10	122nd Ave (from eb)
9	I-205, S to Salem, N to Seattle, to [airport], (to 102nd Ave from eb)
8	I-205 N (from eb), N [O] to [airport]
7	Halsey St (from eb), Gateway Dist
6	I-205 S (from eb)
5	OR 213, to 82nd Ave (eb only), N [lodging] Days Inn, S [food] Eastern Cathay [lodging] Comfort Inn
4	68th Ave (from eb), to Halsey Ave
3	58th Ave (from eb), S [gas] 76, Shell/dsl [O] [H], Fred Meyer
2	43rd Ave, 39th Ave, Halsey St, N [gas] 76 [food] Burger King, Panera Bread, Starbucks [lodging] Banfield Motel [O] Rite Aid, Trader Joe's, S [O] [H], same as 1
1	33rd Ave, Lloyd Blvd (eb only), downtown, N [gas] Shell/dsl [food] Burger King, Starbucks [O] AT&T, S [food] Wendy's [O] Schwab Tire, same as 2
1	to downtown (wb only), N [food] Applebee's [lodging] Doubletree, Residence Inn [O] $Tree, Macy's, Marshall's, Nordstrom, Safeway, Sears, S [O] Cadillac

I-84 begins/ends on I-5, exit 301.

PORTLAND AREA

INTERSTATE 205 (PORTLAND)

Exit #	Services
37mm	**I-205 begins/ends on I-5. Exits 36-27 are in Washington.**
36	NE 134th St (from nb), E [gas] Chevron/dsl [lodging] Holiday Inn Express [O] [H], W [gas] 7-11, Arco, Mobil, Shell [food] Applebee's, Baskin-Robbins, Billygan's Roadhouse, Burger King, Burgerville, El Tapatio, Jack-in-the-Box, McDonald's, Muchas Gracias, Panda Express, Papa Murphy's, PizzaSchmitzza, Round Table Pizza, Starbucks, Subway, Taco Bell [lodging] La Quinta, Shilo Inn, Vancouver Inn [O] 99 RV Park, Albertson's, Fred Meyer, Safeway/dsl, Verizon, Walgreens
32	NE 83rd St, Andreson Rd, Battle Ground, W [gas] Shell/dsl/24hr [food] Burger King, Emporor Chinese, Krispy Kreme, Panda Express, Starbucks, Subway, Taste of China, Weinerschnitzel, Wendy's [O] Costco/gas, Home Depot, vet
30c b a	WA 500, Orchards, Vancouver, E [gas] 76, Shell, Shell, USA [food] ABC Buffet, Applebee's, Burger King, Burgerville, DQ, Imperial Palace, KFC, McDonald's, Papa Murphy's, Subway, Wendy's [O] 7-11, GNC, Jo-Ann Crafts, Midas, Office Depot, PetCo, repair, Sportsman's Whse, Toyota/Scion, Walgreens, W [gas] 7-11/dsl, Chevron/dsl, Shell/dsl [food] Burgerville, ChuckeCheese, Golden Tent BBQ, Great Taste Chinese, Hometown Buffet, IHOP, Jack-in-the-Box, Jamba Juice, LaCosta Mexican, Muchas Gracias, Olive Garden, Outback Steaks, Popeyes, Red Lobster, Red Robin, RoundTable Pizza, Shari's, Starbucks, Subway, Taco Bell [lodging] Best Western, Comfort Suites, Day's Inn, Heathman Lodge, Holiday Inn Express, Howard Johnson's, Residence Inn, Staybridge Inn [O] $Tree, Americas Tire, auto repair, Barnes&Noble, GNC, JC Penney, Macy's, mall, Old Navy, Petsmart, Ross, Sears/auto, Target, TJ Maxx, URGENT CARE, Verizon, Walmart Mkt
28	Mill Plain Rd, E [gas] 76, Chevron [food] Applebee's, Baskin-Robbins, Breakfast At Valerie's, Burger King, Burgerville, DQ, Elmer's Rest., Irishtown Grill, Jimmy John's, Kings Buffet, McDonald's, McGrath's Fish House, Muchas Gracias Mexican, Pizza Hut, Shari's, Starbucks, Starbucks, Sweet Tomatoes, Taco Bell,
28	Continued Yummy Mongolian [lodging] Best Western, DoubleTree Hotel, Extended Stay America, The Guesthouse Motel [O] $Tree, 7-11, Fred Meyer/dsl, O'Reilly Parts, PetCo, Schwab Tire, Trader Joe's, W [gas] 7-11, 76 [food] Arby's, Jack-in-the-Box, Little Caesar's, Subway [O] [H], auto/tire repair, Walgreens, Walmart/McDonald's
27	WA 14, Vancouver, Camas, Columbia River Gorge
25mm	Oregon/Washington state line. Columbia River. **Exits 27-36 are in Washington.**
24	122nd Ave, Airport Way, E [gas] 7-11/dsl [food] Burger King, China Wok, Dutch Bros Coffee, Jack-in-the-Box, McDonald's, Panera Bread, Shari's, Subway [lodging] Candlewood Suites, Clarion, Comfort Suites, Courtyard, Fairfield Inn, Hilton Garden, Holiday Inn Express, La Quinta, Shilo Inn/rest., SpringHill Suites, Staybridge Suites, Super 8 [O] Home Depot, Michaels, W [food] Buffalo Wild Wings, Famous Dave's, Red Robin [lodging] Embassy Suites, Hampton Inn, Hyatt Place, Loft Hotel, Red Lion Hotel, Residence Inn, Sheraton/rest. [O] [airport], Best Buy, Marshall's, PetsMart, Ross, Staples
23b a	US 30 byp, Columbia Blvd, E [gas] Leather's Fuel/dsl, Shell/dsl [food] Bill's Steaks, Elmer's Rest. [lodging] Best Western, Comfort Inn, Econolodge, Quality Inn, Rodeway Inn, W [lodging] Best Value Inn, Holiday Inn, Rádisson, Ramada Inn
22	I-84 E, US 30 E, to The Dalles
21b	I-84 W, US 30 W, to Portland
21a	Glisan St, E on NE 102nd St [gas] 76, Arco [food] Applebee's, Carl's Jr, Izzy's Pizza, Jamba Juice, Starbucks, Subway [O] Fred Meyer, Kohl's, Office Depot, Ross, WinCo Foods
20	Stark St, Washington St, E [gas] 76/7-11, Chevron/dsl [food] Arby's, Baja Fresh, Burger King, Denny's, Elmer's Rest., Hometown Buffet, Jack-in-the-Box, McMenamin's Rest., Old Chicago Pizza, Olive Garden, Panda Express, Portland Seafood Co, Red Robin, Saylor's, Starbucks, Subway, Village Inn [lodging] Chestnut Tree Inn, Ramada [O] $Tree, Big Lots, Home Depot, Target, Tuesday Morning, Verizon, W [food] Stark St Pizza, Taco Bell [lodging] Motel 6 [O] 7-11
19	US 26, Division St, E [gas] Space Age/dsl [O] [H], W [gas] Shell [food] Burgerville, Campbell's BBQ, ChuckeCheese, McDonald's [O] Jo-Ann Fabrics, Walmart
17	Foster Rd, **1 mi** W [gas] Chevron [food] Copper Penney Grill
16	Johnson Creek Blvd, W [gas] 76, Arco [food] Applebee's, Bajio, Burger King, Carl's Jr, Five Guys, Hog Wild BBQ, Jack-in-the-Box, Jimmy John's, Krispy Kreme, McDonald's, McDonald's, Outback Steaks, Panda Express, RoundTable Pizza, Starbucks, Taco Bell [O] 7-11, Best Buy, Dick's, Firestone/auto, Fred Meyer/dsl, Home Depot, Knecht's Parts, O'Reilly Parts, PetsMart, Radio Shack, RV Ctrs, Trader Joe's, Walgreens, Walmart/Subway
14	Sunnyside Rd, E [gas] 76/dsl [food] A&W/KFC, Baja Fresh, Domino's, Garlic Jim's Pizza, Gustav's Grill, McMenamin's, Starbucks, Subway, TCBY, Thai BBQ [lodging] Days Inn, Motel 6 [O] [H], Office Depot, W [gas] Chevron/dsl [food] Burger King, CA Pizza Kitchen, Chipotle, Claim Jumper, Dave&Buster's, Denny's, DQ, Jimmy John's, McDonald's, Muchas Gracias, Noodles&Co, Old Spaghetti Factory, Olive Garden, Panera Bread, Pieology Pizzaria, Pizza Hut, RAM Rest., Red Robin, Stanford's Rest., Wendy's [lodging] Courtyard, Monarch Hotel/rest. [O] America's Tire, Barnes&Noble, JC Penney, Kohl's, Macy's, mall, Nordstroms, Old Navy, PetCo, REI, Sears/auto, Target, U-Haul, Verizon, Walgreens, World Mkt
13	OR 224, to Milwaukie, W [O] CarMax, Lowe's

OR

INTERSTATE 205 (PORTLAND) Cont'd

Exit #	Services
12	OR 213, to Milwaukie, **E** [gas] Chevron/dsl, Pacific Pride, Shell [food] Denny's, Elmer's, KFC, McDonald's, New Cathay Chinese, Pronto Pizza, Subway, Taco Bell, Wendy's [lodging] Clackamas Inn, Hampton Inn [other] $Tree, 7-11, Fred Meyer, USPO, **W** [lodging] Comfort Suites
11	82nd Dr, Gladstone, **W** [gas] Arco, Chevron [food] High Rocks Rest., McDonald's, Starbucks, Subway [lodging] Holiday Inn Express [other] Harley-Davidson, Safeway
10	OR 213, Park Place, **E** [gas] Chevron/dsl [other] H, Home Depot, to Oregon Trail Ctr
9	OR 99E, Oregon City, **E** [gas] 76, Chevron/dsl [food] KFC [other] H, repair, Subaru, **W** [food] La Hacienda Mexican, McDonald's, Shari's, Starbucks, Subway, Thai Rest. [lodging] Best Western/rest
9	Continued [other] $Tree, AT&T, Firestone/auto, Michael's, Rite Aid, Ross, URGENT CARE
8.5mm	Willamette River
8	OR 43, W Linn, Lake Oswego, **E** [gas] 76 [other] museum, **W** [gas] Chevron/dsl, Shell/dsl [food] BJ Willy's Pizza, Starbucks, Taco Del Mar, Thai Linn [other] Mkt of Choice, USPO, Verizon, vet
7mm	hist marker, viewpoint nb
6	10th St, W Linn St, **E** [gas] Chevron/LP [food] 5 Guys Burgers, Ixtapa Mexican, McDonald's, McMenamin's Rest., Papa Murphy's, Shari's/24hr, Wilamet Coffee House [other] Ace Hardware, Les Schwab, Oil Can Henry's, **W** [food] Biscuit's Cafe, Jack-in-the-Box, Starbucks, Subway [other] Albertsons/Sav-On
4mm	Tualatin River
3	Stafford Rd, Lake Oswego, **W** [food] Corner Saloon [other] H
0mm	**I-205 begins/ends on I-5, exit 288.**

PENNSYLVANIA

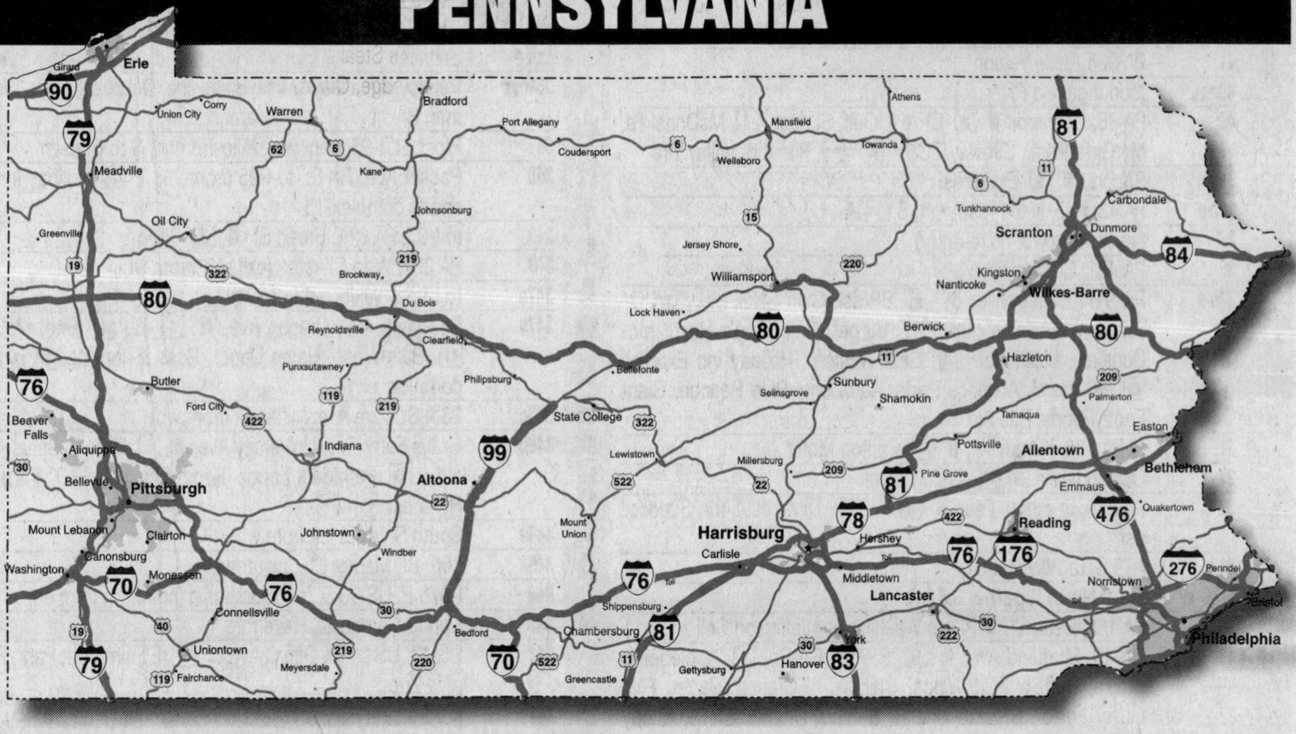

INTERSTATE 70

Exit #	Services
171mm	Pennsylvania/Maryland state line **Welcome Ctr wb, full facilities, info, litter barrels, petwalk, vending**
168	US 522 N, Warfordsburg, **N** [gas] Exxon/dsl, **S** [other] fireworks
163	PA 731 S, Amaranth
156	PA 643, Town Hill, **N** [lodging] Days Inn [other] NAPA
153mm	**[RS] eb, full facilities, litter barrels, petwalk, vending**
151	PA 915, Crystal Spring, **N** [other] auto repair, **S** [other] Country Store/USPO
149	US 30 W, to Everett, S Breezewood (no immediate wb return), **3 mi S** [food] McDonald's [lodging] Penn Aire Motel, Redwood Motel, Wildwood Motel
147	US 30, Breezewood, **services on US 30** [gas] Exxon/dsl, FLYING J/Perkins/dsl/scales/24hr, Sheetz/dsl, Shell/Dunkin Donuts/Subway/dsl, Sunoco/café/dsl, TA/Gateway Rest/dsl/scales/24hr/ @, Valero/dsl [food] Bob Evans, Denny's, DQ,
147	Continued Hardee's, McDonald's, Pizza Hut, Quiznos, Starbucks, Taco Bell, Wendy's [lodging] Best Western, EconoLodge, Holiday Inn Express, Howard Johnson, Penn Aire Motel, Quality Inn, Village Motel, Wiltshire Motel [other] Blue Beacon, camping, museum, Radio Shack, truck/auto repair
	I-70 and I-76/PA Tpk run together 71 mi. See I-76 PA/Tpk exits 148mm-75.
57b a	I-70 W, US 119, PA 66 (toll), New Stanton, **N** [gas] Exxon, Sheetz [food] BBG Grill, Bob Evans, Eat'n Park, McDonald's, Pagano's Rest., Pizza Hut, Subway, Szechuan Wok, Wendy's [lodging] Budget Inn, Comfort Inn, Days Inn, EconoLodge, Express Inn, Fairfield Inn, Garden Inn, Super 8, **S** [gas] BP/dsl, Sunoco/dsl [food] Cracker Barrel, La Tavola Ristorante, TJ's Rest. [other] USPO
54	Madison, **N** [other] KOA, **S** [other] truck repair
53	Yukon
51b a	PA 31, West Newton, **S** [other] Volvo/Mack

BREEZEWOOD

OR

PA

F A Y E T T E C I T Y

W A S H I N G T O N

INTERSTATE 70 Cont'd

Exit #	Services
49	Smithton, N 🅖 Citgo/rest./dsl/scales/ @, ⭘FLYING J/Denny's/dsl/LP/scales/24hr/ @
46b a	PA 51, Pittsburgh, N 🅖 Sunoco/dsl 🅕 Burger King 🅛 Comfort Inn 🅞 Buick/Cadillac/Chevrolet, Ford/Kia, Honda, S 🅖 GetGo/dsl, PP/dsl 🅕 Clubhouse Grille 🅛 Belle Vernon Hotel, Budget Inn 🅞 golf
44	Arnold City
43b a	(43 from eb)PA 201, to PA 837, Fayette City, S 🅖 Exxon/dsl 🅕 A&W/LJ Silver, Burger King, Denny's, Domino's, Eat'n Park, Hibachi Buffet, Hoss' Rest., KFC, Little Bamboo, McDonald's, Old Mexico, Pizza Hut, Rita's Custard, Sonny's Grille, Starbucks, Subway, Taco Bell, Wendy's 🅛 Hampton Inn, Holiday Inn Express 🅞 $General, $Tree, Advance Parts, Aldi Foods, AT&T, BigLots, CVS Drug, Giant Eagle Foods, GNC, Jo-Ann Fabrics, K-Mart, Lowe's, NAPA, Radio Shack, Rite Aid, Staples, URGENT CARE, Verizon, Walmart
42a	Monessen
42	N Belle Vernon, S 🅖 BP/McDonald's/7-11, Sunoco/dsl 🅕 DQ
41	PA 906, Belle Vernon
40mm	Monongahela River
40	PA 88, Charleroi, N 🅖 BP/dsl, Gulf, Sunoco 🅕 McDonald's, My Girl's Rest., Subway/TCBY 🅞 🏪 Rite Aid, Valley Tire
39	Speers, S 🅖 Exxon/dsl
37b a	PA 43 (toll), N to Pittsburgh, S to CA
36	Lover (from wb, no re-entry)
35	PA 481, Centerville
32b a	PA 917, Bentleyville, S 🅖 BP/dsl, Gain CNG, 🚚/DQ/Subway/dsl/scales/24hr 🅕 Burger King, King's Rest., McDonald's, Pizza Hut 🅛 Best Western, Holiday Inn Express 🅞 $General, Advance Parts, AutoZone, Blue Beacon, Giant Eagle Foods, Rite Aid
31	to PA 136, Kammerer, N 🅛 Carlton Motel
27	Dunningsville, S 🅛 Avalon Motel
25	PA 519, to Eighty Four, S 🅖BP/7-11 Diner/dsl/24hr, Sunoco/dsl
21	I-79 S, to Waynesburg
I-70 W and I-79 N run together 3.5 mi.	
20	PA 136, Beau St, S 🅞 to Washington&Jefferson Coll
19b a	US 19, Murtland Ave, N 🅖 BP/dsl, GetGo 🅕 Applebee's, Arby's, Buffalo Wild Wings, Chick-fil-A, Cracker Barrel, Five Guys, Fusion Steaks, Ichiban Steaks, Jimmy John's, Krispy Kreme, Longhorn Steaks, Max&Erma's, McDonald's, Moe's SW Grill, Noodles&Co, Olive Garden, Outback Steaks, Panera Bread, Penn Sta Subs, Ponderosa, Red Lobster, Red Robin, Rita's Custard, Starbucks, Subway, TGIFriday's, TX Roadhouse, Wong's Wok 🅛 SpringHill Suites 🅞 $Tree, Aldi Foods, AT&T, Dick's, Field&Stream, Ford, Giant Eagle Foods, GNC, Hobby Lobby, Honda, Hyundai, Kohl's, Lowe's, Mercedes, Michael's, Nissan, PetCo, Petsmart, Radio Shack, Sam's Club/gas, Save-A-Lot Foods, Target, Toyota/Scion, URGENT CARE, Verizon, Walmart/McDonald's, S 🅖 BP/dsl, Exxon/dsl, Sunoco, Valero/dsl 🅕 A&W/LJ Silver, Bob Evans, Donut Connection, Eat'n Park, Grand China, KFC, Old Mexico, Papa John's, Pizza Hut, Waffle House 🅛 Hampton Inn, Motel 6 🅞 🏪 BigLots, Buick/GMC, Chevrolet, Firestone/auto, Home Depot, Jo-Ann Fabrics, Mazda, Pepboys, Staples, Subaru
18	I-79 N, to Pittsburgh.
I-70 E and I-79 S run together 3.5 mi.	
17	PA 18, Jefferson Ave, Washington, N 🅖 GetGo/dsl 🅕 DQ, McDonald's 🅞 Family$, Rite Aid, S 🅖 Valero/dsl 🅕 4Star

Exit #	Services
17	Continued Pizza, Burger King, China Express, Domino's, Little Caesars, Subway 🅞 $General, Advance Parts, AutoZone, CarQuest, CVS Drug, Shop'n Save Foods, USPO, Walgreens
16	Jessop Place, N 🅖 Citgo 🅛 Extended Stay America, S 🅞 auto/truck repair
15	US 40, Chesnut St, Washington, N 🅞 Food Land, S 🅖 BP/7-11, Exxon/dsl, Sunoco/dsl, Valero 🅕 Angello's, Bob Evans, Denny's, Garfield's Rest., James Grill, McDonald's, Taco Bell, Wendy's 🅛 Best Value Inn, Comfort Suites, Days Inn, Ramada Inn, Red Roof Inn 🅞 BonTon, Gander Mtn, Jo-Ann, Macy's, mall, Marshalls, Rite Aid, Ross, Sears/auto
11	PA 221, Taylorstown, N 🅖 BP/dsl 🅞 repair
6	PA 231, to US 40, Claysville, N 🅖 Exxon/dsl
5mm	**Welcome Ctr eb, full ♿ facilities, litter barrels, petwalk 🅿️ vending**
1	W Alexander
0mm	Pennsylvania/West Virginia state line

P H I L A D E L P H I A

INTERSTATE 76

Exit #	Services
354mm	Pennsylvania/New Jersey state line, Delaware River, Walt Whitman Br
351	Front St, I-95 (from wb), N to Trenton, S to Chester
350	Packer Ave, 7th St, to I-95 (fromeb), S 🅛 Holiday Inn 🅞 to sports complex
349	to I-95, PA 611, Broad St, N 🅖 Citgo
348	PA 291, W to Chester (exits left from wb)
347a	to I-95 S (exits left from wb)
347b	Passyunk Ave, Oregon Ave, N 🅕 Burger King, McDonald's 🅞 BJ's Whse, Home Depot, Ross, ShopRite, S 🅞 sports complex
346c	28th St, Vare Ave, Mifflin St (from wb)
346b	Grays Ferry Ave, University Ave, N 🅕 Little Caesars, McDonald's 🅞 PathMark Foods, Radio Shack, USPO, S 🅖 Citgo, Hess/dsl 🅞 🏪
346a	South St (exits left from wb)
345	30th St, Market St, downtown
344	I-676 E, US 30 E, to Philadelphia (no return from eb)
343	Spring Garden St, Haverford
342	US 13, US 30 W, Girard Ave, S 🅞 E Fairmount Park, Philadelphia Zoo
341	Montgomery Dr, W River Dr, W Fairmount Park, S 🅞 W Fairmount Park
340b	US 1 N, Roosevelt Blvd, to Philadelphia
339	US 1 S, S 🅕 CA Pizza Kitchen, Chipotle Mexican, Houlihans, PeiWei Asian, Potbelly's, Starbucks, TGIFriday's 🅛 Crowne Plaza 🅞 Target, Verizon
340a	Lincoln Dr, Kelly Dr, to Germantown
338	Belmont Ave, Green Lane, S 🅖 Sunoco 🅞 St Police, WaWa
337	Hollow Rd (from wb), Gladwyne
332	PA 23 (from wb), Conshohocken, N 🅛 Marriott
331b a	I-476, PA 28 (from eb), to Chester, Conshohocken
330	PA 320, Gulph Mills, S 🅞 to Villanova U
329	Weadley Rd (from wb), N 🅖 Exxon
328b a	US 202 N, to King of Prussia, N 🅖 Citgo, Exxon/dsl, Lukoil, Shell, Sunoco, WaWa 🅕 Bahama Breeze, Baja Fresh, Burger King, CA Pizza Kitchen, Capital Grille, Champp's, Cheesecake Factory, Chili's, Fox&Hound, Gino's, Joe's Crabshack, Lonestar Steaks, Maggiano's, Morton's Steaks, Panera Bread, Red Lobster, Ruby's Diner, Sullivan's Steaks, TGIFriday's, Uno Grill 🅛 Best Western, Clarion, Comfort Inn, Crowne Plaza, Fairfield

INTERSTATE 76 Cont'd

328b a Continued
Inn, Hampton Inn, Holiday Inn, Hotel Sierra, Motel 6 Acme Foods, Best Buy, Bloomingdale's, Costco, Home Depot, JC Penney, Lord&Taylor, Macy's, mall, Neiman Marcus, Nordstrom, Old Navy, Sears/auto, vet

327 US 202 S, to US 420 W, Goddard Blvd, Valley Forge Park, Valley Forge Park

326 **I-76 wb becomes I-76/PA Tpk to Ohio.**

For I-76 westbound to Ohio, see I-76/PA Turnpike.

INTERSTATE 76 (TURNPIKE)

Exit # Services

PA Tpk runs wb as I-276.

359 Pennsylvania/New Jersey state line, Delaware River Bridge. **I-276 runs eb to NJ Tpk.**

358 US 13, Delaware Valley, **N** BP, WaWa Dallas Diner Comfort Inn, Day's Inn, Ramada Inn 7-11, auto repair, U-Haul, vet, **S** LukOil/dsl, Sunoco/dsl, Valero Burger King, Gigi's Pizza, Golden Eagle Diner, Italian Family Pizza Villager Lodge $General, Buick, Mr. Transmission

352mm **Neshaminy Service Plaza,** Sunoco/dsl/24hr Breyer's, Burger King, HotDog Co, McDonald's, Nathan's, Starbucks, **Welcome Ctr wb**

351 US 1, to I-95, to Philadelphia, **N** 99, Bob Evans, Chick-fil-A, Cracker Barrel, Longhorn Steaks, On The Border, Red Robin, Ruby Tuesday, Starbucks, Wendy's Courtyard, Hampton Inn, Holiday Inn Select Buick/GMC, Home Depot, Lowes Whse, Macy's, mall, Sears/auto, Target, Walmart, **S** Exxon/Subway, LukOil, Sunoco/dsl Dunkin Donuts Comfort Inn, Howard Johnson, Knight's Inn, Neshaminy Inn, Radisson, Red Roof Inn, Sunrise Inn Toyota/Scion

343 PA 611, Willow Grove, **N** Shell Carrabba's Candlewood Suites (5mi), Courtyard , **S** Hess/dsl, Shell, Sunoco Bonefish Grill, China Garden, Domino's, Dunkin Donuts, Friendly's, McDonald's, Nino's Pizza, Ooka Japanese, Starbucks, Williamson Rest. Hampton Inn 7-11, Audi/Infiniti, Best Buy, PepBoys, repair, Staples, transmissions

340 to VA Dr, EZ tagholder only, no return eb, no trucks

339 PA 309, Ft Washington, **N** Gulf, LukOil/dsl Dunkin Donuts, Friendly's, Subway Best Western, Hilton Garden, Holiday Inn BMW, Mercedes, Volvo, WaWa

334 PA Tpk NE Extension, I-476, S to Philadelphia, N to Allentown

333 Germantown Pike, to Norristown, **N** LukOil/dsl, Sunoco/Dunkin Donuts California Pizza Kitchen, Houlihan's, PF Chang's, Red Stone Grill, Starbucks Courtyard, DoubleTree, Extended Stay America, SpringHill Suites , Boscov's, Macy's, **S** LukOil

328mm **King of Prussia Service Plaza wb,** Sunoco/dsl/24hr Breyer's, McDonald's

PA Tpk runs eb as I-276, wb as I-76.

326 I-76 E, to US 202, I-476, Valley Forge, **N** Shell Burger King, Cracker Barrel, Hooters, Hoss' Rest. MainStay Suites, Radisson, Sleep Inn, **S** Exxon, LukOil, Shell, Sunoco, WaWa CA Pizza Kitchen, Cheesecake Factory, Chili's, Denny's, Houlihan's, Lone Star Steaks, Maggiano's, McDonald's, Red Lobster, Ruth's Chris Steaks, Sullivan Steaks Best Western, Clarion, Comfort Inn, Hampton Inn, Holiday Inn Express, Motel 6 Best Buy, Costco, Home Depot, JC Penney, Macy's, mall, Neiman Marcus, Nordstrom, Sears/auto, Walmart

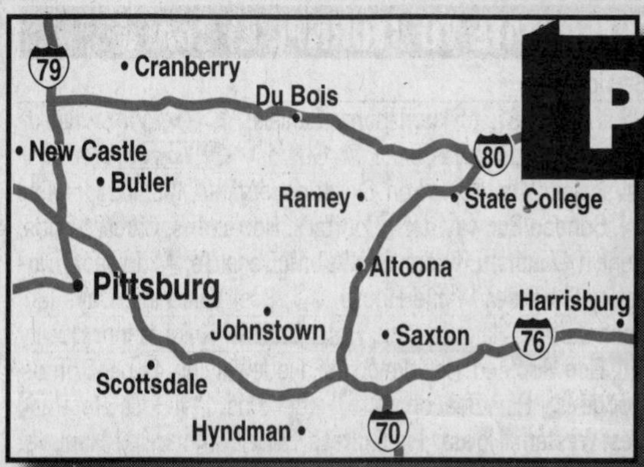

325mm **Valley Forge Service Plaza eb,** Sunoco/dsl/24hr Burger King, Starbucks

312 PA 100, to Downingtown, Pottstown, **N** WaWa/dsl CarSense, Harley-Davidson, **S** Sunoco/dsl, WaWa Applebee's, Chick-fil-A, Hoss's, Isaac's Deli, Red Robin, Starbucks, Uno Grill Comfort Suites, Extended Stay America, Fairfield Inn, Hampton Inn, Residence Inn , Genuardi's Foods, Giant Foods, Walgreens

305mm **Camiel Service Paza wb,** Sunoco/dsl/24hr Roy Rogers, Sbarro's, Starbucks

298 I-176, PA 10, to Reading, Morgantown, **N** Arby's, DQ, Dunkin Donuts, Sonic, Subway Economy Lodge, Heritage Motel/rest. , $Tree, GNC, Lowe's, Verizon, Walmart, **S** Exxon, Sheetz Heritage Rest., McDonald's, Rita's Custard Holiday Inn Chevrolet, Rite Aid

290mm **Bowmansville Service Plaza eb,** Sunoco/dsl/24hr Burger King, Hershey's, Starbucks

286 US 322, PA 272, to Reading, Ephrata, **N** Citgo/dsl, Turkey Hill Baskin-Robbins/Dunkin Donuts, Subway Black Horse Inn/rest., Comfort Inn, Red Carpet Inn, Red Roof Inn, **S** Hampton Inn (11mi)

266 PA 72, to Lebanon, Lancaster, **N** Hess/Blimpie/dsl, Sunoco/Chester's Farmer's Hope Inn Rest Holiday Inn Express (17 mi), Penns Woods Inn, Red Carpet Inn , auto repair, Harley-Davidson, NAPA, **S** Hitz Mkt/deli Hampton Inn Mt Hope Winery, Pinch Pond Camping

259mm **Lawn Service Plaza wb,** Sunoco/dsl/24hr Burger King, Starbucks RV dump

HARRISBURG

250mm **Highspire Service Plaza eb,** Sunoco/dsl/24hr Hershey's Ice Cream, Sbarro's, Starbucks

247 I-283, PA 283, to Harrisburg, Harrisburg East, Hershey, **N** Exxon/dsl, Sunoco Bob Evans, Capitol Diner, Eat'n Park, McDonald's, Taco Bell, Wendy's Best Western, Courtyard, Days Inn, EconoLodge, Holiday Inn Express, Howard Johnson, La Quinta, Red Roof Inn, Rodeway Inn, Sheraton, Super 8, Travelodge, Wingate Inn, Wyndham Harrisburg East Camping, JC Penney, Kia, Target

246mm Susquehannah River

242 I-83, Harrisburg West, **N** Hess/Dunkin Donuts, Shell/dsl Bob Evans, Doc Holliday's Rest, John's Diner, McDonald's, Pizza Hut Best Western, Comfort Inn, Fairfield Inn, Holiday Inn, Motel 6, Quality Inn, Rodeway Inn, Travel Inn vet, **S** Days Inn, Keystone Inn

236 US 15, to Gettysburg, Gettysburg Pike, Harrisburg, **N** Exxon, Gulf/dsl Isaac's Rest, McDonald's, Papa John's, Peppermill Rest, Subway Comfort Inn, Country Inn&Suites, Courtyard, EconoLodge, Hampton Inn/rest., Holiday Inn, Homewood Suites , U-Haul, vet, **S** Sheetz Arby's, Burger King, Cracker Barrel, Quiznos, Wendy's Best Western, Wingate Inn Giant Food/gas, GNC, Rite Aid

INTERSTATE 76 (TURNPIKE) Cont'd

Exit #	Services
226	US 11, to I-81, to Harrisburg, Carlisle, N FLYING J/Denny's/dsl/LP/scales/24hr/ @, Gulf/dsl, Loves/Wendy's/dsl/scales/24hr, Petro/Iron Skillet/dsl/scales/24hr/ @, Pioneer/dsl, Sunoco/Subway/dsl Arby's, Bob Evans, Carelli's Subs, Dunkin Donuts, Embers Steaks, McDonald's, Middlesex Diner, Rte 11 Diner, Waffle House Best Value Inn, Days Inn, EconoLodge, Hampton Inn, Hotel Carlisle, Knights Inn, Quality Inn, Red Roof Inn, Residence Inn, Rodeway Inn, Super 8, Travelodge Blue Beacon, S Rutter's/dsl Hoss' Rest. Best Western, Holiday Inn Express, Motel 6 , U-Haul, vet
219mm	**Plainfield Service Plaza eb,** Sunoco/dsl/24hr Hershey's Ice Cream, Roy Rogers gifts
203mm	**Blue Mtn Service Plaza wb,** Sunoco/dsl/24hr Hershy's Ice Cream, Nathan's, Roy Rogers, Uno
201	PA 997, to Shippensburg, Blue Mountain, S Johnnie's Motel/rest., Kenmar Motel
199mm	Blue Mountain Tunnel
197mm	Kittatinny Tunnel
189	PA 75, Willow Hill, S Willow Hill Motel/rest.
187mm	Tuscarora Tunnel
180	US 522, Mt Union, Ft Littleton, N Gulf/dsl, Noname/dsl The Family Rest. Downes Motel , st police
172mm	**Sideling Service Plaza both lanes,** Sunoco/dsl/24hr Burger King, Famiglia Pizza, Hershey's, Popeye's, Starbucks
161	US 30, Breezewood, **Services N on US 30** Exxon/dsl, FLYING J/Perkins/dsl/scales/24hr, Sheetz/dsl, Shell/Dunkin Donuts/Subway/dsl, Sunoco/café/dsl, TA/Gateway Rest/dsl/scales/24hr/ @, Valero/dsl Bob Evans, Denny's, DQ, Hardee's, McDonald's, Pizza Hut, Quiznos, Starbucks, Taco Bell, Wendy's Best Western, EconoLodge, Holiday Inn Express, Howard Johnson, Penn Aire Motel, Quality Inn, Village Motel, Wiltshire Motel Blue Beacon, camping, museum, Radio Shack, truck/auto repair
161mm	**I-70 W and I-76/PA Turnpike W run together.**
148mm	**Midway Service Plaza both lanes,** Sunoco/dsl/24hr Hershey's Ice Cream, Quiznos, Sbarro's, Starbucks gifts
146	I-99, US 220, Bedford, N GetGo/McDonald's/dsl, PP/dsl, Sheetz/dsl/24hr, Shell/Subway/dsl Bedford Diner, Clara's Place, Denny's, Ed's Steaks, Hoss' Rest., LJ Silver, Pizza Hut, Salsa's Mexican, Wendy's Best Value Inn, Budget Host, Fairfield Inn, Quality Inn, Rodeway Inn, Travelodge Blue Knob SP (15mi), to Shawnee SP (10mi), S Hampton Inn
123mm	Allegheny Tunnel
112mm	**Somerset Service Plaza both lanes,** Sunoco/dsl/24hr Famiglia Pizza, Hershey's Ice Cream, Quiznos, Roy Rogers, Starbucks gifts
110	PA 601, to US 219, Somerset, N KwikFill/dsl, Sheetz Hog Father's BBQ, Hoss' Rest., King's Rest., Pizza Hut $Inn, Economy Inn Advance Parts, Chrysler/Jeep, Ford, tires, S Somerset TravelCtr/dsl/ @, Turkey Hill Arby's, Bruster's Ice Cream, Donut Connection, DQ, Eat'n Park, KFC, LJ Silver, Maggie Mae's Café, McDonald's, Pine Grill, Ruby Tuesday, Starbucks, Subway, Summit Diner, Wendy's Best Value Inn, Best Western, Budget Host, Budget Inn, Comfort Inn, Days Inn, Hampton Inn, Holiday Inn, Quality Inn, Super 8 Dodge, Harley-Davidson, Volvo
91	PA 711, PA 31, to Ligonier, Donegal, N Tall Cedars Rest., S BP/McDonald's, Exxon/Subway/dsl, Sunoco/dsl DQ Days Inn camping, golf
78mm	**New Stanton Service Plaza wb,** Sunoco/dsl/24hr Burger King, Hershey's Ice Cream, Quiznos, Starbucks

I-70 E runs with I-76/PA Turnpike eb.

Exit #	Services
75	I-70 W, US 119, PA 66 (toll), New Stanton, S BP/7-11/dsl, Exxon, Sheetz, Sunoco Bob Evans, Campy's Pizza, Cracker Barrel, Eat'n Park, La Tavola Risorante, McDonald's, Pagano's Rest., Pizza Hut, Subway, Szechuan Wok, TJ's Rest., Wendy's Best Value Inn, Budget Inn, Comfort Inn, Days Inn, EconoLodge, Fairfield Inn, Howard Johnson, Super 8 USPO
74.6mm	**Hemphill Service Plaza eb,** Sunoco/dsl/24hr Breyer's, McDonald's atm
67	US 30, to Greensburg, Irwin, N BP/dsl, Sheetz/24hr , Ford, tires, vet, S Marathon/7-11, Sunoco/24hr Arby's, Bob Evans, Burger King, CiCi's Pizza, Denny's, DQ, Dunkin Donuts, Eat'n Park, KFC, LJ Silver, Los Campesinos Mexican, McDonald's, Panera Bread, Pizza Hut, Subway, Taco Bell, Teddy's Rest., Wendy's Conley Inn, Holiday Inn Express $Tree, Advance Parts, Aldi Foods, CarQuest, Giant Eagle Foods/24hr, GNC, Kohl's, Radio Shack, Rite Aid, Target
61mm	**parking area eb**
57	I-376, US 22, to Pittsburgh, Monroeville, S Citgo/dsl, Exxon, Sheetz, Sunoco A&W/LJ Silver, Arby's, Baskin-Robbins, Bob Evan's, Chick-fil-A, China Palace, ChuckeCheese, CiCi's Pizza, Damon's, Denny's, Golden Corral, Honeybaked Ham, Max&Erma's, McDonald's, Olive Garden, Outback Steaks, Panera Bread, Park Diner, Pizza Hut, Primanti Bro's, Quizno's, Red Lobster, Starbucks, Taco Bell, TGIFridays, Wendy's Comfort Suites, Courtyard, Day's Inn, Extended Stay America, Hampton Inn, Holiday Inn, Radisson Inn, Red Roof Inn, Springhill Suites , Aamco, Big Lots, Firestone/auto, Honda, Jaguar/Land Rover, Jo-Ann Fabrics, Lowes Whse, Marshall's, Michael's, NTB, Office Depot, Old Navy, Pet Land, PetCo, Radio Shack, Rite Aid, to Three Rivers Stadium
49mm	**Oakmont Service Plaza eb,** Sunoco/dsl/24hr Food-Court litter barrels, phone, picnic tables
48.5mm	Allegheny River
48	PA 28, to Pittsburgh, Allegheny Valley, New Kensington, N Shell/24hr, Sunoco Pizza Hut, Subway CarQuest, Rite Aid, S Exxon/dsl, GetGo Bob Evans, Bruster's, Denny's, Gino Bro's Pizza, KFC, King's Rest., McDonald's, Ponderosa, Primanti Bro's, Subway, Taco Bell, Wendy's Comfort Inn, Day's Inn, Holiday Inn Express, Super 8, Valley Motel Advance Parts, Ford, Target
41mm	**parking area/call box eb**
39	PA 8, to Pittsburgh, Butler Valley, **0-1 mi N** Exxon/7-11/dsl, GetGo, Sheetz/24hr, Sunoco Applebees, Atria's Rest., Bruno's Pizza, Buffalo Wild Wings, Eat'n Park, King's Rest., Max&Erma's, McDonald's, Sonic, Starbucks, Taco Bell, Wendy's Comfort Inn, Pittsburgh N Motel/rest $Tree, Advance Parts, Curves, Dodge, Giant Eagle Foods, GNC, Kohl's, Lowes Whse, Rite Aid, Shop'n Save Foods, Target, TJ Maxx, Walmart/auto/drugs, S BP, Sunoco/dsl Arby's, Brusters, Burger King, China Bistro, KFC, McDonald's, Panera Bread, Pasquales Pizza, Pizza Hut, Subway, Vocelli Pizza, Wendy's , AutoZone, Firestone/auto, Goodyear/auto, Home Depot, Mr. Tire, Radio Shack, Rite Aid, USPO
31mm	**toll plaza wb**
28	to I-79, to Cranberry, Pittsburgh, N BP/dsl, Exxon/dsl/24hr, GetGo, Sheetz/24hr, Sunoco/dsl 5 Guys Burgers, A&W/LJ Silver, Adrian's Pizza, Arby's, Bob Evans, Boston Mkt, Bravo Italian, Burger King, Chipotle Mexican, CiCi's Pizza, Denny's, Dominichi's Rest., DQ, Dunkin Donuts, Dynasty, Eat'n Park, Hartner's Rest., HotDog Shoppe, Houlihan's, Ichiban Steakhouse, King's Rest., Krispy Kreme, LoneStar Steaks, Mad Mex,

PITTSBURGH

INTERSTATE 76 (TURNPIKE) Cont'd

28	Continued Max&Erma's, McDonald's, Montecello's Grill, Panera Bread, Perkins, Pizza Hut, Pizza Roma, Primanti Bros, Quaker Steak, Saga Steaks, Subway, UNO, Vocelli Pizza, Wendy's Comfort Inn, Fairfield Inn, Hampton Inn, Holiday Inn Express, Hyatt Place, Motel 6, Red Roof Inn, Residence Inn, Sheraton, Super 8 $Tree, Barnes&Noble, Best Buy, Costco/gas, Dick's, Giant Eagle Foods, GNC, Home Depot, Jo-Ann Fabrics, Kuhn's Foods, mall, Marshall's, Michael's, NAPA, Old Navy, PepBoys, PetCo, Radio Shack, Rite Aid, Toyota/Scion, transmissions, Tuesday Morning, USPO, vet, Walgreens, Walmart
23.5mm	pulloff eb
22mm	**Zelienople Service Plaza eb, Welcome Ctr,** Sunoco/dsl/24hr FoodCourt crafts, gifts
17mm	**parking area eb**
13.4mm	**parking area eb**
13mm	Beaver River
13	PA 8, to Ellwood City, Beaver Valley, N Al's Corner Subway Alpine Inn, Beaver Falls Motel, HillTop Motel, Holiday Inn, Lark Motel , S Super 8
10	PA 60 (toll), to New Castle, Pittsburgh, S to airport, services (6mi)
6mm	**pulloff eb**
2mm	**pulloff eb**
1mm	**toll plaza eb,** call boxes located at 1 mi intervals
0mm	Pennsylvania/Ohio state line

INTERSTATE 78

Exit #	Services
77mm	Pennsylvania/New Jersey state line, Delaware River
76mm	**Welcome Ctr wb, full facilities, litter barrels, petwalk vending, toll booth wb**
75	to PA 611, Easton, N TurkeyHill/dsl Dunkin Donuts, McDonald's (1mi), Subway Quality Inn Crayola Factory, CVS Drug, S Exxon/dsl
71	PA 33, to Stroudsburg, **1 mi N on Freemansburg Ave** CJT Asian, Frank's Pizza, Panera Bread, Ruby Tuesday, TGIFriday's, TX Roadhouse, Wayback Burgers Courtyard Barnes&Noble, Best Buy, Dick's, H, Lowe's, Michael's, Pet Supplies+, ShopRite Mkt, Staples
67	PA 412, Hellertown, N TurkeyHill/gas Wendy's Comfort Suites (3mi) H, Chevrolet, S Citgo/dsl, Exxon/dsl, Sunoco Bella's Ristorante, Dunkin Donuts, Papa John's, Rocco's Pizza, Roma Pizza, Vassi's Drive-In, Waffle House Holiday Inn Express 7-11, CVS Drug, repair
60b a	PA 145 N, PA 309 S, South Fort St, Quakertown
59	to PA 145 (from eb), Summit Lawn
58	Emaus St (from wb), S Gulf $General
57	Lehigh St, N Sunoco/dsl, WaWa/dsl China House, IHOP, Palumbo Pizza, Queen City Diner, Subway, Willy Joe's Rest. Best Value Inn $Tree, AAA, BigLots, CVS Drug, Family$, Ford/Lincoln, Home Depot, Infiniti, Kia, Radio Shack, Redner's Whse, STS Tires/repair, Toyota/Scion, VW, S Sunoco, TurkeyHill, Valero A1 Japanese, Bangkok, Brass Rail Rest., Domino's, Dunkin Donuts, McDonald's, Papa John's, Perkins, Pizza Hut/Taco Bell, Rodizio Grill, Rossi's Pizza, Starbucks, Subway, Tilted Kilt Eatery, Wendy's Acura, AT&T, Audi/Mercedes/Porsche, BonTon, Bottom$ Mkt, Buick/GMC, Cadillac/Chevrolet, Chrysler/Dodge/Jeep, Honda, Hyundai,

ALLENTOWN

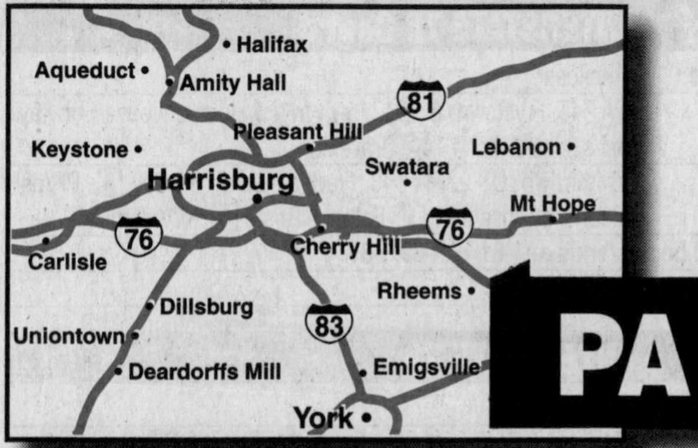

57	Continued Kost Tire, Mazda, Midas, Ross, Staples, SteinMart, Verizon, Volvo, Williams Tire/auto
55	PA 29, Cedar Crest Blvd, N Shell, S H
54b a	US 222, Hamilton Blvd, N Hess Bamboo Asian, Baskin-Robbins/Dunkin Donuts, Boston Mkt, Carrabba's, Friendly's, Gourmet Buffet, Ice Cream World, McDonald's, Menchie's, Perkins, Pistachio Cafe, Pizza Hut, Subway, Teppan Steaks, TGIFriday's, Wendy's Comfort Suites/rest., Holiday Inn Express, Howard Johnson Bottom$ Mkt, Dorney Funpark, Dorneyville Drug, Office Depot, Rite Aid, Weis Foods, S WaWa Dunkin Donuts, Hunan Springs Wingate Inn Queen City Tire, repair, Subaru
53	PA 309 (wb only)
51	to I-476, US 22 E, PA 33 N (eb only), Whitehall
49b a	PA 100, Fogelsville, N Arby's, Cracker Barrel, Joe's Pizza, LJ Silver, Panda&Fish Chinese, Pizza Hut, Winger Deli Comfort Inn, Hawthorn Inn KOA (7mi), Rite Aid, STS Tire/repair, S Shell/Dunkin Donuts, Sunoco, WaWa/dsl Boston's Grill, Burger King, Florence Italian, Starlite Diner, Taco Bell, Yocco's Hotdogs Hampton Inn, Hilton Garden, Holiday Inn, Sleep Inn, Staybridge Suites Clover Hill Winery, st police, Toyota/Scion
45	PA 863, to Lynnport, N Exxon/Subway/dsl, Sunoco/New Smithville Diner/dsl truck service, S Super 8
40	PA 737, Krumsville, N Pine Hill Campground, Robin Hill RV Park (4mi)
35	PA 143, Lenhartsville, 3 mi S Robin Hill Park
30	Hamburg, S Hamburg Mkt
29b a	PA 61, to Reading, Pottsville, N Shell//Subway/dsl, WaWa/dsl Baskin-Robbins/Dunkin Donuts, Burger King, Cracker Barrel, Five Guys, JA Buffet, LJ Silver/Taco Bell, Logan's Roadhouse, McDonald's, Pappy T's, Pizza Hut, Red Robin, Wendy's Microtel $Tree, Advance Parts, AT&T, Boat'n RV Ctr RV, Cabela's Outdoor, GNC, Harley-Davidson (8mi), Hyundai, Lowe's, Pet Supplies+, Russell Stover, Toyota/Scion, Verizon, Walmart/Subway
23	Shartlesville, N Chromeshop/dsl, Loves/McDonald's/Subway/dsl/scales/24hr Dunkin Donuts Dutch Motel Appalachian Campsites, S Blue Mtn Family Rest. Scottish Inn antiques, camping, Dutch Haus/gifts, USPO
19	PA 183, Strausstown, N Lukoil Sheepskin Motel, S Power/dsl
17	PA 419, Rehrersburg, N Best truck/tire repair
16	Midway, N Exxon/dsl, Sunoco/dsl J&S Pizza, Midway Diner Comfort Inn, S auto/truck repair
15	Grimes
13	PA 501, Bethel, N Valero/dsl, S Bethel/dsl dsl repair

= gas = food = lodging = other = rest stop

INTERSTATE 78 Cont'd

Exit #	Services
10	PA 645, Frystown, S FLYING J/Huddle House/Subway/dsl/scales/24hr/ @ Travel Inn
6	(8 from wb, US 22)PA 343, Fredricksburg, 1 mi S PP/dsl, Redner's Whse/mkt Esther's Rest. KOA (5mi)

I-78 begins/ends on I-81, exit 89, I-81.

INTERSTATE 79

ERIE

Exit #	Services
183b a	PA 5, 12th St, Erie, E Valley Tire, W Country Fair/dsl, GetGo, Sunoco/dsl Applebee's, Bob Evans, Bruster's, Dunkin Donuts, Eat'n Park, El Canelo Mexican, Five Guys, Hibachi Japanese, KFC, McDonald's, Moe's SW Grill, Panera Bread, Pizza Hut, Serafini's, Taco Bell, Tim Hortons, Wendy's Comfort Inn (2mi) $General, $Tree, Advance Parts, Aldi Foods, BigLots, CVS Drug, Dunn Tire, Family$, Giant Eagle Foods, GNC, Save-a-Lot Foods, Tires-4-Less, to Presque Isle SP, Tuesday Morning, U-Haul, Verizon, vet
182	US 20, 26th St, E Country Fair/dsl, KwikFill Subway , CVS Drug, Family$, Tops Foods/gas/24hr, W Country Fair/dsl, GetGo/dsl Arby's, Burger King, DQ, Hong Kong Chinese, Hoss's Steaks, Hungry Howie's, Little Caesar's, LJ Silver, McDonald's, Subway, Tim Hortons Glass House Inn $General, AT&T, AutoZone, Ford, Giant Eagle Foods, K-Mart, Monro, O'Reilly Parts, TrueValue, URGENT CARE, USPO, vet, Volvo
180	US 19, to Kearsarge, E Aoyama Japanese, Arby's, Buffalo Wild Wings, Cheddars, Coldstone, Firebirds Grill, Fox&Hound, KFC, Mad Mex, Max&Erma's, McDonald's, Moe's SW Grill, O'Charley's, Olive Garden, Outback Steaks, Primanti Bros, Red Lobster, Smokey Bones BBQ, Starbucks, Wendy's Candlewood Suites, Fairfield Inn, Homewood Suites, SpringHill Suites, TownePlace Suites , Audi/Cadillac, Barnes&Noble, Bon-Ton, Chrysler/Dodge/Jeep, Dick's, Field & Stream, Firestone/auto, Gander Mtn, JC Penney, Macy's, mall, Michael's, Petco, PetCo, Rite Aid, Ross, Sears/auto, TJ Maxx, Toyota/Scion, Verizon, W Country Fair/dsl camping
178b a	I-90, E to Buffalo, W to Cleveland
174	to McKean, E access to gas/dsl, W KOA
166	US 6N, to Edinboro, E Country Fair/dsl, Sheetz McDonald's (3mi), Perkins (2mi), Subway, Wendy's Comfort Suites Advance Parts, Verizon, vet, Walmart
163mm	**both lanes, full facilities, litter barrels, petwalk vending**
154	PA 198, to Saegertown, Conneautville, Erie NWR (17mi)
147b a	US 6, US 19, US 322, to Meadville, E All American Gas/wash, Country Fair, GetGo, Sheetz/dsl 5 Guys Burgers, Applebee's, Arby's, Chovy's Italian, Cracker Barrel, DQ, Hoss's Rest., KFC, Perkins, Pizza Hut, Super Buffet, Taco Bell Days Inn/rest., EconoLodge, Holiday Inn Express , Advance Parts, Eddie's Hotdogs, Family$, Giant Eagle Foods, Home Depot, Jo-Ann Fabrics, Radio Shack, Save-a-Lot Foods, W Sheetz/dsl Burger King, Compadres Mexican, King's Rest., McDonald's, Red Lobster, Subway, Tim Hortons, Yuen's Garden Hampton Inn, Quality Inn $Tree, Aldi Foods, AutoZone, Buick/Cadillac/GMC, Chevrolet, GNC, K-Mart, st police, Staples, to Pymatuning SP, Toyota/Scion, URGENT CARE, Verizon, visitor info, Walmart
141	PA 285, to Geneva, E to Erie NWR (20mi), W Aunt Bee's Rest./dsl, Citgo/dsl

MEADVILLE

PA

Exit #	Services
135mm	**both lanes, full facilities, litter barrels, petwalk vending**
130	PA 358, to Sandy Lake, W (13mi), to Goddard SP
121	US 62, to Mercer, E Valley Tire, W Sunoco/dsl st police
116b a	I-80, E to Clarion, W to Sharon
113	PA 208, PA 258, to Grove City, E BP, Country Fair/dsl Compadres Mexican , W KwikFill/Subway, Sheetz/dsl Eat'n Park, Elephant&Castle Rest., Hoss' Rest., King's Rest., McDonald's, My Bro's Place, Primanti Bros, Taco Bell, Wendy's Best Western, Comfort Inn, Hampton Inn, Holiday Inn Express, Microtel, Super 8 KOA (3mi), Premium Outlets/famous brands, tires
110mm	**/weigh sta sb, full facilities, litter barrels, petwalk vending**
107mm	**/weigh sta nb, full facilities, litter barrels, petwalk vending**
105	PA 108, to Slippery Rock, E DQ Evening Star Motel Slippery Rock Camping, to Slippery Rock U
99	US 422, to New Castle, E to Moraine SP, W Pilot/McDonald's/Subway/dsl/scales/24hr Coopers Lake Camping, to Rose Point Camping
96	PA 488, Portersville, E Bear Run Camping, Moraine SP, W Brown's Country Kitchen, gas/dsl, McConnell's Mill SP (3mi)
88	(87 from nb) US 19, PA 68, Zelienople, E Log Cabin Inn Rest., W BiLo/dsl Burger King, Pizza Hut
85	(83 from nb), PA 528 (no quick return), to Evans City, W Buick
80mm	**weigh sta both lanes**
78	(76 from nb, exits left from nb), US 19, PA 228, to Mars, access to I-76, PA TPK, E GetGo/dsl, Gulf/7-11/dsl Applebee's, Chick-fil-A, Coldstone, DiBella's Subs, Echo Rest., Jimmy Wan's Chinese, Longhorn Steaks, McDonald's, Moe's SW Grill, Noodles&Co, Olive Garden, On-the-Border, Red Robin, Smokey Bones BBQ, Starbucks, Subway Courtyard, Hilton Garden, Marriott , AT&T, Dick's, GNC, Kohl's, Lowe's, Petsmart, Staples, Target, TJ Maxx, W on US 19 5 Guys Burgers, A&W/LJ Silver, Alladin's Eatery, Arby's, Bob Evans, Boston Mkt, Bravo Italian, Buffalo Wild Wings, Burger King, Chipotle Mexican, Denny's, DQ, Dunkin Donuts, Dynasty, Eat'n Park, Emiliano's Mexican, Firehouse Subs, HotDog Shoppe, Houlihan's, Ichiban Steakhouse, Jimmy John's, LoneStar Steaks, Mad Mex, Max&Erma's, McDonald's, Monte Cello's Grill, Panera Bread, Perkins, Pizza Roma, Primanti Bros, Quaker Steak, Saga Steaks, Sports Grille, Subway, Wendy's Candlewood Suites, Comfort Inn, Fairfield Inn, Hampton Inn, Holiday Inn Express, Hyatt Place, Motel 6, Red Roof Inn, Residence Inn, Sheraton, Super 8 $Tree, AAA, AT&T, Autozone, Barnes&Noble, Best Buy, BP/dsl, Costco/gas, Firestone/auto, GetGo, Giant Eagle Foods, GNC, Home Depot, Jo-Ann Fabrics, Kuhn's Foods, mall, Marathon/dsl, Marshall's, Michael's, NAPA, Old Navy, PepBoys, PetCo, Radio Shack, Rite Aid, Sheetz, Sunoco/dsl, Toyota/Scion, transmissions, Tuesday Morning, USPO, Verizon, vet, Walgreens, Walmart
77	I-76/Tpk, to Youngstown
75	US 19 S (from nb), to Warrendale, services on US 19
73	PA 910, to Wexford, E BP Eat'n Park, King's Family Rest., Starbucks EconoLodge, W Exxon/Subway/dsl Carmody's Rest.
72	I-279 S (from sb, exits left), to Pittsburgh
68	Mt Nebo Rd, E Sheetz/dsl, W
66	to PA 65, Emsworth

CRANBERRY

INTERSTATE 79 Cont'd

PITTSBURGH

Exit #	Services
65	to PA 51, Coraopolis, Neville Island, E Kings Grille Fairfield Inn Penske Trucks, W Subway
64.5mm	Ohio River
64	PA 51 (from nb), to Coraopolis, McKees Rocks
60	PA 60, Crafton, E King's Rest, Primanti Bros Comfort Inn, EconoLodge, Motel 6, Travelodge , W Juliano's Rest. Meineke
59b	I-376 W, US 22 W, US 30 (from nb), W airport
59a	I-376 E, to Pittsburgh
57	to Carnegie
55	PA 50, to Heidelberg, **E on PA 50** BP, Marathon, Sunoco Arby's, Bob Evans, ChuckeCheese, Damon's, Eat'n Park, Firestone/auto, KFC, LJ Silver, McDonald's, Pizza Hut, Sonic, Starbucks, Taco Bell, TX Roadhouse, Wendy's $Tree, BigLots, Ford, Giant Eagle Foods, GNC, Home Depot, Jo-Ann Fabrics, K-Mart/Little Caesar's, Lowe's, Mr Tire, Pepboys, Radio Shack, Rite Aid, TJ Maxx, Walgreens, Walmart
54	PA 50, to Bridgeville, E BP/dsl, Fuel Stop/dsl, GetGo King's Rest., McDonald's Holiday Inn Express , Chevrolet, Midas, Monro, NAPA, Rite Aid, USPO, W Sunoco/dsl Hampton Inn, Knights Inn
50mm	**both lanes, full facilities, litter barrels, petwalk vending**
48	South Pointe, W Jackson's Rest. Hilton Garden, Homewood Suites
45	to PA 980, Canonsburg, E Sheetz, W BP, Citgo Hogfathers BBQ, KFC/Taco Bell, LJ Silver, McDonald's, Papa John's, Pizza Hut, Quiznos, Starbucks, Subway, WaiWai Grill, Wendy's Super 8 $General, Advance Parts, auto/transmission repair, Verizon, Walgreens
43	PA 519, Houston, E BP/dsl, W Sunoco Freightliner
41	Race Track Rd, E Marathon/dsl Buger King, McDonald's, Waffle House, Wendy's Cambria Suites, Candlewood Suites, Comfort Inn, Country Inn&Suites, Courtyard, Doubletree, Hampton Inn, Holiday Inn Audi, Old Navy, racetrack, Tanger Outlets/famous brands, W BP/dsl Microtel Trolley Museum
40	Meadow Lands, W golf, racetrack, Trolley Museum (3mi)
38	I-70 W, to Wheeling
I-79 and I-70 run together 3.5 mi. See I-70, exits 19b a-20.	
34	I-70 E, to Greensburg
33	US 40, to Laboratory, W KOA
31mm	**weigh sta sb**
30	US 19, to Amity, W Exxon/Subway/dsl
23	to Marianna, Prosperity
19	US 19, to PA 221, Ruff Creek, W BP/dsl
14	PA 21, to Waynesburg, E BP Bob Evans Comfort Inn, Microtel Walmart/Subway, W BP/7-11/dsl, Exxon/dsl, GetGo, Marathon, Sheetz, Sunoco Burger King, DQ, Golden Wok, Hardee's, KFC, Little Caesars, McDonald's, Pizza Hut, Scotty's Pizza, Subway, Vocelli Pizza, Wendy's EconoLodge, Hampton Inn, Super 8 , $General, $Tree, Ace Hardware, Advance Parts, Aldi Foods, AT&T, AutoZone, BigLots, Cadillac/Chevrolet/Subaru, Chrysler/Dodge/Jeep, CVS Drug, Family$, Giant Eagle Foods, Radio Shack, Rite Aid, st police, Verizon, Walgreens
7	to Kirby
6mm	**Welcome Ctr/weigh sta nb, full facilities, litter barrels, petwalk vending**
1	Mount Morris, E Sunoco/Huddle House/dsl/scales/24hr Honda/Mazda, W BFS/dsl Mt Morris Campground

WAYNESBURG

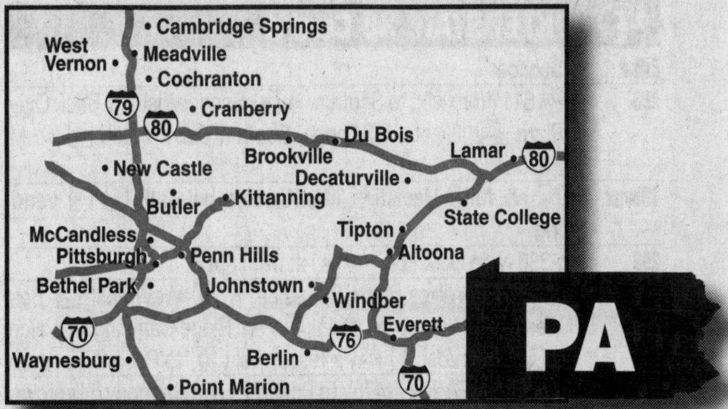

Exit #	Services
0mm	Pennsylvania/West Virginia state line

INTERSTATE 80

STROUDSBURG

Exit #	Services
311mm	Pennsylvania/New Jersey state line, Delaware River
310.5	**toll booth wb**
310	PA 611, Delaware Water Gap, **S Welcome Ctr/ , full services, info** Fuel On, Gulf Apple Pie Bakery, Doughboys Pizza, Water Gap Diner,
309	US 209 N, PA 447, to Marshalls Creek, N Gulf Blue Tequila Mexican, DQ, Dunkin Donuts, Landmark Cafe, Wendy's (2mi) Days Inn, Staybridge Suites
308	East Stroudsburg, N Exxon/Subs Now , vet, WaWa, **1 mi S** Arby's, Burger King, CiCi's, Friendly's, Holy Guacamole, Ichiban Asian, KFC, McDonald's, Roasted Tomato Grill Budget Motel, Super 8 K-Mart, Radio Shack, ShopRite Foods, Walmart/McDonald's
307	PA 191, Broad St, N Hampton Inn , S Sunoco Compton's Rest. EconoLodge
306	Dreher Ave (from wb, no EZ return), N WaWa
305	US 209, Main St, N Gulf/dsl, Shell Perkins Quality Inn, S Exxon/dsl Holiday Inn Express
304	US 209, to PA 33, 9th St (from wb)
303	9th St, (from eb), N 5 Guys Burgers, Burger King, Dunkin Donuts, Fume Asin, Garfield's Rest., McDonald's, Olive Garden, Panera Bread, Popeye's, Ruby Tuesday, TX Roadhouse, Wendy's $Tree, Best Buy, BJ's/Subway/gas, Bon Ton, Buick/GMC, Chevrolet, CVS Drug, Home Depot, Hyundai, JC Penney, Kia, Michaels, Midas, Old Navy, Petsmart, Radio Shack, Staples, Target, Target, TJ Maxx, URGENT CARE, Walgreens, Weis Foods/gas
302	PA 611, to Bartonsville, N Exxon/dsl Big Daddy's BBQ, Chili's, Dickey's BBQ, Dunkin Donuts, East Gourmet Buffet, Frank's Pizza, Ichiban Steaks, Longhorn Steaks, Moe's SW Grill, Red Lobster, Red Robin, Sonic, Studebaker's, Subway Comfort Inn, Hampton Inn, Howard Johnson $Tree, Advance Parts, AT&T, Dick's, Giant Foods/gas, Kohl's, Lowe's, URGENT CARE, Verizon
299	PA 715, Tannersville, N Citgo/dsl, Mobil/Burger King/dsl, Turkey Hill DQ, Dunkin Donuts, FoodCout, Friendly's, Pocono Diner Ramada Ltd, Scotrun Motel $General, CVS Drug, The Crossing Factory Outlet/famous brands, Weis Foods, S Sunoco/dsl Tannersville Diner Days Inn, Summit Resort to Big Pocono SP, to Camelback Ski Area

PA

INTERSTATE 80 Cont'd

Exit #	Services
298	PA 611 (from wb), to Scotrun, N 🅿 Sunoco/dsl 🍴 Brick Oven Pizza 🏨 Great Wolf Lodge, Scotrun Diner/motel 🅾 to Mt Pocono
295mm	🆁🆂 eb, full ♿ facilities, litter barrels, petwalk 🚻 🅰 vending
293	I-380 N, to Scranton, (exits left from eb)
284	PA 115, to Wilkes-Barre, Blakeslee, N 🅿 WaWa/dsl 🏨 Best Western, Blakeslee Inn (2mi) 🅾 Fern Ridge Camping, st police, S 🅿 Exxon/dsl 🍴 Ray's Tuscan Villa 🅾 to Pocono Raceway
277	PA 940, to PA Tpk (I-476), to Pocono, Lake Harmony, Allentown, N 🅿 WaWa 🍴 A&W/LJ Silver, Arby's, McDonald's, Subway 🏨 Comfort Inn, EconoLodge, Holiday Inn Express, Mtn Laurel Resort, Pocono Inn/Resort, Quality Inn, Split Rock Resort
274	PA 534, N 🅿 Hickory Run/Valero/rest./dsl/scales/24hr, Sunoco/Subs Now/dsl/24hr 🅾 towing/repair, S 🅾 to Hickory Run SP (6mi)
273mm	Lehigh River
273	PA 940, PA 437, to Freeland, White Haven, N 🅿 Exxon, Fuel One, S 🍴 Forks Rest., Powerhouse Eatery
270mm	🆁🆂 eb, full ♿ facilities, info, litter barrels, petwalk 🚻 🅰 RV dump, vending
262	PA 309, to Hazleton, Mountain Top, N 🅿 Citgo 🍴 Mary's Rest., Wendy's 🏨 EconoLodge 🅾 auto/truck repair, S 🅿 Valero/dsl 🏨 Holiday Inn Express 🅾 Nescopeck SP (5mi)
260b a	I-81, N to Wilkes-Barre, S to Harrisburg
256	PA 93, to Nescopeck, Conyngham, N 🅿 Pilot/Subway/dsl/scales/24hr, Sunoco/repair, S 🍴 Tom's Kitchen (2mi) 🏨 Best Value Inn, Hampton Inn (4mi) 🅾 🔁, towing/truck repair
251mm	Nescopeck River
246mm	🆁🆂/weigh sta both lanes, full ♿ facilities, litter barrels, petwalk 🚻 🅰 vending, weather info
242	PA 339, to Mainville, Mifflinville, N 🅿 Love's/Arby's/dsl/scales/24hr, Sunoco/Subway/dsl 🍴 McDonald's 🏨 Super 8, S 🅿 Exxon/dsl 🏨 Comfort Inn
241mm	Susquehanna River
241b a	US 11, to Berwick, Lime Ridge, Bloomsburg, N 🏨 Red Maple Inn (2mi) 🅾 🔁, 2-5 mi S 🅿 Sheetz/dsl, Sunoco/Subs Now/dsl 🍴 Applebee's, Arby's, Burger King, Domino's, Dunkin Donuts, Kemlar's Rest., Marley's Grill, McDonald's, Morris Rest., Oliran Japanese, Pizza Hut, Rita's Custard, Subway, Taco Bell, Taste of Italy, Wendy's 🏨 Budget Host, Relax Inn 🅾 AAA, Ace Hardware, Advance Parts, BigLots, Buick/GMC, Cadillac/Chevrolet, CVS Drug, Ford/Honda, Giant Foods/gas, Kost Tire, Rite Aid, Staples, U-Haul, Weis Foods/gas
236	PA 487, to Bloomsburg, Lightstreet, S 🅿 Sunoco 🍴 Denny's 🏨 Hampton Inn, Relax Inn (2mi), Turkey Hill Inn 🅾 🔁, to Bloomsburg U
232	PA 42, Buckhorn, N 🅿 Exxon/Subs Now, TA/Country Pride/Subway/dsl/scales/24hr/ @ 🍴 Burger King, Cracker Barrel, KFC, Perkins, Quaker Steak&Lube, Ruby Tuesday, Wendy's 🏨 EconoLodge, Holiday Inn Express 🅾 AT&T, BonTon, Home Depot, JC Penney, mall, Sears/auto, S 🍴 Carini's Italian, Gourmet Buffet, Olive Garden, Panera Bread 🏨 Comfort Suites 🅾 $Tree, Indian Head Camping (3mi), Lowe's, PetCo, Verizon, Walmart/McDonald's
224	PA 54, to Danville, N 🅿 Exxon/Subway/dsl 🏨 Quality Inn, S 🍴 Friendly's, McDonald's, Mom's Dutch Kitchen 🏨 Best Western, Hampton Inn, Red Roof Inn, Super 8 🅾 🔁
219mm	🆁🆂 both lanes, full ♿ facilities, info, litter barrels, petwalk 🚻 🅰 vending
215	PA 254, Limestonevill, N 🅿 Milton 32 Trkstp/rest./dsl/24hr, S 🅿 ⓕFLYING J/Penn 80 Rest./Subway/dsl/scales/24hr/ @ 🅾 Eagle Truckwash
212b a	I-180 W, PA 147 S, to Muncy, Williamsport, S 🅿 Sunoco (1mi)
210.5mm	Susquehanna River
210 a	US 15, to Williamsport, Lewisburg, S 🅿 Sunoco/dsl 🍴 Bonanza 🏨 Comfort Inn, Holiday Inn Express 🅾 🔁, KOA (5mi)
199	Mile Run
194mm	🆁🆂/weigh sta both lanes, full ♿ facilities, litter barrels, petwalk 🚻 🅰 vending
192	PA 880, to Jersey Shore, N 🅿 Sunoco/dsl 🅾 🔁, S 🅿 Valero/dsl 🅾 towing/truck repair
185	PA 477, Loganton, N 🅿 Valero 🅾 camping, S 🍴 RB Winter SP (12mi), Twilight Diner
178	US 220, Lock Haven, 5 mi N 🅿 KwikFill/dsl, Sheetz/dsl 🍴 Little Caesar's, Pizza Hut, Ruby Tuesday 🅾 🔁, $General, $Tree, Advance Parts, K-Mart, Lowe's, Walmart/Subway, Weis Foods
173	PA 64, Lamar, N 🅿 Pilot/Subway/dsl/scales/24hr 🍴 Cottage Rest., McDonald's 🏨 Comfort Inn/rest., Hampton Inn 🅾 repair, S 🅿 ⓕFLYING J/Denny's/dsl/LP/scales/24hr/, TA/Country Pride/dsl/scales/24hr/ @, Valero
161	I-99, US 220 S, PA 26, to Bellafonte, N 🅾 Bellefonte Camping, KOA (2mi), S 🅾 to PSU
158	US 220 S, PA 150, to Altoona, Milesburg, N 🅿 Bestway/rest./dsl/motel/24hr/ @, Shell/Subway, TA/Country Pride/dsl/scales/24hr/ @, Valero/dsl 🍴 McDonald's 🏨 Quality Inn, S st police
147	PA 144, to Snow Shoe, N 🅿 Exxon/dsl/repair/24hr, Sunoco/dsl/24hr 🍴 Snow Shoe Rest., Snow Shoe Sandwich Shop, Subway 🅾 Hall's Foods, USPO
146mm	🆁🆂 both lanes, full ♿ facilities, litter barrels, petwalk 🚻 🅰 vending
138mm	Moshannon River
133	PA 53, to Philipsburg, Kylertown, N 🅿 KwikFill/motel/dsl/scales 🍴 Roadhouse Rest. 🅾 Black Moshannon SP (9mi), dsl repair, Mtn View Mkt, USPO, S 🅾 🔁
123	PA 970, to Shawville, Woodland, N 🅾 Woodland Camping, S 🅿 Gio's BBQ/dsl (2mi), PP/dsl 🅾 st police, USPO
120mm	Susquehanna River, W Branch
120	PA 879, Shawville, Clearfield, N 🅿 Sapp Bros/rest./dsl/scales/24hr/ @ 🏨 EconoLodge 🅾 Peterbilt, S 🅿 BP/dsl, Sheetz, Snappy's 🍴 Arby's, Burger King, Chinese buffet, Dunkin Donuts, Dutch Pantry, KFC/Taco Bell, McDonald's 🏨 Best Western, Comfort Inn, Hampton Inn, Holiday Inn Express, Super 8, Travelodge 🅾 🔁, Lowe's, Walmart/Subway
111mm	2250 ft, highest point on I-80 east of Mississippi River
111	PA 153, to Penfield, N 🅾 to Parker Dam, to SB Elliot SP, S 🅾 🔁
101	PA 255, Du Bois, N 🅿 Snappy's/Quiznos/dsl 🅾 camping, 1-2 mi S 🅿 Sheetz/dsl 🍴 A&W/LJ Silver, Arby's, Burger King, Dubois Buffet, Eat'n Park, Italian Oven, Japan One, McDonald's, Napoli Pizzeria, Perkins, Pizza Hut, Ponderosa, Red Lobster, Ruby Tuesday, Station 101 Grill, Subway, Taco Bell, Valley Dairy Rest., Wendy's 🏨 Fairfield Inn, Hampton Inn, Homewood Suites 🅾 🔁, $General, $Tree, Aldi Foods, BigLots, BonTon, CVS Drug, JC Penney, Jo-Ann Fabrics, K-Mart, Lowe's, mall, Old Navy, PetCo, Radio Shack, Rite Aid, Ross, Sears/auto, Shop'n Save Foods, st police, Staples, TJ Maxx, URGENT CARE, Verizon, Walmart/Subway
97	US 219, to Brockway, Du Bois, 2 mi S 🅿 Pilot/Arby's/dsl/scales/24hr, Sheetz/dsl/24hr 🍴 Dutch Pantry Rest., Hoss'

Side labels: HAZLETON · PA · LAMAR · DU BOIS

B R O O K V I L L E C L A R I O N

INTERSTATE 80 Cont'd

97	Continued Rest. Best Western, Clarion, Holiday Inn Express, Advance Parts, Freightliner, st police
90	PA 830 E, N Du Bois Regional
87.5mm	**both lanes, full facilities, litter barrels, petwalk vending**
86	PA 830, to Reynoldsville
81	PA 28, to Brookville, Hazen, S Brookville, hist dist (2mi)
78	PA 36, to Sigel, Brookville, N *FLYING J*/Denny's/dsl/LP/scales/24hr, TA/BP/Taco Bell/dsl/scales/Howard Johnson/24hr/@ DQ, McDonald's, Pizza Hut Super 8 NAPA, to Cook Forest SP, S GetGo/dsl, Oring CNG, Sheetz Arby's, Burger King, China Wok, Plyler's Buffet, Subway Gold Eagle Inn, Quality Inn Chrysler/Dodge/Jeep, Family$, truckwash
73	PA 949, Corsica, N to Clear Creek SP, S USPO
70	US 322, to Strattanville
64	PA 66 S, to New Bethlehem, Clarion, N to Clarion U
62	PA 68, to Clarion, N BP, KwikFill/dsl A&W/LJ Silver, Applebee's, Arby's, Eat'n Park, Hunan King, McDonald's, Perkins, Pizza Hut, RRR Roadhouse, Sakura Buffet, Subway, Taco Bell Comfort Inn, Hampton Inn, Holiday Inn/rest., Microtel, Quality Inn, Super 8 , $Tree, Advance Parts, Aldi Foods, AT&T, AutoZone, JC Penney, K-Mart, Verizon, Walmart/Subway
61mm	Clarion River
60	PA 66 N, to Shippenville, N Jiffy/dsl camping, to Cook Forest SP
56mm	**weigh sta both lanes**
53	to PA 338, to Knox, N Satterlee Gas/dsl (cardlock) BJ's Eatery Countryside Crafts/Quilts, Wolf's Camping Resort, S Good Tire Service
45	PA 478, to St Petersburg, Emlenton, **4 mi** S Golf Hall of Fame
44.5mm	Allegheny River
42	PA 38, to Emlenton, N Exxon/Subway/dsl, Shell/Trkstp/rest./dsl/scales/24hr Emlenton Motel Gaslight RV Park, truck/RV repair
35	PA 308, to Clintonville
30.5mm	**both lanes, full facilities, litter barrels, petwalk vending**
29	PA 8, to Franklin, Barkeyville, N Arby's, Burger King, King's Rest. Motel 6, Quality Inn Freightliner, S Heath/dsl, KwikFill/dsl/scales/motel/24hr, TA/BP/Subway/dsl/scales/24hr/@ to Slippery Rock U, truckwash
24	PA 173, to Grove City, Sandy Lake, S , Grove City Coll, Wendell August Forge/gifts (3mi)
19b a	I-79, N to Erie, S to Pittsburgh
15	US 19, to Mercer, N PP/dsl, Shell Burger King, Margarita King Mexican, McDonald's/rv parking Comfort Inn st police, **2 mi** S Iron Bridge Rest., Springfield Grill KOA (4mi)
4b a	I-376, PA 60, to PA 18, to Sharon-Hermitage, New Castle, N Sheetz/dsl, Sunoco/Subway/dsl EconoLodge, Hampton Inn, Holiday Inn Express, Park Inn, Quality Inn, Red Roof Inn, Super 8, S DQ, MiddleSex Diner $General
2.5mm	Shenango River
1mm	**Welcome Ctr eb, full facilities, litter barrels, petwalk vending**
0mm	Pennsylvania/Ohio state line

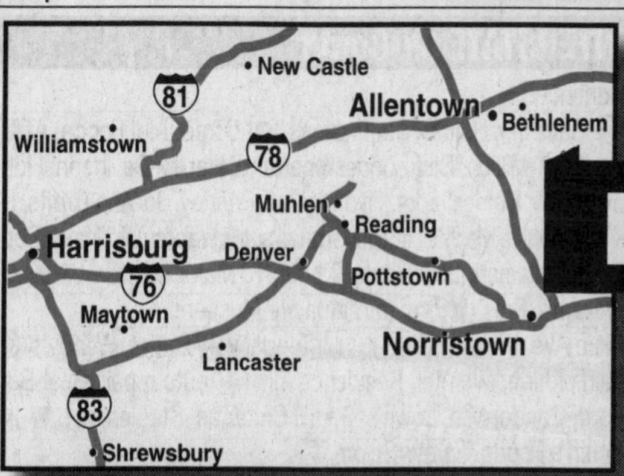

INTERSTATE 81

Exit #	Services
233mm	Pennsylvania/New York state line
232mm	**Welcome Ctr/weigh sta sb, full facilities, litter barrels, petwalk**
230	PA 171, Great Bend, E Valero Lakeside Camping (5mi), W Exxon/Tim Hortons/dsl, Sunoco/dsl Burger King, Dobb's Country Kitchen, Dunkin Donuts, McDonald's, Subway Colonial Brick Motel Family$, Reddon's Drugs, Rob's Foods
223	PA 492, New Milford, E East Lake Camping/RV Park (3mi), W Gulf/dsl, Sunoco, Valero Green Gables Rest. Blue Ridge Motel, Lynn Lee B&B (1.5mi)
219	PA 848, to Gibson, E Sunoco/Burger King/dsl, W *FLYING J*/Denny's/dsl/scales/24hr, Exxon/McDonald's/dsl/24hr Holiday Inn Express, st police
217	PA 547, Harford, E Exxon/Subway/dsl/24hr, Mobil/dsl/24hr
211	PA 92, Lenox, E Elk Mtn Ski Area, Shady Rest Camping (3mi), W Pump-N-Pantry/dsl, Shell/dsl Bingham's Rest., Lenox Rest. Lenox Drug
209mm	**sb, full facilities, litter barrels, petwalk vending**
206	PA 374, to Glenwood, Lenoxville, E Sunoco/dsl to Elk Mountain Ski Resort
203mm	**nb, full facilities, litter barrels, petwalk vending**
202	PA 107, to Fleetville, Tompkinsville
201	PA 438, East Benton, W Duchniks/dsl/repair B&B Rest.
199	PA 524, Scott, E Mobil/dsl, W Exxon/Subway Motel 81 to Lackawanna SP
197	PA 632, Waverly, E Rite Aid, Weis Foods, W Sunoco/Doc's Deli Camelot Inn/rest
194	US 6, US 11, to I-476/PA Tpk, Clarks Summit, W Exxon/dsl, Sheetz/dsl, Sunoco/dsl, Valero Burger King, Damon's, Dino&Francesco's, Domino's, Dunkin Donuts, Krispy Kreme, Kyoto Japanese, La Tonalteca, McDonald's, Moe's SW Grill, New Century Chinese, Starbucks, Subway, Sunny Chinese, Taco Bell, Waffle House, Wendy's Comfort Inn, EconoLodge, Hampton Inn, Nichols Village Inn, Ramada Inn Ace Hardware, Advance Parts, Kost Tire, Monro, Radio Shack, Rite Aid, Verizon, Weis Foods
191b a	US 6, US 11, to Carbondale, E Sheetz/dsl, Sunoco A&W/LJ Silver, Applebee's, Burger King, China Palace, Chipotle, ChuckECheese, Denny's, Dunkin Donuts, Five Guys, HoneyBaked Ham, Kobe Japanese, La Tonalateca, McDonald's, Old Country Buffet, Olive Garden, Panera Bread, Perkins, Quaker Steak&Lube, Red Lobster, Red Robin, Rita's Custard, Roma Pizza, Royal Buffet, Ruby Tuesday, Starbucks, Subway, TCBY, TGIFriday's, TX Roadhouse, Uno Grill, Viewmont Diner

PA

INTERSTATE 81 Cont'd

SCRANTON

191b a Continued
Days Inn, Holiday Inn Express $Tree, Aldi Foods, AT&T, Books-A-Million, Dick's, Firestone/auto, Harley-Davidson, Hobby Lobby, Home Depot, Hyundai, JC Penney, Jo-Ann Crafts, K-Mart, Kohl's, Macy's, mall, Marshall's, Michael's, Old Navy, Pep-Boys, Petsmart, Sears/auto, Target, TJ Maxx, Verizon, Walmart, William's Tires, W to Anthracite Museum

190 Main Ave, Dickson City, E Teppanyaki Buffet, Wendy's Fairfield Inn, Microtel, Residence Inn auto repair, Best Buy, Ford, Gander Mtn, Lowe's, Sam's Club/gas, Staples, vet, W Schiff's Foods, Toyota/Scion

188 PA 347, Throop, E Sheetz/dsl, Sunoco/dsl McDonald's, Wendy's Dunmore Inn, Quality Inn, Scottish Inn, Sleep Inn Advance Parts, BigLots, Kost Tire, Monro, Nissan, PriceChopper Foods, st police, URGENT CARE, W Exxon/Subway/dsl Burger King, Dunkin Donuts, Friendly's

187 to I-84, I-380, US 6 (no return from nb)

186 PA 435, Drinker St (from nb), E Valero/dsl, W Exxon/dsl

185 Central Scranton Expwy (exits left from nb), W

184 to PA 307, River St, W Exxon/Subway/dsl, Valero, Vamco Asian Taste, Dunkin Donuts Sheraton , $Tree, CVS Drug, Gerrity Foods

182 Davis St, Montage Mtn Rd, E Exxon/Coldstone/Subway/dsl Doc's Oyster House, Gourmet Slice Pizza, Johnny Rockets Cafe, Longhorn Steaks, Nonno's Pizza, Panchero's Mexican, Panera Bread, Quiznos, Ruby Tuesday, Starbucks Comfort Suites, Courtyard, Hampton Inn, Springhill Suites, TownePlace Suites AT&T, GNC, Verizon, W Sunoco Dunkin Donuts, Waffle House, Wendy's EconoLodge CVS Drug, USPO

180 to US 11, PA 502, to Moosic, (exits left from nb), **W on US 11** Exxon/dsl, Sunoco Subway

178b a to US 11, Avoca, E Holiday Inn Express, W Petro/Valero/Iron Skillet/dsl/scales/24hr/ @

175b a PA 315 S, to I-476, Dupont, E Exxon/Subway/dsl, Sunoco/dsl Arby's, McDonald's, Perkins Knights Inn Volvo, W Pilot/Wendy's/dsl/scales/24hr Burger King, Star Asia Buffet, Uncle Joe's Pizza Comfort Inn truck repair, Verizon, Walmart/Subway

WILKES BARRE

170b a PA 115, PA 309, Wilkes-Barre, E Exxon/Subway/dsl, Sunoco/dsl Holiday Inn to Pocono Downs, W Citgo, Sunoco/dsl Buffalo Wild Wings, Burger King, Denny's, Dunkin Donuts, Friendly's, Grotto Pizza, Jersey Mike's, LJ Silver, Longhorn Steaks, McDonald's, Moe's SW Grill, Red Lobster, Sonic, Taco Bell, TGIFriday's, Wendy's Days Inn, Extended Stay America, Fairfield Inn, Holiday Inn Express, Host Inn, Quality Inn, Red Roof Inn , $General, BonTon, Chevrolet, Goodyear, Harley-Davidson, JC Penney, Macy's, mall, Sears/auto

168 Highland Park Blvd, Wilkes-Barre, W Sheetz/dsl, Sunoco, TurkeyHill Applebee's, Bob Evans, Chili's, Chipotle, Chuck-eCheese, Cracker Barrel, Five Guys, King's Buffet, La Tolteca Mexican, Logan's Roadhouse, Lucky's SportHouse, Mizu Steaks, Nello's Pizza, Olive Garden, Outback Steaks, Panera Bread, Popeye's, Red Robin, Smokey Bones BBQ, Starbucks, Subway, Wendy's Courtyard, Hampton Inn, Hilton Garden, Motel 6 AT&T, Barnes&Noble, Best Buy, Dick's, Firestone/auto, Home Depot, Kohl's, Kost Tire, Lowe's, Marshall's, Michael's, Nissan, Old Navy, PepBoys, PetCo, Petsmart, PriceChopper, Radio Shack, Ross, Sam's Club/gas, Staples, Target, TJ Maxx, U-Haul, URGENT CARE, Verizon, Walgreens, Walmart/Subway, Wegman's Foods

HAZLETON

165b a PA 309 S, (exits left from nb), Wilkes-Barre, W Citgo/dsl, Gulf Dunkin Donuts, McDonald's, Perkins, Taco Bell Comfort Inn, EconoLodge $Tree, Advance Parts, K-Mart, Rite Aid

164 PA 29, to Nanticoke, Ashley

159 Nuangola, W Valero/Subs Now/dsl camping (10mi)

157mm **/weigh sta sb, full facilities, litter barrels, petwalk vending**

156mm **/weigh sta nb, full facilities, litter barrels, petwalk vending**

155 to Dorrance, E Sunoco/dsl EconoLodge (2mi), W Blue Ridge Plaza/dsl

151b a I-80, E to Mountaintop, W to Bloomsburg

145 PA 93, W Hazleton, E Sunoco/dsl, TurkeyHill/dsl Applebee's, Arby's, Bonanza, Damon's, Denny's, Five Stars Chinese, Friendly's, LJ Silver, McDonald's, Perkins, Pizza Hut, Taco Bell, Wendy's Best Western (2mi), Comfort Inn, Fairfield Inn, Forest Hill Inn, Ramada Inn (2mi) , $Tree, Advance Parts, Aldi Foods, AT&T, Big Lots, Boscov's, Buick/Cadillac/GMC, Chrysler/Dodge/Jeep, JC Penney, K-Mart, Lowe's, Mazda, Michael's, Old Navy, Petsmart, Radio Shack, st police, Staples, Weis Foods, W Shell, Top of the 80's Candlewood Suites, Hampton Inn

143 PA 924, to Hazleton, W Fuelon/Subs Now/dsl/scales, Sunoco/Subway, TurkeyHill/dsl Burger King, Sonic Residence Inn

141 PA 424, S Hazleton Beltway, E Mt Laurel Motel

138 PA 309, to McAdoo, **2 mi E** Pines Motel

134 to Delano

132mm **parking area/weigh sta both lanes**

131b a PA 54, Mahanoy City, E to Tuscarora/Locust Lake SP, W Shell/dsl, Sunoco/dsl Mainstay Suites

124b a PA 61, to Frackville, E Cracker Barrel, McDonald's Holiday Inn Express BigLots, BonTon, mall, W Exxon, Gulf/dsl, Speedway Anthony's Pizza, Dutch Kitchen, Subway EconoLodge, Granny's Motel, Rodeway Inn , Goodyear/auto, Rite Aid, st police

119 High Ridge Park Rd, to Gordon, E Country Inn&Suites

116 PA 901, to Minersville, E 901 Rest.

112 PA 25, to Hegins, W camping

107 US 209, to Tremont

LEBANON

104 PA 125, Ravine, E Exxon/Burger King/dsl/scales/24hr Echo Valley Campground

100 PA 443, to Pine Grove, E Exxon/dsl Arby's, McDonald's Comfort Inn, EconoLodge $General, W Pilot/DQ/Subway/dsl/scales/24hr Gooseberry Farms Diner Hampton Inn KOA (5mi), truckwash

90 PA 72, to Lebanon, E Exxon/Subway, Love's/McDonald's/dsl/scales/24hr, Speedway/Blimpie/Dunkin Donuts/dsl DQ, Wendy's Best Western, Days Inn KOA, repair, st police, W Comfort Inn

89 I-78 E, to Allentown

85b a PA 934, to Annville, **2 mi W** Exxon/dsl Funck's Rest. to IndianTown Gap Nat Cem

80 PA 743, Grantville, E Shell/dsl Days Inn, Hampton Inn, W Exxon/dsl Italian Delight Comfort Suites, Holiday Inn camping, racetrack

79mm **/weigh sta both lanes, full facilities, litter barrels, petwalk vending**

77 PA 39, to Hershey, E Exxon/dsl, Pilot/Pizza Hut/dsl/scales/24hr, Valero/dsl Hershey Rd Rest. Country Inn&Suites, EconoLodge, La Quinta, Motel 6, Scottish Inn st police, to Hershey Attractions, W Exit 77 TP/Subway/

PA

INTERSTATE 81 Cont'd

HARRISBURG

77 Continued
dsl, TA/Country Pride/dsl/scales/24hr/ @, Wilco/Hess/Perkins/Stuckey's/dsl/24hr/ @ McDonald's Holiday Inn Express Goodyear, SpeedCo, truck repair

72 to US 22, Linglestown, E Hess/dsl, Sheetz/dsl, Sunoco/dsl 5 Guys Burgers, Burger King, Chipotle Mexican, McDonald's, Red Robin, Starbucks, Subway, Tonino's Pizza Comfort Inn, Quality Inn Advance Parts, Chrysler/Dodge/Jeep, Costco/gas, CVS Drug, Giant Foods, Harley-Davidson, Karn's Foods, Target, Toyota/Scion, U-Haul, W Turkey Hill Mikado Japanese, Sindbaad Diner, Subway Candlewood Suites, Ramada Inn $General

70 I-83 S, to York, airport

69 Progress Ave, E Cracker Barrel, Dunkin Donuts, Harvest Grill, Macaroni Grill, Starbucks, Tonino's Grill AT&T, CVS Drug, st police, Susquehanna Shoppes, W Turkey Hill/dsl Arby's, YP Rest. Clarion, Hampton Inn, Red Roof Inn, SpringHill Suites

67b a US 22, US 322 W, PA 230, Cameron St, to Lewistown

66 Front St, E , W Exxon, Sunoco Bro's Pizza, Front St Diner, McDonald's, Pizza Hut, Simply Turkey, Taco Bell, Wendy's Best Value, Days Inn

65 US 11/15, to Enola, **1 mi** E Sunoco/dsl, Tom's Al's Pizza, China Taste, DQ, Dunkin Donuts, McDonald's, Subway, Summerdale Diner, Wendy's Quality Inn $Tree, Advance Parts, Fischer Parts, K-Mart, Rite Aid, Sure Fine Foods

61 PA 944, to Wertzville, E Holiday Inn Express , Giant/dsl, Weiss Mkt, W Turkey Hill/dsl Microtel

59 PA 581, to US 11, to I-83, Harrisburg, **3 mi** E on Carlisle Pk Sheetz/dsl, Sunoco Applebee's, Bob Evans, Burger King, Carrabba's, Denny's, Dunkin Donuts, McDonald's, Outback Steaks, Quaker Steak, TGIFriday's, Wayback Burger, Wendy's Park Inn AutoZone, Buick/GMC, Dick's, GNC, Home Depot, Hyundai, K-Mart, Lowe's, Nissan, NTB, Pepboys, Petsmart, Staples, TJ Maxx

57 PA 114, to Mechanicsburg, **2 mi** E Sheetz/dsl Alfredo's Pizza, Arby's, Dickey's BBQ, Great Wall Chinese, Isaac's Rest., KFC/LJ Silver, McDonald's, Olive Garden, Pizza Hut, Red Robin, Silver Spring Diner, Subway, Taco Bell Baymont Inn CarMax, Giant Foods/gas, Marshall's, Sam's Club/gas, Verizon, Walmart

CARLISLE

52b a US 11, to I-76/PA Tpk, Middlesex, E FLYING J/Denny's/dsl/scales/24hr/ @, Pioneer/dsl Bob Evans, Dunkin Donuts, Ember's Steaks, Middlesex Diner Best Value Inn, Days Inn, Hotel Carlisle, Red Roof Inn, Super 8 , W Gulf, Loves/Wendy's/dsl/24hr, Petro/Iron Skillet/dsl/24hr/@ @, Sunoco/Subway/dsl Arby's, Carelli's Subs, McDonald's, Rte 11 Diner, Waffle House Best Western, EconoLodge, Hampton Inn, Holiday Inn Express, Knights Inn, Motel 6, Quality Inn, Quality Inn, Residence Inn, Rodeway Inn, Travelodge , Blue Beacon

49 PA 74 (no EZ sb return), E Sheetz/dsl same as 48, W Trindle Grill AAA

48 PA 74, York Rd (no EZ nb return), E Gulf/dsl Asian Cafe, Red Robin, Starbucks, Subway $Tree, Aldi Foods, Hancock Fabrics, Kohl's, Michael's, Petsmart, Rite Aid, Target, Verizon, W Speedway Burger King, Little Caesars, McDonald's, Pizza Hut, Taco Bell BonTon, CVS Drug, Dunkin Donuts, Ford, Lowe's, Midas, Weis Foods

47 PA 34, Hanover St, E Chili's, Cracker Barrel Sleep Inn Home Depot, W Al's Pizza, Applebee's, Bruster's/Nathan's, DQ, Palace China, Panera Bread, Papa John's,

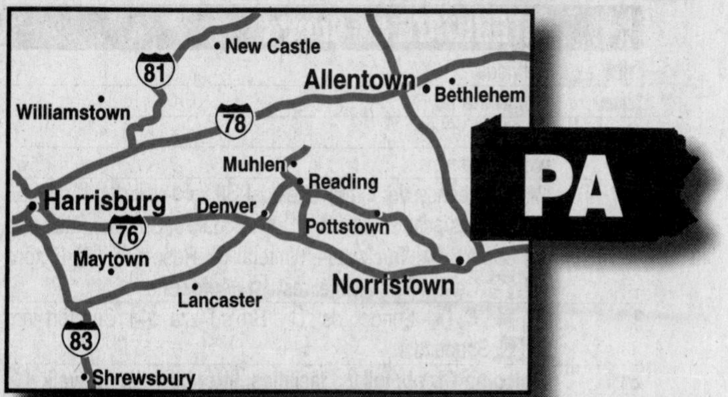

CHAMBERSBURG

47 Continued
Rita's Custard, Subway, Super Buffet, Vinny's Rest, Wendy's AT&T, CVS Drug, Rite Aid, Staples, TJ Maxx, Walmart/McDonald's

45 College St, E Gulf/dsl Alfredo Pizza, Arby's, Great Wall Buffet, McDonald's, Subway, Walnut Bottom Diner Days Inn, Super 8 , K-Mart, Nell's Foods, Tire Pros, Verizon

44 PA 465, Allen Rd, to Plainfield, E Country Inn&Suites, Fairfield Inn , st police, W Sheetz/dsl Subway

38.5mm **both lanes, full facilities, litter barrels, petwalk vending**

37 PA 233, to Newville, E Pine Grove Furnace SP, W Col Denning SP

29 PA 174, King St, E Sunoco/dsl Rodeway Inn, W Gulf, Rutter's/dsl Bros Pizza, Burger King, Domino's, KFC, Little Caesar's, Subway, Taco Bell, Wendy's Best Western, Holiday Inn Express, Theo's Motel $General, Advance Parts, Aldi Foods, AT&T, Cadillac/Chevrolet, CVS Drug, Ford, Lowe's, Verizon, vet, Walmart

24 PA 696, Fayette St, W Pacific Pride/dsl

20 PA 997, Scotland, E Bonanza, McDonald's Comfort Inn, Super 8 BonTon, Gander Mtn, JC Penney, mall, W Sunoco Sleep Inn

17 Walker Rd, W Sheetz/dsl Aki Steaks, Bruster's/Nathan's, Cafe del Sol, Chipotle Mexican, Fuddrucker's, Longhorn Steaks, Olive Garden, Panera Bread, Red Robin, Sonic, Subway, TGIFriday's, TX Roadhouse Candlewood Suites, Country Inn&Suites AT&T, BJ's/dsl, Buick/Chevrolet/GMC, Ford, Giant Foods/gas, Kohl's, Michael's, Mr Tire, Petsmart, Staples, Target, URGENT CARE, Verizon

16 US 30, to Chambersburg, E Fuel Ctr, Sheetz Arby's, Broadway Deli, Bro's Pizza, Burger King, Dunkin Donuts, Hoss's Rest., KFC, Little Caesars, Perkins, Popeye's, Rita's Custard, Rte 30 Rest., Ryan's, Supreme Buffet, Waffle House, Wendy's Days Inn $Tree, AAA, Aldi Foods, Dick's, Harley-Davidson, Hobby Lobby, Jo-Ann Fabrics, Lowe's, Midas, NAPA, Nissan/Toyota/Scion, Petco, TJ Maxx, U-Haul, Verizon, vet, Walmart/Subway, W Speedway/dsl Big Oak Cafe, Burger King, Chambersburg Diner, Copper Kettle, LJ Silver, McDonald's, Pizza Hut, Ruby Tuesday, Starbucks, Subway, Taco Bell Best Western, Clarion, La Quinta , Advance Parts, AutoZone, Lincoln, URGENT CARE, Walgreens

14 PA 316, Wayne Ave, E Sheetz/dsl Bob Evans, Cracker Barrel Fairfield Inn, Hampton Inn, Red Carpet Inn, W KwikFill, Shell Applebee's, Arby's, China Buffet, China Wok, Denny's, Mario's Italian, Montezuma Mexican, Papa John's, Red Lobster, Stoney's Rest., Subway, Twin Dragon Chinese, Volcano Japanese, Wendy's Holiday Inn Express, Quality Inn, Red Roof Inn $Tree, CVS Drug, Giant Foods/gas, GNC, K-Mart, Mr Tire, Save-a-Lot Foods, Verizon, Weis Foods

INTERSTATE 81 Cont'd

Exit #	Services
12mm	**weigh sta sb**
10	PA 914, Marion
7mm	**weigh sta nb**
5	PA 16, Greencastle, E Shell/dsl, Sunoco/grill/dsl, TA/Country Pride/dsl/scales/24hr/@ McDonald's, Subway, Taco Bell Super 8 Truckwash, Whitetail Ski Resort, W Exxon/dsl Castle Green Motel/rest AutoZone
3	US 11, E Sunoco/dsl Bro's Pizza Comfort Inn, W Sheetz/dsl
2mm	**Welcome Ctr nb, full facilities, litter barrels, petwalk vending**
1	PA 163, Mason-Dixon Rd, W Stateline Inn, Stateline Motel Keystone RV Ctr
0mm	Pennsylvania/Maryland state line, Mason-Dixon Line

INTERSTATE 83

HARRISBURG

Exit #	Services
51b a	**I-83 begins/ends on I-81, exit 70.**
50b a	US 22, Jonestown Rd, Harrisburg, E Hess/dsl, Sunoco/dsl, USA 5 Guys Burgers, Applebee's, Arby's, Buffalo Wild Wings, Chipotle Mexican, Cold Stone, Colonial Park Diner, Domino's, El Rodeo Mexican, Gilligan's Grill, Hibachi Grill, LJ Silver, Longhorn Steaks, McDonald's, Old Country Buffet, Olive Garden, Panera Bread, Pizza Hut, Red Lobster, Red Robin, Shogun Asian, Starbucks, Subway, Taco Bell, Tonino's Pizza, Wendy's Aamco, Advance Parts, AutoZone, Best Buy, Bon-Ton, Boscov's, Coscto/gas, Dick's, Ford, Gander Mtn, Giant Foods, Goodyear/auto, Home Depot, Jo-Ann, K-Mart, Kohl's, mall, Marshall's, Meineke, Michael's, NTB, Old Navy, PepBoys, PetCo, Radio Shack, Ross, Sears/auto, Shannon Tire/auto, Target, Tires+, U-Haul, Verizon, vet, Weis Foods, William's Tires/repair, W Sunoco/dsl DQ, Dunkin Donuts, Friendly's, Gabriella's Italian, KFC, Roberto's Pizza Rite Aid
48	Union Deposit Rd, E Sunoco Arby's, Burger King, Infinito's Buffet, Panera Bread Best Western, Hampton Inn $Tree, Giant Foods/gas, Rite Aid, Staples, URGENT CARE, W Gulf/dsl, Sheetz/dsl ChuckeCheese, Empire Asian Bistro, Great Wall Chinese, Jimmy John's, JoJo's Pizza, McDonald's, Naples Pizza, New China, Outback Steaks, Rita's Ice Cream, Starbucks, Subway, TGIFriday's, TX Roadhouse, Waffle House, Wendy's Country Inn&Suites, EconoLodge, Fairfield Inn, Holiday Inn Express $Tree, BigLots, Family$, Hancock Fabrics, Lowe's, PriceRite Foods, Tuesday Morning, Weis Foods
47	(46b from nb), US 322 E, to Hershey, Derry St, E Hess Papa John's, Pizza Hut Home Depot, Petsmart
46b a	I-283 S, to I-76/PA Tpk, W Taco Bell, Wendy's Days Inn, **services E off I-283 S** Exxon/dsl, Sunoco/dsl Bob Evans, Capitol Diner, Chili's, Five Guys, Friendly's, Lancaster Brewing Rest., Leeds Rest., McDonald's, Moe's SW Grill, Subway Courtyard, EconoLodge, Holiday Inn, Howard Johnson, La Quinta, Red Roof Inn, Sheraton, Sleep Inn, Super 8, Wyndham Garden $General, GNC, JC Penney, Kia, Target, Verizon
45	Paxton St, E Sheetz/dsl Applebees, Burger King, Cafe Fresco, Fiesta Mexico, Hibachi Buffet, Isaac's Rest., McDonald's, Melting Pot, Papa Joe's Pizza, Pizza Hut, Qdoba, Ruby Tuesday, Starbucks, Tomato Pie Cafe Hilton Garden, Homewood Suites, Towneplace Suites Advance Parts, Bass Pro Shops, Macy's, mall, Mazda/Subaru, Meineke, Nissan, Toyota/Scion
44b	17th St, 19th St, E Sunoco, Turkey Hill Benihana Japanese, Dunkin Donuts, Hardee's Advance Parts, AutoZone, Buick/GMC, Firestone/auto, Honda, Hyundai, Midas
44a	PA 230, 13th St, Harrisburg, E Family$, W Chevrolet, VW, downtown
43	2nd St, Harrisburg, W Crowne Plaza, Hilton st capitol, downtown
42.5mm	Susquehanna River
42	Lemoyne
41b	Highland Park, E Turkey Hill Burger King, KFC, W Sunoco Papa Joe's Ace Hardware, Weis Foods
41a	US 15, PA 581 W, to Gettysburg
40b	New Cumberland, W Gulf/dsl Cedar Cliff Pizza, McDonald's, New China, Subway $General, CVS Drug

LEWISBERRY

Exit #	Services
40a	Limekiln Rd, to Lewisberry, E Shell/dsl, Sunoco Bob Evans, John's Diner, McDonald's, Pizza Hut Budget Inn, Clarion, Comfort Inn, Fairfield Inn, Quality Inn, W Hess Best Western, Motel 6, Scottish Inn vet
39b	I-76/PA Tpk
39a	PA 114, Lewisberry Rd, E Rutter's/dsl Days Inn, Highland Inn, Red Carpet Inn
38	Reesers Summit
36	PA 262, Fishing Creek, E Hess/Dunkin Donuts Bruster's, Mamma's Pizza CVS Drug
35	PA 177, Lewisberry, E 601 Pizzaria, W Exxon Francescos, Summit Rest. Alpine Inn
34mm	**parking area/weigh sta sb**
34	Valley Green (from nb), same as 33
33	PA 392, Yocumtown, E Hess/Dunkin Donuts/dsl, Rutter's Brothers Pizzaria, Burger King, Golden Plate Diner, Hong Kong Buffet, KFC/Taco Bell, Maple Donuts, McDonald's, New China Buffet, Subway Super 8 $Tree, Advance Parts, Darrenkamp's Mkt, GNC, Radio Shack, Rite Aid, Verizon, Walmart/Subway
33mm	**parking area/weigh sta nb**
32	PA 382, Newberrytown, E Rutter's/deli/dsl/24hr, Sunoco/dsl, W Exxon/dsl
28	PA 295, Strinestown, W Rutter's/24hr 83 Diner, Wendy's
24	PA 238, Emigsville, W Sunoco/dsl 4 Bros Rest.
22	PA 181, N George St, E Rutter's Comfort Inn, Homewood Suites, W same as 21b

YORK

Exit #	Services
21b a	US 30, Arsenal Rd, to York, E Sheetz/dsl Cheddar's, Clock Diner, Qdoba, San Carlo's Rest., Starbucks Days Inn, EconoLodge, Motel 6, Sheraton AT&T, Buick/GMC, W Royal Farms/dsl, Rutter's/dsl, Sheetz/dsl 5 Guys Burgers, Arby's, Bob Evans, Burger King, Chick-fil-A, Chili's, China Buffet, CiCi's, Denny's, Domino's, DQ, Dunkin Donuts, El Rodeo Mexican, Friendly's, Great Wall, Hardee's, Hoss's, Jimmy John's, KFC, Little Caesars, LJ Silver, Logan's Roadhouse, Lyndon Diner, Maple Donuts, McDonald's, Mission BBQ, Old Country Buffet, Olive Garden, Panera Bread, Pizza Hut, Quaker Steak, Rita's Custard, Ruby Tuesday, Smokey Bones BBQ, Subway, Taco Bell, Wendy's Best Western, Motel 6, Super 8, Wingate Inn $General, $Tree, Acura, Advance Parts, Aldi Foods, AutoZone, BJ's Whse/gas, BMW, Cadillac/Chevrolet, Chrysler/Dodge/Jeep, CVS Drug, Dick's, Gander Mtn, Giant Foods/gas, Harley-Davidson, Honda, Kia, Kohl's, Lowe's, Macy's, NTB, Old Navy, PepBoys, PetCo, Petsmart, Radio Shack, Ross, Staples, Subaru, Target, TJ Maxx, URGENT CARE, Verizon, Walmart/McDonald's, Weis Foods/gas

INTERSTATE 83 Cont'd

Exit #	Services
19	PA 462, Market St, **E** [gas] Rutter's/dsl [food] Applebee's, Arby's, Aroma Buffet, Buffalo Wild Wings, Chick-fil-A, Chuck-ECheese's, DQ, Fiesta Mexico, Fuddruckers, Jimmy John's, KFC, Outback Steaks, Panera Bread, Papa John's, Perkins, Red Lobster, Rita's Custard, Starbucks, Taco Bell, Tokyo Diner, Wendy's [lodging] Quality Inn [other] $General, $Tree, Aamco, Advance Parts, Aldi Foods, Burlington Coats, Firestone/auto, Giant Foods/gas, Goodyear/auto, Home Depot, Lowe's, Nissan, NTB, Petco, Sam's Club/gas, Volvo, Walgreens, Walmart, Weis Foods, **W** [other] [airport]
18	PA 124, Mt Rose Ave, Prospect St, **E** [gas] Pacific Pride/dsl, Rutters [food] 5 Guys Burgers, Arooga's Grille, Burger King, Nino's Pizza, Parma Pizza Grill, Pizza Hut, Subway, Sweet House Chinese [other] Amelia's Groceries, K-Mart, Nello Tire
16b a	PA 74, Queen St, **E** [gas] Sunoco [food] Baskin-Robbins/Dunkin Donuts, Cracker Barrel, Imperial Gourmet, Isaac's Rest., John's Pizza Shop, Maple Donuts, Ruby Tuesday, Starbucks, Stone Grill [lodging] Country Inn&Suites, Hampton Inn [other] Giant Foods/gas, **W** [gas] Sheetz/dsl [food] Chipotle, Infinito's Pizza, Jimmy John's, Little Caesar's, McDonald's, Pizza Hut/Taco Bell, S Yorke Diner, Subway, Wendy's [other] $General, $Tree, AT&T, BonTon, CVS Drug, Jo-Ann Fabrics, Price Rite Foods, Tuesday Morning, vet, Walgreens, Weis Mkt
15	S George St, I-83 spur into York, **W** [other] [airport]
14	PA 182, Leader Heights, **E** [food] Arby's, Domino's, First Wok, Subway [other] vet, **W** [gas] Rutter's [food] McDonald's [lodging] Holiday Inn Express [other] Rite Aid
10	PA 214, Loganville, **W** [gas] Rutter's/dsl [food] Mamma's Pizza [lodging] Midway Motel [other] st police, TrueValue
8	PA 216, Glen Rock, **W** [other] Shrewsbury Mkt (2mi)
4	PA 851, Shrewsbury, **E** [gas] Tom's/dsl/24hr [food] Bill Bateman's Grill, Cracker Barrel, Papa John's, Ruby Tuesday [lodging] Hampton Inn [other] Home Depot, TrueValue, **W** [gas] Exxon/dsl [food] Arby's, Chick-fil-A, Coachlight Rest., Emerald Garden Chinese, Ginza Japanese, KFC/Taco Bell, McDonald's, Rita's Custard, Sons of Italy Pizzaria, Starbucks, Subway, Wendy's [other] $Tree, AAA, Advance Parts, Giant Foods, GNC, Mr Tire, Radio Shack, Saubel's Foods, Verizon, Walmart
2mm	**Welcome Ctr nb, full [handicapped] facilities, litter barrels, petwalk [phone] [picnic] vending**
0mm	Pennsylvania/Maryland state line

S H R E W S B U R Y

INTERSTATE 84

Exit #	Services
54mm	Pennsylvania/New York state line, Delaware River
53	US 6, PA 209, Matamoras, **N Welcome Ctr both lanes, full [handicapped] facilities, litter barrels, petwalk [phone] [picnic] vending,** [gas] Go24, Shell, TurkeyHill/dsl [food] Polar Bear Rest, Stewart's Drive-Inn, The Grill [lodging] Appl Inn [other] auto repair, AutoZone, fireworks, PriceChopper, **S** [gas] Sunoco/dsl [food] Dunkin Donuts, McDonald's, Perkins, Roma Pizza, Subway, Village Diner, Wendy's [lodging] Best Western, Hampton Inn, Scottish Inn [other] $Tree, Advance Parts, Home Depot, K-Mart, Lowe's, Staples, Tristate RV Park, Walmart/Subway
46	US 6, to Milford, **N** [gas] Sunoco/dsl, **0-2 mi S** [gas] Exxon/dsl, Gulf, TurkeyHill, Xtra [food] Apple Valley Rest., Chang Mao Chinese, China Buffet [lodging] Black Walnut B&B, Red Carpet Inn [other] Grand Union Foods, NAPA, Rite Aid, USPO

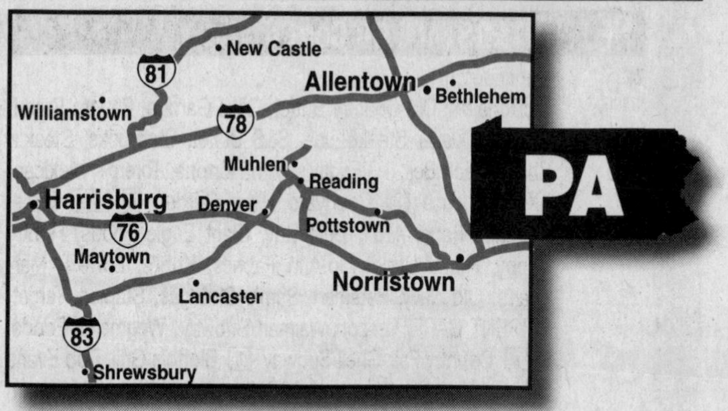

Exit #	Services
34	PA 739, to Lords Valley, Dingmans Ferry, **S** [gas] Sunoco/Dunkin Donuts/dsl, Xtra/dsl [food] Bruno's Pizza, McDonald's, Panda Chinese, Subway [other] Family$, Rite Aid, USPO, Weis Foods
30	PA 402, to Blooming Grove, **N** [other] st police, to Lake Wallenpaupack
26	PA 390, to Tafton, **N** [gas] Exxon/dsl [other] Tanglewood Ski Area (4mi), to Lake Wallenpaupack, **S** [other] to Promised Land SP
26mm	**[rest stop] both lanes, full [handicapped] facilities, litter barrels, petwalk [phone] [picnic] vending**
20	PA 507, Greentown, **N** [gas] Exxon/dsl, Shell/Subway [food] John's Italian [other] Animal Park (5mi)
17	PA 191, to Newfoundland, Hamlin, **N** [gas] Howe's/Exxon/dsl/scales/24hr [food] Twin Rocks Diner [lodging] Comfort Inn [other] dsl repair
8	PA 247, PA 348, Mt Cobb, **N** [gas] Gulf/dsl, Sunoco/Burger King/Tim Hortons/dsl, **S** [gas] Exxon/Subway/dsl
4	I-380 S, to Mount Pocono
2	PA 435 S, to Elmhurst
1	Tigue St, **S** [gas] Valero/dsl

I-84 begins/ends on I-81, exit 54.

INTERSTATE 90

Exit #	Services
46mm	Pennsylvania/New York state line, **Welcome Ctr/weigh sta wb, full [handicapped] facilities, litter barrels, petwalk [phone] [picnic] vending**
45	US 20, to State Line, **N** [gas] KwikFill/dsl/scales [food] McDonald's, **S** [gas] Shell/Subway/dsl [lodging] Red Carpet Inn [other] fireworks, Niagara Falls Info
41	PA 89, North East, **N** [gas] Shell/repair [food] New Harvest Rest. [lodging] Holiday Inn Express, Vineyard B&B, **S** [other] Family Affair Camping (4mi), winery
37	I-86 E, to Jamestown
35	PA 531, to Harborcreek, **N** [gas] TA/Country Pride/Pizza Hut/Subway/dsl/scales/24hr/ @ [other] Blue Beacon, dsl repair
32	PA 430, PA 290, to Wesleyville, **N** [gas] Country Fair, GetGo/dsl, st police, **S** [other] camping
29	PA 8, to Hammett, **N** [gas] Country Fair [food] Wendy's [other] [airport], **S** [lodging] Best Value [other] dsl repair, Peterbilt
27	PA 97, State St, Waterford, **N** [gas] Country Fair/dsl, Kwikfill [food] Arby's, Barbato's Italian, Doc Holiday's Grill, McDonald's [lodging] Days Inn, La Quinta, Red Roof Inn, Tallyho Inn [other] [airport], **S** [gas] Pilot/Subway/dsl/scales/24hr, Sheetz/dsl, Shell/Tim Hortons/dsl [food] Taco Bell [lodging] Baymont Inn, Quality Inn, Super 8 [other] casino
24	US 19, Peach St, to Waterford, **N** [gas] Country Fair/dsl, Delta Sonic/Subway, GetGo/dsl, KwikFill [food] Applebee's, Burger King, Chick-fil-A, Chipotle Mexican, ChuckeCheese, Cracker Barrel, Dunkin Donuts, Eat'n Park, Famous Dave's BBQ, Five Guys, Golden Corral, KFC, Krispy Kreme, Longhorn Steaks,

INTERSTATE 90 Cont'd

ERIE

24 Continued
McDonald's, Old Country Buffet, Olive Garden, Panera Bread, Qdoba, Quaker Steak&Lube, S&S Buffet, Starbucks, Steak'n Shake, Taco Bell, TGIFriday's, Tim Hortons, Torero's Mexican, TX Roadhouse [lodging] Courtyard, Hilton Garden [other] $Tree, Advance Parts, AT&T, Best Buy, Giant Eagle Foods, Hobby Lobby, Home Depot, Jo-Ann Fabrics, Kohl's, Lowe's, Marshall's, Old Navy, Petsmart, Sam's Club/gas, Staples, Target, URGENT CARE, Verizon, Walmart/Subway, Wegman's Foods, **S** [gas] Country Fair, Shell/Subway [food] Blotto's Grill, Bob Evans [lodging] Comfort Inn, Country Inn&Suites, EconoLodge, Hampton Inn, Holiday Inn Express, Home 2 Suites, Microtel, Residence Inn, Wingate Inn [other] waterpark

22b a I-79, N to Erie, S to Pittsburgh, **3-5 mi N** services in Erie

18 PA 832, Sterrettania, **N** [gas] Marathon/dsl [food] Burger King [other] Presque Passage RV Park, to Presque Isle SP, Waldameer Park (8mi), **S** [food] Beechwood Rest. [lodging] Quality Inn [other] golf, KOA, West Haven RV Park/camping

16 PA 98, to Franklin Center, Fairview, **S** [other] Follys Camping (2mi), Mar-Da-Jo-Dy Camping (5mi)

9 PA 18, to Girard, Platea, **N** [other] Fiesler's Service/repair/tires, Langer's Automotive, st police, **S** [lodging] Green Roof Inn (2mi)

6 PA 215, to Albion, East Springfield, **N** [lodging] lodging

3 US 6N, to Cherry Hill, West Springfield, **N** [lodging] lodging on US 20, **S** [gas] State Line/deli/dsl/scales/24hr

2.5mm [rest stop] **eb, full facilities, info, litter barrels, petwalk [picnic] vending**

0mm Pennsylvania/Ohio state line

INTERSTATE 95

LEVITTOWN

Exit # Services

51mm Pennsylvania/New Jersey state line, Delaware River

51 PA 32, to New Hope, **W** Washington Crossing Hist Park

50mm **Welcome Ctr sb, full facilities, litter barrels, petwalk [picnic] vending**

49 PA 332, to Yardley, Newtown, **W** [food] Dunkin Donuts [lodging] Hampton Inn [other] to Tyler SP

46b a US 1 to I-276, PA TPK, Langhorne, Oxford Valley, **E** [other]

44 US 1, PA 413, to Penndel, Levittown, **E** [gas] Shell/7-11/dsl [food] Arrano Hibachi Steaks, Blue Fountain Diner, Buffalo Wild Wing, ChuckECheese's, Dunkin Donuts, Friendly's, Great American Diner, Hong Kong Pearl, Langhorne Ale House, Ming's Asian, Olive Garden, Panera Bread, Red Lobster, Ruby Tuesday, Subway, Wendy's [lodging] Sheraton [other] $Tree, Acura, Chrysler/Dodge/Jeep, Firestone/auto, Ford, Goodyear/auto, Harley-Davidson, Honda, Hyundai/Suzuki, Kia, K-Mart, Lincoln, Lowe's, Marshall's, Mazda, PepBoys, Redner's Whse Mkt, Sam's Club, Staples, Subaru, Target, TJ Maxx, VW/Volvo, **W** [gas] LukOil/dsl [food] Denny's, McDonald's [other] Toyota/Scion, U-Haul

40 PA 413, I-276, to Bristol Bridge, Burlington, **E** [gas] Hess/Dunkin Donuts/dsl, WaWa [food] Fish Factory Rest., Golden Eagle Diner, KFC, McDonald's [other] Chevrolet

37 PA 132, to Street Rd, **W** [gas] BP/dsl, Sunoco/dsl [food] Burger King, Chili's, China Sun Buffet, Dunkin Donuts, Gino's Burgers/Chicken, Golden Corral, IHOP, McDonald's, Old Country Buffet, Popeye's, Sonic, TX Roadhouse, Wendy's [other] $Tree, 7-11, Advance Parts, Aldi Foods, Giant Foods, GNC, Goodyear/auto, K-Mart, Kohl's, PepBoys, Radio Shack, Ross, Save-A-Lot, U-Haul, Walgreens, WaWa

PHILADELPHIA AREA

35 PA 63, to US 13, Woodhaven Rd, Bristol Park, **1 mi W** [gas] BP, Exxon, Liberty, LukOil, Sunoco/dsl [food] Arby's, Bob Evans, Boston Mkt, Burger King, Champs Pizza, Dave&Buster's, Dunkin Donuts, Dynasty Rest., Grand China Buffet, Hibachi Buffet, Joe Santucci's, KFC, McDonald's, McDonald's, Mr V's Steaks, Old Haven Pizza, Panda King, Pizza Hut, Rita's Custard, Ruby Tuesday, Supreme Buffet, Taco Bell, Uno, Wendy's [lodging] Hampton Inn [other] $Tree, Acme Foods, BigLots, Burlington Coats, Dick's, Home Depot, Marshall's, NTB, Old Navy, Pathmark Foods, Rite Aid, Sam's Club, Tires+, Verizon, Walmart, WaWa

32 Academy Rd, **W** [other] K-Mart

30 PA 73, Cottman Ave, **W** [gas] Sunoco

27 Bridge St, **W** [gas] 7-11, BP, Exxon, LukOil [food] Dunkin Donuts [other] Rite Aid

26 to NJ 90, Betsy Ross Brdg, **W** [gas] BP, Hess, Sunoco/dsl [food] Applebee's, Burger King, KFC, McDonald's, Wendy's [other] Home Depot, Lowe's, ShopRite Foods, Target

25 Allegheny Ave, **W** [gas] Sunoco [other] WaWa

23 Lehigh Ave, Girard Ave, **E** casino, **W** [gas] Exxon [food] Applebee's, Arby's, Coldstone, Dunkin Donuts, Pizza Hut, Rita's Custard [other] AutoZone, CVS Drug, Family$, GNC, PepBoys, Radio Shack, Rite Aid, WaWa

22 I-676, US 30, to Central Philadelphia, Independence Hall

20 Columbus Blvd, Penns Landing, **1-2 mi E on Columbus** [gas] BP, Liberty/WaWa/dsl, LukOil/dsl [food] Burger King, Champp's Rest., ChartHouse Rest., Chick-fil-A, Dave&Buster's, Famous Dave's BBQ, IHOP, La Veranda Italian, Longhorn Steaks, McDonald's, Moshulu Rest., Ruby Buffet, Wendy's [lodging] Comfort Inn, Hyatt Hotel (1mi), Sheraton [other] $Tree, Best Buy, Home Depot, Lowe's, Marshall's, PepBoys, ShopRite Foods, Staples, Target, Verizon, Walmart

19 I-76 E, to Walt Whitman Bridge, **E** [gas] BP, Exxon/dsl, Sunoco [food] Burger King, Dunkin Donuts, KFC, Little Caesars, McDonald's, Pizza Hut [lodging] Holiday Inn, to stadiums [other] Aldi Foods

17 PA 611, to Broad St, Pattison Ave, **W** [other] to Naval Shipyard, to stadium

15mm Schuykill River

15 Enterprise Ave, Island Ave (from sb)

14 Bartram Ave, Essington Ave (from sb)

13 PA 291, to I-76 W (from nb), to Central Philadelphia, **E** [gas] Exxon/dsl [lodging] Days Inn, Guest Quarters, Hilton, Marriott, Renaissance Inn, Residence Inn, Sheraton, Sheraton Suites, Westin Suites

12 **E** Philadelphia Intl [other] services same as 10

10 PA 291, Bartrom Ave, (from nb), Cargo City, **E** [lodging] Marriott, Renaissance Hotel, **W** [gas] WaWa/dsl [food] Ruby Tuesday [lodging] Courtyard, Embassy Suites, Extended Stay America, Extended Stay Deluxe, Fairfield Inn, Hampton Inn, Microtel, Studio+ [other] Heins NWR

9b a PA 420, to Essington, Prospect Park, **E** [gas] Sunoco/dsl, Valero/dsl [food] Denny's, Lehmans Rest., Mel's Diner, Philly Diner [lodging] Comfort Inn, Motel 6, Ramada Inn, Red Roof Inn, Residence Inn, SpringHill Suites, Wyndham Garden [other] USPO, WaWa

8 to Chester Waterfront, Ridley Park, **W on US 13** [food] Stargate Diner

7 I-476 N, to Plymouth, Meeting

6 PA 352, PA 320, to Edgmont Ave, **1 mi E on US 13** [food] McDonald's, Popeye's [other] Radio Shack, Walmart/Subway

5 Kerlin St (from nb), **W** [lodging] Days Inn/Dawn's Diner

4 US 322 E, to NJ, to Barry Bridge, **W** [lodging] Highland Motel

3 (from nb, no EZ return) US 322 W, Highland Ave, **E** [gas] Sunoco/dsl [other] Ford, Goodyear

INTERSTATE 95 Cont'd

2	PA 452, to US 322, Market St, Exxon McDonald's, Subway
1	Chichester Ave, E Sunoco fireworks, W BP transmissions, WaWa
0mm	Pennsylvania/Delaware state line, **Welcome Ctr/weigh sta nb, full facilities, litter barrels, petwalk**

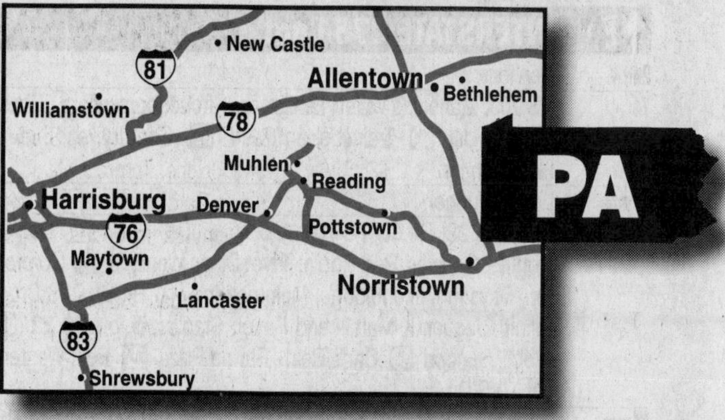

INTERSTATE 99

Exit #	Services
I-99 begins/ends on I-80, exit 161	
83	PA 350, Bellefonte, Bellafonte, E Weis Foods/gas, W Lyken's Mkt Bonfatto's Rest., Burger King, Pizza Hut Rite Aid, TrueValue
81	PA 26 S, to PA 64, to Pleasant Gap
80	Harrison Rd (from nb, no re-entry)
78b a	PA 150, to Bellafonte, W Sheetz/dsl Bro's Pizza, Colts Rest. EconoLodge auto repair, Ford
76	Shiloh Rd, E Sheetz/dsl Garfields, McDonald's, Perkins, Quaker Steak, Rey Azteca Best Western $Tree, AAA, Advance Parts, Barnes&Noble, BigLots, BonTon, Chevrolet, JC Penney, Jo-Ann Fabrics, Macy's, Office Depot, Ross, Sam's Club, Sears, Subaru, Walmart/Subway
74	Innovation Park,, Beaver Stadium, Penn State U
73	US 322 E, Lewiston, State College
71	Woodycrest, Tofftrees, E Applebee's, Chick-fil-A, Cracker Barrel, Eat'n park, McDonald's, Olive Garden, Outback Steaks, Red Lobster, Starbucks, TX Roadhouse Hampton Inn, Holiday Inn Express, SpringHill Suites $Tree, Best Buy, Dick's, Kohl's, Michael's, PetCo, Radio Shack, Target, Verizon, Walmart, Wegman's Foods, W Down Under Cafe Marriott Golf Resort
69	US 322 E, Valley Vista Dr, E Sheetz/dsl Home Depot, Lowe's
68	Skytop Mtn Rd, Grays Woods, Waddle
62	US 322 W, to Phillipsburg (from sb)
61	to US 322 W, Port Matilda, E Lykens Mkt/Sub Express/dsl Brother's Pizza Port Matilda Hotel USPO
52	PA 350, W Snappy's/Subway/dsl
48	PA 453, Tyrone, W Sheetz/dsl Burger King, Nino's Pizza, Subway a USPO, Rite Aid
45	Tipton, Grazierville, W Rossi's Aunt Nettie's Cafe DelGrosso's Funpark, Ford
41	PA 865 N, Bellwood, E Ft Roberdeau HS (6mi), W Martin Gen Store/dsl, Sheetz/dsl DelGrosso's Funpark (3 mi)
39	PA 764 S, Pinecroft, W La Scalia Rest. Comfort Inn, Days Inn Martin's Foods, Oak Spring Winery
33	17th St, Altoona, E same as 32, W Sheetz/dsl Aldi Foods, Lowe's, Railroader Museum, U-Haul
32	PA 36, Frankstown Rd, Altoona, E GetGo, Sheetz/dsl Chili's, Chipotle, DQ, Millie's Pizza, Panera Bread, Subway, TX Roadhouse Barnes&Noble, Best Buy, Boscov's, Canoe Cr SP, Dick's, Giant Eagle Foods, GNC, Home Depot, Kohl's, Michael's, PetCo, Ross, Staples, Verizon, W Sheet/dsl ChuckeCheese, Dunkin Donuts, El Campesino Mexican, Five Guys, Honeybaked Ham, HongKong Buffet, McDonald's, Olive Garden, Papa John's, Perkins, Pizza Hut, Red Lobster, Subway, Wendy's EconoLodge, Holiday Inn Express, Super 8 $Tree, AT&T, AutoZone, Chrysler/Dodge/Jeep, CVS Drug, Jo-Ann Fabrics, Nissan, Rite Aid, Save-A-Lot, URGENT CARE, USPO, Walgreens
31	Plank Rd, Altoona, E Friendly's, Jethro's Rest., King's Rest., Montezuma Mexican, Outback Steaks, TGIFriday's Altoona Grand Hotel Field&Stream, Firestone/auto, Radio Shack, Sam's Club/gas, st police, Target, TJ Maxx, Walmart/McDonald's, W GetGo Applebee's, Arby's, Bob Evans, Burger King, Casa Valadez, Champs Grill, Coldstone, Cracker Barrel, Denny's, Eat'n Park, Gourmet Buffet, KFC, Little Ceasars, LJ Silver, Longhorn Steaks, Taco Bell Hampton Inn, Motel 6 Advance Parts, BigLots, Buick/GMC, Hobby Lobby, JC Penney, K-Mart, Macy's, Martin's/gas, Petco, Sears/auto, Verizon, Weis Foods
28	US 22, to Ebensburg, Holidaysburg
23	PA 36, PA 164, Roaring Spring, Portage, E GetGo/dsl, Sheetz/24hr, Turkey Hill Backyard Burger , truck repair, Walmart/Subway
15	Claysburg, King, Claysburg, King, W Sheetz/dsl Subway $General
10	to Imler, W Slick's Ivy Stone Rest. (2mi), Blue Knob SP (8mi)
7	PA 869, Osterburg, St Clairsville, W Slick's Ivy Stone Rest. (2mi), Blue Knob SP
3	PA 56, Johnstown, Cessna, E st police, truck parts
1	I-70/76, E GetGo/McDonald's/dsl, Pacific Pride/dsl, Sheetz/dsl, Shell/Subway/dsl Bedford Diner, Clara's Place, Denny's, Ed's Steaks, Hoss' Rest, LJ Silver, Pizza Hut, Salsa's Mexican, Wendy's Best Value, Budget Host, Fairfield Inn, Hampton Inn, Quality Inn, Rodeway Inn, Travelodge
I-99 begins/ends on US 220.	

STATE COLLEGE

ALTOONA

INTERSTATE 476

Exit #	Services
131	US 11, US 6. **I-476 begins/ends on I-81. Services same as I-81, exit 194.**
122	Keyser Ave, Old Forge, Taylor
121mm	toll plaza
115	I-81, PA 315, Wyoming Valley, Pittston, W Exxon/Subway/dsl, Pilot/Wendy's/dsl/scales/24hr, Sunoco/dsl Arby's, Burger King, McDonald's, Perkins Comfort Inn, Knight's Inn, Walmart/Subway Volvo
112mm	**toll plaza**
105	PA 115, Wilkes-Barre, Bear Creek, E Exxon, Mobil
97mm	**parking areas both lanes**
95	I-80, PA 940, Pocono, Hazleton, W WaWa A&W/LJ Silver, Arby's, McDonald's, Subway Comfort Inn, EconoLodge, Holiday Inn Express, Mtn Laurel Resort, Pocono Inn/Resort, Quality Inn, Split Rock Resort
90mm	parking area sb
86mm	**Hickory Run Service Plaza both lanes** Sunoco/dsl Breyer's, hot dogs, McDonald's

INTERSTATE 476 Cont'd

Exit #	Services
74	US 209, Mahoning Valley, Lehighton, Stroudsburg, W 🅖 Shell/Subway/dsl 🍴 Trainer's Inn Rest. 🛏 Country Inn&Suites, Hampton Inn
71mm	Lehigh Tunnel
56	I-78, US 22, PA 309, Lehigh Valley, E 🅖 Gulf 🍴 Dunkin Donuts, Quiznos, Red Robin, Trivet Diner, Wendy's 🛏 Comfort Inn, Days Inn, Econolodge, McIntosh Inn Ⓞ BMW, CVS Drug, Infiniti, Jaguar, K-Mart, Land Rover, Staples, W on US 22 🅖 Mobil, Sunoco 🍴 Chris Rest., Parma Pizza 🛏 Best Western Ⓞ CVS Drug
56mm	**Allentown Service Plaza both lanes** 🅖 Sunoco/dsl 🍴 Big Boy, Hershey's Ice Cream, Pizza Hut, Roy Rogers
44	PA 663, Quakertown, Pottstown, E 🅖 BP, Mobil/dsl 🍴 Avanti Grill, Faraco's Pizza 🛏 Best Western (3mi), Comfort Suites, Hampton Inn, Holiday Inn Express, Rodeway Inn Ⓞ 🖼
37mm	**parking area sb**
31	PA 63, Lansdale, E 🅖 Exxon, Lukoil, WaWa 🍴 Bones Grill 🛏 Best Western, Courtyard, Lansdale Motel, Residence Inn Ⓞ 🖼
20	Germantown Pike W, to I-276 W, PA Tpk W
19	Germantown Pike E

Exit #	Services
18b a	(18 from sb), Conshoshocken, Norristown, E 🅖 Lukoil, Sunoco 🍴 Andy's Diner, Baja Fresh, Burger King, Domino's, Dunkin Donuts, Illiano's Pizza, McDonald's, Outback Steaks, Panera Bread, Rita's Ice Cream, Salad Works, Starbucks 🛏 Hampton Inn Ⓞ Barnes&Noble, Best Buy, Cracker Barrel, Dick's, Genuradi's Foods, Giant Foods, Giant Foods, Lowe's, Marshall's, Office Depot, Old Navy, Petsmart, Ross, Ruby Tuesday, Target, Toyota/Scion, W 🍴 Papa John's, Uno, Wendy's Ⓞ BJ's Whse, Ford, Home Depot, Honda, Hyundai, Kia, Mazda, Michael's, Nissan, Porsche
16b a	(16 from sb), I-76, PA 23, to Philadelpia, Valley Forge
13	US 30, E 🅖 Shell 🍴 Campus Pizza, Nova Grill, Winger's Ⓞ 🖼, Staples, to Villanova U, USPO
9	PA 3, Broomall, Upper Darby, E 🍴 Barnaby's Rest Ⓞ 🖼
5	US 1, Lima, Springfield, E 🍴 Dragon Garden, Mesa Mexican Ⓞ AT&T, Giant Foods, Jo-Ann Fabrics, Marshall's, Old Navy, Petsmart, Verizon, Walmart
3	Baltimore Pike, Media, Swarthmore, E 🅖 Lukoil 🍴 Ruby Tuesday Ⓞ 🖼, Macy's, Swarthmore Coll, Target
1	McDade Blvd, E 🅖 Exxon 🍴 Dunkin Donuts, KFC, McDonald's, Panda Chinese Ⓞ CVS Drug, Rite Aid
I-476 begins/ends on I-95, exit 7.	

RHODE ISLAND

INTERSTATE 95

Exit #	Services
43mm	Rhode Island/Massachusetts state line
30 (42)	East St, to Central Falls, E 🍴 Dunkin Donuts, Subway
29 (41)	US 1, Cottage St, W 🍴 d'Angelo's
28 (40)	RI 114, School St, E 🅖 Sunoco Ⓞ Ⓗ Car Pros, to hist dist, Yarn Outlet
27 (39)	US 1, RI 15, Pawtucket, W 🅖 Shell/repair, Sunoco/dsl/24hr 🍴 Burger King, Dunkin Donuts, Ground Round 🛏 Comfort Inn
26 (38)	RI 122, Lonsdale Ave (from nb), E Ⓞ U-Haul
25 (37)	US 1, RI 126, N Main St, Providence, E 🅖 Gulf, Hess, Shell 🍴 Chili's, Dunkin Donuts, Gregg's Rest., Subway Ⓞ Ⓗ PepBoys, Rite Aid, URGENT CARE, Walgreens, W 🅖 Gulf/dsl, Hess 🍴 Burger King, Chelo's Rest Ⓞ AAA, Aamco, Suzuki
24 (36.5)	Branch Ave, Providence, W 🅖 Mobil 🍴 Wendy's Ⓞ Stop&Shop, URGENT CARE, Walmart/Subway, downtown
23 (36)	RI 146, RI 7, Providence, E 🅖 Mobil/dsl 🛏 Marriot Ⓞ Ⓗ W Ⓞ USPO
22 (35.5)	US 6, RI 10, Providence, E 🍴 Cheesecake Factory, Dave&Buster's Ⓞ CVS Drug, JC Penney, Macy's, mall, Nordstrom's
21 (35)	Broadway St, Providence, E 🛏 Hilton, Regency Plaza
20 (34.5)	I-195, to E Providence, Cape Cod
19 (34)	Eddy St, Allens Ave, to US 1, W 🍴 Dunkin Donuts, Wendy's Ⓞ Ⓗ
18 (33.5)	US 1A, Thurbers Ave, W 🅖 Shell/dsl 🍴 Burger King Ⓞ Ⓗ
17 (33)	US 1 (from sb), Elmwood Ave, W Ⓞ Cadillac, Tires Whse
16 (32.5)	RI 10, Cranston, W Ⓞ Williams Zoo/park
15 (32)	Jefferson Blvd, E 🅖 Mobil 🍴 Bugaboo Creek Steaks, Dunkin Donuts, Shogun Steaks 🛏 Courtyard, La Quinta, Motel 6, W Ⓞ Ryder Trucks
14 (31)	RI 37, Post Rd, to US 1, W 🅖 Shell, Sunoco 🍴 Burger King Ⓞ Ⓗ CVS Drug, Ford/Lincoln, Mazda, Volvo

Exit #	Services
13 (30)	1 mi E 🅖 Shell, Sunoco/Dunkin Donuts 🍴 Chelo's Grill, Legal Seafood, Wendy's 🛏 Best Western, Comfort Inn, Hampton Inn, Hilton Garden, Holiday Inn Express, Homestead Suites, Homewood Suites, Radisson, Residence Inn Ⓞ TF Green Airport
12b (29)	RI 2, I-295 N (from sb)
12a	RI 113 E, to Warwick, E 🅖 Shell/Dunkin Donuts/dsl 🛏 Crowne Plaza Hotel Ⓞ Lowe's, Stop&Shop, W 🅖 Sunoco 🍴 ChuckeCheese, Wendy' Ⓞ Kohl's, mall, Sears/auto, Walmart/Subway
11 (29)	I-295 N (exits left from nb), to Woonsocket
10b a (28)	RI 117, to Warwick, W Ⓞ Ⓗ
9 (25)	RI 4 S, E Greenwich
8b a (24)	RI 2, E Greenwich, E 🅖 Shell/dsl 🍴 China Buffet, Coldstone, Dunkin Donuts, McDonald's, Outback Steaks, Panera Bread, Ruby Tuesday, TX Roadhouse 🛏 Extended Stay America Ⓞ AT&T, CVS Drug, Dave's Mkt, Walgreens, **0-2 mi** W 🅖 Citgo, Sunoco/dsl 🍴 5 Guys Burgers, Agave's Mexican, Applebee's, Carrabba's, Chili's, Denny's, KFC, Olive Garden, PapaGino's Pizza, Smokey Bones BBQ, TGIFriday's, Wendy's 🛏 Spring Hill Suites Ⓞ Acura, Aldi Foods, Arlington RV Ctr, Audi/Bentley/BMW/Inifinti/Lexus/Mini/Porsche/Smart, Barnes&Noble, Best Buy, Cadillac, Dick's, GNC, Goodyear/auto, Home Depot, Honda, Hyundai, Jaguar, Jo-Ann Fabrics, Land Rover, Lowe's, mall, Mercedes, Michael's, Nissan, PepBoys, Petco, Petsmart, Staples, Stop&Shop, Target, vet, VW
7 (21)	to Coventry, E 🅖 Mobil/dsl, W 🍴 Applebee's, Cilantro Mexican, Cracker Barrel, Denny's, Dunkin Donuts, Honeydew Donuts, Riccotti's Subs, Wendy's 🛏 Fairfield Inn, Hampton Inn, Residence In Ⓞ BJ's Whse/gas, CVS Drug, GNC, Home Depot, Radio Shack, Walmart/Subway
6a (20)	Hopkins Hill Rd, W 🍴 Dunkin Donut Ⓞ park&ride
6 (18)	RI 3, to Coventry, W 🅖 Lukoil, Shell/dsl/24hr, Sunoco/dsl 🍴 Dunkin Donuts, Europa Pizza, Gentleman Farmer Diner, Subway, Venus Pizza 🛏 Best Western, Super 8 Ⓞ TrueValue

Sidebar: **P R O V I D E N C E** **E G R E E N W I C H** **PA** / **RI**

 = gas = food = lodging = other = rest stop

INTERSTATE 95 Cont'd

Exit #	Services
5b a (15)	RI 102, W R.I.'s Only Trkstp/dsl/scales/24hr Dan's Rest. Classic Motor Lodge
10mm	**rest area/weigh sta both lanes**
4 (9)	RI 3, to RI 165 (from nb), Arcadia, W Arcadia SP, camping
3b a (7)	RI 138 E, to Kingston, Wyoming, E Dunkin Donuts, McDonald's, Wendy's Rite Aid, Stop&Shop/gas, vet, W Gulf, Hess, Mobil Bali Village Chinese, Dragon Palace, Subway, Village Pizza, Wood River Inn Rest. Stagecoach House B&B CVS Drug, Family$, NAPA, USPO, Walgreens
6mm	**Welcome Ctr nb, full facilities, litter barrels, petwalk vending**
2 (4)	Hope Valley
1 (1)	RI 3, to Hopkinton, Westerly, E beaches, RV camping, to Misquamicut SP
0mm	Rhode Island/Connecticut state line

INTERSTATE 295 (PROVIDENCE)

Exit #	Services
2b a (4)	I-95, N to Boston, S to Providence. **I-295 begins/ends on I-95, exit 4 in MA. Exits 2-1 are in MA.**
1b a (2)	US 1, E Mobil/Dunkin Donuts/dsl 99 Rest., Chicago Grill, ChuckeCheese, d'Angelo's, Friendly's, Hearth'n Kettle, Longhorn Steaks, Panera Bread, PapaGino's Italian, Ruby Tuesday, TGIFriday's $Tree, Best Buy, BJ's Whse, Buick/Chevrolet/GMC, CVS Drug, Dick's, JC Penney, Jo-Anne Fabrics, Lowe's, Macy's, mall, Marshalls, Michael's, Office Depot, Old Navy, Petsmart, Sears/auto, Staples, Stop&Shop, Target, TJMaxx, Walmart, W Emerald/dsl, Gulf, Shell/ds Applebee's, Dunkin Donuts Holiday Inn Express, Pineapple Inn, Super 8 CVS Drug, Nissan, Toyota/Scion
0mm	Rhode Island/Massachusetts state line, **exits 1-2 are in MA.**
11 (24)	RI 114, to Cumberland, E Shell/dsl, Sunoco Dunkin Donuts, HoneyDew Donuts CVS Drug, Dave's Foods, USPO, W J's Deli, Pizza Pasta&More, Saki's Pizza/subs Diamond Hill SP
10 (21)	RI 122, E Gulf, Lukoil Burger King, Dunkin Donuts, Forno Pizza, Jacky's Rest., McDonald's, Ronzio Pizza Verizon, W Forno Pizza, Fortune House Chinese, Pamfilios Deli, Subway Ace Hardware, Curves, CVS Drug, Rite Aid, Seabra Foods, URGENT CARE
20mm	Blackstone River
19.5mm	**weigh sta/rest area (full facilities) nb** Baskin-Robbins/Dunkin Donuts
9b a (19)	RI 146, Woonsocket, Lincoln, E Courtyard
8b a (16)	RI 7, N Smithfield, E European Cafe, W 7-11/dsl, Shell Decarlo's Italian, Dunkin Donuts, House of Pizza, Parentes Rest. Comfort Suites, Hampton Inn, Holiday Inn Express Smith-Appleby House
7b a (13)	US 44, Centerdale, E Hess, Valero Ball's Grill, Cancun Mexican, La Cocina Italian CarQuest, NAPA, repair, W Gulf/dsl, Mobil, Shell A&W, Applebee's, Burger King, Chelo's Grill, Chicago Grill, Chili's, D'angelo's, Dominos, Dunkin Donuts, KFC/Taco Bell, McDonald's, Panera Bread,

PROVIDENCE

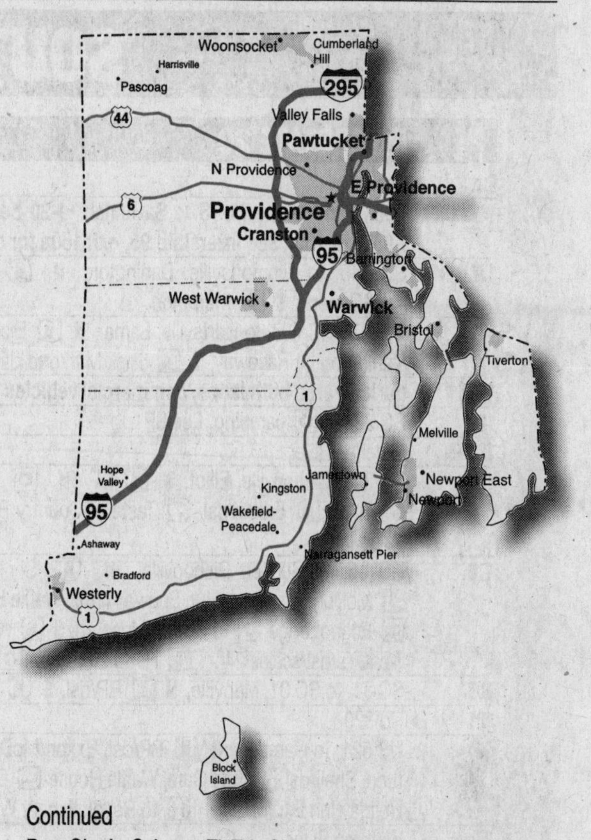

Exit #	Services
7b a (13)	Continued PapaGino's, Subway, TinTsin Chinese, Wendy's, Yamato Steaks $Tree, AAA, AT&T, Barnes&Noble, Curves, CVS Drug, Dave's Foods, Dick's, Home Depot, Kohl's, Michael's, Old Navy, Radio Shack, Rite Aid, Staples, Stop&Shop, Target, TJ Maxx, to Powder Mill Ledges WR, URGENT CARE, Verizon
6b c (10)	US 6, to Providence, E 7-11, Shel Atwood Grill, Burger King, D'Angelo's, Dunkin Donuts, Jacky's Rest., KFC, Newport Creamery, Noble House Chinese, Ruby Tuesday, Subway, Wendy's AT&T, BJ's Whse, Buick/Chevrolet/GMC, Chrysler/Dodge/Jeep, CVS Drug, Honda, Kia, Office Depot, PetsMart, Rite Aid Stop&Shop, USPO
6a (9)	US 6 E Expswy, **1 mi** E McDonald's, Ribs&Co, Ruby Tuesday, Taco Bell BJ's Whse, Home Depot, Petsmart
5 (8)	RI Resource Recovery Industrial Park
4 (7)	RI 14, Plainfield Pk, E Hess, W Gulf, Mobil/dsl/24hr Dunkin Donuts, Palmieri Pizz CVS Drug, repair
3b a (4)	Rd 37, Phenix Ave, E TF Green Airport
2 (2)	RI 2 S, to Warwick, E Chicago Grill, Longhorn Steaks, Red Robin JC Penney, Macy's, mall, Marshalls, Old Navy, Verizon, Walgreens, W Mobil, Sunoco Burger King, Chili's, Chipotle Mexican, ChuckeCheese, Dunkin Donuts, Hometown Buffet, McDonald's/playplace, Olive Garden, On-the-Border, Panera Bread, Starbucks, Subway, Taco Bell, Wendy's AT&T, Barnes&Noble, Best Buy, Chrysler/Dodge/Keep/Kia, Home Depot, Jaguar, Kohl's, mall, PetsMart, Price Rite Foods, Rite Aid, Sears/auto, Staples, Subaru, Target, TJMaxx, TownFair Tire, Trader Joe's, Verizon, Walmart/Subway
1 (1)	RI 113 W, to W Warwick, same as 2
0mm	**I-295 begins/ends on I-95, exit 11**

🅖 = gas 🍴 = food 🛏 = lodging 🅞 = other 🆁🆂 = rest stop Copyright 2016 - The Next EXIT

SOUTH CAROLINA

🅴 INTERSTATE 20

Exit #	Services
141b a	I-95, N to Fayetteville, S to Savannah. **I-20 begins/ends on I-95, exit 160. See Interstate 95, exit 160a for services.**
137	SC 340, to Timmonsville, Darlington, N 🅖 BP/dsl (1mi) 🅞 $General, S 🍴 Marathon
131	US 401, SC 403, to Hartsville, Lamar, N 🅖 Exxon/dsl 🅞 to Darlington Int Raceway, S 🅖 Shell/Markette/dsl
129mm	parking area both lanes, commercial vehicles only
123	SC 22, N 🅞 camping, Lee SP
121mm	Lynches River
120	SC 341, Bishopville, Elliot, N 🅖 BP/dsl 🅞 to Cotton Museum, S 🅖 Exxon/dsl 🍴 Taste of Country Rest. 🛏 Best Value Inn
116	US 15, to Sumter, Bishopville, N 🅖 Shell/KFC/dsl/24hr 🍴 McDonald's, Pizza Hut, Subway (1mi), Waffle House, Zaxby's 🛏 EconoLodge 🅞 to Cotton Museum, S 🅖 Wilco/Hess/DQ/Wendy's/dsl/scales/24hr 🍴 Huddle House, 🅞 Shaw AFB
108	SC 34, to SC 31, Manville, N 🅖 BP/dsl, S 🅖 Exxon/dsl
101	Rd 329
98	US 521, to Camden, N 🅖 BP/dsl, Exxon/McDonald's, Marathon, Shell/dsl 🍴 Fatz Cafe, Waffle House 🛏 Comfort Suites, Holiday Inn Express 🅞 🚻, to Revolutionary War Park
96mm	Wateree River
93mm	🆁🆂 both lanes, full ♿ facilities, litter barrels, petwalk 🕭 🖼 vending
92	US 601, to Lugoff, N 🅖 Marathon, Pilot/DQ/Subway/dsl/scales/24hr, Shell/Bojangles/dsl 🍴 Hardee's, Waffle House 🛏 EconoLodge, Ramada Ltd
87	SC 47, to Elgin, N 🅖 BP/dsl, Shell/dsl
82	SC 53, to Pontiac, N 🅖 Mobil, Shell 🍴 Blimpie, Burger King, Egg Roll Express, Quaker Steak & Lube 🛏 ValuePlace Inn 🅞 $General, Harley-Davidson, vet, S 🅖 BP/dsl 🅞 Clothing World Outlet
80	Clemson Rd, N 🅖 Circle K, Exxon/dsl, Shell/Bojangles/dsl 🍴 China Garden, D's, Dunkin Donuts, Groucho's Deli, Henry's, Krispy Kreme, Maurice's BBQ, McDonald's, San Jose Mexican, Subway, Sumo Japanese, Travinia Italian, Waffle House, Zaxby's 🛏 Hampton Inn, Holiday Inn Express 🅞 CVS Drug, Firestone/auto, S 🍴 Wendy's 🅞 Chevrolet, Ft Jackson Nat Cem, Hyundai
76b	Alpine Rd, to Ft Jackson, N 🅞 Sesquicentennial SP
76a	(76 from eb), I-77, N to Charlotte, S to Charleston
74	US 1, Two Notch Rd, to Ft Jackson, N 🅖 Mobil/dsl 🍴 Chili's, Fazoli's, Hooters, IHOP, Lizard's Thicket, Outback Steaks, Waffle House 🛏 Best Western, Comfort Suites, EconoLodge, Fairfield Inn, Hampton Inn, La Quinta, Microtel, Motel 6, Red Roof Inn 🅞 Home Depot, to Sesquicentennial SP, USPO, S 🅖 BP, Exxon, Shell 🍴 Applebee's, Bojangles, Brickhouse, China Garden, Church's, Harbor Inn Seafood, Hardee's, Honeybaked Ham, Jasmine Buffet, Maurice's BBQ, McDonald's, Monterrey Mexican, Substaion II 🛏 Days Inn 🅞 Advance Parts, AT&T, AutoZone, Best Buy, Firestone/auto, K-Mart, Lowe's, mall, Marshalls, Sears/auto, Verizon
73b	SC 277 N, to I-77 N
73a	SC 277 S, to Columbia, S 🅞 🚻
72	SC 555, Farrow Rd
71	US 21, N Main, to Blythewood, Columbia, N 🅖 Citgo/dsl, Save-a-Ton/dsl, TravelPlaza/Subway/dsl/scales/24hr/@

71	Continued 🍴 McDonald's 🛏 Days Inn 🅞 tires/repair, truckwash S 🅖 Shell
70	US 321, Fairfield Rd, S 🅖 ⊕FLYING J/Denny's/dsl/LP/24hr, Exxon 🍴 Hardee's 🛏 Super 8 🅞 Blue Beacon, truck repa
68	SC 215, Monticello Rd, to Jenkinsville, N 🅖 Exxon/dsl, Shel dsl, S 🅖 Shell/dsl
66mm	Broad River
65	US 176, Broad River Rd, to Columbia, N 🅖 BP, El Cheapo, Exxon, Shell/Circle K 🍴 Applebee's, Bojangles, Rush's BBQ, Sonic, Subway, Waffle House 🛏 Economy Inn 🅞 $Tree Aamco, CVS Drug, U-Haul, Walgreens, S 🅖 Hess/Godfather Pizza, RaceWay/dsl 🍴 Arby's, Atlantic Seafood, Baskin-Rob bins/Dunkin Donuts, Chick-fil-A, Church's, KFC, Lizard's Thick et, McDonald's, Nick's, Ocean View Seafood, Ruby Tuesda Sandy's HotDogs, Scholtzsky's, Taco Bell, Wendy's, Zaxby's 🛏 American Inn, InTown Suites, Quality Inn, Ramada Ltd, Roy Inn 🅞 $General, Advance Parts, Belk, Office Depot, PepBoy Rite Aid
64b a	I-26, US 76, E to Columbia, W to Greenville, Spartanburg
63	Bush River Rd, N 🅖 Shell/Circle K 🍴 Burger King, Cracke Barrel, Real Mexican, Subway 🛏 Travelodge 🅞 CVS Drug S 🅖 Marathon, Murphy USA/dsl, RaceWay, Sunoco/d 🍴 Fuddrucker's 🛏 Best Western, DoubleTree, Knights In Sleep Inn 🅞 Hamrick's, Walmart
61	US 378, W Cola, N 🅖 Exxon/Hardee's 🍴 Chick-Fil-A, Chili's McDonald's, Taco Bell 🛏 Wingate Inn 🅞 Honda, S 🅖 BP dsl, Shell/Burger King/dsl 🍴 Waffle House
58	US 1, W Columbia, N 🅖 Exxon, Shell/Subway/dsl 🍴 Waff House, S 🅖 Murphy Express/dsl 🍴 Bojangles, San Jos Mexican 🛏 ValuePlace Inn 🅞 auto repair, County Tire
55	SC 6, to Lexington, N 🅖 Shell/dsl 🍴 Chicken Shack Hampton Inn (2mi) 🅞 CarQuest, John's RV Ctr, S 🅖 BP/ds Kangaroo/DQ/dsl, Pops 🍴 Bojangles, Dunkin Donuts, Grea Wall Chinese, Maurice's BBQ, McDonald's, Waffle House, Wer dy's 🛏 Ramada Ltd 🅞 $General, CVS Drug, Piggly Wiggly
52.5mm	weigh sta wb
51	SC 204, to Gilbert, N 🅖 Exxon/dsl, Shell/Subway/dsl/24h 🍴 Burger King, S 🅖 ♥Loves/Chester's/McDonald's/ds scales/24hr, Mobil/dsl 🅞 $General
44	SC 34, to Gilbert, N 🅖 44Trkstp/rest/dsl/24hr, BP/Blimpie/d
39	US 178, to Batesburg, N 🅖 Exxon/dsl, S 🅖 Marathon/ds scales 🍴 Hillview Rest.
35.5mm	weigh sta eb
33	SC 39, to Wagener, N 🅖 Cheapway/dsl, S 🅖 KK/Hudd House/dsl/scales
29	SC 49, Wire Rd
22	US 1, to Aiken, S 🅖 BP/dsl, RaceWay/dsl, Shell/Circle K/d 🍴 Baynham's, Hardee's, McDonald's, Waffle House 🛏 Day Inn, Quality Inn 🅞 $General, Palmetto Lake RV Camping, t USC Aiken
20mm	parking area both lanes (commercial vehicles only)
18	SC 19, to Aiken, S 🅖 Exxon/Subway/dsl, Shell 🍴 Waff House 🛏 Deluxe Inn, Guesthouse Inn 🅞 🚻
11	Bettis Academy Rd, SC 144, Graniteville, N 🅖 BP/Hudd House/dsl/scales/24hr, S 🅖 Wilco/Hess/Dunkin Donuts/Sub way/dsl/scales/24hr
6	I-520 to N Augusta
5	US 25, SC 121, N 🅖 BP/repair/dsl, Circle K/dsl, Shell/Circ K/dsl 🍴 Bojangles, Burger King, Checkers, Little Caesars

COLUMBIA (vertical, left margin)

COLUMBIA (vertical, right margin)

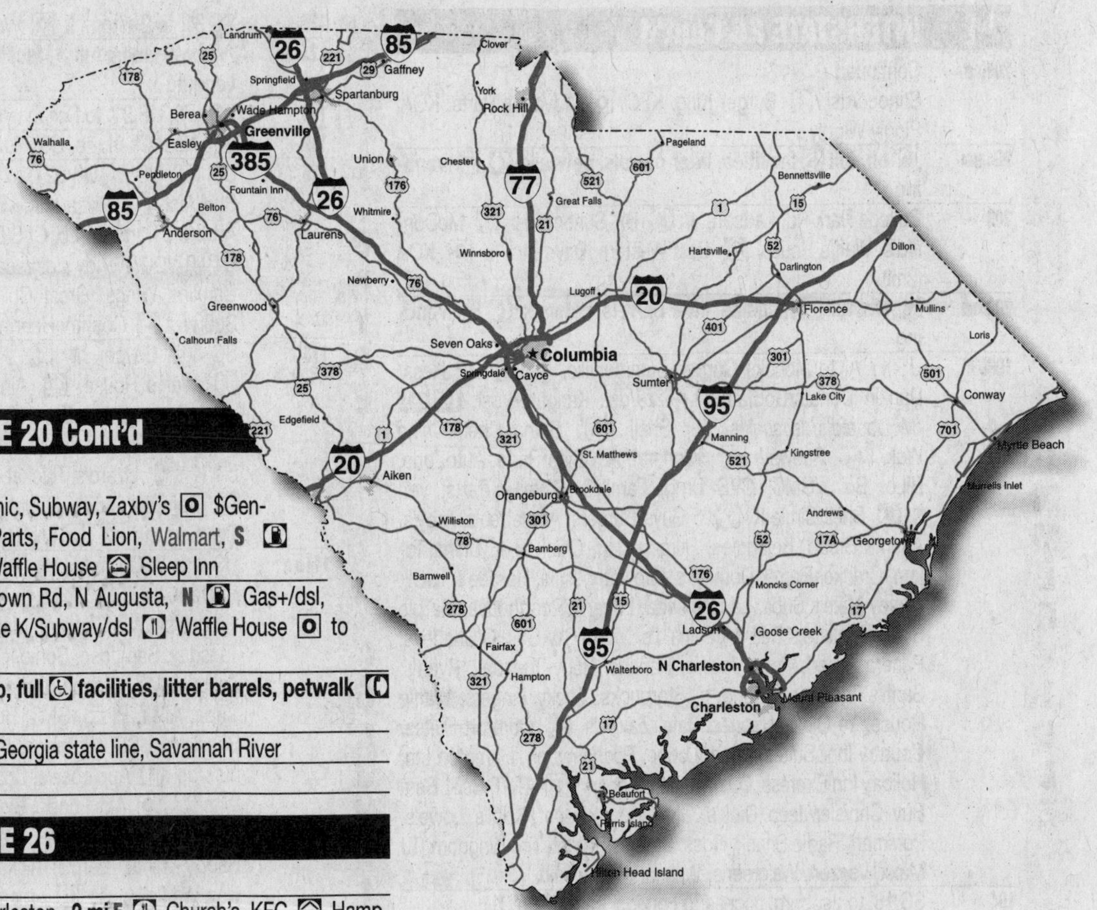

INTERSTATE 20 Cont'd

5	Continued McDonald's, Sonic, Subway, Zaxby's $General, Advance Parts, Food Lion, Walmart, S Marathon Waffle House Sleep Inn
1	SC 230, Martintown Rd, N Augusta, N Gas+/dsl, S Shell/Circle K/Subway/dsl Waffle House to Garn's Place
.5mm	**Welcome Ctr eb, full facilities, litter barrels, petwalk vending**
0mm	South Carolina/Georgia state line, Savannah River

INTERSTATE 26

CHARLESTON

Exit #	Services
221	Meeting St, Charleston, **2 mi E** Church's, KFC Hampton Inn Family$, Piggly Wiggly, Visitors Ctr
221b	US 17 N, to Georgetown
	I-26 begins/ends on US 17 in Charleston, SC.
221a	US 17 S, to Kings St, to Savannah, N
220	Romney St (from wb)
219b	Morrison Dr, East Bay St (from eb), N Exxon
219a	Rutledge Ave (from eb, no EZ return), to The Citadel, College of Charleston
218	Spruill Ave (from wb), N Charleston
217	N Meeting St (from eb)
216b a	SC 7, Cosgrove Ave, to US 17 S
215	SC 642, Dorchester Rd, N Charleston, N El Cheapo/dsl Clarion, S BP/dsl Alex's Rest Rodeway Inn
213b a	Montague Ave, Mall Dr, N Piccadilly's, Red Lobster Courtyard, Sheraton, ValuePlace Charles Towne Square, S BP/dsl, Mobil, Spinx/dsl 5 Guys Burgers, Arby's, Big Billy's Burgers, Bufflo Wild Wings, Burger King, Chick-fil-A, CiCi's Pizza, Fatz Cafe, Firehouse Subs, Golden Corral, Grand Buffet, Gringos, Hardee's, IHOP, Jimmy John's, Jim'N Nick's BBQ, Kamille's Cafe, La Hacienda, McAlister's Deli, McDonald's, Panda Express, Panera Bread, Qdoba, Rita's Custard, Sake Japanese, Starbucks, Steak'n Shake, Waffle House ALoft, Crowne Plaza, Days Inn, EconoLodge, Embassy Suites, Extended Stay Deluxe, Fairfield Inn, Hampton Inn, Hilton Garden, Holiday Inn Express, HomePlace Suites, Homestead Suites, Homewood Suites, Hyatt Place, InTown Suites, N Charleston Inn, Residence Inn, Sleep Inn $Tree, AT&T, Old Navy, Radio Shack, Sam's Club/gas, Staples, Tanger Outlet/Framous Brands, Verizon, vet, Walmart/Subway
212c b	I-526, E to Mt Pleasant, W to Savannah,
212a	Remount Rd, Hanahan, **N on US 52/78** KFC, Taco Bell Advance Parts, AutoZone, Ford, Suzuki

NORTH CHARLESTON

211b a	Aviation Pkwy, **N on US 52/78** Citgo, Exxon Arby's, Burger King, Capt D's, Church's, KFC, McDonald's, Papa John's, Popeye's, Sonic, Subway, Super Buffet, Taco Bell, Zaxby's Masters Inn, Radisson O'Reilly Parts, PepBoys, PetCo, U-Haul, USPO, S Kangaroo/dsl Waffle House Budget Inn
209	Ashley Phosphate Rd, to US 52, N Exxon, Kangaroo Applebee's, Cane's, Carrabba's, Chick-fil-A, China Buffet, Chipotle Mexican, ChuckEcheese, Denny's, Hardee's, Hooters, Jason's Deli, Jersey Mike's Subs, Jimmy John's, King Street Grill, Longhorn Steaks, Los Reyes, Moe's SW Grill, O'Charley's, Olive Garden, Outback Steaks, Perkins, Smokey Bones BBQ, Starbucks, Taco Bell, Waffle House, Wendy's, Wild Wing Cafe Candlewood Suites, Country Hearth Inn, Country Inn&Suites, Hawthorn Inn, Holiday Inn Express, InTown Suites, Red Roof Inn, Studio+ , $General, $Tree, AT&T, Barnes&Noble, Belk, Best Buy, BigLots, Books-A-Million, Dillard's, Firestone/auto, GNC, Hancock Fabrics, Home Depot, JC Penney, Lowe's, Marshalls, Michael's, Nissan, Office Depot, Old Navy, Ross, Sears/auto, Target, Tire Kingdom, Toyota/Scion, Verizon, Walgreens, Walmart, S BP, Hess/dsl, RaceWay/dsl Bojangles, Cracker Barrel, IHOP, McDonald's, Osaka Asian, Ruby Tuesday, Waffle House Best Western, Hampton Inn, Hyatt Place, InTown Suites, La Quinta, Motel 6, Quality Inn, Relax Inn, Residence Inn, Sleep Inn, Staybridge Suites, Value Place Inn
209a	to US 52 (from wb), to Goose Creek, Moncks Corner
205b a	US 78, to Summerville, N BP, Hess/dsl Arby's, Atl Bread Co, Bruster's, Cook-Out, Dunkin Donuts, Fortune Garden, Sonic, Subway, Waffle House, Wendy's, Zaxby's Fairfield Inn, Hampton Inn, Holiday Inn Express, Wingate Inn , Charleston Southern U, CVS Drug, S Hess/dsl,

INTERSTATE 26 Cont'd

SUMMERVILLE

205b a Continued
Sunoco/dsl [food] Burger King, KFC [O] Advance Parts, KOA, Piggly Wiggly

204mm **[Rs] eb, full [handicap] facilities, litter barrels, petwalk [phone] [picnic] vending**

203 College Park Rd, Ladson, N [gas] BP, Sunoco/dsl [food] McDonald's, Waffle House [lodging] Best Western, Days Inn, S [O] KOA (2mi)

202mm **[Rs] wb, full [handicap] facilities, litter barrels, petwalk [phone] [picnic] vending**

199b a US 17 A, to Moncks Corner, Summerville, N [gas] BP, Hess/Dunkin Donuts/Godfather's Pizza/dsl, Kangaroo/dsl, Pilot/McDonald's/dsl/scales/24hr, Shell [food] China Chef, China Wok, KFC, Subway [O] $General, Advance Parts, AutoZone, BiLo, Buick/GMC, CVS Drug, Family$, O'Reilly Parts, vet, S [gas] Shell/Circle K [food] 5 Guys Burgers, Applebee's, Arby's, Atlanta Bread, Bojangles, Burger King, Chick-fil-A, China Token, Cracker Barrel, Domino's, Firewater Grille, Hardee's, IHOP, Jersey Mike's Subs, La Hacienda, Logan's Roadhouse, Marble Slab, McAlisters Deli, McDonald's, Moe's SW Grill, O'Charleys, Panera Bread, Papa John's, Perkins, Ruby Tuesday, Ryan's, Santi's Taqueria, Shoney's, Starbucks, Sticky Fingers, Waffle House, Ye Ole Fashioned Cafe, Zaxby's [lodging] Comfort Suites, Country Inn&Suites, EconoLodge, Economy Inn, Hampton Inn, Holiday Inn Express, Quality Inn, Sleep Inn [O] AT&T, Belk, Best Buy, Chrysler/Jeep, Dick's, GNC, Home Depot, Kohl's, Lowe's, Petsmart, Radio Shack, Ross, Staples, Target, Tire Kingdom, TJ Maxx, Verizon, Walgreens, Walmart, World Mkt

194 SC 16, to Jedburg, access to Foreign Trade Zone 21

187 SC 27, to Ridgeville, St George, N [gas] Shell, S [gas] BP/dsl [O] Francis Beidler Forest (10mi)

177 SC 453, to Holly Hill, Harleyville, S [gas] Shell/dsl [lodging] Ashley Lodge

174mm **weigh sta both lanes**

172b a US 15, to Santee, St George, S [gas] Horizon/Domino's/Subway/dsl/e-85/scales/24hr

169b a I-95, N to Florence, S to Savannah

165 SC 210, to Bowman, N [gas] Exxon/dsl, S [gas] **BP/dsl**

159 SC 36, to Bowman, N [gas] Pilot/McDonald's/dsl/scales/24hr/@, S [gas] Exxon

ORANGEBURG

154b a US 301, to Santee, Orangeburg, N [lodging] Days Inn, S [gas] Exxon, Loves/Chesters/Subway/dsl/scales/24hr, Shell/dsl [food] Waffle House

152mm **[Rs] wb, full [handicap] facilities, litter barrels, petwalk [phone] [picnic] vending**

150mm **[Rs] eb, full [handicap] facilities, litter barrels, petwalk [phone] [picnic] vending**

149 SC 33, to Cameron, to SC State Coll, Orangeburg, [O] Claflin Coll

145b a US 601, to Orangeburg, St Matthews, S [gas] BP/dsl, Exxon, Shell, Sunoco/dsl, United/dsl [food] Burger King, Chick-fil-A, Cracker Barrel, Fatz Café, Hardee's, McDonald's, Ruby Tuesday, Seafood Academy, Subway, Waffle House, Wendy's, Zaxby's [lodging] Carolina Lodge, Comfort Inn, Country Inn&Suites, Days Inn, Fairfield Inn, Hampton Inn, Holiday Inn Express, Howard Johnson, Quality Inn, Sleep Inn, Southern Lodge [O] [H], $General, Cadillac/Chevrolet, Chrysler/Dodge/Jeep, Ford, Nissan, Toyota/Scion

139 SC 22, to St Matthews, S [gas] Horizon/e-85, Mobil, Wilco/Hess/Arby's/dsl/scales/24hr [O] Sweetwater Lake Camping (2.5mi)

136 SC 6, to North, Swansea, N [gas] Exxon/dsl

129 US 21, N [gas] Shell/dsl

CAYCE

125 SC 31, to Gaston, N [O] Wolfe's Truck/trailer repair

123mm **[Rs] both lanes, full [handicap] facilities, litter barrels, petwalk [phone] [picnic] vending**

119 US 176, US 21, to Dixiana, S [gas] BP/Subway/dsl, Exxon/dsl

116 I-77 N, to Charlotte, US 76, US 378, to Ft Jackson

115 US 176, US 21, US 321, to Cayce, N [gas] BP, Gulf, RaceWay, Shell/dsl [food] Pizza Hut, Waffle House [O] $General, $Tree, Advance Parts, Bi-Lo, CVS Drug, Family$, Reid's Foods, S [gas] Pilot/DQ/Wendy's/dsl/scales/24hr, Shell/dsl [food] Bojangles, Carolina Wings, Great China, Hardee's, McDonald's, Sonic, Subway [lodging] Country Hearth Inn [O] Firestone, Piggly Wiggly

113 SC 302, Cayce, N [gas] A1, Mobil/Burger King, Sunoco/dsl [food] Waffle House [lodging] Airport Inn, Knights Inn, Masters Inn [O] $General, AutoZone, O'Reilly Parts, Rite Aid, Save-A-Lot, Toyota/Scion, Walgreens, S [gas] BP/dsl, RaceWay, Shell/Circle K [food] Lizard's Thicket, Shoney's, Subway, Waffle House [lodging] Carolina Lodge, Country Inn&Suites, Days Inn, Sleep Inn, Travelers Inn [O] [airport], NAPA

COLUMBIA

111b a US 1, to W Columbia, N [gas] Murphy USA/dsl, RaceWay, Shell/Circle K/dsl [food] Chick-fil-A, Domino's, Dragon City Chinese, Hardee's, Little Caesars, Maurice's BBQ, Moe's SW Grill, Ruby Tuesday, San Jose, Sonic, Subway, Tokyo Grill, Waffle House, Zaxby's [lodging] Clarion, Delta Motel, Quality Inn [O] $General, $Tree, AT&T, Bi-Lo, GNC, Hobby Lobby, Pet Supplies+, Radio Shack, to USC, Walgreens, Walmart, S [gas] Hess/Dunkin Donuts/dsl [food] Applebee's, China Chef, Fat Boy Greek, Popeye's, Wendy's [O] Aldi Foods, BigLots, Family$, Lowe's, U-Haul

110 US 378, to W Columbia, Lexington, N [food] Grecian Gardens, Happy China, Lizard's Thicket, McDonald's, Rush's Rest., Subway, Waffle House [lodging] America's Inn, Hampton Inn, Holiday Inn [O] CVS Drug, Family$, Food Lion, Toyota, S [gas] Mobil/dsl, Shell/Circle K [food] Atlanta Bread, Bojangles, China Dragon, Firehouse Subs, La Fogata, Pizza Hut [lodging] Executive Inn [O] [H], URGENT CARE

108b a I-126 to Columbia, Bush River Rd, N [gas] BP, Exxon/dsl, Shell/dsl [food] Capt D's, Chick-fil-A, Hardee's, Ruby Tuesday, Schlotzsky's, Waffle House, Wendy's, Zaxby's [lodging] Comfort Inn, Embassy Suites, Extended Stay America, Homewood Suites [O] $General, Advance Parts, Belk, Chrysler/Jeep/Dodge, Dodge/Ram, Firestone/auto, Ford/Lincoln, Hyundai, Kia, Mazda, Midas, Office Depot, Rite Aid, Verizon, S [gas] City Gas, Murphy USA/dsl, RaceWay/dsl, Sunoco/dsl [food] Bamboo House, Fuddrucker's, Pizza Hut, Tokyo Grill [lodging] Baymont Inn, Best Western, DoubleTree, Knights Inn, Sleep Inn [O] GNC, Hamrick's, Radio Shack, Riverbanks Zoo, Walmart

107b a I-20, E to Florence, W to Augusta

106b a St Andrews Rd, N [gas] Exxon/dsl [food] ChuckECheese, IHOP, Papa John's, Sonic, Top China Buffet [lodging] Motel 6 [O] $Tree, Bi-Lo, Camping World RV Ctr, CVS Drug, Infiniti, Jaguar, Nissan, Walgreens, S [gas] BP/dsl, Hess/Dunkin Donuts/dsl, Shell [food] Domino's, King Buffet, Maurice's BBQ, McDonald's, Nick's Grill, Pizza Hut, Sandy's Hot Dogs, Substation II, Waffle House, WG's Wings, Zaxby's [lodging] EconoLodge, Red Roof Inn [O] $General, KJ's IGA, Tire Kingdom, vet

104 Piney Grove Rd, N [gas] Sunoco/dsl [food] Hardee's, San Jose Mexican, Waffle House [lodging] Quality Inn [O] Sportsmans Whse, vet, S [gas] Exxon, Shell/dsl [lodging] Country Inn&Suites, Microtel [O] Carmax, Land Rover

103 Harbison Blvd, N [food] Applebee's, Hooters, Wendy's [lodging] Hampton Inn [O] Chevrolet, funpark, Home Depot, Lowe's, S [gas] Hess/Dunkin Donuts/dsl, Shell/Circle K [food] 5 Guys Burgers, Bojangles, BoneFish Grill, Buffalo Wild Wings, Carolina Alehouse, Carrabba's, Casa Linda, Chick-fil-A, Chili's, Chipotle

INTERSTATE 26 Cont'd

Exit	Services
103	Continued Mexican, Coldstone, Copper River Grill, Denny's, Fazoli's, Firehouse Subs, Flaming Grill, Honey Baked Ham, Huhot Mongolian, Jimmy John's, Longhorn Steaks, Macaroni Grill, Marble Slab, McAlister's Deli, McDonald's, Miyabi Japanese, Miyo's, Olive Garden, Outback Steaks, Panera Bread, Rioz Brazilian, Rita's Custard, Ruby Tuesday, Rush's BBQ, Ryan's, Sonic, Starbucks, Subway, Tilted Kilt, Tokyo Grill, Tsunami Steaks, TX Roadhouse, Which Wich, Wild Wing Cafe, Yamato Japanese Comfort Suites, Fairfield Inn, Hilton Garden, Holiday Inn Express, Home Towne Suites, InTown Suites, Wingate Inn $Tree, AT&T, Belk, Best Buy, Buick/GMC, Dick's, Dillard's, Firestone/auto, Goodyear/auto, Hancock Fabrics, JC Penney, Kohl's, mall, Marshalls, Michael's, Midas, Old Navy, Petsmart, Publix, Ross, Sam's Club/dsl, Staples, SteinMart, Target, Tire Kingdom, TJ Maxx, Verizon, Walmart
102	SC 60, Ballentine, Irmo, N Cracker Barrel Extended Stay Deluxe, Hyatt Place H, S JP/dsl, Shell Arby's, Bellacino's Pizza, Dunkin Donuts, Groucho's Deli, Marco's Pizza, Maurice's BBQ, Moe's SW Grill, Papa John's, Smashburger, Taco Bell, Zaxby's, Zoe's Kitchen Residence Inn AAA, CVS Drug, Jiffy Lube, same as 103
101b a	US 76, US 176, to N Columbia, **1/2 mi** N Exxon/Subway/dsl Bojangles, China House, Fatz Café, Fuji Cafe, HotDog Heaven, Jersey Mike's Subs, Zorba's $General, AutoZone, Food Lion, Harley-Davidson, Publix, Rite Aid, Walgreens, S BP, Hickory Point/dsl, Mobil, Shell/dsl Burger King, Lucky's BurgerShack, Waffle House $General, Bi-Lo, Toyota/Scion
97	US 176, to Ballentine, Peak, N China 1, Subway Food Lion, S Exxon/dsl
94mm	**weigh sta wb**
91	SC 48, to Chapin, S BP/dsl, Exxon/Taco Bell/dsl, Shell/dsl Bojangles, Farm Boys BBQ, McDonald's, Waffle House to Dreher Island SP, URGENT CARE
85	SC 202, Little Mountain, Pomaria, S to Dreher Island SP
82	SC 773, to Prosperity, Pomaria, N Marathon/Kangaroo/Subway/dsl/24hr, Wilco/Hess/Wendy's/dsl/scales/24hr Waffle House
81mm	**weigh sta eb**
76	SC 219, to Pomaria, Newberry, N Love's/McDonald's/Chester's/dsl/scales/24hr, **0-2 mi** S BP, Murphy USA Burger King, Wendy's Hampton Inn (4mi), Holiday Inn Express to Newberry Opera House, Walmart
74	SC 34, to Newberry, N BP/dsl, Shell/dsl Bill&Fran's Café, **2-4 mi** S Citgo/dsl Arby's, Capt D's, Hardee's, McDonald's, Waffle House Days Inn, EconoLodge, Economy Inn H, to NinetySix HS
72	SC 121, to Newberry, S Citgo/dsl H, to Newberry Coll
66	SC 32, to Jalapa
63.5mm	**both lanes, full facilities, litter barrels, petwalk vending**
60	SC 66, to Joanna, S BP/dsl Magnolia RV Park
54	SC 72, to Clinton, N BP/dsl, S Citgo/dsl Fatz Cafe Hampton Inn H, to Presbyterian Coll
52	SC 56, to Clinton, N Pilot/Subway/dsl/scales/24hr Blue Ocean Rest., McDonald's Comfort Suites, Quality Inn, S Citgo/dsl Hardee's, Waffle House, Wendy's Days Inn H
51	I-385, to Greenville (from wb)
45.5mm	Enoree River
44	SC 49, to Cross Anchor, Union

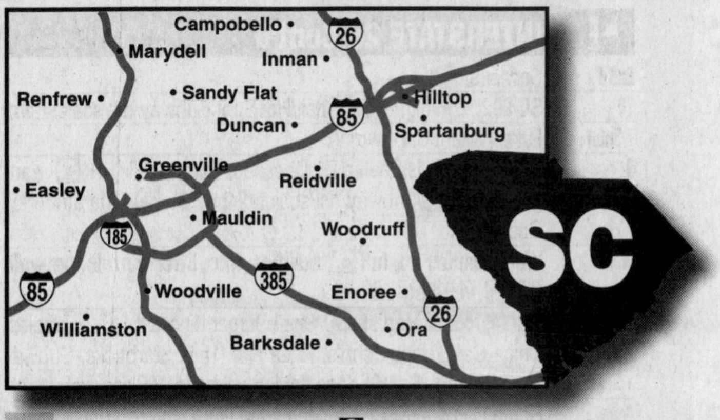

SPARTANBURG

Exit	Services
41	SC 92, to Enoree, N Valero
38	SC 146, to Woodruff, N HotSpot/Shell/Hardee's/Stuckey's/dsl/scales/24hr
35	SC 50, Walnut Grove Rd, to Woodruff, S BP/dsl
33mm	S Tyger River
32mm	N Tyger River
28	US 221, to Spartanburg, N Kangaroo/dsl/24hr, Shell/Subway/dsl Bojangles, Burger King, Italian Pizza, Waffle House H, Pine Ridge Camping (3mi), to Walnut Grove Plantation
22	SC 296, Reidville Rd, to Spartanburg, N Exxon/dsl, Marathon/Kangaroo/dsl, Spinx/dsl Arby's, Blue Bay Rest., Bruster's, Chief's Rest., Fatz Cafe, Fuddrucker's (1mi), Little Caesars, McDonald's, Outback Steaks, Substation II, Waffle House, Wasabi Japanese, Wayback Burger, Zaxby's $General, Advance Parts, to Croft SP, USPO, vet, S 7-11/dsl, Sunoco/dsl Clock Rest., Denny's, Domino's, Dunkin Donuts, El Limon Mexican, Hardee's, Hong Kong Express, Hunan K, Panda Garden, Papa John's, Subway Sleep Inn, Southern Suites, Super 8 $General, Abbott Farms, Bi-Lo, CVS Drug, Hyundai, Midas, Rite Aid, Toyota/Scion, vet, VW, Walgreens
21b a	US 29, to Spartanburg, N Marathon/Kangaroo, Spinx/dsl A&W/LJ Silver, Bojangles, Brasilia Steaks, Buffalo Wild Wings, Burger King, Chick-fil-A, Chipotle Mexican, ChuckECheese, CiCi's, City Range Steaks, Corona Mexican, DQ, Firehouse Subs, FoodCourt, Golden Corral, Jack-in-the-Box, Jason's Deli, Jin Jin Buffet, Kanpai Tokyo, KFC, La Taverna Italian, Longhorn Steaks, McAlister's Deli, Moe's SW Grill, O'Charley's, Olive Garden, Panera Bread, Pizza Hut, Red Bowl Asian, Red Lobster, Ruby Tuesday, Ryan's, Starbucks, Subway, Wendy's Comfort Suites, Hampton Inn, Holiday Inn Express AT&T, Barnes&Noble, Belk, Best Buy, Costco/gas, Dick's, Dillard's, Discount Tire, Firestone/auto, Hamrick's, Home Depot, JC Penney, Jo-Ann Fabrics, Lowe's, mall, Meineke, Michael's, Office Depot, Old Navy, Petsmart, Rite Aid, Ross, Sears/auto, TJ Maxx, Tuesday Morning, USPO, Verizon, Walmart/McDonald's, S Marathon/dsl, Shell/dsl Apollo's Pizza, Applebee's, Compadre's TexMex, IHOP, McDonald's, Shogun Japanese, Starbucks, Taco Bell, Waffle House $Tree, Advance Parts, CarQuest, Hobby Lobby, Ingles Foods/gas, Kohl's, Sam's Club/gas, Target, TrueValue
19b a	Lp I-85, Spartanburg, N BP/dsl, Valero Cracker Barrel, Subway Residence Inn, S Valero Brookwood Inn
18b a	I-85, N to Charlotte, S to Greenville
17	New Cut Rd, S BP/dsl, Virk/dsl Burger King, Fatz Café, McDonald's, Waffle House Days Inn, EconoLodge, Howard Johnson, Rodeway Inn
16	John Dodd Rd, to Wellford, N Marathon/Kangaroo/Aunt M's/dsl Camping World RV Ctr
15	US 176, to Inman, N Breakers, Shell/Circle K/dsl/scales Waffle House H, S Citgo/dsl

INTERSTATE 26 Cont'd

Exit #	Services
10	SC 292, to Inman, N Shell/Hot Spot/Subway/dsl/scales/24hr
7.5mm	Lake William C. Bowman
5	SC 11, Foothills Scenic Dr, Chesnee, Campobello, N Kangaroo/Pilot/Subway/dsl/scales/24hr, S Marathon/Li'l Cricket/dsl
3mm	**Welcome Ctr eb, full facilities, info, litter barrels, petwalk vending, wifi**
1	SC 14, to Landrum, S Shell/Burger King/dsl Bojangles, China Cafe, Papa John's, Pizza Hut (1mi), Starbucks, Subway $General, Bi-Lo Foods, Ingles/café/gas, Verizon, vet
0mm	South Carolina/North Carolina state line

INTERSTATE 77

Exit #	Services
91mm	South Carolina/North Carolina state line
90	US 21, Carowinds Blvd, E Gulf/Quizno's/dsl, Kangaroo/dsl, QT/dsl Bojangles, McDonald's H, Carowinds Camping (4mi), fireworks, W Exxon/7-11, Kangaroo/Subway, Shell/Circle K/Wendy's/dsl Cracker Barrel, Culver's, KFC, La Unica Mexican Best Western, Clarion, Comfort Inn, EconoLodge, Motel 6, Quality Inn Carowinds Funpark
89.5mm	**Welcome Ctr sb, full facilities, info, litter barrels, petwalk vending, weigh sta nb**
88	Gold Hill Rd, to Pineville, E URGENT CARE, W QT/dsl, Shell/dsl, Valero/dsl Hardee's WingBonz Cantina Chrysler/Dodge/Jeep, Fiat, Ford, Hyundai, KOA, Publix
85	SC 160, Ft Mill, Tega Cay, E Exxon Subway Bi-Lo, Ft Mill Drug, The Drug Store, W BP/dsl, QT/dsl, Shell/Circle K/dsl Akahana Asian, Beef O'Brady's, Big Wok, Burger King, Charanda Mexican, Chick-fil-A, Empire Pizza, Fratelli's Italian, Jimmy John's, McAlister's Deli, Moe's SW Grill, Papa John's, Pizza Hut, Starbucks, Wendy's, Zaxby's CVS Drug, Firestone/auto, Goodyear/auto, Harris-Teeter, Lowe's, Meineke, vet, Walgreens
84.5mm	**weigh sta sb**
83	SC 49, Sutton Rd, W Love's/Chester/Subway/dsl/scales/24hr
82.5mm	Catawba River
82c	US 21, SC 161, Rock Hill, Ft Mill, E Exxon IHOP, Sonny's BBQ, Steak'n Shake, Zaxby's Home Depot, Petsmart, W Corner Stop, Kangaroo/dsl, QT/dsl, Shell/Circle K, Shell/dsl Big Wok, Chinese Bistro Deli, Empire Grill, Hooters, Krispy Kreme, McDonald's, Outback Steaks, Sonic, Starbucks Courtyard H, $General, Food Lion, TreadQtrs Auto, Walgreens
82b a	E Exxon Ramada Inn, W Kangaroo, RaceWay Arby's, Bojangles, Burger King, Chick-fil-A, China Kitchen, CiCi's Pizza, Cookout, Golden Corral, HoneyBaked Ham, HongKong Chinese, Italian Island Pizza, Jack-in-the-Box, Little Caesar's, Luigi& Sons Italian, Mario's Pizza, McDonald's, Penn Sta. Subs, Pizza Hut, Popeyes, Sake Express, Sakura Japanese, Señor Nachos Mexican, Subway, Taco Bell, Waffle House, Wendy's Baymont Inn, Best Way, Country Inn&Suites, Days Inn, EconoLodge, Economy Express Inn, Howard Johnson, Microtel, Motel 6, Quality Inn, Regency Inn, Super 8 $General, Advance Parts, Aldi Foods, AutoZone, BigLots, Cadillac/Chevrolet, city park, Family$, Firestone/auto, Hancock Fabrics, K-Mart, Midas, NAPA, Office Depot, O'Reilly Parts, PepBoys, Publix, Verizon, York Co Museum
79	SC 122, Dave Lyle Blvd, to Rock Hill, E BP/dsl, Murphy USA/dsl Amber Buffet, Applebee's, Buffalo Wild Wings, Charanda Mexican, Chick-fil-A, Cracker Barrel, Five Guys, Hardee's, Jersey Mike's, Longhorn Steaks, Newk's Eatery, O'Charley's, Ruby Tuesday, TX Roadhouse Comfort Suites, Hampton Inn, Holiday Inn, TownePlace Suites, Wingate Inn $Tree, Belk, Discount Tire, Food Lion, Hobby Lobby, Honda, JC Penney, Kohl's, Lowe's, mall, Meineke, Nissan, Sam's Club/dsl, Sears/auto, Staples, Tire Kingdom, Toyota/Scion, Verizon, Walmart, W Kangaroo/dsl Bob Evans, Chili's, DQ, Jack-in-the-Box, McAlister's Deli, McDonald's, Mellow Mushroom Pizza, Moe's SW Grill, Olive Garden, Panera Bread, Pizza Cafe, Quiznos, Subway, Taco Bell, Wendy's Hilton Garden Best Buy, Books-A-Million, Dick's, Ford, Michael's, Ross, Target, TJ Maxx, URGENT CARE, visitor ctr
77	US 21, SC 5, to Rock Hill, E BP/Subway/dsl, Wilco/Hess/dsl to Andrew Jackson SP (12mi), W Exxon/dsl, Valero/dsl Waffle House to Winthrop Coll
75	Porter Rd, E Sunoco/dsl
73	SC 901, to Rock Hill, York, E FLYING J/Denny's/dsl/scales/LP/24hr, Exxon/dsl, W H
66mm	**both lanes, full facilities, litter barrels, petwalk vending**
65	SC 9, to Chester, Lancaster, E BP/dsl, Citgo/dsl, Liberty/Subway/dsl Bojangles, China Wok, Waffle House Days Inn, EconoLodge, Relax Inn $General, IGA Foods/gas, W Exxon/dsl Burger King, Country Omelette, Front Porch Cafe, KFC/Taco Bell, McDonald's, Zaxby's Comfort Inn, Motel 6, Super 8 H, vet
62	SC 56, to Fort Lawn, Richburg
55	SC 97, to Chester, Great Falls, E Exxon/dsl, W H, to Chester SP
48	SC 200, to Great Falls, E Shell/Grand Central Rest./dsl/ @, W Wilco/Hess/DQ/Wendy's/dsl/scales/24hr/
46	SC 20, to White Oak
41	SC 41, to Winnsboro, E to Lake Wateree SP
34	SC 34, to Winnsboro, Ridgeway, E Am Pm/dsl Ridgeway Motel (1mi) Bryan's Auto/tire, Ridgeway Camping (1mi), W Exxon/dsl Waffle House Ramada Ltd
32	Peach Rd, Ridgeway, Little Cedar Creek Camping (2mi)
27	Blythewood Rd, E BP/Dunkin Donuts, Exxon/Bojangles/dsl/24hr Carolina Wings, China King, Hardee's, KFC/Pizza Hut, McDonald's, San Jose Mexican, Subway, Valentina's Greek, Waffle House, Wendy's Comfort Inn, Days Inn, Holiday Inn Express $General, IGA Foods, repair/tires, USPO, vet, W Lizard's Thicket Food Lion, Groucho's Deli
24	US 21, to Wilson Blvd., E BP/dsl, Shell/Subway/dsl auto repair, W Exxon/dsl
22	Killian Rd, E Mobil/Burger King/dsl, Murphy Express/dsl Bojangles, McDonald's, Taco Bell, Zaxby's Acura, Aldi Foods, AutoZone, CVS Drug, Discount Tire, Firestone, Honda, Kia, Lowe's, Mazda, Rite Aid, Toyota/Scion, VW, Walgreens, W China Dragon, Monterrey's Mexican AT&T, Lexus/Buick/GMC/Cadillac, Verizon, Walmart/McDonald's
19	SC 555, Farrow Rd, E BP/dsl, Exxon, Shell/dsl Bojangles, Cracker Barrel, Sonic, Wendy's Courtyard, Hilton Garden, Residence Inn H, Carquest, Longs Drug, W Shell/dsl Waffle House SC Archives
18	to SC 277, to I-20 W (from sb), Columbia
17	US 1, Two Notch Rd, E BP, Citgo, Kangaroo, Shell/Circle K Arby's, Burger King, TX Roadhouse, Waffle House Holiday Inn, InTown Suites, Quality Inn, Wingate Inn Bi-Lo, Family$, Rite Aid, to Sesquicentennial SP, U-Haul, USPO, vet,

ROCK HILL

INTERSTATE 77 Cont'd

COLUMBIA

Exit #	Services
17	Continued Walgreens, **W** [gas] Mobil [food] Chili's, Fazoli's, Hooters, IHOP, Lizard's Thicket, Outback Steaks, Waffle House [lodging] Best Western, Comfort Suites, EconoLodge, Fairfield Inn, Hampton Inn, La Quinta, Microtel, Red Roof Inn [other] Home Depot
16b a	I-20, W to Augusta, E to Florence, Alpine Rd
15b a	SC 12, to Percival Rd, **W** [gas] Shell
13	Decker Blvd (from nb), **W** [gas] El Cheapo, Spinx/dsl
12	Forest Blvd, Thurmond Blvd, **E to Ft Jackson, W** [gas] BP/dsl, Shell/dsl/24hr [food] Chick-fil-A, Cookout, Domino's, Eastern Buffet, Fatz Café, Golden Corral, McDonald's, Pancho's, Sonic, Subway, Wendy's [lodging] Extended Stay America, Super 8 [other] [H], $Tree, AT&T, Hobby Lobby, museum, Radio Shack, Sam's Club/gas, Tuesday Morning, Verizon, vet, Walmart
10	SC 760, Jackson Blvd, **E** to Ft Jackson, **2 mi W** [gas] Shell [food] Applebee's, Bojangles, Buffalo Wild Wings, Maurices BBQ, Moe's SW, Ruby Tuesday, Smashburger, Subway [lodging] EconoLodge [other] Bilo, Staples, Walgreens, Whole Foods Mkt
9b a	US 76, US 378, to Sumter, Columbia, **0-2 mi E** [gas] BP, Citgo, Murphy USA/dsl, Shell, Shell/Burger King, Sunoco/dsl [food] Arby's, Bojangles, Capt D's, Chick-fil-A, Domino's, Ichiban, KFC, McDonald's, Pizza Hut, Popeye's, Ruby Tuesday, Rush's Rest., Shoney's, Subway, Taco Bell, Waffle House, Waffle House, Wendy's, Zaxby's [lodging] Baymont Inn, Candlewood Suites, Comfort Inn, Country Inn&Suites, Days Inn, Hampton Inn, Hampton Inn, Holiday Inn Express, La Quinta, Microtel, Quality Inn, Sleep Inn, TownePlace Suites [other] $Tree, Advance Parts, Aldi Foods, AutoZone, CVS Drug, Family$, Firestone/auto, Interstate Batteries, Lowe's, O'Reilly Parts, Tire Kingdom, URGENT CARE, USPO, Verizon, Walgreens, Walmart, **W** [gas] Circle K, Shell [food] CiCi's Pizza, Eric's Mexican, Hardee's, Jimmy John's, Krispy Kreme, Panera Bread, Sonic, Starbucks, Sub Station, Wendy's [lodging] Best Value Inn [other] [H], $General, BigLots, GNC, Goodyear/auto, Radio Shack, Rite Aid, Sav-A-Lot Foods, Target
6b a	Shop Rd, **W** [other] fairgrounds, to USC Coliseum
5	SC 48, Bluff Rd, **W** [gas] Shell/Burger King/dsl [food] Bojangles (2mi) [other] $General
3mm	Congaree River
2	Saxe Gotha Rd
1	US 21, US 176, US 321 (from sb), Cayce, **W** same as SC I-26, exit 115.

I-77 begins/ends on I-26, exit 116.

INTERSTATE 85

Exit #	Services
106.5mm	South Carolina/North Carolina state line
106	US 29, to Grover, **E** [gas] BP/dsl, **W** [gas] Exxon/dsl, Hickory Point/gas, Mobil/dsl/fireworks, Wilco/Hess/DQ/Wendy's/dsl/scales/24hr
104	SC 99, Tribal Rd, **E** [gas] Loves/McDonald's/Subway/dsl/scales/24hr, **W** [other] fireworks
103mm	**Welcome Ctr sb full [handicapped] facilities, info, litter barrels, petwalk [phone] [picnic] vending**
102	SC 198, to Earl, **E** [gas] BP/dsl, Shell [food] Hardee's, **W** [gas] FLYING J/Denny's/dsl/scales/LP/24hr, Citgo/dsl [food] McDonald's, Waffle House
100mm	Buffalo Creek
100	SC 5, to Blacksburg, Shelby, **W** [gas] Citgo, Subway/dsl/scales/24hr

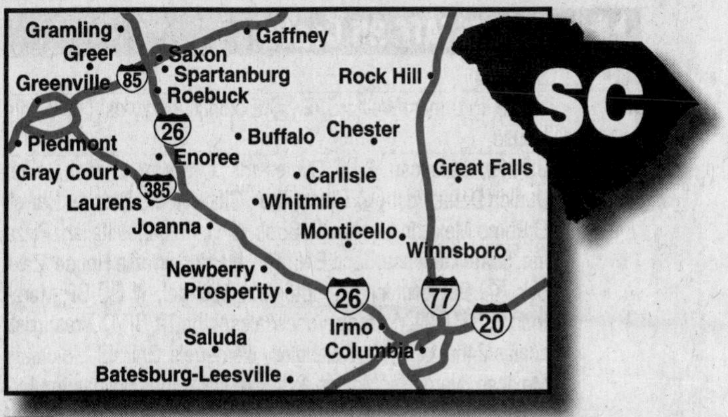

GAFFNEY

Exit #	Services
98	Frontage Rd (from nb)
97mm	Broad River
96	SC 18, **E** [gas] Kangaroo/Krystal/dsl
95	SC 18, to Gaffney, **E** [gas] Kangaroo/Aunt M's Rest/dsl, Petro-Max/dsl [food] Italian Grill/Pizzaria, Mr Waffle [lodging] Gaffney Inn, Shamrock Inn [other] [H], to Limestone Coll
92	SC 11, to Gaffney, **E** [gas] Fast Point/dsl, Marathon/Subway/dsl, Murphy USA/dsl [food] Aegean Pizza, Applebee's, Bojangles, Burger King, Chick-fil-A, China Express, CookOut, Daddy Joe's BBQ, Domino's, Firehouse Subs, KFC, Little Caesars, McDonald's, Olive Garden, Papa John's, Pizza Hut, Sagebrush Steaks, Sonic, Taco Bell, Waffle House, Wendy's, Zaxby's [lodging] Baymont Inn, Super 8 [other] $General, $Tree, Advance Parts, Aldi Foods, Belk, BigLots, BiLo, Ingles Foods, Lowe's, O'Reilly Parts, Radio Shack, Rite Aid, to Limestone Coll, USPO, Verizon, Walgreens, Walmart, **W** [gas] BP [food] Fatz Cafe [lodging] Homestead Lodge, Quality Inn [other] Chevrolet, Foothills Scenic Hwy, to The Peach
90	SC 105, SC 42, to Gaffney, **E** [gas] Marathon/Kangaroo/DQ/dsl, Pilot/Arby's/dsl/scales/24hr, QT/dsl [food] Bojangles, Bronco Mexican, Clock Rest., Starbucks, Subway, Waffle House [lodging] Red Roof Inn, Sleep Inn, **W** [gas] Citgo/dsl, Kangaroo/Burger King [food] Cracker Barrel, Cruisers, Food Court, Outback Steaks [lodging] Hampton Inn [other] fruit stand, Hamrick's, Prime Outlets/famous brands
87	SC 39, **E** KOA
83	SC 110, **E** [other] fruit stand, **W** [gas] Westar/dsl/scales/24hr @ [other] fruitstand, to Cowpens Bfd
82	Frontage Rd (from nb)
80.5mm	Pacolet River
80	SC 57, to Gossett, **E** [gas] Hot Spot/Shell/dsl

SPARTANBURG

Exit #	Services
78	US 221, Chesnee, **E** [gas] Citgo/dsl [food] Hardee's [lodging] Motel 6, **W** [gas] QT/dsl, RaceWay/dsl, Sunoco/Burger King/dsl [food] Arby's, Bojangles, McDonald's, Southern BBQ, Subway, Waffle House, Wendy's [lodging] Hampton Inn, Holiday Inn Express [other] $General, Advance Parts, Harley-Davidson, Ingles Foods/cafe/dsl
77	Lp 85, Spartanburg, services along Lp 85 exits E
75	SC 9, Spartanburg, **E** [food] Denny's [lodging] Best Value Inn, **W** [gas] Marathon/Burger King/dsl, Pure, QT/dsl, RaceWay/dsl [food] Bruster's, Capri's Italian, CookOut, Copper River Grill, Fatz Café, Grapevine Rest, Jade House Asian, La Paz Mexican, McDonald's, Pizza Hut, Waffle House, Zaxby's [lodging] Comfort Inn, Days Inn [other] CVS Drug, Ingles/cafe/gas, Parr 3 Automotive, USPO
72	US 176, to I-585, **E** [other] to USCS, Wofford/Converse Coll, **W** [gas] Kangaroo/dsl, RaceWay/dsl [food] China Fun, El Limon Mexican, Subway, Waffle House [other] $General, Ingles Foods/cafe/gas
70b a	I-26, E to Columbia, W to Asheville
69	Lp 85, SC 41 (from nb), to Fairforest
68	SC 129, to Greer
67mm	N Tyger River

INTERSTATE 85 Cont'd

Exit #	Services
66	US 29, to Lyman, Wellford, E Exxon/Subway/dsl Waffle House
63	SC 290, to Duncan, E Circle K/dsl, Citgo/dsl, QT/dsl, Spinx/Dunkin Donuts/dsl Chick-Fil-A, Clock Rest., Cracker Barrel, El Primo Mexican, Firehouse Subs, KFC, Paisanos Italian, Pizza Inn, Sake Japanese, Taco Bell, Thai Garden, Waffle House, Zaxby's Baymont Inn, Hampton Inn, Microtel, W BP, Marathon/dsl, Pilot/Wendy's/dsl/scales/24hr, TA/BP/DQ/rest./dsl/scales/24hr/ @ Bojangles, Demetre's Grill, El Molcajete Mexican, Hardee's, McDonald's Day's Inn, Holiday Inn Express, Quality Inn, ValuePlace Inn Blue Beacon, Sonny's RV Ctr, Speedco
62.5mm	S Tyger River
60	SC 101, to Greer, E Citgo/dsl, Marathon, Sunoco/dsl Landmark Diner, Subway, Theo's Rest, W Spinx/Burger King/dsl Bojangles, Waffle House Super 8 BMW Visitor Ctr
58	Brockman-McClimon Rd
57	W Greenville-Spartanburg Airport
56	SC 14, to Greer, E Citgo/dsl H, W QT/dsl, Spinx/dsl Goodyear Truck Tires, Ledford's Adventure RV Ctr
55mm	Enoree River
54	Pelham Rd, E Marathon/Kangaroo, Stop-A-Minute/dsl Burger King, Corona Mexican, Skin's Hotdogs, Waffle House Best Western, W BP/dsl 5 Guys Burgers, Acapulcos Mexican, Atlanta Bread Co, Bellacino's, Bertolos Pizza, Bojangles, California Dreaming Rest., Chick-fil-A, China Kitchen, Chophouse 47, Dunkin Donuts, Firehouse Subs, Frankie's Pizza, Hardee's, Joe's Crabshack, Joy of Tokyo, Logan's Roadhouse, Macaroni Grill, McDonald's, Moe's SW Grill, On the Border, Palmetto Alehouse, Papa Murphy's, PDQ Rest., Ruby Tuesday, Schlotzsky's, Starbucks, Subway Courtyard, EconoLodge, Extended Stay America, Fairfield Inn, Hampton Inn, Holiday Inn Express, Home2 Suites, MainStay Suites, Marriott, Quality Inn, Residence Inn, Wingate Inn Advance Parts, Bi-Lo, CVS Drug, EarthFare Foods, Goodyear/auto, Radio Shack, Verizon, Walgreens, Walmart
51	I-385, SC 146, Woodruff Rd, E Brixx Pizza, Buffalo Wild Wings, Chipotle Mexican, Coldstone, Cracker Barrel, Fuddrucker's, IHOP, Lieu's Bistro, Longhorn Steaks, Monterrey Mexican, Oriental House, Panera Bread, PF Chang's, Red Robin, Sticky Fingers Drury Inn, Hampton Inn, Hilton Garden, Homewood Suites, Staybridge Suites Barnes&Noble, Best Buy, Dick's, Goodyear/auto, Hamrick's Outlet, Lowe's, Marshalls, PetCo, Petsmart, Ross, Verizon, vet, Whole Foods Mkt, W Marathon/Kangaroo, QT/dsl, RaceWay/dsl Bad Daddy's Burger, Carolina Alehouse, Carrabba's, Cheddars, Chuy's Mexican, Dave&Busters's, Firebirds, HuHot Mongolian, Krystal, Krystal, McDonald's, MidTown Deli, Ruby Tuesday, Ruth's Chris Steaks, Starbucks, Subway, TGIFriday's, Tucanos Brazilian Grill, Twin Peaks Rest, Waffle House, Yardhouse Rest., Zoe's Kitchen Candlewood Suites, Comfort Inn, Crowne Plaza, Days Inn, Embassy Suites, Holiday Inn Express, La Quinta, Micotel AT&T, Cabela's, Costco/gas, Firestone/auto, Home Depot, Old Navy, Target, Trader Joe's
48b a	US 276, Greenville, E BP/dsl Waffle House Red Roof Inn BMW/Mini, CarMax, to ICAR, W Exxon/dsl Arby's, Bojangles, Burger King, Happy China, Hooters, McDonald's, Olive Garden, Pizza Hut/Taco Bell, Ryan's, Subway Comfort Inn, Embassy Suites $Tree, Acura, Audi/Porsche/VW, Bi-Lo, Buick/GMC, Chevrolet/Cadillac, Chrysler/
48b a	Continued Dodge/Jeep, CVS Drug, Ford/Lincoln, GNC, Hancock Fabrics, Honda, Infiniti, Jaguar, Kia, Lexus, Mazda, Meineke, Mercedes, Michael's, Nissan, Office Depot, Old Time Pottery, PepBoys, Petsmart, SteinMart, Subaru, Toyota/Scion, Volvo
46c	Rd 291, Pleasantburg Rd, Mauldin Rd, W Citgo/dsl Jack-in-the-Box, Papa John's, Subway InTown Suites, Quality Inn, Super Lodge, ValuePlace Aamco, Advance Parts, Bi-Lo/gas, CVS Drug, Home Depot, same as 46ba, Tire Kingdom
46b a	US 25 bus, Augusta Rd, E Mike&Jack/dsl, QT/dsl, Spinx/dsl, Vgo Burger King, Waffle House Country Hearth Inn, Southern Suites, W Economy Inn, Traveler's Inn Home Depot, same as 46c
44	US 25, White Horse Rd, E Spinx/Subway/dsl, W Citgo/McDonald's, RaceWay/dsl Waffle House H, Freightliner
44a	SC 20 (from sb), to Piedmont
42	I-185, to Greenville, I-185 S (**toll**), Columbia, W H
40	SC 153, to Easley, E BP/dsl Waffle House, W Citgo/dsl, RaceWay/dsl, Spinx/dsl Arby's, Bojangles, Burger King, Cracker Barrel, El Sureno Mexican, Huddle House, KFC, Little Caesars, Los Amigos, McDonald's, Pizza House, Pizza Hut/Taco Bell, Sonny's BBQ, Subway, Zaxby's Best Western, Executive Inn, Hampton Inn (4mi), Super 8 $General, Advance Parts, Bi-Lo, CVS Drug, GNC, Rite Aid, Verizon, Walgreens, N 7-11/dsl, QT/dsl Chick-Fil-A, Firehouse Subs Walmart
39	SC 143, to Piedmont, E Vgo/dsl, W Shell/dsl
35	SC 86, to Easley, Piedmont, E BP/Subway (1.5mi), Pilot/McDonald's/dsl/scales/24hr Cancun Mexican, Hardee's (1.5mi), Millhouse Rest., Tony' Pizza O'Reilly Parts, repair/tires, Rite Aid, W Spinx/Pete's Grill/dsl Bojangles
34	US 29 (from sb), to Williamston
32	SC 8, to Pelzer, Easley, E 7-11/dsl, Shell/dsl
27	SC 81, to Anderson, E BP/dsl, Exxon/dsl Arby's, Fiesta Rodeo Mexican, McDonald's, Waffle House Hampton Inn, Holiday Inn Express H
23mm	**sb, full facilities, litter barrels, petwalk RV dump, vending**
21	US 178, to Anderson, **2 mi** E BP/dsl, QT/dsl Applebee's, Chick-fil-A, Chili's, Longhorn Steaks, O'Charley's, Waffle House Publix/deli
19b a	US 76, SC 28, to Anderson, **2 mi** E Exxon/dsl, QT/dsl, Shell/dsl, Stop A Minit/dsl Applebee's, Barbarito's, Bojangles, Carson Steaks, Chick-fil-A, Chili's, Chipotle, CookOut, Denny's, Five Guys Burgers, Fuddruckers, Golden Corral, Golden Corral, Grand China, Hardee's, Hardee's, Hibachi Grill, Jack-in-the-Box, Logan's Roadhouse, Longhorn Steaks, O'Charley's, Olive Garden, Panera Bread, Red Lobster, Sake Japanese, Starbucks, Tucker's Rest., TX Roadhouse, Zaxby's Best Value Inn, Days Inn, Hilton Garden, Holiday Inn, Rodeway Inn, Super 8 $General, $Tree, Advance Parts, Aldi Foods, AT&T, Best Buy, Chrysler/Dodge/Jeep, Dick's, Ford/Mazda, GNC, Goodyear, Hancock Fabrics, Harley-Davidson, Hobby Lobby, Home Depot, Honda, K-Mart, Kohl's, Lowe's, Meineke, Michael's, Nissan, Office Depot, Old Navy, O'Reilly Parts, Petsmart, Publix/deli, Ross, Russell Stover, Sam's Club, Staples, Target, TJ Maxx, Toyota/Scion, Verizon, vet, Walmart/Subway, W RaceWay/dsl, Shell/McDonald's Arby's, Cracker Barrel, Fatz Cafe, Hooters, J Peters Grill, Outback Steaks, Subway, Waffle House, Wendy's, Wild Wing Cafe Baymont Inn, Comfort Suites,

GREENVILLE

ANDERSON

INTERSTATE 85 Cont'd

19b a	Continued Country Inn&Suites, Fairfield Inn, Hampton Inn, Holiday Inn Express, Microtel [other] to Clemson U (11mi)
18mm	**[rest stop] nb, full [handicap] facilities, litter barrels, petwalk [phone] [picnic] RV dump, vending**
15mm	Lake Hartwell
14	SC 187, to Clemson, Anderson, E [gas] Marathon/dsl [food] Huddle House [other] camping (1mi), W [gas] Hickory Point/dsl [food] Famous Pizza Grill [lodging] Budget Inn [other] to Clem Research Pk
12mm	Lake Hartwell, Seneca River
11	SC 24, SC 243, to Townville, E [gas] Exxon/dsl [food] Subway [other] to Savannah River Scenic Hwy, W [gas] Shell/dsl [food] Townville Cafe [other] RV camping
9mm	**weigh sta nb**
4	SC 243, to SC 24, Fair Play, E [gas] Love's/Arby's/dsl/scales/24hr
2	SC 59, to Fair Play, W [other] fireworks
1	SC 11, to Walhalla, W [food] Gazebo Rest. [other] fireworks, to Lake Hartwell SP
.5mm	**Welcome Ctr nb, full [handicap] facilities, info, litter barrels, petwalk [phone] [picnic] vending**
0mm	South Carolina/Georgia state line, Tugaloo River, Lake Hartwell

INTERSTATE 95

Exit #	Services
198mm	South Carolina/North Carolina state line
196mm	**Welcome Ctr sb, full [handicap] facilities, info, litter barrels, petwalk [phone] [picnic] vending**
195mm	Little Pee Dee River
193	SC 9, SC 57, to N Myrtle Beach, Dillon, E [gas] Exxon/dsl, Mobil/dsl, Murphy Express/dsl, Sunoco/dsl [food] B&C Steak/BBQ, Burger King, Huddle House, Papa John's, Pizza Hut, Popeyes, Shoney's, Subway, Tokyo Cafe, Waffle House, Wendy's, Zaxby's [lodging] Best Value Inn, Days Inn, Quality Inn, Red Roof Inn, Royal Regency Inn [other] [H], $General, $Tree, Advance Parts, CVS Drug, fireworks, Food Lion, O'Reilly Parts, SaveALot Foods, Walgreens, Walmart, W [food] Eastern Cafe Chines [lodging] EconoLodge, Super 8 [other] Bass Lake RV Camp/LP
190	SC 34, to Dillon, W [gas] Love's/Arby's/dsl/scales/24hr
181	SC 38, Oak Grove, E [gas] FLYING J/dsl/LP/scales/24hr, BP/Subway/dsl/24hr, Shell/McDonald's/dsl/24hr [other] fireworks, W [gas] Wilco/Hess/DQ/Wendy's/dsl/scales/24hr [lodging] Best Western
175mm	Pee Dee River
170	SC 327, E [gas] BP, Pilot/Wendy's/dsl/scales/24hr [food] McDonald's, Subway, Waffle House, Zaxby's [lodging] Holiday Inn Express [other] Missile Museum, to Myrtle Beach
169	TV Rd, to Florence, E [other] dsl repair, Florence RV Park, W [gas] BP, Petro/Shell/Iron Skillet/dsl/scales/24hr/ @ [lodging] Best Value Inn [other] Blue Beacon, dsl repair, Peterbilt
164	US 52, to Darlington, Florence, E [gas] Exxon/dsl, RaceWay, Shell/Huddle House/dsl [food] Angelo's Seafood Rest., Cracker Barrel, McDonald's, Quincy's, Quiznos, Ruby Tuesday, Waffle House, Wendy's [lodging] Baymont Inn, Best Western, EconoLodge, Motel 6, Ramada Inn, Suburban Lodge, Super 8, Travel Inn [other] [H], Chrysler/Dodge/Jeep, Hyundai, W [gas] Pilot/Subway/Taco Bell/dsl, TA/BP/Popeye's/dsl/scales/ @ [food] Arby's, Calabria Mexican, Dickey's BBQ, Dunkin Donuts, Fatz Café, Hardee's, Krispy Kreme, Shoney's, Young's Pecans, Zaxby's [lodging] Comfort Suites, Country Inn&Suites, Days Inn, Hampton Inn,

DILLON

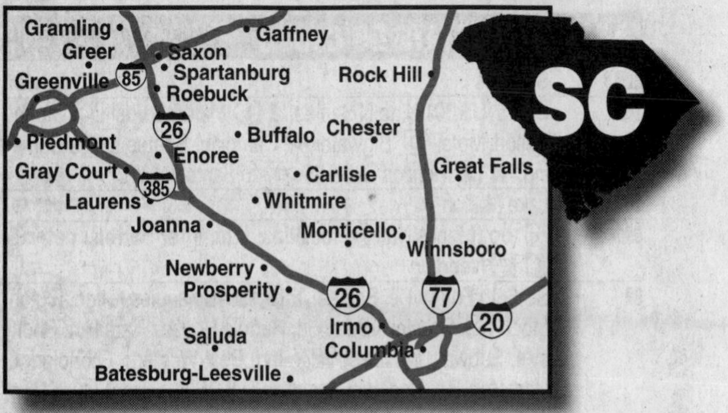

164	Continued Howard Johnson, La Quinta, Microtel, Sleep Inn, Thunderbird Inn, Travel House Inn [other] to Darlington Raceway, transmissions
160b	I-20 W, to Columbia
160a	Lp 20, to Florence, E [gas] Exxon/dsl [food] Arby's, Bruster's Ice Cream, Buffalo Wild Wings, Burger King, Chick-fil-A, Chili's, Chipotle, ChuckeCheese, Firehouse Subs, Golden Corral, Hibachi Grill, IHOP, La Bamba Mexican, Longhorn Steaks, Mellow Mushroom, Olive Garden, Outback Steaks, Percy & Willy, Red Bowl Asian, Red Lobster, Ruby Tuesday, San Jose's, Waffle House, Western Sizzlin [lodging] Courtyard, Fairfield Inn, Hampton Inn, Hilton Garden, Holiday Inn Express, Home2 Hilton, Quality Inn, Red Roof Inn, Residence Inn, SpringHill Suites [other] $Tree, AT&T, Barnes&Noble, Belk, Best Buy, Big Lots, Dick's, Hamricks, Hobby Lobby, Home Depot, JC Penney, Kohl's, Lowes Whse, mall, Petsmart, Sam's Club/gas, Sears/auto, Target, Walmart
157	US 76, Timmonsville, Florence, E [gas] Citgo/dsl, Kangaroo/dsl, Marathon/dsl, Shell/McDonald's [food] Peking Asian, Waffle House [lodging] Florence Inn, Travelodge [other] Abbott Farms Peaches, W [gas] Bull/dsl [lodging] Ramada/rest., Swamp Fox Camping (1mi), Tree Top Inn [other] auto repair
153	Honda Way, W [gas] Exxon/dsl [other] Honda Plant
150	SC 403, to Sardis, E [gas] BP/dsl/scales [food] Hotplate Cafe [lodging] Budget Inn, W [gas] Exxon/dsl
147mm	Lynches River
146	SC 341, to Lynchburg, Olanta, E [lodging] Relax Inn
141	SC 53, SC 58, to Shiloh, E [gas] Exxon [other] DonMar RV Ctr, to Woods Bay SP, W [gas] Shell
139mm	**[rest stop] both lanes, full [handicap] facilities, litter barrels, petwalk [phone] [picnic] vending**
135	US 378, to Sumter, Turbeville, E [gas] BP/dsl, Citgo/dsl/24hr [food] Compass Rest. [lodging] Day's Inn, W [gas] Exxon/Subway/dsl
132	SC 527, to Sardinia, Kingstree
130mm	Black River
122	US 521, to Alcolu, Manning, W [gas] Exxon/dsl
119	SC 261, to Paxville, Manning, **0-1 mi** E [gas] Mobil, Murphy USA/dsl, Shell/dsl, TA/BP/Pizza Hut/Popeye's/dsl/scales/24hr/ @ [food] Arby's, Bojangles, Golden Chick, Huddle House, Mariachi's Mexican, McDonald's, Shoney's, Sonic, Subway, Waffle House, Wendy's, Yucatan Mexican, Zaxby's [lodging] Baymont Inn, Days Inn, Hampton Inn, Quality Inn, Ramada Inn [other] [H], $General, AutoZone, Chrysler/Dodge/Jeep, CVS Drug, Ford, O'Reilly Parts, Radio Shack, truckwash, Verizon, Walmart, W [gas] Horizon/dsl/e-85, Paxville [lodging] Super 8 [other] auto repair
115	US 301, to Summerton, Manning, W [gas] Shell/dsl [food] Georgio's Rest [lodging] Knights Inn
108	Rd 102, Summerton, E [gas] BP/DQ, Travel Depot/dsl [other] Taw-Caw Camping (6m), W [lodging] Days Inn, Deluxe Inn

FLORENCE

MANNING

INTERSTATE 95 Cont'd

SANTEE

Exit #	Services
102	US 15, US 301 N, to N Santee, E Marathon/dsl Santee Resort/Motel Bigwater RV Camping, Santee Lakes Camping, W Horizon/dsl/e-85 to Santee NWR
100mm	Lake Marion
99mm	**both lanes, full facilities, info, litter barrels, petwalk vending**
98	SC 6, to Eutawville, Santee, E BP/Bojangles, Citgo, Exxon, Mobil Coaster's Seafood, Huddle House, Pizza Hut, Shoney's, Subway Best Value Inn, Best Western, Econolodge, Hampton Inn, Rodeway Inn, Super 8, Whitten Inn $General, IGA Foods, W Hess/dsl, Horizon/dsl/e-85, Shell Burger King, Cracker Barrel, Domino's, Maurice's BBQ, McDonald's, Waffle House, Wendy's Clark Inn/rest., Comfort Inn, Holiday Inn, Howard Johnson, Lake Marion Inn, Quality Inn CarQuest, CVS Drug, Family$, Food Lion, Rivers Country Store, to Santee SP (3mi), USPO
97	US 301 S (from sb, no return), to Orangeburg
93	US 15, to Santee, Holly Hill
90	US 176, to Cameron, Holly Hill, W Exxon/dsl
86b a	I-26, W to Columbia, E to Charleston
82	US 178, to Bowman, Harleyville, E Horizon/Subway, Wilco/Hess/Stuckey's/Wendy's/DQ/dsl/scales/24hr Peachtree Inn, W Shell/dsl tires/truck repair
77	US 78, to Bamberg, St George, E FLYING J/Denny's/dsl/scales/24hr, Horizon/Subway/dsl/e-85, Monoco, Sunoco Georgio's Rest., Hardee's, KFC, McDonald's, Pizza Hut, Skynyrd's Grill, Waffle House Best Value Inn, Comfort Inn/RV Park, EconoLodge, Quality Inn $General, Ace Hardware, BiLo, Chevrolet/GMC, CVS Drug, Family$, Ford, USPO, W BP, Shell/Taco Bell/dsl Country Hearth Inn, Knights Inn
74mm	**weigh sta nb, parking area commercial vehicles only sb**
68	SC 61, Canadys, E BP, Crosco Express, Shell/Subway/dsl to Colleton SP (3mi), truck lube/repair
62	McLeod Rd
57	SC 64, Lodge, Walterboro, E Citgo/dsl, Horizon/e85, Shell/DQ, Sunoco/dsl Arby's, Bojangles, Burger King, Capt D's, Dimitrio's Rest., Domino's, Dunkin Donuts, Hardee's, Huddle House, KFC, McDonald's, Olde House Café, Subway, Taco Bell, Waffle House, Wendy's Carolina Lodge, Sleep Inn, Southern Inn H, $General, Ace Hardware, Advance Parts, AutoZone, Belk, Family$, Ford, GNC, O'Reilly Parts, Rite Aid, W Murphy USA/dsl China Buffet, Zaxby's Super 8 $Tree, AT&T, PetCo, Verizon, Walmart
53	SC 63, to Varnville, Walterboro, Hampton, E BP/McDonald's, El Cheapo, Exxon, Petro Express/dsl, Shell/DQ Ruby Tuesday, Shoney's, Waffle House Best Western, Comfort Inn, EconoLodge, Palms Inn, Quality Inn, Ramada Inn, Red Roof Inn, Rice Planter's Inn fireworks, W Horizon/dsl Cracker Barrel Country Hearth Inn, Days Inn, Hampton Inn, Holiday Inn Express, Microtel Green Acres Camping
47mm	**both lanes, full facilities, litter barrels, petwalk vending**
42	US 21, to Yemassee, Beaufort
40mm	Combahee River
38	SC 68, to Hampton, Yemassee, E Horizon/dsl/e-85 Family$, W BP/Subway/TCBY, Exxon/dsl, Shell/dsl Rodeway Inn
33	US 17 N, to Beaufort, E BP/dsl, Exxon/McDonald's, Marathon/Subway/TCBY, Shell Denny's, Waffle House, Wendy's Best Western, Knights Inn, Point South Hotel, Red Roof Inn Confederate Railroad Museum, KOA, The Oaks RV Camping

WALTERBORO

HARDEEVILLE

Exit #	Services
30.5mm	Tullifinny River
29mm	Coosawhatchie River
28	SC 462, to Coosawhatchie, Hilton Head, Bluffton, W E Cheapo, Tiger Express/dsl
22	US 17, Ridgeland, W Sunoco H
21	SC 336, to Hilton Head, Ridgeland, E Citgo/dsl, Liberty/dsl McDonald's, Wendy's Boat'n RV Whse, W BP/DQ/dsl, Exxon, Gulf/dsl, Shell BBQ Buffet, Bella Pizza Burger King, Hong Kong Chinese, KFC, Subway, Waffle House Carolina Lodge, EconoLodge, Quality Inn, Travelodge H, $General, Harvey's Foods, Rite Aid
18	SC 13, to US 17, US 278, to Switzerland, Granville, Ridgeland
17mm	**parking area both lanes, commercial vehicles only**
8	US 278, to Bluffton, Hardeeville, E BP/Burrito/dsl/scales Exxon, Kangaroo/McDonald's Waffle House H, Hilton Head info, W Horizon/Subway/dsl, Shell/dsl Holiday Inn Express, Motel 6
5	US 17, US 321, to Savannah, Hardeeville, E Citgo/dsl Exxon/Blimpie, Shell, Speedway/DQ/Subway/dsl/scales/24h Mi Tierrita Mexican, Waffle House Days Inn, Economy Inn, Sleep Inn fireworks, to Savannah NWR, W Butlers/dsl/repair, Octane/dsl, Speedway/dsl, Sunoco/dsl Burger King, Wendy's Best Western+, Deluxe Inn, Knights Inn, Magnolia Motel, Quality Suites, Red Roof Inn, Rodeway Inn, Stay Express Inn, Super 8 $General, Advance Parts, Family$, fireworks, NAPA
4.5mm	**Welcome Ctr nb, full facilities, info, litter barrels, petwalk vending**
4mm	**weigh sta both lanes**
0mm	South Carolina/Georgia state line, Savannah River

INTERSTATE 385 (GREENVILLE)

GREENVILLE

Exit #	Services
42	US 276, Stone Ave, to Travelers Rest, **I-385 begins/ends on US 276.** E CarQuest, vet, **1-2 mi** W Spinx/dsl multiple services on US 276, to Greenville Zoo, I-385 begins/ends on US 276.
40b a	SC 291, Pleasantburg Dr, E Sunoco Jack-in-the-Box, Little Caesar's, Olive Tree, S&S Cafeteria, Sonic, Starbucks Subway, Taco Casa, Wendy's $Tree, CVS Drug, Family$, Furman U, to BJU, Walgreens, W Citgo/dsl, QT/dsl Domino's, Krispy Kreme Phoenix Inn/Rest., Sleep Inn Cottman Transmissions, Midas
39	Haywood Rd, E Spinx Noodleville, Outback Steaks, Portofino's, Tony's Pizzeria Clarion, Courtyard, Hawthorn Inn, Hilton, Hyatt Place, La Quinta Firestone/auto, USPO, W Spinx/dsl Applebee's, Backyard Burger, Burger King, Chick-fil-A, Chili's, Chipotle, ChuckeCheese, CiCi's Pizza, CityRange Steaks, Clock Rest., Copper River Grill, Don Pablo, Firehouse Subs, Five Guys, Fried Green Tomatoes, Grille 33, Habiba Mediterranean, Halton Country Buffet, Harbor Inn Seafood, Jason's Deli, Jimmy John's, Kanpai Tokyo, McAlister's Deli, Miyabi Japanese, Moe's SW Grill, Monterrey Mexican, Panera Bread, Papa's&Beer, Rafferdi's, Saskatoon Rest,, Starbucks, Stax Grill, Steak'n Shake, Waffle House Baymont Inn, Extended Stay America, Hampton Inn AT&T, Barnes&Noble, Belk, Dillard's, Discount Tire, JC Penney, Jo-Ann, Macy's, mall, Sears/auto, TJ Maxx, Verizon, vet
37	Roper Mtn Rd, W Marathon/Kangaroo/dsl, QT/dsl, RaceWay/dsl Carrabba's, Cheddar's, Chuy's Mexican, Dave&Busters, HuHot Mongolian, Krystal, McDonald's, MidTown Deli, Ruby Tuesday, Ruths Chris Steaks, Starbucks,

INTERSTATE 385 (GREENVILLE) Cont'd

37 Continued
Strossner's Cafe, Subway, TGI Friday's, Tucnos Brazilian Grill, Twin Peaks Rest., Waffle House, Yardhouse Rest. Candlewood Suites, Comfort Inn, Crowne Plaza, Days Inn, Embassy Suites, Holiday Inn Express, La Quinta, Microtel AT&T, Cabela's, Costco/gas, Firestone/auto, Home Depot, Hyundai, Old Navy, Target, Trader Joe's

36b a I-85, N to Charlotte, S to Atlanta

35 SC 146, Woodruff Rd, **0-2 mi E** Marathon, QT/dsl, Spinx Applebee's, Bojangles, Bone Fish Grill, Boston Pizzeria, Bruster's, Chick-fil-A, Chili's, China Buffet, CookOut, Culver's, Dunkin Donuts, Epic Curean Rest., Firehouse Subs, Great Harvest Bread, Green Tomato Buffet, Hardee's, Hibachi Grill, Jersey Mike's, JP's 4 Corners SW Rest., KFC, Krispy Kreme, Little Caesar's, McAlister's Deli, McDonald's, Mimi's Japanese Steaks, Moe's SW Grill, Pizza Inn, Sonic, Starbucks, Stevi B's, Subway, Taco Bell, Topper's Rest., Travinia Italian, Waffle House, Wendy's, Your Pizza Pie, Zaxby's $Tree, AAAAZ, Ace Hardware, Aldi Foods, BigLots, Bi-Lo Foods, Discount Tire, GNC, Hobby Lobby, Kohl's, O'Reilly Parts, Publix, Radio Shack, Rite Aid, Sam's Club/gas, Save-a-Lot Foods, Staples, Tire Kingdom, URGENT CARE, USPO, Walmart, **W** Red Robin Brixx Pizza, Buffalo Wild Wings, Chipotle Mexican, Coldstone, Cracker Barrel, Fuddrucker's, Genghis Grill, IHOP, La Parrilla Mexican, Lieu's Bistro, Longhorn Steaks, Monterrey Mexican, Oriental House, Panera Bread, PF Chang's, Red Robin, Salsarita's, Sticky Fingers, Which Wich? Drury Inn, Hampton Inn, Hilton Garden, Homewood Suites, Staybridge Suites Barnes&Noble, Best Buy, Dick's, Goodyear/auto, Hamrick's Outlet, Lowe's, Marshall's, Petco, Petsmart, REI, Ross, Verizon, vet, Whole Foods Mkt, World Mkt

34 Butler Rd, Mauldin, **E** Spinx/dsl Arby's, **W** Bojangles, Dino's Rest., Moretti's Pizzeria, Sub Sta. 2 $General

33 Bridges Rd, Mauldin

31 I-185 toll, SC 417, to Laurens Rd, **E** Marathon, Shell/dsl Hardee's, McDonald's, Subway BiLo, SaveALot Foods, **W** Spinx/dsl

30 **I-185 toll**, US 276, Standing Springs Rd

29 Georgia Rd, to Simpsonville, **W** ValuePlace Inn

27 Fairview Rd, to Simpsonville, **E** Shell Carolina Rest., CoachHouse Rest., JB's BBQ, Little Caesar's, McDonald's, Milano Pizzeria, Subway Palmetto Inn H, $General, Advance Parts, AutoZone, Big Lots, CVS Drug, O'Reilly Parts, **W** Exxon, Murphy USA, Spinx/dsl 5 Guys Burgers, Anthony's Pizza, Applebee's, Arby's, AZ Steaks, Baskin-Robbins, Bellacino's, Bruster's, Burger King, Chick-fil-A, Cracker Barrel, Epic Buffet, Firehouse Subs, Hibachi House, Hungry Howie's, IHOP, Jack-in-the-Box, Jersey Mike's, KFC, La Fogata Mexican, Mad Cuban, McDonald's, Mei Mei House, Moe's SW Grill, O'Charley's, Panera Bread, Pizza Hut, Ruby Tuesday, Sonic, Starbucks, Subway, Taco Bell, Tequila's Mexican, Waffle House, Wendy's, Zaxby's Comfort Suites, Days Inn, Hampton Inn, Holiday Inn Express, Motel 6, Quality Inn $Tree, AT&T, Belk, Bi-Lo, CVS Drug, GNC, Goodyear/auto, Home Depot, Ingles Foods, Kohl's, Lowe's, Publix, Radio Shack, Ross, Target, Tire Kingdom, TJ Maxx, URGENT CARE, USPO, Verizon, Walgreens, Walmart

SIMPSONVILLE

26 Harrison Bridge Rd, **W** 7-11/dsl, same as 27

24 Fairview St, **E** Marathon Hardee's, Waffle House

23 SC 418, to Fountain Inn, Fork Shoals, **E** Exxon/pizza/subs/dsl Bojangles $General, O'Reilly Parts, USPO, **W** Sunoco/dsl

22 SC 14 W, Old Laurens Rd, to Fountain Inn

19 SC 14 E, to Gray Court, Owings

16 SC 101, to Woodruff, Gray Court

10 Rd 23, Barksdale, Ora

9 US 221, to Laurens, Enoree, **E** Citgo/Subs/dsl Waffle House Budget Inn, **W** Walmart Dist Ctr

6mm **both lanes (both lanes exit left), full facilities, litter barrels, petwalk vending**

5 SC 49, to Laurens, Union

2 SC 308, to Clinton, Ora, **W** H, to Presbyterian Coll in Clinton

0mm I-26 S to Columbia, **I-385 begins/ends on I-26 at 52mm.**

INTERSTATE 526 (CHARLESTON)

Exit # Services

33mm **I-526 begins/ends.**

32 US 17, **0-1 mi N** Hess/dsl, Shell Atl Bread, Bojangles, Burger King, Burton's Grill, Cane's, Five Guys, Grimaldi's Brick Oven, IHOP, PF Chang's, Qdoba, Sonic, Taco Bell, TGIFriday, Zoe's Kitchen Courtyard, Hampton Inn Advance Parts, AT&T, Barnes&Noble, Belk, BiLo, Chevrolet, CVS Drug, GNC, Lowes Whse, Midas, Old Navy, Rite Aid, Tire Kingdom, TrueValue, Verizon, Walgreens, **0-1 mi S** Shell/Circle K, Sunoco/dsl Applebees, Arby's, Chick-fil-A, Cici's, Firehouse Subs, Hardee's, Huddle House, Jimmy John's, La Hacienda Mexicana, Liberty Rest., McDonald's, Melvin's Ribs& Cue, Moe's SW Grill, Momma Goldberg's Deli, Outback Steaks, Sticky Fingers, Subway, Wendy's, Zeus Grill Best Western, Clarion, Day's Inn, Extended Stay America, Hampton Inn, Hilton Garden, Holiday Inn, Holiday Inn Express, Mainstay Suites, Quality Inn, Red Roof Inn, Sleep Inn $Tree, Bi-Lo, CVS Drug, Firestone/auto, Harris Teeter, Jiffy Lube, Marshall's, Michaels, NAPA, Office Depot, O'Reilly Parts, Petco, Publix, Radio Shack, Staples, TJ Maxx, Trader Joe's, USPO, Verizon, vet, VW, Walmart, Whole Foods Mkt

28 Long Point Rd, **N** BP, Exxon Bamboo Garden, Beef'o Brady's, McAlister's, Moe's SW Grill, Sonic, Starbucks, Subway, Waffle House, Wendy's Charles Pinckney NHS, CVS Drug, Food Lion, Harris Teeter Foods, PetsMart, Ross, Steinmart

26mm Wando River

24 Daniel Island, **S** Texaco Dragon Palace, Lana's Mexican, Queen Anne's Steaks/seafood, Subway Hampton Inn Publix

23b a Clements Ferry Rd

21mm Cooper River

20 Virginia Ave (from eb), **S** Hess Depot

19 N Rhett Ave, **N** Hess, Kangaroo/Subway/dsl Hardee's Family$, Food Lion, Rite Aid, **S** BP

C H A R L E S T O N

▲E INTERSTATE 526 (CHARLESTON) Cont'd

Exit #	Services
18b a	US 52, US 78, Rivers Ave, **N** 🅿 BP/dsl, Hess, Kangaroo/dsl 🍴 KFC, Peking Gourmet, Pizza Hut/Taco Bell 🅾 auto repair, AutoZone, Dodge, Family$, Ford, H&L Foods, **S** 🅿 Exxon
17b a	I-26, E to Charleston, W to Columbia
16	Montague Ave, Airport Rd, **S** 🍴 Bonefish Grill, Chili's, Denny's, Jersey Mike's, La Hacienda, Panera Bread, Starbucks, Wendy's 🛏 Embassy Suites, Hilton Garden, Holiday Inn, Homewood Suites, Residence Inn 🅾 Sam's Club/gas, Staples, Tanger Outlet/famous brands, Walmart/Subway
15	SC 642, Dorchester Rd, Paramount Dr, **N** 🅿 Shell/Circle K 🅾 auto service, Family$, **S** 🅿 Citgo/dsl, Sunoco 🍴 Burger King, Checker's, Domino's, East Bay Deli, Huddle House, Little Caesars, Pizza Hut, Subway 🛏 Airport Inn 🅾 Advance Parts, Bi-Lo Foods, CVS Drug, Family$, Food Lion, Harley-Davidson, U-Haul
14	Leeds Ave, **S** 🛏 Value Place Inn 🅾 boat marina
13mm	Ashley River

11b a	SC 61, Ashley River Rd, **N** 🍴 Baron's Pizza, Chick-fil-A McDonald's, O'Charley's 🅾 🅷 Food Lion, Home Depot, Jo-Ann, Kohl's, Lowes Whse, Marshall's
10	US 17, SC 7, **E services from US 17** 🅿 BP 🍴 5 Guys Burgers, Bessinger's BBQ, Capt D's, Chick-fil-A, CookOut, Dunkin Donuts, Hopsing's Asian, IHOP, King St Grille, Krispy Kreme, La Fontana Italian, McDonald's, Panera Bread, Red Lobster, Ruby Tuesday, Taco Bell 🛏 Best Western, Evergreen Motel, Holiday Inn Express, Motel 6, Sleep Inn, Town & Country Suites 🅾 AutoZone, Belk, BiLo, BMW/Mini, Buick/GMC/Cadillac, Chevrolet, Chrysler/Dodge/Jeep, Dick's, Dillard's, Ford/Lincoln, Honda, Hyundai, Hyundai, Infiniti, Jaguar/Range Rover/Porsche, JC Penney, Maserati, Mercedes, Nissan, Pepboys, Petsmart, Ross, Sears/auto, Smart, Target, Tire Kingdom, vet, Volvo, **W services from US 17** 🅿 AMFlag, Hess/dsl, Shell/Circle K 🍴 China Fun, Hardees, Inyabi Japanese, Subway, Waffle House 🛏 Comfort Suites, Econolodge, Hampton Inn, Hawthorn Suites, InTown Suites 🅾 Acura, Advance Parts, Audi, Carmax, Costco/gas, CVS Drug, DriveTime, Family$, Food Lion, Kia, Lexus, Toyota
9	**I-526 begins/ends on US 17.**

SOUTH DAKOTA

S I S S E T O N

▲N INTERSTATE 29

Exit #	Services
253mm	South Dakota/North Dakota state line
251mm	**Welcome Ctr sb, full ♿ facilities, info, litter barrels, petwalk 🐾 📶**
246	SD 127, to Rosholt, New Effington, **3 mi W** 🅿 gas 🍴 food 🅾 RV camping, Sica Hollow SP (24mi)
242	no services
235mm	**weigh sta sb**
232	SD 10, Sisseton, **E** 🅿 Dakota Connection/dsl/casino/24hr 🍴 Crossroads Cafe, **1-3 mi W** 🅿 Amstar/dsl, FuelMax/dsl, Sinclair/dsl/E-85, Tesoro 🍴 Cottage Rest, DQ, Pizza Hut, Subway, Taco John's 🛏 Holiday Motel, I-29 Motel, Super 8 🅾 🅷, Alco, Buick, Camp Dakotah, Family$, Ft Sisseton SP (35mi), NAPA, ShopKO, SuperValu Foods/gas, Teals Mkt, to Roy Lake SP (25mi)
224	Peever, Sioux Tribal Hqtrs, **E** 🅿 I-29 Food'n Fill/dsl, **W** 🅾 Pickerel Lake (16mi)
213	SD 15, to Wilmot, **7 mi E** 🆁🆂 **both lanes, full ♿ facilities, litter barrels, petwalk 🐾 📶 RV dump,** 🅿 🍴 🅾, to Hartford Beach SP (17mi), st patrol
207	US 12, Summit, **E** 🅿 Sinclair/dsl/24hr 🍴 County Line Rest (1mi), **W** 🅾 Blue Dog Fish Hatchery (15mi), Waubay NWR (19mi)
201	to Twin Brooks
193	SD 20, to South Shore, Stockholm
185	to Waverly, **4 mi W** 🅾 Dakota Sioux Casino/rest.
180	US 81 S, to Watertown, **5 mi W** 🅿 Sinclair 🅾 📶, Bramble Park Zoo
177	US 212, Watertown, **E** 🅿 Tesoro/Grainery Cafe/dsl/24hr 🛏 Holiday Inn Express 🅾 fireworks, truck repair, truck wash, WW Tires, **0-2 mi W** 🅿 Cenex/Subway/dsl, Clark/dsl, Freedom/dsl, Sinclair/dsl, Tesoro/dsl 🍴 Applebee's, Arby's, Buffalo Wild Wings, Burger King, China Buffet, Culver's, Domino's, DQ, Godfather's, Guadalajara Mexican, Italian Garden, Jimmy John's,

W A T E R T O W N

B R O O K I N G S

177	Continued KFC, McDonald's, Papa Murphy's, Perkins, Pizza Hut, Quiznos, Senor Max's Mexican, Starbucks, Subway, Taco John's 🛏 Days Inn, Hampton Inn, Quality Inn, Rodeway Inn, Travelers Inn 🅾 $Tree, Advance Parts, AT&T, Chrysler/Dodge/Jeep, Ford/Lincoln, Goodyear/auto, Harley-Davidson, Herberger's, Hy-Vee Foods, JC Penney, Menards, NAPA, O'Reilly Parts, Radio Shack, ShopKO, Target, Tires+, to Sandy Shore RA (10mi) Verizon, Walgreens, Walmart/Subway
164	SD 22, to Castlewood, Clear Lake, **9 mi E** 🅿 Cenex/dsl 🅾 🅷
161mm	🆁🆂 **both lanes, full ♿ facilities, litter barrels, petwalk 🐾 📶 vending**
157	to Brandt
150	SD 28, SD 15 N, to Toronto, **7 mi W** 🅿 gas 🍴 food 🛏 lodging 🅾 Lake Poinsett RA, SD Amateur Baseball Hall of Fame
140	SD 30, to White, Bruce, **W** 🅾 Oakwood Lakes SP (12mi)
133	US 14 byp, Brookings, **E** 🅾 WW Tires, **W** 🅾 Laura Ingalls Wilder Home, museums, to SD St U
132	US 14, Lp 29, Brookings, **E** 🅿 Cenex/dsl 🍴 Applebee's 🛏 Fairfield Inn, Hampton Inn, Holiday Inn Express, Super 8, **W** 🅿 BP 🍴 Arby's, Buffalo Wild Wings, Burger King, Culver's, DQ, Ground Round, Guadalajara Mexican, Hardee's, Jimmy John's, KFC, King's Wok, McDonald's, Papa John's, Papa Murphy's, Perkins, Pizza Ranch, Qdoba Mexican, Subway 🛏 Comfort Inn, Days Inn, Staurolite Inn 🅾 🅷, Advance Parts, Buick/Chevrolet/GMC, CarQuest, city park, Lowe's, Radio Shack, Walmart/Subway
127	SD 324, to Elkton, Sinai
124mm	Big Sioux River
121	to Nunda, Ward, **E** 🆁🆂 **both lanes, full ♿ facilities, litter barrels, petwalk 🐾 📶 RV dump, st patrol, vending, W** 🍴 RV camping

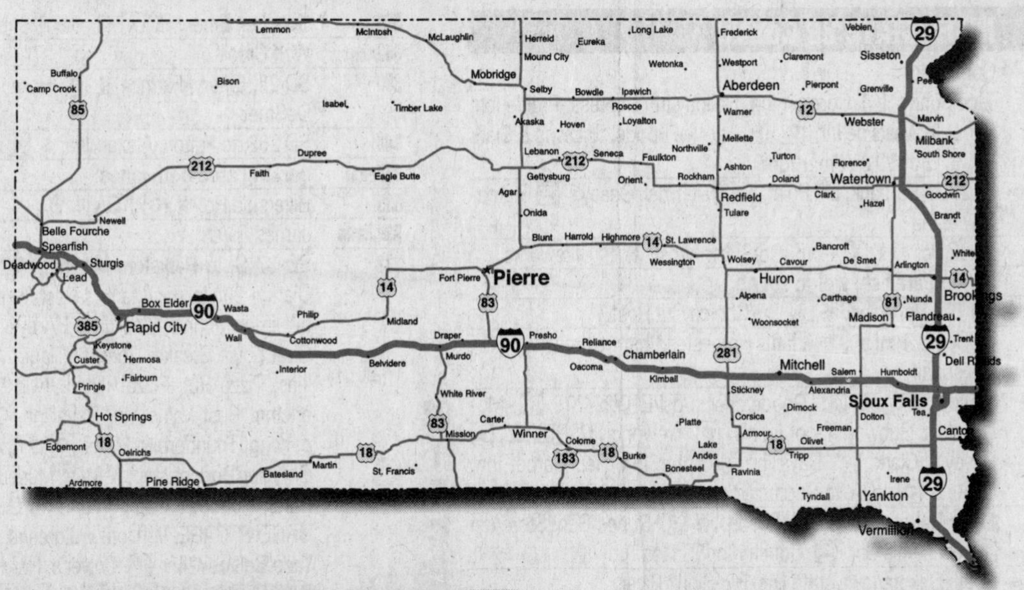

INTERSTATE 29 Cont'd

SIOUX FALLS

Exit #	Services
114	SD 32, to Flandreau, 7 mi E Cenex Subway Sioux River Motel/RV park Royal River Casino/hotel, Santee Tribal Hqtrs
109	SD 34, to Madison, Colman, W BP/rest/dsl, Shell/rest/dsl Dakota St U, museum, to Lake Herman SP
104	to Trent, Chester
103mm	**parking area both lanes**
98	SD 115 S, Dell Rapids, 3 mi E Cenex, Shell DQ, Pizza Ranch Bilmar Inn H, Chevrolet
94	SD 114, to Baltic, 10 mi E to EROS Data Ctr, US Geological Survey
86	to Renner, Crooks
84b a	I-90, W to Rapid City, E to Albert Lea
83	SD 38 W, 60th St, E FLYING J/Denny's/dsl/LP/scales/24hr/ @ Quality Suites Freightliner, Harley-Davidson, Indian Motorcycles, Truckwash, W fireworks, hwy patrol, Walmart/Subway
82	Benson Rd, E BeefOBrady's Fairfield Inn
81	SD 38 E, Russell St, Sioux Falls, E BP, Food'n Fuel/Quiznos Roll'n Pin Rest. Arena Motel, Best Western/Ramkota, Dakotah Lodge, Guesthouse Inn, Motel 6, Ramada Inn, Sheraton, Sioux Falls Inn, Sleep Inn, Super 8 golf, Schaap's RV Ctr, W Subway
80	Madison St, E Sinclair/dsl to fairgrounds
79	SD 42, 12th St, E BP, Freedom Burger King, Burger Time, Fry'n Pan, Golden Harvest Chinese, KFC, McDonald's, Pizza Hut, Sneaky's Chicken, Subway, Taco Bell, Taco John's, Tomacelli's Pizza, Wendy's Ramada, ValuePlace Inn H, $General, Ace Hardware, BMW/Cadillac/Mercedes, Chevrolet, city park, K-Mart, Lewis Drug, NAPA, Nissan, to Great Plains Zoo/museum, Toyota/Scion, USPO, Walgreens, W BP/dsl, Cenex/Chester's/dsl, Food'n Fuel Hardee's Meineke, Tower RV Park
78	26th St, Empire St, E BP/dsl/E85 Buffalo Wild Wings, Carino's Italian, Carnaval Brazillian Grill, Chevy's Mexican, ChuckeCheese, Coldstone, Cracker Barrel, Culver's, Domino's, Granite City Rest, Outback Steaks, Puerto Vallarta, Ruby Tuesday, Sonic ClubHouse Suites, Hampton Inn, Holiday Inn Express, StayBridge Suites BigLots, Home Depot, Michael's, Petsmart, Sam's Club/gas, USPO, World Mkt, W
78	Continued DQ, Papa John's, Starbucks TownePlace Suites Hy-Vee Foods/gas, Lowe's, Tuffy Auto, Verizon
77	41st St, Sioux Falls, E BP, SA/dsl, Shell, Sinclair/dsl Applebee's, Arby's, Burger King, Chili's, Firehouse Subs, Fry'n Pan Rest., Fuddrucker's, HuHot Mongolian, KFC, Lonestar Steaks, McDonald's, Old Chicago Pizza, Olive Garden, Pancake House, Panda Express, Papa Murphy's, Perkins, Pizza Hut, Pizza Ranch, Qdoba Mexican, Red Lobster, Starbucks, Subway, Szechwan Chinese, Taco Bell, Taco John's, TX Roadhouse, Valentino's, Wendy's Best Western, Comfort Suites, Courtyard, Fairfield Inn, Microtel, MyPlace Hotel, Red Rock Inn, Residence Inn, SpringHill Suites, Super 8 Advance Parts, Barnes&Noble, Best Buy, Dick's, Ford/Lincoln, Goodyear/auto, Gordman's, Hyundai, Hy-Vee Foods/dsl, JC Penney, Kohl's, Macy's, Mazda, Menards, Old Navy, PetCo, Radio Shack, Sears/auto, ShopKO, Target, Tires+, TJ Maxx, Verizon, Walgreens, Walmart/Subway, Younkers, W Shell/dsl Burger King, Godfather's, IHOP, Little Caesars, Perkins, Subway AmericInn, Baymont Inn, Days Inn Lewis Drug, USPO
75	I-229 E, to I-90 E
73	Tea, E Sinclair/dsl Marlin's Rest, 1.5 mi W Red Barn Camping
71	to Harrisburg, Lennox, E repair, W RV camping
68	to Lennox, Parker
64	SD 44, Worthing, W Buick/Chevrolet, Great Plains RV Ctr
62	US 18 E, to Canton, E Shell/pizza/dsl Countryside RV park/motel
59	US 18 W, to Davis, Hurley
56	to Fairview, E to Newton Hills SP (12mi)
53	to Viborg
50	to Centerville, Hudson
47	SD 46, to Irene, Beresford, E BP/Burger King, Casey's/dsl, Sinclair/dsl Emily's Café, Subway Crossroads Motel, Super 8 $General, Chevrolet, Fiesta Foods, Jet Auto Repair, W Clark/Godfather's/dsl/scales/24hr
42	to Alcester, Wakonda
41mm	**truck check (from sb)**
38	to Volin, E to Union Grove SP (3mi)
31	SD 48, to Akron, Spink
26	SD 50, to Vermillion, E **Welcome Ctr/ both lanes, full facilities, info, litter barrels, petwalk** , W BP/dsl Burger King, Godfather's Pizza, Red Steakhouse, Subway,

[gas] = gas [food] = food [lodging] = lodging [other] = other [rest stop] = rest stop

SD

INTERSTATE 29 Cont'd

26	Continued Taco John's [lodging] Comfort Inn, Holiday Inn Express, Prairie Inn, Super 8, Westside Inn [other] [H], Hy-Vee Foods, to Lewis & Clark RA, to U of SD, Walmart/deli
18	Lp 29, to Burbank, Elk Point, E [gas] A-1/dsl, Casey's [lodging] Home-Towne Inn
15	to Elk Point, E [gas] Kum&Go/Subway/dsl, W [other] fireworks
13mm	**parking area sb, weigh sta nb**
9	SD 105, Jefferson, E [gas] BP/Choice Cut Rest.
4	McCook, 1 mi W [other] Adams Homestead/nature preserve, KOA (seasonal)
2	N Sioux City, E [gas] Goode/casino/dsl/E10/20/30 [food] McDonald's, Subway, Taco John's [other] fireworks, USPO, W [gas] Casey's, Clark [lodging] Days Inn, Hampton Inn, Red Carpet Inn, Super 8 [other] KOA, to Sodrac Dogtrack
1	E [other] Dakota Dunes Golf Resort, W [gas] Dunes Gen. Store/dsl [food] Graham's Grill [lodging] Country Inn&Suites
0mm	South Dakota/Iowa state line, Big Sioux River

INTERSTATE 90

Exit #	Services
412.5mm	South Dakota/Minnesota state line
412mm	**Welcome Ctr wb/[rest stop] eb, full [handicapped] facilities, info, litter barrels, petwalk [phone] [picnic] RV dump (wb), weigh sta (wb)**
410	Valley Springs, N [other] Palisades SP (7mi), S [gas] gas [food] food [other] Beaver Creek Nature Area
406	SD 11, Brandon, Corson, N [other] Palisades SP (10mi), S [gas] BP/dsl, Holiday/McDonald's/dsl, Local [food] Brandon Steaks, DQ, Great Wall, Pizza Hut, Pizza Ranch, Subway, Taco John's, Tailgater's Grill [lodging] Comfort Inn, Holiday Inn Express [other] Ace Hardware, Lewis Drug, Sturdevant's Parts, Sunshine Foods, to Big Sioux RA (4mi), Verizon
402	EROS Data Ctr, N [other] Jellystone RV Park, tires
400	I-229 S
399	SD 115, Cliff Ave, Sioux Falls, N [gas] TC's/BP/dsl [other] KOA, Spader RV Ctr, S [gas] BP, Get'n Go/DSL, Holiday/dsl/e-85, Love's/Grandma Max's/Subway/dsl/scales/24hr/ @, Sinclair [food] Arby's, Burger King, McDonald's/truck parking, Perkins, Taco Bell, Taco John's [lodging] Cloud Nine Motel, Days Inn, EconoLodge, Super 8 [other] [H], Graham Tire, Kenworth, Peterbilt, Volvo
398mm	Big Sioux River
396b a	I-29, N to Brookings, S to Sioux City
395	Marion, S [other] Walmart/Subway
390	SD 38, Hartford, N [food] Pizza Ranch (3mi) [other] Camp Dakota RV Park, Goos RV Ctr, S [gas] Cowboy Town/dsl
387	Rd 17, Hartford, N [gas] BP/dsl [food] Midway Grill, Pizza Ranch (1.6mi) [lodging] AmericInn
379	SD 19, Humboldt, N [gas] Clark/dsl [other] USPO
375mm	E Vermillion River
374	to SD 38, Montrose, 5 mi S [other] Battle Creek Res., Lake Vermillion RA, RV camping
368	Canistota, 4 mi S [lodging] Best Western, Canistota Depot Inn, Ortman Hotel
364	US 81, to Yankton, Salem, 1 mi N [gas] Cenex [lodging] Home Motel [other] Camp America
363.5mm	W Vermillion River
363mm	**[rest stop] both lanes, full [handicapped] facilities, litter barrels, petwalk [phone] [picnic] RV dump, st patrol, vending**
357	to Bridgewater, Canova
353	Spencer, Emery, S [gas] FuelMart/Subway/dsl/casino/24hr
352mm	Wolf Creek
350	SD 25, Emery, Farmer, N [other] Home of Laura Ingalls Wilder, DeSmet
344	SD 262, to Fulton, Alexandria, S [gas] Shell/dsl
337mm	**parking area both lanes**
335	Riverside Rd, N [other] KOA (1mi)
334.5mm	James River
332	SD 37 S, to Parkston, Mitchell, N [gas] Cenex/Chester's/ds Clark, I-90/Holiday/Marlin's Rest./Subway/dsl/scales/24hr, Mo bil/Jimmy John's, Sinclair [food] Arby's, Cattleman's Club Steak Chef Louie Steaks, Corona Village Mexican, McDonald's, Pe kins, Pizza Hut, Pizza Ranch, Twin Dragon Chinese [lodging] Am ericInn, Best Value Inn, Days Inn, Quality Inn, Super 8/truc parking, Thunderbird Motel [other] [H], Advance Parts, AutoZon Chrysler/Dodge/Jeep, K-Mart, Museum of Pioneer Life, O'Reil Parts, Rondee's Campground, to Corn Palace, transmission URGENT CARE, Verizon, Walgreens, S [gas] Shell/Godfather's Taco Bell/dsl/24hr [food] Culver's, Hardee's, Quiznos, Ruby Tues day, Whiskey Creek Grill [lodging] Comfort Inn, Hampton Inn, Holida Inn Express, Kelly Inn [other] $Tree, AT&T, Cabela's, Menards, Ve rizon, Walmart/Subway
330	SD 37 N, Mitchell, N [gas] Cenex/Chester's/dsl, Shell/ds Sinclair/dsl [food] DQ, Phoenix & Dragon Chinese [lodging] Bud get Inn, EconoLodge, Motel 6, Ramada Inn, Siesta Motel [other] [H], County Fair Foods, Jack's Campers/RV Ctr, Lewis Drug, M Tire, museum, to Corn Palace, weigh sta, S [other] Dakota RV Par
325	Betts Rd, S [other] Famil-e-Fun Camping
319	Mt Vernon, 1 mi N [gas] Sinclair/dsl, Westey's One Stop/dsl
310	US 281, to Stickney, S [gas] Sinclair/Deli Depot/dsl/24hr [other] t Ft Randall Dam
308	Lp 90, to Plankinton, N [gas] Sinclair/Al's Cafe/dsl [lodging] Cabi Fever Motel/RV Park, Smart Choice Inn [other] Gordy's Camping Hills RV Park, repair, USPO
301.5mm	**[rest stop] both lanes, full [handicapped] facilities, litter barrels [phone] [picnic] R dump**
296	White Lake, 1 mi N [gas] Hillman's/dsl [lodging] A-Z Motel [other] USPO S [other] Siding 36 Motel/RV Park
294mm	Platte Creek
289	SD 45 S, to Platte, S [other] to Snake Cr/Platte Cr RA (25mi)
284	SD 45 N, Kimball, N [gas] Clark, Conoco/Ditty's/Diner/dsl [food] Frosty King [lodging] Dakota Winds Motel, Regency Inn [other] Parkwa Campground, repair/tires, S [other] tractor museum
272	SD 50, Pukwana, 2 mi N [gas] [food] [lodging], S [other] Snake/Platte Creek Rec Areas (25mi)
265	SD 50, Chamberlain, N [gas] Cenex/DQ/dsl [lodging] AmericInn [other] [H], Alco, St Joseph Akta Lakota Museum (4mi), vet, S [gas] SA dsl [other] Happy Camper Campground
264mm	**[rest stop] both lanes, full [handicapped] facilities, litter barrels, petwalk [phone] [picnic] scenic view**
263	Chamberlain, N [gas] Sinclair/dsl [food] McDonald's, Pizza Hut, Subway (1mi), Taco John's [lodging] Bel Aire Motel (1mi), Best Western (1mi), Riverview Inn, Super 8 [other] Crow Creek Sioux Tribal Hqtrs, SD Hall of Fame
262mm	Missouri River
260	SD 50, Oacoma, N [gas] Cenex/Arby's/dsl, Clark/dsl, Shell/dsl [lodging] Al's Oasis/Motel/Camping/cafe/mkt, Cedar Shore Motel/Camping (3mi), Days Inn, Howard Johnson, Quality Inn [other] antiques, Buick/Chevrolet, Dakota Camping, Oasis Camping, Old West Museum
251	SD 47, to Winner, Gregory
248	SD 47, Reliance, N [gas] Cenex (1mi), Farmer's Union/dsl (1mi) [other] Sioux Tribal Hqtrs, to Big Bend RA

SIOUX FALLS

MITCHELL

CHAMBERLAIN

SD

INTERSTATE 90 Cont'd

Exit #	Services
241	to Lyman
235	SD 273, Kennebec, N Clark/dsl Hot Rods Steaks Budget Host, Kings Inn auto repair, KOA, USPO
226	US 183 S, Presho, N Cenex/dsl, Sinclair/dsl Hutch's Motel/café New Frontier RV Park, pioneer museum, repair, vet
225	lp 90, Presho, same as 226
221mm	**wb, full facilities, info, litter barrels, petwalk RV dump, RV dump**
220	no services
218mm	**eb, full facilities, info, litter barrels, petwalk RV dump, RV dump**
214	Vivian
212	US 83 N, SD 53, to Pierre, N Sinclair/dsl (34mi)
208	no services
201	Draper
194mm	**parking area both lanes**
192	US 83 S, Murdo, N Pilot/Subway/dsl/Lp/scales/24hr, Pioneer/dsl Buffalo Rest., Murdo Drive-In, Prairie Pizza, Rusty Spur Steaks, Star Rest., The Diner American Inn, Anchor Inn, Best Western, Iversen Inn, Range Country Lodge, Sioux Motel, Super 8 American RV Park/camping, auto museum, city park, Ford, Murdo Foods, USPO, S Country Inn to Rosebud
191	Murdo, N same as 192
188mm	**parking area both lanes, litter barrels**
183	Okaton, S Ghost Town
177	no services
175mm	central/mountain timezone
172	to Cedar Butte
170	SD 63 N, to Midland, N Shell/dsl 1880's Town, KOA
167mm	**wb, full facilities, litter barrels, petwalk RV dump**
165mm	**eb, full facilities, litter barrels, petwalk RV dump**
163	SD 63, Belvidere, S Belvidere Store/dsl JR's Grill
152	Lp 90, Kadoka, N Conoco/rest./dsl/24hr, S Badlands Petrified Gardens, camping
150	SD 73 S, Kadoka, N Dakota Inn/rest., S Conoco/dsl, Sinclair/pizza/dsl Subway, Sunset Grill Best Value Inn, Budget Host, Ponderosa Motel/RV Park, Rodeway Inn, Wagon Wheel Motel Kadoka Kampground, repair, to Buffalo Nat Grasslands
143	SD 73 N, to Philip, **15 mi** N
138mm	scenic overlook wb
131	SD 240, N Minuteman Missle NHS, S Conoco Badlands Inn (9mi), Cedar Pass Lodge/rest. (9mi) Circle 10 Camping, KOA (11mi), Prairie Home NHS, to Badlands NP
129.5mm	scenic overlook eb
127	no services
121	Bigfoot Rd
116	239th St
112	US 14 E, to Philip
110	SD 240, Wall, N Conoco/dsl, Exxon, Phillips 66/Subway Cactus Cafe, DQ, Red Rock Rest., Roadtrip Cafe, Wall Drug Rest. Ann's Motel, Best Value Inn, Best Western, Days Inn, EconoLodge, Fountain Hotel, Motel 6, Sunshine Inn, Super 8, The Wall Motel, Welsh Motel Ace Hardware, Arrow Campground, Harley Davidson, National Grasslands Visitor Ctr, Pronto Parts, Sleepy Hollow RV Park/Camping, Wall Drug, Wall

MURDO

KADOKA

WALL

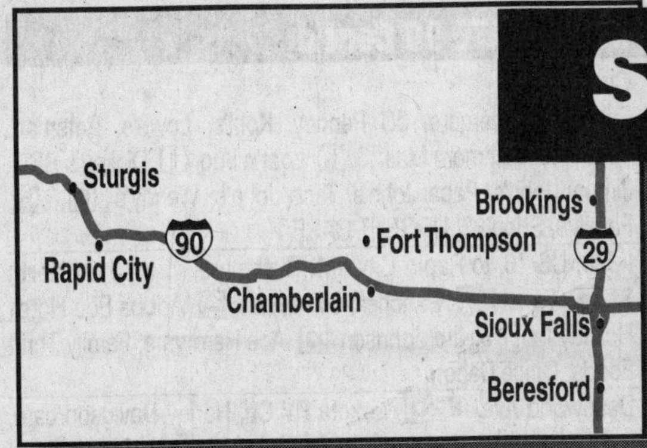

Exit #	Services
110	Continued Foods, Wounded Knee Museum, S Frontier Cabins Motel RV camping, to Badlands NP
109	W 4th Ave, Wall, **1-2 mi** N access to same as 110
107	Cedar Butte Rd
101	Jensen Rd, to Schell Ranch
100mm	**both lanes, full facilities, info, litter barrels, petwalk RV dump, vending**
99.5mm	Cheyenne River
98	Wasta, N Mobil/dsl 24 Express RV Camping, USPO
90	173rd Ave, to Owanka
88	171st Ave (from eb, no re-entry)
84	167th Ave, N Olde Glory Fireworks
78	161st Ave, New Underwood, S Sinclair/dsl, Steve's General Store/dsl/motel/rest. Harry's Hideaway Rest, BJ's Motel Boondocks Camping
69mm	**parking area both lanes**
67	to Box Elder, N Loves/Subway/dsl/scales/24hr Air&Space Museum, Ellsworth AFB
63	(eb only), Ellsworth AFB, to Box Elder
61	Elk Vale Rd, N FLYING J/Conoco/CountryMkt/dsl/e-85/LP/RV dump/scales/24hr/@ Quaker Steak Cambrian Suites, MainStay Suites Black Hills Visitor Ctr, Cabela's, Dakota RV Ctr, S Conoco/dsl, Mobil/dsl/e-85 Arby's, Dakotah Steakhouse, Marco's Pizza, McDonalds Baymont Inn, Comfort Suites, Fairfield Inn, La Quinta, Residence Inn, Sleep Inn KOA (2mi seasonal)
60	Lp 90, to Mt Rushmore, Rapid City, N Buick/GMC, Chevrolet, Ford, Great Western Tire, Kenworth/Volvo, Toyota, S Blaze Pizza, Culver's, Famous Dave's, Five Guys, Fuji Japanese Steaks, HuHot Mongolian, Longhorn Steaks, On the Border, Pizza Ranch, Popeyes, Qdoba Mexican, Smiling Moose Deli, Starbucks H, $Tree, Aamco, Gordman's, Menards, Michael's, Nat Coll of Mines/Geology, PetCo, Sam's Club/dsl, Scheel's Sports, Target, TJ Maxx, Verizon
59	La Crosse St, Rapid City, N Mobil/dsl, Phillips 66 Boston's Rest., Burger King, Denny's, Fuddrucker's, Minerva's Rest., Outback Steaks, Starbucks, TGIFriday's, TX Roadhouse Best Western, Country Inn&Suites, EconoLodge, Hilton Garden, Holiday Inn Express, Super 8 Herberger's, Hobby Lobby, mall, Sears/auto, st patrol, S Exxon/24hr, Sinclair Arnold's Diner, China Wok, Golden Corral, Little Caesar's, MillStone Rest., Mongolian Grill, Pacific Rim Cafe, Perkins, Philly Ted's, Subway AmericInn, Comfort Inn, Days Inn, Fair Value Inn, Foothills Inn, Grand Gateway Hotel, Hampton Inn, Microtel, Motel 6, Ramada, Travelodge AT&T, URGENT CARE, Walgreens, Walmart/McDonald's
58	Haines Ave, Rapid City, N Fresh Start/dsl Applebee's, Chili's, Hardee's, IHOP, Olive Garden, Red Lobster Best Value Inn, Grand Stay Motel BAM!, Best Buy, Hancock

RAPID CITY

🅖 = gas 🍴 = food 🛏 = lodging 🅞 = other 🆁🆂 = rest stop Copyright 2016 - The Next EXIT ®

S T U R G I S

S P E A R F I S H

	⬆E INTERSTATE 90 Cont'd
58	Continued
Fabrics, Herbergers, JC Penney, Kohl's, Lowe's, Petsmart, Tires+, to Rushmore Mall, **S** 🅖 Loaf'n Jug 🍴 Dickey's BBQ, Jimmy John's, Papa John's, Taco John's, Wendy's 🅞 🅷, Family$, ShopKO, URGENT CARE	
57	I-190, US 16, to Rapid City, Mt Rushmore, **1 mi S on North St** 🅖 Exxon 🍴 Panchero's Mexican 🛏 Adoba Eco Hotel, Holiday Inn, Howard Johnson 🅞 Ace Hardware, Family Thrift Foods, Office Depot
55	Deadwood Ave, **N** 🅞 Dakota RV Ctr, Harley-Davidson/cafe, **S** 🅖 ⛽/Subway/dsl/scales/24hr/ @ 🍴 Marlin's Rest. 🅞 Cadillac/Chevrolet, dsl repair
52	Peaceful Pines Rd, Black Hawk, **N** 🅞 Lazy JD RV Park (4mi), Three Flags Camping (1mi), **S** 🍴 BJ's/dsl, Godfather's Pizza, Longhorn Rest. 🅞 Family$, USPO
48	Stagebarn Canyon Rd, **N** 🅞 RV camping, **S** 🅖 Conoco/Haggar's Mkt/food, PitStop/dsl 🍴 Pizza Hut 🛏 Ramada 🅞 Mid-States RV Ctr
46	Piedmont Rd, Elk Creek Rd, **N** 🍴 Elk Creek Steakhouse 🅞 Elk Creek RV Park, to Petrified Forest, **S** 🅖 Mobil/Country Corner Cafe/Papa John's/dsl 🍴 Sacora Sta Rest. 🅞 Sacora Sta Camping
44	Bethlehem Rd, **S** 🅞 Jack's RV Ctr (2mi)
42mm	🆁🆂 both lanes, full ♿ facilities, info, litter barrels, petwalk 🅲 🚿 RV dump, vending
40	Tilford, **S** 🅞 RV Park
39mm	weigh sta eb
37	Pleasant Valley Rd, **N** 🅞 Elkview Camp, **S** 🅞 Bulldog Camping, Rush-No-More Camping
34	**S** 🅞 Black Hills Nat Cemetary, No Name City RV Park
32	SD 79, Jct Ave, Sturgis, **N** 🅖 Conoco/dsl, Exxon/dsl 🍴 Caddy's Grill, Taco John's 🛏 Best Western, Knight's Inn 🅞 🅷, Ford, Grocery Mart, NAPA, to Bear Butte SP, vet
30	US 14A W, SD 34E, to Deadwood, Sturgis, **N** 🅖 Cenex/dsl, Fresh Start/dsl 🍴 McDonald's, Pizza Hut, Shanghai Chinese 🅞 CarQuest, Day's End Camping, Famliy$, Indian Motorcycles, Mr Tire, O'Reilly Parts, ShopKo, USPO, **S** 🅖 Conoco/dsl, RanchMart 🍴 Burger King, DQ, Kangeroo San Asian, Pizza Ranch, Subway 🛏 Days Inn, Holiday Inn Express, Super 8 🅞 BMW Motorcycles, Chevrolet, Verizon
23	SD 34 W, to Belle Fourche, Whitewood, **N** 🅞 Northern Hills RV Ctr, **S** 🍴 Howdy's/dsl, Sonset Sta/dsl 🍴 Hideaway Diner 🛏 Tony's Motel 🅞 USPO
17	US 85 S, to Deadwood, **9-17 mi S in Deadwood** 🍴 Brown Rock, Deadwood Grill, Silverado Café 🛏 Deadwood Lodge, Elkhorn Ridge Motel, Holiday Inn Express, Mineral Palace Motel, SpringHill Suites, Super 8 🅞 Deadwood NLH, Elkhorn Ridge RV Resort, Whistler Gulch Camping
14	US 14A, Spearfish Canyon, **N** 🅖 FreshStart/dsl 🍴 Applebee's, Culver's, Subway 🛏 Fairfield Inn, Hampton Inn, Holiday Inn/rest., Quality Inn 🅞 AutoZone, Verizon, Walmart, **S** 🅖 Phillips 66/dsl 🍴 KFC/LJ Silver, Perkins, Pizza Ranch, Roma's Rest. 🛏 Howard Johnson, Rodeway Inn, Super 8 🅞 Ace Hardware, camping, Ford/Lincoln, K-Mart, transmissions
12	Jackson Blvd, Spearfish, **S** 🅖 Conoco/dsl, Exxon, Loaf'n Jug, Phillips 66/dsl 🍴 Arby's, Barbacoa's, Domino's, Jade Palace Chinese, McDonald's, Millstone Rest., Papa Murphy's, Pizza Hut, Taco John's 🛏 Best Western 🅞 🅷, Black Hills St U,

12	Continued
CarQuest, Chrysler/Dodge/Jeep, historic fish hatchery, Radio Shack, same as 10	
10	US 85 N, to Belle Fourche, **S** 🍴 Burger King, Cedar House Rest., Golden Dragon Chinese, Little Caesar's, McDonald's, Philly Ted's, Subway, Taco Bell 🛏 Days Inn 🅞 🅷, Buick/Chevrolet, Cadillac/GMC, KOA, Safeway/dsl, same as 12, USPO, Walgreens
8	McGuigan Rd, W Spearfish, **S** 🅞 KOA (1mi)
2	**1 mi N** 🅞 McNenny St Fish Hatchery
1mm	Welcome Ctr eb, full ♿ facilities, info, litter barrels, petwalk 🅲 🚿 RV dump
0mm	South Dakota/Wyoming state line

S I O U X F A L L S

	⬆N INTERSTATE 229 (SIOUX FALLS)
Exit #	Services
10b a	I-90 E and W. **I-229 begins/ends on I-90, exit 400.**
9	Benson Rd, **W** 🅖 Sinclair/pizza/dsl 🍴 DQ, Jimmy John's, Marlin's Rest. 🅞 Ford Trucks, Western Star
7.5mm	Big Sioux River
7	Rice St, **E** winter sports, **W** to stockyards
6	SD 38, 10th St, **E** 🅖 Sinclair 🍴 A&W, Applebee's, Arby's, Denny's, Domino's, DQ, Fryn' Pan Rest., Jimmy John's, KFC, Pizza Hut, Pizza Ranch, Taco Bell, Tokyo Hibachi, Tomacelli's Italian 🛏 Super 8 🅞 AT&T, AutoZone, Family$, Hy-Vee Foods, K-Mart, O'Reilly Parts, ShopKO, Sturdevant's Parts, USPO, Valvoline, vet, **W** 🅖 BP/dsl, Casey's/dsl, Shell 🍴 Burger King, BurgerTime, Hardee's, Little Caesar's, McDonald's, Pita Pit, Pizza Inn, Pizza Man, Puerto Vallarta, Qdoba Mexican, Subway, Taco John's 🛏 Rushmore Motel 🅞 Lewis Drug, vet
5.5mm	Big Sioux River
5	26th St, **E** 🅖 Holiday/dsl 🍴 Burger King, Cherry Creek Grill, Dario's Pizza, McDonald's, SaiGon Panda 🅞 city park, **W** 🅞 🅷
4	Cliff Ave, **E** 🅖 BP
3	SD 115, Lp 229, Minnesota Ave, **E** 🅞 city park, **W** 🅖 BP/dsl, Sinclair 🍴 Arby's, Burger King, Camilles Cafe, Culver's, DQ, Famous Dave's BBQ, Golden Bowl Chinese, Hardee's, Little Caesar's/TCBY, McDonald's, Subway 🅞 $Tree, Ace Hardware, Acura, Buick/GMC, Costco/gas, Hy-Vee Foods/dsl, Kia, Lewis Drug, Staples, tires, USPO, ver
2	Western Ave, **E** 🅖 Holiday/dsl 🍴 Bracco Cafe, DQ, Scooters Coffee, Starbucks, **W** 🅖 Cenex/dsl, Holiday 🍴 Buck's Roadhouse, Burger King, China Buffet, Huhot Mongolian, Lone Star Steaks, Papa Murphy's, PepperJax Grill, Perkins, Qdoba Mexican, Redrossa Pizza, Scheel's, Valentino's 🅞 🅷, Advance Parts, AutoZone, Best Buy, Goodyear/auto, Hancock Fabticks, Radio Shack, Tuesday Morning
1.5mm	Big Sioux River
1c	Louise Ave, **E** 🅖 Holiday/dsl 🛏 Comfort Suites, Holiday Inn Express, Homewood Suites 🅞 🅷, Chrysler/Dodge/Jeep, Fiat, Lewis Drug, **W** 🅖 BP 🍴 Burger King, Jimmy John's, Marco's Pizza, McDonald's, Noodles&Co, Panera Bread, Qdoba Mexican, Royal Palace, Spezia's Rest, Taco John's, Wendy's 🛏 Hilton Garden Inn 🅞 Barnes&Noble, Dick's, Honda, Hy-Vee Foods/dsl, JC Penney, Jo-Ann Fabrics, Kohl's, mall, Target, Verizon, Walgreens
1b a	I-29 N and S. **I-229 begins/ends on I-29, exit 75.**

TENNESSEE

TN

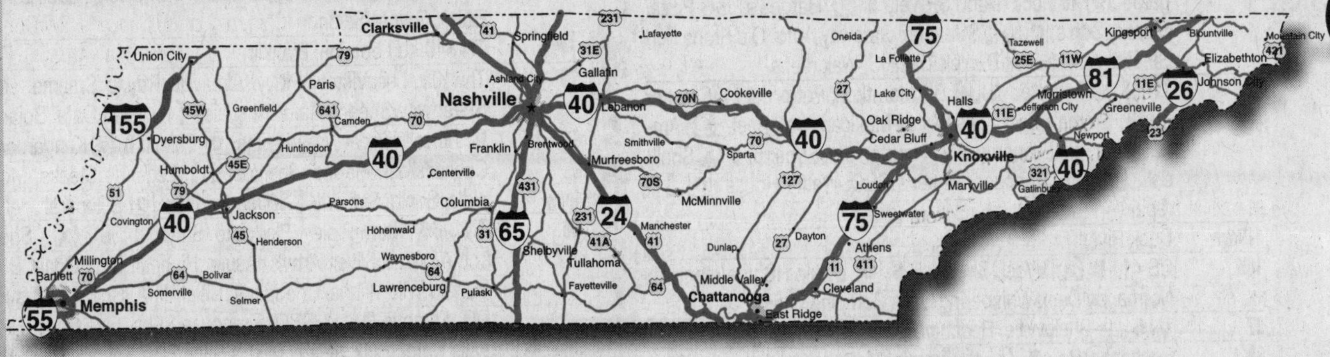

INTERSTATE 24

CHATTANOOGA

Exit #	Services
185b a	I-75, N to Knoxville, S to Atlanta. **I-24 begins/ends on I-75, exit 2 in Chattanooga.**
184	Moore Rd, S Chef Lin's Buffet, Provino's Italian $Tree, URGENT CARE
183	(183a from wb), Belvoir Ave, Germantown Rd
181a	US 41 S, to East Ridge (from eb), S Sugar's Ribs, Underdog's Grill King's Lodge
181	Fourth Ave, to TN Temple U, Chattanooga, N Citgo/dsl, Exxon/dsl, Hi-Tech Fuel, Stop'n Save Bojangles, Burger King, Capt D's, Hardee's, Krystal, Subway, Waffle House Chatt Inn $General, BiLo, Family$, Mack/Volvo Trucks, NAPA, O'Reilly Parts, repair, vet, S Mystik
180b a	US 27 S, TN 8, Rossville Blvd, N Best One Tires/service, to UT Chatt, S Mapco/dsl, RaceWay/dsl Hamilton Inn auto repair, Family$, NTB, to Chickamauga Battlefield
178	US 27 N, Market St, to Lookout Mtn, Chattanooga, N BP/dsl, Citgo Country Hearth Inn, La Quinta, Marriott, Staybridge Suites Chevrolet, Ford/Lincoln, Midas, Nissan, to aquarium, to Chattanooga ChooChoo, U-Haul, S Race-Way/dsl KFC Comfort Suites, Motel 6, Red Roof Inn
175	Browns Ferry Rd, to Lookout Mtn, N BP, Spirit/dsl China Gourmet, El Rey Mexican Best Value Inn, La Quinta CVS Drug, vet, S Mapco/dsl Hardee's, McDonald's Comfort Inn, EconoLodge, Quality Inn $General
174	US 11, US 41, US 64, Lookout Valley, N Waffle House Days Inn Racoon Mtn Camping (1mi), st patrol, S BP/dsl, Kangaroo Cracker Barrel, Diamond Pizza, Logan's Roadhouse, Los 3 Amigos, New China, Taco Bell, Waffle House, Wendy's Baymont Inn, Best Western, Budget Motel, Clarion, Country Inn&Suites, Fairfield Inn, Hampton Inn, Holiday Inn Express, Knights Inn, Ramada Ltd, Super 8 $Tree, Ace Hardware, AT&T, Lookout Valley Camping, URGENT CARE, Verizon, Walmart/Subway
172mm	**eb, full facilities, litter barrels, petwalk vending**
171mm	Tennessee/Georgia state line
169	GA 299, to US 11, N Mapco/dsl, S BP/Krispy Chicken/dsl/24hr, Citgo, Pilot/Subway/dsl/scales/24hr $General, repair
167	I-59 S, to Birmingham
167mm	Central/Eastern time zone, Tennessee/Georgia state line
161	TN 156, to Haletown, New Hope, N Anchor Inn/dsl (1mi) Hales Bar RV Park (2.5mi), S Chevron/fireworks
160mm	Tennessee River/Nickajack Lake
159mm	**Welcome Ctr wb/ eb, full facilities, litter barrels, petwalk vending**
158	US 41, TN 27, Nickajack Dam, N Loves/McDonald's/Subway/dsl/scales/24hr, S Shellmound Camping (2.5mi), Citgo/dsl/fireworks
155	TN 28, Jasper, N Hi-Tech/dsl Hardee's, Western Sizzlin Quality Inn, S BP/Quiznos/dsl H
152	US 41, US 64, US 72, Kimball, S Pittsburg, N Phillips 66/fireworks, RaceWay/dsl, Shell/dsl A&W/LJ Silver, Arby's, China Buffet, Cracker Barrel, Domino's, El Toril, KFC, Krystal, Little Caesar's, McDonald's, Pizza Hut, Shoney's, Subway, Taco Bell, Waffle House, Wendy's Best Value Inn, Comfort Inn, Hampton Inn, Holiday Inn Express, Super 8 $Tree, Buick/Chevrolet/GMC, GNC, Lowe's, Walmart, **3 mi S** Lodge Cast Iron, to Russell Cave NM

MONTEAGLE

Exit #	Services
143	Martin Springs Rd, N Citgo/dsl
135	US 41 N, Monteagle, N BP/dsl, Wilco/Hess/Wendy's/dsl/scales/24hr High Point Rest., Rocky Top Rest., Shan Chinese Family$, Monteagle Parts, USPO, S Motel 6
134	US 64, US 41A, to Sewanee, Monteagle, N BP/Mapco/McDonald's/dsl Sonic American Eagle Inn CVS Drug, to S Cumberland SP, S Marathon/Kangaroo, Shell/dsl Hardee's, Pizza Hut, Smokehouse BBQ, Subway, Waffle House Best Western, Mountain Inn, Super 8 $General, Auto/tire repair, Fred's, Piggly Wiggly, to U of The South
133mm	**both lanes, full facilities, litter barrels, petwalk vending**
128mm	Elk River
127	US 64, TN 50, to Winchester, Pelham, N Marathon/dsl, Phillips 66, S Gulf/dsl to Tims Ford SP/RV camping
119mm	trucks only parking area both lanes
117	to Tullahoma, USAF Arnold Ctr, UT Space Institute
116mm	**weigh sta both lanes**

MANCHESTER

Exit #	Services
114	US 41, Manchester, N Exxon/24 Truckers/scales/dsl, Marathon/dsl, Murphy USA/dsl, Shell/dsl Great Wall Chinese, Logan's Roadhouse, O'Charley's, Potrillos Mexican, Starbucks Comfort Suites, Holiday Inn Express, Motel 6, Quality Inn, Scottish Inn, Sleep Inn, Truckers Inn $Tree, Home Depot, KOA, Nissan, tire/truck repair, Toyota, Verizon, Walmart/Subway, S Marathon, RaceWay/dsl Arby's, Baskin-Robbins, Burger King, Capt D's, Hong Kong Buffet, KFC, Krystal, McDonald's/playplace, Papa John's, Pizza Hut, Rafael's Italian, Subway, Taco Bell, Waffle House, Wendy's Country Inn&Suites, Days Inn, Microtel, Regency Inn, Royal Inn Advance Parts, AutoZone, Family$, Ford/Lincoln, O'Reilly Parts, Russell Stover, USPO, vet

= gas = food = lodging = other = rest stop

TN

INTERSTATE 24 Cont'd

Exit #	Services
111	TN 55, Manchester, N BP/dsl, Co-op/dsl, Marathon/Kangaroo to Rock Island SP, vet, S Hardee's, J&G Pizza/Steaks, Sonic H, $General, Gateway Auto, Old Stone Fort SP, Rite Aid, to Jack Daniels Dist HS, Walgreens
110	TN 53, Manchester, N BP, Marathon, Petro/dsl Cracker Barrel, Emma's Rest., Las Fajitas Mexican, Oak Rest. Ambassador Inn, Economy Inn, Hampton Inn, Super 8, S Shell/dsl Los 3 Amigos, Prater's BBQ, Waffle House H, repair
110mm	Duck River
105	US 41, N BP/dsl, Shell/dsl, S Dickle HS, tire/repair, to Normandy Dam, Whispering Oaks Camping (1.5mi)
97	TN 64, to Shelbyville, Beechgrove, S BP/dsl
89	Buchanan Rd, N Loves/McDonald's/dsl/scales/24hr Subway, S Shell/dsl $General, A&L RV Ctr
84	Joe B. Jackson Pkwy, N Subway
81	US 231, Murfreesboro, N Exxon, Gulf/dsl, Mapco, Shell Cathay Asian, Cracker Barrel, Krystal, Parthenon Grille, Shoney's, Sports Seasons Grill, Wendy's Best Value Inn, Knights Inn, Quality Inn, Ramada Ltd, Regal Inn H, Chrysler/Dodge/Jeep, Honda, S Kangaroo, Kangaroo, Mapco/dsl, Pilot/Arby's/scales/dsl/24hr Bojangles, Burger King, La Siesta Mexican, McDonald's/playplace, Pizza Hut, Rick's BBQ, Sonic, Starbucks, Subway, Taco Bell, Waffle House, Whitt's BBQ, Zaxby's Select Inn, Vista Suites $General, Advance Parts, AutoZone, Discount Tire, Gateway Auto, Kroger/dsl, O'Reilly Parts, Rite Aid, Toyota/Scion, vet
80	New Salem Hwy, Rd 99, S Speedway/Speedy's Cafe/DSL Domino's, Marco's Pizza, Subway
78	TN 96, to Franklin, Murfreesboro, N Marathon, Murphy USA/dsl, Phillips 66/Church's/White Castle/dsl, Shell/Jack-in-the-Box Arby's, Baskin-Robbins, Bonefish Grill, Buffalo Wild Wings, Carrabba's, Cheddar's, Chick-fil-A, Chipotle, Chophouse, ChuckECheese, Coconut Bay Cafe, Cracker Barrel, Egg&I Cafe, Fazoli's, Firehouse Subs, Five Guys, IHOP, Jason's Deli, Jimmy John's, Jim'n Nick's BBQ, KFC, McDonald's, Mi Patria, Moe's SW Grill, Old Chicago, Olive Garden, Outback Steaks, Panda Express, Panera Bread, Red Lobster, Red Robin, Sam's Grill, Samurai's Cuisine, Sandwich Factory, SmashBurger, Starbucks, Steak'n Shake, Subway, TGIFriday's, Waffle House, Wendy's, Zaxby's Baymont Inn, Best Western, Candlewood Suites, Clarion, Comfort Suites, Country Inn&Suites, Days Inn, DoubleTree, EconoLodge, Fairfield Inn, Hampton Inn, Holiday Inn Express, Microtel, Motel 6, Red Roof Inn, Sleep Inn, Super 8 $Tree, Aldi Foods, AT&T, Books-A-Million, Dillard's, Discount Tire, Firestone, Hobby Lobby, Home Depot, JC Penney, Jo-Ann Fabrics, Lowe's, Marshalls, NTB, Petsmart, Ross, Sears/auto, Staples, SteinMart, Target, TJ Maxx, to Stones River Bfd, Verizon, vet, Walgreens, Walmart, S Kangaroo/dsl, Mapco, Marathon/dsl, Shell/dsl Camino Real Mexican, Capt D's, China Garden, Dos Rancheros, DQ, Hardee's, Jersey Mike's Subs, McDonald's, O'Charley's, Papa Murphy's, Pizza Garden, Pizza Hut, Sonic, Subway, Taco Bell, Waffle House, Wasabi Japanese ValuePlace Inn $General, auto repair, AutoZone, Kohl's, Kroger/dsl, Old Time Pottery, O'Reilly Parts, Rite Aid, Sam's Club/gas, vet, Walgreens
76	Fortress Blvd, Manson Pike, Medical Center Pkwy, N Thornton's/dsl Bar Louie, Chili's, Culver's, Genghis Grill, Longhorn Steaks, Macaroni Grill, Mimi's Cafe, Newk's Eatery, Peter D's, Starbucks, Subway, Which Wich? Embassy Suites, Hilton Garden, Holiday Inn, Residence Inn H,

MURFREESBORO

NASHVILLE

Exit #	Services
76	Continued Barnes&Noble, Belk, Best Buy, Dick's, GNC, Michael's, Old Navy, Petco, Tire Discounters, to Stones River Nat. Bfd, World Mkt, S Exxon/dsl Sonic Chevrolet/Cadillac/GMC/Buick, Toyota/Scion
74b a	TN 840, to Lebanon, Franklin
70	TN 102, Lee Victory Pkwy, Almaville Rd, to Smyrna, N Speedway/Speedy Cafe/dsl/scales Asian Cafe, Bojangles, Mi Tierro Mexican, Naked Fish Publix, S Kangaroo/Little Caesar's/dsl, Mapco, Shell/dsl Legends Steaks, McDonald's, Sonic, Subway Deerfield Inn $General
66	TN 266, Sam Ridley Pkwy, to Smyrna, N Shell/dsl A&W/LJ Silver, Arby's, Asuka Hibachi, Blue Coast Burrito, Buffalo Wild Wings, Cheddar's, Chick-fil-A, Chili's, CiCi's Pizza, DQ, Famous Dave's BBQ, Firehouse Subs, Five Guys, Hickory Falls Cafe, IHOP, Jersey Mike's Subs, Jim'n Nick's BBQ, Krispy Kreme, La Siesta Mexican, Logan's Roadhouse, Longhorn Steaks, Panda Express, Panera Bread, Papa Murphy's, Pollo Tropical, Razz Grill, Smoothie King, Sonic, Starbucks, Subway, Waffle House, Wendy's, Zaxby's H, $General, $Tree, AT&T, CVS Drug, Discount Tire, Firestone/auto, GNC, Home Depot/gas, Kohl's, Kroger/dsl, Lowe's, Nashville I-24 Camping (3mi), Petsmart, Publix, Ross, Staples, Target, Tire Discounters, URGENT CARE, Verizon, Walgreens, S Cracker Barrel, O'Charley's, Ruby Tuesday Candlewood Suites, Comfort Suites, Fairfield Inn, Hampton Inn, Hilton Garden, Holiday Inn Express, La Quinta, Sleep Inn
64	Waldron Rd, to La Vergne, N Kangaroo, Kwik Sak, Pilot/Subway/dsl/scales/24hr Arby's, Hardee's, Krystal, McDonald's, Waffle House Comfort Inn, Quality Inn, Ramada Inn, S Mapco/dsl $General
62	TN 171, Old Hickory Blvd, N Citgo/Subway/dsl, Shell/dsl, TA/BP/Burger King/Popeye's/dsl/scales/24hr @ Acapulco Burrito Rodeway Inn
60	Hickory Hollow Pkwy, N Exxon/dsl, Mapco, Thornton's/dsl 360 Burger, Burger King, ChuckECheese, KFC/LJ Silver, Logan's Roadhouse, McDonald's/Playplace, New Century Buffet, O'Charley's, Red Lobster, Starbucks, Subway, Taco Bell, Wendy's, Zaxby's Country Inn&Suites, Hampton Inn, Holiday Inn Express Chevrolet, Chrysler/Dodge/Jeep, Family$, Firestone/auto, Kroger/gas, Mazda, Office Depot, S BP/Quiznos/dsl, Shell/Dunkin Donuts Camino Real Mexican, Casa Fiesta Mexican, IHOP, Olive Garden, Shoney's, Steak'n Shake Antioch Qtrs, Knights Inn, Super 8 Home Depot, Kia, vet
59	TN 254, Bell Rd, same as 60
57	Haywood Lane, N Kwik Sak/dsl Hardee's, Whitt's BBQ $General, Walgreens, S Kangaroo, Shell
56	TN 255, Harding Place, N Delta/dsl, Exxon, Shell/dsl Applebee's, Bar-B-Cutie, Chicago Gyros, Dunkin Donuts, KFC, McDonald's, Mikado Japanese, Pizza Hut/Taco Bell, Subway, Waffle House, Wendy's Executive Inn, M Motel, Stay Lodge, Thrifty Inn $Tree, Sam's Club/gas, S Delta/dsl, Shell/dsl Burger King, Hooters, Jack-in-the-Box, La Fiesta Best Value Inn, Travelodge H
54b a	TN 155, Briley Pkwy, to Opryland
53	I-440 W, to Memphis
52	US 41, Murfreesboro Rd, N Phillips 66/dsl, Shell Waffle House Best Western, Days Inn, Holiday Inn Express, Rodeway Inn, Super 8, S Mapco/dsl, SpeedCo/dsl/e85 BP/dsl NAPA
52b a	I-40, E to Knoxville, W to Memphis

I-24 and I-40 run together 2 mi. See I-40, exits 212-213.

INTERSTATE 24 Cont'd

Exit #	Services
50b	I-40 W
49	Shelby Ave, (from wb only), S [gas] Exxon [other] to LP Field
48	James Robertson Pkwy, N [gas] Citgo, S [gas] Exxon, TA/Country Pride/dsl/24hr/ @ [food] Gerst Haus Rest., Shoney's [lodging] Ramada, Stadium Inn [other] LP Stadium, st capitol
47a	US 31E
47	N 1st St, Jefferson St, N [gas] BP, Citgo, Zmart/dsl [other] Family$, S [gas] Mystic Gas [lodging] Clarion, Knights Inn [other] U-Haul
I-24 and I-65 run together. See I-65, exit 87 b a.	
44b a	I-65, N to Louisville, S to Nashville
43	TN 155, Briley Pkwy, Brick Church Pike
40	TN 45, Old Hickory Blvd, N [gas] BP/Subway/dsl, Phillips 66/dsl, Shell/dsl [food] El Rey Azteca [lodging] Super 8
35	US 431, to Joelton, Springfield, N [other] [H], S [gas] Heritage TC/DQ/Subway/dsl, Shell/dsl [food] Family Rest., Mazatlan Mexican, McDonald's [lodging] Days Inn [other] $General, auto repair, Family$, OK Camping
31	TN 249, New Hope Rd, N [gas] Shell/Taco Tico/dsl, S [gas] Marathon/dsl, Shell/dsl
24	TN 49, to Springfield, Ashland City, N [gas] BP/Pizza Hut/dsl, Mapco/Quiznos/dsl, Phillips 66/dsl [other] [H], repair, S [gas] Shell/dsl, SS/Dunkin Donuts/Wendy's/dsl [food] Dragon Buffet, KFC/Taco Bell, Sonic, Subway [other] $General Mkt, city park, Hill Foods, USPO, vet
19	TN 256, Maxey Rd, to Adams, N [gas] Phillips 66/dsl, S [gas] Shell/dsl [other] $General
11	TN 76, to Adams, Clarksville, N [gas] Shell/dsl, S [gas] Citgo, Exxon/dsl [food] McDonald's, Pancho Villa Grille, Subway, Waffle House [lodging] Baymont Inn, Comfort Inn, Days Inn, Super 8 [other] [H], $General, vet
9mm	Red River
8	TN 237, Rossview Rd, S [other] Dunbar Cave SP
4	US 79, to Clarksville, Ft Campbell, N [gas] BP/dsl, Exxon/dsl [food] Cracker Barrel [lodging] Best Western, Hilton Garden [other] Sam's Club/gas, Spring Creek Camping (2mi), S [gas] BP/dsl, Murphy USA/dsl, Shell/Subway/dsl [food] Applebee's, Arby's, Baskin-Robbins, Buffalo Wild Wings, Burger King, Canela Mexican, Capt D's, Cheddar's, Chick-Fil-A, Chili's, China King, Chipotle, ChuckeCheese, Church's/White Castle, DQ, Fazoli's, Firehouse Subs, Golden Corral, Harbor Cafe, IHOP, Jersey Mike's, KFC, Krispy Kreme, Krystal, LJ Silver, Logan's Roadhouse, Longhorn Steaks, McDonald's, Moe's SW Grill, Noodles&Co, O'Charley's, Old Chicago Pizza, Olive Garden, Outback Steaks, Panera Bread, Rafferty's, Red Lobster, Shogun Japanese, Shoney's, Starbucks, Steak'n Shake, Subway, Taco Bell, Tilted Kilt, TX Roadhouse, Waffle House, Wendy's, Zaxby's [lodging] Baymont Inn, Best Inn, Best Value Inn, Candlewood Suites, Country Inn&Suites, Courtyard, Days Inn, EconoLodge, Fairfield Inn, Gateway Inn, Guesthouse Inn, Hampton Inn, Hometowne Suites, La Quinta, Mainstay Suites, Microtel, Quality Inn, Ramada Ltd, Red Roof Inn, Rodeway Inn, Super 8, ValuePlace Hotel [other] [H], $Tree, AT&T, Belk, Best Buy, Books-A-Million, Buick/GMC, Dick's, Firestone/auto, Goodyear/auto, Hancock Fabrics, Hobby Lobby, Home Depot, Hyundai, JC Penney, K-Mart, Kohl's, Kroger/dsl, Lowe's, mall, Mazda, Office Depot, Petco, Petsmart, Ross, Sears/auto, Subaru, Target, TJ Maxx, to Austin Peay St U, to Land Between the Lakes, Toyota, U-Haul, Verizon, Walmart/McDonald's
1	TN 48, to Clarksville, Trenton, N [gas] Exxon/dsl, Shell/dsl [other] Clarksville RV Camping, S [gas] Exxon/dsl, Shell/dsl [food] Bojangles, Burger King, Coldstone, Dunkin Donuts, El Bracero

CLARKSVILLE

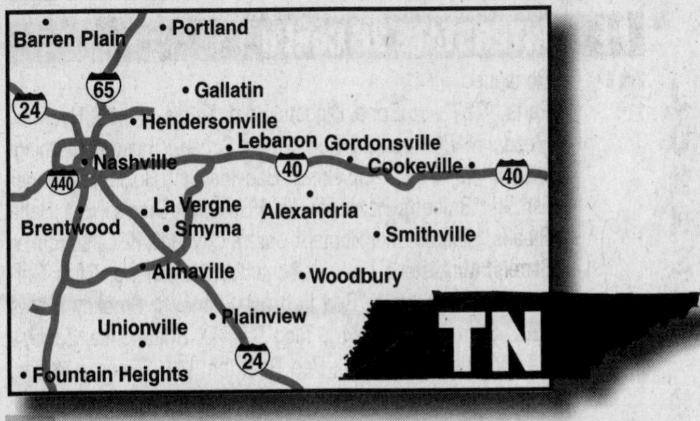

Exit #	Services
1	Continued Mexican, Little Caesar's, Marco's Pizza, McDonald's, Sonic, Subway, Taco del Mar, Wendy's, Zaxby's [other] $General, AT&T, AutoZone, Walgreens
0.5mm	**Welcome Ctr eb, full [handicapped] facilities, litter barrels, petwalk [phone] [picnic] vending**
0mm	Tennessee/Kentucky state line

INTERSTATE 26

Exit #	Services
54.5mm	Tennessee/North Carolina state line
54mm	**runaway truck ramp wb**
52mm	**runaway truck ramp wb, scenic overlook eb (no trucks)**
50	Flag Pond Rd
47.5mm	scenic overlook wb (no trucks)
46mm	**N [RS]/Welcome Ctr both lanes, full [handicapped] facilities, litter barrels, petwalk [phone] [picnic] vending**
44mm	Higgins Creek
43	US 19 W, Rd 352, Temple Hill Rd
42mm	S Indian Creek
40	Jackson-Love Hwy, Erwin, Jonesborough, N [gas] Valero/dsl [lodging] Mtn Inn [other] [H], Nolichucky Gorge Camping (2mi)
37	TN 81, Rd 107, Erwin, Jonesborough, N [gas] Shell [food] Bojangles, Huddle House, McDonald's, Pal's Drive-Thru, Taco Bell [other] [H], USPO, Walgreens, S [lodging] Super 8 [other] A. Johnson NHS (31mi), River Park Camping (5mi)
36	Main St, Erwin, N [gas] BP/dsl, Exxon/dsl/e-85 [food] Azteca Mexican, Hardee's, KFC, Little Caesars, Pizza Hut, Subway, Wendy's [other] $General, Advance Parts, AutoZone, Firestone, Rite Aid
34	Tinker Rd, N [gas] Murphy USA/dsl [food] Los Jalapenos, Primo's Pizza [other] Walmart
32	Rd 173, Unicoi Rd, to Cherokee NF, N [gas] Jerry's Mkt [food] Clarence's Drive-In, Whistle Stop Deli [other] $General, Grandview Ranch Camping (7mi), USPO, S [other] Woodsmoke Camping
27	Rd 359 N, Okolona Rd, N [gas] BP [lodging] Budget Inn (3mi) [other] truck repair
24	US 321, TN 67, Elizabethton, N [gas] Shell/Dunkin Donuts/dsl [other] Roan Mtn SP, S [gas] BP/dsl [food] Arby's, Burger King, Fox's Pizza, Little Caesars, LJ Silver, Subway [lodging] Comfort Inn [other] [H], Advance Parts, CVS, Food City/gas, Price Less Foods, to ETSU, Walgreens
23	Rd 91, Market St, N [food] DQ, McDonald's, S [other] museum
22	Rd 400, Unaka Ave, Watauga Ave
20b a	US 11 E, US 19 N, to Roan St, N [gas] Shell/dsl, Sunoco/dsl [food] Arby's, Cootie Brown's Rest., Harbor House Seafood, Hardee's, Little Caesars, LJ Silver, Mellow Mushroom Pizza, Moto Japanese, Peerless Rest., Perkins, Popeye's, Sonic [lodging] Best Western, Holiday Inn, Ramada Ltd, Super 8 [other] Acura, Advance

ERWIN

TN

🅐 = gas 🍴 = food 🛌 = lodging Ⓞ = other 🅟ₛ = rest stop Copyright 2016 - The Next EXIT ®

TN

J O H N S O N C I T Y

🔼🔽Ⓔ INTERSTATE 26 Cont'd

20b a	Continued Parts, AT&T, AutoZone, BigLots, Ford, Fred's, Honda, Hyundai, Mazda, NAPA Repair, O'Reilly Parts, Subaru, Tuesday Morning, UHaul, VW, **S** 🍴 Applebees, Babylon Grill, Bojangles, Bonefish Grill, Brusco's Pizza, Fazoli's, Five Guys, Greg's Pizza, Hana Steaks, Hibachi Grill, Hooters, Jack's City Grill, KFC, Longhorn Steaks, McAlister's Deli, McDonald's, O'Charley's, Olive Garden, Papa Murphy's, Red Lobster, Shoney's, Smokey Bones BBQ, Starbucks, Subway, Taco Bell, TX Roadhouse, Zaxby's 🛌 Doubletree, Motel 6, Red Roof Inn Ⓞ $General, $Tree, Belk, Books-A-Million, CVS, Dick's, FreeService Tire/auto, Hancock Fabrics, JC Penney, Kroger, Office Depot, Sears/auto, Target, TJ Maxx, Verizon, Walgreens
19	TN 381, to St of Franklin Rd, to Bristol, **N** 🅐 Murphy USA/dsl, Valero/McDonald's 🍴 Golden Corral, Honeybaked Ham, Logan's Roadhouse, Outback Steaks, Subway 🛌 Comfort Suites Ⓞ Walmart, **0-2 mi S** 🍴 Amigo Mexican, Barberito's Grille, Buffalo Wild Wings, Carrabba's, Cheddar's, Chick-fil-A, Chili's, ChuckECheese's, East Coast Wings, Fuddruckers, IHOP, Jason's Deli, Mad Greek, Ming's Asian, Panera Bread, Rita's Custard, Wendy's, Which Wich? 🛌 Courtyard, Hampton Inn, Sleep Inn Ⓞ 🏥, AT&T, Barnes&Noble, Best Buy, Home Depot, K-Mart, Kohl's, Lowe's, Michael's, Natural Foods Mkt, Old Navy, PetsMart, Ross, Sam's Club/gas, Steinmart, USPO, Verizon, vet
17	Boone St, **N** 🅐 BP, QP/dsl 🍴 Beef'o Brady's, Bob Evans, Giovanni's Italian, Hardee's, McDonald's, Pal's Drive-in, Pizza+ Ⓞ $General, Ingles Foods/dsl, **S** 🅐 Exxon/e-85, Shell/Subway/dsl 🍴 Cracker Barrel, Domino's, Poblano's Mexican, Waffle House, Wendy's 🛌 Holiday Inn Express, Quality Inn, Value Place
13	Rd 75, Bobby Hicks Hwy, **N** 🅐 BP, Shell 🍴 Burger King, China Luck, DQ, La Carreta, McDonald's, Pal's Drive-Thru, Papa John's, Pizza Hut, Sicily Italian, Subway, Taco Bell, Yong Asian Ⓞ $General, Advance Parts, Food City/gas, O'Reilly Parts, USPO, Walgreens, **S** 🅐 Exxon/dsl
10	Eastern Star Rd, **N** 🍴 Phil's Dream Pit BBQ
8b a	I-81, to Bristol, Knoxville
6	Rd 347, Rock Springs Rd, **S** 🅐 Rite Quik/dsl
5mm	Welcome Ctr/🅟ₛ, **full** ♿ **facilities both lanes, litter barrels, petwalk** 🅿
4	TN 93, Wilcox Dr, **N** 🅐 BP/Subway, Mobil/McDonald's/dsl 🍴 Burger King, Hardee's, La Carreta Mexican, Pizza Hut, Wendy's 🛌 Comfort Suites, Hampton Inn, Holiday Inn Express, Quality Inn Ⓞ $General, Cave's Drug, Price Less Foods, **S** 🅐 Exxon, Mobil/Arby's/dsl/e-85 🍴 Pizza+
3	Meadowview Pkwy, **N** 🛌 Marriott
1	US 11 W, West Stone Dr, **N** 🅐 Shell 🍴 Little Caesars, Molcajete's Mexican 🛌 Super 8 Ⓞ 🏥, Walgreens, **S** 🅐 Exxon, Murphy USA/dsl 🍴 Bojangles, China Star, Fatz Cafe, Sonic, Subway Ⓞ $Tree, Lowe's, Walmart

I-26 begins/ends on US 23.

K I N G S P O R T

🔼🔽Ⓔ INTERSTATE 40

Exit #	Services
451mm	Tennessee/North Carolina state line
451	Waterville Rd
447	Hartford Rd, **N** 🅐 Citgo/dsl, **S** 🅐 BP/dsl 🍴 Bean Tree Cafe, Pigeon River Smokehouse Ⓞ Foxfire Camping, Shauan's Riverside RV Park, USPO, whitewater rafting

N E W P O R T

D A N D R I D G E

446mm	Welcome Ctr wb, full ♿ facilities, litter barrels, petwalk Ⓒ 🅿 vending, no trucks
443	Foothills Pkwy, to Gatlinburg, **S** Ⓞ camping, Ⓞ Great Smoky Mtns NP
443mm	Pigeon River
440	US 321, to Wilton Spgs Rd, Gatlinburg, **N** 🅐 440 Trkstp/cafe/dsl, **S** 🅐 Marathon 🍴 Broasted Chicken Ⓞ Arrow Creek Camping (14mi), CrazyHorse Camping (14mi), Jellystone Camping (12mi)
439mm	Pigeon River
435	US 321, to Gatlinburg, Newport, **N** 🅐 Exxon/Biodsl/e-85, Marathon, Mobil, Shell/dsl, Weigel/dsl 🍴 Arby's, Burger King, Hardee's, KFC, Lois' Country Kitchen, McDonald's, Pizza Hut, SageBrush Steaks, Subway, Taco Bell 🛌 Motel 6, Parkway Inn Ⓞ 🏥, CVS Drug, O'Reilly Parts, Town&Country Drug, USPO, Walgreens, **S** 🅐 Mobil/dsl, Murphy USA/dsl 🍴 Bojangles, Brooklyn Pizza, Cracker Barrel, Monterrey Mexican, New China, Papa John's, Ruby Tuesday, Waffle House, Wendy's 🛌 Best Western, Days Inn, Family Inn, Holiday Inn Express, Super 8 Ⓞ $General, $Tree, AT&T, Lowe's, Save-A-Lot Foods, Verizon, Walmart/Subway
432b a	US 70, US 411, US 25W, to Newport, **N** 🅐 Exxon/dsl, Marathon/dsl, TimeOut TC/BP/Huddle House/dsl/scales 🍴 Brandywine Creek Steaks 🛌 Comfort Inn, Relax Inn Ⓞ Buick/Chevrolet, Chrysler/Dodge/Jeep, Ford, KOA (2mi), Tana-See RV Park, truck service, Westgate Tire, **S** 🅐 BP/pizza, Citgo/dsl, Marathon/dsl, Shell/dsl 🛌 Family Inn/rest. Ⓞ $General
426mm	🅟ₛ wb, full ♿ facilities, litter barrels, petwalk Ⓒ 🅿 vending
425mm	French Broad River
424	TN 113, Dandridge, **N** 🅐 Marathon/dsl
421	I-81 N, to Bristol
420mm	🅟ₛ eb, full ♿ facilities, litter barrels, petwalk Ⓒ 🅿 vending
417	TN 92, Dandridge, **N** 🅐 Marathon/dsl, Pilot/Subway/dsl/scales/24hr/ @ 🍴 Capt's Galley, Hardee's, McDonald's, Perkins, Ruby Tuesday, Taste of Dandridge 🛌 EconoLodge, **S** 🅐 Marathon/dsl, Shell/Wendy's/dsl, Weigel's/dsl 🍴 Arby's, Bojangles, LJ Silver/Taco Bell, Shoney's, Waffle House 🛌 Hampton Inn, Holiday Inn Express, Jefferson Inn, Quality Inn, Super 8 Ⓞ Advance Parts
415	US 25W, US 70, to Dandridge, **S** 🅐 Marathon/dsl 🍴 Sonic (3mi)
412	Deep Sprgs Rd, to Douglas Dam, **N** 🅐 Loves/Chester's/Subway/dsl/scales/24hr
407	TN 66, to Sevierville, Pigeon Forge, Gatlinburg, **N** 🅐 Shell/Subway/dsl 🍴 Chophouse, Cracker Barrel, McDonald's, Uncle Buck's Grill 🛌 Best Value Inn, Fairfield Inn, Hampton Inn, Holiday Inn Express Ⓞ Bass Pro Shops, RV Camping, Smoky Mtn Visitor's Ctr, **S** 🅐 BP/Subway/dsl, Exxon/Subway/dsl, Mobil/Dunkin Donuts/dsl, Shell/Krystal/dsl 🍴 Burger King, FlapJack's, Wendy's 🛌 Comfort Suites, Days Inn, Motel 6, Quality Inn Ⓞ Chrysler/Dodge/Jeep, flea mkt, Russell Stover, RV Camping, TN Tourist Info, USPO, multiple services/outlets
402	Midway Rd
398	Strawberry Plains Pk, Strawberry Plains Pk, **N** 🅐 BP/dsl, Citgo/dsl, Exxon/dsl, Shell/dsl 🍴 Aubrey's Rest., McDonald's, Outback Steaks, Waffle House, Wendy's 🛌 EconoLodge, Hampton Inn, Holiday Inn Express, Knight's Inn, Quality Inn, Red Roof Inn, Rodeway Inn, Super 8 Ⓞ TN RV Ctr, **S** 🅐 Pilot/Subway/dsl/scales/24hr, Weigel's 🍴 Arby's, Burger King, Cracker Barrel, Golden Wok Chinese, KFC, Krystal, Puleo's Grille, Taco

 = gas = food = lodging = other = rest stop

INTERSTATE 40 Cont'd

398	Continued
	Bell Best Western, Comfort Suites, Fairfield Inn, La Quinta, Motel 6
395mm	Holston River
394	US 70, US 11E, US 25W, Asheville Hwy, N Pilot/dsl, Shell/Quizno's/dsl Papa John's, Subway, Wendy's Gateway Inn Advance Parts, AutoZone, city park, S Exxon, Mapco/dsl Habaneros Mexican, Pizza Hut, Scott's Place, Waffle House Relax Inn $General, CVS Drug, Family$, Kroger/gas, vet, Walgreens
393	I-640 W, to I-75 N
392	US 11W, Rutledge Pike, N Citgo/dsl $General, truck repair, U-Haul, S Shell Buddy's BBQ, Hardee's, Shoney's NAPA, Save-A-Lot Foods, to Knoxville Zoo, transmissions
390	Cherry St, Knoxville, N Marathon/dsl, Top Fuel Mart, Weigel's/Subway Happy Garden Chinese Knoxville Inn tires, S Exxon Arby's, Little Caesar's, LJ Silver, McDonald's Regency Inn Advance Parts, Family$, O'Reilly Parts, vet, Walgreens
389	US 441 N, Broadway, 5th Ave, N Pilot/dsl, Shell/dsl, Star Burger King, KFC, Krystal, McDonald's, Sonic, Subway, Taco Bell, Wendy's $General, Ace Hardware, Belew Drug, CVS Drug, Family$, Firestone/auto, Kroger/dsl, Radio Shack, Save-A-Lot Foods, USPO, Walgreens/24hr
388	US 441 S (exits left from wb), S Crowne Plaza, Hilton, Holiday Inn downtown, to Smokey Mtns, to U of TN
387a	I-275 N, to Lexington
387	TN 62, 17th St, N Gas'N Go, Pilot/dsl Hamilton Inn, Royal Inn $General, Food City, vet
386b a	US 129, University Ave, to UT
385	I-75 N, I-640 E

I-40 W and I-75 S run together 17 mi.

383	Papermill Rd, N Red Roof Inn, S Exxon/dsl, Pilot/dsl Barberitos, Buddy's BBQ, Burger King, Five Guys, Krispy Kreme, Sonic, Twin Peaks, Waffle House Courtyard, Hampton Inn, Holiday Inn Express, Travelodge Food City, same as 380, Walgreens
380	US 11, US 70, West Hills, S Delta Express, Mapco/dsl Arby's, Brazeiro's Brazilian Steaks, Brixx Pizza, Burro Flojo Mexican, Cheesecake Factory, Chick-fil-A, Chili's, Cookout, Doc's Grille, Dunkin Donuts, Firehouse Subs, Hardee's, Honeybaked Ham, Hooters, IHOP, Jets Pizza, Jimmy John's, Longhorn Steaks, McAlister's Deli, McDonald's, Mooyah Burger, Mr Gatti's, O'Charley's, Olive Garden, Papa John's, Penn Sta Subs, Petro's Chili, PF Chang's, Pizza Hut, PlumTree Chinese, Qdoba Mexican, Red Lobster, Salsarita's Cantina, Starbucks, Subway, Taco Bell, Tropical Smoothie Cafe, TX Roadhouse, Zaxby's Extended Stay America, Ramada Inn $Tree, AT&T, Barnes&Noble, Belk, Dillards, Food City, JC Penney, Kohl's, mall, Office Depot, Old Navy, O'Reilly Parts, Petsmart, REI, Ross, Sears/auto, Steinmart, Target, TJ Maxx, Trader Joe's, U-Haul, Walgreens, Whole Foods Mkt
379	Bridgewater Rd, N Exxon/Subway/dsl, Pilot/McDonald's/dsl Taco Bell Sam's Club/gas, Walmart/Subway, S Conoco/dsl, Marathon/dsl Asia Kitchen, Buddy's BBQ, Burger King, Cheddar's, ChuckeCheese, CiCi's Pizza, Makino Japanese, Misaki Japanese, Shoney's, Sonic, Wendy's InTown Suites Aamco, Advance Parts, AutoZone, Books-A-Million, Buick/GMC, Chrysler/Dodge/Jeep, Firestone/auto, Ford/Lincoln, Hyundai/Subaru, Mazda, Nissan, NTB, Tire Barn, Transmission World

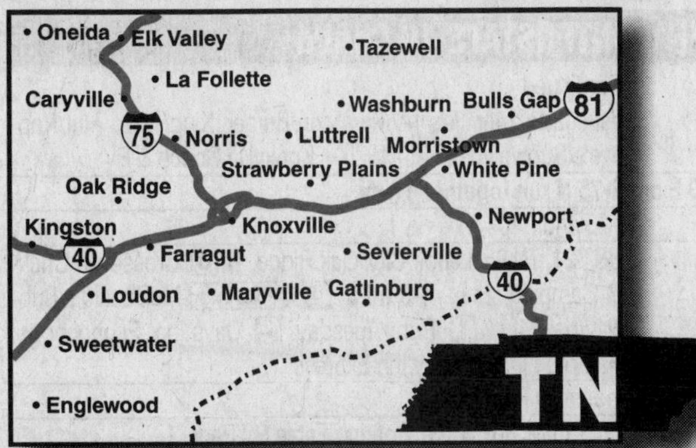

KNOXVILLE

378	Cedar Bluff Rd, N Pilot/Taco Bell/dsl, Shell, Weigel's/dsl Arby's, Burger King, Cracker Barrel, Dunkin Donuts, KFC, Little Caesar's, McDonald's, Old Mill Bread Co., Papa John's, Starbucks, Subway, Waffle House, Wendy's Country Inn&Suites, Days Inn, Hampton Inn, Holiday Inn, Quality Inn H, $General, S Exxon Applebee's, Blaze Pizza, Cancun Mexican, Capt D's, Carrabba's, Chipotle, Chuy's Mexican, Famous Dave's BBQ, Firehouse Subs, Fuddrucker's, Hardee's, Jason's Deli, Koko Japanese, Krystal, La Rosa's, Lenny's Subs, Newk's Cafe, Outback Steaks, Panera Bread, Parkside Grill, Peerless Grill, Penn Sta. Subs, Pizza Hut, Puleo's Grill, Rafferty's, Salsarita's, Starbucks, Which Wich?, Zaxby's Baymont Inn, Best Western, Comfort Inn, Courtyard, Embassy Suites, Extended Stay America, Hilton Garden, Home 2 Suites, Microtel, Motel 6, Red Roof Inn, Residence Inn, Towne Place Suites $Tree, Aldi Foods, AT&T, Best Buy, Cadillac, Chevrolet, CVS Drug, Dick's, Fiat, Ford/Lincoln, GNC, Home Depot, Jo-Ann Fabrics, Kia, Kroger/dsl, Lowe's, Pepboys, Radio Shack, Staples, Tuesday Morning, Volvo, Walgreens
376	I-140 E, TN 162 N, to Maryville, N to Oak Ridge Museum
374	TN 131, Lovell Rd, N Shell/dsl, Speedway/Speedy Cafe/dsl/scales/24hr, TA/Country Pride/dsl/scales/24hr/@ Bojangles, Subway, Waffle House Econolodge Harley-Davidson, S Pilot/Wendy's/dsl/24hr Abuelo's Mexican, Arby's, Baskin-Robbins, Bonefish Grill, Brixx Pizza, Buffalo Wild Wings, Calhoun's Rest., Chick-fil-A, Chipotle, Connor's Rest., Egg&I Cafe, Flemings, Hurricane Grill, IHOP, Jimmy John's, Kabuki Japanese, Krystal, Lenny's Subs, McAlister's Deli, McDonald's, Mimi's Cafe, Moe's SW Grill, Noodles&Co, O'Charley's, Olive Garden, Panera Bread, Pei Wei, Red Robin, Salsarita's Cantina, Smokey Mtn Brewery, Sonic, Starbucks, Steak'n Shake, Taco Bell, TX Roadhouse, Wasabi Japanese, Zoe's Kitchen Budget Inn, Candlewood Suites, Homewood Suites, SpringHill Suites H, $Tree, Advance Parts, AutoZone, Belk, Best Buy, BMW/Mini, CarMax, Costco/gas, EarthFare Foods, GNC, Hobby Lobby, Honda, Land Rover, Lexus, Marshall's, Mercedes, Old Navy, Petsmart, Ross, Target, Toyota/Scion, Walgreens, Walmart/Subway, World Mkt
373	Campbell Sta Rd, N Marathon/dsl, Shell/dsl Comfort Suites, Country Inn&Suites, Fairfield Inn, Holiday Inn Express, Super 8 Buddy Gregg RV Ctr, S Exxon/dsl, Pilot/dsl, Weigel's Bad Daddy's Burger, Cracker Barrel, Dunkin Donuts, Hardee's, La Parrilla, Longhorn Steaks, Mellow Mushroom, Newk's Grill, Panda Express, Potbelly, Seasons Grille, Taco Boy, Wild Wing Cafe, Zaxby's Clarion, Hampton Inn, Staybridge Suites AT&T, Gander Mtn, JC Penney, Publix, Verizon, Walgreens
372mm	**weigh sta both lanes**
369	Watt Rd, N FLYING J/Denny's/dsl/LP/scales/RV dump/24hr, Speedco Blue Beacon, S Petro/Iron Skillet/

TN

INTERSTATE 40 Cont'd

369 Continued
dsl/scales/24hr/ @, TA/Marathon/Burger King/Pizza Hut/Popeye's/Subway/dsl/24hr/ @ 🅞 Knoxville Coach & RV

I-40 E and I-75 N run together 17 mi.

368 I-75 and I-40

364 US 321, TN 95, Lenoir City, Oak Ridge, N 🅞 Crosseyed Cricket Camping (2mi), **4-5 mi** S 🅖 ♥Loves/McDonald's/Subway/dsl/24hr 🅕 Ruby Tuesday 🅛 Days Inn, EconoLodge, Hampton Inn, Holiday Inn Express

362 Industrial Park Rd

360 Buttermilk Rd, N 🅞 Soaring Eagle RV Park

356 TN 58 N, Gallaher Rd, to Oak Ridge, N 🅖 Marathon/dsl, Weigels/dsl 🅛 Motel 6 🅞 $General, 4 Seasons Camping

355 Lawnville Rd, N 🅖 🚂/Subway/dsl

352 TN 58 S, Kingston, N 🅖 Lakeview Inn, S 🅖 Exxon/dsl, Mobil/dsl, RaceWay 🅕 Buddy's BBQ, Hardee's, Little Caesar's, McDonald's, Sonic, Subway, Taco Bell 🅛 Super 8 🅞 $General, Cash Saver Foods, Family$, Marina RV Park, to Watts Bar Lake, USPO

351mm Clinch River

350 US 70, Midtown, S 🅖 Weigel's/dsl 🅕 Bojangles, Gondolier Italian, Subway, Zaxby's 🅞 🅗, AT&T, Caney Creek Camping (3mi), Kroger, Lowe's, Walgreens

347 US 27, Harriman, N 🅖 Phillips 66/dsl 🅕 Hardee's, KFC, LJ Silver, Los Primos Mexican, McDonald's, Pizza Hut, Ruby Tuesday, Subway, Taco Bell, Wendy's 🅛 Days Inn 🅞 Big S Fork NRA, to Frozen Head SP, Verizon, **2-3 mi** S 🅖 Murphy USA/dsl, Shell/Krystal/dsl/24hr, Sunoco/dsl 🅕 Cancun Mexican, Capt D's, China King, Cracker Barrel, Domino's, McDonald's, Shoney's, Sonic 🅛 Comfort Inn, Holiday Inn Express, Quality Inn, Rodeway Inn 🅞 🅗, Ace Hardware, BigLots, vet, Walmart

340 TN 299 N, 🚻 Rd

339.5mm eastern/central time zone line

338 TN 299 S, Westel Rd, N 🅖 Marathon/dsl, S 🅖 Exxon/dsl, Sunoco/dsl 🅞 Boat-N-RV Ctr/Park

336mm parking area/weigh sta eb, litter barrels

329 US 70, Crab Orchard, N 🅖 Liberty/dsl, Marathon/dsl 🅞 KOA (4mi), S 🅞 Cumberland Trails SP, Wilson SP

327mm 🆁🆂 wb, full 🅰 facilities, litter barrels, petwalk 🅲 🅰 vending

324mm 🆁🆂 eb, full 🅰 facilities, litter barrels, petwalk 🅲 🅰 vending

322 TN 101, Peavine Rd, Crossville, N 🅖 Exxon/Subway/dsl, Volunteer/dsl 🅕 Hardee's, McDonald's 🅛 Holiday Inn Express 🅞 Deer Run RV Resort, KOA Camping, Roam-Roost RV Campground, to Fairfield Glade Resort, S 🅖 Shell/dsl 🅕 Cancun Mexican, Taco Bell 🅛 Comfort Suites, Hampton Inn, Super 8 🅞 🅗, Chestnut Hill Winery, Cumberland Mtn SP

320 TN 298, Crossville, N 🅖 🚂/Wendy's/dsl/scales/24hr 🅕 Butcher's Block Rest., Lefty's BBQ 🅞 antiques, winery, S 🅖 Shell/DQ/dsl, Speedway/dsl 🅕 Log Cabin Rest. 🅞 🅗, auto repair/tires, Crossville Outlet/famous brands, Save-A-Lot Foods

318mm Obed River

317 US 127, Crossville, N 🅖 Exxon/dsl, Shell/Circle K/dsl 🅕 Shoney's, Subway 🅛 Baymont Inn, Motel 6, Quality Inn 🅞 repair, to Big South Fork RA, to York SP, **0-2 mi** S 🅖 Jiffy, Marathon/dsl, Murphy USA/dsl, Shell 🅕 Arby's, Bojangles, Burger King, Cancun Mexican, Cracker Barrel, La Costa Mexican, McDonalds, Papa John's, Romo's Mexican, Ruby Tuesday, Ryan's, Sonic, Subway, Taco Bell, Tokyo Steaks, Vegas Steaks, Waffle House, Zaxby's 🅛 Economy Inn, Red Roof Inn 🅞 🅗, $General, $Tree, Buick/Cadillac/Chevrolet/GMC, Chrysler/

317 Continued
Dodge/Jeep, Ford, GNC, Lowe's, Rite Aid, Shadden Tires, Staples, to Cumberland Mtn SP, Verizon, Walgreens, Walmart

311 Plateau Rd, N 🅖 Sunoco/Papa Lorenzo's Pizza/dsl, S 🅖 BP/dsl, Exxon/Hunt Bros Pizza

307mm parking area/weigh sta wb, litter barrels

301 US 70 N, TN 84, Monterey, N 🅖 Shell 🅕 Burger King, DQ, Rocky Pops BBQ/Catfish, Subway 🅛 Bethel Inn

300 US 70, Monterey, N 🅖 Citgo/dsl 🅕 DQ, Hardee's

291mm Falling Water River

290 US 70, Cookeville, S 🅖 Super/dsl 🅕 Fiesta Cancun 🅛 Alpine Suites

288 TN 111, to Livingston, Cookeville, Sparta, N Hull SP, S 🅖 Sunoco/dsl, Super Truck&TravelCtr/dsl/24hr 🅕 Subway 🅛 Fall Creek Inn

287 TN 136, Cookeville, N 🅖 Marathon/dsl, Murphy USA/dsl, Shell/dsl 🅕 Applebee's, Arby's, Baskin-Robbins, Blue Coast Burrito, Buffalo Wild Wings, Bully's Rest., Burger King, Capt D's, Cheddars, Chick-fil-A, Chili's, Cookout, Cracker Barrel, Dunkin Donuts, Fazoli's, Firehouse Subs, Fuji Japanese, Golden Corral, Hibachi Buffet, IHOP, Krystal, LJ Silver, Logan's Roadhouse, Longhorn Steaks, Marco's Pizza, McDonald's, Nick's Rest., O'Charley's, Olive Garden, Outback Steaks, Papa Murphy's, Pizza Hut, Red Lobster, Ruby Tuesday, Shoney's, Sonic, Starbucks, Steak'n Shake, Subway, Taco Bell, Wendy's 🅛 Best Value Inn, Best Western, Clarion, Comfort Inn, Comfort Suites, Days Inn, Hampton Inn, Red Roof Inn 🅞 Aldi Foods, BigLots, Firestone/auto, Harley-Davidson, JC Penney, K-Mart, Kroger/gas, Lowe's, Nissan, Radio Shack, st patrol, transmissions, Verizon, Walmart, S 🅖 Marathon/Godfather's/dsl, Pilot/dsl 🅕 Gondola, KFC, Waffle House 🅛 Country Inn&Suites, Fairfield Inn, Holiday Inn Express, La Quinta, Motel 6 🅞 Sam's Club/gas, URGENT CARE

286 TN 135, Burgess Falls Rd, N 🅖 Exxon, Gulf, RaceWay/dsl, Shell/dsl 🅕 Arby's, Hardee's, Waffle House 🅞 🅗, Chrysler/Dodge/Jeep, Ford/Lincoln, Goodyear/auto, Hyundai, Kia, to TTU, Toyota/Scion, USPO, S 🅖 Sunoco/dsl 🅛 Star Motor Inn 🅞 Burgess Falls SP (8mi)

280 TN 56 N, Baxter, N 🅖 ♥Loves/McDonalds/Subway/dsl/scales/24hr, Speedway/dsl/24hr 🅕 Huddle House 🅞 Camp Discovery (2mi), Twin Lakes RV Park (2mi)

276 Old Baxter Rd

273 TN 56 S, to Smithville, S 🅖 Gulf 🅕 Rose Garden Rest. 🅞 USPO

268 TN 96, Buffalo Valley Rd, N Grandville Marina Camping (11mi), S to Edgar Evins SP/RV camping

267mm Caney Fork River

267mm 🆁🆂 both lanes, full 🅰 facilities, info, litter barrels, petwalk 🅲 🅰 vending

266mm Caney Fork River

263mm Caney Fork River

258 TN 53, Gordonsville, N 🅖 Exxon/KFC/Taco Bell, Shell/dsl 🅕 McDonald's, Subway, Timberloft Café, Waffle House 🅛 Comfort Inn 🅞 to Cordell Hull Dam, S 🅖 Hess/Wendy's/dsl/scales/24hr, Mobil/dsl 🅕 Arby's, Cornerstone Cafe, El Corral Mexican, KFC/Taco Bell 🅞 $General

254 TN 141, to Alexandria

252mm parking area/truck sta both lanes, litter barrels, 🅰

245 Linwood Rd

239 US 70, Lebanon, N 🅖 RaceWay/dsl, Shell 🅞 $General, S 🅖 Phillips 66/Uncle Pete's/dsl/scales 🅕 Jalisco Mexican

238 US 231, Lebanon, N 🅖 Exxon, Mapco/dsl, Murphy Express/dsl, Shell/dsl 🅕 Applebee's, Arby's, Chick-fil-A, Cici's Pizza,

Vertical text left margin: HARRIMAN, CROSSVILLE

Vertical text right margin: COOKEVILLE, NASHVILLE

INTERSTATE 40 Cont'd

LEBANON

238 Continued
Cracker Barrel, Demo's Steaks, El Molino Mexican, Hardee's, Jack-in-the-Box, KFC, Logan's Roadhouse, Los Compadres, McDonald's, Panda Express, Pizza Hut, Ryan's, Shoney's, Starbucks, Subway, Sunset Rest., Taco Bell, Waffle House, Wendy's, White Castle, Whitt's BBQ, Zaxby's Days Inn, EconoLodge, Executive Inn, Holiday Inn Express, Quality Inn, Ramada H, $Tree, Aldi Foods, AT&T, Discount Tire, Lowe's, to Bledsoe SP (23mi), Verizon, Walgreens, Walmart/Subway, **S** Citgo/Pizza Inn/Quiznos/dsl, LNG, Pilot/Subway/DQ/dsl/scales/24hr, Shell/dsl, Speedway/dsl/e85 O'Charley's, Sonic Comfort Suites, Knights Inn, La Quinta, Travel Inn Family RV Ctr, Lebanon Outlets/famous brands, Shady Acres Camping, Timberline Campground, to Cedars of Lebanon SP

236 S Hartmann Dr, **N** Mapco/dsl, Shell/dsl Chili's, Outback Steaks, Subway H, Buick/Chevrolet/GMC, Hampton Inn, Home Depot, Rose Tire

235 TN 840 W, to Murfreesboro

232 TN 109, to Gallatin, **N** Mapco/Quiznos/dsl, Shell/McDonald's/dsl/24hr, Speedway/dsl, Thornton's/dsl Bellacino's Pizza, Coach's Grill, Sonic, Subway, Waffle House, Wendy's Sleep Inn, ValuePlace Inn, **S** KOA (3mi)

228mm **truck sta, wb only**

226mm **truck sta**

229b a Beckwith Rd

226 TN 171, Mt Juliet Rd, **N** BP/McDonald's/dsl, Exxon/dsl, Murphy Express/dsl, Shell/dsl Arby's, Capt D's, Cheddars, Don Pancho Mexican, Far East Buffet, Five Guys, Longhorn Steaks, Subway Comfort Suites $Tree, Aldi Foods, Firestone/auto, Lowe's, NTB, URGENT CARE, Walmart, **S** Mapco/Quiznos/dsl Blue Coast Burrito, Bonfire Japanese Steaks, Buffalo Wild Wings, Chick-fil-A, ChuckECheese, Cori's Dog House, Cracker Barrel, Firehouse Subs, Fulin's Asian, Jonathan's, Logan's Roadhouse, Marble Slab, Martin's BBQ, McDonald's, Mi Casa Mexican, NY Pizza, O'Charley's, Olive Garden, Panera Bread, Penn Sta Subs, Pizza Hut, Red Lobster, Red Robin, Salsarita's Cantina, Sonic, Steak'n Shake, Taco Bell, Taziki's Cafe, Waffle House, Wasabi Steaks, Wendy's, Which Wich?, Zaxby's Hampton Inn, Holiday Inn Express, Quality Inn AT&T, Belk, Best Buy, Books-A-Million, Dick's, Discount Tire, Ford, Gander Mtn, GNC, JC Penney, JoAnn Fabrics, Kroger/dsl, Old Navy, Petsmart, Publix, Ross, Staples, Target, Tire Discounters, TJ Maxx, to Long Hunter SP, Verizon, vet, Walgreens

NASHVILLE

221 TN 45 N, Old Hickory Blvd, to The Hermitage, **0-2 mi N** BP, Delta/dsl, Exxon, RaceWay/dsl Applebee's, Baskin-Robbins/Dunkin Donuts, Buffalo Wild Wings, Burger King, Chick-fil-A, Chili's, Cinco de Mayo, Domino's, DQ, Famous Dave's, Fazoli's, Firehouse Subs, Golden Corral, Hardee's, IHOP, Jack-in-the-Box, Jets Pizza, Las Palmas Mexican, O'Charley's, Outback Steaks, Panera Bread, Penn Sta Subs, Pizza Hut, Qdoba Mexican, Starbucks, Steak'n Shake, Subway, Taziki's Cafe, Waffle House Best Value Inn, Suburban Lodge, Super 8, Vista Inn H, Home Depot, Kroger, Lowe's, PetCo, Staples, Verizon, Walgreens, **S** Kwik Sak/dsl, Marathon/dsl, Phillips 66/White Castle, Shell/McDonald's

219 Stewart's Ferry Pike, **N** Mapco/dsl, **S** Mapco/Subway/dsl, Shell/dsl, Thornton's/dsl China King, Cracker Barrel, La Hacienda Mexican, Sal's Pizza, Subway, Waffle House Comfort Suites, Country Inn&Suites, Days Inn, EconoLodge, Family Inn, Motel 6, Sleep Inn $General, Food Lion, Fred's, vet

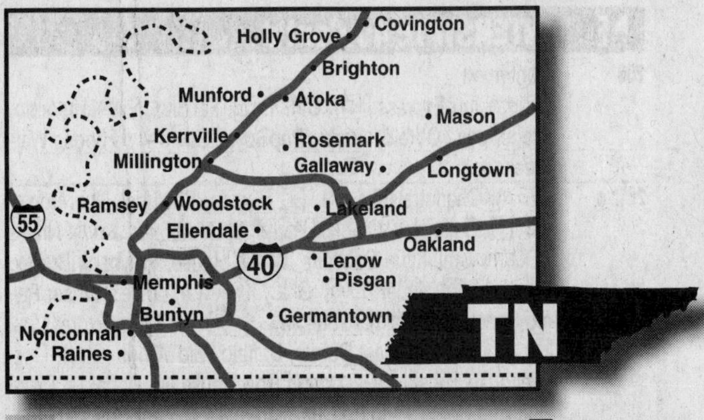

TN

216 (216 c from eb) TN 255, Donaldson Pk, **N** BP/dsl, Mapco, RaceWay/dsl, Shell/dsl Arby's, Backyard Burger, Bar-B-Cutie, Darfon's, Jalisco Mexican, KFC, McDonald's, Panera Bread, Ruby Tuesday, Shoney's, Sonic, Subway, Taco Bell, Waffle House, Wendy's BNA Inn, Country Inn&Suites, Drury Inn, Hampton Inn, Holiday Inn Express, Hyatt Place, La Quinta, Radisson, Red Roof Inn, Sheraton, SpringHill Suites, Super 8 Advance Parts, K-Mart, USPO, Walgreens, **S**

216b a (from eb), **S** Nashville Intn'l

215b a TN 155, Briley Pkwy, to Opryland, **N on Elm Hill** Citgo, Mapco Jack-in-the-Box, Waffle House Alexis Inn, Baymont Inn, Club Hotel, Comfort Suites, Courtyard, Doubletree, Extended Stay, Hilton Garden, Holiday Inn, Homewood Suites, La Quinta, Marriott, Nashville Inn, Quality Inn, Residence Inn, TownePlace Suites URGENT CARE, **S** Phillips 66/dsl Dunkin Donuts, Mazatlan Mexican, Panda House, Subway Hamilton Inn, Hotel Preston

213 US 41 (from wb no return), to Spence Lane, **N** CNG Kenworth, **S** Phillips 66/dsl, Shell Waffle House Best Western, Days Inn, Holiday Inn Express, Rodeway Inn, Super 8 same as 212

213b I-24 W

213a I-24 E/I-440, E to Chattanooga

212 Fessler's Lane (from eb, no return), **N** Freightliner, Harley-Davidson, **S** BP/dsl, Mapco/dsl, Shell/Dunkin Donuts, SpeedCo/dsl/e85 Burger King, McDonald's, Sonic, Wendy's Scottish Inn Chevrolet, NAPA, same as 213

211mm Cumberland River

211b I-24 W

211a I-24E, I-40 W

210c US 31 S, US 41A, 2nd Ave, 4th Ave, **N** Hilton, Renaissance Hotel, Sheraton, **S** museum

210b a I-65 S, to Birmingham

209b a US 70 S, Charlotte Ave, Nashville, **N** Exxon McDonald's Sheraton Conv Ctr, Country Music Hall of Fame, Firestone, Mazda, **S** Exxon Burger King, Jack Cauthon's BBQ, Krystal, Sonic, Subway, White Castle Comfort Inn, Hilton Garden Buick/GMC, Hyundai, Toyota/Scion, URGENT CARE, Walgreens

208b a I-65, N to Louisville

207 28th Ave, Jefferson St, Nashville, **N** BP Subway, Wendy's Family$, to TN St U, **S** H

206 I-440 E, to Knoxville

205 46th Ave, W Nashville, **S** Shell/dsl M L Rose Burgers, McDonald's USPO

204 TN 155, Briley Pkwy, **S** BP/dsl Burger King, China Buffet, Church's/White Castle, Cinco De Mayo, Domino's, Hattie B's Chicken, Jack-in-the-Box, KFC, Las Palmas, Papa John's, Shoney's, Subway, Waffle House, Wendell Smith's Rest., White Castle, Whitt's BBQ Best Western, Comfort Inn, Days Inn,

🅖 = gas 🍴 = food 🛌 = lodging 🅞 = other 🅡ﬆ = rest stop Copyright 2016 - The Next EXIT ®

TN

INTERSTATE 40 Cont'd

204	**Continued** Holiday Inn Express 🅞 CVS Drug, Family$, Firestone/auto, Kroger/gas, O'Reilly Parts, PepBoys, Sav-a-lot Foods, Walgreens
201b a	US 70, Charlotte Pike, **N** 🅖 Exxon, Shell/dsl, Thornton's/dsl 🍴 Bojangles, Cracker Barrel, El Sombrero, Jim 'N Nick's BBQ, Krystal, Little Caesar's, Waffle House, Wayback Burger, Wendy's 🛌 Super 8 🅞 GNC, Kwik Kar, Lowe's Whse, Radio Shack, vet, Walmart/Subway, **S** 🍴 BP, Delta Express/dsl 🍴 Arby's, Blue Coast Burrito, Buffalo Wild Wings, Chick-fil-A, Firehouse Subs, IHOP, Logan's Roadhouse, McDonald's, Pizza Hut, Red Robin, Taco Bell 🅞 $Tree, AT&T, Best Buy, Big Lots, Books-A-Million, Costco/gas, Dick's, Firestone/auto, GNC, Marshall's, Old Navy, PetsMart, Publix, Ross, Target, Uhaul, URGENT CARE, Verizon, World Mkt
199	Rd 251, Old Hickory Blvd, **N** 🅖 Shell/dsl 🅞 $General, **S** 🅖 BP, Mapco/dsl 🍴 Sonic, Subway 🅞 Sam's Club/gas
196	US 70, to Bellevue, Newsom Sta, **N** 🅖 Mapco/dsl 🍴 Shoney's, **S** 🅖 BP, Mapco/dsl, Shell/dsl 🍴 Arby's, Asihi Asian, Baskin Robbins, El Agavero, Jonathan's Grill, O'Charley's, Pizza Hut, Sir Pizza, Sonic, Subway, Taco Bell, Waffle House, Wendy's 🛌 Hampton Inn, Microtel 🅞 $Tree, AutoZone, Firestone/auto, Home Depot, Michael's, PetCo, Publix, Sears/auto, Staples, USPO, Verizon, Walgreens
195mm	Harpeth River
192	McCrory Lane, to Pegram, **N** 🅖 Eddie's Mkt (1mi), **4 mi S** 🍴 Loveless Cafe 🅞 Natchez Trace Pkwy
190mm	Harpeth River
188mm	Harpeth River
188	Rd 249, Kingston Springs, **N** 🅖 BP, Mapco/Quiznos/dsl, Shell/Arby's/dsl 🍴 El Jardin Mexican, McDonald's/playplace, Sonic, Subway 🛌 Best Western, Mid-Town Inn, Relax Inn 🅞 USPO, **S** 🅖 Petro/BP/Quick Skillet/dsl/scales/showers/24hr/ @ 🅞 vet
182	TN 96, to Dickson, Fairview, **N** 🅖 BP/dsl 🛌 Fairview Inn 🅞 M Bell SP (16mi), **S** 🅖 ⛽FLYING J/Denny's/dsl/LP/scales/24hr, Citgo/Backyard Burger/Dunkin Donuts/dsl 🛌 Deerfield Inn
176	TN 840
172	TN 46, to Dickson, **N** 🅖 Exxon/dsl, Marathon/dsl, 🅿🅸🅻🅾🆃/Wendy's/dsl/scales/24hr, Shell/Dunkin Donuts/Taco Bell/dsl 🍴 Arby's, Cracker Barrel, Logan's Roadhouse, McDonald's, Ruby Tuesday, Waffle House 🛌 Best Western, Comfort Inn, EconoLodge, Hampton Inn, Motel 6, Rodeway Inn, South-Aire Inn, Super 8 🅞 🏥, $General, auto repair, Chappell's Foods, Chevrolet/Buick/GMC, Dickson RV Park, Ford, Nissan, to M Bell SP, truck repair, **S** 🅖 BP/dsl, Shell/dsl 🍴 Colton's Steaks, O'Charley's, Sonic 🛌 Days Inn, Holiday Inn Express, Mega Inn
170	🅡ﬆ **both lanes, full ♿ facilities, litter barrels, petwalk 🅒 🅐 vending**
166mm	Piney River
163	Rd 48, to Dickson, **N** 🅖 Loves/McDonald's/Subway/dsl/scales/24hr, Phillips 66/dsl 🅞 tire repair, **S** 🅖 Shell 🅞 Pinewood Camping (7mi), Tanbark Camping
152	Rd 230, Bucksnort, **N** 🅖 Sunoco/dsl 🛌 Travel Inn
149mm	Duck River
148	Rd 50, Barren Hollow Rd, to Turney Center
143	TN 13, to Linden, Waverly, **N** 🅖 Marathon/Subway/dsl, 🅿🅸🅻🅾🆃/Arby's/dsl/scales/24hr, Shell 🍴 Log Cabin Rest., Loretta Lynn's Kitchen, McDonald's, Rochelle's BBQ 🛌 Best Western, Days Inn, Holiday Inn Express, Knights Inn 🅞 KOA/LP, **S** 🛌 Scottish Inn

DICKSON

PARKERS CROSSROADS

141mm	Buffalo River
137	Cuba Landing, **N** 🅞 TN River RV Park, **S** 🍴 Cuba Landing Rest./gas
133mm	Tennessee River
133	Rd 191, Birdsong Rd, **9 mi N** 🛌 Birdsong RV Resort/marina, Good Sam RV Park
131mm	🅡ﬆ **both lanes, full ♿ facilities, litter barrels, petwalk 🅒 🅐 vending**
126	US 641, TN 69, to Camden, **N** 🅖 Marathon/Subway/dsl, Phillips 66/North 40/dsl, Shell/dsl 🅞 Paris Landing SP, tire/truck repair, to NB Forrest SP, **S** 🅖 BP/dsl, Shell/dsl 🛌 Days Inn 🅞 🏥, Mouse-tail Landing SP (24mi)
116	Rd 114, **S** 🅞 RV camping, to Natchez Trace SP
110mm	Big Sandy River
108	TN 22, to Lexington, Parkers Crossroads, **N** 🅖 Citgo/dsl/24hr, Phillips 66/dsl, Shell/McDonald's/dsl 🍴 Bailey's Rest., DQ, Subway 🛌 Knights Inn 🅞 city park, USPO, **S** 🅖 Exxon 🍴 Becky's Kitchen, Patty's Rest. 🛌 Best Value Inn 🅞 🏥, Parkers Crossroads Bfd Visitors Ctr, RV camping, to Shiloh NMP (51mi)
103mm	**parking area/truck sta eb, litter barrels**
102mm	**parking area/truck sta wb, litter barrels**
101	Rd 104, **N** 🅖 101 TP/Real Food/dsl/tires/24hr 🅞 golf (3mi)
93	Rd 152, Law Rd, **N** 🅖 Phillips 66/deli/dsl/24hr, **S** 🅖 Super Way/dsl
87	US 70, US 412, Jackson, **N** 🅖 Gulf/dsl, **S** 🅖 BP/dsl, Loves/Hardee's/dsl/scales/24hr, Speedway/dsl
85	Christmasville Rd, to Jackson, **N** 🅖 Exxon/dsl, 🅿🅸🅻🅾🆃/Denny's/dsl/scales/24hr, Shell/dsl, Speedway/dsl 🛌 Comfort Inn 🅞 $General, **S** 🅖 Shell/Pizza Pro/dsl 🍴 Jiang Jun Chinese, Lenny's Subs, Los Portales, McDonald's, Reggi's BBQ, Sonic, Sparky's, Taco Bell 🛌 Holiday Inn Express 🅞 $Tree, Food Giant
83	Campbell st, **N** 🅖 Shell/Old Madina Mkt/dsl 🛌 Residence Inn, **S** 🛌 Courtyard, Hampton Inn
82b a	US 45, Jackson, **N** 🅖 BP 🍴 Cracker Barrel 🛌 Best Value Inn, Knights Inn 🅞 Batteries+Bulbs, Smallwoods RV Ctr (4mi), **S** 🅖 Exxon 🍴 Baskin-Robbins, Burger King, Catfish Galley, ChuckeCheese, DQ, KFC, Krystal, Little Caesar's, LJ Silver, Los Portales Mexican, McDonald's/playplace, Pizza Hut, Popeye's, Rafferty's, Sakura Japanese, Sonic, Starbucks, Subway, Taco Bell, Tulum Mexican, Waffle House, Wendy's 🛌 Executive Inn, La Quinta, Ramada Ltd, Scottish Inn, Travellers Motel 🅞 $General, $Tree, Advance Parts, AT&T, AutoZone, Belk, BigLots, Firestone/auto, Fred's, Goodyear/auto, JC Penney, Kroger/dsl, Macy's, Office Depot, Radio Shack, Sears/auto, TJ Maxx, vet
80b a	US 45 Byp, Jackson, **0-2 mi N** 🅖 Exxon, Shell/DSL 🍴 Applebee's, Arby's, Asahi Japanese, Backyard Burger, Baskin-Robbins, Buffalo Wild Wings, Casa Adobe, Cheddar's, Chick-fil-A, Chili's, Coyote Blues, Don Pancho, DQ, Dunkin Donuts, Fazoli's, Firehouse Subs, Five Guys, Flat Iron Grill, Fujiyama Japanese, Genghis Grill, HoneyBaked Ham, IHOP, Jason's Deli, Jimmy John's, Lenny's Subs, Longhorn Steaks, Maggie Moo's, Marco's Pizza, McAlisters Deli, Moe's SW Grill, Olive Garden, Outback Steaks, Panda Express, Panera Bread, Perkins, Popeye's, Quiznos, Red Lobster, Red Robin, Snappy Tomato, Sonic, Starbucks, Steak'n Shake, Subway, TGIFriday's, Wendy's, Zaxby's 🛌 Baymont Inn, Fairfield Inn, Howard Johnson 🅞 $Tree, Aldi Foods, AT&T, AutoZone, Best Buy, Books-A-Million, Buick/Cadillac/Chevrolet/GMC, CarMax, Dick's, Firestone/auto, Gateway Tires/repair, Hobby Lobby, Home Depot, JoAnn Fabrics, Kia, Kohl's, Lowe's, Marshall's, Mazda, Nissan, Old Navy, Petsmart, Ross, Sam's Club/gas, SteinMart, Target, TJ Maxx,

JACKSON

TN

INTERSTATE 40 Cont'd

80b a Continued
Toyota/Scion, Verizon, Walmart/gas, S BP, G/dsl, Phillips 66/dsl, Shell/dsl Arby's, Asia Garden, Barnhill's Buffet, Baudo's Rest., Burger King, Heavenly Ham, Logan's Roadhouse, McDonald's, O'Charley's, Old Hickory Steakhouse, Old Town Spaghetti, Pizza Hut, Red Bones Grill, Subway, Taco Bell, Waffle House, Wingery All Suites Hotel, Best Western, Casey Jones Motel, Comfort Suites, Days Inn, DoubleTree, EconoLodge, Jackson Hotel, Motel 6, Old Hickory Inn, Quality Inn, Super 8 H, $General, Chickasaw SP, Chrysler/Dodge/Jeep, Ford/Lincoln, Harley-Davidson, Honda, Hyundai, K-Mart, to Pinson Mounds SP, Tuesday Morning

79 US 412, Jackson, N Gander Mtn., S BP/dsl, Citgo/Subway/dsl, Exxon, Phillips 66 Rodeway Inn Jackson RV Park

78mm Forked Deer River

76 Rd 223, S McKenzie BBQ (2.5mi) McKellar-Sipes, Whispering Pines RV Park

74 Lower Brownsville Rd

73mm **both lanes, full facilities, info, litter barrels, petwalk vending**

68 Rd 138, Providence Rd, N BP/dsl Ole South Inn, S TA/Shell/Subway/dsl/scales/24hr/ @, Valero/dsl Joy-O RV Park

66 US 70, to Brownsville, N Ft Pillow SHP (51mi), S Exxon/dsl Motel 6

60 Rd 19, Mercer Rd

56 TN 76, to Brownsville, N Marathon, Shell/dsl DQ, KFC, McDonald's/playplace, Pizza Hut, Taco Bell Comfort Inn, Days Inn, Econolodge, Travelers Best Inn, S Exxon/Breakfast Cove/dsl, Valero

55mm Hatchie River

52 TN 76, Rd 179, Koko Rd, to Whiteville, S Koko Mkt

50mm phone, **weigh sta both lanes**

47 TN 179, to Stanton, Dancyville, S Exit 47 Trkstp/dsl

42 TN 222, to Stanton, S Exxon/dsl, Pilot/Chester's/Subway/dsl/scales/24hr Deerfield Inn

35 TN 59, to Somerville, S Shelldsl/scales Longtown Rest.

29.5mm Loosahatchie River

25 TN 205, Airline Rd, to Arlington, N Shell/dsl, S Exxon/Taco bell/dsl vistor ctr

24 I-269, TN 385, Rd 204, to Arlington, Millington, Collierville

20 Canada Rd, Lakeland, N BP/McDonald's, Shell/dsl Cracker Barrel, Waffle House Motel 6, Relax Inn, Super 8, S Exxon/Subway/dsl fireworks, Memphis East Camping

18 US 64, to Bartlett, N Shell/Burger King Abuelo's, Bob Evans, Buffalo Wild Wings, El Porton Mexican, Firebird's Grill, Hooters, Longhorn Steaks, McAlister's Deli, O'Charley's, Olive Garden, Panera Bread, Steak'n Shake, TGI Friday's, TX Roadhouse Best Western, Fairfield Inn, Holiday Inn, La Quinta, SpringHill Suites Buick/GMC, Firestone/auto, Goodyear/auto, Lowe's, same as 16, Sam's Club/gas, Walmart, S BP, Circle K/dsl, Citgo Backyard Burger, Dunkin Donuts, KFC, Lenny's Subs, Papa John's, Papa Murphy's, Pizza Hut, Subway AT&T, Family$, Kroger/dsl, Walgreens, Zaxby's

16b a TN 177, to Germantown, N BP/Circle K, Shell/Circle K Abuelo's, Arby's, Bahama Breeze, Baskin Robbins, Burger King, Casa Mexicana, Chick-fil-A, Chili's, Colton's Steaks, Danver's, IHOP, J. Alexander's, Joe's Crabshack, Logan's Roadhouse, Macaroni Grill, McDonald's/playplace, On-the-Border, Red Lobster, Red Sun Buffet, Starbucks, Subway, Taco Bell, TCBY, Tellini's Italian, Waffle House, Wendy's Extended

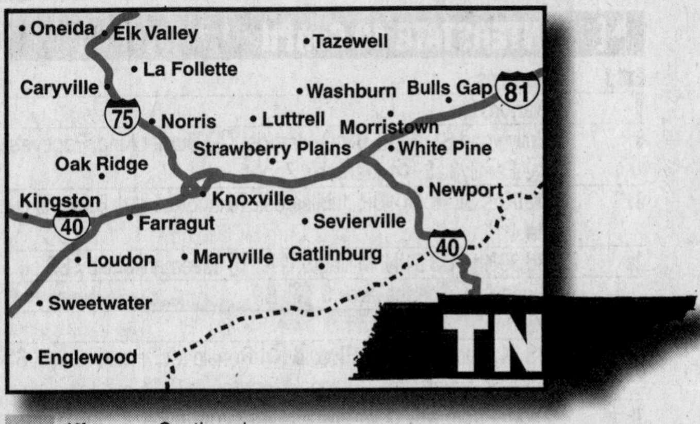

16b a Continued
Stay America, Hampton Inn, Hyatt Place H, $Tree, Barnes&Noble, Best Buy, BigLots, CarMax, Chevrolet, Chrysler/Dodge/Jeep, Dillard's, Ford, Hancock Fabrics, Hobby Lobby, Home Depot, Honda, Hyundai, JC Penney, Macy's, mall, Michael's, Nissan, Office Depot, Old Navy, Petsmart, Sears/auto, Target, TJ Maxx, Walgreens, **0-2 mi** S BP/Circle K, Shell/Circle K Abbay's Rest., Arby's, Backyard Burger, Burger King, Cheddar's, ChuckeCheese, Corky's BBQ, El Porton Mexican, Genghis Grill, Honeybaked Ham, Howard's Donuts, Jason's Deli, Jimmy John's, Jim'n Nick's BBQ, La Hacienda, Little Caesar's, McDonald's, Newk's Cafe, Osaka, Pei Wei Chinese, Pyros Pizza, Shogun Japanese, Waffle House, Wendy's Comfort Suites, Hilton Garden, Microtel, Quality Suites, Wingate Inn Aldi Foods, AT&T, AutoZone, Costco/gas, Dick's, GNC, Gordman's, Kohl's, Kroger/gas, Marshall's, Rite Aid, Ross, Steinmart, Toyota/Scion, Tuesday Morning, URGENT CARE, Verizon, vet

15b a Appling Rd, N BP/Circle K/dsl, Shell/dsl H

14 Whitten Rd, N Mapco, Shell/Burger King, Texaco/dsl McDonald's, Sidecar Café Firestone/auto, Harley-Davidson, S BP/Circle K, Shell/Backyard Burger/dsl Dunkin Donuts, Subway, Supreme Hot Wings Family$, Walgreens

12 Sycamore View Rd, N Citgo/dsl, Murphy Express/dsl, Texaco/dsl Applebee's, Cajun Catfish Co., Capt D's, Church's, Cracker Barrel, IHOP, Krystal, McDonald's, Mrs Winner's, Perkins, Ruby Tuesday, Shoney's, Sonic, Starbucks, Taco Bell, Waffle House Baymont Inn, Best Value Inn, Drury Inn, EconoLodge, Extended Stay America, GardenTree Hotel, Motel 6, Quality Inn, Red Roof Inn $General, AT&T, AutoZone, Family$, Fred's, Walgreens, S BP/Circle K/dsl, Exxon, Mapco Beijing Chinese, Burger King, Dos Amigos, Pizza Hut, Popeye's, Subway, Tops BBQ, Wendy's Budgetel, Comfort Inn, Days Inn, Econolodge, Fairfield Inn, La Quinta, Memphis Inn, Rodeway Inn, Super 8 Bass Pro Shops

10.5mm Wolf River

10b a (from wb) I-240 W around Memphis, I-40 E to Nashville

12c (from eb) I-240 W, to Jackson, I-40 E to Nashville

12b Sam Cooper Blvd (from eb)

12a US 64/70/79, Summer Ave, N Mapco/dsl, Shell/dsl Asian Palace, Waffle House Welcome Inn U-Haul, S Exxon McDonald's, Subway $Tree, Firestone/auto, Fred's, Sav-A-Lot Foods

10 TN 204, Covington Pike, N BP/Circle K McDonald's, Wendy's Audi/VW, Buick/GMC, Chevrolet, Chrysler/Dodge/Jeep, Honda, Hyundai, Kia, Mazda, Nissan, Sam's Club, Subaru, SuperLo Food/gas, VW

8b a TN 14, Jackson Ave, N Citgo/dsl Motel 6, Sleep Inn Raleigh Tire, S Citgo/dsl, Mapco AutoZone, Family$, O'Reilly Parts, transmissions

MEMPHIS

R = gas ⑪ = food ⌂ = lodging ⊡ = other RS = rest stop Copyright 2016 - The Next EXIT ®

TN

▲E INTERSTATE 40 Cont'd

Exit #	Services
6	Warford Rd
5	Hollywood St, **N** R BP, Q-Mart/dsl ⑪ Burger King, Popeye's ⊡ Family$, **S** ⊡ Memphis Zoo
3	Watkins St, **N** R BP, Jubilee/dsl, Texaco/dsl ⊡ Family$, U-Haul
2a	Rd 300, to US 51 N, Millington, **N** ⊡ Meeman-Shelby SP
2	Smith Ave, Chelsea Ave, **S** R BP
1e	I-240 E
1d c b	US 51, Danny Thomas Blvd, **N** ⊡ Ronald McDonald House, St Jude Research Ctr
1a	2nd St (from wb), downtown, **S** ⌂ Crowne Plaza, Holiday Inn, Marriott, Sheraton ⊡ Conv Ctr
1	Riverside Dr, Front St (from eb), Memphis, **S** ⌂ Comfort Inn, Courtyard, Sleep Inn ⊡ Conv Ctr, Riverfront, Visitors Ctr
0mm	Tennessee/Arkansas state line, Mississippi River

▲N INTERSTATE 55

Exit #	Services
13mm	Tennessee/Arkansas state line, Mississippi River
12c	Delaware St, Memphis
12b	Riverside Dr, **E** TN Welcome Ctr, downtown Memphis
12a	E Crump Blvd (from nb), **E** R Exxon ⑪ Capt D's, KFC, LJ Silver, Taco Bell, Wendy's ⊡ Family$, museum
11	McLemore Ave, Presidents Island, industrial area
10	S Parkway, 1/2 mi **E** R Marathon/dsl
9	Mallory Ave, industrial area
8	Horn Lake Rd (from sb)
7	US 61, 3rd St, **E** R Exxon, Shell ⑪ Church's, Interstate BBQ, McDonald's ⊡ $Tree, AutoZone, Family$, Kroger, NAPA, Roses, Save-A-Lot Foods, Walgreens, **W** R MapCo, Marathon/Chester's/dsl ⑪ KFC, McDonald's, Subway ⌂ Rest Inn ⊡ Fuller SP, Indian Museum
6b a	I-240
5b	US 51 S, Elvis Presley Blvd, to Graceland, **0-2 mi W on US 51** R BP, Citgo/dsl, Dodge's/dsl, Exxon, Shell/dsl ⑪ Baskin-Robbins, BJ's Wings, Burger King, Checker's, Exline Pizza, KFC, Krispy Kreme, Little Caesars, McDonald's, Piccadilly's, Subway, Taco Bell ⌂ American Inn, Days Inn, EconoLodge, Heartbreak Hotel/RV Park, Value Place Inn ⊡ Ḥ, $General, $Tree, Advance Parts, Aldi Foods, D&N RV Ctr, Family$, Memphis Visitors Ctr, Presley RV Park, Radio Shack, to Graceland, Walgreens
5a	Brooks Rd, **E** R BP, Exxon, Mapco/dsl ⑪ Blimpie, Burger King, Popeye's ⌂ ✈ Inn, Best Value Inn, Budget Lodge, Clarion, Motel 6 ⊡ Freightliner, Peterbilt
2b a	TN 175, Shelby Dr, Whitehaven, **E** R BP/dsl, Citgo/Subway, Exxon, Shell/dsl, Texaco ⌂ Colonial Inn, **W** R BP, Exxon/dsl, Shell/dsl ⑪ Burger King, Dixie Queen Burgers, IHOP, McDonald's, Popeye's ⊡ $General, Family$, Goodyear/auto, Kroger/gas, Macy's, Save-a-Lot Foods, Sears/auto, Toyota/Scion, U-Haul, Walgreens
0mm	Tennessee/Mississippi state line

▲N INTERSTATE 65

Exit #	Services
121.5mm	Tennessee/Kentucky state line
121mm	**Welcome Ctr sb, full** ♿ **facilities, litter barrels, petwalk** Ⓒ 🚹 **vending**

MEMPHIS (vertical text, left margin)

NASHVILLE (vertical text, right margin)

119mm	weigh/insp sta both lanes
117	TN 52, Portland, **E** R BP/Godfather's/Quiznos/dsl, Shell/dsl/fireworks ⌂ Comfort Suites ⊡ Ḥ, Bledsoe Cr SP, **W** R BP/dsl ⌂ Budget Host ⊡ fireworks
116mm	Red River
113mm	Red River
112	TN 25, Cross Plains, **E** R BP/dsl ⑪ Sad Sam's Deli ⊡ antiques, Bledsoe Cr SP, fireworks, **W** R Mapco/dsl, Shell/Godfather's/dsl ⑪ Sweet&Savory Diner
108	TN 76, White House, **E** R Nervous Charlie's/dsl, Shell ⑪ A&W/KFC, China Spring, Cracker Barrel, Hardee's, Little Caesars, Los Agave's, McDonald's, Mr Wok, Sonic, Subway, Taco Bell, Waffle House, Wendy's ⌂ Best Western, Comfort Inn, Holiday Inn Express, Quality Inn ⊡ $Tree, Ace Hardware, city park/playground, Kroger/gas, O'Reilly Parts, Rite Aid, USPO, Walgreens, Walmart/Subway, **W** R BP/dsl ⑪ Greek Gyro ⌂ Days Inn
104	Rd 257, Bethel Rd, **E** R BP/rest./dsl, **W** R Shell/dsl ⊡ Owl's Roost Camping
98	US 31 W, Millersville, **E** R Citgo/dsl, RaceWay, Shell/dsl ⑪ Subway, Waffle House ⊡ $General, auto repair, Nashville Country RV Park, **W** R BP ⌂ Economy Inn ⊡ fireworks
97	Rd 174, Long Hollow Pike, **E** R BP/dsl, Exxon, Mapco ⑪ Arby's, Capt D's, China Express, Cracker Barrel, Domino's, Kabuto Japanese, KFC, McDonald's, Papa Murphy's, Quiznos, Shoney's, Subway, Waffle House, Wendy's ⌂ Best Western, Courtyard, Days Inn, Executive Inn, Hampton Inn, Quality Inn, Red Roof Inn ⊡ K-Mart, Kroger, Walgreens, **W** R Shell/dsl ⑪ Buck's BBQ, DQ, Hardee's, Krystal, Poncho Villa Grill, Sonic ⌂ Holiday Inn Express, Motel 6 ⊡ Rite Aid, vet, Walgreens
96	Rivergate Pky, **E** R Citgo/dsl, Shell/dsl ⑪ Bailey's Grill, Dougie Ray's Grill, El Chico, Fuji Steaks, HoneyBaked Ham, Hooters, Las Palmas Mexican, McDonald's, Pizza Hut, Subway, Waffle House, Wendy's ⌂ Baymont Inn, Best Value Inn, Comfort Suites, Rodeway Inn ⊡ Ḥ, Best One Tires, Dillard's, JC Penney, Macy's, mall, Sears/auto, **W** R Marathon, Volunteer, **E on Gallatin N** ⑪ A&W/LJ Silver, Arby's, Bar-B-Cutie, Burger King, Calhoun's Cafe, Checker's, Chick-fil-A, Chili's, Chuck-eCheese, Fazoli's, IHOP, Krispy Kreme, Las Fiestas, Logan's Roadhouse, Longhorn Steaks, Olive Garden, Outback Steaks, Panera Bread, Popeye's, Rafferty's, Ryan's, Sonic, Starbucks, Steak'n Shake, Taco Bell, TGI Friday's ⊡ $General, AAA, AT&T, Best Buy, Books-A-Million, CarMax, Chevrolet, Chrysler/Dodge/Jeep, CVS Drug, Dick's, Discount Tire, Firestone/auto, Goodyear/auto, Harley-Davidson, Hobby Lobby, Home Depot, Honda, Jo-Ann's Etc, Kia, Lexus, Lincoln, Lowe's, Mazda, Michael's, Nissan, Office Depot, Old Navy, PepBoys, Petsmart, Sam's Club/gas, Staples, Target, TJ Maxx, Toyota/Scion, URGENT CARE, Verizon, VW, Walgreens, Walmart
95	TN 386, Vietnam Veterans Blvd (from nb)
92	Rd 45, Old Hickory Blvd, **E** ⊡ Ḥ, to Old Hickory Dam
90b	TN 155 E, Briley Pkwy, **E** ⊡ to Opreyland
90a	US 31W, US 41, Dickerson Pike, **E** R Citgo/dsl, Exxon/dsl, Mapco/dsl, Shell ⑪ Arby's, Capt D's, Chicago Gyros, China King, Church's, Domino's, Jay's Rest., KFC, McDonald's, Pizza Hut, Subway, Taco Bell, Waffle House, Wendy's ⌂ Days Inn, EconoLodge, Sleep Inn, Super 8 ⊡ $General, Advance Parts, AutoZone, CVS Drug, Family$, Kroger, O'Reilly Parts, Walgreens, **W** ⊡ Lowe's, Walmart
88b a	I-24, W to Clarksville, E to Nashville
87b a	US 431, Trinity Lane, **E** R BP, Loves/Subway/dsl/scales/24hr ⑪ Church's/White Castle, Krystal, Sonic ⌂ Cumberland Inn, Delux Inn ⊡ Piggly Wiggly, **W** R BP,

INTERSTATE 65 Cont'd

Exit	Services
87b a	Continued Exxon, Shell/dsl, Victory/dsl [food] Fat Mo's, Jack-in-the-Box, Jack's BBQ, McDonald's, Subway, Taco Bell, Waffle House [lodging] Best Value Inn, Days Inn, EconoLodge, Halmark Inn, Howard Johnson, King's Inn, Magnuson Hotel, Ravin Hotel, Red Roof Inn, Regency Inn, Rodeway Inn [other] $General, Family$
86	I-24 E, to I-40 E, to Memphis
86mm	Cumberland River
85	US 41A, 8th Ave, **E** [gas] BP [other] O'Reilly Parts, tires, to st capitol, **W** [gas] Exxon [food] Arby's, Jersey Mike's, McDonald's, Pizza Hut, Starbucks, Subway, Taco Bell, Wendy's, Wise Burger [lodging] Millennium Hotel, SpringHill Suites [other] Cadillac/Honda
84b a	I-40, E to Knoxville, W to Memphis
209 [I-40]	US 70, Charlotte Ave, Church St, **E** [gas] Exxon [food] McDonald's [other] Firestone, **W** [gas] Exxon, Shell [food] Burger King, Krystal, Sonic, Subway, White Castle [lodging] Comfort Inn [other] URGENT CARE, Walgreens
82b a	I-40, W to Memphis, E to Nashville
81	Wedgewood Ave, **W** [gas] BP, Exxon, Shell [food] Burger King, Subway [other] $General, U-Haul
80	I-440, to Memphis, Knoxville
79	Armory Dr, **E on Powell** [gas] Shell [food] Applebee's, Jersey Mike's, Logan's Roadhouse, Panda Express, Panera Bread, Rafferty's, Subway, Wendy's [other] BMW, CarMax, Home Depot, Michael's, Petsmart, Ross, Staples, TJ Maxx
78b a	Rd 255, Harding Place, **E** [gas] Mapco, Pure, Shell [food] Beijing Chinese, Cracker Barrel, Mama Mia's Italian, Sub House, Waffle House [lodging] La Quinta, Red Roof Inn, Traveler's Rest Hist Home [other] CVS Drug
74	TN 254, Old Hickory Blvd, to Brentwood, **E** [food] Capt D's, Coldstone, Longhorn Steaks, Panera Bread, Qdoba Mexican, Shoney's, Waffle House [lodging] Best Western, Holiday Inn Express, Hyatt Place, Sheraton [other] GNC, Target, **W** [gas] BP, Gulf, Shell/dsl [food] 5 Guys Burgers, Backyard Burger, Chick-fil-A, Chili's, Chipotle Mexican, Church's, Corky's BBQ, Jimmy John's, Maggie Moo's, Mazatlan Mexican, McAlister's Deli, McDonald's, Moe's SW Grill, Mrs Winner's, O'Charley's, Papa John's, Pei Wei, Pizza Hut, Ruby Tuesday, Starbucks, Subway, Taco Bell, Wendy's [lodging] Courtyard, Extended Stay America, Hampton Inn, Hilton Suites, Homestead Suites, Studio+ [other] Cadillac, CVS Drug, Fresh Mkt Foods, Harris-Teeter, Land Rover, Office Depot, PetCo, Publix, Rite Aid, SteinMart, TJ Maxx, USPO, Walgreens
71	TN 253, Concord Rd, to Brentwood
69	Rd 441, Moores Lane, Galleria Blvd, **E** [gas] MapCo/dsl, Shell [food] Amerigo's Grill, Baskin-Robbins, Cozymel's, Dunkin Donuts, Fuji Japanese, Greek Cafe, Outback Steaks, Papa Murphy's, Shogun Japanese, Sonic, Starbucks [lodging] Hilton Garden, Hyatt Place, Red Roof Inn, Wingate Inn [other] Acura/Lexus, CVS Drug, Home Depot/gas, Michael's, Petsmart, Publix, Walgreens, **W** [gas] BP, Shell/dsl [food] Backyard Burger, Buca Italian, Burger King, Capt D's, Chili's, Cracker Barrel, Famous Dave's, HoneyBaked Ham, J Alexander's Rest., Krispy Kreme, Logan's Roadhouse, Macaroni Grill, McDonald's, Peking Palace, Pizza Hut/Taco Bell, Red Lobster, Schlotzsky's, Stoney River Steaks [lodging] Sleep Inn [other] $Tree, Barnes&Noble, Belk, Best Buy, Costco/gas, Dillard's, Discount Tire, JC Penney, Macy's, mall, NTB, Old Navy, Ross, Sears/auto, Target
68b a	Cool Springs Blvd, **E** [food] Jersey Mike's [lodging] Courtyard, Embassy Suites, Marriott, Residence Inn, **W** [gas] Exxon, Shell [food] 5 Guys Burgers, BoneFish Grill, Bread&Co, Canton Buffet, Carrabba's, Chick-fil-A, ChuckeCheese, Chuy's Mexican, Genghis Grill, Golden Corral, Greek Cafe, J Christopher's, Jack-in-the-

B R E N T W O O D

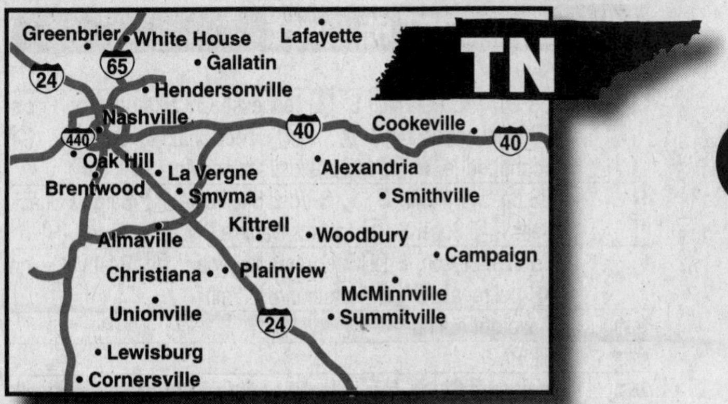

Exit	Services
68b a	Continued Box, Jason's Deli, Jersey Mike's, KFC, McAlister's Deli, McDonald's, Moe's SW Grill, Newk's Cafe, Omikoshi Japanese, Otter's Chicken Tenders, Panera Bread, PF Chang's, Pizza Hut, Quiznos, Royal Thai, Starbucks, Subway, TGIFriday's, Wendy's [lodging] ALoft, Country Inn&Suites, Hampton Inn [other] Acura, AT&T, Dick's, GNC, Harley-Davidson, Jo-Ann Fabrics, Kohl's, Kroger, Lowe's, Marshall's, Office Depot, Sam's Club/gas, Staples, TJ Maxx, to Galleria Mall, Verizon, Walgreens
67	McEwen Dr, [food] Blue Coast Burrito, Brick Top's, Little Caesars, Marco's Pizza, Sonic, Subway, Tazikis Mediterranean Cafe [lodging] Drury Inn [other] Toyota/Scion, Walmart/Blimpie, Whole Food Mkt
65	TN 96, to Murfreesboro, Franklin, **E** [gas] Mapco, Shell/Krystal [food] Cracker Barrel, Sonic, Steak'n Shake [lodging] Best Value Inn, Comfort Inn, Days Inn, Holiday Inn Express, La Quinta, Ramada Inn [other] auto repair, Buick/GMC, Chevrolet, Honda, Kia, Subaru, URGENT CARE, Volvo, Walgreens, **W** [gas] BP/dsl, Shell, Shell/dsl [food] Arby's, Backyard Burger, Bar-B-Cutie, Bleachers Sports Grill, Franklin Chophouse, Hardee's, IHOP, KFC, La Terraza Mexican, McDonald's, Nashville Pizza, O'Charley's, Pancho's Mexican, Papa John's, Shoney's, Starbucks, Subway, Taco Bell, Waffle House, Wendy's, Whitts BBQ, Zaxby's [lodging] Best Western, Best Western, Quality Inn [other] $General, $Tree, Aldi Foods, BigLots, Chrysler/Dodge/Jeep, Discount Tire, Fiat, Ford/Lincoln, Hobby Lobby, Home Depot, K-Mart, Kroger/gas, Publix/gas, Radio Shack, Rite Aid, SteinMart, to Confederate Cem at Franklin, Tuesday Morning, Verizon, vet, Walgreens
64mm	Harpeth River
61	TN 248, Peytonsville Rd, to Spring Hill, **E** [gas] TA/BP/Country Pride/dsl/scales/24hr/@ @, **W** [gas] Mapco, Shell/dsl [lodging] Goose Creek Inn
59b a	TN 840, to Nashville
58mm	W Harpeth River
53	TN 396, Saturn Pkwy, Spring Hill, Columbia, **W** TN Scenic Pkwy
48mm	litter barrels, truck insp/weigh sta nb
46	US 412, TN 99, to Columbia, Chapel Hill, **E** [gas] BP/dsl, Loves/Arbys/dsl/scales/24hr [other] Harley-Davidson, Henry Horton SP, **W** [gas] Citgo/dsl, Phillip 66/Subway/dsl, Shell, TJ's/Burger King [food] Cracker Barrel, McDonald's, Stan's Rest, Waffle House [lodging] Best Value Inn, Comfort Inn, Fairfield Inn, Hampton Inn, Holiday Inn Express, Relax Inn, Super 8 [other] [H]
40.5mm	Duck River
37	TN 50, to Columbia, Lewisburg, **E** [other] [H], TN Walking Horse HQ, **W** [gas] Phillips 66dsl [other] to Polk Home
32	Rd 373, to Lewisburg, Mooresville
27	Rd 129, to Lynnville, Cornersville, **E** [other] Texas T Camping
25mm	**W parking area sb, litter barrels**
24mm	**E parking area nb, litter barrels**

F R A N K L I N

INTERSTATE 65 Cont'd

Exit #	Services
22	US 31A, to Pulaski, E Tennesseean Trkstp/Exxon/Pop's BBQ/dsl/scales/24hr/ @ McDonald's, Subway EconoLodge, W Pilot/dsl/scales/24hr, Shell/dsl
14	US 64, to Pulaski, E BP/dsl, Shell/dsl Sarge's Shack Rest. Super 8 to Jack Daniels Distillery, W H
6	Rd 273, Bryson, E Shell/rest./dsl/repair Best Value Inn dsl repair, W Marathon/dsl (2mi)
5mm	**E weight sta nb**
4mm	Elk River
3mm	**Welcome Ctr nb, full facilities, info, litter barrels, petwalk**
1	US 31, Rd 7, Ardmore, **1-2 mi** E Chevron/dsl, Exxon/dsl, Shell $General, El Olmeca Mexican, Hardee's, KFC/Taco Bell, McDonald's, Pizza Hut, Sonic, Subway, Whitts BBQ $General Mkt, Ardmore Tire, O'Reilly Parts
0	Tennessee/Alabama state line

INTERSTATE 75

Exit #	Services
161.5mm	Tennessee/Kentucky state line
161mm	**Welcome Ctr sb, full facilities, litter barrels, petwalk vending**
160	US 25W, Jellico, E Exxon/dsl, Marathon/dsl, W BP/Wendy's/dsl, Shell/Arby's/dsl Hardee's, Heritage Pizza, McDonald's, Subway Days Inn, Parkway Inn H, camping, fireworks, to Indian Mtn SP
156	Rarity Mtn Rd
144	Stinking Creek Rd, **4 mi** E Ride Royal Blue Camping
141	TN 63, to Royal Blue, Huntsville, E Shell/dsl El Rey Azteca, W Pilot/Subway/dsl/scales/24hr, Shell/dsl Comfort Inn fireworks, repair/truckwash, to Big South Fork NRA
134	US 25W, TN 63, Caryville, E Shell Takumi Japanese, Waffle House Hampton Inn, Holiday Inn Express, Super 8, Travelodge H, $General, Cumberland Gap NHP, to Cove Lake SP, W BP/dsl Scotty's Hamburgers, Shoney's Budget Host USPO
129	US 25W S, Lake City, W Exxon/dsl, Marathon/Sonic/dsl, Pilot/dsl, Shell/dsl Cracker Barrel, Domino's, Glen's Pizza, KFC/Taco Bell, La Fiesta Mexican, McDonald's, Subway Blue Haven Motel, Days Inn, Lamb's Inn/rest., Scottish Inn $General, Family$, fireworks, same as 128
128	US 441, to Lake City, E Sunoco Mtn Lake Marina Camping (4mi), W Exxon/dsl, Marathon, Weigel's/dsl Blue Haven Motel $General, Advance Parts, antique cars, Family$, same as 129, to Norris Dam SP
126mm	Clinch River
122	TN 61, Bethel, Norris, E Shell/dsl, Wiegel's/dsl Shoney's antiques, KOA, Museum of Appalachia, Toyota/Scion, W BP/dsl, Exxon/Burger King/Subway/dsl, Git'n Go/dsl, Phillips 66/dsl, Shell/Baskin-Robbins Arby's, Bojangles, Golden Girls Rest., Gondolier Italian, Hardee's, Harrison's Grill, Krystal, LJ Silver, McDonald's, Waffle House, Wendy's, Zaxby's Comfort Inn, Country Inn&Suites, Hampton Inn, Holiday Inn Express, Red Roof Inn, Super 8 AT&T, Big Pine Ridge SP, Ford, Verizon, Walgreens, Walmart/McDonald's
117	Rd 170, Racoon Valley Rd, E Pilot/dsl/scales/24hr, W Valley Inn Racoon Valley RV Park, Volunteer RV Park
112	Rd 131, Emory Rd, to Powell, E Marathon/Buddy's BBQ/dsl, Pilot/DQ/Taco Bell/dsl 5 Guys Burgers, Arby's, Aubrey's Rest., Bruster's, Chick-fil-A, Firehouse Subs, Jets Pizza, Krystal, McDonald's/playplace, Petro's Cafe, Ruby Tuesday, Starbucks, Steak'n Shake, Subway, Wendy's, Zaxby's Comfort Inn, Country Inn&Suites, Holiday Inn Express H, CVS Drug, Ingles/gas, O'Reilly Parts, Rigg's Drug, Verizon, W Exxon/dsl, Shell/dsl, Weigel's/dsl Hardee's, Shoney's, Waffle House Super 8
110	Callahan Dr, E Weigel's/dsl Archer's BBQ, Asian Cafe Express Inn, Knights Inn Honda, W Scottish Inn Kia, Mack/Volvo
108	Merchants Dr, E Delta/dsl, Marathon/dsl, Mobil/dsl, Pilot/dsl Applebee's, Cracker Barrel, El Chico, Hooters, Monterrey Mexican, O'Charley's, Pizza Hut, Puelo's Grill, Starbucks, Waffle House Best Western, Comfort Suites, Days Inn, Hampton Inn, Mainstay Suites, Quality Inn, Relax Inn, Sleep Inn Ingles, Valvoline, W Exxon/dsl, Pilot/Domino's/dsl Austin's Steaks, Burger King, Capt D's, IHOP, Mandarin House, McDonald's, Nixon's Deli, Outback Steaks, Red Lobster, Subway, Taco Bell Best Value Inn, Clarion Inn, EconoLodge, Motel 6, Super 8 CVS Drug, Radio Shack, Walgreens
107	I-640 & I-75
3b [I-640]	US 25W, (from nb), W Chevrolet, Ford, Nissan
1 [I-640]	Rd 62, Western Ave, E Hardee's, Krystal Advance Parts, Family$, O'Reilly Parts, W Exxon/dsl, Marathon/dsl, RaceWay/dsl Central Park, Firehouse Subs, KFC, Little Caesars, LJ Silver, McDonald's, Panda Chinese, Shoney's, Subway, Taco Bell, Wendy's CVS Drug, Kroger/dsl, Walgreens
I-75 and I-40 run together 17 mi. See I-40, exits 369 through 385.	
84 [368]	I-40, W to Nashville, E to Knoxville
81	US 321, TN 95, to Lenoir City, E BP/Buddy's BBQ/TCBY/dsl, Exxon/Subway/dsl, Marathon/dsl, Mobil, Murphy USA/dsl, Shell/dsl, Weigel's/dsl Arby's, Aubrey's Rest., Bojangles, Burger King, Capt D's, Chick-fil-A, Chili's, China Buffet, Cinco Amigos Mexican, Cracker Barrel, Domino's, Dunkin Donuts, Firehouse Subs, Gondolier Italian, Hardee's, KFC, McDonald's, Papa John's, Pizza Hut, Shoney's, Taco Bell, Tako Yaki Steaks, Waffle House, Wendy's, Zaxby's Days Inn, Hampton Inn, Holiday Inn Express, King's Inn/rest. H, $General Mkt, $Tree, Advance Parts, AT&T, AutoZone, Big Lots, CVS Drug, Food City/gas, Ford, Ft Loudon Dam, GNC, Great Smokies NP, Home Depot, Ingles, Lazy Acres RV Park (7mi), O'Reilly Parts, Verizon, Walgreens, Walmart/Subway, W Citgo/dsl Krystal, Ruby Tuesday Comfort Inn, EconoLodge, Knights Inn Crosseyed Cricket Camping (6mi), Matlock Tires/Repair
76	Rd 324, Sugar Limb Rd, W to TN Valley Winery
74mm	Tennessee River
72	TN 72, to Loudon, E BP/McDonald's, Exxon/Wendy's/dsl, Weigel's/dsl Bojangles, Cabin Rest., KFC, Taco Bell Country Inn&Suites, Inn of Loudon to Ft Loudon SP, W Marathon Best Value Inn Express RV Park
68	Rd 323, to Philadelphia, E Marathon/dsl cheese factory/store (2mi)
62	Rd 322, Oakland Rd, to Sweetwater, E Dinner Bell Rest., W KOA
60	TN 68, Sweetwater, **0-2 mi** E BP/dsl, RaceWay, Sunoco A&W/LJ Silver, Bradley's BBQ, Burger King, Hardee's, KFC, Little Caesar's, McDonald's, Mexi Wings, Pizza Hut, Sonic, Subway, Taco Bell Days Inn, Economy Inn, Hilltop Motel, Quality Inn H, $General, Ace Hardware, Advance Parts, Family$, Ford/Lincoln, K-Mart, O'Reilly Parts, to Lost Sea

BETHEL

SWEETWATER

TN

INTERSTATE 75

ATHENS

60	Continued Underground Lake, Verizon, Walgreens, W Kangaroo/dsl, Marathon Holiday Inn Express, Super 8 flea mkt, to Watts Bar Dam
56	Rd 309, Niota, E Wilco/Stuckey's/Wendy's/dsl/scales/24hr TN Country Camping, W repair
52	Rd 305, Mt Verd Rd, to Athens, E Marathon/dsl (2mi) Subway (2mi) Overniter RV Park, W BP Athens Lodge
49	TN 30, to Athens, E Exxon, Kangaroo, Marathon, Mobil/dsl, Murphy USA/dsl Applebee's, Arby's, Buddy's BBQ, Burger King, Capt D's, China Wok, Dunkin Donuts, Firehouse Subs, Hardee's, KFC, Krystal, Little Caesar's, McDonald's, Mexi Wing, Ming Dynasty, Papa John's, Pizza Hut, Ruby Tuesday, Shoney's, Sonic, Subway, Subway, Taco Bell, Waffle House, Wendy's, Western Sizzlin, Zaxby's Days Inn, Hampton Inn, Holiday Inn Express, Homestead Inn, Motel 6, Scottish Inn, Super 8 H, $General, $Tree, Advance Parts, Athens I-75 Camping, Belk, BigLots, GNC, K-Mart, Russell Stover, Staples, to TN Wesleyan Coll, URGENT CARE, Verizon, Walgreens, Walmart/Subway, W Mobil/dsl, Speedway/dsl Cracker Barrel Best Value Inn, Comfort Inn
45mm	**both lanes, full facilities, litter barrels, petwalk vending**
42	Rd 39, Riceville Rd, E Citgo/dsl Relax Inn, Rice Inn (2mi)
36	Rd 163, to Calhoun, E Hardee's (3mi) Hiwassee/Ocoee River SP
35mm	Hiwassee River
33	Rd 308, to Charleston, E Marathon/dsl Hardee's, W Loves/McDonald's/Subway/dsl/scales/24hr

CLEVELAND

27	Paul Huff Pkwy, **1 mi** E Murphy USA, Shell/dsl Applebee's, Buffalo Wild Wings, Capt D's, Chili's, CiCi's, DQ, Fazoli's, Firehouse Subs, Five Guys, Golden Corral, IHOP, Little Caesar's, Longhorn Steaks, McDonald's, O'Charley's, Olive Garden, Outback Steaks, Panera Bread, Papa Murphy's, Pita Pit, Pizza Hut, Royal Buffet, Santa Fe Steaks, Six Happiness, Sonic, Starbucks, Steak'n Shake, Subway, Taco Bell Baymont Inn, Holiday Inn Express $Tree, Aldi Foods, auto repair/tires, AutoZone, Belk, Buick/Cadillac/GMC, CVS Drug, Discount Tire, Food Lion, Hobby Lobby, Home Depot, JC Penney, K-Mart, Lowe's, mall, PetCo, Publix, Radio Shack, Rite Aid, Staples, TJ Maxx, Verizon, Walgreens, Walmart, W Exxon/dsl, Orbit/dsl, Shell/Subway Denny's, Fulin's Asian, Hardee's, Honeybaked Ham, Shane's Ribshack, Stevi B's Pizza, Waffle House, Wendy's Clarion, Classic Suites, Hampton Inn, Quality Inn, Royal Inn, Super 8, Travelodge AT&T, Books-A-Million, Kohl's, Michael's, Ross, Target
25	TN 60, Cleveland, E Chevron/dsl, RaceWay/dsl, Shell/dsl, Sunoco/dsl Bojangles, Burger King, Checkers, Cracker Barrel, Dunkin Donuts, Hardee's, Las Margaritas, McDonald's, Old Fort Rest., Sonic, Waffle House, Wendy's, Zaxby's Colonial Inn, Days Inn, Douglas Inn, EconoLodge, Economy Inn, Fairfield Inn, Howard Johnson, Knights Inn, Travel Inn H, $General, Ace Hardware, BigLots, Cherokee Drug, NAPA, Rite Aid, to Lee Coll, Tuesday Morning, W BP Comfort Inn, La Quinta, Mtn View Inn, Wingate Inn
23mm	truck/weigh sta nb
20	US 64 byp, to Cleveland, **1-4 mi** E FuelMart Ford, Honda, Kia, W Exxon/dsl, Pilot/McDonald's/Subway/dsl/scales/24hr fireworks, KOA (1mi), Toyota/Scion
16mm	scenic view sb

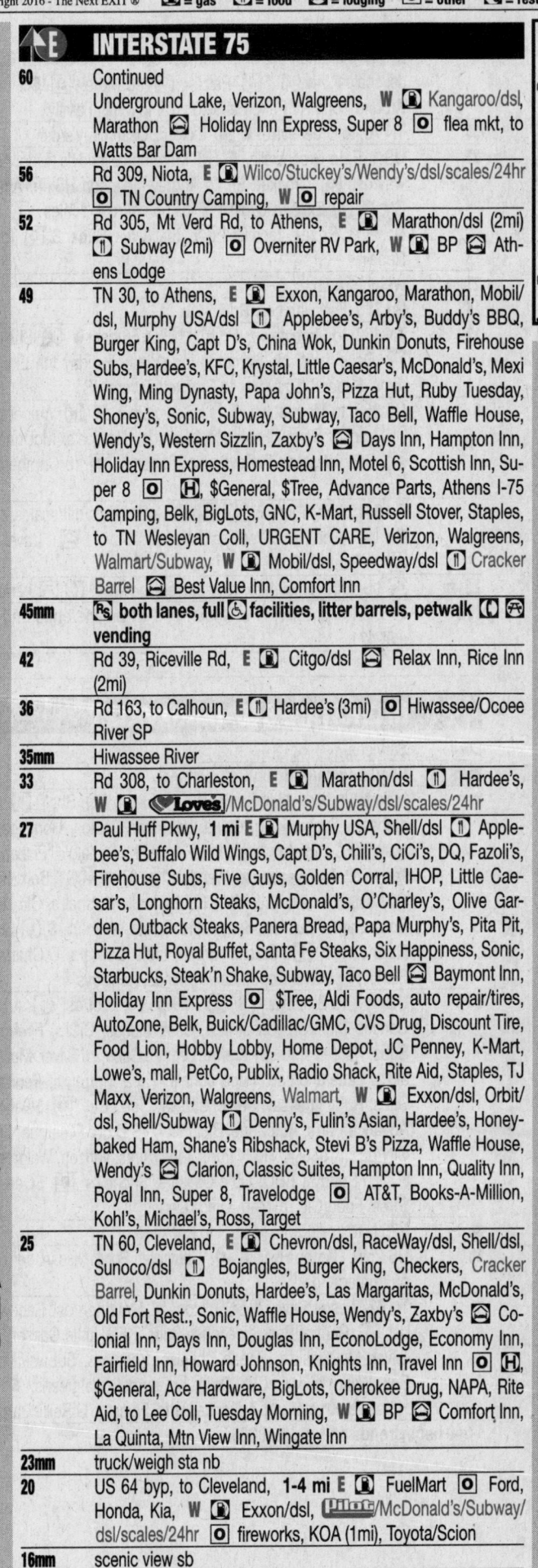

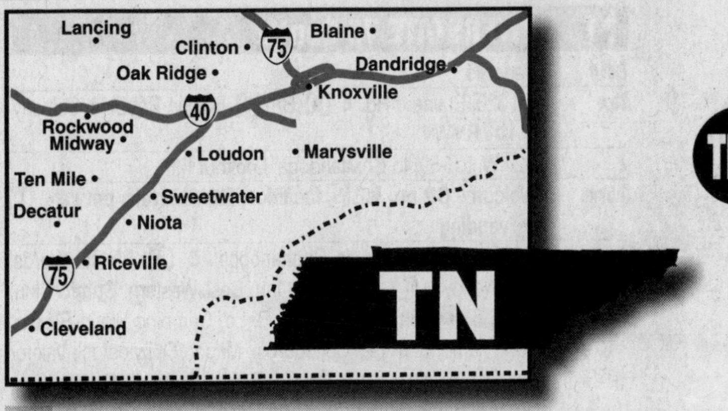

CHATTANOOGA

13mm	**truck/weigh sta, litter barrels sb**
11	US 11 N, US 64 E, Ooltewah, E BP, Mapco, Murphy USA/dsl, RaceWay/dsl Arby's, Bojangles, Burger King, China Rose, Cracker Barrel, El Matador Mexican, Hardee's, Little Caesars, McDonald's, Pizza Hut, Sonic, Subway, Taco Bell, Wendy's, Western Sizzlin, Zaxby's Hampton Inn, Holiday Inn Express $General, Ace Hardware, BiLo, GNC, O'Reilly Parts, Verizon, Walgreens, Walmart/Subway, W BP/dsl, Shell/dsl Beef'o Brady's, Krystal, Waffle House Super 8 Publix, to Harrison Bay SP
9	TN 317, Apison Pk, Volkswagen Dr, E Shell
7b a	US 11, US 64, Lee Hwy, E Shell/dsl, W BP, Speedway/dsl City Cafe, Waffle House Inn, Best Inn, Best Value Inn, Best Western, EconoLodge, Motel 6, Rodeway Inn, ValuePlace Inn Denton's Repair, Harley-Davidson, Jaguar/Land Rover/Porsche/Infiniti
5	Shallowford Rd, E Arby's, CiCi's, Famous Dave's, Forbidden City Chinese, Imperial Garden, J. Alexanders, Jersey Mike's, Krystal, Logan's Roadhouse, Macaroni Grill, McAlister's Deli, McDonald's, Mellow Mushroom Pizza, Melting Pot, Outback Steaks, Panda Express, Ruth's Chris Steaks, Smokey Bones BBQ, Souper Salad, Starbucks, Steak'n Shake, Taco Bell, Zaxby's Courtyard, Embassy Suites, Quality Inn, Wingate Inn Best Buy, Firestone/auto, FreshMkt Foods, Hobby Lobby, Home Depot, Lowe's, Office Depot, Old Navy, Petco, Petsmart, SteinMart, Target, Walgreens, Walmart/Subway, World Mkt, W BP, Citgo/dsl, Exxon/dsl, Shell, Speedway/dsl Applebee's, Cracker Barrel, Fazoli's, Firebox Grill, Fuji Steaks, O'Charley's, Papa John's, Shoney's, Sonic, Subway, TX Roadhouse, Waffle House, Wendy's Comfort Inn, Country Inn&Suites, Days Inn, Fairfield Inn, Guesthouse Inn, Hampton Inn, Hilton Garden, Holiday Inn, Homewood Suites, Knights Inn, La Quinta, MainStay Suites, Red Roof Inn, Residence Inn, Sleep Inn, Staybridge Suites, Super 8, Travelodge H, Bi-Lo, CarMax, CVS Drug, Family$, Goodyear/auto, same as 4a, SaveALot, U of TN/Chatt
4a	(from nb) Hamilton Place Blvd, E Shell Abuelo's, Acropolis, Bar Louie Grill, Big River Grille, BoneFish Grill, Capt D's, Carrabba's, Cheddar's, Chick-fil-A, Chili's, Chop House, DQ, El Meson Mexican, Firebird's, Firehouse Subs, Five Guys, Fox&Hound Grille, Golden Corral, Honeybaked Ham, Jason's Deli, Kanpai of Tokyo, McDonald's, Moe's SW Grill, Olive Garden, Outback Steaks, Panera Bread, PF Chang's, Red Lobster, Red Robin, Salsarita's Mexican, Shogun Japanese, Starbucks, Sticky Fingers BBQ, Taziki's Cafe Hampton Inn, InTown Suites $Tree, AAA, AT&T, Barnes&Noble, Belk, Big Lots, Dick's, Dillard's, Earthfare, Firestone/auto, JC Penney, Jo-Ann, Kohl's, mall, Marshall's, Michael's, Pepboys, Ross, same as 5, Sears/auto, Staples, Target, TJ Maxx, Verizon, World Mkt
4	TN 153, Chickamauga Dam Rd,

= gas = food = lodging = other = rest stop

INTERSTATE 75 Cont'd

Exit #	Services
3b a	TN 320, Brainerd Rd, E BP Baskin-Robbins, Subway, W BMW
2	I-24 W, to I-59, to Chattanooga, Lookout Mtn
1.5mm	**Welcome Ctr nb, full facilities, litter barrels, petwalk vending**
1b a	US 41, Ringgold Rd, to Chattanooga, E BP, Texaco/dsl Wendy's Best Value Inn, Best Western, Comfort Inn, Motel 6 Bass Pro Shops, Bi-Lo, Camping World RV Ctr/park, Family$, W Conoco/dsl, Mapco/Quiznos/dsl, Valero/dsl A&W/LJ Silver, Arby's, Baskin-Robbins, Burger King, Cracker Barrel, Hardee's, Krystal, McDonald's, Popeyes, PortoFino Italian, Sonic, Subway, Taco Bell, Teriyaki House, Waffle House, Wally's Rest. Fairfield Inn, Holiday Inn Express, Super 8, Superior Creek Lodge, Waverly Motel $General, Advance Parts, AutoZone, Family$, O'Reilly Parts, Rite Aid, U-Haul, Walgreens
0mm	Tennessee/Georgia state line

INTERSTATE 81

Exit #	Services
75mm	Tennessee/Virginia state line, **Welcome Ctr sb, full facilities, info, litter barrels, petwalk vending**
74b a	US 11W, to Bristol, Kingsport, E Fairfield Inn, Hampton Inn H, W Valero/dsl Brusco's Pizza, Chick-fil-A, Hambino's Cafe, Jersey Mike's, McDonald's, Pal's Drive-Thru, Steak'n Shake, Zaxby's AT&T, Bass Pro Shops, Belk, Dick's, GNC, Marshall's, Michael's
69	TN 394, to Blountville, E BP/Subway/dsl Arby's, Domino's Advance Parts, Bristol Int Speedway, Lakeview RV Park (8mi), Shadrack Camping
66	Rd 126, to Kingsport, Blountville, W Shell/dsl McDonald's
63	Rd 357, E BP/Krystal/dsl, Shell/Subway/dsl Cracker Barrel, Wendy's La Quinta, Sleep Inn Hamricks, Tri-Cities, W Citgo/dsl Econolodge dsl repair, KOA, Rocky Top Camping
60mm	Holston River
59	Rd 36, to Johnson City, Kingsport, E Marathon/dsl Super 8, W Exxon/dsl, Marathon, Shell/dsl, Sunoco Arby's, Fisherman's Dock Rest., Hardee's, HotDog Hut, Jersey Mike's Subs, La Carreta Mexican, Little Caesars, McDonald's, Moto Japanese, Pal's Drive-Thru, Perkins, Pizza Hut, Plum Tree Rest., Raffaele's Pizza, Sonic, Subway, The Shack BBQ, Zachary's Steaks Colonial Inn, Comfort Inn $General, $Tree, Advance Parts, CVS Drug, Firestone/auto, Ingles/deli, O'Reilly Parts, to Warrior's Path SP, URGENT CARE, USPO, Verizon, Walgreens
57b a	I-26
56	Tri-Cities Crossing, E regional shopping complex
50	TN 93, Fall Branch, W auto auction, st patrol
44	Jearoldstown Rd, E Marathon
41mm	**sb, full facilities, litter barrels, petwalk vending**
38mm	**nb, full facilities, litter barrels, petwalk vending**
36	Rd 172, to Baileyton, E Pilot/Subway/dsl/scales/24hr W Marathon/dsl, Shell/Subway/dsl/24hr, TA/Country Pride/dsl/scales/24hr/ @ Pizza+ 36 Motel $General Around Pond RV Park, Baileyton Camp (2mi), Family$
30	TN 70, to Greeneville, E Exxon/DQ/Stuckey's/dsl
23	US 11E, to Greeneville, E Marathon/Wendy's, Mobil/Subway/dsl Crockett SP, to Andrew Johnson HS, Tri-Am RV Ctr, W Exxon/DQ/dsl, Phillips 66/dsl/rest./scales McDonald's, Pizza+, Taco Bell Quality Inn, Super 8 Tony's Repair
21mm	**weigh sta sb**
15	Rd 340, Fish Hatchery Rd
12	TN 160, to Morristown, E Phillips 66/dsl, W Shell/dsl Days Inn (6mi), Hampton Inn (12mi), Holiday Inn Express (5mi), Super 8 (5mi) to Crockett Tavern HS
8	US 25E, to Morristown, E Sonic (2mi), W Weigel's/dsl Cracker Barrel, Fastop/Subway/dsl, Hardee's, McDonald's Best Western, Parkway Inn, Super 8 to Cumberland Gap NHP
4	Rd 341, White Pine, E Pilot/McDonald's/dsl/scales/24hr, W Wilco/Hess/Wendy's/dsl/scales/24hr Travel Inn to Panther Cr SP
2.5mm	**sb, full facilities, litter barrels, petwalk vending**
1b a	I-40, E to Asheville, W to Knoxville. **I-81 begins/ends on I-40, exit 421.**

INTERSTATE 640 (KNOXVILLE)

Exit #	Services
9mm	**I-640 begins/ends on I-40, exit 393.**
8	Millertown Pike, Mall Rd N, N Exxon/DQ, Shell Applebee's, Burger King, China Wok, Don Pablos, Honeybaked Ham, KFC, Krystal, Mandarin Palace, McDonald's, Pizza Hut, Taco Bell, TX Roadhouse, Wendy's $Tree, AT&T, Belk, Food City/dsl, JC Penney, Jo-Ann, Kohl's, mall, Marshall's, Old Navy, Ross, Sam's Club/dsl, Sears/auto, Target, Walmart, S Shell/Quiznos/dsl Cracker Barrel, Little Caesars, O'Charley's, Sonic Home Depot, Lowe's Whse, PepBoys
6	US 441, to Broadway, N Phillips 66, Pilot/dsl Arby's, Cancun Mexican, Chick-fil-A, Chop House, CiCi's, Firehouse Subs, Hardee's, Krispy Kreme, Lenny's Subs, LJ Silver, McDonald's, Panera Bread, Papa John's, Papa Murphy's, Penn Sta Subs, Ruby Tuesday, Sonic, Subway, Taco Bell $General, Advance Parts, AutoZone, BigLots, CVS Drug, Firestone, Food City/gas, Kroger, O'Reilly Parts, repair/tires, Verizon, Walgreens, S Buddy's BBQ, Little Caesars, Shoney's $General, $Tree, Food City, K-Mart, Office Depot
3a	I-75 N to Lexington, I-275 S to Knoxville
3b	US 25W, Clinton Hwy, N Chevrolet, Ford, Nissan, services on frontage rds
1	TN 62, Western Ave, N Exxon/dsl, Marathon/dsl, Raceway/dsl Central Park, Firehouse Subs, KFC, Little Caesars, LJ Silver, McDonald's, Panda Chinese, Shoney's, Subway, Taco Bell, Wendy's CVS Drug, Kroger/dsl, Walgreens, S Hardee's, Krystal Advance Parts, Family$, O'Reilly Parts

I-640 begins/ends on I-40, exit 385.

TEXAS

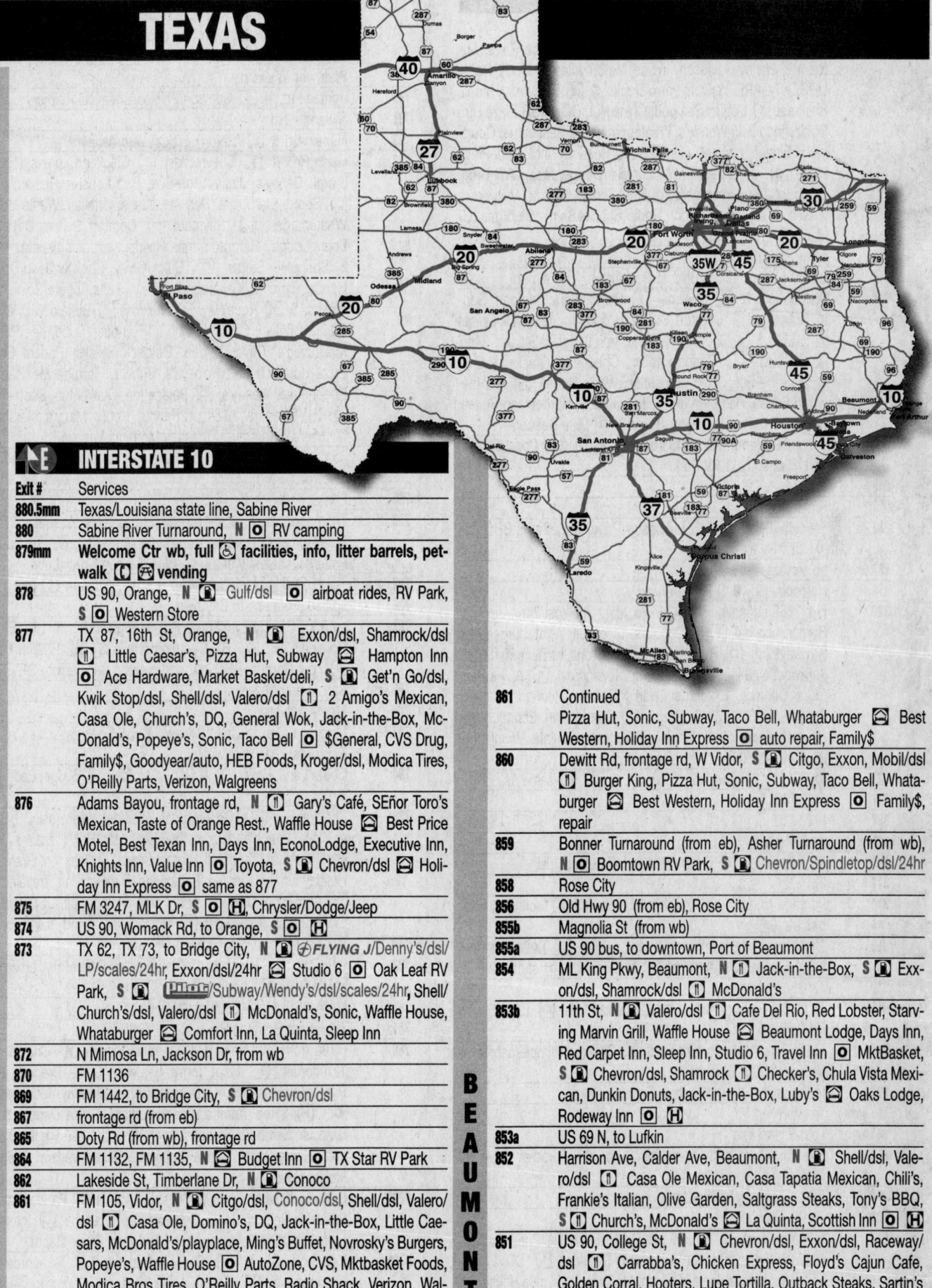

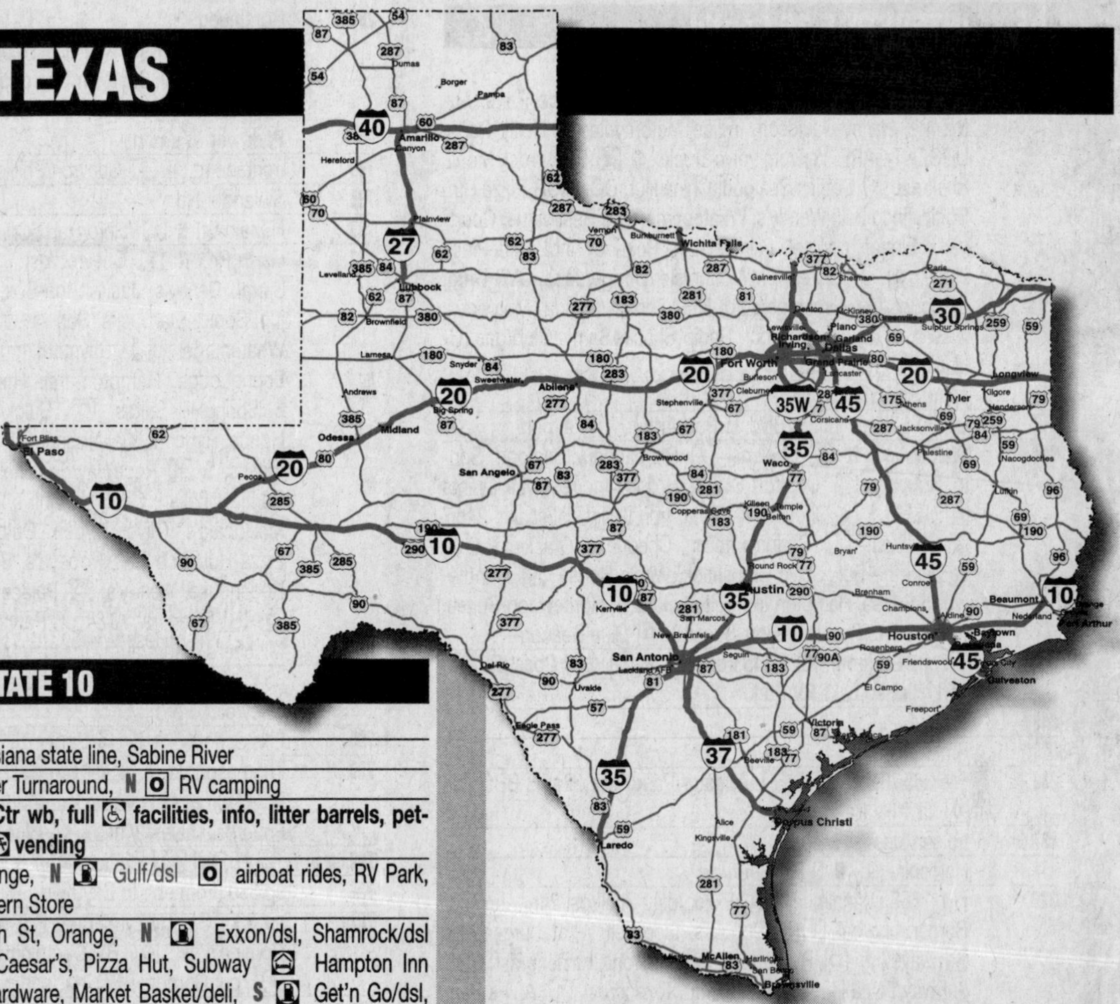

TX

INTERSTATE 10

Exit #	Services
880.5mm	Texas/Louisiana state line, Sabine River
880	Sabine River Turnaround, N RV camping
879mm	**Welcome Ctr wb, full facilities, info, litter barrels, petwalk vending**
878	US 90, Orange, N Gulf/dsl airboat rides, RV Park, S Western Store
877	TX 87, 16th St, Orange, N Exxon/dsl, Shamrock/dsl Little Caesar's, Pizza Hut, Subway Hampton Inn Ace Hardware, Market Basket/deli, S Get'n Go/dsl, Kwik Stop/dsl, Shell/dsl, Valero/dsl 2 Amigo's Mexican, Casa Ole, Church's, DQ, General Wok, Jack-in-the-Box, McDonald's, Popeye's, Sonic, Taco Bell $General, CVS Drug, Family$, Goodyear/auto, HEB Foods, Kroger/dsl, Modica Tires, O'Reilly Parts, Verizon, Walgreens
876	Adams Bayou, frontage rd, N Gary's Café, SEñor Toro's Mexican, Taste of Orange Rest., Waffle House Best Price Motel, Best Texan Inn, Days Inn, EconoLodge, Executive Inn, Knights Inn, Value Inn Toyota, S Chevron/dsl Holiday Inn Express same as 877
875	FM 3247, MLK Dr, S H, Chrysler/Dodge/Jeep
874	US 90, Womack Rd, to Orange, S H
873	TX 62, TX 73, to Bridge City, N FLYING J/Denny's/dsl/LP/scales/24hr, Exxon/dsl/24hr Studio 6 Oak Leaf RV Park, S Pilot/Subway/Wendy's/dsl/scales/24hr, Shell/Church's/dsl, Valero/dsl McDonald's, Sonic, Waffle House, Whataburger Comfort Inn, La Quinta, Sleep Inn
872	N Mimosa Ln, Jackson Dr, from wb
870	FM 1136
869	FM 1442, to Bridge City, S Chevron/dsl
867	frontage rd (from eb)
865	Doty Rd (from wb), frontage rd
864	FM 1132, FM 1135, N Budget Inn TX Star RV Park
862	Lakeside St, Timberlane Dr, N Conoco
861	FM 105, Vidor, N Citgo/dsl, Conoco/dsl, Shell/dsl, Valero/dsl Casa Ole, Domino's, DQ, Jack-in-the-Box, Little Caesars, McDonald's/playplace, Ming's Buffet, Novrosky's Burgers, Popeye's, Waffle House AutoZone, CVS, Mktbasket Foods, Modica Bros Tires, O'Reilly Parts, Radio Shack, Verizon, Walgreens, Walmart, S Citgo/dsl, Exxon/dsl Burger King,
861	Continued Pizza Hut, Sonic, Subway, Taco Bell, Whataburger Best Western, Holiday Inn Express auto repair, Family$
860	Dewitt Rd, frontage rd, W Vidor, S Citgo, Exxon, Mobil/dsl Burger King, Pizza Hut, Sonic, Subway, Taco Bell, Whataburger Best Western, Holiday Inn Express Family$, repair
859	Bonner Turnaround (from eb), Asher Turnaround (from wb), N Boomtown RV Park, S Chevron/Spindletop/dsl/24hr
858	Rose City
856	Old Hwy 90 (from eb), Rose City
855b	Magnolia St (from wb)
855a	US 90 bus, to downtown, Port of Beaumont
854	ML King Pkwy, Beaumont, N Jack-in-the-Box, S Exxon/dsl, Shamrock/dsl McDonald's
853b	11th St, N Valero/dsl Cafe Del Rio, Red Lobster, Starving Marvin Grill, Waffle House Beaumont Lodge, Days Inn, Red Carpet Inn, Sleep Inn, Studio 6, Travel Inn MktBasket, S Chevron/dsl, Shamrock Checker's, Chula Vista Mexican, Dunkin Donuts, Jack-in-the-Box, Luby's Oaks Lodge, Rodeway Inn H
853a	US 69 N, to Lufkin
852	Harrison Ave, Calder Ave, Beaumont, N Shell/dsl, Valero/dsl Casa Ole Mexican, Casa Tapatia Mexican, Chili's, Frankie's Italian, Olive Garden, Saltgrass Steaks, Tony's BBQ, S Church's, McDonald's La Quinta, Scottish Inn H
851	US 90, College St, N Chevron/dsl, Exxon/dsl, Raceway/dsl Carrabba's, Chicken Express, Floyd's Cajun Cafe, Golden Corral, Hooters, Lupe Tortilla, Outback Steaks, Sartin's Seafood, Tokyo Japanese, Waffle House Howard Johnson

VIDOR

BEAUMONT

TX

INTERSTATE 10 Cont'd

851 Continued
Quality Inn, Ramada, Red Roof Inn [O] Advance Parts, AutoZone, Harley-Davidson, Indian Motorcycles, O'Reilly Parts, URGENT CARE, Verizon, Volvo Trucks, **S** [gas] Exxon/dsl, Mobil, Shell/dsl [food] Catfish Seafood, China Hut, DQ, IHOP, Pizza Hut, Sonic, Taco Bell, Wendy's, Whataburger [lodging] Best Value, Courtyard, Elegante Motel, Fairfield Inn, Regency Inn, ValuePlace Hotel [O] [H], $Tree, BMW, Chrysler/Dodge/Jeep, CVS Drug, Discount Tire, Firestone/auto, HEB Foods, Honda, Mercedes, Nissan, NTB, Office Depot, Radio Shack, Sam's Club/gas, U-Haul, VW, Walgreens

850 same as 851, wb only

849 US 69 S, Washington Blvd, to Port Arthur, [O] airport

848 Walden Rd, **N** [gas] Shell/dsl [food] Pappadeaux Seafood, Sonic, Subway [lodging] Comfort Suites, Holiday Inn/rest., La Quinta [O] USPO, **S** [gas] Chevron/dsl, Petro/Iron Skillet/dsl/scales/24hr/@, Shell/dsl [food] Carino's Italian, Cheddar's, Cracker Barrel, Jack-in-the-Box, Joe's Crabshack, Waffle House [lodging] Candlewood Suites, Hampton Inn, Hilton Garden, Homewood Suites, Knights Inn, Residence Inn, Super 8 [O] Blue Beacon

847 Brooks Rd (from wb), (845 from eb), **S** [O] Gulf Coast RV Resort, Hidden Lake RV Park

845 TX 364

843 Smith Rd

838 FM 365, Fannett, **N** [food] Alligator Park/Rest., Bar-H BBQ/gas [O] T&T RV Park

837.5mm no services

833 Hamshire Rd, **N** [gas] Chevron/dsl

WINNIE

829 FM 1663, Winnie, **N** [gas] Exxon/dsl, Shell/dsl/24hr, Texaco/Burger King/dsl [food] McDonald's, Taco Bell, Whataburger/24hr [lodging] Days Inn [O] RV Park, **S** [gas] Chevron/Chester's/dsl, Gulf/Subway/Pizza Hut/dsl/scales/24hr, Texaco/dsl [food] Al-T's Seafood, Denny's, Exxon/dsl, Hart's Chicken, Hunan Chinese, Jack-in-the-Box, Waffle House [lodging] Comfort Inn, EconoLodge, Hampton Inn, Holiday Inn, Home Suites, La Quinta, Winnie Inn/RV Park [O] [H], Chrysler/Jeep/Dodge

828 TX 73, TX 124 (from eb), to Winnie, **S** [O] [H], same as 829

827 FM 1406

822 FM 1410

821 **insp sta wb**

819 Jenkins Rd, **S** [gas] Exxon/Stuckey's/Chester's/dsl

817 FM 1724

814 frontage rd, from eb, [RS] **both lanes, full [handicap] facilities, litter barrels** [picnic]

813 TX 61 (from wb), Hankamer, **N** [gas] Shell/dsl [lodging] TX Country Inn, **S** [gas] Exxon/DJ's Diner/dsl [food] McDonald's [O] same as 812

812 TX 61, Hankamer

811 Turtle Bayou Turnaround, **S** [gas] Gator Jct/dsl [O] Turtle Bayou RV Park

810 FM 563, to Anahuac, Liberty, **S** [gas] Chevron/Blimpie/dsl, Texaco/Jack-in-the-Box/dsl

807 to Wallisville, **S** [O] Heritage Park

BAYTOWN

805.5mm Trinity River

804mm Lost Rivers, Old

803 FM 565, Cove, Old River-Winfrey, **N** [O] Paradise Cove RV Park, **S** [gas] Valero/dsl

800 FM 3180, **N** [gas] Exxon/dsl

799 TX 99, Grand Pkwy

797 (798 from wb) TX 146, 99 toll, Baytown, **N** [gas] Chevron/Subway/dsl/scales, Conoco/dsl/scales, Shell/dsl [food] DQ, El Hacendado, Iguana Joe's Mexican, McDonald's, Waffle House [lodging] Crystal Inn, Motel 6, Super 8 [O] L&R RV Park, Value RV Park,

797 Continued
S [gas] Exxon, RaceWay/dsl, Stripes/Taco Co/dsl, Texaco/Popeye's/dsl [food] Baytown Seafood, Jack-in-the-Box, KFC/Taco Bell, Sonic [lodging] Magnuson Hotel [O] [H], Houston East RV Park, vet, Walmart

796 frontage rd, **N** [gas] Chevron/Phillips/Chemical Refinery

795 Sjolander Rd

793 N Main St, **S** [gas] Valero/Hartz Chicken/dsl/24hr

792 Garth Rd, **N** [gas] Chevron/dsl [food] Chicken Express, Cracker Barrel, Denny's, Jack-in-the-Box, Red Lobster, Richard's Cajun, Sonic, Starbucks, Subway, Tuscany Italian, Waffle House, Whataburger [lodging] Baymont Inn, Comfort Suites, Days Inn, EconoLodge, Hampton Inn, Holiday Inn, La Quinta, Motel 6, SpringHill Suites [O] Buick/GMC, Chrysler/Jeep/Dodge, Honda, Hyundai, Kia, Nissan, O'Reilly Parts, Toyota/Scion, Walgreens, **S** [gas] RaceWay/dsl, Shell/dsl [food] Buffalo Wild Wings, Carino's Italian, Carl's Jr, Chili's, Firehouse Subs, Lee Palace, McDonald's, Olive Garden, Outback Steaks, Panera Bread, Pizza Hut/Taco Bell, Popeye's, Subway, Tortuga Mexican, TX Rodehouse, Wendy's [lodging] Palace Inn, Quality Inn, Scottish Inn [O] [H], $General, AT&T, JC Penney, Kohl's, Macy's, Marshall's, Michael's, Sears/auto, Tuesday Morning, Verizon

791 John Martin Rd, **S** [food] Cheddars [lodging] ValuePlace [O] Cadillac/Chevrolet, Ford

790 Ellis School Rd, **N** [lodging] Super 8

789 Thompson Rd, **N** [gas] Love's/McDonald's/dsl/scales/24hr@, **S** [gas] FLYING J/Denny's/dsl/scales/24hr@, TA/Country Pride/dsl/scales/24hr@ [O] Blue Beacon, Truck Lube

788.5mm [RS] **eb, full [handicap] facilities, litter barrels, petwalk** [phone] [picnic]

788 sp 330 (from eb), to Baytown

787 sp 330, Crosby-Lynchburg Rd, to Highlands, **N** [gas] Exxon/Domino's/dsl [O] RV Camping (1mi), **S** [gas] Phillips 66/dsl [food] Four Corners BBQ [O] camping, to San Jacinto SP

786.5mm San Jacinto River

786 Monmouth Dr

785 Magnolia Ave, to Channelview, **N** [gas] Shell/dsl/scales, **S** [gas] Exxon/dsl [O] truckwash

784 Cedar Lane, Bayou Dr, **N** [gas] Valero/dsl [lodging] Budget Lodge, TX Inn

783 Sheldon Rd, **N** [gas] Chevron/dsl, Shell/dsl, Valero/dsl [food] Burger King, Church's, Jack-in-the-Box, Pizza Hut, Pizza Inn, Popeye's, Subway, Taco Bell, Whataburger [lodging] Days Inn, Grand Inn, Holiday Inn, Leisure Inn, Palace Inn, Parkway Inn, Travelers Inn [O] AutoZone, Discount Tire, Family$, FoodFair, USPO, **S** [gas] Chevron/dsl, Texaco/dsl [food] McDonald's, Wendy's [lodging] Deluxe Inn, Fairfield Inn, Scottish Inn [O] auto repair

782 Dell-Dale Ave, **N** [gas] Exxon/dsl [lodging] Dell-Dale Motel, Luxury Inn [O] [H], **S** [O] Channelview RV Ctr

781b Market St, **N** [lodging] Clarion [O] [H]

781a TX 8, Sam Houston Pkwy, **S** [gas] Gulf/dsl

780 (779a from wb)Uvalde Rd, Freeport St, **N** [gas] Chevron/dsl, Texaco/dsl [food] Capt Tom's Seafood, China Dragon, IHOP, Panda Express, Shipley Donuts, Sonic, Subway, Taco Cabana [O] [H], $Tree, Aamco, Ace Hardware, Office Depot, **S** [food] Baytown Seafood, Golden Corral, Whataburger [O] Firestone/auto, Home Depot, Sam's Club/gas, U-Haul, Verizon, Walmart/McDonald's

779b **N** [gas] Gulf, Valero/dsl [food] China Dragon, IHOP, Panda Express, Shipley's Donuts, Sonic, Subway, Taco Cabana [lodging] Interstate Motel [O] $Tree, Aamco, Ace Hardware, Office Depot

778b Normandy St, **N** [gas] Shell/Jack-in-the-Box, Texaco/dsl [lodging] La Quinta, **S** [gas] Citgo/dsl [food] Cafe Ko, Church's [lodging] Normandy Inn

INTERSTATE 10 Cont'd

HOUSTON

Exit #	Services
778a	FM 526, Federal Rd, Pasadena, N Burger King, Casa Ole Mexican, KFC/Taco Bell, Pizza Hut, Popeye's, Subway, S Shell/dsl James Coney Island, Pappadeaux Seafood Kitchen, Pappas BBQ, Pappa's Seafood, Peking Bo Chinese, Saltgrass Steaks, Sonic, Swamp Shack Rest. Lamplight Inn, Super 8 AutoZone, Discount Tire, O'Reilly Parts, Scottish Inn
776b	John Ralston Rd, Holland Ave, N Chevron/dsl, Exxon, Texaco Chulas Mexican, Denny's, Fuddruckers, Luby's, Mambo Seafood, Pappasito's Cantina, Subway Candlewood Suites, Comfort Inn, Day Inn, Palace Inn, Regency Inn Family$, Fiesta Foods, NTB, URGENT CARE, S same as 778
776a	Mercury Dr, N Aranda's Mexican, Burger King, McDonald's, Tepatillan Mexican, TX Grill Best Western, Hampton Inn, Motel 6, Premier Inn, Quality Inn Volvo Trucks, S Shell/dsl, Valero/dsl Chili's, Cici's Pizza, Murphy's Deli Holiday Inn Express CVS Drug, URGENT CARE
775b a	I-610
774	Gellhorn (from eb) Blvd, S Anheuser-Busch Brewery
773b	McCarty St, N Chevron/dsl, Shell
773a	US 90A, N Wayside Dr, N Speedy/dsl Jack-in-the-Box, Whataburger, S Chevron/dsl, Shell/dsl, Valero Church's, Subway
772	Kress St, Lathrop St, N Conoco, Exxon Popeye's, S 7 Mares Seafood, Burger King
771b	Lockwood Dr, N Chevron/Subway/dsl McDonald's Family$, Walgreens, S Shell/dsl Palace Inn
771a	Waco St
770c	US 59 N
770b	Jenson St, Meadow St, Gregg St
770a	US 59 S, to Victoria
769c	McKee St, Hardy St, Nance St, downtown
769a	Smith St (from wb), to downtown
768b a	I-45, N to Dallas, S to Galveston
767b	Taylor St
767a	Studemont Dr, Yale St, Heights Blvd, S Shell/dsl Chick-fil-A, Chili's, Dickey's BBQ, KFC/Taco Bell, Panda Express, Subway AT&T, Petsmart, Staples, Target
766	(from wb), Heights Blvd, Yale St
765b	N Durham Dr, N Shepherd Dr, N Shell/dsl Wendy's Howard Johnson vet, S Valero/dsl Saltgrass Steaks
765a	TC Jester Blvd, S Exxon/dsl, Texaco/dsl Golden Hunan, Starbucks vet
764	Westcott St, Washington Ave, Katy Rd, N Denny's Hampton Inn, S Chevron IHOP, McDonald's Scottish Inn
763	I-610
762	Silber Rd, Post Oak Rd, N Chick-fil-A, Dave&Buster's, Jimmy John's, Panda Express, Red Robin, SteaKountry Chrysler/Dodge/Jeep, Fiat, Firestone/auto, IKEA, Walmart, S Jack-in-the-Box, Shipley Donuts Crowne Plaza, Holiday Inn Express
761b	Antoine Rd, S Exxon/dsl CVS Drug
761a	Wirt Rd, Chimney Rock Rd, S Exxon/dsl CVS Drug
760	Bingle Rd, Voss Rd, N Burger Shack, Hunan Chef, Pueblo Viejo, Starbucks, Subway AT&T, Home Depot, S Shell/dsl Sweet Tomatoes
759	Campbell Rd (from wb), N Ranch Mkt, same as 758b
758b	Blalock Rd, Campbell Rd, N Sonic H, Lowe's, S Chevron/McDonald's/dsl Baskin-Robbins, Goode Co TX

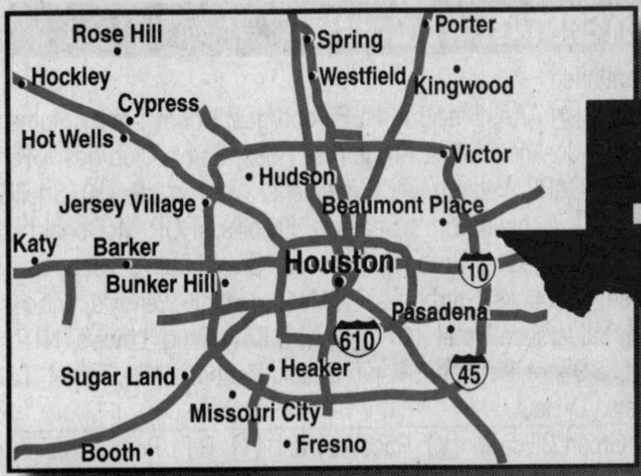

HOUSTON

Exit #	Services
758b	Continued BBQ, Pappy's Cafe, Saltgrass Steaks, Starbucks cleaners, Kroger, Walgreens
758a	Bunker Hill Rd, N Boudreaux's Cajun, Dennys, Egg&I, Five Guys, Freebirds Burritos, Genghis Grill, Jimmy John's, Marble Slab, Olive Garden, Panda Express, Which Wich? Best Buy, Costco/gas, GNC, HEB Foods/dsl, Jo-Ann, Lowe's, Michael's, PepBoys, S American Island Grill, Buffalo Wild Wings, Ciro's Italian, Corner Bakery Cafe, Denis Seafood, Firehouse Subs, Guadalajara Mexican, Kobe Japanese, Longhorn Steaks, Lupe Tortilla, Russo's NY Pizza, Subway Memorial Inn Marshall's, Ross, Verizon
757	Gessner Rd, N Chili's, Chulas Grill, McDonald's, Murphy's Deli, Taco Bell, Wendy's, Whataburger AT&T, CVS Drug, Hobby Lobby, Home Depot, Honda, Radio Shack, Sam's Club/gas, U-Haul, S 59 Diner, Cheesecake Factory, Fuddrucker's, Goode Co. Seafood, Jason's Deli, Pappadeaux Seafood, Pappasito's, Perry's Steaks Westin Hotel H, Firestone/auto, Ford, Macy's, mall, Office Depot, Target
756	TX 8, Sam Houston Tollway
755	Willcrest Rd, N Discount Tire, Lincoln, Mazda, NTB, U-Haul, S Citgo/dsl, Exxon/dsl Brenner's Steaks, Denny's, IHOP, McDonald's, Subway, Taste of TX Candlewood Suites, Extended Stay America, Hampton Inn, Sheraton
754	Kirkwood Rd, N Embassy Suites Audi/Porsche, Lincoln, Toyota/Scion, S Shell/dsl Carrabba's, Prince's Burgers, Shipley Do-Nuts, Spicy Pickle, Starbucks, Taco Cabana, Twin Peaks, Whataburger Chevrolet
753b	Dairy-Ashford Rd, N Infiniti, Lexus, Nissan, Volvo, S Exxon/dsl Chili's, Hibachi Grill, Subway, TX Cattle Steaks Courtyard, Hilton Garden, Holiday Inn Express Cadillac, URGENT CARE
753a	Eldridge Pkwy, N Conoco/dsl Omni Hotel, S Valero/dsl Kwik Kar
751	TX 6, to Addicks, N Shell Bros Pizza, Cattlegard Rest., Quiznos, Waffle House Drury Inn, Homewood Suites, Studio 6, Wyndham, S North China, Salata, Subway Beat Value, Extended Stay America, Fairfield Inn, Hyatt House, La Quinta, Motel 6, TownePlace Suites USPO
750	Park Ten Blvd, eb only, N Red Roof Inn, S Marriott Acura, BMW, Buick/GMC, Hoover RV Ctr
748	Barker-Cypress Rd, N Exxon/Subway BurgerTex Grill, Coaches Grill, El Rancho Mexican, Firehouse Subs, Popeyes, Smoothie Factory, Tony's Mexican Residence Inn H, S Cracker Barrel Hyundai, Subaru, vet, VW
747b a	Fry Rd, N Gulf/dsl, Shell/dsl 5 Guys Burgers, Applebee's, Arby's, Buffalo Wild Wings, Burger King, Chipotle, Denny's, DQ, Jimmy John's, McDonald's, Panda Express, Panera Bread, Pizza Hut, Smoothie King, Sonic, Souper Salad, Subway, Taco Bell, Waffle House, Whataburger Candlewood

TX

[gas icon] = gas [food icon] = food [lodging icon] = lodging [other icon] = other [RS] = rest stop

TX

INTERSTATE 10 Cont'd

747b a Continued Suites AAA, Best Buy, HEB Food/gas, Hobby Lobby, Home Depot, Jo-Ann, Kohl's, Kroger/dsl, Ross, Sam's Club/gas, URGENT CARE, Verizon, vet, Walgreens, Walmart, S Shell/dsl Captain Tom's Seafood, Fazoli's, IHOP, McDonald's, Outback Steaks, Potbelly, Quiznos, Smashburger, Star Chinese, Starbucks, Starbucks, TX Mesquite Grill, Wendy's, Willie's ValuePlace Hotel H, A&T, Katy Drug, Lowe's, NTB, Office Depot, Petsmart, Radio Shack, Randall's Mkt, Target, TJ Maxx, U-Haul

746 W Green Blvd, N RaceWay/dsl BJ's Rest., Chang's Chinese, Cheddar's, Chuy's Mexican, Firehouse Subs, Kublai Khan Stirfry, Longhorn Steaks, Nagoya Japanese, Olive Garden, Orleans Seafood Kitchen, Springcreek BBQ, Stadia Grill, Steak'n Shake, TX Roadhouse, Wild Wings Cafe Holiday Inn Express, Palace Inn, S Carl's Jr, Jimmy Changas Tex-Mex Home2 Christian Bros Automotive, CVS Drug, Ford, Honda

745 Mason Rd, N CarMax, S Shell/dsl, Valero/dsl Babin's Seafood, Blackeyed Pea, Burger King, Carino's Italian, Chick-fil-A, Chili's, CiCi's, Dickey's BBQ, DQ, El Patron Mexican, Freebirds Burrito, Hooters, Jack-in-the-Box, Jason's Deli, KFC, Landry's Seafood, Luby's, McDonald's, Panda Express, Papa John's, Pizza Hut, Popeye's, Rudy's BBQ/gas, SaltGrass Steaks, Schlotzsky's, Subway, Taco Bell, Taco Cabana, Whataburger, Which Wich? Comfort Inn&Suites, Hampton Inn, La Quinta, Motel 6, Super 8 $Tree, 99c Store, AutoZone, Chevrolet, Chrysler/Dodge/Jeep, Discount Tire, Fiesta Foods, Firestone/auto, Goodyear/auto, Hancock Fabrics, HEB Food/gas, Kia, Toyota/Scion, transmissions, Walgreens

743 TX 99, Grand Pkwy, Peek Rd, N La Madeleine, Red Robin H, JC Penney, S Freddy's Steakburgers, Subway Costco/gas, URGENT CARE

741 (742 from wb)Katy-Fort Bend County Rd, Pin Oak Rd, S Murphy USA/dsl, Shell/dsl, Texaco/dsl Alegra Brazilian, Alicia's Mexican, Antonia's Rest, Chick-fil-A, ChuckECheese, CiCi's Pizza, Denny's, Fuddruckers, Jack-in-the-Box, Jimmy John's, JoJo's Mongolian Grill, KFC, LJ Silver/Taco Bell, Los Cucos, Pizza Hut, Popeyes, Rainforest Cafe, Red Lobster, Smashburger, Starbucks, Subway, Subway, TGIFriday's, Whataburger Best Western, Comfort Suites, Coumtry Inn & Suites, Hilton Garden, Residence Inn, SpringHill Suites H, $Tree, AT&T, BassPro Shops, BooksAMillion, Discount Tire, HEB/dsl, Katy Mills Outlet/famous brands, Marshall's, Nissan, Ross, URGENT CARE, Verizon, Walgreens, Walmart/McDonald's

740 FM 1463, N Exxon/dsl, S Shell/McDonald's/dsl

737 Pederson Rd, N Loves/Arby's/dsl/scales/24hr, S Camping World RV Super Ctr, Holiday World RV Ctr

735 Igloo Rd

734 Woods Rd

732 FM 359, to Brookshire, N FLYING J/Denny's/dsl/LP/scales/24hr/ @, Exxon/Chester's/dsl, Shell Church's, Orlando's Pizza, Subway Executive Inn RV camping, S Chevron/dsl, Shell/McDonald's/dsl Burger King, Jack-in-the-Box, Popeyes, Taco Bell Super 8 truck lube, truckwash

731 FM 1489, to Koomey Rd, N Exxon/dsl Ernesto's Mexican Brooke Hotel RV Park, S La Quinta

729 Peach Ridge Rd, Donigan Rd (730 from wb)

726 Chew Rd (from eb), S golf

725 Mlcak Rd (from wb)

SEALY

723 FM 1458, to San Felipe, N Exxon/Subway/dsl/scales/24hr Peterbilt, to Stephen F Austin SP (3mi), S Riverside Tire

721 (from wb) US 90, N Shell/Chester's/dsl Ford

720a Outlet Ctr Dr, N Shell/Chester's/dsl

720 TX 36, to Sealy, N Shell/dsl China Buffet, DQ, Hartz Chicken, McDonald's, Sonic, Tony's Rest. $General, Jones RV Ctr, O'Reilly Parts, Walgreens, S Chevron/dsl, Murphy USA/dsl, Shell/dsl, Texaco/dsl Cazadore's Mexican, Hinze's BBQ, Jack-in-the-Box, Jin's Asian, Maribelli Italian, Pizza Hut, Subway, Whataburger Best Value Inn, Countryside Inn, Holiday Inn Express, Super 8 Verizon, Walmart/Subway

718 US 90 (from eb), to Sealy

716 Pyka Rd, N Exxon/dsl/rest./showers/24hr/ @

713 Beckendorff Rd

709 FM 2761, Bernardo Rd

704 FM 949, N Happy Oaks RV Park (3mi)

699 FM 102, to Eagle Lake, N Happy Oaks RV Park, S Eagle Lake SP (14mi)

698 Alleyton Rd, N Mikeska's BBQ Lone Star Inn, S Shell/Taco Bell/BBQ/dsl Chrysler/Dodge/Jeep, Ford

697mm Little Colorado River

COLUMBUS

696 TX 71, Columbus, N Chevron/dsl, Shell/dsl #1 Buffet, Cantus Rest., El Rey Mexican, Jack-in-the-Box, Pizza Hut, Schobel's Rest., Whataburger Columbus Inn, Holiday Inn Express H, AT&T, AutoZone, HEB Foods, Walmart, S Conoco/Church's/Subway/dsl, Phillips 66/dsl, Valero/dsl Los Cabos Mexican, McDonald's, Nancy's Steaks, Sonic Best Value, Comfort Inn, LaQuinta Columbus RV Park

695 TX 71 (from wb), to La Grange

693 FM 2434, to Glidden

692mm **RS both lanes, full facilities, litter barrels, petwalk RV dump, vending**

689 US 90, to Hattermann Lane, N Whispering Oaks RV Park

682 FM 155, to Wiemar, N Shell/dsl, Valero/dsl DQ, McDonald's, Subway/Texas Burger Scottish Inn H, $General, Lowe's Mkt, Tire Pros, S Chevron/Church's/dsl/24hr, Loves/Chester's/Wendy's/dsl/scales/24hr Buick/Chevrolet/GMC

678mm E Navidad River

677 US 90

674 US 77, Schulenburg, N Exxon/dsl, Stripes/Taco Co McDonald's, Oak Ridge Smokehouse Executive Inn, Oak Ridge Motel Ford, Potter Country Store, S Shell/dsl, Valero/Subway Chez Grill, DQ, Frank's Rest., Guadalajara Mexican, Whataburger Best Western, Holiday Inn Express $General, Family$, Schulenberg RV Park

672mm W Navidad River

668 FM 2238, to Engle

661 TX 95, FM 609, to Flatonia, N Citgo/dsl Joel's BBQ, Robert's Steaks, San Jose Mexican Flatonia RV Ranch (1mi), S Exxon/dsl, Shell/McDonald's/Grumpy's Rest./motel/dsl, Valero DQ, Subway Carefree Inn, Hampton Inn $General, NAPA

658mm **both lanes, litter barrels**

653 US 90, Waelder, N Shell/dsl

649 TX 97, to Waelder

642 TX 304, to Gonzales

637 FM 794, to Harwood

632 US 90/183, to Gonzales, N Loves/Subway/dsl/scales/24hr Best Western, Coachway Inn (2mi), S Buc-ee's/dsl camping, to Palmetto SP (5mi)

630mm San Marcos River

INTERSTATE 10 Cont'd

Exit #	Services
628	TX 80, to Luling, N 🔲 Citgo (2mi), Valero/pizza/dsl/24hr 🍴 DQ (2mi) 🔲 H, Riverbend RV Park
625	Darst Field Rd
624.5mm	Smith Creek
621mm	both lanes, weigh sta
620	FM 1104
618mm	🆁🆂 both lanes, full 🦽 facilities, litter barrels, petwalk 🔲 🏧
617	FM 2438, to Kingsbury
614	toll 130 N, to Austin, Waco, 🔲 no services
612	US 90
611mm	Geronimo Creek
610	TX 123, to San Marcos, N 🔲 Exxon/dsl, Shell/Subway/dsl 🍴 Bella Sera Italian, Chili's, IHOP, Los Cucos Mexican 🛏 Comfort Inn, Days Inn, Hampton Inn, Holiday Inn Express, Towne-Place Suites 🔲 Carters Tires, S 🔲 Valero/dsl 🍴 Taco Cabana 🔲 H
609	TX 123, Austin St, S 🔲 Phillips 66/dsl 🔲 Chevrolet, Home Depot
607	TX 46, FM 78, to New Braunfels, N 🔲 Valero/Jack-in-the-Box/dsl 🛏 Motel 6 🔲 Ford, S 🔲 Chevron/dsl, Exxon/dsl 🍴 Bill Miller BBQ, Dixie Grille, McDonald's, Subway, Whataburger 🛏 La Quinta, Super 8 🔲 Chrysler/Dodge/Jeep
605	FM 464, N 🔲 Twin Palms RV Park
605mm	Guadalupe River
604	FM 725, to Lake McQueeney, N 🔲 Loves/Arby's/dsl/scales/24hr 🔲 Explore USA RV Ctr, Twin Palms RV Park
603	US 90 E, US 90A, to Seguin, N 🔲 D&A RV Park, Seguin RV Ctr
601	FM 775, to New Berlin, N 🔲 Chevron/Subway/dsl/scales/24hr
600	Schwab Rd
599	FM 465, to Marion
599mm	Santa Clara Creek
597	Santa Clara Rd, N 🔲 auto racetrack
595	Zuehl Rd
594mm	Cibolo Creek
593	FM 2538, Trainer Hale Rd, N 🔲 Texaco/dsl 🔲 tires, S 🔲 Exxon/Lucille's Rest./dsl/24hr
593mm	Woman Hollering Creek
591	FM 1518, to Schertz, N 🔲 Alamo Trvl Ctr/Shell/dsl 🔲 repair
589	Pfeil Rd, Graytown Rd
589mm	Salatrillo Creek
587	LP 1604, Randolph AFB, to Universal City
585.5mm	Escondido Creek
585	FM 1516, to Converse, N 🔲 Shell/Church's/dsl/scales/24hr 🛏 Best Western, S 🔲 Kenworth, Peterbilt/GMC/Freightliner
585mm	Martinez Creek
583	Foster Rd, N 🔲 FLYING J/Denny's/dsl/LP/scales/24hr/ @, Valero/Subway/dsl/24hr 🍴 Jack-in-the-Box 🛏 La Quinta 🔲 Blue Beacon, Speedco Lube, Tire Mart, S 🔲 TA/Chevron/Burger King/Pizza Hut/Popeye's/dsl/24hr/ @
582.5mm	Rosillo Creek
582	Ackerman Rd, Kirby, N 🔲 Pilot/Subway/dsl/scales/24hr, S 🔲 Petro/Iron Skillet/dsl/scales/24hr/ @ 🍴 El Rodeo Mexican 🛏 Knights Inn 🔲 Blue Beacon, Petrolube
581	I-410
580	LP 13, WW White Rd, N 🔲 Chevron/dsl 🍴 El Jacalito, La Playa Seafood, Wendy's 🛏 Motel 6, Red Roof Inn, Rodeway Inn 🔲 tires, S 🔲 Exxon/7-11 🍴 Bill Miller BBQ, El Rodeo Mexican, Lazaritas Mexican, McDonald's, Pizza Hut, Popeye's, Sonic, Subway 🛏 Best Value, EconoLodge, Super 8 🔲 $General, Ford/Volvo Trucks, tires/repair

Exit #	Services
579	Houston St, N 🔲 Valero/dsl 🛏 Travelodge 🔲 Penske, S 🔲 Chevron 🛏 Comfort Inn, Days Inn, Passport Inn
578	Pecan Valley Dr, ML King Dr, S 🔲 Shell/Subway/dsl
577	US 87 S, to Roland Ave, S 🍴 Whataburger 🛏 Super 8
576	New Braunfels Ave, Gevers St, S 🔲 Valero 🍴 McDonald's
575	Pine St, Hackberry St, S 🍴 Little Red Barn Steaks
574	I-37, US 281
573	Probandt St, N 🍴 Jack-in-the-Box, Miller's BBQ, S 🔲 Valero 🔲 tires/repair, to SA Missions HS
	I-10 and I-35 run together 3 miles. See I-35, exits 156-154a.
569c	Santa Rosa St, 🔲 to Our Lady of the Lake U, downtown
568	spur 421, Culebra Ave, Bandera Ave, S 🔲 to St Marys U
567	Lp 345, Fredericksburg Rd (from eb upper level accesses I-35 S, I-10 E, US 87 S, lower level accesses I-35 N)
566b	Fresno Dr, S 🔲 Exxon/dsl 🛏 Galaxy Inn
566a	West Ave, N 🔲 Exxon/7-11 🍴 DQ, Subway, Whataburger 🔲 CarCare
565c	(from wb), access to same as 565 a b, S 🔲 Shell 🍴 Jimador Mexican, Starbucks 🛏 La Quinta
565b	Vance Jackson Rd, N 🔲 Murphy USA/dsl 🍴 Bill Miller BBQ, IHOP 🛏 Comfort Inn, Days Inn, EconoLodge 🔲 Walmart, S 🔲 Shell/dsl 🛏 Holiday Inn Express
565a	Crossroads Blvd, Balcone's Heights, N 🔲 Shell/dsl 🛏 Howard Johnson 🔲 vet, S 🔲 Valero/dsl 🍴 Crossroads BBQ, Dave&Buster's, Denny's, El Pollo Loco, McDonald's, Whataburger 🛏 SpringHill Suites 🔲 Firestone/auto, Hobby Lobby, mall, Mazda, Office Depot, Target
564b a	I-410, services off of I-410 W, Fredericksburg Rd
563	Callaghan Rd, N 🔲 Valero 🍴 Las Palapas Mexican, Subway 🛏 Embassy Suites, Marriott 🔲 $General, Ford, Sprouts Mkt, Toyota/Scion, S 🔲 Exxon/7-11 🍴 Mamacita's Rest. 🔲 Lowe's
561	Wurzbach Rd, N 🔲 Texaco/dsl 🍴 Bolo's Grille, Broadway 5050 Grill, County Line BBQ, Egg&I, Firehouse Subs, Fuddrucker's, Honeybaked Ham, Jason's Deli, Pappasito's Cantina, Popeye's, Sea Island Shrimphouse, Taste Of China, TX Land&Cattle, Wasabi Grill 🛏 Extended Stay America, Homewood Suites, Hyatt Place, Motel 6, Staybridge Suites 🔲 AutoZone, BigLots, HEB Food/gas, Office Depot, Porsche, Tuesday Morning, S 🔲 Shell/dsl 🍴 210 Ceviche Seafood, Alamo Café, Arby's, Chester's Burgers, China Sea, Church's, Denny's, El Taco Tote, Jack-in-the-Box, Mamma Margie's Mexican, McDonald's, Pizza Hut, Ruby Tuesday, Sumo Japanese, Taco Bell, Wendy's 🛏 Baymont Inn, Best Western, Candlewood Suites, Drury Inn, Hawthorn Suites, La Quinta, Motel 6, Sleep Inn 🔲 H, CarMax
560b	frontage rd (from eb), same as 561
560a	Huebner Rd, N 🍴 CA Pizza Kitchen, Chipotle, Fare Wok, Genghis Grill, La Madeleine, Macaroni Grill, Panera Bread, Pericos Mexican, Salata, SaltGrass Steaks 🔲 Cadillac, Chrysler/

SAN ANTONIO (vertical side tab)

KIRBY (vertical side tab)

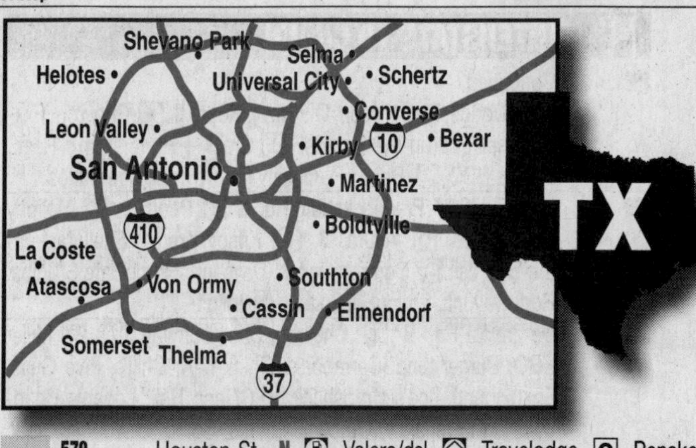

E INTERSTATE 10 Cont'd

SAN ANTONIO

560a Continued
Jeep/Dodge, Fiat, Nissan, Old Navy, Ross, **S** [gas] Chevron, Exxon, Shell/Jack-in-the-Box/dsl [food] Cracker Barrel, Jim's Rest., Miller's BBQ [lodging] Days Inn, Quality Inn, TownePlace Suites

559 Lp 335, US 87, Fredericksburg Rd, **N** [food] Pearl Inn [lodging] Holiday Inn Express [other] Acura, **S** [food] Krispy Kreme, Shell/Jack-in-the-Box/dsl [lodging] Comfort Suites, Days Inn, HomeGate Studios, Rodeway Inn, SpringHill Suites [other] Infiniti

558 De Zavala Rd, **N** [gas] Chevron, Shell/Subway [food] Bill Miller BBQ, Burger King, Carrabba's, Chick-fil-A, Chili's, Five Guys, Fox&Hound, Joe's Crabshack, KFC/Taco Bell, Logan's Roadhouse, McDonald's, Outback Steaks, Sonic, Starbucks, Taco Cabana, The Earl of Sandwich, Wendy's [other] HEB Foods, Home Depot, Marshall's, PetCo, Petsmart, Steinmart, Target, **S** [food] IHOP, Popeyes, Schlotzsky's [lodging] Days Inn, SpringHill Suites, Studio6 [other] Discount Tire, Sam's Club/gas, Verizon, Walmart

557 Spur 53, **N** [gas] Exxon/dsl [food] Cheddar's, Chuy's Mexican [lodging] Best Western, EconoLodge, Howard Johnson, Super 8 [other] Audi, Chevrolet, Hyundai, Jaguar/Mazerati/Ferrari, **S** [gas] Valero/Subway/dsl [food] A&W/LJ Silver, Cici's Pizza, Huhot Chinese, IHOP, Matamoro's Cantina, Quiznos, Twin Peaks, Whataburger, Zio's Italian [lodging] Holiday Inn [other] Costco/gas, Land Rover, Sams Club/gas, Univ of TX at San Antonio, Walmart

556b frontage rd

556a to Anderson Lp, **S** [other] to Seaworld, Six Flags

555 La Quintera Pkwy, **N** [food] 54th St Rest., BJ's Rest., Bob's Chophouse, Chick-fil-A, Coldstone, Freddy's Steakburger, Hofbrau at the Rim, Islamorada Rest., Maggiano's Little Italy, McDonald's/playplace, Mimi's Cafe, Popeyes, Red Robin, Starbucks, TGIFriday's, Tiago's, Whataburger [lodging] Courtyard, Hilton Garden, Residence Inn [other] $Tree, AT&T, Bass Pro Shops, Best Buy, Dick's, GNC, JC Penney, Lowe's, Michaels, Old Navy, Ross, Staples, Target, TJ Maxx, World Mkt, **S** [food] Applebee's, Longhorn Steaks, Olive Garden, Red Lobster [lodging] Drury Inn, La Quinta, Motel 6 [other] Honda, to La Cantera Pkwy

554 Camp Bullis Rd, **N** [gas] Texaco/dsl [other] Russell CP, **S** [gas] Shell/dsl [lodging] Rodeway Inn

551 Boerne Stage Rd (from wb), to Leon Springs, **N** [gas] Shamrock/dsl [food] Rudy's BBQ, Sonic, **S** [food] Bourbon St Seafood, Las Palapas Mexican, Longhorns Rest., Papa Nacho's, Starbucks, Subway [other] CarX, GNC, HEB Foods/dsl

550 FM 3351, Ralph Fair Rd, **N** [gas] Exxon/McDonald's/dsl, Valero/dsl [food] Willie's Cafe [lodging] La Quinta, **S** [gas] Shell/Domino's/dsl [food] Schlotsky's, Taco Cabana [other] Walgreens

546 Fair Oaks Pkwy, Tarpon Dr, **N** [food] Papa John's [other] American Dream RV Ctr, Harley-Davidson, vet, **S** [gas] Chevron/dsl/café, Exxon/dsl/café [other] Fair Oaks Automotive, Goodyear/auto, Hoover RV Ctr

543 Boerne Stage Rd, to Scenic LP Rd, **N** [gas] Valero/Subway/dsl [lodging] Fairfield Inn [other] Ancira RV Ctr, Buick/GMC, Chevrolet, Chrysler/Dodge/Jeep, Ford, NAPA, tires/repair, to Cascade Caverns/camping (3mi), **S** [other] Explore USA RV Ctr, Mercedes, Nissan, Toyota/Scion

542 (from wb), **N** [gas] Shamrock [food] Domino's, Pizza Hut, Subway, Wendy's [other] $Tree, Alamo Fiesta RV Park, same as 540, Verizon

540 TX 46, to New Braunfels, **N** [gas] Exxon/Taco Bell/dsl, Murphy USA/dsl, Shell/dsl [food] Burger King, Centinela Mexican, Church's, Denny's, DQ, Guadalajara Mexican, Little Caesars, Papa Murphy's, Pizza Hut, Shanghai Chinese, Sonic, Subway, Taco Cabana, Wendy's [lodging] Best Value, Comfort Inn, Motel 6 [other] AutoZone, HEB Food/dsl, Radio Shack, Verizon, vet, Walgreens,

540 Continued
Walmart, **S** [food] Chili's, Starbucks, Whataburger [lodging] Hampton Inn [other] [H], Home Depot

539 Johns Rd, **N** [lodging] La Quinta, **S** [gas] Valero/dsl/LP

538mm Cibolo Creek

538 Ranger Creek Rd

537 US 87, to Boerne

533 FM 289, Welfare, **N** [food] PoPo Family Rest. [other] Top of the Hill RV Park (1mi)

532mm Little Joshua Creek

531mm **[picnic] wb, litter barrels**

530mm Big Joshua Creek

529.5mm **[picnic] eb, litter barrels**

527 FM 1621 (from wb), to Waring

526.5mm Holiday Creek

524 TX 27, FM 1621, to Waring, **N** [other] vet, **1mi S** [gas] Chevron, Shell/dsl

523.5mm Guadalupe River

523 US 87 N, to Comfort, **N** [gas] Chevron/Chicken Express/dsl, Loves/McDonald's/Subway/dsl/scales/24hr, **S** [gas] Exxon/dsl [food] DQ [lodging] Executive Inn [other] $General, RV Park/LP

521.5mm Comfort Creek

520 FM 1341, to Cypress Creek Rd

515mm Cypress Creek

514mm **[RS] both lanes, full [handicapped] facilities, litter barrels, petwalk [phone] [picnic] playground, RV dump, vending, wireless internet**

KERRVILLE

508 TX 16, Kerrville, **N** [gas] Exxon/dsl [other] Buick/Cadillac/Chevrolet, **0-2 mi S** [gas] Exxon, Shell/McDonald's/dsl/24hr, Stripes/Taco Co, Valero/dsl/e-85 [food] Bamboo Asian, Bella Sera Italian, Chicken Express, Cracker Barrel, DQ, IHOP, Jack-in-the-Box, Little Caesars, McDonald's, Schlotzsky's, Sonic, Taco Bell, Taco Casa, Valentino's Italian [lodging] Best Value Inn, Best Western, Big Texas Inn, Days Inn, Hampton Inn, Holiday Inn Express, La Quinta, Motel 6, Quality Inn, Super 8, Yo Ranch Hotel [other] [H], $Tree, Advance Parts, BigLots, Hastings Books, Home Depot, Kerrville RV Ctr, Lowe's, O'Reilly Parts, vet, Walgreens

505 FM 783, to Kerrville, **S** [gas] Exxon/dsl, **3 mi S on TX 27** [gas] Exxon/dsl, Phillips 66/dsl, Stripes/Taco Co/dsl [food] Billy Gene's Rest., Chili's, CiCi's, Culver's, Del Norte Rest., Dickey's BBQ, DQ, Fuddruckers, Mamacita's, McDonald's, Pizza Hut, Popeyes, Sonic, Starbucks, Subway, Taco Casa, Wendy's, Whataburger [lodging] Inn of the Hills [other] $General, AT&T, AutoZone, Chrysler/Dodge/Jeep, CVS Drug, Discount Tire, HEB Foods/gas, Take It Easy RV Resort, Tuesday Morning, Walmart/McDonald's

503.5mm **scenic views both lanes, litter barrels**

501 FM 1338, **N** [other] Buckhorn RV Resort, **S** [other] KOA (2mi)

497mm **picnic area both lanes, tables, litter barrels**

492 FM 479

490 TX 41

488 TX 27, to Ingram, Mountain Home

484 Midway Rd

477 US 290, to Fredericksburg

476.5mm service Rd eb

472 Old Segovia Rd

465 FM 2169, to Segovia, **S** [gas] Phillips 66/rest./dsl [lodging] EconoLodge/RV park

464.5mm Johnson Fork Creek

462 US 83 S, to Uvalde

461mm **[picnic] eb, litter barrels**

460 (from wb), to Junction

459mm **[picnic] wb, litter barrels**

 = gas = food = lodging = other = rest stop

INTERSTATE 10 Cont'd

JUNCTION

Exit #	Services
457	FM 2169, to Junction, N Shell/dsl, S Days Inn RV camping, S. Llano River SP
456.5mm	Llano River
456	US 83/377, Junction, N Alon/dsl, Chevron/dsl, Valero/McDonald's/dsl/24hr Cooper's BBQ, Tia Nina's Mexican Motel 6, S Big Star/dsl, Conoco/dsl, Exxon/Church's/dsl, Shell/Quizno's/dsl DQ, Isaack Rest., La Familia Mexican, Lum's BBQ, Sonic Best Western, Lazy T Motel, Legends Inn, Rodeway Inn, Sun Valley Motel, The Hills Motel H, $General, Best Hardware, CarQuest, Family$, Lowe's Mkt, Plumley's Store, Radio Shack, S Llano RV Park, to S Llano River SP
452.5mm	Bear Creek
451	RM 2291, to Cleo Rd
448mm	North Creek
445	RM 1674, S camping
444.5mm	Stark Creek
442mm	Copperas Creek
442	RM 1674, to Ft McKavett, N to Ft McKavett SHS
439mm	N Llano River
438	Lp 291 (from wb), to Roosevelt, same as 437
437	Lp 291 (from eb, no EZ return), to Roosevelt, **1 mi** N Simon Bros Mercantile/dsl USPO
429	RM 3130, to Harrell
423mm	**parking area both lanes, litter barrels**
420	RM 3130, to Baker Rd
412	Allison Rd, RM 3130
404	RM 3130, RM 864, N to Ft McKavett St HS, **3 mi** S Stripes/Taco Co Holiday Host Motel H

SONORA

Exit #	Services
400	US 277, Sonora, N Shell/dsl Sutton Co Steaks Days Inn, S Alon/7-11/dsl, Chevron/dsl, Stripes/dsl DQ, La Mexicana Rest., Pizza Hut, Sonic, Taco Grill Best Western, Comfort Inn, Economy Inn Alco, Family$, USPO
399	(from eb)LP 467, Sonora, N Days Inn, S Chevron/dsl, Stripes/Taco Co DQ H, RV camping
394mm	**both lanes, full facilities, litter barrels, petwalk RV dump**
392	RM 1989, Caverns of Sonora Rd, **8 mi** S Caverns of Sonora Camping
388	RM 1312 (from wb)
381	RM 1312 (from eb)
372	Taylor Box Rd, N Exxon/rest./dsl/scales/24hr Super 8 auto museum, Circle Bar RV Park
368	LP 466, N same as 365 & 363

OZONA

Exit #	Services
365	TX 163, Ozona, N Chevron/dsl, Stripes/Godfather's/Taco Co/dsl, Valero/dsl Cafe Next Door, DQ, Sonic, Subway Best Value Inn, Best Western, Economy Inn/RV Park, Hillcrest Inn, Holiday Inn Express H, $General, dsl/auto repair, NAPA, to David Crockett Mon, S Chevron, Pilot/dsl El Chato's city park
363	Lp 466, to Ozona
361	RM 2083, Pandale Rd
357mm	Eureka Draw
351mm	Howard Draw
350	FM 2398, to Howard Draw
349mm	**parking area wb, litter barrels**
346mm	**parking area eb, litter barrels**
343	TX 290 W, S Ft. Lancaster Historic Site
337	Live Oak Rd
336.5mm	Live Oak Creek
328	River Rd, Sheffield
327.5mm	Pecos River

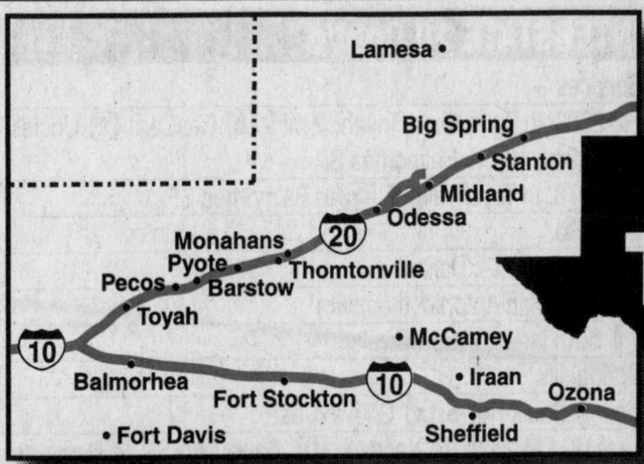

FT STOCKTON

Exit #	Services
325	TX 290, TX 349, to Iraan, Sheffield, N H
320	frontage rd
314	frontage rd
309mm	**both lanes, full facilities, litter barrels, petwalk wireless internet**
307	US 190, FM 305, to Iraan, N H
298	RM 2886
294	FM 11, Bakersfield, N Exxon, S Chevron/café/dsl phone
288	Ligon Rd, N many windmills
285	McKenzie Rd, S Domaine Cordier Ste Genevieve Winery
279mm	litter barrels, picnic area eb, tables
277	FM 2023
273	US 67/385, to McCamey, **picnic area wb, tables, litter barrels**
272	University Rd
264	Warnock Rd, N Fort Stockton RV Park/Roadrunner Cafe
261	US 290 W, US 385 S, N Exxon/dsl, S Loves/Carl's Jr/dsl/scales/24hr, Shell/dsl, Stripes/dsl DQ, Pizza Hut, Sonic, Subway All Inn, Budget Inn, Deluxe Inn, Executive Inn H, RV camping, to Big Bend NP
259b a	(259 from eb)TX 18, FM 1053, Ft Stockton, N Alon/dsl, Apache Fuel Ctr/dsl, Shell/Burger King/dsl John Chihuahua's Mexican I-10 RV Park, tires, S FLYING J/Subway/dsl/scales/24hr H
257	US 285, to Pecos, Ft Stockton, N Stripes/Exxon/Taco Co/dsl/scales24hr Comanche Land RV Park, golf, S Alon/dsl, Chevron/dsl, Exxon/dsl, Shell/dsl DQ, KFC/Taco Bell, McDonald's, Pecos Roadhouse, Pizza Hut, Pizza Pro, Sonic, Steak House, Subway Atrium Inn, Best Western, Candlewood Suites, Days Inn, Hampton Inn, La Quinta, Quality Inn, Texan Inn $General, Ace Hardware, AutoZone, Buick/Chevrolet, CarQuest, Family$, Firestone/auto, Lowe's Foods, McKissick Tires, O'Reilly Parts
256	to US 385 S, Ft Stockton, N HillTop RV, **1 mi** S Shell/dsl Dragon Buffet, Howard's Drive-In, K-Bob's Steaks, Subway Comfort Suites, Holiday Inn Express, Motel 6, Sleep Inn, Super 8 auto/RV repair, Big Bend NP, Ford, to Ft Stockton Hist Dist, vet, Walmart
253	FM 2037, to Belding
248	US 67, FM 1776, to Alpine, S to Big Bend NP
246	Firestone
241	Kennedy Rd
235	Mendel Rd
233mm	**both lanes, full facilities, litter barrels, petwalk**
229	Hovey Rd
222	Hoefs Rd
214	(from wb), FM 2448
212	TX 17, FM 2448, to Pecos, N **picnic area, litter barrels,** S I-10 Fuel/café/dsl, Saddleback RV Camping
209	TX 17, S Ft Davis NHS, to Balmorhea SP, to Davis Mtn SP

TX

VAN HORN

EL PASO

INTERSTATE 10 Cont'd

Exit #	Services
206	FM 2903, to Balmorhea, Toyah, **2 mi** S 🚗 GasCard 🍴 Uncles Rest. (2mi) ⊙ to Balmorhea SP
192	FM 3078, to Toyahvale, S ⊙ to Balmorhea SP
188	Giffin Rd
187	I-20, to Ft Worth, Dallas
186	I-10, E to San Antonio (from wb)
185mm	🚮 **both lanes, litter barrels**
184	Springhills
181	Cherry Creek Rd, S 🚗 Chevron/dsl
176	TX 118, FM 2424, to Kent, S ⊙ Davis Mtn SP, Ft Davis, to McDonald Observatory
173	Hurd's Draw Rd
166	Boracho Sta
159	Plateau, N 🚗 Exxon/rest./dsl/24hr
153	Michigan Flat
146	Wild Horse Rd
146mm	**weigh sta wb**
145mm	🅿 **both lanes, full ♿ facilities, litter barrels, petwalk** 🚮 **wireless internet**
140b	Ross Dr, Van Horn, N 🚗 Chevron/dsl, Exxon/dsl, ◆Loves/Subway/dsl/scales/24hr 🛏 Days Inn, Desert Inn, Sands Motel/rest. ⊙ Desert Willow RV Park, repair, S ⊙ Mountain View RV Park/dump
140a	US 90, TX 54, Van Horn Dr, N 🛏 Hotel El Capitan ⊙ 🅷, NAPA, S 🚗 ▦/Wendy's/dsl/scales/24hr, Valero/dsl 🍴 Papa's Pantry ⊙ dsl/tire repair, KOA, RV Dump
138	Lp 10, to Van Horn, N 🍴 Chuy's Rest. 🛏 Budget Inn, EconoLodge, King's Inn, Knights Inn, Motel 6, Red Roof Inn, Value Inn, Whitten Inn ⊙ $General, auto/dsl repair, city park, Eagles Nest RV Park, Oasis RV Park, Porter Foods, UPSO, visitor info, S 🚗 Chevron/dsl/24hr 🍴 McDonald's 🛏 Hampton Inn, Quality Inn, Super 8 ⊙ tires/repair
137mm	**weigh sta eb**
136mm	**scenic overlook wb** 🚮 **litter barrels**
135mm	Mountain/Central time zone line
133	(from wb) frontage rd
129	to Hot Wells, Allamore
108	to Sierra Blanca (from wb), same as 107
107	FM 1111, Sierra Blanca Ave, N 🚗 Exxon/Subway/dsl/24hr 🍴 Delfina's Mexican ⊙ to Hueco Tanks SP, truck/tire repair, USPO, S 🚗 Chevron/dsl 🛏 Americana Inn ⊙ Stagecoach Trading Post
105	(106 from wb)Lp 10, Sierra Blanca, same as 107
102.5mm	**insp sta eb**
99	Lasca Rd, N 🚮 **both lanes, litter barrels, no restrooms**
98mm	🚮 **eb, litter barrels, no restrooms**
95	frontage rd (from eb)
87	FM 34, S 🚗 gas/dsl
85	Esperanza Rd
81	FM 2217
78	TX 20 W, to McNary
77mm	**truck parking area wb**
72	spur 148, to Ft Hancock, S 🚗 Shell/dsl 🍴 Angie's Rest. 🛏 Ft Hancock Motel ⊙ USPO
68	Acala Rd
55	Tornillo
51mm	🅿 **both lanes, full ♿ facilities, litter barrels, petwalk** 🚮
49	FM 793, Fabens, S 🚗 FastTrak/dsl 🍴 Church's, Little Caesar's, McDonald's, Subway 🛏 Fabens Inn/Cafe ⊙ Family$, San Eli Foods
42	FM 1110, to Clint, S 🚗 Express/dsl 🍴 Cotton Eyed Joe's, Mamacita's Rest. 🛏 Adobe Inn, Best Western, Cotton Valley Motel/RV Park/rest./dump
37	FM 1281, Horizon Blvd, N 🚗 ⊕FLYING J/Denny's/dsl/scales/24hr/ @, ◆Loves/Chester's/Subway/dsl/scales/24hr/ @ 🛏 Americana Inn ⊙ Freightliner, RV Camping, Speedco Lube, S 🚗 Petro/Valero/Iron Skillet/Subway/dsl/scales/24hr/ @ 🍴 McDonald's 🛏 Deluxe Inn ⊙ Blue Beacon
35	Eastlake Blvd.
34	TX 375, Americas Ave, N 🚗 Chevron/dsl, Valero/Subway/dsl 🛏 Microtel, ValuePlace ⊙ Mission RV Camping, Peterbilt, U-Haul, S ⊙ El Paso Museum of Hist
32	FM 659, Zaragosa Rd, N 🚗 Alon/7-11 🍴 Applebee's, Barrigos Mexican, BJ's Rest., Cheddar's, Chico's Tacos, Chipotle Mexican, Corner Bakery Cafe, Famous Dave's, Five Guys, Furr's Buffet, Genghis Grill, Great American Steaks, IHOP, Jaci-in-the-Box, Jason's Deli, Krispy Kreme, La Malinche Mexican, Logan's Roadhouse, Macaroni Grill, Mama Fu's Asian, McDonald's, Outback Steaks, Pei Wei, Peter Piper Pizza, Potbelly, Sonic, Starbucks, Taco Bell, Village Inn, Whataburger 🛏 Courtyard, Hampton Inn, Holiday Inn Express ⊙ AT&T, Chevrolet, Discount Tire, GNC, Kohl's, Lowe's, Michaels, Nissan, Office Depot, Ross, Walgreens, Which Wich, World Mkt, S 🚗 Valero/dsl 🍴 Gallego's Mexican ⊙ city park, vet, Volvo/Mack
30	Lee Trevino Dr, N 🚗 Exxon 🍴 Denny's, Los Canarios Mexican, Whataburger 🛏 La Quinta, Motel 6, Red Roof Inn, Studio 6 ⊙ Discount Tire, Firestone/auto, Ford, Home Depot, Kenworth/Ford Trucks, Lexus, Mazda, Toyota/Scion, S ⊙ Chrysler/Dodge/Jeep
29	Lomaland Dr, S 🚗 Alon/7-11 🛏 Ramada ⊙ Harley-Davidson
28b	Yarbrough Dr, El Paso, N 🚗 Murphy USA, Shell/Coldstone/dsl, Texaco 🍴 Buffalo Wild Wings, Burger King, ChuckECheese, Corner Bakery, Dunkin Donuts, Grandy's, Hayashi Japanese, Hong Kong Buffet, LJ Silver, McDonald's, Peter Piper Pizza, Sonic, Subway, TX Roadhouse, Wendy's, Whataburger, Wienerschnitzel 🛏 Days Inn ⊙ 🅷, AT&T, Big Lots, Office Depot, Radio Shack, Ranch Mkt, Ross, Walmart, S 🚗 Rudy's BBQ, Valero/dsl 🍴 Applebee's, Fuddrucker's, Julio's Cafe, La Malinche Mexican, Lin's Buffet, Pizza Hut, Rudy's BBQ/gas, Shangri-La, Villa Del Mar 🛏 Comfort Inn, InTown Suites, La Quinta ⊙ 🅷
28a	FM 2316, McRae Blvd, N 🚗 Texaco/dsl, Valero 🍴 Pizza Hut 🛏 La Quinta ⊙ 🅷, Jo-Ann Fabrics, K-Mart, Murphy USA/dsl, S 🚗 Circle K/dsl 🍴 Fuddruckers, Gabriel's Mexican, Pizza Hut 🛏 La Quinta, Quality Inn ⊙ NAPA, vet
27	Hunter Dr, Viscount Blvd, N 🚗 Alon/7-11, Valero/dsl 🍴 Grand China Buffet, Taco Bell 🛏 La Quinta ⊙ $General, $Tree, Jo-Ann, S 🚗 Alon/7-11, Exxon/dsl 🍴 Whataburger ⊙ Family$, Food City
26	Hawkins Blvd, El Paso, N 🚗 Shamrock, Shell 🍴 Arby's, Chipotle Mexican, Firehouse Subs, Five Guys, Landry's Seafood, Luby's, Olive Garden, Starbucks, Twin Peaks ⊙ AT&T, Barnes&Noble, Best Buy, Dick's, Dillard's, JC Penney, Macy's, Old Navy, Petsmart, Sam's Club/gas, Sears/auto, Steinmart, TJ Maxx, Verizon, Walgreens, Walmart, S 🚗 Valero/dsl 🍴 McDonald's, Village Inn 🛏 Super 8 ⊙ Tony Lama Boots
25	Airway Blvd, N 🚗 Shell/dsl 🍴 Carino's, Famous Dave's, Starbucks, Whataburger 🛏 Comfort Inn, Courtyard, Hampton Inn, Holiday Inn, Residence Inn ⊙ El Paso ✈, VW/Volvo/Mercedes, S 🚗 Chevron/Subway/dsl/24hr 🛏 Holiday Inn Express, Staybridge Suites

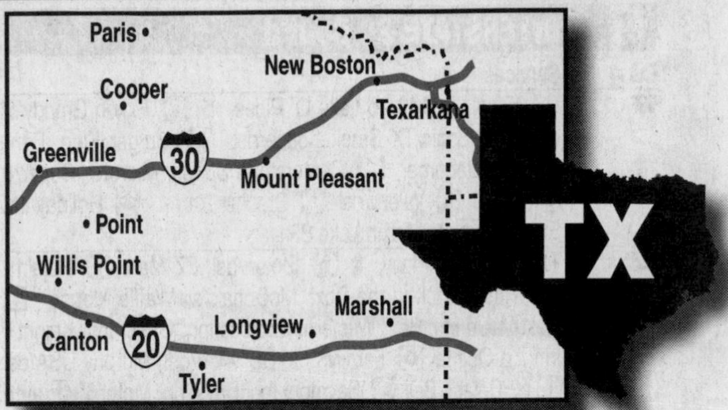

TX

INTERSTATE 10 Cont'd

EL PASO

Exit #	Services
24b	Geronimo Dr, N [food] El Taco Tote, Taco Cabana [lodging] Wingate Inn [other] $Tree, Costco/gas, Kohl's, Marshall's, Office Depot, Ross, Target, Walgreens, S [gas] Alon/7-11/dsl, Circle K [food] Denny's, IHOP [lodging] Embassy Suites, Hilton Garden, Homewood Suites, Hyatt Place, La Quinta [other] URGENT CARE
24a	Trowbridge Dr, N [food] Luby's, McDonald's, Whataburger [other] Ford, Nissan, Walgreens
23b	US 62/180, to Paisano Dr, N [food] Jack-in-the-Box, McDonald's, Whataburger [lodging] Budget Inn, Soluna Inn [other] Ford, to Carlsbad, U-Haul
23a	Raynolds St, S [food] Arby's [lodging] Best Value Inn, Motel 6 [other] [H]
22b	US 54, Patriot Fwy
22a	Copia St, El Paso, N [gas] Alon/7-11, Shamrock [food] KFC
21	Piedras St, El Paso, N [food] Burger King, McDonald's [other] Family$
20	Dallas St, Cotton St, N [gas] Valero [food] Church's, Subway
19	TX 20, El Paso, downtown, N [gas] Chevron, S [lodging] Camino Real Hotel, DoubleTree Inn, Holiday Inn Express
18b	Franklin Ave, Porfirio Diaz St
18a	Schuster Ave, N [other] Sun Bowl, S [other] to UTEP
16	Executive Ctr Blvd, N [gas] Valero [lodging] Best Value Inn
13b a	US 85, Paisano Dr, to Sunland Park Dr, N [gas] Valero [food] 5 Guys Burgers, Barrigo's Café, Buffalo Wild Wings, Carino's Italian, ChuckECheese, Corner Bakery Cafe, Grand China, IHOP, Olive Garden, PF Chang's, Red Lobster, Sonic, Whataburger [other] $Tree, AT&T, Barnes&Noble, Best Buy, Dillard's, JC Penney, K-Mart, Macy's, mall, Marshall's, Michael's, Office Depot, Old Navy, Petsmart, Ross, Sears/auto, Sprouts Mkt, Target, URGENT CARE, Verizon, vet, S [gas] Shamrock/dsl, Shell [food] Bob-O's Funpark, La Malinche Mexican, Little Caesars, McDonald's, Sonic, State Line BBQ, Subway [lodging] Best Western, Comfort Suites, Extended Stay America, Holiday Inn, Sleep Inn [other] Buick/GMC, Chrysler/Dodge/Jeep, Family$, Vista Mkt
12	Resler Dr (from wb)
11	TX 20, to Mesa St, Sunland Park, N [gas] Chevron/dsl, Circle K, Mobil/dsl, Valero/dsl [food] AJ's Diner, Chick-fil-A, Chili's, CiCi's, Coldstone, Cracker Barrel, El Taco Tote, Famous Dave's BBQ, Golden Corral, Krispy Kreme, Leo's Mexican, PacoWong's Chinese, Panda Express, Pei Wei, Popeye's, Schlotsky's, Souper Salad, Subway, Taco Bell, TX Roadhouse, Wendy's, Wienerschnitzel [lodging] Comfort Suites, EconoLodge, Fairfield Inn, La Quinta, LaQuinta, Red Roof Inn, SpringHill Suites [other] $General, Albertson's, BigLots, Family$, Firestone/auto, GNC, Home Depot, PepBoys, SteinMart, TirePros, USPO, Verizon, Walmart/McDonald's, S [gas] Chevron/dsl, Valero/dsl [food] Ay Caramba Mexican, Burger King, Church's, Golden Buddha, Jack-in-the-Box, KFC, McDonald's, Pizza Hut, Starbucks, Subway, Taco Cabana, Village Inn [lodging] Days Inn, Motel 6, Travelodge [other] $General, $Tree, AutoZone, Big 8 Foods, Hobby Lobby, Martin Tires, Radio Shack, Sam's Club/gas, Walgreens
9	Redd Rd, N [gas] Valero [food] Applebee's, Burger King, Double Dave's Pizza, Peter Piper Pizza, Starbucks, Subway [other] Albertson's, Ford, Kohl's, Lowe's, O'Reilly Parts, S [gas] Circle K/dsl, Valero [other] Chevrolet, Honda, Mazda, VW, Walmart Mkt
8	Artcraft Rd, S [gas] Shell/dsl [food] Carl's Jr, Church's, Rudy's BBQ/dsl [lodging] Guesthouse Inn, Hampton Inn, Holiday Inn Express
6	Lp 375, to Canutillo, N [gas] Shell/DQ/dsl [other] Franklin Mtns SP, to Trans Mountain Rd, S [gas] Chevron/McDonald's [food] Pizza Hut, Starbucks, Whataburger [other] Discount Tire, El Paso Shops/Famous Brands, Martin Tire, RV camping

ANTHONY

Exit #	Services
5mm	truck check sta eb
2	Westway, Vinton, N [gas] Petro/Valero/Subway/dsl/scales/24hr/@ [other] American RV Park, Camping World (1mi), PetroLube/tires, S [other] truck repair/tires
1	**S Welcome Ctr eb, full [handicapped] facilities, info, litter barrels, petwalk** [phone] [picnic] [gas] Great American Steaks [other] Anthony RV Ctr, funpark,
0	FM 1905, Anthony, N [gas] FLYING J/Denny's/dsl/LP/RV dump/24hr, Love's/Chester's/McDonald's/dsl/scales/24hr [food] Carl's Jr [lodging] Best Value Inn, S [gas] Alon/7-11/dsl, Pilot/Subway/Wendy's/dsl/24hr/@ [food] Burger King, KFC/Taco Bell [lodging] Best Western [other] $General, $Tree, Anthony RV Ctr, Big 8 Foods, funpark, tires, truckwash, Walgreens
0mm	Texas/New Mexico state line

INTERSTATE 20

MARSHALL

Exit #	Services
636mm	Texas/Louisiana state line
635.5mm	**Welcome Ctr/[rest stop] wb, full [handicapped] facilities, info, litter barrels, petwalk** [phone] [picnic]
635	TX 9, TX 156, to Waskom, N [gas] Chevron/Burger King/dsl, Exxon/dsl [food] DQ, Jim's BBQ [other] Family$, USPO
633	US 80, FM 9, FM 134, to Waskom, N [gas] Shell [food] Catfish Village Rest., S [other] Miss Ellie's RV Park
628	to US 80, to frontage rd
624	FM 2199, to Scottsville
620	FM 31, to Elysian Fields, N [other] Timberline RV Park (3mi)
617	US 59, Marshall, **0-2 mi** N [gas] Exxon/dsl, Shell [food] Applebee's, Burger King, Cafe Italia, Catfish Express, Golden Chick, Golden Corral, IHOP, In Japan Steaks, Jalapeño Tree, KFC, Little Caesars, LJ Silver, McDonald's, Pizza Hut, Porky's Smokehouse, Sonic, Subway, Taco Bell, Waffle House, Wendy's, Whataburger [lodging] Baymont Inn, Best Western, Best Western, Comfort Suites, Days Inn, Fairfield Inn, Hampton Inn, Quality Inn [other] $General, Chevrolet, Chrysler/Dodge/Jeep, Ford/Lincoln, JC Penney, NAPA, Save-A-Lot Foods, Toyota/Scion, S [gas] Chevron/dsl, Conoco/Pony Express/dsl/scales/@, Rudy's/dsl, Valero/dsl [food] JW's Diner [lodging] Best Value Inn, EconoLodge, Holiday Inn Express, La Quinta, Motel 6, Super 8 [other] Holiday Springs RV Park (2mi)
614	TX 43, to Marshall, S [other] to Martin Creek Lake SP
610	FM 3251
604	FM 450, Hallsville, N [gas] Valero/dsl [other] 450 Hitchin' Post RV Park, to Lake O' the Pines
600mm	Mason Creek
599	FM 968, Longview, N [other] Kenworth, S [gas] Exxon/Sonic/dsl, Valero Travel Plaza @ [other] Cowboy RV Park (5mi), Goodyear Truck Tire, truck repair, truck/rv wash

TX

INTERSTATE 20 Cont'd

Exit #	Services
596	US 259 N, TX 149, to Lake O' Pines, N [gas] Exxon/Grandy's/dsl, Shell/Sonic/TX Smokehouse/dsl [food] Burger King, Denny's, Whataburger [lodging] Centerstone Suites, Microtel, Super 8 [other] [H], S [gas] Valero/dsl [food] Cracker Barrel [lodging] Holiday Inn Express [other] to Martin Lake SP
595b a	TX 322, Estes Pkwy, N [gas] Exxon/dsl, EZ Mart [food] Hajalmer's Rest., Jack-in-the-Box, McDonald's, Waffle House [lodging] Best Value Inn, Best Western, Express Inn, Guest Inn, Knight's Inn, La Quinta [other] Family$, S [gas] Alon/dsl, Murphy USA/dsl [food] KFC/Taco Bell [lodging] Baymont Inn, Days Inn, Motel 6 [other] auto repair, Walmart/Subway
593mm	Sabine River
591	FM 2087, FM 2011, S [other] Fernbrook RV Park (2mi)
589b a	US 259, TX 31, Kilgore (exits left from wb), **1-3 mi** S [gas] Chevron/dsl, Exxon/dsl [food] Chili's, Kilgore Café, Mazzio's, McDonald's, Taco Bueno [lodging] Best Value Inn, Comfort Suites, Hampton Inn, Holiday Inn Express [other] AutoZone, Chevrolet, E Texas Oil Museum, Ford, O'Reilly Parts
587	TX 42, Kilgore, N [gas] Exxon/dsl [food] Bodacious BBQ, S [gas] Shell/Wendy's/dsl [food] Denny's [lodging] Days Inn [other] Big Rig Lube, E TX Oil Museum, Walmart (3mi)
583	TX 135, to Kilgore, Overton, N [gas] EZmart/dsl [other] Liberty City RV Park, Shallow Creek RV Resort
582	FM 3053, Liberty City, N [gas] Mobil/Subway/dsl, Shell/Whataburger/dsl [food] Bob's BBQ, DQ, Los Enchiladas, Pizza Boy, Sonic
579	Joy-Wright Mtn Rd
575	Barber Rd
574mm	**picnic area both lanes, handicapped accessible, litter barrels, picnic tables**
571b	FM 757, Omen Rd, to Starrville
571a	US 271, to Gladewater, Tyler, S [gas] Shell/Sonic/Texas Smokehouse/dsl/scales/24hr
567	TX 155, Winona, N [gas] Valero/dsl/24hr, S [food] DQ (2mi) [lodging] Best Value Inn [other] [H], Freightliner
565	FM 2015, to Driskill-Lake Rd
562	FM 14, N [food] Bodacious BBQ [other] to Tyler SP, S [gas] Pilot/McDonald's/dsl/scales/24hr [other] Northgate RV Park (4mi)
560	Lavender Rd, S [other] 5 Star RV Park (2 mi)
557	Jim Hogg Rd, N [gas] Shell/dsl [other] TX Rose RV Park
556	US 69, to Tyler, N [gas] Murphy USA/dsl, RaceWay/dsl, Shamrock/dsl [food] Burger King, Chicken Express, Chili's, Domino's, Eastern Buffet, IHOP, KFC\LJ Silver, McDonald's, Pizza Hut, Pizza Inn, Posado's Cafe, Sonic, Subway, Taco Bell [lodging] Best Western, Comfort Suites, Days Inn, Hampton Inn, La Quinta [other] $General, Family$, Fred's, Kwik Kar, Lowe's, Verizon, Walmart/Subway, S [gas] Chevron/DQ, Exxon/dsl [food] Cracker Barrel, Wendy's [lodging] Best Value Inn
554	Harvey Rd
553	TX 49 S (toll), CR 411
552	FM 849, N [gas] Valero/dsl [food] Collin St Bakery, Subway [other] vet
548	TX 110, to Grand Saline, N [gas] Exxon/dsl, S [gas] Valero/dsl
546mm	**cmv insp sta both lanes**
544	Willow Branch Rd, N [other] Willow Branch RV Park
540	FM 314, to Van, N [gas] Loves/Carl's Jr/dsl/scales/24hr [food] DQ, Farmhouse Rest, Sonic, Soul Mans BBQ [lodging] Van Inn
538mm	[rest stop] **both lanes, full [handicapped] facilities, litter barrels, petwalk [phone] [picnic] vending**
537	FM 773, FM 16
536	Tank Farm Rd
533	Oakland Rd, to Colfax, N [gas] Shell/Pilot/A&W/LJ Silver/dsl

TYLER

CANTON

Exit #	Services
530	FM 1255, Canton
528	FM 17, to Grand Saline
527	TX 19, N [gas] Exxon/dsl [food] Burger King, Denny's, Papadales Grill, Whataburger [lodging] Motel 6, Quality Inn, Super 8, S [gas] Circle K/dsl/24hr, Shell/dsl [food] Dairy Palace, DJ's BBQ, DQ, Juanita's Mexican, KFC/Taco Bell, McDonald's [lodging] Best Western, Days Inn [other] Ford, Mill Creek Ranch RV Resort, to First Monday SP
526	FM 859, to Edgewood, N [other] water park
523	TX 64, Wills Point, N [gas] Shell/dsl/24hr [food] Taco Casa [other] Bluebird RV Park, repair
521	Myrtle Springs Rd, S [other] Explore USA RV Ctr, repair, RV camp/dump
519	Turner-Hayden Rd, S [other] Canton RV Park
516	FM 47, to Wills Point, N [food] Fourwinds Steaks, to Lake Tawakoni, S [gas] Texaco/dsl [food] Robertson's Café/gas [lodging] Interstate Motel
512	FM 2965, Hiram-Wills Point Rd
512mm	[other] cmv inspection sta both lanes
509	Hiram Rd, S [gas] Shell/dsl/cafe/24hr
506	FM 429, FM 2728, College Mound Rd, N [other] Blue Bonnet Ridge RV Park
503	Wilson Rd, S [gas] TA/Shell/Country Fare/Pizza Hut/Subway/dsl/LP/24hr/ @
501	TX 34, to Terrell, N [gas] Exxon/dsl, QT/dsl, Shell/Subway/dsl [food] Church's, Italrican Cafe, Schlotzsky's, Sonic, Starbucks, Steak&Grill, Waffle House [lodging] Best Value Inn, Best Western, Comfort Inn, Days Inn, La Quinta, Motel 6 [other] [H], Home Depot, S [gas] Circle K/dsl, Valero/dsl/24hr [food] Applebee's, Carmona's Cantina, IHOP, McDonald's, Wendy's [lodging] Holiday Inn Express, Super 8 [other] Old Navy, Tanger Outlet/famous brands
499b	Rose Hill Rd, to Terrell
499a	to US 80, W to Dallas, same as 498
498	FM 148, to Terrell, N [gas] Exxon/Denny's/Subway/dsl, Shell/dsl [food] Soulman's BBQ, S [gas] Terrell RV Park
493	FM 1641, S [gas] Exxon/Pizza Inn/Taco Mayo/dsl [food] Sonic
491	FM 2932, Helms Tr, to Forney, N [gas] Shell/Subway/dsl
490	FM 741, to Forney
487	FM 740, to Forney, S [other] Forney RV park
483	Lawson Rd, Lasater Rd
482	Belt Line Rd, to Lasater, N [gas] Exxon/dsl [food] Smokehouse BBQ, Sonic, S [gas] Shell/KFC/Pizza Hut/Subway [other] RV park
481	Seagoville Rd, N [gas] Shell/Church's/Dickey's BBQ, Valero/dsl [lodging] La Quinta, S [food] Lindy's Rest.
480	I-635, N to Mesquite
479b a	US 175, S [gas] Marlow/dsl
477	St Augustine Rd, S [gas] Shell/dsl [food] Sonic
476	Dowdy Ferry Rd
474	TX 310 N, Central Expsy
473b a	JJ Lemmon Rd, I-45 N to Dallas, S to Houston
472	Bonnie View Rd, N [gas] Flying J/Denny's/dsl/LP/24hr, Shell [food] Jack-in-the-Box [lodging] Ramada Ltd [other] Blue Beacon, Kenworth, Speedco Lube, S [gas] TA/Exxon/Burger King/Taco Bell/dsl/scales/24hr/ @
470	TX 342, Lancaster Rd, N [gas] Chevron/dsl, USA/Popeye's/Subway/dsl/scales/24hr [food] Soulman's BBQ, S [gas] Pilot/Wendy's/dsl/scales/24hr, Shell [food] LJ Silver/Taco Bell, McDonald's, Sonic, Whataburger, William's Chicken [lodging] Days Inn
468	Houston School Rd, S [gas] Exxon/dsl [food] Whataburger
467b a	I-35E, N to Dallas, S to Waco, **1 mi N off of I-35E** [gas] Chevron, Shell [food] McDonald's
466	S Polk St, N [gas] Exxon/dsl, Texaco/dsl [food] DQ, Sonic, Subway [other] Family$, S [gas] Loves/Carl's Jr/dsl/scales/24hr

TERRELL

DALLAS

INTERSTATE 20 Cont'd

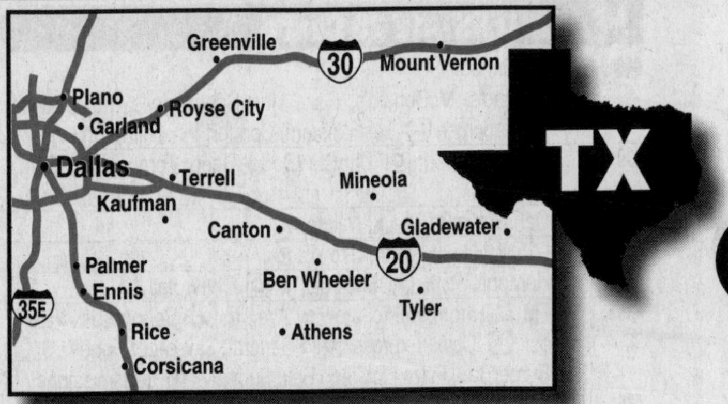

Exit #	Services
465	Wheatland/S Hampton Rds, N [gas] Shell/Subway [food] Chick-fil-A, Chili's, Furr's Cafeteria [other] $Tree, Aldi Foods, CVS Drug, GNC, Office Depot, Petsmart, Ross, Target, S [gas] Chevron/McDonald's, Murphy USA/dsl, QT/dsl, RaceWay/dsl [food] Arby's, Burger King, Cheddar's, Jack-in-the-Box, Panda Express, Popeye's, Sonic, Spring Creek BBQ, Taco Bell, Wendy's [lodging] Super 8 [other] [H], Home Depot, Honda, Hyundai, Kia, Lowe's, Nissan, Sam's Club/gas, Toyota/Scion, Walmart
464b a	US 67, Love Fwy
463	Camp Wisdom Rd, N [gas] Chevron/7-11, Exxon [food] Catfish King Rest., Denny's, Taco Bell/LJ Silver, Taco Cabana [lodging] Best Value Inn, Royal Inn, Super 7 [other] $Tree, Chrysler/Dodge/Jeep, S [gas] Shamrock [food] Burger King, Chubby's Rest., Dave's BBQ, Olive Garden, Red Lobster, Subway, Tortilla Factory
462b a	Duncanville Rd (no EZ wb return), S [gas] QT, Shell/dsl [food] Church's, Jack-in-the-Box, Los Lupes Mexican, Popeye's, Whataburger [lodging] Hilton Garden, Motel 6 [other] Firestone/auto, Kroger, Radio Shack
461	Cedar Ridge Rd, S [gas] RaceWay/dsl
460	TX 408
458	Mt Creek Pkwy
457	FM 1382, to Grand Prairie, N [gas] Shell/7-11/dsl, Valero/dsl [food] Waffle House, S [gas] RaceTrac/dsl [food] Jack-in-the-Box [other] to Joe Pool Lake
456	Carrier Pkwy, to Corn Valley Rd, N [gas] QT [food] Chick-fil-A, Dickey's BBQ, Domino's, Don Pablo, Popeyes, Sonic, Starbucks, Taco Cabana, Whataburger [other] AutoZone, Home Depot, Kohl's, Radio Shack, Target, S [gas] Shell [food] Baskin-Robbins, Boston Mkt, Chapp's Cafe, Cheddar's, Chili's, Chipotle, Denny's, IHOP, Little Caesar's, McDonald's, Spring Creek BBQ, Subway [lodging] Holiday Inn Express [other] Albertsons/gas, CVS Drug, GNC, Tom Thumb Foods/gas, Verizon, vet, Walgreens
455	TX 151
454	Great Southwest Pkwy, N [gas] Chevron/7-11/dsl, Exxon/dsl [food] Beto's, Carino's Italian, China Dragon, ChuckeCheese, DQ, Golden Corral, KFC, McDonald's, Pizza Hut/Taco Bell, Taco Bueno, TX Roadhouse, Waffle House, Wendy's, Wienerschnitzel [lodging] Comfort Suites, Heritage Inn, Quality Inn [other] [H], Firestone/auto, Harley-Davidson, U-Haul, S [gas] 7-11, Shell/Subway/dsl, Valero/dsl [food] Applebee's, Arby's, Buffalo Wild Wings, Burger King, Schlotzsky's, Sonic [lodging] La Quinta, Super 8 [other] $Tree, AT&T, Discount Tire, Kroger, Office Depot, Petsmart, RaceTrac/dsl, Sam's Club, to Joe Pool Lake, Walgreens, Walmart/McDonald's
453b a	TX 360
452	Frontage Rd
451	Collins St, New York Ave, N [gas] Exxon/dsl, RaceTrac/dsl, Rudy's Store/BBQ/dsl [food] Cotton Patch Cafe, Golden Corral, Jack-in-the-Box, Whataburger [other] Chrysler/Dodge/Jeep, Gander Mtn, Kia/Mazda/VW, URGENT CARE, S [gas] QT, Shell, Valero/dsl [food] Chicken Express, KFC/Taco Bell, McDonald's, Sonic, Subway, Taco Bueno [lodging] Hampton Inn [other] Buick/GMC, Nissan
450	Matlock Rd, N [food] Abuelo's Mexican, Bar Louie, BJ's Rest., Black-eyed Pea, Bone Daddy's, Boomer Jack's Grill, Chuy's Mexican, Coldstone, Dave&Buster's, Genghis Grill, Houlihan's, India Grill, Jason's Deli, Kincaide's Burgers, McAlister's Deli, Melting Pot, Mercado Juarez, Mimi's Cafe, PF Changs, Pluckers's Wings, Potbelly, Red Robin, Starbucks, Sweet Tomatoes, The Keg Steaks, Wendy's, Which Wich [lodging] Courtyard, Quality Inn, Residence Inn [other] [H], AT&T, Costco/gas, Jo-Ann Fabrics, Lowe's, Old Navy, Petsmart, Staples, World

FT WORTH

Exit #	Services
450	Continued Mkt, S [gas] 7-11, RaceWay/dsl, Shell/7-11 [food] Joe's Pizza, Pizza Patron, Starbucks [other] Fry's Electronics, O'Reilly Parts
449	FM 157, Cooper St, N [gas] Shell/dsl [food] Cane's, Cheesecake Factory, Chili's, Corner Bakery, Grandy's, Honeybaked Ham, IHOP, In-N-Out, McDonald's, Nagoya Japanese, On-the-Border, Outback Steaks, Pei Wei, Razzoo's Cajun Café, Red Lobster, Rockfish Seafood, Salt Grass Steaks, Souper Salad, Spaghetti Whse, Spring Creek BBQ, Whataburger [lodging] Best Western, Days Inn, Holiday Inn Express, La Quinta, Studio 6, Super 8 [other] Barnes&Noble, Best Buy, Dick's, Dillard's, Discount Tire, JC Penney, Macy's, mall, Michael's, Office Depot, Sears/auto, Target, TJ Maxx, Verizon, S [gas] Shell [food] Applebee's, Arby's, Boston Mkt, Burger St, Carl's Jr, Chick-fil-A, Chipotle, Denny's, El Arroyo, El Fenix Mexican, Lin's Buffet, LJ Silver, Macaroni Grill, McDonald's, Olive Garden, Panda Express, Peter Piper Pizza, Schlotsky's, Starbucks, Subway, Taco Bueno, Taco Cabana, TGIFriday [lodging] InTown Suites, Microtel [other] $Tree, AAA, Acura, Chevrolet, Ford, Hobby Lobby, Home Depot, Honda, Hyundai, NTB, Ross, Suzuki, Toyota, Walmart/McDonald's
448	Bowen Rd, N [gas] QT, RaceTrac/dsl [food] Cracker Barrel, Sonic, S [gas] Shell
447	Kelly-Elliott Rd, Park Springs Blvd, N [gas] 7-11, Valero, S [gas] Exxon/Subway [other] city park
445	Green Oaks Blvd, N [gas] Conoco/dsl, Shell/7-11/dsl [food] Arby's, Boston Mkt, Braum's, Burger St, Cafe Acapulco, Chapp's Cafe, Chick-fil-A, Church's, CiCi's, Colter's BBQ, Fuzzy's Tacos, Hooters, Jack-in-the-Box, Jay Jay Rest., Joe's Pizza, Mijo's Cafe, Quizno's, Schlotzsky's, Starbucks, Taco Bell, Taco Cabana, Taco Casa, Tai-Pan, Wendy's, Whataburger [other] $Tree, Ace Hardware, Albertsons, AT&T, CVS Drug, Firestone, Kroger/dsl, Meineke, Office Depot, Radio Shack, Verizon, Walgreens, S [gas] 7-11, Murphy Express/dsl, QT/dsl, Valero/dsl [food] Cheddar's, Corky's Pizza, Golden Buffet, IHOP, McDonald's, Pancho's Mexican, Panda Express, Sonic, Subway, Taco Bueno, Waffle House [other] $General, AutoZone, BigLots, Discount Tire, O'Reilly Parts, Tuesday Morning, vet, Walmart/Subway
444	US 287 S, to Waxahatchie, from eb, same as 445
443	Bowman Springs Rd (from wb)
442b a	I-820 to Ft Worth, US 287 bus, N [gas] Valero [lodging] Great Western Inn, Knights Inn, S [gas] QT/dsl
441	Anglin Dr, Hartman Lane, N [lodging] ValuePlace Inn, S [gas] Conoco/dsl
440b	Forest Hill Dr, S [gas] Shell/7-11/dsl [food] Braum's, Capt D's, CiCi's Pizza, Jack-in-the-Box, Luby's, Sonic, Starbucks, Subway, Taco Bell [lodging] La Quinta [other] $General, $Tree, AutoZone, CVS Drug, Discount Tire, O'Reilly Parts, Super 1 Foods, Walgreens
440a	Wichita St, N [gas] Chevron/dsl [food] #1 Chinese, Taco Casa, Wendy's, S [gas] Texaco/dsl, Valero [food] Chicken Express, Denny's,

TX

INTERSTATE 20 Cont'd

440a Continued
Domino's, McDonald's, Pizza Hut, Schlotzsky's, Taco Bueno, Whataburger Best Western, Comfort Inn, Hampton Inn

439 Campus Dr, N Chrysler/Dodge/Jeep, Ford, S Sam's Club/gas

438 Oak Grove Rd, S Valero

437 I-35W, N to Ft Worth, S to Waco

436b Hemphill St, N Shell/dsl, S Chevrolet

436a FM 731 (from eb), to Crowley Ave, N Conoco/dsl, Valero/dsl China Express $General, Sav-a-Lot Foods, S BurgerBox, Pizza Hut/Taco Bell, Subway transmissions

435 McCart St, N Shamrock, Shell/dsl, S Mobil/dsl

434b Trail Lakes Dr, S Shell Sonic, Starbucks, Subway, Wendy's CVS Drug, Family$

434a Granbury Rd

433 Hulen St, N Shell/dsl Chef Chen, ChuckECheese, Honeybaked Ham, Hooters, Olive Garden, Papa Murphy's, Souper Salad, Subway, TX Roadhouse TownePlace Suites Albertsons, Home Depot, NTB, Petsmart, Sprouts Mkt, TJ Maxx, S Abuelo's Mexican, BJ's Rest., Denny's, Five Guys, In-N-Out, Jack-in-the-Box, Kincaide's Burgers, McDonald's, Panera Bread, Pizza Inn, Potbelly, Red Lobster, Red Robin Hampton Inn Barnes&Noble, Dillard's, Hobby Lobby, Macy's, mall, Michael's, Office Depot, Old Navy, Ross, Sears/auto

431 (432 from wb), TX 183, Bryant-Irvin Rd, N Chevron Chipotle Mexican, Genghis Grill, Keg Steaks, Mimi's Café, On-the-Border, Taste of Asia Best Buy, Cavender's Boots, Kohl's, Lowe's, Petsmart, Sam's Club/gas, S Chevron, Shell/dsl Blackeyed Pea, Chicken Express, Chick-fil-A, Cousin's BBQ, Fox & Hound, Fuddruckers, IHOP, Jimmy John's, Lonestar Oysters, Outback Steaks, Pei Wei, Pizza Hut, Razzoo's Cajun, Rio Mambo, SaltGrass Steaks, Schlotzsky's, Sonic, Starbucks, Subway, Szechuan Courtyard, Extended Stay America, Holiday Inn Express, Homewood Suites, Hyatt Place, La Quinta H, AT&T, Costco/gas, Firestone/auto, Ford, Goodyear/auto, Infiniti, Kwik Kar, Lexus, Mazda, PetCo, Staples, Target, Verizon, Walgreens

430mm Clear Fork Trinity River

429b Winscott Rd, N Circle K/dsl Cracker Barrel Best Western, Comfort Suites

429a US 377, to Granbury, S QT/dsl, RaceTrac/dsl, Shell/dsl, Valero 7-11/dsl, Arby's, Braum's, Burger King, Chicken Express, Chick-fil-A, Domino's, Golden Chick, Jack-in-the-Box, KFC/Taco Bell, McDonald's, NY Pizza, Panda Express, Pizza Hut, Ricky's BBQ, Sonic, Starbucks, Subway, Taco Casa, Taco Villa, Waffle House, Waffle House, Whataburger Motel 6 $General, Albertsons, AutoZone, CVS Drug, O'Reilly Parts, USPO, Walgreens, Walmart

428 I-820, N around Ft Worth

426 RM 2871, Chapin School Rd

425 Markum Ranch Rd

421 I-30 E (from eb), to Ft Worth

420 FM 1187, Aledo, Farmer, parking & ride

419mm **weigh sta eb**

418 Ranch House Rd, Willow Park, Willow Park, N Exxon/Taco Casa, Shell/dsl Pizza Hut, Sonic, Subway, Whataburger, S Shell/ChickenExpress/dsl Domino's, McDonald's, Milano's Italian, Mr Jim's Pizza, Railhead BBQ Knights Inn $General, Ace RV Ctr., Brookshire Foods, Cowtown RV Park

417mm no services

415 FM 5, Mikus Rd, Annetta, S Shell/dsl, Signature/dsl 415 RV Ctr

WEATHERFORD

413 (414 from wb), US 180 W, Lake Shore Dr, N Murphy USA/dsl, RaceTrac/dsl, Shell/dsl DQ, Golden Chick, McDonald's, Sonic, Subway, Taco Bell, Waffle House Buick/Cadillac/Chevrolet/GMC, Ford, Hyundai, Lincoln, Nissan, Suzuki, Toyota/Scion, Walgreens, Walmart/Subway, S Valero/dsl

410 Bankhead Hwy, S Loves/Subway/dsl/24hr

409 FM 2552 N, Clear Lake Rd, N Petro/Valero/Iron Skillet/dsl/24hr/ @ Antonio's Mexican, Granny's Kitchen, Jack-in-the-Box, Little Panda Chinese, Popeyes Heritage Inn, SleepGo Motel H, Blue Beacon, S Shell/dsl

408 TX 171, FM 1884, FM 51, Tin Top Rd, Weatherford, N Exxon, Mobil, Murphy USA/dsl Applebee's, Baker's Ribs, Braum's, Buffalo Wild Wings, Chicken Express, China Harbor, CiCi's Pizza, Cotton Patch Cafe, IHOP, Kincade's Burgers, LJ Silver, Logan's Roadhouse, McAlister's Deli, McDonald's, MT Rest., Olive Garden, Rosa's Cafe, Schlotzsky's, Starbucks, Subway, Taco Bell, Taco Bueno, Taco Cabana, Whataburger, Wild Mushroom Steaks La Quinta, Sleep Inn, Super 8 $Tree, AT&T, AutoZone, Belk, Christian Bros Auto, Discount Tire, Firestone/auto, JC Penney, Just Brakes, Michael's, Radio Shack, TJ Maxx, Verizon, Walgreens, Walmart/Subway, S Exxon/Subway/dsl, Shell/Burger King/dsl Chick-fil-A, Chili's, Cracker Barrel, Honey Bee Ham, On-the-Border, Tokyo Japanese Steaks, Waffle House, Whataburger Best Western, Candlewood Suites, Comfort Suites, Fairfield Inn, Hampton Inn, Holiday Inn Express, Motel 6, Quality Inn, Super Value Inn Best Buy, GNC, Kohl's, Lowe's, NTB, Petsmart, Ross, Target, URGENT CARE

407 Tin Top Rd (from eb), N Home Depot, S KOA, same as 408

406 Old Dennis Rd, N Truck&Travel/dsl Chuck Wagon Rest. Quest Inn, S Pilot/Wendy's/dsl/scales/24hr EconoLodge, Quality 1 Motel Boss Shop Repair

404 Williams Memorial Dr

402 (403 from wb), TX 312, to Weatherford

397 FM 1189, to Brock, N Valero/dsl Oak Creek RV Park

394 FM 113, to Millsap

393mm Brazos River

391 Gilbert Pit Rd

390mm **both lanes, full facilities, litter barrels, petwalk vending**

386 US 281, to Mineral Wells, Stephenville, N Shell/Subway/dsl Gilbert Pecans, S Chevron/Maverick TC/Taco Casa/dsl, Sunoco/Stripes/Taco Co/dsl DQ

380 FM 4, Santo, S RV Park

376 Blue Flat Rd, Panama Rd

373 TX 193, Gordon

370 TX 108 S, FM 919, Gordon, N Texaco/Bar-B/dsl, S Exxon/dsl Cactus Rose RV Park, Longhorn Inn/Country Store

367 TX 108 N, Mingus, N Smoke Stack Café Thurber Sta, S NY Hill Rest.

364mm Palo Pinto Creek

363 Tudor Rd litter barrels

362mm **Bear Creek, both lanes, litter barrels,**

361 TX 16, to Strawn

358 (from wb), frontage rd

356mm Russell Creek

354 Lp 254, Ranger

353 **S eb, full facilities, litter barrels vending**

351 (352 from wb), College Blvd

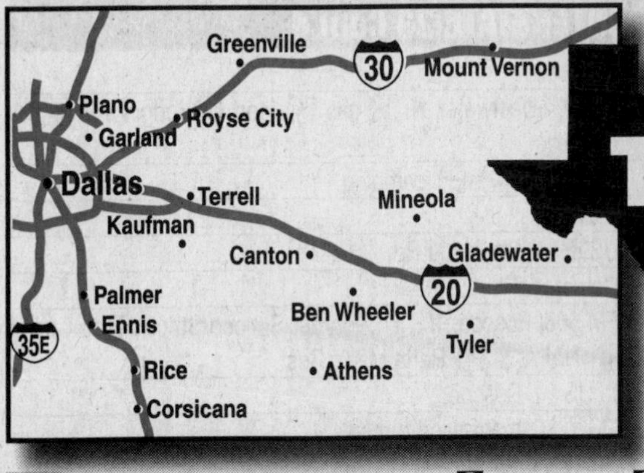

TX

INTERSTATE 20 Cont'd

Exit #	Services
349	FM 2461, Ranger, N Loves/Godfather's/Subway/dsl/scales/24hr DQ Best Inn RL RV Park, S Phillips 66/dsl repair
347	FM 3363 (from wb), Olden, S TX Steakhouse
345	FM 3363 (from eb), Olden, S TX Steakhouse
343	TX 112, FM 570, Eastland, Lake Leon, N Alon/7-11/Subway, Murphy USA/dsl, Shell/dsl Chicken Express, DQ, Golden Chick, McDonald's, Pizza Heaven, Sonic, Taco Bell Holiday Inn Express, La Quinta, Super 8/RV park $General, AT&T, AutoZone, Buick/Cadillac/Chevrolet/GMC, Chrysler/Dodge/Jeep, Ford, O'Reilly Parts, TrueValue, Walmart, S Exxon/dsl Pulido's Mexican Budget Host, Days Inn
340	TX 6, Eastland, N Valero/dsl H, S Shell/dsl
337	spur 490, N The Wild Country RV Park
332	US 183, Cisco, N Alon/Allsups/dsl, Cow Pokes/dsl Chicken Express, DQ, Pizza Heaven, Sonic, Subway Cisco Inn, Executive Inn/RV Park $General, Family$, Hilton Mon (1mi), NAPA
330	TX 206, Cisco, N Sunoco/Stripes/Tacos/dsl/scales/24hr Best Value Inn H, S FLYING J/Denny's/dsl/scales/24hr
329mm	**wb, litter barrels, accessible**
327mm	**eb, litter barrels, accessible**
324	Scranton Rd
322	Cooper Creek Rd
320	FM 880 N, FM 2945 N, to Moran
319	FM 880 S, Putnam, N Fillin Sta/café USPO
316	Brushy Creek Rd
313	FM 2228
310	Finley Rd
308	Lp 20, Baird
307	US 283, Clyde, N Loves/Chester's/Subway/dsl/scales/24hr DQ Baird Motel/RV park/dump, S Alon/Allsups/7-11, Conoco/dsl Robertson's Café
306	FM 2047, Baird, N Chevrolet/GMC, Hanner RV Ctr
303	Union Hill Rd
301	FM 604, Cherry Lane, N Exxon/dsl McDonald's, Sonic, Whataburger, S Alon/7-11/dsl, Shell/dsl Chicken Express, Pizza House, Subway Family$, Lawrence Bros Mkt
300	FM 604 N, Clyde, N Chrysler/Dodge/Jeep, S Conoco/dsl White's RV Park/dump
299	FM 1707, Hays Rd
297	FM 603, Eula Rd
296.5mm	**both lanes, full facilities, litter barrels, petwalk wireless internet**
294	Buck Creek Rd, N Big Counry RV Ctr/park, Buck Creek RV Park/dump, S Abilene RV Park
292b	Elmdale Rd
292a	Lp 20 (exits left from wb)
290	TX 36, Lp 322, S airport, zoo
288	TX 351, N Alon/7-11/dsl, Alon/7-11/dsl, Murphy USA/dsl Chick-fil-A, Chili's, Cracker Barrel, DQ, Golden Chick, Jason's Deli, Oscar's Mexican, Panda Express, Subway, Taco Casa, Wendy's Comfort Suites, Courtyard, Days Inn, Executive Inn, Holiday Inn Express, Knights Inn, Quality Inn, Residence Inn, TownePlace Suites, Whitten Inn $Tree, AT&T, Lowe's, Radio Shack, Walmart/Subway, S Super 8 H
286c	FM 600, Abilene, N Alon/7-11/dsl, Alon/Allsups/dsl Denny's Best Western, Hampton Inn, Holiday Inn, La Quinta, S Alon/7-11/dsl Sleep Inn

ABILENE

Exit #	Services
286	US 83, Pine St, Abilene, S Alon/Allsups Frontier Inn H
285	Old Anson Rd, S Alon/Allsups/dsl Best Value Inn
283b	N US 277, U83, Anson
283a	US 277 S, US 83 (exits left from wb)
282	FM 3438, Shirley Rd, S Motel 6 KOA
281	Fulwiler Rd, to Dyess AFB, to Dyess AFB
279	US 84 E, to Abilene, **1-3 mi** S access to services
278	Lp 20, N Conoco/dsl/24hr dsl repair, S Westgo TC/Conoco/Huddle House/dsl/scales/24hr/ @ Mack Trucks/Volvo
277	FM 707, Tye, N FLYING J/Denny's/dsl/LP/24hr Peterbilt, truck lube, Tye RV Park, S Alon/7-11/dsl Southern Tire Mart, USPO
274	Wells Lane
272	Wimberly Rd
270	FM 1235, Merkel, N Conoco/dsl, Shell/dsl/24hr
269	FM 126, N Sonic, Subway Scottish Inn Walmart Mkt/dsl, S Alon/7-11/dsl, Phillips 66/dsl DQ, Skeet's BBQ CarQuest, Family$
267	Lp 20, Merkel, **1 mi** S
266	Derstine Rd
264	Noodle Dome Rd
263	Lp 20, Trent, N RV Park
262	FM 1085, S Alon/7-11/dsl
261	Lp 20, Trent
259	Sylvester Rd
258	White Flat Rd, oil wells
257mm	**both lanes, full facilities, litter barrels, petwalk vending**
256	Stink Creek Rd
255	Adrian Rd
251	Eskota Rd
249	FM 1856, N Lonestar RV Park
247	TX 70 N, Sweetwater
246	Alabama Ave, Sweetwater
245	Arizona Ave (from wb), same as 244
244	TX 70 S, Sweetwater, N Alon/7-11/dsl/24hr, Chevron/Subway/dsl, Murphy USA/dsl Dickey's BBQ, Domino's, DQ, Golden Chick, McDonald's, Subway, Wendy's Best Western, Budget Inn, La Quinta, Motel 6 H, AT&T, AutoZone, Medicine Place Drug, Verizon, Walmart, S Shell/dsl Big Boy's BBQ, Buck's BBQ, Great Wall Buffet, Schlotzsky's, Skeet's Grill, Taco Bell Country Hearth Inn, Hampton Inn, Holiday Inn Express, Ranch House Motel/rest., Stay Express Inn Chaparral RV Park, Ford, K-Mart, Rainbolt RV Park
243	Hillsdale Rd, Robert Lee St, N Family RV Ctr
242	Hopkins Rd, N Loves/Arby's/dsl/scales/24hr Microtel, S TA/Pizza Hut/Popeye's/dsl/scales/24hr/ @ Rolling Plains RV Park, truck wash, truck/tire repair

SWEETWATER

= gas = food = lodging = other = rest stop

TX

INTERSTATE 20 Cont'd

Exit #	Services
241	Lp 20, Sweetwater, N gas food lodging, S RV camping
240	Lp 170, N , camping
239	May Rd
238b a	US 84 W, Blackland Rd
237	Cemetery Rd
236	FM 608, Roscoe, N Alon/dsl, Sunoco/Stripes/Taco Co/dsl NAPA, S Retta Mae's Rest
235	to US 84, Roscoe
230	FM 1230, many wind turbines
229mm	**wb, litter barrels, accessible**
228mm	**eb, litter barrels, accessible**
227	Narrell Rd
226b	Lp 20 (from wb), Loraine
226a	FM 644 N, Wimberly Rd
225	FM 644 S, **1 mi** S
224	Lp 20, to Loraine, **1 mi** S
223	Lucas Rd, S 223 RV Park
221	Lasky Rd
220	FM 1899
219	Lp 20, Country Club Rd, Colorado City
217	TX 208 S, N Sunoco/Stripes/Taco Co/DSL/scales/24hr
216	TX 208 N, N Chevron/Subway/dsl DQ Days Inn, S Sunoco/Stripes/Taco Co/dsl Golden Chick, Pizza Hut, Sonic American Inn, Hotel Texas, Super 8 H, $General, City RV Park, Parts+
215	FM 3525, Rogers Rd, **2 mi** S access to gas food H
214.5mm	Colorado River
213	Lp 20, Enderly Rd, Colorado City
212	FM 1229
211mm	Morgan Creek
210	FM 2836, S camping, picnic area, to Lake Colorado City SP
209	Dorn Rd
207	Lp 20, Westbrook
206	FM 670, to Westbrook
204mm	**N wb, full facilities, litter barrels, petwalk**
200	Conaway Rd
199	Iatan Rd
195	frontage rd (from eb)
194a	E Howard Field Rd
192	FM 821, many oil wells
191mm	**eb, full facilities, litter barrels, petwalk**
190	Snyder Field Rd
189	McGregor Rd
188	FM 820, Coahoma, N Sunoco/Stripes/Taco Co/dsl DQ Coahoma Inn Coahoma RV Park, USPO
186	Salem Rd, Sand Springs
184	Moss Lake Rd, Sand Springs, N Alon/dsl $General, S RV camping
182	Midway Rd
181b	Refinery Rd, N Alon Refinery
181a	FM 700, N airport, RV camping, **2 mi** S H
179	US 80, Big Spring, S Alon/7-11 Denny's Camlot Inn, Quality Inn, Super 8 $General, Buick/Cadillac/Chevrolet
178	TX 350, Big Spring, N Shell/dsl tire/truck service, S Pilot/McDonald's/dsl/scales/24hr
177	US 87, Big Spring, N Exxon/dsl, TA/Subway/Popeye's/dsl/scales/24hr/ @ Texas Cajan Cafe Advantage Inn, La Quinta, Motel 6, Plaza Inn, S Alon/dsl, Sunoco/Stripes/dsl

BIG SPRING

Exit #	Services
177	Continued Casa Blanca Mexican, DQ Best Western, Hampton Inn, Holiday Inn Express
176	TX 176, Andrews
174	Lp 20 E, Big Springs, S Shell/dsl H, airport, Big Spring SP
172	Cauble Rd
171	Moore Field Rd
169	FM 2599
168mm	**both lanes, litter barrels**
165	FM 818
158	Lp 20 W, to Stanton, N RV camping
156	TX 137, Lamesa, S Phillips 66/Stripes/Subway/dsl/24hr Sonic Cobblestone Inn, Comfort Inn, Super 8
154	US 80, Stanton, **2 mi** S
151	FM 829 (from wb)
144	Loop 250, **2-3 mi** N services in Midland
143mm	frontage rd (from eb)
142mm	**both lanes, litter barrels, hist. marker**
140	FM 307 (from eb)
138	TX 158, FM 715, Greenwood, N Pilot/dsl, Valero/dsl KD's BBQ, Whataburger, S FLYING J/Moe's/dsl/scales/24hr, Sunoco/Stripes/Subway/dsl, Sunoco/Stripes/Taco Co/dsl Comfort Inn
137	Old Lamesa Rd, N Mainstay Suites
136	TX 349, Midland, N Murphy USA/dsl, Sunoco/Stripes/Taco Co/dsl Cici's Pizza, Domino's, IHOP, Jack-in-the-Box, Little Caesars, McAlister's Deli, McDonald's, Sonic, Starbucks Best Western, Candlewood Suites, Comfort Inn, Country Inn&Suites, Holiday Inn Express, Microtel, Quality Inn, Super 8, West Texas Inn $General, $Tree, Advance Parts, AutoZone, Chavez Tires, Discount Tire, Family$, Petroleum Museum, Verizon, Walmart/Subway, S Daves Gas/NAPA/dsl, Exxon/Burger King/dsl, Pilot/dsl, Stripes/Taco Co/dsl
135	Cotton Flat Rd, S H
134	Midkiff Rd, **0-1 mi (Wall St)** N Alon/7-11, Exxon/dsl, Shell, Sunoco/Stripes/Subway/dsl Denny's, DQ Best Value Inn, Bradford Inn, Days Inn, Executive Inn, La Quinta, Studio 6, Super 8 H, Chevrolet, Chrysler/Dodge/Jeep, Ford/ Lincoln, Honda, Midland RV Park, Subaru
131	TX 158, Midland, N Motel 6, S Loves/Carl's Jr/dsl/scales/24hr Midland RV Park
126	FM 1788, N Pilot/McDonald's/dsl/scales/24hr, Sunoco/Stripes/Taco Co/dsl, Warfield/Texaco/Subway/dsl/scales/@ Steak'n Shake, Subway airport, Carquest, museum, Mwin Street Mkt/dsl, Western Auto
121	Lp 338, Odessa, **0-3 mi** (TX 191) N Alon/7-11, Stripes/Taco Co/dsl Carino's, Casa Ole, Cheddar's, Chili's, Dickey's BBQ, Domino's, Fazoli's, Five Guys, Fuddruckers, Genghis Grill, Golden Corral, Harigan's Grill, Hooters, IHOP, KFC, Logan's Roadhouse, McDonald's, Panda Express, Pizza Hut, Red Lobster, Rosa's Cafe, Schlotzsky's, Sonic, Subway, Twin Peaks Rest, Wendy's, Whataburger Comfort Suites, Days Inn, Elegante Hotel, Fairfield Inn, Hampton Inn Express, Hilton Garden, Holiday Inn, Holiday Inn Express, La Quinta, Parkway Inn, Quality Inn, Sleep Inn, Studio 6, Super Inn $Gerneral, $Tree, AT&T, Buick/GMC, Chevrolet, Dillard's, Hobby Lobby, Home Depot, Honda, Hyundai, JC Penney, Lowe's, Mazda, Mkt Street, Nissan, Sam's Club/gas, Sears/auto, Staples, Target, Toyota/Scion, U of TX Permian Basin, USPO, Walmart/Subway, S FLYING J/McDonald's/dsl/scales/24hr
120	JBS Pkwy, N Candlewood Suites, Comfort Inn, Super 8 Mack/Volvo

MIDLAND

ODESSA

INTERSTATE 20 Cont'd

Exit #	Services
118	FM 3503, Grandview Ave, N Alon/dsl Freightliner/ Peterbilt
116	US 385, Odessa, N Chevron/dsl, Stripes/Taco Co/dsl DQ, La Margarita Delux Inn, Ramada, Villa West Inn H, $General, city park, Family$, S Alon/dsl, Valero/dsl MainStay Suites, Motel 6
115	FM 1882, N Sunoco/Stripes/Taco Co/dsl, S Loves /McDonald's/Subway/dsl/scales/24hr
113	TX 302, Odessa
112	FM 1936, Odessa, N Red X Trkstp/dsl
108	Moss Ave, Meteor Crater, Meteor Crater, N Road Ranger/ Church's/Subway/dsl/scales/24hr
104	FM 866, Meteor Crater Rd, Goldsmith, N RV park
103.5mm	**weigh sta both directions**
101	FM 1601, to Fenwell, Penwell
93	FM 1053, to Ft Stockton
86	TX 41, N camping, Monahans Sandhills SP
83	US 80, Monahans, **2 mi** N H, RV camping
80	TX 18, Monahans, N Chevron/dsl Bar-H Steaks, DQ, Great Wall Buffet, McDonald's, Pappy's BBQ, Pizza Hut, Sonic Candlewood Suites, Holiday Inn Express H, $General, Alco, Family$, Lowe's Foods, O'Reilly Parts, repair/tires, Verizon, S Alon/dsl, Sunoco/Stripes/Subway/dsl, Texaco/ Huddle House/dsl/24hr Huddle House Best Value Inn, Best Western, Comfort Inn, Texan Inn Buick/Chevrolet/ GMC, Chrysler/Dodge/Jeep, RV Park, vet
79	Lp 464, Monahans, S La Quinta
76	US 80, Monahans, **2 mi** N RV camping, to Million Barrel Museum
73	FM 1219, Wickett, N Alon/Allsup's/dsl
70	TX 65
69.5mm	**both lanes, full facilities, litter barrels, petwalk wifi**
66	TX 115, FM 1927, to Pyote
58	frontage rd, multiple oil wells
52	Lp 20 W, to Barstow
49	FM 516, to Barstow
48mm	Pecos River
44	Collie Rd
42	US 285, Pecos, N FLYING J/Denny's/dsl/scales/24hr, Alon, Sunoco/Stripes/dsl/e85 Alfredo's Mexican, DQ, El Rodeo Mexican, Golden Palace Chinese, Pizza Hut Holiday Inn Express, Motel 6, OakTree Inn, Quality Inn AutoZone, museum, tire repair, Walmart, S Loves/McDonald's/ Subway/Chester's/dsl/scales/24hr @ Microtel
40	Country Club Dr, N Comfort Suites st patrol, S Stripes/Subway Alpine Lodge Rest Best Western/rest., LaQuinta municipal park, Pecos Park/Zoo, RV camping
39	TX 17, Pecos, N H, S Hampton Inn Buick/Chev- rolet/GMC, Pecos Tire, Trapark RV Park
37	Lp 20 E, **2 mi** N Sonic Pecos Economy Inn
33	FM 869
29	Shaw Rd, S to TX AM Ag Sta
25mm	**both lanes, litter barrels, accessible**
22	FM 2903, to Toyah
13	McAlpine Rd
7	Johnson Rd
3	Stocks Rd
0mm	**I-20 begins/ends on I-10, 187mm.**

MONAHANS

PECOS

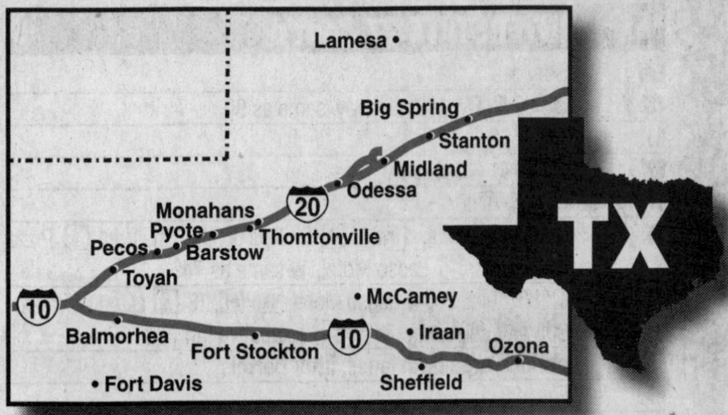

TX

INTERSTATE 27

Exit #	Services
	I-27 begins/ends on I-40, exit 70 in Amarillo.
123b	I-40, W to Albuquerque, E to OK City
123a	26th Ave, E Discount Gas
122c	from sb only
122a	34th Ave, Tyler St, E Valero Sonic $General
122b	FM 1541, Washington St, Parker St, Moss Lane, W Hungry Howie's, Taco Bell, Thai Express
121a	Hawthorne Dr, Austin St, E Amarillo Motel, W Scottie's Transmissions
121b	Georgia St, E Murphy USA/dsl Buick/GMC, Honda, Mazda, Subaru, Walmart/McDonald's
120b	45th Ave, E Waffle House O'Reilly Parts, repair, W Toot'n Totum, Valero Abuelo's Mexican, Burger King, Donut Stop, Gatti's Pizza, Grandma's Cocina, McDonald's, Whata- burger $General, Advance Parts, BMW, Chrysler/Dodge/ Jeep, Drug Emporium, vet, Walgreens
120a	Republic Ave
119b a	(from sb) Western St, 58th Ave, E Phillips 66/dsl Sonic, Subway $General, W Valero/dsl Arby's, Braum's, LJ Silver, Pizza Hut, Thai Palace, Wendy's Aamco, U-Haul, USPO, Walgreens
119a	(from nb) W Hillside
117	Bell St, Arden Rd, W Valero/dsl Popeye's, Sonic $General
116	Lp 335, Hollywood Rd, E Loves/Subway/dsl/ scales/24hr, Phillips 66/dsl McDonald's, Waffle House, Whataburger Comfort Suites, Motel 6, W Holiday Inn Express H (8mi)
115	Sundown Lane
113	McCormick Rd, E $General, Ford, W Family Camping Ctr
112	FM 2219, E Stater's RV Ctr
111	Rockwell Rd, W Buick/GMC
110	US 87 S, US 60 W, Canyon
109	Buffalo Stadium Rd, W stadium
108	FM 3331, Hunsley Rd
106	TX 217, to Palo Duro Cyn SP, Canyon, E Palo Duro Can- yon SP (10mi), Palo Duro RV Park, **3 mi** W McDonald's Best Western, Holiday Inn Express Plains Museum, to W TX A&M
103	FM 1541 N, Cemetery Rd
99	Hungate Rd
98mm	**parking area both lanes, litter barrels**
96	Dowlen Rd
94	FM 285, to Wayside
92	Haley Rd
90	FM 1075, Happy, W gas/dsl

AMARILLO

INTERSTATE 27 Cont'd

Exit #	Services
88b a	US 87 N, FM 1881, Happy, same as 90
83	FM 2698
82	FM 214
77	US 87, Tulia
75	NW 6th St, Tulia, 1 mi E ⓡ Phillips 66/dsl, Shell/dsl ⓕ Pizza Hut, Sonic ⓛ Lasso Motel, W same as 74
74	TX 86, Tulia, E ⓛ Lasso Motel ⓞ Ⓗ, W ⓡ Pilot/Valero/Subway/dsl/scales/24hr ⓛ Executive Inn
70mm	**parking area both lanes, litter barrels**
68	FM 928
63	FM 145, Kress, 1 mi E ⓞ ⓕ Ⓒ
61	US 87, County Rd
56	FM 788
54	FM 3183, to Plainview
53	Lp 27, Plainview, E ⓞ Ⓗ, ⓕ Ⓒ ⓛ camping
51	Quincy St
50	TX 194, Plainview, E ⓡ Valero/dsl ⓞ Ⓗ, to Wayland Bapt U, W ⓛ Reddy Hotel
49	US 70, Plainview, E ⓡ AllStar/dsl, Alon/dsl, Cefco/dsl, Conoco, Stripes/dsl ⓕ A&W/LJ Silver, Carlito's Mexican, China Dragon, Cotton Patch Café, Domino's, Furr's Café, Leal's Mexican, Pizza Hut, Tokyo Japanese, Woodfire Grill ⓛ Comfort Suites, Days Inn, Quality Inn ⓞ $Tree, AutoZone, Beall's, Ford/Lincoln, GNC, NAPA, O'Reilly Parts, Radio Shack, Toyota, United Foods, W ⓡ Murphy USA/dsl, Phillips 66/dsl, Valero/dsl ⓕ Burger King, Chicken Express, Chili's, Empire Buffet, IHOP, Little Mexico, McDonald's, Mia's Italian, Sonic, Subway, Taco Bell ⓛ Holiday Inn Express, Plainview Inn, Super 8 ⓞ Verizon, Walmart/McDonald's
48	FM 3466, Plainview (from nb), E ⓞ Chevrolet
45	Lp 27, to Plainview
43	FM 2337
41	County Rd
38	Main St
37	FM 1914, Cleveland St, W ⓡ Conoco/dsl ⓞ city park, Family$, Lowe's Foods
36	FM 1424, Hale Center
32	FM 37 W
31	FM 37 E
29mm	ⓡˢ **both lanes, full ♿ facilities, litter barrels, petwalk Ⓒ 🖼 tornado shelter, vending**
27	County Rd
24	FM 54, W ⓞ RV park/dump
22	Lp 369, Abernathy
21	FM 597, Main St, Abernathy, W ⓡ Conoco/dsl ⓕ DQ ⓞ $General, USPO
20	FM 597, Abernathy (from nb)
17	CR 53
15	Lp 461, to New Deal, same as 14
14	FM 1729, E ⓡ Alon/rest./dsl/scales/24hr
13	Lp 461, to New Deal
12	access rd (from nb)
11	FM 1294, Shallowater
10	Keuka St, E ⓞ Fed Ex
9	🛩 Rd, E ⓞ airport, W ⓞ Lubbock RV Park/LP/dump
8	FM 2641, Regis St, E ⓞ airport, W ⓡ Loves/Subway/Chester's/dsl/scales/24hr
7	Yucca Lane, E ⓡ Pharr RV Ctr
6b a	Lp 289, Ave Q, Lubbock, E ⓞ Pharr RV
5	B. Holly Ave, Municipal Dr, E ⓞ Mackenzie SP, W ⓞ Civic Ctr

PLAINVIEW

LUBBOCK

4	US 82, US 87, 4th St, to Crosbyton, E ⓞ funpark, W ⓡ ⊕FLYING J/Subway/dsl/LP/scales/24hr ⓞ to TTU
3	US 62, TX 114, 19th St, Floydada
2	34th St, E ⓡ Phillips 66/dsl ⓕ Pete's Drive Inn, W ⓡ Valero ⓕ Josie's #5, Phillips 66, Subway ⓞ AutoZone, Raff&Hall Drug, U-Haul
1c	50th St, E ⓡ Buddy's ⓕ El Charro ⓞ Family$, W ⓡ Alon/7-11, Bolton Fuel/dsl, Valero/dsl ⓕ A&W/LJ Silver, Bryan's Steaks, Burger King, China Star, Church's, Domino's, KFC, McDonald's, McDonald's, Pizza Hut/Taco Bell, Subway, Taco Villa, Tech Cafe, Whataburger, Wienerschnitzel ⓛ Howard Johnson ⓞ $General, O'Reilly Parts, United Food/gas, USPO, Walgreens
1b	US 84, E ⓛ Best Value Inn, Days Inn, W ⓛ Best Western, Comfort Inn, Country Inn Suites, Holiday Inn Express, Motel 6, Quality Inn, Red Roof Inn, Super 8, Value Place
1a	Lp 289
1	82nd St. W ⓡ Phillips 66/dsl **I-27 begins/ends on US 87 at 82nd St in S Lubbock.**

INTERSTATE 30

Exit #	Services
223mm	Texas/Arkansas state line
223b a	US 59, US 71, State Line Ave, Texarkana, N ⓡ Exxon/dsl, EZ Mart, Shell/dsl ⓕ Denny's, IHOP, Los Agaves, Naaman's BBQ, Pizza Inn, Waffle House ⓛ Best Western, Clarion, Holiday Inn Express, Howard Johnson, La Quinta, Quality Inn, Ramada Inn, Regency Inn, Super 8, Texarkana Inn, Wyndham Garden ⓞ Cooper Tire, KOA, S ⓡ Chevron/dsl, Exxon, Murphy USA/dsl, RaceWay/dsl, Shell ⓕ Burger King, Cattleman's Steaks, China Inn, China King, El Chico, Fuzzy's Tacos, Hooters, KFC, Little Caesar's, LJ Silver, Marble Slab, McDonald's, Papa John's, Popeye's, Schlotzsky's, Slim Chickens, Sonic, Starbucks, Subway, Taco Bell, Wendy's, Whataburger ⓛ Ambassador Inn, Best Value Inn, Days Inn, EconoLodge, Executive Inn, La Quinta, Motel 6, Rodeway Inn ⓞ $General, $Tree, Albertson's/Sav-On, AutoZone, CVS Drug, Hancock Fabrics, O'Reilly Parts, VW, Walgreens, Walmart/Subway
223mm	**Welcome Ctr wb, full ♿ facilities, info, litter barrels, petwalk Ⓒ 🖼 vending**
222	TX 93, FM 1397, Summerhill Rd, N ⓡ Shell, Valero/Subway/dsl ⓕ Applebee's, McDonald's, The One Buffet, Waffle House ⓛ Motel 6 ⓞ AT&T, Goodyear Truck Tire, Hyundai, URGENT CARE, S ⓡ Shell/dsl ⓕ Bryce's Rest., Catfish King, Sonic ⓞ Ford, Gateway Tires, Nissan, Walmart Mkt/dsl
220b	FM 559, Richmond Rd, N ⓡ Shell ⓕ Buffalo Wild Wings, Burger King, Cane's, Carino's Italian, Chick-fil-A, Chipotle, CiCi's Pizza, Coldstone Creamery, Cracker Barrel, Domino's, DQ, Fuji Grill, Genghis Grill, Gusano's Pizza, Jason's Deli, Jimmy John's, Little Caesar's, Longhorn Steaks, McAlister's Deli, Mooyah Burgers, On-the-Border, Osaka Japanese, Papa Murphy's, Pizza Hut, Red Lobster, Reggie's Cafe, Ruby Tuesday, Schlotzsky's, Silver Star Smokehouse, Smashburger, Sonic, Starbucks, Steak'n Shake, Taco Bell, TaMolly's Mexican, TX Roadhouse, Wendy's, Wing Stop ⓛ Comfort Suites, Courtyard, Residence Inn, TownePlace Suites ⓞ $General, $Tree, AT&T, Best Buy, Chevrolet, Discount Tire, Home Depot, Honda, Kohl's, Kwik Kar, Meineke, Office Depot, Old Navy, Petsmart, Sam's Club/gas, Super 1 Food/gas, Target, TJ Maxx, Verizon, Walmart Mkt/dsl, S ⓡ Valero/dsl ⓕ Arby's, Chili's, ChuckeCheese, Firehouse Subs, Golden Chick, Golden Corral, Grandy's, Lee's China, McDonald's, Olive Garden, Outback Steaks, Subway, Taco Bueno

TEXARKANA

INTERSTATE 30 Cont'd

220b Continued
[lodging] Candlewood Suites, Hampton Inn, Hilton Garden/Conv Ctr, Holiday Inn Express [other] Albertson's/Sav-On, AT&T, Books-A-Million, Cavender's Boots, CVS Drug, Dillard's, Hobby Lobby, JC Penney, mall, Michael's, Ross, Sears/auto, Tuesday Morning, Walgreens

220a US 59 S, Texarkana

219 Pecan St, University Ave, N [other] Gander Mtn, S [gas] Exxon, Murphy USA [food] Subway, Wendy's [lodging] Country Inn&Suites, Fairfield Inn [other] Buick/GMC, Cadillac, Chrysler/Dodge/Jeep, Harley-Davidson, Kia, Lowe's, Mazda, Mercedes, vet, Walmart

218 FM 989, Nash, N [gas] Road Runner/dsl [food] Dixie Diner, Papa Poblano's, S [gas] Exxon/Burger King/dsl [food] Sonic [other] GMC/Peterbilt, to Lake Patman, Toyota/Scion, USPO

213 FM 2253, Leary, S [gas] Love's/McDonald's/Subway/dsl/scales/24hr

212 spur 74, S [gas] Shell/dsl [other] Lone Star Army Ammo Plant

208 FM 560, Hooks, S [gas] Truckstp/dsl/scales/24hr [food] DQ, Sonic [other] $General, Family$, Hooks Tire

NEW BOSTON

207 no services

206 TX 86, S [other] Red River Army Depot

201 TX 8, New Boston, N [gas] Shell/dsl, Valero/dsl [food] Pitt Grill [lodging] Tex Inn [other] Chevrolet, Chrysler/Dodge/Jeep, S [gas] Murphy USA/dsl, Shell/dsl [food] Amigo Juan, Catfish King, Church's, Domino's, DQ, KFC/Taco Bell, McDonald's, Pizza Hut, Randy's BBQ, Sonic [lodging] Best Value Inn, Bostonian Inn, Holiday Inn Express [other] Brookshire's Foods/gas, Ford, O'Reilly Parts, Walmart/Subway

199 US 82, New Boston, **1/2 mi** N [gas] VP/dsl

198 TX 98, **1/2 mi** N [gas] VP/dsl

193mm Anderson Creek

192 FM 990, N [food] Culpeppers Rest.

186 FM 561

181mm Sulphur River

178 US 259, to DeKalb, Omaha

174mm White Oak Creek

170 FM 1993

165 FM 1001

MT PLEASANT

162b a US 271, FM 1402, FM 2152, Mt Pleasant, N [gas] Exxon/dsl [food] Applebee's, Blalock BBQ [lodging] Holiday Inn Express, Super 8 [other] $General, KOA, S [gas] Shell/dsl, Valero/Subway/dsl [food] Burger King, McDonald's, Sonic [lodging] Best Western [other] H, $General, Cadillac/Chevrolet, Chrysler/Dodge/Jeep, Family$, Ford, vet

160 US 271, FM 1734, Mt Pleasant, N [gas] Texaco/dsl [food] Senorita's Mexican [lodging] La Quinta [other] Buick/GMC (1mi), Lowe's, Ramblin Fever RV Park (2mi), Toyota, S [gas] Exxon/dsl, Shell/dsl [food] El Chico, IHOP [lodging] Days Inn, Hampton Inn, Motel 6, Quality Inn [other] Sandlin SP

158mm **weigh sta both lanes**

156 frontage rd

153 spur 185, to Winfield, Miller's Cove, N [gas] Crazy 8, Winfield/dsl, S [gas] Shamrock/dsl

150 Ripley Rd, N [other] Lowe's Distribution

147 spur 423, N [gas] Love's/Chester's/Subway/dsl/scales/24hr [lodging] American Inn, Economy Inn [other] tires/repair

146 TX 37, Mt Vernon, N [food] Sonic [other] H, $General, auto repair, Brookshire Foods/gas, O'Reilly Parts, S [gas] Cefco/Huddle House/dsl/24hr, Exxon/dsl [food] Burger King, DQ, McDonald's, Mi Casita [lodging] Super 8 [other] auto/dsl repair, to Lake Bob Sandlin SP

143 **[RS] both lanes, full [handicapped] facilities, litter barrels, petwalk [phone] [picnic] vending**

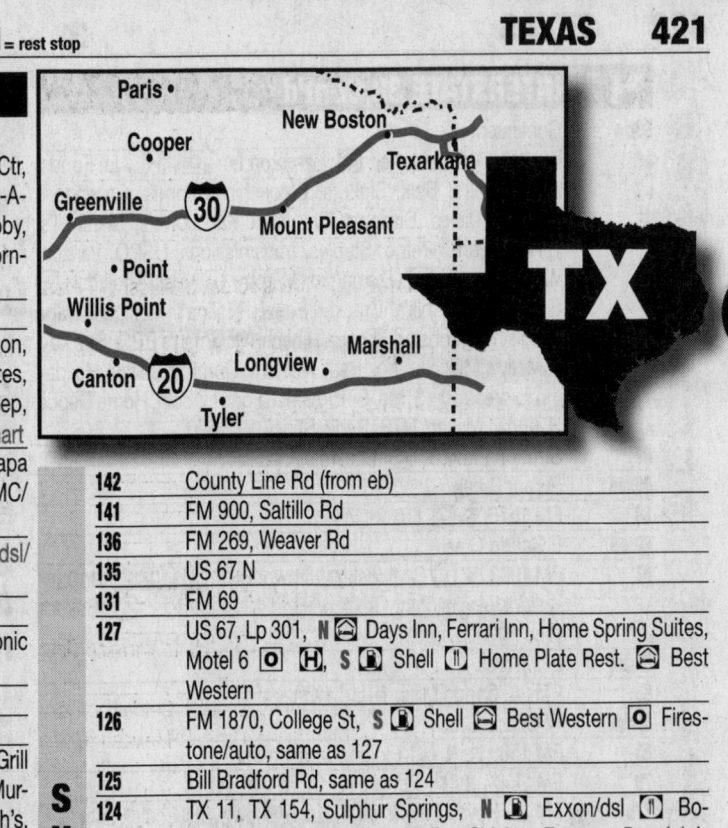

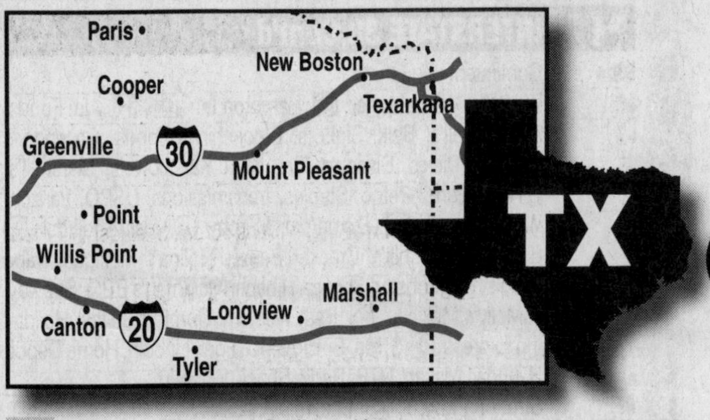

142 County Line Rd (from eb)

141 FM 900, Saltillo Rd

136 FM 269, Weaver Rd

135 US 67 N

131 FM 69

127 US 67, Lp 301, N [lodging] Days Inn, Ferrari Inn, Home Spring Suites, Motel 6 [other] H, S [gas] Shell [food] Home Plate Rest. [lodging] Best Western

126 FM 1870, College St, S [gas] Shell [lodging] Best Western [other] Firestone/auto, same as 127

SULPHUR SPGS

125 Bill Bradford Rd, same as 124

124 TX 11, TX 154, Sulphur Springs, N [gas] Exxon/dsl [food] Bodacious BBQ, Broadway Buffet, Chicken Express, Don lalo's Mexican, IHOP, Juan Pablo's Mexican, Metro Diner, Pizza Hut, Subway, Wendy's [lodging] Hampton Inn, Holiday Inn Express, Royal Inn [other] H, $General, AutoZone, Brookshire's Foods/gas, CVS Drug, Family$, Ford/Lincoln, FSA Outlet/famous brands, O'Reilly Parts, USPO, VF Outlet/famous brands, Walgreens, S [gas] Exxon/dsl, Murphy USA/dsl, Shell/dsl [food] Braum's, Burger King, Chili's, Domino's, Furr's Rest., Jack-in-the-Box, McDonald's, Panda Express, Pizza Inn, Sonic, Taco Bell/LJ Silver, Whataburger [other] AT&T, Cody Drug, Discount Wheel&Tire, Lowe's, Verizon, Walmart/Subway

123 FM 2297, League St, N [gas] Shamrock/dsl, Shell

122 TX 19, to Emory, N [gas] Shamrock/dsl [other] H, Chrysler/Dodge/Jeep, to Cooper Lake SP, Travel Time RV Ctr, S [gas] CNG, Pilot/Arby's/dsl/scales/24hr, Valero/Zinga's/dsl [other] dsl repair, RV Park

120 US 67 bus

116 FM 2653, Brashear Rd, S [other] USPO

112 FM 499 (from wb)

110 FM 275, Cumby, N [gas] Phillips 66/dsl, S [gas] Shell

104 FM 513, FM 2649, Campbell, S to Lake Tawakoni

101 TX 24, TX 50, FM 1737, to Commerce, N [gas] Valero/dsl [other] to TX A&M-Commerce, S [food] TX Beach Club Grill

97 Lamar St, N [gas] Exxon/dsl [lodging] Budget Inn, S [other] vet

96 Lp 302

95 Division St, S [other] H

94b US 69, US 380, Greenville, N [gas] Valero/dsl [food] Collin St Bakery, Golden Chick, Senorita's Mexican [lodging] Days Inn, Royal Inn [other] H, S [gas] Exxon, QT/dsl [food] Arby's, McDonald's, Racho Viejo [lodging] Economy Inn, Express Inn, Guest Inn, Motel 6, Super 8

94a US 69, US 380, Greenville, S [gas] QT/dsl, Valero/Subway/dsl [other] Chrysler/Dodge/Jeep

93b a US 67, TX 34 N, N [gas] Chevron/Taco Casa/dsl, Exxon/dsl, Shell/dsl, Texaco [food] Applebee's, Braum's, Chicken Express, Chick-fil-A, CiCi's, Cotton Patch Cafe, DQ, Grandy's, IHOP, Jack-in-the-Box, KFC, Little Caesar's, Pizza Hut, Schlotzsky's, Sonic, Starbucks, Subway, Taco Bell, Taco Bueno, Tony's Italian,

⯅E	**INTERSTATE 30 Cont'd**

GREENVILLE

TX

93b a	Continued
	Wendy's, Whataburger ⊟ Hampton Inn Ⓞ Ⓗ, Aldi Foods, AT&T, Beall's, Belk, BigLots, Brookshire's Foods, Cavender's Outfitter, Dick's, Discount Tire, Kwik Kar, Lowe's, Marshall's, O'Reilly Parts, Petco, Staples, transmissions, USPO, Verizon, Walgreens, **S** ■ Exxon/dsl, Murphy USA/dsl, Shell/dsl Ⓕ Burger King, Chili's, Cracker Barrel, Molina's Mexican, Papa John's, Red Lobster, Shogun Hibachi, Soulman's BBQ, Subway, TaMolly's Mexican ⊟ Best Western, Comfort Suites, Holiday Inn Express Ⓞ $Tree, Buick/GMC, Ford/Lincoln, Home Depot, Hyundai, Nissan, NTB, Radio Shack, Walmart
92	Stratton Pkwy, **S** Ⓞ Chevrolet/Cadillac
90mm	Farber Creek
89	FM 1570, **S** ⊟ Luxury Inn
89mm	E Caddo Creek
87	FM 1903, **N** ■ Shell/dsl Ⓞ fireworks, **S** ■ ▦/McDonald's/dsl/scales/24hr, Texaco/Huddle House/dsl Ⓕ Baker's Ribs Ⓞ tire repair
87mm	Elm Creek
85	FM 36, Caddo Mills, **N** Ⓞ KOA
85mm	W Caddo Creek
83	FM 1565 N, **N** ■ Exxon/Pizza Inn/dsl
79	FM 2642, **N** Ⓞ Budget RV Ctr, **S** Ⓞ vet
77b	FM 35, Royse City, **N** ■ Texaco/Subway/dsl/scales/24hr Ⓕ Soulman's BBQ Ⓞ Family$
77a	TX 548, Royse City, **N** ■ Shell/dsl Ⓕ Jack-in-the-Box, McDonald's ⊟ American Inn Ⓞ AutoZone, tires, **S** ■ Exxon Ⓕ Denny's, Pizza Hut, Rice Express, Sonic, Taco Bell ⊟ Holiday Inn Express
76	Campbell Blvd, **N** Ⓞ CVS Drug, Walmart
73	FM 551, Fate
70	FM 549, **N** Ⓞ Happy Trails RV Ctr, McLains RV Ctr, **S** ■ ♥Loves/Carl's Jr./dsl/scales/24hr Ⓞ Kia
69	(from wb), frontage rd, **N** ⊟ Super 8, **S** Ⓞ Honda, Hyundai, Nissan, Nissan, Toyota/Scion
68	TX 205, to Rock Wall, **N** ■ 7-11/dsl, Murphy USA/dsl, QT/dsl, Shell Ⓕ Braum's, Chicken Express, Domino's, Joe Willy's Grill, Luigi's Italian, Starbucks, Subway, Taco Casa, Whataburger ⊟ Best Western, Super 8, Value Place Ⓞ Buick/GMC, Chevrolet, Chrysler/Dodge/Jeep, Ford, Hobby Lobby, vet, Walmart/Subway, **S** ■ RaceTrac/dsl, TA/Burger King/Starbucks/dsl/24hr/scales/ @ Ⓕ Cane's, Firehouse Subs, Freebird Burritos, In-N-Out, Luby's, Rosa's Cafe, Soulman's BBQ Ⓞ Belk, Costco/gas, Jo-Ann Fabrics, Toyota/Scion
67b	FM 740, Ridge Rd, **N** ■ Chevron, Murphy USA/dsl Ⓕ Buffet City, Culver's, Denny's, Edohana Hibachi, Grandy's, IHOP, LJ Silver, Logan's Roadhouse, McDonald's, Mellow Mushroom Pizza, Popeye's, Schlotzsky's, Steak'n Shake, Taco Bueno, Taco Cabana, Waffle House, Wendy's ⊟ Hampton Inn Ⓞ Firestone/auto, Goodyear/auto, **S** ■ Exxon, Kroger/dsl, Shell Ⓕ Applebee's, Bahama Buck's Ice Cream, Blackeyed Pea, Buffalo Wild Wings, Carino's Italian, Chick-fil-A, Chili's, Chipotle Mexican, ChuckeCheese, CiCi's, Cotton Patch Cafe, Dickey's BBQ, El Chico, Firehouse Subs, Five Guys, Freebirds Burrito, Jack-in-the-Box, Jimmy John's, La Madelein, Mi Cocina, Mooyah Burgers, Olive Garden, On-the-Border, Panda Express, Pizza Hut, Sonic, Soulman's BBQ, Starbucks, Subway, Taco Bell, Which Wich? ⊟ La Quinta Ⓞ Ⓗ, $Tree, AT&T, Beall's, Belk, Best Buy, CVS Drug, Dick's, Discount Tire, Home Depot, JC Penney, Jo-Ann, Kohl's, Lowe's, Michael's, NTB, Old Navy, PetCo, Petsmart, Radio Shack, Ross, Staples, SteinMart, Target, TJ Maxx, to Lake Tawakoni, URGENT CARE, Verizon, vet

ROCKWALL

GARLAND

DALLAS

67a	Horizon Rd, Village Dr, **N** Ⓕ Genghis Grill, Kyoto Japanese, Saltgrass Steaks, Snuffer's Rest, Starbucks ⊟ Hampton Inn, **S** Ⓕ Culpepper Steaks, Oar House ⊟ Hilton
66mm	Ray Hubbard Reservoir
64	Dalrock Rd, Rowlett, **N** ■ Shell/dsl, Valero/dsl Ⓕ Alejandro's Grill, Church's, Dickey's BBQ ⊟ Comfort Suites Ⓞ Ⓗ
63mm	Ray Hubbard Reservoir
62	Bass Pro Dr, **N** ⊟ Quality Inn Ⓞ to Hubbard RA, **S** ■ Shell/dsl, Texaco, Valero/dsl Ⓕ CiCi's Pizza, Flying Saucer Grill, Islamadora Fish Co, Primo's Grille, TX Land&Cattle, Whataburger ⊟ Holiday Inn Express Ⓞ Bass Pro Shops
61b	Bush Tpk
61a	Zion Rd (from wb), **N** ■ Exxon/dsl ⊟ Discovery Inn
60b	Bobtown Rd (eb only), **N** ■ 7-11/dsl Ⓕ Jack-in-the-Box ⊟ La Quinta, **S** ■ Shell Ⓕ Subway
60a	Rose Hill Dr
59	Beltline Rd, Garland, **N** ■ 7-11/dsl, QT Ⓕ Chili's, China City, Denny's, IHOP, KFC, Little Caesar's, McDonald's, McDonald's, Moe's SW, Papa John's, Starbucks, Subway, Taco Bell, Taco Cabana, Taco Casa, Wendy's, Whataburger Ⓞ Albertson's, Discount Tire, GNC, Tuesday Morning, Walgreens, Walmart, **S** ■ RaceTrac/dsl Ⓕ Baker's Ribs, Carl's Jr, DQ, Sonic, Waffle House, Williams Chicken ⊟ Best Value Inn, Motel 6, Super 8 Ⓞ AT&T, Kroger
58	Northwest Dr, **N** ■ Shell, Valero/dsl Ⓞ Hyundai, Nissan, **S** ■ Exxon/dsl, QT/dsl, Texaco Ⓕ Jack-in-the-Box Ⓞ Lowe's
56c b	I-635 S-N
56a	Galloway Ave, Gus Thomasson Dr (from eb), **N** ■ Star USA, Texaco, Valero/dsl Ⓕ Golden Chick, KFC, McDonald's, Sonic, Taco Bell Ⓞ AutoZone, USPO, Walgreens, **S** ■ 7-11, Chevron Ⓕ Dicky's BBQ, Domino's, El Fenix, Grandy's, Hooters, Jack-in-the-Box, King Buffet, Luby's, Olive Garden, Outback Steaks, Posado's Cafe, Razzoo's Cajun, Red Lobster, Sports City Cafe, Subway, TGIFriday's, Wendy's ⊟ Courtyard, Crossland Suites, Delux Inn, Fairfield Inn Ⓞ Aldi Foods, BigLots, Celebration Sta Funpark, Firestone/auto, Kroger/dsl, NTB, RV Max
55	Motley Dr, **N** ■ Shell/dsl ⊟ Astro Inn Ⓞ to Eastfield Coll, **S** ■ Exxon/7-11 ⊟ Microtel
54	Big Town Blvd, **N** ■ Valero/dsl ⊟ Mesquite Inn, **S** Ⓞ Explore RV Ctr, Holiday World RV Ctr
53b	US 80 E (from eb), to Terrell
53a	Lp 12, Buckner, **N** ⊟ Holiday Inn Express, Super 8 Ⓞ Chevrolet, Toyota/Scion, **S** Ⓕ Panda Express, Taco Cabana, Whataburger Ⓞ $Tree, Sam's Club/gas, Staples, Walmart
51	(52 a from wb), Highland Rd, Jim Miller Blvd, **N** ■ Exxon/7-11 Ⓕ Country China, Denny's, McDonald's, Waffle House ⊟ Holiday Inn Express, Quality Inn, **S** ■ RaceWay/dsl, Shell/dsl Ⓕ Burger King, Capt D's, CiCi's Pizza, Furr's Cafe, Grandy's, KFC, Popeye's, Subway, Taco Bell, Wendy's ⊟ Motel 6, Super 7 Inn Ⓞ AutoZone, CVS Drug, O'Reilly Parts
50b a	Longview, Ferguson Rd, **N** ■ Texaco, **S** Ⓞ Brake-O, U-Haul
49b	Dolphin Rd, Lawnview Ave, Samuell Ave, **N** ■ Shell ⊟ Best Value Inn
49a	Winslow St, **N** ■ Circle K, Shell/dsl Ⓕ Jack-in-the-Box, McDonald's, **S** ■ Circle K, Shell/dsl Ⓞ tires
48b	TX 78, E Grand, **N** Ⓞ arboretum, **S** Ⓞ fairpark
48a	Carroll Ave, Central Ave, Peak St, Haskell Ave, **N** ■ 7-11, Shamrock, Valero Ⓞ Ⓗ, Hamm's Tires, **S** Ⓕ Joe's Rest
47	2nd Ave, **S** ■ Shell Ⓕ McDonald's Ⓞ Cotton Bowl, fairpark
46b	I-45, US 75, to Houston
46a	Central Expswy, downtown

INTERSTATE 30 Cont'd

Exit #	Services
45	I-35E, N to Denton, to Commerce St, Lamar St, Griffin St, S Gulf/dsl McDonald's Ambassador Inn
44b	I-35E S, Industrial Blvd
44a	I-35E N, Beckley Ave (from eb)
43b a	Sylvan Ave (from wb), N Valero/dsl H, Family$, USPO
42	Hampton Rd
41	Westmoreland Ave
39	Cockrell Hill Rd, N Shell/dsl Grand China, IHOP, KFC/ Taco Bell, Pollo Campero, Sonic, Wing Stop Comfort Suites, Fairfield Inn, Hampton Inn Staples, S Murphy USA/dsl Burger King, Chick-fil-A, Chili's, CiCi's, Dickey's BBQ, Golden Corral, Little Caesar's, Lucky Rice, McDonald's, New Buffet, Panda Express, Starbucks, Subway, Taco Cabana, Wendy's, Whataburger Holiday Inn Express $Tree, Best Buy, Lowe's, Ross, Walmart/McDonald's
38	Lp 12, **1 mi** N Exxon/7-11, Texaco/dsl, VP/dsl Burger King
36	MacArthur Blvd, S U-Haul
34	Belt Line Rd, N QT/dsl, RaceTrac/dsl Studio 6, Super 8 Ford, Ripley's Museum, S RaceTrac/dsl, Shell/Subway/ dsl, Valero/dsl Burger King, Popeye's, Schlotzsky's, Starbucks city park, vet
32b a	George Bush Tpk, toll, N Valero/dsl
30	TX 360, Six Flags Dr, Arlington Stadium, N Shell, Valero/dsl Boston's, Cracker Barrel, Grand Buffet, Saltgrass Steaks, Steak'n Shake, The Rock Grill, Wendy's Best Inn, Budget Suites, Candlewood Suites, Crowne Plaza, Extended Stay America, Extended Stay America, Fairfield Inn, Hawthorn Suites, Hilton, Hilton Garden, Hyatt Place, Motel 6, Residence Inn, Studio 6, Wingate Inn, S Shell/7-11/dsl, Valero Denny's, Humperdink's Rest., Jack-in-the-Box, Mariano's Mexican, McDonald's, Red Neck Heaven Rest, Subway Baymont Inn, Holiday Inn Express, Homewood Suites, Hyatt Place, Knight's Inn, La Quinta, Quality Inn, Ranger Inn, Sleep Inn Ford/Lincoln, Six Flags Funpark
29	Ball Park Way, N Chevron/7-11, QT, Valero/dsl Dicky's BBQ, Rio Mambo, Sonic Hampton Inn, Springhill Suites, Towneplace Suites Auto Nation/Toyota/Scion, USPO, S On-the-Border, Vila Brazil Howard Johnson, Sheraton Six Flags Funpark
28b a	FM 157, Collins St, N Chevron/dsl Chipotle, IHOP, Mooyah Burgers, Pei Wei, Potbelly, Starbucks, Waffle House EconoLodge, Holiday Inn BMW, Cadillac, Chrysler/ Dodge/Jeep, Mini, Walmart, Whole Foods Mkt, S Arby's, Asian Buffet, Blackeyed Pea, Blue Mesa Grill, Buffalo Wild Wings, Cane's, Chili's, El Chico, Gino's East Pizzaria, Hooters, Jason's Deli, Joe's Crab Shack, Lupe's Grill, Olive Garden, Panda Express, Panera Bread, Pappadeaux, Pappasito's Cantina, Popeye's, Sherlock's Grill, Subway, Taco Bell, Taco Bueno, TGIFriday's, TX Land&Cattle, Wendy's, Which Wich? Comfort Suites, Courtyard, Days Inn $Tree, GNC, Home Depot, Michael's, Office Depot, PepBoys, Petsmart, Ross, SteinMart, TX Stadium, Walgreens
27	Lamar Blvd, Cooper St, N Gulf Jack-in-the-Box, Subway BigLots, Family$, Kroger/dsl, vet, S 7-11, QT/dsl, Shell/dsl Burger King, Pappasito's Cantina, Tom's Burgers Comfort Suites
26	Fielder Rd, S to Six Flags (from eb)
25mm	Village Creek
24	Eastchase Pkwy, N Jack-in-the-Box, Panda Express La Quinta CarMax, Lowe's, Sam's Club/gas, Verizon,

ARLINGTON

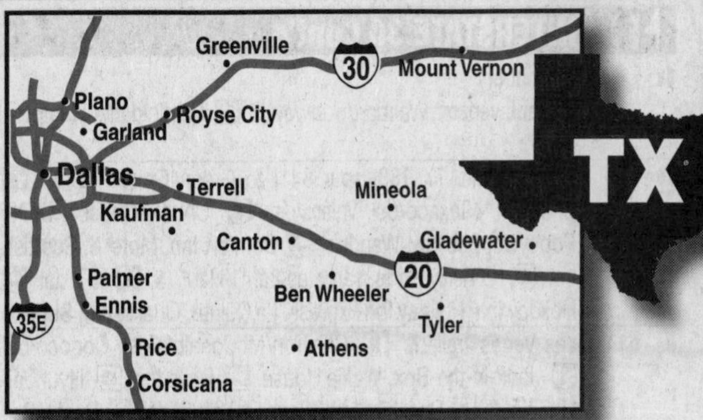

Exit #	Services
24	Continued Walmart/McDonald's, S Chevron/7-11/dsl, RaceTrac/dsl, Shell/7-11/dsl Burger King, Chicken Express, CiCi's Pizza, IHOP, McDonald's, No Frills Grill, Pizza Hut, Schlotzsky's, Subway, Taco Bell, Wendy's, Whataburger $Tree, Aldi Foods, AT&T, GNC, Marshall's, Office Depot, Radio Shack, Ross, Target
23	Cooks Lane, S Shell/dsl
21c b	I-820
21a	Bridgewood Dr, N Chevron/dsl Braum's, Dickey's BBQ, Jack-in-the-Box, KFC, Luby's, Subway, Taco Casa, Wendy's $General, Albertson's, Discount Tire, Firestone/auto, Home Depot, U-Haul, S Conoco, Phillips 66/dsl, QT Taco Bueno, Whataburger/24hr
19	Brentwood Stair Rd (from eb), N Shell, S Shamrock, Texaco Family$
18	Oakland Blvd, N Circle K, Shell/dsl Taco Bell, Waffle House Motel 6
16c	Beach St, S 7-11 Motel 6, Stay Express Hotel
16b a	Riverside Dr (from wb), S Great Western Inn
15b a	I-35W N to Denton, S to Waco
14b	Jones St, Commerce St, Ft Worth, downtown
14a	TX 199, Henderson St, Ft Worth, downtown
13b	TX 199, Henderson St, N Holiday Inn Express, Omni, Sheraton
13a	8th Ave, N Holiday Inn Express
12b	Forest Park Blvd, N Pappadeaux Café, Pappa's Burgers, Pappasito's, S H, URGENT CARE
12a	University Dr, City Parks, S SpringHill Suites
11	Montgomery St, S Shell/7-11/dsl Railhead BBQ, Taco Bell, Whataburger
10	Hulen St, Ft Worth, S Buttons Rest., Chick-fil-A, McDonald's, Mi Cocina, Potbelly, Smoothie King, Starbucks Central Mkt, WorldMkt
9b	US 377, Camp Bowie Blvd, Horne St, N Uncle Julio's Mexican, S 7-11, Exxon/7-11, Texaco/dsl Campisi's Italian, Chipotle, Jack-in-the-Box, Jason's Deli, Jersey Mike's, Jimmy John's, McDonald's, Mexican Inn Cafe, Schlotzsky's, Smashburger, Sonic, Starbucks, Subway, Taco Bueno, Wendy's AT&T, Batteries+Bulbs, URGENT CARE, Walgreens
9a	Bryant-Irvin Rd, S Shell same as 9b
8b	Ridgmar, Ridglea
8a	TX 183, Green Oaks Rd, N Applebee's, Arby's, Asia Bowl, Cane's, Chick-fil-A, Chipotle, Cowtown BBQ, Del Taco, Don Pablo's, Firehouse Subs, Grand Buffet, Jack-in-the-Box, McDonald's, Olive Garden, Panda Express, Papa Murphy's, Sonic, Subway, Taco Bueno, Whataburger, Woody Creek BBQ Courtyard $Tree, Albertson's, Aldi Foods, AT&T, Best Buy, BigLots, Dillard's, Firestone/auto, JC Penney, Jo-Ann Fabrics, Lowe's, Macy's, Neiman Marcus, NTB, Office Depot, Old Navy, PetCo, Petsmart, Ross, Sam's Club/gas, Sears/auto, Target,

FT WORTH

INTERSTATE 30 Cont'd

8a	Continued
	U-Haul, Verizon, Walmart/Subway, **S** 🛏 Fairfield Inn, Hampton Inn
7b a	Cherry Lane, TX 183, spur 341, to Green Oaks Rd, **N** 🅖 Shell/7-11, Texaco/dsl, Valero/dsl 🍴 ChuckECheese, IHOP, Popeye's, Subway, Wendy's 🛏 Comfort Inn, Motel 6, Scottish Inn 🅞 O'Reilly Parts, same as 8a, U-Haul, **S** 🅖 QT/dsl 🛏 Holiday Inn, Holiday Inn Express, La Quinta, Quality Inn, Super 8
6	Las Vegas Trail, **N** 🅖 Chevron/McDonald's/dsl, Conoco/dsl 🍴 Jack-in-the-Box, Waffle House 🛏 Days Inn 🅞 Hyundai, Lincoln, **S** 🅖 Shell/7-11/dsl, Texaco, Valero/dsl 🛏 Best Value Inn, Knights Inn, Relax Inn 🅞 AutoZone, Kia, vet
5b c	I-820 N and S
5a	Alemeda St (from eb, no EZ return)
3	RM 2871, Chapel Creek Blvd, **S** 🅖 Exxon/Church's/Subway/dsl 🍴 Sonic
2	spur 580 E
1b	Linkcrest Dr, **S** 🅖 Gulf/dsl
0mm	I-20 W. **I-30 begins/ends on I-20, exit 421.**

INTERSTATE 35

G A I N E S V I L L E

Exit #	Services
504mm	Texas/Oklahoma state line, Red River
504	frontage rd, **access to Texas Welcome Ctr**
503mm	**parking area both lanes**
502mm	**TX Tourist Bureau/info, Welcome Ctr sb, full ♿ facilities, litter barrels 🚻 📶 wireless internet**
501	FM 1202, Prime Outlets Blvd, **E** 🅞 Chrysler/Dodge/Jeep, Ford, **W** 🅖 Conoco/café/dsl 🍴 Applebee's, Cracker Barrel, Serna's Mexican 🛏 Hampton Inn, La Quinta 🅞 Prime Outlets/famous brands, RV camping, Western Outfitter
500	FM 372, Gainesville, **W** 🅖 Hitchin' Post/Shell/dsl
498b a	US 82, to Wichita Falls, Gainesville, Sherman, **E** 🅖 Chevron/dsl, Exxon, Shell/dsl, Valero/dsl 🍴 TX Border Rest, Waffle Inn 🛏 12 Oaks Inn, Bed&Bath Inn, Budget Host, Super 8 🅞 🅷, **W** 🅖 Exxon/dsl 🛏 Atria Inn, Comfort Suites, Days Inn
497	frontage rd, **W** 🅖 Valero/dsl
496b	TX 51, FM 51, California St, Gainesville, **E** 🍴 Arby's, Braum's, Fera's Mexican, IHOP, McDonald's, Sonic, Starbucks, Starbucks, Taco Bell, Taco Casa, Wendy's 🛏 Holiday Inn Express, Quality Inn 🅞 Goodyear/auto, N Central TX Coll, **W** 🅖 Valero 🍴 Chili's
496a	to Weaver St
496mm	Elm Fork of the Trinity River
495	frontage rd
494	FM 1306
492mm	🏞 sb, litter barrels
491	Spring Creek Rd
490mm	🏞 nb, litter barrels
489	FM 1307, to Hockley Creek Rd
487	FM 922, Valley View, **W** 🅖 Valero/dsl/24hr 🍴 DQ 🅞 USPO
486	Fm 1307, **W** 🅖 Texaco/dsl 🛏 Motel 6 🅞 $General
485	frontage rd (from sb)
483	FM 3002, Lone Oak Rd, **E** 🅖 Shell/Church's/Subway/dsl 🅞 Roberts Lake SP
482	Chisam Rd
481	View Rd, **W** 🅞 McClain's RV Ctr
480	Lois Rd, **E** 🅞 Walmart Dist Ctr
479	Belz Rd, Sanger, same as 478

D E N T O N

478	FM 455, to Pilot Pt, Bolivar, **E** 🅖 QuickTrack, Shell 🍴 DQ, Fuzzy's Tacos, Miguelitos, Sonic, Subway, Taco Bell 🛏 Sange Inn 🅞 RV park, USPO, **W** 🅖 Chevron/dsl, Fuel 4 TX/Chicke Express/dsl 🍴 Jack-in-the-Box, McDonald's 🅞 Chevrole Family$, IGA Foods, Kwik Kar Lube, O'Reilly Parts, Ray Rober Lake and SP, RV Park
477	Keaton Rd, **E** 🅖 Exxon 🅞 Curves
475b	Rector Rd
475a	FM 156, to Krum (from sb)
474	Cowling rd (from nb)
473	FM 3163, Milam Rd, **E** 🅖 ❤Loves/Subway/dsl/scales/24h
472	Ganzer Rd, **W** 🅞 Best Value RV Ctr, Crandell RV Ctr
471	US 77, FM 1173, Lp 282, to Denton, Krum, **E** 🅖 TA/Pizza Hut Taco Bell/dsl/scales/24hr/ @ 🅞 🅷, **W** 🅞 Foster's Wester Shop, to Camping World RV Supply, truckwash
470	Lp 288, same services as 469 from sb
469	US 380, University Dr, to Decatur, McKinney, **E** 🅖 Chevror Subway, RaceTrac/dsl 🍴 Braum's, Catfish King, Chick-fil-A ChinaTown Café, Cowboy Chicken, Cracker Barrel, Freebird Burrito, Luigi's Pizza, McDonald's, Panda Express, Taco Casa Villa Grande, Whataburger, Which Wich, Wing Stop 🛏 Bes Western, Fairfield Inn 🅞 Albertson's/Sav-On, AT&T, GNC, Jo Ann Fabrics, Kohl's, Kwik Kar, PetCo, Ross, Sam's Club/gas Walmart/McDonald's, **W** 🅖 QT/dsl, Shell/dsl 🍴 Denny's DQ, Sonic, Waffle House 🛏 Comfort Inn, Days Inn, Holida Inn Express, Howard Johnson, La Quinta, Motel 6, ValuePlac Inn 🅞 🅷, Camping World RV Supply, I-35 RV Ctr, to TX Woman's U
468	FM 1515, 🔀 Rd, W Oak St, **E** 🅞 🅷
467	I-35W, S to Ft Worth
I-35 divides into E and W sb, converges into I-35 nb. See Texas I-35 W	
466b	Ave D, **E** 🅖 Exxon/dsl 🍴 IHOP, McDonald's, Pancho's Mex can, Taco Cabana 🛏 Comfort Suites 🅞 $General, Sack' Save Foods, to NTSU
466a	McCormick St, **E** 🅖 EKon, Shell/7-11/dsl 🍴 Pon cho's Mexican, Taco Cabana 🛏 Comfort Suites, Royal In 🅞 Sack&Save, **W** 🅖 Fina/dsl
465b	US 377, Ft Worth Dr, **E** 🅖 RaceTrac/dsl, Valero 🍴 Michael' Kitchen, Taco Bell, Taco Bueno, Whataburger 🛏 La Quinta **W** 🅖 EKon, QuickTrack 🍴 Outback Steaks, Soni 🛏 Knights Inn
465a	FM 2181, Teasley Ln, **E** 🅖 7-11 🍴 Applebee's, Braum's, Ca rino's, ChuckeCheese, Domino's, Hooters, KFC, Little Caesars Pizza Hut 🛏 Hampton Inn, Holiday Inn, Quality Inn 🅞 bank Brookshires Foods, PepBoys, U-Haul, **W** 🅖 Exxon, Shell 🍴 La Milpa Mexican, Rudy's BBQ/gas 🛏 Best Value Inn, Super 🅞 vet
464	US 77, Pennsylvania Dr, Denton, same as 463
463	Lp 288, to McKinney, **E** 🍴 Arby's, Buffet King, Burger King CiCi's Pizza, El Chico, El Fenix, Golden Corral, Grandy's, Ja son's Deli, McAlister's Deli, Olive Garden, On-the-Border, Pizz Hut/Taco Bell, Red Lobster, Starbucks, TX Roadhouse, Wen dy's 🛏 Best Western, Courtyard, Hilton Garden 🅞 $Tre AT&T, Barnes&Noble, BigLots, Burlington Coats, Dillards, Dis count Tire, Goodyear, Hastings Books, Hobby Lobby, Hom Depot, JC Penney, Macy's, Office Depot, Old Navy, PetCo Ross, Sears/auto, Staples, Target, Verizon, **W** 🅖 Chevron/ds 🍴 Blackeyed Pea, Chili's, Chuy's Mexican, Genghis Grill, Ita lia Cafe, Jack-in-the-Box, Schlotzsky's 🛏 Homewood Suite 🅞 same as 464, vet
462	State School Rd, Mayhill Rd, **E** 🅖 QT 🍴 Dickey's BBQ 🅞 🅷, URGENT CARE, **W** 🅖 Exxon 🍴 Shogun Japanese, Son

INTERSTATE 35 Cont'd

462 Continued
[other] Buick/GMC, Cadillac, Chevrolet, Curves, Dodge, Honda, Toyota/Scion

461 Sandy Shores Rd, Post Oak Dr, E [other] Explore USA RV Ctr, Ford, Hyundai, vet, W [other] Christian Bros Auto, Chrysler/Dodge/Jeep, Kia, Mazda, Nissan, Subaru

460 Corinth Pkwy, E [gas] Chevron/dsl [other] camping, McClains RV Ctr, W [other] Harley-Davidson

459 frontage rd, W [other] Destiny RV Resort

458 FM 2181, Swisher Rd, E [gas] Circle K, QT/dsl, Shell [lodging] Best Western, Comfort Inn [other] O'Reilly Parts, W [gas] Chevron/McDonald's, Exxon/7-11, Murphy USA/dsl [food] Burger King, Chicken Express, Chick-fil-A, IHOP, IHOP, Jack-in-the-Box, KFC/Taco Bell, Little Caesars, McDonald's, Sonic, Starbucks, Subway, Wendy's, Whataburger [other] Albertson's, AutoZone, Discount Tire, GNC, Kwik Kar, Radio Shack, URGENT CARE, Walgreens, Walmart

457b Denton Rd, Hundley Dr, Lake Dallas, W [food] Chili's, Hickory Creek BBQ, TX L&C Steaks

457a Hundley Dr (from nb), Lake Dallas

456 Highland Village

456mm Lewisville Lake

454b Garden Ridge Blvd, W [gas] Fuel4TX [other] city park

454a FM 407, Justin, E [gas] Valero [food] Old House BBQ, W [gas] QT, Valero [food] McDonald's

453 Valley Ridge Blvd, E [other] Ford, May's RV, W [gas] Chevron [food] Burger King, Subway [other] Home Depot, Kohl's, Lowe's, Staples

452 FM 1171, to Flower Mound, E [food] IHOP, Taco Bueno [lodging] Select Inn [other] [H], W [gas] Shell [food] Buffet Palace, Cane's, Chick-fil-A, Chipotle Mexican, CiCi's Pizza, Corner Cafe, Grandy's, McDonald's, Panda Express, Taco Bell, Taco Cabana, Whataburger [other] Albertson's, Midas, PetCo, Radio Shack, same as 451, Sam's Club/gas, Staples, transmissions, U-Haul, URGENT CARE, Walmart

451 Fox Ave, E [gas] Shell/dsl [food] Braum's, W [gas] Chevron [food] Cracker Barrel [lodging] EconoLodge, Hampton Inn [other] Family$, VW

450 TX 121, Grapevine, E [gas] 7-11 [lodging] Texan Inn [other] $General, Chrysler/Dodge/Jeep, Oliver's Automotive, W [gas] Chevron, Conoco/dsl, Fina/dsl [food] Burger King, Church's, LJ Silver, McDonald's, Subway, Taco Bell, Waffle House [other] Firestone/auto, Kroger, Kwik Kar, Nissan, Toyota/Scion, transmissions

LEWISVILLE

449 Corporate Drive, E [gas] Valero/dsl [food] Awshucks Oyster Bar, Fox&Hound, Hooters, On-the-Border, Wild Ginger Steaks [lodging] Extended Stay America, Motel 6 [other] Cavender's Boots, Chevrolet, Honda, Just Brakes, transmissions, W [gas] Valero [food] Cantina Loredo, Chili's, Denny's, El Fenix, Outback Steaks [lodging] Best Western, La Quinta [other] $Tree, Jo-Ann Fabrics, Marshall's, NTB, Petsmart

448b a FM 3040, Round Grove Rd, E [gas] 7-11, Citgo [food] A&W, Abuelo's Mexican, Cane's, ChuckeCheese, Dickey's BBQ, Frankie's Grill, Jack-in-the-Box, Joe's Crabshack, LJ Silver, Mimi's Cafe, Olive Garden, Pei Wei, Saltgrass Steaks, Souper Salad, Starbucks, Subway, Tilted Kilt [lodging] Homewood Suites [other] Honda, Radio Shack, Ross, Target, W [gas] Exxon/7-11, RaceTrac [food] 5 Guys Burgers, Applebee's, BJ's Grill, Buffalo Wild Wings, Carino's Italian, Chick-fil-A, Chipotle Mexican, Cotton Patch Rest, Denny's, Firehouse Subs, IHOP, Jason's Deli, La Madeline Bakery, Logan's Roadhouse, Macaroni Grill, McDonald's, Panda Express, Red Lobster, Redneck Heaven BBQ, Schlotzsky's, Sonic, Spring Creek BBQ, Starbucks, Steak'n Shake, Taco Bueno, Taco Cabana, TGIFriday's, Twin Peaks [lodging] Comfort

TX

DALLAS

448b a Continued
Suites, Country Inn&Suites, Courtyard, Fairfield Inn, Hampton Inn, Hilton Garden, Holiday Inn Express, Old Country Inn [other] AT&T, Barnes&Noble, Best Buy, Costco/gas, Dillard's, Discount Tire, JC Penney, Macy's, mall, Michael's, Office Depot, Old Navy, Sears/auto, Verizon

446 Frankford Rd, E [gas] RaceTrac [food] La Hacienda Ranch Grill [other] Volvo

445b a Pres Geo Bush Tpk

444 Whitlock Lane, Sandy Lake Rd, E [gas] Shell [food] Bros Pizza, El Paisa, La Hacienda [lodging] Rodeway Inn [other] Buick/GMC, Kia, RV camping, W [food] McDonald's, Starbucks [lodging] Delux Inn [other] Harley-Davidson

443 Belt Line Rd, Crosby Rd, E [gas] RaceTrac [other] Ford, Hyundai, NTB, W [gas] Shell [other] Chevrolet, U-Haul

442 Valwood Pkwy, E [gas] Chevron/Subway [food] Abby's Mexican, DQ, Grandy's, Jack-in-the-Box, Redline Burgers, Taco Bueno, Waffle House [lodging] Guest Inn, LoneStar Inn, Royal Inn, Super 8 [other] Hill Tire, W [gas] Fina/dsl [other] transmissions

441 Valley View Lane, W [gas] Chevron, Shell [food] Michael's Rest. [lodging] Best Value Inn, Days Inn, La Quinta

440b I-635 E

440c I-635 W, [other] to DFW [airport]

439 Royal Lane, E [gas] Shamrock, Shell [food] McDonald's, W [gas] Chevron, Exxon/dsl [food] Jack-in-the-Box

438 Walnut Hill Lane, E [gas] Chevron/dsl, Shell, Valero/dsl [food] Burger King, Church's, Denny's, Trail Dust Steaks, Wild Turkey Grill [lodging] Comfort Inn, Hampton Inn, La Quinta [other] Suzuki, W [gas] Shell/dsl

437 Manana Rd (from nb), same as 438

436 TX 348, to DFW, Irving, E [gas] Shell/dsl [food] IHOP, Rucas Cantina, Starbucks, Waffle House [lodging] Courtyard, Elegante Hotel, Holiday Inn Express, SpringHill Suites, Studio 6, Suburban Lodge, W [gas] Exxon, Valero [food] Chili's, Ghengis Grill, Humperdinks, Jack-in-the-Box, Jason's Deli, Joe's Crabshack, McDonald's, Olive Garden, Papadeaux Seafood, Pappa's BBQ, Pappasito's Mexican, Red Lobster, Taco Bell/Pizza Hut, TX L&C, Wendy's [lodging] Best Value Inn, Budget Suites, Century Inn

435 Harry Hines Blvd (from nb)

434b Regal Row, E [gas] Texaco/Grandy's [food] Denny's, Whataburger [lodging] Motel 6, W [lodging] Ramada Inn

434a Empire, Central, E [gas] Shell/McDonald's [food] Kay's Rest, Sonic, Wendy's [lodging] Budget Suites, Candlewood Suites, InTown Suites, Wingate Inn [other] Office Depot, W [gas] Texaco [food] Burger King, Pizza Hut/Taco Bell, Schlotzsky's

433b Mockingbird Lane, E [gas] Shell/dsl [food] Jack-in-the-Box [lodging] Budget Suites, Comfort Inn, Crowne Plaza, Park Inn, Radisson, Residence Inn, Sheraton, [other] Love Field [airport]

433a (432b from sb)TX 356, Commonwealth Dr, W [lodging] Delux Inn

TX

DALLAS

⬆🅽	**INTERSTATE 35 Cont'd**
Exit #	**Services**
432a	Inwood Rd, E 🅖 Exxon/7-11 🄾 🄷, Chevrolet, W 🅖 Shell, Texaco/Subway/dsl 🅕 Whataburger 🄰 Embassy Suites, Holiday Inn Express, Homewood Suites
431	Motor St, E 🅖 Chevron 🅕 Denny's 🄾 🄷, W 🅖 Shell/7-11 🅕 Alamo Rest 🄰 Marriott Suites
430c	Wycliff Ave, E 🅕 JoJo's Rest. 🄰 Holiday Inn, Renaissance Hotel 🄾 Intn'l Apparel Mart, W 🄰 Hilton Anatole, Hilton Garden
430b	Mkt Ctr Blvd, E 🄾 World Trade Ctr, W 🅖 Shell 🅕 Denny's 🄰 Courtyard, DoubleTree, Fairfield Inn, Ramada Inn, Sheraton Suites, Wyndham Garden
430a	Oak Lawn Ave, E 🄰 Holiday Inn, W 🅖 Shell, Texaco/dsl 🅕 Denny's, Medieval Times Rest. 🄾 to Merchandise Mart
429c	HiLine Ave (from nb)
429b	Continental Ave, Commerce St W, E 🅕 Hooters, W 🅖 Exxon, Shell 🅕 McDonald's, downtown
429a	to I-45, US 75, to Houston
428e	Commerce St E, Reunion Blvd, Dallas, downtown
428d	I-30 W, to Ft Worth
428a	I-30 E, to I-45 S
428b	Industrial Blvd, E 🅖 Exxon, W 🅖 Gulf/dsl, Shamrock
427b	I-30 E
427a	Colorado Blvd, E 🄾 🄷
426c	Jefferson Ave, E 🅖 Shell/dsl
426b	TX 180 W, 8th St, E 🅖 Shell/dsl
426a	Ewing Ave, E 🅕 McDonald's, Popeye's
425c	Marsalis Ave, W 🅖 Chevron, Valero 🅕 Jack-in-the-Box
425b	Beckley Ave, 12th St, sb only, W 🅖 Shell, Valero 🅕 Wendy's
425a	Zang Blvd, same as 425b
424	Illinois Ave, E 🅖 Chevron 🅕 William's Chicken 🄾 🄷, W 🅖 Exxon/7-11 🅕 Church's, Jack-in-the-Box, Pancake House, Sonic, Subway, Taco Bell 🄰 Oak Tree Inn 🄾 Kroger, Ross, Walgreens
423b	Saner Ave
423a	(422b from nb)US 67 S, Kiest Blvd, W 🅖 Shell/repair 🅕 McDonald's, Subway, Taco Del Mar 🄰 Dallas Inn
421b	Ann Arbor St, W 🅖 Exxon/dsl 🄾 L&L Repair
421a	Lp 12E W, E 🅖 RaceWay 🄰 Delux Inn
420	Laureland, W 🅖 Exxon/dsl, Texaco 🄰 Linfield Inn
419	Camp Wisdom Rd, E 🅖 Exxon 🅕 Jack-in-the-Box 🄰 Oak Cliff Inn, W 🅖 Chevron, Shell 🅕 McDonald's 🄰 Grand Inn 🄾 U-Haul
418c	Danieldale Rd (from sb)
418b	I-635/I-20 E, to Shreveport
418a	I-20 W, to Ft Worth
417	Wheatland Rd (from nb)
416	Wintergreen Rd, E 🄾 repair, W 🅖 7-11 🅕 Cracker Barrel, Waffle House 🄰 Days Inn, Grande Hotel, Hampton Inn, Holiday Inn Express
415	Pleasant Run Rd, E 🅖 Chevron, Shell/dsl 🅕 Bienvenidos Mexican, Chili's, Chubby's, CiCi's Pizza, Evergreen Buffet, Grandy's, IHOP, In-N-Out, Logan's Roadhouse, Subway, Taco Cabana, Waffle House 🄰 Great Western Inn, Hwy Express Inn, Motel 6, Royal Inn, Spanish Trails Motel 🄾 Home Depot, Kia, NAPA, W 🅖 Chevron 🅕 Burger King, Dicky's BBQ, El Chico, KFC, LJ Silver, Luby's, McDonald's, On the Border, Outback Steaks, Starbucks, Taco Bueno, Wendy's 🄰 Best Value Inn, Best Western, La Quinta 🄾 🄷, AT&T, Chevrolet, Discount Tire, Firestone/auto, Ford, Kroger, Office Depot, Ross

WAXAHATCHIE

HILLSBORO

414	FM 1382, Desoto Rd, Belt Line Rd, E 🅖 Murphy USA/dsl 🅕 Taco Bell, Whataburger 🄾 Radio Shack, Walmart/McDonald's, W 🅖 QT, Shell
413	Parkerville Rd, W 🅖 Exxon/Subway 🄾 U-Haul
412	Bear Creek Rd, W 🅖 Shell/dsl 🅕 Jack-in-the-Box, Whataburger 🄾 HiHo RV Ctr, transmissions, vet
411	FM 664, Ovilla Rd, E 🅖 Exxon, RaceTrac 🅕 Denny's, DQ, LJ Silver/Taco Bell, McDonald's, Whataburger 🄰 Comfort Inn 🄾 Brookshire's Foods, CVS Drug, Walmart, W 🅖 Exxon/Subway, Shamrock
410	Red Oak Rd, E 🅖 Shell/Pizza Inn/Subway/dsl, Valero 🄰 Best Value Inn, W 🄾 Hilltop Travel Trailers
408	US 77, TX 342, to Red Oak, E 🄾 golf
406	Sterrett Rd, E 🄾 fireworks
405	FM 387, E 🅖 Phillips 66/dsl
404	Lofland Rd, industrial area
403	US 287, to Ft Worth, E 🅖 RacTrac, Valero 🅕 A&W/LJ Silver, Carino's, Chick-fil-A, Chili's, DQ, El Fenix, IHOP, Jack-in-the-Box, KFC, Logan's Roadhouse, McDonald's, Panda Express, Pizza Hut, Taco Bell, Taco Bueno, Waffle House, Wendy's 🄰 Comfort Suites, Hampton Inn, Holiday Inn Express 🄾 Belk, Best Buy, Cadillac/Chevrolet, Discount Tire, Home Depot, Lowe's, Office Depot, Ross, Target, Walmart, W 🄾 Buick/GMC, Chrysler/Dodge/Jeep, Ford
401b	US 287 bus, Waxahatchie, E 🄰 Best Value Inn, Super 8
401a	Brookside Rd, E 🄰 American Suites, Executive Inn, W 🄾 vet
399b	FM 1446
399a	FM 66, FM 876, Maypearl, E 🄰 Texas Inn, W 🅖 Exxon/dsl
397	to US 77, to Waxahachie
393mm	🆁ˢ both lanes, full 🦽 facilities, litter barrels, petwalk 🅲 🅰 vending
391	FM 329, Forreston Rd
386	TX 34, Italy, E 🅖 Shell/Smokehouse BBQ/dsl 🅕 Sonic 🄾 $General, W 🅖 Exxon/Grandy's/McDonald's/dsl/scales 🅕 Pizza Inn, Subway 🄰 Italy Inn 🄾 truckwash
384	Derrs Chapel Rd
381	FM 566, Milford Rd
377	FM 934
374	FM 2959, Carl's Corner, W 🅖 Petro/Exxon/Dunkin Donuts/Iron Skillet/dsl/scales/24hr
373	I-35E
371	I-35 W. **I-35 divides into E and W nb, converges sb. See Texas I-35 W.**
370	US 77 N, FM 579, Hillsboro
368b	FM 286 (from sb), E 🅕 LoneStar Café, LoneStar Café, Taco Bell, Taco Bell, Wendy's, Wendy's 🄰 Hampton Inn, Hampton Inn, W 🅖 Exxon, Valero/dsl 🅕 Braum's, El Conquistador Mexican, El Taco Jalisco, Pizza Hut 🄰 Best Value Inn, Comfort Inn, EconoLodge, La Quinta 🄾 🄷
368a	TX 22, TX 171, to Whitney, E 🅖 7-11, ♥Loves/Chester's/Subway/dsl/scales/24hr 🅕 Arby's, Blackeyed Pea, DQ, Harvest Buffet, IHOP, McDonald's, Starbucks 🄰 Comfort Suites, Days Inn, Holiday Inn Express, Motel 6, Super 8 🄾 Hillsboro Outlets/Famous Brands, W 🅖 7-11, Chevron/dsl, Mobil, Murphy USA/dsl 🅕 Chicken Express, Jack-in-the-Box, KFC, Schlotzsky's, Whataburger 🄰 Thunderbird Motel/rest. 🄾 Chrysler/Dodge/Jeep, Ford, Walmart/Subway
367	Old Bynum Rd (from nb), same as 368
364b	TX 81 N, to Hillsboro (from nb, exits left)
364a	FM 310 (from sb)
362	CR 3111
361mm	🆁ˢ both lanes, full 🦽 facilities, litter barrels, petwalk 🄰
359	FM 1304, W 🅖 Mobil/dsl/24hr 🄾 truckwash

 = gas = food = lodging = other = rest stop

INTERSTATE 35 Cont'd

Exit #	Services
358	FM 1242 E, Abbott, E Up in Smoke BBQ
356	Co Rd 3102
355	County Line Rd, E Waco North RV Park
354	Marable St, E Waco North RV Park
353	FM 2114, West, E Chevron/dsl, Shell/Czech Bakery Bush's Chicken, Sonic, Subway Ford, W Czech Inn auto repair, Chevrolet
351	FM 1858, E tires/repair
349	Wiggins Rd
347	FM 3149, Tours Rd
346	Ross Rd, W Exxon/Church's/dsl/24hr antiques, I-35 RV Park/LP
345	Old Dallas Rd, E antiques, W I-35 RV Park/LP
345a	frontage rd, same as 345
343	FM 308, Elm Mott, E Exxon/DQ, Shell/Jct Cafe/dsl/scales/24hr, W $General
342b	US 77 bus, W North Crest RV Park
342a	FM 2417, Crest Dr, W Valero/dsl Bush's Chicken, DQ Everyday Inn auto repair, Family$
341	Craven Ave, Lacy Lakeview, W Chevron, Shell
340	Myers Lane (from nb)
339	to TX 6 S, FM 3051, Lake Waco, E Valero/dsl Casa Ole, Cici's Pizza, Domino's, El Conquistador, Jack-in-the-Box, Luby's, Pizza Hut, Popeye's, Sonic, Subway, Wendy's, Whataburger, WingStop Holiday Inn $General, Advance Parts, Discount Tire, Home Depot, Walmart, W Chevron, Shell Burger King, Cracker Barrel, Heitmiller Steaks, KFC, McDonald's, Starbucks, Taco Bell Fairfield Inn, Hampton Inn AT&T, to airport, URGENT CARE
338b	Behrens Circle (from nb), E Jack-in-the-Box, same as 339, Sonic, W Shell/dsl/LP Cracker Barrel Comfort Inn, Country Inn&Suites, Days Inn, Delta Inn, Hampton Inn, Knights Inn, Motel 6
338a	US 84, to TX 31, Waco Dr, E Phillips 66 Subway Value Place Suites AutoZone, Family$, HEB Food/gas, O'Reilly Parts, Sam's Club/gas, W Orchid Hotel H
337	US 77 business
335c	Lake Brazos Dr, MLK Blvd, W Buzzard Billy's Scottish Inn, Victorian Inn H
335mm	Brazos River
335b	FM 434, University Parks Dr, E Chili's, Starbucks Baylor U, TX Ranger Museum, W Arby's, Jack-in-the-Box, Magic China Best Value Inn, Residence Inn
335a	4th St, 5th St, E Exxon/Subway/dsl Denny's, IHOP, Pizza Hut Best Western, La Quinta Baylor U, W Chevron/dsl, Valero/dsl Fazoli's, LJ Silver, McDonald's, Taco Bell, Taco Bueno, Taco Cabana, Wendy's, Whataburger Clarion
334b	US 77 S, 17th St, 18th St, E Phillips 66, Shell/dsl Burger King, Popeye's, Schlotzsky's, Vitek's BBQ Budget Inn, Magnuson Hotel, Super 8, W Phillips 66/dsl, Shell Arranda's Mexican H
333a	Lp 396, Valley Mills Dr, E El Chico, Elite Café, Rudy's BBQ, Trujillo's Mexican, TX Roadhouse Comfort Suites, La Quinta, Motel 6 Kia, Mazda, Suzuki, W RaceWay, Valero Bush's Chicken, Catfish King, Church's, Jack-in-the-Box, Little Caesars, Papa John's, Sonic, Subway Aamco, Advance Parts, AutoZone, CVS Drug, Family$, HEB Foods, Lincoln, Walgreens
331	New Rd, E Phillips 66 New Road Inn, Relax Inn, Rodeway Inn, W FLYING J/Denny's/dsl/scales/24hr

WACO

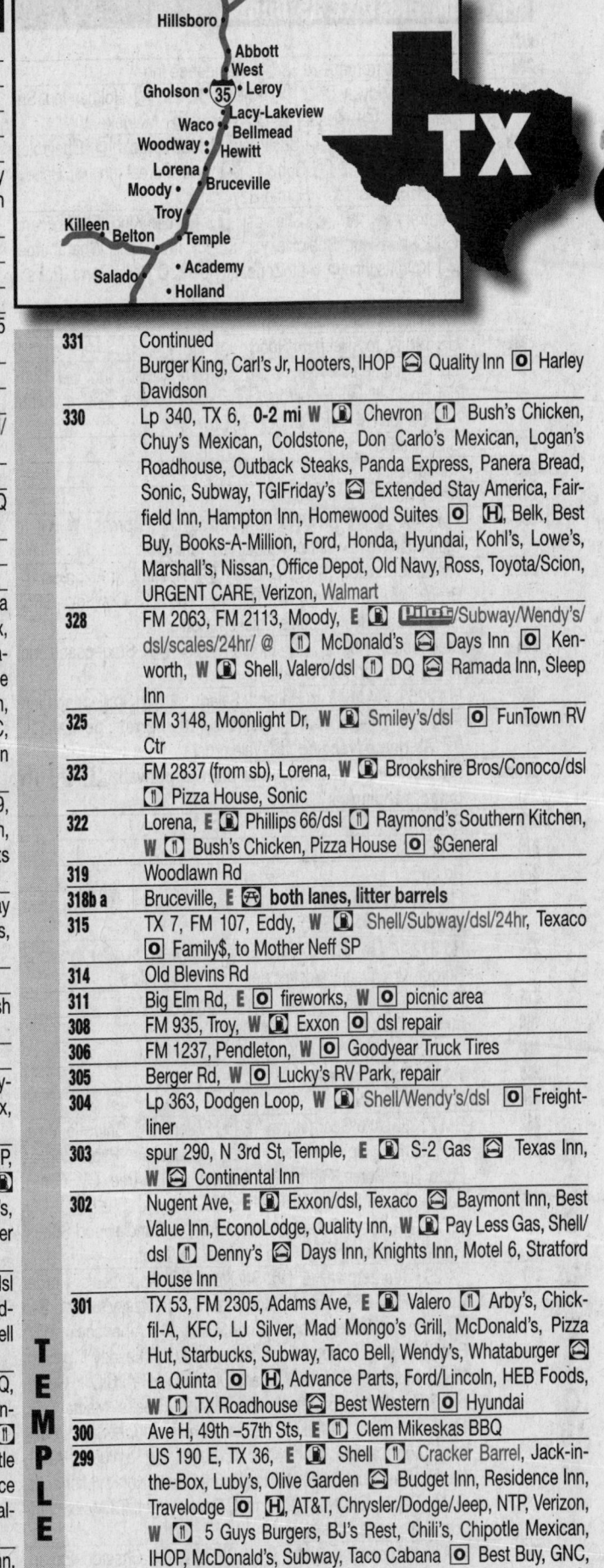

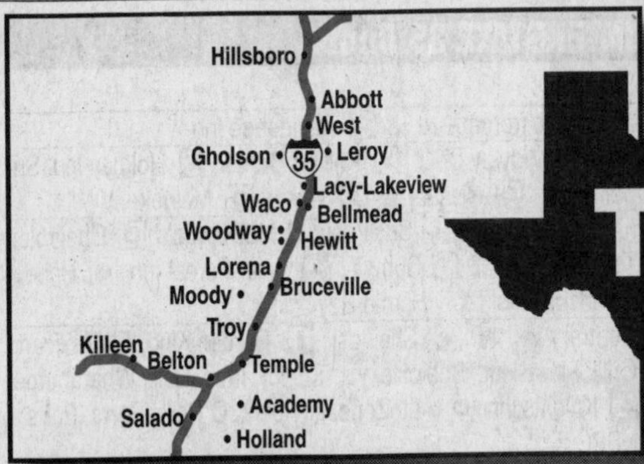

Exit #	Services
331	Continued Burger King, Carl's Jr, Hooters, IHOP Quality Inn Harley Davidson
330	Lp 340, TX 6, **0-2 mi** W Chevron Bush's Chicken, Chuy's Mexican, Coldstone, Don Carlo's Mexican, Logan's Roadhouse, Outback Steaks, Panda Express, Panera Bread, Sonic, Subway, TGIFriday's Extended Stay America, Fairfield Inn, Hampton Inn, Homewood Suites H, Belk, Best Buy, Books-A-Million, Ford, Honda, Hyundai, Kohl's, Lowe's, Marshall's, Nissan, Office Depot, Old Navy, Ross, Toyota/Scion, URGENT CARE, Verizon, Walmart
328	FM 2063, FM 2113, Moody, E Pilot/Subway/Wendy's/dsl/scales/24hr/ @ McDonald's Days Inn Kenworth, W Shell, Valero/dsl DQ Ramada Inn, Sleep Inn
325	FM 3148, Moonlight Dr, W Smiley's/dsl FunTown RV Ctr
323	FM 2837 (from sb), Lorena, W Brookshire Bros/Conoco/dsl Pizza House, Sonic
322	Lorena, E Phillips 66/dsl Raymond's Southern Kitchen, W Bush's Chicken, Pizza House $General
319	Woodlawn Rd
318b a	Bruceville, E **both lanes, litter barrels**
315	TX 7, FM 107, Eddy, W Shell/Subway/dsl/24hr, Texaco Family$, to Mother Neff SP
314	Old Blevins Rd
311	Big Elm Rd, E fireworks, W picnic area
308	FM 935, Troy, W Exxon dsl repair
306	FM 1237, Pendleton, W Goodyear Truck Tires
305	Berger Rd, W Lucky's RV Park, repair
304	Lp 363, Dodgen Loop, W Shell/Wendy's/dsl Freightliner
303	spur 290, N 3rd St, Temple, E S-2 Gas Texas Inn, W Continental Inn
302	Nugent Ave, E Exxon/dsl, Texaco Baymont Inn, Best Value Inn, EconoLodge, Quality Inn, W Pay Less Gas, Shell/dsl Denny's Days Inn, Knights Inn, Motel 6, Stratford House Inn
301	TX 53, FM 2305, Adams Ave, E Valero Arby's, Chick-fil-A, KFC, LJ Silver, Mad Mongo's Grill, McDonald's, Pizza Hut, Starbucks, Subway, Taco Bell, Wendy's, Whataburger La Quinta H, Advance Parts, Ford/Lincoln, HEB Foods, W TX Roadhouse Best Western Hyundai
300	Ave H, 49th –57th Sts, E Clem Mikeskas BBQ
299	US 190 E, TX 36, E Shell Cracker Barrel, Jack-in-the-Box, Luby's, Olive Garden Budget Inn, Residence Inn, Travelodge H, AT&T, Chrysler/Dodge/Jeep, NTP, Verizon, W 5 Guys Burgers, BJ's Rest, Chili's, Chipotle Mexican, IHOP, McDonald's, Subway, Taco Cabana Best Buy, GNC, Home Depot, Michael's, Petsmart, Target

TEMPLE

TX

= gas = food = lodging = other = rest stop

TX

INTERSTATE 35 Cont'd

Exit #	Services
298	nb only, to frontage rd, E Residence Inn
297	FM 817, Midway Dr, E Phillips 66/dsl Holiday Inn, Super 8/rest. Nissan, W Valero Meineke, VW
294b	FM 93, 6th Ave, E Shell/dsl McDonald's Chevrolet, Toyota/Scion, W Subway River Forest Inn Harley-Davidson, U of Mary Hardin Baylor
294a	Central Ave, W Shell/dsl Burger King, El Mexicano Grill, Pizza Hut, Schlotzsky's, Sonic, Taco Bell, Whataburger Knights Inn AutoZone, city park, O'Reilly Parts, Parts+, USPO
293b	TX 317, FM 436, Main St
293a	US 190 W, to Killeen, Ft Hood
292	Lp 121 (same as 293a), E Valero/rest./dsl/24hr Budget Host, W Mobil/dsl Oxbow Steaks La Quinta Belton RV Park, Sunbelt RV Ctr
290	Shanklin Rd
289	Tahuaya Rd
287	Amity Rd
286	FM 2484, E Best Western, Holiday Inn Express, W to Stillhouse Hollow Lake, Tranquil RV Park (2mi)
285	FM 2268, Salado, E Subway Holiday Inn Express Brookshire Foods/gas, W Pay Less Cowboys BBQ, Robertson's Rest., Rush's Chicken, Sonic
284	Stagecoach Rd, E Exxon/Arby's Stagecoach Inn, W DQ, Johnny's Steaks
283	FM 2268, FM 2843, to Holland, Salado, E Stagecoach Inn
282	FM 2115, E **sb, full facilities, litter barrels, petwalk RV dump, vending** Valero/dsl
281mm	**nb, full facilities, litter barrels, petwalk RV dump, vending**
280	Prairie Dell
279	Hill Rd
277	Rd 305
275	FM 487, to Florence, Jarrell, E Exxon/dsl $General, W Shell USPO
274	Rd 312, E Chevron/dsl, Exxon/Subway/dsl, FLYING J/Burger King/Denny's/dsl/scales McDonald's
271	Theon Rd, Rd 311, W Shell/Subway/dsl/24hr
268	fm 972, Walburg, E Crestview RV Ctr
266	TX 195, E Phillips 66/dsl, W Shell/dsl
265	TX 130 Toll S, to Austin
264	Lp 35, Georgetown
262	RM 2338, Lake Georgetown, E Valero Chipotle Mexican, Duke's Smokehouse, KFC, McDonald's, Papa John's, Pizza Hut, Sonic, Starbucks, Subway $Tree, CVS Drug, Parts+, Radio Shack, URGENT CARE, W Shell DQ, La Tapatia, Placa Greek, Whataburger Candlewood Suites, Georgetown Inn, Holiday Inn Express, La Quinta
261	TX 29, Georgetown, E Shell/dsl Applebee's, Burger King, Chili's, KFC, Luby's, McDonald's, Schlotzsky's, Taco Bell Comfort Suites, Country Inn&Suites Albertson's, HEB Foods, Hobby Lobby, Midas, same as 262, Tuesday Morning, W Murphy USA/dsl Casa Ole, Chick-fil-A, CiCi's, Genghis Grill, Ichyban Buffet, IHOP, Longhorn Steaks, Mama Fu's, McAlister's Deli, MT Mike's, Panda Express, Souper Salad, Subway, Taco Cabana, Wendy's, Zio's Italian antiques, AT&T, Beall's, Best Buy, Discount Tire, Home Depot, Kohl's, Michael's, Office Depot, Old Navy, Petsmart, Ross, Target, TJ Maxx, Verizon, Walgreens, Walmart
260	RM 2243, Leander, E H, USPO, W Chevron, Exxon, Texaco Jack-in-the-Box Quality Inn
259	Lp 35, W RV Outlet Ctr, to Interspace Caverns
257	Westinghouse Rd, E Buick/Chevrolet, Chrysler/Dodg Jeep, Ford/Lincoln, Mazda, Subaru/Volvo, VW
256	RM 1431, Chandler Rd, E BJ Rest, Chili's, Jamba Juic La Madeline, Mimi's Cafe, Panda Express JC Penney, J Ann Fabrics, Mazda, Mazda, Petsmart, REI, Ross, Round Roc Outlet/famous brands, Volvo
254	FM 3406, Round Rock, E Chevron Arby's, Gatti's Pizz La Tapatia, McDonald's Best Western $General, CV Drug, Firestone/auto, Harley-Davidson, Honda, Hyundai, Sma Car, Toyota/Scion, W Phillips 66/dsl, Shell Blue Oa Grill, Carino's Italian, Chuy's Mexican, Cracker Barrel, Dave Pizza, Denny's, Mesa Rosa Mexican, Rudy's BBQ/gas, Sal Grass Steaks Country Inn&Suites, Courtyard, Hilton Ga den, Holiday Inn Express, La Quinta, Red Roof Inn, SpringH Suites, ValuePlace CVS Drug, GMC, Nissan
253b	US 79, to Taylor, E Chevron, Shell, Texaco Arby's Baskin-Robbins, Casa Garcia's, DQ, Fuddrucker's, KFC, L Silver, Pizza Hut, Short Stop Dogs, Sirloin Stockade Bes Western, Wingate Inn H, $General, AutoZone, Beall's CarQuest, Cottman Transmissions, Just Brakes, vet, W Exxon/dsl, Shell/dsl Gatti's Pizza, Hunan Lion, IHOP, L Margarita, Popeye's, Starbucks, Taco Bell, Westside Ale Hous Best Value Inn, Country Inn&Suites, Fairfield Inn, La Quin ta, Red Roof Inn, Sleep Inn, ValuePlace $Tree, CVS Drug USPO
253a	Frontage Rd, same as 253 b
252b a	RM 620, E Shell/dsl Candlewood Suites, Extende Stay America NAPA, W Texaco/dsl Freddy' Steakburgers, Little Caesars, McDonald's, Starbucks, Wendy' Comfort Suites, Staybridge Suites
251	Lp 35, Round Rock, E Valero CiCi's Pizza, Outbac Steaks, Whataburger Residence Inn $General, Aam co, BigLots, Brake Check, Tuesday Morning, W She Burger King, China Wall, Jack-in-the-Box, Luby's, Luck Dog Grill, Taco Cabana Days Inn, Mariott, Sleep Inn GNC, NTB, transmissions, Walgreens
250	FM 1325, E 5 Guys Burgers, Chick-fil-A, Chili's, Jason's Deli, Joe's Crabshack, Macaroni Grill, McDonald's, Panda Ex press, Subway, Twin Peaks Rest. Hampton Inn, Homewoo Suites, Residence Inn $Tree, AT&T, Best Buy, Discour Tire, Home Depot, Michael's, Petsmart, Radio Shack, Ross Steinmart, Target, URGENT CARE, Walmart, W Shell An tonio's Cantina, ChuckeCheese, Fast Eddie's, Hooters, Jimm John's, Mongolian Grill, Olive Garden, Schlotzsky's, Starbuck Extended Stay America, La Quinta Barnes&Noble, Hob by Lobby, Kohl's, Lowe's, Marshall's, Old Navy, PetCo, Ross Sam's Club, World Mkt
248	Grand Ave Pkwy, E Citgo, Shell, Texaco/Subway/ds Chucho's Mexican, Posados Cafe, Thundercloud Subs, T Roadhouse Comfort Suites Firestone, URGENT CARE W Chevron/McDonald's
247	FM 1825, Pflugerville, E Texaco Cheddar's, Fish Daddy's Grill, Jack-in-the-Box, Sonic, Subway, Taco Cabana Wendy's Comfort Suites Firestone/auto, HEB Foods gas, W Exxon, Shell/Church's KFC, Miller's BBQ, Sonic Holiday Inn Express Goodyear, Tires4Less
246	Howard Lane, E Citgo, Shell/dsl Arby's, Baby Acapulco, McDonald's, Subway, Wings'n More Home Depot, Kohl's, NTB, W Valero/dsl IHOP, Whataburge Sleep Inn
245	FM 734, Parmer Lane, to Yager Lane (244 from nb), E Carino's, Chick-fil-A, Chili's, Golden Wok, Jimmy John's, Pei Wei

GEORGETOWN

ROUND ROCK

INTERSTATE 35 Cont'd

245 Continued
Schlotzsky's, Souper Salad, Subway, Zed's Rest Courtyard $Tree, HEB Food/E-85, Hobby Lobby, JC Penney, Kohl's, Office Depot, PetCo, Petsmart, Ross, Sears Grand, Target, Verizon, W Conoco/dsl, Exxon, Murphy USA/dsl Buffalo Wild Wings, Golden Corral, Hoho Chinese, Red Robin, Starbucks Courtyard, Fairfield Inn, Hilton Garden, Residence Inn, SpringHill Suites AT&T, CarMax, Discount Tire, Lowe's, Walmart

243 Braker Lane, E Valero Jack-in-the-Box, Whataburger U-Haul, W Citgo, Shell/dsl Austin Motel, Value-Place $General

241 Rundberg Lane, E Exxon Grand China Buffet, Jack-in-the-Box, Mr Gatti's, Old San Francisco Steaks Extended Stay Deluxe, Ramada Inn $General, Albertson's, Chevrolet, U-Haul, Walmart, W Chevron, Conoco, Shell, Texaco Austin Suites, Budget Inn, Budget Lodge, Economy Inn, Holiday Inn Express, Motel 6, Red Roof Inn, Super 8, Wingate Inn

240a US 183, Lockhart, E Exxon DQ, Jack-in-the-Box, Old San Francisco Steaks Days Inn, Ramada Inn, W Chevron/dsl, Texaco/dsl Motel 6, Red Roof Inn, Super 8, Wingate Inn

239 St John's Ave, E Shell Burger King, Chili's, Japon Japanese, Pappadeaux, Pappasito's Mexican Crowne Plaza, Days Inn, DoubleTree, Drury Inn, Hampton Inn, North Austin Plaza, Studio 6 USPO, W Conoco/dsl, Exxon, Valero/dsl Antonio's Texmex, Applebee's, Buffalo Wild Wings, Carrabba's, Denny's, IHOP, Panda Express, Quiznos, Verona Italian, Wendy's Baymont Inn, Best Value Inn, Comfort Inn, Country Inn&Suites, Courtyard, Holiday Inn Express, Hyatt Place, La Quinta, Radisson, Ramada Inn, Sheraton, Sumner Suites Ford, Office Depot

238b US 290 E, RM 222, frontage rds connect several exits, same as 238a

238a 51st St, E Chevron/dsl, Exxon, Shell Buffet King, Burger King, Church's, McDonald's, TX Steaks DoubleTree Hotel, Drury Inn, EconoLodge, Embassy Suites, North Austin Suites $Tree, Advance Parts, AutoZone, Best Buy, Firestone, FoodLand, Home Depot, Jo-Ann Crafts, Marshall's, Old Navy, Petsmart, Ross, Staples, Target, Walgreens, W Baby Acapulco, Capt Benny's Seafood Capital Inn, Courtyard, Fairfield Inn, Hilton, Motel 6, Super 8 Dillard's

237b 51st St, same as 238a

237a Airport Blvd, E BBQ, W Jack-in-the-Box, Quiznos, Wendy's GNC, Goodyear, HEB Foods, Old Navy, PetCo, Sears/auto

236.7 lower level accesses downtown, upper level is I-35 thru

236b 39th St, E Chevron/dsl Short Stop Burgers, Subway Fiesta Foods, O'Reilly Parts, U-Haul, W Shell/dsl tires, to U of TX, Tune&Lube

236a 26th-32nd Sts, E Los Altos Mexican, Subway Days Inn, W Rodeway Inn H

235b Manor Rd, E Denny's DoubleTree, W Rodeway Inn st capitol, U of TX, vet, same as 236a

235a MLK, 15th St, W H

234.9 lower level accesses downtown, upper level is I-35 thru

234c 11th St, 12th St, E Chevron/dsl, Shell/dsl Denny's, Wendy's DoubleTree Hotel, Super 8 CVS Drug, W Chevron, Shell, Texaco Wendy's Crowne Plaza, Hilton Garden, La Quinta, Marriott, Omni Motel, Radisson, Sheraton H, museum, st capitol, downtown

234b 8th-3rd St, W IHOP

A U S T I N

TX

234a Cesar Chavez St, Holly St, downtown

233 Riverside Dr, Town Lake, E Shell/dsl, W Chevron/dsl Holiday Inn

232mm Little Colorado River

232b Woodland Ave

232a Oltorf St, E Gulf, Shell/dsl Luby's, Sonic Country Garden Inn, Garden West, Howard Johnson, La Quinta, Motel 6, Parkwest Inn, W Conoco/dsl, Exxon Denny's, Starbucks Clarion

231 Woodward St, E Shell/dsl same as 232, Wyndham Garden, W Home Depot

230b a US 290 W, TX 71, Ben White Blvd, St Elmo Rd, E Shell Domino's, Jim's Rest., McDonald's, Sigon Kitchen, Subway, Western Choice Steaks Baymont Inn, Best Western, Comfort Suites, Courtyard, Fairfield Inn, Hampton Inn, Marriott, Omni Hotel, Red Roof Inn, Residence Inn, SpringHill Suites Acura, W Burger King, Furr's Cafeteria, IHOP, Pizza Hut Candlewood Suites, Days Inn, La Quinta H, Audi, CarMax, Chrysler/Dodge/Jeep, Ford, Hyundai, Kia, Mazda, Nissan, NTB, Suzuki, Toyota/Scion

229 Stassney Lane, W Buffalo Wild Wings, Chili's, Krispy Kreme, Logan's Roadhouse, Macaroni Grill, Pizza Hut, Rockfish Grill, Twin Peaks Rest., TX Cattle Co Steaks Albertson's/gas, Fiesta Foods/gas, Kia, Lowe's

228 Wm Cannon Drive, E Exxon, Valero Applebee's, McDonald's, Taco Bell Brake Check, Chrysler, Discount Tire, HEB Foods, Mitsubishi, Nissan, Radio Shack, Target, W Shell/dsl, Texaco Arby's, Burger King, China Harbor, Gatti's Pizza, Jack-in-the-Box, KFC, LJ Silver, Peter Piper Pizza, Taco Cabana, Wendy's, Whataburger $General, Advance Parts, BigLots, Chevrolet, CVS Drug, Firestone, Hyundai/Subaru

227 Slaughter Lane, Lp 275, S Congress, E Shell/dsl Don Dario's, IHOP Home Depot, Lone Star RV Resort, U-Haul, W Murphy USA/dsl, Texaco, Valero/dsl Carino's, Chick-fil-A, Chili's, Chipotle Mexican, Gatti's, Jack-in-the-Box, Jason's Deli, Longhorn Steaks, Mama Fu's, Miller BBQ, Panda Express, Sonic, Starbucks, Steak'n Shake, Subway, Taco Bell, TGIFriday's, TX Roadhouse, Wendy's, Whataburger Best Buy, Firestone/auto, GNC, Hobby Lobby, JC Penney, Marshall's, Petsmart, Ross, Sam's Club/gas, Target, Walgreens, Walmart

226 Slaughter Creek Overpass

225 FM 1626, Onion Creek Pkwy, E Texaco, Valero Subway Harley-Davidson

224 frontage rd (from nb)

223 FM 1327, Rd 45 toll

221 Lp 4, Buda, E Chevron/McDonald's, Shell/dsl Starbucks Best Value Inn, Comfort Suites, Holiday Inn Express Ford, Kenworth, W Chevron, Murphy USA/dsl, Shell Arby's, Chili's, Cracker Barrel, Dan's Burgers, Jack-in-the-Box, KFC/LJ Silver, Little Caesars, Logan's Roadhouse, Miller

[gas] = gas [food] = food [lodging] = lodging [other] = other [RS] = rest stop

TX

INTERSTATE 35 Cont'd

SAN MARCOS

221 Continued
BBQ, Papa John's, Pizza Hut, Sonic, Subway, Taco Bell, Whataburger [lodging] Hampton Inn, Microtel [other] AT&T, Cabela's, HEB Food/dsl/E-85, O'Reilly Parts, Radio Shack, USPO, Walgreens, Walmart

220 FM 2001, Niederwald, E [gas] Shell [other] Camper Clinic RV Ctr, Marshall's RV Park, W [other] Crestview RV Ctr/Park, Peterbilt

217 Lp 4, Buda, E [gas] Conoco/dsl/24hr [lodging] La Quinta [other] Mack/Volvo, W [gas] Valero/dsl [food] Burger King [lodging] Best Western [other] Christian Bros Auto, Home Depot

215 Bunton Overpass, E [gas] Exxon/KFC/LJ Silver [other] [H], AT&T, Discount Tire, Lowe's, Walgreens, W [gas] Shell/dsl [food] Jack-in-the-Box, McDonald's, Papa Murphy's, Starbucks, Subway, Whataburger [other] $Tree, Explore USA RV Ctr, GNC, HEB Foods/dsl, Kohl's, PetCo, Target

213 FM 150, Kyle, E [gas] Valero/dsl [food] DQ [other] AutoZone, Goodyear/auto, W [gas] Conoco/dsl [food] Casa Maria Mexican [other] CVS Drug, repair

210 Yarrington Rd, E [other] Hyundai, W [other] Buick/Chevrolet/GMC, Plum Creek RV Park

209 weight sta (sb only)

208mm Blanco River

208 Frontage Rd, Blanco River Rd, W [other] Buick/Chevrolet/GMC

206 Lp 82, Aquarena Springs Rd,. E [gas] Conoco, Valero [other] San Marcos RV Park, W [gas] Citgo/dsl, Exxon/dsl, Shell, Texaco [food] Pancake House, Popeye's, Sonic [lodging] Best Value Inn, Howard Johnson, La Quinta, Motel 6, Ramada Ltd, Rodeway Inn, Summit Inn, Super 8, Travelodge [other] to SW TX U

205 TX 80, TX 142, Bastrop, E [gas] Exxon, Quix, RaceWay, Shell/dsl, Valero/dsl [food] Arby's, China Palace, DQ, Fazoli's, Jason's Deli, Subway, Wing Stop [lodging] Executive Inn [other] $General, AutoZone, CVS Drug, Hastings Books, Hobby Lobby, Kwik Kar, Verizon, vet, Walmart, W [gas] Valero [food] A&W/LJ Silver, Burger King, Church's, KFC, Kobe Japanese, Logan's Roadhouse, McDonald's, Pizza Hut, Taco Cabana, Wendy's [lodging] Best Western, Budget Inn, Days Inn, Gateway Inn, Knights Inn, Red Roof Inn, Rodeway Inn [other] Brake Check, city park, GNC, HEB Foods, JC Penney, Office Depot, Radio Shack, Walgreens

204mm San Marcos River

204b CM Allen Pkwy, W [gas] Shell/dsl, Spirit [food] DQ, Krispy Kreme, La Fonda Rest, Mazatlan Mexican, Plucker's Grill, Sonic [lodging] Best Western, EconoLodge [other] AutoZone, O'Reilly Parts, transmissions

204a Lp 82, TX 123, to Seguin, E [gas] Conoco, Exxon/dsl, Valero [food] Burger King, Carino's, Chicken Express, Chili's, Golden Corral, Luby's, McDonald's, Red Lobster, Whataburger [lodging] Comfort Suites, Hampton Inn, Holiday Inn Express [other] [H], Aamco, Ford

202 FM 3407, Wonder World Dr, E [gas] Exxon, Shell/Church's [food] Carl's Jr, Chick-fil-A, Fuschaks BBQ, Jack-in-the-Box, Taco Bueno, Taste of China, Wienerschnitzel [other] [H], $Tree, Best Buy, Discount Tire, Lowe's, Marshall's, Petsmart, Ross, Sams Club/gas, W [gas] Valero/dsl [food] TX Roadhouse [lodging] Candlewood Suites, Country Inn&Suites [other] repair

201 McCarty Lane, E [lodging] Embassy Suites, W [food] Panda Express, Sonic [other] AT&T, Beall's, Chrysler/Dodge/Jeep, Firestone/auto, JC Penney, Nissan, Target

200 Centerpoint Rd, E [food] Cracker Barrel, Food Court, Outback Steaks, River City Grill, Subway, Taco Bell, Wendy's [other] GNC, Old Navy, San Marcos Outlets/famous brands, Tanger Outlet/famous brands, VF Outlets/famous brands, W [gas] Valero/dsl [food] McDonald's, Quiznos, Starbucks, Whataburger [lodging] Baymont Inn [other] Honda

NEW BRAUNFELS

199 Posey Rd, E [other] same as 200, Tanger Outlets/famous brands, Toyota/Scion

196 FM 1106, York Creek Rd, W [other] Canyon Trail RV Park

195 Watson Lane, Old Bastrop Rd

193 Conrads Rd, Kohlenberg Rd, W [gas] TA/Country Fare Rest/Popeye's/Subway/dsl/scales/24hr/ @ [other] Camping World RV Ctr

191 FM 306, FM 483, Canyon Lake, E [gas] Buc-ee's [food] BJ's Rest, Longhorn Steaks, Subway, Whataburger [other] AT&T, Best Buy, Dick's, I-35 RV Camping, JC Penney, Petsmart, Ross, Target, URGENT CARE, Verizon, Walmart Dist Ctr, W [gas] Chevron, Exxon/dsl [food] Burger King, Quiznos [lodging] Wingate Inn [other] transmissions

190c Post Rd

190b frontage rd, New Braunfels

190a frontage rd, same as 189

189 TX 46, Seguin, E [gas] Shell/dsl [food] Chili's, Denny's, Golden Corral, Logan's Roadhouse, Olive Garden, Peter Piper Pizza, Taco Bueno [lodging] Best Value Inn, EconoLodge, Hampton Inn, La Quinta, Super 8 [other] Discount Tire, Home Depot, Kohl's, Office Depot, vet, W [gas] Texaco, Valero [food] Applebee's, Chili's, Chipotle Mexican, El Tapatio, IHOP, Mama Fu's, McDonald's, MT Mike's, Pizza Hut, Subway, Taco Bell, Taco Cabana, TJ's Burgers, Wendy's [lodging] Baymont, Best Western, Comfort Suites, Days Inn, Edelweiss Inn, Fairfield Inn, Hilton Garden, Howard Johnson, Microtel, Motel 6, Quality Inn, Ramada Inn, Rodeway Inn, Sleep Inn [other] [H], Walgreens

188 Frontage Rd, W [food] Garden Buffet, HoneyBaked Ham, Mamacita's Rest. [lodging] River Ranch Resort [other] Hastings Books, Tuesday Morning

188mm Guadalupe River

187 FM 725, Lake McQueeny Rd, E [food] A&W/LJ Silver, Arby's, Burger King, CiCi's, Schobell's Rest., Subway, Whataburger [other] Aamco, BigLots, Chevrolet, Family$, Ford/Lincoln, Hobby Lobby, Jeep, Meineke, W [food] Adobe Café, DQ, Jack-in-the-Box, Jason's Deli, Steaks to Go [lodging] Budget Inn [other] [H], CVS Drug, River Ranch RV Resort

186 Walnut Ave, E [gas] Exxon/Subway, Murphy USA/dsl, Valero [food] Carl's Jr, Chick-fil-A, McDonald's, Popeye's, Schlotzsky's, Taco Bell [lodging] Red Roof Inn [other] Lowe's, Walmart, W [gas] Shell/dsl [food] Baskin-Robbins, Bonzai Japanese, KFC, Mr Gatti's, Panda Express, Papa John's, Starbucks [other] $Tree, AT&T, AutoZone, Brake Check, Ford/Lincoln, GNC, HEB Foods/gas, Radio Shack, U-Haul, Walgreens

185 FM 1044

184 FM 482, Lp 337, Rueckle Rd, E [gas] Shell/dsl [other] Hill Country RV Park, Kia, Mazda, W [gas] Pilot/McDonald's/Subway/dsl/scales [food] Jack-in-the-Box [other] Suzuki

183 Solms Rd, W [gas] Exxon/dsl

182 Engel Rd, E [other] Stamann RV Ctr

180 Schwab Rd

179mm **[RS] both lanes, full [handicapped] facilities, litter barrels, petwalk [phone] [picnic] vending**

178 FM 1103, Cibolo Rd, Hubertus Rd, E [gas] Shell/dsl [other] Walgreens

177 FM 482, FM 2252, W [other] Stone Creek RV Park

176 Weiderstein Rd, same as 175

175 FM 3009, Natural Bridge, E [gas] Valero/dsl [food] Chili's, IHOP, La Pasadita Mexican, McDonald's, Miller's BBQ, Schlotzsky's, Sonic, Taco Cabana [lodging] Fairfield Inn, Hampton Inn [other] HEB Food/dsl/E-85, Lowe's, Radio Shack, Verizon, W [gas] Murphy USA/dsl, Shell/dsl, Valero/Subway/dsl [food] Abel's Diner, Arby's, Denny's, Domino's, Jack-in-the-Box, KFC/Pizza Hut/Taco Bell,

INTERSTATE 35 Cont'd

SAN ANTONIO

175 Continued McDonald's, Panda Express, Quiznos, Starbucks, Wendy's, Whataburger, Wing Stop Atrium Inn, La Quinta AT&T, URGENT CARE, Walmart/McDonald's

174b Schertz Pkwy, E Shell Crestview RV Ctr

174a FM 1518, Selma, E Phillips 66/dsl Ruddy's BBQ Honda, Subaru, W Comfort Inn Crestview RV Ctr

173 Old Austin Rd, Olympia Pkwy, E 5 Guys Burgers, Baskin Robbins, Charlie's Subs, Cheddar's, Chick-fil-A, Chili's, Chipotle Mexican, CiCi's, Firehouse Subs, Freddy's Custard, Freddy's Steakburgers, Genghis Grill, Hooters, IHOP, Las Palapas, Outback Steaks, Panda Express, Panera Bread, Papouli's Greek, Peter Piper Pizza, Red Robin, Sea Island Srimp, Starbucks, Subway, Taste of China, Wendy's Holiday Inn Express AT&T, Beall's, Best Buy, Costco/gas, Discount Tire, GNC, Hobby Lobby, Home Depot, Kohl's, Michael's, NTB, Old Navy, Petsmart, Ross, Target, TJ Maxx, Verizon, WorldMkt, W ChuckeCheese, Chuy's Mexican, Freebirds Burritos, Houlihan's Hampton Inn Office Depot

172 TX 218, Anderson Lp, P Booker Rd, E Buffalo Wild Wings, Coldstone, IHOP, Krystal, On-the-Border, TX Roadhouse, Zio's Comfort Inn, ValuePlace Nissan, to Randolph AFB, W to SeaWorld

171 Topperwein Rd, same as 170

170 Judson Rd, to Converse, E Carl's Jr, Denny's, Subway, Whataburger Great Value Inn, La Quinta (H), Buick/GMC, Chevrolet, Ford, GMC, Hyundai, Nissan, W Exxon Best Western Kia, Mazda, Sam's Club/gas

169 O'Conner Rd, Wurzbach Pkwy, E Exxon/dsl McDonald's, Quiznos, Subway, Taco Cabana Comfort Suites CarMax, Chrysler/Dodge/Jeep, Lowe's, Walgreens, W Shell/dsl, Valero Jack-in-the-Box, Jim's Rest., Mi Casa Mexican, Sonic Mazda

168 Weidner Rd, E Citgo/dsl Comfort Suites, Days Inn, W Chevron Quality Inn, Super 8 Harley-Davidson, Volvo Trucks

167b Thousand Oaks Dr, Starlight Terrace, E Valero/dsl

167a Randolph Blvd, E Valero, W Days Inn, Midtowne Suites, Motel 6, Ruby Inn

166 I-410 W, Lp 368 S, W to Sea World

165 FM 1976, Walzem Rd, E Shell, Valero/dsl Applebee's, Burger King, China Harbor, Church's, Firehouse Grill, IHOP, Jack-in-the-Box, KFC/Taco Bell, Las Palapas Mexican, Little Caesars, LJ Silver, Luby's, Marie Callender's, McDonald's, Miller's BBQ, Olive Garden, Pizza Hut, Red Lobster, Shoney's, Starbucks, Subway, Taco Cabana, Whataburger Drury Inn 99c Store, AutoZone, CVS Drug, Discount Tire, Firestone/auto, Home Depot, Michael's, Office Depot, PepBoys, Petsmart, Radio Shack, W Sonic NTB

164b Eisenhauer Rd, E Exxon/dsl Hampton Inn, La Quinta, Mainstay Suites, ValuePlace Inn $General

164a Rittiman Rd, E Exxon, Shell/dsl, Valero/dsl Burger King, Church's, Cracker Barrel, Denny's, Guadalajara Mexican, Jack-in-the-Box, McDonald's, Taco Cabana, Whataburger Best Western, Comfort Suites, La Quinta, Motel 6, Rittiman Inn, Travel Inn, ValuePlace Inn dsl repair, HEB Foods, W Chevron/dsl, Valero Bill Miller BBQ, Popeye's, Sonic, Subway

163 I-410 S (162 from nb, exits left from sb)

161 Binz-Engleman Rd (from nb), same as 160

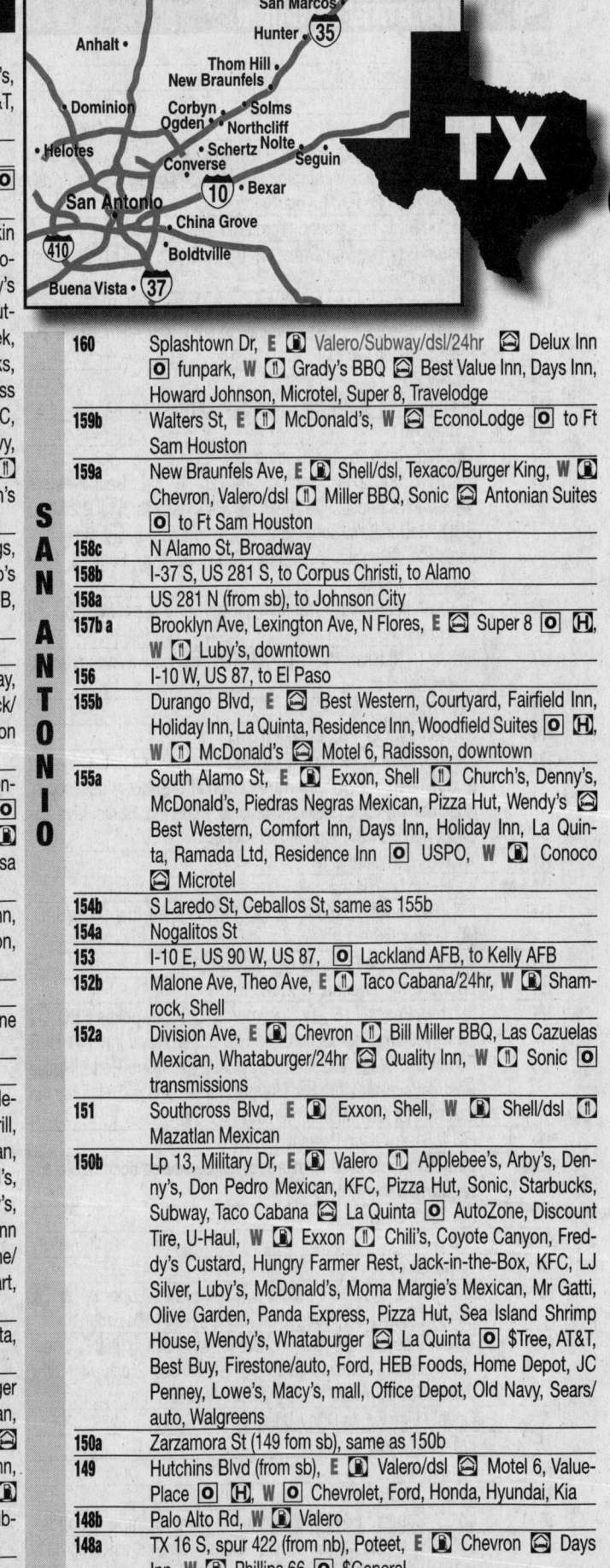

SAN ANTONIO

160 Splashtown Dr, E Valero/Subway/dsl/24hr Delux Inn funpark, W Grady's BBQ Best Value Inn, Days Inn, Howard Johnson, Microtel, Super 8, Travelodge

159b Walters St, E McDonald's, W EconoLodge to Ft Sam Houston

159a New Braunfels Ave, E Shell/dsl, Texaco/Burger King, W Chevron, Valero/dsl Miller BBQ, Sonic Antonian Suites to Ft Sam Houston

158c N Alamo St, Broadway

158b I-37 S, US 281 S, to Corpus Christi, to Alamo

158a US 281 N (from sb), to Johnson City

157b a Brooklyn Ave, Lexington Ave, N Flores, E Super 8 (H), W Luby's, downtown

156 I-10 W, US 87, to El Paso

155b Durango Blvd, E Best Western, Courtyard, Fairfield Inn, Holiday Inn, La Quinta, Residence Inn, Woodfield Suites (H), W McDonald's Motel 6, Radisson, downtown

155a South Alamo St, E Exxon, Shell Church's, Denny's, McDonald's, Piedras Negras Mexican, Pizza Hut, Wendy's Best Western, Comfort Inn, Days Inn, Holiday Inn, La Quinta, Ramada Ltd, Residence Inn USPO, W Conoco Microtel

154b S Laredo St, Ceballos St, same as 155b

154a Nogalitos St

153 I-10 E, US 90 W, US 87, Lackland AFB, to Kelly AFB

152b Malone Ave, Theo Ave, E Taco Cabana/24hr, W Shamrock, Shell

152a Division Ave, E Chevron Bill Miller BBQ, Las Cazuelas Mexican, Whataburger/24hr Quality Inn, W Sonic transmissions

151 Southcross Blvd, E Exxon, Shell, W Shell/dsl Mazatlan Mexican

150b Lp 13, Military Dr, E Valero Applebee's, Arby's, Denny's, Don Pedro Mexican, KFC, Pizza Hut, Sonic, Starbucks, Subway, Taco Cabana La Quinta AutoZone, Discount Tire, U-Haul, W Exxon Chili's, Coyote Canyon, Freddy's Custard, Hungry Farmer Rest, Jack-in-the-Box, KFC, LJ Silver, Luby's, McDonald's, Moma Margie's Mexican, Mr Gatti, Olive Garden, Panda Express, Pizza Hut, Sea Island Shrimp House, Wendy's, Whataburger La Quinta $Tree, AT&T, Best Buy, Firestone/auto, Ford, HEB Foods, Home Depot, JC Penney, Lowe's, Macy's, mall, Office Depot, Old Navy, Sears/auto, Walgreens

150a Zarzamora St (149 fom sb), same as 150b

149 Hutchins Blvd (from sb), E Valero/dsl Motel 6, ValuePlace (H), W Chevrolet, Ford, Honda, Hyundai, Kia

148b Palo Alto Rd, W Valero

148a TX 16 S, spur 422 (from nb), Poteet, E Chevron Days Inn, W Phillips 66 $General

147 Somerset Rd, E Shell/dsl, W Chrysler/Dodge/Jeep

TX

Exit #	Services
	▲N INTERSTATE 35 Cont'd
146	Cassin Rd (from nb)
145b	Lp 353 N
145a	I-410, TX 16
144	Fischer Rd, **E** ☐ Valero/Subway/dsl/scales/24hr ☐ D&D Motel ☐ lube, RV camping, **W** ☐ ♥**Loves**/Carl's Jr/dsl/scales/24hr/ @ ☐ Toyota/Scion
142	Medina River Turnaround (from nb)
141	Benton City Rd, Von Ormy, **E** ☐ USPO, **W** ☐ Shell/dsl/Parador Café
140	Anderson Lp, 1604, **E** ☐ Exxon/dsl/24hr ☐ Burger King, **W** ☐ Valero/Church's/dsl/scales/24hr ☐ Alamo River RV Resort, to Sea World
139	Kinney Rd
137	Shepherd Rd, **E** ☐ truck repair, **W** ☐ gas/dsl ☐ dsl repair
135	Luckey Rd
133	TX 132 S (from sb), Lytle, same as 131
131	FM 3175, FM 2790, Benton City Rd, **E** ☐ Best Western ☐ Chuck's Repair, NAPA, **W** ☐ Pico/dsl/24hr ☐ Bill Miller BBQ, McDonald's, Sonic, Subway, Whataburger ☐ Days Inn/cafe ☐ $General, AutoZone, Crawford Drug, Family$, HEB Food/dsl, USPO
129mm	☐ both lanes, full ☐ facilities, litter barrels, petwalk ☐ ☐ vending
127	FM 471, Natalia, **W** ☐ ♥**Loves**/Subway/Wendy's/dsl/scales/24hr/ @
125	FM 770
124	FM 463, Bigfoot Rd, **E** ☐ Ford
122	TX 173, Divine, **E** ☐ Exxon/dsl ☐ Chevrolet, Chrysler/Dodge/Jeep, **W** ☐ Chevron/McDonald's/Subway/dsl, Exxon, Shell/dsl ☐ CCC Steaks, Church's, Pizza Inn, Sonic, Viva Zapatas Mexican ☐ Country Corner Inn
121	TX 132 N, .Devine
118.5mm	weigh sta both lanes
114	FM 462, Yancey, Bigfoot, **W** ☐ Shell/Subway/dsl ☐ USPO, ☐ Lucky/dsl
111	US 57, to Eagle Pass, **W** ☐ Valero/dsl
104	Lp 35, **E** ☐ Gilendo RV Park
101	FM 140, Pearsall, **E** ☐ Chevron/dsl ☐ Cowpokes BBQ ☐ Best Western, Pearsall Inn, Rio Frio Motel, Royal Inn ☐ HEB Foods/dsl, **W** ☐ Exxon/Subway/dsl/24hr, Valero/Porter House Rest/dsl/scales/24hr ☐ Hungry Hunter Grill ☐ Holiday Inn Express, La Quinta, Southern Inn ☐ ☐
99	FM 1581, to Divot, Pearsall
93mm	parking/picnic area both lanes, handicapped accessible, litter barrels
91	FM 1583, Derby
90mm	Frio River
86	Lp 35, Dilley
85	FM 117, **E** ☐ Garcia Café ☐ Relax Inn, Super 8, **W** ☐ Exxon ☐ DQ ☐ Budget Inn, Sona Inn ☐ RV park
84	TX 85, Dilley, **E** ☐ Conoco/Burger King/dsl ☐ ☐, Chevrolet, Super S Foods/dsl, **W** ☐ Shell/Pollo Grande/dsl/24hr, Valero/Subway/dsl/24hr ☐ Executive Inn
82	County Line Rd, to Dilley, Dilley
77	FM 469, Millett
74	Gardendale
69	Lp 35, Cotulla
65	Lp 35, Cotulla, **E** ☐ Phillips 66 ☐ Family$, Super S Foods
67	FM 468, to Big Wells, **E** ☐ Exxon/Wendy's/dsl/24hr, JJ's/dsl, Valero/deli/dsl/24hr ☐ DQ, Golden Chick, Subway, Taco Palenque ☐ Executive Inn, Extended Stay, Holiday·Inn Ex

P E A R S A L L (vertical sidebar)

67	Continued press, Village Inn ☐ tire repair, **W** ☐ Chevron/McDonald's dsl/scales/24hr ☐ Best Western ☐ RV park
63	Elm Creek Interchange
59mm	☐ both lanes, full ☐ facilities, litter barrels, petwalk ☐ ☐ vending
56	FM 133, Artesia Wells
48	Caiman Creek Interchange
39	TX 44, Encinal, **E** ☐ ♥**Loves**/Chester Fried/Subway/dsl scales/24hr, **W** ☐ Exxon/dsl
38	TX 44 (from nb), Encinal
32	San Roman Interchange
29mm	inspection sta nb
27	Callaghan Interchange
24	**255 toll**, Camino Colombia toll rd, to Monterrey
22	Webb Interchange
18	US 83 N, to Carrizo Springs, **E** **TX Travel Info Ctr (8am-5pm)** ☐, full ☐ facilities, litter barrels, petwalk ☐ wireless internet, **W** RV Camping
14mm	**parking area, sb**
12b	(13 from sb) Uniroyal Interchange, **E** ☐ ☐☐☐/McDonald's Subway/dsl/scales/24hr ☐ Blue Beacon, **W** ☐ *FLYING J*/Denny's/dsl/scales/24hr, TA/Burger King/Subway/Taco Bell dsl/scales/24hr/ @
12a	Port Loredo
10	Port Laredo Carriers Dr (from nb)
9	Industrial Blvd, to Bob Bullock Lp (from sb only)
8b	Lp 20 W, to Solidarity Bridge
8a	Lp 20 W, to to World Trade Bridge, Milo
5	San Isidro Pkwy
4b	Las Cruces Dr, **E** ☐ Valero/dsl ☐ El Pescador
4a	FM 1472, new exit
4	FM 1472, Del Mar Blvd, **E** ☐ Exxon/Burger King/dsl ☐ Applebee's, Carino's Italian, CiCi's, IHOP, Jack-in-the-Box, McDonald's, Quiznos, Whataburger ☐ Extended Stay America, Hampton Inn ☐ Best Buy, BigLots, HEB Foods/gas Marshall's, Old Navy, Radio Shack, Target, **W** ☐ Shell/ds ☐ Days Inn ☐ Harley-Davidson
3b	Mann Rd, **E** ☐ Buffalo Wild Wings, Krispy Kreme, Lin's Chinese ☐ Residence Inn ☐ Buick/Cadillac/GMC, Ford/Lincoln, Honda, Kia, Lowe's, mall, Mazda, URGENT CARE, **W** ☐ Chili's, Danny's Rest, Golden Corral, Hayashi Japanese, Kettle Pancake House, Subway, Taco Palenque, TX Roadhouse Whataburger ☐ Best Value, Family Garden Inn, Gateway Inn La Hacienda Motel, Monterey Inn, Motel 6, Red Roof Inn, SpringHill Suites ☐ $Tree, AT&T, Home Depot, Kohl's, Michael's Office Depot, PetCo, Ross, Verizon, Walmart/McDonald's
3a	San Bernardo Ave, **E** ☐ Shell ☐ Chick-fil-A, ChuckeCheese El Taco Tote, Emperor Garden, Fuddrucker's, LJ Silver, Logan's Roadhouse, Luby's, Olive Garden, Peter Piper Pizza, Red Lobster, Sirloin Stockade, Tony Roma's ☐ Fairfield Inn ☐ Advance Parts, Dillards, HEB Foods/gas, K-Mart, Macy's, mall NAPA, PepBoys, Sears/auto, SteinMart, **W** ☐ Valero ☐ Arby's, Burger King, DQ, McDonald's, Pizza Hut, Popeye's, Taco Bell, Taco Palenque, Wendy's ☐ O'Reilly Parts, Sam's Club/gas
2	US 59, Saunders Rd, **E** ☐ Conoco, Shell ☐ Jack-in-the-Box ☐ ☐, **W** ☐ Exxon/Burger King/dsl, Shell ☐ Church's Denny's ☐ Courtyard, Holiday Inn, La Quinta, Super8 ☐ Advance Parts, AutoZone, Mexico Insurance
1b	Park St, to Sanchez St, **W** ☐ Conoco/dsl ☐ La Mexicana Rest., Pizza Hut, Popeye's

L A R E D O (vertical sidebar)

INTERSTATE 35 Cont'd

Exit #	Services
1a	Victoria St, Scott St, Washington St (from sb), E Shell, Valero, W Exxon/dsl, Valero Mariachi Express, McDonald's, Wendy's Firestone/auto

I-35 begins/ends in Laredo at Victoria St access to multiple services

INTERSTATE 35 (WEST)

Exit #	Services
	I-35W begins/ends on I-35, exit 467.
85b	W Oak St, E H
85a	I-35E S
84	FM 1515, Bonnie Brae St, E H
82	FM 2449, to Ponder
79	Crawford Rd
76	FM 407, to Justin, Argyle, W Exxon/dsl Paradise Mkt, Paradise RV Park
76mm	**picnic area both lanes, picnic tables, litter barrels**
74	FM 1171, to Lewisville
72	Dale Earnhardt Way, W Marriott TX Motor Speedway
70	TX 114, to Dallas, Bridgeport, E Shell/Subway/dsl, Valero/dsl Motel 6, Sleep Inn North Lake RV Park, to DFW, W Marriott TX Motor Speedway
68	Eagle Pkwy, W airport
67	Alliance Blvd, W FedEx, to Alliance
66	to Westport Pkwy, Keller-Haslet Rd, E Hampton Inn, Hilton Garden, Residence Inn, W 7-11/Wendy's/dsl Bryan's BBQ, Schlotzsky's, Snooty Pig, Subway, Taco Bueno USPO
65	TX 170 E, E Pilot/McDonald's/dsl/scales/24hr IHOP Cabela's/cafe
64	Golden Triangle Blvd, to Keller-Hicks Blvd, E Chrysler/Dodge/Jeep
63	Heritage Trace, Park Glen, E 7-11 BJ's, Cheddar's, Chick-fil-A, Free Birds Burritos, Houlihan's, Jason's Deli, McDonald's, Smoothie King, Starbucks, Subway, Tutti Frutti, Which Wich, Zoe's Kitchen Belk, Best Buy, Hobby Lobby, JC Penney, Kroger/dsl, Petsmart, Verizon
62	North Tarrant Pkwy, E 5 Guys Burgers, Firehouse Subs, Fuzzy's Tacos, HaNaBi Hibachi, Mi Cocina, Olive Garden, Pizza Inn, Thai Fusion H, Tuesday Morning
60	US 287 N, US 81 N, to Decatur
59	Basswood (sb only), E Chevron/Jack-in-the-Box/dsl Sonic Home Depot, NTB
58	Western Ctr Blvd, E 7-11, Shell/Church's Braum's, Casa Rita, Chili's, Denny's, Dublin Square Rest., Flips Grill, Genghis Grill, Jimmy John's, Macaroni Grill, On-the-Border, Posados Cafe, SaltGrass Steaks, Shady Oak Grill, Wendy's, Which Wich, Wing Stop, Zio's Italian Best Western, Residence Inn AT&T, Kauffman Tire, W Boston's, Firehouse Subs, Joe's Crabshack, McDonald's, Popeye's, Rosa's Cafe, Salad Bowl, Smoothie King, Starbucks, Subway, Waffle House, Whataburger Comfort Inn, Holiday Inn Express repair, URGENT CARE
57b a	I-820 E&W
56b	Melody Hills Dr
56a	Meacham Blvd, E Shell/7-11 Hilton Garden, Knights Inn, La Quinta, W Texaco/dsl Cracker Barrel, McDonald's, Subway Holiday Inn, Quality Inn, Radisson, Super 8 USPO
55	Pleasantdale Ave (from nb)

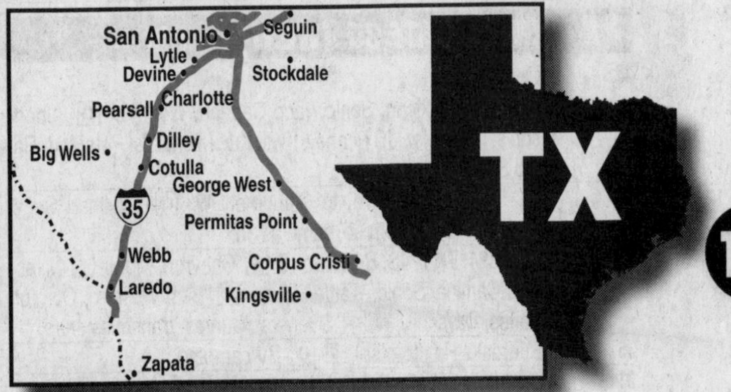

TX

FT WORTH

Exit #	Services
54c	33rd St, Long Ave (from nb), W Conoco/dsl, Valero/dsl Motel 6
54b a	TX 183, NE 28th St, E Lisa's Chicken/dsl, W QT/dsl Stockyards Inn
53	North Side Dr, Yucca Dr, E Shell/7-11/dsl, W Mercado Juarez Café Country Inn&Suites
53mm	Trinity River
52e	Carver St (from nb)
52d	Pharr St (exits left from nb)
52b	US 377N, Belknap
52a	US 377 N, TX 121, to DFW
51a	I-30 E, to Avalene (from nb), downtown Ft Worth
50c a	I-30 W, E to Dallas
50b	TX 180 E (from nb)
49b	Rosedale St, E 7-11/dsl Jack-in-the-Box, W H
49a	Allen Ave, E Valero, W H
48b	Morningside Ave (from sb), same as 48a
48a	Berry St, E Chevron/McDonald's Autozone, El Rio Grande Foods, Family$, W RaceTrac/dsl U-Haul, zoo
47	Ripy St, E transmissions, W Astro Inn
46b	Seminary Dr, E RaceWay Grandy's, Jack-in-the-Box, Taco Cabana, Whataburger Days Inn, Delux Inn, Regency Inn, Super 7 Inn NAPA, W Shell, Valero Denny's, Sonic, Wendy's Firestone/auto, Pepboys
46a	Felix St, E Valero Dalworth Inn, W Cesar's Tacos, McDonald's Family$
45b a	I-20, E to Dallas, W to Abilene
44	Altamesa, E Radisson, W Prism Rig Steaks, Waffle House Baymont Inn, Best Western, Comfort Suites, Motel 6, South Lp Inn
43	Sycamore School Rd, W Exxon Chicken Express, Jack-in-the-Box, Sonic, Subway, Whataburger $General, Home Depot, Radio Shack, repair
42	Everman Pkwy, W QT/dsl/scales, Shell
41	Risinger Rd, W Camping World RV Service/Supplies, McClain's RV Ctr
40	Garden Acres Dr, E Love's/Subway/dsl/scales/24hr Microtel H, W Taco Bell
39	FM 1187, McAlister Rd, E H, W Shamrock/dsl/24hr, Shell Buffalo Wild Wings, Firehouse Subs, Logan's Roadhouse, Olive Garden, Panda Express, Red Lobster, TGIFriday's, Waffle House Howard Johnson Best Buy, Kohl's, Staples, Verizon
38	Alsbury Blvd, E Chevron/24hr, Mobil/dsl Chili's, Cracker Barrel, Hibachi Japanese, IHOP, McDonald's, Mexican Inn Cafe, On-the-Border, Outback Steaks, Over Time Grill, Spring Creek BBQ Hampton Inn, Holiday Inn Express, La Quinta, Super 8 Discount Tire, Ford, Lowe's Whse, W RaceTrac, Shamrock, Shell/24hr Applebees, Arby's, Burger King, Chick-fil-A, Coldstone Creamery, Cotton Patch Cafe, Denny's,

= gas = food = lodging = other = rest stop

INTERSTATE 35 (WEST) Cont'd

38	Continued Pancho's Mexican, Sonic, Taco Cabana, Wendy's Albertson's, Chevrolet, JC Penney, Kwik Kar, Michael's, PetsMart, Radio Shack, Ross, vet
37	TX 174, Wilshire Blvd, to Cleburne, W Walmart Super Ctr/24hr, (2mi), from sb, same as 36
36	FM 3391, TX 174S, Burleson, E Chevron, Mobil Miranda's Cantina, Sonic, Waffle House Best Western, Comfort Suites, Days Inn, W $General, Curves, transmissions
35	Briaroaks Rd (from sb), W RV camping
33mm	**sb, full facilities, litter barrels**
32	Bethesda Rd, E Valero Best Value Inn RV Ranch Park, W Mockingbird Hill RV Park
31mm	**nb, full facilities, litter barrels**
30	FM 917, Mansfield, E Shell/Sonic/dsl, W Shell/dsl RanchHouse Rest.
27	Rd 604, Rd 707
26b a	US 67, Cleburne, E Chevron/KFC/dsl Chicken Express, DQ, McDonald's, Pizza Hut, Sonic, Waffle House, Whataburger Best Western, Days Inn, La Quinta, Super 8 $General, Ancira RV Ctr, AutoZone, Brookshire Foods, Family$, Motor Home Specialist, Parts+, Walmart
24	FM 3136, FM 1706, Alvarado, E Shell/Grandy's/dsl/scales/24hr Longhorn Grill
21	Rd 107, to Greenfield
17	FM 2258
16	TX 81 S, Rd 201, Grandview
15	FM 916, Maypearl, W Chevron/dsl, Mobil/dsl Subway
12	FM 67
8	FM 66, Itasca, E Valero/dsl/café/24hr, W DQ Ford, litter barrels, picnic tables
7	FM 934, E **picnic tables, litter barrels,** W Exxon/dsl Golden Chick Cafe
3	FM 2959, E to Hillsboro Airport

I-35W begins/ends on I-35, 371mm.

INTERSTATE 37

Exit #	Services
142b a	I-35 S to Laredo, N to Austin. **I-37 begins/ends on I-35 in San Antonio.**
141c	Brooklyn Ave, Nolan St (from sb), downtown
141b	Houston St, E Comfort Suites, Red Roof Inn tires, W Shell Denny's Crockett Hotel, Crowne Plaza, Days Inn, Drury Inn, Fairfield Inn, Hampton Inn, Hyatt Hotel, La Quinta, Marriott, Residence Inn, SpringHill Suites Macy's, to The Alamo
141a	Commerce St, E Staybridge Suites, W Denny's La Quinta, Marriott Macy's
140b	Durango Blvd, E Bill Miller BBQ to Alamo Dome, downtown
140a	Carolina St, Florida St, E Shell/dsl
139	I-10 W, US 87, US 90, to Houston, W to Sea World
138c	Fair Ave, Hackberry St, E DQ, Jack-in-the-Box, La Tapatia Mexian, Las Margarita's, Popeye's Brake Check, Family$, Home Depot, W Exxon, Shell
138b	E New Braunfels Ave (from sb), E IHOP, Little Caesars, McDonald's, Taco Cabana, Wendy's, Whataburger Beall's, HEB/dsl, Marshall's, W Exxon Sonic
138a	Southcross Blvd, W New Braunfels Ave, E McDonald's, Taco Cabana, Wendy's, W Exxon Sonic

SAN ANTONIO

137	Hot Wells Blvd, W IHOP Motel 6, Super 8
136	Pecan Valley Dr, E Citgo/dsl KFC/Taco Bell, Pizza H Pecan Valley Inn AutoZone, O'Reilly Parts, W H
135	Military Dr, Lp 13, E Shell, Valero Jack-in-the-Box Quality Inn Mission Trail RV park, W Valero/Subway/d A&W/LJ Silver, Buffalo Wild Wings, Burger King, Carino Italian, Chaba Thai, Chick-fil-A, Chili's, Cracker Barrel, IHO Little Caesars, Longhorn Cafe, Panda Express, Papa John's Peter Piper Pizza, Sonic, Starbucks, Subway, Whataburger La Quinta H, $Tree, Advance Parts, AT&T, Best Buy, B gLots, Discount Tire, Hancock Fabrics, HEB Food/gas, Hom Depot, Lowe's, Office Depot, PetCo, Radio Shack, Ross, Targe to Brooks AFB, Walgreens, Walmart/McDonald's
133	I-410, US 281 S
132	US 181 S, to Floresville, E Shell $General
130	Donop Rd, Southton Rd, E Valero/dsl Tom's Burger Days Inn Braunig Lake RV Resort, W Shell/ds car/truckwash
127	San Antonio River Turnaround (from nb), Braunig Lake
127mm	San Antonio River
125	FM 1604, Anderson Lp, E Conoco/dsl/24hr Burge King fireworks, W Exxon/dsl, Shell/dsl Miller's BBQ, Whataburger fireworks, tires
122	Priest Rd, Mathis Rd, E Valero
120	Hardy Rd
117	FM 536
113	FM 3006
112mm	**both lanes, litter barrels**
109	TX 97, to Floresville, E Chevron/dsl Portrillo's Mexicar Chrysler/Dodge/Jeep
106	Coughran Rd
104	spur 199, Leal Rd, to Pleasanton (no immediate sb return), same as 103
103	US 281 N, Leal Rd, to Pleasanton, E Valero/dsl DQ, K&K Cafe Kuntry Inn
98	TX 541, McCoy
92	US 281A, Campbellton
88	FM 1099, to FM 791, Campbellton
83	FM 99, Whitsett, Peggy, E Shell/cafe/dsl, W Chevron/dsl, Exxon/dsl Choke Canyon BBQ
82mm	**sb, full facilities, litter barrels RV dump**
78mm	**nb, full facilities, litter barrels RV dump**
76	US 281A, FM 2049, Whitsett
75mm	**truck weigh sta sb**
74mm	**truck weigh sta nb**
72	US 281 S, Three Rivers, **4 mi** W Loves/McDonald's/Subway/dsl/scales/24hr/ @, Valero DQ, Staghorn Rest, Van's BBQ Best Western, EconoLodge to Rio Grande Valley
69	TX 72, Three Rivers, W Valero/café/dsl/24hr RV park, tires, to Choke Cyn SP
65	FM 1358, Oakville, E Van's BBQ
59	FM 799
56	US 59, George West, E Valero/dsl/24hr, W Shell/Subway/dsl/24hr, Valero/Burger King/dsl/24hr
51	Hailey Ranch Rd
47	FM 3024, FM 534, Swinney Switch Rd, W Swinney Switch Cafe Mike's Mkt/gas (1mi), to KOA (4mi)
44mm	**parking area sb**
42mm	**parking area nb**
40	FM 888

INTERSTATE 37 Cont'd

Exit #	Services
36	TX 359, to Skidmore, Mathis, W Citgo/Subway/dsl, Shell/ McDonald's/dsl, Valero/dsl (1mi) Pizza Hut Mathis Inn Lake Corpus Christi SRA
34	TX 359 W, E Adventure TX RV Ctr/LP, W Shell, Valero/ dsl DQ, Pizza Hut $General, O'Reilly Parts, to Lake Corpus Christi SP
31	TX 188, to Sinton, Rockport
22	TX 234, FM 796, to Odem, Edroy
20b	Cooper Rd
19.5mm	**both lanes, litter barrels**
17	US 77 N, to Victoria
16	LaBonte Park, W **info, litter barrels**
15	Sharpsburg Rd (from sb), Redbird Ln
14	I-69, US 77 S, Redbird Ln, to Kingsville, Robstown, **1 mi W on FM 624** RaceWay/dsl, Shell/dsl, Valero/Burger King/dsl Chili's, CiCi's, Denny's, Good'n Crisp Chicken, Miller's BBQ, Papa John's, Pizza Hut, Popeye's, Sonic, Subway, Whataburger, Wienerschnitzel Comfort Inn, Holiday Inn Express H, $General, $Tree, AT&T, AutoZone, Beall's, CVS Drug, Discount Tire, Firestone/auto, GNC, Hobby Lobby, Home Depot, O'Reilly Parts, Radio Shack, Walmart/McDonald's
13b	Sharpsburg Rd (from nb)
13a	FM 1694, Callicoatte Rd, Leopard St
11b	FM 24, Violet Rd, Hart Rd, E Citgo/Subway/dsl Chicken Shack, W Exxon/dsl, Valero/dsl DQ, Fliz Amancer Mexican, KFC/LJ Silver, Little Caesars, McDonald's, Pizza Hut, Schlotzsky's, Sonic, Subway, Taco Bell, Whataburger Best Western, Hampton Inn AutoZone, HEB Food/gas, O'Reilly Parts, vet, Walgreens
11a	McKinzie Rd, E Shell Jack-in-the-Box La Quinta, W Valero/dsl
10	Carbon Plant Rd
9	FM 2292, Up River Rd, Rand Morgan Rd, W Valero/dsl Whataburger
7	Suntide Rd, Tuloso Rd, Clarkwood Rd, W CC RV Ctr, Freightliner
6	Southern Minerals Rd, E refinery
5	Corn Products Rd, Valero Way, E Kenworth/Mack, W PetroFleet Jalisco II Rest. Howard Johnson, Travelodge, ValStay
4b	Lantana St, McBride Lane (from sb), W Airport Inn, Motel 6
4a	TX 358, to Padre Island, W Holiday Inn, Plaza Inn, Quality Inn (4mi), Walmart
3b	McBride Lane (from nb), W Gulf Coast Racing
3a	Navigation Blvd, E Valero/dsl Rodeway Inn, W Exxon/dsl Denny's, La Milpas, Miller BBQ Days Inn, Hampton Inn, Holiday Inn Express, La Quinta, Super 8 CarQuest
2	Up River Rd, E refinery
1e	Lawrence Dr, Nueces Bay Blvd, E refinery, W Valero Church's Red Roof Inn Aamco, AutoZone, Firestone, HEB Foods, USPO
1d	Port Ave (from sb), W Coastal, Shell Vick's Burgers, Whataburger EconoLodge Port of Corpus Christi, Radio Shack
1c	US 181, TX 286, Shoreline Blvd, Corpus Christi, W H
1b	Brownlee St (from nb), Shell
1a	Buffalo St (from sb), **0-1 mi W on Shoreline** Valero/dsl Burger King, Joe's Crabshack, Landry's Seafood, Subway, Waterstreet Seafood, Whataburger Bayfront Inn, Best

CORPUS CHRISTI

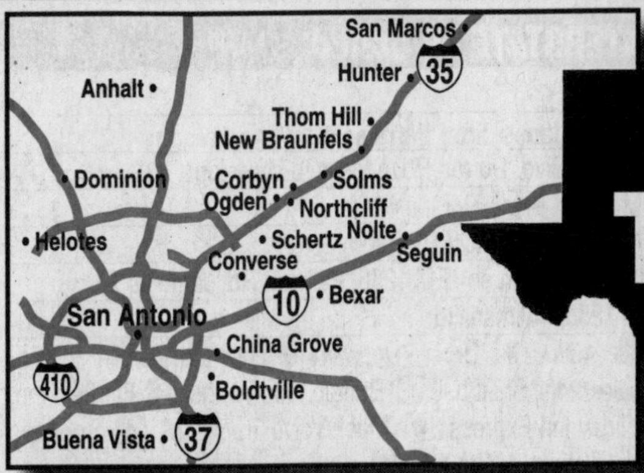

TX

Exit #	Services
1a	Continued West ern, Omni Hotel, Super 8 U-Haul, USPO **I-37 begins/ ends on US 181 in Corpus Christi.**

INTERSTATE 40

Exit #	Services
177mm	Texas/Oklahoma state line
176	spur 30 (from eb), to Texola
169	FM 1802, Carbon Black Rd
167	FM 2168, Daberry Rd
165mm	**check sta wb**
164	Lp 40 (from wb), to Shamrock, **1 mi S** EconoLodge H, **check sta eb**, museum
163	US 83, to Wheeler, Shamrock, N Chevron/Taco Bell/dsl Mitchell's Rest. Best Western, Motel 6 Ace Hardware, S Conoco/dsl, Valero/Subway/dsl DQ, McDonald's EconoLodge, Holiday Inn Express, Sleep Inn, Western Motel Family$
161	Lp 40, Rte 66 (from eb), to Shamrock
157	FM 1547, Lela, **1 mi S** West 40 RV Camping
152	FM 453, Pakan Rd
148	FM 1443, Kellerville Rd
146	County Line Rd
143	Lp 40 (from wb), to McLean, to Phillips 66/dsl
142	TX 273, FM 3143, to McLean, N Phillips 66/dsl Red River Steaks Cactus Inn RV Camping/dump, USPO
141	Rte 66 (from eb), McLean, same as 142
135	FM 291, Rte 66, Alanreed, S Conoco/motel/café/RV park/ dump USPO
132	Johnson Ranch Rd, ranch access
131mm	**wb, full facilities, litter barrels, petwalk**
129mm	**eb, full facilities, litter barrels, petwalk**
128	FM 2477, to Lake McClellan, N Lake McClellan RA/RV Dump
124	TX 70 S, to Clarendon, S RV camping/dump (11mi)
121	TX 70 N, to Pampa
114	Lp 40, Groom, N dsl repair
113	FM 2300, Groom, S Phillips 66/dsl DQ Chalet Inn
112	FM 295, Groom, S gas Biggest Cross
110	Lp 40, Rte 66
109	FM 294
108mm	**parking area wb, litter barrels**
106mm	**parking area eb, litter barrels**
105	FM 2880, grain silo
98	TX 207 S (from wb), to Claude
96	TX 207 N, to Panhandle, N Loves/Subway/dsl/24hr, S Conway Inn/cafe, Executive Inn
89	FM 2161, to Rte 66
87	FM 2373

SHAMROCK

= gas = food = lodging = other = rest stop

TX

INTERSTATE 40 Cont'd

AMARILLO

Exit #	Services
87mm	**both lanes, litter barrels**
85	Amarillo Blvd, Durrett Rd, access to camping
81	FM 1912, N Phillips 66/dsl
80	FM 228, N AOK RV Park
78	US 287 S (from eb), FM 1258, Pullman Rd, same as 77
77	FM 1258, Pullman Rd
76	spur 468, N FLYING J/Denny's/dsl/LP/RV dump/scales/24hr, Shell/dsl Buffalo Wild Wings Fairfield Inn, Holiday Inn Express Mack/Volvo Trucks, S Speedco Custom RV Ctr, TX info
75	Lp 335, Lakeside Rd, N Pilot/McDonald's/dsl/scales/24hr/ @ Hampton Inn, Knights Inn, Super 8 KOA (2mi), Overnite RV Park, S Petro/dsl/rest./scales/@, Valero/dsl Blue Beacon
74	Whitaker Rd, N Big Texan Inn RV camping, S Love's/Subway/dsl/scales/ @, TA/Exxon/FoodCourt/dsl/scales/24hr/ @ Blue Beacon, Eagle Truckwash, Peterbilt
73	Eastern St, Bolton Ave, Amarillo, N TT/dsl Express Inn, Motel 6, Value Place, S Valero/dsl Best Western
72b	Grand St, Amarillo, N Valero/dsl Henk's BBQ Value Inn O'Reilly Parts, S Murphy USA/dsl, Phillips 66, Valero Braum's, Chicken Express, McDonald's, Pizza Hut, Sonic, Starbucks, Subway, Taco Villa, Whataburger Best Value Inn $Tree, Advance Parts, Amigo's Foods, AutoZone, BigLots, GNC a, Meineke, same as 73, URGENT CARE, Walmart
72a	Nelson St, N Cracker Barrel Ashmore Inn, Comfort Inn, La Kiva Hotel, Luxury Inn, Sleep Inn, Super 8 Qtrhorse Museum, S Valero/dsl Camelot Suites transmissions
71	Ross St, Osage St, Amarillo, N Shell/dsl, Valero A&W/LJ Silver, Burger King, IHOP, KFC, McDonald's, Schlotsky's, Subway, Wienerschnitzel Clarion, Comfort Inn, Days Inn, Microtel, Quality Inn Discount Tire, S Arby's, Denny's, Fiesta Grande Mexican, Sonic, Taco Bell, Wendy's Baymont Inn, La Quinta, Red Roof Inn Chevrolet, Ford, Hyundai, Sam's Club/gas, USPO
70	I-27 S, US 60 W, US 87, US 287, to Canyon, Lubbock, to downtown Amarillo
69b	Washington St, Amarillo, S TT/dsl DQ CVS Drug
69a	Crockett St, access to same as 68b
68b	Georgia St, N TT/dsl Dyer's BBQ, Schlotzky's, Sharky's Burrito Co Wyndham Garden, S Valero Baker Bro's Deli, Burger King, Church's Chicken, Coldstone, Denny's, Furr's Café, Jersey Mike's, Pizza Hut, Sonic, Starbucks, TX Roadhouse, Whataburger Holiday Inn Express Hastings Books, Home Depot, Office Depot, Radio Shack, Walgreens
68a	Julian Blvd, Paramount Blvd, N Chili's, Rosa's Cafe same as 67, Wyndham Garden, S Valero Baker Bro's Deli, Burger King, Chick-Fil-A, Chipotle, Furr's Buffet, Hayashi Japanese, Kushiyama, Panda Express, Popeyes, Red Lobster, Ruby Tequila's Mexican, TX Roadhouse Holiday Inn Express, Motel 6, Super 8, Travelodge Home Depot, Office Depot
67	Western St, Amarillo, N Phillips 66 Braum's, Burger King, McAlister's Deli, McDonald's, Papa Murphy's, Sonic, Subway, Taco Bell, Wendy's, S Murphy Express/dsl, Rudy's/BBQ/dsl, Valero Blue Sky Rest., Cheddar's, IHOP, Jimmy John's, Olive Garden, Waffle House, Wienerschnitzel Baymont Inn, Candlewood Suites, Comfort Suites, Staybridge
67	Continued Suites Discount Tire, Firestone/auto, Michael's, O'Reil Parts, Petco, same 68
66	Bell St, Amarillo, N Cefco/dsl Fairfield Inn, Red Ro Inn, Relax Inn, Residence Inn Harley-Davidson, S De nut Stop, King & I Chinese, Taco Bueno CashSaver
65	Coulter Dr, Amarillo, N Phillips 66/dsl Arby's, Carino Italian, Golden Corral, Kabuki Japanese, Logan's Roadhous SaltGrass Steaks, Subway, Taco Bell, Waffle House Cour yard, Days Inn, Executive Inn, Extended Stay America, Holida Inn, Holiday Inn Express, La Quinta H, Cadillac/Chevrole Cavender's Boots, Chrysler/Dodge/Jeep, Discount Tire, Fires tone/auto, S Chevron/Chicken Express/dsl ChinaSta CiCi's, Hoffbrau Steaks, McDonald's, Outback Steaks, Pizz Hut, Wendy's, Whataburger 5th Season Inn, Hampton Inn Sleep Inn AT&T, Goodyear/auto, Verizon
64	Soncy Rd, to Pal Duro Cyn, N Famous Dave's BBQ, Furr Buffet, Jimmy John's, Lin's Chinese, Plaza Rest., Red Robin Comfort Inn, Country Inn&Suites, Drury Inn, Hilton Garden, Holi day Inn, Homewood Suites USPO, S Valero/dsl/24h Applebee's, Baker Bros Deli, ChuckeCheese, DQ, Fazoli's Hooters, Marble Slab Creamery, McAlisters Deli, McDon ald's, On-the-Border, Pei Wei, Starbucks, Subway $Tree Barnes&Noble, Best Buy, Dillard's, Ford, Home Depot, JC Pen ney, Jo-Ann Fabrics, Kohl's, Lincoln, mall, Old Navy, PetsMart Ross, Sears/auto, Target, Verizon, World Mkt
62b	Lp 40, Amarillo Blvd, N Gander Mtn, S Sundown RV Resort
62a	Hope Rd, Helium Rd, S Cadillac RV camping
60	Arnot Rd, S Love's/Subway/dsl Oasis RV Resort dump
57	RM 2381, Bushland, N Falcon Stop/dsl grain silos S Phillips 66/dsl Bushland Burger, Joe's Pizza USPO, vet
55mm	**parking area wb**
54	Adkisson Rd
53.5mm	**parking area eb, litter barrels**
49	FM 809, Wildorado, S Crist Fuel/dsl/LP Royal Inn
42	Everett Rd
37	Lp 40 W, to Vega, **1 mi** N Bonanza Motel same as 36, Walnut RV Park
36	US 385, Vega, N Alon/dsl, Conoco/dsl/24hr, Shamrock DQ, Subway Days Inn RV Park, S Shell/cafe/dsl
35	to Rte 66, to Vega, N Best Value Inn, Bonanza Motel (1mi) same as 36, Walnut RV Park (1mi)
32mm	**both lanes, litter barrels**
28	to Rte 66, Landergin
23	to Adrian, Vega, same as 22
22	TX 214, Adrian, N Midpoint Cafe auto repair, USPO, S Phillips 66/dsl/Tommy's Café
18	FM 2858, Gruhlkey Rd
15	Ivy Rd
13mm	**both lanes, litter barrels**
5.5mm	turnout
0	Lp 40, to Glenrio
0mm	Texas/New Mexico state line, Central/Mountain time zone

AMARILLO

VEGA

INTERSTATE 44

Exit #	Services
15mm	Texas/Oklahoma state line, Red River
14	Lp 267, E 3rd St, W historical marker, KOA
13	Glendale St, W Subway Beall's

🅴 INTERSTATE 44 Cont'd

Exit #	Services
12	Burkburnett, **E** 🛢 Valero/dsl 🏨 Red River Inn, **W** 🛢 Alon/7-11/dsl 🍴 Braum's, Chicken Express, Feedlot Rest., Lite Pan Asian, McDonald's, Whataburger ⊙ Chevrolet, Ford
11	FM 3429, Daniels Rd
9mm	🅟 **both lanes, petwalk, litter barrels**
7	East Rd
6	Bacon Switch Rd
5a	FM 3492, Missile Rd, **E** 🍴 El Mejicano Rest., Hunan Chinese, Marco's Pizza ⊙ st patrol, **W** 🛢 Exxon/dsl
5	Access Rd
4	City Loop St
3c	FM 890, **W** 🛢 Murphy USA/dsl 🍴 Cracker Barrel, Jack-in-the-Box, KFC/Taco Bell, Parkway Grill, Subway ⊙ Walmart/Subway
3b	sp 325, Sheppard AFB
3a	US 287 N, to Amarillo, **W** 🛢 Shell/dsl 🍴 Carl's Jr 🏨 Howard Johnson
2	Maurine St, **E** 🛢 Alon/7-11/dsl, Shell/dsl 🏨 Best Value Inn, Executive Inn, Motel 6, Quality Inn ⊙ Chevrolet, Mazda/VW, **W** 🛢 Alon/7-11 🍴 Denny's, El Chico, LJ Silver, Whataburger 🏨 Candlewood Suites, Comfort Inn, La Quinta, Red Roof Inn, Super 8
1d	US 287 bus, Lp 370, **W** 🛢 FuelStop/dsl 🏨 Travelodge
1c	Texas Travel Info Ctr, **E** 🛢 $Saver
1b	Scotland Park (from nb)
1a	US 277 S, to Abilene, **W** 🍴 Arby's 🏨 EconoLodge
1	Holliday St, **W** 🛢 Valero/dsl 🍴 Arby's, Burger King, Carl's Jr, IHOP, McDonald's, Subway 🏨 EconoLodge, Motel 6 ⊙ 🅗 Family$, Walgreens
0mm	Witchita Falls, **I-44 begins/ends on US 287**

WICHITA FALLS

🅽 INTERSTATE 45

Exit #	Services
286	to I-35 E, to Denton. **I-45 begins/ends in Dallas.**
285	Bryan St E, US 75 N
284b a	I-30, W to Ft Worth, E to Texarkana, access to 🅗
283b	Pennsylvania Ave, to MLK Blvd, **E** 🛢 Shamrock
283a	Lamar St
281	Overton St (from sb), **W** 🛢 Chevron
280	Illinois Ave, Linfield St, **E** 🏨 Star Motel, **W** 🛢 Exxon, Shell/dsl
279b a	Lp 12
277	Simpson Stuart Rd, **W** ⊙ to Paul Quinn Coll
276b a	I-20, W to Ft Worth, E to Shreveport
275	TX 310 N (from nb, no re-entry)
274	Dowdy Ferry Rd, Hutchins, **E** 🛢 Exxon/Subway/dsl, Shell/McDonald's/dsl 🏨 Gold Inn, La Quinta, Motel 6 ⊙ auto repair, **W** 🍴 DQ, Jack-in-the-Box, Whataburger
273	Wintergreen Rd, 🛢 QT/dsl/scales/24hr
272	Fulghum Rd, **E** 🛢 ⬥Loves/Carl's Jr/dsl/scales/24hr, **W** 🛢 **weigh sta, both lanes**
271	Pleasant Run Rd
270	Belt Line Rd, to Wilmer, **E** 🛢 Texaco/Pizza Inn/dsl, **W** 🛢 Exxon/Sonic/dsl, Shell/Church's/Subway/dsl ⊙ $General, Family$, USPO
269	Mars Rd
268	Malloy Bridge Rd
267	Frontage Rd

DALLAS

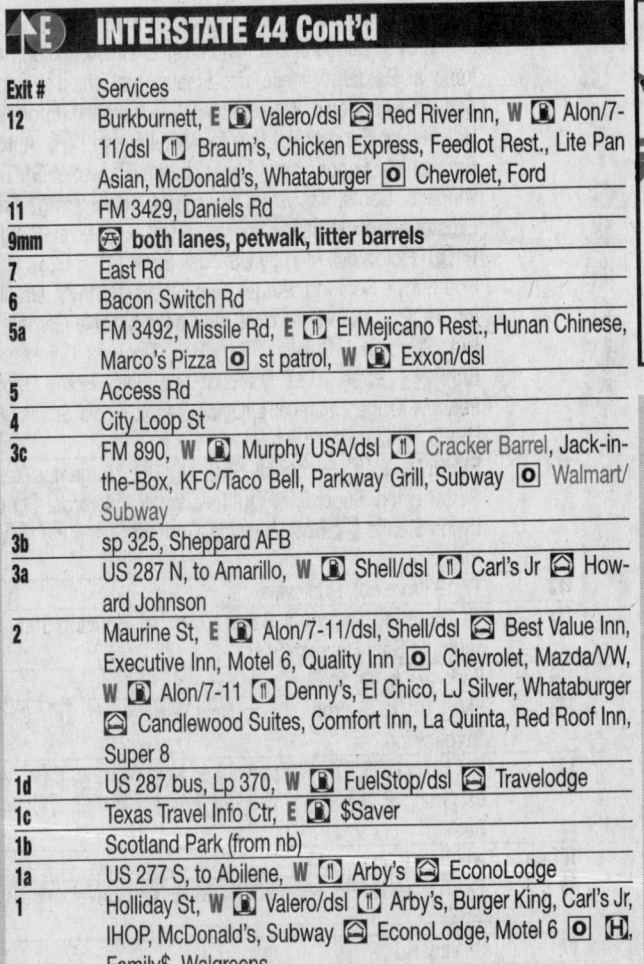

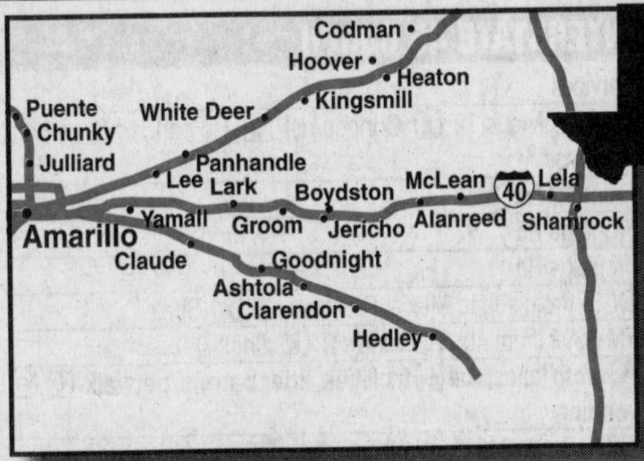

Exit #	Services
266	FM 660, **E** 🍴 Jack-in-the-Box, **W** 🛢 Shamrock/dsl 🍴 DQ, Pizza Hut
265	Lp 45, Ferris, nb only
263a b	Lp 561
262	frontage rd
260	Lp 45, **E** 🍴 Trailor RV Park, **W** 🛢 Shell/Sonic/dsl
259	FM 813, FM 878, Jefferson St, **W** ⊙ Goodyear
258	Lp 45, Palmer, **E** 🛢 Chevron/Subway/dsl/scales/24hr ⊙ golf
255	FM 879, Garrett, **E** 🛢 Exxon/dsl, **W** 🛢 Chevron/dsl
253	Lp 45, **W** 🛢 Shell/Subway/dsl
251b	TX 34, Ennis, **E** 🛢 Fina/dsl, Shell/dsl, Valero/dsl 🍴 Bubba's BBQ, McDonald's 🏨 Baymont Inn, Comfort Suites, Days Inn, Holiday Inn Express ⊙ Ford, **W** 🛢 Chevron/dsl, Exxon/dsl/24hr, Murphy USA/dsl, Valero 🍴 Braum's, Burger King, Chili's, Denny's, Domino's, DQ, Golden Chick, Grand Buffet, Hilda's Kitchen, IHOP, Jack-in-the-Box, Jungle Jack's Pizza, KFC, Little Caesars, Sonic, Starbucks, Subway, Taco Bell, Taco Cabana, Waffle House, Wall Chinese, Wendy's, Whataburger 🏨 Ennis Inn, Quality Inn ⊙ 🅗, $Tree, AutoZone, Beall's, Chevrolet, Chrysler/Dodge/Jeep, Radio Shack, RV camping, Walmart/McDonald's
251a	Creechville Rd, FM 1181, Ennis, **W** ⊙ 🅗
249	FM 85, Ennis, **E** 🏨 Budget Inn, **W** 🛢 Exxon/Subway ⊙ Blue Beacon, repair
247	US 287 N, to Waxahatchie
246	FM 1183, Alma, **W** 🛢 Chevron
244	FM 1182
243	Frontage Rd
242	Calhoun St, Rice, **W** 🛢 Shell/Sonic/dsl
239	FM 1126, **W** 🛢 45 Kwik Stop ⊙ Rendell RV Ctr
238	FM 1603, **E** 🛢 Exxon/rest/dsl/24hr ⊙ Casita RV Trailers
237	Frontage Rd
235b	Lp I-45 (from sb), to Corsicana
235a	Frontage Rd
232	Roane Rd, E 5th Ave
231	TX 31, Corsicana, **E** 🛢 Phillips 66/dsl 🍴 Jack-in-the-Box 🏨 Best Western, Colonial Inn, La Quinta ⊙ Buick/Cadillac/Chevrolet/GMC, **W** 🛢 Exxon/Subway/dsl, Shell/Arby's 🍴 Bill's Fried Chicken, DQ, McDonald's 🏨 Comfort Inn ⊙ 🅗, Chrysler/Dodge/Jeep, Ford/Lincoln, to Navarro Coll
229	US 287, Palestine, **E** 🛢 Exxon/Wendy's/dsl, Shell/dsl 🍴 Applebee's, Chili's, Collin St Bakery, Denny's, Sonic, Subway, Taco Bell 🏨 Hampton Inn, Holiday Inn Express ⊙ Corsicana Outlets, Gander Mtn, Home Depot, Office Depot, Russell Stover Candies, **W** 🍴 Waffle House 🏨 Corsicana Inn, EconoLodge, Motel 6, Traveler's Inn
228b	Lp 45 (exits left from nb), Corsicana, **2 mi** **W** services in Corsicana
228a	15th St, Corsicana, ⊙ Scion/Toyota

ENNIS

CORSICANA

[gas] = gas [food] = food [lodging] = lodging [other] = other [RS] = rest stop

TX

INTERSTATE 45 Cont'd

FAIRFIELD

Exit #	Services
225	FM 739, Angus, E [gas] Conoco/dsl [other] RV park, to Chambers Reservoir
221	Frontage Rd
220	Frontage Rd
219b	Frontage Rd
219a	TX 14 (from sb), to Mexia, Richland, W [gas] Shell
218	FM 1394 (from nb), Richland, W [gas] Shell
217mm	**[RS] both lanes, full [handicapped] facilities, litter barrels, petwalk [phone] [picnic] vending**
213	TX 75 S, FM 246, to Wortham, W [gas] Exxon/dsl
211	FM 80, to Streetman, Kirvin
206	FM 833, **3 mi**, I-45 RV Park
198	FM 27, to Wortham, E [gas] Shell/Cole's BBQ [food] Gilberto's Mexican [lodging] La Quinta [other] [H], W [gas] Cooper Farms/dsl, Loves/Burger King/dsl/scales/24hr [lodging] Budget Inn [other] I-45 RV Park (4mi)
197	US 84, Fairfield, E [gas] Chevron/dsl, Exxon/dsl, Shell/dsl [food] Bush's Chicken, DQ, Jack-in-the-Box, McDonald's, Sam's Rest., Something Different Rest, Sonic, Subway/TX Burger [lodging] Days Inn, Holiday Inn Express, Super 8 [other] Brookshire Foods/gas, Chevrolet, Chrysler/Dodge/Jeep, Fred's Store, W [gas] Exxon/dsl, Shell/dsl, Texaco/dsl [food] I-45 Rest., KFC/Taco Bell, Lonestar Grill, Pizza Hut, Ponte's Diner [lodging] Best Value Inn, Regency Inn [other] Ace Hardware, Ford
189	TX 179, to Teague, E [gas] Citgo/Shirley's Cafe/dsl, Exxon/Dinner Bell Rest/dsl
180	TX 164, to Groesbeck
178	US 79, Buffalo, E [gas] Chevron, Conoco/dsl, Shell/dsl [food] Pizza Hut, Subway/TX Burger [other] $General, Brookshire Foods/gas, Family$, W [gas] Exxon/Church's/Subway/dsl/scales, Shamrock/dsl/24hr, Texaco/dsl [food] Dickey's BBQ, DQ, Mexican, Pitt Grill, Rancho Viejo, Sonic [lodging] Comfort Inn, Craig's Inn, Economy Inn, Hampton Inn
175mm	Bliss Creek
166mm	weigh sta sb
164	TX 7, Centerville, E [gas] Chevron, Shell/Woody's BBQ/dsl [food] Country Cousins BBQ, Subway/TX Burger [lodging] Days Inn, W [gas] Exxon/dsl, Shell/Woody's BBQ/dsl [food] DQ, Jack-in-the-Box, Roble's Mexican
160mm	**[picnic] sb, litter barrels**
159mm	Boggy Creek
156	FM 977, to Leona, W [gas] Exxon/dsl
155mm	**picnic area nb, picnic tables, litter barrels**
152	TX OSR, to Normangee, W [gas] Chevron/dsl, Shell/Arby's/dsl
146	TX 75
142	US 190, TX 21, Madisonville, E [gas] Exxon/BBQ/dsl, Shell/Buc-ees/dsl [lodging] Best Western, Carefree Inn, W [gas] Chevron/Church's/dsl, Shell/Subway [food] Castanedas Mexican, Jack-in-the-Box, Lakeside Rest, McDonald's, Pizza Hut, Sonic, Taco Bell, TX Burger [lodging] Budget Motel, Western Lodge [other] [H], Ford, Toyota
136	spur 67, E [food] Shrimpy's Seafood [other] Home on the Range RV camping/LP (3mi)
132	FM 2989
124mm	**[RS] both lanes, full [handicapped] facilities, litter barrels, petwalk [phone] [picnic] vending**
123	FM 1696
118	TX 75, E [gas] Shell/Hitchin Post/dsl/24hr/ @ [other] Texas Prison Museum, truckwash, W [gas] Pilot/Wendy's/dsl/scales/24hr, Shell/Dickey's BBQ/Subway/dsl [food] Chicken Express

HUNTSVILLE

Exit #	Services
116	US 190, TX 30, E [gas] Conoco/dsl, Phillips 66/dsl, Valero/dsl [food] Arby's, Bandera Grill, Church's, El Chico, Golden Corral, Imperial Garden Chinese, Jct Steaks, McDonald's, Popeye's, Schlotzsky's, Sonic, Whataburger [lodging] Days Inn, EconoLodge, Holiday Inn Express, La Quinta, Motel 6 [other] [H], AutoZone, Brookshire Foods/gas, Buick/Cadillac/Chevrolet/GMC, Cavander's Boots, Chrysler/Dodge/Jeep, CVS Drug, Family$, Firestone/auto, Hastings Books, O'Reilly Parts, vet, Walgreens, W [gas] Exxon/dsl, Murphy USA/dsl, Shell [food] 5 Guys Burgers, Bob Luby's Seafood, Burger King, Chili's, Denny's, Grand Buffet, IHOP, Jack-in-the-Box, Little Caesars, Olive Garden, Pizza Hut, Starbucks, Subway, Taco Bell, Tinsley's Chicken, Wing Stop [other] $Tree, AT&T, Discount Tire, GNC, Home Depot, JC Penney, Kroger, Marshall's, Office Depot, Radio Shack, Target, USPO, Verizon, Walmart
114	FM 1374, E [gas] Exxon/dsl, Shell [food] DQ, Margaritas Rest. [lodging] Gateway Inn, Super 8, W [gas] Texaco/dsl, Valero/dsl [food] Country Inn Steaks [lodging] Best Value Inn, Comfort Suites [other] [H], Ford, Hyundai
113	TX 19 (from nb), Huntsville
112	TX 75, E [gas] Citgo [lodging] Baker Motel [other] Houston Statue, museum, to Sam Houston St U
109	Park 40, W [other] to Huntsville SP
103	FM 1374/1375 (from sb), to New Waverly, W [gas] Chevron/Burger King/dsl
102	FM 1374/1375, TX 150 (from nb), to New Waverly, E [gas] Valero/dsl (1mi), W [gas] (1mi), Chevron/Burger King/dsl [food] Waverly Rest.
101mm	**weigh sta nb**
98	TX 75, Danville Rd, Shepard Hill Rd, E [other] Convenience RV Ctr/repair
97	Calvary Rd
95	Longstreet Rd, Calvary Rd, Willis, W [gas] Loves/Subway/Wendy's/dsl/scales/24hr
94	FM 1097, Longstreet Rd, to Willis, E [gas] Kwik Stop/dsl [food] Jack-in-the-Box, Sonic, Taco Bell [other] $General, AutoZone, W [gas] Chevron/Popeye's, Shell/dsl [food] Burger King, Chick-fil-A, Little Caesars, McDonald's, Pizza Hut, Rico's Grill, Scholtzsky's, Subway, Whataburger [lodging] Best Western [other] Kroger/dsl, vet, Walgreens
92	FM 830, Seven Coves Dr, W [other] Omega Farms RV Park, RV Park on the Lake (3mi), Thousand Trails Resort
91	League Line Rd, E [gas] Chevron/McDonald's, Shell/dsl [food] Mamma Juanita's Mexican, Waffle House, Wendy's [lodging] Comfort Inn, Days Inn, La Quinta [other] Conroe Outlets/famous brands, W [gas] Shell/Jack-in-the-Box [food] Cracker Barrel
90	FM 3083, Teas Nursery Rd, Montgomery Co Park, E [gas] Exxon/dsl [food] Applebee's, Buffalo Wild Wings, Popeye's, Red Lobster, Smokey Mo's BBQ [lodging] Fairfield Inn [other] AT&T, convention center (4mi), Kohl's, Old Navy, Petsmart, Ross, TJ Maxx, W [food] Firehouse Subs, Olive Garden, Subway, Wings Wok [lodging] Value-Place Inn [other] JC Penney, Verizon
88	Lp 336, to Cleveland, Navasota, E [gas] Mobil/Chester's/dsl, Shell/dsl, Valero/dsl [food] A&W/LJ Silver, Arby's, Burger King, Chili's, China Delight, Denny's, Domino's, Los Cucos Mexican, Marble Slab Creamery, Margarita's Mexican, McDonald's, Papa John's, Pizza Hut, Quizno's, Sonic, TX Roadhouse, Whataburger, Wing Stop [lodging] Hampton Inn, Holiday Inn Express [other] $Tree, Advance Parts, Buick, CVS Drug, Discount Tire, GNC, HEB Foods/gas, Hobby Lobby, Just Brakes, Kroger/gas, Michael's, vet, Walgreens, W [gas] Chevron/24hr [food] Blackeyed Pea, Casa Ole Mexican, Culver's, Dickie's BBQ, El Bosque Mexican, Jack-in-the-Box, KFC, Ryan's, Subway [other] 99Cent Store, Hancock

CONROE

INTERSTATE 45 Cont'd

88 Continued
Fabrics, Lowe's, PetCo, Sam's Club/gas, Tuesday Morning, Walmart

87 TX 105, Conroe, E Burger King, Jack-in-the-Box, Kettle, Luther's BBQ, McDonald's, Outback Steaks, Popeye's, Saltgrass Steaks, Sonic, Taco Bell, Tast of China Super 8 H, $General, CVS Drug, Firestone/auto, Hyundai, Kia, NTB, W Exxon Chick-fil-A, Coney Island, Luby's, Panda Express, Panera Bread, Quizno's, Schlotzsky's, Shogun Japanese, Smoothie King, Starbucks, Subway, Taco Bell, Taco Bueno, Whataburger Best Buy, Buick/GMC, Hastings Books, Home Depot, Office Depot, Radio Shack, Target, Tiremaxx

85 FM 2854, Gladstell St, E Citgo/dsl Motel 6 H, Honda, Nissan, W Shell/dsl, Valero IHOP Baymont Inn, Days Inn Cadillac, Chrysler/Dodge/Jeep, Fun Country RV Ctr, Mazda, Scion/Toyota

84 TX 75 N, Frazier St, E Chevron Corporate Inn, Ramada Ltd Ford, U-Haul, W Shell China Buffet, Incredible Pizza, Subway, Taco Cabana, Waffle House H, Albertson's, Discount Tire, K-Mart, Kroger

83 Crighton Rd, Camp Strake Rd

82 River Plantation Dr

82mm San Jacinto River

81 FM 1488, to Hempstead, Magnolia, E Citgo, W Valero/Subway CamperLand RV Ctr

80 Needham Rd (from sb)

79 TX 242, Needham, E Shell/McDonald's Mama Juanita's Mexican, Quizno's Best Western Batteries+, W Chevron, Murphy USA/dsl Adobe Cafe, Arby's, Burger King, ChuckeCheese, Domino's, Outback Steaks, Popeye's, Sonic, Subway, Taco Cabana, Wendy's, Whataburger, Willie's Grill, Wings'N More Country Suites, Fairfield Inn, TownPlace Suites H, BMW/Mini, Firestone/auto, Kohl's, Lowe's Whse, Walgreens, Walmart

78 Needham Rd (from sb), Tamina Rd, access to same as 77

77 Woodlands Pkwy, Robinson, Chateau Woods, E Chevron, Conoco/dsl Babin's Seafood, Buca Italian, Buffalo Wild Wings, Church's, Chuy's, Hooters, Lupe Tortilla, Melting Pot, Pancho's Mexican, Pappadeaux, Pappa's BBQ, PeiWei, Pizza Hut, Red Robin, Saltgrass Steaks, Subway, Tom's Steaks Best Value Inn, Budget Inn Discount Tire, funpark, Home Depot, Jo-Ann Fabrics, Michael's, NTB, Office Depot, Old Navy, Petsmart, Sam's Club/gas, SteinMart, vet, Walgreens, W Exxon, Shell, Texaco, Valero/dsl A&W/KFC, Blackeyed Pea, Cane's, Chick-fil-A, Chili's, Chipotle Mexican, Culver's, Denny's, El Bosque Mexican, Guadalajara Mexican, Jack-in-the-Box, Jason's Deli, Jimmy John's, Kabab House, Kirby's Steakhouse, La Madeliene, Landry's Seafood, Luby's, Macaroni Grill, Olive Garden, Red Lobster, Sweet Tomatos, TGIFriday's Comfort Suites, Days Inn, Drury Inn, Hampton Inn, Homewood Suites, La Quinta, Marriott, Shenandoa Inn H, auto repair, Best Buy, Dillard's, HEB Foods, Macy's, mall, Marshall's, Ross, Sears, Target, World Mkt

HOUSTON

76 Research Forest Dr, Tamina Rd, E Chevron/dsl LJ Silver, Pappa's BBQ Firestone/auto, JustBrakes, Tiremaxx, URGENT CARE, vet, W Shell Carrabba's, Denny's, El Chico, IHOP, Jack-in-the-Box, Kyoto Japanese, Macaroni Grill, Olive Garden, TGIFriday's, Tortuga Mexican Courtyard, Crossland Suites, Residence Inn Goodyear/auto, JC Penney, Sears/auto, Woodlands Mall

73 Rayford Rd, Sawdust Rd, E Conoco, Shell, Valero Hartz Chicken, Jack-in-the-Box, McDonald's, Popeye's, Sonic,

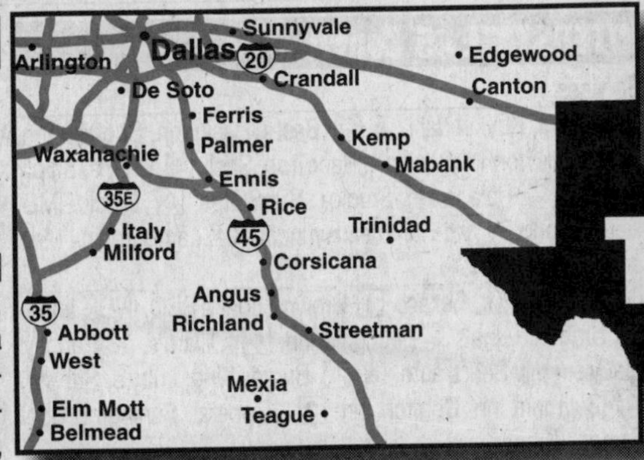

TX

73 Continued
Taqueria Arandas, Thomas BBQ Holiday Inn Express, La Quinta Aamco, AutoZone, O'Reilly Parts, U-Haul, W Mobil/dsl, Shell, Texaco Carrabba's, Cici's Pizza, Grand Buffet, IHOP, Subway, Taipei Chinese, Tortuga Extended Stay America, Red Roof Inn, Super 8 Brake Check, Discount Tire, GNC, Goodyear/auto, Harley-Davidson, HEB Foods, Kroger, Walgreens

72a Spring Crossing Dr, W Texaco/dsl

72b to Hardy Toll Rd from sb

70b Spring-Stuebner Rd, E Vaughn RV Ctr

70a FM 2920, to Tomball, E Exxon, Murphy USA/dsl, Rudy's BBQ/dsl, Shell Arby's, Chick-fil-A, El Palenque Mexican, Godfather's Pizza, Golden Jade Chinese, Hartz Chicken, McDonald's, Pizza Hut, Quizno's, Subway, Taco Cabana, Wendy's, Whataburger $General, $Tree, BigLots, Kohl's, Kroger, Lincoln, Michael's, O'Reilly Parts, Radio Shack, Ross, Scion/Toyota, transmissions, Vaughn's RV Ctr, Walmart/24hr, W Chevron, RaceTrac, Texaco Burger King, Taco Bell, Tuscan Sun Coffee, Whataburger/24hr Travelodge Ford, U-Haul

68 Holzwarth Rd, Cypress Wood Dr, E Texaco/dsl Burger King, Pizza Hut/Taco Bell, Sonic, Starbucks, Wendy's Albertson's, AT&T, Gander Mtn, GNC, Tiremaxx, W Chevron/dsl Cheddar's, Denny's, Jack-in-the-Box, Lenny's Subs, Pizza Hut, Popeye's, Starbucks Motel 6, Spring Lodge Advance Parts, Best Buy, Chrysler/Dodge/Jeep, Firestone/auto, Ford, Home Depot, Lowe's Whse, Office Depot, PetCo, Target, Walgreens

66 FM 1960, to Addicks, E Chevron, RaceTrac, Shell Hick's Rest., Jack-in-the-Box, Sonic, Subway, TX Roadhouse Acura, AT&T, BMW, Chevrolet, Honda, Mercedes, Mistubishi, Petsmart, Radio Shack, Subaru, W Exxon, Shell/dsl/24hr, Texaco/dsl, Valero Cici's Pizza, Hooters, Jack-in-the-Box, James Coney Island, McDonald's, Outback Steaks, Panda Express, Red Lobster, Subway, Taco Bell, Taquiera Arendas Baymont Inn, Comfort Suites, Fairfield Inn, Hampton Inn, Studio 6 H, Audi, Infiniti, Jaguar/LandRover, Lexus, mall, NTB, U-Haul

64 Richey Rd, E Atchafalaya River Café Best Value Inn, Holiday Inn, Lexington Suites, Rmada CarMax, Discount Tire, Sam's Club/gas, W FLYING J/Denny's/dsl/scales/24hr Cracker Barrel, House of Creole, Jack-in-the-Box, Joe's Crabshack, Lupe Tortilla, Mamacita's Mexican, Michoacan Rest, SaltGrass Steaks, Tokyohana, Whataburger, Wings'n More, Zio's Italian Jones RV Ctr

63 Airtex Dr, E Texaco/Subway, Valero/Church's China Bear, Pappasito's Cantina ValuePlace Inn Acura, Cadillac, LoneStar RV Ctr, Nissan, W Cracker Barrel, Jack-in-the-Box, Whataburger Best Western, Guesthouse Suites

= gas = food = lodging = other = rest stop Copyright 2016 - The Next EXIT

TX

INTERSTATE 45 Cont'd

HOUSTON

Exit #	Services
62	Rankin Rd, Kuykendahl, E Best Classic Inn, Scottish Inn, W Chevron/McDonald's, RaceTrac, Shell Luby's, Shiply Donuts Palace Inn, Studio+, SunSuites Buick/GMC, Demontrono RV Ctr, Hummer, Hyundai, Kia, Lamborghini, Mercedes, Volvo, VW
61	Greens Rd, E Texaco Brown Sugar's BBQ, IHOP, Imperial Dragon, Luna's Knights Inn Dillard's, JC Penney, Macy's, mall, Sears/auto, W Burger King, Luby's, Subway Baymont Inn, Comfort Inn $General, Burlington Coat Factory, Kroger
60c	Beltway E
60	(b a from nb) TX 525, W Pappas Seafood U-Haul
59	FM 525, West Rd, E Shell/dsl A&W/LJ Silver, Burger King, China Border, Denny's, Domino's, Mambo Seafood, McDonald's, Michoacan Rest, Moon Palace Chinese, Pizza Hut, Taco Cabana CarQuest, Chrysler/Dodge/Jeep, Firestone, Honda, Office Depot, W Exxon, Shell Chili's, Jalisco's Mexican, Panda Express, Papa John's Pizza, Quizno's, Starbucks, Subway, Taco Bell, Taco Cabana, Wendy's, Whataburger, Wing Stop Best Value Inn, Best Western $Tree, AT&T, Best Buy, Discount Tire, Fry's Electronics, Home Depot, NTB, Office Depot, PepBoys, Radio Shack, Ross, Verizon, Walmart/24hr
57	(b a from nb) TX 249, Gulf Bank Rd, Tomball, E Chevron, Mobil/dsl, Texaco/Church's Wings'n More, W Shell Sonic, Tombico Seafood Greenchase Motel, La Quinta, Quality Inn CVS Drug, Family$, Giant$, Mas Club/dsl
56	Canino Rd, E Taj Inn Suites, W Shell, Texaco Capt D's, Denny's, Jack-in-the-Box, KFC, Luby's Best Value Inn, EconoLodge, Gulfwind Motel, Passport Inn Ford, Isuzu, USPO
55	(b a from nb) Little York Rd, Parker Rd, E Chevron, Texaco Burger King, China Panda, McDonald's, Whataburger Advance Parts, Family$, FoodTown, W Shell Popeye's Symphony Inn H, Family$, Walgreens
54	Tidwell Rd, E Exxon/dsl Aunt Bea's Rest, Burger King, Chacho's Mexican, China Border, Frenchys, Pancho's Mexican, Subway, Thomas BBQ, Wings'N More CVS Drug, Discount Tire, Radio Shack, transmissions, W Chevron McDonald's Guest Motel, Scottish Inn, Southwind Motel, Town Inn U-Haul
53	Airline Dr, E Citgo Popeye's Fiesta Foods/drug, W Citgo, Shell Little Mexico, Wendy's Luxury Inn, Palace Inn
52	(b a from nb) Crosstimbers Rd, E Baskin-Robbins, Burger King, Chick-fil-A, China Star, ChuckeCheese, Cici's, IHOP, Jack-in-the-Box, James Coney Island, KFC, Pappas BBQ, Pizza Hut, Pollo Rico, Sonic, Subway, Taco Bell $Tree, AT&T, CVS Drug, Discount Tire, Firestone, GNC, mall, Marshall's, Office Depot, Ross, Verizon, Walmart, W Chevron/dsl Whataburger/24hr Texan Inn
51	I-610
50	(b a from nb) Patton St, Calvacade St, Link Rd, E Citgo, Exxon, Loves/Wendy's/dsl/scales/24hr, Shell Best Value Inn, Luxury Inn, W Astro Inn NAPA
49b	N Main St, Houston Ave, E Citgo Casa Grande Mexican Best Value Inn, Luxury Inn, W Exxon/dsl Domino's, McDonald's, Subway, Whataburger/24hr Sleep Inn O'Reilly Parts
48b a	I-10, E to Beaumont, W to San Antonio
47d	Dallas St, Pierce St (from sb), E H
47c	McKinney St (from sb, exits left)
47b	Houston Ave, Memorial Dr, W Double Tree Hotel, downtow
47a	Allen Pkwy (exits left from sb)
46b a	US 59, N to Cleveland, S to Victoria, E Chevron, W Texaco McDonald's, Taco Bell BMW
45b a	South St, Scott St, Houston, E Shell/Blimpie, to TSU
44	Cullen Blvd, Houston, E to U of Houston, Valero/dsl
43b	Telephone Rd, Houston
43a	Tellepsen St, E Luby's, W U of Houston
41b	US 90A, Broad St, S Wayside Dr, E Phillips 66 Arranda's Mexican Houston Inn, Red Carpet Inn, W Chevron, Exxon, Mobil Jack-in-the-Box, McDonald's, Monterrey Mexican, Subway, Taquiera Mexican, Wings and More $Tree, K-Mart, Sellars Foods
41a	Woodridge Dr, E Shell Bonnie's Rest., China Star Denny's, James Coney Island, McDonald's, Pappa's Seafood House, Schlotsky's King$, W Citgo BoneBreak BBQ, IHOP, Pappas BBQ, Sonic, Subway, Wendy's, Whataburger Chevrolet/Buick, Dillard's, HEB Food/gas, Home Depot, Lowe's, mall, Marshall's, Office Depot, Old Navy, Radio Shack, Ross
40c	I-610 W
40b	I-610 E, to Pasadena
40a	Frontage Rd (from nb)
39	Park Place Blvd, Broadway Blvd, E Shell/dsl, W Shell Kelley's Rest., Papa John's, Red Panda, Subway Chevrolet/Dodge/Jeep, Family$, transmissions
38b	Howard Dr, Bellfort Dr (from sb), E Shell Jack-in-the-Box, Wendy's, W Citgo, Shell, Texaco Chilo's Seafood Camelot Inn, Moonlight Inn, Mustang Inn, Palace Inn PepBoys
38	TX 3, Monroe Rd, E Chevron/dsl, Shell/dsl, Valero DQ, Jack-in-the-Box, Ninfa, Starbucks, Wendy's Family$, Firestone, NTB, TX Campers, U-Haul, W Chevron/dsl, Texaco/dsl Manny's Seafood, Pappa's BBQ, Subway Holiday Inn Express, Sheraton Firestone, U-Haul
36	College Ave, Airport Blvd, E Valero Arranda's Bakery, Burger House, DQ, Jack-in-the-Box, Shipley Do-Nuts, Waffle House Knights Inn, W Shell/dsl, Valero/dsl Denny's, Paco Joe's, Taco Cabana Baymont Inn, Comfort Suites, Courtyard, Days Inn, Drury Inn, Hampton Inn, La Quinta, Marriott, Motel 6, SpringHill Suites, Super 8, Travel Inn Discount Tire
35	Edgebrook Dr, E Chevron, RaceWay Arranda's Mexican, Burger King, Chilo's Rest., Jack-in-the-Box, KFC, Popeye's, Subway, Taco Bell Airport Inn Family$, Fiesta Foods, Firestone, Office Depot, vet, W Mobil James Coney Island, Mambo Seafood, McDonald's, Pizza Hut, Whataburger Verizon
34	S Shaver Rd, E Conoco McDonald's Island Suites Ford, Kia, Nissan, Toyota/Scion, W MurphyUSA/dsl Arby's, China Star Buffet, Chopstix, KFC, Pancho's Mexican, Piccadilly's, Pizza Patron, Starbucks, Subway, Taco Bell, Wendy's AT$T, Discount Tire, Firestone, GNC, Honda, Macy's, Marshall's, PetsMart, Ross, Staples, Walmart/McDonald's
33	Fuqua St, E Chili's, Denny's, Fuddrucker's, Las Haciendas, Luby's, Olive Garden, Schlotzky's, TGIFriday's Studio 6, Sun Suites Hyundai, Lincoln, Volvo, W Bayou City Wings, Blackeyed Pea, Boudreaux's, Casa Ole, Cici's Pizza, Fox&Hound, Golden Corral, Gringo's Mexican, IHOP, Joe's Crabshack, Kimhai Asian, McDonald's, Murphy's Deli, Outback Steaks, Subway, Taco Cabana, TX Land&Cattle Steaks, Whataburger, Wings&More Buick/GMC, CarMax, Chevrolet,

HOUSTON

INTERSTATE 45 Cont'd

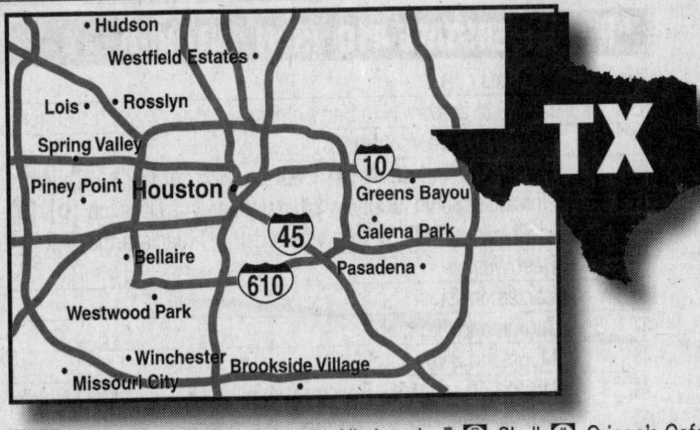

TX

33 Continued
Home Depot, JC Penney, mall, Old Navy, Radio Shack, Sam's Club/gas, Subaru

32 Sam Houston Tollway

31 FM 2553, Scarsdale Blvd, W [other] Chevrolet

30 FM 1959, Dixie Farm Rd, Ellington Field, E [gas] Shell/dsl [food] El Nopalito, Subway [lodging] Howard Johnson [other] [H], Chrysler/Dodge/Jeep, Fiat, Infiniti, W [gas] RaceWay, Shell/dsl [food] McDonald's, Popeye's [lodging] Palace Inn [other] Lonestar RV, VW

29 FM 2351, Clear Lake City Blvd, to Clear Lake RA, Friendswood, W [other] Hyundai

27 El Dorado Blvd, E [gas] Exxon, Shell [food] Taco Bell [other] Home Depot, W [food] Sonic, TX Roadhouse, Whataburger [other] Cadillac, Kohl's, Lexus, Radio Shack, Sam's Club/gas, Walmart/McDonald's

26 Bay Area Blvd, E [gas] Chevron [food] Chick-fil-A, Panera Bread, Peiwei, Potbelly's, Red Lobster, TGIFriday's, Zio's Kitchen [other] [H], Barnes&Noble, Best Buy, Lowe's, Michael's, Staples, to Houston Space Ctr, World Mkt, W [food] 5 Guys, Cafe Adobe, Chick-fil-A, ChuckeCheese, Denny's, McDonald's, Olive Garden, Panda Express [lodging] Holiday Inn Express [other] AT&T, Dillard's, JC Penney, Jo-Ann Fabrics, Macy's, mall, Marshall's, Office Depot, Old Navy, Sears/auto, Target, U of Houston, Verizon

25 FM 528, NASA Rd 1, E [gas] Chevron, Conoco [food] Big Ben Rest., Cheddar's, Chili's, Chuy's Mexican, Las Hacienda Mexican, Marble Slab, McAlister's Deli, Michiru Asian, Pappa's Seafood, Pappasito's Cantina, Rudy's BBQ/gas, Saltgrass Steaks, Steak'n Shake, Twin Peaks Rest., Vito's, Waffle House [lodging] Motel 6, Springhill Suites [other] [H], BigLots, Fry's Electronics, Hobby Lobby, Home Depot, Honda, Mazda, Volvo, W [food] Cici's Pizza, Floyd's Cajun, Han's BBQ, Hooters, Hot Wok Chinese, James Coney Island, Pappa's Cafe, Subway [other] Tuesday Morning

LEAGUE CITY

23 FM 518, League City, E [gas] RaceWay/dsl [food] Center Buffet, KFC, La Brisa, Subway, Sudie's Seafood [other] Just Brakes, Kroger, W [gas] Chevron/dsl, Valero [food] Cracker Barrel, McDonald's, Taco Bell, Waffle House, Wendy's [lodging] Super 8 [other] Discount Tire, Space Ctr RV Park, U-Haul

22 Calder Dr, Brittany Bay Blvd, E [food] Wings'n More [other] BMW/Mini, Mercedes, Nissan, Toyota/Scion, URGENT CARE, W [other] Acura, Holiday World RV Ctr

20 FM 646, Santa Fe, Bacliff, E [gas] MurphyUSA/dsl [food] 5 Guys, Chick-fil-A, Cici's Pizza, Denny's, Jack-in-the-Box, Logan's Roadhouse, Marble Slab, McDonald's, Panda Express, Schlotzky's, Spring Creek BBQ, Subway, Whataburger [lodging] Candlewood Suites, Hampton Inn [other] $Tree, Best Buy, Hobby Lobby, Home Depot, JC Penney, Lowe's, Michael's, NTB, PetsMart, Radio Shack, Ross, Staples, Target, TJ Maxx, Walmart/McDonald's, W [gas] Chevron/dsl [food] Badabing, Chili's, Chinese Rest., Subway, Taco Cabana [other] HEB Foods/gas, Kohl's, PetCo, Verizon

19 FM 517, Dickinson Rd, Hughes Rd, E [food] Jack-in-the-Box, Monterey Mexico, Shipley Do-Nuts [other] Buick/GMC, CVS Drug, Due's RV Ctr, Family$, Kia, W [gas] Conoco/dsl, Shell/dsl [food] Burger King, Dickenson's Seafood, KFC, McDonald's, Pizza Hut, Sonic, Subway, Taco Bell, Wendy's, Whataburger/24hr [lodging] Days Inn, Economy Inn [other] Chrysler/Dodge/Jeep, Curves, Ford, Kroger, Walgreens

17 Holland Rd, W [other] Tanger Outlets/Famous Brands, to Gulf Greyhound Park

16 FM 1764 E (from sb), Texas City, same as 15

15 FM 2004, FM 1764, Hitchcock, E [gas] Shell [food] Gringo's Cafe, Jack-in-the-Box, Olive Garden, Popeye's, Ryan's, Uncle Chan's [lodging] Best Western, Fairfield Inn, Hampton Inn, Holiday Inn Express, Value Place Inn [other] [H], Chevrolet/Toyota/RV Ctr, DeMontrond RV Ctr, Dillard's, JC Penney, Lowe's, Macy's, mall, Sam's Club/gas, Sears/auto, Toyota/Scion, W [gas] Gulf/Subway, MurphyUSA/dsl, Shell [food] IHOP, Little Caesars, Pizza Hut, Sonic, Waffle House, Wendy's, Whataburger, WingStop [other] AT&T, Gulf Greyhound Park, Radio Shack, Verizon, Walmart/McDonald's

13 Century Blvd, Delany Rd, W [food] Barcema's Mexican [lodging] Best Value Inn, Super 8 [other] Lazy Days RV Park, VF Factory Outlet/famous brands

12 FM 1765, La Marque, E [gas] Chevron/24hr [food] Domino's, Jack-in-the-Box, Kelley's Rest., Sonic, W [gas] Texaco [other] Little Thicket RV Park

11 Vauthier Rd

10 E [gas] Exxon, Valero [food] KFC, McDonald's, PitStop BBQ, Subway, W [gas] Shell/dsl [other] Hoover RV Ctr, Oasis RV Park

9 Frontage Rd (from sb, no return/turnaround)

8 Frontage Rd (from nb)

7c Frontage Rd

7b TX 146, TX 6 (exits left from nb), Texas City

7a TX 146, TX 3

6 Frontage Rd (from sb)

5 Frontage Rd

4 Frontage Rd, Village of Tiki Island, W [gas] Valero [other] public boat ramp, Welcome Ctr

4mm West Galveston Bay

1c TX 275, FM 188 (from nb), Port Ind Blvd, Teichman Rd, Port of Galveston, E [gas] Citgo, Exxon, Valero [lodging] Motel 6 [other] Buick/Chevrolet/GMC, Ford, Toyota/Scion

1b 71st St (from sb), E [gas] EZ Mart/gas, same as 1c

GALVESTON

1a TX 342, 61st St, to W Beach, E [food] WingStop [lodging] Candlewood Suites [other] BigLots, Home Depot, NTB, PetsMart, Target, **0-2 mi W** [gas] Chevron, Citgo, Exxon, RaceWay, Valero [food] Cici's Pizza, Happy Buddah, Healthy Chinese, Hibachi Grill, Jack-in-the-Box, KFC, Little Caesars, Mario's, McDonald's, Pizza Hut, Popeye's, Quiznos, Sonic, Starbucks, Subway, Taco Bell, Taco Cabana, Wafflehouse, Whataburger, Yamato Japanese [lodging] Best Western, Comfort Inn, Days Inn, Quality Inn, Springhill Suites, Super 8 [other] $Tree, AT&T, AutoZone, CVS Drug, Family$, Firestone, Kroger/dsl, KwikCar, Marshall's, Office Depot, O'Reilly Parts, Randall's Food/gas, Ross, Tuesday Morning, USPO, Verizon

I-45 begins/ends on TX 87 in Galveston.

INTERSTATE 410 (SAN ANTONIO)

SAN ANTONIO

Exit #	Services
53	I-35, S to Laredo, N to San Antonio
51	FM 2790, Somerset Rd
49	TX 16 S, spur 422, N Chevron, Texaco/dsl Church's, Domino's, Sonic, Subway, Whataburger Days Inn H, to Palo Alto Coll, S Valero/dsl Jack-in-the-Box Best Western
48	Zarzamora St
47	Turnaround (from eb)
46	Moursund Blvd
44	US 281 S, spur 536, Roosevelt Ave, N Shell/McDonald's/dsl, Valero/dsl, S Holiday Inn Express
43	Espada Rd (from eb)
42	spur 122, S Presa Rd, S Citgo/dsl, to San Antonio Missions Hist Park
41	I-37, US 281 N
39	spur 117, WW White Rd
37	Southcross Blvd, Sinclair Rd, Sulphur Sprs Rd, N Valero Capparelli's Pizza H
35	US 87, Rigsby Ave, E Exxon, Murphy USA/dsl, Valero/dsl A&W, BorderTown Mexican, Cici's Pizza, Denny's, Jack-in-the-Box, LJ Silver, McDonald's, Subway, Taco Bell $Tree, Radio Shack, Walmart/24hr, W Chevron Barnacle Bill's Seafood, Bill Miller BBQ, Domino's, El Tapito Mexican, Luby's, Sonic, Taco Cabana, Whataburger Days Inn $General, Aamco, Advance Parts, auto/dsl repair, O'Reilly Parts, U-Haul, vet, Walgreens
34	FM 1346, E Houston St, W Valero/dsl
33	I-10 E, US 90 E, to Houston, I-10 W, US 90 W, to San Antonio
32	Dietrich Rd (from sb), FM 78 (from nb), to Kirby
31b	Lp 13, WW White Rd
31a	FM 78, Kirby, Citgo, Valero/dsl Family$
30	Binz-Engleman, Space Center Dr (from nb)
I-410 and I-35 run together 7 mi. See I-35, exits 161 thru 165.	
27	I-35, N to Austin, S to San Antonio
26	Lp 368 S, Alamo Heights
25b	FM 2252, Perrin-Beitel Rd, N Chevron/dsl, Valero Carl's Jr, KFC/Taco Bell, Quizno's, Schlotsky's, Tastee-Freez/Wienerschnitzel, Wendy's Best Value Inn Brake Check, S Jim's Rest.
25a	Starcrest Dr, N Valero Jack-in-the-Box, Los Patios Mexican H, Toyota
24	Harry Wurzbach Hwy, N Taco Cabana, S Chevron BBQ Sta. VW
23	Nacogdoches Rd, N Shell Bill Miller BBQ, Church's, IHOP, Jack-in-the-Box, Luby's, Mamma's Cafe, Pizza Hut, Sonic, Wendy's Crowne Plaza, S Chevron
22	Broadway St, N Shell/dsl Chili's, Las Palapas, McDonald's Cambria Suites, Courtyard vet, S Citgo, Valero Chesters Hamburgers, Jim's Rest., Little Caesar's, Martha's Mexican, Quizno's, Taco Palenque, Whataburger Residence Inn, TownHouse Motel
21	US 281 S, Airport Rd, Jones Maltsberger Rd, N Applebee's, Bubba's Rest Best Western, Drury Suites, Hampton Inn, Holiday Inn, Holiday Inn Express, PearTree Inn, S Murphy USA/dsl Pappadeaux, Red Lobster, Texas Land&Cattle, Whataburger Best Western, Courtyard, Days Inn, Fairfield Inn, La Quinta, Renaissance Hotel, Staybridge Suites, TownePlace Suites Hyundai/Kia, Mitsubishi, Subaru, Target, TJ Maxx, Walmart/McDonald's/24hr
20	TX 537, N Valero Arby's, Chick-fil-A, Jack-in-the-Box, Jason's Deli, McDonald's, Subway, TGIFriday's DoubleTree Hotel, Hilton Barnes&Noble, Bealls, Best Buy, Brake Check Cavender's Boots, Chevrolet, Honda, Jo-Ann Fabrics, Lexus Lincoln, Marshall's, Mazda, Office Depot, PetCo, Ross, World Mkt, S Cheesecake Factory, El Pollo Loco, La Madeleine Luby's, Taco Cabana AT&T, CVS Drug, Dillard's, Dodge, JC Penney, Macy's, mall, Saks 5th, Sears/auto, Target, Verizon
19b	FM 1535, FM 2696, Military Hwy, N Guajillos Mexican Souper Salad, S Denny's, Jim's Rest.
19a	Honeysuckle Lane, Castle Hills
17b	(18 from wb), S Shell Bill Miller BBQ, Subway Firestone/auto, HEB Foods/gas
17	Vance Jackson Rd, N Valero/dsl Jack-in-the-Box McDonald's, Sonic, Taco Cabana, Whataburger Embassy Suites, Marriott Aamco, Discount Tire, S Citgo, Shell Church's, Subway U-Haul
16b a	I-10 E, US 87 S, to San Antonio, I-10 W, to El Paso, US 87 N
15	Lp 345, Fredericksburg Rd, E Citgo Church's, Dave&Buster's, Denny's, El Pollo Loco, Jack-in-the-Box, Jim's Rest., Luby's, McDonald's, Taco Cabana, Wendy's, Whataburger Best Value Inn, SpringHill Suites AT&T, Family$, Firestone/auto, Hobby Lobby, Jo-Ann Fabrics, SteinMart, Target, transmissions, W Chevron/dsl CVS Drug
14	(c b a from sb) Callaghan Rd, Babcock Ln, E Chevron/dsl, Valero Marie Callender's, Popeye's Comfort Inn, Hampton Inn, Travelodge Suites AT&T, GMC, Hyundai, W Shell, Valero Burger King, Chili's, ChopSticks Chinese, DingHow Chinese, Golden Corral, Henry's Tacos, IHOP, Jack-in-the-Box, Jim's Rest, Joe's Crabshack, Las Palapas Mexican, McDonald's, Quizno's, Red Lobster, Taco Cabana, Wendy's H, Cavander's Boots, Chevrolet, Home Depot, NTB, Petsmart, Sam's Club/gas, vet, Walmart/Subway/24hr
13	(b a from sb) TX 16 N, Bandera Rd, Evers Rd, Leon Valley, E Outback Steaks, Panda Express Audi, HEB Foods/dsl, Office Depot, Old Navy, Toyota, U-Haul, W Bill Miller BBQ, Henry's Tacos, Jim's Rest., Schlotzsky's, Sea Island Rest, Taco Cabana BigLots, Chevrolet
12	(from sb) W Fortune Cookie Chinese, Jason's Deli, Sea Island Shrimp House, Starbucks $Tree, AT&T, Barnes&Noble, Best Buy, Marshall's, Michael's, Ross
11	Ingram Rd, E Shell/dsl KFC/Taco Bell, Krystal, Panda Buffet, TX Roadhouse Comfort Suites, Courtyard, Days Inn, EconoLodge, Holiday Inn Express, Red Roof Inn, Residence Inn Aamco, BrakeCheck, Chrysler/Dodge/Jeep, Mazda, W Applebee's, Casa Real Mexican, Chick-fil-A, ChuckeCheese, Denny's, Fuddrucker's, Jack-in-the-Box, Whataburger Best Western Dillard's, Firestone/auto, JC Penney, Macy's, mall, Sears/auto
10	FM 3487, Culebra Rd, E Bill Miller BBQ, Denny's, J Anthony's Seafood, McDonald's, Wendy's La Quinta, Ramada Ltd Harley-Davidson, to St Mary's U, W Phillips 66 Ford, Mitsubishi
9	(b a from sb) TX 151, W Murphy USA/dsl Buffalo Wild Wings, Carino's Italian, Cheddar's, Chili's, Chipotle Mexican, Cracker Barrel, IHOP, McAlister's Deli, Panda Express, Starbucks, Taco Bueno, TGIFriday's Alamo City Hotel, Quality Inn, Sleep Inn Home Depot, Lowe's Whse, Office Depot, Petsmart, Ross, Target, to Sea World, Verizon, Walmart/24hr
7	(8 from sb) Marbach Dr, E Exxon Church's, IHOP PepBoys, W Chevron/dsl, Shell Acadiena Café, Asia Kitchen, Burger King, Coyote Canyon, Golden Wok, Jack-in-the-Box, Jim's Rest., KFC, LJ Silver, McDonald's, Mr Gatti's,

SAN ANTONIO

INTERSTATE 410 (SAN ANTONIO) Cont'd

7	Continued Pancho's Mexican, Peter Piper Pizza, Pizza Hut, Red Lobster, Sonic, Subway, Taco Bell, Taco Cabana, Whataburger/24hr Motel 6, Super 8 $General, $Tree, Advance Parts, Bealls, BigLots, BrakeCheck, Discount Tire, Firestone/auto, HEB Foods/gas
6	US 90, E Country Inn Motel, W Shell/dsl, Valero/dsl Andrea's Mexican Best Western Explore USA RV Ctr, to Lackland AFB
4	Valley Hi Dr, to Del Rio, San Antonio, E Valero Burger King, Church's, McDonald's, Pizza Hut, Sonic AutoZone, HEB Food/gas, Radio Shack, W Valero Jack-in-the-Box to Lackland AFB, Walgreens
3	(b a from sb) Ray Ellison Dr, Medina Base, E Chevron/dsl, W Valero/Subway/dsl
2	FM 2536, Old Pearsall Rd, E Shell/dsl, Valero/dsl Bill Miller BBQ, Church's, McDonald's, Mexico Taqueria, Sonic, Subway O'Reilly Parts
1	Frontage Rd, Scion/Toyota

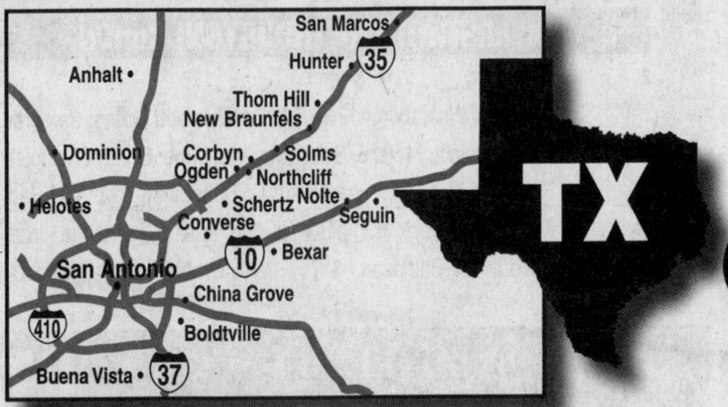

INTERSTATE 610 (HOUSTON)

HOUSTON

Exit #	Services
38c a	TX 288 N, access to zoo, downtown
37	Scott St, N Citgo, Valero
36	FM 865, Cullen Blvd, N Crystal Inn, S Chevron/McDonald's, Mobil, Shell, Valero Timmy Chan Crown Inn, Cullen Inn
35	Calais Rd, Crestmont St, MLK Blvd, N Exxon, Valero Burger King
34	S Wayside Dr, Long Dr, N Chevron, Phillips 66, Shell Church's, Wendy's, S Shell, Valero NAPA
33	Woodridge Dr, Telephone Rd, N Shell/dsl Chuck-eCheese, Cici's Pizza, IHOP, KFC/Taco Bell, McDonald's, Papa John's, Starbucks, Wendy's South Lp Inn Best Buy, Brake Check, HEB Foods, Lowe's, Marshall's, Old Navy, Ross, Staples, S Texaco/dsl Burger King, Gabby's BBQ, KFC, Piccadilly's Cafeteria, Spanky's Pizza, Whataburger Dodge, Ford, mall
32b a	I-45, S to Galveston, N to Houston, to airport
31	Broadway Blvd, S Texaco/dsl, Valero/dsl
30c b	TX 225, to Pasadena, San Jacinto Mon
29	Port of Houston Main Entrance
28	Clinton Dr, to Galina Park
27	Turning Basin Dr, industrial area
26b	Market St
26a	I-10 E, to Beaumont, I-10 W, to downtown
24	(b a from sb) US 90 E, Wallisville Rd, E Citgo/dsl, Loves/Arby's/dsl/scales/24hr, Pilot/McDonald's/dsl/scales, Texaco/dsl, Valero/Heart's Chicken/dsl/scales/24hr Luby's, Wendy's Blue Beacon, W Citgo/dsl
23b	N Wayside, N Valero
23a	Kirkpatrick Blvd
22	Homestead Rd, Kelley St, N Shell/dsl Whataburger Super 8, S Chevron/Subway/dsl/scales
21	Lockwood Dr, N Chevron/McDonald's, Shell Church's, Popeye's, Timmy Chan Chinese H, Family$, Fiesta Foods
20a b	US 59, to downtown
19b	Hardy Toll Rd
19a	Hardy St, Jensen Dr (from eb)
18	Irvington Blvd, Fulton St, N Chevron, S Shell/dsl
17b c	I-45, N to Dallas, S to Houston
17a	(eb only) Airline Dr, S Shell Jack-in-the-Box Western Inn
16	(b a from eb) Yale St, N Main St, Shamrock, N Exxon Harley-Davidson, S Texaco Burger King, Church's, KFC/Taco Bell, Starbucks
15	TX 261, N Shepherd Dr, N Sonic, Taco Cabana, S Chevron, Shell Wendy's, Whataburger Home Depot, PepBoys
14	Ella Blvd, N Exxon, Texaco A&W, KFC, McDonald's, Popeye's, Taco Bell, S Shell Thomas BBQ H, BrakeCheck, Lowe's Whse, Office Depot
13c	TC Jester Blvd, N Mobil, Shell Denny's, Juanita's Mexican, Po' Boys Sandwiches Courtyard, SpringHill Suites, S Phillips 66/dsl
13b a	US 290 (exits left from nb)
12	W 18th St, E Applebee's, Whataburger, W Shell Burger King Sheraton
11	I-10, W to San Antonio, E to downtown Houston
10	Woodway Dr, Memorial Dr, W Chevron/Pizza Inn/dsl, Shell/dsl Goodyear
9b	Post Oak Blvd, E Drury Inn, Hampton Inn, La Quinta, W Champp's Rest., McCormick&Schmick's Café
9a	San Felipe Rd, Westheimer Rd, FM 1093, E Mobil, Shell Omaha Steaks Courtyard, Extended Stay America, Hampton Inn, La Quinta CVS Drug, NTB, Target, W Shell Jamba Juice, Luke's Burgers Crowne Plaza Hotel, HomeStead Suites, Marriott, Sheraton Best Buy, Dillard's, Nieman-Marcus
8a	US 59, Richmond Ave, E Extended Stay America, Holiday Inn CVS Drug, W Shell Dillards
7	Bissonet St, West Park Dr, Fournace Place, E Beudreax's Kitchen Candlewood Suites Home Depot, W Shell/dsl/repair
6	Bellaire Blvd
5b	Evergreen St
5a	Beechnut St, E Chevron Boston Mkt, IHOP, Lowe's, McDonald's, Outback Steaks, W Citgo, Shell Escalante Mexican Grill, James Coney Island, Saltgrass Steaks, Smoothie King GNC, mall, Marshall's, Ross
4a	S Post Oak Rd, Brasswood, E Citgo Outback Steaks Days Inn, W Target, Walmart
3	Stella Link Rd, N Chevron Jack-in-the-Box Discount Tire, Food City, Radio Shack, S Exxon, Phillips 66/dsl, Shell, Valero Brake Check
2	US 90A, N Chevron, Conoco, Valero Arby's, Burger King, Church's, Denny's/24hr, KFC, McDonald's, Shoney's, Taco Bell, Wendy's Grand Plaza Hotel, Howard Johnson, Villa Motel CVS Drug, Discount Tire, Ford, Honda, Walgreen, S Chevron, Shell Golden Corral, Pizza Hut/

HOUSTON

TX
UT

INTERSTATE 610 (HOUSTON) Cont'd

2	Continued Taco Bell, Whataburger/24hr Candlewood Suites, CareFree Inn, La Quinta, Motel 6, Speedway Inn, Super 8 Chevrolet, Firestone, Mazda, Nissan, to Buffalo Speedway, Toyota, U-Haul
1c	Kirby Dr (from eb), N Burger King, Shell Crowne Plaza, Holiday Inn, Radisson, S Joe's Crabshack, Pappadeaux
1c	Continued Seafood, Pappasito's Cantina Cavender's Boots, Chevrolet, NTB, Toyota/Scion
1b a	FM 521, Almeda St, Fannin St, N Chevron, Shell Burger King Scottish Inn Astro Arena, S Shell McDonald's Aamco, Chrysler/Dodge/Jeep, Sam's Club, to Six Flags

UTAH

INTERSTATE 15

Exit #	Services
400.5mm	Utah/Idaho state line
398	Portage
392	UT 13 S, Plymouth, E United/A&W/dsl
385	UT 30 E, to Riverside, Fielding, **1 mi E** Sinclair/Riverside Grill/dsl
381	Tremonton, Garland, **2 mi E** (H), food, gas, lodging
379	I-84 W, to Boise
376	UT 13, to Tremonton, **2-3 mi E** Texaco/Arby's/dsl/scales/24hr Arctic Circle, JC'S Diner, Subway, Taco Time Marble Motel, **N** Sandman Motel (3mi)
372	UT 240, to UT 13, to rec area, Honeyville, **E** Crystal Hot Springs Camping
370mm	**sb, full facilities, litter barrels, info, petwalk RV dump, vending**
365	UT 13, Brigham City, **W** to Golden Spike NHS
363	Forest St, Brigham City, **W** Bear River Bird Refuge
362	US 91, to US 89, Brigham City, Logan, **E** Chevron/dsl, Exxon, Phillips 66/dsl, USA Arby's, Burger King, China Hua Guan, Domino's, Floriberto's Mexican, Hunan Chinese, J&D's Rest., KFC/Taco Bell, McDonald's, Old Grist Mill Bread, Pizza +, Pizza Hut, Sonic, Subway, Taco Time, Wendy's, Wingers Crystal Inn, Howard Johnson Express (H), Verizon, $General, $Tree, 7-11, AT&T, AutoZone, Buick/Cadillac/Chevrolet, Family$, Golden Spike RV Park, John Watson DC (5mi), KOA (4mi), O'Reilly Parts, Schwab Tires, ShopKO, to Yellowstone NP via US 89, Walmart/Subway, **W** Pilot/DQ/dsl/scales/24hr Days Inn
361mm	**nb, full facilities, litter barrels, petwalk RV dump, vending**
359	**Port of Entry both lanes**
357	UT 315, to Willard, Perry, **E** FLYING J/Subway/dsl/LP/scales/24hr KOA (2mi), Willard Peak Camping
351	UT 126, to US 89, to Utah's Fruit Way, Willard Bay, **W** Smith & Edwards Hardware
349	UT 134, N Ogden, Farr West, **E** 7-11, Exxon/Wendy's/dsl, Maverik/dsl Arby's, Bella's Mexican, Del Taco, Domino's, Jumbo Burger, McDonald's, Subway Comfort Inn Jiffylube, **W** Chevron/dsl Wasatch View RV park
346	to Harrisville, **W** Chevron/Subway/dsl, dsl repair, Maverik/dsl GriDeli's, Taco Time, Zhang's Chinese Cal Store
344	UT 39, 12th St, Ogden, **E** 7-11/dsl, Chevron/dsl, Old Frontier Best Western/rest. to Ogden Canyon RA, **W** Pilot/Subway/Taco Bell/dsl/24hr Uncle Lee's Cafe Sleep Inn Sierra RV Ctr
343	UT 104, 21st St, Ogden, **E** FLYING J/Denny's/dsl/LP/24hr, Phillips 66/dsl Big Z Rest, Cactus Red's SW Grill,
343	Continued McDonalds Comfort Suites, Holiday Inn Express, Motel 6, ValuePlace Inn RV Repair, **W** Texaco/Blimpie/dsl Super 8 Bideaux RV Ctr, Century RV Park
342	(from nb, no return) UT 53, 24th St, Ogden
341b a	UT 79 W, 31st St, Ogden, **E** Longhorn Steaks Ford, **1-2 mi E on Wall St** (H), Big O Tires, Chevrolet, Costco/gas, Dillard's, Firestone/auto, Hyundai, mall, to Weber St U **W**
340	I-84 E (from sb), to Cheyenne, Wyo
339	UT 26 (from nb), to I-84 E, Riverdale Rd, **E** Exxon/dsl, Sinclair/dsl Applebee's, Arby's, Bajio Grill, Buffalo Wild Wings, Carl's Jr, Chili's, Honeybaked Ham, IHOP, Jamba Juice, Lucky Buffet, McDonald's, Starbucks, Subway, Wendy's Motel 6 $Tree, Best Buy, Buick/GMC, Cadillac, Chrysler/Dodge/Jeep, Good Earth Natural Foods, Gordman's, Harley-Davidson, Home Depot, Honda, Jo-Ann Fabrics, Kia, Mazda, Nissan, Petsmart, Sam's Club/gas, Schwab Tire, Target, Toyota/Scion, Verizon, Walmart
338	UT 97, Roy, Sunset, **E** Air Force Museum, **W** 7-11, Exxon/dsl, Maverik/dsl, Sinclair/dsl A&W/KFC, Arby's, Beez Cafe, Blimpie, Chinese Gourmet, Five Star Chinese, Greek Island Broiler, Japanese Wasabi, La Frontera Mexican, McDonald's, Panda Express, Papa Murphy's, Rancherito's Mexican, Subway, Taco Bell, Village Inn Rest., Warren's Drive-In, Wendy's AutoZone, Citte RV Ctr, CVS Drug, Discount Tire, Family$, Firestone/auto, Harmon's Mkt, Midas, O'Reilly Parts, RiteAid, Sacco's Fresh Mkt, Schwab Tires, Smith's/dsl, transmissions, vet, vet, Walgeens
335	UT 103, Clearfield, **E** Starbucks Hill AFB, **W** Conoco, Phillips 66/dsl, Tesoro/dsl, Texaco/dsl Carl's Jr, KFC, McDonald's, Subway, Taco Bell, Winger's Days Inn, EconoLodge C&M Tires
334	UT 193, Clearfield, **E** Chevron/dsl, Maverik to Hill AFB, **W** 7-11, Maverik/dsl Domino's AutoZone
332	UT 108, Syracuse, **E** Applebee's, Bandidos Border Grill, Boston's Rest., Brick Oven, Cafe Rio, Carl's Jr., Chick-fil-A, Chili's, Cracker Barrel, Famous Dave's, Five Guys, Golden Corral, Jimmy John's, Koi Asian, MacCool's Grill, Marie Callender's, Mimi's Cafe, Noodles&Co, Outback Steaks, Panda Express, Papa Murphy's, Red Robin, Rumbi Island Grill, Sonic, Tepanyaki, Zupas Cafe Courtyard, Fairfield Inn, Hampton Inn, Hilton Garden, Holiday Inn Express, Home2Home, La Quinta, TownePlace Suites Barnes&Noble, Big O Tires, Lowe's Whse, Michaels, Office Depot, Petco, Ross, Target, URGENT CARE, Walgreens, **W** Conoco/dsl Arby's, Burger King, Crown Burger, McDonald's (H), 7-11, Ford, Kmart, to Antelope Island

BRIGHAM CITY
OGDEN
ROY

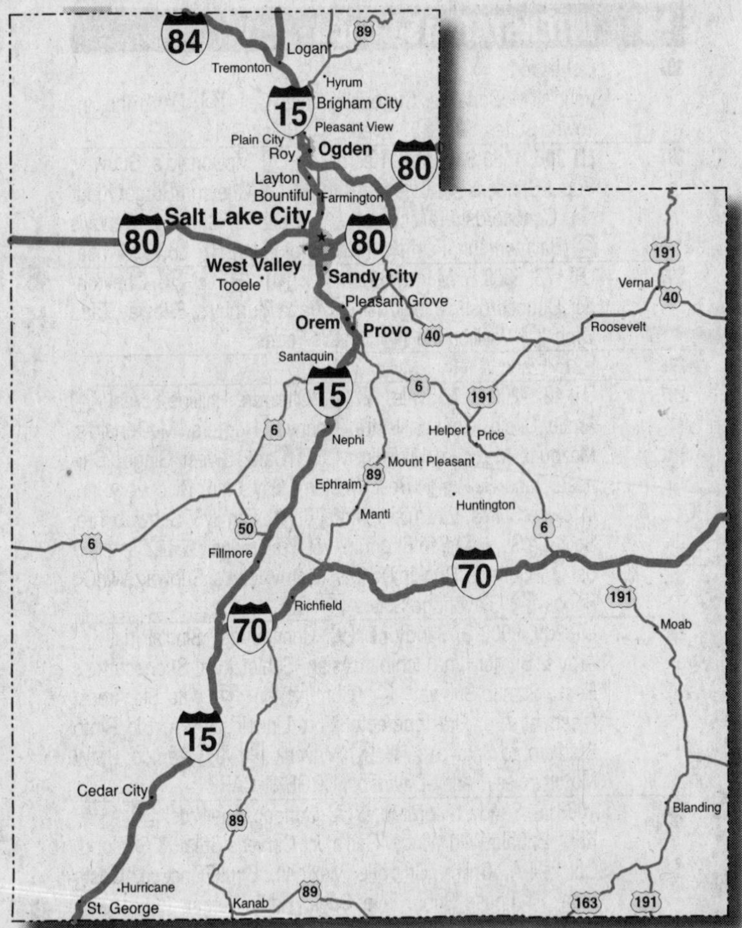

UT

INTERSTATE 15 Cont'd

LAYTON

KAYSVILLE

N SALT LAKE

SALT LAKE

Exit #	Services
331	UT 232, UT 126, Layton, E [food] Buffalo Wild Wings, Costa Vida, Denny's, Garcia's, McDonald's, Olive Garden, Red Lobster, Sizzler, Training Table Rest., TX Roadhouse, Wendy's [lodging] Best Western, Comfort Inn [other] $Tree, Dick's, JC Penney, Macy's, mall, to Hill AFB S Gate, Tuesday Morning, W [gas] Exxon/dsl [food] Asian Buffet, Bajio Mexican, Burger King, Cantina SW Grill, ChuckeCheese, Coldstone, Del Taco, IHOP, KFC, Krispy Kreme, La Puente Mexican, Maid Rite Diner, Moon Dog Cafe, Pace's Rest., Rancheritos Mexican, Starbucks, Taco Bell, Taco Time [other] AT&T, Batteries+Bulbs, Big Lots, Buick/GMC, Chevrolet, Chrysler/Dodge/Jeep, Discount Tire, Hancock Fabrics, Hobby Lobby, Home Depot, Petsmart, Sam's Club/gas, ShopKO, Staples, Verizon, Walmart/McDonald's, [food] Iggy's Grill
330	Layton Pkwy, to UT 126, Layton, E [food] Little Orient Chinese [other] Tire Pros, W [other] Camping World RV Ctr
328	UT 273, Kaysville, E [gas] 7-11/dsl, Chevron/McDonald's [food] Arby's, Big Daddy's Pizza, Domino's, Dylan's Drive-In, Granny Annie's Rest., Pizza Hut, Subway, Taco Time, Wendy's, Winger's [other] AutoZone, Big O Tire, Fresh Mkt Foods, O'Reilly Parts, Schwab Tire, USPO, Walgreens, W [other] Camping World, Kia
325mm	**parking area both lanes**
325	UT 225, Lagoon Dr, Farmington, E [food] Subway [other] camping, funpark, W [food] Costa Vida, Dickey's BBQ, Habit Burger, Panda Express, Starbucks, Subway, Zupas [other] Cabela's, Gordmans, Harmon's Mkt, Marshalls, Old Navy, Petco, Ross
324	US 89 N, UT 225, Legacy Pkwy (from sb), **1 mi** E [gas] Maverik/dsl, Smith's Foods/dsl [food] Burger King, Chevron/dsl, Chopstix Chinese, Javier's Mexican, Papa John's, Subway [lodging] Hampton Inn [other] Aunt Pam's, Burt Bros/Goodyear/auto, RV Park, to I-84
322	UT 227 (from nb), Lagoon Dr, to Farmington, E [food] Subway [other] Lagoon Funpark/RV Park
319	UT 105, Parrish Lane, Centerville, E [gas] 7-11/dsl, Chevron/dsl, Phillips 66/dsl [food] Arby's, Carl's Jr, Chick-fil-A, Chili's, Costa Vida, DQ, Iggy's Grill, IHOP, In-N-Out, La Puente Mexican, Little Caesar's, McDonald's, Papa Murphy's, Ruby River Steaks, Starbucks, Subway, Taco Bell, TacoMaker, Wendy's [other] $Tree, Ace Hardware, Big O Tire, Dave's Auto Repair, Dick's Mkt, GNC, Home Depot, Jo-Ann, Kohl's, Land Rover, O'Reilly Parts, Petsmart, Schwab Tire, Target, Walmart
317	US 89 S (exits left from sb), UT 131, 500W, S Bountiful, E [gas] Chevron/dsl, Exxon/dsl, Sinclair/7-11/dsl [food] Starbucks [lodging] Country Inn Suites [other] Chrysler/Dodge/Jeep, Costco/gas, Office Depot, Parts+, PetCo
316	UT 68, 500 S, W Bountiful, Woods Cross, E [gas] Texaco [food] Applebee's, Barbacoa Mexican, Cafe Rio, Carl's Jr, Chipotle, ChuckaRama, Coldstone, Del Taco, Five Guys, Jimmy John's, KFC, McDonald's, Mikado Japanese, Panda Express, Pei Wei, Pizza Factory, Pizza Hut, Sizzler, Starbucks, Subway, Taco Bell, TX Roadhouse, Wendy's [other] [H], $Tree, AT&T, AutoZone, Barnes&Noble, Costco/gas, Firestone/auto, GNC, Lowe's, Michael's, Midas, Office Depot, O'Reilly Parts, Petco, Radio Shack, Ross, ShopKO, Tire Pros, TJ Maxx, Walgreens, W [gas] Phillips 66/A&W/dsl [lodging] InTown Suites [other] vet
315	26th S, N Salt Lake, E [gas] Chevron/dsl, Tesoro, Texaco [food] Arby's, Best Burger, Empire Chinese, Kneaders Bakery Cafe,
315	Continued Mc Donald's, Nielsen's Frozen Custard, Pappa's Steaks, Subway, Taco Time, Village Inn, Wendy's [lodging] Best Western, Comfort Inn [other] Buick/GMC, Burt Bros Tires, Chevrolet, Discount Tire, Ford/Lincoln, Honda, Mazda, Nissan, Schwab Tire, Smith's Foods, Southfork Hardware, Toyota/Scion, Tunex, U-Haul, Walgreens, W [food] Lorena's Mexican [lodging] Hampton Inn, Motel 6
314	Center St, Cudahy Lane (from sb), N Salt Lake, E [gas] gas
313	I-215 W (from sb), [other] to [airport]
312	US 89 S, to Beck St, N Salt Lake
311	2300 N
310	900 W (from sb), W [lodging] Salt City Motel
309	600 N, E [other] [H], downtown, LDS Temple, to UT State FairPark
308	I-80 W, to Reno, [other] [airport]
307	400 S, downtown
306	600 S, SLC City Ctr, **1 mi** E [gas] Chevron, Phillips 66/dsl, Sinclair [food] Alberto's Mexican, Denny's, McDonald's, Starbucks, Subway, Wendy's [lodging] Chrystal Inn, Comfort Inn, DoubleTree, Grand America, Hampton Inn, Hilton Garden, Little America, Motel 6, Red Lion Inn, Rodeway Inn, Sheraton, SpringHill Suites [other] Hyundai, LDS Church Offices, to Temple Square, Toyota
305c-a	1300 S, 2100 S UT 201 W, SLC, downtown, E [gas] Chevron/Subway/dsl, Shell [food] Carl's Jr, ChuckECheese, Dickey's BBQ, IHOP, Jimmy John's, McDonald's, Starbucks, Tepanyaki Japanese [other] $Tree, Best Buy, Costco/gas, Home Depot, Office Depot, PetsMart, Sams Club/dsl, U-Haul, Walmart, W [gas] FLYING J/Denny's/dsl/LP/24hr [food] El Pasa Mexican [other] Blue Beacon, Kia
304	I-80 E, to Denver, Cheyenne
303	UT 171, 3300 S, S Salt Lake, E [gas] 7-11, Maverik/dsl, Sinclair/dsl [food] Apollo Burgers, Burger King, Crown Burger, Jimmy

= gas = food = lodging = other = rest stop

UT

INTERSTATE 15 Cont'd

303 Continued
John's, McDonald's, Starbucks, Taco Bell Day's Inn, InTowne Suites, **W** Maverik Buick/GMC

301 UT 266, 4500 S, Murray, Kearns, **E** McDonald's, Subway, Super Grinders Discount Tire, **W** Chevron/Burger King/dsl, Conoco/dsl, Texaco/dsl Denny's, Subway, Wendy's Baymont Inn, Fairfield Inn, Hampton Inn Lowe's Whse

300 UT 173, 5300 S, Murray, Kearns, **E** (H), **W** Chevron/dsl, Conoco/dsl, Sinclair/dsl Papa Murphy's, Subway, Taco Time Pavilion Inn Smith's Foods

298 I-215 E and W

297 UT 48, 7200 S, Midvale, **E** Chevron, Phillips 66/dsl Arctic Circle, Cafe Silvestre, Denny's, Hooters, McDonald's, Mezquite Mexican, Midvale Mining Cafe, Sweet Ginger Chinese, Taco Bell Best Western, Day's Inn, Discovery Inn, InTowne Suites, La Quinta, Motel 6 Family$, Schwab Tire, Solitude Ski Areas, to Brighton, vet, Walgreens, **W** Sinclair/dsl Culver's, Dunkin Donuts, Jimmy John's, Subway, WinCo Foods Staybridge Suites GNC

295 UT 209, 9000 S, Sandy, **E** Chevron/dsl, Sinclair/dsl Arby's, Burger King, Ichiban Asian, Schlotzky's, Sconecutter's Rest., Sizzler, Subway Comfort Inn Alta Ski Areas, Discount Tire, Firestone/auto, Ford/Lincoln, NAPA, Rio Rinto Stadium, to Snowbird, **W** Maverik (H), Aamco, BMW Motorcycles, Harley-Davidson, URGENT CARE

SANDY

293 106th S, Sandy, S Jordan, **E** Conoco, Shell//dsl A&W/KFC, Buffalo Wild Wings, Carl's Jr., Carver's Steak & Seafood, Chick-fil-A, Chili's, Chipotle Mexican, ChukECheese, Costa Vida, Firehouse Subs, Five Guys, Habit Burger, Iggy's Grill, IHOP, Jim's Rest., La Frontera, Los Cucos Mexican, McDonald's, McGrath's Fishhouse, Mimi's Cafe, Olive Garden, Pei Wei, Rumbi Island Grill, Sampan Chinese, Starbucks, Subway, Sweet Tomatoes, Taco Bell, TGIFriday, Training Table, TX Roadhouse, Village Inn, Wendy's Best Western, Courtyard, Extended Stay America, Hampton Inn, Hilton Garden, Holiday Inn Express, Hyatt Summerfield, Marriott, Residence Inn, TownePlace Suites Best Buy, Chevrolet, Chrysler/Dodge/Jeep, Costco/gas, Dillard's, Goodyear/auto, Home Depot, Honda, Hyundai, JC Penney, Macy's, mall, Petsmart, Scheels Sports, Staples, Subaru, Target, USPO, **W** Denny's Country Inn Suites, Sleep Inn, Super 8 Buick/GMC/Kia, CarMax, Nissan, Sam's Club/dsl, VW, Walmart

DRAPER

291 UT 71, 12300 S, Draper, Riverton, **E** Chevron, Common Cents/dsl Arby's, Arctic Circle, Café Rio Mexican, Carl's Jr, Del Taco, Fazoli's, Guadalahonky's Mexican, In-N-Out, Jamba Juice, KFC, McDonald's, Panda Express, Pizza Hut, Quizno's, Ruby Tuesday, Sonic, Teriyaki Express, Wendy's, Wienerschnitzel, Wingers Diner Comfort Inn, Fairfield Inn, Ramada Ltd Brown RV, Camping World RV Supplies (1mi), Discount Tire, FSA Outlets/famous brands, Goodyear/auto, Greenbax, Kohl's, Mountain Shadows Camping, Smith's Foods, **W** Phillips 66 Sam's Club/gas, Walmart

289 Bangerter Hwy, **W** Exxon/Quiznos/dsl McDonald's 7-11, IKEA

288 UT 140, Bluffdale, **E** Chevron/dsl Camping World RV Supplies (2mi), Kohl's, Quality RV Ctr, **W** 7-11, Common Sense/gas st prison

284 UT 92, Timpanogas Hwy, to Alpine, Highland, **E** McDonald's Hyatt Place Cabela's, to Timpanogas Cave, Traverse Mtn Outlets/famous brands, **W** 7-11/Subway/dsl, Maverik/dsl Arby's, Carl's Jr, Costa Vida, Cubby's Cafe, Del Taco, Dickey's BBQ, Firehouse Subs, JCW Burgers, Popeye's,

284 Continued
Smashburger, Starbucks, Zaxby's, Zupas Kitcken Courtyard, Hampton Inn, Home 2 Suites, SpringHill Suites Lon Peak RV Ctr, Thanksgiving Point/café

LEHI

282 US 89 S, 12th W, to UT 73, Lehi, **W** Tesoro/dsl

279 UT 73, to Lehi, **E** Texaco/dsl Buffalo Wild Wings, Caf Rio, Chili's, ChuckARama, Culver's, Del Taco, Denny's, El Poll Loco, Hibachi House, Jimmy John's, One Man Band Dine Panda Express, TX Roadhouse, Which Wich?, Wienerschnitze Motel 6 Costco/gas, Home Depot, Lowe's Whse Petsmart, Schwab Tire, Verizon, Walgreens, Walmart/Burge King, **W** Chevron/dsl, CNG, Phillips 66/Wendy's Arcti Circle, KFC/Pizza Hut, McDonald's, Moochie's, Papa Murphy's Subway, Tepanyki Japanese Best Western, Day's Inn, Super 8 7-11, Big O Tire, Dave's Chiropractic, GNC, Macey's O'Reilly Parts, USPO, vet

278 Main St, American Fork, **E** Phillips 66/dsl, Texaco Chili's, Cobblestone Pizza, Del Taco, In-N-Out, Ottavio's Italian Pier 49, Sonic, Wendy's (H), $Tree, Chevrolet, Chrysler Dodge/Jeep, Home Depot, K-Mart, Kohl's, Office Depot, Old Navy, Smith's Foods, Subaru/Suzuki, Target, Walmart, **W** Value Place

276 5th E, Pleasant Grove, **1-2 mi E** Circle K, Conoco/Blimpie Phillips 66, Texaco Arby's, Carl's Jr, Del Taco, Denny's, Golden Corral, Hardee's, KFC, McDonald's, Subway, Taco Bell Wendy's Quality Inn (H), American Camping, Chevrolet, Stewart's RV Ctr, **W** Buick/GMC, Ford, Land Rover

275 Pleasant Grove, **E** Bajio Grill, Panda Express, Sonic, Wienerschnitzel BMW, Macey's Foods

OREM

273 Orem, Lindon, **E** Exxon/dsl, Holiday Costa Vida Mexican, Del Taco Discount Tire, Home Depot, Lexus, Mercedes, Schwab Tire, **W** Harley-Davidson

272 UT 52, to US 189, 8th N, Orem, **1 mi E** Maverik, Phillips 66 Arby's, Cafe Rio, Denny's, DQ, Sonic La Quinta to Sundance RA

271 Center St, Orem, **E** 7-11, Conoco Burger King, Cafe Rio, KFC, Panda Express, Taco Bell, Wendy's (H), funpark, **W** Tesoro La Casita Blanca Mexican Econolodge LP

269 UT 265, 12th St S, University Pkwy, **1-3 mi E** Chevron, Sinclair, Texaco/Wendy's/dsl Applebee's, Arby's, Carrabba's, Chili's, Fuddrucker's, Golden Corral, HoneyBaked Ham, IHOP, Krispy Kreme, McDonald's, Noodles & Co., Outback Steaks, Pizza Hut, Sakura Japanese, Sizzler, Starbucks, Subway, Thai Evergreen, Village Inn Best Western, Comfort Inn, Courtyard, Hampton Inn, La Quinta Barnes&Noble, Best Buy, Ford, Honda, JC Penney, JiffyLube, Jo-Ann Fabrics, Lowe's Whse, mall, many services on US 89, Mazda, Mazda, Michael's, Nissan, Office Depot, Old Navy, Petsmart, Ross, Subaru, TJ Maxx, to BYU, Toyota/Scion, VW, Walmart, **W** Chevron

PROVO

265b a UT 114, Center St, Provo, **E** 7-11, Conoco, Phillips 66/Wendy's, Shell, Sinclair/dsl Marriott, Travelers Inn, Travelodge (H), Albertson's, auto repair, Checker Parts, Firestone/auto, **W** Chevron, Shell/dsl Great Steak Rest., Subway Econolodge KOA, Lakeside RV, to Utah Lake SP

263 US 189 N, University Ave, Provo, **E** Chevron, Conoco/dsl, Maverik, Sinclair A&W/KFC, Arby's, Burger King, ChuckaRama, Fazoli's, Hogi Yogi, Los Three Amigos Mexican, McDonald's, Papa Murphy's, Ruby River Steaks, Sizzler, Taco Bell, Taco Time, Village Inn Rest., Wendy's Best Western, Colony Inn, Fairfield Inn, Hampton Inn, La Quinta, Motel 6, National 9 Inn, Safari Motel, Sleep Inn, Super 8, Western Inn auto repair, CarQuest, Curves, Dillard's, GoodEarth Foods, Home De

INTERSTATE 15 Cont'd

SPRINGVILLE

Exit	Services
263	Continued pot, JC Penney, K-Mart, Les Schwab, mall, NAPA, Sam's Club/gas, Sears/auto, Silver Fox RV Camping, Staples, to BYU, VW/Audi
261	UT 75, Springville, E FLYING J/Denny's/dsl/scales/24hr, Maverik McDonald's (1mi) Best Western, Holiday Inn Express KOA, RS
260	UT 77, Springville, Mapleton, E Phillips 66/7-11/dsl Del Taco, IHOP, Mongolian Grill, Papa John's, Pizza Hut, Wendy's Big O Tire, JiffyLube, Walmart/Subway, W Chevron/Subway/dsl, Loves/Chester's/McDonald's/dsl/scales/24hr Cracker Barrel Days Inn Quality RV Ctr
257b a	US 6 E, UT 156, Spanish Fork, E Chevron/dsl, Sinclair, Tesoro/dsl, Texaco/dsl/LP Amber Rest., Arby's, Burger King, Cafe Rio, Carl's Jr, China Wok, Costa Vida, Cubby's Cafe, Culver's, Five Guys, Italian Place, Jimmy John's, KFC, Kneaders, Little Caesar's, McDonald's, One Man Band Diner, Papa Murphy's, Pizza Factory, Rita's, Sonic, Starbucks, Subway, Taco Bell, Taco Time, Wendy's, Zupas Kitchen $Tree, AT&T, AutoZone, Big O Tire, Cal Store, Costco/gas, Fresh Mkt/gas, GNC, Good Earth Mkt, Jo-Ann Fabrics, K-Mart, Macey's Foods, O'Reilly Parts, ShopKO, Verizon, Walmart/Subway, W Chevrolet
253	UT 164, to Spanish Fork

NEPHI

Exit	Services
250	UT 115, Payson, E Chevron/dsl McDonald's, Subway Comfort Inn H, Checker Parts, dsl repair, Mt Nebo Loop, Payson Foods, RiteAid
248	Payson, Salem, E Chevron, Texaco/Arby's/dsl Hunan City, Papa John's, Pizza Hut, Subway, Taco Bell, Tsing Tao Asian $Tree, AutoZone, Walmart, W Phillips 66/Wendy's/dsl
244	US 6 W, Santaquin, E Maverik/dsl DQ Tire Factory, TrueValue, W Conoco/dsl, Sinclair Family Tree Rest., One Man Band Diner, Santa Queen Burgers, Subway, Taco Time auto/tire care, Family$, Ford, Main St Mkt, Nat Hist Area, USPO
242	to S Santaquin, W Chevron/dsl
233	UT 54, Mona
228	UT 28, to Nephi, **2-4 mi** W services
225	UT 132, Nephi, E Tesoro/dsl/LP Main St Pizza, One Man Band Diner, Taco Time, W Chevron/Arby's/dsl, Phillips 66/7-11/Wendy's/dsl Economy Inn H, Big O Tire
222	UT 28, to I-70, Nephi, E Chevron/dsl, Sinclair/Hogi Yogi/scales/dsl/24hr, Texaco/dsl Burger King, Mickelson's Rest., Subway Motel 6, National 9 Inn, Super 8 dsl repair, W FLYING J/Denny's/dsl/LP/scales/24hr Lisa's Country Kitchen Best Western, Safari Motel H, dsl repair, High Country RV Park
207	to US 89, Mills
202	Yuba Lake, access to boating, camping, phone, rec services

FILLMORE

Exit	Services
188	US 50 E, to I-70, Scipio, E Chevron/Subway/dsl, Texaco/dsl Scipio Hotel, W FLYING J/DQ/dsl/rest stop/24hr
184	ranch exit
178	US 50, to Delta, W gas phone, to Great Basin NP
174	to US 50, Holden, to great Basin NP
167	Lp 15, Fillmore, E Chevron/dsl, Sinclair/dsl 5 Buck Pizza Best Western/rest. H, CarQuest, city park, golf, Goodyear, KOA (3mi), WagonsWest RV Park, W Chevron/Subway/rest stop/dsl, Texaco/dsl Carl's Jr tires/repair
163	Lp 15, to UT 100, Fillmore, E Conoco/Burger King/Costa Vida/dsl, Maverik/dsl Hong Kong Chinese, Larry's Drive-In Comfort Inn H, KOA, W Texaco/dsl Travel & Rest Inn

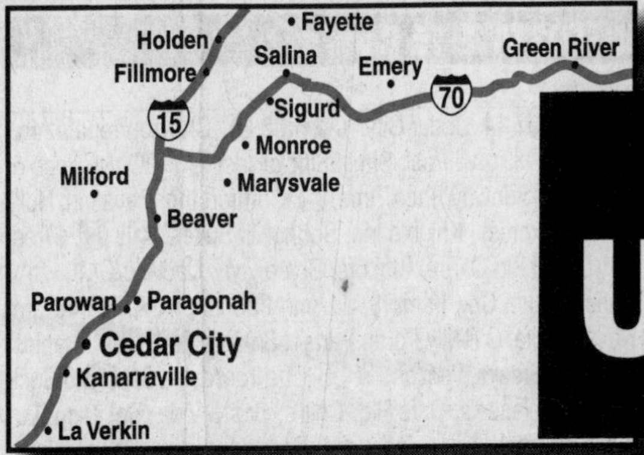

UT

BEAVER

Exit	Services
158	UT 133, Meadow, E Conoco/dsl, Shell/dsl
153mm	view area sb
151mm	view area nb
146	Kanosh, **2 mi** E gas chainup area
138	ranch exit
135	Cove Fort Hist Site, E Chevron/Subway/rest stop/dsl repair/tires
132	I-70 E, to Denver, Capitol Reef NP, Fremont Indian SP
129	Sulphurdale, **chainup area**
125	ranch exit
120	Manderfield, **chainup area nb**
112	to UT 21, Beaver, Manderfield, E Chevron/dsl, Conoco/dsl, Sinclair/dsl Arshel's Café, Crazy Cow Cafe, Hunan Chinese, McDonald's, Subway Beaver Lodge, Best Western, Country Inn, De Lano Motel/RV Park, Motel 6 H, Alco, auto/RV/dsl repair, Family$, KOA (1mi), W FLYING J/cafe/dsl/scales/24hr Wendy's Days Inn, Super 8 to Great Basin NP
109	to UT 21, Beaver, E Phillips 66/dsl, Shell/Burger King/dsl/RV dump, Spirit/dsl Best Western, Comfort Inn H, auto repair, Cache Valley Cheese, Mike's Foodtown, NAPA, United Camping, W Blu LNG, Chevron/DQ/dsl KanKun Mexican, Timberline Rest. Quality Inn to Great Basin NP, truck wash
100	ranch exit
95	UT 20, to US 89, to Panguitch, Bryce Canyon NP
88mm	**RS both lanes, full facilities, hist site, litter barrels, petwalk**
82	UT 271, Paragonah
78	UT 141, **1 mi** E Chevron/dsl, Maverik Days Inn NAPA, ski areas, W TA/Subway/Taco Bell/LP/dsl/scales/24hr/ @
75	UT 143, **2 mi** E Chevron, Maverik Days Inn Parowan Mkt, to Brian Head/Cedar Breaks Ski Resorts
71	Summit
62	UT 130, Cedar City, E Loves/Carl's Jr/Subway/dsl/scales/24hr, Phillips 66/dsl Allberto's Mexican H, Country Aire RV Park, KOA (2mi), st patrol, W Maverik/dsl, Shell/dsl/24hr/dsl repair @ Travelodge
59	UT 56, Cedar City, **0-2 mi** E Chevron/dsl, Maverik, Phillips 66/dsl/LP, Texaco A&W/KFC, Arby's, Burger King, China Kitchen, Denny's, Great Harvest Bread Co., Hermie's Drive-In, Hong Kong Buffet, IHOP, Jimmy John's, Little Caesars, McDonald's/playplace, Papa Murphy's, Pizza Factory, Roberto's Tacos, Sizzler, Sonny Boy's BBQ, Subway, Taco Bell, Wendy's Abbey Inn, Best Value Inn, Best Western, Quality Inn, Stratford Hotel $Tree, Buick/Chevrolet, Goodyear/auto, Lin's Mkt, NAPA, Tire Co., USPO, Verizon, W Maverik/dsl, Sinclair/dsl Bard's Cafe, Subway Crystal Inn, Motel 6, Super 8

UT

INTERSTATE 15 Cont'd

CEDAR CITY

Exit #	Services
57	Lp 15, to UT 14, Cedar City, **0-2 mi** E gas Chevron/repair/24hr, Maverik, Phillips 66/dsl, Shell, Sinclair/dsl food DQ, Mi Pueblo, Pizza Hut, Subway, Taco Time lodging Comfort Inn, Days Inn, Holiday Inn Express, Knights Inn, SpringHill Suites other H, $Tree, AutoZone, Big O Tire, BigLots, Bryce Cyn, Cadillac/GMC, CAL Ranch, Duck Crk, Family$, Jo-Ann Fabrics, KOA, NAPACare, Navajo Lake, O'Reilly Parts, Parts+, Smith's Food/gas, Staples, to Cedar Breaks, Verizon, W gas Chevron/dsl, USA food 5 Buck Pizza, Applebee's, Cafe Rio, Chili's, Costa Vida, Del Taco, Lupita's Mexican, Ninja Japanese, Panda Express, Papa John's, Quiznos, Starbucks, Subway, Winger's lodging Hampton Inn other GNC, Home Depot, Jiffy Lube, Radio Shack, Tunex, Verizon, Walgreens, Walmart/McDonald's
51	Kanarraville, Hamilton Ft
44mm	**RS both lanes, full facilities, hist site, litter barrels, petwalk**
42	New Harmony, Kanarraville, W gas Texaco/dsl
40	to Kolob Canyon, E other scenic drive, tourist info/phone, Zion's NP
36	Black Ridge
33	Snowfield
31	Pintura
30	Browse
27	UT 17, Toquerville, E other Grand Canyon, Lake Powell, to Zion NP
23	Leeds, Silver Reef (from sb), **3 mi** E other hist site, Leed's RV Park/gas, museum
22	Leeds, Silver Reef (from nb), same as 23
16	UT 9, to Hurricane, E gas Texaco/dsl lodging Holiday Inn Express other Harley-Davidson, Walmart Dist Ctr
13	Washington Pkwy, E gas Maverik/dsl
10	Middleton Dr, Washington, E gas Phillips 66/dsl, Sinclair/dsl, USA food Alvero's Mexican, Arby's, Arctic Circle, Benja's Thai, Bishop's Cafe, Buca Italian, Burger King, Costa Vida, Del Taco, Dickey's BBQ, Don Pedro's Mexican, El Pollo Loco, Freddy's, Hungry Howie's, IHOP, In-N-Out, Jack-in-the-Box, Jimmy John's, Little Caesars, Mad Pita, McDonald's, Peppers Cantina, Pizza Factory, Pizza Hut, Red Robin, Royal Thai, Sonic, Subway, TX Roadhouse, Wendy's lodging Country Inn&Suites, Quality Inn other AAA, Albertsons/Sav-On, AutoZone, Barnes&Noble, Best Buy, Costco/gas, Dillard's, Discount Tire, Home Depot, JC Penney, Jo-Ann Fabrics, Kohl's, Natural Grocers, O'Reilly Parts, PetCo, Sears/auto, Tunex, Verizon, vet, Walmart/Subway, W gas Chevron/dsl/LP, Texaco/dsl other auto repair, St George RV Park/camping
8	St George Blvd, St George, E gas Chevron/Subway/dsl, Texaco/dsl food 5 Guys Burgers, Apollo Burger, Applebee's, Brick Oven, Buffalo Wild Wings, Carl's Jr, Chick-fil-A, Chili's, Chuck-aRama, Coldstone, Firehouse Subs, Golden Corral, Habit Burger, Iggy's Grill, Jimmy John's, Mongolian BBQ, Olive Garden, Outback Steaks, Panda Express, Paradise Bakery & cafe, Red Lobster, Smashburger, Starbucks, Subway, Village Inn Rest., Winger's lodging Best Inn, Courtyard, Hampton Inn, Ramada Inn, TownePlace Suites other H, $Tree, AT&T, Dick's, Harmon's Foods, Lowe's, Old Navy, Petsmart, Ross, Staples, Sunrise Tire, Target, TJ Maxx, Tuesday Morning, Verizon, Zion Outlets/famous brands, W gas Conoco/dsl, Maverik, Shell/dsl, Sinclair/dsl, Texaco/dsl food A&W/KFC, Burger King, Cafe Rio, Denny's, Iceberg Drive-In, Larsen's Drive-In, McDonald's, Ocean Buffet, Panda Garden, Papa John's, Port of Subs, Red Ginger Asian, Sakura Japanese, Taco Bell, Taco Time, Tropical Smoothie,

ST GEORGE

Exit #	Services
8	Continued Wendy's lodging Best Western, Chalet Motel, Coronada Inn, Days Inn, EconoLodge, Economy Inn, Knights Inn, Motel 6, Rodeway Inn, Sands Motel, SunTime Inn, Super 8 other Auto Tech/tires, Big O Tire, Desert Coach RV Ctr, NAPA, O'Reilly Parts, Rite Aid, to LDS Temple, vet
6	UT 18, Bluff St, St George, E gas Chevron/dsl, Sinclair/dsl, Texaco/dsl food Cracker Barrel, Culver's, Jack-in-the-Box, Player's Grill, Rib Chop House, Subway lodging Ambassador Inn, Comfort Inn, Fairfield Inn, Hilton Garden other Buick/GMC, Hyundai, Kia, museum, Subaru, VW, W gas Shell, Texaco food Arby's, Beijing Buffet, Black Bear Diner, Burger King, Denny's, Domino's, DQ, Jimmy John's, McDonald's, Pizza Hut, Ricardo's Rest., SF Pizza lodging Best Value Inn, Best Western, Claridge Inn, Clarion Suites, Crystal Inn, Howard Johnson, Lexington Hotel, Quality Inn, St George Inn other H, auto/truck repair, AutoZone, Big O Tire, Cadillac/Chevrolet, Camping World RV Ctr, Chrysler/Dodge/Jeep, Ford/Lincoln, funpark, Goodyear/auto, Honda, K-Mart, Mazda, Nissan, Radio Shack, TempleView RV Park, Toyota, U-Haul
5	Dixie Dr
4	Brigham Rd, Bloomington, E gas Pilot/Burger King/dsl/scales/24hr lodging La Quinta, W gas Chevron/Subway/Taco Time/dsl, USA/dsl food Dickey's BBQ, Hungry Howie's, Peppers Cantina, Wendy's lodging Wingate Inn other Walmart/Subway
2	UT 7 E, Southern Pkwy, E other
1	Port of Entry/**weigh sta both lanes**
0mm	Utah/Arizona state line

INTERSTATE 70

GREEN RIVER

Exit #	Services
232mm	Utah/Colorado state line
228mm	view area wb, litter barrels
227	Westwater
221	ranch exit
214	to Cisco
204	UT 128, to Cisco
193	Yellowcat Ranch Exit
190mm	**Welcome Ctr wb, full facilities, info, litter barrels vending**
187	Thompson, N gas Shell/dsl other Ballard RV Park
185mm	**parking area eb**
182	US 191 S, Crescent Jct, to Moab, N gas Papa Joe's, S other to Arches/Canyonlands NP
181mm	**RS eb, full facilities, litter barrels scenic view**
175	ranch exit
164	UT 19, Green River, **1-3 mi** N gas Phillips 66/Burger King/dsl, Pilot/Westwinds/rest/dsl/scales/24hr, Silver Eagle/Blimpie/dsl food Tamarisk Rest. lodging Best Value Inn, Comfort Inn, Holiday Inn Express, Knights Inn, Motel 6, River Terrace Inn, Super 8 other KOA, Powell River Museum, same as 160, tires/repair
160	UT 19, Green River, **0-2 mi** N gas Chevron/Subway/dsl, Conoco/Arby's/dsl food Cathy's Pizza, Chowhound, La Veracruzana, Ray's Rest. lodging Budget Inn, Robbers Roost, Sleepy Hollow Motel other Ace Hardware, city park, Green River SP, NAPA/repair, same as 164, Shady Acres RV Park, USPO
157	US 6 W, US 191 N, to Price, Salt Lake
149	UT 24 W, to Hanksville, to Capitol Reef, Lake Powell, other Goblin Valley SP
146	view area, restrooms wb
144mm	**runaway truck ramp eb**
143mm	view area both lanes, restrooms
142mm	**runaway truck ramp eb**

UT

INTERSTATE 70 CONT'D

Exit #	Services
138mm	**brake test area, restrooms eb**
131	Temple Mt Rd
122mm	Ghost Rock View Area both lanes, restrooms
116	to Moore, N view area both lanes
115	N view area eb
108	ranch exit
105mm	Salt Wash View Area both lanes
99	ranch exit
91	UT 10 N, UT 72, to Emery, Price, **12 mi** N [gas] gas, S [other] to Capitol Reef NP
86mm	**S [rest stop] both lanes, full [handicapped] facilities, litter barrels, petwalk**
73	ranch exit
63	Gooseberry Rd
56	US 89 N, to Salina, US 50 W, to Delta, NEXT SERVICES 109 MI EB, **0-1 mi** N [gas] Conoco/dsl, Maverik/dsl, Phillips 66/Carl's Jr/dsl, Sinclair/Burger King/dsl [food] Denny's, El Mexicano Mexican, Losta Motsa Pizza, Mom's Cafe, Subway [lodging] EconoLodge, Rodeway Inn, Super 8 [other] Barretts Foods, Butch Cassidy RV Camp, Family$, NAPA, Peterbilt, truck/RV/auto repair, S [gas] Loves/Arby's/dsl/scales/24hr
48	UT 24, to US 50, Sigurd, Aurora, **1-2 mi** S [gas] gas [food] food [other] Capitol Reef NP, to Fishlake NF
40	Lp 70, Richfield, **0-2 mi** S [gas] FLYING J/Pepperoni's/dsl/LP/rest./24hr, Chevron/dsl, Maverik/dsl, Texaco/dsl [food] Arby's, Frontier Village Rest., Papa Murphy's, Subway, Taco Time [lodging] Best Western, Budget Host, Days Inn/rest., Holiday Inn Express, Super 8 [other] [H], Big O Tire, Buick/Cadillac/Chevrolet/GMC, Chrysler/Dodge/Jeep, city park, Fresh Mkt, IFA Store, NAPA, RV/truck repair, USPO
37	Lp 70, Richfield, **1-2 mi** S [gas] Phillips 66/Wendy's/dsl, Silver Eagle/Burger King/dsl [food] Dickey's BBQ, KFC/Taco Bell, Little Caesar's, Lotsa Motsa Pizza, McDonald's, Pizza Hut, Steve's Steaks, Wingers [lodging] Comfort Inn, Fairfield Inn, Hampton Inn, Motel 6, New West Motel, Quality Inn, Royal Inn [other] $Tree, Ace Hardware, AutoZone, Ford, golf, Home Depot, K-Mart, KOA, O'Reilly Parts, Pearson Tire, st patrol, to Fish Lake/Capitol Reef Parks, Verizon, Walmart/Subway
31	Elsinore, Monroe, S [gas] Silver Eagle/DQ/dsl
25	UT 118, Joseph, Monroe, S [other] Flying U Country Store/dsl/RV park
23	US 89 S, to Panguitch, Bryce Canyon
17	N [other] camping, **chain-up area (wb)**, Fremont Indian SP, info, museum, phone
13mm	**brake test area eb**
7	Ranch Exit
3mm	Western Boundary Fishlake NF
1	N [gas] Chevron/Subway/rest stop (2mi) [other] Historic Cove Fort
0mm	I-15, N to SLC, S to St George.

I-70 begins/ends on I-15, exit 132.

RICHFIELD

INTERSTATE 80

Exit #	Services
197mm	Utah/Wyoming state line
191	Wahsatch
187	ranch exit
185	Castle Rock
182mm	**Port of Entry/weigh sta wb**
178	Emery (from wb)
170	**Welcome Ctr wb, [rest stop] eb, full [handicapped] facilities, litter barrels, petwalk [phone] [picnic] RV dump, vending**
169	Echo
168	I-84 W, to Ogden, I-80 E, to Cheyenne
166	view area both lanes, litter barrels
162	164 Coalville, N [gas] Phillips 66/dsl/mart [lodging] Best Western [other] CamperWorld RV Park, Holiday Hills RV Camp/LP, S [gas] Chevron/dsl, Sinclair/dsl [food] Polar King, Subway [other] Griffith's Foods, NAPA, to Echo Res RA, USPO
155	UT 32 S, Wanship, S [gas] Sinclair/dsl [other] to Rockport SP
150	[other] toll gate promontory
146b a	US 40 E, to Heber, Provo, N [gas] Sinclair/Blimpie/Pizza Hut/dsl, S [gas] Phillips 66/7-11/dsl [other] Burt Bros Tires, Home Depot
146	view area/**chain up wb**
145	UT 224, Kimball Jct, to Park City, N [other] Chevrolet, Ford, Park City RV Park, vet, S [gas] Chevron/dsl [food] Arby's, Cafe Rio, Coldstone, Del Taco, Five Guys, Freebirds Burrito, Ghidottis Italian, Great Harvest Bread Co, Jimmy John's, Loco Lizard Cantina, McDonald's, Panda Express, Papa John's, Pizza Hut, Red Rock Cafe, Ruby Tuesday, Starbucks, Subway, Szechwan Chinese, Taco Bell, Wendy's, Whole Foods Mkt [lodging] Best Western, Hampton Inn, Holiday Inn Express [other] Best Buy, Best Buy, GNC, Michaels, Outlet Mall/famous brands, Petco, RV camping, Smith's Foods/dsl, Staples, TJ Maxx, to ski areas, USPO, visitors info, Walmart
144mm	view area eb
141	ranch exit, N [gas] Phillips 66/Subway/dsl [other] Burt Bros Tires, to Jeremy Ranch, S [food] Billy Blanco Mexican [other] camping, Fresh Mkt, ski area
140	Parley's Summit, Parley's Summit, S [gas] Sinclair/dsl [food] No Worries Café
137	Lamb's Canyon
134	UT 65, Emigration Canyon, East Canyon, [other] Mountaindale RA
133	utility exit (from eb)
132	ranch exit
131	(from eb) Quarry
130	I-215 S (from wb)
129	UT 186 W, Foothill Dr, Parley's Way, N [other] [H]
128	I-215 S (from eb)
127	UT 195, 23rd E St, to Holladay
126	UT 181, 13th E St, to Sugar House, N [gas] Chevron [food] A&W/KFC, Cael's Jr, Chick-fil-A, Olive Garden, Red Lobster, Sizzler, Taco Bell, Training Table, Wendy's [lodging] Extended Stay America [other] ShopKO, Verizon
125	UT 71, 7th E St, N [food] Dee's Rest., Jimmy John's, Little Caesar's, Olympian Rest., Starbucks [other] AT&T, Firestone, Pepboys
124	US 89, S State St, N [gas] 7-11 [food] Astro Burgers, Burger King, Starbucks, Subway, Taco Bell [other] Access RV Ctr, Chrysler/Dodge/Jeep, Discount Tire, vet, S [food] A&W/KFC [lodging] Ramada Inn
123mm	I-15, N to Ogden, S to Provo

KIMBALL JCT

UT

SALT LAKE CITY

INTERSTATE 80 Cont'd

Exit #	Services
I-80 and I-15 run together approx 4 mi. See I-15, exits 308-310.	
121	600 S, to City Ctr
120	I-15 N, to Ogden
118	UT 68, Redwood Rd, to N Temple, **0-1 mi N on N Temple** Chevron/Subway/dsl, Loves/Arby's/dsl/scales/24hr, Shell/dsl A&W/KFC, Apollo Burger, Burger King, Carls Jr, Denny's, Taco Bell, Wendy's Airport Inn, Baymont Inn, Candlewood Suites, Comfort Suites, Holiday Inn Express, Motel 6, Radisson, Salt Lake Inn, S Maverik/dsl H
117	I-215, N to Ogden, S to Provo
115b a	Bangerter Hwy, N to Salt Lake
114	Wright Bros Dr (from wb), N same as 113
113	5600 W (from eb), N Phillips 66/dsl Perkins, Port of Subs, Subway Comfort Inn, Courtyard, DoubleTree, Fairfield Inn, Hampton Inn, Hilton Garden, Holiday Inn, Hyatt Place, La Quinta, Microtel, Quality Inn, Ramada Inn, Residence Inn, SpringHill Suites, Super 8
111	7200 W
104	UT 202, Saltair Dr, to Magna, N beaches, Great Salt Lake SP
102	UT 201 (from eb), to Magna
101mm	view area wb
99	UT 36, to Tooele, S FLYING J/Denny's/dsl/scales/LP/24hr, Chevron/Subway/dsl, TA/Burger King/Taco Bell/dsl/scales/24hr/ @, Texaco/dsl Del Taco, McDonald's Comfort Inn/Suites, Oquirrh Motel/RV Park H, Mamie's Place, SpeedCo
88	to Grantsville
84	UT 138, to Grantsville, Tooele
77	UT 196, to Rowley, Dugway
70	to Delle, S Delle/Tesoro/café/dsl
62	to Lakesid e, Eagle Range, military area
56	to Aragonite
55mm	**both lanes, full facilities, litter barrels, petwalk vending**
49	to Clive
41	Knolls
26mm	architectural point of interest
10mm	**both lanes, full facilities, litter barrels, observation area, petwalk vending**
4	Bonneville Speedway, N Sinclair/dsl/café/24hr
3mm	**Port of Entry, weigh sta both lanes**
2	UT 58 (no EZ wb return), Wendover, S Shell/Taco Time/dsl, Sinclair/dsl Subway Best Western, Bonneville Inn, Knights Inn, Motel 6, Nugget Hotel/casino, Quality Inn, Super 8, Western Ridge Motel auto repair, Carquest, Family$, KOA, Montego Bay Hotel/Casino, USPO
0mm	Utah/Nevada state line, Mountain/Pacific time zone

INTERSTATE 84

RIVERDALE

Exit #	Services
120	**I-84 begins/ends on I-80, exit 168 near Echo, Utah.**
115	Ut 65 S, to Henefer, Echo, to Henefer, Echo, **1/2 mi S** Grump's Gen Store/gas, to E Canyon SP, USPO
112	UT 86 E, Henefer, S
111	Croydon
111mm	Devil's Slide Scenic View
108	Taggart
106	ranch exit
103	UT 66, Morgan, N Ford, S Phillips 66/7-11/dsl, Texaco/dsl J's Drive-in, Spring Chicken Café, Subway Ace Hardware, city park, E Canyon SP, Family$, Ridley's Mkt, URGENT CARE, USPO
96	Peterson, N Sinclair/dsl (3mi) Nordic Valley Ski Areas, Powder Mtn, to Snow Basin, S Phillips 66/dsl
94mm	**wb, full facilities, litter barrels, petwalk**
92	UT 167 (from eb), to Huntsville, N Sinclair/dsl (2mi) city park (2mi), to ski areas
91mm	**S eb, full facilities, litter barrels, petwalk**
87b a	US 89, to Ogden, Layton, Ogden, N McDonald's (2mi), Wendy's (2mi) Best Western Cheese Outlet, Goodyear/auto, S to Hill AFB
85	S Weber, Uintah
81	to I-15 S, UT 26, Riverdale Rd, N Exxon/dsl, Sinclair/dsl Applebee's, Arby's, Bajio Grill, Buffalo Wild Wings, Carl's Jr, Chili's, Honeybaked Ham, IHOP, Jamba Juice, Lucky Buffet, McDonald's, Starbucks, Subway, Wendy's $Tree, Best Buy, Buick/GMC, Cadillac, Good Earth Foods, Gordman's, Harley-Davidson, Home Depot, Honda, Jo-Ann, Kia, Lowe's Whse, Mazda, Nissan, PepBoys, Petsmart, Sam's Club/gas, Schwab Tire, Target, Toyota/Scion, Verizon, Walmart/McDonald's, S Motel 6 Chrysler/Dodge/Jeep
I-84 and I-15 run together. See I-15, exits 344 through 379.	
41	I-15 N to Pocatello
40	UT 102, Tremonton, Bothwell, **1 mi N** Chevron/Poblano's/dsl/wash/24hr, Maverik/dsl, Sinclair/Burger King/dsl/scales/ @ Denny's, Grille Rest., McDonald's, Wendy's Hampton Inn, Western Inn Alco, C&R Rv Ctr, H (4mi), O'Reilly Parts, RV/truck/tire repair, S to Golden Spike NHS
39	to Garland, Bothwell, N H
32	ranch exit
26	UT 83 S, to Howell, S to Golden Spike NHS
24	to Valley
20	to Blue Creek
17	ranch exit
16	to Hansel Valley (from wb)
12	ranch exit
7	Snowville, N FLYING J/Pepperoni's/dsl/LP/24hr, Sinclair/dsl Mollie's Café, Ranch House Diner Outsiders Inn city park, Lotti-Dell RV camping, USPO
5	UT 30, to Park Valley
0mm	Utah/Idaho state line

INTERSTATE 215

Exit #	Services
29	**I-215 begins/ends on I-15.**
28	UT 68, Redwood Rd, E Pony Express RV Park, W FLYING J/Pepperoni's/dsl/LP/24hr/ @, Maverik/dsl Lotus Chinese
26	Legacy Pkwy
25	22nd N
23	7th N, E Exxon/dsl, Loves/Arbys/dsl/scales/24hr (1.5 mi), Maverik Denny's, KFC, McDonald's, Papa Murphy's, Subway, Taco Bell, Wendy's Motel 6 $Tree, Family$, Super Saver Mkt, W Airport Inn, Baymont Inn, Candlewood Suites, Comfort Suites, Holiday Inn Express, Radisson
22b a	I-80, W to Wendover, E to Cheyenne
21	California Ave, E Sapp Bros/Sinclair/Burger King/dsl/ @, Tesoro/7-11/dsl RV/Truckwash, W Chevron/dsl Port of Subs

SALT LAKE CITY

INTERSTATE 215 Cont'd

Exit #	Services
20b a	UT 201, W to Magna, 21st S, W Maverik/dsl Del Taco Goodyear, Kenworth
18	UT 171, 3500 S, W Valley, E 7-11 Applebee's, Chili's, Costa Vida Mexican, Cracker Barrel, Greek Souvlaki, IHOP, Kowloon Cafe Baymont Inn, Country Inn Suites, Crystal Inn, Extended Stay America, Holiday Inn Express, La Quinta, Sleep Inn, Staybridge Suites H, PepBoys, W Cafe Rio, In-N-Out, Jimmy John's, Olive Garden, Pizza Hut, Red Robin, Smashburger, TGIFriday's, Wendy's, Winger's, Zupas Embassy Suites AT&T, Big O Tire, Costco/gas, CVS Drug, JC Penney, Macy's, Office Depot, Petco, Ross, Staples, Verizon
15	UT 266, 47th S, E 7-11, Conoco/dsl Dee's Rest., KFC, Mad Greek, Pizza Hut, Taco Time, Village Inn, Wendy's Fresh Mkt, Goodyear/auto, Rite Aid, Walgreens, W Chevron/dsl Arby's, Arctic Circle, Tammie's Diner vet, Sinclair/dsl
13	UT 68, Redwood Rd, E Chevron, Shell/dsl Apollo Burger, Applebee's, Arby's, Burger King, Carl's Jr, City Buffet, Dickey's BBQ, Domino's, Francesco's Rest., Freebirds Burrito, Honey Baked Ham, McDonald's/playplace, Panda Express, Starbucks, Subway, TX Roadhouse Extended Stay America $Tree, AT&T, Harmon's Mkt, Jo-Ann Fabrics, PetsMart, Radio Shack, Ross, ShopKO, Verizon, Walmart/McDonald's
12	I-15, N to SLC, S to Provo
11	same as 10 (from eb)
10	UT 280 E, E Tesoro Papa John's AutoZone, Sam's Club/gas, W A&W/KFC, Applebee's, Arby's, Braza Grill, Brio Grill, CA Pizza, Cheesecake Factory, ChuckARama,
10	Continued Corner Bakery Cafe, Jason's Deli, Macaroni Grill, McDonald's, Olive Garden, Panda Express, Red Lobster, Red Robin, RedRock Cafe, Starbucks, Subway, Taco Bell, Village Inn H, Dillard's, Firestone/auto, Honda, Marshalls, Midas, Nordstrom, Pepboys, ShopKO, Sprouts Mkt, Verizon
9	Union Park Ave, E Applebee's, Bucca Italian, Buffalo Wild Wings, Cafe Rio, Carl's Jr, Chick-fil-A, Chili's, Chipotle, Denny's, Dickey's BBQ, Famous Dave's BBQ, Firehouse Subs, Five Guys, Longhorn Steaks, Noodles&Co, Panda Express, Pei Wei, Smashburger, Subway, Wendy's Hawthorn Suites, Super 8 $Tree, Barnes&Noble, Dick's, GNC, Gordman's, Home Depot, Michaels, Old Navy, Petco, Ross, Smith's Foods, Target, TJ Maxx, Verizon, Walmart/Subway, W Shell Crystal Inn, Motel 6 Extended Firestone/auto, Office Depot
8	UT 152, 2000 E, E Chevron KFC, McDonald's, Sonic, Taco Bell Whole Foods Mkt, W Phillips 66/dsl Subway, Wendy's Discount Tire
6	6200 S, E Jimmy John's, Luna Blanca, Pie Five, Starbucks, Trio Cafe, Zupas Hyatt Place, Residence Inn Alta, Brighton, Snowbird, Solitude/ski areas
5	UT 266, 45th S (from sb), Holladay, W Sinclair
4	39th S, E Chevron/dsl, Sinclair/dsl Barbacoa Grill, Rocky Mtn Pizza, Subway Ace Hardware, Dan's Mkt, W H
3	33rd S, Wasatch, W Smith's/dsl Cafe Rio, Five Guys, KFC/Taco Bell, McDonald's, Shivers Burgers, Wendy's Petsmart, REI, Smith's Mkt
2	I-80 W
0	**I-215 begins/ends on I-80, exit 130.**

UT VT

VERMONT

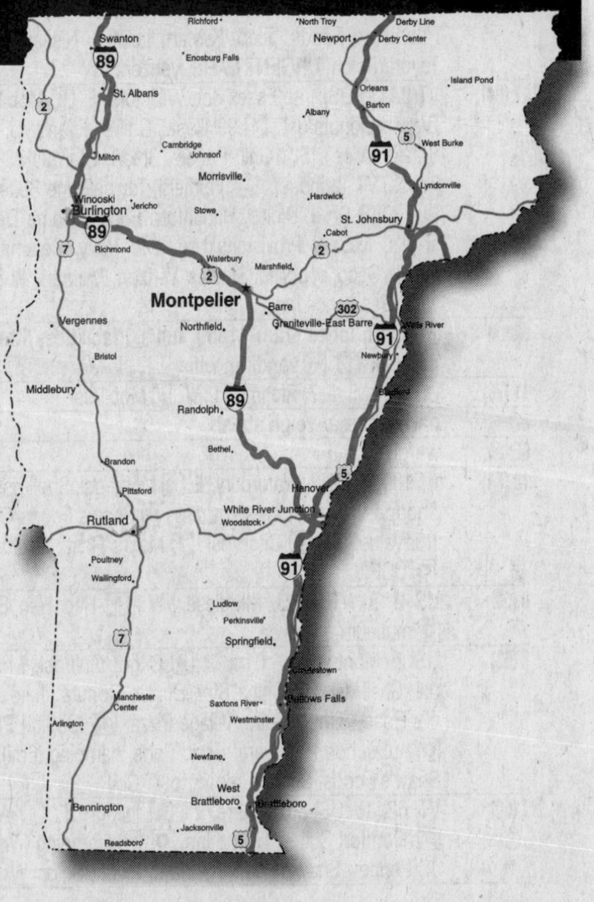

ST ALBANS

INTERSTATE 89

Exit #	Services
130mm	US/Canada Border, Vermont state line, I-89 Begins/Ends
22 (129)	US 7 S, Highgate Springs, E Irving/dsl DutyFree
129mm	Latitude 45 N, midway between N Pole and Equator
128mm	Rock River
21 (123)	US 7, VT 78, Swanton, E Shell/dsl, W Mobil/Subway/dsl, Shell, Sunoco/dsl Dunkin Donuts, McDonald's, Pam's Pizza, Shaggy's Snack Bar Aubuchon Hardware, Hannaford Foods, NAPA
20 (118)	US 7, VT 207, St Albans, E Chevrolet, Toyota, W Mobil/Subway/dsl, Sunoco Burger King, Dunkin Donuts, Hibachi Buffet, KFC/Taco Bell, McDonald's, Oriental Kitchen, Pizza Hut H Advance Parts, AT&T, Aubuchon Hardware, Buick/GMC/Cadillac, Ford, Hannaford Foods, Jo-Ann Fabrics, Kinney Drug, PriceChopper Foods, Radio Shack, Staples, TJ Maxx, Verizon, Walmart/Subway
19 (114)	US 7, VT 36, VT 104, St Albans, W Mobil/dsl, Shell/dsl Dunkin Donuts, Subway La Quinta H st police, vet
111mm	**both lanes, full facilities, info, litter barrels, petwalk vending, wifi**
18 (107)	US 7, VT 104A, Georgia Ctr, E Mobil/dsl, Shell GA Farmhouse Rest. GA Auto Parts, Homestead RV Park, repair, USPO
17 (98)	US 2, US 7, E Mobil, Shell/dsl camping (4mi), W camping (6mi), to NY Ferry, Lake Champlain Islands

INTERSTATE 89

Exit #	Services
96mm	**weigh sta both lanes**
16 (92)	US 7, US 2, Winooski, E Mobil Lighthouse Rest. Hampton Inn Costco, CVS Drug, Osco Drug, Shaw's Foods, W Citgo, Irving, Shell/dsl Athens Diner, Burger King, Jr's Italian, McDonald's, Subway Motel 6, Quality Inn
15 (91)	VT 15 (from nb no return), Winooski, E Days Inn, Handys Extended Stay Suites to St Michael's Coll., W Mobil/dsl, Shell USPO
90mm	Winooski River
14 (89)	US 2, Burlington, E Gulf, Mobil, Shell/dsl, Sunoco, Valero Al's Cafe, Applebee's, Chicken Charlie's, Dunkin Donuts, Hana Japanese, Leonardo's Pizza, McDonald's, Moe's SW Grill, Outback Steaks, Pulcinella's, Quiznos, Rotisserie, Starbucks, Subway, Trader Dukes, Wind Jammer Rest., Zachary's Pizza Anchorage Inn, Best Western, Comfort Inn, DoubleTree Hotel, Holiday Inn, Homewood Suites, La Quinta Aubuchon Hardware, Barnes&Noble, BonTon, Hannaford Foods, Healthy Living Mkt, JC Penney, Jo-Ann Fabrics, Kohl's, mall, Midas, PriceChopper, Rite Aid, Sears/auto, Trader Joe's, USPO, W Mobil/dsl, Shell Sheraton H Advance Parts, Michael's, PetCo, Staples, to UVT, Verizon
13 (87)	I-189, to US 7, Burlington, N Citgo/dsl, Sunoco/dsl Buffalo Wild Wings, China Express, Five Guys, Starbucks, Subway $Tree, GNC, Hyundai/Subaru, Kinney Drug, PriceChopper Foods, Radio Shack, Shaw's Foods, TJ Maxx, USPO, Walgreens, **2 mi** W on US 7 S Gulf, Irving, Mobil/dsl, Shell/dsl, Sunoco Burger King, Chicago Grill, Denny's, Koto Japanese, Lakeview House Rest., McDonald's, Olive Garden, Panera Bread, Pauline's Cafe, Subway, Zen Garden Comfort Suites, Ho-Hum Hotel, Holiday Inn Express, Maple Leaf Motel, North Star Motel, Travelodge Acura/Audi/VW, Advance Parts, Buick/Cadillac/GMC, Chevrolet, Chrysler/Dodge, Ford, Hannaford Foods, Jeep, K-Mart, Lowe's, Nissan, Tire Whse, Toyota/Scion, URGENT CARE, Verizon, VW
12 (84)	VT 2A, to US 2, to Essex Jct, Williston, E Mobil, Sunoco/Dunkin Donuts/dsl 99 Rest., Chili's, Friendly's, Longhorn Steaks, Moe's SW Grill, Panera Bread, Starbucks, TX Roadhouse, VT Taphouse Fairfield, TownePlace Suites Best Buy, CVS Drug, Dick's, Hannaford Foods, Home Depot, Marshall's, Natural Provisions Mkt, Old Navy, Petsmart, Shaws Foods/Osco, st police, Staples, Verizon, Walmart, W Courtyard, Residence Inn
82mm	**[RS] both lanes (7am-11pm), full facilities, litter barrels, petwalk vending, wifi**
11 (79)	US 2, to VT 117, Richmond, W Mobil/dsl
67mm	**parking area/weigh sta sb**
66mm	**weigh sta nb**
10 (64)	VT 100, to US 2, Waterbury, E Mobil/dsl, Shell/dsl Pizza Shoppe Best Western/rest Shaws Foods/Osco Drug, TrueValue, W Citgo/dsl Maxi's Rest., Zachary's Pizza USPO
9 (59)	US 2, to VT 100B, Middlesex, W Red Hen Baking Co museum, st police
8 (53)	US 2, Montpelier, **1 mi** E Citgo, Gulf/dsl, Mobil, Shell/dsl, Shell/dsl China Star, Dunkin Donuts, Julio's, Sarducci's Rest., Simply Subs, Village Pizza Capitol Plaza Hotel Aubuchon Hardware, Bond Parts, camping (6mi), Rite Aid, Shaw's Foods, Sunoco/repair, to VT Coll
7 (50)	VT 62, to US 302, Barre, E Irving/dsl Applebee's Comfort Suites, Hilltop Inn H camping (7mi), Honda, JC Penney, Shaw's Foods, Subaru, Toyota/Scion, Walmart
6 (47)	VT 63, to VT 14, S Barre, **4 mi** E camping, info
5 (43)	VT 64, to VT 12, VT 14, Williamstown, **6 mi** E camping, /dsl W to Norwich U
41mm	1752 ft, highest elevation on I-89
34.5mm	**weigh sta both lanes**
4 (31)	VT 66, Randolph, E RV camping (seasonal 1mi), W Mobil/dsl lodging (3mi), McDonald's H RV camping (5mi)
30mm	**parking area sb**
3 (22)	VT 107, Bethel, E Mobil/dsl Eaton's Rest., Village Pizza to Jos Smith Mon (8mi), **1 mi** W Irving/dsl/LP Rite Aid, st police, vet
14mm	White River
2 (13)	VT 14, VT 132, Sharon, W Gulf/dsl Jos Smith Mon (6mi), Sharon Country Store, USPO
9mm	**[RS]/weigh sta both lanes (7am-11pm), full facilities, info, litter barrels vending, wifi**
7mm	White River
1 (4)	US 4, to Woodstock, Quechee, **3 mi** E Irving Hampton Inn, Holiday Inn Express, Super 8, **3 mi** N Fairfield Inn
1mm	I-91, N to St Johnsbury, S to Brattleboro
0mm	Vermont/New Hampshire state line, Connecticut River

INTERSTATE 91

Exit #	Services
178mm	US/Canada Border, Vermont state line, US Customs, **I-91 begins/ends.**
29 (177)	US 5, Derby Line, E Dutyfree, **1 mi** W Irving/Circle K/dsl city park
176.5mm	**Welcome Ctr sb full facilities, info, litter barrels, Midpoint between the Equator and N Pole, petwalk vending, wifi**
28 (172)	US 5, VT 105, Derby Ctr, E Gulf, Shell/dsl, Sunoco/repair Cow Palace Rest. auto/tire service, USPO, W Irving/Hoagie's Pizza, Mobil/dsl China Moon, McDonald's, Penn's Rest., Pizza Hut, Roasters Cafe, Village Pizza, VT Pie&Pasta 4 Seasons, Pepin's Motel H $Tree, Advance Parts, Bond Parts, Chrysler/Dodge/Jeep, CVS Drug, Family$, Kinney Drug, Parts+, PriceChopper Foods, Rite Aid, RV camping, Shaw's Foods, st police, Verizon
27 (170)	VT 191, to US 5, VT 105, Newport, **3 mi** W H Border Patrol, camping, info
167mm	**parking area/weigh sta both directions**
26 (161)	US 5, VT 58, Orleans, E Irving, Sunoco Subway Austin's Drugs, Family$, Thibaults Mkt, TrueValue, USPO, W camping (5mi)
156.5mm	Barton River
25 (156)	VT 16, Barton, **1 mi** E Gulf, Irving/Circle K/dsl Ming's Chinese, Parson's Corner Rest. C&C Foods, camping (2mi), Kinney Drug, USPO
154mm	**parking area nb**
150.5mm	1856 ft, highest elevation on I-91
143mm	**scenic overlook nb**
141mm	**[RS] sb, full facilities, info, litter barrels vending**
24 (140)	VT 122, Wheelock, **2 mi** E
23 (137)	US 5, to VT 114, Lyndonville, E Gulf/dsl, Mobil/Dunkin Donuts Hoagie's Pizza, Lyndon Buffet, McDonald's, Miss Lyndonville Diner, Pizza Man Colonnade Inn $General, CarQuest, Kinney Drug, Rite Aid, TrueValue, White Mkt Foods, W Lyndon Motel
22 (132)	to US 5, St Johnsbury, **1-2 mi** E Sunoco/dsl KFC/Taco Bell, Kham's Cuisine, Pizza Hut H Aubuchon Hardware,

BURLINGTON

DERBY CTR

INTERSTATE 91 CONT'D

ST JOHNSBURY

22 (132)	Continued Bond Parts, Buick/GMC, Kinney Drug, NAPA, PriceChopper Foods, repair, Subaru
21 (131)	US 2, to VT 15, St Johnsbury, **1-2 mi E** services
20 (129)	US 5, to US 2, St Johnsbury, **E** Irving/dsl, Mobil, Shell/dsl Anthony's Diner, Dunkin Donuts, East Garden Chinese, McDonald's, Subway, Winegate Rest. Family$, Kevin's Repair, museum, Rite Aid, welcome ctr, **W** Comfort Inn st police
19 (128)	I-93 S to Littleton NH
122mm	**scenic view nb**
18 (121)	to US 5, Barnet, **E** camping (5mi), **W** camping (5mi)
115mm	**parking area sb**
113mm	**parking area nb**
17 (110)	US 302, to US 5, Wells River, NH, **W** P&H Trkstp/rest./dsl/scales/24hr camping (9mi), (5mi)
100mm	**nb , sb parking area, full facilities, info, litter barrels, petwalk vending**
16 (98)	VT 25, to US 5, Bradford, **E** Mobil/dsl/LP/café Hungry Bear Grill, Oasis Grill Bradford Motel Bond Parts, Family$, Hannafords Foods, Kinney Drug, NAPA, Pierson Farm Mkt, **W** st police
15 (92)	Fairlee, **E** Gulf, Irving/dsl, Sunoco/dsl Fairlee Diner, Subway camping, USPO, Wings Mkt/deli, **W** golf
14 (84)	VT 113, to US 5, Thetford, **1 mi E** camping **W** camping
13 (75)	US 5, VT 10a, Hanover, NH, **E** to Dartmouth, **W** Citgo Norwich Inn Rest. Subaru, USPO
12 (72)	US 5, White River Jct, Wilder, **E** Gulf/dsl, Mobil
11 (71)	US 5, White River Jct, **E** Mobil/dsl, Shell/Subway/dsl China Moon, Crossroads Country Café, McDonald's Comfort Inn Ford/Lincoln, Hyundai, Toyota, USPO, **W** Citgo, Irving/Dunkin Donuts, Sunoco/dsl Fairfield Inn, Hampton Inn, Holiday Inn Express, Super 8, White River Inn
10N (70)	I-89 N, to Montpelier
10S	I-89 S, to NH,
68mm	**weigh sta both lanes**
9 (60)	US 5, VT 12, Hartland, **E** **W** Mobil (1mi) Hartland Diner info
8 (51)	US 5, VT 12, VT 131, Ascutney, **E** Citgo/dsl, Gulf/dsl, Irving/Circle K, Sunoco/Dunkin Donuts/dsl Ascutney House Rest.,

BRATTLEBORO

8 (51)	Continued Mr G's Rest. Yankee Village Motel Getaway Camping (2mi), USPO, **W** auto repair/tires
7 (42)	US 5, VT 106, VT 11, Springfield, **W** Irving/Circle K/Subway/dsl/scales/24hr Holiday Inn Express camping, (5mi)
39mm	**weigh sta sb**
6 (34)	US 5, VT 103, to Bellows Falls, Rockingham, **E** Shell/dsl Leslie's Rest. Rodeway Inn, **W** Sunoco/dsl st police (6mi)
5 (29)	VT 121, to US 5, to Bellows Falls, Westminster, **3 mi E**
24mm	**parking area both lanes**
22mm	**weigh sta sb**
20mm	**parking area nb**
4 (18)	US 5, Putney, **W** Rod's/repair, Sunoco/dsl/LP/24hr Katy's Cafe, Putney Diner, Putney Food Coop/deli, Putney Village Pizza camping (3mi), Putney Gen Store/deli, USPO
3 (11)	US 5, VT 9 E, Brattleboro, **E** Agway/dsl, Citgo/dsl, Mobil/dsl, Sunoco 99 Rest., China Buffet, Dunkin Donuts, Fast Eddy Cafe, House of Pizza, KFC, McDonald's, Panda North, Taco Bell, Thin Crust Pizzaria, Village Pizza, Wendy's Best Inn, Colonial Motel, Hampton Inn, Holiday Inn Express, Motel 6, Quality Inn, Super 8 Advance Parts, Aldi Foods, AT&T, Bond Parts, Buick/Chevrolet/GMC, Chrysler/Dodge/Jeep, Family$, Ford, GNC, Hannaford Foods, Radio Shack, Rite Aid, Staples, Subaru, TrueValue, USPO, Verizon
2 (9)	VT 9 W, to rd 30, Brattleboro, **W** VT Country Deli st police, to Marlboro Coll
1 (7)	US 5, Brattleboro, **E** Gulf/dsl, Irving/Circle K/dsl, Mobil/Dunkin Donuts, Shell/Subway/dsl Burger King, FC Chinese, Georgio's Pizza, VT Inn Pizza EconoLodge PriceChopper Foods, Rite Aid, to Ft Dummer SP, vet, Walgreens
6mm	**Welcome Ctr nb, full facilities, info, litter barrels, petwalk playground, vending, wifi**
0mm	Vermont/Massachusetts state line

INTERSTATE 93

See New Hampshire Interstate 93

VT VA

VIRGINIA

INTERSTATE 64

NORFOLK

Exit #	Services
299b a	I-264 E, to Portsmouth. **I-64 begins/ends on I-264.**
297	US 13, US 460, Military Hwy, **N** 7-11, Exxon McDonald's
296b a	US 17, to Portsmouth, **N** 7-11 Hardee's, McDonald's, Papa John's, Subway, Zino's Cafe Comfort Inn $General, Food Lion, USPO, vet
294mm	S Br Elizabeth River
292	VA 190, to VA 104 (from eb, no EZ return), Dominion Blvd, **S** 7-11 #1 China, Burger King, Royal China, Subway Family$, Food Lion
291b a	I-464 N, VA 104 S, to Elizabeth City, Outer Banks, same services as 292
290b a	VA 168, Battlefield Blvd, to Nag's Head, Manteo, **N** Burger King ValuePlace $General, BigLots, Hancock Fabrics,
290b a	Continued K-mart, Merchant's Auto Ctr, NAPA, **S** 7-11, BP/DQ, Shell 5 Guys Burgers, Applebee's, Baskin-Robbins, Burger King, Carrabba's, Chick-fil-A, ChuckECheese's, Denny', Dunkin Donuts, Firehouse Subs, Golden Corral, Grand China Buffet, Hardee's, Hunan Wok, Jade Garden, McDonald's, Salsarita's Cantina, Sonic, Starbucks, Taco Bell, TGIFriday's, Tropical Smoothie Café, TX Roadhouse, Waffle House, Wendy's, Wildwing Café, Woodchick's BBQ Days Inn, Hampton Inn, Quality Inn, Savannah Suites , $Tree, Goodyear/auto, Home Depot, Kohl's, Lowe's, Nissan, Rite Aid, Sam's Club/gas, USPO, vet, Walgreens, Walmart
289b a	Greenbrier Pkwy, **N** 7-11, Citgo, WaWa Burger King, Cugini's Pizza, McDonald's, Subway, Taco Bell, Wendy's Cedar Tree Inn, Extended Stay, Hampton Inn, Marriott, Red Roof Inn, Staybridge Suites, Wingate Inn Acura, auto repair,

VA

E INTERSTATE 64 Cont'd

289b a Continued
Chevrolet, Chrysler/Jeep, Dodge, Ford, Hyundai, JoAnn Fabrics, Kia, Lincoln, Mazda, Scion/Toyota, U-Haul, vet, **S** 7-11 Abuelo's Mexican, Baker's Crust, Boston Mkt, Buffalo Wild Wings, Chipotle, Coldstone, Cracker Barrel, Fazoli's, Firehouse Subs, Friendly's, Greenbrier Buffet, Hooters, Jason's Deli, Jersey Mike's Subs, Jimmy John's, Joe's Crabshack, Kyoto Japanese, LoneStar Steaks, McDonald's, Olive Garden, Panera Bread, Paradocks Grill, Pizza Hut, Pop's Diner, Qdoba, Red Robin, Ruby Tuesday, Smokey Bones BBQ, Starbucks, Subway, Zero's Subs, Zoot's Cafe Aloft Hotel, Comfort Suites, Courtyard, Extended Stay America, Fairfield Inn, Hilton Garden, Homewood Suites, Residence Inn, SpringHill Suites, Sun Suites AT&T, Barnes&Noble, Best Buy, Dillard's, Food Lion, Harris Teeter, Macy's, mall, Marshall's, Michael's, Office Depot, Old Navy, Petsmart, Ross, Sears/auto, Steinmart, Target, TJ Maxx, Verizon, Walgreens

286b a Indian River Rd, **N** BP/dsl, Gulf, Hess/dsl, SkyMart/dsl Dunkin Donuts, Golden China, Hardee's CVS, **S** Sunoco/dsl Capt D's, Oriental Cuisine, Shoney's, Top's China, Waffle House 7-11

285mm E Branch Elizabeth River

284a I-264, to Norfolk, to VA Beach (exits left from eb)

284b Newtown Rd

282 US 13, Northampton Blvd, **N** Quality Inn, Sleep Inn to Chesapeake Bay Br Tunnel

281 VA 165, Military Hwy (no EZ eb return), **N** Shell/dsl EconoLodge Aamco, Chysler/Dodge/Jeep, Fiat, **S** 7-11, Citgo Burger King, Chick-fil-A, Cook-Out, Frank'n Bubba's BBQ, Hooters, IHOP, Jersey Mike's Subs, Jimmy John's, KFC, Logan's Roadhouse, Max&Erma's, Panera Bread, Qdoba, Sonic, Starbucks, Taco Bell, Wendy's Candlewood Suites, Hampton Inn, Hilton, Holiday Inn, Holiday Inn Express, La Quinta, Ramada, Residence Inn, Savannah Suites BJ's Whse, FarmFresh Foods, Firestone/auto, Food Lion, Home Depot, Lowe's, Nissan, Pep Boys, Petco, Petsmart, Target, TJ Maxx, Verizon, Walgreens, Walmart/Subway

279 Norview Ave, **N** K Express, Shell/repair, WaWa China House, Franco's Italian, Golden Corral, Pizza Hut, Wendy's $General, $Tree, 7-11, Food Lion, K-Mart/gas, Tire City, to airport & botanical garden

278 VA 194 S (no EZ return)

277b a VA 168, to Tidewater Dr, **N** 7-11, Shell Bojangles, Hardee's, Ruby Tuesday Advance Parts, Food Lion, Radio Shack, Walmart/Subway, **S** BP

276c to US 460 W, VA 165, Little Creek Rd, (from wb only), **N** Race Coast Gas, **S** BP, Shell KFC, McDonald's, Papa John's, Pizza Hut, Starbucks, Taco Bell, Wendy's AutoZone, FarmFresh Foods, Kroger, Rite Aid, USPO, Walgreens

276b a I-564 to Naval Base (exits left from wb)

274 Bay Ave (from wb), to Naval Air Sta

273 US 60, 4th View St, Oceanview, **N** 7-11 Economy Inn Oceanview Pier, **S** info, to Norfolk Visitors Ctr

272 W Ocean View Ave, **N** Willoughby Seafood, **S** Sunset Grill

270mm Chesapeake Bay Tunnel

269mm **weigh sta eb**

268 VA 169 E, to Buckroe Beach, Ft Monroe, **N** Citgo Hardee's, McDonald's to VA Air&Space Ctr

267 US 60, to VA 143, Settlers Ldg Rd, **S** Golden City Chinese, Subway, Tropical Smoothie **H**, to Hampton U

265c (from eb), **N** Armistead Ave, to Langley AFB

HAMPTON

265b a VA 134, VA 167, to La Salle Ave, **N** Citgo, RaceWay Super 8 Home Depot, **S** BP KFC/Taco Bell, McDonald's **H**, Advance Parts, Family$

264 I-664, to Newport News, Suffolk

263b a US 258, VA 134, Mercury Blvd, to James River Br, **N** 7-11, BP, Exxon/dsl, Shell 5 Guys Burgers, Abuelo's Mexican, Applebee's, Bojangles, Boston Mkt, Burger King, Chick-fil-A, Chili's, China Wok, Chipotle Mexican, Denny's, Dog House, El Azteca, Firehouse Subs, Golden Corral, Hooters, IHOP, Jason's Deli, KFC, McDonald's, New Garden Buffet, Olive Garden, Outback Steaks, Panera Bread, Parklane Rest., Pizza Hut, Quizno's, Rally's, Red Lobster, Starbucks, Subway, Taco Bell, Tokyo Japanese, Waffle House, Wendy's Comfort Inn, Courtyard, Days Inn, Embassy Suites, Holiday Inn Express, Quality Inn, Red Roof Inn, Rodeway Inn $Tree, AT&T, Chevrolet/Mazda, FarmFresh Foods, Food Lion Ford, GNC, Goodyear/auto, JC Penney, Jo-Ann Fabrics, Macy's, Marshall's, Michael's, NAPA, Nissan, Office Depot, PetCo, Ross, Target, U-Haul, USPO, Verizon, Volvo, Walgreens, Walmart, **S** Citgo/dsl, Miller's Chick-fil-A, CiCi's Pizza, Coldstone, Cracker Barrel, Domino's, Joe's Crabshack, Lonestar Steaks, Longhorn Steaks, Pizza Hut, Rita's, Sonic, Sports Grill, Waffle House, Zaxby's Hampton Bay Suites, Hilton Garden, La Quinta, Relax Inn, Savannah Suites, SpringHill Suites 7-11, Aamco Advance Parts, BassPro Shop, BigLots, BJ's Whse/Subway/gas, CVS Drug, Firestone/auto, Hancock Fabrics, Lowe's, PepBoys, Radio Shack, Toyota/Scion

262 VA 134, Magruder Blvd (from wb, no EZ return), **N** 7-11, Exxon Country Inn&Suites, Suburban Lodge Hyundai, Mercedes

261b a Center Pkwy, to Hampton Roads, **N** Hampton Inn (2mi), **S** 7-11, Shell Anna's Italian, ChuckECheese's, Fortune Garden Chinese, McDonald's, Peking Chinese, Pizza Hut/Taco Bell, Plaza Azteca, Ruby Tuesday, Subway $Tree, FarmFresh Foods, Food Lion, GNC, Rite Aid, TJMaxx

258b a US 17, J Clyde Morris Blvd, **N** BP, Shell/dsl Domino's, Fiorello Italian, New China, Waffle House BudgetLodge, Country Inn&Suites, Holiday Inn, Host Inn, PointPlaza Hotel, Quality Inn 7-11, Advance Parts, Family$, Food Lion, **S** BP, Kangaroo, WaWa Angelo's Steaks, Burger King, DQ, KFC/Taco Bell, McDonald's, Papa John's, Starbucks, Subway, Vinny's Pizza, Wendy's Motel 6 **H**, museum, Rite Aid, Subaru, VW

256b a Victory Blvd, Oyster Point Rd, **N** BP, Citgo/dsl, Murphy USA/dsl 3 Amigos Mexican, Arby's, Burger King, Chick-fil-A, China Ocean, Hardee's, McDonald's, NY Pizza, Pizza Hut, Ruby Tuesday, Saisaki Asian, Sonic, Starbucks, Subway, TX Roadhouse, Uno Grill CandleWood Suites, Courtyard, Hampton Inn, Hilton Garden, Staybridge Suites, TownePlace Suites $Tree, FarmFresh Foods, GNC, Goodyear, K-Mart, Kroger, RadioShack, Walgreens, Walmart, **S** Crestwood Suites, Jameson Inn

255b a VA 143, to Jefferson Ave, **N** Shell/dsl 5 Guys Burgers, Chili's, Cookout, Donato's Pizza, Firehouse Subs, Golden Corral, HoneyBaked Ham, Hooters, Jason's Deli, Longhorn Steaks, McDonald's, Moe's SW Grill, Olive Garden, Panera Bread, Papa John's, Red City Buffet, Red Lobster, Smokey Bones BBQ, Starbucks Comfort Suites **H**, Acura, airport, Buick/Cadillac/GMC, Chrysler/Dodge/Jeep, FarmFresh Foods/deli, Fiat, GNC, Home Depot, Kohl's, Lincoln, Lowe's, Michael's, PetCo, Ross, Sam's Club/gas, TJ Maxx, Trader Joe's, Tuesday Morning, Walmart, **S** BP/dsl, Citgo/dsl, Exxon/dsl Applebee's, Bailey's Grille, Buffalo Wild Wings,

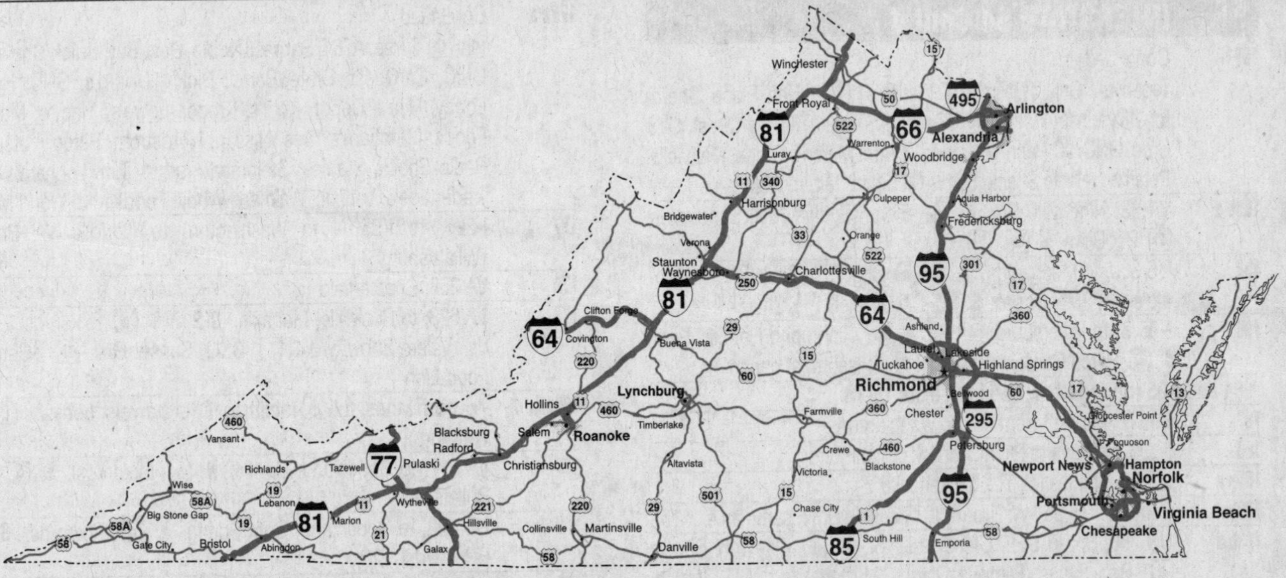

E INTERSTATE 64 Cont'd

WILLIAMSBURG

255b a Continued
Carrabba's, Cheddar's, Cheeseburger Paradise, Chick-fil-A, Chipotle Mexican, Coldstone, Cracker Barrel, KFC, McDonald's, Outback Steaks, Red Robin, Starbucks, Subway, Taco Bell, TGIFriday's, Waffle House, Wendy's [lodging] Best Western, Comfort Inn, Courtyard, Extended Stay America, Hampton Inn, Microtel, Residence Inn [other] 7-11, Barnes&Noble, Best Buy, Costco, Dick's, Dillard's, Fresh Mkt, JC Penney, Macy's, mall, Petsmart, Sears Auto Ctr, Target, Verizon, World Mkt

250b a to US Army Trans Museum, **N** [gas] 7-11/gas, Dodge's Store, Exxon/dsl, Sunoco [food] China Dragon, Hardee's, Little Italy, Subway [other] B&L Auto Repair, to Yorktown Victory Ctr, **S** [lodging] Ft Eustis Inn, Holiday Inn Express, Mulberry Inn [other] 7-11, Newport News Campground/Park (1mi)

247 VA 143, to VA 238 (no EZ return wb), **N** [gas] 7-11/gas [other] to Yorktown, **S** [other] to Jamestown Settlement

243 VA 143, to Williamsburg, exits left from wb, **S** same as 242a

242b a VA 199, to US 60, to Williamsburg, **N** [lodging] Day's Hotel/rest. [other] Best Buy, Dick's, JC Penney, Kohl's, Target, to Yorktown NHS, water funpark, **1 mi S** [gas] 7-11/gas, Shell, Sunoco [food] China's Cuisine, Doraldo's Italian, KFC, McDonald's, Sportsmans Grille, Starbucks, Subway, Taco Bell, Wendy's, Whaling Co Rest. [lodging] Country Inn&Suites, Courtyard, Marriott/rest., Quality Inn [other] Busch Gardens, camping, to Jamestown NHS, to William& Mary Coll

238 VA 143, to Colonial Williamsburg, Camp Peary, **2-3 mi S on US 60** [gas] 7-11/gas, Shell, Sunoco [food] 5 Guys Burgers, Aberdeen Barn Rest., Applebee's, Arby's, Chili's, Chipotle Mexican, Cracker Barrel, DQ, Firehouse Subs, Golden Corral, Hooters, IHOP, Jefferson Steaks, KFC, Kyoto, McDonald's, Pancake House, Pizza Hut, Plaza Azteca, Red Hot&Blue, Ruby Tuesday, Sal's Rest., Seafare Rest, Smokehouse Grill, Subway, Taco Bell, Uno Grille, Wendy's [lodging] 1776 Hotel, America's Inn, Best Western, Comfort Inn, Comfort Suites, Country Inn&Suites, Days Inn, EconoLodge, Embassy Suites, Fairfield Inn, Hampton Inn, Hilton Garden, Holiday Inn Express, Holiday Inn/rest., Homewood Suites, La Quinta, Quality Inn, Sleep Inn, SpringHill Suites, Travelodge [other] H, Anvil Camping (4mi), CVS Drug, Goodyear, K-Mart

234 VA 646, to Lightfoot, **1-2 mi N** [other] KOA, **2-3 mi S** [gas] BP/dsl, Exxon/dsl, Shell/dsl [food] Burger King, Chick-fil-A, China

234 Continued
Wok, Hardee's, IHOP, McDonald's, Quiznos, Sonic, Starbucks, Subway [lodging] Greatwolf Lodge, Holiday Inn Express, Super 8 [other] H, $Tree, Ford, Home Depot, Lowe's, PetCo, Pottery Camping (3mi), Ross, Toyota/Scion, USPO, Walmart

231b a VA 607, to Norge, Croaker, **N** [gas] 7-11/gas [other] to York River SP, **1-3 mi S on US 60** [gas] Shell/dsl [food] Candle Light Kitchen, China Star, Daddy-O's Pizza, Jimmy's Grill, Pizza Hut [lodging] EconoLodge [other] American Heritage RV Park, CVS Drug, FarmFresh Deli/gas, Food Lion, Honda, Hyundai, USPO

227 VA 30, to US 60, to West Point, Toano, **S** [gas] BP/dsl (2mi), Shell/dsl, Star/Subway/dsl [food] McDonald's

220 VA 33 E, to West Point, **N** [gas] Exxon/dsl, Mobil/Circle K/dsl

214 VA 155, to New Kent, Providence Forge, **S** [gas] Exxon/DQ/dsl [food] Antonio's Pizza, Tops China [other] camping (8mi), Colonial Downs Racetrack

213mm **[rest stop] both lanes, full [handicapped] facilities, litter barrels, petwalk [phone] [picnic] vending**

211 VA 106, to Talleysville, to James River Plantations, **S** [gas] Pilot/Subway/dsl/scales/24hr

RICHMOND

205 VA 33, VA 249, to US 60, Bottoms Bridge, Quinton, **N** [gas] Exxon/dsl, Star Express, Valero [food] Julio's Mexican, Maria's Italian, Panda Garden, Pizza Hut, Subway, Wendy's [other] Food Lion, **S** [gas] FasMart, Shell/dsl [food] Bojangle's, McDonald's [lodging] Star Motel (3mi) [other] Food Lion, Rite Aid

204mm Chickahominy River

203mm **weigh sta both lanes**

200 I-295, N to Washington, S to Rocky Mount, to US 60

197b a VA 156, [airport] Dr, to Highland Springs, **N** [gas] Shell/dsl, Valero [food] Antonio's Pizza, Domino's, Hardee's, Subway, Tops China [other] 7-11, Advance Parts, CVS Drug, Farmers Foods, **S** [gas] 7-11, BP, Chubby's/dsl, WaWa [food] Arby's, Aunt Sarah's Pancakes, Burger King, Mexico Rest., Pizza Hut, The Patron, Waffle House [lodging] Best Value Inn, Best Western, Comfort Inn, Courtyard, EconoLodge, Hampton Inn, Hilton Garden, Holiday Inn, Holiday Inn Express, Homewood Suites, Microtel, Motel 6, Quality Inn, Red Roof Inn, Super 8 [other] $General, to airport

195 Laburnum Ave, **N** [gas] Citgo [other] auto repair, **S** [gas] 7-11, BP, Exxon, WaWa [food] 5 Guys Burgers, Applebee's, Capt D's, Chick-fil-A, China King, CiCi's Pizza, Cracker Barrel, Firehouse Subs, Hardee's, IHOP, KFC, Little Caesars, Longhorn Steaks, McDonald's, Olive Garden, Panera Bread, Papa John's, Qdoba Mexican, Red Lobster, Steak'n Shake, Subway, Taco Bell,

[gas] = gas [food] = food [lodging] = lodging [other] = other [RS] = rest stop Copyright 2016 - The Next EXIT ®

VA

INTERSTATE 64 Cont'd

RICHMOND

195 Continued
Tepanyaki Grill, TGIFriday's, Wendy's [lodging] Hyatt Place, Sheraton, Wyndham Hotel [other] $General, $Tree, AT&T, CarQuest, CVS Drug, GNC, JC Penney, Kroger, Lowe's, Martin's Foods, Michael's, Petsmart, Radio Shack, Sam's Club/gas, Target, Walgreens

193b a VA 33, Nine Mile Rd, **N** [gas] Exxon/Subway/dsl, Sunoco/dsl [other] PepBoys, **S** [other] [H]

192 US 360, to Mechanicsville, **N** [gas] Citgo/dsl, Shell [food] McDonald's [other] Tuffy Repair, **S** [gas] Citgo, Shell [food] Church's

190 I-95 S, to Petersburg, 5th St, **N** [other] Richmond Nat Bfd Park, **S** [lodging] Hilton Garden, Marriott [other] coliseum, st capitol

I-64 and I-95 run together. See I-95, exits 76-78.

187 I-95 N (exits left from eb), to Washington.

186 I-195, to Powhite Pkwy, from wb, Richmond

185b a US 33, Staples Mill Rd, Dickens Rd

183c from wb, US 250 W, Broad St, Glenside Dr N, same as exit 183

183b a US 250, Broad St E, Glenside Dr S., **N** [gas] Chevron, Sheetz [food] Bob Evans, Famous Dave's, McDonald's, Olive Garden, Pizza Hut, Taco Bell, TGIFriday's, Waffle House [lodging] Baymont Inn, Best Western, Embassy Suites, Hampton Inn, Super 8, ValuePlace [other] AutoZone, Honda, Hyundai, K-Mart, same as 181, vet, Volvo, **S** [food] Denny's, Plaza Azteca [lodging] Courtyard, Sheraton, Westin [other] [H], Home Depot, Target, to U of Richmond

181b a Parham Rd **2 mi N on Broad** [gas] BP/dsl, Citgo [food] Arby's, Bailey's Grill, Buffalo Wild Wings, Burger King, Casa Grande Mexican, Chick-fil-A, ChuckeCheese, CiCi's Pizza, Coldstone, Domino's, Friendly's, Gyros & Subs, Hooters, KFC, LoneStar Steaks, Ma Ma Wok, McDonald's, Nanking Rest., Outback Steaks, Penn Sta Subs, Piccadilly, Quaker Steak, Red Lobster, Shoney's, Starbucks, Superking Buffet, Valacino's, Wendy's, Zorba's Rest. [lodging] Country Inn&Suites, EconoLodge, Quality Inn, Rodeway Inn, Suburban Lodge [other] [H], $General, $Tree, Aamco, Acura, Audi/VW, BigLots, BMW/Mini, Books-A-Million, Cadillac, Chrysler/Dodge/Jeep, CVS Drug, Food Lion, Hancock Fabrics, Infiniti, Jo-Ann Fabrics, KIA, Marshall's, Mercedes, Merchant's Tire, NAPA, PepBoys, Scion/Toyota, Steinmart, Subaru, TJ Maxx, Tuffy Repair, Verizon, Walgreens, Exxon, Hess, Shell, Wawa

180 Gaskins Rd, **N** [gas] BP, Shell/dsl [food] Applebee's, Cracker Barrel, Golden Corral, IHOP, McDonald's, O'Charley's, Pizza Hut, Qdoba, Ruby Tuesday, Starbucks, Subway, Taco Bell, Tripp's Rest. [lodging] 7-11, East Coast, Exxon, Fairfield Inn, Holiday Inn Express, SpringHill Suites [other] $Tree, Advance Parts, AutoZone, Costco/gas, Goodyear/auto, Kroger/gas, Lowe's, Martin's Foods, Mazda, Michael's, Sam's Club/gas

RICHMOND

178b a US 250, Broad St, Short Pump, **N** [gas] 7-11, Exxon, Wawa [food] 5 Guys Burgers, BurgerWorks, Capital Alehouse, Chipotle Mexican, DQ, Firehouse Subs, Hondo's Rest., Joey's Hotdogs, Leonardo's Pizza, Moe's SW Grill, Panera Bread, Silver Diner, Starbucks [lodging] Comfort Suites, Courtyard, Extended Stay America, Hampton Inn, Hilton Garden, Homestead Suites, Hyatt Place, Marriott, Residence Inn [other] CarMax, CVS Drug, Firestone/auto, Ford, Kia, Marshall's, Ross, Verizon, **S** [gas] 7-11, Shell [food] Arby's, Bertucci's, Bonefish Grill, Buffalo Wild Wings, Burger King, Capt D's, Cheesecake Factory, Chick-fil-A, Chili's, Chipotle Mexican, Chuy's Mexican, Dave&Buster's, Domino's, Genghis Grill, HoneyBaked Ham, Jason's Deli, Jersey Mike's Subs, Jimmy John's, Kanpai, KFC, Kona Grill, LJSilver, Longhorn Steaks, Maggiano's Italian, McAlister's Deli, McDonald's, Mexico Rest., Mimi's Cafe, Olive Garden, Panera Bread, Plaza Azteca, Quiznos, Shula's Steaks, Sonic, Starbucks, Taco Bell, TGIFriday's, Wendy's [lodging] Candlewood Suites, Hilton, Wingate

178b a Continued
Inn [other] $Tree, AT&T, Barnes&Noble, Best Buy, Buick/Chevrolet/GMC, CarQuest, Crate&Barrel, Dick's, Dillard's, GNC, Hobby Lobby, Home Depot, Kohl's, Kroger, Lowe's, Macy's, Martin's Foods, Merchant's Tires, Nissan, Nordstrom, Petco, Petsmart, Radio Shack, Staples, Steinmart, Target, Tom Leonard's Mkt, Trader Joe's, Verizon, Walmart, Whole Foods Mkt, World Mkt

177 I-295, to I-95 N to Washington, to Norfolk, VA Beach, Williamsburg

175 VA 288, Chesterfield

173 VA 623, to Rockville, Manakin, **0-2 mi S** [gas] Exxon/dsl, Shell/dsl, Valero/Subway/dsl [food] BBQ, Sunset Grill [other] $General, Food Lion

169mm **[RS] both lanes, full [handicapped] facilities, litter barrels, petwalk [phone] [picnic] vending**

167 VA 617, to Goochland, Oilville, **N** [gas] Exxon/dsl, **S** [gas] BP/Bullets/dsl

159 US 522, to Goochland, Gum Spring, **N** [gas] Exxon/dsl, **S** [gas] BP/DQ/dsl, Citgo

152 VA 629, Hadensville, **1 mi S** [gas] BP, Liberty [other] repair

148 VA 605, Shannon Hill

143 VA 208, to Louisa, Ferncliff, **7 mi N** [other] Small Country Camping, **S** [gas] Citgo/dsl, Exxon/dsl

136 US 15, to Gordonsville, Zion Crossroads, **N** [gas] Sheetz/dsl [food] Arby's, IHOP, Subway [lodging] Best Western [other] Lowe's, Walmart, **S** [gas] BP/McDonald's/dsl/24hr, Exxon/Burger King/dsl, Shell/Blimpie/dsl/scales [food] Crescent Rest.

CHARLOTTESVILLE

129 VA 616, Keswick, Boyd Tavern

124 US 250, to Shadwell, **2 mi N** [gas] BP, Exxon, Hess, Shell [food] Applebee's, Burger King, Guadalajara Mexican, Hardee's, McDonald's, Quiznos, Starbucks, Taco Bell, TipTop Rest., Topeka's Steaks [lodging] Hilton Garden [other] [H], Audi/VW, BMW, CarMax, Ford, Giant Foods, KIA, Mercedes, Porsche, Rite Aid, Toyota/Scion, **S** [lodging] Comfort Inn

123mm Rivanna River

121 VA 20, to Charlottesville, Scottsville, **N** [gas] BP/Blimpie, **S** [other] KOA (10mi), to Monticello

120 VA 631, 5th St, to Charlottesville, **N** [gas] Exxon/dsl [food] Burger King, Domino's, Hardee's, Pizza Hut/Taco Bell, Waffle House [lodging] Holiday Inn, Sleep Inn [other] CVS Drug, Food Lion, vet

118b a US 29, to Lynchburg, Charlottesville, **N** [gas] BP [other] [H], services N on US 220, to UVA

114 VA 637, to Ivy

113mm **[RS] wb, full [handicapped] facilities, litter barrels, petwalk [phone] [picnic] vending**

111mm Mechum River

108mm Stockton Creek

107 US 250, Crozet, **1 mi N** [gas] Citgo, Shell/dsl, **1 mi S** [other] Misty Mtn Camping

105mm **[RS] eb, full [handicapped] facilities, litter barrels, petwalk [phone] [picnic] vending**

WAYNESBORO

104mm scenic area eb, litter barrels, no truck or buses,

100mm scenic area eb, hist marker, litter barrels, no trucks or buses,

99 US 250, to Waynesboro, Afton, **N** [lodging] Colony Motel [other] ski area, Skyline Drive, to Blue Ridge Pkwy, to Shenandoah NP, **S** [lodging] Afton Inn

96 VA 622, to Lyndhurst, Waynesboro, **3 mi N** [gas] Hess, Shell [food] Tastee Freez [lodging] Quality Inn [other] Waynesboro Camping

95mm South River

94 US 340, to Stuarts Draft, Waynesboro, **N** [gas] 7-11/dsl, Exxon/dsl [food] Applebee's, Buffalo Wild Wings, Cracker Barrel, Giovanni's Pizza, Golden Corral, KFC, King Garden, Logan's Roadhouse, Outback Steaks, Panera Bread, Plaza Azteca, Ruby

INTERSTATE 64 Cont'd

LEXINGTON

94	Continued Tuesday, Shoney's, Sonic, Starbucks, Waffle House, Wendy's Best Western, Comfort Inn, Days Inn, Holiday Inn Express, Residence Inn, Super 8 H, Home Depot, Lowe's, Martin's Food/Drug, Radio Shack, vet, Walmart, Waynesboro N 340 Camping (9mi), S Shell/dsl Chick-fil-A, McAlister's Deli, McDonald's Books-A-Million, GNC, Kohl's, Michael's, museum, Petsmart, Ross, Target, Verizon
91	Va 608, to Stuarts Draft, Fishersville, N Exxon/Subway (1mi), Shell/dsl Hampton Inn H, Eaver's Tires, S Sheetz/dsl McDonald's, Wendy's Shenadoah Acres Camping (8mi), Walnut Hills Camping (9mi)
89mm	Christians Creek
87	I-81, N to Harrisonburg, S to Roanoke
I-64 and I-81 run together 20 miles. See I-81, exits 195-220.	
55	US 11, to VA 39, N Exxon Burger King, Crystal Chinese, Naples Pizza, Ruby Tuesday, Waffle House Best Western, Sleep Inn, Super 8, Wingate Inn $Tree, Lowe's, Radio Shack, Stonewall Jackson Museum, Verizon, Walmart, S BP/DQ, Marathon/7-11/Subway Applebee's, Country Cookin, Redwood Rest. Best Western, Comfort Inn, Country Inn&Suites, Holiday Inn Express, Motel 6 Cool Spring Mkt/cafe
50	US 60, Rd 623, to Kerrs Creek, Lexington, **5 mi** S Days Inn
43	Rd 780, to Goshen
35	VA 269, Rd 850, Longdale Furnace
33mm	**truck rest area eb**
29	VA 269, VA 42 E, S Sunoco/dsl
27	US 60 W, US 220 S, VA 629, Clifton Forge, N to Douthat SP, S BP/dsl, Exxon Bella Pizza, Pizza Hut (2mi) Alleghany Highlands Arts/crafts
24	US 60, US 220, Clifton Forge, **1 mi** S Shell/dsl DQ, Hardee's, Vick's Cafe
21	to Rd 696, Low Moor, S Exxon Penny's Diner, Quiznos Oak Tree Inn H
16	US 60 W, US 220 N, to Hot Springs, Covington, N BP/Subway, Exxon/dsl, Shell Burger King, Cucci's, Mtn View Rest., Western Sizzlin Best Value Inn, Best Western, Holiday Inn Express, Pinehurst Hotel to ski area, S McDonald's Compare Inn K-Mart, Radio Shack
14	VA 154, to Hot Springs, Covington, N Exxon/Arby's, Sunoco Hong Kong Chinese, KFC, Little Caesars, LJ Silver, Subway, Wendy's $General, Advance Parts, AutoZone, CVS Drug, Family$, Food Lion, S Applebee's, China House, Petron Mexican, Trani's Grille $Tree, Walmart
10	US 60 E, VA 159 S, Callaghan, S Marathon/dsl/LP
7	Rd 661
2.5mm	**Welcome Ctr eb, full facilities, litter barrels, no trucks, petwalk**
1	Jerry's Run Trail, N to Allegheny Trail
0mm	Virginia/West Virginia state line

COVINGTON

INTERSTATE 66

Exit #	Services
77mm	Constitution Ave, to Lincoln Mem. **I-66 begins/ends in Washington, DC.**
76mm	Potomac River, T Roosevelt Memorial Bridge
75	US 50 W (from eb), to Arlington Blvd, G Wash Pkwy, I-395, US 1, S Iwo Jima Mon

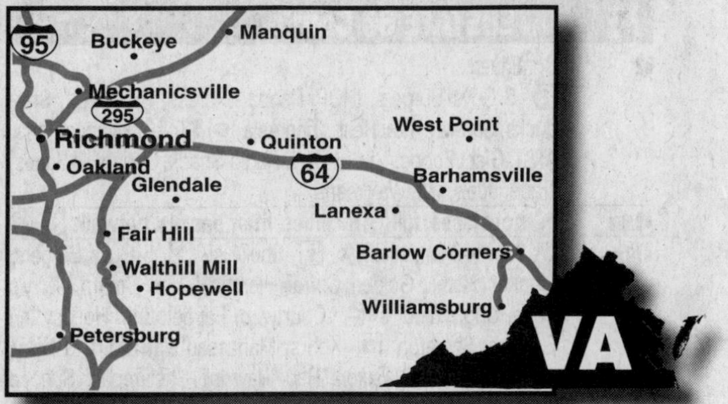

DC AREA

73	US 29, Lee Hwy, Key Bridge, to Rosslyn, N Marriott, S Holiday Inn
72	to US 29, Lee Hwy, Spout Run Pkwy (from eb, no EZ return), N Shell Virginia Inn, S Starbucks, Tarbouch Grill CVS Drug, Giant Foods, Rite Aid, Starbucks, Walgreens
71	VA 120, Glebe Rd (no EZ return from wb), N H, S Sunoco Booeymonger Grill, IHOP, Melting Pot, PF Chang's Comfort Inn, Holiday Inn
69	US 29, Sycamore St, Falls Church, N Exxon/7-11, S Rock Cafe EconoLodge
68	Westmoreland St (from eb), same as 69
67	to I-495 N (from wb), to Baltimore, Dulles
66b a	VA 7, Leesburg Pike, to Tysons Corner, Falls Church, N Exxon, Sunoco Jason's Deli, Ledo's Pizza, Olive Garden (2mi), Starbucks, Subway, Tara Thai 7-11, Trader Joe's, Whole Foods Mkt, S Citgo Baja Fresh, LJ Silver, McDonald's, Starbucks CVS Drug, Giant Foods, GNC, Kia, Staples, vet, Volvo
64b a	I-495 S, to Richmond
62	VA 243, Nutley St, to Vienna, S Citgo Chick-fil-A, Dunkin Donuts, IHOP, McDonald's, Starbucks, **1 mi S on Lee Hwy** , 7-11, Advance Parts, Chrysler/Dodge/Jeep, Citgo, CVS Drug, Harley-Davidson, Home Depot, Jeep, Liberty, Michael's, Radio Shack, Safeway Foods/gas, Shell, Subaru, Sunoco/dsl, Walgreens
60	VA 123, to Fairfax, S Exxon, Shell, Sunoco 29 Diner, Denny's, Freddy's Steakburgers, Fuddruckers, Hooters, McDonald's, Outback Steaks, Panera Bread, Papa John's, Red Lobster, Smashburger, Subway Best Western, Hampton Inn, Holiday Inn Express, Residence Inn Chevrolet, CVS Drug, Kia, Mazda, Rite Aid, Subaru, to George Mason U, Toyota/Scion
57b a	US 50, to Dulles , N Cheesecake Factory Extended Stay America, Marriott access to same as 55, JC Penney, Lord&Taylor, Macy's, mall, Sears/auto, S BP, Shell/dsl Ruby Tuesday, Wendy's Comfort Inn/rest., Courtyard, SpringHill Suites Ford, Giant Foods, Honda, K-Mart, NRA Museum, Volvo, VW, Walmart
55	Fairfax Co Pkwy, to US 29, N Exxon, Sunoco Applebees, Blue Iguana Café, Burger King, Cantina Italiana, Cooker Rest., Joe's Crabshack, Logan's Roadhouse, Malibu Grill, Olive Garden, Pizza Hut/Taco Bell, Red Robin, Sakura Japanese, Starbucks, Wendy's Hyatt Hotel, Residence Inn H, Best Buy, BJ's Whse, Bloom's Foods, GNC, Kohl's, Michael's, Petsmart, Radio Shack, Target, Walmart, Whole Foods Mkt, World Mkt, 4 Lakes Mall
53b a	VA 28, to Centreville, S same as 52, Dulles , Manassas Museum
52	US 29, to Bull Run Park, Centreville, N Sunoco/dsl Bull Run Park/RV Dump, Goodyear/auto, S Exxon, Sunoco/dsl

VA

INTERSTATE 66 Cont'd

MANASSAS

52 Continued
[food] 5 Guys Burgers, IHOP, Panda Express, Pizza Hut, Starbucks, Subway, Thai Rest., Tien Asia [other] $Tree, Advance Parts, AT&T, Giant Foods, Grand Mart, Radio Shack, SpringHill Suites, Trader Joe's, vet, Walgreens

49mm **[RS] both lanes, full [handicap] facilities, litter barrels, petwalk [phone] [picnic]**

47b a VA 234, to Manassas, N [gas] Shell/dsl [food] 5 Guys Burgers, Cracker Barrel, Golden Corral, Hershey's Ice Cream, Jerry's Subs, Uno, Wendy's [lodging] Courtyard, Fairfield Inn, Holiday Inn Express, Sheraton [other] Kohl's, Manassas Nat Bfd, Old Navy, S [gas] 7-11, BP, Exxon, RaceWay/dsl, Shell/repair, Sunoco [food] Arby's, Backyard Grill, Baja Fresh, Bob Evans, Burger King, CA Tortilla, Cafe Rio, Casa Chimayo, Checker's, Chick-fil-A, Chili's, China Jade, Chipotle Mexican, ChuckECheese's, City Grille, Coldstone, Denny's, Domino's, Don Pablo's, El Tolteca, Firehouse Subs, Great American Buffet, Hibachi Buffet, Hooters, KFC, Logan's Roadhouse, Marlin Ray's Grill, McDonald's, Olive Garden, Panda Express, Panera Bread, Papa John's, Pizza Hut, Pollo Campero, Popeye's, Potbelly's, Red Hot&Blue BBQ, Red Lobster, Starbucks, Subway, Taco Bell, TGIFriday's, Wendy's, Wok'n Roll [lodging] Best Western, Comfort Suites, Hampton Inn, Holiday Inn, Quality Inn, Red Roof Inn, Residence Inn, Super 8 [other] $Tree, Advance Parts, Aldi Foods, AT&T, AutoZone, Barnes&Noble, Best Buy, Bottom$ Foods, Buick/GMC, Burlington Coats, Chevrolet, Costco/gas, CVS Drug, Dick's, Family$, Giant Foods, Home Depot, Honda, Jo-Ann Fabrics, K-Mart, Lowe's, Macy's, Marshall's, Merchant Auto Ctr, Michael's, NTB, Office Depot, PepBoys, PetCo, Petsmart, Radio Shack, Reines RV Ctr, Ross, Sears/auto, Shopper's Foods, Staples, Toyota, Tuesday Morning, Verizon, vet, Walgreens, Walmart

44 VA 234 S, Manassas, N to Bristoe Sta Bfd SP

43b a US 29, to Warrenton, Gainesville, N [gas] WaWa, S [gas] 7-11, Sunoco/dsl, WaWa [food] 5 Guys Burgers, Burger King, Chick-fil-A, Chili's, Coldstone, Domino's, IHOP, Joe's Pizza/Subs, KFC/Pizza Hut/Taco Bell, McDonald's, Mimi's Cafe, MVP Grill, Papa John's, PeiWei, Potbelly, Qdoba, Subway, Wendy's [lodging] Hampton Inn, ValuePlace [other] Best Buy, CVS Drug, Giant Food/drug, GNC, Goodyear/auto, Lowe's, Petsmart, Target/food, Walgreens

40 US 15, Haymarket, N [other] Greenville Farms Camping, S [gas] Sheetz/dsl [food] Foster's Grill, Giuseppe's Italian, McDonald's, Papa John's, Subway, Young Chow Cafe [other] Bloom Foods, CVS Drug

31 VA 245, to Old Tavern, **1 mi** N [gas] BP [other] USPO

28 US 17 S, Marshall, N [gas] 7-11, BP/McDonald's/dsl [food] Anthony's Pizza, Foster's Grille, Great Wall Chinese, Subway [other] [H], Bloom Foods, Radio Shack, vet

27 VA 55 E, Rd 647, Marshall, **1 mi** N [gas] Citgo, Exxon/dsl/LP [food] Marshall Diner [other] IGA Foods

23 US 17 N, VA 55, Delaplane (no re-entry from eb)

20mm Goose Creek

18 VA 688, Markham

13 VA 79, to VA 55, Linden, Front Royal, S [gas] Exxon/dsl, Shell/7-11 [food] Applehouse Rest./BBQ/gifts [other] Skyline Drive, to Shenandoah NP

11mm Manassas Run

7mm Shenandoah River

6 US 340, US 522, to Winchester, Front Royal, N [gas] 7-11, Quarle's/Bullet's/dsl [food] Applebee's, Checkers, Cracker Barrel, Foster's Grille, Ledo's Pizza, Los Potrillo's, McAlister's Deli, Mikado, Panda Express, Quiznos, Starbucks, TGIFriday's, Vocelli Pizza [other] $Tree, Buick/GMC, Ford, GNC, Lowe's, PetCo, Staples, Target,

6 Continued
Walmart, S [gas] 7-11, Exxon/Dunkin Donuts, Shell [food] McDonald's [lodging] Hampton Inn [other] Poe's Southfork Camping (2mi)

1b a I-81, N to Winchester, S to Roanoke

I-66 begins/ends on I-81, exit 300.

INTERSTATE 77

WYTHEVILLE

Exit # Services

67mm Virginia/West Virginia state line, East River Mtn

66 VA 598, to East River Mtn

64 US 52, VA 61, to Rocky Gap

62 VA 606, to South Gap

62mm **Welcome Ctr sb, full [handicap] facilities, info, litter barrels, petwalk [phone] [picnic] vending**

59mm **Welcome Ctr nb, full [handicap] facilities, info, litter barrels, petwalk [phone] [picnic] vending**

58 US 52, to Bastian, E [gas] BP/Front Porch Cafe/dsl, W [gas] Marathon/Kangaroo

56mm **runaway ramp nb**

52 US 52, VA 42, Bland, E [gas] Sunoco [food] Subway [other] $General, W [gas] Kangaroo/DQ/dsl [lodging] Big Walker Motel

51.5mm **weigh sta both lanes**

48mm Big Walker Mtn

47 VA 717, **6 mi** W [other] to Deer Trail Park/NF Camping

41 VA 610, Peppers Ferry, Wytheville, E [food] Sagebrush Steaks [lodging] Best Western, Sleep Inn, Super 8, W [gas] Kangaroo/dsl/scales/24hr, TA/BP/Country Pride/Popeye's/Subway/Taco Bell/dsl/scales/24hr/ @ [food] Southern Diner [lodging] Comfort Suites, Country Inn&Suites, Fairfield Inn, Hampton Inn, Ramada Inn

40 I-81 S, to Bristol, US 52 N

I-77 and I-81 run together 9 mi. See I-81, exits 73-80.

32 I-81 N, to Roanoke

26mm New River

24 VA 69, to Poplar Camp, E [other] New River Trail Info Ctr, to Shot Tower HP, W [gas] Marathon/Kangaroo/Subway/dsl

19 VA 620, airport

14 US 58, US 221, to Hillsville, Galax, E [gas] Citgo/Subway [food] Peking Palace [lodging] Red Carpet Inn [other] [H], LakeRidge RV Resort (14mi), W [gas] BP, Exxon/dsl, Gulf/dsl/24hr [food] McDonald's, Pizza Inn, Shoney's, TCBY, Wendy's [lodging] Best Western, Comfort Inn, Hampton Inn, Holiday Inn Express, Quality Inn, Super 8 [other] Carrollwood Camping, Chevrolet

8 VA 148, VA 775, to Fancy Gap, E [gas] Gulf [food] Fancy Gap Cafe (2mi) [lodging] Lakeview Motel/rest., Mountain Top Motel [other] $General, Chance's Creek RV Ctr, to Blue Ridge Pkwy, USPO, W [gas] BP, Marathon/Kangaroo/dsl [lodging] Countryview Inn, Days Inn [other] KOA (2mi)

6.5mm **runaway truck ramp sb**

4.5mm **runaway truck ramp sb**

3mm **runaway truck ramp sb**

1 VA 620, E [gas] Loves/McDonald's/Subway/dsl/scales/24hr

.5mm **Welcome Ctr nb, full [handicap] facilities, info, litter barrels, petwalk [phone] [picnic]**

0mm Virginia/North Carolina state line

INTERSTATE 81

Exit # Services

324mm Virginia/West Virginia state line

323 Rd 669, to US 11, Whitehall, E [gas] Exxon, W [gas] FLYING J/Denny's/Subway/dsl/LP/scales/24hr

INTERSTATE 81 Cont'd

WINCHESTER

Exit #	Services
321	Rd 672, Clearbrook, E [gas] Citgo/Old Stone Cafe/dsl [food] Woolen Mills Grill
320mm	**Welcome Ctr sb, full [handicapped] facilities, litter barrels, petwalk [phone] [picnic] vending**
317	US 11, Stephenson, E [food] Chick-fil-A, Guan's Garden, Las Trancas, McDonald's, Subway, Tropical Smoothie Café, TX Roadhouse [other] AT&T, Lowe's, Petsmart, Target, Verizon, W [gas] Exxon/Dunkin Donuts/dsl, Sheetz, Shell/7-11/Burger King, Sunoco/dsl [food] Denny's, Pizza Hut/Taco Bell [lodging] Comfort Inn, EconoLodge, Holiday Inn Express (3mi) [other] [H], Candy Hill Camping
315	VA 7, Winchester, E [gas] Exxon, Sheetz/dsl [food] Bamboo Garden, Ledo's Pizza, Little Caesars, Sonic, Starbucks, Waffle House [lodging] TownePlace Suites [other] $Tree, Chrysler/Dodge/Jeep, GNC, Goodyear/auto, Martin's Foods/gas, PetCo, URGENT CARE, Walgreens, W [gas] Exxon/Dunkin Donuts/Subway, Liberty/dsl, Shell/dsl [food] 5 Guys Burgers, Apple Blossom Diner, Arby's, Camino Real Mexican, KFC, McDonald's, NIK Italian, Pizza Hut, Wendy's [lodging] Hampton Inn, Winchester Inn [other] AutoZone, CVS Drug, Family$, Food Lion, Food Maxx, Sharp Shopper Mkt, TrueValue
314mm	Abrams Creek
313	US 17/50/522, Winchester, E [gas] Exxon/Baskin-Robbins/Dunkin Donuts/Subway, Liberty/dsl, Mobil/7-11/dsl, Shell/dsl [food] Apple Valley Diner, Chinatown, Cracker Barrel, Golden Corral, Hibachi Grill, IHOP, Los Tolteco's Mexican, TX Steaks, Umberto's Pizza [lodging] Aloft Hotel, Candlewood Suites, Fairfield Inn, Holiday Inn, Red Roof Inn, Sleep Inn, Super 8, Travelodge [other] BigLots, Costco/gas, Food Lion, Jo-Ann Fabrics, Nissan, vet, W [gas] Sheetz/dsl [food] Bob Evans, Buca Italian, Chili's, China Jade, China Wok, Chipotle Mexican, ChuckECheese's, CiCi's, Coldstone, Dickey's BBQ, Five Guys, Glory Days Grill, Ichiban Japanese, Jimmy John's, KFC, Longhorn Steaks, McDonald's, Okinawa Steaks, Olive Garden, Panera Bread, Perkins, Rancho Mexican, Red Lobster, Roy Rogers, Ruby Tuesday, Subway, Taco Bell, TGIFriday's, Waffle House, Wendy's [lodging] Best Western, Hampton Inn, Hilton Garden, Wingate Inn [other] $Tree, AT&T, Belk, Best Buy, Books-A-Million, Dick's, Hobby Lobby, Home Depot, JC Penney, Kohl's, Lowe's, mall, Martin's Foods, Merchants Tire, Michael's, Old Navy, PepBoys, Petsmart, Ross, Sears/auto, Staples, Target, TJ Maxx, to Shenandoah U, URGENT CARE, Verizon, Walgreens, Walmart
310	VA 37, to US 50W, W [gas] Citgo/dsl, Shell/7-11/dsl [food] Carrabba's, McDonald's, Outback Steaks, Subway [lodging] Country Inn&Suites [other] [H], Aldi Foods, Camping World, Candy Hill Camping (6mi), CarQuest, Gander Mtn, Honda, Volvo, VW
307	VA 277, Stephens City, E [gas] Liberty/dsl, Shell/Burger King/dsl, Shell/Subway/dsl [food] Arby's, China House, Del Rio Mexican, Domino's, Ginger Asian, KFC/Taco Bell, McDonald's, Pizza Hut, Roma Italian, Waffle House, Wendy's [lodging] Comfort Inn, Holiday Inn Express [other] $General, 7-11, Advance Parts, AutoZone, Food Lion, Martin's Foods/gas, Rite Aid, Verizon, W [gas] Exxon/Dunkin Donuts, Sheetz
304mm	**weigh sta both lanes**
302	Rd 627, Middletown, E [gas] Exxon/dsl, W [gas] 7-11, Liberty/dsl [food] McDonald's [lodging] Econolodge [other] $General, to Wayside Theatre
300	I-66 E, to Washington, Shenandoah NP, Skyline Dr
298	US 11, Strausburg, E [gas] Exxon/McDonald's/dsl/LP, Shell/7-11/dsl [food] Anthony's Pizza, Arby's, Burger King, Castiglia Italian, Ciro's Pizza, Denny's, Golden China, Great Wall Buffet [lodging] Fair

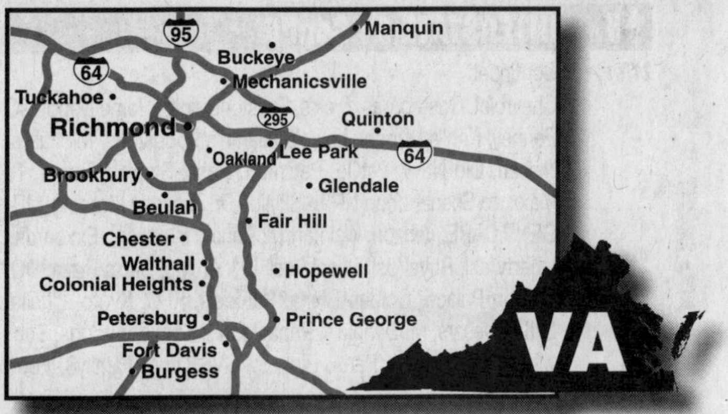

VA

HARRISONBURG

Exit #	Services
298	Continued field Inn, Ramada Inn [other] Advance Parts, Family$, Food Lion, Verizon, W [other] Battle of Cedar Grove Camping, to Belle Grove Plantation
296	US 48, VA 55, Strausburg, E [other] museums
291	Rd 651, Toms Brook, E [lodging] Budget Inn (3mi), W [gas] Loves/Arby's/dsl/scales/24hr, Pilot/DQ/Stuckey's/Subway/dsl/scales/24hr [other] truckwash/repair
283	VA 42, Woodstock, E [gas] Liberty/7-11, Sheetz, Shell/Dunkin Donuts [food] Arby's, Burger King, China Wok, KFC, Las Trancas, McDonald's, Pizza Hut, Sunrise Cafe, Taco Bell, Tony's Pizza, Wendy's [lodging] Comfort Inn, Hampton Inn, Holiday Inn Express [other] [H], CVS Drug, Family$, Food Lion, Rite Aid, to Massanutten Military Academy, W [gas] Exxon/dsl, Sunoco [food] China Wok, Cracker Barrel, Domino's, Paisano's Pizza, Subway [other] $Tree, Ford, Lowe's, NAPA Care, Radio Shack, Walmart
279	VA 185, Rd 675, Edinburg, E [gas] Exxon/dsl, Shell/dsl [food] Sal's Italian Bistro [other] auto repair, Creekside Camping (2mi), USPO
277	Rd 614, Bowmans Crossing
273	VA 292, Rd 703, Mt Jackson, E [gas] 7-11, Exxon/dsl, Liberty/dsl/scales/24hr, Sheetz/dsl/scales/24hr [food] Burger King, China King, Denny's, Italian Touch, Subway [lodging] Super 8 [other] $General, Food Lion, to Mt Jackson Hist Dist, USPO
269	Rd 730, to US 11, Shenandoah Caverns, E [gas] Shell/dsl
269mm	N Fork Shenandoah River
264	US 211, New Market, E [gas] Exxon/Subway/dsl, Liberty/dsl, Mobil/dsl, Shell/dsl [food] Appleseed's Rest., Burger King, Italian Job, McDonald's [lodging] Quality Inn [other] Endless Caverns Camping, Skyline Dr, to Shenandoah NP, W [gas] 7-11 [lodging] Days Inn [other] to New Market Bfd SHP
262mm	**[rest stop] both lanes, full [handicapped] facilities, litter barrels, petwalk [phone] [picnic] vending**
257	US 11, VA 259, to Broadway, **3-5 mi** E [gas] Liberty/7-11/Burger King/dsl [other] Endless Caverns Camping, KOA
251	US 11, Harrisonburg, W [gas] Exxon/dsl, Pilot/Subway/dsl/scales/24hr [lodging] Economy Inn
247b a	US 33, Harrisonburg, E [gas] Citgo/dsl, Exxon/dsl, Royal/dsl, Sheetz/dsl, Shell/dsl, Walmart [food] Applebee's, Aroma Buffet, Bob Evans, Bravo Italian, Bruster's, Buffalo Wild Wings, Burger King, Chick-fil-A, Chili's, Chipotle, CiCi's Pizza, Cook Out, Domino's, Dunkin Donuts, El Charro Mexican, Firehouse Subs, Five Guys, Franco's Pizza, Golden Corral, Great Wok, IHOP, Jess' Lunch, Jimmy John's, McAlister's Deli, McDonald's, O'Charley's, O'Neill's Grill, Outback Steaks, Panera Bread, Qdoba, Quaker Steak&Lube, Red Lobster, Ruby Tuesday, South Fork BBQ, Subway, Taco Bell, Tilted Kilt, TX Roadhouse, Waffle House, Wendy's, Which Wich?, Wood Grill Buffet [lodging] Best Western, Candlewood Suites, Comfort Inn, Courtyard, EconoLodge, Fairfield Inn, Hampton Inn, Holiday Inn, Motel 6, Quality Inn, Residence Inn, Sleep Inn [other] $Tree, AT&T, Barnes&Noble, Belk, Best Buy, Books-A-Million, Cadillac/

INTERSTATE 81 Cont'd

HARRISONBURG

247b a Continued
Chevrolet, Costco/gas, Dick's, Firestone/auto, Home Depot, JC Penney, Kohl's, Kroger, Lowe's, Martin's Foods/gas, Michael's, Nissan, Old Navy, PetCo, Petsmart, Ross, Staples, Target, TJ Maxx, to Shenandoah NP, to Skyline Dr, Tuesday Morning, URGENT CARE, Verizon, Walmart/McDonald's, **W** Exxon/dsl, Liberty/dsl, Royal/dsl, Sheetz/dsl Arby's, Ciro's Pizza, DQ, Dragon Palace, Golden China, Hardee's, KFC, Kyoto, L'Italia, Little Caesars, McDonald's, Papa John's, Sam's Hotdogs, Subway Advance Parts, BigLots, CVS Drug, Family$, Food Lion, URGENT CARE

245 VA 659, Port Republic Rd, **E** Campus Corner, Exxon/dsl, Liberty/dsl, Royal/dsl China Express, Corgan's Publick House, El Charro, McDonald's, Subway, Tropical Smoothie, Vito's Italian Days Inn H, CVS Drug, Food Lion, **W** Asian City, Jimmy John's, Starbucks to James Madison U

243 US 11, to Harrisonburg, **0-2 mi W** Exxon/dsl, Harrisonburg Travel Ctr/diner/dsl/scales, Liberty, Sheetz/dsl, Shell/7-11/dsl Burger King, Cracker Barrel, Griddle&Grill, McDonald's, Pano's Rest., Pizza Hut, Subway, Taco Bell Country Inn Suites, Hampton Inn, Holiday Inn Express, Microtel, Motel 6, Ramada Inn, Super 8 $General, Advance Parts, AutoZone, CarMax, Family$, Ford, Honda, Hyundai, Kia, Lincoln, Subaru, Toyota/Scion, USPO

240 VA 257, Rd 682, Mount Crawford, **E** Shell/7-11/dsl McDonald's, **W** Exxon/Burger King/dsl (1mi)

235 VA 256, Weyers Cave, **E** Shell/dsl, **W** BP/Subway/dsl, Exxon/dsl Freightliner, to Grand Caverns

232mm **both lanes, full facilities, litter barrels, petwalk vending**

STAUNTON

227 Rd 612, Verona, **E** BP/Subway/dsl Waffle Inn, **W** 7-11/Wendy's, Exxon, Shell/dsl Burger King, Ciro's Pizza, Hardee's, McDonald's Knights Inn $General, antiques, Food Lion, Good Sam RV Park (3mi), Rite Aid

225 VA 262, Woodrow Wilson Pkwy, **E** Motel 6, **W** Days Inn, Holiday Inn/rest.

222 US 250, Staunton, **E** BP, Royal/dsl Cracker Barrel, Hometown Grill, McDonald's, Mrs Rowe's Rest., TX Steaks Best Western, Red Roof Inn, Sleep Inn, **W** Hess/dsl, Sheetz Baskin-Robbins/Dunkin Donuts, Burger King, Chili's, Country Cookin, Firehouse Subs, KFC, Massaki Japanese, Pizza Hut, Starbucks, Waffle House Comfort Inn, EconoLodge American Frontier Culture Museum, AT&T, auto repair, AutoZone, Lowe's, Martin's Foods/gas, Toyota/Scion, URGENT CARE, Walmart/Subway

221 I-64 E, to Charlottesville, Skyline Dr, Shenandoah NP

220 VA 262, to US 11, Staunton, **1 mi W** Citgo, Exxon, Shell A&W/LJ Silver, Applebee's, Arby's, Burger King, CiCi's Pizza, El Puerto, Jimmy John's, Kathy's Rest., Kline's Dairy Bar, Maria's Italian, McDonald's, Papa John's, Red Lobster, Sam's HotDogs, Sauced Grill, Subway, Taco Bell, Wendy's Budget Inn, Hampton Inn $General, $Tree, Advance Parts, Belk, Buick/GMC, Cadillac/Chevrolet, Chrysler/Dodge/Jeep, CVS Drug, Food Lion, Ford/Lincoln, Harley-Davidson, Honda, Hyundai, JC Penney, Kia/Mazda, Kroger/dsl, Merchant's Tire/auto, Nissan, Obaugh RV Ctr, Petco, Staples, Subaru, TJ Maxx, Verizon, vet, VW

217 Rd 654, to Mint Spring, Stuarts Draft, **E** BP/Subway/dsl Days Inn, **W** Liberty/LP, Marathon/Kangaroo/dsl/24hr Relax Inn KOA

213b a US 11, US 340, Greenville, **E** BP/Subway, Pilot/Arby's/scales/dsl/24hr, Shell Edelweiss Rest. Hometown Inn KOA (3mi)

205 Rd 606, Raphine, **E** Fuel City/Smiley's BBQ/dsl/24hr, Petro/Exxon/Burger King/dsl/scales/24hr/ @, Sunoco/dsl Blue Beacon, **W** Pilot/Wendy's/dsl/scales/24hr Comfort Inn/rest. Peterbilt

200 Rd 710, Fairfield, **E** BP/McDonald's/dsl, Pure Frank's Pizza, **W** Exxon/Subway/dsl, Shell/dsl

199mm **sb, full facilities, litter barrels, petwalk vending**

LEXINGTON

195 US 11, Lee Hwy, **E** Maple Hall Country Inn, **W** Exxon/dsl, TA/Shell/Berky's Rest./dsl/scales/24hr/ @ Days Inn, Howard Johnson, Quality Inn Lee-Hi Camping, repair

191 I-64 W (exits left from nb), US 60, to Charleston

188b a US 60, to Lexington, Buena Vista, **3-5 mi E** BP, Exxon Burger King, Hardee's Buena Vista Inn H, $General, Family$, Food Lion, Marshall Museum, to Blue Ridge Pkwy, to Glen Maury Park, to Stonewall Jackson Home, **W** Exxon/dsl to Washington&Lee U, VMI

180 US 11, Natural Bridge, **E** Relax Inn Cave Mtn NF, Jellystone Camping, **W** Shell/dsl Pink Cadillac Diner Budget Inn (180a exits left from sb), KOA

175 US 11 N, to Glasgow, Natural Bridge, **E** Exxon Natural Bridge Hotel/rest. (2mi) Jellystone Camping (6.5mi), to James River RA

168 VA 614, US 11, Blue Ridge Pkwy, Arcadia, **E** Shell/dsl Mtn View Rest. Wattstull Inn Middle Creek Camping (6mi), **2 mi W** Exxon Burger King, Rancho Veijo

167 US 11 (from sb), Buchanan

162 US 11, Buchanan, **E** Exxon/dsl to BR Pkwy, **W** Citgo/Subway

158mm **sb, full facilities, litter barrels, petwalk vending**

156 Rd 640, to US 11, **E** Exxon/Brugh's Mill/dsl

150 US 11/220, to Fincastle, **E** Dodge's/dsl, Marathon/Kangaroo/dsl/24hr, Pilot/Subway/dsl/24hr, TA/BP/Country Pride/dsl/scales/24hr/ @ Bella Pizza, Country Cookin, Cracker Barrel, Hardee's, McDonald's, Shoney's, Taco Bell, Waffle House Comfort Inn, Holiday Inn Express, Quality Inn, Red Roof Inn, Travelodge $General Mkt, Berglund RV Ctr, truckwash, **W** BP/dsl, Exxon/dsl, Sunoco 3 Lil Pigs BBQ, Bojangles, Little Caesars, Pizza Hut, Rancho Viejo Mexican, Three Lil' Pigs BBQ, Wendy's Howard Johnson, Super 8 Kroger/dsl, Verizon, vet

149mm **weigh sta both lanes**

ROANOKE

146 VA 115, Cloverdale, **E** BP/dsl, Exxon, Shell/dsl El Rodeo Mexican, Hardees, McDonald's, Subway Country Inn&Suites, Days Inn/rest., Fairfield Inn, Hampton Inn Camping World, CVS, Gander Mtn, to Hollins U

143 I-581, US 220, to Roanoke, Blue Ridge Pkwy (exits left from sb), **1 mi E** Kroger/dsl El Toreo, Subway, Waffle House Howard Johnson, Motel 6, Quality Inn, Super 8 Honda, **2-3 mi E on Hershberger** Abuelo's Mexican, Applebee's, Buffalo Wild Wings, Carrabba's, Cheddar's, Chick-fil-A, Hardee's, IHOP, Logan's Roadhouse, Longhorn Steaks, O'Charley's, Olive Garden, Panera Bread, Penn Sta Subs, Red Palace Chinese, Red Robin, Ruby Tuesday, Shaker's, Smokey Bones BBQ, Starbucks, TGIFriday's, Zaxby's Best Western, Comfort Inn, Courtyard, Extended Stay America, Hampton Inn, Holiday Inn, Hyatt Place, MainStay Suites, Residence Inn, Sheraton $Tree, AT&T, Barnes&Noble, Belk, Best Buy, BigLots, Dick's, Exxon, Home Depot, JC Penney, Macy's, mall, Murphy USA/dsl,

INTERSTATE 81 Cont'd

SALEM

143 Continued
NTB, Old Navy, Petsmart, Sears/auto, Shell, Staples, Target, U-Haul, Verizon, Walmart

141 VA 419, Salem, **E** BP, Liberty/7-11/dsl, Marathon/Burger King Hardee's, IHOP, Starbucks Baymont Inn, Days Inn, Holiday Inn Express, La Quinta H, Chevrolet, GNC, Kroger/gas, **W** BP/Subway/dsl, Citgo Subway

140 VA 311, Salem, **1 mi E** Mac&Bob's Cafe, **1 mi W** BP/Subway/dsl, Citgo Billy's Barn Rest., Hanging Rock Grill/golf

137 VA 112, VA 619, Salem, **E** BP, Citgo/dsl, Exxon/dsl, Go-Mart, Marathon, Sheetz/dsl Anthony's Cafe, Applebees, Arby's, Bojangles, Burger King, Chick-fil-A, Denny's, Dynasty Buffet, El Rodeo Mexican, Firehouse Subs, Hardee's, Jimmy John's, K&W Cafeteria, KFC, Mamma Maria Italian, McDonald's, Omelette Shoppe, Pizza Hut, Quiznos, Rancho Viejo, Starbucks, Subway, Taco Bell, Tokyo Express, Wendy's, Zaxby's Comfort Suites, Quality Inn, Stay At Inn, Super 8 $General, $Tree, Aamco, Advance Parts, AutoZone, BigLots, Food Lion, Goodyear, K-Mart, Kroger/dsl, Lowe's, Merchant's Tire, O'Reilly Parts, Snyder's RV, Verizon, vet, Walgreens, Walmart/Subway, **W** Holiday Inn, Howard Johnson

132 VA 647, to Dixie Caverns, **E** Citgo/dsl, Shell (2mi) Blue Jay Hotel Dixie Caverns Camping, st police

129mm **nb, full facilities, litter barrels, petwalk vending**

128 US 11, VA 603, Ironto, **E** Shell, **W** Exxon/Dixie's/Subway/dsl/24hr

118c b a US 11/460, Christiansburg, **E** Shell/dsl Cracker Barrel, Denny's Days Inn, Fairfield Inn, Holiday Inn Express, Quality Inn, Super 8, **W** Exxon/dsl, Liberty/7-11/dsl, Shell Country Cookin, Hardee's, LJ Silver, McDonald's, Pizza Hut, Ruby Tuesday, Waffle House, Wendy's EconoLodge, Shayona Inn H, $General, Advance Parts, Chevrolet, Chrysler/Dodge/Jeep, Food Lion, Ford, Honda, Hyundai, Kia, Subaru, to VA Tech, Toyota/Scion

114 VA 8, Christiansburg, **E** to Blue Ridge Pkwy, **0-1 mi W** Citgo/dsl Burger King, Pizza Inn, Subway Budget Inn $General Mkt, tires, USPO

109 VA 177, VA 600, **E** H, **0-2 mi W** Marathon, Sunoco/dsl Best Western, Comfort Inn, La Quinta, Super 8 (2mi) Buick/Cadillac/Chevrolet

107mm **both lanes, full facilities, litter barrels, petwalk vending**

105 VA 232, Rd 605, to Radford, **2-4 mi W** Citgo, Marathon/dsl Sal's Italian Executive Motel museum

101 Rd 660, to Claytor Lake SP, **E** Claytor Lake Inn, Sleep Inn repair, **W** Marathon/DQ/dsl, Shell/Omelette Shoppe/Taco Bell/dsl/scales/ @

98 VA 100 N, to Dublin, **E** Exxon/Subway/dsl, Marathon Bojangles, Shoney's Hampton Inn, Holiday Inn Express, Quality Inn, **W** Liberty/Blimpie/dsl, Marathon/dsl Arby's, Burger King, El Ranchero Mexican, Fatz Cafe, McDonald's, Subway, Waffle House, Wendy's Super 8 $General, NAPA, O'Reilly Parts, to Wilderness Rd Museum, vet, Walmart/Subway

94b a VA 99 N, to Pulaski, **0-3 mi W** BP, Exxon/dsl, Hess China Wall, Compadre's Mexican, Domino's, Hardee's, KFC, Kimono Japanese, Little Caesars, McDonald's, Pizza Hut, Sonic, Subway, Taco Bell, Wendy's H, $General, Advance Parts, CVS, Family$, Food Lion, Goodyear/auto, O'Reilly Parts, Rite Aid

92 Rd 658, to Draper, **E** BP to New River Trail SP

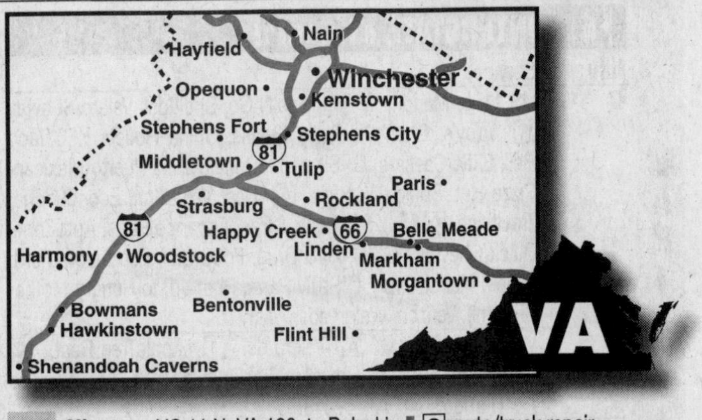

WYTHEVILLE

89b a US 11 N, VA 100, to Pulaski, **E** auto/truck repair

86 Rd 618, Service Rd, **W** Sunoco/Appletree Rest./dsl repair

84 Rd 619, to Grahams Forge, **W** Kangaroo/DQ/dsl/24hr, Loves/Chester Fried/Subway/dsl/scales/24hr Josey's Cafe Fox Mtn Inn, Trail Motel

81 I-77 S, to Charlotte, to Blue Ridge Pkwy. I-81 S and I-77 N run together 9 mi., Galax

80 US 52 S, VA 121 N, to Ft Chiswell, **E** FLYING J/Denny's/dsl/scales/24hr/ @, BP/Burger King/dsl Wendy's Hampton Inn, Super 8 Blue Beacon, Ft Chiswell RV Park, NAPA, **W** Marathon/dsl, Valero Judy's Diner, McDonald's Comfort Inn Speedco

77 Service Rd, **E** FLYING J/Denny's/dsl/scales/LP/RV Dump/24hr, Marathon/Subway/dsl/24hr, Wilco/Hess/dsl/LP Burger King KOA, **W** Exxon/dsl, Pilot/Arby's/DQ/dsl/scales/24hr IA 80 Truck'o Mat Truckwash, st police

73 US 11 S, Wytheville, **E** Go-Mart, Kangaroo/dsl Applebee's, Bob Evans, Cracker Barrel, El Puerto Mexican, Hardee's, LJ Silver, Papa John's, Peking Chinese, Shoney's, Smokey's BBQ, Sonic, The Ville Rest., Waffle House, Wendy's Best Value Inn, Budget Host, Days Inn, EconoLodge, Holiday Inn Express, Kingston Inn, La Quinta, Motel 6, Quality Inn, Red Roof Inn H, $General, AutoZone, Buick/Chevrolet/GMC, CVS Drug, Food Lion, Ford, Goodyear/auto, Harley-Davidson, K-Mart, Nissan, Rite Aid

I-81 N and I-77 S run together 9 mi.

72 I-77 N, to Bluefield, **1 mi N, I-77 exit 41 E** Sagebrush Steaks Best Western, Sleep Inn, Super 8, **1 mi N, I-77 exit 41 W** Kangaroo/dsl/24hr, TA/Country Pride/Popeye's/Subway/Taco Bell/dsl/scales/24hr/ @ Southern Diner Comfort Suites, Country Inn&Suites, Fairfield Inn, Hampton Inn, Ramada/rest.

70 US 21/52, Wytheville, **E** BP/dsl, Sheetz/dsl Bojangles, China Wok, El Patio Mexican, KFC/Taco Bell, Little Caesars, McDonald's, Ruby Tuesday, Starbucks, Subway, Tokyo Japanese, Wendy's H, $Tree, AT&T, Food Lion, GNC, Lowe's, PetCo, Verizon, Walmart/Subway, **W** Kangaroo Comfort Inn

67 US 11 (from nb, no re-entry), to Wytheville

61mm **nb, full facilities, litter barrels, No Trucks, petwalk vending**

60 VA 90, Rural Retreat, **E** Shell/dsl Dutch Pantry, McDonald's $General, camping, to Rural Retreat Lake

54 Rd 683, to Groseclose, **E** Exxon, Sunoco/dsl The Barn Rest. Relax Inn Settler's Museum

53.5mm **sb, full facilities, litter barrels, petwalk vending**

50 US 11, Atkins, **W** Exxon, Marathon/Subway/dsl/24hr Comfort Inn NAPA Care

VA

⬆N INTERSTATE 81 Cont'd

Exit #	Services
47	US 11, to Marion, **W** 🅖 Gas'N Go, Shell/dsl, Valero/Subway 🍴 Arby's, Charley's Philly Steaks, China House, KFC/Taco Bell, Little Caesars, LJ Silver, McDonald's, Mi Puerto Mexican, Pizza Hut, Sonic, Wendy's 🛏 Best Value Inn, EconoLodge, Travel Inn 🅞 🅷, $General, $Tree, Advance Parts, AutoZone, Buick/Chevrolet/GMC, CVS Drug, Food City, Food Lion, Ford, Ingles, Marion Drug, O'Reilly Parts, Rite Aid, to Hungry Mother SP (4mi), Verizon, Walgreens, Walmart
45	VA 16, Marion, **E** 🅖 Valero/dsl 🍴 AppleTree Rest. 🅞 Mt Rogers NRA, to Grayson Highlands SP, **W** 🅖 Sunoco 🍴 Hardee's 🅞 NAPA, USPO
44	US 11, Marion, **W** 🅞 $General, Vet
39	US 11, Rd 645, Seven Mile Ford, **W** 🅞 Interstate Camping
35	VA 107, Chilhowie, **E** 🍴 Chilhowie Pizza, Hardees 🛏 Knights Inn, **W** 🅖 Exxon/dsl, Gas'N Go, Mobil/Main St Mkt, Shell/dsl 🍴 McDonald's, Riverfront Rest., Subway, Taco Bell 🛏 Budget Inn (1mi) 🅞 $General, Food City, Greever's Drugs, USPO
32	US 11, to Chilhowie
29	VA 91, to Damascus, Glade Spring, **E** 🅖 Marathon/Subway/dsl, Petro/Iron Skillet/dsl/24hr/ @, Valero/Wendy's 🍴 Giardino's Italian, Pizza+ 🛏 EconoLodge, Knights Inn 🅞 $General, Peterbilt, **W** 🅖 Exxon, Shell/dsl, Spirit 🍴 El Burrito Loco 🅞 CarQuest, vet
26	Rd 737, Emory, **W** 🍴 Macado's (1mi) 🅞 to Emory&Henry Coll, USPO (1mi)
24	VA 80, Meadowview Rd, **W** 🅞 auto/truck repair
22	Rd 704, Enterprise Rd, **E** 🅖 Brown's Pantry/dsl 🅞 🅷
19	US 11/58, to Abingdon, **E** 🅖 Shell/Subway/Dunkin Donuts/dsl 🍴 DQ, McDonald's, Pizza+ 🅞 Lowe's, to Mt Rogers NRA, URGENT CARE, vet, **W** 🅖 BP/dsl, Citgo/Huddle House, Exxon/dsl 🍴 Bella's Pizza, Burger King, Cracker Barrel, Harbor House Seafood, Pita's, Wendy's 🛏 Alpine Motel, Best Value Inn, Holiday Inn Express, Quality Inn 🅞 $General
17	US 58A, VA 75, Abingdon, **E** 🅖 Mobil/dsl 🍴 Domino's, LJ Silver 🛏 Hampton Inn, **W** 🅖 Exxon, Gas'n Go 🍴 Arby's, Charley's Subs, China Wok, Hardee's, Little Caesar's, Los Arcos, McDonald's, Papa John's, Pizza Hut, Shoney's, Subway, Taco Bell, Wendy's 🛏 Super 8 🅞 🅷, Advance Parts, Food City, GNC, K-Mart, Kroger/dsl, Radio Shack
14	US 19, VA 140, Abingdon, **W** 🅖 BP/dsl, Exxon, Shell/dsl 🍴 McDonald's, Milano's Italian, Moon Dog Cafe, Subway 🛏 Comfort Inn, Comfort Suites 🅞 Chevrolet, Ford/Lincoln, Riverside Camping (10mi)
13.5mm	🅡ˢ nb, full 🚻 facilities, litter barrels 🅒 🔌 vending, Truckers Only
13	VA 611, to Lee Hwy, **W** 🅖 Shell/dsl 🅞 Kenworth, Mack, Volvo
10	US 11/19, Lee Hwy, **W** 🅖 Exxon, Shell/dsl 🛏 Deluxe Inn, Economy Inn, Evergreen Inn, Red Carpet Inn
7	Old Airiport Rd, **E** 🅖 Shell/dsl 🍴 Bojangles, Cheddar's, Cracker Barrel, Sonic 🛏 Baymont Inn, Hilton Garden, **W** 🅖 Marathon, Sunoco/Wendy's, Valero/dsl 🍴 Chick-fil-A, Chili's, Cook-Out, Domino's, DQ, El Patio Mexican, Five Guys, Golden Corral, IHOP, Jersey Mike's Subs, Kobe Japanese, Logan's Roadhouse, Los Arcos, Mellow Mushroom, O'Charley's, Olive Garden, Outback Steaks, Pal's Drive-In, Perkins, Pizza Hut, Red Lobster, Ruby Tuesday, Salsarita's, Starbucks, Subway, Taco Bell 🛏 Courtyard, Holiday Inn, Motel 6, Quality Inn 🅞 $General, $Tree, Advance Parts, AutoZone, Best Buy, Books-A-Million, Food City/gas, Home Depot, Lowe's, Office Depot,

M A R I O N

A B I N G D O N

Exit #	Services
7	Continued Old Navy, Petsmart, Ross, Sam's Club/gas, Sugar Hollow Camping, Target, TJ Maxx, Tuesday Morning, Verizon, Walmart
5	US 11/19, Lee Hwy, **E** 🅖 Shell 🍴 Arby's, Burger King, Hardee's, KFC, LJ Silver, McDonald's, Shoney's 🛏 Budget Inn, Travel Inn 🅞 Family$, Harley-Davidson, Price Less Foods, USPO, **W** 🅖 Exxon/dsl 🛏 Comfort Inn 🅞 Buick/GMC, Cabela's, Kings Tire
3	I-381 S, to Bristol, **1 mi E** 🅖 Shell/dsl, Zoomers/dsl 🍴 Applebee's, Arby's, Krystal 🛏 EconoLodge
1b a	US 58/421, Bristol, **1 mi E** 🅖 5 Mart/dsl, Exxon/dsl, Shell 🍴 Burger King, Capt D's, Chinese Family Buffet, KFC, McDonald's, Pizza Hut, Sonic, Subway, Taco Bell, Wendy's 🛏 Knights Inn 🅞 🅷, Chrysler/Dodge/Jeep, CVS Drug, Family$, K-Mart, Kroger/dsl, Sears/auto, Toyota/Scion, UHaul, URGENT CARE, Verizon, vet, Walgreens
0mm	Virginia/Tennessee state line **Welcome Ctr nb, full** 🚻 **facilities, info, litter barrels, petwalk** 🅒 🔌 **vending No Trucks,**

⬆N INTERSTATE 85

Exit #	Services
	I-85 begins/ends on I-95.
69	US 301, I-95 N, Wythe St, Washington St, Petersburg
68	I-95 S, US 460 E, to Norfolk, Crater Rd
65	Squirrel Level Rd, **E** 🅞 to Richard Bland Coll, **W** 🅖 BP
63b a	US 1, to Petersburg, **E** 🅖 Chubby's/dsl, Exxon/KFC/dsl, Shell 🍴 Burger King/dsl 🍴 Hardee's, Waffle House 🛏 Holiday Inn Express, **W** 🅖 BP 🍴 McDonald's
61	US 460, to Blackstone, **E** 🅖 EastCoast/Subway/dsl/LP/e85 🍴 Huddle House, **W** 🍴 Giuseppe's Pizza 🅞 airport, auto repair
55mm	🅡ˢ both lanes, full 🚻 facilities, litter barrels, petwalk 🅒 🔌 vending
53	VA 703, Dinwiddie, **W** 🅖 Exxon/dsl 🍴 Fats BBQ 🅞 to 5 Forks Nat Bfd
52mm	Stony Creek
48	VA 650, DeWitt
42	VA 40, McKenney, **W** 🅖 Citgo, Exxon 🅞 auto repair
40mm	Nottoway River
39	VA 712, to Rawlings, **W** 🅖 Davis TC/Exxon/Dunkin Donuts/Subway/dsl/scales/24hr, Racine 🛏 Nottoway Motel/rest.
34	VA 630, Warfield, **W** 🅖 Exxon/dsl
32mm	🅡ˢ both lanes, full 🚻 facilities, litter barrels, petwalk 🅒 🔌 vending
28	US 1, Alberta, **W** 🅖 Exxon 🅞 Family Dollar
27	VA 46, to Lawrenceville, **E** 🅞 to St Paul's Coll
24	VA 644, to Meredithville
22mm	weigh sta both lanes
20mm	Meherrin River
15	US 1, to South Hill, **E** 🅖 Citgo, **W** 🅖 Loves/Subway/McDonald's/dsl/scales/24hr, Valero/dsl 🍴 Kahill's Rest.
12	US 58, VA 47, to South Hill, **E** 🅖 BP/Quizno's/Stucky's/dsl, RaceWay, Shell/dsl 🍴 Applebee's, Arby's, Bojangles, Domino's, Glass House Grill, Sonic 🛏 Best Western, Comfort Inn, Fairfield Inn, Hampton Inn 🅞 $Tree, Verizon, Walmart/Subway, **W** 🅖 Exxon/dsl, Kangaroo/dsl 🍴 Brian's Steaks, Burger King, Cracker Barrel, Down Home Buffet, Hardee's, KFC/Taco Bell, McDonald's, New China, Pizza Hut, Subway, Wendy's 🛏 Quality Inn 🅞 🅷, $General, AutoZone, CVS Drug, Family$, Food Lion, Home Depot, Roses

P E T E R S B U R G

S O U T H H I L L

INTERSTATE 85 Cont'd

Exit #	Services
4	VA 903, to Bracey, Lake Gaston, E BP/Subway/dsl, Exxon/Simmon's/dsl/scales/24hr/ @ Huddle House, K St. Café Americamps Camping (5mi), W Shell/Pizza Hut/Quizno's Lake Gaston Inn
3mm	Lake Gaston
1mm	**Welcome Ctr nb, full facilities, litter barrels, petwalk vending**
0mm	Virginia/North Carolina state line

INTERSTATE 95

DC AREA

Exit #	Services
178mm	Virginia/Maryland state line, Potomac River, W Wilson Mem Br
177c b a	US 1, to Alexandria, Ft Belvoir, E Great American Steaks Budget Host, Hampton Inn, Red Roof Inn, Relax Inn Chevrolet, Chrysler/Dodge/Jeep, W Hess, Liberty/repair
176b a	VA 241, Telegraph Rd, E Hess/dsl, W Courtyard, Holiday Inn, Homestead Suites Staples
174	Eisenhower Ave Connector, to Alexandria
173	Rd 613, Van Dorn St, to Franconia, E Comfort Inn, **1 mi** W Exxon, Shell Dunkin Donuts, Jerry's Subs, McDonald's, Quizno's, Red Lobster Aamco, Giant Foods, NTB
170a	I-495 N, **I-495 & I-95 N run together to MD, to Rockville**
170b	I-395 N, to Washington
169b a	Rd 644, Springfield, Franconia, E Bertucci's, Dunkin Donuts, Houlihan's, Silver Diner, Starbucks, Subway, TGIFriday's Best Western, Comfort Inn, Courtyard, Extended Stay America, Hampton Inn, Hilton H, AT&T, Barnes&Noble, Best Buy, Dick's, Firestone/auto, Ford, Home Depot, JC Penney, Macy's, mall, Michael's, Nissan, Old Navy, Petsmart, Staples, Subaru, Target, W BP, Shell, Sunoco 5 Guys Burgers, Blue Pearl Buffet, Chick-fil-A, Chipotle Mexican, Deliah's Grill, Domino's, Dunkin Donuts, Hard Times Cafe, KFC, McDonald's, Noodles&Co, Outback Steaks, Panda Express, Popeye's, Starbucks, Subway Holiday Inn Express, Homewood Suites, Motel 6, Residence Inn, TownePlace Suites 7-11, Advance Parts, CarQuest, Chrysler/Dodge/Jeep, CVS Drug, Giant Foods, GNC, Goodyear/auto, K-Mart, Mr Tire, Radio Shack, Toyota/Scion, Trader Joe's, USPO, Verizon, vet, VW
167	VA 617, Backlick Rd (from sb), W InterFuel/dsl
166b a	VA 7100, Newington, to Ft Belvoir, E Pkwy Express Wendy's Embassy Suites NTB, Toyota/Scion, U-Haul, W Exxon/7-11/dsl McDonald's Costco
163	VA 642, Lorton, E Shell/repair, Sunoco/dsl auto repair, W Shell/dsl Antoneli's Pizza, Burger King, Gunston Wok, Kabob Factory Rest. Comfort Inn
161	US 1 S (exits left from sb, no reentry nb), to Ft Belvoir, Mt Vernon, Woodlawn Plantation, Gunston Hall
160.5mm	Occoquan River
160b a	VA 123 N, Woodbridge, Occoquan, E Sunoco Taco Bell Hampton Inn, Quality Inn Aldi Foods, Food Lion, Mr Transmissions, W Exxon/repair/dsl, Fast Fuels, Shell/dsl KFC, Madigan's Waterfront Rest., McDonald's, VA Grill, Wendy's 7-11, same as 161
158b a	VA 294, Prince William Pkwy, Woodbridge, W 7-11, Exxon, Shell, Sunoco/dsl Bonefish Grill, Boston Mkt, Bungalow Alehouse, Chick-fil-A, Chipotle Mexican, ChuckeCheese, Coldstone, Famous Dave's BBQ, Firehouse Subs, Hooters, IHOP, Macaroni Grill, McDonald's, Noodles&Co, Old Country Buffet, On-the-Border, Panda Express, Panera Bread, Qdoba, Red

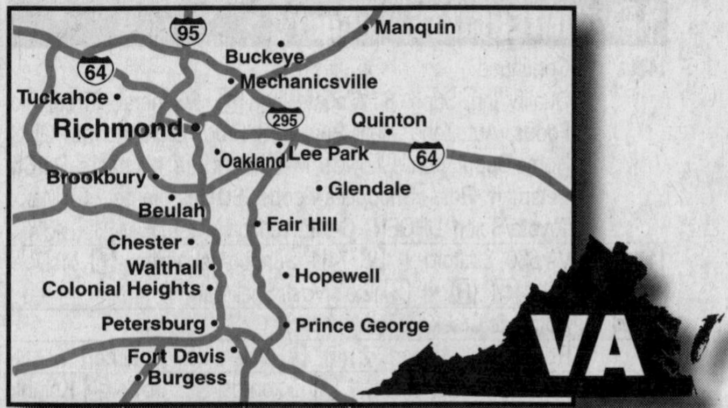

VA

DUMFRIES

Exit #	Services
158b a	Continued Lobster, Red Robin, Smokey Bones BBQ, Starbucks, Taco Bell, TGIFriday's, Wendy's Country Inn&Suites, Courtyard, Fairfield Inn, Holiday Inn Express, Residence Inn, SpringHill Suites $Tree, Advance Parts, Best Buy, CarMax, Dick's, GNC, JC Penney, Lowe's, Michael's, Office Depot, Petsmart, Sam's Club/gas, Shopper's Foods, Target, Verizon, Walmart/Subway
156	VA 784, Potomac Mills, E Brixx Woodfired Grill, Firebirds Grill, PF Chang's, Potbelly, Starbucks, Travinia Italian, Uncle Julio's Grill, Zoe's Kitchen Hilton Garden, Homewood Suites H, AT&T, Old Navy, REI, to Leesylvania SP, Wegman's Mkt, W Mobil/dsl, Shell/dsl, Sunoco/dsl Bahama Breeze, Bob Evans, Bobby's Burger, Buffalo Wild Wings, Burger King, Char Broil Grill, Cheesecake Factory, Chili's, China King Buffet, Denny's, Domino's, DQ, Guapo's, Hard Times Cafe, Los Amigos, McDonald's, Olive Garden, Outback Steaks, Paisano's, Popeye's, Sakura Japanese, Silver Diner, Subway, Wendy's Best Western, Wytestone Suites Costco/gas, Family$, Firestone/auto, IKEA, Jo-Ann Fabrics, K-Mart, Marshalls, Nordstrom Rack, NTB, Potomac Mills Outlets/Famous Brands, Staples, Tuesday Morning, U-Haul, vet
154mm	**/weigh sta both lanes**
152	VA 234, Dumfries, to Manassas, E BP/dsl, Express, Exxon/dsl, Shell/dsl, Valero/Subway Applebee's, China One, KFC, McDonald's, Ruby Tuesday, Taco Bell Sleep Inn, Super 8 7-11, Food Lion, Meineke, NAPA Autocare, Walmart, Weems-Botts Museum, W 7-11, Exxon Asian Pan, Chick-fil-A, Cracker Barrel, Five Guys, IHOP, Jerry's Subs, MontClair Rest., Panera Bread, Starbucks, Subway, Tiziano Italian, Waffle House Comfort Inn, Days Inn, EconoLodge, Hampton Inn, Holiday Inn AT&T, Prince William Camping, Rite Aid, Shoppers Foods, Target, URGENT CARE
150	VA 619, Quantico, to Triangle, E Dunkin Donuts, McDonald's Ramada Inn 7-11, to Marine Corps Base, W Prince William Forest Park
148	to Quantico, (2mi) E Gulf/dsl Subway Courtyard to Marine Corps Base
143b a	to US 1, VA 610, Aquia, E 7-11, Exxon/Circle K/dsl, Valero Carlos O'Kelly's, El Gran Charro, KFC, McDonald's, Mick's Rest., Papa John's, Pizza Hut, Ruby Tuesday, Subway Best Western, Fairfield Inn, Hampton Inn, Staybridge Suites, Suburban Extended Stay, Towne Place Suites Aquia Pines Camping, Nissan, Rite Aid, Tires+, W 7-11, Exxon/dsl, Kangaroo, WaWa 5 Guys Burgers, Applebee's, Baskin-Robbins/Dunkin Donuts, Bob Evans, Buffalo Wild Wings, Burger King, Chick-fil-A, Chili's, China Wok, CiCi's, Firehouse Subs, Hardee's, Hibachi Buffet, IHOP, Jersey Mike's, Jimmy the Greek, Kobe Japanese, Little Caesar's, McDonald's, Moe's SW Grill, Outback Steaks, Pancho Villa, Panera Bread, Popeye's, Starbucks, Taco Bell, Umi Japanese, Wendy's Comfort Inn, Country Inn&Suites,

= gas = food = lodging = other = rest stop

INTERSTATE 95 Cont'd

143b a Continued
Quality Inn, Super 8, Wingate Inn [O] $General, $Tree, Aldi Foods, AutoZone, Best Buy, CVS Drug, Giant Foods, GNC, Home Depot, Kohl's, Lowe's, Merchant's Tire, Michael's, PetCo, Petsmart, Ross, Shopper's Foods, Staples, Target, TJ Maxx, Toyota/Scion, URGENT CARE, Verizon, Walmart/McDonald's

140 VA 630, Stafford, E [gas] 7-11, Sunoco/dsl, Valero [food] McDonald's [O] [H], W [gas] Exxon/dsl, Shell/dsl

137mm Potomac Creek

136 Rd 8900, Centreport, **2 mi** E [gas] Valero/dsl, W airport

133b a US 17 N, to Warrenton, E [gas] Exxon/dsl [food] Arby's [lodging] Knights Inn, Motel 6 [O] 7-11, auto/truck repair, CarQuest, W [gas] EastCoast/Subway/dsl, Shell/dsl, WaWa/dsl [food] Aladin Grill, Burger King, Dunkin Donuts, Hardee's, McDonald's, Pancho Villa Mexican, Panera Bread, Perkins, Ponderosa, Popeye's, Sam's Pizza&Subs, Subway, Taco Bell, Waffle House, Wendy's [lodging] Best Value Inn, Clarion, Comfort Suites, Country Inn&Suites, Days Inn, Holiday Inn Express, Quality Inn, Sleep Inn, Super 8, Super Value Inn, Wingate Inn [O] Advance Parts, AutoZone, Blue Beacon, Food Lion, Honda, Petsmart, Target, Verizon

132.5mm Rappahannock River

132mm [RS] **sb, full [handicapped] facilities, litter barrels, petwalk [phone] [picnic] vending**

130b a VA 3, to Fredericksburg, E [gas] BP/dsl, Gulf/dsl, Shell/dsl, Wawa [food] Aladin Cafe, Arby's, Bob Evans, Dixie Bones BBQ, Dunkin Donuts, Friendly's, Honeybaked Ham, KFC, Lonestar Steaks, McDonald's, Pizza King, Popeye's, Shoney's, Starbucks, Subway, Teppanyaki Buffet, Wendy's [lodging] Best Western, Quality Inn [O] [H], AutoZone, Batteries+Bulbs, BigLots, Home Depot, PepBoys, Staples, Tuesday Morning, U-Haul, Verizon, W [gas] Exxon/dsl, Murphy USA, Sheetz/dsl, Valero, WaWa [food] 5 Guys Burgers, A&W/LJ Silver, Applebee's, BoneFish Grill, Bravo!, Buffalo Wild Wings, Burger King, Cancun Mexican, Carrabba's, Checker's, Cheeburger Cheeburger, Chick-fil-A, Chili's, Chipotle Mexican, ChuckeCheese, CiCi's Pizza, Cracker Barrel, Dunkin Donuts, Firebirds Grill, Firehouse Subs, Hibachi Buffet, IHOP, Jimmy John's, Joe's Crabshack, Krispy Kreme, Logan's Roadhouse, McDonald's, Melting Pot, Noodles&Co, O'Charley's, Olive Garden, Outback Steaks, Pancho Villa, Panda Express, Panera Bread, Park Lane Grill, Peter Chang, Potbelly, Qdoba, Quaker Steak, Red Lobster, Ruby Tuesday, Ryan's, Sam's Pizza, Santa Fe Grill, Shane's Ribshack, Smokey Bones BBQ, Starbucks, Subway, Taco Bell, TGIFriday's, Tito's Diner, TX Roadhouse [lodging] Best Western, Hampton Inn, Hilton Garden, Homewood Suites, Hospitality House, Residence Inn, Super 8, ValuePlace Inn [O] $General, $Tree, AAA, Aldi Foods, AT&T, AutoZone, Barnes&Noble, Belk, Best Buy, BJ's Whse, Books A Million, Costco/gas, CVS Drug, Dick's, Food Lion, Gander Mtn, GNC, Hancock Fabrics, Hobby Lobby, JC Penney, K-Mart, Kohl's, Lowe's, Macy's, mall, Meineke, Mercedes, Merchants Tire, Michael's, NTB, Office Depot, Old Navy, Petsmart, Radio Shack, Sears/auto, Target, Verizon, vet, Volvo, Walmart, Wegman's Foods, Yankee Candle

FREDERICKSBURG

126 US 1, US 17 S, to Fredericksburg, E [gas] 7-11/dsl, BP/dsl, Exxon/Circle K, Gulf/dsl, Shell/dsl, Wawa [food] Arby's, Denny's, DQ, Friendly's, Golden Corral, Hardee's, Hooters, McDonald's, Pizza Hut, Poncho Villa Mexican, Ruby Tuesday, Subway, Taco Bell, Vita Felice Italian, Waffle House [lodging] Best Value Inn, Country Inn&Suites, Days Inn/rest., EconoLodge, Fairfield Inn, Hampton Inn, Howard Johnson, Knights Inn, Motel 6, Royal Inn, TownePlace Suites [O] [H], $General, $Tree, Advance Parts, Aldi Foods, AutoZone, BMW Cycles, Buick/GMC, Chrysler/Dodge/

FREDERICKSBURG

126 Continued
Jeep, CVS Drug, Family$, Fiat, Food Lion, Hyundai, Kia, Little Tires, Mazda, Midas, Nissan, Rite Aid, Subaru, Tires+, VW, W [gas] 7-11, 95 Fuel Stop/dsl, Exxon/Circle K, WaWa/dsl [food] 5 Guys Burgers, Applebee's, Arby's, Asian Diner, Bob Evans, Buffalo Wild Wings, Burger King, Chick-fil-A, Chili's, China King, Chipotle Mexican, Coldstone Creamery, Cracker Barrel, Dickey's BBQ, El Charro Mexican, Famous Dave's BBQ, Firehouse Subs, Golden China, KFC, Kobe Japanese, Legends Grill, Longhorn Steaks, Mad Crab Grill, McDonald's, Mexico Rest., Mimi's Cafe, Panera Bread, Papa John's, Red Robin, Salsarita's Cantina, Sonic, Starbucks, Steak'n Shake, Subway, Taco Bell, Wendy's [lodging] Candlewood Suites, Holiday Inn Express, Sleep Inn, WyteStone Suites [O] AT&T, Carmax, CVS Drug, Dick's, Firestone/auto, GNC, Jo-Ann Fabrics, Kohl's, Lowe's, Marshalls, Merchant Tire/auto, Petsmart, Radio Shack, Rite Aid, Ross, Staples, Target, URGENT CARE, USPO, Verizon, vet, Walmart/Subway, World Mkt

118 VA 606, to Thornburg, E [gas] Shell/dsl [O] Safford RV Ctr, to Stonewall Jackson Shrine, W [gas] 7-11, Citgo/dsl, Exxon, Shell/DQ/dsl, Valero [food] Angela's Italian, Burger King, Domino's, McDonald's, Subway [lodging] Holiday Inn Express, Quality Inn [O] $General, Family$, Food Lion, KOA (7mi), to Lake Anna SP, USPO

110 VA 639, to Ladysmith, E [gas] Citgo, Shell/dsl, W [gas] Citgo/dsl, Exxon/dsl [food] Domino's, Guiseppe's Rest., Lin's Gourmet, McDonald's, Subway, Timbers Rest. [O] $General, Family$, Food Lion, Lady Smith Drug, Lady Smith Tire/repair, Verizon

108mm [RS] **both lanes, full [handicapped] facilities, litter barrels, petwalk [phone] [picnic] vending**

104 VA 207, to US 301, Bowling Green, E [gas] Exxon/dsl, FLYING J/Golden Corral/dsl/Lp/scales/24hr/ @, Gulf/7-11/dsl, Loves/DQ/Subway/dsl/scales/24hr, Mr Fuel/dsl, Valero/dsl [food] Arby's, McDonald's, Wendy's [lodging] Knights Inn, Super 8 [O] Blue Beacon, SpeedCo, to Ft AP Hill, W [gas] FLYING J/Denny's/dsl/scales/RV dump/24hr, Exxon/dsl [food] Waffle House [lodging] City Studio, Comfort Inn, Days Inn/rest., EconoLodge [O] CarQuest, USPO

98 VA 30, Doswell, E [gas] 7-11, Doswell TP/motel/dsl/scales/24hr/ @, Exxon [food] Burger King, Denny's [lodging] Best Western, Country Inn&Suites, Days Inn, La Quinta [O] Camp Wilderness, King's Dominion Camping, to King's Dominion Funpark, truckwash/service

92 VA 54, Ashland, E [gas] Sunoco, W [gas] 7-11/dsl, EC/Krispy Kreme/dsl, Exxon/Subway, Kangeroo/dsl, Shell/dsl, Sunoco/Circle K/dsl, TA/Valero/Country Pride/dsl/scales/24hr/ @ [food] Anthony's Pizza, Applebee's, Arby's, Brickoven Rest., Burger King, Capt D's, Chick-fil-A, China Wok, Cracker Barrel, DQ, El Azteca, GNC, Hardee's, Jersey Mike's Subs, KFC/LJ Silver, McDonald's, New China Buffet, Pizza Hut, Ponderosa, Ruby Tuesday, Starbucks, Taco Bell, Tops China, Waffle House, Wendy's [lodging] Apple Garden Inn, Ashland Inn, Days Inn, EconoLodge, Hampton Inn, Holiday Inn Express, Howard Johnson, Motel 6, Sleep Inn, Super 8 [O] $General, $Tree, Ace Hardware, Advance Parts, AutoZone, Buick/GMC, CarQuest, CVS Drug, Family$, Food Lion, Martin's Foods/dsl, O'Reilly Parts, Radio Shack, Rite Aid, Tuesday Morning, Verizon, Walmart/Subway

89 VA 802, to Lewistown Rd, E [gas] Shell, TA/Pizza Hut/Popeye's/dsl/scales/24hr/ @ [O] Americamps RV Camp, W [food] Bojangles, Dunkin Donuts, Subway, Wendy's [lodging] Country Inn Suites [O] Bass Pro Shops, Harley Davidson, Kosmo Village Camping, McGeorge's RV Ctr

86b a VA 656, Elmont, to Atlee, E [gas] Sheetz/dsl, Valero/dsl [food] Burger King, Mario's Italian, McDonald's, Pizza Hut, Subway

INTERSTATE 95 Cont'd

ELMONT

Exit	Services
86b a	Continued CVS Drug, Food Lion, tire/auto repair, vet, W Wawa/dsl Applebee's, Arby's, BBQ, Buffalo Wild Wings, Chick-fil-A, Chili's, Chipotle Mexican, CiCi's Pizza, Coldstone Creamery, Famous Dave's BBQ, Firehouse Subs, Halligan BBQ, Jade Chinese, Jersey Mike's Subs, McDonald's, O'Charley's, O'Dragon Buffet, Panera Bread, Papa John's, Pizzaro, Plaza Azteca Mexican, Red Robin, Roda Japanese, Shoney's, Sonic, Starbucks, Subway, TX Roadhouse, Wendy's Candlewood Suites, Comfort Suites, Courtyard, Hampton Inn, SpringHill Suites $Tree, 7-11, AT&T, Barnes&Noble, Best Buy, Burlington, Dick's, Firestone/auto, GNC, Goodyear/auto, Home Depot, JC Penney, Macy's, mall, Martin's Foods, Merchant's Tire, Michael's, Petsmart, Ross, Sears/auto, Shell/dsl, Target, Tire America, Walgreens
84b a	I-295 W, to I-64, to Norfolk
83b a	VA 73, Parham Rd, W 7-11, Exxon/DQ, Shell/dsl, Wawa Aunt Sarah's, Burger King, Firehouse Subs, Frida's Cafe, Hardee's, Hawks BBQ, KFC/Taco Bell, McDonald's, Popeyes, River City Diner, Starbucks, Subway, Waffle House, Wendy's Best Value Inn, Best Western, Cavalier Motel, Days Inn, EconoLodge, Knights Inn, Quality Inn, Sleep Inn $Tree, BigLots, Food Lion, Lowe's, Verizon, Walmart
82	US 301, Chamberlayne Ave, E BP/dsl, Sunoco/dsl, Valero/dsl, Wawa KFC, McDonald's, Pizza Hut/Taco Bell, Subway Super 8 $Tree, Family$, Food Lion, USPO, W Exxon/Circle K
81	US 1, Chamberlayne Ave (from nb), same as 82
80	Hermitage Rd, Lakeside Ave (from nb, no return), W Citgo/Subway Ginter Botanical Gardens, Goodyear/auto
79	I-64 W, to Charlottesville, I-195 S, to U of Richmond
78	Boulevard (no EZ nb return), E BP Clarion, W H, stadium, to VA HS
76	Chamberlayne Ave, Belvidere, E H, VA Union U
75	I-64 E, VA Beach, to Norfolk, airport
74c	US 33, US 250 W, to Broad St, W H, Museum of the Confederacy, st capitol
74b	Franklin St, E Richmond Nat Bfd Park
74a	I-195 N, to Powhite Expswy, downtown
73.5mm	James River
73	Maury St, to US 60, US 360, industrial area
69	VA 161, Bells Rd, E Port of Richmond, W Exxon/dsl, Shell/dsl McDonald's, Subway Candlewood Suites, Hampton Inn, Holiday Inn, Red Roof Inn
67b a	VA 895 (toll E), VA 150, to Chippenham Pkwy, Falling Creek, W BP/dsl, RaceWay/dsl, Shell/dsl Burger King, Hardee's Food Lion, U-Haul
64	VA 613, to Willis Rd, E BP, Exxon/Circle K/dsl Waffle House Best Value Inn, EconoLodge, W 7-11, Citgo/dsl, Shell/dsl, Sunoco Burger King, Maury's BBQ, McDonald's, Subway Country Inn&Suites, La Quinta, Sleep Inn, VIP Inn Drewry's Bluff Bfd, flea mkt
62	VA 288 N, to Chesterfield, Powhite Pkwy, to airport
61b a	VA 10, Chester, E RaceWay/dsl Don Pepe Mexican, Hardee's Comfort Inn, Courtyard, Hampton Inn, Holiday Inn Express, Homewood Suites, Quality Inn H, City Point NHS, Petersburg NBF, to James River Plantations, W Exxon/Circle K/dsl, Gulf/dsl, Mobil/Circle K/dsl, Shell/dsl, Sunoco/dsl Applebee's, Bojangles, Brass Monkey Grill, Buffalo Wild Wings, Burger King, Capt D's, Chili's, Chipotle, CiCi's Pizza, Cracker Barrel, Denny's, Don Papa Mexican, Friendly's,

RICHMOND

CHESTER

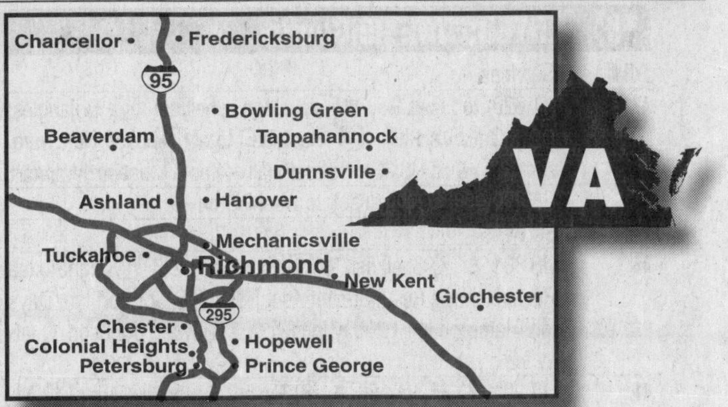

Exit	Services
61b a	Continued Hardee's, Hooters, IHOP, KFC, Logan's Roadhouse, McDonald's, O'Charley's, Panera Bread, Peking Chinese, Pizza Hut, Shoney's, Sonic, Starbucks, Subway, Taco Bell, The Patron Cantina, Wendy's Country Inn&Suites, Days Inn, Fairfield Inn, InTowne Suites, Suburban Lodge, Super 8 $General, $Tree, Aamco, AT&T, Big Lots, Chevrolet, CVS Drug, Food Lion, GNC, Home Depot, K-Mart, Kohl's, Kroger/gas, Lowe's, Martin's Foods, NAPA, PetCo, Radio Shack, Rite Aid, Target, to Pocahontas SP, Verizon
58	VA 746, to Ruffinmill Rd, E Pilot/Wendy's/dsl/scales/24hr Honda, Hyundai, Kia, Nissan, Toyota/Scion, VW, W 7-11, Exxon/Subway/dsl, Wawa/dsl McDonald's Candlewood Suites, Days Inn, EconoLodge Family$
54	VA 144, Temple Ave, Hopewell, to Ft Lee, E Exxon/Subway, Sheetz/dsl, Shell/Burger King, Sunoco/Circle K/dsl, Wawa/dsl 5 Guys Burgers, Applebee's, Arby's, Buffalo Wild Wings, Chick-fil-A, China Buffet, Chipotle, CiCi's Pizza, Denny's, Firehouse Subs, Golden Corral, Great China, IHOP, Jimmy John's, LoneStar Steaks, McDonald's, Olive Garden, Outback Steaks, Panera Bread, Picadilly, Pizza Hut, Quiznos, Red Lobster, Ruby Tuesday, Sagebrush Steaks, Sonic, Starbucks, Subway, Taco Bell, TX Roadhouse, Wendy's Comfort Suites, Hampton Inn, Hilton Garden, Holiday Inn, ValuePlace Inn $Tree, AAA, AT&T, Best Buy, BooksAMillion, Dick's, Home Depot, JC Penney, Jo-Ann Fabrics, K-Mart, Macy's, mall, Marshall's, Merchant's Tire, Michael's, Old Navy, Petsmart, Radio Shack, Sam's Club/gas, Sears/auto, Staples, Target, Verizon, Walmart/Subway W Kangaroo/dsl DQ, Hardee's, Hardee's, Waffle House to VSU, U-Haul
53	S Park Blvd, E same as 54
52.5mm	Appomattox River
52	Washington St, Wythe St, E Exxon/dsl, Valero/dsl Jade Garden Knights Inn, Royal Inn, Super 8 Petersburg Nat Bfd, W Liberty Neptune's Rest. H
51	I-85 S, to South Hill, US 460 W
50d	Wythe St, (from nb), same as 52
50b c	E 7-11 Flagship Inn
50a	US 301, US 460 E, to Crater Rd, County Dr, E BP, RaceWay/dsl, Star Express Hardee's American Inn, Budget Inn, California Inn, EconoLodge H
48b a	Wagner Rd, W on Crater Rd Gulf/dsl, Wawa Arby's, Bojangles, Burger King, Capt D's, KFC, King's BBQ, Little Caesar's, Pizza Hut, Plaza Mexico, Subway, Taco Bell, Taste of China Country Inn&Suites, Super 8 $General, $Tree, Advance Parts, Martin's Foods, O'Reilly Parts, PepBoys, Radio Shack, USPO, Verizon, Walgreens, Walmart

PETERSBURG

VA

= gas = food = lodging = other = rest stop

VA

INTERSTATE 95 Cont'd

Exit #	Services
47	VA 629, to Rives Rd, W Citgo, Shell/dsl Bojangles, KFC, Outlaw's Rest. Heritage Motel Ace Hardware, same as 48 on US 301, Softball Hall of Fame Museum, Walmart
46	I-295 N (exits left from sb), to Washington
Exit #	Services
45	US 301, E Shell/dsl, W Exxon/Circle K Lighthouse Rest., Nanny's Rest., Steven Kent Rest. Comfort Inn, Days Inn, Hampton Inn, Holiday Inn Express, Howard Johnson, Quality Inn
41	US 301, VA 35, VA 156, E Exxon/dsl/scales/24hr Nino's N Italian Rest. EconoLodge South 40 camp resort, W Travelers Inn
40mm	**weigh sta both lanes**
37	US 301, Carson, W BP/dsl, Shell/dsl
36mm	**nb, full facilities, litter barrels, petwalk vending**
33	VA 602, W Davis/Exxon/Subway/Starbucks/dsl/scales/24hr Burger King, Denny's, Little Italy Hampton Inn, Sleep Inn
31	VA 40, Stony Creek, to Waverly, W Shell/dsl, Sunoco/dsl Tastee Hut Family$
24	VA 645
20	VA 631, Jarratt, W Exxon/Blimpie/Pizza Hut/dsl/24hr, Race-in/dsl $General, Ford
17	US 301, 1 mi E Knights Inn, Reste Motel Jellystone Park Camping
13	VA 614, to Emporia, E Exxon/Chester's/dsl, Shell/dsl
12	US 301 (from nb)
11b a	US 58, Emporia, to South Hill, E Citgo/Burger King, Exxon/Blimpie/LJ Silver, Shell/dsl Applebee's, Arby's, Carolina BBQ, Cracker Barrel, Domino's, Hardee's, KFC, McDonald's, Pizza Hut, Taco Bell, Wendy's, Wong's Garden Country Inn&Suites, Fairfield Inn, Rodeway Inn H, Advance Parts, Buick/Chevrolet/GMC, CVS Drug, Family$, Food Lion, NAPA, O'Reilly Parts, Rite Aid, Verizon, Walmart, W Exxon, Pilot/Sadler/5 Guys Burgers/dsl/scales/24hr/ @, Race-In/Quiznos/dsl Bojangles, Pino's Pizza, Shoney's Best Western, Days Inn, Hampton Inn, Holiday Inn Express, Quality Inn, Sleep Inn
8	US 301, E Citgo, Simmons/Exxon/Huddle House/dsl/scales/24hr Motel 6, Red Carpet Inn truck repair
4	VA 629, to Skippers, E Love's/McDonald's/dsl/scales/24hr, Wilco/Hess/Dunkin Donuts/Subway/dsl/scales/24hr, W Foodmart/gas AmericanInn camping (3mi)
3.5mm	Fountain's Creek
0.5mm	**Welcome Ctr nb, full facilities, litter barrels, petwalk vending**
0mm	Virginia/North Carolina state line

EMPORIA

INTERSTATE 264 (NORFOLK)

Exit #	Services
23mm	**I-264 begins/ends.** BP, Shell convention ctr
22	Birdneck Rd, S Shell/dsl LJ Silver, Max&Erma's, McDonald's/playplace, Subway Double Tree Family$, Food Lion, museum
21	VA Beach Blvd, First Colonial Rd, N BP, Shell 5 Guys Burgers, Applebee's, Arby's, Burger King, Burton's Grill, Chick-fil-A, China Wok, DQ, IHOP, KFC, McDonald's, Moe's SW Grill, Otani Japanese, Outback Steaks, Panera Bread, Pizza Hut, Plaza Azteca, Qdoba, Schlotzsky's, Shogun Japanese, Sonic,
21	Continued Starbucks, Subway, Taco Bell, Virginian Steaks, Wendy's Advance Parts, CVS, GNC, Infiniti, JoAnn Fabrics, K-Mart, Kroger/dsl, Michael's, Office Depot, Petsmart, Radio Shack, Rite Aid, SteinMart, Target, Toyota/Scion, Trader Joe's, USPO, vet, Whole Foods Mkt, S Shell, Wawa/dsl 7-11, CarQuest, NAPA
20	US 58 E, to VA Beach Blvd (eb only), N Citgo, Kangaroo, Wawa Bojangle's, Capt. George's Seafood, China Moon, Hardee's, Ruby Tuesday, Subway 7-11, Family$, Food Lion, KIA/Lincoln, Lowe's, PepBoys, TJ Maxx, Tuesday Morning, vet
19	Lynnhaven Pkwy, N 7-11, Wawa Ensenda Mexican, Iggle's, Lucky Express, Subway Audi, Chevrolet, FarmFresh Foods, Ford, Hyundai, Jaguar, Porsche, Subaru, URGENT CARE, VW, S McDonald's
18	Rosemont, N Exxon Bonefish Grill, Burger King, Denny's, Hardee's, Jade Garden, KFC, LJ Silver, McDonald's, Mi Casita Mexican, Papa John's, Starbucks, Taco Bell, Wendy's, Zero's Subs EconoLodge $Tree, Acura, AutoZone, BJ's Whse/gas, CarMax, Chrysler/Dodge/Jeep, Food Lion, Harris Teeter, Home Depot, Honda, Kroger, Merchant's Tire/Auto, Nissan, Petsmart, Radio Shack, Rite Aid, Sam's Club/gas, Walgreens, S Hess/dsl, Wawa 4 Seasons Chinese $General, CVS
17.5mm	wb only, inspection sta
17a b	Independance Blvd, N Exxon Cheesecake Factory, Chipotle, IHOP, Jason's Deli, Macaroni Grill, Max&Erma's, McDonald's, Panera Bread, PF Chang's, Ruby Tuesday, Smokey Bones BBQ, Starbucks, Taco Bell, Tripps Rest., Village Inn, Wendy's Candlewood Suites, Crowne Plaza, Days Inn, Extended Stay, Hilton Garden, Motel 6, Westin Barnes&Noble, Best Buy, Dick's, K-Mart, Kohl's, Michael's, Old Navy, Sears/auto, Steinmart, Target, Walgreens, S 7-11, Exxon, Wawa Arby's, Azteca Mexican, Domino's, Firehouse Subs, Golden Corral, Hardee's, KFC, Panda China, Quiznos, Starbucks, Subway, TX Roadhouse, Zero Subs InTown Suites $General, auto repair, Food Lion, Mazda, Rite Aid, vet
16	Witchduck Rd
15a b	Newtown Rd, N BP, Citgo McDonald's, Shoney's, Wendy's Homewood Suites, TownePlace Suites AutoZone, S BP, Shell Denny's, Ruby Tuesday Courtyard, Hampton Inn, Holiday Inn, La Quinta, Red Roof Inn, SpringHill Suites 7-11, Rite Aid
14b a	I-64. US 13, to Military Hwy
13	US 13, Military Hwy, N Shell Arby's, Boston Mkt, Lonestar Steaks, Mongolian BBQ, Norfolk Garden Korean, Piccadilly, Schlotzsky's Days Inn, EconoLodge, Motel 6, Ramada Ltd CVS, Firestone/auto, JC Penney, Macy's, Ross
12	Ballentine Blvd, N H, Norfolk SU
11b a	US 460, VA 166/168, Brambleton Ave, Campostello Rd, N 7-11, Shell
10	Tidewater Dr, City Hall Ave, exits left from eb, 7-11, Shell
9	St Paul's Blvd, Waterside Dr, to Harbor Park Stadium
8	I-464 S, to Chesapeake
7.5mm	tunnel
7b a	VA 141, Effingham St, Crawford St, N Shell Naval H, S Shipyard
6.5mm	**weigh sta eb**
6	Des Moines Ave (from eb)
5	US 17, Frederick Blvd, N H, S BP Harley-Davidson, Midtown Tunnel
4	VA 337, Portsmouth Blvd

INTERSTATE 264 (NORFOLK) Cont'd

Exit #	Services
3	Victory Blvd, N [gas] 7-11, Exxon, Shell, WaWa [food] Bojangles, Capt D's, Domino's, DQ, Firehouse Subs, KFC, McDonald's, Pizza Hut, Ruby Tuesday, Taco Bell, Wendy's [other] $Tree, Advance Parts, AutoZone, BigLots, Lowe's, PepBoys, Radio Shack, Walgreens, S [gas] Valero/dsl
2b a	Greenwood Dr
0mm	**I-264 begins/ends on I-64, exit 299.**

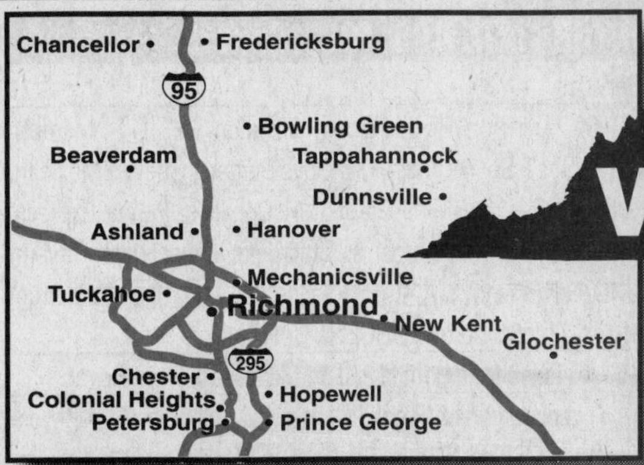

INTERSTATE 295 (RICHMOND)

MECHANICSVILLE

Exit #	Services
53b a	I-64, W to Charlottesville, E to Richmond, to US 250, **I-295 begins/ends.**
51b a	Nuckols Rd, **1 mi N** [gas] Miller's/dsl, Valero [food] Bruster's, Casa Grande, Cheeburger, Chen's Chinese, Home Team Grill, McDonald's, Nonna's Pizzaria, Rico's Mexican, Samurai Japanese, Starbucks, Subway, Tropical Smoothie Cafe [other] CVS Drug, Food Lion, vet, Walgreens, S [gas] Exxon/Mkt Cafe [other] USPO
49b a	US 33, Richmond, **2 mi S** [food] Carvel's Ice Cream, Little Szechuan, Quiznos [other] 7-11, Martin's Foods
45b a	Woodman Rd, **1-2 mi S** [gas] 7-11, Valero [food] Little Caesar's [other] $General, CVS Drug, Meadow Farm Museum
43	I-95, US 1, N to Washington, S to Richmond (exits left from nb), **N on US 1** [gas] Shell/dsl [food] Applebee's, Arby's, BBQ, Buffalo Wild Wings, Chick-fil-A, Chili's, Chipotle Mexican, Coldstone, Famous Dave's BBQ, Firehouse Subs, McDonald's, O'Charley's, O'Dragon buffet, Panera Bread, Papa John's, Pizzaro, Plaza Azteca Mexican, Red Robin, Roda Japanese, Shoney's, Starbucks, Subway, TX Roadhouse, Wendy's [lodging] Candlewood Suites, Comfort Suites, Courtyard, Hampton Inn, SpringHill Suites [other] $Tree, AT&T, Barnes&Noble, Best Buy, Burlington, Dick's, Firestone/auto, GNC, Goodyear/auto, Home Depot, JC Penney, Macy's, mall, Martin's Foods, Merchant's Tire, Michael's, Petsmart, Ross, Sears/auto, Target, Tire America, Walgreens, **1-2 mi S** [gas] 7-11, Shell, WaWa [food] Aunt Sarah's, Burger King, Frida's Mexican, Hardee's, KFC/Taco Bell, McDonald's, Ming's Dynasty, Starbucks, Subway, Waffle House, Wendy's [lodging] Best Value Inn, Cavalier Motel, Days Inn, EconoLodge, Knights Inn, Sleep Inn [other] $Tree, Food Lion, Lowe's, Walmart
41b a	US 301, VA 2, E [gas] BP/dsl, Valero/dsl, WaWa/dsl [food] Burger King, McDonald's, Popeye's, Tropical Smoothie Cafe, Zheng's Chinese [other] $General, Kroger/gas, Walgreens, **0-4mi W** [gas] Exxon/dsl [food] Friendly's [lodging] Holiday Inn, Super 8, Travelodge
38b a	VA 627, Pole Green Rd, **0-1mi E** [gas] 7-11, BP/Miller's Mkt/dsl, Exxon [food] Antonio's Pizza, Bruster's, Chen's Rest., Coffee Lane, Mimmo's Rest., Plaza Tapatia, Subway [other] Curves, Food Lion, vet, W [gas] 7-11, Valero [food] Padon's Hams
37b a	US 360, **1 mi E** [gas] BP, Shell/dsl, Valero [food] Applebee's, Arby's, Buffalo Wild Wings, Burger King, Chick-fil-A, China Buffet, Cracker Barrel, DQ, Gus' Italian, IHOP, KFC, McDonald's, Mexico Rest., Moe's SW Grill, Noodles&Co, Outback Steaks, Panera Bread, Papa John's, Pizza Hut, Ruby Tuesday, Shoney's, Starbucks, Taco Bell, Waffle House, Wendy's [lodging] Hampton Inn, Holiday Inn Express [other] $Tree, AT&T, Best Buy, BJ's Whse/gas, GNC, Home Depot, Kohl's, Marshall's, Martin's Foods, Old Navy, Petsmart, Radio Shack, Target, Verizon, Walmart, W [gas] 7-11, Sunoco/dsl, Valero/dsl [other] $General, to Mechanicsville
34b a	VA 615, Creighton Rd, E [gas] 7-11, Valero

HOPEWELL

Exit #	Services
31b a	VA 156, E [gas] Citgo/dsl [other] to Cold Harbor Bfd, **4 mi W** [gas] Shell, Valero [food] Hardee's [lodging] Courtyard, EconoLodge, Holiday Inn Express, Motel 6
28	I-64, to US 60, W [other] museum
25	Rd 895 W (**toll**), to Richmond
22b a	VA 5, Charles City, E [gas] Exxon/dsl [food] DQ [other] Shirley Plantation, W [gas] Valero/dsl [food] China Taste, Portabella's Cafe [other] Food Lion, Richmond Nat Bfd, Rite Aid
18mm	James River
16	Rivers Bend Blvd
15b a	VA 10, Hopewell, E [gas] BP/dsl [other] [H], James River Plantations, W [gas] EC/Subway/dsl, Exxon/McDonald's/dsl, Sheetz, WaWa [food] Cesare's Ristorante, Chen's Rest., Jalapeno's, Wendy's, Wing's Pizza [lodging] Hyatt Place, Residence Inn [other] 7-11, Curves, CVS Drug, Food Lion
13mm	Appomattox River
9b a	VA 36, Hopewell, E [gas] Gulf, Petrol, WaWa [food] A&W, Bojangles, El Nopal Mexican, Hardee's, Hong Kong's Rest., Huddle House, KFC, Little Caesar's, LJ Silver, McDonald's, Rosa's Italian [lodging] Best Western, EconoLodge, Fairfield Inn, StayOver Suites [other] Advance Parts, AutoZone, Family$, O'Reilly Parts, vet, Walgreens, W [gas] BP/dsl/24hr, Shell, Valero/dsl [food] Burger King, Denny's, DQ, Dragon Express, Dunkin Donuts, Kanpai Japanese, McDonald's, Papa John's, Pizza Hut, Ruby Tuesday, Shoney's, Subway, Taco Bell, Top's China, Waffle House, Wendy's [lodging] Baymont Inn, Candlewood Suites, Hampton Inn, Quality Inn [other] $General, Chevrolet, Family$, Farmer's Foods, Food Lion, Rite Aid, to Petersburg Nat Bfd, U-Haul, US Army Museum
5.5mm	Blackwater Swamp
3b a	US 460, Petersburg, to Norfolk, E [gas] EC/Subway/dsl, Wilco/Hess/Wendy's/dsl/scales/24hr [food] Prince George BBQ, **1-2 mi W** [gas] BP/dsl [food] McDonald's
	I-95, N to Petersburg, S to Emporium, **I-295 begins/ends.**

INTERSTATE 495 (DC)

Exit #	Services
57	I-95 S, I-395 N, I-95 N. **I-495 & I-95 N run together. See MD I-95, exits 25b a-2b a.**
54b a	VA 620, Braddock Rd, S [gas] Sunoco [food] Hong Kong Express [other] 7-11, Ctr for the Arts, Geo Mason U, NTB, Rite Aid, Safeway Foods, USPO
52b a	VA 236, Little River Tpk, Fairfax, E [gas] Liberty/dsl, Sunoco/repair [food] Chicken Loco, KFC/Taco Bell, Little Caesar's, McDonald's, Wendy's [other] $Tree, 7-11, Advance Parts, GNC, Petco, Safeway Foods
51	VA 657, Gallows Rd, W [gas] Exxon [other] [H], 7-11

= gas = food = lodging = other = rest stop

VA

WASHINGTON DC AREA

INTERSTATE 495 (DC) Cont'd

Exit #	Services
50b a	US 50, Arlington Blvd, Fairfax, Arlington, E Marriott, W Shell, Sunoco/dsl 5 Guys Burgers, Chevy's Mexican, Grevey's Rest, Jasmine Garden, McDonald's, Panda Express, Panera Bread, Papa John's, Starbucks, Sweetwater Tavern, UNO Grill, Wendy's Residence Inn O H, CVS Drug, Midas, Staples, Target, URGENT CARE, vet
49c b a	I-66 (exits left from both lanes), to Manassas, Front Royal
47b a	VA 7, Leesburg Pike, Tysons Corner, Falls Church, E Westin, W BP/dsl, Exxon, Shell/dsl BJ's Rest., Chili's, Jimmy John's, McDonald's, Olive Garden, On-the-Border, Panera Bread, Silver Diner, Starbucks, Subway, Wendy's Embassy Suites, Hilton Garden O AT&T, Best Buy, Bloomingdale's, Buick/Chevrolet/GMC, Chrysler/Dodge/Jeep, CVS Drug, mall, Marshall's, Mr Tire, PetCo, Petsmart, Radio Shack, Staples, Subaru/VW, TJ Maxx
46b a	VA 123, Chain Bridge Rd, W Gulf/dsl, Sunoco/dsl Cheesecake Factory, Maggiano's, PF Chang's Courtyard, Crowne Plaza O Macy's
45b a	VA 267 W (**toll**), to I-66 E, to Dulles
44	VA 193, Langley
43	G Washington Mem Pkwy, no trucks
42mm	Virginia/Maryland state line, Potomac River. **Exits 41-27 are in Maryland.**
41	Clara Barton Pkwy, Carderock, Great Falls, no trucks
40	Cabin John Pkwy, Glen Echo (from sb), no trucks
39	MD 190, River Rd, Washington, Potomac
38	I-270, to Frederick
36	MD 187, Old Georgetown Rd, S O H
35	I-270 (from wb)
34	MD 355, Wisconsin Ave, Bethesda
33	MD 185, Connecticut Ave, N O LDS Temple, S Citgo/repair, Giant/dsl, Liberty Chevy Chase Mkt, Starbucks
31b a	MD 97, Georgia Ave, Silver Spring, N O H, S BP/dsl, Exxon/dsl, Shell, W Express/dsl Armand's Pizza, Domino's, Mayflower Chinese O CVS Drug, Snider's Foods, Staples, vet
30b a	US 29, Colesville, N BP/dsl, Citgo, Shell Chipotle, McDonald's, Papa John's, Red Maple Asian, Starbucks, Subway O 7-11/Jerry's Subs, CVS Drug, Safeway Foods
29b a	MD 193, University Blvd
28b a	MD 650, New Hampshire Ave, N BP, Exxon/dsl, Shell/repair Domino's, Quizno's, Starbucks, Urban BBQ O 7-11, CVS Drug, Radio Shack, Safeway Foods
27	I-95, N to Baltimore, S to Richmond.

I-495 & I-95 S run together. See VA I-95, exits 173-177.

PORTSMOUTH

INTERSTATE 664 (NORFOLK)

Exit #	Services
15b a	I-64 to Chesapeake, I-264 E to Portsmouth & Norfolk. **I-664 begins/ends on I-64, exit 299.**
13b a	US 13, US 58, US 460, Military Hwy, E Shell/dsl Bowers Hill Inn
12	VA 663, Dock Landing Rd
11b a	VA 337, Portsmouth Blvd, E 7-11, Citgo, Exxon/dsl, Hess, Shell/dsl 5 Guys Burgers, Applebee's, Arby's, Buffet City, Burger King, Chick-fil-A, ChuckECheese, Golden Corral, IHOP, Jalapeno's, McDonald's, Olive Garden, Outback Steaks, Piccadilly, Pizza Hut, Plaza Azteca, Red Lobster, Red Robin, Rita's Custard, Subway, Taco Bell, Wendy's Extended Stay 4 Less, Hampton Inn, Holiday Inn Express O $Tree, $Tree Mkt, AutoZone, Best Buy, BJ's Whse/gas, Buick, Firestone Auto, Food Lion, Ford, Home Depot, JC Penney, K-Mart, Macy's, Merchant's Auto Ctr, Michael's, Old Navy, Petsmart, Ross, Sam's Club/gas, Sears/auto, Target, Tuesday Morning, Walmart, W 7-11 Burger King, Cracker Barrel, Subway, Waffle House Baymont Inn, Candlewood Suites O Lowe's
10	VA 659, Pughsville Rd, E 7-11, Shell O Food Lion, Rite Aid
9b a	US 17, US 164, E 7-11, Hess, Wawa Burger King, Capt D's, Domino's, DQ, Dunkin Donuts, Great Wall Chinese, KFC, McDonald's, Pizza Hut, Sonic, Taco Bell, Waffle House, Wendy's Best Western, Budget Lodge, Extended Stay America, Sleep Inn, Super 8 O $Tree, Advance Parts, Chevrolet, FarmFresh Foods, Honda, Hyundai, NAPA, Nissan, O'Reilly Parts, tires, Toyota/Scion, W Buffalo Wild Wings, Subway Comfort Suites, Hilton Garden O H, Harris Teeter, museum, to James River Br
8b a	VA 135, College Dr, E 7-11, Exxon Applebee's, Arby's, Chick-fil-A, Firehouse Subs, McDonald's, Panera Bread, Ruby Tuesday, Subway, Wendy's O Dick's, Food Lion, GNC, Kohl's, Petsmart, Radio Shack, TJ Maxx, Walmart, W Riverstone Chophouse Courtyard, TownePlace Suites
11.5mm	**insp sta nb**
9mm	James River
8mm	tunnel
7	Terminal Ave
6	25th St, 26th St, E 7-11 McDonald's
5	US 60 W, 35th St, Jefferson Ave, E Fast&Easy #1 Chinese, Church's, King's Pizza O Hornsby Tire
4	Chesnut Ave, Roanoke Ave
3	Aberdeen Rd, W 7-11 Hardee's, McDonald's, Wendy's
2	Powhatan Pkwy, E 7-11, **1-2 mi** W Coldstone, Joe's Crabshack, Lonestar Steaks Hilton Garden, SpringHill Suites O Bass Pro Shop, BJ's Whse/gas, Lowe's
1b a	I-64, W to Richmond, E to Norfolk. **I-664 begins/ends on I-64.**

NOTES

WASHINGTON

INTERSTATE 5

Exit #	Services
277mm	USA/Canada Border, Washington state line, customs
276	**BLAINE** WA 548 S, Blaine, E Shell/dsl, Tank'n Tote/dsl, Texaco/dsl, USA/dsl Big Al's Diner Northwoods Motel Duty Free, NAPA, to Peace Arch SP, W Chevron/dsl/repair Black Forest Steaks, Chada Thai, Little Red Caboose Cafe, Ocean Bay Chinese, Pasa Del Norte, Pizza Factory, Seaside Bakery Cafe, Subway, Tony's Cafe Anchor Inn, Bay Side Motel, Cottage by the Bay B&B, International Motel, Sunset Inn Blaine Marine Park, USPO
275	WA 543 N (from nb, no return), E Chevron/dsl, Mkt/dsl, Shell/dsl Burger King, Little Caesars, Subway $Tree, Ace Hardware, Border Tire, CostCutter Foods, Rite Aid, vet, truck customs
274	Peace Portal Drive (from nb, no return), Blaine, W Shell/dsl camping, Semi-ah-moo Resort
270	Birch Bay, Lynden, W Shell/Domino's/Subway/dsl Bob's Burgers, Jack-in-the-Box, Subway Semi-ah-moo Resort Birch Bay Mkt, Thousand Trails Camping, vet
269mm	**Welcome Ctr sb, full facilities, info, litter barrels, petwalk vending**
267mm	**Welcome Ctr nb full facilities, info, litter barrels, petwalk vending**
266	WA 548 N, Grandview Rd, Custer, W Arco Birch Bay SP
263	Portal Way, E Pacific Pride/dsl, Shell/dsl El Nopal Mexican AA RV Park, Cedars RV Park
263mm	Nooksack River
262	Main St, Ferndale, E Chevron/dsl, Pilot/Subway/dsl/scales/24hr Denny's, McDonald's Super 8 RV Park, TDS Tires, vet, W Gull/dsl, Shell/dsl Bob's Burgers, Domino's, DQ, Jack-in-the-Box, Papa Murphy's, Quiznos, Sonic, Starbucks Scottish Lodge $Tree, Costcutter Foods, Haggen's Foods, NAPA, O'Reilly Parts, Schwab Tire, Verizon, vet, Walgreens
260	Slater Rd, Lummi Island, E Arco/dsl antiques, El Monte RV Ctr, **4 mi** W Silver Reef Hotel/Casino Lummi Ind Res
258	**BELLINGHAM** Bakerview Rd, E 5 Guys Burgers, Asian Fusion, Baskin-Robbins, Jack-in-the-Box, Papa Murphy's, Starbucks, Subway La Quinta Fred Meyer/dsl, Verizon, W 76/7-11, Arco, Mkt/dsl Mykono's Greek Rest. Hampton Inn, Shamrock Motel airport, Bellingham RV Park, st patrol
257	Northwest Ave, E Home 2 Hilton, SpringHill Suites, TownePlace Suites Cadillac/Chevrolet
256b	Bellis Fair Mall Pkwy, E JC Penney, mall, Target
256a	WA 539 N, Meridian St, E Shell/dsl, Super Gas/dsl Arby's, Asian 1, Boston's Rest., Buffalo Wild Wings, Burger King,
256a	Continued China Palace, Chipotle Mexican, Coldstone, Denny's, DQ, Lorenzo's Mexican, McDonald's, Mi Mexico, Old Country Buffet, Olive Garden, Quiznos, Red Robin, Shari's, Starbucks, Subway, Taco Bell, Taco Time, Thai House Rest., Wendy's, Wonderful Buffet Baymont Inn, Best Western, Comfort Inn, Holiday Inn Express, Oxford Suites, Quality Inn $Tree, AAA, AT&T, Barnes&Noble, Best Buy, Costco/gas, Home Depot, JC Penney, Kohl's, Macy's, mall, Marshall's, Michael's, Midas, Office Depot, O'Reilly Parts, PetCo, Petsmart, Rite Aid, Ross, Schwab Tire, st patrol, Target, TJ Maxx, to Nooksack Ind Res, U-Haul, vet, Walgreens, Walmart/McDonald's, WinCo Foods, W Slo Pitch Grill EconoLodge, Rodeway Inn, Super Buffet
255	WA 542 E, Sunset Dr, Bellingham, E 76, Chevron/dsl, Shell/Subway/Domino's/dsl A&W/KFC, Applebee's, El Gitano Mexican, Hawaii BBQ, Jack-in-the-Box, Panda Express, Panda Palace, Port of Subs, RoundTable Pizza, Starbucks, Taco Bell Jo-Ann Fabrics, K-Mart, Lowe's, Rite Aid, Safeway, to Mt Baker, Tuesday Morning, USPO, Walgreens, W H
254	Iowa St, State St, Bellingham, E 76, Valero Audi/VW, Chrysler/Dodge/Jeep, Honda, Hyundai, Kia, Mercedes, Nissan, Subaru/Buick/GMC, Toyota/Scion, VacationLand RV Ctr, Volvo, W Chevron/dsl, Shell DQ, McDonald's, Subway AutoZone, Ford/Lincoln, Midas, NAPA, O'Reilly Parts
253	Lakeway Dr, Bellingham, E Little Caesars, Papa Murphy's, Port of Subs, Rhodes Cafe, Sol de Mexico, Subway Best Western, Guesthouse Inn 7-11, Discount Tire, Fred Meyer/dsl, Radio Shack, W same as 252
252	Samish Way, Bellingham, E same as 253, W 76, Chevron, SuperGas/dsl Boomers Drive-In, Busara Thai Cuisine, Diego's Mexican, Domino's, El Agave, El Albanil Mexican, Kyoto Steaks, McDonald's, Pizza Hut, Sehome Diner, Starbucks, Subway, Taco Time, Wendy's Aloha Motel, Bay City Motel, Bellingham Lodge, Cascade Inn, Coachman Inn, Days Inn, Motel 6, Villa Inn $Tree, 7-11, Ace Hardware, AT&T, Haggen Foods, REI, Rite Aid, vet
250	WA 11 S, Chuckanut Dr, Bellingham, Fairhaven Hist Dist, W Arco, Shell/repair to Alaska Ferry, to Larrabee SP, True Value
246	N Lake Samish, E Lake Padden RA, W Shell/dsl RV camping
242	Nulle Rd, S Lake Samish

WA

WA

BURLINGTON

MT VERNON

INTERSTATE 5 Cont'd

Exit #	Services
240	Alger, E [gas] Shell/dsl/LP/RV dump [food] Alger Grille [lodging] Whispering Firs Motel/RV Parking
238mm	**[RS] both lanes, full [handicap] facilities, litter barrels, petwalk [phone] [picnic] vending**
236	Bow Hill Rd, E [other] Skagit Hotel Casino/rest./dsl/LP
235mm	**weigh sta sb**
234mm	Samish River
232	Cook Rd, Sedro-Woolley, E [gas] 76/dsl, Shell/dsl [food] Bob's Burgers, Jack-in-the-Box, Starbucks, Subway [lodging] Fairfield Inn [other] [H], KOA (3mi)
231	WA 11 N, Chuckanut Dr, E [other] Camping World RV Ctr, Dreamchasers RV Ctr, Kia, W [other] st patrol, to Larrabee SP (14mi)
230	WA 20, Burlington, E [gas] Chevron, Shell/dsl [food] Applebee's, Carino's Italian, Jack-in-the-Box, Mi Mexico, Outback Steaks, Papa Murphy's, Pizza Factory, Pizza Hut/Taco Bell, Popeye's, Red Robin [lodging] Cocusa Motel, Sterling Motel [other] [H], $Tree, 7-11, AutoZone, Fred Meyer/dsl, Haggen Foods, JC Penney, Macy's, mall, Schwab Tire, Sears/auto, Skagit Transmissions, Target, to N Cascades NP, Verizon, Walgreens, W [gas] Pacific Pride/dsl [food] McDonald's [lodging] Holiday Inn Express [other] Harley-Davidson, Hyundai, to San Juan Ferry
229	George Hopper Rd, E [gas] Arco, USA/dsl [food] Chipotle Mexican, Five Guys, Jamba Juice, McDonald's, Olive Garden, Panera Bread, Sakura Japanese, Shari's, Starbucks, Subway, Taco Del Mar, Wendy's [lodging] Candlewood Suites, Hampton Inn [other] Best Buy, Costco/gas, Dick's, Discount Tire, Home Depot, K-Mart/Little Caesars, Kohl's, Michael's, Old Navy, Outlet Shops/famous brands, Petsmart, Ross, See's Candies, Verizon, vet, W [other] Chrysler/Jeep/Dodge, Ford/Lincoln, Honda, Mazda, Nissan, Subaru, Suzuki, Toyota/Scion, VW
228mm	Skagit River
227	WA 538 E, College Way, Mt Vernon, E [food] A&W, Big Scoop Rest., Cocina 18 Mexican, Denny's, Dragon Inn, El Gitano, Hong Kong Rest., Jack-in-the Box, Jersey Mike's, KFC, Max Dale's Steak Chops, Moreno's Mexican, Papa Murphy's, Pizza Hut/Taco Bell, Riverside Cafe, RoundTable Pizza, Sahara Pizza, Starbucks, Subway, Taco Time [lodging] Days Inn, West Winds Motel [other] $Tree, Ace Hardware, AT&T, AutoZone, Goodyear/auto, Grocery Outlet, Hobby Lobby, Jo-Ann Fabrics, Midas, Office Depot, O'Reilly Parts, PetCo, Rite Aid, Safeway/dsl, Tire Factory, W [gas] APP/dsl, Shell/dsl [food] Arby's, Burger King, Cranberry Tree Rest., DQ, Fortune Chinese, IHOP, Los Compadres, Panda Express, Royal Star Buffet [lodging] Best Western, Quality Inn, Tulip Inn [other] Blade RV Ctr, Chevrolet, Lowe's, Riverbend RV Park, URGENT CARE, Walmart/Subway
226	WA 536 W, Kincaid St, E [other] [H], RV camping, W [food] Old Towne Grainery Rest., Skagit River Brewing Co [other] City Ctr, NAPA, Red Apple Mkt, visitor info
225	Anderson Rd, E [gas] 76/dsl, Fuel Express/dsl [other] CarQuest, Country Motorhomes, vet, W [gas] Chevron, Truck City Trkstp/dsl [other] Evert's RV Ctr, Freightliner, Poulsbo RV Ctr, Poulsbo RV Ctr
224	WA 99 S (from nb, no return), S Mt Vernon, E [food] [gas]/dsl
221	WA 534 E, Conway, Lake McMurray, E [gas] 76/dsl [other] farmers mkt, W [gas] 76/dsl, Chevron/dsl/LP [food] Conway Deli [lodging] Channel Lodge/Rest. (11mi) [other] Blake's RV Park/marina (6mi), USPO
218	Starbird Rd
215	300th NW, W [gas] Interstate/dsl
214mm	**weigh sta nb**
212	WA 532 W, Stanwood, Bryant, W [gas] 76/dsl, Shell/Burger Stop/dsl [other] Camano Island SP (19mi)
210	236th NE, E [other] Angel Winds Casino, River Rock/dsl
209mm	Stillaguamish River
208	WA 530, Silvana, Arlington, E [gas] 76, A1/dsl, Arco/dsl, Tesoro/dsl [food] Denny's, Patty's Eggnest&Turkeyhouse, Subway [lodging] Arlington Motel [other] to N Cascades Hwy, W [gas] 76/dsl
207mm	**[RS] both lanes, coffee, full [handicap] facilities, litter barrels, petwalk [phone] [picnic] RV dump, vending**
206	WA 531, Lakewood, E [gas] 7-11, 76/dsl, 76/dsl, Arco, Shell [food] Alfy's Pizza, Buzz Inn Steaks, Domino's, Jack-in-the-Box, Jersey Mike's, Jersey Mike's, Jimmy John's, Jimmy John's, KFC, Little Caesar's, Little Caesar's, McDonald's, Moose Creek BBQ, Olympia Pizza, Olympia Pizza, Panda Express, Panda Express, Papa Murphy's, Papa Murphy's, Peking Palace, Peking Palace, Starbucks, Subway, Taco Del Mar, Taco Time, Wendy's [lodging] Best Western, Best Western, Medallion Hotel, Quality Inn, Quality Inn, Smokey Point Motel [other] $Tree, AT&T, Chrysler/Dodge/Jeep, Ford, Ford, Harley-Davidson, Honda, Honda, Jo-Ann Fabrics, Lowe's, O'Reilly Parts, Radio Shack, Radio Shack, Rite Aid, Safeway/dsl, Schwab Tire, Smokey Point RV Park, vet, Walmart/Subway, W [food] 5 Guys Burgers, Boston's, Buffalo Wild Wings, Burger King, Coldstone, Hot Iron Mongolian, IHOP, Jamba Juice, Pizza Hut, Red Robin, Starbucks, Subway, Taco Bell, Teriyaki Wok, Wonderful Buffet [other] AT&T, Best Buy, Costco/gas, Discount Tire, Firestone/auto, Marshall's, Michael's, Office Depot, PetCo, Target, to Wenburg SP, Verizon
202	116th NE, E [gas] Shell/dsl [food] Blazing Onion Burger, Carl's Jr, Magic Dragon Chinese, Papa John's, Starbucks, Subway, Taco Bell, Tres Hermanos Mexican [other] Kohl's, Petsmart, Rite Aid, Ross, Verizon, WinCo Foods, W [gas] Chevron/dsl, Donna's Trkstp/Gull/dsl/scales/24hr/ @ [food] McDonald's, Olive Garden, Ram Rest. [other] Seattle Outlets/famous brands, st patrol, Tulalip Resort/Casino
200	88th St NE, Quil Ceda Way, E [gas] 7-11, Shell/dsl/LP [food] Applebee's, Mkt St Cafe, Starbucks [lodging] Holiday Inn Express [other] Haggen's Foods, W [gas] USA [food] Bob's Burgers, Port of Subs, Taco Del Mar [other] Cabela's, casino, Home Depot, Walmart/McDonald's
199	WA 528 E, Marysville, Tulalip, E [gas] 76, Arco, Chevron/dsl, Shell/dsl [food] Burger King, Don's Rest./24hr, DQ, Jack-in-the-Box, Las Margaritas Mexican, Maxwell's Rest., Subway [lodging] Village Motel/Rest. [other] Albertson's, Big Lots, JC Penney, O'Reilly Parts, PepBoys, Petco, Rite Aid, Staples, Verizon, Walgreens, W [gas] 76, Chevron/dsl [food] Arby's, McDonald's, Taco Time, Wendy's [lodging] Comfort Inn [other] casino, Chevrolet, Robinson RV Ctr, Subaru, to Tulalip Indian Res
198	Port of Everett (from sb), Steamboat Slough, st patrol
195mm	Snohomish River
195	Port of Everett (from nb), Marine View Dr
194	US 2 E, Everett Ave, W [gas] Shell/dsl [other] Schwab Tire, City Ctr
193	WA 529, Pacific Ave (from nb), W [gas] 76 [food] Denny's, Hunan Palace [lodging] Best Western, Holiday Inn, Travelodge [other] [H], Lowe's
192	Broadway, to 41st St, W [gas] 76/dsl, Chevron, Shell [food] Buzz Inn Steaks, IHOP, Little Caesars, Quiznos, Starbucks, Subway [lodging] Travelodge [other] City Ctr
189	WA 526 W, WA 527, Everett Mall Way, Everett, E [gas] Arco, Chevron, Shell/dsl [food] Alfy's Pizza, Burger King, Buzz Inn Steaks, Subway, Wendy's [lodging] EconoLodge, Extended Stay America [other] Costco/gas, vet, WinCo Foods, W [gas] Shell/dsl [food] Bob's Burgers, Famous Dave's, Jack-in-the-Box, Jimmy John's, Olive Garden [lodging] Days Inn, Extended Stay America

INTERSTATE 5 Cont'd

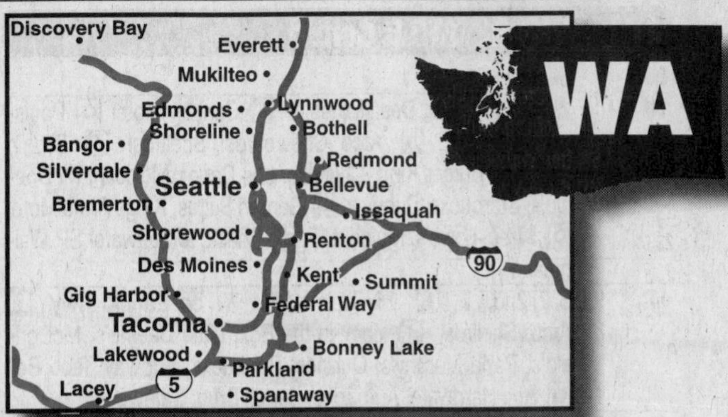

SEATTLE

189 Continued
[other] Best Buy, Goodyear/auto, Macy's, mall, Michaels, Petsmart, Sears/auto, TJ Maxx, Verizon, Walmart

188mm [RS] /weigh sta sb, coffee, full [handicapped] facilities, info, litter barrels, [phone] [picnic] RV dump

186 WA 96, 128th SW, E [gas] 76/dsl, Shell/dsl, Texaco [food] O'Donnells Rest. [lodging] Quality Inn [other] Lakeside RV Park, W [gas] Arco, Chevron, Shell [food] A&W/KFC, Acropolis Pizza, Denny's, Dickey's BBQ, DQ, McDonald's, Ming Dynasty, Papa John's, Pizza Hut, Skipper's, Starbucks, Subway, Taco Bell, Taco Time [lodging] Holiday Inn Express, La Quinta, Motel 6 [other] $Tree, Albertson's/Sav-on, Goodyear/auto, Maple RV Park, vet

183 164th SW, E [gas] Arco, Shell/dsl [food] Jack-in-the-Box, Panda Express, Quiznos, Starbucks, Subway, Taco Del Mar, Taco Time [other] Walgreens, Walmart, W [gas] Chevron/dsl [food] 5 Guys Burgers, MOD Pizza, Subway [other] Fred Meyer/dsl, vet

182 WA 525, Alderwood Mall Blvd, to Alderwood Mall, E I-405 S, to Bellevue, W [gas] Arco [food] Anthony's SeafoodGrill, Azteca Mexican, Buffalo Wild Wings, Cafe Rio, Claim Jumper, Fatburger, Jersey Mike's, Keg Steaks, Macaroni Grill, Panera Bread, PF Chang's, Qdoba Mexican, Red Robin, TCBY [lodging] Homewood Suites, Residence Inn [other] JC Penney, Kohl's, Macy's, Nordstrom, REI, Rite Aid, Ross, Sears/auto, See's Candies, Target, vet, World Mkt

181 44th Ave W, to WA 524, Lynnwood, E [gas] 76/dsl, Arco, Shell [food] Jimmy John's, Little Caesar's, McDonald's/playplace, Old Spaghetti Factory, Starbucks [lodging] Embassy Suites, Extended Stay America, Hampton Inn, Holiday Inn Express [other] Albertson's, Barnes&Noble, Best Buy, Jaguar, Land Rover, Lowe's, Old Navy, O'Reilly Parts, PetCo, Staples, Verizon, vet, Whole Foods Mkt, W [gas] 76/dsl, Arco, Chevron, Shell/repair [food] Applebee's, Arby's, Black Angus, Buca Italian, Chipotle Mexican, ChuckeCheese, Denny's, Ezell's Chicken, IHOP, Jack-in-the-Box, KFC, McDonald's, Old Country Buffet, Olive Garden, Panda Express, Red Lobster, Rock Woodfire Pizza, Starbucks, Subway, Taco Bell, Taco del Mar, Todo Mexico, Wendy's [lodging] Best Western, Courtyard, Days Inn, La Quinta [other] 7-11, Fred Meyer/dsl, Goodyear/auto, Radio Shack, Schwab Tire, Tuesday Morning, URGENT CARE, USPO, vet

179 220th SW, Mountlake Terrace, W [gas] Shell/dsl [food] Azteca Mexican, Port of Subs, Subway [other] [H], vet

178 236th St SW (from nb), Mountlake Terrace

177 WA 104, Edmonds, E [gas] Chevron/dsl, Shell/dsl [food] Gabriel's Fire BBQ, Mazatlan Mexican, McDonald's/playplace, Pagliacchi Pizza, Starbucks, Subway, Time Out Burger, Todo Mexico [lodging] Motel 6 [other] Office Depot, O'Reilly Parts, RiteAid, Thriftway Foods, URGENT CARE

176 NE 175th St, Aurora Ave N, to Shoreline

175 WA 523, NE 145th, 5th Ave NE

174 NE 130th, Roosevelt Way

173 1st Ave NE, Northgate Way, E [gas] 76 [food] 5 Guys Burgers, Azteca Mexican, BlueFin Grill, CA Pizza Kitchen, Chipotle Mexican, Domino's, Jimmy John's, Macaroni Grill, Mama Sportini's, Marie Callender's, Panera Bread, Quiznos, Ram Rest., Red Robin, Stanford's Rest., Super Buffet [other] Barnes&Noble, Best Buy, Discount Tire, JC Penney, Macy's, mall, Nordstrom, Old Navy, Ross, Target, Verizon, W [gas] 76, Chevron, Shell/dsl [food] Arby's, McDonald's, Saffron Grill, Starbucks [lodging] Hotel Nexus [other] 7-11

172 N 85th, Aurora Ave

171 WA 522, Lake City Way, Bothell

170 Ravenna Blvd, E [gas] Shell/dsl

SEATTLE

169 NE 45th, NE 50th, E [gas] 76, Shell [food] Subway [other] [H], PetCo, U of WA, vet, W [other] to Seattle Pacific U, zoo

168b WA 520, to Bellevue

168a Lakeview Blvd, downtown

167 Mercer St (exits left from nb), Fairview Ave, Seattle Ctr

166 Olive Way, Stewart St, E [other] [H], W [lodging] SpringHill Suites [other] Honda

165a Seneca St (exits left from nb), James St, E [other] [H]

165b Union St, E [lodging] Homewood Suites, W [food] Ruth's Chris Steaks [lodging] Renaissance Inn, Sheraton

164b 4th Ave S, to Kingdome, downtown

164a I-90 E, to Spokane, downtown

163 6th Ave, S Spokane St, W Seattle Br, Columbian Way, **1 mi W** on 4th Ave S [gas] Arco/dsl, Gull/dsl, Shell [food] Arby's, Burger King, Denny's, Jack-in-the-Box, KFC, McDonald's, Starbucks, Subway, Taco Bell [other] Costco/gas, Pepboys, USPO

162 Corson Ave, Michigan St (exits left from nb), same as 161

161 Swift Ave, Albro Place, W [gas] 76/dsl, Shell/dsl [food] Arby's, Starbucks, Thai Rest. [lodging] Georgetown Inn

158 Pacific Hwy S, E Marginal Way, W [gas] Chevron/dsl [other] NAPA

157 ML King Way

156 WA 539 N, Interurban Ave (no EZ return to sb), Tukwila, E [gas] Pacific Pride/dsl [food] Billy Baroos Rest., W [gas] 76/dsl, Shell/dsl [food] Jack-in-the-Box, Quiznos, Starbucks, Sunny Teriyaki [lodging] Days Inn

154b WA 518, Burien, W [lodging] Extended Stay America

154a I-405, N to Bellevue

153 S Center Pkwy, (from nb), E [gas] Chevron/dsl [food] Applebee's, Azteca Mexican, Bahama Breeze, BJ's Rest., Buffalo Wild Wings, Burger King, CA Pizza Kitchen, Cheesecake Factory, Chipotle Mexican, ClaimJumper, Coldstone, Duke's ChowderHouse, Famous Dave's, Five Guys, Grazie Ristorante, IHOP, Jamba Juice, Mayflower of China, McDonald's, Mizuki Buffet, Mizuki Japanese Steaks, Mongolian Grill, Old Spaghetti Factory, Olive Garden, Outback Steaks, Panda Express, Panera Bread, Qdoba Mexican, Red Robin, Simply Thai, Sizzler, Stanford's Rest., Starbucks, Subway, Thai Cuisine, Zoopa [lodging] DoubleTree Inn [other] $Tree, Acura, AT&T, Barnes&Noble, Best Buy, Big Lots, Firestone/auto, JC Penney, Jo-Ann Fabrics, Kohl's, Macy's, mall, Michael's, Nordstrom, Nordstrom Rack, Office Depot, Old Navy, PetCo, Petsmart, REI, Ross, Sears/auto, See's Candies, Target, Tuesday Morning, Verizon, World Mkt

152 S 188th, Orillia Rd, W [gas] 76/dsl [food] Dave's Diner, Denny's, Jack-in-the-Box, Taco Bell [lodging] DoubleTree Hotel, Hampton Inn, La Quinta, Motel 6 [other] city park, to airport

151 S 200th, Military Rd, E [gas] 76/Subway/dsl [lodging] Motel 6, W [gas] 7-11, 76, Chevron [food] IHOP [lodging] Best Value Inn, Best Western, Comfort Inn, Days Inn, Fairfield Inn, Hampton Inn, Holiday Inn Express, Sleep Inn, Super 8 [other] AutoZone, city park, NAPA, O'Reilly Parts, U-Haul

WA

INTERSTATE 5 Cont'd

Exit #	Services
149	WA 516, to Kent, Des Moines, E Century Motel Poulsbo RV Ctr, W Arco, Chevron/dsl, Shell/dsl Baskin Robbins, Burger King, Church's, Los Cabos Mexican, McDonald's, Starbucks, Subway Garden Suites, Kings Arms Motel $Tree, Lowe's, Meineke, Radio Shack, to Saltwater SP, Walgreens
147	S 272nd, E 76/Circle K/dsl, W **on Pacific Hwy** Arco, Shell/dsl Jack-in-the-Box, Little Caesar's, McDonald's, Papa Murphy's, Quiznos, Starbucks, Subway, Taco Bell Ace Hardware, AutoZone, Bartell Drug, Safeway
143	S 320th, Federal Way, W 76/dsl, Arco, Shell/dsl Applebee's, Azteca Mexican, Black Angus, Black Bear Diner, Buffalo Wild Wings, Chipotle Mexican, Church's, Coldstone, Costa Vida, Denny's, Domino's, Grand Buffet, Grand Peking, Ivar's Seafood, Jasmine Mongolian, Jimmy John's, McDonald's, McGrath's Fishouse, Mika Japanese Buffet, Old Country Buffet, Outback Steaks, Panda Express, Panera Bread, Papa Murphy's, Qdoba Mexican, Ram Rest., Red Lobster, Red Robin, Starbucks, Subway, Taco Time, Tokyo Japanese Steaks, Village Inn, Wendy's Best Western, Clarion, Comfort Inn, Courtyard, Extended Stay America, Hampton Inn Albertson's, AT&T, Barnes&Noble, Best Buy, Dick's, Jo-Ann Fabrics, Kohl's, Macy's, mall, Marlene's Natural Mkt, Michael's, O'Reilly Parts, PetCo, Petsmart, Radio Shack, Rite Aid, Ross, Safeway/dsl, Sears/auto, See's Candies, Target, TJ Maxx, to Dash Point SP, Trader Joe's, Tuesday Morning, Verizon, Walmart/McDonald's
142b a	WA 18 E, S 348th, Enchanted Pkwy, E funpark, W Chevron, Shell/dsl Arby's, Biscuits Cafe, Burger King, Del Taco, Denny's, Fatburger, Jack-in-the-Box, Jamba Juice, Jimmy Mac's Roadhouse, KFC, LJ Silver, McDonald's, Olive Garden, Panda Express, Popeye's, Puerta Vallarta, Quiznos, RoundTable Pizza, Shari's, Starbucks, Subway, Taco Bell, Taco Del Mar, Taco Time, Thai Bistro, The Rock Pizza, Time Out Grill Day's Inn, Quality Inn, Red Lion Inn H, Chevrolet, Costco/gas, Discount Tire, Hobby Lobby, Home Depot, Lowe's, Office Depot, O'Reilly Parts, Pepboys, Schwab Tire, UHaul, Verizon, Walmart/Subway
140mm	**both lanes, full facilities, litter barrels, nb, petwalk RV dump, weigh sta**
137	WA 99, Fife, Milton, E Chevron/dsl, Shell, Tahoma Express/dsl DQ, Johnny's Rest., Warthog BBQ Motel 6 Acura, Cadillac, Evert's RV Ctr, visitor info, W 76/dsl, Shell/dsl A&W/KFC, Arby's, Denny's, Fife Thai Rest., McDonald's, Mitzel's Kitchen, Pick Quick Burgers, Pizza Hut, Pizza Hut/Taco Bell, Poodle Dog, Quiznos, Sapporo Japanese, Starbucks, Subway, Taco Time, Wendy's Days Inn, EQC Motel/casino, Quality Inn 7-11, Audi/Porsche, Infiniti, Mercedes, O'Reilly Parts, Schwab Tire, Sumner RV Ctr, Sunset RV Ctr, Tacoma RV Ctr, Verizon
136b a	Port of Tacoma, E CFN/dsl Baydos RV Ctr, BMW, Costco, Honda, I-5 Motors, Mini, Peterbilt, Tacoma RV Ctr, W Chevron/dsl, Gull/dsl, Loves/Chester's/Subway/dsl/scales/LP/RV dump/24hr, Shell/dsl Jack-in-the-Box Best Night Inn, EconoLodge, Extended Stay America, Rodeway Inn, Sunshine Motel, Travelodge Fife RV Ctr, Goodyear/biodsl, Harley-Davidson, Land Rover/Jaguar/Lexus, Meineke, NAPA, Nissan, Poulsbo RV Ctr, truck repair, Volvo
135	Bay St, Puyallup, E Shell/Tahoma Express Majestic RV Park (4mi), W Chevron/dsl/scales Subway La Quinta to Tacoma Dome
134	Portland Ave (from nb), same as 135
133	WA 7, I-705, W Best Western, Courtyard, Holiday Inn Express museum, Tacoma Dome, City Ctr
132	WA 16 W, S 38th, Gig Harbor, to Bremerton, W Adriatic Grill, BJ's Rest., Buffalo Wild Wings, Chipotle, Five Guys, Jamba Juice, Jimmy John's, Krispy Kreme, Panera Bread, Red Robin, Wendy's $Tree, Best Buy, Costco/gas, Firestone/auto, Ford/Toyota, Goodyear/auto, JC Penney, JoAnn Fabrics, Macy's, mall, Nordstrom, Old Navy, PetCo, REI, Sears/auto, to Pt Defiance Pk/Zoo, Verizon, World Mkt
130	S 56th, Tacoma Mall Blvd, W Shell/dsl Axteca Mexican, ChuckeCheese, Jack-in-the-Box, Subway, Wingers Extended Stay America
129	S 72nd, S 84th, E Chevron, Valero Applebee's, Burger King, DQ, Elmer's, Famous Dave's, IHOP, Jack-in-the-Box, Mongolian Grill, Olive Garden, Popeyes, Red Lobster, RoundTable Pizza, Shari's, Starbucks, Subway Motel 6, Shilo Inn Bass Pro Shops, WinCo Foods, W Hooters Days Inn Home Depot, to Steilacoom Lake
128	S 84th St (from nb) same as 129, E 76, Shell/dsl Denny's, Ginger Palace, Greatwall Chinese, Subway American Lodge, Comfort Inn, Crossland Suites, Econolodge, Hampton Inn, Holiday Inn Express, Howard Johnson, Red Lion Hotel, Rothem Inn, W Shell/dsl Discount Tire
127	WA 512, S Tacoma Way, Puyallup, Mt Ranier, W 7-11, 76/7-11, Arco/dsl, Eagle AAA Buffet, DQ, Ivar's Seafood, Mazatlan Mexican, McDonald's, Sizzler, Starbucks, Subway, Taco Guaynas, Taco Time, Wendy's Candlewood Suites, Western Inn Grocery Outlet, O'Reilly Parts
125	to McChord AFB, Lakewood, W 76/Circle K/dsl, Chevron, Shell A&W/KFC, Carr's Rest., Church's, Denny's, Greek Cafe, Pizza Hut, Subway, Wendy's Holiday Inn Express, Home Motel H, 7-11, Aamco, Ford, NAPA, O'Reilly Parts, tires/repair, U-Haul
124	Gravelly Lake Dr, W 76/Circle K, Arco/repair El Toro Mexican, Pizza Casa, Red Robin (2mi), same as 125
123	Thorne Lane, Tillicum Lane
122	Berkeley St, Camp Murray, W Chevron/repair Gertie's Grill, Jack-in-the-Box, KFC, McDonald's, Papa John's, Pizza Hut, Popeyes, Subway, Taco Bell, Teryaki House, Wok In Wok Out 7-11, AutoZone
120	Ft Lewis, E Ft Lewis Military Museum
119	Du Pont Rd, Steilacoom, E to Ft Lewis, W 76 Happy Teriyaki, Starbucks, Subway Hampton Inn
118	Center Dr, W Chevron/dsl Domino's, Farrelli's Pizza, Fortune Cookie Chinese, Jack-in-the-Box, Koko's Wok, McDonald's, McNamara's Eatery, Quiznos, Starbucks, Subway, Super Buffet, Viva Mexico GuestHouse Inn, Liberty Inn
117mm	**weigh sta nb**
116	Mounts Rd, Old Nisqually, E golf, W Caddy Shack Grill
115mm	Nisqually River
114	Nisqually, E Arco/dsl, Chevron/repair/Lp Nisqually Grill, Norma's Burgers Nisqually Auto Repair, Nisqually RV Park, River Bend RV Park (3mi), WLYH RV Park (2mi)
111	WA 510 E, Marvin Rd, to Yelm, E 76/Circle K, Chevron/dsl, Shell/dsl Burger King, Coldstone, Hawk's Prairie Rest./casino, Jack-in-the-Box, Jamba Juice, KFC/LJ Silver, Lemon Grass Rest., Little Caesar's, McDonald's, Panda Express, Panera Bread, Papa Murphy's, Popeyes, Puerto Vallarta, RAM Rest., Red Robin, RoundTable Pizza, Starbucks, Subway, Super Buffet, Taco Del Mar, Taco Time, Vinny's NY Pizza Best Western, Day's Inn $Tree, AT&T, Best Buy, BigLots, Costco/gas, Grocery Outlet, Harley Davidson, Home Depot, O'Reilly Parts, PetCo, Radio Shack, Rite Aid, Safeway/gas, Schwab Tire, Verizon,

WA

TACOMA

INTERSTATE 5 Cont'd

OLYMPIA

111 Continued
Walgreens, Walmart/Subway, WLYH RV Park (2mi), W 7-11/dsl Mayan Mexican, Meconi's Subs Cabela's, RV camping, Tolmie SP (5mi)

109 Martin Way, Sleator-Kenny Rd, E Main Chinese Buffet, Subway, Taco Bell, The Rock Pizza Discount Tire, ShopKO, W 76/dsl, Shell/dsl Brewery City Pizza, Burger King, Casa Mia, Denny's, El Serape Mexican, Jimmy John's, Red Lobster, Shari's, Subway Comfort Inn, La Quinta, Quality Inn, Ramada Inn, Super 8 H, Tire Factory

108 Sleater-Kinney Rd, E Shell/dsl Applebee's, Arby's, Carl's Jr, McDonald's/playplace, Pizza Hut/Taco Bell, Starbucks, Wendy's $Tree, Firestone/auto, Fred Meyer/dsl, GNC, Kohl's, Marshall's, Michael's, Office Depot, Petsmart, Radio Shack, Rite Aid, Sears/auto, Target, Tuesday Morning, Verizon, W Arco/dsl, Shell Casa Mia, Dirty Dave's, El Sarape Mexican, Jack-in-the-Box, Panda Express, Starbucks, Subway Ramada Inn H, AT&T, Lowe's, Safeway/gas, same as 109, Tire Factory

107 Pacific Ave, E Shell/dsl/E-85 DQ, Fajita a Grill, Izzy's Pizza, Jimmy's Thai/Chinese, Shari's, Subway, Taco Time H, Albertson's, Home Depot, Ross, vet, W Coumbs RV Ctr, Ford

105 St Capitol, W 76/Subway/dsl, Chevron/dsl Quality Inn to St Capitol

104 US 101 N, W Olympia, to Aberdeen, W 7-11, Chevron/dsl, Shell/Oly Burger/dsl Jack-in-the-Box Extended Stay America, Red Lion Hotel Buick/GMC, Chevrolet/Cadillac, Ford, Honda, Hyundai, Kia, Lincoln/Mazda, Nissan, Subaru, to Capitol Mall, Toyota/Scion, VW

103 2nd Ave, Deschutes Ave, to hist dist

102 Trosper Rd, Black Lake, E Shell Brewery City Pizza, Burger King, DQ, El Sarape Mexican, Happy Teriyaki, Jack-in-the-Box, KFC, McDonald's, Plaza Jalisco Mexican, Starbucks, Subway, Taco Bell, Taco Time Best Western, Tumwater Inn Ace Hardware, Goodyear/auto, O'Reilly Parts, Schwab Tire, Verizon, W Chevron, Mobil Best Buffet, Nickelby's Rest., Panda Express, Papa Murphy's, Pizza Hut, Starbucks, Subway, Taco Del Mar, The Brick Rest. Albertson's, Alderbrook RV Park, AutoZone, Costco/gas, Fred Meyer/dsl, GNC, Home Depot, Radio Shack, Tumwater Auto Repair, Walgreens, Walmart

101 Tumwater Blvd, E Chevron, Shell/dsl DQ (1mi), Inferno's Pizza, Meconi's Pizza, Red Wagon Burgers Comfort Inn, GuestHouse Inn, Olympia Camping 7-11, USPO

99 WA 121 S, 93rd Ave, Scott Lake, E Pilot/McDonald's/Subway/dsl/scales/24hr Ace Hardware, American Heritage Camping, Olympia Camping

95 WA 121, Littlerock, 3 mi E Millersylvania SP, RV camping, W Chevron/dsl (3mi) Farmboy Drive-In Freightliner

93.5mm **both lanes, coffee, full facilities, info, litter barrels, petwalk vending**

91mm **both lanes, coffee, full facilities, info, litter barrels, petwalk vending**

88 US 12, Rochester, E Blair's I-5 RV Ctr, I-5 Truckwash, W Arco, CFN/dsl, Chevron/dsl, Shell Burger Claim, DQ, Figaro's Pizza, Jack-in-the-Box, Mariachi Mexican, McDonald's, Quiznos, Starbucks Great Wolf Lodge auto repair, Outback RV Park (2mi)

82 Harrison Ave, Factory Outlet Way, Centralia, E Arco Burger King, Burgerville, Casa Ramos Mexican, Centralia Deli, DQ, Panda Chinese, Papa Pete's Pizza, Peking House

CENTRALIA

82 Continued
Chinese, Pizza Hut, Quiznos, Thai Dish, Wendy's Centralia Inn, King Oscar Motel, Quality Inn, Travelodge AutoZone, VF/famous brands, W Chevron/dsl, Shell/dsl, Texaco Arby's, Bill&Bea's, Country Cousin Rest., Denny's, Domino's, Jack-in-the-Box, McDonald's, Papa Murphy's, Starbucks, Subway, Taco Bell Motel 6 AT&T, Centralia Outlets/famous brands, Midway RV Park, O'Reilly Parts, Rite Aid, Safeway/dsl, Schwab Tire, Verizon, city park

82mm Skookumchuck River

81 WA 507, Mellen St, E Chevron/dsl, Shell/dsl Subway Empress Inn, Lakeview Inn, Pepper Tree Motel/RV Park/dump, W H

79 Chamber Way, E Shell/dsl Jalisco Mexican Goodyear/auto, museum, vet, visitor info, W Texaco/dsl/LP/e85 Applebee's, McDonald's, Starbucks, Subway, Taco Del Mar, Wendy's $Tree, GNC, Grocery Outlet, Home Depot, K-Mart/Little Caesar's, Michael's, O'Reilly Parts, Radio Shack, st patrol, Toyota/Scion, Verizon, Walgreens, Walmart/McDonald's

77 WA 6 W, Chehalis, E 76/dsl, Cenex/dsl/LP Dairy Bar, Jeremy's Cafe Holiday Inn Express NAPA, Schwab Tire, USPO, W Rainbow Falls SP (16mi), truck parts, veterans museum

76 13th St, E Arco, Chevron/dsl Denny's, Jack-in-the-Box, Kit Carson Rest., South Pacific Bistro, Subway Best Western, Econolodge, Relax Inn Baydo's RV Ctr, Ford, Uhlmann's I-5 RV Ctr/RV dump, W RV park/dump

74 Labree Rd, W Emerald RV Ctr

72 Rush Rd, Napavine, E Shell/dsl/scales Burger King, McDonald's, RibEye Rest., Subway Country Canopy RV Ctr/repair, RV park, W Loves/Carl's Jr/dsl/scales/24hr, Shell/dsl Starbucks

72mm Newaukum River

71 WA 508 E, Onalaska, Napavine, E 76/dsl KC Truck Parts

68 US 12 E, Morton, E Arco/dsl, Texaco/dsl Spiffy's Rest. Gateway RV Ctr, Mt Ranier NP, RV Park, to Lewis&Clark SP, W 76/rest./dsl

63 WA 505, Winlock, W Shell/Chesters/dsl/LP

60 Toledo Vader Rd, Toledo

59 WA 506 W, Vader, E Shell/dsl Beesley's Cafe RV Park, W Chevron/Subway/dsl Country House Rest.

59mm Cowlitz River

57 Jackson Hwy, Barnes Dr, E R&R Tires, W Texaco/GeeCee's/café/dsl/scales/24hr/ @ repair, RV camping

55mm **both lanes, full facilities, litter barrels, petwalk vending**

52 Barnes Dr, Toutle Park Rd, E Paradise Cove RV Park/general store, W Toutle River RV Resort

50mm Toutle River

🅖 = gas 🍴 = food 🛏 = lodging ⊙ = other 🆁 = rest stop Copyright 2016 - The Next EXIT ®

N INTERSTATE 5 Cont'd

Exit #	Services
49	WA 504 E, Castle Rock, **E** 🅖 Chevron/dsl/LP, Shell/dsl 🍴 49er Diner, Burger King, C&L Burgers, El Compadre Mexican, Papa Pete's Pizza, Parker's Rest., Subway 🛏 7 West Motel, Mt St Helens Motel, Timberland Inn ⊙ Seaquest SP (5mi), **W** 🍴 McDonald's
48	Castle Rock, **E** ⊙ Cedars RV Park/dump, **W** ⊙ city park
46	Pleasant Hill Rd, Headquarters Rd, **E** ⊙ Cedars RV Park/dump
44mm	weigh sta sb 🍴
42	Bridge Dr, Lexington, **W** 🅖 Chevron/dsl 🍴 Subway ⊙ auto repair
40	to WA 4, Kelso-Longview, **W** 🅖 Texaco 🛏 Econolodge
39	WA 4, Kelso, to Longview, **E** 🅖 Arco, Shell 🍴 Denny's, Jack-in-the-Box, McDonald's, Shari's, Starbucks, Subway, Taco Time 🛏 Motel 6, Red Lion Hotel, Super 8 ⊙ Brook Hollow RV Park, city park, Rite Aid, Verizon, **W** 🍴 Burger King, DQ, Fiesta Bonita Mexican, Izzy's Pizza, Red Lobster, Taco Bell 🛏 Comfort Inn, GuestHouse Inn ⊙ JC Penney, Macys, mall, museum, Safeway/dsl, Target
36	WA 432 W, to WA 4, to US 30, Kelso, **E** ⊙ U-Neek RV Ctr, **W** ⊙ RV Camping, Toyota/Scion
32	Kalama River Rd, **E** 🍴 Fireside Café ⊙ Camp Kalama RV Park/camping/gifts
31mm	Kalama River
30	Kalama, **E** 🅖 Chevron/dsl 🍴 Burger Bar, Columbia Rest., Lucky Dragon Chinese, Playa Azul Mexican, Poker Pete's Pizza, Subway 🛏 Kalama River Inn ⊙ antiques, Godfrey's Drug, USPO, **W** 🅖 Spirit/dsl ⊙ RV camping
27	Todd Rd, Port of Kalama, **E** 🅖 Rebel/Shell/café/dsl/24hr
22	Dike Access Rd, **W** ⊙ Columbia Riverfront RV Park, O'Reilly Parts, Schwab Tire, Walmart/Subway
21	WA 503 E, Woodland, **E** 🅖 Arco/dsl, Chevron, Pacific Pride/dsl, Shell/LP/dsl 🍴 America's Diner, Burgerville, Casa Tapatia, DQ, Fat Moose Grill, Guilliano's Pizza, Mali Thai, OakTree Rest., Rosie's Rest. 🛏 Lewis River Inn, Motel 6, Quality Inn ⊙ Ace Hardware, Hi-School Drug, Woodland Shores RV Park, **W** 🅖 Astro, Shell/dsl 🍴 Antony's Pizzaria, Guadalajara Mexican, Los Pepes Mexican, McDonald's, Papa Murphy's, Starbucks, Subway 🛏 Hansen's Motel ⊙ $Tree, NAPA, Oil Can Henry's, repair/tires, Safeway/dsl, Verizon
20mm	N Fork Lewis River
18mm	E Fork Lewis River
16	NW La Center Rd, La Center, **E** 🅖 Shell/dsl 🍴 Twin Dragons Rest. (2mi) ⊙ Paradise Point SP, Tri-Mountain Golf/rest.
15mm	weigh sta nb
14	WA 501 S, Pioneer St, Ridgefield, **E** 🅖 Arco 🍴 Country Café, Papa Pete's Pizza, Subway, Teriyaki Thai ⊙ Big Fir RV Park (4mi), Ridgefield WR, to Battleground Lake SP (14mi), Tri-Mountain RV Park, vet, **W** 🅖 Chevron/dsl
13mm	🆁 sb, full ♿ facilities, info, litter barrels, petwalk 🍴 ♻ RV dump, vending
11	WA 502, Battleground, 🆁 nb, full ♿ facilities, info, litter barrels, petwalk 🍴 ♻ RV dump, vending
9	NE 179th St, **E** 🍴 Jollie's Rest., **W** 🅖 Chevron/dsl ⊙ RV Park
7	I-205 S (from sb), to I-84, WA 14, NE 134th St, **E** 🅖 7-11, Arco, Mobil 🍴 Applebee's, Billygan's Roadhouse, Burger King, Burgerville, Jack-in-the-Box, McDonald's, Muchas Gracias, Panda Express, Round Table Pizza, Starbucks, Subway, Taco Bell 🛏 Holiday Inn Express, Shilo Inn, Vancouver Inn ⊙ 🄷, 99 RV Park, Albertson's, Safeway/dsl, Verizon, Walgreens,

7	Continued **W** 🅖 Shell 🍴 Baskin-Robbins, Bruchi's, El Tapatio, Garlic Jim's Pizza, Papa Murphy's, PizzaSchmitzza, Planet Thai, Starbucks, Subway 🛏 La Quinta ⊙ AT&T, Fred Meyer, URGENT CARE
5	NE 99th St, **E** 🍴 Burgerville, Carl's Jr, Del Taco, Domino's, Fat Dave's Rest., Popeyes, Quiznos ⊙ 7-11, AutoZone, Harley-Davidson, Walgreens, Walmart/Subway, Winco Foods/gas **W** 🅖 Arco/dsl, Chevron/dsl 🍴 Applebee's, Bortolami's Pizza, McDonald's, Subway, Taco Del Mar ⊙ $Tree, Grocery Outlet, Kohl's, Office Depot, PetCo, Target, Verizon
4	NE 78th St, Hazel Dell, **E** 🅖 7-11, 76 🍴 Baja Fresh, Baskin Robbins, Burger King, Canton Chinese, Don Pedro Mexican, Dragon Buffet, Izzy's Grill, KFC, McDonald's, Muchas Gracias Mexican, PeachTree Rest., Pizza Hut, Skipper's, Starbucks, Subway, Taco Bell 🛏 Quality Inn ⊙ Aamco, AT&T, CarQuest, CostLess Parts, Firestone, Fred Meyer, Jo-Ann, O'Reilly Parts, Radio Shack, Tire Factory, U-Haul, **W** 🅖 Shell/dsl/LP 🍴 Buffalo Wild Wings, Chipotle Mexican, Five Guys, Jack-in-the-Box, Jazzy John's BBQ, Jimmy John's, Little Caesar's, Panda Express, Pita Pit, RoundTable Pizza, Starbucks, Wendy's ⊙ GNC, Hancock Fabrics, Natural Grocers, Petsmart, Ross, Safeway, Tuesday Morning
3	NE Hwy 99, Main St, Hazel Dell, **E** 🅖 7-11 🍴 Muchas Gracias Mexican, Pizza Hut, Skippers, **W** 🅖 Arco/dsl, Chevron/dsl 🍴 Papa Murphy's ⊙ Safeway, transmissions
2	WA 500 E, 39th St, to Orchards
1d	E 4th, Plain Blvd W, to WA 501, Port of Vancouver
1c	Mill Plain Blvd, City Ctr, **E** ⊙ Clark Coll, **W** 🅖 Chevron 🍴 Black Angus 🛏 Comfort Inn ⊙ st patrol
1b	6th St, **E** 🍴 Joe's Crabshack, Who Song & Larry's Mexican, **W** 🛏 EconoLodge, Hilton, Red Lion Hotel
1a	WA 14 E, to Camus, **E** ⊙ 🄷, **W** 🛏 EconoLodge, Hilton
0mm	Washington/Oregon state line, Columbia River

E INTERSTATE 82

Exit #	Services
11mm	I-82 Oregon begins/ends on I-84, exit 179.
10	Westland Rd, **E** ⊙ to Umatilla Army Depot
5	Power Line Rd
1.5mm	Umatilla River
1	US 395/730, Umatilla, **E** 🍴 Jack-in-the-Box (5mi) 🛏 Best Western (8mi), Motel 6 (8mi), Oxford Inn (5mi), Quality Inn/rest. (2mi) ⊙ Hatrock Camping (8mi), to McNary Dam, **W** 🅖 Shell/Crossroads Trkstp/dsl/rest./24hr, Tesoro/Subway/dsl, Texaco/dsl 🛏 Tillicum Motel, Umatilla Inn ⊙ Harvest Foods, st police, Umatilla Marina/RV Park, USPO, weigh sta, Welcome Ctr
132mm	Columbia River, Washington/Oregon state line
131	WA 14 W, Plymouth, **N** ⊙ RV camping, to McNary Dam
130mm	weigh sta wb
122	Coffin Rd
114	Locust Grove Rd
113	US 395 N, to I-182, Kennewick, Pasco, st patrol, **2-4 mi N** 🅖 Exxon/Circle K/dsl, Metro/dsl, USA/dsl 🍴 A&W/KFC, Azteca Mexican, Bob's Burgers, Burger King, Carl's Jr, Costa Vida, Denny's, Dickey's BBQ, DQ, Fujiyama Japanese, Jack-in-the-Box, Little Caesars, McDonald's, Osaka Asian, Panda Express, Starbucks, Subway, Taco Bell, Tesoro/dsl, The Rock Kitchen 🛏 Baymont Inn, Best Western, Comfort Suites, Days Inn, La Quinta ⊙ 🄷, AT&T, Blue Dog RV Ctr, Fred Meyer/dsl, GNC, Harley-Davidson, Home Depot, PetCo, Radio Shack, Rite Aid,

Side vertical text: **VANCOUVER** | **KENNEWICK** | **KELSO** | **KALAMA** | **WA**

INTERSTATE 82 Cont'd

113	Continued Safeway/dsl, st patrol, Traveland RV Ctr, Verizon, vet, Walgreens, Walmart/Subway
109	Badger Rd, W Kennewick, N Exxon/Subway/dsl Country Gentleman's Rest. Guesthouse Suites, Quality Inn, Red Lion Hotel, Super 8, S RV Park
104	Dallas Rd, 3 mi N Conoco/dsl
102	I-182, US 12 E, to US 395, Spokane, H, Pasco, services in Richland
96	WA 224 E, Benton City, N Conoco/cafe/dsl Beach RV Park
93	Yakitat Rd
88	Gibbon Rd
82	WA 22, WA 221, Mabton, S Conoco/dsl H, museum, to WAS U Research, to Wine Tasting
82mm	Yakima River
80	Gap Rd, S **both lanes, full facilities, litter barrels RV dump, wireless internet** Chevron/dsl, Pacific Pride/dsl, Shell/dsl/scales Barn Rest., Burger King, El Rancho Alegre, Garcia's Mexican, Golden Horse Chinese, KFC/Taco Bell, McDonald's, Starbucks, Subway Best Western, Vintners Inn H, Ford, Schwab Tire, Verizon, Wine Country RV Park
76mm	**weigh sta eb**
75	County Line Rd, Grandview, S Cenex/dsl, Conoco/dsl (1mi) Country Deli, Papa Murphy's O'Reilly Parts, same as 73
73	Stover Rd, Wine Country Rd, Grandview, S Chevron/Subway/dsl, Conoco/dsl 10-4 Café, DQ, Eli&Kathy's Rest., Garcia's Mexican, New Hong Kong Apple Valley Motel, Grandview Motel Chrysler/Dodge/Jeep, IGA Mercado, RV park/dump, Safeway/dsl, Schwab Tire
69	WA 241, to Sunnyside, N Arco/dsl, Shell/dsl/scales/24hr, USA/dsl A&W, Burger King, China Buffet, El Charrito Mexican, Green Olive Cafe, KFC, Little Caesars, McDonald's, Mongolian BBQ, Panda Garden, Papa Murphy's, Pizza Hut, Skipper's, Subway, Taco Bell Best Western, Quality Inn $Tree, AT&T, auto repair, AutoZone, Buick/Chevrolet, Fiesta Foods, GNC, JC Penney, Nissan, O'Reilly Parts, Radio Shack, Rite Aid, Walmart/Subway
67	Sunnyside, Port of Sunnyside, N Chevron/CFN/dsl, Conoco/dsl/e85 Jack-in-the-Box H, BiMart Foods, S DariGold Cheese
63	Outlook, Sunnyside, 3 mi N Snipe's Rest. Country Inn&Suites, Travel Inn Sunnyside RV Park
58	WA 223 S, to Granger, S Arco/dsl/tacos, Conoco/dsl
54	Division Rd, Yakima Valley Hwy, to Zillah, S Teapot Dome NHS
52	Zillah, Toppenish, N 76/dsl, Chevron/Circle K/dsl, Shell/Circle K/dsl El Porton Mexican, McDonald's, Pizza Hut, Subway Vintage Valley Inn
50	WA 22 E, to US 97 S, Toppenish, 3-4 mi S Legends Buffet/casino, McDonald's Days Inn, Quality Inn H, Murals Museum, RV Park, to Yakima Nation Cultural Ctr
44	Wapato, N Shell/dsl
40	Thorp Rd, Parker Rd, Yakima Valley Hwy, N Sagelands Vineyard/Winery, S Windy Point Vineyard
39mm	Yakima River
38	Union Gap (from wb), 1 mi S museum
37	US 97 (from eb), S Conoco/dsl, Shell
36	Valley Mall Blvd, Yakima, S Arco/dsl, Cenex/dsl, Shell/Gearjammer/Subway/dsl/scales/24hr/ @ A&W/KFC, Applebee's, Burger King, Carl's Jr, Denny's, El Porton Mexican,

SUNNYSIDE

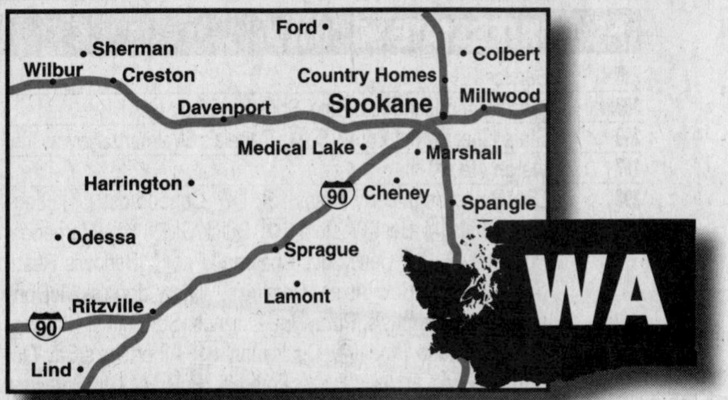

36	Continued Famous Dave's, Jack-in-the-Box, McDonald's, Miner's Drive-In, Old Country Buffet, Old Town Sta Rest., Outback Steaks, Sea-Galley Rest., Shari's, Starbucks, Subway, Taco Bell Best Western, Quality Inn, Super 8 AT&T, Best Buy, Cabela's, Canopy RV Ctr, Costco/gas, dsl/repair, Gap Autoparts, Hobby Lobby, Home Depot, JC Penney, Kohl's, Lowe's, Macy's, mall, Michaels, Office Depot, Old Navy, PetCo, Petsmart, Rite Aid, Ross, Sears/auto, ShopKO, st patrol, Tire Factory, TJ Maxx, Toyota/Scion, Verizon
34	WA 24 E, Nob Hill Blvd, Yakima, N dsl/repair, K-Mart, Sportsman SP, S 7-11, 76/dsl, Arco/dsl, CFN/dsl, Time/dsl H, 19th Hole RV Park, Fiesta Foods, Freightliner, Kenworth, O'Reilly Parts, Peterbilt, Volvo
33	Yakima Ave, Yakima, N Chevron/dsl, Shell/dsl Burger King, El Mirador Mexican Oxford Inn&Suites Chevrolet, Honda, Mazda, Walmart/McDonald's, S 7-11, Arco Bob's Burgers, Domino's, DQ, Pizza Hut, Taco Bell Fairfield Inn, Guesthouse Suites, Hilton Garden, Holiday Inn, Holiday Inn Express, Howard Johnson, Ledgestone Hotel, Red Lion Hotel $Tree, BigLots, Schwab Tire, Target
31b a	US 12 W, N 1st St, to Naches, S Arco/dsl, Conoco/dsl, Shell Black Angus Steaks, El Rinconsito, Golden Moon Chinese, Jack-in-the-Box, Mel's Diner, NY Teryaki, Peking Palace, Red Lobster, Subway, Tammy's Mexican, Waffle's Cafe, Yakima Rest. Best Western, Budget Inn, Days Inn, Economy Inn, Holiday Lodge, Red Apple Motel, Sun Country Inn, Sunshine Motel, Yakima Inn, Yakima Valley Hotel Harley-Davidson, Trailer Inns RV Park
30	WA 823 N, Rest Haven Rd, to Selah
29	E Selah Rd, N fruits/antiques
26	WA 821 N, to WA 823, Canyon Rd, N Chevrolet/Noble Romans/Subway/dsl
24mm	**eb, full facilities, litter barrels RV dump**
23mm	Selah Creek
22mm	**wb, full facilities, litter barrels RV dump**
21mm	2265 elev, S Umptanum Ridge
19mm	Burbank Creek
17mm	2315 elev, N Umptanum Ridge
15mm	Lmuma Creek
11	Military Area, Military Area
8mm	2672 elev, Manastash Ridge, view point both lanes
3	WA 821 S, Thrall Rd
0mm	I-90, E to Spokane, W to Seattle. **I-82 begins/ends on I-90, exit 110.**

YAKIMA

WA

= gas = food = lodging = other = rest stop

WA

INTERSTATE 90

Exit #	Services
300mm	Washington/Idaho state line, Spokane River
299	State Line, Port of Entry, N Cabela's, Walmart/Subway
297	**weigh sta wb**
296	Otis Orchards, Liberty Lakes, N Conoco/dsl Legend's Grill Best Western Buick/GMC, Kia, Mercedes, Porsche, S Cenex/dsl, Chevron/LP Barlow's Rest., Carl's Jr, Ding How Asian, Domino's, Jimmy John's, McDonald's, Papa Murphy's, Pizza Hut, Quiznos, Starbucks, Subway, Taco Bell, Taco Time Quality Inn Albertson's/Sav-On, Home Depot, O'Reilly Parts, Peterbilt, RnR RV Ctr, Safeway, TireRama, URGENT CARE, Verizon, vet, Walgreens
294	Country Vista Dr, Appleway Ave
293	Barker Rd, Greenacres, N Chevron/Trkstp/dsl/scales, Conoco/dsl Wendy's Camping World RV Ctr, Freedom RV Ctr, Harley-Davidson, S Exxon/Subway/dsl, Mobil/dsl NW RV Ctr, repair, USPO
291b	Sullivan Rd, Veradale, N Arby's, Hong Kong Buffet, Krispy Kreme, Outback Steaks Hampton Inn, My Place, Oxford Suites, Residence Inn AT&T, Barnes&Noble, Best Buy, JoAnn Fabrics, mall, Verizon, S Chevron/dsl, Conoco/dsl, Tesoro/dsl 5 Guys Burgers, DQ, Jack-in-the Box, Jimmy John's, KFC, Little Caesars, Max' Rest., McDonald's, Mongolian BBQ, Noodle Express, Panda Express, Pizza Hut, Pizza Pipeline, RoundTable Pizza, Schlotzsky's, Shari's, Starbucks, Subway, Taco Bell, Wendy's, Zelia's Cafe Mirabeau Park Hotel, Ramada Inn $Tree, Ace Hardware, Fred Meyer/dsl, GNC, Hancock Fabrics, Hastings Books, Kohl's, Lowe's, Michael's, NAPA, PetCo, Petsmart, Ross, Schwab Tire, USPO, Walgreens, Walmart/McDonald's
291a	Evergreen Rd, N Azteca Mexican, Black Angus, Boston's Rest, Buffalo Wild Wings, Cafe Rio, Honeybaked Ham, IHOP, Red Robin, Twigs Bistro Dick's, Hobby Lobby, JC Penney, Macy's, mall, Old Navy, Sears/auto, Staples, TJ Maxx, S Exxon/dsl, Maverik/dsl
289	WA 27 S, Pines Rd, Opportunity, N Sam's/dsl Black Pearl Rest., Subway 7-11, S Cenex, Conoco/dsl, Holiday/dsl Applebee's, DQ, Jack-in-the-Box, Qdoba Mexican, Quiznos Comfort Inn H, NW Auto, repair, Walgreens
287	Argonne Rd, Millwood, N Holiday/dsl, Tesoro/dsl Burger King, Caruso's Sandwiches, Denny's, Domino's, DQ, Jack-in-the-Box, Longhorn BBQ, McDonald's, Panda Express, Papa Murphy's, Pizza Hut, Starbucks, Subway, Taco Time, Timber Creek Grill, Wendy's Motel 6, Super 8 $Tree, Albertson's, O'Reilly Parts, Savon, URGENT CARE, Verizon, vet, Walgreens, Yoke's Foods, S Cenex/dsl, Conoco Casa de Oro Mexican, Jimmy John's, Little Caesars, Starbucks Holiday Inn Express, Quality Inn Ace Hardware, Rite Aid, Safeway
286	Broadway Ave, N FLYING J/Conoco/rest./dsl/LP/scales/24hr/ @, Chevron/dsl Goodyear, Smacky's Cafe, Zip's Burgers Rodeway Inn International Trucks, Kenworth, Schwab Tire, S 7-11
285	Sprague Ave, N Dragon Garden Chinese, IHOP, Jack-in-the-Box, McDonald's, Panda Express, Starbucks, Subway, Wendy's ParkLane Motel/RV Park $Tree, AT&T, AutoZone, Costco/gas, Grocery Outlet, Home Depot, K-Mart/Little Caesars, Lowe's, O'Reilly Parts, Radio Shack, Verizon, Volvo Trucks, Walmart, S Conoco Bag of Burgers, Cottage Cafe, Puerta Vallarta Mexican, Starbucks, Taco Time Acura, CarMax, Chevrolet, Chrysler/Dodge, Ford, Honda, Hyundai, Mazda, Nissan, Toyota/Scion, transmissions, vet
284	Havana St (from eb, no EZ return), N Tesoro/dsl Wolf Lodge Steaks, S Conoco/dsl Fred Meyer/dsl
283b	Freya St, Thor St, N Chevron/dsl, Tesoro/dsl Wolf Lodge Steaks, S Conoco/dsl Fred Meyer/dsl
283a	Altamont St, S Cenex
282b	2nd Ave, N Conoco/dsl Comfort Inn Office Depot
282a	WA 290 E, Trent Ave, Hamilton St, N Conoco/dsl Comfort Inn Office Depot
281	US 2, US 395, to Colville, N 7-11, Conoco, Exxon, Tesoro/dsl Arby's, Dick's Hamburgers, Frankie Doodles Rest., Starbucks, Subway, Taco Time Days Inn, FairBridge Inn Firestone/auto, Schwab Tire, U-Haul, S Quality Inn H, URGENT CARE
280b	Lincoln St, N Chevron, Conoco/dsl Atilano's Mexican, Carl's Jr, Chapala Mexican, Domino's, Jack-in-the-Box, McDonald's, Molly's Rest., Taco Bell, Thai Cuisine, Zip's Burgers Tradewinds Motel Fiat, Honda, Lexus, Toyota/Scion, Troy's Tire, S H
280a	Spokane, downtown, N Chevron/McDonald's/dsl, Conoco/dsl Frank's Diner, Pizza Hut, Subway AAA, Grocery Outlet
279	US 195 S, Pullman, to Colfax, no facilites
277b a	US 2 W (no ez wb return), to Grand Coulee Dam, N Blvd Motel, EconoLodge, Hampton Inn, Knight's Inn Fairchild AFB
276	Geiger Blvd, N FLYING J/dsl/LP/24hr Denny's, Subway Airway Express Inn, Best Western st patrol, USPO, S Conoco/dsl
272	WA 902, Medical Lake, N Mobil/dsl Overland Sta/RV Park, S Exxon/Subway/dsl, Petro/Iron Skillet/dsl/scales/24hr/ @ McDonald's Super 8 Freightliner, Ponderosa Falls RV Resort, truck repair
270	WA 904, Cheney, Four Lakes, S 76 Holiday Inn Express (4mi), Willow Springs Motel (6mi) E WA U, Peaceful Pines RV Park (7mi)
264	WA 902, Salnave Rd, to Cheney, Medical Lake, **2 mi** N camping
257	WA 904, Tyler, to Cheney, S Peaceful Pines RV Park (10mi), to Columbia Plateau Trail SP, Tyler RV Park
254	Fishtrap, S Fishtrap RV camping/tents
245	WA 23, Sprague, S Chevron/dsl Viking Drive-In Sprague Motel/RV park 4 Seasons RV Park (6mi), Sprague Lake Resort/RV Park
242mm	**both lanes, full facilities, litter barrels, petwalk RV dump (eb), tourist/weather info**
231	Tokio, N **weigh sta both lanes**, S Templin's Café/CFN/dsl RV Park
226	Schoessler Rd
221	WA 261 S, Ritzville, City Ctr, N Chevron/McDonald's, Conoco/dsl, Exxon/Circle K/Subway/dsl Cow Creek Cafe/gifts, Ritz Roadhouse, Starbucks, Taco Del Mar, Zip's Rest. Best Western, Cedars Inn/RV park, Empire Motel, Top Hat Motel H, hist dist, S Loves/Carl's Jr/dsl/scales/24hr
220	to US 395 S, Ritzville, N Pacific Pride/dsl, Texaco/Jake's Rest./dsl Jake's Rest. Top Hat Motel Cedars Inn RV Park, Harvest Foods, NAPA, Schwab Tire, st patrol
215	Paha, Packard
206	WA 21, Odessa, to Lind
199mm	**both lanes, full facilities, info, litter barrels, petwalk vending**
196	Deal Rd, to Schrag
188	U Rd, to Warden, Ruff
184	Q Rd

VERADALE

SPOKANE

CHENEY

INTERSTATE 90 Cont'd

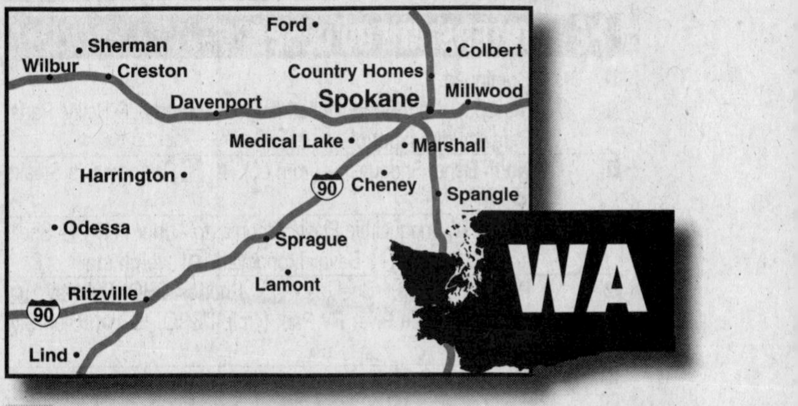

Exit #	Services
182	O Rd, to Wheeler
179	**MOSES LAKE** WA 17, Moses Lake, **1 mi** **N** [gas] Conoco/Subway/dsl, Ernie's Trkstp/Chevron/café/dsl/24hr, Sunval/dsl, Texaco/dsl [food] Arby's, Bob's Cafe, Burger King, DQ, McDonald's, Shari's, Starbucks, Subway, Taco Bell, Y Guy's Grill [lodging] Comfort Suites, El Rancho Motel, Holiday Inn Express, Moses Lake Inn, Ramada Inn, Shilo Inn [other] [H], $Tree, Chevrolet, Chrysler/Dodge/Jeep, Ford/Lincoln, Honda, Lowe's, Toyota/Scion, vet, **S** [other] I-90 RV, Mardon RV Park (15mi), Potholes SP (22mi), Willows RV Park (2mi)
177mm	Moses Lake
176	WA 171, Moses Lake, **N** [gas] 76/dsl, Cenex/dsl, Chevron/dsl, Conoco, Exxon/dsl, Sunval/dsl [food] El Rodeo Mexican, Michael's Rest., Subway, Taco Del Mar [lodging] Best Western/rest., Interstate Inn, Motel 6, Oasis Motel, Super 8 [other] [H], AAA RV Park, Ace Hardware, auto repair, Harvest Foods, Lake Front RV Park, transmissions, vet, **S** [lodging] Lakeshore Motel
175	Westshore Dr (from wb), to Mae Valley, **N** [other] Moses Lake SP, **S** [other] st patrol
174	Mae Valley, **N** [other] Suncrest Resort/RV, **S** [gas] Conoco/dsl [other] Pier 4 RV Park, st patrol
169	Hiawatha Rd
164	Dodson Rd, **N** [other] Sunbasin RV park/camp (1mi)
162mm	**[RS] wb, full [handicap] facilities, litter barrels, petwalk [phone] [picnic] RV dump**
161mm	**[RS] eb, full [handicap] facilities, litter barrels, petwalk [phone] [picnic] RV dump**
154	Adams Rd
151	WA 281 N, to Quincy, **N** [gas] Shell/pizza/subs/dsl [other] [H] (12mi), Shady Grove RV park, to Grand Coulee Dam
149	WA 281 S, George, **N** [other] [H] (12mi), **S** [gas] BW&M/DSL, Shree's Trkstp/Subway/dsl/scales/24hr [other] RV camp
143	Silica Rd, **N** [other] to The Gorge Ampitheatre
139mm	**N** [other] Wild Horses Mon, scenic view both lanes
137	WA 26 E, to WA 243, Othello, Richland
137mm	Columbia River
136	Huntzinger Rd, Vantage, **N** [gas] Spirit, Texaco/dsl [food] Blustery's Burger Drive-in, Golden Harvest Rest. [other] auto repair, Riverstone Vantage Resort/RV Park, to Ginkgo SP, Vantage Gen. Store, **S** [other] to Wanapum SP (3mi)
126mm	Ryegrass, elev 2535, **[RS] both lanes, full [handicap] facilities, litter barrels, petwalk [phone] [picnic]**
115	Kittitas, **N** [gas] Shell/dsl/LP [food] Main Stop Rest. [other] Olmstead Place SP, UHaul
110	**ELLENSBURG** I-82 E, US 97 S, to Yakima
109	Canyon Rd, Ellensburg, **N** [gas] 76, Astro/dsl, Chevron, Exxon/Circle K [food] Arby's, Baskin Robbins, Burger King, Carl's Jr, Fiesta Mexican, KFC, Los Cabos Mexican, McDonald's, Oyama Japanese, Papa Murphy's, Quiznos, RanchHouse Rest., Roadhouse Grill, Rodeo City BBQ, Starbucks, Subway, Taco Del Mar, Teriyaki Wok, Wendy's [lodging] Best Western, Comfort Inn, Holiday Inn Express, Quality Inn, Super 8 [other] [H], AutoZone, CarQuest, Chevrolet, NAPA, O'Reilly Parts, Rite Aid, Schwab Tire, Super 1 Foods, TrueValue, **S** [gas] Conoco/FLYING J/Sak's/dsl/scales/LP/24hr [food] Buzz Inn Steaks [lodging] Days Inn/RV park
106	US 97 N, to Wenatchie, **N** [gas] 76/dsl, Chevron/dsl, Conoco/dsl, Loves/Subway/dsl/scales/24hr [food] DQ, IHOP, Perkins [lodging] Cedars Inn, Hampton Inn [other] Buick/Cadillac/GMC, Canopy Country RV Ctr, Chrysler/Dodge/Jeep, Truck/RV Wash, **S** [other] KOA, st patrol
101	Thorp Hwy, **N** [gas] Arco/dsl [other] antiques/fruits/vegetables
93	Elk Heights Rd, Taneum Creek
92.5mm	Elk Heights, elev 2359,
89mm	Indian John Hill, elev 2141, **[RS] both lanes, full [handicap] facilities, info, litter barrels, petwalk [phone] [picnic] vending**
85	**CLE ELUM** WA 970, WA 903, to Wenatchie, **N** [gas] 76/dsl, Gas Save/dsl, Shell/dsl [food] Cottage Café, Giant Burger, Homestead BBQ [lodging] Aster Inn, Chalet Motel, Cle Elum Traveler's Inn, EconoLodge [other] vet
84	Cle Elum (from eb, return at 85), **N** [gas] Chevron/dsl, Shell/Subway/dsl, Warrior's/dsl [food] Beau's Pizza, Burger King, Caboose Grill, DQ, El Caporal Mexican, Los Cabos Mexican, MaMa Vallones, McDonald's, New Cam Chinese, Sahara Pizza, Sunset Café, Taco Bell [lodging] Best Western Snowcap, Stewart Lodge, Timber Lodge Inn [other] Cle Elum Drug, Cle Elum Hardware, museum, Radio Shack, Safeway/dsl, Trailer Corral RV Park, URGENT CARE, USPO
81mm	Cle Elum River
80	Roslyn, Salmon la Sac, **N** [lodging] Suncadia Resort/rest. (4mi)
80mm	**weigh sta both lanes**
78	Golf Course Rd, **S** [other] Sun Country Golf/RV Park
74	W Nelson Siding Rd
71	Easton, **S** [gas] Easton Store/dsl/LP [lodging] Easton Motel [other] Iron Horse SP, John Wayne Tr, USPO
71mm	Yakima River
70	Sparks Rd, Easton, Lake Easton SP, **N** [gas] Shell/RV Town/dsl/café [food] Backwoods Cafe, Mtn High Burger [other] repair, Silver Ridge Ranch RV Park, **S** [other] Lake Easton RV Camping, Lake Easton SP
63	Cabin Creek Rd
62	Stampede Pass, elev 3750, to Lake Kachess, **N** Lake Kachess Lodge
54	Hyak, Gold Creek, **S** Ski Area
53	Snoqualmie Pass, elev 3022, **S** [gas] Chevron [food] Summit Pancake House [lodging] Summit Lodge [other] info, Lee's Summit Mkt, to rec areas
52	W Summit (from eb), same as 53
47	Tinkham Rd, Denny Creek, Asahel Curtis, **N** [other] chain area, **S** [other] RV camping/dump
45	USFS Rd 9030, **N** to Lookout Point Rd
42	Tinkham Rd
38	**N** fire training ctr
35mm	S Fork Snoqualmie River
34	468th Ave SE, Edgewick Rd, **N** [gas] Gull/dsl/deli, Shell/dsl, TA/Country Pride/Popeyes/dsl only/24hr/ @ [lodging] Edgewick Inn [other] Norwest RV Park
32	436th Ave SE, **1 mi** **N** [other] Snoqualmie Ranger Sta, gas, lodging, **S** [food] Riverbend Cafe, Iron Horse SP (3mi)
31	WA 202 W, North Bend, Snoqualmie, **N** [gas] Chevron/dsl, Shell/dsl [food] Arby's, Blimpie, Burger King, Los Cabos, McDonald's, Mongolian Grill, Papa Murphy's, Starbucks, Subway, Taco Time [lodging] North Bend Motel, Sallish Lodge, Sunset Motel [other] [H],

WA

ISSAQUAH

SEATTLE

INTERSTATE 90 Cont'd

Exit	Services
31	Continued museum, NorthBend Outlets/famous brands, O'Reilly Parts, Safeway/dsl, st patrol
27	North Bend, Snoqualmie (from eb), N [food] Woodman's Steaks [other] [H]
25	WA 18 W, Snoqualmie Pkwy, Tacoma, to Auburn, N [gas] Shell/dsl/e85 (1.5mi) [food] Bayan Mongolian [other] **weigh sta**
22	Preston, N [gas] Shell/dsl [food] Rhodes BBQ, Subway [other] LP, Snoqualmie River RV Park (4mi), USPO, S [other] Blue Sky RV Park
20	High Point Way
18	E Sunset Way, Issaquah, S [gas] Shell (1mi) [food] Flying Pie Pizza, Jak's Grill, Mandarin Garden, Stan's BBQ, Sunset Alehouse [other] Front St Mkt
17	E Sammamish Rd, Front St, Issaquah, N [gas] 76 [food] Coho Cafe, Coldstone, Fatburger, Jamba Juice, Krispy Kreme, McDonald's, Panda Express, Papa John's, Qdoba Mexican, Starbucks, Subway [other] AT&T, Bartell Drug, Best Buy, Fred Meyer, Home Depot, URGENT CARE, Walgreens, S [gas] Arco/dsl, Cenex/dsl, Chevron/dsl, Shell/dsl [food] Boehms Chocolates, Domino's, Shanghai Garden Rest., Stan's BBQ, Subway, XXX Rootbeer [other] Big O Tire, Staples, transmissions
15	WA 900, Issaquah, Renton, N [gas] Arco/dsl, Chevron [food] Georgio's Subs, IHOP, O'Char Thai, Red Robin, Taco Time, Tully's Coffee [lodging] Holiday Inn, Motel 6 [other] Barnes&Noble, Big Lots, Costco/gas, Lowe's, Michael's, Office Depot, PCC Natural Mkt, Petsmart, to Lk Sammamish SP, S [gas] Shell/dsl [food] 12th Ave Cafe, Baskin-Robbins, Burger King, Cascade Garden Chinese, Chipotle Mexican, Denny's, Five Guys, Franky's Pizza, Issaquah Cafe, Jack-in-the-Box, Jamba Juice, KFC/Taco Bell, La Venadita, McDonald's, Panera Bread, Papa Murphy's, Potbelly, RoundTable Pizza, Starbucks, Subway, Taco Time, The Egg&Us Rest., Tuttabella Pizza, WildFin Grill [lodging] Hilton Garden, Homewood Suites [other] Chevrolet, Firestone/auto, Ford, GNC, O'Reilly Parts, PetCo, QFC Foods, Radio Shack, REI, Rite Aid, Ross, Safeway, See's Candies, Target, Trader Joe's, USPO, Verizon
13	SE Newport Way, W Lake Sammamish, S [gas] 76/dsl [food] Starbucks, Subway [other] Matthew's Thriftway Mkt, vet
11	SE 150th, 156th, 161st, Bellevue, N [gas] Shell [food] Dalian House Chinese, DQ, Jack-in-the-Box, Lil' Jon Rest., McDonald's, Starbucks, Subway, Tulley's Coffee [lodging] Days Inn, Embassy Suites, Hyatt House, Silver Cloud Inn [other] 7-11, LDS Temple, Subaru/VW, Toyota/Scion, vet, S [gas] 76, Chevron, Shell/dsl, Standard/dsl [food] Baskin-Robbins, Domino's, Outback Steaks, Pizza Hut [lodging] Larkspur Landing Suites [other] Albertson's, Honda, O'Reilly Parts, Rite Aid, RV Park
10	I-405, N to Bellevue, S to Renton, exit 10. Services located off I-405 S, exit 10
9	Bellevue Way
8	E Mercer Way, Mercer Island
7c	80th Ave SE (exits left from wb)
7b a	SE 76th Ave, 77th Ave, Island Crest Way, Mercer Island, S [gas] Chevron/dsl, Shell/dsl [food] McDonald's, Qdoba, Starbucks, Subway, Thai Rest., Tully's Coffee [other] Albertson's, TrueValue, Walgreens
6	W Mercer Way (from eb), same as 7
5mm	Lake Washington
3b a	Ranier Ave, Seattle, downtown, N [gas] Shell/dsl [other] Vet
2c b	I-5, N to Vancouver, S to Tacoma
2a	4th Ave S, to King Dome

I-90 begins/ends on I-5 at exit 164.

RICHLAND

INTERSTATE 182 (RICHLAND)

Exit #	Services
	I-182 begins/ends on US 395 N.
14b a	US 395 N, WA 397 S, OR Ave, N [gas] *FLYING J*/ds scales/24hr, King City/Shell/rest/dsl/@ [food] Burger King, Subway [other] Freightliner, Peterbilt, RV Park, S [lodging] Motel 6
13	N 4th Ave, Cty Ctr, N [gas] CFN/dsl [lodging] Airport Motel, Starli Motel, S [gas] 76/dsl, Chevron/dsl [other] [H], museum, RV par Tire Pros, vet
12b	N 20th Ave, N [lodging] Best Western, Red Lion Hotel
12a	US 395 S, Court St, S **on Court St** [gas] Chevron, Conoco Exxon/Jack-in-the-Box, Mobil/Circle K/dsl, Shell/dsl, Texaco USA [food] A&W/KFC, Andy's Rest., Baskin-Robbins, Burger King, Domino's, El Mirador Mexican, Little Caesars, McDonald's, Oriental Express, Papa Murphy's, Pizza Hut, Quiznos RoundTable Pizza, Subway, Taco Bell, Wendy's [other] $Tree, Albertson's, AutoZone, Cadillac/Chevrolet, Chief RV Ctr, Dean R Ctr, Ford, Hyundai, Mazda, Nissan, Rite Aid, Subaru, U-Hau USPO, Walgreens
9	Rd 68, Trac, N [gas] Exxon/Circle K/dsl, Maverik/dsl, Tesoro dsl [food] Antonio's Pizza, Applebee's, Arby's, Bruchi's, Cousin Rest., DQ, Fiesta Mexican, Figaro's Pizza, Hacienda del So IHOP, Jack-in-the-Box, Little Caesar's, McDonald's, Pand Express, Pier 39 Seafood, Pita Pit, Pizza Hut, Shakey's Pizza Sonic, Starbucks, Subway, Taco Bell, Teryaki Grill [lodging] Holida Inn Express, MyPlace [other] AT&T, Discount Tire, Firestone/auto Franklin County RV Park, Lowe's, O'Reilly Parts, Schwab Tire URGENT CARE, Verizon, Walgreens, Walmart/Subway, Yoke Foods, S [gas] Maverik/dsl
7	Broadmoor Blvd, N [lodging] Sleep Inn [other] GNC, vet, S [gas] Exxon dsl [other] Broadmoor RV Ctr, KOA
6.5mm	Columbia River
5b a	WA 240 E, Geo Washington Way, to Kennewick, N [gas] Conoco/dsl [food] Anthony's Rest., Applebee's, Jack-in-the-Box, Starbucks [lodging] Courtyard, Days Inn, Economy Inn, Hampton Inn Red Lion Hotel, Shilo Inn, TownePlace Suites [other] $Tree, AT&T Winco Foods
4	WA 240 W, N [gas] Shell/dsl [food] El Porton Mexican, McDonald's Starbucks [other] BMW, Fred Meyer/dsl, vet
3.5mm	Yakima River
3	Keene Rd, Queensgate, N [gas] Exxon/Circle K, Maverik/dsl USA/dsl [food] A&W/KFC, Bob's Burgers, Burger King, Costa Vida, El Rancho Alegre, Five Guys, Fujiyama Steaks, LJ Silver McDonald's, Panda Express, Starbucks, Stick+Stone Pizza Subway, Taco Bell [other] GNC, Home Depot, Marshall's, PetCo Schwab Tire, Target, Tire Factory, Verizon, Walmart/Subway S [gas] Chevron/dsl [other] RV Park (3mi), tires/repair

I-182 begins/ends on I-82, exit 102.

INTERSTATE 405 (SEATTLE)

Exit #	Services
30	I-5, N to Canada, S to Seattle, **I-405 begins/ends on I-5, exit 182.**
26	WA 527, Bothell, Mill Creek, E [food] Canyon's Rest., McDonald's [lodging] Extended Stay America [other] Lake Pleasant RV Park, W [gas] Shell/dsl [food] Applebee's, Arby's, Bamboo House, Baskin-Robbins, Bonefish Grill, Crystal Creek Cafe, D.Thai, Denny's, Five Guys, Grazie Ristorante, Imperial Wok, Jack-in-the-Box, Jimmy John's, Little Caesar's, Mongolian Grill, Outback Steaks, Papa Murphy's, Qdoba Mexican, Quiznos, Starbucks, Subway, Taco Bell, Taco Time, Tully's Coffee, Wendy's, Zeek's Pizza

SEATTLE

INTERSTATE 405 (SEATTLE) Cont'd

26	Continued ComfortInn, Extended Stay America, Hilton Garden, Holiday Inn Express 7-11, Bartell Drug, Goodyear/auto, QFC Foods, Radio Shack, Rite Aid, URGENT CARE, vet
24	NE 195th St, Beardslee Blvd, E Shell/Quiznos/dsl Subway, Teryaki Etc. Country Inn&Suites, Residence Inn, SpringHill Suites Exotic vet
23b	WA 522 W, Bothell
23a	WA 522 E, to WA 202, Woodinville, Monroe
22	NE 160th St, E Chevron, Shell/dsl Top Mkt/deli
20	NE 124th St, E Arco, Chevron, Shell/dsl Brown Bag Cafe, Cafe Veloce, Chan's Place, Denny's, Jack-in-the-Box, KFC, Pizza Hut, Santa Fe Mexican, Shari's, Subway, Taco Bell, Thai Kitchen Baymont Inn, Comfort Inn, Motel 6 H, 7-11, AutoZone, Big O Tire, Chrysler/Dodge/Jeep, Discount Tire, Fiat, Firestone/auto, Ford, Hyundai, Infiniti, NAPA, O'Reilly Parts, Radio Shack, Rite Aid, Ross, Schwab Tire, Toyota/Scion, Trader Joe's, Verizon, VW, W 76/dsl Azteca Mexican, Burger King, Five Guys, Hunan Wok, Izumi Japanese, Jimmy John's, McDonald's, Mediterranean Kitchen, Olive Garden, Papa Murphy's, Picnics Hotdogs, Romio's Pizza, Starbucks, Subway, Taco Del Mar, Taco Time, Wendy's Courtyard AT&T, Buick/GMC, Fred Meyer/dsl, GNC, QFC Foods
18	WA 908, Kirkland, Redmond, E 76/Circle K/dsl, Chevron, Shell/dsl Baskin-Robbins, Garlic Jim's, Little Caesar's, McDonald's, Outback Steaks, Pegasus Grill, Starbucks, Subway, Taco Time, Tres Hermanos, Valhalla Grill Chevrolet, Costco, Goodyear/auto, Hancock Fabrics, Honda, Kia, Mazda, O'Reilly Parts, PetCo, Safeway, Tuesday Morning, U-Haul, URGENT CARE, vet, Walgreens, W Shell/dsl Acropolis Pizza, Original Pancakes, Papa John's, Starbucks, Subway, Wendy's QFC Foods, Tire Factory
17	NE 70th Pl
14b a	WA 520, Seattle, Redmond
13b	NE 8th St, E Arco, Chevron/dsl, Shell/dsl Burger King, Taco del Mar Coast Hotel H, Bartell Drugs, Best Buy, Cadillac, Chevrolet, Ford, Home Depot, Mercedes, Nissan, Porsche, Volvo, Whole Foods Mkt, W Starbucks, Subway Courtyard, Hyatt
13a	NE 4th St, E Extended Stay America, Hampton Inn Chrysler/Dodge/Jeep, Lexus, W Azteca Mexican, Subway Hilton, Hotel Bellevue, Marriott, Red Lion/Bellevue Inn, Residence Inn, Sheraton
12	SE 8th St, W Residence Inn
11	I-90, E to Spokane, W to Seattle
10	Cold Creek Pkwy, Factoria, E **on Factoria Blvd** 76, Chevron Applebee's, Burger King, Coldstone, El Tapatio Mexican, Goldberg's Rest., Great Harvest Bread, Jamba Juice, Jimmy John's, Keg Steaks, KFC, McDonald's, Novilhos Brazilian Steaks, Old Country Buffet, Panda Express, Panera Bread, Peking Wok, Ricardo's Mexican, Romio's Pizza, Shanghai Cafe, Starbucks, Subway, Taco Bell, Taco Time, Thai Ginger, Tokyo Japanese, Tony Maroni's Pizza 7-11, AT&T, Bartell Drug, Midas, Old Navy, O'Reilly Parts, PetCo, QFC Foods, Radio Shack, Rite Aid, Safeway, Target, TJ Maxx, Verizon, vet, Walmart
9	112th Ave SE, Newcastle, phone
7	NE 44th St, E Denny's, McDonald's, Starbucks, Subway, Teriyaki Wok EconoLodge
6	NE 30th St, E Arco, W Chevron/dsl, Shell/dsl 7-11
5	WA 900 E, Park Ave N, Sunset Blvd NE, W Jimmy John's, Panda Express, Panera Bread, Potbelly, Red Robin, Torero's Mexican Dick's, Fry's Electronics, GNC, Lowe's, Marshall's, Petsmart, Ross, Staples, Target, Verizon, World Mkt
4	WA 169 S, Wa 900 W, Renton, E Shari's Quality Inn Aqua Barn Ranch Camping, W Burger King, Pizza Dudes, Stir Rest., Subway Renton Inn $Tree, 7-11
2	WA 167, Rainier Ave, to Auburn, E Hilton Garden, Larkspur Landing, SpringHill Suites, TownePlace Suites H, W Arco/dsl, Chevron, Chevron, Mobil/dsl, Shell/dsl A&W/KFC, Applebee's, Baskin-Robbins, IHOP, Jack-in-the-Box, Jimmy John's, Jimmy Mac's Roadhouse, King Buffet, Little Caesar's, Mazatlan Mexican, McDonald's, Papa Murphy's, Pizza Hut, Popeyes, Starbucks, Subway, Taco Bell, Taco Time, Wendy's, Yankee Grill Red Lion Hotel AutoZone, Buick/Cadillac/GMC, Chevrolet, Chrysler/Dodge/Jeep, Fiat, Firestone/auto, Ford, Fred Meyer/dsl, Honda, Hyundai, Kia, Mazda, Midas, O'Reilly Parts, Radio Shack, Safeway/gas, Sam's Club/gas, Schwab Tire, Subaru, Toyota/Scion, vet, Walgreens, Walmart
1	WA 181 S, Tukwila, E 76/dsl Jack-in-the-Box, Taco Bell, Teriyaki Wok Courtyard, Embassy Suites, Extended Stay America, Hampton Inn, Ramada, Residence Inn 7-11, mall, W 76 Subway Comfort Suites, Homewood Suites fun center
0mm	I-5, N to Seattle, S to Tacoma, WA 518 W. **I-405 begins/ends on I-5, exit 154.**

WA WV

WEST VIRGINIA

INTERSTATE 64

LEWISBURG

Exit #	Services
184mm	West Virginia/Virginia state line
183	VA 311, (from eb, no reentry), Crows (from eb)
181	US 60, WV 92 (no ez wb return), White Sulphur Springs, **0-2 mi N** BP/Godfather's, Exxon/Quiznos, Shell April's Pizzaria, Hardee's Budget Inn, Greenbrier Resort, Old White Motel Family$, Food Lion, Rite Aid, ski area, to Midland Trail, USPO, S Black Bear Lodge Twilight Camping
179mm	**Welcome Ctr wb, full facilities, info, litter barrels, petwalk**
175	US 60, WV 92, Caldwell, N Exxon, Mountaineer Mart/dsl, Shell/Subway/dsl Carlitos, McDonald's, Wendy's Village Inn $General, S Greenbrier SF, Mountainaire Camping
173mm	Greenbrier River
169	US 219, Lewisburg, Hist Dist, N Shell Biscuit World Federated Parts, S Exxon/dsl, Gomart, Shell Applebee's, Arby's, Bob Evans, China Palace, Hardee's, Papa John's, Ruby Tuesday, Shoney's, Subway, Taco Bell Fairfield Inn, Hampton Inn, Holiday Inn Express, Quality Inn, Super 8 H, $Tree, AT&T, AutoZone, Buick/Chevrolet, Ford, Lowe's, URGENT CARE, Verizon, Walmart

= gas = food = lodging = other = rest stop

WV

CHARLESTON

INTERSTATE 64 Cont'd

Exit #	Services
169	US 219, Lewisburg, Hist Dist, N Shell Biscuit World Federated Parts, S Exxon/dsl, Gomart, Shell Applebee's, Arby's, Bob Evans, China Palace, Hardee's, Papa John's, Ruby Tuesday, Shoney's, Subway, Taco Bell Fairfield Inn, Hampton Inn, Holiday Inn Express, Quality Inn, Super 8 H, $Tree, AT&T, AutoZone, Buick/Chevrolet, Ford, Lowe's, URGENT CARE, Verizon, Walmart
161	WV 12, Alta, S Citgo/dsl Alta Sta/cafe Greenbrier River Camping (14mi)
156	US 60, Midland Trail, Sam Black Church, N Citgo/dsl, Shell/dsl
150	Rd 29, Rd 4, Dawson, S Exxon Cheddar's Cafe Dawson Inn RV camping
147mm	**runaway truck ramp wb**
143	WV 20, Green Sulphur Springs, N Liberty/dsl
139	WV 20, Sandstone, Hinton, S Citgo/dsl Blue Stone SP (16mi), Richmonds Store/USPO, to Pipestem Resort Park (25 mi)
138mm	New River
136mm	**runaway truck ramp eb**
133	WV 27, Pluto Rd, Bragg, S RV camping, **mandatory truck stop eb**, Sandstone Mtn (Elev. 2765)
129	WV 9, Shady Spring, N to Grandview SP, S Exxon/dsl, Shell/dsl Subway Little Beaver SP
125	WV 307, Airport Rd, Beaver, N Shell/dsl Biscuit World Sleep Inn, **1 mi S** BP/dsl, GoMart/gas, Sheetz/dsl Bellacino's, DQ, El Mariachi, Hardee's, KFC, Little Caesars, LJ Silver, McDonald's, Pizza Hut, Subway, Wendy's Advance Parts, Adventure RV Ctr, CVS Drug, Family$, Kroger, Radio Shack, USPO, Walgreens
124	US 19, Eisenhower Dr, E Beckley, **1-2 mi N** GoMart/gas Capt D's, Huddle House Green Bank Motel, Microtel H, $General, **last exit before toll Rd wb**
121	I-77 S, to Bluefield
I-64 and I-77 run together 61 mi. See I-77, exits 42 through 100.	
59	I-77 N (from eb), to I-79
58c	US 60, Washington St, N BP, Exxon, GoMart/dsl Family$, S 5th Quarter Steaks, Capt D's, Panera Bread, Shoney's, Wendy's Courtyard, Embassy Suites, Hampton Inn, Holiday Inn Express, Marriott H, civic ctr, Goodyear/auto, Macy's, mall, Sears
58b	US 119 N (from eb), Charleston, downtown, same as 58c
58a	US 119 S, WV 61, MacCorkle Ave
56	Montrose Dr, N Exxon/dsl, Marathon/dsl, Speedway/dsl Hardee's, Los Agaves Mexican Holiday Inn, Microtel, Wingate Inn $General, Acura, Advance Parts, Chevrolet, Dodge, Hyundai, KIA, NAPA, Rite Aid, VW
55	Kanawha Tpk (from wb)
54	US 60, MacCorkle Ave, N Burger King, Casa Garcia, Graziano's Pizza, Krispy Kreme, Subway $Tree, AT&T, Kroger/dsl, TJ Maxx, S Bob Evans, Husson's Pizza, KFC, LJ Silver, McDonald's, Pizza Hut, Schlotzsky's, Taco Bell, Wendy's H, Aamco, Family$, Harley-Davidson, Honda, Mazda, URGENT CARE
53	Roxalana Rd, to Dunbar, S GoMart/dsl BiscuitWorld, Capt D's, Gino's Pizza, Graziano's Pizza, Los Agaves, McDonald's, Subway, Wendy's Dunbar Plaza Motel, Super 8 $General, Advance Parts, Aldi Foods, CVS Drug, Family$, Jo-Ann Fabrics, Kroger/dsl, NTB, Rite Aid
50	WV 25, Institute, S GoMart/dsl
47b a	WV 622, Goff Mtn Rd, N Exxon/dsl, GoMart, Speedway/dsl BiscuitWorld, Bob Evans, Capt D's, Domino's, Gino's Pizza, Little Caesar's, McDonald's, Papa John's, Pizza Hut, Subway, Taco Bell, Wendy's Motel 6 Advance Parts, AT&T, Autozone, Family$, Kroger/gas, Rite Aid, Save-a-Lot, URGENT CARE, Walgreens, S Arby's, Asian Buffet, Barnyard BBQ, Buffalo Wild Wings, Burger King, Cracker Barrel, Golden Corral, HoneyBaked Ham, La Roca Mexican, Sakura Japanese, TGIFriday's Comfort Inn, Holiday Inn Express, Sleep Inn $Tree, Lowe's, Radio Shack, Staples, Walmart
45	WV 25, Nitro, N Pilot/Arby's/dsl/scales/24hr Chevrolet, S Exxon/dsl, GoMart, Speedway/dsl Biscuit-World, Checker's, DQ, Gino's Pizza, McDonald's, Subway, Wendy's $General
44.3mm	Kanawha River
44	US 35, St Albans, S Shell/7-11/dsl
40	US 35 N, Winfield, Pt Pleasant, S Sheetz/dsl, Speedway/dsl DQ
39	WV 34, Winfield, N BP/Arby's, GoMart/dsl Applebee's, Bob Evans, Rio Grande Mexican, Taste of Asia Holiday Inn Express, Red Roof Inn $General, $Tree, Advance Parts, Aldi Foods, BigLots, Elder-Beerman, GNC, Home Depot, Radio Shack, USPO, S GoMart, TA/Country Pride/dsl/scales/24hr/@ Biscuit World, Burger King, Capt D's, China Chef, El Rancho Grande, Fat Patty's, Fireside Grille, Gino's Pizza, Graziano's Pizza, KFC, McDonald's, Penn Sta., Subway, Taco Bell, TCBY, Wendy's Hampton Inn AT&T, AutoZone, K-Mart, Kroger/dsl, Rite Aid, URGENT CARE, Verizon
38mm	**weigh sta both lanes**
35mm	**both lanes, full facilities, litter barrels, petwalk vending**
34	WV 19, Hurricane, N Arby's, KFC, Taco Bell $Tree, Chevrolet, Chrysler/Dodge/Jeep, Ford, Martin RV Ctr, Walmart/Subway, S Exxon/Dunkin Donuts, Go-Mart, Sheetz/dsl BiscuitWorld/Gino's Pizza, China Wok, Little Caesar's, McDonald's, Mi Pueblito, Pizza Hut, Subway American Inn, Budget Inn Rite Aid, USPO, vet, Walgreens
28	US 60, Milton, **0-2 mi S** Exxon, Go-Mart, Marathon/dsl, Sheetz/dsl Biscuit World, McDonald's, Pizza Hut, Subway, Taco Bell, Wendy's $General, Advance Parts, AutoZone, CVS Drug, Family$, Jim's Camping (2mi), KOA (3mi), NAPA, Piggly Wiggly, Rite Aid, Save-A-Lot foods, USPO
20	US 60, Mall Rd, Barboursville, N Applebee's, Bob Evans, Buffalo Wild Wings, Burger King, Chick-fil-A, Chili's, Chipotle, IHOP, Logan's Roadhouse, McDonald's, Olive Garden, Panera Bread, Qdoba Mexican, Ruby Tuesday, Super China, Wendy's Comfort Inn BAM!, Best Buy, Dick's, Drug Emporium, Elder-Beerman, Firestone/auto, Hobby Lobby, JC Penney, Jo-Ann Fabrics, Kohl's, Lowe's, Macy's, mall, Michael's, NTB, Old Navy, Sears/auto, Walmart/Subway, S BP/dsl, Sheetz/dsl Cracker Barrel, Fat Patty's, Outback Steaks, Shogun Japanese, Sonic, Steak&Shake, Subway, Taco Bell Best Western, Hampton Inn, Holiday Inn Toyota
18	US 60, to WV 2, Barboursville, N Bellacino's, O'Charley's, Starbucks $Tree, Home Depot, Marshall's, Office Depot, Petco, Target, S Shell/7-11 Biscuit World, Gino's, Giovanni's Pizza, Hardee's, Papa John's Food Fair, Kia, Kroger/gas, NAPA, Rite Aid, Walgreens
15	US 60, 29th St E, N GoMart/dsl, Shell/dsl, Speedway/dsl #1 Kitchen, Arby's, Biscuit World, Burger King, Honeybaked Ham, Ponderosa, Subway, Waffle House, Wendy's Huntington Motel, Quality Inn H, $General, AT&T, BigLots, NAPA, Save-a-Lot Foods, st police, Verizon, Walmart/McDonald's,

INTERSTATE 64 Cont'd

HUNTINGTON

15	Continued S Exxon Fazoli's, Golden Corral, KFC, Little Caesar's, Marco's Pizza, McDonald's, Penn Sta., Taco Bell Days Inn, Red Roof Inn Buick/Cadillac/GMC, CVS Drug, Honda, Nissan, Subaru, VW
11	WV 10, Hal Greer Blvd, **0-2 mi** N Marathon/Subway Arby's, Baskin-Robbins, Biscuit World, Bob Evans, El Ranchito Mexican, Frostop Drive-In, McDonald's, Papa John's, Ritzy's Cafe, Wendy's Hampton Inn, Ramada Ltd, Super 8, TownePlace Suites H, AutoZone, Chrysler/Dodge/Jeep, Rite Aid, S Beech Fork SP (8mi)
10mm	**Welcome Ctr eb, full facilities, litter barrels, petwalk vending**
8	WV 152 S, WV 527 N, N URGENT CARE, vet, S GoMart/dsl, Speedway/dsl
6	US 52 N, W Huntington, Chesapeake, N Sheetz/dsl, Speedway/dsl Pizza Hut, Shoney's, Wendys H, $General, AutoZone, BigLots, Family$, Save-A-Lot Foods
1	US 52 S, Kenova, **0-1 mi** N Exxon, Shell/dsl Burger King, Evaroni's Pizza, Gino's Pizza, Hermanos Nunez Mexican, McDonald's, Stewart's Hotdogs, Taco Bell Hollywood Motel $General, Advance Parts, CVS Drug, NAPA, Save-A-Lot, USPO
0mm	West Virginia/Kentucky state line, Big Sandy River

INTERSTATE 68

MORGANTOWN

Exit #	Services
32mm	West Virginia/Maryland state line
31mm	**Welcome Ctr wb, full facilities, litter barrels, petwalk vending**
29	Rd 5, Hazelton Rd, N Sunoco/dsl Microtel (1mi), S Big Bear Camping (3mi), Pine Hill RV Camp (4mi)
23	WV 26, Bruceton Mills, N BFS/Subway/dsl/24hr, Sunoco/Little Sandy's Rest./dsl/24hr Mill Place Rest. Maple Leaf Motel antiques, Bumper Parts, Family$, Hostetler's Store, USPO
18mm	Laurel Run
17mm	runaway truck ramp eb
16mm	**weigh sta wb**
15	WV 73, WV 12, Coopers Rock, N Chestnut Ridge SF, Sand Springs Camping (2mi)
12mm	**runaway truck ramp wb**
10	WV 43 N, to Rd 857, Fairchance Rd, Cheat Lake, N BFS/Charlie's/Little Caesar's/dsl, Exxon/dsl Anthony's Pizza, Dragon Cafe, Subway Lakeview Resort USPO, vet, S Burger King
9mm	Cheat Lake
7	Rd 705, Pierpont Rd, N BFS/Little Caesar's/Subway/TCBY, Exxon/Taco Bell/dsl Bob Evans, Fujiyama Steaks, Honeybaked Ham, IHOP, McDonald's, Outback Steaks, Ruby Tuesday, Wendy's Holiday Inn Express, Super 8 H, Books-A-Million, Family$, GNC, Lowe's, Michael's, Shop'n Save Foods, to WVU Stadium, Verizon, S Sunoco/dsl Don Patron Mexican, Fox's Pizza Den, Provoloni's Italian, Rita's Custard Chrysler/Dodge

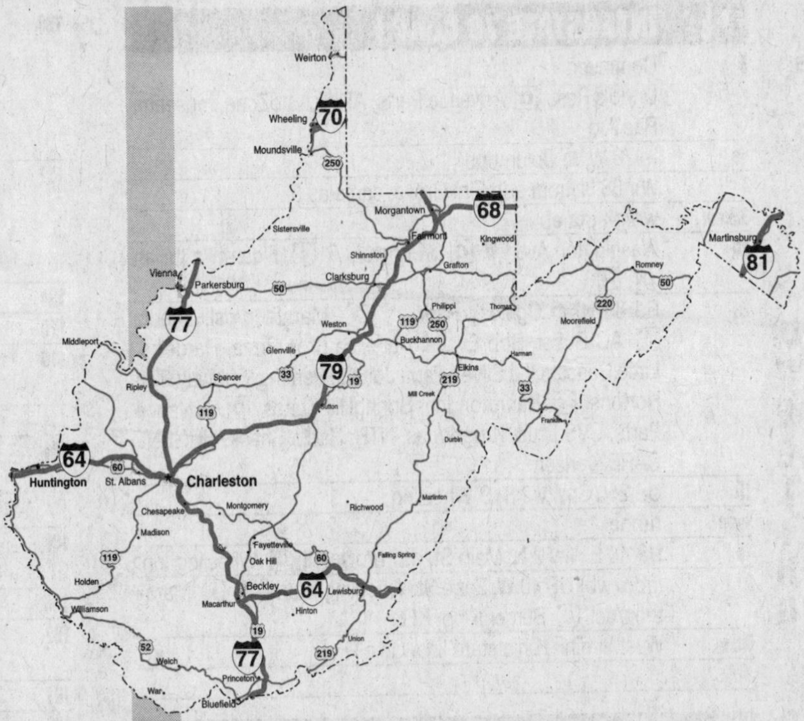

4	Rd 7, to Sabraton, N BFS/Subway/dsl, Sheetz/dsl Arby's, Burger King, Dunkin Donuts, Hardee's, KFC, LJ Silver, McDonald's, Shoney's, Wendy's SpringHill Suites, Suburban Lodge $General, Advance Parts, AutoZone, CVS Drug, Family$, Ford/Lincoln, Kroger/dsl, NAPA, Save-A-Lot Foods, USPO, Walgreens, S Marathon/Circle K, Sunoco/dsl China City
3mm	Decker's Creek
1	US 119, Morgantown, N Go-Mart/dsl Comfort Inn, Ramada Inn/rest. tires, S Mariachi Loco $Tree, to Tygart L SP, Walmart/Subway
0mm	I-79, N to Pittsburgh, S to Clarksburg. **I-68 begins/ends on I-79, exit 148.**

INTERSTATE 70

Exit #	Services
14mm	West Virginia/Pennsylvania state line
13.5mm	**Welcome Ctr wb, full facilities, litter barrels, petwalk vending**
11	WV 41, Dallas Pike, N TA/Country Pride/dsl/scales/24hr/@ Comfort Inn, S Exxon, Marathon/DQ/dsl EconoLodge RV camping
10	Rd 65, to Cabela Dr, N Sheetz/dsl Applebee's, Bob Evans, Cheddar's, Coldstone, Cracker Barrel, Eat'n Park, El Paso Mexican, Fusion Steaks, Logan's Roadhouse, McDonald's, Olive Garden, Panera Bread, Primanti Bros, Quaker Steak, TX Roadhouse, Wendy's Hampton Inn, Hawthorn Suites, Microtel AT&T, Best Buy, Books-A-Million, Cabela's, JC Penney, Kohl's, Michael's, Old Navy, PetCo, Russell Stover Candies, Target, TJ Maxx, Verizon, Walmart/Subway, S Holiday Inn Express, Suburban Lodge Buick/GMC, Chevrolet, Ford/Lincoln, Honda, Hyundai, Nissan, Toyota/Scion
5	US 40, WV 88 S, Tridelphia, N Marathon/dsl Pizza Hut, Subway, Wendy's Super 8 Chrysler/Dodge/Jeep, Family$, Riesbeck's Foods, Subaru, URGENT CARE, vet, S Marathon/dsl Arby's, DQ, McDonald's,

WV

= gas = food = lodging = other = rest stop

WV

INTERSTATE 70 Cont'd

WHEELING

5	Continued Undo's Rest. Advance Parts, AT&T, AutoZone, museum, Rite Aid
5a	I-470 W, to Columbus
4	WV 88 N (from eb), Elm Grove, same as 5
3.5mm	**weigh sta eb**
2b	Washington Ave, **N** $General, **S** Figaretti's Italian
2a	Rd 88 N, to Oglebay Park, **N** Marathon/dsl, Sheetz AC Buffet, Bob Evans, DeFelice Bros Pizza, Hardee's, Little Caesars, LJ Silver, Papa John's, Perkins, Subway, Tim Hortons Hampton Inn, SpringHill Suites Advance Parts, CVS Drug, Kroger/gas, NTB, Radio Shack, URGENT CARE, Verizon
1b	US 250 S, WV 2 S, S Wheeling
1mm	**tunnel**
1a	US 40 E, WV 2 N, Main St, downtown, **S** Wheeling Inn
0	(from wb) US 40 W, Zane St, Wheeling Island, **N** Marathon/dsl Burger King, KFC
0mm	West Virginia/Ohio state line, Ohio River

INTERSTATE 77

PARKERSBURG

Exit #	Services
186mm	West Virginia/Ohio state line, Ohio River
185	WV 14, WV 31, Williamstown, **W** **Welcome Ctr/, full facilities, info, litter barrels**, Clark, GoMart/dsl, Shell (1mi) Dutch Pantry Econolodge/Rodeway Inn Glass Factory Tours
179	WV 2 N, WV 68 S, to Waverly, **E** Exxon/dsl airport, **W** BP/dsl Burger King, Hardee's (3mi) Red Carpet Inn, Sleep Inn
176	US 50, 7th St, Parkersburg, **E** to North Bend SP, **W** BP/7-11, GoMart Domino's, DQ, Hardee's, Little Caesar's, McDonald's, Mountaineer Rest./24hr, Omelette Shoppe, Wendy's Economy Inn, Travelodge Advance Parts, AutoZone, Chrysler/Dodge/Jeep, CVS Drug, Family$, Ford/Lincoln, Honda, Hyundai, Kroger/dsl, Mercedes, NAPA, Rite Aid, to Blennerhassett Hist Park, Toyota
174	WV 47, Staunton Ave, **1 mi E** GoMart/Sub Express/dsl $General
174mm	Little Kanawha River
173	WV 95, Camden Ave, **E** Marathon/dsl, **1-4 mi W** BP Hardee's Blennerhassett Hotel
170	WV 14, Mineral Wells, **E** BP/dsl/repair, GoMart/Taco Bell/dsl, Liberty Trkstp/dsl/24hr McDonald's, Wendy's Comfort Suites, Hampton Inn, **W** Cracker Barrel, Napoli's Pizza Holiday Inn Express, Microtel, Mineral Wells Inn
169mm	**weigh sta both lanes**
166mm	**both lanes, full facilities, litter barrels, petwalk vending**
161	WV 21, Rockport, **W** Marathon/dsl
154	WV 1, Medina Rd
146	WV 2 S, Silverton, Ravenswood, **E** Ruby Lake Camping (4mi), **W** Exxon/DQ, Marathon/dsl McDonald's (3mi), Subway (4mi), Wendy's (3mi) Scottish Inn
138	US 33, Ripley, **E** BP/dsl, Marathon/dsl, Murphy USA/dsl, Sheetz/dsl Arby's, KFC, Las Trancas Mexican, LJ Silver, McDonald's, Pizza Hut, Taco Bell, Wendy's

CHARLESTON

138	Continued Holiday Inn Express, Super 8 $Tree, AutoZone, Family$, Kroger/dsl, NAPA, Rite Aid, Sav-A-Lot Foods, Verizon, Walmart/Subway, **W** Exxon/dsl Bob Evans, Ponderosa, Shoney's, Subway Quality Inn
132	WV 21, Fairplain, **E** BP/7-11/dsl, GoMart/dsl, Speedway/dsl/24hr Burger King, Fratello's Italian $General, Ford, Statts Mills RV Park (6mi), **W** Loves/Chester's/McDonald's/dsl/scales/24hr
124	WV 34, Kenna, **E** Exxon Your Family Rest.
119	WV 21, Goldtown, same as 116
116	WV 21, Haines Branch Rd, Sissonville, **4 mi E** Rippling Waters Camping
114	WV 622, Pocatalico Rd, **E** BP/dsl $General
111	WV 29, Tuppers Creek Rd, **W** BP/Subway/dsl Gino's (2mi), McDonald's (2mi), Tudor's Biscuit World, Wendy's (2mi)
106	WV 27, Edens Fork Rd, **W** Marathon/dsl/country store Sunset Motel (3mi)
104	I-79 N, to Clarksburg
102	US 119 N, Westmoreland Rd, **E** BP/7-11, GoMart Hardee's Foodland/gas
101	I-64, E to Beckley, W to Huntington
100	Broad St, Capitol St, **W** Subway Best Western, Charleston Capitol Hotel, Marriott , Cadillac/GMC, Firestone, Rite Aid, USPO
99	WV 114, Capitol St, **E** airport, **W** BP/7-11, Exxon/Noble Roman's Domino's, McDonald's, Wendy's st capitol, to museum
98	35th St Bridge (from sb), **W** Shell/7-11/dsl Husson's Pizza, KFC, McDonald's, Steak Escape, Subway, Taco Bell, Wendy's , Rite Aid, to U of Charleston
97	US 60 W (from nb), Kanawha Blvd
96	US 60 E, Midland Trail, Belle, **W** Anchor Pizza, Biscuit World, Gino's Budget Host
96mm	W Va Turnpike begins/ends
95.5mm	Kanawha River
95	WV 61, to MacCorkle Ave, **E** GoMart/dsl/24hr, Marathon/Subway/dsl Bob Evans, IHOP, Lonestar Steaks, McDonald's, TX Steaks, Wendy's Country Inn&Suites, Days Inn, Holiday Inn Express, Knights Inn, Motel 6, Red Roof Inn Advance Parts, AutoZone, K-Mart, **W** Exxon/dsl, GoMart, Shell/7-11/dsl Applebee's, Arby's, Capt D's, China Buffet, Cracker Barrel, Firehouse Subs, Fujiyama Japanese, Hooters, La Carreta's, Little Caesar's, Pizza Hut, Taco Bell $Tree, AT&T, Drug Emporium, Foodland, GNC, Kings Tire, Kroger/dsl, Lowe's, Radio Shack, URGENT CARE, vet
89	WV 61, WV 94, to Marmet, **E** Exxon/Subway/dsl/24hr, GoMart/dsl, Sunoco/dsl BiscuitWorld, Gino's Pizza, Hardee's, LJ Silver, Wendy's $General, Family$, Family$, Ford, Kroger/dsl, NAPA, Rite Aid, USPO
85	US 60, WV 61, East Bank, **E** Marathon/dsl, She'll/Arby's/dsl Gino's Pizza, McDonald's, Shoney's $General, Chevrolet, Rite Aid
82.5mm	**toll booth**
79	Cabin Creek Rd, Sharon
74	WV 83, Paint Creek Rd
72mm	**Morton Service Area nb,** Exxon/dsl Burger King, Hershey's Ice Cream, KFC, Pizza Hut, Starbucks
69mm	**sb, full facilities, litter barrels**
66	WV 15, to Mahan, **1/2 mi W** Sunoco/dsl/24hr

INTERSTATE 77 Cont'd

Exit #	Services
60	WV 612, Oak Hill, to Mossy, **1/2 mi** E Exxon/dsl RV camping
56.5mm	**toll plaza**
54	Rd 2, Rd 23, Pax, E Citgo/dsl
48	US 19, N Beckley, **1-4 mi E on US 19/WV 16** Exxon/Subway, Sheetz/dsl Bob Evans, Buffalo Wild Wings, Burger King, Cheddar's, Chick-fil-A, Chili's, Dickey's BBQ, Five Guys, Honeybaked Ham, LJ Silver, Logan's Roadhouse, McDonald's, Olive Garden, Panera Bread, Peking Buffet, Qdoba, Rally's, Ryan's, Starbucks, Subway, Taco Bell, Wendy's Days Inn $General, $Tree, Advance Parts, AT&T, AutoZone, Belk, BigLots, Buick/GMC, Chevrolet, Chrysler/Dodge/Jeep, CVS Drug, Dick's, Food Lion, Goodyear/auto, Hobby Lobby, Honda, Hyundai, JC Penney, Jo-Ann Fabrics, Kia/Subaru, K-Mart, Kohl's, Kroger/gas, Lowe's, NAPA, Nissan, Petsmart, Radio Shack, Rite Aid, RV Ctr, Sam's Club/gas, Sears/auto, Staples, TJ Maxx, Toyota, U-Haul, Walgreens, Walmart
45mm	**Tamarack Service Area both lanes**, W Exxon/dsl Burger King, Hershey's Ice Cream, Quiznos, Sbarro's, Starbucks gifts
44	WV 3, Beckley, E Exxon/dsl, Marathon/dsl, Shell/Dickey's BBQ Applebee's, Burger King, Campestre Mexican, DQ, Fujiyama Japanese, Hooters, IHOP, McDonald's, Omelet Shoppe, Outback Steaks, Pizza Hut Courtyard, EconoLodge, Fairfield Inn, Howard Johnson, Quality Inn/rest., Super 8, Travelodge H, Advance Parts, CVS Drug, Kroger/gas, Rite Aid, Tires, URGENT CARE, W BP/Subway/dsl, Go-Mart/dsl Bob Evans, Cracker Barrel, Pasquale Italian, Ruby Tuesday, Sam's Hotdogs, TX Steaks, Wendy's Baymont Inn, Comfort Inn, Country Inn&Suites, Hampton Inn, Holiday Inn, Microtel
42	WV 16, WV 97, to Mabscott, **2 mi** E H, W BP/dsl, Go-Mart Arby's, Gino's Pizza/Biscuit World, Subway AutoValue Repair, O'Reilly Parts, USPO, Walmart/Subway
40	I-64 E, to Lewisburg
30mm	**toll booth**
28	WV 48, to Ghent, E Exxon/dsl, Marathon/dsl Subway Appalachian Resort Inn (12mi), Glade Springs Resort (1mi) to ski area, W Knight's Inn
26.5mm	Flat Top Mtn, elevation 3252
20	US 19, to Camp Creek, E Exxon/dsl, W Camp Creek SP/RV camping
18.5mm	Bluestone River, scenic overlook/parking area/**weigh sta sb**
17mm	**Bluestone Service Area/weigh sta nb, full facilities scenic view** Exxon/dsl Blimpie, Hershey's Ice Cream, Starbucks, Uno Pizza atm/fax
14	WV 20, Athens Rd, E Pipestem Resort SP, to Concord U
9mm	**WV Turnpike begins/ends**
9	US 460, Princeton, E **Welcome Ctr/ both lanes, full facilities, litter barrels, petwalk** , Walmart/dsl Campestre Mexican, Kimono Japanese, Outback Steaks, Ryan's Country Inn&Suites, Fairfield Inn $Tree, AT&T, URGENT CARE, Verizon, Walmart/Subway, W BP/dsl, Exxon, Sheetz/dsl, Shell/Subway Applebee's, Arby's, Bob Evans, Bojangles, Capt D's, Chili's, Cracker Barrel, DQ, Hardee's, McDonald's, Omelet Spot, Shoney's, Starbucks, TX Steaks, Wendy's Comfort Inn, Days Inn,

BECKLEY

PRINCETON

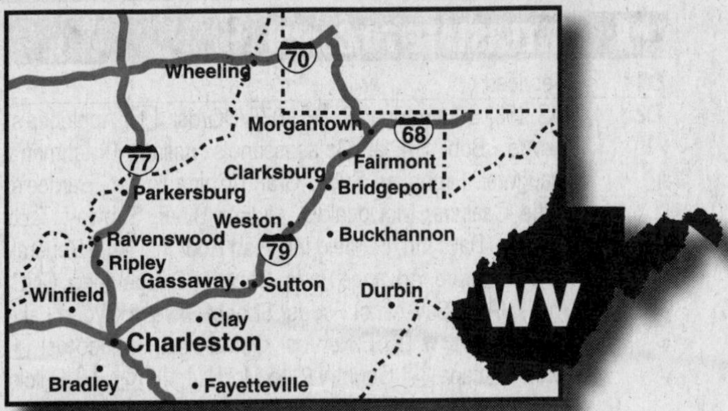

Exit #	Services
9	Continued Eden Rock Motel, Hampton Inn, Holiday Inn Express, Microtel, Sleep Inn, Turnpike Motel H, Hyundai, Lowe's
7	WV 27, Twelve Mile Rd
5	WV 112 (from sb, no re-entry), to Ingleside
3mm	East River
1	US 52 N, to Bluefield, **4 mi** W KFC/LJ Silver, Wendy's EconoLodge, Quality Inn H, to Bluefield St Coll
0mm	West Virginia/Virginia state line, East River Mtn

WV

INTERSTATE 79

Exit #	Services
160mm	West Virginia/Pennsylvania state line
159	**Welcome Ctr sb, full facilities, info, litter barrels, petwalk vending**
155	US 19, WV 7, **0-3 mi** E GetGo, Sheetz/dsl Cheddars, Chili's, CiCi's Pizza, Cracker Barrel, Evergreen Buffet, Golden Corral, Longhorn Steaks, McDonald's, Olive Garden, Red Lobster, Shoney's, TX Roadhouse Best Western, EconoLodge, Fairfield Inn, HM Hotel H, $Tree, Barnes&Noble, Best Buy, Buick/Chevrolet/GMC, CVS Drug, Dick's, Giant Eagle Foods, Old Navy, PetCo, Sam's Club/gas, Target, TJ Maxx, to WVU, Walmart, W Harley-Davidson
152	US 19, to Morgantown, E BFS/dsl, Exxon, Getty Arby's, China Wok, McDonald's, Pizza Hut, Subway, Taco Bell EconoLodge Advance Parts, BigLots, Monro, URGENT CARE, W Bob Evans, Burger King, Garfield's Rest. Microtel Belk, Elder-Beerman, JC Penney, K-Mart, Lowe's, mall, Sears/auto
150mm	Monongahela River
148	I-68 E, to Cumberland, MD, **1 mi** E Go-Mart/dsl Mariachi Loco, Subway Comfort Inn, Morgantown Motel, Ramada Inn $Tree, tires, to Tygart Lake SP, Walmart
146	WV 77, to Goshen Rd, W Pilot/deli/dsl/scales/24hr
141mm	**weigh sta both lanes**
139	WV 33, E Fairmont, E Sunoco, W (1 mi), Exxon, K&T/BP/dsl/scales repair, RV camping, to Prickett's Ft SP
137	WV 310, to Fairmont, E Exxon/dsl, Sunoco Clarion to Valley Falls SP, vet, W Shell/dsl Domino's, KFC, McDonald's, Subway, Wendy's H, $General, Advance Parts, Family$, Shop'n Save Foods
136	Rd 273, Fairmont
135	WV 64, Pleasant Valley Rd
133	Kingmont Rd, E Exxon/Fazoli's/dsl, Marathon/Subway/dsl Cracker Barrel Holiday Inn Express, Super 8, W Shell/Quiznos/dsl DJ's Diner Comfort Inn

MORGANTOWN

= gas = food = lodging = other = rest stop Copyright 2016 - The Next EXIT

WV

CLARKSBURG

CHARLESTON

INTERSTATE 79 Cont'd

Exit #	Services
132	US 250, S Fairmont, E BFS/DQ/dsl Applebee's, Arby's, Bob Evans, Colasessano's Italian, Dutchman's Daughter, Firehouse Subs, Grand China Buffet, Hardee's, Little Caesars, McDonald's, Oldie's Diner, Subway, Taco Bell Days Inn, Fairfield Inn, Red Roof Inn $General, Ace Hardware, Advance Parts, Chrysler/Dodge/Jeep, GNC, mall, NAPA, Sav-A-Lot Foods, Shop'n Save, to Tygart Lake SP, Walmart, W Exxon/dsl, GoMart/dsl, Sunoco/dsl Steak Escape Country Club Motel (4mi) H, Buick/GMC, Ford/Lincoln, Toyota/Scion, Trailer City RV Ctr
125	WV 131, Saltwell Rd, to Shinnston, E Oliverio's Rest. (4mi), W Exxon/Circle K/Dunkin Donuts/Subway/dsl
124	Rd 279, Jerry Dove Dr, E BFS, Exxon/Dunkin Donuts/dsl Buffalo Wild Wings, DQ, Little Caesars Microtel, Wingate Inn, W Sheetz/dsl IHOP, Subway Courtyard, Holiday Inn Express H
123mm	**both lanes, full facilities, info, litter barrels, petwalk RV dump, vending**
121	WV 24, Meadowbrook Rd, E GoMart, Sheetz Biscuit World, Bob Evans, Gino's Pizza Hampton Inn Hyundai/Subaru, URGENT CARE, W Exxon/dsl Burger King, Garfield's Rest., Outback Steaks Super 8 Dick's, JC Penney, Jo-Ann Fabrics, mall, Marshall's, NTB, Old Navy, Sears/auto, Target
119	US 50, to Clarksburg, E A&W/LJ Silver, Brickside Grille, Chick-fil-A, Coldstone, Denny's, Eat'n Park, Grand China, Hank's Deli, KFC, Las Trancas, Little Caesar's, Maxey's Rest., McDonald's, Panera Bread, Pizza Hut, Red Hot Buffet, Starbucks, Taco Bell, TX Roadhouse, Wendy's Best Western, Days Inn, Sleep Inn, Sutton Inn, Townplace Suites, Travelodge H, Advance Parts, Autozone, BigLots, Family$, GNC, Home Depot, K-Mart, Kohl's, Kroger/dsl, Lowe's, Monro, Radio Shack, Sam's Club/gas, USPO, Walgreens
117	WV 58, to Anmoore, E BFS/dsl Applebee's, Arby's, Burger King, Honeybaked Ham, Ruby Tuesday, Ryan's, Subway Hilton Garden Aldi Foods, AT&T, Kia, Staples, Walmart
115	WV 20, Nutter Fort, to Stonewood, E BP/7-11/dsl, Exxon/dsl Stonewood Bulk Foods, W Greenbrier Motel (5mi)
110	Lost Creek, E BP/dsl
105	WV 7, to Jane Lew, E Jane Lew Trkstp/dsl/rest., Valero/dsl/rest Plantation Inn, W GoMart, Shell $General, glass factory tours, Kenworth/Mack/Volvo
99	US 33, US 119, to Weston, E Marathon/DQ/Little Caesars/dsl, Sheetz/dsl Burger King, Gino's Pizza, McDonald's, Patron Mexican, Peking Buffet, Steer Steakhouse, Subway Comfort Inn/rest., Hampton Inn (9mi), Holiday Inn Express, Super 8 Advance Parts, Curves, Family$, GNC, Kroger/dsl, Radio Shack, Walmart, **0-2 mi W** Exxon, Go-Mart, Shell/7-11 Domino's, Giovanni's, Hardee's, KFC, LJ Silver, Pizza Hut, Subway, Wendy's H, $General, Blackwater Falls, Chrysler/Dodge, CVS Drug, Ford, NAPA, NAPACare, Rite Aid, Save-a-Lot, to Canaan Valley Resort
96	WV 30, to S Weston, E Broken Wheel Camping, to S Jackson Lake SP
91	US 19, to Roanoke, E Marathon/dsl Stillwaters Rest camping, to S Jackson Lake SP
85mm	**both lanes, full facilities, info, litter barrels, pet walk RV dump, vending**
79.5mm	Little Kanawha River
79	WV 5, Burnsville, E Exxon 79er Motel/rest. Burnville Dam RA, W GoMart Cedar Cr SP
76mm	Saltlick Creek
67	WV 4, to Flatwoods, E BP/Arby's/dsl, Exxon, Go-Mar dsl, Shell/dsl Custard Stand, KFC/Taco Bell, McDonald's, Subway Day's Hotel, Sutton Lake Motel antiques, Buick/Chevrolet, camping, to Sutton Lake RA, W Pilot/Moe's SW Grill/dsl/scales/24hr, Sunoco Chin Buffet, Shoney's, Wendy's Bulk Foods, farmer's mk Flatwood Factory Stores
62	WV 4, Gassaway, to Sutton, E Elk Motel Sutto Lake Camping, W GoMart LJ Silver, Pizza Hut Microtel H, Chrysler/Dodge/Jeep, CVS Drug, Forc Kroger/deli
57	US 19 S, to Beckley
52mm	Elk River
51	WV 4, to Frametown, E antiques, food
49mm	**both lanes, full facilities, litter barrels, petwalk RV dump, vending**
46	WV 11, Servia Rd
40	WV 16, to Big Otter, E GoMart/dsl, W Exxon/dsl
34	WV 36, to Wallback, **10 mi E** BiscuitWorld, Gino's Dine Subway
25	WV 29, to Amma, E Exxon/dsl
19	US 119, VW 53, to Clendenin, E BP/dsl Biscuit World, Gino's Diner 7-11, Shafer's Superstop
9	WV 43, to Elkview, E GoMart/dsl Burger Kin AutoZone, W Exxon/Arby's/dsl, Speedway/dsl Bob Evans, La Carreta, McDonald's, Pizza Hut, Ponderosa Subway Inn&Suites $Tree, Advance Parts, CVS Drug, K-Mart, Kroger/dsl, Radio Shack
5	WV 114, to Big Chimney, **1 mi E** Exxon Hardee's Rite Aid, Smith's Foods
1	US 119, Mink Shoals, E Harding's Family Rest. Sleep Inn
0	I-77, S to Charleston, N to Parkersburg. **I-79 begins/ends on I-77, exit 104.**

INTERSTATE 81

Exit #	Services
26mm	West Virginia/Maryland state line, Potomac River
25mm	**Welcome Ctr sb, full facilities, info, litter barrels, petwalk**
23	US 11, Marlowe, Falling Waters, E Exxon/AC&T/Subway/dsl Kings Rest., Red Lantern Chinese $General, Falling Waters Camping (1mi), Food Lion, W BP/dsl 7-11, Outdoor Express RV Ctr
20	WV 901, Spring Mills Rd, E Sheetz/dsl China Spring, Cinco de Mayo, Little Caesar's, McDonald's, Pizza Montese, Tokyo Cafe Motel 6 $Tree, Advance Parts, Walmart/Subway, W Shell/dsl Burger King, Domino's Quality Inn
16	WV 9, N Queen St, Berkeley Springs, E Crown/dsl, Exxon/Subway/dsl, Sheetz Arby's, China King, Domino's, Dunkin Donuts, Hoss's, KFC, La Trattoria, LJ Silver, McDonald's, Meridian Cafe, Mrs McCracken's Diner, Pizza Hut, Popeye's, Rita's Custard, Subway, Taco Bell, Waffle House Care Free Inn, Comfort Inn, Knights Inn, Super 8

M A R T I N S B U R G

INTERSTATE 81 Cont'd

16 Continued
[other] Advance Parts, Aldi Foods, AutoZone, BigLots, Carquest, CVS Drug, Family$, Food Lion, URGENT CARE, USPO, Walgreens, **W** [gas] Shell/Subway/dsl

14 Rd 13, Dry Run Rd, **E** [other] [H], **W** [other] Butler's Farm Mkt (1mi)

13 Rd 15, Kings St, Martinsburg, **E** [gas] BP/Subway/dsl, Sheetz/dsl [food] Applebee's, Buffalo Wild Wings, Burger King, Cracker Barrel, Daily Grind, Fiesta Tapatia, Golden Corral, Jerry's Subs, Kobe Japanese, Las Trancas, Outback Steaks, Pizza Hut, Wendy's [lodging] Courtyard, Days Inn, Holiday Inn/rest. [other] [H], Chevrolet/Scion/Toyota, Walmart

12 WV 45, Winchester Ave, **E** [gas] Sheetz/dsl, Shell/dsl, Sunoco/dsl [food] Arby's, Asian Garden, Bob Evans, Chick-fil-A, China City Buffet, McDonald's, Olive Garden, Papa John's, Ruby Tuesday, Ryan's, Taco Bell, Waffle House [lodging] Hampton

12 Continued
Inn [other] Advance Parts, AutoZone, BonTon, Food Lion, JC Penney, K-mart/Little Caesars, Lowe's, Martin's Foods/gas, Nahkeeta Camping, **W** [food] Ledo Pizza, Logan's Roadhouse, Subway, Tropical Smoothie [lodging] Hilton Garden [other] $Tree, AT&T, Best Buy, Books-A-Million, Dick's, GNC, Michael's, Petsmart, Target, TJ Maxx, URGENT CARE

8 Rd 32, Tablers Sta Rd, **E** [gas] Sheetz/dsl

5 WV 51, Inwood, to Charles Town, **E** [gas] 7-11, BP, Liberty, Sheetz/dsl, Shell/dsl [food] Burger King, Domino's, DQ, KFC, McDonald's, Pizza Hut, Pizza Oven, Subway, Waffle House [lodging] Hampton Inn [other] Advance Parts, CVS Drug, Family$, Food Lion, NAPA, Rite Aid, URGENT CARE, USPO, **W** [other] Lazy-A Camping (9mi)

2mm **Welcome Ctr/weigh sta nb, full [handicapped] facilities, info, litter barrels, petwalk [phone] [picnic] vending**

0mm West Virginia/Virginia state line

WISCONSIN

WV WI

INTERSTATE 39

Exit #	Services
211	US 51, Rd K, Merrill, **2 mi W** [gas] Cenex [food] Chip's Burgers, Hardee's, Pizza Hut [other] [airport]
208	WI 64, WI 17, Merrill, **E** [food] KFC, Taco Bell, **W** [gas] Cenex/dsl, KwikTrip/dsl, Mobil/dsl [food] 3's Company Rest., Culver's, Los Mezcales, McDonald's, Pine Ridge Rest., Pizza Now, Subway [lodging] Americinn, Best Inn, EconoLodge [other] [H], $Tree, Chrysler/Dodge/Jeep, O'Reilly Parts, Piggly Wiggly, to Council Grounds SP, Walmart
206mm	Wisconsin River
205	US 51, Rd Q, Merrill, **E** [gas] BP/Hwy 51/rest./dsl/24hr [other] Buick/Cadillac/Chevrolet, fireworks
197	Rd WW, to Brokaw
194	US 51, Rd U, Rd K, Wausau, **E** [gas] F&F/dsl, KwikTrip/dsl [food] McDonald's, Taco Bell, **W** [food] BP/Arby's [other] Ford, Nissan, Subaru, Toyota/Scion
193	Bridge St, **E** [other] CVS Drug, **W** [other] [H]
192	WI 29 W, WI 52 E, Wausau, to Chippewa Falls, same as 191 b
191b	Sherman St, **E** [gas] BP [food] Applebee's, Dickey's BBQ, Great Dane Rest., Hudson's Grill, Jimmy John's, King Buffet, Little Caesars, McDonald's, Noodles&Co, Panera Bread, Papa Murphy's, Qdoba, Starbucks, Subway, Toppers Pizza [lodging] Courtyard, Days Inn, Hampton Inn, La Quinta, Plaza Hotel, Super 8 [other] County Mkt Foods, ShopKo, Trig's Foods, Walgreens, **W** [gas] KwikTrip/dsl [food] 2510 Deli, Hardee's [other] [H], Cadillac, Home Depot, Honda, Menards
191a	WI 29, Chippewa Falls
190mm	Rib River
190	Rd NN, **E** [gas] Mobil/Burger King [food] Bo-Jo's Grill, IHOP, Krumbee's Bakery [lodging] Howard Johnson, **W** [gas] The Store/

W A U S A U

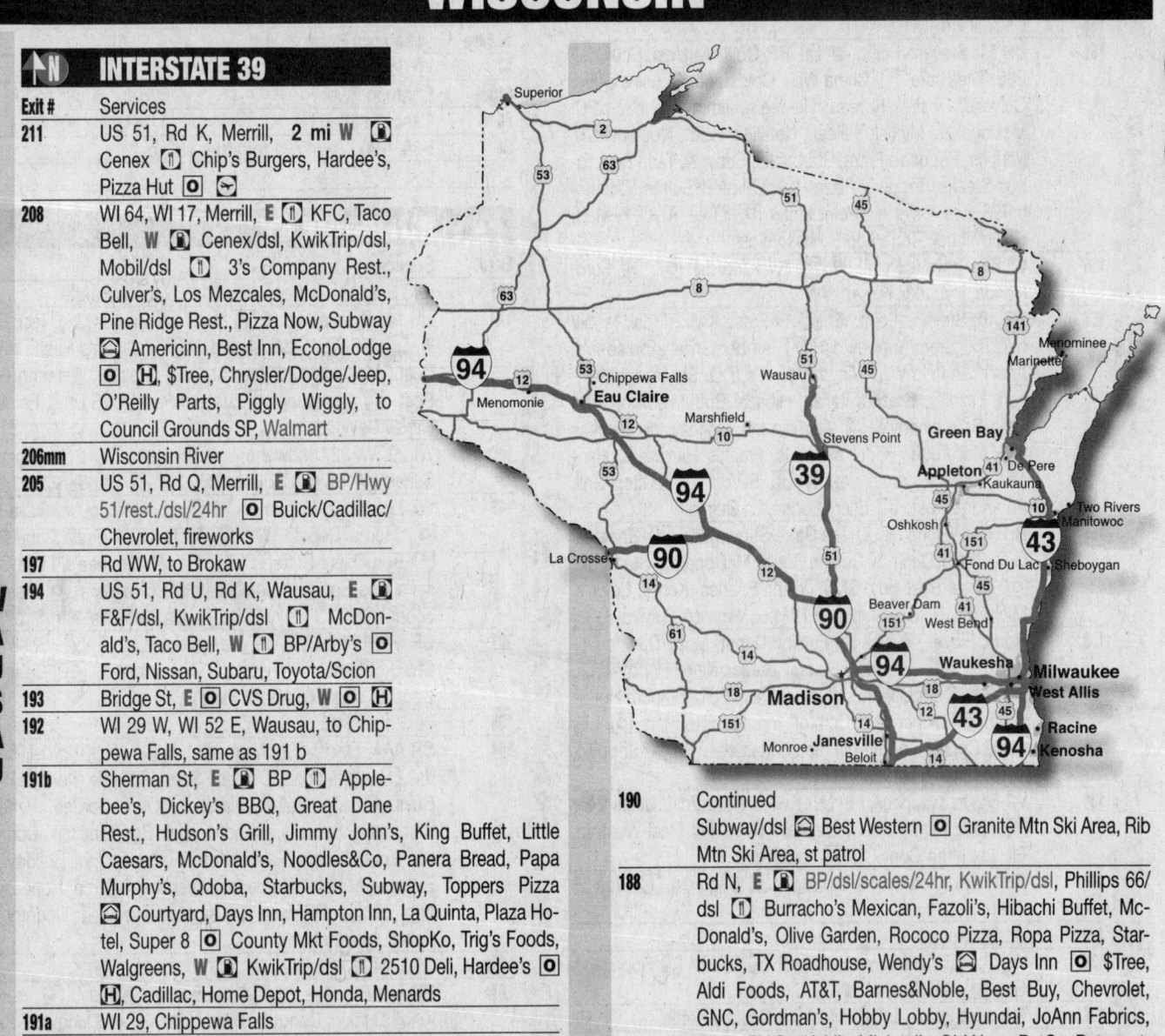

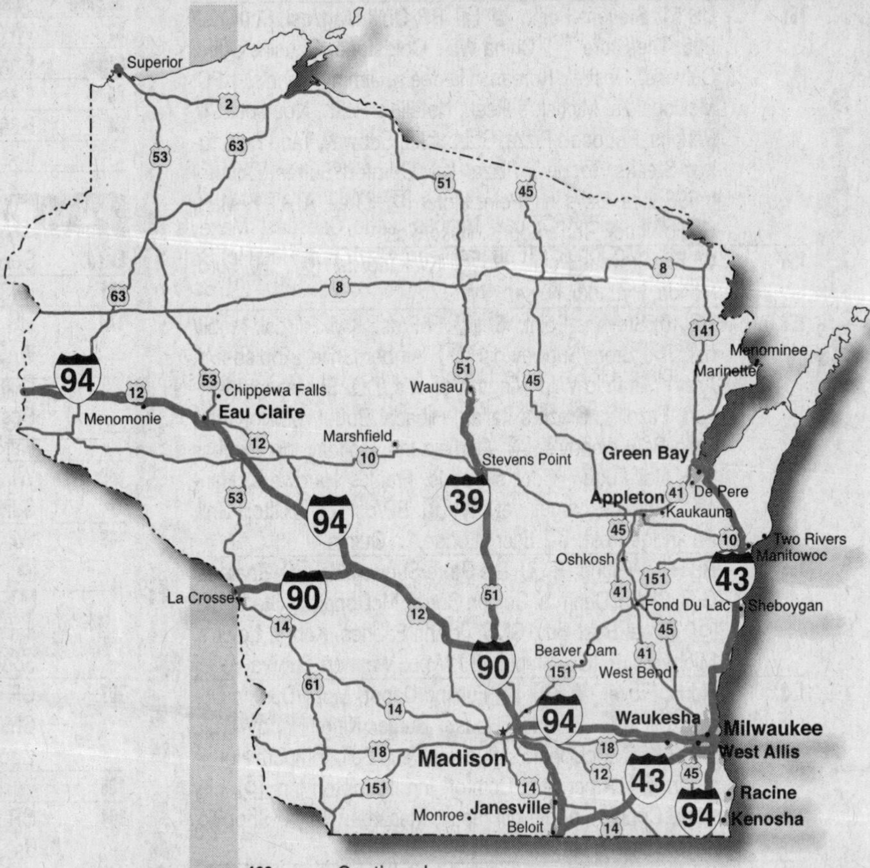

190 Continued
Subway/dsl [lodging] Best Western [other] Granite Mtn Ski Area, Rib Mtn Ski Area, st patrol

188 Rd N, **E** [gas] BP/dsl/scales/24hr, KwikTrip/dsl, Phillips 66/dsl [food] Burracho's Mexican, Fazoli's, Hibachi Buffet, McDonald's, Olive Garden, Rococo Pizza, Ropa Pizza, Starbucks, TX Roadhouse, Wendy's [lodging] Days Inn [other] $Tree, Aldi Foods, AT&T, Barnes&Noble, Best Buy, Chevrolet, GNC, Gordman's, Hobby Lobby, Hyundai, JoAnn Fabrics, King's RV Ctr, Kohl's, Michael's, Old Navy, PetCo, Petsmart, Radio Shack, Sam's Club/gas/dsl, Tires+, TJ Maxx, Tuesday Morning, Volvo, Walmart/Subway, **W** [other] Rib Mtn SP

INTERSTATE 39 Cont'd

WV

STEVENS PT

Exit #	Services
187mm	**I-39 begins/ends. Freeway continues N as US 51.**
187	WI 29 E, to Green Bay
186mm	Wisconsin River
185	US 51, Rothschild, Kronenwetter, E [gas] BP/dsl [food] Arby's, Culver's, Denny's, Green Mill Rest., Master Buffet, Subway [lodging] Candlewood Suites, Cedar Creek Lodge, EconoLodge, Holiday Inn, Motel 6, Stoney Creek Inn [other] Cedar Creek Factory Stores/famous brands, Gander Mtn, Harley-Davidson, mall, Pick'n Save Foods, visitor ctr
181	Maple Ridge Rd, Kronenwetter, Mosinee, E [other] Peterbilt, vet, Volvo, W Kenworth
179	WI 153, Mosinee, W [gas] BP/Subway/dsl, KwikTrip, Shell/dsl [food] McDonald's, StageStop Rest. [lodging] Quality Inn
175	WI 34, Knowlton, to WI Rapids, **1 mi** W [other] Mullins Cheese Factory
171	Rd DB, Knowlton, E Rivers Edge Camping, W [other] camping, [food] [lodging], to [gas]
165	US 10 W, to Marshfield (no nb re-entry)
163	Casimir Rd
161	US 51, Stevens Point, W [gas] BP, Quik Mart/dsl, Shell/dsl/E85, The Store [food] China Wok, Coldstone, Cousins Subs, Culver's, Dosirak Korean, Hardee's, Jimmy John's, KFC, McDonald's, Michele's Rest., Natalie's Rest., Noodles&Co, Perkins, Rococo's Pizza, Starbucks, Subway, Taco Bell, Tokyo Steaks, Topper's Pizza [lodging] Comfort Suites, Country Inn&Suites, Days Inn, Point Motel [other] $Tree, AT&T, K-Mart, Radio Shack, Trig's Foods, visitors ctr
159	WI 66, Stevens Point, W [gas] KwikTrip/dsl [other] [H], Ford, Honda, Hyundai, Nissan, VW
158	US 10, Stevens Point, E [gas] F&F/dsl, KwikFill/dsl, Mobil/dsl, The Store/Subway/dsl [food] Amber Grille, Applebee's, Arby's, Buffalo Wild Wings, Culver's, DQ, El Mezcal Mexican, Fazoli's, Grazie's Italian, Hibachi Buffet, McDonald's, Taco Bell, Wendy's [lodging] Fairfield Inn, Holiday Inn Express [other] Aldi Foods, Copp's Foods, Frank's Hardware, Hancock Fabrics, Target, vet, W [gas] BP/dsl [food] Hilltop Grill, Parkridge Rest. [lodging] EconoLodge, La Quinta
156	Rd HH, Whiting, E [gas] The Store/Subway/dsl [food] Charcoal Grill, Chili's, Denny's, Golden Corral, McDonald's, Starbucks [other] $Tree, Best Buy, GNC, JoAnn Fabrics, Kohl's, Lowe's, Michael's, PetCo, Staples, TJ Maxx, Walmart/Subway
153	Rd B, Plover, W [gas] BP, Fueling Depot, Mobil/Dunkin Donuts/dsl [food] Bamboo House, Burger King, Happy Wok, IHOP, KFC, McDonald's, Subway, Taco Bell, Tempura House Asian [lodging] AmericInn, Comfort Inn, Hampton Inn [other] city park, Copp's Foods, dsl repair, Menards, NAPA, ShopKo, Toyota/Scion, vet, Younkers
151	WI 54, to Waupaca, E [gas] KwikTrip/rest./dsl/scales/24hr [food] 4Star Family Rest., Shooter's Rest. [lodging] Best Western, Elizabeth Inn/Conv Ctr [other] tires/repair
143	Rd W, Bancroft, to WI Rapids, E [gas] Citgo/dsl [food] Area 51 Rest.
139	Rd D, Almond
136	WI 73, Plainfield, to WI Rapids, E [gas] BP/dsl [food] Hooligan's Grill [other] NAPA Care, W [gas] Citgo/dsl
131	Rd V, Hancock, E [gas] Citgo [food] Country Kettle
127mm	weigh sta both lanes (exits left)
124	WI 21, Coloma, E [gas] Mobil/A&W/dsl [food] Subway [lodging] Mecan Inn [other] Buick/Chevrolet, Caloma Camping, W [gas] BP/dsl
120mm	**[RS] sb, full [disabled] facilities, litter barrels, petwalk [phone] [picnic] RV dump, vending**
118mm	**[RS] nb, full [disabled] facilities, litter barrels, petwalk [phone] [picnic] RV dump, vending**
113	Rd E, Rd J, Westfield, W [gas] BP/Burger King, Marathon, Mobil/dsl [food] McDonald's, Subway [lodging] Pioneer Motel/rest. [other] city park, Curves, Family$
106	WI 82 W, WI 23 E, Oxford, E [lodging] Crossroads Motel, W [gas] Citgo/dsl
104	(from nb, no EZ return) rd D, Packwaukee
100	WI 23 W, Rd P, Endeavor, E [gas] BP/dsl [food] KW's Grill
92	US 51 S, Portage, E [gas] KwikTrip/dsl, Mobil [food] Chi-pan Asian, Culver's, Dino's Rest., Golden Cup 2 Cafe, Jimmy John's, KFC, La Tolteca Mexican, McDonald's, Papa Murphy's, Pizza Ranch, Subway, Suzy's Steaks, Taco Bell, World Buffet [lodging] Best Western, Ridge Motel, Sunset Motel, Super 8 [other] [H], $Tree, Ace Hardware, AutoZone, Chrysler/Dodge/Jeep, Curves, Ford/Lincoln, GNC, K-Mart, Pierce's Foods, Radio Shack, Staples, Verizon, Walgreens, Walmart
89b a	WI 16, to WI 127, Portage, E [gas] BP/dsl [food] Hitching Post Eatery, Murph's Chop Shop
88.5mm	Wisconsin River
87	WI 33, Portage, W ski area
86mm	Baraboo River
85	Cascade Mt Rd
84	**I-39, I-90 & I-94 run together sb/eb**

PORTAGE

INTERSTATE 41

GREEN BAY

Exit #	Services
171	I-43 S, to Milwaukee, US 41/141 N, to Marinette
170	US 141 S, Velp Ave, E [gas] Mobil [food] Burger King, Taco Bell, W [gas] BP/A&W/dsl, Shell/dsl [food] Gilligan's Rest., Julie's Rest., McDonald's, River St Grill, Subway, Watering Hole Rest. [lodging] AmericInn [other] Bumper Parts, CVS Drug, Family$, Harley Davidson
168c b	WI 29, WI 32, Shawano Ave, Dousman St, E [lodging] Comfort Suites [other] Buick/Cadillac/GMC, W [other] Gander Mtn
168	WI 32, WI 54, Mason St, E [food] Burger House, Pizza Hut [other] Home Depot, W [gas] Mobil, Shell/Papa John's/dsl [food] Bon Orient Buffet, Chili's, Fazoli's, Hardee's, Little Caesar's, Los Banditos, McDonald's, Schlotsky's [other] Festival Foods, GNC, O'Reilly Parts, Sam's Club, Walmart/Subway
167	CR VK, Lombardi Ave, Hazelwood Ln, E [gas] Shell [food] ChuckeCheese, Margaritas, Red Lobster [other] Cabela's, Copp's Foods, Lambeau Field
165	WI 172, to I-43
164	CR AAA, Oneida St, Waube Ln, E [gas] KwikTrip/dsl, Shell/dsl [food] Applebee's, Cousins Subs, Culver's, Denny's, Five Guys, Grazie's Italian, Hardee's, Olive Garden, Perkins, Starbucks, Subway, Wendy's [lodging] Baymont Inn, Comfort Inn, EconoLodge, Fairfield Inn, Hampton Inn, Holiday Inn Express, Motel 6, Ramada, Super 8 [other] $Tree, Honda, JoAnn, W [gas] BP/dsl [food] Los Magueyes [lodging] Country Inn Suites, Microtel
163b	WI 32 N, Green Bay
163a	CR G, Main Ave, E [gas] Mobil/dsl, Shell/dsl [food] Burger King, Dunkin Donuts, Jimmy John's, McDonald's, Papa John's, Papa Murphy's, Starbucks, Subway [other] $General, AutoZone, CVS Drug, Festival Foods, Peterbilt, USPO, Walgreens, W [gas] BP/A&W/Taco Bell/dsl/scales

INTERSTATE 41 Cont'd

Exit #	Services
161	CR F, Scheuring Rd, De Pete, E [gas] Mobil/Arby's/dsl, Shell/dsl [food] Culver's, DQ, Plank Road Rest. [lodging] Sleep Inn [other] $Tree, Menard's, Verizon, Walmart/Subway
157	CR S, Freedom, W [gas] BP/Chester's/Godfather's/dsl
154	CR U, Wrightstown
153	**weigh sta nb**
150	CR J, Kaukauna, E [other] Chrysler/Dodge/Jeep, W [gas] BP/dsl [other] Freightliner
148	WI 55, Seymour, Kaukauna, E [gas] KwikTrip/dsl, Shell/Arby's/dsl [lodging] Days Inn, W [other] Chevrolet/Buick/GMC
146	CR N, Little Chute, Kimberly, E [gas] Mobil/McDonald's/Subway/dsl, Shell/dsl, Sunoco [food] Burger King, Culver's, Tom's Drive In [lodging] Country Inn Suites, W [other] Simon's Cheese Store
145	WI 441 S
144	CR E, Ballard Rd, E [gas] Shell/dsl [food] Baskin Robbins, Hardee's, McDonald's [other] [H], W [lodging] AmericInn, Cambria Suites
142	WI 47, Richmond St, Black Creek, E [gas] Mobil [food] Fazoli's, Jimmy John's, Little Caesar's, McDonald's, Starbucks, Taco Bell [lodging] Snug In Motel [other] Kohl's, Walgreens, W [gas] KwikTrip/dsl, [food] Arby's
139	WI15, CR OO, Northland Ave, Greenville, Hortonville, W [gas] KwikTrip/dsl [other] Acura, BMW, Hyundai, Infiniti, Land Rover/Jaguar/Porsche, Lexus, Mazda, Mercedes, Nissan, Volvo, VW/Audi
138	WI 96, Wisconsin Ave, Fremont, E [gas] KwikTrip/dsl [food] Arby's, Famous Dave's, Golden Corral, Stevi B's, Wendy's [lodging] Comfort Suites [other] CarX, Home Depot, Petsmart, Sam's Club, W [gas] Mobil [food] Atl Bread, Buca Italian, Chili's, IHOP, Jimmy John's, Noodles&Co, Olive Garden, Osaka Japanese, Papa Murphy's, Qdoba, Red Lobster, Schlotsky's, Solea Mexican Grill, Starbucks, Walmart/Subway [other] $Tree, AT&T, Costco/dsl, Dick's, Discount Tire, Hancock Fabrics, JC Penney, Jo-Ann, Macy's, Menard's, Michael's, Petco, Scheel's, Sears, Target, Tires+, TJ Maxx, Verizon, Walgreens
137	WI 125, College Ave, E [gas] BP/dsl, Express, KwikTrip [food] Applebee's, Burger King, Denny's, HuHot, McDonald's, Panda Express, Panera Bread, Parma Italian, Perkins, Pizza Hut, Starbucks, Subway, Taco Bell, TX Roadhouse [lodging] Best Western, La Quinta, Motel 6, Quality Inn, Super 8 [other] Big Lots, Chrysler/Dodge/Jeep, Firestone/auto, Ford, Goodyear/auto, Honda, Kia, Office Depot, Subaru, Woodman's Gas, W [gas] KwikTrip/dsl [food] Buffalo Wild Wings, Chipotle, ChuckECheese, Fazoli's, Five Guys, Fuddrucker's, Machine Shed Rest., Outback Steaks, TGIFriday's [lodging] Candlewood Suites, Country Inn Suites, Fairfield Inn, GrandStay Suites, Hampton Inn, Holiday Inn, Microtel, Residence Inn [other] Barnes&Noble, Gordman's, Hobby Lobby, Old Navy, USPO
136	CR BB, Prospect Ave, W [gas] BP, Mobil/Subway [other] Van Zealand Autocare
134	US 10 E, WI 441 N
133	CR II, Winchester Rd
132	Main St, Oak Ridge Rd (no return nb or sb), E [gas] BP/dsl, Citgo/dsl [food] Bradke's Rest. [other] Chevrolet/Buick/Cadillac
131	WI 114, CR JJ, Winneconne Ave, Hilbert, Sherwood, E [gas] Citgo/dsl, Express, KwikTrip/dsl [food] Burger King, Ground Round, Hardee's, KFC, Little Caesar's, McDonald's, Papa Murphy's, Pizza Hut, Starbucks, Subway [lodging] Best Western,

APPLETON

Exit #	Services
131	Continued Days Inn [other] $Tree, Advance Parts, CVS Drug, Festival Foods, Firestone/auto, Ford/Lincoln, GNC, Pick'n Save, Shopko, W [food] A&W, Applebee's, Arby's, Culver's, Jimmy John's, Perkins, Qdoba, Taco Bell [other] Kohl's, Verizon, Walgreens, Walmart/Subway
129	Bell St, Breezewood Ln, W [gas] Mobil [food] Solea Mexican
124	WI 76, Jackson St, E [gas] Mobil, W [gas] KwikTrip/dsl/CNG, Sunoco [other] truck repair
120	US 45, US 10 W, New London
119	WI 21, Omro Rd, Oshkosh, E [food] DQ [lodging] La Quinta, W [gas] KwikTrip/dsl, Shell/McDonald's [food] Cousins Subs, Culver's, Panera Bread, Papa Murphy's, Rocky Rococo Pizza, Subway, Wendy's [lodging] Holiday Inn Express [other] Chevrolet/Buick/GMC/Cadillac, Dick's, Festival Foods, [H], Lowe's, Menard's, Verizon
117	9th Ave, E [gas] KwikTrip/dsl [food] Benvenuto's Italian, Buffalo Wild Wings, China King, Cousins Subs, Golden Corral, IHOP, Jimmy John's, Little Caesar's, McDonald's, Olive Garden, Pizza Hut, Qdoba, Red Robin, Starbucks, Subway, Taco Bell [lodging] Comfort Suites [other] AT&T, Best Buy, CVS Drug, Duluth Trading, Hobby Lobby, Jo-Ann, Ross, Shopko, Staples, TJ Maxx, Verizon, Walgreens, W [food] Burger King, Domino's, Perkins, Pizza Ranch [other] NAPA, Walmart/Subway
116	WI 44, WI 91, S Park Ave, Ripon Rd, E [gas] BP/dsl, Mobil/dsl [food] Applebee's, Arby's, Charcoal Pit, Fazoli's, Friar Tuck's Rest., Hardee's, Noodles&Co, Subway [lodging] AmericInn, Fairfield Inn, Hilton Garden, Super 8 [other] $Tree, Advance Parts, air museum, [airport], Aldi Foods, CarX, GNC, Petco, Pick'n Save, Target, Tires+, W [gas] KwikTrip/dsl, Shell/dsl [food] Johnny Rockets [lodging] Hawthorn Suites [other] Honda, Kia, Nissan, Oshkosh Outlets/famous brands, Subaru, Toyota/Scion, vet, VW
113	WI 26, CR N, Rosendale, Waupun, Pickett, E [other] Sleepy Hollow Camping (2mi), W [gas] Planeview/Subway/dsl/scales/24hr [lodging] Cobblestone Inn
106	CR N, Van Dyne
101	CR OO, Winnebago St, E [gas] BP/Rest./dsl/scales [other] Mack/Volvo, truck wash
99	WI 23, Johnson St, Rosendale, Ripon, E [food] Ala Roma Pizza, Applebee's, Buffalo Wild Wings, Burger King, DQ, Faro's Rest., Fazoli's, Hardee's, KFC, McDonald's, Panda Express, Panera Bread, Pizza Hut, Qdoba, Rocky Rococo Pizza, Schriener's Rest., Starbucks [lodging] Days Inn, Hampton Inn, Super 8 [other] AT&T, AutoZone, Best Buy, Jo-Ann, Kohl's, Pick'n Save, Shopko, Staples, TJ Maxx, W [gas] KwikTrip/dsl, Shell/Subway/dsl [food] Arby's, Culver's [other] $Tree, Aldi Foods, CarX, Chevrolet/Buick/GMC/Cadillac, Ford, Harley Davidson, Mazda, Menard's, Petsmart, Target, Verizon, Walmart/Subway

OSHKOSH

RIPON

Ⓖ = gas Ⓕ = food Ⓛ = lodging Ⓞ = other Ⓡ**S** = rest stop Copyright 2016 - The Next EXIT ®

⬆N INTERSTATE 41 Cont'd

Exit #	Services
98	CR D, Military Rd, **E** Ⓕ McDonald's Ⓛ Microtel Ⓞ F&F/dsl, Schiek's Camoers, **W** Ⓖ BP/dsl Ⓕ Rolling Meadows Rest. Ⓛ Comfort Inn, Holiday Inn, Holiday Inn Express Ⓞ Chrysler/Dodge/Jeep, Merz RV Ctr, st patrol
97	CR VVV, Hickory St, **E** Ⓖ KwikTrip/dsl, Shell/dsl, **W** Ⓖ Loves/Subway/dsl/scales/24hr, Marathon/dsl Ⓛ Country Inn Suites
95	US 152, Madison, Manitowoc, **E** Ⓞ Ⓗ
92	CR B, Oakfield, Eden, **E** Ⓞ Breezy Hill Camping (2 mi)
87	WI 49, CR KK, Brownsville, Waupun
85	WI 67, Lomira, Campbellsport, **E** Ⓖ Exxon/dsl, **W** Ⓖ BP/Taco Bell/dsl, Shell/Subway/dsl Ⓕ Bublitz's Rest., McDonald's Ⓛ Country Hearth Inn Ⓞ $General, Ford, Piggly Wiggly
82.5mm	Ⓡ**S** both lanes, full ♿ facilities, litter barrels, petwalk 🐾
81	WI 28, Mayville, Kewaskum
76	CR D, **W** Ⓞ fireworks
72	WI 33, CR W, West Bend, Allenton, **W** Ⓖ BP/dsl, Mobil Ⓕ Alma's Cafe, Subway
68	CR K, **W** Ⓖ Mobil/dsl Ⓕ MJ Stevens Rest. Ⓞ USPO
66	WI 144, West Bend, Slinger, **W** Ⓞ Freedom RV Ctr, Held's Cheese/sausage, Slinger Speedway
64	WI 60, to Jackson, Slinger, Hartford, **E** Ⓞ Scenic RV Ctr, **W** Ⓖ BP/dsl, Citgo, KwikTrip/dsl Ⓕ Burger King Ⓞ Chevrolet, Chrysler/Dodge/Jeep, Ⓗ, Piggly Wiggly, Schaefer's Service Ctr
60	CR FD, to WI 145, Richfield, **E** Ⓖ Mobil/dsl/e85 Ⓞ Cabela's, **W** Ⓖ BP/McDonald's/dsl/scales/24hr
59	(from nb) US 45 W
57	WI 167, Holy Hill Rd, **E** Ⓖ Mobil/Subway/dsl, **W** Ⓖ Exxon/Rest./dsl/scales
54	WI 167, CR Y, Lannon Rd, Germantown, **E** Ⓖ KwikTrip/dsl Ⓛ Best Western, Country Inn Suites Ⓞ Gander Mtn
52	CR Q, County Line Rd, **E** Ⓕ Briscoe Co Wood Grill, **W** Ⓖ Mobil/dsl, Speedway/dsl Ⓕ Applebee's, Arby's, Buffalo Wild Wings, Burger King, Cracker Barrel, Jimmy John's, KFC, McDonald's, Panda Express, Pizza Hut/Taco Bell, Starbucks, Wendy's Ⓛ Holiday Inn Express, Super 8 Ⓞ AT&T, Best Buy, Costco/dsl, Kohl's, Target
51b a	Pilgrim Rd, **W** Ⓖ KwikTrip Ⓕ Kramerz Burgers, Toppers Ⓞ AutoZone, Wamart Mkt
50b a	WI 74 W, WI 100 E, Menomonee Falls, **E** Ⓞ Buick/GMC, Ford car repair VW, **W** Ⓖ Mobil Ⓛ De Martinis Pizza, Radisson Ⓞ Monro
48	WI 145, **E** Ⓞ Sam's Club/gas, Woodman's Mkt/gas
47b	CR PP, Good Hope Rd, **E** Ⓕ Point Burger Bar, Ruby Tuesday Ⓛ Comfort Suites, Hilton Garden Ⓞ CarMax, Chevrolet, Mazda, Nissan, Toyota/Scion
47	WI 175, Appleton Ave
46	CR E, Silver Spring Dr, **E** Ⓖ Marathon/dsl, Mobil/dsl Ⓕ Arby's, Athens Rest., Cousins Subs, KFC, McDonald's, Subway, Taco Bell, Wendy's Ⓛ Hampton Inn, La Quinta Ⓞ Goodyear/auto, Harley Davidson, Petro Mart, **W** Ⓖ Speedway/dsl
45	CR EE, Hampton Ave, **E** Ⓖ Citgo, **W** Ⓖ BP/dsl
44	WI 190, Capitol Dr, **E** Ⓕ Subway Ⓞ Walgreens, **W** Ⓖ BP Ⓕ Arby's, Burger King, Chick-fil-A, Chipotle, Culver's, Jimmy John's, McDonald's, Noodles&Co, Potbelly's, Qdoba, Starbucks Ⓞ Advance Parts, GNC, Home Depot, Petco, Pick'n Save, Ross, Target, Walmart Mkt

MILWAUKEE

43	Burleigh St, **E** Ⓕ Corner Bakery Cafe, Osgood's Rest., Pizza Man Ⓞ Dick's, Ⓗ, Meijer, Old Navy, TJ Maxx, **W** Ⓕ Dickey's BBQ, Wendy's Ⓛ Cousins Subs Ⓞ Aldi Foods, Firestone/auto, Lowe's
42b	North Ave W, **E** Ⓖ BP Ⓕ Applebee's, Buffalo Wild Wings, Cheesecake Factory, Dave&Buster's, Denny's, Five Guys, Maggiano's, McCormick&Schmick, Panera Bread, PF Chang's Ⓛ Extended Stay America, Holiday Inn Express, Radisson Ⓞ Barnes&Noble, Best Buy, Macy's, Nordstrom's, Walgreens
42a	WI 100, Mayfair Rd, North Ave E (from nb), **E** Ⓕ Dave&Buster's, **W** Ⓕ Firehouse Subs Ⓛ Crowne Plaza Ⓞ Kia, Pick'n Save, USPO
40	Watertown Plank Rd, Swan Blvd, **E** Ⓞ Ⓗ, **W** Ⓛ Crowne Plaza
39	US 18, Wisconsin Ave, Bluemound Rd, **E** Ⓞ Ⓗ
1b a	I-94
1d	WI 53, Greenfield Ave, **E** Ⓕ Subway Ⓞ CVS Drug, Family$, **W** Ⓖ BP/dsl, Speedway/dsl Ⓕ Griddlers Cafe, Las Fajitas, McDonald's, Starbucks Ⓞ O'Reilly Parts, Sam's Club, Walgreens
1e	(from sb) Lincoln Ave, **E** Ⓞ same as 2 E
2a	(from sb) National Rd (wb)
2b	(from sb) Oklahoma Ave, **E** Ⓖ Citgo Ⓞ auto repair, Ⓗ
3	Beloit Rd
4mm	**I-41 S runs with I-43 N/I-894 E, then I-94 E. See I-43 exits 5-9 and I-94 exits 316-347**
1.5mm	Wisconsin/Illinois state line
1b a	**I-41 begins/ends on I-94 IL**, Tri State tollway, Russell Rd

⬆N INTERSTATE 43

Exit #	Services
192mm	**I-43 begins/ends at Green Bay on US 41.**
192b	US 41 S, US 141 S, to Appleton, services on Velp Ave, **1 mi** **S** Ⓖ BP/A&W/dsl, Express/dsl, Mobil, Shell/dsl Ⓕ Burger King, Gilligan's Rest., Julie's Cafe, McDonald's, Riverstreet Grill, Subway, Taco Bell, Watering Hole Rest Ⓛ AmericInn Ⓞ Bay Parts, Bumper Parts, CVS Drug, Family$, Harley-Davidson, Trans Motive Auto
192a	US 41 N, US 141 N
189	Atkinson Dr, to Velp Ave, Port of Green Bay, **W** Ⓖ Shell/dsl
188mm	Fox River
187	East Shore Dr, Webster Ave, **W** Ⓖ Shell/dsl/24hr Ⓕ McDonald's, Subway, Wendy's Ⓛ Hampton Inn, Hyatt Ⓞ Ⓗ
185	WI 54, WI 57, University Ave, to Algoma, **E** Ⓞ U of WI GB, **W** Ⓖ Mobil, Shell/A&W Ⓕ Green Bay Pizza, Subway, Taco Bell Ⓞ Family$, University Foods, Walgreens
183	Mason St, Rd V, **E** Ⓕ Culver's, Mackinaw's Grill Ⓛ Country Inn&Suites, Super 8 Ⓞ Ⓗ, URGENT CARE, **1 mi** **W** Ⓖ BP, Mobil/dsl, Shell Ⓕ Applebee's, Arby's, Burger King, China Buffet, Fazoli's, KFC, Little Caesar's, McDonald's, Noodles&Co, Papa John's, Papa Murphy's, Perkins, Pizza Hut, Pizza Ranch, Qdoba, Sonic, Starbucks, Taco Bell Ⓞ $General, Advance Parts, Aldi Foods, AutoZone, Batteries+Bulbs, Chevrolet, Chrysler/Dodge/Jeep, Copps Foods, Family$, Hobby Lobby, Kohl's, Mazda, Nissan, O'Reilly Parts, PetCo, ShopKO, Subaru, Tires+, Walgreens, Walmart/Subway

GREEN BAY

WI

INTERSTATE 43 Cont'd

MANITOWOC

MILWAUKEE

Exit #	Services
181	Eaton Rd, Rd JJ, E BP/McDonald's/dsl Hardee's, Jimmy John's, Luigi's, Sgambati's Pizza, Taco John's Ford/Kia, Home Depot, W Mobil/Subway/dsl, Shell A&W, Ravine Grill AmericInn Farm&Fleet/gas, Festival Foods, Menards
180	WI 172 W, to US 41, **1 exit** W BP/Taco Bell/24hr, Citgo/Country Express/dsl/scales/24hr, KwikTrip/dsl, Shell/Subway/dsl Burger King, McDonald's, Tuscon's Rest. Holiday Inn Express H, AT&T, Copps Foods, Costco/gas, GNC, Target, to stadium, Verizon, Walgreens, multiple services
178	US 141, to WI 29, Rd MM, Bellevue, E Shell/Arby's/dsl, W repair
171	WI 96, Rd KB, Denmark, E BP/dsl deGrande Rest, McDonald's, Steve's Cheese, Subway Shady Acres Camping
168mm	**both lanes, full facilities, litter barrels, petwalk vending**
166mm	Devils River
164	WI 147, Rd Z, Maribel, W BP/dsl
160	Rd K, Kellnersville
157	Rd V, Hillcrest Rd, Francis Creek, E Citgo/Subway/dsl, Marathon/diner/dsl
154	US 10 W, WI 310, Two Rivers, to Appleton, E H
153mm	Manitowoc River
152	US 10 E, WI 42 N, Rd JJ, Manitowoc, E TimeOut Grill H, antiques, maritime museum
149	US 151, WI 42 S, Manitowoc, E BP, Citgo/dsl, KwikTrip/dsl, Mobil, Shell/dsl A&W, Applebee's, Arby's, Buffalo Wild Wings, Burger King, Charcoal Grill, China Buffet, Culver's, DQ, Fork&Knife Rest, Four Seasons Rest., Frier Tuck's Sandwiches, Hardee's, Jimmy John's, KFC, Little Caesar's, McDonald's, Panda Express, Papa Murphy's, Perkins, Pizza Ranch, Qdoba, Starbucks, Taco Bell, Wendy's Birch Creek Inn, Harbor Town Inn, Holiday Inn, Quality Inn H, $Tree, Advance Parts, Aldi Foods, AutoZone, Buick/Cadillac/Chevrolet/GMC, Chrysler/Dodge/Jeep, Copps Foods, Family$, Festival Foods, GNC, Goodyear/auto, Hobby Lobby, Kohl's, Lowe's, O'Reilly Parts, PetCo, ShopKO, Tires+, USPO, Verizon, vet, Walgreens, Walmart/Subway, W Shell/McDonald's Subway AmericInn Harley-Davidson, Menards
144	Rd C, Newton, E Mobil/dsl antiques
142mm	**weigh sta sb**
137	Rd XX, Cleveland, E Citgo/Subway/dsl Wildflower Cafe Kessler's Old World Guesthouse Wagner's RV Ctr
128	WI 42, Howards Grove, E BP/dsl/24hr, KwikTrip/dsl Culver's, Hardee's, Harry's Diner, Shuff's Rest., TX Roadhouse Quality Inn Gander Mtn, Pomp's Tire, W Mobil/dsl/scales Menards, Walmart/Subway
126	WI 23, Sheboygan, E BP, KwikTrip/dsl, Tesla EVC Applebee's, Cousins Subs, Culver's, McDonald's, New China, Noodles&Co, Pizza Hut/Taco Bell, Pizza Ranch La Quinta, Super 8 H, Aldi Foods, Batteries+Bulbs, BigLots, Festival Foods, Firestone/auto, Ford/Kia, Goodyear/auto, Hobby Lobby, Honda/Mazda, Hyundai/Mazda, Kohl's, NAPA, ShopKO, Subaru, Toyota/Scion
123	WI 28, Rd A, Sheboygan, E Citgo/dsl/24hr, Mobil/McDonald's/dsl Coldstone, Cruisers Cafe, Jimmy John's,

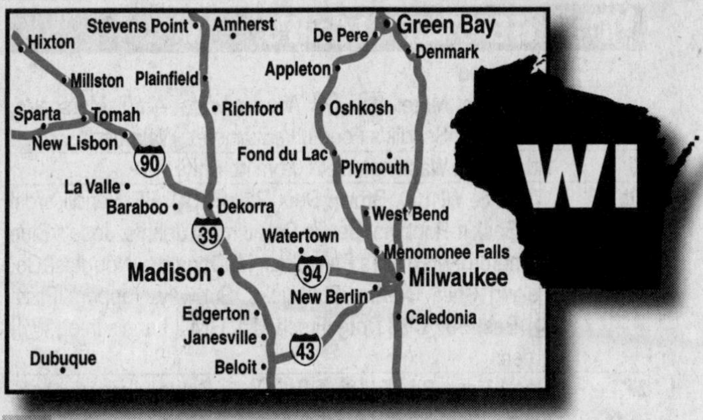

Exit #	Services
123	Continued Perkins, Qdoba, Starbucks, Subway, Wendy's AmericInn, Holiday Inn Express CarX, Harley-Davidson/Cruisers Burgers, Walmart/Subway, W Arby's, Buffalo Wild Wings, Chili's $Tree, AT&T, Best Buy, Boston's Store, GNC, Home Depot, Jo-Ann Fabrics, Petsmart, Target, TJ Maxx
120	rds OK, V, Sheboygan, E Citgo/dsl Hwy Ridge Rest. Sleep Inn camping, Nissan, to Kohler-Andrae SP, VW, **1 mi** W Horn's RV Ctr
116	Rd AA, Foster Rd, Oostburg, **1 mi** W Judi's Place Rest., Pizza Ranch, Subway Piggly Wiggly/gas
113	WI 32 N, Rd LL, Cedar Grove, W Citgo/dsl/repair, Mobil/dsl, Sunoco/Fueling Depot Country Grove Rest. (1mi), Cousins Subs Lakeview Motel
107	Rd D, Belgium, E Lake Church Inn/grill Harrington Beach SP, W BP/McDonald's/dsl/24hr, How-Dea Trkstp/Hobo's Korner Kitchen/dsl/scales, Mobil/dsl/24hr Bic's Place, Say Cheese Outlet, Subway Rodeway Inn repair, USPO
100	WI 32 S, WI 84 W, Port Washington, E Citgo/dsl, Mobil Arby's, McDonald's, Pizza Hut, Subway Country Inn&Suites, Holiday Inn (2mi) Allen-Edmonds Shoes, Goodyear/auto, Sentry Foods, ShopKO Express, True Value, vet, W Nisleit's Country Rest.
97	(from nb, exits left), WI 57, Fredonia
96	WI 33, to Saukville, E Citgo Culver's (1mi), KFC/LJ Silver Best Hardware, Buick/Cadillac/Chevrolet, Camping World RV Ctr, Chrysler/Dodge/Jeep, Ford, O'Reilly Parts, Piggly Wiggly, Walgreens, Walmart, W Exxon/McDonald's, KwikTrip/dsl Domino's, DQ, La Chimenea Mexican, Lam's Chinese, Lam's Chinese, Papa Murphy's, Subway, Taco Bell Motel 6 repair/tires
93	WI 32 N, WI 57 S, Grafton, **2 mi** E BP George Webb Rest. vet, W Flannery's Cafe (2mi)
92	WI 60, Rd Q, Grafton, E BP/dsl GhostTown Rest., Water St Rest. Hampton Inn, W Citgo/DQ/dsl Charcoal Grill, Noodles&Co, Qdoba, Quiznos, Starbucks, Subway Comfort Inn H, Aldi Foods, AT&T, Best Buy, Costco/gas, Dick's, Home Depot, Kohl's, Meijer, Michael's, Petsmart, Target, Verizon
89	Rd C, Cedarburg, W Mobil/dsl Cedar Crk Settlement Café (6mi) StageCoach Inn (3mi), Washington House Inn (3mi) H
85	WI 57 S, WI 167 W, Mequon Rd, W BP, Mobil, QStop/dsl, Shell Caribou Coffee, Chancery Rest., Cousins Subs, Culver's, DQ, First Watch Cafr, Jimmy John's, Leonardo's Pizza, McDonald's, Noodles&Co, Panera Bread, Papa Murphy's, Pizza Hut, Starbucks, Subway, Taco Bell

INTERSTATE 43 Cont'd

85 Continued
Chalet Motel H, Ace Harware, AT&T, Marshall's, Metro Mkt, Sendik's Foods, Verizon, vet, Walgreens

83 Rd W, Port Washington Rd (from nb only)

82b a WI 32 S, WI 100, Brown Deer Rd, E BP, Sendik's/dsl Baskin-Robbins, Benji's Deli, Jimmy John's, Jose's Blue Sombrero, Maxfield's Pancakes, McDonald's, Noodles&Co, Peking Chef, Qdoba, Starbucks, Subway, Toppers Pizza Best Buy, CVS Drug, Fresh Mkt, GNC, Land's Inlet, Walgreens

80 Good Hope Rd, E BP Dr Dawg, Jimmy John's, King's Wok, Samurai Japanese North Shore Suites, Radisson Pick'n Save Foods, to Cardinal Stritch U

78 Silver Spring Dr, E BP, Citgo Applebee's, Bar Louie, BD Mongolian, Boston Mkt, Bravo Italian, Buffalo Wild Wings, Burger King, CA Pizza Kitchen, Cheesecake Factory, Cousins Subs, Devon Steaks, Fiddleheads Coffee, Five Guys, Food Court, McDonald's, Panera Bread, Papa Murphy's, Perkins, Pizza Hut, Qdoba, Sprecher's Rest., Subway, Taco Bell La Quinta, La Quinta, Motel 6 AT&T, Barnes&Noble, Batteries+Bulbs, Goodyear/auto, Kohl's, mall, Nissan, Trader Joe's, USPO, Verizon, Walgreens, W H

77b a (from nb), E Anchorage Rest., Solly's Grille Holiday Inn

76b a WI 57, WI 190, Green Bay Ave, E Home Depot, W BP/dsl Burger King

75 Atkinson Ave, Keefe Ave, E Mobil, W BP

74 Locust St

73c North Ave (rom sb), E Wendy's, W McDonald's

73b North Ave (from nb), downtown

73a WI 145 E, 4th St (exits left from sb), Broadway, downtown

72c Wells St, E Hilton H, Civic Ctr, museum

72b (from sb), I-94 W, to madison

72a (310c from nb, exits left from sb), I-794 E, I-94 W to Madison, to Lakefront, downtown

311 WI 59, National Ave, 6th St, downtown

312a Lapham Blvd, Mitchell St, W BP, Citgo

312b (from nb), Becher St, Lincoln Ave

314a Holt Ave, E SP Mart/dsl Applebee's, Arby's, China King, Jimmy John's, Little Caesar's, Starbucks, Subway, Taco Bell, Wendy's $General, Family$, Home Depot, Pick'n Save Foods, Piggly Wiggly, Target, vet, W H, to Alverno Coll

314b Howard Ave

10b I-94 S to Chicago, E

9b a WI 241, 27th St, E Clark, Supreme/dsl Arby's, Benny's Cafe, Burger King, Famous Dave's, Pizza Hut, Sonic, Subway Suburban Motel AutoZone, Subaru, Target, USPO, Walgreens, W Boston Mkt, Buffalo Wild Wings, Chipotle Mexican, Denny's, Jimmy John's, McDonald's, New China, Omega Rest., Panda Express, Papa John's, Rich's Cakes, Starbucks, Taco Bell, Wong's Wok, Zebb's Rest Quality Inn, Rodeway Inn H, $Tree, AAA, Advance Parts, Chevrolet, CVS Drug, Firestone/auto, Ford, Goodyear/auto, Kohl's, Marshall's, Michael's, Pick'n Save Foods, Save-A-Lot Foods, Walgreens, Walmart

8a WI 36, Loomis Rd, E BP/dsl, Paul's Gas Los Mariachi's Aldi Foods, Walgreens, W Griddler's Cafe to Alverno Coll

7 60th St, E Speedway/dsl Subway, Wendt's Grille Harley-Davidson, W Speedway/dsl URGENT CARE

5b 76th St (from sb, no EZ return), E Applebee's, Bakers Square, Buca Italian, Burger King, Carrabba's Italian, Chick-fil-A, Cousins Subs, El Beso, Griddler's Cafe, Hooters, Jersey Mike's, Jimmy John's, Kopp's Burgers, Kyoto Japanese, Longhorn Steaks, McDonald's, Noodles&Co, Old Country Buffet, Olive Garden, Outback Steaks, Panera Bread, Qdoba, Red Lobster, Red Robin, Ruby Tuesday, Starbucks, TGIFriday's, Topper's Pizza, Traditional Pancake House, Wendy's $Tree, AT&T, Barnes&Noble, Best Buy, Firestone/auto, Goodyear, JC Penney, Jo-Ann Fabrics, Kohl's, Macy's, Midas, PetCo, Petsmart, Sears/auto, Sendik's Food Mkt, Tuesday Morning, Verizon, Walmart, W Arby's, Pizza Hut, Subway Advance Parts, Family$, Pick'n Save Foods, TJ Maxx, USPO, Walgreens, Panda Express

5a WI 24 W, Forest Home Ave, E Citgo/dsl Boerner Botanical Gardens, Welk's Auto

61 (4 from sb), I-894/US 45 N, I-43/US 45 S

60 US 45 S, WI 100, 108th St (exits left from sb), E BP, Hometown, Kwik Pantry, Marathon A&W, Amore Italian, Ann's Italian, Chipotle Mexican, Confucious Chinese, Cousins Subs, Culver's, DQ, Dunkin Donuts, Fortune Chinese, George Webb Rest., McDonald's, McGuire's Grill, Noodles&Co, Open Flame Grill, Papa Murphy's, Pizza Hut, Starbucks, Subway, Taco Bell $Tree, AutoZone, Chevrolet, O'Reilly Parts, Pick'n Save, USPO, vet, Walgreens, W Andy's/dsl Forum Rest., McDonald's, Organ Piper Pizza, Subway Aldi Foods, Badger Transmissions, Goodyear, NAPA, Nissan, vet, Walgreens, Walmart/Subway

59 WI 100, Layton Ave (from nb, exits left), Hales Corner, W BP/Cousins Subs same as 60

57 Moorland Rd, E KwikTrip/dsl Applebee's, Stonefire Pizza Co, TX Roadhouse, Zaffiro's Pizza La Quinta Costco/dsl, W Speedway/dsl Arby's, Buffalo Wild Wings, Cusina Real, Panera Bread, Pap John's, Quaker Steak&Lube, Subway Holiday Inn Express Firestone/auto, GNC, Michael's, Target

54 Rd Y, Racine Ave, **1-2 mi** E BP/dsl, KwikTrip Cousins Subs, Culver's, McDonald's, Piggly Wiggly, Walgreens

50 WI 164, Big Bend, W KwikTrip/dsl/e85 McDonald's

44mm Fox River

43 WI 83, Mukwonago, E BP/dsl Aldi Foods, Chevrolet, Chrysler/Dodge/Jeep, Home Depot, H, Walmart, W Citgo Boneyard Grille, Chen's Kitchen, Domino's, DQ, Taco Bell Rodeway Inn

38 WI 20, East Troy, W BP/dsl, Pilot/Road Ranger/Subway/dsl/24hr, Shell/McDonald's Burger King, Cousins Subs, Dos Amigos, Genoa Pizza, Grist Mill Rest., LD's BBQ $General, Carquest, Chrysler/Dodge/Jeep

36 WI 120, East Troy, E Alpine Valley Resort, W Quality Inn Suites

33 Bowers Rd, E to Alpine Valley Music Theatre

32mm **both lanes, full facilities, litter barrels, petwalk vending**

29 WI 11, Elkhorn, W fairgrounds

27b a US 12, to Lake Geneva, E H

25 WI 67, Elkhorn, E Mobil/dsl AmericInn Buick/Chevrolet/GMC, Chrysler/Dodge/Jeep, vet, W Speedway/dsl/24hr Burger King, Subway Hampton Inn (2mi) Dehaan Auto/RV Ctr

INTERSTATE 43 Cont'd

Exit #	Services
21	WI 50, Delavan, **E** [food] Brodie's Beef, Chili's, China 1, Culver's, Domino's, Jimmy John's, Panera Bread, Papa Murphy's, Starbucks, Subway, Yoshi Japanese [other] Aldi Foods, AT&T, F&F Tires, golf, Kohl's, Lowe's, Petsmart, Radio Shack, Staples, Verizon, Walmart, **W** [gas] Mobil/Dunkin Donuts/dsl [food] KFC, McDonald's, Perkins, Pizza Hut, Taco Bell, Wendy's [lodging] Comfort Suites, Super 8 [other] $Tree, AutoZone, Cadillac/Chevrolet, Ford/Lincoln, GNC, NAPA, Piggly Wiggly, ShopKO, Walgreens
17	Rd X, Delavan, Darien, **W** [gas] BP/dsl
15	US 14, Darien, **E** [gas] Mobil/dsl [food] West Wind Diner
6	WI 140, Clinton, **E** [gas] Citgo/Subway/TCBY/dsl [other] $General, Ford
2	Rd X, Hart Rd, **E** [food] Butterfly Fine Dining
1b a	I-90, E to Chicago, W to Madison, **S** [gas] Mobil/McDonald's, Pilot/Taco Bell/dsl/scales/24hr, Shell, Speedway/dsl [food] Applebee's, Arby's, Asia Buffet, Buffalo Wild Wings, Culver's, Doc's Rest., Jimmy John's, Little Caesar's, Little Mexico, Papa Murphy's, Qdoba, Road Dawg Rest., Starbucks, Subway, Wendy's [lodging] Baymont Inn, Fairfield Inn, Hampton Inn, Holiday Inn Express, Quality Inn, Rodeway Inn [other] $Tree, Aldi Foods, AT&T, Buick/GMC, Cadillac/Chevrolet, GNC, Menards, NTB, O'Reilly Parts, Radio Shack, Staples, Walmart
0	**I-43 begins/ends on I-90, exit 185 in Beloit.**

DELAVAN · BELOIT

INTERSTATE 90

Exit #	Services
187mm	Wisconsin/Illinois state line, **I-90 & I-39 run together nb.**
187mm	**Welcome Ctr wb, full [handicapped] facilities, info, litter barrels, petwalk [phone] [picnic] vending**
185b	I-43 N, to Milwaukee
185a	WI 81, Beloit, **S** [gas] Mobil/McDonald's/dsl, Pilot/Taco Bell/dsl/scales/24hr, Shell, Speedway/dsl [food] Applebee's, Arby's, Asia Buffet, Buffalo Wild Wings, Culver's, Doc's Rest., Jimmy John's, Little Caesars, Little Mexico, Papa Murphy's, Qdoba, Road Dawg Rest, Starbucks, Subway, Wendy's [lodging] Baymont Inn, Fairfield Inn, Hampton Inn, Holiday Inn Express, Quality Inn, Rodeway Inn [other] $Tree, Aldi Foods, AT&T, Buick/GMC, Cadillac/Chevrolet, GNC, Menards, NTB, O'Reilly Parts, Radio Shack, Staples, Walmart
183	Shopiere Rd, Rd S, to Shopiere, **S** [gas] BP/Rollette/dsl/24hr [other] [H], camping, repair
181mm	**weigh sta wb**
177	WI 11 W, Janesville, **2 mi S** [gas] KwikTrip/dsl [other] S WI Airport, to Blackhawk Tec Coll
175b a	WI 11 E, Janesville, to Delavan, **N** [gas] BP/Subway/dsl [lodging] Baymont Inn [other] [H], bet, **S** [lodging] Lannon Stone Motel [other] city park
171c b	US 14, WI 26, Janesville, **N** [gas] TA/Mobil/Wendy's/dsl/scales/24hr/@ [food] Coldstone, Cozumel Mexican, Fuddruckers, HomeTown Buffet, IHOP, Quaker Steak, Starbucks, Subway, TX Roadhouse [lodging] Holiday Inn Express, Microtel [other] Aldi Foods, Best Buy, Gander Mtn, GNC, Home Depot, Michael's, NTB, Old Navy, PetCo, Staples, TJ Maxx, **S** [gas] Citgo, Exxon/dsl, Kwik Trip/dsl [food] Applebee's, Arby's, Buffalo Wild Wings, Burger King, Chipotle, ChuckeCheese, Culver's, Dunkin Donuts, Famous Dave's, Fazoli's, Fuji Steaks, Hacienda Real, Hardee's, Hooters,

BELOIT · JANESVILLE

Exit #	Services
171c b	Continued Jimmy John's, KFC, Mac's Pizza, McDonald's, Milio's Sandwiches, Milwaukee Grill, Noodles&Co, Olive Garden, Panda Express, Panera Bread, Papa Murphy's, Peking Chinese, Perkins, Pizza Hut, Prime Quarter Steaks, Qdoba Mexican, Red Robin, Road Dawg Eatery, Subway, Taco Bell, Taco John's, Toppers Pizza, World Buffet [lodging] EconoLodge, Super 8 [other] [H], $Tree, Aldi Foods, AT&T, AutoZone, Big Lots, CarQuest, CVS Drug, F&F, Festival Foods, Ford/Lincoln, Harley-Davidson, Hobby Lobby, Hyundai, JC Penney, K-Mart/Little Caesar's, Kohl's, mall, Mazda, Menards, Nissan/Kia/Subaru, O'Reilly Parts, Sears/auto, ShopKO, Target, Toyota/Scion, USPO, Verizon, Walgreens
171a	WI 26, **N** [gas] BP/dsl [food] Cracker Barrel [lodging] Hampton Inn, Motel 6, Ramada/rest. [other] Chrysler/Dodge/Jeep, Sam's Club, URGENT CARE, VW, Walgreens, Walmart, **S** same as 171c b
168mm	**[RS] eb, full [handicapped] facilities, litter barrels, petwalk [phone] [picnic] vending**
163.5mm	Rock River
163	WI 59, Edgerton, to Milton, **N** [gas] Mobil/Subway/dsl, Shell/Dunkin Donuts/Taco John's/dsl [food] Blue Gilly's Rest., Culver's, McDonald's, WI Cheese Store [lodging] Comfort Inn [other] marina
160	US 51S, WI 73, WI 106, Oaklawn Academy, to Deerfield, **S** [gas] BP/dsl/scales/24hr/ @ [other] [H], Creek View Camping (2mi)
156	US 51N, to Stoughton, **S** [lodging] Coachman's Inn/rest. [other] [H]
147	Rd N, Cottage Grove, to Stoughton, **S** [gas] BP/Arby's/dsl, Road Ranger/Pilot/Subway/dsl/scales [other] Lake Kegonsa SP
146mm	**weigh sta eb**
142b a	(142a exits left from wb) US 12, US 18, Madison, to Cambridge, **N** [gas] BP/dsl [food] Roadhouse Rest [lodging] Best Value Inn, Magnuson Grand Hotel [other] casino, Harley-Davidson, **S** [gas] Citgo/dsl, Phillips 66/Arby's/dsl, Shell/dsl [food] Denny's [lodging] Days Inn, Sleep Inn [other] [H], Menards, UWI
138a	I-94, E to Milwaukee, W to La Crosse
	I-90 W and I-94 W run together for 93 miles, (exits left from eb)
138b	WI 30, Madison, **S** [airport]
135c b	US 151, Madison, **N** [gas] BP/dsl [food] Erin's Cafe, Happy Wok, Milio's Sandwiches, Uno Grill [lodging] Cambria Suites, Courtyard, Fairfield Inn, GrandStay Suites, Holiday Inn, Staybridge Suites [other] Buick/GMC, Chrysler/Dodge/Jeep, Ford, Honda, Hyundai, Kia, Mazda, Nissan, Subaru, Toyota/Scion
135a	US 151, Madison, **S** [gas] BP, Citgo, Mobil, Shell [food] Applebee's, Arby's, Buffalo Wild Wings, Chili's, Chipotle Mexican, Cracker Barrel, Culver's, Denny's, Dickey's BBQ,

MADISON

WI

[gas] = gas [food] = food [lodging] = lodging [other] = other [RS] = rest stop

INTERSTATE 90 Cont'd

MADISON

135a Continued
DoLittle's Woodfire Grill, Fazoli's, Hardee's, Hometown Buffet, Hooters, IHOP, Imperial Garden, Jimmy John's, KFC, McDonald's, Milio's, Noodles&Co, Olive Garden, Outback Steaks, Panera Bread, Perkins, Pizza Hut, Potbelly, Qdoba, Red Lobster, Red Robin, Rocky's Pizza, Starbucks, Taco Bell, Takumi Japanese, TGIFriday's, Toppers's Pizza, TX Roadhouse, Wendy's [lodging] Best Western, Comfort Inn, Crowne Plaza Hotel/rest., EconoLodge, Hampton Inn, Howard Johnson, Microtel, Motel 6, Red Roof Inn, Residence Inn, Rodeway Inn, Super 8 [other] $Tree, Aldi Foods, AT&T, Barnes&Noble, Best Buy, Burlington Coats, city park, Dick's, Firestone/auto, Goodyear/auto, Gordman's, Hobby Lobby, Home Depot, Hy-Vee Foods, JC Penney, JoAnn Fabrics, Kohl's, mall, Marshalls, Menards, Michaels, Office Depot, Old Navy, Petsmart, Savers, Sears/auto, ShopKO, st patrol, Target, Verizon

132 US 51, Madison, De Forest, N [gas] Shell/Pinecone Rest/dsl/24hr [other] Camping World RV Ctr, Gander Mtn, S [gas] TA/BP/Subway/Taco Bell/dsl/scales/24hr/ @ [other] Freightliner/GMC/Volvo/White, Goodyear, Peterbilt, WI RV World

131 WI 19, Waunakee, N [gas] Kwik Trip/dsl, Mobil/dsl, Speedway/dsl [food] A&W, McDonald's, Rodeside Grill [lodging] Days Inn, Super 8 [other] fireworks, Kenworth, Mousehouse Cheesehaus, truckwash

WI

126 Rd V, De Forest, to Dane, N [gas] BP/A&W/Rococo's/dsl, Phillips 66/Arby's/dsl [food] Burger King, Culver's, McDonald's, Subway, Taco Bell [lodging] Holiday Inn Express [other] Cheese Chalet, KOA, S [gas] Exxon, Shell [lodging] Comfort Inn [other] dsl repair

119 WI 60, Arlington, to Lodi, S [gas] Mobil/A&W/Cousins Subs/dsl [food] A&W, Rococo's Pizza [lodging] Quality Inn [other] dsl/tire repair

115 Rd CS, Poynette, to Lake Wisconsin, N [gas] BP/dsl [food] McDonald's, Subway [other] auto repair, dsl truck/trailer repair, Smokey Hollow Camping, trout fishing

113mm **[RS] both lanes, full [handicapped] facilities, litter barrels, petwalk [phone] [picnic] vending**

111mm Wisconsin River

108b a I-39 N, WI 78, to US 51 N, Portage, N [other] [H], to WI Dells, S [gas] BP, Mobil, Petro/Iron Skillet/DQ/Subway/dsl/24hr/ @ [lodging] Comfort Suites, Days Inn [other] Blue Beacon

106mm Baraboo River

106 WI 33, Portage, N [other] [H], S [gas] BP [other] Circus World Museum, Devil's Lake SP, Kamp Dakota, SkyHigh Camping, to Cascade Mtn Ski Area, Wayside Park

92 US 12, to Baraboo, N [gas] BP/dsl, Citgo/Subway/dsl, Exxon, Mobil/Dunkin Donuts/dsl/24hr [food] Buffalo Phil's Grille, Burger King, Cheese Factory Rest, Cracker Barrel, Culver's, Denny's, Domino's, Famous Dave's BBQ, Field's Steaks, Green Owl Pizza, Marley's Rest., McDonald's, Milio's, Monk's Grill, Noodles&Co, Pizza Ranch, Ponderosa, R Place Italian, Sarento's Italian, Starbucks, Taco Bell, Uno Grill, Wintergreen Grill [lodging] Alakai Hotel, Country Squire Motel, Dell Creek Motel, Glacier Canyon Lodge, Grand Marquis Inn, Great Wolf Lodge, Holiday Inn Express, Kalahari Resort, Ramada, Wilderness Hotel, Wintergreen Hotel [other] Mkt Square Cheese, museum, Tanger Outlets Famous Brands, URGENT CARE, Verizon, S [lodging] Motel 6 [other] [H], Jellystone Camping, Mirror Lake SP, Red Oak Camping, Scenic Traveler RV Ctr

WISCONSIN DELLS

89 WI 23, Lake Delton, N [gas] Phillips 66, Shell/dsl [food] Bra thouse Grill, Denny's Diner, Howie's Rest., KFC, Moosejaw Pizza [lodging] Hilton Garden, Kings Inn, Malibu Inn, Olympia Motel, Travelodge [other] Crystal Grand Music Theatre, Jellystone Camping, Springbrook Camping, USPO, S [food] McDonald's [other] $Tree, Country Roads RV Park, Home Depot, Jo-Ann, Kohl's, Walmart/Subway

87 WI 13, Wisconsin Dells, N [gas] Citgo/dsl, Mobil/Arby's/dsl, Shell/Dunkin Donuts [food] Applebee's, Bunyan's Rest., Burger King, Coldstone, Culver's, Denny's, IHOP, Jimmy John's, McDonald's, Mexicali Rose Rest., Perkins, Starbucks, Taco Bell, Wei's Chinese [lodging] Ambers Resort, AmericInn, Baymont Inn, Best Western, Econolodge, Polynesian Hotel, Quality Inn, Super 8 [other] golf, info, KOA, Sherwood Forest Camping, Walgreens, waterpark

85 US 12, WI 16, Wisconsin Dells, N [lodging] Fairway Motel [other] KOA, Sherwood Forest Camping, Standing Rock Camping, to Rocky Arbor SP, S [gas] BP [food] Piccadilly's [lodging] Arrowhead Camping, Days End Motel, Edge-O-the-Dell RV Camping, Summer Breeze Resort

79 Rd HH, Lyndon Sta, S [gas] BP/Subway/dsl/24hr

76mm **[RS] wb, full [handicapped] facilities, litter barrels, petwalk [phone] [picnic] RV dump, vending**

74mm **[RS] eb, full [handicapped] facilities, litter barrels, petwalk [phone] [picnic] RV dump, vending**

69 WI 82, Mauston, N [gas] Mauston TP/BP/Taco Bell/24hr, Pilot/Wendy's/dsl/scales/24hr, Shell/24hr [food] China Buffet, Family Rest. [lodging] Best Western Oasis, Quality Inn, Super 8 [other] Carr Valley Cheese, to Buckhorn SP, S [gas] KwikTrip/Hearty Platter Rest/dsl/scales/24hr, Mobil [food] Culver's, Log Cabin Deli, McDonald's, Pizza Hut, Roman Castle Rest., Subway [lodging] Alaskan Inn [other] [H], $General, Buick/Chevrolet, Family$, Festival Foods, K-Mart, Verizon, vet, Walgreens

61 WI 80, New Lisbon, to Necedah, N [gas] Mobil/A&W/Subway/dsl/scales/24hr [lodging] Edge O' the Woods Motel, Travelers Inn [other] Buckhorn SP, Chrysler/Dodge/Jeep, fireworks, Ford, S [gas] KwikTrip/24hr [other] city park, Elroy-Sparta ST Tr, USPO

55 Rd C, Camp Douglas, N [other] to Camp Williams, Volk Field wayside, S [gas] BP/dsl, Mobil/Home Front Cafe/dsl [lodging] K&K Motel [other] to Mill Bluff SP

48 Rd PP, Oakdale, N [gas] Road Ranger/Pilot/Subway/dsl/scales/24hr [other] antiques, Granger's Camping, KOA, truck/car wash, S [gas] Loves/Hardee's/dsl/scales/24hr [other] Mill Bluff SP, repair

45 I-94 W, to St Paul

I-90 E and I-94 E run together for 93 miles

TOMAH

43 US 12, WI 16, Tomah, N [gas] BP/dsl, KwikTrip/dsl/24hr [food] Burnstadt's Café, DQ [lodging] Daybreak Inn, Rest Well Motel [other] [H], Burnstadt's Mkt, vet

41 WI 131, Tomah, to Wilton, N [gas] KwikTrip/dsl/24hr, Mobil/dsl [food] Burnstadts Cafe [lodging] Daybreak Inn [other] vet, S [other] st patrol

28 WI 16, Sparta, Ft McCoy, N [gas] BP/diner/dsl/scales [lodging] Best Western [other] [H]

25 WI 27, Sparta, to Melvina, N [gas] Cenex/dsl, KwikTrip/dsl, Mobil/Taco Bell, Shell/dsl [food] Burger King, Culver's, DQ, KFC, McDonald's, Pizza Hut, Sparta Rest., Subway [lodging] Country Inn, Super 8 [other] [H], $General, Buick/Chevrolet, Family$, Ford, Hansens IGA, O'Reilly Parts, Walgreens, Walmart/Subway, S [other] camping

22mm **[RS] wb, full [handicapped] facilities, litter barrels, petwalk [phone] [picnic] RV dump, vending**

INTERSTATE 90 Cont'd

LA CROSSE

Exit #	Services
20mm	**eb, full facilities, litter barrels, petwalk RV dump, vending**
15	WI 162, Bangor, to Coon Valley, N gas, S Chevrolet
12	Rd C, W Salem, N Cenex/cafe/dsl/24hr Coulee Region RV Ctr, NAPA, Neshonoc Camping, S BP/Subway/dsl AmericInn
10mm	**weigh sta eb**
5	WI 16, La Crosse, N BA Burrito, Buffalo Wild Wings, Ciatti's Italian, Coldstone, Manny's Mexican, Outback Steaks Baymont Inn, Hampton Inn, Microtel $Tree, Aldi Foods, Freightliner, Home Depot, Walmart/Subway, Woodman's Foods/gas/lube, S Kwik Trip/dsl/24hr Bamboo House, Burracho's Mexican Grill, Carlos O'Kelly's, ChuckeCheese, Culver's, Fazoli's, Hong Kong Buffet, HuHot Grill, Jimmy John's, McDonald's, Old Country Buffet, Olive Garden, Perkins, Starbucks, TGIFriday's, TX Roadhouse Holiday Inn Express H, Barnes&Noble, Best Buy, Chevrolet, Dick's, F&F, Ford/Lincoln, Hobby Lobby, JC Penney, Kohl's, Macy's, mall, Michael's, Sears/auto, ShopKO, Target, Walgreens
4	US 53 N, WI 16, to WI 157, La Crosse, N Harley-Davidson, S Kwik Trip, TO Applebee's, Burger King, Caribou Coffee, China Inn, Cousins Subs, Famous Dave's BBQ, Grizzly's Rest, Panera Bread, Papa Murphy's, Red Lobster, Rococo's Pizza, Shogun Hibachi, Subway, Taco Bell, Wendy's Comfort Inn H, Festival Food/24hr, Gander Mtn, GNC, Goodyear/auto, Hancock Fabrics, La Crosse River St Trail, Office Depot, Old Navy, PetCo, Petsmart, Sam's Club, Tires+, TJ Maxx, Verizon
3	US 53 S, WI 35, to La Crosse, S Clark/dsl, Kwik Trip Burger King, Coney Island, Edwardo's Pizza, Hardee's, KFC, La Crosse Rest., McDonald's, North Country Steaks, Perkins, Pizza Hut, Subway Best Value Inn, Best Western, Motel 6, Quality Inn, Settle Inn, Super 8 ShopKo, to Great River St Trail, U-Haul, Viterbo Coll, Walgreens
2.5mm	Black River
2	Rd B, French Island, N , S BP/dsl Days Inn/rest. IGA Foods
1mm	**Welcome Ctr eb, full facilities, info, litter barrels, petwalk vending**
0mm	Wisconsin/Minnesota state line, Mississippi River

INTERSTATE 94

KENOSHA

Exit #	Services
349mm	Wisconsin/Illinois state line, **weigh sta nb**
348.5mm	**weigh sta wb**
347	WI 165, Rd Q, Lakeview Pkwy, E **Welcome Ctr nb, full facilities, litter barrels, petwalk vending,** BP/dsl Chancery Rest., Culver's, McDonald's Radisson Old Navy, Premium Outlets/famous brands,
345	Rd C, E Holiday Inn Express (1mi)
345mm	Des Plaines River
344	WI 50, Lake Geneva, to Kenosha, **1 mi** E Buffalo Wild Wings, Cheddar's, Cousins Subs, Dickey's BBQ, Famous Dave's, Mobil/dsl, Noodles&Co, Olive Garden, Panda Express, Perkins, Pizza Hut, Shell/Dunkin Donuts/dsl, Sparti's Gyros, Starbucks, Subway, Tuscany Bistro, TX Roadhouse, White Castle, Woodman's/gas Candlewood Suites, Holiday Inn Express, La Quinta, Super 8 H, AT&T,

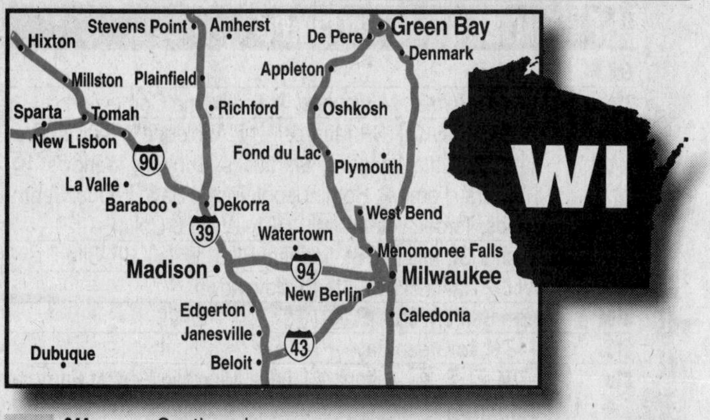

Exit #	Services
344	Continued Best Buy, Chevrolet, Dick's, Gander Mtn, GNC, JC Penney, Petsmart, Target, Verizon, Walgreens, W BP/dsl, Speedway/dsl Arby's, Birchwood Grill, Cracker Barrel, KFC, McDonald's, Phoenix Rest., Wendy's Best Western, Comfort Inn, Country Inn&Suites, Hampton Inn, Value Inn BratStop Cheese Store, CarMax, Honda, Nissan, Subaru, Toyota/Scion
342	WI 158, to Kenosha, E Harley-Davidson, W antiques
340	WI 142, Rd S, to Kenosha, E Kenosha TP/BP/Subway/dsl/E85/LP/scales/24hr H, W Mars Cheese Castle Rest. Oasis Inn Fun Time RV Ctr, to Bong RA
339	Rd E
337	Rd KR, to Mt Pleasant, W Apple Holler Rest./orchard
335	WI 11, to Mt Pleasant, Burlington, to Racine
333	WI 20, Waterford, to Racine, E KwikTrip/dsl/24hr, Shell/Cousins Subs/dsl Burger King, McDonald's Days Inn, Excel Inn, Holiday Inn Express H, Toyota/Scion, W Citgo/Wendy's/dsl/24hr, Petro/Mobil/Iron Skillet/dsl/scales/24hr/ @ Chicken'n Waffles, Culver's, Route 20 Outhouse Grill, Subway Quality Inn Burlington RV Ctr, visitor info
329	Rd K, Thompsonville, to Racine, E Pilot/Arby's/Subway/dsl/scales/24hr A&W dsl repair
328mm	weigh sta eb
327	Rd G, W fireworks
326	7 Mile Rd, E BP, Mobil/dsl Jellystone Park, W Seven Mile Fair
325	WI 241 N (from wb) , to 27th St
322	WI 100, to Ryan Rd, E KwikTrip/dsl McDonald's, Wendy's dsl repair, W Loves/Denny's/dsl/LP/scales/RV dump/24hr, Mobil, Pilot/Subway/dsl/LP/scales/24hr, Shell/A&W/KFC/dsl Arby's, Cousins Subs, Dish Bakery, Dunkin Donuts, Perkins, Starbucks, Yen Hwa Chinese Staybridge Suites, Value Inn AutoZone, Blue Beacon, Freightliner/repair, H, Pick'n Save, vet, Walgreens
321	Drexel Ave
320	Rd BB, Rawson Ave, E BP/7-11/dsl, Mobil Applebee's, Burger King La Quinta
319	Rd ZZ, College Ave, E Shell/Subway, Speedway/dsl Branded Steer Rest., McDonald's Candlewood Suites, Comfort Suites, Country Inn&Suites, Crowne Plaza, Days Inn, EconoLodge, Fairfield Inn, Hampton Inn, Holiday Inn Express, MainStay Suites, Motel 6, Red Roof Inn Burlington Coats, W Royal
318	WI 119, E
317	I-43, I-894 (from wb)
316	I-43 S, I-894 W (I-94 exits left from eb) , to Beloit, E Clark/dsl Martino's Hotdogs

WI

INTERSTATE 94 Cont'd

MILWAUKEE

Exit #	Services
314b	Howard Ave, to Milwaukee, W to Alverno Coll
314a	Holt Ave, E [gas] SP Mart/dsl [food] Applebee's, Arby's, China King, Little Caesar's, Starbucks, Subway, Wendy's [other] $General, Family$, Home Depot, Pick'n Save Foods, Sentry Foods, Target, vet, W [other] [H], to Alverno Coll
312b a	Becher St, Mitchell St, Lapham Blvd, W [gas] BP, Citgo
311	WI 59, National Ave, 6th St, downtown
310a	13th St (from eb), E [other] [H]
310b	I-43 N, to Green Bay
310c	I-794 E, E [lodging] Hilton [other] Lake Michigan Port of Entry, to downtown
309b	26th St, 22nd St, Clybourn St, St Paul Ave, N [other] [H], to Marquette U
309a	35th St, N [other] URGENT CARE
308c b	US 41
308a	VA Ctr, S [other] Miller Park
307b	68th-70th St, Hawley Rd
307a	68th-70th St
306	WI 181, to 84th St, N [other] [H], S [other] Olympic Training Facility
305b	I-41 N, US 45 N, to Fond du Lac, N [other] [H]
305a	I-41 S, I-894 S, US 45 S, to Chicago, S [other] to [airport]
304b a	WI 100, N [gas] 7-11, Amstar/dsl, BP, Shell/dsl [food] Cousins Subs, Domino's, Ghengis Khan BBQ, Habanero's Mexican, HoneyBaked Cafe, Jimmy John's, Mo's Irish Grill, Peony Chinese, Qdoba, Rococo's, Starbucks, Subway, Taco Bell [lodging] Crowne Plaza, Forty Winks Inn [other] [H], zoo, S [gas] Amstar, BP/dsl, Speedway/dsl [food] Culver's, DQ, Fazoli's, McDonald's, Pallas Rest., Starbucks, Toppers Pizza, Wendy's [lodging] Days Inn [other] Aldi Foods, Midas, O'Reilly Parts, Sam's Club, U-Haul, Walgreens
301b a	Moorland Rd, N on US 18 [gas] BP/dsl, Mobil [food] Bakers Square, Bravo Italiano, Buffalo Wild Wings, Chipotle, CiCi's, Cooper's Hawk, Culver's, Five Guys, Fleming's Rest., Food Court, Fuddrucker's, Hooters, Jamba Juice, Jersey Mike's, Marty's Pizza/subs, McDonald's, Mitchell's Fish Mkt, Noodles&Co, Original Pancake House, Qdoba, Red Robin, Starbucks, Stir Crazy, Subway, TGIFriday's [lodging] Courtyard, Sheraton, TownePlace Suites [other] AT&T, Barnes&Noble, CVS Drug, F&F Tire, Firestone/auto, Fresh Mkt Foods, Goodyear/auto, JC Penney, Jo-Ann Fabrics, mall, Metro Mkt, Michael's, Office Depot, PetCo, Petsmart, Sears/auto, SteinMart, TJ Maxx, Verizon, vet, Walgreens, World Mkt, S [food] Champp's Grill, Outback Steaks, Panera Bread, Starbucks [lodging] Best Western Midway, Brookfield Suites, Country Inn&Suites, Residence Inn [other] golf, Pick'n Save Foods, Walgreens, Walmart
297	WI 164 S, US 18, Rd JJ, Blue Mound Rd, Barker Rd, **0-2 mi** N [gas] BP, Clark [food] Applebee's, BoneFish Grill, Boston Mkt, Brookfield Rest., Bullwinkle's Rest., Carrabba's, Chili's, ChuckECheese's, Cousins Subs, Emperors Kitchen, George Webb Rest., Hom Woodfired Grill, Jimmy John's, Jose's Mexican, KFC, Kopp's Custard, Laredo's Mexican, Mama Mia's, McDonald's, Melting Pot, Olive Garden, Perkins, Potbelly, Starbucks, Subway [lodging] DoubleTree, Extended Stay America, Hampton Inn, La Quinta, Motel 6, Quality Inn [other] [H], $Tree, Acura, Advance Parts, Aldi Foods, Best Buy, GNC, Hobby Lobby, Lexus/Mazda/VW, Meineke, Metro Mkt, S [gas] Clark, PDQ [food] Arby's, Burger King, Chancery Rest., Cousin's Subs, Culver's, Famous Dave's BBQ,
297	Continued La Fuente Mexican, McDonald's, Meiji Chinese, New China, Oscar's Burgers, Papa Murphy's, Sonic, Starbucks, Subway, Taco Bell, Topper's Pizza, TX Roadhouse, Wendy's [lodging] Baymont Inn, Extended Stay America, Super 8 [other] AT&T, Buick/GMC, Cadillac, CarMax, Chevrolet, Farm&Fleet, Firestone/auto, Ford, Gander Mtn, Home Depot, Honda, Hyundai, Infiniti/Maserati/Mercedes/Porsche, Jaguar/Land Rover/Volvo, Kia, Kohl's, Menards, Midas, Nissan, Sam's Club, st patrol, Subaru, Target, Tires+, Walgreens, Woodman's/[gas]

WAUKESHA

Exit #	Services
295	Rd F, to WI 74, Waukesha, N [gas] KwikTrip/dsl [food] Jimmy John's [lodging] Marriott, S [other] [H], to Carroll U
294	WI 164, Rd J S, to Waukesha, N [gas] Mobil/Subway/dsl [food] Machine Shed Rest., Thunder Bay Grille [lodging] Holiday Inn, Wildwood Lodge, S [other] Expo Ctr, Peterbilt
293c	WI 16 W, Pewaukee (from wb), N [other] GE Plant
293b a	Rd T, Wausheka, Pewaukee, S [gas] KwikTrip/dsl, Mobil [food] Arby's, Asian Fusion, Canyon City Wood Grill, Cousins Subs, Culver's, Denny's, Dunkin Donuts, Feng's Kitchen, Jimmy John's, McDonald's, Mr. Wok, Papa Murphy's, Qdoba, Rococo's Pizza, Spring City Rest., Subway, Taco Amigo, Topper's Pizza, Weissgerber's Gasthaus Rest., Wendy's [lodging] Best Western [other] $Tree, AutoZone, CVS Drug, Firestone/auto, GNC, Goodharvest Mkt, Jo-Ann Fabrics, Office Depot, Pick'n Save Foods, Verizon, Walgreens
291	Rd G, Rd TT, N [lodging] Country Springs Inn
290	Rd SS, Pewaukee
287	WI 83, Hartland, to Wales, N [food] Applebee's, Five Guys, Hardee's, McDonald's, Noodles&Co, Panera Bread, Perkins, Qdoba, Starbucks, Water St Brewery/rest. [lodging] Country Pride Inn, Holiday Inn Express [other] Albrecht's Mkt, Best Buy, GNC, Kohl's, Marshalls, Verizon, Walgreens, S [gas] BP, PDQ/dsl/24hr [food] Burger King, Coldstone, DQ, Jimmy John's, Marty's Pizza, Pacific Asian Bistro, Pizza Hut, Rocky Rococo Pizza, StoneCreek Coffee, Subway [lodging] La Quinta [other] $Tree, Ace Hardware, Home Depot, PetCo, Target, Tires+, vet, Walmart/Subway
285	Rd C, Delafield, N [gas] BP/dsl, Mobil/deli [lodging] Delafield Hotel [other] to St John's Military Academy, S [other] to Kettle Moraine SF
283	Rd P, to Sawyer Rd
282	WI 67, Dousman, to Oconomowoc, **0-2 mi** N [gas] KwikTrip/dsl, Mobil [food] Chili's, Cousins Subs, Culver's, Eat Smart Cafe, Feng's Kitchen, Jimmy John's, Pizza Hut, Qdoba, Quiznos, Rococo's Pizza, Rosati's Pizza, Starbucks, Stone Creek Coffee, Subway [lodging] Hilton Garden, Olympia Resort [other] Ace Hardware, Aldi Foods, AT&T, Brennan's Mkt, Ford, GNC, K-Mart, Pick'n Save, Radio Shack, vet, Walgreens, S [lodging] Staybridge Suites [other] [H], Harley-Davidson, Old World WI HS (13mi), to Kettle Moraine SF (8mi)
277	Willow Glen Rd (from eb, no return)
275	Rd F, Ixonia, to Sullivan, N [gas] Mobil/dsl [other] Concord Gen Store, S [other] camping
267	WI 26, Johnson Creek, to Watertown, N [gas] BP/McDonald's/dsl, Shell/dsl/rest./scales/24hr [food] Arby's, Hwy Harry's Cafe [lodging] Comfort Suites, Days Inn [other] Goodyear/auto, Johnson Creek Outlet Ctr/famous brands, Old Navy, S [gas] KwikTrip/dsl [food] Culver's, Midpoint Eatery, Subway, Taco Bell [other] [H], Kohl's, Menards, to Aztalan SP
266mm	Rock River
264mm	**[RS] wb, full [handicapped] facilities, litter barrels, petwalk [phone] [picnic] RV dump, vending**
263mm	Crawfish River

WI

INTERSTATE 94 Cont'd

Exit #	Services
261mm	eb, full facilities, litter barrels, petwalk RV dump, vending
259	WI 89, Lake Mills, to Waterloo, N Mobil/rest/dsl/24hr Best Value Inn truck repair, S BP/dsl/E85, Kwik-Trip/dsl Jimmy John's, McDonald's, Pizza Pit, Subway Pyramid Motel/RV park Ace Hardware, Buick/Chevrolet, Country Campers, to Aztalan SP, URGENT CARE, vet, Walgreens
250	WI 73, Deerfield, to Marshall
244	Rd N, Sun Prairie, Cottage Grove, N BP/dsl Subway, S BP/dsl, KwikTrip Arby's
240	I-90 E.
I-94 & I-90 run together for 93 mi. See I-90 exits 48-138.	
147	I-90 W, to La Crosse
143	US 12, WI 21, Tomah, N Mobil/dsl A&W/LJ Silver, Perkins AmericInn, Best Western, Microtel, Super 8 Humbird Cheese/gifts, truckwash, S to Ft McCoy (9mi), BP, KwikTrip/rest./dsl/scales/24hr Arby's, China Buffet, Culver's, Ground Round, KFC, McDonald's, Pizza Hut, Subway, Taco Bell Cranberry Lodge, EconoLodge, Hampton Inn, Quality Inn H, $Tree, Ace Hardware, Advance Parts, Aldi Foods, U-Haul, Verizon, Walmart/Subway S on US 12 Burger King, Ace Hardware, Chrysler/Dodge/Jeep, Firestone/auto, Ford, GMC, NAPA, O'Reilly Parts
135	Rd EW, Warrens, N Cenex/dsl 3 Bears Resort Jellystone Camping, S Bog Rest.
128	Rd O, Millston, N Black River SF, camping, S Cenex/dsl USPO
123mm	/scenic view both lanes, full facilities, litter barrels, petwalk RV dump, vending
116	WI 54, N Cenex/Subway/Taco Johns/dsl/LP Perkins Best Western Arrowhead/rest., Comfort Inn, Super 8 Black River RA, casino, Parkland Camp, S FLYING J/Denny's/dsl/24hr/ @, KwikTrip/dsl Burger King, Culver's, McDonald's, Oriental Kitchen, Pizza Hut Days Inn $General, Buick/Chevrolet/GMC, Walmart/Subway
115mm	Black River
115	US 12, WI 27, Black River Falls, to Merrillan, S BP, Holiday/dsl Hardee's, KFC, Subway, Sunrise Rest. H, Ace Hardware, Harley-Davidson, vet
105	to WI 95, Hixton, to Alma Center, N Motel 95/camping KOA (3mi), S Cenex/dsl, Clark/dsl/24hr Timber Valley Rest. city park
98	WI 121, Northfield, Pigeon Falls, to Alma Center, S Cenex/dsl Crazy Jerry's Burgers
88	US 10, Osseo, to Fairchild, N BP/DQ, Exxon/Webb Rest./dsl/scales/24hr, Mobil/dsl Hardee's, Moe's Diner 10-7 Inn, Super 8 Chevrolet, Ford, Stoney Cr RV Park, S SA/dsl McDonald's, Subway, Taco John's Osseo Inn H, Family$
81	Rd HH, Rd KK, Foster, S BP/dsl/LP Foster Cheesehaus
70	US 53, Eau Claire, N off Golf Rd Mobil/dsl Applebee's, Asia Palace, Buffalo Wild Wings, Burracho's Mexican, Caribou Coffee, Chipotle, Coldstone, Culver's, Fazoli's, Firehouse Subs, Fuji Steaks, Grizzly's Grill, HuHot Chinese, Jade Garden, Jimmy John's, Mancino's, Manny's Grill, McDonald's, Noodles&Co, Olive Garden, Panera Bread, TGIFriday's, TX Roadhouse Baymont Inn, Country

TOMAH

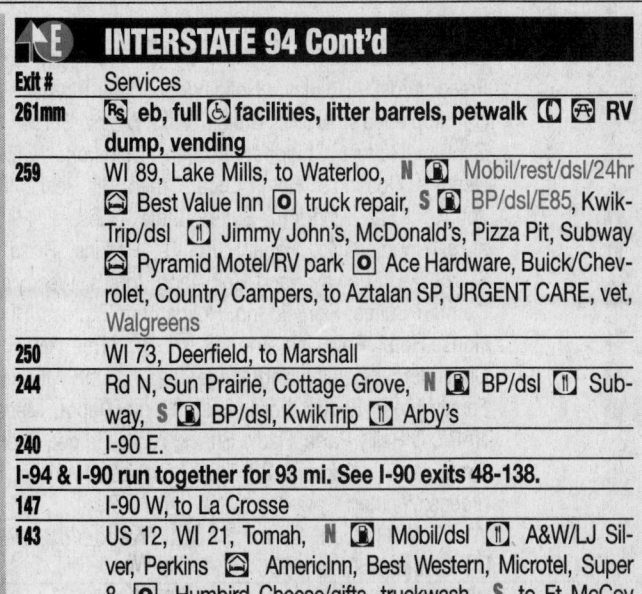

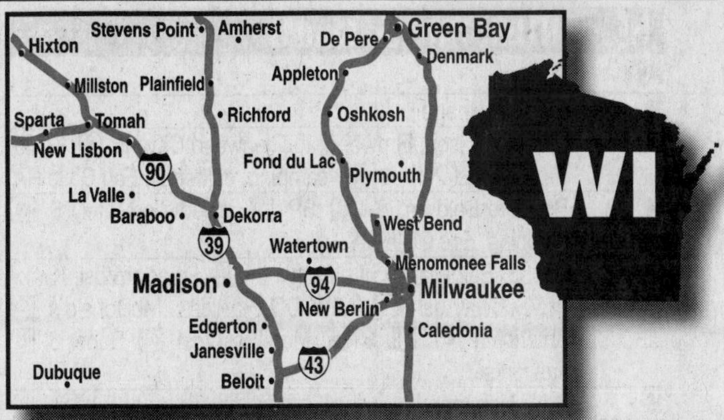

Exit #	Services
70	Continued Inn&Suites, Grandstay, Holiday Inn $Tree, Aldi Foods, AT&T, Bam!, Best Buy, Hancock Fabrics, JC Penney, Jo-Ann Fabrics, Kohl's, Macy's, mall, Menards, Michael's, Office Depot, PetCo, Petsmart, Sam's Club, Scheel's Sports, Sears/auto, Target, TJ Maxx, Tuesday Morning, Verizon, Walmart/Subway, Younkers, S Gander Mtn, st police,
68	WI 93, to Eleva, N Holiday, KwikTrip/dsl Burger King, Cousins Subs, DQ, Famous Dave's BBQ, Quiznos, Red Robin EconoLodge BigLots, Chrysler/Dodge/Jeep, County Mkt Foods, Festival Foods, Firestone/auto, Goodyear/auto, Kia, NAPA, Nissan, Subaru, Suzuki, transmissions, vet, S Holiday/dsl Metropolis Resort Audi/VW, Ford/Lincoln, Honda, Hyundai
65	WI 37, WI 85, Eau Claire, to Mondovi, N Exxon, Holiday/dsl, KwikTrip/dsl Arby's, Godfather's Pizza, Green Mill Rest., Hardee's, Jimmy John's, Mancino's, McDonald's, Pizza Hut, Randy's Rest., Red Lobster, Starbucks, Subway, Taco Bell Best Value Inn, Best Western, Clarion, Comfort Inn, Days Inn/rest., Hampton Inn, Highlander Inn, Plaza Hotel, Super 8 H, County Mkt Foods, dsl repair, Radio Shack, ShopKo, Verizon, Walgreens
64mm	Chippewa River
59	to US 12, Rd EE, to Eau Claire, N Holiday/Burger King/dsl/24hr, Holiday/Subway/dsl/24hr Dana's Grill, El Mariachi, McDonald's AmericInn, Days Inn, Knights Inn H, auto repair/towing, Freightliner, Mack/Volvo Trucks, Peterbilt, S dsl repair
52	US 12, WI 29, WI 40, Elk Mound, to Chippewa Falls, S U-Fuel/E85
49mm	**weigh sta wb**
45	Rd B, Menomonie, N Cenex/Subway/dsl/scales/24hr, Loves/Hardee's/dislike/scales/24hr, S KwikTrip/dsl/scales/24hr Red Cedar Steaks Quality Inn H, AOK RV Ctr, dsl repair, Kenworth, truckwash, Walmart Dist Ctr
44mm	Red Cedar River
43mm	**both lanes, full facilities, litter barrels, petwalk vending, weather info**
41	WI 25, Menomonie, N Cenex/E85 Applebee's, Caribou Coffee, China Buffet, Los Cabos Mexican, Pizza Hut, Subway H, $Tree, Aldi Foods, AT&T, Radio Shack, Twin Springs Camping, Walmart/Subway, S F&F/dsl, Holiday, SA/dsl Arby's, Denny's, Dickey's BBQ, Jimmy John's, McDonald's, Perkins, Taco Bell, Taco John's, Wendy's AmericInn, Country Inn&Suites, EconoLodge, Motel 6, Super 8 Advance Parts, Buick/GMC, Chevrolet, Chrysler/Dodge/Jeep, K-Mart, Mkt Place Foods, O'Reilly Parts, to Red Cedar St Tr, Walgreens

MENOMONIE

WI

INTERSTATE 94 Cont'd

HUDSON

Exit #	Services
32	Rd Q, to Knapp
28	WI 128, Wilson, Elmwood, to Glenwood City, N [gas] KwikTrip/rest./dsl/24hr, S [other] camping, dsl repair, Eau Galle RA
24	Rd B, to Baldwin, N [gas] BP [lodging] Woodville Motel, S [other] camping, Eau Galle RA
19	US 63, Baldwin, to Ellsworth, N [gas] Freedom/dsl, KwikTrip/Subway/dsl [food] A&W, DQ, Hardee's, McDonald's [lodging] AmericInn [other] [H], S [gas] Mobil/rest./dsl [lodging] Super 8 [other] fireworks
16	Rd T, Hammond
10	WI 65, Roberts, to New Richmon, [gas] BP/dsl (2mi), FLYING J/McDonald's/dsl/scales/24hr [food] Barnboard Rest. (2mi), Freightliner
8mm	**weigh sta eb**
4	US 12, Rd U, Somerset, N [gas] BP/dsl, TA/Country Pride/dsl/scales/24hr/ @ [lodging] Regency Inn [other] to Willow River SP, vet
3	WI 35 S, to River Falls, U of WI River Falls
2	Rd F, Carmichael Rd, Hudson, N [gas] BP/repair, F&F/dsl, Freedom/dsl, Holiday, Holiday/dsl, KwikTrip/dsl, Shell [food] Applebee's, Arby's, Buffalo Wild Wings, Burger King, Caribou Coffee, Chipotle Mexican, Coldstone, Culver's, Denny's, Domino's, Fiesta Loca, Green Mill Rest., Jimmy John's, KFC, Kingdom Buffet, Little Caesars, McDonald's, Noodles&Co, Papa Murphy's, Perkins, Pizza Hut, Starbucks, Subway, Taco Bell, Taco John's, Wendy's [lodging] Comfort Suites, Fairfield Inn, Holiday Inn Express, Hudson House Hotel, Royal Inn, Super 8 [other] [H], $Tree, Aldi Foods, Chevrolet/GMC, Chrysler/Dodge/Jeep, County Mkt Foods, Family Fresh Foods, Ford, GNC, Home Depot, Menards, NAPA, O'Reilly Parts, Radio Shack, repair, Target, TirePros, Tires+, to Kinnickinnic SP, USPO, Verizon, Verizon, Walgreens, Walmart
1	WI 35 N, Hudson, **1 mi** N [gas] Freedom/dsl, Holiday [food] Carbones Pizzeria, DQ
0mm	Wisconsin/Minnesota state line, St Croix River

WYOMING

WI WY

INTERSTATE 25

BUFFALO

CASPER

Exit #	Services
300	I-90, E to Gillette, W to Billings. **I-25 begins/ends on I-90, exit 56.**
299	US 16, Buffalo, E [gas] Cenex/dsl, Exxon/dsl, Maverik/dsl [food] Winchester Steaks [lodging] Buffalo Inn, Comfort Inn, Hampton Inn, Holiday Inn Express [other] Bighorn Tire, Deer Park Camping, KOA, vet, W [gas] Cenex/dsl/24hr [food] Bozeman Tr Steaks, Dash Inn Rest., Hardee's, McDonald's, Pizza Hut, Sub Shop, Subway, Taco John's [lodging] Days Inn, Quality Inn, Rodeway WYO Motel, Super 8 [other] [H], Ace Hardware, Family$, Indian RV Camp, O'Reilly Parts, to Yellowstone, Verizon
298	US 87, Buffalo, W Nat Hist Dist Info
291	Trabing Rd
280	Middle Fork Rd
274mm	parking area both lanes, litter barrels
265	Reno Rd
254	Kaycee, E [gas] Exxon/dsl [food] Country Inn Diner, Invasion Rest. [lodging] Cassidy Inn Motel, Siesta Motel [other] Kaycee Gen. Store, museum, NAPA Repair, Powder River RV Park, USPO, W [Rs] **both lanes, full [handicapped] facilities, litter barrels, petwalk** [phone] [picnic], [gas] Sinclair/pizza/subs/dsl/LP/motel [other] KC RV Park
249	TTT Rd
246	Powder River Rd
235	Tisdale Mtn Rd
227	WY 387 N, Midwest, Edgerton, Oil Field Museum
223	no services
219mm	**parking area both lanes, litter barrels**
216	Ranch Rd
210	Horse Ranch Creek Rd, Midwest, Edgerton
197	Ormsby Rd
191	Wardwell Rd, to Bar Nunn, W [gas] Loaf'N Jug/dsl [other] KOA
189	US 20, US 26 W, to Shoshone, W [other] [airport], Port of Entry
188b	WY 220, Poplar St, E [food] McDonald's, The Fort Eatery [lodging] Best Western, Hampton Inn, Hilton Garden, La Quinta,
188b	Continued
	Motel 6, Quality Inn, W [gas] Exxon [food] Burger King, Casper's Rest., DQ [other] Harley-Davidson, to Ft Casper HS
188a	Center St, Casper, E [gas] Conoco/dsl, Shell/dsl [food] Poor Boys Steaks, Taco John's [lodging] National 9 Inn, Ramada, Showboat Motel, W [food] La Cocina, Starbucks, Subway [lodging] Days Inn, Parkway Plaza Motel/cafe [other] USPO
187	McKinley St, Casper, E [gas] Loaf'N Jug/dsl [lodging] Ranch House Motel
186	US 20, US 26, US 87, Yellowstone St, E [other] city park, dsl repair, transmissions/repair, W [gas] Exxon [other] [H], auto repair, Chevrolet/Subaru, Kia, O'Reilly Parts
185	WY 258, Wyoming Blvd, E Casper, E [gas] Kum&Go/dsl, Loaf'n Jug/dsl [food] Applebee's, Hacienda Mexican, IHOP, Outback Steaks, Southern BBQ HQ, TX Roadhouse [lodging] Baymont Inn, C'mon Inn, Comfort Inn, Hotel [other] bet, Murdoch's Ranch Store, RV camping, Smith RV Ctr, W [gas] FLYING J/Conoco/Subway/dsl/LP/scales/24hr, Exxon/dsl, Loaf'n Jug [food] Arby's, Buffalo Wild Wings, Burger King, Denny's, DQ, Five Guys, Golden Corral, Hamburger Stand, Hardee's, KFC/LJ Silver, McDonald's, Mongolian Grill, Old Chicago Grill, Olive Garden, On The Border, Perkins, Pizza Hut, Pizza Ranch, Qdoba, Red Lobster, Sanford's Cafe, Starbucks, Taco Bell, Taco John's, Village Inn, Wendy's [lodging] 1st Interstate Motel, Candlewood Suites, Courtyard, Holiday Inn Express [other] AutoZone, Best Buy, Dick's, Home Depot, JC Penney, K-Mart, Macy's, mall, Natural Grocers, Nissan, PetCo, Plains Tire, Ross, Safeway Foods/dsl, Sam's Club/gas, Sears/auto, Staples, Target, to Oregon Tr, Verizon, Walgreens, Walmart
182	WY 253, Brooks Rd, Hat Six Rd, E [gas] Sinclair/Lou's Rest/dsl [food] Sonic [lodging] Sleep Inn [other] Rivers Edge Camping, to Wilkins SP, W [food] Famous Dave's BBQ, FireRock Rest., Keg&Cork Rest., Subway [lodging] Best Western, Holiday Inn, Mainstay Suites [other] [H], Buick/Cadillac/GMC, Chrysler/Dodge/Jeep, Kohl's, Marshall's, Menards, Toyota, VW
171mm	**parking area both lanes, litter barrels**
Exit #	Services

INTERSTATE 25 Cont'd

165	Glenrock, **E** dinosaur museum, same as 160
160	US 87, US 20, US 26, E Glenrock, **E** [food] G-Rock's, Paisley Shawl [lodging] All American Inn, Hotel Higgins B&B [other] Deer Creek Village Camping, to Johnston Power Plant
156	Bixby Rd
154	Barber Rd
153mm	**parking area both lanes, litter barrels**
151	Natural Bridge
150	Inez Rd
146	La Prele Rd
140	WY 59, Douglas, **E** [gas] Conoco/Subway/dsl, Maverik/dsl, Shell/dsl [food] Arby's, La Costa Mexican, McDonald's, Taco John's [lodging] Douglas Inn, Holiday Inn Express, La Quinta, Sleep Inn, Super 8 [other] [H], Chrysler/Dodge/Jeep, city park, Ford, KOA, Lone Tree Village RV Park, Pioneer Museum, vet, WY St Fair
135	US 20, US 26, US 87, Douglas, **E** [gas] Loaf'n Jug/dsl, Sinclair/dsl, Sinclair/rest./dsl/24hr [food] 4 Seasons Chinese, Pizza Hut, Plains Trading Post Rest., Village Inn [lodging] 1st Interstate Inn, 4 Winds Motel, Budget Inn Express, Plains Motel [other] [H], auto repair, Douglas Hardware, Family$, O'Reilly Parts, Safeway Foods/dsl, Shopko, Verizon
129mm	parking area both lanes
126	US 18, US 20 E, Orin, **E Orin Jct** [rest stop] **both lanes, full** [accessible] **facilities, litter barrels, petwalk** [gas] [phone] [picnic] **RV dump** [gas] Sinclair/Orin Jct Trkstp/dsl/café
125mm	N Platte River
111	Glendo, **E** [gas] Sinclair/dsl [food] Glendo Marina Café [other] Glendo Lakeside RV camping, to Glendo SP, USPO
104	to Middle Bear
100	Cassa Rd
94	El Rancho Rd
92	US 26 E, Dwyer, **E** [rest stop] **both lanes, full** [accessible] **facilities, litter barrels, petwalk** [picnic] **RV dump**, Ft Laramie NHS, to Guernsey SP
87	Johnson Rd
84	Laramie River Rd
84mm	Laramie River
80	US 87, Laramie Power Sta, Wheatland, Laramie Power Sta, **E** [gas] Sinclair/A&W/Chester's/dsl [food] Pizza Hut [lodging] Best Western, Super 8 [other] Arrowhead RV Park, Buick/Cadillac/Chevrolet, CarQuest, Chrysler/Dodge/Jeep, Family$, Ford, museum, Safeway Foods, same as 78, ShopKo
78	US 87, Wheatland, **E** [gas] Cenex/dsl, Maverik/dsl, Shell/dsl [food] Arby's, Burger King, Subway, Taco John's, Western Sky's Diner [lodging] All American Motel, Motel 6, West Winds Motel, WY Motel [other] [H], visitors ctr, Wheatland Country Store, **W** [gas] Exxon/dsl, Pitstop/dsl [other] Mtn View RV Park
73	WY 34 W, to Laramie
70	Bordeaux Rd
68	Antelope Rd
66	Hunton Rd

DOUGLAS

WHEATLAND

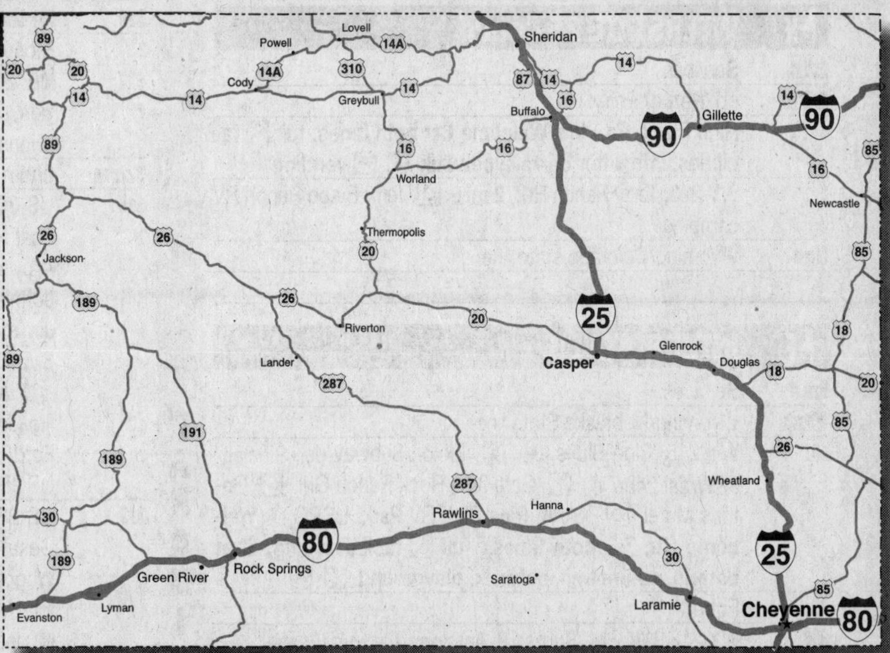

65.5mm	**parking area both lanes, litter barrels**
65	Slater Rd
64mm	Richeau Creek
57	TY Basin Rd, Chugwater
54	Lp 25, Chugwater, **E** [rest stop] **both lanes, full** [accessible] **facilities, litter barrels, petwalk** [phone] [picnic] **RV dump,** [lodging] Buffalo Lodge/Grill
47	Bear Creek Rd
39	Little Bear Community
36mm	Little Bear Creek
34	Nimmo Rd
33mm	Horse Creek
29	Whitaker Rd
25	ranch exit
21	Ridley Rd
17	US 85 N, to Torrington, **W** [food] Little Bear Rest. (2mi)
16	WY 211, Horse Creek Rd
13	Vandehei Ave, **E** [gas] Loaf'n Jug/Subway, Maverik/dsl [food] Mr Gem's Pizza, Silvermine Subs, **W** [gas] Shamrock/dsl
12	Central Ave, Cheyenne, **E on Yellowstone Rd** [gas] Exxon/dsl, Loaf'n Jug [food] Arby's, Godfather's, Godfather's, Great Harvest Bread, McDonald's, Pizza Hut, Starbucks, Subway, Taco John's [lodging] Rodeway Inn [other] [H], Albertsons, Big O Tire, Frontier Days Park, museum, Peerless Tire
11b	Warren AFB, Gate 1, Randall Ave, **E** [other] museum, to WY St Capitol
10b d	Warren AFB, Gate 2, Missile Dr, WY 210, HappyJack Rd, **W** [other] to Curt Gowdy SP
9	US 30, W Lincolnway, Cheyenne, **E** [gas] Exxon/Downhome Diner/dsl [food] Outback Steaks, Village Inn [lodging] Best Value Inn, Candlewood Suites, Days Inn, Hampton Inn, Holiday Inn Express, La Quinta, Luxury Inn, Motel 6, My Place, Super 8, Towne Place Suites [other] Buick/Cadillac/GMC, Chevrolet, Ford/Lincoln, Home Depot, Honda, Hyundai, Mazda, Nissan, Subaru, Toyota, **W** [gas] Little America/Sinclair/dsl/rest./motel/ @
8d b	I-80, E to Omaha, W to Laramie
7	WY 212, College Dr, **E** [gas] Loves/Wendy's/dsl/scales/24hr/ @, Shamrock/Subway/dsl/24hr [food] Arby's [other] A-B RV Park (2mi) , **W** [gas] FLYING J/Denny's/dsl/LP/scales/24hr/ @ [food] McDonald's [lodging] Quality Inn

CHEYENNE

WY

INTERSTATE 25 Cont'd

Exit #	Services
6.5mm	nb, Port of Entry
4	High Plains Rd, **WY Welcome Ctr both lanes, full facilities, info, litter barrels, petwalk vending**
2	WY 223, Terry Ranch Rd, **2 mi** E Terry Bison Ranch RV camping
0mm	Wyoming/Colorado state line

INTERSTATE 80

CHEYENNE

Exit #	Services
402mm	Wyoming/Nebraska State line
401	WY 215, Pine Bluffs, N Exxon/Subway/dsl, Sinclair/A&W/dsl/24hr/ @ Cafe 307, Rock Ranch Grill Gator's Motel NAPA, Pine Bluff RV Park, USPO, S **Welcome Ctr, both lanes, full facilities, info, litter barrels, nature trail, petwalk, playground**
391	Egbert
386	WY 213, WY 214, Burns, N Antelope Trkstp/dsl/cafe
377	WY 217, Hillsdale, N TA/Burger King/Taco Bell/dsl/scales/24hr/ @ Wyo RV Camping
372mm	Port of Entry wb, **truck insp**
370	US 30 W, Archer, N Sapp Bros/Sinclair/T-Joe's Rest./dsl/scales/24hr/ @ Rodeway Inn fireworks, repair, RV park
367	Campstool Rd, N Pilot/Subway/dsl/scales/24hr Best Western KOA (seasonal), Volvo Trucks, S to Wyoming Hereford Ranch
364	WY 212, to E Lincolnway, Cheyenne, S AB Camping (4mi), Peterbilt, **1-2 mi N on Lincolnway** Exxon/dsl, Kum&Go/dsl, Loaf'n Jug/Subway Burger King, KFC, McDonald's, Shari's Rest., Subway, Taco Bell, Wendy's H, $Tree, AutoZone, Big O Tire, BigLots, Family$, Harley-Davidson, Hobby Lobby, Murdoch's Ranch Store, O'Reilly Parts, Sierra Trading Post, Walgreens
362	US 85, I-180, to Central Ave, Cheyenne, Greeley, **1 mi** N Kum&Go/dsl Arby's, Carls' Jr, Hacienda Mexican, Jimmy John's, Los Abuelo's Mexican, Papa John's, Quiznos, Village Inn H, CarQuest, Family$, museum, st capitol, Verizon, S Exxon/dsl, Loaf'n Jug/dsl, Shamrock/dsl Burger King, Little Caesar's, Pizza Hut, Sonic, Subway, Taco John's Comfort Inn, Holiday Inn, Roundup Motel, SpringHill Suites Family$, Hideaway RV Village, Safeway Foods/gas, transmissions
359c a	I-25, US 87, N to Casper, S to Denver
358	US 30, W Lincolnway, Cheyenne, N Exxon/dsl/24hr, Little America/Sinclair/dsl/motel/ @ Outback Steaks, Village Inn Best Value Inn, Candlewood Suites, Days Inn, Hampton Inn, Holiday Inn Express, La Quinta, Luxury Inn, My Place Inn, Super 8, TownPlace Suites H, Buick/GMC/Cadillac, Chevrolet, Ford/Lincoln, Home Depot, Honda, Hyundai, Mazda, Nissan, Subaru, Toyota
357	Wy 222, Roundtop Rd
348	Otto Rd
345	Warren Rd, N truck parking
342	Harriman Rd
339	Remount Rd
335	Buford, S Phin Deli/dsl
333mm	parking area both lanes, point of interest

LARAMIE

Exit #	Services
329	Vedeauwoo Rd, N camping, S Nat Forest RA, to Ames Monument
323	WY 210, Happy Jack Rd, N **both lanes, full facilities,** elev. 8640, Lincoln Monument, litter barrels, petwalk, phone, picnic tables, to Curt Gowdy SP
322mm	**chain up area both lanes**
316	US 30 W, Grand Ave, Laramie, **0-2 mi** N Exxon/dsl, Loaf'N Jug, USA Gas Almanza's Mexican, Applebee's, Arby's, Burger King, Chili's, Hong Kong Buffet, Jimmy John's, Luciano's Italian, McAlister's Deli, McDonald's, Mr Jim's Pizza, Papa Murphy's, Perkins, Sonic, Starbucks, Subway, Taco Bell, Taco John's, Village Inn, Wendy's AmericInn, Comfort Inn, Hampton Inn, Hilton Garden, Holiday Inn H, $Tree, AT&T, Buick/Chevrolet/GMC, Ford/Lincoln, GNC, Ridley's Mkt, Staples, to UW, Toyota, URGENT CARE, Verizon, Walgreens, Walmart/Subway
313	US 287, to 3rd St, Laramie, Port of Entry, N Exxon, GasaMat, Loaf'N Jug, Phillips 66/dsl, Shell/dsl Chuck Wagon Rest., Corona Village Mexican Laramie Valley Inn, Motel 8, Sunset Inn H, Honda, Laramie Plains Museum, NAPA, Nissan, S Motel 6, Ramada Inn USPO
312mm	Laramie River
311	WY 130, WY 230, Snowy Range Rd, Laramie, N WY Terr Park, S Conoco/dsl, Phillips 66/dsl, Sinclair/dsl/LP McDonald's, Subway Best Value Inn repair/tires, to Snowy Range Ski Area
310	Curtis St, Laramie, N Pilot/Wendy's/dsl/scales/24hr/ @, Shamrock/café/dsl Best Western, Days Inn, EconoLodge, Super 8 H, KOA, repair, S Blue Beacon, Petro/Iron Skillet/dsl/scales/24hr/ @ Fairfield Inn, Quality Inn Chrysler/Dodge/Jeep
307mm	**parking area both lanes, litter barrels**
297	WY 12, Herrick Lane
290	Quealy Dome Rd, S A&C Truckstop/dsl
279	Cooper Cove Rd
272mm	Rock Creek
272	WY 13, to Arlington, N RV camping
267	no services
262mm	**parking area both lanes**
260	CR 402
259mm	E Fork, Medicine Bow River
257mm	Medicine Bow River
255	WY 72, Elk Mtn, to Hanna, N Conoco/dsl, S Elk Mtn Hotel/rest
238	Peterson Rd
235	WY 130, S US 30/87, N Shell/dsl
229mm	N Platte River
228	no services

RAWLINS

Exit #	Services
221	E Sinclair, N Sinclair/rest/dsl/24hr camping, to Seminoe SP
219	W Sinclair, N camping, to Seminoe SP
215	Cedar St, Rawlins, N Conoco/dsl, Shell/KFC/Taco Bell/dsl, Sinclair/dsl Burger King, China House, McDonald's, Penny's Diner, Pizza Hut, Subway, Taco John's 1st Choice Inn, Comfort Inn, Days Inn, Fairfield Inn, Hampton Inn, Holiday Inn Express, OakTree Inn, Rodeway Inn, The Key Motel $Tree, Alco, Buick/Chevrolet/GMC, CarQuest, Chrysler/Dodge/Jeep, City Mkt/dsl, Do-It Hardware, Frontier Prison NHS, museum, O'Reilly Parts, ShopKO, to Yellowstone/Teton NP, Walmart/dsl

WY

INTERSTATE 80 Cont'd

Exit #	Services
214	Higley Blvd, Rawlins, N Pronghorn Suites KOA, S TA/Shell/Subway/dsl/scales/24hr/ @ Best Value Inn
211	WY 789, to US 287 N, Spruce St, Rawlins, N Conoco/dsl, Exxon/dsl, Loaf'n Jug, Sinclair/dsl Cappy's Rest., Dragon Gate Chinese Best Western, EconoLodge, Express Inn, La Bella, Motel 7, Sunset Motel, Super 8, Travelodge H, Family$, Ford, RV World Camping, V1/LP, Verizon
209	Johnson Rd, N FLYING J/Denny's/dsl/LP/scales/24hr
206	Hadsell Rd (no return)
205.5mm	continental divide, elev 7000
204	Knobs Rd
201	Daley Rd
196	Riner Rd
190mm	**parking area wb, litter barrels**
189mm	**parking area wb, litter barrels**
187	WY 789, Creston, Baggs Rd
184	Continental Divide Rd
173	Wamsutter, N Loves/Chester's/Subway/dsl/24hr/ @, S Conoco/dsl/repair/café/24hr, Phillips 66/dsl Broadway Café, Southern Comfort Cafe Wamsutter Motel
165	Red Desert
158	Tipton Rd, continental divide, elev 6930
156	GL Rd
154	BLM Rd
152	Bar X Rd
150	Table Rock Rd
146	Patrick Draw Rd
144mm	**both lanes, full facilities, litter barrels, petwalk**
143mm	**parking area both lanes, litter barrels**
142	Bitter Creek Rd
139	Red Hill Rd
136	Black Butte Rd
133mm	parking area both lanes
130	Point of Rocks, N Conoco/dsl RV Park
122	WY 371, to Superior
111	Airport Rd, Baxter Rd, S
107	Pilot Butte Ave, Rock Springs, S Kum&Go/dsl/e-85, Mobil/dsl Pizza Hut, Pizza Hut Sands Inn/cafe, Springs Motel
104	US 191 N, Elk St, Rock Springs, N FLYING J/Denny's/dsl/LP/24hr, Conoco/dsl, Exxon, Kum&Go/dsl/e-85, Phillips 66/dsl, Texaco/Burger King/dsl McDonald's, Renegade Rest., Santa Fe SW Grill, Subway, Taco Time Best Western, EconoLodge/rest. Buick/GMC, to Teton/Yellowstone Nat Parks via US 191, truck repair, S Exxon/dsl Days Inn
103	College Dr, Rock Springs, S Loaf'n Jug/dsl Domino's H, W WY Coll
102	WY 430, Dewar Dr, Rock Springs, N Exxon, Loaf'N Jug/dsl, Sinclair/dsl Applebee's, China King, KFC/LJ Silver, Taco Time Best Value Inn, Comfort Inn, LaQuinta, Motel 6 $Tree, Cadillac/Chevrolet, Chrysler/Dodge, Herberger's, Home Depot, JC Penney, Jo-Ann, K-Mart, Murdoch's, Smith's Foods, S Dickey's BBQ, Kum&Go/dsl, Loaf'N Jug/dsl, Mobil Arby's, Bonsai Chinese, Burger King, Cafe Rio, Chopstix Chinese, Costa Vida, Dickey's BBQ,

ROCK SPGS

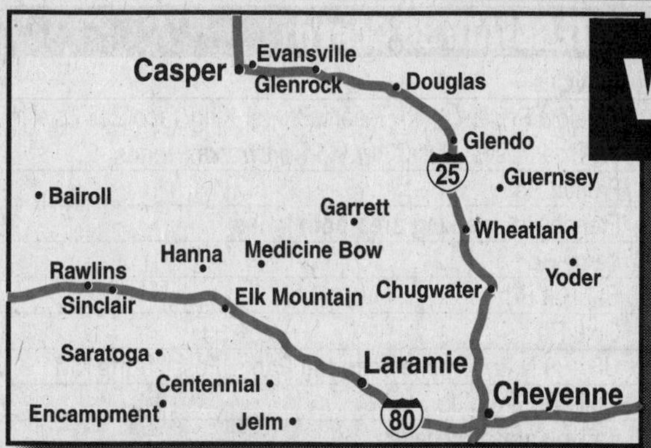

Exit #	Services
102	Continued Golden Corral, IHOP, Jimmy John's, Little Caesar's, McDonald's, Papa Murphy's, Pizza Hut, Quizno's, Sonic, Starbucks, Subway, Taco Bell, Village Inn, Wendy's, Winger's, Wonderful House Chinese Hampton Inn, Holiday Inn, Holiday Inn Express, Homewood Suites, Motel 8, My Place, Quality Inn, Super 8, Western Inn H, Albertsons/Savon, AutoZone, Big O Tire, Family$, Ford/Lincoln, Hastings Books, NAPA, Nissan, O'Reilly Parts, Radio Shack, Staples, Verizon, Walgreens, Walmart/Subway
99	US 191 S, E Flaming Gorge Rd, N KOA (1mi), S Sinclair/dsl/rest./24hr/ @ Log Inn Rest., Ted's Rest. fireworks, truck repair
94mm	Kissing Rock
91	US 30, to WY 530, Green River, **2 mi** S Loaf'N Jug/dsl, Maverik/dsl Arctic Circle, McDonald's, Pizza Hut, Subway, Taco Time Coachman Inn, Mustang Inn, Super 8 Expedition NHS, Family$, same as 89, to Flaming Gorge NRA
89	US 30, Green River, S Exxon/dsl, Sinclair/dsl Penny's Diner, Pizza Hut Hampton Inn, OakTree Inn, Super 8, Western Inn Adam's RV Service, The Travel Camp, to Flaming Gorge NRA
87.5mm	Green River
85	Covered Wagon Rd, S Adams RV parts/service, The Travel Camp
83	WY 372, La Barge Rd, N to Fontenelle Dam
78	(from wb)
77mm	Blacks Fork River
72	Westvaco Rd
71mm	parking area both lanes
68	Little America, N Sinclair/Little America Hotel/rest./dsl/24hr @ RV camping
66	US 30 W, to Teton, Yellowstone, Fossil Butte NM, Kemmerer
61	Cedar Mt Rd, to Granger
60mm	**parking area both lanes, litter barrels**
54mm	**parking area eb, litter barrels**
53	Church Butte Rd
49mm	**parking area wb, litter barrels**
48	Lp 80, Lyman, Ft Bridger, Hist Ft Bridger
45mm	Blacks Fork River
41	WY 413, Lyman, N **both lanes, full facilities, litter barrels, petwalk**, Gas'n Go/cafe/dsl, S Taco Time Gateway Inn (2mi), KOA (1mi)
39	WY 412, WY 414, to Carter, Mountain View
34	Lp 80, to Ft Bridger, S Wagon Wheel Motel Ft Bridger NHS, Ft Bridger RV Camp, to Flaming Gorge NRA
33.5mm	**parking area eb, litter barrels**
33	Union Rd

GREEN RIVER

WY

= gas = food = lodging = other = rest stop

INTERSTATE 80 Cont'd

Exit #	Services
30	Bigelow Rd, **N** TA/Tesoro/Burger King/Taco Bell/Fork In the Road/dsl/scales/24hr/ @, **S** fireworks
28	French Rd
28mm	French Rd, **parking area both lanes**
24	Leroy Rd
23	Bar Hat Rd
21	Coal Rd
18	US 189 N, to Kemmerer, to Nat Parks, Fossil Butte NM
15	Guild Rd (from eb)
14mm	parking area both lanes
13	Divide Rd
10	Painter Rd, to Eagle Rock Ski Area, to Eagle Rock Ski Area
6	US 189, Bear River Dr, Evanston, **N** Pilot/Subway/dsl/scales/24hr, Sinclair/dsl Jody's Diner Econolodge, Motel 6, Prairie Inn, Vagabond Motel Phillips RV Park, repair/tires, truck wash, Wyo Downs Racetrack (10mi), **S** **Welcome Ctr both lanes, full facilities, litter barrels, petwalk playground, RV dump (seasonal),** Bear River SP
5	WY 89, Evanston, **N** Chevron/Taco Time/dsl, Maverik/dsl Arby's, DragonWall Chinese, McDonald's, Papa Murphy's, Subway, Wendy's EconoLodge H, $Tree, AutoZone, Chevrolet, GNC, Jiffy Lube, Murdoch's, NAPA, O'Reilly Parts, Verizon, Walmart/Subway, **S** WY St H
3	US 189, Harrison Dr, Evanston, **N** FLYING J/Subway/dsl/scales/24hr, Chevron/dsl, Shell, Sinclair JB's, Lotty's Rest., TC's Rest., Wally's Burgers Best Western/rest., Comfort Inn, Days Inn, Hampton Inn, HillCrest Motel, Holiday Inn Express, Howard Johnson, Quality Inn, Super 8 Chrysler/Dodge/Jeep, USPO, **S** KFC/Taco Bell H, fireworks
.5mm	**Port of Entry eb, weigh sta wb**
0mm	Wyoming/Utah state line

EVANSTON

WY

INTERSTATE 90

Exit #	Services
207mm	Wyoming/South Dakota state line
205	Beulah, **N** Sinclair/dsl/LP Buffalo Jump Rest. Sand Creek Trading Post/gas/cafe, USPO, **S** Ranch A NHP (5mi)
204.5mm	Sand Creek
199	WY 111, to Aladdin, **N** **Welcome Ctr both directions, full facilities, litter barrels, petwalk** , Red Water Creek RV Park, to Devil's Tower NM, to Vore Buffalo Jump NHP
191	Moskee Rd
189	US 14 W, Sundance, **N** Conoco/dsl/24hr Best Western H, Mt View Camping, museum, to Devil's Tower NM, **S** **both lanes, full facilities, info, litter barrels, petwalk playground, RV dump, port of entry/weigh sta**
187	WY 585, Sundance, **N** Fresh Start/dsl, Sinclair/dsl Aro Rest., Higbee's Cafe, Subway Bear Lodge, Best Western, Budget Host Arrowhead, Rodeway Inn H, auto repair, Decker's Foods, museum, NAPA, to Devil's Tower
185	to WY 116, to Sundance, **2 mi S** Conoco/dsl, same as 187
178	Coal Divide Rd
177mm	**parking area both lanes**
172	Inyan Kara Rd
171mm	**parking area both lanes, litter barrels**
165	Pine Ridge Rd, to Pine Haven, **N** Cedar Ridge RV Park (10mi), to Keyhole SP
163mm	**parking area both lanes**
160	Wind Creek Rd
154	US 14, US 16, **S** Cenex/dsl Donna's Diner, Subway Cozy Motel, Moorcourt Motel, Rangerland Motel/RV Park, Wyo Motel city park, Diehl's Foods/gas, museum, USPO
153	US 16 E, US 14, W Moorcroft, **N** **both lanes, full facilities, litter barrels, petwalk** , **S** same as 154
152mm	Belle Fourche River
141	Rozet, **S** All Seasons RV Park (3.5mi)
138mm	**parking area both lanes**
132	Wyodak Rd
129	Garner Lake Rd, **S** Arbuckle Lodge auto repair, Crazy Woman Camping (3mi) , Harley-Davidson, High Plains Camping
128	US 14, US 16, Gillette, **N** Conoco/Papa John's/dsl, Kum&Go, Maverik/dsl Mona's American/Mexican, Taco John's, Village Inn Howard Johnson, Mustang Motel, National 9 Inn Crazy Woman Camping (2mi) , East Side RV Ctr., Port of Entry, **S** Arbuckle Lodge High Plains Camping
126	WY 59, Gillette, **N** Cenex/dsl, Conoco/Papa John's/dsl, Loaf'N Jug China King Buffet, Hardee's, Little Caesar's, McDonald's, Pokey's BBQ, Prime Rib Rest., Starbucks, Subway Best Value Inn city park, Family$, Radio Shack, Smith's Foods, Tire Factory, Verizon, **S** FLYING J/dsl/24hr, Exxon, Loaf'N Jug/dsl A&W/LJ Silver, Adriano's Italian, Applebee's, Arby's, Buffalo Wild Wings, Burger King, DQ, Goodtimes Grill/Taco John's, Great Wall Chinese, Hibachi Buffet, Ice Cream Cafe, Jimmy John's, Jordan's Rest., KFC, Las Margarita's Mexican, Old Chicago Grill, Papa Murphy's, Perkins, Pizza Hut, Qdoba Mexican, Quiznos, Smiling Moose Deli, Subway, Taco Bell, Wendy's Candlewood Suites, Clarion, Country Inn&Suites, Days Inn, Fairfield Inn, Holiday Inn Express, Wingate Inn $Tree, Albertson's, AT&T, AutoZone, bet, Big O Tire, city park, GNC, Goodyear Truck Tire, Hastings Books, Home Depot, Jo-Ann, K-Mart, Midas, Office Depot, O'Reilly Parts, Osco Drug, Petco, Plains Tire, Tire-O-Rama, Verizon, Walgreens, Walmart/Subway
124	WY 50, Gillette, **N** Conoco/Papa John's/dsl, Kun&Go/dsl, Shell/Burger King/dsl Hong Kong Rest., Los Compadres Mexican, Pizza Hut, Rooster's Rest., Subway Best Western/rest., Budget Inn, Comfort Inn, Hampton Inn, Motel 6, Super 8 H, Crazy Woman Camping, Don's Foods, Ford, **S** Kum&Go/dsl McDonald's Bighorn Tire, Buick/Chevrolet/GMC, Chrysler/Dodge/Jeep
116	Force Rd
113	Wild Horse Creek Rd
106	Kingsbury Rd
102	Barber Creek Rd
91	Dead Horse Creek Rd
89mm	Powder River
88	Powder River Rd, **N** **both lanes, full facilities, litter barrels, petwalk** , **RV Park**
82	Indian Creek Rd

SUNDANCE

GILLETTE

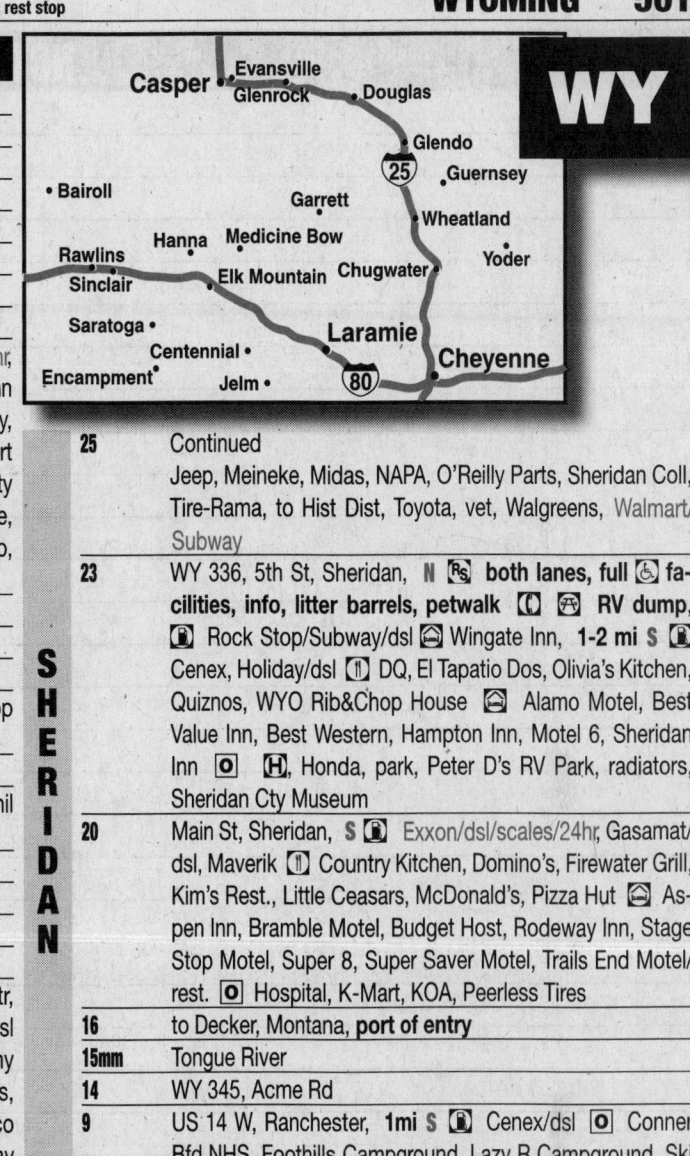

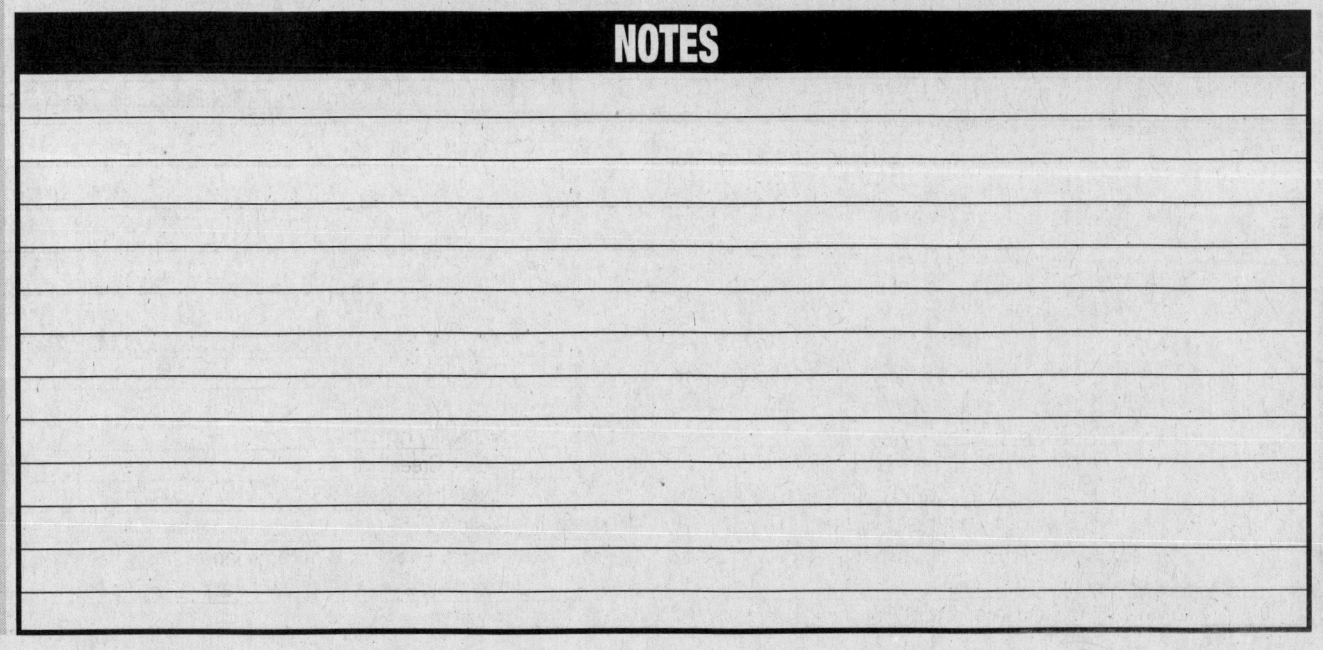

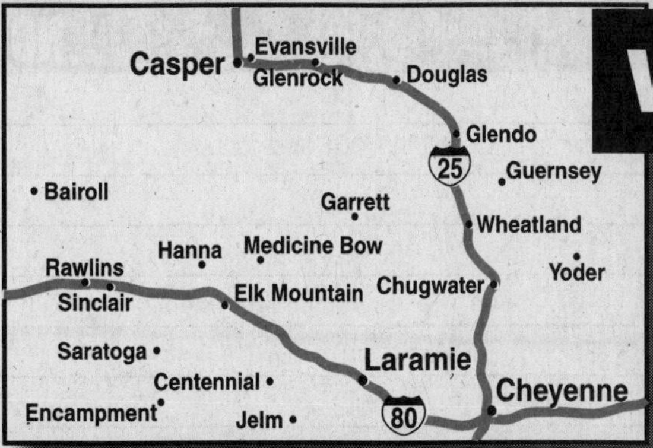

INTERSTATE 90 Cont'd

BUFFALO

Exit #	Services
77	Schoonover Rd
73.5mm	Crazy Woman Creek
73	Crazy Woman Creek Rd
69	Dry Creek Rd
68.5mm	**parking area wb, litter barrels (wb only)**
65	Red Hills Rd, Tipperary Rd
60mm	**parking area both lanes, litter barrels**
58	US 16, to Ucross, Buffalo, **0-3 mi** S Cenex/dsl/24hr, Exxon/dsl, Maverik/dsl Bozeman Tr Steaks, Dash Inn Rest., Hardee's, McDonald's, Pizza Hut, Sub Shop, Subway, Taco John's, Winchester Steaks Buffalo Inn, Comfort Inn, Days Inn, Hampton Inn, Holiday Inn Express, Quality Inn, Rodeway WYO Motel, Super 8 H, Ace Hardware, Bighorn Tire, Deer Park Camping, Family$, Indian RV Camp, KOA, Nat Hist Dist, O'Reilly Parts, Verizon, vet
56b	I-25 S, US 87 S, to Buffalo
56a	25 Bus, 90 Bus, to Buffalo, **services 2mi S (from eb)**
53	Rock Creek Rd
51	Lake DeSmet, **1 mi** N Lake De Smet RV park, Lake Stop gas/motel/cafe
47	Shell Creek Rd
44	US 87 N, Piney Creek Rd, to Story, Banner, N Ft Phil Kearney, museum, **5 mi** S Wagon Box Cabins/Rest.
39mm	scenic turnout wb
37	Prairie Dog Creek Rd, to Story
33	Meade Creek Rd, to Big Horn
31mm	**parking area eb**
25	US 14 E, Sheridan, N Quality Inn Dalton's RV Ctr, S Exxon/dsl, Holiday/dsl, Loaf'n Jug/dsl, Maverik/dsl Arby's, Burger King, Goodtimes/Taco John's, JB's, Jimmy John's, Los Agaves, McDonald's, Ole's Pizza, Papa John's, Papa Murphy's, Perkins, Qdoba, Starbucks, Subway, Taco Bell, Wendy's Candlewood Suites, Days Inn, Holiday Inn, Holiday Lodge, Mill Inn $Tree, Ace Hardware, Albertson's/Osco Drug, Buick/GMC, Chrysler/Dodge/Jeep, Firestone/auto, Ford/Lincoln, Goodyear/auto, Home Depot,

SHERIDAN

Exit #	Services
25	Continued Jeep, Meineke, Midas, NAPA, O'Reilly Parts, Sheridan Coll, Tire-Rama, to Hist Dist, Toyota, vet, Walgreens, Walmart/Subway
23	WY 336, 5th St, Sheridan, N **both lanes, full facilities, info, litter barrels, petwalk RV dump,** Rock Stop/Subway/dsl Wingate Inn, **1-2 mi** S Cenex, Holiday/dsl DQ, El Tapatio Dos, Olivia's Kitchen, Quiznos, WYO Rib&Chop House Alamo Motel, Best Value Inn, Best Western, Hampton Inn, Motel 6, Sheridan Inn H, Honda, park, Peter D's RV Park, radiators, Sheridan Cty Museum
20	Main St, Sheridan, S Exxon/dsl/scales/24hr, Gasamat/dsl, Maverik Country Kitchen, Domino's, Firewater Grill, Kim's Rest., Little Ceasars, McDonald's, Pizza Hut Aspen Inn, Bramble Motel, Budget Host, Rodeway Inn, Stage Stop Motel, Super 8, Super Saver Motel, Trails End Motel/rest. Hospital, K-Mart, KOA, Peerless Tires
16	to Decker, Montana, **port of entry**
15mm	Tongue River
14	WY 345, Acme Rd
9	US 14 W, Ranchester, **1mi** S Cenex/dsl Conner Bfd NHS, Foothills Campground, Lazy R Campground, Ski Area, Teton NPs, to Yellowstone, Western Motel
1	Parkman
0mm	Wyoming/Montana state line

WY

NOTES

NOTES

Assist A Fellow Traveler with...

the Next EXIT®

Published annually, the Next EXIT® provides the best USA Interstate Highway Information available. Use this form to order another copy of the Next EXIT® for yourself or for someone special.

Please send ______ copies of the Next Exit® to the address below.
I've enclosed my check or money order for ***$23.95 US ($26.95 Canadian)*** *per copy.*

Name: ____

Address: ______________________________ Apt./Suite #______________

City: ___________________________ State: ______ Zip: ______________

THREE EASY ORDER OPTIONS:

1. ***MAIL ORDER FORM TO:*** the Next EXIT®, Inc.
PO Box 888
Garden City, Utah 84028

2. ***ORDER ON THE WEB AT:*** ***www.theNextExit.com***

3. ***Give Us A Call & Use Your Charge Card:*** **1-800-NEX-EXIT** or **1-800-639-3948**

More digital options are available at www.theNextExit.com

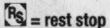